The WORLD DIRECTORY of DIPLOMATIC REPRESENTATION

The WORLD DIRECTORY of DIPLOMATIC REPRESENTATION

1st edition

EUROPA PUBLICATIONS LIMITED

First published 1992

18 Bedford Square, London, WC1B 3JN, England

Australia and New Zealand
James Bennett (Collaroy) Pty Ltd, 4 Collaroy Street, Collaroy, NSW 2097, Australia

Japan
Maruzen Co Ltd, POB 5050, Tokyo International 100-31

British Library Cataloguing in Publication Data
World Directory of Diplomatic
Representation 327

ISBN 0-946653-78-X
ISSN 0965-3783

Printed and bound in England by
Staples Printers Rochester Limited
Neptune Close, Medway City Estate, Frindsbury, Rochester, Kent ME2 4LT

FOREWORD

This first edition of THE WORLD DIRECTORY OF DIPLOMATIC REPRESENTATION provides listings of the names, job titles, addresses and telephone, telex and fax numbers of over 33,000 ambassadors, high commissioners, consuls and other diplomatic staff in every country of the world. Information is also included on missions to and from international organizations such as the United Nations and the European Communities.

The book covers the whole range of diplomatic personnel, from senior to junior staff, whatever their specialist field: for example, commerce, culture, defence, tourism, agriculture, immigration, labour, social welfare, customs, shipping and energy, among others, are listed.

At the end of the book an extensive index lists the principal members of the diplomatic corps of every country in the world, enabling the reader to trace individuals to their particular positions and addresses.

The book can be used in a variety of ways. For example, if the reader wishes to contact foreign commercial attachés in Paris, then the chapter on France will supply the relevant information. Alternatively, if the requirement was to contact French commercial attachés abroad, the index section on France should be consulted.

The editor is most grateful to all those people working in foreign ministries and embassies around the world who supplied us with information by replying to our questionnaires and other correspondence.

March 1992.

CONTENTS

INTERNATIONAL TELEPHONE CODES

To use this table:

Select the International Code for the country from which the call is to be made (column 2), then the Country Code for the country to which the call is going (column 1). To make the call, dial the International Code plus the Country Code plus the number required (adding area codes provided in the entries where necessary). For example, to call a person at the American Embassy in Brussels from the USA, the following numbers would have to be dialled: 011 (International Code from the USA) + 32 (Country Code for Belgium) + (2) (area code) + 513-20-87 (Embassy's number).

	Column 1 Country Code To	Column 2 International Code From
Afghanistan	93	*
Albania	42	*
Algeria	213	00
Andorra	33 628	0
Angola	244	*
Antigua and Barbuda	1 809	011
Argentina	54	*
Armenia	7	810
Australia	61	0011
Australian External Territories:		
Christmas Island	672 4	*
Cocos (Keeling) Islands	672 2	*
Norfolk Island	672 3	*
Austria	43	00
Azerbaidzhan	7	810
Bahamas	1 809	011
Bahrain	973	*
Bangladesh	880	*
Barbados	1 809	011
Belarus	7	810
Belgium	32	00
Belize	501	*
Benin	229	*
Bhutan	*	*
Bolivia	591	*
Botswana	267	*
Brazil	55	00
Brunei	673	*
Bulgaria	359	00
Burkina Faso	226	*
Burundi	257	*
Cambodia	*	*
Cameroon	237	*
Canada	1	011
Cape Verde	238	*
Central African Republic	236	*
Chad	235	*
Chile	56	00
China, People's Republic	86	*
China (Taiwan)	886	*
Colombia	57	90
Comoros	*	*
Congo	242	*
Costa Rica	506	*
Côte d'Ivoire	225	*
Cuba	53	*
Cyprus	357	00
'Turkish Republic of Northern Cyprus'	905	99
Czechoslovakia	42	00
Denmark	45	009
Danish External Territories:		
Faeroe Islands	298	*
Greenland	299	*
Djibouti	253	*
Dominica	1 809 44	0
Dominican Republic	1 809	*
Ecuador	593	01
Egypt	20	*
El Salvador	503	0
Equatorial Guinea	240	*
Estonia	7	810
Ethiopia	251	*
Fiji	679	*
Finland	358	990
France	33	19
French Overseas Departments:		
French Guiana	594	*
Guadeloupe	590	*
Martinique	596	*
Réunion	262	*
French Overseas Collectivités Territoriales:		
Saint Pierre and Miquelon	508	*
French Overseas Territories:		
French Polynesia	689	*
New Caledonia	687	*
Wallis and Futuna Islands	*	*
Gabon	241	*
Gambia	220	*
Georgia	7	810
Germany	49	00
Ghana	233	*
Greece	30	00
Grenada	1 809	011
Guatemala	502	00
Guinea	224	*
Guinea-Bissau	245	*
Guyana	592	*
Haiti	509	*
Honduras	504	00
Hungary	36	00
Iceland	354	90
India	91	00
Indonesia	62	*
Iran	98	*
Iraq	964	*
Ireland	353	16
Israel	972	00
Italy	39	00
Jamaica	1 809	011
Japan	81	001
Jordan	962	*
Kazakhstan	7	810
Kenya	254	*
Kiribati	686	*

INTERNATIONAL TELEPHONE CODES

	Column 1 Country Code To	Column 2 International Code From
Korea, Democratic People's Republic (North Korea)	*	*
Korea, Republic (South Korea)	82	001
Kuwait	965	*
Kyrgyzstan (Kirghizia)	7	810
Laos	*	*
Latvia	7	810
Lebanon	961	*
Lesotho	266	*
Liberia	231	*
Libya	218	*
Liechtenstein	41 75	*
Lithuania	7	810
Luxembourg	352	00
Madagascar	261	*
Malawi	265	*
Malaysia	60	*
Maldives	960	*
Mali	223	*
Malta	356	0
Marshall Islands	692	*
Mauritania	222	*
Mauritius	230	*
Mexico	52	98
Micronesia	691	*
Moldavia (Moldova)	7	810
Monaco	33 93	19
Mongolia	*	*
Morocco	212	00
Mozambique	258	*
Myanmar	95	*
Namibia	264	*
Nauru	674	*
Nepal	977	*
Netherlands	31	09
Netherlands Dependencies:		
Aruba	297	*
Netherlands Antilles	599	*
New Zealand	64	00
New Zealand's Associated Territories:		
Cook Islands	682	*
Niue	*	*
Nicaragua	505	*
Niger	227	*
Nigeria	234	*
Norway	47	095
Oman	968	*
Pakistan	92	*
Panama	507	*
Papua New Guinea	675	*
Paraguay	595	*
Peru	51	*
Philippines	63	*
Poland	48	00
Portugal	351	00 (07 Porto)
(Madeira	351 91)	
Portuguese Overseas Territory:		
Macau	853	*
Qatar	974	*
Romania	40	*
Russia	7	810
Rwanda	250	*
Saint Christopher and Nevis	1 809	011
Saint Lucia	1 809 45	0
Saint Vincent and the Grenadines	1 809 45	0
San Marino	39 549	0
São Tomé and Príncipe	239	*

	Column 1 Country Code To	Column 2 International Code From
Saudi Arabia	966	*
Senegal	221	*
Seychelles	248	*
Sierra Leone	232	*
Singapore	65	005
Solomon Islands	677	*
Somalia	252	*
South Africa	27	*
Spain	34	07
Sri Lanka	94	*
Sudan	249	*
Suriname	597	*
Swaziland	268	*
Sweden	46	009
Switzerland	41	00
Syria	963	*
Tadzhikistan	7	810
Tanzania	255	*
Thailand	66	001
Togo	228	*
Tonga	676	*
Trinidad and Tobago	1 809	01
Tunisia	216	00
Turkey	90	99
Turkmenistan (Turkmenia)	7	810
Tuvalu	*	*
Uganda	256	*
Ukraine	7	810
United Arab Emirates	971	*
United Kingdom	44	010
United Kingdom Crown Dependencies	44	010
British Dependent Territories:		
Anguilla	1 809 497	011
Ascension Island	247	*
Bermuda	1 809	011
British Virgin Islands	1 809	011
Cayman Islands	1 809 94	0
Falkland Islands	500	*
Gibraltar	350	*
Hong Kong	852	001
Montserrat	1 809 491	011
Pitcairn Islands	*	*
Saint Helena	*	*
Turks and Caicos Islands	1 809 946	0
United States of America	1	011
United States External Territories:		
American Samoa	684	*
Guam	671	*
Northern Mariana Islands	670	*
Palau	680	*
Puerto Rico	1 809	135
United States Virgin Islands	1 809	011
Uruguay	598	*
Uzbekistan	7	810
Vanuatu	678	*
Vatican City (Holy See)	39	00
Venezuela	58	00
Viet-Nam	*	*
Western Samoa	685	*
Yemen	967	*
Yugoslavia	38	99
Zaire	243	*
Zambia	260	*
Zimbabwe	263	*

* No Information/Contact International Operator

LATE INFORMATION

India

ISRAEL

Embassy: New Delhi.
Chargé d'affaires: Giora Becher.
Consulate: Bombay.

Latvia

CHINA (TAIWAN)

Consulate: Riga.

FINLAND

Embassy: Teatra iela 9, 226050 Riga.
Chargé d'affaires: Anja Bomen.

GERMANY

Embassy (temporary): Hotel Ridzene, Endrupa iela 1, 226050 Riga; tel (0132) 32-59-82.
Ambassador: Hagen Graf Lambsdorf v. d. Wenge.

ITALY

Embassy (temporary): Hotel Ridzene, Endrupa iela 1, 226050 Riga; tel (0132) 32-59-82.
Ambassador: Umberto Pestalozzi.

NORWAY

Embassy (temporary): Hotel Riga, Aspazijas bulvaris 2, 226050 Riga.
Ambassador: Torbjorn Aalbu.

SWEDEN

Embassy: Lačpleša iela 13, 226050 Riga.
Ambassador: Karl Vidal Hellners.

USA

Embassy (temporary): Hotel Ridzene, Endrupa iela 1, 226050 Riga; tel (0132) 32-59-82.
Ambassador: Ints Siliņš.

Russia

SOUTH AFRICA

Embassy: Moscow.

South Africa

RUSSIA

Embassy: Pretoria.

Yugoslavia

HOLY SEE

Apostolic Nunciature: Zagreb.
Apostolic Nuncio: Mgr Giulio Einaudi.

For information on diplomatic representation in the newly-independent state of **CROATIA,** please refer to the details of the consulates in Zagreb (the capital of Croatia), Dubrovnik, Rijeka and Split. See pages 418–420.

For information on diplomatic representation in the newly-independent state of **SLOVENIA,** please refer to the details of the consulates in Ljubljana (the capital of Slovenia). See pages 418–419.

The United Nations

Armenia, Azerbaidzhan, Kazakhstan, Kyrgyzstan (Kirghizia), Moldavia (Moldova), San Marino, Tadzhikistan, Turkmenistan (Turkmenia) and Uzbekistan were formally admitted to the United Nations on 2 March 1992.

The
WORLD DIRECTORY
of
DIPLOMATIC REPRESENTATION

AFGHANISTAN

AUSTRIA

Embassy: POB 24, Zarghouna Wat, Kabul; tel (93) 32720; telex 218.
Chargé d'affaires a.i.: Heinz Mayer.
Economic Attaché: Josef Prelec.

BANGLADESH

Embassy: POB 510, House 19, Sarak 'H', Wazir Akbar Khan Mena, Kabul; tel (93) 25783.
Chargé d'affaires a.i.: Mahmood Hasan.

BULGARIA

Embassy: Wazir Akbar Khan Mena, Kabul; tel (93) 22996.
Ambassador: Ivan Ivanov Mateev.

CHINA, PEOPLE'S REPUBLIC

Embassy: Shah Mahmud Wat, Shar-i-Nau, Kabul; tel (93) 20446.
Chargé d'affaires: Zhang Deliang.

CUBA

Embassy: Shar Rahi Haji Yaqub, opp. Shar-i-Nau Park, Kabul; tel (93) 30863.
Ambassador: Regino Farinas Cantero.

CZECHOSLOVAKIA

Embassy: Taimani Wat, Kala-i-Fatullah, Kabul; tel (93) 32082.
Ambassador: Bohuslav Handl.

DENMARK

Embassy: Kabul.

FRANCE

Embassy: ave Djadi Solh, Shar-i-Nau, Kabul; tel (93) 23631.
Chargé d'affaires: Thierry Bernadac.
Economic Section: POB 62; tel (93) 23171; telex 233.

GERMANY

Embassy: Ghazi Ayub Khan Wat, Shar-i-Nau, Kabul; tel (93) 20782; telex 249.
Ambassador: Horst Lindner.

HUNGARY

Embassy: POB 830, Sin 306-308, Wazir Akbar Khan Mena, Kabul; tel (93) 24281.
Ambassador: Mihály Golub.
Commercial Counsellor: Imre Gyöngyösi.
Administrative Attaché: Samuel Kiss.

INDIA

Embassy: Malalai Wat, Shar-i-Nau, Kabul; tel (93) 30557.
Ambassador: Vijay K. Nambiar.

INDONESIA

Embassy: POB 532, Wazir Akbar Khan Mena, District 10, House 93, Kabul; tel (93) 23334; telex 239.
Chargé d'affaires a.i.: Hafiz Abdol Ghani.

IRAN

Embassy: Shar-i-Nau, Kabul; tel (93) 26255.
Chargé d'affaires a.i.: Ahmad Khudadadi.

IRAQ

Embassy: POB 523, Wazir Akbar Khan Mena, Kabul; tel (93) 24797.
Ambassador: Burhan Khalil Ghazal.

ITALY

Embassy: POB 606, Khoja Abdullah Ansari Wat, Kabul; tel (93) 24624; telex 55.
Chargé d'affaires a.i.: Mr Calamai.

JAPAN

Embassy: POB 80, Wazir Akbar Khan Mena, Kabul; tel (93) 26844; telex 216.
Chargé d'affaires a.i.: Keiki Hiraga.

KOREA, DEMOCRATIC PEOPLE'S REPUBLIC

Embassy: Wazir Akbar Khan Mena, House 28, Sarak 'H' House 103, Kabul; tel (93) 22161.
Ambassador: Oh In-Yong.

LIBYA

Embassy: 103 Wazir Akbar Khan Mena, Kabul; tel (93) 25947.
Secretary: Salem A. el-Huni.

MONGOLIA

Embassy: Wazir Akbar Khan Mena, Sarak 'T' House 8714, Kabul; tel (93) 22138.

PAKISTAN

Embassy: Zarghouna Wat, Shar-i-Nau, Kabul; tel (93) 21374.
Chargé d'affaires a.i.: S. Fida Yunas.

POLAND

Embassy: POB 78, Guzargah St, Kabul; tel (93) 42461.
Chargé d'affaires: Andrzej Wawrzyniak.
Commercial Attaché: Edmund Napiorkowski.

RUSSIA

Embassy: Darulaman Wat, Kabul; tel (93) 41541.
Ambassador: Boris Nikolayevich Pastukhov.
Consular Section: POB 228; tel (93) 21922; telex 383.
Consulate-General: Mazari-Sharif, Kude-Bark.

SWEDEN

Embassy: Kabul.

TURKEY

Embassy: Shar-i-Nau, Kabul; tel (93) 20072.
Chargé d'affaires a.i.: Salih Zeki Karaca.

UNITED KINGDOM

Embassy: Karte Parwan, Kabul; tel (93) 30511.
Chargé d'affaires a.i.: Ian W. Mackley.

USA

Embassy: Wazir Akbar Khan Mena, Kabul; tel (93) 62230.
Chargé d'affaires a.i.: Jon D. Glassmann.

VIET-NAM

Embassy: 3 Nijat St, Wazir Akbar Khan Mena, Kabul; tel (93) 26596.

YUGOSLAVIA

Embassy: POB 53, 923 Main Rd, Wazir Akbar Khan Mena, Kabul; tel (93) 61671; telex 272.
Chargé d'affaires a.i.: Velibor Dulović.
Attaché: Darko Ninković.

ALBANIA

BULGARIA

Embassy: Rruga Skënderbeu 12, Tirana; tel (42) 22672.
Ambassador: Stefan Naumov.

CHINA, PEOPLE'S REPUBLIC

Embassy: Rruga Skënderbeu 57, Tirana; tel (42) 22600; telex 2148.
Ambassador: Gu Maoxuan.

CUBA

Embassy: Rruga Kongresi i Përmetit 13, Tirana; tel (42) 25176; telex 2155.
Ambassador: Julio C. Cancio Ferrer.

CZECHOSLOVAKIA

Embassy: Rruga Skënderbeu 10, Tirana; tel (42) 22552; telex 2162; fax (42) 32159.
Ambassador: Jindřich Manďák.
First Secretary: Imrich Sedlák.
Third Secretary: Ivan Šveda.

EGYPT

Embassy: Rruga Skënderbeu 43, Tirana; tel (42) 23013; telex 2156.
Ambassador: Manzur Ahmad al-Dali.

FRANCE

Embassy: Rruga Skënderbeu 14, Tirana; tel (42) 22804; telex 2150.
Ambassador: Michel Boulmer.
Economic Section: Rruga Skënderbeu 24; tel (42) 9158; telex 2150.

GERMANY

Embassy: Rruga Skënderbeu, Tirana; tel (42) 23481; telex 2254.
Ambassador: Friedrich Kroneck.

GREECE

Embassy: Rruga Frederick Shiroka 3, Tirana; tel (42) 26850.
Ambassador: Spyridon A. Dokianos.

HUNGARY

Embassy: Rruga Skënderbeu 16, Tirana; tel (42) 22004; telex 2257; fax (42) 33211.
Ambassador: Ferenc Póka.
Counsellor: Károly Laincsek.
Commercial Counsellor: György Tausz.
Third Secretary: Antal Heizer.

ITALY

Embassy: Rruga Labinoti 103, Tirana; tel (42) 22800; telex 2166.
Ambassador: Torquato Cardilli.

KOREA, DEMOCRATIC PEOPLE'S REPUBLIC

Embassy: Rruga Skënderbeu 55, Tirana; tel (42) 22258.
Ambassador: Kim U-Chong.

POLAND

Embassy: Rruga Kongresi i Përmetit 123, Tirana.
Ambassador: Władysław Ciaston.

ROMANIA

Embassy: Rruga Themistokli Gërmenji 2, Tirana; tel (42) 22259.
Ambassador: Gheorghe Miku.

RUSSIA

Embassy: Tirana.
Ambassador: Victor Yefimovich Nerubaylo.

TURKEY

Embassy: Rruga Konferenca e Pezës 31, Tirana; tel (42) 22449.
Ambassador: Teoman Sürenkök.
Third Secretary: Ali Kemal Aydin.
Attaché: Bilal Çamlik.
Attaché: Hasan Keçeci.

UNITED KINGDOM

Embassy: Tirana.

VIET-NAM

Embassy: Rruga Lek Dukagjini, Tirana; tel (42) 22556; telex 2253.
Ambassador: Nguyen Chi Thanh.

YUGOSLAVIA

Embassy: Rruga Kongresi i Përmetit 192-196, Tirana; tel (42) 23042; telex 2167.
Ambassador: Novak Pribicević.

ALGERIA

ALBANIA

Embassy: 19 bis rue Abdelkarim Lagoune, el-Mouradia, Algiers.
Ambassador: Dhimitër Stamo.

ANGOLA

Embassy: 34 chemin Abd al-Kader, el-Mouradia, Algiers; tel (2) 56-15-24; telex 62204.
Ambassador: Henrique Teles Carreira.

ARGENTINA

Embassy: 7 rue Hamani, 16000 Algiers; tel (2) 64-74-08; telex 67485; fax (2) 64-14-15.
Ambassador: Eduardo M. de L. Airaldi.
First Secretary: Hector G. Fassi.
Second Secretary: Pedro A. Real.
Economic and Commercial Secretary: Jorge Riccombeni.

AUSTRALIA

Embassy: 12 ave Emile Marquis, Djenane-el-Malik, Hydra, Algiers; tel (2) 60-28-46; telex 66105; fax (2) 59-20-81.
Ambassador: M. P. F. Smith.

AUSTRIA

Embassy: Les Vergers, rue 2, Villa 9, DZ-16330 Bir Khadem, Algiers; tel (2) 56-26-99; telex 62302.
Ambassador: Dr Hans G. Knitel.
First Secretary: Dr Thomas Buchsbaum.
Economic Secretary: Giorgio Nushi.

BANGLADESH

Embassy: 14 ave des Frères Oughlis le Golf, el-Mouradia, Algiers; tel (2) 59-48-05; telex 66363; fax (2) 59-46-16.
Ambassador: Mahbubul Huq.
First Secretary: Nasim Firdous.

BELGIUM

Embassy: 22 chemin Youcef Tayebi, el-Biar, Algiers; tel (2) 78-57-12; telex 61365.
Ambassador: André Adam.

BENIN

Embassy: rue 3, Villa no. 4, Beaulieu, el-Harrach, Algiers; telex 52447.
Ambassador: Antoine Laleye.

BRAZIL

Embassy: 48 blvd Muhammad V, Algiers; telex 52470.
Ambassador: Ronald L. M. Small.

BULGARIA

Embassy: 13 blvd Col Bougara, Algiers; tel (2) 60-15-14; telex 67309; fax (2) 74-22-32.
Ambassador: Grigor Todorov Kruchmarski.
Counsellor (Political/Cultural Affairs): Boris Petzev.
Counsellor (Commercial/Economic Affairs): Stefan Stefanov.
Military, Naval and Air Attaché: Lieut Col Roumen Popov.
First Secretary (Consular Affairs): Krassin Domostchiev.
First Secretary (Commercial Affairs): Nikolay Todorov.
Third Secretary (Commercial Affairs): Borislav Gueorguiev.
Attaché (Administrative Affairs): Petko Paguelski.

BURUNDI

Embassy: 116 bis blvd des Martyrs, Algiers; telex 53501.
Ambassador: André Nadayirage.

CAMEROON

Embassy: 26 chemin Cheikh Bachir Ibrahimi, el-Biar, Algiers; telex 52421.
Ambassador: Simon Nko'o Etoungou.

CANADA

Embassy: 27 bis rue d'Anjou, Hydra, Algiers; BP 225, Alger-Gare, Algiers; tel (2) 60-66-11; telex 66043; fax (2) 60-59-20.
Ambassador: Marc C. Lemieux.
Counsellor and Consul: C. Anstis.
Counsellor (Commercial): R. J. A. Goulet.
Counsellor (Development): M. Cadieux.
First Secretary (Development): D. Marcheterre.
First Secretary (Commercial) and Consul: A. Guindi.
Second Secretary (Administration) and Vice-Consul: H. Huard.

CHAD

Embassy: 6 rue Sylvain Fourastier, Le Golf, Algiers; telex 52642.
Ambassador: Mbailaou Naimbaye Lossimian.

CHILE

Embassy: Algiers.

CHINA, PEOPLE'S REPUBLIC

Embassy: 34 blvd des Martyrs, Algiers; tel (2) 60-27-24; telex 53233.
Ambassador: An Huihou.
Counsellor: Li Jinren.
Counsellor: Chen Lianhe.
First Secretary (Head of Chancery and Consular Affairs): Zhang Fuxia.
Second Secretary (Political Affairs): Wang Yong.
Second Secretary (Political Affairs): Gao Youzhen.
Second Secretary (Administrative Affairs): Zhang Mingxiang.
Second Secretary (Political Affairs): Liang Dingding.
Second Secretary (Consular Affairs): Chen Fenglian.
Second Secretary (Administrative Affairs): Du Yuhe.
Office of Military Attaché: tel (2) 60-31-24.
Military, Naval and Air Attaché: Col Zhang Jiazhen.
Cultural Office: tel (2) 60-52-60.
Cultural Counsellor: Chen Boxiang.
First Secretary (Cultural Affairs): Sun Xuebin.
Commercial Office: tel (2) 60-53-62; telex 66193.
Commercial Counsellor: Chen Yiqing.
First Secretary (Commercial Affairs): Qian Changan.
First Secretary (Commercial Affairs): Xu Chongshan.
Economic Office: tel (2) 60-31-89.
Economic Counsellor: Liu Wenzha.
First Secretary (Economic Affairs): Chen Jinsui.
First Secretary (Economic Affairs): Yin Zuozhi.

CONGO

Embassy: 13 rue Rabah Noël, Algiers; telex 52069.
Ambassador: Benjamin Bounkoulou.

COTE D'IVOIRE

Embassy: Immeuble 'Le Bosquet', Le Paradou, Hydra, Algiers; telex 52881.
Ambassador: Lambert Amon Tamoh.

CUBA

Embassy: 22 rue Larbi Alik, Hydra, Algiers; telex 66163.
Ambassador: Ulises Estrada Lescaille.

CZECHOSLOVAKIA

Embassy: 7 chemin du Zyriab, Dar Malika, BP 999, Algiers; tel (2) 60-05-25; telex 66281.
Ambassador: Jiri Osvald.
First Secretary: Michal Svantner.
Commercial Counsellor: Josef Koci.
Military and Air Attaché: Col Romeo Horak.
Second Secretary: Ivan Kalus.
Third Secretary: Milan Kral.
Commercial Attaché: Jozef Marcina.
Commercial Attaché: Jiri Jirous.
Commercial Attaché: Vladimir Horovitz.

DENMARK

Embassy: 12 ave Emile Marquis, DZ-16035 Hydra, Algiers; tel (2) 60-19-65; telex 66270; fax (2) 64-51-52.
Ambassador: Preben Hansen.
Attaché and Consul: Hubert Svoldgaard.

EGYPT

Embassy: 16300, Algiers; tel (2) 60-16-73; telex 66058.
Ambassador: Dr Hussain Ahmad Amin.

FINLAND

Embassy: Lot Djenane El Malik, face Cité des PTT, 16035 Hydra, Algiers; BP 256, DZ-16035 Hydra, Algiers; tel (2) 59-32-93; telex 66296; fax (2) 59-46-37.
Ambassador: Jan Groop.
First Secretary: Risto Piipponen.
Administrative Attaché: Riitta Nikkanen.
Administrative Attaché: Taija Mikkola.
Commercial Section: telex 66273.

FRANCE

Embassy: Parc Peltzer, 6 rue Larbi Alik, Hydra, Algiers; tel (2) 60-44-88; telex 52644; fax (2) 60-53-69.
Ambassador: Jean Audibert.
Minister-Counsellor: Hadelin de la Tour du Pin.
Second Counsellor: André Pierrot.
First Secretary: Danièle Dupraz.
First Secretary: Nicolas Galey.
Second Secretary: Bruno Aubert.
Press Attaché: P. Vladimir Glasman.
Defence Attaché: Claude Liautaud.
Naval Attaché: Denis Richard.

Commercial Attaché: Olivier Remond.
Financial Attaché: Frédéric Visnovsky.
Counsellor (Culture/Science/Co-operation): Pierre Père.
Director of the University and Culture Office: Christian Pellaumail.
Counsellor for Social Affairs: Jean André Carreno.

Economic Section: 12 chemin du Réservoir; tel (2) 60-05-22; telex 66117.
Minister-Counsellor (Economic/Financial): Philippe Doyon.

Consulate-General: 1 rue du Professeur Vincent, Algiers; tel (2) 64-59-93; telex 66565; fax (2) 74-57-55.
Consul-General: Jean-Paul Angelier.

Consulate-General: 3 sq. Cayla, Oran; tel (6) 33-53-00; telex 22890; fax (6) 33-18-67.
Consul-General: Claude Losguardi.

Consulate-General: rue Gouta Sebti, 23000 Annaba; tel (8) 82-63-91; telex 81875.
Consul-General: Pierre Marchal.

GABON

Embassy: 136 bis blvd Salah Bouakouir au 80 rue Allili, BP 85, Algiers; tel (2) 72-02-64; telex 52242.
Ambassador: Yves Ongollo.

GERMANY

Embassy: 165 chemin Sfindja, BP 664, Algiers; tel (2) 74-19-41; telex 67343; fax (2) 74-05-21.
Ambassador: Dr Rudolf Koppenhöfer.

Visa Section: telex 66573.

GHANA

Embassy: 62 rue des Frères Bénali Abdellah, Hydra, Algiers; tel (2) 60-64-44; telex 62234.
Ambassador: Isaac O. Twum-Ampofo.

GREECE

Embassy: 31 rue A. les Crêtes, DZ-16035 Hydra, Algiers; tel (2) 60-08-55; telex 66071.
Ambassador: Georges Helmis.

GUINEA

Embassy: 43 blvd Central Said Hamdine, Hydra, Algiers; telex 53451.
Ambassador: Fode Berete.

GUINEA-BISSAU

Embassy: Cité DNC, rue Ahmad Kara, Hydra, Algiers; tel (2) 60-01-51.
Ambassador: Dr Lionel Vieira.

HOLY SEE

Nunciature: 1 rue Nourredine Mekiri, 16090 Bologhine, Algiers; tel (2) 62-34-30.
Pro-Nuncio: Mgr Edmond Farhat.

HUNGARY

Embassy: 18 ave des Frères Oughlis, BP 68, el-Mouradia, Algiers; tel (2) 60-77-09; telex 62217.
Ambassador: Zoltán Zsigmond.

ICELAND

Embassy: Algiers.

INDIA

Embassy: 119 ter rue Didouche Mourad, Algiers; tel (2) 59-46-00; telex 66138.
Ambassador: V. K. Nambiar.

INDONESIA

Embassy: 6 rue Muhammad Chemlal, BP 62, 16070 el-Mouradia, Algiers; tel (2) 60-20-51; telex 62214.
Ambassador: Muhammad Singgih Hadipranowo.

IRAN

Embassy: 60 rue Didouche Mourad, Algiers; telex 52880.
Ambassador: Siavash Zargaran Yaqoubi.

IRAQ

Embassy: 4 rue Arezki Abri, Hydra, Algiers; telex 53067.
Ambassador: Ibrahim Shujaa Sultan.

ITALY

Embassy: 18 rue Muhammad Ouidir Amellal, el-Biar, Algiers; tel (2) 78-33-99; telex 61357.
Ambassador: Michelangelo Jacobucci.

JAPAN

Embassy: 1 chemin Macklay, el-Biar, BP 80, Algiers; tel (2) 78-62-00; telex 61389; fax (2) 79-22-93.
Ambassador: Nishiyama Takehiko.

JORDAN

Embassy: 6 rue du Chenoua, Algiers; telex 52464.
Ambassador: Yasin Istanbuli.

KOREA, DEMOCRATIC PEOPLE'S REPUBLIC

Embassy: 49 rue Hamlia, Bologhine, Algiers; telex 53929.
Ambassador: Li Man-Sok.

KOREA, REPUBLIC

Embassy: Algiers.

KUWAIT

Embassy: 1 ter rue Didouche Mourad, Algiers; telex 52267.
Ambassador: Abdel-Latif Hamad al-Salih.

LEBANON

Embassy: 9 rue Kaïd Ahmad, el-Biar, Algiers; telex 52416.
Ambassador: Salhad Nasri.

LIBYA

Embassy: 15 chemin Cheikh Bachir Ibrahimi, Algiers; telex 52700.
Ambassador: Abdel-Fattah Naas.

MADAGASCAR

Embassy: 22 rue Abd al-Kader Aouis Bologhine, Algiers; tel (2) 62-31-96; telex 61156.
Ambassador: Samuel Lahady.

MALI

Embassy: Villa no. 15, Cité DNC/ANP, chemin du Kaddous, Hydra, Algiers; tel (2) 60-61-16; telex 52631.
Ambassador: Sinaly Coulibaly.
First Counsellor: Mamby Diabate.
Counsellor (Cultural): Kalilou Maguiraga.

MALTA

Embassy: 'el Aurassi', ave Dr Frantz Fanon, Algiers; tel (2) 63-19-74; telex 67373.
Ambassador: Alfred A. Zarb (resident in Malta).
First Secretary and Chargé d'affaires a.i.: John Scerri.

MAURITANIA

Embassy: BP 276, el-Mouradia, Algiers; telex 53437.
Ambassador: Ould Muhammad Mahmoud Muhammadou.

MEXICO

Embassy: 8 chemin du Kaddous, BP 880, DZ-16300 Alger-Gare, Algiers; tel (2) 59-12-13; telex 66090.
Ambassador: Jorge Palacios.

MONGOLIA

Embassy: 4 rue Belkacem Amani, Cité Sellier, Hydra, Algiers; tel (2) 60-26-12.
Ambassador: Burenjargalyn Orsoo.
Attaché: Sharavdorjiin Bayarkhuu.

MOROCCO

Embassy: Algiers.
Ambassador: Prof. Abd al-Latif Berbiche.

NETHERLANDS

Embassy: 23 chemin Cheikh Bachir Ibrahimi, BP 72, el-Biar, Algiers; tel (2) 78-28-29; telex 61364; fax (2) 78-07-70.
Ambassador: Dr Patrick S. J. Rutgers.

NIGER

Embassy: 54 rue Vercors Rostamia Bouzareah, Algiers; telex 52625.
Ambassador: Moustapha Tahi.

NIGERIA

Embassy: 27 bis rue Blaise Pascal, BP 629, Algiers; tel (2) 60-60-50; telex 52523.
Ambassador: B. A. Oki.

OMAN

Embassy: 126 rue Didouche Mourad, BP 543, Alger-Gare, Algiers; tel (2) 79-26-55; telex 61335; fax (2) 79-90-10.
Ambassador: Roched Ben Nacer al-Lamki.
First Secretary: Ali Ben Ahmed al-Ojaili.
First Secretary: Hamad Bin Rashid al-Madilwi.
Diplomatic Attaché: Abdullah al-Houtti.

PAKISTAN

Embassy: 14 ave Souidani Boudjemâa, el-Mouradia, BP 1023, Alger-Gare, Algiers; tel (2) 60-57-81; telex 66277.
Ambassador: Karamatullah Khan Ghori.
Second Secretary and Head of Chancery: Akhtar Ali Sulehri.

PHILIPPINES

Embassy: Algiers.
Ambassador: Pacifico Castro.

POLAND

Embassy: 37 ave Mustafa Ali Khodja, el-Biar, Algiers; telex 52562.
Ambassador: Stanisław Pichla.

PORTUGAL

Embassy: 67 chemin Muhammad Gacem, Algiers; tel (2) 56-61-95; telex 62202.
Ambassador: Fernando Andresen Guimarães.

QATAR

Embassy: 25 bis allée Centrale, BP 118, Clairval, Algiers; tel (2) 79-80-56; telex 52224.
Ambassador: Khalifa Sultan al-Assiry.

ROMANIA

Embassy: 24 rue Si Arezki, Hydra, Algiers; telex 52915.
Ambassador: Tudor Zamfira.

RUSSIA

Embassy: impasse Boukhandoura, el-Biar, Algiers; telex 52511.
Ambassador: Vasiliy Taratouta.

Consular Section: tel (2) 78-52-12; telex 61561.

Consulate-General: 42 blvd de l'Armée de Libération Nationale, Oran; tel (6) 39-79-10; telex 22153.

Consulate-General: 1 blvd Fellah Rachid, Annaba; tel (8) 82-78-10; telex 81750.

SAUDI ARABIA

Embassy: 4 rue Arezki Abri, Hydra, Algiers; telex 53039.
Ambassador: Hasan Faqqi.

SENEGAL

Embassy: 1 rue Arago, Algiers; tel (2) 60-32-85; telex 52133.
Ambassador: Ibrahima Wone.

SOMALIA

Embassy: 11 impasse Tarting, blvd des Martyrs, Algiers; telex 52140.
Ambassador: Abd al-Hamid Ali Youcef.

SPAIN

Embassy: 10 rue Azil Ali, Algiers; telex 67330.
Ambassador: Gumersindo Rico y Rodríguez Villar.

SWEDEN

Embassy: rue Olof Palme, Nouveau Paradou, Hydra, Algiers; BP 623, DZ-16035 Hydra, Algiers; tel (2) 59-43-00; telex 66046; fax (2) 59-17-17.
Ambassador: Tom G. R. Tscherning.
Counsellor: Lars Ahlstrand.
Second Secretary: Anna Block.
Chancellor: Kerstin Helena Viktoria Ferroukhi.

SWITZERLAND

Embassy: 27 blvd Zirout Youcef, BP 482, DZ-16000 Alger-Gare, Algiers; tel (2) 63-39-02; telex 67342; fax (2) 63-79-77.
Ambassador: O. Uhl.
First Secretary: Christian Schmed.
Attaché and Head of Chancery: Pierre-Alain Rebetez.

SYRIA

Embassy: Domaine Tamzali, chemin A. Gadouche, Hydra, Algiers; telex 52572.
Ambassador: Ahmad Madaniya.

TUNISIA

Embassy: 11 rue du Bois de Boulogne, Hydra, Algiers; telex 52968.
Ambassador: M'Hedi Baccouche.

TURKEY

Embassy: Villa dar el Ouard, chemin de la Rochelle, blvd Col Bougara, Algiers; tel (2) 60-12-57; telex 66244.
Ambassador: Omer Ersun.

UNITED ARAB EMIRATES

Embassy: 26 rue Aouis Mokrane, BP 454, el-Mouradia, Algiers; tel (2) 56-46-47; telex 62208.
Ambassador: Muhammad I. al-Jowaied.

UNITED KINGDOM

Embassy: Résidence Cassiopée, Bâtiment B, 7 chemin des Glycines, BP 43, DZ-16000 Alger-Gare, Algiers; tel (2) 60-50-38; telex 66151; fax (2) 60-44-10.
Ambassador: Christopher C. R. Battiscombe.
Counsellor, Consul-General and Deputy Head of Mission: K. G. Bloomfield.
Counsellor: G. L. St L. Rolleston.
Cultural Attaché (British Council Director): D. Monro.
First Secretary (Commercial): R. Shaw.
Assistant Defence Attaché: Lieut Col I. P. Howard-Harwood.
Second Secretary (Commercial): R. I. Drummond.
Consul and Second Secretary (Management): P. A. S. Holmes.
Second Secretary (Immigration) and Consul: J. A. Chiswell.

Consular/Visa Section: telex 66266.

USA

Embassy: 4 chemin Cheikh Bachir el-Ibrahimi, BP 549, Alger-Gare, 16000 Algiers; tel (2) 60-11-86; telex 66047; fax (2) 60-39-79.
Deputy Chief of Mission: Steven J. Coffey.
Political Section: Gerald J. Loftus.
Economic Section: Christopher White Webster.
Consular Section: George Kopf.
Administrative Section: John L. Mack.
Regional Security Officer: Robert J. Reca.
Office of the Defence Attaché: Col Allan Ingalls.
Communications Programme Officer: David Patterson.

Commercial Section: fax (2) 60-18-63.
Commercial Section: Terence Flannery.

Information Service: fax (2) 60-74-88.
Public Affairs Officer: Yolande Veron-Sullivan.

Agricultural Trade Office: fax (2) 78-61-45.
Agricultural Trade Officer: Paul Hoffman.

Consulate: 14 sq. de Bamako, Oran; tel (6) 33-45-09; telex 22310.
Principal Officer: David M. Hess.
Consular Section: Diane W. Shelby.

VENEZUELA

Embassy: impasse Ahmed Kara, BP 813, 16000 Alger-Gare, Algiers; tel (2) 59-28-46; telex 66642; fax (2) 60-75-55.
Ambassador: José Rafael Domínguez.
Minister-Counsellor: Zoed Karam Duaiji.

VIET-NAM

Embassy: 30 rue de Chenoua, Hydra, Algiers; telex 52147.
Ambassador: Vo Toan.

YEMEN

Embassy: 74 rue Bouraba, Algiers; telex 53582.
Ambassador: Hamod Muhammad Bayder.

YUGOSLAVIA

Embassy: 7 rue des Frères Benhafid, BP 662, Hydra, Algiers; tel (2) 60-47-04; telex 66076.
Ambassador: Borislav Milošević.

ZAIRE

Embassy: 12 rue A, Les Crêtes, Hydra, Algiers; telex 52749.
Ambassador: Ikolo Bolelama W'okondola.

ZIMBABWE

Embassy: 24 rue Arab Si Ahmad, Birkhadem, Algiers.
Ambassador: Solomon Rakobe Nkomo.

International Organizations

EUROPEAN COMMUNITIES

External Delegation: 36 rue Arezki Abri, 16035 Hydra, Algiers; tel (2) 59-08-22; telex 66067; fax (2) 59-39-47.

ANDORRA

GERMANY

Consulate-General: 338 ave du Prado, 13295 Marseilles Cedex 8, France; tel 91-77-08-98; telex 401335.
Consul-General: Joachim-Richard Vogel.

SWEDEN

Consulate-General: Avda Diagonal 601, 4°, 08028 Barcelona, Spain; Apdo 30210, 08034 Barcelona; tel (3) 4101108; telex 5251725; fax (93) 4102501.
Consul-General: Göte Lönnmar.

UNITED KINGDOM

Consulate-General: Edif. Torre de Barcelona, Avda Diagonol 477, 13°, Apdo 12111, 08036 Barcelona, Spain; tel (3) 3222151; telex 52799.

ANGOLA

ALGERIA

Embassy: Luanda.
Ambassador: Hanafi Oussedik.

BELGIUM

Embassy: CP 1203, Luanda; tel (2) 336437; telex 3356.
Ambassador: Guido Vansina.

BRAZIL

Embassy: Avda Houari Boumedienne 132, CP 5428, Miramar, Luanda; tel (2) 343275; telex 3365.
Ambassador: Ruy Antonio Neves Pinheiro de Vasconcellos.
Counsellor: Sebastião Neves.

BULGARIA

Embassy: Luanda; telex 3375.
Ambassador: Boyan Mihaylov.

CANADA

Consulate: Rua Rei Katyavalla 113, Luanda; tel (2) 343754; telex 4072; fax (2) 343754.
Honorary Consul: A. Cain.

CAPE VERDE

Embassy: Luanda; telex 3247.

CHINA, PEOPLE'S REPUBLIC

Embassy: Luanda.
Ambassador: Hu Lipeng.

CONGO

Embassy: Luanda.
Ambassador: Anatole Khondo.

COTE D'IVOIRE

Embassy: Rua Karl Marx 43, Luanda.
Ambassador: Jean-Marie Kacou Gervais.

CUBA

Embassy: Luanda; telex 3236.
Ambassador: Narcisco Martín Mora.

CZECHOSLOVAKIA

Embassy: Rua Amílcar Cabral 5, CP 2691, Luanda; tel (2) 334456.
Ambassador: Jaroslav Suttner.
Consul and Cultural Attaché: Vojtěch Nagy.
Military Attaché: Milan Bachan.
Commercial Counsellor: Vladimír Piša.

DENMARK

Embassy: Luanda.
Ambassador: Per W. Frellesvig (resident in Denmark).

Consulate-General: Avda 4 de Fevereiro 24, c/o Hull Blyth (Angola) Ltd, CP 1214, Luanda; tel (2) 373184; telex 3053.
Consul-General: John Scott Nicolson.
Vice-Consul: Virginia Victor.

EGYPT

Embassy: Luanda; telex 3380.
Ambassador: Anwar Dakroury.

FRANCE

Embassy: Rua dos Enganos 1, CP 584, Luanda; tel (2) 334841; telex 3361.
Ambassador: Jacques Gasseau.

Economic Section: CP 5609; tel (2) 38019; telex 3327.

GABON

Embassy: Avda 4 de Fevereiro 95, Luanda; tel (2) 372614; telex 3263.
Ambassador: Raphaël Nkassa-Nzogho.

GERMANY

Embassy: Avda 4 de Fevereiro 120, CP 1295, Luanda; tel (2) 334516; telex 3372.
Ambassador: Hans Helmut Freundt.

GHANA

Embassy: Rua Vereador Castelo Branco 5, CP 1012, Luanda; telex 3331.
Ambassador: Dr Keli Nordor.

GUINEA

Embassy: Luanda; telex 3177.

HOLY SEE

Apostolic Delegation: Rua Luther King 123, CP 1030, Luanda; tel (2) 336289; fax (2) 332378.
Apostolic Delegate: Most Rev. Fortunato Baldelli, Titular Archbishop of Mevania (Bevagna).

HUNGARY

Embassy: Rua Vereador Jaime de Amorim 22-28, Alvalade, CP 2977, Luanda; telex 3084.
Ambassador: József Németh.

INDIA

Embassy: Hotel Turismo, Rua Rainha Ginga, Luanda; tel (2) 393681; telex 4098.
Ambassador: Vaman Sardesai.

ITALY

Embassy: Luanda; tel (2) 393533; telex 3265.
Ambassador: Francesco Lanata.

KOREA, DEMOCRATIC PEOPLE'S REPUBLIC

Embassy: Luanda.
Ambassador: Kim Chung Nam.

NETHERLANDS

Embassy: CP 3624, Luanda; telex 3051.
Ambassador: Cornelis De Sroot.

NIGERIA

Embassy: CP 479, Luanda; tel (2) 340084; telex 3014.
Ambassador: L. O. C. Agubuzu.

POLAND

Embassy: CP 1340, Luanda; telex 3222.
Ambassador: Jan Bojko.

PORTUGAL

Embassy: Rua Karl Marx 50, CP 1346, Luanda; tel (2) 333027; telex 3370.

Ambassador: António d'Oliveira Pinto da França.

ROMANIA

Embassy: Rua 5 de Outubro 68, Luanda; tel (2) 336757; telex 3022.
Ambassador: Marin Iliescu.

RUSSIA

Embassy: CP 3141, Luanda; tel (2) 345028.

Consular Section: Rua H. Boumedienne 172.

Consulate-General: 1 Avda da Independencia, Lobito; tel (2) 22578.

SÃO TOMÉ AND PRÍNCIPE

Embassy: Luanda.
Ambassador: Ariosto Castelo David.

SPAIN

Embassy: Rua 4 de Fevereiro 95, 1°, CP 3061, Luanda; tel (2) 391166; telex 3526; fax (2) 391188.
Ambassador: Antonio Sánchez Jara.
First Secretary: José Maria Ridao.

SWEDEN

Embassy: rua Garcia Neto 9, CP 1130, Luanda; tel (2) 339482; telex 3126.
Ambassador: Per Lindström.
First Secretary: Martin Rosén.
Second Secretary: Margareta Kristianson-Auffredou.
Head of Aid Office: Dag Ehrenpreis.

SWITZERLAND

Embassy: Rua 4 de Fevereiro 129, 2°, CP 3163, Correio central, Luanda; tel (2) 336878; telex 3172.
Chargé d'affaires and Counsellor: Giambattista Mondada.

TANZANIA

Embassy: Luanda.
Ambassador: Crispin Mbadila.

UNITED KINGDOM

Embassy: Rua Diogo Cão 4, CP 1244, Luanda; tel (2) 392991; telex 3130; fax (2) 333331.
Ambassador: John Gerrard Flynn.
Consul and Deputy Head of Mission: G. A. Pirie.
First Secretary (Chancery): S. M. Noakes.
Second Secretary (Commercial/Aid): B. R. Jones.
Third Secretary (Management) and Vice-Consul: A. J. Marshall.

Commercial Section: tel (2) 392998; telex 4016.

VIET-NAM

Embassy: Luanda; telex 3226.
Ambassador: Nguyen Huy Loi.

YUGOSLAVIA

Embassy: Luanda; telex 3234.
Ambassador: Zivadin Jovanović.

ZAIRE

Embassy: Luanda.
Ambassador: Mr Ilangwa-e-Yoka.

ZAMBIA

Embassy: CP 1496, Luanda; tel (2) 331145; telex 3439.
Ambassador: Boniface Zulu.

ZIMBABWE

Embassy: Avda 4 de Fevereiro 42, CP 428, Luanda; tel (2) 332337; telex 3275; fax (2) 332339.
Ambassador: Dr Neville Ndondo.
Counsellor: Gideon G. Gapare.
First Secretary: Cyril Musasike.
First Secretary: Charles Wenyeve.
Second Secretary: Fortune Tamburayi.
Third Secretary: Ronald Kushamba.
Third Secretary: Venus Showa.

International Organizations

EUROPEAN COMMUNITIES

External Delegation: Rua Rainha Jinga 6, 1°, CP 2669, Luanda; tel (2) 393038; telex 3397; fax (2) 392531.
Commission Delegate: Carlos Gil Renaux.
Technical Adviser: Jaime Diez-Canseco.
Technical Adviser: Franco Nulli.
Economic Adviser: Carla Montesi.
Agricultural Adviser: Jacques Roman.
Administration and Finance Adviser: Vittorio Guandalini.

ANTIGUA AND BARBUDA

CHINA, PEOPLE'S REPUBLIC

Embassy: St John's.
Ambassador: Zhou Wenzhong.

DENMARK

Consulate-General: St John's.

Consulate: 54 High St, POB 104, St John's; tel 462-0182; telex 2138; fax 462-0183.
Consul: John R. Anjo.

GERMANY

Consulate: Ocean View, Hodges Bay, POB 1259, St John's; tel 462-3174; telex 2145.
Honorary Consul: Carsten Biel.

UNITED KINGDOM

High Commission: Price Waterhouse Centre, 11 Old Parham Rd, POB 483, St John's; tel 462-0008; telex 2113; fax 462-2806.
First Secretary and Resident Representative: I. D. March.
Third Secretary (Immigration): D. W. Platt.
Third Secretary (Immigration): A. A. Howard.

USA

Embassy: Queen Elizabeth Highway, St John's; tel 462-3505; telex 2140; fax 462-3516.
Political/Economic Section: David L. Gandle.
Commercial Section: Tom Moore.
Administrative Section: Lysbeth J. Rickerman.
Legal Attaché: Paul F. Nolan.

VENEZUELA

Embassy: Cross and Redcliffe Sts, POB 1201, St John's; tel 462-1574; telex 2161; fax 462-1570.
Ambassador: Daniela F. Szokoloczi H.
First Secretary: Alberto Molina Sanchez.

International Organizations

EUROPEAN COMMUNITIES

External Delegation (Sub-Office of Delegation to Barbados): Alpha Bldg, 2nd Floor, Redcliffe St, POB 1392, St John's; tel 462-2970; fax 462-2970.
Resident Adviser: John Simpson.

ARGENTINA

ALBANIA

Embassy: Olazábal 2060, 1428 Buenos Aires; tel (1) 781-7740; telex 22658.
Ambassador: Piro Andoni.

ALGERIA

Embassy: Montevideo 1889, 1021 Buenos Aires; tel (1) 22-1271; telex 22467.
Ambassador: Abdallah Feddal.

AUSTRALIA

Embassy: Swiss Air Bldg, Avda Santa Fé 846, 8°, 1059 Buenos Aires; tel (1) 312-6841; telex 21946; fax (1) 311-1219.
Ambassador: Robert Henry Robertson.
Counsellor: William John Alexander Rigg.
First Secretary: David Jeffrey Schramm.
First Secretary (Consular and Administrative): Paul Christopher Hogan.
First Secretary (Immigration): Jonathan Christian Willoughby-Thomas.
Second Secretary: Gordon Brodrick Matthews.
Second Secretary (Immigration): Paisley Claire Nugent.
Attaché: Thomas Nicholas O'Brien.
Third Secretary (Consular and Administrative): Roberto Gallagher.

AUSTRIA

Embassy: French 3671, Casilla 4889, 1425 Buenos Aires; tel (1) 802-1400; telex 18853; fax (1) 805-4016.
Ambassador: Dr Gerhard Heible.
Counsellor: Dr Rudolf Lennkh.
Counsellor (Administrative Affairs) and Consul: Gertraud Borges da Gama.
Commercial Delegate: Dr Walter Höfle.

Consulate: Jerónimo Cortez 636, 5000 Córdoba; tel (51) 72-0450.
Honorary Consul: Federico Scherzer.

Consulate: Posadas.
Honorary Consul: Lia Elena Dlugoszewski-Breitegger.

Consulate: 24 de Septiembre 230, 8400 San Carlos de Bariloche; tel (944) 24-873; telex 80702.
Honorary Consul: Franz Pirker.

BELGIUM

Embassy: Defensa 113, 8°, 1065 Buenos Aires; tel (1) 331-0066; telex 22070.
Ambassador: Thierry Muuls.

BOLIVIA

Embassy: Corrientes 545, 2°, 1043 Buenos Aires; tel (1) 394-6042; telex 24362.
Ambassador: Agustín Saavedra Weise.

BRAZIL

Embassy: Calle Cerrito 1350, 1007 Buenos Aires; tel (1) 812-0035; telex 21158; fax (1) 814-4035.
Ambassador: Francisco Thompson-Flôres Netto.
Minister-Counsellor: Luciano Ozorio Rosa.
Minister (Economic Affairs): Jayro Coelho.
Counsellor and Head of Political Sector: Carlos Alfredo Lazary Teixeira.
Counsellor and Head of Economic and Finance Sector: Carlos Eduardo Sette Câmara da Fonseca Costa.
Counsellor and Head of Trade Promotion Sector: Antônio José Maria de Souza e Silva.
Counsellor and Head of Cultural Sector: Maria da Graça Nunes Carrion.
First Secretary and Head of Science and Technology Sector: Durval Carvalho de Barros.
Second Secretary and Head of Administrative Sector: Francisco Carlos Soares Luz.

Consulate-General: Carlos Pellegrini 1363, 5°; tel (1) 394-5227; telex 21158.
Consul-General: Roberto Soares-de-Oliveira.

BULGARIA

Embassy: Manuel Obarrio 2967, 1425 Buenos Aires; tel (1) 802-9251; telex 21314.
Ambassador: Parvan Alexandrov Chernev.

CANADA

Embassy: Edif. Brunetta 25°, Suipacha 1111, Casilla 1598, Suipacha and Santa Fé, 1368 Buenos Aires; tel (1) 312-9081; telex 21383; fax (1) 312-9775.
Ambassador: Clayton G. Bullis.
Counsellor (Commercial and Economic): G. M. Kostyrsky.
Counsellor and Consul: R. Beaulieu.

Counsellor (Immigration) and Consul: B. K. LeConte.
First Secretary and Consul: D. E. Gillett.
Second Secretary (Commercial): G. Harquail.
Second Secretary (Administration): G. Ogaick.
Third Secretary (Immigration) and Vice-Consul: S. Wiebe.

Commercial Office: Casilla 3898.

CHILE

Embassy: Tagle 2762, 1425 Buenos Aires; tel (1) 802-7020; telex 21669.
Ambassador: Carlos Figueroa Serrano.

CHINA, PEOPLE'S REPUBLIC

Embassy: Avda Crisólogo Larralde 5349, 1425 Buenos Aires; tel (1) 543-8862; telex 22871.
Ambassador: Li Guoxin.

COLOMBIA

Embassy: Avda Santa Fé 782, 1°, 1059 Buenos Aires; tel (1) 325-0258; telex 22254.
Ambassador: Hernando Pastrana Borrero.

COSTA RICA

Embassy: Lavalle 507, 4°, 1048 Buenos Aires; tel (1) 325-6022; telex 21394.
Ambassador: Fernando Salazar Navarrete.

COTE D'IVOIRE

Embassy: Ugarteche 3069, 1425 Buenos Aires; tel (1) 802-3982.
Ambassador: Gaston Ouassenan Kone.

CUBA

Embassy: Virrey del Pino 1810, 1426 Buenos Aires; tel (1) 782-9049; telex 22433.
Ambassador: Santiago Díaz Paz.

CZECHOSLOVAKIA

Embassy: Figueroa Alcorta 3240, 1425 Buenos Aires; tel (1) 801-3804; telex 22748.
Ambassador: Jaroslav Pavlicek.

DENMARK

Embassy: Avda Leandro N. Alem 1074, 1001 Buenos Aires; tel (1) 312-6901; telex 22173; fax (1) 312-7857.
Ambassador: Karl-Frederik Hasle.
Secretary: Lisbeth Arne Pedersen.
Attaché and Consul: Jørn P. Andersen.
Consul-General and Honorary Counsellor: Dr Oscar Cuper.
Social Attaché: Pastor Steen Lerfeldt.

Consulate: Calle 1, Muelle Carga General 8103, Ing. White, Casilla 335, 8000 Bahía Blanca, Prov. de Buenos Aires; tel (91) 71-590; telex 81861; fax (91) 70-653.
Consul: Arturo Cesar Hosch.

Consulate: Calle 51 1840, 7630 Necochea, Prov. de Buenos Aires; tel (262) 22-982.
Consul: Birgitte Sally Andersen.

Consulate: Sarratea 450, 2000 Rosario, Prov. de Santa Fé; tel (41) 81-5295; telex 41540.
Consul: Mogens Christian Christensen.

Consulate: Avda Moreno 114, of. 10, 7500 Tres Arroyos, Prov. de Buenos Aires; tel (983) 26-286.
Consul: Poul Petersen Dam.
Vice-Consul: Edvard Sønderup Dam.

DOMINICAN REPUBLIC

Embassy: Avda Santa Fé 1206, 2°, 1059 Buenos Aires; tel (1) 41-4669; fax (1) 361-6298.
Ambassador: Dr Victor Gómez Borges.
Minister-Counsellor and Consul-General: Marilyn Baloguer de Tortecolo.
Attaché: Dr Giancarlo Hernández.
Medical Attaché: Dr Milogros Almonte Alonso.
Administrative Assistant (Consular): Georgina Santiago.
Secretary (Consular): Cristina Melo Stoczkac.

EGYPT

Embassy: Juez Tedín 2795, 1425 Buenos Aires; tel (1) 801-6145.
Ambassador: Hassan I. Abdel Hadi.

EL SALVADOR

Embassy: Avda Santa Fé 882, 12° 'A', 1059 Buenos Aires; tel (1) 311-1864; fax (1) 311-1864.
Ambassador: Manuel Arturo Calderon.
Consul: Mauricio Suárez Escalante.

FINLAND

Embassy: Avda Santa Fé 846, 5°, 1059 Buenos Aires; tel (1) 312-0600; telex 21702; fax (1) 312-0670.
Ambassador: Pertti A. O. Kärkkäinen.

Consulate: Bv. Chacabuco 716, 5000 Cordoba; tel (51) 60-5049; telex 51988; fax (51) 69-0232.
Consul: Fulvio Salvador Pagani.

Consulate: Boulogne sur Mer 631, 5500 Mendoza; tel (61) 97-3844; telex 55285; fax (61) 97-3737.
Consul: Carlos Alberto Pulenta.

Consulate: Gobernador Barreyro 947, 3360 Oberá, Misiones; tel (755) 81-153.
Consul: Hugo E. Sand.

Consulate: Sarmiento 819, 2000 Rosario, Santa Fé; tel (41) 44-900; telex 41856.
Consul: Jorge Weskamp.

Consulate: Gobernador Paz 1569, 9410 Ushuaia, Terr. Nac., Tierra del Fuego; tel (901) 22-122; telex 88624.
Consul: Gustavo Adelfo Giro.

FRANCE

Embassy: Cerrito 1399, 1010 Buenos Aires; tel (1) 393-1071.
Ambassador: Pierre Guidoni.

Economic Section: telex 24300.

Consulate-General: Avda Santa Fé 846, 1059 Buenos Aires; tel (1) 312-2409.

GABON

Embassy: Avda Figueroa Alcorta 3221, 1425 Buenos Aires; tel (1) 393-1071; telex 18577.
Ambassador: J.-B. Eyi-Nkoumou.

GERMANY

Embassy: Villanueva 1055, Casilla 2979, 1426 Buenos Aires; tel (1) 771-5054; telex 21668; fax (1) 775-9612.
Ambassador: Dr Herbert Limmer.

Consulate: Calle Ambrosio Olmos 501, Casilla 283, 5000 Córdoba; tel (51) 33-962; telex 51876.
Consul: Hans-Dietrich Bernhard.

Consulate: Avda General San Martin 3552, Casilla 301, 3380 Eldorado, Misiones; tel (751) 21-632.
Honorary Consul: Frithjof Weström.

Consulate: Formosa 550, Casilla 1375, 7600 Mar del Plata; tel (23) 51-3053; telex 39960.
Honorary Consul: Dr Joachim Werner.

Consulate: Calle Montevideo 127, 1°, Dept. 6, 5500 Mendoza; tel (61) 24-2539.
Honorary Consul: Frederico Werner Hilbing.

Consulate: Córdoba 2251, 3300 Posadas, Misiones; tel (752) 30-508.
Honorary Consul: Dr Roland Kegler.

Consulate: Saavedra 185, 3500 Resistencia, Prov. Chaco; tel (722) 22-269; telex 41855.
Honorary Consul: Werner Nothardt.

Consulate: Córdoba 1437, 5°, of. 3, Casilla 225, 2000 Rosario; tel (41) 66-546.
Honorary Consul: Rodolfo Herfarth.

Consulate: Gral Gülmes 1156, Casilla 7, 4400 Salta; tel (87) 22-0916.
Honorary Consul: Walter Gutbrod.

Consulate: Ruiz Moreno 65, 8400 San Carlos de Bariloche, Rió Negro; tel (944) 25-695; telex 80728.
Honorary Consul: Jorge Borchert.

Consulate: Rivadavia 105, of. 311, Casilla 109, 4000 San Miguel de Tucumán; tel (81) 21-9102.*Honorary Consul:* Francisco Steinmetz.

Consulate: Tucumán 3828, 3000 Santa Fé; tel (42) 40-225.
Honorary Consul: Carlos Enrique Meissner.

Consulate: Triunvirato 516, 9410 Ushuaia; tel (901) 22-778.
Honorary Consul: Rodolfo Wantz.

GREECE

Embassy: Avda Pte Roque Sáenz Peña 547, 4°, 1035 Buenos Aires; tel (1) 34-0528; telex 22102.
Ambassador: Apostolos D. Anninos.
Counsellor: Georges Papadopoulos.
Naval Attaché: Capt. Nicolaos Kypriadakis.
First Secretary and Head of Consular Office: Eleftherios Kouvaritakis.

GUATEMALA

Embassy: Avda Santa Fé 830, 5°, 1059 Buenos Aires; tel (1) 313-9180; fax (1) 313-9180.
Ambassador: Leslie Mishaan de Kirkvoorde.

HAITI

Embassy: Avda Figueroa Alcorta 3297, 1425 Buenos Aires; tel (1) 802-0211.
Ambassador: Frank Paul.

HOLY SEE

Apostolic Nunciature: Avda Alvear 1605, 1014 Buenos Aires; tel (1) 742-9697; telex 17406; fax (1) 742-1109.
Apostolic Pro-Nuncio: Mgr Ubaldo Calabresi.
Secretary: Claudio Mondino.

HONDURAS

Embassy: Avda Santa Fé 1385, 4°, 1059 Buenos Aires; tel (1) 42-1643; telex 18008.
Ambassador: Edgardo Paz Barnica.

HUNGARY

Embassy: Coronel Díaz 1874, 1425 Buenos Aires; tel (1) 824-5845; telex 22843; fax (1) 805-3918.
Ambassador: László Major.
Counsellor and Consul: Tamás Toth.
Economic Counsellor: Miklós Bányai.

ICELAND

Consulate-General: San Martin 320, 1004 Buenos Aires; tel (1) 325-8303; telex 23792; fax (1) 325-8304.
Consul-General: Walter R. Koltonski.
Consul: Daniel Koltonski.

INDIA

Embassy: Córdoba 950, 4°, 1054 Buenos Aires; tel (1) 393-4001; telex 23413; fax (1) 393-4063.
Ambassador: A. N. Ram.
First Secretary: S. Rajagopalan.
Second Secretary: K. K. Sachdev.

Third Secretary: A. M. Padar.
Attaché: Dilbag Singh.
Attaché: G. D. Ratti.
Attaché: S. Venkataraman.

INDONESIA

Embassy: M. Ramón Castilla 2901, 1425 Buenos Aires; tel (1) 801-6622; telex 21781.
Ambassador: Pudisanto Sadarjoen.

IRAN

Embassy: Figueroa Alcorta 3229, 1425 Buenos Aires; tel (1) 802-1470; telex 21288.
Ambassador: Hossein Tajgardon.

IRAQ

Embassy: Villanueva 1400, 1426 Buenos Aires; tel (1) 771-5620; telex 17134.
Ambassador: Sahib Hussain Tahir.

IRELAND

Embassy: Suipacha 1380, 2°, 1008 Buenos Aires; tel (1) 325-0849; telex 17654; fax (1) 325-7572.
Ambassador: Bernard Davenport.
Secretary: Jacqueline O'Halloran.

ISRAEL

Embassy: Arroyo 916, 1007 Buenos Aires; tel (1) 325-2502; telex 17106.
Ambassador: Itshak Shefi.

ITALY

Embassy: Billinghurst 2577, 1425 Buenos Aires; tel (1) 802-0071; telex 21961.
Ambassador: Ludovico Incisa di Camerana.

JAMAICA

Consulate: Avda Corrientes 127, 4°, Suites 407-8, Buenos Aires; tel (1) 311-4872.
Honorary Consul: G. Uhlfelder.
Honorary Vice-Consul: R. Uhlfelder.

JAPAN

Embassy: Avda Paseo Colón 275, 9°, 1063 Buenos Aires; tel (1) 30-2561; telex 22516; fax (1) 334-5203.
Ambassador: Agustin Yoshio Fujimoto.

KOREA, REPUBLIC

Embassy: Avda Libertador 2257, 1425 Buenos Aires; tel (1) 802-9665; telex 22294.
Ambassador: Sang Chin Lee.

LEBANON

Embassy: Avda Libertador 2354, 1425 Buenos Aires; tel (1) 801-7267; telex 22866.
Ambassador: Jihad Mortada.

LIBYA

Embassy: Alejandro M. de Aguado 2885, 1425 Buenos Aires; tel (1) 801-7267; telex 22682.
Ambassador: Gibreel Mansoury.

MALAYSIA

Embassy: Sheraton Hotel, 20°, San Martín 1225, 1104 Buenos Aires; tel (1) 311-6311.
Ambassador: Hee K. Hor.

MEXICO

Embassy: Larrea 1230, 1117 Buenos Aires; tel (1) 826-2161; telex 21869.
Ambassador: Jesús Puente Leyva.

MOROCCO

Embassy: Calle Mariscal Ramón Castilla No. 2952, 1425 Buenos Aires; tel (1) 801-8154; telex 18161.
Ambassador: Mohammed Boucetta.

NETHERLANDS

Embassy: Edif. Holanda 2°, Maipú 66, 1084 Buenos Aires; tel (1) 331-6066; telex 21824.
Ambassador: Schelto van Heemistar.

NEW ZEALAND

Consulate: Echeverria 2140, Buenos Aires; tel (1) 787-0593; fax (1) 787-0593.
Honorary Consul: Arturo Mayer.

NICARAGUA

Embassy: Villanueva 1080, 1426 Buenos Aires; tel (1) 772-2268; telex 23481.
Ambassador: Ariel Ramón Granera Sacasa.

NIGERIA

Embassy: 11 de Setiembre 839, 1426 Buenos Aires; tel (1) 771-6541; telex 23565.
Ambassador: Okon Edet Uya.

NORWAY

Embassy: Esmerelda 909, 3°, 1007 Buenos Aires; Casilla 2286, Correo Central, 1000 Buenos Aires; tel (1) 312-1904; telex 22811.
Chargé d'affaires: Dr Lars Vaagen.

PAKISTAN

Embassy: 3 de Febrero 1326, 1426 Buenos Aires; tel (1) 782-7398; telex 19032.
Ambassador: Raja Tridiv Roy.
First Secretary: Iftikhar Hussein Kazmi.

PANAMA

Embassy: Avda Santa Fé 1461, 5°, 1019 Buenos Aires; tel (1) 42-8543.
Ambassador: María Esther Villalaz de Arias.

PARAGUAY

Embassy: Las Heras 2545, 1425 Buenos Aires; tel (1) 802-4948; telex 21687.
Ambassador: Miguel Bestard.

PERU

Embassy: Avda Libertador 1720, 1425 Buenos Aires; tel (1) 802-6824; telex 17807.
Ambassador: Alfonso Grados Bertorini.

PHILIPPINES

Embassy: Juramento 1945, 1428 Buenos Aires; tel (1) 781-4170.
Ambassador: Sime D. Hidalgo.

POLAND

Embassy: Alejandro María de Aguado 2870, 1425 Buenos Aires; tel (1) 802-9681.
Ambassador: Janusz Bałewski.

PORTUGAL

Embassy: Córdoba 3154, 3°, 1054 Buenos Aires; tel (1) 311-2586; telex 22736.
Ambassador: António Baptista Martins.

ROMANIA

Embassy: Arroyo 962, 1007 Buenos Aires; tel (1) 393-0883; telex 24301.
Ambassador: Muntean Mihail.

RUSSIA

Embassy: Avda Rodríguez Peña 1741, 1021 Buenos Aires; tel (1) 42-1552; telex 22147.
Ambassador: Vladimir V. Nikitin.

SAN MARINO

Consulate-General: Parana 791, 6° B, 1017 Buenos Aires; tel (1) 46-9057.
Consul-General: Carlo Maria Busignani.

SAUDI ARABIA

Embassy: Alejandro María de Aguado 2881, 1425 Buenos Aires; tel (1) 802-4735; telex 23291.
Ambassador: Fuad A. Nazir.

SOUTH AFRICA

Consulate: Avda Marcelo T. de Alvear 590-8°, Buenos Aires; tel (1) 311-8991; telex 24549; fax (1) 111-475.
Vice-Consul: P. R. Dietrichsen.
Vice-Consul: M. van Dyk.
Vice-Consul: P. J. R. G. Maassen.
Vice-Consul: J. M. Nieman.
Vice-Consul (Administration): H. J. Swanepoel.
Vice-Consul (Maritime): R. A. S. Hauter.
Vice-Consul (Trade): W. W. Mentz.
Vice-Consul (Trade): S. G. S. Kruger.
Vice-Consul (Agriculture): Dr. J. Grobbelaar.

Consulate: Carrero Patagonico 2915, 9000 Comodoro Rivadavia, Chubut; tel 26-195.
Honorary Vice-Consul: M. Blackie.

SPAIN

Embassy: Mariscal Ramón Castilla 2720, 1425 Buenos Aires; tel (1) 802-6031; telex 21660.
Ambassador: Raimundo Bassols Jacas.

SWEDEN

Embassy: Corrientes 330, 3°, 1378 Buenos Aires; Casilla 3599, Correo Central, 1000 Buenos Aires; tel (1) 311-3080; telex 21340; fax (1) 311-8052.
Ambassador: Anders Sandström.
Counsellor: John-Olof Dahlstein.
Second Secretary: Britt Ericsson de Oliva.
Second Secretary: Ewa Polano.
Chancellor: Olga Marta Persson-Linde.

Consulate: Avda Marcelo T. de Alvear 10, 5000 Córdoba; tel (51) 24-0086; telex 51906; fax (51) 24-0111.
Consul: Jorge Osvaldo García Velazco.

Consulate: Calle Gustavo Erasmie 131, 3360 Oberá, Misiones; tel (755) 21-003.
Consul: Gunnar Erik Wilhelm Erasmie.

Consulate: Avda Islas Malvinas, Ruta Provincial 302, Km 11, Colombres, 4000 San Miguel de Tucumán, Dep. Cruz Alta; Casilla 3, Correo Central, 4000 San Miguel de Tucumán; tel (81) 26-0455; telex 61105; fax (81) 31-1748.
Consul: Anders Spåre.

SWITZERLAND

Embassy: Avda Santa Fé 846, 12°, 1059 Buenos Aires; Casilla 4895, Correo Central, 1000 Buenos Aires; tel (1) 311-6491; telex 22418; fax (1) 313-2998.
Ambassador: Dr Karl Fritschi.
Counsellor (Economic Affairs): Robert Reich.
Third Secretary: Ivana Bezucha.
Attaché and Head of Chancery: Yvonne Daucourt.

Consulate: Rioja 1474, 1°, 2000 Rosario de Santa Fé; Casilla 766, Correo Central, 2000 Rosario de Santa Fé; tel (41) 67-272; telex 41429.
Honorary Consul: Marcelo J. Martin.

SYRIA

Embassy: Calloa 956, 1023 Buenos Aires; tel (1) 42-2113.

Ambassador: Abdul Hassib Itswani.

THAILAND

Embassy: Virrey del Pino 2458, 6°, 1426 Buenos Aires; tel (1) 785-6504; fax (1) 785-654.
Ambassador: Vichien Chatsuwan.

TURKEY

Embassy: Juez Tedín 2728, 1425 Buenos Aires; tel (1) 802-3676; telex 21135.
Ambassador: Sekih Belen.

UNITED KINGDOM

Embassy: Dr Luis Agote 2412, Casilla 2050, 1425 Buenos Aires; tel (1) 803-7070; fax (1) 803-1731.
Ambassador: Humphrey Maud.
Deputy Head of Mission: L. G. Faulkner.
Defence Attaché: Group Capt. P. S. E. Tootal.
Military Attaché: Col J. G. Neeve.
Consul: R. J. A. Golland.
Cultural Attaché (British Council Director): H. Fish.
First Secretary (Commercial): M. H. McIntosh.
Second Secretary (Economic): E. C. Evans.
Second Secretary (Chancery): E. M. Scholes.
Second Secretary (Information): J. M. Ingamells.
Second Secretary (Works): D. M. Corfield.
Second Secretary (Management) and Vice-Consul: A. Greatrix.

USA

Embassy: Avda Colombia 4300, Palermo, 1425 Buenos Aires; tel (1) 774-7611; telex 18156; fax (1) 775-4205.
Ambassador: Terence A. Todman.
Deputy Chief of Mission: James D. Walsh.
Political Section: Donald R. Knight.
Economic Section: James M. Derham.
Commercial Section: Rafael Fermoselle.
Consular Section: Barbara Hemingway.
Administrative Section: Bernardo Segura Giron.
Regional Security Officer: Victor G. Dewindt, Jr.
Public Affairs Officer: Ernesto Uribe.
Communications Programme Officer: Robert N. Mansfield.
Information Systems Manager: Vincent J. Ryan.
Scientific Attaché: Paul C. Maxwell.
Office of the Defence Attaché: Col Kenneth J. Monroe.
Military Group: Col George A. Carpenter.
Agricultural Section: Marvin L. Lehrer.
Labour Officer: Donald R. Knight.

URUGUAY

Embassy: Avda Las Heras 1907, 1127 Buenos Aires; tel (1) 803-6030; telex 25526.
Ambassador: Adolfo Castells Mendivil.

VENEZUELA

Embassy: Avda Santa Fé 1461, 2°/7°, 1060 Buenos Aires; tel (1) 442-0033; telex 21089; fax (1) 111-2310.
Ambassador: Reinaldo Leandro R.
Minister-Counsellor: Clemente Segovia.
Counsellor: Luis Perez Velasquez.
Second Secretary: Paul Simon Hernandez Gomez.
First Attaché: Lautaro Ovalles.
Second Attaché: Beatriz Rojas.
Third Attaché: Aura Dubuc Araujo.

Consulate-General: Esmeralda 909, 4°, 1007 Buenos Aires; tel (1) 311-0450.
First Consul-General: Basilio Quiñones P.
Second Consul-General: Samuel Almosny B.

YUGOSLAVIA

Embassy: Marcelo T. de Alvear 1705, 1060 Buenos Aires; tel (1) 41-2860; telex 21479.
Ambassador: Rudolf Hazuran.

ZAIRE

Embassy: Calle Villanueva 1356, 2°, Casilla 5589, 1426 Buenos Aires; tel (1) 771-0075; telex 22324.
Ambassador: Bavassa ba Maduka.
Minister-Counsellor Plenipotentiary: Omadikandja Kandula.
Second Counsellor: Siongo Luambo.
Attaché: Ngabu Ndolumingu.

ARMENIA

FRANCE

Embassy: Yerevan.

USA

Embassy: Yerevan.
Ambassador: Nelson Ledsky.

AUSTRALIA

ALGERIA

Embassy: 3 Stromlo Park, Crowder St, Stirling, ACT 2611; tel (6) 288-0628.
Chargé d'affaires a.i.: Abdelkader Boutaine.

ARGENTINA

Embassy: MLC Tower, Suite 102, 1st Floor, POB 262, Woden, Canberra, ACT 2606; tel (6) 282-4555; telex 62195; fax (6) 285-3062.
Ambassador: Dr Juan Carlos Beltramino.
Counsellor: Fernando Segre-Carman.
First Secretary: Angel Villanueva Moure.

Consulate-General: Suite 6, Level 30 Northpoint, 100 Miller St, North Sydney, NSW 2060; tel (2) 922-7272; telex 70751; fax (2) 923-1798.
Consul-General: Carlos Eduardo Rospide.
Consul: Eduardo A. Varela.

Commercial Office: Suite 195, Level 19, 1 York St, Sydney, NSW 2000; POB N37, Grosvenor St, Sydney, NSW 2000; tel (2) 241-1571; telex 27846; fax (2) 251-4963.
Consul (Commercial): Carlos Abel Martese.

AUSTRIA

Embassy: 12 Talbot St, Forrest, Canberra, ACT 2603; POB 3375, Manuka, ACT 2603; tel (6) 295-1376; telex 62726; fax (6) 239-6751.
Ambassador: Dr Walter Hietsch.
Counsellor (Administration): Eva-Maria Moss-Mottl.

Consulate-General: 2 Kingsland Rd, Bexley, Sydney, NSW 2207; tel (2) 567-1008; telex 26100; fax (2) 597-4587.
Honorary Consul-General: Luis Hupfau.
Honorary Consul: Nicholas Michael Stead.

Commercial Office: 19th Floor, 1 York St, Sydney, NSW 2000; tel (2) 247-8581; telex 24641; fax (2) 251-1038.
Consul (Commercial): Dr Heinz Seitinger.

Consulate: Suite 2, 30 Argyle St, Breakfast Creek, Brisbane, Queensland 4010; POB 357, Albion, Brisbane, Queensland 4010; tel (7) 262-8955; fax (7) 262-8082.
Honorary Consul: David Macalister Henderson.

Consulate: 95 Lefevre Terrace, POB 25, North Adelaide, South Australia 5006; tel (8) 267-5748; fax (8) 239-0714.
Honorary Consul: Dr Peter Steidl.

Consulate-General: 1st Floor, 897 High St, Armadale, Melbourne, Victoria 3143; POB 219, Armadale, Melbourne, Victoria 3143; tel (3) 509-0360.
Honorary Consul-General: Alexander T. Simon.

Consulate: 8th Floor, 95 St George's Terrace, Perth, Western Australia 6000; POB 7216, Cloisters Square, Perth, Western Australia 6000; tel (9) 481-3622.
Honorary Consul: Timothy Alastair Holmes.

BANGLADESH

High Commission: 11 Molineaux Place, Farrer, Canberra, ACT 2607; POB 197, Mawson, ACT 2607; tel (6) 286-1200; telex 61729; fax (6) 286-1400.
High Commissioner: Air Vice-Marshal (retd) Sultan Mahmud.
Counsellor: Mohammed Farooq.
Counsellor (Press): Abdul Matin.
Second Secretary: Golam Mohammad.

Consulate-General: Suite 303, 40 Miller St, North Sydney, NSW 2060; tel (2) 954-4256; telex 176182.
Consul-General: S. M. Rashed Ahmed.
Consul (Commercial): Tajuddin Ahmed Khondkar.

BARBADOS

Consulate-General: 49th Floor, MLC Centre, Martin Place, Sydney, NSW 2000; tel (2) 238-2216.
Honorary Consul-General: John William Cunningham.

Consulate: Singapore Airlines House, 1st Floor, 414 Collins St, Melbourne, Victoria 3000; POB 388D, Melbourne, Victoria 3001; tel (3) 605-2538.
Honorary Consul: John MacKinnon.

BELGIUM

Embassy: 19 Arkana St, Yarralumla, ACT 2600; tel (6) 273-2501; telex 62601; fax (6) 273-3392.
Ambassador: Dr Jacques Scavée (designate).
Counsellor: Nancy Rossignol.

Consulate-General: 12A Trelawney St, Woollahra, Sydney, NSW 2025; tel (2) 327-8377; telex 25671; fax (2) 327-8386.
Consul-General: Luc K. W. Teirlinck.
Vice-Consul: Genevieve Pearson-Verbeek.
Vice-Consul (Commercial): Hubert Cooleman.

Consulate: 12 Brookes St, Bowen Hills, Brisbane, Queensland 4006; POB 1130, Fortitude Valley, Brisbane, Queensland 4006; tel (7) 854-1920; fax (7) 854-1705.
Honorary Consul: Lester T. Padman.

Consulate: Commonwealth Banking Corporation, 4th Floor, 96 King William St, Adelaide, South Australia 5000; tel (8) 206-4211; fax (8) 206-4134.
Honorary Consul: John Edward Newland.

Consulate: 45-71 Bathurst St, Hobart, Tasmania 7000; POB 1358P, Hobart, Tasmania 7001; tel (02) 34-7666; fax (02) 31-0327.
Honorary Consul: Graham Woodward.

Consulate: Fawkner Centre, 5th Floor, 499 St Kilda Rd, Melbourne, Victoria 3004; tel (3) 867-4966; telex 25671; fax (3) 820-9568.
Vice-Consul (Commercial): Alexandre Somers.

Consulate: 16 St George's Terrace, St George's Court, Perth, Western Australia 6000; tel (9) 325-4233; fax (9) 221-3554.
Honorary Consul: Lucien Baee.
Vice-Consul (Commercial): Jacques Raoul Bury.

Consulate: 98 Wood St, Darwin, Northern Territory 0800; POB 2140, Darwin, Northern Territory 0801; tel (89) 81-8848; fax (89) 41-1364.
Honorary Consul: Peter Martin Barr.

BOLIVIA

Consulate: 2nd Floor, Gemini House, 65 Belmore Rd, Randwick, Sydney, NSW 2031; tel (2) 398-4311; fax (2) 398-9708.
Honorary Consul: Antonio Moron Nava.

Consulate-General: 5th Floor, Penneys Bldg, 210 Queen St, Brisbane, Queensland 4000; POB 53, Brisbane, Queensland 4001; tel (7) 221-1606; fax (7) 229-7175.
Honorary Consul-General: Allan Campbell.

Consulate: 23 Nitschke St, Elizabeth Grove, Adelaide, Southern Australia 5108; POB 795, Salisbury, Adelaide, Southern Australia 5108; tel (8) 255-9744.
Honorary Consul: Juan Carlos Roncal Rodriguez.

BRAZIL

Embassy: 19 Forster Crescent, Yarralumla, Canberra, ACT 2600; GPO Box 1540, Canberra City, ACT 2601; tel (6) 273-2372; telex 62327; fax (6) 273-2375.
Ambassador: Marcos Henrique Camillo Côrtes.
First Secretary: Matias A. S. Vilhena.
Second Secretary and Head of Chancery: Paulo Medeiros.

Consulate: AMP Centre, 16th Floor, 50 Bridge St, Sydney, NSW 2000; tel (2) 231-5077; telex 122337.
Vice-Consul: Sergio de Moraes Ramos.

BRUNEI

High Commission: 16 Bulwarra Close, O'Malley, ACT 2606; tel (6) 290-1801; telex 61216; fax (6) 290-1832.
High Commissioner: Dato Paduka Haji Abdullah Haji Mohamad Jaafar.
First Secretary: Mrs Pengiran Basmillah Pengiran Haji Abbas.
Second Secretary: Mr Sulia Haji Nayan.
Third Secretary (Administration and Finance): Haji Abdul Majid Haji Abdul Hamid.
Third Secretary (Consular): Haji Mohamad Noor Haji Badarudin.

BULGARIA

Consulate-General: Unit 2, 4 Carlotta Rd, Double Bay, Sydney, NSW 2028; tel (2) 327-7581; telex 27755; fax (2) 327-8067.
Consul-General: Stoil Krentchev.
Consul: Kapka Voutchkova.
Vice-Consul: Ilia Terziev.

Commercial Office: 1/4 Carlotta Rd, Double Bay, Sydney, NSW 2028; tel (2) 327-4440.
Consul (Commercial): Boris Tanushev.

CANADA

High Commission: Commonwealth Ave, Canberra, ACT 2600; tel (6) 273-3844; telex 62017; fax (6) 273-3285.
High Commissioner: R. Allen Kilpatrick.
Deputy High Commissioner: Nicholas H. R. Etheridge.
Counsellor (Commercial and Economic): Graham Lochhead.
Counsellor (Agriculture and Fisheries): David A. Roberts.
Counsellor: Marc Cousineau.
Forces Adviser: Col W. R. Kirkwood.
First Secretary (Consular and Administration): Edward J. Laughren.
First Secretary: Joseph A. Makin.
First Secretary: Gregory D. Pattinson.

Consulate: 6th Floor, 1 Collins St, Melbourne, Victoria 3000; tel (3) 654-1433; telex 30501; fax (3) 650-5939.
Consul and Senior Trade Commissioner: Graham B. Rush.

Consulate-General: 8th Floor, AMP Centre, 50 Bridge St, Sydney, NSW 2000; tel (2) 231-6522; telex 20600; fax (2) 223-4230.
Consul-General: Roger B. Blake.
Consul and Senior Trade Commissioner: P. W. Bélanger.
Consul (Immigration): T. M. Ryan.
Consul and Trade Commissioner: B. C. Cox.

Consulate: 11th Floor, National Mutual Centre, 111 St George's Terrace, Perth, Western Australia 6000; tel (9) 322-7930; fax (9) 321-1151.
Honorary Consul: Jeannie Lyall.

CHILE

Embassy: 10 Culgoa Circuit, O'Malley, ACT 2606; POB 69, Monaro Crescent, ACT 2603; tel (6) 286-2430; telex 62685; fax (6) 286-1289.
Ambassador: Juan Salazar Sparks.
Counsellor: Jorge Dupouy.
First Secretary: Alfredo Garcia.
Second Secretary: Enrique Barriga.

Consulate-General: Level 24, National Mutual Centre, 44 Market St, Sydney, NSW 2000; tel (2) 299-2533; telex 72440.
Consul-General: Felipe du Monceau de Bergendal.
Honorary Consul: Albert P. Cramley.

Commercial Office: tel (2) 299-2770; fax (2) 299-2868.
Consul (Commercial): Marcelo Salas.

Consulate: 26 St Leonard's St, Coorparoo, Brisbane, Queensland 4151; tel (7) 847-1122.
Honorary Consul: Raquel Sanhueza Redmond.

Consulate-General: Level 43, Nauru House, 80 Collins St, Melbourne, Victoria 3000; POB 1674N, Melbourne, Victoria 3001; tel (3) 654-4479; fax (3) 650-8290.
Consul-General: Celso Moreno.

Consulate: 33 Grant St, Cottesloe, Perth, Western Australia 6011; tel (9) 328-7877.
Honorary Consul: Leo Gatica-Evans.

CHINA, PEOPLE'S REPUBLIC

Embassy: 15 Coronation Drive, Yarralumla, ACT 2600; tel (6) 273-4780; telex 62489; fax (6) 273-4878.
Ambassador: Shi Chunlai.
Counsellor: Liang Jianming.
Defence Attaché: Maj.-Gen. Yu Jianzhong.
Counsellor (Commercial): Guo Yimin.
Counsellor (Scientific): Yuan Zhongli.
Counsellor (Education): Cai Peiyi.
Counsellor (Consular): Wang Wenzhu.
Counsellor (Cultural): Lou Xiaoyan.
First Secretary (Consular): Ni Zhuocheng.
First Secretary (Scientific): Zhao Xucai.
First Secretary: Zheng Hekang.
First Secretary (Commercial): Zheng Yongmian.
First Secretary: Wu Ronghe.
First Secretary: Xie Jue.
First Secretary: Liu Huanxing.
Deputy Defence Attaché: Wang Zhiyong.

Cultural Office: 6 Terrigal Crescent, O'Malley, ACT 2606; tel (6) 286-2465.

Education Office: 2 Dalman Crescent, O'Malley, ACT 2606; tel (6) 286-4351.

Consulate-General: 539 Elizabeth St, Surry Hills, Sydney, NSW 2010; tel (2) 698-7373; telex 27931; fax (2) 319-2430.
Consul-General: Xu Guangjian.
Deputy Consul-General: Wu Hanquan.
Consul (Science and Technology): Song Guangyao.
Consul (Commercial): Cai Wenju.
Consul (Education): Gao Liqun.
Consul (Administrative): Li Xiufeng.

Consulate-General: 75-77 Irving Rd, Toorak, Melbourne, Victoria 3142; tel (3) 822-0605; telex 135026; fax (3) 822-0320.
Deputy Consul-General: Yang Chong.
Deputy Consul-General: Keshan Ruan.
Consul (Cultural): Li Dongwen.
Consul (Education): Zhou Qun.
Consul (Education): Dai Chengtai.

COLOMBIA

Embassy: 2nd Floor, 101 Northbourne Ave, Turner, POB 2892, Canberra City, ACT 2601; tel (6) 257-2027; telex 62055; fax (6) 257-1448.
Ambassador: Dr Antonio Puerto.
First Secretary: Guillermo Mejía Castillo.

Consulate-General: 5th Floor, 220 Pacific Highway, POB 1322, Crows Nest, Sydney, NSW 2065; tel (2) 955-0311; fax (2) 922-6688.
Consul-General: Dr Ciro Arévalo Yepes.

Consulate: c/o 37th Level, South Tower, Rialto, 525 Collins St, Melbourne, Victoria 3000; tel (3) 629-1722; fax (3) 614-6972.
Honorary Consul: Michael Hamson.

COSTA RICA

Consulate-General: 11th Floor, de la Sala House, 30 Clarence St, Sydney, NSW 2000; POB 2513, Sydney, NSW 2001; tel (2) 261-1177; telex 20275; fax (2) 261-2953.
Honorary Consul: Robert Perez de Lasala.

CUBA

Consulate-General: Suite 804, 9/13 Bronte Rd, POB 625, Bondi Junction, Sydney, NSW 2022; tel (2) 389-0966; telex 26823.
Consul-General: Francisco A. Marchante Castellano.

CYPRUS

High Commission: 37 Endeavour St, Red Hill, Canberra, ACT 2603; tel (6) 295-2120; telex 62499; fax (6) 295-2892.
High Commissioner: Andreas Pirishis.
Second Secretary: Stavrakis Loizides.
Attaché (Press): Michalis Andreou.
Attaché (Administration): Michael Michael.

Consulate-General: 280 Sir Fred Schonell Drive, St Lucia, Brisbane, Queensland 4067; POB 156, Kenmore, Brisbane, Queensland 4069; tel (7) 371-5105; fax (7) 870-3466.
Honorary Consul-General: Constantine M. Philippides.
Honorary Vice-Consul: Anthe I. Philippides.

CZECHOSLOVAKIA

Embassy: 47 Culgoa Circuit, O'Malley, ACT 2606; tel (6) 290-1516; telex 61807.
Ambassador: Dr Peter Kadlec.
First Secretary: Dr Jan Dufek.
Second Secretary: Petr Sedláček.
Attaché: Tomas Krejčí.

Consulate-General: 169 Military Rd, Dover Heights, Sydney, NSW 2030; tel (2) 371-8878; telex 171091; fax (2) 371-9635.
Consul-General: Josef Sládek.
Consul: Dr Viera Jaresová.

Commercial Office: Level 20, Suite 2001B, Bondi Junction Plaza 2, 500 Oxford St, Bondi Junction, NSW 2022; tel (2) 369-1091; telex 20655; fax (2) 387-1083.
Vice-Consul (Commercial): Dusan Tomcik.
Vice-Consul (Commercial): Miroslav Bolkovec.
Vice-Consul (Commercial): Lubomir Malinsky.

DENMARK

Embassy: 15 Hunter St, Yarralumla, Canberra, ACT 2600; tel (6) 273-2195; telex 62661; fax (6) 273-3864.
Chargé d'affaires a.i. and Attaché: Torben Edsberg.

Consulate-General: 21st Floor, Goldfields House, Circular Quay, Sydney, NSW 2000; tel (2) 247-2224; telex 24666; fax (2) 251-7504.
Consul-General: Per Lassen.
Consul: Else Tullin.

Consulate: 633 Wickham St, Fortitude Valley, Brisbane, Queensland 4006; POB 1136, Brisbane, Queensland 4001; tel (7) 854-1855; telex 40712; fax (7) 252-4953.
Honorary Consul: Frank Nissen-Wiis.

Consulate: Chartered Account Bldg, 10th Floor, 26 Flinders St, Adelaide, South Australia 5000; tel (8) 212-4903; telex 82947; fax (8) 231-6896.
Honorary Consul: John Gilbert Branson.

Consulate-General: 341 Elizabeth St, North Hobart, Tasmania 7000; POB 84, North Hobart, Tasmania 7002; tel (02) 34-9474; telex 57085; fax (02) 34-9301.
Honorary Consul-General: J. O. Cogan.

Consulate-General: 1279 Nepean Highway, Cheltenham, Melbourne, Victoria 3192; POB 177, Southland Centre, Melbourne, Victoria 3192; tel (3) 581-4499; telex 35148; fax (3) 581-4498.

Honorary Consul-General: Erik Jens Jensen.

Consulate: 19 Phillimore St, POB 393, Fremantle, Perth, Western Australia 6160; tel (9) 335-5122; telex 92106; fax (9) 430-4141.
Honorary Consul: Sven Lysgaard Jørgensen.

Consulate: 849 Wellington St, West Perth, POB 401, Nedlands, Western Australia 6009; tel (9) 322-1888; fax (9) 336-1886.
Honorary Vice-Consul: Axel Handevitt Haar.

DOMINICAN REPUBLIC

Consulate-General: 48 Beresford Rd, Rose Bay, Sydney, NSW 2029; POB 652, Double Bay, Sydney, NSW 2028; tel (2) 327-3900.
Honorary Consul-General: Colin W. Mansell.
Honorary Vice-Consul: Gordon V. Stewart.

Consulate: 83 Kensington Rd, Norwood, Adelaide, South Australia 5067; tel (8) 332-8200; fax (8) 332-7001.
Honorary Consul: Peter H. D. Lathlean.

Consulate: 242A Kooyong Rd, Toorak, Melbourne, Victoria 3142; tel (3) 822-5917.
Honorary Consul: Dr John Levin.

ECUADOR

Consulate: American Express Tower, 388 George St, Suite 1702A, Sydney, NSW 2000; tel (2) 223-3248; telex 178275.
Consul: Dr Beatriz Cocíos de Duran.

Consulate: 30th Floor, Nauru House, 80 Collins St, Melbourne, Victoria 3000; POB 2291U, Melbourne, Victoria 3001; tel (3) 640-9027; fax (3) 654-1294.
Honorary Consul: John P. Young.

EGYPT

Embassy: 1 Darwin Ave, Yarralumla, Canberra, ACT 2601; tel (6) 273-4437; telex 62497; fax (6) 273-4279.
Ambassador: Adel A. M. Elkhedry (designate).
Counsellor: Adel A. Elmeligy.
Counsellor (Commercial): Ayoub Mahmoud Ayoub.
Counsellor (Press and Information): Abdel Hamid Mohamed Khalil Shawky.
Attaché (Press and Information): Mohsem Amin Rohaim.

Commercial Bureau: 216 La Perouse St, Red Hill, ACT 2603; tel (6) 295-0748; telex 61603; fax (6) 295-1105.

Press and Information Bureau: 1 Darwin Ave, Yarralumla, ACT 2600; tel (6) 273-4260; telex 61443; fax (6) 273-4629.

Consulate-General: 335 New South Head Rd, Double Bay, Sydney, NSW 2028; tel (2) 362-3483; telex 74460; fax (2) 327-1096.
Consul-General: Adel Sadek Abdel-Shahid.
Consul: Hassan Salem.
Vice-Consul: Mortada Lashin.
Vice-Consul: Mahmoud Fawzy A. Dounya.

Commercial Office: Suite 708, 251 Oxford St, Bondi Junction, Sydney, NSW 2022; tel (2) 389-6066; fax (2) 387-4138.
Consul (Commercial): Kamal Selim.

Consulate-General: 9th Floor, 124 Exhibition St, Melbourne, Victoria 3000; tel (3) 654-8634; fax (3) 650-8362.
Consul-General: Ahmed Salah E. Nafeh.
Consul: Sobhi Adel.
Consul: Napoleon Elrahim.

FIJI

Embassy: 9 Beagle St, Red Hill, ACT 2603; POB E159, Queen Victoria Terrace, ACT 2600; tel (6) 239-6872; fax (6) 295-3283.
Ambassador: Dr T. M. Biumaiwai.
First Secretary: Vincent Thomas Rajalingam.

Consulate-General: 10th Floor, 225-233 Clarence St, Sydney, NSW 2000; POB C94, Clarence St, Sydney, NSW 2001; tel (2) 290-1615.
Vice-Consul: Sitiveni Yavalanavanua.

FINLAND

Embassy: 10 Darwin Ave, Yarralumla, Canberra, ACT 2600; tel (6) 273-3800; telex 62713; fax (6) 273-3603.
Ambassador: Ulf-Erik Slotte.
Counsellor: Timo Karmakallio.
Second Secretary: Risto Piipponen.

Consulate-General: 537 New South Head Rd, Double Bay, Sydney, NSW 2028; tel (2) 327-5672; telex 123388; fax (2) 327-7528.
Honorary Consul-General: Paul T. C. Wenham.
Consul (Commercial): William A. Leikola.
Consul (Commercial): Holger Standertskjöld-Nordenstam.

Consulate: Level 7, Waterfront Place, 1 Eagle St, Brisbane, Queensland 4000; POB 7888, Waterfront Place, Brisbane, Queensland 4001; tel (7) 229-8733; fax (7) 229-1227.
Honorary Consul: Raymond Howard Peldan.
Honorary Vice-Consul: Mikko Mäki-Neste.

Consulate: c/o Bennett & Fisher, 12 Currie St, Adelaide, South Australia 5000; tel (8) 212-3687; telex 88630.
Honorary Consul: Anthony Gilbert Summers.

Consulate: 159 Harrington St, Hobart, Tasmania 7000; POB 608F, Hobart, Tasmania 7001; tel (02) 30-0322.
Honorary Consul: Andrew Carrington Kemp.

Consulate-General: 313 Montague St, Albert Park, Melbourne, Victoria 3206; tel (3) 699-1388; telex 35501; fax (3) 690-8480.
Honorary Consul-General: Peter Harold Sleigh.
Honorary Vice-Consul: Lionel Ernest Davidson.

Consulate: 1/85 MacLeod Rd, Applecross, Perth, Western Australia 6153; tel (9) 316-1929.
Honorary Consul: Peter Kingsley Howard.

Consulate: Mallum Chambers, 26 Mitchell St, Darwin, Northern Territory 0800; POB 884, Darwin, Northern Territory 0801; tel (89) 81-2715; fax (89) 81-5205.
Honorary Consul: E. B. M. James.

FRANCE

Embassy: 6 Perth Ave, Yarralumla, ACT 2600; tel (6) 270-5111; telex 62141; fax (6) 273-3193.
Ambassador: Roger Duzer.
Counsellor: Rémy Perraud.
Defence Attaché: Capt. Yves le Borgne.
Counsellor (Cultural): Prof. Daniel Leuwers.
Counsellor (Scientific): Laurent d'Ozouville.
First Secretary: Jean-Louis Puig.
Second Secretary (Press and Information): Kostia Sakow.
Third Secretary (Communication): Sylvain Lamotte.

Economic Section: Level 2, 24 Marcus Clarke St, Canberra City, ACT 2601; tel (6) 257-2500; telex 61206.

Consulate-General: 20th Floor, St Martin's Tower, 31 Market St, Sydney, NSW 2000; tel (2) 261-5779; telex 72620; fax (2) 267-2467.
Consul-General: Xavier Driencourt.
Consul: Jean Magnière.
Consul: Dominique A. Caton.
Consul (Press): Laurence Oxenberg.

Commercial Office: BNP Bldg, 11th Floor, 12 Castlereagh St, Sydney, NSW 2000; tel (2) 223-8011; telex 20070; fax (2) 223-7829.
Deputy Consul-General (Commercial): Pierre Letocart.
Consul (Commercial): Thierry P. Laloux.
Consul (Commercial): Lise Driencourt.
Consul (Commercial): Jacques Ardoin.

Consulate: 3/21 Campbell St, Wollongong, NSW 2500; tel (42) 297-808.
Honorary Consul: George Ackaoui.

Consulate: Floor 2, National Bank House, cnr Creek and Adelaide Sts, Brisbane, Queensland 4000; POB 606, Brisbane, Queensland 4001; tel (7) 229-8201; fax (7) 229-1579.
Honorary Consul: Samuel Winston-Smith.

Consular Agency: 95 Currie St, Adelaide, South Australia 5000; tel (8) 231-8633.
Honorary Consul: William Corneloup.

Consular Agency: 728 Sandy Bay Rd, Sandy Bay, Hobart, Tasmania 7005; tel (02) 25-2086.
Honorary Consul: Prof. I. H. Smith.

Consulate-General: 4th Floor, 492 St Kilda Rd, Melbourne, Victoria 3004; tel (3) 820-0209; telex 38968; fax (3) 820-9363.
Consul-General: Joseph Géara.
Consul (Consular): Marcel Fontaine.
Vice-Consul: Jean-Raymond Albiges.

Commercial Office: 14/500 Collins St, Melbourne, Victoria 3000; tel (3) 614-4255; telex 37521; fax (3) 614-2404.
Consul (Commercial): Robert van Keerbergen.

Consulate: Suite 21, Mount Hospital Medical Centre, 146 Mounts Bay Rd, Perth, Western Australia 6000; tel (9) 321-1940; fax (9) 322-1209.
Honorary Consul: Dr Robert Pearce.

Commercial Office: 5th Floor, 231 Adelaide Terrace, Perth, Western Australia 6000; tel (9) 325-8707.
Consul (Commercial): Pierre Chouard.

Consulate: 25 Daly St, Darwin, Northern Territory 0800; tel (02) 81-5351.
Honorary Consul: Anthony Maryon.

GABON

Consulate: 42 Quinton Rd, Manly, Sydney, NSW 2095; tel (2) 977-0599; fax (2) 977-0185.
Honorary Consul: Brian Kirk.

GERMANY

Embassy: 119 Empire Circuit, Yarralumla, ACT 2600; tel (6) 270-1911; telex 62035; fax (6) 273-4386.
Ambassador: Dr Hans Schauer.
Minister-Counsellor: Dr Otto Roever.
Defence Attaché: Lieut Col Heinrich Wall.
Counsellor (Press and Cultural Affairs): Dr Elke Maria Schmitz.
Counsellor: Peter Hoffmann.
First Secretary: Dr Michael Gimmerthal.
Second Secretary (Administration): Rolf Potent.
Third Secretary (Consular and Economic): Detlef Küster.

Consulate-General: 13 Trelawney St, POB 204, Woollahra, Sydney, NSW 2025; tel (2) 328-7733; telex 25966; fax (2) 327-9649.
Consul-General: Dr Ditrich Gescher.
Deputy Consul-General: Rolf Meyer-Olden.
Consul: Klaus Meskendahl.

Consulate: 32nd Floor, AMP Place, 10 Eagle St, Brisbane, Queensland 4000; tel (7) 221-7819; fax (7) 229-7675.
Honorary Consul: Christopher R. Featherstone.

Consulate: Mercedes House, 62-72 Flinders St, POB 1867, Adelaide, South Australia 5000; tel (8) 223-5107.
Honorary Consul: Sir Bruce Roy Macklin.

Consulate: 348 Sandy Bay Rd, Sandy Bay, Hobart, Tasmania 7005; tel (02) 23-1814.
Honorary Consul: Barry Darrell Hedley Fisher.

Consulate-General: 480 Punt Rd, South Yarra, POB 76, Melbourne, Victoria 3141; tel (3) 828-6888; telex 35911; fax (3) 820-2414.

Consul-General: Hans-Georg Fein.
Deputy Consul-General: Johannes Müllers.
Consul: Kuno Boppré.
Vice-Consul (Consular): Michael Geiken.
Vice-Consul (Cultural): Janina Low.
Vice-Consul (Consular): Thomas Bittner.

Consulate: 8th Floor, St George's Court, 16 St George's Terrace, Perth, Western Australia 6000; tel (9) 325-8851.
Honorary Consul: Alan Eric Blanckensee.
Vice-Consul: Joachim Colell.

Consulate: 2 Sheppard St, POB 38995, Winnelle, Darwin, Northern Territory 0821; tel (02) 84-3769; fax (02) 47-0037.
Honorary Consul: Harry Maschke.

GREECE

Embassy: 9 Turrana St, Yarralumla, Canberra, ACT 2600; tel (6) 273-3011; telex 62724; fax (6) 273-2620.
Ambassador: V. S. Zafiropoulos.
Defence Attaché: Brig. Ioannis Stouras.
First Secretary: George P. Chatzimichelakis.
Attaché (Administration): Ermioni Patsiouri.
Attaché (Administration): Theodore Karakassides.

Consulate-General: Level 20, 15 Castlereagh St, Sydney, NSW 2000; tel (2) 221-2388; telex 23505; fax (2) 221-1423.
Consul-General: Constantine Pischinas.
Consul: Theocharis Lalacos.
Consul (Education): Nicholas Tsarouchis.
Vice-Consul (Press): Andreas Papageorgopoulos.
Vice-Consul (Press): N. Karakatsanis.

Commercial and Economic Affairs Office: Third Floor, 51 Pitt St, Sydney, NSW 2000; tel (2) 272-334; fax (2) 251-7208.
Consul (Commercial and Economic): Anastasios Kouroussis.

Mercantile Marine Office: 29 Manning Rd, Double Bay, Sydney, NSW 2028; tel (2) 327-6905.
Consul (Shipping): Constantinos Prevedourakis.

Consulate: 215 Newcastle Rd, POB 135, East Maitland, NSW 2323; tel (49) 336-467; fax (49) 341-517.
Honorary Consul: A. Antoniades.

Consulate-General: 25th Floor, 215 Adelaide St, Brisbane, Queensland 4000; POB 1309, Brisbane, Queensland 4001; tel (7) 228-5811; fax (7) 229-3709.
Honorary Consul-General: Alexander Freeleagus.
Honorary Vice-Consul: Demetrius Diacaris.

Consulate-General: 1st Floor, 366 King William St, Adelaide, South Australia 5000; tel (8) 211-8066; fax (8) 211-8820.
Consul-General: Dionyssios Coundoureas.
Consul: Ioannis Andreades.
Consul (Education): Efstathia Dimopoulou.

Consulate: 37B Derwentwater Ave, Sandy Bay, Hobart, Tasmania 7005; tel (02) 20-2118.
Honorary Consul: Dr A. C. Pittas.

Consulate-General: 8th Floor, Stanhill House, 34 Queen's Rd, Melbourne, Victoria 3004; tel (3) 866-4524.
Consul-General: Emmanuel Wlandis.

Education Service: 9th Floor; tel (3) 266-4660.

Press and Information Service: 1st Floor, Suite 103; tel (3) 267-2737.
Consul (Press and Information): Achilles Paparsenos.

Consulate: 16 St George's Terrace, Perth, Western Australia 6000; tel (9) 325-6608; fax (9) 325-2940.
Consul: Ioannis Raptakis.

Consulate: Pan Hellenic Cultural Centre, 17 Chapman Rd, Nightcliff, Darwin, Northern Territory 5794; POB 2091, Darwin, Northern Territory 0801; tel (89) 81-6083; fax (89) 48-0259.
Honorary Consul: Peter Paroulakis.

HAITI

Consulate: 73 Cliff Ave, Northbridge, Sydney, NSW 2063; tel (2) 958-0516.
Honorary Consul: H. C. Brierley.

HOLY SEE

Apostolic Nunciature: 2 Vancouver St, Red Hill, ACT 2603; POB 3633, Manuka, ACT 2603; tel (6) 295-3876; fax (6) 95-3690.
Apostolic Pro-Nuncio: Most Rev. Franco Brambilla, Titular Archbishop of Viminacium.
Counsellor: Mgr Dr Thomas Yeh Sheng-Nan.

HONDURAS

Consulate-General: 7th Level, 19-31 Pitt St, Sydney, NSW 2000; POB H6, Australia Square, Sydney, NSW 2000; tel (2) 252-3779; telex 171590; fax (2) 247-6384.
Honorary Consul-General: K. H. Goddard.

Consulate-General: 23 Margarita St, Brighton Beach, Melbourne, Victoria 3188; tel (3) 598-8878.
Honorary Consul-General: P. F. Sherman.

Consulate: 44 Troy Terrace, Daglish, Perth, Western Australia 6008; tel (9) 382-2695.
Honorary Consul: Eugenia de Newmann.

HUNGARY

Embassy: 17 Beale Crescent, Deakin, ACT 2600; tel (6) 282-2555; telex 62737; fax (6) 285-3012.
Ambassador: Dr László Pordány.
Second Secretary: Dr Istvan Horvath.

Consulate-General: Unit 6, 351/A Edgecliff Rd, Edgecliff, Sydney, NSW 2027; tel (2) 328-7859; telex 23262; fax (2) 327-1829.
Consul-General: Dr Sándor Varga.

Commercial Section: Suite 201, Piccadilly Court, 356-366 New South Head Rd, Double Bay, Sydney, NSW 2028; tel (2) 327-4878; telex 123262; fax (2) 327-4311.
Consul (Commercial): Maria Csaki.
Vice-Consul (Commercial): Zoltan Czako.

Consulate: 3rd Floor, Austral House, 115-119 Collins St, Melbourne, Victoria 3000; tel (3) 650-8636; fax (3) 654-6462.
Honorary Consul: T. H. Lustig.

ICELAND

Embassy: c/o Ministry of Foreign Affairs, Hverfisgötu 115, 150 Reykjavík, Iceland; tel (1) 623-000; telex 2225.
Ambassador: Benedikt Gröndal.

Consulate-General: 1/10 Kennedy St, POB 4631, Kingston, Canberra, ACT 2604; tel (62) 227-4307; fax (62) 227-4216.
Honorary Consul-General: Ross L. Gibson.

Consulate-General: 4 Wiston Gardens, Double Bay, Sydney, NSW 2028; tel (2) 327-1814; fax (2) 327-5818.
Honorary Consul-General: Sigrún K. Baldvinsdóttir.

Consulate-General: 44 St George's Rd, Toorak, Melbourne, Victoria 3142; tel (3) 827-7819; fax (3) 670-4889.
Honorary Consul-General: R. Renshaw-Jones.

INDIA

High Commission: 3-5 Moonah Place, Yarralumla, ACT 2600; tel (6) 273-3774; telex 62362; fax (6) 273-3328.
High Commissioner: Madan Lall (acting).
Military, Naval and Air Adviser: Capt. S. K. K. Krishnan.
Attaché: Kidar Singh.
Attaché: C. R. Ahloyan.
Attaché: R. Rajagopalan.

Consulate-General: 153 Walker St, North Sydney, NSW 2060; tel (2) 955-7055; telex 24010; fax (2) 929-6058.
Consul-General: Arif Qamarain.
Deputy Consul-General: Lal Dingliana.
Consul (Commercial): V. S. Kohli.

Consulate: 258 Bell St, Coburg, Melbourne, Victoria 3058; tel (3) 350-4684; fax (3) 350-6614.
Honorary Consul: T. J. Rao.

INDONESIA

Embassy: 8 Darwin Ave, Yarralumla, ACT 2600; tel (6) 273-3222; telex 62525; fax (6) 273-3748.
Chargé d'affaires a.i.: Abdul Irsan.
Minister-Counsellor: Ismodirdjo Susanto.
Defence Attaché (Naval and Air): Col Yuswaji.
Counsellor (Economic): Buchari Effendi.
Counsellor (Information): Soekamto Wienardi.
Counsellor: Yusuf Ibrahim.
Attaché (Education and Cultural): Prof. Dr Samuel Ferdinand Poli.
Military Attaché: Col T. P. Sihombing.
Attaché (Trade): Anwar Wahab.
First Secretary (Administration): Mr Gunawan.
First Secretary: Sutan Bagindo Nasrun.
First Secretary (Consular): Mohammad Tojib Hadiprawira.
Second Secretary: Masdur Kasdana.
Third Secretary (Political): Nasri Gustaman.

Consulate-General: 236-238 Maroubra Rd, Maroubra, Sydney, NSW 2035; tel (2) 344-9933.
Consul-General: Basoeki Slamet.
Consul: Satria Djambek.
Consul (Administration): Maimunah Vera Syafick.
Vice-Consul (Economic): Rudhito Widagdo.
Vice-Consul (Information): Wiwiek Setyowati Kemas Firman-Samadi.
Vice-Consul (Immigration): Mochamad Iman Santoso.

Commercial Office: tel (2) 29-7741.

Consulate: 32 Brand St, Beulah Park, Adelaide, South Australia 5067; tel (8) 31-8108.
Honorary Consul: Richard Rungkat.

Consulate: 3rd Floor, 52 Albert Rd, South Melbourne, Victoria 3205; tel (3) 690-7811; telex 35223; fax (3) 696-0863.
Consul: Gunawan Tjiptosumiarso.
Vice-Consul (Economic and Protocol): Irandra Anwar.
Vice-Consul (Consular, Cultural and Information): Robertus Broto Utomo.
Vice-Consul: Sugiarti Chusnul Ardhiah.

Consulate: 2 Norfolk House, 85 Forrest St, Cottesloe, Perth, Western Australia 6011; tel (9) 385-1472; fax (9) 385-1426.
Honorary Consul: R. C. H. (Don) Manser.

Consulate: 22 Coronation Drive, Stuart Park, Darwin, Northern Territory 0800; POB 1953, Darwin, Northern Territory 0801; tel (89) 81-8627; fax (89) 41-2709.
Vice-Consul (Administration): Julia Ratnaningsih Hassan.
Vice-Consul (Cultural and Information): Rachmat Murni.
Vice-Consul (Protocol and Consular): Soelfan S. Danoerahardja.

IRAN

Embassy: 14 Torres St, Red Hill, Yarralumla, ACT 2603; POB 3219, Manuka, ACT 2603; tel (6) 295-2243; telex 62490; fax (6) 295-2882.
Ambassador: Mehdi Khandaghabadi.
First Secretary: Ahmad Alamolhoda.
Attaché (Consular): Aboulghassem Shahrzad.
Attaché (Administration): Kazem Shamkhali.
Third Secretary: Abbas Golriz.
Third Secretary: Taghi Baethi.

IRAQ

Embassy: 48 Culgoa Circuit, O'Malley, Canberra, ACT 2606; tel (6) 286-1333; telex 61520.
Chargé d'affaires a.i.: Ismail K. H. Ahmed.

IRELAND

Embassy: 20 Arkana St, Yarralumla, Canberra, ACT 2600; tel (6) 273-3022; telex 62720; fax (6) 273-3741.
Ambassador: Martin B. Burke.
First Secretary: Dr John Raymond Bassett.
Second Secretary: Dr Seán Ó Riain.

Consulate-General: 10 Lilika Rd, City Beach, Perth, Western Australia 6015; POB 20, Aberdeen St, Northbridge, Perth, Western Australia 6000; tel (9) 244-1499; fax (9) 446-4555.
Honorary Consul-General: George Michael Nolan.

ISRAEL

Embassy: 6 Turrana St, Yarralumla, ACT 2600; tel (6) 273-1300; telex 62224; fax (6) 273-4273.
Ambassador: Zvi Kedar.
Counsellor: David Goren.
Attaché (Technological Affairs): Abraham Harel.
Attaché (Administration): Nimrod Shani.

Consulate-General: 6th Floor, 37 York St, Sydney, NSW 2000; tel (2) 264-7933; telex 26124; fax (2) 390-2259.
Consul-General: Raphael Goren.
Consul: Aharon Ram.
Consul (Economic Affairs): Gil Kaynan.
Vice-Consul: Arik Almog.

Commercial Office: tel (2) 262-3943.

ITALY

Embassy: 12 Grey St, Deakin, ACT 2601; POB 360, Canberra City, ACT 2601; tel (6) 273-3333; telex 62028; fax (6) 273-4223.
Ambassador: Dr Francesco Cardi.
First Counsellor: Dr Domenico Pedata.
First Secretary: Dr Giulio Timoni.
Second Secretary: Dr Eugenio Sgro'.
Education Attaché: Prof. Antonio Moreño.

Consulate-General: 1st Floor, ICI House, 61-69 Macquarie St, Sydney, NSW 2000; tel (2) 247-8442; telex 73021; fax (2) 252-4830.
Consul-General: Dr Fabio Claudio de Nardis.

Commercial Office: tel (2) 357-3104.

Consular Agency: 102 Yambil St, Griffith, Wagga Wagga, NSW 2680; tel (69) 62-6333; fax (69) 62-6951.
Honorary Consular Agent: A. del Gigante.

Consular Agency: 97 Keen St, Lismore, NSW 2480; tel (66) 21-7306; fax (66) 22-1554.
Honorary Consular Agent: F. Volpato.

Consular Agency: 35 King's Rd, New Lambton, Cessnock, NSW 2305; tel (49) 52-4754.

Consular Agency: 238 Couper St, Warrawong, NSW 2502; tel (42) 74-0612; fax (42) 75-1425.
Honorary Consular Agent: S. Chiodo.

Consulate: Oxford Place, Level 2, 133 Leichhardt St, Spring Hill, Brisbane, Queensland 4005; tel (7) 832-0099; telex 142775; fax (7) 832-0058.
Consul: Dr Paolo Scartozzoni.

Consulate: 91 Grafton St, Cairns, Queensland 4870; tel (70) 51-6472.
Honorary Vice-Consul: Mary Meoli.

Consular Agency: cnr Marion and Camooweal Sts, Mt Isa, Townsville, Queensland 4825; tel (77) 43-3024.
Honorary Consular Agent: Giuseppe Vaiente.

Consular Agency: Shop 12, Venture Plaza, 345 Flinders St, Mall, Townsville, Queensland 4810; tel (77) 72-4488.

Consulate: 398 Payneham Rd, Glynde, Adelaide, Southern Australia 5070; tel (8) 337-0777; telex 87058; fax (8) 365-1540.
Consul: Dr Francesco Azzarello.

Consulate: 1st Floor, 147 Liverpool St, Hobart, Tasmania 7000; tel (02) 34-5458.
Honorary Vice-Consul: Nerea Bini-Maluta.

Consulate-General: 34 Anderson St, South Yarra, Melbourne, Victoria 3141; tel (3) 867-5744; telex 154569; fax (3) 866-3932.
Consul-General: Dr Mario Alberto Montecalvo.

Consulate: 31 Labouchere Rd, South Perth, Western Australia 6151; tel (9) 367-3603; telex 95503; fax (9) 474-1320.
Consul: Dr Vincenzo Schioppa.

Consular Agency: 114 Bourke St, Alice Springs, Darwin, Northern Territory 0870; tel (89) 52-4644.
Honorary Consular Agent: Dino Diano.

JAMAICA

Consulate-General: 16 Josephine St, Oak Park 3046, Melbourne, Victoria 3046; tel (3) 306-7417; fax (3) 306-8466.
Honorary Consul-General: Valerie Y. Lamb.

JAPAN

Embassy: 112 Empire Circuit, Yarralumla, Canberra, ACT 2600; tel (6) 273-2272; telex 62034; fax (6) 273-1848.
Ambassador: Hiromu Fukada.
Minister: Sadaaki Numata.
Counsellor (Agriculture and Fisheries): Kazutoshi Ito.
Counsellor (Economic): Kenji Inaba.
First Secretary (Economic): Haruhiro Kikugawa.
First Secretary (Consular): Hidekazu Naganuma.
First Secretary (Press and Information): Minoru Ishida.
First Secretary (Administration): Sahei Sekine.
First Secretary (Defence): Capt. Takao Nakai.
First Secretary (Cultural): Fumio Isoda.
First Secretary: Mizuhiro Kuroda.
First Secretary (Scientific): Shinichi Kawarada.
First Secretary (Economic): Yoshikazu Ono.

Consulate-General: Level 34, State Bank Centre, 52 Martin Place, Sydney, NSW 2000; POB 4125, Sydney, NSW 2001; tel (2) 231-3455; telex 121118; fax (2) 221-6157.
Consul-General: Michihiko Ikeda.

Consulate-General: 17th Floor, Comalco Place, 12 Creek St, Brisbane, Queensland 4000; tel (7) 221-5188; telex 41339; fax (7) 229-0878.
Consul-General: Shigetaka Ishihara.
Consul: Yoshiharu Araki.
Consul: Seijiro Shirahama.

Consulate-General: 1028-1042 South Rd, Edwardstown, Adelaide, South Australia 5039; tel (8) 372-0598.
Honorary Consul-General: Ronald Ross Johnson.

Consulate-General: 40 Melville St, Hobart, Tasmania 7000; POB 333D, Hobart, Tasmania 7001; tel (02) 38-0200; fax (02) 38-0209.
Honorary Consul-General: A. A. Ashbolt.

Consulate-General: 3rd Floor, Holland House, 492 St Kilda Rd, Melbourne, Victoria 3004; tel (3) 867-3244; telex 31957; fax (3) 867-2871.
Consul-General: Masao Kawase.
Consul: Koji Moriyama.
Consul (Economic): Katsufumi Urushibara.
Consul (Economic): Katsura Oikawa.
Vice-Consul (Consular): Shigeyuki Hirakawa.

Consulate-General: 21st Floor, The Forrest Centre, 221 St George's Terrace, Perth, Western Australia 6000; POB 7347, Cloisters Sq, Perth, Western Australia 6000; tel (9) 321-7816; telex 92752; fax (9) 321-2030.
Consul-General: Hirayoshi Sakuma.
Consul (Politics/Economics): Kazuyoshi Yamaguchi.
Consul: Takenori Yamazaki.

Consulate-General: 19 Lindsay St, Darwin, Northern Territory 1800; tel (89) 81-8722.
Honorary Consul-General: Richard Morris.

JORDAN

Embassy: 20 Roebuck St, Red Hill, ACT 2603; tel (6) 295-9951; telex 62551.
Ambassador: Saad Batainah.
Third Secretary: Mohamed el-Kayed.
Attaché: Ali al-Kayed.

KENYA

High Commission: QBE Bldg, 6th Floor, 33-35 Ainslie Ave, Canberra, ACT 2601; POB 1990, Canberra City, ACT 2601; tel (6) 247-4311; telex 61929; fax (6) 257-6613.
Ambassador: Maj.-Gen. Joseph Mbyati Musomba.
Counsellor: John W. K. Mukuriah.

KIRIBATI

High Commission: c/o Ministry of Foreign Affairs, POB 68, Bairiki, Tarawa, Kiribati; tel 21342; telex 77054; fax 21466.

Consulate-General: 35 Dover Rd, POB 376, Rose Bay, Sydney, NSW 2029; tel (2) 371-7808; fax (2) 371-0248.
Honorary Consul-General: W. Franken.

KOREA, REPUBLIC

Embassy: 113 Empire Circuit, Yarralumla, ACT 2600; tel (6) 273-1050.
Ambassador: Lee Chang Soo.
Minister: Yang Dong Chil.
Defence Attaché: Col Kim In Sung.
Counsellor: Chang Dong Chul.
Counsellor: Yoon Jong Heon.
Attaché (Cultural): Lee Moon Cho.
First Secretary: Kim Ji Young.
Attaché (Commercial): Kim Chil Doo.
Second Secretary: Hwang Seung Hyun.

Consulate-General: Level 8, Challenge Bank House, 32 Martin Place, Sydney, NSW 2000; POB 1601, Sydney, NSW 2001; tel (2) 221-3866; fax (2) 223-4903.
Consul-General: Sae Hoon Ahn.
Consul: Hyun Bae Shin.
Consul: Bon Young Jin.
Consul: Jong-Hyun Choi.
Vice-Consul: Yeoung Shik Lee.

LAOS

Embassy: 1 Dalman Crescent, O'Malley, Canberra, ACT 2606; tel (6) 286-4595; telex 61627; fax (6) 290-1910.
Ambassador: Vang Rattanavong.
Third Secretary: Douangdy Khanthavilay.

LATVIA

Consulate: 38 Longstaff St, East Ivanhoe, Melbourne, Victoria 3079; POB 23, Kew, Melbourne, Victoria 3101; tel (3) 499-6920; fax (3) 499-7008.

Honorary Consul: Emils Delins.
Honorary Vice-Consul: Janis Roberts Delins.

LEBANON

Embassy: 27 Endeavour St, Red Hill, Canberra, ACT 2603; tel (6) 295-7378; telex 61762.
Ambassador: Latif Abul-Husn.
First Secretary: Mansour Abdallah.

Consulate-General: 2 Trelawney St, Woollahra, Sydney, NSW 2025; tel (2) 326-1611; telex 72412; fax (2) 327-4776.
Consul-General: Sleiman Rassi.

Consulate-General: Unit 4, 83-87 Wellington St, Windsor, Melbourne, Victoria 3181; tel (3) 529-4498; telex 151135.
Consul-General: Tony Badaoui.

LESOTHO

Consulate-General: 56 Wentworth St, Randwick, Sydney, NSW 2031; tel (2) 398-3798.
Honorary Consul-General: John B. Crane.

LIBERIA

Consulate: 34 Hunter St, Sydney, NSW 2000; tel (2) 233-1155; fax (2) 221-6771.
Honorary Consul-General: F. J. Church.

Consulate: 3/32 Cooper Place, Beaumont, Adelaide, South Australia 5066; tel (8) 79-9121.
Honorary Consul: William B. Coombs.

Consulate-General: 36 Yarravale Rd, Kew, Melbourne, Victoria 3101; tel (3) 862-1392; fax (3) 862-3563.
Honorary Consul-General: Ronald David Silverstein.

LUXEMBOURG

Consulate: Level 18, Royal Exchange Bldg, 56 Pitt St, Sydney, NSW 2000; tel (2) 259-0222; telex 24850; fax (2) 259-0345.
Honorary Consul: Geoffrey D. Dunstan.

MADAGASCAR

Consulate-General: 7th Level, Jardine-Fleming House, 19-31 Pitt St, Sydney, NSW 2000; tel (2) 252-3770; telex 171590; fax (2) 247-6384.
Honorary Consul-General: F. I. L. Barnes.

MALAYSIA

High Commission: 7 Perth Ave, Yarralumla, ACT 2600; tel (6) 273-1543; telex 62032; fax (6) 273-2496.
High Commissioner: Dato' Abdul Karim Marzuki.
Deputy High Commissioner: Lily Zachariah.
Defence Adviser: Col Amir bin Baharudin.
Counsellor: Mohd Yusof bin Abdul Aziz.
First Secretary (Information): Hussain Abu Bakar.
Second Secretary (Head of Chancery): Muhammad Husni bin Mohd Jazri.
Assistant Defence Adviser: Lieut Commdr Ismail bin Hamzah.
Second Secretary (Administration): Tuan Syed Majid M. T. Hussain.
Third Secretary (Consular): Rosli bin Osman.

Consulate: 67 Victoria Rd, Bellevue Hill, Sydney, NSW 2023; tel (2) 327-7565; telex 17705; fax (2) 363-1257.
Senior Consul: Muhammad Kaddyran Haji Abdul Salam.
Consul: Abdol Rahman Moharam.
Consul: Rahimah Bt Yeop.
Consul: Othman Muda.
Consul: Mohd Yusof Mohd Saleh.

Trade Commission: 11th Floor, R & W House, 92 Pitt St, Sydney, NSW 2000; tel (2) 231-1377; telex 26936; fax (2) 223-4515.
Trade Commissioner: Mohd Sidek bin Haji Hassan.

Consulate: 6th Floor, CML Bldg, 300 Queen St, Brisbane, Queensland 4000; POB 2249, Brisbane, Queensland 4001; tel (7) 231-5222; fax (7) 229-0005.
Honorary Consul: Hon. Paul Everingham.

Consulate: 9th Floor, TAA Bldg, 144 North Terrace, Adelaide, South Australia 5034; tel (8) 212-2236.
Consul: Mohd Yasin bin Maarup.
Honorary Consul: Hassan bin Mohamed Salleh.

Consulate: 1st Floor, 434 St Kilda Rd, Melbourne, Victoria 3004; tel (3) 867-5339; fax (3) 820-3469.
Consul: Mahmad Amir bin Radzali.

Consulate: 4th Floor, Airways House, 195 Adelaide Terrace, Perth, Western Australia 6004; tel (9) 325-9146.
Consul: Ayub Haji Talib.

MALTA

High Commission: 261 La Perouse St, Red Hill, Canberra, ACT 2603; tel (6) 295-1586; telex 62817; fax (6) 239-6084.
High Commissioner: Victor J. Gauci.
Deputy High Commissioner: Dr Paul Pullicino.
First Secretary: Michael A. Debono.
First Secretary: Nicholas Aquilina.

Consulate: Malta House, Suite 713, 7th Floor, Mirvac Trust Bldg, 185 Elizabeth St, Sydney, NSW 2000; tel (2) 267-3633; telex 75003; fax (2) 264-2874.
Consul and Senior Trade Commissioner: Anthony Scibberas.

Consulate: 57 Clifton St, Camden Park, Adelaide, South Australia 5038; tel (8) 295-8811.
Honorary Consul: Gaetan A. Grech.

Consulate-General: Suite 414, 343 Little Collins St, Melbourne, Victoria 3000; tel (3) 670-8427; fax (3) 670-9415.
Consul-General: Clemente Zammit.
Honorary Consul: Dr Victor G. Borg.

Consulate: 16 Evans St, Morwell, Moe, Victoria 3840; tel (51) 34-8963.
Honorary Vice-Consul: Mario A. Sammut.

Consulate: Bassendean Medical Centre, 1 Old Perth Rd, Bassendean, Perth, Western Australia 6054; tel (9) 378-3777.
Honorary Consul: Dr Anthony Victor Sciberras.

MAURITIUS

High Commission: 43 Hampton Circuit, Yarralumla, Canberra, ACT 2600; tel (6) 281-1203; telex 62863; fax (6) 282-3235.
High Commissioner: Gian Nath.
Deputy High Commissioner: Parrwiz Cassim Hossen.
First Secretary: Seeneevasen Ponnusamy.
Attaché: M. C. Florise Prele.

Consulate: POB 25, Northbridge, Sydney, NSW 2063; tel (2) 958-0378.
Honorary Consul-General: James L. B. Cowan.

Consulate: 11 St George's Rd, Toorak, Melbourne, Victoria 3142; tel (3) 241-4112.
Honorary Consul: Donald George Osborne.

MEXICO

Embassy: 14 Perth Ave, Yarralumla, Canberra, ACT 2600; tel (6) 273-3905; telex 62329; fax (6) 273-3488.
Ambassador: Alejandro Morales.
Minister: Everardo Suarez.
First Secretary: Eduardo Villarreal.
Second Secretary: Jorge Chapero.

Consulate-General: Level 1, 135-153 New South Head Rd, Edgecliff, Sydney, NSW 2027; tel (2) 326-1292; telex 74468; fax (2) 327-1110.
Consul-General: Enrique Buj-Florres.
Consul: Arturo Chavarria-Balleza.
Vice-Consul: Luis F. Vilches.

Consulate: 26 Aston St, Toowong, Brisbane, Queensland; tel (7) 870-9188.
Honorary Consul: Marney Dunn.

Consulate: 967 Glenhuntly Rd, POB 63, South Caulfield, Melbourne, Victoria 3162.
Honorary Consul: David J. Aarons.

Consulate: 16 Gladstone Rd, Rivervale, Perth, Western Australia 6103; POB 1618, Perth, Western Australia 6001; tel (9) 362-2031.
Honorary Consul: Robert Charles Hemery.

MONACO

Consulate: Fairwater, 560 New South Head Rd, Double Bay, Sydney, NSW 2028; tel (2) 327-2030; fax (2) 327-2647.
Honorary Consul: Lady Fairfax.

Consulate-General: 22nd Floor, National Bank House, 500 Bourke St, Melbourne, Victoria 3000; tel (3) 602-3088; fax (3) 670-2629.
Honorary Consul-General: Sir Rupert Clarke.
Honorary Consul: Rupert G. A. Clarke.

MOROCCO

Consulate: 11 West St, North Sydney, NSW 2060; tel (2) 922-4999; telex 176821; fax (2) 923-1053.
Honorary Consul: Terence J. Mullane.

MYANMAR

Embassy: 22 Arkana St, Yarralumla, Canberra, ACT 2603; tel (6) 273-3751; telex 61376.
Ambassador: U Thane Myint.
First Secretary: U Tin Aung Cho.
Third Secretary: Soe Aung.
Attaché: U Aye Lwin.

NAURU

Consulate: Suite 502, Level 5, 17 Castlereagh St, Sydney, NSW 2000; POB 4487, Sydney, NSW 2001; tel (2) 233-8044; telex 73503; fax (2) 221-7032.
Honorary Consul: Ken Walker.

Consulate-General: Nauru House, Level 50, 80 Collins St, Melbourne, Victoria 3000; tel (3) 653-5709; telex 31158; fax (3) 654-4738.
Consul-General: Theodore Conrad Moses.

NEPAL

Consulate-General: Suite 2A, 48 Mitchell St, McMahons Point, Sydney, NSW 2060; tel (2) 956-8815; telex 73315; fax (2) 956-8767.
Honorary Consul-General: Christine M. Gee.

Consulate-General: 2/51 Douglas St, Milton, Brisbane, Queensland 4064; POB 1097, Toowong, Brisbane, Queensland 4066; tel (7) 378-0124; fax (7) 368-4035.
Honorary Consul-General: Dr L. D. Griffith.

Consulate-General: Suite 23, 18-20 Bank Place, Melbourne, Victoria 3000; tel (3) 602-1271; telex 151035; fax (3) 670-6480.
Honorary Consul-General: W. A. Johns.

Consulate-General: Suite 2, 16 Robinson St, Nedlands, Perth, Western Australia 6009; tel (9) 386-2102; fax (9) 386-3087.
Honorary Consul General: H. L. Roberts.

NETHERLANDS

Embassy: 120 Empire Circuit, Yarralumla, ACT 2600; tel (6) 273-3089; telex 62047; fax (6) 273-3206.

Ambassador: J. Cornelius T. Bast.
Counsellor: Karel H. Birkman.
First Secretary: Pieter J. Langenberg.
Attaché (Agriculture and Emigration): Alfred Evers.
Attaché (Consular and Administration): Wout Aartsen.

Consulate-General: 19th Floor, Bondi Junction Plaza, 500 Oxford St, POB 261, Bondi Junction, Sydney, NSW 2022; tel (2) 387-6644; telex 171209; fax (2) 387-3962.
Consul-General: R. T. Derksen.
Vice-Consul: A. J. Wagemakers.

Emigration Bureau: tel (2) 389-6622.

Consulate: Suite 71/72, 11th Floor, North Point Bldg, 231 North Quay, Brisbane, Queensland 4000; tel (7) 236-1612; fax (7) 236-2152.
Consul: Willem Johannes Hilgeman.

Consulate: 71 Fullarton Rd, Kent Town, Adelaide, South Australia 5067; tel (8) 31-2111; fax (8) 31-5018.
Honorary Consul: Willem Ouwens.

Consulate: 62 Rosny Esplanade, Rosny, Hobart, Tasmania 7018; tel (02) 44-3449; fax (02) 73-0718.
Honorary Consul: Pieter Kapinga.

Consulate-General: 11th Floor, Fawkner Centre, 499 St Kilda Rd, Melbourne, Victoria 3004; tel (3) 867-7933; telex 13517; fax (3) 867-1186.
Consul-General: Arnold A. M. Hermans.
Vice-Consul: Johan C. van Drecht.

Consulate: The Mill Point Centre, Suite 4, 83 Mill Point Rd, South Perth, Western Australia 6151; tel (9) 474-1282; telex 93706.
Honorary Consul: Thomas C. Dercksen.
Vice-Consul: Willy B. Burchartz.

NEW ZEALAND

High Commission: Commonwealth Ave, Canberra, ACT 2600; tel (6) 273-3611; telex 62019; fax (6) 273-3194.
High Commissioner: Edward A. Woodfield.
Deputy High Commissioner: Wade M. V. Armstrong.
Counsellor: Bronwen Chang.
Counsellor (Administration): Donald J. Robertson.
First Secretary: W. Mark Sinclair.
First Secretary (Economic): Rachel Fry.
Communications Officer: Kathryn Stevens.
Defence and Military Adviser: Brig. Michael J. Dudman.
Naval Adviser: Capt. Alan J. Peck.
Air Adviser: Group Capt. Frank S. Sharp.
Assistant Military Adviser: Lieut Col B. A. Stewart.
Assistant Defence Adviser: Capt. Angela M. Fitzsimons.

Consulate-General: Level 25, State Bank Centre, 52 Martin Place, POB 365, Sydney, NSW 2001; tel (2) 233-8388; telex 24190; fax (2) 231-6369.
Consul-General: Paul Cotton.
Consul (Commercial): John Jenner.
Consul (Commercial): Ian Mustchin.
Consul (Customs): David F. Davenport.
Consul (Liaison Officer): Quentin Doig.

Tourism Department Office: AMEV-UDC House, 84 Pitt St, POB 614, Sydney, NSW 2000; tel (2) 233-6633; telex 20781; fax (2) 235-0737.
Director: Gowan Patton.
Marketing Manager: Nick Marks.
Promotions Manager: Kevin Gough.

Consulate-General: Jetset Centre, 288 Edward St, POB 62, Brisbane, Queensland 4001; tel (7) 221-9933; fax (7) 229-7495.
Consul-General: John Kenneth Bryan.
Consul (Commercial): Tony J. Pervan.
Consul (Commercial): Kerry Francis McKewen.

Consulate-General: 6th Floor, 60 Albert Rd, South Melbourne, Victoria 3205; POB 7275, Melbourne, Victoria 3004; tel (3) 696-0399; fax (3) 696-0391.
Consul-General: Derek P. Morris.
Consul (Commercial): John Nicholson.
Vice-Consul (Defence Liaison): Lieut Commdr G. T. Purcell.

Consulate: 4th Floor, St George's Court, 16 St George's Terrace, POB X2227, Perth, Western Australia 6001; tel (9) 325-7877; telex 93700; fax (9) 325-2820.
Consul and Trade Commissioner: David J. Robertson.

Trade Development Board Office: 213 Greenhill Rd, POB 229, Eastwood, Adelaide, South Australia 5063; tel (8) 274-3705; fax (8) 274-3795.
Trade Commissioner: Anthony Mackay.

NICARAGUA

Consulate: 24 Centreway, East Keilor, Melbourne, Victoria 3036; POB 209, Niddrie, Melbourne, Victoria 3042; tel (3) 336-2411.
Honorary Consul: P. W. B. Millar.

NIGERIA

High Commission: 7 Terrigal Crescent, O'Malley, Canberra, ACT 2606; POB 241, Civic Square, ACT 2608; tel (6) 286-1044; fax (6) 286-5335.
High Commissioner: Prof. Jonathan O. Ndagi.
Counsellor: E. A. Balogun.
First Secretary: O. A. E. Negwa.
Second Secretary: Adesegun Olateru-Olagbegi.
Finance Attaché: A. N. Esedebe.

NORWAY

Embassy: 17 Hunter St, Yarralumla, Canberra, ACT 2600; tel (6) 273-3440; telex 62569; fax (6) 273-3669.
Ambassador: Per Thelin Haugestad.
Attaché: Espen Larsen.

Consulate-General: Third Level, 5 Gresham St, Sydney, NSW 2000; tel (2) 251-6628; telex 177058; fax (2) 247-4460.
Honorary Consul-General: Trygve Amundsen.
Vice-Consul: Aase Gerda Aasen.

Trade Commission: tel (2) 251-2388; fax (2) 251-7661.
Trade Commissioner: Carolyn Humble.

Consulate: 633 Wickham St, POB 1252, Fortitude Valley, Brisbane, Queensland 4006; tel (7) 854-1855; telex 40712; fax (7) 252-4953.
Consul: Robert H. Smith.

Consulate: 1st Floor, 124 Waymouth St, Adelaide, South Australia 5000; POB 212, Adelaide, South Australia 5001; tel (8) 231-8711; fax (8) 231-1929.
Honorary Vice-Consul: Margaret A. Bonesmo.

Consulate: 40 Melville St, Hobart, Tasmania 7000; POB 333D, Hobart, Tasmania 7001; tel (02) 38-0200; fax (02) 38-0208.
Honorary Consul: R. Noel Hopkins.

Consulate-General: 15th Floor, 469 La Trobe St, Melbourne, Victoria 3000; tel (3) 600-1591; fax (3) 670-4772.
Honorary Consul-General: Baard Solnordal.

Consulate: 11 Cliff St, POB 497, Fremantle, Perth, Western Australia 6160; tel (9) 430-0400; fax (9) 430-0423.
Honorary Consul: Peter Geoffrey Lynn.
Honorary Vice-Consul: David G. Lynn.

Consulate: 27 Victoria St, POB 4, Bunbury, Western Australia 6230; tel (97) 21-4866; telex 93045.
Honorary Vice-Consul: John Willinge.

Consulate: POB 39513, Winnellie, Darwin, Northern Territory 0821; tel (89) 84-3677; fax (89) 84-3508.
Honorary Consul: Arne Furre.

PAKISTAN

High Commission: 59 Franklin St, Forrest, Canberra, ACT 2603; POB 3198, Manuka, ACT 2603; tel (6) 295-0021; fax (6) 295-2707.
High Commissioner: M. Bashir Khan Babar.
Minister: Khalid Nizami.
Counsellor: Muhammad Khaleel Khan.
Attaché (Press and Information): Malik Muhammad Ashraf.

Consulate-General: 10th Floor, Shaw House, 49-51 York St, Sydney, NSW 2000; POB 5256, Sydney, NSW 2001; tel (2) 267-7066; telex 76571; fax (2) 299-7319.
Consul-General: Zaheer Ahmed.

Consulate: 707 Owen Dixon Chambers, 205 William St, Melbourne, Victoria 3000; tel (3) 608-7153; telex 36782; fax (3) 608-7153.
Honorary Consul: J. Rupert Balfe.

Consulate: 26 Carnarvon Crescent, Mount Lawley, Perth, Western Australia 6050; tel (9) 444-3648.
Honorary Consul: Mohammad Ayub Khan.

PANAMA

Consulate-General: 11th Floor, 30 Clarence St, Sydney, NSW 2000; POB 2513, Sydney, NSW 2001; tel (2) 261-1177.

Consulate: 40 Jijaws St, Sumner Park, Brisbane, Queensland 4074; tel (7) 376-6270.

PAPUA NEW GUINEA

High Commission: Forster Crescent, Yarralumla, ACT 2600; POB 572, Manuka, ACT 2603; tel (6) 273-3322; telex 62592; fax (6) 273-3732.
High Commissioner: Paul Bernard Songo.
Counsellor (Deputy Head of Mission): Frank M. Miro.
Defence Adviser: Col David N. Josiah.
Third Secretary: Barbara Burode Mimino.

Consulate-General: Somare Haus, 100 Clarence St, Sydney, NSW 2000; POB 4201, Sydney, NSW 2001; tel (2) 29-5151; telex 120263.
Consul-General: William N. Nindim.
Consul: Joseph Konu.
Consul (Commercial): Longas C. Solomon.

Consulate: 16th Floor, Capita House, 307 Queen St, POB 220, Brisbane, Queensland 4000; tel (7) 221-7915.
Consul: Thomas N. Polume.
Consul: Age Kila.

PERU

Embassy: Qantas House, Suite 1, 9th Floor, 197 London Circuit, Canberra City, ACT 2601; POB 971, Civic Square, ACT 2608; tel (6) 257-2953; telex 61664; fax (6) 257-5198.
Ambassador: Gonzalo Bedoya.
Counsellor: Fernando Montero.
Second Secretary: Alfredo Pareja-Lecaros.

Consulate: Level 2, 140 William St, Sydney, NSW 2011; tel (2) 358-2311; fax (2) 358-4855.
Honorary Consul: Ricardo Zalapa Rouse.

Consulate: 965-967 Glenhuntly Rd, POB 63, Caulfield South, Melbourne, Victoria 3162; tel (3) 571-1088; telex 31561; fax (3) 563-6220.
Honorary Consul: J. T. Stacey.
Honorary Vice-Consul: Gary R. Sauvarin.

PHILIPPINES

Embassy: 1 Moonah Place, Yarralumla, Canberra, ACT 2600; POB 3297, Manuka, ACT 2603; tel (6) 273-2535; telex 62665; fax (6) 273-3984.
Ambassador: Rora Navarro-Tolentino.
Minister-Counsellor: Jorge V. Arizabal.
Consul-General: Ben Hur C. Ong.
Third Secretary and Vice-Consul: Gilberto G. B. Asuque.
Third Secretary and Vice-Consul: Maria Cleofe R. Natividad.
Attaché and Administrative Officer: Antonia A. Arizabal.
Attaché and Consular Assistant: Rolando M. Mendoza.
Attaché and Cultural Officer: Lilia G. Bayod.
Attaché and Protocol Officer: Lucille I. Torres.
Attaché and Finance Officer: Cecilia S. Tomas.
Defence Attaché: Col Arturo G. Tagamolila, Jr.
Agricultural Attaché: Dr Dalmacio S. Salting.

Consulate-General: Suite G-2, 8-12 Bridge St, POB R608, Sydney, NSW 2000; tel (2) 247-9377.
Consul-General: Juan A. Ona.
Consul (Legal): Fernando G. Santos.
Consul (Commercial): Bruno Y. Cuenca, Jr.

Consulate-General: 482 Kingsford Smith Drive, Hamilton, Brisbane, Queensland 4007; POB 72, Hamilton Central, Brisbane, Queensland 4007; tel (7) 268-8235; telex 40377; fax (7) 268-8286.
Honorary Consul-General: Trevor Hagen Bryans.

Consulate-General: 7 Hamilton St, Erindale, Adelaide, South Australia 5066; POB 86, Burnside, Adelaide, South Australia 5066; tel (8) 31-7423.
Honorary Consul-General: Thomas Peter Fowler.

Consulate: 55 Sandy Bay Rd, Hobart, Tasmania 7004; POB 558F, Hobart, Tasmania 7001; tel (02) 34-9211; fax (02) 23-2510.
Honorary Consul: Ronald T. Banks.

Consulate-General: 25th Floor, 500 Collins St, Melbourne, Victoria 3000; tel (3) 629-3375; telex 32459; fax (3) 629-7406.
Honorary Consul-General: Jerome Patrick Nugent-Smith.
Honorary Consul: Rick A. Henson.

Consulate: 2 Coolibah St, Nightcliff, Darwin, Northern Territory 0810; POB 10, Berrimah, Darwin, Northern Territory 0828; tel (89) 84-4411; fax (89) 84-4715.
Honorary Consul: Robert W. Matthewson.
Honorary Vice-Consul: Dr Renato R. Penaloza.

POLAND

Embassy: 7 Turrana St, Yarralumla, ACT 2600; tel (6) 273-1208; telex 62584; fax (6) 273-3184.
Ambassador: Antoni Pierzchala.
Counsellor: Josef Jendrych.
Third Secretary: Roman Iwanicki.

Consulate-General: 10 Trelawney St, Woollahra, Sydney, NSW 2025; tel (2) 363-9816; telex 25546; fax (2) 327-8568.
Consul-General: Dr Grzegorz Pieńkowski.
Consul: Maciej Krych.
Consul: Jozef Kaminski.

Commercial Office: tel (2) 363-9821.
Consul (Commercial): Waclaw Kosicki.
Consul (Commercial): Zdzislaw Sieczek.

PORTUGAL

Embassy: 6 Campion St, 1st Floor, Deakin, Canberra, ACT 2600; tel (6) 285-2084; telex 62649; fax (6) 282-3705.
Ambassador: Dr José Pacheco Luiz-Gomes.
Counsellor: João Manuel Pina Perestrelo Cavaco.

Consulate-General: 132 Ocean St, Edgecliff, Sydney, NSW 2027; POB 4219, Sydney, NSW 2011; tel (2) 326-1844; fax (2) 326-2325.
Consul-General: Dr Alexandro Lindin Vassalo.

Consulate: 379 Queen St, Brisbane, Queensland 4000; POB 94, Brisbane, Queensland 4001; tel (7) 229-2233; fax (7) 229-2264.
Honorary Consul: D. Johnson.

Consulate: Burns Cuming House, 25 Peel St, Adelaide, South Australia 5000; POB 8070, Hindley St, Adelaide, South Australia 5000; tel (8) 212-1666; fax (8) 231-3673.
Honorary Consul: Dr Raymond F. Walters.

Consulate: 1st Floor, 413 Brunswick St, Fitzroy, Melbourne, Victoria 3065; tel (3) 417-5573; telex 151063; fax (3) 419-5772.
Honorary Consul: Dr Carlos Pereira de Lemos.

Consulate: 242 South Terrace, POB 780, Fremantle, Perth, Western Australia 6160; tel (9) 335-9458; fax (9) 430-6448.
Honorary Consul: Manuel Zarcos Palma.

Consulate: 15 Colster Crescent, Wagaman, Darwin, Northern Territory 0810; tel (89) 27-1956; fax (89) 27-7288.
Honorary Consul: Maria dos Anjos da Vidigal de Castro.

ROMANIA

Consulate-General: 333 Old South Head Rd, Bondi, Sydney, NSW 2026; tel (2) 30-5714; telex 122312; fax (2) 30-5714.
Consul-General: Pavel Platona.
Consul (Commercial): Emil Cazacu.

RUSSIA

Embassy: 78 Canberra Ave, Griffith, ACT 2603; tel (6) 295-9033; telex 61365; fax (6) 295-1847.
Ambassador: Vyacheslav I. Dolgov.
Minister-Counsellor: Vadim Kouznetsov.
Counsellor (Commercial): Mikhail Nesterov.
Counsellor: Viatcheslav Kouzmin.
Counsellor: Andrei Trofimov.
Attaché (Agriculture): Yuri Fomitchev.
Counsellor: Yuri Yartsev.
First Secretary: Valeri Morozov.
First Secretary: Yevgeny Popov.
Second Secretary (Commercial): Vladimir Klinskikh.

Consulate-General: 7-9 Fullerton St, Woollahra, Sydney, NSW 2025; tel (2) 326-1188; telex 73606; fax (2) 327-5065.

Commercial Office: 3/313 Edgecliff Rd, Woollahra, Sydney, NSW 2025; tel (2) 327-6318; telex 72448; fax (2) 362-3556.
Consul-General: Igor Shtcherbakov.
Consul (Commercial): Oleg Kouznetsov.

SAN MARINO

Consulate-General: 1 Charles St, Carlton, Melbourne, Victoria 3053; tel (3) 688-3742; telex 07130625.
Honorary Consul-General: Molly José Oliver.

SAUDI ARABIA

Embassy: 12 Culgoa Circuit, O'Malley, Canberra, ACT 2606; POB 63, Garran, ACT 2605; tel (6) 286-2099; telex 61454; fax (6) 290-1835.
Ambassador: A. Rahman N. Alohaly.
Second Secretary: Mohammed S. al-Hedan.
Third Secretary: Abdulaziz Ali Alghamdi.
Third Secretary: Nayef D. S. al-Rasheed.
Attaché: Abdullah al-Ajroush.
Attaché: Abdullah M. al-Aql.

SEYCHELLES

High Commission: c/o Ministry of Planning and External Relations, POB 656, National House, Victoria, Seychelles; tel 24041; telex 2260; fax 24845.
High Commissioner: Callixte d'Offay.

Consulate: Level 10, 60 Park St, Sydney, NSW 2000; tel (2) 283-1414; fax (2) 264-5299.
Honorary Consul: J. I. Charody.

Consulate-General: 23 Marri Crescent, Lesmurdie, Perth, Western Australia 6076; tel (9) 291-6570; fax (9) 291-9154.
Honorary Consul-General: Guy Francis Robert.

SINGAPORE

High Commission: 17 Forster Crescent, Yarralumla, Canberra, ACT 2600; tel (6) 273-3944; telex 62192; fax (6) 273-3260.
High Commissioner: Tan Seng Chye.
First Secretary: Tay Kuan Yan.
Defence Adviser: Col Clarence Tan.
Third Secretary: Lim Chin Chin.

SOLOMON ISLANDS

High Commission: c/o Ministry of Foreign Affairs, POB G10, Honiara, Solomon Islands; tel 21250; telex 66311.

Consulate-General: National Australia Bank Bldg, cnr Adelaide and Creek Sts, Brisbane, Queensland 4000; tel (7) 221-7899; fax (7) 221-2296.
Consul-General: Hugh Kauvaka Paia.
Vice-Consul (Commercial): Moses Mose Kouni.
Vice-Consul: Faye Wright Mose.

Consulate: Level 2, 72 Campbell St, Surry Hills, Sydney, NSW 2010; POB 3949, Sydney, NSW 2001; tel (2) 281-7955; telex 23290; fax (2) 281-5026.
Honorary Consul: Henry Cumines.

SOUTH AFRICA

Embassy: cnr State Circle and Rhodes Place, Yarralumla, ACT 2600; tel (6) 273-2424; telex 62734; fax (6) 273-3543.
Ambassador: F. D. Tothill.
Counsellor: André Pelser.
Counsellor (Agriculture): Jacobus A. Swart.
First Secretary: Timo Beukes.
First Secretary (Administration): Johanna van Vuuren.
Third Secretary: Jan Hough.
Third Secretary: Jacques D. G. Malan.
Attaché (Administration): Sieg Kuschke.

SPAIN

Embassy: 15 Arkana St, Yarralumla, Canberra, ACT 2600; POB 76, Deakin, ACT 2600; tel (6) 273-3555; telex 62485; fax (6) 273-3918.
Ambassador: Dr José Luis Pardos.
Counsellor: Alvaro de Salas.
Counsellor (Education): Fernando Gomez.
Counsellor (Labour): Santiago Villalta.
Attaché (Administration): Miguel Carrasco.

Consulate-General: 7th Floor, 50 Park St, Sydney, NSW 2000; POB E441 St James, Sydney, NSW 2000; tel (2) [illegible]1-2433; telex 176957; fax (2) 283-1695.
Consul-General: Don Antonio Soler Algaba.

Commercial Office: Edgecliff Centre, Suite 408, 203 New South Head Rd, Edgecliff, Sydney, NSW 2027; tel (2) 362-4212; telex 22194; fax (2) 362-4057.
Consul (Commercial): Don Federico Povedano Alonso.
Vice-Consul (Commercial): Carmen Garcia.

Consulate: 2nd Floor, Perry House, 131 Elizabeth St, Brisbane, Queensland 4000; POB 375, Mount Gravatt, Brisbane, Queensland 4122; tel (7) 221-8571.
Honorary Consul: Jacinto Perez Torralba.

Consulate: 81 Sheridan St, Cairns, Queensland 4870; tel (70) 51-6640.
Honorary Vice-Consul: Amador Calahorra Martinez de Moentin.

Consulate: 19 Menkens St, Fulham Gardens, Adelaide, South Australia 5024; tel (8) 353-1469.
Honorary Consul: Joaquin Artacho.

Consulate-General: 3rd Floor, 766 Elizabeth St, Melbourne, Victoria 3000; tel (3) 347-1966.
Consul-General: Ramon Alvarez-Novoa.
Honorary Consul: Manuel Jimenez.

Consulate: 1st Floor, 181 St George's Terrace, Perth, Western Australia 6000; tel (9) 322-4522; fax (9) 321-4351.
Honorary Consul: Angel Quintela.

SRI LANKA

High Commission: 35 Empire Circuit, Forrest, Canberra, ACT 2603; tel (6) 239-7041; telex 61620; fax (6) 239-6166.
High Commissioner: Edwin Loku Bandara Hurulle.
Deputy High Commissioner: Sarath Perera.
Attaché: M. D. Wilton.

Consulate: Suite 701, 7th Floor, 191 Clarence St, Sydney, NSW 2000; tel (2) 262-5944; fax (2) 290-2335.
Consul (Commercial): S. A. M. W. R. Senanayoke.
Consular Officer: J. A. C. Jayasuriaarachchi.

Consulate: 139 Roghan Rd, Taigum, Brisbane, Queensland 4034; tel (7) 265-3693.
Honorary Consul: Anton Swan.

Consulate: 30 Prosperity Way, Athlestone, Adelaide, South Australia 5076; tel (8) 337-0639.
Honorary Consul: Radley Lorenz Claessen.

Consulate: 8 Sutton Parade, Box Hill North, Melbourne, Victoria 3129; POB 125, Surrey Hills, Melbourne, Victoria 3127; tel (3) 898-6760.
Honorary Consul: Rodney A. Arambewela.

Consulate: Suite 2, 66 Mill Point Rd, South Perth, Western Australia 6151; POB 386, Victoria Park, Perth, Western Australia 6100; tel (9) 474-2288; telex 94690; fax (9) 474-1507.
Honorary Consul: Major Wilton White.

Consulate: POB 36955, Winnellie, Darwin, Northern Territory 0821; tel (89) 82-5300.
Honorary Consul: Upali Ranasinghe.

SWEDEN

Embassy: 5 Turrana St, Yarralumla, Canberra, ACT 2600; tel (6) 273-3033; telex 62303; fax (6) 273-3298.
Ambassador: Bo Heinebäck.
Counsellor: Bo Eriksson.
Defence Attaché: Capt. Anders Timdahl.
Second Secretary: Ing Britt Roche.

Consulate-General: National Mutual Centre Bldg, 18th Floor, 44 Market St, Sydney, NSW 2000; tel (2) 299-1951; telex 126745; fax (2) 290-1019.
Consul-General: Jacob Ankarcrona.

Commercial Office: 25th Floor; tel (2) 262-1077; telex 178166; fax (2) 290-3907.
Consul (Commercial): Rutger Engsäll.

Consulate: 1st Floor, Suncorp House, 30-36 Hershel St, Brisbane, Queensland 4000; POB 54, Indooroopilly, Brisbane, Queensland 4068; tel (7) 236-2797; fax (7) 236-2440.
Honorary Consul: James Sinclair Stodart.

Consulate: c/o Peat Marwick, 13th Floor, National Mutual Tower Bldg, 15 Lake St, POB 7200, Cairns, Queensland 4870; tel (70) 51-7322; fax (70) 51-0116.
Honorary Consul: Graham Ernest Cook.

Consulate: 256 Stanley St, POB 596, North Adelaide, South Australia 5006; tel (8) 267-4977; fax (8) 267-1801.
Honorary Consul: David George Seaton.

Consulate: 164 Campbell St, Hobart, Tasmania 7000; POB 1024K, Hobart, Tasmania 7001; tel (02) 34-2477; fax (02) 34-5484.
Honorary Consul: John Richard Harris.

Consulate: 61 Riggall St, POB 192, Broadmeadows, Melbourne, Victoria 3047; tel (3) 301-1888; telex 30555; fax (3) 301-1361.
Honorary Consul: Athol Dennis Lapthorne.
Chancellor: Elsbeth Doolan.

Consulate: c/o Courier Australia, 23 Walters Drive, Herdsman, Perth, Western Australia 6016; POB J680, Perth, Western Australia 6001; tel (9) 244-3699; fax (9) 244-3723.
Honorary Consul: Harry Morgan.

Consulate: c/o Ward Keller Barristers and Solicitors, 19 The Mall, Darwin, Northern Territory 0800; POB 330, Darwin, Northern Territory 5790; tel (89) 81-2971; fax (89) 81-1253.
Honorary Consul: Hugh B. Bradley.

SWITZERLAND

Embassy: 7 Melbourne Ave, Forrest, ACT 2603; tel (6) 273-3977; telex 62275; fax (6) 273-3428.
Ambassador: Dr Arnold Hugentobler.
Counsellor: Dr Urs Stemmler.
Attaché and Head of Chancery: Wulf Leuz.

Consulate-General: Edgecliff Centre, 203-233 New South Head Rd, POB 82, Edgecliff, Sydney, NSW 2027; tel (2) 328-7511; telex 170315; fax (2) 327-7097.
Consul-General: Hans-Peter Egger.
Consul: Werner Dill.

Consulate: 15 Corowa St, Wavell Heights, Brisbane, Queensland 4012; tel (7) 266-9782.
Honorary Consul: W. A. Brunner.

Consulate: 504 Glynburn Rd, POB 70, Burnside, Adelaide, South Australia 5066; tel (8) 333-2977; fax (8) 364-1685.
Honorary Consul: Paul A. Richter.

Consulate: 1 Cedar Court, Sandy Bay, Hobart, Tasmania 7005; tel (02) 20-2019.
Honorary Consul: Prof. J. H. Tisch.

Consulate-General: 6th Floor, 3 Bowen Crescent, Melbourne, Victoria 3004; POB 7026, St Kilda Rd PO, Melbourne, Victoria 3004; tel (3) 867-2266; telex 39395; fax (3) 867-5318.
Consul-General: Leo Renggli.
Vice-Consul and Chancellor: Elisabeth Pfister.

Consulate: 5 Marie Way, Kalamunda, Perth, Western Australia 6076; tel (9) 293-2704.
Honorary Consul: Rudolf Abplanalp.

Consulate: 46 Wells St, Ludmilla, Darwin, Northern Territory 0820; tel (89) 81-8225.
Honorary Consul: P. H. Fuchs.

SYRIA

Consulate: 9 Belmore St, Arncliffe, Sydney, NSW 2205; tel (2) 597-7714; fax (2) 597-2226.
Honorary Consul: Dr Victor Ghannoum.

Consulate: 41 Alexandra Ave, South Yarra, Melbourne, Victoria 3141; tel (3) 867-5131.
Honorary Consul: Dr Nasseh Mirza.

THAILAND

Embassy: 111 Empire Circuit, Yarralumla, Canberra, ACT 2600; tel (6) 273-1149; telex 62533; fax (6) 273-1518.
Ambassador: Dr Chawan Chawanid.
Minister: Suriya Rochanabuddhi.
Defence and Air Attaché: Group Capt. Prapat Vinagupt.
Army Attaché: Col Teera Yoosook.
Naval Attaché: Capt. Kiat Korbsook.
Education Counsellor: Udom Mungkasem.
Agricultural Counsellor: Dr Adisak Sreesenpagit.
Commercial Counsellor: Rhat Chanthongkaew.
First Secretary (Commercial): Pramote Natisupalak.
First Secretary (Education): Sini Chareonpojana.
First Secretary (Agriculture): Chan Chiumkanokchai.

Consulate-General: 2nd Floor, 75-77 Pitt St, Sydney, NSW 2000; tel (2) 241-2542; fax (2) 247-9312.
Consul-General: Samroeng Laksanasut.

Commercial Office: 12th Floor, Royal Exchange Bldg, 56 Pitt St, Sydney, NSW 2000; tel (2) 241-1075; telex 23467; fax (2) 251-5981.
Deputy Consul-General (Commercial): Somjin Plengkhum.
Consul (Commercial): Kanya Amorntheerakul.

Consulate: 5th Floor, Silverton Place, 101 Wickham Terrace, Brisbane, Queensland 4000; tel (7) 832-1999; fax (7) 831-2191.
Honorary Consul: William J. Dunn.

Consulate-General: North Terrace House, 19 North Terrace, Hackney, Adelaide, South Australia 5069; tel (8) 363-0771.
Honorary Consul-General: Joan M. Walton.

Consulate-General: 6th Floor, 277 Flinders Lane, Melbourne, Victoria 3000; tel (3) 650-1714; fax (3) 650-1726.
Honorary Consul: Dr Simon A. Wallace.

Consulate-General: 135 Victoria Ave, Dalkeith, Perth, Western Australia 6009; tel (9) 386-8092; fax (9) 221-1635.
Honorary Consul-General: Brig. W. D. Jamieson.
Honorary Consul: William J. D. Jamieson.

Visa Section: 3rd Floor, 8 Victoria Ave, Perth, Western Australia 6000; tel (9) 221-3237.

TONGA

Consulate-General: 158 Pacific Highway, North Sydney, NSW 2060; POB 238, North Sydney, NSW 2060; tel (2) 929-8794; fax (2) 929-6778.
Honorary Consul-General: William Stanley Waterhouse.

TRINIDAD AND TOBAGO

Consulate: 6/18 Serpentine Parade, Vaucluse, Sydney, NSW 2030; POB 109, Rose Bay, Sydney, NSW 2029; tel (2) 337-4391; fax (2) 337-4564.
Honorary Consul: Michael George Agostini.

TUNISIA

Consulate: 15 Transvaal Ave, POB 805, Double Bay, Sydney, NSW 2028; tel (2) 327-3296.
Honorary Consul: Maurice Moubarak.

Consulate: 37 Miller Crescent, POB 181, Mount Waverley, Melbourne, Victoria 3149; tel (3) 807-5023; fax (3) 807-3876.
Honorary Consul: Bernard B. S. Robertson.

TURKEY

Embassy: 60 Mugga Way, Red Hill, Canberra, ACT 2603; tel (6) 295-0227; telex 62764; fax (6) 239-6592.
Ambassador: Ergün Pelit.
First Secretary: Ahmet S. Arda.
Counsellor (Education): Muzaffer Duygu.
Attaché (Education): Emel Latifaoglu.
Attaché: Ayse Energin.
Attaché: Haydar Irmak.

Consulate-General: 66 Ocean St, Woollahra, Sydney, NSW 2025; tel (2) 326-1897; telex 27341; fax (2) 362-4533.
Consul-General: Oral Akyün.
Deputy Consul-General: Bilge Erol.

Consul (Commercial): Monad Balkan.
Consul (Labour and Social Affairs): Ahmet Kapusiz.
Consul (Commercial): Kemal Sinan Tuzun.

Consulate-General: 12 Blyth St, Brunswick, Melbourne, Victoria 3056; POB 73, Brunswick East, Melbourne, Victoria 3057; tel (3) 387-0746; telex 136173; fax (3) 388-1431.
Consul-General: Attila Sunay.
Consul: Oguz Ates.
Vice-Consul: Gül Balci.

TUVALU

Consulate-General: 11 Becket Ave, East Bentleigh, Melbourne, Victoria 3165; tel (3) 570-6000.
Honorary Consul-General: Pravin Sundarjee.

UNITED KINGDOM

High Commission: Commonwealth Ave, Yarralumla, Canberra, ACT 2600; tel (6) 270-6666; telex 62222; fax (6) 270-6653.
High Commissioner: R. J. Smith.
Deputy High Commissioner: I. W. Mackley.
Defence and Naval Adviser and Head of Defence Liaison Staff: Cdre A. C. G. Wolstenholme.
Counsellor and Director of Trade Promotion: Thomas N. Young.
Military Adviser: Col C. David McCarthy.
Air Adviser: Group Capt. J. G. Sheldon.
First Secretary (Management): Derek Moorhouse.
First Secretary: William C. Patey.
First Secretary: David G. Blunt.
First Secretary (Defence Export Services): Michael R. Maiden.
First Secretary: K. F. Harding.
First Secretary (Information): M. R. Eastburn.
First Secretary (Commercial and Agricultural): Graham L. Minter.
Head of Defence Research and Supply Staff: Graham J. Burrows.
Assistant Naval Adviser: Lieut Commdr G. Ewen MacDonald.
Second Secretary (Consular): Kevin A. Casey.
Second Secretary (Works): John David Warrener.
Second Secretary (Economic): Judith M. Slater.

Passport/Visa/Consular Section: Level 10, CBS Tower, cnr Akuna and Bunda Sts, Canberra City, ACT 2601; tel (6) 257-1982; telex 62690; fax (6) 257-5857.
Third Secretary (Passports): J. Taylor.

Consulate-General: Level 16, The Gateway, 1 MacQuarie Place, Sydney Cove, NSW 2000; tel (2) 247-9731; telex 20680; fax (2) 233-1826.
Consul-General: R. S. Reeve.
Cultural Adviser and British Council Director: M. S. Foot.

Commercial and Trade Section: tel (2) 247-7521.
Deputy Consul-General (Commercial): A. J. Ward.
Vice-Consul (Commercial): P. J. Hughes.

Consulate-General: BP House, 193 North Quay, Brisbane, Queensland 4000; tel (7) 236-2575; telex 40556; fax (7) 236-2576.
Consul-General: Barrie S. Jones.
Consul (Commercial): David G. Reader.

Consulate-General: c/o Hassell Pty Ltd, Level 5, 70 Hindmarsh Sq, Adelaide, South Australia 5000; tel (8) 224-0033; fax (8) 223-4989.
Honorary Consul-General: John Neville Morphett.

Consulate-General: 17th Floor, 90 Collins St, Melbourne, Victoria 3000; telex 30660; fax (3) 650-2990.
Consul-General: Stephen D. R. Brown.

Commercial and Trade Section: tel (3) 650-3699.
Deputy Consul-General (Commercial): Donald Hunter Cairns.
Vice-Consul (Commercial Management): Richard Webb.

Passport, Consular and Immigration Section: tel (3) 650-4155.

Consulate-General: Prudential Bldg, 6th Floor, 95 St George's Terrace, Perth, Western Australia 6000; tel (9) 322-3200; telex 92493; fax (9) 481-4755.
Consul-General: J. B. Noss.
Consul: J. Maguire.
Vice-Consul and Management Officer: Robert J. Andrews.

Commercial Section: tel (9) 322-5952.
Consul (Commercial): John Maguire.

Wireless Relay Station: POB 39670, Winnellie, Darwin, Northern Territory 0821; POB 3670, Darwin, Northern Territory 0801; tel (89) 83-1039; telex 85114.
Manager: P. Hart.
Deputy Manager: R. S. Nutt.

USA

Embassy: Moonah Pl., Yarralumla, Canberra, ACT 2600; tel (6) 270-5000; telex 62104; fax (6) 270-5970.
Ambassador: Melvin F. Sembler.
Deputy Chief of Mission: E. Gibson Lanpher.
Political Section: John E. Kelley.
Economic Section: Tain P. Tompkins.
Commercial Section: Michael J. Hand (resident in Sydney).
Consular Section: Elizabeth A. Schoppe.
Regional Security Officer: David R. Haag.
Public Affairs Officer: Lewis R. Luchs.
Communications Programme Officer: Nicodemo Romeo.
Information Systems Manager: Robert E. Arthurs.
Scientific Attaché: Donald R. Cleveland.
Office of the Defence Attaché: Col Max M. Morosko, Jr.
Agricultural Section: John E. Riesz.
Labour Officer: Robert E. Snyder.

Consulate-General: 553 St Kilda Rd, Melbourne, Victoria 3004; tel (3) 526-5900; fax (3) 510-4646.
Consul-General: J. Richard Bock.
Consular Section: Sandra A. Stevens.
Branch Public Affairs Officer: John M. Keller.
Communications Programme Officer: Carol P. Burris.

Information Service: fax (3) 510-4686.

Commercial Section: fax (3) 510-4660.
Commercial Section: Daniel J. Young.

Consulate-General: 36th Floor, Electricity House, Hyde Park Sq., cnr Park and Elizabeth Sts, Sydney, NSW 2000; tel (2) 261-9200; fax (2) 264-9908.
Consul-General: Philip T. Lincoln, Jr.
Consular Section: Donald R. Tyson.
Branch Public Affairs Officer: Margaret A. Eubank.
Communications Programme Officer: Bruce F. Hoof, Jr.
Internal Revenue Service: William Voyzey.
Consul (Tourism): Thomas J. Quinn.

Commercial Section: fax (2) 261-8148.
Commercial Section: Gary L. Gallagher.

Consulate: 383 Wickham Terrace, Brisbane, Queensland 4000; tel (7) 839-8955; telex 145695; fax (7) 832-6247.
Principal Officer: M. Patricia Wazer.

Consular Agency: Level 24, State Bank Centre, 91 King William St, Adelaide, South Australia 5000; tel (8) 233-5819; fax (8) 233-5858.
Consular Agent: Raymond W. Hollis.

Consulate-General: 553 St Kilda Rd, POB 6722, Melbourne, Victoria 3004; tel (3) 526-5900; fax (3) 510-4646.
Consul-General: J. Richard Bock.
Consul (Public Affairs): John M. Keller.
Consul (Commercial): Daniel Young.

Consulate-General: 13th Floor, St George's Court, 16 St George's Terrace, Perth, Western Australia 6000; POB 6044, East Perth, Western Australia 6004; tel (9) 221-1177; fax (9) 325-3569.
Consul-General: Jane Whitney.
Commercial Section: Charles M. Reese.
Consular Section: James B. Gray.
Branch Public Affairs Officer: Anne T. Callaghan.
Representative (Commdr of Seventh Fleet): Commdr J. J. Gorman, Jr.

URUGUAY

Embassy: Bonner House, Suite 5, POB 318, Woden, Canberra, ACT 2606; tel (6) 282-4418; telex 61486.
Chargé d'affaires a.i.: Julio Giambruno.

Consulate-General: 10th Floor, American Express Tower, 388 George St, Sydney, NSW 2000; POB 717, Sydney, NSW 2001; tel (2) 232-8029; telex 73051.
Consul-General: Dr Carlos A. Mora.

Consulate: 26A Curtin Ave, Eagle Farm, Brisbane, Queensland 4007; POB 760, Hamilton, Brisbane, Queensland 4007; tel (7) 868-1181; fax (7) 268-7241.
Honorary Consul: Ben MacDonald.

VANUATU

High Commission: c/o Ministry of Foreign Affairs and Judicial Services, Private Mail Bag 051, Port Vila, Vanuatu; tel 2347; telex 1041; fax 3142.
High Commissioner: Nikenike Vurobaravu.

VENEZUELA

Embassy: MLC Tower, Suite 106, 1st Floor, POB 37, Woden, Canberra, ACT 2606; tel (6) 282-4827; telex 62110; fax (6) 281-1969.
Ambassador: Dr Eduardo Morreo Bustamante.
Minister-Counsellor: Marco Anibal Requena.

VIET-NAM

Embassy: 6 Timbarra Crescent, O'Malley, Canberra, ACT 2606; tel (6) 286-6059; fax (6) 286-4534.
Ambassador: Tran Tuan Anh.
Counsellor (Commercial): Nguyen Ngoc Thanh.
First Secretary: Nguyen Dinh Thu.
Third Secretary: Ho Xuan Phong.
Third Secretary: Tran Van Hinh.
Third Secretary: Tran Van Lien.
Attaché: Nguyen Hong Cuong.
Attaché: Le Ba Phon.
Attaché: Le Huy Hoang.

WESTERN SAMOA

High Commission: 33 Murray Crescent, POB 3274, Manuka, ACT 2603; tel (6) 239-6996; fax (6) 239-6252.
High Commissioner: Feesago Siaosi Fepulea'i.

YEMEN

Embassy: 13 Culgoa Circuit, O'Malley, ACT 2606; POB 672, Woden, ACT 2606; tel (6) 290-1679; telex 61612; fax (6) 290-1682.

Ambassador: Dr Abdul Jalil Abdul Aziz Homarah.
Minister: Mohamed Hasson Thabet.
Second Secretary: Mohamed M. al-Ashabi.

YUGOSLAVIA

Embassy: 11 Nuyts St, Red Hill, Canberra, ACT 2603; POB 3161, Manuka, Canberra, ACT 2603; tel (6) 295-1458; telex 62317; fax (6) 239-6178.
Ambassador: Dr Boris Cizelj.
Counsellor: Dusan Vukasinovic.
First Secretary: Zlatko Gluhbegovic.
First Secretary: Krunoslav Kukoc.
Attaché: Ljubisa Micic.

Consulate-General: 12 Trelawney St, Woollahra, Sydney, NSW 2025; POB 190, Edgecliff, Sydney, NSW 2027; tel (2) 362-3003.
Consul-General: Zoran Veljic.
Consul: Miodrag Ilickovic.
Vice-Consul: Saso Brazanski.

Consulate-General: 58 Lisson Grove, POB 147, Hawthorn, Melbourne, Victoria 3122; tel (3) 818-2254; telex 33342; fax (3) 818-0054.
Consul-General: Trajan Bavtirovski.
Consul: Zoran Popovic.
Vice-Consul: Ivica Dronjic.

Consulate: 24 Colin St, West Perth, Western Australia 6005; tel (9) 321-4539; fax (9) 321-3664.
Consul: Dragan Tomisic.
Vice-Consul: Kostadin Ruzic.
Vice-Consul: Miodrag Zivkovic.

ZAMBIA

High Commission: 28 Guilfayle St, Yarralumla, Canberra, ACT 2600; POB 289, Civic Square, Yarralumla, Canberra, ACT 2600; tel (6) 281-0111; telex 61796.
High Commissioner: Jason C. Mfula.
Deputy High Commissioner: R. S. Sikazwe.
First Secretary: George M. Mwanza.
First Secretary (Finance): Godfrey M. Simfukwe.
First Secretary (Commerce and Trade): George Zulu.

ZIMBABWE

High Commission: 11 Culgoa Circuit, O'Malley, Canberra, ACT 2606; tel (6) 286-2700; telex 62211; fax (6) 290-1680.
High Commissioner: Lucas Pande Tavaya.
Counsellor: Chitsaka Chipaziwa.
First Secretary: Vusumuzi Ntonga.
First Secretary: Marshall Mututu.
Second Secretary: Stenford Chitaunhike.

International Organizations

COMMISSION FOR THE CONSERVATION OF ANTARCTIC MARINE LIVING RESOURCES—CCAMLR

Office: 25 Old Wharf, Hobart, Tasmania 7000; tel (02) 31-0366; telex 57236; fax (02) 23-2714.
Executive Secretary: Dr Darry L. Powell.

EUROPEAN COMMUNITIES

External Delegation: 18 Arkana St, Yarralumla, Canberra, ACT 2600; tel (6) 271-2777; telex 62762; fax (6) 273-4445 .
Head of Delegation: Ove Juul Jørgensen (also responsible for New Zealand).
Deputy Head of Delegation: Roderick M. Skinner.
Administration Attaché: Bruno Kruijer.
Secretary to Head of Delegation: Alison Walker.

SOUTH PACIFIC FORUM SECRETARIAT—SPFS

Office: Level 6, 50 Park St, Sydney, NSW 2000; tel (2) 283-5933; telex 170342; fax (2) 283-5948.
Director: William T. McCabe.

UNITED NATIONS

Information Centre: Suite 1, 2nd Floor, 125 York St, Sydney, NSW 2000; POB 4045, NSW 2001; tel (2) 283-1144; telex 25777; fax (2) 283-1319.
Director: Thelma O'Con-Solorzano.

UNITED NATIONS CHILDREN'S FUND—UNICEF

Office: Suite 2, 2nd Floor, 125 York St, POB Q143, Sydney, NSW 2000; tel (2) 283-1344; telex 170202; fax (2) 283-1347.

UNITED NATIONS HIGH COMMISSIONER FOR REFUGEES—UNHCR

Regional Office: 10 Moore St, POB 1983, Canberra City, ACT 2601; tel (62) 257-2055; telex 61741; fax (62) 247-8331.
Regional Representative: Per Johannessen.
Deputy Representative (Legal): Henry Domzalski.

AUSTRIA

AFGHANISTAN

Embassy: 1010 Vienna, Doblhoffgasse 3/4; tel (1) 43-24-01; telex 111891.
Chargé d'affaires a.i. and Counsellor: Abdul Habib Majid.
Second Secretary: Abdul Rahman Zadran.

ALBANIA

Embassy: 1190 Vienna, Blaastr. 24; tel (1) 36-91-229; telex 133248; fax (1) 36-14-83.
Ambassador: Engjëll Kolaneci.
Counsellor: Alfred Papuciu.
Counsellor (Commercial): Thanas Milo.
First Secretary and Consul: Ilir Cepani.
Second Secretary: Miltiadh Vevecka.
Attaché: Arban Iliriani.
Attaché: Ahmet Kucani.
Attaché (Commercial): Lacka Pirro.

ALGERIA

Embassy: 1010 Vienna, Rudolfinergasse 18; tel (1) 36-88-53; telex 134163.
Ambassador: Ahmed Amine Kherbi.
Counsellor (Commercial): Ghouti Kaouadji.
Counsellor: Fatiha Selmane.
First Secretary: Sid Ali Abdel Bari.
Second Secretary: Nourredine Avadi.
Attaché: Abdallah Arzour.
Attaché: Ahmed Arab.
Attaché (Finance): Mohamd Amorkane Benmokhtar.

ANGOLA

Consulate: 1010 Vienna, Gonzagag. 2/5/1; tel (1) 63-92-18.
Honorary Consul: Walter Neubauer.

ARGENTINA

Embassy: 1010 Vienna, Goldschmiedgasse 2/1; tel (1) 533-85-77; telex 114512; fax (1) 63-87-97.
Ambassador: Dr Jorge Alberto Taiana.
Counsellor: Eduardo Maria Blanchet.
Counsellor: Silvia Elena Mira.
Second Secretary: Marcelo Joaquin Puio.
Second Secretary: Maria de los Milagros Domma Raballo.
Second Secretary: Carlos Alberto Hernandez.
Trade and Economic Sections: 1020 Vienna, Untere Donaustr. 13-15; tel (1) 26-96-71.
Counsellor (Commercial): Honorio Pueyrredon.
Second Secretary (Trade/Economic): Guillermo F. Kreckler.

AUSTRALIA

Embassy: 1040 Vienna, Mattiellistr. 2-4/III; tel (1) 512-85-80; telex 114313; fax (1) 513-29-08.
Ambassador: Michael John Wilson.
Counsellor: John A. Tileman.
Counsellor (Commercial): John William Warnock.
Counsellor (Nuclear Energy): Dr Garth Richard Hogg.
First Secretary (Economic/Consular): Stephen M. Conan-Davies.
First Secretary: John Malcolm Page.
First Secretary: Jeffrey R. Hart.
First Secretary (Commercial): Peter Trandafilovic.
First Secretary (Immigration): Richard L. Greenaway.
Second Secretary (Immigration): Sarah Ruth Dinning.

BANGLADESH

Consulate-General: 1190 Vienna, Probusgasse 1; tel (1) 37-36-01.
Honorary Consul-General: Reinhard F. Grünberger.

BARBADOS

Consulate-General: 1040 Vienna, Brucknerstr. 4; tel (1) 505-74-55.
Honorary Consul-General: Kurt Mach.

BELGIUM

Embassy: 1040 Vienna, Operngasse 20B; tel (1) 56-75-79; telex 133004; fax (1) 56-75-88.
Ambassador: Vicomte Georges Vilain XIIII.
First Secretary: L. Carbonez.
Attaché: Line Vreven.
Attaché (Consular): Victor Ottoy.
Attaché (Commercial): Alexandre Khoudokormoff.
Attaché (Commercial): Jan Pajecki.
Attaché (Cultural): George Englebert.
Attaché: Jean Janssens.
Attaché: Victor Wei.
Office of Military Attaché: 1040 Vienna, Schönburgstr. 8; tel (1) 65-75-69.
Military and Air Attaché: Col Willy Koeken.
Deputy Military and Air Attaché: François Louis Verstraeten.
Consulate: 8020 Graz, Keplerstr. 105; tel (316) 91-13-61.
Honorary Consul: Gerhard Franz.
Consulate: 6020 Innsbruck, Gilmstr. 6; tel (512) 533-31-11.
Honorary Consul: Otto Kaspar.
Consulate: 4020 Linz, Roseggerstr. 38/1; tel (732) 66-56-10.
Honorary Consul: Klaus Czempirek.
Consulate: 5020 Salzburg, Fischergasse 17; tel (662) 313-55-13.
Honorary Consul: Hannes Erhardt.

BENIN

Consulate: 1130 Vienna, Anatourgasse 62; tel (1) 56-78-88.
Honorary Consul: Anton Traunfellner.

BOLIVIA

Embassy: 1010 Vienna, Bauernmarkt 6/6; tel (1) 535-04-91; telex 135555; fax (1) 535-04-92.
Ambassador: Dr A. Gastón Ponce Caballero.
Minister-Counsellor and Deputy Head of Mission: Jaime Aliaga.
Counsellor and Deputy Head of Mission: Roberto Calzadilla Sarmiento.
Consulate: 1050 Vienna, Pilgramgasse 20; tel (1) 56-32-57.
Honorary Consul: Klaus Zahradnik.
Consulate: 4020 Linz, Hauptpl. 14; tel (732) 27-13-01.
Honorary Consul: Cecilia Baldivieso Pardo de Witzany.
Consulate: 8020 Graz, Pluddemanngasse 73; tel (316) 46-16-07.
Honorary Consul: Leopold Heimlich.

BRAZIL

Embassy: 1010 Vienna, Lugeck 1/V/15; tel (1) 512-06-310; telex 111925.
Ambassador: João Tabajara de Oliveira.
Counsellor (Commercial): Alfredo Carlos de Oliveira Tavares.
First Secretary: Sergio Sanginito Novaes da Silva.
Second Secretary: Paulo Mendes de Carvalho.
Consulate: 8010 Graz, Glacisstr. 67/I; tel (316) 82-11-65.
Honorary Consul: Rudolf Griss.
Honorary Vice-Consul: Gunter Griss.
Consulate: 4010 Linz, Kalsergasse 17, Postfach 166; tel (732) 27-31-33.
Honorary Consul: Roland Goblirsch-Urban.
Consulate: 5081 Salzburg, Amf 175; tel (6246) 22-03.
Honorary Consul: Gotelinde Nekola.

BULGARIA

Embassy: 1040 Vienna, Schwindgasse 8; tel (1) 505-64-44; telex 131794; fax (1) 505-14-23.
Ambassador: Dr Toschko Toschkov.
Counsellor (Commercial): Georgi Dimov.
Counsellor: Stoyan Evtimov.
Counsellor: Nikola Balkanski.
Counsellor: Todor Atanassov.
Counsellor and Head of Cultural Section: Lubomir Stoytchev.
Counsellor and Head of Trade Section: Emil Doynov.
Military, Naval and Air Attaché: Col Dimiter Ivanov.
First Secretary: Stefan Enev.
First Secretary: Raschko Iltschev.
First Secretary: Christo Maleev.
First Secretary: Stefan Tsevetanov.
Attaché (Economic): Nedeliu Nedelev.

BURKINA FASO

Consulate-General: 1060 Vienna, Mittelgasse 16; tel (1) 597-83-01; telex 11-4293.
Honorary Consul-General: Bruno Buchweiser.
Honorary Consul: Petrus Zehndorfer.
Honorary Consul: Franz Madl.

BURUNDI

Consulate: 1190 Vienna, Schegargasse 5/17; tel (1) 312-22-93.
Honorary Consul: Ernst Zachmann.

CANADA

Embassy: 1010 Vienna, Dr Karl Lüger Ring 10/IV; tel (1) 533-36-91; telex 115320; fax (1) 535-44-73.
Ambassador: Edward G. Lee.
Deputy Permanent Representative (UN) and Counsellor: P. McRae.
Head of Delegation (CSBM/CFE): H. David Peel.
Counsellor (Science and Technology): J. D. Sainsbury.
Counsellor (CSBM/CFE): I. Mundell.
Counsellor (CSBM/CFE): J. D. Bryson.
Counsellor (Immigration) and Consul: E. H. A. Bergbusch.
Counsellor (Commercial): D. R. Punter.

Counsellor and Consul: C. A. Lacharité.
Military Adviser (CSBM/CFE): Col W. K. Megill.
Military Adviser (CSBM/CFE): A. P. Rasiulis.
First Secretary (UN): S. Moran.
First Secretary: D. S. Murphy.
Second Secretary (CSBM/CFE): A. Ouellette.
Attaché (Medical): Dr T. D. Jeyachandran.

CAPE VERDE

Consulate: 1060 Vienna, Lanke Wienzeile 4; tel (1) 587-31-66.
Honorary Consul: Wolfgang Meixner.

CHILE

Embassy: 1010 Vienna, Lugeck 1/III/10; tel (1) 512-92-08; telex 115952; fax (1) 512-92-08-33.
Ambassador: Hernán Gutiérrez Leyton.
Counsellor and Deputy Head of Mission: Ramiro Riobo Piñones.
Counsellor (Science): Alberto Niño de Zepeda Schele.
First Secretary: José Miguel de la Cruz Cross.
First Secretary: Hernán Mena Taboada.
Attaché: Ximena V. Vasquez Flores.

Consulate: 1010 Vienna, Lugeck 1/III/8; tel (1) 512-23-53.
Third Secretary and Consul: Francisco Javier Berguño Hurtado.

Consulate: 1190 Vienna, Blaasstr. 13; tel (1) 34-71-78.
Honorary Consul: Armin G. Fehle.

Consulate: 4020 Linz, Kaplanhofstr. 3; tel (732) 28-14-41.
Honorary Consul: Dieter Fuchshuber.

Consulate: 5020 Salzburg, Bärengäßchen 11; tel (662) 32-5-82.
Honorary Consul: Hans Günter.

CHINA, PEOPLE'S REPUBLIC

Embassy: 1030 Vienna, Metternichgasse 4; tel (1) 75-31-49; telex 135794; fax (1) 713-68-16.
Ambassador: Hu Benyao.
Counsellor: Chen Liangquing.
Counsellor: Cao Quining.
Counsellor (Trade): Zhu Jianhua.
Military Attaché: Liu Xige.
Assistant Military Attaché: Zhenhan Wang.
First Secretary: Lin Zhaorum.
First Secretary: Gu Yongliang.
First Secretary: Zhang Yuexin.
First Secretary: Yulin Zeng.
First Secretary: Wang Ximan.
First Secretary: Liu Zhaoming.
First Secretary (Scientific/Technical): Chen Wenxin.

COLOMBIA

Embassy: 1010 Vienna, Stadiongasse 6-8; tel (1) 42-42-49; telex 116798; fax (1) 48-83-03.
Ambassador: Dr Mario Laserna Pinzón.
Counsellor and Head of Trade Section: Jorge Dela Mora.
Counsellor (Economic): Maria Isabel Segura Acevedo.
First Secretary and Head of Consular Section: Patricia Koppel Durau.
Second Secretary: Dr Mario Leonel Rodriguez Vargas.
Attaché (Cultural): Carlos Orlando Rengifo Vasquez.

CONGO

Consulate-General: 1203 Vienna, Weberg 30; tel (1) 33-25-56.
Honorary Consul-General: Friedrich Babak.

COSTA RICA

Embassy: 1030 Vienna, Paulusgasse 13/1/5; tel (1) 713-05-40; fax (1) 713-05-41.
Ambassador and Permanent Representative (UN/UNIDO): Prof. Dr Manuel A. Constenla.
Permanent Representative (IAEA): Dr Félix Przedborski.
Counsellor (Trade): Oscar Acuna-Blanco.

COTE D'IVOIRE

Embassy: 1090 Vienna, Alser Str. 28/12; tel (1) 408-37-21; telex 111108.
Ambassador: Adonit Manouan.
Counsellor: Georges Aboua.
Counsellor: Sallah Ben Abdelkader Hamza.
Second Secretary: Emmanuel N'da Yao.

Consulate-General: 2441 Mitterndorf, Mitterndorferstr. 1; tel (2234) 84-02.
Honorary Consul-General: Peter Landesmann.

CUBA

Embassy: 1130 Vienna, Eitelbergergasse 24; tel (1) 82-81-98; telex 131398.
Ambassador: Gustavo Mazorra Hernández.
Counsellor: Conrado Valdivia.
Counsellor (Economic/Trade): Alberto Tutor.
Third Secretary: Crescenciano Ramirez.
Attaché: Nery Rodriguez.

CYPRUS

Consulate: 1010 Vienna, Singerstr. 27; tel (1) 512-75-55; telex 135171; fax (1) 513-75-88.
Honorary Consul: Dr Werner Masser.

CZECHOSLOVAKIA

Embassy: 1140 Vienna, Penzinger Str. 11-13; tel (1) 894-21-26; telex 131702.
Ambassador: Magdaléna Vášáryová.
Counsellor: Augustin Hubka.
Counsellor: Oldrich Vaca.
Counsellor (Trade): Emil Volee.
Military and Air Attaché: Maj.-Gen. Oldrich Frank.
Deputy Military and Air Attaché: Maj. Jan Brada.
First Secretary: Dr Jan Mika.
First Secretary: Ivan Bacina.
First Secretary (Consular): Josef Kavin.
Second Secretary and Head of Consular Section: Ladislav Jaros.
Second Secretary (Consular): Jan Marx.

DENMARK

Embassy: 1015 Vienna, Führichgasse 6, Postfach 298; tel (1) 512-79-04; telex 113261; fax (1) 513-81-20.
Ambassador: Henrik Munck Netterstrøm.
Counsellor: Hugo Østergaard-Andersen.
Counsellor: Peter Taksöe-Jensen.
Counsellor (Special Adviser): Mogens Bruhn.
Counsellor (Trade): Jorgen Elholm.
Counsellor (Fisheries): Holger Bak Andersen.

Consulate-General: 1090 Vienna, Ferstelgasse 3/4; tel (1) 42-22-97; telex 115258.
Honorary Consul-General: Richard Peter Kwizda.

Consulate: 8011 Graz, Grieskai 12-4; tel (316) 91-38-01; telex 311284; fax (316) 913-80-88.
Honorary Consul: Hans Helmut Weitzer.

Consulate: 6020 Innsbruck, Maria Theresien Str. 42; tel (512) 58-29-71; fax (512) 573-95-14.
Honorary Consul: Markus Putscher.

Consulate: 4020 Linz, Figulystr. 27; tel (732) 51-4-14.
Honorary Consul: Erich Wöhrle.

Consulate: 5020 Salzburg, Imbergstr. 15; tel (662) 71-4-85; fax (662) 71-69-86.
Honorary Consul: Norman Dick.

DOMINICAN REPUBLIC

Consulate: 1190 Vienna, Leopold Steinergasse 12; tel (1) 32-21-46.
Honorary Consul: Hans Sommer.

ECUADOR

Embassy: 1010 Vienna, Goldschmiedgasse 10/II/24; tel (1) 535-32-08; telex 134958; fax (1) 535-08-97.
Ambassador: Jorge E. Pareja Cucalón.
Counsellor (Commercial): Dr Fernando Flores Marcias.
First Secretary and Head of Consular Section: Dr Maria del Carmen Gonzales-Cabal.

EGYPT

Embassy: 1190 Vienna, Gallmeyergasse 5; tel (1) 36-11-34; telex 115623; fax (1) 36-63-21.
Ambassador: Mervat Tallawy.
Counsellor: Mohamed Ezz Eldine Abdel-Moneim.
Counsellor: Allem Mohmoud Mohamed.
Counsellor (Commercial/Trade): Soliman el-Gohary.
Counsellor: Maha Kamel Fahmi.
Defence Attaché: Brig.-Gen. Mohamed Ibrahim Emam.
Deputy Defence Attaché: Capt. Hany Moustafa Kamel.
Second Secretary: Taher Ahmed Farahat.
Attaché (Economic): Ahmad Mohamed Ahmad.
Attaché (Economic): Mohamed Reda Mobarek.
Attaché (Economic): Basem Mohamed Labib Mohamed Abdullah.
Attaché (Economic): Shewell Saad Eldin Fath Allah.
Attaché (Economic): Mostafa Elsayed Ahmed.
Attaché (Economic): Salah Youssef Mohamed.
Attaché (Economic): Mohamed Fahti Abbas.
Attaché (Press): Mona Hamouda.

Cultural Section: 1010 Vienna, Dobhoffgasse 3/4; tel (1) 43-24-01.
Counsellor (Cultural): Dr Hazem Ahmed Attiatallah.

FINLAND

Embassy: 1010 Vienna, Gonzagagasse 16/2; tel (1) 53-15-90; telex 135230; fax (1) 535-57-03.
Ambassador: Alec Aalto.
Minister-Counsellor: Antti Sierla.
First Secretary: Merja Lindroos-Binham.
Second Secretary: Anne Sipiläinen.
Second Secretary: Ilkka-Pekka Similä.
Commercial Counsellor: Heikki Masalin.
Commercial Counsellor: Jukka Orispää.
Industrial Attaché: Jukka Anttila.

Consulate-General: 1070 Vienna, Richtergasse 1; tel (1) 93-14-94; fax (1) 93-24-91.
Honorary Consul-General: Walter Kollin.

Consulate: 1070 Vienna, Neubaugasse 4; tel (1) 93-35-00; telex 132929.
Honorary Consul: Gottfried Merckens.

Consulate: 7000 Eisenstadt, Rochusstr. 7; tel (2682) 42-57.
Honorary Consul: Prof. Dr Egon Presoly.

Consulate: 8021 Graz, Waagner-Biró-Str. 39-41; tel (316) 51-5-11; telex 311232; fax (316) 51-5-51.
Honorary Consul: Johannes Hornig.

Consulate: 5400 Hallein, Am Weinberg 1; tel (6245) 32-94; telex 631047; fax (6245) 32-94.
Honorary Consul: Jan Wessel Cappelen.
Honorary Vice-Consul: Marion W. Cappelen.

Consulate: 6020 Innsbruck, Bozner Platz 6; tel (512) 52-09-40; telex 533798; fax (512) 52-0-94.
Honorary Consul: Mario Stedile-Foradori.

Consulate: 9020 Klagenfurt, Villacher Str. 1; tel (463) 51-15-27; telex 422227; fax (463) 56-38-5.
Honorary Consul: Ernst Göß.

Consulate: 4050 Linz, Traun, Postfach 444, Eduard Haasstr. 25; tel (732) 84-2-44; telex 21000.
Honorary Consul: Eduard Haas.

Consulate: 6961 Bregenz/Wolfurt, Rickenbacherstr. 8-11; tel (5574) 35-6-41; telex 57711; fax (5574) 35-5-90.
Honorary Consul: Artur Doppelmayr.

FRANCE

Embassy: 1040 Vienna, Technikerstr. 2; tel (1) 505-47-47; telex 131333; fax (1) 505-63-92-91.
Ambassador: Jean François Noiville.
Counsellor: Francis Bellanger.
Defence, Military and Air Attache: Col Jean Paul Kieffer.
Assistant Defence Attaché: Daniel Blaise.
Second Secretary: Sophie Giami.
Second Secretary and Head of Press and Information: Georges Guiblet.

Trade Section: 1030 Vienna, Reisnerstr. 50; tel (1) 712-63-57.
Trade and Finance Representative: Bertrand Fessard de Foucault.
Assistant Trade Representative: Jacques Chincholle.

Cultural Office: 1090 Vienna, Währinger Str. 30; tel (1) 316-77-60.
Counsellor (Cultural): Michel Guerin.
Counsellor (Cultural/Scientific): Jean-Luc Bredel.

Tourist Office: 1030 Vienna, Hilton Center 2; tel (1) 75-70-62.
Attaché (Tourism): Lucien Dell'Agata.

Consular Section: 1010 Vienna, Wipplingerstr. 24-6; tel (1) 535-62-09.
Head of Consular Section: François Penot.
Attaché and Deputy Head of Consular Section: Geoffroy Muller.

Consular Agency: 9020 Klagenfurt, Hirshchstr. 5; tel (4222) 32-4-23.
Honorary Consular Agent: Hermann Hirsch.

Consular Agency: 4020 Linz, Landstr. 49/I; tel (732) 28-52-21.
Honorary Consular Agent: Ute Pastl-Hippmann.

Consular Agency: 5020 Salzburg, Mozart Pl. 5/7; tel (662) 42-5-01.
Honorary Consular Agent: Günther Klimitsch.

Consular Agency: 6845 Hohenems, Rudolf von Emsstr. 41; tel (5576) 20-12.
Honorary Consular Agent: Anton Fend.

GABON

Consulate: 1010 Vienna, Kärntner Str. 17; tel (1) 512-45-35; telex 111360.
Honorary Consul: Wilhelm Hendricks.

GAMBIA

Consulate-General: 1130 Vienna, Larocheg 30; tel (1) 82-62-45.
Honorary Consul-General: Johanna Huber.

GERMANY

Embassy: 1030 Vienna, Metternichgasse 3; tel (1) 71-1-54; telex 134261; fax (1) 713-83-66.
Ambassador: Philipp Jenninger.
Counsellor: Dietrich Steiner.
Counsellor (Trade): Kirsten Siebold.
Counsellor: Morst Meyer.
Counsellor (Press): Olaf Nichelsen.
Military and Air Attaché: Col Manfred Vieweg.
Assistant Military and Air Attaché: Lieut Col Günter Schmidt.
First Secretary (Science/Research): Gerd Hartmann.
First Secretary (Cultural): Irmgard Nickelsen.
Head of Transport Section: Günter Thiele.
Head of Consular Section: Horst Richel.

Consulate-General: 8011 Graz, Hamerlinggasse 6/I, Postfach 368; tel (316) 82-14-01.
Consul-General: Karl Bellmann.

Consulate-General: 6020 Innsbruck, Adamgasse 5/V; 6021 Innsbruck, Postfach 644; tel (512) 59-6-65; telex 533087.
Consul-General: Richard Louis.

Consulate-General: 5020 Salzburg, Bürgerspitapl. 1; tel (662) 84-15-91.
Consul-General: Karl Reinhard Marks.

Consulate: 6900 Bregenz, Kaspar Hagenstr. 2; tel (5574) 23-1-80; fax (5574) 47-0-83.
Honorary Consul: Wilhelm Otten.

Consulate: 7000 Eisenstadt, Haupstr. 52a; tel (2682) 55-15.
Honorary Consul: Eugen Horvath.

Consulate: 9020 Klagenfurt, Miestalerstr. 14; tel (463) 56-1-60.
Honorary Consul: Dieter Kern.

Consulate: 4020 Linz, Schillerstr. 53/III; tel (732) 66-26-76.
Honorary Consul: Hermann Bell.

GREECE

Embassy: 1040 Vienna, Argentinierstr. 14; tel (1) 505-57-91; telex 133176; fax (1) 505-62-17.
Ambassador: Antonios J. Coundakis.
Counsellor: Vassilios Ikossipentarchos.
Military Attaché: Lieut Andreas Goudas.
First Secretary: Fotios-Jean Xydas.
First Secretary and Head of Consular Section: Dimitros Letsios.
Attaché: Maria Makaratzi.
Attaché and Consul: Georgios Androutsopoulos.
Attaché: Erifili Kontopoulou.
Attaché: Constantin Andriotis.
Attaché: Lais Lambrou.
Attaché: Nicolaos Zaravellas.

Tourism Office: 1010 Vienna, Opernring 8; tel (1) 512-53-17.
Attaché (Tourism): Anastosios Vafiadis.

Trade Section: 1030 Vienna, Bayerng. 3/13; tel (1) 715-41-68.
Counsellor (Trade/Economy): Dr Theodores Karavias.
Second Secretary: Rallou-Evangelia Papazoglou-Xyda.
Attaché: Marianthi Kasparian.

Press Office: 1040 Vienna, Schwindg. 20/3/6; tel (1) 65-81-25.
Counsellor (Press): Joannis Tzortzis.
Head of Press Office: Nikolaos Zervos.

Consulate-General: 5016 Salzburg, Reichenhaller Str. 7; tel (662) 84-31-00.
Honorary Consul-General: Dimitri Z. Pappas.
Honorary Vice-Consul: Georges Z. Pappas.

GUATEMALA

Embassy: 1010 Vienna, Opernring I/R/4/407; tel (1) 56-91-01.
Ambassador: Eduardo Castillo Arriola.

HAITI

Consulate: Vienna.
Honorary Consul: Nikolaus Dreihann-Holenia.

Consulate: 9010 Klagenfurt, Dr Franz Pallagasse 4; tel (463) 55-2-33.
Honorary Consul: Walter Rossmann.

HOLY SEE

Apostolic Nunciature: 1040 Vienna, Theresianumgasse 31; tel (1) 505-13-27.
Apostolic Nuncio: Most Rev. Donato Squicciarini, Titular Archbishop of Tiburnia.
Secretary: Mgr Thomas E. Gullickson.

HONDURAS

Consulate: 1235 Vienna, Breitenfurter Str. 380 A/8; tel (1) 88-70-77.
Honorary Consul: Ewald Kloser.
Honorary Vice-Consul: Klaus Stanglmayer.

HUNGARY

Embassy: 1010 Vienna, Bankgasse 4-6; tel (1) 533-26-31; telex 135546.
Ambassador: János Nagy.
Counsellor (Press): Jenó Batha.
Counsellor: Jószef Kovács.
Counsellor: György Krausz.
Counsellor: Lajos Dezsó.
Counsellor and Head of Consular Section: János Biro.
Counsellor (Consular): Ottó Lelovies.
Military and Air Attaché: Lieut Col István Horváth.
Assistant Military and Air Attaché: Lieut Col Tamás Tóth.
First Secretary (Consular): Márta Horváth Fekszi.
Second Secretary (Science/Technology): László Stoklász.

Press Office: 1010 Vienna, Teinfaltstr. 4; tel (1) 63-03-76.
Second Secretary (Press): Zoltán Imecs.

Cultural Institute: 1020 Vienna, Hollandstr. 4; tel (1) 24-05-81.
Counsellor and Head of Cultural Institute: Ferenc Grossmann.

Trade Office: 1010 Vienna, Parkring 12/III; tel (1) 512-66-41; telex 1622.
Counsellor and Head of Trade Office: Gyula Kovács.
Counsellor (Trade): Jószef Czeglédi.

ICELAND

Consulate-General: Vienna, Naglergasse 2/5; tel (1) 533-24-98; fax (1) 875-03-35.
Honorary Consul-General: Dr Cornelia Schubrig.
Vice-Consul: Alfred Schubrig.

Consulate: 5020 Salzburg, Ursulinenplatz 4; tel (662) 84-35-91; telex 632036; fax (662) 84-35-11.
Honorary Consul: Erich Eibl.

INDIA

Embassy: 1015 Vienna, Kärntner Ring 2; tel (1) 505-86-66; telex 113721; fax (1) 505-92-19.
Ambassador: Peter L. Sinai.
Counsellor and Deputy Head of Mission: Saurabh Kumar.
Counsellor (Commercial): S. K. Gupta.
Counsellor: Dr Ashok Mohan.
First Secretary (Economic): P. N. G. Subramanian.
First Secretary and Head of Chancery: D. R. Pradhan.

INDONESIA

Embassy: 1180 Vienna, Gustav-Tschermak-Gasse 5-7; tel (1) 34-25-34; telex 75579.
Ambassador: Johannes Petrus Louhanapessy.
Counsellor (Commercial): Hanny Rehem T. Situmorang.
Counsellor (Commercial): Dadang Sukander.
Counsellor (Commercial): Zulkarnain Afri Pane.
Counsellor: Jacky Djumantara Wahyu.
Counsellor (Economic): Sri Narjadi.
First Secretary: Susanto Martokusumo.
Second Secretary: Djismun Kasri.

Second Secretary: Mr Nurhadi.
Second Secretary (Economic): Abdullah Rustam.
Attaché (Science): Jasif Iljas.
Attaché (Industrial): Mohammad Chunsaeni Bambang Djatmiko.
Attaché (Trade): Doddy Hidajat.

IRAN

Embassy: 1030 Vienna, Jaurèsgasse 3; tel (1) 72-26-57; telex 131718; fax (1) 713-57-33.
Ambassador: Hossein Noghrehkar Shirazi.
Counsellor (Commercial): Mohammad Reza Mobarhan.
Second Secretary and Head of Consular Section: Hassan Yousefi Soumeh Sarace.
Third Secretary: Mohammed Ali Sadeghi Nyaraki.
Third Secretary: Farhad Mamdouhi.
Attaché: Vahab Banaee Kalkhouran.
Attaché: Majid Eslami.
Attaché: Ramezan Karami.
Attaché: Mohammed Hossein Bakshizadeh Moghaddam.
Attaché (Press/Culture): Ali Sadeghi.
Attaché: Ahmad Aghighi.
Attaché: Morteza Khonssari.

IRAQ

Embassy: 1010 Vienna, Johannesgasse 26; tel (1) 713-81-95; telex 135397; fax (1) 713-67-20.
Ambassador: Dr Rahim Abid Alkital.
Counsellor: Ghaleb Fahad.
Counsellor: Matooq A. Muhammad al-Matooq.
Second Secretary: Abdul Razzak Hamoud Ahmed.
Attaché: Abd al-Mushin Subhi.
Attaché: Sabah T. Fayadh.

IRELAND

Embassy: 1030 Vienna, Hilton Centre, 16th Floor, POB 139; tel (1) 75-42-46; telex 136887; fax (1) 713-60-04.
Ambassador: Joseph Small.
First Secretary: Kathleen White.
Secretary: Michael Sanfey.

ISRAEL

Embassy: 1180 Vienna, Anton Frank-Gasse 20; tel (1) 31-15-06; telex 4005; fax (1) 31-70-09.
Chargé d'affaires a.i.: Gideon Yarden.
Counsellor: Gershon Gorev.
Counsellor (Economic) and Head of Consular Section: Uriel Itzhaki.
First Secretary: Jacob-David Hadas-Handelsman.
Second Secretary: Daniel Tamuz.
Second Secretary: Itzhak Efrat.
Attaché: Andras Zer.
Attaché: Ruth Cohan Dar.
Attaché: Avraham Koren.
Attaché: Shimon Zamir.
Attaché: David Zohary.
Attaché: Joel Zaloman.

ITALY

Embassy: 1030 Vienna, Rennweg 27; tel (1) 712-51-21; telex 132620; fax (1) 713-97-19.
Ambassador: Dr Alessandro Quaroni.
First Counsellor: Fabrizio de Agostini.
Counsellor: Mario Musella.
Counsellor: Faiti Salvadori.
Counsellor (Commercial): Dr Franco Tempesta.
Counsellor: Dr Gianfranco Giorgolo.
Military and Air Attaché: Col Natalino Vivaldi.
First Secretary (Economic): Enrico Fazio.
Attaché (Cultural): Dr Lorenzo Gabetti.
Administrative Inspector: Dr Marina Livadiotti.
Scientific Attaché: Dr Vittorio Manno.
Consulate: 1030 Vienna, Ungargasse 43; tel (1) 713-56-71.
Consul: Marco del Panta Ridolfi.
Consulate-General: 6020 Innsbruck, Conradstr. 9A; tel (512) 58-13-33.
Consul-General: Silvestro Scimonelli.
Consulate-General: 9010 Klagenfurt, Karfreitstr. 24; tel (463) 51-30-55; fax (463) 51-32-46.
Consul-General: Nicola di Tullio.
Consular Agency: 9500 Villach, Hauptpl. 19.
Honorary Consular Agent: Dante Buzzi.
Consulate: 3010 Graz, Elisabethstr. 16; tel (316) 32-1-53.
Honorary Consul: Salvatore Corsaro.
Consulate: 6900 Bregenz, Maurachgasse 19; tel (5574) 22-2-43.
Honorary Vice-Consul: Ivo Fischer.
Consulate: 1000 Eisenstadt, Haydngasse 17; tel (2682) 31-55.
Honorary Vice-Consul: Margarete Gati.
Consulate: 4010 Linz, Hessenpl. 19; tel (732) 276-54-30.
Honorary Vice-Consul: Norbert Bemkofer.
Consulate: 5020 Salzburg, Alpenstr. 102; tel (662) 25-2-33.
Honorary Vice-Consul: Nicola Nicolelli Fulgenzi.

JAMAICA

Consulate: 1050 Vienna, Rüdigergasse 22; tel (1) 587-13-13.
Honorary Consul: Herbert Haberl.

JAPAN

Embassy: 1040 Vienna, Argentinierstr. 21; tel (1) 501-71-02; telex 135810; fax (1) 505-45-37.
Ambassador: Kazutoshi Hasegawa.
Counsellor: Teruyoshi Inagawa.
First Secretary (Health): Dr Tetsuro Nakamura.
First Secretary: Yoshikazu Takeuchi.
First Secretary: Masayoshi Kamohara.
First Secretary: Masaho Nishihara.
First Secretary: Masato Kaji.
First Secretary (Consular): Seishi Tashiro.
First Secretary (Administrative): Takao Kitamoto.
First Secretary (Administrative): Fumihiko Matsumi.
Cultural Section: 1040 Vienna, Mattiellstr. 2/4; tel (1) 512-32-49.
Second Secretary (Cultural): Seisuke Narumiya.
Consulate-General: 5020 Salzburg, Ernest-Thun Str. 8; tel (662) 78-58-1.
Honorary Consul-General: Thomas Wassibauer.

JORDAN

Consulate-General: 1010 Vienna, Rotenturmstr. 25; tel (1) 533-02-33; telex 114701.
Honorary Consul-General: Prof. Hannes Lintl.
Honorary Consul: Christian Lintl.

KENYA

Consulate: 1190 Vienna, Hohe Warte 7A; tel (1) 36-51-73.
Honorary Consul: Ingrid Seeman-Pelicon.

KOREA, DEMOCRATIC PEOPLE'S REPUBLIC

Embassy: 1140 Vienna, Beckmanngasse 10-12; tel (1) 894-23-11; telex 131750.
Ambassador: Chou In Chan.
Counsellor: Kil Gyong Chil.
Counsellor: Li Myong Gun.
Second Secretary: Kim Tschol Ryong.
Second Secretary (Trade): Myong Gil Hyon.
Third Secretary: O Won Chang.
Third Secretary (Trade): Chon Chol Ho.

KOREA, REPUBLIC

Embassy: 1020 Vienna, Praterstr. 31; tel (1) 215-34-41; telex 131252.
Ambassador: Lee Chang-Choon.
Counsellor (Commercial): Park Wang Kyu.
Counsellor (Commercial): Hahm Myung-Chul.
Counsellor: Lee Tae Sik.
Military Attaché: Col Lee Jin Young.
First Secretary: Chang Young Dai.
Second Secretary: Kim Jong Hae.
Second Secretary and Consul: Yong Kyu Kwon.
Attaché and Vice-Consul: Lee In Yong.
Attaché (Science): Nam Ho.
Attaché (Trade): Jung Si Kyung.
Attaché (Cultural/Information): Son Wie Soo.
Consulate: 5020 Salzburg, Getreideg 2; tel (662) 42-2-98.
Honorary Consul: Peter Malata.

KUWAIT

Embassy: 1010 Vienna, Universitätstr. 5; tel (1) 42-56-46; telex 135898.
Ambassador: Abdul-Hamid Abdullah al-Awadhi.
Counsellor: Zaid Sherida Zaid al-Sherida.
Attaché: Mohammad Sulaiman Abdul-Aziz al-Fraih.
Attaché: Ali Sulaiman al-Saeid.

LEBANON

Embassy: 1010 Vienna, Schwedenplatz 2/15; tel (1) 63-88-21; telex 115273.
Chargé d'affaires: Christiane Gezrawi-Bassile.
First Secretary: Ishaya el-Khoury.

LIBERIA

Consulate: 1030 Vienna, Reisnerstr. 20; tel (1) 713-65-58.
Honorary Consul: Christiane Knoblich.

LIBYA

People's Bureau: 1170 Vienna, Dornbacherstr. 27; tel (1) 45-36-11; telex 116267.
Secretary of People's Bureau: Enbeia Mansur Wadi.
First Secretary and Consul: M. B. Khalifa Fergiani.
Second Secretary (Finance): Hassan Ayyad Hamed.
Attaché (Economic): Mohamed B. Bashir Nagi.
Attaché (Health): Ibrahem K. Almantaser.
Attaché (Health): Dr Attia Taher Gieaay.
Attaché (Press/Cultural): Elmahdi Saleh Merjbi.

LIECHTENSTEIN

Embassy: 1014 Vienna, Ballhausplatz 2.

LUXEMBOURG

Embassy: 1190 Vienna, Hofzeile 27; tel (1) 36-21-86; telex 115276; fax (1) 369-26-97.
Ambassador: Jacques Reuter.
Attaché and Vice-Consul: Stan Myck.
Consulate-General: 1210 Vienna, Divischgasse 4; tel (1) 39-35-27.
Honorary Consul-General: Georg Fürstenberg.
Consulate: 6020 Innsbruck, Falkstr. 1; tel (512) 34-3-40.
Honorary Consul: Herbert Braunsteiner.
Consulate: 5412 Puch/Salzburg, 262; tel (6245) 26-82.
Honorary Consul: Dieter Usner.

MADAGASCAR

Consulate-General: 1184 Vienna, Pötzleinsdorfer Str. 94/6; tel (1) 47-12-73.
Honorary Consul-General: Robert Krapfenbauer.

MALAWI

Consulate: 1190 Vienna, Saarpl. 17; tel (1) 369-26-28.
Honorary Consul: Friedrich Wimmer.

MALAYSIA

Embassy: 1040 Vienna, Prinz Eugen-Str. 18; tel (1) 505-10-42; telex 133830; fax (1) 505-79-42.
Ambassador: Abdul Halim bin Ali.
Counsellor: Hussin Nayan.
Counsellor (Trade): Samad bin Kassim.
Third Secretary: Alias Mohd Isa.
Third Secretary: Khahl bin Musa.
Attaché (Science): Fatimahj Mohd Amin.

MALTA

Consulate-General: 1140 Vienna, Kienmayergasse 15; tel (1) 92-26-01; telex 133170.
Honorary Consul-General: Alfred Klima.

Consulate: 5020 Salzburg, Getreideg. 37; tel (662) 84-85-11.
Honorary Consul: Johannes Walderdorff.

Consulate: 6029 Innsbruck, Amraser Seestr. 56a; tel (512) 43-3-11.
Honorary Consul: Walter Hess.

MAURITANIA

Consulate: 5541 Altenmarkt, Im Pongau; tel (6452) 60-01.
Honorary Consul: Engelbert Steiner.

MEXICO

Embassy: 1040 Vienna, Renngasse 4; tel (1) 535-17-76; telex 115660; fax (1) 535-17-76.
Ambassador: Eugenio Anguiano Roch.
Counsellor (Commercial): Dr Maria Cristina de la Garza Sandoval.
First Secretary: Javier Ramon Brito Moncada.
Attaché: Porfirio Thierry Munoz Ledo.
Attaché: Roberto Trevino Arizpe.
Attaché: Rosa Maria Castro Valle.
Attaché: Maripilar Alcala Arrando.

Trade Section: 1010 Vienna, Passauer Pl. 5; tel (1) 63-72-60.
Counsellor (Trade): Licenciado Joaquin Eversbusch von Loebecke.

Consulate: 6020 Innsbruck, Südtiroler Pl. 6/VI; tel (512) 58-00-21.
Honorary Consul: Manfred Swarovski.

MONACO

Consulate-General: 1184 Vienna, Khevenhüllerstr. 9a; tel (1) 44-14-61.
Honorary Consul-General: Isabelle Hild.
Honorary Vice-Consul: Herbert Hild.

MOROCCO

Embassy: 1020 Vienna, Untere Donaustr. 13-15; tel (1) 24-25-68; fax (1) 216-79-84.
Ambassador: Taoufik Kabbaj.
Counsellor: Ahmed Bakhat.
Counsellor: Mohamed Rida el-Fasi.
Secretary: Abdallah Zegrani.
Secretary: Ahmed el-Ghernougui.
Secretary: Mohamed Ait Hmid.
Attaché: Brahim el-Atmani.
Attaché: Ahmed Taki.
Attaché: Mohamed Aouad.

NETHERLANDS

Embassy: 1020 Vienna, Untere Donaustr. 13-15/VIII; tel (1) 24-85-87; telex 135462; fax (1) 216-57-22.
Ambassador: Lodewijk H. J. B. van Gorkom.
Counsellor (Commercial): Cornelius M. M. H. R. van Hanswijck de Jonge.
Counsellor (Transport/Post/Telecommunications): Willem Adrianus van den Toorn.
First Secretary (UN): David A. H. van Iterson.
First Secretary (IAEA): Pieter de Klerk.
Second Secretary (Trade): Saskia E. de Lang.
Attaché (Economic) and Head of Consular Section: Herman F. L. M. Timmermans.

Agricultural Office: 1020 Vienna, Untere Donaustr. 13-15/7; tel (1) 24-85-87.
Counsellor (Agriculture): F. J. Guerten.
Attaché (Agriculture): Jean Frédéric Rummenie.

Consulate: 8020 Graz, Lastenstr. 11; tel (316) 91-15-65.
Honorary Consul: Michael Mayer-Rieckh.

Consulate: 6020 Innsbruck, Salurner Str. 1; tel (512) 27-4-92.
Honorary Consul: Andreas Trentini.

Consulate: 9020 Klagenfurt, Alter Pl. 1; tel (4222) 55-0-06.
Honorary Consul: Heinrich Orsini-Rosenberg.

Consulate: 4020 Linz, Kapuzinerstr. 84; tel (732) 28-40-06.
Honorary Consul: Hugo Wagner.

Consulate: 5020 Salzburg, Lastenstr. 20; tel (662) 73-3-23.
Honorary Consul: Werner Winzer.

NEW ZEALAND

Embassy: 1010 Vienna, Lugeck 1, Postfach 1471; tel (1) 512-66-36; telex 136582; fax (1) 512-66-39.
Ambassador: Barry Hewitt Brooks.
Second Secretary: Maree Johnson.
Second Secretary: Deborah Jackson.
Trade Commissioner: Stephen Diver.

NICARAGUA

Embassy: 1070 Vienna, Neustiftgasse 66, Rothensteiner Apts; tel (1) 93-96-43.
Ambassador: Humberto Carrion McDonough.

Consulate: 6700 Bludenz, Herrengasse 23; tel (5552) 62-2-35.
Honorary Consul: Josef Bertsch.

NIGER

Consulate: 1040 Vienna, Fleischmanngasse 9/2; tel (1) 587-35-43; telex 133104; fax (1) 587-20-81.
Honorary Consul: Hermann Mörtendorfer.

NIGERIA

Embassy: 1030 Vienna, Rennweg 25; tel (1) 72-66-85; telex 131583.
Ambassador: Timothy Anaele Mgbokwere.
Counsellor (Commercial): Abiodun O. Bashua.
Counsellor (Commercial): M. M. Bauchi.
First Secretary: Sylvia Ekpo.
Second Secretary: I. Jack.
Second Secretary: Abdullahi Tukur.
Attaché (Finance): Michael O. Idowu.
Attaché (Economic): Grace O. N. Nduonofit.
Attaché (Economic): S. O. Braide.

NORWAY

Embassy: 1030 Vienna, Bayerngasse 1/3; tel (1) 715-66-92; telex 132768; fax (1) 72-65-52.
Ambassador: Knut Hedemann.
Counsellor (Commercial): Ralf Olaf Berg.
First Secretary: And Marit Wiig.
Attaché: Karin Rager.
Defence Attaché: Brig.-Gen. Alf Hammer.

Consulate-General: 1010 Vienna, Dr Karl Lueger-Ring 6; tel (1) 53-468.
Honorary Consul-General: Johann Kwizda.

Consulate: 1010 Vienna, Schotteng 6; tel (1) 53-1-31.
Honorary Consul: Rudolf Schneider.

Consulate: 8010 Graz, Geidorfgürtel 20/II; tel (316) 32-5-25.
Honorary Consul: Heinz Scheidbach.

Consulate: 5020 Salzburg, Alter Markt 10; tel (662) 84-63-33.
Honorary Consul: Herbert Vogel.

Consulate: 6020 Innsbruck, Erlersstr. 9; tel (512) 53-33.
Honorary Consul: Gerhard Moser.

Consulate: 6840 Götzis, Breite 12; tel (5523) 25-83.
Honorary Consul: Herwig Rhomberg.

OMAN

Embassy: 1090 Vienna, Währingerstr. 2-4/24-25; tel (1) 31-64-52; telex 116662.
Chargé d'affaires: Yahya S. H. al-Wahaibi.
First Secretary: Jaifer Sahim Ali al-Said.
Second Secretary: Jamal bin Amer bin Nasser al-Yahmadi.

PAKISTAN

Embassy: 1190 Vienna, Hofzeile 13; tel (1) 36-73-81; telex 135634; fax (1) 36-73-76.
Chargé d'affaires a.i. and First Secretary: Iftikhar A. Arain.
Third Secretary: Amjad Hussain B. Sial.
Attaché (Commercial/Atomic Energy): Jawad A. Hashimi.

PANAMA

Embassy: 1030 Vienna, Strohgasse 35/6; tel (1) 713-46-33.
Ambassador: Ernesto Koref.
Counsellor: Diana Chavez Centeno.

Consulate-General: 5020 Salzburg, Ziegeleistr. 26; tel (662) 77-3-76.
Honorary Consul-General: Leonhard Voithofer.

PARAGUAY

Consulate: 1080 Vienna, Trautsong 6; tel (1) 48-86-29.
Honorary Consul: Josef Moser.

PERU

Embassy: 1030 Vienna, Gottfried-Keller-Gasse 2; tel (1) 713-43-77; telex 135524; fax (1) 712-77-04.
Ambassador: Dr Alejandro San Martín Caro.
Counsellor (Commercial): Walter P. Negreiros.
Counsellor: Alberto Salas Barahona.
Counsellor: Dr Paul Andres Paredes Portella.
Counsellor (Commercial): Martha Chavarri-Dupuy.
Third Secretary: Manuel Torres Franco.

Consulate-General: 5020 Salzburg, Linzer Gasse 42; tel (662) 72-3-56.
Honorary Consul-General: Erwin Apfler.

PHILIPPINES

Embassy: 1190 Vienna, Nedergasse 34; tel (1) 36-84-48; telex 132740.
Ambassador: Nelson D. Laviña.
Counsellor (Commercial): Eloy Bello III.
First Secretary: Linglingay F. Lacanlale.
Attaché (Finance): Susan T. Hebreo.
Attaché: Eriberto C. Castillo.
Attaché: Emiliana P. Dulay.
Assistant Attaché: Carolina A. Constantino.

Consulate-General: 5016 Salzburg, Moosstr. 195; tel (662) 84-43-58.
Honorary Consul-General: Peter Franz Wagner.

Consulate: 8041 Graz, Liebenauer Haupstr. 64; tel (316) 413-33-77.
Honorary Consul: Axel Brandner.

POLAND

Embassy: 1130 Vienna, Hietzinger Hauptstr. 42c; tel (1) 82-74-44; fax (1) 82-92-68.
Ambassador: Stanisław Bejger.
Counsellor and Chargé d'affaires: Miroslaw Wojtkowski.
Counsellor and Head of Polish Institute: Prof. Dr Boleslaw Faron.
Counsellor: Konrad Biczyk.
Counsellor: Anna Betkowska.
Military and Air Attaché: Lieut Col Tadeuz Lesniowski.
Deputy Military and Air Attaché: Capt. Jerzy Zadora.
First Secretary and Head of Consular Section: Jerzy Szustakievicz.
First Secretary: Jerzy Kawiak.
First Secretary: Jan Kniaz.
First Secretary: Marek Wagner.
First Secretary (Press): Marek Pietraszewski.

Trade Office: 1130 Vienna, Titlgasse 15; tel (1) 82-63-43.
Counsellor (Trade): Dr Adam S. Martowski.
Counsellor (Economic): Slaw Milewski.
Assistant Attaché (Finance): Arkadiusz Kaczor.

Cultural and Scientific Section: 1010 Vienna, Am Gestade 7; tel (1) 63-89-61.
Second Secretary and Head of Cultural and Scientific Section: Andrjez Placzynski.

PORTUGAL

Embassy: 1040 Vienna, Operngasse 20B; tel (1) 56-75-36; telex 113237; fax (1) 587-58-39.
Ambassador: Carlos Ary-dos-Santos.
Counsellor (Commercial): José Barbosa Ferreira.
Counsellor: Dr Frederico Alcantara de Melo.
First Secretary: Dr Vera Fernandez.

Trade Office: 1010 Vienna, Stubenring 16; tel (1) 513-26-70.
Counsellor (Trade): Dr Luis Henrique Lasso de la Vega Charters.
Attaché (Trade): Luis Felipe d'Oliveira Pereira.

Consulate: 4020 Linz, Mozartstr. 11/31; tel (732) 27-22-81.
Honorary Consul: Rudolf Ungar.

Consulate: 5020 Salzburg, Faberstr. 2b; tel (662) 73-9-02.
Honorary Consul: Hans Werner Ebner.

QATAR

Embassy: 1090 Vienna, Strudlhofgasse 10; tel (1) 31-66-39; telex 131306; fax (1) 31-70-86.
Ambassador: Jasim Yousof Jamal.
Counsellor: Abdulrahman al-Muftah.
Second Secretary: Mohamed Ahmed al-Haiyki.
Third Secretary: Mohamed Jaber Abdullah al-Sulaiti.

ROMANIA

Embassy: 1040 Vienna, Prinz Eugen-Str. 60; tel (1) 505-32-27; telex 133335.
Ambassador: Constantin Georgescu.
Counsellor: Vasile Todoran.
Trade Counsellor: Nicolae Jantea.
Counsellor: Florian Murg.
Military and Air Attaché: Col Ion Arcadie Sasu.
First Secretary: Andrei Sanda.
First Secretary: Corneliu Găvăneanu.
First Secretary: Dr Gheorghe Bivol.

RUSSIA

Embassy: 1030 Vienna, Reisnerstr. 45-47; tel (1) 72-12-29; telex 136278; fax (1) 72-33-88.
Ambassador: Valeri N. Popov.
Counsellor (Commercial) and Chargé d'affaires: Piotr A. Smidovich.
Counsellor: Dr Vladimir Matlatch.
Counsellor: Henrique W. Kokorev.
Counsellor: Vladimir Gubernov.
Counsellor: Janis Zakenfeld.
Counsellor: Yuri W. Aljokhin.
Counsellor: Oleg J. Raevich.
Counsellor: Boris A. Leonov.
Counsellor: Ivan I. Alekhnovich.
Counsellor: Alexandre Stupak.
Military and Air Attaché: Col Yuri N. Belaev.
Assistant Military Attaché: Lieut Col Victor A. Telechev.
Assistant Military and Air Attaché: Col Yuri S. Klytschichin.
Assistant Military Attaché: Lieut Col Alexandre O. Lossik.
First Secretary: Mikhail P. Tavokin.
First Secretary: Lev Ivanovich Chilov.
First Secretary: Valeri Dimitrievich Onichtchenko.
First Secretary: Vladimir V. Lejen.
First Secretary: Alexandre S. Koulin.
First Secretary: Vladimir Galitski.
First Secretary: Alexandre V. Blagov.
Attaché (Science/Technology): Vladimir V. Azarenkov.

Trade Section: 1040 Vienna, Argentinierstr. 27; tel (1) 505-26-68.
Counsellor and Head of Trade Section: Oleg N. Korounv.
Counsellor (Trade): Dmitri D. Dontsov.
Third Secretary (Trade): Viktor A. Kozirev.

Consulate-General: 5020 Salzburg, Bürglsteinstr. 2; tel (66) 22-41-84.
Consul-General: Genrich E. Lapin.
Consul: V. I. Sobolev.

RWANDA

Consulate: 1070 Vienna, Burggasse 60; tel (1) 93-46-79.
Honorary Consul: Viktor Wagner.

SAN MARINO

Embassy: 1090 Vienna, Spitalgasse 17A; tel (1) 42-42-47; telex 113792; fax (1) 48-76-13.
Ambassador: Giovanni Vito Marcucci.

Consulate-General: 1090 Vienna, Spitalgasse 17A; tel (1) 42-26-65; telex 113792.
Honorary Consul-General: Helmut Petsch.

SAUDI ARABIA

Embassy: 1190 Vienna, Formanekgasse 38; tel (1) 36-23-16; telex 115757.
Ambassador: Essa A. al-Nowaiser.
Counsellor (Science/Atomic Energy): Dr Mohammed Hassan Kattan.
First Secretary: Kassem al-Hejin.
First Secretary: Nasir A. al-Hooti.
First Secretary: Fahad al-Zeid.
Second Secretary: Nabil Hussain Ashri.
Second Secretary: Abdullah S. al-Subaihi.
Third Secretary: Abdulmomen M. Sharaf.
Attaché: Saud Ali Abu-Najafa.

Cultural Section: 1030 Vienna, Rennweg 17; tel (1) 713-91-97.
Attaché (Cultural): Abdullah A. Alhussain.
Attaché: Abdulaziz al-Jybllam.

SENEGAL

Consulate-General: 6020 Innsbruck, Kapuzinergasse 10; tel (512) 58-89-57.
Honorary Consul-General: Helmut P. Lerch.

Consulate-General: 5020 Salzburg, Getreidegasse 22; tel (662) 84-57-20.
Honorary Consul: Fritz Kutscha.

Consulate: 4020 Linz, Bethlehemstr. 3; tel (732) 28-19-51.
Honorary Consul: Bernhard Lobnig.

SIERRA LEONE

Consulate: 1070 Vienna, Sigmundsgasse 16; tel (1) 93-51-00
Honorary Vice-Consul: Michael Schilling.

Consulate-General: 5071 Wals bei Salzburg, Wals Nr 257, Postfach 47.
Honorary Consul-General: Hans Harrer.

SINGAPORE

Consulate: 1030 Vienna, Am Stadtpark 9; tel (1) 71-7-07.
Honorary Consul: Klaus Liebscher.

SOUTH AFRICA

Embassy: 1190 Vienna, Sandgasse 33; tel (1) 32-64-93; telex 116671.
Ambassador and Permanent Representative (UN/IAEA): Cecilia Johanna Schmidt.
Counsellor and Alternate Permanent Representative (UN/IAEA): Pieter J. S. Bezuidenhout.
Counsellor (Cultural): Prof. Richard Herman Behrens.
First Secretary: Christian Frederik Pool.
First Secretary: Petrus Jacobus Viviers.
First Secretary (Trade): Gerhardus Stander.
First Secretary: Wolf Joachim Rothkegel.
First Secretary (Economic): Richard Badenhorst.
First Secretary (UN) and Adviser (IAEA): M. I. Heyns.
First Secretary (UN) and Adviser (IAEA): J. Kellerman.
Third Secretary (Consular): Ingrid Brummerhoff.

Consulate: 8020 Graz, Villefortgasse 13/II; tel (316) 32-5-48; telex 3927115.
Honorary Consul: Herbert Depisch.

SPAIN

Embassy: 1040 Vienna, Argentinierstr. 34; tel (1) 505-57-80; telex 131545; fax (1) 650-90-59.
Ambassador: Dr Jesús Núñez.
Counsellor (Commercial): Javier Urzáiz y Azlor de Aragon.
Counsellor (Economic): Gonzalo Bescos Ferraz.
Counsellor: Juan Manuel Molina Lamothe.
Attaché (Tourism): Fernando Gayo de Aranzana.

Trade Office: 1010 Vienna, Stubenring 16/1, Postfach 604; tel (1) 513-39-33.

Cultural Section: 1040 Vienna, Goldeggasse 7; tel (1) 505-25-35.
Counsellor (Cultural/Press): Dr Xavier Selles Ferrando.
Attaché (Cultural): Prof. Jaime Siles.

Consulate: 5024 Salzburg, Schwarzstr. 19; tel (662) 70-5-71.
Honorary Consul: Günter Daghofer.

Consulate: 4060 Linz-Leonding, Kremstal-Bundesstr., Peintnerstr. 2a; tel (732) 67-45-45.
Honorary Consul: Carl Rosenauer.

Consulate: 6832 Feldkirch, Muntlix 181; tel (5522) 42-3-23.
Honorary Consul: Franz Bischof.

SRI LANKA

Consulate-General: 1010 Vienna, Wiesingerstr. 8; tel (1) 513-17-48.
Honorary Consul-General: Kurt Hawlicek.

SUDAN

Embassy: 1090 Vienna, Spittelauer Platz 4/1-4; tel (1) 34-46-40; telex 114385.
Ambassador: Ali Yassin Gaili.
Counsellor: Hashim Abdel Rahman.
Attaché (Economic): Mahmoud Ibrahim Mohamed.
Second Secretary: Salwa Dallalah.
Military and Air Attaché: Brig. Faisal Mohamed Sinada.

SWEDEN

Embassy: 1020 Vienna, Obere Donaustr. 49-51; tel (1) 33-45-45; telex 114720; fax (1) 35-75-82.
Ambassador: Curt Lidgard.
Minister: Sten Ask.
Counsellor: Agneta Bohman.
First Secretary: Eva Walder Brundin.
First Secretary and Consul: Björn Hagström.

Trade Section: 1010 Vienna, Universitätsstr. 5; tel (1) 402-35-15.
Counsellor (Trade): Sten Sture Wallin.

Consulate: 6850 Dornbirn, Oberdorfer Str. 2, Postfach 2; tel (5572) 64-5-61; telex 59181; fax (5572) 39-94-60.
Honorary Consul: Hanno Hämmerie.
Chancellor: Angelika Wittwer.

Consulate: 7001 Eisenstadt, Julius-Raab-Str. 1; tel (2682) 25 86 55; telex 17739.
Consul: Hans Hahnenkamp.
Chancellor: Peter Wrann.

Consulate: 8010 Graz, Beethovenstr. 19; tel (316) 34-2-52; telex 311619; fax (316) 821-687-17.
Honorary Consul: Erhard Wressnig.
Chancellor: Wendela Birgitta Gogg.

Consulate: 6020 Innsbruck, Andreas Hofer Str. 43; tel (512) 57-18-71; telex 61352-2230; fax (512) 57-98-65.
Honorary Consul: Helmut Marsoner.
Chancellor: Margarethe Zankl.

Consulate: 9020 Klagenfurt, Dr Arthur Lemisch Pl. 5; tel (463) 58-58; telex 422220; fax (463) 511-555-255.
Honorary Consul: Maximilian Meran.
Chancellor: Roswitha Smrekar.

Consulate: 4020 Linz, Hessenpl. 3, Handelskammer; tel (732) 280-02-01; telex 02-1230.
Honorary Consul: Arnold Richter.
Chancellor: Friederike Trinker-Gronau.

Consulate: 5020 Salzburg, Max Ott Pl. 6; tel (662) 88-20-21; telex 633616.
Honorary Consul: Othmar Horwath.
Chancellor: Ines Vrabel.

SWITZERLAND

Embassy: 1030 Vienna, Prinz Eugen-Str. 7; tel (1) 78-45-21; telex 132960; fax (1) 78-45-21.
Ambassador: Jean-Pierre Ritter.
Counsellor (Commercial): Pierre Luciri.
Counsellor and Head of Consular Section: Fred Jenny.
Defence Attaché: Col Charles Ott.
Deputy Defence Attaché: Maj. Samuel Hunziker.
First Secretary: Beat Loeliger.
Attaché and Vice-Consul: Eric Pfändler.

Consulate: 6900 Bregenz, Römer Str. 35; tel (5574) 23-2-32.
Consul: Ernst Bänziger.
Chancellor: Jost Schmid.

Consular Agency: 6020 Innsbruck, Höhenstr. 107; tel (512) 33-1-93.
Honorary Consular Agent: Heribert Berger.

Consular Agency: 4020 Linz, Eisenhandstr. 15; tel (732) 28-37-41.
Honorary Consular Agent: L. Dionys Lehner.

Consular Agency: 5020 Salzburg, Alpenstr. 85; tel (662) 22-5-30.
Honorary Consular Agent: Rudolf Frey.

Consular Agency: 9100 Völkermarkt, Wildstr. 4; tel (4232) 25-27.
Honorary Consular Agent: Hanspeter Brutschy.

THAILAND

Embassy: 1180 Vienna, Weimarer-Str. 68; tel (1) 310-16-30; telex 133893; fax (1) 310-39-35.
Ambassador: Sawanit Kongsiri.
Counsellor: Vichien Chensavacdijai.
First Secretary: Yupadi Wattanalai.
First Secretary (Industry): Kanokpan Chancharaswat.
Second Secretary: Dr Thanes Sucharikul.
Attaché (Industry): Soodsakorn Putho.

Trade Office: 1030 Vienna, Dampfschiffstr. 6/1; tel (1) 712-59-56.
Counsellor (Trade): Manoon Saenghiruna.
First Secretary (Trade): Inthorn Wankeao.
First Secretary (Trade): Chanchai Nokdhes.

Consulate-General: 1190 Vienna, Formanekgasse 12-4; tel (1) 36-53-43.
Honorary Consul-General: Claudius R. Walter.

Consulate: 6850 Dornbirn, Bahnhoferstr. 28; tel (5572) 65-6-14.
Honorary Consul: Peter Ambros Fitz.

Consulate: 6020 Innsbruck, Bozner Pl. 2; tel (512) 20-4-61; telex 653507.
Honorary Consul: Armin Sautter.

Consulate: 5020 Salzburg, Arenbergerstr. 2; tel (662) 71-6-69.
Honorary Consul: Alfons Coreth.

TOGO

Consulate: 1070 Vienna, Siebensterngasse 19; tel (1) 96-13-29.
Honorary Consul: Gerhard Zinsler.

TUNISIA

Embassy: 1030 Vienna, Ghegastr. 3; tel (1) 78-65-52; telex 111748; fax (1) 78-73-41.
Ambassador: Habib Ammar.
Counsellor (Commercial): Ali Chtioui.
Counsellor (Tourism): Saida Chtioui.
Counsellor: Taoufik el-Gueyed.
First Secretary: Mohamed Ridha Hamada.
First Secretary: Dr Zouheir Allagui.
First Secretary: Khaled el-Fendri.
Attaché (Social Affairs): Fethi ben Messaoud.

Consulate: 1010 Vienna, Opernring 1, 8 Opernringerhofgesellschaft; tel (1) 587-15-65.
Honorary Consul: Norbert Zimmer.

Consulate: 6850 Dornbirn, Moosmahdstr. 1; tel (5572) 65-5-41.
Honorary Consul: Oskar Rhomberg.

Consulate: 9010 Klagenfurt, Kohldorferstr. 98; tel (463) 21-5-51.
Honorary Consul: Gaston Kugler.

Consulate: 4010 Linz, Promenade 11/3; tel (732) 23-91.
Honorary Consul: Hansjörg Rigele.

Consulate: 7000 Eisenstadt, Julius Raab Str. 1; tel (2682) 25-8-60.
Honorary Consul: Karl Heinz Jeschko.

Consulate: 6134 Innsbruck, Vomp 51; tel (5242) 22-64.
Honorary Consul: Fritz Heiss.

Consulate: St Pölten.
Honorary Consul: Ernst Leopold Gruber.

TURKEY

Embassy: 1040 Vienna, Prinz Eugen-Str. 40; tel (1) 505-55-59; telex 131927; fax (1) 505-36-60.
Ambassador: Ayhan Kamel.
Minister-Counsellor: Şule Soysal.
First Counsellor: Murat Ersavci.
Counsellor: Atillâ Uzer.
Counsellor: Tanju Sümer.
Counsellor: Kemâl Asya.

Economic and Commercial Section: 1030 Vienna, Gottfried Kellergasse 2/12; tel (1) 712-43-82.
Counsellor: Doğan Togay.
Counsellor: Değer Berkol.
Deputy Counsellor: Yildiz Soykan.

Tourism Section: 1010 Vienna, Singer Str. 2/8; tel (1) 512-21-28; fax (1) 513-83-26.
Counsellor: Mehmet Gündüz.

Press Section: Embassy Chancery; tel (1) 650-92-47; fax (1) 505-46-75.
Counsellor: Can Evcen.

Consulate-General: 5020 Salzburg, Rudolfs Kai 54; tel (662) 84-36-72; telex 632460.
Consul-General: Deniz Uzmen.
Vice-Consul: Cemal Erbay.

Consulate-General: 6900 Bregenz, St Anna Str. 1; tel (5574) 42-0-83; telex 57408.
Consul-General: Ülkü Başsoy.
Vice-Consul: Artemis Erbeyli.

UKRAINE

Embassy: Vienna.
Ambassador: Yuri Kostenko.

UNITED ARAB EMIRATES

Embassy: 1190 Vienna, Peter-Jordan-Str. 66; tel (1) 36-14-55; telex 114106.
Ambassador: Abdul Aziz al-Owais.
Counsellor: Mohammad Jasim al-Nawis.
Attaché: Ahmed Rashed Fahed al-Dosari.

UNITED KINGDOM

Embassy: 1030 Vienna, Jaurèsgasse 12; tel (1) 713-15-75; telex 132810; fax (1) 75-78-24.
Counsellor, Consul-General and Deputy Head of Mission: R. P. Nash.
Counsellor (Chancery): N. H. McMillan.
Defence Attaché: Lieut Col P. W. L. Hughes.
First Secretary: S. J. O'Flaherty.
First Secretary and Consul: J. B. Moorby.
First Secretary (Commercial): S. G. Ratcliffe.
First Secretary (Management): A. N. King.
First Secretary (Chancery/Information): R. E. Dear.
Second Secretary (Economic): S. G. Berry.
Second Secretary (Chancery/Information): M. Alessandri.

Consular Section: 1030 Vienna, Jaurèsgasse 10; tel (1) 75-61-17.

Mission to IAEA, UNIDO and UN: fax (1) 713-58-99.
Permanent Representative: G. E. Clark.
First Secretary and Deputy Permanent Representative: M. R. McIntosh.
First Secretary (Management): A. N. King.
First Secretary (IAEA): M. H. Clements.
First Secretary (IAEA): W. A. Dickson.
Second Secretary (UN/UNIDO): A. J. Hennessey.
Third Secretary (Management): J. M. Green.

Delegation to Negotiations on Conventional Arms Control in Europe: fax (1) 75-78-24.
Head of Delegation: P. Lever.
Deputy Head of Delegation: B. E. Cleghorn.
Counsellor: D. J. Bowen.
Senior Military Adviser: Brig. R. F. Baly.
Deputy Military Adviser: Group Capt. R. E. Holliday.
First Secretary (Management): A. N. King.

Consulate: 6923 Lauterach/Bregenz, Bundesstr. 110; tel (5574) 38-5-86; telex 057733; fax (5574) 30-92-8.
Honorary Consul: P. Senger-Weiss.

Consulate: 8010 Graz, Schmiedgasse 8-12; tel (316) 82-61-05; telex 031718; fax (316) 821-61-64.
Honorary Consul: K. D. Brühl.

Consulate: 6021 Innsbruck, Matthias-Schmid-Str. 12; tel (512) 58-83-20; telex 053402; fax (512) 58-61-51.
Honorary Consul: Hellmut Buchroithner.
Honorary Pro-Consul: H. Reinisch.

Consulate: 5020 Salzburg, Alter Markt 4; tel (662) 84-81-33; telex 0633811; fax (662) 85-04-98.
Honorary Consul: M. M. Kaindl.
Honorary Pro-Consul: H. Danmayr.

USA

Embassy: 1091 Vienna, Boltzmanngasse 16; tel (1) 31-55-11; telex 114634; fax (1) 31-00-682.
Ambassador: Roy Michael Huffington.
Deputy Chief of Mission: Michael J. Habib.
Political Section: Joseph C. Snyder III.
Economic Section: Edward B. O'Donnell.
Commercial Section: Benjamin N. Brown.
Administrative Section: Warren P. Nixon.
Regional Security Officer: Timothy W. Fountain.
Public Affairs Officer: Thomas E. O'Connor.
Communications Programme Officer: David T. Jacks.
Information Systems Manager: Paul A. Converti.
Office of the Defence Attaché: Col Peter S. Hoffmann.
Agricultural Section: Robert J. Svec.
Labour Officer: Francis T. Scanlon.
Immigration and Naturalization Service: Robert V. Looney.
Customs Service: Ivan E. Taborsky.
Drug Enforcement Agency: Dennis J. Silvestri.

Consular Section: 1010 Vienna, Gartenbaupromenade 2, 4th Floor; (1) 51-4-51.
Consular Section: Thomas J. Rice.

Mission to International Organizations in Vienna (UNVIE): 1190 Vienna, Obersteinergasse 11; tel (1) 36-31-52; fax (1) 369-15-85.
Chief of Mission: Michael H. Newlin.
Deputy Chief of Mission: John A. Buche.
Political Adviser: Richard W. Hoover.
Narcotics Adviser: Gregory B. Sprow.
Senior Scientific Adviser: Marvin Peterson.
Scientific Attaché: Michael L. von Grey.

Mission to International Atomic Energy Agency: fax (1) 36-83-92.
International Atomic Energy Agency: Frederick F. McGoldrick.
International Atomic Energy Agency: Maurice J. Katz.

Delegation for Negotiation on Conventional Armed Forces in Europe (CFE): 1190 Vienna, Obersteinergasse 11; fax (1) 36-63-85.
Representative: R. James Woolsey.
Deputy Representative: Philip S. Kaplan.
Political Section: Thomas R. Maertens.
Administrative Section: Elizabeth J. Agnew.
Communications Programme Officer: David Jacks.

Delegation to Negotiations on Confidence/- and Security-Building Measures (CSBM): 1014 Vienna, Wallnerstr. 3; tel (1) 535-08-13; fax (1) 535-08-24.
Chairman: John J. Maresca.
Deputy Chairman: Rudolf V. Perina.
Executive Secretary: Scott N. Thayer.
Political Adviser: William T. Harris.
Administrative Section: Kathy A. Johnson.

Consulate-General: 5020 Salzburg, Am Giselakai 51; tel (662) 28-6-01; telex 633164; fax (662) 27-49-46.
Consul-General: John K. Bauman.

URUGUAY

Embassy: 1010 Vienna, Krugerstr. 3/1/4-6; tel (1) 513-22-40; telex 112589.
Ambassador: José D. Lissidini.
First Secretary: Daniel Pérez del Castillo.
Third Secretary: Gabriela Ricaldoni.

Consulate: 5033 Salzburg, Alpenstr. 75; tel (662) 20-5-16.
Honorary Consul: Arthur Weillinger.

VENEZUELA

Embassy: 1030 Vienna, Marokkanergasse 22; tel (1) 75-32-19; telex 136219; fax (1) 72-26-38.
Ambassador: Dr Reinaldo Pabón García.
Counsellor (Commercial): Francisco Alvarez-Gorsira.
First Secretary: Beatriz Davila Barrios.
Second Secretary: Jacqueline Petersen.
Attaché (Cultural): Petro Liendo.

YUGOSLAVIA

Embassy: 1030 Vienna, Rennweg 3; tel (1) 713-25-95; telex 135398.
Ambassador: Dr Ivan Brnelić.
Counsellor: Alfonz Naberznik.
Counsellor (Trade): Djorde Misajlovski.
Counsellor (Social Affairs): Muharem Adanalic.
Counsellor (Press/Cultural): Ivana Vrhovcak.
Counsellor: Petar Tasic.
Counsellor (IAEO/UNIDO): Dr Miroljub Savic.
Military and Air Attaché: Col Ivan Umek.

Consulate-General: 8010 Graz, Hilmteichstr. 10; tel (316) 33-1-80.
Consul-General: Vladimir Rajh.

Consulate-General: 9020 Klagenfurt, Radetzkystr. 26; tel (4222) 57-8-50.
Consul-General: Borut Miklaveic.
Consul: Ivan Jecl.
Consul: Franz Miksa.

Consulate-General: 5020 Salzburg, Widmannstr. 11; tel (662) 84-52-54.
Consul-General: Bosko Vranes.
Consul: Zarije Stojanovic.
Consul: Boro Supat.

ZAIRE

Embassy: 1030 Vienna, Marokkanergasse 22/1/6; tel (1) 713-88-75; telex 133565.
Ambassador: Bokonga Ekanga Botombele.
Counsellor: Ndjoko Mulopo Nku.
Counsellor: Elebe Lisembe.
First Secretary: Lulu Mulasi.
Attaché (Finance): Kalimira Asonga.

International Organizations

EUROPEAN COMMUNITIES

External Delegation: 1040 Vienna, 5 Hoyosgasse; tel (1) 505-33-797; telex 133152; fax (1) 505-33-797.
Head of Delegation: Dietrich Hammer.
Counsellor: Gerhard Weingärtner.
Counsellor: Norbert Jousten.
Attaché: David Tyson.
Attaché: Anton Leicht.

UNITED NATIONS

Delegation: 1400 Vienna, POB 500, Vienna Informational Centre; tel (1) 211-31-0; telex 135612.
Director-General: Margaret J. Anstee.

AZERBAIDZHAN

IRAN

Embassy: 370001 Baku, Bouniad Sardarof 4; tel (892) 92-30-83.
Ambassador: Abdulghasen Olad Damechghi.
Vice-Consul: Mehdi Abbass Paidar.

IRAQ

Consulate-General: Baku, Khagani ul. 9; tel (892) 92-82-83.

TURKEY

Consulate-General: Baku.
Consul-General: Altan Karamanoglu.
Vice-Consul: Mehmet Ali Bayar.
Attaché: Siya Onder.

USA

Embassy: Baku.

BAHAMAS

AUSTRIA

Consulate: POB SS-6519, Nassau; tel (32) 363-2929; fax (32) 363-2308.
Honorary Consul: Heinz Robert Kloihofer.

CANADA

Consulate: 21 Out Island Traders Bldg, POB SS-6371, Nassau; tel (32) 393-1305.
Honorary Consul: D. Tomlinson.

DENMARK

Consulate-General: Nassau.

Consulate: c/o United Shipping Co. Ltd, Beaumont House Arcade, Bay St, POB 4005, Nassau; tel (32) 322-1340; telex 29120160; fax (32) 323-8779.
Consul: Berlin Wilbert Key.

FRANCE

Embassy: Nassau.
Ambassador: Patrick Amiot.

GERMANY

Consulate: Colony Investments Ltd, Horseshoe Drive, Oaksfield, POB N-3035, Nassau; tel (32) 322-8032; fax (32) 322-8033.
Honorary Consul: Ernst Brokmeier.

ICELAND

Consulate-General: G. K. Symonette Bldg, Shirley St, POB N-7525, Nassau; tel (32) 322-8956.
Consul-General: C. R. Julian Maynard.

JAMAICA

Consulate: POB 3451, Nassau; tel (32) 323-5771; telex 20571.
Honorary Consul: Patrick Hanlan.

SWEDEN

Consulate: Cable Beach Manor Hotel, Prospect Ridge Rd, Skyline Hight, POB CB-11000, Nassau; tel (32) 327-7785; fax (32) 327-7782.
Consul: Sten Anders Wiberg.

SWITZERLAND

Consulate: Scotiabank Bldg, POB N-4928, Nassau; tel (32) 322-8349.
Honorary Consul: Franz Jolidon.

UNITED KINGDOM

High Commission: 3rd Floor, Bitco Bldg, East St, POB N-7516, Nassau; tel (32) 325-7471; telex 20112; fax (32) 323-3871.
High Commissioner: M. E. J. Gore.
Deputy High Commissioner: R. G. Church.
Defence Adviser: Capt. A. J. S. Taylor.
Commercial/Information Officer: M. A. Ansell.

USA

Embassy: Mosmar Bldg, Queen St, POB N-8197, Nassau; tel (32) 322-1181; telex 20138; fax (32) 328-7838.
Ambassador: Jacob Hecht.
Deputy Chief of Mission: Lino Gutierrez.
Political Section: Bruce E. Thomas.
Economic/Commercial Section: Jessica Webster.
Administrative Section: Jacquelyn O. Briggs.
Regional Security Officer: Darwin Cadogan.
Public Affairs Officer: Mary K. Reeber.
Communications Programme Officer: Jerry C. Oliver.
Narcotics Assistance Unit: Denise Malczewski.
Labour Officer: Anthony Kern.
Internal Revenue Service: Louis Hobbie.

International Organizations

EUROPEAN COMMUNITIES

External Delegation (Sub-Office of Delegation to Jamaica): Frederick House, 2nd Floor, Frederick St, POB 3246, Nassau; tel (32) 325-5850; telex 310.

BAHRAIN

ALGERIA

Embassy: POB 26402, Adiliya 336, Villa 579, Rd 3622, Manama; tel 713783; telex 2775.
Ambassador: Belaid Mohand Oussaid.

BANGLADESH

Embassy: POB 26718, House 159, Rd 2004, Area 320, Hoora, Manama; tel 293371; telex 7029; fax 291272.
Ambassador: Abdul Momen Choudhury.
First Secretary: Mohammed Nurul Bashir.
Third Secretary: Monir Ahmad Choudhury.

BELGIUM

Consular Agency: c/o Banque Française de l'Orient, POB 5820, Manama; tel 251822; fax 261685.
Consular Agent: Herman Dom.

DENMARK

Consular Agency: POB 45, Maersk Line, Manama; tel 727896; telex 8676; fax 728797.
Consular Agent: Søren Graversen.

EGYPT

Embassy: POB 818, Adiliya; tel 720005; telex 8248.
Ambassador: Nabil Mustafa Ibrahim.

FRANCE

Embassy: POB 11134, King Faisal Rd, Diplomatic Area, Manama; tel 291734; telex 9281.
Ambassador: Pierre Boillot.

Economic Section: POB 10487; telex 9281.

GERMANY

Embassy: POB 10306, Diplomatic Area 317, Al-Hasan Bldg, Sheikh Hamad Causeway, Bldg 668, Manama; tel 530210; telex 8340; fax 536282.
Chargé d'affaires a.i.: Manfred Ahlbrecht.

ICELAND

Embassy: Manama.

INDIA

Embassy: POB 26106, Bldg 182, Rd 2608, Qudhaibiya, Area 326, Adliya, Manama; tel 712785; telex 9047; fax 715527.
Ambassador: Nathu Ram Verma.

IRAN

Embassy: POB 26477, Sheikh Isa Rd 2709, Manama; tel 712151; telex 8238.
Chargé d'affaires: Hussain Naraqian.

IRAQ

Embassy: Ar-Raqeeb Bldg, No 17, Rd 2001, Comp 320, King Faisal Rd, Manama; tel 290999; telex 9620.
Ambassador: Taha M. Allawi al-Qaisi.

JAPAN

Embassy: POB 23720, House 403, Rd 915, Salmaniya, Area 309, Manama; tel 243364; telex 7002; fax 230694.
Ambassador: Toshiro Ogushi.

JORDAN

Embassy: POB 5242, Villa 43, Rd 1901, Al-Fatih Ave, Manama; tel 291109.
Ambassador: Amjad al-Majali.

KOREA, REPUBLIC

Embassy: POB 11700, Manama; Bldg No. 69, Road No. 1901, Block No. 319, Al Hoora; tel 291629; telex 8736.
Ambassador: Kwak Hoi-Jung.
Counsellor: Kim Jong-Yong.
Vice-Consul: Park Seung-Gyoo.
Secretary: G. C. Merrick.

KUWAIT

Embassy: POB 786, 76 Rd 1703, Diplomatic Area, Manama; tel 242330; telex 8830.
Ambassador: Faisal M. al-Haji.

NEW ZEALAND

Consular Agency: Yateem Centre 2, 2nd Floor, POB 5881, Manama; tel 271600; telex 8748; fax 274654.
Consular Agent: Don Harwood.

NORWAY

Consular Agency: POB 10580, Manama; tel 531480; telex 9714; fax 530158.
Consular Agent: Knut Gunnar Borgen.

OMAN

Embassy: POB 26414, Bldg 37, Rd 1901, Diplomatic Area, Manama; tel 293663; telex 9332.
Ambassador: Ghalib bin Abdullah bin Jubran.

PAKISTAN

Embassy: POB 563, House 75, Rd 3403, Area 334, Mahooz, Manama; tel 712470.
Ambassador: Muhammad Khan Junejo.

SAUDI ARABIA

Embassy: POB 1085, Bldg 1450, Rd 4043, Jufair, Manama; tel 727223.
Ambassador: Dr Ghazi Abd ar-Rahman al-Gosaibi.

SWEDEN

Consular Agency: c/o Gulf Agency Co. Ltd, al-Moosa Bldg, Ground Floor, Diplomatic Area, Manama; POB 412, Manama; tel 530022; telex 8211; fax 530063.
Consular Agent: Per Bruno Zachrisson.

SWITZERLAND

Consular Agency: POB 795, Manama; tel 250811; telex 8222; fax 257988.
Consular Agent: Claus Büchi.

TUNISIA

Embassy: POB 26911, al-Mahouz, Manama; tel 721431.
Ambassador: Nourreddin Hamdane.

UNITED KINGDOM

Embassy: POB 114, 21 Government Ave, Manama 306; tel 534404; telex 8213; fax 531273.
First Secretary (Commercial), Consul and Deputy Head of Mission: W. I. Rae.
First Secretary (Political): J. C. A. Rundall.
Second Secretary (Commercial): D. J. Holder.
Second Secretary (Works): D. G. Wright.
Third Secretary (Chancery/Information): S. T. Harrison.

USA

Embassy: POB 26431, Bldg 979, Rd 3119, Area 331, Manama; tel 273300; telex 9398; fax 272594.
Ambassador: Charles W. Hostler.
Deputy Chief of Mission: Jay P. Freres.
Political Section: Calvin A. Mitchell III.
Political/Military Section: David Vanell.
Economic/Commercial Section: Steven M. Brattain.
Consular Section: Stephanie A. Kronenburg.
Administrative Section: Lyle A. Dittmer.
Regional Security Officer: David R. Bettis.
Communications Programme Officer: Burdette R. Hammitt.
Security Assistance Office: Col Larry Crumrine.

Information Service: tel 276180; fax 270547.
Public Affairs Officer: Ricky L. Roberts.

Agricultural Trade Office: tel 270331.
Agricultural Trade Office: Philip A. Letarte.

Office of Military Co-operation: tel 274023; fax 276046.

Agricultural Section: fax 274233.

BANGLADESH

AFGHANISTAN

Embassy: House CWN(C)-2A Gulshan Ave, Gulshan Model Town, Dhaka 12; tel (2) 603232.
Chargé d'affaires a.i.: Abdul Ahad Wolasi.

ALGERIA

Embassy: 4 CWN(C) Gulshan Ave, Gulshan Model Town, Dhaka 12; tel (2) 605021.
Ambassador: Muhammad Chadly.

AUSTRALIA

High Commission: 184 Gulshan Ave, Gulshan Model Town, Dhaka 12; tel (2) 600091; telex 642317.
High Commissioner: Susan J. D. Boyd.

AUSTRIA

Consulate: 107 Motijheel Commercial Area, Dhaka; tel (2) 257616; telex 642425.
Honorary Consul: Islam Abdul Khair Mohammad Mainul.

BELGIUM

Embassy: House 40, Rd 21, Block B, Banani, Dhaka; tel (2) 600138; telex 642304.
Ambassador: Baron Olivier Gilles.

BHUTAN

Embassy: House 58, Rd 3A, Dhanmandi R/A, POB 3141, Dhaka; tel (2) 505418.
Ambassador: D. K. Chhetri.

BRAZIL

Embassy: House 23, Rd 5, Baridhara Model Town, Dhaka 1212; tel (2) 605390; telex 642334.
Chargé d'affaires a.i.: Bernardino Raimundo da Silva.

CANADA

High Commission: House CWN 16/A, Rd 48, Gulshan Model Town, POB 569, Dhaka 12; tel (2) 883639; telex 642328; fax (2) 883043.
High Commissioner: Emile Gauvreau.
Counsellor (Development): S. Gibbons.
Counsellor: Y. P. A. Oxley-Young.
Counsellor (Development): S. Brown.
First Secretary (Development): S. E. Rayfield.
First Secretary (Development): N. E. Mussell.
First Secretary (Development): B. Proskurniak.
Second Secretary (Administration): R. N. Flanagan.

CHINA, PEOPLE'S REPUBLIC

Embassy: Plot NE(L)6, Rd 83, Gulshan Model Town, Dhaka 12; tel (2) 601037.
Ambassador: Chen Songlu.
Political Counsellor: Zhu Luchang.
Cultural Counsellor: Wang He.
Economic Counsellor: Sun Zhongqian.
Military, Naval and Air Attaché: Col Lu Quangen.
Commercial Counsellor: Su Junlu.
First Secretary (Administration): Wang Youtu.
Deputy Military, Naval and Air Attaché: Col Geng Kepu.
First Secretary (Economic): Huang Zhaohong.
Second Secretary (Political): Chai Xi.

CZECHOSLOVAKIA

Embassy: House 3A NE(O), Rd 90, Gulshan Model Town, Dhaka 12; tel (2) 601673; telex 65730.
Ambassador: Jiří Majsajdr.

DENMARK

Embassy: House NW(H)1, Rd 51, Gulshan Model Town, POB 2056, Dhaka 12; tel (2) 600108; telex 642320.
Ambassador: Jørn Krogbeck.
Attaché: Knud Jensen.
Minister-Counsellor and Head of Aid Mission: Finn Thilsted.
Aid Counsellor: Jens Peter Pedersen.
Aid Counsellor: Mogens Laumand Christensen.
Aid Attaché: Johnny Flentø.
Project Co-ordinator: Anders Qvortrup.

EGYPT

Embassy: House NE(N)-9, Rd 90, Gulshan Model Town, Dhaka 12; tel (2) 600158.
Ambassador: Muhammad Mustafa Badr.

FINLAND

Consulate-General: c/o Orioxi Ltd, Chamber Bldg, 122-124 Motijheel CA, Dhaka 2; tel (2) 231927; telex 642403.
Consul-General: Zeaul Huq.

FRANCE

Embassy: House 18, Rd 108, Gulshan Model Town, POB 22, Dhaka 12; tel (2) 605890; telex 642300; fax (2) 883612.
Ambassador: Serge Degallaix.
Counsellor: Michel Penaud.
First Secretary: Bernard Lelarge.
Consul: Christian Nguyen Huu.
Counsellor (Development/Culture/Flood Prevention): Alain Vanden Abeele.
Commercial Counsellor: Bernard François.

Economic Section: POB GN6095; tel (2) 604320; telex 642312.

GERMANY

Embassy: 178 Gulshan Ave, Gulshan Model Town, POB 108, Dhaka 12; tel (2) 600166; telex 642331.
Ambassador: Dr Karl-Heinz Scholtyssek.

HOLY SEE

Apostolic Nunciature: Plot 1-2, Baridhara Model Town, POB 6003, Dhaka 1212; tel (2) 882018; fax (2) 883574.
Apostolic Pro-Nuncio: Most Rev. Piero Biggio, Titular Archbishop of Otricoli.

HUNGARY

Embassy: 80 Gulshan Ave, Gulshan Model Town, POB 6012, Dhaka 1212; tel (2) 608101; telex 642314; fax (2) 883117.
Chargé d'affaires and Head of Mission: I. B. Buday.
Commercial Secretary: L. Nemes.

ICELAND

Embassy: Dhaka.

Consulate-General: Chamber Bldg, 122-124 Motijheel C. A., Dhaka 2; tel (2) 231937; telex 642403.
Consul-General: Zeaul Huq.

INDIA

High Commission: House 120, Rd 2, Dhammandi R/A, Dhaka 1205; tel (2) 503606; telex 642336.
High Commissioner: K. Srinivasan.

INDONESIA

Embassy: 75 Gulshan Ave, Gulshan Model Town, Dhaka 12; tel (2) 600131; telex 632309.
Ambassador: Air Vice-Marshal (retd) Iswadi Soemakno.
Counsellor (Political and Economic): Wasdjoed Sisworo.
Second Secretary (Information and Socio-Cultural Affairs): Muhammad Ischak.
Second Secretary (Administration): Suprijadi Oding.
Second Secretary (Administration/Protocol/Consular): S. Sukowibowo Lestario.
Defence Attaché: Col Munawar.

Consulate: Agrabad Hotel, Chittagong; tel (31) 500111; telex 66237; fax (31) 225572.
Consul: Hakim Ali.

IRAN

Embassy: CWN(A)-12 Kamal Ataturk Ave, Gulshan Model Town, Dhaka 12; tel (2) 601432; telex 65714.
Ambassador: Muhammad Ganjidoost.

IRAQ

Embassy: 112 Gulshan Ave, Gulshan Model Town, Dhaka 12; tel (2) 600298; telex 642307.
Ambassador: Zuhair Muhammad Alomar.

ITALY

Embassy: House NWD(4), Rd 58/62, Gulshan Model Town, Dhaka 12; tel (2) 603161; telex 642313.
Ambassador: Dr Sandro Maria Siggia.

JAPAN

Embassy: Plot 110, Rd 27, Block A, Banani Model Town, POB 458, Dhaka 12; tel (2) 608191; telex 65872; fax (2) 412265.
Ambassador: Takeo Iguchi.

KOREA, DEMOCRATIC PEOPLE'S REPUBLIC

Embassy: House 6, Rd 7, Baridhara Model Town, Dhaka; tel (2) 601250.
Ambassador: Kang Tal-Son.

KOREA, REPUBLIC

Embassy: House NW(E)17, Rd 55, Gulshan Model Town, Dhaka 12; tel (2) 604921.
Ambassador: Man Soon Chang.

KUWAIT

Embassy: Plot 39, Rd 23, Block J, Banani, Dhaka 13; tel (2) 600233; telex 65600.

Ambassador: Ahmad Murshed al-Suliman.

LIBYA

People's Committee: NE(D), 3A, Gulshan Ave (N), Gulshan Model Town, Dhaka 12; tel (2) 600141.
Secretary of People's Committee: Musbah Ali A. Maimoon (acting).

MALAYSIA

High Commission: House 4, Rd 118, Gulshan Model Town, Dhaka 12; tel (2) 600291.
High Commissioner: Zainuddin A. Rahman.

MYANMAR

Embassy: 89(B), Rd 4, Banani, Dhaka; tel (2) 601915.
Ambassador: U Soe Myint.

NEPAL

Embassy: United Nations Rd 2, Baridhara Model Town, Dhaka; tel (2) 601790; telex 65643.
Ambassador: Dr Mohan Prasad Lohani.

NETHERLANDS

Embassy: House 49, Rd 90, Gulshan Model Town, Dhaka 12; tel (2) 600278.
Ambassador: J. H. J. Jeurissen.

PAKISTAN

High Commission: House NEC-2, Rd 71, Gulshan Model Town, Dhaka 12; tel (2) 600276.
High Commissioner: Anwar Kemal.

PHILIPPINES

Embassy: House NE(L) 5, Rd 83, Gulshan Model Town, Dhaka 12; tel (2) 605945.
Ambassador: Reynaldo O. Archilla.

POLAND

Embassy: 53 Gulshan Ave, Gulshan Model Town, Dhaka 12; tel (2) 606098; telex 642316.
Ambassador: Edward Baradziej.

QATAR

Embassy: House 23, Rd 108, Gulshan Model Town, Dhaka 12; tel (2) 604477.
Chargé d'affaires a.i.: Abdullah al-Mutawa.

ROMANIA

Embassy: House 33, Rd 74, Gulshan Model Town, Dhaka 12; tel (2) 601467; telex 65739.
Chargé d'affaires a.i.: Alexandru Voinea.

RUSSIA

Embassy: NE(J) 9, Rd 79, Gulshan Model Town, Dhaka 12; tel (2) 601050.
Ambassador: Vitaly Stepanovich Smirnov.

Consulate-General: Zakir Hussain Rd, Khulshi R/A, Plot A4/A5, Chittagong; tel (31) 205723.

SAUDI ARABIA

Embassy: House SW(A)-25, Rd 10, Gulshan Ave, Dhaka 12; tel (2) 600221; telex 642305.
Ambassador: Abdul Latif Abdullah Ibrahim al-Maimanee.

SRI LANKA

High Commission: House 22 (NW), Rd 56, Gulshan Model Town, Dhaka 12; tel (2) 604009; telex 642321.
High Commissioner: A. K. David.

SWEDEN

Embassy: 73 Gulshan Ave, Gulshan Model Town, POB 304, Dhaka 12; tel (2) 600278; telex 642303; fax (2) 883948.
Ambassador: Carl Olof Cederblad.
First Secretary: Sören Freij.
Head of Aid Office: Bengt Liljenroth.

SWITZERLAND

Embassy: House 5, Rd 104, Gulshan Model Town, POB 928, Dhaka 12; tel (2) 600181; telex 642308; fax (2) 883497.
Chargé d'affaires a.i. and Counsellor: Heinz Wey.
Attaché (Development Co-operation and Humanitarian Aid): Dr Urs Heierli.

THAILAND

Embassy: House NW(E)12, Rd 59, Gulshan Model Town, Dhaka; tel (2) 601475.
Ambassador: Chaiya Chindawongse.

TURKEY

Embassy: House 7, Rd 62, Gulshan Model Town, Dhaka 12; tel (2) 602198.
Ambassador: Muammer Tuncer.

UNITED ARAB EMIRATES

Embassy: House CEN(H)41, Rd 113, Gulshan Model Town, Dhaka 12; tel (2) 604775; telex 642301.
Ambassador: Ibrahim Jawad al-Ridha.

UNITED KINGDOM

High Commission: Abu Bakr House, Plot 7, Rd 84, Gulshan Model Town, POB 6079, Dhaka 12; tel (2) 600133; telex 671066; fax (2) 883437.
High Commissioner: Colin Henry Imray.
Deputy High Commissioner: G. Finlayson.
Defence Adviser: Col G. M. Longdon.
First Secretary and Head of Political and Information Sections: G. P. R. Boon.
First Secretary (Consular and Immigration): E. Loader.
First Secretary (Aid): B. W. Hefferon.
First Secretary (Medical Officer): Dr S. M. C. Michelson.
First Secretary (Commercial): D. E. Donald.
First Secretary (Management): B. D. Adams.
First Secretary (Natural Resources): L. Brown.
First Secretary (Health and Population): Dr J. B. W. Lob-Levyt.
First Secretary (Works): D. C. Grant.
First Secretary (Works): J. K. Medlen.

Consular and Immigration Sections: House 42, Rd 135, Gulshan, Dhaka; tel (2) 600224.

Visa Office: House 3, Rd 2, Gulshan, Dhaka; tel (2) 603027.

Management Section: House 8, Rd 83, Gulshan, Dhaka; tel (2) 603640.

British Council: telex 642470.

USA

Embassy: Diplomatic Enclave, Madani Ave, Baridhara Model Town, POB 323, Dhaka 1212; tel (2) 884700; telex 642319; fax (2) 883648.
Ambassador: William B. Milam.
Deputy Chief of Mission: Lee O. Coldren.
Political Section: Stephen R. Snow.
Economic/Commercial Section: Michael E. McNaull.
Consular Section: Ruth E. Bright.
Administrative Section: Kenneth W. Parent.
Regional Security Officer: Daniel R. McCarthy.
Communications Programme Officer: Harold Jimerson.
Information Systems Manager: Kevin J. Dempsey.
Agency for International Development: Mary C. Kilgour.
Office of the Defence Attaché: Lieut Col James A. Dunn, Jr.

Information Service: Jiban Bima Bhaban, 5th Floor, 10 Dilkusha CA, Dhaka 1000; tel (2) 234480; fax (2) 833987.
Public Affairs Officer: Ray Peppers.

YUGOSLAVIA

Embassy: House 10, Rd 62, Gulshan Model Town, Dhaka 12; tel (2) 601505.
Ambassador: Kalman Feher.

International Organizations

EUROPEAN COMMUNITIES

External Delegation: House CES(E) 19, Rd 128, Gulshan, Dhaka 12; tel (2) 607016; telex 642501; fax (2) 883118.
Head of Delegation: Jacques Bailly.
First Secretary (Economics and Development): Sean Doyle.
Second Secretary (Development): N. de Joncheere.

BARBADOS

ARGENTINA

Embassy: Bridgetown; tel 429-4782.

AUSTRIA

Consulate: Bridgetown; tel 427-8880.
Honorary Consul: Richard Glen Cunningham.

BELGIUM

Consulate: Bridgetown; tel 425-2594.

BRAZIL

Embassy: Sunjet House, Independence Square, Bridgetown; tel 427-1735; telex 2434.
Ambassador: Amaury Bier.

CANADA

High Commission: Bishops Court Hill, St Michael; POB 404, Bridgetown; tel 429-3550; telex 2247; fax 429-3780.
High Commissioner: Janet P. Zukowsky.
Counsellor: S. Wade.
Counsellor (Development): A. M. Saper.
Counsellor (Development): M. Lepage.
Counsellor (Development): A. McCabe.
Counsellor (Commercial): S. Potvin.
Counsellor (Development): I. Thomson.
Counsellor (Development): T. Tuong.
First Secretary (Immigration): N. Scott-Hankey.
First Secretary (Development): M. Kurus.
First Secretary (Development): J. A. Langevin.
First Secretary (Development): K. J. Olson.
First Secretary (Development): H. W. Powles.
First Secretary (Development): J. J. Loubser.
First Secretary (Development): P. Marion.
First Secretary (Development): D. Testelin.
First Secretary (Administration): M. J. Dennis.
First Secretary (Development): T. Carroll.
Second Secretary (Immigration): C. A. Turner.

CHINA, PEOPLE'S REPUBLIC

Embassy: 17 Golf View Terrace, Rockley, Christ Church; tel 436-6042; telex 2363.
Ambassador: Lu Zongqing.

COLOMBIA

Embassy: 'Rosemary', Dayrells Rd, Rockley, Christ Church; tel 429-6821; telex 2499.
Ambassador: Ligia Londoño (designate).

COSTA RICA

Embassy: 'Highbury House', Sandy Lane Estate, St James; tel 432-1164; telex 2203; fax 429-4854.
Chargé d'affaires a.i.: Dr Luis Carlos Mora Corrales.

CYPRUS

Consulate: Bridgetown; tel 427-7478.

DENMARK

Consulate: Goddard Food Fairs Bldg, Kensington, Fontabelle, St Michael, POB 304, Bridgetown; tel 426-0720; telex 2267.
Consul: Patrick David Patterson.

DOMINICAN REPUBLIC

Consulate: Bridgetown; tel 426-0200.

ECUADOR

Consulate: Bridgetown; tel 426-6799.

FINLAND

Consulate-General: c/o Da Costas Ltd, POB 103, Carlinle House, Hinks St, Bridgetown W1; tel 426-0850; telex 2237; fax 436-9870.
Consul-General: Peter Desmond Bowen Short.

FRANCE

Embassy: Bridgetown.

Consulate: Bridgetown; tel 429-6361.

GERMANY

Consulate: Banyan Court, Bay St, Bridgetown; tel 427-1876.
Honorary Consul: Peter Lehmann.

HAITI

Consulate: Bridgetown; tel 427-3111.

HOLY SEE

Mission: Bridgetown.
Apostolistic Nuncio: Mgr Manuel Monteiro de Castro.

ICELAND

Embassy: Bridgetown.
Ambassador: Ingvi S. Ingvarsson.

ISRAEL

Consulate: Bridgetown; tel 426-4764.

ITALY

Consulate: Bridgetown; tel 425-3122.

JAMAICA

Consulate: 6 Cross Roads, St Philip; tel 423-6706.
Honorary Consul: Dr Alfred Ralston.

JAPAN

Consulate: Bridgetown; tel 437-7929.

KOREA, REPUBLIC

Embassy: Bridgetown; tel 429-9650.

MEXICO

Consulate: Bridgetown; tel 426-0489.

NETHERLANDS

Consulate: Bridgetown; tel 428-0034.

NORWAY

Consulate: Bridgetown; tel 427-5131.

PERU

Consulate: Bridgetown; tel 427-7224.

SWEDEN

Consulate: Leo Leacock & Co. Ltd, Sunjet House, Fairchild St, Bridgetown; POB 629C, Bridgetown; tel 426-2482; telex 2277; fax 436-9261.
Consul: Leo Cecil Leacock.

TRINIDAD AND TOBAGO

High Commission: Cockspur House, Nile St, Bridgetown; tel 429-9600; telex 2326.
High Commissioner: Mervyn Williams.

UNITED KINGDOM

High Commission: Lower Collymore Rock, POB 676, St Michael, Bridgetown; tel 436-6694; telex 2219; fax 436-5398.
High Commissioner: Emrys Thomas Davies.
Deputy High Commissioner: J. A. Noakes.
First Secretary (Chancery): R. C. Wilkin.
First Secretary (Chancery): S. R. Morley.
Naval Adviser and Assistant Defence Adviser, Caribbean: Commdr H. M. Humphreys.
Second Secretary (Management/Consular): J. Eastwood.
Second Secretary (Chancery/Information): P. G. McCrudden.
Second Secretary (Technical Works): I. Agnew.
Third Secretary (Immigration): D. W. Platt.
Third Secretary (Immigration): A. A. Howard.

Development Division in the Caribbean: Lower Collymore Rock, POB 167, Bridgetown; tel 436-9873; telex 2236; fax 426-2194.
Head of Division: J. Bawden.
Senior Natural Resources Adviser: J. B. Warren.
Senior Engineering Adviser: M. F. Sergeant.
Programme Manager: G. H. Malley.
Programme Manager: I. Stuart.
Senior Economic Assistant: F. Lappin.
Economic Adviser: P. J. Dearden.
Regional Natural Resources Adviser: Dr J. Fergusson.
Registrar and Assistant Management Officer: D. Collingwood.
Regional Legal Adviser: Sir Clifford Hammett.
Regional Education Adviser: M. Ratcliffe.
Regional Auditor: J. Stratfull.
Regional Architectural Adviser: A. McOnegal.
Regional Police Adviser: B. Graves.
Regional Computer Adviser: A. Howcroft.
Financial Services Adviser: R. M. Gallagher.

USA

Embassy: Canadian Imperial Bank of Commerce Bldg, Broad St, POB 302, Bridgetown; tel 436-4950; telex 2259; fax 429-5246.
Ambassador: G. Philip Hughes.
Deputy Chief of Mission: Barbro A. Owens.
Political/Economic Section: Richard Miller.
Economic Section: Raymond Brown.
Consular Section: Thomas Cairns.
Administrative Section: Alexander Kirkpatrick.
Regional Security Officer: George W. Goodrich III.
Public Affairs Officer: Katherine Lee.
Communications Programme Officer: Duane R. Bredeck.
Agency for International Development: Mosina Jordan.
Office of the Defence Attaché: Lieut Col Armand P. Haynes.
Military Liaison Office: Commdr Don Waylett.
Labour Officer: Mary Ann Singlaub.
Legal Attaché: Paul F. Nolan.

VENEZUELA

Embassy: El Sueño, Worthing, Christ Church; tel 435-7619; telex 2339.
Ambassador: Orestes di Giacomo.

International Organizations

EUROPEAN COMMUNITIES

External Delegation: Sunset House, Fairchild St, POB 654 C, Bridgetown; tel 427-4362; telex 2327; fax 427-8687.
Commission Delegate: Eberhard Stahn.

BELARUS

BULGARIA

Consulate-General: Minsk, Bronevoy per. 3; tel (17) 22-55-00.
Consul-General: Stoil Ferdov.

GERMANY

Consulate-General: Minsk, ul. Sakharova 26; tel (17) 33-07-52; telex 252273.
Consul-General: Reinhart Kraus.
Consul: Dr Hans Haubold.
Consul: Horst Dierenfeld.
Vice-Consul: Georg Stenz.

POLAND

Consulate-General: Minsk, Omsky per. 6; tel (17) 33-13-13.
Consul-General: Elżbieta Smułek.
Consul: Henryk Kalinowski.
Consul: Eugeniusz Zarzycki.
Consul: Kazimierz Dunaj.
Attaché: Andrzej Tomczynski.

USA

Embassy: Minsk.
Ambassador: David H. Swartz.

BELGIUM

ALGERIA

Embassy: 209 ave Molière, 1060 Brussels; tel (2) 343-50-78; telex 64142.
Ambassador: Nourredine Kerroum.

ANGOLA

Embassy: 182 rue Franz Merjay, 1180 Brussels; tel (2) 344-49-80; telex 63170.
Ambassador: Emilio Carvalho Guerra.

ARGENTINA

Embassy: 225 ave Louise, BP 6, 1050 Brussels; tel (2) 647-78-12.
Ambassador: Dr Victor Massuh.

AUSTRALIA

Embassy: 6-8 rue Guimard, 1040 Brussels; tel (2) 231-05-00; telex 21834; fax (2) 230-68-02.
Ambassador: Peter Campbell John Curtis.

AUSTRIA

Embassy: 47 rue de l'Abbaye, 1050 Brussels; tel (2) 649-91-70; telex 22463; fax (2) 648-94-17.
Ambassador: Dr Heinz Weinberger.
Counsellor: Leopold Radauer.
Consul: Gertrude Betzner.

Consulate: 176-178 Mechelsestweg, 2018 Antwerp; tel (3) 247-14-11; telex 72329.
Honorary Consul: Lucainus J. M. Boelens.

Consulate: Floraliapaleis, 5e étage, 9000 Ghent; tel (91) 22-96-69; telex 12666.
Honorary Consul: Henri P. Persin.

Consulate: c/o Banque O. de Schaetzen & Cie, 4-6 blvd d'Avroy, 4000 Liège; tel (41) 23-79-60; telex 41283.
Honorary Consul: Baron Bertrand de Schaetzen.

Consulate: c/o Cockerill Sambre SA, 1 rue de l'Usine, 6090 Couillet/Charleroi; tel (71) 44-43-03; telex 51226.
Honorary Consul: Philippe Delaunois.

Consulate: 8 Plantijnstraat, 8400 Ostende; tel (59) 80-70-60.
Honorary Consul: F. Ghesquiere.

BANGLADESH

Embassy: 29-31 rue Jacques Jordaens, 1050 Brussels; tel (2) 640-55-00; telex 63189.
Ambassador: A. K. M. Kamaluddin Choudhury.

BARBADOS

Embassy: 162 ave Louise, 1e étage, 1050 Brussels; tel (2) 648-13-58; telex 63926; fax (2) 646-23-97.
Ambassador: Rashid Orlando Marville.

BENIN

Embassy: 5 ave de l'Observatoire, 1180 Brussels; tel (2) 374-91-92; telex 24568; fax (2) 375-83-26.
Ambassador: Edmond Cakpo-Tozo.
Minister-Counsellor: Albert Agossou.
Minister-Counsellor: Omer de Souza.
First Counsellor: Awahou Labouda.
First Counsellor: Christophe Gbegbo.
Second Secretary: Emile Djidohokpin.
Attaché: Marcellin Yevide.
Attaché: Joseph Domingo.
Attaché: Ramanatou Saka.

Consulate: 59 chemin de Liège, 5200 Huy, Liège; tel (85) 21-24-67.
Honorary Consul: Albert Charles Charlier.

BOLIVIA

Embassy: 176 ave Louise, BP 6, 1050 Brussels; tel (2) 647-27-18; telex 63494; fax (2) 647-47-82.
Ambassador: Eduardo Ruíz García.
First Secretary: Rut Corina Ybarnegaray Urquidi.

Consulate: 87 Olympiadelaan, 7e étage, 2020 Antwerp; tel (3) 827-50-86.
Honorary Consul: J. V. G. Stappaerts.

BOTSWANA

Embassy: 169 ave de Tervueren, 1150 Brussels; tel (2) 735-20-70; telex 22849; fax (2) 735-63-18.
Ambassador: Sipho Ernest Mpofu.
Counsellor: L. C. Lekoa.
Second Secretary: M. B. Sebele.
Commercial Attaché: F. N. S. Mogatusi.
Second Secretary: A. M. Matsheka.
Administrative Attaché: P. S. Bale.

BRAZIL

Embassy: 350 ave Louise, BP 5, 1050 Brussels; tel (2) 640-20-15; telex 26758; fax (2) 640-81-34.
Ambassador: Marco César Meira Naslausky.

BULGARIA

Embassy: 58 ave Hamoir, 1180 Brussels; tel (2) 374-59-63; telex 22473.
Ambassador: Atanas Gueorguiev Guinev.

BURKINA FASO

Embassy: 16 place Guy d'Arezzo, 1060 Brussels; tel (2) 345-99-11; telex 22252; fax (2) 345-06-12.
Ambassador and Head of Mission: Salifou Rigobert Kongo.
First Counsellor: Alain Francis Gustave Ilboudo.
Commercial Counsellor: Brigitte Marie Thérèse Kongo.
Economic Counsellor: Daniel Ouedraogo.
Financial Attaché: Hati Alexis Ouedraogo.

BURUNDI

Embassy: 46 square Marie-Louise, 1040 Brussels; tel (2) 230-45-35; telex 23572; fax (2) 230-78-83.
Ambassador: Julien Nahayo.

CAMEROON

Embassy: 131 ave Brugmann, 1060 Brussels; tel (2) 345-18-70; telex 24117.
Ambassador: Isabelle Bassong-Akoumba-Monneyang.

CANADA

Embassy: 2 ave de Tervueren, 1040 Brussels; tel (2) 735-60-40; telex 21613; fax (2) 735-33-83.
Ambassador: Jacques J. A. Asselin.
Minister-Counsellor: L. I. Friedlaender.
Counsellor and Consul: R. P. Bersma.
Counsellor (Cultural Affairs and Information) and Consul: J. Fredette.
Counsellor (Science and Technology): J. H. Prinsen.
Counsellor (Administration) and Consul: R. J. P. Renaud.
Counsellor (Commercial/Economic): B. Picard.
Forces Attaché: Col F. S. Carpenter.
Attaché (Agriculture/Food): D. Cumming.
Second Secretary (Immigration) and Vice-Consul: L. Pouliot.

CENTRAL AFRICAN REPUBLIC

Embassy: 416 blvd Lambermont, 1030 Brussels; tel (2) 242-28-80; telex 22493.
First Counsellor: Victor Wayne.
Counsellor (Economic and Commercial): Maurice Epelaki.
Counsellor (Agro-Economics): Jacky-Alphonse Tchabassimy.
Attaché (Administration and Finance): Virginie Modave.

CHAD

Embassy: 52 blvd Lambermont, 1030 Brussels; tel (2) 215-19-75.
Ambassador: Abdoulaye Lamana.

CHILE

Embassy: 17 rue Montoyer, 1040 Brussels; tel (2) 512-46-00; telex 61955.
Ambassador: Juan Luis González Reyes.

CHINA, PEOPLE'S REPUBLIC

Embassy: 443-445 ave de Tervueren, 1150 Brussels; tel (2) 771-33-09.
Ambassador: Xia Daosheng.

COLOMBIA

Embassy: 44 rue Van Eyck, BP 5-6, 1050 Brussels; tel (2) 649-56-79; telex 25254; fax (2) 649-42-39.
Ambassador: Manuel José Cárdenas.

CONGO

Embassy: 16-18 ave F. D. Roosevelt, 1050 Brussels; tel (2) 648-38-56; telex 23677; fax (2) 648-42-13.
Ambassador: Ambroise Gambouele.
First Counsellor and Head of Chancery: Roger-Julien Menga.
Economic Counsellor (Bilateral Relations): Jacques Obia.
Economic Counsellor (Multilateral Relations): Henri Calixte Dimi.
First Secretary: Alphonsine Kouyokila-Soumina.
Secretary (Cultural Affairs): Angelique Gassiere.
Secretary (Consular Affairs): Guy Leon Ongagna.
Secretary (Telecommunications): Xavier-François Dassoa.
Financial Attaché: Raphaël Desiré Bopacah Locelet.
Administrative Attaché: Thérèse Gabrielle Peya.

COSTA RICA

Embassy: 489 ave Louise, BP 23, 1050 Brussels; tel (2) 640-55-41; fax (2) 648-31-92.
Ambassador: Guillermo Jiménez Ramírez.

Counsellor: Maria-Eugenia Cortes de Bourla.
Commercial Minister-Counsellor: Felix Przedborski.
Counsellor and Consul-General: Rodrigo Gerardo Redondo Gómez.
First Secretary: Eugenia Maria Zawadzki Montes de Oca.
Honorary Consul: Guy Roggen.

Consulate: Hoveniersstraat 50-52, 2018 Antwerp; tel (3) 232-84-41.
Honorary Consul: Charles Berkovic.

COTE D'IVOIRE

Embassy: 234 ave F. D. Roosevelt, 1050 Brussels; tel (2) 672-23-57; telex 21993.
Ambassador: Charles Valy Tuho.

CUBA

Embassy: 77 rue Roberts-Jones, 1180 Brussels; tel (2) 343-00-20; telex 21945; fax (2) 344-96-91.
Ambassador: Teresita Averhoff Purón.

CYPRUS

Embassy: 83 rue de la Loi, 4e étage, 1040 Brussels; tel (2) 230-12-95; telex 25172.
Ambassador: Nicos Agathocleous.

'TURKISH REPUBLIC OF NORTHERN CYPRUS'

Embassy: 284-286 ave Louise, BP 10, 1050 Brussels; tel (2) 648-48-70; fax (2) 48-70-88.
Ambassador: Ayer Kaşif.
First Secretary: Zeki Gazioğlu.

CZECHOSLOVAKIA

Embassy: 152 ave Adolphe Buyl, 1050 Brussels; tel (2) 647-68-09; telex 64565; fax (2) 647-91-81.
Ambassador: Karel Lukáš.
Counsellor: Ján Varšo.
First Secretary: Václav Vondrášek.
Second Secretary: Igor Keblúšek.
Second Secretary: Bohuslav Matucha.
Second Secretary: Ivana Susová.
Third Secretary: Petr Vecek.
Third Secretary: Miloš Posád.
Military and Air Attaché: Alois Petr.
Military and Air Attaché: Miroslav Galaš.

Commercial Section: 118 ave Brugmann, 1050 Brussels; tel (2) 343-35-05; fax (2) 343-67-30.
Commercial Counsellor: František Martiňák.
Deputy Commercial Attaché: Karel Kohout.

DENMARK

Embassy: 221 ave Louise, BP 7, 1050 Brussels; tel (2) 648-25-25; telex 22591; fax (2) 647-07-09.
Ambassador: Carl Ernst Wilhelm Ulrichsen.
Commercial Counsellor: F. Folmer Petersen.
Attaché and Consul: Birthe Vase.
Export Assistant: Margrethe Kirk.
Commercial Assistant: Nadine Pochez.
Commercial Assistant: Jan Verleysen.
Agricultural Counsellor: Jens Hauge Pedersen.
Fisheries Counsellor: Flemming Reislev.
Chaplain: Mogens Lindhardt Pedersen.

Consulate-General: Antwerp Tower, 5 De Keyserlei, BP 4, 2018 Antwerp; tel (3) 232-01-98; telex 33135; fax (3) 232-88-22.
Consul-General: Ove Jensen.
Secretary and Vice-Consul: Marie-Thérèse de Boungne.

Consulate: 68-70 Pathoekeweg, 8000 Bruges; tel (50) 31-51-41; telex 81153; fax (50) 31-40-59.
Consul: Jan van den Abeele.

Consulate: 34 Fiévéstraat, 9000 Ghent; tel (91) 24-24-02; telex 11322; fax (91) 24-35-70.
Consul: Henri Georges Jacques Ghislain Wagemans.

Consulate-General: 53 blvd d'Avroy, 4000 Liège; tel (41) 23-22-93; telex 41402; fax (41) 22-02-26.
Consul-General: Pierre Gaston Julien Latteur.

DJIBOUTI

Embassy: 24 ave F. D. Roosevelt, 1050 Brussels; tel (2) 646-41-51; telex 27242; fax (2) 646-44-59.
Ambassador: Hassan Idriss Ahmed.
First Counsellor: Ahmed Mohamed Ismael.
Second Counsellor: Doualeh Ali Ahmed.
Counsellor: Hassan Said Idriss.
Financial Attaché: Mohamed Ali Barreh.
Attaché: Mohamed Ismaël Ali.
Press Attaché: Tina Antonsen.

European Promotion Office: tel (2) 646-27-77.
Director: A. M. Ismaël.
Secretary-General: Francis Henrion.
External Relations: Tina Antonsen.
Culture, Co-operation and Development and Consul: Elisabeth Speeckaert-Cornet d'Elzius.

Consulate: 53 blvd Saint-Michel, 1040 Brussels; tel (2) 736-36-07; fax (2) 732-10-52.

Consulate: Antwerp.

DOMINICA

Embassy: 12 rue des Bollandistes, 1040 Brussels; tel (2) 733-43-28; telex 29380; fax (2) 735-72-37.
Ambassador: Charles Angelo Savarin.
Second Secretary: Alcid Joseph.

DOMINICAN REPUBLIC

Embassy: 106A ave Louise, bte 19, 1050 Brussels; tel (2) 646-08-40; fax (2) 640-95-61.
Chargé d'affaires a.i. and Minister-Counsellor: Renso Herrera Franco.
Attaché (Economic Affairs): Escipion Joaquin Oliveira Gomez.

Consulate-General: 190 Mechelsesteenweg, 2018 Antwerp; tel (3) 216-10-58.
Consul-General: Moira Suro.

ECUADOR

Embassy: 70 chaussée de Charleroi, 1060 Brussels; tel (2) 537-91-30; telex 63292; fax (2) 537-90-66.
Ambassador: Xavier Pérez Martínez.

EGYPT

Embassy: 44 ave Léo Errera, 1180 Brussels; tel (2) 345-50-15; telex 23716; fax (2) 343-65-33.
Ambassador: Hussein Mohamed Elkamel.
Minister Plenipotentiary: Mohamed Chérif Sadek.
Minister Plenipotentiary: Samiha Abou-Steit.
Counsellor: Mokhless Kotb.
Second Secretary: Yasser Morad Hossny.
Third Secretary: Ashraf Hamdy Saad.
Third Secretary: Alaa El Din Youssef.

Commercial Section: 522 ave Louise, 1050 Brussels; tel (2) 647-32-27; telex 64809; fax (2) 646-45-09.
Minister Plenipotentiary: Fikry el-Kallini.
Counsellor (Commercial Affairs): Kamal Eldin Aly Rezk.
Attaché (Commercial Affairs): Ahmed Tallat Mohamed.

Press and Information Section: 42 blvd Général Jacques, 1050 Brussels; tel (2) 640-35-01; fax (2) 646-45-32.
Counsellor (Press): Asma el-Meligui.

EL SALVADOR

Embassy: 3 blvd Saint-Michel, 1150 Brussels; tel (2) 732-35-66; fax (2) 735-02-11.
Ambassador: Ana Cristina Sol.
Minister-Counsellor: Luis Menendez Castro.
Minister-Counsellor (Consular Affairs): Mathilde Abastado de Craik.
Third Secretary: Astrid W. de Amador.

ETHIOPIA

Embassy: 32 blvd Saint-Michel, 1040 Brussels; tel (2) 733-98-18; telex 62285; fax (2) 732-18-51.
Ambassador: Hailu Wolde Amanuel.

FIJI

Embassy: 66-68 ave de Cortenberg, 7e étage, BP 7, 1040 Brussels; tel (2) 736-90-50; telex 26934; fax (2) 736-14-58.
Ambassador: Kaliopate Tavola.
Counsellor: Josaia Maivusaroko.
Commercial Counsellor: Sung Kangwai.
First Secretary: Waisale Rai.
Third Secretary: Munesh Naidu.

FINLAND

Embassy: 489 ave Louise, 5e étage, 1050 Brussels; tel (2) 648-84-84; telex 23099; fax (2) 640-18-58.
Ambassador: Ensio Helaniemi.

Commerce, Science and Technology Section: 475 ave Louise; tel (2) 647-67-64; telex 63865; fax (2) 648-96-31.
Commercial Secretary: Tapio Wento.
Secretary for Science and Technology: Matti Supponen.

Consulate-General: 7 ave des Gaulois, 1040 Brussels; tel (2) 735-40-98.
Consul-General: Antti Majorin.

Consulate-General: 139 Noorderlaan, 2030 Antwerp; tel (3) 543-73-33; telex 34000; fax (3) 541-23-09.
Consul: Jan Gelens.
Vice-Consul: Kauko Hyytiä.

Consulate: Charleroi.

Consulate: 32 Stapelplein, 9000 Ghent; tel (91) 23-96-86; telex 12691.
Consul: Jacques Emile Paul Pauwelyn.

Consulate: 10 rue des Renards, 4040 Tilff., Liège; tel (41) 68-68-62.
Consul: Francis M. Festraets.

Consulate: 8 Strandschelplaan, 8400 Ostend; tel (59) 70-86-03.
Consul: Yvan Deswaef.

FRANCE

Embassy: 65 rue Ducale, 1000 Brussels; tel (2) 512-17-15; telex 21478.
Ambassador: Alain Pierret.

Economic Section: 42 blvd du Régent, 1000 Brussels; tel (2) 513-90-12; telex 22250.

Consulate-General: 4 ave des Arts, 1040 Brussels; tel (2) 217-24-63.

Consulate-General: 24 Bosmanslei, 2018 Antwerp; tel (3) 238-23-91.

Consulate-General: 33 Sint-Annaplem, 9000 Ghent; tel (91) 25-97-30.

Consulate-General: 1 rue Saint-Rémy, 4000 Liège; tel (41) 23-42-45.

Consulate-General: 19 rue Terre-du-Prince, 7000 Mons; tel (65) 35-23-04.

GABON

Embassy: 112 ave W. Churchill, 1180 Brussels; tel (2) 343-00-55; telex 23383.

Ambassador: Michel Leslie Taele.

GAMBIA

Embassy: 126 ave F. D. Roosevelt, 1050 Brussels; tel (2) 640-10-49; telex 24344; fax (2) 646-32-77.
Ambassador: Mamadu Kalifo Bojang.

GERMANY

Embassy: 190 ave de Tervueren, 1150 Brussels; tel (2) 770-58-30; telex 21382; fax (2) 772-36-92.
Ambassador: Renate Finke-Osiander.

Consulate-General: 5 de Keyserlei, bus 26, 2018 Antwerp; tel (3) 226-01-30; telex 35556.
Consul-General: Wedigo Graf von Wedel-Gödens.

Consulate-General: 7a ave Rogier, 4000 Liège; tel (41) 23-59-95; telex 42295.
Consul-General: Dr Walter Fröwis.

Consulate: 11 blvd Tirou, 6000 Charleroi; tel (71) 27-17-11; telex 51136.
Honorary Consul: Albert Frère.

Consulate: 82 Doornzelestraat, 9000 Ghent; tel (91) 25-91-68.
Honorary Consul: Robert Lalemant.

Consulate: 18 Kunstlaan, 3500 Hasselt; tel (11) 22-57-06.
Honorary Consul: Marcel Dierckx.

Consulate: 12 Henri Baelskaai, 8400 Ostende; tel (59) 32-28-65.
Honorary Consul: Charles Decrop.

GHANA

Embassy: 7 blvd Général Wahis, 1030 Brussels; tel (2) 245-82-20; telex 22572; fax (2) 245-64-53.
Ambassador: Alex N. Abankwa.
Counsellor: Kingsley Ebow Derby.
First Secretary: Beatrice Rosa Brobey.
First Secretary: Robert Kofi Badu.
Second Secretary: Stephen Yaw Ofori.
Second Secretary: Daniel Komla Alifo.
Third Secretary: Elizabeth Modey.

GREECE

Embassy: 430 ave Louise, 3e étage, 1050 Brussels; tel (2) 648-17-30; telex 25521.
Ambassador: Constantin Eliopoulos.
First Secretary: Jean Christofilis.
Second Secretary: Catherine Loupas.

Consulate-General: 204-206 Mechelse Steenweg, 2018 Antwerp; tel (3) 248-17-32.
Consul-General: V. Simantirakis.

Consulate: 41 ave Blonden, 4000 Liège; tel (41) 52-65-65.
Consul: K. Loukakis.

Consulate: 20 blvd Rirou, 6000 Charleroi; tel (71) 31-43-51.

GRENADA

Embassy: 24 ave des Arts, 7e étage, BP 2, 1040 Brussels; tel (2) 230-62-65; telex 64015; fax (2) 230-39-63.
Minister-Counsellor and Chargé d'affaires a.i.: Samuel Orgias.

GUATEMALA

Embassy: 53 blvd Général Wahis, 1030 Brussels; tel (2) 736-03-40; telex 25130.
Ambassador: Carlos Humberto Jiménez Licona.

GUINEA

Embassy: 75 ave Roger Vandendriessche, 1150 Brussels; tel (2) 771-01-26; telex 64731.
Ambassador: Mamadou Bobo Camara.

GUINEA-BISSAU

Embassy: 70 ave F. D. Roosevelt, 1050 Brussels; tel (2) 647-08-90; telex 63631; fax (2) 640-43-12.
Ambassador: Bubacar Turé.

GUYANA

Embassy: 13-17 rue de Praetere, 1050 Brussels; tel (2) 646-61-00; telex 26180; fax (2) 646-55-13.
Ambassador: James Henry Edward Matheson.
First Secretary: Neil O. Pierre.
First Secretary (Commercial): James Ramsahoye.
Attaché (Finance): Dianne J. Abel.
Attaché: Debra A. L. Collins.

HAITI

Embassy: 160A ave Louise, BP 25, 1050 Brussels; tel (2) 649-73-81; fax (2) 649-62-47.
Chargé d'affaires a.i.: Maryse Penette.

HOLY SEE

Apostolic Nunciature: 5-9 ave des Franciscains, 1150 Brussels; tel (2) 762-20-05; fax (6) 762-20-32.
Apostolic Nuncio: Most Rev. Giovanni Moretti, Titular Archbishop of Vartana.
Secretary: Mgr Joseph Chennoth.

HONDURAS

Embassy: 3 ave des Gaulois, 5e étage, 1040 Brussels; tel (2) 734-00-00; telex 63175.
Chargé d'affaires a.i.: Edith Glynn.

HUNGARY

Embassy: 41 rue Edmond Picard, 1180 Brussels; tel (2) 343-67-90; telex 26650; fax (2) 347-60-28.
Ambassador and Consul-General: György Granasztói.
First Counsellor and Deputy Head of Mission: Tibor Kiss.
First Counsellor (Security and Political Affairs): László Ság.
Counsellor (Economic Affairs): Gyula Braun.
Counsellor (Cultural Affairs and the Media): László Csejdy.
Counsellor (Information and the Press): Tibor Gubcsi.
Second Secretary: Miklós Nott.
Military and Air Attaché: Lieut Col Zoltán Papp.
Assistant Military and Air Attaché: Maj. István Fekete.

Consulate-General: 45 rue Edmond Picard, 1180 Brussels; tel (2) 343-94-47.
Consul and First Secretary: Jenő Ambrus.

ICELAND

Embassy: 5 rue Archimède, 8e étage, 1040 Brussels; tel (2) 231-03-95; telex 29459; fax (2) 230-81-46.
Ambassador: Einar Benediktsson.
Minister-Counsellor: Gunnar Snorri Gunnarsson.
Secretary: Thórdur B. Gudjónsson.
Counsellor: Tómas Óli Jónsson.
Secretary: Petrína Bachmann.

Consulate-General: 27 Galerie Ravenstein, 1000 Brussels; tel (2) 512-59-65; telex 21299; fax (2) 513-33-80.
Consul-General: Jacques Tasiaux.
Consul: Philippe Tasiaux.
Vice-Consul: Jean B. Godts.

Consulate: 13 Keizerstraat, 2000 Antwerp; tel (3) 223-04-45.
Consul: Maurice Velge.

INDIA

Embassy: 217 chaussée de Vleurgat, 1050 Brussels; tel (2) 640-91-40; telex 22510; fax (2) 648-96-38.
Ambassador: Dr A. K. Sengupta.
Deputy Chief of Mission: S. S. Gill.
Counsellor: O. P. Goel.
Counsellor: A. K. Pandey.
First Secretary: M. Raghupathi.
First Secretary: A. Dasgupta.
First Secretary: S. P. Mann.
First Secretary: K. Sharma.
Second Secretary: S. Prakash.
Third Secretary: V. Misri.

Consulate-General: 11 G. Willemotlaan, 9030 Ghent; tel (91) 26-34-23.
Consul-General: Chevalier R. Desprechins de Gaesebek.

Consulate-General: ADC Bldg, B517, 2 Hovenierstraat, 2018 Antwerp; tel (3) 234-11-22.
Consul-General: Paul Meeus.

INDONESIA

Embassy: 294 ave de Tervueren, 1150 Brussels; tel (2) 771-20-14; telex 21200.
Ambassador: Atmono Suryo.

IRAN

Embassy: 415 ave de Tervueren, 1150 Brussels; tel (2) 762-37-45; telex 24083; fax (2) 762-39-15.
Ambassador: Mohammad Reza Bakhtiari.
Minister-Counsellor: Hassan Tajik.
First Secretary: Ahmad Shahvary.
Third Secretary: Moradali Gholami Nohouji.
Third Secretary: Gholamreza Ebrahimpour.
Third Secretary: Said Kholoozadeh.
Consul: Hussein Filsouf.
Attaché: Hassan Teymouri Ashtiani.

IRAQ

Embassy: 131 ave de la Floride, 1180 Brussels; tel (2) 374-59-92; telex 26414.
Ambassador: Zaïd Hwaishan Haidar.

IRELAND

Embassy: 19 rue du Luxembourg, 3e étage, 1040 Brussels; tel (2) 513-66-33; telex 24598; fax (2) 513-21-73.
Ambassador: Gearoid Ó Clerigh.
First Secretary: Isolde Moylan McNally.

Consulate-General: Koffie F. Rombouts NV, 16-40 Rudolfstraat, 2000 Antwerp; tel (3) 238-25-90; telex 31031; fax (3) 216-08-40.
Honorary Consul-General: Ivan Rombouts.

ISRAEL

Embassy: 40 ave de l'Observatoire, 1180 Brussels; tel (2) 374-90-80; telex 24290; fax (2) 374-98-20.
Ambassador: Avraham Primor.

ITALY

Embassy: 28 rue Emile Claus, 1050 Brussels; tel (2) 649-97-00; telex 23950; fax (2) 648-54-85.
Chargé d'affaires a.i. and First Counsellor (Political Affairs): Ferruccio Marri Caciotti.
First Counsellor (Emigration and Social Affairs): Valeria Spinelli-Catani.
Counsellor (Economic and Commercial): Giorgio Trabattoni.
Scientific Attaché: Giorgio Velo.

Consulate-General: 5 Nationalestraat, bte 36, 2000 Antwerp; tel (3) 233-81-75.
Consul: F. Galante.

Consulate-General: 24 blvd Audent, 6000 Charleroi; tel (71) 32-86-50.
Consul: B. Carloni.

Consulate-General: 31 place Xavier Neujean, 4000 Liège; tel (41) 23-59-03.
Consul: G. F. d'Alessandro.

Consulate: 38 rue de Livourne, 1050 Brussels; tel (2) 537-19-34.
Consul: G. B. Campagnola.

JAMAICA

Embassy: 83-85 rue de la Loi, 5e étage, 1040 Brussels; tel (2) 230-11-70; telex 26644; fax (2) 230-37-09.
Ambassador: Leslie Armon Wilson.
Minister-Counsellor: Yvette Cross.

JAPAN

Embassy: 58 ave des Arts, 7e étage, 1040 Brussels; tel (2) 513-92-00; telex 22174; fax (2) 513-15-56.
Ambassador: Atsuhiko Yatabe.

JORDAN

Embassy: 104 ave F. D. Roosevelt, 1050 Brussels; tel (2) 640-77-55; telex 62513.
Chargé d'affaires a.i.: Nabil Masarweh.

KENYA

Embassy: 1-5 ave de la Joyeuse Entrée, 1040 Brussels; tel (2) 230-30-65; telex 62568.
Ambassador: Francis Kirimi Muthaura.

KOREA, REPUBLIC

Embassy: 3 ave Hamoir, 1180 Brussels; tel (2) 375-39-80; telex 26256.
Ambassador: Chung Woo Young.

KUWAIT

Embassy: 43 ave F. D. Roosevelt, 1050 Brussels; tel (2) 647-79-50; telex 62904; fax (2) 646-12-98.
Ambassador: Ahmad A. al-Ebrahim.

LEBANON

Embassy: 2 rue Guillaume Stocq, 1050 Brussels; tel (2) 649-94-60; telex 22547.
Ambassador: Dr Saïd al-Assaad.

LESOTHO

Embassy: 66 ave de Cortenbergh, BP 5, 1040 Brussels; tel (2) 736-39-76; telex 25852.
Ambassador: Mabotse Lerotholi.

LIBERIA

Embassy: 55 ave F. D. Roosevelt, 1050 Brussels; tel (2) 648-13-49; telex 61384.
Chargé d'affaires a.i.: Jarjar Kamara.

LIBYA

People's Bureau: 28 ave Victoria, 1050 Brussels; tel (2) 649-21-12.
Secretary of People's Bureau: Dr Mohamed Saraf Edin Alfaituri.

LUXEMBOURG

Embassy: 211 rue du Noyer, 1040 Brussels; tel (2) 733-99-77; telex 21707; fax (2) 736-14-29.
Ambassador: Guy de Muyser.
First Counsellor and Consul-General: Jean-Paul Munchen.
Attaché and Vice-Consul: Antoine Bernardy.

MADAGASCAR

Embassy: 276 ave de Tervueren, 1150 Brussels; tel (2) 770-17-26; telex 61197.
Ambassador: Christian Rémi Richard.

MALAWI

Embassy: 13 rue de la Loi, 1040 Brussels; tel (2) 231-09-80; telex 24128.
Ambassador: Lawrence P. Anthony.

MALAYSIA

Embassy: 414A ave de Tervueren, 1150 Brussels; tel (2) 762-67-67; telex 26396; fax (2) 762-50-49.
Ambassador: Dato Dali Mahmud Hashim.
Minister-Counsellor: Kamal Ismaun.
Minister-Counsellor (Customs): Wan Yeop Abdul Shukor Bin Wan Din.
Minister-Counsellor (Trade): Kalsom B. Abdul Rahman.
First Secretary: Fauziah Mohd Taib.
First Secretary: Mohd Hatta Abdul Aziz.
Trade Commissioner: Abdul Kabur Bin Mohd Ibrahim.
Second Secretary (Administration): Abu Bakar Bin Hanif.
Attaché (Administration): Ahmad Apandi Bin Samsudin.

MALI

Embassy: 487 ave Molière, 1060 Brussels; tel (2) 345-74-32; telex 22508; fax (2) 344-57-00.
Ambassador: Lamine Keïta.
First Counsellor: Amadou Tidiané Dia.
First Counsellor: Demba Macalou.
Secretary: Dioflo Coulibaly.

Consulate: 1 Maria Henriettalei, 2018 Antwerp; tel (3) 231-36-55.
Honorary Consul: Mr Wijffels.

MALTA

Embassy: 44 rue Jules Lejeune, 1060 Brussels; tel (2) 343-01-95; telex 26616; fax (2) 343-01-06.
Ambassador: Dr Joseph Licari.
First Secretary: Charles Inguanez.
First Secretary: Dr Paul Saliba.
Consul-General: Anthony J. B. Soler.

Consulate: 14 Welkomstraat, Wonnelgem, 2000 Antwerp; tel (3) 353-40-80; telex 72246; fax (3) 353-18-99.
Honorary Consul: Dr Baudouin C. M. P. G. Franck.

MAURITANIA

Embassy: 127 ave Gustave Demey, 1160 Brussels; tel (2) 672-47-47.
Ambassador: Ely Ould Allaf.

MAURITIUS

Embassy: 68 rue des Bollandistes, 1040 Brussels; tel (2) 733-99-88; telex 23114; fax (2) 734-40-21.
Ambassador: Raymond Chasle.

MEXICO

Embassy: 164 chaussée de la Hulpe, 1170 Brussels; tel (2) 676-07-11; telex 22355; fax (2) 672-93-12.
Ambassador: Adolfo Hegewisch.

MONACO

Embassy: 17 place Guy d'Arezzo, BP 7, 1060 Brussels; tel (2) 347-49-87; fax (2) 343-49-20.
Ambassador: Jean Gréther.

Consulate: 14 ave de la Ferme Rose, BP 7, 1180 Brussels; tel (2) 344-28-38.
Consul: Chevalier Gilson de Rouvreux.

Consulate: 22 rue Forgeur, 4000 Liège; tel (4) 22-02-71.
Consul: Jacques Deruelle.

Consulate: 25 Van Breestraat, 2018 Antwerp; tel (3) 232-10-70.
Consul: Guy van Doosselaere.

Consulate: 21 Leopold II Laan, 8400 Ostend; tel (59) 50-66-99.
Consul: Rosette Porta.

MOROCCO

Embassy: 29 blvd Saint-Michel, 1040 Brussels; tel (2) 736-11-00; telex 21233; fax (2) 734-64-68.
Ambassador and Head of Mission: Abdellah Lahlou.
First Counsellor and Deputy Head of Mission: Jaafar H. Alj.
First Counsellor: Abdesslam Alem.
Counsellor: Mina Tounsi.

Consulate-General: 52 rue P. E. Janson, 1050 Brussels; tel (2) 649-60-10.
Consul-General: A. Assouli.

Consulate: 35 Berkenlaan, Wilrijk, 2610 Antwerp; tel (3) 830-57-51.
Consul: A. Medbouhi.

Consulate: 54 quai St Léonard, 4000 Liège; tel (41) 27-41-24.
Consul: M. Zouaoui.

MOZAMBIQUE

Embassy: 97 blvd Saint-Michel, 1040 Brussels; tel (2) 736-25-64; telex 65478; fax (2) 735-62-07.
Ambassador: Frances Victoria Velho Rodrigues.

NETHERLANDS

Embassy: 35 rue de la Science, 1040 Brussels; tel (2) 230-30-20; telex 21311.
Ambassador: Hubert Joseph Marie van Nispen tot Sevenaer.

NEW ZEALAND

Embassy: 47-48 blvd du Régent, 1000 Brussels; tel (2) 512-10-40; fax (2) 513-48-56.
Ambassador: David Le Preu Gamble.
Counsellor and Consul-General: Maarten L. Wevers.
First Secretary: John N. Goodman.
First Secretary: Deborah L. Broome.
Attaché: Pam J. Dalton.
Attaché: Karen L. Wong.
Counsellor (Veterinary): Dr Barry D. O'Neil.
First Secretary (Customs): Michael A. Spong.

Consulate: 9 Grote Markt, 2000 Antwerp; tel (3) 233-16-08; fax (3) 226-29-69.
Honorary Consul: Alexander P. van Heeren.

NICARAGUA

Embassy: 55 ave de Wolvendael, 1180 Brussels; tel (2) 375-64-34; telex 63553; fax (2) 375-71-88.
Ambassador: Sergio Mario Blandon Lanzas.
Minister-Counsellor: Lester Mejia Solis.

NIGER

Embassy: 78 ave F. D. Roosevelt, 1050 Brussels; tel (2) 648-61-40; telex 22857.
Ambassador: Adamou Zada.

NIGERIA

Embassy: 288 ave de Tervueren, 1150 Brussels; tel (2) 762-98-31; telex 22435.
Ambassador: Maurice B. Ekpang.

NORWAY

Embassy: 17 rue Archimède, 1040 Brussels; tel (2) 230-78-65; telex 62563; fax (2) 230-36-81.

Ambassador: Knut Sverre.

PAKISTAN

Embassy: 57 ave Delleur, 1170 Brussels; tel (2) 673-80-07; telex 61816; fax (2) 675-31-37.
Ambassador: Munir Akram.
Minister and Head of Chancery: Toheed Ahmad.
Minister (Economic): Shuja Shah.
Minister (Customs): Tahir Mahmood.
First Secretary: Mr Sanaullah.
First Secretary: Fauzia M. Sana.

PANAMA

Embassy: 8 blvd Brand Whitlock, 1050 Brussels; tel (2) 733-90-89; telex 25169; fax (2) 733-77-79.
Ambassador: Roberto Alemán.

PAPUA NEW GUINEA

Embassy: 17-19 rue Montoyer, 1040 Brussels; tel (2) 512-31-27; fax (2) 512-86-43.
Chargé d'affaires a.i.: Lucy B. Bogari.
First Secretary: Ageauka Kila.
Third Secretary (Administrative Affairs): Hitolo Heagi.

PARAGUAY

Embassy: 42 ave de Saturne, 1180 Brussels; tel (2) 374-87-48; telex 26535.
Ambassador: Dido Florentín-Bogado.

PERU

Embassy: 179 ave de Tervueren, 1150 Brussels; tel (2) 733-33-19; telex 24577.
Ambassador: Julio Ego-Aguirre Alvarez.

PHILIPPINES

Embassy: 85 rue Washington, 1050 Brussels; tel (2) 533-18-11; telex 23631; fax (2) 538-35-40.
Ambassador: Roberto R. Romulo.
Minister: Jose A. Zaide, Jr.
Second Secretary and Consul: Ricardo M. Endaya.
Second Secretary and Consul: Libran N. Cabactulan.
Second Secretary and Consul: Alejandrino A. Vicente.
Administrative Officer and Attaché: Reynaldo G. Cardenas.
Property/Records Officer and Attaché: Virgilio G. Cajaljal.
Finance Officer and Attaché: Norma C. Tuiza.
Secretary to Ambassador and Attaché: Maria Victoria V. Ortiz-Dony.
Special Trade Representative and Counsellor: Cristina G. Ortega.
Agricultural Attaché: Horacio M. Carandang.
First Secretary (Information): Alejandro D. del Rosario.

POLAND

Embassy: 126 ave des Gaulois, 1050 Brussels; tel (2) 735-72-12; telex 21562.
Ambassador: Tadeusz Olechowski.

PORTUGAL

Embassy: 115 rue Defacqz, 5e étage, 1050 Brussels; tel (2) 539-38-50; telex 24570.
Ambassador: António Augusto de Medeiros Patricio.

QATAR

Embassy: 71 ave F. D. Roosevelt, 1050 Brussels; tel (2) 640-74-06; telex 63754; fax (2) 648-40-78.
Chargé d'affaires a.i.: Ali Hassan al-Hamadi.

ROMANIA

Embassy: 105 rue Gabrielle, 1180 Brussels; tel (2) 345-26-80; telex 21859.
Ambassador: Ovidiu Popescu.

RUSSIA

Embassy: 66 ave de Fré, 1180 Brussels; tel (2) 374-34-06; telex 65272.
Ambassador: Nikolai N. Afanasyevsky.

Consular Section: 78 rue Robert Jones, 1180 Brussels; tel (2) 373-35-69; telex 65272; fax (2) 374-26-13.

Consulate-General: 20 Della Faillelaan, 2020 Antwerp; tel (3) 829-16-11; telex 35779.

RWANDA

Embassy: 1 ave des Fleurs, 1150 Brussels; tel (2) 763-07-05; telex 26653.
Ambassador: François Ngarukiyintwali.

SAN MARINO

Embassy: 44 ave Brugman, BP 6, 1060 Brussels; tel (2) 344-60-67; fax (2) 347-17-08.
Ambassador: Gian Nicola Filippi Balestra.

Consulate-General: tel (2) 343-31-36.
Honorary Consul-General: Emmanuel Noël.
Honorary Vice-Consul: Henry Brouwers-Tits.

SÃO TOMÉ AND PRÍNCIPE

Embassy: 42 ave Brugman, 1060 Brussels; tel (2) 347-53-75; telex 65313.
Chargé d'affaires a.i.: Carlos Gustavo dos Anjo.
First Secretary: Antonio Albertino Afonso Dias.
Second Secretary: Horacio Fernandes da Fonseca.
Third Secretary: Rosa da Silva Simao.

SAUDI ARABIA

Embassy: 45 ave F. D. Roosevelt, 1050 Brussels; tel (2) 649-57-25; telex 64626.
Chargé d'affaires a.i.: Omar Bamanie.

SENEGAL

Embassy: 196 ave F. D. Roosevelt, 1050 Brussels; tel (2) 673-08-87; telex 63951.
Ambassador: Falilou Kane.

SIERRA LEONE

Embassy: 410 ave de Tervueren, 1150 Brussels; tel (2) 771-11-80; telex 63624.
Ambassador: Marian Judith Tanner Kamara.

SINGAPORE

Embassy: 198 ave F. D. Roosevelt, 1050 Brussels; tel (2) 660-30-98; telex 26731.
Ambassador: Jayalekshimi Mohideen.

SOMALIA

Embassy: 66 ave F. D. Roosevelt, 1050 Brussels; tel (2) 640-16-69; telex 24807.
Ambassador: Ali Hassan Ali.

SOUTH AFRICA

Embassy: 26 rue de la Loi, BP 7/8, 1040 Brussels; tel (2) 230-68-45; telex 23495; fax (2) 30-13-36.
Ambassador: Marinus Leonard te Water Naudé.
Counsellor: J. H. P. Castelyn.
Counsellor (Administration): Z. J. Prinsloo.
Counsellor (Customs): H. J. D. Rudman.
First Secretary: Dr P. G. W. du Plessis.
First Secretary: S. F. Engelbrecht.
First Secretary: W. E. de Groot.
First Secretary: D. J. Steenkamp.
First Secretary (Trade): P. A. Hattingh.
First Secretary (Consular): F. A. Booijse.
Attaché (Agriculture): G. J. Joubert.

Consulate: 9 Eiken Straat, 2000 Antwerp; tel (3) 31-49-60.
Honorary Consul: L. K. Rochtus.

Consulate: Quai de Condroz 21/011, 4020 Liège; tel (41) 42-80-84.
Honorary Consul: J.-M. Mesters.

SPAIN

Embassy: 19 rue de la Science, 1040 Brussels; tel (2) 230-03-40; telex 22092.
Ambassador: Nicolás Martínez-Fresno y Pavia.

SRI LANKA

Embassy: 21-22 ave des Arts, 1040 Brussels; tel (2) 230-48-90; telex 26927.
Ambassador: Tyrrel Derric Samuel Alaric Dissanayaka.

SUDAN

Embassy: 124 ave F. D. Roosevelt, 1050 Brussels; tel (2) 647-94-94; telex 24370.
Ambassador: Saeed Saad Mahgoub Saad.

SURINAME

Embassy: 379 ave Louise, BP 20, 1050 Brussels; tel (2) 640-11-72; telex 62680.
Ambassador: Donald Aloysius McLeod.

SWAZILAND

Embassy: 71 rue Joseph II, 5e étage, 1040 Brussels; tel (2) 230-00-44; telex 26254; fax (2) 230-50-83.
Ambassador: J. B. J. S. Dhlamini.

SWEDEN

Embassy: 148 ave Louise, 1050 Brussels; tel (2) 641-66-11; telex 21148; fax (2) 641-66-20.
Ambassador: Henrik Liljegren.
Counsellor: Karl-Gunnar Lidström.
Counsellor: Fredrik Vahlquist.
Press Counsellor: Christian Andersson.
First Secretary: Leif Krusberg.
Chancellor: Kristina Laanen.
Labour Counsellor: Margit Wallsten.

Trade Office: Trade Council, 33 blvd de la Cambre, 1050 Brussels; tel (2) 648-46-04; telex 21112; fax (2) 648-80-71.
Commercial Secretary: Ingemar Ehlin.

Consulate-General: c/o Westerlund Corp nv, 8 Oude Leeuwenrui, 2000 Antwerp; tel (3) 231-27-01; telex 32344; fax (3) 224-18-88.
Consul-General: Jean Jacques Willy Westerlund.
Vice-Consul: Monique Renée Hendrikx.

Consulate: c/o SV Metalunion, Krakeleweg s/n, 8000 Bruges; tel (50) 32-09-11; telex 81141.
Consul: François Marie-Joseph Gaston Tytgadt.

Consulate: 57 ave Sixième, 6001 Marcinelle/Charleroi; tel (71) 43-81-85.
Consul: André Felix Maurice Ghislain Baugnée.

Consulate: c/o W. Lippens nv, 22 Sint-Antoniuskaai, 9000 Ghent; tel (91) 24-19-91; telex 11781.
Consul: Wilfried Adrien Romain Maurice Lippens.

Consulate: c/o Banque Nagelmackers, 18 place de la Cathédrale, 4000 Liège; tel (41) 20-02-11; telex 41271.
Consul: Alain Paul Jean Marie Léopold Nagelmackers.

SWITZERLAND

Embassy: 26 rue de la Loi, BP 9, 1040 Brussels; tel (2) 230-61-45; telex 63711; fax (2) 230-37-81.

Ambassador: Gaspard Bodmer.
Counsellor: Erich Imm.
Consul and Head of Chancery: Margareta Aeschlimann-Blaser.

Consulate-General: 18 Schoenmarkt, 2000 Antwerp; tel (3) 233-53-42; telex 32259.
Honorary Consul-General: Frédéric Bohner.

SYRIA

Embassy: 3 ave F. D. Roosevelt, 1050 Brussels; tel (2) 648-01-35; telex 26669.
Ambassador: Siba Nasser.

TANZANIA

Embassy: 363 ave Louise, 7e étage, 1050 Brussels; tel (2) 640-65-00; telex 63616.
Ambassador: Prof. Abdi Hassan Masangama.

THAILAND

Embassy: 2 square du Val de la Cambre, 1050 Brussels; tel (2) 640-68-10; telex 63510; fax (2) 648-30-66.
Ambassador: Danai Tulalamba.

TOGO

Embassy: 264 ave de Tervueren, 1150 Brussels; tel (2) 770-17-91; telex 25093; fax (2) 771-50-75.
Ambassador: Assiongbon A. Agbenou.
First Counsellor: Déma Codjo.
Attaché: Kafui Agbossou.
Financial Attaché: Alangba Talboussouma.
Attaché: Appoh Amabley.
Attaché: Latré-Kayi Amabley.

TRINIDAD AND TOBAGO

Embassy: 14 ave de la Faisanderie, 1150 Brussels; tel (2) 762-94-00; telex 23539; fax (2) 772-27-83.
Ambassador: Terrence Baden-Semper.
Counsellor: Rawlston Gonourie.
First Secretary: Carl Francis.
Commercial Attaché: Richardson Andrews.
Financial Attaché: Suresh Balliram.
Administrative Attaché: Angela Blake.

TUNISIA

Embassy: 278 ave de Tervueren, 1150 Brussels; tel (2) 771-73-95; telex 22078.
Ambassador: Rachid Sfar.

TURKEY

Embassy: 4 rue Montoyer, 1040 Brussels; tel (2) 513-40-93; telex 24677; fax (2) 514-07-48.
Ambassador: Ecmel Barutçu.

UGANDA

Embassy: 317 ave de Tervueren, 1150 Brussels; tel (2) 762-58-25; telex 62814.
Ambassador: Charles Kakuru Katungi.

UNITED ARAB EMIRATES

Embassy: 73 ave F. D. Roosevelt, 1050 Brussels; tel (2) 640-60-00; telex 26559.
Ambassador: Salem Rached Salem al-Agroobi.

UNITED KINGDOM

Embassy: Britannia House, 28 rue Joseph II, 1040 Brussels; tel (2) 217-70-41; telex 22703; fax (2) 217-67-63.
Ambassador: Robert James O'Neill.
Counsellor and Deputy Head of Mission: N. M. McCarthy.
Counsellor (Commercial): B. Attewell.
Counsellor: J. W. B. Richards.
Defence and Military Attaché: Col K. Woodrow.
Naval and Air Attaché: Wing Commdr B. A. Horton.
Cultural Counsellor (British Council Director): K. McGuinness.
First Secretary (Labour): A. Tyson.
First Secretary (Chancery): C. P. D. Harvey.
First Secretary (Commercial): W. A. Kelly.
First Secretary (Chancery): A. J. Stafford.
First Secretary (Information): J. C. Northover.
First Secretary and Consul: N. J. Morris.
Second Secretary (Chancery and European Community Affairs): M. T. Stollery.

Joint Management Office: 1 rue Marie-Thérèse, 1040 Brussels; tel (2) 217-90-00; fax (2) 217-67-63.
Counsellor (Management) and Consul-General: G. C. Fedrick.
First Secretary (Management): M. W. Growcott.
Third Secretary (Management) and Accountant: S. J. Hildersley.

Hong Kong Government Office: 228 ave Louise, 1050 Brussels; tel (2) 648-38-33.
Minister: S. A. Webb-Johnson.
Counsellor: S. P. C. Wu.
Counsellor: J. K. Wilson.
First Secretary (Industrial Promotion): J. A. White.

Consulate-General: 7 Korte Klarenstraat, 2000 Antwerp; tel (3) 232-69-40; telex 34981; fax (3) 231-69-75.
Honorary Consul-General: P. A. Knight.

Consulate: 45 rue Beeckmann, 4000 Liège; tel (41) 23-58-32.
Honorary Consul: J. M. Delfosse.

USA

Embassy: 27 blvd du Régent, 1000 Brussels; tel (2) 513-20-87; telex 21336; fax (2) 511-27-25.
Ambassador: Maynard Wayne Glitman.
Deputy Chief of Mission: Donald J. McConnell.
Political Section: Randolph M. Bell.
Economic Section: Arnold J. Croddy, Jr.
Commercial Section: Jean Gardner.
Consular Section: John M. Jones.
Administrative Section: Nicholas S. Baskey, Jr.
Regional Security Officer: Richard M. Gannon.
Public Affairs Officer: John P. Harrod.
Communications Programme Officer: John W. Channel.
Information Systems Manager: R. Peter Price.
Office of the Defence Attaché: Col Raymond K. Bluhm, Jr.
Office of Defence Co-operation: Col Alfred K. Muelhoefer.
Agricultural Section: John M. Beshoar.
Labour Officer: Jean Gardner.
Federal Aviation Administration: Benjamin Demps, Jr.

Consulate-General: Rubens Centre, 5 Nationalestraat, 2000 Antwerp; tel (3) 225-00-71; telex 31966; fax (3) 234-36-98.
Consul-General: Sheldon I. Krebs.
Political Section: Alison Pentz.
Economic/Commercial Section: Jerome B. Neal.
Consular Section: Lois A. Price.

European Logistical Support Office: 147 Noorderlaan, bus 12A, 2030 Antwerp; tel (3) 542-47-75; telex 34964; fax (3) 542-65-67.
Director: Clifford W. Mecklenburg.
Deputy Director: John Kwiatkowski.

URUGUAY

Embassy: 437 ave Louise, 1050 Brussels; tel (2) 640-11-69; telex 24663; fax (2) 648-29-09.
Ambassador: José Maria Araneo.

VENEZUELA

Embassy: 6 rue Paul Emile Janson, 1050 Brussels; tel (2) 647-52-12; telex 61742; fax (2) 647-88-20.
Ambassador: Júlio César Gil.
Minister-Counsellor: Antonio J. Rodríguez Yturbe.
Minister-Counsellor: José Egidio Rodríguez.
Counsellor: Paula Barrios de Dávila.
Counsellor: Amadeo Volpe Giacoboni.
Second Secretary: Juan Luis Pietri Rivas.
Second Secretary: María Milagros Gil Quintero.

WESTERN SAMOA

Embassy: 95 ave F. D. Roosevelt, 1050 Brussels; tel (2) 660-84-54; telex 25657; fax (2) 675-03-36.
Ambassador: Afamasaga Fa'Amatala Toleafoa.
First Secretary: Tina Hellesoe.

YUGOSLAVIA

Embassy: 11 ave Emile de Mot, 1050 Brussels; tel (2) 647-26-52; telex 26156.
Ambassador: Kuzman Dimcevski.

ZAIRE

Embassy: 30 rue Marie de Bourgogne, 1040 Brussels; tel (2) 513-66-10; telex 21983.
Ambassador: Kimbulu Moyanso wa Lokwa.

ZAMBIA

Embassy: 469 ave Molière, BP 2, 1060 Brussels; tel (2) 345-56-49.
Ambassador: Kapembe N'Singo.

ZIMBABWE

Embassy: 21-22 ave des Arts, BP 5/6, 1040 Brussels; tel (2) 230-85-35; telex 24133.
Ambassador: Dr Andrew H. Mtetwa.

International Organizations

EUROPEAN COMMUNITIES

Bureau: 73 rue Archimède, 1040 Brussels; tel (2) 235-38-44; telex 26657; fax (2) 235-01-66.
Director: Joseph van den Broeck.

BELIZE

BELGIUM

Embassy: Belize City.
Ambassador: Willy Verriest.

CANADA

Consulate: 120-A New Rd, Belize City; tel (2) 31060.
Honorary Consul: L. Young.

CHINA (TAIWAN)

Embassy: 7 Cork St, POB 1020, Belize City; tel (2) 78744; fax (2) 31890.
Ambassador: David Hong.

COSTA RICA

Embassy: POB 922, Belize City; tel (2) 45635; telex 1154.
Ambassador: Roberto Francisco Angleda Soler.

DENMARK

Consulate: 13 Southern Foreshore, POB 233, Belize City; tel (2) 72172; telex 238.
Consul: James Matthew Dunnachie Murphy.

GERMANY

Consulate: c/o 123 Albert St, POB 1248, Belize City; tel (2) 3343; telex 211; fax (2) 9316.
Honorary Consul: Dr Nils Grüber.

HONDURAS

Embassy: 91 North Front St, POB 285, Belize City; tel (2) 45889; telex 103.
Chargé d'affaires: Gustavo Milla Bermúdez.

JAMAICA

Consulate-General: 16A Pickstock St, POB 524, Belize City; tel (2) 45284; telex 243.
Consul-General: Richard Coombs.

JORDAN

Embassy: Belize City.
Ambassador and Representative (EC): Talal al-Hassan.

MEXICO

Embassy: 20 North Park St, Belize City; tel (2) 44301; telex 277.
Ambassador: Federico Uruchua.

PANAMA

Embassy: 79 Unity Blvd, Belmopan; tel (8) 22714.
Chargé d'affaires: José de la Cruz Paredes.

SWEDEN

Embassy: Belmopan.

Consulate-General: Queen and Handyside Sts, POB 763, Belize City; tel (2) 77234; telex 227.
Consul-General: Frank Adam Kuylen.

UNITED KINGDOM

High Commission: Embassy Sq., POB 91, Belmopan; tel (8) 22146; telex 284; fax (8) 22761.
High Commissioner: David P. R. MacKilligin.
Deputy High Commissioner: G. H. W. Morgan.
Third Secretary (Management/Consular): T. J. Hines.
Third Secretary (Aid): D. F. Partridge.

USA

Embassy: Gabourel Lane and Hutson St, POB 286, Belize City; tel (2) 77161; fax (2) 30802.
Ambassador: Eugene L. Scassa.
Deputy Chief of Mission: Joseph E. Hayes.
Political Section: Alexander Featherstone.
Economic/Commercial Section: Katherine Christensen.
Consular Section: Rudolph F. Boone.
Administrative Section: Charles H. Grover.
Communications Programme Officer: Joseph H. Johnson.
Voice of America: Frederick Haney.
Office of the Defence Attaché: Lieut Col Randall R. Parish.
Military Liaison Office: Maj. Jerry R. Croghan.

Agency for International Development: tel (2) 31067; fax (2) 30215.
Agent for International Development: Mosina Jordan.

VENEZUELA

Embassy: 18-20 Unity Blvd, POB 49, Belmopan; tel (8) 22384; telex 249; fax (8) 22022.
Ambassador: Dr José Tineo Farillas.
Second Secretary: Lucymar Rivas Acosta.

International Organizations

EUROPEAN COMMUNITIES

External Delegation (Sub-office of Delegation to Jamaica): 1 Eyre St, POB 907, Belize City; tel (2) 72785; telex 106; fax (2) 72785.
Representative: Glauco Calzuola.

BENIN

ALGERIA

Embassy: Les Cocotiers, BP 1809, Cotonou; tel 30-04-54; telex 5030.
Ambassador: Hanafi Oussedik.

BULGARIA

Embassy: BP 7058, Cotonou; tel 30-03-66; telex 1110.
Chargé d'affaires a.i.: Petur Jordanov Krastev.

CHAD

Embassy: BP 080359, Cotonou; tel 33-08-51.
Chargé d'affaires a.i.: Darkou Ahmat Kalabassou.

CHINA, PEOPLE'S REPUBLIC

Embassy: BP 196, Cotonou; tel 30-12-92.
Ambassador: Zhu Yourong.

CUBA

Embassy: BP 948, Cotonou; tel 31-47-92; telex 5277.
Ambassador: José Felipe Suárez Gómez.

DENMARK

Consulate-General: 65A ave Proche, BP 296, Cotonou; tel 31-25-74.
Consul-General: Arnold Lotsu.

EGYPT

Embassy: BP 1215, Cotonou; tel 30-08-42; telex 5274.
Ambassador: Mohsen Amin Khalifa.

FRANCE

Embassy: route de l'Aviation, BP 966, Cotonou; tel 30-08-24; telex 5209.
Ambassador: Guy Azaïs.

Economic Section: BP 2033; tel 31-28-72; telex 5327.

Consulate: ave du Général de Gaulle, BP 605; tel 31-26-38.

GERMANY

Embassy: 7 route Inter-Etats, BP 504, Cotonou; tel 31-29-67; telex 5224.
Ambassador: Fritz Hermann Flimm.

GHANA

Embassy: Les Cocotiers, BP 488, Cotonou; tel 30-07-46.
Ambassador: Christian T. K. Quarshie.

KOREA, DEMOCRATIC PEOPLE'S REPUBLIC

Embassy: BP 317, Cotonou.
Ambassador: An Gui-Bok.

LIBYA

People's Bureau: Les Cocotiers, BP 405, Cotonou; tel 30-04-52; telex 5254.
People's Bureau Representative: Ali Sahli.

NIGER

Embassy: derrière Hôtel de la Plage, BP 352, Cotonou; tel 31-40-30; telex 5005.
Ambassador: Salou Yaroh.

NIGERIA

Embassy: blvd de la France Marina, BP 2019, Cotonou; tel 30-11-42; telex 5247.
Ambassador: Philip B. Koroye.

RUSSIA

Embassy: BP 2013, Cotonou; tel 31-28-34.
Ambassador: Valentin Pavlov.

Consular Section: 4km from Airport; tel 31-28-35.

SWEDEN

Consulate-General: Cotonou.

SWITZERLAND

Embassy: BP 08-0123, Cotonou; tel 30-14-68; telex 5348; fax 30-08-96.
Attaché (Development Co-operation, Humanitarian Aid and Consular Affairs): François Roduit.

UNITED KINGDOM

Embassy: Cotonou.
Minister-Counsellor, Consul-General and Deputy Head of Mission: R. S. Gorham.
Counsellor (Commercial): D. Broad.
First Secretary (Chancery and Information): P. R. Sizeland.
First Secretary (Economic and Technical Co-operation): C. B. Jennings.
First Secretary and Consul: F. J. Savage.
Second Secretary (Chancery): F. Cochrane-Dyet.
Second Secretary (Consular): N. A. Starkey.

Consulate: SOBEPAT, BP 147, Cotonou; tel 31-20-58; telex 5047.
Honorary Consul: D. Inchelin.

USA

Embassy: rue Caporal Anani Bernard, BP 2012, Cotonou; tel 30-06-50; fax 30-19-74.
Ambassador: Harriet W. Isom.
Economic/Commercial Section: Michele J. Sison.
Consular Section: Lance C. Rennie.
Administrative Section: Betsy Ross Peters.
Public Affairs Officer: Herman W. Henning.
Communications Programme Officer: John W. McManus.

ZAIRE

Embassy: BP 130, Cotonou; tel 30-19-83.

International Organizations

EUROPEAN COMMUNITIES

External Delegation: ave Roume, Bâtiment Administratif, BP 910, Cotonou; tel 31-26-84; telex 5257; fax 312-53-28.
Commission Delegate: Lorenzo Antón Santos.

BHUTAN

BANGLADESH

Embassy: POB 178, Thorilam, Thimphu; tel 22539.

INDIA

Embassy: India House Estate, Lungtenzampa, Thimphu; tel 22162; telex 890211.
Ambassador: Vinod Kumar Chandranarain Khanna.

BOLIVIA

ARGENTINA

Embassy: Calle Aspiazu 497, La Paz; tel (2) 32-2172; telex 3300; fax (2) 39-1083.
Ambassador: Eduardo Héctor Iglesias.

AUSTRIA

Consulate-General: Edif. Petrolero, 7°, of. 1, Avda 16 de Julio 1616, Casilla 83, La Paz; tel (2) 32-6601; telex 2433; fax (2) 36-9863.
Honorary Consul-General: Dr Dietrich Hausherr.
Honorary Consul: Werner Kautsch.

BELGIUM

Embassy: Avda Hernando Siles 5290, Casilla 2433, La Paz; tel (2) 78-4925; telex 3274.
Ambassador: Philippe Jottard.

BRAZIL

Embassy: Avda 20 de Octubre 2038, Edif. Foncomin, 9°, 10° and 11°, La Paz; tel (2) 35-0718; telex 2432; fax (2) 39-1258.
Ambassador: Luiz Orlando Carone Gelio.
Counsellor: João Batista Cruz.
Naval Attaché: Commdt Ronaldo da Silva.
Military Attaché: Col Janir Loreto de Moraes.
Air Attaché: Col Waldomiro Bezerra de Melo.
Second Secretary: Paulo Roberto Caminha de Castilhos França.
Second Secretary: Alfredo José Cavalcanti Jordão de Camargo.
Second Secretary: David Silveira da Mota Neto.
Second Secretary: Regina Celia de Oliveira Bittencourt.

CANADA

Consulate: 2342 Avda Arce, La Paz; tel (2) 37-5224; telex 3271; fax (2) 32-9435.
Honorary Consul: B. Canedo Patino.

CHINA, PEOPLE'S REPUBLIC

Embassy: La Paz; telex 5558.
Ambassador: Xie Rumao.

COLOMBIA

Embassy: Calle 20 de Octubre 2427, Casilla 1418, La Paz; tel (2) 35-9658; telex 3593.
Ambassador: Carlos Eduardo Lozano Tovar.

COSTA RICA

Embassy: Avda Vera 6870, Casilla 2780, La Paz.
Ambassador: Guillermo Gago Pérez.

CUBA

Embassy: Avda Arequipa 8037, Calacoto, La Paz; tel (2) 79-2616; telex 2447.
Ambassador: Gustavo Brugués-Pérez.

CZECHOSLOVAKIA

Embassy: Urb. Las Colinas, Calle 24, No 6, Calacoto, Casilla 2780, La Paz; telex 2530.
Ambassador: Stanislav Novotný.

DENMARK

Consulate-General: Edif. Castilla, Calle Loayza 250, of. 508, Casilla 662, La Paz; tel (2) 36-0655; telex 2337; fax (2) 37-6380.
Consul-General: Fernando Rojas.

Consulate: Avda Cañoto 252, Casilla 2005, Santa Cruz; tel (33) 92-34531; telex 4369.
Consul: Niels Axel Boserup.
Vice-Consul: Hector Renato Laguna Moreno.

ECUADOR

Embassy: Edif. Herrman 14°, Plaza Venezuela, Casilla 406, La Paz; tel (2) 32-1208; telex 3388.
Ambassador: Olmedo Monteverde Paz.

EGYPT

Embassy: Avda Ballivián 599, Casilla 2956, La Paz; tel (2) 78-6511; telex 2612.
Ambassador: Dr Gaber Sabra.

FINLAND

Consulate-General: CIBO SA, Mercado 1004, La Paz; Casilla 954, La Paz; tel (2) 35-0900; telex 2399.
Consul-General: Johnny Gelernter H.

FRANCE

Embassy: Avda Hernando Silés 5390, esq. Calle 8, Obrajes, Casilla 824, La Paz; tel (2) 78-6114; telex 2484.
Ambassador: Pierre Mutter.

Economic Section: Calle 5 590, Casilla 4817; tel (2) 78-6610; telex 2267.

GERMANY

Embassy: Avda Arce 2395, Casilla 5265, La Paz; tel (2) 39-0850; telex 3303; fax (2) 39-1297.
Ambassador: Dr Hermann Saumweber.

Consulate: Calle España N-0149, Casilla 174, Cochabamba; tel (42) 25-529.
Honorary Consul: Jürgen Berodt.

Consulate: Adolfo Mier esq. Soria Calvarro, Casilla 256, Oruro; tel (53) 50-220; telex 2252.
Honorary Consul: Rosemarie Cederberg.

Consulate: Buenos Aires esq. Cañoto, Casilla 370, Santa Cruz; tel (3) 34-4569; telex 4288.
Honorary Consul: Hanns Hiller.

Consulate: Calle Arenales 215-219, Casilla 208, Sucre; tel (64) 18-62.
Honorary Consul: Guillermo Schütt Hodgkinson.

Consulate: Sucre 665, Casilla 139, Tarija; tel (66) 20-62.
Honorary Consul: Karl-Heinz Methfessel.

HOLY SEE

Apostolic Nunciature: Avda Arce 2990, Casilla 136, La Paz; tel (2) 37-5007; telex 2393; fax (2) 39-2122.
Apostolic Nuncio: Most Rev. Giovanni Tonucci, Titular Archbishop of Torcello.
Secretary: Mgr Antonio Arcari.

ISRAEL

Embassy: Edif. Esperanza 10°, Avda Mariscal Santa Cruz, Casilla 1309, La Paz; tel (2) 32-5463; telex 3297.
Ambassador: Berl Zerubavel.

ITALY

Embassy: Avda 6 de Agosto 2575, Casilla 626, La Paz; tel (2) 32-3597; telex 2654; fax (2) 39-1075.
Ambassador: Dr Giovanni Mingazzini.
First Secretary: Domenico La Spina.

Consulate: Calle La Paz 532, Santa Cruz de la Sierra; tel (3) 32-2949.
Honorary Consul: Fausto Barbonari.

Consulate: Calle Ayacucho, Galería Cochabamba, 1°, Cochabamba; tel (42) 27-223.
Honorary Consul: Carlo Schiavi.

Consulate: Calle Dalence 33, Sucre; tel (64) 24-280.
Honorary Vice-Consul: Luis Poggi Bastida.

JAPAN

Embassy: Calle Rosendo Gutiérrez 497, esq. Sanchez Lima, Casilla 2725, La Paz; tel (2) 36-6859; telex 2548; fax (2) 39-1052.

Consulate: Calle Saavedra 314, esq. Cochabamba, Casilla 543, Santa Cruz; tel (3) 32-2516; fax (3) 35-1022.
Consul: Minoru Yokokawa.

KOREA, DEMOCRATIC PEOPLE'S REPUBLIC

Embassy: La Paz.
Ambassador: Kim Chan Sik.

KOREA, REPUBLIC

Embassy: Avda 6 de Agosto 2592, Casilla 1559, La Paz; tel (2) 36-4485; telex 3262.
Ambassador: Cho Kab-Dong.

MEXICO

Embassy: Avda 6 de Agosto 2652, San Jorge, Casilla 430, La Paz; tel (2) 39-2337; telex 3316; fax (2) 39-1136.
Ambassador: Enrique Fernandez Zapata.
Minister and Head of Chancery: Jorge Alfonso Fuentes Mendez.
Head of Consular Section: Juan Carlos Briz Figueroa.

PANAMA

Embassy: Calle Potosí 1270, Casilla 678, La Paz; tel (2) 37-1277; telex 2314.
Chargé d'affaires a.i.: Lic. José Rodrigo de la Rosa.

PARAGUAY

Embassy: Edif. Venus, Avda Arce esq. Montevideo, Casilla 882, La Paz; tel (2) 32-2018.
Ambassador: Gen. Ramón Duarte Vera.

PERU

Embassy: Calle Rosendo Gutiérrez 113 esq. Capitán Ravelo, Casilla 668, La Paz; tel (2) 35-3550; telex 2475.
Ambassador: Jaime Cacho Sousa.

PHILIPPINES

Consulate: Calle Montevideo 176, La Paz; tel (2) 32-4710; fax (2) 39-1846.
Honorary Consul: Juan Carlos Valdivia.

ROMANIA

Embassy: Calle Capitán Ravelo (Pasaje Isaac G. Eduardo) 2173, Casilla 20879, La Paz; tel (2) 37-8632; telex 3260.
Ambassador: Ion Flores.

RUSSIA

Embassy: Avda Arequipa 8128, Casilla 5494, La Paz; tel (2) 79-2048; telex 2480.
Ambassador: Takhir Byashimovich Durdiyev.

Consular Section: tel (2) 78-6419.

SOUTH AFRICA

Embassy: Calle 22, Calacoto No. 7810, Casilla 6018, La Paz; tel (2) 79-2101; telex 3279.

Consulate: Rosendo Gutierrez 482, Casilla 11511, La Paz; tel (2) 36-7754; telex 2300; fax (2) 32-1768.
Honorary Consul: P. I. Habegger.

SPAIN

Embassy: Avda 6 de Agosto 2860, Casilla 382, La Paz; tel (2) 34-3518; telex 3304.
Ambassador: Carmelo Angulo Barturen.

SWEDEN

Consulate-General: Avda Arce 2856, Casilla 852, La Paz; tel (2) 32-7535; telex 2307; fax (2) 39-1006.
Consul-General: Carlos Fernando Romero Moreno.
Vice-Consul: Maria Bertha Arduz.

Consulate: Calle Casto Rojas Quezada s/n, Casilla 1627, Cochabamba; tel (42) 46-289.
Vice-Consul: Eva Margareta Arvidsson.

SWITZERLAND

Embassy: Edif. Petrolero, 6°, Avda 16 de Julio 1616, Casilla 657, La Paz; tel (2) 32-0697; telex 2325; fax (2) 37-5042.
Chargé d'affaires a.i. and Counsellor: Fermo Gerosa.
Attaché and Head of Chancery: Ghislaine Henrioud.
Attaché (Development Co-operation and Humanitarian Aid): Adrian Schläpfer.
Assistant to Attaché (Development Aid): Markus Hügli.

UNITED KINGDOM

Embassy: Avda Arce 2732-2754, Casilla 694, La Paz; tel (2) 39-1301; telex 2341; fax (2) 39-1063.
Ambassador: R. Michael Jackson.
First Secretary (Commercial), Consul and Deputy Head of Mission: A. W. Shave.
Second Secretary (Aid/Information): J. McGhee.
Third Secretary (Management), Vice-Consul and Accountant: R. J. Shackell.

Consulate: Calle Parapeti 28-2°, Casilla 3181, Santa Cruz; tel (3) 33-6415; telex 4220; fax (3) 32-9154.
Honorary Consul: F. R. Taendler.

USA

Embassy: Edif. Banco Popular del Perú, cnr Calles Mercado and Colón, Casilla 425, La Paz; tel (2) 35-0120; telex 3268; fax (2) 35-9875.
Ambassador: Robert Sidney Gelbard.
Deputy Chief of Mission: Marilyn McAfee.
Political Section: Stephen G. McFarland.
Economic/Commercial Section: J. Michael Shelton.
Consular Section: Roger J. Daley.
Administrative Section: Russell F. King.
Regional Security Officer: Jeffrey Pursell.
Public Affairs Officer: Robert J. Callahan.
Communications Programme Officer: Kenneth L. Hill.
Information Systems Manager: Thomas R. Barnes.
Agency for International Development: Carl H. Leonard.
Office of the Defence Attaché: Col David Hunt.
Military Group: Col James D. Hallums.
Labour Officer: Robert J. Featherstone.
Inter-American Geodetic Survey: Charles E. Klimicek.
Narcotics Assistance Unit: Harold A. Burgess.

URUGUAY

Embassy: Avda Arce 2985, Casilla 441, La Paz; tel (2) 35-3857; telex 2378.
Ambassador: José M. Alvarez.

VENEZUELA

Embassy: Avda Arce, esq. Campos, Edif. Jllimani, 4°, La Paz; tel (2) 35-1365; telex 2383; fax (2) 32-0872.
Ambassador: Gilberto Barradas F.
Counsellor: Alida Rodriguez.
Counsellor (Technical): Maria Luisa Cadenas.

YUGOSLAVIA

Embassy: Benito Juárez 315, La Florida, Casilla 1717, La Paz; tel (2) 79-2148.
Chargé d'affaires: Svetislav Rajević.

BOTSWANA

ANGOLA

Embassy: Private Bag 111, Gaborone; tel 352599.
Ambassador: Agnelo da Conceicão Pereira de Silva.

BELGIUM

Consulate: Tirelo House, 1st Floor, The Mall, POB 160, Gaborone; tel 352364; telex 2427; fax 352061.
Consul: Richard Lyons.

CANADA

High Commission: Equity Bldg, 1 The Mall, POB 245, 4377 Gaborone; tel 314377; telex 2703; fax 356564.
First Secretary (Development): C. Tovee.

CHINA, PEOPLE'S REPUBLIC

Embassy: POB 1031, Gaborone; tel 352209; telex 2428.
Ambassador: Zhi Chengxun.

DENMARK

Consulate: Mengwe Close, House 142, POB 367, Gaborone; tel 353770; telex 2404.
Consul: Henning Kjaer.

GERMANY

Embassy: IGI House, The Mall, POB 315, Gaborone; tel 353143; telex 2225; fax 353038.
Ambassador: Egon Katzki.

INDIA

High Commission: Tirelo House, 4th Floor, The Mall, Private Bag 249, Gaborone; tel 372676; telex 2622; fax 374636.
High Commissioner: Satyabrata Pal.
First Secretary: P. K. Bhutiani.
First Secretary: Parminder Singh.
Attaché: Ramesh Kumar.
Attaché: Anil Kumar.
Attaché: K. P. S. Sharma.

LIBYA

People's Bureau: POB 180, Gaborone; tel 352481; telex 2501; fax 356928.
Secretary of People's Bureau: Taher Ettoumi.
Cultural Attaché: Mohammad Hamed.
Financial Attaché: S. Bazen.
Administrative Attaché: Hakim Saied.

NETHERLANDS

Consulate: Shell Depot Station, Industrial Site, Haile Selassie Rd, POB 457, Gaborone; tel 357335; telex 2748; fax 357335.
Consul: P. L. Steenkamp.

NIGERIA

Embassy: POB 274, Gaborone; tel 313561; telex 2415.
High Commissioner: Mallam M. Dauru.

POLAND

Embassy: Private Bag 00209, Gaborone; tel 352501.
Chargé d'affaires: Dr Jan Rudkowski.

RUSSIA

Embassy: 4711 Twana Close, POB 81, Gaborone; tel 353389; telex 2595; fax 352930.
Ambassador: Boris Asoyan.
Commercial Counsellor: Alexander S. Filippov.
First Secretary: Kakajan J. Berdiev.
First Secretary: Vladimir R. Streltsov.
First Secretary: Karen D. Chalian.
Second Secretary: Nikolai A. Strizhov.
Second Secretary: Vitaly V. Markovsky.
Second Secretary: Anatoly G. Pavochka.
Second Secretary: Gennady V. Vorontsov.

SWEDEN

Embassy: Development House, The Mall, Private Bag 0017, Gaborone; tel 353912; telex 2421; fax 353942.
Ambassador: Folke Löfgren.
First Secretary: Suzanne Malmberg.
Head of DCO Office (SIDA): Astrid Dufborg.

UNITED KINGDOM

High Commission: Private Bag 0023, Gaborone; tel 352841; telex 2370; fax 356105.
Deputy High Commissioner and Chargé d'affaires: P. Newman.
Second Secretary (Commercial and Information): K. Clark.
Third Secretary (Development): J. M. Cairns.
Third Secretary (Consular and Management): C. J. R. Moore.

USA

Embassy: POB 90, Gaborone; tel 353982; telex 2554; fax 356947.
Ambassador: David Passage.
Deputy Chief of Mission: Jimmy J. Kolker.
Political/Economic Section: Douglas R. Kramer.
Consular/Commercial Section: Ken McGhee.
Administrative Section: Mark M. Boulware.
Regional Security Officer: Kim T. Starke.
Public Affairs Officer: Alice C. Lemaistre.
Communications Programme Officer: Ron Wildermuth.
Agency for International Development: Howard R. Handler.
Office of Military Co-operation: Maj. Gary Walker.

ZAMBIA

High Commission: POB 362, Gaborone; tel 351951; telex 2416.
High Commissioner: Kasonde P. Kasuto.

ZIMBABWE

High Commission: IGI Bldg, The Mall, POB 1232, Gaborone; tel 314495; telex 2701.
High Commissioner: Dr Nick George Gideon Makura.
Counsellor (Political) and Head of Chancery: Nicholas Mhute.
Counsellor (Commercial): F. A. Zembe.
Counsellor (Press, Information and Tourism): Dennis Takaidzwa Rwafa.
Counsellor (Defence) and Defence Attaché: Lieut Col Harold Chirenda.
First Secretary (Political): Kudakwashe Robert Musara.
First Secretary (Commercial): Kurayi Brian Chiutsi.
Second Secretary (Administration): Mukai Abigail Dube.

International Organizations

EUROPEAN COMMUNITIES

External Delegation: 68 North Ring Rd, POB 1253, Gaborone; tel 314455; telex 2403; fax 313626.
Commission Delegate: Jean-Paul Jacquemin.

BRAZIL

ALGERIA

Embassy: SHIS, Q1 09, Conj. 13, Casa 01, Lago Sul, 71.600 Brasília, DF; tel (61) 248-4039; telex (61) 1278.
Ambassador: Abdelouahab Keramane.

ANGOLA

Embassy: SHIS, Q1 09, Conj. 16, Casa 23, Brasília, DF; tel (61) 248-3362; telex (61) 4971.
Ambassador: Francisco Romão de Oliveira e Silva.

ARGENTINA

Embassy: SEPN, Av. W-3 Quadra 513, Bloco D, Edif. Imperador, 4° andar, 70.442 Brasília, DF; tel (61) 273-3737; telex (61) 1013.
Ambassador: Héctor Alberto Subiza.

AUSTRALIA

Embassy: SHIS, QI 09, Conj. 16, Casa 01, Lago Sul, 70.469 Brasília, DF; tel (61) 248-5569; telex (61) 1025; fax (61) 248-1066.
Ambassador: Warwick Robinson Pearson.
First Secretary: Peter Brian Rayner.
First Secretary (Administration) and Consul: John Wilson Sinclair.
Third Secretary: Eric Justus van der Wal.

Consulate-General: Av. Morvan Dias de Figueiredo 1400, Parque Novo Mundo, 02.178 São Paulo; tel (11) 954-4517; fax (11) 954-7914.
Honorary Consul: Talito Endler.

AUSTRIA

Embassy: SES, Av. das Nações, Lote 40, CP 07-1215, 70.426 Brasília, DF; tel (61) 243-3111; telex (61) 1202.
Ambassador: Dr Nikolaus Horn.
First Secretary: Marianne da Costa de Moraes.
Economic Counsellor: Ingrid Harzallah-Stenutz.

Consulate: Rua José Americo Cancado Bahia 199, Cidade Industrial, 32.200 Contagem/Belo Horizonte, MG; tel (31) 333-3622; telex (31) 1969.
Honorary Consul: Rüdiger Maria Goblirsch-Urban.

Consulate: Rua Marechal Floriano Peixoto 228, Edif. Banrisul, 17°, conj. 1706/1707, CP 2473, 80.000 Curitiba, PR; tel (41) 224-6795; telex (41) 5704; fax (41) 225-2032.
Honorary Consul: Walter Jiraschek.

Consulate: Rua Tirol 29, 89.650 Treze Tilias, SC; tel (495) 37-101.
Honorary Vice-Consul: Ricardo Tennenberg.

Consulate: Rua Luiz Delfino 31, Apdo 501, CP 132, 88.000 Florianópolis; tel 22-5952.
Honorary Consul: Ivo Federico Schmithausen.

Consulate: Av. Carlos Gómes 111, conj. 303, CP 1771, 90.430 Porto Alegre, RS; tel (512) 45-1566.
Honorary Consul: Dr Carlos Lang.

Consulate-General: Av. Atlantica 3804, 22.070 Rio de Janeiro, RJ; tel (21) 227-0040; telex (21) 32576.
Consul-General: Emanuel Helige.

Consulate-General: Av. Almirante Marques Leao 46 (ex-1), Apdo 33, CP 4032, 40.000 Salvador, BA; tel (71) 247-6013.
Honorary Consul-General: Eva Adler.

Consulate-General: Rua Augusta 2516, 10°, 01.412 São Paulo, SP; tel (11) 282-6223; telex (11) 22711.
Consul-General: Otto Heller.

BANGLADESH

Embassy: SHIS, QL 10, Conj. 10, Casa 17, 70.468 Brasília, DF; tel (61) 248-4830; telex (61) 1287; fax (61) 248-4830.
Minister and Chargé d'affaires a.i.: S. H. M. B. Nur Chowdhury.
Second Secretary: M. Sayedazzaman.

BELGIUM

Embassy: Av. das Nações, Lote 32, 70.422 Brasília, DF; tel (61) 243-1133; telex (61) 1261; fax (61) 243-1219.
Ambassador: Christian de Saint Hubert.
Counsellor: Christian van Driessche.

Consulate-General: Av. Visconde de Albuquerque 694, 22.450 Rio de Janeiro, RJ; tel (21) 274-3722.
Consul-General: Philippe Dartois.

Consulate-General: Av. Paulista 2073, Ed. Horsa I, Conj. 1303, 01.311 São Paulo, SP; tel (11) 287-7892.
Consul-General: Jean Lint.

BOLIVIA

Embassy: SHIS, QL 20, Conj. 05, Casa 17, Lago Sul, 70.470 Brasília, DF; tel (61) 366-1441; telex (61) 1946.
Ambassador: Jaime Balcazar Aranibar.

BULGARIA

Embassy: SEN, Av. das Nações, Lote 8, 70.432 Brasília, DF; tel (61) 223-5193; telex (61) 1305.
Ambassador: Georgi Jekov Geurov.

BURKINA FASO

Consulate: Rua Arizona 1256, sala 4, Brooklin, 04.567 São Paulo, SP; tel (11) 241-9590; fax (11) 542-2419.
Honorary Consul: Harry Serge Lugros.

CAMEROON

Embassy: QI 3, Conj. 5, Casa 2, Lago Sul, 71.600 Brasília, DF; tel (61) 248-4433; telex (61) 2235.
Ambassador: Martin Nguele Mbarga.

CANADA

Embassy: SES, Av. das Nações, Lote 16, CP 07-0961, 70.410 Brasília, DF; tel (61) 223-7515; telex (61) 1296; fax (61) 225-5233.
Ambassador: William L. Clarke.
Counsellor and Consul: Terrence Lonergan.
Counsellor (Commercial/Economic): Frederick J. N. Spoke.
First Secretary (Commercial): D. A. Fortney.
First Secretary (Development): N. Asselin.
First Secretary and Consul: Conrad L. Sheck.
First Secretary (Development): R. Thivierge.
First Secretary: C. McDermott.
Second Secretary (Administration) and Vice-Consul: E. Loughlin.
Second Secretary and Vice-Consul: Alison Leclaire.

Consulate-General: Edif. Top Center, Av. Paulista 854, 5°, CP 22002, São Paulo, SP; tel (11) 287-2122; telex (11) 23230; fax (11) 251-5057.
Consul-General: C. William Ross.
Consul: J. J. Deschênes.
Consul and Trade Commissioner: P. Pichette.
Consul (Medical): Dr K. B. Kennedy.

Consulate: Rua Dom Gerardo 46, Rooms 1109/1110, Centro, 20.090 Rio de Janeiro, RJ; tel (21) 233-9286.
Honorary Consul: F. C. Williams.

CHILE

Embassy: SES, Av. das Nações, Lote 11, 70.407 Brasília, DF; tel (61) 226-5545; telex (61) 1075.
Ambassador: Raúl Schmidt Dussaillant.

CHINA, PEOPLE'S REPUBLIC

Embassy: SES, Av. das Nações, Lote 51, 70.443 Brasília, DF; tel (61) 244-8695; telex (61) 1300.
Ambassador: Shen Yunao.

COLOMBIA

Embassy: SES, Av. das Nações, Lote 10, 70.444 Brasília, DF; tel (61) 226-8902; telex (61) 1458.
Ambassador: Germán Rodríguez Fonnegro.

COSTA RICA

Embassy: SCS, Edif. Ceará 501/502, 70.303 Brasília, DF; tel (61) 226-7212; telex (61) 1690.
Ambassador: Miguel Angel Campos Sandi.

COTE D'IVOIRE

Embassy: SEN, Av. das Nações, Lote 09, 70.473 Brasília, DF; tel (61) 321-4656; telex (61) 1095.
Ambassador: Gen. Bertin Zeze Baroan.

CUBA

Embassy: QI 05, Conj. 18, Casa 01, Lago Sul, 71.600 Brasília, DF; tel (61) 248-2018.
Ambassador: René Rodríguez.

CZECHOSLOVAKIA

Embassy: SES, Av. das Nações, Lote 21, 70.414 Brasília, DF; tel (61) 243-1263; telex (61) 1073.
Ambassador: Vladimir Gulla.

DENMARK

Embassy: SES, Av. das Nações, Lote 26, CP 07-0484, 70.416 Brasília, DF; tel (61) 242-8188; telex (61) 1494; fax (61) 242-1577.
Ambassador: Erik B. Lyrtoft-Petersen.
Attaché: Else Kruse.

Consulate-General: Av. das Américas 3333, salas 803-806, 22.631 Rio de Janeiro, RJ; tel (21) 431-1395; telex (21) 22311; fax (21) 326-2275.
Honorary Consul-General: Ib John Hornemann.
Honorary Vice-Consul: Jan Nikolaj Jensen.

Consulate-General: Av. Indianópolis 381, 04.063 São Paulo, SP; tel (11) 570-2769; telex (11) 23556; fax (11) 570-3416.
Honorary Consul-General: Jørgen Bjørn Kullmann.
Honorary Vice-Consul: Knud Eriksen.

Consulate: Rua Manoel Barata 704, sala 1503, Edif. Paes de Carvalho, CP 826, 66.020 Belém,

PA; tel (91) 241-1588; telex (91) 1601; fax (91) 224-7275.
Honorary Consul: Arne Hvidbo.

Consulate: Rua Prof. Jerson Martins 166, Bairro Aeroporto, 31.270 Belo Horizonte, MG; tel (31) 441-2822; telex (31) 1421; fax (31) 443 6040.
Honorary Consul: Hermano Neto Barbosa.

Consulate: Av. Alberto Nepomuceno 77, 6°, CP 1025, 60.055 Fortaleza, CE; tel (85) 221-4070; telex (85) 1118; fax (85) 228-3445.
Honorary Consul: Humberto Fontenele.

Consulate: Rua Miranda Leão 45 (altos), Centro, CP 218, 69.003 Manaus, AM; tel (92) 622-1365; telex (92) 2387; fax (92) 234-3190.
Honorary Consul: Saul Benchimol.

Consulate: Rua Marechal Floriano 741, Bairro Costeira, CP 155, 83.200 Paranaguá, PR; tel (41) 422-1674; telex (41) 4141; fax (41) 422-1043.
Honorary Consul: Ole Dam.

Consulate: Av. Ipiranga 321, 5°, Bairro Menino Deus, CP 500, 90.060 Pôrto Alegre, RS; tel (512) 33-4600; telex (512) 1054; fax (512) 33-6423.
Honorary Consul: Frank Edward Cranston Woodhead.

Consulate: Av. Marquês de Olinda 85, 2°, Edif. Alberto Fonseca, CP 34, 50.030 Recife, PE; tel (81) 224-0311; telex (81) 1343; fax (81) 224-0997.
Honorary Consul: Fernando Lauria Santos.

Consulate: Rua Marechal Floriano 122, CP 92, 96.200 Rio Grande, RS; tel (532) 32-4422; telex (532) 128; fax (532) 32-4288.
Honorary Consul: James George Kerr.

Consulate: Av. Sete de Setembro 3959, 2°, Bairro Barra, 40.160 Salvador, BA; tel (71) 242-3616; telex (71) 1516; fax (71) 247-9667.
Honorary Consul: Luiz Raymundo Tourinho Dantas.

Consulate: Rua Frei Gaspar 22, 10°, sala 106, CP 726, 11.010 Santos, SP; tel (132) 32-8752; telex (132) 1185; fax (132) 32-8752.
Honorary Consul: Gunnar Henningsen.

Consulate: Rua do Sol 141, Edif. Colonial, sala 210, 65.020 São Luis, MA; tel (98) 222-4075.
Honorary Consul: Kleber Moreira.

Consulate: Rua Amélia Tartuce Nasser 265, Camburi, 29.060 Vitória, ES; tel (27) 227-3807.
Consul: Sergio Nasser.

DOMINICAN REPUBLIC

Embassy: QI 17, Conj. 03, Casa 13, Lago Sul, 70.000 Brasília, DF; tel (61) 248-1405.
Ambassador: Oscar Hazim Subero.

ECUADOR

Embassy: QI 11, Conj. 09, Casa 24, 71.600 Brasília, DF; tel (61) 248-5560; telex (61) 1290.
Ambassador: Jernán Veintimilla S.

EGYPT

Embassy: SEN, Av. das Nações, Lote 12, 70.435 Brasília, DF; tel (61) 225-8517; telex (61) 1387.
Ambassador: Medhat Ibrahim Tewfik.

EL SALVADOR

Embassy: QI 07, Conj. 12, Casa 01, Lago Sul, 71.600 Brasília, DF; tel (61) 248-6409; telex (61) 2763; fax (61) 248-6409.
Ambassador: Mauricio Castro Aragon.

FINLAND

Embassy: SES, Av. das Nações, Lote 27, 70.417 Brasília, DF; CP 13.2093, 70.259 Brasília, DF; tel (61) 242-8011; telex (61) 1155; fax (61) 244-9620.
Ambassador: Risto Kauppi.

Consulate: Rua Paissandu 7, 4°, 22.210 Rio de Janeiro, RJ; CP 16-028, 22.210 Rio de Janeiro, RJ; tel (21) 225-6145; telex (21) 21192.
Consul-General: Arnoldo Niskier.

Consulate: Rodovia Arthur Bernandes 1393, 66.000 Belém, Bairro Telegrato, PA; CP 582, 66.000 Belém, PA; tel (91) 233-0333; telex (91) 1217.
Consul: Joaquim Borges Gomes.

Consulate: Av. Contorno 6283, Sala 604, Savassi, 30.130 Belo Horizonte, MG; tel (31) 223-7277; telex (31) 2216.
Consul: Ruben José de Oliveira.

Consulate: Rua Marcílio Dias 131-133, 69.000 Manaus, AM; tel (92) 234-5084; telex (92) 2543.
Consul: Jacob Fortunato Cohen.

Consulate: Rua Comendador Azevedo 244, CP 402, 90.000 Pôrto Alegre, RS; tel (51) 222-7188.
Consul: Ingo Gerhard Kley Hertz.

Consulate: Av. Conde da Boa Vista 708, 50.000 Recife, PE; tel (81) 221-4377; telex (81) 3042.
Consul: Sérgio Lôbo Jardim.

Consulate: Largo das Aflitos s/n, 4°, Ed. FIEB, 40.000 Salvador, BA; tel (71) 245-4811; telex (71) 1837.
Consul: José Vieira Nascimento.

Consulate: Praça da Republica 87, 12°, Conj. 121, 11.100 Santos, SP; tel (132) 33-1115; telex (132) 1123.
Consul: Liberato Carioni.

Consulate-General: Praça Ramos da Azevedo 206-15, 01.037 São Paulo, SP; tel (11) 223-5428; telex (11) 37835.
Consul-General: Taavi Siuko.

Consulate: Praça Costa Pereira 52, 9°, Sala 907, CP 307, 29.000 Vitória, ES; tel (27) 223-6366; telex (27) 2156.
Consul: Gilberto Michelini.

FRANCE

Embassy: SES, Av. das Nações, Lote 4, 70.404 Brasília, DF; tel (61) 321-5354; telex (61) 1078.
Ambassador: Jean-Bernard Ouvrieu.

Economic Section: CP 07-0499, 70.000 Brasília, DF; tel (61) 225-0662; telex (61) 1720.

Consulate-General: Av. Presidente Antonio Carlos 58, 20.020 Rio de Janeiro, RJ; tel (21) 210-1272; telex (21) 22599.

Consulate-General: Edif. San Diego, Av. Dantas Barreto 1200, 9°, CP 681, 50.020 Recife, PE; tel (81) 224-6722.

Consulate-General: Conj. Nacional-Horsa, Av. Paulista I-2073, 17°, 01.311 São Paulo, SP; tel (11) 287-9522.

Consulate: Av. Presidente Pernambuco 269, 66.000 Belém, PA; tel (91) 224-6818; telex (91) 1518.

GERMANY

Embassy: SES, CP 07-0752, Av. das Nações, Lote 25, 70.415 Brasília, DF; tel (61) 243-7234; telex (61) 1198; fax (61) 244-6063.
Ambassador: Heinz Dittmann.

Consulate-General: Av. João Gualberto 1237, CP 764/CP 2281, 80.000 Curitiba, PR; tel (41) 252-4244; telex (41) 5065.
Consul-General: Dorothee Boden.

Consulate-General: Rua Prof. Annes Dias 112, 11°, CP 2552, 90.020 Porto Alegre, RS; tel (512) 24-9255; telex (512) 1374.
Consul-General: Dr Dietrich Schellert.

Consulate-General: Av. Dantas Barreto 191, Edif. Santo António, 4°, CP 1604, 50.000 Recife, PE; tel (81) 424-1840; telex (81) 1382.

Consulate-General: Rua Presidente Carlos de Campos 417, CP 64, 22.231 Rio de Janeiro, RJ; tel (21) 285-2333; telex (21) 22579; fax (21) 205-0184.
Consul-General: Dr Hans Joachim Dunker.

Consulate-General: Av. Brigadeiro Faria Lima 1383, 12°, Jardim Paulistano, CP 20944, 01.451 São Paulo, SP; tel (11) 814-6644; telex (11) 83923; fax (11) 815-7538.
Consul-General: Wilfried Richter.

Consulate: Travessa Campos Sales 63, Edif. Comendador Pinho, 4°, CP 2, 66.000 Belém, PA; tel (91) 222-5634.
Honorary Consul: Helena Steffen.

Consulate: Edif. 'WALMAP', Rua Carijós 244, 8°, CP 2011, 30.000 Belo Horizonte, MG; tel (31) 222-3411.
Honorary Consul: Joachim Boerger.

Consulate: Rua Caetano Deeke 20, Edif. Hering, 11°, salas 1105/6, CP 1002, 89.100 Blumenau; tel (473) 22-1172; telex (473) 156.
Honorary Consul: Hans Prayon.

Consulate: Mercedes Benz do Brasil SA, Av. Mercedes Benz 679, Distrito Industrial, CP 1834, 13.001 Campinas, SP; tel (192) 47-1343; telex (11) 44157; fax (192) 59-3633.
Honorary Consul: Dr Gerhard Hoffmann-Becking.

Consulate: Rua Pedro Borges 33, Edif. Palácio Progresso, Conj. 1135, CP 1.115, 60.000 Fortaleza, CE; tel (85) 231-4366; telex (85) 1073.
Honorary Consul: Gerhard Wichmann.

Consulate: Av. Goiás 623, sala 1402, 14°, CP 1196, 74.000 Goiânia, GO; tel (62) 224-0122.
Honorary Consul: Jürgen Axel Schulze-Gabler.

Consulate: Rua Princesa Isabel 238, Conj. 716, Edif. Principe de Joinville, CP 1197, 89.200 Joinville, SC; tel (474) 22-7383; telex (474) 264.
Honorary Consul: Wolfgang Voigt.

Consulate: c/o Amazonas Timber, Rua Barroso 335, 1°, sala A, CP 741, 69.000 Manaus, AM; tel (92) 232-0890; telex (92) 2238.
Honorary Consul: Otto Oesterle.

Consulate: Rua Carlos Ernesto Knorr 28, CP 352, 18.280 Panambi, RS; tel (55) 375-2812.
Honorary Consul: Annemarie Wegermann.

Consulate: Av. Arthur de Abreu 29, 8.0°, s/n, 83.200 Paranaguá, PR; tel (41) 422-6455; telex (41) 4234; fax (41) 422-2784.
Honorary Consul: Werner Bohling.

Consulate: Rua Ma Andréa 269, CP 16, 96.200 Rio Grande, RS; tel (536) 32-6677; telex (536) 2100.
Honorary Consul: Hermann Werner Hädrich.

Consulate: Av. Tiradentes 689, CP 70, 86.600 Rolândia, PR; tel (432) 56-1931.
Honorary Consul: Vera Tkotz.

Consulate: Rua da Graca 32, Apto 1001, 40.000 Salvador, BA; tel (71) 237-2929; telex (71) 3015.
Honorary Consul: Wolfgang Roddewig.

Consulate: Rua Frei Gaspar 22, 10°, Santos, SP; tel (132) 34-4069.
Honorary Consul: Joachim Stuth-Timm.

Consulate: Harms & Cia Ltda, Praça Goncalves Dias 301, CP 234, 65.000 São Luis, MA; tel (98) 221-2294; telex (98) 2148; fax (98) 221-2233.
Honorary Consul: Ernst Otto Pflüger.

Consulate: Edif. 'Moyses', Av. Jerônimo Monteiro 331, sala 24, CP 495, 29.000 Vitória, ES; tel (27) 229-0912.
Honorary Consul: Frederico Herdmann Seide.

GHANA

Embassy: SHIS QL 10, Conj. 08, Casa 02, 71.600 Brasília, DF; tel (61) 248-6047.

GREECE

Embassy: SHIS, QL 04, Conj. 1, Casa 18, 70.461 Brasília, DF; tel (61) 248-1127; telex (61) 1843.
Ambassador: Stefanos Potamianos.

GUATEMALA

Embassy: SHIS, QL 08, Conj. 05, Casa 11, 70.460 Brasília, DF; tel (61) 248-3318; fax (61) 248-4383.
Ambassador: Carlos Alberto Prera.

GUYANA

Embassy: Edif. Venâncio III, salas 410-414, 70.438 Brasília, DF; tel (61) 224-9229.
Ambassador: Hubert O. Jack.

HAITI

Embassy: SHIS, QI 7, Conj. 16, Casa 13, Lago Sul, 70.465 Brasília, DF; tel (61) 248-6860.
Ambassador: Raymond Mathieu.

HOLY SEE

Apostolic Nunciature: SES, Av. das Nações, Lote 1, CP 07-0153, 70.401 Brasília, DF; tel (61) 223-0794; telex (61) 2125.
Apostolic Nuncio: Most Rev. Carlo Furno, Titular Archbishop of Abari.
Auditor: Mgr Christophe Pierre.
Auditor: Fernando Filoni.
Secretary: Pierre Nguyen van Tot.

HONDURAS

Embassy: SBN, Edif. Eng. Paulo Mauricio Sampaio, 13°, salas 1311/15, 70.040 Brasília, DF; tel (61) 223-2773; telex (61) 3736; fax (61) 321-7809.
Ambassador: Rigoberto Arriaga Chinchilla.
Counsellor: Edgardo Paz-Barnica Sierke.
Minister-Counsellor (Consular Affairs): Edna Rossina Sagastume de Gonzaga.
Cultural Attaché: Rosa María Arriaga Gallo.

Consulate-General: Travessa Santa Leocadia 20, Copacabana, 22.061 Rio de Janeiro, RJ; tel (21) 255-2247.
Consul-General: Magaly Funes.

Consulate: Plaça Rui Barbosa 537, Curitiba, PR; tel (41) 232-9911.
Honorary Consul: Newton Parodi.

Consulate: Rua Barão de Itapetiniga 50, 1°, sala 122, 01.042 São Paulo, SP; tel (11) 255-2336.
Honorary Consul: Ruy Teixeira.

HUNGARY

Embassy: SES, Av. das Nações, Lote 19, 70.413 Brasília, DF; tel (61) 243-0822; telex (61) 1285; fax (61) 244-3426.
Ambassador: János Benyhe.
Second Secretary: János Balla.

Commercial Section: SQS 314, bl. F, ap. 604, 70.383 Brasília, DF; tel (61) 245-5437; telex (61) 1253; fax (61) 245-4839.
Commercial Counsellor: Sándor Bagó.

Consulate-General: Rua André Ampere 153, Conj. 43, 04.562 São Paulo, SP; tel (11) 535-5011; telex (11) 54199; fax (11) 842-0444.
Consul-General: György Bernád.

Commercial Section: Rua Desembargador Paulo Passalacqua 110, 01.248 São Paulo, SP; tel (11) 262-4422; telex (11) 83424.

Commercial Section: Av. Rui Barbosa 460, ap. 606, 22.250 Rio de Janeiro, RJ; tel (21) 551-2247; telex (21) 21955; fax (21) 551-1278.

ICELAND

Consulate-General: Praia do Flamengo 66, Bloco B, Gr. 1015, 22.210 Flamengo, Rio de Janeiro, RJ; CP 1773, 20.001 Rio de Janeiro, RJ; tel (21) 285-1795; telex (21) 22663.
Consul-General: Kaare Ringseth.

Consulate-General: Rua Conde d'Eu 618, 04.738 Santo Amaro, São Paulo, SP; tel (11) 548-4016.
Consul-General: Arne S. Arnesen.

INDIA

Embassy: SDS, Edif. Denasa, 13° andar, CP 11-1097, Brasília, DF; tel (61) 226-1585; telex (61) 1245.
Ambassador: Avaduth Raoji Kakodkar.

INDONESIA

Embassy: SES, Av. das Nações Quandra 805, Lote 20, 70.200 Brasília, DF; tel (61) 243-0102; telex (61) 2541.
Ambassador: Alex Rumamby.

IRAN

Embassy: SES, Av. das Nações, Lote 31, 70.421 Brasília, DF; tel (61) 242-5733; telex (61) 1347; fax (61) 244-9640.
Ambassador: Ali Nematollahi.
Counsellor: Mohammad Abbaszadeh.
Second Secretary: Gholam Ali Rajabi Yazdi.
Cultural Attaché: Abbas Nazari.
Consular Attaché: Mohammad Reza Saadatmand.

IRAQ

Embassy: SES, Av. das Nações, Lote 64, Brasília, DF; tel (61) 243-1804; telex (61) 1331.
Ambassador: Oais Tawfig Almukhfar.

IRELAND

Consulate: Av. Princesa Isabel 323/1208, 22.011 Rio de Janeiro, RJ; tel (21) 275-0196; telex 21791; fax (21) 275-6299.
Honorary Consul: Paul Crean.

Consulate: Av. Paulista 2006-5, 01.310 São Paulo, SP; tel (11) 287-6362; telex (11) 22289.
Honorary Consul: Thomas F. O'Keeffe.

ISRAEL

Embassy: SES, Av. das Nações, Lote 38, 70.424 Brasília, DF; tel (61) 244-7675; telex (61) 1093.
Ambassador: Itzhak Sarfaty.

ITALY

Embassy: SES, Av. das Nações, Lote 30, 70.420 Brasília, DF; tel (61) 244-0044; telex (61) 1488.
Ambassador: Antonio Ciarrapico.

JAPAN

Embassy: SES, Av. das Nações, Lote 39, CP 07-0891, 70.425 Brasília, DF; tel (61) 242-6866; telex (61) 1376; fax (61) 242-0738.
Ambassador: Harunory Kaya.

Consulate-General: Rua Marechal Deodoro, 630 Edif. CCI, 18°, CP 6028, 80.000 Curitiba, PR; tel (41) 224-3861; telex (41) 6308; fax (41) 222-0499.
Consul-General: Kato Shizuya.

Consulate-General: Av. Paulista 475, 5°-8°, CP 361, 01.311 São Paulo, SP; tel (11) 287-0100; telex (11) 21095; fax (11) 288-9460.
Consul-General: Shunji Maruyama.

Consulate-General: Travessa Padre Eutiquio 2112, CP 912, 66.010 Belém, PA; tel (91) 222-1691; telex (91) 1005; fax (91) 224-3821.
Consul-General: Izumi Takayama.

Consulate-General: Av. João Obino 467, Bairro Petrópolis, CP 1022, 90.000 Porto Alegre, RS; tel (242) 34-1125; telex (51) 1072; fax (242) 34-1742.
Consul-General: Kazunori Uno.

Consulate General: Rua Ferreira Pena 92, CP 307, 69.000 Manaus, AM; tel (92) 232-2000; telex (92) 2260; fax (92) 232-6073.
Consul-General: Keiji Hamada.

Consulate-General: Praia do Flamengo 200, 10°, 22.210 Rio de Janeiro, RJ; tel (21) 245-1714; telex (21) 21967; fax (21) 245-9185.
Consul-General: Toshiaki Tanabe.

Consulate-General: Av. Dantas Barreto 191, Edif. Santo Antonio, 3°, CP 502, 50.010 Recife, PE; tel (81) 224-1930; telex (81) 1166; fax (81) 424-3230.
Consul-General: Tatsuo Noguchi.

KOREA, REPUBLIC

Embassy: SEN Av. das Nações, Lote 14, 70.436 Brasília, DF; tel (61) 223-3466; telex (61) 1085.
Ambassador: Tae Woong Kwon.

KUWAIT

Embassy: SHI-Sul, QI 5, Ch. 30, 70.467 Brasília, DF; tel (61) 248-1634; telex (61) 1367.
Ambassador: Faisal Rashed al-Glais.

LEBANON

Embassy: SES, Av. das Nações, Q.805, Lote 17, 70.411 Brasília, DF; tel (61) 242-4801; telex (61) 1295.
Ambassador: Samir Hobeica.

LIBYA

Embassy: SHIS, QI 15, Chácara 26, CP 3505, 71.462 Brasília, DF; tel (61) 248-6710; telex (61) 1099.
Ambassador: Ali Suleiman al-Aujali.

MALAYSIA

Embassy: SHIS, QI 05, Chácara 62, Lago Sul, 70.477 Brasília, DF; tel (61) 248-5008; telex (61) 3666.
Ambassador: M. M. Sathiah.

MALTA

Consulate-General: Av. Graça Aranha, 416-GR, 701/7, 20.030 Rio de Janeiro, RJ; tel (21) 274-0683; telex (21) 23375.
Honorary Consul-General: Delio Aloisio de Mattos Santos.
Honorary Consul: Germana Helen Guinle.

Consulate: Rua Xavier de Almeida 227, 1 Piranga, 04.211 São Paulo, SP; tel (11) 914-4420; telex (11) 22807; fax (11) 914-4420.
Honorary Consul: Dr Italo Baggio.

MEXICO

Embassy: SES, Av. das Nações, Lote 18, 70.412 Brasília, DF; tel (61) 244-1011; telex (61) 1101.
Ambassador: Jesús Cabrera Muñoz-Ledo.

MOROCCO

Embassy: SHIS, QI 11, Conj. 05, Casa 13, Lago Sul, 71.600 Brasília, DF; tel (61) 248-3543; telex (61) 1381.
Ambassador: Mohamed Larbi Messari.
Counsellor: Amar el-Mars.
Secretary: Hassan Lamzouak.
Secretary: Tariq Louajri.
Attaché: Mohamed Bekkal.
Accountant: El Hadj Chaairat.

NETHERLANDS

Embassy: SES Av. das Nações, Lote 05, 70.405 Brasília, DF; CP 07-0098, 70.000 Brasília, DF; tel (61) 223-2025; telex (61) 1492.
Ambassador: Jonkheer Hubert van Nispen.

NEW ZEALAND

Consulate-General: Rua Hungria 888, 6°, CEP 01.455 São Paulo, SP; tel (11) 212-2288; telex (11) 81017; fax (11) 212-7728.
Honorary Consul-General: Brian Sinclair.

NICARAGUA

Embassy: SCS, Edif. Venâncio da Silva 1301/1310, 70.302 Brasília, DF; tel (61) 225-0283; telex (61) 2495.

NIGERIA

Embassy: SEN, Av. das Nações, Lote 05, CP 11-1190, 70.432 Brasília, DF; tel (61) 226-1717; telex (61) 1315; fax (61) 226-1717.
Ambassador: J. J. Lewu.

NORWAY

Embassy: SES, Av. das Nações, Lote 28, CP 07-0670, 70.351 Brasília, DF; tel (61) 243-8720; telex (61) 1265; fax (61) 242-7989.
Ambassador: Sigurd Endresen.

Consulate-General: Rua da Gloria 122, CP 436, 20.241 Rio de Janeiro, RJ; tel (21) 242-2033; telex (21) 21702; fax (21) 224-4464.

Commercial Office: Sala 102; tel (21) 242-9742; fax (21) 224-4564.

PAKISTAN

Embassy: SCS, Edif. Central, 5°, 70.458 Brasília, DF; tel (61) 224-2922; telex (61) 2252; fax (61) 223-5875.
Ambassador: Touqir Hussain.
Second Secretary: Jauhar Saleem.
Commercial Secretary: Azam Muhammad.

Commercial Section: Av. Paulista 2073, Horsa II, CJ 141, 01.311 São Paulo, SP; tel (11) 283-2373; telex (11) 32166.

PANAMA

Embassy: SCS, Edif. JK, 13° andar, 132/133, CP 13-2334, 70.449 Brasília, DF; tel (61) 225-0859.
Ambassador: Víctor Manuel Barleta Millán.

PARAGUAY

Embassy: SES, Av. das Nações, Lote 42, CP 14-2314, 70.427 Brasília, DF; tel (61) 242-3723; telex (61) 1845.
Ambassador: Juan Esteban Aguirre.

PERU

Embassy: SES, Av. das Nações, Lote 43, 70.428 Brasília, DF; tel (61) 242-9435; telex (61) 1108.
Ambassador: Hugo Palma Valderrama.

PHILIPPINES

Embassy: SEN, Av. das Nações, Lote 1, CP 14-2295, 70.431 Brasília, DF; tel (61) 223-5143; telex (61) 1420.
Ambassador: Lauro L. Baja, Jr.

POLAND

Embassy: SES, Av. das Nações, Lote 33, 70.423 Brasília, DF; tel (61) 243-3438; telex (61) 1165.
Ambassador: Stanisław Pawliszewski.

PORTUGAL

Embassy: SES, Av. das Nações, Lote 2, 70.402 Brasília, DF; tel (61) 321-3434; telex (61) 1033.
Ambassador: Adriano de Carvalho.

ROMANIA

Embassy: SEN, Av. das Nações, Lote 6, 70.456 Brasília, DF; tel (61) 226-0746; telex (61) 1283.
Ambassador: Constantin Dumitrescu.

RUSSIA

Embassy: SES, Av. das Nações, Lote A, 70.476 Brasília, DF; tel (61) 223-3094; telex (61) 1273.
Ambassador: Leonid Filippovich Kuzmin.

Consular Section: tel (61) 223-5094.

Consular Agency: Rua Prof. Azevedo Márques 50, Rio de Janeiro, RJ; tel (21) 274-0097.

Consular Agency: Rua Traipu 831, São Paulo, SP; tel (11) 262-3765; telex (11) 23324.

SAN MARINO

Consulate-General: Rua Bueno Brandao 226, São Paulo, SP; tel (11) 542-8011; telex (11) 21573.
Consul-General: Giuseppe Lantermo di Montelupo.

SAUDI ARABIA

Embassy: SHI-Sul, QL 10, Conj. 9, Casa 20, 70.471 Brasília, DF; tel (61) 248-3523; telex (61) 1656.
Ambassador: Abdullah Saleh Hababi.

SENEGAL

Embassy: SEN, Av. das Nações, Lote 18, 70.437 Brasília, DF; tel (61) 226-4405; telex (61) 1377.
Ambassador: El Hadj Diouf.

SOUTH AFRICA

Embassy: SES, Av. das Nações, Lote 6, CP 11-1170, 70.406 Brasília, DF; tel (61) 223-4873; telex (61) 1683; fax (61) 224-9367.
Ambassador: R. von Gernet.
First Secretary: P. J. Kruger.
Third Secretary: R. Scherman.
Third Secretary (Administration): G. D. Frieslaar.

Consulate-General: Rua Lauro Muller 116/1107, (Torre Rio Sul), Botafogo, CP 21-182, Rio de Janeiro, RJ; tel (21) 542-6191; telex (21) 21554; fax (21) 542-6244.
Consul-General: D. O. Gericke.
Consul: E. Theron.
Consul (Minerals/Energy): D. H. Klopper.
Vice-Consul (Administration): P. J. C. Jonas.
Vice-Consul (Trade): K. A. Ponter.

Consulate-General: Av. Paulista 1754, 12° andar, CP 82-29, 01.501 São Paulo, SP; tel (11) 285-0433; telex (11) 24449; fax (11) 288-8262.
Consul-General: J. J. Spies.
Consul: K. E. Cilliers.
Consul (Trade): J. Stopforth.
Vice-Consul (Administration): M. Naughton.

Consulate: Av. Bras de Aguiar 85/501, Edif. INA, CP 931, 66.000 Belém, PA; tel (91) 223-2789; telex (91) 1139.
Honorary Consul: J. Sláma.

SPAIN

Embassy: SES, Av. das Nações, Lote 44, 70.429 Brasília, DF; tel (61) 242-1074; telex (61) 1313.
Ambassador: José Luis Crespo de Vega.

SURINAME

Embassy: QI 07, Conj. 1, Casa 6, 70.457 Brasília, DF; tel (61) 248-1210; telex (61) 1414; fax (61) 248-3791.
Ambassador: Dr Siegfried Edmund Werners.
Counsellor: Otmar George Bottse.
First Secretary: Johan Andre Alspeer.
Second Secretary: Guno Lackin.
Administrative Attaché: Frederik Flamingo.

SWEDEN

Embassy: SES, Av. das Nações, Lote 29, CP 07-0419, 70.419 Brasília, DF; tel (61) 243-1444; telex (61) 1225; fax (61) 243-1187.
Ambassador: Gunnar Hultner.
First Secretary: Björn Nellhede.
Second Secretary: Barbro Zewoldi.
Second Secretary: Carl Johan Åsenius.

Consulate-General: Praia do Flamengo 344, 22.210 Rio de Janeiro, RJ; tel (21) 552-2422; telex (21) 21486; fax (21) 551-9091.
Consul-General: Lars Arnö.
Chancellor: Mailie Kristina Fjällgren.

Consulate: Rua Santo Antonio 316, Conj. 604, 66.020 Belém, PA; tel (91) 222-4788; telex (91) 1555.
Consul: Mario Lenzi Silvestre.

Consulate: Rua Dezenove 117, Cidade Industrial, Contagem, CP 2001, 30.161 Belo Horizonte, MG; tel (31) 331-1146; telex (31) 1061; fax (31) 333-5000.
Consul: Göran Fredrik Wallgren.

Consulate: Rua Boris 90, CP 29, 60.000 Fortaleza, CE; tel (85) 231-0177; telex (85) 1063; fax (85) 221-6837.
Consul: Francis Joseph Bloc-Boris.

Consulate: Av. Senador Salgado Filho 327, ap. 1303, CP 670, 90.001 Porto Alegre, RS; tel (512) 27-1289.
Consul: Mário Siegfried Landgraf.

Consulate: Av. Marques de Olinda 126, 1°, 50.030 Recife, PE; tel (81) 224-1222; telex (81) 3107; fax (81) 224-4142.
Consul: Armin Albrecht Adalbert Werner.

Consulate: Rua Quintino de Carvalho 153, ap. 601, Jardim Apipema, 40.160 Salvador, BA; tel (71) 242-3544; telex (71) 2579.
Consul: Olav Gran.

Consulate: Praça da República 36, 2°, sala 8, CP 404, 11.100 Santos, SP; tel (132) 32-9052; telex (132) 1186.
Consul: Elmar José Braun.
Chancellor: Marianne Anna de Pauly.

Consulate-General: Rua Oscar Freire 379, 3°, CP 51626, 01.499 São Paulo, SP; tel (11) 883-3322; telex (11) 24009; fax (11) 883-3607.
Consul-General: Per-Gunnar Kalborg.
Vice-Consul: Ulla Birgitta Wilhelmina Weichert.

SWITZERLAND

Embassy: SES, Av. das Nações, Lote 41, CP 04.0171, 70.448 Brasília, DF; tel (61) 244-5500; telex (61) 1135; fax (61) 244-5711.
Ambassador: Dr Charles Henry Bruggmann.
Counsellor: Dr Oscar Knapp.
Third Secretary: Kurt Kunz.
Attaché and Head of Chancery: Jean-François Lichtenstern.

Consulate: Av. Marechal Floriano Peixoto 228, 11°, Conj. 1104/5, Edif. BANRISUL, 80.017 Curitiba, PR; CP 1783, 80.001 Curitiba, PR; tel (41) 223-7553.
Consul: Ettore Domeniconi.

Consulate-General: Rua Cândido Mendes 157, 11°, 20.241 Rio de Janeiro, RJ; CP 744, 20.001 Rio de Janeiro, RJ; tel (21) 242-8035; telex (21) 22440; fax (21) 252-3991.
Consul-General: François Pillonel.
Vice-Consul and Chancellor: Marc Gerber.

Consulate-General: Av. Paulista 1754, 4°, Edif. Grande Avenida, 01.310 São Paulo, SP; CP

22021, 01.499 São Paulo, SP; tel (11) 289-1033; telex (11) 31553; fax (11) 288-0370.
Consul: Hans Dürig.
Chancellor: Roland Viotti.

SYRIA

Embassy: SEN, Av. das Nações, Lote 11, 70.434 Brasília, DF; tel (61) 226-0970; telex (61) 1721.
Ambassador: Ghassoub Rifai.

THAILAND

Embassy: SEN, Av. das Nações Norte, Lote 10, CP 10-2460, 70.433 Brasília, DF; tel (61) 224-6943; telex (61) 3763.
Ambassador: Pradeep Sochiratna.

TOGO

Embassy: SHIS QI 11, Conj. 9, Casa 10, CP 13-1998, 71.259 Brasília, DF; tel (61) 248-4752; telex (61) 1837.
Ambassador: Lambana Tchaou.

TRINIDAD AND TOBAGO

Embassy: SHIS, QL 8, Conj. 4, Casa 5, 71.600 Brasília, DF; tel (61) 248-1922; telex (61) 1844; fax (61) 248-1533.
Ambassador: Babooram Rambissoon.

TURKEY

Embassy: SES, Av. das Nações, Lote 23, Q805, 70.452 Brasília, DF; tel (61) 242-1448; telex (61) 1663; fax (61) 242-1448.
Ambassador: Ergun Sav.
First Counsellor: Sadik Toprak.
Attaché: Emel Eryilmaz.
Attaché: Mustafa Ay.
Attaché: Ismet Yilmaz.
Attaché: Erdin Katan.

UNITED KINGDOM

Embassy: SES, Quadra 801, Conj. K, CP 07-0586, 70.408 Brasília, DF; Av. das Nações, Lote 8, 70.359 Brasília, DF; tel (61) 225-2545; telex (61) 1360; fax (61) 225-1777.
Ambassador: Michael John Newington.
Minister-Counsellor, Consul-General and Deputy Head of Mission: Philip Morrice.
Counsellor: Alastair W. Crooke.
Defence, Military and Air Attaché: Col David Keith W. Farrant.
Naval Attaché: Capt. James R. Luard.
First Secretary (Political): J. D. F. Holt.
First Secretary (Commercial and Economic): Michael D. Aron.
First Secretary (Management) and Consul: George Michael Johnson.
Second Secretary (Economic): N. D. Sutcliffe.

Consulate: Agencias Mundiais, Rua Gaspar Viana 490, CP 98, 66.000 Belém, PA; tel (91) 224-4822; telex (91) 1184.
Honorary Consul: R. J. Burnett.

Consulate: Wilson & Sons Ltd, Av. Eduardo Ribeiro 520, 12° andar S/1202, CP 1091, 69.000 Manáus, AM; tel (92) 234-1018; telex (92) 1046.
Honorary Vice-Consul: G. R. Clarke.

Consulate-General: Praia do Flamengo, 284, 2°, Rio de Janeiro, RJ; CP 669, CEP 20.010; tel (21) 552-1422; telex (21) 21577; fax (21) 552-5796.
Consul-General: Pat M. Kelly.
Consul (Commercial): V. B. M. O'Hara.
Vice-Consul (Economic): D. B. Keegan.
Vice-Consul: G. D. Hart.

Consulate: Edif. Guimarães, 5°, Av. Alfonso Pena 952, CP 576, CEP 30.000 Belo Horizonte, MG; tel (31) 222-6318.
Honorary Consul: R. A. Gough.
Vice-Consul: R. Pacheco.

Consulate: c/o Grupo Edson Queiroz, Praça da Imprensa, Aldeota, 60.000 Fortaleza, CE; tel (85) 244-8888; telex (85) 3701.
Honorary Consul: A. T. Y. Reeves de Castro.

Consulate: Av. Domingos Ferreira 2222, Sala 203, 51.0201 Recife, PE; tel (81) 326-3733; telex (81) 4014; fax (81) 326-4880.
Honorary Consul: A. E. Fiore.
Vice-Consul: R. J. M. Guedes.

Consulate: Av. Estados Unidos 4, salas 1109/13, Edif. Visconde de Cayru, CP 38, CEP 40.010 Salvador, BA; tel (71) 243-9222; telex (71) 1050.
Honorary Consul: W. N. Lee.

Consulate-General: Av. Paulista 1938, 17°, CP 846, 01.310 São Paulo, SP; tel (11) 287-7722; telex (11) 21384; fax (11) 287-7637.
Consul-General: Michael Perceval.
Consul (Commercial): G. S. Cowling.
Consul (Commercial): B. M. Biscoe.
Vice-Consul (Commercial): P. Ashworth.

Consulate: Edif. Montreal, Rua Itapeva 110, Conj. 505, Bairro Passo D'Areia, CEP 91.350 Pôrto Alegre, RS; tel (512) 31-6602.
Honorary Consul: G. J. Powell.

Consulate: Rua Francisco Marques 163, CP 455, Centro, 96.200 Rio Grande, RS; tel (532) 32-1575; telex (532) 191.
Honorary Consul: R. V. Wigg.

Consulate: Rua Tuiuti 58, 2°, CP 204, 11.010 Santos, SP; tel (132) 33-6111; telex (132) 1013.
Honorary Consul: C. M. Marote.

Consulate: Rua Marechal Deodoro 421, 80.020 Curitiba, PR; tel (41) 232-5067; telex (41) 5166; fax (41) 232-5935.
Honorary Consul: P. R. ter Poorten.

USA

Embassy: SES, Av. das Nações, Lote 3, 70.403 Brasília, DF; tel (61) 321-7272; telex (61) 1091; fax (61) 225-9136.
Ambassador: Richard H. Melton.
Deputy Chief of Mission: Robert E. Service.
Political Section: John F. Keane.
Economic Section: M. Gordon Jones.
Commercial Section: Kevin C. Brennan.
Consular Section: Edwin L. Beffel.
Administrative Section: Jeremy Nice.
Regional Security Officer: Thomas C. Allsbury.
Public Affairs Officer: Robert F. Jordan.
Communications Programme Officer: Mark J. Pero.
Information Systems Manager: Hector Morales Colon.
Scientific Attaché: Barbara J. Tobias.
Agency for International Development: Howard B. Helman.
Office of the Defence Attaché: Brig.-Gen. Joseph S. Stringham.
Military Liaison Office: Col Billie R. Carpenter.
Agricultural Section: John Reddington.
Narcotics Assistance Unit: John W. Corris, Jr.

Consulate-General: Av. Presidente Wilson 147, Rio de Janeiro, RJ; tel (21) 292-7117; telex (21) 22831; fax (21) 220-0439.
Consul-General: A. Donald Bramante.
Political Section: Daniel A. Strasser.
Economic Section: V. Edward Olson.
Commercial Section: Walter Hage.
Consular Section: Clyde Bishop.
Administrative Section: Manuel F. Acosta.
Regional Security Officer: Craig P. Decampli.
Communications Programme Officer: Ronald P. DeBrosse.
Office of the Defence Attaché: Philip E. Cather.
Military Liaison Office: Robert J. McDonough.
Resources: Gilbert M. Johnson.
Agricultural Section: John Reddington (resident in Brasília).
Federal Aviation Administration: Santiago Garcia.

Information Service: telex (21) 21466.
Branch Public Affairs Officer: David P. Wagner.

Consulate-General: Rua Padre João Manoel 933, CP 8063, 01.411 São Paulo; tel (11) 881-6511; telex (11) 31574; fax (11) 852-5154.
Consul-General: James F. Creagan.
Political Section: Donald B. Harrington.
Economic Section: Ralph M. Buck.
Commercial Section: Arthur A. Alexander.
Consular Section: Sandra L. Mendyk.
Administrative Section: Edmund E. Atkins.
Communications Programme Officer: James H. Porter.
Labour Officer: Charles B. Smith, Jr.
Internal Revenue Service: Stanley Newman.

Information Service: telex (21) 21466.
Branch Public Affairs Officer: C. Sigrid Maitrejean.

Trade Centre: Edif. Eloy Chaves, Av. Paulista 2439, São Paulo, SP; tel (11) 853-2011; telex (11) 25274.
Director: Arthur A. Alexander.
Agricultural Section: Marcus E. Lower.

Consulate: Rua Coronel Genuino 421, 9°, Porto Alegre, RS; tel (512) 26-4288; telex (512) 292.
Principal Officer: Roger A. McGuire.
Consular Section: Jane B. Buchmiller.
Branch Public Affairs Officer: Merrie D. Blocker.

Consulate: Rua Goncalves Maia 163, Recife, PE; tel (81) 221-1412; telex (81) 1190; fax (81) 231-1906.
Principal Officer: Leslie V. Rowe.
Consular Section: Marc J. Meznar.
Branch Public Affairs Officer: Martin E. Adler.

URUGUAY

Embassy: SES, Av. das Nações, Lote 14, 70.450 Brasília, DF; tel (61) 224-2415; telex (61) 1173.
Ambassador: Dr Roberto Vivo Bonomi.

VENEZUELA

Embassy: SES, Av. das Nações, Lote 13, Q-803, 70.451 Brasília, DF; tel (61) 223-9325; telex (61) 1325; fax (61) 226-5633.
Ambassador: Sebastian A. Alegrett R.
Minister-Counsellor: Carlos Cristancho R.
Second Secretary: Ilba Lucia Cismeros.
Second Secretary: Elvia Elena Jimenez M.
Second Secretary: Neiza Pineda Viloria.
Second Secretary: Eduardo Pastor Spadaro Alvarez.
Third Secretary: Ruben Pacheco H.

Consulate: Transversal Benjamin Constant 1303, Farid Apto 104, Belèm, DP; tel (91) 222-6396; telex (91) 2782.
Consul: Felix Mendez Correa.
Attaché: José E. Bruestlen A.

Consulate-General: Av. Benjamin Constant 525, esq. Barao de Rio Branco, CP 206, Boa Vista; tel (95) 224-2182; telex (95) 2042; fax (95) 224-8859.
Consul-General: José Andres Adarmes Perez.

Consulate-General: Rua Recife 1620, Adrianopolis, CP 3241, 69.075 Manaus, AM; tel (92) 236-5074; telex (92) 1209; fax (92) 236-0414.
Consul-General: Francisco Chacin Medina.
Consul: Ana Cazzadore.
Consul: Mario Liani Ripoll.

Consulate-General: Praia de Botafogo 242, 5°, CP 9056-2C-02, 22.250 Botafogo/Rio de Janeiro, RJ; tel (21) 551-5698; telex (21) 30680.
Consul-General: Carlos Porras Rodrigo.

Consul: Ilenia Medina Carrasco.

Consulate-General: Rua Italia 539, Dardin Europa, 01.449 São Paulo, SP; tel (11) 46-2388; telex (11) 32649.
Consul-General: Ricardo E. Kamel Ache.
Vice-Consul: Trina Nohemi Coviella.

YEMEN

Embassy: Brasília, DF.

YUGOSLAVIA

Embassy: SES, Av. das Nações, Q-803, Lote 15, CP 07-1240, 70.409 Brasília, DF; tel (61) 223-7272; telex (61) 2053.
Ambassador: Branko Trpenovski.

ZAIRE

Embassy: SHIS, QI 9, Conj. 8, Casa 20, Lago Sul, CP 07-0041, 71.600 Brasília, DF; tel (61) 248-3348; telex (61) 1435.
Ambassador: Ngoie Kampeng Kamakanga.

International Organizations

EUROPEAN COMMUNITIES

External Delegation: SHIS QI 7, Bloco A, Lago Sul, 71.615 Brasília, DF; tel (61) 248-3122; telex (61) 2517; fax (61) 248-0700.
Head of Delegation: Amândio de Azevedo.
First Secretary: Leonello Gabrici.
Administrative Assistant: Robert van der Bilt.

BRUNEI

AUSTRALIA

High Commission: 4th Floor, Teck Guan Plaza, cnr Jalan Sultan and Jalan McArthur, Bandar Seri Begawan 2085; tel (2) 229435; telex 2582.
High Commissioner: Philip Moulton Knight.

AUSTRIA

Consulate-General: 5 Taman Jubli, Simpang 75, Jalan Subok, Bandar Seri Begawan 2180; tel (2) 23083; telex 2447; fax (2) 223083.
Consul-General: Alfred Flaim.

BELGIUM

Consulate: 3rd Floor, 146 Jalan Pemancha, POB 65, Bandar Seri Begawan 1900; tel (2) 20895; fax (2) 220615.
Honorary Consul: David Kenneth Davies.

FRANCE

Embassy: Komplex Jalan Sultan, Units 301-306, 3rd Floor, 51-55 Jalan Sultan, Bandar Seri Begawan 2085; POB 3027, Bandar Seri Begawan; tel (2) 220960; telex 2743; fax (2) 243373.
Ambassador: Jean-Marie Momal.
First Secretary: Jean-Luc Wertheimer.
Head of Cultural Office: Alain Lepresle.

Economic Expansion Office: Units 504-505, Teck Guan Plaza, 50-60 Jalan Sultan, Bandar Seri Begawan 2085; POB 1268, Bandar Seri Begawan 1912; tel (2) 240924; telex 2837; fax (2) 240926.
Economic Expansion Officer: Jean-Pierre Rouzo.

GERMANY

Embassy: 6th Floor, UNF Bldg, 49-50 Jalan Sultan, POB 3050, Bandar Seri Begawan 2085; tel (2) 225547; telex 2742; fax (2) 225583.
Ambassador: Friedrich Krekeler.

INDONESIA

Embassy: Simpang 528, 4498 Sungai Hanching Baru, Jalan Maura, Bandar Seri Begawan 3890; POB 3013, Bandar Seri Begawan 1930; tel (2) 330180; fax (2) 330646.
Chargé d'affaires a.i.: Dr Haji Rizal Charis.

JAPAN

Embassy: 1/7/3 Jalan Jawatan Dalam, Kampong Maboahi, POB 3001, Bandar Seri Begawan 1930; tel (2) 229265; telex 2564; fax (2) 229481.
Ambassador: Shigenobu Yoshida.

KOREA, REPUBLIC

Embassy: No. 9, Lot 21652, Kampong Beribi, Jalan Gadong, Bandar Seri Begawan 3188; POB 2169, Bandar Seri Begawan; tel (2) 650471; telex 2615; fax (2) 650299.
Ambassador: Huh Se-Lin.

MALAYSIA

High Commission: 6th Floor, Darussalam Bldg, Jalan Sultan, POB 2826, Bandar Seri Begawan 1928; tel (2) 228410; telex 2401; fax (2) 228412.
High Commissioner: Zainal Abidin bin Mokhtar.

NEW ZEALAND

Consulate: c/o Truebridge Callender, Beach (B) Sdn Bhd, 35A Seri Lambak Complex, Jalan Berekas, Bandar Seri Begawan; tel (2) 331010; fax (2) 331612.
Consul: G. Walker.

NETHERLANDS

Consulate: c/o Brunei Shell Petroleum, 7082 Seria, Bandar Seri Begawan; tel (3) 72176; telex 3313; fax (3) 72040.
Honorary Consul: Anton Barendregt.

OMAN

Embassy: Lot 5446, 323 Simpang 402, Kampong Telanai, Jalan Tutong, Bandar Seri Begawan 2686; POB 2875, Bandar Seri Begawan 1928; tel (2) 651069; telex 2215.
Chargé d'affaires a.i.: Fuad Mubarak al-Hinai.

PAKISTAN

High Commission: LB 277, Kampong Telanai, Mile 3, Jalan Tutong; tel (2) 651623.
High Commissioner: Saquib Mawaz-Khan.

PHILIPPINES

Embassy: 4th-5th Floors, Badi-ah Bldg, Mile 1, Jalan Tutong, POB 3025, Bandar Seri Begawan 1930; tel (2) 228241; telex 2673.
Ambassador: Eusebio A. Abaquin.

SINGAPORE

High Commission: 5th Floor, RBA Plaza, Jalan Sultan, Bandar Seri Begawan 2085; POB 2159, Bandar Seri Begawan 1921; tel (2) 227583; telex 2385; fax (2) 220957.
High Commissioner: Tan Keng Jin.
First Secretary: Geoffrey Singham.
Third Secretary: Lee Kam Kong.

SWEDEN

Consulate: Suite 1-2, 3rd Floor, Tumasek Plaza, Jalan Tutong, Bandar Seri Begawan 2682; POB 278, Seri Kompleks, Bandar Seri Begawan 2602; tel (2) 223918; telex 2447; fax (2) 241492.
Consul: Sulaiman Haji Ahai.

THAILAND

Embassy: LB 241, Jalan Elia Fatimah, Kampong Kiarong, POB 2989, Bandar Seri Begawan 1929; tel (2) 229653; telex 2607; fax (2) 221775.
Ambassador: Somchit Insingha.

UNITED KINGDOM

High Commission: 3rd Floor, Hongkong and Shanghai Bank Chambers, Jalan Pemancha, POB 2197, Bandar Seri Begawan 2085; tel (2) 222231; telex 2211; fax 226002.
High Commissioner: A. J. Sindall.
Deputy High Commissioner and First Secretary (Commercial): W. Whitton.
Second Secretary (Chancery/Information): J. C. A. Clephane.
Third Secretary (Management and Consular): J. Fong.

USA

Embassy: 3rd Floor, Teck Guan Plaza, cnr Jalan Sultan and Jalan McArthur, Bandar Seri Begawan 2085; tel (2) 229670; telex 2609; fax (2) 225293.
Ambassador: Christopher H. Phillips.
Economic/Commercial Section: James P. Wojtasiewicz.
Consular/Administrative Section: Omar A. Bsaies.
Communications Programme Officer: David V. Merritt.

BULGARIA

AFGHANISTAN

Embassy: Sofia, L. Karavelov St 34; tel (2) 66-12-45.
Ambassador: Mehrabuddin Paktiawal.

ALBANIA

Embassy: Sofia, Dimitur Polyanov St 10; tel (2) 44-33-81.
Ambassador: Bashkim Rama.

ALGERIA

Embassy: Sofia, Slavyanska St 16; tel (2) 87-56-83; telex 22519.
Ambassador: Zine el-Abidine Hachichi.

ARGENTINA

Embassy: Sofia, Blvd Klement Gottwald 42; tel (2) 44-38-21.
Ambassador: Raúl Medina Muñoz.

AUSTRIA

Embassy: 1000 Sofia, Rusky St 13; tel (2) 52-28-07; telex 22566.
Ambassador: Dr Manfred Kiepach.
Counsellor: Gabriel Kramaries.
Economic Counsellor: Johann Rapp.

BELGIUM

Embassy: Sofia, Ul. Frédéric Joliot-Curie 19; tel (2) 72-35-27; telex 22455.
Ambassador: Michael Dooms.

BRAZIL

Embassy: Sofia, Blvd Rusky 27, 2nd Floor; tel (2) 44-17-01; telex 22359.
Ambassador: Guy M. de Castro Brandão.
Counsellor: Sonia Maria de Castro.
Second Secretary: Ana Souza Cartaxo de Sá.

CAMBODIA

Embassy: Sofia, Mladost 1, Blvd Salvador Alliende, Res. 2; tel (2) 75-51-35.
Chargé d'affaires a.i.: Chum Sounry.
Third Secretary: Chea Sam Nang.

CHINA, PEOPLE'S REPUBLIC

Embassy: Sofia, Blvd Rusky 18; tel (2) 87-87-24; telex 22545.
Ambassador: Li Fenlin.

COLOMBIA

Embassy: Sofia, Vasil Aprilov St 17; tel (2) 44-61-77; telex 23393.
Ambassador: Evelio Ramírez Martínez.

CONGO

Embassy: Sofia, Blvd Klement Gottwald 54; tel (2) 44-65-18; telex 23828.
Chargé d'affaires a.i.: Pierre Adoua.

CUBA

Embassy: Sofia, Mladezhka St 1; tel (2) 72-09-96; telex 22428.
Ambassador: Manuel Pérez Hernández.

CZECHOSLOVAKIA

Embassy: Sofia, Blvd Vladimir Zaimov 9; tel (2) 44-62-81.
Ambassador: Václav Janoušek.

DENMARK

Embassy: 1000 Sofia, Blvd Rusky 10, 4 sal, POB 1393; tel (2) 88-04-55; telex 22099.
Ambassador: S. G. Mellbin.
Commercial Secretary: Rima Mirska.

EGYPT

Embassy: Sofia, Shesti Septemvri St 5; tel (2) 87-02-15; telex 22270.
Ambassador: Mohamed el-Etreby.

ETHIOPIA

Embassy: Sofia, Vasil Kolarov St 28; tel (2) 88-39-24.
Chargé d'affaires a.i.: Ayelle Makonen.

FINLAND

Embassy: 1126 Sofia, Volokolamsko St 57, Res. 3; tel (2) 68-32-37; telex 22776; fax (2) 68-35-26.
Ambassador: Pekka Artturi Oinonen.

FRANCE

Embassy: Sofia, Oborishte St 29; tel (2) 44-11-71; telex 22336.
Ambassador: Jacques Rummelhardt.

Trade Promotion Office: 1000 Sofia, POB 831; tel (2) 72-22-50; telex 22926.

GERMANY

Embassy: 1113 Sofia, Henri Barbusse St 7, POB 869; tel (2) 72-03-08; telex 22590; fax (2) 71-80-41.
Ambassador: Karl Walter Lewalter.

Visa, Legal and Consular Sections: Sofia, Schipha St 48; tel (2) 43-01-81; telex 24214.

Economic Section and Trade Promotion Office: Sofia, Ul. Frédéric Joliot-Curie 25; tel (2) 65-04-51.

GHANA

Embassy: 1113 Sofia, Pierre Degeyter St 9, Apt 37-38; tel (2) 70-65-09.
Ambassador: Coffi Akuwa-Harrison.

GREECE

Embassy: Sofia, Blvd Klement Gottwald 68; tel (2) 44-37-70; telex 22458.
Ambassador: Georgios Christoyannis.

HUNGARY

Embassy: Sofia, Shesti Septemvri St 57; tel (2) 66-20-21; telex 22459.
Ambassador: Sándor Szabó.

Cultural Institute: 1000 Sofia, Blvd Rusky 8; tel (2) 87-83-29.
Director of Cultural Institute: Zoltán Király.

INDIA

Embassy: Sofia, Blvd Patriyarkh Evtimii 31; tel (2) 87-39-44; telex 22954.
Ambassador: Girish Dhume.

INDONESIA

Embassy: 1504 Sofia, Veliko Turnovo St 32; tel (2) 44-23-49; telex 22358.
Ambassador: Abdel Kobir Sasradipoera.

IRAN

Embassy: Sofia, Blvd Klement Gottwald 70; tel (2) 44-10-13; telex 22303.
Ambassador: Sayyed Homayun Amir-Khalili.

IRAQ

Embassy: Sofia, Anton Chekhov St 21; tel (2) 87-00-13; telex 22307.
Ambassador: Fawsi Dakir al-Ani.

ITALY

Embassy: Sofia, Shipka St 2; tel (2) 88-17-06; telex 22173.
Ambassador: Paolo Taroni.

JAPAN

Embassy: Sofia, Lyulyakova Gradina St 14; tel (2) 71-90-22; telex 22397; fax (2) 72-25-15.
Ambassador: Takashi Tajima.

KOREA, DEMOCRATIC PEOPLE'S REPUBLIC

Embassy: Sofia, Mladost 1, Blvd S. Aliende, Res. 4; tel (2) 77-53-48.
Ambassador: Kim Pyong Il.

KOREA, REPUBLIC

Embassy: Sofia, Blvd Anton Ivmon; tel (2) 624-51.
Ambassador: Kim Choe-Su.

KUWAIT

Embassy: Sofia, Blvd Klement Gottwald 47; tel (2) 44-19-92; telex 23586.
Ambassador: Talib Jalal ad-Din al-Naqib.

LAOS

Embassy: Sofia, Ovcha Kupel, Buket St 80; tel (2) 56-55-08.
Ambassador: Thaleune Warrintrasak.

LEBANON

Embassy: Sofia, Ul. Frédéric Joliot-Curie 19; tel (2) 72-04-31; telex 23140.
Ambassador: Hussein Moussawi.

LIBYA

People's Bureau: Sofia, Oborishte St 10; tel (2) 44-19-21; telex 22180.
Secretary of People's Bureau: Omar Muftah Dallal.

MALTA

Embassy: Palazzo Parisio, Merchants St, Valletta, Malta; tel 222407; telex 1100; fax 237822.
Ambassador: Dr Joseph Cassar.

MEXICO

Embassy: Sofia, Todor Strashimirov St 1; tel (2) 44-32-82; telex 22087.
Ambassador: Jaime Fernández-MacGregor.

MONGOLIA

Embassy: Sofia, Ul. Frédéric Joliot-Curie 52; tel (2) 65-84-03; telex 22274.

Ambassador: Lhamyn Tserendondog.

MOROCCO

Embassy: Sofia, Blvd Klement Gottwald 44; tel (2) 44-27-94; telex 23515.
Ambassador: Abdelhamid Bennani.

MOZAMBIQUE

Embassy: Sofia.
Ambassador: Gonçalves Rafael Sengo.

NETHERLANDS

Embassy: 1000 Sofia, Denkoglu St 19a, POB 91; tel (2) 87-41-86; telex 22686; fax (2) 87-76-46.
Ambassador: Vivian H. Meertins.
Counsellor: H. J. Nijhof.
Third Secretary (Economic and Commercial Affairs): R. Swartbol.

NICARAGUA

Embassy: Sofia, Mladost 1, Blvd Aliende, Res. 1; tel (2) 75-41-57 .
Ambassador: Roger Vásquez Barrios.

PERU

Embassy: Sofia, Ul. Frédéric Joliot-Curie 19, Apt. 20; tel (2) 70-32-63; telex 23182.
Chargé d'affaires: Julio Vega Erausquín.

POLAND

Embassy: Sofia, Khan Krum St 46; tel (2) 88-51-66; telex 22595; fax (2) 87-36-45.
Ambassador: Tadeusz Wasilewski.
Counsellor and Minister Plenipotentiary: Jerzy Bauer.
Counsellor (Consular Affairs): Edward Waszczuk.
Counsellor (Economic Affairs): Andrzej Sokołowski.
First Secretary: Bogusław Gorszewski.
First Secretary: Anna Kamińska.
First Secretary (Consular Affairs): Paweł Piątkowski.
First Secretary (Press Affairs): Marian Orlikowski.
Commercial Section: Sofia, Blvd Klement Gottwald 48; tel (2) 44-16-86.
Counsellor (Commercial Affairs): Aleksander Filasiewicz.
Cultural Institute: Sofia, Blvd Rusky 12; tel (2) 87-51-88.
Counsellor and Head of Cultural Institute: Maksymilian Celeda.
Consulate-General: Varna, Blvd Tchervenoarmeiski 43; tel (52) 22-55-86.
Consul-General and Minister Plenipotentiary: Jerzy Mąkosa.
Consul: Antoni Gruca.

PORTUGAL

Embassy: Sofia, Ivats Voivoda St 6; tel (2) 44-35-48; telex 22082.
Ambassador: Luiz Gonzaga Ferreira.

ROMANIA

Embassy: Sofia, Sitnyakovo St 4; tel (2) 70-70-47; telex 22321.
Ambassador: Vasile Pungan.

RUSSIA

Embassy: Sofia, Blvd Bulgaro-Savetska, Druzhba 28; tel (2) 66-88-19.
Ambassador: Victor Vasilevich Sharapov.
Consular Section: tel (2) 66-57-32.
Consulate-General: Ruse, Nish St 1; tel (82) 50-23-81.
Consulate-General: Varna, Macedonia St 53; tel (52) 22-35-46.
Consulate-General: Plovdiv, Vazov St 20; tel (32) 22-67-61.

SOUTH AFRICA

Interests Section: Sofia.
Minister-Counsellor and Head of Interests Section: A. P. Burger.

SPAIN

Embassy: Sofia, Oborishte St 47; tel (2) 43-00-17; telex 22308.
Ambassador: Joaquín Pérez Gómez.

SWEDEN

Embassy: 1113 Sofia, Shiptchenski Prokhod 16, POB 620; tel (2) 72-22-89; telex 22373; fax (2) 70-55-31.
Ambassador: Hans-Olle Olsson.
Second Secretary: Ingemar Dolfe.
Commercial Section: Sofia, Neofit Rilski 45, POB 620; tel (2) 66-14-31; telex 23956; fax (2) 80-05-09.

SWITZERLAND

Embassy: 1504 Sofia, Shipka St 33; 1000 Sofia, POB 244; tel (2) 44-31-98; telex 22792; fax (2) 44-39-47.
Ambassador: Harald Borner.
First Secretary: Ulrich Gubler.
Attaché and Head of Chancery: Gérald Délèze.

SYRIA

Embassy: Sofia, Hristo Georgiev 10; tel (2) 44-15-85; telex 23464.
Chargé d'affaires: Ahmad Omran.

TURKEY

Embassy: Sofia, Blvd Tolbukhin 23; tel (2) 87-23-06; telex 22199.
Ambassador: Yalçin Oral.

UNITED KINGDOM

Embassy: Sofia, Blvd Marshal Tolbukhin 65-67; tel (2) 87-95-75; telex 22363; fax (2) 46-20-65.
Ambassador: Richard Thomas.
First Secretary, Consul and Deputy Head of Mission: J. Leslie Buchanan.
First Secretary (Economic and Press) and Head of Political Section: Keith I. Malin.
First Secretary (Commercial and Economic): Christine M. Laidlaw.
First Secretary (Management): Gillian Pegler.
First Secretary (Medical Adviser): Dr H. M. Carpenter.
Second Secretary (Know-How Fund): Peter J. W. Hardman.
Second Secretary (Management): A. F. Gee.
Third Secretary (Political, Information and Press): Sarah J. Lampert.
Defence Attaché: Col Nicholas A. King.
British Council: Sofia, Todor Strashimirov 7; tel (2) 24-21-2.
Cultural Attaché and British Council Director: David G. Stokes.
Assistant Cultural Attaché and British Council Director: C. W. Rennie.

USA

Embassy: Sofia, Blvd A. Stamboliisky 1; tel (2) 88-48-01; telex 22690; fax (2) 88-48-06.
Ambassador: H. Kenneth Hill.
Deputy Chief of Mission: William D. Montgomery.
Political/Economic Section: Douglas Ray Smith.
Economic/Commercial Section: Michael Gelner.
Consul: Philip H. Egger.
Administrative Section: Eva J. Groening.
Communications Programme Officer: Ricardo Chiarella.
Informations Systems Manager: Gary Price.
Press/Cultural Officer: John Menzies.
Office of the Defence Attaché: Col John M. Handley.

URUGUAY

Embassy: Sofia, Tsar Ivan Asen II St 91, POB 213; tel (2) 44-19-57; telex 23087.
Ambassador: Guido M. Yerlas.

VENEZUELA

Embassy: Sofia, Todor Strashimiro 1; tel (2) 44-32-82; telex 22087.
Counsellor: Ignacio Carrasquero.

VIET-NAM

Embassy: Sofia, Ilya Petrov St 1; tel (2) 72-08-79; telex 22717.
Ambassador: Nguyen Tien Thong.

YEMEN

Embassy: Sofia, Blvd S. Aliende, Res. 3; tel (2) 75-61-63.
Ambassador: Ali Munassar Muhammad.

YUGOSLAVIA

Embassy: Sofia, G. Gheorghiu-Dej St 3; tel (2) 44-32-37; telex 23537.
Ambassador: Milenko Stefanović.

BURKINA FASO

ALGERIA

Embassy: BP 3893, Ouagadougou; telex 5359.

CANADA

Office of the Canadian Embassy: Centre de la Coopération Canadienne, BP 548, Ouagadougou; tel 30-00-39; telex 5264; fax 30-10-80.
Counsellor (Development) and Consul: G. Barchechat.
Counsellor (Development) and Consul: A. W. Bain.
First Secretary (Development): S. Moreau.
First Secretary (Development): Y. Perrier.
First Secretary (Development): J. Gauvin.
Second Secretary (Development): R. Langlois.
Second Secretary (Development): C. Nadeau.

CHINA, PEOPLE'S REPUBLIC

Embassy: quartier Rotonde, BP 538, Ouagadougou.
Ambassador: Wu Jiasen.

CUBA

Embassy: BP 3422, Ouagadougou; telex 5360.
Ambassador: Reme Remigio Ruiz.

DENMARK

Consulate: c/o Voltaique du Métal, BP 1200, Ouagadougou; tel 33-31-13; telex 5328.
Consul: Jean-Baptiste Tapsoba.

EGYPT

Embassy: BP 668, Ouagadougou; telex 5289.
Ambassador: Dr Mohamad Aley el-Kordy.

FINLAND

Embassy: Ouagadougou.
Ambassador: Osmo Väinölä (resident in Finland).

FRANCE

Embassy: 902 ave de l'Indépendance, 01 BP 504, Ouagadougou 01; tel 30-67-71; telex 5211.
Ambassador: Alain Deschamps.

Trade Promotion Office: BP 4382, Ouagadougou; tel 33-55-81; telex 5393.

GERMANY

Embassy: 01 BP 600, Ouagadougou 01; tel 30-67-31; telex 5217.
Ambassador: Jürgen Dröge.

GHANA

Embassy: BP 212, Ouagadougou; tel 33-28-75.

KOREA, DEMOCRATIC PEOPLE'S REPUBLIC

Embassy: BP 370, Ouagadougou.
Ambassador: Kim Sun-che.

LIBYA

People's Bureau: BP 1601, Ouagadougou; telex 5311.

NETHERLANDS

Embassy: BP 1302, Ouagadougou; telex 5303.
Ambassador: P. R. Brouwer.

NIGERIA

Embassy: BP 132, Ouagadougou; tel 33-42-41; telex 5236.
Chargé d'affaires a.i.: A. K. Alli Assayouti.

RUSSIA

Embassy: Secteur 4, BP 7041, Ouagadougou; tel 30-66-33; telex 5299; fax 31-24-60.
Ambassador: Yevgeni Nikolayevich Korendyasov.
First Counsellor: Sergei Nenachev.
Commercial Counsellor: Stanislav Roumiantsev.
First Secretary: Andrei Deuidov.
First Secretary: Vladimir Zyssov.
Second Secretary and Consul: Valery Gorbatko.
Second Secretary: Valery Zyssounkin.
Second Secretary and Head of Cultural Centre: Anatoly Fedoutinos.
Press Attaché: Akyl Aripov.
Head of Protocol and Economic Attaché: Dmitri Boukin.

SWEDEN

Consulate: BP 218, Ouagadougou; tel 30-62-97; telex 5243; fax 30-62-99.
Consul: Zouhair Michel Fadoul.

SWITZERLAND

Embassy Office: ave Président Guillaume Ouedraogo, BP 578, Ouagadougou; tel 30-67-29; telex 5371; fax 31-04-66.
Attaché (Development Co-operation and Consular Affairs): Pascal Fellay.

UNITED KINGDOM

Consulate: BP 1918, Ouagadougou; tel 33-63-63.

USA

Embassy: 01 BP 35, Ouagadougou 01; tel 30-67-23; telex 5290; fax 31-23-68.
Ambassador: Edward P. Brynn.
Deputy Chief of Mission: Robert M. Beecroft.
Political/Economic/Commercial Section: Stuart M. Smith.
Political/Military Section: Roger A. Frazier.
Consul: Jacqueline R. Moyer.
Administrative Section: Sharon A. Lavorel.
Public Affairs Officer: Thomas R. Genton.
Communications Programme Officer: Larry D. Moyer.
Agency for International Development: Wilbur J. Thomas.
Labour Officer: Ollie P. Anderson, Jr (resident in the USA).

International Organizations

EUROPEAN COMMUNITIES

External Delegation: BP 352, Ouagadougou; tel 30-73-85; telex 5242; fax 30-89-66.
Commission Delegate: Uwe Werblow.

BURUNDI

BELGIUM

Embassy: 9 ave de l'Industrie, BP 1920, Bujumbura; tel (2) 23676; telex 5033.
Ambassador: Denis Banneel.

CANADA

Consulate: Siruco, Bujumbura; tel (2) 22520; fax (2) 22816.
Honorary Consul: J. M. A. Persoons.

CHINA, PEOPLE'S REPUBLIC

Embassy: BP 2550, Bujumbura; tel (2) 24307.
Ambassador: Wang Jianbang.

DENMARK

Consulate: 52 ave de la Poste, BP 2880, Bujumbura; tel (2) 26099; telex 5089.
Consul: Michael Andersen.

EGYPT

Embassy: 31 ave de la Liberté, BP 1520, Bujumbura; tel (2) 23161; telex 5040.
Ambassador: Resk Aladdin.
Diplomatic Attaché: Mohamed Salah el-Din.

FINLAND

Consulate: Bujumbura.
Consul: Daniel Paul Louis Parisse.

FRANCE

Embassy: 60 ave de l'UPRONA, BP 1740, Bujumbura; tel (2) 26464; telex 5044.
Ambassador: Robert Rigouzzo.

Trade Promotion Office: 155 ave de l'UPRONA, BP 1740, Bujumbura; tel (2) 22518; telex 5143.

GERMANY

Embassy: 22 rue du 18 septembre, BP 480, Bujumbura; tel (2) 26412; telex 5068.
Ambassador: Karl Flittner.

HOLY SEE

Apostolic Nunciature: 46 chaussée Prince Louis-Rwagasore, BP 1068, Bujumbura; tel (2) 22326; fax 23176.
Apostolic Pro-Nuncio: Most Rev. Pietro Sambi, Titular Archbishop of Belcastro.
Secretary: Wojciech Zaluski.

KOREA, DEMOCRATIC PEOPLE'S REPUBLIC

Embassy: BP 1620, Bujumbura; tel (2) 22881.
Ambassador: Ahn Jae Bu.

ROMANIA

Embassy: rue Pierre Ngendandumwe, BP 2770, Bujumbura; tel (2) 24135.
Chargé d'affaires a.i.: Alexandra Andrei.

RUSSIA

Embassy: 9 ave de l'UPRONA, BP 1034, Bujumbura; tel (2) 26098.
Ambassador: Vtsevolod Sofinsky.

Consular Section: 76 ave de l'UPRONA, BP 1034, Bujumbura; tel (2) 22984; telex 5164.

RWANDA

Embassy: 24 ave du Zaïre, BP 400, Bujumbura; tel (2) 23140; telex 5032.
Ambassador: Emmanuel Ruzindana.

SPAIN

Consulate: chaussée Rwagasore, Appt CTB s/n, BP 1762, Bujumbura; tel (2) 25524.
Honorary Consul: Ma Isabel Pintado.

SWEDEN

Consulate: c/o Old East, chaussée Rwagasore 1-3, BP 330, Bujumbura; tel (2) 22026; telex 5064.
Consul: Daniel Parisse.

SWITZERLAND

Consulate: 40 ave des Travailleurs, BP 1284, Bujumbura; tel (2) 23686; telex 5126; fax (2) 26603.
Honorary Consul: Gertrud Vann-Amberg.

TANZANIA

Embassy: BP 1653, Bujumbura.
Ambassador: Nicholas J. Maro.

UNITED KINGDOM

Consulate: 43 ave Bubanza, BP 1344, Bujumbura; tel (2) 23711; telex 5126.

USA

Embassy: ave des Etats-Unis, BP 1720, Bujumbura; tel (2) 23454; fax 22926.
Ambassador: Cynthia Shepard Perry.
Deputy Chief of Mission: David B. Dunn.
Economic/Commercial Section: Edwin P. Brown, Jr.
Consul: Emily E. Jeffers.
Administrative Section: James E. Paige, Jr.
Regional Security Officer: Joseph Davison.
Public Affairs Officer: Walter Theurer.
Communications Programme Officer: Kanikar N. Daly.

Agency for International Development: fax 986.
Agent for International Development: Glenn G. Slocum.

ZAIRE

Embassy: 5 ave Olsen, BP 872, Bujumbura; tel (2) 23492.
Ambassador: Ikolo Mboloko.

International Organizations

EUROPEAN COMMUNITIES

External Delegation: ave du 13 octobre, BP 103, Bujumbura; tel (2) 23426; telex 5031; fax (2) 24612.
Commission Delegate: Patrick Towers Picton.

CAMBODIA

AFGHANISTAN

Embassy: Phnom-Penh.
Ambassador: Mohammed Ismail Mahshook.

BULGARIA

Embassy: 227 blvd Tou Samouth, Phnom-Penh; tel 23181.
Ambassador: Gantcho Christov Gantchev.
Counsellor: Tsvetelin Vassilev Tsolov.

CUBA

Embassy: 98 Voi 2140 Router 214, Phnom-Penh; tel 24181.
Ambassador: Viriato Mora Iaz.

CZECHOSLOVAKIA

Embassy: 102 rue Tou Samouth, Phnom-Penh; tel 23781.

FRANCE

Embassy: Phnom-Penh.
Ambassador: Philippe Coste.

HUNGARY

Embassy: 771-773 blvd Achar Mean, Phnom-Penh; tel 22781.
Ambassador: Lajos Tamás.
Second Secretary: Béla Fazekas.
Attaché: Péter Noszko-Horváth.

INDIA

Embassy: Villa No. 177, blvd Achar Mean, Phnom-Penh.
Chargé d'affaires: Rinzing Wangdi.

LAOS

Embassy: 19 rue Tito, Phnom-Penh; tel 25182.
Ambassador: Phuonsavat Thongsoukkhoun.

MONGOLIA

Embassy: Phnom-Penh.
Ambassador: Gelegiyn Adiya.

NICARAGUA

Embassy: Phnom-Penh.
Ambassador: Olga Ailes López.

POLAND

Embassy: 767 blvd Achar Mean, Song Ngoc Minh, Phnom-Penh; tel 23582.
Chargé d'affaires a.i.: Sławomir Nestorowicz.

RUSSIA

Embassy: 213 rue Lénine, Phnom-Penh; tel 22081.
Ambassador: Yuri Myakotnykh.

UNITED KINGDOM

Office: Phnom-Penh.
Envoy: David Burns.

USA

Embassy: Phnom-Penh.
Chargé d'affaires a.i.: Charles Twining, Jr.

VIET-NAM

Embassy: blvd Achar Mean, Phnom-Penh; tel 25482.

YEMEN

Embassy: Phnom-Penh.
Ambassador: I. Abdulla Saidi.

CAMEROON

ALGERIA

Embassy: BP 1619, Yaoundé; tel 23-06-65; telex 8517.
Ambassador: Missoum Sbih.

AUSTRIA

Consulate: Douala.

BELGIUM

Embassy: BP 816, Yaoundé; tel 22-27-88; telex 8314.
Ambassador: Franz Michils.

BRAZIL

Embassy: BP 348, Yaoundé; tel 23-19-57; telex 8587.
Ambassador: Annunciata Salgado dos Santos.

CANADA

Embassy: Immeuble Stamatiades, place de l'Hôtel de Ville, BP 572, Yaoundé; tel 22-16-00; telex 8209; fax 22-10-90.
Ambassador: Anne Leahy.
Counsellor (Development): Laval Gobeil.
First Secretary (Development): Yvan R. Lapointe.
First Secretary (Development) and Consul: Réjean Hamel.
Second Secretary (Administration) and Vice-Consul: Donald G. Viner.
Third Secretary (Political) and Vice-Consul: Isabelle Roy.
Consular Affairs/Archives: Joseph Champagne.
Information Officer: Joseph Peyo.

Consulate and Centre Canadien de Coopération Industrielle (CCCI): BP 2373, Douala; tel 42-24-60; telex 5474; fax 42-70-69.
Consul and Counsellor (Development): Michel Roy.

CENTRAL AFRICAN REPUBLIC

Embassy: BP 396, Yaoundé; tel 22-51-55.
Ambassador: Basile Akelelo.

CHAD

Embassy: BP 506, Yaoundé; tel 22-06-24; telex 8352.
Ambassador: Neatobei Bidi.

CHINA, PEOPLE'S REPUBLIC

Embassy: BP 1307, Yaoundé; tel 23-00-83.
Ambassador: Shen Lianrui.

CONGO

Embassy: BP 1422, Yaoundé; tel 23-24-58; telex 8379.
Ambassador: Bernadette Bayonne.

COTE D'IVOIRE

Embassy: Immeuble Ndende, quartier Bastos, BP 203, Yaoundé; tel 22-09-69; telex 8388.
Ambassador: Antoine Konan Koffi.

DENMARK

Consulate-General: Immeuble Scanwater, Face 'Palais Royal', Nylon (Nlongkak), BP 1967, Yaoundé; tel 23-29-62; telex 8613.
Consul-General: Hans Winther Nielsen.

Consulate: Zone des Professions Maritimes, Vallée de Tokoto, BP 215, Douala; tel 42-98-65; telex 5252.
Consul: Edmund Dupuy.

EGYPT

Embassy: BP 809, Yaoundé; tel 22-39-22; telex 8360.
Ambassador: Mohamed al-Khazindar.

EQUATORIAL GUINEA

Embassy: BP 277, Yaoundé; tel 22-41-49.
Ambassador: Alfredo Abeso Mveno Onguene.

FINLAND

Consulate: BP 4324, Yaoundé; tel 23-15-28; telex 8694.
Consul: Alix Elisabeth Suzanne Betayene.

Consulate: BP 4344, Douala; tel 42-76-59; telex 1134; fax 42-77-03.
Consul: Kauko Malin.

FRANCE

Embassy: Plateau Atémengué, BP 1631, Yaoundé; tel 22-02-33; telex 8233.
Ambassador: Yvon Omnès.

Consulate-General: ave Ahmadou-Ahidjo, BP 309, Yaoundé; tel 22-09-01.

Trade Promotion Office: BP 102, Yaoundé; tel 22-25-65; telex 8302.

Consulate-General: ave des Cocotiers, BP 869, Douala; tel 42-53-70.

Consulate: route de l'Aviation, BP 127, Garoua; tel 27-14-75.

GABON

Embassy: BP 4130, Yaoundé; tel 22-29-66; telex 8265.
Ambassador: Yves Ongollo.

GERMANY

Embassy: rue Charles de Gaulle, BP 1160, Yaoundé; tel 22-05-66; telex 8238.
Ambassador: Eberhard Nöldeke.

Consular Section: 14 ave du Général de Gaulle, BP 509, Douala-Bonanjo; tel 42-86-00.

GREECE

Embassy: BP 82, Yaoundé; tel 22-39-36; telex 8364.
Chargé d'affaires a.i.: Dimitri Karabalis.

HOLY SEE

Apostolic Nunciature: rue du Vatican, BP 210, Yaoundé; tel 22-04-75; telex 8382.
Apostolic Pro-Nuncio: Most Rev. Santos Abril y Castelló, Titular Archbishop of Tamada.
Secretary: Sérapion Bambonanire.

ISRAEL

Embassy: BP 5934, Yaoundé; tel 22-16-44; telex 8632.
Ambassador: Yaacov Keinan.

ITALY

Embassy: quartier Bastos, BP 827, Yaoundé; tel 22-33-76; telex 8305.
Ambassador: Margherita Costa.

JAPAN

Embassy: Yaoundé.
Ambassador: Hideo Kakinuma.

KOREA, DEMOCRATIC PEOPLE'S REPUBLIC

Embassy: Yaoundé.
Ambassador: Kil-Moun Yeung.

KOREA, REPUBLIC

Embassy: BP 301, Yaoundé; tel 23-32-23; telex 8241.
Ambassador: Nam-Cha Hwang.

LIBERIA

Embassy: Ekoudou, Quartier Bastos, BP 1185, Yaoundé; tel 23-12-96; telex 8227.
Ambassador: Carlton Alexwyn Karpeh.

LIBYA

People's Bureau: BP 1980, Yaoundé; telex 8272.
Head of People's Bureau: Hamdi Fannoush.

MALTA

Consulate: rue Joseph Clerc, BP 11834, Yaoundé; tel 22-37-34; telex 8907; fax 22-17-85.
Honorary Consul: Paul Kammogne Fokam.

MOROCCO

Embassy: BP 1629, Yaoundé; tel 22-50-92; telex 8347.
Ambassador: Mimoun Mehdi.

NAMIBIA

Embassy: Yaoundé.

NETHERLANDS

Embassy: BP 310, Yaoundé; tel 22-05-44; telex 8237.
Ambassador: Georges-Albert Wehry.

NIGERIA

Embassy: BP 448, Yaoundé; tel 22-34-55; telex 8267.
Ambassador: George Bello.

RUSSIA

Embassy: blvd de l'URSS, quartier Bastos, BP 488, Yaoundé; tel 22-17-14.
Ambassador: Vitalya Yakovlievich Litvin.

Consular Section: tel 22-47-64.

SAUDI ARABIA

Embassy: BP 1602, Yaoundé; tel 22-39-22; telex 8336.
Ambassador: Hamad al-Toaimi.

SENEGAL

Embassy: Plateau 'Bastos', BP 1716, Yaoundé; tel 22-03-08; telex 8303.
Ambassador: Saloum Kande.

SPAIN

Embassy: BP 877, Yaoundé; tel 20-35-43; telex 8287.

Ambassador: Manuel Piñeiro-Souto.
First Secretary and Consul: Emilio de Miguel Calabia.
Chancellor: Antonio Laveda Martínez.
Attaché: Ma del Carmen Peche González.
Attaché: Blandine Laveda Ralisoa.

Consulate: 3 rue G. Duboit de Saigny, Douala; tel 42-82-95.
Honorary Consul: Félix Cabrejas Blanco.

Commercial Bureau: blvd de la Liberté, Douala; tel 42-73-46; telex 6093; fax 42-35-31.
Deputy Commercial Attaché: José García Cuenca.

SWEDEN

Consulate: Ste Mory, SOAEM, BP 280, Yaoundé; tel 23-34-77; telex 8235; fax 22-26-63.
Consul: Jacques Charles Marcel Duchene-Marullaz.

Consulate-General: SOAEM, blvd de la Liberté, Bonanjo, BP 4057, Douala; tel 42-02-88; telex 5220.
Consul-General: Jean-Louis Greciet.

SWITZERLAND

Embassy: Villa Zogo Massy, route du Mont Fébé, Quartier Bastos, BP 1169, Yaoundé; tel 23-28-96; telex 8316.
Ambassador: Jürg Streuli.
Second Secretary and Head of Chancery: Jean-Jacques Leutenegger.

TUNISIA

Embassy: rue du Rotary, Quartier Bastos, BP 6074, Yaoundé; tel 20-33-68; telex 8370; fax 21-05-07.
Ambassador: Mohamed Saïd el-Kateb.
First Counsellor: Mohamed Kemicha.
First Secretary (Economic and Cultural): Farah Hafsa.
Second Secretary (Administrative and Financial): Abdellatif el-Ouni.

UNITED KINGDOM

Embassy: ave Winston Churchill, BP 547, Yaoundé; tel 22-05-45; telex 8200; fax 22-01-48.
Ambassador and Consul-General: William E. Quantrill.
Deputy Head of Mission, First Secretary (Commercial) and Consul: B. Donaldson.
Second Secretary (Commercial/Aid) and Vice-Consul: R. W. Hyde.
Pro-Consul and Accountant: J. Rumiel.

Consulate: 2e étage, Résidence La Rose, 16 rue de l'Hôtel de Ville, BP 1016, Douala; tel 42-21-77; telex 5353; fax 42-88-96.
Consul: D. A. Pearce.

USA

Embassy: rue Nachtigal, BP 817, Yaoundé; tel 23-40-14; telex 8223; fax 23-07-53.
Ambassador: Frances D. Cook.
Deputy Chief of Mission: Tibor B. Nagy, Jr.
Political Section: Timothy D. Andrews.
Economic/Commercial Section: Robert F. Godec.
Consul: Gerry W. Fuller.
Administrative Section: Richard E. Kramer.
Regional Security Officer: George F. Rodman, Jr.
Public Affairs Officer: Mary Roberta Jones.
Communications Programme Officer: Aurel Manupella.
Agency for International Development: Jay P. Johnson.
Office of the Defence Attaché: Lieut Col Steven A. Lovasz.

Consulate: 21 ave du Général de Gaulle, BP 4006, Douala; tel 42-06-88; telex 5233; fax 42-77-90
Principal Officer: William R. Gaines.
Political/Economic Section: George M. Frederick.
Communications Programme Officer: Allan Jeffries.

ZAIRE

Embassy: BP 632, Yaoundé; tel 22-51-03; telex 8317.
Ambassador: Kutendakana Bumbulu.

International Organizations

EUROPEAN COMMUNITIES

External Delegation: Quartier Bastos, BP 847, Yaoundé; tel 22-13-87; telex 5402; fax 22-21-49.
Commission Delegate: Agostino Trapani.

CANADA

ALGERIA

Embassy: 435 Daly Ave, Ottawa K1N 6H3; tel (613) 232-9453; telex 053-3625; fax (613) 232-9099.
Ambassador: Mohammed Ghoualmi.

ANTIGUA AND BARBUDA

High Commission: Place de Ville, Tower B, 112 Kent St, Suite 205, Ottawa K1P 5P2; tel (613) 234-9143; fax (613) 232-0539.
High Commissioner: Deborah-Mae Lovell (acting).

Consulate-General: 60 St Clair Ave East, Toronto M4T 1N5; tel (416) 961-3085.
Consul-General: Madeline Blackman.

ARGENTINA

Embassy: 90 Sparks St, Suite 620, Ottawa K1P 5B4; tel (613) 236-2351; telex 053-4293; fax (613) 235-2659.
Ambassador: Oscar Fernández.

AUSTRALIA

High Commission: 50 O'Connor St, Suite 710, Ottawa K1P 6L2; tel (613) 236-0841; telex 053-3391; fax (613) 236-4376.
High Commissioner: David H. Spencer.
Deputy High Commissioner: Michael Jonathan Thwaites.
First Secretary: Arthur Tansley.
Assistant Army Adviser: Lieut Col Colin Sharp.
First Secretary (Public Affairs): Robert E. Pounds.

Commercial Section: tel (613) 236-2684.
Counsellor (Commercial): Richard D. Ryan.
First Secretary (Commercial): Philip Lowday.

Consular and Administrative Section: tel (613) 236-4278.
First Secretary (Consular and Administrative): Jon Hundloe.
Third Secretary (Administrative) and Vice-Consul: William Carolan.

Consulate-General: 175 Bloor St East, Suites 314/316, Toronto M4W 3R8; POB 69, Commerce Court, Postal Station, Toronto; tel (416) 323-1155; telex 06-219762; fax (416) 323-3910.
Consul-General: Terry Hunt.
Consul (Visas and Immigration): Ahmet Ali.

Consulate-General: World Trade Centre Office Complex, 999 Canada Pl, Suite 602, Vancouver V6C 3E1; POB 12519, Vancouver V6E 3X1; tel (604) 684-1177; telex 045-07580; fax (604) 684-1856.
Consul-General: William Meehan.
Vice-Consul (Consular and Administration): T. Willis.
Vice-Consul (Immigration): G. Dival.
Marketing Officer: K. Lamb.
Trade Officer: K. Tate.

AUSTRIA

Embassy: 445 Wilbrod St, Ottawa K1N 6M7; tel (613) 563-1444; telex 053-3290; fax (613) 563-0038.
Ambassador: Dr Kurt Herndl.
Minister-Counsellor: Dr Christian Krepela.
Counsellor (Press and Cultural): Dr Artur Bablok.
Counsellor (Administrative) and Consul: Ursula E. Rose.

Consulate-General: 1350 Sherbrooke St W, Suite 1030, Montréal H3G 1J1; tel (514) 845-8661.
Consul-General: Ulrike Billard.

Trade Commission: 1010 Sherbrooke St W, Suite 1410, Montréal H3A 2R7; tel (514) 849-3708; fax (514) 849-9577.
Trade Commissioner: Richard Voh.

Consulate-General: 390 Bay St, Suite 2018, Toronto M5H 2Y2; tel (416) 863-0649.
Consul-General: Dr Hans Günther Abromeit.

Trade Commission: 2 Bloor St East, Suite 3330, Toronto M4W 1A8; tel (416) 967-3348; telex 062-3196; fax (416) 967-4101.
Trade Commissioner: Dr Georg Canisius.

Consulate: 525 Seymour St, Suite 716, Vancouver V6B 3H9; tel (604) 683-7571.
Consul: Graham P. Clarke.

Trade Commission: 200 Granville St, Suite 1380, Vancouver V6C 1S4; tel (604) 683-5808; fax (604) 662-8528.
Trade Commissioner: Dr Wolfgang Harwalik.

Consulate: 1131 Kensington Rd, NW, Calgary T2N 3P4; tel (403) 283-6526; fax (403) 283-4909.
Consul: Hans Ockermueller.

Consulate: 1718 Argyle St, Suite 710, Halifax B3J 3N6; tel (902) 429-8200; fax (902) 425-0581.
Consul: Michael Marcelino Novac.

Consulate: 2401 Saskatchewan Dr. Plaza, Suite 100, Regina S4P 4H9; tel (306) 359-7777; fax (306) 522-3299.
Consul: E. F. Anthony Merchant.

BAHAMAS

High Commission: 360 Albert St, Suite 1020, Ottawa K1R 7X7; tel (613) 232-1724; telex 053-3793; fax (613) 232-0097.
High Commissioner: Idris G. Reid.
Counsellor: Sheila Carey.

BANGLADESH

High Commission: 85 Range Rd, Suite 402, Ottawa K1N 8J6; tel (613) 236-0138; telex 053-4283.
High Commissioner: A. N. M. Nuruzzaman.

BARBADOS

High Commission: 151 Slater St, Suite 210, Ottawa K1P 5H3; tel (613) 236-9517; telex 053-3375; fax (613) 230-4362.
High Commissioner: Sir James Cameron Tudor.
Counsellor: Nigel O. Harper.
First Secretary: Dolores M. Watson.
Attaché: Betty Callender.

Consulate-General: 20 Queens St West, Suite 1508, POB 18, Toronto M5H 3R3; tel (416) 979-2643; fax (416) 979-8726.
Consul-General: Wendell H. Kellman.

Liaison Service: City Centre North York, Suite 700, 5160 Yonge St, North York, Ontario M2N 6L9; tel (416) 512-2533; fax (416) 250-5629.
Head of Liaison Service: Ronald J. Rock.

BELGIUM

Embassy: 85 Range Rd, Suites 601-604, Ottawa K1N 8J6; tel (613) 236-7267; telex 053-3568; fax (613) 236-7882.
Ambassador: Jean-François de Liederkerke.

BELIZE

High Commission: Ottawa.
High Commissioner: Rudolph I. Castillo.

BENIN

Embassy: 58 Glebe Ave, Ottawa K1S 2C3; tel (613) 233-4429; telex 053-3630.
Ambassador: Bernardine de Régo.

BOLIVIA

Embassy: 77 Metcalfe St, Suite 608, Ottawa K1P 5L6; tel (613) 236-8237.
Ambassador: Luis Peláez Rioja.

BRAZIL

Embassy: 450 Wilbrod St, Ottawa K1N 6M8; tel (613) 237-1090; telex 053-3176; fax (613) 237-6144.
Ambassador: Paulo Pires do Rio.
Minister-Counsellor: Luiz Augusto de Castro Neves.
Counsellor: Américo Dyott Fontenelle.
First Secretary: Paulo Cordeiro de Andrade Pinto.
First Secretary: Luís Henrique Sobreira Lopes.
First Secretary: Francisco Mauro Brasil de Holanda.

Consulate-General: 2000 Mansfield St, Suite 1700, Montreal H3A 3A5; tel (514) 499-0968; telex 052-4470.
Consul-General: José Maurício Bustani.

Consulate-General: 77 Bloor St West, Suite 1109, Toronto M5S 1M2; tel (416) 922-2503; telex 062-3730; fax (416) 922-1832.
Consul-General: Regis Novaes de Oliveira.

Consulate-General: 1140 West Pender St, Suite 1300, Vancouver V6E 4G1; tel (604) 687-4589; telex 045-8631; fax (604) 681-6534.
Consul-General: João Gualberto Marques Porto.

BULGARIA

Embassy: 325 Stewart St, Ottawa K1N 6K5; tel (613) 232-3215; telex 053-4386; fax (613) 232-9547.
Ambassador: Chavdar Damianov.
Counsellor: Peter Karlukovski.
Second Secretary: Venelin Stoytchkov.

Consulate-General: 100 Adelaide St West, Suite 1410, Toronto M5H 1S3; tel (416) 363-7307; telex 062-3535; fax (416) 368-3505.
Consul-General: Tchavdar Mladenov.
Consul: Branimir Radev.

Trade Mission: 100 Adelaide St West, Suite 1405, Toronto M5H 1S3; tel (416) 368-1034; telex 062-3535; fax (416) 368-3505.
Consul: Ivan Dragnevski.

BURKINA FASO

Embassy: 48 Range Rd, Ottawa K1N 8J4; tel (613) 238-4796; telex 053-4413; fax (613) 238-3812.
Ambassador: Léandre B. Bassole.

First Counsellor: Lamoussa Ambroise Balma.
Economic and Commercial Counsellor: Fati Balma.
Financial Attaché: Yacouba Traore.
Attaché: Catherine Traore.

Consulate: 485 rue McGill, 11e étage, Montréal H2Y 2H4; tel (514) 982-3377; telex 05-825571; fax (514) 982-9416.
Honorary Consul: Pierre Bastien.

Consulate: 372 Bay St, Suite 610, Toronto M5H 2W9; tel (416) 867-8669; fax (416) 867-3079.
Honorary Consul: Peter K. Large.

BURUNDI

Embassy: 151 Slater St, Suite 800, Ottawa K1P 5H3; tel (613) 236-8483; telex 053-3393; fax (613) 563-1827.
Ambassador: Philippe Kanonko.

CAMEROON

Embassy: 170 Clemow Ave, Ottawa K1S 2B4; tel (613) 236-1522; telex 053-3736.
Ambassador: Philémon Yang Yunji.

CHILE

Embassy: 151 Slater St, Suite 605, Ottawa K1P 5H3; tel (613) 235-4402; telex 053-3774; fax (613) 235-1176.
Ambassador: Francisco Rivas.
Military Attaché: Col Juan Lucar.
Counsellor: Luis Palma.
First Secretary (Economic and Commercial): Hernán Brantes.
Third Secretary (Consular): María Paula González.

Consulate-General: 1010 Sherbrooke St West, Suite 710, Montréal H3A 2R7.
Consul-General: Patricio Maturana.

Consulate-General: 1240 Bay St, Suite 700, Toronto M5R 3L9.
Consul-General: Magdalena Balduzzi.

Consulate-General: 666 Burrard St, Place Bldg, Suite 1300, Vancouver V6C 3J8.
Consul-General: Fernando Cousiño.

Consulate: POB 22079, Bankers' Hall, Calgary T2P 4J1.
Honorary Consul: Daniel Mondaca.

CHINA, PEOPLE'S REPUBLIC

Embassy: 511-515 St Patrick St, Ottawa K1N 5H3; tel (613) 234-2706; telex 053-3770; fax (613) 230-9794.
Ambassador: Wen Yezhan.
Minister-Counsellor: Zha Peixin.
Counsellor (Administration): Tang Maohua.
Counsellor (Cultural): Sun Weixue.
Counsellor (Consular): Yang Zongliang.
Counsellor (Science and Technology): Quan Jinguan.
Counsellor (Education): Li Shunxing.
Counsellor (Commercial): Yu Zhiting.
Military, Naval and Air Attaché: Col Yu Huadong.
First Secretary: Chen Guangcai.
First Secretary: Chen Wenzhao.

Consulate-General: 3380 Granville St, Vancouver V6H 3K3; tel (604) 736-3910; fax (604) 737-0154.
Consul-General: An Wenbin.

Consulate-General: 240 George St, Toronto M5R 2P4; tel (416) 964-7260; fax (416) 324-6468.
Consul-General: Tang Fuquan.

COLOMBIA

Embassy: 150 Kent St, Suite 404, Ottawa K1P 5P4; tel (613) 230-3760; telex 053-3786; fax (613) 230-4416.
Ambassador: German Montoya.
Minister-Counsellor: Alejandro Borda.
First Secretary: Sofia de Gomez.

Consulate-General: 1 Dundas St, Suite 2108, Toronto M5G 1Z3; tel (416) 977-0098; fax (416) 977-1025.
Consul-General: Eduardo Osorio.
Vice-Consul: Edith Andrade.

Consulate-General: 1010 Sherbrooke St West, Montreal H3A 2R7; tel (514) 849-4852; fax (514) 849-4324.
Consul-General: Jaime Martínez.

Consulate: 5476 Alberta St, Vancouver V5Y 3M3; tel (604) 325-3061; fax (604) 325-1934.
Honorary Consul: Beatriz Horry.

COSTA RICA

Embassy: 150 Argyle Ave, Suite 115, Ottawa K2P 1B7; tel (613) 234-5762; telex 053-4398; fax (613) 230-2656.
Ambassador: Carlos E. Miranda.
Minister-Counsellor and Consul-General: Rodrigo Delgado.
Minister-Counsellor and Consul: Edwin Salas.
Counsellor: Maria de los Angeles Chacon.

Consulate: 894 Bellerive, Longueil, Montreal; tel (514) 651-0472.
Consul: Montserrat Romero.

Consulate: Downtown Fine Cars, 164 Av Rd, Toronto; tel (416) 961-6773.
Consul: Peter Kircher.

Consulate: 1550 Alberni St, Suite 804, Vancouver; tel (604) 669-0797.
Consul: William Dow.

COTE D'IVOIRE

Embassy: 9 Marlborough Ave, Ottawa K1N 8E6; tel (613) 236-9919; telex 053-3794; fax (613) 563-8287.
Ambassador: Julien Kacou.

CUBA

Embassy: 388 Main St, Ottawa K1S 1E3; tel (613) 563-0141; telex 053-3135; fax (613) 563-0068.
Ambassador: Carlos Castillo.
Counsellor: Aurora Gramatges.
First Secretary: José Miguel Hidalgo.
Third Secretary: José Ramon Cabañas.

Consulate-General: 1415 Pine Ave West, Montréal H3G 1B2; tel (514) 843-8897; telex 052-5228; fax (514) 735-8765.
Consul-General: Jesus Fernández Ponce.

Consulate-General: 2340 Dundas St West, Unit G-35, Toronto M6P 4A9; tel (416) 535-2664; telex 062-2226; fax (416) 535-1520.
Consul-General: Alfredo Armenteros.

CZECHOSLOVAKIA

Embassy: 50 Rideau Terrace, Ottawa K1M 2A1; tel (613) 749-4442; telex 053-4224; fax (613) 749-4989.
Ambassador: Ján Janovič.

DENMARK

Embassy: 85 Range Rd, Suite 702, Ottawa K1N 8J6; tel (613) 234-0116; telex 053-3114; fax (613) 234-7368.
Ambassador: Bjørn Olsen.
Counsellor: Ole Løwe.

Consulate-General: 151 Bloor St West, Suite 310, Toronto M5S 1S4; tel (416) 962-5661; telex 06-22032; fax (416) 962-3668.
Consul-General: Erling Harild Nielsen.
Commercial Counsellor and Consul: Flemming Crawfurd.
Export Assistant: Peder Bærenholdt.

Consulate: 1235 11th Ave SW, Calgary T3C 0M5; tel (403) 245-5755.
Consul: Kai Mortensen.

Consulate: 10235 101st St, Suite 1112, Oxford Tower, Edmonton T5J 3G1; tel (403) 426-1457.
Consul: Donn Larsen.

Consulate: 1525 Birmingham St, POB 3550, Halifax B3J 3J3; tel (902) 429-5680; telex 019-21771.
Consul: Harry Isaac Mathers.

Consulate: 2020 University St, Bureau 1527, Montréal H3A 2A5; tel (514) 849-5391; fax (514) 288-3704.
Consul: Michel Blouin.

Consulate: 5400 blvd des Galéries, Québec City G2K 2B5; tel (418) 624-3333; fax (418) 624-0404.
Consul: Jacques Ewart Fortier.

Consulate: 22 Millar Rd, Regina S4S 1N2; tel (306) 586-1442.
Consul: Gordon Allen Rasmussen.

Consulate: Harbour Bldg, Suite 306, 133 Prince William St, POB 6639, Station A, St John E2L 4S1; tel (506) 634-7320.
Consul: Eric Lawrence Teed.

Consulate: Kenmount Rd, POB 8220, Station A, St John's A1B 3N6; tel (709) 722-6910; fax (709) 739-0924.
Consul: Peter Norman Outerbridge.

Consulate: 475 Howe St, Suite 1102, Vancouver V6C 2B3; tel (604) 684-5171; fax (604) 682-8054.
Consul: Finn Karlo Petersen.

Consulate: 111 Mountbatten Ave, Winnipeg R3P 0P5; tel (204) 837-1099.
Consul: Anders Bruun.

DOMINICA

High Commission: Place de Ville, Tower B, 112 Kent St, Suite 1050, Ottawa K1P 5P2; tel (613) 236-8952; telex 053-4476; fax (613) 236-3042.
High Commissioner: Dr J. Bernard Yankey.

ECUADOR

Embassy: 50 O'Connor St, Suite 1311, Ottawa K1N 6L2; tel (613) 563-8206; fax (613) 235-5776.
Ambassador: Dr Alfonso Barrera.

EGYPT

Embassy: 454 Laurier Ave East, Ottawa K1N 6R3; tel (613) 234-4931; telex 053-3340; fax (613) 234-9347.
Ambassador: Mohamed Adel Elsafty.
Minister Plenipotentiary: Teymour Moustapha Sirry.
Counsellor/Consul: Abla Abdel-Rahman.
Third Secretary: Hesham Youssef.
Administrative Attaché: Eitedal Moussa.
Administrative Attaché: Dawlat Omran.
Administrative Attaché: Farouk Mostafa Montasser.
Administrative Attaché: Teymour Rostom Ahmed.

Press and Information Office: No. 905, 85 Range Rd, Ottawa K1N 8J6; tel (613) 563-1248.
Head of Press and Information Office: Ahmed Nasr Said.

Commercial Office: No. 207, 85 Range Rd, Ottawa K1N 8J6; tel (613) 238-6263; telex 053-4863; fax (613) 238-2578.
Head of Commercial Office: Abdel Moneim El-Erksousey.

Consulate-General: 3754 Côte des Neiges, Montréal H3H 1V6; tel (514) 937-7781; telex 524846; fax (514) 937-0588.
Consul-General: Sherif Sharara.

Egyptian Tourist Authority: Place Bonaventure, 40 Frontenac East, POB 304, Montréal H5A 1B4; tel (514) 861-4420; telex 055-62447; fax (514) 861-8071
Head of Tourist Authority: Ayden Noor.

Egyptian Commercial Affairs: POB 246, Floor F, 48 Frontenac, Place Bonaventure, Montréal H5A 1B2; tel (514) 861-6340.
Head of Commercial Affairs: Ezzat El-Kolaly.

International Civil Aviation Organization (ICAO): Suite 776, 1000 Sherbrooke St West, Montréal H3A 3G4; tel (514) 285-8219.

Egyptair Office: Suite 300, 151 Bloor St W, Toronto M5S 1S4; tel (416) 960-0009; telex 062-3604.
Head of Office: Ezzat El-Alayli.

ESTONIA

Consulate-General: 958 Broadview Ave, Toronto M4K 2R6; tel (416) 461-0764; fax (416) 461-0448.
Honorary Consul-General: Ilmar Heinsoo.

FIJI

Consulate: 130 Slater St, Suite 750, Ottawa K1P 6E2; tel (613) 233-9252; fax (613) 694-8705.
Consul: Dr D. Elaine Pressman.

Consulate: 1840 Clark Drive, Vancouver V5N 3G4; tel (604) 254-5544.
Consul: Raj Gopal Pillai.

FINLAND

Embassy: 55 Metcalfe St, Suite 850, Ottawa K1P 6L5; tel (613) 236-2389; telex 053-4462; fax (613) 238-1474.
Ambassador: Erkki Mäentakanen.

Consulate-General: 1200 Bay St, Suite 604, Toronto M5R 2A5; tel (416) 964-0066; telex 062-2513; fax (416) 964-1524.
Consul: Peter von der Pahlen.

Commercial Section: tel (416) 964-7400.
Consul and Senior Trade Commissioner: Olavi Pöllänen.
Consul and Industrial Attaché: Erkki Sirkkola.

Consulate-General: 1176 West Georgia St, Suite 1120, Vancouver V6E 4A2; tel (604) 688-4483; telex 045-5703; fax (604) 687-4888.
Honorary Consul-General: Keijo Seppälä.

Commercial Section of Vancouver Consulate-General: tel (604) 687-6366.
Consul and Trade Commissioner: Aarne T. Hildén.

Consulate: 900-350 7th Ave SW, Calgary T2P 3N9; tel (403) 260-1400; telex 038-22631; fax (403) 233-7151.
Honorary Consul: Judith M. Romanchuk.

Consulate: Westin Hotel, Lower Level, 10135 100th St, Edmonton T5J 0N7; tel (403) 426-7865; telex 037-2966; fax (403) 425-0329.
Honorary Consul: Christian Graefe.

Consulate: Halifax.

Consulate: 1 Place Ville Marie, Suite 3725, Montreal H3B 3P4; tel (514) 878-9641; telex 052-5610; fax (514) 878-1450.
Honorary Consul: John B. Claxton.

Consulate: Edifice Mérici, Bureau 200, 801 Chemin St-Louis, Québec G1S 1C1; tel (418) 683-3000; telex 051-3786; fax (418) 683-8784.
Honorary Consul: Henri Grondin.

Consulate: 700 Royal Bank Bldg, 2010 11th Ave, Regina S4P 0J3; tel (306) 757-1641; telex 071-2518; fax (306) 359-0785.
Honorary Consul: Gordon Joseph Kuski.

Consulate: 133 Prince William St, Saint John E2L 4G8; POB 7174, Postal Station A, Saint John E2L 4S6; tel (506) 634-7450; fax (506) 634-3612.
Honorary Consul: Thomas L. McGloan.

Consulate: 29 Pageant Drive, Sault Ste Marie P6B 5J7; tel (705) 942-6196.
Honorary Consul: Raimo Matias Viitala.

Consulate: 219 Pine St, Sudbury P3C 1X4; tel (705) 674-4289; fax (705) 671-1047.

Consulate: 76 Algoma St North, POB 2870, Thunder Bay P7B 5G3; tel (807) 344-9161; fax (807) 345-5348.
Honorary Consul: Seppo Kalevi Päiväläinen.

Consulate: 5 Birch St, Timmins P4N 6C8; tel (705) 264-7857; fax (705) 264-9977.
Consul: Margaret Kangas.

Consulate: 500-360 Main St, Winnipeg R3C 3Z4; tel (204) 942-7458; telex 075-7818; fax (204) 943-5448.
Honorary Consul: Robert Purves.

FRANCE

Embassy: 42 Sussex Drive, Ottawa K1M 2C9; tel (613) 232-1795; fax (613) 232-4302.
Ambassador: François Bujon de L'Estang.

Trade Promotion Office: 10 John St, Ottawa K1M 1P5; tel (613) 233-5681; telex 053-4410.

Consulate-General: 300 Highfield Place, 10010 106 St, Edmonton T5I 3L8; tel (403) 428-0235.

Consulate-General: 250 Lutz St, POB 1109, Moncton E1C 8P6; tel (506) 8574191.

Consulate-General: 2 Elysée, place Bonaventure, BP 202, Montréal H5A 1B1; tel (514) 878-4381; telex 052-4890.

Representation on Council of International Civil Aviation Organization: Suite 852, 1000 Sherbrooke St West, Montréal H3A 3G4; tel (514) 285-8269; telex 052-67578; fax (514) 284-3308.

Consulate-General: 1110 ave des Laurentides, Québec City G1S 3C3; tel (418) 668-0430.

Consulate-General: 130 Bloor St West, Suite 400, Toronto M5S 1N5; tel (416) 925-3076.

Consulate-General: 1201-736 Granville St, Vancouver V6Z 1H9; tel (604) 681-2301.

GABON

Embassy: 4 Range Rd, Ottawa K1M 8J5; tel (613) 232-5301; telex 053-4295; fax (613) 232-6916.
Ambassador: Simon Ombegue.

GERMANY

Embassy: 1 Waverley St, Ottawa K2P 0T8; POB 379, Postal Station A, Ottawa K1N 8V4; tel (613) 232-1101; telex 053-4226; fax (613) 594-9330.
Ambassador: Wolfgang Behrends.

Consulate-General: 1220 Manulife Pl., 10180 101 St, Edmonton T5J 3S4; POB 363, Edmonton T5J 2J6; tel (403) 422-6175; telex 037-3056; fax (403) 425-9768.
Consul-General: Dr Wolfgang Schanz.

Consulate-General: 3455 rue de la Montagne, Montréal H3G 2A3; tel (514) 286-1820; telex 052-4483; fax (514) 286-0175.
Consul-General: Dr Michael Schmidt.

Consulate-General: 77 Admiral Rd, Toronto M5R 2L4; POB 523, Postal Station P, Toronto M5S 2T1; tel (416) 925-2813; telex 062-2866; fax (416) 925-2818.
Consul-General: Dr Henning Leopold von Hassell.

Consulate-General: World Trade Centre, 999 Canada Pl., Suite 704, Vancouver V6C 3E1; tel (604) 684-8377; telex 450-7769; fax (604) 684-8334.
Consul-General: Siegfried Haller.

Consulate: 840 6th Ave SW, Suite 337-338, Calgary T2P 3E5; tel (403) 269-5900; telex 082-6703; fax (403) 265-3783.
Honorary Consul: Osmar Beltzner.

Consulate: Bank of Commerce Bldg, 1809 Barrington St, Suite 708, Halifax B3J 3K8; tel (902) 420-1599.
Honorary Consul: Dr Edgar Gold.

Consulate: 370 Frederick St, Kitchener N2H 2P3; tel (519) 576-8650.
Honorary Consul: Peter D. Kruse.

Consulate: 3534 Argyle Rd, Regina S4S 2B8; tel (306) 586-8762.
Honorary Consul: Dr Günter Kocks.

Consulate: 22 Poplar Ave, St John's A1C 6H5; tel (709) 753-7777.
Honorary Consul: Guenter K. Sann.

Consulate: 208-310 Donald St, Winnipeg R3B 2H4; POB 876, Winnipeg R3C 2S1; tel (204) 947-0958.
Honorary Consul: Gerhard Spindler.

GHANA

High Commission: 1 Clemow Ave, Ottawa K1S 2A9; tel (613) 236-0871; telex 053-4276; fax (613) 236-0874.
High Commissioner: Daniel O. Agyekum.

GREECE

Embassy: 80 MacLaren St, Ottawa K2P 0K6; tel (613) 2386271; telex 053-3852; fax (613) 238-6273.
Ambassador: Leonidas Mavro-Michalis.

GRENADA

High Commission: Place de Ville, Tower B, 112 Kent St, Suite 1050, Ottawa K1P 5P2; tel (613) 236-8952; telex 053-4476; fax (613) 236-3042.
High Commissioner: Dr J. Bernard Yankey.

Consulate-General: Phoenix House, 439 University Ave, Suite 830, Toronto M5G 1Y8; tel (416) 595-1343; telex 065-24033; fax (416) 595-8278.
Consul-General: Canute Burke.

GUATEMALA

Embassy: 294 Albert St, Suite 500, Ottawa K1P 6E6; tel (613) 237-3941; telex 053-3065; fax (613) 237-0492.
Ambassador: Federico Urruela-Prado.

GUINEA

Embassy: 483 Wilbrod St, Ottawa K1N 6N1; tel (613) 232-1133.
Ambassador: Thomas Curtis.

GUYANA

High Commission: 151 Slater St, Suite 309, Ottawa K1P 5H3; tel (613) 235-7249; telex 053-3684; fax (613) 235-1447.
High Commissioner: Hubert O. Jack.

HAITI

Embassy: Place de Ville, Tower B, 112 Kent St, Suite 1308, Ottawa K1P 5P2; tel (613) 238-1628; telex 053-3688; fax (613) 238-2986.
Chargé d'affaires a.i.: Jean Gateau.

HOLY SEE

Apostolic Nunciature: 724 Manor Ave, Rockcliffe Park, Ottawa K1M 0E3; tel (613) 746-4914; telex 053-3380; fax (613) 746-4786.
Apostolic Pro-Nuncio: Most Rev. Carlo Curis, Titular Archbishop of Medeli.
Counsellor: Rt. Rev. Dante Pasquinelli.

HONDURAS

Embassy: 151 Slater St, Suite 300A, Ottawa K1P 5H3; tel (613) 233-8900; telex 053-4528.
Ambassador: Juan Ramón Molina Cisneros.
Counsellor and Consul: Felipe S. Paredes.
Cultural Attaché: Nora Bueso.
Attaché: Mario Castejon.

Consulate: 1650 De-Maisonneuve West, Suite 306, Montréal H3H 2P3; tel (514) 937-1138.
Consul: Jenny Melgar de Schmidt.

Consulate: 222 The Esplanade, No. 820, Toronto M5H 1M8; tel (416) 867-9087.
Consul: Elia Maria Crespo.

Consulate: 1334 Marecha Foch, Québec City G1S 2C4; tel (418) 643-6912.
Consul: Thérèse Lacroix.

Consulate: POB 3654, Vancouver V6B 3Y8; tel (604) 685-7711.
Consul: Enrique González Calvo.

HUNGARY

Embassy: 7 Delaware Ave, Ottawa K2P 0Z2; tel (613) 232-1711; telex 053-3251; fax (613) 232-5620.
Ambassador: Dr Kálmán Kulcsár.

Consulate: Vancouver.
Honorary Consul: András Molnár.

ICELAND

Consulate-General: 116 Lisgar St, Suite 700, Ottawa K2P 0C2; tel (613) 238-1744; fax (613) 238-1441.
Consul-General: M. Ellen Lahey.
Vice-Consul: Roderick Ian Lahey.

Consulate: 140 Strathaven Circle SW, Apt 20, Calgary T3H 2N5; tel (403) 220-7555.
Consul: Clifford A. Marteinsson.

Consulate: 14434 McQueen Rd, Edmonton T5N 3L6; tel (403) 455-7946.
Consul: Guđmundur A. Arnason.

Consulate: Dover Mills Ltd, Terminal Rd, POB 2185, Halifax B3J 3C4; tel (902) 429-0622; telex 019-21506; fax (902) 423-9075.
Consul: Lawrence John Cooke.

Consulate: 21 Military Rd, St John's A1C 2C5; tel (709) 754-2292.
Consul: Avalon M. Goodridge.

Consulate-General: Montréal.

Consulate: 20 Queen St West, Suite 3000, POB 30, Toronto M5H 1V5; tel (416) 979-6740; fax (416) 979-1234.
Consul: Jón Ragnar Johnson.

Consulate: 4709 Paton St, Vancouver V6Z 2H9; tel (604) 261-0973.
Consul: Harold S. Sigurdsson.

Consulate-General: 200 Augusta Drive, Winnipeg R3T 4G5; tel (204) 275-0878; telex 075-87559; fax (204) 947-3789.
Consul: Birgir Brynjólfsson.

INDIA

High Commission: 10 Springfield Rd, Ottawa K1M 1C9; tel (613) 744-3751; telex 053-4172; fax (613) 744-0913.
High Commissioner: Surbir Jit Singh Chhatwal.

INDONESIA

Embassy: 287 MacLaren St, Ottawa K2P 0L9; tel (613) 236-7403; telex 053-3119; fax (613) 563-2858.

Consulate: 425 University Ave, 9th Floor, Toronto M5G 1T6.

Consulate: 1455 West Georgia St, 2nd Floor, Vancouver V6G 2T3.

IRAN

Embassy: 245 Metcalfe St, Ottawa K2P 2K2; tel (613) 235-4726; telex 053-4229; fax (613) 232-5712.
Ambassador: Mohammad Hossein Lavassani.
First Secretary: Alireza Shirmohammadi.
First Secretary: Kourosh Ahmadi.
Attaché: Mohammad Javad Rezayat.

IRAQ

Embassy: 215 McLeod St, Ottawa K2P 0Z8; tel (613) 236-9177; telex 053-4310; fax (613) 567-1101.
Ambassador: Hisham al-Shawi.

IRELAND

Embassy: 170 Metcalfe St, Ottawa K2P 1P3; tel (613) 233-6281; telex 053-4240; fax (613) 233-5835.
Ambassador: Declan M. Kelly.
First Secretary: Tom Brady.

ISRAEL

Embassy: 410 Laurier Ave West, Suite 601, Ottawa K1R 7T3; tel (613) 237-6450; telex 053-4858; fax (613) 237-8865.
Ambassador: Israel Gur-Arieh.

ITALY

Embassy: 275 Slater St, 21st Floor, Ottawa K1P 5H9; tel (613) 232-2401; telex 053-3278; fax (613) 233-1484.
Ambassador: Sergio Silvio Balanzino.

JAMAICA

High Commission: 275 Slater St, Suite 402, Ottawa K1P 5H9; tel (613) 233-9311; telex 053-3287; fax (613) 233-0611.
High Commissioner: H. Dale Anderson.
Deputy High Commissioner: Norma Taylor-Roberts.

Consulate-General: 214 King St West, Suite 216, Toronto M5H 1K4; tel (416) 598-3008; telex 062-19738.
Vice-Consul: Ray Baxter.

Consulate: 36 Windermere Crescent, St Albert T8N 3S5; tel (403) 429-3019.
Honorary Consul: H. M. Booth.

Consulate: 11 Wadham Way, Winnipeg P3T 3K2; tel (204) 269-0094.
Honorary Consul: Prof. Donald Keith Gordon.

JAPAN

Embassy: 255 Sussex Drive, Ottawa K1N 9E6; tel (613) 236-8541; telex 053-4220; fax (613) 563-9047.
Ambassador: Hiroshi Kitamura.

Consulate-General: 900 Board of Trade Tower, 1177 West Hastings St, Vancouver V6E 2K9; tel (604) 684-5868; telex 045-1402; fax (604) 684-6939.
Consul-General: Shigenobu Yoshida.

Consulate-General: 730-215 Garry St, Credit Union Central Plaza, Winnipeg R3C 3P3; tel (204) 943-5554; telex 075-7533; fax (204) 957-0374.
Consul-General: Yuzuki Kaku.

Consulate-General: 2480 ManuLife Place, 10180 101st St, Edmonton T5J 3S4; tel (403) 422-3752; telex 037-3404; fax (403) 424-1635.
Consul-General: Tetsuo Nonogaki.

Consulate-General: Toronto Dominion Centre, Suite 2702, POB 10, Toronto M5K 1A1; tel (416) 363-7038; telex 065-24187; fax (416) 367-9392.
Consul-General: Tadashi Masui.

Consulate-General: 600 rue de la Gauchetièrée Ouest, Suite 1785, Montréal H3B 4L8; tel (514) 866-3429; telex 052-5376; fax (514) 395-6000.
Consul-General: Masahiko Iwasaki.

JORDAN

Embassy: 100 Bronson Ave, Suite 701, Ottawa K1N 6R4; tel (613) 238-8090; telex 053-4538.
Ambassador: Hani Khalifeh.

KENYA

High Commission: 415 Laurier Ave East, Ottawa K1P 6R4; tel (613) 563-1773; telex 053-4873; fax (613) 233-6599.
High Commissioner: Peter M. Nyamweya.

KOREA, REPUBLIC

Embassy: 151 Slater St, 5th Floor, Ottawa K1P 5H3; tel (613) 232-1715; fax (613) 232-0928.
Ambassador: Soo Gil Park.

LEBANON

Embassy: 640 Lyon St, Ottawa K1S 3Z5; tel (613) 236-5825; telex 053-3571; fax (613) 232-1609.
Ambassador: Dr Assem Salman Jaber.
Counsellor: Gilbert Ghazi.
First Secretary: Michel Haddad.

Consulate-General: 40 Côte Ste Catherine, Montréal H2V 2A2; tel (514) 276-2638; telex 055-61105; fax (514) 276-0090.
Consul-General: Elyse Alam.

LESOTHO

High Commission: 202 Clemow Ave, Ottawa K1S 2B4; tel (613) 236-9449; telex 053-4563.
High Commissioner: Raphael Ramaliehe Kali.

MALAWI

High Commission: 7 Clemow Ave, Ottawa K1S 2A9; tel (613) 236-8931; telex 053-3365; fax (613) 236-1054.
High Commissioner: M. W. Machinjili.

MALAYSIA

High Commission: 60 Boteler St, Ottawa K1N 8Y7; tel (613) 237-5182; telex 053-3064; fax (613) 237-4852.
High Commissioner: Tan Sri Datuk Thomas Jayasuria.

MALI

Embassy: 50 Goulburn Ave, Ottawa K1N 8C8; tel (613) 232-1501; telex 053-3361; fax (613) 232-7429.
Ambassador: Ousmane Dembele.
First Counsellor: Moussa Diakite.
First Secretary: Aliou N'Diaye.

Consulate: 1770 blvd René-Levesque Ouest, No. 1001, Montréal H3H 2S9; tel (514) 939-1267; fax (514) 939-1296.
Honorary Consul: Paul Fortin.

Consulate: 1 St John's Rd, Toronto M6P 4C7; tel (416) 766-8957.
Honorary Consul: Paul J. Tuz.

MALTA

Commercial Office: 1 St John's Rd, Suite 305, Toronto M6P 4C7; tel (416) 767-2901; telex 06-984767; fax (416) 767-0563.
Commercial Counsellor and Honorary Consul-General: Milo Vassallo.

Consulate-General: POB 186, Station C, Crosbie Bldg, Crosbie Rd, St John's A1C 5J2; tel (709) 722-2744; telex 016-3333; fax (709) 739-7352.
Honorary Consul-General: Charles Puglisevich.

Consulate: 3461 Northcliffe, Montréal H4A 3K8; tel (514) 284-3627; fax (514) 284-1860.
Honorary Consul: Edward G. Abela.

MEXICO

Embassy: 130 Albert St, Suite 1800, Ottawa K1P 5G4; tel (613) 233-8988; telex 053-4520.
Ambassador: Alfredo Phillips O.

MOROCCO

Embassy: 38 Range Rd, Ottawa K1N 8J4; tel (613) 236-7391; telex 053-3683; fax (613) 236-6164.
Ambassador: Maati Jorio.

MYANMAR

Embassy: 85 Range Rd, Suite 902, Ottawa K1N 8J6; tel (613) 232-6434; telex 053-3334; fax (613) 232-6435.
Chargé d'affaires a.i.: U Hla Pe Than.

NETHERLANDS

Embassy: 275 Slater St, 3rd Floor, Ottawa K1P 5H9; tel (613) 237-5030; telex 053-3109; fax (613) 237-6471.
Ambassador: J. F. E. Breman.

NEW ZEALAND

High Commission: Metropolitan House, 99 Bank St, Suite 801, Ottawa K1P 6G3; tel (613) 238-5991; telex 053-4282; fax (613) 238-5707.
High Commissioner: Bruce Brown.
Deputy High Commissioner: Sarah Dennis.
Second Secretary: Pam Wilkinson.
Second Secretary: Rosemary Lawrence.
Defence Adviser: Col I. J. Duthie.

Consulate: 60 Bloor St West, Suite 1002, Toronto M4W 3B8; tel (416) 975-0544; fax (416) 975-0571.
Consul and Trade Commissioner: Kathe Huse.

Consulate: 701 West Georgia St, Suite 1260, IBM Tower, POB 10071, Pacific Centre, Vancouver V7Y 1B6; tel (604) 684-7388; telex 045-5186; fax (604) 684-1265.
Consul and Trade Commissioner: Paul Voigt.
Trade Commissioner: Vicki Wogan.
Regional Tourism Director: Barry Eddington.

NICARAGUA

Embassy: 170 Laurier Ave West, Suite 908, Ottawa K1P 5V5; tel (613) 234-9361; telex 053-4338; fax (613) 238-7666.
Ambassador: René Sandino.
Counsellor (Political): Susan Grigsby.
Counsellor (Commercial): Mayra Zeledon-Neal.
First Secretary (Consular): Maria Matilde Robelo.

NIGER

Embassy: 38 Blackburn Ave, Ottawa K1N 8A2; tel (613) 232-4291; telex 053-3757; fax (613) 230-9808.
Ambassador: Abdubacar Abdou.

NIGERIA

High Commission: 295 Metcalfe St, Ottawa K2P 1R9; tel (613) 236-0521; telex 053-3285; fax (613) 236-0529.
High Commissioner: G. O. George.

NORWAY

Embassy: Royal Bank Centre, 90 Sparks St, Suite 532, Ottawa K1P 5B4; tel (613) 238-6570; telex 053-4239; fax (613) 238-2765.
Ambassador: Jan E. Nyheim.

Trade Commission: 1200 Bay St, Suite 702, Toronto M5R 2A5; tel (416) 920-0434; telex 062-3492; fax (416) 920-5982.

Consulate-General: 1 place Ville Marie, Suite 3825, Montréal H2Y 2G3; tel (514) 874-9087; telex 06-1916; fax (514) 875-9000.

Consulate-General: Suite 1800, Pacific Centre South, 700 West St, Vancouver V6C 2G8; fax (604) 682-8376.

PAKISTAN

High Commission: 151 Slater St, Suite 608, Ottawa K1P 5H3; tel (613) 238-7881; telex 053-4428; fax (613) 238-7296.
High Commissioner: S. M. A. Khairi.

PERU

Embassy: 170 Laurier Ave West, Suite 1007, Ottawa K1P 5V5; tel (613) 238-1777; telex 053-3754; fax (613) 232-3062.
Ambassador: Jorge Gordillo.

PHILIPPINES

Embassy: 130 Albert St, Suite 606, Ottawa K1P 5G4; tel (613) 233-1121; telex 053-4537; fax (613) 233-4165.
Ambassador: Ramón A. Diaz.
Minister-Counsellor: Marcellama G. Desales.
Second Secretary and Consul: Leoncio R. Cardenas.
Third Secretary and Vice-Consul: Rosendo Villamayor.
Attaché: Josefina A. Villamayor.
Attaché: Maria B. Paraiso.
Attaché: Asunción C. Fuentes.
Attaché: Edna L. Pataunia.
Attaché: Bayani G. Sibug.

Consulate-General: 151 Bloor St, Suite 365, Toronto M5S 1S4; tel (416) 922-7181.
Consul-General: Hermenegildo B. Garcia.

Consulate-General: 301-308 Roger's Bldg, 470 Granville St, Vancouver V6C 1V5; tel (604) 685-7645.
Consul-General: Eufronia M. Recaido.

POLAND

Embassy: 443 Daly Ave, Ottawa K1N 6H3; tel (613) 236-0468; telex 053-3133; fax (613) 232-3463.
Ambassador: Alojzy Bartoszek.

PORTUGAL

Embassy: 645 Island Park Drive, Ottawa K1Y 0B8; tel (613) 729-0883; telex 053-3756.
Ambassador: João Uva de Matos Proença.

ROMANIA

Embassy: 655 Rideau St, Ottawa K1N 6A3; tel (613) 232-5345; telex 053-3101.
Ambassador: Dr Emilian Rodean.

RUSSIA

Embassy: 285 Charlotte St, Ottawa K1N 8L5; tel (613) 235-4341; telex 053-3332; fax (613) 236-6342.
Ambassador: Richard S. Ovinnikov.
Minister-Counsellor: Vassili D. Sredin.
Military, Naval and Air Attaché: Col Valeri I. Romanenko.

Press Office: 400 Stewart St, Suite 1108-1110, Ottawa K1N 6L1; tel (613) 236-7228; fax (613) 231-3921.
Counsellor (Press and Information): Igor V. Lobanov.

Consular Section: 52 Range Rd, Ottawa K1N 8J5; tel (613) 236-6215.
Counsellor (Consular): Gennadi N. Tchebotarenko.

Trade Mission: 95 Wurtemburg St, Ottawa K1N 8Z7; tel (613) 236-1222; fax (613) 238-2951.
Counsellor (Commercial): Vladimir P. Pletnev.

Consulate-General: 3655 ave du Musée, Montréal H3G 3E1; tel (514) 842-5343; fax (514) 842-2012.
Consul-General: Evgeni Kochetkov.

RWANDA

Embassy: 121 Sherwood Drive, Ottawa K1Y 3V1; tel (613) 722-5835; telex 053-4522; fax (613) 729-3291.
Ambassador: Dr Maximin Segasayo.
First Counsellor: Faustin Kanyamibwa.
Embassy Secretary: Juvénal Kambanda.

Consulate-General: 1600 rue De Lorimier, Montréal H2K 3W5; tel (514) 526-1392; fax (514) 521-7081.
Consul-General: Pierre Valcourt.

Consulate: 200 Consumers, Suite 500, Willowdale M2J 4R4; tel (416) 493-5474; fax (416) 493-5824.
Consul: Ronald Heynneman.

SAINT CHRISTOPHER AND NEVIS

High Commission: Place de Ville, Tower B, 112 Kent St, Suite 1050, Ottawa K1P 5P2; tel (613) 236-8952; telex 053-4476; fax (613) 236-3042.
High Commissioner: Dr J. Bernard Yankey.

SAINT LUCIA

High Commission: Place de Ville, Tower B, 112 Kent St, Suite 1050, Ottawa K1P 5P2; tel (613) 236-8952; telex 053-4476; fax (613) 236-3042.
High Commissioner: Dr J. Bernard Yankey.

SAINT VINCENT AND THE GRENADINES

High Commission: Place de Ville, Tower B, 112 Kent St, Suite 1050, Ottawa K1P 5P2; tel (613) 236-8952; telex 053-4476; fax (613) 236-3042.
High Commissioner: Dr J. Bernard Yankey.

SAN MARINO

Consulate-General: 615 blvd Dorchester Ouest, Suite 1010, Montréal H3B 1P9; tel (514) 871-3838; telex 24456; fax (514) 876-4217.
Consul-General: Raymond Lette.

Consulate: 15 McMurrich St, Suite 1104, Toronto M5R 3M6; tel (416) 925-7777.
Consul: Germano Valle.
Vice-Consul: Bernard Lette.

SAUDI ARABIA

Embassy: 99 Bank St, Suite 901, Ottawa K1P 6B9; tel (613) 237-4100; telex 053-4285; fax (613) 237-0567.
Chargé d'affaires a.i.: Redha M. A. Mokhtar.

SENEGAL

Embassy: 57 Marlborough Ave, Ottawa K1N 8E8; tel (613) 238-6392; telex 053-4531.

SOMALIA

Embassy: 130 Slater St, Suite 1000, Ottawa K1P 6E2; tel (613) 563-4541; telex 053-4739.
Ambassador: Abdikarim Ali Omar.

SOUTH AFRICA

Embassy: 15 Sussex Drive, Ottawa K1M 1M8; tel (613) 744-0330; telex 053-4185; fax (613) 741-1639.
Ambassador: Johannes Hendrik de Klerk.
Counsellor: Gerrit Pretorius.
Second Secretary: Robert D. Stone.
Second Secretary (Administration): T. E. Matthysen.
Third Secretary: Erney Breytenbach.
Third Secretary: Ilse E. Scholtz.

Consulate: 1 Place Ville Marie, Suite 2615, Montréal H3B 4S3; tel (514) 878-9217; telex 055-61745; fax (514) 878-3973.
Consul: Jacques de Villiers.

Consulate: Stock Exchange Tower, Suite 2515, 2 First Canadian Place, cnr York and King St West, POB 424, Toronto M5X 1E3; tel (416) 364-0314; telex 062-3733; fax (416) 363-8974.
Consul: Johan B. van Rooyen.
Consul (Trade): A. J. van Zyl.

SPAIN

Embassy: 350 Sparks St, Suite 802, Ottawa K1R 7S8; tel (613) 237-2193; telex 053-4510.
Ambassador: Antonio José Fournier.

SRI LANKA

High Commission: 85 Range Rd, Suites 102-104, Ottawa K1N 8J6; tel (613) 233-8449; telex 053-3668; fax (613) 238-8448.
High Commissioner: Walter G. Rupesinghe.

SUDAN

Embassy: 457 Laurier Ave East, Ottawa K1N 6R4; tel (613) 235-4000.
Ambassador: Nuri Khalil Siddiq.

SWEDEN

Embassy: Mercury Court, 377 Dalhousie St, Ottawa K1N 9N8; tel (613) 236-8553; telex 053-3331; fax (613) 236-5720.
Ambassador: Håkan Berggren.
Counsellor: Lennart Linnér.
Counsellor: Gunn Axelsson.
Press Attaché: Claes Jernaeus.
Chancellor: Katarina de la Rocq.
Defence Attaché: Lieut Col Nils Alstermark.
Defence Attaché: Commdr Nils Bruzelius.
Agricultural Counsellor: Anders Lundin.
Attaché (Working Conditions): Eric Jannerfeldt.

Consulate-General: 1155 blvd René Lévesque Ouest, Suite 800, Montréal H3B 2H7; tel (514) 866-4019; telex 055-60751; fax (514) 393-3432.
Consul-General: Karin Ahrland.

Consulate-General: 1 Queen St East, Suite 2010, POB 85, Toronto M5C 2W5; tel (416) 367-8768; telex 06-218131; fax (416) 367-8809.
Consul-General: Mats Marling.
Chancellor: Lisbet Margareta Fabricius Jakobsen.
Commercial Secretary: Staffan Englund.

Consulate-General: 1177 West Hastings St, Suite 1106, Vancouver V6E 2K3; tel (604) 683-5838; telex 045-1451; fax (604) 687-8237.
Honorary Consul-General: Magnus Ericson.

Consulate: 420 47th Ave SW, Calgary T2S 1C4; tel (403) 243-1093; telex 038-21172; fax (403) 237-0201.
Honorary Consul: Armilda Anne Zoumer.

Consulate: 11523-100 Ave, Suite 305, Edmonton T5K 0J8; tel (403) 482-2561.
Honorary Consul: Lars Göran Fahlström.

Consulate: 11 Briar Place, Clayton Park, Halifax B3M 2X3; tel (902) 443-6888; fax (902) 443-6868.
Honorary Consul: Gunnar Knut Gustaf Jennegren.

Consulate: c/o Le Soleil, 390 St-Vallier Est, Québec G1K 7J6; tel (418) 647-3352; telex 051-3755; fax (418) 647-3434.
Honorary Consul: Robert Normand.

Consulate: c/o Furncan Marine Ltd, 560 Main St, Bldg A, Hilyard Place, POB 6340, Station A, Saint John E2L 3Z5; tel (506) 632-1090; telex 014-47212; fax (506) 636-8924.
Honorary Consul: Gerard Andrew McGillivray.

Consulate: Harvey & Co Ltd, Kenmount Rd, POB 8220, Station A, St John's A1B 3N6; tel (709) 722-6910; fax (709) 739-0924.
Honorary Consul: Peter Norman Outerbridge.

Consulate: c/o Robertson Stromberg, 700-1867 Hamilton St, Regina S4P 2C2; tel (306) 359-1733; fax (306) 757-6443.
Honorary Consul: Dale Robert Doan.

Consulate: c/o Robertson Stromberg, 700-122 First Ave South, Saskatoon S7K 7E5; tel (306) 652-7575; fax (306) 652-2445.
Honorary Consul: Dale Robert Doan.

Consulate: 1035 Mission St, Winnipeg R2J 0A4; tel (204) 233-0671; fax (204) 233-6938.
Honorary Consul: Neil Edwin Carlson.

SWITZERLAND

Embassy: 5 Marlborough Ave, Ottawa K1N 8E6; tel (613) 235-0958; telex 053-3648; fax (613) 563-1394.
Counsellor: Thomas Feller.
Attaché and Head of Chancery: Urs Müller.

Consulate-General: 1572 Ave Dr Penfield, Montréal H3G 1C4; tel (514) 932-7005; telex 055-60026; fax (514) 932-9028.
Consul-General: Hermann Buff.
Consul: Charly Teuscher.
Vice-Consul and Chancellor: Hans Wirz.

Consulate-General: 154 University Ave, Suite 601, Toronto M5H 3Y9; tel (416) 593-5371; telex 065-24624; fax (416) 593-5083.
Consul-General: Ernst Keller.
Chancellor: Evelyne Stampfli.

Consulate-General: World Trade Centre, 999 Canada Place, Suite 790, Vancouver V6C 3E1; tel (604) 684-2231; telex 045-1184; fax (604) 684-2806.
Consul-General: Max Inhelder.
Consul and Chancellor: Kurt Mägli.

TANZANIA

High Commission: 50 Range Rd, Ottawa K1N 8J4; tel (613) 232-1509; telex 053-3569.
High Commissioner: Dr P. K. Palangyo.

THAILAND

Embassy: 180 Island Park Drive, Ottawa K1Y 0A2; tel (613) 722-4444; telex 053-3975; fax (613) 722-6624.
Ambassador: Chawat Arthayukti.

Office of Commercial Counsellor: 396 Cooper St, Suite 310, Ottawa K2P 2H7; tel (613) 238-4002; telex 053-4883; fax (613) 238-6226.

TOGO

Embassy: 12 Range Rd, Ottawa K1N 8J3; tel (613) 238-5916; telex 053-4564; fax (613) 235-6425.
Ambassador: Kossivi Osseyi.
First Counsellor (Economic and Cultural): Folly-Glidjito Akakpo.
First Secretary (Information and Cultural): Nyatéfé K. Sokpor.
Attaché (Consular): Tondoma Lalle.
Attaché (Finances): Kouassi W. Salakor.
Attaché: Afua Wolou.

Consulate: 1207 11th Ave SW, Calgary T3C 0M5; tel (403) 229-0103.
Consul: Garry Tarrant.

Consulate: 484 5th Ave, Verdun, Montreal H4C 2K1; tel (514) 769-4888.
Consul: Gérard Shanks.

Consulate: 1 St John's Rd, Suite 403, Toronto M6P 4C7; tel (416) 766-5744.
Consul: Paul Tuz.

TRINIDAD AND TOBAGO

High Commission: 75 Albert St, Suite 508, Ottawa K1P 5E7; tel (613) 232-2418; telex 053-4343; fax (613) 232-4349.
High Commissioner: Laila Valere.

Consulate-General: 2005 Sheppard Ave East, Suite 303, Willowsdale, Toronto M2J 5B4; tel (416) 495-9442; telex 218199; fax (416) 495-6934.
Consul-General: Dean Aziz.

Consulate: 252 Rochester Ave, Winnipeg R3T 3W2; tel (204) 269-5169.
Honorary Consul: Harridial Siew Maharaj.

TUNISIA

Embassy: 515 O'Connor St, Ottawa K1S 3P8; tel (613) 237-0330; telex 053-4161; fax (613) 237-7939.
Ambassador: Sadok Bouzayen.

TURKEY

Embassy: 197 Wurtemburg St, Ottawa K1N 8L9; tel (613) 232-1577; telex 053-3716; fax (613) 232-5498.
Ambassador: Ali Tuygan.

UGANDA

High Commission: 231 Cobourg St, Ottawa K1N 8J2; tel (613) 233-7797; telex 053-4469; fax (613) 232-6689.
High Commissioner: Joseph Tomusange.
First Secretary: Charles W. G. Wagaba.
Second Secretary: Florence Bakulumpagi-Wamala.
Attaché: Regina Muwanga.

UNITED KINGDOM

High Commission: 80 Elgin St, Ottawa K1P 5K7; tel (613) 237-1530; telex 053-3318; fax (613) 237-7980.
High Commissioner: Frederick Eaton.
Deputy High Commissioner: P. M. Newton.
Counsellor (Economic and Commercial): R. J. Fell.
Counsellor (Cultural Affairs/British Council Director): M. A. Evans.
Counsellor: M. G. B. Greig.
Defence and Military Adviser: Brig. T. D. V. Bevan.
Naval Adviser: Capt. P. J. Bootherstone.
Air Adviser: Group Capt. J. R. Legh-Smith.
First Secretary: D. Scrafton.
First Secretary: N. A. Penrhys-Evans.
First Secretary (Management and Consular): R. V. Welborn.

First Secretary: A. Jordan.
First Secretary (Economic and Commercial): I. D. Kydd.
Assistant Military Adviser (Technical): Lieut Col C. E. E. Sloan.
Assistant Defence Adviser: Maj. B. R. Lawson.
Head of Secretariat: Sqn Ldr G. A. Clyde.
Head of Secretariat: Lieut Commdr A. Menzies.
Second Secretary (Chancery/Information): A. P. Penrith.
Third Secretary (Political): P. A. Hadley.

Consulate: Suite 1501, Purdy's Wharf Bldg, 1959 Upper Water St, Halifax B3J 2X1; POB 310, Halifax; tel (902) 429-4230; telex 019-21587; fax (902) 423-8548.
Honorary Consul: L. Straughan.

Consulate: 34 Glencoe Drive, POB 8833, St John's; tel (709) 364-1200; telex 016-4596; fax (709) 364-3550.
Honorary Consul: F. D. Smith.

Consulate-General: Suite 1404, 10025 Jasper Ave, Edmonton T5J 1S6; tel (403) 428-0375; telex 037-2421; fax (403) 426-0624.
Consul-General: P. Johnstone.

Consulate: 111 Aldershot Bldg, Winnipeg R3P 0E2; tel (204) 896-1380; fax (204) 774-4053.
Honorary Consul: J. R. Hignell.

Consulate-General: Suite 901, 1155 University St, Montréal H3B 1R6; tel (514) 866-5863; telex 055-61224; fax (514) 866-0202.
Consul-General: A. R. Clark.
Consul (Commercial): D. Herbert.

Consulate-General: Suite 1910, College Park, 777 Bay St, Toronto M5G 2G2; tel (416) 593-1290; telex 065-24486; fax (416) 593-1229.
Consul-General and Director-General of Trade Promotion in Canada: P. D. R. Davies.
Deputy Consul-General: P. J. Smith.
Vice-Consul (Commercial): F. J. Marshall.
Vice-Consul (Commercial, Consular and Management): M. J. Dwyer.

Consulate-General: Suite 800, 1111 Melville St, Vancouver V6E 3V6; tel (604) 683-4421; telex 045-1287; fax (604) 681-0693.
Consul-General: A. A. Joy.
Consul (Commercial): C. R. Boardman.

Representation on Council of the International Civil Aviation Organization: Suite 928, 1000 Sherbrooke St W, Montréal H3A 3G4; tel (514) 285-8302; telex 055-61404; fax (514) 285-8001.
Representative: F. A. Neal.
Alternate Representative: V. Singh.

USA

Embassy: 100 Wellington St, Ottawa K1P 5T1; tel (613) 238-5335; telex 053-3582; fax (613) 233-8511.
Ambassador: Edward N. Ney.
Deputy Chief of Mission: John Todd Stewart.
Political Section: Stephen W. Buck.
Economic Section: Lawrence P. Taylor.
Commercial Section: George Mu.
Consul: Leonard F. Willems.
Administrative Section: A. Lucille Thomas.
Regional Security Officer: Steven L. Cox.
Public Affairs Officer: Dell F. Pendergrast.
Communications Programme Officer: Christopher B. Barrett.
Scientific Attaché: Thomas J. Walda.
Office of the Defence Attaché: Col George Manolis.
Agricultural Section: Bryant H. Wadsworth.
Labour Officer: Arlen R. Wilson.
Customs Service: William Laverty.
Internal Revenue Service: Joe D. Hook.

Consulate-General: Suite 1050, 615 Macleod Trail, SE, Calgary T2G 4T8; tel (403) 265-2116; fax (403) 264-6630.
Consul-General: William N. Witting.
Economic Section: Patricia Foran.
Administrative Section: Cecile Shea.

Consulate-General: Suite 910, Cogswell Tower, Scotia Sq., Halifax B3J 3K1; tel (902) 429-2480; fax (902) 423-6861.
Consul-General: George C. Lannon.

Consulate-General: BP 65, Postal Station Desjardins, Montréal H5B 1G1; tel (514) 398-9695; fax (514) 398-0973.
Consul-General: Andrew F. Antippas.
Economic Section: John P. Riley.
Commercial Section: Geoffrey Walser.
Administrative Section: Melvin T. Spence.
Branch Public Affairs Officer: Veda Wilson.
Communications Programme Officer: James E. Balsitis.

Consulate-General: 2 place Terrasse Dufferin, CP 939, Québec City G1R 4T9; tel (418) 692-2095; fax (418) 692-4640.
Consul-General: William C. McCahill, Jr.

Consulate-General: 360 University Ave, Toronto M5G 1S4; tel (416) 595-1700; fax (416) 595-0051.
Consul-General: Michael L. Durkee.
Economic Section: Leonard A. Hill.
Commercial Section: Dale V. Slaght.
Administrative Section: Daniel Santos, Jr.
Communications Programme Officer: Marvin C. Hardebeck.
Branch Public Affairs Officer: John Quintus.

Consulate-General: 1075 West Georgia St, Vancouver V6E 4E9; tel (604) 685-4311; fax (604) 685-5285.
Consul-General: David T. Johnson.
Economic Section: Jack P. Orlando.
Commercial Section: Stephan Wasylko.
Branch Public Affairs Officer: Michael Betcher.

International Civil Aviation Organization (ICAO): 1000 Sherbrooke St, W, Suite 753, Montréal H3A 3G4; tel (514) 285-8304; fax (514) 285-8021.
Representative: Don M. Newman.
Alternate Representative: Robert D. Cook.
Alternate Finance Committee and Joint Support Committee Representative: David L. Schiele.

URUGUAY

Embassy: 130 Albert St, Suite 1905, Ottawa K1P 5G4; tel (613) 234-2727.
Chargé d'affaires a.i.: Dr Zulma Guelmán.

VENEZUELA

Embassy: 32 Range Rd, Ottawa K1N 8J4; tel (613) 235-5151; telex 053-4729; fax (613) 235-3205.
Ambassador: Santiago Ochoa Antich.
Counsellor: Rosa Esther Lisboa.
Second Attaché: Nelson González C.
Third Attaché: Beatriz Arias.
Third Attaché: Sergio Ramírez Osio.
Third Attaché: Teresa Requena.

Consulate-General: 2055 Peel St, Suite 400, Montréal H3A 1V4; tel (514) 842-3417; telex 052-67523; fax (514) 287-7101.
Consul-General: Francisco Iturbe R.
Consul: Elena Czisky de R.
Consul: Pablo Gaudnik.
Consul: Judith Parada de C.
Consul: Alejandro Kaufman.

Consulate-General: 2 Carlton St, Suite 703, Toronto M5B 1J3; tel (416) 977-6809; telex 065-24519; fax (416) 977-6811.
Consul-General: Manuel Angarita Soules.

International Civil Aviation Organization (ICAO): Suite 826, 1000 Sherbrooke St W, Montréal H3A 3G4; tel (514) 285-8362; telex 055-61912; fax (514) 285-1032.
Representative: Luisa Elena Vera Barrios.
Counsellor: Miguel Manrique.
Second Secretary: Manuel Rodríguez M.

YUGOSLAVIA

Embassy: 17 Blackburn Ave, Ottawa K1N 8A2; tel (613) 233-6289; telex 053-4203; fax (613) 233-7850.
Ambassador: Goran Kapetanović.

ZAIRE

Embassy: 18 Range Rd, Ottawa K1N 8J3; tel (613) 236-7103; telex 053-4314.
Ambassador: K. Bukasa-Muteba.

ZAMBIA

High Commission: 130 Albert St, Suite 1610, Ottawa K1P 5G4; tel (613) 563-0712; telex 053-4418; fax (613) 235-0430.
High Commissioner: Kebby S. K. Musokotwane.

ZIMBABWE

High Commission: 332 Somerset St West, Ottawa K2P 0J9; tel (613) 237-4388; telex 053-4221; fax (613) 563-8269.
High Commissioner: Munyaradzi S. Kajese.
Counsellor: Pavelyn Tendai Musaka.
Counsellor (Education): Solomon Mhlanga.
First Secretary (Press and Information): Albert Mombeshora.
First Secretary (Political and Economic): E. P. Chiutsi.
First Secretary (Commercial): W. Dumba.
Second Secretary: E. H. Chikwanha.
Third Secretary: Edward Madziire.
Third Secretary: Lorraine Ncube.
Third Secretary: Maryline Mutepfa.

International Organizations

EUROPEAN COMMUNITIES

External Delegation: Office Tower, Suite 1110, 350 Sparks St, Ottawa K1R 7S8; tel (613) 238-6464; telex 053-4544; fax (613) 238-5191.
Head of Delegation: Jacques Lecomte.
First Secretary: Pedro Martínez.
Administrative Attaché: Stephen Andrews.
Press and Information: Roy Christensen.

CAPE VERDE

BRAZIL

Embassy: Rua Guerra Menoes, CP 93, Praia, São Tiago; tel 61-13-85; telex 6075.
Ambassador: Fernando Buarque Franco Nette.

CHINA, PEOPLE'S REPUBLIC

Embassy: Praia, São Tiago.

CUBA

Embassy: Público CV, Praia, São Tiago; tel 61-14-65; telex 6087.
Ambassador: Gilberto García Alonso.

DENMARK

Consulate: CP 12, Mindelo, São Vicente; tel 31-51-50; telex 3049.
Consul: Argo André Rocheteau.

FRANCE

Embassy: Quartier Prainha, CP 192, Praia, São Tiago; tel 61-16-93; telex 6064.
Ambassador: Claude Thullier.

GERMANY

Consulate: Largo 5 de Outubro, Praia, São Tiago; tel 61-15-19; telex 6039; fax 61-24-66.
Honorary Consul: Aquilino de Azevedo Camacho.

PORTUGAL

Embassy: Achada de Santo António, CP 160, Praia, São Tiago; tel 61-37-09; telex 6055; fax 61-39-26.
Ambassador: João Manuel Guerra Salgueiro.
First Secretary: Antonio de Almeida Ribeiro.
Defence Attaché: Adelio Villas-Buas Dias.
Counsellor for Co-operation: Fernando Ribeiro Rosa.
Counsellor (Commercial Section): João Novais Fonseca.

RUSSIA

Embassy: Achada de Santo Antonio, CP 31, Praia, São Tiago; tel 61-21-32; telex 6016.
Ambassador: Pavel Mikhailovich Shmelkov.

SENEGAL

Embassy: Preinha Babylone, CP 269, Praia, São Tiago; tel 61-20-24; telex 6085.
Ambassador: Omar ben Khatab Sokhna.
Counsellor: Nicolas Diagne.
First Secretary: Marcel Minkilane.
First Secretary: Assane Samb.
Attaché: Ndiouma Diouf.
Attaché: Youkhoupe Gueye.

SWEDEN

Consulate: Praça Didjikiti, CP 53, Mindelo, São Vicente; tel 31-52-16; telex 3040.
Consul: Verissimo Lima dos Santos.

USA

Embassy: Rua Hoji Ya Henda 81, CP 201, Praia, São Tiago; tel 61-42-53; telex 6068; fax 61-13-55.
Ambassador: Francis Terry McNamara.
Consul: Bernice Powell.
Administrative Section: David C. Joyce.
Communications Programme Officer: Todd Roe.
Agency for International Development: Thomas C. Luche.

International Organizations

EUROPEAN COMMUNITIES

External Delegation: Achada de Santo Antonio, CP 122, Praia, São Tiago; tel 61-37-50; telex 6071; fax 61-34-67.
Commission Delegate: Martino Meloni.

THE CENTRAL AFRICAN REPUBLIC

CAMEROON

Embassy: BP 935, Bangui; telex 5249.
Ambassador: Christopher Nsahlai.

CHAD

Embassy: BP 461, Bangui; telex 5220.
Ambassador: El Hadj Mouli Seid.

CONGO

Embassy: BP 1414, Bangui; telex 5292.
Chargé d'affaires: Antoine Delica.

COTE D'IVOIRE

Embassy: BP 930, Bangui; telex 5279.
Ambassador: Jean-Marie Agnini Bile Malan.

DENMARK

Consulate: CFAO, ave du Tchad, BP 837, Bangui; tel 61-10-69; telex 5286; fax 61-32-87.
Consul: Philippe Le Ber.

EGYPT

Embassy: BP 1422, Bangui; telex 5284.
Ambassador: Sameh Samy Darwiche.

FRANCE

Embassy: blvd du Général de Gaulle, BP 784/884/914, Bangui; tel 61-30-00; telex 5218.
Ambassador: Antoine Frasseto.

Consulate-General: blvd du Général de Gaulle, BP 784, Bangui; tel 61-01-76.

GABON

Embassy: BP 1570, Bangui; tel 61-29-97; telex 5234.
Ambassador: François de Paule Moulengui.

GERMANY

Embassy: ave du Président Gamal Abdel Nasser, BP 901, Bangui; tel 61-07-46; telex 5219.
Ambassador: Ulrich Dreesen.

HOLY SEE

Apostolic Nunciature: ave Boganda, BP 1447, Bangui; tel 61-26-54.
Apostolic Pro-Nuncio: Most Rev. Beniamino Stella, Titular Archbishop of Midila.
Secretary: Rev. Claudio Mondino.
Attaché: Rev. Battista Ricca.

IRAQ

Embassy: Bangui; telex 5287.
Chargé d'affaires: Abdul Karim Aswad.

JAPAN

Embassy: ave des Martyrs, BP 1367, Bangui; tel 61-06-68; telex 5204.
Chargé d'affaires: Shoji Sakamaki.

KOREA, DEMOCRATIC PEOPLE'S REPUBLIC

Embassy: BP 1816, Bangui.
Ambassador: Y. Yong-Hak.

LIBYA

Mission: BP 1732, Bangui; telex 5317.
Head of Mission: El-Senuse Abdallah.

NIGERIA

Embassy: BP 1010, Bangui; tel 61-39-00; telex 5269.
Chargé d'affaires: T. A. O. Odegbile.

ROMANIA

Embassy: BP 1435, Bangui.
Chargé d'affaires a.i.: Mihai Gaftoniuc.

RUSSIA

Embassy: Bangui.
Ambassador: Yuri I. Balabanov.

SWEDEN

Consulate: Banque Internationale pour l'Afrique Occidentale, place de la République, BP 910, Bangui; tel 61-38-99; telex 5233.
Ambassador: Bengt Rösiö (resident in Sweden).
Consul: François Epaye.

UNITED KINGDOM

Consulate: c/o SOCACIG, BP 728, Bangui; tel 61-03-00; telex 5258.
Honorary Consul: X. Lambert.

USA

Embassy: blvd David Dacko, BP 924, Bangui; tel 61-02-00; telex 5287; fax 61-44-94.
Ambassador: Daniel H. Simpson.
Deputy Chief of Mission: Mary B. Marshall.
Political Section: Mark Zamkov.
Economic/Commercial Section: Mary Townswick.
Consul: Lisa J. Peterson.
Administrative Section: Christopher E. Wittmann.
Regional Security Officer: Brent Bohne.
Public Affairs Officer: Chris Rochester.
Communications Programme Officer: Alberto Rodriguez.
Agency for International Development: Stephen G. Brundage.

ZAIRE

Embassy: BP 989, Bangui; telex 5232.
Ambassador: Embe Isea Mbambe.

International Organizations

EUROPEAN COMMUNITIES

External Delegation: rue de Flandre, BP 1298, Bangui; tel 61-30-53; telex 5231; fax 61-65-35.
Commission Delegate: Henri Duret.

CHAD

ALGERIA

Embassy: N'Djamena; tel 51-38-15; telex 5216.
Ambassador: Mami Abderrahmane.

CENTRAL AFRICAN REPUBLIC

Embassy: BP 115, N'Djamena; tel 51-32-06.
Ambassador: Martin Koyou-Koumbele.

CHINA, PEOPLE'S REPUBLIC

Embassy: ave Président Blanchart, BP 1133, N'Djamena; tel 51-37-72; telex 5235.
Ambassador: Zhou Zhendong.

DENMARK

Consulate: Tchami Toyota, rue Félix Eboué, BP 455, N'Djamena; tel 51-57-38; telex 5205; fax 51-59-41.
Consul: Jean-Louis Bourdiau.

EGYPT

Embassy: BP 1094, N'Djamena; tel 51-36-60; telex 5216.
Ambassador: Aziz M. Nour el-Din.

FRANCE

Embassy: rue du Lieut-Franjoux, BP 431, N'Djamena; tel 51-25-75; telex 5202.
Ambassador: Yves Aubin de la Messuzière.

Consulate: BP 913, N'Djamena; tel 51-25-76.

GERMANY

Embassy: ave Félix Eboué, BP 893, N'Djamena; tel 51-30-90; telex 5246.

IRAQ

Embassy: N'Djamena; tel 51-22-57; telex 5339.
Chargé d'affaires: Ali Mahmoud Hashim.

LIBYA

Embassy: N'Djamena.
Ambassador: Gaith Salem an-Nasser.

NIGERIA

Embassy: 35 ave Charles de Gaulle, BP 752, N'Djamena; tel 51-24-98; telex 5242.
Ambassador: Prof. Dandati Abdulkadir.

SUDAN

Embassy: BP 45, N'Djamena; tel 51-34-97; telex 5235.
Ambassador: Taha Makkawi.

SWEDEN

Consulate: N'Djamena.

SWITZERLAND

Embassy Office: Quartier Sabangali, 1102 N'Djamena; tel 51-53-40; telex 5328.
Attaché (Development Co-operation, Humanitarian Aid and Consular Affairs): Marc Vielle.

UNITED KINGDOM

Embassy: Foreign and Commonwealth Office, Downing St, London SW1A 2AL; tel (71) 270-3000.
Chargé d'affaires a.i.: J. Cummings (resident in the United Kingdom).
Third Secretary: C. Longdon (resident in the United Kingdom).

Consulate: ave Charles de Gaulle (opposite Air Chad Office), BP 877, N'Djamena; tel 51-30-64; telex 5235.
Honorary Consul: E. Abtour.

USA

Embassy: ave Félix Eboué, BP 413, N'Djamena; tel 51-40-09; telex 5203; fax 51-33-72.
Ambassador: Richard W. Bogosian.
Deputy Chief of Mission: Barbara L. Schell.
Political/Consular Section: Michael L. Bajek.
Political/Military Section: Bruce Held.
Economic/Commercial Section: Alexander Bolling.
Administrative Section: Terrence P. McCulley.
Regional Security Officer: Jon Meyers.
Public Affairs Officer: Mark B. Krischik.
Communications Programme Officer: Georgia A. Smith.
Agency for International Development: Bernard Wilder.
Office of the Defence Attaché: Lieut Col Dale B. Flora.

ZAIRE

Embassy: ave du 20 août, BP 910, N'Djamena; tel 51-59-35; telex 5322.
Ambassador: Gen. Malu-Malu Dhanda.

International Organizations

EUROPEAN COMMUNITIES

External Delegation: Concession de la Caisse de Coton, route de Farcha, BP 552, N'Djamena; tel 51-22-76; telex 5245; fax 51-21-05.
Commission Delegate: Andrew Barron.
Counsellor for Civil Engineering: Francisco Sastre.
Counsellor for Rural Development: Patrice Pillet.
Economic Counsellor: Pierre Hennebert.
Administrative and Financial Attaché: Alain Le Mintier.

CHILE

ARGENTINA

Embassy: Miraflores 285, Santiago; tel (2) 33-1076; telex 240280.
Ambassador: José María Alvarez de Toledo.

AUSTRALIA

Embassy: Gertrudis Echeñique 420, Casilla 33, Correo 10, Las Condes, Santiago; tel (2) 228-5065; telex 240855; fax (2) 48-1707.
Ambassador: Malcolm J. Dan.
Second Secretary (Consular and Administration): T. B. Middleton.

AUSTRIA

Embassy: Barros Errázuriz 1968, 3°, Providencia, Casilla 16196, Santiago 9; tel (2) 223-4281; telex 240528; fax (2) 204-9382.
Ambassador: Dr Wolfgang Jilly.
Third Secretary and Vice-Consul: Harald Ulbrich.
Honorary Consul: Dr Paul Sommer.

Commercial Section: Ismael Valdés Vergara 368, Depto. 51, Santiago; tel (2) 39-1151.
Commercial Counsellor: Helmut Wagner.

Consulate: 7 Norte 1107, Viña del Mar, Casilla 3-D, Valparaíso; tel (32) 97-1200.
Honorary Consul: Paul Kulka.

BELGIUM

Embassy: Avda Providencia 2653, 11°, Of. 1104, Santiago; tel (2) 232-1070; telex 440088.
Chargé d'affaires: Michel Godfrind.

BRAZIL

Embassy: Alonso Ovalle 1665, Santiago; tel (2) 698-2486; telex 340350; fax (2) 671-5961.
Ambassador: Guilherme Leite Ribeiro.
Minister-Counsellor: Stelio Marcos Amarante.
Counsellor: Flavio Roberto Bonzanini.
First Secretary: Carlos Henrique Cardim.
First Secretary: Luiz Alberto Figueiredo Machado.
Second Secretary: Antonio José Ferreira Simões.
Second Secretary: Nelson Antonio Tabajara de Oliveira.

BULGARIA

Interests Section: c/o Embassy of Austria.

CANADA

Embassy: Ahumada 11, 10°, Casilla 427, Santiago; tel (2) 696-2256; telex 240341; fax (2) 696-0738.
Ambassador: Michael T. Mace.
Counsellor and Consul: D. Bickford.
First Secretary (Immigration) and Consul: W. N. Brockenshire.
Second Secretary (Immigration) and Vice-Consul: S. Hesse.
Second Secretary (Administration) and Vice-Consul: M. Edwards.

Commercial Office: Casilla 771, Santiago.
Counsellor (Commercial): D. R. Turner.
First Secretary (Commercial): P. Alarie.

CHINA, PEOPLE'S REPUBLIC

Embassy: Pedro de Valdivia 550, Santiago; tel (2) 25-0755; telex 240863.
Ambassador: Huang Shikang.

COLOMBIA

Embassy: Darío Urzúa 2080, Santiago; tel (2) 74-7570; telex 340401.
Ambassador: Jorge E. Rodríguez.

COSTA RICA

Embassy: Barcelona 2070, Santiago; tel (2) 231-8915.
Ambassador: Fabio Cruz Briceño.

DENMARK

Embassy: Sucursal 21, Avda Santa María 0182, Casilla 13430, Santiago; tel (2) 37-6056; telex 440032.
Chargé d'affaires and Attaché: Bent Roll.

Consulate: POB 242, Antofagasta, Latorre 2274; tel (83) 22-1452; telex 325034.
Consul: Camilo Hurtado Cortes.

Consulate: 21 de Mayo 399, Arica; tel (80) 23-2250.
Consul: Emilio Gutiérrez Bonelli.

Consulate: Colón 409, Punta Arenas; tel (61) 22-2716.
Consul: A. J. Gibbons MacLeay.

Consulate-General: Casilla 416, Blanco 951, Valparaíso; tel (32) 21-3942; telex 230016.
Consul: Lars Dan Sørensen Halse.

Consulate: Torre 'Arturo Prat', Calle Aníbal Pinto 222, Ofs 11/12, Casilla 517, Talcahuano; tel (41) 54-1731; telex 260197; fax (41) 54-1731.
Consul: Hector Manuel Castro Araya.

DOMINICAN REPUBLIC

Embassy: Mariscal Petain 125, Santiago; tel (2) 228-8083.
Ambassador: Rafael Váldez Hicario.

ECUADOR

Embassy: Avda Providencia 1979, 5°, Santiago; tel (2) 23-5742; telex 240717.
Ambassador: César Valdivieso Chiriboga.

EGYPT

Embassy: Roberto del Río 1871, Santiago; tel (2) 274-8881; telex 440156.
Ambassador: Adel Ahmad El-Samawi.

EL SALVADOR

Embassy: Calle Noruega 6595, Las Condes, Santiago; tel (2) 25-1096.
Ambassador: Dr José Horacio Trujillo.

FINLAND

Embassy: Mons. Sótero Sanz 55, Of. 71, Providencia, Santiago; Apdo 16657, Santiago 9; tel (2) 232-4573; fax (2) 232-0456.
Chargé d'affaires a.i.: Ilpo Manninen.

Consulate-General: Torre Antonio Varas, Avda 11 de Septiémbre 1480, 7°, Of. 73, Santiago 9; tel (2) 223-5980; telex 242380; fax (2) 223-7695.
Consul-General: James Peter O'Shea.

Consulate: José Menendéz 1147, Casilla 1237, Punta Arenas; tel (61) 22-3498; telex 34-280025; fax (61) 22-3498.
Consul: Juan Mauricio Rosenfeld.

Consulate: Valparaíso.

FRANCE

Embassy: Avda Condell 65, Providencia, Casilla 38-D, Santiago; tel (2) 225-1030; telex 240535.
Ambassador: Daniel Lequertier.

Trade Promotion Office: CC 1/9; tel (2) 32-5020; telex 341088.

GERMANY

Embassy: Agustinas 785, 7° y 8°, Casilla 9949, Santiago; tel (2) 33-5031; telex 240583; fax (2) 33-6119.
Ambassador: Dr Wiegand Pabsch.

Consulate: Calle O'Higgins 445, 2°, Casilla 41-C, Concepción; tel (41) 23-0621; telex 260096; fax (41) 24-2591.
Counsellor to Legation: Horst Kriegler.

Consulate: Calle Bolivar 374, Casilla 454, Antofagasta; tel (83) 25-1691; telex 225064.
Honorary Consul: Hans Schaefer.

Consulate: Calle 21 de Mayo 639, Of. 8, Casilla 907, Arica; tel (80) 23-1551; fax (80) 23-1234.
Honorary Consul: Klaus Eitner.

Consulate: Calle Mackenna 987, entrepiso Of. 4, Casilla 419, Osorno; tel (64) 23-2151.
Honorary Consul: Ameli Schilling.

Consulate: Calle Chorillos 1582, Casilla 12-D, Puerto Montt; tel (65) 25-4222; telex 370023.
Honorary Consul: Oscar Weil.

Consulate: Independencia 875, Casilla 44-D, Punta Arenas; tel (61) 23-781; telex 280007.
Honorary Consul: Peter Füssel.

Consulate: Aldunate 285, Temuco; tel (45) 21-2510.
Honorary Consul: Oswald Frindt.

Consulate: Avda Prat 243, Casilla 4, Valdivia; tel (63) 21-5701.
Honorary Consul: Arnold Michaelis.

Consulate: Blanco 1215, Edif. Nautilus, 11°, Of. 1102, Casilla 167-V, Valparaíso; tel (32) 25-6749.
Honorary Consul: Dr Herbert Karlsruher.

GUATEMALA

Embassy: Los Españoles 2155, Pedro de Valdivia Norte, Providencia, Santiago; tel (2) 231-7367; fax (2) 232-4494.
Ambassador: Julio Gándara Valenzuela.

HAITI

Embassy: Avda 11 de Septiembre 2155, Of. 801, Torre B, Santiago; tel (2) 231-8233.
Ambassador: Max Jadotte.

HOLY SEE

Apostolic Nunciature: Calle Nuncio Sótero Sanz 200, Casilla 507, Santiago; tel (2) 231-2020; telex 241035; fax (2) 231-0868.
Auditor: Mgr Orlando Antonini.

HONDURAS

Embassy: Avda 11 de Septiembre 2155, Of. 303, Santiago; tel (2) 231-4161; telex 440456.

Ambassador: Carlos H. Reyes.

HUNGARY

Embassy: Coyancura 2241, Of. 74, Correo 34, Casilla 179, Santiago.

ICELAND

Consulate: Mathiesen SAC, Nuncio Sótero Sanz 102, Casilla 9495, Santiago; tel (2) 231-1803; telex 240586; fax (2) 231-8160.
Consul: Michael Boettiger.

INDIA

Embassy: Triana 871, Casilla 10433, Santiago; tel (2) 223-1548; telex 340046; fax (2) 274-3240.
Ambassador: Jawahar Lal.
Second Secretary: T. N. Arora.
Attaché: J. M. Uppal.
Attaché (Private Secretary to Ambassador): B. K. Kishnani.
Personal Assistant to Second Secretary: S. Vasudev.
Accountant: Sanjay Datta.

ISRAEL

Embassy: San Sebastián 2812, 5°, Casilla 1224, Santiago; tel (2) 246-1570; telex 240627.
Ambassador: Daniel Mokady.

ITALY

Embassy: Clemente Fabres 1050, Santiago; tel (2) 225-9029; telex 440321.
Chargé d'affaires: Armando Sanguini.

JAPAN

Embassy: Avda Providencia 2653, 19°, Casilla 2877, Santiago; tel (2) 232-1807; telex 440132; fax (2) 232-1812.
Ambassador: Rikio Shikama.

JORDAN

Embassy: Los Militares 4280, Las Condes, Casilla 10431, Santiago; tel (2) 228-8989; telex 346196.
Ambassador: Wael D. Tuqan.
Counsellor: Ihsan S. Amr.

KOREA, REPUBLIC

Embassy: Alcántara 74, Casilla 1301, Santiago; tel (2) 228-4214; telex 340380.
Ambassador: Suh Kyung-Suk.

LEBANON

Embassy: Isidoro Goyenechea 3607, Casilla 3667, Santiago; tel (2) 232-5027; telex 440118.
Ambassador: Ibrahim Kraidy.

NETHERLANDS

Embassy: Las Violetas 2368, Casilla 56-D, Santiago; tel (2) 223-6825; telex 340381.
Ambassador: Robert Fruin.

NEW ZEALAND

Embassy: Avda Isidora Goyenechea 3516, Casilla 112, Las Condes, Santiago; tel (2) 231-4204; telex 3440066; fax (2) 231-9040.
Ambassador: Paul J. A. Tipping.
Second Secretary and Vice-Consul: Peter J. MacIntyre.
Attaché: Julie G. Haack.

NORWAY

Embassy: Américo Vespucio Norte 548, Casilla 2431, Santiago; tel (2) 228-1024; telex 440150.
Ambassador: Helge Vindenes.

PANAMA

Embassy: Bustos 2199, Correo 9892, Santiago; tel (2) 225-0147.
Ambassador: Ricardo Moreno Villalaz.

PARAGUAY

Embassy: Huérfanos 886, 5°, Ofs 514-515, Santiago; tel (2) 39-4640; telex 645357.
Ambassador: Dr Fabio Rivas Araujo.

PERU

Embassy: Avda Andrés Bello 1751, Providencia, Santiago 9, Casilla 16277, Santiago; tel (2) 223-8883; telex 440095.
Ambassador: Luis Marchand Stens.

PHILIPPINES

Embassy: La Gloria 17 (Esquina Apoquindo), Las Condes, Santiago; tel (2) 208-1313; telex 340412; fax (2) 208-1400.
Ambassador: Hermenegildo C. Cruz.
Attaché (Administrative/Legal Officer) and Acting Head of Consular Post: Alonzo R. Tinagan.
Attaché (Trade Promotion Officer): Phebe K. Lat.
Attaché (Finance Officer): Cynthia A. Adajar.

ROMANIA

Embassy: Benjamín 2955, Casilla 290, Las Condes, Santiago; tel (2) 231-1893; telex 241320.
Ambassador: Constantin Tunsanu.
First Secretary: Constantin Eftimie.
First Secretary: Eugen Ionele.
Third Secretary: Paul Stanciu.

RUSSIA

Embassy: Santiago.
Ambassador: Yuri I. Pavlov.

SOUTH AFRICA

Embassy: Avda 11 de Septiembre 2353, 16°, Torre San Ramón, Providencia, Casilla 16189, Santiago 9; tel (2) 231-2860; telex 341522; fax (2) 231-3185.
Ambassador: Lieut-Gen. Pieter W. van der Westhuizen.
First Secretary: L. Pienaar.
First Secretary (Administration): D. A. Abroue.
Second Secretary: H. J. H. Fourie.
Armed Forces Attaché: Col G. F. Snyman.
Army Attaché: Col A. de S. Hendrikz.
Naval Attaché: Commdr J. J. Viljoen.

Trade Section: Pedro de Valdivia 800, Santiago 9; tel (2) 223-2319; telex 340713.
First Secretary (Trade): H. G. A. Breytenbach.

Consulate-General: Philips 16, 3°, Dept Y, Casilla 2134, Santiago; tel (2) 33-6394; telex 340676.
Honorary Consul-General: J. D. Carr-Rollitt.

SPAIN

Embassy: Avda Andrés Bello 1895, Casilla 16456, Santiago; tel (2) 74-2021; telex 340253.
Ambassador: Pedro Bremejo Marín.

SWEDEN

Embassy: Torre San Ramón, Avda 11 de Septiembre 2353, 4°, Providencia, Santiago; tel (2) 231-2733; telex 440153; fax (2) 232-4188.
Ambassador: Staffan Wrigstad.
Counsellor: Gunvor Gonçalves.
Counsellor: Åke Wadstein.
Second Secretary: Jenny Malmquist.
Chancellor: Inga Berit Palmén.

Consulate: Antofagasta.

Consulate: Camino Boca Sur s/n, San Pedro, Casilla 357, Concepción; tel (41) 37-1911; telex 265507; fax (41) 37-1974.
Consul: Stig Georg Blomström.

Consulate: Avda Costanera 841, Edif. Andacollo, Casilla 227, Coquimbo; tel (51) 31-1063.
Vice-Consul: Patricio Campos Lira.

Consulate: Calle Zegers 231, Casilla 379, Iquique; tel (81) 21-873; telex 223001.
Vice-Consul: Syers Bertram Outram Kelsall Dawson.

Consulate: Errázuriz 891, Casilla 499, Punta Arenas; tel (61) 22-4862; telex 280336; fax (61) 22-4107.
Vice-Consul: Walter Enrique Bärthold Molkenbuhr.

Consulate: Edif. Nautilus, Blanco 1215, Of. 1002, Casilla 3232, Valparaíso; tel (32) 25-6507.
Consul: Carl Christer Åkeson Wiberg.

SWITZERLAND

Embassy: Edif. Forum, Avda Providencia 2653, 16°, Of. 1602, Casilla 3875, Santiago; tel (2) 231-5341; telex 340870; fax (2) 232-1872.
Ambassador: Paul Wipfli.
Counsellor: Michel Coquoz.
Consul: Dieter Gruber.

SYRIA

Embassy: Carmencita 111, Casilla 12, Correo 10, Santiago; tel (2) 232-7471; telex 240095.
Ambassador: Hisham Hallaj.

TURKEY

Embassy: N. Sotéro Sanz 136, Casilla 16182-9, Providencia, Santiago; tel (2) 231-8952; telex 340278.
Ambassador: Nurettin Karaköylü.

UNITED KINGDOM

Embassy: La Concepción 177, Casilla 72 D or Casilla 16552, Santiago 9; tel (2) 223-9166; telex 340483; fax (2) 223-1917.
Ambassador: Richard A. Neilson.
Counsellor, Consul-General and Deputy Head of Mission: R. D. Lavers.
Defence, Naval and Military Attaché: Capt. J. A. Finnigan.
Air Attaché: Group Capt. B. J. Hall.
First Secretary (Commercial): J. V. Everard.
First Secretary (Chancery): P. H. C. Harris.
First Secretary (Economic): J. E. Stephenson.
Cultural Attaché (British Council Director): W. Campbell.
Consul and Second Secretary (Management): A. S. Whitmore.
Second Secretary (Commercial): P. A. Thornton.
Second Secretary (Chancery and Information): K. D. Lyne.
Assistant Cultural Attaché (British Council): S. Milner.

Consulate: Baquedano 653, Casilla 653, Arica; tel (80) 23-1960.
Honorary Consul: G. H. Hulse.

Consulate: Chacabuco 1205, Casilla 452, Concepción; tel (41) 22-5655.
Honorary Consul: J. F. B. Pomeroy.

Consulate: Lautaro Navarro 398, Calle Sarmiento 780, Casilla 327, Punta Arenas; tel (61) 22-4275; telex 280004; fax (61) 22-2251.
Honorary Consul: R. W. Matheson.

Consulate: Errázuriz 730, Casilla 82V, Valparaíso; tel (32) 25-6117; fax (32) 25-5365.
Honorary Consul: E. C. Kenrick.

USA

Embassy: Codina Bldg, Agustinas 1343, 5°, Santiago; tel (2) 71-0133; telex 240062; fax (2) 699-1141.
Ambassador: Charles A. Gillespie, Jr.
Deputy Chief of Mission: David N. Greenlee.
Political Section: Nancy M. Mason.
Economic Section: Glen R. Rase.
Commercial Section: Ricardo Villalobos.
Consul: Laurence M. Kerr.
Administrative Section: Daniel A. Johnson.
Regional Security Officer: Laurence H. Liptak.
Public Affairs Officer: James T. L. Dandridge II.
Communications Programme Officer: Cliff Brozowski.
Information Systems Manager: Timothy J. Cook.
Office of the Defence Attaché: Capt. Thomas H. Smith.
Agency for International Development: Paul W. Fritz.
APHIS: Herbert L. Murphy.
Agricultural Section: Robert H. Curtis.
Labour Officer: Arnold A. Chacon (acting).

URUGUAY

Embassy: Avda Pedro de Valdivia 711, Casilla 2636, Santiago; tel (2) 74-3569; telex 340371.
Ambassador: Alfredo Bianchi Palazzo.

VENEZUELA

Embassy: Bustos No 20-21, Providencia, Santiago; Casilla 16577, Santiago 9; tel (2) 218-1041; telex 440170; fax (2) 49-9117.
Ambassador: Ignacio Arcaya Smith.
Minister-Counsellor: Otto Veitia Matos.
First Secretary: Héctor Quintero M.
First Secretary: Juan Rodríguez Guaje.
First Secretary: Maria del R. Rojas de Pabon.
Second Secretary: Mario Alejandro Aguzzi Duran.
Second Secretary: Luis José Carpio Govea.
Counsellor (Technical Affairs): Yolanda Parra Yanez.
First Attaché: Roberto Hernández B.
First Attaché: Nicomedes Zuloaga.

YUGOSLAVIA

Embassy: Santiago.
Ambassador: Franc Krnic.

ZAIRE

Consulate: Casilla 144, Correo 10, Las Condes, Santiago; tel (2) 220-1464; telex 340260; fax (2) 698-4127.
Consul: Gonzalo Beltran Repetto.

International Organizations

EUROPEAN COMMUNITIES

External Delegation: Avda Américo Vespucio Sur 1835, Santiago 9; Casilla 10093; tel (2) 228-2484; telex 340344; fax (2) 228-2571.
Head of Office: Vittorino Allocco.

THE PEOPLE'S REPUBLIC OF CHINA

AFGHANISTAN

Embassy: 8 Dong Zhi Men Wai Dajie, Chao Yang Qu, Beijing; tel (1) 5321582.

ALBANIA

Embassy: 28 Guang Hua Lu, Beijing; tel (1) 5321116; telex 211207.
Ambassador: Justin Niko Papajorgji.

ALGERIA

Embassy: Dong Zhi Men Wai Dajie, 7 San Li Tun, Beijing; tel (1) 5321231; telex 22437.
Ambassador: Mourad Bencheikh.

ARGENTINA

Embassy: Bldg 11, 5 Dong Jie, San Li Tun, Beijing; tel (1) 5322090; telex 22269.
Ambassador: Arturo Enrique Ossorio Arana.

AUSTRALIA

Embassy: 15 Dong Zhi Men Wai Dajie, San Li Tun, Beijing 100600; tel (1) 5322331; telex 22263; fax (1) 5324605.
Ambassador: Michael Lightowler.
Minister: Colin Heseltine.
Minister (Commercial): Robin Dulfer-Hyams.
Counsellor (Political): John Courtney.
Counsellor (Economic): Edward Sulikowski.
Counsellor (Administration): Kenneth Cowden.
Counsellor (Cultural Affairs): Peter Brown.
Counsellor (Commercial): Michael Newton.
Public Affairs Officer: Grant Thompson.
Technical Co-operation Section: East Lakes Centre Office Bldg, 4th Floor, 35 Dong Zhi Men Wai, San Li Tun, Beijing; tel (1) 4081907; fax (1) 4082050.
Counsellor (Technical Co-operation): Gary Quayle.
Immigration Section and Overseas Student Office: Tayuan Office Bldg, 14th Floor, West Block, San Li Tun, Beijing; tel (1) 5321724; fax (1) 5324349.
Counsellor (Immigration): Maureen Chong.
Consulate-General: 17 Fuxing Rd West, Shanghai 200031; tel (21) 4334604; telex 3312; fax (21) 4331732.
Consul-General: Murray McLean.

AUSTRIA

Embassy: 5 Xiu Shui Nan Jie, Jian Guo Men Wai, Beijing; tel (1) 5321505; telex 22258.
Chargé d'affaires: Jutta Stefan-Bastl.
First Secretary: Roland Hauser.
Economic Secretary: Horst Redl.

BANGLADESH

Embassy: 42 Guang Hua Lu, Beijing; tel (1) 5321819; telex 22143; fax (1) 5324346.
Ambassador: Farooq Sobhan.

BELGIUM

Embassy: 6 San Li Tun Lu, Beijing 100600; tel (1) 5321736; telex 22260; fax (1) 5325097.
Ambassador: Willy De Valck.
Counsellor: Guy Trouveroy.
First Secretary (Economic and Commercial): Dirk N. Loncke.
Chancellor and Consul: Jean-Marie Van Strydonck.
Commercial Attaché: Howard Wei.
Commercial Attaché: André Mathieu.
Cultural Attaché: Eliane Longly.
Attaché: Andrée Kerremans.
Attaché: Katrien Costenoble.
Attaché: Sylvie Gerard.
Attaché: Christel Van Laere.
Attaché: Hilde Mertens.

BENIN

Embassy: 38 Guang Hua Lu, Beijing; tel (1) 5322741; telex 22599; fax (1) 5325103.
Ambassador: Auguste Alavo.
Minister-Counsellor: Gustave Savoeda.
Minister-Counsellor: Lucie Savoeda.
Attaché (Finances): Barthélémy Hounsa.
Attaché: Comlan Ade.

BOLIVIA

Embassy: Ta Yuan Diplomatic Office Bldg, 14 Liang Ma He Nan Lu, 3-1-142, Beijing; tel (1) 5324370; telex 210415; fax (1) 5324686.
Ambassador: Carlos Böhrt I.
Minister-Counsellor: Roberto Castro P.

BRAZIL

Embassy: 27 Guang Hua Lu, Beijing; tel (1) 5322881; telex 22117; fax (1) 5322751.
Ambassador: Roberto Abdenur.

BULGARIA

Embassy: 4 Xiu Shui Bei Jie, Jian Guo Men Wai, Beijing; tel (1) 5322231.
Ambassador: Filip Markov.

BURKINA FASO

Embassy: 9 Dong Liu Jie, San Li Tun, Beijing 100600; tel (1) 5322492; telex 22666; fax (1) 5323343.
Ambassador: W. Raymond Edouard Ouedraogo.
First Counsellor: Marcel Guigma.
Attaché (Finance): Siriki Koulybari.

BURUNDI

Embassy: 25 Guang Hua Lu, Beijing 100600; tel (1) 5321801; telex 22271; fax (1) 5322381.
Ambassador: Tharcisse Ntakibirora.
Second Counsellor: Charles Imwiyitire.
Administrative Secretary: Anastasie Imwiyitire.
Attaché: Georges Niyonzima.

CAMEROON

Embassy: 7 San Li Tun, Dong Wu Jie, Beijing; tel (1) 5321771; telex 22256.
Ambassador: Eleih Elle Etian.

CANADA

Embassy: 10 San Li Tun Lu, Chao Yang Qu, Beijing; tel (1) 5323536; telex 22717; fax (1) 5321684.
Trade Section: Ta Yuan Bldg, No. 4 South Liang Ma He Rd, Apt 2-4-1, Chao Yang District, Beijing; tel (1) 5323031.
Ambassador: Fred Bild.
Minister (Commercial): R. Craig.
Minister-Counsellor and Consul: B. Jutzi.
Counsellor and Consul: D. G. Myatt.
Counsellor (Commercial): M. M. Abou-Guendia.
Counsellor (Development): H. S. Tsé.
Counsellor (Development): A. Desjardins.
Counsellor (Commercial): R. Collette.
Canadian Forces Attaché: Col W. Trimble.
First Secretary (Commercial): J. B. Clapp.
First Secretary and Consul: R. J. Briggs.
First Secretary (Development): M. Collette.
First Secretary (Administration) and Consul: K. M. Pearson.
First Secretary: R. E. S. Hayhoe.
First Secretary (Development) and Consul: H.-P. Normandin.
First Secretary (Development): S. Poohkay.
First Secretary and Consul: M. Tessier.
Consulate-General: Union Bldg, 4th Floor, 100 Yan'an Rd (East), Shanghai; tel (21) 3202822; telex 33608; fax (21) 3203623.
Consul-General: Normand H. Mailhot.
Consul: G. E. Benson.

CHAD

Embassy: 21 Guang Hua Lu, Jianguo Men Wai, Beijing; telex 22287.
Ambassador: Issa Abbas Ali.

CHILE

Embassy: 1 Dong Si Jie, San Li Tun, Beijing; tel (1) 5321641; telex 22252; fax (1) 5323170.
Ambassador: Eduardo Bravo.
Counsellor: Carlos Dinator.
Military, Naval and Air Attaché: Brig. Arno Wenderoth.
Second Secretary: Roberto Alvarez.
Third Secretary: Roberto Nieto.
Third Secretary and Head of Consular Section: Eduardo Calleja.

COLOMBIA

Embassy: 34 Guang Hua Lu, Beijing; tel (1) 5323166; telex 22460; fax (1) 5321969.

CONGO

Embassy: 7 San Li Tun, Dong Si Jie, Beijing; tel (1) 5321387; telex 20428.
Ambassador: Gabriel Emouengué.
First Counsellor: Yves Motandeau-Monghot.
First Secretary: Jem Ayoulove.
Second Secretary: Felix N'goma.
Secretary: François-Xavier Nzinga.
Secretary: Eugene Boussougou.
Attaché: Edgard Pounguy.
Attaché: Celestin Boussougou.

COTE D'IVOIRE

Embassy: Beijing; tel (1) 5321482; telex 22723.
Ambassador: Amoakon Ejampan Thiemele.

CUBA

Embassy: 1 Xiu Shui Nan Jie, Jian Guo Men Wai, Beijing; tel (1) 5322822; telex 22249; fax (1) 5322129.
Ambassador: José Armando Guerra Menchero.
Counsellor: Esteban Lobaina Romero.
Commercial Counsellor: Eugenio Deus Casuso.
Second Secretary: Lazaro Herrera Martínez.
Attaché (Commercial): Armando Menendez.
Information Officer: F. Nuñez.
Consulate-General: New Town Mansion, Shanghai; tel (21) 2753078; fax (21) 2751745.
Consul-General: Orlando Valdez Viera.

CYPRUS

Embassy: 2-13-2, Tayuan Diplomatic Office Bldg, Liang Ma He Nan Lu 14, Chao Yang Qu, Beijing 100600; tel (1) 5325057; fax (1) 5325060.
Ambassador: Sotirios C. Zackheos.
Second Secretary: Pantelakis Eliades.

CZECHOSLOVAKIA

Embassy: Ri Tan Lu, Jian Guo Men Wai, Beijing; tel (1) 5321531; telex 22553.
Ambassador: Borivoj Cuda.

DENMARK

Embassy: 1 Dong Wu Jie, San Li Tun, 100600 Beijing; tel (1) 5322431; telex 22255; fax (1) 5322439.
Ambassador: William Friis-Møller.
Counsellor: Ole Christofferson.
Counsellor: Mogens Poulsen.
Commercial Attaché: Bo Bjerregaard Rasmussen.
Attaché: Ib Norin Larsen.
Commercial Attaché: C. Abildgaard Jensen.
Secretary-Archivist: Jane J. Severinsen.

ECUADOR

Embassy: 2-41 San Li Tun, Beijing; telex 22710.
Ambassador: Dr Rodrigo Váldez Baquero.

EGYPT

Embassy: 2 Ri Tan Dong Lu, Beijing; tel (1) 5322541; telex 22134.
Ambassador: Badr Hammam.

EQUATORIAL GUINEA

Embassy: 2 Dong Si Jie, San Li Tun, Beijing; tel (1) 5323679.
Ambassador: Lino-Sima Ekua Avomo.
First Secretary: Candido Oyono Ela Eyang.

ETHIOPIA

Embassy: 3 Xiu Shui Nan Jie, Jian Guo Men Wai, Beijing; tel (1) 5321721; telex 22306.
Ambassador: Philippos Wolde-Mariam.
Attaché: Tsegereda Seleshi.

FINLAND

Embassy: Liang Ma He Nan Lu 14, Tayuan Diplomatic Office Bldg, 1-10-1, Beijing 100600; tel (1) 5321806; telex 22129; fax (1) 5321884.
Ambassador: Arto Mansala.
Commercial Section and Office of Science and Technology: 0718 China World Tower, China World Trade Centre, No. 1 Jian Guo Men Wai Da Jie, Beijing 100020; tel (1) 5052288; telex 222512; fax (1) 5053543.
Commercial Secretary: Juha Itkonen.
Commercial Secretary: Tuomo Jussila.
Scientific Attaché: Markku Kavonius.
Office of the Commercial Attachés: Qijiayuan 7-3-51, Beijing 100600; tel (1) 5321503; telex 22294; fax (1) 5323123.
Commercial Attaché: Annikki Antila.
Commercial Attaché: Eija Pöytäkivi.
Commercial Attaché: Jukka Rapeli.

FRANCE

Embassy: 3 Dong San Jie, San Li Tun, Beijing; tel (1) 5321331; telex 22183.
Ambassador: Claude Martin.
Trade Promotion Office: Bang Gong Lou 141, San Li Tun, Beijing; tel (1) 522631; telex 22296.
Consulate-General: 1431 Huai-hai Zhong Lu, Shanghai; tel (21) 332639.

GABON

Embassy: 36 Guang Hua Lu, Beijing; tel (1) 5322810; telex 22110.
Ambassador: Hubert Okouma.

GERMANY

Embassy: 5 Dong Zhi Men Wai Dajie, Chaoyang District, Beijing 100600; tel (1) 5322161; telex 22259; fax (1) 5325336.
Ambassador: Dr Hannspeter Hellbeck.
Trade Promotion and Visa Sections: tel (1) 5321181; telex 210250.
Consulate-General: Yong Fu Lu 151/181, Shanghai; tel (21) 4336951; telex 33140; fax (21) 4714448.
Consul-General: Dr Hannelore Theodor.

GHANA

Embassy: 8 San Li Tun Lu, Beijing; tel (1) 5322288.
Ambassador: Jonas Awuku Afari.

GREECE

Embassy: 19 Guang Hua Lu, Beijing; tel (1) 5321317; telex 22267.
Ambassador: Emmanuel E. Megalokonomos.
First Counsellor: Panay Otis Makris.
Attaché: George Zissis.

GUINEA

Embassy: 7 Dong San Jie, San Li Tun, Beijing; tel (1) 5323649; telex 22706.
Ambassador: Abou Camara.
Counsellor: Dominique Koly.
Attaché: Mohamed Bangoura.

GUYANA

Embassy: 1 Xiu Shui Dong Jie, Jian Guo Men Wai, Beijing; tel (1) 5321601; telex 22295.
Ambassador: Peter W. Denny.

HUNGARY

Embassy: 10 Dong Zhi Men Wai Dajie, Beijing; tel (1) 5321683; telex 22679.
Ambassador: Dr Iván Németh.
Consulate-General: Shanghai.

ICELAND

Embassy: Beijing.
Ambassador: Benedikt Gröndal.

INDIA

Embassy: 1 Ri Tan Dong Lu, Beijing; tel (1) 5321927; telex 22126.
Ambassador: Chetput Venkatasubban Ranganathan.

INDONESIA

Embassy: Beijing.
Ambassador: Abdurrahman Gunadirdja.

IRAN

Embassy: No. 13, Dong Liu Jie, San Li Tun, Chaoyang District, Beijing; tel (1) 5322040; telex 22253; fax (1) 5321403.
Ambassador: Ala ed-Din Broujerdi.

IRAQ

Embassy: 3 Ri Tan Dong Lu, Chao Yang Qu, Beijing; tel (1) 5321950; telex 22288.
Ambassador: Mohamed Amin Ahmed al-Jaf.

IRELAND

Embassy: 3 Ri Tan Dong Lu, Qui Jia Yuan, Beijing; tel (1) 5322691; telex 22425; fax (1) 5322280.
Ambassador: Gearoid O'Broin.
First Secretary: Anne Webster.
Secretary: Eamonn Robinson.

ITALY

Embassy: 2 Dong Er Jie, San Li Tun, Beijing 100600; tel (1) 5322131; telex 22414; fax (1) 5324676.
Ambassador: Oliviero Rossi.
Minister-Counsellor: Attilio Massimo Iannucci.
First Counsellor: Alberto Bradanini.
Counsellor: Enrico Gambacorta.
Army and Defence Attaché: Col Pasqualino Verdecchia.
Air Attaché: Col Franco Vito Ferrara.
Naval Attaché: Commdr Giancarlo Schiavoni.
First Secretary: Lucia Fiori.
First Secretary: Mario Palma.
Second Secretary: Giovanni Pugliese.

Consulate-General: 127 Wu Yi Lu, Shanghai; tel (21) 2524373; telex 33502; fax (21) 2511728.
Consul: Pietro Ballero.

JAPAN

Embassy: 7 Ri Tan Lu, Jian Guo Men Wai, Beijing; tel (1) 5322361; telex 22275; fax (1) 5324625.
Ambassador: Hiroshi Hasimoto.

Consulate-General: Garden Tower, 368 Huanshi, Dong Lu, Guangzhou; tel (20) 338999; telex 44333; fax (20) 338972.
Consul-General: Takashi Arinobu.

Consulate-General: 1517 Huaihai Rd Central, Shanghai; tel (21) 4336639; telex 33061; fax (21) 4331008.
Consul-General: Yoshihiro Hasumi.

Consulate-General: 50 Shisi Wei Lu, He Ping, Qu Shenyang, Liaoning; tel (24) 290155; telex 80010; fax (24) 720727.
Consul-General: Michi Takahashi.

JORDAN

Embassy: 54 Dong Liu Jie, San Li Tun, Beijing; tel (1) 5323906; telex 22651.
Ambassador: Walid al-Sadd al-Batayneh.

KAZAKHSTAN

Embassy: Beijing.

KENYA

Embassy: 4 Xi Liu Jie, San Li Tun, Beijing; tel (1) 5323381; telex 22311.
Ambassador: Jelani Habib.

KOREA, DEMOCRATIC PEOPLE'S REPUBLIC

Embassy: Ri Tan Bei Lu, Jian Guo Men Wai, Beijing; telex 20448.

KUWAIT

Embassy: 23 Guang Hua Lu, Beijing; tel (1) 5322216; telex 22127.

LAOS

Embassy: 11 Dong Si Jie, San Li Tun, Chao Yang Qu, Beijing 100600; tel (1) 5321224; telex 22144.
Ambassador: Phongsavath Boupha.
Military and Air Attaché: Col Khamphouang Chanthaphomma.
Deputy Military Attaché: Lieut Col Sonxay Savangchit.
Second Secretary: Vichith Xindavong.
Deputy Military Attaché: Maj. Visay Chanthamath.

LEBANON

Embassy: 51 Dong Liu Jie, San Li Tun, Beijing; tel (1) 5322770; telex 22113.
Ambassador: Farid Samaha.

LIBYA

People's Bureau: 55 Dong Liu Jie, San Li Tun, Beijing; telex 22310.
Secretary of the People's Bureau: Abd al-Hamid al-Zintani.

LUXEMBOURG

Embassy: 21 Nei Wu Bu Jie, 100600 Beijing; tel (1) 556175; telex 22638; fax (1) 5137268.
Ambassador: Paul Schuller.

MADAGASCAR

Embassy: 3 Dong Jie, San Li Tun, Beijing; tel (1) 5321353; telex 22140.
Ambassador: Jean-Jacques Maurice.

MALAYSIA

Embassy: 13 Dong Zhi Men Wai Dajie, San Li Tun, Beijing; tel (1) 5322531; telex 22122.
Ambassador: Dato Noor Adlan Yahayauddin.

MALI

Embassy: 8 Dong Si Jie, Road 4, San Li Tun, Beijing; tel (1) 5321687; telex 22257.
Ambassador: Nakounté Diakité.
First Counsellor: Bounafou Sidibe.
First Secretary: Fousseini Sy.
Secretary: Ahmadou Frantao Cisse.

MALTA

Embassy: Ta Yuan Diplomatic Compound, 2-1-22, Beijing; tel (1) 5323114; telex 22670.
First Secretary and Chargé d'affaires a.i.: Olaf Terribile.

MAURITANIA

Embassy: 9 Dong San Jie, San Li Tun, Beijing; tel (1) 5321346; telex 22514.
Ambassador: Taki Ould Sidi.

MEXICO

Embassy: 5 Dong Wu Jie, San Li Tun, Beijing 100600; tel (1) 5322070; telex 22262; fax (1) 5323744.
Ambassador: Jorge Eduardo Navarrete.
Counsellor: Ignacio Rios.
Third Secretary: Cuauhtémoc Villamar.
Third Secretary: Amparo Anguiano.
Consular Attaché: Juan Cerda.
Military Attaché: Col Mario Fuentes.
Commercial Counsellor: Arturo Mejia.

MONGOLIA

Embassy: 2 Xiu Shui Bei Jie, Jian Guo Men Wai, Beijing; tel (1) 5321203; telex 22262.

MOROCCO

Embassy: 16 San Li Tun Lu, Beijing; tel (1) 5321489; telex 22268.
Ambassador: Abderrahim Bouchaara.

MOZAMBIQUE

Embassy: San Li Tun, Entrance No. L, 8th Floor, Beijing; tel (1) 523664; telex 22705.
Ambassador: Daniel Banze.

MYANMAR

Embassy: 6 Dong Zhi Men Wai Dajie, Chao Yang Qu, Beijing; tel (1) 5321584; telex 10416.
Ambassador: U Tin Aung Tun.

NEPAL

Embassy: 1 San Li Tun, Xi Liu Jie, Beijing 100600; tel (1) 5321795; telex 210408; fax (1) 5323251.
Minister: Mukunda P. Dhungel.
First Secretary: Pushkar Man Singh Rajbhandari.
Military Attaché: Lieut Col Kamud Rimal.
First Secretary: Shambhu P. Pyakurel.
Attaché: Prem Bahadur Shrestha.
Attaché: M. R. Mishra.
Attaché: K. P. Lamsal.

Consulate-General: Norbulingka Rd 13, Lhasa, Xizang (Tibet); tel 22880; telex 68015.
Consul-General: Dr Rana B. Thapa.

NETHERLANDS

Embassy: 1-15-2 Tayuan Diplomatic Office Bldg, 14 Liang Ma He Nan Lu, Beijing; tel (1) 5321131; telex 22277.
Ambassador: Dr Roland Van den Berg.

NEW ZEALAND

Embassy: 1 Ri Tan, Dong Er Jie, Chaoyang Qu, Beijing 100600; tel (1) 5322731; telex 22124; fax (1) 5324317.
Ambassador: Michael J. Powles.
Counsellor: Heather Baigent.
First Secretary: Michelle Slade.
Second Secretary: Brian Johnstone.
Second Secretary: Greg Rumney.
Attaché: Annette Swaysland.
Attaché: Shelley Murphy.
Trade Commissioner: Bill Sharp.
Trade Commissioner: Mark Lewis.

NIGER

Embassy: 50 Dong Liu Jie, San Li Tun, Beijing; tel (1) 5321616; telex 22133.
Ambassador: Issoufou Mayaki.

NIGERIA

Embassy: 2 Dong Wu Jie, San Li Tun, Beijing; tel (1) 5321650; telex 22274.
Ambassador: Emmanuel Nwachukwu Oba.
Minister: P. A. Kuyoro.
First Secretary: A. Modibbo.
First Secretary: J. C. Ejinaka.
First Secretary: O. C. Cocodia.
Second Secretary: S. O. Worlu.
Finance Attaché: P. A. Ogundele.
Administrative Attaché: B. S. Hassan.
Administrative Attaché: J. A. Obute.

NORWAY

Embassy: 1 San Li Tun, Dong Yi Jie, Beijing; tel (1) 5322261; telex 22266; fax (1) 5322392.
Ambassador: Jan Tore Holvik.

OMAN

Embassy: 6 Liang Ma He Nan Lu, San Li Tun, Beijing; tel (1) 5323956; telex 22192.

Ambassador: Mushtaq bin Abdullah bin Jaffer al-Saleh.

PAKISTAN

Embassy: 1 Dong Zhi Men Wai Dajie, San Li Tun, Beijing; tel (1) 5322504; telex 22673; fax (1) 5322715.
Ambassador: Khalid Mahmood.
Minister: Tariq Fatemi.
Defence and Army Attaché: Brig. Sher Zaman Malik.
Counsellor: Asma Anisa.
Commercial Counsellor: Zaigham Mahmood.
Counsellor: Dr Tariqur Rehman.
Press and Cultural Attaché: M. Yousuf Aziz.

PERU

Embassy: 2-82 San Li Tun, Beijing; tel (1) 5324658; telex 22278; fax (1) 5322178.
Ambassador: Roberto Villarán Koechlin.

PHILIPPINES

Embassy: 23 Xiu Shui Bei Jie, Jian Guo Men Wai, Beijing; tel (1) 5323420; telex 22132.
Ambassador: Felipe H. Mabilangan.

POLAND

Embassy: 1 Ri Tan Lu, Jian Guo Men Wai, Beijing; tel (1) 5321235; telex 210288.
Ambassador: Zbigniew Dembowski.
Minister Plenipotentiary and Counsellor: Dr Zdzisław Góralczyk.
Minister Plenipotentiary and Counsellor (Commercial): Tadeusz Kowalski.
Military, Naval and Air Attaché: Col Henryk Dunal.
Counsellor (Cultural and Press): Bogusław Maciborski.
Counsellor (Economic/Scientific/Technological): Tadeusz Gołacki.
Counsellor (Political/Scientific/Education): Kazimierz Rurka.
First Secretary (Consular): Tomasz Nowacki.
First Secretary (Administrative): Andrzej Musiał.
Deputy Financial Attaché: Janusz Janicki.

Consulate: 618 Jianguo Xi Lu, 200-031 Shanghai; tel (21) 4339228.
Consul-General: Józef Sołtysiewicz.

Consulate: 63 Shamian Dajie, 510-130 Guangzhou; tel (20) 862872.
Consul-General: Jan Nowak.

PORTUGAL

Embassy: 2-72 San Li Tun, Beijing; tel (1) 5323220; telex 22326; fax (1) 5324637.
Ambassador: José Manuel Villas-Boas.

QATAR

Embassy: Beijing.
Ambassador: Mohamed Saad al-Fahid.

ROMANIA

Embassy: Jian Guo Men Wai, Xiushui, Beijing; tel (1) 5323255; telex 22250.
Ambassador: Angelo Miculescu.

RUSSIA

Embassy: 4 Dong Zhi Men Wai Zhong Jie, Beijing; tel (1) 5321267; telex 22247.
Ambassador: Nikolai N. Solovyev.

Consulate-General: 20 Huang Pu Lu, Shanghai; tel (21) 240221; telex 30220.

RWANDA

Embassy: 30 Xiu Shui Bei Jie, Beijing; tel (1) 5321762; telex 22104.
Ambassador: Karamage Augustin.
First Counsellor: Leon Ngarukiye.
Third Secretary: Gabriel Ntawiheba.

SAUDI ARABIA

Embassy: Beijing.
Ambassador: Tawfiq al-Alamdar.

SENEGAL

Embassy: 1 Ri Tan Dong Yi Jie, Jian Guo Men Wai, Beijing; tel (1) 5322576; telex 22100.
Ambassador: Mady Ndao.

SIERRA LEONE

Embassy: 7 Dong Zhi Men Wai Dajie, Beijing; tel (1) 5321222; telex 22166.
Ambassador: Sheku Badara Bastru Dumbuya.

SINGAPORE

Embassy: 4 Liang Ma He Nan Lu, San Li Tun, Beijing 100600; tel (1) 5323926.

SOMALIA

Embassy: 2 San Li Tun Lu, Beijing; tel (1) 5321742; telex 22121.
Ambassador: Mohamed Hassan Said.
Counsellor: Ahmed Adan Liban.
Second Secretary: Abdullahi Warsame Ali.
Third Secretary: Mohamed Haji Aweis.

SPAIN

Embassy: 9 San Li Tun Lu, Beijing; tel (1) 5323629; telex 22108; fax (1) 5323401.
Minister-Counsellor: Antonio F. Mazarambroz.
First Secretary: Jorge Romeu.

SRI LANKA

Embassy: 3 Jian Hua Lu, Jian Guo Men Wai, Beijing 100600; tel (1) 5321861; telex 22136; fax (1) 5325426.
Ambassador: Suhita Gautamadasa.
First Secretary: Kumara Ranjith Arachchi.
First Secretary: Tissa Wijeratne.
Attaché: Abdul Cader Mohamed Ibrahim.

SUDAN

Embassy: 1 Dong Er Jie, San Li Tun, Beijing; tel (1) 5322205; telex 22116; fax (1) 5321280.
Ambassador: Dr Anwar el-Hadi Abdel-Rahman.
Minister Plenipotentiary: B. Mohammed El-Hassan.
Military Attaché: Lieut Gen. Ahmad Ali Salih.
Minister Plenipotentiary: Charles Manyang D'Awol.
First Secretary: Musa Abdel-Rahm.
Second Secretary: Mohammed Abdalla.
Administrative Attaché: Mohammed Beshir.
Financial Attaché: Mohammed Osman Sherif.
Administrative Attaché: Fadol El-Mula al-Sawi.

SWEDEN

Embassy: 3 Dong Zhi Men Wai Dajie, San Li Tun, Chaoyang District, Beijing 100600; tel (1) 5323331; telex 22261; fax (1) 5325008.
Ambassador: Björn Ingvar Skala.
Minister: Nils Eliasson.
Counsellor: Per Ström.
Counsellor (Commercial Affairs): Jan Söderberg.
Second Secretary: Annika Hahn-Englund.
Second Secretary: Elisabet Sjöbom.
Third Secretary (Translation): Peter Sivam.

SWITZERLAND

Embassy: 3 Dong Wu Jie, San Li Tun, Beijing 100600; tel (1) 5322736; telex 22251; fax (1) 5324353.
Ambassador: Erwin Schurtenberger.
First Secretary: Hans Jakob Roth.
First Secretary (Economic Affairs): Rolf Lenz.
Attaché: Marie-Louise Scherer.
Attaché and Head of Chancery: Verena Raffaeli-Jost.

SYRIA

Embassy: 6 Dong Si Jie, San Li Tun, Beijing; tel (1) 5321347; telex 22138.
Ambassador: Loutof Allah Haydar.
Minister Plenipotentiary: Dr Issam Hayani.
Attaché: Mohamed Dablah.
Attaché: Kamel Osman.

TADZHIKISTAN

Embassy: Beijing.

TANZANIA

Embassy: 53 Dong Liu Jie, San Li Tun, Beijing; tel (1) 5321408; telex 22749.
Ambassador: Ferdinand K. Ruhinda.
Minister Plenipotentiary: Isaya B. Chialo.
Second Secretary: M. P. Kaducha.
Second Secretary: Rajubu H. Gamaha.
Attaché: D. P. Kassolo.
Attaché: R. B. Kalumanzilah.
Attaché: C. Mahundi.

THAILAND

Embassy: 40 Guang Hua Lu, Beijing 100600; tel (1) 5321903; telex 22145; fax (1) 5323986.
Ambassador: Tej Bunnag.

TOGO

Embassy: 11 Dong Zhi Men Wai Dajie, Beijing; tel (1) 5322202; telex 22130.
Ambassador: Yao Bloua Agbo.

TUNISIA

Embassy: 1 Dong Jie, San Li Tun, Beijing; tel (1) 5322435; telex 22103.
Ambassador: Salah Jebali.
First Secretary: Mohamed Ben Salah.
Secretary: Zohra Ben Hamida.
Attaché: Ali Hakimi.
Attaché: Mohamed Raouf Bahi.

TURKEY

Embassy: 9 Dong Wu Jie, San Li Tun, Beijing; tel (1) 5322650; telex 210168; fax (1) 5323268.
Ambassador: Resat Arim.
Counsellor: Cengiz Sanay.
Military, Naval and Air Attaché: Lieut Col Adem Demir.
Economic and Commercial Counsellor: Hasan Aka.
Economic and Commercial Counsellor: Osman Yasar Bekaroglu.
Assistant Economic and Commercial Counsellor: Feridum Ozkazanc.
Third Secretary and Head of Consular Section: Mehmet Ogutcu.

UGANDA

Embassy: 5 Dong Jie, San Li Tun, Beijing 100600; tel (1) 5321708; telex 22272; fax (1) 5322242.
Ambassador: William Wycliffe Rwetsiba.
First Secretary: Catherine Sebitosi.
Second Secretary: David A. Simbwa.
Second Secretary: Henry Picho-Okello.
Administrative Attaché: G. L. Bosa.

UKRAINE

Embassy: Beijing.

UNITED KINGDOM

Embassy: 11 Guang Hua Lu, Jian Guo Men Wai, Beijing; tel (1) 5321930; telex 211216; fax (1) 5321961.
Ambassador: Sir Robin J. T. McLaren.
Counsellor (Political) and Deputy Head of Mission: D. Coates.
Counsellor (Commercial): A. Kerfoot.
Counsellor (Cultural/British Council Director): A. D. Johnson.
Defence, Military and Air Attaché: Col C. A. Lees.
Naval Attaché: Commdr A. P. B. Armstrong.
Consul-General: Dr J. E. Hoare.
First Secretary (Management) and Consul: G. R. Duff.
First Secretary and Consul: P. B. Davies.
First Secretary (Chancery): P. Clark.
First Secretary (Chancery): S. C. Riordan.
First Secretary (Energy): J. M. Candlish.
First Secretary (Cultural ELO): J. D. Stoddart.
First Secretary (Cultural Affairs and Science): Dr G. Alexander.
First Secretary (Cultural - Books): C. C. Edwards.
First Secretary (Commercial): Dr L. Bristow-Smith.
Second Secretary (Cultural - Scholarships): A. Hadley.
Second Secretary (Cultural - Exchanges): Dr P. W. C. Hart.
Second Secretary (Cultural - Administration and Arts): C. Lindsley.
Second Secretary (Cultural - Assistant ELO): G. Slaven.
Second Secretary (Chancery and Information): B. J. Davidson.
Third Secretary (Accommodation): J. Allan.
Third Secretary (Immigration): M. A. Russell.
Third Secretary (Immigration): C. Murphy.

Consulate-General: 244 Yong Fu Lu, Shanghai; tel (21) 4330508; telex 33476; fax (21) 4333115.
Consul-General: J. W. MacDonald.
Consul (Commercial): I. B. Wellfare.
Vice-Consul (Management): J. W. Short.

USA

Embassy: 3 Xiu Shui Bei Jie, Beijing 100600; tel (1) 5323831; telex 22701; fax (1) 5323178.
Ambassador: James Roderick Lilley.
Deputy Chief of Mission: B. Lynne Pascoe.
Political Section: Donald W. Keyser.
Economic Section: Stephen A. Schlaikjer.
Commercial Section: Timothy P. Stratford.
Administration Section: Michael Bart Flaherty.
Regional Security Officer: Frederic C. Brandt.
Public Affairs Officer: McKinney H. Russell.
Communications Programme Officer: George A. McKinney.
Information Systems Manager: Larry J. Kozak.
Scientific Attaché: Andres D. Onat.
Office of the Defence Attaché: Rear Adm. Eric A. McVadon, Jr.
Agricultural Section: Edwin A. Bauer.
Agricultural Trade Office: Jonathan P. Gressel.

Consulate-General: Dong Fang Hotel, Liu Hua Rd, Guangzhou; tel (20) 669900; telex 44439.
Consul-General: Dennis G. Harter.
Political Section: Gary Williams.
Economic Section: John T. Tkacik, Jr.
Commercial Section: Todd N. Thurwachter.
Administrative Section: Roberto Brady.
Branch Public Affairs Officer: Richard Stites.
Communications Programme Officer: Steven M. Derrick.
Information Systems Manager: Sharon Weiss.
Agricultural Trade Office: Philip A. Shull.

Consulate-General: 1469 Huai Hai Middle Rd, Shanghai; tel (21) 4336880; telex 33383; fax (21) 4334122.
Consul-General: Frank P. Wardlaw.
Political Section: Jonathan M. Aloisi.
Economic Section: John J. Norris, Jr.
Commercial Section: Nora Sun.
Administrative Section: John B. Hitchcock.
Branch Public Affairs Officer: Norma F. Harris.
Regional Security Officer/GSO: David G. Kidd.

Consulate-General: 40 Lane 4, Section 5, Sanjing St, Heping District, Shenyang; tel (24) 290000; telex 80011; fax (24) 290074.
Consul-General: Morton J. Holbrook III.
Economic Section: Paul D. Stephenson.
Commercial Section: Richard Mohr.
Consular/Political Section: Laurent D. Charbonnet.
Administrative Section: Robert Wilson.
Branch Public Affairs Officer: Ruth A. Kurzbauer.
Communications Programme Officer: Thomas A. Trainer.

Consulate-General: Jinjiang Hotel, 180 Renmin Rd, Chengdu, Sichuan; tel (28) 582222; telex 60128; fax (28) 583520.
Consul-General: Marshall P. Adair.
Political Section: Kenneth H. Jarrett.
Administrative Section: Bryan Chastain.
Branch Public Affairs Officer: Barbara A. Zigli.

URUGUAY

Embassy: 2-7-2 Tayuan Bldg, Beijing; tel (1) 5324445; telex 211237; fax (1) 5324357.
Ambassador: Guillermo Valles Galmes.

UZBEKISTAN

Embassy: Beijing.

VENEZUELA

Embassy: 14 San Li Tun Lu, Beijing; tel (1) 5321295; telex 22137; fax (1) 5323817.
Ambassador: Eduardo Casanova Sucre.
Second Secretary: Leong Pui.

VIET-NAM

Embassy: 32 Guang Hua Lu, Jian Guo Men Wai, Beijing.
Ambassador: Dang Nghiem Hoanh.

YEMEN

Embassy: 4 Dongzhi Men Wai Dajie, Beijing; tel (1) 5321362.
Ambassador: Ghaleb Saeed al-Adoofi.
Minister Plenipotentiary: Ahmed M. Al-Habshi.
Economic Counsellor: Ahmed Mohamed Ali Daer.
First Secretary: Ali Ali Mohamed Al-Soswa.
Attaché: Abadu Alhamid A. Besbas.

YUGOSLAVIA

Embassy: 1 Dong Liu Jie, San Li Tun, Beijing; tel (1) 5323016; telex 22403; fax (1) 5321207.
Ambassador: Ilija Djukić.
Minister-Counsellor: Radoslav Maksimovic.
Armed Forces Attaché: Col Tomislav Simunovic.
Counsellor: Cedica Nikolic.
First Secretary: Istvan Janik.
Second Secretary: Branko Marjanac.
Third Secretary: Bozidar Jovanovic.
Attaché: Miroslav Virovkic.
Attaché: Milorad Milicevic.

ZAIRE

Embassy: 6 Dong Wu Jie, San Li Tun, Beijing; tel (1) 421966; telex 22273.
Ambassador: Lombo Lo Mangamanga.
Minister-Counsellor: Bukasa Mulumba.
Second Counsellor: Mabela Lukoki Mayala.
Second Counsellor and Head of Co-operation Section: Alluma Idolua Mulamba.
First Secretary and Deputy Head of Co-operation Section: Nzapalaye Ndagbia.

ZAMBIA

Embassy: 5 Dong Si Jie, San Li Tun, Beijing; tel (1) 5321550; telex 22388; fax (1) 5321891.
Ambassador: Peter Lesa Kasanda.
Counsellor: Marty Bwalya Kalamba.
First Secretary (Political): Patson Victor Robert Lwenje.
Second Secretary (Administration and Finance): Ernest Kabila Ilubala.
Third Secretary (Communications): Atanasio Lungu.
Third Secretary (Personal Secretary to Ambassador): Ruth Namukonda.

ZIMBABWE

Embassy: 7 Dong San Jie, San Li Tun, Beijing; tel (1) 5321652; telex 22671; fax (1) 5325383.
Ambassador: B. G. Chidyausiku.
Counsellor: C. Mlambo.
Defence Attaché: Lieut Col D. Chiweza.
First Secretary: G. Machengete.
First Secretary: D. Dzvuke.
Deputy Defence Attaché: Sqn Ldr Kadziyanike.
Second Secretary: E. Goniwa.
Second Secretary: M. Mashingaidze.
Secretary: P. Parwada.

International Organizations

EUROPEAN COMMUNITIES

External Delegation: Ta Yuan Diplomatic Offices Bldg, Apt. No 2-6-1, Liang Ma He Nan Lu 14, Beijing; tel (1) 5324443; telex 222690; fax (1) 5324342.
Head of Delegation: Pierre Duchateau.

CHINA (TAIWAN)

COSTA RICA

Embassy: Tulip Bldg, 1st Floor, 108 Chung Cheng Rd, Sec. 2, Taipei; tel (2) 8712422.
Ambassador: Francisco Tacsan Lam.

DOMINICAN REPUBLIC

Embassy: 110 Chung Cheng Rd, 1st Floor, Sec. 2, Tien Mou, Taipei; tel (2) 8717938; telex 19873.
Ambassador: José Manuel López Balaguer.

EL SALVADOR

Embassy: 15 Lane 34, Ku Kung Rd, Shih Lin 11102, Taipei; tel (2) 8819887; fax (2) 8817995.
Ambassador: Francisco Ricardo Santana Berrios.
Defence Attaché: Rafael Eduardo Argueta Montes.

GUATEMALA

Embassy: 6 Lane 88, Chien Kuo North Rd, Sec. 1, Taipei; tel (2) 5077043; fax (2) 5060577.
Ambassador: Carlos Oriol Jiménez Quiroa.

HAITI

Embassy: 246 Chungshan North Rd, 3rd Floor, Sec. 6, Taipei; tel (2) 8317086.
Ambassador: Raymond Perodin.

HOLY SEE

Apostolic Nunciature: 87 Ai Kuo East Rd, Taipei 10605; tel (2) 3216847; fax (2) 3911926.
Counsellor and Chargé d'affaires a.i.: Mgr Adriano Bernardini.

HONDURAS

Embassy: 142 Chung Hsiao East Rd, Room 701, Sec. 4, Taipei; tel (2) 7518737; telex 14224.
Ambassador: Agripino Flores Aguilar.

KOREA, REPUBLIC

Embassy: 345 Chung Hsiao East Rd, Sec. 4, Taipei; tel (2) 7619363 .
Ambassador: Han Chul-Soo.

LATVIA

Consulate: Taipei.

NAURU

Consulate: 247 Chung Cheng Rd, 9th Floor, C, Sec. 2, Tien Mou, Taipei; tel (2) 8736121; fax (2) 8736125.
Consul: Miniva Depaune.

PANAMA

Embassy: 13 Te Huei St, 5th Floor, Taipei; tel (2) 5968563.
Ambassador: Carlos Yap Chong.

PARAGUAY

Embassy: 20 Lane 38 Tien Yee St, 2nd Floor, Tien Mou, Taipei; tel (2) 8728932; telex 13744.
Ambassador: Angel Juan Souto Hernández.

SOUTH AFRICA

Embassy: Bank Tower, 13th Floor, 205 Tun Hua North Rd, POB 540, Taipei; tel (2) 7153251; telex 21954; fax (2) 7123214.
Ambassador: Alan McAllister Harvey.
Minister: J. H. Kotze.
Counsellor (Administration): A. F. Venter.
Counsellor (Trade): S. P. Pretorius.
First Secretary: M. N. S. Wilson.
First Secretary: J. L. Nel.
First Secretary (Trade): R. I. S. Moodie.
Second Secretary (Trade): P. J. Steenkamp.
Armed Forces Attaché: Col D. E. Page.
Army and Naval Attaché: Commdt C. S. Harrison.
Assistant Armed Forces Attaché: Maj. J. J. Huysamen.

COLOMBIA

ARGENTINA

Embassy: Avda 40A, 13-09, 16°, Bogotá, DE; tel (1) 288-0900; telex 44576.
Ambassador: Daniel Olmos.

AUSTRIA

Embassy: Carrera 11, No 75-29, Bogotá, DE; Apdo Aéreo 075651, Bogotá 8, DE; tel (1) 211-9735; telex 41489.
Ambassador: Arthur Schuschnigg.
Economic Counsellor: Heidemarie Glantschnig.
Counsellor (Commercial): Wolfgang Entmayr.
Attaché (Commercial): Martin Pilser.
Attaché: Kathrin Kapusta.

Consulate: Calle 65 B No. 41-68, Apdo Aéreo 1317, Barranquilla; tel (58) 32-0953; telex 33431.
Honorary Consul: Oswald Loewy.

Consulate-General: Edif. Portachuelo, Calle No. 5-60, Apdo 703, Bogotá, DE; Apdo Aéreo 075679, Bogotá 8, DE; tel (1) 249-3139.
Honorary Consul-General: Koloman Brunner-Lehenstein.

Consulate: Calle 12, No. 1-12, Of. 408, Apdo Aéreo 2126, Cali; tel (23) 64-4646; telex 55724; fax (23) 64-4657.
Honorary Consul: Janek Harold Zangen.

Consulate: Edif. Concasa, 10°, Apdo Aéreo 1626, Cartagena; tel (53) 64-7450; telex 37791; fax (53) 65-1809.
Honorary Consul: Hermann Schwyn.

Consulate: Calle 30, No. 46-65, Apdo Aéreo 1453, Medellín; tel (4) 232-0500; telex 65210.
Honorary Consul: Hans Michael Widhalm.

BELGIUM

Embassy: Calle 26, No 4A-45, 7°, Bogotá, DE; tel (1) 282-8881; telex 41203.
Ambassador: Willy J. Stevens.

BOLIVIA

Embassy: Calle 78, No 9-57, Of. 1103, Bogotá, DE; tel (1) 211-8962; telex 45583.
Ambassador: Guillermo Riveros Tejada.

BRAZIL

Embassy: Calle 93, No 14-20, 8°, Bogotá, DE.
Ambassador: Alvaro da Costa Franco.

BULGARIA

Embassy: Calle 81, No 7-71, Apdo Aéreo 89751, Bogotá, DE; tel (1) 212-8028; telex 41217.
Ambassador: Dimitar Petkov Popov.

CANADA

Embassy: Calle 76, No 11-52, Apdo Aéreo 53531, Bogotá 2, DE; tel (1) 217-5555; telex 44568; fax (1) 235-6253.
Ambassador: Dean J. Browne.
Counsellor and Consul: G. Charlebois.
Counsellor (Commercial): P. Zalite.
Counsellor (Development): D. Smart.
First Secretary (Commercial): B. J. Wassink.
Second Secretary (Administration) and Vice-Consul: K. C. Beach.
Second Secretary: L. Beaulne.

Immigration Section: Apdo Aéreo 052978, Bogotá 2.
First Secretary (Immigration) and Consul: P. A. Lancefield.

Consulate: Calle de la Inquisicion con, Santo Domingo Esquina No. 33-08, Apto 201, Cartagena; tel (53) 648-250.
Honorary Consul: E. Dager.

CHILE

Embassy: Calle 100, No 11B-44, Bogotá, DE; tel (1) 214-7926; telex 44404.
Ambassador: Carlos Negri Chiorrini.

CHINA, PEOPLE'S REPUBLIC

Embassy: Calle 71, No 2A-41, Bogotá, DE; tel (1) 255-8548; telex 45387.
Ambassador: Yusheng Wang.

COSTA RICA

Embassy: Carrera 15, No 80-87, Of. 401, Apdo Aéreo 11354, Bogotá, DE; tel (1) 236-1098.
Ambassador: Rafael A. Chinchilla Fallas.

CZECHOSLOVAKIA

Embassy: Avda 13, No 104A-30, Bogotá, DE; tel (1) 214-2240; telex 44590.
Ambassador: René Hanousek.

DENMARK

Consulate-General: Cra. 10, No. 96-29, of. 611-612, Apdo Aéreo 250313, Bogotá 8, DE; tel (1) 610-0798; fax (1) 610-0829.
Consul-General: Vagn Aage Knudsen.
Commercial Officer and Vice-Consul: José Guatama.

Consulate: Carrera 45, No. 34-44, Edif. Libertad No. 503, Apdo Aéreo 3089, Barranquilla; tel (58) 32-8785; telex 31112; fax (58) 41-2065.
Consul: Julio Zakzuk Villadiego.

Consulate: Avda 4 Norte No. 4n-46, Barrio Centenario, Apdo Aéreo 99, Cali; tel (23) 614368.
Consul-General: Knud Henry Jensen.

Consulate: Edif. Banco de Bogotá, Of. 601, Apdo Aéreo 3040, Cartagena; tel (53) 64-3669; telex 037666; fax (53) 68-5162.
Consul: Rafael Espinosa Gray.

Consulate: Calle 51, No. 42-61, Apdo Aéreo 9039, Medellín; tel (4) 239-7696.
Consul-General: Alfredo Mora de la Hoz.

DOMINICAN REPUBLIC

Embassy: Calle 87, No 16-27, 3°, Bogotá, DE; tel (1) 218-8673.
Ambassador: Rodolfo Leyba Polanco.

ECUADOR

Embassy: Calle 89, No 13-07, Bogotá, DE; tel (1) 257-0066; telex 45776; fax (1) 257-9799.
Ambassador: Dr Fernando Córdova.

EGYPT

Embassy: Carrera 19A, No. 98-17, Bogotá, DE; tel (1) 236-4832.
Ambassador: Ahmed Fathi Abulkheir.

EL SALVADOR

Embassy: Carrera 9A, No 80-15, Of. 503, Apdo 089394, Bogotá, DE; tel (1) 212-5932; telex 42072.
Ambassador: José Roberto Andino Salzar.

FINLAND

Embassy: Calle 72, No 8-56, 7°, Apdo Aéreo 75155, Bogotá, DE; tel (1) 212-6111; telex 44304; fax (1) 212-6106.
Ambassador: Risto Rekola.
Commercial Secretary: Raimo Kehusmaa.
First Secretary: Kristina Pingoud-Fred.

Consulate-General: Carrera 7a, No 35-33, 7°, Apdo Aéreo 4990, Bogotá, DE; tel (1) 232-1202; telex 44578; fax (1) 285-7752.
Consul-General: Erkki Alhanko.

Consulate: Carrera 10, No 95-26, Of. 223, Apdo Aéreo 250529, Bogotá, DE; tel (1) 610-1830; fax (1) 610-1830.
Consul: Antti Aro.

Consulate: Via 40 de Las Flores, Cementos del Caribe, Apdo Aéreo 2739, Barranquilla; tel (58) 35-0080; telex 33373.
Consul: Juan Manuel Ruiseco Vieira.

Consulate: Avda 3B, No 7A-02, Barrio las Mercedes, Cruz Roja Colombiana, Apdo Aéreo 675, Buenaventura; tel (32) 24-475.
Consul: Eduardo Diaz Ruíz.

Consulate: Calle 4 Norte No 1N-52, 3°, Barrio Centanario, Apdo Aéreo 5793, Cali; tel (23) 61-1145; fax (23) 67-3004.
Consul: Alfonso Holguín Beplat.

Consulate: Edif. Banco Bogotá, Of. 602, Apdo Aéreo 30-40, Cartagena; tel (53) 43-500; telex 37666.
Consul: Rafael Espinosa Gray.

Consulate: Carrera 46, No 52-82, Edif. Camera de Comercio, 6°, Apdo Aéreo 1468, Medellín; tel (4) 31-6222; telex 66809.
Consul: Jorge Alberto Uribe Echavarria.

Consulate: Edif. de los Bancos, Carrera 3, No 14-21, Of. 605, Apdo Aéreo 946, Santa Marta; tel (54) 27-589; telex 38888.
Consul: Luis Díaz-Granados Alzamora.

FRANCE

Embassy: Avda 39, No 7-84, Apdo Aéreo 29611, Bogotá, DE; tel (1) 285-4311; telex 44558.
Ambassador: Charles Crettien.

Consular Section: Carrera 7, No 38-91, Bogotá, DE; tel (1) 285-5534; telex 44558.

Trade Promotion Office: Calle 37, No 7-43, Bogotá, DE; tel (1) 287-9121; telex 45534.

GERMANY

Embassy: Carrera 4, No 72-35, 6°, Edif. Sisky, Apdo Aéreo 91808, Bogotá, DE 8; tel (1) 212-0511; telex 44765; fax (1) 210-4256.
Ambassador: Dr Heribert Wöckel.

Consulate: Calle 80, No 79-79, Edif. Tealco, Apdo Aéreo 668, Barranquilla, Atlántico; tel (58) 45-8308.
Honorary Consul: Dierk Schnabel.

Consulate: Carrera 33, No 70-78, Apdo Aéreo 0343, Bucaramanga, Santander del Sur; tel (7) 71-102.

Honorary Consul: Siegfried Markert.

Consulate: Avda 4a Norte, No 14-107, Barrio Granada, Apdo Aéreo 1788, Cali, Valle del Cauca; tel (23) 68 5361.
Honorary Consul: Peter Niessen.

Consulate: Calle 5a, No 12-76, Castillogrande, Of. 8D, Apdo Aéreo 1043, Cartagena, Bolívar; tel (53) 65-1901.
Honorary Consul: Frank Bolle.

Consulate: Calle 7, No 4-55, Apdo Aéreo 581, Cúcuta, Santander del Norte; tel (70) 22-455.
Honorary Consul: Eugenio Hugo Wittenzellner.

Consulate: Calle 23, No 21-41, Apdo Aéreo 2558, Manizales, Caldas; tel (68) 84-1261.
Honorary Consul: Guillermo Sanint Botero.

Consulate: Calle 52, No 47-28, Edif. la Ceiba, Of. 1302, Apdo Aéreo 51666, Medellín, Antioquia; tel (4) 251-6316; telex 65208.
Honorary Consul: Hellmuth E. Lücker.

GUATEMALA

Embassy: Transversal 29, Apdo 139A-41, Bogotá, DE; tel (1) 259-1496; fax (1) 274-5365.
Ambassador: Hugo Cerezo Arévalo.

HAITI

Embassy: Calle 67, No 10-18, 4°, Bogotá, DE; tel (1) 217-6209.
Chargé d'affaires: Carlo Toussaint.

HOLY SEE

Apostolic Nunciature: Carrera 15, No 36-33, Apdo Aéreo 3740, Bogotá, DE; tel (1) 245-4260; fax (1) 285-1817.
Apostolic Nuncio: Most Rev. Paolo Romeo, Titular Archbishop of Vulturia.
First Secretary: Mgr Ivan Jurkovič.

HONDURAS

Embassy: Carrera 13, No 63-51, Bogotá, DE; tel (1) 235-3158; telex 45540.
Ambassador: Ricardo Arturo Pineda Milla.

HUNGARY

Embassy: Carrera 6A, No 77-46, Bogotá, DE; tel (1) 217-8578; telex 43244.
Ambassador: Dr Vince Kóczián.

ICELAND

Consulate-General: Carrera 10, No 92-56, Apdo 9712, Bogotá, DE; tel (1) 610-2149; fax (1) 236-5254.
Consul-General: Sleiman Turk.

INDIA

Embassy: Calle 93B, No 13-44, Bogotá, DE; tel (1) 236-9821; telex 41380; fax (1) 218-5393.
Ambassador: G. D. Atuk.

IRAN

Embassy: Transversal 20, No 114-20A, Bogotá, DE; tel (1) 215-8262; telex 42252.
Ambassador: Ali Asghar Almousavi.

ISRAEL

Embassy: Calle 35, No 7-25, 14°, Bogotá, DE; tel (1) 287-7782; telex 44755.
Ambassador: Gideon Tadmor.

ITALY

Embassy: Calle 70, No 10-25, Bogotá, DE; tel (1) 235-4300; telex 45588.
Ambassador: Filippo Anfuso.

JAMAICA

Consulate: Calle 30A, No 6-22, Office 1903, Bogatá; tel (1) 232-8856.
Honorary Consul: Alberto Byfield.
Honorary Vice-Consul: E. Byfield.

JAPAN

Embassy: Carrera 7, No 74-21, 8° y 9°, Edif. Seguros Aurora, Apdo Aéreo 7407, Bogotá, DE; tel (1) 217-6950; telex 43327; fax (1) 212-3226.
Ambassador: Chihiro Tsukada.

KOREA, REPUBLIC

Embassy: Calle 94, No 9-39, Bogotá, DE; tel (1) 236-1616; telex 41468.
Ambassador: Yong Chol Ahn.

LEBANON

Embassy: Calle 74, No 12-44, Bogotá, DE; tel (1) 212-8360; telex 44333.
Ambassador: Joseph Akl.
First Secretary (Consular Affairs): Hassan Muslimani.

MEXICO

Embassy: Calle 99, No 12-08, Bogotá, DE; tel (1) 256-6121; telex 41264.
Ambassador: Rodulfo Figueroa.

MOROCCO

Embassy: Carrera 13A, No 98-33, Bogotá, DE; tel (1) 218-7147; telex 43468.
Ambassador: Youssef Fassi Fihri.

NETHERLANDS

Embassy: Carrera 9, No 74-08, Bogotá, DE; tel (1) 211-9600; telex 44629; fax (1) 211-9855.
Ambassador: Reijnier Flaes.

NEW ZEALAND

Consulate: Apdo Aéreo 30402, Calle 106, No. 25-41, Bogotá, DE; tel (1) 215-8949; fax (1) 215-1190.
Honorary Consul: Annette Pearson de González.

NICARAGUA

Embassy: Transversal 19A, No 108-77, 2°, Bogotá, DE; tel (1) 214-1445; fax (1) 215-9582.
Ambassador: Donald Castillo Rivas.
Minister-Counsellor: Manuel S. Abaunza Gutierrez.

PANAMA

Embassy: Calle 92, No 7-70, Bogotá, DE; Apdo Aéreo 90094, Bogotá, DE; tel (1) 257-5067; telex 44970; fax (1) 257-5068.
Ambassador: Jaime Ricardo Fernández Urriola.
Chargé d'affaires a.i. and Second Secretary: Orlando S. Bethancourt T.
Head of Consular Affairs: Itzel Marie Pretto Lugo.
Attaché and Administrative Secretary: Diana Elizabeth Gaitán De Maldonado.
Commercial Attaché: Emely E. Chiari Ortega.
Cultural Attaché: Vielka Arosemeda De Avendaño.
Legal Attaché: Erick Daniel Bravo Dutary.

PARAGUAY

Embassy: Calle 57, No 7-11, Of. 702, Apdo Aéreo 20085, Bogotá, DE; tel (1) 255-4160.
Ambassador: Rubén Ruiz Gómez.

PERU

Embassy: Calle 94A, No 7A-26, Bogotá, DE; tel (1) 257-3753; telex 44453; fax (1) 18-0133.

POLAND

Embassy: Calle 104A, No 23-48, Bogotá, DE; tel (1) 214-0854; telex 44591.
Ambassador: Mieczysław Biernacki.
Chargé d'affaires: Andrzej Podkowinski.

PORTUGAL

Embassy: Calle 71, No 11-10, Of. 703, Bogotá, DE; tel (1) 212-4223.
Ambassador: António Syder Santiago.
Counsellor (Commercial): Dr João Rodriguez.

ROMANIA

Embassy: Carrera 7, No 92-58, Bogotá, DE; tel (1) 256-6438; telex 41238.
Ambassador: Gheorghe Fulea.

RUSSIA

Embassy: Carrera 4, No 75-00, Apdo Aéreo 90600, Bogotá, DE; tel (1) 235-7960; telex 44503.
Ambassador: Igor Dmitrievich Bubnov.

Consular Section: tel (1) 235-7980.

SPAIN

Embassy: Calle 92, No 12-68, Bogotá, DE; tel (1) 236-2154; telex 44779.
Ambassador: Salvador Bermúdez de Castro y Bernales.

SWEDEN

Embassy: Calle 72, 5-83, 9°, Edif. Avda de Chile, Apdo Aéreo 52966, Bogotá, DE; tel (1) 255-3777; telex 44626; fax (1) 210-3401.
Ambassador: Fredrik Bergenstråhle.
Counsellor: Sven-Olof Johansson.
Second Secretary: Björn Häggmark.

Consulate: Calle 77, No 74-111, Apdo Aéreo 939, Barranquilla; tel (58) 58-0222; telex 31311; fax (58) 56-0095.
Consul: Carlos José Recio Munck.

Consulate: Edif. Gerleinco, Calle 8A, No 3-133, Apdo Aéreo 528, Buenaventura; tel (32) 22-797; telex 52373.
Consul: Rafael Antonio Ibarra Luna.

Consulate: Carrera 1, No 52-41, Apdo Aéreo 9545, Cali; tel (23) 46-4455; telex 51261; fax (23) 46-4967.
Consul: Gunnar Knutsson Lindahl.

Consulate: Calle San Pedro Claver No 31-7, 2°, Apdo Aéreo 20160, Cartagena; tel (53) 64-2197; telex 37669; fax (53) 65-5417.
Consul: Humberto Benedetti Lecompte.

Consulate: Edif. Banco Caldas, 14°, Calle 21, No 21-45, Apdo Aéreo 2008, Manizales; tel (68) 82-2232; telex 83584; fax (68) 84-1473.
Consul: Hernán Arango Uribe.

Consulate: Edif. Multicentro Aliadas, Of. 312, Calle 9, No 43A-33, El Poblado, Apdo Aéreo 51000, Medellín; tel (4) 268-0647; telex 66768; fax (4) 268-0501.
Consul: Oscar Llano Escobar.

Consulate: Edif. Los Bancos, Of. 804, Apdo Aéreo 1396, Santa Marta; tel (56) 23-3739; telex 38888; fax (56) 32-168.
Consul: Eduardo Agaton Díaz Granados Alzamora.

SWITZERLAND

Embassy: Carrera 9a, No 74-08/1101, Edif. Profinanzas, Apdo Aéreo 4304, Bogotá, DE; tel (1) 255-3945; telex 41230; fax (1) 217-0026.
Ambassador: Peter Niederberger.
Counsellor: Heinrich Gattiker.
Attaché and Head of Chancery: Siegfried Zurbrügg.

Consulate: Edif. Beneficencia del Valle, Carrera 4a, No 8-50, Of. 205, Apdo Aéreo 2183, Cali; tel (23) 79-1024; telex 55719.

Honorary Consul: Ruedi Schmid.

UNITED KINGDOM

Embassy: Torre Propaganda Sancho, Calle 98, No 9-03, 4°, Apdo 4508, Bogotá, DE; tel (1) 218-5111; telex 44503; fax (1) 218-2460.
Ambassador: Keith E. H. Morris.
First Secretary, Consul and Deputy Head of Mission: J. W. Forbes-Meyler.
Defence Attaché: Col J. D. Griffiths-Eyton.
Second Secretary (Chancery and Technical Co-operation): A. F. Bedford.
Third Secretary (Management) and Vice-Consul: D. E. Gordon.

Consulate: Carrera 44, No 45-57, Apdo 706, Barranquilla; tel (58) 32-6936; telex 33559.
Vice-Consul: M. Hutchinson.

Consulate: Edif. Garces, Calle 11 No 1-07, Office No 409, Apdo 1326, Cali; tel (23) 83-2752.
Honorary Consul: A. E. B. Laurence.

Consulate: Calle 9 No 43B-93, Medellín; tel (4) 246-3114; telex 65375; fax (4) 266-7318.
Honorary Consul: F. Osorio.

USA

Embassy: Calle 38, No 8-61, Bogotá, DE; tel (1) 285-1300; telex 44843; fax (1) 288-5687.
Ambassador: Thomas E. McNamara.
Deputy Chief of Mission: J. Phillip McLean.
Political Section: David L. Hobbs.
Economic Section: Robert B. McMullen.
Commercial Section: Arthur Trezise.
Administrative Section: George M. Lowe, Jr.
Regional Security Officer: Wallace Ray Williams.
Public Affairs Officer: Louis P. Falino.
Communications Programme Officer: Mary Dingler (acting).
Information Systems Manager: Leon Galanos.
Agency for International Development: James F. Smith.
Office of the Defence Attaché: Col James S. Roach.
Military Assistance Advisory Group: Col Arturo Rodríguez.
Agricultural Section: Larry M. Senger.
Labour Officer: Charlotte E. Roe.
Narcotics Assistance Unit: James V. Doane, Jr.

Consulate: Calle 77 Carrera 68, Centro Comercial, Mayorista; tel (58) 45-7088; telex 33482; fax (58) 45-9464.
Principal Officer: Ross E. Benson.
Administrative/Consular Section: Anne E. Pforzheimer.

URUGUAY

Embassy: Carrera 9A, No 80-15, 11°, Apdo Aéreo 01466, Bogotá, DE; tel (1) 235-2968; telex 43377.

VENEZUELA

Embassy: Calle 33, No 6-94, Edif. La Lonja, Propiedad Raiz, 10°, 11° y 12°, Bogotá, DE; tel (1) 285-2035; telex 44504; fax (1) 285-7372.
Ambassador: Fernando Gerbasi.
Minister-Counsellor: Rafael C. Rangel Vargas.
Counsellor: Héctor Cassy Azocar.
Counsellor: Rocio Maneyro G.
First Secretary: Enrique X. Badillo Sposito.
First Secretary: Rafael Quevedo.
Second Secretary: Robert Noriega Moreno.
Second Secretary: Sonia Belisario.
Second Secretary: Ricardo Peraza.
Military Attaché: Emilio Fuentes L.
Naval Attaché: Simon José Salas.
Air Attaché: Hugo Fernández.
Attaché (National Guard): Wenceslao García.
Cultural Affairs Attaché: Marco Miliani.
Labour Attaché: Juan Rafael Marval.

Consulate: Avda Olaya Herrera, esq. Con Cauca, Calle 26-A, 2°, Arauca; tel (8180) 52-246.
Consul: Mario Padilla Gilly.

Consulate-General: Calle 70, No. 53-74, 4°, Edif. Centro Financiero El Prado, Barranquilla, Atlántico; tel (58) 58-0048.
Consul-General: Edwing José Chiriquez.

Consulate-General: Carrera 35-A, No. 54-41, Apdo Aéreo 3923, Bucaramanga, Santander del Sur; tel (7) 37-1272; telex 77622.
Consul-General: María Jara de Parra.
Consul: Ciro Augusto Peñaloza.

Consulate-General: Carrera 12, No. 5-75, Castillo Grande, Apdo Aéreo 1178, Cartagena, Bolívar; tel (53) 65-0382; telex 37859.
Consul-General: Jesús González Guerra.

Consulate-General: Avda 0 con Calle 8, No 8-23, Esquina, Cúcuta, Santander del Norte; tel (70) 72-3983; telex 76613; fax (70) 71-2107.
Consul-General: Rosa López de Ramos.
Consul: Enrique Prieto Hopkins.
Consul: Gonzalo Briceño Barrios.

Consulate-General: Calle 32-B, No. 69-59, Barrio Malibú, Apdo Aéreo 8804, Medellín, Antioquia; tel (4) 235-1020; telex 56012; fax (4) 235-9930.
Consul-General: Aquiles Yibirín.

Consulate: Calle Orinoco s/n, Puerto Carreño, Vichada; tel (816) 54-057.
Consul: Jorge Méndez Montilla.

Consulate: Puerto Inírida, Guainía; tel (816) 56-117.
Consul: Francisco A. Torres González.

Consulate: Carrera 7, No. 308, Edif. El Ejecutivo, 7B°, Riohacha, La Guajira; tel (54) 27-4076.
Consul: Alfredo Jesus Mijares Meza.

YUGOSLAVIA

Embassy: Calle 93A, No 9A-22, Apdo 91074, Bogotá, DE; tel (1) 257-0290; telex 45155.
Ambassador: Radomir Zecević.

THE COMOROS

BELGIUM

Consulate: BP 880, Moroni; tel 73-28-39; telex 212921.
Consul: Francis Deprez.

CHINA, PEOPLE'S REPUBLIC

Embassy: Moroni; tel 73-27-21.
Ambassador: Wei Dong.

FRANCE

Embassy: blvd de Strasbourg, BP 465, Moroni; tel 73-06-15; telex 220.
Ambassador: Jean-Luc Sibiude.

ITALY

Consulate: Moroni.

MAURITIUS

Embassy: Moroni.

SOUTH AFRICA

Consulate: BP 1392, Moroni; tel 73-18-12 (calls must be booked - dial 0900).
Consul: M. Boni.
Vice-Consul: Dr E. Kruger.

SWEDEN

Embassy: Moroni.
Ambassador: Lars Schönander (resident in Sweden).

USA

Embassy: BP 1318, Moroni; tel 73-22-03; telex 257.
Ambassador: Kenneth N. Peltier.
Deputy Chief of Mission: Karl I. Danga.
Administrative/Consular Section: Peter X. Harding.

International Organizations

EUROPEAN COMMUNITIES

External Delegation (Sub-office of Delegation to Mauritius): BP 559, Moroni; tel 73-23-06; telex 212; fax 73-21-90.
Representative: Benoît M. J. T. Aubenas.
Counsellor: Charles Goes.

THE CONGO

ALGERIA

Embassy: BP 2100, Brazzaville; tel 83-39-15; telex 5303.
Ambassador: Mohamed Nacer Adjali.

ANGOLA

Embassy: BP 388, Brazzaville; tel 81-14-71; telex 5321.
Ambassador: José Agostinho Neto.

BELGIUM

Embassy: BP 225, Brazzaville; tel 83-29-63; telex 5216.
Ambassador: Lothar G. E. Versyck.
Attaché: Luc Muylle.

Consulate: c/o Satrans SA, BP 220, Pointe-Noire; tel 94-06-24; fax 94-06-24.
Consul: Mr Vigoureux.

CAMEROON

Embassy: BP 2136, Brazzaville; tel 83-34-04; telex 5242.
Ambassador: Jean-Hilaire Mbea Mbea.

CENTRAL AFRICAN REPUBLIC

Embassy: BP 10, Brazzaville; tel 83-40-14.
Ambassador: Charles Guerebangbi.

CHAD

Embassy: BP 386, Brazzaville; tel 81-22-22.
Chargé d'affaires: Neato-bei Bidi.

CHINA, PEOPLE'S REPUBLIC

Embassy: BP 213, Brazzaville; tel 83-11-20.

CUBA

Embassy: BP 80, Brazzaville; tel 81-20-91; telex 5308.
Ambassador: Diego Ernesto González Pérez.

CZECHOSLOVAKIA

Embassy: BP 292, Brazzaville; tel 82-08-37.
Ambassador: Lubomír Haluska.

DENMARK

Consulate-General: ave Amilcar Cabral, BP 34, Brazzaville; tel 83-10-22; telex 5317; fax 83-11-91.
Ambassador: Per W. Frellesvig (resident in Denmark).
Consul-General: Leopold Louis Germain Annoyer.

Consulate: SOAEM, 35 rue Zéphirin Lassy, BP 674, Pointe-Noire; tel 94-10-16; telex 8214.
Consul: Pierre Lions.

EGYPT

Embassy: BP 917, Brazzaville; tel 83-44-28; telex 5248.
Ambassador: Mohamed Abdel Rahman Diab.

FINLAND

Embassy: Finland.
Ambassador: Osmo Väinölä (resident in Finland).

FRANCE

Embassy: rue Alfassa, BP 2089, Brazzaville; tel 83-14-23; telex 5239.
Ambassador: Robert Delos Santos.

Consulate-General: rue Alfassa, BP 72, Brazzaville; tel 83-10-86.

Trade Promotion Office: BP 2012; tel 83-05-64; telex 5239.

Consulate-General: 4 allée Nicolau, BP 720, Pointe-Noire; tel 94-00-02.

GABON

Embassy: ave Fourneau, BP 2033, Brazzaville; tel 81-05-90; telex 5225.
Ambassador: Constant Tsoumou.

GERMANY

Embassy: place de la Mairie, BP 2022, Brazzaville; tel 83-11-27; telex 5235.
Ambassador: Georg Merten.

Consulate: blvd Stephanopoulos, BP 1136, Pointe-Noire; tel 94-05-07; telex 8337.
Honorary Consul: Jørgen Filskov.

GUINEA

Embassy: BP 2477, Brazzaville; tel 81-24-66.
Ambassador: Bonata Dieng.

HOLY SEE

Apostolic Nunciature: rue Colonel Brisset, BP 1168, Brazzaville; tel 83-15-46.
Apostolic Pro-Nuncio: Most Rev. Beniamino Stella, Titular Archbishop of Midila.

Secretary: Rev. Claudio Mondino.
Attaché: Battista Ricca.

ITALY

Embassy: 2-3 blvd Lyautey, BP 2484, Brazzaville; tel 83-40-47; telex 5251.
Ambassador: Tibor Hoor Tempis Livi.

KOREA, DEMOCRATIC PEOPLE'S REPUBLIC

Embassy: BP 2032, Brazzaville; tel 83-41-98.
Ambassador: Yu Kwan-chin.

LIBYA

People's Bureau: BP 920, Brazzaville.
Secretary of People's Bureau: Saad Abdessalem Baaiu.

NIGERIA

Embassy: BP 790, Brazzaville; tel 83-13-16; telex 5263.
Ambassador: Lawrence Olufolahan Oladejo Oyelakin.

ROMANIA

Embassy: BP 2413, Brazzaville; tel 81-32-79; telex 5259.
Chargé d'affaires a.i.: Diaconesco Milcea.

RUSSIA

Embassy: rue Amilcar Cabral, BP 2132, Brazzaville; tel 81-44-39; telex 5455; fax 83-69-17.
Ambassador: Anatoly Safronovich Zaitsev.

Consulate-General: BP 848, Pointe-Noire; tel 94-09-42.

SPAIN

Consulate: 715 rue Williams Guynet, BP 784, Brazzaville; tel 83-36-48.
Honorary Consul: José Luis Carretero.

SWEDEN

Consulate: c/o SOAEM, rue Emile Jacob, BP 284, Brazzaville; tel 83-02-71; telex 5292.
Ambassador: Bengt Rösiö (resident in Sweden).
Consul: Yves-Maric Dulioust.

Consulate: c/o SOAEM, 16-18 ave Zéphirin Lassy, BP 674, Pointe-Noire; tel 94-09-53; telex 8214.
Consul: Pierre Lions.

TOGO

Consulate: BP 2476, ave Louis Portella, Mvoumvou; tel 94-07-95.
Consul: Adalbert Kouassi.

UNITED KINGDOM

Embassy: ave du Général de Gaulle, Plateau, BP 1038, Brazzaville; tel 83-25-69; telex 5385; fax 83-49-45.
Ambassador and Consul: Peter Warren Chandley.

Consulate: Président Directeur Général, British Petroleum Development Ltd, ave Marien Ngouabi, BP 1181, Pointe Noire; tel 94-39-88; telex 8443; fax 94-39-90.
Honorary Consul: J. Perry.

USA

Embassy: ave Amílcar Cabral, BP 1015, Brazzaville; tel 83-20-70; telex 5367; fax 83-63-38.
Ambassador: James D. Phillips.
Deputy Chief of Mission: Roger A. Meece.
Political Section: Walter M. Hughey.
Economic Section: Alexander G. Andrews, Jr.
Consul: Lynn Gutensohn.
Administrative Section: Elizabeth D. Thompson.
Public Affairs Officer: Mary H. Johnson.
Communications Programme Officer: Dennis L. Watson.
Agency for International Development: Glissa A. McKiernan.
Office of the Defence Attaché: Maj. Ambrous Jacobs.

VIET-NAM

Embassy: BP 988, Brazzaville; tel 83-26-21.
Ambassador: Bui Van Thanh.

YUGOSLAVIA

Embassy: BP 2062, Brazzaville; tel 83-42-46; telex 5316.
Chargé d'affaires a.i.: Ibrahim Djikić.

ZAIRE

Embassy: 130 ave de l'Indépendance, BP 2450, Brazzaville; tel 83-29-38.

International Organizations

EUROPEAN COMMUNITIES

External Delegation: ave Lyautey, BP 2149, Brazzaville; tel 83-38-78; telex 5257; fax 83-60-74.
Commission Delegate: Antonio Marongiu.

COSTA RICA

ARGENTINA

Embassy: Calle 27, Avda Central, Apdo 1.963, San José; tel 21-3438; telex 2117.
Ambassador: Rubén Antonio Vela.

AUSTRIA

Consulate-General: De la Toyota en el Paseo Colón, 200 metros al sur y 50 al oeste, frente a Parque de Mata Redonda, Casa No. 3650, San José; Apdo Postal 683-1007, Centro Colón, San José; tel 55-0767.
Honorary Consul-General: Tomas Nagel-Schlesinger.

BELGIUM

Embassy: 4A, entrada de Los Yoses, Apdo 3.725, 1000 San José; tel 25-6255; telex 2909.
Ambassador: Frans M. J. Hintjens.
First Secretary (Co-operation): François Bochkoltz.
Attaché: Agnes Scheers.
Attaché (Cultural/Press/Information): Victor Valembois.
Attaché: Madeline Claude.
Assistant Attaché: Valerie de Bruyen.
Assistant Attaché (Commercial): Hugues Delannoy.
Assistant Attaché (Commercial): Ana Cristina Guier de Picado.

BRAZIL

Embassy: Edif. Plaza de la Artillería 7°, Calle 4, Avda Central y 1, Apdo 10.132, San José; tel 23-4325; telex 2270.
Ambassador: R. B. Denys.

BULGARIA

Embassy: Edif. Delcoré 3°, 100 metros Sur Hotel Balmoral, Apdo 4.752, San José.
Ambassador: Kiril Slatkov Nikolov.

CANADA

Embassy: Edif. Cronos, 6°, Avda Central, Calle 3, Apdo 10.303, 1000 San José; tel 55-3522; telex 2179; fax 23-2395.
Ambassador: Henry G. Pardy.
Counsellor (Commercial) and Consul: C. Don Caldwell.
Counsellor (Development): Marcel A. Custeau.
Counsellor (Development): Leonard Matton.
Counsellor (Development): Gaston Grenier.
First Secretary (Political) and Consul: Peter M. Boehm.
First Secretary (Immigration) and Consul: A. M. Rita Beauchamp.
First Secretary (Adminstration) and Consul: Peter G. Hunt.
Second Secretary (Commercial) and Vice-Consul: Danielle Ayotte-Rivard.

CHILE

Embassy: De la Pulpería La Luz 125 metros Norte, Casa 116, Apdo 10.102, San José; tel 24-4243; telex 2207.
Ambassador: Pedro Palacios Camerón.

CHINA (TAIWAN)

Embassy: Edif. Mendiola 3°, Avda Central 917, Apdo 907, San José; tel 21-3752; telex 2174.
Ambassador: Shao Hsioh-Kwen.

COLOMBIA

Embassy: Apdo 3.154, 1000 San José; tel 21-0725; telex 2918; fax 55-1705.
Ambassador: María Cristina Zuleta de Patiño.

CZECHOSLOVAKIA

Embassy: 200 metros sur del Rótulo de la Plaza del Sol, Residencial El Prado, Carretera a Curridabat, Apdo 3.910, 1000 San José; telex 2323.
Chargé d'affaires a.i.: Václav Malý.

DENMARK

Consulate-General: Apdo 276, Escazú, 1250; From McDonalds la Sabana 150 Metros Este, Contiguo Barberia Bonaparte, San José; tel 31-6283; fax 31-6283.
Consul-General: Palle Paaby.
Vice-Consul: Bodil Paaby.

DOMINICAN REPUBLIC

Embassy: Frente costado al norte de la Nunciatura Apostólica, Barrio Rohrmoser, Apdo 4.746, San José; telex 3210.
Ambassador: José Marcos Iglesias Iñigo.

ECUADOR

Embassy: Edif. de la esquina sureste del Museo Nacional, 125 metros al este, Avda 2°, entre calles 19 y 21, Apdo 1.374, 1000 San José; tel 23-6281; telex 2601.
Ambassador: Lic. Andrés Córdova Galarza.

EL SALVADOR

Embassy: Edif. Trianón 3°, Avda Central y Calle 5A, Apdo 1.378, San José; tel 22-5536; telex 2641.
Ambassador: Carlos Matamoros Guirola.

FINLAND

Embassy: Centro Colón, Apto 9-10, Paseo Colón, San José; Apdo 547-1150, La Uruca, San José; tel 55-2515; fax 55-2662.
Counsellor (Development Co-operation): Pertti Majanen.

Consulate-General: Centro Colón, 7°, Apdo 2506, San José; tel 57-0210; telex 3463.
Consul-General: Klaus Reher.

Consulate: Calle 13, Avdas 8 y 10, Casa 843, Apdo 5597, San José; tel 21-3912.
Vice-Consul: Ulf Bjarne Kvist.

Consulate: Costado Oeste plaza Mora y Canas, Apdo 10, Puntarenas; tel 61-0812.
Vice-Consul: Miquel Alvarez Montenegro.

FRANCE

Embassy: Carretera a Curridabat Del Indoor Club, 200 al Sur y 25 al Oeste, Apdo 10.177, 1000 San José; tel 25-0733; telex 2191; fax 53-7027.
Ambassador: Hélène Dubois.
First Counsellor: Philippe Barbry.
Consul: Colette Dueso.
Counsellor (Technical/Scientific Co-operation): Philippe Cujo.
Press Attaché: Daniel Cassieula.

Trade Promotion Office: Apdo 3164, Correo Central, 1000 San José; tel 22-1149; telex 2212.

GERMANY

Embassy: de la Residencia de España 200 metros al norte, 50 metros al oeste, Apdo 4.017, 1000 San José; tel 32-5450; telex 2183; fax 31-6403.
Ambassador: Dr Dieter Zeisler.

GUATEMALA

Embassy: Avda Primera detrás Más y Menos del Paseo Colón, Avda 2, Apdo 328-1000, San José; tel 31-6654; fax 31-6645.
Ambassador: Lic. Ramiro Leal E.

HOLY SEE

Apostolic Nunciature: Urbanización Rohrmoser, Sabana Oeste, Apdo 992, Centro Colón, San José; tel 32-2128.
Apostolic Nuncio: Most Rev. Pier Giacomo De Nicolò, Titular Archbishop of Martana.
Secretary: Mgr Vicente Juan Segura.

HONDURAS

Embassy: Yoses Sur (De Farmacia Montealegre 200 norte y 100 este), San José; tel 34-9502; telex 2784; fax 53-2209.
Ambassador: Edgardo Sevilla Idiaquez.
Counsellor and Head of Consular Section: Maximiliano Cruz Navarrete.
First Secretary: Argentina Wellerman de Sanchez.
First Secretary: Ricardo Cardona López.
Commercial Attaché: Carlos Young Torres.
Civil Attaché: Rosalía Suárez Carias de Siercke.
Civil Attaché: Marta Montis de Martínez.
Commercial Attaché: Mike Canavati.

Consular Section: Apdo 2.239, 1000 San José; tel 34-9504.
Head of Consular Section: Maximiliano Cruz Navarrete.

ISRAEL

Embassy: Edif. Parque Central, Calle 2, Avdas 2 y 4, Apdo 5.147, San José; tel 21-6011; telex 2258; fax 57-0867.
Ambassador: Nehemia Tevell.
Second Secretary: Talya David.

ITALY

Embassy: 5° entrada del Barrio Los Yoses, Apdo 1.729, San José; tel 24-6574; telex 2769.
Ambassador: Dr Rosario Guido Nicosia.

JAMAICA

Consulate-General: Apdo 2.234, San José; tel 28-0802.
Consul-General: Neville Clarke.
Honorary Consul: Milton Clarke.
Honorary Vice-Consul: Grace Manhertz.

JAPAN

Embassy: De la 1a entrada del Barrio Rohrmoser (Sabana Oeste) 500 metros Oeste y 100 Norte, Apdos 501 y 10.145, San José; tel 32-1255; telex 2205; fax 31-3140.
Ambassador: Chusaka Nomura.

KOREA, REPUBLIC

Embassy: Calle 28, Avda 2, Barrio San Bosco, Apdo 3.150, San José; tel 21-2398; telex 2512.

Ambassador: Kim Jae Hoon.

MEXICO

Embassy: Avda 7, No 1371, Apdo 10.107, San José; tel 22-5485; telex 2218; fax 22-6080.
Ambassador: Jesús Cabrera Muñoz Ledo.

NETHERLANDS

Embassy: 2a entrada de Los Yoses, 100 metros al sur, Avda 8, Calle 37, Apdo 10.285, San José; tel 25-3516; telex 2187.
Ambassador: Jan-Willem Bertens.

NICARAGUA

Embassy: Edif. Trianón, Calle 25 y 27, Avda Central, San José; tel 22-4749; telex 2316.
Ambassador: Claudia Chamorro Barriose.

NORWAY

Embassy: Apdo 941, 1007 Centro Colón, San José; tel 57-1414; telex 2245; fax 33-8113.

PANAMA

Embassy: 200 metros al sur, 25 metros al este de Higueron, La Granja, San Pedro de Montes de Oco, San José; tel 25-3401.
Ambassador: Walter Myers.

PERU

Embassy: Del Automercado de Los Yoses, 300 Sur y 75 oeste, Casa blanca de patio rojo, Apdo 4.248, 1000 San José; tel 25-9145; telex 3515; fax 53-0457.
Minister-Counsellor and Chargé d'affaires a.i.: Eduardo Barandiaran Barandiaran.
Second Secretary and Head of Consular Affairs: Maria del Pilar Castro Barreda.
Civil Attaché: Elena González Vega.

ROMANIA

Embassy: Urbanización Rohrmoser, frente al costado este del Parque La Favorita, Apdo 10.321, San José; tel 31-0813; telex 2337.
Ambassador: Nicolae Turturea.
Minister-Counsellor: Augustin Berindeau.

RUSSIA

Embassy: Curridabad, Barrio González Montealegre, Avda 2A este, Calle Ondres, Apdo 6.340, San José; tel 25-5780; telex 2299.
Ambassador: Valery Nikolaevich Kalmyk.
Consular Section: tel 24-9441; telex 2309.

SPAIN

Embassy: c/32, Paseo Colón, Avda 2, Apdo 10.150, 1000 San José; tel 221-1933; telex 2438.
Ambassador: J. A. Ortiz Ramos.

SWEDEN

Consulate-General: Almacén Font, Carretera Nacional 1, La Uruca, Apdo 10.295, 1000 San José; tel 32-8222; telex 2216; fax 20-1854.
Consul-General: Francisco Font Ulloa.

SWITZERLAND

Embassy: Edif. Centro Colón, 4°, Paseo Colón, San José; Apdo 895, 1007 San José; tel 21-4829; telex 2521; fax 55-2831.
Ambassador: Dr Johann Bucher.
First Secretary and Head of Chancery: Werner Dill.

UNITED KINGDOM

Embassy: Edif. Centro Colón, 11°, Apdo 815, 1007 San José; tel 21-5566; telex 2169; fax 33-9938.
Ambassador and Consul-General: William Marsden.
First Secretary, Consul and Deputy Head of Mission: M. C. Ramscar.
First Secretary (Commercial) and Director of Trade Promotion for Central America: A. J. M. Walter.
Second Secretary (Technical Assistance Management Officer) and Vice-Consul: E. A. McEwan.

USA

Embassy: Pavas Frente Centro Comercial, Apdo 920-1200 Pavas, San José; tel 20-3939; fax 20-2305.
Chargé d'affaires: Robert O. Homme.
Political Section: John R. Hamilton.
Economic Section: Stephen V. Noble.
Commercial Section: Judith Henderson.
Consul: Donna J. Hamilton.
Administration Section: Robert L. Graninger.
Regional Security Officer: Richard J. Watts.
Public Affairs Officer: Louise K. Crane.
Communications Programme Officer: Gilbert M. Harcum.
Information Systems Manager: Lynn E. Crammer.
Agency for International Development: Ronald F. Venezia.
Office of Defence Co-operation: Lieut Col Raul J. Colon.
Agricultural Section: David B. Young.

URUGUAY

Embassy: Calle 2, Avda 1, San José; tel 23-2512.
Ambassador: Jorge Justo Boero-Brian.

VENEZUELA

Embassy: Avda Central 5A entrada Los Yoses, 100 metros al Sur y 50 Oeste, Apdo 10.230, San José; tel 25-5813; telex 2413; fax 53-8710.
Ambassador: Dr Francisco Salazar Martínez.
Second Secretary: Jaime Velazquez Bello.
Third Attaché: Gisela Tucci Salvino.

YUGOSLAVIA

Embassy: Calles 30 y 32, Paseo Colón, San José; tel 22-0619.

International Organizations

EUROPEAN COMMUNITIES

External Delegation: Centro Calon, Apdo 836, 1007 San José; tel 33-2755; telex 3482; fax 21-0893.
Head of Delegation: Fernando Cardesa García.

COTE D'IVOIRE

ALGERIA

Embassy: 53 blvd Clozel, 01 BP 1015, Abidjan 01; tel 21-23-40; telex 23243.

ARGENTINA

Embassy: 08 BP 860, Abidjan 08; tel 44-41-78; telex 26100.
Ambassador: Federico Mirre.

AUSTRIA

Embassy: Immeuble N'Zarama, 6e étage, blvd Lagunaire-Charles de Gaulle, Plateau, 01 BP 1837, Abidjan 01; tel 21-25-00; telex 22664; fax 22-19-23.
Ambassador: Dr Georg Znidaric.
Second Secretary: Gerhard Dedic.
Secretary: Margit Mandl.
Secretary: Andrea Schmid.

BELGIUM

Embassy: Immeuble Alliance, ave Terrasson de Fougères, 01 BP 1800, Abidjan 01; tel 21-00-88; telex 23633.
Ambassador: Jacques de Montjoye.

BENIN

Embassy: rue des Jardins, 09 BP 238, Abidjan 09; tel 41-44-14; telex 23922.
Ambassador: Jonas Gbogbohoundada.

BRAZIL

Embassy: Immeuble Alpha 2000, rue Gourgas, 01 BP 3820, Abidjan 01; tel 22-23-41; telex 23443.
Ambassador: Italo M. A. Mastrogiovanni.

BURKINA FASO

Embassy: 2 ave Terrasson de Fougères, 01 BP 908, Abidjan 01; tel 21-13-13; telex 23453.
Ambassador: Bernard Nabare.

CAMEROON

Embassy: 01 BP 2886, Abidjan 01.
Ambassador: Paul Kamga Njike.

CANADA

Embassy: Immeuble Trade Centre, 23 ave Nogues, Plateau, 01 BP 4104, Abidjan 01; tel 21-20-09; telex 23593; fax 32-77-28.
Ambassador: Jean-Guy St-Martin.
Counsellor (Development) and Consul: C. Francoeur.
Counsellor (Commercial): R. Ledoux.
Counsellor and Consul: Y. Bouthillette.
Counsellor (Immigration) and Consul: A. E. Arsenault.
Counsellor (Development): D. Potvin.
Counsellor (Education): J. Veilleux.
Attaché (Medical): Dr J. St-Germain.
First Secretary (Administration) and Consul: M. H. Desloges.

CENTRAL AFRICAN REPUBLIC

Embassy: rue des Combattants, 01 BP 3387, Abidjan 01; tel 21-36-46; telex 22102.
Ambassador: Antoine Kezza.

CHILE

Embassy: 06 BP 380, Abidjan 06; tel 21-92-37; telex 22173.
Ambassador: Félix Cabezas.

CHINA, PEOPLE'S REPUBLIC

Embassy: 01 BP 3691, Abidjan 01; tel 41-32-48; telex 22104.
Ambassador: Cai Zaidu.

COLOMBIA

Embassy: Tour BIAO, 16e étage, 01 BP 3874, Abidjan 01; tel 33-12-44; telex 22576; fax 32-47-31.
Ambassador: Octavio Gallón Restrepo.
First Secretary: Clemencia Izquierdo de Schloss.

CZECHOSLOVAKIA

Embassy: Immeuble Tropique III, rue Jesse Owens, Abidjan-Plateau; 01 BP 1349, Abidjan 01; tel 21-20-30; telex 22110; fax 22-19-06.
Chargé d'affaires a.i. and Commercial Counsellor: Petr Poštulka.

DENMARK

Embassy: Immeuble Le Mans, 5e étage, blvd Boitreau Roussel, angle ave Noguès, Plateau, 01 BP 4569, Abidjan 01; tel 33-17-65; telex 23871; fax 32-41-89.
Minister-Counsellor and Chargé d'affaires: Johan Otto Stephensen.
Attaché: Anne-Grethe Jørgensen.

EGYPT

Embassy: Immeuble El Nasr, ave du Général de Gaulle, 01 BP 2104, Abidjan 01; tel 32-79-25; telex 23537.
Ambassador: Nosrat Ali Fahmi Naim.

ETHIOPIA

Embassy: Immeuble Nour Al-Hayat, 01 BP 3712, Abidjan 01; tel 21-33-65; telex 23848.

FINLAND

Office of the Commercial Attaché: Deux Plateaux, Vallon, BP 1835, Abidjan 01; tel 41-50-01; telex 27157.
Ambassador: Osmo Väinölä (resident in Finland).

Consulate-General: 53 blvd Alchalme, Abidjan (Marcory); BP 1379, Abidjan 01; tel 35-55-29.
Consul-General: Michel Keller.

Consulate: tel 35-35-86.
Consul: David José Pairaud.

FRANCE

Embassy: rue Lecoeur, quartier du Plateau, 17 BP 175/176, Abidjan 17; tel 21-67-49; telex 23699.
Ambassador: Michel Dupuch.

Consulate-General: 01 BP 1385, Abidjan 01; tel 32-25-66.

Trade Promotion Office: 17 BP 151, Abidjan 17; tel 32-93-12; telex 23846.

Consulate: quartier Nimbo, BP 1465, Bouaké; tel 63-24-63.

GABON

Embassy: Cocody Danga Nord, derrière la Direction de la Géologie, 01 BP 3765, Abidjan 01; tel 41-51-54; telex 27188.
Ambassador: Aboubakar Bokoko.

GERMANY

Embassy: Immeuble Le Mans, blvd Boitreau Roussel, ave Nogues, 01 BP 1900, Abidjan 01; tel 32-47-27; telex 23642; fax 32-47-29.
Ambassador: Roland Zimmermann.

GHANA

Embassy: Résidence de la Corniche, blvd du Général de Gaulle, 01 BP 1871, Abidjan 01; tel 21-11-24.
Ambassador: J. E. A. Kotei.

GUINEA

Embassy: Immeuble Crosson Duplessis, 08 BP 2280, Abidjan 08; tel 21-86-00; telex 22865.
Ambassador: Richard Haba.

HOLY SEE

Apostolic Nunciature: 08 BP 1347, Abidjan 08; tel 44-38-35; telex 26182; fax 44-72-40.
Apostolic Nuncio: Most Rev. Janusz Bolonek, Titular Archbishop of Madauro.
Secretary: Rev. Luciano Suriani.

INDIA

Embassy: Lot 36, Impasse, Ablaha Pokou, Cocody Danga Nord, 06 BP 318, Abidjan 06; tel 44-52-31; telex 28103; fax 44-01-11.
Ambassador: Beni Prasad Agarwal.

ISRAEL

Embassy: Immeuble Nour Al-Hayat, 01 BP 1877, Abidjan 01; tel 21-49-53.
Ambassador: Menahem Carmon.

ITALY

Embassy: 16 rue de la Canebière, Cocody, 01 BP 1905, Abidjan 01; tel 44-61-70; telex 26123.

JAPAN

Embassy: Immeuble Alpha 2000, Tour A, 18ème étage, angle ave Chardy et rue Gourgas, 01 BP 1329, Abidjan 01; tel 21-28-63; telex 23400; fax 21-30-51.
Ambassador: Masaki Yagi.

KOREA, DEMOCRATIC PEOPLE'S REPUBLIC

Embassy: Cocody Danga, 9 rue des Jasmins; 01 BP V48, Abidjan 01; tel 44-22-75.
Ambassador: Ri Djai Rim.
First Secretary: Ri Myong Tcheul.

KOREA, REPUBLIC

Embassy: Immeuble Le Général, 01 BP 3950, Abidjan 01; tel 21-22-90; telex 23638.
Ambassador: Lee Joung-Soo.

LEBANON

Embassy: 01 BP 2227, Abidjan 01; tel 21-28-24; telex 22245.

Ambassador: Nizar Chamas.

LIBERIA

Embassy: Immeuble La Symphonie, 30 ave du Général de Gaulle, Abidjan; tel 22-23-59; telex 23535.
Ambassador: Harold Tarr.

MALI

Embassy: Maison du Mali, rue du Commerce, 01 BP 2746, Abidjan 01; tel 21-31-47; telex 23429.
Ambassador: Modibo Diarra.

MAURITANIA

Embassy: 01 BP 2275, Abidjan 01; tel 44-16-43; telex 27181.
Ambassador: Col Ahmedou Oum Abdallah.

MOROCCO

Embassy: 24 rue de la Canebière, Cocody, 01 BP 146, Abidjan 01; tel 44-58-78; telex 26147.
Ambassador: Mohamed Bennis.

NETHERLANDS

Embassy: Immeuble Les Harmonies, blvd Carde, 01 BP 1086, Abidjan 01; tel 22-77-12; telex 23694.

NIGER

Embassy: 01 BP 2743, Abidjan 01; tel 35-50-98; telex 43185.
Ambassador: Madou Mahamadou.

NIGERIA

Embassy: 35 blvd de la République, 01 BP 1906, Abidjan 01; tel 21-38-17; telex 23532.
Ambassador: Dr J. O. Coker.

NORWAY

Embassy: Immeuble N'Zarama, blvd du Général de Gaulle, 01 BP 607, Abidjan 01; tel 22-25-34; telex 23355; fax 32-91-99.
Ambassador: Kjell Østrem.

POLAND

Embassy: 04 BP 308, Abidjan 04; tel 44-12-25; telex 26114.
Chargé d'affaires: Andrzej Kulesza.

RUSSIA

Embassy: Riviera SQ-1 Sud, 01 BP 7646, Abidjan 01; tel 43-09-59.
Ambassador: Boris Minakov.
Consular Section: tel 32-43-19; telex 22381.

RWANDA

Embassy: 01 BP 3905, Abidjan 01; tel 41-38-31; telex 27152; fax 41-05-37.
Ambassador: Ismaïl Amri Sued.
First Counsellor: Faustin Kanyamibwa.

SENEGAL

Embassy: Résidence Nabil, blvd du Général de Gaulle, 08 BP 2165, Abidjan 08; tel 21-28-76; telex 23897.
Ambassador: Abdourahmane Touré.

SOUTH AFRICA

Mission: Abidjan; tel 44-59-63; fax 44-59-63.
Representative: C. E. Paterson.
Deputy Representative: A. D. Crowther.
Assistant Representative (Administration): E. E. Kruger.

SPAIN

Embassy: 01 BP 2589, Abidjan 01; tel 44-48-50; telex 28120; fax 33-28-48.
Ambassador: Fernando Castillo.

SWEDEN

Embassy: Immeuble Alpha 2000, rue Gourgas, Tour A1, 18e étage, 04 BP 992, Abidjan 04; tel 21-24-10; telex 23293; fax 21-21-07.
Ambassador: Arne Ekfeldt.
First Secretary: Wilhelm von Warnstedt.
Second Secretary: Per Carlsson.

SWITZERLAND

Embassy: Immeuble Alpha 2000, 12e étage, rue Gourgas, 01 BP 1914, Abidjan 01; tel 21-17-21; telex 23492; fax 21-27-70.
Ambassador: Jacques Reverdin.
Second Secretary: André Regli.
Attaché and Head of Chancery: Claude Duvoisin.

THAILAND

Embassy: Immeuble CCI, 13e étage, 01 BP 6471, Abidjan 01; tel 33-19-59; telex 22276.

TUNISIA

Embassy: Immeuble Shell, 48 ave Lamblin, 01 BP 3906, Abidjan 01; tel 21-23-04; telex 23709.
Ambassador: Abdel Aziz al-Ayadhi.

UNITED KINGDOM

Embassy: Immeuble Les Harmonies, 3e étage, angle blvd Carde et ave Dr Jamot, Plateau, 01 BP 2581, Abidjan 01; tel 21-82-09; telex 23706; fax 22-32-21.
Ambassador and Consul-General: Margaret Irene Rothwell.
Deputy Head of Mission, First Secretary (Commercial) and Consul: Dermot Richard Francis Flanagan.
Second Secretary (Chancery and Information): Alistair William Jackson Kerr.
Third Secretary (Management) and Vice-Consul: Wendy Paula Freeman.
Archivist: Sarah Marguerite Weeks.
Representation at African Development Bank: rue Joseph Anoma, 01 BP 1387, Abidjan 01; tel 20-40-23; telex 22203.
Executive Director: Dr H. M. Schmidt.
Alternate Executive Director: G. Duyfjes.
Assistant to Executive Director: S. Mattinson.

USA

Embassy: 5 rue Jesse Owens, 01 BP 1712, Abidjan 01; tel 21-09-79; telex 23660; fax 21-09-79.
Ambassador: Kenneth L. Brown.
Deputy Chief of Mission: Hugh G. Hamilton, Jr.
Political Section: Fred Kaplan.
Economic Section: Janice Price.
Commercial Section: Gene Harris.
Consul: Steve Voien.
Administrative Section: Elaine B. Schunter.
Regional Security Officer: Berne M. Indahl.
Public Affairs Officer: Robert B. Peterson.
Communications Programme Officer: John C. Conner.
Information Systems Manager: Terrence Williamson.
Agency for International Development/Regional Economic Development Services Office: Frederick E. Gilbert.
Agency for International Development/Regional Housing and Urban Development Office: Stephen W. Giddings.
Office of the Defence Attaché: Col Jerry R. Fry.
Agricultural Section: Randy Zeitner.
Representation at African Development Bank/Fund: ave Joseph Anoma, 01 BP 1387 Abidjan 01; tel 20-40-15.
Executive Director: Mima S. Nedelcovych.
Alternate Director: Stephen P. Donovan.

ZAIRE

Embassy: 29 blvd Clozel, 01 BP 3961, Abidjan 01; tel 22-20-80; telex 23795.
Ambassador: Louya Londoale.

International Organizations

EUROPEAN COMMUNITIES

External Delegation: Immeuble 'Azur', 18 blvd Crozet, 01 BP 1821, Abidjan 01; tel 32-24-28; telex 23729; fax 21-40-89.

CUBA

AFGHANISTAN

Embassy: Calle 24, No 106, entre 1 y 3, Miramar, Havana; tel (7) 22-1145; telex 511207.
Ambassador: Nur Ahmad Nur.
First Secretary: Sayed Wahdat Shah Ahmadzadah.

ALBANIA

Embassy: Calle 13, No 851, esq. 4, Vedado, Havana; tel (7) 30-2788; telex 511587.
Ambassador: Clirim Cepani.
Attaché: Aleksander Avduli.
Attaché: Gezim Senka.

ALGERIA

Embassy: 5a Avda, No 2802 esq. 28, Miramar, Havana; tel (7) 2-6538.
Ambassador: Abdelhamid Latreche.
First Secretary: Omar Guetarni.
Attaché: Ali Bessa.
Attaché: Laoucine Chabane.
Attaché: Mohamed Abbes.

ANGOLA

Embassy: Avda 5, No 1012, entre 10 y 12, Miramar, Havana; tel (7) 22-3473; telex 511105.
Ambassador: Luís Dokuy Paolo de Castro.
First Secretary: Osvaldo Dos Santos Varela.
First Secretary: Jorge Inocencio Dombolo.
Military Attaché: Col Rafael Sapilinha.
Third Secretary: Manuel Pedro da Rocha.
Third Secretary (Consular Affairs): Samuel da Cunha Ferreira.
Cultural Attaché: Victor N. de Oliveira Guilherme N.
Deputy Military Attaché: Maj. Rui A. de Gouveia do Nascimento.
Deputy Military Attaché: Maj. Luís Diogos de Carvalho.
Financial Attaché: Isabel Maria S. F. Pereira.
Attaché: Jorge Catala.
Attaché: Kinanga García.
Attaché: Manuel Miguel Kuende.
Attaché: Pedro Lemos Alves dos Santos.

ARGENTINA

Embassy: Calle 36, No 511, entre 5a y 7a, Miramar, Havana; tel (7) 22-5540; telex 511138.
Ambassador: Juan Carlos Olima.
Economic and Commercial Minister-Counsellor: Atilio Tomas Audisio.
Counsellor: José Gutierrez Maxwell.
Counsellor and Head of Consular Section: Daniel Samaniego.
Attaché: Osvaldo Narciso Caeiro.

AUSTRIA

Embassy: Calle 4, No 101 entre 1 y 3, Miramar, Havana; tel (7) 22-4394; telex 511415.
Ambassador: Heide Keller.
Economic Secretary: Gerhard Gerlza.
Commercial Section: Calle Cero, No 114, entre 1 y 3, Miramar, Havana; tel (7) 22-1430.
Commercial Counsellor: Georg Krauchenberg.

BAHAMAS

Embassy: 767 Third Ave, 9th Floor, New York, NY 10017, USA; tel (212) 421-6925; fax (212) 759-2135.

BELGIUM

Embassy: Avda 5a, No 7408, esq. 76, Miramar-Playa, Havana; tel (7) 29-6440; telex 511482.
Ambassador: Count Louis M. C. A. Cornet d'Elzius du Chenoy.
Second Secretary and Head of Chancery: Willy F. M. Leeman.
Commercial Attaché: Werner Claes.
Attaché: Françoise Vandercruyssen.

BENIN

Embassy: Avda 7a, No 3205, entre 32 y 34, Miramar, Havana; tel (7) 29-6142.
Ambassador: Cosme Ahannon Duguenon.
Minister-Counsellor: Falilou Sanya.
Cultural Counsellor: Sabitou Kegnide Alao-Fary.
Second Counsellor: Joseph Victor Menard.
First Secretary: Claude Houndeffo.
Attaché (Administrative): Alfred Dossou Houegnissode.
Attaché: Jean-Bosco Degbedji.

BOLIVIA

Embassy: Calle 26, No 109 entre 1 y 3, Miramar, Havana; tel (7) 22-7829.
Ambassador: Oscar Peña Franco.
Counsellor (Consular Affairs): Hugo Guzman Iturri.
Cultural Counsellor: Roberto Echazu Mavahas.

BRAZIL

Embassy: Calle 16, No 503, entre 5 y 7, Miramar, Havana; tel (7) 22-5617.
Second Secretary: Arthur Henrique Villanova Noguiera.
Second Secretary: Maria E. Teofilo de Luna Nogueira.
Second Secretary: Fernando José Marroni de Adreu.

BULGARIA

Embassy: Calle B, No 252, entre 11 y 13, Vedado, Havana; tel (7) 30-0212; telex 1920.
Ambassador: Kiril Zlatkov.
Minister-Counsellor: Pavel Peychev.
Economic Counsellor: Gueorgui Rachkov.
Military, Naval and Air Attaché: Col Vladimir Naydenov.
First Secretary (Consular Affairs): Dimitar Stoyanov.
First Secretary: Konstantin Zafirov.
Second Secretary (Cultural Affairs): Valentin Modev.
Third Secretary (Press): Emil Savov.
Attaché (Administrative Affairs): Boris Efremov.
Attaché (Administrative Affairs): Gueorgui Minchev.
Commercial Section: Calle 21, esq. 0, Edif. ICP (Mezzanine), Vedado, Havana; tel (7) 32-5586; telex 1354.
Commercial Counsellor: Boris Pamayotov.

BURKINA FASO

Embassy: Calle 7a, No 8401 entre 84 y 84a, Miramar, Havana; tel (7) 22-8295; telex 512423.
Ambassador: Timothée Some.
Cultural Counsellor: Guy Yameogo.
First Secretary: François Oubida.
Attaché: Marie Claude Yameogo.
Attaché: Edouard Ouangre.
Attaché: Jacqueline Oubida.

CAMBODIA

Embassy: Avda 5a, No 7001, entre 70 y 72, Miramar, Havana; tel (7) 2-8045.
Ambassador: Him Smoeurk (designate).
Second Secretary: Lay Yem.
Third Secretary: Muong Sowath.
Third Secretary: Heng Sovannary.

CANADA

Embassy: Calle 30, No 518, esq. a 7a, Miramar, Havana; tel (7) 2-6516; telex 511586; fax (7) 22-7044.
Ambassador: Robert M. Middleton.
Counsellor (Commercial) and Consul: Donald Harvard Leavitt.
Counsellor and Consul: Georges J. Béchard.
First Secretary (Commercial) and Consul: Edward C. Wang.
First Secretary and Consul: Paul G. Willox.
Second Secretary (Administration) and Vice-Consul: John Michael Legault.
Second Secretary (Immigration) and Vice-Consul: J.-F. Hubert-Rouleau.
Attaché: Dan W. Barnes.
Attaché: Leger Roy.
Attaché: Francine Cyr.
Attaché: Catriona Ann Foster.
Attaché: Robert Kennedy.
Attaché: Donald W. Drennan.
Attaché: Tom Ray Kozel.
Attaché: Ronald Phillip Kinney.
Attaché: Michel Dusablon.
Attaché: Alan John Hauser.

CAPE VERDE

Embassy: Calle 98, No 508, entre 5 y 5b, Miramar, Havana; tel (7) 21-8912; telex 512462.
Counsellor and Chargé d'affaires a.i.: Mário Ferreira Lopes Camões.
Attaché (Administrative Affairs): Jorge Borges Silva.

CHINA, PEOPLE'S REPUBLIC

Embassy: Calle C, entre 13 y 15, Vedado, Havana; tel (7) 32-5205.
Ambassador: Chen Jiuchang.
Political Counsellor: Li Jinzhang.
Military, Naval and Air Attaché: Col Chu Fugen.
First Secretary (Press): Zhang Hongfa.
First Secretary (Consular Affairs): Wang Yanghai.
Second Secretary: Bai Yunqi.
Second Secretary: Han Xiaoyan.
Second Secretary: Huang Minhui.
Second Secretary: Nan Mengjie.
Third Secretary: Wu Lili.
Third Secretary: Wang Kanhu.
Commercial Section: Calle 42, No 313, esq. 5, Miramar, Havana
Commercial Counsellor: Si Xiuzhang.
Second Secretary (Commercial Affairs): Ding Mingxin.
Cultural Section: tel (7) 32-7236.
Cultural Counsellor: Li Zhihua.
First Secretary (Cultural): Xu Jiquong.

COLOMBIA

Interests Section: c/o Embassy of Switzerland.

CONGO

Embassy: Avda 5, No 1003, entre 10 y 12, Miramar, Havana; tel (7) 22-6116; telex 512306.
Ambassador: Marcel Touanga.
Political Counsellor: Barthélémy Dzambeya.
Military, Naval and Air Attaché: Col Bernard Oyeka.
Economic Counsellor: Rigobert Itoua.
Counsellor: Paul Sita.
Counsellor: Gilbert Kingamba Ngoya.
First Secretary (Political/Economic): Eric Gakegne.
Second Secretary (Cultural): Marie Louise Dambendzet.
Attaché (Consular/Administrative/Financial): Joseph Amboulou.

CZECHOSLOVAKIA

Embassy: Avda Kohly, No 259, entre 41 y 43, Nuevo Vedado, Havana; tel (7) 30-0002; telex 512325.
Ambassador: Jaroslav Balaz.
Counsellor: Dr Jan Domok.
Economic Counsellor: Miroslav Holub.
Military and Air Attaché: Lieut Col Jiri Mecas.
First Secretary: Michal Davidek.
First Secretary and Head of Cultural Institute: Josef Strouhal.
Second Secretary (Press): Lubomir Hladik.
Third Secretary and Deputy Head of Cultural Institute: Vilen Sebek.
Third Secretary (Consular Affairs): Milan Vrba.
Attaché (Administrative Affairs): Zdemek Novotny.

Commercial Section: Edif. ENE, 12°, Calle N, No 266, entre 21 y 23, Vedado, Havana; tel (7) 32-2377; telex 512386.
Commercial Counsellor: Pavel Bires.
Commercial Attaché: Karel Maly.

Consular Section: Calle 66, No 521, 5B y 7, Miramar, Havana; tel (7) 2-5994.
Third Secretary (Consular Affairs): Milan Vrba.

DENMARK

Consulate: Paseo de Martí (Prado) No 20, Apto 4-C, Zona 2, 10200 Havana; tel (7) 32-7969; telex 511100; fax (7) 32-7013.
Consul: Mario Emilio Arredondo Gómez.

ECUADOR

Embassy: Avda 5a-A, No 4407, entre 44 y 46, Miramar, Havana; tel (7) 29-2934; telex 511770; fax (7) 22-6468.
Ambassador: Gustavo Jarrín Ampudia.
Minister: Dr Leonardo Ruilova.
Third Secretary (Consular Affairs): Ivan Oña Velez.
Civil Attaché: Roxana Patricia Velazquez de Cabrera.

EGYPT

Embassy: Avda 5, No 1801, esq. 18, Miramar, Havana; tel (7) 22-2541; telex 511551.
Ambassador: Esmat Abdel Halim Mohammad.
Counsellor (Political/Economic): Hazem Mohamed Taher.
Third Secretary (Consular/Press/Cultural): Cherif Fouad Mustafa Maguib.
Attaché (Administrative): Mohamed Moustafa A. El-Zant.
Attaché (Administrative): Youssef Abbas Bayoumi.
Attaché (Administrative): Abdel Raouf Ragheb Hussein.

ETHIOPIA

Embassy: Calle 6, No 318, entre 3 y 5, Miramar, Havana; tel (7) 33-2641; telex 511593.
Chargé d'affaires a.i.: Yilekal Denekew.
Counsellor (Political/Economic/Social/Press): Taye Abayere Giorgis.
Counsellor (Education and Culture)): Nega Leku Afework.

FINLAND

Embassy: Avda 5a, No 9202, esq. 92, Miramar, Playa, Apdo. 3304, Havana; tel (7) 22-4098; telex 511485.
Ambassador: Heikki Puurunen.
Attaché: Gun Soderlund.

FRANCE

Embassy: Calle 14, No 312, entre 3a y 5a Avdas, Miramar, Havana; tel (7) 29-3792; telex 511195.
Ambassador: Philippe Peltier.
Counsellor: Jeanne Texier.
Counsellor (Cultural/Scientific/Technical Collaboration): Michel Jena Bibard.
Second Secretary and Press Attaché: Annie Mari.
Third Secretary: Roland Pouliquen.
Attaché: Pierre Olivier.
Attaché: Larbi Sefsaf.
Assistant Cultural Attaché: Didier Bourven.
Assistant Cultural Attaché: Jean Luc Bertolino.

Consular Section: tel (7) 29-3532.
Second Secretary (Consular/Administrative): Jean Marc Lamadieu.

Trade Promotion Office: Calle 21, No 104, entre L y M, Vedado, Havana; tel (7) 32-9475; telex 511884.
Economic and Commercial Counsellor: Bernard Paulien.
Commercial Attaché: Antonio Avila.

GERMANY

Embassy: Calle 28, No 313, entre 3a y 5a, Miramar, Havana; tel (7) 22-2560; telex 511433.
Ambassador: Dr Georg Trefftz.
Counsellor: Peter Schaller.
Counsellor: Peter Wurzburg.
Second Secretary and Head of Chancery: Horst Schroder.
Second Secretary: Siegfried Eisenreich.
Third Secretary: Joachim Flock.
Attaché: Guido Meyer.
Attaché: Angelika Flock.
Attaché: Dagmar Zimmermann.
Attaché: Wolfgang Amm.
Attaché: Wolfgang Veith.
Attaché: Bernd Engelgeh.
Attaché: Siegfried Heine.
Attaché: Petra Heine.
Attaché: Klaus Schultz.

GHANA

Embassy: Avda 5a, No 1808, esq. A Calle 20, Miramar, Havana; tel (7) 2-7640; telex 512108; fax (7) 22-2117.
Counsellor (Political/Economic) and Chargé d'affaires a.i.: Kodjo Asimeng Wadee.
Counsellor (Education): Paul Wentum-Kitcher.
Second Secretary (Administrative Affairs): Nixon K. Semador.
Second Secretary: Phileta Odonkor.

GREECE

Embassy: Avda 5a, No 7802, esq. 78, Miramar; CP 11600, Havana; tel (7) 22-6854; telex 512377.
Ambassador: Marinos Raftopoulos.
First Secretary: Panayotis Stournaras.
Attaché: Maria Choursoulidou.

GRENADA

Embassy: Ave 6a, No 8409, Calle 84, Miramar, Havana.

GUINEA

Embassy: Calle 20, No 504, entre 5 y 7, Miramar, Havana; tel (7) 2-6003; telex 511896.
Ambassador: Lamine Sougoulé.
Counsellor: Amara Djoubar Soumah.
First Secretary: Blaise Pascal Keita.
Cultural Attaché: Lounseny Dore.
Attaché (Financial/Consular): Pascal Selly Onivogui.
Attaché: Mamadou Alpha Barry.
Attaché: Sayon Sidibe.
Attaché: Ibrahima Conte.

GUINEA-BISSAU

Embassy: Calle 14, No 313 entre 3 y 5, Miramar, Havana; tel (7) 29-0096.
Ambassador: Constantino Lopes da Costa.
Minister-Counsellor: Liberato Gomes.
Attaché: Palmira M. Romano Ferreira.

GUYANA

Embassy: Calle 18, No 506, entre 5 y 7, Miramar, Havana; tel (7) 22-1249; telex 511498.
Ambassador: Oscar E. Clarke.
Counsellor: Rita R. Ramlall.
Attaché: Enid Garrett.
Attaché: Joycelyn V. Dasilva.

HOLY SEE

Apostolic Nunciature: Calle 12, No 514, entre 5 y 7, Miramar Marianao 13, Havana 11300; tel (7) 2-5296; telex 512267.
Apostolic Pro-Nuncio: Most Rev. Faustino Sáinz Muñoz, Titular Archbishop of Novaliciana.
First Secretary: Mgr Michael Courtney.

HUNGARY

Embassy: Calle G, No 458, entre 19 y 21, Vedado, Havana; tel (7) 32-6520; telex 511360.
Ambassador: Béla Bardócz.
Counsellor: Sándor Almási.
First Secretary (Consular and Cultural Affairs and the Press): Karoly Scherczer.

Commercial Section: Edif. ENE, Calle N, No. 266, Vedado, Havana; tel (7) 32-3581.
Commercial Counsellor: T. Endre Sult.
Second Secretary (Commercial): Tihamer Mudlicz.
Second Secretary (Commercial Affairs): Laszlo Glatz.

ICELAND

Consulate-General: Havana.

INDIA

Embassy: Calle 21, No 202, esq. K, Vedado, Havana; tel (7) 32-5169; telex 511414.
Ambassador: Mukur Kanti Khisha.
First Secretary (Political/Commercial): Kocheril V. Bhagirath.
First Secretary (Cultural/Press): Hemalata Chandramouli.

IRAN

Embassy: Avda 5a, No 3002, esq. a 30, Miramar, Havana; tel (7) 2-6597; telex 512186.
Ambassador: Seyed Mahmoud Sadrid Tabaee Zavareh.
First Secretary: Mehdi Mohammadzadeh Miri.
Third Secretary: Ardeshir Ghahremani Choobeh.
Attaché (Cultural Affairs): Hossein Maghsoudi.

IRAQ

Embassy: Avda 5a, No 8201, entre 82 y 84, Miramar, Havana; tel (7) 2-6426; telex 511413.
Ambassador: Waleed Aboud Abbass.
First Secretary: Sadah Kamil Said.
Attaché: Sadah Salch Mehdi.
Attaché: Ibrahim K. Ibrahim.
Attaché: Khaled Ismail Nowman.

ITALY

Embassy: Calle Paseo, No 606, entre 25 y 27, Vedado, Havana; tel (7) 30-0334; telex 511352.
Ambassador: Carlo Civiletti.
Counsellor: Dr Cesare A. Corti.
First Secretary (Commercial and Consular Affairs): Dr Renato Varriale.
Attaché (Consular Affairs): Valdiniro Bianchi.
Attaché (Administrative Affairs): Dr Pietro De Santi.
Attaché (Commercial Affairs): Maria Cristina Corsi.
Attaché: Benito Merolli.
Attaché: Aroldo Preite.
Attaché: Alberto Spina.
Attaché (Administrative Affairs): Giuseppe Occhiuto.
Attaché: Antonietta Franza.
Attaché: Luciano Campoli.
Attaché (Consular Affairs): Gianni Sforza.
Attaché: Luciano Cappelletti.
Attaché: Giovanni Potente.
Attaché: Giuseppe Costantini.

JAMAICA

Embassy: Havana.
Ambassador: Peter Carlysle Black (designate, resident in Jamaica).

JAPAN

Embassy: Calle N, No 62, esq. 15, Vedado, Apdo 752, Havana; tel (7) 32-3507; telex 511260; fax (7) 32-4172.
Ambassador: Nobuo Miyamoto (designate).
Minister-Counsellor: Katsuya Shidata.
First Secretary: Toshimi Takahashi.
Second Secretary: Shigeo Maruyama.
First Secretary: Hidetaka Ogura.
Attaché: Masamitsu Sanada.
Attaché: Masahiro Iwasaki.
Attaché: Akira Tadano.

KOREA, DEMOCRATIC PEOPLE'S REPUBLIC

Embassy: Calle 17, No 752, esq. a Paseo, Vedado, Havana; tel (7) 30-5132; telex 511553.
Ambassador: Pak Zung Guk.
Counsellor: Che Je Ryong.
Counsellor: Che Biong Ik.
Commercial Counsellor: Che Gi Ryong.
First Secretary: Che Ki Bok.
First Secretary: Jong Min Chol.
Second Secretary: Wong Gi Yong.
Second Secretary (Commercial Affairs): Che Ryong Sam.
Third Secretary: Che Sung Jyon.
Third Secretary: Pak Myong Hon.
Third Secretary: Cho Bon Su.
Third Secretary: Li Gyong Mu.
Military, Naval and Air Attaché: Col Che Song Su.

LAOS

Embassy: Avda 5a, No 2808, esq. 30, Miramar, Havana; tel (7) 2-6198; telex 511500.
Ambassador: Ponmek Delaloy.
Third Secretary: Somlith Khantivong.
Attaché: Bounthieng Boupha.

LEBANON

Embassy: Calle 174, No 1707, entre 17 y 17a, Siboney, Havana; tel (7) 21-8087; telex 1671.
Ambassador: Dr Wafic Jaber.

LIBYA

People's Bureau: Calle 8, No 309, entre 3 y 5, Miramar, Havana; tel (7) 2-3192; telex 511570.
Chargé d'affaires a.i. (Consular): Saleh Khalifa Saleh.
Attaché (Cultural Affairs/Information): Said Hamali Galfala.
Attaché (Financial Affairs): Hasem Mohamed Labiedi.
Attaché (Economic/Commercial): Ali Mahmud Dagez.

LUXEMBOURG

Interests Section: c/o Embassy of the Netherlands.

Economic and Consular Affairs: c/o Embassy of Belgium.

MEXICO

Embassy: Calle 12, No 518, entre 5 y 7, Miramar, Havana; tel (7) 22-1142; telex 511298; fax (7) 29-4717.
Ambassador: Mario Noya Palencia.
Minister: Carlos Ferrer Argote.
Counsellor and Head of Consular Section: Roberto Ramírez Vargas.
Counsellor: Maria Carmen Oñáte de Cuevas.
Cultural Attaché: Francisco Valdes Treviño.
Naval Attaché: Vice-Adm. Sergio Loperena García.
Military and Air Attaché: Brig.-Gen. José Luis Trejo Bonilla.
Assistant Naval Attaché: Rear Adm. Casimiro A. Martínez.
Civil Attaché: Maria de los A. Samaniego Caraza.

Commercial Section: Avda 5a, No 6604, entre 66 y 68, Miramar, Havana; tel (7) 22-4162.
Commercial Counsellor: Carlos Sanchez Lara Tajonar.

MONGOLIA

Embassy: Calle 66, No 505, esq. 5A, Miramar, Havana; tel (7) 22-2346; telex 511957.
Ambassador: Osoryn Erdene.
First Secretary: Tserendorzh Balbaryn.

MOZAMBIQUE

Embassy: 7a Avda, No 2203, entre 22 y 24, Miramar, Havana; tel (7) 22-8332; telex 512394.
Ambassador: Amour Zacarias Kupela.
Second Secretary (Political): Cesar Francisco de Gouveia Junior.
Second Secretary (Economic): Fernanda Eugenio Moises Lichale.
Attaché (Consular): Armando Fietines.
Attaché (Financial/Administrative): Paulo Filipe Chinguvo.

NETHERLANDS

Embassy: Calle 8, No 307, entre 3 y 5, Miramar, Havana; tel (7) 22-2534; telex 511279; fax (7) 29-0254.
Ambassador: Gerhard Johan van Hattum.
Agricultural Counsellor: Jan Jaap Hooft.
Third Secretary and Head of Chancery: Willem Rutger Veldhuijzen van Zanten.
Attaché: Helene J. Kerlen.

NICARAGUA

Embassy: Avda 7a, No 1402, esq. 14, Miramar, Havana; tel (7) 22-1212; telex 511727.
Counsellor and Chargé d'affaires a.i.: Aura Estela Cano Aragon.
Minister-Counsellor: Roger Salomon López Rojas.
Counsellor: Guillermo Martinica Osorio.
Economic Counsellor: Graciela del Carmen Silva Rois.
Second Secretary: Cairo Arevalo.
Second Secretary: Carmen Argeñal.
Second Secretary: Hugo Ramon Norory Pallavicini.
Attaché: Lenin Adolfo Perez Ramos.
Attaché: José Antonio Arce Vado.

NIGERIA

Embassy: Avda 5a, No 1401, entre 14 y 16, Apdo 6232, Miramar, Havana; tel (7) 22-3196; telex 511589.
Ambassador: Solomon Kikiowo Omojokun.
Counsellor and Head of Chancery: Anthony Onelli Chikezie.
First Secretary (Economic/Consular/Student Affairs): Ibrahim Kayode Laro.
First Secretary (Political): Musa Jonathan Zakari.
First Secretary (Political/Cultural/Information): Chris Oshoke Erwat.
Financial Attaché: Ijona Oziegbu Maduka.
Attaché (Administrative): Edmund Alakwen Akobundu.

PANAMA

Embassy: Calle 26, No 109, Miramar, Havana; tel (7) 22-4096.

PERU

Embassy: Calle 36, No 109, entre 1 y 3, Miramar, Havana; tel (7) 22-8363; telex 511289; fax (7) 2-8636.
Ambassador: José Torres Muga Jiménez (designate).
Minister-Counsellor: Luis W. Sandiga Cabrera.
First Secretary (Economic/Commercial/Co-operation) and Head of Consular Section: Manuel Eduardo Loyola Sotil.
Second Secretary: Cesar Jordan Palomino.
Civil Attaché: Lilia Margot Moreno Hilares.
Civil Attaché: Carlos Vera Acevedo.

PHILIPPINES

Embassy: Calle 28, No 705, entre 7 y 9, Miramar, Havana; tel (7) 2-6177; telex 511081.
Ambassador: Ophelia A. Gonzáles y San Agustin.
Deputy Head of Mission and Consul-General: Erlinda F. Basilio.
Administrative Officer and Attaché: Emiliana P. Dulay (acting).
Finance Officer and Attaché: Brigido Achas.
First Secretary and Consul: Ariston E. Barsama.

POLAND

Embassy: Avda 5, No 4405, entre 44 y 46, Miramar, Havana; tel (7) 22-3322; telex 511037.
Ambassador: Wojciech Baranski.
Counsellor: Stanislaw Szafraniec.
Military, Naval and Air Attaché: Brig.-Gen. Tadeusz Gembicki.
Second Secretary (Press Affairs): Janusz Seczys.
Economic Attaché: Boguslaw Gajdamowicz.
Attaché: Kazimierz Cieniak.
Attaché: Krzysztof Wielgus.
Attaché: Janusz Chodniewicz.

Commercial Section: Calle 6, No 106, entre 1 y 3, Miramar, Havana; tel (7) 22-4453; telex 511717.
Commercial Counsellor: Andrzej Kamieniarz.

Consular Section: Calle 46, no 503, entre 5 y 5A, Miramar, Havana.

Counsellor (Head of Consular Section): Stanislaw Raczka.

PORTUGAL

Embassy: Avda 5a, No 6604, entre 66 y 68, Miramar, Havana; tel (7) 22-2593; telex 511411.
Ambassador: Fernão Manuel H. de Gouveia Favila Vieira.
Attaché (Administrative Affairs): Maria Helena Lópes Cardoso.

ROMANIA

Embassy: Calle 21, No 307, entre H y I, Vedado, Havana; tel (7) 32-1671; telex 512123.
Ambassador: Nicolae Petrut.
Counsellor: Cornel Margauan.
First Secretary: Ion Vasile.

Economic Section: tel (7) 32-4158.
Commercial Counsellor: Daniel Spirache.

RUSSIA

Embassy: 5ta Avda, No 6402, entre 62 y 66, Miramar, Havana; tel (7) 22-5042; telex 511281.
Ambassador: Yuri Vladimirovich Petrov.
Minister-Counsellor: Vladimir I. Kiseliov.
Minister-Counsellor (Economic Affairs): Boris P. Sokolov.
Counsellor: Dmitri Kanunnikov.
Counsellor: Nikolai E. Babich.
Counsellor: Mikhail P. Torshin.
Counsellor (Cultural Affairs): Oleg P. Smolensky.
Counsellor: Vladimir N. Isaev.
Counsellor: Victor I. Gnilosyrov.
Counsellor (Press and Information): Boris S. Ivanochkin.
Military, Naval and Air Attaché: Capt. Oleg A. Shevchenko.
First Secretary: Eugenio G. Gliok.
First Secretary: Victor I. Kurianov.
First Secretary: Alexandr Smirnov.
First Secretary: Valery A. Pogrushevsky.
First Secretary: Vladimir O. Korolkov.
First Secretary: Alexandr V. Gladzkov.
First Secretary (Economic): Evgeny S. Kuznetsov.
First Secretary: Vladimir V. Fiodorov.
First Secretary: Vladimir M. Ponedilko.
First Secretary: Evgeny N. Efinov.
Assistant Military Attaché: Capt. Victor V. Zaikin.
Assistant Military Attaché: Col Andrei G. Marshankin.

Commercial Section: Calle 3 y Final, La Puntilla, Miramar, Havana; tel (7) 2-3859.
Commercial Representative: Piotr I. Kormilitsin.
Principal Commercial Representative: Vladislav V. Martinov.

Representation of the State Planning Committee (GOSPLAN): Avda 5A, No 6617, entre 66 y 70, Miramar, Havana; tel (7) 22-5752.
Counsellor and Representative of the State Planning Committee: Valery F. Paulman.

Consular Section: Calle 13, No 651, entre B y C, Vedado, Havana; tel (7) 3-3934.
First Secretary and Consul-General: Alexandr I. Sandyrev.
First Secretary: Vladimir I. Kotov.

Consulate-General: Calle 4, No 202, esq. 7, Vista Alegre, Santiago de Cuba; tel 4-2346.
Consul-General: Alexandr M. Medvedev.
Consul: Victor A. Zavialov.
Consul: Viacheslav I. Levkov.

Consulate-General: Avda 64, No 11103, Buena Vista, Cienfuegos; tel 5395.
Consul-General: Victor P. Chukov.
Consul: Alexandr A. Sazonov.
Consul: Alexandr A. Safronov.

Consulate-General: Calle 4, No 129, entre 1 y 7, RPTO Rollo Monterrey, Moa; tel 6-8282.
Consul: Vladimir T. Kuraev.
Consul: Nikolai M. Grigorichev.

SEYCHELLES

Embassy: Havana.
Ambassador: Danielle Jorre de St Jorre (resident in Seychelles).

SPAIN

Embassy: Cárcel No 51, esq. Zulueta, Havana; tel (7) 62-6061; telex 511367.
Ambassador: Gunersindo Rico Rodríguez.
Counsellor: Ignacio Ruperez Rubio.
First Secretary: Fidel Sendagorta y Gómez del Campillo.
Attaché: Ignacio Estevez Vila.
Attaché: Alfredo Vicente Former.
Attaché: José Antonio Alaez Fernandez.
Attaché: Juan Antonio Moral Gutierrez.
Attaché: Carlos José Barbachano García.

Commercial Section: tel (7) 62-6063; telex 512435; fax (7) 62-2691.
Commercial Counsellor: Dario José Saez Mendez.

Co-operation Section: tel (7) 62-6064.
Attaché (Head of Co-operation): Angel San Juan Marciel.

Consular Section: Zulueta No 2, esq. Cárcel, Havana; tel (7) 62-6065; telex 512469.
Minister Plenipotentiary and Consul-General: Antonio García Abad.
Attaché: José Manuel Fernandez Arce.

Consulate: Calle 6, No 158, Vista Alegre, Santiago de Cuba; tel 4-2871.
Honorary Vice-Consul: Maria Dolores Martínez Palencia.

SRI LANKA

Embassy: Calle 32, No 307, entre 3 y 5, Miramar, Havana; tel (7) 22-7992; telex 512310.
Ambassador: N. Kanagaratnam Rajalingam.
Attaché (Administrative Affairs): Chandradasa Rupage.

SWEDEN

Embassy: Avda 31, No 1411, entre 14 y 18, Miramar, Havana; tel (7) 33-2563; telex 511208.
Ambassador: Karin Oldfelt Hjertonsson.
Second Secretary: Olof Skoog.
Second Secretary: Johanna Brismar Skoog.
Assistant Secretary: Hanna Rooth.

SWITZERLAND

Embassy: Avda 5, No 2005, entre 20 y 22, Miramar-Playa, Havana; Apdo 3328, Havana 3; tel (7) 22-1129; telex 511194.
Ambassador: Marcus Kaiser.
First Secretary: Katharina Zahnd.
Attaché and Head of Chancery: Dominique Uldry.

SYRIA

Embassy: Avda 5, No 7402, entre 74 y 76, Miramar, Havana; tel (7) 22-5266; telex 511394.
Minister Plenipotentiary and Chargé d'affaires a.i.: Aref Al-Jajeh.
Attaché (Administrative Affairs): Ahmad Takrouni.

TURKEY

Embassy: Calle 20, No 301, entre 3 y 5, Miramar, Havana; tel (7) 22-3037; telex 511724.
Ambassador: Mehmet Güney.
Minister-Counsellor: Haluk Akman.
Attaché: Selahaddin Senel.

UGANDA

Embassy: Calle 14, No 125, esq. 3, Miramar, Havana; tel (7) 29-3985; fax (7) 29-3985.
First Secretary and Chargé d'affaires a.i.: Edward Kamurasi Kapiriisa.
Commercial Attaché: Peter Elimu Elyetu.
Attaché (Financial and Administrative Affairs): Silvester Tibanyendere.

UNITED KINGDOM

Embassy: Edif. Bolívar, Carcel No 101-103, e Morro y Prado, Apdo 1069, Havana; tel (7) 62-3071; telex 511656.
Ambassador: A. L. S. Coltman.
Counsellor and Deputy Head of Mission: Nicholas R. Jarrold.
First Secretary (Commercial) and Consul: Robert Daly.
Second Secretary (Management/Consular): G. W. Brown.
Third Secretary (Chancery): J. Knott.
Attaché: Carol May Massingham.
Attaché: David A. Sherwood.
Attaché: Ian Brebner.
Attaché: P. Scott.
Attaché: Barry I. Rees.

USA

Interests Section: Calzada entre L y M, Vedado Seccion, Havana; tel (7) 32-0543; telex 512206.
Counsellor and Principal Officer: Alan H. Flanigan.
First Secretary and Deputy Principal Officer: L. Bradley Hittle.
First Secretary and Consul: Deborah A. Bolton.
First Secretary (Administrative Section): Nancy H. Cady.
Attaché and Regional Security Officer: Frederick A. Byron.
First Secretary (Cultural Affairs) and Public Affairs Officer: David L. Evans.
Communications Programme Officer: Walter Myers.
First Secretary (Consular Affairs): Dennis P. Harrington.
Second Secretary: Timothy N. Howard.
Second Secretary: Fulton T. Armstrong.
Second Secretary: Lisa Bobbie Schreiber Hughes.
Third Secretary (Consular Affairs): Stephen J. Carrig.
Third Secretary (Consular Affairs): Wallis S. Haynes.
Third Secretary (Consular Affairs): Benito M. Krawczyk.

URUGUAY

Embassy: Calle 14, No 506 entre 5 y 7, Miramar, Havana; tel (7) 22-0218; telex 511103.
Ambassador: Alberto Voss Rubio.
First Secretary and Consul: Maria Del C. Gonzalez de Dorelo.
Attaché (Administrative Affairs): Carlos Fernando Jardi.

VANUATU

Embassy: Havana.
Ambassador: Nikenike Vurdbaravu (resident in Vanuatu).

VENEZUELA

Embassy: Calle 36-A, No 704, entre 7 y 42, Miramar, Havana; tel (7) 22-1362; telex 511384.
Ambassador: Maria Clemencia López-Jiménez.
Minister-Counsellor: Milena Santana Bolivar.
First Secretary (Consular Affairs): Gabriel Armand Navarro.
First Secretary (Cultural Affairs): Asunta Paolini Valderrana.

Second Secretary: Ricardo Peraza Sanchez.
First Attaché: Oscar Angulo Mata.
First Attaché: Victor José Pérez Almeida.
Third Attaché: Belkys Zambrano de Pacheco.
Third Attaché: Ilona Torrealba Sierra.

VIET-NAM

Embassy: Avda 5a, No 1802, esq. 18, Miramar, Havana; tel (7) 2-3532; telex 512480.
Ambassador: Do Van Tai.
Counsellor: Tran Quang Hoan.
First Secretary (Economic/Scientific/Technical): Nai Thao.
First Secretary (Political/Consular): Nguyen Van Khan.
First Secretary (Political): Trinh Huy Ouang.
Second Secretary (Political/Press): Nguyen Xuan Vuong.
Third Secretary (Administrative): Nguyen Thi Xuan Ha.
Attaché (Cultural): Le Thu Son.

Commercial Section: Calle 16, No 514, entre 5 y 7, Miramar, Havana; tel (7) 2-3540; telex 511514.
Commercial Counsellor: Nguyen Thai Binh.

Military Section: Avda 1A, No 15215, esq. 154, Náutico, Havana; tel (7) 21-8597.
Military, Naval and Air Attaché: Col Tran Ngoc Que.
Assistant Military Attaché: Lieut Col Bui Trong Whu.

YEMEN

Embassy: Avda 7a, No 2207 esq. 24, Miramar, Havana; tel (7) 22-2594; telex 511488.
Ambassador: Muhammad Abdulrahman Hussein.
Minister Plenipotentiary: Ahmed Ali Alakwaa.
Counsellor: Omar Hussein Thabet.
First Secretary: Aidroos Zein Hasson Assakkaf.
Attaché: Ali Abdullah A. Honied.
Attaché: Abdullah Saleh Alawi.

YUGOSLAVIA

Embassy: Calle 42, No 115, entre 1 y 3, Miramar, Havana; tel (7) 22-6588; telex 512137.
Ambassador: Milutin Stojanović.
Counsellor (Political and Press Affairs): Milorad Ivanović.
First Secretary (Economic and Cultural Affairs): Slobodan Milić.
Attaché: Miroslav Jevtić.

ZAIRE

Embassy: Calle 36, No 716 entre 7 y 9, Miramar, Havana; tel (7) 2-4653.
Ambassador: Simba Ndombe.
Second Counsellor: Mr Baza-Boko.
First Secretary: Kafinga Mukoko.

ZIMBABWE

Embassy: Avda 3, No 1001 entre 10 y 12, Miramar, Havana; tel (7) 29-0468.
Ambassador: Amos Bernard Muvengwa Midzi.
Counsellor: Rafael R. S. Ndawana.
Political Counsellor: Ignatius K. Mutsinze.
First Secretary: Kennedy Samaneka.
Second Secretary: Stewart H. Shayamapiki.
Third Secretary: Sheila Murimba.
Third Secretary: Lennie Shayamapiki.

International Organizations

FOOD AND AGRICULTURE ORGANIZATION—FAO

Representation: Calle B, No. 15201, esq. a 152 Nautico, Havana; tel (7) 21-9155; telex 512110; fax (7) 21-8289.
Permanent Representative (FAO): Augusto Simoes Lopes Meto.

UNITED NATIONS DEVELOPMENT PROGRAMME—UNDP

Offices: Calle 18, No 110, 1 y 3 Avda Playa, Miramar, Havana; tel (7) 22-2504; telex 511477.
Representative (UN and UNDP): Joachim Von Braunmuhl.
Assistant Representative: Guido Ordoñez.
Associated Programme Officer: Govert Visser.
Associated Programme Officer: Ralf Schroder.

UNITED NATIONS EDUCATIONAL, SCIENTIFIC AND CULTURAL ORGANIZATION—UNESCO

Office: Calzada no 551, esq. D, Vedado, Havana; tel (7) 32-7741, 32-2840; telex 512154; fax (7) 32-5478.
Director of Regional Office and UNESCO Representative: Herman Crespo Toral.
Regional Counsellor (Cultural): Rafael Ricart Nouel.
Assistant Representative (UNESCO): Ada Penton Pedrera.

Other Organizations

AFRICAN NATIONAL CONGRESS—ANC

Embassy: Avda 21A, No 20617, esq. 214, Reparto Atabey, Havana; tel (7) 21-9894.
Permanent Representative: Kingsley Xuma.

PALESTINE LIBERATION ORGANIZATION—PLO

Embassy: Calle 20, No 714, entre 7 y 9, Miramar, Havana; tel (7) 22-6868; telex 511590.
Ambassador: Imad Jada'a.
First Secretary: Walid Salim Abdel-Rahim.
Third Secretary (Administrative Affairs): Mohamed Yousef Kazzaz.
Third Secretary (Cultural Affairs and the Press): Abdullah Younes.
Third Secretary: Ahmed E. Ata.
Attaché: Ziad Al-Najar.

CYPRUS

AUSTRALIA

High Commission: 4 Annis Komninis St, 2nd Floor, Nicosia; tel (2) 473001; telex 2097; fax (2) 366486.
High Commissioner: Edward John Stevens.
Counsellor (Commercial): Geoff Spears.
First Secretary (Consular/Administrative): Raymond G. Tuckfield.
Attaché: F. G. Egan.

AUSTRIA

Consulate-General: 33 Demosthenous Severis, POB 3961, Nicosia; tel (2) 451994; telex 2844.
Honorary Consul-General: Andreas Avraamides.
Honorary Vice-Consul: Christakis George Christofides.

BELGIUM

Consulate: Dramas 6, POB 1653, Nicosia; tel (2) 476244; telex 2206; fax (2) 451584.
Honorary Vice-Consul: Marios E. Lanitis.

Consulate: 113 Arch. Makarios III Ave, Cyprus Popular Bank Bldg, POB 1445, Limassol; tel (5) 338204; telex 3315.
Honorary Consul: Andreas P. Lanitis.

BRAZIL

Consulate: Lombard House, Stylianos Lenas Sq., POB 1425, Nicosia; tel (2) 463871; telex 3499; fax (2) 457870.
Honorary Consul: Hagop M. Keheyan.
Honorary Vice-Consul: Garo M. H. Keheyan.

BULGARIA

Embassy: 15 St Paul St, Nicosia; tel (2) 472486; telex 2188.
Ambassador: Peter Evtimov.
Counsellor: Kostadin Barakov.
Military, Naval and Air Attaché: Col Evtim Saparevsky.
Assistant Military Attaché: Maj. Ilia Peykov.
First Secretary (Political/Press): Filip Filev.
Attaché (Administrative): Stefan Stoilov.

Trade Representation: 13 Constantinou Paleologou St, Engomi, Nicosia; tel (2) 472740; telex 2188; fax (2) 456598.
Counsellor (Commercial): Damian Kounev.
Second Secretary (Commercial): Stoyan Stoyanov.

Cultural Centre: 24A Dorieon St, Nicosia; tel (2) 461791; fax (2) 472350.
Second Secretary (Cultural/Consular): Georgi Bourkov.

BURUNDI

Consulate: 4-6 Romanou St, Nicosia; tel (2) 461366; telex 2899; fax (2) 443551.
Honorary Consul: Tassos Anastassiades.

CANADA

Consulate: 15 Themistocles Dervis St, Margarita House, Suite 403, POB 2125, Nicosia; tel (2) 451630; telex 2110.
Honorary Consul: Michael Ioannides.

CHILE

Consulate-General: 5 Medhondos St, Nicosia; tel (2) 465424; fax (2) 456447.
Honorary Consul: George Zachariades.

CHINA, PEOPLE'S REPUBLIC

Embassy: 28 Archimedes St, POB 4531, Engomi, Nicosia; tel (2) 358182; telex 6376; fax (2) 353530.
Ambassador: Lin Aili.
Counsellor: Li Binghong.
First Secretary: Zhou Mingrui.
Second Secretary: Wang Yongqin.
Second Secretary: Wang Zeshan.
Second Secretary: Zhao Yali.
Third Secretary (Administrative): Zeng Weigan.

Commercial Section: 3 Korinthou St, Acropolis, Nicosia; tel (2) 313533; telex 4910; fax (2) 313479.
Counsellor (Commercial): Wang Guiyi.
Third Secretary (Commercial): Lu Yaxin.
Third Secretary (Commercial): Li Liansheng.

COLOMBIA

Consulate: Verengaria Bldg, 5th floor, 25 Sp. Araouzos St, POB 407, Limassol; tel (5) 364163; telex 2436; fax (5) 365269.
Honorary Consul: Pantelis C. Tsanos.

COSTA RICA

Consulate-General: 143E Chr. Haggipavlou St, POB 17, Limassol; tel (5) 362223; telex 2253; fax (5) 374534.
Honorary Consul-General: Costas Economou.
Honorary Consul: George C. Economou.
Honorary Consul: Yiannakis C. Economou.

CUBA

Embassy: 39 Regas Phereos St, Acropolis, Nicosia; tel (2) 427211; telex 2306; fax (2) 429390.
Ambassador: Jorge Rodriguez Grillo.
Third Secretary: Osvaldo Cobacho.
Attaché (Commercial): Ignacio Leon Llera.

CZECHOSLOVAKIA

Embassy: 7 Kastorias St, POB 1165, Acropolis, Nicosia; tel (2) 311681; telex 2490.
Ambassador: Emil Keblušek.
First Secretary: Jaroslav Roman.
Attaché: Frantisek Krivosudsky.
Attaché: Pavol Kucmas.

Commercial Section: 47 Aphrodite St, POB 5202, Aglanjia, Nicosia; tel (2) 348035; telex 6107; fax (2) 348133.
Counsellor (Commercial): Jaroslav Mulac.

DENMARK

Consulate: 39 Artemis Ave, POB 739, Larnaca; tel (4) 152027; telex 3180.
Consul-General: Nadina N. Dimitriou.
Vice-Consul (Commercial Affairs): Loukis C. Loucaides.

ECUADOR

Consulate: 38 Nicou Pattichi St, POB 167, Limassol; tel (5) 334245; telex 3112; fax (5) 336402.
Honorary Consul: Maximos Michaelides.

EGYPT

Embassy: 3 Egypt Ave, POB 1752, Nicosia; tel (2) 465144; telex 2102.
Ambassador: Nasr Mostafa Mahdy.
Minister: Taher Osman Dinana.
Counsellor: Yehya Saleh el-Din.
Counsellor: Mahmoud Mohamed Ismail.
Second Secretary: Yasser Reda Said.
Attaché (Administrative): Mohamed Ahmed Megahed.
Attaché (Administrative): Mokhtar Hussein Sayed.
Attaché (Administrative): Mohamed Mohamed Hassan.

FINLAND

Consulate-General: 9 Archbishop Makarios III Ave, POB 1139, Nicosia; tel (2) 444277; telex 2398; fax (2) 444897.
Consul-General: Demosthenis Z. Severis.
Vice-Consul: Costas Z. Severis.

FRANCE

Embassy: 6 Ploutarchou St, Engomi, POB 1671, Nicosia; tel (2) 465258; telex 2389; fax (2) 452289.
Ambassador: Daniel Husson.
Counsellor: Paul Ortholan.
First Secretary (Consular): Jean-Claude Marize.
Third Secretary: Denis Borrot.
Attaché (Finance): Bruno Cabrillac.
Attaché (Administrative): Patrick Beaufour.
Attaché (Administrative): Lucien Mimaud.
Attaché (Administrative): Michel Soulier.

Military Section: 6 Ploitarchou St, Engomi, POB 1671, Nicosia; tel (2) 457334.
Assistant Defence Attaché: Sqn Ldr Hughes Costes.

Trade Promotion Office: 19 Demosthenous St, cnr Evanthous St, Ayios Andreas, POB 1784, Nicosia; tel (2) 451388; telex 3756.
Counsellor (Commercial): Maxime Leport.
Attaché (Commercial): Elizabeth Modercin.

Cultural Section: 3 Jean Moreas St, POB 1713, Nicosia; tel (2) 443071.
Counsellor (Cultural): Jean-Louis Depierris.
Attaché (Cultural): Françoise Benedetti.
Attaché (Cultural): André Platbrood.
Attaché (Cultural): Brunehilde Imhaus.

Consulate: 140 Franklin Roosevelt St, POB 1682, Limassol; tel (5) 369000; telex 2882; fax (5) 352640.
Honorary Consul: Takis Solomonides.

Consulate: Eol Court, Flat 8, Halkidos St, Larnaca; tel (4) 656959.
Honorary Consul: Jacques E. A. Murat.

GERMANY

Embassy: 10 Nikitaras St, POB 1795, Ayii Omologhitae, Nicosia; tel (2) 444037; telex 2460; fax (2) 365694.
Ambassador: Dr Thilo Rötger.
Counsellor: Jörg Metger.
Second Secretary (Press/Administrative): Eckart Harmsen.
Third Secretary (Commercial): Wolfgang Polak.
Third Secretary: Erwin Altmann.
Third Secretary: Hartmut Mayer.
Third Secretary: Rainer Harms.
Attaché (Consular): Angela Ganninger.
Attaché (Administrative): Wolfgang Lehmann.
Attaché: Annegret Faust.
Attaché: Liane Leppla.

Consulate: 21 Archbishop Kyprianos St, POB 203, Limassol; tel (5) 166230; telex 2339; fax (5) 141361.
Honorary Consul: Costas Lanitis.

GREECE

Embassy: 8/10 Byron Ave, POB 1799, Nicosia; tel (2) 441880; telex 2394; fax (2) 473990.
Ambassador: Yannis Fotopoulos.
Counsellor: Constantine Kokossis.
Counsellor: Christos Panagopoulos.
Counsellor (Press): Nicolaos Spyridopoulos.
Second Secretary and Consul: Aikaterini A. Boura.
Second Secretary: Anna Korka.
Attaché (Consular): Margarita Mina.
Attaché (Administrative): Michalis Polyzopoulos.
Attaché (Consular/Education): Nicolaos Pitsikas.
Attaché (Administrative): Demetrios Doukas.
Attaché (Press): Eleni Alexandrou-Sapouna.
Attaché (Maritime): Commdr Greg Tsiambokalos.

Economic and Commercial Section: Evagoras Ave and King Paul's St, Nicosia; tel (2) 442219.
Attaché (Commercial): Georgios Lelis.
Secretary (Economic/Commercial): Paraskevi Tasakou.

GUYANA

Consulate: 13 Posidonos St, POB 3900, Nicosia; tel (2) 429250.
Honorary Consul: George Economides.

HOLY SEE

Apostolic Nunciature: Paphos Gate, Paphos St, POB 3751, Nicosia; tel (2) 462132.

Mission: St Catherine's Catholic Church, 2 Jerusalem St, Limassol; tel (5) 362946.
Attaché: Rev. Fr Umberto Barato.

HUNGARY

Embassy: 6 Vasileos Tefkrou St, Ayios Dhometios, Nicosia; tel (2) 472010; telex 2537; fax (2) 472011.
Ambassador: Dr Imre Uranovicz.
Counsellor (Consular): Maria Szekely-Nemeth.

Commercial Section: POB 6640, Limassol; tel (5) 136341; telex 6129; fax (5) 132129.
Commercial Advisor: Andreas Kereszetes.

Consulate-General: 54-8 Evagoras A' Ave, POB 1301, Nicosia; tel (2) 442114; telex 4929; fax (2) 459800.
Honorary Consul-General: Costas Loizou.

ICELAND

Embassy: c/o Ministry for Foreign Affairs, Hverfisgt. 115, 150 Reykjavik, Iceland; tel (1) 623000; telex 2050; fax (1) 622373.
Secretary: Inga Cleaver (resident in Iceland).

Consulate: 11 Acharnon St, POB 1820, Nicosia 145; tel (2) 348484; telex 5877; fax (2) 347870.
Consul: Michael Psomas.

INDIA

High Commission: 3 Indira Gandhi St, Engomi, POB 5544, Nicosia; tel (2) 351741; telex 4146; fax (2) 350402.
High Commissioner: Rajendra Gopalaswami Parthasarathy.
Second Secretary: Vishnu Dutta.
Military and Naval Attaché: Col Mammohan Bharadwaj.

Consulate-General: 7 Spyros Araouzos St, POB 125, Limassol; tel (5) 362093; telex 3308; fax (5) 442724.
Honorary Consul-General: Felix Cirilli de Nores (resident in Nicosia).

IRAN

Embassy: 1 cnr Santa Rosa-Avlanos St, Nicosia; tel (2) 450020; telex 6416.
Chargé d'affaires a.i.: Mohammad Reza Karshenas.
First Secretary: Mohamed Reza Rauf Sheibani.
Third Secretary: Masoud Kazemi.
Attaché: Houshang Dinarvandi.
Attaché: Mossayeb Aliyary.

IRAQ

Embassy: c/o Minister for Foreign Affairs, Salhiah-Karkh, Baghdad, Iraq; tel 537-0091; telex 2313.
Ambassador: Fuad Fityan al-Rawi (resident in Iraq).

IRELAND

Consulate: St Etienne Enterprises Ltd, Flat 301, cnr Calypso and Armenias Sts, POB 523, Nicosia; tel (2) 499554; telex 3974; fax (2) 312658.
Honorary Consul: Stephanos A. Stephanou.

ISRAEL

Embassy: 4 I. Gryparis St, POB 1049, Nicosia; tel (2) 445195; telex 5978.
Ambassador: Aharon Lopez.
Second Secretary: Daniel Meron.
Second Secretary and Head of Consular Section: Eliahu Levi.
Attaché: Gideon Avrami.
Attaché: Eyal Kotzer.
Attaché: Reuven Rosen.
Attaché: Rafi Levy.

ITALY

Embassy: Margarita House, 15 Themistoklis Dervis St, POB 1452, Nicosia; tel (2) 473183; telex 3847.
Ambassador: Guido Rizzo Venci.
Counsellor: Fabrizio Pignatelli Della Leonessa.
Attaché: Col Rino Stanig.
Attaché (Press/Information): Sebastiano Cipriano.
Attaché (Administrative): Maria Antonietta Scocchi.
Attaché (Consular): Alvaro Manni.
Attaché (Commercial): Vanda Spataro Gianola.
Attaché: Massimo Gianola.
Attaché: Gennaro Di Lorenzo.
Attaché: Andrea Fontanella.
Attaché: Mario Carapacchio.

Consulate: 130 Sp. Araouzos St, POB 1, Limassol; tel (5) 362045; telex 2413; fax (5) 377842.
Honorary Consul: Benito A. Mantovani.

Consulate: 1 King Paul Sq., POB 109, Lanarca; tel (4) 652024; telex 2412; fax (4) 652393.
Honorary Consul: Victor Mantovani.

JAPAN

Consulate-General: 130 Sp. Araouzos St, POB 1, Limassol; tel (5) 362045; telex 2413; fax (5) 377842.
Honorary Consul-General: Umberto V. Mantovani.

JORDAN

Consulate: 9 Demitsanis St, Galeria Bldg, Flat 101, POB 4862, Nicosia; tel (2) 473988; telex 2561.
Honorary Consul: Michael G. Leptos.

LEBANON

Embassy: 1 Vasilissis Olgas St, POB 1924, Nicosia; tel (2) 442216; telex 3056.
Ambassador: Zaidan Zaidan.
Counsellor: Leila Chehab.
Secretary (Consular): Micheline Baz.

LIBERIA

Consulate: 2 Aristides Charalambous St, Mykonos Bldg, 3rd Floor, Nicosia; tel (2) 499096; telex 3405.
Honorary Consul: Loizos A. Karageorges.

Consulate: c/o 20 Costi Palama St, Aspelia Court, Office B3, 2nd Floor, Nicosia; tel (2) 451127; telex 6025; fax (2) 477485.
Honorary Consul: Kyriacos J. Koushos.

LIBYA

People's Bureau: 14 Estias St, POB 3669, Nicosia; tel (2) 496511; telex 3277; fax (2) 316152.
Secretary of People's Bureau: Ali Abdulhamed al-Saghaier.
Member (Political): Mustafa Filali.
Member (Political): Ghaleb A. Dalla.
Finance Controller: Salem Y. el-Hannashi.
Member (Commercial): Emhemmed el-Wkai.
Member (Administrative): Bashir Mohamed Gaffar.
Member (Administrative): Mohamed Arrir.
Member (Administrative): Omar Mohamed Hagerrs.
Secretary (Cultural): Mohamed Kashada.
Assistant Secretary (Cultural): Mohamed L. Ali.

LUXEMBOURG

Consulate: 22 Hera St, Offices 9/10, POB 2411, Nicosia; tel (2) 450832; telex 3960; fax (2) 457996.
Honorary Consul: Christos M. Triantafyllides.

MALI

Consulate: Libra House, 21 P. Catelaris St, POB 5001, Nicosia; tel (2) 466766; telex 2687; fax (2) 448777.
Honorary Consul: Acis Montagnos.

MALTA

Consulate-General: 101A Sp. Araouzos St, POB 145, Limassol; tel (5) 362642; telex 2344.
Honorary Consul-General: John M. Louisides.
Honorary Consul: Michael J. Louisides.

MEXICO

Consulate: Shacolas House, POB 1744, Nicosia; tel (2) 482880; telex 4627; fax (2) 482847.
Honorary Consul: Nicolas Shakolas.

NETHERLANDS

Consulate: cnr Athens and O'Connor Sts, Cyprus Popular Bank Bldg, POB 203, Limassol; tel (5) 366230; telex 2339; fax (5) 341361.
Honorary Consul: Evagoras C. Lanitis.
Honorary Vice-Consul: Plato E. Lanitis.

Consulate: New Port Rd, POB 1490, Limassol; tel (5) 342294; telex 2985; fax (5) 367246.
Honorary Consul: Nicos H. Stephanou.

NORWAY

Consulate-General: 4 Meletiou Metaxaki St, POB 1012, Nicosia; tel (2) 472024; telex 2426; fax (2) 459359.
Honorary Consul-General: Solon A. Triantafyllides.

Consulate: 16 Princess de Tyras, Karantokis Bldg, 7th Floor, POB 1012, Nicosia; tel (2) 449760; telex 3849; fax (2) 365011.
Honorary Consul: Polyvios G. Polyviou.

OMAN

Consulate: 1E Menandrou St, 4th Floor, POB 4670, Nicosia; tel (2) 453311; telex 5188.

Honorary Consul: Marcos P. Spanos.

PANAMA

Consulate-General: Nicosia Tower Centre, 8th Floor, 36 Byron Ave, POB 1341, Nicosia; tel (2) 444455; telex 3843; fax (2) 444040.
Honorary Consul-General: Polakis K. Sarris.
Honorary Consul: Constantinos S. Dalitis.

PERU

Consulate: Asteria Beach Hotel, Potamos Yermasoyias, POB 1261, Limassol; tel (5) 321177; telex 2370.
Honorary Consul: Chritis E. Doritis.

PHILIPPINES

Consulate: 7 Androcleous St, Office 22, POB 1216, Nicosia; tel (2) 472060; telex 5797; fax (2) 367053.
Honorary Consul: John P. Erotocritou.

PORTUGAL

Consulate: Larnaca Industrial Estate, POB 142, Larnarca; tel (4) 637766; telex 2749; fax (4) 636992.
Honorary Consul: Stelios J. Dimitriou.

ROMANIA

Embassy: 37 Tombazis St, Nicosia; tel (2) 445845; telex 2431.
Counsellor and Chargé d'affaires a.i.: Ioan Sbarna.
Military, Naval and Air Attaché: Col Marin-Dumitru Manea.
First Secretary: Teodor Sterian.

RUSSIA

Embassy: 4 Gladstone St, POB 1845, Nicosia; tel (2) 472141; telex 5808; fax (2) 472230.

New Premises: Ayios Prokopios, Archbishop Makarios III St, Engomi, Nicosia; tel (2) 464622; telex 5808; fax (2) 464854.
Ambassador: Boris G. Zenkov.
Minister-Counsellor: Valentin V. Markov.
Counsellor: Viatcheslav I. Frolov.
Military, Naval and Air Attaché: Col Victor P. Gradoselsky.
Assistant Military, Naval and Air Attaché: Capt. Arkadi A. Palkine.
Assistant Military, Naval and Air Attaché: Lieut Col Igor V. Kirsanov.
First Secretary (Cultural): Gennady A. Pivovarov.
First Secretary: Vladimir A. Chizhov.
First Secretary: Valeri I. Gusev.
First Secretary: Gennady P. Naianov.
First Secretary: Boris G. Urunov.
First Secretary: Vadim L. Maiatski.
Second Secretary: Yuri D. Pianykh.
Second Secretary: Yuri V. Cherchavov.
Second Secretary: Vladimir P. Liziaev.
Second Secretary: Sergei V. Martynov.
Second Secretary: Oleg P. Sosnovsky.

Consular Section: Ayios Prokopios, Archbishop Makarios III St, Engomi, Nicosia; tel (2) 464622; tel 5808; fax (2) 464854.

Trade Representation: 10 Gladstone St, POB 1755, Nicosia; tel (2) 474285; telex 3090.
Trade Representative: Vladimir P. Iline.
Deputy Trade Representative: Boris K. Stalnov.
Deputy Trade Representative: Vladislav A. Artemiev.

RWANDA

Consulate: 12 Themistoclis Dervis St, POB 1255, Nicosia; tel (2) 462925; telex 3828; fax (2) 450620.
Honorary Consul: Marcos S. Kyprianou.

SAN MARINO

Consulate-General: 14 Regas Fereos St, POB 27, Limassol; tel (5) 362341; telex 3396.
Honorary Consul-General: Petros A. Anastassiades.

SIERRA LEONE

Consulate-General: Oriana Court, 4th Floor, 225 Archbishop Makarios III Ave, POB 4080, Limassol; tel (5) 366363; telex 3318.
Honorary Consul-General: Phaedon T. Economides.

SPAIN

Consulate-General: cnr Polaodomias and Phedras Sts, Kaimakli, POB 1244, Nicosia; tel (2) 433151; telex 2282; fax (2) 430880.
Honorary Consul-General: Spyros A. Araouzos.

SRI LANKA

Consulate: 126 Franklin Roosevelt St, Limassol; tel (5) 363933; telex 2444; fax (5) 374229.
Honorary Consul: Doros A. Jeropoulos.

SWEDEN

Consulate-General: Princess Zena de Tyras Bldg, POB 5487, Nicosia; tel (2) 442483; telex 2597; fax (2) 466412.
Consul-General: Demetrakis Zeno Pierides.
Consul: George Polycarpou Vryonides.

SWITZERLAND

Consulate-General: Commercial Union Tower, 101 Archbishop Makarios III Ave, POB 729, Nicosia; tel (2) 446261; telex 5694; fax (2) 446008.
Counsellor and Chargé d'affaires a.i.: Rudolf Stauch.
Honorary Consul-General: Dimitri Shukuroglou.
Attaché and Head of Chancery: Norbert Arnold.

SYRIA

Embassy: cnr Androcleous and Thoukidides Sts, POB 1891, Nicosia; tel (2) 474481; telex 2030; fax (2) 446963.
First Secretary and Chargé d'affaires a.i.: Abdul al-Fattah Ammourah.
Third Secretary: Ali Ghazi.
Attaché (Press): Yaroub al-Sayed.
Attaché: Yassin Ali.
Attaché: Mohammed id Abou al-Dahab.

THAILAND

Consulate: Park Tower 2, Flat 403, Ipatias St, POB 415, Limassol; tel (5) 352333.
Honorary Consul: John Voyias.

UNITED KINGDOM

High Commission: POB 1978, Alexander Pallis St, Nicosia; tel (2) 473131; telex 2208; fax (2) 367198.
High Commissioner: David John Michael Dain.
Counsellor and Deputy High Commissioner: Michael C. Clements.
Defence Adviser: Col John I. Pocock.
First Secretary (Commercial): Derek Reed.
First Secretary (Information): Richard W. Potter.
First Secretary (Consular): Jenny M. Taylor.
First Secretary (Chancery): Christopher N. M. James.
First Secretary (Chancery): N. P. Westgate.
Second Secretary (Commercial): Gavin A. Mackay.
Second Secretary (Chancery): D. H. Craig.
Second Secretary (Chancery): P. McGee.
Assistant Management Officer: J. P. Banks.

USA

Embassy: Dositheos St and Therissos St, Lykavitos, Nicosia; tel (2) 465151; telex 4160; fax (2) 459571.
Ambassador: Robert E. Lamb.
Deputy Chief of Mission: Carolyn Huggins.
Political Section: Eric Tunis.
Economic/Commercial Section: Michael Meigs.
Consul: John Spiegel.
Administrative Section: Gregory Engle.
Regional Security Officer: Roger Brown.
Public Affairs Officer: Lane Cubstead.
Communications Programme Officer: Marty Myers.
Office of the Defence Attaché: Col Stephen R. Norton.

YEMEN

Embassy: 25 Thermopylon St, POB 2002, Acropolis, Nicosia; tel (2) 494598; telex 3640; fax (2) 447837.
Ambassador: Ahmad Mohammad al-Moutawakil.
Minister-Counsellor: Dr Abdul G. S. Thabet.
Counsellor: Mohamed Awad Alawi.

YUGOSLAVIA

Embassy: 2 Vasilissis Olgas St, POB 1968, Nicosia; tel (2) 445511; fax (2) 445910.
Ambassador: Petar Bosković.
Secretary: Alenka Vipotnik-Kopanja.
Attaché (Administrative): Mirko Miljus.
Attaché: Strahimir Ilic.

International Organizations

EUROPEAN COMMUNITIES

External Delegation: Iris Tower, 2 Agapinor St, Archbishop Makarios III Ave, POB 3480, Nicosia; tel (2) 369202; telex 4960; fax (2) 368926.
Head of Delegation: Jean-Pierre Derisbourg.
Third Secretary: Llewellyn Edwards.
Attaché: Sonia Dixon.

FOOD AND AGRICULTURE ORGANIZATION—FAO

Office: c/o Ministry of Agriculture and Natural Resources, Nicosia; tel (2) 302730; telex 4660.
Representative (FAO): Axel Baille.

UNITED NATIONS DEVELOPMENT PROGRAMME—UNDP

Office: Govt House, 22 Dem. Severis Ave, POB 3521, Nicosia; tel (2) 303188; telex 4861; fax (2) 366125.
Representative (UNDP): Jan Swietering.
Deputy Representative (UNDP): Adel M. Khalifa.

UNITED NATIONS PEACE-KEEPING FORCE IN CYPRUS—UNFICYP

Representation: POB 1642, Nicosia; tel (2) 359000; telex 2329; fax (2) 359053.
Special Representative (UNFICYP): Oscar Camilion.
Commander (UNFICYP): Maj.-Gen. Clive Milner.
Chief of Staff (UNFICYP): Brig. Niels L. Fredenslund.

Other Organizations

PALESTINE LIBERATION ORGANIZATION—PLO

Representation: 41 Aristokyprou St, POB 4669, Acropolis, Nicosia; tel (2) 315010; telex 2086; fax (2) 315013.
Representative: Samir Abu Ghazala.
Counsellor: Malath M. Abdo.
First Secretary (Press): Fayez Younes.
First Secretary: Sanih A. O. Khader.
First Secretary: Mohammed Fawzi Suleiman.
First Secretary (Finance): Basman Ali Khateb.
Second Secretary: Saleh M. Zakout.

'TURKISH REPUBLIC OF NORTHERN CYPRUS'

TURKEY

Embassy: Bedreddin Demirel Ave, Nicosia, Mersin 10, Turkey; tel (520) 72314.
Ambassador: Ertuğrul Kumcuoğlu.

CZECHOSLOVAKIA

AFGHANISTAN

Embassy: U Vorlíku 17, 125 01 Prague 6; tel (2) 381532.
Ambassador: Mohammad Araf Sakhra.

ALBANIA

Embassy: Pod Kaštany 22, Bubeneč, 160 00 Prague 6; tel (2) 379329; fax (2) 379329.
Political Counsellor and Chargé d'affaires a.i.: Vangjel Mita.
Commercial Counsellor: Fiqirete Elmazi.
Head of Consular Section: Fejzi Kodra.

ALGERIA

Embassy: Korejská 16, 125 21 Prague; tel (2) 322021.
Ambassador: Abdelhamid Latreche.

ARGENTINA

Embassy: Washingtonova 25, 3rd Floor, 125 22 Prague 1; tel (2) 223803; telex 121847.
Ambassador: Abel Parentini Posse.
Attaché: Marcelo D. Bottini.

Consular Section: tel (2) 260320.
Counsellor and Head of Consular Section: Ricardo H. Forrester.

Commercial Section: Sokolská 29, 120 00 Prague 2; tel (2) 293939; telex 121778.
Secretary and Head of Commercial Section: Mario Quinteros.

AUSTRIA

Embassy: Viktora Huga 10, 125 43 Prague 5; tel (2) 546550; telex 121849; fax (2) 549626.
Ambassador: Karl Peterlik.
Minister: Wolfgang Paul.
Counsellor: Jakub Forst-Battaglia.
Economic Counsellor and Consul: August Zotter.
Economic Secretary: Alexander Scheller.
Military and Air Attaché: Col Helmut Dorner.
Press and Cultural Counsellor: Rainer Lustig-Leignitz.
Cultural Attaché: Christine Dollinger.

Consulate-General: Holubyho 11, 811 03 Bratislava; tel (7) 311103; telex 93272.
Consul-General: Walter Swatosch.
Vice-Consul: Heribert Quirchmayer.

BELGIUM

Embassy: Valdštejnská 6, 125 24 Prague 1; tel (2) 534051; telex 122362.
Ambassador: Baron Henry Beyens.

BOLIVIA

Embassy: Ve Smečkách 25, 125 59 Prague 1; tel (2) 263209; telex 122402.
Ambassador: Carlos Costa du Rels.
First Secretary and Consul: Juan Carlos Quiroga.

BRAZIL

Embassy: Bolzanova 5, 125 01 Prague 1; tel (2) 229254; telex 122292.
Ambassador: Carlos Eduardo de Affonseca Alves de Souza.

BULGARIA

Embassy: Krakovská 6, 125 00 Prague 1; tel (2) 264310; telex 121381; fax (2) 2361781.
Ambassador: Prof. Boyan Nichev.
Counsellor (Economic/Commercial): Svobodan Kalaydjiev.
Counsellor (Political): Ognyan Gurkov.
Counsellor (Cultural): Vutyo Rakovsky.
Military Attaché: Col Nikola Nochev.
First Secretary (Economic/Commercial): Milcho Pavlov.
First Secretary (Political): Radko Vlaykov.
Second Secretary (Protocol/Press): Valentin Russev.
Second Secretary (Education/CSCE): Lilia Zakharieva.
Second Secretary and Consul: Marin Yovchevsky.

Consulate-General: Kuzmaniho 1, Bratislava; tel (7) 315308; telex 92126.
Consul-General: Nicola Kirkov.
Consul: Yordan Gerassimov.

CAMBODIA

Embassy: Na Hubálce 1, 169 00 Prague 6; tel (2) 352603.
Ambassador: Ung Sean.

CANADA

Embassy: Mickiewiczova 6, 125 33 Prague 6; tel (2) 3120251; telex 121061; fax (2) 3112791.
Ambassador: Alan P. McLaine.
Counsellor (Immigration): Denis G. J. Létourneau.
Canadian Forces Attaché: Col James D. Hunter.
First Secretary and Consul: Robert G. McRae.
Second Secretary (Administration) and Vice-Consul: R. Wallace L. Brown.
Third Secretary and Vice-Consul: Carmel A. Whelton.

Commercial Section: Na Petynce 120, 169 00 Prague 6; tel (2) 3579665; fax (2) 355476.
Counsellor (Commercial): Ross N. Miller.
Third Secretary (Commercial): Jennifer A. Daubeny.

CHINA, PEOPLE'S REPUBLIC

Embassy: Majakovského 22, 160 00 Prague 6.
Ambassador: Wang Xingda.

COLOMBIA

Embassy: Příčná 1, 110 00 Prague 1; tel (2) 291330.
Ambassador: Camilo Reyes Rodríguez.

COSTA RICA

Embassy: Dlouhá 36, 110 00 Prague 1; tel (2) 2619073; telex 121726; fax (2) 2320878.
Ambassador: Carlos E. Fernández García.

CUBA

Embassy: Sibiřské nám. 1, 125 35 Prague 6; tel (2) 341341; telex 93184.
Ambassador: Mario Rodríguez Martínez.

DENMARK

Embassy: U Havličkových sadu 1, POB 54, 120 21 Prague 2; tel (2) 254715; telex 122209; fax (2) 254715.
Ambassador: Vigand Lose.
Secretary: Ole Egberg Mikkelsen.
Commercial Officer: Jaroslav Kubát.

ECUADOR

Embassy: Opletalova 43, 125 01 Prague 1; tel (2) 261258; telex 123286.
Ambassador: Oswaldo Ramírez Landazuri.

EGYPT

Embassy: Majakovského 14, 125 46 Prague 6; tel (2) 341051; telex 123552.
Ambassador: Nabil Helmy.
Military, Naval and Air Attaché: Capt. Hany Mostafa Kamel.

ETHIOPIA

Embassy: V Průhledu 9, 125 01 Prague 6; tel (2) 3120479; telex 122067; fax (2) 3123464.
Ambassador: Teferra Shiawl.
First Secretary: Belay Girmay.
Counsellor (Education): Shibabaw Belay Workneh.
Attaché (Administrative/Financial): Assefa Mengesha.

FINLAND

Embassy: Dřevná 2, 125 01 Prague 2; tel (2) 205541; telex 121060; fax (2) 296098.
Ambassador: Pauli Opas.
Counsellor: Markku Kauppinen.
Military and Air Attaché: Lieut Col Matti Lehtonen.
Counsellor (Commercial Affairs): Pertti Peltoranta.
Attaché (Consular Affairs): Kaija Pesonen.
Attaché (Industrial Affairs): Taavi Hiltunen.

Office of the Commercial Attaché: Gorkeho 15, 801 00 Bratislava; tel (7) 330829; telex 93200.
Commercial Attaché: Markku Rantalainen.

Consulate: U Sitkova 1, 110 00 Prague 1; tel (2) 294100; telex 121917.
Consul: Jana Matejovská.

FRANCE

Embassy: Velkopřevorské nám. 2, 110 00 Prague 1; tel (2) 533042; fax (2) 539926.
Ambassador: Jean Guéguinou.

Trade Promotion Office: tel (2) 533047; telex 121317.

GERMANY

Embassy: Vlašská 19, 125 60 Prague 1; tel (2) 532351-6; telex 122814; fax (2) 531231.
Ambassador: Hermann Huber.

Visa Section: telex 121542.

Consulate-General: Palisàdy 47, Bratislava; tel (7) 315300; telex 92686.

GHANA

Embassy: V Tišině 4, 160 00 Prague 6; tel (2) 373058; telex 122263.
Ambassador: Moses Kwasi Ahmad Agyeman.
Second Secretary: Georgina Hackman.

GREECE

Embassy: Na Ořechovce 19, 125 45 Prague 6; tel (2) 354279.
Ambassador: Constantin Politis.

HUNGARY

Embassy: Mičurinova 1, 125 37 Prague 6; tel (2) 365041; telex 122655; fax (2) 329425.
Ambassador: György Varga.
Counsellor: Pál Benyo.
Military and Air Attaché: Lieut Col András Nagy.
Counsellor: László Fendrik.
Consul: Sándor Lilienberg.
First Secretary: Dr Pál Belyó.
Second Secretary: Lajos Szénási.
Second Secretary: Dr Sándor Kása.
Commercial Counsellor: Dr Gergely Mezö.
Commercial Secretary: Miklós Czimer.

Cultural Centre: Rytirska 25, 110 00 Prague 1; tel (2) 2361249.
Cultural Counsellor and Director of Cultural Centre: Klára Gindeléné Bencskó.

Consulate-General and Cultural Centre: Palisády 54, 811 06 Bratislava; tel (7) 335601.
Consul-General: Dr Jenö Boros.
Director of Cultural Centre: László Honti.

INDIA

Embassy: Valdštejnská 6, 125 28 Prague 1; tel (2) 532642; telex 121901.
Ambassador: Bhupatray Oza.

INDONESIA

Embassy: Nad Budánkami II/7, 125 29 Prague 5; tel (2) 526041; telex 121443.
Ambassador: H. R. Enap Suratman.

IRAN

Embassy: Nám. Družby 9, Prague 6; tel (2) 322745; telex 122732.
Ambassador: Hamid Reza Hosseini.

IRAQ

Embassy: Na Zátorce 10, 125 01 Prague 6.
Ambassador: Munther Ahmed al-Mutlak.

ITALY

Embassy: Nerudova 20, 125 31 Prague 1; tel (2) 530666; telex 122704.
Ambassador: Giovanni Castellani Pastoris.

JAPAN

Embassy: Maltézské nám. 6, 1 Malá Str., 125 32 Prague 1; tel (2) 535751; telex 121199; fax (2) 539997.
Ambassador: Tisati Cato.

KOREA, DEMOCRATIC PEOPLE'S REPUBLIC

Embassy: R. Rollanda 10, 160 00 Prague 6; tel (2) 373953.
Ambassador: Kim Kwang Sop.

KOREA, REPUBLIC

Embassy: Prague.
Ambassador: Son Chun-Yong.

LEBANON

Embassy: Gottwaldovo nábřeží 14, 110 00 Prague 1; tel (2) 293633; telex 123583.

LIBYA

People's Committee: Na baště sv. Jiří 7, 160 00 Prague 6.
Secretary of People's Committee: Muhammad Musbah Khalifa.

MEXICO

Embassy: Nad Kazankou 8, 171 00 Prague 7; tel (2) 8555554; telex 121947; fax (2) 8550477.
Ambassador: José Caballero Bazán.

MONGOLIA

Embassy: Korejská 5, 160 00 Prague 6; tel (2) 328992; telex 121921.
Ambassador: Djamsragiyn Dulma.

MOROCCO

Embassy: Petrska 24, 124 47 Prague 1; tel (2) 310935.
Ambassador: Tajeddine Baddou.

MYANMAR

Embassy: Romaina Rollanda 3, 125 23 Prague 6; tel (2) 381140; telex 122519; fax (2) 370646.
Ambassador: U Than Tun.
First Secretary: U Ko Ko.
Third Secretary: U Aung Kyi.

NETHERLANDS

Embassy: Maltézské nám. 1, 110 00 Prague 1; tel (2) 531378; telex 122643; fax (2) 531368.
Ambassador: Count Lambert D'Ansembourg.

NICARAGUA

Embassy: Na Baště sv. Jiří 3, 125 46 Prague 6; tel (2) 324410; telex 123336.
Ambassador: Mayra Pasos Marciaq.

NIGERIA

Embassy: Před Bateriemi 18, 160 00 Prague 6; tel (2) 354294; telex 123575.
Ambassador: Dr Musa Otigba.

NORWAY

Embassy: Na Ořechovce 69, 162 00 Prague 6; tel (2) 353437; telex 122200; fax (2) 3123797.
Ambassador: Knut Taraldset.

Commercial Section: Parizska 28, POB 102, 110 01 Prague 6; tel (2) 3123617; telex 122200.

PERU

Embassy: Hradecká 18, 125 01 Prague 3; tel (2) 742024; telex 123345.
Ambassador: Igor Velázquez Rodríguez.

POLAND

Embassy: Valdštejnská 8, 125 42 Prague 1; tel (2) 536951; telex 121841; fax (2) 536427.
Ambassador: Jacek Baluch.

PORTUGAL

Embassy: Bubenská 3, 3rd Floor, 170 00 Prague 7; tel (2) 802188; telex 121354; fax (2) 802624.
Ambassador: Luís Quartin.
Counsellor: Paulo Rufino.
Cultural and Press Attaché: Luís Machado.
Attaché (Consular Affairs): João Miranda.

ROMANIA

Embassy: Nerudova 5, 125 44 Prague; tel (2) 533059.
Ambassador: Ion Ciubotaru.

RUSSIA

Embassy: Pod Kaštany 1, 160 00 Prague 6; tel (2) 373323.

Consulate-General: U Godrova 4, 801 00 Bratislava; tel (7) 313468.

Consulate-General: Glinky 142-B, 603 00 Brno; tel (5) 334427.

Consulate-General: U Petra Velikeho 18, 360 01 Karlovy Vary; tel (17) 22609.

SOUTH AFRICA

Consulate-General: Prague.
Consul-General: N. W. du Bois.

SPAIN

Embassy: Pevnostní 9, 162 00 Prague 6; tel (2) 327124; telex 121974; fax (2) 323573.
Ambassador: José Luis Dicenta Ballester.

SUDAN

Embassy: Malostranské nábřeží 1, 125 01 Prague; tel (2) 536547.
Ambassador: Sayyid Abd al-Mutasim.

SWEDEN

Embassy: Úvoz 13, 125 52 Prague 1; tel (2) 533344; telex 121840; fax (2) 532213.
Ambassador: Lars-Åke Nilsson.
First Secretary: Sven Nylander.
Second Secretary: Mats Foyer.

Swedish Trade Council: Štěpánská 57, 110 00 Prague 1; tel (2) 220190; telex 121458; fax (2) 224741.
Commercial Secretary: Karl-Gustaf Gustafsson.

Consulate: Rázusovo nábr 4, 811 02 Bratislava; tel (7) 333534; telex 92460; fax (7) 315462.
Consul and Head of Commercial Section: Ruben Arne Kemeny.

SWITZERLAND

Embassy: Pevnostní 7, 162 00 Prague 6; tel (2) 3121805; telex 121095; fax (2) 3123058.
Ambassador: Maurice Jeanrenaud.
Counsellor: Clemens Birrer.
Attaché and Head of Chancery: Peter Oberhänsli.

SYRIA

Embassy: Pod Kaštany 16, 125 01 Prague 6; tel (2) 326231; telex 121532.
Ambassador: Subhi Haddad.

TUNISIA

Embassy: Nad Kostelem 8, 125 01 Prague 4; tel (2) 460652; telex 122512; fax (2) 460825.
Ambassador: Noureddine Boujellabia.
Counsellor: Arbia Ben Ajmia.
First Secretary: Abdeljelil Ben Ajmia.
Secretary: Habib Hachicha.

TURKEY

Embassy: Pevnostní 3, 160 00 Prague 6; tel (2) 320597; fax (2) 320597.
Ambassador: İnal Batu.

UNITED KINGDOM

Embassy: Thunovská 14, 125 50 Prague 1; tel (2) 533340; telex 121011; fax (2) 250986.
Ambassador: A. David Brighty.
Deputy Head of Mission and Counsellor: J. S. Laing.
Counsellor: G. J. Garrett.
First Secretary: A. B. Gundersen.
First Secretary: W. J. C. Meath-Baker.
First Secretary (Management) and Consul: J. A. Holder.
Second Secretary (Chancery/Information): M. H. Tatham.
Second Secretary (Works): J. G. Darlington.
Second Secretary: M. J. Gunnett.
Second Secretary (Consular/Information): P. D. Broom.
Third Secretary (Know-How Fund): C. F. M. Blair.
Defence and Military Attaché: Col W. J. Chesshyre.
Air Attaché: Wing Commdr R. Foster.

Commercial Section: Blanická 13/11, 120 00 Prague; tel (2) 252907; telex 122926; fax (2) 250986.
First Secretary (Commercial): S. J. Davey.
Second Secretary (Commercial): H. R. Nellthorp.

Cultural Section: Jungmannova 30, 110 00 Prague; tel (2) 224501.
Cultural Attaché: W. H. Jefferson.

USA

Embassy: Tržiště 15, 125 48 Prague 1; tel (2) 536641; telex 121196; fax (2) 532457.
Ambassador: Shirley Temple Black.
Deputy Chief of Mission: Theodore E. Russell.
Political Section: Timothy M. Savage.
Economic Section: Harvey D. Lampert.
Commercial Section: Robert Shipley.
Consul: Mary McAteer.
Administrative Section: Frank J. Coulter.
Regional Security Officer: James D. Gleeson.
Public Affairs Officer: Thomas Hull.
Communications Programme Officer: Frank E. Morgan.
Information Systems Manager: Paul D. Lane.
Office of the Defence Attaché: Col Edwin J. Motyka.

Consulate: Hviezdoslavovo nám. 4, Bratislava; tel (7) 330861.
Principal Officer: Paul Hacker.
Branch Public Affairs Officer: Beth Richie.

URUGUAY

Embassy: Václavské námestí 64; POB 1046, 111 21 Prague 1; tel (2) 351587; telex 121291.
Ambassador: Antonio L. Camps Valgoi.
Counsellor: Dr María Amalia Sereno de Terrenoire.

VENEZUELA

Embassy: Janáčkovo nábřeží 49, 150 00 Prague 5; POB 123, Prague; tel (2) 536051; telex 122146; fax (2) 538323.
Ambassador: José Francisco Sucre Figarela.
Officer: Maria Isabel Arocha.
Officer: Carlos Espert S.

VIET-NAM

Embassy: Holečková 6, 125 55 Prague; tel (2) 536127; telex 121824.
Ambassador: Nguyen Phu Soai.

YEMEN

Embassy: Washingtonova 17, 125 22 Prague 1; tel (2) 222411; telex 123300.
Ambassador: Abd al-Latif Muhammad Dhaif Allah.

YUGOSLAVIA

Embassy: Mostecká 15, 118 00 Prague; tel (2) 531443; telex 123284.
Ambassador: Dusan Rodić.

DENMARK

ARGENTINA

Embassy: Store Kongensgade 45, 1st Floor, 1264 Copenhagen K; tel 33-15-80-82; telex 27182; fax 31-15-55-74.
Ambassador: Jorge Horacio Mauhourat.
Counsellor: María Isabel Rendón.

Economic and Commercial Section: Kastelsvej 15, 2100 Copenhagen Ø; tel 31-38-52-11; telex 27444; fax 31-38-46-59.
First Secretary and Head of Economic and Commercial Section: María Teresa Delgado.

AUSTRALIA

Embassy: Kristianiagade 21, 2100 Copenhagen Ø; tel 31-26-22-44; telex 22308; fax 35-43-22-18.
Ambassador: John Robson Burgess.
First Secretary: Hamish John McPherson McCormick.
Consul and First Secretary (Administration): Trevor John Spring.
Secretary: Karin Rietdijk.
Secretary: Alison Smith.

AUSTRIA

Embassy: Grønningen 5, 1st and 3rd Floors, 1270 Copenhagen K; tel 33-12-46-23; telex 27023; fax 33-32-15-42.
Ambassador: Dr Franz Wunderbaldinger.
First Secretary: Dr Johann Spitzer-Zöpfl.
Attaché (Administrative) and Vice-Consul: Robert Franz Zeichmann.

Consulate: Frue Kirkaplads 4, 8100 Århus; tel 86-12-55-11; telex 64793; fax 86-18-27-66.
Honorary Consul: Ejler Munch Andersen.

BANGLADESH

Consulate-General: Henrikshave 4, 2950 Vedbæk; tel 42-89-07-53.
Consul-General: Frands Fridberg.

BELGIUM

Embassy: Øster Allé 7, 2100 Copenhagen Ø; tel 31-26-03-88; telex 22624; fax 35-43-01-02.
Ambassador: Erik Bal.
Ambassador's Secretary: Jan Luykx.
Second Secretary (Administrative/Consular): Joseph Bultynck.

Consulate: Aalborg.
Honorary Consul: Ole Bjørn.

Consulate: Århus.
Honorary Consul: S. Salling-Petersen.

Consulate: Esbjerg.
Honorary Consul: Flemming Rønn.

Consulate: Haderslev.
Honorary Consul: Carl Damgaard Engel.

Consulate: Odense.
Honorary Consul: Leif Poul Ladbye-Hansen.

Consulate: Thorshavn, Faroe Islands.
Honorary Consul: Eivind Fosaa.

BOLIVIA

Consulate-General: Kohavevej 3, 2950 Vedbæk; tel 42-89-46-77; fax 42-89-00-24.
Consul-General: Anton Holtmann Kryger (acting).

BRAZIL

Embassy: Ryvangs Allé 24, 2100 Copenhagen Ø; tel 31-20-64-78; telex 19322; fax 39-27-36-07.
Ambassador: Luiz Antonio Jardim Gagliardi.
Minister-Counsellor: Antonio Augusto Dayrell de Lima.
First Secretary: Mitzi Gurgel Valente da Costa.
Second Secretary: João Carlos Belloc.

Consulate: Århus.
Honorary Consul: Robert Herluf.

Consulate: Thorshavn, Faroe Islands.
Honorary Vice-Consul: Demmus Hentze.

BULGARIA

Embassy: Gamlehave Allé 7, 2920 Charlottenlund; tel 31-63-56-34; telex 27020; fax 31-63-49-23.
Ambassador: Svetla Dmitrova Popova.
Counsellor (Commercial/Economic): Ivan Tsonev.
First Secretary: Boyko Stoyanov Gurov.
Third Secretary: Kiril Todorov Dimitrov.

Economic and Commercial Section: Kildegårdsvej 36, 2900 Hellerup; tel 31-68-22-10; telex 27020; fax 31-65-22-30.

BURKINA FASO

Embassy: Svanemøllevej 20, 2100 Copenhagen Ø; tel 31-18-40-22; telex 19375; fax 39-27-18-86.
Ambassador: Anne Konaté.
First Secretary: Dieudonné Kere.
Attaché (Finance): Ouanza Maurice Domboue.

BURUNDI

Consulate: c/o Sellmore A/S, Frederiksberggade 12, 2nd Floor, 1459 Copenhagen K; tel 33-32-31-81.
Honorary Consul: Stig E. Eriksen.

CAMEROON

Consulate: Gladsaxevej 363, 2860 Søborg; tel 31-69-02-22.
Honorary Consul: Sherif el-Ayouty.

CANADA

Embassy: Kr. Bernikowsgade 1, 1105 Copenhagen K; tel 33-12-22-99; telex 27036; fax 33-14-05-85.

Ambassador: Ronald S. MacLean.
Counsellor (Commercial): John N. Grantham.
First Secretary and Consul: J. David Duinker.
Attaché: Sylvia Hunter.

Consulate: Godthåb/Nuuk.
Honorary Consul: Povl Brandt.

CHILE

Embassy: Kastelsvej 15 (3), 2100 Copenhagen Ø; tel 31-38-58-34; telex 15099; fax 31-38-42-01.
Ambassador: Mario Valenzuela.
First Secretary and Consul: Ricardo Benavente.
Attaché (Culture/Press): Silvia Rivera.
Attaché (Social Affairs): Aldo Verdugo.

Consulate: c/o Fa. C. J. Knudsen, Vedbæk Strandvej 350, 2950 Vedbæk; tel 42-89-18-15.
Honorary Consul: Hans Jørgen Christensen.

CHINA, PEOPLE'S REPUBLIC

Embassy: Øregårds Allé 25, 2900 Hellerup; tel 31-62-58-06; telex 27019; fax 31-62-54-84.
Ambassador: Zheng Yaowen (designate).
Counsellor: Zhou Hufei.
Counsellor (Commercial): Ma Meili.
Counsellor (Cultural): Yi Rucheng.
Military Attaché: Col Qin Shouren.
First Secretary: Hu Xigu.
First Secretary: Zhou Yongming.
First Secretary: Liu Huafang.
First Secretary: Zhang Xiankong.
First Secretary: Yang Dexing.
Second Secretary: Wang Xiaoping.
Second Secretary (Commercial): Zhu Jingdong.

Commercial Section: Øregårds Allé 12, 2900 Hellerup; tel 31-61-10-13; telex 19106.

COLOMBIA

Embassy: Kastelsvej 15, 2100 Copenhagen Ø; tel 31-26-22-97; telex 27072; fax 31-26-22-97.
Second Secretary, Consul and Chargé d'affaires a.i.: Norella Mesa de Mutis.

Consulate: Berlingsbakke 14 C, 2920 Charlottenlund; tel 31-64-22-49.
Honorary Consul: Arne Vittrup Christensen.

COSTA RICA

Consulate-General: Amaliegade 9, 1256 Copenhagen K; tel 33-14-42-82; fax 33-32-31-22.
Consul-General: Bent Jørgensen.
Consul: Mads Marstrand Jørgensen.

COTE D'IVOIRE

Embassy: Gersonsvej 8, 2900 Hellerup; tel 31-62-88-22; telex 22351; fax 31-62-01-62.
Ambassador: François Konan Banny (designate).
First Counsellor (Political): Marcel N'Guessan Konan.
Counsellor (Economic/Commercial): Digbé Tui.
First Secretary (Consular/Cultural/Protocol): Aba Yapo.
Second Secretary (Finance): Aman oi Aman Lazare.

Consulate: Arenvangen 3, 2840 Holte; tel 42-80-20-80.
Honorary Consul: Tage Dalsgaard Jensen.

CYPRUS

Consulate: 2200 Copenhagen, 33 Heimdalsgade; tel 31-85-17-00; fax 31-85-31-10.
Honorary Consul: Max Fodgaard.
Honorary Vice-Consul: Ove Linde.

CZECHOSLOVAKIA

Embassy: Ryvangs Allé 14, 2100 Copenhagen Ø; tel 31-29-15-98; fax 31-29-09-30.
Ambassador: Hana Ševčíková.
Counsellor: Vladislav Doležal.
Counsellor (Commercial): Jaroslav Černohlávek.
Third Secretary: Zdeněk Lyčka.
Attaché (Commercial): Pavel Mašek.
Attaché: Stanislav Balun.

Visa and Consular Section: Ryvangs Allé 16, 2100 Copenhagen Ø; tel 31-29-16-64.

Commercial Section: Vesterled 26, 2100 Copenhagen Ø; tel 31-20-99-11; telex 27112; fax 31-20-99-13.

EGYPT

Embassy: Nyropsgade 47, 1602 Copenhagen V; tel 33-12-76-41; telex 19892; fax 33-12-04-07.
Ambassador: Ahmed Amin Waly.
Counsellor: Ossama Mohamed Hamdy.
Counsellor (Commercial): Mohamed Said Mohamed Bayoumy.
Third Secretary: Ahmed Mohamed Fadel Yacoub.
Third Secretary (Commercial): Ahmed Ibrahim Ali.
Attaché (Administrative): Salah Hafez el-Sayed.
Attaché (Administrative): Nasef el-Said al-Morsy.
Attaché (Administrative): Badr Abd el Mooty Sharaf el-Din.

ESTONIA

Embassy: H. C. Andersens Blvd 38, 1153 Copenhagen; tel 33-93-34-62; fax 33-91-30-99.
Ambassador: Arvo Alas.

FINLAND

Embassy: Skt. Annæ Plads 24, 1250 Copenhagen K; tel 33-13-42-14; telex 27084; fax 33-13-43-41.
Ambassador: Johannes Bäckström.
Counsellor: Veikko Soralhti.
Counsellor (Press/Culture): Kristofer Gräsbeck.
Second Secretary: Anna Wickström-Nøjgaard.
Secretary (Commercial): Hannu Lehtomäki.
Secretary (Commercial): Leila-Mari Ryynänen.
Secretary (Commercial): Olli Brotherus.
Attaché (Administrative): Yrjö von Lüders.

Consulate-General: Strandagervej 10, 2900 Hellerup; tel 31-61-05-55.
Consul-General: Leif Aandahl.
Consul: Ralf Yngve Cornelius Petersen.

Consulate: Åbenrå.
Honorary Consul: Jørgen Cleeman.

Consulate: Aalborg.
Honorary Consul: Hugo Viktor Eriksen.

Consulate: Århus.
Honorary Consul: T. Bjerglund Andersen.

Consulate: Esbjerg.
Honorary Consul: Henning Georg Kruse.

Consulate: Fredericia.
Honorary Consul: Niels Jørgen Andersen.

Consulate: Frederikshavn.
Honorary Consul: Knud Uggershøj (designate).

Consulate: Godthåb/Nuuk.
Honorary Consul: Jens K. Lyberth.

Consulate: Helsingør.
Honorary Consul: Ebbe H. Kristiansen.

Consulate: Herning.
Honorary Consul: Henrik Bjørn-Jepsen.

Consulate: Korsør.
Honorary Consul: Svend Johan Repsdorph Mogensen.

Consulate: Nyborg.
Honorary Consul: Carl A. Schmidt.

Consulate: Nykøbing.
Honorary Consul: Jørgen A. P. Jeppesen.

Consulate: Odense.
Honorary Consul: Kirsten Inge Hennings.

Consulate: Randers.
Honorary Consul: Vagn Hesseldahl.

Consulate: Rønne.
Honorary Consul: Svend-Erik Larsen.

Consulate: Svendborg.
Honorary Consul: Per Munch Glente.

Consulate: Thorshavn, Faroe Islands.
Honorary Consul: Thorolf Ingemar Björklund.

Consulate: Vejle.
Honorary Consul: Holger Bagger-Sørensen.

FRANCE

Embassy: Kongens Nytorv 4, 1050 Copenhagen K; tel 33-15-51-22; telex 27029; fax 33-93-97-52.
Ambassador: Michel Drumetz.
Counsellor: Bernadette Lefort.
Counsellor (Culture/Science/Co-operation): Roland Goeldner.
Counsellor (Commercial): Pierre Herly.
Military Attaché: Col Jean-Paul Laudet.
First Secretary: Nicolas Dally.
Second Secretary (Consular): Michel Didier.
Third Secretary: Bernard Faucher.
Attaché: Marc Bombardier.
Attaché (Press): Ellen Nissen.
Attaché (Commercial): Eric Duedal.
Attaché (Agriculture): Daniel Blanc.

Consular Section and Visa Office/Press and Information Section: Ny Øtergade 3, 2nd Floor, 1101 Copenhagen K; tel 33-32-50-90.

Cultural Section: Rosenvængets Allé 38, 2100 Copenhagen Ø; tel 31-26-55-82; fax 31-26-62-13.

Consulate: Aalborg.
Honorary Consul: Harald Klitgaard.

Consulate: Århus.
Honorary Consul: Niels Blæsbjerg.

Consulate: Esbjerg.
Honorary Consul: Knud Svarrer.

Consulate: Fredericia.
Consular Agent: Niels Bröchner-Mortensen.

Consulate: Frederikshavn.
Consul: Per Qvist.

Consulate: Haderslev.
Vice-Consul: Niels Arkil.

Consulate: Odense.
Consul: Niels Christian Larsen.

Consulate: Randers.
Vice-Consul: Tage Dybdahl Østergård.

Consulate: Ribe.
Consular Agent: Torben Bisgaard.

Consulate: Rønne.
Honorary Vice-Consul: Finn Thomassen.

Consulate: Thorshavn, Faroe Islands.
Honorary Consul: Valdemar Lützen.

GAMBIA

Consulate-General: Høffingsvej 22, 2500 Valby; tel 31-37-43-44.
Consul-General: Poul Henning Kjær-Hansen.

GERMANY

Embassy: Stockholmsgade 57, POB 2712, 2100 Copenhagen Ø; tel 31-26-16-22; telex 27166; fax 31-26-71-05.
Ambassador: Hermann Gründel.
Minister-Counsellor: Dr Johst Wilmanns.
Counsellor (Press/Culture): Ove Schlichting.
Counsellor (Economic): Jens-Peter Voss.
Defence Attaché: Lieut Col Peter Haessler.
First Secretary: Hartmut Lenz.
First Secretary (Agriculture): Dr Elke Günther.
Second Secretary (Administrative): Manfred Laun.

Second Secretary (Commercial): Hans-Günter Clausen.
Third Secretary (Consular): Erich Lewandrowski.
Third Secretary: Hermann Forster.
Third Secretary (Consular): Uwe Meerkötter.

Consulate-General: Kystvej 18, POB 149, 6200 Åbenrå; tel 74-62-14-64; telex 52136.
Consul-General: Hugo Fehrenbach.

Consulate: Rings Møbler, Danmarksgade 58-64, 9000 Aalborg; tel 98-12-56-33; fax 98-12-61-69.
Honorary Consul: Jørn Astrup Bertelsen.

Consulate: Havnegade 4, 8100 Århus; tel 86-12-32-11; telex 64336.
Honorary Consul: Sven Erik Nørholt.

Consulate: A/S J. Lauritzen's Eftf., Amerikavej 1, 6700 Esbjerg; tel 75-12-31-33; telex 54133.
Honorary Consul: Lars Lindinger.

Consulate: Frederikshavn.
Honorary Consul: Mogens C. Madsen.

Consulate: Korsør.
Honorary Consul: Else Kathrine Poulsen.

Consulate: A/S Dan-Bunkering Ltd, Brogade 2A-B, POB 71, 5500 Middelfart; tel 41-54-01; telex 58253.
Honorary Consul: Torben Østergaard Nielsen.

Consulate: Merkurgården, Frisegade 26, 4800 Nykøbing; tel 54-85-27-00; fax 54-32-27-72.
Honorary Consul: Knud Almegaard Hansen.

Consulate: Vestre Kaj 6, 4700 Næstved; tel 53-72-20-00; telex 46220.
Honorary Consul: Peter Mønsted.

Consulate: Slotsgade 18-22, 5000 Odense; tel 60-14-14-14; fax 60-14-80-14.
Honorary Consul: Knud Thybo.

Consulate: Store Torv 12, 3700 Rønne; tel 53-95-22-11.
Honorary Consul: Erik Ipsen.

Consulate: Kuopivej 11, 5700 Svenborg; tel 62-21-15-15; telex 58151.
Honorary Consul: Caj Eric Carstens.

Consulate: P/F Jákup á Dul, POB 1, 110 Thorshavn, Faroe Islands; tel 14-94-9; telex 81314; fax 29-11-33-0.
Honorary Consul: Ása á Dul Jacobsen.

Consulate: Sydkajen 12, 7100 Vejle; tel 82-00-11; telex 61102; fax 82-08-39.
Honorary Consul: Poul Melgaard Olesen.

GHANA

Embassy: Egebjerg Allé 13, 2900 Hellerup; tel 31-62-82-22; telex 19471; fax 31-62-16-52.
Ambassador: Christine Oduro.
Counsellor: Ferdinand Ofosu Somuah.
Second Secretary: Victoria Akosua Geyi.

GREECE

Embassy: Borgergade 16, 1300 Copenhagen K; tel 33-11-45-33; telex 27279.
Ambassador: Stelios Rocanas.
First Counsellor: Christos Karapanos.
Second Secretary (Consular): Andreas Papadakis.
Attaché: Constantin Kanakis.

Economic and Commercial Section: Gothersgade 12-14, 4th Floor, 1123 Copenhagen K; tel 33-14-84-86; telex 15355; fax 33-14-02-35.
Attaché (Economic/Commercial): Ioannis Glinos.

Consulate: Aalborg.
Honorary Vice-Consul: Ib Elsøe.

Consulate: Århus.
Honorary Consul: Knud Friis.
Honorary Vice-Consul: Christian Bunde.

Consulate: Thorshavn, Faroe Islands.
Honorary Consul: Birgir Danielsen.

GUINEA

Consulate: c/o Fa. I. Krüger, Gladsaxevej 363, 2860 Søborg; tel 31-69-02-22.
Honorary Consul: Sherif el-Ayouty.

HOLY SEE

Apostolic Nunciature: Immortellevej 11, 2950 Vedbæk; tel 42-89-35-36; fax 45-66-17-71.
Apostolic Pro-Nuncio: Most Rev. Henri Lemaître, Titular Archbishop of Tongeren.
Counsellor: Mgr Edward Joseph Adams.

HONDURAS

Consulate-General: Telegrafvej 5, 2750 Ballerup; tel 42-97-36-26.
Honorary Consul-General: Carl G. Sander.

HUNGARY

Embassy: Strandvejen 170, 2920 Charlottenlund; tel 31-63-16-88; telex 27186; fax 31-63-00-52.
Ambassador: Dr László Demus.
Counsellor: Dr Pál Éliás.
Counsellor (Economic/Agricultural): Tamás Bokor.
Consul and First Secretary (Cultural/Consular): Dr András Back.

Commercial Office: Landemaerket 10, 1119 Copenhagen K; tel 33-13-36-82; fax 33-11-56-17.
Counsellor (Commercial): Dr László Kőósvőlgyi.

ICELAND

Embassy: Dantes Plads 3, 1556 Copenhagen V; tel 33-15-96-04; telex 15954; fax 33-93-05-06.
Ambassador: Ingvi S. Ingvarsson.
Minister-Counsellor: Birgir Möller.
Counsellor (Commercial): Bjørn Gudmundsson.
Chaplain: Lárus T. Gudmundsson.

Consulate: Aalborg Vaerft A/S, Gasvaerksvej 28, POB 659, 9100 Aalborg; tel 98-10-33-99; telex 69693; fax 98-12-29-91.
Honorary Consul: Knud-Erik Bengtsen.

Consulate: Århus Stiftstidende, Olof Palmes Allé 39, 8200 Århus N; tel 86-78-40-00; telex 64321; fax 86-78-44-00.
Honorary Consul: Erling Zanchette.

Consulate: Esbjerg Varehandel A/S, POB 2100, Staerevej 2, 6705 Esbjerg; tel 75-12-51-00.
Honorary Consul: Svend Aage Villemoes.

Consulate: Fredericia Skibsvaerft A/S, Vaerftsvej, 7000 Fredericia; tel 75-92-00-00; telex 51135; fax 75-93-34-30.
Honorary Consul: Knud Andersen.

Consulate: Stengade 14A, 3000 Helsingør; tel 31-62-73-19.
Honorary Consul: Elinor Brammer.

Consulate: Godsbanegade 2, 8700 Horsens; tel 75-62-48-11; telex 61614.
Honorary Consul: Leif Hede Nielsen.

Consulate: Hr. Finnur Erlendsson, Danmarksgade 23, 9900 Frederikshavn; tel 98-43-40-22.
Honorary Vice-Consul: Finnur Erlendsen.

Consulate: Norgeskajen, Havnen, POB 34, 9850 Hirtshals; tel 98-94-23-33; telex 67756.
Honorary Vice-Consul: Niels Jensen.

Consulate: Fjordvej 116, Strandhuse, 6000 Kolding; tel 75-52-34-50; fax 75-50-65-11.
Honorary Vice-Consul: Aage I. Vestergaard.

Consulate: Gerthasvej 14, 5000 Odense C; tel 66-13-18-00.
Honorary Vice-Consul: Harald Hansen.

Consulate: Ostervold 40, POB 11, 8900 Randers; tel 86-42-55-55; telex 65109; fax 86-42-88-82.
Honorary Vice-Consul: Henning Ove Knudsen.

Consulate: J. C. Svabosgöta 31, Box 65, 100 Thorshavn, Faroe Islands; tel 11-15-5.
Honorary Consul: Poul Mohr.

Consulate: Jörundsgöta 46, 700 Klaksvig, Faroe Islands; tel 55-47-7.
Honorary Vice-Consul: Samuel Aksel Thorsteinsson.

Consulate-General: Anders Olsensvej B900, 3920 Julianehåb/Qaqortoq, Greenland; tel 38-27-7; telex 90201; fax 38-83-3.
Honorary Consul-General: Henrik Aqqalooraq Lund.

Consulate-General: Skibshavnsvej 24, POB 1057, 3900 Godthåb/Nuuk, Greenland; tel 24-41-1; telex 90674; fax 22-98-6.
Honorary Consul-General: Anders Bröns.

INDIA

Embassy: Vangehusvej 15, 2100 Copenhagen Ø; tel 31-18-28-88; telex 15964; fax 39-27-02-18.
First Counsellor and Chargé d'affaires: R. Lobo.
Attaché: Srinivasan Raghavan.
Attaché: Padmanabhan Ajithakumar.

INDONESIA

Embassy: Ørehøj Allé 1, 2900 Hellerup; tel 31-62-44-22; telex 16274; fax 31-62-44-39.
Ambassador: Haringun Hardjotanojo.
First Secretary (Political): Isnianto Sudjono.
Second Secretary (Administrative): A. Nano Harsihono.
Second Secretary (Culture/Protocol): Mariati Urni Lestari Suhartono.
Third Secretary (Economic): Ronald Yosef Pariaman Manik.
Third Secretary (Consular): Dewi Anggraeni Wahyudati.
Attaché (Commercial): Rod Enis Brahamana.

Consulate-General: POB 196, Holbæk; tel 53-43-38-20.
Honorary Consul-General: Vagn Ulsted-Jørgensen.

IRAN

Embassy: Grønningen 5, 1270 Copenhagen K; tel 33-14-12-38; telex 16979; fax 33-14-98-94.
Ambassador: Mansour Gharavi.
First Secretary: Ataollah Mobarhani.
Third Secretary: Alireza Rajabalizadeh Pakdel.
Attaché (Consular): Majid Jarrahi.
Attaché: Majid Assadi.

IRELAND

Embassy: Østbanegade 21, 2100 Copenhagen Ø; tel 31-42-32-33; telex 22995; fax 35-43-18-58.
Ambassador: Andrew O'Rourke.
First Secretary: Gerald O'Connor.
Third Secretary and Consul: Carol Baxter.

ISRAEL

Embassy: Lundevangsvej 4, 2900 Hellerup; tel 31-62-62-88; telex 27136; fax 31-62-19-38.
Ambassador: Nathan Meron.
Counsellor: Michael Arbel.
Counsellor: Shimshon Issaki.
Counsellor and Consul: Joseph Alfassy.
Defence Attaché: Capt. Dan-Erik Melamed-Lemkow.
Third Secretary: Yakir Nirgad.
Third Secretary: Asaf Shalev.
Attaché: Rafi Saadon.
Attaché: Doron Nagar.
Attaché: Dror Sitner.
Attaché: Eran Tzebary.
Attaché: Moshe Adri.
Attaché: Rami Nir.

ITALY

Embassy: Gammel Vartov Vej 7, 2900 Hellerup; tel 31-62-68-77; telex 27078; fax 31-62-25-99.
Ambassador: Mario Manca.
Counsellor: Alberto Cabassi.

Consular Section and Visa Office: Engskiftevej 7, 2100 Copenhagen Ø; tel 31-18-34-44.
Counsellor (Commercial) and Head of Consular Section: Mario Cospito.

Cultural Section: Gjørlingsvej 11, 2900 Hellerup; tel 31-62-06-96.
Cultural Officer: Gaetano Gangi.

Consulate: Aalborg.
Honorary Vice-Consul: Virgilio Zennaro.

Consulate: Thorshavn, Faroe Islands.
Honorary Vice-Consul: Renate Ruth Simonsen.

JAPAN

Embassy: Pilestræde 61, 1112 Copenhagen K; tel 31-11-33-44; telex 27082; fax 33-11-33-77.
Ambassador: Yoshifumi Matsuda.
Counsellor: Masahiko Horie.
First Secretary: Mizue Nakajima.
First Secretary: Takashi Ono.
Second Secretary: Koji Oshiman.
Second Secretary: Atsushi Kawabe.
Third Secretary: Hisanobu Mochizuki.
Third Secretary: Satoshi Takaya.
Attaché: Hiroshi Tsuchiya.
Attaché: Keiichi Suda.

Consulate-General: Århus.

KOREA, DEMOCRATIC PEOPLE'S REPUBLIC

Embassy: Skelvej 2, 2900 Hellerup; tel 31-62-50-70; fax 31-62-50-70.
Ambassador: O Ung Gwon.
Second Secretary: Kim Jin Hae.
Third Secretary: Ha Sin Guk.

KOREA, REPUBLIC

Embassy: Svanemøllevej 104, 2900 Hellerup; tel 39-40-12-33; fax 39-40-18-18.
Ambassador: Kim Sai-Taik.
Counsellor: Choo Yeon-Gon.
Counsellor: Chun Ju Pyong.
Attaché (Consular): Han Joon-Ki.

Consulate: Århus.
Honorary Consul: Jørn B. Jansen.

KUWAIT

Consulate: Lundtoftevej 150, POB 280, Lyngby; tel 42-88-50-20.
Honorary Consul: Børge Hansen.

LESOTHO

Embassy: Østerkildevej 14, 2820 Gentofte; tel 31-65-14-42; telex 16687; fax 31-65-33-64.
Ambassador: Bishop Victor Teboho N'Dobe.
Counsellor (Political): Simon Mphosi Nkheche.
Third Secretary (Finance): Moepi Winston Sematlane.
Attaché: Lintle Motsabi Mosala.
Attaché: Tholoana Ntsoele.

Consulate-General: Birkebakken 19, 3210 Vejby; tel 42-11-50-66.
Honorary Consul-General: Jørgen Madsen.

LIBERIA

Consulate-General: St Konegensgade 110 A, 1264 Copenhagen K; tel 33-91-15-25; fax 33-32-25-35.
Honorary Consul-General: Willi Gottlieb.
Vice-Consul: Søren Heintzelmann.

LIBYA

People's Bureau: Rosenvængets Hovedvej 4, 2100 Copenhagen Ø; tel 31-26-36-11; telex 22652; fax 31-26-56-06.
Chargé d'affaires a.i. (Political/Information): Aref A. Abuhajar.
Member of Bureau (Consular): Giumaa Ismael el-Sherif.
Member of Bureau (Finance): Hamad Hard el-Mountaser.

LITHUANIA

Embassy: H. C. Andersens Blvd 38, 1553 Copenhagen V; tel 33-15-18-62; fax 33-91-30-99.
Counsellor and Chargé d'affaires: Dalius Cekuolis.

LUXEMBOURG

Embassy: Copenhagen.
Ambassador: Julien Alex.
Attaché: Paul Kirtz.

Consulate-General: Rådhuspladsen 59, 1550 Copenhagen V; tel 33-12-12-71.
Honorary Consul-General: Ole Olsen.

MALAWI

Consulate: Jægersborg Allé 16, 2920 Charlottenlund; tel 31-64-49-99.
Honorary Consul: Niels Jørgen Beckmann.

MALAYSIA

Consulate: Amaliegade 35, 1256 Copenhagen K; tel 33-11-23-11.
Honorary Consul: Finn Frandsen.

MALI

Consulate: Skodsborqvej 188, 2850 Nærum; tel 42-80-53-33.
Honorary Consul: Jørgen Galst.

MALTA

Consulate: c/o Eskofot, Industriparken 35-7, POB 222, 2750 Ballerup; tel 42-97-44-00; telex 35156; fax 42-97-62-66.
Honorary Consul: Børge S. Nielsen.

Consulate: Jernet 17, 6000 Kolding; tel 75-52-55-33; telex 51364; fax 75-52-88-77.
Honorary Consul: Christian Vejen Hindkjær.

MAURITANIA

Consulate-General: Hoerkaer 32, 2730 Herlev; tel 42-91-00-73.
Honorary Consul-General: Ove Andersen.

MEXICO

Embassy: Gammel Vartov Vej 18, 2900 Hellerup; tel 31-20-86-00; telex 27503; fax 31-20-82-48.
Ambassador: Mario Ruíz Massieu.
Second Secretary: Jorge Anastacio Stergios Gómez.
Second Secretary: Raúl Millán González.
Attaché: Rodrigo Mauricio Puentes Alvárez.

MONACO

Consulate-General: Aurehøjvej 11, 2900 Hellerup; tel 31-62-63-58.
Honorary Consul-General: Vagn Jespersen.

MOROCCO

Embassy: Øregårds Allé 19, 2900 Hellerup; tel 31-62-45-11; telex 22913; fax 31-62-24-49.
Ambassador: Mokhtar Anegay.
Counsellor: Chaib Lalouh.
First Secretary: Mahfoud Bahbouhi.
Attaché: Abderrazak Tahir.
Attaché: Mohammed Mouloudi.

NEPAL

Consulate-General: Taglgårdstræde 2, 1452 Copenhagen K; tel 33-14-31-75.
Honorary Consul-General: Ole Janus Larsen.

NETHERLANDS

Embassy: Toldbodgade 33, 1253 Copenhagen K; tel 33-15-62-93; telex 27093; fax 33-14-03-50.
Ambassador: Willem Sinninghe Damsté.
Counsellor: Johannes M. Corijn.
Counsellor (Agriculture): Albert van der Struik.
Second Secretary (Economic): Pieter Nordermeer.
Attaché (Administrative/Consular): Gonny Charlotte van Grunsven.

Consulate: Aalborg.
Honorary Consul: Morten D. Jacobsen.

Consulate: Århus.
Honorary Consul: Bent Vagner.

Consulate: Esbjerg.
Honorary Consul: Ernst Moth Nielson.

Consulate: Fredericia.
Honorary Vice-Consul: Jan Bonfils.

Consulate: Nakskov.
Honorary Vice-Consul: P. Brøndtved.

Consulate: Odense.
Honorary Consul: Vagn Sinius-Clausen.

Consulate: Rønne.
Honorary Vice-Consul: Mogens Mannering.

Consulate: Thorshavn, Faroe Islands.
Honorary Consul: Julianna Leonsson.

NICARAGUA

Consulate: Marielundvej 34 A, 2730 Herlev; tel 42-91-37-00.
Honorary Consul: Ditz Peschardt.

NIGER

Consulate: c/o I. Krüger A/S, Gladsaxevej 363, 2869 Søborg; tel 31-69-02-22.
Honorary Consul: Jean-Pierre Zafiryadis.

NORWAY

Embassy: Trondhjems Plads 4, 2100 Copenhagen Ø; tel 31-38-89-85; telex 27114; fax 31-38-09-15.
Ambassador: Arne Arnesen.
Minister: Thomas J. Ronneng.
Counsellor (Press/Culture): Lars Albert Wensell.
Counsellor (Commercial): Audun Midtgaard.
First Secretary: Victor Conrad Rønneberg.
Second Secretary: Kaja Lene Brundtland.
Attaché: Anne-Cathrine Glavas.
Attaché: Roy Odd Schøyen.
Chaplain: Ragnvald Seierstad.
Consul (Consular Section): Erling H. C. Korch.
Vice-Consul (Consular Section): Elisabeth Thomsen.

Consulate: Åbenrå.
Honorary Consul: Carsten Andersen.

Consulate: Aalborg.
Honorary Consul: Arne Friis Budtz.

Consulate: Århus.
Honorary Consul: Bent Clausen.

Consulate: Esbjerg.
Honorary Consul: Torben Skot-Hansen.

Consulate: Fredericia.
Honorary Consul: Hans Flemming Jørgensen.

Consulate: Frederikshavn.
Honorary Consul: Aage Erling Jensen.

Consulate-General: Godthåb/Nuuk, Greenland.
Honorary Consul-General: Svend Erik Danielsen.

Consulate: Helsingør.
Honorary Consul: John Finderup.

Consulate: Horsens.
Honorary Consul: Axel Schur.

Consulate: Kalundborg.
Honorary Consul: Jørgen Møller.

Consulate: Korsør.
Honorary Consul: Arne Sylow Rasmussen.

Consulate: Naksov.
Honorary Consul: Finn Christensen.

Consulate: Nykøding F.
Honorary Consul: Arne Juhl Olsen.

Consulate: Odense.
Honorary Consul: Steen Haustrup.

Consulate: Randulf.
Honorary Consul: Fritz Wulf.

Consulate: Rønne.
Honorary Consul: Mogens Edmund Andersen.

Consulate: Thisted.
Honorary Consul: Jørgen Pedersen.

Consulate: Thorshavn, Faroe Islands.
Honorary Consul: Dánjal Magnussen.

PAKISTAN

Embassy: Valeursvej 17, 2900 Hellerup; tel 31-62-11-88; telex 19348; fax 39-40-10-70.
Minister and Chargé d'affaires a.i.: Eitizaz Hussain.
Counsellor and Attaché (Community Welfare): Syed Aqeel Zafar-ul-Hasan.

PANAMA

Consulate: Grønttorvet 226, 2500 Valby; tel 31-17-68-06.
Honorary Consul: Klaus Lembcke.

PARAGUAY

Consulate-General: Vester Voldgade 96, 1552 Copenhagen V; tel 33-15-01-78.
Honorary Consul: Poul Krogh (designate).

PERU

Consulate-General: Rosenvængets Allé 20, 2100 Copenhagen Ø; tel 31-38-38-75.
Honorary Consul-General: Héctor Cabada Barrios.
Honorary Vice-Consul: Elena Iturrizaga de Lesziák.

Consulate: Kolding.
Honorary Consul: Mercedes Cabada de Ohmeyer.

PHILIPPINES

Consulate-General: Snorregade 20, 2300 Hellerup; tel 31-62-77-02.
Honorary Consul-General: Arne Simonsen.

POLAND

Embassy: Richelieus Allé 12, 2900 Hellerup; tel 31-62-72-44; telex 19264; fax 31-62-71-20.
Ambassador: Jerzy S. Sito.
Military Attaché: Lieut Col Władysław Gapys.
Deputy Military Attaché: Maj. Andrzej Turek.
Counsellor: Stanisław Borek.
First Secretary (Agriculture): Edward Golebiowski.
Second Secretary (Administrative): Aleksander Jędraszko.
Third Secretary (Cultural): Elżbieta Wykretowicz.
Third Secretary: Zbigniew Czarkowski.

Consular Section: Richelieus Allé 10, 2900 Hellerup; tel 31-62-80-28.
Counsellor and Head of Consular Section: Ryszard Liczmanski.
First Secretary (Consular): Ewa Maria Malgorzata Bylinska.
Second Secretary (Consular): Antoni J. Wręga.

Commercial Section: Ryvangs Allé 46, 2900 Hellerup; tel 31-62-26-33; telex 19264; fax 31-62-25-54.
Counsellor (Commercial): Anatol Nowik.
Attaché (Commercial): Mieczyslaw Kaminski.
Attaché (Commercial): Ryszard Skaut.

PORTUGAL

Embassy: Hovedvagtsgade 6, Mezz., 1103 Copenhagen K; tel 33-13-13-01; telex 16586; fax 33-13-24-87.
Ambassador: Alexandre Eduardo Lencastre de Veiga.
Counsellor (Commercial): José Estrela Leão.
First Secretary: António Luis Peixoto Cotrim.

Commercial Section: Frederiksborggade 1, 1360 Copenhagen K; tel 33-12-76-32; telex 22936; fax 33-93-88-85.

ROMANIA

Embassy: Strandagervej 27, 2900 Hellerup; tel 31-62-42-04; telex 27017.
Counsellor and Chargé d'affaires: Vasile Stoian.
Counsellor (Commercial/Economic): Gheorghe Ilinca.
First Secretary and Consul: Mihai Basa.
Second Secretary (Economic): Valentin Brebenel.

RUSSIA

Embassy: Kristianiagade 3-5, 2100 Copenhagen Ø; tel 31-42-55-85; telex 16943; fax 31-42-37-41.
Ambassador: Gennadi Georgiyevich Vedernikov.
Minister-Counsellor: Yuri Ouchakov.
Counsellor: Nikolai A. Chatskikh.
Counsellor: Viatcheslav M. Timofeev.
Counsellor (Science): Vitali Vechniakov.
Defence Attaché: Col Victor A. Kolegov.
Assistant Defence Attaché: Col Alexander K. Grichko.
Assistant Defence Attaché: Capt. Sergei Lvovich.
Assistant Defence Attaché: Commdr Gennadi A. Reviakov.
First Secretary (Culture): Yuri Kolesnikov.
First Secretary: Yuri Kazarian.
First Secretary: Vladimir I. Sourodine.
First Secretary and Consul: Kirill Khorevich.
First Secretary: Sergueis Tseplis.
Attaché (Fisheries): Victor Belolraguine.
Attaché (Agriculture): Kheino Veldi.

Commercial Representation: Viyerslev Allé 161, 2500 Valby; tel 31-46-28-11; telex 27152.
Commercial Representative: Vladimir Petrovski.
Assistant Commercial Representative: Andrei Mekhanikov.

Press Office: Vestagervej 7, 2100 Copenhagen Ø; tel 31-20-04-44; telex 15618; fax 31-20-19-42.
First Secretary (Press): Vladimir Koptelov.

SAUDI ARABIA

Embassy: Lille Strandvej 27, 2900 Hellerup; tel 31-62-12-00; telex 15931; fax 31-62-60-09.
First Secretary and Chargé d'affaires a.i.: Abdul Rahman A. Owaidah.
Third Secretary: Mahmood A. Bahrawi.
Attaché (Administrative): Fahd H. al-Johani.

SENEGAL

Consulate-General: Vejlesøparken 16, 2840 Holte; tel 42-42-07-01.
Honorary Vice-Consul and Acting Consul-General: Bjørn Rosenvinge-Thürmer.

SEYCHELLES

Consulate-General: Vejleøparken 16, 2840 Holte; tel 42-42-07-01.
Honorary Consul-General: Erling Starup.
Honorary Vice-Consul: Henrik Starup.

SIERRA LEONE

Consulate: Henningsens Allé 8, 2900 Hellerup; tel 31-62-24-44.
Honorary Consul: J. Rath Jørgensen.

SOMALIA

Consulate-General: Snorresgade 20, 2300 Copenhagen S; tel 31-54-40-11.
Honorary Consul-General: J. C. Weinrich.

SOUTH AFRICA

Embassy: Gammel Vartov Vej 8, Box 128, 2900 Hellerup; tel 31-18-01-55; telex 16333; fax 31-18-28-59.
Ambassador: Conrad Johannes Sidego.
First Secretary: Eli Bitzer.
Second Secretary (Administration): Leonard Bands.
Third Secretary: Daniela Fourie.

SPAIN

Embassy: Upsalagade 26, 2100 Copenhagen Ø; tel 31-42-47-00; telex 27145; fax 31-26-30-99.
Ambassador: Carlos Fernández-Longoria.
Minister-Counsellor: Jesús Maria Obregón Saracho.
Counsellor (Labour): Bernardo Díez Rodríguez.
First Secretary (Culture): Aurora Mejía Errasquín.
First Secretary: Pascual Ignacio Navarro Ríos.
Attaché: Fernando Gayo de Arenzana.

Commercial and Economic Office: Vesterbrogade 10, 3, 1620 Copenhagen V.; tel 31-31-11-42; telex 27322; fax 31-21-33-90.
Counsellor (Economic/Commercial): Leopardo Ceballos Lopéz.
Counsellor (Commercial): Alberto Alonso Díaz.

Social Affairs (Labour) Office: Købmagergade 43/1, 1150 Copenhagen K; tel 33-93-12-90; telex 22188; fax 33-93-21-55.

Consulate: Aalborg.
Honorary Consul: Kresten Dyhrberg Nielsen.

Consulate: Århus.
Honorary Vice-Consul: Erik Aaen.

Consulate: Vejle.
Honorary Vice-Consul: Jes Christian Langager.

Consulate: Thorshavn, Faroe Islands.
Honorary Vice-Consul: Hans Hansen.

SRI LANKA

Consulate: Amager Strandvej 112, 2300 Copenhagen; tel 31-58-92-11; telex 31216; fax 31-59-57-94.
Honorary Consul: Jørgen Bjørnbak Hallstein.

SWAZILAND

Embassy: Kastelsvej 19, 2100 Copenhagen Ø; tel 31-42-61-11; telex 15810; fax 31-42-63-00.
Ambassador: Mpumelelo Joseph Ndumiso Hlophe.
Counsellor: John Mfondo Simelane.
First Secretary (Finance): Mabili D. Dlamini.
First Secretary (Information): Alfred M. Dlamini.
Third Secretary: Philemon Mzingeleni Magongo.

Consulate: Stranvejen 100, 2900 Hellerup; tel 31-62-65-00.
Honorary Consul: Flemming J. Jørgensen.

SWEDEN

Embassy: Skt. Annæ Plads 15A, 1250 Copenhagen K; tel 33-14-22-42; telex 22933; fax 33-32-90-35.
Ambassador: Carl-Johan Groth.
Minister: Lars Lönnback.
Counsellor: Håkon Damm.
Counsellor (Commercial): Jörgen Wiklund.
Defence Attaché: Lieut Col Lars Alveskog.
First Secretary (Political/Press): Thomas Belius.
First Secretary: Sven-Olov Carlsson.
Attaché (Social): Helena Alring.
Attaché (Customs): Malte Eriksson.
Consul-General: Karlerik Nordenquist.
Chaplain: Olle Ek.

Commercial Section: Ny Østergade 20, 1101 Copenhagen K; tel 33-15-55-22; fax 33-32-94-99.

Social Affairs Section: Ingerslevsgade 4, 1705 Copenhagen V; tel 31-21-41-83.

Consulate: Åbenrå; tel 74-62-20-00; telex 52131.
Honorary Consul: Erling Hansen.

Consulate: Aalborg; tel 98-13-36-66; telex 69699.
Honorary Consul: Jørgen Brix Steby.

Consulate: Århus; tel 86-13-63-11; fax 86-12-30-87.
Honorary Consul: Jørgen Geday.

Consulate: Esbjerg; tel 75-14-42-22; telex 54145.
Honorary Consul: Niels Giversen Nielsen.

Consulate: Fredericia; tel 75-94-21-13.
Honorary Consul: Hans Cohr.

Consulate: Frederikshavn; tel 98-42-29-22; telex 67104.
Honorary Consul: Hans Emil Larsen.

Consulate-General: Godthåb/Nuuk, Greenland; tel 24-41-1; telex 90674.
Honorary Consul-General: Hans Pavia Egede.

Consulate: Grenå; tel 86-32-03-00; telex 63490.
Honorary Consul: Johan Peter Lyngdorf.

Consulate: Haderslav; tel 74-52-10-11.
Honorary Consul: Hans Valdemar Thyssen.

Consulate: Helsingør; tel 42-10-16-61.
Honorary Consul: Bent Faurholdt.

Consulate: Hirtshals; tel 98-94-11-00; telex 67740.
Honorary Consul: Niels C. Espersen.

Consulate: Holbæk; tel 53-43-73-00; fax 53-44-20-58.
Honorary Consul: Viggo Finn Christiansen.

Consulate: Kalundborg; tel 53-51-00-51.
Honorary Consul: Hans Meredin Petersen.

Consulate: Kolding; tel 75-52-27-11.
Honorary Consul: Ove Grønborg.

Consulate: Korsør; tel 53-57-06-19.
Honorary Consul: Poul Christiansen.

Consulate: Nakskov; tel 53-92-14-08; telex 47545.
Honorary Consul: Kaj Anker Rasmussen.

Consulate: Nyborg; tel 65-31-01-06.
Honorary Consul: Niels Klindt Jørgensen.

Consulate: Nykøbing F; tel 54-85-25-11.
Honorary Consul: Flemming Saunte.

Consulate: Næstved; tel 53-72-14-78.
Honorary Consul: Henrik Meding.

Consulate: Odense; tel 66-11-83-83; telex 59863.
Honorary Consul: Hans Erik Hempel-Hansen.

Consulate: Randers.
Honorary Consul: Jørgen Semler-Jørgensen.

Consulate: Rønne; tel 53-95-76-55.
Honorary Consul: Niels Villy Rask.

Consulate: Skagen; tel 98-44-14-38.
Honorary Consul: Hemming Nibe-Hansen.

Consulate: Stege; tel 55-81-50-06.
Honorary Consul: Erik Lehn Thisted Simonsen.

Consulate: Svendborg; tel 62-21-24-31.
Honorary Consul: Jørgen Nielsen.

Consulate: Thisted; tel 97-92-33-11.
Honorary Consul: Jørgen P. Bornerup.

Consulate-General: Thorshavn, Faroe Islands; tel 11-36-0.
Honorary Consul: Aksel Emil Hansen.

Consulate: Vejle; tel 75-82-33-55.
Honorary Consul: Ingemar C. Schjøth.

SWITZERLAND

Embassy: Amaliegade 14, 1256 Copenhagen K; tel 33-14-17-96; telex 16239; fax 33-33-75-51.
Ambassador: Daniel P. Dayer.
Defence Attaché: Lieut Col Adolf Ludin.
Assistant Defence Attaché: Capt. Martin Schmid.
Second Secretary: Hans-Jürg Dové.
Attaché (Administrative/Consular): Beat Kaser.

THAILAND

Embassy: Norgesmindevej 18, 2900 Hellerup; tel 31-62-50-10; telex 16216; fax 31-62-50-59.
Ambassador: Dr Chawan Chawanid (designate).
Minister-Counsellor: Krabaun Pornsobhon.
Counsellor (Commercial): Nivat Jinuntuya.
First Secretary (Commercial): Nalin Krairiksh.
First Secretary: Somchai Powcharoen.
First Secretary: Pornprapai Ganjanarintr.
Third Secretary: Seri Moottatarn.
Third Secretary: Panida Supa.

Commercial Section: H. C. Andersens Blvd 39, 1553 Copenhagen V; tel 33-13-53-54; telex 27172; fax 33-91-12-62.

Consulate-General: Tordenskjoldsgade 22, 1055 Copenhagen K; tel 33-11-33-49.
Consul-General: Henning Hempel Spasø.
Honorary Consul: Peer Rosenfeldt.

Consulate: Otto Peders Vej 1, 6960 Hvide Sande; tel 97-31-15-22.
Honorary Consul: Ib Thomsen.

TUNISIA

Consulate-General: Kejsergade 2, 1155 Copenhagen K; tel 33-91-92-93.
Honorary Consul-General: Laue Traberg Smidt.

TURKEY

Embassy: Vestagervej 16, 2100 Copenhagen Ø; tel 31-20-55-00; telex 27476; fax 31-18-00-31.
Ambassador: Baki Ilkin.
First Counsellor: Yavuz Ergüven.
Counsellor (Social Affairs/Labour): Mehemt Karaduman.
Counsellor (Social Affairs): Hasan Uysal.
Counsellor: Necat Özdemiroglu.
Counsellor (Economic/Commercial): Tulay Ulu.
Counsellor (Economic/Commercial): Günay Bascinar.
Third Secretary (Consular): Mehmet Bilir.
Attaché (Social Affairs/Labour): Halûk Sahin.
Attaché (Administration/Culture/Information): Derya Sarar.
Assistant Attaché (Social Security/Labour): Ali Riza Levent Genc.

Consular Section: Vestagervej 18, 2100 Copenhagen Ø; tel 31-20-55-00.

Commercial and Economic Section: Borgergade 42, 1300 Copenhagen K; tel 33-12-29-20; telex 19537; fax 33-14-63-46.

Information and Culture Section: Vesterbrogade 11A, 1620 Copenhagen V; tel 31-22-31-00; fax 31-22-90-68.

Consulate-General: Rønvangen 85, 8302 Hinnerup.
Honorary Consul-General: Jens Hultmann Pedersen.

UGANDA

Embassy: Sofievej 15, 2900 Hellerup; tel 31-62-09-66; telex 15689; fax 31-61-01-48.
Ambassador: Edith Grace Ssempala.
Second Secretary: Deborah Nsimbi Kamenya.
Third Secretary: Amooti Asaaba-Winyi.
Attaché (Administrative): Mary Ruth Kiwanuka.

UNITED KINGDOM

Embassy: Kastelsvej 36-40, 2100 Copenhagen Ø; tel 31-26-46-00; telex 19908; fax 31-38-10-12.
Ambassador: Nigel C. R. Williams.
Counsellor and Deputy Head of Mission: Philip S. Astley.
Counsellor (Economic/Commercial): Anthony M. Layden.
Defence Attaché: Commdr Robert E. Woolgar.
First Secretary (Political/EC): Kevin Cullen.
First Secretary (Political/Information): Dick Thomson.
First Secretary (Political): Roger P. Hamilton.
First Secretary (Management) and Consul: Brian Robertson.
First Secretary (Commercial): Christopher P. Haslam.
First Secretary (Economic): Stephen Christopher Parris.
Assistant Defence Attaché: Maj. Robert R. P. Milton.
Second Secretary (Political): H. A. Christian Haig-Thomas.
Second Secretary (Political): Robert J. Dean.
Attaché (Culture) and British Council Director: Michael G. Holcroft.
Attaché and Vice-Consul: Nicholas J. K. Stucley-Houghton.

Consulate: Søndergade 24, 62000 Åbenra; tel 74-62-30-85; telex 52115; fax 74-62-92-87.
Honorary Consul: Carlo Daus-Petersen.

Consulate: Stationmestervej 85, 92000 Aalborg SV; tel 98-18-16-00; telex 69888; fax 98-18-18-55.
Honorary Consul: Jørgen Bladt.

Consulate: Havnegade 8, 8100 Århus C; tel 86-12-88-88; fax 86-13-50-98.
Honorary Consul: Claus Robert Herluf.

Consulate: Kanalen 1, 6700 Esbjerg; tel 75-13-05-11; telex 54391; fax 75-13-03-19.
Honorary Consul: Gert Kragelund.

Consulate: Vesthavnen, POB 235, 7000 Fredericia; tel 75-92-20-00; telex 51126; fax 75-91-02-13.
Honorary Consul: Moerten Rahbek Hansen.

Consulate: Orebygaardvej 3-7, 7400 Herning; tel 97-26-88-01; fax 97-26-88-26.
Honorary Consul: Niels Christian Jensen.

Consulate: Albanitorv 4, 5000 Odense C; tel 66-14-47-14.
Honorary Consul: Frits Niegel.

Consulate: Fiskerivej 1, 3700, Rønne; tel 53-95-21-11; telex 48137; fax 53-95-25-67.
Honorary Consul: Henrik Espersen.

Consulate: Yviri vid Strond 19, POB 49, 100 Thorshavn, Faroe Islands; tel 13-51-0; telex 81259; fax 11-31-8.
Honorary Consul: Johan Mortensen.

Consulate: Proeks, Vestervig 45, POB 1073, 3900 Greenland; tel 24-42-2; telex 90437; fax 22-40-9.
Honorary Consul: O. G. Ramlau-Hansen.

USA

Embassy: Dag Hammarskjölds Allé 24, 2100 Copenhagen Ø; tel 31-42-31-44; telex 22216; fax 35-43-02-23.
Ambassador: Richard B. Stone (designate).
Counsellor (Economic): Dennis A. Sandberg.
Counsellor and Head of Information Service: Charles R. Dickerman.
Political Section: Gregory M. Suchan.
Commercial Section (FCS): Stephen Helgesen.
Counsellor (Economic): Jeffrey R. Cunningham.
Labour Officer: Marc E. Northern.
First Secretary (Consular): Robert L. Fretz.
Administrative Section: Peter W. Bodde.
Regional Security Officer: Tony R. Bell.
Agricultural Section (USDA/FAS): Robert C. Tetro.
Public Affairs Officer (USIS): Mary Ellen Connell.
Defence, Naval and Air Attaché: Capt Michael C. Tiernan.
Air Attaché: Col John E. Long.
Military Attaché: Col Lionel R. Ingram, Jr.
Office of Defence Co-operation: Col Robert E. Bryan.
Communications Programme Officer: Robert Cummings.

VENEZUELA

Embassy: Hammerensgade 3, Second Floor, 1267 Copenhagen K; tel 33-93-63-11; telex 15309; fax 33-15-69-11.
Ambassador: Gerardo E. Wills.
Minister-Counsellor: Dr Luis Sosa-Vaamonde.
Counsellor: Carmen Matos-Azócar.
Attaché: Edith Mayora-Román.

YEMEN

Embassy: Strandvejen 153, First Floor, 2900 Hellerup; tel 31-62-30-40; telex 40990; fax 31-62-30-45.
Ambassador: Salem Abdo Alsheikh Fares.
First Counsellor: Abdul-Salem Qasim Said al-Awadi.
Second Secretary: Mohamed Hussain Hussain al-Faqeeh.

YUGOSLAVIA

Embassy: Svanevænget 36, 2100 Copenhagen Ø; tel 31-29-71-61; fax 31-29-79-19.
Ambassador: Nada Filipović.
First Secretary: Slobodan Gojkov.

International Organizations

EUROPEAN COMMUNITIES

Bureau: Højbrohus, 61 Østergade, POB 144, 1004 Copenhagen K; tel 33-14-41-40; telex 16402; fax 33-11-12-03.
Director: Per Vinther.

UNITED NATIONS CHILDREN'S FUND—UNICEF

Representation: UNICEF Plads, 2100 Copenhagen Ø; tel 35-27-35-27; telex 19813; fax 31-26-94-21.
Representative: David J. Halliday (designate).
Deputy Representative: Jean Wasselin.

WORLD HEALTH ORGANIZATION—WHO

Office: Scherfigsvej 8, 2100 Copenhagen Ø; tel 39-17-17-17; telex 15348; fax 31-18-11-20.
Regional Director: Dr Jo E. Asvall (designate).

DJIBOUTI

BELGIUM

Consulate: BP 105, Djibouti; tel 351027; telex 5864; fax 355309.
Consul: S. Remon.

CHINA, PEOPLE'S REPUBLIC

Embassy: Djibouti; tel 352246; telex 5926.
Ambassador: Xu Chenghua.

DENMARK

Consulate: 8 rue Marchand, POB 2601, Djibouti; tel 351150; telex 5827; fax 355623.
Consul: Michel Izzo.

EGYPT

Embassy: BP 1989, Djibouti; tel 351231; telex 5880.
Ambassador: Mohsen T. Azmi.

ETHIOPIA

Embassy: BP 230, Djibouti; tel 350718.
Ambassador: Berhanu Dinka.

FRANCE

Embassy: 45 blvd du Maréchal Foch, BP 2039, Djibouti; tel 350325; telex 5861.
Ambassador: Claude Soubeste.

Consulate-General: Villa Normandie, blvd du Maréchal Lyautey, BP 75, Djibouti; tel 352096.

GERMANY

Consulate-General: rue des Bruxelles, BP 2617, Djibouti; tel 355735; telex 5704.
Honorary Consul-General: Pierre Guicheney.

IRAQ

Embassy: BP 1983, Djibouti; tel 353469; telex 5877.
Ambassador: Abdel Aziz al-Gailani.

LIBYA

Embassy: BP 2073, Djibouti; tel 353339; telex 5874.
Ambassador: Jalal Muhammad al-Daghely.

OMAN

Embassy: BP 1996, Djibouti; tel 350852; telex 5876.
Ambassador: Saoud Salem Hassan al-Ansi.

RUSSIA

Embassy: BP 1913, Djibouti; tel 352051; telex 5906.
Ambassador: Poulat Abdoullaiev.
Counsellor: Raat Issakov.
First Secretary: Alexei Machkine.
Second Secretary: Vladimir Martynov.

SAUDI ARABIA

Embassy: BP 1921, Djibouti; tel 351645; telex 5865; fax 352284.
Chargé d'affaires: Mowaffak al-Doligane.

SOMALIA

Embassy: BP 549, Djibouti; tel 353521; telex 5815.
Ambassador: Muhammad Shek Muhammad Malingur.

SUDAN

Embassy: Djibouti; tel 351483.
Ambassador: Tag el-Sir Muhammad Abass.

SWEDEN

Consulate: c/o Ets. Marill, 8 rue Marchand, BP 2601, Djibouti; tel 351150; telex 5827; fax 355623.
Consul: Michel Izzo.

UNITED KINGDOM

Consulate: Gellatly Hankey & Co., POB 81, Djibouti; tel 355718; telex 5843; fax 353294.
Honorary Consul: E. Vandendriessche.
Honorary Vice-Consul: P. Arthur.

USA

Embassy: Villa Plateau du Serpent, blvd Maréchal Joffré, BP 185, Djibouti; tel 353995; fax 353940.
Ambassador: Robert S. Barrett IV.
Deputy Head of Mission: Jay L. Dehmlow.
Political Officer: John H. Winant.
Economic and Commercial Officer: Thomas M. Murphy.
Administrative Officer: David W. Ball.
Administrative and Consular Officer: Sharon A. Lavorel.
Regional Security Officer: Gary M. Gibson.
Liaison Officer: Maj. Lyle G. Radebaugh.
Public Affairs Officer: C. Robert Dickerman.

Communications Programme Officer: Kenneth Lamkins.

YEMEN

Embassy: BP 194, Djibouti; tel 352975.
Ambassador: Muhammad Abdoul Wassi Hamid.

International Organizations

EUROPEAN COMMUNITIES

External Delegation: 11 blvd du Maréchal Joffre, BP 2477, Djibouti; tel 352615; telex 5894; fax 350036.
Commission Delegate: Emilio Pérez Porras.

DOMINICA

CHINA (TAIWAN)

Embassy: Morne Daniel, POB 56; tel 91385; telex 8661; fax 92085.
Chargé d'affaires: George Chan.

SWEDEN

Consulate: c/o H. H. V. Whitchurch & Co. Ltd, Old St, POB 71, Roseau; tel 82181; telex 8614; fax 85787.
Consul: Gerald Leonard Aird.

VENEZUELA

Embassy: 3rd Floor, 37 Cork St, POB 70, Roseau; tel 83348; telex 8643; fax 86198.
Ambassador: Hector M. Griffin.

THE DOMINICAN REPUBLIC

ARGENTINA

Embassy: Avda Máximo Gómez 10, Santo Domingo, DN; tel 682-2977; telex 346-0154.
Ambassador: Jorge Vásquez.

AUSTRIA

Consulate-General: José Desiderio Valverde 103, Zone 7, Apdo 1333, Santo Domingo, DN; tel 685-4114; telex 346-0093.
Honorary Consul-General: Pedro James Ostreicher.

BRAZIL

Embassy: Avda Winston Churchill 32, Edif. Franco-Acra y Asociados, 2°, Apdo 1655, Santo Domingo, DN; tel 532-0868; telex 346-0155.
Ambassador: P. G. Vilas-Bôas Castro.

CANADA

Consulate: Maximo Gomez 30, 1°, Apdo 2054, Santo Domingo, DN; tel 685-1136; telex 346-0270; fax 682-2691.
First Secretary and Consul: Russell W. Stubbert.

Consulate: Beller 51, Suite 3, Puerto Plata; tel 586-3305; telex 346-2022; fax 586-5762.
Honorary Consul: T. Hall.

CHILE

Embassy: Avda Anacaona 11, Mirador del Sur, Santo Domingo, DN; tel 532-7800; telex 346-0395; fax 532-7979.
Ambassador: Ricardo Lira Gómez.

CHINA (TAIWAN)

Embassy: Edif. Palic, 1°, Avda Abraham Lincoln, esq. José Amado Soler, Santo Domingo, DN; tel 562-5555; fax 541-5207.
Ambassador: Wang Meng-Hsien.

COLOMBIA

Embassy: Avda Abraham Lincoln 502, 2°, Santo Domingo, DN; tel 567-6836; telex 346-0448.
Ambassador: Dr Ernesto Torres Díaz.

COSTA RICA

Embassy: Andrés Julio Aybar 15, Santo Domingo, DN; tel 565-7294.
Chargé d'affaires: Odalisca Aued Rodríguez.

CYPRUS

Consulate: Avda Isabel Aguiar esq. Calle K, Zona Industrial de Herrera, Apdo 1296, Santo Domingo, DN; tel 530-8350; telex 4380; fax 530-1311.
Honorary Consul: Francisco Zacarias Bendek.

DENMARK

Consulate-General: Autopista Duarte Km. 6 1/2, zona 9, Apdo 856, Santo Domingo, DN; tel 562-1333; telex 346-0022.
Vice-Consul: Jaak E. Rannik.

Consulate: Calle 12 de Julio 6, Apdo 322, Puerto Plata; tel 586-2317.
Vice-Consul: Andrés Emilio Bournigal Nunez.

ECUADOR

Embassy: Gustavo M. Ricart 90, Santo Domingo, DN; tel 565-0822; telex 326-4556.
Ambassador: Adaiberto Ortiz Q.

EL SALVADOR

Embassy: Calle José A. Brea Peña 12, Ensanche Evaristo Morales, Santo Domingo, DN; tel 565-4311; fax 541-7503.
Ambassador: Dr Byron Fernando Larios López.
First Secretary and Consul-General: Idalia Gertrudis Menjivar Campos.
Cultural Attaché: Linda Azucena Chacon Reyes.
Commercial Attaché: Evelyn Safie de Zacarias Bendek.

FINLAND

Consulate: Rodríguez Objío 9, Santo Domingo, DN; tel 687-9240; fax 567-8909.
Consul: Juan Alfredo Du-Breil Bancalari.

Consulate: Anibal Espinosa 65, Apdo 20107, Santo Domingo, DN; tel 565-1260; fax 566-5029.
Vice-Consul: Ramón José Puig Ordeix.

FRANCE

Embassy: Edif. Heinsen, 2°, Avda Jorge Washington 353, Apdo 780, Santo Domingo, DN; tel 689-2161; telex 346-0392.
Ambassador: Claude Fouquet.

GERMANY

Embassy: Calle Lic. Juan Tomás Mejía y Cotes 37, Santo Domingo, DN; tel 565-8811; telex 326-4125.
Ambassador: Dr Robert Laub.

GUATEMALA

Embassy: Zona No 8, Naco, Santo Domingo, DN; tel 566-8881.

HAITI

Embassy: Cub Scouts 11, Naco, Santo Domingo, DN; tel 567-2511; telex 346-0851.
Ambassador: Albert Chassagne.

HOLY SEE

Apostolic Nunciature: Máximo Gómez No 27, Apdo 312, Santo Domingo, DN; tel 682-3773; fax 687-0287.
Apostolic Nuncio: Most Rev. Fortunato Baldelli, Titular Archbishop of Bevagna.
Secretary: Rev. Mgr Hans J. Kothius.

HONDURAS

Embassy: Calle Porfirio Herrera No 9 esq. Respaldo Federico Geraldino Ensanche Piantini, Santo Domingo, DN; tel 566-5707; telex 346-4104.
Ambassador: Iván Romero Martínez.

ISRAEL

Embassy: Pedro Henríquez Ureña 80, Santo Domingo, DN; tel 686-7359; fax 687-7888.
Ambassador: Gavriel Levy.

ITALY

Embassy: Rodríguez Objío 4, Santo Domingo, DN; tel 689-3684; telex 346-0543.
Ambassador: Roberto Rosellini.

JAMAICA

Consulate-General: Jose Contreras 98, Edif. Santa Maria, Apdo 306, Santo Domingo, DN; tel 532-1079; telex 4390.
Honorary Consul-General: T. Allan Marley.

JAPAN

Embassy: Torre BHD, 8°, Avda Winston Churchill esq. Luis F. Thomén, Apdo 1236, Santo Domingo, DN; tel 566-8023; telex 4154; fax 566-8013.
Ambassador: Katsuhiko Tsunoda.

KOREA, REPUBLIC

Embassy: Avda Sarasota 98, Santo Domingo, DN; tel 532-4314; telex 326-4368.
Ambassador: Kim Sung-Shik.

MEXICO

Embassy: Rafael Hernández 11, Ensanche Naco, Santo Domingo, DN; tel 565-2744; telex 326-4187.
Ambassador: Humberto Lira Mora.

NICARAGUA

Embassy: El Recodo, Santo Domingo, DN; tel 532-8846; telex 326-4542.
Ambassador: Dr Danilo Valle Martínez.

PANAMA

Embassy: E. de Marchena 36, Santo Domingo, DN; tel 685-6950.
Chargé d'affaires a.i.: Cristóbal Sarmiento.

PERU

Embassy: Cancillería, Winston Churchill, Santo Domingo, DN; tel 565-5851.
Ambassador: Raúl Gutiérrez.

ROMANIA

Embassy: Santo Domingo, DN.

SPAIN

Embassy: Independencia 1205, Santo Domingo, DN; tel 533-1424; telex 346-0158; fax 535-7001.
Ambassador: Fernando González-Camino.

SWEDEN

Embassy: Sweden.
Ambassador: Lennart Klackenberg (resident in Sweden).

Consulate-General: Avda Máximo Gómez 31, Apdo 916, Santo Domingo, DN; tel 685-2121; telex 346-0117.
Consul-General: Maximo Antonio Pellarano Romano.

Consulate: Edif. Industria Cartonera Dominicana, Avda John F. Kennedy Km 5, Apdo 641, Santo Domingo, DN; tel 562-4500; telex 346-0161.
Consul: José del Carmen Ariza Gómez.

SWITZERLAND

Consulate-General: José Gabriel Garcia 26, Apdo 941, Santo Domingo, DN; tel 689-4131; telex 346-0403.
Honorary Consul-General: Robert Alexander.

Chancellor: Marzio Tartini.

UNITED KINGDOM

Consulate: St George School, Abraham Lincoln 552, Santo Domingo, DN; tel 562-5010; telex 346-0781; fax 562-5015.
Honorary Consul: M. Tejede.

Consulate (Commercial): Apdo Postal 30341, Avdo Rómulo Betancourt 1302, Apdo 202, Santo Domingo, DN; tel 532-4216; fax 541-1100.
Honorary Vice-Consul (Commercial): F. G. Nicolás.

Consulate: Beller 51, No 2, Apdo 312, Puerto Plata; tel 586-4244; fax 586-3096.
Honorary Vice-Consul: D. M. Salem.

USA

Embassy: cnr Calle César Nicolás Pensón and Calle Leopoldo Navarro, Apdo 34041-0008, Santo Domingo, DN; tel 541-2171; telex 346-0013.
Ambassador: Paul D. Taylor.
Deputy Head of Mission: Mark J. Platt.
Political Section: David E. Randolph.
Economic Section: William R. Falkner.
Commercial Section: Dan A. Wilson.
Consular Section: Harry E. Jones.
Administrative Section: Roland W. Bullen.
Regional Security Officer: Christopher D. Lyons.
Public Affairs Officer: Sheldon H. Avenius.
Communications Programme Officer: Michael F. Soares.
Informations System Manager: Otho Neil Harbison.
Agency for International Development: Raymond F. Rifenburg.
Office of Defence Attaché: Lieut Col Garry R. Wright.
Agricultural Section: Forrest K. Geerken.

URUGUAY

Embassy: Avda México 169, Santo Domingo, DN; tel 565-2669; telex 346-0442.
Ambassador: Jaime Wolfson Kot.

VENEZUELA

Embassy: Avda Bolívar 832, Santo Domingo, DN; tel 687-5066; telex 326-4279; fax 688-9962.
Ambassador: Hector Vargas Acosta.
Minister-Counsellor: Luis Navarro F.
First Secretary: Alexis Curiel Quintero.
First Secretary: Gustavo Adolfo Matheus Jugo.

Consulate: Prolongación Ave, México 105, Santo Domingo, DN; tel 567-4527; telex 346-0218; fax 531-0968.
Consul-General: Jesus Marquez Moreno.
Consul: Maria E. Mancini Lozada.

ECUADOR

ARGENTINA

Embassy: Avda Amazonas 477, Apdo 2937, Quito; tel (2) 562-292.
Ambassador: Ricardo H. Illia.

AUSTRIA

Embassy: Avda Patria y Amazonas, Edif. Cofiec, 11°, Casilla 179A, Quito; tel (2) 545-336; telex 22588; fax (2) 564-560.
Ambassador: Artur Schuschnigg.

Consulate-General: Avda Coruña 1224, Edif. 'Austria', 3°, Casilla 167, Quito; tel (2) 239-660.
Honorary Consul-General: Gerhard Ruess.
Honorary Consul: Mathias Baumann.
Honorary Consul: Peter Juris.

Consulate: 9 de Octubre 1310 y Quito, Apdo 742, Guayaquil; tel (4) 282-303.
Honorary Consul: Astudillo Orlando Molina.

BELGIUM

Embassy: Austria 219 e Irlanda, Quito; telex 2767.
Ambassador: F. Franz.

BOLIVIA

Embassy: Quito.
Ambassador: Eusebio Moreira.

BRAZIL

Embassy: Calle Amazonas 1429 y Colón, Apdo 231, Quito; tel (2) 563-846; telex 22218.
Ambassador: Adolpho Benevides.

BULGARIA

Embassy: Calle Colina 331 y Orellana, Quito; tel (2) 552-553; telex 22047.
Chargé d'affaires: Lubomir Ivanov.

CANADA

Consulate: Edif. Joseuth Gonzalez, Avda 6 de Diciembre 2186 y James Orton, Quito; tel (2) 543-214; telex 22044.
Honorary Consul: G. Vorbeck Pachano.

Consulate: General Cordova 802 y Victor Manuel Rendon, Edif. Torres de la Merced, 21°, Of. 6, Guayaquil; tel (4) 303-580.
Honorary Consul: F. J. Costa Echeverria.

CHILE

Embassy: Edif. Rocafuerte 4° y 5°, Avda Amazonas 325 y Washington, Quito; telex 2167.
Ambassador: Gabriel van Schouwen Figueroa.

CHINA, PEOPLE'S REPUBLIC

Embassy: Quito.
Ambassador: Pang Ganghua.

COLOMBIA

Embassy: Calle San Javier 169, Casilla 2923, Quito; telex 2156.
Ambassador: Laureano Alberto Arellano.

COSTA RICA

Embassy: Quito.
Ambassador: Félix Córtez.

CUBA

Embassy: Quito.
Ambassador: Carlos Zamora.

CYPRUS

Consulate: Avda Colombia 1573, Edif. Computec-Penthouse, Apdo 1229, Quito; tel (2) 540-214; telex 2817.
Honorary Vice-Consul: Maria Cardenas de Perez.

CZECHOSLOVAKIA

Embassy: Calle General Salazar 459 y Coruña, Quito; telex 2478.
Ambassador: Julius Stang.

DENMARK

Consulate-General: Edif. Gabriela 3, Avda República del Salvador 733 y Portugal, Apdo 3086, Quito; tel (2) 437-163; telex 22336; fax (2) 436-942.
Consul-General: Per A. Vorbeck.

Consulate: General Córdoba 604 y Mendiburu, 3°, Of. 304, Apdo 1118, Guayaquil; tel (4) 308-020; telex 3474.
Consul: Flemming Bo Falkentoft.

DOMINICAN REPUBLIC

Embassy: Avda 6 de Diciembre 4629, Quito.
Ambassador: Mario Pena.

EGYPT

Embassy: Edif. Araucaria, 9°, Baquedano 222 y Reina Victoria, Apdo 9355, Sucursal 7, Quito; tel (2) 235-046; telex 2154.
Ambassador: Khairat Issa.

EL SALVADOR

Embassy: Avda de los Shyris 1240 y Portugal, Edif. Albatros, Apdo 8386, Quito; tel (2) 433-823; telex 22931.
Ambassador: Byron Fernando Larios L.

FINLAND

Consulate: Avda 18 de Setiembre 368 y Amazonas, Edif. 'Suárez', 3°, Quito; tel (2) 523-493; telex 2617.
Consul: René Cruz Silva.

Consulate: Luis Urdaneta 212 y Córdova, Apdo 4848, Guayaquil; tel (4) 304-381; telex 3519.
Consul: Humberto Mata Salvador.

FRANCE

Embassy: Plaza 107 y Avda Patria, Apdo 536, Quito; tel (2) 560-789; telex 2146.

Ambassador: Jean-Michel Gaussot.

GERMANY

Embassy: Avda Patria y 9 de Octubre, Edif. ETECO, 5°, Casilla 1701537, Quito; tel (2) 232-660; telex 2222; fax (2) 563-697.
Ambassador: Dr Johann-Joachim Graf Schirndinger von Schirnding.

Consulate-General: Avda 9 de Octubre 109 y Malecón, 2°, Casilla 4721, Guayaquil; tel (4) 512-700; telex 3229.
Honorary Consul-General: Gunter Lisken.

Consulate: c/o Pasamaneria S.A., Avda Huayana Capac 12-24, Casilla 60 SC 2, Cuenca; tel (7) 832-388; telex 48578; fax (7) 833-610.
Honorary Consul: Otto Schneewind.

Consulate: c/o Sefman CA, Avda 102, Casilla 4872, Manta; tel (4) 614-051; telex 6162.
Honorary Consul: Wolf-Rüdiger Harten.

GUATEMALA

Embassy: Avda La República 192 y Diego de Almagro, Edif. 'Casa Blanca', 4-B, Apdo 17-03-294, Quito; tel (2) 501-389; fax (2) 501-927.
Ambassador: Aurora Valle Valdizán.
Third Secretary: Rafael Aguilar Saravia.

HOLY SEE

Apostolic Nunciature: Apdo 17-03-4543, Avda Orellana 692, Apdo 4543-A, Quito; tel (2) 528-783; telex 2053; fax (2) 564-810.
Apostolic Nuncio: Most Rev. Francesco Canalini, Titular Archbishop of Gratiana.
First Secretary: Most Rev. Charles D. Balvo.

HONDURAS

Embassy: Cordero 279 y Plaza, Quito; telex 2805.
Ambassador: Antonio Molina O.

HUNGARY

Embassy: Edif. Gabriela, 3°, Of. 301, Avda República de El Salvador 733 y Avda Portugal, Quito; tel (2) 459-700; telex 2255.
Ambassador: Vince Kóczián.

IRELAND

Consulate-General: Edif. Jerico 14-B, Avda 12 de Octubre 2449 y Orellana, Apdo 633, Suc. 12, Quito; tel (2) 235-713; telex 22935; fax (2) 501-444.
Honorary Consul-General: Edward J. Kennedy.

ISRAEL

Embassy: Avda Eloy Alfaro 969 y Avda Amazonas, Quito; tel (2) 565-509; telex 2174.
Ambassador: Abraham Setton.

ITALY

Embassy: Calle La Isla 111, Apdo 072-A, Quito; tel (2) 561-077; telex 22715.
Ambassador: Giovanni Battista Crosetti.

JAPAN

Embassy: Calle Juan León Mera 130 y Avda Patria, Edif. de la Corporación Financiera Nacional, 8°, Apdo 3031, Quito; tel (2) 561-899; telex 22185; fax (2) 503-670.
Ambassador: Akira Nakayama.

KOREA, REPUBLIC

Embassy: Calle Reina Victoria 1539 y Avda Colón, Edif. Banco de Guayaquil, 11°, Quito; tel (2) 560-573; telex 2868.
Ambassador: Hae Yung Chung.

LEBANON

Consulate: Apdo 8860, Quito; tel (2) 500-523.
Honorary Consul: Sami el-Khoury.

Consulate: Apdo 5686, Guayaquil; tel (4) 324-079.
Honorary Consul: Juan M. Saade.

MEXICO

Embassy: Avda 6 de Diciembre 4843 y Naciones Unidas, Casilla 6371, Quito; tel (2) 457-820; telex 2395.
Ambassador: Ignacio Villaseñor.

NETHERLANDS

Embassy: Edif. Club de Leones Central, 3°, Avda de las Naciones Unidas entre Avdas 10 de Agosto y Amazonas, Apdo 2840, Quito; telex 2576.
Ambassador: Dr J. Weidema.

PANAMA

Embassy: Calle Pazmiño 245 y Avda 6 de Diciembre, Quito.
Ambassador: Roberto Samuel Fábrega Goytia.

PARAGUAY

Embassy: Avda Gaspar de Villarroel 2013 y Avda Amazonas, Casilla 139-A, Quito; tel (2) 245-871; telex 2260.
Ambassador: Dr Gilberto Caniza Sánchiz.

PERU

Embassy: Edif. España Pent-House, Avda Colón y Amazonas, Quito; tel (2) 520-134; telex 2864; fax (2) 562-349.
Ambassador: Eduardo Ponce Vivanco.
Minister: César Castillo Ramírez.
Counsellor and Consul-General: Luis Hernández Ortíz.

Consulate-General: 9 de Octubre y Chile, Edif. Finansa, Guayaquil; tel (4) 322-738; fax (4) 327-637.
Minister and Consul-General: Vicente Azula de la Guerra.

Consulate: Bolivar y Colon esq., Machala; tel (4) 930-680; fax (4) 930-680.
Counsellor and Consul: José Miguel Cuadros.

Consulate: L. Lasso y Zoilo Rodriguez, Loja; tel 961-668; fax 963-051.
Counsellor and Consul: Amador Velásquez.

POLAND

Embassy: Quito.
Chargé d'affaires a.i.: Czesław Bugajski.

ROMANIA

Embassy: Avda República del Salvador 482 e Irlanda, Quito; telex 2230.
Ambassador: Gheorghe Dobra.

RUSSIA

Embassy: Reina Victoria 462 y Roca, Casilla 3868, Quito; tel (2) 526-361.
Ambassador: German E. Shliapnikov.

SPAIN

Embassy: La Pinta 455 y Amazonas, Casilla 17-01-9322, Quito; tel (2) 564-373; telex 22816; fax (2) 500-826.
Ambassador: Juan Manuel Egea Ibáñez.
Counsellor: Manuel Pradas Romaní.
Counsellor (Commercial): Ramón Santos Martínez.

Consulate: Victor Manuel Rendon 120, Guayaquil; tel (4) 304-860.
Consul: Enrique Novas A.

Consulate: Avda del Estado y Manuel J. Calle, Cuenca; tel (7) 810-211.
Vice-Consul: Gerardo Martínez.

SWEDEN

Embassy: Edif. Las Cámaras, 2°, Avda República y Amazonas, Apdo 17-03-420-A, Quito; tel (2) 441-445; telex 2396; fax (2) 445-973.
Ambassador: Christer Manhusen.
First Secretary: Agneta Landorf.

Consulate: Km. 6 1/2 Via a Daule, Apdo 1317, Guayaquil; tel (4) 254-111; telex 43205; fax (4) 254-159.
Consul: Bo Assar Bohman.

SWITZERLAND

Embassy: Edif. Xerox, Avda Amazonas 3617 y Juan Pablo Sanz, 2°, Casilla 4815, Quito; tel (2) 434-113; telex 2592; fax (2) 449-314.
Chargé d'affaires a.i. and Counsellor: Gian Frederico Pedotti.
Third Secretary and Office Manager: Andreas Mathys.

Consulate: Casilla 397, Guayaquil; tel (4) 363-607; telex 043386; fax (4) 372-574.
Honorary Consul: Fritz Gfeller.

UNITED KINGDOM

Embassy: González Suárez 111, Casilla 314, Quito; tel (2) 560-669; telex 2138; fax (2) 560-730.
Ambassador: Frank B. Wheeler.
Consul and Deputy Head of Mission: G. J. C. Pirnie.
Defence Attaché: Group Capt. J. V. Bell.
First Secretary (Commercial): M. J. McLoughlin.
Third Secretary (Chancery/Economic): C. R. Blake.
Third Secretary (Management) and Vice-Consul: J. C. Chick.
Attaché (Culture) and British Council Director: D. F. M. Lauder.

Consulate: General Córdova 623 y Urdaneta (Casilla 8598), Guayaquil; tel (4) 300-400; telex 3379.
Honorary Consul: C. R. Armstrong.

Consulate: Plazoleta Pedro Toulop, Pasaje San Alfonso, Planta Baja, Cuenca; tel (7) 831-996; telex 48565; fax (7) 832-430.
Honorary Consul: T. Jerves Núñez.

Consulate: c/o Etica Office, Barrio Estrada, Puerto Ayora, Isla Santa Cruz, Gálapagos; tel (4) 284-666.
Honorary Consul: D. E. Balfour.

USA

Embassy: Avda 12 de Octubre y Avda Patria 120, Quito; tel (2) 562-890; telex 2329; fax (2) 502-052.
Ambassador: Paul C. Lambert.
Deputy Head of Mission: Adolph H. Eisner.
Political Section: Hugh Simon, Jr.
Economic Section: John R. Savage.
Commercial Section: Jerry M. Dabbs.
Labour Office: Laurie Tracy.
Administrative Section: J. Richard Mason.
Regional Security Officer: Linda K. Fleetwood-Kincer.
Agency for International Development: Charles E. Costello.
Public Affairs Officer: Gregory Lagana.
Office of Defence Attaché: Col Michael E. Ryan.
Military Group: Col Steven Hightower.
Narcotics Assistance Unit: Yvonne F. Thayer.
Communications Programme Officer: Harold M. Muroaka.
Information Systems Manager: Stephen A. Jasak.

Consulate-General: 9 de Octubre y Garcia Moreno, Apdo 34039, Guayaquil; tel (4) 323-570; fax (4) 325-286.
Consul-General: Ralph T. Jones.
Administrative Section: Ann Michelle Deney.
Communications Programme Officer: John E. Alston.

URUGUAY

Embassy: Tamayo y Lisardo Garcia, Quito; tel (2) 541-968; telex 22657; fax (2) 503-474.
Ambassador: Aldofo Castells.
Minister: Ruben H. Diaz.
Second Secretary: Eduardo Bouzout.
Attaché: Giselle Hontou.
Consulate: Guayaquil; tel (4) 320-658.
Consul: Atilio Areco.

VENEZUELA

Embassy: Coruña 1733 y Belo Horizonte, Apdo 688, Quito; tel (2) 564-626; telex 22160; fax (2) 502-630.
Ambassador: Miguel Bellorin.
Minister-Counsellor: Maria Salazar S.
Third Secretary: Carmen Elena Montaño Rigual.
Consulate-General: Chile 329 y Aguirre, Edif. Rond's, 2°, Quito; tel (2) 517-053; tel 42453; fax (2) 320-751.
Second Secretary: Vladimir Gonzalez G.
Consul-General: Juan José Castillo.

YUGOSLAVIA

Embassy: Gen. Francisco Salazar 958 y 12 de Octubre, Quito; tel (2) 526-218; telex 2633.
Ambassador: Samuilo Protić.

EGYPT

AFGHANISTAN

Interests Section: c/o Embassy of India, 39 Sharia Orouba, Cairo (Heliopolis); tel (2) 666653.

ALBANIA

Embassy: 29 Sharia Ismail Muhammad, Cairo (Zamalek); tel (2) 3415651.
Ambassador: Alkyz Cerga.

ALGERIA

Interests Section: c/o Embassy of India, 14 Sharia Brasil (Zamalek), Cairo; tel (2) 3402466.

ANGOLA

Embassy: 12 Midan en-Nasr, Cairo (Dokki); tel (2) 707602.
Ambassador: Kamu d'Almeida.

ARGENTINA

Embassy: 8 Sharia as-Saleh Ayoub, Cairo (Zamalek); tel (2) 3401501.
Ambassador: Jorge H. de Belausbegui.

AUSTRALIA

Embassy: 5th Floor, South Bldg, Cairo Plaza Annexe, Corniche-en-Nil, Boulac 11111, Cairo; tel (2) 777900; telex 92257; fax (2) 768220.
Ambassador: John H. Crighton.
Information Officer: Louise O'Keefe.

AUSTRIA

Embassy: Sharia El-Nil, cnr of Sharia Wissa Wassef, Riyadh Tower, 5th Floor, Cairo (Giza); tel (2) 737602; telex 92258; fax (2) 730935.
Ambassador: Dr Peter Pramberger.
Minister-Counsellor: Dr Rudolf Agstner.
Counsellor (Culture): Dr Brigitte Agstner-Gehring.
Counsellor (Commercial): Dr Heinrich Kaufmann.
Third Secretary (Administrative) and Vice-Consul: Michael Jan Swoboda.
Attaché (Culture): Georg Bittner-Buddenbrock-Hettersdorff.
Attaché (Commercial): Dr Martin Pilser.
Consulate-General: 8 rue Eglise, Debbané, Alexandria; tel (3) 808888; telex 54588.
Honorary Consul-General: Vahan Dikran Alexanian.

BAHRAIN

Interests Section: c/o Embassy of Pakistan, 8 Sharia Jamaiat an-Nisr, Cairo (Dokki); tel (2) 705052; telex 2084.

BANGLADESH

Embassy: 47 Sharia Ahmed Heshmat, Cairo (Zamalek); tel (2) 3412642.
Ambassador: M. Nurun Nabi Chowdhury.

BELGIUM

Embassy: 20 Sharia Kamel esh-Shennawi, Cairo (Garden City); tel (2) 3547494; telex 92264.
Ambassador: Alain Rens.

BOLIVIA

Embassy: Cairo; tel (2) 3550917.
Chargé d'affaires a.i.: Enrique Soria Nau.

BRAZIL

Embassy: 1125 Corniche en-Nil, 11561 Cairo (Maspiro); tel (2) 756938; telex 92044.
Ambassador: Ivan Velloso da Silveira Batalha.

BRUNEI

Embassy: 26 Sharia Gezirat al-Arab, Mohandessine, Dokki, Cairo; tel (2) 3471109; telex 22068; fax (2) 3466014.

BULGARIA

Embassy: 141 Sharia Tahrir, Cairo (Dokki); tel (2) 982691.

BURKINA FASO

Embassy: Ramses Centre, 3 Sharia Abd al-Khawi Ahmad, POB 306, Cairo; tel (2) 3440301; telex 93871.
Ambassador: Yaya Gnessien.

BURUNDI

Embassy: 22 rue El Nakhil, Cairo (Dokki); tel (2) 708431; telex 20091.
Ambassador: Lieut Col Gervais Ndikumagenge.
Second Counsellor: Gérard Nduwayo.

CAMBODIA

Embassy: 2 Sharia Tahawia, Cairo (Giza); tel (2) 3489436.
Ambassador: In Sopheap.
Minister-Counsellor: In Sivuth.
Second Secretary: Poc Dany.
Attaché: Yao Kim Li.

CAMEROON

Embassy: POB 2061, 15 Sharia Israa, Madinet el-Mohandessin, Cairo (Dokki); tel (2) 341101; telex 92088.
Ambassador: Mouchili Nji Mfouayo.

CANADA

Embassy: 6 Sharia Muhammad Fahmi el-Sayed, POB 2646, Cairo (Garden City); tel (2) 3543110; telex 92677; fax (2) 3557276.
Ambassador: Jacques T. Simard.
Counsellor (Commercial/Economic) and Consul: G. J. Shannon.
Counsellor and Consul: J. F. Gould.
Counsellor (Immigration) and Consul: J. P. Delisle.
Counsellor (Development) and Consul: V. R. Carvell.
Counsellor (Development): F. Mes.
Forces Attaché: Col J. L. Orr.
First Secretary (Administrative) and Consul: N. K. Flynn.
First Secretary (Development): J. M. Touzel.
First Secretary: R. A. Sawyer.

CENTRAL AFRICAN REPUBLIC

Embassy: 13 Sharia Chehab, Madinet el-Mohandessin, Cairo (Dokki); tel (2) 713291.
Ambassador: Pierre Fidèle Bakri.

CHAD

Embassy: POB 1869, 12 Midan el Rifaï, Cairo (Dokki) 11511; tel (2) 703232; telex 92285.
Ambassador: Mahmoud Adji.

CHILE

Embassy: 5 Sharia Chagaret ed-Dorr, Cairo (Zamalek); tel (2) 3408711; telex 92519.

CHINA

Embassy: 14 Sharia Bahgat Aly, Cairo (Zamalek); tel (2) 3417691.
Ambassador: Zhan Shiliang.

COLOMBIA

Embassy: 20/A Gamal ed-Din Aboul Mahassen, Cairo (Garden City); tel (2) 3546152; telex 3036; fax (2) 3557087.
Chargé d'affaires a.i.: Dr Jairo Montes Moreno.

COTE D'IVOIRE

Embassy: 39 Sharia el-Kods esh-Sherif, Madinet el-Mohandessin, Cairo (Dokki); tel (2) 699009; telex 2334.
Ambassador: Gen. Félix Ory.

CUBA

Embassy: 6 Fawakeh St, Madinet el-Mohandessin, Cairo (Dokki); tel (2) 710525; telex 93966.
Ambassador: Jorge Cubiles Hernández.

CYPRUS

Embassy: 23A Sharia Ismail Muhammad, 1st Floor, Cairo (Zamalek); tel (2) 3411288; telex 92059; fax (2) 3415299.
Ambassador: George Georgiades.
Secretary: Costas Miltiadous.
Attaché (Press): Michalakis Michail.

Consulate-General: Alexandria; tel (3) 4825898.
Attaché (Consular/Administrative): George Vias.

CZECHOSLOVAKIA

Embassy: 4 Sharia Dokki, Cairo (Giza); tel (2) 3485469; telex 92295; fax (2) 3485892.
Ambassador: Ivan Voleš.
Counsellor: Josef Fogl.
Counsellor (Commercial): Vladimír Loskot.
Military Attaché: Jan Vašíček.
First Secretary: Josef Mikulka.
Second Secretary: Ján Bóry.

Consulate-General: 26 Rushdy St, Alexandria; tel (3) 840582; telex 5004; fax (3) 850209.
Consul-General: Antonín Hrůza.

DENMARK

Embassy: 12 Sharia Hassan Sabri, 11111 Cairo (Zamalek); tel (2) 3402502; telex 92254; fax (2) 3411780.
Ambassador: Jørgen Bøjer.
First Secretary: Sophie Kisling.
Attaché (Commercial): Hans Jørgen Ipland.
Attaché: Annette Madsen.
Commercial Correspondent: Mohamed Abou Alam.
Commercial Correspondent: Ruth Abdallah.
Attaché (Aid): Ole E. Moesby.

Consulate-General: 20 Patrice Lumumba St, Bab Sharki, POB 622-21131, Alexandria; tel (3) 4906000; telex 54133; fax (3) 4920909.
Consul-General: Abdel Kader el-Naggar.

Consulate: c/o Seaman's Service, Sultan Hussein 30, 4th Floor, POB 539, Port Said; tel (66) 227514; telex 63174.

Consulate: Saad Zagloul St 11, Suez; tel (62) 225667.
Consul: Mahmoud Ali Gomaa Fattouh.

DJIBOUTI

Embassy: 157 Sharia Sudan, Madinet el-Mohandessin, Cairo (Dokki); tel (2) 709787; telex 93143.

ECUADOR

Embassy: 93 rue el-Malek Abdel Aziz al-Seoud, el-Manial, Cairo; tel (2) 3639229; telex 93464; fax (2) 3406667.
Ambassador: Uribe Lasso.

Consular Section: tel (2) 3637246.
First Secretary (Consular): Eugenio va Quez.

ETHIOPIA

Embassy: 12 Midan Bahlawi, Cairo (Dokki); tel (2) 705372.
Ambassador: Ato Betrou Kidane Mariam.

FINLAND

Embassy: 3 Abu el-Feda St, 13th Floor, 11511 Cairo (Zamalek); tel (2) 3411487; telex 92328; fax (2) 3405170.
Ambassador: Elisabeth Tigerstedt-Tähtelä.
Secretary (Commercial): Timo Manninen.
Attaché (Commercial): Ari Huttunen.

Consulate-General: 2 ave el-Horreya, BP 250, Alexandria; tel (3) 4824482; telex 55881.
Consul-General: Omar Ali el-Hadidi.

Consulate: 11 Saad Zaghloul St, Suez; tel (62) 25667.
Consul: Mahmoud Ali Gomaa.

FRANCE

Embassy: 29 ave de Guizeh, BP 1777, Cairo (Giza); tel (2) 728033; telex 92032.
Ambassador: Patrick Leclercq.

Consulate: 5 rue el Fadl, BP 1777, Cairo; tel (2) 3934316.

Consulate-General: 2 place Ahmed Orabi, BP 474, Alexandria; tel (3) 483-5613.

GABON

Embassy: 15 Sharia Mossadek, Cairo (Dokki); tel (2) 702963; telex 92323.
Ambassador: Alain Maurice Mayombo.

GERMANY

Embassy: 8b Sharia Hassan Sabri, Cairo (Zamalek); tel (2) 3410015; telex 92023; fax (2) 3410530.
Ambassador: Dr Heinz Fiedler.
First Counsellor and Chargé d'affaires: Dr Christoph Brümmer.

Consulate-General: 5 Sharia Mina, Roushdy, Alexandria 21511; tel (3) 5455999.
Consul-General: Franz Josef Meurer.

GHANA

Embassy: 24 Sharia el-Batal Ahmad Abd al-Aziz, Cairo (Dokki); tel (2) 704275.
Ambassador: Dr W. C. Yaw Anoff.

GREECE

Embassy: 18 Sharia Aicha et-Taimouria, Cairo (Garden City); tel (2) 3550443; telex 92036.
Ambassador: Pandeus Menglidis.

GUATEMALA

Embassy: 8 Mohamed Fahmy al-Mohdar St, Madinet Nasr, Cairo; tel (2) 2611813; telex 93242; fax (2) 2611814.
Ambassador: Rodolfo Rosales Muralles.
First Secretary and Consul: Josefina E. de León.
Administrative Secretary: Laila Abdel-Rahman.

GUINEA

Embassy: 46 Sharia Muhammad Mazhar, Cairo (Zamalek); tel (2) 3411088.
Ambassador: Amirou Diallo.

GUINEA-BISSAU

Embassy: 37 Sharia Lebanon, Madinet el-Mohandessin, Cairo (Dokki).

HOLY SEE

Apostolic Pro-Nunciature: Safarat al-Vatican, 5 Sharia Muhammad Mazhar, Cairo (Zamalek); tel (2) 3402250; fax (2) 3406152.
Apostolic Pro-Nuncio: Most Rev. Antonio Magnoni, Titular Archbishop of Boseta.

HUNGARY

Embassy: 55 Sharia Muhammad Mazhar, Cairo (Zamalek); tel (2) 3405091.
Ambassador: Dr Ernő Simonyi.

ICELAND

Consulate-General: 1282 Immobelia Bldg, Cairo; tel (2) 3925573; telex 22366; fax (2) 3931101.
Consul-General: Nadia Niazi Mostafa.

INDIA

Embassy: 5 Sharia Aziz Abaza, Cairo (Zamalek); tel (2) 3413051; telex 92081.
Ambassador: Pascal Alan Nazareth.

INDONESIA

Embassy: POB 1661, 13 Sharia Aicha el-Taimouria, Cairo (Garden City); tel (2) 3547200.
Ambassador: R. Achmad Djumiril.

IRAQ

Interests Section: c/o Embassy of Yugoslavia, 33 Sharia Mansour Muhammad, Cairo (Zamalek); tel (2) 3404061; telex 21046.

IRELAND

Embassy: POB 2681, 3 Sharia Abu el-Feda, Cairo (Zamalek); tel (2) 3408254; telex 92778; fax (2) 3412863.
Ambassador: Eamonn O'Tuathail.
First Secretary: Justin Carroll.

Consulate: 36 Kafr-Abdo St, Rochdy, Alexandria; tel (3) 5460081; telex 54048; fax (3) 5460081.
Honorary Consul: Hisham G. Helmy.

ISRAEL

Embassy: 6 Sharia ibn el-Malek, Cairo (Giza); tel (2) 729329; telex 93363.
Ambassador: Ephraim Dubek.

ITALY

Embassy: 15 Sharia Abd ar-Rahman Fahmi, Cairo (Garden City); tel (2) 3543194; telex 94229; fax (2) 3540657.
Ambassador: Patrizio Schmidlin.
Minister-Counsellor: Vitaliano Napoleone.
Counsellor (Commercial): Gherardo La Francesca.
Counsellor: Pia Bertini Malgarini.

Consular Section: 14 Champollion St, Cairo; tel (2) 751398.
Head of Consular Section: Francesco Piccione.

Consulate-General: 25 Midan Saad Zaghlul, Alexandria; tel (3) 4827292.
Consul-General: Enzo Bocchia.

Consulate: Shara Salah Salem, Port Said; tel (66) 23756.
Consul: Lolita Cartareggia.

JAPAN

Embassy: Immeuble Cairo Centre, 3rd Floor, 2 Sharia Abd al-Kader Hamza, 106 Kasr el-Eini, Cairo; tel (2) 3551477; telex 92226; fax (2) 3563540.
Ambassador: Hiroshi Hashimoto.

Consular Office: 41 Moustafa Abu Heif St, Saba Pasha Ramleh, POB 2434, Alexandria; tel (3) 5879966.
Consul: Toyoshige Munemoto.

JORDAN

Embassy: 6 Sharia Juhaini, Cairo; tel (2) 3487543.
Ambassador: Nabih an-Nimr.

KENYA

Embassy: POB 362, 7 Sharia Mohandes Galal, Mohandessine, Cairo (Dokki); tel (2) 3453628; telex 92021.
Ambassador: Ali Mohamed Abdi.
Counsellor: W. L. N'dege.
Defence Attaché: Brig. E. G. Kihia.
Second Secretary: Alloys P. Mauda.
Attaché (Finance): Rosemary A. Onam.
Attaché (Administrative): Ahmed Olat Odawa.
Attaché (Administrative): Florence A. Odero.

KOREA, DEMOCRATIC PEOPLE'S REPUBLIC

Embassy: 6 Sharia es-Saleh Ayoub, Cairo (Zamalek); tel (2) 650970.
Ambassador: O Chang Rim.

KOREA, REPUBLIC

Embassy: 6 Sharia el-Hesn, Cairo (Giza); tel (2) 729162.

KUWAIT

Embassy: 12 Sharia Nabil el-Wakkad, Cairo (Dokki); tel (2) 701611.

LEBANON

Embassy: 5 Sharia Ahmad Nessim, Cairo (Giza); tel (2) 728454; telex 92227.
Ambassador: Abdel Rachman.

LIBERIA

Embassy: 11 Sharia Brasil, Cairo (Zamalek); tel (2) 3419864; telex 92293.
Ambassador: Gabriel G. Farngalo.
Consul and Counsellor: E. Cosby Sherman.

MALAYSIA

Embassy: 7 Sharia Wadi en-Nil, Mohandessin, Cairo (Agouza); tel (2) 699162.
Ambassador: Abdullah Zawawi bin Haji Muhammad.

MALI

Embassy: 3 Sharia al-Kawsar, Cairo (Dokki); tel (2) 701641.
Ambassador: Muphtah ag-Hairy.

MALTA

Embassy: 7A Sharia 20, Cairo (Maadi); tel (2) 3754453; fax (2) 3503014.
Ambassador: Ives de Barro.

MAURITANIA

Embassy: 31 Sharia Syria, Cairo (Dokki); tel (2) 707229; telex 92274.

MAURITIUS

Embassy: 72 Sharia Abd el-Moneim Riad, Agouza 11111, Cairo (Giza); tel (2) 3470929; telex 93631; fax (2) 3452425.
First Secretary and Chargé d'affaires a.i.: Dooladren Pillay Tirvengadum.

MEXICO

Embassy: 5 Sharia Dar es-Shifa, Cairo; tel (2) 3543422; telex 92277; fax (2) 3557953.
Ambassador: Prof. Graciela de la Lama.

MONGOLIA

Embassy: 3 Midan en-Nasr, Cairo (Dokki); tel (2) 650060.
Ambassador: Sonomdorjin Dambadarjaa.

MOROCCO

Interests Section: c/o Embassy of Senegal, 10 Sharia Salah ed-Din Ayoub, Cairo (Zamalek); tel (2) 3458479; telex 92047.

MYANMAR

Embassy: 24 Sharia Muhammad Mazhar, Cairo (Zamalek); tel (2) 3404176.
Ambassador: U Aye Thein.

NEPAL

Embassy: 9 Sharia Tiba, Cairo (Dokki); tel (2) 704447.
Ambassador: Krishna Bahadur Monandhar.

NETHERLANDS

Embassy: 18 Sharia Hassan Sabri, Cairo (Zamalek); tel (2) 3406434; telex 2028; fax (2) 3415249.
Ambassador: L. J. Hanrath.

NIGER

Embassy: 28 Sharia Pahlaw, Cairo (Dokki); tel (2) 987740; telex 2880.
Ambassador: Sory Mamadou Diallo.

NIGERIA

Embassy: 13 Sharia Gabalaya, Cairo (Zamalek); tel (2) 3406042; telex 92038.
Ambassador: Mustafa Sam.

NORWAY

Embassy: 8 Sharia el-Gezireh, Cairo (Zamalek); tel (2) 3403340; telex 92259; fax (2) 3420709.
Ambassador: Knut Morkved.

OMAN

Embassy: 30 Sharia el-Montazah, Cairo (Zamalek); tel (2) 3407811; telex 92272.
Ambassador: Ghaleb Abdullah Joubran.

PAKISTAN

Embassy: 8 Sharia el-Salouli, Cairo (Dokki); tel (2) 3487677; fax (2) 3480310.
Ambassador: Gul Haneef.

PANAMA

Embassy: 5 Shagaret el-Dorr St, Cairo (Zamalek); tel (2) 3411093; telex 92776; fax (2) 3411092.
Chargé d'affaires a.i.: Dr E. Monterrey.

PERU

Embassy: 8 Sharia Kamel el-Shenawi, Cairo (Garden City); tel (2) 3562973; telex 93663; fax (2) 3557985.
Ambassador: Claudio Enrique Sosa V.
Minister: Alberto Tamayo B.
Third Secretary and Head of Consular Section: Cesar Salinas O.

Consulate: 7 Sharia Saint Saba, Alexandria; tel (3) 4832843; telex 54795; fax (3) 4832198.
Honorary Consul: Basil Marco.

PHILIPPINES

Embassy: 5 Sharia Ibn el-Walid, Cairo (Dokki); tel (2) 3480393; telex 92446.
Ambassador: Kasan A. Marohombsar.

POLAND

Embassy: 5 Sharia el-Aziz Osman, Cairo (Zamalek); tel (2) 3417456.
Ambassador: Roman Czyzycki.

PORTUGAL

Embassy: 15A Sharia Mansour Muhammad, Cairo (Zamalek); tel (2) 3405583; telex 20325.
Ambassador: José de Mattos-Parreira.

QATAR

Embassy: 10 Sharia ath-Thamar, Midan an-Nasr, Madinet al-Mohandessin, Cairo; tel (2) 704537; telex 92287.

ROMANIA

Embassy: 6 Sharia Kamel Muhammad, Cairo (Zamalek); tel (2) 3409546; telex 93807.
Ambassador: Ion Cozma.

RUSSIA

Embassy: Sharia Sad al-Asman, Cairo (Giza); tel (2) 3489356.
Ambassador: Vladimir Polyakov.

Consulate-General: Sharia Tag al-Rusa 9, Alexandria; tel (3) 5873534.

Consulate-General: Abdel Salem, Port Said; tel (66) 225628.

RWANDA

Embassy: 9 Sharia Ibrahim Osman, Mohandessin, POB 485, Cairo; tel (2) 3413224; telex 92552; fax (2) 3461079.
Ambassador: Célestin Kabanda.
Second Counsellor: Antoine Habiyaremye.
Second Secretary: Jean-Baptiste Zikamabahali.

SAUDI ARABIA

Embassy: 12 Sharia al-Kamel Muhammad, Cairo (Zamalek); tel (2) 819111.
Ambassador: M. Jalloh.

SENEGAL

Embassy: 46 Sharia Abd al-Moneim Riad, Mohandessin, Cairo (Dokki); tel (2) 3458479; telex 92047.
Ambassador: Shams ed-Dine Ndoye.

SIERRA LEONE

Interests Section: c/o Embassy of Saudi Arabia, 12 Sharia al-Kamel Muhammad, Cairo (Zamalek); tel (2) 819111.

SINGAPORE

Embassy: POB 356, 40 Sharia Babel, Cairo (Dokki); tel (2) 704744; telex 21353.
Ambassador: Tan Keng Jin.

SOMALIA

Embassy: 38 Sharia esh-Shahid Abd el-Moneim Riad, Cairo (Dokki); tel (2) 704038.
Ambassador: Hussein Hassan Fareh.

SPAIN

Embassy: 9 Hod el-Laban, Cairo (Garden City); tel (2) 3547069; telex 92255.
Ambassador: Carlos Fernández-Longoria.

SRI LANKA

Embassy: POB 1157, 8 Sharia Sri Lanka, Cairo (Zamalek); tel (2) 3400047; telex 23375.
Ambassador: Ronnie Weerakoon.
Minister-Counsellor (Commercial): Asoka Gnanapala Dharmawardhane.

Second Secretary: Karunatilaka Amunugama.
Attaché: Don Bernard Kalidasa Withanage.

SUDAN

Embassy: 4 Sharia el-Ibrahimi, Cairo (Garden City); tel (2) 3549661.
Ambassador: al-Amin Abd al-Latif.

SWEDEN

Embassy: 13 Sharia Muhammad Mazhar, POB 131, 11212 Cairo (Zamalek); tel (2) 3414132; telex 92256; fax (2) 3404357.
Ambassador: Jan Ståhl.
Counsellor: Stig Elvemar.
Second Secretary: Lisbeth Ekelöf.
Second Secretary: Magnus Hellgren.

Consulate: 57 Sharia 26th of July, POB 1261, Alexandria; tel (3) 4833855; telex 55577.
Vice-Consul: Maryse Pauline Khalil.

Consulate: 30 Sharia Sultan Hussein, 4th Floor, POB 539, Port Said; tel (66) 227514; telex 63174.

Consulate: 11 Sharia Saad Zagloul, Suez; tel (62) 225667.
Consul: Mahmoud Ali Gomaa Fattouh.

SWITZERLAND

Embassy: 10 Sharia Abd al-Khalek Saroit, POB 633, Cairo; tel (2) 758133; telex 92267; fax (2) 745236.
Ambassador: Ernst Thurnheer.
Counsellor: Adrien Evequez.
Defence Attaché: Jürg Fivaz.
Second Secretary: Martin Aeschbacher.
Head of Chancery: Bruno Schmid.

SYRIA

Embassy: 14 Ahmad Hechmar St, Cairo (Zamalek).

TANZANIA

Embassy: 9 Sharia Abd al-Hamid Lotfi, Cairo (Dokki); tel (2) 704155; telex 23537.
Ambassador: Muhammad A. Foum.

THAILAND

Embassy: 2 Sharia al-Malek el-Afdal, Cairo (Zamalek); tel (2) 3408356; telex 94231.
Ambassador: Chamras Chombhubol.

TUNISIA

Embassy: 26 Sharia el-Jazirah, Cairo (Zamalek); tel (2) 3404940.
Ambassador: Mahmoud Mestiri.

TURKEY

Embassy: ave en-Nil, Cairo (Giza); tel (2) 726115.
Ambassador: Berduk Olgaçay.

UGANDA

Embassy: 9 Midan el-Messaha, Cairo (Dokki); tel (2) 3485544; telex 92087.
Ambassador: Daudi M. Taliwaku.

UNITED ARAB EMIRATES

Interests Section: c/o Embassy of Turkey, 4 Sharia ibn Sina, al-Gezira, Cairo; tel (2) 729955.

UNITED KINGDOM

Embassy: Sharia Ahmad Raghab, Cairo (Garden City); tel (2) 3540852; telex 94188; fax (2) 3540859.
Ambassador: Sir James Adams.
Counsellor and Deputy Head of Mission: A. F. Goulty.
Counsellor (Commercial): A. P. Ceurvorst.
Counsellor: D. T. Handley.
Defence and Military Attaché: Col E. A. J. Gardener.
Naval Attaché: Commdr M. Maddox.
Air Attaché: Wing Cmdr B. C. Hunt.
Attaché (Culture) and British Council Director: J. J. Barnett.
First Secretary and Head of Political Section: A. Aitken.
First Secretary: J. M. J. Darke.
First Secretary and Consul: A. M. M. Sheldon.
First Secretary (Arab League): A. A. S. Lines.
First Secretary (Management): S. N. Lee.
First Secretary (Culture): Dr D. J. F. Burton.
Second Secretary (Commercial/Aid): H. Lattin-Rawstrone.
Second Secretary (Chancery/Information): J. L. Sharp.
Second Secretary (Technical): J. Ritchie.
Second Secretary (Culture): D. Codling.
Third Secretary (Economic/Aid): G. Briggs.
Deputy Management Officer and Claims Attaché: A. T. Holmes.

Consulate-General: 3 Mina St, Kafre Abdou, Roushdi, Alexandria 21529; tel (3) 5467001; telex 54578; fax (3) 5467177.
Consul-General: M. J. Copson.
Consul (Culture): D. K. E. Scott.

Consulate: 1 Nile St, Luxor; tel (95) 382374; telex 23604.
Honorary Consular Agent: M. H. Y. el Haggagy.

Consulate: HS Supply Co., 9 el-Galaa St, Suez; tel (62) 220145; telex 66112.
Honorary Consul: Dr Hussein Samir.

Consulate: Hilton Compound Complex, 6 Room 623, Port Said; tel (66) 231155; telex 63400.
Honorary Consul: Fathi Atout.

USA

Embassy: Lazougi St, Cairo (Garden City); tel (2) 3557371; telex 93773; fax (2) 3357375.
Ambassador: Frank G. Wisner.
Deputy Head of Mission: Wesley W. Egan, Jr.
Political Office: Stanley T. Escadero.
Economic Office: G. Paul Balabanis.
Commercial Section: Norman D. Glick.
Labour Officer: Gina Abercrombie-Winstanley.
Agricultural Section: Frank D. Lee.
Administrative Section: James McGunnigle.
Regional Security Officer: Peter Bergin.
Agency for International Development: Marshall D. Brown.
Public Affairs Officer: Kenton Keith.
Office of the Defence Attaché: Col David L. Lemon.
Office of Military Co-operation: Maj. William A. Fitzgerald, Jr.
Communications Programme Officer: Joseph Devlin.
Information Systems Manager: Alec M. Peltier.

Consulate-General: 110 ave Horreya, Alexandria; tel (3) 4821911; fax (3) 4838830.
Consul-General: Robert M. Maxim.
Consular and Political Sections: Jonathan Fishbein.
Administrative Section: Jeffrey D. Levine.
Branch Public Affairs Officer: Anne O'Leary.
Agency for International Development: Judi A. Shane.
Communications Programme Officer: Glenn T. Jones.

URUGUAY

Embassy: 6 Sharia Lotfallah, Cairo (Zamalek); tel (2) 3415137; telex 92435.
Ambassador: Ramiro Piriz Ballón.

VENEZUELA

Embassy: 15A Sharia Mansour Muhammad, Cairo (Zamalek); tel (2) 3413517; telex 93638.
Ambassador: Dr José A. Martínez-Ramírez.
Minister-Counsellor: Miguel Raidi Raidi.

VIET-NAM

Embassy: 47 Sharia Ahmad Hishmat, Cairo (Zamalek); tel (2) 3402401.
Ambassador: Vu Bach Mai.

YEMEN

Embassy: Cairo.

YUGOSLAVIA

Embassy: 33 Sharia Mansour Muhammad, Cairo (Zamalek); tel (2) 3404061; telex 21046.
Ambassador: Dr Ivan Iveković.

ZAIRE

Embassy: 5 Sharia Mansour Muhammad, Cairo (Zamalek); tel (2) 3403662; telex 92294.
Ambassador: Ngandu Mwalba.

ZAMBIA

Embassy: POB 253, 10 Gomhouriya Mutahada Sq., Madinet el-Mohandessin, Cairo; tel (2) 3610282; telex 92262; fax (2) 3610833.
Ambassador: Kalenga Kangwa.

International Organizations

EUROPEAN COMMUNITIES

External Delegation: 6 Ibn Zanki St, Zamalek, Cairo; tel (2) 3419393; telex 94258; fax (2) 3400385.
Head of Delegation: Francine Henrich.

EL SALVADOR

ARGENTINA

Embassy: 79 Avda Norte 704, Colonia Escalón, Apdo 01-384, San Salvador; tel 24-4238; telex 20221.
Ambassador: Juan Carlos Ibáñez.

AUSTRIA

Consulate-General: Alameda Deininger, Antiguo Cuscatían, Apdo 167, San Salvador; tel 23-8993.
Honorary Consul-General: Ehrentraud Katstaller-Schott.

BRAZIL

Embassy: Edif. la Centroamericana, 5°, Alameda Roosevelt 3107, San Salvador; tel 23-1214; telex 20096.
Ambassador: Mario Loureiro Dias Costa.

CANADA

Consulate: 111 Avda Las Palmas, Apdo 3078, Colonia San Benito, San Salvador; tel 74-4993.
Honorary Consul: J. D. Hunter.

CHILE

Embassy: Pasaje Belle Vista 121, Entre 9a C.P. y 9a C.P. bis, Colonia Escalón, San Salvador; tel 23-7132; telex 20377; fax 23-4751.
Ambassador: Pedro Alfonso Medrano Rojas.
Consul and Third Secretary: Christian von Loebenstein.
Honorary Consul: Yolanda Baños Breucop.

CHINA (TAIWAN)

Embassy: 89a Avda Norte 335, Colonia Escalón, San Salvador; tel 23-6920; telex 20152.
Ambassador: Gen. Lo Yu-Lum.

COLOMBIA

Embassy: Edif. Inter-Capital, 2°, Paseo General Escalón y Calle La Ceiba, Colonia Escalón, San Salvador; tel 23-0126; telex 20247.
Ambassador: Dr Luis Guillermo Vélez Trujillo.

COSTA RICA

Embassy: Edif. La Centroamericana, 3°, Alameda Roosevelt 3107, San Salvador; tel 23-8283; telex 20171.
Ambassador: Jesús M. Fernández.

DENMARK

Consulate-General: Apdo 01-43, San Salvador; tel 206-9519; telex 20359; fax 23-4137.
Consul-General: René Valiente Vides.

DOMINICAN REPUBLIC

Embassy: San Salvador; tel 23-6636.
Ambassador: Alberto Emilio Despradel Cabral.

ECUADOR

Embassy: Blvd Hipódromo 803, Colonia San Benito, San Salvador; tel 24-5921; telex 20445.
Ambassador: Jaime Sánchez Lemos.

FINLAND

Consulate: Edif. Las Américas, 2°, 203-A, Blvd Tutunichapa y Avda Las Américas, Apdo 06-383, San Salvador; tel 26-3335; fax 23-9276.
Vice-Consul: Manuel Salvador del Valle Menéndez.

FRANCE

Embassy: Pasaje A 41-46, Colonia La Mascota, Casilla 474, San Salvador; tel 23-0728; telex 20243.
Ambassador: Gaston le Paudert.

GERMANY

Embassy: 3a Calle Poniente 3831, Colonia Escalón, Apdo 693, San Salvador; tel 23-6140; telex 20149; fax 23-6173.
Ambassador: Guido Heymer.

GUATEMALA

Embassy: 15 Avda Norte 135, San Salvador; tel 21-6097.
Ambassador: Brig.-Gen. Luis Federico Fuentes Corado.

HOLY SEE

Apostolic Nunciature: 87a Avda Norte y 7a Calle Poniente, Colonia Escalón, Apdo 01-95, San Salvador; tel 23-2454; fax 23-7607.
Apostolic Nuncio: Most Rev. Francesco de Nittis, Titular Archbishop of Tunis.
First Secretary: Peter Gerard.

HONDURAS

Embassy: 7a Calle Poniente 4326, Colonia Escalón, San Salvador; tel 98-0524; fax 79-0545.
Ambassador: Francisco Zepeda.
Minister-Counsellor: Miguel A. Erazo.
Defence Attaché: Cesar Zelaya.
First Consul: Reinery David Amador.

IRELAND

Consulate: Quinonez Hermanos SSAP (01), Carr. Panamericana 3525, Colonia Roma, San Salvador; tel 23-1111; telex 20182.
Honorary Consul: Brian L. Coughlin Q.

ISRAEL

Embassy: 85 Avda Norte 619, Colonia Escalón, Apdo 1776, San Salvador; tel 23-8770; telex 20777.
Ambassador: Aryeh Amir.

ITALY

Embassy: Blvd del Hipódromo 330 y Avda La Capilla 1, Colonia San Benito, San Salvador; tel 23-7325; telex 20418.
Ambassador: Dr Arrigo López Celly.

JAPAN

Embassy: Avda La Capilla 615, Colonia San Benito, San Salvador; tel 24-4597; telex 20099; fax 24-4597.
Chargé d'affaires a.i.: Chusaku Nomura.

MEXICO

Embassy: Paseo General Escalón 3832, San Salvador; tel 98-1084; telex 20070; fax 98-1178.
Ambassador: Hermilio López-Bassols.

NICARAGUA

Embassy: 71a Avda Norte y 1a, Calle Poniente 164, Colonia Escalón, San Salvador; tel 23-7729; telex 20546; fax 23-7201.
Ambassador: Luis G. Cardenal A.
Minister-Counsellor and Consul-General: Roger Aviles Icaza.
Counsellor: Lilliam Roman de González.
Counsellor: Martha Salinas de Cardenal.
First Secretary: Lincoln Escobar Reyes.
Cultural Attaché: Manuel J. Aguilar Trujillo.

PANAMA

Embassy: Edif. Balam Quitzé 68-1, Calle Circunvalación y 89a Avda Sur, Colonia Escalón, San Salvador; tel 23-7893.

PARAGUAY

Embassy: Avda La Capilla 414, Colonia San Benito, San Salvador; tel 23-5951.
Ambassador: Juan Alberto Llánez.

PERU

Embassy: Edif. La Centroamericana, 2°, Alameda Roosevelt 3107, Apdo 1620, San Salvador; tel 23-0008; telex 20791; fax 23-5672.
Ambassador: Dr Max de la Fuente Prem.
Minister-Counsellor: Carlos González Elías.
Civil Attaché and Head of Consular Section: Pedro Mayta Rodríguez.

SOMALIA

Interests Section: c/o Embassy of Italy, Blvd del Hipódromo 330 y Avda La Capilla 1, Colonia San Benito, San Salvador; tel 23-7325; telex 20418.

SPAIN

Embassy: 51 Avda Norte 138, San Salvador; tel 23-7961; telex 20372.
Ambassador: Francisco Cádiz.

SWEDEN

Consulate-General: Blvd Tutunichapa y Avda Las Américas, Local 201 B, Apdo 856, San Salvador; tel 25-3144.
Consul-General: Oscar Lacayo Rosales.

UNITED KINGDOM

Embassy: Edif. Inter Inversión, Paseo General Escalón 4828, Apdo 1591, San Salvador; tel 23-9047; telex 20033; fax 23-5817.
Chargé d'affaires a.i., First Secretary and Consul: I. R. Murray.
Third Secretary and Vice-Consul: D. J. B. Torrence.

Consulate: Apdo 242, San Salvador; tel 71-1026; telex 20174.
Honorary Consul: W. H. J. Chippendale.

USA

Embassy: 25 Avda Norte 1230, San Salvador; tel 26-7100; telex 20648; fax 26-5839.
Ambassador: William G. Walker.
Deputy Head of Mission: William J. Dieterich.
Political Section: Phillip T. Chicola.
Economic and Commercial Sections: Richard M. Bash.

Labour Officer: Kevin M. Johnson.
Administrative Section: Guido A. Del Prado.
Regional Security Officer: James F. Bermingham.
Agency for International Development: Henry H. Bassford.
Public Affairs Officer: Pamela Corey-Archer.
Office of the Defence Attaché: Col George Utter.
Military Group: Col Mark Hamilton.
Communications Programme Officer: Richard L. Gunn.
Information Systems Officer: Heywood Miller.

URUGUAY

Embassy: Edif. Intercapital, 1°, Calle La Ceiba y Paseo General Escalón, San Salvador; tel 24-6661; telex 20391.
Ambassador: Alfredo Lafone.

VENEZUELA

Embassy: 93 Avda Norte 619, Colonia Escalón, San Salvador; tel 23-5809; telex 20388; fax 23-0925.
Ambassador: Luis Rodriguez M.
Minister-Counsellor: Elba Luna Cisneros.
Second Secretary: Gilberto Ramon Plaza Moreno.

EQUATORIAL GUINEA

CAMEROON

Embassy: BP 292, Malabo; tel 22-63; telex 1111.
Ambassador: John Nchotu Akum.

CHINA, PEOPLE'S REPUBLIC

Embassy: Malabo.
Ambassador: Dai Shiqi.

CUBA

Embassy: Malabo.

FRANCE

Embassy: Carreterra del Aeropuerto, Malabo; tel 20-05.
Ambassador: Jacques Gazon.

GABON

Embassy: Apdo 648, Douala, Malabo; tel 420; telex 1125.
Ambassador: Jean Baptiste Mbatchi.

KOREA, DEMOCRATIC PEOPLE'S REPUBLIC

Embassy: Malabo.
Ambassador: Chi Yong-Ho.

NIGERIA

Embassy: 4 Paseo de los Cocoteros, Apdo 78, Malabo; tel 23-86.
Ambassador: John Shinkame.

RUSSIA

Embassy: Calle Acacio Mane 3, Malabo; tel 32-22.
Ambassador: Lev Aleksandrovich Vakhramayev.

SPAIN

Embassy: Malabo.
Ambassador: Manuel Alabart Fernández Cabada.

SWEDEN

Embassy: Malabo.
Ambassador: Bengt Rösiö (resident in Sweden).

UNITED KINGDOM

Consulate: World Bank Compound, Apdo 801, Malabo; tel 24-00; telex 913103.

USA

Embassy: Calle de Los Ministros, POB 597, Malabo; tel 24-06.
Chargé d'affaires a.i.: William Mithoefer, Jr.
Political and Economic Sections: Edgar Embrey.
Administrative and Consular Sections: Nathan M. Bluhm.
Communications Programme Officer: Josh J. Hromatka.

International Organizations

EUROPEAN COMMUNITIES

External Delegation: Apdo 779, Malabo; tel 29-44; telex 5402.
Commission Delegate: Roger Leenders.

ESTONIA

CANADA

Embassy: Tolli 3, Tallinn 200001; tel (0142) 31-08-76.
Ambassador: Peter Roose.

DENMARK

Embassy: Vana-Viru 4, Tallinn 200100; tel (0142) 44-47-61; telex 173134; fax (0142) 60-12-47.
Ambassador: Sven Nordberg.
Secretary: Silvi Teesalu.

FINLAND

Embassy: Liivalaia 12, Tallinn 200001; tel (0142) 44-95-22; telex 173186; fax (0142) 446-392.
Ambassador: Jaakko Kaurinkoski.

FRANCE

Embassy: c/o Hotel Palace, Vabaduse väljak 3, Tallinn 200001; tel (0142) 44-47-61.
Ambassador: Jacques Huntzinger.

GERMANY

Embassy: Rävala 9, Tallinn 200100; tel (0142) 69-14-72.
Ambassador: Henning von Wistinghausen.

ITALY

Embassy: c/o Hotel Palace, Vabaduse väljak 3, Tallinn 200001; tel (0142) 44-47-61.
Ambassador: Carlo Siano.

LATVIA

Embassy: Tõnismägi 10, Tallinn; tel (0142) 68-16-68.
Ambassador: Aldis Beržinš.

LITHUANIA

Embassy: Vabaduse väljak 10, Tallinn 200001; tel (0142) 44-89-17.
Ambassador: Sigitas Kudarauskas.

NORWAY

Embassy: c/o Hotel Palace, Vabaduse väljak 3, Tallinn 200001; tel (0142) 44-47-61.
Ambassador: Brit Løvseth.

RUSSIA

Embassy: Pikk 19, Tallinn; tel (0142) 71-83-94.
Ambassador: Artur Kuznetsov.

SWEDEN

Embassy: Endla 4a, Tallinn 200001; tel (0142) 45-03-50; telex 173124; fax (0142) 45-06-76.
Ambassador: Lars Arne Grundberg.

UNITED KINGDOM

Embassy: c/o Hotel Palace, Vabaduse väljak 3, Tallinn 200001; tel (0142) 44-47-61.
Ambassador: Brian Buik Low.

USA

Embassy: c/o Hotel Palace, Rm 507, Vabaduse väljak 3, Tallinn 200001; tel (0142) 44-47-61.
Ambassador: Robert C. Frasure.

ETHIOPIA

ALGERIA

Embassy: POB 5740, Addis Ababa; tel (1) 441334; telex 21302.
Ambassador: Hocine Mesloub.

ARGENTINA

Embassy: Addis Ababa; telex 21172.
Ambassador: Dr H. R. M. Mogues.

AUSTRALIA

Embassy: POB 5798, Addis Ababa; tel (1) 114500; telex 21488.
Ambassador: J. P. C. Sheppard.

AUSTRIA

Embassy: Old Airport Area, POB 1219, Addis Ababa; tel (1) 712144; telex 21060.
Ambassador: Dr Horst-Dieter Rennau.
Secretary (Economic): Monika Mag Stanek.

BELGIUM

Embassy: Fikre Mariam St, Higher 16, Kebele, POB 1239, Addis Ababa; tel (1) 611643; telex 21157.
Ambassador: Michel Carlier.
First Secretary: Gunther Sleeuwagen.

BULGARIA

Embassy: Jomo Kenyatta St, H-17, K-13, POB 987, Addis Ababa; tel (1) 610032; telex 21450.
Ambassador: Boris Ivanov Pavlov.
Counsellor (Commercial): Svetoslav Dinishev.
Second Secretary (Political/Consular/Cultural): Vladimir Ratchev Moutafov.
Attaché (Administrative): Valentin Nikolov.

BURUNDI

Embassy: POB 3641, Addis Ababa; tel (1) 651300; telex 21069.
Ambassador: Tharcisse Midonzi.
Second Counsellor: Egide Ndikuriyo.
First Secretary: Barnabé Bugera.
Attaché: Marie-Claire Nahimana.

CAMEROON

Embassy: Bole Rd, POB 1026, Addis Ababa; telex 21121.
Ambassador: Dominique Yong.

CANADA

Embassy: 6th Floor, African Solidarity Insurance Bldg, Churchill Ave, POB 1130, Addis Ababa; tel (1) 511319; telex 21053; fax (1) 512818.
Ambassador: Francis M. Filleul.
Counsellor and Consul: F. E. K. Chandler.
Counsellor (Development) and Consul: F. Stapenhurst.
First Secretary (Development): M. Florida.
First Secretary (Development) and Consul: Y. Banks.

CHAD

Embassy: Addis Ababa; telex 21419; fax (1) 612050.
Ambassador: J. B. Laokole.

CHINA, PEOPLE'S REPUBLIC

Embassy: POB 5643, Addis Ababa; telex 21145.
Ambassador: Gu Jiaji.

CONGO

Embassy: POB 5571, Addis Ababa; tel (1) 154331; telex 21406.
Ambassador: C. Stanislas Batheas-Mollomb.

COTE D'IVOIRE

Embassy: POB 3668, Addis Ababa; tel (1) 711213; telex 21061.
Ambassador: Antoine Kouadio-Kirine.
First Counsellor: James Badou.
Second Counsellor: Yao Koffi Gaston.
First Secretary: Pierre Nemlin Guirobo.
Second Secretary (Consular): N'da Koussan.
Second Secretary (Administrative/Financial): Gahou Teti.

CUBA

Embassy: Jimma Rd Ave, POB 5623, Addis Ababa; tel (1) 202010; telex 21306.
Ambassador: Antonio Pérez Herrero.

CZECHOSLOVAKIA

Embassy: POB 3108, Addis Ababa; tel (1) 516382; telex 21021.
Ambassador: Dušan Rovensky.

DJIBOUTI

Embassy: POB 1022, Addis Ababa; tel (1) 183200; telex 21317.
Chargé d'affaires: Djibril Djama Elabe.

EGYPT

Embassy: POB 1611, Addis Ababa; tel (1) 113077; telex 21254.
Ambassador: Samir Ahmed.

EQUATORIAL GUINEA

Embassy: POB 246, Addis Ababa.
Ambassador: Salvador Ela Nseng Abegue.

FINLAND

Embassy: Tedla Desta Bldg, Bole Rd, POB 1017, Addis Ababa; tel (1) 513854; telex 21259; fax (1) 513900.
Chargé d'affaires a.i.: Erik Brehmer.

FRANCE

Embassy: Kabana, POB 1464, Addis Ababa; tel (1) 550066; telex 21040; fax (1) 551793.
Ambassador: Gérald Pavret de la Rochefordière.
Second Counsellor: René Revoltier.
Counsellor (Culture): Joël Mahe.
Defence Attaché: Col Troadec.
First Secretary: Alain Le Seac'h.
Vice-Consul and Head of Chancery: Jean-Claude Olivie.
Attaché (Commercial): René Cochard.
Attaché (Co-operation): André Maximin.

GABON

Embassy: POB 1256, Addis Ababa; tel (1) 181075; telex 21208.
Ambassador: Denis Dangue Rewaka.

GERMANY

Embassy: Kabana, POB 660-1267, Addis Ababa; tel (1) 550433; telex 21015; fax (1) 551311.
Ambassador: Dr Kurt Stöckl.

GHANA

Embassy: POB 3173, Addis Ababa; tel (1) 711402; telex 21249.
Ambassador: Boniface Kwame Atepor.

GREECE

Embassy: Africa Ave, POB 1168, Addis Ababa; tel (1) 110612; telex 21092.
Chargé d'affaires: M. Diamantopoulos.

GUINEA

Embassy: POB 1190, Addis Ababa; tel (1) 449712.
Ambassador: Pierre Bassamba Camara.

HOLY SEE

Apostolic Nunciature: Makanissa Rd, POB 588, Addis Ababa; tel (1) 712100; telex 21815.
Apostolic Pro-Nuncio: Most Rev. Patrick Coveney, Titular Archbishop of Satriano.
First Secretary: Rev. Mgr Paul Tschang.

HUNGARY

Embassy: Abattoirs Rd, POB 1213, Addis Ababa; tel (1) 651850; telex 21176.
Ambassador: Dr Sándor Róbel.

INDIA

Embassy: Kabana, POB 528, Addis Ababa; tel (1) 552100; telex 21148; fax (1) 552521.
Ambassador: K. P. Balakrishnan.

INDONESIA

Embassy: Mekanisa Rd Higher 23, Kebele 13, House 1816, POB 1004, Addis Ababa; tel (1) 202104; telex 21264.
Ambassador: T. M. Mochtar Mohamad Thajeb.

IRAN

Embassy: 317/02 Jimma Rd, Old Airport Area, POB 1144, Addis Ababa; tel (1) 200369; telex 21118.
Chargé d'affaires: Hassen Dabir.

ISRAEL

Embassy: New Tafari Makonnen School, POB 1075, Addis Ababa.
Chargé d'affaires: Meir Yafe.

ITALY

Embassy: Villa Italia, POB 1105, Addis Ababa; tel (1) 551565; telex 42312; fax (1) 550218.
Ambassador: Sergio Angeletti.

Commercial Section: tel (1) 550120.
Counsellor and Head of Commercial Section: Pasquale D'Avino.

Consular Section: tel (1) 551212.
Second Secretary and Head of Consular Section: Arturo Luzzi.

Cultural Section: Italian Cultural Institute, POB 1635, Addis Ababa; tel (1) 552670.
Head of Cultural Section: Prof. Nadir Morosi.

JAMAICA

Embassy: National House, Africa Ave, POB 5633, Addis Ababa; tel (1) 613656; telex 21137.

Ambassador: Owen A. Singh.

JAPAN

Embassy: Finfinne Bldg, 2nd Floor, Revolution Sq., POB 5650, Addis Ababa; tel (1) 448215; telex 21108; fax (1) 511350.
Ambassador: Chuichio Ito.

KENYA

Embassy: Fikre Mariam Rd, POB 3301, Addis Ababa; tel (1) 610303; telex 21103.
Ambassador: Mude Dae Mude.

KOREA, DEMOCRATIC PEOPLE'S REPUBLIC

Embassy: POB 2378, Addis Ababa.
Ambassador: Sok Tae Uk.

KOREA, REPUBLIC

Embassy: Jimma Rd, Old Airport Area, POB 2047, Addis Ababa; tel (1) 444490; telex 21140.
Ambassador: Deuk Po Kim.

LIBERIA

Embassy: POB 3116, Addis Ababa; tel (1) 513655; telex 21083.
Ambassador: Thomas C. T. Bestman.
Counsellor: David J. Saryee, Jr.
First Secretary and Consul: Genevieve A. Kennedy.

LIBYA

Embassy: POB 5728, Addis Ababa; telex 21214.
Secretary of People's Bureau: K. Bazelya.

MALAWI

Embassy: POB 2316, Addis Ababa; tel (1) 44829536; telex 21087.
Ambassador: D. P. W. Kachikuwo.

MEXICO

Embassy: Tsige Mariam Bldg 292/21, 4th Floor, Churchill Rd, POB 2962, Addis Ababa; tel (1) 443456; telex 21141.
Ambassador: Carlos Ferrer.

MOZAMBIQUE

Embassy: Addis Ababa; telex 21008.
Ambassador: Alberto Sithole.

NETHERLANDS

Embassy: Old Airport Area, POB 1241, Addis Ababa; tel (1) 711100; telex 21049.
Ambassador: A. Heldring.

NIGER

Embassy: POB 5791, Addis Ababa; tel (1) 161175; telex 21284.
Ambassador: Abdourahamane Hama.

NIGERIA

Embassy: POB 1019, Addis Ababa; tel (1) 550644; telex 21028.
Ambassador: Segun Olusola.
Senior Counsellor: B. K. Alabi.
Counsellor and Head of Chancery: B. A. Banjoko.
First Secretary: I. D. Faransi.
Finance Attaché: P. A. Ogundele.
Information Attaché and Head of Information Service Centre: D. T. Orjiako.

POLAND

Embassy: Bole Rd, POB 1123, Addis Ababa; tel (1) 610068; telex 21185.
Ambassador: Tadeusz Wujek.
Counsellor: Kazimierz Kurowski.
Counsellor (Commercial): Boguslow Kamola.
Attaché: Ryszard Zuchowski.

ROMANIA

Embassy: Africa Ave, POB 2478, Addis Ababa; tel (1) 610156; telex 21168.
Ambassador: Ion Mirescu.
Second Secretary (Economic): Traian Popescu.

RUSSIA

Embassy: POB 1500, Higher 16, Kebele 01, Addis Ababa; tel (1) 21404; telex 21534; fax (1) 613795.
Ambassador: Lev D. Mironov.
Minister-Counsellor: Yuri Merzliakov.
Minister-Counsellor (Economic Affairs): Boris Andrianov.
Military Attaché: Col Valery Diomin.
Trade Representative: Vatter Zinovkin.
Head of Protocol: Dmitry Suslov.
Consular Section: tel (1) 612054.
First Secretary and Head of Consular Section: Ivan Isachenko.

RWANDA

Embassy: Africa House, Higher 17 Kebele 20, POB 5618, Addis Ababa; tel (1) 610300; telex 21199; fax (1) 610411.
Ambassador: Jean-Marie Vianney Ndagijimana.

SAUDI ARABIA

Embassy: Old Airport Area, POB 1104, Addis Ababa; tel (1) 448010; telex 21194.
Chargé d'affaires: Hassan M. Attar.

SENEGAL

Embassy: Africa Ave, POB 2581, Addis Ababa; tel (1) 611376; telex 21027.
Ambassador: Papa Louis Fall.

SIERRA LEONE

Embassy: Old Airport (Jimma) Rd, POB 5619, Addis Ababa; tel (1) 710033; telex 21144.
Ambassador: Abdul Gadrie Koroma.
Counsellor and Head of Chancery: William Sebana Bangura.

SOMALIA

Embassy: Addis Ababa.
Ambassador: Abrahim Haji Nur.

SPAIN

Embassy: Entoto St, POB 2312, Addis Ababa; tel (1) 550222; telex 21107.
Ambassador: A. Martínez-Morcillo.

SUDAN

Embassy: Kirkos, Kabele, POB 1110, Addis Ababa; tel (1) 21293.
Ambassador: Uthman Adam.

SWEDEN

Embassy: Ras Tesemma Sefer, POB 1029, Addis Ababa; tel (1) 516699; telex 21039; fax (1) 515830.
Ambassador: Birgitta Karlström-Dorph.
Counsellor: Fredrik Schiller.
Second Secretary: Ulla Baudin.
Head of Aid: Karl-Gunnar Hagström.

SWITZERLAND

Embassy: Jimma Rd, Old Airport Area, POB 1106, Addis Ababa; tel (1) 710577; telex 21123.
Ambassador: Gaudenz B. Ruf.
First Secretary and Office Manager: Peter Hof.

TANZANIA

Embassy: POB 1077, Addis Ababa; tel (1) 441064; telex 21268.
Ambassador: Fatuma Tatu Nuru.

TUNISIA

Embassy: Kesetegna 20, Kebele 39, POB 10069, Addis Ababa.
Ambassador: Mohamed Bachrouch.

TURKEY

Embassy: Africa Ave, POB 1506, Addis Ababa; tel (1) 612321; telex 21257; fax (1) 611688.
Ambassador: Erhan Öğüt.

UGANDA

Embassy: POB 5644, Addis Ababa; tel (1) 513088; telex 21143; fax (1) 514355.
Ambassador: Swaib Matumbwe Musoke.

UNITED KINGDOM

Embassy: Fikre Mariam Abatechan St, POB 858, Addis Ababa; tel (1) 612354; telex 21299; fax (1) 610588.
Ambassador: M. J. C. Glaze.
First Secretary and Deputy Head of Mission: J. C. W. Kidd.
First Secretary: A. J. Barber.
First Secretary (Commercial): S. Murphy.
Second Secretary (Management) and Consul: S. C. Blake.
Second Secretary (Development): C. E. Cooper.
Second Secretary (Chancery/Information): Caroline J. Barber.
Cultural Attaché (British Council Director): M. B. L. Nightingale.

USA

Embassy: Entoto St, POB 1014, Addis Ababa; tel (1) 550666; telex 21282; fax (1) 551166.
Chargé d'affaires a.i.: Robert G. Houdek.
Deputy Head of Mission: Joseph M. DeThomas.
Economic and Political Sections: Mark C. Eaton.
Political Section: L. Scott Harrison.
Administrative Section: Edward M. Alford.
Public Affairs Officer: James M. Haley.
Agency for International Development: Willard J. Pearson.
Regional Security Officer: Vance Witmer.
Communications Programme Officer: Thomas J. Zuraw.

VENEZUELA

Embassy: Dedre Zeit Rd, POB 5584, Addis Ababa; tel (1) 654790; telex 21102.
Chargé d'affaires: Alfredo Hernández-Rovati.

VIET-NAM

Embassy: POB 1288, Addis Ababa.
Ambassador: Nguyen Duy Kinh.

YEMEN

Embassy: POB 664, Addis Ababa; telex 21346.
Ambassador: Lieut-Col Hussein Mohasin al-Ghaffari.

YUGOSLAVIA

Embassy: Marshal Tito Ave, POB 1341, Addis Ababa; tel (1) 517804; telex 21233.
Ambassador: Igor Jovovic.
First Secretary: Ognen Maleski.

ZAIRE

Embassy: Makanisa Rd, POB 2723, Addis Ababa; tel (1) 204385; telex 21043.

Ambassador: Waku Yizila.

ZAMBIA

Embassy: POB 1909, Addis Ababa; tel (1) 711302; telex 21065.
Ambassador: Basil R. Kabwe.

ZIMBABWE

Embassy: POB 5624, Addis Ababa; tel (1) 183872; telex 21351.
Ambassador: Tichaona J. B. Jokonya.

International Organizations

EUROPEAN COMMUNITIES

External Delegation: Tedla Desta Bldg, 1st Floor, Africa Ave (Bole Rd), POB 5570, Addis Ababa; tel (1) 512511; telex 21135; fax (1) 514119.
Commission Delegate: Benno Haffner.

FIJI

AUSTRALIA

Embassy: Dominion House, POB 214, Suva; tel 312844; telex 2126; fax 300900.
Ambassador: Robert Cotton.

CANADA

Consulate: Suva.

CHINA, PEOPLE'S REPUBLIC

Embassy: 147 Queen Elizabeth Drive, Suva; tel 322425; telex 2136.
Ambassador: Xu Mingyuan.

DENMARK

Consulate: 7th Floor, Air Pacific House, Butt St, Suva; tel 315199; telex 2147; fax 313947.
Consul: Adam Dickson.

FINLAND

Consulate: Fiji's Employers' Consultative Association, POB 575, Suva; tel 25688; telex 2589.
Consul: Kenneth Adrian John Roberts.

FRANCE

Embassy: 1st Floor, Dominion House, Thomson St, Suva; tel 300991; telex 2326; fax 301925.
Ambassador: Henri Jacolin.

JAPAN

Embassy: 2nd Floor, Dominion House, POB 13045, 1 Suva; tel 302122; telex 2253; fax 301452.
Chargé d'affaires a.i.: Yasuo Takahashi.

KOREA, REPUBLIC

Embassy: 8th Floor, Vanua House, PMB, Suva; tel 311977; telex 2175.
Ambassador: Hyon Chin Kim.

MALAYSIA

Embassy: Air Pacific House, Suva; tel 312166; telex 2295; fax 303350.
Ambassador: Syed Ariff Fadzillah.

MARSHALL ISLANDS

Embassy: Suva.

MICRONESIA

Embassy: Suva.
Ambassador: Alik L. Alik.

NAURU

Consulate: Ratu Sukuna House, 7th Floor, McArthur St, Suva; tel 313566; fax 302861.
Consul: Ross Cain.

NEW ZEALAND

Embassy: 10th Floor, Reserve Bank of Fiji Bldg, POB 1378, Pratt St, Suva; tel 311422; telex 2161; fax 300842.
Ambassador: Brian William Peter Absolum.
Counsellor: Carl Robinson Worker.
Trade Commissioner: Ian Stanley Grooby.
First Secretary: Donald Grant Will.
First Secretary: Mark James Gibb.
First Secretary: Kerry Arthur Ridgway.

NORWAY

Consulate: POB 149, Suva; tel 314188; fax 302672.
Consul: Barrie Sweetman.

PAPUA NEW GUINEA

Embassy: 6th Floor, Ratu Sukuna House, POB 2447, Suva; tel 325420; telex 2113.
Ambassador: Maimu Raka-Nou.

SWEDEN

Consulate: Honson Bldg, 7th Floor, Thompson St, POB 575, Suva; tel 313188; telex 2589; fax 302183.
Consul: Kenneth Adrian John Roberts.

TUVALU

Embassy: 8 Mitchell St, POB 14449, Suva; tel 300697; telex 2297; fax 301023.
Ambassador: Saufatu Sopoanga.
First Secretary: Tine Leuelu.
Executive Officer (Accounts): Ioata Tauialia.

UNITED KINGDOM

Embassy: Victoria House, 47 Gladstone Rd, POB 1355, Suva; tel 311033; telex 2129; fax 301406.
Ambassador: A. B. Peter Smart.
First Secretary, Consul and Deputy Head of Mission: R. C. B. Jones.
Second Secretary (Aid): A. C. Hamilton-Walker.
Vice-Consul (Consular/Management): R. Hamilton.

USA

Embassy: 31 Loftus St, POB 218, Suva; tel 314466; telex 2255; fax 300081.
Ambassador: Evelyn I. H. Teegen.
Deputy Head of Mission: Michael P. Owens.
Political Section: Liam J. Humphreys.
Economic Section: Glen B. Miller.
Administrative Section: Craig S. Tymeson.
Agency for International Development: John B. Woods.
Public Affairs Officer: Judith A. Moon.
Office of Defence Attaché: Lieut Col Craig L. Mayer.
Communications Programme Officer: Herman H. Beckham II.

International Organizations

EUROPEAN COMMUNITIES

External Delegation: Dominion House, 3rd Floor, Private Mail Bag, GPO, Suva; tel 313633; telex 2311; fax 300370.
Commission Delegate: Nikolas Alexandrakis.

FINLAND

ARGENTINA

Embassy: Bulevardi 10A 14, 00120 Helsinki; tel (0) 607630; telex 122794.
Ambassador: Nereo Ignacio Melo Ferrer.

AUSTRIA

Embassy: Eteläesplanadi 18, 00130 Helsinki; tel (0) 171322; telex 121340; fax (0) 665084.
Ambassador: Manfred Ortner.
First Secretary: Helmut Bernhard Koller.
Second Secretary: Christine Kivinen.

Consulate-General: Erottajankatu 4C, 00120 Helsinki; tel (0) 604208.
Consul-General: Klaus Cederberg.

Consulate: Hämeenkatu 24, 33101 Tampere; (31) 192033; fax (31) 381642.
Consul: Sakari Haukka.

Consulate: Mallastie 7, 90520 Oulu; tel (81) 543919; fax (81) 543655.
Consul: Ilkka Lantto.

Consulate: Untamonkatu 2, 20520 Turku; tel (21) 603111; fax (21) 332734.
Consul: Heikki Sippolainen.

BELGIUM

Embassy: Kalliolinnantie 5, 00140 Helsinki; tel (0) 170412; telex 121390; fax (0) 628842.
Ambassador: Jacques Ivan d'Hondt.

BRAZIL

Embassy: Mariankatu 7A 3, 00170 Helsinki; tel (0) 177922.
Ambassador: Carlos Luzilde Hildebrandt.

BULGARIA

Embassy: Itäinen Puistotie 10, 00140 Helsinki; tel (0) 661707; fax (0) 663723.
Ambassador: Valeri Pchelintsev.
Counsellor (Commercial): Vladimir Zankov.
Second Secretary: Andrey Zhishev.
Second Secretary: Valentin Dobrev.
Attaché: Tchavdar Grigorov.

CANADA

Embassy: Pohjoisesplanadi 25B, POB 779, 00100 Helsinki 10; tel (0) 171141; telex 121363; fax (0) 601016.
Ambassador: Mary E. Vandenhoff.
Counsellor (Commercial) and Consul: C. C. Charland.
Second Secretary (Administrative) and Vice-Consul: J.-P. Laframboise.

CHILE

Embassy: Fredrikinkatu 16 A 22, 00120 Helsinki; tel (0) 631600; telex 122119; fax (0) 631505.
Ambassador: Lucio Parada Dagnino.
Second Secretary: Samuel Ossa.

Consulate-General: Eteläranta 4, 00130 Helsinki; tel (0) 134511; telex 124447; fax (0) 611684.
Honorary Consul-General: Harry B. Berner.
Honorary Consul: George Berner.

CHINA, PEOPLE'S REPUBLIC

Embassy: Vanha Kelkkamäki 9-11, 00570 Helsinki; tel (0) 6848371; fax (0) 6849551.
Ambassador: Yu Lixuan.

COLOMBIA

Embassy: Fredrikinkatu 61, 00100 Helsinki; tel (0) 6931255; telex 126210.
Ambassador: Nicolás Salom-Franco.

CUBA

Embassy: Paasivuorenkatu 3, 00530 Helsinki; tel (0) 766199; telex 121017.
Ambassador: Oscar Fernández Mell.

CYPRUS

Consulate-General: Vattuniemenkatu 10, 00210 Helsinki; tel (0) 673341; telex 122113; fax (0) 692-2369.
Honorary Consul-General: Erkki Eino Salo.

CZECHOSLOVAKIA

Embassy: Armfeltintie 14, 00150 Helsinki 15; tel (0) 171051; telex 121804; fax (0) 630655.
Ambassador: Peter Kerlik.
Counsellor: Miroslav Mára.
First Secretary: Ľubomír Kopaj.
First Secretary: Oľga Bakossová.
Second Secretary: Josef Bajer.

Commercial Section: Annankatu 25, 00100 Helsinki; tel (0) 640101; fax (0) 640105.
Commercial Counsellor: Vladimír Nováček.

DENMARK

Embassy: Georgsgatan 9, POB 178, 00121 Helsinki; tel (0) 641948; telex 124782; fax (0) 608169.
Ambassador: E. Krog-Meyer.
Counsellor: Jørgen V. Andersen.
Secretary (Commercial): Berni Antell.
Attaché (Commercial): Therkild Therkildsen.
Attaché (Commercial) and Vice-Consul: Gunni Busck-Nielsen.

Consulate: Mäntyluoto, 28880 Pori-Björneborg 88; tel (39) 443122; telex 66398.
Consul: Arto Alarik Illman.

Consulate: c/o Sparbanken, Mannerheimgatan 11, 06100 Porvoo-Borgå 10; tel (15) 143122.
Consul: Kai Erik Rosendahl.

Consulate: Enso-Gutzeit Ab, Summa Bruk, 49420 Hamina-Frederikshamn 2; tel (52) 295111; telex 5416.
Consul: Kimmo Risto Erkki Kalela.

Consulate: Brunnsgatan 10, 10900 Hangö; tel (11) 86495; telex 13137.
Consul: Axel Eric Liljefors.

Consulate: Storgatan 14, POB 7, 68601 Jakobstad; tel (67) 30958.
Consul: Leif Eklund.

Consulate: c/o Postbanken, Karleby Kontor, Torggatan 31, 67007 Karelby.
Consul: Jussi Suves.

Consulate: Kemi Oy, Mekanisk Skogsindustri, 94200 Kemi 20; tel (698) 191301; telex 3611.
Consul: Tero Ilmari Paajanen.

Consulate: Södra Kymmene Sparbank, Liikekeskus, Kirkkodatu 7, 48100 Kotka 10; tel (52) 294111.
Consul: Ragnar Backström.

Consulate: Oy Finncarriers Ab, Kumpusaaren Syväsatana, 70620 Kuopio; tel (71) 123750; telex 123709.
Consul: Auvo Sulevi Muraja.

Consulate: c/o Ålands Aktiebank, Nygatan 2, 22100 Mariehamn; tel (28) 29011; telex 63119.
Consul: Karl Thorvald Eriksson.

Consulate: Peuratie 29, 26200 Rauma; tel (38) 3161; telex 65128.
Consul: Jukka Jalmar Paasikivi.

Consulate: Otavalankatu 3A, POB 466, 33101 Tampere-Tammerfors; tel (31) 113333; fax (31) 132280.
Consul: Vilhelm Franck.

Consulate: c/o Rettig Ab, POB 14, Koskitie 10, 90501 Oulu-Uleåborg 50; tel (81) 345344; telex 32260.
Consul: Nils Gustav Granholm.

Consulate: Hovrättspl. 11, 65100 Vaasa-Vasa 10; tel (61) 255111; telex 74222.
Consul: Kaj Ericsson.

Consulate: Vasavägen 18 POB 148, 20101 Turku-Åbo 10; tel (21) 604111; telex 62239.
Consul: Tor Linblom.

EGYPT

Embassy: Stenbäckinkatu 22A, 00250 Helsinki; tel (0) 413288; telex 124216.
Ambassador: Hosny Saad el-din el-Agizy.

ESTONIA

Consulate: Fabianinkatu 13 A 2, 13 Helsinki; tel (0) 663548; fax (0) 669615.
Consul: Kulle Raig.

FRANCE

Embassy: Itäinen Puistotie 13, 00140 Helsinki; tel (0) 171521; fax (0) 6933514.
Ambassador: Marcel Maître.

GERMANY

Embassy: Fredrikinkatu 61, 00100 Helsinki; tel (0) 6943355; telex 124568; fax (0) 6932564.
Ambassador: Hans Peter Bazing.

Consulate: Kirkkokatu 1, POB 44, 48100 Kotka 10; tel (52) 190111; telex 53128.
Honorary Consul: Hartmut Zimmermann.

Consulate: Metsä-Serla Oy, Savon Sellun tehtaat, POB 57, 70101 Kuopio; tel (71) 341255; telex 42168; fax (71) 342049.
Honorary Consul: Vilho Rautalahti.

Consulate: c/o Viking Line, Storagatan 2, POB 35, 22101 Mariehamn; tel (28) 16270; telex 63122.
Honorary Consul: Thor-Alf Ellasson.

Consulate: Schaumann Wood Oy, 52420 Pellosniemi; tel (55) 41010; telex 55123; fax (55) 41237.
Honorary Consul: Kari Mennander.

Consulate: Nokia Kaapeli, Kaapelitie 6, 90630 Oulu; POB 269, 90101 Oulu; tel (81) 502011; telex 32166.
Honorary Consul: Reijo Lehtonen.

Consulate: Tampereen Aluesäästöpankki, Hämeenkatu 12, 33100 Tampere; POB 38, 33101 Tampere; tel (31) 194111; telex 22194.
Honorary Consul: Paavo Prepula.

Consulate: c/o Oy Silja Line Ab, Käsityöläskatu 4a, POB 210, 20101 Turku; tel (21) 652211; telex 62251; fax (21) 652337.
Honorary Consul: Ralf Sandström.

Consulate: Strömberg Oy, Strömberginkatu 1, 65320 Vaasa; POB 69, 65101 Vaasa; tel (61) 162111; telex 12440550.
Honorary Consul: Topi Nieminen.

GREECE

Embassy: Lönnrotinkatu 15C 26, 00120 Helsinki; tel (0) 645202; fax (0) 6801038.
Ambassador: Anastássios Sideris.

HOLY SEE

Apostolic Pro-Nunciature: Bulevardi 5 as. 12, 00120 Helsinki; tel (0) 644664.

HUNGARY

Embassy: Kuusisaarenkuja 6, 00340 Helsinki; tel (0) 484144; fax (0) 480497.
Ambassador: Béla Javorszky.

ICELAND

Consulate-General: Salomonsgt. 17A, 00100 Helsinki 10; tel (0) 90693911; telex 124444; fax (0) 488545.
Consul-General: Kai Juranto.
Vice-Consul: Kai E. Juranto.

Consulate: Hangö.
Consul: Lars Eskil Strömstén.

Consulate: Runeberginkatu 24A, 48200 Kotka 20; tel (52) 12177; fax (52) 12100.
Consul: Jean Bengt Fröjd.

Consulate: Skarpansgården, Skarpansvägen, 22100 Mariehamn; tel (28) 11845.
Consul: William Waldemar Nordlund.

Consulate: Oy Silja Line AB, Hantverkargr. 4a, 20100 Åbo 10; tel (21) 516196; telex 5762251.
Consul: Harry V. Österberg.

Consulate: Hovrättsesplanaden 11, lok. 17, 65100 Vaasa-Vasa.
Consul: Holger Strandberg.

Consulate: Keskikankaantie 8, 15860 Hollola 2; tel (18) 801334; telex 16308; fax (18) 803238.
Vice-Consul: Pertti Mikko Juhani Lindqvist.

INDIA

Embassy: Satamakatu 2A 8, 00160 Helsinki; tel (0) 608927; telex 125202; fax (0) 6221208.
Ambassador: Thangkima Cherpoot.

INDONESIA

Embassy: Berikinkatu 37, 00180 Helsinki; tel (0) 6947744; fax (0) 6949394.
Ambassador: Rochsid Setyoko.

IRAN

Embassy: Bertel Jungintie 4, 00570 Helsinki; tel (0) 6847133; fax (0) 6849412.
Ambassador: M. Mohammad Reza Dokhanchi.

IRAQ

Embassy: Lars Sonckintie 2, 00570 Helsinki; tel (0) 6849177.
Ambassador: Anwar Abdul Kadir Mohammed al-Hadithi.

IRELAND

Consulate-General: Yritystieto Oy, Kalevankatu 45 AI, POB 148, 00181 Helsinki 18; tel (0) 648292; telex 121394; fax (0) 648250.
Honorary Consul-General: Borje Thilman.

Consulate: Markkinointi Topitorma Oy, Fredrikinkatu 48A, 00100 Helsinki; tel (0) 6941600; telex 121713; fax (0) 6940280.
Honorary Consul: Erkki Yrjola.

ISRAEL

Embassy: Vironkatu 5A, 00170 Helsinki; tel (0) 1356177; fax (0) 1356959.
Ambassador: Yosef Haseen.

ITALY

Embassy: Fabianinkatu 29C 4, 00100 Helsinki; tel (0) 175144; telex 121753; fax (0) 175976.
Ambassador: Giancarlo Carrara Cagni.

JAPAN

Embassy: Yrjönkatu 13, 00120 Helsinki; tel (0) 644206; fax (0) 611344.
Ambassador: Hisami Kurokochi.

KOREA, DEMOCRATIC PEOPLE'S REPUBLIC

Embassy: Kulosaaren Puistotie 32, 00570 Helsinki; tel (0) 6848195; fax (0) 6848995.
Ambassador: Dr Sung Chol Ryo.
Counsellor: Song Lim Yun.
Second Secretary: Ui Nam Won.
Third Secretary: Jae Won Chon.

KOREA, REPUBLIC

Embassy: Mannerheimintie 76A 7, 00250 Helsinki; tel (0) 498955; telex 122589.
Ambassador: Sang Jin Choi.

LATVIA

Consulate: Helsinki.
Honorary Consul: Sauli Pillamaa.

MALTA

Consulate: c/o Scan Pacific Line, Itatuuiclenkuja 10, 02100 Espoo; tel 4553539; telex 124342; fax 4553518.
Honorary Consul: Paul Eric Grunstroem.

MAURITANIA

Consulate: Nortamonkatu 18, 26100 Rauma; tel (38) 221418.
Consul: Kauko Nikko.

MEXICO

Embassy: Fredrikinkatu 51-53a, 00100 Helsinki; tel (0) 640637; telex 122021; fax (0) 6801227.
Ambassador: Ricardo Villanueva Hallal.

NETHERLANDS

Embassy: Raatimiehenkatu 2A 7, 00140 Helsinki; tel (0) 661737; telex 121779; fax (0) 654734.
Ambassador: Egbert Frederik Jacobs.

NORWAY

Embassy: Rehbinderintie 17, 00150 Helsinki; tel (0) 171234; telex 124707; fax (0) 657807.
Ambassador: Kjell Rasmussen.

PERU

Embassy: Fredrikinkatu 16A 22, 00120 Helsinki; tel (0) 631354; telex 123650.
Ambassador: Alberto Montagne.

POLAND

Embassy: Armas Lindgrenintie 21, 00570 Helsinki; tel (0) 6848077; telex 124642; fax (0) 6848907.
Chargé d'affaires a.i. and Minister-Counsellor: Mirosława Wiklik.
Counsellor (Commercial): Andrzej Dorosz.
Military Attaché: Col Władysław Staluszka.
First Secretary and Head of Consular Section: Ryszard Wojtal.
First Secretary: Joanna Trzcińska-Mejor.
Second Secretary: Jolanta Krasińska-Sokołowska.
Attaché (Economic): Janusz Strzelecki.

PORTUGAL

Embassy: Itäinen Puistotie 11B, 00140 Helsinki; tel (0) 171717; telex 121877.
Ambassador: Fernando da Costa Figueirinhas.

ROMANIA

Embassy: Stenbäckinkatu 24, 00250 Helsinki; tel (0) 413624; telex 121041; fax (0) 413272.
Ambassador: Vasile Florea.
Counsellor (Political): Ioan Agaficioaia.
Second Secretary (Finance): Ion Serban.
Second Secretary (Press/Culture): Mircea Ciobanu.
Second Secretary (Technical/Scientific/Consular): Vasile Cringanu.

RUSSIA

Embassy: Tehtaankatu 1B, 00140 Helsinki; tel (0) 661876.
Ambassador: Boris Ivanovich Aristov.

Consulate-General: Vartiovuorenkatu 2, Turku; tel (21) 336441.

Consulate: Norra Esplandankatu 11, Mariehamn; tel (28) 11524.

SAN MARINO

Consulate-General: Marsalkanpolku 5, 00570 Helsinki; tel (0) 6849216.
Consul-General: Michele Wainstein.
Consul: Peter Stenius.

SOUTH AFRICA

Embassy: Rahapajankatu 1A 5, 00160 Helsinki; tel (0) 658288; telex 123605; fax (0) 655884.
Ambassador: Connie M. Swart.
First Secretary: W. H. Lotze.
Third Secretary: Philip Riley.
Third Secretary (Administration): C. R. M. Reyneke.

SPAIN

Embassy: Bulevardi 10A 8, 00120 Helsinki; tel (0) 647351; telex 122193; fax (0) 601742.
Ambassador: Luis Jordana de Pozas Fuentes.

SRI LANKA

Consulate: Kuortaneenkatu 13, 00520 Helsinki; tel (0) 718188; telex 121487; fax (0) 738437.
Honorary Consul: Goran Ahman.

SWEDEN

Embassy: Norra Esplanaden 7B, POB 329, 00171 Helsinki; tel (0) 651255; telex 124538; fax (0) 655285.
Ambassador: Knut Thyberg.
Minister: Katarina Brodin.
Counsellor (Press): Orwar Roberntz.
Military Attaché: Col Vulf Hessaulf.
Defence Attaché: Maj. Folke Benjamin.
First Secretary: Jan Janonius.
Second Secretary: Teppo Taurianen.
Secretary (Commercial): Per-Olof Dahllöf.
Chancellor: Anja Marjatta Ikonen.
Chancellor: Laila Pitkänen.
Attaché (Cultural): Thomas Henrikson.

Consulate: Rauma-Repola Oy, Antinkatu 2, POB 51, 28100 Pori-Björneborg; tel (39) 823041; telex 66115.
Consul: Rolf Hjalmar Modeen.

Consulate: Brahegt. 19, 92100 Brahestad; tel (82) 37007.

Consul: Carl Ossian August Swanljung.

Consulate: Kungdgt. 7, POB 44, 10601 Ekenäs; tel (11) 13200.
Consul: Kurt Bruno Lindström.

Consulate: Pikkuympyräkatu 14, POB 67, 49401 Frederikshamn; tel (52) 54600; telex 5410.
Consul: Jaakko Armas Aalto.

Consulate: O/Y Wilh. Schauman AB, POB 42, 68601 Jakobstad; tel (67) 862102; telex 7554; fax (67) 12483.
Consul: Martin Gustav Granholm.

Consulate: Kauppakatu 17-B, 80100 Joensuu; tel (73) 21311; fax (73) 127678.
Consul: Mauri Heimo Kalervo Vänskä.

Consulate: Varassaari 40800; POB 121, 40101 Jyväskylä 10; tel (41) 263411; telex 28296; fax (41) 665485.
Consul: Timo Heikki Anton Frederikson.

Consulate: Änsgt. 2-4, Oy Auto-Haro Ab, POB 22, 67101 Karleby; tel (68) 14633; fax (68) 200870.
Consul: Per-Ole Valentin Holm.

Consulate: Kemi Oy, Karihaara, 94200 Kemi; tel (698) 1911; telex 3613; fax (698) 191246.
Consul: Erik Allan Volmari.

Consulate: c/o Steveco Oy, Ruukinkatu 9, POB 44, 48101 Kotka; tel (52) 190111; telex 53181; fax (52) 190505.
Consul: Toivo Juhani Forss.

Consulate: Haapaniemenkatu 28, POB 145, 70101 Kuopio 10; tel (71) 124222.
Consul: Lauri Matti Birger Hallman.

Consulate: Starckjohann-Telko Oy, Neljänkaivonkatu 28, POB 54, 15101 Lahti; tel (18) 28911; telex 16142; fax (18) 514951.
Consul: Erik Hermann Starckjohann.

Consulate: Rauma-Repola Oy, POB 94, 26101 Raumo; tel (38) 3311; fax (38) 335009.
Consul: Esko Ilmari Immonen.

Consulate: Oy Pohjoiskalotti Ab, Hallitie 11, POB 8146, 96101 Rovaniemi; tel (60) 20361; telex 37114; fax (60) 311950.
Consul: Osmo Antero Ikäheimo.

Consulate: Porrassalmenkatu 17, 50100 St Michel 10; tel (55) 360777; telex 55120.
Consul: Heimo Olavi Heikkilä.

Consulate: c/o Tamfelt Oy Ab, Yrittäjäankatu 21, 33710 Tammerfors; POB 427, 33101 Tammerfors; tel (31) 560120; telex 22169.
Consul: Axel Viktor Folkern Cedercreutz.
Chancellor: Riitta Charlotta Salvén.

Consulate: Oy Hartwall AB Lapin Kulta, Oravaisenkatu 6, 95400 Torneå; tel (698) 41751; telex 3526.
Consul: Leo Torsti Andelin.

Consulate: Käyttöauto Oy, Konetie 4, 90630 Uleåborg; tel (81) 542211; telex 32155; fax (81) 542751.
Consul: Veikko Olavi Hulkko.

Consulate: Halli Oy, Vasaesplanaden 18, 65100 Vaasa-Vasa 10; tel (61) 113927.
Consul: Tauno Emil Oskar Rewell.

Consulate: Turun Sanomat-Hus, Köpmansgt. 5, POB 95, 20101 Turku-Åbo 10; tel (21) 331310; telex 62213; fax (21) 693469.
Consul: Arvo Mikko Olavi Ketonen.
Chancellor: Kristiina Ketonen.
Chancellor: Lisbeth Veso.

Consulate: Norragt. 44, 22100 Mariehamn, Åland; tel (28) 11624; fax (28) 17624.
Consul: Nils Gösta Damberg.

SWITZERLAND

Embassy: Uudenmaankatu 16A, 00120 Helsinki 12; tel (0) 649422; fax (0) 6801343.
Ambassador: Othmar Uhl.
Counsellor: Dr Peter Sutter.
Assistant Defence Attaché: Capt. Martin Schmid.
Attaché and Office Manager: Urs Bühler.

TURKEY

Embassy: Topeliuksenkatu 3B A 1-2, 00260 Helsinki; tel (0) 406058.
Ambassador: Tuncer Topur.

UNITED KINGDOM

Embassy: Itäinen Puistotie 17, 00140 Helsinki; tel (0) 661293; telex 121122; fax (0) 661342.
Ambassador: G. Neil Smith.
Counsellor (Commercial) and Deputy Head of Mission: N. A. Thorne.
Defence, Naval, Military and Air Attaché: Lieut Col F. A. B. Clement.
First Secretary: V. J. Henderson.
First Secretary (Political): R. M. F. Kelly.
First Secretary (Commercial): W. Hamilton.
First Secretary, Consul and Management Officer: N. J. Kelly.
Second Secretary (Information/Chancery): P. R. Ivey.

Consulate: Valmet Paper Machinery Inc., POB 587, SF 40101 Jyväsklä; tel (41) 295211; telex 28213.
Honorary Consul: E. A. Leivo.

Consulate: Port Authority of Kotka, Laivurinkatu 7, 48100 Kotka 10; tel (52) 274280; telex 53144.
Honorary Consul: E. I. Elo.

Consulate: Kuopio Chamber of Commerce, Kasarmikatu 2, 70100 Kuopio; tel (71) 220291; fax (71) 223304.
Honorary Consul: O. Jääskeläinen.

Consulate: Södragatan 16 B4, 22100 Mariehamm Aland Islands; tel (28) 16620; fax (28) 16901.
Honorary Consul: Dr P. Darby.

Consulate: Rautaruukki Oy, POB 217, Kiilakiventie 1, SF 90101 Oulu; tel (81) 327711; telex 32109.
Honorary Consul: A. V. A. Saarinen.

Consulate: Repola Oy, PL51, Antinkatu 2, POB 69, 28101 Pori; tel (39) 823007; telex 66155.
Honorary Consul: T. J. Hiillos.

Consulate: Oy Finlayson Ab, PL 407, 33101 Tampere; tel (31) 35222; telex 22170.
Honorary Consul: H. C. Sucksdorff.

Consulate: Turun Kauppakamari, Puolalankatu 1, 20101 Turku; tel (21) 501440; telex 62114.
Honorary Consul: S. O. Hansen.

Consulate: Royal Vaasa Hotel, Hoviokeudenpuistikko 18, 65100 Vaasa-Vasa; tel (61) 278111; telex 74193.
Honorary Consul: R. Grönblom.

USA

Embassy: Itäinen Puistotie 14A, 00140 Helsinki; tel (0) 171931; telex 121644; fax (0) 171931.
Ambassador: John Giffen Weinmann.
Deputy Head of Mission: Max M. Robinson.
Political Section: William J. Kushlis.
Economic Section: Lawrence E. Butler.
Commercial Section: Richard J. Newquist.
Labour Officer: John P. Fernandez.
Administrative Section: William J. Burke, Jr.
Regional Security Officer: James W. Holt.
Public Affairs Officer: William P. Kiehl.
Office of Defence Attaché: Col William A. J. Mackie.
Communications Programme Officer: Dennis R. Thatcher.

VENEZUELA

Embassy: Mannerheimintie 14B, 00100 Helsinki; tel (0) 641522; fax (0) 640791.
Ambassador: Germán de Pérez Castillo.
Counsellor: Carmen Matos Azocar.
Second Secretary: Perla Marina Iribarren P.

YUGOSLAVIA

Embassy: Kulosaarentie 36, 00570 Helsinki; tel (0) 6848522; telex 122099.
Ambassador: Mito Pejovski.

FRANCE

AFGHANISTAN

Embassy: 32 ave Raphaël, 75016 Paris; tel (1) 45-27-66-09.
Chargé d'affaires a.i.: M. Wahidullah.
First Secretary: Kadir Mahboub.
Third Secretary: Abdul Aziz.

ALBANIA

Embassy: 131 rue de la Pompe, 75116 Paris; tel (1) 45-53-51-32; telex 611534.
Ambassador: Ksenofon Nushi.

ALGERIA

Embassy: 50 rue de Lisbonne, 75008 Paris; tel (1) 42-25-70-70.

ANGOLA

Embassy: 19 ave Foch, 75116 Paris; tel (1) 45-01-58-20; telex 649847.
Ambassador: Elisio de Figueiredo.

ARGENTINA

Embassy: 6 rue Cimarosa, 75116 Paris; tel (1) 45-53-14-69; telex 613819.
Ambassador: Fernando Gelbard.

ARMENIA

Embassy: Paris.

AUSTRALIA

Embassy: 4 rue Jean Rey, 75724 Paris Cédex 15; tel (1) 45-75-62-00; telex 202313.
Ambassador: Edward Robert Pocock.

AUSTRIA

Embassy: 6 rue Fabert, 75007 Paris; tel (1) 40-59-33-00; telex 200708; fax (1) 45-55-63-65.
Ambassador: Wolfgang Schallenberg.
Counsellor (Commercial): Karl Vetter von der Lille.
Counsellor: Benita Waldner.
Counsellor (Press): Helene Lamesch.
Counsellor (Cultural): Rudolf Altmüller.
Counsellor (Social Affairs): Gerhard Antonik.
Defence Attaché: Brig. Richard Bondi.
Second Secretary: Walter Rochel.

Consular Section: 12 rue Edmont Valentin, 75007 Paris; tel (1) 47-05-27-17.
Consul-General: Gerda Meyer.
Consul: Aloisia Schmidt.

Consulate-General: 29 ave de la Paix, 67000 Strasbourg; tel 88-35-13-94; telex 870976.
Consul-General: Erich Buttenhauser.
Vice-Consul: Michael Ian Swoboda.

Consulate: 86 cours Balguerie-Stuttenberg, 33300 Bordeaux; tel 56-00-00-70; telex 550766.
Honorary Consul: Emile Castéja.

Consulate: 17 blvd des Belges, 69006 Lyon; tel 78-93-21-86.
Honorary Consul: Charles Mérieux.

Consulate: 27 cours Pierre Puget, 13006 Marseille; tel 91-53-02-08; telex 401457.
Honorary Consul: Jean Leopold Renard.

Consulate: 6 ave de Verdun, 06000 Nice; tel 93-87-01-31; telex 461624.
Honorary Vice-Consul: Patrick Maître Rizzo.

Consulate: 22 blvd de la Gare, 31500 Toulouse; tel 61-54-50-04.
Honorary Consul: Jacques Metzler.

BAHRAIN

Embassy: 15 ave Raymond Poincaré, 75116 Paris; tel (1) 45-53-01-19; telex 620924.
Ambassador: Abd al-Aziz Buali.

BANGLADESH

Embassy: 5 sq. Pétrarque, 75016 Paris; tel (1) 45-53-41-20; telex 630868.
Ambassador: Dr A. Tozammel Huq.

BELGIUM

Embassy: 9 rue de Tilsit, 75840 Paris Cédex 17; tel (1) 43-80-61-00; telex 650484.
Ambassador: Alfred Cahen.

BENIN

Embassy: 87 ave Victor Hugo, 75116 Paris; tel (1) 45-00-98-82; telex 610110.
Ambassador: Souler Issifou Idrissou.

BOLIVIA

Embassy: 12 ave Président Kennedy, 75016 Paris; tel (1) 42-24-93-44; telex 611879; fax (1) 45-25-86-23.
Chargé d'affaires a.i.: Fernando Laredo.

BRAZIL

Embassy: 34 cours Albert 1er, 75008 Paris; tel (1) 45-25-92-50; telex 650063; fax (1) 42-89-03-45.
Ambassador: João Hermes Pereira de Araújo.

BRUNEI

Embassy: 4 rue Logelbach, 75017 Paris; tel (1) 42-67-49-29; fax (1) 42-67-49-47.

BULGARIA

Embassy: 1 ave Rapp, 75007 Paris; tel (1) 45-51-89-90.
Ambassador: Milan Milanov.

BURKINA FASO

Embassy: 159 blvd Haussmann, 75008 Paris; tel (1) 43-59-90-63; telex 641870; fax (1) 42-56-50-07.
Ambassador: Serge Théophile Balima.
First Counsellor: Léon Yougbare.
Counsellor (Economic): Xavier Niodogo.
Counsellor (Culture): Robert Korahire.
Counsellor (Consular Affairs): Yamba Antoine Bougma.
Counsellor (Financial Affairs): Félix L. P. Ouedraogo.
Deputy Cultural Counsellor (Head of Centre for Administration of students): N. D. Félix Compaore.
Deputy Counsellor (Financial Affairs): Souleymane Doussa.
Military Attaché: Mr Zagre.
First Secretary: Michel Guenguere.
Second Secretary: Augustine Anasthasie Bonogo.
Attaché (Social Affairs): Sylviane Sango.
Attaché (Consular Affairs): Kotoa Hubert Mantoro.

Consulate: 25 rue Jean Mieg, 68051 Mulhouse Cédex.
Consul: Georges Wetterer.

Consulate: 22 rue Paul Helbronner, 38100 Grenoble.
Consul: René Guichard.

Consulate: Villa Marie-Anne, 44 ave Raquel Miler, 06 Villefranche-sur-Mer.
Consul: René Gentil.

Consulate: 60 rue du Tondu, 33000 Bordeaux.
Consul: Col Jean-Pierre Petit.

Consulate: 473 rue Paradis, 13008 Marseille.
Consul: Paul Roubaud.

Consulate: 68 rue Boileau, 69006 Lyon.
Consul: Jean-Paul Grollemund.

BURUNDI

Embassy: 3 rue Octave Feuillet, 75116 Paris; tel (1) 45-20-60-61; telex 611463.
Chargé d'affaires a.i.: Pasteur Nzinahora.

CAMEROON

Embassy: 73 rue d'Auteuil, 75016 Paris; tel (1) 47-43-98-33; telex 620312.
Ambassador: Simon Nko'o Etoungou.

CANADA

Embassy: 35 ave Montaigne, 75008 Paris; tel (1) 47-23-01-01; telex 280806; fax (1) 47-23-56-28.
Ambassador: Claude T. Charland.
Minister: J. A. Malone.
Minister-Counsellor (Commercial/Economic): R. Frenette.
Minister-Counsellor: M. R. Lortie.
Counsellor (Finance): S. Kennedy.
Counsellor (Immigration): A. A. Jurkovich.
Counsellor (Immigration) and Consul: H. Raymond.
Counsellor (Immigration): C. Labelle.
Counsellor (Commercial/Agriculture/Fisheries): R. H. Davidson.
Counsellor (Administrative) and Consul: C. Thibault.
Counsellor and Consul: R. E. Lapointe.
Counsellor (Commercial): L. R. Poisson.
Counsellor (Commercial): R. Lecoq.
Counsellor (Defence Research): P. Twardawa.
Counsellor (Science/Technology): J. Y. Tremblay.
Counsellor: J. J. R. Crête.
Counsellor: P. A. Lortie.
Counsellor: R. Roy.
Defence Attaché: Brig.-Gen. J. J. R. Parent.
Naval Attaché: Lieut Commdr D. L. Sing.
Air Attaché: Lieut Col J. J. A. R. Aubry.
First Secretary and Consul: L. de Lorimer.
First Secretary (Immigration): N. P. Martel.
First Secretary: P. Fauteux.
First Secretary: C. Tait.
First Secretary: A. J. A. Nadon.
Attaché (Investment): P. Bélanger.

Cultural Office: 5 rue de Constantine, 75007 Paris; tel (1) 45-51-35-73; fax (1) 47-05-43-55.
Minister-Counsellor (Cultural/Information): E. Martel.

Permanent Delegation to UNESCO: 1 rue Miollis, 75015 Paris; BP 307, 75007 Paris; tel (1) 45-68-35-17; telex 280806; fax (1) 43-06-87-27.

Permanent Representative (UNESCO): Jean Drapeau.
Deputy Permanent Representative (UNESCO) and Minister-Counsellor: M. Meunier.

Consulate: Edifice Bonnel, Par-Dieu, coin Bonnel et Garibaldy, 74 rue de Bonnel, 3e étage, 69003 Lyon; tel 72-61-15-25; fax 78-62-09-36.
Consul: B. Goulet.

Consulate: Polysar France, rue du Ried, CP 7, 67610 La Wantzenau; tel 88-96-26-54; telex 870043; fax 88-96-64-54.
Honorary Consul: J.-P. Andrieux.

CENTRAL AFRICAN REPUBLIC

Embassy: 29 blvd de Montmorency, 75116 Paris; tel (1) 42-24-42-56; telex 611908.
Ambassador: Joseph Hetman-el-Roosalem.

CHAD

Embassy: 65 rue des Belles Feuilles, 75116 Paris; tel (1) 45-53-36-75; telex 610629.
Ambassador: Ahmed Allam-Mi.

CHILE

Embassy: 2 ave de la Motte-Piquet, 75007 Paris; tel (1) 45-51-46-68; telex 260075.
Ambassador: José-Miguel Barros.

CHINA, PEOPLE'S REPUBLIC

Embassy: 11 ave George V, 75008 Paris; tel (1) 47-23-34-45; telex 270114.
Ambassador: Zhou Jue.

COLOMBIA

Embassy: 22 rue de l'Elysée, 75008 Paris; tel (1) 42-65-46-08; telex 640935.
Ambassador: Fernando Rey.

COMOROS

Embassy: 20 rue Marbeau, 75116 Paris; tel (1) 40-67-90-54; telex 651390; fax (1) 40-67-72-96.
Ambassador: Ali Mlahaili (designate).
First Counsellor: Bourhane Abdourazak.
Counsellor (Political): Salim Djohar.
Counsellor (Culture): Ahmed Kalidanse.
Counsellor (Finance): Said Amadi.
Accountant: Said Oussoufa.

CONGO

Embassy: 37 bis rue Paul Valéry, 75016 Paris; tel (1) 45-00-60-57; telex 611954.
Ambassador: Jean-Marie Ewengué.

COSTA RICA

Embassy: 135 ave de Versailles, 75116 Paris; tel (1) 45-25-52-23; telex 648046.
Ambassador: Enrique Castillo.

COTE D'IVOIRE

Embassy: 102 ave Raymond Poincaré, 75116 Paris; tel (1) 45-01-53-10; telex 611915.
Ambassador: Eugène Aidara.

CUBA

Embassy: 16 rue de Presles, 75015 Paris; tel (1) 45-67-55-35; telex 200815.
Ambassador: Fernando Flórez Ibarra.

CYPRUS

Embassy: 23 rue Galilée, 75116 Paris; tel (1) 47-20-86-28; telex 610664; fax (1) 40-70-13-44.
Ambassador: Georges Lycourgos.

Consulate: 35 rue Sainte Hélène, 69002 Lyon; tel 78-37-75-56; fax 72-40-08-38.
Honorary Consul: Gabriel-Michael Dhikeos.

Consulate: Sudcarges, 17 ave Robert Schuman, POB 2478, 13218 Marseille 2; tel 91-08-69-00; telex 440448; fax 91-08-69-27.
Honorary Consul: Nicolaos Boyadjis.

Consulate: 78 rue d'Ignauval, 76310 Le Havre; tel 35-54-21-94; fax 35-54-13-57.
Honorary Consul: Anthony Doucas.

CZECHOSLOVAKIA

Embassy: 15 ave Charles Floquet, 75007 Paris; tel (1) 47-34-29-10; telex 611032; fax (1) 47-83-50-78.
Ambassador: Jaroslav Šedivý.

DENMARK

Embassy: 77 ave Marceau, 75116 Paris; tel (1) 47-23-54-20; telex 620172; fax (1) 47-20-03-90.
Ambassador: Gunnar Riberholdt.
Counsellor (Commercial): Dan Larsen.
Counsellor (Culture/Press): Uffe Andreasen.
Counsellor (Agriculture/Government): Børge Schou Pedersen.
Counsellor: Birgitte Lindsay-Poulsen.
Economic Adviser: Claus Grube.
Attaché (Consular) and Consul: Bent Andersen.
Attaché (Administrative) and Consul: Henrik H. Sørensen.
Attaché (Commercial): Viggo Thomas Wilhelmsen.
Attaché (Agriculture): Hans Erik Dylmer.
Attaché (Social Affairs) and Chaplain: Steffen Ravn Jørgensen.
Press Correspondent: Merete Soussan.
Export Assistant: Tine Haakonsen.

Consulate-General: 97 quai des Chartrons, BP 133, 33027 Bordeaux Cédex; tel 56-81-24-10; telex 550138; fax 56-44-56-39.
Consul-General: Jean-Henri Schÿler-Schröder.

Consulate-General: 62 rue Paul-Cazeneuve, 69008 Lyon; tel 78-72-55-38; telex 340003; fax 72-73-48-19.
Consul-General: Henri Chiara.

Consulate: 166 rue Vanheeckhoët, BP 387, 62205 Boulogne-sur-Mer; tel 21-87-88-00.
Consul: Marie-Edith Charles Mylius.

Consulate: 5 et 7 blvd Sainte Barbe, 59140 Dunkerque; tel 28-63-33-00; telex 160932.
Consul: Edouard de Clebsattel.

Consulate: 17 place de Suède, BP 851, 62225 Calais Cédex; tel 21-34-44-00; telex 810098.
Consul: Jean Mulard.

Consulate: 1 rue du Duc, 17003 La Rochelle; tel 46-41-10-66; telex 791462.
Consul: Jacques Godet.

Consulate: 7 rue Pierre Brossolette, BP 114, 76051 Le Havre Cédex; tel 35-21-11-22; telex 190159.
Consul: Claude Henri Joseph Colin-Olivier.

Consulate: 13 quai de la Vicomté, 76400 Fécamp; tel 35-29-22-86; telex 190202.
Consul: François André Jean Ledun.

Consulate: parc de la Côte-Joire, 44 à 48 ave de la Marne, 59290 Wasquehal; tel 20-26-49-19; telex 820662; fax 20-26-54-05.
Consul: Ole Gregersen.

Consulate: 22 place des Bancs, 87000 Limoges; tel 55-32-42-62.
Consul: Hans Andersen Prisak.

Consulate: place du Château, 74200 Thonon-les-Bains; tel 50-71-78-97; telex 385084.
Consul: Annelise Petersen.

Consulate-General: 2 rue Henri-Barbusse, BP 2136, 13205 Marseille; tel 91-90-80-23; telex 400312; fax 91-91-35-00.
Consul-General: Hans Henrik Liljeborg.
Vice-Consul and Secretary: Lis Vendel Petersen.
Export Assistant: Bettina Charlotte Berhoft.

Consulate: New Holiday Management S.A., Le Statège, Z.A. du Millenaire, 34000 Montpellier; tel 67-69-74-85; telex 485470; fax 67-69-74-69.
Consul: Georges Pagès.

Consulate: 'Nice Etoile', 30 ave Jean Médecin, Bureau 411, 06000 Nice; tel 93-85-35-49; telex 462783; fax 93-85-07-91.
Consul: John Brown Thomsen.
Vice-Consul: Jan Raffel.

Consulate: 13 rue du Docteur Grenier, 66000 Perpignan; tel 68-85-02-58.
Consul: Joseph Henri Martin Armangué.

Consulate: 20 cours Landrivon, 13110 Port de Bouc; tel 42-06-09-89; telex 420555.
Consul: Paul A. L. Girard.

Consulate: 3 quai de la République, 34200 Sète; tel 67-74-30-20; telex 480036.
Consul: Gérard Seguin.

Consulate: 12 rue du Chêne Lassé, 44800 St Herblain; tel 40-92-16-05; telex 711130.
Consul: Freddie Svend Pedersen.

Consulate: 38 quai de la Duoanne, 29283 Brest; tel 98-44-49-95; telex 940522.
Consul: Jean Pierre Caradec.

Consulate: 17 blvd Abbé Le Cam, 56100 Lorient; tel 97-37-25-77; telex 950071; fax 97-37-58-22.
Consul: Jean-Maurice Besnard.

Consulate: c/o Cobrecaf, quai du Moros, BP 182, 29183 Concarneau Cédex; tel 98-97-35-88; telex 940130.
Consul: Yves Cariou.

Consulate: 2 chaussée des Corsaires, BP 179, 35400 St-Malo Cédex; tel 99-56-07-21.
Consul: Yves Delamaire.

Consulate: SCAC Transport International, Z.I. Portuaire, 44550 Montoir de Bretagne; tel 40-90-47-47; telex 700998; fax 40-90-46-15.
Consul: Annie Ollivaud.

Consulate: c/o Transcap, 28 quai Gaston Boulet, BP 570, 76000 Rouen; tel 35-07-29-29; telex 770858.
Consul: Xavier Edmond Pierre Lesage.

Consulate: Zone Caen Canal, BP 53, 14011 Caen Cédex; tel 31-72-35-30; telex 170268.
Consul: Landry Julien Georges Valette.

Consulate: 48 rue Alfred Rossel, 50100 Cherbourg; tel 33-44-00-22.
Consul: Rémi Marie Jean Mauger.

Consulate: 1 rue du Bassin d'Austerlitz, 67100 Strasbourg; tel 88-84-20-11; telex 870016.
Consul: Laurent Charles Seegmuller.

Consulate: 32 place Mage, 31000 Toulouse; tel 61-52-87-65; telex 520592.
Consul: Jacques Dary.

DJIBOUTI

Embassy: 26 rue Emile Ménier, 75116 Paris; tel (1) 47-27-49-22; telex 614970.
Ambassador: Ahmed Omar Farah.
Counsellor: Youssouf Omar Doualeh.

DOMINICAN REPUBLIC

Embassy: 2 rue Georges-Ville, 75116 Paris; tel (1) 45-01-88-81; telex 615333.
Chargé d'affaires a.i.: Caonabo Fernández Naranjo.

ECUADOR

Embassy: 34 ave de Messine, 75008 Paris; tel (1) 45-61-10-21; telex 641333; fax (1) 42-56-06-64.
Ambassador: Juan Cueva.
Counsellor: Carlos Abad.
Second Secretary: Alfonso Morales.
Consul: Ramiro Escudero.

EGYPT

Embassy: 56 ave d'Iéna, 75116 Paris; tel (1) 47-20-97-70; telex 611691; fax (1) 47-23-06-43.
Ambassador: Ahmed Sidky.
Counsellor (Cultural): Ahmed el Sayed.

Office of Military Attaché: 53 rue Dumont d'Urville, 75016 Paris; tel (1) 45-00-94-10.
Military, Naval and Air Attaché: Naeim el-Khawaga.

Tourism Office: 90 ave des Champs Elysées, 75008 Paris; tel (1) 45-62-94-42.
Counsellor (Tourism): Amin Atwa.

EL SALVADOR

Embassy: 12 rue Galilée, 75116 Paris; tel (1) 47-20-42-02; fax (1) 40-70-01-95.
Ambassador: Ana Christina Sol.

EQUATORIAL GUINEA

Embassy: 6 rue Alfred de Vigny, 75008 Paris; tel (1) 47-66-44-33.
Ambassador: Faustino Nguema Esono.

ESTONIA

Embassy: 11 rue Cadet, 75009 Paris; tel (1) 40-22-95-87; fax (1) 40-22-95-87.
Ambassador: Malle Talvet.

ETHIOPIA

Embassy: 35 ave Charles Floquet, 75007 Paris; tel (1) 47-83-83-95; telex 260008; fax (1) 43-06-52-14.
Ambassador: Habtemariam Seyoum.
Minister-Counsellor: Assefa Tessema.
Counsellor: Alemayehu Rameto.
First Secretary: Bolcho Hotesso.
Third Secretary: Amdemichael Tekle.
Attaché: Belaynech Yirgu.

FINLAND

Embassy: 2 rue Fabert, 75007 Paris; tel (1) 47-05-35-45; telex 200054; fax (1) 45-51-63-23.
Ambassador: Matti Häkkänen.
Counsellor (Commercial): Lauri Parikka.
Secretary (Commercial): Taina Kärkkäinen.
Secretary (Commercial): Seppo Seppänen.
Attaché (Scientific): Antti Joensuu.

Consulate-General: 18 bis rue d'Anjou, 75008 Paris; tel (1) 42-65-33-65; telex 650297; fax (1) 42-65-20-25.
Consul-General: Kristian Packalen.

Consulate: Hôtel Consulaire, quai l'Herminier, 20000 Ajaccio; tel 95-21-34-65; telex 460084.
Consul: Edouard Cuttoli.

Consulate: 10 rue Albert 1, 64100 Bayonne; tel 59-59-06-19; telex 570027.
Consul: André Labat.

Consulate: 59 cours Xavier Arnozan, 33000 Bordeaux; tel 56-44-94-45; telex 541337.
Consul: Lionel Cruse.

Consulate: Boulogne Terminal, quai Amiral Huguet, BP 241, 62204 Boulogne Cédex; tel 21-30-44-55; telex 110056.
Consul: Robert Desarbres.

Consulate: 25 rue de Luc, 14830 Langrune, Caen; tel 31-97-33-27; telex 77140.
Consul: Jean-Hans Gruneberg.

Consulate: 12 blvd des Alliés, BP 817, 62225 Calais Cédex; tel 21-96-55-03; telex 810713.
Consul: Henri Ravisse.

Consulate: 36 ave du Maréchal Juin, 06400 Cannes; tel 93-43-37-44; telex 470029.
Consul: Louis Rival.

Consulate: 26 rue Chabot Charny, 21000 Dijon; tel 80-67-13-24.
Consul: Michel Guyon.

Consulate: 11 rue des Arbres, 59383 Dunkerque; tel 28-66-33-33; telex 820911.
Consul: Serge Dewulf.

Consulate: Société Allemande, 38140 Rives, 38000 Grenoble; tel 76-91-01-33; telex 320746.
Consul: Christian Rettmeyer.

Consulate: 37 rue de Chagnolet, Perigny, 17000 La Rochelle; tel 46-44-15-07; telex 790852.
Consul: André Barraud.

Consulate: 192 rue de la Vallée, 76600 Le Havre; tel 35-25-22-18; telex 190012.
Consul: Eric Bardinet.

Consulate: National Westminster Bank S.A., 32 ave Foch, BP 6403, 69413 Lyon Cédex 06; tel 78-89-60-50; telex 370623.
Consul: Philippe de Varax.

Consulate: 22 quai du Lazaret, BP 397, 13215 Marseille Cédex 1; tel 91-91-91-62; telex 440602.
Consul: François Jean Le Bars.

Consulate: 37 blvd de Scarpone, 54000 Nancy; tel 83-98-64-40; telex 960040.
Consul: Yvan Cauwe.

Consulate: Nice.
Consul: René Marie Claude Léonce Calvy.

Consulate: 12 rue Saint-Amant, 66000 Perpignan; tel 68-34-61-47; telex 500865.
Consul: Ludovic Pams.

Consulate: Sodipan-Nokia S.A., blvd Industriel, Z.I., 76800 St Etienne du Rouvray; BP 202, 76304 Sotteville les Rouen; tel 35-65-24-24; telex 180517.
Consul: Harry Forssel.

Consulate: 2 ave de la 2e Division Blindée, 67300 Schiltigheim, Strasbourg; BP 142, 67303 Schiltigheim Cédex; tel 88-33-211-57; telex 870795.
Consul: Henri Nied.

Consulate: Banque Populaire Toulouse Pyrénées, 'Le Castera' C.D. 64, 31130 Balma; tel 61-48-11-12; telex 520780.
Consul: Yves Bernard.

Consulate: 38 quai de la Douane, 29283 Brest Cédex; tel 98-80-24-42; telex 940522.
Vice-Consul: Max Caillé.

Consulate: 5 rue de Noyon, BP 20, 50102 Cherbourg Cédex; tel 33-43-50-80; telex 170690.
Vice-Consul: Daniel Surget.

Consulate: 8 quai Paul Riqeut, 34200 Sète; tel 67-48-63-16; telex 480017.
Vice-Consul: Gilles Suquet.

GABON

Embassy: 26 bis ave Raphaël, 75016 Paris; tel (1) 42-24-79-60; telex 610146.
Ambassador: François Banga Eboumi.
Counsellor (Cultural): Théophile Loungo.
Counsellor (Protocol): Fidèle-Tristan Eboumy.
Counsellor (Press): Roger Dominique Nkazengani.
Counsellor (Economic): Marie-Geneviève Charpentier.
Counsellor (Education): Ludwyne Perrois.
Counsellor (Economic/Commercial): François Oyabi.
Counsellor (Protocol): Polycarpe Ndjelassili Alongo.
Counsellor (Cultural): Pierre Mounanga-Loundou.
Counsellor: Antoine Timothé Poulissi.
Counsellor: Amélie Félicité Banga Ebouri.
Counsellor: Marie-Thérèse Heau.
Counsellor (Protocol): Damien Mahicka.
Counsellor: Jacques Mba Dirabou.

GERMANY

Embassy: 13-15 ave Franklin D. Roosevelt, 75008 Paris; tel (1) 42-99-78-00; telex 280136; fax (1) 43-59-74-18.
Ambassador: Dr Franz Pfeffer.

Consulate-General: 377 blvd du Président Wilson, 33200 Bordeaux; tel 56-08-60-20; telex 540662; fax 56-42-32-65.

Consulate-General: 22 place du Maréchal Leclerc, 59046 Lille; tel 20-93-84-63; telex 160293.
Consul-General: Franz-Walter Pyroth.

Consulate-General: 33 blvd des Belges, 69458 Lyon Cédex 06; tel 78-93-54-73; telex 370517.
Consul-General: Peter Schoenwaldt.

Consulate-General: 338 ave du Prado, 13295 Marseille Cédex 8; tel 91-77-60-90; telex 401335.
Consul-General: Joachim-Richard Vogel.

Consulate-General: 15 rue de Buthégnémont, 54052 Nancy Cédex; tel 83-96-12-43; telex 850805.
Consul-General: Johann Stenglein.

Consulate-General: 15 rue des Francs Bourgeois, 67081 Strasbourg Cédex; tel 88-32-61-86; telex 880390.

Consulate: c/o ADAC Avignon, Z.Z. Courtine, 185 ave des Rémouleurs, 84000 Avignon; tel 90-82-98-71.
Honorary Consul: Bettina Buckwell.

Consulate: Immeuble Rivoli C, ave de la Libération, 20600 Bastia; tel 95-33-85-41; telex 460072.
Honorary Consul: Franz Meindl.

Consulate: 7-11 rue de Verdun, 62200 Boulogne-sur-Mer; BP 78, 62201 Boulogne-sur-Mer; tel 21-33-92-33; telex 11039.
Honorary Consul: Philippe Delpierre.

Consulate: 9 square Commandant l'Herminier, 29200 Brest; tel 98-44-35-59.
Honorary Consul: Wolfgang Barfuss.

Consulate: Ets. Breillon, 17-9 ave de la Gare, BP 6, 73800 Montmelian; tel 79-84-21-45; telex 980074; fax 79-84-14-49.
Honorary Consul: Philibert Braillon.

Consulate: 47 rue d'York, 21100 Dijon; tel 80-71-52-34.
Honorary Consul: Jean Georges Brunner.

Consulate: 6 rue de Beaumont, 59140 Dunkerque; BP 2/100, 59376 Dunkerque Cédex; tel 28-59-35-59; telex 820947.
Honorary Consul: Laurent Lemaire.

Consulate: 7 rue Pierre-Brossolette, 76051 Le Havre Cédex; tel 35-21-11-22; telex 190159.
Honorary Consul: Alexis Lobadowsky.

Consulate: 2 rue Esnoult des Châtelets, 56100 Lorient; tel 97-21-18-94.
Honorary Consul: Raymond Horel.

Consulate: 3 rue Fournarié, 34000 Montpellier; tel 67-60-47-43.
Honorary Consul: Martin Andersch.

Consulate: 22 rue Crébillon, 44000 Nantes; BP 336, 44011 Nantes Cédex 01; tel 40-69-76-37; telex 700182; fax 40-69-25-15.
Honorary Consul: Dominique Houitte de la Chesnais.

Consulate: 22 ave Notre Dame, 06000 Nice; tel 93-62-22-26; telex 461624.
Honorary Consul: Gerd Ziegenfeuter.

Consulate: 12 blvd Wilson, 66000 Perpignan; tel 68-51-15-49.
Honorary Consul: André Dauner.

Consulate: 9 place Royale, 51100 Reims; tel 26-45-12-34; telex 830486.
Honorary Consul: Christian Lefebvre.

Consulate: 22 rue Mustel, 76000 Rouen; BP 651, 76007 Rouen Cédex; tel 35-88-48-88; telex 77905.
Honorary Consul: Francis C. Humann.

Consulate: 24 rue de Metz, 31000 Toulouse; tel 61-52-35-56.
Honorary Consul: Yves Barthez.

GHANA

Embassy: 8 Villa Said, 75116 Paris; tel (1) 45-00-09-50; telex 611020.
Ambassador: Thérèse Striggner Scott.

GREECE

Embassy: 17 rue Auguste Vacquerie, 75116 Paris; tel (1) 47-23-72-28; telex 612747; fax (1) 47-23-33-57.
Ambassador: Alexandre Raphaël.
Minister-Counsellor: Georges Yennimatas.
First Counsellor: Spyros Georgiles.
First Secretary: Alexis-Platon Hadjimichalis.
First Secretary: Nicolaos Pazios.
Second Secretary: Maria-Louisa Marinakis.
Attaché (Culture): Stamatina Tolia.
Attaché: Panayota Anagnostopoulou.
Attaché: Stéfanos Petinakis.

Consulate-General: 23 rue Galilée, 75116 Paris; tel (1) 47-23-72-23; fax (1) 47-20-42-64.
Consul-General: Lazaros Nanos.

Consulate-General: 538 rue Paradis, 13008 Marseille; tel 91-77-54-01; fax 91-71-55-54.
Consul-General: Georges Gabrielides.

GUATEMALA

Embassy: 73 rue de Courcelles, 75008 Paris; tel (1) 42-27-78-63; telex 650850; fax (1) 47-54-02-06.
Ambassador: Guillermo Putzeis-Alvarez.

GUINEA

Embassy: 51 rue de la Faisanderie, 75016 Paris; tel (1) 47-04-81-48; telex 648497.
Ambassador: Marcel Martin.

HAITI

Embassy: 10 rue Théodule Ribot, 75017 Paris; tel (1) 47-63-47-78.
Chargé d'affaires a.i.: Serge Vieux.

HOLY SEE

Apostolic Nunciature: 10 ave du Président Wilson, 75116 Paris; tel (1) 47-23-58-34; fax (1) 47-23-65-44.
Apostolic Nuncio: Most Rev. Lorenzo Antonetti, Titular Archbishop of Roselle.
Counsellor: Mgr Osvaldo Padilla.
Counsellor: Mgr Mario Giordana.
Secretary: Mgr Giacomo Ottonello.

HONDURAS

Embassy: 6 place Vendôme, 75001 Paris; tel (1) 42-61-34-75; fax (1) 42-61-12-99.
Chargé d'affaires a.i.: Sonia Mendieta de Badaroux.

HUNGARY

Embassy: 5 bis sq. de l'ave Foch, 75116 Paris; tel (1) 45-00-41-59; telex 610822.
Ambassador: János Szávai.

ICELAND

Embassy: 124 blvd Haussmann, 75008 Paris; tel (1) 45-22-81-54; telex 290314; fax (1) 42-93-42-95.
Ambassador: Albert Gudmundsson.
Counsellor: Benedikt Jónson.
Secretary: Hannes Heimisson.
Secretary: Charlotta María Hjaltadóttir.

Consulate-General: Hôtel Terminus-Gruber, 10-1 place de la Gare, 67000 Strasbourg; tel 88-32-87-00; telex 870998.
Consul-General: Jean-Noël Riehm.

Consulate: Les Vins de Crus, 58-60 blvd Pierre 1er, 33000 Bordeaux; tel 56-48-22-39; telex 540300; fax 56-44-81-01.
Consul: Herman Mostermans.

Consulate: 8 ave Maréchal Foch, 06000 Nice; tel 93-80-61-83; fax 93-62-43-94.
Consul: Maurice Dumas-Lairolle.

Consulate: Algoe S.A., 9 bis route de Campagne, 69134 Ecully Cédex; tel 78-33-14-30; telex 380020.
Consul: Gerard H. N. Debrinay.
Vice-Consul: William Withnell.

Consulate: c/o Cie Chambon, 147 rue Sainte, BP 48, 13262 Marseille; tel 91-54-92-29; telex 430255; fax 91-55-65-58.
Consul: Jeanne-Marie de Gaudemar.
Vice-Consul: Eric Jokumsen.

Consulate: Résidence le Beaugency, 6 rue de Vielleville, 57000 Metz; tel 87-75-34-52.
Consul: Bernard Schmitt.

INDIA

Embassy: 15 rue Alfred Dehodencq, 75016 Paris; tel (1) 45-20-39-30; telex 610621.
Ambassador: Soonu Kochar.

INDONESIA

Embassy: 47-49 rue Cortambert, 75116 Paris; tel (1) 45-03-07-60; telex 648031; fax (1) 45-04-50-32.
Ambassador: Doddy A. Tisna Amidjaja.

Consulate: 25 blvd Carmagnole, 13008 Marseille.

IRAN

Embassy: 4 ave d'Iéna, 75116 Paris; tel (1) 47-23-61-22; telex 610600.
Ambassador: Dr Ali Ahani.

IRAQ

Embassy: 53 rue de la Faisanderie, 75116 Paris; tel (1) 45-01-51-00; telex 613706.
Ambassador: Abd ar-Razzak Gassem al-Hashimi.

IRELAND

Embassy: 12 ave Foch, 75116 Paris; tel (1) 45-00-20-87; telex 620557; fax (1) 45-00-84-17.
Ambassador: Tadhg O'Sullivan.
Counsellor (Political): Proinsias Gallagher.
Counsellor (Economic): John Lawton.
First Secretary: John Morahan.
First Secretary: Orla O'Hanrahan.
First Secretary: Donal Kelly.
Third Secretary: Aidan O'Hara.

Consulate-General: 152 blvd J. F. Kennedy, 06600 Antibes; tel 93-61-50-63; fax 93-67-96-08.
Honorary Consul-General: Pierre Joannon.

ISRAEL

Embassy: 3 rue Rabelais, 75008 Paris; tel (1) 42-56-47-47; telex 650831; fax (1) 42-25-64-15.
Ambassador: Ovadia Sofer.

ITALY

Embassy: 51 rue de Varenne, 75007 Paris; tel (1) 45-44-38-90; telex 270827.
Ambassador: Giacomo Attolico.
Military Attaché: Col Antonio Lombardo.

JAMAICA

Consulate: 60 ave Foch, 75116 Paris; tel (1) 05-00-62-25; telex 270105.
Honorary Consul: Albert Bickel.

JAPAN

Embassy: 7 ave Hoche, 75008 Paris; tel (1) 47-66-02-22; telex 660493; fax (1) 42-27-50-81.
Ambassador: Akitane Takeuchi.
Minister: Terusuku Terada.
Counsellor (Political): Norio Haltori.

Consulate-General: 70 ave de Hambourg, 13008 Marseille; tel 91-73-45-55; telex 401939; fax 91-72-55-46.
Consul-General: Takashi Miyazaki.
Consul: Shigeya Hatta.

JORDAN

Embassy: 80 blvd Maurice Barrès, 92200 Neuilly-sur-Seine; tel (1) 46-24-23-78; telex 630084.
Chargé d'affaires a.i.: Awad al-Khalidi.

KENYA

Embassy: 3 rue Cimarosa, 75116 Paris; tel (1) 45-53-35-00; telex 620825.
Ambassador: Simon B. Arap Bullut.

KOREA, REPUBLIC

Embassy: 125 rue de Grenelle, 75007 Paris; tel (1) 47-53-01-01.
Chargé d'affaires a.i.: Young Chan Lo.

KUWAIT

Embassy: 2 rue de Lubeck, 75016 Paris; tel (1) 47-23-54-25; telex 620513.
Ambassador: Tarek Razzouqi.

LAOS

Embassy: 74 ave Raymond Poincaré, 75116 Paris; tel (1) 45-53-02-98; telex 610711; fax (1) 47-27-57-89.
Ambassador: Phoune Khammounheuang.
Minister-Counsellor: Sèngchanh Soukhaseum.
Counsellor (Commercial/Economic): Mongkhol Sasorith.
First Secretary: Siphan Malivarn.
Second Secretary (Commercial/Economic): Sèngthong Thonesengsy.
Attaché: Vatthana Souvannachak.

LEBANON

Embassy: 3 villa Copernic, 75116 Paris; tel 45-00-22-25; telex 611087.
Ambassador: Johnny Abdou.

LIBERIA

Embassy: 8 rue Jacques Bingen, 75017 Paris; tel (1) 47-63-58-55; telex 290288.
Ambassador: Aaron J. George, II.

LIBYA

People's Bureau: 2 rue Charles Lamoureux, 75116 Paris; tel (1) 47-04-71-60; telex 620643.
Secretary of People's Bureau: Saad Mujber.

LUXEMBOURG

Embassy: 33 ave Rapp, 75007 Paris; tel (1) 45-55-13-37; telex 204711; fax (1) 45-51-72-29.
Ambassador: Pierre Wurth.
Assistant Counsellor: Pierre Gramegna.
Secretary and Consul: Fernand Schritz.

MADAGASCAR

Embassy: 4 ave Raphaël, 75016 Paris; tel (1) 45-04-62-11; telex 610394.

Ambassador: François de Paul Rabotoson.
First Counsellor (Military Affairs): Jean Pierre Totobesola.
Counsellor and Deputy Permanent Representative to UNESCO: Robertine Raonimahary.
Counsellor (Training, Co-operation and French-speaking Communities): Pierre Rakotoson.
Counsellor (Maritime Affairs): Louis Fenomanana Rakotomavo.
Counsellor (Economic and Commercial): Benjamin Rakotofamola.
Counsellor (Banking): Richard Randriamaholy.
Counsellor (Industrial Affairs): Xavier Rakotonirina.
Counsellor (Consular Affairs): Armand Edouard Tsimiante.
Counsellor (Social/Medical): Desiré Andrianananjanirina.
Counsellor (Cultural Affairs and Documentation): Arisoa Razafitrimo.
Secretary (Protocol): Maxime Ralaiarison.
Secretary (Consular Affairs): Mizarinala Ralaimiaramanana.
Secretary (French-speaking Communities): Marie Angeline Justin.
Secretary (Information/Press): Florine Injerona.
Secretary (Economy): Angeline Mahajy.
Secretary (Visas): Marie-Annick Dahy.
Secretary (Financial): Rochel Rakotonarivo.
Secretary (Commercial): Parfait Raoelina.
Attaché (Training and Co-operation): Justine Totobesola.

Consulate-General: 234 blvd Périer, 13008 Marseille.

Consulate-General: 21 rue Michelet, 42000 Saint-Etienne.

Consulate: 24 blvd Eugène Réguillon, 69100 Villeurbanne.

Consulate: 39 rue Alphonse Tourres, 76071 Le Havre Cédex.

Consulate: 19 rue Thiac, 33000 Bordeaux.

MALAWI

Embassy and Permanent Delegation to UNESCO: 20 rue Euler, 75008 Paris; tel (1) 47-20-20-27; telex 642804; fax (1) 47-23-62-48.
Ambassador and Permanent Delegate to UNESCO: Willie S. Khoza.
First Secretary (Administration): Emmanuel H. Lozo.
Second Secretary: Richard B. Segula.
Third Secretary (General Duties): Alice Horea.

MALAYSIA

Embassy: 2 bis rue Bénouville, 75116 Paris; tel (1) 45-53-11-85.
Ambassador: Datuk Ismail Ambia.

MALI

Embassy: 89 rue du Cherche-Midi, 75006 Paris; tel (1) 45-48-58-43; telex 260002.
Ambassador: H'Fagnanama Kone.

MALTA

Embassy: 92 ave des Champs Elysées, 75008 Paris; tel (1) 45-62-53-01; telex 641023; fax (1) 45-62-00-36.
Ambassador: Joseph Licari.
First Secretary: Tanya Camilleri.
First Secretary (Political/Cultural/Press/Information): John Borg Micallef.
First Secretary (Administrative/Commercial/Consular): Giovanni Miceli.
Third Secretary: Elizabeth Pace.
Attaché: Josephine Busuttil.

Consulate: 30 ave Robert Schuman, Worms Services Maritime Bldg, 13002 Marseille; tel 91-56-40-40; telex 440067; fax 91-56-01-47.
Honorary Consul: Claud Bietron.

MAURITANIA

Embassy: 5 rue de Montévideo, 75116 Paris; tel (1) 45-04-88-54; telex 620506.
Ambassador: Muhammad el Hauchi Ould Muhammad Saleh.

MAURITIUS

Embassy: 68 blvd de Courcelles, 75017 Paris; tel (1) 42-27-30-19; telex 644233; fax (1) 40-53-02-91.
Ambassador: Eddy Joseph Changkye.
First Secretary: Balmookoond Taposeea.
First Secretary: Jagdeesh Goopt Fokeer.

Consulate: Bordeaux; tel 56-52-17-50.
Honorary Consul: Maurice Dubois.

Consulate: Lille; tel 20-55-32-62.
Honorary Consul: Pierre Galichon.

Consulate: Lyon; tel 74-62-12-74.
Honorary Consul: Christian Dupond.

MEXICO

Embassy: 9 rue de Longchamp, 75116 Paris; tel (1) 45-53-76-43; telex 645332; fax (1) 47-55-65-29.
Ambassador: Manuel Tello.
Minister: Francisco Del Rio.
Counsellor (Science): Samuel Ramos.
Counsellor (Economic): Maria Elena Espinosa.
Counsellor (Culture): Alvaro Uribe.
Counsellor (Press): Salvador Del Rio.
Military Attaché: Brig. Ignacio Sanchez Ortiz.
Deputy Military Attaché: Lieut Col Leobardo Quezada.
Deputy Military Attaché: Maj. Carlos García López.
Naval Attaché: Vice-Adm. Gandhi Zilli.
Deputy Naval Attaché: Capt. José Duarte.
First Secretary (Political): Socorro Rovirosa.
First Secretary (Head of Cultural Centre): Yuriria Iturriaga.
Second Secretary (Head of 'Maison de Mexique'): Enrique Riva Palacio.

Consulate-General: 4 rue Notre Dame des Victoires, 75002 Paris; tel (1) 42-61-51-80; fax (1) 49-26-02-78.
Consul-General: Fernando del Paso.

Tourist Bureau: 4 rue Notre Dame des Victoires, 75002 Paris; tel (1) 42-61-51-80; fax (1) 42-86-05-80.
Counsellor (Tourist Affairs): Benito Echeverría.

Bancomext Commercial Section: fax (1) 42-61-52-95.

Consulate: 7 ave Porfirio Díaz, 04400 Barcelonnette.
Honorary Consul: Pierre Audibert.

Consulate: Domaine de Fleurenne, BP 513, 33291 Blanquefort, Bordeaux.
Honorary Consul: Joël Clavières.

Consulate: 58 rue de Mulhouse, 76600 Le Havre.
Honorary Consul: Brice Vatinel.

Consulate: 39 rue du 22 novembre, 67000 Strasbourg.
Honorary Consul: Raymond Leissner.

Consulate: 3 rue du Président Carnot, 69002 Lyons.
Honorary Consul: Patrick Bertrand.
Honorary Vice-Consul: Anne Bertrand.

Consulate: 274 chemin du Littoral, 13015 Marseilles.
Honorary Consul: Yves Magnan.
Honorary Vice-Consul: Harvey Haight.

Consulate: 35 rue Ozenne, 31000 Toulouse.
Honorary Consul: Raymond de Las Casas de Saint Martin.

MONACO

Embassy: 22 blvd Suchet, 75116 Paris; tel (1) 45-04-74-54; telex 611088.
Ambassador: Christian Orsetti.
Minister-Counsellor: Jacques Boisson.
First Secretary: Jean Fissore.
Attaché: Geneviève Vatrican.

Consulate-General: 93 rue Ducau, 33000 Bordeaux; tel 56-44-16-55.
Consul-General: Jean-Pierre Calamel.

Consulate-General: 12 cours Aristide Briand, 69300 Lyon; tel 78-08-65-05.
Consul-General: Patrick de Grossouvre.

Consulate-General: 38 cours d'Estienne d'Orves, 13008 Marseille; tel 91-33-30-21.
Consul-General: Bruno Grand-Dufay.

Consulate: 5 place Léon-Meyer, BP 103, 76050 Le Havre Cédex; tel 35-21-07-77.
Consul: François Le Chevalier.

Consulate: 3 rue Maguelone, 34000 Montpelier; tel 67-92-69-54.
Consul: Jean Fabre.

Consulate: 17 rue Alexandre-Mari, 06300 Nice; tel 93-85-60-86.
Consul: Paul Hancy.

Consulate: 10 place Gutenburg, 67000 Strasbourg; tel 88-32-12-55.
Consul: Roland Wagner.

Consulate: 82 rue du Général de Gaulle, BP 33, Papeete, Tahiti; tel 25-32-9.
Consul: Paul-Emile Victor.

MONGOLIA

Embassy: 5 ave Robert Schuman, 92100 Boulogne-Billancourt; tel 46-05-28-12; telex 200656.
Ambassador: Luvsandorjiin Mundagbaatar.
First Secretary: Pagamjavyn Boudragtchaa.
Attaché: Oyun Pavdanguin.

Consular Section: tel 46-05-23-18.
Third Secretary and Head of Consular Section: Oidovyn Tchimidregzen.

MOROCCO

Embassy: 3-5 rue Le Tasse, 75016 Paris; tel (1) 45-20-69-35; telex 611025.
Ambassador: Abbes el-Fassi.

MOZAMBIQUE

Embassy: 82 rue Laugier, 75017 Paris; tel (1) 47-64-91-32; telex 641527.
Ambassador: Murade Isaac Miguigy Murargy.

MYANMAR

Embassy: 60 rue de Courcelles, 75008 Paris; tel (1) 42-25-56-95; telex 642190.
Ambassador: U Saw Tun.

NEPAL

Embassy: 45 bis rue des Acacias, 75017 Paris; tel (1) 46-22-48-67; fax (1) 42-27-08-65.
Ambassador: Kalyana Birkam Adhikary.
First Secretary and Chargé d'affaires: R. B. P. Bichwakarma.
Attaché: Ram Khatri.

NETHERLANDS

Embassy: 7-9 rue Eblé, 75007 Paris; tel (1) 43-06-61-88; telex 200070; fax (1) 40-56-01-32.
Ambassador: Henry Wijnaendts.

NEW ZEALAND

Embassy: 7 ter., rue Léonard de Vinci, 75116 Paris; tel (1) 45-00-24-11; fax (1) 45-01-26-39.
Ambassador: Judith C. Trotter.

Minister: Peter Heenan.
Counsellor (Economic): George Troup.
Counsellor: Darryl Dunn.
First Secretary (Agriculture): Neil Fraser.
First Secretary (Administration): Godfrey Payne.
Attaché: Robyn Madden.
Trade Commissioner: Tim Sheppard.
Trade Commissioner: Stephen Jacobi.

NICARAGUA

Embassy: 11 rue de Sontay, 75116 Paris; tel (1) 45-00-35-42; telex 612017.
Ambassador: Roberto Argüello Hurtado.

NIGER

Embassy: 154 rue de Longchamp, 75116 Paris; tel (1) 45-04-80-60; telex 611080.
Ambassador: Yacouba Sandi.

NIGERIA

Embassy: 173 ave Victor Hugo, 75116 Paris; tel (1) 47-04-68-65; telex 620106.
Ambassador: Oluyemi Adeniji.

NORWAY

Embassy: 28 rue Bayard, 75008 Paris; tel (1) 47-23-72-78; telex 280947; fax (1) 47-23-97-40.
Ambassador: Arne Langeland.

OMAN

Embassy: 50 ave d'Iéna, 75116 Paris; tel (1) 47-23-01-63; telex 613765; fax (1) 47-23-77-10.
Ambassador: Munir Abdulnabi Youssuf Makki.
First Secretary: Ghazi al-Rawas.
Second Secretary: Abdullah al-Sadi.

PAKISTAN

Embassy: 18 rue Lord Byron, 75008 Paris; tel (1) 45-62-23-32; telex 644000; fax (1) 45-62-89-15.
Ambassador: Dr Tanvir Ahmed Khan.
Minister: Khalid Mahmood.
Information Officer: Zafar Masud.

Consulate-General: 10 blvd Jules Favre, 69006 Lyon; tel 78-24-68-46; fax 78-52-96-80.
Consul-General: Marcel Cuzin.

PANAMA

Embassy: 145 ave de Suffren, 75015 Paris; tel (1) 47-83-23-32; telex 205970; fax (1) 45-67-99-43.
Ambassador: Antonia de Roux Arosemena.

PARAGUAY

Embassy: 8 ave Charles Floquet, 75007 Paris; tel (1) 47-83-54-77.
Ambassador: Aníbal Filartiga Caraillo.

PERU

Embassy: 50 ave Kléber, 75116 Paris; tel (1) 47-04-34-53; telex 611081.
Chargé d'affaires a.i.: Norah Nalvarte.

PHILIPPINES

Embassy: 39 ave Georges Mandel, 75116 Paris; tel (1) 47-04-65-50; telex 611572; fax (1) 47-04-49-92.
Ambassador: Felicidad Bengzon-Gonzales.

POLAND

Embassy: 1-3 rue Talleyrand, 75007 Paris; tel (1) 45-51-60-80; telex 611029.
Ambassador: Jerzy Lukaszewski.

PORTUGAL

Embassy: 3 rue de Noisiel, 75116 Paris; tel (1) 47-27-35-29; telex 620905.
Ambassador: Luís Gaspar da Silva.

QATAR

Embassy: 57 quai d'Orsay, 75007 Paris; tel (1) 45-51-90-71; telex 270074.
Ambassador: Abd ar-Rahman al-Attıyah.

ROMANIA

Embassy: 5 rue de l'Exposition, 75007 Paris; tel (1) 47-05-57-64.
Chargé d'affaires a.i.: Sabin Pop.

RUSSIA

Embassy: 40-50 blvd Lannes, 75116 Paris; tel (1) 45-04-05-50; telex 611761.
Ambassador: Yuri Ryjov.

Consulate-General: 3 ave Ambroise-Pare, Marseille; tel 91-77-15-25; telex 440272.

RWANDA

Embassy: 12 rue Jadin, 75017 Paris; tel (1) 42-27-36-31; telex 650930.
Ambassador: Denis Magira-Bigirimana.

SAN MARINO

Embassy: 19 ave Franklin Roosevelt, 75008 Paris; tel (1) 49-53-08-85; telex 643445; fax (1) 49-53-01-26.
Ambassador: Camillo de Benedetti.
Counsellor (Culture): Maria Teresa Chiantore-Seragnoli.
Counsellor: Countess Isa Corinaldi.
Secretary: Rolf Spier-Donati.

Consulate-General: 50 rue du Colisée, 75000 Paris; tel (1) 43-59-82-89.
Consul-General: Pier Marino Barulli.

Consulate: 10 rue de Belgrade, Grenoble; tel 76-46-36-82.
Consul: Eliane Rastelli.

Consulate: 94 chemin du Littoral, Marseille; tel 91-69-44-49.
Consul: Regis Teisseire.

Consulate: 18 place du Forum, Metz; tel 87-75-15-31.
Consul: Michel Nicoletta.

Consulate: 23 rue Verdi, Nice; tel 93-88-01-49.
Consul: Emile Lemire.

SAUDI ARABIA

Embassy: 5 ave Hoche, 75008 Paris; tel (1) 47-66-02-06; telex 641508.
Ambassador: Jamil al-Hejailan.

SENEGAL

Embassy: 14 ave Robert Schuman, 75007 Paris; tel (1) 47-05-39-45; telex 611563.
Ambassador: Massamba Sarre.

SEYCHELLES

Embassy: 53 bis rue François 1er, 75008 Paris; tel (1) 47-23-98-11; telex 649634; fax (1) 47-23-77-02.
Ambassador: Callixte F.-X. d'Offay.
Secretary: Renette Nicette.

Consulate-General: tel (1) 47-20-26-26; telex 650055; fax (1) 47-23-09-65.
Honorary Consul-General: Adil Iskaros.
Honorary Consul-General: Adil Iskaros.

SINGAPORE

Embassy: 12 sq. de l'ave Foch, 75116 Paris; tel (1) 45-00-33-61; telex 630994; fax (1) 45-00-61-79.
Ambassador: David Saul Marshall.

SOMALIA

Embassy: 26 rue Dumont d'Urville, 75116 Paris; tel (1) 45-00-76-51; telex 611828.
Ambassador: Said Hagi Muhammad Farah.

SOUTH AFRICA

Embassy: 59 quai d'Orsay, 75383 Paris Cédex 07; tel (1) 45-55-92-37; telex 200280; fax (1) 45-51-88-12.
Ambassador: Dr A. W. M. Burger.
Counsellor (Administrative Affairs): D. Robbertse.
Counsellor (Commercial Affairs): G. Gleimius.
Counsellor (Mining and Energy Affairs): A. Dykes.
Counsellor (Technical/Agricultural Affairs): G. J. Carstens.
Counsellor (Technical/Agricultural Affairs): S. Visser.
Counsellor (Technical Affairs): D. R. Spring.
Counsellor: P. L. U. Viljoen.
Counsellor: H. A. Van Dalsen.
Air Attaché: Col D. Du Toit.
Naval Attaché: Capt. S. Stead.
First Secretary (Commercial Affairs): P. E. Nortje.
First Secretary: Mr Faure.
First Secretary: Mr du Preez.
First Secretary: J. Russouw.
First Secretary: E. Dry.
Attaché (Immigration): J. J. B. Hewetson.
Attaché (Immigration): M. du Plessis.

Consulate: 408 ave du Prado, 13008 Marseille; tel 16-91-22-66.
Consul: L. Conradie.

Consulate-General: BP 1259, 76063 Le Havre; tel 35-22-81-81.
Honorary Consul: E. P. J. Balguerie.

Consulate-General: 104 rue Nationale, 59800 Lille; tel 20-57-54-73; telex 120112.
Honorary Consul-General: L. G. Tharin.

SPAIN

Embassy: 13 ave Georges V, 75008 Paris; tel (1) 47-23-61-83; telex 280689.
Ambassador: Juan Durán-Lóriga Rodrigáñez.

SRI LANKA

Embassy: 15 rue d'Astorg, 75008 Paris; tel (1) 42-66-35-01; telex 642337.
Chargé d'affaires a.i.: Dr Ananda W. P. Gurugé.

SUDAN

Embassy: 56 ave Montaigne, 75008 Paris; tel (1) 47-20-07-34; telex 660268.
Ambassador: Awad el-Karim Fadulalla.

SWEDEN

Embassy: 17 rue Barbet-de-Jouy, 75007 Paris; tel (1) 45-55-92-15; telex 204675; fax (1) 45-50-26-43.
Ambassador: Carl Lidbom.
Minister: Christofer Gyllenstierna.
Minister-Counsellor: Steen Hohwü-Christensen.
Counsellor (Press): Gösta Grassman.
Counsellor: Carl-Göran Nylén.
Second Secretary: Krestin Charlier.
Second Secretary: Jan Knuttson.
Second Secretary: May Ann Ramsey.
Second Secretary: Caroline Wergens.
Third Secretary: Barbro Alsén-Crétien.
Vice-Consul: Monica Thomas.
Chancellor: Gunilla Benneberg-Jannier.
Chancellor: Solveig Bonnet.
Chancellor: Liselott Vivi-Anne Linberg.
Chancellor: Hildur Elisabet Maunoury-Isaksson.
Counsellor (Agricultural): Jerzy Glücksman.

Counsellor (Labour): Margit Wallsten.
Counsellor (Labour): Christer Dahlberg.
Attaché (Technical Contracts): Kurt Nordsfor.

Consulate-General: 376 ave du Prado, 13008 Marseille; tel 91-76-30-14; telex 42430273; fax 91-76-16-48.
Consul-General: Ragnar Dromberg.

Consulate: 20 rue de Beauvais, 80000 Amiens; tel 56-39-33-33; telex 560031.
Consul: Patrick Pierre Dominique Thomas.

Consulate: 38 quai de la Douanne, 29283 Brest Cédex; tel 98-44-49-95; telex 940522; fax 98-43-30-20.
Consul: Loïc Emile François-Marie Morice.

Consulate: 198 rue des Quatres Coins, BP 261, 62105 Calais Cédex; tel 21-34-77-34; telex 130114; fax 21-96-71-49.
Consul: Edmond Marie Jacques Paignez.

Consulate: Le Mont Maigre, route de Montreuil, 50570 Marigny; tel 33-05-51-61.
Consul: Michel Paul Eugène Robert Yvon.

Consulate: 11 quai de la Citadelle, BP 31177, 59377 Dunkerque Cédex; tel 28-66-74-00; telex 820983.
Consul: Ola Sätren.
Chancellor: Gilbert Nicloux.

Consulate: 106 blvd Emile Delmas, BP 2038, 17009 La Rochelle Cédex; tel 46-42-13-44; telex 790742.
Consul: Yves Eugène Desiré Thomas.

Consulate: 182 rue de Paris, BP 133, 76051 Le Havre Cédex; tel 35-42-23-54; telex 190923.
Consul: Gérard Jacques Spicq.

Consulate: 1 blvd de la Liberté, 59800 Lille; tel 20-54-27-80.
Consul: Jacques Victor Charles Mollet.

Consulate: 103 cours Emile Zola, 69100 Villeurbanne; tel 78-93-11-77; telex 300585.
Consul: Raymond Villiers.
Chancellor: Claude Le Moël.

Consulate: 70 quai de la Fosse, BP 779, 44029 Nantes Cédex 04; tel 40-73-85-59; telex 700578.
Consul: Serge Gilbert Marie Naudin.

Consulate: Société Mumm, 29 rue du Champs de Mars, 51100 Reims; tel 26-40-22-73; telex 830001.
Consul: Paul Alain Coureau.

Consulate: 22 rue Mustel, BP 4013, 76021 Rouen Cédex; tel 35-89-81-81; telex 770905.
Consul: Lionel Marcel Philippe Taconet.
Chancellor: Hélène Lucie Verdure.

Consulate: 11 rue du Canal, 67400 Illkirch-Graffenstaden, BP 271, 67007 Strasbourg Cédex; tel 88-39-43-91.
Consul: Pierre-Etienne Weiss.

Consulate: 27-9 ave Jean-Médecin, Europole C., 06000 Nice; tel 93-88-14-40; fax 93-87-19-00.
Chancellor: Boel Eleonora Obadia.

Consulate: 26 rue Paul Fort, 66000 Perpignan; tel 68-61-07-44.
Consul: Laurent Emile Jean Cornella.

Consulate: 8 quai Paul Riquet, BP 48, 34201 Sète Cédex; tel 67-48-63-16; telex 480017; fax 67-48-65-50.
Consul: Laurent Henri Léon Suquet.

Consulate: 10 allée Paul Sabatier, 31000 Toulouse; tel 61-55-45-20; fax 61-25-71-41.
Consul: Bernard de Costecaude de Saint-Victor.

SWITZERLAND

Embassy: 142 rue de Grenelle, 75007 Paris; tel (1) 45-50-34-46; telex 270969; fax (1) 45-51-34-77.
Ambassador: Carlo Jagmetti.
Minister: Jean-Marc Boulgaris.
Counsellor (Press): Christian Dunant.
Counsellor (Economic): Dante Martinelli.
Counsellor (Space): Viktor Christen.
Defence Attaché: Brig. Bruno Deslarzes.
First Secretary (Culture): Paul Koller.
First Secretary: Pierre Helg.
Consul and Office Manager: Urs Badertscher.
Consul: Claude Péclard.
Vice-Consul: Jean-Jacques Mayor.
Vice-Consul: Roland Rietmann.

UNESCO Delegation: 1 rue Miollis, 75732 Paris Cédex 15; tel (1) 47-83-28-39; telex 270969; fax (1) 43-83-28-97.
Ambassador: François Nordmann.
Counsellor: Michel Pache.
Attaché and Head of Chancery: Josette Decaillet.

Consulate-General: 14 cours Xavier, Arnozan, 33080 Bordeaux Cédex; tel 56-52-18-65; fax 56-44-08-65.
Consul-General: Francis Cousin.
Vice-Consul and Chancellor: Claude-André Berberat.

Consulate-General: 8 rue Godefroy, 69453 Lyon Cédex 06; BP 6408, 69413 Lyon Cédex 06; tel 78-93-51-34; fax 78-93-50-49.
Consul-General: Hansjörg Säuberli.
Consul and Chancellor: Werner von Deschwanden.

Consulate-General: 65 ave du Prado, 13006 Marseille; tel 91-78-51-61; telex 402599; fax 91-79-04-22.
Consul-General: Alfred Bähler.
Chancellor: Jean-Daniel Crausaz.

Consulate: 25 rue Royale, Annecy; BP 70, 74002 Annecy Cédex; tel 50-51-18-82; fax 50-45-18-02.
Consul: Egmund Frei.
Vice-Consul and Chancellor: Ursula Winzler.

Consulate: 25 rue Proudhon, Besançon; BP 107, 25013 Besançon Cédex; tel 81-81-00-10; fax 81-81-19-89.
Consul: Günter Britschgi.
Vice-Consul and Chancellor: Nelly Ryser.

Consulate: 124 blvd de Strasbourg, 76600 Le Havre; CP 108, 76050 Le Havre Cédex; tel 35-42-27-09; fax 35-21-42-08.
Consul: Osvaldo Casoni.
Vice-Consul and Chancellor: Beat Bürgi.

Consulate: 19b rue de Sauvage, 68100 Mulhouse; CP 1027, 68050 Mulhouse Cédex; tel 89-45-32-12; fax 89-56-46-25.
Consul: Walter Baumann.
Chancellor: Angelo Stucker.

Consulate: 4 ave Georges Clemenceau, 06000 Nice; tel 93-88-85-09; fax 93-88-52-47.
Consul: Charles Gilliéron.
Vice-Consul and Chancellor: Adele Scherrer-Cortesi.

Consulate: 11 blvd du Président Edwards, 67083 Strasbourg Cédex; tel 88-35-00-70; telex 880086; fax 88-35-55-31.
Consul: Victor Lauper.
Chancellor: Georges Croisier.

Consulate: 18 rue Audra, 21000 Dijon; tel 80-30-81-00.
Honorary Consul: Pierre Oechslin.
Vice-Consul and Chancellor: Arlette Graber.

Consulate: 24 rue Desrousseaux, 59800 Lille; tel 20-52-65-26.
Honorary Consul: Michel Joseph.

SYRIA

Embassy: 20 rue Vaneau, 75007 Paris; tel (1) 45-50-24-90.
Ambassador: Honein Hatem.

TANZANIA

Embassy: 70 blvd Péreire, 75017 Paris; tel (1) 47-66-21-77; telex 643968.
Ambassador: Tatu Nuru.

THAILAND

Embassy: 8 rue Greuze, 75116 Paris; tel (1) 47-04-32-22; telex 611626; fax (1) 47-55-67-13.
Ambassador: Thep Devakula.
Minister: Phoonphol Thevit.
Minister-Counsellor: Kanya Chaiman.
Counsellor (Education): Kobkul Yamali.
Defence and Naval Attaché: Capt. Roongrat Boonyaratapan.
Military Attaché: Col Sunshine Rajatawan.
First Secretary: Vanida Kuttawas.
First Secretary: Pichal Israbhakdi.
Second Secretary: Boonsom Chankitisakoon.
Second Secretary: Busaya Ongsulee.
Second Secretary: Prayoon Chatphaisal.
Second Secretary: Suphorn Pholmani.
Second Secretary: Chanchai Jiamboonsri.

Commercial Office: 184 rue de l'Université, 75007 Paris; tel (1) 45-51-73-43; fax (1) 45-51-66-59.
Counsellor (Commercial): Suraphol Jaovisidha.

UNESCO Delegation: Bureau S.233, 1 rue Moillis, 75015 Paris; tel (1) 45-68-25-66.
Permanent Delegate: Srinoi Povatong.

Consulate-General: 1 traverse Mardirossain, 13015 Marseille; tel 91-60-96-46.
Honorary Vice-Consul-General: François Biget.

Consulate: 2 quai Général Sarrail, 69006 Lyon; tel 78-24-99-37.
Honorary Consul: Marquis Jean de Leusse.

TOGO

Embassy: 8 rue Alfred Roll, 75017 Paris; tel (1) 43-80-12-13; telex 290497.
Ambassador: Boumbéra Alassounouma.

TUNISIA

Embassy: 25 rue Barbet de Jouy, 75007 Paris; tel (1) 45-55-95-98; telex 200639; fax (1) 45-56-02-64.
Ambassador: Ibrahim Turki.

TURKEY

Embassy: 16 ave de Lamballe, 75016 Paris; tel (1) 45-24-52-24; telex 611784; fax (1) 45-20-41-91.
Ambassador: Ilter Türkmen.

UGANDA

Embassy: 13 ave Raymond Poincaré, 75116 Paris; tel (1) 47-27-46-80; telex 630028; fax (1) 47-27-46-80.
Ambassador: Francis Xavier Sentole Hatega.
First Secretary and Chargé d'affaires a.i.: Winnifred Karagwa Byanyima.
First Secretary and Head of Chancery: Jackson Big Ocana.
First Secretary: Joyce Claire Banya.
Third Secretary: Beatrice Baruga.

UKRAINE

Embassy: Paris.

UNITED ARAB EMIRATES

Embassy: 3 rue de Lota, 75116 Paris; tel (1) 45-53-94-04; telex 620003.
Chargé d'affaires a.i.: Ali Moubarak al-Mansouri.

UNITED KINGDOM

Embassy: 35 rue du Faubourg Saint Honoré, 75383 Paris Cédex 08; tel (1) 42-66-91-42; telex 650264; fax (1) 42-66-95-90.
Ambassador: Sir Ewen Fergusson.
Minister: J. R. Young.
Counsellor and Head of Chancery: J. M. MacGregor.
Counsellor (Information): B. P. Noble.
Counsellor (Finance and EC): C. D. Crabbie.
Counsellor (Management): P. A. McDermott.
Counsellor (Culture) and British Council Director: D. T. Ricks.
Counsellor (Technology): Dr R. A. Pullen.
Defence and Air Attaché: Air Cdre. C. R. Adams.
Military Attaché: Brig. J. F. Rickett.
Naval Attaché: Capt. J. G. F. Cooke.
Assistant Naval Attaché (Technical): Commdr P. A. C. Lockwood.
Assistant Military Attaché (Technical): Lieut Col T. J. W. Robertson.
Assistant Air Attaché (Technical): Wing Commdr J. L. Davies.
First Secretary (Aviation/Defence Supply): S. T. Lindsay.
First Secretary (Economic/Financial): D. G. Roberts.
First Secretary (Commercial): M. Hodge.
First Secretary (Labour): A. R. I. Wilkins.
First Secretary (Technology): H. M. Boyle.
First Secretary (Technology): M. J. Hentley.
First Secretary (Technology): K. Walker.
First Secretary (Agriculture): W. F. G. Strang.
First Secretary (Management): A. J. Smith.
First Secretary (Works): J. I. S. McLean.
First Secretary and Consul-General: M. E. Hunt.
First Secretary and Consul: J. H. L. Lacey.
First Secretary: Dr V. Caton.
First Secretary: M. J. Lyall-Grant.
First Secretary: N. E. Trapé.
First Secretary: N. Marden.
First Secretary: M. A. Runacres.
First Secretary: P. R. Jenkins.
First Secretary: C. A. MacQueen.
Second Secretary (Commercial): B. W. West.
Second Secretary (Science/Technology): M. J. Ward.
Second Secretary (Visa) and Vice-Consul: F. Jones.
Third Secretary (Visits): D. M. Spires.
Attaché and British Council Deputy Director: P. D. R. Ellwood.

Consulate-General: 16 rue d'Anjou, 75008 Paris; tel (1) 42-66-91-42; telex 281715.
Consul-General: G. C. T. Styles.

Consulate-General: 353 blvd du Président Wilson, 33073 Bordeaux Cédex; tel 56-42-34-13; telex 570440; fax 56-08-33-12.
Consul-General: R. J. Langridge.
Vice-Consul (Commercial): A. Roberts.

Consulate-General: 11 sq. Dutilleul, 59800 Lille; tel 20-57-87-90; telex 120169; fax 20-54-88-16.
Consul-General: D. M. Bell.
Vice-Consul (Commercial): D. A. Hinchliffe.
Vice-Consul (Commercial): J. P. Gleave.

Consulate-General: 24 rue Childebert, 69002 Lyon; tel 78-37-59-67; telex 330254; fax 72-40-25-24.
Consul-General: B. Sparrow.
Vice-Consul (Commercial): G. B. Romaine.
Vice-Consul (Commercial): H. L. J. Burlet.

Consulate-General: 24 ave du Prado, 13006 Marseille; tel 91-53-43-32; telex 420307; fax 91-37-47-06.
Consul-General: J. Illman.
Vice-Consul (Commercial): J. J. Patanchon.

Consulate: Barclays Bank SA, 7 ave Edward VII, BP 98, 64202 Biarritz Cédex; tel 59-24-04-60; telex 570004; fax 59-24-46-34.
Honorary Consul: R. F. M. Hope.

Consulate: c/o Lucas Areospace Victoria Centre, Bâti. Didier Daurat, 20 chemin de Laporte, 31300 Toulouse; tel 61-15-02-02; fax 61-15-08-92.
Honorary Consul: R. H. Virnuls.

Consulate: c/o Cotrama, Tour Administrative, Hoverport, 62200 Boulogne-sur-Mer Cédex; tel 21-87-16-80; telex 135585; fax 21-83-10-85.
Honorary Consul: S. G. Ellis.

Consulate: c/o P & O European Ferries, 41 place d'Armes, 62100 Calais; tel 21-96-33-76; telex 810750; fax 21-96-97-57.
Honorary Consul: J. M. Inglis.

Consulate: c/o L. Dewulf, Cailleret & Fils, 11 rue des Arbres, BP, 59383 Dunkerque; tel 28-66-11-98; telex 820911.
Honorary Consul: C. R. Baker.

Consulate: 2 rue de Congress, 06000 Nice; tel 93-82-32-04.
Honorary Consul: R. W. Challoner.

Consulate: Townsend Thoresen, Gare Maritime, 50101 Cherbourg; tel 44-20-13; telex 170765.
Honorary Consul: G. R. Caron.

Consulate: Lloyds Register of Shipping, 7 rue Pierre Brossolette, 76000 Le Havre; tel 35-42-42-15; telex 771303; fax 35-21-47-56.
Honorary Consul: K. R. Dagnall.

Consulate: L'Aumarière, 43220 Couëron, Nantes; tel 40-62-16-02.
Honorary Consul: M. C. V. Chevalier.
Honorary Vice-Consul: E. Chevalier.

Consulate: 'La Hulotte', 8 ave de la Libération, 35800 Dinard, St Malo-Dinard; tel 99-46-26-64; telex 950311.
Honorary Consul: R. Frankel.

Consulate: 16 ave Président Monnerville, Cayenne, French Guyana; tel 31-10-34; telex 910365; fax 30-40-94.
Honorary Consul: G. Nouh-Chaia.

Consulate: Propriété Boubée, route Tuterai Tane, Pirae - Tihiti, BP 1064 Papeete, Tahiti; tel 42-84-57; telex 537; fax 41-08-47.
Honorary Consul: R. J. Withers.

Consulate: Route du Phare, 97200 Fort de France, Martinique; tel 61-56-30; telex 912729; fax 61-33-89.
Honorary Consul: A. J. Ernoult.

Consulate: BP 2041, Zone Industrielle de Jarry, 97192 Pointe à Pitre Cédex, Guadeloupe; tel 26-64-29; telex 019779.
Honorary Consul: W. G. A. Boyd.

Consulate: 136 chemin Neuf, 97417 Montagne Réunion, Réunion; tel 21-06-19; telex 916104.
Honorary Consul: J. M. P. Gaud.

USA

Embassy: 2 ave Gabriel, 75382 Paris Cédex 08; tel (1) 42-61-80-75; telex 650221; fax (1) 42-66-97-83.
Ambassador: Mr Curley.
Deputy Head of Mission: Stephen M. Ecton.
Political Section: Miles S. Pendleton, Jr.
Economic Section: Janice F. Bay.
Commercial Section: Gus Maffry.
Labour Officer: John J. Muth.
Consul: Diane Dillard.
Administrative Section: Bruce W. Clark.
Regional Security Officer: William D. Clarke.
Attaché (Science): Daniel D. Dolan.
Agricultural Section: Herbert F. Rudd.
Public Affairs Officer: James M. Roberts.
Office of Defence Attaché: Rear Adm. Philip A. Dur.
Office of Defence Co-operation: Col Richard J. Beauregard.
Federal Aviation Administration: Robert T. Francis II.
Internal Revenue Service: William Connett.
Attaché (Finance): John D. Lange.
Communications Programme Officer: John Kennedy.
Information Systems Officer: Durwood L. Franke.
Agency for International Development: Martin V. Dagata.
Security Trade Control: Ronald D. Flack.
Department of Energy: Peter P. Jodoin.

Consulate-General: 22 cours du Maréchal Foch, 33080 Bordeaux Cédex; tel 56-52-65-95; telex 540918; fax 56-51-60-42.
Consul-General: Judith M. Heimann.

Consulate-General: 7 quai General Sarrail, 69454 Lyon Cédex 3; tel 78-24-68-49; telex 380597.
Consul-General: Ann L. Stanford.

Consulate-General: 12 blvd Paul Peytral, 13286 Marseille Cédex; tel 91-54-92-00; telex 430597; fax 91-55-09-47.
Consul-General: R. Susan Wood.
Communications Programme Officer: Shirley E. Kern.

Consulate-General: 15 ave d'Alsace, 67082 Strasbourg Cédex; tel 88-35-31-04; telex 870907.
Consul-General: Ints M. Silins.

URUGUAY

Embassy: 15 rue Le Sueur, 75116 Paris; tel (1) 45-00-81-37; telex 610564.
Ambassador: Horacio Terra Gallinal.

VENEZUELA

Embassy: 11 rue Copernic, 75116 Paris; tel (1) 45-53-29-98; telex 610683.
Ambassador: Isidro Morales-Paul.
Minister-Counsellor: Adriana Paula Pulido.
First Secretary: Jacqueline Mora V.
Second Secretary: Rafael Casado Lezama.
First Attaché: Maria A. Borjas R.
First Attaché: Teresa Flores Petit.
First Attaché: Victoria Heredia de H.
First Attaché: Carmen Mistaje de B.
Second Attaché: Nery Mariño.
Third Attaché: Luis Fernando Perez Segnini.
Third Attaché: Antonio Maria Leon.
Vice-Consul: Damian Giuliani.

VIET-NAM

Embassy: 62-66 rue Boileau, 75016 Paris; tel (1) 45-24-50-63; telex 613240.
Ambassador: Pham Binh.

YEMEN

Embassy: 25 rue Georges Bizet, 75016 Paris; tel (1) 47-23-61-76; telex 645241; fax (1) 47-23-69-41.
Ambassador: Ali Muthana Hasson.
Ambassador: Mohammad Abo Lohom.
Minister: Mohamed Nasser Ali H'Nbalh.
Counsellor (Commercial): Abdul Aziz Almekhlafi.
Counsellor (Cultural): Mustafa Abood.
Counsellor (Consular): Tareq Ghaleb Yehya.
Third Secretary (Aministrative/Financial): Abdulrazq al-Amrani.

YUGOSLAVIA

Embassy: 54 rue de la Faisanderie, 75116 Paris; tel (1) 45-04-05-05; telex 645846; fax (1) 45-04-09-85.

Minister-Counsellor (Consular Affairs): Ivan Mladenovic.
Minister-Counsellor (Economic Affairs): Taib Bekto.
Minister-Counsellor: Milivoj Pisar.
Counsellor (Press and Cultural Affairs): Vladimir Prvulovic.
Counsellor (Social Affairs): Petar Mijic.
Military, Naval and Air Attaché: Lieut Col Jovan Kordic.
First Secretary (Consular Affairs): Mara Dimitrijevic Vucinic.
First Secretary: Srdjan Dizdarevic.
Second Secretary (Consular Affairs): Mirjana Nikolic.

Consulate-General: 15 blvd Gambetta, 67000 Strasbourg; tel 88-35-39-80; fax 88-36-09-49.
Consul-General: Andrej Novak.

Consulate: 5 cours Franklin Roosevelt, 69006 Lyons; tel 78-89-22-02; fax 78-93-30-69.
Consul: Mico Stupar.

ZAIRE

Embassy: 32 cours Albert 1er, 75008 Paris; tel (1) 42-25-57-50; telex 280661.
Ambassador: Ramazani Baya.

ZAMBIA

Embassy: 76 ave d'Iéna, 75116 Paris; tel (1) 47-23-43-52; telex 610483.
Minister-Counsellor: Tadumi On'Okoko.

ZIMBABWE

Embassy: 5 rue de Tilsit, 75008 Paris; tel (1) 47-63-48-31; telex 643505.
Ambassador: Ben Kufakunesu Jambga.

International Organizations

EUROPEAN COMMUNITIES

Bureau: 288 blvd Saint-Germain, 75007 Paris; tel (1) 40-63-40-99; fax (1) 45-56-94-17.
Director: Jean-Michel Baer.

Sub-Office: CMCI, 2 rue Henri-Barbusse, 13241 Marseille Cédex 01; tel 91-91-46-00; telex 402538; fax 90-90-98-07.
Director: Charles André.

GABON

ALGERIA

Embassy: BP 4008, Libreville; tel 73-23-18; telex 5313.
Ambassador: Benyoucef Baba-Ali.

ANGOLA

Embassy: BP 4884, Libreville; tel 73-04-26; telex 5565.
Ambassador: Bernardo Dombele M'Bala.

ARGENTINA

Embassy: BP 4065, Libreville; tel 74-05-49; telex 5611.
Ambassador: Hugo Hurtubei.

BELGIUM

Embassy: BP 4079, Libreville; tel 73-29-92; telex 5273.
Ambassador: Paul de Wulf.

BRAZIL

Embassy: 'Indépendance 76', blvd de l'Indépendance, BP 3899, Libreville; tel 76-05-35; telex 5492.
Ambassador: Jaime Villa-Lobos.
Second Secretary: Jorge Karl de Sá Earp.

CAMEROON

Embassy: blvd Léon Mba, BP 14001, Libreville; tel 73-28-00; telex 539660.
Chargé d'affaires a.i.: Isaac Nyemb Nguene.
First Secretary: Simon Khoam Chuinkam.

CANADA

Embassy: BP 4037, Libreville; tel 74-34-64; telex 5527; fax 74-34-66.
Ambassador: Jean Nadeau.
Counsellor (Development) and Consul: Y. L. Valiquette.
Attaché (Administrative) and Vice-Consul: M. Barrenger.

CENTRAL AFRICAN REPUBLIC

Embassy: BP 2096, Libreville; tel 72-12-28; telex 5323.
Ambassador: François Diallo.

CHINA, PEOPLE'S REPUBLIC

Embassy: BP 3914, Libreville; tel 74-32-07; telex 5376.
Ambassador: Yang Shanghuh.

CONGO

Embassy: BP 269, Libreville; tel 73-29-06; telex 5541.
Ambassador: Pierre Obou.

COTE D'IVOIRE

Embassy: BP 3861, Libreville; tel 72-05-96; telex 5317.
Ambassador: Jean-Obeo Coulibaly.

DENMARK

Consulate: Ceca-Gadis, BP 89, Libreville; tel 710971; telex 5230.
Consul: Jean-Pierre Juilla.

EGYPT

Embassy: BP 4240, Libreville; tel 73-25-38; telex 5425.
Ambassador: Effat Reda.

EQUATORIAL GUINEA

Embassy: BP 14262, Libreville; tel 76-30-15.
Ambassador: Crisantos Ndongo Aba Messian.

FRANCE

Embassy: blvd de l'Indépendance, Pont-Pirah, BP 2125, Libreville; tel 76-20-31; telex 5249.
Ambassador: Louis Dominici.

Consulate-General: rue de la Mairie, BP 2161, Libreville; tel 74-34-20.

Consulate-General: ave Savorgnan de Brazza, BP 511, Port-Gentil; tel 75-20-86.

GERMANY

Embassy: Immeubles les Frangipaniers, blvd de l'Indépendance, BP 299, Libreville; tel 76-01-88; telex 5248.
Ambassador: Jürgen Goldschmidt.

GUINEA

Embassy: BP 4046, Libreville; tel 70-11-46.
Chargé d'affaires: Mamadi Koly Kourouma.

IRAN

Embassy: BP 2158, Libreville; tel 73-05-33; telex 5502.
Ambassador: Dr Abbasse Safarian.

ITALY

Embassy: Immeuble Personnaz et Gardin, rue de la Mairie, BP 2251, Libreville; tel 74-28-92; telex 5287.
Ambassador: Alfredo Matacotta.

JAPAN

Embassy: blvd du Bord de Mer, BP 2259, Libreville; tel 73-22-97; telex 5428; fax 73-60-60.
Ambassador: Hideo Kakinuma.

KOREA, DEMOCRATIC PEOPLE'S REPUBLIC

Embassy: BP 4012, Libreville; tel 73-26-68; telex 5486.
Ambassador: Yim Kun Chun.

KOREA, REPUBLIC

Embassy: BP 2620, Libreville: tel 73-40-00; telex 5356; fax 73-00-79.
Ambassador: Park Chang Il.

LEBANON

Embassy: BP 3341, Libreville; tel 73-14-77; telex 5547.
Ambassador: Mamlouk Abdellatif.

MAURITANIA

Embassy: BP 3917, Libreville; tel 74-31-65; telex 5570.
Ambassador: El Hadj Thiam.

MOROCCO

Embassy: BP 3983, Libreville; tel 73-31-03; telex 5434.
Chargé d'affaires a.i.: Tagma Moha Ouali.

NIGERIA

Embassy: BP 1191, Libreville; tel 73-22-03; telex 5605.
Ambassador: Joe-Effiong Udoh Ekong.

PHILIPPINES

Embassy: BP 1198, Libreville; tel 72-34-80; telex 5279.
Chargé d'affaires: Arcadio Herrera.

RUSSIA

Embassy: BP 3963, Libreville; tel 73-27-46; telex 5797.
Ambassador: Yuri Shmanevski.

SÃO TOMÉ AND PRÍNCIPE

Embassy: BP 409, Libreville; tel 72-15-46; telex 5557.
Ambassador: Joseph Fret Lau Chong.

SENEGAL

Embassy: Quartier Sobraga, BP 3856, Libreville; tel 73-26-87; telex 5332.
Ambassador: Oumar Wélé.
First Counsellor: Ousmane Bá.

SPAIN

Embassy: BP 2105, Libreville; tel 72-12-64; telex 5258.
Ambassador: Germán Zurita y Sáenz de Navarrete.
Secretary: Alfonso Barnuevo Sebastián de Erice.

SWEDEN

Embassy: Libreville.

Consulate-General: c/o SOAEM, Zone Portuaire, route d'Owendo, BP 72, Libreville; tel 70-20-82; telex 5205; fax 70-00-91.
Consul-General: Gérard Michel Henri Trotereau.

TOGO

Embassy: BP 14160, Libreville; tel 73-29-04; telex 5490.
Ambassador: Ahlonko Koffi Aquereburu.
Second Secretary: Anani Kokou Nyawouame.
Second Secretary: Bama Lare.

TUNISIA

Embassy: BP 3844, Libreville; tel 73-48-21.
Ambassador: Ezzedine Kerkeni.

USA

Embassy: blvd de la Mer, BP 4000, Libreville; tel 76-20-03; telex 5250; fax 74-55-07.
Ambassador: Keith L. Wauchope.
Deputy Head of Mission: Paul L. Smith.
Political Section: Alexander G. Andrews.
Economic and Commercial Sections: Matthew M. Rooney.
Administrative Section: James R. Reid.
Regional Security Officer: Christopher Amyes.
Public Affairs Officer: Jan Hartman.
Communications Programme Officer: Melvin T. Kolb.

URUGUAY

Embassy: BP 5556, Libreville; tel 74-30-44; telex 5646.
Ambassador: Dr Alvaro Alvarez.

VENEZUELA

Embassy: Hôtel Dialogue, blvd du Bord de Mer, BP 3854, Libreville; tel 73-31-18; telex 5264; fax 73-30-67.
Ambassador: Victor Croquer-Vega.
Second Secretary: Olga Fonseca Jimenez.

YUGOSLAVIA

Embassy: BP 930, Libreville; tel 73-30-05; telex 5329.
Ambassador: Čedomir Strbac.

ZAIRE

Embassy: BP 2257, Libreville; tel 74-32-54; telex 5335.
Ambassador: Kabangi Kaumbu Bula.

ZIMBABWE

Embassy: Libreville.

International Organizations

EUROPEAN COMMUNITIES

External Delegation: Quartier Batterie IV, Lotissement des Cocotiers, BP 321, Libreville; tel 73-22-50; telex 5511; fax 73-65-54.
Commission Delegate: Pierre Protar.

THE GAMBIA

CHINA, PEOPLE'S REPUBLIC

Embassy: Fajara, Banjul; tel 23835.
Chargé d'affaires: An Yongyu.

DENMARK

Consulate: 3 Leman St, POB 268, Banjul; tel 28345; telex 2255; fax 28887.
Consul: Peter Smith.

NIGERIA

High Commission: Garba Jahumpa Ave, Banjul; tel 95805.
High Commissioner: Mark Nnabugwu Eze.

SENEGAL

Embassy: 10 Cameron St, Banjul; tel 27469.
Ambassador: Saliou Cissé.

SIERRA LEONE

High Commission: 67 Hagan St, Banjul; tel 28206.
High Commissioner: H. R. S. Bultman.

SWEDEN

Embassy: Banjul.
Ambassador: Bengt Homquist (resident in Sweden).
Consulate: 20th St West, Fajara, POB 883, Banjul; tel 95299; telex 2300; fax 96042.
Consul: Nils Robert Hardmark.

UNITED KINGDOM

High Commission: 48 Atlantic Rd, Fajara, POB 507, Banjul; tel 95133; telex 2211; fax 96134.
High Commissioner: Alan J. Pover.
Deputy High Commissioner: R. W. Saunders.
Third Secretary (Management/Consular): C. J. Jones.
Third Secretary (Aid): M. R. Goodwin.

USA

Embassy: Kairaba Ave, Fajara, POB 19, Banjul; tel 92856; telex 2300; fax 92475.
Ambassador: Arlene Render.
Deputy Head of Mission: Ruth Wagoner.
Economic, Commercial and Consular Sections: Janet Beik.
Political Section: Steven P. Coffman.
Administrative Section: Ruth D. Wagoner.
Agency for International Development: Jimmie Stone.
Communications Programme Officer: Robert E. Claus.

International Organizations

EUROPEAN COMMUNITIES

External Delegation: 10 Cameron St, POB 512, Banjul; tel 27777; telex 2233; fax 26219.
Commission Delegate: Alan Waddams.

GEORGIA

TURKEY

Consulate-General: Batumi, Svobodi Prospekt 8; tel 339-09.
Consul-General: Okhan Atakan.
Attaché: Ergüven Kuthu.
Attaché: Mete Eryasa.

GERMANY

AFGHANISTAN

Embassy: 5300 Bonn 1, Liebfrauenweg 1A; tel (228) 251927; telex 885270; fax (228) 255310.
First Secretary and Chargé d'affaires a.i.: Dr Makhan Shinwari.
First Secretary: Mir Enayatullah Sadat.
Second Secretary: Mohammad Daud Farkhari.

Consulate-General: 1080 Berlin, Otto-Grotewohl-Str. 3A; tel (2) 2202071; telex 114204.
Consul-General: Mohammad Shafi.

ALBANIA

Embassy: 5300 Bonn 2, Dürenstr. 35-37; tel (228) 351044; telex 8869669; fax (228) 351048.
Ambassador: Andon Berxholi.

ALGERIA

Embassy: 5300 Bonn 2, Rheinallee 32-4; tel (228) 82070; telex 885723.
Ambassador: Kamel Hacene.

ANGOLA

Embassy: 5300 Bonn 1, Kaiser-Karl-Ring 20c; tel (228) 555708; telex 885775; fax (228) 659282.
Ambassador: Hermínio Joaquim Escórcio.
Counsellor: Filipe Manuel Martins.
Counsellor: Augusto Caetano Joao.
Counsellor: Maria Elizabeth Augusto Simbrao.
Third Secretary: António Van-Dúnem Ferreira.
Third Secretary: Eliseu Bumba.
Attaché (Administrative/Financial): Miguel Bento.
Attaché (Press): Maria Fernanda Neves Fernandes.

Consulate: 1157 Berlin, Ehrlichstr. 54; tel (2) 5099064; telex 069114271.
Consul: Mateus de Almeida.

ANTIGUA AND BARBUDA

Consulate: 2000 Hamburg 1, Amsinckstr. 43-3; tel (40) 230446; telex 2162022; fax (40) 231977.
Honorary Consul: Eike F. Malling.

Consulate: 6000 Frankfurt-am-Main, Freiherr-vom-Stein-Str. 24-6; tel (69) 17000010; telex 413926; fax (69) 17000140.
Honorary Consul: Fritz K. Wolf.

ARGENTINA

Embassy: 5300 Bonn 1, Adenauerallee 50-52; tel (228) 222011; telex 886478; fax (228) 229636.
Ambassador: Dr Carlos Alfredo Mandry.

Consulate-General: 2000 Hamburg 36, Neuer Jungfernstieg 6a; tel (40) 342051.
Consul-General: Juan A. Pardo.

Consulate-General: 4000 Dusseldorf, Graf-Adolf-Str. 16-2; tel (211) 324004.
Consul-General: José M. Berro Madero.

Consulate-General: 6000 Frankfurt-am-Main 1, Wiesenhüttenplatz 26-8; tel (69) 233644.
Consul-General: Jorge Stok-Capella.

Consulate-General: 8000 Munich 2, Kaufingerstr. 7/IV; tel (89) 263787.
Consul-General: José María Cantilo.

AUSTRALIA

Embassy: 5300 Bonn 2, Godesberger Allee 105-7; tel (228) 81030; telex 885466; fax (228) 376268.
Ambassador: John Stewart Bowan.
First Secretary: Gregory Rice.

Consulate-General: 6000 Frankfurt-am-Main 1, Postfach 160113, Gutleutstr. 85-4; tel (69) 273909; telex 413821; fax (69) 232631.
Consul-General: John Garran.

AUSTRIA

Embassy: 5300 Bonn 1, Johanniterstr. 2; tel (228) 53006; telex 886780; fax (228) 5300645.
Ambassador: Dr Herbert Grubmayr.
Counsellor (Culture and Science): Dr Christa Sauer.
Counsellor: Dr Alfons Kloss.
Counsellor: Dr Christoph Thun-Hohenstein.
Defence Attaché: Brig. Peter-Erik Czák.
First Secretary (Administration and Consular Affairs): Walter Portisch.
Second Secretary: Mag. Marina Chrystoph.

Consulate-General: 1080 Berlin, Otto-Grotewohl-Str. 5/III; 1000 Berlin 11, Postfach 110509; tel (30) 3915418; telex 114275; fax (30) 3915904.
Consul-General: Gabriele Matzner-Holzer.

Consulate-General: 2000 Hamburg 36, Alsterufer 37; tel (40) 446004; telex 213221; fax (40) 452907.
Consul-General: Dr Jörg Schubert.

Consulate-General: 4000 Düsseldorf 10, Cecilienallee 43A; tel (211) 434141; telex 8584672; fax (211) 453651.
Consul-General: Dr Robert Karas.

Consulate-General: 6000 Frankfurt-am-Main 90, Am Weingarten 25; tel (69) 772066; telex 412859; fax (69) 777013.
Consul-General: Dr Heinrich Winter.

Consulate-General: 8000 Munich 80, Ismaninger Str. 136; 8000 Munich 86, Postfach 860640; tel (89) 9210900; telex 529372; fax (89) 9810225.
Consul-General: Dr Anton Segur-Cabanac.

Consulate: 3000 Hannover 1, Podbielskistr. 7; tel (511) 6083662; telex 922252; fax (511) 6083670.
Honorary Consul: Hermann Bahlsen.

Consulate: 5000 Cologne 1, Glockengasse 1; tel (221) 247475; telex 8873441.
Honorary Consul: Dr John-Werner Madaus.

Consulate: 7000 Stuttgart 1, Augustenstr. 4; tel (711) 626260.
Honorary Consul: Alexander Grupp.

Consulate: 2300 Kiel 1, Lorentzendamm 22; tel (431) 552505; telex 299864; fax (431) 5194234.
Honorary Consul: Dr Fritz Süverkrüp.

Consulate: 2400 Lübeck 1, Postfach 1227, Gertrudenstr. 15; tel (451) 310050; telex 26749.
Honorary Consul: Joachim Brüggen.

Consulate: 2800 Bremen 1, Postfach 101044, Friedrich-Ebert-Str. 26; tel (421) 8096; telex 246055; fax (421) 558097.
Honorary Consul: Robert O. Drewes.

Consulate: 4600 Dortmund 1, Joseph-Scherer-Str. 3; tel (231) 122019; telex 826842.
Honorary Consul: Rolf Hasenclever.

Consulate: 4800 Bielefeld 17, Striegauer Str. 1; tel (521) 207272; telex 932476.
Honorary Consul: Rudolf Miele.

Consulate: 6500 Mainz, Lotharstr. 36; tel (6131) 223947; telex 4187112.
Honorary Consul: Dr Folkert Bellstedt.

Consulate: 6600 Saarbrücken 2, Im Rotfeld; tel (681) 47701.
Honorary Consul: Alexander Rugge.

BANGLADESH

Embassy: 5300 Bonn 2, Bonner Str. 48; tel (228) 352525; telex 885640; fax (228) 354142.
Ambassador: Anwar Hossain.

Consulate: 1000 Berlin 51, Waldstr. 23-5; tel (30) 4109516.
Honorary Consul: Gerd Petrik.

Consulate-General: 2000 Hamburg 11, Ost-West-Str. 69; tel (40) 36081; telex 211347.
Honorary Consul-General: Hubert G. Waldow.

Consulate-General: 6000 Frankfurt-am-Main, Frankfurt Airport Centre; tel (69) 070607; telex 411215.
Honorary Consul-General: Dr Horstmar Stauber.

Consulate-General: 8000 Munich 2, Wittelsbacherplatz 1; tel (89) 235004; telex 529763.
Honorary Consul-General: Dr Wolf Schwarz.

Consulate-General: 2800 Bremen, Martinistr. 58; tel (421) 1760244; telex 244219.
Honorary Consul-General: Karl Hillard Geuther.

BARBADOS

Consulate: 6000 Frankfurt-am-Main, Rathenplatz 1a; tel (69) 294782; telex 414068.
Consul: Kyle Hutson Inniss.

Consulate: 2850 Bremerhaven, Borriesstr. 6-10; tel (471) 28388; telex 238794.
Honorary Consul: Dr Axel Schultze-Petzold.

BELGIUM

Embassy: 5300 Bonn 1, Kaiser-Friedrich-Str. 7; tel (228) 212001; telex 886777; fax (228) 220857.
Ambassador: Georges vander Espt.
Counsellor (Economic): Jan Mutton.
Envoy (Political): Johan Verkercke.
Envoy (Commercial/Economic): Jan de Bock.
Defence Attaché: Col Roger Heyman.
First Secretary (Political/Press): Philippe Coessens.
First Secretary (Commercial): Werner Walravens.
First Secretary (Commercial/Economic): Christine Detaille.
First Secretary (Consular): Jean-Louis Flament.
Second Secretary (Political): Paul Vanheessen.

Agricultural Section: tel (228) 213903.
Counsellor (Agriculture): Romain de Vylder.

Consulate-General: 1000 Berlin 12, Mommsenstr. 45, Postfach 191340; tel (30) 3244031; telex 182773.
Consul-General: André Mernier.

Passport and Visa Office: 5000 Cologne 1, Cäcilienstr. 46; tel (221) 215364.

Cultural Section: tel (221) 218216.

Consulate-General: 4000 Düsseldorf 30, Jägerhofstr. 31; tel (211) 488987; telex 8581498.
Consul-General: Dr Louis de Clerck.

Consulate-General: 2000 Hamburg 13, Mittelweg 87; tel (40) 417075; telex 215779.
Consul-General: Willy de Valck.

Consulate-General: 8000 Munich 40, Franz-Josef-Str. 15; tel (89) 397096; telex 5216044.
Consul-General: Michel Godfrind.

Consulate-General: 6000 Frankfurt-am-Main, Fellnerstr. 5; tel (69) 590578; telex 412849.
Consul-General: Paul Ponjaert.

Consulate: 3000 Hannover, Hans-Böckler-Allee 20; tel (511) 8572554; telex 922755.
Honorary Consul: Günther Tilk.

Consulate: 5000 Cologne 71, Edsel-Ford-Str., Postfach 714444; tel (221) 7197243.
Honorary Consul: Denis de Groof.

Consulate: 8500 Nuremberg 11, Mülgasse 8, Postfach 9122; tel (911) 221886; telex 622070.
Honorary Consul: Gerhard Wöhrl.

Consulate: 2800 Bremen, Herrlichkeit 5; tel (421) 5907134; telex 245740.
Honorary Consul: Michael Grobein.

Consulate: 5100 Aachen, Kapuzinergraben 12-6, Dresdner Bank; tel (241) 467205.
Honorary Consul: Carlita Grass-Talbot.

Consulate: 4100 Duisburg 1, Schifferstr. 26; tel (203) 314399.
Honorary Consul: Heribert Becker.

Consulate: 5650 Solingen, Langansstr. 6; tel (2122) 704556.
Honorary Consul: Cyrille A. van Lierde.

BELIZE

Consulate: 7120 Bietigheim, Lindenstr. 46-8, Bissengen; tel (7142) 3924; fax (7142) 33225.
Honorary Consul: Wolf Kahles.

BENIN

Embassy: 5300 Bonn 2, Rüdigerstr. 10, Postfach 200254; tel (228) 344031; telex 8869656; fax (228) 857192.
Ambassador: Saturnin K. Soglo.
First Counsellor: Séraphin Lissassi.
Minister-Counsellor: Raymond Dominique Vivenagbo.
Second Counsellor: Jean Francis Zinsou.
Second Counsellor: Lucien René Pognon.
Third Secretary: Djahougbo Emile Houwanou.

Consulate: 1000 Berlin 44, Richardplatz 24; tel (30) 6870709; fax (30) 6867524.
Honorary Consul: Dr E. Stegenwallner.

Consulate: 4000 Düsseldorf 1, Ubierstr. 52-54, Postfach 7120; tel (211) 155095; telex 8581892; fax (211) 156155.
Honorary Consul: Horst Markgraf.

Consulate: 2000 Hamburg 11, bei St. Annen 1; tel (40) 3088370; telex 2161209; fax (40) 3088355.
Honorary Consul: Helmuth Kern.

Consulate: 7000 Stuttgart 80, Rübezahlweg 63; tel (711) 714608; telex 0781107.
Honorary Consul: Herbert Reiss.

Consulate: 8000 Munich 40, Tengstr. 27; tel (89) 2716406; fax (89) 2725835.
Honorary Consul: Dr Wilhelm Bezold.

Consulate: 2800 Bremen 1, Langenstr. 52-4; tel (421) 31631.
Honorary Consul: Jürgen Willhöft.

BOLIVIA

Embassy: 5300 Bonn 2, Konstantinstr. 16; tel (228) 362038; telex 885785; fax (228) 355952.
Ambassador: Bernardo Bauer Kyllmann.
Envoy: Jaime Lazcano.
First Secretary (Economic/Commercial/Tourism): Carlos-Rodrigo Zapata.
Second Secretary (Cultural): Lorena Kempff.

Consulate-General: 2000 Hamburg 20, Heilwigstr. 125; tel (40) 476437.
Consul-General: Ana María de Bumüller.

Consulate: 4000 Düsseldorf, Kasernenstr. 21; tel (211) 320990.
Honorary Consul: Erich Gall.

Consulate: 8000 Munich 22, Widenmayerstr. 17; tel (89) 2913800; telex 5214047; fax (89) 2913844.
Honorary Consul: Rüdiger von Kaufmann.

Consulate: 2820 Bremen 70, Weserstr. 73E, Postfach 700203; tel (421) 661230; fax (421) 654103.
Honorary Consul: Franz Meinen.

BOTSWANA

Consulate: 2000 Hamburg 74, Berzeliusstr. 45; tel (40) 7313344.
Honorary Consul: Paul Eckler.

Consulate: 4030 Düsseldorf, Berliner Str. 1; tel (211) 473211.
Honorary Consul: Wolf von Bila.

BRAZIL

Embassy: 5300 Bonn 2, Kennedyallee 74; tel (228) 376976; telex 885471; fax (228) 373696.
Ambassador: João Carlos Pessoa Fragoso.

Consulate-General: 1000 Berlin 15, Kurfürstendamm 11; tel (30) 8831208; telex 184492.

Consulate-General: 2000 Hamburg 36, Große Theaterstr. 42, II; tel (40) 440651; fax (40) 351829.
Consul-General: Francisco de Lima e Silva.

Consulate-General: 6000 Frankfurt-am-Main, Stephanstr. 3-4, Postfach 100961; tel (69) 290708; telex 412003.

Consulate-General: 8000 Munich 22, Widenmayerstr. 47; tel (89) 227985; telex 529013.
Consul-General: Romeo Zero.

Consulate: 3000 Hannover, Hohenzollernstr. 22; tel (511) 7984206; telex 0923923.
Honorary Consul: Dr Hans Ewald Krüger.

Consulate: 7000 Stuttgart, Königstr. 5; tel (711) 20613323.
Honorary Consul: Dr Walther Zügel.

Consulate: 6500 Mainz, Kappelstr. 30; tel (6131) 41234.
Honorary Consul: Reinhard L. Jagdt.

Consulate: 2820 Bremen 70, Am Sedanplatz 2; tel (421) 663816.
Honorary Consul: Dr Ludwig Lohsin.

Consulate: 5100 Aachen, Reichsweg 19-42; tel (241) 508041.
Honorary Consul: Klaus-Peter Pavel.

BRUNEI

Embassy: 5300 Bonn 2, Koblenzer Str. Be 99, 4th Floor; tel (228) 26970; telex 885693; fax (228) 2697777.
Ambassador: Othman Ghafar.

BULGARIA

Embassy: 5300 Bonn 2, Auf der Hostert 6; tel (228) 363061; telex 885739; fax (228) 358215.
Ambassador: Dr Stojan Shivkov Stalev (designate).
Envoy: Andrej Karaslawov.
Counsellor and Head of Press Section: Simeon Nikolov.
Counsellor (Culture): Jvor Sachariev.
Counsellor: Ivan Alexiev.
Defence Attaché: Lieut Col Todor Daraktschiev.
Deputy Defence Attaché: Maj. Plamen Nestorov.
First Secretary: Ivan Starkov.
First Secretary: Krassimir Petrov.
Second Secretary (Press): Ivan Dimitrov.
Second Secretary: Peter Dischliev.
Third Secretary (Politics): Zlatko Ivanov.
Third Secretary (Protocol): Boris Usunov.

Economic and Commercial Section: 5300 Bonn 2, Am Büchel 17; tel (228) 363061.
Counsellor and Head of Economic and Commercial Section: Neno Mitev.
Counsellor (Economic): Georgi Georgiev.

Consular Affairs Section: tel (228) 351071.
Counsellor and Head of Consular Section: Ilia Krastelnikov.

Passport and Visa Section: 8000 Munich 50, Wintrichring 85; tel (89) 174056.
Envoy and Head of Passport and Visa Section: Dimiter Peev.

Branch Office: 1080 Berlin, Leipziger Str. 20; tel (2) 000922; telex 114101; fax (2) 086283.
Envoy and Head of Branch: Metodi Peev.
Envoy: Vassil Petrov.
Counsellor (Economic): Panayot Radkov.
Counsellor (Cultural): Christo Tuparov.
Counsellor: Stantscho Kazakin.
Second Secretary (Political): Plamen Petkov.
Third Secretary (Legal): Milen Ljuzkanov.
Third Secretary (Press): Valentin Valev.
Third Secretary (Consular): Valentin Samsarov.

Consulate-General: 1000 Berlin 33, Max-Eyth-Str. 8; tel (30) 8234108.

BURKINA FASO

Embassy: 5300 Bonn 2, Wendelstadtallee 18; tel (228) 332063; telex 885508.
Ambassador: Moumouni Fabré.

Consulate: 1000 Berlin 45, Kyllmannstr. 20; tel (30) 8337101.
Honorary Consul: Helga Exner.

Consulate-General: 8000 Munich 2, Mozartstr. 18; tel (89) 5309421; telex 528207.
Honorary Consul-General: Walter Heubl.

Consulate: 3000 Hannover 1, Hildesheimer Str. 9/5 O.G.; tel (511) 858836.
Honorary Consul: Klaus Dieter Wolf.

Consulate: 4000 Düsseldorf, 4330 Mülheim/Ruhr, Kohlenkamp 14; tel (208) 44151; telex 856522.
Honorary Consul: Helmut Troitzsch.

Consulate: 7000 Stuttgart 1, Vaihinger Landstr. 48; tel (711) 696910; telex 07255656.
Honorary Consul: Hellmut Niethammer.

Consulate: 6500 Mainz, Kaiserstr. 76-8; tel (6131) 229536; telex 0451209.
Honorary Consul: Dr Dieter Spiess.

BURUNDI

Embassy: 5307 Wachtberg-Niederbachem/Bonn, Drosselweg 2; tel (228) 345032; telex 885745.
Ambassador: Sébastien Ntahuga.

Consulate: 6230 Frankfurt-am-Main 80, Mainzer Landstr. 683; tel (69) 390010; telex 176990925.
Honorary Consul: Bardo Stieffenhofer.

CAMEROON

Embassy: 5300 Bonn 2, Rheinallee 76; tel (228) 356037; telex 885480.
Ambassador: Jean Melaga.
Counsellor (Economic): Maurice Sil Mabouang.
Counsellor: André Marie Atangana-Zang.
Counsellor: Mr Ntamack.
First Secretary: Mathieu Messi Mbarga.
First Secretary: Messac Joseph Linjouom.
First Secretary: Lucien Fouda.
First Secretary: Hamidou Mahonde.
Second Secretary: Thaddée Mefiro.

Military Section: tel (228) 351458.
Defence Attaché: Col Marc Guillaume Nguidjol.

Cultural Section: tel (228) 356463.

First Secretary (Culture): Daniel Mepin.

Consulate-General: 2000 Hamburg.
Consul-General: George A. Tamanji.

Consulate: 4000 Düsseldorf, Kreuzbergstr. 38; tel (211) 403055.
Honorary Consul: Dr Hans Walter.

Consulate: 6000 Frankfurt-am-Main, Mainzer Landstr. 41; tel (69) 2542311.
Honorary Consul: Dr Frank Niethammer.

CANADA

Embassy: 5300 Bonn 1, Friedrich-Wilhelm-Str. 18; tel (228) 231061; telex 886421; fax (228) 230857.
Ambassador: William Thomas Delworth.
Minister: Gary J. Smith.
Minister-Counsellor (Commercial/Economic)): Duane D. van Beselaere.
Counsellor (Economic): Stephen Woollcombe.
Counsellor: Michel Duval.
Counsellor (Investment): Ottfried von Finckenstein.
Counsellor (Commercial): Wayne Robinson.
Counsellor (Press/Public Relations): Peter Roman Lishchynski.
Counsellor (Cultural): Anthony Advokaat.
Counsellor (Financial/Defence): Edmund Carroll Whiteside.
Counsellor (Political): Robert Walter Poetschke.
Counsellor (Science): Dr Walter Fraser Davidson.
Counsellor: Alexander Malcom Leith.
Counsellor: Michael T. Horn.
Defence Attaché: Col Colin W. Wilson.
First Secretary (Financial): Euhen Daniel Ciuriak.

Consular and Immigration Section: 5300 Bonn 2, Godesberger Allee 119; tel (228) 810060; telex 886421.
Counsellor (Immigration): R. Albert Naumann.
Counsellor (Immigration): William van der Stoel.

Consulate-General: 1000 Berlin 30, Europa-Center; tel (30) 2611161; telex 93803; fax (30) 2629206.
Consul-General: Franco D. Pillarella.

Consulate-General: 4000 Düsseldorf 1, Immermann Hof, Immermannstr. 65D, Postfach 4729; tel (211) 353471; telex 8587144; fax (211) 359165.
Consul-General: Dennis S. M. Baker.

Consulate-General: 8000 Munich 2, Maximiliansplatz 9; tel (89) 222661; telex 5214139; fax (89) 2285987.
Consul-General: George E. B. Blackstock.
Consul and Trade Commissioner: D. A. Rosenthal.
Consul and Trade Commissioner: R. Clynick.

CAPE VERDE

Embassy: 5300 Bonn 1, Meckenheimer Allee 113; tel (228) 651604; telex 885505; fax (228) 630588.
Ambassador: António Rodrigues Pires.

Consulate: 2000 Hamburg 36, Jungfernstieg 34; tel (40) 344859.
Honorary Consul: Heinz Georg Kremer.

Consulate: 6000 Frankfurt, 6236 Eschborn, Mergenthaler Allee 45-7; tel (6196) 472711; telex 4072734.
Honorary Consul: José Medina Alves.

Consulate: 7000 Stuttgart 1, Hauptmannsreute 93/1; tel (711) 294157.
Honorary Consul: Helmut Schweimler.

Consulate: 6600 Saarbrücken, Feldmannstr. 72; tel (681) 51006; telex 4421395.
Honorary Consul: Frithjof Wundrack.

CENTRAL AFRICAN REPUBLIC

Embassy: 5300 Bonn 3, Rheinaustr. 120; tel (228) 469724; telex 8861166.
Ambassador: Christian Lingama-Tolequé.

Consulate: 1000 Berlin 33, Hubertusallee 18; tel (30) 8915326.
Honorary Consul: Engelbert Klein.

Consulate-General: 7000 Stuttgart, Herdweg 16; tel (711) 293631.
Honorary Consul-General: Hans Langensiepen.

Consulate: 2000 Hamburg 1, Kleiner Pulverteich 17-21; tel (40) 241431.
Honorary Consul: Walter Harms.

CHAD

Embassy: 5300 Bonn 2, Basteistr. 80; tel (228) 356025; telex 8869305; fax (228) 355887.
First Counsellor and Chargé d'affaires: Taher Abderraman Haggar.
Counsellor (Economic): Bamanga Abbas Malloum.
First Secretary: Khamis Gody.
Second Secretary: Moyana Ndilbe Bindi.

Consulate: 5484 Bad Breisig, Bachstr. 45; tel (2633) 97663.
Honorary Consul: Walter Tauffenbach.

CHILE

Embassy: 5300 Bonn 2, Kronprinzenstr. 20; tel (228) 363089; telex 885403; fax (228) 353766.
Ambassador: Dr Carlos Huneeus.
Minister-Counsellor: Fernando Soro (resident in Hamburg).

Consulate-General: 1000 Berlin 31, Bundsplatz 12; tel (30) 8532193.
Consul-General: Hans Betzhold.

Consulate-General: 2000 Hamburg 13, Harvesthuder Weg 7; tel (40) 457585; telex 213712.

Consulate-General: 6000 Frankfurt-am-Main 1, Humboldstr. 94; tel (69) 550194; telex 413982.
Honorary Consul-General: Bruno Schubert.

Consulate-General: 8000 Munich 22, Mariannenstr. 5; tel (89) 294835.

Consulate: 7000 Stuttgart 1, Etzelstr. 9; tel (711) 604722.
Honorary Consul: Georg Kieferle.

Consulate: 2800 Bremen, Große Weserbrücke 1; tel (421) 323731.
Honorary Consul: Klaus E. Momm.

Consulate: 2300 Kiel, Uferstr. 72; tel (431) 337879.
Honorary Consul: Oswald Dreyer-Eimbcke.

CHINA, PEOPLE'S REPUBLIC

Embassy: 5300 Bonn 2, Kurfürstenallee 12; tel (228) 361095; telex 885655; fax (228) 361635.
Ambassador: Mei Zhaorong.

Consulate-General: 2000 Hamburg 13, Harvestehuder Weg 39; tel (40) 448851; telex 212811; fax (40) 440170.
Consul-General: Wang Taizhi.

COLOMBIA

Embassy: 5300 Bonn 1, Friedrich-Wilhelm-Str. 35; tel (228) 234565; telex 886305; fax (228) 236845.
Ambassador: Luis Guillermo Giraldo Hurtado.

Consulate: 1000 Berlin 15, Kurfürstendamm 62; tel (30) 8819038; telex 184336; fax (30) 8825385.
Honorary Consul: Mohr von Chamier-Glisczinski.

Consulate-General: 2000 Hamburg 13, Hochallee 89; tel (40) 452812; telex 214244.
Consul-General: Ernesto Silva Vasquez.

Consulate-General: 6000 Frankfurt-am-Main, Rudolfstr. 13-7, 5 Stock; tel (69) 251650.
Consul-General: Martha Beatriz Nino de Stand.

Consulate-General: 8000 Munich 40, Ohmstr. 8; tel (89) 347759.
Consul-General: José Joaquim Gori Cabrera.

Consulate: 7000 Stuttgart 1, Eberhardstr. 12; tel (711) 232202; telex 722825; fax (711) 232202.
Honorary Consul: Herbert Hillebrand.

COMOROS

Consulate: 5000 Cologne 41, Löwenburgstr. 10; tel (221) 462161.
Honorary Consul: Dr Karl-Hans Körbel.

CONGO

Embassy: 5300 Bonn 2, Rheinallee 45; tel (228) 357085; telex 886690.
Counsellor: Daniel Eyeni-Sinomono.
First Secretary: Mr Essami-Khaullot.
Second Secretary: Barthélémy Olandzobo.
Third Secretary: Jean-Alexis Boleko.
Attaché: Michel Bakinga.

Branch Office: 1080 Berlin, Clara Zetkinstr. 97; tel (2) 2292768.
Head of Office: François Nguie.

Consulate-General: 2000 Hamburg 76, Armgartstr. 2; tel (40) 2201141.
Consul-General: Klaus Günther Dahms.

COSTA RICA

Embassy: 5300 Bonn 1, Borsigallee 2; tel (228) 252940; telex 8869961; fax (228) 252950.
Ambassador: Arnoldo Amrhein.
Envoy: Isabel Montero de Meissner.
Envoy-Counsellor: Eloy Alfaro Altamirano.
Counsellor: Alvaro Arguedas.
Counsellor: Lucy Argüello.

Consulate: 1000 Berlin 45, Ostpreussendamm 72/74; tel (30) 7123011.
Honorary Consul: Dr Wolfgang Steiner.

Consulate-General: 2000 Hamburg 52, Meyerhofstr. 8; tel (40) 801395; telex 214401; fax (40) 66961910.
Honorary Consul-General: Joachim Ulrich.

Consulate: 3000 Hannover, Marienstr. 8; tel (511) 281127; fax (511) 2834111.
Honorary Consul: Dr Hans Wolf Sievert.

Consulate: 5000 Cologne 1, Am Neumarkt 47; tel (221) 546890.
Honorary Consul: Horst Berndorff.

Consulate: 7000 Stuttgart 70, Chemnitzerstr. 13; tel (711) 721064.
Honorary Consul: Jürgen Hunzelmann.

Consulate: 8000 Munich 2, Neuhauser Str. 16 (Augustiner Haus); tel (89) 266646.
Honorary Consul: Hans Inselkammer.

Consulate: 2800 Bremen 33, Oberneulander Heerstr. 26-28; tel (421) 255131; fax (421) 255591.
Honorary Consul: Helmut Scheffler.

Consulate: 4040 Neuss 1, Am Roettgen 48; tel (2101) 35480.
Honorary Consul: Harry Walter.

Consulate: 6600 Saarbrücken 1, Gutenbergstr. 11-23; tel (681) 502302.
Honorary Consul: Uwe Jacobsen.

Consulate: 6900 Heidelberg, Albert-Überle-Str. 24; tel (6221) 44221.
Honorary Vice-Consul: Maria Krebs.

COTE D'IVOIRE

Embassy: 5300 Bonn 1, Königstr. 93; tel (228) 212098; telex 886524; fax (228) 217313.
Ambassador: Lambert Amon-Tanoh.

Consulate: 1000 Berlin 30, Reichpeitschufer 20, bei Dr R. Weiss Nachfolger GmbH; tel (30) 2628618; telex 184245; fax (30) 2628688.
Honorary Consul: Werner Lütgenau.

Consulate: 2000 Hamburg 11, Beim Neuen Krahn 2; tel (40) 362487; telex 215666; fax (40) 364894.
Honorary Consul: Wilfried Helmcke.

Consulate: 4000 Düsseldorf 13, Am Trippelsberg 105; tel (211) 790196; telex 8588529; fax (211) 796199.
Honorary Consul: Christoph Zimmerman.

Consulate: 8000 Munich 70, Fürstenrieder Str. 276; tel (89) 7141063; fax (89) 716402.
Consul: Ludwig Bauer.

CUBA

Embassy: 5300 Bonn 2, Kennedyallee 22-24; tel (228) 3091; telex 885733.
Ambassador: Raúl Barzaga Navas.

CYPRUS

Embassy: 5300 Bonn 2, Kronprinzenstr. 58; tel (228) 363336; telex 885519; fax (228) 353626.
Ambassador: Andreas J. Jacovides.
Counsellor (Commercial): Costas Shekeris.
Counsellor: Pavlos Hadjitofis.
Second Secretary: Kornelios Korneliou.
Attaché (Administrative): Agathi Koukoulli.
Attaché (Press): Demetrios Hasikos.
Attaché (Commercial): Antonios D. Antoniades.

Consulate: 1000 Berlin 30, Kurfürstenstr. 75; tel (30) 250008; telex 185380; fax (30) 2628408.
Honorary Consul: André Dujardin.

Consulate-General: 2000 Hamburg 13, Rothenbaumchaussee 3; tel (40) 4107497; fax (40) 4107246.
Consul-General: Charalambos Ioannides.

Consulate-General: 6000 Frankfurt-am-Main, Theaterplatz 2; tel (69) 232821; telex 413425.
Honorary Consul-General: Gotthard Häcker.

Consulate-General: 8000 Munich 22, Kardinal-Faulhaber-Str. 15; tel (89) 227920; telex 523426; fax (89) 2393455.
Honorary Consul-General: Wolfgang Wunder.

Consulate: 6231 Sulzbach a. Ts., Wiensenstr. 17; tel (6196) 701411; fax (6196) 74173.
Honorary Consul: Gotthard Häcker.

CZECHOSLOVAKIA

Embassy: 5300 Bonn 1, Im Rheingarten 7; tel (228) 284765; telex 8869322; fax (228) 284369.
Ambassador: Dr Milan Kadnár.

Consulate and Military Mission: 1000 Berlin 33, Podbielskiallee 54; tel (30) 8324084.

DENMARK

Embassy: 5300 Bonn 1, Pfälzer Str. 14, Postfach 180220; tel (228) 729910; telex 886892; fax (228) 7299131.
Ambassador: Knud Erik Tygesen.
Counsellor (Commercial): Kay R. D. Gad.
Counsellor (Press/Culture): Knud Plougmann Nielsen.
Counsellor (Agriculture/Government): Martin Hermansen.
Counsellor: Søren Haslund Jensen.
Defence Attaché: Col Steen Søndergaard Jensen.
Secretary: Franz-Michael Skjold Mellbin.
Secretary: Peter Munk Jensen.
Attaché (Labour): Henning Gade.
Economic Adviser: Tom Risdahl Jensen.
Consul (Consular/Administrative): Claus Petersen.
Commercial Correspondent: Karl Hardt.
Press Correspondent: Dr Bernd Kretschmer.

Consular Section: 1000 Berlin 33, Bitterstr. 23; tel (30) 8324001; telex 183547; fax (30) 8316152.

Consulate-General: 2000 Hamburg 13, Heimhuderstr. 77; tel (40) 4140050; telex 214727; fax (40) 4104057.
Consul-General: Flemming Mørch.
Consul and Counsellor (Commercial): Hans Ingemann Larsen.
Consul: Ruth Mathiesen.
Export Assistant: Mikael Gotlieb Hansen.

Consulate-General: 6000 Frankfurt-am-Main 90, Am Leonhardsbrunn 20; tel (69) 770391; telex 4189452; fax (69) 7071876.
Consul-General and Counsellor (Commercial): Bent Brogaard.
Export Assistant: Hans Ole Larsen.

Consulate-General: 8000 Munich 2, Sendlinger-Tor-Platz 10/IV; tel (89) 595831; telex 528107; fax (89) 597815.
Consul-General and Counsellor (Commercial): Tom Jensen.
Export Assistant: Mike Dittmann.

Consulate-General: 2390 Flensburg, Nordergraben 19; Postfach 2028; tel (461) 23305; telex 22646; fax (461) 17928.
Consul-General: Jørgen Peder Hansen.
Vice-Consul and Chancellor: Hanne Eder.

Consulate: 3000 Hannover 1, Norddeutsche Genossenschaftsbank, Schiffgraben 55; tel (511) 311231; telex 0922751; fax (511) 1227155.
Consul: Gerhard Barner.

Consulate: 4000 Düsseldorf, Königsallee 4; Postfach 1107; tel (211) 131400; telex 8587055; fax (211) 88620225.
Consul: Friedrich Otto Wendt.

Consulate: 7000 Stuttgart, Bolzstr. 6, Postfach 102722; tel (711) 290137; telex 722348; fax (711) 290137.
Consul: Dietrich Weller.

Consulate: 2800 Bremen 1, Schlachte 15/8; tel (421) 17681; telex 244266; fax (421) 1768400.
Consul: Rita Dubbers-Albrecht.

Consulate: 2300 Kiel 1, Kehdenstr. 26; Postfach 1340; tel (431) 970102; telex 292726.
Consul: Wulf Rauno.

Consulate: 2400 Lübeck 1, Fackenburger Allee 67; Postfach 1805; tel (451) 41603; telex 026473; fax (451) 46255.
Consul: Erik Flindt-Hansen.

Consulate: 2190 Cuxhaven, c/o Cuxhavener Schiffahrtskontor, Uwe Trulsen, Färhafen; tel (4721) 38021; telex 232149; fax (4721) 38023.
Vice-Consul: Yvonne Trulsen.

DJIBOUTI

Consulate: 2800 Bremen, Alter Postweg 173 C-H; tel (421) 450006; fax (421) 455006.
Honorary Consul: Hans R. Marquart.

DOMINICAN REPUBLIC

Embassy: 5300 Bonn 2, Burgstr. 87; tel (228) 364956; fax (228) 352576.
Ambassador: Dr Santiago Cruz Lopez.
Attaché (Culture): Dr Magaly Bello de Kemper.

Consulate: 1000 Berlin 30, Tauentzienstr. 16; tel (30) 2112758.
Honorary Consul: George E. Dobbs.

Consulate-General: 2000 Hamburg, Heilwigst. 125; tel (40) 474084; fax (40) 4605197.
Consul-General: Carmen Rosa Hernándes.

Consulate: 4000 Dusseldorf, Rheinallee 46; tel (211) 53234.
Honorary Consul: Franz Wilhelm Dommel.

Consulate: 6000 Frankfurt-am-Main 50, Fuchshohl 59; tel (69) 521035.
Honorary Consul: Horst Wolfgang Dettmer.

Consulate: 8000 Munich 2, Pacellistr. 7 II; tel (89) 29386162.
Honorary Consul: Hans Schubert.

ECUADOR

Embassy: 5300 Bonn 2, Koblenzer Str. 37-9; tel (228) 352544; telex 8869527; fax (228) 361765.
Ambassador: Dr Miguel Espinosa Páez.
Counsellor: Dr Diego Stacey Moreno.
Second Secretary: César Montano Huerta.

Consulate: 1080 Berlin, Clara Zetkin Str. 89; tel (2) 2291258; telex 112755.
Consul: Dr Edwin Johnson.

Consulate: 1000 Berlin 20, Zitadellenweg 20 D-F; tel (30) 3320377.
Honorary Consul: B. Stephan.

Consulate-General: 2000 Hamburg 13, Rothenbaumchaussee 221; tel (40) 443135.
Consul-General: Dr Manuel Granzio.

Trade Mission: 2000 Hamburg, an der Alster 84; tel (40) 249845; telex 211304; fax (40) 245001.
Trade Officer: Claudio Luque.

Consulate-General: 8000 Munich 5, Fraunhoferstr. 2; tel (89) 265658; fax (89) 23701269.
Consul-General: Dr Max Schlereth.

Consulate: 6000 Frankfurt-am-Main 1, Berlinerstr. 56-8; tel (69) 1332295; telex 413173; fax (69) 1332474.
Honorary Consul: Dr Jur Wolfgang Kuhn.

EGYPT

Embassy: 5300 Bonn 2, Kronprinzenstr. 2; tel (228) 364008; telex 885719; fax (228) 364304.
Ambassador: Ahmed Raouf Mansour Ghoneim.
Minister Plenipotentiary: Hassan Salem.
Minister Plenipotentiary (Trade): Ahmed Medhat Elgoweni.
Counsellor (Culture): Dr Kamal Moursi Radwan.
Counsellor (Press and Information): Laila Wassef.
Counsellor (Press and Information): Abdel Hamid Rashed.
Counsellor: Hala Hassan Ismail.
Counsellor: Hamdi Abdel Fattah.
Counsellor: Ahmed Hani Attia Ibrahim.
Counsellor: Fayez Mostafa Nozeir.
Second Secretary (Trade): Amin Sabry Abdel Maguid.
Second Secretary: Ibrahim Mostafa Hafez.

Consulate-General: 2000 Hamburg 13, Harvestehuder Weg 50; tel (40) 4101031.
Consul-General: Anwar Abd el-Massih Bishai.

Consulate-General: 6000 Frankfurt-am-Main 1, Eysseneckstr. 52; tel (69) 590557.
Consul-General: Abdelhamid Ismail.

EL SALVADOR

Embassy: 5300 Bonn 1, Burbacherstr. 2; tel (228) 221351; fax (228) 218824.
Ambassador: José Saguer Saprissa.
Minister (Consular/Economic): Mario Castro Grande.
Third Secretary (Press): Alicia Margerit.
Third Secretary (Cultural): Rhina Rehmann.

Consulate: 1000 Berlin 13, Saatwinkler Damm 42-43; tel (30) 310441.
Honorary Consul: Ernst Schilling.

Consulate: 2000 Hamburg 11, Sandtorkai 5; tel (40) 37001279.
Honorary Consul: Cuno Rothfos.

Consulate: 5000 Cologne, Richard-Strauß-Str. 2; tel (221) 400840.
Honorary Consul: Paul Ernst Bauwens.

Consulate: 6000 Frankfurt-am-Main, Stresemannallee 35-7; tel (69) 638511.

Consul: Franz Otto Kern.

Consulate: 6050 Offenbach/Main, Schillstr. 2; tel (69) 8099338.
Honorary Consul: Dr Lothar Winkler.

Consulate: 7000 Stuttgart 1, Postfach 102721; tel (711) 2579190.
Honorary Consul: Otto H. Appelt.

Consulate: 2800 Bremen 33, Rockwinkeler Landstr. 49; tel (421) 382421.
Honorary Consul: Helmut Werner.

ESTONIA

Embassy: 5300 Bonn 1, Bertha-von-Suttner-Platz 1-7; tel (228) 658276; fax (228) 691251.
Ambassador: Tiit Matsulevitch.

ETHIOPIA

Embassy: 5300 Bonn 1, Brentanostr. 1; tel (228) 233041; telex 8869498; fax (228) 233045.
Ambassador: Tibebu Bekele.

FINLAND

Embassy: 5300 Bonn 2, Friesdorferstr. 1; tel (228) 382980; telex 885626; fax (228) 3829850.
Ambassador: Kai Helenius.
Counsellor (Commercial): Pekka Wuoristo.

Consulate-General: 1000 Berlin 15, Am Kurfürstendamm 183; tel (30) 8827727; telex 308149; fax (30) 8831439.
Consul-General: Erkki Kivimäki.
Consul: Pia Pankamo-Miettinen.

Consulate-General: 2000 Hamburg 36, Esplanade 41; Postfach 301726; tel (40) 3508070; telex 211980; fax (40) 340700.
Consul-General: Unto Tanskanen.
Consul: Hilkka Nenonen.
Consul: Anneli Koch.

Consulate-General: 6000 Frankfurt-am-Main, Lessingstr. 5; Postfach 170255; tel (69) 728148; telex 414698; fax (69) 721150.
Consul-General and Counsellor (Commercial): Peter von Koskull.

Consulate-General: 8000 Munich 2, Löwengrube 12 & 18; tel (89) 2285322; telex 5214589; fax (89) 298875.
Consul-General: Rudolf Alexander Bayer.
Secretary (Commercial): Harri Salmi.

Consulate: 3000 Hannover 1, Hildesheimerstr. 53; Postfach 6547; tel (511) 8071142; telex 922766; fax (511) 8071299.
Consul: Hans Georg Rüdiger.

Consulate: 4000 Dusseldorf, Tonhallenstr. 14-5; Postfach 3729; tel (211) 3672; telex 08582809; fax (211) 3672264.
Consul: Detmar Grolman.

Consulate: 7000 Stuttgart-Mitte 1, Torstr. 15; 7000 Stuttgart 10, Postfach 100463; tel (711) 2148218; telex 2148200; fax (711) 2148200.
Consul: Friedrich Wilhelm Hofmann.

Consulate: 2300 Kiel 1, Sartori & Berger, Wall 49-51; tel (431) 9810; telex 292611; fax (431) 96108.
Consul: Volkert Knudsen.

Consulate: 2400 Lübeck 1, Große Altefähre 20-2; Postfach 1934; tel (451) 15070; telex 26815; fax (451) 150729.
Consul: Claus-Achim Eschke.

Consulate: 2800 Bremen 1, Hafenhochhaus, Überseehafen; tel (421) 3981; fax (421) 398763.
Consul: Hans-Heinrich Pöhl.

Consulate: 2940 Wilhelmshaven, Friedrich-Paffrath-Str. 116; tel (4421) 8021; telex 253416; fax (4421) 802100.
Consul: Friedrich August Meyer.

Consulate: 2970 Emden, Schweckendieckplatz 1; tel (4921) 28800; telex 27840; fax (4921) 21721.

Consul: Fokko Walter Geerds.

FRANCE

Embassy: 5300 Bonn 2, Kapellenweg 1A; tel (228) 362031; telex 885445; fax (228) 351832.
Ambassador: Serge Boidevaix.

Consulate-General: 1000 Berlin 15, Kurfürstendamm 211; tel (30) 8818028; telex 183414.
Consul-General: Raoul Calvignac.

Consulate-General: 2000 Hamburg 13, Pöseldorferweg 32; tel (40) 414106; telex 2164271; fax (40) 41410660.

Consulate-General: 4000 Dusseldorf 30, Cecilenallee 10; tel (211) 499077; telex 8588051.
Consul-General: Jacques Nizart.

Commercial Section: 5000 Cologne 1, Hohenstaufenring 62; tel (221) 204000; telex 8881846; fax (221) 2040077.

Consulate-General: 6000 Frankfurt-am-Main 1, Bettinastr. 62; tel (69) 740137; telex 414494.
Consul-General: Bernard Pottier.

Consulate-General: 7000 Stuttgart 1, Richard Wagner Str. 53; tel (711) 235566; telex 721866.
Consul-General: Joseph Muller.

Consulate-General: 8000 Munich 80, Möhlstr. 5; tel (89) 475016; telex 522007; fax (89) 475016.
Consul-General: Jean-Claude Moreau.

Consulate-General: 6600 Saarbrücken, Johannisstr. 2; tel (681) 30626; telex 4421387; fax (681) 31028.
Consul-General: Paul Copigneaux.

Consulate: 3000 Hannover 1, Kabelkamp 20; Postfach 260; tel (511) 6763271; telex 0922711; fax (511) 6763311.
Honorary Consul: Wolfgang G. Plinke.

Consulate: 2800 Bremen, Töferbohmstr. 8; tel (421) 3053110; telex 244983; fax (421) 3053110.
Honorary Consul: Wilhelm Meier.

Consulate: 4400 Münster, Bismarckallee 1; tel (251) 52030.
Honorary Consul: Paul Schnitker.

Consular Agency: 6800 Mannheim, P2, 12, Dresdner Bank AG; tel (621) 1790.
Honorary Consular Agent: Hans Pfaff.

Consulate: 7800 Freiburg-im-Breisgau, Lessingstr. 13; tel (761) 72383; telex 772799.
Consul: Jean Forlot.

Consulate: 8500 Nuremberg 20, Rathenauplatz 16-8; tel (911) 5312180; telex 622163.
Honorary Consul: Dr Georg Bayer.

Consulate: 6630 Saarlouis, Bathaus-Pavillonstr.; tel (6831) 2936.
Honorary Consul: Odile Villeroy de Galhau.

Consulate: 7570 Baden-Baden, Solmstr. 1; tel (7221) 23750; telex 781424.
Consul: Jacques Agar.

GABON

Embassy: 5300 Bonn 2, Kronprinzenstr. 52; Postfach 200164; tel (228) 352239; telex 885520; fax (228) 356096.
First Counsellor and Chargé d'affaires a.i.: Henri Mbira-Nze.
Counsellor (Economic/Social): E. William Messan.
Counsellor (Culture): Eugénie Mbira-Nze.
Counsellor (Chancery): Henri Igondjo.

Consulate: Berlin.
Honorary Consul: W. Brosch.

Consulate: 4000 Dusseldorf, Roseggerstr. 5; tel (211) 611288.
Honorary Consul: Dr Hans Zahn.

Consulate: 8000 Munich 40, Postfach 221249; tel (89) 989022; fax (89) 9810261.
Honorary Consul: Dr Karl Herrligkoffer.

GAMBIA

Consulate: 1000 Berlin 31, Kurfürstendamm 103; tel (30) 8923121; fax (30) 8911401.
Honorary Consul: Gerhard Bartels.

Consulate: 4000 Dusseldorf 1, Königstr. 9; tel (211) 326537; telex 8881083.
Honorary Consul: Rolf Becker.

Consulate: 8000 Munich 22, Widenmayerstr. 18; Postfach 221249; tel (89) 989022; fax (89) 9810261.
Honorary Consul: Freda Treutlein von Stackelberg.

GHANA

Embassy: 5300 Bonn 2, Rheinallee 58; tel (228) 352011; telex 885660; fax (228) 363498.
Ambassador: Kwame Samuel Adusei-Poku.

Consulate-General: 2000 Hamburg 11, Deichstr. 48-50; tel (40) 372266; telex 161138.
Honorary Consul-General: Willi O. Bührich.

Consulate-General: 4000 Dusseldorf 1, Lindemannstr. 43; tel (211) 682858.
Honorary Consul-General: Manfred O. Schröder.

Consulate-General: 6000 Frankfurt-am-Main 1, Schillerstr. 31; tel (69) 289758.
Honorary Consul-General: Alois Bromkamp.

GREECE

Embassy: 5300 Bonn 2, Koblenzerstr. 103; tel (228) 83010; telex 885636; fax (228) 353284.
Ambassador: Alexandros Zafiriou.

Consulate-General: 1000 Berlin 30, Batreutherstr. 3; tel (30) 2137033.

Consulate-General: 2000 Hamburg 13, Abteistr. 33; tel (40) 440772.
Consul-General: Alexios Christopoulos.

Consulate-General: 3000 Hannover, Podbielskistr. 34; tel (511) 628356.
Consul-General: Jean Vavvas.

Consulate-General: 4000 Dusseldorf, Kaiserstr. 30a; tel (211) 499246.
Consul-General: Dennis Lellos.

Consulate-General: 5000 Cologne, Tunisstr. 19; tel (221) 132008.
Consul-General: Panayotis Karakasis.

Consulate-General: 6000 Frankfurt-am-Main, Cronstettenstr. 64; tel (69) 595750.
Consul-General: Nicolas Vamvounakis.

Consulate-General: 7000 Stuttgart 1, Firnhaberstr. 5a+b; tel (711) 221056.
Consul-General: Evangelos Karokis.

Consulate-General: 8000 Munich 80, Dingolfingerstr. 6; tel (89) 492061.
Consul-General: Kyriakos Rodoussakis.

Consulate-General: 4600 Dortmund, Hansastr. 101-3; tel (231) 142063.
Consul-General: Georgios Veis.

Consulate: 8500 Nuremberg, Königstr. 34; tel (911) 221231.
Honorary Consul: Grete Schickedanz.

Consulate: 8700 Würzburg, Hofstr. 10; tel (931) 52532.
Honorary Consul: Werner Matzdorf.

GRENADA

Consulate: 1000 Berlin.
Honorary Consul: Ronald Bauermeister.

GUATEMALA

Embassy: 5300 Bonn 2, Zietenstr. 16; tel (228) 351579; telex 8869983; fax (228) 354940.
Ambassador: Lucrecia Rivera de Ampuero.

Consulate: 1000 Berlin 15, Lietzenburgerstr. 96; tel (30) 8826793.
Honorary Consul: Reinhart Wieser.

Consulate-General: 2000 Hamburg 76, Lessingstr. 7; tel (40) 2505434; telex 2164426.
Consul-General: Sergio Lionel Amado Monroy.

Consulate: 7000 Stuttgart 30; 7257 Ditzingen, Panoramastr. 3; tel (7156) 6817; telex 355121.
Honorary Consul: Walter Neuer.

Consulate: 8000 Munich 80, Grafingerstr. 2; tel (89) 406214.
Honorary Consul: Otto Eckart.

GUINEA

Embassy: 5300 Bonn 1, Rochusweg 50; tel (228) 231097; telex 886448.
Ambassador: Jean Delacroix Camara.
Counsellor (Political): Amirou Sanoussi.
Counsellor (Economic): Alexis Louis Gomez.
First Secretary: Sanoussi Diallo.
Attaché: Oumar Cissé.
Attaché (Cultural): Abdoulaye Barry.
Attaché (Commercial): Yamory Keita.
Attaché: Mamadou Touré.

Consulate-General: 4100 Duisburg 13, Krausstr. 1a; tel (203) 804235.
Honorary Consul-General: Heinrich Stomberg.

Consulate: 8025 Munich-Unterhaching, Bilbergerstr. 89; tel (89) 611030.
Consul-General: Paul Böhringer.

GUINEA-BISSAU

Consulate: 2820 Bremen, Am Wall 142; Postfach 100305; tel (421) 15122.
Honorary Consul: Karsten-Uwe Koepke.

HAITI

Embassy: 5300 Bonn 2, Schlossallee 10; tel (228) 340351; fax (228) 856829.
Minister and Chargé d'affaires a.i.: Waner Cadet.

Consulate: 1000 Berlin 31, Paulsbornerstr. 2; tel (30) 890030.
Honorary Consul: W. J. E. Böttger.

Consulate: 6000 Frankfurt-am-Main, Hynspergstr. 4; tel (69) 551586.
Honorary Consul: Karl Heinz Arnold.

Consulate: 7000 Stuttgart, Zollamtsgebäude, Hauptgüterbahnhof; tel (711) 225040; telex 722989.
Honorary Consul: Dr Edgar Scherer.

Consulate: 8000 Munich 2, Sonnenstr. 6; tel (89) 553067.
Honorary Consul: Dr Halvor Jaeger.

Consulate: 2820 Bremen 70, Retbergweg 8, 2800 Bremen 33; tel (421) 259588; telex 0244719.
Honorary Consul: Günther Brinkmann.

Consulate: 6500 Mainz, Schillerplatz 7; tel (6321) 30054.
Honorary Consul: Horst Sobirey.

HOLY SEE

Apostolic Nunciature: 5300 Bonn 2, Turmstr. 29; Postfach 200152; tel (228) 376901; telex 8869794; fax (228) 379180.
Apostolic Nuncio: Mgr Giuseppe Uhač, Titular Archbishop of Tharros.
Counsellor: Mgr Fouad Twal.
Secretary: Mgr Mario Zenari.

HONDURAS

Embassy: 5300 Bonn 2, Ubierstr. 1; tel (228) 356394; telex 889496; fax (228) 351981.
Ambassador: Rafael Aguilar Paz C.
Counsellor: Fabrizia Velasquez.
First Secretary (Consular): Marco Tulio Gutierrez.

Consulate: 1000 Berlin 33, Humboldstr. 35; tel (30) 8924044.
Honorary Consul: Heinz Kroh.

Consulate-General: 2000 Hamburg 1, An der Alster 21; tel (40) 2802205.
Honorary Consul-General: Maria Antonia Gonzales-Valladares.

Consulate: 6000 Frankfurt-am-Main 1, Kaiserstr. 4; tel (69) 287644.
Honorary Consul: Heinz Ludwig Bickerle.

Consulate: 8000 Munich, Blütenstr. 9; tel (89) 272902.
Honorary Consul: Carl Peter Söhnges.

Consulate: 2800 Bremen, Breitenweg 29-33; tel (421) 3092560.
Honorary Consul: Friedrich Otto Gellerich.

HUNGARY

Embassy: 5300 Bonn 2, Turmstr. 30; tel (228) 376797; telex 886501; fax (228) 374994.
Ambassador: Dr István Horváth.

Consulate: 8000 Munich 81, Vollmannstr. 2; tel (89) 911032.
Consul: Pál Gresznaryk.

ICELAND

Embassy: 5300 Bonn 2, Kronprinzenstr. 6; tel (228) 364021; telex 885690; fax (228) 361398.
Ambassador: Hjálmar W. Hannesson.
First Secretary: Guňi Bragason.

Consulate: 1000 Berlin 15, Kurfürstendamm 57; tel (30) 323061; telex 17308084; fax (30) 3249840.
Honorary Consul: Andreas Howaldt.

Consulate: 2000 Hamburg, Raboisen 5, 1 Eimbcke-Haus; tel (40) 336696; telex 2163223; fax (40) 331347.
Honorary Consul: Oswald Dreyer-Eimbcke.

Consulate: 5000 Cologne 41, Spitzwegstr. 16; tel (221) 487878.
Honorary Consul: Dr Max Adenauer.

Consulate: 6000 Frankfurt-am-Main, Rossmarkt 10; tel (69) 299978; fax (69) 7505444.
Honorary Consul: Helmut K. Holz.

Consulate: 7000 Stuttgart, Westbahnhof 79; tel (711) 6572031; telex 721822; fax (711) 659065.
Honorary Consul: Emilia G. Hartmann.

Consulate: 8000 Munich 80, Mühldorfstr. 15; tel (89) 41292214; telex 5237030; fax (89) 41292213.
Honorary Consul: Friedrich Schwarz.

Consulate: 2400 Lübeck, Körnerstr. 18; tel (451) 54075; telex 26293; fax (451) 51337.
Honorary Consul: Franz Siemsen.

Consulate: 2850 Bremerhaven; tel (471) 71055; telex 238661; fax (471) 77027.
Honorary Consul: Ludwig Janssen.

Consulate: 2190 Cuxhaven, Leuchtturmweg 5; tel (4721) 36037; telex 2322139; fax (4721) 37765.
Honorary Consul: Wolf-Rüdiger Dick.

Consulate: 4006 Erkrath, Otto-Hahn-Str. 2; tel (211) 25094416; telex 8586603; fax (211) 2509461.
Honorary Consul: Ernst O. Hesse.

Consulate: 3003 Ronnenberg, Lägenfeldstr. 8; tel (5109) 05114609; telex 922979; fax (5109) 4609120.
Honorary Consul: Wolf Grütter.

INDIA

Embassy: 5300 Bonn 1, Baunscheidstr. 7; tel (228) 5405131; telex 8869301; fax (228) 5405153.
Ambassador: Anantanarayan Madhavan.

Consulate-General: 1000 Berlin 12, Bismarckstr. 91; tel (30) 3134091; telex 186562; fax (30) 3136692.
Consul-General: S. R. Choudhuri.

Consulate-General: 2000 Hamburg 1, Burchardstr. 14/VI (Sprinkehof), Zimmer 603/5; tel (40) 338036; telex 2163585; fax (40) 323757.
Consul-General: R. P. Dua.

Consulate-General: 6000 Frankfurt-am-Main, Wilhelm-Leuschner-Str. 93; tel (69) 271040; telex 4170182; fax (69) 237816.
Consul-General: Sudhir T. Devare.

Consulate-General: 7000 Stuttgart, Charlottenplatz 17; tel (711) 297078.
Honorary Consul-General: Helmut Nanz.

INDONESIA

Embassy: 5300 Bonn 2, Bernkasteler Str. 2; tel (228) 382990; telex 886352; fax (228) 311393.
Ambassador: Dr Hasjim Djalal.
Minister and Deputy Head of Mission: Dr Izher Ibrahim.
Minister-Counsellor (Consular): Syamsuddin Shobari.
Minister-Counsellor (Political): Dody Sutano.
Minister-Counsellor (Economic): Zainudin Nasution.
Minister-Counsellor (Press/Information): Ridwan Yahya.
Counsellor: Suryo Suyitno.
Defence Attaché: Lieut Col G. Susanto Darus.
Assistant Air Attaché: Lieut Col Suprihadi.
First Secretary (Administrative): Dewa Putu Arga.
Second Secretary (Economic): Z. H. Matamiang.
Second Secretary (Political): Putri Reno Oesman.
Attaché (Trade): Sumarjono Gunarjo.
Attaché (Immigration): Willy Wekuyahti.
Attaché (Culture/Education): Girindro Pringgodigdo.

Consulate-General: 1000 Berlin 33, Rudeloffweg 7; tel (30) 8315076; telex 183010.
Consul-General: Mr Oetorjo.

Consulate-General: 2000 Hamburg 60, Bebelallee 15; tel (40) 512071; telex 212906.
Consul-General: Noor Handono.

Consulate: 3000 Hannover 1, Georgsplatz 1; tel (511) 1032150; telex 921620.
Honorary Consul: Günther Karl Willi Nerlich.

Consulate: 8000 Munich 22, Widenmayerstr. 24; tel (89) 294609; telex 0524481.
Honorary Consul: Wolfgang Schoeller.

Consulate: 2300 Kiel, Sophienblatt 33; tel (431) 6032010; telex 299850.
Honorary Consul: Walter Hans Hermann Dethloff.

Consulate: 2800 Bremen, Domhof 26; tel (421) 325058; telex 244702.
Honorary Consul: Dr Manfred Nies.

Consulate: 6082 Waldorf bei 6000 Frankfurt-am-Main, Nordenstr. 44; tel (6105) 76003; telex 4185712.
Honorary Consul: Klaus Schramböhmer.

IRAN

Embassy: 5300 Bonn 2, Godesberger Allee 133-137; tel (228) 8100521; telex 885697.
Ambassador: Mehdi Ahary Mostafavi.

Consulate-General: 2000 Hamburg 13, Abteistr. 25; tel (40) 4140930.
Consul-General: Bagher Golzarnia.

Consulate-General: 6000 Frankfurt-am-Main 1, Guiollettstr. 56; tel (69) 7140050.
Consul-General: Rasoul Ghassab-Gharaie.

Consulate-General: 8000 Munich 80, Mauerkircherstr. 59; tel (89) 984322.
Consul-General: Moh. Taghi Mashayekh.

IRAQ

Embassy: 5300 Bonn 2, Dürenstr. 33; tel (228) 82031; telex 8869471.
Ambassador: Abdul Jabbar Omar Ghani.

IRELAND

Embassy: 5300 Bonn 2, Godesberger Allee 119; tel (228) 376937; telex 885588; fax (228) 373500.
Ambassador: Kester W. Heaslip.
Counsellor: Marie Cross.
First Secretary (Press/Information): Tom Bolster.
First Secretary (Agriculture): Seamus Carroll.
First Secretary: Tom Hanney.
Secretary: John McCullagh.

Consulate: 1000 Berlin 10, Ernst Reuter Platz 10; tel (30) 34800822; telex 181794; fax (30) 34800863.
Honorary Consul: Karl H. Pepper.

Consulate-General: 8000 Munich, Thomas-Mann-Allee 1, Mauerkircherstr. 1a; tel (89) 981841; fax (89) 481841.
Honorary Consul-General: Liselotte Linnebach.

Consulate: 2800 Bremen 1, Außer der Schleifmühle 29; Postfach 100725; tel (421) 321373; telex 2385; fax (421) 325978.
Honorary Consul: Heinz Robert Vesshoff.

ISRAEL

Embassy: 5300 Bonn 2, Simrockallee 2; tel (228) 8231; fax (228) 356093.
Ambassador: Benjamin Navon.

ITALY

Embassy: 5300 Bonn 2, Karl-Finkelnburg-Str. 51; tel (228) 8220; telex 885450; fax (228) 822169.
Ambassador: Marcello Guidi.
Minister-Counsellor: Raniero Avogadro.
Counsellor (Political Section): Pierandrea Magistrati.
Secretary (Political Section): Dr Marco Marsilli.
Secretary (Political Section): Dr Francesco Barbaro.
Secretary (Political Section): Dr Placido Vigo.
Counsellor (Economic Section): Alessandro Merola.
Counsellor (Social Section): Giovanni Polizzi.
Secretary (Economic Section): Dr Michele Esposito.
Defence and Air Attaché: Gen. Leonardo Tricarico.
Military Attaché: Col Primo Gadia.
Naval Attaché: Capt. Claudio De Polo.
Secretary (Cultural Section): Prof. Bruno Mocci.
Attaché (Scientific Section): Prof. Wolfgang Alles.

Consulate: 1000 Berlin, Graf-Spee-Str. 1-7; tel (30) 2611591; telex 186248; fax (30) 2628590.
Consul and Minister: Giovanni Ferrari.

Consulate-General: 2000 Hamburg 13, Feldbrünnenstr. 54; tel (40) 4140070; telex 212903; fax (40) 41400739.
Consul-General and Counsellor: Maurizio Zanini.

Consulate-General: 3000 Hannover 1, Bischofsholer Damm 62; tel (511) 281036; telex 921122; fax (511) 858643.
Consul-General and Counsellor: Renzo Pennacchioni.

Consulate: 5000 Cologne 41, Universitätstr. 81; tel (221) 400870; telex 8883343; fax (221) 4060350.
Consul and Counsellor: Ugo Aldrighetti.

Consulate: 6000 Frankfurt-am-Main, Beethovenstr. 17; tel (69) 75310; telex 411682; fax (69) 7531143.
Consul and Counsellor: Gianfranco Benito Volpi.

Consulate: 7000 Stuttgart, Lenzhalde 69; tel (711) 222710; telex 722616; fax (711) 2563136.
Consul and Counsellor: Enrico Guicciardi.

Consulate: 8000 Munich 80, Möhlstr. 3; tel (89) 4180030; telex 17898474; fax (89) 477999.
Consul and Minister: Sergio Valacchi.

Consulate: 2800 Bremen, Siewall 54; tel (421) 702030.
Honorary Consul: Inge Beutler.

Consulate: 4600 Dortmund, Göbenstr. 14; tel (231) 577960; telex 8227514.
Consul: Dr Mario Sammartino.

Consulate: 7800 Freiburg, Schreiberstr. 4; tel (761) 36292; telex 772435; fax (761) 381766.
Consul: Romano Camastra.

Consulate: 8500 Nuremberg, Gleisbühlstr. 10; tel (911) 204721; telex 626799.
Consul: Anna Panciera.

Consulate: 6600 Saarbrücken, Preussenstr. 19; tel (681) 65033; telex 4428695.
Consul: Dr Romano Rocci.

Consular Agency: 6800 Mannheim 1; tel (621) 414148; telex 462698.
Head of Consular Agency: Corrado Cozze.

Consular Agency: 3180 Wolfsburg, Porschestr. 74; tel (5361) 23077; telex 958339.
Head of Consular Agency: Salvatore Bonaventura.

JAMAICA

Embassy: 5300 Bonn 2, Am Kreuter 1; tel (228) 354045; telex 885493.
Ambassador: M. Patricia Durrant.

Consulate: 2000 Hamburg 1, Ballindamm 1; tel (40) 302990; telex 2161444.
Honorary Consul: Reinhard Schönberg.

Consulate: 8000 Munich 80, Ismaninger Str. 98; tel (89) 981855; telex 5216353.
Honorary Consul: Gloria Elmendorff.

JAPAN

Embassy: 5300 Bonn 1, Bonn-Center, H1 701, Bundeskanzlerplatz; tel (228) 5001; telex 886878.
Ambassador: Keizo Kimura.

Consulate-General: 1000 Berlin 33, Wachtelstr. 8; tel (30) 8327026; telex 183006.
Consul-General: Terno Kirjima.

Consulate-General: 2000 Hamburg 1, Rathausmarkt 5; tel (40) 3330170; telex 214885.
Consul-General: Toshiyuki Kawakami.

Consulate-General: 4000 Dusseldorf 1, Immermannstr. 45; tel (211) 353311; telex 8587188.
Consul-General: Noriaki Owada.

Consulate-General: 6000 Frankfurt-am-Main, Hamburger Allee 2-10; tel (69) 770351; telex 416408.
Consul-General: Dr Tadao Araki.

Consulate-General: 8000 Munich 80, Prinzregentenplatz 10; tel (89) 471043; telex 529796.
Consul-General: Shigeru Tsumori.

JORDAN

Embassy: 5300 Bonn 2, Beethovenallee 21; tel (228) 354051; telex 885401; fax (228) 353951.
Ambassador: Khaled F. Madadha.
Minister-Counsellor: Moh'd Amin A. Shahankari.
Counsellor (Cultural): Ismail Awad.
Counsellor (Press): Nayef Mutlaq.
Second Secretary: Nayef F. Zidan.

Consulate: 1000 Berlin 20, Pichelswerderstr. 3-5; tel (30) 3311152.
Honorary Consul: Dr Helmut Schleicher.

Consulate: 3000 Hannover, Andreae-Str. 1; tel (511) 321218.
Honorary Consulate: Kurt Uihlein.

Consulate: 4000 Dusseldorf, Poststr. 7; tel (211) 1380602.
Honorary Consul: Carl Gielisch.

Consulate: 8000 Munich 40, Barerstr. 37; tel (89) 282953.
Honorary Consul: Rudolf Neumeister.

Consulate: 6200 Wiesbaden, An der Ringkirche 6; tel (611) 495251.
Honorary Consul: Dr Helmut Hildebrand.

Consulate: 7015 Stuttgart-Korntal, ASK-Kugellagerfabrik, beim Bahnhof; tel (711) 837077; telex 723307.
Honorary Consul: Dr Roland Seyfert.

KENYA

Embassy: 5300 Bonn 2, Villichgasse 17; tel (228) 353066; telex 885570.
Ambassador: Vincent John Ogutu-Obare.

Consulate-General: 6000 Frankfurt-am-Main, Hochstr. 53; tel (69) 2825512.
Consul-General: James N. Orina.

KIRIBATI

Consulate: 2000 Hamburg, Rödingsmarkt 16; tel (40) 361460; telex 215274; fax (40) 365571.
Honorary Consul: Frank Leonhardt.

KOREA, REPUBLIC

Embassy: 5300 Bonn 1, Adenauerallee 124; tel (228) 267960; telex 8869508.
Ambassador: Shin Dong-Won.
Military, Naval and Air Attaché: Col Lee Kwang-Woo.
Assistant Military Attaché: You Buel-Jun.

Consulate-General: 1000 Berlin 30, Ansbacher Str. 5; tel (30) 243079.
Consul-General: Dong Kyu Park.

Consulate-General: 2000 Hamburg 13, Hagedornstr. 53; tel (40) 4102031.
Consul-General: Joon Ho Choi.

Consulate-General: 4000 Dusseldorf 30, Immermannstr. 65a; tel (211) 365939.
Honorary Consul-General: Hermann Storm.

Consulate-General: 6000 Frankfurt-am-Main, Eschersheimer Landstr. 327; tel (69) 563051; telex 417382.
Consul-General: Sung Ku Kang.

Consulate-General: 7000 Stuttgart 80, Sigmaringer Str. 107; tel (711) 719155; fax (711) 7203368.
Honorary Consul-General: Dr Clauspeter Göhring.

KUWAIT

Embassy: 5300 Bonn 2, Godesberger Allee 77-81; tel (228) 378081; telex 886525.
Ambassador: Khalid al-Babtain.

LEBANON

Embassy: 5300 Bonn 2, Rheinallee 27; tel (228) 352075; telex 8869339.
Ambassador: Souheil Chammas.

Consulate: 4000 Dusseldorf 30, Kaiserwerther Str. 166; tel (211) 431512.
Honorary Consul: Adel Ardati.

LESOTHO

Embassy: 5300 Bonn 2, Godesberger Allee 50; tel (228) 376868; telex 8869370.
Ambassador: Mokheseng Reginald Tekateka.

Consulate: 3000 Hannover 1, Alexanderstr. 2; tel (511) 326674.
Honorary Consul: A. David Grojnowski.

Consulate: 6000 Frankfurt-am-Main, Hofheimer Str. 14; tel (69) 361001; telex 4189411.

Honorary Consul: Jürgen Lorenz.

LIBERIA

Embassy: 5300 Bonn 1, Hohenzollernstr. 73; tel (228) 352394; telex 886637.
Ambassador: Nathaniel Eastman.

Consulate: 1000 Berlin 33, Pockler Str. 8; tel (30) 8313053.
Honorary Consul: Joachim Meier.

Consulate-General: 2000 Hamburg 1, An der Alster 15; tel (40) 244574.

Consulate-General: 6000 Frankfurt-am-Main, Bernusstr. 7; tel (69) 7072409.
Honorary Consul-General: Dr Gerhard Holland.

Consulate: 4000 Dusseldorf 30, Golzheimer Platz 3; tel (211) 4541770; telex 8587916.
Honorary Consul: Dr Ernst Wilhelm Handschumacher.

Consulate: 8000 Munich 40, Frankfurter Ring 220; tel (89) 3232555.
Honorary Consul: Konrad Stroebel.

Consulate: 2800 Bremen 1, Schlachte 31; tel (421) 170291.
Honorary Consul: Bernd Hansing.

Consulate: 7800 Freiberg im Breisgau, Kirchenhölzle 9; tel (761) 507051.
Honorary Consul: Hellmuth Dettinger.

LIBYA

People's Committee: 5300 Bonn 2, Beethovenallee 12A; tel (228) 820090; telex 885738; fax (228) 364260.
Secretary of the People's Committee: Ali Mahmoud el- Gheriani.

LUXEMBOURG

Embassy: 5300 Bonn 1, Adenauerallee 108; tel (228) 214008; telex 886557; fax (228) 222920.
Ambassador: Adrien Ferdinand Josef Meisch.
Secretary: Marc Court.
Attaché and Vice-Consul: Esther Mertes.

Consulate: 1000 Berlin 12, Haus der Wirtschaft, Am Schillertheater 2; tel (30) 31005130; telex 184366; fax (30) 31005120.
Honorary Consul: Klaus Osterhof.

Consulate-General: 6000 Frankfurt-am-Main 1, Neckarstr. 7; tel (69) 236611.
Honorary Consul-General: Meinhard Carstensen.

Consulate: 2000 Hamburg 52, Klein-Flottbeker Weg 4; tel (40) 8804055; telex 2165639; fax (40) 8811617.
Honorary Consul: Volker Neumann-Schniedewind.

Consulate: 3000 Hannover 61, Karl-Wiechart-Allee 4; tel (511) 563035; telex 922828; fax (511) 5661996.
Honorary Consul: Erwin Möller.

Consulate: 4000 Dusseldorf 30, Jägerhofstr. 10; tel (211) 4981336; telex 8587437.
Honorary Consul: Helmut Nieland.

Consulate: 7000 Stuttgart 1, Uhlandstr. 2; tel (711) 245591; telex 723801.
Honorary Consul: Peter Adolff.

Consulate: 8000 Munich 5, Klenzestr. 101; tel (89) 20242202; fax (89) 2014233.
Honorary Consul: Hanns Maier.

Consulate: 2800 Bremen 1, Markstr. 3, Börsenhof C; tel (421) 3660052; fax (421) 3660099.
Honorary Consul: Joachim Theye.

Consulate: 5100 Aachen, Haus Löwenstein, Am Markt 39-41; tel (241) 403656; fax (241) 28121.
Honorary Consul: Ottmar Braun.

Consulate: 5500 Trier, Hosenstr. 24; tel (651) 40401; telex 472862; fax (651) 7101228.
Honorary Consul: Heinrich Holzenbrink.

Consulate: 6600 Saarbrücken; 6620 Völklingen, Bismarckstr. 57; Postfach 1724; tel (6898) 103498; telex 4424110; fax (6898) 104001.
Honorary Consul: Michel Obertin.

MADAGASCAR

Embassy: 5300 Bonn 2, Rolandstr. 48; Postfach 200 251; tel (228) 331057; telex 885781; fax (228) 334628.
Ambassador: Samuël Lahady (designate).
Counsellor and Chargé d'affaires a.i: René Fidèle Rajaonah.
Counsellor (Consular): Roger Rabehanta.
Counsellor (Cultural): Mr Assoumany.
Counsellor (Economic/Commercial): Alfred Léonard Ratovonirina.
Attaché (Public Relations): Brigitte Razafindramiandra.
Attaché (Social Affairs): Jocelyne Rajaonah.

Consulate-General: 4000 Dusseldorf, Schadowplatz 14; tel (211) 84011.
Honorary Consul-General: Hans Heil.

Consulate: 8000 Munich 40, Akademiestr. 7 (bei Bayr. Elektrizitätswerke GmbH); tel (89) 3819020; fax (89) 897399.
Honorary Consul: Ingo Wallner.

Consulate: 6500 Mainz, Große Bleiche 15; Postfach 1669 (Dresdner Bank AG); tel (6131) 4041.
Honorary Consul: Werner Wolz.

Consulate: 6600 Saarbrücken, 6623 Völklingen-Luisenthal, Str. des 13 Januar 273; tel (6898) 81100.
Honorary Consul: Eric Ruffing.

Consulate: 7800 Freiburg-im-Breisgau, Goethestr. 66; tel (761) 74363.
Honorary Consul: Helmut W. Dyllick-Brenzinger.

MALAWI

Embassy: 5300 Bonn 2, Mainzer Str. 124; tel (228) 343016; telex 8869689; fax (228) 340619.
Counsellor: Trevor Andie Vincent Chande.
First Secretary (Administrative): Snechen Norves Dzama.
Third Secretary: Beautie Aretha Kabvina.

Consulate: 2000 Hamburg 36, Große Bleichen 12-4; tel (40) 353778.
Honorary Consul: Manfred Mehr.

Consulate: 4000 Dusseldorf 31, Angermünderstr. 64; tel (203) 741224.
Honorary Consul: Wolfgang Bernhard Schaar.

Consulate: 7000 Stuttgart 60, Am Westkai 25; tel (711) 329313.
Honorary Consul: Rudi Ernst Karl Bieller.

Consulate: 8021 Munich-Icking; tel (8178) 7492.
Honorary Consul: Hanns Reich.

MALAYSIA

Embassy: 5300 Bonn 2, Mittelstr. 43; tel (228) 376803; telex 885683; fax (228) 376584.
Ambassador: Dato' Zainal Abidin bin Ibrahim.
Counsellor: Ali bin Abdullah.
First Secretary (Information): Aini Mohd Yusof.
First Secretary (Economic): Nik Mustapha Kamal bin Nik Ahmad.
Third Secretary (Administrative): Mohd Noor bin Pitt.

Consulate: 1000 Berlin 30, Genthinerstr. 41; tel (30) 269211; telex 183169; fax (30) 372172.
Honorary Consul: Achim E. Turklitz.

Consulate: 2000 Hamburg, Kajen 2; tel (40) 372172; fax (40) 3687249.
Honorary Consul: Edgar E. Nordmann.

Consulate: 8000 Munich 2, Promenadeplatz 7; tel (89) 2139; fax (89) 21392375.
Honorary Consul: Jürgen Heidemann.

MALI

Embassy: 5300 Bonn 2, Basteistr. 86; tel (228) 357048; telex 885680; fax (228) 361922.
Ambassador: Modibo Keïta.
Counsellor: Moussa Coulibaly.
First Secretary: Marcel Ky.

Consulate-General: 2000 Hamburg 36, Valentinskamp 88-90, Berolina Haus; tel (40) 341150; telex 2173430.
Honorary Consul-General: Hans-Georg Graichen.

Consulate-General: 8000 Munich 40, Georgenstr. 104; tel (89) 377814.
Honorary Consul-General: Heinz Wirth.

MALTA

Embassy: 5300 Bonn 2, Viktoriastr. 1; tel (228) 363017; telex 885748; fax (228) 363019.
Ambassador: Richard Lapira.
First Secretary: Edwin Abela.
Second Secretary: Manuel Mifsud.
Attaché (Press/Culture): Dr Francis Cachia.

Consulate: 1000 Berlin 15, Kurfürstendamm 50; tel (30) 8813813.
Honorary Consul: Ingrid Christine Möbus.

Consulate-General: 2000 Hamburg 1, Raboisen 5/13; tel (40) 330421; telex 2163067.
Honorary Consul-General: Otto Techau.

Consulate-General: 4000 Dusseldorf, Schadowstr. 59 (Gold Kraemer Haus); tel (211) 358266.
Honorary Consul-General: Paul R. Kraemer.

Consulate-General: 8000 Munich 19, Adamstr. 4; tel (89) 184522; telex 5212098; fax (89) 184271.
Honorary Consul-General: Joachim Hietzig.

Consulate-General: 6500 Mainz 21, Orchideenweg 3; tel (6131) 473100.
Honorary Consul-General: Hannetraud Schultheiss.

Consulate: 7000 Stuttgart 80, Robert-Leicht-Str. 43; tel (711) 732213.
Honorary Consul: Viktor Dulger.

Consulate: 2800 Bremen 1, Westerstr. 17; tel (421) 505250; fax (421) 591059.
Honorary Consul: Thomas Stöcker.

MAURITANIA

Embassy: 5300 Bonn 2, Bonnerstr. 48; Postfach 200261; tel (228) 364024; telex 885550; fax (228) 361788.
Ambassador: Dr Youssouf Diagana.
First Counsellor: Senny Ould Khyar.
First Counsellor: N'Diaye Kane.
First Counsellor (Press): Ahmed Salem Ould Abdi.
Second Counsellor: Khalil Balla Gueye.
First Secretary: Ahmed Mahmoud Ould Mohamed.

Consulate: 4000 Dusseldorf 30, Münster Str. 306; tel (211) 623047.
Honorary Consul: Hubertus Spieker.

MAURITIUS

Consulate-General: 4000 Dusseldorf, Jacobstr. 7; tel (211) 35674; telex 8582395; fax (211) 365659.
Honorary Consul-General: Herbert Gottlieb.

Consulate-General: 8000 Munich 2, Sendlinger Str. 64; tel (89) 2607240; telex 529030.
Honorary Consul-General: Johannes Kneifel.

MEXICO

Embassy: 5300 Bonn 1, Adenauerallee 100; tel (228) 217577; telex 886819; fax (228) 211113.
Ambassador: Juan José Bremer.

Consulate-General: 1000 Berlin 31, Kurfürstendamm 72; tel (30) 3249047; fax (30) 3249843.
Consul-General: José Luis Martinez Hernandez.

Consulate-General: 2000 Hamburg 13, Hallerstr. 70 I; tel (40) 448774; telex 2173499.
Consul General: Roberto Friedrich-Heinze.

Consulate: 3000 Hannover, Am Marstall 18-24; tel (511) 327321.
Honorary Consul: Walter Koch.

Consulate: 6000 Frankfurt-am-Main, Neue Mainzer Str. 57; tel (69) 235709; telex 411166; fax (69) 236134.
Consul: Astrid Galindo Sardoz.

Consulate: 8000 Munich 80, Vogelweidstr. 5/I; tel (89) 981617.
Honorary Consul: Siegfried Otto.

Consulate: 2800 Bremen 1, Präsident-Kennedy-Str. 1; tel (421) 324946; telex 244830; fax (421) 3678232.
Honorary Consul: Peter W. Lampke.

MONACO

Embassy: 5300 Bonn 1, Zitelmannstr. 16; tel (228) 232007.
Ambassador: René Bocca.

Consulate: 1000 Berlin 12, Fasanenstr. 5; tel (30) 3133042; telex 183708.
Honorary Consul: Günther Follmer.

Consulate: 2000 Hamburg 36, Neuer Jungfernstieg 20; tel (40) 34961.
Honorary Consul: Heinrich Freiherr von Berenberg-Gossler.

Consulate: 4000 Dusseldorf 30, Freiligrathstr. 1; tel (211) 4979141; telex 8587027.
Honorary Consul: Bernd Kunth.

Consulate: 7000 Stuttgart 1, Uhlandstr. 13; tel (711) 234591.
Honorary Consul: Simon van Kempen.

Consulate: 8000 Munich 22, Von-der-Tann-Str. 14; tel (89) 282718; telex 523143.
Honorary Consul: Alfred Liegl.

MONGOLIA

Embassy: 5310 Troesdorf-Siegler, Siebengebirgsblick 4-6; tel (228) 402727.
Ambassador: Agvaanborjeen Tsolnon.

MOROCCO

Embassy: 5300 Bonn 2, Gotenstr. 7-9; tel (228) 355044; telex 885428; fax (228) 357894.
Ambassador: Abdel Aziz Benjelloun.
First Counsellor: Mustapha Cherkaoui.
Counsellor (Economic): Abdellah M'Sahi.
Defence Attaché: Col Moulay Hachem el Amrani.
First Secretary (Press Section): Farhat Bouazza.
First Secretary (Cultural Section): Hamidan Bouziani.
Second Secretary (Consular Section): Bouchta Issaad.

Consulate-General: 2000 Hamburg, Kajen 10; tel (40) 367003; telex 21110.
Honorary Consul-General: Peter Hansen.

Consulate-General: 4000 Dusseldorf, Cäcilienallee 14; tel (211) 451041.
Consul-General: Boutahar Lhaj.

Consulate-General: 6000 Frankfurt-am-Main, Adickesallee 63/65; tel (69) 559887.
Consul-General: Hassan Bennani.

Consulate: 8000 Munich, Prinzregentenstr. 89; tel (89) 476004.
Honorary Consul: Hans Bäumler.

Branch Office: 1000 Berlin, Kuckhoffstr. 116; tel (2) 4829703.

MOZAMBIQUE

Embassy: 5300 Bonn 1, Adenauerallee 46a; tel (228) 224024.
Ambassador: Amadeo Paul Samuel da Conceição.

MYANMAR

Embassy: 5300 Bonn 1, Schumann Str. 112; tel (228) 210091; telex 8869560; fax (228) 219316.
Ambassador: U Win Aung.
Counsellor: U Nyi Nyi Than.
First Secretary: U Kyaw Nyunt Hman.
Second Secretary: Daw Maw Maw.
Attaché: U Sein Nyunt.

NEPAL

Embassy: 5300 Bonn 2, Im Hag 15; tel (228) 343097; telex 8869297; fax (228) 856747.

Consulate: 1000 Berlin 15, Uhlandstr. 171-2; tel (30) 8814049; fax (30) 8825917.
Honorary Consul: Ulrich Schmidt.

Consulate-General: 6000 Frankfurt-am-Main 60, Flinschstr. 63; tel (69) 4087.
Honorary Consul-General: Hans Viktor Howaldt.

Consulate: 7000 Stuttgart 80, Handswerkstr. 5-7; tel (711) 7864614; telex 725511.
Honorary Consul: Margot Busak.

Consulate: 8000 Munich 21, Landsberger Str. 191; tel (89) 5704406; telex 5213058.
Honorary Consul: Ludwig Alexander Greissl.

NETHERLANDS

Embassy: 5300 Bonn 1, Strässchensweg 10; tel (228) 5305; telex 886826; fax (228) 238621.
Ambassador: Jan Gerard van der Tas.

Consulate and Military Mission: 1000 Berlin 15, Meierotto-Str. 7; Postfach 31-1029; tel (30) 8835173; telex 184805.
Consul-General: A. H. J. M. Speekenbrink.

Consulate-General: 2000 Hamburg 1, Pelzerstr. 2, Ecke Rathausstr.; tel (40) 324411; telex 2161023; fax (40) 336272.
Consul-General: Willhelm Hendrik Simonsz.

Consulate-General: 4000 Dusseldorf, Oststr. 10 (Wehrhahn-Center, 6 Stock); tel (211) 3613055; telex 8585541; fax (211) 359040.
Consul-General: Jacob Schoen.

Consulate-General: 6000 Frankfurt-am-Main, Beethovenstr. 5; tel (69) 752021; fax (69) 746036.
Consul-General: Adolf D. H. Simonsz.

Consulate-General: 7000 Stuttgart 1, Herdweg 60; tel (711) 297080.
Honorary Consul-General: Manfred Prechtl.

Consulate-General: 8000 Munich 2, Nymphenburger Str. 1; tel (89) 594103; telex 5212154; fax (89) 594634.

Consulate: Hannover-Kirchrode, Bünteweg 2; tel (511) 5249406.
Honorary Consul: Ralf E. E. H. J. Zimmermann von Siefart.

Consulate: 5000 Cologne 51, Sechtemer Str. 12, Postfach 510665; tel (221) 371423; telex 8882382; fax (221) 388034.
Honorary Consul: Hans A. H. Meerloo.

Consulate: 2800 Bremen, Altenwall 2-5; tel (421) 323726.
Honorary Consul: Frans Peter Wethmar.

Consulate: 4100 Duisburg, Franz-Haniel-Platz 6-8; 4100 Duisburg 13 Ruhrort; tel (203) 86688.
Honorary Consul: Gerd Wilhelm Hulsman.

Consulate: 4400 Münster/Westf., Bogenstr. 11-2; tel (251) 45260.
Honorary Consul: Hermann Hallermann.

Consulate: 4500 Osnabrück, Neuer Graben 38; tel (541) 24363.
Honorary Consul: Hans-Georg Gallenkamp.

Consulate: 5100 Aachen, Theaterstr. 6-8; tel (241) 33253; fax (241) 438259.
Honorary Consul: Otto Escweiller.

Consulate: 6600 Saarbrücken 3, Ursulinenstr. 63; tel (681) 30401; telex 4421300.
Honorary Consul: Hugo Bonk.

Consulate: 2370 Rendsberg, Hollesenstr. 21; Anwaltskanzlei Dr Fürsen, Postfach 44, 2374 Fockbek-Rendsburg; tel (4331) 61065.
Honorary Consul: Dr Ernst J. Fürsen.

Consulate: 4190 Kleve, Bahnhofstr. 19; tel (2821) 24006.
Honorary Consul: Carl Hans von Gimborn.

NEW ZEALAND

Embassy: 5300 Bonn 1, Bonn-Center, HI 902, Bundeskanzlerplatz 2-10; tel (228) 228070; fax (228) 221687.
Ambassador: Dr Richard Grant.
Counsellor: Phil Bennet.
Second Secretary: Penelope Ridings.
Trade Commissioner: Len Donaldson.
Trade Commissioner: Helen Williams.
Senior Immigration Officer: Alan Moran.
Tourism Director: Jenny Burgess (resident in Frankfurt-am-Main).

NICARAGUA

Embassy: 5300 Bonn 2, Konstantinstr. 41; tel (228) 362505; telex 885734.
Chargé d'affaires a.i.: Ramón-Alfonso Estrada Centeno.

Consulate-General: 2000 Hamburg 13, Mittelweg 143; tel (40) 4104434.
Honorary Consul-General: Jürgen Gotthardt.

Consulate: 8000 Munich 40, Osterwaldstr. 69A.
Honorary Consul: Horst Engler-Hamm.

Consulate: 5600 Wuppertal 2, Winchenbachstr. 49; tel (202) 50542.
Honorary Consul: Ursula Schulz.

NIGER

Embassy: 5300 Bonn 2, Dürenstr. 9; tel (228) 356057; telex 885572; fax (228) 363246.
Ambassador: Youssofa Mamadou Maiga.
Counsellor: Aminata Maiga Djibrilla.
Second Secretary (Administration/Finance): Hiya Chekaraou.

Consulate: 1000 Berlin 19, Badenallee 12-3; tel (30) 3046309.
Honorary Consul: Heinz-Günther Schmidt.

Consulate: Munich, 8022 Grünwald, Ludwig-Thoma-Str. 13; tel (89) 6492082; telex 5218826; fax (89) 6492346.
Honorary Consul: Carl Wiedmeier.

Consulate: 2300 Kiel 1, Duesternbrooker Weg 130; tel (431) 85021; telex 292245; fax (431) 82674.
Honorary Consul: Joachim Krumhoff.

Consulate: 6800 Mannheim 1, Gottlieb-Daimler-Str. 12a; tel (621) 403974.
Honorary Consul: Heinz B. Braun.

NIGERIA

Embassy: 5300 Bonn 2, Goldbergweg 13; tel (228) 322071; telex 885522.
Ambassador: Asuquo Eta Hogan Emenyi.

NORWAY

Embassy: 5300 Bonn 2, Mittelstr. 43; tel (228) 8199740; telex 885491; fax (228) 373498.
Ambassador: Per Martin Ølberg.

Consulate: 1000 Berlin 15, Pfalzburgerstr. 74; tel (30) 8821224; telex 186171; fax (30) 8817926.

Honorary Consul: Horst Sandner.

Consulate-General: 2000 Hamburg 36, Neuer Jungfernstieg 7/8; tel (40) 343455; telex 211329; fax (40) 342998.
Consul-General: Per G. Schöyen.

Consulate-General: 7000 Stuttgart, Nordbahnhofstr. 41; tel (711) 2568949; telex 723351; fax (711) 2578661.
Honorary Consul-General: Hans Joachim Schmidtgen.

Consulate: 3000 Hannover, Herrenhäuser Str. 83; tel (511) 79070; telex 922978; fax (511) 79072.
Honorary Consul: Jürgen Middendorff.

Consulate: 6000 Frankfurt-am-Main, Hanauer Landstr. 330; tel (69) 411040; telex 417138; fax (69) 4019388.
Honorary Consul: Hans Messer.

Consulate: 8000 Munich 2, Promenadeplatz 7; tel (89) 224170; telex 5210521; fax (89) 21392622.
Honorary Consul: Christian Seidel.

Consulate: 2300 Kiel 1, Lorentzendamm 28; tel (431) 5921050; telex 292936; fax (431) 592051.
Honorary Consul: Thieß Beiderwieden.

Consulate: 2400 Lübeck, Göniner Str. 249; tel (451) 5302211; telex 26839; fax (451) 5302492.
Honorary Consul: Rudolf G. Baader.

Consulate: 2800 Bremen 1, Faulenstr. 2-12; tel (421) 3034293; telex 0244825; fax (421) 3034290.
Honorary Consul: Hans Specht.

Consulate: 2970 Emden, Am Borkumkai, Postfach 1154; tel (4921) 890723; telex 27833; fax (4921) 890746.
Honorary Consul: Maximilian Graf von Spee.

OMAN

Embassy: 5300 Bonn 2, Lindenallee 11; tel (228) 357031; telex 885688; fax (228) 357045.
Ambassador: Saud bin Suliman al-Nabhani.
First Secretary: Hafidh Salim Mohammed B. Omar.
First Secretary: Awadh bin Said al-Shanfari.
Second Secretary: Hafidh Hamed Sulaiman al-Rawahi.

Consulate: 6000 Frankfurt-am-Main 1, Mainzer Landstr. 46; tel (69) 721036; telex 416581; fax (69) 727695.
Honorary Consul: Friedhelm Jost.

PAKISTAN

Embassy: 5300 Bonn 2, Rheinallee 24; tel (228) 352004; telex 885787.
Ambassador: Najmuddin A. Shaikh.

Consulate: 1000 Berlin 33, Miquelstr. 20; tel (30) 8232601.
Honorary Consul: Erich Springer.

Consulate-General: 2000 Hamburg 1, Nordkanalstr. 30; tel (40) 2231779.
Honorary Consul-General: Hermann Schnabel.

Consulate-General: 4000 Dusseldorf, Königsallee 30; tel (211) 329265.
Honorary Consul-General: Herbert Schnapka.

Consulate-General: 6000 Frankfurt-am-Main 1, Börsenstr. 14; tel (69) 287489.
Honorary Consul-General: Matthias Ohms.

Consulate-General: 8000 Munich 2, Rückerstr. 1; tel (89) 534880.
Honorary Consul-General: Sieglinde Heckelmann.

Consulate: 2800 Bremen 1, Präsident-Kennedy-Platz 1; tel (421) 3678231.
Honorary Consul: Peter Koopmann.

PANAMA

Embassy: 5300 Bonn 2, Lützowstr. 1; tel (228) 361036; telex 885600; fax (228) 363558.
Ambassador: Maximiliano E. Jiménez.
Attaché (Consular/Administrative): Catalina Raquel Pereira Duclias.

Consulate-General: 2000 Hamburg 36, Gänsemarkt 44 V; tel (40) 343616; telex 214101.

Consulate-General: 6000 Frankfurt-am-Main, Kennedy-Allee 99; tel (69) 636663.
Honorary Consul-General: Peter Michael Stoll.

Consulate-General: 6500 Mainz, Viermorganweg 4; tel (6131) 476872; telex 4187828.
Honorary Consul-General: Hans Dieter Klenk.

Consulate: 4000 Dusseldorf 1, Hebbelstr. 20; tel (211) 684486.
Honorary Consul: Franz-Josef Fieger.

Consulate: 2800 Bremen 1, Domhof 14-5; tel (421) 3630014; telex 244899; fax (421) 3630060.
Honorary Consul: Klaus F. Müller-Leiendecker.

PAPUA NEW GUINEA

Embassy: 5300 Bonn 2, Gotenstr. 163; tel (228) 376855; telex 886340; fax (228) 375103.
Ambassador: Andrew M. D. Yauieb.
Counsellor: Nilip P. Nakikus.
Consular Trade Officer: Vera Linden.
Administrative/Accounts Officer: Nigel Tandy.
Third Secretary: Margaret Charlie.

Consulate: 8000 Munich 40, Academiestr. 7 III; tel (89) 3817080; telex 5215575; fax (89) 38170826.
Honorary Consul: Dr Walter Schöll.

Consulate: 2000 Hamburg 1, Bergstr. 11; tel (40) 234110; fax (40) 234647.
Honorary Consul: Horst-Joachim Hoertelmann.

PARAGUAY

Embassy: 5300 Bonn 2, Plittersdorfer Str. 32; tel (228) 356727; fax (228) 354963.
Ambassador: Dr Nicólas Lüthold.
First Secretary: Luis Esteban Páez.

Consulate-General: 2000 Hamburg 20, Heilwigstr. 123; tel (40) 474741; fax (40) 4802337.
Consul-General: Felix Gerardo von Glasenapp.

Consulate-General: 6000 Frankfurt-am-Main, Mainzer Landstr. 46, 32 Stock.; tel (69) 720170; telex 4186872.
Honorary Consul-General: Rudolf Justus Hambach.

Consulate-General: 8000 Munich 60, Fritz-Reuter-Str. 25; tel (89) 882757.
Honorary Consul-General: Dr Hubert Krier.

Consulate: 2300 Kiel 17, Düppelstr. 19; tel (431) 83198.
Honorary Consul: Horst Menck.

Consulate: 4030 Ratingen, Waldseestr. 31; tel (2102) 18440; telex 2102356; fax (2102) 18441.
Honorary Consul: Heinrich F. Kreyenberg.

Consulate: 6200 Wiesbaden, Wandermannstr. 68; tel (611) 711361; fax (611) 712490.
Honorary Consul: Rudolf Justus Hambach.

Consulate: 7000 Stuttgart 1, Gaustr. 74b; tel (711) 654151.
Honorary Vice-Consul: Herrmann Walter Sieger.

PERU

Embassy: 5300 Bonn 2, Godesbergerallee 127; tel (228) 373045; telex 886325; fax (228) 379475.
Ambassador: Gabriel García Pike.

Consulate-General: 2000 Hamburg, Blumenstr. 28; tel (40) 476745; telex 2164119.
Consul-General: Javier Gaonzales Terrones.

Consulate-General: 6000 Frankfurt-am-Main, Am Roßmarkt 16; tel (69) 20301.
Consul-General: Ernesto Pinto-Bazurco Rittler.

Consulate: 3000 Hannover 82, Deutsche Messen AG, Messegelände 3000; tel (511) 8931000.
Honorary Consul: Klaus Goehrmann.

Consulate: 4000 Dusseldorf 1, Grafenberger Allee 100; tel (211) 667839.
Honorary Consul: Engelbert Heitkamp.

Consulate: 7000 Stuttgart, Leuschnerstr. 41-7; tel (711) 6665103.
Honorary Consul: Hans Wolfgang Fein.

Consulate: 2800 Bremen, Martinstr. 58; Postfach 105449; tel (421) 315629; telex 244219.
Honorary Consul: Artur Schnitger.

PHILIPPINES

Embassy: 5300 Bonn 1, Argelanderstr. 1; tel (228) 267990; telex 8869571; fax (228) 221968.
Ambassador: Bienvenido A. Tan, Jr.
Minister-Counsellor: Milagros R. Perez.
Military Attaché: Commdr Justo Manlongat.
First Secretary and Consul-General: Phoebe A. Gomez.
First Secretary and Consul: Fe Pangilinan-Klingert.
Second Secretary and Consul: Antonio C. Modena.
Attaché (Administrative): Violeta V. David.
Attaché (Consular): Carmencita H. Maack.
Attaché (Financial): Fernando Clavecilla.
Attaché (Consular): Lazaro Garcia.
Vice Consul (Berlin): Domingo Lucenario.
Trade Representative: Roman Baltazar.

Consulate: 1000 Berlin, Europa-Center/18.OG.; tel (30) 2619188; telex 183694; fax (30) 2628832.
Honorary Consul: Heinz H. Pietsch.

Consulate-General: 2000 Hamburg 13, Jungfrauthal 13; tel (40) 442952; telex 213822.
Consul-General: Lolita R. Haney.

Consulate-General: 7000 Stuttgart, Hohenzollernstr. 14; tel (711) 6401670; telex 721768; fax (711) 6491545.
Honorary Consul-General: Lothar Strobel.

Consulate: 4000 Dusseldorf, Elizabethstr. 52a; tel (211) 370366; fax (211) 383201.
Honorary Consul: Karl-Heinz Stockheim, Jr.

Consulate: 6000 Frankfurt-am-Main 70, Dreieichstr. 59, 4 Stock.; tel (69) 627538; telex 4189047.
Honorary Consul: Peter Merck.

Consulate: 8000 Munich 81, Pienzenaustr. 88; tel (89) 982269; fax (89) 981748.
Honorary Consul: Friedrich Karl Eugen Haberl.

Consulate: 6600 Saarbrücken 3, Mainzer Str. 180-4; tel (681) 814008; telex 4428808.
Honorary Consul: Helmut Wagner.

POLAND

Embassy: 5000 Cologne 51, Lindenallee 7; tel (221) 380261; telex 8881040; fax (221) 343089.
Ambassador: Janusz Reiter.

Consulate: 1000 Berlin 33, Lassenstr. 19-21.

PORTUGAL

Embassy: 5300 Bonn 2, Ubierstr. 78; tel (228) 363011; telex 885577; fax (228) 352864.
Ambassador: Dr António d'Oliveira Pinto da França.
Minister-Counsellor: Dr João António Silveira de Lima Pimentel.
Counsellor: Dr João José Gomes Caetano da Silva.
First Secretary: Dr Jorge Tito Dias Cabral.

Consulate: 1000 Berlin B-61, Otto-Grotewohl-Str. 3A; tel (30) 3922366.
Consul: Dr António B. Sousa.

Consulate-General: 2000 Hamburg 36, Gänsemarkt 21; tel (40) 343478.

Consulate-General: 4000 Dusseldorf, Graf-Adolf-Str. 16; tel (211) 80633.
Consul-General: Dr António Queiróz.

Consulate-General: 6000 Frankfurt-am-Main, Zeppelinallee 15; tel (69) 702066.
Consul-General: Dr João Versteeg.

Consulate-General: 7000 Stuttgart, Königstr. 20; tel (711) 225013.
Consul-General: Dr M. José Monteiro.

Consulate-General: 4500 Osnabrück, Schloßwall 2; tel (541) 48046.
Consul-General: Fernando Cardosa.

Consulate: 8000 Munich, Thomas-Wimmer-Ring 9/III; tel (89) 299932; telex 5218226.
Honorary Consul: Joachim Vielmetter.

QATAR

Embassy: 5300 Bonn 2, Brunnenallee 6; tel (228) 351074; telex 885476; fax (228) 351170.
Ambassador: Ahmed Abdulla al-Khal.

ROMANIA

Embassy: 5300 Bonn 1, Legionsweg 14; tel (228) 555860; telex 8869791; fax (228) 680247.
Ambassador: Dr Radu Comşa.
Envoy (Political): Constantin Parvu.
Envoy (Economic/Commercial): Ilie Panescu.
Counsellor (Political): Vasile Croicu.
Defence, Air and Naval Attaché: Doru Vasilescu.
First Secretary (Economic/Commercial): Victor Spulber-Todosciuc.
First Secretary (Cultural/Scientific): Ion Corneliu Iorgulescu.
First Secretary (Economic/Commercial): Andrei Balan.
First Secretary (Press): Toma Ciugudean.
First Secretary (Cultural): Mihai Botorog.
Second Secretary (Social): Donciu Ramiro Mihai.

Consular Section: tel (228) 678697.
Counsellor and Consul-General: Gheorghe Juganaru.

Consulate-General: 1000 Berlin 38, Matterhornstr. 79; tel (30) 8033019.

RUSSIA

Embassy: 5300 Bonn 2, Waldstr. 42; tel (228) 312086; telex 41885615; fax (228) 364561.
Ambassador: Vladislav Petrovich Terekhov.

Consulate-General: 100 Berlin 33, Reichensteinerweg 34-6; tel (30) 8327004.
Consul-General: Rudolf Fiodorowitsch.

Consulate-General: 2000 Hamburg 76, am Feenteich 20; tel (40) 2295301; telex 41211927.
Consul-General: Wladlen I. Kusnezow.

Consulate-General: 8000 Munich 2, Seidlstr. 28; tel (89) 592528.
Consul-General: Nikolaj Michejlowitsch Obertyschew.

RWANDA

Embassy: 5300 Bonn 2, Beethovenallee 72; tel (228) 355058; telex 885604; fax (228) 351922.
Ambassador: Oswald Rukashaza.
Second Counsellor: Raphäel Mutombo.
Second Counsellor: Jean Bosco Uwihangange.
First Secretary: Claude Rulibikiye.

Consulate-General: 8045 Ismaning bei Munich, Adalperostr. 20; tel (89) 960901.
Honorary Consul-General: Norbert Handwerk.

Consulate: 2000 Hamburg.
Honorary Consul: Walter Bouchard.

Consulate: 6500 Mainz-Mombach, An der Brunnenstube 33-5; tel (6131) 687051.
Honorary Consul: Otto Meyer.

SAINT LUCIA

Consulate: 6000 Frankfurt-am-Main, Steinberger, Frankfurter Hof, Am Kaiserplatz; tel (69) 215801; telex 411806; fax (69) 215900.
Honorary Consul: Bernd O. Ludwig.

SAUDI ARABIA

Embassy: 5300 Bonn 2, Godesberger Allee 40-42; tel (228) 379013; telex 885442; fax (228) 375593.
Ambassador: Abbas Faig Ghazzawi.

SENEGAL

Embassy: 5300 Bonn 1, Argelanderstr. 3; tel (228) 218008; telex 8869644.
Ambassador: Faye Gassama.

Consulate: 1000 Berlin 31, Sächsische Str. 39; tel (30) 8610124; telex 17308268.
Honorary Consul: Otto Meissner.

Consulate-General: 7000 Stuttgart 1, Feuerbacher Heide 49; Postfach 2891; tel (711) 2579191; telex 723917.
Honorary Consul-General: Manfred Ulmer.

Consulate: 2000 Hamburg 11, Vorsetzen 54; tel (40) 31101200; telex 211380.
Honorary Consul: Oscar Herwig.

Consulate: 3000 Hannover, Rathenaustr. 3/I, Zimmer 29-30; tel (511) 16630.
Honorary Consul: Heinrich Pfingsten.

Consulate: 6000 Frankfurt-am-Main 1, Große Bockenheimer Str. 41; tel (69) 288187.
Honorary Consul: Günther Luedecke.

Consulate: 8000 Munich 21, Rüdesheimer Str. 11; tel (89) 570702; telex 5212808.
Honorary Consul: Max Gierke.

SEYCHELLES

Consulate: 2000 Hamburg 36, Jungfernstieg 7; tel (40) 346606; fax (40) 352529.
Honorary Consul: Hans-Joachim Worms.

SIERRA LEONE

Embassy: 5300 Bonn 2, Rheinallee 20; tel (228) 352001; telex 885651; fax (228) 364269.
Ambassador: Dauda Suleiman Kamara.
Counsellor: Sarah A. A. Lewis.

Consulate-General: 2000 Hamburg 13, Jungfrauenthal 51; tel (40) 4104072.
Honorary Consul-General: Dr R. Trede.

Consulate: 6000 Frankfurt-am-Main 60, Am Bächelchen; tel (69) 685637.
Honorary Consul: Walther M. Bessler.

Consulate: 8000 Munich 40, Frankfurter Ring 220; tel (89) 222388.
Honorary Consul: Ruth M. Ströbel.

SINGAPORE

Embassy: 5300 Bonn 2, Südstr. 133; tel (228) 312007; telex 885642; fax (228) 310527.
Ambassador: Tony K. Siddique.

SOMALIA

Embassy: 5300 Bonn 2, Hohenzollernstr. 12; tel (228) 355084; telex 885724.
Ambassador: Dr Hassan Abshir Farah.

Consulate-General: 7000 Stuttgart, Pleninger Str. 100; tel (711) 7206501; telex 7111507.
Honorary Consul-General: Rolf Deyhle.

SOUTH AFRICA

Embassy: 5300 Bonn 2, Auf der Hostert 3; tel (228) 82010; telex 885720; fax (228) 352579.
Ambassador: Albert Erich van Niekerk.
Minister: W. Scholtz.
Minister (Trade): A. J. S. van der Merwe.
Counsellor: D. van Schoor.
Counsellor: Dr J. J. Roelofse.
Counsellor: P. R. Mackay.
Counsellor (Administrative): A. H. Nel.
Counsellor (Industry): H. H. Beckurts.
Counsellor (Cultural): R. E. Chernis.
Counsellor (Science/Technology): Dr R. U. Biesenbach.
First Secretary: C. van den Berg.
First Secretary: A. C. Steenkamp.
First Secretary: T. Albrecht.
First Secretary: E. D. du Preez.
Second Secretary (Consular): J. F. Janse van Rensburg.
Second Secretary (Trade): P. J. Preiss.
Attaché (Agricultural Economics): G. R. Müller.

Consulate-General: 2000 Hamburg 13, Harvestehuder Weg 37; tel (40) 412961; telex 213979.
Consul-General: Stephanus Willem Wentzel.
Consul (Trade): P. S. Buys.

Consulate-General: 8000 Munich 2, Sendlinger Tor-Platz 5; tel (89) 2605081; telex 528364.
Consul-General: Christian Martin van Niekerk.
Consul (Administrative): G. J. van Niekerk.
Consul (Trade): R. Siefert.

Consulate: 3000 Hannover 61 (Kleefeld), an der breiten Wiese 3/5; tel (511) 5702.
Honorary Consul: Gerhard Syrbius.

Consulate: 6000 Frankfurt-am-Main 1, Ulmenstr. 37-9, 18 Stock.; tel (69) 723741; telex 416738.
Consul: David Jacobs.
Vice-Consul (Administrative): C. Rademeyer.

Consulate: 7000 Stuttgart 1, Johannesstr. 41-5; tel (711) 611885.
Honorary Consul: Andreas Franz Vogt.

Consulate: 2300 Kiel, Speckenbeker Weg 143; tel (431) 68921.
Honorary Consul: Klaus Richter.

Consulate: 2400 Lübeck, Hinter den Kirchkaten 75-9; tel (451) 530050.
Honorary Consul: K. Richter.

Consulate: 2800 Bremen 41, Sonneberger Str. 18; tel (421) 4677081; telex 245294.
Honorary Consul: August Jaekel.

Consulate: 6604 Saarbrücken-Fechingen, An der Heringsmühle 16; tel (6893) 2470.
Honorary Consul: Karl-Heinz Reintgen.

SPAIN

Embassy: 5300 Bonn 1, Schlossstr. 4; tel (228) 217094; telex 886792; fax (228) 223405.
Ambassador: Eduardo Foncillas.

Consulate-General: 1000 Berlin 30, Lichtensteinallee 1; tel (30) 2616081; telex 181862; fax (30) 1624032.
Consul-General: Enrique Iranzo Arques.

Consulate-General: 2000 Hamburg 13, Mittelweg 37; tel (40) 443620; telex 2166341.
Consul-General: Anibal Julio Jiménez Abascal.

Consulate-General: 3000 Hannover 1, Wedekindstr. 32; tel (511) 311085; telex 922211.
Consul-General: Salvador Barbera Fraguas.

Consulate-General: 4000 Dusseldorf, Homberger Str. 16; tel (211) 434777; telex 8586297; fax (211) 453768.
Consul-General: Juan Manuel de la Vega.

Consulate-General: 6000 Frankfurt-am-Main, Steinlestr. 6; tel (69) 638071; telex 4170152; fax (69) 6314085.
Consul-General: Francisco Monforte López.

Consulate-General: 7000 Stuttgart 1, Lenzhalde 61; tel (711) 225091; telex 722882; fax (711) 225927.
Consul-General: Pablo Bravo Lozano.

Consulate-General: 8000 Munich 81, Oberföhringer Str. 45; tel (89) 985027; telex 5218876.

Consul-General: Vicente Fernández Trelles.

Consulate-General: 2800 Bremen, Scwachhauser Ring 124; tel (421) 344090.

Consulate: 6500 Mainz, Drususwall 72; tel (6131) 22455.
Vice-Consul: Joachim Bech de Careda.

SRI LANKA

Embassy: 5300 Bonn 2, Rolandstr. 52; tel (228) 332055; telex 885612; fax (228) 331829.
Ambassador: Irangani Manel Abeysekera.

Consulate-General: 2000 Hamburg 11, Pickhuben 9; tel (40) 367140; telex 212315.
Honorary Consul-General: Carl-Olav Ellerbock.

SUDAN

Embassy: 5300 Bonn 2, Koblenzerstr. 99; tel (228) 363074; telex 885478.
Ambassador: Ahmed Eltayeb Yousif Elkordofani.

SURINAME

Consulate-General: 8000 Munich 2, Adolf-Kolping-Str. 16; tel (89) 594369; telex 5215341; fax (89) 597064.
Honorary Consul-General: Edwin Matt.

SWAZILAND

Consulate-General: 4000 Dusseldorf, Worringer Str. 59; tel (211) 350866; telex 8517391; fax (211) 0673351.
Honorary Consul-General: Hermann J. Raths.

SWEDEN

Embassy: 5300 Bonn 1, Allianzplatz, Haus I, Heussallee 2-10; tel (228) 260002; telex 886667; fax (228) 223837.
Ambassador: Torsten Örn.
Minister: Ingmar Karlsson.
Minister-Counsellor: Bengt Lundborg.
Counsellor (Press): Sture Stiernlöf.
Counsellor: Jan Thorbjörnson.
Counsellor (Cultural): John Walldén.
Counsellor (Labour Market): Uno Westerlund.
Military Attaché: Col Nils Förander.
First Secretary: Krister Bringéus.
First Secretary: Michael Odevall.
Chancellor: Irmgard Elfriede Growitz.
Attaché (Press): Veronika Bard Bringéus.
Attaché (Technical Contracts): Staffan Johansson.

Consulate-General: 1000 Berlin 31, Kurfürstendamm 151; Postfach 310809; tel (30) 8917091; telex 41183398; fax (30) 8916369.
Consul-General: Jan Lundvik.
Chancellor: Bärbel Roswitha Nowka.

Consulate-General: 2000 Hamburg 36, Alsterufer 15; Postfach 304950; tel (40) 448453; telex 41212461; fax (40) 459917.
Consul-General: Arne Lundquist.
Chancellor: Cecilia Ann-Margreth Ljundqvist.
Chancellor: Brunhilde Elisabeth Wriedt.

Consulate-General: 4000 Dusseldorf 1, Königsallee 46; Postfach 200604; tel (211) 324632; telex 8588294; fax (211) 320216.
Consul-General: Hans-Georg Paffrath.
Chancellor: Kerstin Anna Elizabeth Enzenauer.
Secretary (Commercial): Ulf Öhrwall.

Consulate-General: 6000 Frankfurt-am-Main, Gutleutstr. 45; Postfach 160751; tel (69) 230479; telex 416367; fax (69) 235304.
Consul-General: Bertil Lund.

Consulate-General: 8000 Munich 2, Marieplatz 21/IV; tel (89) 264089; telex 5216038; fax (89) 266481.
Consul-General: Mats Elgqvist.
Chancellor: Anna-Greta Ericson.
Chancellor: Margareta Floss.

Consulate: 3000 Hannover 71, Tiergartenstr. 130; Postfach 710430; tel (511) 5100525; telex 5118516.
Consul: Carl Ludwig Wilkening.
Chancellor: Maud Birgitta Wulf.

Consulate: 7000 Stuttgart 1, Bolstr. 4, Haus Marquardt; tel (711) 290600; telex 41722180.
Consul: Michael Klett.
Chancellor: Carla Grazia Wiig-Buchwald.
Chancellor: Mabel Katarina Engberg.

Consulate: 7000 Stuttgart 1, Bolstr. 4, Haus Marquardt; tel (711) 290600; telex 41722180.
Consul: Michael Klett.
Chancellor: Klaus Pegler.

Consulate: 2400 Lübeck 1, Beckergrube 38-52; tel (451) 78099; telex 26849; fax (451) 148255.
Consul: Dietrich Schulz.
Chancellor: Heinke Burmeister.

Consulate: 2800 Bremen 1, Am Wall 114/5; tel (421) 3592134; fax (421) 3592733.
Consul: Günther Czichon.
Chancellor: Karin Viveka Schneider.

Consulate: 6600 Saarbrücken, Gebäude C, Altenkesseler Str. 17, c/o Saarländische Energie Agentur GmbH; tel (681) 7931280; telex 4421500; fax (681) 7931175.
Consul: Peter Karl Wilhelm Waltzinger.

Consulate: 2970 Emden, Postfach 1133, Kranstr. 10; tel (4921) 21904; telex 27862.
Consul: Friedrich-Karl Johann Ernst Hassel.

SWITZERLAND

Embassy: 5300 Bonn 2, Gotenstr. 156; Postfach 200255; tel (228) 810080; telex 885646; fax (228) 8100819.
Ambassador: Alfred Hohl.
Minister: Dr Jürg Leutert.
Counsellor (Economic): Eric Martin.
Counsellor: Dr Johannes Kunz.
Defence Attaché: Commdr Walter Zimmermann.
Assistant Defence Attaché: Maj. Bernard von Muralt.
First Secretary (Cultural): Christian Mühlethaler.
Third Secretary: Dr Phil Burkhard.
Attaché and Office Manager: Martin Bruhin.

Consulate-General: 1000 Berlin 21, Fürst Bismarckstr. 4; tel (30) 3944021; telex 181814.
Consul-General: Edwin Trinkler.
Vice-Consul and Chancellor: Eduard Zaugg.

Consulate-General: 2000 Hamburg 1, Rathausmarkt 5; tel (40) 321581; telex 215153; fax (40) 323616.
Consul-General: Alphons Müggler.
Chancellor: Claude Gander.

Consulate-General: 4000 Dusseldorf 30, Cecilienallee 17; tel (211) 434601; telex 8584398.
Consul-General: Robert Wenger.
Vice-Consul and Chancellor: Paul Margreth.

Consulate-General: 6000 Frankfurt-am-Main 1, Zurich Haus am Opernplatz, Bockenheimer; 6000 Frankfurt-am-Main 17, Postfach 170561; tel (69) 755941; telex 411814.
Consul-General: Friedrich Vogel.
Vice-Consul and Chancellor: Michel Failletaz.

Consulate-General: 7000 Stuttgart 1, Hirschstr. 22; tel (711) 293995; fax (711) 2262525.
Consul-General: Emanuel Dubs.
Chancellor: Peter Eisenhut.

Consulate-General: 8000 Munich 40, Leopoldstr. 33; 8000 Munich 44, Postfach 440165; tel (89) 347063; telex 523465; fax (89) 393958.
Consul-General: Paul Studer.
Vice-Consul and Chancellor: Rudolf Bloch.

Consulate: 7800 Freiburg, Zurich Haus, 3 Og, Schreiberstr. 4; Postfach 1507; tel (761) 36642; fax (761) 39103.
Consul: Heinz Gerhard.
Vice-Consul and Chancellor: Erika Grossenbacher.

SYRIA

Embassy: 5300 Bonn 1, Andreas-Hermes-Str. 5; tel (228) 819920; telex 885757; fax (228) 8199299.
Ambassador: Suleyman Haddad.
Minister: Mohamed Anwar Chaykhouni.
Minister: Dr Joseph Raad.
Second Secretary: Mamoun Hariri.
Third Secretary: Radwan Loufti.

TANZANIA

Embassy: 5300 Bonn 2, Theaterplatz 26; tel (228) 358051; telex 885569; fax (228) 358226.
Ambassador: James L. Kateka.
Minister-Counsellor: Mike A. Urio.
Counsellor: Richard Tibandebage.
Third Secretary: Paul B. Ndayeze.

Consulate: 5000 Cologne, Justinianstr. 16; tel (221) 811561; telex 8873481.
Honorary Consul: Albert Löhr.

Consulate: 6000 Frankfurt-am-Main, Bettinaplatz 2; tel (69) 745989; telex 4186268.
Honorary Consul: Ludwig C. Fritz.

THAILAND

Embassy: 5300 Bonn 2, Ubierstr. 65; tel (228) 355065; telex 886574; fax (228) 363702.
Ambassador: Sokol Vanabriksha.

Office of Air Attaché: Rudiger Str. 58; tel (228) 342727; fax (228) 865476.
Air Attaché: Col Krit Asvananda.

Consulate-General: 1000 Berlin 33, Podbielskiallee 1; tel (30) 8312715.
Consul-General: Bandit Sotipalalit.

Consulate-General: 6000 Frankfurt-am-Main, Roßmarkt 14; tel (69) 20110.
Honorary Consul-General: Günter Langer.

Consulate: 2000 Hamburg 1, An der Alster 85; tel (40) 24839118.
Honorary Consul: Wolfgang Krohm.

Consulate: 4000 Dusseldorf, Königsallee 27; tel (211) 8382247.
Honorary Consul: Michael Thomas Giradet.

Consulate: 8000 Munich 71, Meglingerstr. 19; tel (89) 781997.
Honorary Consul: Barbara Steinle.

TOGO

Embassy: 5300 Bonn 2, Beethovenallee 13; tel (228) 355091; telex 885595; fax (228) 351639.
Ambassador: Dr Fousseni Mamah.
First Secretary: Awoyo Djisa Senaya.
Third Secretary: Kodjo Kodjoto Alade.
Attaché (Finance): Kossi Agbégnon Samotu.

Consulate: 1000 Berlin 20, Markt 5; tel (30) 3336087; telex 182718; fax (30) 3336088.
Honorary Consul: Heinz Fahrenkrog-Petersen.

Consulate: 2000 Hamburg 11, Baumwall 7; tel (40) 2790732; telex 164776.
Honorary Consul: Joachim Haase.

Consulate: 4000 Dusseldorf 1, Lindemannstr. 35; tel (211) 681014.
Honorary Consul: Hans Imhoff.

Consulate: 8000 Munich 2, Mathidenstr. 1; tel (89) 591860.
Honorary Consul: Franz Hochreiter.

Consulate: 2800 Bremen, Schlachte 32; Postfach 105467; tel (421) 31641; telex 245537.
Honorary Consul: Heinz Glahr.

Consulate: 3006 Hannover-Burgwedel 1, Raiffeisenstr. 2; tel (5139) 7054; telex 92186.
Honorary Consul: Gerd Nelke.

TONGA

Consulate: 2000 Hamburg 11, Ost-West-Str. 59; tel (40) 37050.
Honorary Consul: Erwin M. Ludewig.

Consulate: 4000 Dusseldorf 31, Angermunder Str. 64; tel (203) 741211; telex 8551300.
Honorary Consul: Alexander Müller.

TUNISIA

Embassy: 5300 Bonn 2, Godesberger Allee 103; tel (228) 376981; telex 885477; fax (228) 374223.
Ambassador: Muhammad Karboul.

Consulate-General: 8000 Munich 19, Adamstr. 4; tel (89) 180012; telex 5216263; fax (89) 183811.
Consul-General: Abdelaziz Joulak.

Consulate: 2000 Hamburg 76, Overbeckstr. 19; tel (40) 2201756; telex 2173880; fax (40) 2279786.
Consul: Tahar Belkhodja.

Consulate: 4000 Dusseldorf 1, Graf-Adolf-Platz 7-8; tel (211) 371007; telex 8581912; fax (211) 7304005.
Consul: Abderrazak Jouini.

TURKEY

Embassy: 5300 Bonn 2, Ute Str. 47; tel (228) 346052; telex 885521.
Ambassador: Reşat Arim.

Consulate-General: 1000 Berlin 33, Kurfürstendamm 142-3; tel (30) 8925033; telex 183896.
Consul-General: Akin Emregül.

Consulate-General: 2000 Hamburg 13, Tesdorpfstr. 18; tel (40) 443041; telex 2164281.
Consul-General: Ecvet Tezcan.

Consulate-General: 3000 Hannover, an der Christuskirche 3; tel (511) 17708; telex 922060.
Consul-General: Erdinç Ulumlu.

Consulate-General: 4000 Dusseldorf, Cecilienallee 41; tel (211) 450999; telex 8584654.
Consul-General: Bozkurt Aran.

Consulate-General: 6000 Frankfurt-am-Main, Zeppelinallee 17; tel (69) 772048; telex 4170615.
Consul-General: Umur Apaydin.

Consulate-General: 7000 Stuttgart 1, Kerner Str. 19B; tel (711) 283271; telex 721479.
Consul-General: Ahmet Ertay.

Consulate-General: 8000 Munich 19, Menzingerstr. 3; tel (89) 176093; telex 523764.
Consul-General: Aydin Idil.

Consulate-General: 2800 Bremen 61, Ahkler-Dorf-Str. 9; Postfach 610224; tel (421) 841128; fax (421) 841115.
Honorary Consul-General: Karl Grabbe.

Consulate-General: 4300 Essen, Alfredstr. 307; tel (201) 42931; telex 8579066.
Consul-General: Önder Alaybeyi.

Consulate-General: 4400 Münster, Lotharingerstr. 25-7; tel (251) 47007; telex 892624.
Consul-General: Sanli Topçuoğlu.

Consulate-General: 5030 Hürth, Luxemburger Str. 285; tel (2233) 78091; telex 8882146.
Consul-General: Nurettin Nurkan.

Consulate-General: 6500 Mainz 1, an der Karlschanze 7, am Rosengarten; tel (6131) 82025; telex 4187403.
Consul-General: Yaşar Togo.

Consulate-General: 7500 Karlsruhe, Kriegstr. 123; tel (721) 848046; telex 7825201.
Consul-General: Burhanettin Muz.

Consulate-General: 8500 Nuremberg, Regensburger Str. 69; tel (911) 49523; telex 623906.
Consul-General: Turgut Serdaroğlu.

TUVALU

Consulate: 2000 Hamburg 56, Grete-Nevermann-Weg 20; tel (40) 810508; telex 811016.
Honorary Consul: Peter Feist.

UGANDA

Embassy: 5300 Bonn 2, Dürenstr. 44; tel (228) 355027; telex 885578; fax (228) 351692.
Ambassador: Freda Lule Blick.
Minister: Samusoni Bigombe.
First Secretary (Information): Joshua Mutabazi.
Attaché: Annet Kabuye.

Consulate: 2000 Hamburg 11, Brook 1; tel (40) 364549; fax (40) 364235.
Consul: Heinz W. Bonacker.

Consulate-General: 1000 Berlin 38, Reifträgerweg 27-9; tel (30) 8036063; fax (30) 8039172.
Consul-General: Lajos Nagy.

Consulate: 8000 Munich 81, Rosenkavalier Platz 14; tel (89) 919127; fax (89) 911252.
Consul: Dr Wolfgang Wiedmann.

Consulate: 6500 Mainz 1, am Fort Josef 7; tel (6131) 232301; telex 4187716.
Honorary Consul: Alfred Weiß.

Consulate: 5429 Katzenelbogen, Rheinstr. 21; tel (6175) 3649; fax (6486) 61407.
Consul: Alfred Weiss.

UNITED ARAB EMIRATES

Embassy: 5300 Bonn 1, Erste Fährgasse 6; tel (228) 267070; telex 885741; fax (228) 2670714.
Ambassador: Dr Saeed Mohammad al-Shamsi.
Counsellor: Hamed Harib al-Habsi.
Counsellor: Abdul Razzak Hadi.
First Secretary: Ebrahim Mohammed Juma Hassan.

UNITED KINGDOM

Embassy: 5300 Bonn 1, Friedrich-Ebert-Allee 77; tel (228) 234061; telex 886887; fax (228) 234070.
Ambassador: Sir Christopher Mallaby.
Minister: L. P. Neville-Jones.
Counsellor (Labour): J. Franklin.
Counsellor and Head of Chancery: C. R. Budd.
Counsellor (Bilateral Relations): E. J. Mitchell.
Counsellor (Defence Supply): A. Walker.
Counsellor (Economic): D. Broucher.
Counsellor (Management/Consular): P. V. Rollitt.
Counsellor (Science/Technology): Dr R. Escritt.
Counsellor: B. H. Dinwiddy.
Defence Attaché: Brig. A. P. Simm.
Air Attaché: Air Commdr W. M. Craghill.
Naval Attaché: Capt. J. McLees.
Military Attaché: Lieut Col N. S. Hunter.
Assistant Military Attaché (Technical): Lieut Col N. S. Hunter.
Assistant Naval Attaché (Technical): Lieut Cdre J. G. Apps.
First Secretary (Defence Supply): V. J. Evans.
First Secretary (Legal Adviser): P. A. Waterworth.
First Secretary (Economic): R. W. Barnett.
First Secretary (Economic): J. Darby.
First Secretary (Chancery): S. J. Wordsworth.
First Secretary (Chancery): G. B. J. P. Busby.
First Secretary (Information): J. I. Link.
First Secretary (Agriculture): D. J. Greig.
First Secretary (Science/Technology): T. H. Carter.
First Secretary (Management): P. Cunningham.
First Secretary: R. E. Brinkley.
Second Secretary (Accountant): G. Acton.
Second Secretary (Press/Information): R. M. Wills.

Consulate: 1000 Berlin 12, Uhlandstr. 7/8; tel (30) 3095292; telex 184268; fax (30) 3136361.
Director of Trade Promotion: A. R. Nuttall.
Consul: A. E. Sutton.

Consulate-General: 2000 Hamburg 13, Harvesthuder Weg 8a; tel (40) 446071; telex 213562; fax (40) 4107259.
Consul-General: P. Yarnold.
Consul (Commercial): G. E. Mearns.
Vice-Consul (Management/Consular): R. J. Beeson.

Consulate-General: 3000 Hannover 1, Georgsplatz 1; tel (511) 1032220; telex 921634; fax (511) 1034440.
Consul-General: Dr B. Thiemann.

Consulate-General: 4000 Dusseldorf 30, Yorck Str. 19; tel (211) 9448; telex 8584855; fax (211) 486359.
Consul-General and Director of Trade and Investment Promotion: A. C. Hunt.
Consul (Commercial): W. D. Townend.
Consul (Consular/Management/Information): A. A. Windham.
Consul (Commercial): R. Embleton.
Vice-Consul (Immigration): M. J. Carbine.
Vice-Consul (Immigration): G. D. Forrester.
Vice-Consul (Immigration): L. Williams.
Vice-Consul (Immigration): T. J. Burke.

Consulate-General: 6000 Frankfurt-am-Main 1, Bockenheimer Landstr. 42; tel (69) 170002; telex 414932; fax (69) 729553.
Consul-General: C. A. Munro.
Consul (Commercial): M. M. Hall.
Vice-Consul (Consular/Management): M. C. Cross.
Vice-Consul (Investment): Dr S. P. Steiner.
Information Officer: Dr W. Dobler.

Consulate-General: 7000 Stuttgart 1, Breite Str. 2; tel (711) 16269; telex 722397; fax (711) 1626930.
Consul-General: D. R. Thomas.
Commercial Officer: W. R. Seidler.

Consulate-General: 8000 Munich 40, Amalienstr. 62; Postfach 2010; tel (89) 3816280; telex 529959; fax (89) 331848.
Consul-General: A. F. Blake-Pauley.
Consul (Commercial): C. V. Thompson.
Vice-Consul (Consular/Management): M. E. Blake-Pauley.
Information Officer: B. I. Dammert.
Vice-Consul (Investment): Dr S. P. Steiner.

Consulate: 2300 Kiel 17, United Baltic Corporation GmbH Schleuse; Postfach 8080; tel (431) 30632; telex 299829; fax (431) 35895.
Honorary Consul: I. B. Gibson.

Consulate: 2800 Bremen 1, Herrlichkeiten 6; Postfach 103860; tel (421) 59090; telex 244868.
Honorary Consul: Dr H. J. Enge.

Consulate: 7800 Frieburg, Gundelfingen, Buchenstr. 4; tel (761) 583117.
Honorary Consul: A. C. McCarthy.

Consulate: 8500 Nuremberg 10, c/o Schwan-Stabilo Schwanhäusser GmbH & Co., Maxfield Str. 3; Postfach 4553; tel (911) 3609520; telex 623162; fax (911) 3609861.
Honorary Consul: G. Schwanhausser.

USA

Embassy: 5300 Bonn 2, Deichmanns Aue 29; tel (228) 3392053; telex 885452; fax (228) 3392663.
Ambassador: Robert Kimmitt.
Deputy Head of Mission: George F. Ward, Jr.
Office of Defence Attaché: Col Bernard D. McDaniel.
Office of Defence Co-operation: Col Arthur A. Lovgren.
Political Section: Douglas H. Jones.
Economic Section: Donald B. Kursch.

Commercial Section: John W. Bligh, Jr.
Labour Officer: John A. Warnock.
Administrative Section: Harold W. Geisel.
Regional Security Officer: Steven B. Bray.
Attaché (Science): Francis M. Kinnelly.
Attaché (Finance): Carl J. Lohmann.
Agricultural Section: Gerald W. Harvey.
Public Affairs Officer: Cynthia A. Miller.
Customs Service: Viktor Jacobson.
Internal Revenue Service: Larry LaGrand.
Communications Programme Officer: John Hughs.
Information System Manager: Carol Rodley.

Consulate-General: 1000 Berlin 33, Clayallee 170; tel (30) 8324087; telex 0183701.
Consul-General: Diane E. Henshaw.

Commercial Office: 4000 Dusseldorf, Emmanuel-Leutze-Str. 1B; tel (211) 596790; telex 8584246.
Commercial Section: Thomas L. Boam.

Consulate-General: 6000 Frankfurt-am-Main 1, Siesmayerstr. 21; tel (69) 753040; fax (69) 748938.
Consul-General: Pierre Shostal.
Deputy Principal Officer: J. Brayton Redecker.
Commercial Section: Donald Businger.
Administrative Section: Maurice N. Grainek.
Regional Security Officer: Stephen J. Kruchko.
Branch Public Affairs Officer: Craig B. Springer.
Political Adviser: Commdr-in-Chief T. Patrick Killough.
Federal Aviation Administration: James F. Coffey.
Federal Aviation Administration: Gary W. Wirt.
Centres for Disease Control: William F. Simonsen.
Communications Programme Officer: Alvin C. Thomas.
Information Systems Manager: Bradley D. Rohrer.

Consulate-General: 2000 Hamburg 36, Alsterufer 27/8; tel (40) 411710; telex 213777; fax (40) 443004.
Consul-General: James C. Whitlock, Jr.
Commercial Section: James L. Joy.
Political and Economic Sections: Gregory Phillips.
Administrative Section: Virginia I. Kurapka.
Branch Public Affairs Officer: Lynne M. Martin.
Regional Security Officer: John J. Beaudry.
Communications Programme Officer: Michael Chiaventone.

Agricultural Trade Office: 2000 Hamburg 36, Grosse Theaterstr. 42; tel (40) 341207; telex 2163970; fax (40) 341200.
Agricultural Trade Office: Dale L. Good.

Consulate-General: 8000 Munich 22, Koeniginstr. 5; tel (89) 28881; telex 522697; fax (89) 283047.
Political Section and Acting Principal Officer: James E. Jeffrey.
Commercial Section: Edward E. Ruse, III.
Administrative Section: Eugene A. Trahan, Jr.
Regional Security Officer: John J. Stein, Jr.
Branch Public Affairs Officer: Kathryn L. Koob.
Voice of America—EUR: Earl Klitenic.
Voice of America—MRS: George A. Moore.

Consulate-General: 7000 Stuttgart 1, Urbanstr. 7; tel (711) 21450; telex 722945; fax (711) 6494786.
Consul-General: Day O. Mount.
Commercial Section: Camille Sailer.
Administrative Section: Sally L. Lindover.
Branch Public Affairs Officer: Samuel Westgate.
Political and Economic Sections: Elizabeth Montague.
Regional Security Officer: John J. Stein.
Political Adviser: Commdr-in-Chief Diana Smith.
Political Adviser: Commdr-in-Chief Benton G. Moeller.
Communications Programme Officer: J. Michael Suddath.

URUGUAY

Embassy: 5300 Bonn 2, Gotenstr. 1-3; tel (228) 356570; telex 885708.
Ambassador: Dr Augustín Espinosa Lloveras.

Consulate: 1000 Berlin 30, Budapester Str. 24; tel (30) 2611799; telex 186771; fax (30) 2629620.
Honorary Consul: Kurt Rabau.

Consulate-General: 2000 Hamburg 13, Hochallee 76; tel (40) 4106542; telex 213538.
Consul-General: Pedro Dondo.

Consulate: 3000 Hannover, Ständehausstr. 16; tel (511) 17515.
Honorary Consul: Berthold Liebernickel.

Consulate: 4000 Dusseldorf, Wagnerstr. 26; tel (211) 353435.
Honorary Consul: Herbert Liesenfeld.

Consulate: 6000 Frankfurt-am-Main, Eschersheimer Landstr. 532; tel (69) 518510; telex 4189833.
Honorary Consul: Wolfgang Kirsten.

Consulate: 8000 Munich 2, Sedlinger-Tor-Platz 8; tel (89) 591361; fax (89) 591362.
Honorary Consul: Peter Schmalisch.

VENEZUELA

Embassy: 5300 Bonn 3, im Rheingarten 7; Postfach 300224; tel (228) 400920; telex 400920; fax (228) 344057.
Ambassador: Dr Rafael Leon Morales.
Minister-Counsellor (Technical): Dario Bauder.
Counsellor (Technical): Raymundo Garcia Araujo.
First Secretary: Francisco Nieto Guerrero.
Attaché: Ninoska Cuervo.

Branch Office: 1080 Berlin, Otto Grotewohl Str. 5, 4 Stock.; 1000 Berlin, Postfach 610470; tel (2) 2292111; telex 114058; fax (2) 7825725.
Minister-Counsellor: Erick Becker Becker.
First Secretary: Haydee Gomez.

Consulate-General: 2000 Hamburg 13, Rothenbaumchaussee 30; tel (40) 4101241; telex 213341.
Consul-General: Hercilia Briceño de Arciniegas.

Consulate-General: 6000 Frankfurt-am-Main, Brönnerstr. 17; tel (69) 287284; fax (69) 292370.
Consul-General: Avacel Bermudes de Gil.

Consulate: 8000 Munich 22, Prinzregentenstr. 54, Eingang Reitmorstr.; tel (89) 221449.
Honorary Consul: Rolf Simon Schulz.

VIET-NAM

Embassy: 5300 Bonn 2, Konstantinstr. 37; tel (228) 357022; telex 8861122; fax (228) 351866.
Ambassador: Bui Hong Phuc.

WESTERN SAMOA

Consulate: 2000 Hamburg 1, Spaldinstr. 70; Postfach 106021; tel (40) 233818.
Honorary Consul: Hayo Breckwoldt.

YEMEN

Embassy: 5300 Bonn 1, Adenauerallee 77; tel (228) 220273; telex 885765; fax (228) 229364.
Ambassador: Mostafa Ahmed Yacoub.

YUGOSLAVIA

Embassy: 5300 Bonn 2, Schloßallee 5; tel (228) 344051; telex 885530; fax (228) 344057.
Envoy (Economic/Commercial): Ivan Zbašnik.
Envoy: Drago Trbojević.
Counsellor (Press/Culture): Branko Zupanc.
Counsellor (Social/Labour): Dragoljub Ljepoja.
Counsellor (Educational): Stojanka Radenović-Petković.
First Counsellor and Head of Consular Section: Dragutin Knežević.
Counsellor and Head of Consular Section: Vladimir Topic.
Counsellor: Borivoj Crvenic.
Defence Attaché: Lieut Col Dušan Radaković.
First Secretary (Political Affairs): Dušan Bogdanović.

Consulate-General: 2000 Hamburg 13, Harvestehuder Weg 101; tel (40) 444504; telex 213937.
Consul-General: Milivoje Mihić.

Consulate-General: 6000 Frankfurt-am-Main, Thüringer Str. 3; tel (69) 439923; telex 414476; fax (69) 433149.
Consul-General: Petko Stefanovski.

Consulate-General: 7000 Stuttgart, Taubenstr. 4; tel (711) 600646; telex 722618; fax (711) 6494048.
Consul-General: Radovan Milovanović.

Consulate-General: 8000 Munich 80, Böhmerwaldplatz 2; tel (89) 980823; telex 0524840; fax (89) 981319.
Consul-General: Mladjen Rudić.

Consulate: 3000 Hannover, Flüggestr. 21; tel (511) 312058; telex 922076.
Consul: Drago Jović.

Consulate: 4000 Dusseldorf, Lindemannstr. 5; tel (211) 673967; telex 8586827.
Consul: Zvonko Plečaš.

Consulate: 6800 Mannheim, R1, Nr. 1; tel (621) 16012; telex 463005; fax (621) 20914.
Consul: Nikola Radovac.

Consulate: 7800 Freiburg I. Br., Baseler Str. 6; tel (761) 71011; telex 772406; fax (761) 709311.
Consul: Miroljub Milanović.

Consulate: 8500 Nuremberg, Gostenhofer Hauptstr. 21; tel (911) 263221; fax (911) 263291.
Consul: Ibrahim Agić.

ZAIRE

Embassy: 5300 Bonn 2, im Meisengarten 133; tel (228) 346071; telex 885573.
Ambassador: Mabolia Inengo Tra Bwato.

Consulate-General: 4000 Dusseldorf 11, Schiess-Str. 45; tel (211) 5996343; telex 8584478; fax (211) 5996318.
Honorary Consul-General: Peter Jungen.

Consulate-General: 7000 Stuttgart, Robert-Bosch-Str. 4; tel (7111) 291954; telex 722169.
Honorary Consul-General: Karl-Ernst Dietrich.

Consulate-General: 2800 Bremen, Bornstr. 16-7; tel (421) 15820; telex 244140.
Honorary Consul-General: Ansgar Werner.

Consulate: 8000 Munich 40, Siegesstr. 22; tel (89) 331480.
Honorary Consul: Lothar Schmechtig.

ZAMBIA

Embassy: 5300 Bonn 2, Mittelstr. 39; tel (228) 376811; telex 885511; fax (228) 379536.
Ambassador: Charles Chishimba Manyema.
First Secretary: Joseph John Zulu.
First Secretary: Ignacious Ngosa.
First Secretary: Greenfel G. Siuluta.
Second Secretary: Davies Sampa.
Third Secretary: Udie Soko.
Third Secretary: Morgan M. Chibwe.
Third Secretary: Elizabeth N. Nyirenda.
Tourism Manager: Wilfred Sakuhuka.

ZIMBABWE

Embassy: 5300 Bonn 2, Villichgasse 7, Arcadia Centrum; tel (228) 356071; telex 885580.

Ambassador: Prof. Dr George Payne Kahari.
Minister-Counsellor: John Chimbandi.
Counsellor (Commercial): Elijah Chitsike.
Counsellor: Teddy Jamu.
Counsellor: Dudzayi D. Madziwa.
First Secretary (Commercial): Charles A. Chiunye.
First Secretary: Tamuka R. M. Muranga.
Second Secretary: George Ndlovu.

International Organizations

EUROPEAN COMMUNITIES

Bureau: 5300 Bonn, 22 Zitelmannstr.; tel (228) 530090; telex 886648; fax (228) 5300950.
Director: Gird Langguth.

Sub-Office: 1000 Berlin 31, 102 Kurfürstendamm; tel (30) 8924028; telex 184015; fax (30) 8922059.
Director: Eckhard Jaedtke.

Sub-Office: 8000 Munich 2, 27 Erhardtstr.; tel (89) 2021011; telex 5218135; fax (89) 2021015.
Director: Otto Hieber.

GHANA

ALGERIA

Embassy: F606/1, off Cantonments Rd, Christiansborg, POB 2747, Accra; tel (21) 776828.
Ambassador: Hamid Bourki.

BENIN

Embassy: Volta St, 2nd Close H 19, Airport Residential Area, POB 7871, Accra-North; tel (21) 774860.
Ambassador: Georges Nkouéi Timanty.
Second Counsellor (Political): Laitan Grégoire Houde.
Second Counsellor (Information/Interpreting/Translation): Silifatou Gomina.
Attaché (Consular): Djibril Séfou Garba.
Attaché (Administration/Finance): Michel Avoce.

BRAZIL

Embassy: 5 Volta St, Airport Residential Area, POB 2918, Accra; tel (21) 777154; telex 2081.
Ambassador: Carlos Norberto de Oliveira Pares.

BULGARIA

Embassy: 3 Kakramadu Rd, East Cantonments, POB 3193, Accra; tel (21) 772404; telex 2709.
Ambassador: Georgi Kassov.
Counsellor (Commercial): Ianko Kostovski.
Third Secretary: Miroslav Komarov.

BURKINA FASO

Embassy: 772/3 Asylum Down, off Farrar Ave, POB 651, Accra; tel (21) 221988; telex 2108.
Ambassador: Emile Gouba.

CANADA

High Commission: 42 Independence Ave, POB 1639, Accra; tel (21) 228555; telex 2024.
High Commissioner: Douglas Fogerty.
Counsellor: H. P. G. Fraser.
Counsellor (Development): G. Saibel.
First Secretary (Development): R. S. Audette.
First Secretary (Development): G. Chauvet.
Second Secretary (Administrative): J. P. Nadeau.

CHINA, PEOPLE'S REPUBLIC

Embassy: 7 Agostinho Neto Rd, Airport Residential Area, POB 3356, Accra; tel (21) 777073.
Ambassador: Cui Jie.

COTE D'IVOIRE

Embassy: 9 18th Lane, off Cantonments Rd, POB 3445, Christiansborg, Accra; tel (21) 774611; telex 2131.
Ambassador: Konan Nda.

CUBA

Embassy: 10 Ridge Rd, Roman Ridge, Airport Residential Area, POB 9163 Airport, Accra; tel (21) 775842.
Ambassador: Nicolás Rodríguez.

CZECHOSLOVAKIA

Embassy: C260/5, 2 Kanda High Rd, POB 5226, Accra-North; tel (21) 223540; telex 2463.
Ambassador: Dr Ilja Ulrich.
Attaché (Commercial): Blahoslav Matejcek.
Attaché (Press/Cultural/Consular): Pavel Koblizka.

DENMARK

Consulate-General: c/o Scanship Ltd, High St, POB 1705, Accra; tel (21) 666761; telex 2181.
Consul-General: Claus Winther.
Vice-Consul: Grete Toft.

EGYPT

Embassy: 27 Noi Fetreke St, Roman Ridge, POB 2508, Accra.
Ambassador: Bahaa Eldin Mostafa Reda.

ETHIOPIA

Embassy: 6 Adiembra Rd, East Cantonment, POB 1646, Accra; tel (21) 775928.
Chargé d'affaires a.i.: Beide Melaku.

FINLAND

Consulate-General: House Aare, 3rd Rangoon Close, POB 262, Accra; tel (21) 774513; telex 2146.
Consul-General: Hans Rudolf Roth.

FRANCE

Embassy: 12th Rd, off Liberation Ave, POB 187, Accra; tel (21) 228504.
Ambassador: Jean-François Lionnet.
First Counsellor: Jean Graebling.
Counsellor (Economic/Commercial): Louis-Jean l'Hélias.
Counsellor (Culture/Co-operation): Michel Bonnieau.
Consul: Loïc Barreau.

GERMANY

Embassy: Valldemosa Lodge, Plot No. 18, North Ridge Residential Area, 7th Ave Extension, POB 1757, Accra; tel (21) 221311; telex 2025.
Ambassador: Burghart Nagel.

GUINEA

Embassy: 11 Osu Badu St, Dzorwulu, POB 5497, Accra-North; tel (21) 777921.
Ambassador: Dore Diale Drus.

HOLY SEE

Apostolic Nunciature: C 10 Obetsebi Lamptey Ave, POB 9675, Airport, Accra; tel (21) 774019.
Apostolic Pro-Nuncio: Most Rev. Dr Abraham Kattumana.
Secretary: Rev. Mgr Ambrose Madtha.

HUNGARY

Embassy: F582 A/1, Salem Rd, Christiansborg, POB 3027, Accra; tel (21) 774917.
Ambassador: Raymond Tóth.

INDIA

High Commission: 9 Ridge Rd, Roman Ridge, POB 3040, Accra; tel (21) 777916; telex 2154; fax (21) 772176.
High Commissioner: S. K. Uppal.
Counsellor (Economic/Commercial): E. Barwa.
Second Secretary (Political): M. Divakaran.
Attaché (Information/Culture): A. K. Agrawal.
Attaché (Administration): J. R. Sharma.
Attaché (Senior Personal Assistant): G. L. Manocha.

IRAN

Embassy: 10 Agbaamo St, Airport Residential Area, POB 1260073, Accra; tel (21) 74474; telex 2117.
Ambassador: Shameddin Khareghani.

ITALY

Embassy: Jawaharlal Nehru Rd, POB 140, Accra; tel (21) 775621; telex 2039.
Ambassador: Mario Fugazzola.

JAPAN

Embassy: 8 Rangoon Ave, off Switchback Rd, POB 1637, Accra; tel (21) 775616; telex 2068.

Ambassador: Shigeru Kurosawa.

KOREA, DEMOCRATIC PEOPLE'S REPUBLIC

Embassy: 139 Roman Ridge, Ambassadorial Estate, Nortei Ababio Est., POB 13874, Accra; tel (21) 777825.
Ambassador: Yi Hae-Sop.

KOREA, REPUBLIC

Embassy: 3 Abokobi Rd, East Cantonments, POB 13700, Accra; tel (21) 776157; telex 2203.
Ambassador: Jung Il Oh.
Counsellor: Young Sop Song.
Second Secretary and Consul: Young Suck Do.

LEBANON

Embassy: off Cantonments Rd, OSU RE, POB 562, Accra; tel (21) 776727; telex 2118.
Ambassador: Dr Muhammad Issa.

LIBERIA

Embassy: F675/1, off Cantonments Rd, Christiansborg, POB 895, Accra; tel (21) 775641; telex 2071.
Ambassador: T. Boye Nelson.

LIBYA

People's Bureau: 14 Sixth St, Airport Residential Area, POB 6995, Accra; tel (21) 774820; telex 2179.
Secretary of People's Bureau: Abdullah Jibran.

MALI

Embassy: Crescent Rd, Block 1, POB 1121, Accra; tel (21) 666421; telex 2061.
Ambassador: Muphtah Ag Hairy.

NETHERLANDS

Embassy: 89 Liberation Rd, Sankara Circle, POB 3248, Accra; tel (21) 221655; telex 2128.
Chargé d'affaires a.i.: S. H. Bloembergen.

NIGERIA

High Commission: Rangoon Ave, POB 1548, Accra; tel (21) 776158; telex 2051.
High Commissioner: T. A. Olu-Otunla.

PAKISTAN

High Commission: Plot No. 11, Ring Rd East, nr Danquah Circle, POB 1114, Accra; tel (21) 776059; telex 2426.
High Commissioner: Shafqat Ali Shaikh.
Second Secretary: Mohammad Najm Akbar.

POLAND

Embassy: 2 Akosombo St, Airport Residential Area, POB 2552, Accra; tel (21) 775972; telex 2558.
Chargé d'affaires a.i.: Klemens Walkowiak.

ROMANIA

Embassy: North Labone, Ward F, Block 6, House 262, POB M112, Accra; tel (21) 774076; telex 2027.
Chargé d'affaires: Gheorghe V. Ilie.

RUSSIA

Embassy: F856/1, Ring Rd East, POB 1634, Accra; tel (21) 775611; telex 2074.
Ambassador: Yevgeny D. Ostrovenko.

SAUDI ARABIA

Embassy: F868/1, off Cantonments Rd, OSU RE, Accra; tel (21) 776651.
Chargé d'affaires: Anwar Abdul Fattah Abdrabbuh.

SINGAPORE

Embassy: Accra.

SPAIN

Embassy: Airport Residential Area, Lamptey Ave Extension, POB 1218, Accra; tel (21) 774004.
Ambassador: Manuel María González-Haba.

SWEDEN

Consulate-General: F78/51, 11th Lane, OSU RE (opposite US Consulate), POB 4916, Accra; tel (21) 773145; telex 2340; fax (21) 773175.
Consul-General: Amarkai Amarteifio.

SWITZERLAND

Embassy: 9 Water Rd S.I., North Ridge Area, POB 359, Accra; tel (21) 228125; telex 2197.
Ambassador: H. Strauch.
Third Secretary and Office Manager: Michel Bähler.
Attaché (Development Co-operation/Aid): Antoine Brawand.

TOGO

Embassy: Togo House, nr Cantonments Circle, POB 4308, Accra; tel (21) 777950; telex 2166.
Ambassador: Larbli Tchintchibidja.

UNITED KINGDOM

High Commission: Osu Link, off Gamel Abdul Nasser Ave, POB 296, Accra; tel (21) 221665; telex 2323; fax (21) 224572.
High Commissioner: Anthony Michael Goodenough.
Deputy High Commissioner: M. J. Greenstreet.
Defence Advisor: Lieut Col S. D. G. McKinley.
First Secretary (Political): S. C. E. Holt.
First Secretary (Management/Consular): J. A. Stevens.
First Secretary (Commercial): S. S. Strong.
First Secretary (Aid): R. B. Stevenson.
Second Secretary (Chancery/Information): D. J. G. Barton.
Second Secretary (Consular): S. M. Pakes.

USA

Embassy: Ring Rd East, POB 194, Accra; tel (21) 775348; telex 2579; fax (21) 776008.
Ambassador: Raymond C. Ewing.
Deputy Head of Mission: John C. Holzman.
Political, Economic and Labour Sections: David A. Appleton.
Economic and Commercial Sections: Karl H. Fritz.
Consular Section: Donna M. Blair.
Administrative Section: Thomas Cross.
Regional Security Officer: Dennis Bochantin.
Agency for International Development: Joseph Goodwin.
Public Affairs Officer: Daniel McGaffie.
Communications Programme Officer: John B. Davis.

YUGOSLAVIA

Embassy: 47 Senchi St, Airport Residential Area, POB 1629, Accra; tel (21) 775761.
Ambassador: Miroslav Jancic.
Counsellor: Ljubomir Andjelkovic.

International Organizations

EUROPEAN COMMUNITIES

External Delegation: POB 9505, Kotoka International Airport, Accra; tel (21) 774201; telex 2069; fax (21) 774154.
Commission Delegate: Michael McGeever.

GREECE

ALBANIA

Embassy: Odos Karachristou 1, Kolonaki, 115 21 Athens; tel (1) 723-4412; telex 210351; fax (1) 723-1972.
Ambassador: Izedin Hajdini.
Counsellor (Commercial): Gjergj Rrembeci.
First Secretary: Kastriot Robo.
First Secretary: Sino Sinorukaj.
Third Secretary: Demir Kambo.
Attaché: Ilia Stefa.

ALGERIA

Embassy: Leoforos Vassileos Konstantinou 14, 116 35 Athens; tel (1) 751-3560; telex 219992; fax (1) 701-8681.
Ambassador: Mostefa Bouakaz.
Minister-Counsellor: Ahmed Ameur.
Third Secretary: Dine Attalah.
Attaché: Boumediene Belguendouz.
Attaché: Benaouda Khessibi.
Attaché (Consular Affairs): Mohammed Yacine Rezzouk.

ARGENTINA

Embassy: Leoforos Vassilissis Sofias 59, Athens; tel (1) 722-4753; telex 215218; fax (1) 722-7568.
Ambassador: Raúl Bercovich Rodríguez.

AUSTRALIA

Embassy: 37 Dimitriou Soutsou St, Ambelokipi, 115 21 Athens; POB 3070, Ambelokipi, 11510 Athens; tel (1) 644-7303; telex 215815; fax (1) 644-3633.
Ambassador: Kevin Ian Gates.

AUSTRIA

Embassy: Leoforos Alexandras 26, 106 83 Athens 148; tel (1) 821-1036; telex 215938; fax (1) 821-9823.
Ambassador: Dr Georg Calice.
Counsellor (Commercial): Florian Lorenz.
Counsellor (Economic): Mohammad Yusuf Matuska.
Secretary (Economic): Ilse Langmann.

Consulate: Averof 18, 104 33 Athens 148; tel (1) 822-5401.
Honorary Consul: Ioannis Lainopoulos.

Consulate-General: Maoul No. 7, 1 Stock., Nea Krini, Thessaloniki; tel (31) 236500.
Honorary Consul-General: Jannis Koufas.

Consulate: Platia Eleftherius u Dedalou 2, 3 Stock., 712 01 Iraklion, Crete; tel (81) 222213; telex 262385; fax (81) 280608.
Honorary Consul: Roswatha Boduva.

Consulate: 25 Martiou 27-33, POB 69, 851 00 Rhodes; tel (241) 24757; telex 292114.
Honorary Consul: Stefanos Zanettos.

BELGIUM

Embassy: Odos Sekeri 3, 106 71 Athens; tel (1) 361-7886; telex 216422; fax (1) 360-4289.
Ambassador: Gilbert Loquet.

BRAZIL

Embassy: Platia Philikis Etairias 14, 106 73 Athens; tel (1) 721-3039; telex 216604.
Ambassador: Alcides da Costa Guimarães Filho.

BULGARIA

Embassy: Odos Akademias 12, Athens; tel (1) 360-9411.
Ambassador: Petar Iliev Slavtchev.

CANADA

Embassy: Odos Ioannou Gennadiou 4, 115 21 Athens; tel (1) 723-9511; telex 215584; fax (1) 724-7123.
Ambassador: Ernest Hébert.
Counsellor (Commercial): S. B. McDowall.
Counsellor and Consul: K. M. Cook.
Forces Attaché: Col R. J. Rousham.
First Secretary (Immigration): H. Amundsen.
Second Secretary (Administrative) and Vice-Consul: W. G. Skerkowski.
Attaché (Medical): Dr P. Constantinidis.

CHILE

Embassy: Leoforos Vassilissis Sofias 96, Athens; tel (1) 777-5017.
Chargé d'affaires a.i.: Manuel Atria.

CHINA, PEOPLE'S REPUBLIC

Embassy: Odos Krinon 2A, Palaio Psychico, 154 10 Athens; tel (1) 672-3282; telex 214383; fax (1) 672-3819.
Ambassador: Zhu Youwan.
Counsellor: Yang Guangsheng.
Counsellor (Commercial): Liu Bingju.
Military Attaché: Chen Guilin.
Press Officer: Bao Shusheng.

CUBA

Embassy: Odos Davaki 10, Athens; tel (1) 692-5367.
Ambassador: M. F. Alfonso Rodríguez.

CYPRUS

Embassy: Odos Herodotou 16, Athens; tel (1) 723-2727; telex 215642; fax (1) 723-1927.
Ambassador: Frixos Colotas.
Minister: Christodoulos Pashiardis.
Counsellor and Consul-General: Rea Yiordamlis.
First Secretary: Phaedon Anastasiou.

Consulate-General: Odos Aristotelous 9, 6th Floor, Thessaloniki; tel (31) 260611; telex 410858; fax (31) 274984.
Consul-General: George Vyrides.

CZECHOSLOVAKIA

Embassy: Odos Georges Seferi 6, Palaio Psychico, 154 52 Athens; tel (1) 671-3755; telex 214146; fax (1) 671-0675.
Counsellor (Commercial): Jaroslav Matouš.
First Secretary: Lubor Staněk.
Third Secretary: Josef Matějka.
Third Secretary and Consul: Irena Knotková.
Attaché: Libor Blašťák.
Attaché: Ladislav Nykodým.
Attaché: Jiří Kolář.

DENMARK

Embassy: 11 Vassilissis Sofias, 106 71 Athens; tel (1) 360-8315; telex 215586; fax (1) 363-6163.
Ambassador: Skjold Gustav Mellbin.
Counsellor: Kresten Due.
Counsellor (Commercial): Leif Haugsted.
Counsellor (Agriculture/Government): Henrik Curtz.
Chancellor and Vice-Consul: Lone Gad Pilarinou.
Export Assistant: Christoph Wiese.
Export Assistant: Jens Carøe Sørensen.

Consulate: 1 Venizelou St, 841 00 Syros; tel (281) 23714; telex 293172; fax (281) 26262.
Consul: Elias Oikonomopoulis.

Consulate: 58 25th August St, 712 02 Iraklion, Crete; tel (81) 229402; telex 262238; fax (81) 229217.
Consul: Evangelos Georgiou Perakis.

Consulate: Ethnikis Antistasseos 4, 491 00 Corfu; tel (661) 35698; telex 332118.
Consul: Vassilios N. Patras.

Consulate: Koundouriotou St 5 A, Kos; tel (242) 28584; telex 292199.
Consul: Michael C. Stamatiades.

Consulate: 2 Lefkosias, 264 41 Patrai; tel (61) 424382.
Consul: Lise-Lott Wivian Barlas.

Consulate: 93 Akti Miaouli, 185 38 Piraeus; tel (1) 452-4532; telex 211622; fax (1) 418-3006.
Consul: Efstathios Gourdomichalis.

Consulate: 28/30 Iroon Politechniou, Rhodes; tel (241) 20681; telex 292124; fax (241) 28527.
Consul: M. Papathanassis.

Consulate: 26 Komninon St, 546 24 Thessaloniki; tel (31) 284065; telex 412523; fax (31) 283794.
Consul: Christos J. Accas.

Consulate: 118 Dimitriados St, 382 21 Vólos; tel (421) 34332; telex 282146; fax.
Consul: Elizabeth Zografou.

EGYPT

Embassy: Leoforos Vassilissis Sofias 3, Athens; tel (1) 361-8612.
Ambassador: Ahmad Kadry Salamah.

ETHIOPIA

Embassy: Odos Davaki 10, Erythros, 115 26 Athens; tel (1) 692-0483; telex 218548.
Ambassador: Samuel Teferra.

FINLAND

Embassy: Odos Eratosthenous 1, 116 35 Athens; POB 17037, 100 24 Athens; tel (1) 701-1775; telex 215914; fax (1) 751-5064.
Ambassador: Erkki Tiilikainen.

Consulate-General: 17 Valaoritou St, 106 71 Athens; tel (1) 361-8411; telex 215126.
Consul-General: Constantin G. Lazarakis.

Consulate: Riga Fereou St 46, 262 11 Patras; tel (61) 277707.
Consul: Anthony P. Triantaphillopoulos.

Consulate: Notara St 89-91, 185 35 Piraeus; tel (1) 411-7090; telex 211359.
Consul: Alexander P. Pappas.

Consulate: Odos Amerikis 95, 851 00 Rhodes; tel (241) 35780; telex 292132.
Consul: George Carayannis.

Consulate: 4 Jonos Dragoumi St, 6th Floor, Rm 601, 546 24 Thessaloniki; tel (31) 235931; telex 410463.
Consul: Filotas Kazazis.

FRANCE

Embassy: Leoforos Vassilissis Sofias 7, 106 71 Athens; tel (1) 361-1683.
Ambassador: Jacques Thibau.

Consulate-General: 5-7 Ave Vassileos Constantinou, 106 74 Athens; tel (1) 722-0137.

GERMANY

Embassy: POB 61011, Odos Vassilissis Sofias 10, 151 24 Athens; tel (1) 369-4111; telex 215441; fax (1) 802-0523.
Ambassador: Leopold Bill von Bredow.

Consulate-General: Odos Karolou Diehl 4a, 546 23 Thessaloniki; POB 10515, 541 10 Thessaloniki; tel (31) 236315; telex 418299.
Consul-General: Dr Eberhard Schmitt.

Consulate: Odos Daskalogianni 64, POB 1, 731 00 Chania, Crete; tel (821) 57944; telex 291168.
Honorary Consul: Georgios Tsirintanis.

Consulate: Odos Zografou 7, POB 1083, 711 00 Iraklion, Crete; tel (81) 226288; telex 262207; fax (81) 222576.
Honorary Consul: Rolf Haug.

Consulate: Aghiou Georgiou 1, 691 00 Komotini; tel (531) 29325; telex 462184.
Honorary Consul: Polyvios Michaloglou.

Consulate: L. Alexandra 11, 491 00 Corfu; tel (661) 21453; telex 332301.
Honorary Consul: Dimitrios Zervos.

Consulate: Odos Mesonos 98, 262 21 Patras; tel (61) 221943.
Honorary Consul: Georgios Abatzis.

Consulate: Parados Issiodou 12, 851 00 Rhodes; tel (241) 63730.
Honorary Consul: Athanasios Dilanas.

Consulate: Odos Themistoklis Sofoulis 73, 831 00 Samos; tel (273) 27260.
Honorary Consul: Christos Capnoulas.

Consulate: Leoforos Dimitriados 251, POB 1030, Vólos; tel (421) 25379; telex 282136; fax (421) 62766.
Honorary Consul: Günter Scheffel.

HOLY SEE

Apostolic Nunciature: Odos Mavili 2, Palaio Psychiko, 154 52 Athens; tel (1) 647-3598; fax (1) 647-2849.
Apostolic Pro-Nuncio: Most Rev. Luciano Storero.
Secretary: Mgr Steven Otellini.

HONDURAS

Embassy: Leoforos Vassilissis Sofias 86, 115 28 Athens; tel (1) 777-5802; telex 241890; fax (1) 413-6242.
Minister-Counsellor and Chargé d'affaires a.i.: Teodolinda Banegas de Makris.

Consulate: Akti Miaouli 11, 185 35 Piraeus; tel (1) 413-5313; telex 241890; fax (1) 413-6242.
Consul: Lukas Makris.

HUNGARY

Embassy: Odos Kalvou 16, Palaio Psychiko, 154 52 Athens; tel (1) 671-4889.
Ambassador: László Kincses.

ICELAND

Consulate-General: Nikita St 1, Piraeus 185 31; tel (1) 412-2218; telex 212101; fax (1) 418-1947.
Ambassador: Páll Ásgeir Tryggvason.
Consul-General: Constantin J. Lyberopoulos.
Vice-Consul: Emilía Kofoed-Hansen Lyberopoulos.

INDIA

Embassy: Odos Kleanthous 3, 106 74 Athens; tel (1) 721-6481.
Ambassador: Harcharan Singh Dhody.

IRAN

Embassy: Odos Kalari 16, Palaio Psychiko, Athens; tel (1) 647-1436.
Ambassador: Ahmad Ajallooeian.

IRAQ

Embassy: Odos Mazaraki 4, Palaio Psychiko, Athens; tel (1) 671-5012.
Ambassador: Fetah al-Khezreji.

IRELAND

Embassy: 7 Leoforos Vassileos, Konstantinou, 106 74 Athens; tel (1) 723-2771; telex 218111; fax (1) 724-0217.
Ambassador: Bernard McHugh.
First Secretary: Patrick Sammon.
Secretary: Paul Gunning.

ISRAEL

Embassy: Odos Marathonodronou 1, Palaio Psychiko, 154 52 Athens; tel (1) 671-9530; telex 216941; fax (1) 647-9510.
Ambassador: David Sasson.
Counsellor: Emanuel Seri.
Counsellor (Commercial): Moshe Israeli.
First Secretary and Head of Consular Section: Gabriel Levy.

ITALY

Embassy: Odos Sekeri 2, 106 74 Athens; tel (1) 361-1722; telex 210575; fax (1) 362-0740.
Ambassador: Giovanni Dominedo.

JAPAN

Embassy: 21st Floor, Athens A Tower, Leoforos Messoghion 2-4, Ambelokipi, 115 27 Athens; tel (1) 775-8101; telex 214460; fax (1) 770-5964.
Ambassador: Kazuo Kaneko.

JORDAN

Embassy: Odos Palaio Zervou 30, Palaio Psychiko, 154 52 Athens; tel (1) 647-4161; telex 219366; fax (1) 647-0578.
Ambassador: Samir Khalifeh.

KOREA, REPUBLIC

Embassy: Odos Eratosthenous 1, 116 35 Athens; tel (1) 701-2122; telex 216202.
Ambassador: Nam Kyun Park.

KUWAIT

Embassy: Odos Alex. Papanastassiou 55, Athens; tel (1) 647-3593.
Ambassador: Saleh Mohamed al-Mohamed.

LEBANON

Embassy: 6 rue 25 Martiou, Palaio Psychico, 154 52 Athens; tel (1) 685-5873; telex 218572; fax (1) 672-6489.
Ambassador: Elias F. Ghosn.
First Secretary: Christiane Bassile.

LIBYA

Embassy: Odos Vironos 13, Palaio Psychiko, Athens; tel (1) 647-2120.
Ambassador: Abdalla Abumahara.

LUXEMBOURG

Embassy: 2240 Luxembourg, 5 rue Notre-Dame; tel 478777; telex 3405; fax 23144.
Ambassador: Jean-Jacques Kasel (resident in Luxembourg).

MALAYSIA

Consulate: Argyroupolis, 164 52 Athens; tel (1) 992-2774.
Honorary Consul: Thomas A. Haziroglou.

MALTA

Consulate: Odos Efplias 2, 185 37 Piraeus; tel (1) 418-1501; telex 212361; fax (1) 453-9966.
Honorary Consul: Konstadinos Kalogeropoulos.

MEXICO

Embassy: Odos Diamandidou 73a, Palaio Psychiko, 154 52 Athens; tel (1) 647-0852; telex 216172; fax (1) 647-1506.
Ambassador: Hugo Gutiérrez Vega.
Minister: Carlos Gonzalez Magallon.
Second Secretary: Carlos Tirado Zavala.

Consulate: Dodekanisou 17, Thessaloniki 546 26; tel (31) 526397; fax (31) 542189.
Honorary Consul: Byron Antoniadis.

MOROCCO

Embassy: Odos Mousson 14, Palaio Psychiko, 154 52 Athens; tel (1) 647-4209; telex 210925.
Ambassador: Larbi Mouline.

NETHERLANDS

Embassy: Leoforos Vassileos Konstantinou 5-7, 106 74 Athens; tel (1) 723-9701; telex 215971; fax (1) 724-8900.
Ambassador: H. A. L. Vijverberg.

NEW ZEALAND

Embassy: An. Tsoha 15-17, Ambelokipi, 115 21 Athens; tel (1) 641-0311; telex 216630; fax (1) 641-0735.
Chargé d'affaires a.i.: Graham Eskrigge.

NORWAY

Embassy: Leoforos Vassileos Konstantinou 7, 106 74 Athens; tel (1) 724-6173; telex 215109; fax (1) 724-4989.
Ambassador: Nils O. Dietz.

PAKISTAN

Embassy: Odos Loukianou 6, Kolonaki, Athens; tel (1) 729-0122.
Ambassador: Amin Jan Naim.

PANAMA

Embassy: Leoforos Vassilissis Sofias 21, Athens; tel (1) 363-1847.
Ambassador: María Lakas Bahas.

PHILIPPINES

Embassy: Xenofondos 9, Syndagma, 105 57 Athens; tel (1) 324-1615.
Ambassador: Alberto A. Encomienda.

POLAND

Embassy: Odos Chryssanthemon 22, Palaio Psychiko, 154 52 Athens; tel (1) 671-6917.
Ambassador: Janusz Lewandowski.

PORTUGAL

Embassy: Odos Karneadou 44-46, 106 76 Athens; tel (1) 729-0096; telex 214903; fax (1) 723-6784.
Ambassador: Luís Navega.

ROMANIA

Embassy: Odos Emmanuel Benaki 7, Palaio Psychiko, 154 52 Athens; tel (1) 671-8008; telex 215301; fax (1) 671-4860.

Ambassador: Nicolae Stoicescu.
Counsellor (Economic): Grigore Diaconescu.
Military, Naval and Air Attaché: Alexandru Videa.
First Secretary and Head of Press and Cultural Section: Florian Unchiasu.
First Secretary and Head of Consular Section: Gheorghe Diaconu.

RUSSIA

Embassy: Odos Nikiforou Litra 28, Palaio Psychiko, Athens; tel (1) 672-5235.
Ambassador: Anatoly A. Sliusar.

SAN MARINO

Consulate-General: 1 Misthou, 161 21 Athens; tel (1) 722-8061.
Consul-General: Evangelos Antoniou.

SAUDI ARABIA

Embassy: Odos Marathonodromou 71, Palaio Psychiko, 154 52 Athens; tel (1) 671-6911.
Ambassador: Sheikh Abdullah Abdul-Rahman al-Malhooq.

SOUTH AFRICA

Embassy: Leoforos Kifissias 124, 10th Floor, Iatridou St, POB 14281, 115 26 Athens; tel (1) 692-2125; telex 218165; fax (1) 693-0572.
Ambassador: Dr S. G. A. Golden.
Counsellor (Trade): C. J. Gerber.
Counsellor (Minerals/Energy): Prof. N. J. Grobler.
First Secretary: W. A. Drotsky.
First Secretary (Administrative): L. J. Nutt.
Third Secretary (Consular): J. Spangenberg.

Consulate-General: 110 Monastiriou St, 546 27 Thessaloniki; tel (31) 516021.
Honorary Consul-General: G. Gregoriades.

SPAIN

Embassy: Leoforos Vassilissis Sofias 29, Athens; tel (1) 721-4885; telex 215860.
Ambassador: Enrique Mahou Stauffer.

SWEDEN

Embassy: Leoforos Vassileos Konstantinou 7, 5th Floor, 106 74 Athens; tel (1) 729-0421; telex 215646; fax (1) 722-9953.
Ambassador: Karl Anders Wollter.
Counsellor: Kerstin Andersson.
Counsellor: Bertil Jobeus.
Second Secretary (Commercial): Jesper Höstrup.
Chancellor: Christina Bjernevall.

Consulate: Epimenidou 20-2, POB 229, 712 02 Iraklion, Crete; tel (81) 226254; telex 262138; fax (81) 220305.
Consul-General: Tor Finn Ståhl.
Chancellor: Inger Monika Saridaki.

Consulate: Kassandrou 3, 654 03 Kavala; tel (51) 223457; telex 452185.
Consul: Marika Symeon.

Consulate: Donzelotte 7, 491 00 Corfu; tel (661) 39469; telex 332119.
Consul: Spiridion Adam Bogdanos.

Consulate: Parados Bouboulinas, POB 50, 853 00 Kos; tel (242) 23975; telex 292322; fax (242) 24051.
Consul: Andreas Andreadis.

Consulate: Beniamin Lesviou Ave, 811 00 Mytilini; tel (251) 28494; telex 294104.

Consulate: Othonos-Amalias 62, 262 21 Patras; tel (61) 271702; telex 312127.
Consul: Leonidas Sotiropoulos.

Consulate: Notara 89-91, 185 35 Piraeus; tel (1) 411-7090; telex 212042; fax (1) 411-9643.
Consul-General: Alecos P. Pappas.
Chancellor: Monika Sykiotou.

Consulate: Amerikas 50, 851 00 Rhodes; tel (241) 31822; telex 292406.
Consul-General: Epaminondas Solounais.

Consulate: Komninon 26, 546 24 Thessaloniki; tel (31) 284065; telex 412523; fax (31) 283794.
Consul-General: Christos John Accas.
Chancellor: Thurid Ann-Kristen Drakopoulos.

Consulate: Solonos 5, 383 33 Volos; tel (421) 23289.
Consul: Aglaïa Bornozis.

SWITZERLAND

Embassy: Odos Iassiou 2, 115 21 Athens; tel (1) 723-0364; telex 216230; fax (1) 724-9209.
Ambassador: Charles Steinhäuslin.
Counsellor: Rodolphe Imhoof.
First Secretary (Economic): Robert Helfenstein.
Attaché and Office Manager: Eduard Krall.

SYRIA

Embassy: Odos Marathonodromou 79, Palaio Psychiko, Athens; tel (1) 672-5577.
Ambassador: Shahin Farah.

THAILAND

Embassy: Odos Taigetou 23, Palaio Psychiko, 154 58 Athens; tel (1) 671-7969; telex 225856.
Ambassador: S. C. M. Sukri Gajaseni.

TOGO

Consulate: Athens; tel (1) 639152.

TUNISIA

Embassy: Odos Ethnikis Antistaseos 91, Chalandrai, 152 31 Athens; tel (1) 671-7590; telex 223786; fax (1) 647-4244.
Ambassador: Youssef Barkett.

TURKEY

Embassy: Odos Vassileos Gheorghiou B 8, 106 74 Athens; tel (1) 724-5915; telex 216334; fax (1) 722-1778.
Ambassador: Déniz Bolukhasi.

UNITED KINGDOM

Embassy: Odos Ploutarchou 1, 106 75 Athens; tel (1) 723-6211; telex 216440; fax (1) 724-1872.
Ambassador: Sir David Miers.
Counsellor, Consul-General and Deputy Head of Mission: R. N. Culshaw.
Counsellor: W. V. Fell.
Counsellor (Culture) and British Council Director: Dr J. L. Munby.
Defence and Military Attaché: Brig. G. Bulloch.
Naval and Air Attaché: Capt. J. J. Pearson.
First Secretary and Head of Political Section: F. C. Moore.
First Secretary (Management): I. H. Davies.
First Secretary and Consul: D. A. McKellar.
First Secretary (Commercial): M. A. Balmer.
First Secretary (Culture) and British Council Deputy Director: B. P. Chenery.
First Secretary (Economic): P. H. Williams.
First Secretary: T. I. Priest.
First Secretary (Political/Information): M. J. W. Roberts.
Second Secretary (Political/Information): K. L. Smith.
Second Secretary (Technical Works): R. Clarke.

Consulate: 2 Alexandras Ave, Menekratous, 491 00 Corfu; tel (611) 30055; fax (611) 37995.
Consul: P. Hughes.

Consulate: 25th Martiou St, No. 23, POB 47, 851 00 Rhodes; tel (241) 27247; fax (241) 22615.
Honorary Consul: D. E. Demetriades.

Consulate: 8th Floor, 8 Venizelou St, Eleftheria Sq., POB 10332, 541 10 Thessaloniki; tel (31) 278006; fax (31) 286610.
Honorary Consul: G. K. Doucas.

Consulate: 16 Papa Alexandrou St, 712 02 Iraklion; tel (81) 224012; fax (81) 243935.
Vice-Consul: M. R. Tzanaki.

Consulate: 2 Votsi St, 262 21 Patras; tel (61) 277329; fax (61) 225334.
Honorary Vice-Consul: M. J. Morpht-Karatza.

Consulate: 15 Themistocli Sofouli St, Port Vathy, 831 00 Samos; tel (273) 27314; fax (273) 28996.
Honorary Vice-Consul: G. D. L. Marc.

Consulate: B Akti Petrou Ralli, Ermoupolis, 841 00 Syros; tel (281) 22232; fax (281) 23293.
Honorary Vice-Consul: V. Parissi-Thermou.

Consulate: 4 Iolkou St, 382 21 Vólos; tel (421) 24642; fax (421) 26108.
Honorary Vice-Consul: V. Anagnostou.

USA

Embassy: Leoforos Vassilissis Sofias 91, 101 60 Athens; tel (1) 721-2951; telex 215548; fax 646-3450.
Ambassador: Michael George Sotirhos.
Deputy Head of Mission: James A. Williams.
Political Section: Samuel Fromowitz.
Political and Military Sections: Laurel M. Shea.
Economic Section: J. Michael Cleverley.
Commercial Section: John Priamou.
Labour Officer: John L. Klekas.
Consular Section: Danny B. Root.
Administrative Section: Peter S. Flynn.
Regional Security Officer: Arthur A. Maurel.
Agricultural Section: Mollie J. Iler.
Public Affairs Officer: Arthur S. Giuliano.
Office of Defence Attaché: Capt. William Gray.
Office of Defence Co-operation: Brig. Edmond S. Solymosy.
Communications Programme Officer: David Smith.
Information Systems Manager: Henry F. Webb, Jr.

Consulate-General: 59 Leoforos Nikis, 546 22 Thessaloniki; tel (31) 266121.
Consul-General: Larry C. Thompson.
Political and Economic Sections: Donald M. Miller.

URUGUAY

Embassy: Odos Licavitou 1 G, 106 72 Athens; tel (1) 361-3549.
Ambassador: Ulysses Pereira Reverbel.

VENEZUELA

Embassy: Leoforos Vassilissis Sofias 112, 115 27 Athens; tel (1) 770-8769; telex 215845; fax (1) 770-2489.
Ambassador: Olga Lucila Carmona.
Minister-Counsellor (Political and Economic): Maria E. Vivas de Hartmann.
Counsellor: Hugo A. Batista.
Second Secretary: Felix Eloy Torres Roman.

YUGOSLAVIA

Embassy: Leoforos Vassilissis Sofias 106, Athens; tel (1) 777-4344.

Ambassador: Vladimir Sultanović.

ZAIRE

Embassy: Odos Vassileos Konstantinou 2, 116 35 Athens; tel (1) 701-6171; telex 215994.
Ambassador: Bomolo Lokoka.

International Organizations

EUROPEAN COMMUNITIES

Bureau: 2 Vassilissis Sofias, POB 11002, 106 74 Athens; tel (1) 724-3982; telex 219324; fax (1) 724-4620.
Director: Georges Tsouyopoulos.

GRENADA

CHINA (TAIWAN)

Embassy: POB 36, Archibald Ave, St George's; tel (440) 3054; fax (440) 4177.
Ambassador: Liu Po-Lun.
Counsellor: Dr Andrew Wei-te Li.
Second Secretary: Richard R. C. Shih.

FRANCE

Consular Agency: POB 416, St George's; tel (440) 2498.
Consular Agent: Gloria Keens-Douglas.

GUYANA

Consulate: Gore St, POB 213, St George's; tel (440) 2188; telex 3463; fax (440) 4117.
Honorary Consul: Leonard Williams.

NETHERLANDS

Consulate: Huggins Bldg, Grand Etang Rd, St George's; tel (440) 2031.
Honorary Consul: George Menezes.

SWEDEN

Embassy: Sweden.
Ambassador: Lennart Klackenberg (resident in Sweden).

Consulate: Melville St, POB 345, St George's; tel (440) 1832.
Consul: Hermia Angela Smith.

UNITED KINGDOM

High Commission: 14 Church St, St George's; tel (440) 3222; telex 3419; fax (440) 4939.
First Secretary and Resident Representative: A. H. Drury.

USA

Embassy: Point Salines, POB 54, St George's; tel (4440) 1173; fax (4440) 4820.
Ambassador: James Ford Cooper.
Political Section: Mary A. Wright.
Economic Section: William H. Memler.
Consular Section: Charles Jones, Jr.
Administrative Section: Edmee Hawkes Pastore.
Legal Attaché: Paul F. Nolan.
Communications Programme Officer: Shelby Friday.

VENEZUELA

Embassy: 598/1 Archibald Ave, POB 201, St George's; tel (440) 1721; telex 3414.
Ambassador: Efraín Silva Méndez.
First Secretary: Oscar Hernández Bernalette.

International Organizations

EUROPEAN COMMUNITIES

Sub-Office of Delegation to Trinidad and Tobago: POB 5, St George's Old Fort, St George's; tel (440) 3561; telex 3431; fax (440) 4151.
Representative: John Caloghirou.

GUATEMALA

ARGENTINA

Embassy: 2a Avda 11-04, Zona 10, Guatemala City; telex 5285.
Ambassador: Dr Angel Fernando Girardi.

AUSTRIA

Embassy: 6a Avda 20-25, Zona 10, Local 4-1, Apdo 878, Guatemala City; tel (2) 68-2324; telex 5224.
Honorary Consul-General: Ernst Dietrich Glawischnig.
Attaché (Commercial): Bruno Mag Freytag.

BELGIUM

Embassy: Avda Reforma 13-70, Apdo 687-A, Zona 9, Guatemala City; tel (2) 31-5608; telex 5137.
Ambassador: Paul Vermeirsch.

BOLIVIA

Embassy: 12 Avda 15-37, Zona 10, Guatemala City.
Chargé d'affaires a.i.: Dr José Gabina Villanueva G.

BRAZIL

Embassy: 18 Calle 2-22, Zona 14, Apdo 196-A, Guatemala City; tel (2) 37-0949; telex 5200; fax (2) 37-3475.
Ambassador: Mauro M. De Azeredo.
First Secretary: Marcela Maria Nicodemos.
First Secretary: Francisco Catunda Resende.

CANADA

Embassy: Galerías España, 7 Avda 11-59, Apdo 400, Zona 9, Guatemala City; tel (2) 32-1411; telex 5206; fax (2) 32-1419.
Ambassador: Brian Dickson.
Counsellor (Administrative) and Consul: R. J. Edington.
Counsellor and Consul: D. W. McGillivray.
First Secretary and Consul: H. G. Kroll.
First Secretary (Development) and Consul: C. Laviades.

CHILE

Embassy: 13 Calle 7-85, Zona 10, Guatemala City; telex 6162.
Ambassador: Silvio Salgado Ramírez.

CHINA (TAIWAN)

Embassy: Edif. Torrecafe, Of. 1030, 7a Avda 1-20, Zona 4, Guatemala City; telex 5107.
Ambassador: Mao Chi-Hsien.

COLOMBIA

Embassy: Edif. Gemini 10, 12 Calle, 1 Avda, Zona 10, Guatemala City; tel (2) 32-0604.
Ambassador: Laura Ochoa de Ardilla.

COSTA RICA

Embassy: Edif. Galerías Reforma, Of. 320, Avda Reforma 8-60, Zona 9, Guatemala City; tel (2) 32-5768.
Chargé d'affaires: Roberto Chávez Lizano.

DENMARK

Consulate-General: 7a Avda 20-36, Of. 27, Zona 1, Apdo 540, Guatemala City; tel (2) 81091; telex 5415.
Consul-General: Walter Robert Gándara Merlke.
Consul: Rudy Herman Gándara Merkle.

DOMINICAN REPUBLIC

Embassy: 7a Calle 'A' 4-28, Zona 10, Guatemala City.
Ambassador: Pedro Pablo Alvarez Bonilla.

ECUADOR

Embassy: Of. 602, Avda Reforma 12-01, Zona 10, Guatemala City; tel (2) 31-2439; telex 6218.
Ambassador: Diego Paredes-Peña.

EGYPT

Embassy: 12a Calle 6-15, Zona 9, Guatemala City; telex 5157.
Ambassador: Mahmoud Abbas.

EL SALVADOR

Embassy: 12 Calle 5-43, Zona 9, Guatemala City; tel (2) 62-9385; telex 5418.
Ambassador: Agustín Martínez Varela.

FINLAND

Consulate-General: Ruta 2, Calle 24, 0-70, Zona 4, 01004 Guatemala City; tel (2) 31-3116; telex 5697; fax (2) 31-3111.
Consul-General: John M. Willemsen Devlin.
Consul: John M. Willemsen Chacón.

FRANCE

Embassy: 16 Calle 4-53, Edif. Marbella, Zona 10, Apdo 1252, Guatemala City; tel (2) 37-3639; telex 5963.
Ambassador: Paul Poudade.

GERMANY

Embassy: Edif. Plaza Maritima, 20 Calle 6-20, Zona 10, Guatemala City; tel (2) 37-0028; telex 5209.
Ambassador: Dr Henning Dodenberg.

HOLY SEE

Apostolic Nunciature: 10a Calle 4-47, Zona 9, Guatemala City; tel (2) 32-4274; fax (2) 34-1918.
Apostolic Nuncio: Most Rev. Oriano Quilici, Titular Archbishop of Tabla.
Secretary: Kalumbu Gilbert Ngindu.

HONDURAS

Embassy: 16 Calle 8-27, Zona 10, Apdo 730-A, 01909 Guatemala City; tel (2) 37-3919; telex 5865; fax (2) 33-4629.
Ambassador: Guillermo Boquín V.

ISRAEL

Embassy: 13a Avda 14-07, Zona 10, 01010 Guatemala City; tel (2) 33-4624; telex 5218; fax (2) 33-6950.
Ambassador: Jacques Yaacov Deckel.
First Secretary and Consul: Alon Bar.
Attaché: Doron Dagan.

ITALY

Embassy: 5 Avda 8-59, Zona 14, Guatemala City; tel (2) 37-4557; telex 5129.
Ambassador: Francesco Marcello Ruggirello.

JAMAICA

Consulate: 'Costibal', km 13.5, Apdo 38C, Guatemala City; tel (2) 68-2328.
Honorary Consul: Jean Maria Valladares.
Honorary Vice-Consul: Max Holzheu.

JAPAN

Embassy: Ruta 6, 8-19, Apdo 531, Zona 4, Guatemala City; tel (2) 31-9666; telex 5926; fax (2) 31-5462.
Ambassador: Sumio Ono.

KOREA, REPUBLIC

Embassy: 15 Avda 24-51, Zona 13, Apdo 1649, Guatemala City; telex 5369.
Ambassador: Cho Key-Sung.

MEXICO

Embassy: 16a Calle 0-51, Zona 14, Guatemala City; tel (2) 68-0769; telex 5961.
Ambassador: Abraham Talavera López.

NICARAGUA

Embassy: 10 Avda 14-72, Zona 10, Guatemala City; telex 5653.
Ambassador: Ricardo Zambrana.

PARAGUAY

Embassy: 7 Avda 7-78, 8°, Zona 4, Guatemala City.

PERU

Embassy: 2a Avda 9-58, Zona 9, Guatemala City.
Ambassador: Andrés Aramburu Alvarez-Calderón.

PORTUGAL

Embassy: 5 Avda 12-60, Zona 9, Guatemala City.

SOUTH AFRICA

Embassy: 6 Avda 14-75, Zona 9, Guatemala City.
Consulate-General: 10 Avda 30-57, Zona 5, 01005 Guatemala City; tel (2) 32-6890; telex 5254; fax (2) 36-5291.
Honorary Consul: L. F. Monterroso.

SPAIN

Embassy: 10 Calle 6-20, Zona 9, Guatemala City; telex 5393.
Ambassador: Juan Pablo de la Iglesia.

SWEDEN

Embassy: 8a Avda 15-07, Zona 10, Apdo 166, 01901 Guatemala City; tel (2) 68-0621; telex 5916; fax (2) 37-2297.
Ambassador: Ulf Lewin.
First Secretary: Magnus Eriksson.
First Secretary: Michael Frühling.

SWITZERLAND

Embassy: Edif. Seguros Universales, 5°, 4a Calle 7-73, Zona 9, Apdo 1426, 01901 Guatemala City; tel (2) 34-0743; telex 5257; fax (2) 31-8524.
Ambassador: Willy Hold.
First Secretary: Lorenzo Schnyder von Wartensee.
Attaché and Office Manager: Beda Fetz.

UNITED KINGDOM

Embassy: Edif. Centro Financiero, Torre II, 7°, 7a Avda 5-10, Zona 4, Guatemala City; tel (2) 32-1601; telex 5686; fax (2) 34-1904.
Ambassador: Justin P. P. Nason.
First Secretary, Consul and Deputy Head of Mission: Dr P. J. Norris.
Consulate: 7a Calle, entre 3a y 4a Avda, Apdo 399, Puerto Barrios, Izabal; tel 48-0152; telex 726; fax 48-0405.
Honorary Consul: R. O. Vélez.

USA

Embassy: Avda La Reforma 7-01, Zona 10, Guatemala City; tel (2) 31-1541; telex ; fax (2) 31-8885.
Ambassador: Thomas F. Strook.
Deputy Head of Mission: Philip B. Taylor, III.
Political Section: Thomas M. Tonkin.
Economic Section: Rafael L. Marin.
Commercial Section: Charles A. Ford.
Labour Officer: Joseph G. McLean.
Agricultural Section: John Jacobs.
Consular Section: Sue H. Patterson.
Administrative Section: Russell L. Keeton.
Regional Security Officer: Seymour C. DeWitt.
Regional Officer for Central American Programmes: Nadine M. Hogan.
Office of Defence Attaché: Col Allen C. Cornell.
Military Group: Col Armando Lujan.
Communications Programme Officer: Raymond L. Norris.

URUGUAY

Embassy: 20a Calle 8-00, Apdo 2b, Zona 10, Guatemala City.
Chargé d'affaires: Héctor L. Pedetti A.

VENEZUELA

Embassy: 8°, Calle 0-56, Zona 9, Apdo 152, Guatemala City; tel (2) 31-6505; telex 5317; fax (2) 34-1331.
Ambassador: Dr Sadi Garvini di Turno.
Minister-Counsellor: Gisele Sanchez de Camejo.
Attaché (Culture/Press): Cipriano Fuentes.
Attaché (Commercial): Ana Luisa García.

GUINEA

ALGERIA

Embassy: BP 1004, Conakry; tel 44-15-03.
Chargé d'affaires a.i.: Boucherit Naceur.

BENIN

Embassy: BP 787, Conakry.
Ambassador: Jonas Gbouhoundada.

CANADA

Embassy: Corniche Sud, BP 99, Coleah, Conakry; tel 46-23-95; telex 2170; fax 44-42-36.
Chargé d'affaires a.i. and Consul: R. D. Gauthier.
First Secretary (Development) and Consul: J. Lamonde.
First Secretary (Development) and Consul: M. Roussel.
Attaché (Administrative) and Vice-Consul: G. Bisson.

CHINA, PEOPLE'S REPUBLIC

Embassy: BP 714, Conakry.
Ambassador: Jiang Xiang.

CONGO

Embassy: BP 178, Conakry.
Ambassador: C. Eckomband.

COTE D'IVOIRE

Embassy: Conakry; telex 2126.
Chargé d'affaires: Atta Yacouba.

CUBA

Embassy: BP 71, Conakry.
Ambassador: Colman Ferrei.

CZECHOSLOVAKIA

Embassy: BP 1009 bis, Conakry; tel 46-14-37.
Ambassador: Dr Zdenko Hrčka.

DENMARK

Consulate-General: Torréfaction Guinéenne, Import-Export, BP 158, Conakry; tel 44-35-10; telex 22257.
Consul-General: Ossam Moukarim.

EGYPT

Embassy: BP 389, Conakry.
Ambassador: Hussein el-Nazer.

FRANCE

Embassy: Immeuble Chavanel, Babadi Hadiri, BP 373 & 570, Conakry; tel 44-16-55; telex 600.

GERMANY

Embassy: BP 540, Conakry; tel 44-15-08; telex 22479.
Ambassador: Dr Hubert Beemelmans.

GHANA

Embassy: Immeuble Ex-Urbaine et la Seine, BP 732, Conakry; tel 44-15-10.
Ambassador: Larry Bimi.
Counsellor: John Buckner.

GUINEA-BISSAU

Embassy: BP 298, Conakry.
Ambassador: Arafan Ansu Camara.

IRAQ

Embassy: Conakry; telex 2162.
Chargé d'affaires: Munir Chihab Ahmad.

ITALY

Embassy: BP 84, Village Camayenne, Conakry; tel 46-23-32; telex 636.
Ambassador: Fausto Maria Pennacchio.

JAPAN

Embassy: rue Corniche, BP 895, Conakry; tel 44-36-07; telex 22482.
Ambassador: Tsukasa Abe.

KOREA, DEMOCRATIC PEOPLE'S REPUBLIC

Embassy: BP 723, Conakry.
Ambassador: Kim Chang-Sok.

LEBANON

Embassy: BP 342, Conakry; telex 2106.
Ambassador: Mohamed Issa.

LIBERIA

Embassy: BP 18, Conakry; telex 2105.
Chargé d'affaires: Anthony Zezo.

LIBYA

People's Bureau: BP 1183, Conakry; telex 645.
Chargé d'affaires: Muftah Madi.

MALI

Embassy: Conakry; telex 2154.
Chargé d'affaires: Kibili Demba Diallo.

MOROCCO

Embassy: Cité des Nations, Villa No. 12, BP 193, Conakry; tel 44-36-86; telex 22422.
Ambassador: Mohamed Ayouch.

NIGERIA

Embassy: BP 54, Conakry; telex 633.
Ambassador: P. N. Oyedele.

ROMANIA

Embassy: BP 348, Conakry; tel 44-15-68; telex 22450.
Ambassador: Marcel Mamularu.

Counsellor: Traian Teodoru.
Counsellor (Commercial): Valeri Dimitri Gheorghe.

RUSSIA

Embassy: Matat-Port 3, BP 329, Conakry; tel 46-14-64.
Ambassador: Vladimir N. Rayevsky.

SAUDI ARABIA

Embassy: BP 611, Conakry; telex 2146.
Chargé d'affaires: Waheeb Shaikon.

SIERRA LEONE

Embassy: BP 625, Conakry.
Ambassador: Mariam Kamara.

SWEDEN

Embassy: Sweden.
Ambassador: Bengt Homquist (resident in Sweden).
Consulate: route du Niger, BP 1180, Conakry; tel 44-30-16; telex 22230.
Consul: Khalil-Georges Zeidan.

SWITZERLAND

Embassy: Donka, BP 720, Conakry 1; tel 44-31-80; telex 22416.
Chargé d'affaires: Pierre Riem.

SYRIA

Embassy: BP 609, Conakry; tel 46-13-20.
Chargé d'affaires: Bechara Kharouf.

TANZANIA

Embassy: BP 189, Conakry; tel 46-13-32; telex 2104.
Ambassador: Norman Kiondo.

UNITED KINGDOM

Consulate: BP 834, Conakry; tel 44-34-42; telex 22294; fax 44-42-15.
Honorary Consul: V. A. Treitlein.

USA

Embassy: 2nd Blvd and 9th Ave, BP 603, Conakry; tel 44-15-20.
Ambassador: Dane F. Smith, Jr.
Deputy Head of Mission: Gregory T. Frost.
Political Section: David R. Kyzner.
Economic and Commercial Sections: Jonathan S. Turak.
Consular Section: Julianne M. Furman.
Administrative Section: Steven M. Lauterbach.
Public Affairs Officer: Louise Bedichek.
Regional Security Officer: Mark J. Hunter.
Labour Officer: Ollie P. Anderson, Jr (resident in USA).
Agency for International Development: William G. Kushak.
Communications Programme Officer: Arnold Olivo, Jr.

VIET-NAM

Embassy: BP 551, Conakry.
Ambassador: Pham van Son.

YUGOSLAVIA

Embassy: BP 1154, Conakry.
Ambassador: Danilo Milić.
Counsellor: Veselin Davorija.

ZAIRE

Embassy: BP 880, Conakry; telex 632.
Ambassador: B. Kalubye.

International Organizations

EUROPEAN COMMUNITIES

External Delegation: BP 730, Corniche Sud, Madina Dispensaire, Conakry; tel 46-13-25; telex 22479; fax 44-18-74.
Commission Delegate: Guy Petitpierre.

GUINEA-BISSAU

ALGERIA

Embassy: Rua 12 de Setembro 12, CP 350, Bissau; tel 211522.
Ambassador: R. Benchikh el Fegoun.

BRAZIL

Embassy: Rua São Tomé Esquina, CP 29, Bissau; tel 201327; telex 245.
Ambassador: Marcelo Didier.

CAPE VERDE

Embassy: Bissau.
Ambassador: António Lima.

CHINA (TAIWAN)

Embassy: Bissau.

CUBA

Embassy: Rua Joaquim N'Com 1, Bissau; tel 213579.
Ambassador: Diosdado Fernández González.

EGYPT

Embassy: Rua 12 de Setembro, CP 72, Bissau; tel 213642.
Ambassador: Fadel Fadel Atta.

FRANCE

Embassy: Rua Eduardo Mondlane 67-A, CP 95, 1011 Bissau; tel 212633.
Ambassador: Jean Thomas.

GERMANY

Embassy: Avda Osvaldo Vieira 28, Bissau; tel 212992.
Ambassador: Erich Meske.

GUINEA

Embassy: Rua 14, No. 9, CP 396, Bissau; tel 212681.
Ambassador: Guirane Ndiaye.

KOREA, DEMOCRATIC PEOPLE'S REPUBLIC

Embassy: Avda Domingos Ramos 42, Bissau; tel 212885.
Ambassador: Shim Jae-Du.

LIBYA

People's Bureau: Rua 16, CP 362, Bissau; tel 212006.
Representative: Dokali Ali Mustafa.

PORTUGAL

Embassy: Rua Cidade de Lisboa 6, 1108 Bissau Cedex; tel 201261; telex 248; fax 201269.
Ambassador: Augusto Martins Gonçalves Pedro.
Counsellor (Cultural): Mário Matos e Lemos.
Attaché (Co-operation): Domingos Manuel Fonseca de Almeida Machado.

RUSSIA

Embassy: Rua Rui Djassi 17, Bissau; tel 213535.
Ambassador: Aleksandr P. Baryshev.

SENEGAL

Embassy: Bissau; tel 212636.
Ambassador: Ahmed Tijane Kane.

SWEDEN

Embassy: Avda Domingo Ramos, 34-34B, Apdo 52, 1021 Bissau Cedex; tel 201038; telex 243.
Head of Aid Office: Rolf Folkesson.

UNITED KINGDOM

Consulate: Mavegro Int., CP 100, Bissau; tel 211529; telex 259.
Honorary Consul: J. Van Maanen.

USA

Embassy: Avda Domingos Ramos, 1067 Bissau Cedex; tel 201113; fax 201159.
Ambassador: William L. Jacobsen, Jr.

Administrative Section: Thomas F. Scaletta, Jr.
Political, Economic and Consular Sections: Charles A. Stonecipher.
Agency for International Development: Michael F. Lukomski.
Labour Officer: Ollie P. Anderson, Jr (resident in USA).
Communications Programme Officer: James Fletcher.

International Organizations

EUROPEAN COMMUNITIES

External Delegation: 29 rua Eduardo Mondlane, CP 359, Bissau; tel 213360; telex 264; fax 214216.
Commission Delegate: Robert Collingwood.

GUYANA

BRAZIL

Embassy: 308 Church St, Queenstown, POB 10489, Georgetown; tel (2) 57970; telex 2246.
Ambassador: Aderbal Costa.

CANADA

High Commission: High and Young Sts, POB 10880, Georgetown; tel (2) 72081; telex 2215; fax (2) 58380.
High Commissioner: Douglas A. Wardle.
First Secretary: Carolyn Holyoke.
Second Secretary: Danielle Lalonde-Ricordi.
Third Secretary: Cameron Bowes.

CHINA, PEOPLE'S REPUBLIC

Embassy: 108 Duke St, Kingston, Georgetown; tel (2) 71651; telex 2251.
Ambassador: Yang Zengye.

COLOMBIA

Embassy: 306 Church and Peter Rose Sts, Queenstown, Georgetown; tel (2) 71410; telex 2206.
Ambassador: Reynaldo Ospina Caicedo.

CUBA

Embassy: 46 High St, Kingston, Georgetown; tel (2) 66732; telex 2272.
Ambassador: Lázaro Cabezas González.

DENMARK

Consulate: 62 Hadfield & Cross Sts, Werk-en-Rust, Georgetown; tel (2) 64978; fax (2) 57996.
Consul: Robin Mark Sievewright Stoby.

FINLAND

Consulate: 62 Hadfield & Cross Sts, Georgetown, Demerara; tel (2) 64978; telex 2207; fax (2) 57996.
Consul: Richard Berkeley Fields.

GERMANY

Embassy: 70 Murray and Main Sts, Georgetown; tel (2) 61089; telex 2273.

Consulate: 70 Quamina St, POB 10647, Georgetown; tel (2) 61069; telex 211; fax (2) 62299.
Honorary Consul: Winfried Fries.

INDIA

High Commission: 10 Ave of the Republic, POB 101148, Georgetown; tel (2) 63996; telex 3025.
High Commissioner: R. Rajagopalan.
Second Secretary: K. Govindan.

JAMAICA

High Commission: Camp St, Georgetown; tel (2) 69517; telex 226.

Consulate: 70 Quamina St, Georgetown; tel (2) 2553.
Honorary Consul: Jean Pollard.

KOREA, DEMOCRATIC PEOPLE'S REPUBLIC

Embassy: 88 Premniranjan Place, Georgetown; tel (2) 60266; telex 2228.
Ambassador: Chong Jongyu.

LIBYA

People's Bureau: 375 Ganges St, Prashad Nagar, Georgetown; tel (2) 61697; telex 2259.
Chargé d'affaires: Ahmed Ibrahim Ehiwass.

RUSSIA

Embassy: 48 Chandra Nagar St, Prashad Nagar, Georgetown; tel (2) 72975; telex 2277.
Ambassador: Mikhail A. Sobolev.

SURINAME

Embassy: 304 Church St, POB 10508, Georgetown; tel (2) 67844; telex 2282.
Ambassador: John Kolader.

SWEDEN

Embassy: Sweden.
Ambassador: Lennart Klackenburg (resident in Sweden).

Consulate: 61/2 Ave of the Republic and Robb St, Demerara Life Annexe, Georgetown; tel (2) 68470; telex 2249; fax (2) 62628.
Consul: Paul Edward Fredericks.

TRINIDAD AND TOBAGO

High Commission: c/o Ministry of External Affairs, Port of Spain.

UNITED KINGDOM

High Commission: 44 Main St, POB 10849, Georgetown; tel (2) 65881; telex 2221; fax (2) 53555.
High Commissioner: R. Douglas Gordon.
Deputy High Commissioner and First Secretary (Commercial): S. J. Hiscock.
First Secretary (Aid): A. Rowlatt.
Third Secretary (Management): P. Harrington.
Third Secretary (Chancery/Information/Consular): A. J. Ford.

USA

Embassy: 31 Main St, Georgetown; tel (2) 54900; telex 2213; fax (2) 58497.
Deputy Head of Mission: Dennis K. Hays.
Political Section: Russell J. Hanks.
Economic and Commercial Sections: Katharine K. Simonds.
Consular Section: Nicholas M. Williams.
Administrative Section: Edward E. Anderson.
Regional Security Officer: Nick G. Morrow.
Public Affairs Officer: James D. Burns.
Legal Attaché: Paul F. Nolan.
Communications Programme Officer: Carrie A. Ullman.

VENEZUELA

Embassy: 296 Thomas St, POB 10484, Georgetown; tel (2) 61543; telex 2237; fax (2) 53241.
Ambassador: Enrique Peinado Barrios.
Second Secretary: José Antonio Padron Padron.

YUGOSLAVIA

Embassy: 72 Brickdam, POB 10408, Georgetown; tel (2) 71136; telex 2231.
Ambassador: Marin Gersković.

International Organizations

EUROPEAN COMMUNITIES

External Delegation: 72 High St, Kingston, Georgetown; tel (2) 64004; telex 2258; fax (2) 62615.
Commission Delegate: Joël Fessaguet.

HAITI

ARGENTINA

Embassy: impasse Géraud, 20 Bourdon, Port-au-Prince; tel (1) 2-2063; telex 0176.
Chargé d'affaires: Antonio Meri.

AUSTRIA

Consulate-General: 12 rue du Quai, BP 248, Port-au-Prince; tel (1) 2-2042; telex 0372; fax (1) 2-4916.
Honorary Consul-General: Hans-Peter Hackenbruch.

BRAZIL

Embassy: 387 ave John Brown, Bourdon, BP 808, Port-au-Prince; tel (1) 45-6208; telex 20181; fax (1) 45-6206.
Ambassador: Guy Mendes Pinheiro de Vasconcellos.
Counsellor: Paulo Mendes de Carvalho.

CANADA

Embassy: Edif. Banque Nova Scotia, 18 route de Delmas, BP 826, Port-au-Prince; tel (1) 3-2358; telex 20069; fax (1) 3-8720.
Ambassador: Pierre Giguère.
Counsellor and Consul: G. E. Paquet.
Counsellor (Development): R. Carr-Ribeiro.
First Secretary (Immigration) and Consul: D. Jean.
First Secretary (Development): H. Bigras.
First Secretary (Development) and Consul: R. Jodoin.

CHILE

Embassy: 384 route de Delmas, entre rues 42 et 44, Port-au-Prince.
Ambassador: Agustín Rodríguez Pulgar.

CHINA (TAIWAN)

Embassy: 2 rue Rivière, Port-au-Prince.
Ambassador: Lee Nan Hsing.

COLOMBIA

Embassy: 384 route de Delmas, entre rues 42 et 44, Port-au-Prince; tel (1) 6-2599.
Ambassador: Juan Zapata Olivella.

DENMARK

Consulate-General: 105 rue du Quai, BP 1334, Port-au-Prince; tel (1) 2-0317; telex 0398.
Consul-General: Ronald Carl Madsen.
Vice-Consul: Eric Carl Joseph Madsen.

DOMINICAN REPUBLIC

Embassy: Port-au-Prince.
Ambassador: José del Carmen Acosta.

ECUADOR

Embassy: BP 2531, Port-au-Prince; tel (1) 2-4576; telex 0195.
Chargé d'affaires: Adolfo Alvarez.

FINLAND

Consulate: 57 route de l'Aéroport, RTE National 1, Port-au-Prince; BP 488, 4 route de Mais Gaté, Port-au-Prince; tel (1) 6-3661; telex 0296; fax (1) 6-3766.
Consul: Jean-Marie Vorbe.

FRANCE

Embassy: 51 place des Héros de l'Indépendance, BP 1312, Port-au-Prince; tel (1) 2-0951; telex 0049.

GERMANY

Embassy: 8 rue Mangônes, Pétionville, BP 1147, Port-au-Prince; tel (1) 57-0456; telex 0082; fax (1) 57-4131.
Ambassador: Heinrich-Peter Rothmann.

Consulate: 11 rue A, BP 10, Cap Haitien; tel (3) 62-0381.
Honorary Consul: Broder Schütt.

HOLY SEE

Apostolic Nunciature: Morne Calvaire, Pétionville, BP 326, Port-au-Prince; tel (1) 7-3411.
Apostolic Nuncio: Most Rev. Giuseppe Leanza, Titular Archbishop of Lilibeo.
Secretary: Ryszard Szczesny.

ISRAEL

Embassy: 1 route Nationale, Chancerelles, Port-au-Prince; tel (1) 3-8100; telex 0171; fax (1) 2-3767.
Consul: Gilbert Bigio.

ITALY

Embassy: 1 impasse Brave, Delmas 60, BP 886, Port-au-Prince; tel (1) 7-0424; telex 0447.
Ambassador: Luigi Morrone.

JAMAICA

Consulate: 26 rue Pavée, Apt 1, BP 904, Port-au-Prince; tel (1) 4-3452.
Honorary Consul: Robert Tippenhauer.

JAPAN

Embassy: Villa Bella Vista, 2 impasse Tulipe, Desprez, Port-au-Prince; tel (1) 45-3333; telex 20368; fax (1) 45-8834.
Ambassador: Satoshi Aoki.

LIBERIA

Embassy: Port-au-Prince; tel (1) 7-0692.
Ambassador: Henry T. Hoff.

MEXICO

Embassy: Maison Roger Esper, 57A route de Delmas, Port-au-Prince; tel (1) 6-2215; telex 0217.
Ambassador: Sergio Romero Cuevas.

PANAMA

Embassy: 29 rues Met. et Chavannes, Pétionville; tel (1) 7-2260.

PERU

Embassy: 38 Débussy, Turgeau, BP 174, Port-au-Prince; tel (1) 45-4891; telex 20174.
Ambassador: Dr Elmer Schialer-Figueroa.
Second Secretary: Ernesto Delgado-Lizárraga.

SPAIN

Embassy: 11 rue Oscar, Desprez, Port-au-Prince; tel (1) 2-4410.
Ambassador: José Francisco de Castro.

SWEDEN

Embassy: Sweden.
Ambassador: Lennart Klackenberg (resident in Sweden).

Consulate: 41 rue Courbe, Port-au-Prince; tel (1) 2-0332; telex 0017.
Consul: Marie Eugène Georges Maurice Wiener.

SWITZERLAND

Consulate-General: rue Ogé 12, BP 15164, Pétionville; tel (1) 7-0503; telex 0001; fax (1) 7-6377.
Consul-General: Jacqueline Flambert-Viret.

UNITED KINGDOM

Consulate: Hotel Montana, BP 1302, Port-au-Prince; tel (1) 57-3969; telex 0259; fax (1) 57-4048.
Honorary Consul: R. Chenet.
Vice-Consul: M. Guercy.

USA

Embassy: blvd Harry Truman, Cité de l'Exposition, BP 1761, Port-au-Prince; tel (1) 22-0200; telex 0157; fax (1) 23-9007.
Ambassador: Alvin P. Adams, Jr.
Deputy Head of Mission: Douglas K. Watson.
Political Section: Robert M. Holley.
Economic and Commercial Sections: Eugene P. Tuttle.
Consular Section: Dudley G. Siprelle.
Administrative Section: John K. Ivie.
Regional Security Officer: Robert Boyle.
Agency for International Development: David Cohen.
Public Affairs Officer: Christian Filostrat.
Office of Defence Attaché: Col Colin P. Collins.
Military Liaison Officer: Maj. Julius E. Clark.
Communications Programme Officer: Thomas L. Snow (acting).
Information Systems Manager: William E. Croom.

VENEZUELA

Embassy: blvd Harry Truman, Cité de l'Exposition, BP 2158, Port-au-Prince; tel (1) 2-0971; telex 0413; fax (1) 22-3949.
Ambassador: José Gregorio González-Rodríguez.
First Secretary: Abraham Quintero Prieto.

HONDURAS

ARGENTINA

Embassy: Colonia Rubén Darío 2 cuadras al sur del Cenáculo, Apdo 101-C, Tegucigalpa; tel 32-3376; telex 1120.
Ambassador: Luis N. Augusto Sánchez R.

AUSTRIA

Consulate-General: Colonia Miramontes, 8a Avda, Apdo 6, Tegucigalpa DC; tel 31-4788.
Honorary Consul-General: Ricardo Midence.

BRAZIL

Embassy: Paseo República de Argentina, 1930, Colonia Palmira, Apdo 341, Tegucigalpa; tel 32-2021; telex 1151; fax 31-2379.
Chargé d'affaires a.i.: Mariane Bravo Leite.

CANADA

Consulate: Edif. Comercial, Las Castanas, 6°, Blvd Moranan, Tegucigalpa; tel 31-4538; telex 73391; fax 31-5793.
Honorary Consul: S. Gloetzner.

CHILE

Embassy: Edif. Interamericana frente Los Castaños, Blvd Morazán, Apdo 222, Tegucigalpa; telex 1195.
Ambassador: Victoria Eugenia Morales Etchevers.

CHINA (TAIWAN)

Embassy: Avda República de Panamá 2024, Colonia Palmira, Apdo 6-C, Tegucigalpa; tel 32-9490; telex 1383.
Ambassador: Huang Chuam-Li.

COLOMBIA

Embassy: Edif. Palmira, 4°, Colonia Palmira, Apdo 468, Tegucigalpa; tel 32-9300; telex 1336.

COSTA RICA

Embassy: Blvd Morazán, Colonia Palmira, 1a Calle 704, Apdo 512, Tegucigalpa; tel 32-1768; telex 1154.
Ambassador: Maximiliano Oreamuno Brenes.

DENMARK

Consulate-General: Edif. Maduro, 2°, Blvd los Proceres, 2_0 cuadras arriba Hospital San Felipe, Apdo 213, Tegucigalpa; tel 32-5407; telex 1144.
Consul-General: Osmond L. Maduro Joest.

DOMINICAN REPUBLIC

Embassy: Colonia La Granja 402, 4a Calle entre 4a y 5a Avda Comayagüela, Apdo 1460, Tegucigalpa.
Ambassador: Juan Emilio Canó de la Mota.

ECUADOR

Embassy: Avda Juan Lindo 122, Colonia Palmira 3a, Apdo 358, Tegucigalpa; telex 1471.
Ambassador: Fernando Procel Gallegos.

EL SALVADOR

Embassy: 2a Avda 205, Colonia San Carlos, Tegucigalpa; tel 32-1344; telex 1301.
Ambassador: Salvador Trigueros.

FINLAND

Consulate: Apdo 152, final Avda Los Proceres, Frente Cía. Distribuidora, Tegucigalpa; tel 32-1545; telex 1178; fax 32-6740.
Consul: Luis Kafie Larach.

Consulate: Apdo 948, San Pedro Sula; tel 53-1642; telex 5617; fax 52-6426.
Vice-Consul: Raymond Fauzi Maalouf Maalouf.

FRANCE

Embassy: Avda Juan Lindo, Colonia Palmira, Apdo 3441, Tegucigalpa; tel 32-1800; telex 1180.
Ambassador: Pierre Dumon.

GERMANY

Embassy: Edif. Paysen, 3°, Blvd Morazán, Apdo 3145, Tegucigalpa; tel 32-3161; telex 1118.
Ambassador: Dr Walter Eickhoff.

Consulate: c/o Berkling Industrial S.A., Carretera Puerto Cortés, Apdo 588, San Pedro Sula; tel 53-1244.
Honorary Consul: Ruth Berkling.

GUATEMALA

Embassy: Avda Juan Lindo 313, Colonia Palmira, Apdo 34-C, Tegucigalpa; tel 32-5018.
Ambassador: Eunice Lima.

HOLY SEE

Apostolic Nunciature: Palacio de la Nunciatura Apostólica, Colonia Palmira 412, Apdo 324, Tegucigalpa; tel 32-8280; fax 31-4381.
Apostolic Nuncio: Mgr Francisco de Nittis.
Secretary: Francis Assisi Chullikart.

ISRAEL

Embassy: Edif. Palmira, Apdo 1187, Tegucigalpa.
Ambassador: Shlomo Cohen.

ITALY

Embassy: Calle Primera de la Colonia Reforma, Casa 260, Apdo 317, Tegucigalpa; tel 37-5810; telex 1332.
Ambassador: Lodovico Masetti.

Consulate: Edif. La Constancia, San Pedro Sula; tel 52-3672.
Honorary Consul: Giuseppe Voto.

JAMAICA

Consulate: Apdo 1488, Tegucigalpa; tel 22-9411.
Honorary Consul: George L. Schofield.
Honorary Vice-Consul: Gustavo Reyes.

JAPAN

Embassy: Colonia San Conloz, entre 3 y 4, Calle contiguo al Estacionamiento del Supermercado Su Casa, Apdo 3232, Tegucigalpa; tel 31-5511; telex 1141; fax 32-1737.
Ambassador: Kiichi Itabashi.

MEXICO

Embassy: Avda República del Brasil 2028, Apdo 769, Tegucigalpa; tel 32-4039; telex 1143; fax 32-4224.
Ambassador: Manuel Martínez del Sobral.

NICARAGUA

Embassy: Colonia Tepeyac, Bloque M-1, Apdo 392, Tegucigalpa; tel 32-1209; telex 1274.
Ambassador: Lic. Francisco José Lacayo.

PANAMA

Embassy: Edif. Palmira, Apdo 397, Tegucigalpa.
Ambassador: Dr Carlos Alberto de Diego Soriano.

PERU

Embassy: Edif. Palmira, 5°, Apdo 64-C, Tegucigalpa.
Ambassador: Jaime Castro Mendivil.

RUSSIA

Embassy: Tegucigalpa.

SPAIN

Embassy: Colonia Matamoros 801, Apdo 114-C, Tegucigalpa; tel 32-1875; telex 1142.
Ambassador: J. Albi de la Cuesta.

SWEDEN

Consulate-General: Colonia Miramonte, Casa No. 2758, Avda Altiplano retorno Borneo, Apdo 1247, Tegucigalpa; tel 32-7142; telex 1320.
Consul-General: Victor Saúl Sierra Corea.
Vice-Consul: Julio Cesar Bonilla Valle.

SWITZERLAND

Embassy: Apdo 3202, Tegucigalpa; tel 32-8261; telex 1282; fax 31-1242.
Attaché (Development Co-operation/Aid): Dr Martin Pallmann.

UNITED KINGDOM

Embassy: Edif. Palmira, 3°, Colonia Palmira, Apdo 290, Tegucigalpa; tel 32-5429; telex 1234; fax 32-5480.
Ambassador: Peter J. Streams.
Second Secretary and Vice-Consul: C. J. Edge.

Consulate: Terminales de Cortes, Apdo 298, San Pedro Sula; tel 54-2600; telex 5513.
Honorary Consul: F. P. Barber.

USA

Embassy: Avda La Paz, Apdo 26-C, Tegucigalpa; tel 32-3120; fax 32-0027.
Ambassador: Cresencio S. Arcos.
Deputy Head of Mission: Donna J. Hrinak.
Political Section: Alfred R. Barr.
Economic Section: Ward D. Barmon.
Commercial Section: T. Porter Clary.
Labour Officer: Kathleen W. Barmon.
Consular Section: Fernando Sanchez.
Administrative Section: John W. Fuhrer.

Regional Security Officer: Robert E. Benker.
Agency for International Development: John A. Sanbrailo.
Public Affairs Officer: Terrence H. Kneebone.
Office of Defence Attaché: Col Charles E. Hogan, Jr.
Military Group: Col Larry L. Cragg.
Communications Programme Officer: George Solomon.
Information Systems Manager: John F. Carpe.

URUGUAY

Embassy: Edif. Palmira, 4°, Apdo 329, Tegucigalpa.
Ambassador: Alfredo Menini Terra.

VENEZUELA

Embassy: Colonia Palmira 2302, 4°, Calle República de Colombia, Apdo 775, Tegucigalpa; tel 32-1879; telex 1238; fax 32-1016.
Ambassador: Dionssio Teodoro Marcano.

HUNGARY

AFGHANISTAN

Embassy: 1062 Budapest, Lendvay u. 23; tel (1) 132-7187.
Ambassador: Sher Jan Mazdoryar.

ALBANIA

Embassy: 1068 Budapest, Bajza u. 26; tel (1) 122-7251.
Ambassador: Jani Polena.

ALGERIA

Embassy: 1014 Budapest, Dísz tér 6; tel (1) 175-9884; telex 22-6916.
Ambassador: Bachir Rouls.

ARGENTINA

Embassy: 1068 Budapest, Rippl Rónai u. 1; tel (1) 122-8467; telex 22-4128.
Ambassador: Guillermo Jorge Magough.

AUSTRALIA

Embassy: 1062 Budapest, Délibáb u. 30; tel (1) 153-4233; telex 22-7708; fax (1) 153-4866.
Ambassador: Douglas Alan Townsend.
First Secretary and Consul: Anne Quinane-Pys.
Third Secretary: David Peter Morris.
Attaché: Roma Emery.

AUSTRIA

Embassy: 1068 Budapest, Benczúr u. 16; tel (1) 122-9267; telex 22-4447.
Ambassador: Dr Franz Schmid.
Counsellor (Commercial): Gerald Kriechbaum.
Counsellor (Economic): Adolfine Egleston.
Counsellor (Press/Cultural): Gertrude Kothanek.
Military and Air Attaché: Brig. Rudolf Striedinger.
Attaché (Economic): Robert Sereinig.
Consul-General: Franz Bauer.

BELGIUM

Embassy: 1015 Budapest, Donati u. 34; tel (1) 201-1571; telex 22-4664; fax (1) 175-1566.
Consular and Commercial Affairs Section: 1015 Budapest, Toldy Ferenc u. 13.
Ambassador: Willem Verkammen.
Military and Air Attaché: Col W. Koeken.
Embassy Secretary: P. Roland.
Secretary: E. Bogaert.

BOLIVIA

Embassy: Budapest II, Mártírok u. 43-45; tel (1) 116-3019.
Ambassador: Macario Aparicio Burgoa.

BRAZIL

Embassy: 1118 Budapest, Somlói út 3; tel (1) 166-6044; telex 22-5795.
Ambassador: Ivan Velloso da Silveira Batalha.

BULGARIA

Embassy: 1124 Budapest, Levendula u. 15-17; tel (1) 156-6840; telex 22-3032.
Ambassador: Vesselin Filipov Filev.

CAMBODIA

Embassy: 1122 Budapest XII, Ráth György u. 48; tel (1) 155-1128.
First Secretary and Chargé d'affaires a.i.: Seng Lean.
Third Secretary and Consul: Ouk Siphaun.

CANADA

Embassy: 1121 Budapest, Budakeszi út. 32; tel (1) 176-7312; telex 22-4588; fax (1) 176-7689.
Ambassador: Derek R. T. Fraser.
Counsellor (Commercial) and Consul: H. J. Himmelsbach.
Counsellor (Immigration) and Consul: P. Duschinsky.
Forces Attaché: Col P. M. R. Valois.
First Secretary and Consul: J. Paquette.

CENTRAL AFRICAN REPUBLIC

Consulate: 1364 Budapest, Hotel Duna Inter-Continental; tel (1) 117-5122.
Consul: Cornelius van Niekerk Scholtz.

CHILE

Embassy: 1061 Budapest, Diplomatska Kolonija 9; tel (1) 122-4485.
Ambassador: Manuel Sanhueza Cruz.

CHINA, PEOPLE'S REPUBLIC

Embassy: 1068 Budapest, Benczúr u. 17; tel (1) 122-4872.
Ambassador: Dai Bingguo.

COLOMBIA

Embassy: 1024 Budapest, Mártírok u. 43-45; tel (1) 135-2534; telex 22-6012.
Ambassador: Alberto Esteban Rojas Puyo.

COSTA RICA

Embassy: 1118 Budapest, Iglói u. 2 fsz. I; tel (1) 166-4999.
Ambassador: Arnulfo Hernández.

CUBA

Embassy: 1068 Budapest, Benczúr u. 26; tel (1) 121-4037; telex 22-4388.
Ambassador: Faustino Manuel Beato Morejón.

CZECHOSLOVAKIA

Embassy: 1143 Budapest, Népstadion út 22; tel (1) 251-1660; telex 22-4744; fax (1) 251-2568.
Ambassador: Rudolf Chmel.
Envoy: Štefan Oross.
Counsellor (Economic): Ladislav Derian.
Counsellor: Viliam Roth.
Military and Air Attaché: Zoltán Bajkai.
First Secretary (Consular): Vladimír Oláh.
First Secretary: Ladislav Molnár.
Commercial Section: 1046 Budapest, Rózsa F. u. 61; tel (1) 132-5589; fax (1) 122-8621.
Counsellor (Commercial): Ludovit Priecel.
Cultural Office: 1088 Budapest, Rákoczi út 15; tel (1) 118-1308; fax (1) 118-1821.
Counsellor and Head of Cultural Office: Karol Wlachovský.

DENMARK

Embassy: 1122 Budapest, Határör út 37; tel (1) 155-7320; telex 22-4137; fax (1) 175-3803.
Ambassador: Ole Koch.
Counsellor (Commercial): Sven-Aage Andersen.
Attaché: Mette Høyer Larsen.

ECUADOR

Embassy: 1021 Budapest, Budakeszi út 55/D; tel (1) 176-7593.
Ambassador: Galo Rivadeneira.

EGYPT

Embassy: 1016 Budapest, Bérc u. 16; tel (1) 166-5080; telex 22-5184; fax (1) 166-8769.
Ambassador: Mohamed Ali el-Sherei.

FINLAND

Embassy: 1118 Budapest, Kelenhegyi út 16a; 1392 Budapest, POB 352; tel (1) 185-0700; telex 22-4710; fax (1) 185-0772.

Ambassador: Risto Hyvärinen.
Counsellor: Katariina Niemenmaa.
Counsellor (Commercial): Markku Kokkonen.
Military Attaché: Lieut Col Antti Iivonen.
Cultural and Press Attaché: Hannele Malms.

FRANCE

Embassy: 1062 Budapest, Lendvay u. 27; tel (1) 132-4980; telex 22-5143.

GERMANY

Embassy: 1146 Budapest, POB 40, Izsó u. 5; tel (1) 122-3434; telex 22-5951; fax (1) 160-1903.
Ambassador: Dr Alexander Arnot.

Consulate-General: 7633 Pécs, Szántó Kóvacz; 7601 Pécs, POB 301; tel (72) 26-088; telex 12-838; fax (72) 24-664.
Consul-General: Hanns Rehfeld.

GREECE

Embassy: 1063 Budapest, Szegfú u. 3; tel (1) 122-8004; telex 22-4113.
Ambassador: Nicolas Capellaris.

HOLY SEE

Apostolic Nunciature: 1021 Budapest, Budakeszi út 55/D; tel (1) 176-3334.
Apostolic Nuncio: Angelo Acerbi.

INDIA

Embassy: 1025 Budapest, Búzavirág u. 14; tel (1) 115-5211; telex 22-6374.
Ambassador: Surinder Lal Malik.

INDONESIA

Embassy: 1068 Budapest, POB 1442, Gorkij Fasor 26; tel (1) 142-8508; telex 22-5263.
Ambassador: Bustanul Arifin.

IRAN

Embassy: 1062 Budapest, Délibáb u. 29; tel (1) 122-5038; telex 22-4129.
Ambassador: Keyvan Imani.

IRAQ

Embassy: 1145 Budapest, Szántó Béla u. 13; tel (1) 122-6418; telex 22-6058.
Ambassador: Mohammed Ghanim al-Anaz.

ISRAEL

Interests Section: 1026 Budapest, c/o Embassy of Switzerland, Fullánk u. 8; tel (1) 176-7897.
Head of Interests Section: Shlomo Marom.
First Secretary (Economic): Reuben Sharon.

ITALY

Embassy: 1143 Budapest, Népastadion u. 95; tel (1) 121-2450; telex 22-5294.
Ambassador: Joseph Nitti.

JAPAN

Embassy: 1024 Budapest, POB 78, Rómer Flóris u. 56-58; tel (1) 156-4533; telex 22-5048; fax (1) 175-4777.
Ambassador: Eiji Seki.

KOREA, DEMOCRATIC PEOPLE'S REPUBLIC

Embassy: 1068 Budapest, Benczúr u. 31; tel (1) 142-5174; telex 22-6721.
Chargé d'affaires a.i.: Bang Ryong Gab.

KOREA, REPUBLIC

Embassy: 1125 Budapest, Mátyás király u. 14/c; tel (1) 138-3388; telex 22-3370.
Ambassador: Han Tak-Chae.
Counsellor: Lee Wonhyung.
Counsellor: Choi Zihn.
First Secretary and Consul: Lee Han Gon.
Attaché (Press/Culture): Ahn Jay-Hwan.

LAOS

Embassy: 1025 Budapest, Józsefhegyi u. 28-30; tel (1) 115-2891.

LIBYA

People's Bureau: 1443 Budapest, Népstadion út 111, POB 73; tel (1) 122-6076; telex 22-6940.
Head of People's Bureau: Fathi M. al-Misrati.

MEXICO

Embassy: 1021 Budapest, Budakeszi út 55/D, P-5 IX 1; tel (1) 176-7381; telex 22-6633; fax (1) 176-7906.
Ambassador: Luciano Joublanc.
Deputy Head of Mission: Luis Efren Bauza García-Cano.
Counsellor (Commercial): Lajos Szendro.
Consular Affairs: René Gil Romellón.
Cultural Affairs: Taide Navarrete Pellicer.

MONGOLIA

Embassy: 1125 Budapest, Istenhegyi út 59-61; tel (1) 155-7989.
Ambassador: Dergeldalajin Zsambazsancan.

MOROCCO

Embassy: 1026 Budapest, Törökvész Lejto 12/A; tel (1) 115-9251; telex 22-3580.
Ambassador: Mohamed Chahid.

NETHERLANDS

Embassy: 1146 Budapest, Abonyi u. 31; tel (1) 122-8432; telex 22-5562; fax (1) 141-6532.
Ambassador: Hendrik Jan van Oordt.

NICARAGUA

Embassy: 1021 Budapest, Budakeszi út 55/D; tel (1) 176-7953.
Chargé d'affaires a.i.: Gustavo Cruz Moreno.

NORWAY

Embassy: 1122 Budapest, Határör út 35, POB 32; tel (1) 155-1811; telex 22-5867; fax (1) 156-7928.
Ambassador: Leif Edward Edwardsen.

PAKISTAN

Embassy: 1125 Budapest, Adonis u. 3/A; tel (1) 135-9183.
Ambassador: Hamidullah Khan.

PERU

Embassy: 1024 Budapest, Mártírok u. 43-45; tel (1) 115-0292.
Ambassador: José Pablo Morán Val.

PHILIPPINES

Embassy: 1028 Budapest, Hotel Buda Penta; tel (1) 156-6333.
Chargé d'affaires: Marciano A. Paynor, Jr.

POLAND

Embassy: 1025 Budapest, Törökvesz ul. 15; tel (1) 142-5566.
Ambassador: Maciej Kozminski.

PORTUGAL

Embassy: 1024 Budapest, Mártírok u. 43-45; tel (1) 115-5602; telex 22-6509; fax (1) 115-4666.
Ambassador: Antonio Baptista Martins.

ROMANIA

Embassy: 1146 Budapest, Thököly út 72; tel (1) 142-6944; telex 22-5847.
Ambassador: Simion Pop.

RUSSIA

Embassy: 1062 Budapest, Bajza u. 35; tel (1) 132-0911.
Ambassador: Ivan P. Aboimov.

Consulate: 4025 Debrecen, Arany János ul. 3; tel (52) 10-883.
Consul: Nikita Ivanovitch Darcsijev.

SAUDI ARABIA

Embassy: 1026 Budapest, Harangvirág u.3; tel (1) 176-7186.

SOUTH AFRICA

Permanent Mission: Budapest, Apaczaj Cserf. j.i., POB 100; fax (1) 18-4973.
Head of Mission and Minister-Counsellor: C. van N. Scholtz.
Second Secretary (Administrative): I. I. K. von der Ohe.
Third Secretary: G. D. Heydenrych.

SPAIN

Embassy: 1067 Budapest, Eötvös u. 11B; tel (1) 153-1011; telex 22-4130.
Ambassador: Luis de la Torre.

SWEDEN

Embassy: 1146 Budapest, Ajtósi Dürer sor 27/A; tel (1) 122-9880; telex 22-5647; fax (1) 142-6105.
Ambassador: Sten Strömholm.
Counsellor: Göran Ankarberg.
First Secretary: Karin Sundberg.
Secretary (Commercial): Knut-Georg Söderlund.

SWITZERLAND

Embassy: 1143 Budapest, Népstadion út 107; tel (1) 122-9491; telex 22-4528; fax (1) 122-9492.
Ambassador: Paul Wipfli.
Counsellor: Claude Barbey.
Defence Attaché: Col Jean Rossier.
Attaché and Head of Chancery: Françoise Bertschi-Gloor.

SYRIA

Embassy: 1026 Budapest, Harangvirág u. 3; tel (1) 176-7186; telex 22-6605.
Minister Plenipotentiary and Chargé d'affaires a.i.: Mohamad Saleh.
Second Secretary: Issam Haddad.
Attaché: Abdul Salam Mash'hadieh.

THAILAND

Embassy: 1025 Budapest, Józsefhegyi út 28-30 A/3; tel (1) 115-0618; telex 20-2706; fax (1) 115-0606.
Ambassador: Suttiswat Kridakon.
Minister-Counsellor: Thamnoon Thongkhong.
Commercial Counsellor: Inthorn Wankeao.
First Secretary (Commercial): Thiravuthi Bisalbutra.
First Secretary: Nongnuth Phetcharatana.
First Secretary: Apichart Phetcharatana.

TUNISIA

Embassy: 1021 Budapest, Budakeszi út 55/d; tel (1) 176-7595.
Ambassador: Habib Ammar.

TURKEY

Embassy: 1014 Budapest, Uri u. 45; tel (1) 175-0609.
Ambassador: Halit Güvener.

UNITED KINGDOM

Embassy: 1051 Budapest, Harmincad u. 6; tel (1) 118-2888; telex 22-4527; fax (1) 118-0907.
Ambassador: John A. Birch.
Counsellor and Deputy Head of Mission: H. J. S. Pearce.
Defence and Military Attaché: Col W. B. Ibbetson.
Air Attaché: Wing Commdr M. A. Gaynor.
First Secretary and British Council Director: Dr J. P. Grote.
First Secretary (Commercial): S. C. Johns.
First Secretary (Chancery): G. J. Dorey.
First Secretary: P. R. Nelson.
First Secretary (British Council): Dr R. Baker.
First Secretary (British Council): M. H. Thomas.
First Secretary (Management) and Consul: F. A. Blogg.
Second Secretary (Information): Q. J. K. Phillips.

USA

Embassy: 1054 Budapest, Szabadság tér 12; tel (1) 112-6450; telex 22-4222; fax (1) 132-8934.
Ambassador: Charles H. Thomas.
Deputy Head of Mission: Richard L. Baltimore III.
Political Section: Thomas B. Robertson.
Economic Section: Donald E. Grabenstetter.
Commercial Section: David Hughes.
Consular Section: Margaret Higgins.
Press and Culture Officer: Robert McCarthy.
Administrative Section: Mary Jane Thomas.
Regional Security Officer: Richard Gaiani.
Office of Defence Attaché: Col Ruth Anderson.
Attaché (Science): Thomas A. Schlenker.
Communications Programme Officer: Thomas H. Lien.
Information Systems Manager: Joseph Smith.

URUGUAY

Embassy: 1023 Budapest, Vérhalom u. 12-16; tel (1) 136-8333.
Ambassador: Juan B. Oddone Silveira.

VENEZUELA

Embassy: 1023 Budapest, Vérhalom u. 12-16; tel (1) 135-3562; telex 22-6666; fax (1) 115-3274.
Ambassador: Dr Moritz Eiris-Villegas.
Minister-Counsellor: Henry Veliz-Cedeño.

VIET-NAM

Embassy: 1068 Budapest, Benczúr u. 18; tel (1) 142-9943.
Ambassador: Nguyen Van Quy.

YEMEN

Embassy: 1025 Budapest, Tömörkény ul. 3A; tel (1) 176-4048.
Chargé d'affaires a.i.: Mohsen Nagi bin Nagi.

YUGOSLAVIA

Embassy: 1068 Budapest, Dózsa György u. 92/B; tel (1) 142-0566.
Ambassador: Rudolf-Rudi Sova.

Consulate: 7621 Pécs, Rákóczi út 3.
Consul: Emilia Brunner Balla.

International Organizations

EUROPEAN COMMUNITIES

External Delegation: 1014 Budapest, c/o Hilton Hotel, Suite 607, 1/3 Hess Andras tér.; tel (1) 175-1000; telex 22-5984; fax (1) 156-0285.
Head of Delegation: Hans Beck;
Adviser: Jean Trestour.

ICELAND

AUSTRIA

Consulate-General: Austurstræti 17, POB 1389, 121 Reykjavík; tel (1) 24016; telex 2113.
Honorary Consul-General: Ludwig Siemsen.
Honorary Vice-Consul: Arni Siemsen.

CANADA

Consulate-General: Sudurlandsbraut 10, 108 Reykjavík; tel (1) 680820; telex 4879.
Honorary Consul-General: J. H. Bergs.

CHINA, PEOPLE'S REPUBLIC

Embassy: Vidimelur 29, POB 580, Reykjavík; telex 2148.
Chargé d'affaires: Zhai Shixiong.

CYPRUS

Embassy: c/o Ministry of Foreign Affairs, Nicosia, Cyprus.
Ambassador: Taso Panayides.

Consulate: Vatnagardar 20, POB 4240, 124 Reykjavík; tel (1) 681234; telex 2117; fax (1) 686772.
Honorary Consul: Hilmar Fenger.

CZECHOSLOVAKIA

Embassy: Smáragata 16, POB 1443, 101 Reykjavík; tel (1) 19823.

DENMARK

Embassy: Hverfisgata 29, 101 Reykjavík; POB 1540, 121 Reykjavík; tel (1) 621230; telex 2008; fax (1) 623316.
Ambassador: Villads Villadsen.
Counsellor: Claus von Barnekov.
Chancellor and Vice-Consul: Ellen Steindórs.
Export Assistant: Frank Friis Jensen.

Consulate: KEA-Huset, Hafnarstræti 91-5, POB 5000, 600 Akureyri; tel (6) 21400; telex 2195; fax (6) 27588.
Consul: Sigurdur Jóhannesson.

Consulate: Hildartún 41, 780 Höfn; tel (7) 81190.
Consul: Birnir Bjarnason.

Consulate: Adalstræti 24, 400 Isafjord; tel (4) 3226.
Consul: Ruth A. Tryggvason.

Consulate: Melagötu 1, 740 Neskaupstađ; tel (7) 71299.
Consul: Jón E. Lundberg.

Consulate: Öldugata 14, 710 Seydisfjördur; tel (7) 21211; telex 2298; fax (7) 21105.
Consul: Jónas Hallgrímsson.

Consulate: Strandvegur 28, 900 Vestmannaøerne; tel (8) 11100.
Consul: Eyjólfur Martinsson.

FINLAND

Embassy: Túngata 30, 101 Reykjavík; POB 1060, 121 Reykjavík; tel (1) 621577; telex 2373; fax (1) 623880.
Ambassador: Håkan Branders.
Second Secretary: Pirkko Hämäläinen.

Consulate-General: Vatnagardar 4, 104 Reykjavík; tel (1) 688200.
Honorary Consul-General: Haraldur Björnsson.

Consulate: Hamarsstigur 18, Akureyri; tel (6) 23247.
Honorary Consul: Fridrik Thorvaldsson.

Consulate: Tradarstigur 11, 414 Bolungarvik; tel (4) 7350.
Honorary Consul: Jón Fridrik Einarsson.

Consulate: Botnahlid 19, 710 Seydisfjördur; tel (7) 21277.
Honorary Consul: Theodór Blöndal.

Consulate: Hradfrystistöd, Vestmannaeyja hf. Skolavegi 1, 900 Vestmannaeyjar; tel (8) 12301.
Honorary Consul: Sigurdur Einarsson.

FRANCE

Embassy: Túngata 22, POB 1750, Reykjavík; tel (1) 17621; telex 2063.
Ambassador: Jacques Mer.

GERMANY

Embassy: Túngata 18, 101 Reykjavík; POB 400, 121 Reykjavík; tel (1) 19535; telex 2002; fax (1) 25699.
Ambassador: Hans Hermann Haferkamp.

Consulate: Heidarlundur 8A, 600 Akureyri; tel (6) 25338.
Honorary Consul: Svanur Eriksson.

Consulate: Túngata 5, 900 Heimaey/Vestmannaeyjar; tel (8) 1530.
Honorary Consul: Dr Einar Valur Bjarnason.

Consulate: Seljalandsvegur 68, 400 Isafjördur; tel (4) 3345.
Honorary Consul: Ulfur Gunnarson.

Consulate: Urdargata 15, 450 Patreksfjördur; tel (4) 1215.
Honorary Consul: Kristinn Fridhjófsson.

Consulate: 801 Seylar-Ölfusi; POB 45, 800 Selfoss; tel (49) 1815.
Honorary Consul: Dr Magnus Sigurdsson.

Consulate: Túngata 12, 710 Seydisfjördur; tel (7) 2212.
Honorary Consul: Petur Blöndal.

IRELAND

Consulate-General: POB 241, Reykjavík; tel (1) 26300; telex 2085; fax (1) 6244511.
Honorary Consul-General: David S. Thorsteinsson.

NORWAY

Embassy: Fjólugata 17, POB 250, Reykjavík; tel (1) 13065; telex 2163; fax (1) 29553.
Ambassador: Per Aasen.

RUSSIA

Embassy: Garđastræti 33, 101 Reykjavík; tel (1) 15156; telex 2200; fax (1) 620633.
Ambassador: Igor Nikolayevich Krasavin.
Counsellor: Nikolai A. Tolmatchev.
Counsellor and Consul: Vladimir K. Minkevitch.
First Secretary: Victor B. Khorikov.
Commercial Representative: Juri A. Kudinov.
Deputy Commercial Representative: Oleg V. Ermolov.

SOUTH AFRICA

Consulate-General: Hafnarstræti 7, POB 462, 121 Reykjavík; tel (1) 629522; telex 2046.
Honorary Consul-General: J. R. Magnusson.

SWEDEN

Embassy: Lágmúla 7, POB 490, 121 Reykjavík; tel (1) 82022; telex 2087; fax (1) 689615.
Ambassador: Per Olof Forshell.
Counsellor: Arne Nyberg.
Chancellor: Benediktsdottir Elin.

Consulate: Hamarsstigur 12, 600 Akureyri; tel (6) 22721.
Consul: Páll Gunnlaugar Kristinsson.

Consulate: Hafnargata 38, 710 Seydisfjördur; tel (7) 21206.
Consul: Stefan Jóhansson.

Consulate: Sudurgata 56, 580 Siglufjördur; tel (6) 71440.
Consul: Björn Jonasson.

Consulate: Engjavegur 14, 400 Isafjördur; tel (4) 3222.
Consul: Jón Páll.

Consulate: Kirkjuvegur 23, 900 Vestmannaeyjar; tel (8) 12711.
Consul: Páll Zophoníasson.

UNITED KINGDOM

Embassy: Laufásvegur 49, POB 460, 101 Reykjavík; tel (1) 15883; telex 2037; fax (1) 27940.
Ambassador and Consul-General: P. F. M. Wogan.
Second Secretary, Consul and Deputy Head of Mission: A. Mehmet.
Commercial Officer: Orn Valdimarsson.

Consulate: Glerargata 26, Akureyri; tel (6) 21165.
Honorary Vice-Consul: A. Jonsson.

USA

Embassy: Laufásvegur 21, POB 40, Reykjavík; tel (1) 29100; telex 3044; fax (1) 29139.
Ambassador: Charles E. Cobb, Jr.
Deputy Head of Mission: David F. Rogus.
Political Section: Richard P. Rodgers.
Political and Military Sections: Michael H. Schwartz.
Economic and Commercial Sections: Colin S. Helmer.
Consular Section: Michael E. O'Malley.
Administrative Section: Francisca Thomas Helmer.
Public Affairs Officer: Andrew F. Key.
Communications Programme Officer: John R. Corkery.

INDIA

AFGHANISTAN

Embassy: 5/50F Shanti Path, Chanakyapuri, New Delhi 110 021; tel (11) 603331.
Ambassador: Ahmad Sarwar.

ALGERIA

Embassy: E 12/4, Vasant Vihar, New Delhi 110 057; tel (11) 6882029; telex 3170052; fax (11) 6882289.
First Secretary: Rabehi Hassane.
Second Secretary (Commercial/Economic): Milat Toufik.

ARGENTINA

Embassy: B-8/9 Vasant Vihar, Paschimi Marg, New Delhi 110 057; tel (11) 671345; telex 3182007.
Ambassador: Victor E. Beaugé.
First Secretary: Daniel Eduardo Amigo.
Third Secretary: Alberto A. M. Trueba.
Administrative Attaché: Eduardo G. Morales.

Economic and Commercial Section: B-3/21 Vasant Vihar, New Delhi 110 057; tel (11) 678411; telex 3182006; fax (11) 678903.
Second Secretary (Commercial): Oscar A. Aicardi.

AUSTRALIA

High Commission: 1/50-G Shanti Path, Chanakyapuri, POB 5210, New Delhi 110 021; tel (11) 601336; telex 3161156; fax (11) 675088.
High Commissioner: David Wyke Evans.

Consulate-General: 16th Floor, E Block, Makers Tower, Cuffe Parade, Colaba, Bombay; POB 9937, Bombay 400 005; tel (22) 211071; telex 116366.

AUSTRIA

Embassy: EP/13 Chandragupta Marg, Chanakyapuri, New Delhi 110 021; tel (11) 601112; telex 3182014; fax (11) 673929.
Ambassador: Dr Christoph Cornaro.
Minister-Counsellor: Dr Gerhard Deiss.
First Secretary (Administration) and Consul: Walter Kalteis.
Second Secretary (Press and Culture): Dr Johannes Schachinger.
Attaché (Administration) and Vice-Consul: Sybille Pfeiffer.

Consulate-General: Taj Bldg, 210 Dr Dadabhai Naoroji Rd, 3rd Floor, Bombay 400 001; tel (22) 2042044; telex 1182775; fax (22) 2870502.
Honorary Consul-General: Jasu Shah.

Consulate: c/o Kothari Bldg, 20 Nungambakkam High Rd, Madras 600 034; tel (44) 472131; telex 416674; fax (44) 472263.
Honorary Consul: H. C. Kothari.

Consulate: 96/1 Sarat Bose Rd, Calcutta 700 026; tel (33) 752795.
Consul: Anna Mukherji.

BANGLADESH

High Commission: 56M Ring Rd, Lajpat Nagar-III, New Delhi 110 024; tel (11) 6834668; telex 3175218.
High Commissioner: Faruq Ahmed Choudhury.

BELGIUM

Embassy: 50N, Plot 4, Shanti Path, Chanakyapuri, New Delhi 110 021; tel (11) 608195; telex 3161487.
Ambassador: Kamiel Criel.

BENIN

Consulate: B-22, Mayfair Gardens, New Delhi 110 016; tel (11) 660455; telex 3175181; fax (11) 6842307.
Honorary Consul: Sunder T. Vachani.

BHUTAN

Embassy: Chandragupta Marg, Chanakyapuri, New Delhi 110 021; tel (11) 609217; telex 3162263.
Ambassador: Dasho Karma Letho.

BRAZIL

Embassy: 8 Aurangzeb Rd, New Delhi 110 011; tel (11) 3017301; telex 3165277; fax (11) 3015086.
Ambassador: Octavio Rainho da Silva Neves.

BULGARIA

Embassy: 16/17 Chandragupta Marg, Chanakyapuri, New Delhi 110 021; tel (11) 607411; telex 3161490; fax (11) 6876190.
Ambassador: Dr Enyo Savov.
Minister-Counsellor: Bogomil Dojdevski.
Commercial and Economic Counsellor: Nikolai Kalinov.
Counsellor: Dragovest Goranov.
First Secretary: Roumen Sabev.
Third Secretary (Commercial): Gueorgui Tsvetanov.
Attaché (Protocol): Sevdalin Petrov.
Attaché (Administration): Stoyan Pachov.
Attaché (Administration): Ilya Petkov.

CAMBODIA

Embassy: B-47, Soami Nagar, New Delhi 110 017; tel (11) 6423782.
Ambassador: Sok Sath.
First Secretary: Sry Thamarong.
Second Secretary: Kan Pharidh.

CANADA

High Commission: 7/8 Shanti Path, POB 5207, Chanakyapuri, New Delhi 110 021; tel (11) 6876500; telex 3172363; fax (11) 6876500.
Deputy High Commissioner: P. M. Marsden-Dole.
Counsellor (Immigration): A. Lukie.
Counsellor (Commercial): R. R. M. Logie.
Counsellor (Development): A. Labrecque.
Counsellor (Immigration): J. C. LeBane.
Counsellor: A. Pollack.
Counsellor (Development): P. Hoffman.
First Secretary (Commercial): D. B. MacKay.
First Secretary (Immigration): D. R. J. Eales.
First Secretary (Commercial): M. Hough.
First Secretary: J. J. Allen.
First Secretary (Development): J. S. Deyell.
First Secretary (Development): W. Fisher.
First Secretary (Immigration): D. G. Aldworth.
First Secretary (Administration): R. N. Couturier.
First Secretary (Immigration): C. R. Milette.
First Secretary (Immigration): J. F. McEachern.
First Secretary: V. Rakmil.
First Secretary: B. M. Hurst.
Attaché (Medical): Dr E. G. Delios.
Attaché (Medical): Dr C. K. Bridge.

Consulate: Suite 2401, Hotel Oberoi Towers, Nariman Point, Bombay 400 021; tel (22) 2024343; telex 112334; fax (22) 2043282.
Consul and Trade Commissioner: S. M. W. Cartwright.

CHILE

Embassy: 1/13 Shanti Niketan, New Delhi 110 021; tel (11) 671363; telex 3166097.
Ambassador: Eduardo Ortiz.

CHINA, PEOPLE'S REPUBLIC

Embassy: 50D Shantipath, Chanakyapuri, New Delhi 110 021; tel (11) 600328; telex 3172210; fax (11) 675486.
Ambassador: Tu Guowei.
Counsellor (Political): Qian Jinchang.
Counsellor (Commercial): He Wei.
Counsellor (Cultural): Ma Weiguang.
Counsellor (Science/Technology): Liu Guangning.
Military Attaché: Ji Shurang.
First Secretary: Tang Yemen.
First Secretary: Shu Ding.
First Secretary: Fan Mingxig.
First Secretary: Lin Zhenxi.
First Secretary: Liu Yuchun.
First Secretary: Ren Hiukun.
First Secretary: Huang Biao.
First Secretary: Su Yinhaun.
First Secretary: Guo Xiyou.
First Secretary: Wang Wenmin.
First Secretary: Lin Shanglin.
First Secretary: Li Zijie.
First Secretary: Zhare Wangjie.
First Secretary: Li Zhenhua.
First Secretary: Jiang Chunyi.
First Secretary: Li Keju.
First Secretary: Mai Tangyun.
First Secretary: Huang Huikang.

COLOMBIA

Embassy: 82D Malcha Marg, Chanakyapuri, New Delhi 110 021; tel (11) 3012771; telex 3163090.
Ambassador: Luis Guillermo Para.
Counsellor: Carlos Lozano.

CUBA

Embassy: 4 Munirka Marg, Vasant Vihar, New Delhi 110 057; tel (11) 600508; telex 3171395; fax (11) 615338.
Ambassador: Sonia Díaz Llera.

CYPRUS

High Commission: 52 Jor Bagh, New Delhi 110 003; tel (11) 697503; telex 3161788; fax (11) 615338.
High Commissioner: Theophilos V. Theophilou.
Second Secretary: Ioannis Iacovou.
Attaché: Xanthippe Renonos.

Consulate: 14K Dubash Marg, Bombay 400 023; tel (22) 244294; telex 3671.
Honorary Consul: J. M. Chudasama.

CZECHOSLOVAKIA

Embassy: 50M Niti Marg, Chanakyapuri, New Delhi 110 021; tel (11) 608215; telex 3172234.
Ambassador: Dr Miloslav Jezil.

DENMARK

Embassy: 2 Golf Links Area, New Delhi 110 003; tel (11) 616273; telex 3166160; fax (11) 694284.
Ambassador: Jens Ostenfeld.
Minister-Counsellor and Head of Aid Mission: Ole Blicher-Olsen.
Counsellor (Aid): Bjørn Kalmar Hansen.
Counsellor (Aid): Chresten Petersen.
Counsellor (Aid): Preben Gondolf.
Counsellor (Aid): Jens Bastue Jacobsen.
Counsellor: Peter Lysholt Hansen.
Project Co-ordinator: Jens Dybbøl.
Project Administrator: Lars Windfeld Lund.
Attaché (Aid): Peter Jul Larsen.
Attaché and Vice-Consul: Rita A. Nielsen.
Commercial Correspondent: Vinay Capila.

Consulate-General: L & T House, Ballard Estate, POB 278, Bombay 400 038; tel (22) 264462; telex 73346.
Consul-General: N. M. Desai.

Consulate: McLeod House, 3 Netaji Subhas Rd, 3rd Floor, Calcutta 700 001; tel (33) 287476; telex 212882.
Consul: B. P. Bajoria.
Vice-Consul: Shishir Kumar Bajoria.

Consulate: 8 Cathedral Rd, Madras 600 086; tel (44) 473333; telex 417647; fax (44) 477411.
Consul: Narayanan Sankar.
Vice-Consul and Secretary: S. B. Prabhakar Rao.

EGYPT

Embassy: 1/50M Niti Marg, New Delhi 110 021; tel (11) 608904; telex 3162611.
Ambassador: Mohammed Ahmed el-Zoeiby.

ETHIOPIA

Embassy: 7/50G Satya Marg, Chanakyapuri, New Delhi 110 021; tel (11) 604407; telex 3172358.
Ambassador: Gebeyehu Alemneh.

FINLAND

Embassy: E-3 Nyaya Marg, Chanakyapuri, New Delhi 110 021; tel (11) 605409; telex 3165030; fax (11) 671380.
Ambassador: Jyrki Aimonen.
Counsellor (Commercial): Tapio Soveri.
Consul: Pertti Laakso.

Consulate: Bennett, Coleman & Co Ltd, Dr D.N. Rd, Bombay 400 001; tel (22) 2621273; telex 1182699; fax (22) 2620144.
Consul: Ram S. Tarneja.

Consulate: Calland House, 6th Floor, 'Chitrakoot' 230A, Acharya Chandra Bose Rd, Calcutta 700 020; tel (33) 444757; telex 215435.
Consul: Saroj K. Mehera.

Consulate: c/o Travancore Rayon Ltd, 742 Mount Rd, Madras 600 002; tel (44) 87611; telex 418495.
Consul: M. C. Pethachi.

FRANCE

Embassy: 2/50-E Shanti Path, Chanakyapuri, New Delhi 110 021; tel (11) 604004; telex 3172351.
Ambassador: André Lewin.

Consulate-General: Datta Prasad Bldg, 2nd Floor, 10 Nowroji Gamadia Cross Rd, off Pedder Rd, Bombay 400 026; tel (22) 4949808; telex 73934.

Consulate-General: 2 rue de la Marine, Pondicherry 605 001; tel (413) 24058.

GERMANY

Embassy: 6 Block 50G, Shanti Path, Chanakyapuri, New Delhi 110 021; tel (11) 604861; telex 3165670; fax (11) 6873117.
Ambassador: Dr Hans-Georg Wieck.

Consulate-General: Hoechst House, 10th Floor, Nariman Point, 193 Backbay Reclamation, Bombay 400 021; tel (22) 2025493; telex 1182900; fax (22) 2025493.
Consul-General: Hans Wolfgang Schumann.

Consulate-General: 1 Hastings Park Rd, Alipore, POB 16711, Calcutta 700 027; tel (33) 459141; telex 218082; fax (33) 282028.
Consul-General: Richard Giesen.

Consulate-General: 22 Commander-in-Chief Rd, POB 6801, Madras 600 105; tel (44) 471747; telex 418214.
Consul-General: Gudrun Vogel.

GHANA

High Commission: A-42 Vasant Marg, Vasant Vihar, New Delhi 110 057; tel (11) 670788.

GREECE

Embassy: 16 Sundar Nagar, New Delhi 110 003; tel (11) 617800; telex 3165232.
Ambassador: Alexander Philon.

GUYANA

High Commission: 85 Poorvi Marg, Vasant Vihar, New Delhi 110 057; tel (11) 674194; telex 01172167; fax (11) 6874286.
High Commissioner: Balram Raghubir.
First Secretary: Barbara Haley.
Attaché: C. P. P. Singh Ramotar.
Attaché: Verna McCallam.

HOLY SEE

Apostolic Nunciature: 50c Niti Marg, Chanakyapuri, New Delhi 110 021; tel (11) 606520.
Apostolic Pro-Nuncio: Most Rev. George Zur, Titular Archbishop of Sesta.
Secretary: Renato Volante.
Secretary: Pedro Lopéz Quintana.

HUNGARY

Embassy: Plot 2, 50M Niti Marg, Chanakyapuri, New Delhi 110 021; tel (11) 608414; telex 3166038.
Ambassador: Dr András Balogh.

ICELAND

Consulate-General: Speedbird House, 41-2 M-Block, Connaught Circus, New Delhi 110 001; tel (11) 3321122; telex 3166629.
Consul-General: Nand Lal Khemka.

Consulate-General: 38 Western India House, Sir P.M. Rd, Bombay 400 001; tel (22) 2871931; telex 3738; fax (22) 2048411.
Consul-General: Deepnarayan K. Hirlekar.

Consulate: Dhun Bldg, 827 Anna Salai, Madras 600 002; tel (44) 431811; telex 4126023.
Consul: V. Srinivasan.

INDONESIA

Embassy: 50A Chanakyapuri, New Delhi 110 021; tel (11) 602352; telex 3165709.
Ambassador: Ida Bagus Mantra.

Consulate: 19 Altamount Rd, Cumballa Hill, Bombay 400 026.

IRAN

Embassy: 5 Barakhamba Rd, New Delhi 110 001; tel (11) 3329600; telex 3166421.
Ambassador: Ebrahim Rahimpour.

IRAQ

Embassy: 169-171 Jor Bagh, New Delhi 110 003; tel (11) 618011; telex 3166253.
Ambassador: Abdul Wadud ash-Shekhali.

IRELAND

Embassy: 13 Jor Bagh, New Delhi 110 003; tel (11) 617435; telex 3165546; fax (11) 697053.
Ambassador: Margaret Hennessy.
First Secretary: Damien Boyle.
Secretary: Keith McBean.

Consulate-General: Royal Bombay Yacht Club Chambers, Apollo Bunder, Bombay 400 039; tel (22) 2871087; telex 116510.
Honorary Consul-General: Robert W. Leybourne Callaghan.

ITALY

Embassy: 50E Chandragupta Marg, New Delhi 110 021; tel (11) 6873840; telex 3166020.
Ambassador: Gabriele Menegatti.

JAPAN

Embassy: Plots 4-5, 50G Shanti Path, Chanakyapuri, New Delhi 110 021; tel (11) 604071; telex 3172364; fax (11) 670928.
Ambassador: Shunji Kobayashi.

Consulate-General: 12 Pretoria St, Calcutta 700 001; tel (33) 222241; telex 215744; fax (33) 220954.
Consul-General: Toshikazu Kato.

Consulate-General: 1 Babasaheb, Dahanukar Marg, 1 Carmichael Rd, Cumballa Hill, Bombay 400 026; tel (22) 4933857; telex 1173658; fax (22) 4947445.
Consul-General: Tomoji Muto.

Consulate-General: 60 Spur Tank Rd, Chetput, Madras 600 031; tel (44) 865594; telex 417337; fax (44) 478853.
Consul-General: Shosaku Tanaka.

JORDAN

Embassy: 35 Malcha Marg, Chanakyapuri, New Delhi 110 021; tel (11) 3013495; telex 3161963.
Ambassador: Dr Suleiman Dajani.

KENYA

High Commission: E-66 Vasant Marg, Vasant Vihar, New Delhi 110 057; tel (11) 6876538; telex 3172166.
High Commissioner: Benjamin Betts Bore.

KOREA, DEMOCRATIC PEOPLE'S REPUBLIC

Embassy: 42/44 Sundar Nagar, New Delhi 110 003; tel (11) 617140; telex 3165059.
Ambassador: Yu Tae-Sop.

KOREA, REPUBLIC

Embassy: 9 Chandragupta Marg, Chanakyapuri, New Delhi 110 021; tel (11) 601601; telex 315537.
Ambassador: Kim Taezhee.

KUWAIT

Embassy: 5A Shanti Path, Chanakyapuri, New Delhi 110 021; tel (11) 600791; telex 3172211; fax (11) 6873516.
Ambassador: Dharar Abdul Razzak Razzooqi.
Counsellor: Miteb Othman Al-Rumaih.

Attaché: Hamad Khalaf El-Ejel.
Attaché: Faisal Al Hooli.
Consulate: Vaswani Mansions, 120 Dinshaw Vatcha Rd, Bombay 400 020; tel (22) 2871897.
Consul: Kazim Maarafie.

LAOS

Embassy: New Delhi.
Ambassador: Chanpheng Sihaphom.

LEBANON

Embassy: 10 Sardar Patel Marg, Chanakyapuri, New Delhi 110 021; tel (11) 3013174; telex 3161161.
Ambassador: Alexander Ammoun.

LIBERIA

Embassy: 79 Poorvi Marg, Vasant Vihar, New Delhi 110 057; tel (11) 602800; telex 3166686.
Ambassador: Rudolff Kolaco.

LIBYA

People's Bureau: 22 Golf Links, New Delhi 110 003; tel (11) 697717; telex 3165193.
Secretary of People's Bureau: Omar Ahmad Jadollah al-Aukali.

MALAYSIA

High Commission: 50M Satya Marg, Chanakyapuri, New Delhi 110 021; tel (11) 601291; telex 3182056; fax (11) 6872374.
High Commissioner: Mohammed Amir bin Jaafar.
Counsellor and Head of Chancery: Abdullah Sani bin Omar.
Counsellor (Political): Aminuddin bin Abu Bakar.
Counsellor (Information): S. Rajendran.
Defence Adviser: Lieut Col Mohd Ariffin bin Nurudin.
Second Secretary (Administrative): Abdullah H. Hussen.
Office of Assistant High Commissioner: 287 T. T. K. Rd, Madras 600 018; tel (44) 453580; telex 418098.
Assistant High Commissioner: Mahalil H. Baharam.

MALDIVES

High Commission: New Delhi.
High Commissioner: Mohamed Musthafa Hussain.

MALTA

Consulate: 1 Hailey Rd, New Delhi 110 001; tel (11) 3329090; telex 3166409.
Honorary Consul: O. P. Kathpalia.
Consulate: 303 Cumballa Crest, 42 Peddar Rd, Bombay 400 026; tel (22) 365020; telex 115696.
Honorary Consul: Kamla Dua.

MAURITIUS

High Commission: 5 Kautilya Marg, Chanakyapuri, New Delhi 110 021; tel (11) 3011112; telex 3166045; fax (11) 3019925.
High Commissioner: Dr Boodhum Teelock.

MEXICO

Embassy: 10 Jor Bagh, New Delhi 110 003; tel (11) 697991; telex 3166121.
Ambassador: Pedro González-Rubio S.

MONGOLIA

Embassy: 34 Archbishop Makarios Marg, New Delhi 110 003; tel (11) 618921.
Ambassador: Dashdavaagiin Chuluundorj.

MOROCCO

Embassy: 33 Archbishop Makarios Marg, New Delhi 110 003; tel (11) 611588; telex 3166118.
Ambassador: Ahmed Bourzaim.

MYANMAR

Embassy: Burma House, 3/50F Nyaya Marg, Chanakyapuri, New Delhi 110 021; tel (11) 600251; telex 3172224; fax (11) 6877942.
Ambassador: Saw Hlaing.
First Secretary: Kyaw Hein.
Second Secretary: Ngo Kho Pau.
Second Secretary: Hla Aung.
Third Secretary: Daw Yin Yin Oo.

NAURU

Consulate: C/5/4 Safdarjung Development Area, New Delhi 110 016; tel (11) 6863427; fax (11) 6862502.
Consul-General: S. K. Bhalla.

NEPAL

Embassy: Barakhamba Rd, New Delhi 110 001; tel (11) 3328191; telex 3166283.
Ambassador: Bindheswari Shah.

NETHERLANDS

Embassy: 6/50 Shanti Path, Chanakyapuri, New Delhi 110 021; tel (11) 609571; telex 3165070; fax (11) 609327.
Ambassador: E. M. Schoo.

NEW ZEALAND

High Commission: 25 Golf Links, New Delhi 110 003; tel (11) 697296; telex 3165100; fax (11) 693615.
High Commissioner: Priscilla Williams.
First Secretary: Michael Grace.
Attaché: Jane Tate.
Trade Commissioner: Jim Charles.

NICARAGUA

Embassy: E-514 Greater Kailash-II, New Delhi 110 048; tel (11) 6442083; telex 3166034.
Ambassador: César A. Arostegui.

NIGERIA

High Commission: 21 Palam Marg, Vasant Vihar, New Delhi 110 057; tel (11) 670405; telex 3165195.
High Commissioner: E. A. Adeteniwa.

NORWAY

Embassy: 50C Shanti Path, Chanakyapuri, New Delhi 110 021; tel (11) 605982; telex 3182071; fax (11) 6873814.
Ambassador: Jon Atle Gaarder.
Counsellor: Margaret Slettevold.
Second Secretary: Betzy Ellingsen Tunold.
Attaché: Marian Christiansen.
Attaché: Kristin Jokstad.
Consulate-General: Nowroij Mansion, 6th Floor, 31 Nathelal Parekh Marg, Bombay 400 039; tel (22) 242098; telex 1183988; fax (22) 2046576.
Consul-General: George Mathew.
Consulate: Harbour Gate House, 44/45 Rajaji Salai, Madras 600 001; tel (44) 517950; telex 417318.
Consul: C. D. Gopinath.
Consulate: Calland House, Chitrkoot, 6th Floor, 230A Acharya Jagdish Chandra Bose Rd, Calcutta 700 020; tel (33) 474757; telex 215435.
Consul: S. K. Mehera.

OMAN

Embassy: 16 Palam Marg, New Delhi 110 057; tel (11) 670215; telex 3172342.
Ambassador: Ahmed Yousuf al-Harithy.

PAKISTAN

High Commission: 2/50G Shanti Path, Chanakyapuri, New Delhi 110 021; tel (11) 600603; telex 3165270.
High Commissioner: Abdul Sattar.

PANAMA

Embassy: D-129 Panchsheel Enclave, New Delhi 110 017; tel (11) 6438620; telex 3117094.
Ambassador: Horacio J. Bustamante.

PERU

Embassy: D-1/39, Vasant Vihar, New Delhi 110 057; tel (11) 673937; telex 3165274; fax (11) 6876427.
Counsellor and Chargé d'affaires a.i.: Alberto Gutiérrez.
First Secretary: Nelson Ortiz.
Consulate-General: 6 K Dubash Marg, Bombay 400 023; tel (22) 243352.
Honorary Consul-General: Ardeshir B. K. Dubash.

PHILIPPINES

Embassy: 50N Nyaya Marg, Chanakyapuri, New Delhi 110 021; tel (11) 601120; telex 3172397; fax (11) 6876401.
Ambassador: Pablo A. Araque.

POLAND

Embassy: 50M Shanti Path, Chanakyapuri, New Delhi 110 021; tel (11) 608321; telex 3161894.
Ambassador: Juliusz Bialy.
Counsellor: Dr Stefan Stefanski.
Counsellor: Prof. M. Krzysztof Byrski.
Counsellor (Commercial): Stanisław Labis.
Military Attaché: Capt. Stanisław Terlecki.
First Secretary and Consul: Stanisław Ojrzynski.
Second Secretary (Press and Culture): Marcin Górnicki.
Second Secretary (Finance and Administration): Jerzy Sadowski.
Consulate: 36 Ridge Rd, Malabar Hills, Bombay 400 006; tel (22) 8123863.
Consul: W. Kowalski.
Consulate: 3-B Albert Rd, Calcutta 700 017; tel (33) 447144.
Consul: Z. Rejman.

PORTUGAL

Embassy: B-76 Greater Kailash-I, New Delhi 110 048; tel (11) 6441206; telex 3171163.
Ambassador: António Telco de Almeida de Maghalhães Colaco.

QATAR

Embassy: A-3 West End Colony, New Delhi 110 021; tel (11) 601240; telex 3172304.

ROMANIA

Embassy: A-52 Vasant Marg, Vasant Vihar, New Delhi 110 057; tel (11) 670700; telex 3172204.
Ambassador: Julius Ribeiro.
Attaché: Liviu Radu.

RUSSIA

Embassy: Shanti Path, Chanakyapuri, New Delhi 110 021; tel (11) 606026; telex 312802.
Ambassador: Viktor Fedorovich Isakov.

Consulate-General: 42 L. Jagmogandas Marg, Bombay; tel (22) 223627.

Consulate-General: 31 Shakespeare Saranee, Calcutta; tel (33) 444932.

Consulate-General: 14 Santhorne High Rd, Madras; tel (44) 845552.

SAN MARINO

Consulate-General: 15A Aurangzeb Rd, New Delhi 110 011; tel (11) 3016675; telex 3162110.
Consul-General: Bahi Mohan Singh.
Consul: Bhai Manjit Singh.

SAUDI ARABIA

Embassy: S-347 Panchshila Park, New Delhi 110 017; tel (11) 6445419; telex 3171397.
Ambassador: Shaikh Fouad S. Moufti.

SENEGAL

Embassy: New Delhi.
Ambassador: Ahmed el Mansour Diop.

SINGAPORE

High Commission: E-6 Chandragupta Marg, Chanakyapuri, New Delhi 110 021; tel (11) 604162; telex 3172169; fax (11) 677798.
High Commissioner: Michael Cheok Po Chuan.

SOMALIA

Embassy: New Delhi.
Ambassador: Mohamed Osman Omar.

SPAIN

Embassy: 12 Prithviraj Rd, New Delhi 110 011; tel (11) 3013834; telex 3161488.
Ambassador: Santiago Salas.

SRI LANKA

High Commission: 27 Kautilya Marg, Chanakyapuri, New Delhi 110 021; tel (11) 3010201; telex 3161162; fax (11) 3015295.
High Commissioner: Dr F. S. C. P. Kalpagé.

SUDAN

Embassy: New Delhi.

SWEDEN

Embassy: Nyaya Marg, Chanakyapuri, New Delhi 110 021; tel (11) 604961; telex 3162282; fax (11) 676401.
Ambassador: Pår Kettis.
Minister: Sven Julin.
Counsellor: Leif Rensfeldt.
First Secretary: Christina Palm.
First Secretary: Annika Svahnström.
Head of Aid Office: Christina Rehlen.
Attaché (Technical Contracts): Tommy Ahlenbäck.

Consulate-General: Indian Mercantile Chambers, Ramjibhai Kamani Marg, Ballard Estate, Bombay 400 038; tel (22) 262583; telex 1173506.
Consul-General: Fredie Ardeshir Metha.
Consul: Damodar Narashinha Bhat.

Consulate: c/o Flakt India Ltd, 5/2 Russel St, 6 Poonam Bldg, Calcutta 700 071; tel (33) 293639; telex 212082.
Consul: Aloke Mookherjea.
Chancellor: Roshan Jeejeebhoy.

Consulate: 6 Cathedral Rd, Madras 600 086; tel (44) 472040; telex 417865.
Consul: Stina Östlund-Vasu.
Chancellor: Vasantha Radhakrishnan.

SWITZERLAND

Embassy: Nyaya Marg, Chanakyapuri, New Delhi 110 021; tel (11) 604225; telex 3172350; fax (11) 6873093.
Ambassador: Jean-Pierre Zehnder.
Counsellor: Dr Pierre Combernous.
Counsellor (Development) and Head of Swiss Development Co-operation: Laurent Guye.
Defence Attaché: Maj.-Gen. Hans Schlup.
First Secretary (Development): Fritz Schneider.
First Secretary (Development): Alfred Frischknecht.
First Secretary (Development): Christoph Köpfil.
First Secretary: Dr Michael Ambühl.
Attaché (Consular/Administrative) and Head of Chancery: Willy Blaser.

Consulate-General: Manek Mahal, 90 Vir Nariman Rd, Bombay 400 020; tel (22) 2042591; telex 1182608; fax (22) 2029936.
Consul-General: Benedikt Keiser.

SYRIA

Embassy: 28 Vasant Marg, Vasant Vihar, New Delhi 110 057; tel (11) 670233; telex 3172360.
Ambassador: Mohammad Khodar.

TANZANIA

High Commission: 27 Golf Links, New Delhi 110 003; tel (11) 694351; telex 3162977.
High Commissioner: Onesiphorus Henry Tosha.

THAILAND

Embassy: 56N Nyaya Marg, Chanakyapuri, New Delhi 110 021; tel (11) 605985.
Ambassador: Nikorn Praisaengpetch.

TRINIDAD AND TOBAGO

High Commission: 131 Jor Bagh, New Delhi 110 003; tel (11) 618186; telex 3162481; fax (11) 4624581.
High Commissioner: Prem Chand Jagdeo Dass.
Deputy High Commissioner: Chandradath Singh.
Attaché: Patricia Francois.
Attaché (Finance): Anthony Phillip.

TUNISIA

Embassy: 23 Palam Marg, Vasant Vihar, New Delhi 110 057; tel (11) 676204; telex 3172162; fax (11) 674385.
Ambassador: Ali Tekaia.

TURKEY

Embassy: 50N Nyaya Marg, Chanakyapuri, New Delhi 110 021; tel (11) 601921; telex 3172408.
Ambassador: Yalim Eralp.

UGANDA

High Commission: 61 Golf Links, New Delhi 110 003; tel (11) 693584; telex 3166243.
High Commissioner: James Juuco.

UNITED ARAB EMIRATES

Embassy: EP-12 Chandragupt Marg, New Delhi 110 021; tel (11) 670830; telex 3172325.
Ambassador: Ahmed Abdullah al-Musally.

UNITED KINGDOM

High Commission: Shanti Path, Chanakyapuri, New Delhi 110 021; tel (11) 601371; telex 3165125; fax (1) 6872882.
High Commissioner: Sir Nicholas Fenn.
Minister and Deputy High Commissioner: P. J. Fowler.
Defence and Military Adviser: Brig. A. J. MacG. Percival.
Naval Adviser: Capt. J. P. Cardale.
Air Adviser: Group Capt. J. M. Kennell.
Assistant Defence Adviser: Lieut Col K. R. Sinclair.
Counsellor (Economic/Commercial): J. R. James.
Counsellor: G. M. Chittenden.
Counsellor and Head of Chancery: J. E. Holmes.
Counsellor (Management): M. J. Hardie.
First Secretary (Information): D. S. Keeling.
First Secretary (Chancery): C. W. Robbins.
First Secretary (Commercial): G. Thom.
First Secretary (Economic): Dr C. Clift.
First Secretary (Chancery): I. I. McMahon.
First Secretary (Political): S. P. Collis.
First Secretary (Management): R. P. Smith.
First Secretary (Development): J. R. Drummond.
First Secretary (Medical Officer): Dr A. C. E. Stacey.
First Secretary (Defence Supplies): J. P. Bewley.
First Secretary (Immigration): M. G. Hilson.
First Secretary (Commercial/Economic): M. L. Alcock.
First Secretary: P. Corgan.
First Secretary (Natural Resources Adviser): D. Chaffey.
First Secretary (Supplies): A. Shroff.
First Secretary (Works): F. H. Syratt.
Second Secretary (Works): G. C. Mallery.
Second Secretary (Communications): P. C. Salkeld.
Second Secretary (Supplies): P. V. B. George.

Bombay Office: 2nd Floor, Hong Kong Bank Bldg, Mahatma Gandhi Rd, POB 815, Bombay 400 023; tel (22) 274874; telex 112850; fax (22) 2027940.
Deputy High Commissioner: A. E. Furness.
First Secretary (Commercial): L. J. Friston.
First Secretary (Culture): R. A. K. Baker.
First Secretary (Education/Science): Dr K. T. Bailey.
First Secretary (Commercial): P. R. Hagart.
Second Secretary (Management): P. P. Flanagan.
Second Secretary (Consular/Immigration): M. R. Walmsey.

Calcutta Office: 1 Ho Chi Minh Sarani, Calcutta 700 071; tel (33) 445171; telex 215983; fax (33) 283458.
Deputy High Commissioner: I. McCluney.
First Secretary (Commercial): P. J. Cole.
First Secretary (Culture): D. J. Sloan.
First Secretary (Education/Science): P. C. French.
Second Secretary (Consular/Management): I. L. Wilson.

Madras Office: 24 Anderson Rd, Madras 600 006; tel (44) 473136; telex 417169; fax (44) 869004.
Deputy High Commissioner: D. Cockerham.
First Secretary (Culture) and British Council Director: D. N. Sanderson.
First Secretary (Education/Science): A. J. F. Picken.
Second Secretary (Commercial): P. Whiten.
Attaché (Consular/Immigration): J. P. Geddes.

USA

Embassy: Shanti Path, Chanakyapuri, New Delhi 110 021; tel (11) 600651; telex 3182065; fax (11) 6872028.
Ambassador: Thomas R. Pickering.
Deputy Head of Mission: Kenneth C. Brill.
Political Section: Robin L. Raphel.
Economic Section: Louis B. Warren.
Commercial Section: James A. Moorhouse.
Labour Officer: James J. Ehrman.
Consular Section: Richard P. Livingstone.
Administrative Section: Cristobal R. Orozco.
Regional Security Officer: Peter E. Bergin.
Attaché (Science): Peter L. M. Heydemann.
Agricultural Section: Daniel B. Conable.
Agency for International Development: Walter G. Bollinger.
Public Affairs Officer: Stephen F. Dachi.
Office of Defence Attaché: Col Richard J. Crites.

Office of Defence Co-operation: Col Scott Fisher.
Defence Supply Adviser: Col James S. Willoughby.
Communications Programme Officer: Lloyd C. Stevenson.
Information Systems Manager: David C. Pugh.

Consulate-General: Lincoln House, 78 Bhulabhai Desai Rd, Bombay 400 026; tel (22) 8223611; telex 1175425; fax (22) 8220250.
Consul-General: Charles A. Mast.
Political Section: Charles Michael Sayre.
Economic Section: William G. Young.
Commercial Section: Dorothy L. Lutter.
Consular Section: Allen J. Kepchar.
Administrative Section: James D. McGee.
Branch Public Affairs Officer: Roger C. Rasco.
Communications Programme Officer: Marcellus D. Davis.

Consulate-General: 5/1 Ho Chi Minh Sarani, Calcutta 700 071; tel (33) 223611; telex 215982.
Consul-General: Ronald D. Lorton.
Economic and Commercial Sections: James C. Newman.
Consular Section: Kathryn S. R. Berck.
Administrative Section: F. Stephen Malott.
Branch Public Affairs Officer: Bruce J. Kruetzer.

Consulate-General: Mount Rd, Madras 600 006; tel (44) 473040.
Consul-General: Ernestine S. Heck.
Political and Economic Sections: Susan W. Zelle.
Commercial Section: Rajendra K. Dheer.
Consular Section: Gilbert J. Sperling.
Administrative Section: Patricia N. Moller.
Branch Public Affairs Officer: William U. Lawrence.
Communications Programme Officer: Noel Petrin.

VENEZUELA

Embassy: N-114 Panchshila Park, New Delhi 110 017; tel (11) 6436783; telex 3171393; fax (11) 6435264.
Ambassador: Dr Frank Bracho.
Attaché: Sandra Guevara.
Second Officer: Dolores Valbuena.

VIET-NAM

Embassy: 17 Kautilya Marg, Chanakyapuri, New Delhi 110 021; tel (11) 3018059.
Ambassador: Vu Xuan Ang.

YEMEN

Embassy: B-70 Greater Kailash-I, New Delhi 110 048; tel (11) 6414623; telex 3165567.
Ambassador: Mohamed bin Mohamed al-Hubeishi.

YUGOSLAVIA

Embassy: 3/50G Niti Marg, Chanakyapuri, New Delhi 110 021; tel (11) 6872073; telex 3172365.
Ambassador: Dr Ernest Petríc.

ZAIRE

Embassy: 160 Jor Bagh, New Delhi 110 003; tel (11) 619455; telex 3166275.
Ambassador: Beltchika Kalubye.

ZAMBIA

High Commissioner: 14 Jor Bagh, New Delhi 110 003; tel (11) 619328; telex 3166084.
High Commissioner: E. B. Monga (acting).

ZIMBABWE

High Commission: B-8 Anand Niketan, New Delhi 110 021; tel (11) 677460; telex 3172289.
High Commissioner: Tirivafi John Kangai.

International Organizations

EUROPEAN COMMUNITIES

Headquarters of the Delegation for South Asia: YMCA, Cultural Centre Bldg, Jai Singh Rd, New Delhi 110 001; tel (11) 344222; telex 3161315; fax (11) 352706.
Head of Delegation: Robert Houliston.

INDONESIA

AFGHANISTAN

Embassy: Jalan Dr Kusuma Atmaja 15, Jakarta; tel (21) 333169.
Chargé d'affaires: Abdul Ghafur Baher.

ALGERIA

Embassy: Jalan H. R. Rasuna Said, Kav. 10-1, Kuningan, POB 875, Jakarta; tel (21) 514719.
Ambassador: Abdelhak Bererhi.

ARGENTINA

Embassy: Jalan Duren Ban Ka 22, Jakarta 12730; tel (21) 338088; telex 45529.
Ambassador: Gaspar Taboada.

AUSTRALIA

Embassy: Jalan M. H. Thamrin 15, Jakarta 10350; tel (21) 323109; telex 44329; fax (21) 322406.
Ambassador: Philip Flood.
Minister: Anthony J. Hely.
Minister (AUSTRADE): Barbara Higgs.
Counsellor (Political): Judith Pead.
Counsellor (Political): Ronald Ford.
Counsellor (Consular and Administrative): Evan Williams.
Counsellor (Cultural): Dr Jennifer Lindsay.
Counsellor (Development Co-operation): Tony Kelloway.
Counsellor (Public Affairs): Gary Gray.
Counsellor (Medical): Dr Bruce Arthur.
Defence and Army Attaché: Brig. David Cross.
Naval Attaché: Capt. Michael Webster.
Air Attaché: Group Capt. Rick Jones.
First Secretary (Immigration): James O'Callaghan.

Immigration and Information Section: Bank Niaga Bldg, Jelan Thamrin 55, Jakarta; tel (21) 330824; telex 46214; fax (21) 322404.

Consulate: Jalan Raya Sanur 146, Tanjung Bungkak, Sanur, POB 243, Denpasar, Bali; tel (361) 35092; telex 35146; fax (361) 31990.
Consul: J. N. Elliot.

AUSTRIA

Embassy: Jalan Diponegoro 44, Jakarta 10310; POB 2746, Jakarta 10001; tel (21) 338090; telex 46387; fax (21) 4214927.
Ambassador: Herbert Kröll.
Counsellor: Andreas Karabczek.
Counsellor (Administrative) and Consul: Ingeborg Lähr.

Commercial Section: Jalan Jambu 17, Menteng, Jakarta 12960; tel (21) 3105242; telex 61108; fax (21) 327342.
Head of Commercial Section: Wilfried Ferch.

Consulate: 2A, Jalan Prabu, Dimuntur, Bandung; tel (22) 439505.
Honorary Consul: W. H. O. Förster-Romswinckel.

BANGLADESH

Embassy: Jalan Mendut 3, Jakarta; tel (21) 324850.
Ambassador: Maj.-Gen. Moinul Hussein Chowdhury.

BELGIUM

Embassy: Wisma BCA, 15th Floor, Jalan Jenderal Sudirman 22-23, Jakarta 12920; tel (21) 5780510; telex 44413; fax (21) 5700676.
Ambassador: Nestor Cockx.

BRAZIL

Embassy: Jalan Cik Ditiro 39, Menteng, Jakarta 10310; tel (21) 358378; telex 45657.
Ambassador: André Guimarães.

BRUNEI

Embassy: Wisma Bank (Central Asia), 8th Floor, Jalan Jenderal Sudirman, Kav 22-3, Jakarta; tel (21) 5782180; telex 62023; fax (21) 5782205.
Ambassador: Dato Paduka Haji Awang Yahya bin Haji Harris.

BULGARIA

Embassy: Jalan Imam Bonjol 34/36, Jakarta 10310; tel (21) 346725; telex 45106.
Ambassador: Ognyan Mitev.

CANADA

Embassy: Wisma Metropolitan, 5th Floor, Jalan Jenderal Sudirman 29, POB 1052, Jakarta 10010; tel (21) 510709; telex 62131; fax (21) 5782251.
Ambassador: Ingrid M. Hall.
Counsellor (Commercial) and Consul: W. D. Hutton.
Counsellor (Development): A. Volkoff.
Counsellor (Commercial): R. Bélanger.
Counsellor (Development): A. B. Culham.
Counsellor and Consul: E. Whitcomb.
Counsellor (Development): D. L. Keithlin.
Counsellor (Development): M. Renaud.
Counsellor (Development): P. Paradine.
Counsellor (Development): Y. Garneau.
First Secretary (Administrative) and Consul: J. V. Visutkie.

CHILE

Embassy: Bina Mulia Bldg (Revlon), 7th Floor, Jalan H. R. Rasuna Said, Kav. 10, Kuninghan, Jakarta 12950; tel (21) 5201131; telex 62587; fax (21) 5207405.
Ambassador: Raúl Schmidt Dussaillant.
Third Secretary and Consul: Mauricio Hurtado Navia.

CHINA, PEOPLE'S REPUBLIC

Embassy: Jakarta.
Ambassador: Qian Yongnian.

CZECHOSLOVAKIA

Embassy: Jalan Prof. Mohd Yamin 29, POB 319, Jakarta; tel (21) 3101068; fax (21) 3101180.
Ambassador: Izidor Pociatek.
Counsellor: Jindřich Novotný.
First Secretary: Alexej Štěrba.
Second Secretary: Peter Holásek.

DENMARK

Embassy: Bina Mulia Bldg, 4th Floor, Jalan H. R. Rasuna Said, Kav. 10, Kuningan, Jakarta 12950; POB 449, Jakarta 12001; tel (21) 5204349; telex 62123; fax (21) 5201962.
Ambassador: Kris Lund-Jensen.
Counsellor (Commercial): Freddie Per Folmer Peterson.
Attaché and Consul: Per Svanen.
Attaché (Administrative): Ragnhild Kallehauge.

Consulate: Wisma Metropolitan, I, 6th Floor, Jalan Jenderal Sudirman 29, POB 400, Jakarta; tel (21) 516565; telex 62121; fax (21) 5712233.
Honorary Consul: Thomas Thune Andersen.

Consulate: Jalan Serma Gede 5, Sanglah, Denpasar 80114, Bali; tel (361) 35098; telex 34834; fax (361) 23521.
Honorary Consul: I. Gusti Ngurah Bagus.

Consulate: Jalan Hang Jebat 2, Medan, Sumatra; tel (61) 510384; telex 51117; fax (61) 510384.
Honorary Vice-Consul: Gianto Chitra.

EGYPT

Embassy: Jalan Teuku Umar 68, Jakarta; tel (21) 331141.
Ambassador: Muhammad Ali Kamel.

FINLAND

Embassy: Bina Mulia Bldg, 10th Floor, Jalan H. R. Rasuna Said, Kav. 10, Kuningan, Jakarta 12950; tel (21) 516980; telex 62128; fax (21) 512033.
Ambassador: Erik Heinrichs.
Counsellor (Commercial): Sören Lönnberg.

FRANCE

Embassy: Jalan Huski 20, Thamrin, Jakarta; tel (21) 332367; telex 61439; fax (21) 3100504.
Ambassador: Patrick O'Cornesse.

GERMANY

Embassy: Jalan M. H. Thamrin 1, Jakarta; tel (21) 323908; telex 44333; fax (21) 342100.
Ambassador: Theodor Wallau.

Consulate: Tromolpos 7, Medan, Sumatra; tel (61) 324073.
Honorary Consul: Karl Schneider.

Consulate: Jalan Pantal Karang 17, POB 100, Denpasar, Bali; tel (361) 8535.
Honorary Consul: Reinhold Jantzen.

HOLY SEE

Apostolic Nunciature: Jalan Merdeka Timur 18, POB 4227, Jakarta; tel (21) 3841142; fax (21) 3841143.
Apostolic Pro-Nuncio: Mgr Francesco Canalini.
Secretary: Rev. Francis Cao.

HUNGARY

Embassy: 36 Jalan H. R. Rasuna Said, Kav. X/3, Kuningan, Jakarta 12950; tel (21) 5203459; fax (21) 5203461.
Ambassador: Istvan Debreceni.

ICELAND

Consulate-General: Jalan Empang Bahagia 2, Jelambar, Jakarta 11460; tel (21) 5606390; telex 61612.
Consul-General: Djoko Sukendro Notokusumo.

INDIA

Embassy: Jalan H. R. Rasuna Said S-1, Kuningan, Jakarta; tel (21) 5204150; telex 44260; fax (21) 5204160.
Ambassador: R. S. Kalha.

IRAN

Embassy: Jalan Hos Cokroaminoto 110, Jakarta; tel (21) 330623; telex 44433.
Ambassador: Mir Fakhar.

IRAQ

Embassy: Jalan Teuku Umar 38, Jakarta; tel (21) 355017; telex 46280.
Ambassador: Zaki Abdulhamid al-Habba.

IRELAND

Consulate: Lane Moving and Storage, Cilandak Commercial Estate, Facility 408, Jakarta; tel (21) 7800747; telex 62969; fax (21) 7800013.
Honorary Consul: Gerard M. Lane.

ITALY

Embassy: Jalan Diponegoro 45, Jakarta; tel (21) 337440; telex 61546.
Ambassador: Michele Martinez.

JAPAN

Embassy: Jalan Mohammad Hoesni Thamrin 24, Jakarta; tel (21) 324308; telex 46199; fax (21) 325460.
Ambassador: Michihiko Kunihiro.
Consul-General: Kanoo Shiotani.

Consulate-General: Jalan Jenderal Sudirman 31, Ujung Pandang; tel (411) 81030; telex 71123; fax (411) 82323.
Consul-General: Mitsuo Watanabe.

Consulate-General: Jalan Sumatera 93, Surabaya; tel (31) 44677; telex 34196; fax (31) 515872.
Consul-General: Kohei Manabe.

Consulate-General: Jalan Suryo 12, Medan, Sumatra; tel (61) 510533; telex 51177; fax (61) 511447.
Consul-General: Toshihiro Kojima.

KOREA, DEMOCRATIC PEOPLE'S REPUBLIC

Embassy: Jalan Teuku Umar 72/74, Jakarta; tel (21) 3100707.
Ambassador: Han Pong-Ha.

KOREA, REPUBLIC

Embassy: Jalan Jendral Gatot Subroto 57, Jakarta Selatan; tel (21) 512309.
Ambassador: Young-Sup Kim.

LAOS

Embassy: Jalan Kintamani Raya C-17 No. 23, Kuningan Timur, Jakarta 12950; tel (21) 517446; fax (21) 517445.
Ambassador: Phanthong Phommahasai.
First Secretary: Vansy Thithavong.
Second Secretary: Thongphanh Syackhaphom.

MALAYSIA

Embassy: Jalan Imam Bonjol 17, Jakarta 10310; tel (21) 336438; telex 61445.
Ambassador: Dato' Abdullah Zawawi bin Haji Mohammed.

MEXICO

Embassy: Nusantara Bldg, 4th Floor, Jalan M. H. Thamrin 59, Jakarta; tel (21) 337453; telex 61141; fax (21) 331500.
Ambassador: Dr Jesus F. Domene.
Counsellor (Chancery): Miguel García Zamudio.
Attaché (Cultural): Imelda Ortiz Abdala.
Attaché (Protocol): Nadia Mendoza.

MYANMAR

Embassy: Jalan Haji Agus Salim 109, Jakarta; tel (21) 320440; telex 61295.
Ambassador: U Than Hla.

NETHERLANDS

Embassy: Jalan H. R. Rasuna Said, Kav. S-3, Kuningan, Jakarta 12950; tel (21) 511515; telex 62411; fax (21) 5700734.
Ambassador: Baron G. W. de Vos van Steenwijk.

NEW ZEALAND

Embassy: Jalan Diponegoro 41, Menteng, POB 2439, Jakarta; tel (21) 330680; telex 46109; fax (21) 3104866.
Ambassador: Neil D. Walter.
Counsellor: David Kersey.
Counsellor (Commercial): John Bedkober.
Defence Attaché: Col Andrew Renton-Green.
First Secretary: John Mills.
Attaché (Police): Insp. Barry Hunter.
Attaché (Tourism): Fergus Brown.

NIGERIA

Embassy: 15 Jalan Imam Bonjol, POB 3649, Jakarta; tel (21) 327838; telex 61607; fax (21) 3101903.
Ambassador: Tijani Boluri.
Minister-Counsellor: Anthony A. Sekudo.
Counsellor: Adamu Hassan.
First Secretary: Grace Y. Chia.
Second Secretary: Veronica T. Okwechime.
Attaché (Finance): Adams A. O. Ebhomielen.
Attaché (Administrative): Ugo A. Ubosi.

NORWAY

Embassy: Bina Mulia Bldg, 4th Floor, Jalan H. R. Rasuna Said, Kav. 10, Jakarta 12950; tel (21) 511990; telex 62127; fax (21) 5207365.
Ambassador: Torolf Raa.

Secretary: Jan W. Grythe.
Attaché (Administrative): Bjørg Helgesen.

PAKISTAN

Embassy: Jalan Teuku Umar 50, Jakarta; tel (21) 3103945; telex 61739.
Ambassador: M. Abul Fazl.
Defence Attaché: Col Ghulam Nabi Khan.
First Secretary: Kausar Ahsan.
First Secretary (Commercial): S. Anjum Bashir.
Third Secretary: Waheed Ahmed.
Attaché (Press): Ghulum Qadir Khan.

PAPUA NEW GUINEA

Embassy: Panin Bank Centre, 1 Jalan Jenderal Sudirman, Jakarta; tel (21) 711225.
Ambassador: Sebulon Kulu.

PHILIPPINES

Embassy: Jalan Imam Bonjol 6-8, Jakarta; tel (21) 348917.
Ambassador: Oscar G. Valenzuela.

Consulate-General: 3 Jalan Toar, Manado, North Sulawesi; tel (431) 62365.
Consul-General: Dolores B. Sale.

POLAND

Embassy: Jalan Diponegoro 65, Jakarta; tel (21) 320509.
Ambassador: Paweł Cieślar.

ROMANIA

Embassy: Jalan Cik Ditiro 42A, Jakarta; tel (21) 3106240; telex 61208.
Ambassador: Valeriu Georgescu.

RUSSIA

Embassy: Jalan M. H. Thamrin 13, Jakarta; tel (21) 322162.
Ambassador: Valery V. Malygin.

Consulate-General: Karim M. S. 15, Medan, Sumatra; tel (61) 25007.

Consulate-General: 116 Jalan Sumatra, Surabaya; tel (31) 46290.

SAUDI ARABIA

Embassy: Jalan Imam Bonjol 3, Jakarta; tel (21) 346342.
Ambassador: Muhammad Said Basrawi.

SINGAPORE

Embassy: Block X/4, Kav. 2, Jalan H. R. Rasuna Said, Kuningan, Jakarta 12950; tel (21) 5201489; telex 62213; fax (21) 5201486.
Ambassador: Barry Desker.

SPAIN

Embassy: Wisma Kosgoro 12A, Jalan M. H. Thamrin 53, Jakarta; tel (21) 325996; telex 45667.
Ambassador: Leopoldo Stampa.

SRI LANKA

Embassy: Jalan Diponegoro 70, Jakarta; tel (21) 321896; telex 45530; fax (21) 3107962.
Ambassador: Jayanandan Peri Sundaram.
Third Secretary: W. Hettiarachichi.
Attaché and Chancellor: B. Percy Piyasens.

SWEDEN

Embassy: Bina Mulia Bldg, 7th Floor, Jalan H. R. Rasuna Said, Kav. 10, POB 2824, Jakarta 10001; tel (21) 5201551; telex 62714; fax (21) 512652.
Ambassador: Lars-Erik Wingren.
Counsellor: Hans Andersson.
First Secretary: Fredrik Svedäng.
Second Secretary: Jans-Olof Ahlenius.

Consulate: Hotel Segara Village, Jalan Segara Ayu, Sanur, POB 91, Denpasar, Bali; tel (361) 88231; telex 35143; fax (361) 87242.
Consul: Ida Bagus Kompiang.

Consulate: Jalan Hang Jebat 2, Medan, Sumatra; tel (61) 511017; telex 51117; fax (61) 510384.
Consul: Gianto Chitra.

Consulate: Jalan Nusantara 275, Ujung Pandang, Sulawesi; tel (411) 316787; telex 71256.
Consul: Sjamsuddin Daeng Mangawing.

SWITZERLAND

Embassy: Jalan H. R. Rasuna Said, Block X 3/2, Kuningan, Jakarta-Selantan 12950; tel (21) 516061; telex 44113; fax (21) 5202289.
Ambassador: Bernard Freymond.
Counsellor: Kurt M. Höchner.
Attaché (Commercial): Enrico Homberger.
Attaché and Head of Chancery: Bernadette Maritz.
Attaché (Development Co-operation/Aid): George Capt.
Assistant Attaché (Development Co-operation): Ulrich Lutz.

SYRIA

Embassy: 8 Jalan Karang Asem 1, Kuningan Raya, Jakarta; tel (21) 515991; telex 62867.
Ambassador: Nadim Douay.

THAILAND

Embassy: Jalan Imam Bonjol 74, Jakarta; tel (21) 343762; fax (21) 3107469.
Ambassador: Rongpet Subharitikul.

TURKEY

Embassy: Jalan R. S. Kuningan, Kav. I, Kuningan, Jakarta; tel (21) 516258; telex 62506.
Ambassador: Sencer Acena.

UNITED KINGDOM

Embassy: Jalan M. H. Thamrin 75, Jakarta 10310; tel (21) 330904; telex 61166; fax (21) 321824.
Ambassador: Roger J. Carrick.
Counsellor (Commercial/Aid) and Deputy Head of Mission: M. L. H. Hope.
Counsellor, Head of Political Section and Consul-General: Dr P. S. Collecott.
Counsellor (Political): P. B. Preece.
Defence and Military Attaché: Col R. I. L. Ker.
Naval and Air Attaché: Cdre A. C. Moore.
First Secretary: J. I. Malcolm.
First Secretary (Commercial): M. B. E. Plumb.
First Secretary (Aid): D. J. C. Taylor.
First Secretary (Management): D. J. W. Ray.
First Secretary (Defence Sales): C. A. G. Champness.
First Secretary (Political): T. S. A. Follis.
Second Secretary (Works): J. C. P. Evans.
Second Secretary (Political/Information): J. Carroll.

Consulate: 2 Jalan Jend a Yani, Medan, Sumatra; tel (61) 518699; telex 51125; fax (61) 513596.
Honorary Consul: G. E. M. Brown.

Consulate: Kupang Indah VIII 15, POB 854, Surabaya; tel (31) 711604; fax (31) 333598.
Honorary Consul: M. J. Page.

Consulate: Jalan Jenderai Basuki Rahmat 33-37, Surabaya 60011; tel (31) 511200; telex 32151; fax (31) 515200.
Honorary Consul: R. Martin.

USA

Embassy: Medan Merdeka Selatan 5, Jakarta; tel (21) 360360; telex 44218.
Ambassador: John Cameron Monjo.
Deputy Head of Mission: Richard L. Wilson.
Political Section: Thomas P. Hamilton.
Economic Section: Bruce F. Duncombe.
Commercial Section: Theodore F. Villinski.
Labour Officer: Gail P. Scott.
Consular Section: Richard P. Livingston.
Administrative Section: David A. Roberts.
Regional Security Officer: Doyle E. Cooper.
Agency for International Development: Lewis P. Reade.
Agricultural Section: Kenneth L. Murray.
Public Affairs Officer: Michael Yaki.
Office of Defence Attaché: Col John B. Haseman.
Internal Revenue Service: David B. Robison.
Communications Programme Officer: Richard L. Kalla.
Information Systems Manager: Carolyn S. Christian.

Consulate: Jalan Imam Bonjol 13, Medan, Sumatra; tel (61) 322200; telex 51764.
Principal Officer: Bronson E. Percival.
Economic and Consular Sections: Robert S. Wing.
Administrative Section: Floyd S. Cable.
Branch Public Affairs Officer: Kathryn M. Gunning.

Consulate: Jalan Raya Dr Sutomo 33, Surabaya; tel (31) 69287; telex 31334.
Principal Officer: Peter F. Spalding.
Economic and Consular Sections: Andrew C. Rothman.
Administrative and Commercial Sections: Matthew E. Johnson.
Branch Public Affairs Officer: Michael J. Hurley.

VENEZUELA

Embassy: Central Plaza Bldg, 17th Floor, Jalan Sudirman, Jakarta 12930; POB 2727, Jakarta 10002; tel (21) 516885; telex 62701; fax (21) 512487.
Ambassador: Jesús García Coronado.
Counsellor: Ramon Bravo Suarez.
First Secretary: Campos Maritza.

VIET-NAM

Embassy: Jalan Teuku Umar 25, Jakarta; tel (21) 347325.
Ambassador: Do Ngoc Duong.

YUGOSLAVIA

Embassy: Jalan Hos Cokroaminoto 109, Jakarta; tel (21) 333593; telex 45149.
Ambassador: Vjekoslav Koprivnjak.

International Organizations

EUROPEAN COMMUNITIES

External Delegation: Wisma Dharmala Sakti Bldg, 16th Floor, 32 Jalan Jenderal Sudirman, POB 55, Jakarta 10220; tel (21) 5706076; telex 62043; fax (21) 5706075.
Head of Representation: Robert Van Der Meulen.

IRAN

AFGHANISTAN

Embassy: Abbas Abad Ave, Pompe Benzine, cnr 4th St, Teheran; tel (21) 627531.
Ambassador: Mohammad Hamid Ansari.

ALGERIA

Embassy: Vali Asr Ave, Ofogh St, No. 26, Teheran; tel (21) 293482; telex 212393.

ARGENTINA

Embassy: POB 98-164, Ave Mossadegh, Blvd Nahid, No. 35, Tajrish, Teheran.
Chargé d'affaires a.i.: Edelberto J. Lemos.

AUSTRALIA

Embassy: 123 Khaled al-Islambuli Ave, POB 15875-4334, Teheran 15138; tel (21) 626202; telex 212459; fax (21) 626415.
Ambassador: Michael Landle.

AUSTRIA

Embassy: Argentine Sq., No. 78, 3rd Floor, POB 15115-455, Teheran; tel (21) 620180; telex 212872.
Ambassador: Herbert Traxl.
Counsellor (Economic): Herbert Zaforek.
First Secretary: Michael Zimmermann.

BAHRAIN

Embassy: Park Ave, 31st St, No. 16, Teheran.
Ambassador: Yacoub Yousuf Abdulla.

BANGLADESH

Embassy: Gandhi Ave, 5th St, Bldg No. 14, POB 11365-3711, Teheran; tel (21) 682979; telex 212303.
Ambassador: M. M. Rezaul Karim.

BELGIUM

Embassy: Fereshteh Ave, Shabdiz Lane, 3 Babak St, POB 11365-115, Teheran 19659; tel (21) 294574; telex 212446.
Ambassador: Raymond Schrijvers.
First Secretary: P. Kridelka.
Chancellor: W. Achvar.
Attaché (Commercial): J.-J. Manigart.
Attaché (Administrative/Consular): P. Baeten.

BRAZIL

Embassy: Vanak Sq., Vanak St No. 58, Teheran 19964; tel (21) 685175; telex 212392.
Ambassador: Carlos Alberto Pessoa Pardellas.
Defence Attaché: Col Paulo Cesar Romero Castelo Branco.
Head of Commercial Section: Claudio José de Campos.

BULGARIA

Embassy: Vali Asr Ave, Tavanir St, Nezami Ganjavi St No. 82, POB 11365-7451, Teheran; tel (21) 685662; telex 212789.
Ambassador: Stefan Polendakov.

CANADA

Embassy: POB 11365-4647, 57 Shahid Sarafraz (Daryaye-Noor), Osatd-Motahari Ave, Teheran; tel (21) 622623; telex 212337; fax (21) 623202.
Ambassador: Paul S. Dingledine.
Counsellor and Consul: J. A. Sims.
First Secretary (Commercial) and Consul: R. Harwood.
Second Secretary (Administrative) and Vice-Consul: S. E. Dougherty.

CHINA, PEOPLE'S REPUBLIC

Embassy: Pasdaran Ave, Golestan Ave 1, No. 53, Teheran.
Ambassador: Wang Benzuo.

COLOMBIA

Embassy: Teheran.
Ambassador: Antonio Bayona.

CUBA

Embassy: Africa Ave, Amir Parviz St, No. 1/28, Teheran; tel (21) 632953.
Ambassador: Luis Marisy Figueredo.

CZECHOSLOVAKIA

Embassy: Enghelab Ave, Sarshar St, No. 61, POB 11365-4457, Teheran; tel (21) 828168.
Ambassador: Milan Mácha.

DENMARK

Embassy: Intersection Africa and Modaress Expressway, Bidar St No. 40, POB 11365-158, Teheran; tel (21) 297371; telex 212784; fax (21) 294085.
Ambassador: Hans Grunnet.
Counsellor (Commercial): Hans K. Kiil-Nielsen.
Secretary: Lars Andersen.
Export Assistant: Torben Søndergaard.
Commercial Correspondent: Shahrokh Alebooyeh.

FINLAND

Embassy: Vali Asr Ave, Vanak Sq., cnr Nilou St, POB 15115-619, Teheran; tel (21) 684985; telex 212930; fax (21) 1623201.
Ambassador: Tapani Brotherus.
Attaché (Commercial): Jaakko Larma.
Attaché (Commercial): Juha Yrjönen.

FRANCE

Embassy: 85 Neauphle-le-Château St, POB 113-11365, Teheran; tel (21) 676005.
Ambassador: Hubert Colin de Verdière.

GABON

Embassy: POB 337, Teheran; tel (21) 823828; telex 215038.
Ambassador: J. B. Essongue.

GERMANY

Embassy: 324 Ferdowsi Ave, POB 11365-179, Teheran; tel (21) 314111; telex 212488.
Ambassador: Dr Armin Freitag.
First Counsellor: Dr Harald Löschner.
Counsellor (Finance): Klaus Ranner.
Counsellor (Finance): Dr Thomas Bodewig.
Counsellor (Culture and Press): Raymond Dequin.
Counsellor (Chancery): Peter Kuder.
Military Attaché: Reinhold Pense.
Government Adviser: Matthias von Polenz.

GHANA

Embassy: Ghaem Magham Farahani Ave, Varahram St, No. 12, Teheran.
Chargé d'affaires a.i.: Humphrey Okpoti Larsey.

GREECE

Embassy: Africa Expressway (Ex. Jordan Ave), Niloufar St, No. 20, POB 11365-8151, Teheran 19677; tel (21) 4272384.
Ambassador: Dimitri Argyriades.

HOLY SEE

Apostolic Nunciature: Razi Ave, No. 97, ave de France Crossroad, POB 11365-178, Teheran; tel (21) 6403574.
Apostolic Nuncio: Most Rev. Giovanni V. Bulaitis, Titular Archbishop of Narona.
Secretary: Rev. Sébastien Magasani.
Attaché: Rev. Francesco Pirisi.

HUNGARY

Embassy: Abbas Abad Park Ave, 13th St, No. 18, Teheran; tel (21) 622800.
Ambassador: Dr Zsigmond Kázmér.

INDIA

Embassy: Saba-e-Shomali Ave, No. 166, POB 11365-6573, Teheran; tel (21) 894554; telex 212858.
Ambassador: Ramisa Chander Arora.

INDONESIA

Embassy: Ghaem Magham Farahani Ave, No. 210, POB 11365-4564, Teheran; tel (21) 626865; telex 212049.
Ambassador: Mohammad Sabir.

IRAQ

Embassy: Vali Asr Ave, No. 494, Teheran.

IRELAND

Embassy: 8 Razaneh Shomali St, Mirdamad Ave, Teheran; tel (21) 227672; telex 213865; fax (21) 222731.
Ambassador: John Francis Cogan.
First Secretary: Noel Purcell O'Byrne.
Third Secretary: Patrick Bourne.

ITALY

Embassy: 81 Neauphle-le-Château St, POB 11365-7863, Teheran; tel (21) 672107; telex 214171; fax (21) 672374.
Ambassador: Vittorio Amedeo Farinelli.
First Counsellor and Deputy Chief of Mission: Luca Fornari.
Military Attaché: Capt. Giuliano Manzari.
First Secretary (Commercial): Claudio Glaentzer.
First Secretary (Commercial): Luciano Pezzotti.
Attaché (Cultural): Prof. Angelo Michele Piemontese.
Consulate: Neauphle-le-Château St, Kutche Shahid Amir Said Vaezi No 2, Teheran; tel (21) 672333; telex 4150.
Consul: Dr Ettore Francesco Sequi.

JAPAN

Embassy: Bucharest Ave, NW cnr of 5th St, POB 11365-814, Teheran; tel (21) 623396; telex 212757.

Ambassador: Yuhiro Fujimoto.
Chargé d'affaires: Yoshihiro Nakayama.

JORDAN

Embassy: Teheran.

KOREA, DEMOCRATIC PEOPLE'S REPUBLIC

Embassy: Fereshteh Ave, Sarvestan Ave, No. 11, Teheran.
Ambassador: Cho Kyu-il.

KOREA, REPUBLIC

Embassy: 37 Bucharest Ave, Teheran; tel (21) 621125.
Chargé d'affaires a.i.: Sung ku Kang.

KUWAIT

Embassy: Dehkadeh Ave, 3-38 Sazman-Ab St, Teheran; tel (21) 636712.
Ambassador: Ahmad Abd al-Aziz al-Jassim.

LEBANON

Embassy: Teheran.
Ambassador: Ja'far Ma'awi.

LIBYA

People's Bureau: Ostad Motahhari Ave, No. 163, Teheran.
Sec.-Gen. of Committee of People's Bureau: Mahdi al-Mabirash.

MALAYSIA

Embassy: Bucharest Ave, No. 8, Teheran; tel (21) 629523.
Chargé d'affaires a.i.: Sopian bin Ahmad.

MAURITANIA

Embassy: Teheran.

MOROCCO

Embassy: Teheran.

NETHERLANDS

Embassy: POB 11365-138 or Vali Asr Ave, Ostad Motahhari Ave, Sarbederan St, Jahansouz Alley, No. 36, Teheran; tel (21) 896011; telex 212788; fax (21) 4492087.
Chargé d'affaires a.i.: Dr H. Heijnen.
Counsellor: H. van der Goes van Naters.
Second Secretary: A. J. A. Embrechts.

NEW ZEALAND

Embassy: Mirza-ye-Shirazi Ave, Shahid Ali-ye-Mirza, Hassani St, No. 29, POB 11365-436, Teheran; tel (21) 625061; telex 212078.
Ambassador: D. F. Laurie Markes.
Second Secretary: Hamish MacMaster.
Trade Commissioner: Peter MacDonald.

NICARAGUA

Embassy: No 15, Kuhestan 8th, Pasdaran Ave, Teheran 19537; tel (21) 248825; telex 214368; fax (21) 248825.
Chargé d'affaires a.i.: Ramón Antonio Vasquez Espinoza.

NIGERIA

Embassy: Shalid Khaled Islamboli Ave, 31st St, No. 9, POB 11365-7148, Teheran; tel (21) 684921; telex 213151.
Ambassador: Ado Sanusi.
Minister-Counsellor: B. P. Fadumiyo.
Counsellor: Dahiru Adamu.
First Secretary: O. K. Lawal.
First Secretary: R. I. Nwokeabia.
Attaché (Administrative): M. O. Ogunkoya.

NORWAY

Embassy: Bucharest Ave, 6th St, No. 23, POB 15875-4891, Teheran 15146; tel (21) 624644; telex 213009.
Ambassador: Jan Naerby.

OMAN

Embassy: Pasdaran Ave, Golestan 9, No. 5 & 7, POB 41-1586, Teheran; tel (21) 243199; telex 212835.
Chargé d'affaires a.i.: Rashid bin Mubarak bin Rashid al-Odwali.

PAKISTAN

Embassy: Dr Fatemi Ave, Jamshidabad Shomali, Mashal St, No. 1, Teheran; tel (21) 934331.
Ambassador: Tanvir Ahmad Khan.

PHILIPPINES

Embassy: 38 Emdad Gharbi Alley, Sheikh Bahai St, Moullah Sadra Ave, Zafaranieh, POB 19395-4797, Teheran; tel (21) 295840.
Ambassador: Surotani P. Usodan.

POLAND

Embassy: Africa Expressway, Piruz St No. 1/3, Teheran; tel (21) 227262.
Ambassador: Stefan Szymczykiewicz.

PORTUGAL

Embassy: Mossadegh Ave, Tavanir Ave, Nezami Ghanjavi Ave No. 30, Teheran; tel (21) 681380; telex 212588.
Ambassador: Fernando Pinto dos Santos.

QATAR

Embassy: Africa Expressway, Golazin Ave, Parke Davar No. 4, Teheran; tel (21) 221255; telex 212375.
Chargé d'affaires a.i.: I. Muhammad al-Qayed.

ROMANIA

Embassy: Fakhrabad Ave 22-28, Teheran; tel (21) 759841; telex 212791.
Ambassador: Ilie Casu.

RUSSIA

Embassy: 39 Neauphle-le-Château St, Teheran; tel (21) 671161.
Ambassador: Vladimir Gudev.

Consulate-General: Chahar Bahg Pain St, Masjed-e-Sofretchi, Esfahan; tel (31) 22060.

SENEGAL

Embassy: Vozara Ave, 48th St, POB 3217, Teheran; tel (21) 624142.

SOMALIA

Embassy: Shariati Ave, Soheyl Ave, No. 20, Teheran.
Chargé d'affaires a.i.: Muhammad Sheikh Ahmad.

SPAIN

Embassy: Ghaem Maghame Farahani Ave, Varahram St, No. 14, Teheran; tel (21) 624466; telex 212980; fax (21) 624398.
Ambassador: Fernando José Belloso.
First Secretary: Eduardo López Busquets.
Attaché: Adolfo José Moragón.
Attaché: Isabel Timón González.

Commercial Section: Dr Beheshti Ave, Daryaye Noor St, No. 32, 4th Floor, Teheran; tel (21) 621748; telex 213895.
Commercial Counsellor: Miguel Angel Iriso.

SUDAN

Embassy: Khaled Islambouli Ave, 23rd St, No. 10, Teheran; tel (21) 628476; telex 213372.
Ambassador: Ibrahim Ahmad Othman Hamra.

SWEDEN

Embassy: POB 15875-4313, 78 Africa Sq., Teheran; tel (21) 620514; telex 212822.
Ambassador: Håkan Granqvist.
Counsellor: Åke Karlsson.
First Secretary: Åke Lövquist.
Consul-General: Carl-Gustav Åkesson.

SWITZERLAND

Embassy: POB 19395-4683, 13/1 Boustan Ave, Elahieh, Teheran; tel (21) 268226; telex 212851; fax (21) 269448.
Ambassador: Anton Greber.
Counsellor: Jean-Daniel Biéler.
Attaché and Office Manager: Hans Stalder.

Foreign Interests Section: Park Ave, 17th St, No. 5, POB 11365-176, Teheran; tel (21) 625223; telex 213603.
Second Secretary (Foreign Interests): Michel Crot.

SYRIA

Embassy: Bucharest Ave, 10th St, No. 42, Teheran.
Ambassador: Ibrahim Yunis.

THAILAND

Embassy: Baharestan Ave, Parc Amin ed-Doleh, No. 4, POB 11495-111, Teheran; tel (21) 301433; telex 214140.
Ambassador: Waipote Suwanamoli.

TUNISIA

Embassy: Teheran.

TURKEY

Embassy: Ferdowsi Ave, No. 314, Teheran; tel (21) 315299.
Ambassador: Vulkan Vural.

UNITED ARAB EMIRATES

Embassy: Zafar Ave, No. 355-7, Teheran; tel (21) 221333; telex 212697.
Chargé d'affaires a.i.: T. Ahmad al-Haidan.

UNITED KINGDOM

Embassy: 143 Ferdowsi Ave, POB 11365-4474, Teheran; tel (21) 675011; telex 212493; fax (21) 678021.
Chargé d'affaires a.i.: David N. Reddaway.
First Secretary (Commercial): D. J. Hawkes.
Third Secretary (Management/Consular): G. I. Brammer.

VENEZUELA

Embassy: Bucharest Ave, 9th St, No. 31, POB 15875-4354, Teheran; tel (21) 624262; telex 213790; fax (21) 622840.
Ambassador: Jesús García Coronado.
Second Secretary: Leonardo Cañizales.
Third Officer: Belkis Soto de Asgari.

YEMEN

Embassy: Bucharest Ave, No. 26, Teheran.
Chargé d'affaires a.i.: Abdullah ar-Razi.

YUGOSLAVIA

Embassy: Vali Asr Ave, Fereshteh Ave, Amir Teimoor Alley No. 12, POB 11365-118, Teheran 19659; tel (21) 294127; telex 214235; fax (21) 228880.
Ambassador: Trajko Trajkovski.
Minister-Counsellor: Hajrudin Somun.
Counsellor: Dragan Mraović.
Military Attaché: Živojin Djordjević.
Second Secretary: Zoran Bojović.

ZAIRE

Embassy: Vali Asr Ave, Chehrazi St, No. 68, POB 11365-3167, Teheran; tel (21) 222199.
Chargé d'affaires a.i.: N'djate Esele Sasa.

IRAQ

AFGHANISTAN

Embassy: Maghrib St, ad-Difa'ie, 27/1/12 Waziriya, Baghdad; tel (1) 556-0331.
Ambassador: Mohammad Sa'ed.

ALBANIA

Embassy: Baghdad.
Ambassador: Gylani Shehu.

ALGERIA

Embassy: ash-Shawaf Sq., Karradat Mariam, Baghdad; tel (1) 537-2181.
Ambassador: al-Arabi Si Al-Hassan.

ARGENTINA

Embassy: Hay al-Jamia District 915, St 24, No. 142, POB 2443, Baghdad; tel (1) 776-8140; telex 213500.
Ambassador: Gerónimo Cortes-Funes.

AUSTRALIA

Embassy: Masbah 39B/35, POB 661, Baghdad; tel (1) 719-3430; telex 212148.
Ambassador: P. Lloyd.

AUSTRIA

Embassy: POB 294, Hay Babel 929/2/5, Aqaba bin Nafi's Sq., Masbah, Baghdad; tel (1) 719-9033; telex 212383.
Ambassador: Erwin Matsch.
First Secretary: Herbert Krauss.

BAHRAIN

Embassy: al-Mansour, Hay al-Watanabi, POB 27117, Mahalla 605, Zuqaq 7, House 4/1/44, Baghdad; tel (1) 542-3656; telex 213364.
Ambassador: Abd ar-Rahman al-Fadhil.

BANGLADESH

Embassy: 75/17/929 Hay Babel, Baghdad; tel (1) 719-6367; telex 2370.
Ambassador: Mufleh R. Osmarry.

BELGIUM

Embassy: Hay Babel 929/27/25, Baghdad; (1) 719-8297; telex 212450.
Ambassador: Marc Van Rysselberghe.

BRAZIL

Embassy: 609/16 al-Mansour, Houses 62/62-1, Baghdad; tel (1) 541-1365; telex 2240.
Ambassador: Mauro Sergio Conto.

BULGARIA

Embassy: Ameriya, New Diplomatic Quarter, POB 28022, Baghdad; tel (1) 556-8197.
Ambassador: Assen Zlanatov.

CANADA

Embassy: 47/1/7 Hay Al-Mansour, Mahalla 609, St 1, House 33, POB 323 CPO, Baghdad; tel (1) 542-1459; telex 212486.
Ambassador: Christopher J. Poole.
First Secretary and Consul: J. J. Gauthier.
Second Secretary (Administrative) and Vice-Consul: G. Létourneau.

CENTRAL AFRICAN REPUBLIC

Embassy: 208/406 az-Zawra, Harthiya, Baghdad; tel (1) 551-6520.
Chargé d'affaires: René Bissayo.

CHAD

Embassy: 97/4/4 Karradat Mariam, POB 8037, Baghdad; tel (1) 537-6160.
Ambassador: Mahamat Djiber Ahnour.

CHINA, PEOPLE'S REPUBLIC

Embassy: New Embassy Area, International Airport Rd, Baghdad; tel (1) 556-2740; telex 212195.
Ambassador: Zhang Dayong.

CUBA

Embassy: St 7, District 929 Hay Babel, al-Masba Arrasat al-Hindi, Baghdad; tel (1) 719-5177; telex 212389.
Ambassador: Juan Aldama Lugones.

CZECHOSLOVAKIA

Embassy: Dijlaschool St, No. 37, Mansour, Baghdad; tel (1) 541-7136.
Ambassador: Dr Miroslav Kotora.

DENMARK

Embassy: Zukak No. 34, Mahallat 902, Hay al-Wahda, House No. 18/1; POB 2001, Alwiyah, Baghdad; tel (1) 719-3058; telex 212490.
Ambassador: Torben G. Dithmer.
Secretary (Commercial): Mahmoud al-Kaissy.
Export Assistant: Dennis Thomsen.

Consulate-General: POB 29011, House No. 13, St No. 4, 929 Hay Babel, Baghdad; tel (1) 719-2264; telex 212435.
Consul-General: Subhi Muhi al-Khudaira.

DJIBOUTI

Embassy: POB 6223, al-Mansour, Baghdad; tel (1) 551-3805.
Ambassador: Abseia Booh Abdulla.

FINLAND

Embassy: House No. 86, Zuqaq No. 25, Mahallah No. 925, Hay Babel, Jadriyah, Baghdad; POB 2041, Alwiyah, Baghdad; tel (1) 776-6271; telex 212454; fax (1) 776-7922.
Ambassador: Henry Söderholm.
Attaché (Commercial): Ralf Rönns.
Attaché (Commercial): Juhani Nordling.

FRANCE

Embassy: Quartier Abu Nawas, Emplacement 102, St No. 55, House No. 7, POB 118, Baghdad; tel (1) 719-6061.

GERMANY

Embassy: Zuqaq 2, Mahallah 929, Hay Babel (Masbah Sq.), POB 2036, Baghdad; tel (1) 719-2037; telex 212262; fax (1) 718-0340.
Ambassador: Dr Richard Ellerkmann.

GREECE

Embassy: 63/3/913 Hay al-Jamia, al-Jadiriya, Baghdad; tel (1) 776-9511; telex 212479.
Ambassador: Epaminondas Peyos.

HOLY SEE

Apostolic Nunciature: as-Sa'adoun St 904/2/46, POB 2090, Baghdad; tel (1) 719-5183.
Apostolic Pro-Nuncio: Most Rev. Marian Oleś, Titular Archbishop of Ratiaria.

HUNGARY

Embassy: Abu Nuwas St No. 91, House No. 1247/1, az-Zuwiya, POB 2065, Baghdad; tel (1) 776-5000; telex 212293.
Ambassador: Dr Géza Patakai.

INDIA

Embassy: Taha St, Najib Pasha, Adhamiya, Baghdad; tel (1) 422-2014; telex 212248.
Ambassador: K. N. Bakshi.

INDONESIA

Embassy: 906/2/77 Hay al-Wahda, Baghdad; tel (1) 719-8677; telex 2517.
Ambassador: A. A. Murtadho.

IRAN

Embassy: Karradat Mariam, Baghdad.

IRELAND

Embassy: 913/28/101 Hay al-Jamia, Baghdad; tel (1) 776-7355; telex 212541.
Ambassador: Antoin MacUnfraidh.
Secretary: Michael Gaffey.
Secretary: Pat Bourne.

JAPAN

Embassy: 929/17/70 Hay Babel, POB 2369, Masba, Baghdad; tel (1) 719-3840; telex 212241; fax (1) 719-6186.
Ambassador: Taizo Nakamara.

JORDAN

Embassy: House No. 1, St 12, District 609, al-Mansour, POB 6314, Baghdad; tel (1) 541-2892; telex 2805.
Ambassador: Hilmi Lozi.

KOREA, REPUBLIC

Embassy: 915/22/278 Hay al-Jamia, Baghdad; tel (1) 776-5496.
Ambassador: Bong Rhuem Chei.

LEBANON

Embassy: Iwadia Askary St, House 5, Baghdad; tel (1) 416-8092; telex 2263.
Ambassador: Hekmat Aouad.

LIBYA

People's Bureau: Baghdad.
Head of People's Bureau: Abbas Ahmad al-Massrati (acting).

MALAYSIA

Embassy: 6/14/929 Hay Babel, Baghdad; tel (1) 776-2622; telex 2452.
Ambassador: K. N. Nadarajah.

MALTA

Embassy: Malta.
Ambassador: Joseph M. Schembri (resident in Malta).
Commercial Section: 2/1 Zuqaq 49, Mahallat 503, Hai Al Nil, Baghdad; POB 22002 Rassafa PO, Baghdad; tel (1) 772-5032; telex 213019.
Chargé d'affaires a.i.: Nader Salem Rizzo.

MAURITANIA

Embassy: al-Mansour, Baghdad; tel (1) 551-8261.
Ambassador: Muhammad Yehya Walad Ahmad al-Hadi.

MEXICO

Embassy: 601/11/45 al-Mansour, Baghdad; tel (1) 719-8039; telex 2582.
Chargé d'affaires: Víctor M. Delgado.

MOROCCO

Embassy: Hay al-Mansour, POB 6039, Baghdad; tel (1) 552-1779.
Ambassador: Aboleslam Zenined.

NETHERLANDS

Embassy: 29/35/915 Jadiriya, POB 2064, Baghdad; tel (1) 776-7616; telex 212276.
Ambassador: Dr N. van Dam.

NEW ZEALAND

Embassy: 2D/19 az-Zuwiyah, Jadiriyah, Baghdad; POB 2350, Alwiyah, Baghdad; tel (1) 776-8176; telex 212433.
Ambassador: John Clarke.

NIGERIA

Embassy: 2/3/603 Mutanabi, al-Mansour, POB 5933, Baghdad; tel (1) 542-1750; telex 212474.
Ambassador: A. G. Abdullahi.

NORWAY

Embassy: 20/3/609 Hay al-Mansour, POB 6308, Baghdad; tel (1) 541-0097; telex 212715.
Ambassador: Harald Lone.

OMAN

Embassy: POB 6180, 213/36/15 al-Harthiya, Baghdad; tel (1) 551-8198; telex 212480.
Ambassador: Khalifa bin Abdulla bin Salim al-Homaidi.

PAKISTAN

Embassy: 14/7/609 al-Mansour, Baghdad; tel (1) 541-5120.
Ambassador: Khalid Mahmoud.

PHILIPPINES

Embassy: 39/7/35 Hay Babel, Baghdad; tel (1) 719-3228; telex 3463.
Ambassador: Akmad A. Sakkan.

POLAND

Embassy: 30 Zuqaq 13, Mahalla 931, Hay Babel, POB 2051, Baghdad; tel (1) 719-0296.
Ambassador: Dr Witold Jurasz.

PORTUGAL

Embassy: 66/11 al-Karada ash-Sharqiya, Hay Babel, Sector 925, St 25, No. 79, POB 2123, Alwiyah, Baghdad; tel (1) 776-4953; telex 212716.
Ambassador: Gabriel Mesquito de Brito.

QATAR

Embassy: 152/406 Harthiya, Hay al-Kindi, Baghdad; tel (1) 551-2186; telex 2391.
Ambassador: Muhammad Rashid Khalifa al-Khalifa.

ROMANIA

Embassy: Arassat al-Hindia, Hay Babel, Mahalla 929, Zuqaq 31, No. 452/A, Baghdad; tel (1) 776-2860; telex 2268.
Ambassador: Ionel Mihail Cetateanu.

RUSSIA

Embassy: 4/5/605 al-Mutanabi, Baghdad; tel (1) 541-4749.
Ambassador: Viktor V. Posuvalyuk.
Consulate-General: Palestine St 306/8, Basra; tel (40) 213187.

SENEGAL

Embassy: 569/5/10, Hay al-Mansour, Baghdad; tel (1) 542-0806.
Ambassador: Doudou Diop.

SOMALIA

Embassy: 603/1/5 al-Mansour, Baghdad; tel (1) 551-0088.
Ambassador: Issa Ali Mohammed.

SPAIN

Embassy: ar-Riyad Quarter, District 908, St No. 1, No. 21, POB 2072, Alwiyah, Baghdad; tel (1) 719-2852; telex 212239.
Ambassador: Juan López de Chicheri.

SRI LANKA

Embassy: 07/80/904 Hay al-Wahda, POB 1094, Baghdad; tel (1) 719-3040.
Ambassador: N. Navaratnarajah.

SUDAN

Embassy: 38/15/601 al-Imarat, Baghdad; tel (1) 542-4889.
Ambassador: Ali Adam Muhammad Ahmad.

SWEDEN

Embassy: Hay al-Nidhal, Mahalla 103, Zuqaq 41, House 15, POB 720, Baghdad; tel (1) 719-5361; telex 212352.
Ambassador: Henrik Amneus.
Counsellor: Jan Carlson.
Second Secretary: Torkel Stiernlöf.
Consulate-General: Mirjan Bldg, South Gate, Baghdad; tel (1) 888-8639.
Consul-General: Mohammed Makzoumi.

SWITZERLAND

Embassy: Hay Babel, House No. 41/5/929, POB 2107, Baghdad; tel (1) 719-3091; telex 212243.
Ambassador: Hans-Rudolf Hoffmann.
First Secretary: Christoph Bubb.

THAILAND

Embassy: 1/4/609, POB 6062, al-Mansour, Baghdad; tel (1) 541-8798; telex 213345.
Ambassador: Cheuy Suetrong.

TUNISIA

Embassy: Mansour 34/2/4, POB 6057, Baghdad; tel (1) 551-7786.
Ambassador: Larbi Hantous.

TURKEY

Embassy: 2/8 Waziriya, POB 14001, Baghdad; tel (1) 422-2768; telex 214145.
Chargé d'affaires: Sönmez Köksal.

UGANDA

Embassy: 41/1/609 al-Mansour, Baghdad; tel (1) 551-3594.
Ambassador: Swaib M. Musoke.

UNITED ARAB EMIRATES

Embassy: al-Mansour, 50 al-Mansour Main St, Baghdad; tel (1) 551-7026; telex 2285.
Ambassador: Hilal Sa'id Hilal az-Zu'abi.

VENEZUELA

Embassy: al-Mansour, House No. 12/79/601, Baghdad; tel (1) 552-0965; telex 2173.
Ambassador: Freddy Rafael Alvarez Yanes.
Second Secretary: Raul Alfonso González Nava.

VIET-NAM

Embassy: 29/611 Hay al-Andalus, Baghdad; tel (1) 551-1388.
Ambassador: Tran Ky Long.

YEMEN

Embassy: Jadiriya 923/28/29, Baghdad; tel (1) 776-0647.
Ambassador: Mohammed Abdullah ash-Shami.

YUGOSLAVIA

Embassy: 16/35/923 Hay Babel, Jadiriya, POB 2061, Baghdad; tel (1) 776-7887; telex 213521.
Ambassador: Stojan Andov.

IRELAND

ARGENTINA

Embassy: 15 Ailesbury Drive, Dublin 4; tel (1) 2691546; telex 90564.
Ambassador: Nicolás Adrian Sonschein.
Counsellor: Rodolfo Claudio Wolcken.

AUSTRALIA

Embassy: 6th Floor, Fitzwilton House, Wilton Terrace, Dublin 2; tel (1) 761517; fax (1) 685266.
Ambassador: Brian Burke.
Counsellor: Stephen Brady.
First Secretary: Ben Brogan.
First Secretary (Immigration): Robert Malone.
Second Secretary: Cathy Murphy.
HOM Secretary: Carmel O'Dougherty.
Communicator: Laura Pratt.

AUSTRIA

Embassy: 15 Ailesbury Court Apartments, 93 Ailesbury Rd, Dublin 4; tel (1) 691451; telex 30366; fax (1) 830860.
Ambassador: Dr Helga Winkler-Campagna.
First Secretary: Elisabeth Tichy-Fisslberger.
Economic Secretary: Franz Hutegger.

BELGIUM

Embassy: 2 Shrewsbury Rd, Dublin 4; tel (1) 691588; telex 93322; fax (1) 838488.
Ambassador: Luc Putman.

CANADA

Embassy: 4th Floor, 65-68 St Stephen's Green, Dublin 2; tel (1) 781988; telex 93803; fax (1) 781285.
Ambassador: Michael A. Wadsworth.
Counsellor (Commercial): G. Morin.
Counsellor (Immigration): J. P. Scott.
First Secretary and Consul: M. Cleary.

CHINA, PEOPLE'S REPUBLIC

Embassy: 40 Ailesbury Rd, Dublin 4; tel (1) 2691707; telex 30626; fax (1) 2839938.
Ambassador: Han Lili.
First Secretary: Zhao Xingmin.
First Secretary: Wang Jiashou.
First Secretary (Commercial): Wang Lingjun.
Second Secretary: Tao Huicun.

DENMARK

Embassy: 121-122 St Stephen's Green, Dublin 2; tel (1) 756404; telex 93523; fax (1) 784536.
Ambassador: Christoffer Bertelsen.
Commercial Attaché: Peter Wilhelm Jørgensen.

Consulate: Algonquin House, Kilcoolishal, Glanmire, Cork; tel (21) 353535; fax (21) 353399.
Honorary Consul: Richard Anthony Halpin.

Consulate: Security House, 15 Mallow St, Limerick; tel (61) 315315; telex 70711; fax (61) 318164.
Honorary Consul: John Michael Dundon.
Honorary Vice-Consul: John Richard Dundon.

Consulate: 99 The Quay, Waterford; tel (51) 76511; telex 80071; fax (51) 72274.
Honorary Consul: William Douglas Baxter.

EGYPT

Embassy: 12 Clyde Rd, Ballsbridge, Dublin 4; tel (1) 606566; telex 33202.
Ambassador: Hussein Abbas Mesharrafa.

FINLAND

Embassy: Russell House, Stokes Place, St Stephen's Green, Dublin 2; tel (1) 781341; telex 92308; fax (1) 783727.
Ambassador: Osmo Junani Lares.

Commercial Section: fax (1) 781050.
Commercial Counsellor: Lasse Carlsson.

Consulate-General: 43 Mespil Rd, Dublin 4; tel (1) 765153.
Consul-General: John Donnelly.

Consulate: Hainault House, 69 St Stephen's Green, Dublin 2; tel (1) 758291; telex 5154.
Consul: Tom Eklund.

Consulate: 1 Connell St, Cork; tel (21) 275235; telex 75366.
Vice-Consul: Conor Doyle.

Consulate: Security House, 15 Lower Mallow St, Limerick; tel (61) 315315; telex 6911.
Vice-Consul: John Michael Dundon.

Consulate: Waterford.

FRANCE

Embassy: 36 Ailesbury Rd, Ballsbridge, Dublin 4; tel (1) 694777.
Ambassador: Michel Combal.

Economic Section: Marine House, Clanwilliam Place, Dublin 2; tel (1) 680777; telex 93894.

GERMANY

Embassy: 31 Trimleston Ave, Booterstown, Blackrock, Co. Dublin; tel (1) 693011; telex 93809; fax (1) 693946.
Ambassador: Dr Martin Elsasser.

Consulate: Camden House, Camden Quay, Cork; tel (21) 509367; telex 28429.
Honorary Consul: Michael Corkery.

Consulate: Crohane-Fossa, Killarney, Co. Kerry; tel (64) 32628.
Honorary Consul: Klaus Nölke.

GREECE

Embassy: 1 Upper Pembroke St, Dublin 2; tel (1) 767254; telex 30878.
Ambassador: Panayotis A. Tsounis.

HOLY SEE

Apostolic Nunciature: 183 Navan Rd, Dublin 7; tel (1) 380577; fax (1) 380276.
Apostolic Nuncio: Most Rev. Emmanuel Gerada, Titular Archbishop of Nomentum.
Counsellor: Mgr Renato Volante.

HUNGARY

Embassy: Dublin.
Ambassador: Dr István Pataki.

ICELAND

Consulate-General: 6 Monkstown Ave, Monkstown, Dublin; (1) 808103.
Consul-General: Thomas P. Hogan.

INDIA

Embassy: 6 Leeson Park, Dublin 6; tel (1) 970843; telex 30670.
Ambassador: Ramesh Chander Arora.

IRAN

Embassy: 72 Mount Merrion Ave, Blackrock, Co. Dublin; tel (1) 880252; telex 90336.
Ambassador: Mehdi Moeinfar.

ITALY

Embassy: 63/65 Northumberland Rd, Ballsbridge, Dublin 4; tel (1) 601744; telex 93950; fax (1) 682759.
Ambassador: Dr Marcello Salimei.

JAPAN

Embassy: 22 Ailesbury Rd, Dublin 4; tel (1) 694033; telex 93790; fax (1) 838726.
Ambassador: Yuzo Hatano.

KOREA, REPUBLIC

Embassy: 20 Clyde Rd, Ballsbridge, Dublin 4; tel (1) 608280; telex 91776; fax (1) 608716.
Ambassador: Min Hyung-Ki.

LIBYA

Embassy: Dublin.

MALTA

Consulate: 'Traverslea', Glenageary, Co. Dublin; tel (1) 801081; fax (1) 2808807.
Honorary Consul: Noel Judd.

NETHERLANDS

Embassy: 160 Merrion Rd, Ballsbridge, Dublin 4; tel (1) 693444; telex 93561; fax (1) 839690.
Ambassador: Eric Franciscus Charles Niehe.

NIGERIA

Embassy: 56 Leeson Park, Dublin 6; tel (1) 604051; telex 24163.
Ambassador: Wadibra Anyanwn.

NORWAY

Embassy: Hainault House, 69/71 St Stephen's Green, Dublin 2; tel (1) 783133; telex 90173; fax (1) 783277.
Ambassador: Kirsten Ohm.
First Secretary: Tor Wennesland.
Attaché: Karin Rager.

Consulate: James Scott Shipping Ltd Cobh, Scott Bldg, Cobh, Cork; tel (21) 76068; fax (21) 831009.
Consul: Bryan J. Foley.

PORTUGAL

Embassy: Knocksinna House, Knocksinna Rd, Foxrock, Dublin 18; tel (1) 894416; telex 30777; fax (1) 892849.
Ambassador: Pedro José Ribeiro de Menezes.

RUSSIA

Embassy: 184-186 Orwell Rd, Rathgar, Dublin 14; tel (1) 975748; telex 33622.
Ambassador: Gennady Vasilyevich Uranov.

SPAIN

Embassy: 17A Merlyn Park, Dublin 4; tel (1) 691640; telex 93826.
Ambassador: José Antonio de Yturriaga.

SWEDEN

Embassy: Sun Alliance House, 13-17 Dawson St, POB 1313, Dublin 2; tel (1) 715822; telex 93341; fax (1) 6796718.
Ambassador: Margareta Hegardt.
Counsellor: Hans Nicklasson.
First Secretary (Commercial): Jan Lovén.
Third Secretary (Administration): Lena Ström.

Consulate: c/o Sedgwick Dineen Ltd, 55 South Mall, Cork; tel (21) 274236; telex 75830; fax (21) 272444.
Consul: William Hastings Sullivan.

Consulate: Security House, 15 Lower Mallow St, Limerick; tel (61) 315315; telex 70711; fax (61) 318164.
Consul: John Michael Dundon.

SWITZERLAND

Embassy: 6 Ailesbury Rd, Ballsbridge, Dublin 4; tel (1) 2691566; telex 93299; fax (1) 2830344.
Ambassador: Dr Charles Hummel.
Counsellor: Adolf Knöpfel.
Attaché: François Mayor.

SYRIA

Embassy: Dublin.

TURKEY

Embassy: 11 Clyde Rd, Ballsbridge, Dublin 4; tel (1) 601623; telex 31563; fax (1) 685014.
Ambassador: Halil Dag.
Counsellor: Aydin Durusoy.
First Secretary: Deniz Ozmen.
Administrative Attaché: Metin Zoray.
Administrative Attaché: Gulay Kosem.
Attaché: Naci Ugur.
Attaché: Engin Ilcin.

UNITED KINGDOM

Embassy: 31-33 Merrion Rd, Dublin 4; tel (1) 2695211; telex 93717; fax (1) 2838423.
Ambassador: David E. S. Blatherwick.
Counsellor and Deputy Head of Mission: J. W. Thorp.
Defence Attaché: Col S. D. Lambe.
British Council Director: Dr K. T. Churchill.
First Secretary (Commercial): D. F. B. Edye.
First Secretary (Economic): I. R. Whitting.
First Secretary (Political/Information): T. A. Gallagher.
First Secretary (Chancery): G. Fergusson.
First Secretary (Management): D. Harris.
Second Secretary (Agriculture): A. Cobden.
Second Secretary (Commercial): D. S. Marsh.
Second Secretary (Commercial): F. D. Morris.
Third Secretary (Passports/Visas): J. D. Kenny.

USA

Embassy: 42 Elgin Rd, Ballsbridge, Dublin 4; tel (1) 688777; telex 93684; fax (1) 689946.
Ambassador: Richard Anthony Moore.
Deputy Chief of Mission: Brian D. Curran.
Political Section: George T. Dempsey.
Economic Section: Curtis A. Stone.
Commercial Section: John W. Avard.
Consular Section: William H. Griffith.
Administrative Section: Samuel A. Rubino.
Regional Security Officer: Patrick M. McCreary.
Public Affairs Officer: John P. Treacy.
Communications Programme Officer: Rodney G. Painter.
Information Systems Manager: Forrest Partovi.
Office of the Defence Attaché: Col John K. Moon.
Customs Service (Treasury): Paul W. O'Brien.

International Organizations

EUROPEAN COMMUNITIES

Bureau: 39 Molesworth St, Dublin 2; tel (1) 712244; telex 93827; fax (1) 712657.
Head of Office: John Terence Stewart.

ISRAEL

ARGENTINA

Embassy: 112 Rehov Hayarkon, 2nd Floor, Tel-Aviv 63571; tel (3) 5271313; telex 33730; fax (3) 9271150.
Ambassador: Alberto E. Ham.
Counsellor: Alicia de Hoz.
Counsellor (Economic/Commercial): Carlo A. Pezzoni.
Second Secretary (Consular): Eduardo Perez Ibarra.

AUSTRALIA

Embassy: Beit Europa, 4th Floor, 27 Shaul Hamelech Blvd, Tel-Aviv 64928; tel (3) 250451; telex 33777; fax (3) 268404.
Ambassador: John Bruce Cambell.

AUSTRIA

Embassy: 11 Rehov Herman Cohen, POB 11095, Tel-Aviv 61110; tel (3) 5246186; telex 33435; fax (3) 5244039.
Chargé d'affaires: Dr Kurt Hengl.
First Secretary: Dr Willy Kempel.
Attaché (Administration) and Vice-Consul: Robert Landlinger.

Commercial Delegation: 198 Hayarkon St, 63405 Tel-Aviv; tel (3) 5246443; telex 35408; fax (3) 224071.
Commercial Counsellor: Dr Eva Maroscheck.

Consulate: 12 Allenby Rd, Haifa; tel (4) 522498.
Honorary Consul-General: Heinrich Löwenthal Zwi.

Consulate: Hovevei Zionstr. 8, Talbieh, POB 1376, Jerusalem; tel (2) 666161.
Honorary Consul: Isaac Molho.

BELGIUM

Embassy: 266 Rehov Hayarkon, Tel-Aviv 63504; tel (3) 454164; telex 342211.
Ambassador: Michel Adam.

BOLIVIA

Embassy: 73A Rehov Nordau, Herzliya 'B' 46582; tel (52) 582261.
Ambassador: Simón Sejas Tordoya.

BRAZIL

Embassy: 14 Rehov Hei Beiyar, Kikar Hamedina, 5th Floor, Tel-Aviv 62093; tel (3) 219292; telex 33752.
Ambassador: Asdrubal Pinto de Ulyssea.
Second Secretary: João Batista Lanari Bo.

BULGARIA

Embassy: Tel-Aviv.

CAMEROON

Embassy: Dan Panorama Hotel, 10 Rehov Kaufmann, POB 50252, Tel-Aviv 61500.
Chargé d'affaires a.i.: Etonndi Essomba.

CANADA

Embassy: 220 Rehov Hayarkon, Tel-Aviv 63405; POB 6410, Tel-Aviv 61063; tel (3) 228122; telex 341293; fax (3) 5272333.
Ambassador: Michael D. Bell.
Counsellor and Consul: M. de Salaberry.
Canadian Forces Attaché: Col W. H. Minnis.
First Secretary (Immigration): C. A. S. Drapeau.
First Secretary (Commercial): L. L. Léger.
First Secretary and Consul: G. Rioux.
First Secretary (Administration) and Consul: R. I. Hopton.
First Secretary: J. D. MacDonald.

CHILE

Embassy: 54 Rehov Pinkas, Apt 45, Tel-Aviv 62261; tel (3) 440414; telex 342189.
Ambassador: Jorge Massa.

CHINA, PEOPLE'S REPUBLIC

Embassy: Tel-Aviv.

COLOMBIA

Embassy: 52 Rehov Pinkas, Apt 26, Tel-Aviv 62261; tel (3) 449616; telex 342165.
Ambassador: Edmundo Esquenazi.

COSTA RICA

Embassy: 13 Diskin St, Apt 1, POB 1316, Jerusalem 91012; tel (2) 666197; telex 33533; fax (2) 630777.

Ambassador: Isabel Carazo de Saenz.
Minister-Counsellor and Consul-General: Jacob Allaouf.
Minister-Counsellor (Scientific Affairs): Jacob Grunhaus.
Scientific and Technological Attaché: David Moushine.
Counsellor and Consul-General: Jachevet Weinstock.
First Secretary: Gabriela Ramirez-Amaya.

Consulate-General: 6 Rehov Engel, Tel Aviv 65224; tel (3) 5660055; fax (3) 5660365.

COTE D'IVOIRE

Embassy: Dubnov Tower, 3 Rehov Daniel Frisch, POB 14371, Tel-Aviv 64371; tel (3) 262211; telex 341143; fax (3) 262008.
Ambassador: Jean-Pierre Boni.

CZECHOSLOVAKIA

Embassy: POB 16361, Tel-Aviv 61664; tel (3) 218282; fax (3) 218286.
Ambassador: Dr Miloš Pojar.
First Secretary (Consular Affairs): Anton Pinter.
Second Secretary (Press and Cultural Affairs): Dr Leo Pavlat.

DENMARK

Embassy: 23 Rehov Bnei Moshe, POB 21080, Tel-Aviv 62308; tel (3) 440405; telex 33514; fax (3) 454435.
Ambassador: Ellen Margrethe Løj.
Counsellor: Ole A. Petersen.
Vice-Consul: Ruth Gelvan.
Export Assistant: Henrik B. Christiansen.

Consulate: 10 Bnei Brit St, Jerusalem 95146; tel (2) 228083; telex 26144; fax (2) 247403.
Consul: Adin Talbar.

Consulate: c/o Chamber of Commerce, 53 Derech Haazmauth, Haifa 33033; (4) 645428; telex 46653; fax (4) 645428.
Consul: Arie Mehulal.

Consulate: 1153 Los Angeles St, Desert House, 14th Floor, POB 590, Eilat 88104; tel (59) 34277.
Consul: Jakie Pri-Gal.

DOMINICAN REPUBLIC

Embassy: 4 Sderot Shaul Hamelech, Apt 81, Tel-Aviv 64733; tel (3) 6957580; fax (3) 292977.
Ambassador: Alfredo Lebrón-Pumarol.

Consulate-General: 15 Hess St, Tel Aviv; tel (3) 296251; telex 341262; fax (3) 292977.
Honorary Consul-General: Charlotte Matalón.
Honorary Consul: Amnon Matalón.

Consulate: 12 Marcus St, Jerusalem 92233; tel (2) 631354.
Honorary Consul: Ana Nomberg.

Consulate: 1027/17 St, Nazareth; tel (6) 554390.
Honorary Consul: Joseph Jabally.

Consulate: 3 Sweden St, Hod Hacarmel, Haifa; tel (4) 254632; fax (4) 510141.
Honorary Consul: Zaharia Drucker.

ECUADOR

Embassy: 'Asia House', 4 Rehov Weizman, POB 30, Tel-Aviv 64239; tel (3) 258073; telex 342179; fax (3) 269437.
Ambassador: Patricio Palacios.
Second Secretary: Helena Yanez.

EGYPT

Embassy: 54 Rehov Bazel, Tel-Aviv 62744; tel (3) 5464151; telex 361289; fax (3) 5441615.
Ambassador: Muhammad Bassiouni.

EL SALVADOR

Embassy: 16 Kovshei Katamon, POB 4005, Jerusalem 93663; tel (2) 633575.
Ambassador: Enrique Guttfreund Hanchel.

FINLAND

Embassy: Beith Eliahu, 8th Floor, 2 Rehov Ibn Gvirol, Tel-Aviv 64077; POB 20013, 61201 Tel-Aviv; tel (3) 250527; telex 33552; fax (3) 266311.
Ambassador: Pekka J. Korvenheimo.
Second Secretary: Jarmo Viinanen.
Attaché (Consular/Cultural): Sisko Tuomola.
Vice-Consul: Matti Raymond Raatikainen.

B-section: 16 Rehov Moshe Sharett, Tel-Aviv 62092; tel (3) 261307.

Consulate-General: Industrial Development Bank, Asia House, 3rd Floor, 2 Dafna St, Tel-Aviv; tel (3) 216412; telex 33646; fax (3) 253179.
Consul-General: Abraham Friedmann.

Consulate: Lewison Co Ltd, 67 Sderot Rotschild, POB 131, Tel-Aviv 65786; tel (3) 293485; telex 33635; fax (3) 291996.
Consul: Israel A. Harari.

Consulate: c/o Alubin Ltd, 7 Hayovel St, Haifa 35646; tel (4) 338585; fax (4) 338585.
Consul: Abraham Nemes.

FRANCE

Embassy: 112 Tayelet Herbert Samuel, POB 3480, Tel-Aviv 63572; tel (3) 245371; telex 33662; fax (3) 5440062.
Ambassador: Jean-Louis Lucet.

Trade Promotion Office: tel (3) 454244; telex 342697.

Consulate: Immeuble Migdalor, 1/3 Rehov Ben Yehouda, BP 26126, Tel-Aviv 63801; tel (3) 5101415.

Consulate-General: 5 Rehov Paul-Emile Botta, POB 182, Jerusalem 91001; tel (2) 231451.

Consulate: 37 Rehov Hagefen, POB 9539, Haifa 35053; tel (4) 526281.

GERMANY

Embassy: 3 Rehov Daniel Frisch, 19th Floor, Tel-Aviv 64731; POB 16038, Tel-Aviv 61160; tel (3) 5421313; telex 33621; fax (3) 269217.
Ambassador: Otto von der Gablentz.

Consulate: Desert House, Flat 14, Los Angeles St, POB 590, 88100 Eilat; tel (59) 73277; telex 7775.
Honorary Consul: Ya'acov Pri-Gal.

Consulate-General: 105 Ha'Tishbi St, Haifa; POB 6240, Haifa 31061; tel (4) 371354; telex 46400; fax (4) 37153.
Honorary Consul-General: Michael Pappe.

GREECE

Embassy: 65 Shderot Shaul Hamelech, Tel-Aviv; tel (3) 259704; telex 341227.
Ambassador: Petros Anghelakis.

GUATEMALA

Embassy: 74 Rehov Hei Beiyar, Apt 6, Tel-Aviv 62198; tel (3) 5467372.
Ambassador: Stella R. de García-Granados.

HAITI

Embassy: 16 Rehov Bar Giora, Tel-Aviv 64336; tel (3) 280285.
Ambassador: Franck M. Joseph.

HOLY SEE

Apostolic Delegation: POB 19-199, Jerusalem; tel (2) 282298; telex 25648.
Apostolic Delegate: Most Rev. Carlo Curis, Titular Archbishop of Medeli.
Counsellor: Mgr Renzo Fratini.
Cultural Attaché: Mgr Richard Mathes.

HONDURAS

Embassy: 46 Rehov Hei Beiyar, Apt 3, Kikar Hamedina, Tel-Aviv 62093; tel (3) 5469506; telex 361499.
Ambassador: Moises Starkman.

HUNGARY

Embassy: 18 Rehov Pinkas, Tel-Aviv.
Ambassador: Dr János Görög.

ICELAND

Consulate-General: 136 Rothschild Blvd, Tel-Aviv; tel (3) 5617766; telex 33370; fax (3) 5617535.
Consul: Peter G. Naschitz.

ITALY

Embassy: 'Asia House', 4 Rehov Weizman, Tel-Aviv 64239; tel (3) 264223; telex 342664.
Ambassador: Alberto Leoncini-Bartoli.

JAPAN

Embassy: 'Asia House', 4 Rehov Weizman, Tel-Aviv 64239; tel (3) 257292; telex 342202; fax (3) 265069.
Ambassador: Takashi Nakamoto.

LIBERIA

Embassy: 6 Shimeon Frug, Ramat-Gan; tel (3) 728525; telex 361637.
Ambassador: Maj. Samuel B. Pearson, Jr.

MALTA

Consulate: Zim Israel Navigations Co Ltd, 7-9 Pal-Yam Ave, POB 1723, Haifa 31000; tel (4) 652111; telex 46501.
Honorary Consul: Matty Morgenstern.

Consulate: Habonim House, 2 Habonim St, Ramat-Gan 52462; tel (3) 5751833; fax (3) 5751849.
Honorary Consul: Yigal Lotan.

MEXICO

Embassy: 3 Rehov Bograshov, Tel-Aviv 63808; tel (3) 5230367; telex 32352; fax (3) 5237399.
Ambassador: Rogelio Martínez.
First Secretary: Cesar Oscar Ocaranza Castaneda.
First Secretary (Consular): José Ommar Hurtado Contreros.
Second Secretary (Political/Press): Sergio Sierra.

MYANMAR

Embassy: 12 Zalman Schneor St, Ramat Hasharon 47239; tel (3) 5400948; fax (3) 5493866.
Ambassador: U Aung Gyi.
First Secretary: U Ohn Kyaw.

NETHERLANDS

Embassy: 'Asia House', 4 Rehov Weizman, Tel-Aviv 64239; tel (3) 257377; telex 342180.
Ambassador: J. H. R. D. van Roijen.

NORWAY

Embassy: 40 Rehov Namal Tel-Aviv, Tel-Aviv 63506; tel (3) 5442030; telex 33417; fax (3) 5442034.
Ambassador: John Grieg.
Second Secretary: Wegger C. Strömmen.
Attaché (Consular/Administrative): Astrid Gundersen.

Attaché (Consular/Administrative): Anita Hebel.

PANAMA

Embassy: 10 Rehov Hei Beiyar, Kikar Hamedina, Tel-Aviv 62998; tel (3) 256711.
Ambassador: Maj. Rodolfo Castrellón.

PERU

Embassy: 52 Rehov Pinkas, Apt 31, 8th Floor, Tel-Aviv 62261; tel (3) 454065; telex 371351.
Ambassador: Guillermo Fernández-Cornejo.

PHILIPPINES

Embassy: Textile Centre Bldg, 13th Floor, 2 Rehov Kaufmann, POB 50085, Tel-Aviv 68012; tel (3) 5102231; telex 32104; fax (3) 5102229.
Ambassador: Amante R. Manzano.
Third Secretary, Vice-Consul and Acting Adminstrative Officer: Maria Leticia C. Ramos.
Attaché and Finance Officer: Lilian I. Caraos.
Attaché and Assistant: Victor A. Española.
Attaché, Communications Officer and Acting Property Officer: Antonio D. Nalda.

Consulate-General: Bet Yosef, 2 Hanamal St, Haifa; tel (4) 675675.
Honorary Consul: Yehuda Ofer.

Consulate-General: 17 Hatamar St, Caesaria, Jerusalem; tel (63) 62858.
Honorary Consul: Jack Nasser.

POLAND

Embassy: Tel-Aviv.

ROMANIA

Embassy: 24 Rehov Adam Hacohen, Tel-Aviv 64585; tel (3) 247379.
Ambassador: Iulian Bituleanu.

RUSSIA

Embassy: c/o Embassy of Finland; tel (3) 261307.
Ambassador: Aleksandr Ye. Bovin.

SAN MARINO

Consulate-General: 8 Benjamin St, Ramat-Gan, Tel-Aviv 52003; tel (3) 7513495; telex 371327.
Consul-General: Bruno Servadio.

SOUTH AFRICA

Embassy: Yakhin House, 9th Floor, 2 Rehov Kaplan, Tel-Aviv 64734; POB 7138, Tel-Aviv 61071; tel (3) 256147; telex 361208; fax (3) 265532.
Ambassador: Johan L. Viljoen.
Counsellor: G. J. Volschenk.
Counsellor (Administration): V. Nel.
First Secretary: S. Meyer.
First Secretary: B. Harrison.
Second Secretary: J. M. Joubert.
Second Secretary (Consular): J. J. Sims.
Third Secretary: M. A. Rademan.

Commercial Section: fax (3) 251167.
First Secretary (Trade): D. Strydom.

SPAIN

Embassy: Dubnov Tower, 3 Rehov Daniel Frisch, 16th Floor, Tel-Aviv 64731; tel (3) 265210; telex 361415; fax (3) 252505.
Ambassador: Pedro López de Aguirrebengoa.

SWEDEN

Embassy: 'Asia House', 4 Rehov Weizman, Tel-Aviv 64239; tel (3) 258111; telex 33650; fax (3) 258116.
Ambassador: Mats Bergquist.
Counsellor: Lars-Hjalmar Wide.
Second Secretary: Jens Odlander.
Chancellor: Ulla-Britt Sofia Cohen.
Chancellor: Miriam Goldberg.
Chancellor: Marianne Lempert.

Consulate: 1153/14 Bait Hamidbari St, POB 590, Eilat 88104; tel (59) 34277; telex 7712; fax (59) 71796.
Consul: Yaacov Pri-Gal.

Consulate: c/o Israel-Scandinavian Maritime Agency Ltd, Khayat Square 2, POB 33557, Haifa 31334; tel (4) 643162; telex 46440; fax (4) 664902.
Consul: David Castel.

Consulate: 58 Nablus Rd, POB 297, Jerusalem 91002; tel (2) 828117; telex 26572; fax (2) 282801.
Consul: Arnold Hjertström.

SWITZERLAND

Embassy: 228 Rehov Hayarkon, Tel-Aviv 63405; tel (3) 5464455; telex 342237; fax (3) 5464408.
Ambassador: Jean Olivier Quinche.
First Secretary: Martin Georges.
Attaché and Head of Chancery: Marianne Kammermann.

THAILAND

Consulate-General: 57 Pinsker St, Tel-Aviv; tel (3) 5280870; telex 35770.
Consul: Eddy Strod.

TOGO

Embassy: Beit Hatassianim, 29 Rehov Hamered, POB 50222, Tel-Aviv 68125; tel (3) 652206.
Ambassador: Koffi-Mawuenam Kowouvi.

TURKEY

Embassy: 34 Rehov Amos, Tel-Aviv 62495; tel (3) 442315.
Chargé d'affaires a.i.: Ekrem Esat Güvendiren.

UNITED KINGDOM

Embassy: 192 Rehov Hayarkon, Tel-Aviv 63405; tel (3) 5249171; telex 33559; fax (3) 291699.
Ambassador: Mark Elliott.
Defence and Military Attaché: Col E. C. Loden.
Naval and Air Attaché: Wing Commdr J. N. Landeryou.
Cultural Attaché (British Council Director): P. Sandiford.
First Secretary (Chancery). P. D. Orwin.
First Secretary (Chancery/Information): D. Barnes-Jones.
First Secretary (Commercial): P. A. Connolly.
Assistant Cultural Attaché (British Council): C. S. Wade.
Assistant Cultural Attaché (British Council): M. Johnson.
Second Secretary (Management): J. A. T. Sweid.

Consulate-General: Migdalor Bldg, 6th Floor, 1 Ben Yehuda St, Tel-Aviv 63801; tel (3) 5100166; fax (3) 5101167.
Counsellor, Consul-General and Deputy Head of Mission: T. R. V. Phillips.
First Secretary and Consul: A. S. Marshall.

Consulate-General: 19 Nashashibi St, Sheikh Jarrah Quarter, POB 19690, East Jerusalem 97200; tel (2) 828281; telex 26260; Tower House, Kikar Remez, Jerusalem 93541; tel (2) 717724.
Consul-General: D. R. MacLennan.
Consul: J. M. Crane.
Vice-Consul (Management): E. A. Dow.
Cultural Attaché (British Council Director): C. J. Woods-McConville.

Consulate: 14 Tsofit Villas, Eilat 74908; tel (59) 72344.
Honorary Consul: F. Morris.

USA

Embassy: 71 Rehov Hayarkon, Tel-Aviv 63903; tel (3) 654338; telex 33376; fax (3) 663449.
Ambassador: William A. Brown.
Deputy Chief of Mission: Mark R. Parris.
Political Section: John E. Herbst.
Economic Section: Henry L. Clarke.
Commercial Section: Michael J. Mercurio.
Administrative Section: Clarence E. Pegues, Jr.
Regional Security Officer: William L. Adams.
Public Affairs Officer: Christopher Snow.
Communications Programme Officer: Norman R. McKone.
Information Systems Manager: Donald J. McNally.
Office of the Defence Attaché: Col James F. Carney.
Scientific Attaché: Charles A. Lawson.
Labour Officer: Leslie A. Bassett.

Consulate-General: 18 Agron Rd, POB 290, Jerusalem 94190; Consular and Cultural Sections: 27 Nablus Rd, Jerusalem; tel (2) 253288.
Consul-General: Philip C. Wilcox, Jr.
Deputy Principal Officer: David M. Winn.
Political Section: Margaret Scobey.
Economic/Commercial Section: Jonathan R. Cohen.
Administrative Section: Peggy S. Zabriskie.
Regional Security Officer: Jo Ann Moore.
Public Affairs Officer: Gilbert K. Sherman.
Communications Programme Officer: Howard Spake II.

URUGUAY

Embassy: 52 Rehov Pinkas, Apt. 10, 2nd Floor, Tel-Aviv 62261; tel (3) 440411; telex 342669.
Ambassador: Juan Andrés Pacheco.

VENEZUELA

Embassy: Textile Centre, 2 Rehov Kaufmann, 16th Floor, Tel-Aviv 61500; POB 50429, Tel-Aviv; tel (3) 656287; telex 342172; fax (3) 656210.
Ambassador: Nestor Coll Blasini.

YUGOSLAVIA

Interests Section: c/o Embassy of Austria.

ZAIRE

Embassy: 60 He B'eiyar, Kikar Hamedina, Tel-Aviv 62155; tel (3) 452681; telex 371239.
Ambassador: Eluki Monga Aundu.
Minister-Counsellor: Makengo Ma Kimboko.
First Counsellor: Leta Mangasa.
Second Counsellor: Kabangu Wa Kabasele.

International Organizations

EUROPEAN COMMUNITIES

External Delegation: The Tower, 17th Floor, 3 Daniel Frisch St, Tel-Aviv 64731; tel (3) 264166; telex 342108; fax (3) 6951983.
Head of Delegation: J. Gwyn Morgan.
Counsellor: Arne B. Nielsen.
Attaché: Françoise Attal-Daivier.

ITALY

AFGHANISTAN

Embassy: Via Carlo Fea 1, 00161 Rome; tel (6) 8322972.

ALBANIA

Embassy: Via Asmara 9, 00199 Rome; tel (6) 8380725; telex 614169.
Ambassador: Dashnor Dervishi.
Counsellor: Qazim Tepshi.
Counsellor (Commercial): Genci Gjoka.
First Secretary: Mehmet Musollari.
Second Secretary: Spartak Myftiu.
Second Secretary: Luftar Malia.
Second Secretary: Xhevat Lamaj.
Attaché: Flamur Ganaj.
Attaché: Shpetim Pellumbi.

ALGERIA

Embassy: Via Barnaba Oriani 26, 00197 Rome; tel (6) 804141; telex 680846.
Ambassador: Mohammed Rouighi.
Counsellor: Boubakeur Ogab.
Counsellor: Ali Alaoui.
Counsellor: Amina Boudjelti.
Counsellor: Mahmoud Souames.
First Secretary: Ahmed Bouziane.
Attaché: Abdelhafid Debbabi.
Attaché: Bachir Bentayeb.
Attaché: Mourad Namoun.
Attaché: Houria Lalam.

ANGOLA

Embassy: Via Filippo Bernardini 21, 00165 Rome; tel (6) 6374325; telex 614505.
Ambassador: Mawete Jaoa Batista.

ARGENTINA

Embassy: Piazza dell'Esquilino 2, 00185 Rome; tel (6) 4871422; telex 610386; fax (6) 4819787.
Ambassador: Carlos F. Ruckauf.
Minister: Oscar Guillermo Galie.
Second Secretary: Alejandro Antonio Bertolo.

Commercial and Economic Section: Piazza della Rotonda 2, 00184 Rome; tel (6) 6877022; telex 616340; fax (6) 6861745.
Minister-Counsellor (Commercial/Economic): Carlos Arganaraz.
Counsellor (Commercial/Economic): Osvaldo Santiago Pascual.

AUSTRALIA

Embassy: Via Alessandria 215, 00198 Rome; tel (6) 832721; telex 610165; fax (6) 83272300.
Ambassador: Archibald Duncan Campbell.
Counsellor: Michael Ovington.
Counsellor (Agriculture and Minerals): Peter Franklin.
Counsellor (Development Assistance): Ross Brownhall.
First Secretary: Trevor Peacock.
First Secretary (Immigration): John Wimpole.
First Secretary (Consular/Administrative): Alastair Adams.
First Secretary (Legal Affairs): Cliff Foster.
First Secretary: Richard Watts.
First Secretary (Public Affairs): Barbara Whiteman.
Second Secretary (Consular/Administrative): Terry Hobson.
Third Secretary (Consular/Administrative): Joanne Henderson.
Attaché (Legal Affairs): Gianluca Mattioli.
Personal Secretary to Ambassador: Jeanette Dawes.
Registrar: Annette Morris.
Secretary: Louise Swanson.
Communicator: Janette Lynagh.

Consulate-General: Via Borgogna 2, 20122 Milan; tel (2) 76013330; telex 312320; fax (2) 76013350.
Consul-General and Senior Trade Commissioner: Barry Hain.

AUSTRIA

Embassy: Via G. B. Pergolesi 3, 00198 Rome; tel (6) 868241; telex 610139.
Ambassador: Dr Friedrich Frölichsthal.
Chargé d'affaires: Walter Hagg.
Counsellor: Georg Posch.
Counsellor: Maria Kunz.
Economic Secretary: Rudolf Ortner.
Economic Attaché: Hannelore Pawlitschek-Weichselbaumer.
Press Counsellor: Franz Berner.

Consular Section: Viale Liegi 32, interno 1, 00198 Rome; tel (6) 8443509.
Consul: Helmut Feil.
Vice-Consul: Sieglinde Schmidt.

Office of Defence Attaché: Via Giacinta Pezzana 57, 00197 Rome; tel (6) 878372; fax (6) 8543286.
Defence Attaché: Col Jürgen Köberl.

Cultural Institute: Istituto Austriaco di Cultura, Viale Bruno Buozzi 113, 00197 Rome; tel (6) 3224702; telex 624090.
Head of Cultural Institute: Bruno Kunz.
Cultural Counsellor: Manfred Poiger.
Economic Secretary: Andreas Pawlitschek.

Permanent Mission to FAO: Foreign Trade Office, Via Flaminia 158, 00196 Rome; tel (6) 3605913; telex 623058; fax (6) 620138.
Permanent Representative (FAO): Ernst Zimmerl.

Consulate: Via Dalmazia 179, 70121 Bari; tel (80) 331995; telex 810188.
Honorary Consul-General: Bonifacio Pansini.

Consulate: Via Ugo Bassi 13, 40124 Bologna; tel (51) 237506; fax (51) 237506.
Honorary Consul: Maria Letizia Constantini Coccheri.

Consulate: Via dei Servi 9, 50122 Florence; tel (55) 215352; telex 572084.
Honorary Consul: Enrico Ciantelli.

Consulate: Piazza della Vittoria 10, interno 9, 16121 Genova; tel (10) 592680.
Honorary Consul-General: Egon Ploederl.
Honorary Consul: Erich Seiberl.
Honorary Consul: Peter Ploederl.

Consulate-General: Via Tranquillo Cremona 27, primo piano, 20145 Milan; tel (2) 4812066; telex 340053; fax (2) 48009630.

Sub-office: Silbergasse 6, Merkantilgebäude 2 Stock, 39100 Bolzano; tel (471) 970394.
Consul-General: Harald Miltner.
Consul: Imma Oppelik.
Consul (Cultural Affairs): Mario Erschen.

Consulate: Corso Umberto I 275, 80138 Naples; tel (81) 287724.
Honorary Consul: Paolo Ruoppolo.

Consulate: Palermo.

Consulate: Via Otto Geleng 32, 98039 Taormina; tel (942) 24183.
Honorary Consul-General: Walter Tuna.

Consulate-General: Via Fabio Filzi 1, 34132 Trieste; tel (40) 61688; telex 461034; fax (40) 7797427.
Consul-General: Günter Birbaum.
Consul: Gerhart Zaar.

Consulate: c/o SIMU, Corso Giacomo Matteotti 28, 10121 Turin; tel (11) 532222; telex 221208; fax (11) 532226.
Honorary Consul: Riccardo Totta.

Consulate: Piazzale Roma 461/A, 30125 Venice; tel (41) 5200459; telex 420004; fax (41) 5200160.
Honorary Consul-General: Alfredo Bianchini.
Consul: Eleonora Rötzer.

BANGLADESH

Embassy: Via Antonio Bertoloni 14, 00197 Rome; tel (6) 878541; telex 614615.
Ambassador: Waliur Rahman.

BELGIUM

Embassy: Via dei Monti Parioli 49, 00197 Rome; tel (6) 3609441; telex 610425; fax (6) 3226935.
Ambassador: André Rahir.
Minister-Counsellor: Christian Monnoyer.
Counsellor: Danielle Del Marmol.
First Secretary: Isabelle Meert.
Second Secretary: Irene de Hertogh.
Attaché: Jan Peremans.
Attaché: Veronique Siklosi.
Attaché: Rudolphe Croene.
Attaché: Guy Walravens.

Consulate-General: Via A. Vespucci 2, 20124 Milan; tel (2) 6590668; telex 321159.
Consul-General: Walter Lion.

BOLIVIA

Embassy: Via Toscana 30, 00187 Rome; tel (6) 4817438; telex 620221; fax (6) 4821975.
Ambassador: Julio Pantoja Salamanca.

BRAZIL

Embassy: Palazzo Pamphil, Piazza Navona 14, 00186 Rome; tel (6) 650841; telex 610099.
Ambassador: Orlando Soares Carbonar.
Minister-Counsellor: Arnaldo Abilio Godoy Barreira Cravo.
Counsellor: Cezar Augusto de Souza Lima Amaral.
Counsellor: Marcelo Leonardo Vasconcelos.
First Secretary: Alcir Rebello.
First Secretary: Gastão Coimbra.
Second Secretary: Milton Rondó.
Second Secretary: Tarcisio Lumarck de Moura.
Second Secretary: Paulo Estivallet de Mesquita.
Second Secretary: Terezinha Bassani.
Third Secretary: Ricardo Peixoto.

Consulate-General: Via Santa Maria dell'Anima 32, 00186 Rome; tel (6) 6877891; fax (6) 6542883.
Consul-General: José Vicente de S. Pimentel.
Vice-Consul: José Luiz Vieira.

Consulate-General: Corso Europa 12, 20122 Milan; tel (2) 780951; telex 320529.
Consul-General: José Botafogo Gonçalves.

BULGARIA

Embassy: Via Pietro P. Rubens 21, 00197 Rome; tel (6) 3609640; telex 610234.
Ambassador: Rayko Nikolov.
Consul-General: Elena Borislavova Poptodorova.

CAMEROON

Embassy: Via Siracusa 4-6, 00161 Rome; tel (6) 8450451; telex 626873; fax (6) 8553060.
Ambassador: Michael Kima Tabong.
Second Counsellor: Lloyd Nanjor Forbang.
Second Counsellor: Thomas Yanga.
Second Secretary: Marc Aurèle Tang.
Second Secretary: Jasmine Mbida.
Attaché: Joséphine Djongo.

Consulate: Via Einaudi 1, Trieste; tel (40) 366606.
Honorary Consul: Alberto Hesse.

Consulate: Via Montegrappa 18, Novate Milanese; tel (2) 3543798.
Honorary Consul: Luigi Salina.

CANADA

Embassy: Via G. B. de Rossi 27, 00161 Rome; tel (6) 8415341; telex 610056; fax (6) 8848752.
Ambassador: Alan W. Sullivan.
Minister and Consul: J. Fowell.
Minister-Counsellor (Economic/Commercial): D. D. H. Wright.
Counsellor (Commercial/Economic): B. Côté.
Counsellor and Consul: M. Temple.
Counsellor and Consul: Yvon Turcotte.
Canadian Forces Attaché: Col R. J. Rousham.
First Secretary (Commercial): D. K. Daley.
First Secretary (Administration): D. Mysak.
First Secretary (Public Affairs): G. R. Barban.
First Secretary and Consul: R. Doiron.
First Secretary: S. M. Brochez.
First Secretary: A. Sidaros.
Second Secretary (Administration): H. Harris.
Attaché (Medical): Dr M. Emard.

Permanent Mission to FAO: Via Zara 30, 00198 Rome; tel (6) 8441841; telex 610056; fax (6) 4403063.
Minister-Counsellor and Permanent Representative (FAO): E. Weybrecht.
Counsellor (Development) and Alternate Permanent Representative (FAO): S. Robin.

Consular and Immigration Sections: Via Zara 30, 00198 Rome; tel (6) 4403028.
Counsellor (Immigration): M. A. Oppertshauser.
Counsellor (Immigration): R. A. Caldato.
Counsellor (Immigration) and Consul: J. H. J. Drapeau.
Second Secretary (Immigration): P. L. McKenzie.
Second Secretary (Immigration) and Vice-Consul: D. E. Burrows.

Consulate-General: Via Vittor Pisani 19, 20124 Milan; tel (2) 6697451; telex 310368; fax (2) 6704450.
Consul-General: Marie-Andrée Beauchemin.
Consul and Senior Trade Commissioner: C. Fontaine.
Consul and Trade Commissioner: M. Farley.

CHILE

Embassy: Via Nazionale 54, 2nd Floor, 00184 Rome; tel (6) 4742258; telex 611420.
Ambassador: Raul Troncoso Castillo.
Minister-Counsellor: Jorge Bustos Franco.
Counsellor: Ricardo Concha Gazmuri.
Counsellor: Felipe Perez W.
First Secretary: Marcelo Aguirre Dumay.
Third Secretary: Jorge Tagle Canelo.

CHINA, PEOPLE'S REPUBLIC

Embassy: Via Bruxelles 56, 00198 Rome; tel (6) 8448186; telex 680159.
Ambassador: Li Baocheng.

Consulate-General: telex 622051.
Consul-General: Qinshun Zu.

COLOMBIA

Embassy: Via Giuseppe Pisanelli 4, 00197 Rome; tel (6) 6799586; telex 611266.
Ambassador: Dr Oscar Mejía Vallejo.
Second Counsellor: Gloria Alzate.
Attaché: Federico Uribe.

CONGO

Embassy: Via Modena 50, 00184 Rome; tel (6) 4746163; telex 626645.
Ambassador: Joseph Tchicaya.

COSTA RICA

Embassy: Piazza della Torretta 26, 00186 Rome; tel (6) 6871291; telex 623300.
Ambassador: Octavio Torrealba.
Minister: Javier Guerra.

COTE D'IVOIRE

Embassy: Via Lazzaro Spallanzani 4-6, 00161 Rome; tel (6) 868040; telex 610396.
Ambassador: Soulejmane Sako.

CUBA

Embassy: Via Licinia 7/13, 00153 Rome; tel (6) 5755984; telex 610677.
Ambassador: Javier Ardizones Ceballos.
Consul-General: Serafin Gil Rodríguez Valdes.

CYPRUS

Embassy: Via Francesco Denza 15, 00197 Rome; tel (6) 8088365; telex 621033; fax (6) 8088338.
Ambassador: Andros A. Nicolaides.
Counsellor: Charalambos Kapsos.
Attaché (Press): Iacovos S. Giragosian.

Consulate-General: Via Michele Mercati 51, 00197 Rome; tel (6) 879837.
Consul-General: Charalambos Kapsos.

Consulate: Via XX Settembre 29, Genova; tel (10) 54901; telex 271460; fax (10) 562050.
Honorary Consul: George Poulides.

Consulate: Via Ampere 112, Milan; tel (2) 2893479; fax (2) 2896232.
Honorary Consul: Renos A. Michaelides.

Consulate: Via Santa Lucia 90, Naples; tel (81) 418936.
Honorary Consul: Raimondo Rolando.

Consulate: Via Martiri della Libertà 7, Trieste; tel (40) 365442; telex 460407; fax (40) 365445.
Honorary Consul: Sergio Stricca.

CZECHOSLOVAKIA

Embassy: Via Colli della Farnesina 144, 00194 Rome; tel (6) 3278742; telex 610306.
Ambassador: Norbert Židek.

DENMARK

Embassy: Via dei Monti Parioli 50, 00198 Rome; tel (6) 3600441; telex 624696; fax (6) 3610290.
Ambassador: Ib Ritto Andreasen.
Minister-Counsellor: Michael Hjortsø.
Commercial Counsellor: John Idoff Steven Foster.

Agricultural Section: tel (6) 3225436.
Agricultural Counsellor: Tage Jensen.
Permanent Representative (FAO): John Glistrup.
Attaché and Consul: Birgit Poulsen.
Attaché, Consul and Administration Officer: Knud Jerne.
Commercial Attaché: C. F. Jönsson.

Consulate-General: Via San Siro 10, 16124 Genova; tel (10) 297453; telex 270073; fax (10) 5368232.
Consul-General: Giorgio Boesgaard.

Consulate-General: Via L. Ariosto 30, 20145 Milan; tel (2) 4985251; telex 331659; fax (2) 4812445.
Consul-General and Commercial Counsellor: Per Hildebrant.
Commercial Secretary and Vice-Consul: Lars Erik Kruse.
Commercial Officer: Birthe Cristiani.
Export Assistant: Regitze Reeh.

Consular Section: tel (2) 4981441.
Consular Secretary: Anne Lise Ravaglia.

Consulate-General: Via Cervantes 55, 80133 Naples; tel (81) 5515049; telex 710166; fax (81) 5514608.
Consul-General: Oscar Cosulich.

Consulate: Via Cialdini 57, 60100 Ancona; tel (71) 200252; telex 560047; fax (71) 56752.
Consul: Arrigo Archibugi.

Consulate: Via 10 Ottobre 62, 96011 Augusta; tel (931) 978544; telex 972515; fax (931) 977470.
Consul: Gaetano Volpe.

Consulate: Piazza Massari 6, 70122 Bari; tel (80) 5214195; telex 810111; fax (80) 5210513.
Consul: Simeone di Cagno Abbrescia.

Consulate: Via Filomeno Consiglio 59, 72100 Brindisi; tel (831) 21123; telex 813361.
Consul: Mario Plaisant.

Consulate: Via Roma 127, 09124 Cagliari; tel (70) 659394; telex 791040; fax (70) 669150.
Consul: Mario Plaisant.

Consulate: Via dei Servi 13, 50122 Florence; tel (55) 211007; fax (55) 263333.
Consul: Alessandro Berti.

Consulate: Viale Italia 121, 19100 La Spezia; tel (187) 34366; telex 271004; fax (187) 34891.
Vice-Consul: Carlo Laviosa.

Consulate: Via Buontalenti 91, CP 173, 57123 Livorno; tel (586) 884451; telex 500007.
Consul: Alessandro Del Buono.

Consulate: Via Vittorio Emmanuele II 21, 98100 Messina; tel (90) 773719; telex 980037; fax (90) 773719.
Consul: Orazio Giovanni Speciale.

Consulate: c/o STS, Piazza Don Bosco 6, 90143 Palermo; tel (91) 543506; telex 912163; fax (91) 6373378.
Consul: Hanne Elisabeth Frendrup Carstensen Castellucci.

Consulate: c/o Firma Viaggi Condor, Corso d'Augusta 115, 47037 Rimini; tel (541) 27756; telex 551214; fax (541) 54208.
Vice-Consul: Stefano Patacconi.

Consulate: c/o Albatross Viaggi, Piazza Eroi Sanremesi 71, 18038 San Remo; tel (184) 880054; telex 286387; fax (184) 880054.
Consul: Xenia Sibil Stefania Angelastri Cafasso.

Consulate: Via Famagosta 17/1, 17100 Savona; tel (19) 828813; telex 270475; fax (19) 827981.
Vice-Consul: Kaj Erik Pyy.

Consulate: Corso Umberto 143, 98039 Taormina; tel (942) 23052; telex 980116; fax (942) 625367.
Vice-Consul: Antonino Silvestri.

Consulate: Via Beaumont 8, 10143 Turin; tel (11) 543569.

Consul: Valentino Bosso.

Consulate: Viale Miramare 5, 34135 Trieste; tel (40) 7359; telex 460171; fax (40) 44263.
Consul: Francesco Saverio Slocovich.

Consulate: S. Marco Campo Maini 4020, 30124 Venice; tel (41) 5200822; fax (41) 5200822.
Consul: Pier Vettor Grimani.

DOMINICAN REPUBLIC

Embassy: Via Domenico Chelini 9, 00197 Rome; tel (6) 874665.
Ambassador: Guido Emilio d'Alessandro Tavarez.

ECUADOR

Embassy: Via Guido d'Arezzo 14, 00198 Rome; tel (6) 851784; telex 613256.
Ambassador: Roque Cañadas Portilla.

EGYPT

Embassy: 119 Roma Villa Savoia, Via Salaria 267, 00199 Rome; tel (6) 856193; telex 610044.
Ambassador: Hoda El-Marassy.

EL SALVADOR

Embassy: Via Castellini 13, 00197 Rome; tel (6) 3601853.
Ambassador: David Trejo.

ETHIOPIA

Embassy: Via Nicolò Tartaglia 11, 00197 Rome; tel (6) 803057; telex 614414.
Ambassador: Tesfaye Abdi.

FINLAND

Embassy: Via Lisbona 3, 00198 Rome; tel (6) 8415895; telex 625600; fax (6) 8540362.
Ambassador: Ossi Sunell.
Counsellor (Press and Cultural Affairs): Jouni Lilja.
Commercial Secretary: Hannu Kosonen.
Consul-General: Hannu Kalinen.

Consulate-General: Via Turati 18, 20121 Milan; tel (2) 6592608.

Office of the Commercial Secretaries: tel (2) 29004541; telex 320366; fax (2) 6571981.
Commercial Secretary: Markku Mertanen.
Commercial Secretary: Enrico Casagrande.

Office of the Scientific Attaché: tel (2) 6597073; telex 320366; fax (2) 6572084.
Scientific Attaché: Antti Lindgren.

Consulate: Largo Giordano Bruno 30, 70121 Bari; tel (80) 742003; telex 810154.
Consul: Giuseppe Dormio.

Consulate: Via Sonnino 152, 4th Floor, 09100 Cagliari; tel (70) 651699; telex 630565.
Consul: Raffaele Torchiani.

Consulate: Via Anzalone 7, 95131 Catania; tel (95) 326608; telex 970029.
Consul: Oreste C. Geraci.
Vice-Consul: Hellin Paavilainen-Randone.

Consulate: Civitavecchia.

Consulate: Via Strozzi 6, 50123 Florence; tel (55) 293228.
Consul: Giuseppe Jommi.

Consulate-General: Via Assarotti 17/26, 16122 Genova; tel (10) 889495; telex 271380
Consul: Rudolf Walden.

Consulate: La Spezia.

Consulate: Livorno.
Consul: Giovanni Novelli.

Consulate: Via Garibaldi 263, 98100 Messina; tel (90) 47044; telex 980050.
Consul: Aldo Baldassare de Marco.

Consulate: Via Medina 24, 80133 Naples; tel (81) 5512211; telex 710023; fax (81) 5512947.
Consul: Ivan Leif Klingenberg.

Consulate: Via Cristoforo Colombo 24, 90142 Palermo; tel (91) 361290; telex 910070.
Consul: Giulio Adelfio.

Consulate: Societá Aeradria, Via Casalecchio, Rimini; tel (541) 31255; telex 550072.
Consul: Mario Pari.

Consulate: Piazza S. Antonio 4, 34122 Trieste; tel (40) 62960.
Consul: Callisto Gerolimich-Cosulich.

Consulate-General: Corso Massimo d'Azeglio 60, 10126 Turin; tel (11) 688653; telex 221492.
Consul-General: Carlo Bertolotti.

Consulate: Via S. Giuliano 4, 30170 Mestre, Venice; tel (41) 5059912; telex 410414.
Consul: Piero Barbini.

FRANCE

Embassy: Piazza Farnese 67, 00186 Rome; tel (6) 6565241; telex 610093; fax (6) 6547859.
Ambassador: Philippe Cuvillier.
Minister Plenipotentiary and Financial Counsellor: Pierre Achard.
Minister-Counsellor: Pierre Sellal.
Minister-Counsellor for Economic and Commercial Affairs: Guy Carron de la Carrière.
Commercial Counsellor: Olivier Moaligou.
Counsellor for Social Affairs: Sylvie Cohu.
Cultural Counsellor: Xavier North.
Deputy Cultural Counsellor: Sylvie Forbin.
Counsellor for Scientific Affairs: Jean-Louis Basdevant.
Second Counsellor: Patrick Nicoloso.
First Secretary: Pierre Voillery.
First Secretary: Marc Giacomini.
First Secretary: Michel Benard.
Second Secretary: Paul Colombani.
Military and Defence Attaché: Gen. Bernard Messana.
Air Attaché: Col Jean-Pierre Varizat.
Arms Attaché: Marc Prévôt.
Naval Attaché: Capt. Alain Tual.
Attaché (Police Liaison): Jean-Louis Lebas.
Fiscal Attaché: Shirley Avignon.
Agricultural Attaché: Anne Pacquet.

Consulate-General: Via Giulia 251, 00186 Rome; tel (6) 6542152; fax (6) 68601260.
Consul-General: Pierre Delabre.

Trade Promotion Office: Piazza Farnese 44, 00186 Rome; tel (6) 6544241; telex 610521.

Permanent Representation to FAO: Corso del Rinascimento 52, 00186 Rome; tel (6) 6865305.

Consulate-General: Piazza Ognissanti 2, 50123 Florence; tel (55) 213509; telex 580504; fax (55) 2302551.
Consul-General: Paul Copigneaux.
Vice-Consul: Gérard Grall.

Consulate-General: Corso Venezia 42, 20121 Milan; tel (2) 791406; telex 313519; fax (2) 798701.
Consul-General: Olivier de la Baume.

Consulate-General: Via Bogino 8, 10123 Turin; tel (11) 835252; fax (11) 8395859.
Consul-General: Christian Daziano.

Consulate-General: Via Garibaldi 20, 16124 Genova; tel (10) 200879.

Consulate-General: Via Francesco Crispi 31, 80121 Naples; tel (81) 7612275; fax (81) 7614883.
Consul-General: Michel Doucin.

Consulate-General: Palazzo Clary, Zattere 1397, 30123 Venice; tel (41) 5224319; fax (41) 5221798.
Consul-General: Josette Dallant.

GABON

Embassy: No. 31 Largo A. Vessela, 00199 Rome; tel (6) 3012449; telex 612264.
Ambassador: Edouard Teale.

GERMANY

Embassy: Via Po 25C, 00198 Rome; tel (6) 884741; telex 610179; fax (6) 8441812.
Ambassador and Permanent Representative (FAO/IFAD/WFP/WFC): Dr Friedrich Ruth.

Legal and Consular Department: Via F. Siacci 2/C-4, 00197 Rome; tel (6) 805187.

Consulate-General: Via San Vincenzo 4/28, Genova; CP 1296, 16100 Genova; tel (10) 590841; telex 271138; fax (10) 546457.
Consul-General: Dr Manfred Birmelin.

Consulate-General: Via Solferino 40, 20121 Milan; tel (2) 6554434; telex 312444; fax (2) 6554213.
Consul-General: Dr Manfred Steinkühler.

Consulate-General: Via Crispi 69, 80121 Naples; tel (81) 664647; telex 710064; fax (81) 7614687.
Consul-General: Helmut Hehenburger.

Consulate-General: Via Emerico Amari 124, 90139 Palermo; tel (91) 583377; telex 911179; fax (91) 6113798.

Consulate: Corso Italia 205, 52100 Arezzo; tel (575) 22225.
Honorary Consul: Gianfranco Duranti.

Consulate: Corso Cavour 40, 70121 Bari; tel (80) 544395.
Honorary Consul: Dr Angelo D'Addabbo.

Consulate: c/o Istituto di Cultura Germanica, Strada Maggiore 29, 40125 Bologna; tel (51) 225658.
Honorary Consul: Dr Lorenzo Pinotti-Quiri.

Consulate: Via Copenhagen 7, trav. Via Atene (Genneruxi), 09100 Cagliari; tel (70) 307229.
Honorary Consul: Leopold Bruder.

Consulate: Via Milano 10/A, 95128 Catania; tel (95) 386928.
Honorary Consul: Ronald Seifert.

Consulate: Borgo SS Apostoli 22, 50123 Florence; tel (55) 294722.
Honorary Consul: Horst Dedecke.

Consulate: Via S. Francesco 17/I, CP 687, 57100 Livorno; tel (586) 38008.
Honorary Consul: Ermanno Braun.

Consulate: Via San Camillo 16/18, 98100 Messina; tel (90) 364018; telex 98106.
Honorary Consul: Vittorio Misitano.

Consulate: Via Santa Chiara 10, 47037 Rimini; tel (541) 21659.
Honorary Consul: Dr Eugenio della Valle.

Consulate: Via Cellini 3, 34132 Trieste; tel (40) 68453.
Honorary Consul: Dr Roberto Hausbrandt.

Consulate: Via Bruno Buozzi 6, 10121 Turin; tel (11) 531088.
Honorary Consul: Ivana Ariella Bonelli.

Consulate: San Marco 2888, 30124 Venice; tel (41) 25100.
Honorary Consul: Dr Ettore Pietriboni.

GHANA

Embassy: Via Ostriana 4, 00199 Rome; tel (6) 8391200; telex 610270; fax (6) 8319204.
Ambassador and Permanent Representative (FAO): George Odartey Lamptey.
Minister-Counsellor and Alternate Permanent Representative (FAO): Joseph R. Turkson.
Counsellor and Head of Chancery: Leslie K. Christian.
Counsellor (Consular Affairs): J. Bartels-Kodwo.
First Secretary (Accounts): Aaron A. Quaye.

Third Secretary (Adminstration): Adelaide Agyeman.
Consulate-General: Via Soperga 6, 20127 Milan; tel (2) 6696440; telex 334006.
Honorary Consul: Mr Rizzo.

GREECE

Embassy: Via Mercadente 36, 00198 Rome; tel (6) 8549630; telex 610416; fax (6) 8415927.
Ambassador: Konstantinos Georgiou.
Counsellor: Andonios Nicolaidis.
Counsellor (Press): Ioannis Zissimos.
Counsellor (Commercial): Ioannis Tzen.
Counsellor (Cultural): Erifili Maria Sotiropoulou.
First Secretary: Panagis Anninos-Cavalierotos.
Second Secretary: Maria Diamanti.
Attaché (Commercial): Charalambos Coutsoucos.
Consulate-General: Via Turati 6, 20121 Milan; tel (2) 638624.
Consul-General: Michel B. Christides.

GUATEMALA

Embassy: Via dei Colli della Farnesina 128, 00194 Rome; tel (6) 3272632.
Ambassador: Oscar Ernesto Padilla Vidaurre.

GUINEA

Embassy: Via Adelaide Ristori 9/13, 00198 Rome; tel (6) 878989; telex 611487.
Ambassador: Almany Abdoulaye Traore (designate).
Counsellor: Ibrahima Kaba.
First Secretary: Hadiatou Sow.
Second Secretary: Oumar Cisse.
Attaché (Administrative): Soufiane Mohamed Camara.
Attaché (Chancery): Yaya Chérif.
Attaché: Paul Curtis.

HAITI

Embassy: Via Ruggero Fauro 59, 00197 Rome; tel (6) 872777.
Ambassador: Nicholas Lemithe.
Consulate: Via Cerretani 2, 50123 Florence; tel (55) 282683.
Consul: Luigi Masieri.

HOLY SEE

Apostolic Nunciature: Via Po 27-29, 00198 Rome; tel (6) 8546287; fax (6) 8549725.
Apostolic Nuncio: Mgr Luigi Poggi, Titular Archbishop of Forontoniana.
Counsellor: Mgr Alessandro D'Errico.
Office of Permanent Observer (FAO/IFAD/WFP/WFC): Piazza San Calisto 16, 00153 Rome; tel (6) 6987234.
Permanent Observer: Most Rev. Agostino Ferrari-Toniolo, Titular Bishop of Tarasa di Bizacena.
Office of Permanent Observer (World Tourism Organization): Piazza San Calisto 16, 00153 Rome; tel (6) 6987225.
Permanent Observer: Mgr Pietro Fantò.

HONDURAS

Embassy: Via Bafile 5/4, 00195 Rome; tel (6) 3581453; telex 622014.
Ambassador: Arturo Guillermo López Luna.
First Secretary (Consular Affairs): Maria Margarita Duron de Galves.
Second Secretary: Lorna Abelina Calderon Valle.
Third Secretary: Mario Gutierrez Minera.
Attaché: Mayra Aracely Reina Ortega de Titta.

HUNGARY

Embassy: Via dei Villini 12-16, 00161 Rome; tel (6) 860241; fax (6) 4403270.
Ambassador: Dr György Misur.
Counsellor: István Kovacs.
Counsellor (Commercial): Peter Lorincze.
Counsellor (Consular): Ferenc Szocs.
Counsellor (Economic): Janos Pataki.
Second Secretary: Andras Toth.
Consul-General: Ferenc David.
Hungarian Academy: Via Giulia 1, Palazzo Falconieri, 00186 Rome; tel (6) 6542052.
Counsellor (Cultural) and Director of Hungarian Academy: Dr János Kelemen.

ICELAND

Consulate-General: Via Flaminia 441, 00196 Rome; tel (6) 399796; telex 623022; fax (6) 394953.
Consul-General: Antonio La Rocca.
Consulate-General: Via Donatello 21, 3rd Floor, 20131 Milan; tel (2) 2366426.
Consul-General: Giuseppe A. Seeber.
Consulate-General: Via Duomo 348, 80133 Naples; tel (81) 260604; fax (81) 5540064.
Consul-General: Roberto Eminente.
Consulate-General: Via Romana di Quarto 103, 16147 Genova; tel (10) 387429.
Office of Secretary: Via Scottoripa 1/97, Genova; tel (10) 294760.
Consul-General: Carlo Alberto Rizzi.
Vice-Consul: Maria Cristina Rizzi.
Consulate-General: Via Calabria 36, 98100 Messina; tel (90) 718842; telex 980086; fax (90) 718474.
Consul-General: Antonino Strano.
Consulate: Viale Cadorna 37, 98100 Messina; tel (90) 714562.
Consul: Pietro Fama.
Consulate: Via Carcano 26, 10153 Turin; tel (11) 233857; telex 212512; fax (11) 238038.
Consul: Giuseppe Storaci.
Consulate: Corso Vittorio Emanuele 105, 10128 Turin; tel (11) 553438.
Vice-Consul: Luigi Spinelli.

INDIA

Embassy: Via XX Settembre 5, 00187 Rome; tel (6) 464642; telex 611274; fax (6) 4819539.
Ambassador: Kuldip Sahdev.
Consul-General: Muthu Venkataraman.

INDONESIA

Embassy: Via Campania 55, 00187 Rome; tel (6) 4755951; telex 610317.
Ambassador: Rachadi Iskandar.
Minister-Counsellor (Political): Zakaria Soeminta Atmadja.
Minister-Counsellor: Agus Gandakusuma.
Second Secretary: Deddy Sudarman.
Second Secretary (Administrative): Yunus Ali.
Third Secretary: Hertanto Achmad Supandi.
Third Secretary: Kenssy Dwi Ekaningsih.
Third Secretary: Hanggiro Setiabudi.
Third Secretary: Enoa Iskandar Yusuf.
Attaché: Sugianto Brotososanto.
Attaché: Mr Nusjirwan.
Attaché: Paiman Turnip.

IRAN

Embassy: Via della Camilluccia 651, 00135 Rome; tel (6) 3294294; telex 611337; fax (6) 3273757.
Ambassador: Hamid Abutalebi.
First Secretary: Ahmad Vojdani.
Third Secretary: Gholamreza Zangeneh.
Third Secretary: Malkek Sabet Ebrahimi Eshratabadi.
Third Secretary: Hamid Eslamizad.
Attaché: Hossein Mafi Moghaddam.

IRAQ

Embassy: Via della Camilluccia 355, 00135 Rome; tel (6) 346357; telex 622678.
Ambassador: Mohammed Said al-Sahafchali.
Counsellor: Jahid R. Ahmed.
Counsellor (Agriculture): Dr Tawfik Ahmed H. al-Meshhedani.
Counsellor (Cultural): Dr Wagaa Fiarman Mohammed.
Counsellor (Press): Salih Hashim al-Kharkhi.
Assistant Counsellor (Cultural): Abdul Salam B. Yousif.
First Secretary: Ghalib U. M. al-Doori.
Third Secretary: Adnan S. M. al-Robaie.
Attaché (Commercial): Ahmed A. H. al-Khafaji.

IRELAND

Embassy: Largo del Nazareno 3, 00187 Rome; tel (6) 6782541-5; telex 626030; fax (6) 6792354.
Ambassador: Christopher P. Fogarty.
First Secretary: Kieran Dowling.
First Secretary: John Deady.
First Secretary (Agriculture): John Gaule.
Secretary: Stephen Dawson.

ISRAEL

Embassy: Via M. Mercati 12, 00197 Rome; tel (6) 874541; telex 610412; fax (6) 3215762.
Ambassador: Mordechai Drory.
Minister: Gideon ben Ami.
Minister-Counsellor: Zippora Rimon.
Attaché: Avraham-Avi Dadon.
Attaché: David Cohen.
Consulate-General: Corso Europa 12, 20122 Milan; tel (2) 3498606; telex 312315.
Consul-General: Daniel Gal.

JAMAICA

Consulate-General: 1 Via G. Sgambati, 00198 Rome; tel (6) 866626.
Honorary Consul-General: Dr Salvatore Alfano.

JAPAN

Embassy: Via Quintino Sella 60, 00187 Rome; tel (6) 4757151; telex 610063; fax (6) 4740642.
Ambassador: Shinichiro Asao.
Minister: Noritake Kai.
Counsellor: Hisato Maruyama.
Counsellor: Tomoyuki Matsuozawa.
First Secretary: Kunio Kato.
First Secretary: Yosaiyasu Nao.
First Secretary: Masayoshi Kusuda.
First Secretary: Keiji Yamamoto.
First Secretary: Yuri Kodera.
First Secretary: Masa Yuki Takashima.
Second Secretary: Yamaoki Yoshikazu.
Consulate-General: Via 4 Fontane 15, 00184 Rome; tel (6) 460981; telex 616313; fax (6) 4820268.
Consul-General: Giuseppe Guerreri.
Consulate-General: Via F. Turati 16/18, 20121 Milan; tel (2) 6557316; telex 310452; fax (2) 6597201.
Consul-General: Minoru Iida.

JORDAN

Embassy: Via Guido d'Arezzo 5, 00198 Rome; tel (6) 857396; telex 612573.
Ambassador: Tarek K. Madi.

KENYA

Embassy: Via Icilio 14, 00153 Rome; tel (6) 5741512; telex 626537; fax (6) 5742788.
Ambassador: Dr D. D. C. Don Nanjira.
First Secretary: N. E. Kituto.
Second Secretary: P. M. Nzue.
Second Secretary: R. G. S. Solitei.

Second Secretary: D. L. Motindi.
Third Secretary: T. G. Karugu.
Attaché (Financial Affairs): V. O. Oliech.
Attaché (Administrative Affairs): S. G. M. Muriithi.
Attaché (Administrative Affairs): S. M. Minage.

KOREA, REPUBLIC

Embassy: Via Barnaba Oriani 30, 00197 Rome; tel (6) 805292; telex 610182.
Ambassador: Kim Suk Kyu.
Minister: Hwang Boo Hong.
Minister: Song Jae Yoo.
Counsellor: Moon Byung Rok.
First Secretary: Yoo Chul Hyung.
Second Secretary: Park Kang Ho.
Second Secretary and Consul: Kim Kyung Surk.
Attaché (Agriculture): Won Kwang Sik.
Attaché (Cultural): Nam In Kie.
Attaché and Vice-Consul: Kim Mee Ok.
Attaché and Vice-Consul: Cho Min Ho.

KUWAIT

Embassy: Via Archimede 124, 00197 Rome; tel (6) 874419; telex 620426.
Ambassador: Ahmad Ghaith Abdullah.

LEBANON

Embassy: Via Giacomino Carissimi 38, 00198 Rome; tel (6) 8416631; telex 622476; fax (6) 8411794.
Ambassador: Gen. Ahmed el-Hajj.
Counsellor: Dr Mounir Khoraych.
Counsellor: Adnan al-Kadi.

Consulate-General: Via Larga 26, 20121 Milan; tel (2) 8050345.
Consul-General: Saïd Bitar.

LESOTHO

Embassy: Via di Porta Pertusa 4, 00165 Rome; tel (6) 6378183; telex 625838; fax (6) 633490.
Ambassador: Gerard Phirinyane Khojane.
Counsellor: Masuhla Humphrey Leteka.
First Secretary: T. F. Adoro.
Third Secretary: T. M. Pheko.
Attaché: G. M. Leokaoke.

Consulate-General: Ritz Hotel, Rome; tel (6) 803751; fax (6) 633490.
Consul-General: Mr Puccini.

Consulate-General: Milan; tel (2) 7600006.
Consul-General: P. Brambilla.

LIBERIA

Embassy: Viale Bruno Buozzi 64, 00197 Rome; tel (6) 805810; telex 612569.
Ambassador: Gabriel Tarr Myers.

LIBYA

Embassy: Via Nomentana 365, 00162 Rome; tel (6) 830951; telex 611114.
Ambassador: Abd ur-Rahman M. Shalgam.

LUXEMBOURG

Embassy: Via Guerrieri 3, 00153 Rome; tel (6) 5780456; telex 622532; fax (6) 5744874.
Ambassador: Nicolas Mosar.
Secretary and Vice-Consul: Raymond Dutreux.

MADAGASCAR

Embassy: Via Riccardo Zandonai 84A, 00194 Rome; tel (6) 3275183; telex 622526; fax (6) 3294306.
Minister Plenipotentiary and Chargé d'affaires a.i.: René Gilbert Ralison.
Counsellor for Agricultural Affairs: Raphaël Rabe.
Counsellor for Economic and Commercial Affairs: Charles Raharison.
Counsellor for Cultural and Social Affairs: Bruno Joseph.
First Secretary (General Affairs): Folo Jaona.
Attaché (Consular Affairs): Maurice Ravo.
Attaché (Financial Affairs): Angèle Joséphine Ralalanirainy.
Attaché (Administrative Affairs): Daniel Boafa Andriamaharosoa.

Consulate: Via S. Lorenzo 21/9, 16123 Genova; tel (10) 297634; fax (10) 290468.
Honorary Consul: Ermanno Carbone.

Consulate: Via Ariberto 15, 20123 Milan; tel (10) 8321768; fax (10) 8353657.
Honorary Consul: Gianfranco Boveri.

MALAWI

Consulate: Via F. S. Nitti 3, Rome; tel (6) 391942.
Honorary Consul: Franco Musco.

MALAYSIA

Embassy: Via Nomentana 297, 00162 Rome; tel (6) 855764; telex 611035.
Ambassador: Datuk Ismail bin Budin.
Trade Commissioner: Harith bin Ibrahim.

MALI

Consulate: Largo Ponchilli 8, 00198 Rome; tel (6) 8543537.
Honorary Consul: Mr Menaguale.

MALTA

Embassy: Lungotevere Marzio 12, 00186 Rome; tel (6) 6879990; telex 611205; fax (6) 6892687.
Ambassador: Maurice Abela.
Counsellor: Adrian Mercieca.
Second Secretary: Dr Abraham Borg.
Second Secretary and Consul: Anthony Galea.
Attaché: Anthony Bonnici.

Consulate-General: Via Cesare Fracassini 4, 00196 Rome; tel (6) 3273926.
Honorary Consul-General: Dr Michele Pandolfo.

Consulate: Corso Vittorio Emanuele 132, Barletta, Bari; tel (883) 519314; fax (883) 303096.
Honorary Consul: Dr Matteo Bonadies.

Consulate: Corso Martiri della Libertà 14, 95131 Catania; tel (95) 310611; telex 970157; fax (95) 551033.
Honorary Consul: Ferdinando Cali.

Consulate: Via Dell'Orivolo 45, 50122 Florence; tel (55) 217874; fax (55) 2302937.
Honorary Consul: Dr Carlo Pasquinelli.

Consulate: Via XX Settembre 41, 16121 Genova; tel (10) 561103; telex 270086; fax (10) 532809.
Honorary Consul: Dr Paolo U. Cosulich.

Consulate: Portici S. Bernardino 2, 67100 L'Aquila; tel (862) 411068.
Consul-General: Luigi Lombardo.

Consulate: CP 373, Scali d'Azeglio 52, 57123 Livorno; tel (586) 897121; telex 500093; fax (586) 894474.
Honorary Consul: Giorgio Vincenzini.

Consulate-General: Via Larga 7, 20122 Milan; tel (2) 863800; fax (2) 804486.
Honorary Consul-General: Mario Cal.

Consulate: Viale Tunisia 41, 20124 Milan; tel (2) 6595129.
Honorary Consul: Dr Massimo Pini.

Consulate-General: Via Nuova Ponte di Tappia 82, 80133 Naples; tel (81) 5521573; telex 710450; fax (81) 5521183.
Honorary Consul-General: Dr Michele Di Gianni.

Consulate: Via Principe di Belmonte 55, 90139 Palermo; tel (91) 586533; telex 910093.
Honorary Consul: Dr Alfredo Barbaro.

Consulate: Via Gramsci 14/5, 17100 Savona; tel (19) 821404; telex 281184; fax (19) 821403.
Honorary Vice-Consul: Mario Vagnola.

Consulate-General: Corso Stati Uniti 67, 10129 Turin; tel (11) 535551.
Honorary Consul-General: Dr Sebastiano Cossu.
Honorary Consul: Prof. Paul Zammit-Lewis.

Consulate: Via Rittmeyer 5, 34134 Trieste; tel (40) 363324.
Honorary Consul: Dr Aldo Panizzoli.
Honorary Vice-Consul: Armando Panizzoli.

Consulate: Piazzale Europa 1/6, 31046 Odorzo, Venice; tel (41) 5222644.
Honorary Consul: Dr Lorenzo Favero.

MAURITIUS

Consulate: Rome; tel (6) 5037072.
Honorary Consul: Denis Cangy.

MEXICO

Embassy: Via Lazzaro Spallanzani 16, 00161 Rome; tel (6) 4402757; telex 625279; fax (6) 4403876.
Ambassador: Francisco Javier Alejo.
Counsellor: Dr Myriam Zepeda Herrera.
Counsellor: Miguel Angel Caceres.
Counsellor (Cultural): Jaime Nualart Sanchez.
Third Secretary (Commercial): Carlos Garcia de Alba.
Consul: Socrates Gudino Astudillo.
Attaché: Patricia Romandia de Jacchia.
Attaché: Laura Esther Quinianilla Casas.

Consulate-General: Via Cappuccini 4, 20122 Milan; tel (2) 790541; telex 334021.
Consul-General: Alma Patricia Soria Ayuso.

MONACO

Embassy: Via Bertoloni 36, 00197 Rome; tel (6) 8083361; fax (6) 877692.
Ambassador: René Novella.

MOROCCO

Embassy: Via Lazzaro Spallanzani 8/10, 00161 Rome; tel (6) 4402506; telex 620854; fax (6) 4402695.
Ambassador: Zine El Abidine Sebti.
Minister Plenipotentiary: Mohamed Sbihi.
First Counsellor: Mustapha Menouar Sinaceur.
Naval Attaché: Capt. El Mostafa Samir.
First Counsellor: Abdesselam Baita.
Counsellor: Mohamed Ahabchane.
Secretary: Norreddine Radhi.
Secretary: Mohamed Mouadi.
Secretary: Abdellatif El Qamcaoui.
Secretary: Abdesselem Arifi.
Secretary: Fouad Akhrif.
Secretary: Wafaa Zniber.
Attaché: Ahmed Bidara.

Consulate-General: Via Boscovich 31, 20124 Milan; tel (2) 6694521; telex 323512.
Consul-General: Mohamed Benhsain.

MYANMAR

Embassy: Via Bellini 20, 00198 Rome; tel (6) 8549374; telex 625103; fax (6) 8413167.
Ambassador: U Thein Toe.

NETHERLANDS

Embassy: Via Michele Mercati 8, 00197 Rome; tel (6) 873141; telex 610138.
Ambassador: Piet-Hein Houben.
Minister: Hans R. van der Valk.
Counsellor (Economic): Wim Kluft.
Counsellor (Cultural): Ted J. Meijer.

Counsellor (Agriculture): Frans J. B. Bruins.
First Secretary (Consular): P. Uiterlinden.
Second Secretary: Robert in den Bosch.
Second Secretary (Administrative): H. J. Simons.
Attaché: Antoine C. van Arnheim.
Attaché (Agriculture): A. C. van Arnheim.

Consulate-General: Via Cavour 81, 50129 Florence; tel (55) 475249; telex 570130.
Consul-General: Nikolaus Alexander Kamp.

NEW ZEALAND

Embassy: Via Zara 28, 00198 Rome; tel (6) 4402928; telex 626615; fax (6) 4402984.
Ambassador: Peter Robert Bennett.
First Secretary and Vice-Consul: David Luxton.
First Secretary (Commercial): Jane Cunliffe.
Attaché: Norma Sawers.
Public Affairs Officer: A. Giovanardi.

NICARAGUA

Embassy: Via Brescia 16, 00198 Rome; tel (6) 865476; telex 626575.
Ambassador: Orestes Papi.

NIGERIA

Embassy: Via Orazio 14-18, 00198 Rome; tel (6) 6531048; telex 610666.
Ambassador: Judith Attah.
Permanent Representative (FAO): F. Bature.
Minister-Counsellor (Political/Economic): E. Egbara.
Minister-Counsellor (Political): Okun Ayodeji.
Counsellor and Head of Chancery: A. Ladepo.

NORWAY

Embassy: Via delle Terme Deciane 71, 00153 Rome; tel (6) 5755833; telex 610585; fax (6) 5742115.
Ambassador: Torbjørn Christiansen.
Minister-Counsellor: Birger Bye.
First Secretary: Arne Gjermundsen.
First Secretary: Eivind S. Homme.

Commercial Centre: Piazza Castello 20, 20121 Milan; tel (2) 867851; telex 320095; fax (2) 8693015.

OMAN

Embassy: Via Enrico Petrella 4, 00198 Rome; tel (6) 8848038; telex 612524.
Ambassador: Ahmed bin Mohammed bin Rashid.
First Secretary: Aflah Sulieman al-Tai.
Second Secretary: Mohamed Abdulla Khamis al-Sarrai.

PAKISTAN

Embassy: Via della Camilluccia 682, 00135 Rome; tel (6) 3276775; telex 353403; fax (6) 3276936.
Ambassador: Mian Riaz Samee.
Counsellor: Rab Nawaz Khan.
Counsellor (Agriculture): Muhammad Saleem Khan.
Third Secretary: Shah M. Jamal.
Secretary (Press): Ikram Ullah Jan.

Commercial Consulate: Piazzale Giulio Cesare, 20145 Milan; telex 353403.
Consul: Jalil Abbas.

PANAMA

Embassy: Via del Vignola 39, 00196 Rome; tel (6) 3619587; telex 622670.
Minister and Chargé d'affaires a.i.: Mayra Ivankovich Anzola.

PARAGUAY

Embassy: Via Emilio de Cavalieri 12, 00198 Rome; tel (6) 8448236.
Ambassador: Aníbal Fernández.

PERU

Embassy: Via Po 22, 00198 Rome; tel (6) 8417265; telex 612298; fax (6) 8444496.
Ambassador: Manuel A. Roca-Zela.

PHILIPPINES

Embassy: Via di San Valentino 12-14, 00197 Rome; tel (6) 8083530; telex 612104; fax (6) 8084219.
Ambassador: José V. Romero, Jr.
Third Secretary and Vice-Consul: Eleanor L. Jaucian.
Attaché (Legal Affairs): Antonio A. Alon.
Attaché: Erlinda I. Nicolas.
Attaché: Lourdes E. Martínez.
Attaché (Administrative and Cultural Affairs): William G. García.
Attaché (Financial Affairs): Lyrie F. Fulgencio.
Attaché: Orlando J. Panlican.
Attaché: Virginia A. Vicente.
Attaché: Angelica H. Ramos.
Attaché: Titus C. Inton.
Attaché: Amado P. Desiderio.
Attaché (Commercial Affairs): Emmanuel P. Ortencio.
Defence and Armed Forces Attaché: Col Marte S. Chioco.
Labour Attaché: Dante G. Ardivilla.
Agricultural Attaché: Victoriano B. Leviste.
Agricultural Attaché: Horacio M. Carandang.

Consulate-General: Via Cairoli 1, 16124 Genova; tel (10) 200528; fax (10) 202812.
Honorary Consul-General: Dr Filippo Cerruti.

Consulate-General: Via XX Settembre 24, 20123 Milan; (2) 48013099; fax (2) 48013053.
Honorary Consul-General: Dr Camillo Clivio.

Consulate-General: Via dei Fiorentini 21, 80133 Naples; tel (81) 5520489; fax (81) 5524389.
Honorary Consul-General: Dr Giovanni Carrino.

POLAND

Embassy: Via Pietro Paolo Rubens 20, 00197 Rome; tel (6) 3224455; telex 610325; fax (6) 3217895.
Ambassador: Bolesław Michałek.
Counsellor (Political Affairs): Tadeusz Konopka.
Counsellor (Economic Affairs): Kazimierz Klek.
Counsellor (Political Affairs): Jan Ludwik Wdowik.
Counsellor (Press): Elżbieta Jogałła.
Counsellor (Economic Affairs): Marian Minkiewicz.
First Secretary (Cultural Affairs): Alicja Cieżkowska.
First Secretary (Administration): Jerzy Biżewski.
First Secretary (FAO): Tadeusz Strojwas.
Second Secretary (Cultural Affairs): Krzysztof Szczepanik.
Second Secretary (Consular Affairs): Ewa Szapiro.
Third Secretary (Political Affairs): Tadeusz Dadura.

Consulate-General: Via Sporting Mirasole 2, 20090 Noverasco di Opera, Milan; tel (2) 57602241; telex 316472; fax (2) 57602245.
Consul-General: Lucjan Polak.

PORTUGAL

Embassy: Via Giacinta Pezzana 9, 00197 Rome; tel (6) 878016; telex 612304.
First Secretary and Chargé d'affaires a.i.: José Manuel Pessanha Viegas.
Counsellor: Augusto Goncalves Pedro.
Counsellor (Cultural): Eduardo Lovrenco de Faria.
Third Secretary: Henrique M. J. Verdadez Dinis da Gama.
Attaché (Commercial): Alexandre Manuel da Silva.
Attaché (Economic): Jorge Coimbra Martins.

ROMANIA

Embassy: Via Nicolò Tartaglia 36, 00197 Rome; tel (6) 804567; telex 61249.
Chargé d'affaires a.i.: Gheorghe Iu Liu Pancratiu Gheorghu.
Counsellor: Victor Chiujdea.
First Secretary: Ion Negescu.
Attaché: Corneliu A. Fanateanu.
First Secretary: Sorin E. Constantinescu.
First Secretary: Ioan Toma.
First Secretary: Vasile Donea.
Second Secretary: Gheorghe Milosan.

RUSSIA

Embassy: Via Gaeta 5, 00185 Rome; tel (6) 4743989; telex 611286.
Ambassador: Anatoli L. Adamishin.

Consular Section: Via Nomentana 116, Rome; telex 622310.
Consul-General: Valery Keniaiakin.

Consulate-General: Via Sant'Aquilino 3, Milan; tel (2) 4046741; telex 326571.

Consulate-General: Via Ghirardelli Pescetto 16, Nervi, Genova; tel (10) 326047; telex 272899.

SAN MARINO

Embassy: Via Eleonora Duse 35, 00197 Rome; tel (6) 8084567; fax (6) 870072.
Ambassador: Savina Zafferani.
Cultural Adviser: Giorgio Veronesi.

Consulate-General: Via Ermete Novelli 12, 00197 Rome; tel (6) 804567; fax (6) 874582.
First Secretary and Consul-General: Tarcisio Arzilli.

Consulate: Via A. Nini 8, 61032 Ancona; tel (39) 878661.
Consul: Tullio Tonnini.
Chancellor: Nicolò de Vito.

Consulate: Via Putignani 236, 70122 Bari; tel (80) 210554.
Consul: Francesco Saverio Lonero.

Consulate: Via Zamboni 8, 40126 Bologna; tel (51) 269625.
Consul: Gian Emilio Santi.
Vice-Consul: Roberto Nicolini.
Chancellor: Dino Fontana.

Consulate: Via Roma 3, 50123 Florence; tel (55) 280864.
Consul-General: Galliano Boldrini.
Vice-Consul: Luigi Rogantini.

Consulate: Via Avio 2/20, 16151 Genova; tel (10) 414587.
Consul: Roberto Muratori.
Chancellor: Ida Bollina Canepa.

Consulate: Via San Marino 12/A, 20122 Milan; tel (2) 8383; telex 331082; fax (2) 8394594.
Ministerand Consul: Franco Dompe' di Olmeda.

Consulate: Via Monte di Dio 25, 80132 Naples; tel (81) 425540; fax (81) 7623993.
Consul: Vittorio Torino.

Consulate: Via A. Zirardini 24, 48100 Ravenna; tel (544) 37086.
Consul: Marino Forcellini.

Consulate: Via Calatafimi 20, 47037 Rimini; tel (541) 782606.
Consul: Giovanni Conti.
Vice-Consul: Massimo Augusto Corbelli.

Consulate: Corso Duca degli Abbruzzi 69, 10129 Turin; tel (11) 596618.
Consul: Franco Vincenti.

Vice-Consul: Giuliano Giusti.

Consulate: Via delle Milizie 9, 34139 Trieste; tel (40) 942893.
Consul: Fabrizio Silvagni.

Consulate: San Marco 5017/A, 30124 Venice; tel (41) 5228239.
Consul: Giancarlo Mel.
Chancellor: Giuseppina Conti.

SAUDI ARABIA

Embassy: Via G. B. Pergolesi 9, 00198 Rome; tel (6) 868161; telex 613115.
Ambassador: Khaled an-Nasser at-Turki.
Second Secretary: Abdulaziz I. al-Ghadeer.
Second Secretary: Turki al-Madi.

SENEGAL

Embassy: Via Lisbona 3, 00198 Rome; tel (6) 859497; telex 612522.
Ambassador: Youssoupii Baro.
Counsellor: Daouda Maligueye Sene.
Counsellor: Cheikh Tidiane Dieye.
Counsellor: Louis Gomis.
First Secretary: Mayoro Diop.
First Secretary: Jean Jacques Bienvenu.
First Secretary: Abdoulaye Seck.
Secretary: Edgar B. Gueye.
Attaché: Paul Ndour.

SIERRA LEONE

Consulate: Via Francesco Carrara 30, 00196 Rome.
Honorary Consul: Marco Adami.

Consulate: Via Gen. Orsini 42, 80320 Naples.
Honorary Consul-General: Dr Elio Pacifico.

SOMALIA

Embassy: Via dei Villini 9-11, 00161 Rome; tel (6) 853740; telex 613123.
Ambassador: Muhammad Muhamoud Abdullah.

SOUTH AFRICA

Embassy: Via Tanaro 14, 00198 Rome; tel (6) 8419794; telex 621667; fax (6) 8840848.
Ambassador: Glen Babb.
Counsellor (Political): Dennis A. G. Casale.
Counsellor (Administration): Jack La Grange.
Counsellor (Information): Clara Woerner.
First Secretary: J. J. Rankin.
First Secretary: C. H. van Tonder.
Third Secretary (Consular): Estelle Joubert.

Commercial Section: fax (6) 8840848.
Counsellor (Trade): Dana J. du Rand.
Third Secretary (Trade): P. C. Venter.

Consulate-General: Vicolo S. Giovanni Sul Muro 4, CP 1468, 20121 Milan; tel (2) 809036; telex 331699; fax (2) 866402.
Consul-General: Roland W. Darroll.
Vice-Consul (Consular): Ideon Koekemoer.

Commercial Section: fax (2) 72002834.
Consul (Trade): G. S. Scribante.
Vice-Consul (Trade): P. C. Venter.

Consulate: Via Formentini 1, 20121 Milan; tel (2) 861929.
Honorary Consul: M. Smith.

Consulate: Viale Miramare 9, 34100 Trieste; tel (40) 44686; telex 460186; fax (40) 421739.
Honorary Consul: I. Argamante.

Consulate: Via Tommaso Campanella 9/2, 16146 Genova; tel (10) 315129; fax (10) 314416.
Honorary Consul: Dr M. Ercolani.

Consulate: Corso Umberto I 9/11, 80138 Naples; tel (81) 206931; telex 71256.
Honorary Consul: Dr A. Musella.

SPAIN

Embassy: Palazzo Borghese, Largo Fontenella Borghese 19, 00186 Rome; tel (6) 6878172; telex 626126; fax (6) 6872256.
Ambassador: Emilio Menéndez del Valle.

Consulate-General: Via Campo Marzio 34, 00186 Rome; tel (6) 6784673.
Consul-General: Santiago Martínez Caro.

SRI LANKA

Embassy: Via Giuseppe Cuboni 618, 00197 Rome; tel (6) 805362; telex 612602.
Ambassador: Chandra Nawaratne de Zoysa.

SUDAN

Embassy: Via di Porta Ardeatina 1, 00184 Rome; tel (6) 7573344; telex 610302.
Ambassador: Abd al-A'As-Sinada.

SWEDEN

Embassy: CP 7201, 00100 Rome-Nomentano; Piazza Rio de Janeiro 3, 00161 Rome; tel (6) 4402721; telex 610264; fax (6) 4402771.
Ambassador: Ola Ullsten.
Minister: Carl Johan Persson.
Counsellor: Ingemar Börjesson.
Counsellor: Sture Theolin.
First Secretary (Consular and Administrative Affairs): Göran Akander.
Second Secretary: Helena Sångeland.
Counsellor (Agricultural Affairs): Tommie Sjöberg.

Consulate: Via Cialdini 57, 60122 Ancona; tel (71) 200252; telex 560047; fax (71) 56752.
Consul: Arrigo Archibugi.

Consulate: Via Calefati 37, CP 301, 70100 Bari; tel (80) 5244442; telex 810045; fax (80) 5245243.
Consul: Antonio Morfini.

Consulate: Via Sonnino 152, CP 218, 09100 Cagliari; tel (70) 651669; telex 630565.
Consul: Raffaele Torchiani.

Consulate: Via della Scala 4, 50123 Florence; tel (55) 2396865; telex 574369; fax (55) 2396865.
Consul: Manfred Erwin Poettinger.
Vice-Consul: Ulla Annika Lindgren.

Consulate: Via Cogorano 25, 57123 Livorno; tel (586) 894132; telex 590055.
Consul: Guglielmo Capanna.

Consulate: Via G. La Farina 183, 98100 Messina; tel (90) 2932121; telex 980046.
Consul: Ruggero Roberto.

Consulate: Naples.
Vice-Consul: Birgit Margareta Pagnotta.

Consulate: Via Roma 489, 90139 Palermo; tel (91) 581521; telex 910031; fax (91) 581230.
Consul: Salvatore De Luca.

Consulate: Villa San Michele, Via Capodimonte 32, 80071 Anacapri; tel (81) 8371401.
Vice-Consul: Levente András Sandór Erdeös.

Consulate: Villaggio La Serra, 81030 Baia Domizia; tel (823) 930003; telex 710174.
Vice-Consul: Hans Lennart Wikström.

Consulate: Riva del Sole, 58043 Castiglione della Pescaia; tel (564) 933560; telex 500034; fax (564) 935607.
Vice-Consul: Klas Erik Kjällquist.

Consulate: Piazza Vittorio Veneto 6, 91100 Trapani; tel (923) 21121.
Vice-Consul: Carmelo Solina.

Consulate-General: Via Maurizio Gonzaga 7, 20123 Milan; CP 1293, 20100 Milan; tel (2) 8690613; telex 312240; fax (2) 72002426.
Consul-General: Tom Engdahl.
Vice-Consul: Karin Hedgårds.
Chancellor: Maja Lena Alldahl.
Scientific and Technological Attaché: Daniel Mascanzoni.

Swedish Commercial Centre: tel (2) 875268; telex 311420; fax (2) 72001339.
Commercial Secretary: Anna Erlandsson.

Consulate-General: Piazzetta Jacopo da Varagine 1/48B, CP 493, 16100 Genova; tel (10) 293583; telex 281296; fax (10) 282428.
Consul-General: Erik Olof Pihlgren.
Consul: Mario Viali.

Consulate: Via Francesco Crispi 39A/4, 19100 La Spezia; tel (187) 32040; telex 270482; fax (187) 27223.
Consul: Giorgio Santiago Bucchioni.

Consulate: Via Porta Aurea 43, 48100 Ravenna; tel (544) 22639; fax (544) 451730.
Consul: Gian Carlo Marcello Baldini.

Consulate: Corso Marconi 208, c/o Hotel Bobby, 18038 San Remo; tel (184) 60255; telex 271249; fax (184) 60296.
Consul: Eva Gulli Ing-Britt Ghirardelli.

Consulate: Via Famagosta 15/1, CP 200, 17100 Savona; tel (19) 812475; telex 270393; fax (19) 822511.
Consul: Stefano Ami Arecco.

Consulate: Viale Miramare 5, 34135 Trieste; tel (40) 4193155; telex 460171; fax (40) 44263.
Consul: Francesco Stanislao Parisi.

Consulate-General: Corso Vittorio Emanuele 11, 48, 10123 Turin; tel (11) 8126950; fax (11) 8126860.
Consul-General: Gian Mario Rossignolo.
Consul: Sergio Eynard.
Chancellor: Per-Olof Kjellberg.

Consulate: Piazzale Roma 499, 30125 Venice; tel (41) 791611; telex 410068; fax (41) 791661.
Consul: Giancarlo Ligabue.
Vice-Consul: Massimo Casarin.
Chancellor: Renata Nani.

SWITZERLAND

Embassy: Via Barnaba Oriani 61, 00197 Rome; tel (6) 803641; telex 610304; fax (6) 8870510.
Ambassador and Permanent Representative (FAO/WFP/WFC): Francesca Pometta.
Minister and Consul-General: Wilhelm Schmid.
Counsellor (Economic Affairs): Armin Ritz.
Counsellor (Cultural Affairs): Pierre Chrzanovski.
First Secretary: Yvana Enzler.
Consul and Head of Chancery: Ferruccio Beltrametti.
Defence Attaché: Col Silvio Streun.
Permanent Representative (FAO/WFP/WFC): Rudolph De Pourtalès.

Consulate: Piazzale Galileo 5, 50125 Florence; tel (55) 222431; telex 573075.
Honorary Consul: Gerardo Kraft.

Consulate-General: Piazza Brignole 3/6, 16122 Genova; CP 195, 16100 Genova; tel (10) 565620; fax (10) 562632.
Consul-General: Bernard Equey.
Vice-Consul and Chancellor: Giancarlo Fenini.

Consulate-General: Via Palestro 2, 20121 Milan; tel (2) 76009284; telex 353052; fax (2) 76014296.
Deputy Consul-General: Fritz Von Ins.
Vice-Consul and Chancellor: Max Thomann.

Consulate: c/o Pneumofore SpA, Via Sagra S. Michele 66, 10141 Turin; tel (11) 715570; telex 221104; fax (11) 720033.
Honorary Consul: Roberto Hilfiker.

Consulate: Via Pergolesi 1, 80122 Naples; tel (81) 7614390; fax (81) 209440.
Consul: Renzo Meda.
Chancellor: Pierre-Michel Quendoz.

Consulate: Piazza Cavour 36, 95128 Catania; tel (95) 447884.
Honorary Consul: Enrico Ritter.

Consulate: Dorsoduro 810, Campo S. Agnese, 30123 Venice; CP 394, 30100 Venice; tel (41) 5203944.
Consul-General: Giulio Cattaneo.
Vice-Consul and Chancellor: Susanne Amberg.

SYRIA

Embassy: Piazza dell'Ara Coeli, 00186 Rome; tel (6) 6797791; telex 613083.
Ambassador: Burhan Kaial.

TANZANIA

Embassy: Via G. B. Vico 9, 00196 Rome; tel (6) 3610901; telex 612286; fax (6) 3222079.
Ambassador: Abbas Kleist Sykes.

THAILAND

Embassy: Via Nomentana 132, 00162 Rome; tel (6) 8320729; telex 616297; fax (6) 8322275.
Ambassador: Manaspas Xuto.
Minister: Piswong Anukrahanond.
Minister-Counsellor: Powthep Vanachinda.
Consul-General: Colchineepan Chiranond.

Office of the Naval Attaché: tel (6) 5090119.
Naval Attaché: Capt. Nara Seungthaworn.

Office of Agricultural Counsellor: tel (6) 4402234.
Agricultural Counsellor: Vanrob Isarankura.

Office of Commercial Counsellor: Via del Serafico 135, 00142 Rome; tel (6) 5030804; telex 613515; fax (6) 5035225.
Commercial Counsellor: Mongkol Somkanae.

Tourism Authority of Thailand: Ente Nazionale per il Turismo Thailandese, Via Barberini 50, 00187 Rome; tel (6) 4747410; telex 626139; fax (6) 4747660.
Director: Amornsak Pimonmanomai.

Thai Trade Centre: Via Pier Luigi Da Palestrina 4, 20124 Milan; tel (2) 66981756; fax (2) 66981753.
Director of Trade Centre: Wipasri Chalaprawat.

Consulate-General: Viale Berengario 15, 20149 Milan; tel (2) 4988439; fax (2) 4986511.
Consul-General: Cesare Virgilio.

Consulate-General: Via D. Fiasella 4, 16121 Genova; tel (10) 593371; fax (10) 543342.
Consul-General: Franco Novi.

Consulate-General: Viale Virgilio 5, 80132 Naples; tel (81) 7690959; fax (81) 5536107.
Consul-General: Igor Suprina-Petrovic.

Consulate-General: Via della Consolata 8, 10122 Turin; tel (11) 518527; fax (11) 518527.
Consul-General: Bodo di Albaretto.

TUNISIA

Embassy: Via Asmara 7, 00199 Rome; tel (6) 8390748; telex 610190.
Ambassador: Noureddine Mejdoub.

TURKEY

Embassy: Via Palestro 28, 00185 Rome; tel (6) 4941549; telex 612131.
Ambassador: Necdet Tezel.
Counsellor (Press): Selcuk Bakkalbasi.
Counsellor (Cultural): Guman Kiziltan.
Counsellor (Finance): Cevdet Yalcin.
Counsellor (Economic/Commercial): Hilmi Bulent Payasliogl u.
Counsellor (Economic/Commercial): Oktay Elgin.
Counsellor: Bulent Gokay.
First Secretary: Hasan Aygun.
First Secretary: Kemal Demirciler.

Consulate-General: Via S. Barnaba 30, 20122 Milan; tel (2) 5513370.
Consul-General: Ergul Gokcen.

UNITED ARAB EMIRATES

Embassy: Via S. Crescenziano 25, 00199 Rome; tel (6) 8391126; telex 622671; fax (6) 8380844.
Counsellor, Chargé d'affaires a.i.: Mohammed Saeed al-Jarrah.
First Secretary and Consul: Mohammed Salem al-Suweidi.

UNITED KINGDOM

Embassy: Via XX Settembre 80A, 00187 Rome; tel (6) 4825441; telex 626119; fax (6) 4873324.
Ambassador: Sir Stephen Egerton.
Minister: T. C. Wood.
Defence and Military Attaché: Brig. A. R. Jones.
Naval Attaché: Capt. W. C. McKnight.
Air Attaché: Group Capt. A. R. Tolcher.
Counsellor (Political and Management): G. M. Gowlland.
Counsellor (Political): J. P. Watson.
Counsellor (Economic/Commercial): C. R. L. de Chassiron.
Counsellor (British Council Director): K. R. Hunter.
First Secretary (Economic): N. K. Darroch.
First Secretary (Political): J. Ashton.
First Secretary (Economic): J. A. Towner.
First Secretary (Management): C. W. G. Edmonds Brown.
First Secretary (Agriculture/Environment): M. E. Smith.
First Secretary (Social Affairs/Science/Technology): D. J. Hollamby.
First Secretary (Commercial): H. Kershaw.
First Secretary (Consul): G. Roberts.
First Secretary (Information): K. Coombs.
First Secretary (Political): R. J. C. Allen.
Assistant Defence Attaché: Maj. I. W. Jefferson.
Second Secretary (Management): C. J. Ley.
Third Secretary (Chancery): K. J. Stanton.

Consulate: Lungarno Corsini 2, 50123 Florence; tel (55) 212594; telex 570270; fax (55) 219112.
Consul: Mary Louise Croll.
Vice-Consul: Enzo Masi.

Consulate-General: Via San Paolo 7, 20121 Milan; tel (2) 8693442; telex 310528; fax (2) 72020153.
Consul-General and Director General for British Trade Development in Italy: P. H. D. Wetton.
Deputy Consul-General and Consul (Commercial): R. J. Griffiths.
Consul (Commercial): J. L. Blakemore.
Consul (Information): J. H. Halley.
Vice-Consul (Management): D. Lusher.

Consulate: Via XII Ottobre 2/123, 16121 Genova; tel (10) 564833; telex 270689; fax (10) 5531516.
Consul: M. A. Wicks.

Consulate: Corso Massimo d'Azeglio 60, 10126 Turin; tel (11) 683921; telex 221464; fax (11) 6699848.
Consul: D. H. Price.

Consulate: Accademia 1051, Dorsoduro, Venice; POB 679, 30100 Venice; tel (41) 5227207; telex 410283; fax (41) 5222617.
Consul: M. H. Gluckstern.

Consulate: Vicolo delle Ville 16, 34100 Trieste; tel (40) 302884.
Honorary Consul: Maj. N. J. Lister.

Consulate-General: Via Francesco Crispi 122, 80122 Naples; tel (81) 663511; telex 710330; fax (81) 7613720.
Consul-General: R. C. G. Harrison.

Consulate: Anglo-Italian Shipping, Via Montenegro 19, 70121 Bari; tel (80) 5217859; telex 812269; fax (80) 5244024.
Honorary Consul: D. H. Gavan.

Consulate: The British School, Via de Terribile 9, 72100 Brindisi; tel (831) 568340; fax (831) 568340.
Honorary Consul: F. Gentile.

Representation to FAO: Rome.
Permanent Representative (FAO): J. R. Goldsack.

USA

Embassy: Via Vittorio Veneto 119A, 00187 Rome; tel (6) 46741; telex 622322; fax (6) 46742356.
Ambassador: Peter F. Secchia.
Deputy Chief of Mission: Daniel P. Serwer.
Political Section: John S. Brims.
Political/Military Section: Douglas L. McElhaney.
Economic Section: Kevin J. McGuire.
Commercial Section: Emilio Iodice.
Consul: Edward Kreuser.
Administrative Section: Donald R. Schoeb.
Regional Security Officer: Bernhard B. Collins, Jr.
Communications Programme Officer: Robert Hammond.
Information Systems Manager: John Dieffenderfer.
Scientific Attaché: Reno Leon Harrish III.
Office of the Defence Attaché: Capt. James F. Chandler.
Office of Defence Co-operation: Col Joel A. Gruwell.
Agricultural Section: Frank J. Piason.
Labour Officer: William B. Harbin.
Customs Service (Treasury): James P. McShane.
Federal Aviation Administration: James T. Murphy.
Financial Attaché (Treasury): Llewelyn Pascoe.
Internal Revenue Service: Frederick Pablo.

US Information Service: Via Boncompagni 2, 00187 Rome; fax (6) 46742655.
Public Affairs Officer: Jodie Lewinsohn.

Consulate-General: Banca d'America e d'Italia Bldg, Piazza Portello 6, 16124 Genova; tel (10) 282741; telex 270234; fax (10) 290027.
Consul-General: Anthony Leggio.
Branch Public Affairs Officer: Linda Cheatam.

Consulate-General: Via Principe Amedeo 2/10, 20121 Milan; tel (2) 29004559; telex 330208; fax (2) 29001165.
Consul-General: Peter Semler.
Deputy Principal Officer/Economic Section: Sharon J. Mercurio.
Consul: Celio F. Sandate.
Administrative Section: Robert I. Weisberg.
Regional Security Officer: Robert J. Nuernberger.
Communications Programme Officer: Antonio J. González.
Agricultural Section: Stan Cohen.
Customs Service (Treasury): Raphael G. López.

Commercial Section: Centro Cooperazione Internazionale, Piazzale Giulio Cesare, 20145 Milan; tel (2) 4982241; fax (2) 4982241.
Commercial Section: Peter B. Alois.

Information Service: Via Bigli 11/A, 20121 Milan; tel (2) 795051; fax (2) 781736.
Branch Public Affairs Officer: Patrick J. Corcoran.

Consulate-General: Piazza della Repubblica, 80122 Naples; tel (81) 7614303; fax (81) 7611869.
Consul-General: Emil P. Ericksen.
Consul: Nancy Pelletreau.
Administrative Section: Naomi Emerson Lyew.
Branch Public Affairs Officer: James D. O'Callaghan.

Consulate-General: Via Vaccarini 1, 90143 Palermo; tel (91) 343532; telex 910313; fax (91) 343546.
Consul-General: Luciano Mangiafico.
Consul: Fabio M. Saturni.
Branch Public Affairs Officer: Douglas M. Barnes.

Consulate-General: Lungarno Amerigo Vespucci 38, 50123 Florence; tel (55) 217605; telex 570577; fax (55) 284088.

Commercial Section: tel (55) 211676; fax (55) 283780.
Consul-General: Marisa R. Lino.
Consul: Virginia Morris.
Regional Security Officer: Robert J. Nuernberger (resident in Milan).

Information Service: tel (55) 216531; fax (55) 288338.
Branch Public Affairs Officer: Lucille DiPalma.

Mission to United Nations Agencies for Food and Agriculture (FODAG): c/o US Embassy, Villino Pacelli, Via Aurelia 294, 00165 Rome; tel (6) 6390558; telex 622322; fax (6) 6390027.
Representative: Gerald J. Monroe.
Agency for International Development: Richard M. Seifman.
Agricultural Section: J. Dawson Ahalt.

URUGUAY

Embassy: Via Vittorio Veneto 183, 00187 Rome; tel (6) 492796; telex 611201.
Ambassador: Juan Domingo del Campo.

VENEZUELA

Embassy: Viale Bruno Buozzi 109, Apto 6, 00197 Rome; tel (6) 3221998; telex 610361; fax (6) 6799161.
Ambassador: José Francisco Sucre Figarella.
Minister-Counsellor: Myriam Vega Perez.
Counsellor: Carmen Martinez de Grijalva.
Counsellor: Maria Lourdes Vera Mujiga.
Counsellor: Alirio Diaz Leal.
Counsellor (Press): Edith Guzman.
First Secretary: Flor Acconciamessa de Rodriguez.
Second Secretary: Gertrodis Rebecca Guevara.

Permanent Mission to FAO: Via Antonio Gramsci 14-16, 00197 Rome; tel (6) 3305868; telex 614104; fax (6) 3610866.
Permanent Representative (FAO): Mercedes Fermin Gómez.
Technical Counsellor: Alberto Murillo M..

Consulate-General: Via Napo Torriani 31, 20124 Milan; tel (2) 654136; fax (2) 656425.
Consul-General: Ruben Franco Guzman.
Consul: Josefina Puerta Marti.

Consulate-General: Via Santa Lucia 173, 80132 Naples; tel (81) 418550.
Consul-General: Jorge Rondon U.
Consul: Gloria Aguana de M.

VIET-NAM

Embassy: Piazza Barberini 12, 00187 Rome; tel (6) 4754098; telex 610121.
Ambassador: Nguyen Viet.
First Secretary: Le Yan Sinh.
Second Secretary: Tran Van Hai.
Third Secretary: Nguyen Xuan Thu.
Attaché (Commercial): Phaon Van Minh.

YEMEN

Embassy: Via Verona 3, 00161 Rome; tel (6) 4270281; telex 621447; fax (6) 428216.
Ambassador: Dr Mohamed Ben Mohamed Al-Kawsi.
Minister Plenipotentiary: Nasser Saeed Haitham.
Minister Plenipotentiary: Abdulrahman Alhayouti.
Administrative Attaché: Gaffer Mohamed Haidra.

YUGOSLAVIA

Embassy: Via dei Monti Parioli 20, 00197 Rome; tel (6) 3600796; telex 616303.
Ambassador: Dusan Strbac.
Minister-Counsellor: Ranko Bajic.
Counsellor (Consular): Stefan Janevski.
First Secretary: Marinko Domijanovic.
Third Secretary: Nino Maljevic.

ZAIRE

Embassy: Via Annone 71/79, 00199 Rome; tel (6) 8393665; telex 611104.
Ambassador: Kitshodi Nzekele.

ZAMBIA

Embassy: Via Ennio Quirino Visconti 8, 00193 Rome; tel (6) 3213805; telex 611421.
Ambassador: Dr Leonard S. Chivuno.
First Secretary: George R. Nzala.
First Secretary (Finance): C. Siwale.
First Secretary (FAO): J. P. Lungu.
First Secretary: E. F. Sakala.
Third Secretary: M. Nalishuwa.
Third Secretary: Iidephonse S. Mwelwa.
Third Secretary: W. Mbuta.

International Organizations

EUROPEAN COMMUNITIES

Office: Via Poli 29, 00187 Rome; tel (6) 6789722; telex 610184; fax (6) 6791658.
Director: Gerardo Mombelli.

Sub-office: Corso Magenta 59, 20123 Milan; tel (2) 801505; telex 316200; fax (2) 4818543.
Director: Marina Manfredi.

LEAGUE OF ARAB STATES

Delegation: Rome.
Head of Delegation: Aziz Hacene.

UNITED NATIONS HIGH COMMISSIONER FOR REFUGEES—UNHCR

Delegation: Via Caroncini 19, 00197 Rome; tel (6) 877119; telex 622430.
Representative: Waldo Villalpando.

JAMAICA

ARGENTINA

Embassy: Dyoll Bldg, 40 Knutsford Blvd, Kingston 5; tel 926-5588; telex 2107.
Ambassador: Paulino Mussacchio.

AUSTRALIA

High Commission: First Life Bldg, 3rd Floor, 64 Knutsford Blvd, POB 560, Kingston 5; tel 926-3550; telex 2355; fax 929-6480.
High Commissioner: Peter William Rodgers.
First Secretary: Keith Gardner.
Second Secretary (Consular and Administration): J. Scott.

AUSTRIA

Consulate-General: Jamaica Hotel & Tourist Association, 2 Ardenne Rd, Kingston 10; POB 80, Montego Bay; tel 926-3635; telex 5236.
Honorary Consul: Heinz E. W. Simonitsch.

BELGIUM

Embassy: Oxford House, Oxford Rd, Kingston 5; tel 926-6589.
Ambassador: Frans L. Craeninckx.

BOLIVIA

Embassy: Xerox Bldg, 3rd Floor, 53 Knutsford Blvd, Kingston 5; tel 929-7260.
Chargé d'affarires a.i.: Augusto Bedregal.

BRAZIL

Embassy: First Life Bldg, 64 Knutsford Blvd, Kingston 5; tel 929-8607; telex 2221.
Chargé d'affaires a.i.: Victor Manzolillo de Moraes.

CANADA

High Commission: Mutual Security Bank Bldg, 30-36 Knutsford Blvd, Kingston 5; POB 1500, Kingston 10; tel 926-1500; telex 2130; fax 926-1702.
High Commissioner: Jennifer McQueen.
Counsellor (Immigration): E. Donagher.
Counsellor (Development): R. Beadle.
Counsellor: D. C. Korth.
Counsellor (Immigration): P. A. Lilius.
First Secretary (Development): W. Mitchell.
First Secretary (Development): R. L. Noble.
First Secretary (Immigration): L. A. M. Rohringer.
First Secretary (Commercial): J. D. Bonar.
First Secretary: J. Boucher.
Second Secretary (Administration): L. Poirier.
Second Secretary: G. E. Lisk.
Second Secretary (Immigration): J.-C. Gosselin.
Second Secretary (Immigration): G. Spence.
Consulate: 29 Gloucester St, Montego Bay; tel 952-6198.
Honorary Consular Agent: L. Crichton.

CHINA, PEOPLE'S REPUBLIC

Embassy: 8 Seaview Ave, Kingston 10; tel 927-0850; telex 2202.
Chargé d'affaires: Huang Dongbi.

COLOMBIA

Embassy: 53 Knutsford Blvd, Victoria Mutual Bldg, 3rd Floor, Kingston 5; tel 929-1702; telex 2200; fax 929-1701.
Ambassador: Ninon Millan.

COSTA RICA

Embassy: 21 John Wesley Ave, Kingston 6; tel 927-4493.
Ambassador: Dr Roger Churnside.

CUBA

Embassy: Kingston.
Ambassador: Darío de Urra.

DENMARK

Consulate-General: 449 Spanish Town Rd, Kingston 11; tel 923-5051; telex 3508; fax 923-5055.
Consul-General: John Charles Ramson.

DOMINICAN REPUBLIC

Embassy: 7 Ebony Glade, Kingston 5; tel 58338.

FINLAND

Consulate: Deryck A. Gibson Ltd, 7 1/2 Haining Rd, Kingston; POB 11, Kingston 5; tel 926-2250; telex 2171; fax 926-7061.
Consul: Deryck Anthony Gibson.

FRANCE

Embassy: 13 Hillcrest Ave, POB 93, Kingston 6; tel 927-8911; telex 2367.
Ambassador: Michel Reuilard.
Trade Promotion Office: POB 403, Kingston 5; tel 926-2027; telex 2459.

GERMANY

Embassy: 10 Waterloo Rd, POB 444, Kingston 10; tel 926-5665; telex 2146; fax 929-8282.
Ambassador: Dr Nils Grueber.

HAITI

Embassy: 2 Munroe Rd, Kingston 6; tel 927-7595.
Chargé d'affaires a.i.: André A. Rameau.

INDIA

High Commission: 4 Retreat Ave, POB 446, Kingston 6; tel 927-0486.
High Commissioner: Khiangte C. Lalvunga.

ISRAEL

Embassy: Pan Jamaican Bldg, 60 Knutsford Blvd, Kingston 5; tel 926-8768; telex 2466.
Ambassador: Uri Prosor.

JAPAN

Embassy: 3rd Floor, Atrium Bldg, 32 Trafalgar Rd, Kingston 10; POB 8104, Kingston; tel 929-3338; telex 9304; fax 929-7534.
Chargé d'affaires a.i.: Noboru Kawagishi.

KOREA, DEMOCRATIC PEOPLE'S REPUBLIC

Embassy: 18 New Haven Ave, Kingston 6; tel 927-7087; telex 2491.
Ambassador: Shin Myong Ho.

KOREA, REPUBLIC

Embassy: Pan Jamaican Bldg, 2nd Floor, 60 Knutsford Blvd, Kingston 5; tel 929-3035.
Ambassador: Kie Yul Moon.

MEXICO

Embassy: PCJ Bldg, 36 Trafalgar Rd, Kingston 10; tel 926-4242; telex 2255.
Ambassador: Joaquin Mercado.

NETHERLANDS

Embassy: Victoria Mutual Bldg, 3rd Floor, 53 Knutsford Blvd, Kingston 5; POB 390, Kingston 10; tel 926-1247; telex 2177; fax 926-1248.
Chargé d'affaires a.i.: Armand L. Brunings.
First Secretary: Fred A. de Bruin.
Attaché (Administrative/Consular): Karina P. G. Hanssen.
Attaché and Secretary: Annette Otten.

NICARAGUA

Embassy: Kingston.

NIGERIA

High Commission: 5 Waterloo Rd, POB 94, Kingston 10; tel 926-6400; telex 2443.
High Commissioner: Prof. Emmanuel Nweke Ugochukwu.
Minister-Counsellor and Head of Chancery: Taofiq Oseni.
Counsellor: Nnenna Uchegbu.
First Secretary: Muhammadhu Yunusa.
Attaché: Nicholas Asemota.
Attaché: Diana Peterside.

PANAMA

Embassy: 64 Arnold Rd, Kingston 5; tel 928-3861.
Ambassador: Jacinta de Bayard.

PERU

Embassy: Oxford House, 2nd Floor, 6 Oxford Rd, Kingston 5; tel 929-1151; telex 3597.
Ambassador: Víctor Fernández-Dávila.

RUSSIA

Embassy: 22 Norbrook Drive, Kingston 8; tel 924-1048; telex 2216.
Ambassador: Vladimir Aleksandrovich Romantchenko.
Counsellor: Vyatcheslav Semenov.
Trade and Economic Commissioner: Boris Orlov.
First Secretary: Konstantine Kamenev.
First Secretary: Alexandre Koulev.
First Secretary: Eugeni Temiakov.
Second Secretary (Economic): Vladimir Bogdanov.
Second Secretary (Trade): Yuri Souslov.
Attaché (Consular): Alexandre Vilnin.
Attaché (Protocol): Vladislav Ivanov.

SPAIN

Embassy: Xerox Bldg, 3rd Floor, 53 Knutsford Blvd, Kingston 5; tel 929-6710; telex 2364.
Ambassador: Ignacio Masferrer.

SWEDEN

Consulate: c/o Salada Foods Jamaica Ltd, 20 Bell Rd, POB 71, Kingston 11; tel 923-6476; telex 2445.
Ambassador: Lennart Klackenberg (resident in Sweden).

Consul: John Oliver Fletcher.

SWITZERLAND

Consulate-General: 105 Harbour St (entrance on Church St), POB 401, Kingston; tel 922-3347; telex 3553; fax 922-8403.
Honorary Consul-General: Peter R. Bangerter.

TRINIDAD AND TOBAGO

High Commission: Pan-Jamaican Bldg, 60 Knutsford Blvd, Kingston 5; tel 926-5730; telex 2387.
High Commissioner: Carlton K. A. Gomes.

UNITED KINGDOM

High Commission: Trafalgar Rd, POB 575, Kingston 10; tel 926-9050; telex 2110; fax 929-7869.
High Commissioner: Derek Francis Milton.
Deputy High Commissioner: F. Callaghan.
Defence Adviser: Col C. S. Faith.
First Secretary (Chancery): M. Boldt.
First Secretary (Management/Consular): I. F. Powell.
Second Secretary (Commercial/Information): C. Q. G. Jebb.
Second Secretary (Chancery): D. L. Brett.
Second Secretary (Chancery): T. V. D. Manhire.
Second Secretary (Technical Assistance): C. N. Brazier.
Third Secretary (Consular/Passports): C. D. R. Smart.
Third Secretary (Immigration): S. J. Burns.
Information Officer: T. Roberts.

USA

Embassy: Mutual Life Centre, 3rd Floor, 2 Oxford Rd, Kingston 5; tel 929-4850; fax 926-6743.
Ambassador: Glen A. Holden.
Deputy Chief of Mission: Peter D. Whitney.
Political Section: Jennifer C. Ward.
Economic Section: Herman J. Rossi III.
Commercial Section: W. Kelly Joyce, Jr.
Consul: Lois J. Matteson.
Administrative Section: George H. Haines III.
Regional Security Officer: George J. Goldstein.
Public Affairs Officer: Razvigor Bazala.
Communications Programme Officer: Virginia Schrenk.
Information Systems Manager: Anita D. Banks.
Agency for International Development: Robert S. Queener.
Office of the Defence Attaché: Lieut Col Carl T. Hover.
Military Liaison Office: Lieut Col Samuel T. Smith.
Labour Officer: William P. Schofield.

VENEZUELA

Embassy: Petrojam Bldg, 3rd Floor, 36 Trafalgar Rd, POB 26, Kingston 10; tel 926-5510; telex 2179.
Ambassador: Victor Carazo K.
Minister-Counsellor: Vicente Gamboa Marcano.
First Attaché: Mercedes Pons Aponte.
Second Attaché: Odisa Ramos.

International Organizations

EUROPEAN COMMUNITIES

External Delegation: Mutual Life Centre, 2nd Floor, Oxford Rd and Old Hope Rd, POB 435, Kingston 5; tel 929-3030; telex 2391; fax 929-2785.
Commission Delegate: Jean-Claude Heyraud (also responsible for the Bahamas, Belize, the Cayman Islands and the Turks and Caicos Islands).

JAPAN

ALGERIA

Embassy: 10-67, Mita 2-chome, Meguro-ku, Tokyo 153; tel (3) 3711-2661; telex 23260; fax (3) 3710-6534.
Ambassador: Nourredine Yazid Zerhouni.
First Secretary: Abdelmoun'aam Ahriz.
First Secretary: Mohamed Ainseur.
Attaché: Tewfik Azzeddine Boufetta.
Attaché: Kamel Boulhabel.

ARGENTINA

Embassy: Chiyoda House, 2nd and 3rd Floors, 17-8, Nagata-cho 2-chome, Chiyoda-ku, Tokyo 100; tel (3) 3592-0321; telex 22489; fax (3) 3506-8469.
Ambassador: Ernesto de La Guardia.
Minister: José R. Sanchis Muñoz.
Minister (Financial): Virgilio Tedín Uriburu.

Office of the Naval, Military and Air Attaché: tel (3) 3581-6661.
Naval, Military and Air Attaché: Capt. Luis A. García Bourimborde.
Counsellor: Luis Jorge Arregui.
Counsellor: María del Carmen Gilabert.

Economic and Commercial Office: tel (3) 3593-1280; fax (3) 3593-1282.
Counsellor (Commercial): Roberto Read.
First Secretary (Commercial): Jaime Juan Goldaracena.
Second Secretary (Cultural): Silvia A. Raiola.

Consulate-General: Silk Centre Bldg, 1 Yamashita-cho, Naka-ku, Yokohama 231, Kanagawa-ken; tel (45) 641-4194.
Consul-General: Werner R. J. Burghard.

AUSTRALIA

Embassy: 1-12, Shiba Koen 1-chome, Minato-ku, Tokyo 105; tel (3) 3435-0971; telex 22298; fax (3) 3435-1814.
Ambassador: Geoffrey Miller.

Austrade: Sankaido Bldg, 7th Floor, 9-13, Akasaka 1-chome, Minato-ku, Tokyo 107; tel (3) 3582-7231; fax (3) 3582-7239.

Australia-Japan Foundation and Cultural Relations Section: Aoyama Erie Bldg, 5th Floor, 5-1-2 Minami Aoyama, Minato-ku, Tokyo; tel (3) 3498-4141; fax (3) 3498-0794.

Consulate-General: Kojusai Bldg, 23rd Floor, 3-13 Azuchimachi 2-chome, Chuo-ku, Osaka 541; tel (6) 2717071; telex 5225334; fax (6) 2717070.

AUSTRIA

Embassy: 1-20, Moto Azabu 1-chome, Minato-ku, Tokyo 106; tel (3) 3451-8281; telex 26361; fax (3) 3451-8283.
Ambassador: Dr Erich M. Schmid.
Minister: Dr Johannes Skriwan.
First Secretary: Dr Andreas Herdina.
Second Secretary (Cultural): Dr Wolfgang Angerholzer.
Vice-Consul: Josef Knapp.

Trade Commission: 13-3, Moto Azabu 3-chome, Minato-ku, Tokyo 106; tel (3) 3403-1777; telex 28203; fax (3) 3403-3407.
Trade Commissioner: Wolfgang Kueng.
Deputy Trade Commissioner: Walter Koren.

Consulate-General: c/o Itoh & Co Ltd, 1-3, Kyutaro-machi 4-chome, Chuo-ku, Osaka 541-77; tel (6) 241-3011; telex 63260; fax (6) 241-3253.
Consul-General: Teruo Hotta.

Consulate: Senshuan Seika, Kabushiki Kaisha, 17 Banchi, Nishi 3-chome, Minami 3-jo, Chuo-ku, Sapporo City, Hokkaido; tel (11) 261-7964; telex 934525; fax (11) 222-7635.
Consul: Takuji Okabe.

BANGLADESH

Embassy: 7-45, Shirogane 2-chome, Minato-ku, Tokyo 108; tel (3) 3442-1501; telex 28826; fax (3) 3447-3676.
Ambassador: Muhammad Abu Hena.
Minister (Political): M. Mizanur Rahman.
Economic Minister: S. M. Shahjahan.
Counsellor (Political): A. M. Rashed Chowdhury.
Commercial Counsellor: Ahmad Mahmadur Raza Chowdhury.
Press Counsellor: M. A. Awwal.
First Secretary: M. Faroque Amin.

BELGIUM

Embassy: 5, Niban-cho, Chiyoda-ku, Tokyo 102; tel (3) 3262-0191; telex 24979; fax (3) 3262-0651.
Ambassador: Baron Patrick Nothomb.
Minister-Counsellor: Louis Engelen.
First Secretary: Benoît Ryelandt.
Second Secretary: Christine Detaille.

Attaché (Consular/Administrative): Raymond Yans.
Attaché (Industrial/Scientific): Dr Jean-Bernard Aderca.

Consulate-General: Osaka.
Counsellor and Consul General: Michael Goblet d'Alviella.

BOLIVIA

Embassy: Kowa Bldg, No. 38, Room 804, 8th Floor, 12-24, Nishi-Azabu 4-chome, Minato-ku, Tokyo 106; tel (3) 3499-5441; telex 32177; fax (3) 3499-5443.
Ambassador: Gonzalo Montenegro.

BRAZIL

Embassy: 11-12, Kita Aoyama 2-chome, Minato-ku, Tokyo 107; tel (3) 3404-5211; telex 22590; fax (3) 3405-5846.
Ambassador: Carlos Antonio Bettencourt Bueno.
Minister-Counsellor: Jadiel Ferreira de Oliveira.
First Secretary: Paulo Joppert Crissiuma.
First Secretary: Ligia Maria Scherer.
First Secretary: Ricardo Neiva Tavares.
First Secretary: Miguel Junior França de Magalhães.
First Secretary: Ellen Osthoff Ferreira de Barros.
Second Secretary: Renato de Assumção Faria.
Second Secretary: Lys Amayo de Benedek.

BRUNEI

Embassy: 5-2, Kita Shinagawa 6-chome, Shinagawa-ku, Tokyo 141; tel (3) 3447-7997; telex 43931; fax (3) 3447-9260.
Ambassador: Pengiran Dato Paduka Haji Idriss.

BULGARIA

Embassy: 36-3A, Yoyogi 5-chome, Shibuya-ku, Tokyo 151; tel (3) 3465-1021; fax (3) 3465-1031.
Ambassador: Dr Petar Bashikarov.
Minister-Plenipotentiary: Stanislav Baev.
Counsellor: Stoyan Mishev.
Counsellor (Press): Stanoi Karadjov.

Commercial Section: tel (3) 3465-1025.
First Secretary (Commercial): Mirolyub Vutov.
Second Secretary: Mitko Dimitrov.
Second Secretary (Science/Technology): Plamen Nikolov.
Second Secretary (Agriculture): Plamen Boricov.
Third Secretary (Cultural): Gueorgi Kostianev.
Third Secretary (Commercial): Michail Michailov.
Third Secretary (Commercial): Dimo Markov.
Third Secretary (Commercial): Toma Chuparov.
Third Secretary (Commercial): Luchezar Terziyanov.

BURUNDI

Embassy: Tokyo.
Ambassador: Antoine Ntamobwa.

CAMEROON

Embassy: 9-12, Minami Nanpeidai-cho, Shibuya-ku, Tokyo 150; tel (3) 3496-1125; telex 28032.
Ambassador: Etienne Ntsama.

CANADA

Embassy: 3-38, Akasaka 7-chome, Minato-ku, Tokyo 107; tel (3) 3408-2101; telex 22218; fax (3) 3479-5320.

Consular and Information Sections: fax (3) 3470-7278.

Science and Technology Section: fax (3) 3470-7280.

Customs and Excise Section: fax (3) 3408-6933.

Visa Section: tel (3) 3403-9176; fax (3) 3470-7278.
Ambassador: James H. Taylor.
Minister: Stephen H. Heeney.
Minister (Economic/Commercial): J. Swanson.
Minister-Counsellor (Commercial): John H. Treleaven.
Counsellor and Consul: J. Cheh.
Counsellor and Consul: Marie-Isabelle Massip.
Counsellor and Consul: Brian A. Smith.
Counsellor (Science and Technology): Carl B. Kuhnke.
Counsellor and Consul: Bruce L. Barnett.
Counsellor (Commercial): M. G. Stinson.
Counsellor: Eber H. J. Rice.
Counsellor (Immigration) and Consul: John J. Mizobuchi.
Counsellor (Administration) and Consul: D. J. Stimpson.
Counsellor (Commercial): Brian F. Wilkin.
Counsellor (Minerals/Metals/Energy): David E. Wynne.
Counsellor and Consul: David G. Anido.
Canadian Forces Attaché: Capt. Ronald R. Richards.
First Secretary (Commercial/Agriculture/Fisheries): E. Di Emanuele.
Third Secretary (Science and Technology): G. G. Rust.
Attaché (Investment): Russell T. Mark.
Attaché (Customs): James R. Fooks.

Consulate-General: Daisan Shoho Bldg, 12th Floor, 2-3 Nishi Shinsaibashi, 2-chome, Chuo-ku, Osaka 542; POB 150, Osaka Minami 542-91; tel (6) 212-4910; fax (6) 212-4914.
Consul-General: Michael C. Spencer.
Consul and Trade Commissioner: T. Greenberg.

CENTRAL AFRICAN REPUBLIC

Embassy: 32-2, Ohyama-cho, Shibuya-ku, Tokyo 151; tel (3) 3460-8341; telex 24793; fax (3) 3481-6652.
Counsellor and Chargé d'affaires a.i.: Noel Eregani.

CHILE

Embassy: Nihon Seimei Akabanebashi Bldg, 8th Floor, 3-1-14, Shiba, Minato-ku, Tokyo 105; tel (3) 3452-7561; telex 24585; fax (3) 3769-4156.
Ambassador: Italo Zunino Muratori.
Minister-Counsellor: Hernán Tassara Jiménez.
Minister-Counsellor (Head of Commercial Office): Allan Halley-Harris Goñi.
Financial Counsellor: José Luis Daza Narbona.
First Secretary (Commercial): Emilio Brüggemann Abramovich.
Second Secretary and Consul: Jaime Alliende Leiva.
Third Secretary: Marisol Pérez Carranza.

CHINA, PEOPLE'S REPUBLIC

Embassy: 3-4-33, Moto Azabu, Minato-ku, Tokyo 106; tel (3) 3403-3380; telex 28705; fax (3) 3403-3345.
Ambassador: Yang Zhenya.
Minister: Tang Jiaxuan.
Counsellor: Gao Fujin.
Counsellor: Hun Qiufang.
Counsellor: Liu Yongxiang.
Defence Attaché: Miao Changrong.
Counsellor: Xu Yuanhai.
Counsellor: Peng Jiasheng.
Counsellor: Zhao Zhongxin.
Counsellor: Liu Zhigang.
Counsellor: Huang Xing.
Counsellor: Wang Yi.
Military Attaché: Gao Baoxing.
First Secretary: Li Ynxing.
First Secretary (Cultural): Wu Xiehua.
First Secretary: Zong Liangheng.
First Secretary: Wu Delie.
First Secretary: Liu Wangin.
First Secretary: Zhang Guangpei.
First Secretary: Wang Taiping.
First Secretary: Qu Delin.
First Secretary: Zhou Zexing.
First Secretary: Zhou Jiao.

Consular Section: 5-30, Minami Azabu 4-chome, Minato-ku, Tokyo 106; tel (3) 3473-7825.

Commercial Section: 8-16, Minami Azabu 5-chome, Minato-ku, Tokyo 106; tel (3) 3440-2011.
Minister-Counsellor (Commercial): Mou Yongmao.
First Secretary (Commercial): Yu Wenzhong.

Office of Economic Counsellor: 5-30, Minami Azabu 4-chome, Minato-ku, Tokyo 106; tel (3) 3442-2425.
Economic Counsellor: Ma Jinzhu.

Education Section: 2-8, Hirano 2-chome, Koto-ku, Tokyo 135; tel (3) 3643-0305.

COLOMBIA

Embassy: 10-53, Kami Osaki 3-chome, Shinagawa-ku, Tokyo 141; tel (3) 3440-6451; fax (3) 3440-6724.
Ambassador: Fidel Duque Ramírez.

Colombian Govt Trade Bureau: Rm 805, No. 38, Kowa Bldg, 12-24, Nishi Azabu 4-chome, Minato-ku, Tokyo 106; tel (3) 3499-0440.

Office of Commercial Counsellor (Coffee Affairs): 10-54, Kami Osaki 3-chome, Shinagawa-ku, Tokyo 141; tel (3) 3440-6041; fax (3) 3440-6043.
Commercial Counsellor: Fernando Barbosa.
Commercial Attaché: Ricardo Gutiérrez.

COSTA RICA

Embassy: Kowa Bldg, No. 38, Room 901, 12-24, Nishi Azabu 4-chome, Minato-ku, Tokyo 106; tel (3) 3486-1812; fax (3) 3486-1813.
Minister-Counsellor, Consul-General and Chargé d'affaires a.i.: Ana Lucía Nassar Soto.

COTE D'IVOIRE

Embassy: Kowa Bldg, No. 38, Room 701, 12-24, Nishi Azabu 4-chome, Minato-ku, Tokyo 106; tel (3) 3499-7021; telex 26631; fax (3) 3498-4269.
Ambassador: Pierre Nelson Coffi.
First Counsellor: Zoumana Ouattara.
Financial Attaché: Ohoupeu Abale.

CUBA

Embassy: 3-16-23, Higashi-Gotanda, Shinagawa-ku, Tokyo 141; tel (3) 3449-7511; telex 22369; fax (3) 3449-7679.
Ambassador: Amadeo Blanco Valdés-Fauly.
Counsellor: René Castro.

Office of Commercial Counsellor: tel (3) 3449-7054.
Commercial Counsellor: Jorge Dominquez.
First Secretary: María Micaela Ramírez.
Third Secretary: Andrés Maqueira.
Attaché: Angel Moraga.
Attaché: Rolando Fontaina.

CZECHOSLOVAKIA

Embassy: 16-14, Hiroo 2-chome, Shibuya-ku, Tokyo 150; tel (3) 3400-8122; telex 24595; fax (3) 3406-6215.
Ambassador: Jan Winkelhöfer.
Counsellor for Scientific Affairs: Josef Lébl.
First Secretary: Ivan Podzimek.

Second Secretary (Commercial): Viktor Horanský.
Third Secretary: Vladimír Balaník.
Third Secretary (Consular): Igor Hlivka.
Third Secretary: Ferdinand Valent.
Third Secretary: Vladimír Vosecký.
Third Secretary: Vladimír Stárer.
Third Secretary: Pavol Katancik.
Attaché: Josef Venc.
Press Attaché: Jan Levora.

DENMARK

Embassy: 29-6, Sarugaku-cho, Shibuya-ku, Tokyo 150; tel (3) 3496-3001; telex 24417; fax (3) 3496-3440.
Ambassador: William Thune Andersen.
Minister-Counsellor: Kristian Højersholt.
Commercial Counsellor: George D. Rasmussen.
First Secretary (Commercial): Sigurd Schmidt.
Industry Attaché: Jørgen C. Mouridsen.
Attaché and Consul: Bent Carl Lindblad.
Attaché: Svend Aage Laholm.
Industrial Officer: Akira Tanaka.
Commercial Officer: A. Yanagisawa.
Commercial Officer: F. Hisamoto.
Export Assistant: Carsten Nederup-Nielsen.
Agricultural Counsellor: Jorgen Møllegaard Kristensen.

Consulate: 10 Toyo Kaiji Bldg, 31-7 Nishi-Shinbashi 2-chome, Minato-ku, Tokyo 105; POB 432, Tokyo 100-91; tel (3) 459-8230; telex 242-4224; fax (3) 459-8238.
Consul: Klaus Martin Krogh.

Consulate: 3-25-24 Yaoji Bldg, Hakataekimae, Fukuoka 812; tel (92) 474-1101; telex 222-3908; fax (92) 474-1428.
Consul: Yutaka Aso.

Consulate: Hiroshima Andersen Bldg, 3rd Floor, 7-1, Hondori, Naka-ku, Hiroshima 730; tel (82) 247-2403; fax (82) 247-5200.
Consul: Shunsuke Takaki.

Consulate: 1 Nishi 6-chome, Kohyo-cho, Higashinada-ku, Kobe 658; Higashinada POB 60; tel (78) 857-0251; telex 562-2190; fax (78) 857-0850.
Consul: Hiroyuki Kataoka.

Consulate: Suntory Bldg 1-40, Dojimahama 2-chome, Kita-ku, Osaka 530; tel (6) 346-1285; telex 63511; fax (6) 345-1169.
Consul: Shinichiro Torii.

Consulate: Sapporo.

Consulate: Maersk Bldg, 4th Floor, 18 Nihon-odori, Nakaku, Yokohama; POB 244, Yokohama 231; tel (45) 651-1591; telex 382-2384; fax (45) 651-3559.
Consul: Per Jørgensen.
Social Attaché: Rev. Thomas Uhre Fenger.

DOMINICAN REPUBLIC

Embassy: Kowa Bldg, No. 38, Room 904, 12-24, Nishi Azabu 4-chome, Minato-ku, Tokyo 106; tel (3) 3499-6020; telex 33701; fax (3) 3499-6010.
Ambassador: Juan Emilio Canó de la Mota.
Consul-General: Antonio Emilio Ornes.

ECUADOR

Embassy: Kowa Bldg, No. 38, Room 806, 12-24, Nishi Azabu 4-chome, Minato-ku, Tokyo 106; tel (3) 3498-3974; telex 25880; fax (3) 3499-4400.
Ambassador: Marcelo Avila.
Counsellor: Franklin Chávez.

Consular Affairs: tel (3) 3499-2866.
First Secretary (Consular Affairs): Miguel Vasco.
Third Secretary: Cristian Espinosa.

Commercial Section: tel (3) 3498-3974.
Commercial Attaché: Jorge Pazmiño.

Consulate-General: TOC Bldg, 2nd Floor, 7-22-7 Nishi Gotanda, Sinagawa-ku, Tokyo; (3) 3494-2130.
Honorary Consul-General: Dr Kokichi Otani.

Consulate: POB 43 Central Nagoya, Nagoya; tel (52) 781-8295.
Honorary Consul: Hiraku Yamamoto.

EGYPT

Embassy: 5-4, Aobadai 1-chome, Meguro-ku, Tokyo 153; tel (3) 3770-8022; telex 23240; fax (3) 3770-8021.
Ambassador: Wahib Fahmy Elmeniawy.
Minister: Mohamed Yousri El Kouedi.
Counsellor: Abdel Fattah M. Ezzeldin.
First Secretary: Reda Abdel Rahman Bebars.
Second Secretary: Hisham Mohamed Moustafa Badr.
Administrative Attaché: Elsayed Mahmoud Hegazi.
Administrative Attaché: Mohamed Salah El Din Hussein.
Administrative Attaché: Mohamed Khalifa Abdel Baki.

Commercial Section: Kowa Bldg, No. 38, Rm 808, 12-24, Nishi Azabu 4-chome, Minato-ku, Tokyo 106; tel (3) 3409-3361.
Minister (Commercial): Abdel Halim Ali.
Counsellor (Commercial): Mahmoud Nabil Hamed Mansour.
First Secretary (Commercial): Ali Hafez Barrada.
Administrative Attaché (Commercial): Hamed Ibrahim Elmosallami.

Information Office: tel (3) 3770-8401.
Counsellor (Information): Shaker Ibrahim Said.
Administrative Attaché (Information): Fathy Abdel H. M. Radwan.

Cultural Promotion Section: Akasaka 2-chome Annex Bldg, 2nd Floor, 19-8, Akasaka 2-chome, Minato-ku, Tokyo 107; tel (3) 3589-0653.
Counsellor (Cultural Promotion): Rostom El Enani Ali.

EL SALVADOR

Embassy: Kowa Bldg, No. 38, 8th Floor, 12-24, Nishi Azabu 4-chome, Minato-ku, Tokyo 106; tel (3) 3499-4461; telex 25829.
Ambassador: Dr Ernesto Arrieta Peralta.

ETHIOPIA

Embassy: 1-14-15, Midorigaoka, Meguro-ku, Tokyo 152; tel (3) 3585-3151; telex 28402; fax (3) 3586-6780.
Ambassador: Worku Moges.
Economic Counsellor: Kibret Mengistu.
Second Secretary: Aster Abate.
Third Secretary: Eshetu Yisma Nigatu.
Commercial Counsellor: Bekele Engida.
Commercial Attaché: Nigist Berehe.

FIJI

Embassy: Noa Bldg, 10th Floor, 3-5, Azabudai 2-chome, Minato-ku, Tokyo 106; tel (3) 3587-2038; fax (3) 3587-2563.
Ambassador: Charles Walker.
Second Secretary: Apisalome Vuli.

FINLAND

Embassy: 3-5-39, Minami Azabu, Minato-ku, Tokyo 106; tel (3) 3442-2231; telex 26277; fax (3) 3442-2175.
Ambassador: Heikki Kalha.

Commercial Section: telex 32361; fax (3) 3440-6013.
Commercial Counsellor: Paavo Marttila.
Commercial Secretary: Clas-Göran Bystedt.
Commercial Secretary: Heikki Markkanen.

Scientific Section: telex 32361; fax (3) 3442-2336.
Scientific Attaché: Tom Grahn.

Consulate-General: Dojima Bldg, Rm 523, 2-6-8, Nishi-tenma, Kita-ku, Osaka 530; tel (6) 361-0938; telex 523-6858; fax (6) 361-7590.
Honorary Consul-General: Shosaburo Yamamoto.

Consulate: No. 9 Kabuto Bldg, 2nd Floor, 10-1, Hiragashi 2-jo, Toyohira-ku, Sapporo 062; tel (11) 822-7693; fax (11) 814-9620.
Honorary Consul: Masahiko Nakano.

FRANCE

Embassy: 11-44, Minami Azabu 4-chome, Minato-ku, Tokyo 106; tel (3) 3473-0171; fax (3) 3442-9755.
Ambassador: Loïc Hennekinne.
Minister: Jean-Jacques Subrenat.
Counsellor: Jacques Moreau.
Counsellor: Bruno Gain.
First Secretary: Olivier Ansart.
First Secretary: Jacques Maillard.
First Secretary: Jean-Marie Magnien.
Second Secretary: Hugues Nordi.
Third Secretary: Christian Ponge.
Third Secretary: Georges Nguyen Xuan Hop.
Defence Attaché: Capt. Jean-Claude Blanvillain.
Assistant Defence Attaché: Maj. Olivier Lambert.
Assistant Naval Attaché: Lieut Rémi Pagnie.

Office of Financial Counsellor: French Bank Bldg, 1-2, Akasaka 1-chome, Minato-ku, Tokyo 107; tel (3) 3583-9895; fax (3) 3582-0490.
Financial Attaché: Jean-Yves Colin.
Financial Attaché: Jean-Victor Ruault.
Minister-Counsellor (Economic/Commercial): René Ghesquiere.

Office of Commercial Counsellor: Tameike Tokyu Bldg, 1-1-14, Akasaka, Minato-ku, Tokyo 107; tel (3) 3584-8333; telex 22652; fax (3) 3584-8343.
Commercial Counsellor: Bernard Yvetot.
Assistant Commercial Attaché: Patrick de Cazenove.
Customs Attaché: Michel Vermare.
Attaché (Industrial/Technical Information): Patrick Taillandier.
Industrial Affairs Attaché: Jacques Hebrard.
Cultural Counsellor: Jean-Claude Redonnet.
Scientific Counsellor: Christian Delmas.
Scientific Attaché: François Grout.
Nuclear Attaché: Pierre Moriette.

Consulate-General: Ohbayashi Bldg, 24th Floor, 4-33, Kitahama-Higashi, Chuo-ku, Osaka 540; tel (6) 946-6181; fax (6) 949-1887.

GABON

Embassy: 1-12-11, Kami-Osaki, Shinagawa-ku, Tokyo 141; tel (3) 3448-9540; telex 24812; fax (3) 3448-1596.
Ambassador: Patrice Makika.
First Counsellor: Jérôme Obounou-Mbogo.
Economic and Cultural Counsellor: Pascal Youbi-Lagha.
Counsellor and Secretary: Constant Jérôme Leckouta.
First Secretary: Jeanne Obounou-Mbogo.

Consulate: 2-5-8, Bingomachi, Chuo-ku, Osaka City; tel (6) 208-5400.
Consul: K. Zaburo Nishizawa.

GERMANY

Embassy: 5-10, Minami Azabu 4-chome, Minato-ku, Tokyo 106; POB 955, Tokyo 100-91; tel (3) 3473-0151; telex 22292; fax (3) 3473-4243.
Ambassador: Wilhelm Haas.

Minister: Rolf-Eberhard Jung.
First Counsellor (Political): Dr Klaus Platz.
Counsellor (Labour and Social): Rainer G. Czeniek.
Counsellor (Political): Manfred F. Wenzel.
First Counsellor (Press/Information): Dr Manfred Osten.
Counsellor (Press): Dr Wilfried Schulte.
First Counsellor (Economic/Commercial): Dr Werner Kaufmann-Bühler.
First Counsellor (Scientific): Dr Hartmut N. Deyda.
Counsellor (Finance): Kurt Majunke.
Counsellor (Agricultural): Friedrich Distler.
Counsellor (Post/Telecommunications): Udo Moritz.
Counsellor (Economic and Commercial): Holger Green.
First Counsellor (Cultural/Legal/Consular): Wedigo Graf von Wedel.
First Secretary (Political): Dr Martin Hanz.
First Secretary (Economic): Hans Leister.
First Secretary (Economic): Harald Gehrig.
First Secretary (Cultural/Legal/Consular): Dr Ingo Karsten.
First Secretary (Administration): August Adam.
Second Secretary (Political): Stefan Herzberg.
Second Secretary (Press/Information): Angelika Viets.
Attaché (Press/Information): Ingeborg Lohner.
Attaché (Protocol and Scientific): Thomas Triller.
Defence Attaché: Capt. Friedrich Lederer.

Consulate-General: 1-6, Goko-dori 8-chome, Kokusai Kaikan, Chuo-ku, Kobe-shi 651; POB 204, Kobe-ko 651-01; tel (78) 232-1212; telex 78925; fax (78) 232-1215.
Consul-General: Dr Eberhard Baumann.

Consulate: c/o Saibu Gas Kabushiki Kaisha, 17-1, Chigo 1-chome, Hakata-ku, Fukuoka-shi 812-91; Chuo Yubinkyoku POB 41, Fukuoka-shi 810-91; tel (92) 633-2211; fax (92) 633-2291.
Honorary Consul: Yoshiyuki Enya.

Consulate: c/o Chubu Denryoku KK, Toshincho 1, Higashi-ku, Nagoya-shi 461; POB 158, Higashi Yubinkyoku, Nagoya 461-91; tel (52) 951-8211; telex 44405.
Honorary Consul: Seiichi Tanaka.

Consulate: c/o Hokkaido Electric Power Co. (Hokkaido Denryoku Kabushiki Gaisha), 2-banchi, Odori Higashi 1-chome, Chuo-ku, Sapporo; tel (11) 251-1111.
Honorary Consul: Tomoo Nakano.

GHANA

Embassy: Sen Manor A, 5-12-10, Shimomeguro, Meguro-ku, Tokyo 153; tel (3) 3710-8831; fax (3) 3710-8830.
Ambassador: James Leslie Mayne Amissah.
Counsellor (Consular) and Head of Chancery: Kwasi Asante.
First Secretary (Economic/Cultural): Susan Hagan Annobil.
Second Secretary: Constance O. Baadu.

GREECE

Embassy: 16-30, Nishi Azabu 3-chome, Minato-ku, Tokyo 106; tel (3) 3403-0871; fax (3) 3402-4642.
Ambassador: Dr George Lianis.

GUATEMALA

Embassy: 38 Kowa Bldg, Room 905, 4-12-24, Nishi Azabu, Minato-ku, Tokyo 106; tel (3) 3400-1820; fax (3) 3400-1820.
Ambassador: Rodolfo Rosales Muralles.

GUINEA

Embassy: 12-6, Minami Azabu 1-chome, Minato-ku, Tokyo 106; tel (3) 3769-0451; telex 24165; fax (3) 3769-0453.
Ambassador: Boubacar Barry.
First Secretary: Laye Camara.
Financial Attaché (Commercial/Consular): Alpha Amadou Bah.

HAITI

Embassy: Kowa Bldg, No. 38, Room 906, 12-24, Nishi Azabu 4-chome, Minato-ku, Tokyo 106; tel (3) 3486-7070; telex 29601.
Second Secretary, Consul and Chargé d'affaires a.i.: Fritznel Lafontant.

HOLY SEE

Apostolic Nunciature: 9-2, Sanban-cho, Chiyoda-ku, Tokyo 102; tel (3) 3263-6851; fax (3) 3263-6060.
Apostolic Pro-Nuncio: Most Rev. William Aquin Carew, Titular Archbishop of Telde.
First Secretary and Auditor: Mgr Dr Mario Roberto Cassari.

HONDURAS

Embassy: Kowa Bldg, No. 38, Room 802, 8th Floor, 12-24, Nishi Azabu 4-chome, Minato-ku, Tokyo 106; tel (3) 3409-1150; telex 28591; fax (3) 3409-0305.
Ambassador: Aníbal Enrique Quiñónez Abarca.
Counsellor (Consular Affairs): Humberto H. Handal.

HUNGARY

Embassy: 2-17-14, Mita, Minato-ku, Tokyo 108; tel (3) 3476-6061; telex 22688; fax (3) 3798-8812.
Ambassador: András Forgács.
Counsellor: Jenö Molnár.
First Secretary: László Birkás.
Second Secretary: Gyula Turcsányi.
Second Secretary: Gyula Dabrónaki.
Second Secretary: János Rózsa.
Attaché: Zsolt Potondi.

Commercial Office: Mori Bldg, No. 28, 16-13, Nishi-Azabu 4-chome, Minato-ku, Tokyo 106; tel (3) 3499-4951; fax (3) 3499-4918.
First Secretary (Commercial): Péter Gádor.

ICELAND

Consulate-General: Annex Bldg, 4th Floor, 6-1-1 Heiwajima, Ohta-ku, Tokyo 143; tel (3) 5493-8776; telex 2524171; fax (3) 5493-1050.
Honorary Consul-General: Raijiro Nakabe.

INDIA

Embassy: 2-11, Kudan Minami 2-chome, Chiyoda-ku, Tokyo 102; tel (3) 3262-2391; fax (3) 3234-4866.
Ambassador: Arjun Gobindram Asrani.
Minister and Deputy Head of Mission: S. Menon.
Minister (Economic and Commercial): S. C. Tripathi.
Information Section: tel (3) 3239-2485.
Counsellor (Public Relations) and Head of Chancery: G. P. Isser.
Consular Section: tel (3) 3239-2449.
Counsellor (Consular): R. Mathur.
Counsellor (Science and Technology): Dr S. B. Sinha.
Military, Naval and Air Attaché: Capt. S. Kapur.
First Secretary (Economic and Commercial): Om Prakash.
Deputy Military, Naval and Air Attaché: Wing Commdr V. K. Bhatia.
Second Secretary: A. K. Sinha.
Third Secretary: J. Sarkar.
Third Secretary: T. Darlong.
Third Secretary: H. K. Dain.
Attaché (Political): S. S. Rajput.
Attaché (Political): K. N. Rao.

INDONESIA

Embassy: 2-9, Higashi Gotanda 5-chome, Shinagawa-ku, Tokyo 141; tel (3) 3441-4201; telex 22920; fax (3) 3447-1697.
Minister and Chargé d'affaires: Ktut Pageh Nurdhana.
Minister-Counsellor (Head of Political Section): Zainuddin Rahman.
Minister-Counsellor (Head of Information Section): Max F. E. R. Lapod.
Counsellor (Head of Economic Section): Herijanto Suprapto.
Counsellor (Head of Administration Section): Munzy Harmeny Siregar.
First Secretary (Head of Protocol and Consular Section): Mr Hasan.
First Secretary: Djon Sardjono.
Third Secretary (Political): Gary R. M. Yusuf.
Third Secretary (Political): Taufan Adityawarman.
Second Secretary (Economic): Herbangan Napitupulu.
Third Secretary (Economic): Mr Sudirman.
Third Secretary (Information): Bonifatius Agung Herindra.
Third Secretary (Economic): Darmansyah Djumala.
Defence Attaché: Col Prio Utoyo Wardi.
Attaché (Communication): Bonor Leonard Sinaga.
Attaché (Education and Cultural): Siswardojo Sarodja.
Commercial Attaché: Abdul Rachman Fahrul.
Industrial Attaché: Harjanto Ardjunadi Soemarno.
Attaché (Immigration): Freddy Gerung.
Attaché (Agricultural): Saefoeddin Achmad.

Consulate-General: Kato Bldg, 3rd Floor, 76-1, Kyomachi, Ikuta-ku, Chuo-ku, Kobe 650; tel (78) 321-1695.
Consul-General: Johannes Sutantio.

IRAN

Embassy: 10-32, Minami Azabu 3-chome, Minato-ku, Tokyo 106; tel (3) 3446-8011; telex 22753; fax (3) 3446-8023.
Ambassador: Seyed Muhammad Hossein Adeli.
First Secretary: Majid Raeisi Nia.
Second Secretary: Masoud Maleki.
Second Secretary: Behzad Alipour Tehrani.
Third Secretary: Ali Akbar Khosravi Ghassemi.
Attaché: Hossein Aminian.
Attaché: Hadi Harati Sepehr.

IRAQ

Embassy: 4-7, Akasaka 8-chome, Minato-ku, Tokyo 107; tel (3) 3423-1727; telex 28825; fax (3) 3402-8636.
Ambassador: Dr Rashid M. S. al-Rifai.
Attaché: Nawaf S. Taka.
Commercial Attaché: Ahmed Hamid Mahdi.
Attaché: Ali Shakur H. Al-Bakri.
First Secretary: Khalid D. Shebli.
Third Secretary: Jamal A. Al-Gebory.

IRELAND

Embassy: Kowa Bldg, No. 25, 8-7, Sanban-cho, Chiyoda-ku, Tokyo 102; tel (3) 3263-0695; telex 23926; fax (3) 3265-2275.
Ambassador: James A. Sharkey.
First Secretary: Kathryn Coll.
Second Secretary: Peter McIvor.

Counsellor (Education/Training/Science): Declan Collins.

Consulate: Mitsui & Co., Ltd, 1-2-1 Ohtemachi, Chiyoda-ku, Tokyo 100-91; tel (3) 3285-7723; telex 22967; fax (3) 3546-9161.
Honorary Consul: Teruhiko Nishi.

ISRAEL

Embassy: 3, Niban-cho, Chiyoda-ku, Tokyo 102; tel (3) 3264-0911; telex 22636; fax (3) 3261-1138.
Ambassador: Nahum Eshkol.
Minister-Counsellor (Political): Eitan Margalit.
Minister-Counsellor: Arie Arazi.
Minister-Counsellor (Economic): Max Livrat.
Counsellor: David Gabay.
First Secretary (Information): Amos Radian.
First Secretary: Dan Eldar.
Cultural Attaché: Flora Margalit.
Attaché: Ronen Erez.
Counsellor (Economic Affairs): Jacob Pass.
Defence and Armed Forces Attaché: Brig.-Gen. Yuval Daliot.

ITALY

Embassy: 5-4, Mita 2-chome, Minato-ku, Tokyo 108; tel (3) 3453-5291; telex 22433; fax (3) 3456-2319.
Ambassador: Bartolomeo Attolico.
Minister-Counsellor: Francesco Peano.
Counsellor: Salvatore Pinna.
Counsellor (Commercial): Luigi Maccotta.
First Secretary: Francesco Maria Taló.
First Secretary (Commercial): Gianluigi Benedetti.
Attaché: Franco Mazzei.
Attaché (Scientific): Umberto Ratti.
Cultural Attaché: Giorgio de Marchis Bonanni d'Ocre.

Consulate-General: Twin 21 MID Tower 31F, 2-1-61, Shiromi, Chuo-ku, Osaka 540; tel (6) 949-0741; telex 64569; fax (6) 949-2970.
Consul-General: Pierluigi Squillante.

JORDAN

Embassy: 4A, B, Chiyoda House, 4th Floor, 17-8, Nagata-cho 2-chome, Chiyoda-ku, Tokyo 100; tel (3) 3580-5856; telex 23708; fax (3) 3593-9385.
Ambassador: Khaled Madadha.
Second Secretary and Consul: Mohammad K. H. Al-Boukary.
Attaché: Suheil S. J. Haddad.

KENYA

Embassy: 24-3, Yakumo 3-chome, Meguro-ku, Tokyo 152; tel (3) 3723-4006; telex 22378; fax (3) 3723-4488.
Ambassador: Stephen K. Ole Leken.
Counsellor: John D. Odede.
First Secretary (Immigration): Gabriel N. Macharia.
Administrative Attaché: Robert S. Nduati.
Third Secretary (Finance): Gladys O. Okoth.
Attaché: Gladys B. Odera.

KOREA, REPUBLIC

Embassy: 2-5, Minami Azabu 1-chome, Minato-ku, Tokyo 106; tel (3) 3452-7611; telex 22045; fax (3) 3452-2696.

Consular Section: 7-32, Minami Azabu 1-chome, Minato-ku, Tokyo 106; tel (3) 3455-2601.

Cultural Section: Sunshine 60, 5th Floor, 1-1, Higashi Ikebukuro 3-chome, Toshima-ku, Tokyo 170; tel (3) 3988-9271.
Ambassador: Lee Won-kyung.
Minister: Kim Byung Yeon.
Minister: Lee Hahn Choon.
Minister: Kim Hong B.
Minister: Chung Hyung Soo.

KUWAIT

Embassy: 13-12, Mita 4-chome, Minato-ku, Tokyo 108; tel (3) 3455-0361; telex 25501; fax (3) 3456-6290.
Ambassador: Abdul-Aziz Abdullatif al-Sharikh.
First Secretary: Adel Mohammad Hasan.
Second Secretary: Monther Al-Eissa.

LAOS

Embassy: 3-6-2, Minami-magome, Ota-ku, Tokyo 143; tel (3) 3778-1660; fax (3) 3778-1661.
Ambassador: K. Sayakone.
Second Secretary: Chacky Boudtavong.
Attaché: Sisavath Khamsaly.

LEBANON

Embassy: Chiyoda House, 5th Floor, 17-8, Nagata-cho 2-chome, Chiyoda-ku, Tokyo 100; tel (3) 3580-1206; telex 25356; fax (3) 3580-2281.
Ambassador: Samir el-Khoury.

LIBERIA

Embassy: Odakyu Fudosan Minami Aoyama Bldg, 6th Floor, 8-1, Minami Aoyama 7-chome, Minato-ku, Tokyo 107; tel (3) 3499-2451; fax (3) 3499-2453.
Ambassador: Stephen J. Koffa, Sr.
First Secretary and Consul: Harry Tah Freeman, Sr.

LIBYA

People's Bureau: 10-14, Daikanyama-cho, Shibuya-ku, Tokyo 150; tel (3) 3477-0701; telex 22181; fax (3) 3464-0420.
Secretary of the People's Bureau: Muftah R. Naili (acting).
Information and Cultural Affairs: Taher Ali Marwan.
Financial Affairs: Hadi Mohamed Abudib.
Consular Affairs: Nouri Ahmed Mokhtar.
Administrative Affairs: Ali M. Sereti.

LUXEMBOURG

Embassy: Niban-cho TS Bldg, 4th Floor, 2-1, Niban-cho, Chiyoda-ku, Tokyo 102; tel (3) 3265-9621; telex 28822; fax (3) 3265-9624.
Ambassador: Jean-Louis Wolzfeld.

MADAGASCAR

Embassy: 3-23, Moto Azabu 2-chome, Minato-ku, Tokyo 106; tel (3) 3446-7252; telex 25941; fax (3) 3446-7078.
Ambassador: Hubert M. Rajaobelina.
First Counsellor: Norbert Rakotomalala.
Counsellor: Yves Ramiaramanana.
Attaché: Jean Albert Ibia.

MALAYSIA

Embassy: 1-11 Minami Azabu 2-chome, Minato-ku, Tokyo 106; tel (3) 3280-7601; telex 24221; fax (3) 3280-7606.
Ambassador: Datuk H. M. Khatib.
Minister-Counsellor: Hamidon Ali.
Minister-Counsellor: Othman Abdul Razak.
Counsellor: Kamal Ismaun.
Defence Attaché: Capt. Cheah Phee Cheng.
Counsellor (Commercial): Rosli Abdul Shukor.
First Secretary: Salman Ahmad.
First Secretary (Commercial): Abdul Ghafar Musa.
First Secretary (Administration): Othman P. Mohamed.
Second Secretary: Badruddin Ab. Rahman.
Second Secretary: Mohamed Shazili Moris.
Second Secretary (Information): Abdul Aziz Abdul Rahman.
Second Secretary: Amry Mohamed Jamil.
Second Secretary (Administration): Samsudin Mahassan.
Third Secretary (Consular/Immigration): Mohamed Marzuki Mohamed Amin.

MALTA

Consulate-General: Toho Mutual Life Insurance Co, 15-1, Shibuya 2-chome, Shibuya-ku, Tokyo 150; tel (3) 3499-1111; telex 2428069; fax (3) 3797-6782.
Honorary Consul-General: Seizo Ota.

Consulate: Habuki Kyoto Kimono Scholl, 1-15-6, Kita-ohtsuka, Toshima-ku, Tokyo 170; tel (3) 3940-6764; fax (3) 3576-6262.
Honorary Consul: T. Mizushima.

MEXICO

Embassy: 15-1, Nagata-cho 2-chome, Chiyoda-ku, Tokyo 100; tel (3) 3581-1131; telex 26875; fax (3) 3581-4058.
Ambassador: Alfredo Philips.
Minister (Head of Chancery): Abelardo Treviño.
Minister (Economic Affairs): Jorge Efren Domínguez Ramírez.

Office of the Naval Attaché: tel (3) 3581-4802; fax (3) 3581-4802.
Naval Attaché: Vice-Adm. Guillermo Gerardo González Zamudio.

Office of the Commercial Counsellor: tel (3) 3580-0811; fax (3) 3580-9204.
Counsellor (Commercial): Carlos Casas Guerrero.
Counsellor (Economic): José Luis Romero-Hicks.

Tourism Section: tel (3) 3581-2110.
Counsellor (Tourism Affairs): Horacio Reyes.

Press and Information Section: tel (3) 3581-0845.
Counsellor (Press and Information): Alberto López Habib.

Consular Section: tel (3) 3580-2961.
First Secretary and Consul: Enrique Maldonado Diaz.
Second Secretary: Alejandro Madrigal Becerra.
Attaché (Financial Affairs): Alfonso Rodríguez Alvarez.
Attaché (Administration): Carlos Padilla Noriega.

Office of the Cultural Attaché: tel (3) 3581-2150.

MICRONESIA

Embassy: Tokyo.
Ambassador: Masao Nakayama.

MONGOLIA

Embassy: Pine Crest Mansion, 21-4, Shoto, Kamiyama-cho, Shibuya-ku, Tokyo 150; tel (3) 3469-2088; fax (3) 3469-2216.
Ambassador: Buyantyn Dashtseren.
First Secretary: Surenjavyn Ganbold.
Third Secretary (Press and Information): Chultemiin Namchin.

Commercial Section: tel (3) 3469-2092.
Commercial and Economic Attaché: Dejidiin Bayanbat.

MOROCCO

Embassy: Silva Kingdom Bldg, 5th and 6th Floors, 16-3, Sendagaya 3-chome, Shibuya-ku, Tokyo 151; tel (3) 3478-3271; telex 23451; fax (3) 3402-0898.
Ambassador: Saad Eddine Taieb.
Counsellor: Dr Samir Arrour.

MYANMAR

Embassy: 8-26, Kita Shinagawa 4-chome, Shinagawa-ku, Tokyo 140; tel (3) 3441-9291; telex 32289; fax (3) 3447-7394.
Ambassador: U Mya Thein.
Counsellor: U Tun Ngwe.

Office of Military, Naval and Air Attaché: tel (3) 3441-9296.
Military, Naval and Air Attaché: Col Win Sein.
First Secretary: Daw Win Win May.
Third Secretary: U Khin Maung Lynn.
Third Secretary: U Aung Ba Kyu.
Third Secretary: U Soe Maung.
Attaché: U Thet Lwin.
Attaché: U Ave Lwin.

NEPAL

Embassy: 14-9, Todoroki 7-chome, Setagaya-ku, Tokyo 158; tel (3) 3705-5558; telex 23936; fax (3) 3705-8264.
Ambassador: Narayan Prasad Arjal.
Counsellor: Bhanu Prasad Thapliya.
Attaché: Gaurishwor Regmi.

NETHERLANDS

Embassy: 6-3, Shiba Koen 3-chome, Minato-ku, Tokyo 105; tel (3) 3431-5126; telex 22855; fax (3) 3432-7560.

Agricultural Office: Amerex Bldg, 7th Floor, 5-7, Azabudai 3-chome, Minato-ku, Tokyo 106; tel (3) 3582-2500; fax (3) 3505-6360.

Industrial and Scientific Offices: Denmark House, 17-35, Minami Aoyama 4-chome, Minato-ku, Tokyo 107; tel (3) 3403-4261; fax (3) 3403-4230.
Ambassador: Herman C. Posthumus Meyjes.
Minister Plenipotentiary: Dick T. F. van Thessen.
Counsellor (Political/Consular): Dirk T. Schuurman Volker.
Counsellor (Economic/Commercial): Joost C. Dirkzwager.
First Secretary (Press/Cultural): Marion Pennink.
Second Secretary (Economic/Commercial): Aart Jacobi.
Second Secretary (Administrative/Consular): J. E. M. de Bruijn.

Consulate-General: Kobe CIT Bldg, POB 30, Kobe 651; tel (78) 232-3400; fax (78) 231-4787.
Consul-General: W. J. Witkam.

NEW ZEALAND

Embassy: 20-40, Kamiyama-cho, Shibuya-ku, Tokyo 150; tel (3) 3467-2271; fax (3) 3467-2285.
Ambassador: Rodney James Gates.
Minister and Consul-General: Christopher John Elder.
Minister (Commercial): Eugene A. Bowen.
Counsellor: Ian F. Kennedy.
Counsellor (Administration) and Consul: Michael Godfrey.
First Secretary (Commercial): Elizabeth Gollan.
First Secretary (Commercial): D. Brett Douglas.
Second Secretary: Philip A. Turner.
Second Secretary: John Reweti Mataira.

Tourism Dept Office: Toho Twin Tower Bldg, 2nd Floor, 1-5-2 Yurakucho, Chiyoda-ku, Tokyo 100; tel (3) 3508-9902; telex 32427; fax (3) 3501-2326.
Director: Richard Bollard.
Deputy Director: Sarah McLauchlan.

Consulate: 2-12-1 Diamyo-cho, Chuo-ku, Fukuoka 810; tel (92) 751-4429; fax (92) 751-4626.
Honorary Consul: Kazumi Nakayama.

Consulate: 2-2-22 Aoba-cho, Tomakomai-Shi, Hokkaido 053; tel (144) 34-1122; fax (144) 32-3597.
Honorary Consul: Ikuo Matsui.

Consulate: Rinnai Corporation, 2-26 Fukuzumi-cho, Nakagawa-ku, Nagoya 454; tel (52) 361-8211; fax (52) 353-9554.
Honorary Consul: Susunu Naito.

Consulate: Yamanishi Fukushi Kinen Kaikan, 11-12 Kamiyama-cho, Kita-ku, Osaka 530; tel (6) 315-1868; fax (6) 316-1094.
Honorary Consul: Etsuro Yamanishi.

NICARAGUA

Embassy: Kowa Bldg, No. 38, Room 903, 9th Floor, 12-24, Nishi Azabu 4-chome, Minato-ku, Tokyo 106; tel (3) 3499-0400; telex 28119; fax (3) 3499-3800.
Chargé d'affaires a.i., Counsellor and Consul: Salvador E. Stadthagen.

NIGERIA

Embassy: 2-19-7, Uehara, Shibuya-ku, Tokyo 151; tel (3) 3468-5531; telex 24397.
Ambassador: Mai-Bukar Garba Dogon-Yaro.
Minister: Dr J. J. Lewu.
First Secretary: L. A. Ayodele.
Administrative Attaché: A. Adenowo.
Financial Attaché: A. O. Ogundola.

NORWAY

Embassy: 12-2, Minami Azabu 5-chome, Minato-ku, Tokyo 106; tel (3) 3440-2611; telex 26440; fax (3) 3440-2689.
Ambassador: Terje Johannessen.
Minister-Counsellor: Willum Steen.
Counsellor (Science and Technology): Finn Helge Messel.
First Secretary: Aage Grutle.

OMAN

Embassy: Silva Kingdom Bldg, 3rd Floor, 3-16-3, Sendagaya, Shibuya-ku, Tokyo 151; tel (3) 3402-0749; telex 29544; fax (3) 3404-1334.
First Secretary and Chargé d'affaires a.i.: Mohamed Said Rajad Al-Ajeel.
First Secretary: Fakhry Mohamed Said Al-Said.

PAKISTAN

Embassy: 14-9, Moto Azabu 2-chome, Minato-ku, Tokyo 106; tel (3) 3454-4861; fax (3) 3454-4863.
Ambassador: Mansur Ahmed.
Minister and Deputy Head of Mission: Asif Ezdi.
Defence Attaché: Brig. Muhammad Naim Rana.
Minister (Technical): Dr Mohammad Aslam.
Commercial Counsellor: Ashraf M. Hayat.
Press Attaché: Mohammad Sharif.
Third Secretary: Mohammad Raza Otho.

PANAMA

Embassy: Kowa Bldg, No. 38, Room 902, 9th Floor, 12-24, Nishi Azabu 4-chome, Minato-ku, Tokyo 106; tel (3) 3499-3741; telex 22157; fax (3) 5485-3548.
Ambassador: Alberto A. Boyd Arias.
Third Secretary: Enrique Victoria C.

PAPUA NEW GUINEA

Embassy: Mita Kokusai Bldg, Room 313, 3rd Floor, 1-4-28, Mita, Minato-ku, Tokyo 108; tel (3) 3454-7801; telex 25488; fax (3) 3454-7275.
Ambassador: Joseph Kaal Nombri.
Counsellor: Larry Hulo.
First Secretary: C. Wariambu.
Third Secretary: T. Imint.

PARAGUAY

Embassy: Asahi Kami Osaki Bldg, 5th Floor, 5-8, Kami Osaki 3-chome, Shinagawa-ku, Tokyo 141; tel (3) 3447-7496; telex 27496; fax (3) 3447-6184.
Ambassador: Juan Carlos A. Hrase von Bargen.

PERU

Embassy: 4-27, Higashi 4-chome, Shibuya-ku, Tokyo 150; tel (3) 3406-4240; telex 26435; fax (3) 3409-7589.

Commercial Office: Estate MB, 19-3, Tsurumaki 5-chome, Setagaya-ku, Tokyo 154; tel (3) 3439-0261.
Ambassador: Víctor Aritomi Shinto.
Minister: Juan Carlos Capuñay Chávez.
Counsellor: Iván Pinto Román.
Third Secretary: Lanzeth Ludeña López.
Third Secretary: Rubén Espinoza Raymondi.

PHILIPPINES

Embassy: 11-24, Nampeidai-machi, Shibuya-ku, Tokyo 150; tel (3) 3496-2731; telex 22694.
Ambassador: Ramon V. del Rosario.
Minister and Deputy Head of Mission: Benjamin F. Sanvictores.
Minister-Counsellor: Maria Rosario Janolo.
First Secretary and Consul-General: Jesus I. Yabes.
First Secretary and Consul: Maria Zeneida P. Angara-Collinson.
Second Secretary and Consul: Jocelyn B. Garcia.
Second Secretary and Consul: Pedro B. Firmalino.
Second Secretary and Consul: Evan P. Garcia.
Armed Forces Attaché: Col Rodolfo S. Estrellado.
Agricultural Attaché: Joseph Z. Sison.
Economic Attaché: Dativo B. Leyson.
Labour Attaché: Reynaldo B. Parurgao.
Commercial Attaché: Benicio Eusebio, Jr.
Commercial Attaché: Mauino T. Haresco.
Commercial Attaché: Agustin Mangila, Jr.

Consulate-General: Taiwa Bldg, 4th Floor, 18-1 Akashi-mashi, Chou-ku, Kobe; tel (78) 331-9471.
Consul-General: Jesus C. Alvaro.

POLAND

Embassy: 13-5, Mita 2-chome, Meguro-ku, Tokyo 153; tel (3) 3711-5224; telex 23314; fax (3) 3760-3100.
Chargé d'affaires a.i.: Tadeusz Pawlak.
Commercial Counsellor: Nikodem B. Muszynski.
First Secretary: Wieslaw Szczuka.
First Secretary (Consular/Administrative): Waclay Rytel.
Second Secretary: Zbigniew Golebiowski.
Second Secretary: Witld Karp.
Third Secretary: Miroslaw Blaszczak.
Third Secretary: Zbigniew Karczewski.
Commercial Attaché: Eugeniusz Olczak.
Deputy Commercial Attaché: Zbigniew Rucinski.
Deputy Commercial Attaché: Aleksander Jodko.

PORTUGAL

Embassy: Olympia Annex, Apt 304-306, 31-21, Jingumae 6-chome, Shibuya-ku, Tokyo 105; tel (3) 3400-7907; telex 24826; fax (3) 3400-7909.
Ambassador: Dr José Eduardo Mello Gouveia.
Counsellor: Ana Maria Rosa Martins Gomes.
First Secretary: José Costa Pereira.
First Secretary and Head of Consular Section: Manuel Gonçalves de Jesus.
Attaché and Vice-Consul: Maria Joana do Amaral Abranches Pinto.
Cultural Attaché: Eduardo Kol de Carvalho.

Commercial Department: 8-5-8, Akasaka, Minato-ku, Tokyo 107; tel (3) 3470-7162; fax (3) 3470-7164.
Commercial Counsellor: Camilo Martins de Oliveira.
Commercial Counsellor: José Antonio Duarte Preto da Silva.

Consulate: 1-3-18, Sowa-cho, Nada-ku, Kobe; tel (78) 851-9538.
Honorary Consul: Wenceslau José de Couto.

Consulate: The 18th Bank, 1-11, Doza-machi, Nagasaki-shi; tel (958) 24-1818.
Honorary Consul: Shozo Kiyoshima.

Consulate: Sakai-Suji Inabata Bldg, 1-15-14, Minami Semba, Chuo-ku, Osaka 542; tel (6) 267-6090; fax (6) 267-6042.
Honorary Consul: Katsuo Inabata.

Consulate: Kuramaguchi-agaru, Horikawa-dori, Kita-ku, Kyoto; tel (75) 432-5158.
Honorary Consul: Yoshiharu Naya.
Honorary Vice-Consul: Shiro Usui.

Consulate: 3-5, Minamisako 4-bancho, Tokushima-shi; tel (886) 25-2400.
Honorary Consul: Kazusada Nagao.

Consulate: Toyota Motor Corp., Nagoya Office, 1-23-22, Izumi, Higashi-ku, Nagoya-shi; tel (52) 952-2111.
Honorary Consul: Eiji Toyoda.

QATAR

Embassy: 16-22, Shirogane 6-chome, Minato-ku, Tokyo 108; tel (3) 3446-7561; telex 24877; fax (3) 3443-1270.
First Secretary and Chargé d'affaires a.i.: Ahmed Saif Al-Midhadi.

ROMANIA

Embassy: 16-19, Nishi-Azabu 3-chome, Minato-ku, Tokyo 106; tel (3) 3479-0311; telex 22664; fax (3) 3479-0312.
Ambassador: Mircea Mitran.
Counsellor: Ion Scumpieru.
Counsellor: Constantin Tapu.
Military, Air and Naval Attaché: Commdr Marian Ioan.
Commercial Counsellor: Teodor Munteanu.
First Secretary: Dan Tudor Nica.
Second Secretary: Adrian Isac.
Second Secretary (Economic): Catalin Costache.
Second Secretary (Economic): Dan Simion.

RUSSIA

Embassy: 2-1-1, Azabudai, Minato-ku, Tokyo 106; tel (3) 3583-0408; telex 24231; fax (3) 3505-0593.

Press Section: 9-13, Higashi Gotanda 3-chome, Shinagawa-ku, Tokyo 141; tel (3) 3447-3536.

Office of Trade Representative: 6-9, Takanawa 4-chome, Minato-ku, Tokyo 108; tel (3) 3447-3291.
Ambassador: Ludvig Chizhov.
Minister-Counsellor: Yuri D. Kauznetsov.
Minister-Counsellor: Nikolai N. Borisov.
Counsellor: Nikolai A. Sirenko.
Counsellor: Vadim M. Nikolaev.
Counsellor: Vasili N. Dobrovolski.
Counsellor and Consul-General: Victor N. Lizun.
Military and Air Attaché: Col Vitali I. Frolov.
First Secretary: Aleksandr E. Belyaev.
First Secretary: Aleksandr V. Khmelev.
First Secretary: Igor M. Ivanov.
Second Secretary: Vareril I. Nechiporenko.
Second Secretary: Vasili V. Kulakov.
Second Secretary: Mikhail A. Mirolyubov.

Consulate-General: Toyonaka-shi, Nishimidori-gaoka 1-2-2, Osaka; tel (6) 848-3452.

Consulate-General: 064 Nishi 12-chome, Minami 14-jo, Chuo-ku, Sapporo; tel (11) 561-3171; fax (11) 561-8897.

RWANDA

Embassy: Kowa Bldg, No. 38, Room 702, 12-24, Nishi Azabu 4-chome, Minato-ku, Tokyo 106; tel (3) 3486-7800; telex 27701; fax (3) 3409-2434.
Ambassador: Ildephonse Munyeshyaka.
First Counsellor: Ukobizaba Martin.
First Secretary: Sérapion Karera.

Consulate-General: Shinjuku Centre Bldg, POB 4197, 1-25-1, Nishi-Shinjuku, Shinjuku-ku, 163-91; tel 342-2886.
Honorary Consul-General: Masaya Hattori.

SAINT VINCENT AND THE GRENADINES

Consulate: Fugaku Bldg, 5F, 6-15-12, Akasaka, Minato-ku, Tokyo; tel (3) 587-1011.
Honorary Consul: Akira Watanabe.

SAN MARINO

Consulate-General: 802 Shuwa Residence, 4-11-7 Nishi-Azabu, Minato-Ku, Tokyo 106; tel (3) 498-8427; telex 26932; fax (3) 407-6584.
Consul-General: Manlio Cadelo.

SAUDI ARABIA

Embassy: 1-53, Azabu Nagasaka-cho, Minato-ku, Tokyo 106; tel (3) 3589-5241; telex 25731.
Ambassador: Fawzi bin Abdul Majeed Shobokshi.
Third Secretary: Jameel A. Shesha.
Third Secretary: Mohammed A. Al-Othman.
Attaché: Abdulaziz H. H. Al-Harbi.

SENEGAL

Embassy: 3-4, Aobadai 1-chome, Meguro-ku, Tokyo 153; tel (3) 3464-8451; telex 25493; fax (3) 3464-8452.
Ambassador: Kéba Birane Cissé.
First Counsellor: Momar Gueye.
Second Counsellor: Mamadou Diarra.
First Secretary: Papa Yamar Dia.
Attaché: Abdoulaye Latyr Diagne.
Attaché: Doussou Samb.
Attaché: Assiétou Diarra.

SINGAPORE

Embassy: 12-3, Roppongi 5-chome, Minato-ku, Tokyo 106; tel (3) 3586-9111; telex 22404; fax (3) 3582-1085.
Ambassador: Lim Chin Beng.
Counsellor: Robert Chua.
First Secretary: Teng Cheong Thye.
Third Secretary: Goh Keng Swee Milton.

Commercial Section: tel (3) 3584-6032; telex 26354; fax (3) 3584-6135.
First Secretary (Commercial): Ling Ming Chuan.

Industry Section: Imperial Tower, 8th Floor, 1-1-1 Uchisaiwai-cho, Chiyoda-ku, Tokyo 100; tel (3) 3501-6041; telex 33310; fax (3) 3501-6060.
Counsellor (Industry): Chua Taik Him.
First Secretary (Industry): Wong Peng Wai.
First Secretary (Industry): Goh Chao Kuang.

Consulate-General: Osaka Kokusai Bldg 14F, 2-3-13 Azuchimachi, Chuo-ku, Osaka 541.

Commercial Section: tel (6) 262-2662; fax (6) 262-2664.
Consul and Head of Commercial Section: Goh Oon Tong.

Industry Section: tel (6) 261-5131; fax (6) 261-0338.
Consul and Head of Industry Section: Quek Keng Ngak.

SOMALIA

Embassy: 9-10, Shiroganedai 5-chome, Minato-ku, Tokyo 108; tel (3) 3442-7138; telex 33160.
Counsellor and Chargé d'affaires a.i.: Mohamed H. Jama.

SOUTH AFRICA

Consulate-General: 414 Zenkyoren Bldg, 7-9 Hirakawa-cho 2-chome, Chiyoda-ku, Tokyo 102; tel (3) 3265-3366; telex 26208; fax (3) 3237-6458.
Consul-General: A. W. Kuhn.
Consul: E. Grobler.
Consul: S. D. Els.
Consul (Administration): R. J. J. Matthee.
Consul (Commercial): H. S. Schoeman.
Consul (Minerals and Energy): B. J. S. Hornabrook.
Vice-Consul: T. N. Furter.
Vice-Consul (Commercial): G. F. Herselman.

Consulate: Kyoto.

SPAIN

Embassy: 3-29, Roppongi 1-chome, Minato-ku, Tokyo 106; tel (3) 3583-8531; telex 22471; fax (3) 3582-8627.
Ambassador: Antonio Oyarzábal.
Minister-Counsellor: Manuel Villavieja Vega.
First Secretary: Francisco Elías de Tejada Lozano.
First Secretary: Ana Maria Menéndez Pérez.
Commercial Counsellor: Genaro González Palacios.
Commercial Attaché: Antonio García Rebollar.
Attaché: Pablo Muller.

SRI LANKA

Embassy: 14-1, Akasaka 1-chome, Minato-ku, Tokyo 107; tel (3) 3585-7431; telex 24524; fax (3) 3586-9307.
Ambassador: Chithambaranathan Mahendran.
First Secretary (Commercial and Economic): P. D. Fernando.
Second Secretary (Cultural and Information): N. Karunadasa.
Attaché (Administration and Consular Affairs): S. M. U. Sangakkara.

SUDAN

Embassy: Yada Mansion, 6-20, Minami-Aoyama 6-chome, Minato-ku, Tokyo 107; tel (3) 3406-0811; telex 23876; fax (3) 3400-1925.
Ambassador: Dr Musa Mohammed Omer.
Counsellor: Abu El Gasim Abdel Wahid Sheikh Idris.
First Secretary: Nahid Osman Abu Akar.
Administrative Attaché: Omer Mohamed Osman Habib.

SWEDEN

Embassy: 10-3, Roppongi 1-chome, Minato-ku, Tokyo 106; POB 59, Azabu, Tokyo 106; tel (3) 5562-5350; telex 24586; fax (3) 5562-9095.
Ambassador: Ove F. Heyman.
Minister: Vollrath Tham.
Counsellor: Carl-Henrik Hamrin.
First Secretary: Alf Karlsson.
Second Secretary: Magnus Fiskesjö.
Second Secretary: Kaj Reinius.
Press Attaché: Carola Tham.
Second Secretary (Translation): Thomas Östergren.

Office of Science and Technology: Sweden Centre Bldg, 3rd Floor, 11-9 Roppongi, 6-chome, Minato-ku, Tokyo 106; tel (3) 3470-4181; fax (3) 3470-4185.
Scientific and Technical Attaché: Sten Bergman.

Assistant Scientific and Technical Attaché: Peter Hellentin.
Assistant Scientific and Technical Attaché: Lars Hälldahl.

Commercial Section: Sweden Centre Bldg, 2nd Floor; tel (3) 3403-9241; telex 24586; fax (3) 3408-2068.
Commercial Secretary: Göran Edman.

Consulate: c/o Holme Ringer & Co Ltd, Minato-machi 9-9, Moji-ku, Kitakyushi-shi; tel (93) 331-1311; fax (93) 321-2971.
Consul: Noriyuki Yamamoto.

Consulate: c/o Hayashi Daiichi Bldg, 4th Floor, Shimo Yamate-dori 2-13-3, Chuo-ku, Kobe 650; tel (78) 331-4518.
Vice-Consul: Yoshiaki Ohsaki.
Vice-Consul: Ichiro Tanaka.

Consulate: c/o Tokai Bank Ltd, Head Office, 21-24 Nishiki 3-chome, Naka-ku, Nagoya 460; tel (52) 211-1111; fax (52) 211-0947.
Consul: Shigemitsu Miyake.

Consulate: c/o Sapporo Toshi Kaihatsu Kosha (Urban Development) Co. Ltd, 6th Floor, Hinode Bldg, Minami 1, Nishi 4, Chuo-ku, Sapporo 060; tel (11) 231-6060; fax (11) 221-0659.
Consul: Tetsuya Hirase.

Consulate: c/o 77 Bank Ltd, 3-20, 3-chome, Chuo, Aoba-ku, Sendai-shi 980; tel (22) 267-1111.
Consul: Eiichi Ujiie.

Consulate: Park Nova Yokohama One, Rm 904, 1-13-14, Hiranuma, Nishi-ku, Yokohama; POB 117, Central Post Office, Yokohama 220-91; tel (45) 320-5253.
Vice-Consul: Katsumi Yamakawa.

SWITZERLAND

Embassy: 9-12, Minami Azabu 5-chome, Minato-ku, Tokyo 106; Azabu POB 38, Tokyo 106-91; tel (3) 3473-0121; telex 24282; fax (3) 3473-6090.
Ambassador: Roger Bär.
Minister: Dominique Dreyer.
Counsellor (Finance and Economic): Hans-Rudolf Hodel.
Counsellor for Industrial and Scientific Affairs: Jean-Marie Rayroux.
First Secretary (Press and Culture): Peter Reinhardt.
First Secretary (Commercial): Roland Bosshardt.
Attaché (Consular and Administration): Sergio Dini.
Defence: Col Walter Ritzmann.

Consulate-General: 'Dokita-Daibiru' Bldg, 7th Floor, 2-5, Dojima 1-chome, Kita-ku, Osaka 530; POB 1413 Central, Osaka 530-91; tel (6) 344-7671; fax (6) 344-7678.
Consul-General: Hans Meier.
Chancellor: Martin Bienz.

SYRIA

Embassy: Hornat Jade 19-45, Akasaka 6-chome, Minato-ku, Tokyo 107; tel (3) 3586-8977; telex 29405.
Ambassador: Dr Amin Esber.
Minister Plenipotentiary: Jalal Al-Baroudi.
Attaché: Talat Etawn.

TANZANIA

Embassy: 21-9, Kami Yoga 4-chome, Setagaya-ku, Tokyo 158; tel (3) 3425-4531; telex 22121; fax (3) 3425-7844.
Ambassador: Ali Said Mchumo.
Counsellor: Joseph N. Isaka.

THAILAND

Embassy: 14-6, Kami Osaki 3-chome, Shinagawa-ku, Tokyo 141; tel (3) 3441-1386; fax (3) 3442-6750.
Ambassador: M. L. Birabhongse Kasemsri.
Minister-Counsellor: Suchitra Hiranprueck.
Counsellor: Pridi Boonyobhas.
First Secretary: Adul Korwattana.
First Secretary: Wibunsawat Watanawarangkun.
First Secretary and Head of Consular Section: Isinthorn Sornvai.
First Secretary: Somsak Lickanajule.
Second Secretary: Chalermpol Thanchitt.
Second Secretary: Somsak Triamjangarun.
Third Secretary: Vichit Chitvimarn.
Third Secretary: Sompong Chalalai.
Third Secretary: Boonrong Pongstiensak.

Office of Defence, Army, Naval and Air Attachés: 15-21, Shimo Meguro 6-chome, Meguro-ku, Tokyo 153; tel (3) 3712-0950.
Defence and Army Attaché: Col Surapol Pichitka-deepol.
Assistant Army Attaché: Lieut Col Anusorn Teptada.
Naval Attaché: Capt. Sutee Buranasin.
Air Attaché: Group Capt. Xan Raktabtr.

Education Section: 23-12, Kami-Osaki 1-chome, Shinagawa-ku, Tokyo 141; tel (3) 3441-2674.
Counsellor (Education): Weera Chaiyatham.
First Secretary (Education): Chintamai Dhanakom.

Office of Commercial Counsellor: Shuwa Kioicho TBR Bldg, 4th Floor, Rm 401, 7 Koji-machi 5-chome, Chiyoda-ku, Tokyo 102; tel (3) 3221-9482; telex 25733; fax (3) 3221-9484.
Commercial Counsellor: Adul Vinaiphat.
First Secretary (Commercial): Songseen Susevi.
Second Secretary (Commercial): Amparwon Pichalai.

Customs Section: Meguro View Green, Rm 102, 10-58, Kami-Osaki 3-chome, Shinagawa-ku, Tokyo 141; tel (3) 3446-5496.
Counsellor (Customs): Sakda Taevajira.

Office of Economic Counsellor: Akasaka Brighton Bldg, 3rd Floor, 5-2, Akasaka 1-chome, Minato-ku, Tokyo 107; tel (3) 3582-0976; fax (3) 3589-5176.
Economic Counsellor: Somphong Wanapha.
First Secretary (Economic): Chaiyot Santiwong.

Office of Agricultural Counsellor: 27-9 Miyamae 4-chome, Suginami-ku, Tokyo 168; tel (3) 3355-1146; fax (3) 3335-1146.
Agricultural Counsellor: Chote Suvipakit.
First Secretary (Agriculture): Wichian Kamjaipai.

TUNISIA

Embassy: 1-18-8, Wakaba-cho, Shinjuku-ku, Tokyo 160; tel (3) 3353-4111; telex 27146; fax (3) 3225-4387.
Ambassador: Abdelhamid Ben Messaouda.
Second Secretary: Hichem Dhaoui.
Second Secretary: Jamel Boujdaria.
Attaché: Ali El Acheche.

TURKEY

Embassy: 33-6, Jingumae 2-chome, Shibuya-ku, Tokyo 150; tel (3) 3470-5131; telex 22856; fax (3) 3470-5136.
Ambassador: Umut Arik.
Counsellor: Ferit Ergin.
Naval, Military and Air Attaché: Commdr Cengiz Alpözü.

Economic and Commercial Office: tel (3) 3470-6723.
First Counsellor (Economic/Commercial): Kasim Vahap.
Second Counsellor (Economic/Commercial): Ersen Ekren.
Second Counsellor (Economic/Commercial): Ali Urkan.
First Secretary: Ali Riza Çolak.
Third Secretary: Akil Öktem.
Attaché: Ayhan Ecer.
Attaché: Yalçin Alagöz.
Attaché: Fevziye Bulut.
Attaché: Dursun Kerimoglu.

UGANDA

Consulate: c/o Yamato International Inc., 5-1-1 Heiwajiwa, Ohta-ku, Tokyo 143; tel (3) 768-3511; fax (3) 768-3724.
Honorary Consul: Yuichi Kashiwada.

Consulate: c/o Yamato International Inc., 2-3-9, Bakuro-machi, Chuo-ku, Osaka 541; tel (6) 262-1661; fax (6) 261-4343.
Honorary Consul: Fumiko Hannya.

UNITED ARAB EMIRATES

Embassy: Kotsu Anzen Kyoiku Centre Bldg, 7th Floor, 24-20, Nishi Azabu 3-chome, Minato-ku, Tokyo 106; tel (3) 3478-0650; telex 23552.
Ambassador: Hamad Salem al-Makami.
Second Secretary: Ahmed Abdulla Saeed Bin Soaid.

UNITED KINGDOM

Embassy: 1 Ichiban-cho, Chiyoda-ku, Tokyo 102; tel (3) 3265-5511; telex 22755; fax (3) 5275-3164.

Commercial, Information, Science and Technology and Atomic Energy Sections: tel (3) 3265-6340; fax (3) 3265-5580.

Consular Section: tel (3) 3265-6340; fax (3) 5275-0346.

Visa Section: tel (3) 3265-4001; fax (3) 5275-0346.
Ambassador: Sir John Whitehead.
Minister: E. J. Field.
Minister (Financial): J. E. W. Kirby.
Defence and Naval Attaché: Capt. C. M. C. Crawford.
Military and Air Attaché: Group Capt. A. L. Terrett.
Counsellor and Head of Chancery: G. H. Fry.
Counsellor (Commercial): P. S. Dimond.
Counsellor (Economic): C. T. W. Humfrey.
Counsellor: L. C. R. Seeley.
Counsellor (Management) and Consul-General: D. Pragnell.

Office of Cultural Counsellor: The British Council, 2 Kagurazaka 1-chome, Shinjuku-ku, Tokyo 162; tel (3) 3235-8031; telex 27761.
Counsellor (Cultural-British Council Director): R. P. Joscelyne.
Counsellor (Atomic Energy): C. Loughlin.
Counsellor (Science/Technology): Dr R. A. Hinder.
First Secretary (Economic): A. J. Alderson.
First Secretary (Commercial): N. K. Hook.
First Secretary (Commercial): S. J. Plater.
First Secretary (Science/Technology): T. T. Salusbury.
First Secretary (Economic): P. D. Madden.
First Secretary (Cultural-British Council): J. H. G. Foley.
First Secretary (Information): R. E. Coghlan.
First Secretary (Chancery): M. R. Everest-Phillips.
First Secretary (Chancery): D. H. Powell.
First Secretary (Economic): S. L. McNeil-Ritchie.
First Secretary (Economic): S. J. M. Smith.
Second Secretary (Management): J. F. Hogwood.
Second Secretary (Works): B. R. Hooker.

Consulate-General: Hong Kong and Shanghai Bank Bldg, 6-1, 3-chome, Awaji-machi, Choo-

ku, Osaka 541; tel (6) 231-3355; fax (6) 202-4312.
Consul-General and Director of Trade Promotion: G. J. B. Williams.
Consul (Commercial): R. A. Rayner.
Third Secretary (Management) and Vice-Consul: D. Moore.

Consulate: The Nishi-Nippon Bank Ltd, 1-3-6 Hakata-Ekimae, Hakata-ku, Fukuoka City; tel (92) 411-2525; telex 724511.
Honorary Consul: K. Ichikawa.

Consulate: c/o Hiroshima Bank Ltd, 3-8, 1-chome Kamiyacho, Naka-ku, Hiroshima; tel (82) 247-5151; fax (82) 247-3664.
Honorary Consul: O. Hashiguchi.

Consulate: c/o Tokai Bank Ltd, 21-24, 3-chome, Nishiki, Naka-ku, Nagoya; tel (52) 211-1111; fax (52) 211-0920.
Honorary Consul: R. Kato.

USA

Embassy: 10-1, Akasaka 1-chome, Minato-ku, Tokyo 107; tel (3) 3224-5000; telex 22118; fax (3) 35821-0496.
Ambassador: Michael H. Armacost.
Deputy Chief of Mission: William T. Breer.
Political Section: Rust M. Deming.
Economic Section: Joseph A. B. Winder.
Commercial Section: Keith R. Bovetti.
Consul: Nancy H. Sambaiew.
Administrative Section: José J. Cao-García.
Regional Security Officer: Walter H. Sargent.
Public Affairs Officer: Robert L. M. Nevitt.
Communications Programme Officer: Marvin A. Konopik.
Information Systems Manager: William J. Camp III.
Scientific Attaché: Edward M. Malloy.
Office of the Defence Attaché: Capt. Scott A. Van Hoften.
Agricultural Trade Office: Laverne Brabant.
Agricultural Section: James V. Parker.
Labour Officer: John J. La Mazza.
Internal Revenue Service: Dennis Tsujimoto.
Customs Service (Treasury): Gary W. Waugh.
Department of Energy: Milton A. Eaton.
Federal Aviation Administration: Dennis J. Warth.
Financial Attaché (Treasury): John I. Weeks.

Export Development Office: 7th Floor, World Import Mart, 1-3 Higashi Ikebukuro 3-chome, Toshima-ku, Tokyo 170; tel (3) 3987-2441; fax (3) 3987-2447.
Director: Thomas Moore.

Consulate-General: 2564 Nishihara, Urasoe City, Okinawa 90121; tel (98) 876-4211; fax (98) 876-4243.
Consul-General: Lawrence F. Farrar.
Political/Military Section: Hugo Carl Gettinger.
Consular/Administrative Section: Kenneth Shivers.

Consulate-General: 11-5, Nishitenma 2-chome, Kita-ku, Osaka 530; tel (6) 315-5900; telex 5233037; fax (6) 361-5397.
Consul-General: Gregory L. Johnson.
Political/Economic Section: Robert S. Luke.
Commercial Section: Patrick O. Santillo.
Consul: Edward McKeon.
Administrative Section: Peter A. Prahar.
Branch Public Affairs Officer: Laurence D. Wohlers.

Consulate-General: Kita 1-Jo Nishi 28-chome, Chuo-ku, Sapporo 064; tel (11) 641-1115; telex 935338; fax (11) 643-1283.
Consul-General: Roger L. Dankert.
Consul: Gary G. Oba.
Branch Public Affairs Officer: Patrick J. Linehan.

Consulate: 5-26 Ohori 2-chome, Chuo-ku, Fukuoka 810; tel (92) 751-9331; telex 725679; fax (92) 713-9222.
Principal Officer: Evans J. R. Revere.
Economic/Commercial Section: Stanley A. Otto.
Consul: Alec Wilczynski.
Branch Public Affairs Officer: Donna Ann Welton.

URUGUAY

Embassy: Kowa Bldg, No. 38, Room 908, 12-24, Nishi Azabu 4-chome, Minato-ku, Tokyo 106; tel (3) 3486-1888; telex 22843; fax (3) 3486-9872.
Ambassador: Alfredo Giró Pintos.

Consular Section: tel (3) 3486-1750.
First Secretary and Head of Consular Section: Eduardo C. Añon.
First Secretary: Juan Draper.

VENEZUELA

Embassy: Kowa Bldg, No. 38, 7th Floor, Rm 703, 12-24, Nishi Azabu 4-chome, Minato-ku, Tokyo 106; tel (3) 3409-1501; telex 25255; fax (3) 3409-1505.
Ambassador: Fernando Báez-Duarte.
Second Secretary: Roberto Larrazabal T.
Third Attaché: Efrain Vivas Yapur.

Consular Section: tel (3) 3409-1503.

VIET-NAM

Embassy: 50-11, Moto Yoyogi-cho, Shibuya-ku, Tokyo 151; tel (3) 3466-3311; fax (3) 3466-3312.
Ambassador: Vo Van Sung.

Commercial Section: tel (3) 3466-3315; fax (3) 3466-3315.
Commercial Counsellor: Duong Van Thu.
First Secretary: Luu Van Ke.
First Secretary (Economic Affairs): Nguyen Dang Quang.
Second Secretary (Economic Affairs): Nguyen Canh Ruong.
Second Secretary (Visa Affairs): Tran Van Them.
Second Secretary (Protocol Affairs): Nguyen Minh Ha.
Second Secretary (Press/Culture): Vu Duc Chinh.
Third Secretary (Consular Affairs): Pham Quang Toan.

YEMEN

Embassy: Kowa Bldg, No. 38, Room 807, 12-24, Nishi Azabu 4-chome, Minato-ku, Tokyo 106; tel (3) 3499-7151; telex 32431; fax (3) 3499-4577.
Ambassador: Muhammad Abdul Koddos Alwazir.
First Secretary: Abdulrahman Mohamed Alhothi.

YUGOSLAVIA

Embassy: 7-24, Kita Shinagawa 4-chome, Shinagawa-ku, Tokyo 140; tel (3) 3447-3571; telex 22360; fax (3) 3447-3573.
Ambassador: Tarik Ajanović.
Minister-Counsellor: Radoman Jovic.
First Secretary: Rifat Rondic.

ZAIRE

Embassy: Harajuku Green Heights, Room 701, 53-17, Sendagaya 3-chome, Shibuya-ku, Tokyo 151; tel (3) 3423-3981; telex 24211; fax (3) 3423-1984.
Minister Plenipotentiary and Chargé d'affaires a.i.: Ngambani zi Mizele Zingila.
Second Counsellor: Ilanga Bolombo.
Second Counsellor (Co-operation): Kyungu Nyemba.
First Secretary: Kondo Onzege.

ZAMBIA

Embassy: 3-9-19, Ebisu, Shibuya-ku, Tokyo 150; tel (3) 3445-1041; telex 25210; fax (3) 3445-8239.
Ambassador: Boniface Salimu Zulu.
Second Secretary (Political): Lucy M. Mungoma.
Third Secretary: Charles B. Habwanda.
Third Secretary: Rosemary C. Nzala.

ZIMBABWE

Embassy: 5-9-10, Shiroganedai, Minato-ku, Tokyo 108; tel (3) 3280-0331; telex 32075; fax (3) 3280-0466.
Ambassador: Dr Tendai Mutunhu.
Counsellor: Robert Masango.
First Secretary: Spencer Dube.
First Secretary: Charles Mandudzo.
Second Secretary: Allan Ncube.
Third Secretary: Felicity Mukudu.

International Organizations

EUROPEAN COMMUNITIES

External Delegation: Europa House, 9-15 Sanbancho, Chiyoda-ku, Tokyo 102; tel (3) 3239-0441; telex 28567; fax (3) 3261-5194.
Head of Delegation: Jean-Pierre Leng.
Minister-Counsellor: Pierre J. H. Del Grande.
Counsellor (Head of Press/Information): António de Menezes.
Attaché (Deputy Head of Press/Information): Miguel Orozco.
Counsellor (Science/Technology): Maurice Bourène.
Counsellor (Economic/Financial): Seamus Gillespie.
Counsellor (Trade/Industry): Michael Graham.
First Secretary (Agriculture/Transport): Albrecht Rothacher.
Second Secretary (Export Promotion/Aid): João Aguiar Machado.
Second Secretary: Gerard Legris.
Attaché (Administration): Aldo Dalvit.
Attaché (Commercial): Adelheid Hofmann.
Second Secretary: Rüdiger Altpeter.

UNITED NATIONS CHILDREN'S FUND—UNICEF

Representation: Tokyo.
Director: Anwarul Karim Chowdhury.

JORDAN

ALGERIA

Embassy: 3rd Circle, Jabal Amman; tel (6) 641271.
Ambassador: Abderrahman Shrayyet.

AUSTRALIA

Embassy: POB 35201, 4th Circle, Zahran St, Jabal Amman; tel (6) 673246; telex 21743; fax (6) 673260.
Ambassador: G. R. Bowker.

AUSTRIA

Embassy: Hotel Jordan Intercontinental, POB 815368, Amman; tel (6) 644635; telex 22484.
Ambassador: Dr Franz Pernegger.
Economic Counsellor: Helmut Köller.

Visa Section: Hotel Amra, Rm 217, Amman; tel (6) 815071.

BAHRAIN

Embassy: Amman; tel (6) 664148.
Ambassador: Ibrahim Ali Ibrahim.

BELGIUM

Embassy: Andalous St, POB 942, Jabal Amman; tel (6) 675683; telex 22340; fax (6) 697487.
Ambassador: Johan Ballegeer.

BRAZIL

Embassy: POB 5497, Amman; tel (6) 642183; telex 23827.
Ambassador: Félix Baptista de Faria.

BULGARIA

Embassy: POB 950578, Al Mousel St, Um Uzaina al-Janoubi, Amman; tel (6) 818151; telex 23246; fax (6) 818153.
Chargé d'affaires a.i.: Ludmil Spassov.

Trade Representation Section: POB 950344, Dahran St, 6th Circle, Jabal Amman; tel (6) 813193; fax (6) 813194.
Commercial Counsellor: Boris Penev.

CANADA

Embassy: POB 815408, Pearl of Shmeisani Bldg, Shmeisani, Amman; tel (6) 666124; telex 23080; fax (6) 689227.
Ambassador: A. Percy Sherwood.
First Secretary and Consul: M. Chesson.
First Secretary (Commercial) and Consul: W. Pound.
First Secretary: R. A. Sawyer.
First Secretary: C. E. Coghlin.

CHILE

Embassy: 73 Suez St, Abdoun, Amman; tel (6) 814263; telex 21696.
Ambassador: Nelson Hadad-Heresim.

CHINA, PEOPLE'S REPUBLIC

Embassy: Shmeisani, Amman; tel (6) 666139; telex 21770.
Ambassador: Zhang Deliang.

CZECHOSLOVAKIA

Embassy: POB 2213, Amman; tel (6) 665105.
Ambassador: Karel Fiser.

DENMARK

Consulate-General: 24 Abdul Hamid Sharaf St, Shmeisani, POB 222, Amman; tel (6) 603703; telex 21212; fax (6) 672170.
Consul-General: Tawfiq Amin Kawar.
Export Assistant: Peter Bo Andersen.

Consulate: Kawar Bldg, Post Office St, POB 22, Aqaba; tel (3) 313617; telex 62220; fax (3) 313618.
Vice-Consul: Walid Kawar.

EGYPT

Embassy: POB 35178, Zahran St, 3rd Circle, Jabal Amman; tel (6) 641375.
Ambassador: Ihab Seid Wahba.

FINLAND

Consulate-General: Al Waha Square, POB 294, Amman; tel (6) 824607; telex 21695.
Consul-General: Naman Abdul Rahman Rusheidat.
Secretary: Terttu Wegelius.

FRANCE

Embassy: Mutanabi St, POB 374, Jabal Amman; tel (6) 641273; telex 21219.
Ambassador: Patrick Leclercq.

Trade Promotion Office: POB 5101, Amman; tel (6) 644570; telex 21192.

GERMANY

Embassy: 31 Benghazi St, POB 183, Jabal Amman; tel (6) 689351; telex 21235; fax (6) 685887.
Ambassador: Dr Herwig Bartels.

Consulate: tel (6) 689481.

Visa Section: telex 22233.

GREECE

Embassy: POB 35069, Jabal Amman; tel (6) 672331; telex 21566.
Ambassador: Hannibal Velliadis.

HUNGARY

Embassy: Dahiat El-Amir Rashid, 3 Al Baz St, POB 3441, Amman; tel (6) 815614; telex 22815; fax (6) 815836.
Commercial Counsellor and Chargé d'affaires a.i.: Dr Tibor Toth.

INDIA

Embassy: POB 2168, 1st Circle, Jabal Amman; tel (6) 637262; telex 21068; fax (6) 659540.
Ambassador: K. Gajendra Singh.

INDONESIA

Embassy: West of Weibdeh Parcel No. 283, Block 16, Shmeisani, POB 811784, Amman.

IRAN

Embassy: POB 173, Jabal Amman; tel (6) 641281; telex 21218.

IRAQ

Embassy: POB 2025, 1st Circle, Jabal Amman; tel (6) 639331; telex 21277.
Ambassador: Nori al-Wayes.

IRELAND

Consulate: Jordan Insurance Co. Bldg, King Hussain St, POB 1096, Amman; tel (6) 625632; telex 23414; fax (6) 630878.
Honorary Consul: Salim J. Saad.

ITALY

Embassy: POB 9800, Jabal Luweibdeh, Amman; tel (6) 638185; telex 21143; fax (6) 659730.
Ambassador: Francesco de Courten.

JAMAICA

Consulate: POB 1, Amman; tel (6) 604655; telex 21300.
Honorary Consul: Faud T. Kattan.

JAPAN

Embassy: between 4th and 5th Circles, Al-Aqsa St, POB 2835, Jabal Amman; tel (6) 671428; telex 21518; fax (6) 672006.
Ambassador: Tadayuki Nonoyama.

KOREA, DEMOCRATIC PEOPLE'S REPUBLIC

Embassy: Amman; tel (6) 666349.
Chargé d'affaires: Kim Yong Ho.

KOREA, REPUBLIC

Embassy: Al-Burgan St, No. 7, Jabal Amman; POB 3060, Amman; tel (6) 660745; telex 21457.
Ambassador: Tae-Jin Park.
Counsellor: Kim Kewn.
First Secretary: Lee Jong-Cheon.
Consul: Jung Shin-Goo.
Vice-Consul: Kim O-Jong.

KUWAIT

Embassy: POB 2107, Jabal Amman; tel (6) 641235; telex 21377.
Ambassador: Suleiman Salem al-Fassam.

LEBANON

Embassy: 2nd Circle, Jabal Amman; tel (6) 641381.
Ambassador: Pierre Zaidé.

MALTA

Embassy: Palazzo Parisio, Merchants St, Valletta, Malta; tel 222407; telex 1100; fax 237822.
Ambassador: Joseph M. Schembri (resident in Malta).

Consulate: Issam Ajloni St, POB 2259/243, Amman; tel (6) 651321; telex 21271.
Honorary Consul: Yanal K. Bustami.

MOROCCO

Embassy: Jabal Amman; tel (6) 641451; telex 21661.
Chargé d'affaires: Salem Fankhar ash-Shanfari.

NEW ZEALAND

Consulate: Khalaf Bldg, 4th Floor, 99 King Hussein St, POB 586, Amman; tel (6) 625149; telex 21231; fax (6) 634349.
Honorary Consul: Maurice Khalaf.

OMAN

Embassy: Amman; tel (6) 661131; telex 21550.
Ambassador: Khamis bin Hamad al-Batashi.

PAKISTAN

Embassy: Amman; tel (6) 622787.
Ambassador: Prof. Ehsan Rashid.

PHILIPPINES

Embassy: POB 925207, Abbas Aqad St, 2nd Circle, Jabal Amman; tel (6) 645161; telex 23321.
Ambassador: Pacifico A. Castro.
Second Secretary and Consul: Corazon Y. Bahjin.
Third Secretary and Vice-Consul: Walter S. Salmingo.
Attaché: Victoria M. Saldivar.

POLAND

Embassy: 1 Mai Zeyadeh St, 3rd Circle; POB 2124, Jabal Amman; tel (6) 637153; telex 21119; fax (6) 618744.
Counsellor, Minister Plenipotentiary and Chargé d'affaires a.i.: Dr Edmund Pawlak.
Commercial Counsellor: TaduszRóżycki.
Deputy Commercial Attaché: Andrzej Humpich.

QATAR

Embassy: Amman; tel (6) 644331; telex 21248.
Ambassador: Sheikh Hamad bin Muhammad bin Jaber ath-Thani.

ROMANIA

Embassy: Amman; tel (6) 663161.
Ambassador: Teodor Coman.

RUSSIA

Embassy: 28 Zahran St, 3rd Circle, Jabal Amman; tel (6) 641158.
Ambassador: Aleksandr Ivanovich Zinchuk.
Consular Section: tel (6) 649190.

SAUDI ARABIA

Embassy: POB 2133, 5th Circle, Jabal Amman; tel (6) 644154.
Ambassador: Sheikh Ibrahim Muhammad as-Sultan.

SPAIN

Embassy: Jabal Amman; tel (6) 622140; telex 21224.
Ambassador: Ramón Armengod.

SUDAN

Embassy: May Zeiadah St, 3rd Circle, Jabal Amman; POB 3305, Amman; tel (6) 644251; telex 23941; fax (6) 644187.
Ambassador: Abdallah M. Gubarah.
Minister Plenipotentiary: Ismail A. Ismail.
First Secretary: Idris M. Abdulqader.
Second Secretary: Altayeb Abu Algasim Fadl.
Administrative Attaché: Omar Abdulqader Ali.
Administrative Attaché: Mohammed Badawi al-Amin.
Financial Attaché: Mahmoud Mansour Sulaima.

SWEDEN

Embassy: nr 4th Circle, 12 Embassy St, opp. Salah El Din Mosque, POB 830536, Jabal Amman; tel (6) 669177; telex 22039; fax (6) 669179.
Ambassador: Christian Bausch.
Counsellor: Jan Nordlander.
Consulate: POB 22, Aqaba; tel (3) 23619; telex 62220.
Consul: Walid Faddoul Kawar.

SWITZERLAND

Embassy: 4th Circle, nr Salaheldin Mosque, Jabal Amman; POB 5341, Amman; tel (6) 644416; telex 21237.
Ambassador: Dino Sciolli.
Third Secretary and Head of Chancery: Martin Von Arx.

SYRIA

Embassy: POB 1377, 4th Circle, Jabal Amman; tel (6) 641935.
Chargé d'affaires: Majid Abou Saleh.

TUNISIA

Embassy: Jabal Amman; tel (6) 674307; telex 21849.
Ambassador: Mongi Lahbib.

TURKEY

Embassy: POB 2062, Abbas Mahmoud Alaqqad St 31, 2nd Circle, Jabal Amman; tel (6) 641251; telex 23005; fax (6) 612353.
Ambassador: Oktay Aksoy.
Counsellor: Mustafa Vardar.
Military Attaché: Lieut Col Ömer Lutfi Taşcioğlu.
Economic and Commercial Counsellor: İbrahim Ünlü.
Economic and Commercial Counsellor: Hüseyin Şimşek.
First Secretary: Savaş Baydar.
First Secretary (Consular Affairs): Haluk Ağca.
Cultural Centre: POB 2357, Jabal Amman; tel (6) 639777.
Head of Cultural Centre: Şafak Atayman.

UNITED ARAB EMIRATES

Embassy: Jabal Amman; tel (6) 644369; telex 21832.
Ambassador: Abdullah Ali ash-Shurafa.

UNITED KINGDOM

Embassy: POB 87, Abdoun, Amman; tel (6) 823100; telex 22209; fax (6) 813759.
Ambassador: P. H. C. Eyers.
Counsellor, Consul-General and Deputy Head of Mission: H. G. Hogger.
Counsellor: M. J. S. Allen.
Defence, Naval and Military Attaché: Col P. A. Goddard.
Air Attaché: Wing Commdr M. F. Bell.
First Secretary (Commercial): T. M. Ellis.
Consul and First Secretary (Management): M. J. H. Tobin.
Second Secretary (Development): M. A. Ives.
Assistant Defence Attaché: Maj. J. M. Phillips.
Third Secretary (Internal Affairs): K. Wheatley.
Third Secretary (Chancery): B. J. Bucknell.

USA

Embassy: POB 354, Jabal Amman; tel (6) 644371; telex 21510; fax (6) 659720.
Ambassador: Roger G. Harrison.
Deputy Chief of Mission: Patrick N. Theros.
Political Section: Pedro Martínez.
Economic/Commercial Section: Janet A. Sanderson.
Consular Section: Jean D. Bradford.
Administrative Section: Lee R. Lohman.
Regional Security Officer: William N. Kettering.
Public Affairs Officer: Jonathan P. Owen.
Communications Programme Officer: Carl F. Obiden.
Agency for International Development: tel (6) 6604171; fax (6) 604858.
Office of the Defence Attaché: Col Donald A. Dubay.
Federal Aviation Administration: Donald Jones.

YEMEN

Embassy: Amman; tel (6) 642381; telex 23526.
Ambassador: Ali Abdullah Abu Luhoum.

YUGOSLAVIA

Embassy: POB 5227, Amman; tel (6) 665107; telex 21505.
Ambassador: Zoran S. Popović.

International Organizations

EUROPEAN COMMUNITIES

External Delegation: Shmeisani, Wadi Sagra Circle, POB 926794, Amman; tel (6) 668191; telex 22260; fax (6) 686746.
Head of Delegation: Christian Dietrich Falkowski.

KAZAKHSTAN

CHINA, PEOPLE'S REPUBLIC

Embassy: Alma-Ata.

MONGOLIA

Embassy: Alma-Ata.

USA

Embassy: Alma-ta.
Ambassador: William H. Courtney.

KENYA

ARGENTINA

Embassy: POB 30283, Nairobi; tel (2) 335242; telex 22544.
Ambassador: Albino Gómez.

AUSTRALIA

High Commission: Riverside Drive, (off Chiromo Rd), POB 39341, Nairobi; tel (2) 749955; telex 22203; fax (2) 751445.
High Commissioner: D. C. Goss.
Deputy Head of Mission: Peter Hooton.
Senior Trade Commissioner: Julian Watney.
First Secretary and Consul: John Murphy.
First Secretary (Immigration): Barry Boothby.
Second Secretary and Vice-Consul: John Newton.
Second Secretary (Development Assistance): Peter Buckley.
Second Secretary (Immigration): Glen Webster.
Third Secretary: Julia Feeney.
Attaché (Technical): Paul Cameron.

AUSTRIA

Embassy: City House, 2nd Floor, cnr Wabera and Standard Sts, POB 30560, Nairobi; tel (2) 28281; telex 22076.
Ambassador: Dr Walter Siegl.
Counsellor: Franz Horlberger.
Secretary: Martin Kramer.
Honorary Consul-General: Frederick Herbert Gross.

Consulate: Ralli House, 3rd Floor, Nyerere Ave, POB 84045, Mombasa; tel (11) 313386.
Honorary Consul: Tibor Gaal.

BANGLADESH

High Commission: POB 41645, Nairobi; tel (2) 562815; telex 25077.
High Commissioner: Shariful Haq.

BELGIUM

Embassy: Silopark House, Mama Ngina St, POB 30461, Nairobi; tel (2) 741564; telex 22269; fax (2) 741568.
Ambassador: Cristina Funes-Noppen.
First Secretary: M. Ardui.
Consul: A. Cumps.
Trade Commissioner: J. M. Mathelin.
Head of Co-operation: M. Blonnaert.
Deputy Head of Co-operation: T Dumont.
Attaché (Administrative): Mrs Simons.
Attaché (Communication): Mr Lippens.

Consulate: Mombasa.
Consul: M. De Backer.

BRAZIL

Embassy: Jeevan Bharati Bldg, 4th Floor, Harambee Ave, POB 30754, Nairobi; tel (2) 337722; telex 22498; fax (2) 336245.
Ambassador: Luíz Felipe Teixeira Soares.
Second Secretary: Luiz Carlos Galindo De Medeiros.
Third Secretary: Antonio Carlos De Salles Menezes.

BURUNDI

Embassy: Development House, Moi Ave, POB 44439, Nairobi; tel (2) 728340; telex 22425.
Ambassador: Marc Nteturuye.

CANADA

High Commission: Comcraft House, Hailé Sélassie Ave, POB 30481, Nairobi; tel (2) 334033; telex 22198; fax (2) 334090.
High Commissioner and Permanent Representative (HABITAT/UNEP): Lawrence A. H. Smith.
Counsellor and Deputy Permanent Representative (HABITAT/UNEP): O. A. Chistoff.
Counsellor (Immigration): E. E. Allen.
Counsellor (Commercial): M. K. Esselmont.
Counsellor (Development): J. M. Titsworth.
Counsellor (Development): B. Anderson.
Counsellor (Immigration): R. G. Schramm.
First Secretary (Development): N. C. Tresch.
First Secretary (Development): A. Palacios-Hardy.
Second Secretary (Immigration): P. F. Harland.
Second Secretary (Administrative): A. T. Blackwell.
Second Secretary (Development): C. Liebich.
Second Secretary: D. S. Proudfoot.
Attaché (Medical): Dr J. B. Lazarus.
Information Assistant: Nasreen Nurali.

CHILE

Embassy: International House, Mama Ngina St, POB 45554, Nairobi; tel (2) 331320; telex 22348.
Ambassador: Dr Vincente Sánchez.

CHINA, PEOPLE'S REPUBLIC

Embassy: Woodlands Rd, POB 30508, Nairobi; tel (2) 722559; telex 22235.
Ambassador: Wu Minglian.

COLOMBIA

Embassy: No 3, Muthaiga Rd, POB 48494, Nairobi; tel (2) 765927; telex 765911; fax (2) 765911.
Ambassador: Dr German García-Durán.
Counsellor and Consul: Carlos Gamba.

COSTA RICA

Embassy: POB 30750, Nairobi; tel (2) 501501.

CYPRUS

High Commission: Eagle House, Kimathi St, POB 30739, Nairobi; tel (2) 20881; telex 22436.
High Commissioner: Dr Phedon Phedonos-Vadet.

CZECHOSLOVAKIA

Embassy: Milimani Rd, POB 30204, Nairobi; tel (2) 721896; telex 25371.
Ambassador: František Peňažka.
Counsellor (Commercial): Pavol Lešták.
First Secretary: Michal Štanceľ.
First Secretary: Jiří Hlavaček.

DENMARK

Embassy: HFCK Bldg, 11th Floor, Kenyatta Ave and Koinange St, POB 40412, Nairobi; tel (2) 331088; telex 22216; fax (2) 331492.
Ambassador: Eric Fiil.
Minister-Counsellor and Head of Aid Mission: Michael Sternberg.
Counsellor (Aid): Toni Solveig Michelsen.
Counsellor (Aid): Erik Fogh Mortensen.
Secretary: Birgitte Thygesen.
Chancellor and Vice-Consul: Gudrun Jerichau White.
Attaché (Aid): Lars Bruun Rasmussen.
Project Co-ordinator: Henning Frøtland.
Project Co-ordinator: Bo Jensen.
Project Co-ordinator: Jens Rud Larsen.

Consulate: Liwatoni Bay, POB 99543, Mombasa; tel (11) 316776; telex 21469; fax (11) 315558.
Consul: Jørgen Horsbøl Nielsen.

DJIBOUTI

Embassy: POB 59528, Nairobi; tel (2) 339633.

EGYPT

Embassy: 7th Floor, Harambee Plaza, POB 30285, Nairobi; tel (2) 25591; telex 22335.
Ambassador: Marawan Badr.

ETHIOPIA

Embassy: State House Ave, POB 45198, Nairobi; tel (2) 723027; telex 22864.
Ambassador: Assefa Woldie.

FINLAND

Embassy: International House, 2nd Floor, Mama Ngina St, POB 30379, Nairobi; tel (2) 334776; telex 22010; fax (2) 335986.
Ambassador: David Johansson.

Consulate: POB 99543, Mombasa; (11) 316776; telex 21245; fax (11) 315558.
Consul: Jorgen Horsbel Nielsen.

FRANCE

Embassy: Embassy House, Harambee Ave, POB 41784, Nairobi; tel (2) 339783; telex 22279; fax (2) 339421.
Ambassador: Michel de Bonnecorse.

GABON

Embassy: POB 30353, Nairobi; tel (2) 335550; telex 22631.

GERMANY

Embassy: Embassy House, Harambee Ave, POB 30180, Nairobi; tel (2) 26661; telex 22221.
Ambassador: Franz Freiherr von Mentzingen.

Consulate: Palli House, Nyerere Ave, POB 86779, Mombasa; tel (11) 314732; fax (11) 314504.
Honorary Consul: Gerhard Matthiesen.

GREECE

Embassy: IPS Bldg, Kimathi St, POB 30543, Nairobi; tel (2) 340722; telex 22008.
Ambassador: E. Katsareas.

HOLY SEE

Apostolic Nunciature: Manyani Rd, POB 14326, Nairobi; tel (2) 49221; telex 25774.
Aostolic Pro-Nuncio: Mgr Clemente Faccani.
Secretary: Eraldo Fracassi.

HUNGARY

Embassy: City Hall Annexe, 7th Floor, Muindi Mbingu St, POB 30523, Nairobi; tel (2) 226914; telex 22364; fax (2) 569433.
Chargé d'affaires a.i. and Counsellor (Commercial): Zsigmond D. Patay.
Secretary (Commercial): László Pallos.

ICELAND

Consulate-General: Plot L.R., No. 12325/81, Bendera Lane, Spring Valley, POB 45000, Nairobi; tel (2) 338522; telex 25323; fax (2) 740524.
Consul-General: Ingi Thorsteinsson.

INDIA

High Commission: Jeevan Bharati Bldg, Harambee Ave, POB 30074, Nairobi; tel (2) 22566; telex 22079.
High Commissioner: P. Souza.

INDONESIA

Embassy: Utalii House, 3rd Floor, Uhuru Highway, POB 48868, Nairobi; tel (2) 215848; telex 23171; fax (2) 340721.
Ambassador: Dalindra Aman.
Second Secretary (Political): Mizwar Jalaluddin.
Second Secretary (Economic): Mohammad Slamet Hidayat.
Second Secretary (Communications): Raden Bambang Trisoro.
Third Secretary (Information/Culture/Social Welfare): Dalton Sembiring.
Third Secretary (Political): Yoel Rohrohmana.
Attaché (Administration): Mr Adimihardja.

IRAN

Embassy: POB 49170, Nairobi; tel (2) 720343; telex 22563.
Ambassador: Mohammed Shariff Mahdor.

IRAQ

Embassy: Matungulu House, POB 49213, Nairobi; tel (2) 725510; telex 22176.
Ambassador: Abdul al-Jaddorra.

IRELAND

Consulate: POB 30659, O'Washika Rd, Nairobi; tel (2) 562615; telex 22063; fax (2) 540048.
Honorary Consul: Joseph T. O'Brien.

ISRAEL

Embassy: POB 30354, Nairobi; tel (2) 722182; telex 22412.
Ambassador: Arieh Ivtsan.

ITALY

Embassy: International Life House, 9th Floor, POB 30107, Nairobi; tel (2) 337356; telex 22251; fax (2) 337056.
Ambassador: Dr Renato Volponi.
First Secretary: Dr Giorgio Guglielmino.

Consulate: Jubilee Bldg, 1st Floor, Moi Ave, POB 80433, Mombasa; tel (11) 314705; telex 21382; fax (11) 316654.
Honorary Consul: Capt. Michele Esposito.

JAPAN

Embassy: Kenyatta Ave, POB 60202, Nairobi; tel (2) 332955; telex 22286; fax (2) 724445.
Ambassador: Naohiro Kumagai.

KOREA, REPUBLIC

Embassy: Kencom House, Moi Ave, POB 30455, Nairobi; tel (2) 333581; telex 22300.
Ambassador: Na Won-Chan.

KUWAIT

Embassy: Muthaiga Rd, POB 42353, Nairobi; tel (2) 767144; telex 22467.
Chargé d'affaires a.i.: Jaber Salem Hussain Ebraheem.

LESOTHO

High Commission: International House, Mama Ngina St, POB 44096, Nairobi; tel (2) 337493; telex 22489.
High Commissioner: Tokonye Kotelo.

LIBERIA

Consulate: International Construction Ltd, Maendeleo House, POB 41196, Nairobi; tel (2) 229981.
Consul: Ibrahim Zakhem.

MALAWI

High Commission: Standard St, POB 30453, Nairobi; tel (2) 21174; telex 22749.
High Commissioner: C. M. Mkona.

MAURITIUS

High Commission: POB 49326, Nairobi; tel (2) 330215.

MEXICO

Embassy: POB 14145, Nairobi; tel (2) 582850; telex 23065.
Ambassador: J. A. Mateos.

MOROCCO

Embassy: POB 61098, Nairobi; tel (2) 22264; telex 22531.
Ambassador: J. E. Ghazi.

NETHERLANDS

Embassy: Uchumi House, Nkrumah Ave, POB 41537, Nairobi; tel (2) 27111; telex 22285; fax (2) 339155.
Ambassador: L. P. J. Mazairac.

NEW ZEALAND

Consulate: Nanak House, Kimathi St, POB 20-670, Nairobi; tel (2) 331244.
Honorary Consul: Nelson Gillies Wall.

NIGERIA

High Commission: Hurlingham, POB 30516, Nairobi; tel (2) 564116; telex 22194.
High Commissioner: Dr Bawa Saika.

NORWAY

Interests Section: c/o Embassy of Denmark, HFCK Bldg, 11th Floor, Kenyatta Ave and Koinange St, POB 40412, Nairobi; tel (2) 331088; telex 22216; fax (2) 331492.

PAKISTAN

High Commission: St Michel Rd, Westlands, POB 30045, Nairobi; tel (2) 61666; telex 25907.
High Commissioner: Abdul Kadir Sanjrani.

PHILIPPINES

Embassy: Gateway House, State House Rd, POB 47941, Nairobi; tel (2) 725897; telex 22925.
Ambassador: Romeo C. Mendoza.

POLAND

Embassy: Kabernet Rd, POB 30086, Nairobi; tel (2) 566288; telex 22266.
Ambassador: Tadeusz Janicki.

PORTUGAL

Embassy: 10th Floor, Reinsurance Plaza, Taifa Rd, POB 34020, Nairobi; tel (2) 338990; telex 22634; fax (2) 214711.
Ambassador: Dr Paulo Couto Barbosa.
Attaché (Consular): Mário Amaro Barreiros.

RUSSIA

Embassy: Lenana Rd, POB 30049, Nairobi; tel (2) 722462; telex 25261; fax (2) 721888.
Ambassador: Vladimir S. Kitayev.

RWANDA

Embassy: International Life House, Mama Ngina St, POB 48579, Nairobi; tel (2) 334341; telex 22463.
Ambassador: C. Habimana.

SAUDI ARABIA

Embassy: POB 58297, Nairobi; tel (2) 762781; telex 22990.
Chargé d'affaires: Ghaleb A. Samman.

SOMALIA

Embassy: International Life House, Mama Ngina St, POB 30769, Nairobi; tel (2) 24301; telex 22110.
Chargé d'affaires: Ahmed Sheikh Mohmoud.

SPAIN

Embassy: Bruce House, Standard St, POB 45503, Nairobi; tel (2) 336330; telex 22157.
Ambassador: Carlos Abella.

SRI LANKA

High Commission: 8th Floor, International Life House, Mama Ngina St, POB 48145, Nairobi; tel (2) 27577; telex 25081.
High Commissioner: Darsin Serasinghe.
Attaché: K. D. Bandusena.
Administrative and Technical Staff: S. Parameswaran.
Administrative and Technical Staff: S. Daulagala.

SUDAN

Embassy: Minet ICDC House, 7th Floor, POB 48784, Nairobi; tel (2) 720853; telex 22614.
Ambassador: Dr Abdellatif Abdelhamid.
Counsellor: Gaafar Taha Hamza.
Military Attaché: Col Mahjoub Sharfi.
Military Attaché (Administrative): Amir Omer Atta.
First Secretary: Adam Mohamed Jumi.
Second Secretary: Mohammed Elhassan Ibrahim.
Second Secretary: Yasir Abdalla Abdelsalaam.

SWAZILAND

High Commission: Silopark House, POB 41887, Nairobi; tel (2) 339231; telex 22085.
High Commissioner: Harry J. M. Mabuza.

SWEDEN

Embassy: International House, 10th Floor, Mama Ngina St and City Hall Way, POB 30600, Nairobi; tel (2) 229042; telex 22264; fax (2) 723547.
Ambassador: Nils Gunnar Revelius.
Minister: Rolf Lindholm.
Counsellor: Kent Degerfelt.
Second Secretary: Elsa Karlsson.
Head of Aid Office: Carl Bertil Lostelius.

SWITZERLAND

Embassy: International Life House, 7th Floor, Mama Ngina St, POB 30752, Nairobi; tel (2) 228735; telex 22181; fax (2) 728623.
Ambassador: Dr Armin Kamer.
First Secretary (Development Co-operation/Aid): Dominik Langenbacher.
Attaché and Chancellor: Dick Vindayer.

TANZANIA

High Commission: Continental House, POB 47790, Nairobi; tel (2) 331056.
High Commissioner: Job Lusinde.

THAILAND

Embassy: POB 58349, Nairobi; tel (2) 714276; telex 22836; fax (2) 748324.
Ambassador: Somphand Kokilanon.
Minister-Counsellor: Plernpit Potiganond.
Counsellor (Commercial): Manoo Tianniam.
First Secretary: Praphorn Yai-Aroon.
First Secretary: Opas Chantarasap.
First Secretary: Waesong Kumpornlua.

TURKEY

Embassy: Gigiri Rd, off Limuru Rd, POB 30785, Nairobi; tel (2) 520404; telex 22346.
Ambassador: S. Okyar Günden.

UGANDA

High Commission: POB 60853, Nairobi; tel (2) 330801; telex 22732.
High Commissioner: Jotham Kamanyire (acting).

UNITED KINGDOM

High Commission: Bruce House, Standard St, POB 30465, Nairobi; tel (2) 335944; telex 22219; fax (2) 333196.
High Commissioner: Sir Roger Tomkys.
Deputy High Commissioner: H. B. Warren-Gash.
Counsellor: A. J. Hawkes.
Defence and Military Adviser: Col M. H. White.
Naval and Air Attaché: Wing Cmdr C. F. W. Felger.
First Secretary (Political): J. F. Gordon.
First Secretary (Aid): S. M. Bull.
First Secretary (Management): P. A. Heald.
First Secretary (Aid): J. D. Friend.
First Secretary (Chancery): M. E. Webb-Brown.
Second Secretary (Works): B. W. Mitchell.
Second Secretary (Works): W. Southwick.
Second Secretary (Chancery/Information): R. E. C. Denny.
Counsellor and Head of Development Division: D. Sands Smith.

Commercial Section: POB 30133, Nairobi.
First Secretary (Commercial): R. W. Sindon.

Consular Section: POB 48543, Nairobi.
First Secretary (Consular): S. M. G. White.

Mombasa Office: Greenwood Drive, Nyali, POB 84105, Mombasa; tel (11) 471768.
Honorary Consular Representative: B. B. Mitchell.

USA

Embassy: cnr Moi and Haile Selassie Aves, POB 30137, Nairobi; tel (2) 334141; telex 22964; fax (2) 340838.
Ambassador: Smith Hempstone, Jr.
Deputy Head of Mission: Michael E. Southwick.
Political Section: Alan Eastham.
Economic Section: Constance J. Freeman.
Commercial Section: Richard Benson.
Consular Section: Charles L. Stephan III.
Labour Officer: Howard C. Kavaler.
Administrative Section: Terrance M. Day.
Regional Security Officer: Raymond V. Smith.
United Nations Environment Programme: John K. Atchley.
Agricultural Section: David I. Rosenbloom.
Agency for International Development: John R. Westley.
Agency for International Development and Regional Economic Development Services Office: Fred C. Fisher.
Public Affairs Officer: Frederick E. V. La Sor.
Military Liaison Officer: Col Philip D. Riley.
Communications Programme Officer: Lyle H. Rosdahl.
Information Systems Manager: James B. Ditsworth.

Consulate: Palli House, Nyerere Ave, POB 88079, Mombasa; tel (11) 315101; telex 21063.
Consul: Donald E. Stader, Jr.

VENEZUELA

Embassy: International Life House, 3rd Floor, Mama Ngina St, POB 34477, Nairobi; tel (2) 332300; telex 22671.
Ambassador: Edgardo Mondolfi Otero.
First Secretary: Gonzalo Prieto Oliveira.

YEMEN

Embassy: Ngong Rd, POB 44642, Nairobi; tel (2) 564379.
Chargé d'affaires: Awadh Karama Rashid.

YUGOSLAVIA

Embassy: State House Ave, POB 30504, Nairobi; tel (2) 720670; telex 22515.
Ambassador: A. Skerlavaj.

ZAIRE

Embassy: Electricity House, Harambee Ave, POB 48106, Nairobi; tel (2) 29771; telex 22057.
Ambassador: Atenda Mongebe Omwango.

ZAMBIA

High Commission: Nyerere Rd, POB 48741, Nairobi; tel (2) 724796; telex 22193.
High Commissioner: Chibesakunda Bessie Kankasa.

ZIMBABWE

High Commission: Minet ICDC House, Mamlaka Rd, POB 30806, Nairobi; tel (2) 721045; telex 25033.

International Organizations

EUROPEAN COMMUNITIES

External Delegation: National Bank Bldg, Harambee Ave, POB 45119, Nairobi; tel (2) 333592; telex 22302; fax (2) 215925.
Commission Delegate: Tue Rohrsted.
Technical Adviser: Guilluame Rijcken.
Agricultural Adviser: Paul Ceuppens.
Agricultural Adviser: Bas Van Helden.
Administrative and Financial Adviser: Felix Barahona Higes.
Italian Trainee Expert: Giacomo Durazzo.
Personal Assistant to the Delegate: Dianella Moretti.

KIRIBATI

AUSTRALIA

High Commission: POB 77, Bairiki, Tarawa; tel 21184; telex 77060; fax 21440.
High Commissioner: Peter G. Bassett.

NEW ZEALAND

High Commission: POB 53, Bairiki, Tarawa; tel 21400; fax 21402.
High Commissioner: Melvin James Taylor.
Office Manager: Dawn Wardle.

UNITED KINGDOM

High Commission: POB 61, Bairiki, Tarawa; tel 21327; telex 77050; fax 21488.
High Commissioner: Derek Leslie White.
Third Secretary: R. Scott.

THE DEMOCRATIC PEOPLE'S REPUBLIC OF KOREA

AFGHANISTAN

Embassy: Pyongyang.

ALBANIA

Embassy: Pyongyang.
Ambassador: Ismail Nezir Djaloshi.

ALGERIA

Embassy: Munsudong, Pyongyang; tel (2) 90372.
Ambassador: Mokhtar Reguieg.

BENIN

Embassy: Pyongyang.
Ambassador: Taofiqui Maliky.

BULGARIA

Embassy: Munsudong, Pyongyang; tel (2) 380265; telex 35015.
Ambassador: Georgy Stoyanov.
Counsellor (Economic and Commercial): Dimitar Radenkov.
Second Secretary: Chavdar Petkov.

CHINA, PEOPLE'S REPUBLIC

Embassy: Pyongyang; tel (2) 390274.
Ambassador: Zheng Yi.

CUBA

Embassy: Pyongyang; telex 5487.
Ambassador: Juan José León Vega.

CZECHOSLOVAKIA

Embassy: Pyongyang.
Ambassador: Zbyněk Schee.

EGYPT

Embassy: Pyongyang; tel (2) 468; telex 5488.
Ambassador: Bahgat Ibrahim Dessouki.

ETHIOPIA

Embassy: Mun Su Dong, Mun Su District, Pyongyang; tel (2) 532; telex 35034.
Ambassador: Fisseha Geda.
Counsellor and Chargé d'affaires: Girma Mengistu.

GABON

Embassy: Pyongyang.
Ambassador: Aloise Mboumignanou Mbouya.

HUNGARY

Embassy: Haebangsangdong, POB 22, Pyongyang; tel (2) 257.
Ambassador: Mihály Kornidesz.

INDIA

Embassy: Pyongyang.
Ambassador: Shehkholen Kipgen.

INDONESIA

Embassy: 5 Foreigners' Bldg Mon So Dong, Taedongkang District, Pyongyang; tel (2) 297; telex 35030.
Ambassador: Sanadji.

IRAN

Embassy: Pyongyang.
Ambassador: Hassan Dabir.

JORDAN

Embassy: Pyongyang.
Ambassador: Hani Al-Khasawinah.

LIBYA

People's Bureau: Pyongyang.
Secretary of People's Bureau: Asharif G. Al-Kabash.

MALI

Embassy: Pyongyang.
Ambassador: Nakounte Diakité.

MONGOLIA

Embassy: Pyongyang.
Ambassador: Jambaldorjiin Badra.

NICARAGUA

Embassy: Pyongyang.
Ambassador: Víctor Selva Gutiérrez.

NIGERIA

Embassy: Pyongyang.
Ambassador: O. Ashiru.

PAKISTAN

Embassy: Munsudong, Pyongyang; telex 5502.

POLAND

Embassy: Pyongyang.
Ambassador: Mieczysław Deda.

PORTUGAL

Embassy: Munhundang, Pyongyang; ; tel (2) 246; telex 5481.
Ambassador: Aureliu Ioan Lazar.
Counsellor: Marcela Lazar.
Counsellor (Commercial): Ioan Câmpean.
Military, Naval and Air Attaché: Dumitru Bulciu.

ROMANIA

Embassy: Pyongyang; telex 5481.
Ambassador: Nicolae Girba.

RUSSIA

Embassy: Central District, Sinnyangdong, Pyongyang; tel (2) 222.
Ambassador: Aleksandr Semenovich Khapt.
Consulate-General: Chondin; tel 37.

SWEDEN

Embassy: Daedonggang District, Pyongyang; tel (2) 817258; telex 35017; fax (2) 817605.
Counsellor: Göran Wide.

SYRIA

Embassy: Pyongyang.
Ambassador: Yasser al-Farra.

VIET-NAM

Embassy: Pyongyang.
Ambassador: Nguyen Van Trong.

YUGOSLAVIA

Embassy: Pyongyang.
Ambassador: Milan Seslija.

THE REPUBLIC OF KOREA

ARGENTINA

Embassy: 135-53 Itaewon-dong, Yongsan-ku, Seoul; tel (2) 793-4062; telex 24329; fax (2) 792-5820.
Ambassador: Rubén A. Vela.

AUSTRALIA

Embassy: Kyobo Bldg, 11th Floor, 1-1, Chongro 1-ka, Chongro-ku, POB 562, Seoul; tel (2) 730-6490; telex 23663; fax (2) 734-5085.
Ambassador: Darren Gribble.

AUSTRIA

Embassy: Kyobo Bldg, 19th Floor, Chongro, Chongro-ku, Seoul 110-714; tel (2) 732-9071; telex 32447.
Ambassador: Felix Mikl.
Counsellor (Commercial): Gerhard Meschke.
First Secretary and Consul: Marie-Christine Weinberger.
Attaché (Commercial): Christian Gessl.

Consulate: Ssangyong Bldg, 15th Floor, No. 24-1, Juhdong 2-ka, Choong-ku, POB 3708, Seoul; tel (2) 266-6550; telex 27233.
Honorary Consul: Shoul Eisenberg.

BANGLADESH

Embassy: 33-5 Hannam 1-dong, Yongsan-ku, Seoul; tel (2) 796-4056.
Ambassador: Kazi Anwarul Masud.

BELGIUM

Embassy: 1-65 Dongbinggo-dong, Yongsan-ku, Seoul 140230; tel (2) 794-4564; telex 27551; fax (2) 797-1688.
Ambassador: André Mernier.
Second Secretary: Jean-Luc Bodson.
Chancellor: Pascal Vivane.
Attaché (Commercial): Bernard de Guchteneere.

BOLIVIA

Embassy: Garden Tower Bldg, 98-78 Wooni-dong, Chongro-ku, Seoul; tel (2) 742-7170; telex 29271; fax (2) 742-9667.
Ambassador: Jorge Céspedes Toro.

BRAZIL

Embassy: Kum Jung Bldg 301-6, 192-11, 1-ka, Ulchiro, Chung-ku, Seoul; tel (2) 776-4717; telex 27349.
Ambassador: Luiz Mattoso Maia Amado.

BRUNEI

Embassy: 1-94 Dongbinggo-dong, Yongsan-ku, Seoul; tel (2) 796-8643; telex 128644; fax (2) 798-5564.
Ambassador: A. Majid H. A. Rahim.

CANADA

Embassy: Kolon Bldg, 10th Floor, 45 Mugyo-Dong, Jung-ku, Seoul 100-170; tel (2) 735-2605; telex 27425; fax (2) 755-0686.
Ambassador: Brian William Schumacher.
Minister-Counsellor and Consul: K. J. Sunquist.
Counsellor and Consul: H. L. Stephens.
Counsellor (Immigration) and Consul: B. W. Springgay.
Counsellor (Commercial) and Consul: K. Lewis.
Forces Attaché: Col G. Lackonick.
First Secretary (Economic) and Consul: M. R. Bélanger.
First Secretary (Administrative) and Consul: C. Leduc.
First Secretary and Consul: J. B. Gillies.
First Secretary (Commercial): D. M. Grant.
Second Secretary (Commercial) and Vice-Consul: H. J. Kuzner.

CHILE

Embassy: Youngpoong Bldg, 9th Floor, 142 Nonhyun-dong, Kangnam-ku, Seoul; tel (2) 549-1654; telex 28495; fax (2) 549-1656.
Ambassador: Julio Lagarini.

CHINA (TAIWAN)

Embassy: 83, 2-ka, Myung-dong, Chung-ku, Seoul; tel (2) 776-2721; telex 27529.
Ambassador: Charls Shu-Chi King.

COLOMBIA

Embassy: House 125, Namsan Village, Itaewon-dong, Yongsan-ku, Seoul; tel (2) 793-1369; telex 34447.
Ambassador: Virgilio A. Olano B.

COSTA RICA

Embassy: 133, Namsan Village, Itaewon-dong, Yongsan-ku, Seoul; tel (2) 793-0652.
Ambassador: Javier Sancho Bonilla.

DENMARK

Embassy: Namsong Bldg, Suite 701, 260-199 Namsan Kwankwang Rd, Itaewon-dong, Yongsan-ku, Seoul; tel (2) 795-4187; telex 23497; fax (2) 796-0986.
Ambassador: Jan Marcussen.
Counsellor (Commercial): Steen Steensen.
Consul-General: Soon Chai Chun.
Consul: Sam Hyun Lee.
Attaché and Vice-Consul: Lone Spanner.
Commercial Correspondent: Eun Hee Kim.
Export Assistant: Christian Oxholm Winther Juhl.

Consulate: 306-2, Amnam-Dong, Seo-ku, POB 678, Pusan 600-606; tel (51) 244-4849; telex 53115; fax (51) 244-2691.
Consul: Ole Renberg.

DOMINICAN REPUBLIC

Embassy: 1803 Garden Tower Bldg, 98-78 Wooni-dong, Chongro-ku, Seoul 110-350; tel (2) 744-1803.
Ambassador: Bolívar Abreu Fernández.

ECUADOR

Embassy: 133-20 Itaewon-dong, Yongsan-ku, Seoul; tel (2) 795-1278.
Ambassador: Patricio Maldonado Vascóñez.

FINLAND

Embassy: Kyobo Bldg, Suite 1602, 1-1, 1-ka Chongro, Chongro-ku, Seoul 110-714; POB 1518, Seoul 110-615; tel (2) 732-6223; telex 24343; fax (2) 737-3107.
Ambassador: Juha P. Puromies.

Consulate: c/o Kyungbang Ltd, POB 734, Seoul 100-607; tel (2) 678-5241; telex 24273.
Consul: Kak-Choong Kim.

Consulate: c/o Jindo Industries Co Ltd, Jindo Bldg, 3rd Floor, 37 Dohwa-dong, Mapo-ku, Seoul 121-040; tel (2) 719-2045; telex 26541; fax (2) 701-0254.
Consul: Yung Won Kim.

FRANCE

Embassy: 30 Hap-dong, Seodaemun-ku, Seoul; tel (2) 312-3272; telex 27368.
Ambassador: Hubert Forquenot de la Fortelle.

GABON

Embassy: Kunchang Bldg, Room 701, 238-5, Nonhyun-dong, Kangnam-ku, Seoul; tel (2) 548-9912; telex 23211.
Ambassador: Vincent Boule.

GERMANY

Embassy: Daehan Fire and Marine Insurance Bldg, 4th Floor, 51-1 Namchang-dong, POB 1289, Chung-ku, Seoul 100-060; tel (2) 779-3271; telex 23620; fax (2) 756-4562.
Ambassador: Jürgen Kleiner.
Counsellor: Holger Michael.
Defence Attaché: Lieut Col Wulf Ippich.
Second Secretary (Administrative): Rosemarie Salchow.
Second Secretary (Political): Viktor Elbling.
Second Secretary (Scientific/Technical): Thomas Mangartz.
Attaché (Economic): Uwe Janitz.

Consulate: U-I-Dong 956-45, Haeundae-ku, Pusan 612-021; POB 44, Pusan 612-600; tel (51) 742-5929; fax (51) 741-5920.
Honorary Consul: Kurt Karl Schmidtke.

GUATEMALA

Embassy: B-1116, Namsan Village, Itaewon-dong, Yongsan-ku, Seoul; tel (2) 793-1319.
Ambassador: Julio A. Merida C.

HAITI

Embassy: 34-1 Dongbinggo-dong, Yongsan-ku, Seoul; tel (2) 797-9372.
Ambassador: Yves François.

HOLY SEE

Apostolic Nunciature: 2 Koonjung-dong, Chongro-ku, POB 393, Seoul; tel (2) 736-5725; telex 29533; fax (2) 736-5738.
Apostolic Pro-Nuncio: Most Rev. Ivan Dias, Titular Archbishop of Rusubisir.
First Secretary: Mgr James P. Green.

HUNGARY

Embassy: 1-103 Dongbinggo-dong, Yongsan-ku, Seoul 140-230; tel (2) 792-2105; telex 24968; fax (2) 792-2109.
Ambassador: Sándor Etre.
Counsellor: István Torzsa.
Counsellor: András Mócsán.
Third Secretary: Dr István Perosa.

Commercial Office: 9th Floor, Chang Wha Bldg, 1-1, 5-ka, Namdaemunro, Chung-ku, Seoul; tel (2) 752-1626; telex 24794; fax (2) 797-2110.
Counsellor (Commercial): Sándor Csányi.

ICELAND

Consulate-General: Dongsan Bldg, 28-1 Jamwon-dong, Seocho-ku, Seoul 137-030; tel (2) 549-5671; telex 29956; fax (2) 549-0690.
Consul-General: Hai Hyung Cho.

INDIA

Embassy: 37-3 Hannam-dong, Yongsan-ku, Seoul; tel (2) 798-4257; telex 24641.
Ambassador: L. T. Pudaite.

INDONESIA

Embassy: 55 Yoido-dong, Youngdeungpo-ku, Seoul; tel (2) 783-5372; telex 23374.
Ambassador: Kahpi Suriadiredja.

IRAN

Embassy: 726-126 Hannam-dong, Yongsan-ku, Seoul; tel (2) 793-7751; telex 28541.
Ambassador: Hereidoun Entezari.

IRAQ

Embassy: 33-6 Hannam-dong, Yongsan-ku, Seoul; tel (2) 792-6671.
Chargé d'affaires: Kais Mahmood Mousa.

IRELAND

Embassy: Daehan Fire and Marine Insurance Bldg, 51-1 Namchand-Dong, Chung-ku, 100-060 Seoul; tel (2) 774-6455; telex 32611; fax (2) 774-6458.
Ambassador: Richard Ryan.
First Secretary: Peter E. Smyth.

ITALY

Embassy: 1-398 Hannam-dong, Yongsan-ku, Seoul 140-210; tel (2) 796-0491; telex 24619; fax (2) 797-5560.
Ambassador: Dino Volpicelli.

JAMAICA

Consulate: Gohun Bldg, 10th Floor, 646-18, Yoksam-dong, Kangnam-ku, Seoul; tel (2) 554-2191; telex 23376.
Honorary Consul: Lee Chong-Wook.

JAPAN

Embassy: 18-11 Chunghak-dong, Chongro-ku, Seoul; tel (2) 733-5626; telex 23687; fax (2) 734-4528.
Ambassador: Shinichi Yanai.

Consulate-General: 1147-11 Choryang-Dong, Dong-ku, Busan; tel (51) 465-5101; telex 53338; fax (51) 464-1630.
Consul-General: Shigeru Uchio.

LIBERIA

Embassy: 657-42 Hannam-dong, Yongsan-ku, Seoul; tel (2) 793-6704; telex 23999.
Ambassador: Christopher Tugba Minikon.

LIBYA

People's Bureau: 4-5 Hannam-dong, Yongsan-ku, Seoul; tel (2) 797-6001; telex 24322.
Secretary of People's Bureau: Mohamed Ali Abdulssayed.

MALAYSIA

Embassy: 4-1 Hannam-dong, Yongsan-ku, Seoul 140-210; tel (2) 795-9203; telex 27382; fax (2) 794-5488.
Ambassador: Nik Mohamed Hassan.

MALTA

Consulate-General: Marine Centre New Bldg, 21st Floor, 51 Sokong-dong Chung-ku, POB 6228, Seoul; tel (2) 755-6273; telex 24220; fax (2) 753-2442.
Honorary Consul-General: Sooho Cho.

MEXICO

Embassy: Hwan-Kyung Bldg, 3rd Floor, 118 Changchung-dong, 1-ka, Chung-ku, Seoul 100-391; tel (2) 269-4011; telex 23553; fax (2) 742-2682.

Commercial Office: 642 Korea Chamber of Commerce and Industry Bldg, 45, Namdaemunno 4-ka, Seoul 100-743; tel (2) 7555613; fax (2) 775615.
Ambassador: Cassio Luiselli Fernández.
Defence Attaché: Col José Jorge Rodríquez Carbajo.
Assistant Military and Air Attaché: Maj. Marco Antonio Guerrero Corona.
First Secretary: Omar Hurtado Contreras.
First Secretary: Carlos Felix Corona.
Attaché (Commercial): José Flores Diaz.

MOROCCO

Embassy: S-15, UN Village 270-3, Hannam-dong, Yongsan-ku, Seoul; tel (2) 793-6249; telex 22948.
Ambassador: Noureddine Sefiani.

MYANMAR

Embassy: 4-28 Hannam-dong, Yongsan-ku, Seoul; tel (2) 792-3341.
Ambassador: U Aye Kyin.

NETHERLANDS

Embassy: Kyobo Bldg, 14th Floor, 1-1, 1-ka, Chongro, Chongro-ku, Seoul; tel (2) 737-9514; telex 23624; fax (2) 735-1321.
Ambassador: H. G. A. Elink Schuurman.

NEW ZEALAND

Embassy: Rms 1802-1805, 18th Floor, Kyobo Bldg, 1 Chongro 1-ka, Chongro-ku, POB 1059, Seoul; tel (2) 730-7794; telex 27367; fax (2) 737-4861.
Ambassador: Christopher J. Butler.
Counsellor (Commercial): David Leishman.
First Secretary: Brian Wilson.
Second Secretary and Vice-Consul: Guy Lewis.
Attaché: Pam Franks.

Consulate: Rm 202, 84-10 Chungang-Dong 4-ka, Chung-ku, Pusan; tel (51) 462-5055; fax (51) 462-3222.
Honorary Consul: Yoon Seok-Soon.

NIGERIA

Embassy: 158 Hannam-Dong, Yongsan-ku, CPOB 3754, Seoul; tel (2) 797-2370; telex 24695; fax (2) 796-1848.
Ambassador: Eineje Egbadekwu Onobu.
Senior Counsellor: Salihu Ahmed-Sambo.
Counsellor and Head of Chancery: Inalegwu Victor Ogah.
First Secretary: Olaniyi Abiola Mosaku.
Second Secretary: Vincent Ifeanyi Omeokachie.
Attaché (Finance): Ibironke Aina-Alagbala.
Attaché (Administrative): Joy Obioma Egeonu.

NORWAY

Embassy: 124-12 Itaewon-dong, Yongsan-ku, CPOB 355, Seoul; tel (2) 795-6850; telex 25155.
Ambassador: Lars Tangeraas.

OMAN

Embassy: 1-35 Shinmun-no 2-ka, Chongro-ku, Seoul; tel (2) 736-2432.
Chargé d'affaires a.i.: Saleh Arafa Istanbuli.

PAKISTAN

Embassy: 58-1 Shinmun-no, 1-ka, Chongro-ku, Seoul; tel (2) 739-4422; telex 29346; fax (2) 739-0428.
Ambassador: S. Iftikhar Murshed.

PANAMA

Embassy: 1101 Garden Tower Bldg, 98-78 Wooni-dong, Chongro-ku, Seoul; tel (2) 765-0363; fax (2) 742-5874.
Ambassador: Enrique A. Zarak A.

PARAGUAY

Embassy: B-902, Namsan Village, San 1-139, Itaewon-dong, Yongsan-ku, Seoul; tel (2) 794-5553; telex 22289; fax (2) 793-8582.
Ambassador: Aníbal Raúl Casal.
First Secretary: Raul Montiel Gasto.

PERU

Embassy: House 129, Namsan Village, Itaewon-dong, Yongsan-ku, Seoul 140-202; tel (2) 795-2235; telex 28612; fax (2) 797-3736.
Ambassador: Luis Sabogal.
Counsellor (Commercial): Paul Gushiken Nakamura.
First Secretary and Head of the Consular Section: Susana Corbacho Carrillo.
Attaché (Civil): Rosa Gomero Rodríguez.

PHILIPPINES

Embassy: 559-510 Yeoksam-dong, Kangnam-ku, Seoul; tel (2) 568-9131.
Ambassador: Tomas R. Padilla.

PORTUGAL

Embassy: Citicorp Bldg, 89-29, Shinmunno 2-ka, Chongro-ku, Seoul; tel (2) 738-2078.

Ambassador: Luís Soares de Oliveira.

RUSSIA

Embassy: Seoul.
Ambassador: Oleg Sokolov.

Consular Section: c/o Russian Chamber of Commerce & Industry, 159 Samsungdong, Kangnam-ku, Seoul 601; tel (2) 554-9674.

SAUDI ARABIA

Embassy: 1-112, 2-ka, Shinmun-no, Chongro-ku, Seoul; tel (2) 739-0631; telex 26216; fax (2) 732-3110.
Ambassador: Mohammed A. al-Shewaihy.
Second Secretary: Abdulaziz Fahl al-Rebdi.
Third Secretary: Riyadh A. al-Mubaraky.
Attaché: Waheed A. al-Mabi.
Attaché: Abdulrehman A. Alnafisa.

Office of the Military Attaché: 743-18 Hannam-dong, Yongsan-ku, Seoul; (2) 793-3102.
Military Attaché: Brig.-Gen. Saleh Alsaad al-Othman.

SPAIN

Embassy: 726-52 Hannam-dong, Yongsan-ku, Seoul 140-212; tel (2) 794-3581; telex 25067.
Ambassador: Fermin Prieto-Castro.

SRI LANKA

Embassy: Kyobo Bldg, Rm 2004, 1-1, Chongro, 1-ka, Chongro-ku, Seoul; tel (2) 735-2966.
Ambassador: Karunasena Kodituwakku.

SWEDEN

Embassy: 8th Floor, Boyung Bldg, 108-2 Pyung-dong, Chongro-ku, Seoul; tel (2) 738-0846; telex 27231; fax (2) 733-1317.
Ambassador: Christer Sylvén.
First Secretary: Ulf Sörmark.
Second Secretary: Katarina Byrenius.
Second Secretary: Marie-Claire Swärd.

SWITZERLAND

Embassy: 32-10 Songwol-dong, Chongro-ku, Seoul 110-101; POB 2900, Seoul 100-629; tel (2) 739-9511; telex 27201; fax (2) 737-9392.
Ambassador: Dr Walter Fetscherin.
Second Secretary: Karl Hagmann.
Attaché and Office Manager: Ernst Gloor.

THAILAND

Embassy: 653-7 Hannam-dong, Yongsan-ku, Seoul; tel (2) 795-3098; telex 27906; fax (2) 798-3448.
Ambassador: Suchati Chuthasmit.

TURKEY

Embassy: 726-116 Hannam-dong, Yongsan-ku, Seoul; tel (2) 794-0255; telex 26538.
Ambassador: Muammer Akcer.

UNITED ARAB EMIRATES

Embassy: 66 Nonhyun-dong, Kangnam-ku, Seoul; tel (2) 540-4032.
Ambassador: Abdul Kareem Mohammed.

UNITED KINGDOM

Embassy: 4 Chung-Dong, Chung-ku, Seoul; tel (2) 735-7341; telex 27320; fax (2) 733-8368.
Ambassador: David J. Wright.
Counsellor (Economic) and Deputy Head of Mission: P. Longworth.
Defence and Military Attaché: Brig. D. P. de C. Morgan.
Naval and Air Attaché: Group Capt. R. J. Springett.
Assistant Defence Attaché: Maj. M. J. Cartwright.
First Secretary (Defence Supply): P. S. Guest.
First Secretary (Political) and Consul: W. Morris.
First Secretary (Commercial/Information): D. M. Gray.
Second Secretary (Management): R. Hogarth.
Second Secretary (Commercial): S. Buckley.
Second Secretary (Works): J. Collier.
Attaché (Culture) and British Council Director: T. C. White.

Consulate: Chairman's Room, 12th Floor, Yoochang Bldg, 25-2, 4-ka, Chungang-Dong, Chung-ku, POB 75, Pusan; tel (51) 463-0041; telex 53323.
Honorary Consul: S. E. Wang.

USA

Embassy: 82 Sejong-Ro, Chongro-ku, Seoul; tel (2) 732-2601; fax (2) 738-8845.
Ambassador: Donald P. Gregg.
Deputy Head of Mission: Raymond F. Burghardt.
Political Section: E. Mason Hendrickson.
Economic Section: Richard A. Morford.
Commercial Section: Peter Frederick.
Consular Section: Edward H. Wilkinson.
Administrative Section: Oliver P. Garza.
Regional Security Officer: Melvin L. Harrison.
Attaché (Science): Kenneth D. Cohen.
Agricultural Section: George J. Pope.
Agricultural Trade Office: Ralph Gifford.
Public Affairs Officer: John Fredenburg.
Customs Service: Paul W. O'Brien.
Military Assistance Advisory Group: Brig. Robert J. Jellison.
Office of Defence Attaché: Col William R. McKinney.
Director Export Development Office: William M. Yarmy.
Communications Programme Officer: August J. Bleske.
Information Systems Manager: Paige Chilson.

Consulate: 24 2-ka, Dacchung Dong, Chung-ku, Pusan; tel (51) 23-7791.
Principal Officer: Dennis P. Halpin.
Branch Public Affairs Officer: Ann E. Welden.
Consul: Jeffrey M. Zaiser.

URUGUAY

Embassy: Rm 1802, Daewoo Centre Bldg, 541, Namdaemoon 5-ka, Chung-ku, POB 3155, Seoul; tel (2) 753-7893; telex 28242; fax (2) 777-4129.
Ambassador: Alfredo E. Cazes.
First Secretary and Consul: Hector Omar Tortorella.

VENEZUELA

Embassy: Garden Tower Bldg, 18th Floor, 98-78 Wooni-dong, Chongro-ku, POB 10043, Seoul; tel (2) 741-0036; telex 28889; fax (2) 741-0046.
Ambassador: Gaudy Eli Giménez Rodríguez.
Counsellor: Florentina Sapene de S.

International Organizations

EUROPEAN COMMUNITIES

Bureau: 109 1st ga Changchoong-dong 1-ka, Chung-ku, POB 9553, Seoul; tel (2) 271-0781; telex 29135; fax (2) 271-0786.
Head of Delegation: Gilles Anouil.
First Secretary: Angelos Pangratis.
Attaché: Royden Childs.

KUWAIT

AFGHANISTAN

Embassy: POB 33186, 73452 Rawdah, 7 Mishref St, Block 1, House 17, Kuwait City; tel 5396916.
Chargé d'affaires: Tazakhan Wial.

ALGERIA

Embassy: POB 578, 13006 Safat, Istiqlal St, Kuwait City; tel 2519987; telex 44750.
Ambassador: Muhammad Qadri.

AUSTRIA

Embassy: Daiyah, Area No. 3, Shawki St, House 10, Kuwait City; POB 33259, 73453 Rawdah, Kuwait City; tel 2552532; telex 23866.
Ambassador: Johann Demel.
Secretary: Stefan Bagyura.

Consulate: Abdulla Fahad al-Meshan Bldg, 2nd Floor, Flat 7, Bldg No. 4, Soor St, POB 25, 13001 Kuwait City; tel 433667.
Honorary Consul: Marzouk al-Ghunaim.

BAHRAIN

Embassy: POB 196, 13002 Safat, Jabriya, Plot 10, Parcel 312, 5th Ring Rd, Kuwait City; tel 5318530; telex 22649.
Ambassador: Issa Muhammad al-Jama'.

BANGLADESH

Embassy: POB 22344, 13084 Safat, Jabriya, House 3, Street 14, Block 1, Khaldiya, Kuwait City; tel 4834078; telex 22484; fax 4831603.
Ambassador: Khwaja M. Shehabuddin.
Counsellor (Political): Mohsin Ali Khan.
Counsellor (Economic): Khan M. S. A. Kaiser.
First Secretary (Labour): Mir Abul Hossain.

BELGIUM

Embassy: POB 3280, 13033 Safat, Salmiya, Baghdad St, House 15, Block 8, Plot 1; tel 5722014; telex 22535; fax 5722018.
Ambassador: Igance van Steenberge.
Second Secretary: François de Kerchove d'Exaerde.

BHUTAN

Embassy: POB 1510, 13016 Safat, Mishref St, Block 15, St 14, Villa 19, Rd 55, Kuwait City; tel 5382873; telex 30185.
Ambassador: Sangay Dorji.

BOLIVIA

Embassy: POB 3115, 13032 Safat, Yarmouk, Area 3, Ave 16, Block 170, House 7, Kuwait City; tel 5339964; telex 44016; fax 5320046.
Ambassador: Miguel A. Dueri.

BRAZIL

Embassy: POB 21370, 13074 Safat, Istiqlal St, Kuwait City; tel 2549600; telex 22398.
Ambassador: Sergio Seabra de Noronha.

BULGARIA

Embassy: POB 12090, 71651 Shamiya, Salwa, Parcel 10, Plot 312, Kuwait City; tel 5643877; telex 22122.
Ambassador: Angel N. Mantchev.

CANADA

Embassy: Block 4, House 24, Al-Mutawakel, Da Aiyah, POB 25281, 13113 Safat, Kuwait City; tel 2511451; telex 23549; fax 2564167.
Ambassador: Lawrence T. Dickenson.
Counsellor (Commercial) and Consul: R. P. W. Mason.
Counsellor and Consul: W. R. Bowden.
First Secretary (Commercial) and Consul: M. Têtu.
Second Secretary (Commercial) and Vice-Consul: G. E. Luton.
Attaché (Administrative) and Vice-Consul: R. N. Waugh.

CHINA, PEOPLE'S REPUBLIC

Embassy: POB 2346, 13024 Safat, Jabriya, Block 12, Villa 144-145-150, Kuwait City; telex 22688.
Ambassador: Guan Zihuai.

CUBA

Embassy: POB 26385, 13124 Safat, Bayan Block 5, St 5, House 16, Kuwait City; tel 5382024; telex 44703.
Ambassador: Jorge L. Manfugas Lavigne.

CYPRUS

Embassy: POB 22034, 13081 Safat, Mighrab-Mojil Centre, 9th Floor, Abdullah Mubarak St, Kuwait City; tel 2433075; telex 23781; fax 2402971.

Consulate-General: POB 1447, 13081 Safat, Kuwait City.
Honorary Consul: Fahad Abdul Rahman Almojil.

CZECHOSLOVAKIA

Embassy: POB 1151, 13012 Safat, Nuzha, Block 3, Kassima No. 56, St 34, House 13, Kuwait City; tel 2548206; telex 22243.
Ambassador: Tomas Strakos.

DENMARK

Embassy: POB 5452, 13055 Safat, Block 1, Dhahyat, Abdulla al-Salem District, Nisf al-Yousuf St, House 68, Kuwait City; tel 2544988; telex 22670; fax 2553476.
Ambassador: Birger Dan Nielsen.
Attaché and Consul: Ib Norin Larsen.

Consulate-General: POB Safat 5451, Anwar al-Sabah Complex, Block 2 B, 4th Floor, Fahad al-Salem St, Kuwait City; tel 2423376; telex 44378.
Consul-General: Abdulla Yusuf Alghanim.

EGYPT

Embassy: POB 11252, 35153 Ad-Desmah, Istiqlal St, Kuwait City; tel 2519955; telex 22610.
Ambassador: Amin Nammar.

FINLAND

Embassy: POB 26699, 13127 Safat, Surra, St 1, House 8, Block 4, Kuwait City; tel 5312890; telex 44948; fax 5324198.
Ambassador: Tero Lehtovaara.

FRANCE

Embassy: POB 1037, 13011 Safat, Jabriya, Block 12, Parcel 156-158, Kuwait City; tel 5312000; telex 22195.
Ambassador: Jean Bressot.

GABON

Embassy: POB 23956, 13100 Safat, Khaldiya, Block 2, Kuwait City; tel 4830975; telex 22735.

GERMANY

Embassy: Abdullah Salem Area, Plot 1, St 14, Villa 13, Kuwait City; POB 805, 13009 Safat; tel 2520827; telex 20763; fax 2520763.
Ambassador: Claus Sönksen.

GREECE

Embassy: POB 23812, 13099 Safat, Block 2, St 2, House 21, Surra, Kuwait City; tel 5335861; telex 22669.
Ambassador: Constantine L. Tsokos.

HUNGARY

Embassy: POB 23955, 13100 Safat, Shamiya, Block 8, St 84, Villa 6, Kuwait City; tel 4814080; telex 22662.
Ambassador: Balint Gal.

INDIA

Embassy: POB 1450, 13015 Safat, 34 Istiqlal St, Kuwait City; tel 2530600; telex 22273.
Ambassador: Nagendra N. Jha.

INDONESIA

Embassy: POB 21560, 13076 Safat, Nuzha, Nuzha Main St, Block 3, Villa 32, Kuwait City; tel 2514588; telex 22752.
Ambassador: Djamaluddin Joeda.

IRAN

Embassy: POB 4686, 13047 Safat, 24 Istiqlal St, Kuwait City; tel 2533220; telex 22223.
Chargé d'affaires: Hussein Sadeghi.

ITALY

Embassy: POB 4453, 13045 Safat, F. Omar Ben al-Khattab St, al-Mulla Bldgs, Villa 6, Sharq, Kuwait City; tel 2445120; telex 22356; fax 2449773.
Ambassador: Marco Colombo.
Counsellor: Giorgio di Pietrogiacomo.

JAPAN

Embassy: POB 2304, 13024 Safat, Jabriya, Block 9, Plot 496, Kuwait City; tel 5312870; telex 22196; fax 5326165.
Ambassador: Tsuyoshi Kurokawa.

JORDAN

Embassy: POB 15314, 35305 Diiyah, Istiqlal St, Embassies Area, Kuwait City; tel 2533500; telex 30412.
Ambassador: Nabil Tawfiq at-Tahouni.

KOREA, REPUBLIC

Embassy: POB 4272, 13043 Safat, Nuzha, Damascus St, Block 2, Div. 42, Villa 12, Kuwait City; tel 2531816; telex 22353.

Ambassador: Sae Hoon Ahn.

LEBANON

Embassy: POB 253, 13003 Safat, 31 Istiqlal St, Kuwait City; tel 2619765; telex 22330.
Ambassador: Adnan M. Badra.

LIBYA

Embassy: POB 21460, 13075 Safat, Diiyah, Block 1, ar-Roumy St, Plot 2, Kuwait City; tel 2520814; telex 22256.

MALAYSIA

Embassy: POB 4105, 13042 Safat, Villa 1, St 70, Block 7, Faiha, Kuwait City; tel 2546022; telex 22540.
Ambassador: Zainal Abidin bin Alias.

MAURITANIA

Embassy: POB 23784, 13098 Safat, Mishrif, Parcel 6, Villa 37, Kuwait City; tel 5384849; telex 22643.
Ambassador: Muhammad A. Didi.

MOROCCO

Embassy: POB 784, 13008 Safat, Shuwaikh B, Block 5, House 5, Kuwait City; tel 4813912; telex 22074.
Ambassador: Abd al-Wahed ben Masoud.

NETHERLANDS

Embassy: POB 21822, 13079 Safat, Jabriya, Block 9, Parcel 40A, Kuwait City; tel 5312650; telex 22469.
Ambassador: Josephus F. R. M. Veling.

NIGER

Embassy: POB 44451, 32059 Hawalli, Salwa, Area 10, Plot 447, Kuwait City; tel 5652639; telex 23365.
Ambassador: Adamou Zada.

NIGERIA

Embassy: POB 6432, 32039 Hawalli, Surra, Area 1, St 14, House 25, Kuwait City; tel 5320794; telex 22864.
Ambassador: Mustafa Sheikh Saleh.

NORWAY

Embassy: POB 26967, 13130 Safat, Surra, Plot 3, St 13, Kuwait City; tel 5323014; telex 23287; fax 5323053.
Ambassador: Odd Wibeva.
Counsellor (Commercial): Bjorn Eriksen.
First Secretary: Jan Braathu.
Attaché: Guri Bergvoll.

OMAN

Embassy: POB 21975, 13080 Safat, Udailia, Block 3, Parcel 123, House 25, Kuwait City; tel 2561962; telex 22057.
Ambassador: Abdullah bin Muhammad al-Kharusi.

PAKISTAN

Embassy: POB 988, 13010 Safat, Hamza St, Diiyah, Villa 29, Kuwait City; tel 2532101; telex 44117.
Ambassador: Zahid Said Khan.

PARAGUAY

Embassy: POB 886, 13009 Safat, Shuwaikh, Kuwait City; tel 4814462; telex 22071.

PHILIPPINES

Embassy: POB 26288, 13123 Safat, Rawdah, St 34, Area 3, Villa 24, Kuwait City; tel 2524398; telex 22434.
Ambassador: Mauyag M. Tamano.

POLAND

Embassy: POB 5066, 13051 Safat, Rawdah, Block 4, 3rd Ring Rd, Villa 13, Kuwait City; tel 2510355; telex 23211; fax 2524760.
Ambassador: Janusz Dworak.
Counsellor (Commercial): Krzysztof Dąbrowski.
Third Secretary and Consul: Piotr T. Ciećwierz.

QATAR

Embassy: POB 1825, 13012 Safat, Istiqlal St, Diiyah, Kuwait City; tel 2513603; telex 22038; fax 2563428.
Ambassador: Ahmed Ben Ghanem al-Romaihi.
First Secretary: Ali M. M. al-Noami.

ROMANIA

Embassy: POB 11149, Dasmah, 35152 Safat, Zone 4, Muna St, House 34, Kuwait City; tel 4843419; telex 22148; fax 4848929.
Ambassador: Doru Giugariu-Costea.
Counsellor and Chargé d'affaires: Nicolae Iana.
Counsellor (Commercial): Onoriu Nan.

RUSSIA

Embassy: POB 1765, 13018 Safat, Baghdad St, Midan-Hawalli, House 6, Kuwait City; tel 5642711.
Ambassador: Ernest N. Zverev.

SAUDI ARABIA

Embassy: POB 20498, 13065 Safat, Arabian Gulf St, Kuwait City; tel 2531155; telex 23458.
Ambassador: Sheikh Abdullah Abdu-Aziz as-Sudairy.

SENEGAL

Embassy: POB 23892, 13099 Safat, Rawdah, Parcel 3, St 35, House 9, Kuwait City; tel 2542044; telex 22580.
Ambassador: Abdou Lahad Mbacke.

SOMALIA

Embassy: POB 22766, 13088 Safat, Dahiia Abdalla Salim, Block 1, al-Roumi St, Bldg 41, Kuwait City; tel 2555567; telex 23280.
Ambassador: Abdulkader Amin Sheikh Abu.
Counsellor (Commercial): Nimo Ali Yasin.
Second Secretary: Abdulkarim Ibar Shirwa.

SPAIN

Embassy: POB 22207, 13083 Safat, Abdullah Salem District, St 12, Bldg 2, Kuwait City; tel 2512722; telex 22341.
Ambassador: Juan José Arboli.

SRI LANKA

Embassy: POB 16296, 35853 Qadisiah, House 31, Plot 6, Al-Andalus St, Keifan, Kuwait City; tel 4844862; telex 46564.
Ambassador: Latif Sharifdin.

SUDAN

Embassy: POB 1076, 13011 Safat, Rawdah, Block 3, Abu Hayan St 26, Kuwait City; tel 2519299; telex 22528.
Ambassador: Muhammad el-Amin Abdullah.

SWEDEN

Embassy: POB 21448, 13075 Safat, Faiha, Parcel 7, Al Shahbaa St, House 3, Kuwait City; tel 2523588; telex 22508; fax 2564224.
Ambassador: Ingolf Kiesow.
Counsellor: Bo Lundberg.
First Secretary: Lars-Göran Paulsson.

SWITZERLAND

Embassy: POB 23954, 13100 Safat, Udailia, St 32, Area 3, House 12, Kuwait City; tel 2551872; telex 22672; fax 2523596.
Ambassador: Daniel von Muralt.
Counsellor and Chargé d'affaires: Franco Besomi.
Office Manager: Bernhard Bischoff.
Honorary Consul: Yousef Behbehani Morad.

SYRIA

Embassy: POB 25600, 13115 Safat, Rawdah, St 43, Plot 4, Villa 5, Kuwait City; tel 2531164; telex 22270.
Ambassador: Dr Isa Darwish.

THAILAND

Embassy: POB 66647, 43757 Bayan, Surra, Area 3, Block 49, Ali bin Abi-Taleb St, Kuwait City; tel 5314870; telex 44339; fax 5317532.
Ambassador: Vichien Chatsuwan.

TUNISIA

Embassy: POB 5976, 13060 Safat, Faiha, Plot 9, St 91, Villa 10F, Kuwait City; tel 2542144; telex 22518.
Ambassador: Muhammad al-Habib Kaabashi.

TURKEY

Embassy: POB 20627, 13067 Safat, Istiqlal St, Block 16, Plot 10, Kuwait City; tel 2531785; telex 44806.
Ambassador: Guner Oztek.

UNITED ARAB EMIRATES

Embassy: POB 1828, 13019 Safat, Istiqlal St, Plot 70, Kuwait City; tel 2518381; telex 22529.
Ambassador: Yousuf A. as-Sirkal.

UNITED KINGDOM

Embassy: POB 2, 13001 Safat, Arabian Gulf St, Kuwait City; tel 2432046; telex 44614; fax 2407395.
Ambassador: Sir Michael C. S. Weston.
Counsellor and Deputy Head of Mission: L. E. Walker.
First Secretary (Political): A. J. Paice.
First Secretary (Management) and Consul: L. Banks.
First Secretary (Commercial): D. A. R. Macaulay.
First Secretary (Defence): A. D. Young.
Second Secretary (Chancery/Information): B. R. Lowen.

USA

Embassy: POB 77, 13001 Safat, Arabian Gulf St, Kuwait City; tel 2424151; telex 2039; fax 2407368.
Ambassador: Edward W. Gnehm, Jr.
Deputy Head of Mission: Barbara K. Bodine.
Political Section: David D. Pearce.
Economic Section: Emile M. Skodon.
Commercial Section: Paul Scogna.
Consular Section: Gale E. Rogers.
Administrative Section: Wayne K. Logsdon.
Regional Security Officer: Michael C. Bender.
Public Affairs Officer: William B. Armbruster.
Military Assistance Advisory Group: Col John D. Mooneyham.

VENEZUELA

Embassy: POB 24440, 13105 Safat, Surra, Parcel 2, 11 Ali bin Abi-Taleb, Kuwait City; tel 5334578; telex 22782.
Ambassador: Rafael Osuna Lozada.
Counsellor: José Gonzalez C.

YEMEN

Embassy: Ar-Riyad St, Abdullah as-Salam Area, nr School Help, Kuwait City.

YUGOSLAVIA

Embassy: POB 20511, 13066 Safat, Shuwaikh 'B', al-Mansour St, Villa 15, Kuwait City; tel 4813140; telex 46107.
Ambassador: Dr Hasan Dervisbegović.

ZAIRE

Embassy: POB 3998, 13040 Safat, Rawdah, Parcel 3, St 34, Villa 24, Kuwait City; tel 2543688; telex 22460.

KYRGYZSTAN (KIRGHIZIA)

USA

Embassy: Bishtek.
Ambassador: Edward Hurwitz.

LAOS

AFGHANISTAN

Embassy: Vientiane.
Ambassador: Ismail Mohammed Mahshour.

AUSTRALIA

Embassy: rue Pandit J. Nehru, quartier Phone Xay, BP 292, Vientiane; tel 2477; telex 4319.
Ambassador: Philip Allan Jackson.

BULGARIA

Embassy: BP 118, Vientiane; tel 3236.
Chargé d'affaires: Dragomir Cholakov.

CAMBODIA

Embassy: quartier Sophanethong Neua, BP 34, Vientiane.
Ambassador: Thongsoukoun Phounsavan.

CHINA, PEOPLE'S REPUBLIC

Embassy: rue Wat Nak, quartier Sisattanak, Vientiane; tel 9075.
Ambassador: Huang Guocai.
First Secretary: Cai Wencong.
First Secretary (Commercial): Du Zhiguo.
Second Secretary: Pan Guangxue.
Second Secretary: Liu Biwei.
Second Secretary: Li Ying.

CUBA

Embassy: Ban Saphanthong Neua, POB 1017, Vientiane; tel 3150.
Ambassador: José Manuel García Torres.
First Secretary: Maria Ibanez Villar.
Attaché: Arnaldo Ramos Latour.
Attaché: Antonio Fernández Reyes.

CZECHOSLOVAKIA

Embassy: 5 rue Thadeua, BP 508, Vientiane; tel 2705.
Ambassador: Jiří Myslivecek.

EGYPT

Embassy: Vientiane.
Ambassador: Fouad Hamdy Abdul Fattah.

FRANCE

Embassy: ave Setthathirath, BP 6, Vientiane; tel 2347; telex 4308; fax 4866.
Ambassador: Daniel Dupont.
First Counsellor: Olivier Vaysset.
Counsellor (Co-operation): Alain Thiollier.
Attaché (Culture/Co-operation): Alain Faure.

GERMANY

Embassy: rue Pandit J. Nehru, BP 314, Vientiane; tel 2024; telex 4309.
Ambassador: Dr Helmut Arndt.

HUNGARY

Embassy: BP 733, rue Sisangvone, quartier Sisangvone, Vientiane; tel 3111.
Ambassador: Alfred Almasi.

INDIA

Embassy: POB 225, rue Thatluang, Vientiane; tel 2410; telex 4326.
Ambassador: Govind Mahadeo Jambholkar.
First Secretary: S. S. Batish.

INDONESIA

Embassy: ave Phone Keng, BP 277, Vientiane.
Ambassador: Bambang Soemantri.

JAPAN

Embassy: rue Sisangvone, Vientiane; tel 2584; telex 4302.
Ambassador: Hayakawa Teruo.

KOREA, DEMOCRATIC PEOPLE'S REPUBLIC

Embassy: Vientiane.
Ambassador: Chang Yong-Chun.

MALAYSIA

Embassy: quartier Nongbone, place That Luang, BP 789, Vientiane; tel 2662; telex 4316.
Chargé d'affaires: Ng Bak Hai.

MONGOLIA

Embassy: BP 370, Vientiane; tel 2060.
Ambassador: Yumbuugiyn Sandag.

MYANMAR

Embassy: Vientiane.
Ambassador: P. Kyaw Han.

POLAND

Embassy: place That Luang 211, BP 1106, Vientiane; tel 2256.
Ambassador: Marian Fronczek.

ROMANIA

Embassy: Vientiane.
Ambassador: Constantin Potinga.

RUSSIA

Embassy: rue Thadeus, km 3, Vientiane; tel 5012; telex 4323.
Ambassador: Georgi Rudov.

SWEDEN

Embassy: rue Sok Paluang, BP 800, Vientiane; tel 2922; telex 4313.
Head of Aid Office: Per Kökeritz.

THAILAND

Embassy: ave Phone Keng, BP 128, Vientiane; tel 2508; telex 4321.
Ambassador: Nikhom Tantemsap.

USA

Embassy: rue Bartholonie, BP 114, Vientiane; tel 2220; fax 4675.
Chargé d'affaires: Charles B. Salmon, Jr.
Deputy Head of Mission: Karl E. Wycoff.
Political, Economic, Commercial and Consular Sections: R. Wayne Boyls.
Administrative Section: Robert W. Pons.
Communications Programme Officer: Larry Bucher.

VIET-NAM

Embassy: Vientiane.
Ambassador: Nguyen Xuan.

LATVIA

BELGIUM

Embassy: c/o Hotel Ridzene, Endrupa iela 1, 226050 Riga; tel (0132) 32-59-82.
Chargé d'affaires: Jan F. Mutton.

DENMARK

Embassy: c/o Hotel Ridzene, Endrupa iela 1, 226050 Riga; tel (0132) 32-59-82.

FRANCE

Embassy: c/o Hotel Ridzene, Endrupa iela 1, 226050 Riga; tel (0132) 32-59-82.
Ambassador: Jacques de Beausse.

POLAND

Embassy: Riga.
Chargé d'affaires: Jaroslaw Lindenberg.

UNITED KINGDOM

Embassy: c/o Hotel Riga, Aspazijas bulvaris 2, 226050 Riga.
Ambassador: Richard C. Samuels.

LEBANON

ALGERIA

Embassy: Jnah (opp. Coral Beach), Beirut.
Ambassador: Al-Hasnawi al-Khalid.

ARGENTINA

Embassy: Imm. Antoun Saad, 5e étage, rue de l'Eglise Mar Takla, Mar Takla, Hazmieh, Beirut; tel (1) 428960; telex 40687.
Ambassador: Juan Angel Faraldo.
First Secretary: Jaime Sergio Cerda.
Attaché (Administrative): Carlos De Veyga.

AUSTRALIA

Embassy: Farra Bldg, 463 rue Bliss, Beirut; tel (1) 673246; telex 20972.
Ambassador: David Wilson.

AUSTRIA

Embassy: Ras Beirut, rue Sadat, Sadat Tower, BP 3924, Beirut; tel (1) 8015474; telex 20446.
Ambassador: Dr Georg Zindarić.
First Secretary: Michael Linhart.

Consulate: blvd Riad el-Solh, Imm. Wakf Grec-Catholique, 1er étage, POB 114, Saida; tel (7) 720411; telex 20747.
Honorary Vice-Consul: Khalil Fattal.

BAHRAIN

Embassy: Sami Fouad Hamzeh Bldg, Bir Hassan, Beirut.
Chargé d'affaires: Abd al-Youssef al-Ayadi.

BANGLADESH

Embassy: rue Tabet (Verdun), Imm. Said Jaafar, Beirut.
Ambassador: Khondker Golam Mustafa.

BELGIUM

Embassy: BP 5400, 15e étage, Centre Verdun, rue Dunant, Beirut; tel (1) 800857; telex 20612.
Ambassador: Count Louis Cornet d'Elzius.

BOLIVIA

Embassy: Dora, Imm. Tachjian, Beirut.
Chargé d'affaires: Najib Bichara Ghosn.

BRAZIL

Embassy: BP 166175, rue des Antonins, Baabda, Beirut; tel (1) 421136; telex 41330.
Ambassador: Ayrton Dieguez.

BULGARIA

Embassy: rue Australia, Imm. Hibri, Beirut.
Chargé d'affaires a.i.: Todor Dodev.

CHAD

Embassy: blvd Sami Solh, Forêt Kfoury, Imm. Kalot Frères, Beirut.

CHILE

Embassy: rue Taleb Hobeich, quartier Badaro, Imm. Amine Cabbabe, Beirut.
Ambassador: Enrique Guzmán.

CHINA, PEOPLE'S REPUBLIC

Embassy: rue 72, Nicolas Ibrahim Sursock, Ramlet El-Baida, Beirut.
Ambassador: Yang Yihuai.

COLOMBIA

Embassy: BP 1496, Chouran, Imm. Jaber al-Ahmad as-Sabbah, Beirut.
Ambassador: Gustavo Duarte.

CUBA

Embassy: rue Abd as-Sabbah, entre rue Sakiet el-Janzir et rue de Vienne, Imm. Ghazzal, Beirut; tel (1) 805225.
Ambassador: Jorge Cubiles.

CYPRUS

Consulate-General: quartier Sursock, Nagib Trad St, Samaha Bldg, BP 16-5629, Beirut; tel (1) 333886; telex 44401; fax (1) 444382.
Honorary Consul-General: Roger Samaha.

Consulate-General: Villa Omar Jumblat, Bramieh, Saida; BP 11-4895, Jammal Bldg, rue Verdum, Beirut; tel (1) 803270; telex 22449.
Honorary Consul-General: Ziad Chaker Saab.

CZECHOSLOVAKIA

Embassy: BP 1529, ave du 22 Novembre, Beirut.
Ambassador: Karel Fiser.

DENMARK

Consulate: rue de la Douane, BP 2510, Tripoli el Mina; tel (6) 600780.

EGYPT

Embassy: Beirut.
Ambassador: Hassan Shash.

FINLAND

Embassy: BP 113-5966, rue Sadat, 11e étage, Sadat Tower, Beirut; tel (1) 802275; telex 20568.
Secretary: Aune Saad.

Consulate: Imm. Fadel, rue Hôpital St-Joseph, Bouchrieh, BP 11-0444, Beirut; tel (1) 881115; telex 20732.
Consul: Toufic Fadel.

Consulate: Caves de Ksara, Ksara, BP 11-7956, Beirut; tel (1) 860102; telex 20796.
Consul: Zafer Chaoui.

FRANCE

Embassy: rue Clemenceau, Mar-Takla, Beirut; tel (1) 450580.
Ambassador: Daniel Husson.

GERMANY

Embassy: Hôpital Notre Dame du Liban, Jounieh, BP 82, Beirut; tel (1) 830021; telex 45445.
Ambassador: Peter Klewitt.

Consulate: rue el-Mina, BP 82, Tripoli; tel (6) 622112.
Honorary Consul: Hilda Massaad.

GREECE

Embassy: Sadat Tower, rue Sadat, Beirut; tel (1) 349803.
Chargé d'affaires: Mr Bazas.

HAITI

Embassy: rue du Fleuve, Imm. Sarkis, Beirut.

HOLY SEE

Apostolic Nunciature: rue Georges Picot, BP 1882, Beirut; tel (1) 338388; fax (1) 903103.
Apostolic Nuncio: Most Rev. Pablo Puente, Titular Archbishop of Macri.
Secretary: Giovanni D'Aniello.

HUNGARY

Embassy: BP 90618, Imm. Massoud, Beirut-Fanar, Beirut; tel (1) 898840; telex 4404.
Ambassador: József Kertész.

ICELAND

Consulate-General: Almaza Brewery, blvd Dora, BP 90240, Jdeidet-el-Metn, Beirut; tel (1) 883300; telex 44500; fax (1) 884200.
Consul-General: François Jabre.

INDIA

Embassy: rue Kantari, BP 113-5204, Imm. Sahmarani, Beirut; tel (1) 370480; telex 20229.
Ambassador: S. B. Singh.
Military and Air Attaché: Col P. Mehta.
First Secretary and Head of Chancery: A. S. Arya.
First Secretary (Consular): A. K. Kaul.

IRAN

Embassy: Jnah, Imm. Sakina Mattar, Beirut.
Ambassador: Ahmad Distamlitjian.

IRAQ

Embassy: Beirut.
Chargé d'affaires: Sabbar al-Hadithi.

IRELAND

Embassy: Sadat Tower, 3e étage, rue Sadat, BP 113-5980, Beirut; tel (1) 801202; telex 22304.
Ambassador: Patrick McCabe.

Consulate: rue de Chili-Verdun, Koleilat Bldg, BP 11-746, Beirut; tel (1) 814413; telex 43317; fax (1) 860076.
Honorary Consul: Khaled Daouk.

ITALY

Embassy: rue Makdissi, Imm. Cosmidis, BP 211, Beirut; tel (1) 340225; telex 23635.
Ambassador: Antonio Mancini.

JAMAICA

Consulate: Minkara Centre Bldg, 3e étage, rue Mme Curie, Hamra; BP 1481, Beirut; tel (1) 352425; telex 20388.
Honorary Consul: Khalil Zantout.

JAPAN

Embassy: Corniche Chouran, Imm. Olfat Nagib Salha, BP 3360, Beirut; tel (1) 810408; telex 20864.
Ambassador: Natsume Takao.

JORDAN

Embassy: rue Verdun, Imm. Belle-Vue, Beirut; telex 22228.
Ambassador: Mutassem Balbissi.

KOREA, DEMOCRATIC PEOPLE'S REPUBLIC

Embassy: Beirut.
Ambassador: Kim Pong-Kon.

KOREA, REPUBLIC

Embassy: Beirut.
Ambassador: Kim Hyon-Chin.

KUWAIT

Embassy: Bir Hassan, The Stadium Roundabout, Beirut.
Ambassador: Abd al-Hamid Buaijan (no longer resident in Beirut).

LIBERIA

Embassy: rue Clemenceau, Imm. Alpha, Beirut.
Ambassador: Wilmot A. David.

LIBYA

People's Bureau: Jnah, Imm. Cheikh Abdallah Khalifé as-Sabbah, Beirut; telex 20869.
Chair. of People's Bureau: Ashour Abd al-Hamid al-Fourtas.

MALTA

Embassy: Malta.
Ambassador: Joseph M. Schembri (resident in Malta).

Consulate-General: Sarraf Bldg, Independence Ave, Achrafieh, Beirut; tel (1) 322999; telex 21182.
Honorary Consul-General: Jean Bechara.

Consulate: BP 113-5591, Hamra, Beirut; tel (1) 623737.
Honorary Consul: Edmond A. Yazbeck.

MEXICO

Embassy: rue Sadat, Sadat Tower, 6e étage, BP 4332, Beirut; telex 20613.
Ambassador: Víctor M. Rodríguez.

Consulate: rue du Fleuve, Imm. Tyan, Beirut; tel (1) 450206; telex 42278.
Honorary Consul: Joseph Tyan.

MOROCCO

Embassy: Bir Hassan, Beirut; telex 20867.
Chargé d'affaires a.i.: Muhammad Abd ar-Rahman al-Alaoui.

NIGERIA

Embassy: Said Amar Bldg, Corniche Al-Mazraa, rue Malat, Beirut.

NORWAY

Embassy: Taher and Fakhry Bldg, rue Bliss, Ras Beirut, BP 113, Beirut; tel (1) 369594; telex 22690.
Chargé d'affaires a.i.: Petter Ræder.

OMAN

Embassy: Bir Hassan, Beirut.

PAKISTAN

Embassy: Shell Bldg, 11e étage, 1699 rue Lyon, Al-Hamra, Raouche, Beirut; tel (1) 350038.
Ambassador: M. Bashir Babar.

PARAGUAY

Embassy: rue Kantari, Imm. Muhammad ez-Zeben, Beirut.
Chargé d'affaires: Dr Mamdouh H. Agha.

POLAND

Embassy: Ras Beirut, rue Sourati, Imm. Nassif, Beirut.
Ambassador: Janusz Zablocki.

PORTUGAL

Embassy: rue Mme Curie, Green Bldg, Beirut; tel (1) 812070; telex 20312.
Ambassador: Luiz Gonzaga Ferreira

QATAR

Embassy: Dibs Bldg, rue Chouran, Beirut.
Ambassador: Yousef Mohamed Abaidan.

ROMANIA

Embassy: Secteur 3G, Manara, rue 77, Imm. Khaled Abdo, Beirut.
Ambassador: Florea Chitu.

RUSSIA

Embassy: rue Mar Elias et-Tina, Beirut; tel (1) 300041.
Ambassador: Vasili Ivanovich Kolotusha.

SAUDI ARABIA

Embassy: rue Bliss, Manara, Beirut.
Ambassador: Ahmad ibn Mahmoud Mahmoud al-Kaheini.

SPAIN

Embassy: Ramlet el-Baida, Imm. White Sands, Beirut.
Ambassador: Fausto Navarro.

SWEDEN

Consulate: c/o Arida Bros Corpn, Bahsas, BP 38, Tripoli; tel (6) 620158.
Consul: Edgar George Arida.

SWITZERLAND

Embassy: Centre Debs, 9e étage, BP 2008, Kasilik, Beirut; tel (1) 916276; telex 45585.

TOGO

Consulate: BP 798, Beirut; tel (1) 247571.

TUNISIA

Embassy: Ramlet el-Baida, Imm. Rock and Marble, Beirut.

TURKEY

Embassy: Baabda, rue Camille Chamoun, Joseph Yazigi Bldg, Beirut; tel (1) 420582; telex 43331.
Ambassador: Ibrahim Dicleli.

UNITED ARAB EMIRATES

Embassy: Jnah, Face Eden Rock, Imm. Wafic Tanbara, Beirut.
Ambassador: Abd al-Aziz Hadef ash-Shamsi (no longer resident in Beirut).

UNITED KINGDOM

Embassy: Shamna Bldg, Raouché, Beirut; Middle East Airlines Bldg, Tripoli Autostrade, Jal El Dib, North Metn; tel (1) 402035; telex 20465; fax (1) 441251.
Ambassador: David Everard Tatham.
Deputy Head of Mission: John A. Tucknott.

Defence Attaché: Lieut Col Edwin Gould.

Consulate: Daar Al Ain, Tripoli, North Lebanon; tel (6) 661984.
Honorary Consul: Anwar Arida.

Consulate: Jal El Dib, North Metn; tel (1) 411650.
Honorary Consul: William Zard.

USA

Embassy: ave de Paris (Corniche), Antelias, BP 70-840, Imm. Ali Reza, Beirut; tel (1) 417774; telex 20280.
Ambassador: Ryan C. Crocker.
Deputy Head of Mission: Vincent M. Battle.
Political Section: Lois A. Aroin.
Economic and Commercial Sections: James B. Magnor.
Consular Section: Jean Bradford.
Administrative Section: Ralph D. Chiocco.
Regional Security Officer: Patrick M. McCreary.
Agency for International Development: Frederick Machmar.
Office of Defence Attaché and Office of Military Co-operation: Lieut Col Donald Galvanin.
Communications Programme Officer: Michael Monday.

URUGUAY

Embassy: rue Verdun, Fayoumé, Imm. Mohamad Hussein Ben Moutahar, Beirut; tel (1) 803620.
Ambassador: José Vila Dias.

VENEZUELA

Embassy: rue Kantari, Imm. Sahmarani, BP 603, Beirut; tel (1) 452446; telex 44599.
Ambassador: Antonio Pittol.
First Secretary: Nelson E. Castellanos H.

YEMEN

Embassy: blvd Khaldé-Quzai, Imm. Ingénieur Ryad Amaiche, Beirut.
Ambassador: Ahmad Ahmad al-Moudwahi (no longer resident in Beirut).

YUGOSLAVIA

Embassy: Imm. Daouk, rue Khalil Pacha, quartier Arts et Métiers, Beirut; tel (1) 366033.
Ambassador: Bogdan Isoski.
First Secretary: Reuf Hadzihalilovic.
Military, Naval and Air Attaché: Col Strasimir Dasic.
Attaché (Administrative): Aleksandar Sago.
Attaché (Administrative): Zoran Garasevic.

International Organizations

EUROPEAN COMMUNITIES

External Delegation: BP 1640, Centre Saint Paul, Jounieh; tel (9) 937147; telex 45600; fax (9) 937154.

LESOTHO

CANADA

High Commission: 5 Orpen Rd, Mail Bag A-325, Maseru 100; tel 324189; telex 4371; fax 310113.
First Secretary (Development): K. Lotayef.

CHINA (TAIWAN)

Embassy: Maseru.

DENMARK

Consulate: Site 11, Industrial Area, POB 1259, Maseru 100; tel 323630; telex 4252.
Consul: Kai Frode Christensen.

GERMANY

Embassy: 10th Floor, Lesotho Bank Centre, Kingsway, Maseru 100; tel 312750; telex 4379.
Ambassador: Mark-Ulrich von Schweinitz.

IRELAND

Development Co-operation Office: Christie House, Plot 856, Private Mail Bag A67, Maseru 100; tel 314068; telex 4323; fax 310028.
First Secretary: Patrick Curran.

RUSSIA

Embassy: 100 Constitution Rd 243, POB 1640, Maseru; tel 316256.
Ambassador: Yuri Semyonovich Kapralov.

SWEDEN

Embassy: Lesotho Bank Centre, 1st Floor, Private Mail Bag A-175, Maseru 100; tel 311555; telex 4432; fax 310069.
Counsellor and Head of Aid Office: Karin Bosch Roxman.

UNITED KINGDOM

High Commission: POB 521, Maseru 100; tel 313961; telex 4343; fax 310120.
High Commissioner: John C. Edwards.
Deputy High Commissioner: Peter R. Butcher.
Second Secretary (Aid/Commercial): Mary Trough.
Third Secretary (Administrative/Consular): Henry A. J. Bradley.

USA

Embassy: POB 333, Maseru 100; tel 312666; telex 4506; fax 310116.
Ambassador: Leonard H. O. Spearman, Sr.
Deputy Head of Mission: Steven Wagenseil.
Administrative Section: Michael K. St Clair.
Consular Section: Alan J. Hutchings.
Agency for International Development: F. Gary Towery.
Public Affairs Officer: Douglas Ebner.
Communications Programme Officer: Thomas R. Holbrook.
Office of Defence Attaché: Col Michael Ferguson.

International Organizations

EUROPEAN COMMUNITIES

External Delegation: POB MS 518, Maseru 100; tel 313726; telex 4351; fax 310193.
Commission Delegate: Achim Kratz.

LIBERIA

ALGERIA

Embassy: Capitol By-Pass, POB 2032, Monrovia; tel 224311; telex 44475.
Chargé d'affaires: Muhammad Azzedine Azzouz.

CAMEROON

Embassy: 18th St and Payne Ave, Sinlor, POB 414, Monrovia; tel 261374; telex 44240.
Ambassador: Victor E. Ndiba.

CANADA

Consulate: EXCHEM Compound, POB 53, Harbel, Monrovia; tel 721086; telex 44299.
Honorary Consul: M. B. MacGregor.

COTE D'IVOIRE

Embassy: Tubman Blvd, Sinkor, POB 126, Monrovia; tel 261123; telex 44273.
Ambassador: Clement Kaul Meledje.

CUBA

Embassy: 17 Kennedy Ave, Congotown, POB 3579, Monrovia; tel 262600.
Ambassador: M. Gauneano Cardoso Toledo.

DENMARK

Consulate-General: 25 Payne Ave, POB 1587, Monrovia; tel 225360; telex 44258.
Consul-General: Bo Ivan Ansbjerg.

EGYPT

Embassy: POB 462, Monrovia; tel 261953; telex 44308.
Ambassador: Muhammad Saleh el-Din el-Daour.

FINLAND

Consulate: c/o Milton & Richards Inc, 152 Carey St, Monrovia; tel 221615.
Consul: Aaron Barnett Milton.

GERMANY

Embassy: Oldest Congotown, POB 10-0034, 100 Monrovia 10; tel 261460; telex 44230.
Ambassador: Dr Jürgen Gehl.

GHANA

Embassy: cnr 11th St and Gardiner Ave, Sinkor, POB 471, Monrovia; tel 261477.
Ambassador: G. R. Nipah.

GUINEA

Embassy: Tubman Blvd, Sinkor, POB 461, Monrovia; tel 261182.

HOLY SEE

Apostolic Nunciature: POB 4211, Sinkor, Monrovia; tel 262948.
Apostolic Pro-Nuncio: Most Rev. Romeo Panciroli, Titular Archbishop of Noba (temporarily resident at Santanno House, POB 893, Freetown, Sierra Leone).
Secretary: Hans Kothius.

ISRAEL

Embassy: Gardiner Ave, between 11th and 12th Sts, Sinkor, Monrovia; tel 262861; telex 44415.
Ambassador: Moshe Itan.

ITALY

Embassy: Mamba Point, POB 255, Monrovia; tel 224580; telex 44438.
Ambassador: Dr Enric'Angiolo Ferroni-Carli.

JAPAN

Embassy: Kapa House, Liberian Bank for Development and Investment Compound, Tubman Blvd, POB 2053, Congo Town, Monrovia; tel 262468; telex 44209.
Ambassador: Hirosuke Oshima.

KOREA, REPUBLIC

Embassy: 10th St and Payne Ave, Sinkor, POB 2769, Monrovia; tel 261532; telex 44241.
Ambassador: Kim Yong Jip.

LEBANON

Embassy: 12th St, Monrovia; tel 262537; telex 44208.
Ambassador: Michel Bitar.

MOROCCO

Embassy: Tubman Blvd, Congotown, Monrovia; tel 262767; telex 44540.
Chargé d'affaires a.i.: Dr Moulay Abbes al-Kadiri.

NIGERIA

Embassy: Tubman Blvd, Sinkor, POB 366, Monrovia; tel 261093; telex 44278.
Ambassador: A. Ajakaiye.

POLAND

Embassy: cnr 10th St and Gardiner Ave, Sinkor, POB 860, Monrovia; tel 261113.
Chargé d'affaires: Zbigniew Rejman.

ROMANIA

Embassy: 81 Sekou Touré Ave, Sinkor, POB 2598, Monrovia; tel 261508.
Chargé d'affaires: Silvestra Zugrav.

RUSSIA

Embassy: 34 Payne Ave, Sinkor, POB 2010, Monrovia; tel 261304; telex 42210.
Ambassador: Vasili Stepanovich Bebko.

SIERRA LEONE

Embassy: Tubman Blvd, POB 575, Monrovia; tel 261301.
Ambassador: Dennis Ransford Woode.

SPAIN

Embassy: Capitol Hill, POB 275, Monrovia; tel 221299; telex 44538.
Ambassador: Manuel de Luna.

SWEDEN

Embassy: POB 335, Monrovia; tel 261646; telex 44255.
Ambassador: Bengt Homquist (resident in Sweden).
Chargé d'affaires: Ove Svensson.
Consulate-General: c/o Nesstra Inc, 14 Randall St, POB 10559, 1000 Monrovia 10; tel 222617; telex 44284; fax 223762.
Consul-General: David F. Frankfort.

SWITZERLAND

Embassy: 245 Old Sinkor Rd, POB 283, Congotown, 1000 Monrovia 10; tel 261065; telex 44559.
Chargé d'affaires: Charles Haller.
Attaché and Head of Chancery: Anne-Marie Chapuis.

USA

Embassy: 111 United Nations Drive, Mamba Point, POB 98, Monrovia; tel 222991; fax 222450.
Ambassador: Peter J. de Vos.
Deputy Head of Mission: Dennis C. Jett.
Political Section: Robert C. Potter, Jr.
Economic and Commercial Sections: John Garner.
Consular Section: E. J. Fischer.
Regional Security Officer: James Burke.
Administrative Section: Michael J. Adams.
Agency for International Development: Samuel Scott.
Public Affairs Officer: David Krecke.
Voice of America: Wallace Freeman.
Office of Defence Attaché and Military Assistance Advisory Group: Lieut Col Robert Parnell.
Communications Programme Officer: George L. McCumber.
Information Systems Manager: Barbara J. Sullivan.

ZAIRE

Embassy: Spriggs Payne Airport, Sinkor, POB 1038, Monrovia; tel 261326.
Ambassador: Muabi M. S. Kumuanba.

International Organizations

EUROPEAN COMMUNITIES

External Delegation: 34 Payne Ave, Sinkor, POB 3049, 100 Monrovia 10; tel 262278; telex 44358; fax 262266.
Commission Delegate: Robert Kremer.

LIBYA

AFGHANISTAN

Embassy: Sharia Mozhar el-Aftes, POB 4245, Tripoli; tel (21) 75192.
Ambassador: Khayal Muhammad Katawazi.

ALGERIA

Embassy: Sharia Kairauan 12, Tripoli; tel (21) 34631.
Ambassador: Abdullah Fadel.

ARGENTINA

Embassy: Sharia ibn Mufarrej, POB 932, Tripoli; tel (21) 72160; telex 20190.
Ambassador: Dr M. Alberto Alvarez-Pereyra.

AUSTRALIA

Embassy: Beach Hotel, POB 5121, Tripoli.
Chargé d'affaires: Richard Fletcher.

AUSTRIA

Embassy: Sharia Khalid ibn al-Walid, Garden City, POB 3207, Tripoli; tel (21) 43379; telex 20245.
Ambassador: Wilfried Almoslechsner.
Secretary: Harald Ulbrich.

BANGLADESH

Embassy: Hadaba al-Khadra, Villa Omran al-Wershafani, POB 5086, Tripoli; tel (21) 900856; telex 20970.
Ambassador: M. Aminul Islam.
Counsellor: Mohd Abdul Huq.
First Secretary (Labour): Khurshid Alam Chowdhury.

BELGIUM

Embassy: 5th Floor, Tower 4, International Islamic Call Complex, That al-Imad, POB 91650, Tripoli; tel (21) 37797; telex 20564; fax (21) 75618.
Ambassador: Camille Reynkens.

BENIN

Embassy: Tripoli; tel (21) 72914.
Ambassador: El-Hadj Alassane Aboudou.

BRAZIL

Embassy: Sharia ben Ashur, POB 2270, Tripoli; tel (21) 607969; telex 20082.
Chargé d'affaires a.i.: Claudio Roberto Poles.
Attaché: Carlos Eduardo de Campos Armando.
Attaché: Elaine Texeira Gomes.

BULGARIA

Embassy: Sharia Murad Agha 1-3, POB 2945, Tripoli; tel (21) 44260.
Ambassador: Ventzislav Kanev.

BURUNDI

Embassy: Sharia Ras Hassan, POB 2817, Tripoli; tel (21) 608848; telex 20372.
Ambassador: Zacharie Banyiyezako.

CHAD

Embassy: Sharia Muhammad Mussadeq 25, POB 1078, Tripoli; tel (21) 43955.
Ambassador: Ibrahim Mahamat Tidei.

CHINA, PEOPLE'S REPUBLIC

Embassy: Gargaresh M 86, POB 5329, Tripoli; tel (21) 830860.
Ambassador: Wang Houli.

CUBA

Embassy: Sharia ben Ashur/Sharia Essagah, POB 83738, Tripoli; tel (21) 40694; telex 20513.
Ambassador: Enrique Trujillo Rapallo.

CYPRUS

Embassy: Sharia al-Thel, Ben Ashour Area, POB 3284, Tripoli; tel (21) 609728; fax (21) 609547.
Ambassador: Andreas Georgiades.

CZECHOSLOVAKIA

Embassy: Sharia Ahmad Lotfi Sayed, Ben Ashour Area, POB 1097, Tripoli; tel (21) 603444; telex 20111.
Ambassador: Miroslav Belica.
Counsellor (Commercial): František Kurka.
Counsellor: Miloslav Dolejš.

DENMARK

Embassy: 38-40 Sharia Abdulla Irhaem Abeid, Garden City, POB 5149, Tripoli; tel (21) 46018; telex 20244; fax (21) 41865.
Chargé d'affaires a.i. and Minister-Counsellor: Kurt Ebert.
Attaché and Consul: Birte A. Larsen.
Attaché: Jytte R. Rosenkrands.

ETHIOPIA

Embassy: Sharia Jamahiriya, POB 12899, Tripoli; tel (21) 47289.
Chargé d'affaires: Firdyiwek Teklemariam.

FINLAND

Embassy: 7 A, Sharia Ammar Ben Yasser, Garden City, POB 2508, Tripoli; tel (21) 38057; telex 20246; fax (21) 605117.
Ambassador: Antti Lassila.
Attaché and Vice-Consul: Arto Vainiomaki.

FRANCE

Embassy: Sharia Saïd Loufti ben Achour, Gargaresh Area, POB 312, Tripoli; tel (21) 607861; telex 20016.
Ambassador: Jacques Rouquette.

GERMANY

Embassy: Sharia Hassan al-Mashai, POB 302, Tripoli; tel (21) 30554; telex 20298; fax (21) 48968.
Ambassador: Jürgen Hellner.

GHANA

Embassy: Sharia as-Sway Khetumi, POB 4169, Tripoli; tel (21) 44256.
Ambassador: Col Jeff Asmah.

GREECE

Embassy: Sharia Jalal Bayar 18, Tripoli; tel (21) 36978.
Ambassador: Dr Evangelos Hadji-Manolis.

GUINEA

Embassy: Nord-Est de la Mosquée El-Aroussi, quartier Andalous, POB 10657, Tripoli; tel (21) 72793.
Ambassador: Lieut Col Khalifa Kourouma.
Counsellor: Mamadi Traore.

HUNGARY

Embassy: Sharia Talha bin Abdullah, POB 4010, Tripoli; tel (21) 605799; telex 20055.
Ambassador: László Fehervari.

INDIA

Embassy: 16-18 Sharia Mahmud Shaltut, POB 3150, Tripoli; tel (21) 41835; telex 20115.
Chargé d'affaires a.i.: B. R. Ghuliani.

IRAN

Embassy: Sharia Gargaresh, Andalous, Tripoli.
Ambassador: Seyyed Muhammad Qadem Khunsari.

IRAQ

Embassy: Sharia ben Ashur, Tripoli.

ITALY

Embassy: Sharia Uahran 1, POB 912, Tripoli; tel (21) 34131; telex 20602.
Ambassador: Giorgio Reitano.

JAPAN

Embassy: 37 Sharia Ubei ben Ka'ab, POB 3265, Garden City, Tripoli; tel (21) 607462; telex 20094; fax (21) 607462.
Ambassador: Jun Numata.

JORDAN

Embassy: Shara Abdalla Ben Ouf, POB 971, Tripoli; tel (21) 608801; telex 20393; fax (21) 608802.
Ambassador: Hisham al-Mheisin.
First Secretary: Ahmed Ali Jradat.

KOREA, DEMOCRATIC PEOPLE'S REPUBLIC

Embassy: Tripoli.
Ambassador: Li Won-Guk.

KOREA, REPUBLIC

Embassy: Gargaresh 6 km, Travito Project, POB 4781/5160 Tripoli; tel (21) 833484; fax (21) 833503.
Ambassador: Philips Choi.

KUWAIT

Embassy: Sharia Omar bin Yasser, Garden City, POB 2225, Tripoli; tel (21) 40281; telex 20328.
Ambassador: Ahmad Abdel-Aziz al-Jassim.

LEBANON

Embassy: Sharia Omar bin Yasser 20, POB 927, Tripoli; tel (21) 33733; telex 20609.
Ambassador: Raymond Baaklini.

MALAYSIA

Embassy: 32 Trovato Partition, Gargaresh 6km, POB 6309, Andalous, Tripoli; tel (21) 833693; telex 20387.

Ambassador: Mahayuddin Abdul Rahman.
First Secretary: Abd Ghaffar bin Iskandar.
Second Secretary: Mat Dris Yaacob.

MALI

Embassy: Zawia Dahamani, Blvd Djaraba, POB 2008, Tripoli; tel (21) 44924; telex 20697.
Ambassador: Bakary Drame.
Counsellor: Mamby Diabate.
Counsellor: Yacouba Diallo.

MALTA

Embassy: Sharia Ubei ben Ka'ab, POB 2534, Tripoli; tel (21) 38081; telex 20273; fax (21) 48401.
Ambassador: George Saliba.
Consul and First Secretary: Wilfred Zarb Cousin.

MAURITANIA

Embassy: Sharia Eysa Wokwak, Tripoli; tel (21) 43223.
Ambassador: Yahia Muhammad el-Hadi.

MOROCCO

Embassy: Sharia Bashir el-Ibrahim, Garden City, Tripoli; tel (21) 34239.
Chargé d'affaires: Mehdi Masdouki.

NETHERLANDS

Embassy: Sharia Jalal Bayar 20, POB 3801, Tripoli; tel (21) 41549; telex 20279.
Chargé d'affaires: Dr A. J. Quanjer.

NICARAGUA

Embassy: Beach Hotel, Andalous, Tripoli; tel (21) 72641.
Ambassador: Guillermo Espinosa.

NIGER

Embassy: Sharia Bashir Ibrahim, POB 4417, Garden City, Tripoli; tel (21) 43104.
Ambassador: Aliyu Dala Hassan.
Counsellor: Lawal Mohammed Munir.
Attaché (Finance): B. A. A. Awojoula.

NIGERIA

Embassy: Sharia Bashir el-Ibrahim, POB 4417, Garden City, Tripoli; tel (21) 43035; telex 20124.
Ambassador: Prof. Dandatti Abdulkadir.
Minister-Counsellor and Head of Chancery: Lawal Mohammed Munir.
Second Secretary (Consular and Administrative): Abubakar S. Mohammed.
Second Secretary (Political and Economic): B. A. A. Adejinle.
Attaché (Finance): S. O. George.

PAKISTAN

Embassy: Sharia Abdul Karim al-Khattabi 16, Maidan Al Qadisia, POB 2169, Tripoli; tel (21) 40072; telex 20577; fax (21) 44698.
Ambassador: Khawar Rashid Pirzada.
First Counsellor: M. Aslam Rizvi.
Secretary (Commercial): Sarfraz Ahmad.
Attaché (Community Welfare): Mushtaq Ahmad.

PHILIPPINES

Embassy: Sharia ed-Dul, Gargaresh Rd 8 km, POB 12508, Tripoli; tel (21) 831925; telex 2034.
Ambassador: Abdul Ghafuur Madki Alonto.
Minister and Consul-General: Rafael E. Segius.
Third Secretary and Vice-Consul: Pendosina N. Lomondot.
Attaché (Administrative): Abdurrahman D. Macapundag.
Attaché (Finance): Noe L. Nolasco.
Attaché (Consular): Acas T. Bayabao.
Attaché (Communication): Nilo de Guzman.
Attaché (Consular): Sayrads Macalawi.

POLAND

Embassy: Sharia ben Ashur, POB 519, Tripoli; tel (21) 607619; telex 20049.
Ambassador: Stefan Staniszewski.
First Secretary and Deputy Head of Mission: Jósef Osas.
Counsellor (Commercial): Zbigniew Pawlik.
Second Secretary and Head of Consular Section: Zbigniew Smuga.

Consulate-General: Benghazi; tel (61) 28792.
Consul-General: Zbigniew Byszewski.

QATAR

Embassy: Sharia ben Ashur, POB 3506, Tripoli; tel (21) 46660.
Chargé d'affaires: Hasan Ahmad Abu Hindi.

ROMANIA

Embassy: Sharia Ahmad Lotfi Sayed, POB 5085, Tripoli; tel (21) 45570.
Ambassador: Florea Ristache.

RUSSIA

Embassy: Sharia Mustapha Kamel, Tripoli; tel (21) 30545.
Ambassador: Pogos Semenovich Akopov.

Consulate-General: POB 3022, Benghazi; tel (61) 87347; telex 40185.

RWANDA

Embassy: Villa Ibrahim Musbah Missalati, Al-Andalous, POB 6677, Tripoli; tel (21) 72864; telex 20236.
Ambassador: Etienne Sengegera.

SAUDI ARABIA

Embassy: Sharia Kairauan 2, Tripoli; tel (21) 30485.
Chargé d'affaires: Muhammad Hassan Bandah.

SENEGAL

Embassy: Tripoli.

SPAIN

Embassy: Sharia el-Amir Abdel Kader el-Jazairi 36, POB 2302, Tripoli; tel (21) 33275; telex 20184; fax (21) 36797.
Ambassador: Pablo Benavides Orgaz.
First Secretary and Deputy Head of Mission: Gustavo M. de Arístegui.
Counsellor (Commercial): José L. Oterino Navales.
Attaché (Administrative): Juan Luis Marcó Sánchez.

SUDAN

Embassy: Ras Hassan El-Dul, POB 1076, Tripoli; tel (21) 32660; telex 20324.
Minister-Counsellor and Chargé d'affaires a.i.: Salah Mohamed Ali.
Counsellor: Ismail Mohamed Abdeldafie.
First Secretary: Bakri Abdel Hamid Mahir.
Second Secretary: Salwa Awad Bashir.
Third Secretary: Mohamed Eisa Edam.

SWEDEN

Embassy: 5th Floor, Tower No. 5, That al-Imad, POB 437, Tripoli; tel (21) 32343; telex 20154; fax (21) 70357.
Ambassador: Andreas Ådahl.
Counsellor: Bengt Sparre.

Consulate: 4 Sharia El-Arish, Feuhat El-Gharbia, POB 2513, Benghazi; tel (61) 88613; telex 40316; fax (61) 25229.
Consul: Nils Anders Gustav Nilsson.

SWITZERLAND

Embassy: Sharia Jeraba, POB 439, Tripoli; tel (21) 607365; telex 20382.
Chargé d'affaires: Claude Huguenin.
Attaché and Office Manager: Hanspeter Wyss.

SYRIA

Relations Office: Sharia Muhammad Rashid Reda 4, POB 4219, Garden City, Tripoli; tel (21) 31783; telex 20218.
First Secretary and Chargé d'affaires a.i.: Mohammed Kosado.
Second Secretary: Suleiman Aad.
Attaché (Cultural): Mohammoud Ali.
Attaché (Commercial): Mohammed Jaafuri.
Attaché (Information): Mohammed Omer Omer.

TOGO

Embassy: Sharia Khaled bin al-Walid, POB 3420, Tripoli; tel (21) 49565; telex 20373.
Chargé d'affaires a.i.: Woake Koffi Ouyi.
Attaché (Finance): Bakpatina-Batako M'Feguna.
Attaché: Tchacibelle Essoh.

TUNISIA

Embassy: Sharia Bashir Ibrahimi, POB 613, Tripoli; tel (21) 31051; telex 20217; fax (21) 47600.
High Representative: Said ben Mustapha.

TURKEY

Embassy: Sharia Jeraba, POB 947, Tripoli; tel (21) 46528; telex 20031.
Ambassador: Mustafa Aşula.

UGANDA

Embassy: Sharia Jeraba, POB 10978, Tripoli; tel (21) 48006.
Chargé d'affaires: Alli Kiseka.

UNITED KINGDOM

Consulate: c/o Italian Embassy, Sharia Uahran, POB 4206, Tripoli; tel (21) 31191; telex 20296.
Head of British Interests: A. R. Brown.
Second Secretary (Management): D. S. Brown.

VENEZUELA

Embassy: Villa 42, Zanguett Ashour Al Bagi, POB 2584, Tripoli; tel (21) 36652; telex 20532; fax (21) 31496.
Chargé d'affaires a.i. and Counsellor: Alberto Lossada-Sardi.

VIET-NAM

Embassy: Sharia Talha ben Abdullah, POB 587, Tripoli; tel (21) 45753.
Ambassador: Dang San.

YEMEN

Embassy: Sharia ben Ashour, Zenghet Al-Wahshi, POB 4616, Tripoli; tel (21) 605771.
Ambassador: Abdullah Ahmed al-Aoud.
Counsellor: Abdel Karim al-Khamisi.
Counsellor: Abdel Karim Hajar.
Counsellor: Abdel Azziz Awad Salem.

YUGOSLAVIA

Embassy: Sharia Turkia No. 14, Tripoli; tel (21) 34114.
Ambassador: Drago Miršič.

ZAIRE

Embassy: Sharia Aziz al-Masri, POB 5066, Tripoli.

LIECHTENSTEIN

AUSTRALIA

Consulate: Vaduz.

AUSTRIA

Embassy: Austria.
Ambassador: Dietrich Bukowski (resident in Austria).
Consulate: Landstr. 152, 9494 Schann; tel 25477.
Honorary Consul: Werner Tabarelli.

HOLY SEE

Mission: Schann.
Apostolic Nuncio: Mgr Edoardo Rovida.

SWEDEN

Consulate: Altenbach 8, Postfach 367, 9490 Vaduz; tel 24257.
Consul: Anne Marie Olga Charlotte van Eck.

UNITED KINGDOM

Consulate-General: Dufourstr. 56, 8008 Zurich, Switzerland; tel (1) 471520; telex 816467.

According to an arrangement concluded in 1919, Switzerland has agreed to represent Liechtenstein's interests in countries where it has diplomatic missions and where Liechtenstein is not represented in its own right. In so doing, Switzerland always acts only on the basis of mandates of a general or specific nature, which it may either refuse or accept, while Liechtenstein is free to enter into direct relations with foreign states or to establish its own additional missions. Liechtenstein has an embassy in Berne, a non-resident ambassador to Austria and a non-resident ambassador to the Holy See, as well as a permanent representative to the Council of Europe in Strasbourg and a permanent mission to the UN in New York. There are 34 consular representatives accredited to Liechtenstein.

LITHUANIA

ESTONIA

Embassy: 232016 Vilnius, Turmiŝkiu 20; tel (0122) 76-48-96; fax (0122) 61-45-44.
Permanent Representative: Mart Tarmak.
Counsellor: Valki Strikaitiene.

FRANCE

Embassy: Vilnius.
Ambassador: Philippe de Suremain.

ITALY

Embassy: Vilnius.
Ambassador: Franco Tempesta.

POLAND

Consulate-General: Vilnius; tel (0122) 22-44-44.
Consul-General: Zdzisław Kitlinski.

TURKEY

Embassy: Vilnius.

UNITED KINGDOM

Embassy: Vilnius.
Ambassador: Michael J. Peart.

USA

Embassy: Vilnius.
Ambassador: Darryl Johnson.

LUXEMBOURG

AUSTRIA

Embassy: 3 rue des Bains, 1212 Luxembourg; tel 47-11-88; telex 2530; fax 46-39-74.
Ambassador: Klaus Rudolf Ziegler.
Counsellor: Elizabeth Coveos.

BELGIUM

Embassy: 4 rue des Girondins, Luxembourg; tel 44-27-46; telex 2550; fax 45-42-82.
Ambassador: André de Schutter.
Minister-Counsellor: Luc Willemarck.
Military Attaché: Col André Minguet.
First Secretary: René Dillembourg.
Attaché (Commercial): Pierre Leleux.
Attaché: Christine Grégoire.

BULGARIA

Embassy: 47-49 ave Monterey, 2163 Luxembourg; tel 45-16-72; telex 3585.

BURKINA FASO

Consulate: rue de Luxembourg 55, BP 20, 8440 Steinfort; tel 39-08-3; telex 2325; fax 39-09-6.
Honorary Consul: Charles Kieffer.

CANADA

Consulate: c/o Price Waterhouse and Co, 24-6 ave de la Liberté, BP 1443, 1014 Luxembourg; tel 40-24-20; telex 1231; fax 40-24-55.
Honorary Consul: W. Bannerman.

CHINA, PEOPLE'S REPUBLIC

Embassy: 2 rue Van der Meulen, 2152 Luxembourg.
Ambassador: Zhao Liang.
Military Attaché: Zhuang Mingfa.
First Secretary: Du Gaonian.
Second Secretary: Wen Zhen-Shun.

DENMARK

Embassy: 11b blvd Joseph II, 1840 Luxembourg; tel 45-13-11; telex 1705; fax 45-13-31.
Chargé d'affaires a.i. and Minister-Counsellor: Suzanne Rubow.
Consulate: 1 rue Jean Pierre Brasseur, 2015 Luxembourg; tel 45-40-18; telex 3135.
Consul: Robert Kreips.

DJIBOUTI

Consulate: 2 rue des Sapins, 2513 Senningerberg; tel 34-59-4; telex 1463; fax 34-90-01.
Consul: Jean-Paul Strauss.

FINLAND

Consulate-General: 7 rue Alcide de Gasperi, 1615 Luxembourg; tel 43-58-53.
Consul-General: Henri Charles Ahlborn.

FRANCE

Embassy: 9 blvd Prince-Henri, BP 359, 1724 Luxembourg; tel 47-10-91; telex 2744.
Ambassador: Gérard Julienne.
Counsellor: Henri Rouzil.
Counsellor (Commercial): Jean-Marie Bourg.
First Secretary: Jacques Guyot.
Consul: Marcel Samy.
Attaché (Commercial): Jean-Daniel Jond.

GERMANY

Embassy: 20-22 ave Emile Reuter, 2420 Luxembourg; tel 45-34-45; telex 3413; fax 45-56-04.
Ambassador: Dr Goetz-Alexander Martius.
Chargé d'affaires: Horst Uhrig.
First Secretary: Klaus Herzog.
Second Secretary: Ekkehart Wicher.
Second Secretary: Horst Ackermann.

GREECE

Embassy: 117 val Ste Croix, 1371 Luxembourg; tel 44-51-93; telex 2948.
Ambassador: Konstantinos Ivrakis.
First Secretary (Consular): Christos Maniakis-Grivas.
Attaché: Sotrios Théodorou.
Attaché: Dimitrios Toumbas.

ICELAND

Consulate-General: 59 rue Glesener, BP 2102, 1021 Luxembourg; tel 40-27-27-25; telex 3444; fax 40-27-27-37.
Consul-General: Einar Aakrann.

IRELAND

Embassy: 28 route d'Arlon, 1140 Luxembourg; tel 45-06-10; telex 1353; fax 45-88-20.
Ambassador: Liam Rigney.
Secretary: Eamonn Noonan.

ITALY

Embassy: 5 rue Marie-Adélaide, 2128 Luxembourg; tel 44-36-44; telex 2216.
Ambassador: Antonio Napolitano.
Counsellor: Sergio La Tella.
Consul: Mauro Carfagnini.
Attaché (Culture): Salvatore Ettore.
Attaché (Consular): Mauro Celestini.

JAPAN

Embassy: 17 rue Beaumont, BP 1255, 1219 Luxembourg; tel 46-41-51; telex 1870; fax 46-41-76.
Ambassador: Atsuhiko Yatabe.
Chargé d'affaires: Yoshitomo Tsunekawa.
Second Secretary: Takayoshi Hosoya.

MALI

Consulate: 30 rue E. Bérès, 1232 Howald; tel 48-06-65.
Honorary Consul: P. Thilges.

MALTA

Consulate: 3 rue de la Loge, 1945 Luxembourg; tel 20-68-6; telex 60182; fax 46-07-52.
Consul: Rodolphe Redding.

MONACO

Consulate: 42 blvd Joseph II, 1840 Luxembourg; tel 49-92-31.
Consul: Robert Reckinger.

NETHERLANDS

Embassy: 5 rue C. M. Spoo, 2546 Luxembourg; tel 27-57-0; telex 2204; fax 40-30-16.
Ambassador: Johan Gerhard Willem Faber (designate).
Counsellor: Herman G. T. W. Knippenberg.
Attaché (Administrative): Henricus C. P. J. Huijbers.

PORTUGAL

Embassy: 33 allée Scheffer, 2520 Luxembourg; tel 47-39-55; telex 1782.
Ambassador: José Manuel Borges Gama Cornelio da Silva (designate).
Counsellor (Social Affairs): Rui Manuel Dias Costa.
Second Secretary: Francisco Carvalho Sá Martha.
Attaché (Social Affairs): José Sebastião N. C. de Araujo.
Consul-General: José Lages dos Santos.

RUSSIA

Embassy: Château de Beggen, 1719 Luxembourg; tel 42-23-33; telex 60445.
Ambassador: Chingiz Aitmatov.
Counsellor: Nikolaï Solntsev.
First Secretary: Evgeny Plakhotnyï.
First Secretary: Vadim Lukov.

SPAIN

Embassy: 2-4 blvd E. Servais, 2535 Luxembourg; tel 46-02-55; telex 1545; fax 47-48-50.
Ambassador: Luis Javier Casanova Fernández.
Counsellor: Arturo Reig Tapia.
First Secretary: Alberto Moreno Humet.
Attaché (Administrative): Isidoro Rodríguez de Las Parras.

SWEDEN

Consulate-General: c/o Nordbanken, BP 265, blvd Royal 47, 2012 Luxembourg; tel 26-65-1; telex 1558; fax 27-48-9.
Consul-General: Claes Douglas de Neergaard.

SWITZERLAND

Embassy: Résidence 'Royal Bohler', 35 blvd Royal, 2449 Luxembourg; BP 469, 2014 Luxembourg; tel 27-47-74; telex 2299; fax 46-43-93.
Ambassador: André Maillard.
Second Secretary and Office Manager: Werner Ballmer.

TOGO

Consulate: 8065 Bertrange, Luxembourg.
Consul: Paul Hammelmann.

TURKEY

Embassy: 20 rue Marie-Adélaïde, 2128 Luxembourg; tel 44-32-81; telex 2473.
Ambassador: Erdogan Sanalan.
First Secretary: Cem Cetin.
Attaché (Administrative): Semra Güngör.

UNITED KINGDOM

Embassy: 14 blvd Roosevelt, BP 874, 2450 Luxembourg; tel 29-86-4; telex 3443; fax 29-86-7.
Ambassador: Hon. Michael Pakenham.
First Secretary, Consul and Deputy Head of Mission: Sidney H. Palmer.
Second Secretary (Commercial/Information): Christopher James Poole.
Attaché (Management) and Vice-Consul: George Kenneth Hodgson.

USA

Embassy: 22 blvd Emmanuel-Servais, 2535 Luxembourg; tel 46-01-23; fax 46-14-01.
Ambassador: Edward Morgan Rowell.
Deputy Head of Mission: David B. Dlouhy.
Political, Economic and Commercial Sections: Kenneth B. Davis.
Consular Section: Michael A. Raynor.
Administrative Section: Prince A. Terry, Jr.
Communications Programme Officer: Leo J. Cyr.

ZAIRE

Embassy: 6 ave Guillaume, 1650 Luxembourg; tel 44-22-25; telex 3625.
Ambassador: Kinbulu Moyanso.

International Organizations

EUROPEAN COMMUNITIES

Bureau: Bâtiment Jean Monnet, rue Alcide de Gasperi, 2920 Luxembourg; tel 43-01-1; telex 3423; fax 43-01-44-33.
Director: Alphonse Theis.

MADAGASCAR

ALGERIA

Embassy: 5 rue Robert Ducrocq, BP 734, Behorika, 101 Antananarivo; tel (2) 21123; telex 22373.
Ambassador: Muhammad Abdou Abdeddaïm.

AUSTRIA

Consulate: c/o Henry Fraise Fis & Cie, BP 28, Ankorondrano, Antananarivo; tel (2) 22721; telex 22218; fax (2) 28420.
Honorary Consul: John De Jager.

BELGIUM

Consulate: 88 Arabe Ralaimonfo, Analakely, BP 3046, Antananarivo; tel (2) 20984; telex 222118.
Consul: M. Pain.

CANADA

Consulate: c/o QIT-Madagascar Minerals, Lot II-J-169 Villa 3H Ivandry, Antananarivo; CP 4003, Antananarivo 101; tel (2) 42559; telex 22448; fax (2) 42506.
Honorary Consul: P. Lachapelle.

CHINA, PEOPLE'S REPUBLIC

Embassy: Ancien Hôtel Panorama, BP 1658, 101 Antananarivo.
Ambassador: Wei Dong.

DENMARK

Consulate-General: 1 bis rue Patrice Lumumba, BP 679, Antananarivo; tel (2) 22356; telex 22211.
Consul-General: Odd-Gunnar Konow Heffermehl.

Consulate: c/o Codal SA, blvd de l'Ivondro, BP 226, Tamatave; tel (5) 32166; telex 55620.

EGYPT

Embassy: 47 ave Lénine, BP 4082, Ankadifotsy, 101 Antananarivo; tel (2) 25233; telex 22364.
Ambassador: Hussein el-Khazindar.

FINLAND

Consulate: BP 6211, 101 Antananarivo; tel (2) 20565; telex 22340.
Consul: Marcel Ramanandraibe.

GERMANY

Embassy: 101 rue du Pasteur Rabeony Hans, BP 516, Ambodirotra, Antananarivo; tel (2) 21691; telex 22203.
Ambassador: Dr Gottfried Fischer.

HOLY SEE

Apostolic Nunciature: Villa Roma II, Ambonilona Ivandry, BP 650, 101 Antananarivo; tel (2) 42376; telex 22432; fax (2) 43884.
Apostolic Pro-Nuncio: Most Rev. Blasco Francisco Collaço.
Secretary and Chargé d'affaires a.i.: Rev. Bernardito Cleopas Auza.

INDIA

Embassy: 4 làlana Emile Rajaonson, BP 1787, 101 Antananarivo; tel (2) 23334; telex 22484.
Ambassador: Kumud Ranjan Sinha.

INDONESIA

Embassy: 15 rue Radama I Tsaralalana, BP 3969, 101 Antananarivo; tel (2) 24915; telex 22387.
Chargé d'affaires: Widodo Atmosutirto.

IRAN

Embassy: route circulaire, Lot II L43 ter, 101 Antananarivo; tel (2) 28639.
Ambassador: Ahmad Kanani-Bandehkohan.

ITALY

Embassy: 22 rue Pasteur Rabary, BP 16, Ankadivato, Antananarivo; tel (2) 21217; telex 22293.
Ambassador: Carmelo Liotta.

JAPAN

Embassy: 8 rue du Docteur Villette, BP 3863, Isoraka, 101 Antananarivo; tel (2) 26102; telex 22308; fax (2) 21769.
Ambassador: Hideki Harashima.

KOREA, DEMOCRATIC PEOPLE'S REPUBLIC

Embassy: Ambohibao; tel (2) 44442; telex 22494.
Ambassador: Chong Tae Hwa.

LIBYA

People's Bureau: Lot IIB, 37A route circulaire Ampandrana-Ouest, 101 Antananarivo; tel (2) 21892.
Secretary of People's Bureau: Ibrahim ar-Mahdi al-Jaddy.

RUSSIA

Embassy: Ampefiloha, Lot O, BP 4006, Antananarivo; tel (2) 27070.
Ambassador: Pavel Petrik.

Consulate-General: blvd Rastimilaho, BP 129, Toamasina; tel (3) 33197.

SWEDEN

Consulate-General: SEAL, 1 bis rue Patrice Lumumba, BP 679, Antananarivo; tel (2) 22356; telex 22211.
Ambassador: Lars Schönander (resident in Sweden).
Consul-General: Odd-Gunnar Konow Heffermehl.

SWITZERLAND

Embassy: Solombavambahoaka, Frantsay 77, BP 118, 101 Antananarivo; tel (2) 22846; telex 22300; fax (2) 34884.
Counsellor and Chargé d'affaires: Max Heller.
Attaché and Head of Chancery: Pascal Decosterd.
Attaché (Development Co-operation and Humanitarian Aid): Gerhard Pfister.

UNITED KINGDOM

Embassy: Immeuble Ny Havana, 1st Floor, Cité des 67 Hectares, BP 167, 101 Antananarivo; tel (2) 27073; telex 22459; fax (2) 26690.
Ambassador: Denis Oldrieve Amy.
Second Secretary: Jeremy James Macadie.
Third Secretary: C. G. R. Poole.
Commercial Officer: N. Rajaonarivony.

USA

Embassy: 14-16 rue Rainitovo, Antsahavola, BP 620, 101 Antananarivo; tel (2) 20089; telex 22202; fax (2) 34539.
Ambassador: Howard Kent Walker.
Deputy Chief of Mission: Norman H. Frisbie.
Political Section: Cheryl J. Sim.
Economic Section: John W. Davison.
Commercial Section: Stacey G. Kazacos.

Consular Section: Nick Banks.
Administrative Section: Robert T. Yamate.
Regional Security Officer: Peter L. Caton.
Public Affairs Officer: Daniel J. Schuman.
Communications Programme Officer: Jerry T. Scrosia, Jr.
Agency for International Development: Phyllis Dichter-Forbes.
Office of the Defence Attaché: Commdr Richard W. Sim.

VIET-NAM

Embassy: 101 Antananarivo; tel (2) 27651.
Ambassador: Vu Dinh Hoe.

International Organizations

EUROPEAN COMMUNITIES

External Delegation: Immeuble Ny Havana, 67 hectares, BP 746, Antananarivo; tel (2) 24216; telex 222327; fax (2) 32169.
Commission Delegate: Dieter Walter Schmidt.

MALAWI

AUSTRIA

Consulate: Realty House, Churchill Rd, POB 5133, Blantyre-Limbe; tel 605305; telex 4775.
Honorary Consul: Sakker A. S. Sacranie.

BELGIUM

Consulate: c/o AMI Press Ltd, POB 838, Blantyre; tel 671555.
Honorary Consul: Luc Maton.

CANADA

Office of the High Commission: POB 1257, Lilongwe; tel 723732; telex 45386; fax 721553.
Head of Office and First Secretary (Development): S. McCoy.

CHINA (TAIWAN)

Embassy: POB 30221, Capital City, Lilongwe 3; telex 44317.
Ambassador: Dr Yue-Tseng Feng.

DENMARK

Consulate-General: Chilembwe House, Churchill Rd, POB 5095, Limbe; tel 640088; telex 44218.
Consul-General: Andreas Duborg Christiani.

EGYPT

Embassy: POB 30451, Lilongwe 3; tel 730300; telex 44538.
Ambassador: F. M. Y. Elkhadi.

FINLAND

Consulate: POB 5095, Limbe; tel 640088; telex 44218; fax 652485.
Consul: Andreas D. Christiani.

FRANCE

Embassy: Area 40, Road No. 8, POB 30054/30055, Lilongwe 3; tel 730377; telex 44141.
Ambassador: Marcel Rey.
Trade Promotion Office: BP 30119, Lilongwe 3; tel 730377; telex 4347.

GERMANY

Embassy: POB 30046, Lilongwe 3; tel 731266; telex 44124.
Ambassador: Dr Wilfried Rupprecht.

IRELAND

Consulate: POB 462, Downs House, Victoria Ave, Blantyre; tel 620730.
Honorary Consul: Richard F. Fitzsimons.

ISRAEL

Embassy: POB 30319, Lilongwe 3; tel 731333; fax 732246.
Ambassador: Moshe Itan.

KOREA, REPUBLIC

Embassy: POB 30583, Lilongwe 3; telex 44834.
Ambassador: Pak Yong-Chol.

MOZAMBIQUE

Embassy: POB 30579, Lilongwe 3; telex 44793.
Ambassador: Amos Mahanjane.

SOUTH AFRICA

Embassy: Mpico Bldg, City Centre, POB 30043, Lilongwe 3; tel 730888; telex 44255; fax 734205.
Ambassador: George Charles Stroebel.
Counsellor: E. Wolleschak.
First Secretary: S. A. Bonthuys.
Second Secretary (Administration): T. Nieuwoudt.
Third Secretary (Co-operation): J. W. Klopper.
Third Secretary (Consular): L. Keyser.
Third Secretary (Consular): L. Dippenaar.
Attaché (Medical): Dr A. T. van Zyl.
Military Attaché: Col M. S. Ackermann.
Consulate-General: Chayamba Bldg, cnr Victoria Ave and Henderson St, POB 1072, Blantyre; tel 620444; telex 44215; fax 620690.
Consul-General: C. P. Barnard.
Vice-Consul (Administration): M. Pathers.
Trade and Industry Section: fax 620803.
Consul (Trade): L. C. de Jager.

SWEDEN

Consulate: Chilembwe House, Churchill Rd, POB 5095, Limbe; tel 640088; telex 44218; fax 652485.
Consul: Andreas Duborg Christiani.

UNITED KINGDOM

High Commission: Lingadzi House, POB 30042, Lilongwe 3; tel 731544; telex 44727; fax 734163.
High Commissioner: W. Nigel Wenban-Smith.
Deputy High Commissioner and Head of Chancery: G. D. Davies.
First Secretary (Development): P. R. O. Bromley.
Second Secretary (Chancery/Information): A. J. M. Dunlop.
Second Secretary (Commercial): S. J. Seaman.
Second Secretary (Management/Consular): N. Ennescott.
Third Secretary (Consular/Management): Kelvin E. Green.
Third Secretary (Aid Administration/Manpower Liaison): B. Lister-Bins.
British Development Division in Southern Africa: Lingadzi House, POB 30059, Lilongwe 3.
Head of Division: S. E. Unsworth.
Senior Natural Resources Adviser: A. J. Tainsh.
Senior Engineering Adviser: C. I. Ellis.
Senior Economic Assistant: P. Owen.
Senior Education Adviser: M. Seath.
Senior Health Adviser: S. Simmonds.
Natural Resources Adviser: A. T. Barrett.
Manpower and Training Adviser: M. Blunt.

USA

Embassy: Area 40, Flat 18, POB 30016, Lilongwe 3; tel 730166; telex 44627; fax 732282.
Ambassador: George A. Trail III.
Deputy Chief of Mission: George Dragnich.
Economic/Commercial Section: Phillip Carter.
Political Section: Horace Speed.
Administrative Section: Robert L. Kile.
Public Affairs Officer: Donald Creager.
Communications Programme Officer: Danny D. Lockwood.
Agency for International Development: Carol A. Peasley.
Office of the Defence Attaché: Lieut Col Frank B. Bonvillian.

ZAMBIA

High Commission: POB 30138, Lilongwe 3; tel 731911; telex 44181.
High Commissioner: Ammon Umbanda.

ZIMBABWE

High Commission: POB 30183, Lilongwe 3; tel 733988.
High Commissioner: J. S. Mvundura.

International Organizations

EUROPEAN COMMUNITIES

External Delegation: Lingadzi House, POB 30102, Capital City, Lilongwe 3; tel 730255; telex 44260; fax 730593.
Commission Delegate: Hugh Johnstone.

MALAYSIA

ARGENTINA

Embassy: 3 Jalan Semantan Dua, Damansara Heights, 50490 Kuala Lumpur; POB 11200, 50738 Kuala Lumpur; tel (3) 2550176; telex 31854; fax (3) 2552706.
Ambassador: Dr Eduardo Alberto Sadous.
Second Secretary: Alejandro Antonio Aragones.

AUSTRALIA

High Commission: 6 Jalan Yap Kwan Seng, 50450 Kuala Lumpur; tel (3) 2423122; telex 30260; fax (3) 2415773.
High Commissioner: Frank Murray.

AUSTRIA

Embassy: MUI Plaza Bldg, 7th Floor, Jalan P. Ramlee, 50250 Kuala Lumpur; POB 10154, 50704 Kuala Lumpur; tel (3) 2484277; telex 31263; fax (3) 2489813.
Ambassador: Dr Friedrich Posch.
Second Secretary (Economic) and Vice-Consul: Cornelia Hochreiter.

BANGLADESH

High Commission: 204-1 Jalan Ampang, 50450 Kuala Lumpur; tel (3) 2423271; telex 31593.
High Commissioner: Farooq Sobhan.

BELGIUM

Embassy: 12 Lorong Yap Kwan Seng, 50450 Kuala Lumpur; POB 10558, 50718 Kuala Lumpur; tel (3) 2485733; telex 30044; fax (3) 2415922.
Ambassador: Edmond de Wilde.
First Secretary: R. de Bruyne.
Commercial Attaché: P. de Bruyn.

BOLIVIA

Embassy: Kompleks Antarabangsa, Suite 221, 2nd Floor, Jalan Sultan Ismail, 50250 Kuala Lumpur; tel (3) 2425146.
Chargé d'affaires: Dr Francisco Blacutt.

BRAZIL

Embassy: 22 Pesiaran Damansara Endah, Damansara Heights, 50490 Kuala Lumpur; tel (3) 2548607; telex 31574.
Ambassador: Sergio Damasceno Vieira.

BRUNEI

High Commission: MBF Plaza, 16th Floor, Jalan Ampang, 50450 Kuala Lumpur; tel (3) 2612838; telex 32297; fax (3) 2612898.
High Commissioner: Pengiran Haji Abdul Momin.

CANADA

High Commission: Plaza MBF, 7th Floor, 172 Jalan Ampang, 50450 Kuala Lumpur; POB 10990, 50732 Kuala Lumpur; tel (3) 2612000; telex 30269; fax (3) 2611270.
High Commissioner: George W. Seymour.
Counsellor (Commercial): Melvyn L. MacDonald.
Counsellor (Immigration): Dennis R. Scown.
Defence Adviser: Col H. Gregory Leitch.
First Secretary: Gordon Morrison.
First Secretary (Immigration): Caroline M. A. Melis.
Second Secretary (Administration): William J. Hawley.
Second Secretary (Commercial): Judith A. M. St George.

CHINA, PEOPLE'S REPUBLIC

Embassy: 229 Jalan Ampang, 50450 Kuala Lumpur; tel (3) 2428495.
Ambassador: Zhou Gang.

CZECHOSLOVAKIA

Embassy: 32 Jalan Mesra, off Jalan Ampang, 55000 Kuala Lumpur; tel (3) 2427185; telex 30669; fax (3) 2412727.
Chargé d'affaires: Dr Miroslav Jordan.

DENMARK

Embassy: Wisma Angkasa Raya, 22nd Floor, 123 Jalan Ampang, POB 10908, 50728 Kuala Lumpur; tel (3) 2416088; telex 30427; fax (3) 2423732.
Ambassador: Jørgen Holm.
Commercial Counsellor: Finn Mose Mortensen.
Export Assistant: René Frandsen.
Commercial Officer: Yew Choong Wong.
Agricultural Counsellor: Carsten Philipsen.

Consulate: c/o The East Asiatic Co (Malaysia) Berhad, Lot 43 A, Karamunsing Warehouse, 88000 Kota Kinabalu; POB 10705, 88807 Kota Kinabalu, Sabah; tel (88) 240288; telex 80035; fax (88) 235587.
Consul: Ole Sonne.

Consulate: Hongkong Bank Chambers, 3rd Floor, 1 Downing St, 10300 Pulau Pinang; tel (4) 611457; telex 40030.
Consul: Datuk Børge Bek-Nielsen.

Consulate: c/o Nedlloyd EAC Agencies (M) Sdn Bhd, 2A, Persiaran Muda Musa, 42000 Port Kelang, Selangor; POB 5, 42007 Port Kelang; tel 3687101; telex 39521; fax 3685559.
Consul: Niels John Madsen.

EGYPT

Embassy: 28 Lingkungan U Thant, off Jalan U Thant, POB 12004, 55000 Kuala Lumpur; tel (3) 4568184; telex 31196; fax (3) 4573515.
Ambassador: Ahmed Nazmi Moustafa.
Counsellor: Mostafa Mohamed Khadre.
Counsellor: Ibrahim Abdel Salam Youssef.
Counsellor (Commercial): Mohammed Samir Ezzat.
First Secretary: Fathy Guergis Beshara.
Second Secretary: Ali Mohyee el Din M. el-Ashiry.

FINLAND

Embassy: 15th Floor, Plaza MBF, Jalan Ampang, 50450 Kuala Lumpur; POB 10909, 50728 Kuala Lumpur; tel (3) 2611088; telex 31535; fax (3) 2615354.
Ambassador: Pertti Ripatti.
Second Secretary: Bo Lindroos.
Commercial Secretary: Matti Vinha.

Consulate: Peat Tech (M) Sdn Bhd, 18 Jalan Kg Pandan, 55100 Kuala Lumpur; tel (3) 9845620; fax (3) 9853787.
Honorary Consul: Keng-Bin Lee.

Consulate: T. H. Wong & Co, Sdn Bhd, 5 Tanjong Lipat Rd, POB 10185, 88802 Kota Kinabalu, Sabah; tel (88) 52035; telex 80738.
Honorary Consul: Tshen Hin Wong.

FRANCE

Embassy: 192-196 Jalan Ampang, 50450 Kuala Lumpur; POB 10700, 50722 Kuala Lumpur; tel (3) 2484122; telex 30436.
Ambassador: Frédéric Grasset.

Trade Promotion Office: POB 10575, 50718 Kuala Lumpur; tel (3) 2429444; telex 30248.

GERMANY

Embassy: 3 Jalan U Thant, 55000 Kuala Lumpur; POB 10023, 50700 Kuala Lumpur; tel (3) 2429666; telex 30380; fax (3) 2413943.
Ambassador: Wilfried Vogeler.

Consulate: Penang.

ICELAND

Consulate: c/o Diethelm Malaysia Sdn, 74 Jalan University, 46700 Petaling Jaya, POB 77, Selangor; tel (3) 7573745; telex 37683; fax (3) 7559427.
Consul: Hans-Peter Eichenberger.

INDIA

High Commission: Wisma Selangor Dredging, 20th Floor, West Block, 142C, Jalan Ampang, 50450 Kuala Lumpur; tel (3) 261700; telex 30317.
High Commissioner: P. M. S. Malik.

INDONESIA

Embassy: 233 Jalan Tun Razak, POB 10889, 50400 Kuala Lumpur; tel (3) 9842011; telex 30258; fax (3) 9847908.
Ambassador: Sunarso Djajusman.

Consulate-General: Jalan Coastal, Karamunsing, POB 11595, 88817 Kota Kinabalu, Sabah.

Consulate: 467 Jalan Burma, 10350 Pulau Penang; POB 502, Penang.

IRAN

Embassy: 5 and 8 Lorong Mayang, off Jalan Ampang, opp. Wisma Central, 50450 Kuala Lumpur; tel (3) 2433575.
Ambassador: Mohammed-Reza Morshedzadeh.
Counsellor: S. A. Tabatabai.
Second Secretary and Commercial Attaché: S. A. Rezvani.
Attaché: G. R. Jafarpour.
Head of Consular Office: J. Kamyabi.

IRAQ

Embassy: 2 Jalan Langgak Golf, off Jalan Tun Razak, POB 12022, 55000 Kuala Lumpur; tel (3) 2480555; telex 30328; fax (3) 2414331.
Ambassador: Hisham Tabaqchali.

IRELAND

Consulate: Skrine & Co., Straits Trading Bldg, 3rd Floor, 4 Leboh Pasar Besar, 01-23 Kuala Lumpur; tel (3) 2985111; telex 30949; fax (3) 2919552.
Honorary Consul: Peter Mooney.

ITALY

Embassy: 99 Jalan U Thant, 55000 Kuala Lumpur; tel (3) 4565122; telex 30797; fax (3) 4573199.
Ambassador: Luca Daniele Biolato.

JAPAN

Embassy: 11 Pesiaran Stonor, off Jalan Tun Razak, 50450 Kuala Lumpur; tel (3) 2427044; telex 30385; fax (3) 2426570.
Ambassador: Fukuda Hiroshi.

Consulate-General: 2 Biggs Rd, 10350 Penang; tel (4) 368222; telex 40369; fax (4) 365257.
Consul-General: Hiroshi Ikeda.

Consulate: Wisma Yakim, 5th Floor, Jalan Datuk Salleh Sulong, POB 11001, Kota Kinabalu, Sabah; tel (88) 53717; telex 80063; fax (88) 236632.
Consul: Hiroshi Yamaoka.

KOREA, DEMOCRATIC PEOPLE'S REPUBLIC

Embassy: 203 Jalan Ampang, Kuala Lumpur; tel (3) 2420650; telex 30995.
Ambassador: Yu Chae-hwan.

KOREA, REPUBLIC

Embassy: Wisma MCA, 22nd Floor, 163 Jalan Ampang, 50450 Kuala Lumpur; tel (3) 2621385; telex 30324; fax (3) 2623108.
Ambassador: Hong Soon-Young.

LIBYA

People's Bureau: 6 Jalan Madge, Kuala Lumpur; tel (3) 2432112.
Secretary of People's Bureau: Ali Suleiman Alaujali.

MEXICO

Consulate: Jalan Bukit Bintang, Suite 901-2, 9th Floor, (Universal Cable Berhad), Kuala Lumpur Tower, Kuala Lumpur; (3) 2415155; fax (3) 2420950.
Honorary Consul: Dato Lew Sip Hon.

MYANMAR

Embassy: 7 Jalan U Thant, 55000 Kuala Lumpur; tel (3) 2423863.
Ambassador: U Ko.

NETHERLANDS

Embassy: 4 Jalan Mesra, off Jalan Damai, 55000 Kuala Lumpur; POB 10543, 50716 Kuala Lumpur; tel (3) 2421341; telex 30330; fax (3) 2411959.
Ambassador: Bartholomeus de Bruyn Ouboter.
First Secretary: Berend W. van Gorkom.
Second Secretary (Commercial): C. M. Wiedenhof.
Attaché (Administrative): Tom Klos.
Assistant Attaché (Administrative): M. W. M. Broekman.

Consulate: c/o Algemene Bank Nederland, POB 83, 10710 Peneng; tel (4) 622144; fax (4) 628993.
Consul: R. Broedelet.

Consulate: c/o Sarawak Shell Bhd., Locked Bag No. 1, 98009 Miri; tel (85) 452310; fax (85) 452030.
Consul: A. Hartevelt.

NEW ZEALAND

High Commission: 193 Jalan Tun Razak, 50400 Kuala Lumpur; POB 12003, 50764 Kuala Lumpur; tel (3) 2486422; telex 30284; fax (3) 2413094.
High Commissioner: Michael F. Chilton.
Deputy High Commissioner: Warwick A. Hawker.
Attaché: Gerry Cook.
Trade Commissioner: Vic Moss.
Trade Commissioner: Nick Arathimos.
Defence Attaché: Capt. J. E. R. Granville.

NIGERIA

High Commission: Kuala Lumpur.
High Commissioner: Alhaji Abdulrahman Gara.

NORWAY

Embassy: Bangunan Angkasa Raya, 11th Floor, Jalan Ampang, POB 10332, 50710 Kuala Lumpur; tel (3) 2430144; telex 32402; fax (3) 2430363.

PAKISTAN

High Commission: 132 Jalan Ampang, Kuala Lumpur; tel (3) 2483822; telex 33289.
High Commissioner: Syed Azmat Hassan.

PHILIPPINES

Embassy: 1 Changkat Kia Peng, 50450 Kuala Lumpur; tel (3) 2484233.
Ambassador: Rodolfo C. Severino.

POLAND

Embassy: POB 10052, 50704 Kuala Lumpur; No. 495, 4_0 Mile Jalan Ampang, 68000 Ampang, Selangor Darul Ehsan; tel (3) 4576719; telex 33291.
Ambassador: Andrzej Zor.
Second Secretary: Zygmunt Langer.
Third Secretary: Andrzej Reszke.
Secretary: Chong Wei Yin.

Commercial Office: POB 10417, 50712 Kuala Lumpur; No. 8B Jalan Ampang Hilir, 55000 Kuala Lumpur; tel (3) 4560940; telex 31015; fax (3) 4564420.
Commercial Counsellor: Tadeusz Przyborowski.
Commercial Expert: Stanislaw Wszelaki.
Commercial Expert: Eugeniusz Tuzinek.

ROMANIA

Embassy: 114 Jalan Damai, Kuala Lumpur; tel (3) 2423172.
Chargé d'affaires: Gheorghe Savuica.

RUSSIA

Embassy: 263 Jalan Ampang, 50450 Kuala Lumpur; tel (3) 4560009; telex 26073.
Ambassador: Anatoly Ivanovich Khmelnitsky.

SAUDI ARABIA

Embassy: 11 Jalan Ampang, 55000 Kuala Lumpur; tel (3) 4579433; telex 30795.
Ambassador: Sheikh Muhammad al-Hamad al-Shubaili.

SINGAPORE

High Commission: 209 Jalan Tun Razak, 50400 Kuala Lumpur; tel (3) 2616277; telex 30320; fax (3) 2616343.
High Commissioner: Low Choon Ming.
Counsellor: T. Jasudasen.
Defence Adviser: Col Richard Zee Chee Kiong.

SRI LANKA

High Commission: 18 Lorong Yap Kwan Seng, 50450 Kuala Lumpur; tel (3) 2423094.
High Commissioner: H. W. H. Weerasinghe.

SWEDEN

Embassy: Wisma Angkasa Raya, 6th Floor, 123 Jalan Ampang, 50450 Kuala Lumpur; POB 10239, 50708 Kuala Lumpur; tel (3) 2481644; telex 30315; fax (3) 2486325.
Ambassador: Wanja Dougherty Tornberg.
Economic and Commercial Counsellor: Jan Carlson.
Second Secretary: Axel Wernhoff.

Consulate: c/o Plantation Agencies Sdn Bhd, 2nd Floor, Standard Chartered Bank Chambers, Leboh Pantai (Beach St), George Town, 10300 Penang; POB 706, 10790 Penang; tel (4) 625333; telex 40064; fax (4) 622018.
Consul: John William West.

SWITZERLAND

Embassy: 16 Pesiaran Madge, 55000 Kuala Lumpur; POB 12008, 50764 Kuala Lumpur; tel (3) 2431102; telex 31155; fax (3) 2480935.
Ambassador: Charles Steinhäuslin.
First Secretary: Markus Hirsiger.
Attaché and Head of Chancery: Beat Hofmann.

THAILAND

Embassy: 206 Jalan Ampang, 50450 Kuala Lumpur; tel (3) 2488222; telex 31566; fax (3) 2486527.
Ambassador: Dr Chawan Chawanid.

TURKEY

Embassy: 118 Jalan U Thant, 55000 Kuala Lumpur; tel (3) 4572225; telex 31245.
Ambassador: Yalcin Tug.
Economic and Commercial Counsellor: M. Orhan Sagci.
Third Secretary: H. Avni Aksoy.
Attaché (Administration): A. Teoman Dagseven.
Attaché (Administration): Ayla Kansu.
Attaché: Mustafa Coskun.
Attaché: Tuncay Baser.

UNITED KINGDOM

High Commission: 185 Jalan Semantang Ampang, 50450 Kuala Lumpur; POB 11030, 50732 Kuala Lumpur; tel (3) 2482122; telex 35225; fax (3) 2480880.
High Commissioner: Duncan Slater.
Deputy High Commissioner and Counsellor (Commercial/Economic): A. C. Thorpe.
Counsellor: P. R. G. Redshaw.
Defence Adviser: Col G. A. Holt.
Counsellor (Defence Supply): B. Breslin.
First Secretary and Head of Chancery: J. Jenkins.
First Secretary (Commercial): A. C. Gallie.
First Secretary (Management): K. A. Taylor.
First Secretary (Defence Supply): P. J. Sullivan.
Assistant Defence Adviser: Lieut Commdr J. J. Carter.
First Secretary: S. T. O'Connell.
First Secretary: Dr P. G. Topping.
Second Secretary (Aid/Economic): M. Purves.

Office of the Honorary British Representative: Lucas Automotive Sdn Bhd, PLO 17, Senai Industrial Estate, KB 105, 81400 Senai, Johore; tel (7) 591301; telex 60762; fax (7) 594301.
Honorary British Representative: J. W. Bradbury.

Office of the Honorary British Representative: The Hong Kong and Shanghai Banking Corporation, POB 11602, 88817 Kota Kinabalu, Sabah; tel (88) 212622; telex 80065; fax (88) 213041.
Honorary British Representative: M. K. G. Scott.

Office of the Honorary British Representative: c/o Standard Chartered Bank, POB 12, 93900 Kuching, Sarawak; tel (82) 243616; telex 70117; fax (82) 414299.
Honorary British Representative: T. A. McCartney.

Office of the Honorary British Representative: Sarawak Shell Berhad EPS/3, 98100 Lutong, Miri, Sarawak; tel (85) 3408; fax (85) 452030.
Honorary British Representative: G. S. Brown.

Office of the Honorary British Representative: c/o Plantation Agencies Sdn Bhd, Standard Chartered Bank Chambers, Beach St, 10300 Penang; tel (4) 625333; telex 40064; fax (4) 622018.
Honorary British Representative: John William West (designate).

USA

Embassy: 376 Jalan Tun Razak, 50400 Kuala Lumpur; POB 10035, 50700 Kuala Lumpur; tel (3) 2489011; telex 32956; fax (3) 2422207.
Ambassador: Paul M. Cleveland.
Deputy Chief of Mission: W. Scott Butcher.
Political Section: Gene B. Christy.
Economic Section: Douglas A. Hartwick.
Commercial Section: Paul T. Walters.
Consular Section: Peter G. Kaestner.
Administrative Section: Lawrence R. Baer.
Regional Security Officer: John P. Chornyak.
Public Affairs Officer: James C. Pollock.
Communications Programme Officer: Michael McCaffrey.
Information Systems Manager: Kimberley Kaestner.
Office of the Defence Attaché: Col Michael A. McDermott.
Agricultural Section: Jeffrey A. Hesse.

VIET-NAM

Embassy: 4 Pesiaran Stonor, 50450 Kuala Lumpur; tel (3) 2484036.
Ambassador: Tran le Duc.

YUGOSLAVIA

Embassy: Lot 300, Bt 4_0 Jalan Ampang, POB 12357, 50776 Kuala Lumpur; tel (3) 4561087; telex 31219.
Ambassador: Dr Zoran Jasić.

MALDIVES

DENMARK

Consulate: 25 Marine Dr., Malé; tel (32) 2451; telex 66026.
Consul: Abdullah Saeed.

FRANCE

Consular Office: 1/27 Chandhanee Magee, Malé 20-02; tel (32) 3760; telex 66030.
Consular Agent: Ismail Maniku.

INDIA

High Commission: Maafannu Aage, Maafannu, Malé; telex 66044.
High Commissioner: M. P. M. Menon.

PAKISTAN

High Commission: 2 Moonimaage, Galolhu, POB 2006, Malé; tel (32) 2024; telex 66087.
High Commissioner: Mazhar Qayyum Khan.

SRI LANKA

High Commission: Muraka, 5/44 Orchid Magu, Malé 20-02; tel (32) 2845; telex 66061; fax (32) 1652.
High Commissioner: Latif Sheriffdeen.
Third Secretary: Sumith Nakandala.
Attaché: R. S. J. Rambukkana.

SWEDEN

Consulate: c/o Cyprea Ltd, 25 Marine Drive, Malé; tel (32) 2451; telex 66026.
Consul: Abdullah Saeed.

MALI

ALGERIA

Embassy: Derrière le Fleuve, Badalabougou.
Ambassador: Abdelghani Akbi.

BURKINA FASO

Embassy: BP 9022, Bamako.
Ambassador: Hamadou Kone.

CANADA

Office of the Canadian Embassy: route de Koulikoro, BP 198, Bamako; tel 22-22-36; telex 2530; fax 22-43-62.
Counsellor (Development), Consul and Chargé d'affaires: Guy Gagnon.
First Secretary (Development) and Consul: S. Marchand.
First Secretary (Development): M. Piché.
First Secretary (Development): D. Henry.
First Secretary (Development) and Consul: L. Ouimet.
First Secretary (Development) and Consul: M. Lalonde.
First Secretary (Development): G. Robard.
Attaché (Administration) and Vice-Consul: M. Parent.
Attaché (Administration) and Vice-Consul: D. Levasseur.

CHINA, PEOPLE'S REPUBLIC

Embassy: BP 112, Bamako; telex 2455.
Ambassador: Liu Lide.

CUBA

Embassy: BP 40, Korofina; telex 2577.
Ambassador: Eduardo Barbín Martín.

EGYPT

Embassy: BP 44, Badalabougou; tel 22-35-03; telex 2407.
Ambassador: Fathi Draz Moustafa.

FRANCE

Embassy: square Patrice Lumumba, BP 17, Bamako; tel 22-29-51; telex 2569.
Ambassador: Jean-Didier Roisin.

Consulate-General: tel 22-62-46.

Trade Promotion Office: BP 101, Bamako; tel 22-65-43; telex 516.

GERMANY

Embassy: Badalabougou-Est, Lotissement A6, BP 100, Bamako; tel 22-32-99; telex 22529.
Ambassador: Klaus Holderbaum.

GUINEA

Embassy: BP 118, Bamako; tel 22-29-75; telex 2576.
Ambassador: Mamadou Mass Diallo.

IRAN

Embassy: quartier de l'Hippodrome, BP 2136, Bamako.
Ambassador: Mojtaba Shafii.

IRAQ

Embassy: BP 2512, Bamako-Badalabougou; tel 22-38-06; telex 2416; fax 22-51-91.
Ambassador: Homam Hashim al-Alousi.
Attaché: Kadhum Karim A. al-Robaiee.
Attaché: Qasim Sahi Hussein.
Administration Official: Sabah Kadhum Hussain.

KOREA, DEMOCRATIC PEOPLE'S REPUBLIC

Embassy: BP 765, Sogoniko, Bamako.
Ambassador: Pak Chung-Gil.

LIBYA

Embassy: quartier de l'Hippodrome, Bamako; telex 2420.
Ambassador: Ali Moussa Tabass.

MALAYSIA

Embassy: Badalabougou-Ouest, BP 98, Bamako; tel 22-27-83; telex 2423; fax 22-32-32.
Ambassador: Choo Siew-Kioh.

MAURITANIA

Embassy: BP 135, Bamako; telex 2415.
Ambassador: Ahmedou Ould Abdallah.

MOROCCO

Embassy: BP 2013, Bamako; tel 22-21-23; telex 2430.
Chargé d'affaires: Larbi Roudiés.

NIGERIA

Embassy: BP 57, Badalabougou; tel 22-57-71.
Chargé d'affaires: F. F. Adegunloye.

RUSSIA

Embassy: BP 300, Niarela, Bamako; tel 22-51-77; telex 2617.
Ambassador: Yevgeni Nersessov.

SAUDI ARABIA

Embassy: BP 81, Badalabougou; telex 2408.
Chargé d'affaires: Muhammad Rajamiri.

SENEGAL

Embassy: ave Kassé Keïta, Bamako.
Ambassador: Mamadou Laity Ndiaye.

SWEDEN

Consulate: c/o BIAO, ave de l'Indépendance, BP 15, Bamako; tel 22-32-17; telex 2501.

Ambassador: Bengt Holmquist (resident in Sweden).
Consul: Adama Seydou Traore.
Vice-Consul: Bassirou Ba.

SWITZERLAND

Embassy Office: BP 2386, Bamako; tel 22-32-05; telex 2595.
Attaché (Development Co-operation, Humanitarian Aid and Consular Affairs): Markus Müller.

UNITED KINGDOM

Consulate: BP 2069, Bamako; tel 22-20-64; fax 22-42-55.
Honorary Consul: Chasser Jessop.

USA

Embassy: angle rue Rochester NY et rue Mohamed V, BP 34, Bamako; tel 22-54-70; telex 2448; fax 22-37-12.
Ambassador: Herbert Donald Gelber.
Deputy Chief of Mission: John S. Boardman.
Political Section: Mary Curtin.
Economic/Commercial Section: Robert Merrigan.
Consular Section: Steven K. Seigel.
Labour Officer: Ollie P. Anderson, Jr (resident in the USA).
Administrative Section: Peter S. Wood.
Regional Security Officer: Kim O'Connor.
Public Affairs Officer: Linda A. Buggeln.
Communications Programme Officer: Salvador Piazza.
Agency for International Development: Dennis J. Brennan.

YUGOSLAVIA

Embassy: BP 207, Bamako; telex 2463.
Ambassador: Branko Zeković.

International Organizations

EUROPEAN COMMUNITIES

External Delegation: rue Guégau-Badalabougou, BP 115, Bamako; tel 22-23-56; telex 2526; fax 22-36-70.
Commission Delegate: André Van Haeverbeke.

MALTA

AUSTRALIA

High Commission: Ta'Xbiex Terrace, Ta'Xbiex; POB 8, Sliema; tel 338201; telex 1269; fax 319377.
High Commissioner: John Leslie Mahoney.
First Secretary and Consul: Keith Lewis.

AUSTRIA

Consulate-General: 34 Frederick St, Valletta; tel 229182; telex 1294.
Honorary Consul-General: Joseph R. Darmanin.
Honorary Vice-Consul: Michael Darmanin.

BELGIUM

Consulate: 18A/3 Scots House, M.A.Vassalli St, Valletta; tel 230893.
Honorary Consul: S. Gatt.

CANADA

Consulate: Demajo House, 103 Archbishop St, Valletta; tel 233121; telex 1278; fax 235145.
Honorary Consul: J. M. Demajo.

CHINA, PEOPLE'S REPUBLIC

Embassy: Karmnu Court, Lapsi St, St Julian's; tel 334695; telex 1385; fax 344730.
Ambassador: Mei Ping.
Counsellor and Head of Economic Section: Zhang Weizhen.
First Secretary and Head of Commercial Section: Yang Qikai.
Second Secretary: Zhao Jun.
Second Secretary: Li Ruiyu.
Second Secretary (Administration): Chen Sihe.
Third Secretary (Archivist): Zhang Yusheng.
Third Secretary (Economic Section): Wu Gangchen.

COLOMBIA

Consulate: 5 Censu Borg St, Hamrun; tel 237311.
Honorary Consul: Albert V. Rutter.

CYPRUS

Consulate-General: Airways House, 4th Floor, High St, Sliema; tel 341848; telex 1268; fax 310671.
Honorary Consul-General: Dr John Grech.

CZECHOSLOVAKIA

Embassy: 39, Flat 2, Tigne Sea-Front, Sliema; tel 511330; telex 1339.
Minister-Counsellor and Chargé d'affaires a.i.: Dr Zikmund Tobias.
Commercial Section: Flat 2, St Anna Court, Bisazza St, Sliema; tel 311331; telex 1876.
Attaché (Commercial): Jiri Vorac.

DENMARK

Consulate-General: 19 Zachary St, Valletta; tel 232612; telex 1227.
Consul-General: James G. Gollcher.

EGYPT

Embassy: Villa Juliana, Princess Elizabeth St, Ta'Xbiex; tel 314158; telex 1300.
Ambassador: Amin Yousry Ahmed Yousry.
First Secretary: Youssef Kamal Botros.
First Secretary: Magdy Mohamed Ahmad Hashad.
First Secretary: Khaled Farouk Hanafi.
Attaché (Administrative): Hassan Mahmoud Affifi.
Attaché (Administrative): Samira Kerollas Gindi.
Attaché (Administrative): Mahmoud Abdelshakour Fargaly.

FINLAND

Consulate-General: 153 Old Mint St, Valletta; tel 222425; telex 1660.
Consul-General: Edgar E. Arrigo.
Vice-Consul: Paul George Arrigo.

FRANCE

Embassy: Villa Séminia, 12 Sir Temi Zammit St, Ta'Xbiex; POB 408, Valletta; tel 225856; telex 1381; fax 334640.
Ambassador: Samuel Le Caruyer de Beauvais.
First Secretary: Christian Jourde.
Attaché (Cultural): Danièle Harin.
Trade Promotion Office: Flat B, Dolphin Court, Embassy Way, Ta'Xbiex; POB 359, Valletta; tel 334844; telex 1327.
Counsellor (Commercial): Robert Jany.
Attaché (Commercial): Roger Bodin.

GERMANY

Embassy: 'Il-Piazzetta', Entrance B, 1st Floor, Tower Rd, Sliema; POB 48, Valletta; tel 336520; telex 1224; fax 333976.
Ambassador: Dr Gottfried Pagenstert.
Second Secretary: Eberhard Stanizewski.
Attaché (Consular/Cultural): Jorg Resch.
Assistant Attaché (Administrative): Helgard Steinert.

GREECE

Consulate: 48/3 Zachary St, Valletta; tel 237952.
Honorary Consul: Pantelis Mairangas.

HOLY SEE

Apostolic Nunciature: Villa Cor Jesu, Pitkali Rd, Attard; tel 414732; fax 245901.
Apostolic Nuncio: Most Rev. Pier Luigi Celata, Titular Archbishop of Doclea.
First Secretary: Rev. Eliseo Ariotti.

HONDURAS

Consulate: 98 Old Bakery St, Valletta.
Honorary Consul: S. Cauchi.

ICELAND

Consulate: Continental Cars Ltd, Testaferrata St, Msida; tel 339960; telex 371; fax 310480.
Consul: Meurice F. Mizzi.

ITALY

Embassy: 5 Vilhena St, Floriana; tel 233157; telex 1388; fax 221645.

Ambassador: Dott. Giovanni Paolo Tozzoli.
Counsellor: Dott. Marcello Alessio.
Attaché: Dott. Antonio di Blasi.

Cultural Institute: St George's Sq., Valletta; tel 221462.
Attaché (Cultural): Prof. Pietro Insana.

JAPAN

Consulate-General: 311 Republic St, Valletta; tel 232211.
Honorary Consul-General: S. C. Mifsud.

KOREA, DEMOCRATIC PEOPLE'S REPUBLIC

Embassy: Corradino, POB 33, Paola; tel 800003; telex 1492.
Ambassador: Kim Chae Won.
Third Secretary: Li Il Chul.
Attaché: Pak Yong Chol.

KOREA, REPUBLIC

Consulate-General: Exchange Bldgs, Republic St, Valletta; tel 245127.
Honorary Consul-General: Carmel E. Sullivan.
Honorary Consul: John E. Sullivan.

LIBERIA

Consulate-General: 311 Republic St, Valletta; tel 232211.
Honorary Consul-General: S. C. Mifsud.

LIBYA

People's Bureau: Dar il-Jamahariya, Notabile Rd, Balzan; tel 486348; telex 1258.
Secretary: Ahmad Abd an-Nabbi ash-Shahati.
Counsellor (Economic/Cooperation): Attia Omar Mubarak.
Counsellor (Political): Fouad Abubaker Zlitni.
Counsellor (Consular): Mehemmed Ellafi Isa.
Attaché (Administrative): Abdulaziz M. Baisho.
Attaché (Finance): Gama A. Latef.
Attaché (Labour): El-Hadi Khalil.

LUXEMBOURG

Embassy: See Embassy of The Netherlands, Italy.

Financial, Economic and Consular Offices: See Embassy of Belgium, United Kingdom.

Consulate: 52/2 Old Theatre St, Valletta; tel 232271.
Honorary Consul: Dr David Tonna.

MEXICO

Consulate: 150 St Lucia St, Valletta; tel 239497.
Honorary Consul: Salvino J. Sullivan.
Honorary Vice-Consul: David Sullivan.

MONACO

Consulate-General: 12 St Paul's St, Valletta; tel 224128.
Honorary Consul-General: F. X. Zammit Cutajar.

NETHERLANDS

Vice-Consulate: 19 Zachary St, Valletta; tel 233758.
Honorary Vice-Consul: J. G. Golder.

NORWAY

Consulate-General: Notabile Rd, Mriehel; tel 448466.
Honorary Consul-General: Anthony Zammit Cutajar.

PAKISTAN

Consulate-General: 12/25 Strait St, Valletta; tel 237401.
Honorary Consul-General: Joseph C. Mintoff.

PHILIPPINES

Consulate-General: 155 Strait St, Valletta; tel 233446.
Honorary Consul-General: Joseph M. Scicluna.

POLAND

Consulate: 60 South St, Valletta; tel 244306.
Honorary Consul: Stephen Parnis England.

PORTUGAL

Consulate: 35a Archbishop St, Valletta; tel 243149.
Honorary Consul: Dr Austin Sammut.

RUSSIA

Embassy: Anthony Schembri St, Kappara, San Gwann; tel 345111; telex 1545; fax 319195.
Ambassador: Valentina I. Matvienko.
Counsellor: Vladlen V. Diatchenko.
First Secretary: Arkin Akhmetov.
First Secretary: Yuri Ponomarev.
First Secretary: Alexander V. Chirchenko.
Third Secretary: Vladimir V. Lashouk.
Third Secretary: Vladimir A. Yurchenko.

Commercial Section: 'The Lodge', New Rd, Ta'Xbiex; tel 315753; telex 1995.
Counsellor (Commercial): Vladimir I. Petrov.

Cultural Centre: 36 Merchants St, Valletta; tel 222030; fax 244512.
First Secretary (Cultural): Anatoly N. Masko.

Consular Section: Makik Flats, Upper Gardens, St Julian's, Valletta; tel 606394; telex 1545.

SAN MARINO

Consulate-General: St George's Park, St Julians; tel 332312.
Honorary Consul-General: Baron Salvino Testaferrata Moroni Viani.

SENEGAL

Consulate: 38 South St, Valletta; tel 220064.
Honorary Consul: Alfred Calleja.

SPAIN

Embassy: 145/10 Tower Rd, Sliema; tel 314164; telex 1686; fax 333732.
Ambassador: Vicente Ramírez-Montesinos.
Counsellor (Commercial): José Luis Oterino Novales.

Vice-Consulate: 'Scots House', 18 M.A. Vassalli St, Valletta; tel 237606.
Honorary Vice-Consul: S. Gatt.

SWEDEN

Embassy: c/o Ministry for Foreign Affairs, Dept. KSA, POB 16121, 10323 Stockholm, Sweden.
Ambassador: Lars J. Thorwald Bergquist (resident in Sweden).

Consulate-General: 19 Zachary St, Valletta; tel 232612; telex 1227; fax 234195.
Consul-General: James Gustaf Gollcher.
Vice-Consul: Karl Marius Gollcher.
Chancellor: Mark F. Gollcher.

SWITZERLAND

Consulate: 6/7 Zachary St, Valletta; tel 227750.
Honorary Consul: Malcolm Anthony Lowell.

THAILAND

Consulate: 12 Don Rua St, Sliema; tel 338175.
Honorary Consul: W. H. Carbonaro.

TUNISIA

Embassy: Dar Carthage, Qormi Rd, Attard; tel 498853; telex 1835; fax 499973.
Ambassador: Zeinouba Khomsi Maaref (resident in Tunisia).
First Secretary and Chargé d'affaires a.i.: Nooman Jemaiel.
Attaché (Finance): Khemais Amri.

Consulate: Il-Ferries, Ft. 3, Bisazza St, Sliema.
Honorary Consul: Saviour Casapinta.

TURKEY

Consulate-General: 60 South St, Valletta; tel 234059.
Honorary Consul-General: J. Parnis England.

UNITED KINGDOM

High Commission: 7 St Anne St, POB 506, Floriana; tel 233134; telex 1249; fax 242001.
High Commissioner: Peter G. Wallis.
Deputy High Commissioner and First Secretary (Commercial/Economic): Ian Gerken.
Second Secretary (Management): Les R. Dalrymple.
Second Secretary (Consular): Nicholas Johnson.
Third Secretary (Information/Cultural): Elizabeth A. Auld.
Third Secretary (Consular): Diana J. Lees.
Third Secretary (Immigration): Tim J. Dearden.

USA

Embassy: Development House, 2nd Floor, St Anne St, Floriana; POB 535, Valletta; tel 223654; fax 223654.
Ambassador: Sally J. Novetzke.
Deputy Chief of Mission: Howard H. Lange.
Economic/Commercial/Consular Section: Marianne Gustafson.
Political Section: J. Francis Strong.
Administrative Section: Richard V. Davis.
Public Affairs Officer: Sylvia Rifkin.
Communications Programme Officer: Donald J. Ivanich.
Labour Officer: Jack Ferraro.

YUGOSLAVIA

Consulate: 36 Magazine St, Floriana; tel 231450.
Honorary Consul: Nicholas Baldacchino.

International Organizations

EUROPEAN COMMUNITIES

External Delegation: Valletta.

Other Organizations

PALESTINE LIBERATION ORGANIZATION—PLO

Office: 'Villa Serdica', Mensija Rd, St Julian's; tel 338468; fax 339663.
Ambassador: Nuha Tadras.
First Secretary: Samy Ibrahim Baaloushi.
First Secretary: Fathi Hassanian.

MARSHALL ISLANDS

Capital: Majuro.
No information available at time of going to press.

MAURITANIA

ALGERIA

Embassy: Nouakchott; telex 871.
Ambassador: Zerguine Mohamed.

AUSTRIA

Consulate: Nouakchott.

CHINA, PEOPLE'S REPUBLIC

Embassy: BP 196, Nouakchott.
Ambassador: Liu Bai.

DENMARK

Consulate: Ilot K, No. 196, BP 1039, Nouakchott; tel 532-54; telex 564.
Consul: Ahmed Ould Dié.

EGYPT

Embassy: BP 176, Nouakchott; telex 520.

FRANCE

Embassy: BP 231, rue Ahmed Ould M'Hamed, Nouakchott; tel 517-40; telex 582.
Ambassador: Michel Raimbaud.

Trade Promotion Office: BP 574, Nouakchott; tel 522-31; telex 848.

GABON

Embassy: BP 38, Nouakchott; tel 529-19; telex 593.
Ambassador: Jacques Bonaventure Essonghe.

GERMANY

Embassy: BP 372, Nouakchott; tel 510-32; telex 555.

KOREA, REPUBLIC

Embassy: BP 324, Nouakchott; tel 537-86; fax 544-43.
Chargé d'affaires: Kim Won Chol.

LIBYA

Embassy: Nouakchott; telex 534.
Ambassador: Nasser Abass Othmane.

MOROCCO

Embassy: BP 621, Nouakchott; tel 514-11; telex 550.
Ambassador: Abderrahmane El Kouhen.

NIGERIA

Embassy: Ilot P, No. 9, BP 367, Nouakchott; tel 523-04; telex 869.
Chargé d'affaires: Ahmed Mohammed Kele.
First Secretary: Sigismund Adedamola Akinsola.
First Secretary: Olukunle A. Bamgbose.
Third Secretary: Mohammed Bello Muhammed.
Finance Attaché: Paul Boyo.
Administrative Attaché: Elizabeth Olukemi Aderinko.

RUSSIA

Embassy: BP 251, Nouakchott; tel 518-45; telex 974711; fax 552-96.
Ambassador: Vladimir S. Shishov.
Counsellor: Andrei Tareline.
First Secretary: Alexandre Brégadze.
First Secretary: Gennady Poustintsev.
First Secretary and Head of Cultural Centre: Nikolai Chaouline.
Third Secretary: Andrei Bourtsev.
Head of Protocol: Maxime Danilotchkine.

Consular Section: BP 221, Nouakchott.
Third Secretary and Head of Consular Section: Vladimir Novikov.

SAUDI ARABIA

Embassy: Nouakchott; telex 813.
Ambassador: Mohamed Al Fadh El Issa.

SPAIN

Embassy: BP 232, Nouakchott; tel 510-28; telex 563.
Ambassador: Manuel Gómez de Valenzuela.

SWEDEN

Consulate: c/o SMACO, BP 997, Nouakchott; tel 527-03; telex 818.
Ambassador: Bengt Holmquist (resident in Sweden).
Consul: Haiba Ould Hamody.

TUNISIA

Embassy: BP 681, Nouakchott; tel 528-71; telex 857.
Ambassador: Mohamed Gherib.

UNITED KINGDOM

Consulate: Nouakchott.

USA

Embassy: BP 222, Nouakchott; tel 252-660; telex 5558; fax 525-89.
Ambassador: William H. Twaddell.
Deputy Chief of Mission: David C. Bennet.
Political Section: Michael S. Owen.
Economic/Commercial/Consular Section: Mara R. Tekach-Ball.
Administrative Section: Gregory L. McLerran.
Regional Security Officer: Peter D. Ford.
Communications Programme Officer: Thomas Nasetka.
Agency for International Development: William H. Faulkner, Jr.
Labour Officer: Ollie P. Anderson, Jr (resident in the USA).

ZAIRE

Embassy: BP 487, Nouakchott; tel 528-36; telex 812.
Ambassador: Kyalwe Mihambo.

International Organizations

EUROPEAN COMMUNITIES

External Delegation: Ilot V, Lot No 24, BP 213, Nouakchott; tel 527-24; telex 5549; fax 535-24.
Commission Delegate: Jochem Zuidberg.
Counsellor: F. Gosetti.

MAURITIUS

AUSTRALIA

High Commission: Rogers House, 2nd Floor, 5 President John Kennedy St, POB 541, Port Louis; tel 2081700; telex 4414; fax 2088878.
High Commissioner: Gordon K. Miller.
First Secretary: David Combe.
Third Secretary: David Walker.

AUSTRIA

Consulate: c/o Rogers & Co Ltd, Rogers House, 5 President John Kennedy St, POB 60, Port Louis; tel 086801; telex 4312.
Honorary Consul: Jacques D. René Sanson.

BELGIUM

Consulate: Ireland Blyth Ltd, POB 56, Port Louis; tel 2082241.
Consul: J. Desmarais.

CHINA, PEOPLE'S REPUBLIC

Embassy: Royal Rd, Belle Rose, Quatre Bornes, Port Louis; tel 549111.
Ambassador: Shi Nailiang.

DENMARK

Consulate: POB 51, 4 Edith Cavell St, Port Louis; tel 085051; telex 4480.
Consul: Roger Lagesse.

EGYPT

Embassy: King George V Ave, Floreal, Port Louis; tel 65012; telex 4332.
Ambassador: Ayman Abbas Fahmi.

FINLAND

Consulate: Rogers House, 5 President John Kennedy St, POB 60, Port Louis; tel 086801; telex 4221.
Consul: Derek J. A. Taylor.

FRANCE

Embassy: 14 St Georges St, Port Louis; tel 2083755; fax 2088145.
Counsellor: Michel Gardas.
Secretary: Pierre Guillemin.
Deputy Head of Mission: François Leger.
Mission Counsellor: Danielle Robin.
Head of Charles Baudelaire Cultural Centre: Bernard Desoeuvres.
Consul: Gérard Garbay.
Assistant to Head of Cultural Centre: Chérif Alouini.
Deputy Commercial Counsellor: Catherine Bogarit.
Cultural Section and Mission for Co-operation and Cultural Development: tel 2081511; fax 2088863.
Head of Co-operation Mission: Jacques Gérard.
Cultural Counsellor: Jean Lasserre.
Trade Promotion Office: 5 bis rue Champ le Fort, Port Louis; tel 2087984; telex 4233; fax 2088432.
Commercial Counsellor and Head of Trade Promotion Office: Paul Adoue.

GERMANY

Consulate-General: 32 bis rue Saint Georges, Port Louis; tel 2124100; telex 4610; fax 2085330.
Honorary Consul-General: Wilhelm Wolfgang Rieth.

INDIA

High Commission: 5th Floor, Bank of Baroda Bldg, Sir William Newton St, Port Louis; tel 2080031; telex 4523; fax 2086859.
High Commissioner: K. K. S. Rana.
Deputy High Commissioner: A. N. Jha.
Counsellor: A. K. Sen.
First Secretary (Commercial): M. Ganapathy.
First Secretary (Cultural Affairs) and Director (IGCIC): A. Parasnis.
Second Secretary and HOC: V. S. Mehta.
Second Secretary: K. K. Mukerji.
Attaché (Administration): K. Prasanan Pillai.
Attaché and Personal Secretary to High Commissioner: R. S. Narang.

KOREA, REPUBLIC

Embassy: 23 Edith Cavell St, POB 243, Port Louis; tel 2083308.
Ambassador: Chung Kyong Hoon.

MADAGASCAR

Embassy: Queen Mary Ave, Floreal, Port Louis; tel 865015.
Chargé d'affaires: M. Rakotovao.

NEW ZEALAND

Consulate: 29 Edgar Aubert St, POB 687, Port Louis; tel 24920; telex 4487; fax 2084654.
Honorary Consul: Harold Liu Man Hin.

PAKISTAN

High Commission: Anglo-Mauritius House, Intendance St, POB 289, Port Louis; tel 2120359; telex 4609.
Chargé d'affaires a.i.: Tasawar Khan.

RUSSIA

Embassy: Queen Mary Ave, Floreal, POB 509, Port Louis; tel 61545; telex 4826.
Ambassador: Yuri Alekseyevich Kirichenko.

SOUTH AFRICA

Trade Mission: c/o Ireland Blyth Ltd, 10 Dr Ferreire St, POB 158, Port Louis; tel 2128546; telex 4211; fax 2126872.
Trade Representative: C. J. H. van Wyk.
Deputy Trade Representative: R. A. Botha.
Assistant Trade Representative (Administrative): D. Naidoo.
Honorary Trade Representative: J. M. R. Julienne.

SPAIN

Consulate: 10 Dr Ferriere St, POB 58, Port Louis; tel 2082811; telex 4211; fax 2081014.
Honorary Consul: Peter D. Goldsmith.

SWEDEN

Consulate: 5 President John Kennedy St, POB 60, Port Louis; tel 6801; telex 4221; fax 2083646.
Ambassador: Lars Schönander (resident in Sweden).
Consul: Derek James Alexander Taylor.

SWITZERLAND

Consulate: 2 Jules Koenig, POB 437, Port Louis; tel 2088763; telex 4241; fax 2088850.
Honorary Consul: José Poncini.

UNITED KINGDOM

High Commission: King George V Ave, Floreal; POB 186, Curepipe; tel 6865795-9; telex 4266; fax 0865792.
High Commissioner: Michael E. Howell.
Deputy High Commissioner: C. F. Mochan.
Third Secretary (Aid/Chancery): M. B. Harper.
Third Secretary (Management): R. D. Elliott.
Attaché (Immigration/Consular): J. Alexander.
Commercial Section: Ken Lee Bldg, 1st Floor, 20 Edith Cavell St, Port Louis; tel 089850; telex 4861.
Second Secretary (Commercial): J. F. Larner.

USA

Embassy: Rogers House, 4th Floor, President John Kennedy St, Port Louis; tel 2082347; fax 2089534.
Ambassador: Penne Percy Korth.
Deputy Chief of Mission: Susan R. Johnson.
Political Section: Richard C. Jacobson.
Economic/Commercial Section: Peter J. Andrews.
Administrative/Consular Section: John M. Gieseke.
Public Affairs Officer: Philix Aragon.
Communications Programme Officer: Walter W. Sofco.

International Organizations

EUROPEAN COMMUNITIES

External Delegation: 61-63 route Floréal, 'La Mauvraie' Vacoas, POB 10, Vacoas; tel 865061; telex 4282; fax 866318.
Commission Delegate: Leopoldo Schiavo-Campo.

MEXICO

ALBANIA

Embassy: Solón 337, Col. Los Morales, 11510 México, DF; tel (5) 540-0461; telex 1771391.
Ambassador: Clirim Cepani.
First Secretary: Ali Lapa.
Attaché: Kasem Skendaj.

ALGERIA

Embassy: Sierra Madre 540, Col. Lomas de Chapultepec, 11000 México, DF; tel (5) 540-7577; telex 1774310.
Ambassador: Rachid Haddad.
First Secretary: Tayes Sellaoui.
Attaché: Ahmed Rahim.
Attaché: Abdelfettah Tales.
Attaché: Farouk Alioud.

ARGENTINA

Embassy: Avila Camacho 1, 7°, Col. Lomas de Chapultepec, 11000 México, DF; tel (5) 540-4867; telex 1774214.
Ambassador: Facundo Roberto Suárez.

AUSTRALIA

Embassy: Plaza Polanco Torre B, 10°, Jaime Balmes 11, Col. Los Morales, 11510 México, DF; tel (5) 395-0669; telex 1773920; fax (5) 395-7153.
Ambassador: Keith William Baker.
First Secretary: Colin Adams.
First Secretary (Consular/Administrative): John Cornwall.
Third Secretary: Donna Bale.
Third Secretary: Claire McComish.
Information Officer: Cynthia Llanos.

AUSTRIA

Embassy: Campos Elíseos 305, Col. Polanco, 11560 México, DF; Apdo Postal 5552, 06500 México, DF; tel (5) 540-3415; telex 1774448.
Ambassador: Klas Daublebsky.
Minister-Counsellor: Werner Stenzel.
Economic Counsellor: Josef Berinda.
Second Secretary: Stephan Vavrik.
Economic Attaché: Christine Grinschgl.

Consulate: Calle de J. R. Escudero No. 1, despachos 2, 3 y 4, 39300 Acapulco, Gro; tel (748) 22-166.
Honorary Consul: Luis Walton Aburto.

Consulate: Mar Negro 1221, Lomas del Country, 44610 Guadalajara, Jal.; tel (36) 23-0511.
Honorary Consul-General: Erich Coufal.

Consulate: Río Orinoco 105 Pte Col del Valle, Apdo Postal 654, Monterrey, NL; tel (83) 56-4008; telex 382866.
Honorary Consul: Juan Celada Salmón.

Consulate: Blvd Agua Caliente 3401, despacho 803, Fracc. Chapultepec, Apdo Postal 990, 22420 Tijuana, BCN; tel (66) 86-3655.
Honorary Consul: Alberto Limon Padilla.

BELGIUM

Embassy: Musset 41, Col. Polanco, 11550 México, DF; tel (5) 254-3276; telex 1771030.
Ambassador: Willy Verriest.

BELIZE

Embassy: México, DF.
Ambassador: Atlay Morales.

BOLIVIA

Embassy: Campos Elíseos 169, 3°, Col. Polanco, 11560 México, DF; tel (5) 254-1998.
Chargé d'affaires a.i.: Raúl Alfonso García.

BRAZIL

Embassy: Lope de Armendariz 130, Col. Lomas Virreyes, 11000 México, DF; tel (5) 202-7500; telex 1771334; fax (5) 520-4929.
Ambassador: Luis Felipe de Seixas Corrêa.

CANADA

Embassy: Calle Schiller 529 (Rincon del Bosque), Col. Polanco, 11560 México, DF; Apdo 105-05, 11580 México, DF; tel (5) 254-3288; telex 1771191; fax (5) 254-3103.
Ambassador: David J. S. Winfield.
Minister-Counsellor (Commercial/Economic): D. G. Adam.
Counsellor and Consul: H. S. Sterling.
Counsellor (Immigration): R. E. S. Romano.
Counsellor (Commercial): G. Weber.
Attaché (Medical): Dr J. Beltran.
First Secretary (Agriculture): D. A. Gibson.
First Secretary and Consul: A. Charbonneau.
First Secretary and Consul: D. J. Chemla.
First Secretary (Administration) and Consul: T. A. Norris.
First Secretary: H. J. Bourdeau.

Consulate: Hotel Club del Sol, Costera Miguel Aleman, esq. Reyes Catolicos, 39300 Acapulco, Gro; Apdo 691, Acapulco, Gro; tel (748) 56-600; telex 01673; fax (748) 56-595.
Honorary Consul: D. McLean de Huerta.

Consulate: Centro Comercial Plaza Mexico, Local 312, Avda Tulum 200, esq. Agua, 77500 Cancun, Q. Roo; tel (988) 30-733; telex 73330; fax (988) 30-173.
Honorary Consul: D. Lavoie.

Consulate: Hotel Fiesta Americana, Local 30-A, Aurelio Aceves 225, 44100 Guadalajara, Jal.; tel (36) 15-8665; fax (36) 30-3725.
Honorary Consul: A. C. Rose.

Consulate: Hotel Playa Mazatlán, Loaiza 212, Mazatlán, Sin.; Apdo 614, 82110 Mazatlán, Sin.; tel (678) 34-444; fax (678) 40-366.
Honorary Consul: N. J. Gibson.

Consulate: Servitours, Avda Hidalgo 217, Puerto Vallarta, Jal.; tel (322) 25317; telex 065552.
Honorary Consul: N. Gérin de Vazquez.

Consulate: German Gedovius 5-201, Condominio del Parque, Desarrollo Urbano Rio Tijuana, 22320 Tijuana, BCN; tel (66) 84-0461; fax (66) 84-0461.
Honorary Consul: R. Encinas Ripa.

CHILE

Embassy: México, DF.
Ambassador: Hugo Miranda Ramírez.

CHINA, PEOPLE'S REPUBLIC

Embassy: Avda Río Magdalena 172, Villa Alvaro Obregon, 01090 México 20, DF; tel (5) 548-0898; telex 1773907; fax (5) 548-0261.
Ambassador: Huang Shikang.
Counsellor (Political Affairs): Wang Chengjia.
Counsellor (Commercial Affairs): Zhu Ruiqi.
Military Attaché: Shi Hanlin.
Counsellor (Cultural Affairs): Liu Qingdong.
First Secretary: Zhang Chengyi.
First Secretary (Science/Technology Co-operation): Li Qiuchang.
Second Secretary (Information): Xiang Xiong.
Second Secretary (Consular Affairs): Gao Shoujian.
Second Secretary (Educational): Dai Chaofu.

Consulate-General: Avda Jalisco 132, Col. Cacho Tijuana, BCN; tel (66) 84-2756; telex 566594.
Consul-General: Zhang Hongzhao.

COLOMBIA

Embassy: Génova 2-105, Col. Juárez, 06600 México, DF; tel (5) 528-9290; telex 1772951.
Ambassador: Ing. Ignacio Umaña de Brigard.

COSTA RICA

Embassy: Sierra Gorda 89, Col. Lomas Barrilaco, 11010 México, DF; tel (5) 520-1718; telex 1763134.
Ambassador: Angel Edmundo Solano Calderón.

COTE D'IVOIRE

Embassy: Tennyson 67, Col. Polanco, 11550 México, DF; tel (5) 254-4398; telex 1763115.
Ambassador: Ahoussi Julian Kacou.

CUBA

Embassy: Presidente Mazaryk 554, Col. Palmitas, 11560 México, DF; tel (5) 540-6890; telex 1774472.
Ambassador: Dr José Fernández de Cossio Rodríguez.

CYPRUS

Embassy: Sierra Paracaima 1305, Col. Lomas de Chapultepec, 11000 México, DF; tel (5) 596-0960; telex 1763104.
Ambassador: Charalambos Christoforou.

CZECHOSLOVAKIA

Embassy: Cuvier 22, esq. Kepler, Col. Anzures, 11590 México, DF; tel (5) 531-1837; telex 1773092.
Ambassador: Jindřich Tucek.

DENMARK

Embassy: Calle de David Alfaro Siqueiros (Tres Picos) 43, Col. Polanco, Chapultepec, Deleg. M. Hidalgo, 11570 México 5, DF; Apdo 105-105, Col. Polanco, 11580 México, DF; tel (5) 250-8577; telex 1773049; fax (5) 545-5797.
Ambassador: Torben Frost.
First Secretary: Lars-Henrik Worsøe.
Attaché: Torben Antonio Gettermann.

Consulate: Cadete Virgilio Uribe y Tte Azueta 496, Apdo 22, 22800 Ensenada, BC; tel (667) 81315; telex 56404.
Vice-Consul: David Ojeda Ochoa.

Consulate: Avda López Mateos Norte 477, 8°, 44680 Guadalajara, Jal.; tel (36) 52-0293; telex 683202; fax (36) 25-5559.
Consul: Dr Carlos M. Collignon C.

Consulate: Manzanillo, Col.

Consulate: Heriberto Frias 1509-13, 82000 Mazatlán, Sin.; tel (678) 17-642; telex 66778.
Vice-Consul: Alfredo Fuentevilla Ruffo.

Consulate: Calle 32 No.198, 17 Col. García Ginerés, 97070 Mérida, Yuc.; tel (99) 25-4488; telex 753834.
Consul: Bernardo P. Mier y Terán L.

Consulate: Edif. Los Soles C-41, 4°, Desp. 4, Avda Lázaro Cárdenas 2400 Pte., San Pedro Garza García, Monterrey, NL; tel (83) 35-4918; telex 383351; fax (83) 35-4918.
Consul: Alfredo de la Peña Gómez.

Consulate: Calle 30 No. 123, 97320 Progreso, Yuc.; tel (993) 50-029.
Consul: Bernardo P. Mier y Terán L.

Consulate: Edif. Philco Desp. 105, Aduana No. 203 Sur, Apdo 160, 89000 Tampico, Tamps; tel (12) 12-3270; telex 14734.
Consul: Jorge Pulford Nuñez.

Consulate: Independencia 837, 91700 Veracruz, Ver.; tel (29) 32-2417; telex 151855.
Consul: Fernando Delfin Palomba.

DOMINICAN REPUBLIC

Embassy: Avda Insurgentes Sur 216-301, Col. Roma Sur, 06170 México, DF; tel (5) 533-0215.
Ambassador: Alfonso Canto Dinzey.

ECUADOR

Embassy: Tennyson 217, Col. Polanco, 11550 México, DF; tel (5) 545-7041.
Chargé d'affaires: Gustavo Bucheli Garcés.

EGYPT

Embassy: Alejandro Dumas 131, Col. Polanco, 11560 México, DF; tel (5) 531-9028; telex 1775660.
Ambassador: Aziz Seif el-Nasr.

EL SALVADOR

Embassy: Aristóteles 153, Col. Polanco, 11550 México, DF; tel (5) 250-1391; telex 1777399.
Ambassador: Sigfrido Antonio Muñez Cruz.

ETHIOPIA

Embassy: Miguel de Cervantes de Saavedra 465-602, Col. Irrigación, 11500 México, DF; tel (5) 557-2238; telex 1771825.
Chargé d'affaires: Feseha Masresha.

FINLAND

Embassy: Monte Pelvoux No 111, 4°, Col. Lomas de Chapultepec, Deleg. Miguel Hidalgo, 11000 México, DF; tel (5) 202-0495; telex 1771187; fax (5) 540-0114.
Ambassador: Teppo Takala.
Counsellor: Kaija Ilander.
Second Secretary: Hannu Ripatti.

Consulate: Avda Costera Miguel Alemán 500, Acapulco, Gro; tel (748) 40-960; fax (748) 40-475.
Consul: Enrique Carlos Molina Sobrino.

Consulate: Avda Nader 28, Super Manzana 2, Col. Centro, Apdo 1928, 77500 Cancun, Q. Roo; tel 41-238.
Consul: Francisco López Mena.

Consulate: Justo Sierra 2562, Of. 5, Sector Hidalgo, Guadalajara, Jal.; tel (36) 15-8276; fax (36) 41-1431.
Consul: Ignacio García Villaseñor.

Consulate: Avda Roosevelt 136, Col. Centro, Mazatlán, Sin.; tel (678) 13-907; telex 66714; fax (678) 43-422.
Consul: Alejandro A. González Lie.

Consulate: Apdo 2, Cholula 1515, Col. María Luisa, 64040 Monterrey, NL; tel (83) 42-2637; telex 382538; fax (83) 42-4451.
Consul: Guillermo Zambrano, Jr.

Consulate: Avda Chairel 612, Col. Aquila, 89230 Tampico, Tamps; tel (12) 12-1941; telex 14778; fax (12) 12-2391.
Consul: Esther García de González.

Consulate: Avda Revolución 1232, Edif. María Cristina, Of. 123-126, 2°, Col. Centro, 22000 Tijuana, BCN; tel (66) 85-5273; telex 566572; fax (66) 85-6347.
Consul: Carlos Eduardo Moncada Mendoza.

Consulate: Apdo 15, Emparan No. 251, Col. Centro, 91700 Veracruz, Ver.; tel (29) 36-0057; telex 151797; fax (29) 36-0180.
Consul: Manuel Maraboto Gornés.

FRANCE

Embassy: Havre 15, Col. Juárez, 06600 México, DF; tel (5) 533-1360; telex 1771302; fax (5) 514-7311.
Ambassador: Alain Rouquié.

Trade Promotion Office: AP 5-130, 06500 México, DF; tel (5) 533-1657; telex 1775899.

GERMANY

Embassy: Lord Byron 737, Col. Polanco Chapultepec, 11560 México, DF; Apdo M-10762, 06600 México, DF; tel (5) 545-6655; telex 1773089; fax (5) 255-3180.

Consulate: Sebastian Elcano 190, Casa Tres Fuentes, Costa Azul, Apdo Postal C-46, Acapulco, Gro; tel (748) 56-640.
Honorary Consul: Mario Wichtendahl.

Consulate: Agencia Maya de Viajes Turisticos SA, Interior Hotel Club Lagoon, 77500 Cancún, Q. Roo; tel (988) 30-958.
Honorary Consul: Rudolf Bittorf.

Consulate: Blvd Fuentes Mares 8804, Chihuahua, Chih.; Apdo H-11, 31040 Chihuahua, Chih.; tel (14) 20-0357; telex 349664; fax (14) 20-0945.
Honorary Consul: Klaus Herbert Kientzle.

Consulate: Casa Wagner de Guadalajara SA, Avda Ramón Corona 202, Guadalajara, Jal.; Apdo 1-107, 44100 Guadalajara, Jal.; tel (36) 13-1414.
Honorary Consul: Gisela Tiessen.

Consulate: Jacaranda 10, Loma Linda, 82000 Mazatlán, Sin.; tel (678) 12-077.
Honorary Consul: Guillermo Heimpel.

Consulate: Mérida, Yuc.

Consulate: Troa Consultores, SC, Calzada del Valle 400, Local 77, 66220 Col. del Valle, Monterrey, NL; Apdo 436, 66250 Col. del Valle, Monterrey, NL; tel (83) 35-1784.
Honorary Consul: Carlos Ross Schede.

Consulate: Avda Fuentes de San Miguel 5, Club de Golf Las Fuentes, II Sección, 72110 Puebla, Pue.; tel (22) 49-1328; telex 171843; fax (22) 23-299.
Honorary Consul: Gerhard Schreiber.

Consulate: c/o Agencia Naviera de Mexico, SA de CV, 2 de Enero 102-A Sur, 89000 Tampico, Tamps; tel (12) 12-9784.
Honorary Consul: Dieter Schulze.

Consulate: Avda Mérida 221, Col. Hipódromo, Apdo 3272, 22420 Tijuana, BCN; tel (66) 81-8274.
Honorary Consul: Hans-Günter Holtschmitt.

Consulate: Tradver, SC Avda Fco. Madeiro No. 256, 2°, 91700 Veracruz, Ver.; tel (29) 338-0367; telex 151760.
Honorary Consul: Federico Guillermo Chacón y Rábago Voss.

GREECE

Embassy: Paseo de las Palmas 2060, Col. Lomas Reforma, 11020 México, DF; tel (5) 596-6333; telex 1777319.
Ambassador: Nicolaos Ladopoulos.
Counsellor: Dora Grossomanidou.
Counsellor (Press/Information): Charalambos Hatzilambis.
Attaché: Panayota Assimakopoulou.
Attaché: Calliopi Partali de Vives.
Attaché: Anelos Papanicoladu.

GUATEMALA

Embassy: Esplanada 1025, Col. Lomas de Chapultepec, 11000 México, DF; tel (5) 520-2794.
Ambassador: Julio César Méndez Montenegro.

HAITI

Embassy: Taine 229, 4°, Col. Chapultepec Morales, 11570 México, DF; tel (5) 250-7913.
Ambassador: Antoine Bernard.

HOLY SEE

Apostolic Delegation: Calle Felipe Villanueva 118, Col. Guadalupe Inn, Deleg. Alvaro Obregón, 01020 México; tel (5) 660-0542; telex 1772396; fax (5) 660-0571.
Apostolic Delegate: Most Rev. Girolamo Prigione, Titular Archbishop of Lauriaco.
Secretary: Mgr Pietro Parolin.

HONDURAS

Embassy: Paseo Las Palmas No 765-202, Col. Lomas de Chapultepec, 11000 México, DF; tel (5) 658-4855; telex 1762222.

HUNGARY

Embassy: Paseo de Las Palmas 2005, Col. Lomas Reforma, 11020 México, DF; tel (5) 596-0523; telex 1774503.
Ambassador: Dr Vilmos Kopányi.

ICELAND

Consulate-General: Avda Manuel Avila Camacho 80, 3°, México 10, DF; Apdo 1617, 06000 México, DF; tel (5) 557-5544; telex 1773164; fax (5) 395-7903.
Consul-General: David N. Wiesley.

INDIA

Embassy: Musset 325, Col. Polanco, 11560 México, DF; tel (5) 531-1050; telex 1775864.
Ambassador: Kershasp T. Satarawala.

INDONESIA

Embassy: Julio Verne 27, Col. Polanco, 11560 México, DF; tel (5) 540-4167; telex 1772712.
Ambassador: David Napitupulu.
First Secretary: Noer Anna de Bagus Soegito.
Second Secretary (Political): Rahardjo Mustadjab.
Second Secretary (Economic): Sugito Abdulazis.
Second Secretary (Consular): Soeprapto Soerip Puspopanitro.
Second Secretary (Administrative): Siwito Darmosumarto.
Attaché (Cultural/Information): Rahmadi Utomo.

IRAN

Embassy: Paseo de la Reforma 2350, Col. Lomas Altas, 11950 México, DF; tel (5) 596-5399; telex 1774205.
Chargé d'affaires: Mohamed Taherian Allaf.

IRAQ

Embassy: Paseo de la Reforma 1875, Col. Lomas, 11020 México, DF; tel (5) 596-0254; telex 1777680.
Ambassador: Abdul Karim Mohamed Najim al-Tai.

IRELAND

Consulate: Av Chapultepec No. 28, 8°, Col. Doctores, 06724 México, DF; tel (5) 709-3333; telex 1773154; fax (5) 709-6416.
Honorary Consul: Romulo O'Farrell, Jr.

ISRAEL

Embassy: Sierra Madre 215, Del. Miguel Hidalgo, 11000 México, DF; tel (5) 540-6340; telex 1773094.
Ambassador: Dr Dov B. Schmorak.

ITALY

Embassy: Paseo de las Palmas 1994, Col. Lomas de Chapultepec, 11020 México, DF; tel (5) 596-3655; telex 1772717.
Ambassador: Sergio Cattani.

JAMAICA

Embassy: Euken 32, Col. Anzures, 11590 México, DF; tel (5) 250-0011; telex 1771338.
Ambassador: Thomas Alvin Stimpson.
Counsellor: Paul Robotham.

JAPAN

Embassy: Paseo de la Reforma 395, Col. Cuauhtémoc, 06500 México, DF; Apdo 5-101, México, DF; tel (5) 211-0028; telex 1772420; fax (5) 207-7743.
Ambassador: Tsuneo Tanaka.

KOREA, REPUBLIC

Embassy: Lope de Almendariz 110, Col. Lomas Virreyes, 11000 México, DF; tel (5) 596-7131; telex 1773102.
Ambassador: Koo Choong-Whey.

LEBANON

Embassy: Julio Verne 8, Col. Polanco, 11560 México, DF; tel (5) 540-3295; telex 1763169.
Ambassador: Amine el-Khazen.

MALTA

Consulate: Seminario 181, Lomas de La Herradura, 53920 Edo. de México; tel (5) 589-8176; fax (5) 589-2627.
Honorary Consul: Oscar Ernesto De La Fuente Groskorth.

NETHERLANDS

Embassy: Montes Urales Sur 635, 2°, Col. Lomas de Chapultepec, 11000 México, DF; tel (5) 540-7788; telex 1774366; fax (5) 202-6148.
Ambassador: Adriën F. Tieleman.

NEW ZEALAND

Embassy: Homero 229, 8°, Col. Chapultepec Morales, 11570 México, DF; tel (5) 250-5999; telex 1763154; fax (5) 255-4142.
Ambassador: Bruce W. Middleton.
Attaché: Leonie Smith.

NICARAGUA

Embassy: Ahumada Villagrán 36, Col. Lomas de Chapultepec, 11000 México, DF; tel (5) 540-5625; telex 1772381.
Ambassador: Dr Edmundo Jarquín Calderón.

NORWAY

Embassy: Avda Virreyes 1460, Col. Lomas de Chapultepec, Delegación Miguel Hidalgo, 11000 México, DF; tel (5) 540-3486; telex 1772996; fax (5) 202-3019.
Ambassador: John Grieg.

PAKISTAN

Embassy: Hegel 512, Col. Chapultepec Morales, 11570 México, DF; tel (5) 531-2020; telex 1763355; fax (5) 531-6651.
Ambassador: Mansoor Alam.
Counsellor: Pervez Alam Khanzada.
First Secretary: Khalid Hussain Yousfani.

PANAMA

Embassy: Campos Elíseos 111, Col. Bosque de Chapultepec, 11580 México, DF; tel (5) 250-4045.

PARAGUAY

Embassy: Avda Taine 713, Col. Bosque de Chapultepec, 11580 México, DF; tel (5) 545-8155.
Ambassador: Raúl Armin Gómez Núñez.

PERU

Embassy: Paseo de las Palmas 2030, Col. Lomas Reforma, 11020 México, DF; tel (5) 596-0521; telex 1773087.
Ambassador: Dr Juan de la Piedra Villalonga.

PHILIPPINES

Embassy: Calderón de la Barca 240, Colonio Reforma Polanco, 11550 México, DF; tel (5) 254-8055; telex 1772058.
Ambassador: Samuel T. Ramel.
Second Secretary: Anamarie A. Morales.
Second Secretary: Teresa V. Sapinoso.
Attaché: Berth D. Salvador.
Attaché (Cultural): Honorio E. Ybera, Jr.
Attaché (Economic): Visitacio V. Asiddao.

POLAND

Embassy: Cracovia 40, Col. San Angel, Delegación Alvaro Obregón, 01000 México, DF; tel (5) 550-4700; telex 1773090; fax (5) 548-0532.
Ambassador: Irena Gabor-Jatczak.
First Secretary: Dr Stanislaw Górczyński.
Second Secretary and Consul: Miroslaw Kolodziej.
Third Secretary: Andrzej Knyziak.
Attaché: Robert Krzyźanowski.

Commercial Section: Paseo de la Reforma 650, Lomas de Chapultepec, 11000 México, DF; tel (5) 520-1468; fax (5) 540-6836.
Head of Commercial Section: Januz Bieszk.

LOT Aerolineas Polacas: Paseo de la Reforma 87/401, México, DF; tel (5) 592-8551.
Head of Airline Office: María Munko.

AGRPOLAND: Madrid 25, Col. del Carmen Coyoacán, 04100 México, DF; tel (5) 658-2538.
Head of Office: Janusz Grendys.

PORTUGAL

Embassy: Paseo de las Palmas 765-202, Col. Lomas de Chapultepec, 11000 México, DF; tel (5) 540-3396; telex 1772533.
Ambassador: Dr Francisco José Laço Treichler Knopfli.

ROMANIA

Embassy: Sofocles 311, Col. Los Morales, 11510 México, DF; tel (5) 52-0984; telex 1775868.
Ambassador: Constantin Babalau.

RUSSIA

Embassy: José Vasconcelos 204, Col. Condesa, 06170 México, DF; tel (5) 515-6055; telex 1777570.
Ambassador: Rotislav A. Sergeyev.

Consular Section: Carlos B. Setina 12A, Chicontepec, México, DF; tel (5) 515-6970.

Consulate-General: 5 y 6 de Julio, No. 1045, Veracruz, Ver.; tel (29) 35-2560.

SAN MARINO

Consulate: Avda Carlos Dickens 69-3, México, DF; tel (5) 52-05530.
Consul-General: Attila Camisa.

SAUDI ARABIA

Embassy: Reforma 607, Col. Lomas de Chapultepec, 11000 México, DF; tel (5) 540-0240; telex 1775714.
Ambassador: Naji S. Mufti.

SPAIN

Embassy: Parque Vía Reforma 2105, Col. Lomas de Chapultepec, 11000 México, DF; tel (5) 596-1833; telex 1776295; fax (5) 596-0646.
Ambassador: Alberto Aza.

SURINAME

Embassy: Calle Cicerón 609, Col. Los Morales, 11510 México, DF; tel (5) 540-4371; telex 1763120.
Ambassador: Harvey Naarendorp.

SWEDEN

Embassy: Edif. Plaza Comermex, 6°, Blvd Manuel Avila Camacho 1, Col. Lomas de Chapultepec, Delegación Miguel Hidalgo, Apdo 10.726, 11000 México, DF; tel (5) 540-4090; telex 1771115; fax (5) 540-6583.
Ambassador: Bo David Ingvar Wirmark.
Counsellor: Bo Löfgren.
Second Secretary: Margareta Mörn Marrone.
Second Secretary: Charlotte Wrangberg.

Commercial Section: tel (5) 540-6580; telex 1763418.
Commercial Counsellor: Carl-Otto Rydner.

Consulate: Avda Insurgentes No. 2-L-E, Esq. con Cuauhtémoc, 39350 Acapulco, Gro; tel (748) 52-252; fax (748) 50-889.
Consul: Juan Herrera González.

Consulate: Avda Nader No. 34, Super Manzana 2-A, 77500 Cancún, Q. Roo; tel (988) 47-271; fax (988) 47-271.
Consul: Norberto Cozar García.

Consulate: J. Guadalupe Montenegro, 1691 Guadalajara, Jal.; tel (36) 25-6767; telex 683202; fax (36) 25-5559.
Consul: Pedro Guillermo Alberto Collignon.

Consulate: Avda Churubusco 3900 Norte, Focos SA, Apdo 843 y 216, 64000 Monterrey, NL; tel (83) 34-1107; telex 382456.
Consul: Roberto Zambrano Villarreal.

Consulate: Calle Aduana 203 Sur, Des. 105-107, Apdo 160, 89000 Tampico, Tamps; tel (12) 12-3270; telex 14734; fax (12) 12-7078.
Consul: Jorge Pulford Nuñez.

Consulate: Avda Revolución No. 606, Altos 8-A, Apdo 5, 22000 Tijuana, BCN; tel (66) 85-4501; telex 566849.
Consul: Rodolfo González Salazar.

Consulate: Benito Juárez 352, Apdo 151, 91700 Veracruz, Ver.; tel (29) 34-1629; telex 151774; fax (29) 34-1196.
Consul: Joaquín Aguilar Camacho.

SWITZERLAND

Embassy: Calle Hamburgo 66, 4°, Col. Juárez, 06600 México, DF; Apdo 1027, 06000 México, DF; tel (5) 514-1727; telex 1774396; fax (5) 514-7083.
Ambassador: Paul André Ramseyer.
Counsellor: Maria-Luisa Caroni.
Attaché and Head of Chancery: Peter Specker.

THAILAND

Embassy: Sierra Vertientes 1030, Col. Lomas de Chapultepec, 11000 México, DF; tel (5) 596-1290; telex 1772910; fax (5) 596-8236.
Ambassador: Orachun Tanaphong.
Minister-Counsellor: Chamnian Veerasa.
First Secretary (Cultural Affairs): Prasidhi Sochiratna.
First Secretary (Commercial Affairs): Saroj Thanasunti.
Administrative Affairs: Pairoj Saleerat.
Third Secretary (Political Affairs): Ek-Att Thitaram.
Financial Affairs: Vichai Sinkaseam.

TURKEY

Embassy: Paseo de las Palmas 1525, Col. Lomas Barrilaco, 11000 México, DF; tel (5) 520-2344; telex 1774495.
Ambassador: Tanju Ulgen.
First Secretary: Ali Murat Bora.
Attaché: Huseyin Yurtsever.
Attaché: Gulay Turkvan.
Attaché: Nejdet Kutluturk.
Attaché: Hasan Unsal.

UNITED KINGDOM

Embassy: Río Lerma 71, Col. Cuauhtémoc, 06500 México, DF; Apdo 96 bis, Administración de Correos No. 1, 06002 México, DF; tel (5) 207-2089; telex 1773093; fax (5) 207-7672.
Ambassador: Sir Roger Hervey.
Minister-Counsellor and Deputy Head of Mission: Roger Dudley Hart.
Defence, Naval, Military and Air Attaché: Col John Dobson.
First Secretary and Head of Chancery: Tom J. Duggin.
First Secretary (Chancery): Dr Jonathan A. Brewer.
First Secretary (Commercial): Jack F. Thompson.
First Secretary (Management): Frank A. Doherty.
Second Secretary (Commercial): Roger C. Woodward.
Third Secretary (Chancery/Information): Robert D. Aylwin.
Security Officer: Sydney Richardson.
Defence Section: Flight Sgt Anthony Johnson.

Consular Section: Río Usumacinta 30, Col. Cuauhtémoc, 06500 México, DF.
Second Secretary and Consul: Robert E. D. Deffee.

Consulate: Hotal Las Brisas, Carretera Escénica, Apdo 281, Acapulco, Gro; tel (748) 46-605; telex 16837; fax (748) 42-269.
Honorary Consul: Derek Barrington Gore.

Consulate: Calle Fresno 185, Campestre Juárez, Ciudad Juárez, Chih.; tel (161) 75-791.
Honorary Consul: Christian Rex Maingot.

Consulate: Fratteli SA, Calzada González Gallo 1897, Apdo 32-94, Guadalajara, Jal.; tel (36) 35-8295; fax (36) 39-1616.
Honorary Consul: Simon Cohen.

Consulate: Calle 58 y 53, No. 450, Apdo 89, Mérida, Yuc.; tel (99) 16-799; telex 753610.
Honorary Consul: Maj. Alfred Dutton (retd).

Consulate: Privada de Tamazunchale 104, Garza García, Col. del Valle, Apdo 419, NL 66220, Monterrey; tel (83) 56-9114; fax (83) 35-5438.
Honorary Consul: Edward Raymond Lawrence.

Consulate: 2 de Enero 102 Sur-A, Tampico, Tamps; tel (12) 12-9784; fax (12) 14-1147.
Honorary Consul: Dieter Schulze.

Consulate: Lloyds Register of Shipping, Emparan 200, Planta Baja, Apdo 724, Veracruz, Ver.; tel (29) 31-0955; telex 151681.
Honorary Consul: Luis Carbajal.

USA

Embassy: Paseo de la Reforma 305, Col. Cuauhtémoc, 06500 México, DF; tel (5) 211-0042; telex 1773091; fax (5) 511-9980.
Ambassador: John Dimitri Negroponte.
Deputy Chief of Mission: Robert S. Pastorino.
Consul-General: Jon G. Edensword.
Political Section: Allen L. Sessoms.
Economic Section: Donald F. McConville.
Commercial Section: Harrison Sherwood.
Consular Section: Patricia A. Langford.
Administrative Section: Thomas J. Fitzpatrick.
Regional Security Officer: Anthony J. Walters.
Public Affairs Officer: Robert L. Earle.
Communications Programme Officer: William L. Wuensch.
Information Systems Manager: Charles D. Wisecarver, Jr.
Agency for International Development: Gerard R. Bowers.
Office of the Defence Attaché: Brig.-Gen. David L. Cole.
Scientific Attaché: Roy C. Simpkins.
Agricultural Section: William L. Davis.
Labour Officer: John W. Vincent.
Narcotics Assistance Unit: Ross E. Benson.
Customs Service (Treasury): Roberto J. Fernández.
Military Liaison Office: Col Larry N. Looney.
Internal Revenue Service: Daniel R. Dietz.
Financial Attaché (Treasury): Jack V. Sweeney.

US Export Development Office: Liverpool 31, 06600 México, DF; tel (5) 591-0155; telex 1773471; fax (5) 566-1115.
Director of Export Development Office: Carol Murray Kim.

US Travel and Tourism Office: Plaza Comermex, M. Avila Camacho 1-402, 11560 México, DF; tel (5) 520-2101; fax (5) 520-1194.
Director of Travel and Tourism Office: William M. Tappe.

Consulate-General: Ave López Mateos 924N, Ciudad Juárez, Chih.; tel (16) 13-4048; telex 033840; fax (16) 16-9056.
Consul-General: Louis P. Goelz.
Administrative Section: Rufus A. Watkins.
Communications Programme Officer: José A. Perez.

Consulate-General: Progreso 175, Guadalajara, Jal.; tel (36) 25-2700; telex 0682860; fax (36) 26-6549.
Consul-General: Mary Ann Meysenburg.
Political/Economic Section: Manfred G. Schweitzer.
Commercial Section: Americo A. Tadeu.
Administrative Section: Bernard E. Gross.
Regional Security Officer: Mark G. Hoffman.
Branch Public Affairs Officer: Morgan Liddick.
Communications Programme Officer: Robert H. Griego.
Agricultural Section: Nathaniel Perry.

Consulate-General: Avda Constitucion 411, Poniente, 64000 Monterrey, NL; tel (83) 45-2120; telex 0382853; fax (83) 42-0177.
Consul-General: John E. Bennett.
Political Section: Deborah M. Odell.
Economic Section: Paul A. Trivelli.
Commercial Section: Dawn Cooper-Bahar.
Administrative Section: Martha Ann Kelleran.
Regional Security Officer: Edward A. Lennon.
Branch Public Affairs Officer: Robert R. Gibbons.
Communications Programme Officer: Herman Ellington.
Customs Service (Treasury): Dale F. Wisely.

Consulate-General: Tapachula 96, Tijuana, BCN; tel (66) 81-7400; fax (66) 81-8016.
Consul-General: Larry Colbert.
Administrative Section: Joseph L. Warner.
Communications Programme Officer: Joseph L. López.

Consulate: Monterrey 141, Hermosillo; tel (621) 72-375; telex 058829; fax (621) 72-578.
Principal Officer: Robert M. Witajewski.
Communications Programme Officer: Gerald Madewski.

Consulate: Avda Primera 2002, Matamoros; tel (891) 67-270; fax (891) 38-048.
Principal Officer: Janice Jacobs.
Administrative Section: Larry J. Kay.

Consulate: 6 Circunvalacion 120, Centro, Mazatlán, Sin.; tel (678) 52-205; telex 066883; fax (678) 21-454.
Principal Officer: Edward H. Vazquez.
Administrative Section: Michael R. Schimmel.

Consulate: Paseo Montejo 453, Mérida, Yuc.; tel (99) 25-5011; telex 0753885; fax (99) 25-6219.
Principal Officer: Stephanie A. Smith.
Customs Service (Treasury): Andrew F. Soto.

Consulate: Calle Allende 3330, 88260 NL, Col. Jardin; tel (871) 40-696; telex 036849; fax (871) 40-696.
Principal Officer: Ronald J. Kramer.
Communications Programme Officer: Elwood B. Rische III.

URUGUAY

Embassy: Hegel 149, 1°, Col. Chapultepec Morales, 11570 México, DF; tel (5) 531-0880; telex 1771396; fax (5) 531-4029.
Ambassador: Juan Pedro Amestoy.

VENEZUELA

Embassy: Shiller 326, Col. Chapultepec Morales, 11550 México, DF; tel (5) 203-4233; telex 1775813; fax (5) 203-8614.
Ambassador: Rigoberto Henriquez Vera.
Minister-Counsellor: Iris Acosta de F.
Counsellor: Carlos E. Baptista O.
Counsellor: Gustavo Carrasquero H.
Second Secretary: Dulce Maria Parra Fuentes.
First Attaché: Yagor José Medina B.
Third Attaché: Ettey C. Guerrero de R.
Third Attaché: Marielza Izurrieta.
Third Attaché: Josefa E. Volcan de G.
Third Attaché: Eva Maria Zuck.

VIET-NAM

Embassy: Sierra Ventana 255, Col. Lomas de Chapultepec, 11000 México, DF; tel (5) 540-1612; telex 1771079.
Chargé d'affaires: Hoang Hiep.

YUGOSLAVIA

Embassy: Montañas Rocallosas Ote 515, Col. Lomas de Chapultepec, 11000 México, DF; tel (5) 259-1332; telex 1771331; fax (5) 520-9927.
Ambassador: Ignac Golob.

International Organizations

EUROPEAN COMMUNITIES

External Delegation: 1675 Paseo de la Reforma, Lomas de Chapultepec CP, 11000 México, DF; tel (5) 540-3345; fax (5) 540-6564.
Head of Delegation: Erwan Fouere.

MICRONESIA

PHILIPPINES

Embassy: Main St, Kolonia, POB 1300, Pohnpei 96943.
Ambassador: Purisimo A. de Peralta.

MOLDAVIA (MOLDOVA)

ROMANIA

Consulate-General: Kishinyev.
Consul-General: Stefan Dragomir.

MONACO

AUSTRIA

Consulate-General: 19 ave d'Ostende, Monte Carlo, MC 98000; tel 30-08-08; telex 469777.
Honorary Consul-General: Jacques Charles de Beer de Laer.
Honorary Vice-Consul: Bernard Gagelin.

CANADA

Consulate: Monte Carlo.

DENMARK

Consulate-General: 74 blvd d'Italie, Monte Carlo, MC 98000; tel 50-02-03; fax 30-00-57.
Consul-General: Knud Steffen Gam.

FINLAND

Consulate-General: Monte Carlo.

Consulate: 15 rue Louis Notari, Monte Carlo, MC 98000; tel 50-90-21; fax 25-18-08.
Consul: Rainier Boisson.

FRANCE

Consulate-General: Immeuble Monte Carlo Sun, 74 blvd d'Italie, BP 365, Monte Carlo, MC 98006; tel 50-51-67.

GERMANY

Consulate: Villa Les Flots, 2 rue des Giroflées, Monte Carlo, MC 98000; tel 50-58-89.
Honorary Consul: Christine Esswein.

IRELAND

Consulate: Les Lys, 3 rue Louis Aureglia, Monte Carlo, MC 98000; tel 25-73-96; telex 479524; fax 25-72-47.
Honorary Consul: Michael W. J. Smurfit.

MEXICO

Consulate: 10 blvd des Moulins, Esc. des Fleurs, Monte Carlo, MC 98000.
Honorary Consul: Louis Orecchia.

SAN MARINO

Consulate: Résidence les Acanthes, 6 ave des Citronniers, Monte Carlo, MC 98000; tel 25-14-10.
Consul: Marie Claude Bidoire Bunford.

SWEDEN

Consulate: Le Montaigne, 7 ave de Grande-Bretagne, Monte Carlo, MC 98000; tel 50-75-60; telex 489678.
Consul: François Marie Maxime de Monseignat.

UNITED KINGDOM

Consulate-General: 24 ave du Prado, 13006 Marseille, France; tel 91-37-66-95; telex 420307.

MONGOLIA

AFGHANISTAN

Embassy: Jukovyn Örgön Chölöö 68, Ulan Bator; tel 53878.
Ambassador: Amanullah Ostowar.
Second Secretary: Abdul Wase.

BULGARIA

Embassy: Ulan Bator.
Ambassador: Stoyan Pavlov Mikhailov.

CHINA, PEOPLE'S REPUBLIC

Embassy: Ulan Bator; tel 22778.
Ambassador: Zhang Delin.

CUBA

Embassy: Ulan Bator; tel 27008; telex 228.
Ambassador: Manuel Poso Núñez.

CZECHOSLOVAKIA

Embassy: POB 665, Ulan Bator; tel 21886.
Ambassador: Dr Jiří Šíma.
Economic Counsellor: Zdeněk Smejkal.
Economic Counsellor: Václav Hruza.
Attaché: Dr Juraj Martoník.
Economic Counsellor: Jan Volf.
Attaché: František Išković.

GERMANY

Embassy: United Nations St, POB 708, 210613 Ulan Bator; tel 22907; telex 79242.
Ambassador: Dr Reinhard Holubek.

HUNGARY

Embassy: Enh. Tajvani Gudamj 1, Centralpost POB 668, Ulan Bator; tel 23973; telex 244.
Ambassador: Miklós Jaczkovits.
Counsellor: Miklós Bejczi.
Third Secretary: László Kuti.

INDIA

Embassy: Ulan Bator; tel 53167.
Ambassador: Kushok Bakula.

JAPAN

Embassy: Nairamdalyn Gudamj 12, POB 1011, Ulan Bator 13; tel 24408; telex 229.
Ambassador: Hidekazu Takase.

KAZAKHSTAN

Embassy: Ulan Bator.

KOREA, DEMOCRATIC PEOPLE'S REPUBLIC

Embassy: Ulan Bator.
Ambassador: Chong Yun Ho.

KOREA, REPUBLIC

Embassy: Ulan Bator.
Ambassador: Kwong Yong-Sun.

POLAND

Embassy: Sambujgin 1, Ulan Bator; tel 23365.
Ambassador: Stanisław Godziński.
Counsellor: Zbigniew Ostrowski.
Commercial Counsellor: Henryk Kwasowiec.
Second Secretary: Wiesław Mazur.
Commercial Attaché: Jolanta Rydzewska.
Attaché: Wawrzyniec Sakowski.

ROMANIA

Embassy: 18 Enhtaivny St, Ulan Bator; tel 22925; telex 252.
Ambassador: Nicolae Muntean.
Counsellor: Dumitru Albu.
Economic and Commercial Counsellor: Constantin Andrei.
Information Officer: Niţulescu Petruţa.

RUSSIA

Embassy: ul. Mira 64, Ulan Bator; tel 23131.
Ambassador: A. A. Kondratenko.

Consulate-General: ul. Choybalsan 13, Choybalsan; tel 21691.

Consulate-General: District 6, Rm 307, Darhan; tel 5596.

UNITED KINGDOM

Embassy: 30 Enh Tayvny Gudamj, POB 703, Ulan Bator 13; tel 51033.
Ambassador: Anthony B. N. Morey.

Second Secretary: J. L. Hartley.

USA

Embassy: POB 1021, Ulan Bator 13; tel 29095; telex 79253.
Ambassador: Joseph Edward Lake.
Deputy Chief of Mission and First Secretary (Political/ Economic): Michael J. Senko.
Second Secretary (Administrative/Consular): Theodore A. Nist.

VIET-NAM

Embassy: Ulan Bator; telex 249.
Ambassador: Dang Gia Tat.

YUGOSLAVIA

Embassy: Ulan Bator; telex 259.
Ambassador: Vasilie Vasilević.

MOROCCO

ALGERIA

Embassy: 46 blvd Tariq Ibn Ziad, Rabat; tel (7) 65092.

ARGENTINA

Embassy: 12 rue Mekki Bitaouri Souissi, Rabat; tel (7) 55120; telex 31017.
Ambassador: Marcelo Delpeche.

AUSTRIA

Embassy: 2 Zankat Tiddas, BP 135, Rabat; tel (7) 64003; telex 31623.
Ambassador: Robert Marschik.
Economic Secretary: Ingrid Köhn-Dursy.

Consulate-General: Casablanca.

BELGIUM

Embassy: 6 ave de Marrakech, BP 163, Rabat; tel (7) 64746; telex 31087.
Ambassador: Guillaume Metten.

BRAZIL

Embassy: 1 Charia Marrakech, Rabat; tel (7) 65522; telex 31628.
Ambassador: Antonio Sabino Cantuaria Guimarães.
Second Secretary: Hervelter de Mattos.
Attaché: Leticia Godinho Meireles.

BULGARIA

Embassy: 4 ave de Meknès, Rabat; tel (7) 65477; telex 31761.
Ambassador: Kossio Kitipov.
Counsellor: Grozdan Grozdanov.
Economic and Commercial Counsellor: Youry Branitchev.

CAMEROON

Embassy: 20 rue du Rif, BP 1790, Souissi, Rabat; tel (7) 58818; telex 36718; fax (7) 58055.
Ambassador: Mahamat Paba Sale.
Second Counsellor: Masso Ma Biumla.
Military Attaché: Col Eyango Narcisse.
First Secretary: Noumia Emmanuel.
First Secretary: Dr Amougi Appolinaire Tite.
Financial Attaché: Ayafor Konwufine Clement.

CANADA

Embassy: 13 bis, rue Jaâfar as-Sadik, BP 709, Agdal, Rabat; tel (7) 71375; telex 31964; fax (7) 72887.
Ambassador: Guy Wilfred Licari.
Counsellor and Consul: Y. St-Hilaire.
Counsellor (Immigration) and Consul: H. Mathieu.
Counsellor (Commercial): J. Broadbent.
Counsellor (Development): R. Murray.
Second Secretary (Immigration) and Vice-Consul: M.-J. Lebrun.
Third Secretary (Administration) and Vice-Consul: S. Clément.

CENTRAL AFRICAN REPUBLIC

Embassy: Villa 42, ave Pasteur, Agdal, Rabat; tel (7) 70203; telex 31920.
Ambassador: Jules Koualeyaboro.

CHINA, PEOPLE'S REPUBLIC

Embassy: 16 Charia al-Fahs, Rabat; tel (7) 54056; telex 31023.
Ambassador: Wan Yongxian.

COTE D'IVOIRE

Embassy: 21 Zankat Tiddas, BP 192, Rabat; tel (7) 63151; telex 31070.
Ambassador: Amadou Thiam.

CZECHOSLOVAKIA

Embassy: Zankat Ait Melloul, BP 410, Souissi, Rabat; tel (7) 55420; telex 32941.
Ambassador: Václav Pizinger.

DENMARK

Embassy: 4 rue de Khémisset, BP 203, Rabat; tel (7) 67986; telex 31077.
Ambassador: Sven Kuchler Poulsen.

Consulate-General: rue Sidi Belyout, Casablanca 01; tel 316477; telex 23818; fax 316922.
Consul-General: Ebbe Fischer.

Consulate: 3 rue Ibn Rochd (ex rue Henri Regnault), 4e étage, Tangier; tel (9) 38183; telex 33071.
Consul: Saad El Fassi El-Halfaoui.

EGYPT

Embassy: 31 Zankat Al Jazair, Rabat; tel (7) 31833.
Ambassador: Muhammad Beshr.

EQUATORIAL GUINEA

Embassy: 30 ave des Nations Unies, BP 723, Agdal, Rabat; tel (7) 74205; telex 31796.
Ambassador: Resurrección Bita.

FINLAND

Embassy: 18 rue de Khémisset, Rabat; tel (7) 62312; telex 32748; fax (7) 62352.
Chargé d'affaires a.i. and Minister-Counsellor: Antti Koistinen.

Commercial Section: 6 rue Demnate, Rabat; tel (7) 31843; telex 31784; fax (7) 31884.
Commercial Attaché: Stefan Relander.

Consulate: Chambre de Commerce, ave Hassan II, BP 240, Agadir; tel (8) 21794.
Consul: Lahoucine Achengli.

Consulate: Maroc-bureau, 1 place al Yassir, Casablanca 05; tel 243288; telex 25922; fax 244493.
Consul: Abderrahim Zniber.

Consulate: CMCP, BP 94, Kenitra; tel (16) 4295; telex 91039.
Consul: Roger de Weck.

Consulate: ave Mougaouama (Ain El Mouroudi), BP 791, Marrakech; tel (4) 33187; fax (4) 32181.
Consul: Abdelwahed Benabdallah.

Consulate: Conserverie Nord Africaine Consernor, route du Djord, Uniher BP 114, Safi; tel (46) 2546; telex 71783.
Consul: Mohammed Mouncef Kabbaj.

Consulate: Marembal, 3-5 ave de Lisbonne, Tangier; tel (9) 38359; telex 33630; fax (9) 42085.
Consul: M'Hamed Alaoui El M'Hamndi.

FRANCE

Embassy: 3 rue Shahnoun, Agdal, BP 602, Rabat; tel (7) 77822; telex 31013; fax (7) 77752.
Ambassador: Michel Levêque.
Minister-Counsellor: Marie-France Pagnier.
Counsellor: Elizabeth Barbier.
First Secretary: Alexandre Keltchewsky.
First Secretary (Press): Brigitte Collet.
First Secretary (Administration): Alain Migeot.
Press Attaché: Florence Prouverelle.
Defence Attaché: Col Louis Dubois.
Military and Technical Co-operation Counsellor: Col Loïc de Vanssay.
Counsellor (Cultural/Scientific/Co-operative Affairs): Jacques Migozzi.
Counsellor (Economic/Financial): Marc Lautre.

Consulate-General: 49/165 ave Allal Ben Abdallah, BP 139, Rabat; tel (7) 60936.
Consul-General: Sylvie Alvarez.

Trade Promotion Office: BP 552, Rabat-Chellah; tel (7) 77705; telex 31919.

Consulate-General: rue du Prince Moulay Abdallah, BP 15810, Casablanca; tel 220218.
Consul-General: Robert Puissant.

Consulate-General: 1 rue Ibn Khaldoun, BP 518, Marrakech; tel (4) 41748.
Consul-General: Michel Menachemoff.

Consulate-General: 2 place de France, BP 401, Tangier; tel (9) 32039.
Consul-General: Paul Couedor.

Consulate-General: ave Abou Obeida Ibn Jarrah, BP 227, Fes; tel (6) 25547.
Consul-General: Roland Blatmann.

Consulate: blvd Mohamed Cheik Saadi, BP 267, Agadir; tel (8) 222822.

GABON

Embassy: ave des Zaërs, Km 3.5, Rabat; tel (7) 51968; telex 31999.
Ambassador: Claude Roger Qwansango.

GERMANY

Embassy: 7 Zankat Madnine, BP 235, Rabat; tel (7) 709662; telex 36026; fax (7) 706851.
Ambassador: Dr Wilfried Hofmann.
Minister-Counsellor (Economic Affairs): Dr Uwe Neubauer.
Counsellor (Political Affairs): Peter Spies.
Counsellor (Economic Co-operation): Michael Fiebig.
Second Secretary, Consul and Cultural Attaché: Irene Plank.
Second Secretary and Press Attaché: Klaus-Dieter Streicher.
Military Attaché: Lieut-Col Lutz-Herbert Seidel.

Consulate-General: 42 ave de l'Armée Royale, BP 13165, Casablanca; tel 314872; telex 21990; fax 312047.
Consul-General: Günter Fuhrmann.

Consulate: 47 ave Hassan II, BP 195, Tangier; tel (9) 938700; telex 33767.
Vice-Consul: Helmut Piegeler.

GREECE

Embassy: 23 rue d'Oujda, Rabat; tel (7) 23839; telex 31953.
Ambassador: Dimitri Skouroliakos.

GUINEA

Embassy: 2 rue Ibn Mokla, Les Orangers, Rabat; tel (7) 32705; telex 31796.
Ambassador: el Hadj Guirane N'Diaye.
First Counsellor: Dr Camara Abdoul Cheick.
Second Counsellor: el Hadj Soumah Ibrahima.
Military Attaché: Capt. Keita Amara.
First Secretary: Traore Ibrahima Sory.
Chancellery Attaché: Koita Cheick Tidjane.

HOLY SEE

Apostolic Nunciature: rue Béni M'Tir, BP 1303, Souissi, Rabat; tel (7) 72277; fax (7) 56213.
Apostolic Pro-Nuncio: Most Rev. Bernard Jacqueline, Titular Archbishop of Abbir Maius.
Auditor: Mgr Antonio Sozzo.

HUNGARY

Embassy: 190 OLM, Souissi II, Rabat; BP 5026; tel (7) 50757; telex 32718; fax (7) 54123.
Ambassador: Béla Bényei.

Consulate-General: 1 rue Edmond Rostand, Casablanca; tel 200082; telex 24970; fax 233666.
Consul-General: József Bethlen.

INDIA

Interests Section: c/o Embassy of Austria.

INDONESIA

Embassy: 63 rue Béni Boufrah, Route des Zaërs Km 5,9, Souissi, Rabat; BP 5076, Rabat; tel (7) 57860; telex 32783; fax (7) 57859.
Ambassador: Taufiq Rachman Soedarbo.
First Secretary (Political Affairs): Zainal Abidin Sutomo.
Second Secretary (Social/Cultural/Information): Muhammad Maftuh Basyuni.
Third Secretary (Economic Affairs): Heru Wicaksono.
Third Secretary (Protocol): Mas Tata Machron.
Third Secretary (Administrative): Dahroni Abdul Kadir.

IRAN

Embassy: Rabat.

IRAQ

Embassy: 39 rue Béni Iznassen, Souissi, Rabat; tel (7) 54466; telex 31663.
Ambassador: Fadhil al-Shahir.

ITALY

Embassy: 2 Zankat Idriss el-Azhar, BP 111, Rabat; tel (7) 06597; telex 32731; fax (7) 06882.
Ambassador: Giuseppe Panocchia.
Counsellor: Lelio Crivellaro.
Counsellor: Alberto Galluccio.
Military, Naval and Air Attaché: Antonio Mariniello.
Cultural Attaché: Paolo Ghera.

Consulate-General: 21 ave Hassan Souktani, Casablanca; tel 277558.
Consul: Mr di Stolfo.

Consulate: 35 rue Assad ibn Al Farrat, Tangier; tel (9) 31064.
Vice-Consul: Mr Zanetti.

JAPAN

Embassy: 70 ave des Nations Unies, Agdal, Rabat; tel (7) 74163; telex 31901; fax (7) 79274.
Ambassador: Chiyuki Hiraoka.

JORDAN

Embassy: Villa Wafa, No. 65, Logement Militaire, Souissi II, Rabat; tel (7) 51125; telex 31085; fax (7) 58722.
Ambassador: Adnane Bahjat Talhouni.
Consul: Fawaz Kacem El Aitan.
Cultural Counsellor: Mustapha A. Ighnaimat.

Jordanian Cultural Centre: Casablanca; tel 300999.
Head of Commercial Centre: Zouhair Alqdat.

KOREA, REPUBLIC

Embassy: 41 ave Bani Iznassen, Souissi, Rabat; tel (7) 51767; telex 31698.
Ambassador: Lee Jong-Up.
Counsellor: Park Dae Won.
Defence Attaché: Col Seo Hyung Bae.
Attaché: Jung Sung Sub.
Attaché: Lee In Yong.

KUWAIT

Embassy: Rm 413, Charia Iman Malik, Rabat; tel (7) 56423; telex 31955.
Ambassador: Abd al-Muhsin Salem al-Haroun.

LEBANON

Embassy: 19 rue de Fès, Rabat; tel (7) 60728; telex 31060.
Ambassador: Sami Omar Kronfol.
First Secretary: Victor Zmeter.

LIBYA

People's Bureau: 1 rue Chouaïb Doukkali, BP 225, Rabat; tel (7) 68828; telex 31957.
Chargé d'affaires a.i.: Muhammad Zwai.

MALTA

Embassy: Palazzo Parisio, Merchants St, Valletta, Malta; tel 232407; telex 1100; fax 237822.
Ambassador: Alfred A. Zarb (resident in Malta).

MAURITANIA

Embassy: 9 rue Taza, Souissi, Rabat.
Ambassador: Sidna Ould Cheikh Taleb Bouya.

MEXICO

Embassy: 10 ave de Marrakech, Rabat; BP 1789, Rabat; tel (7) 67956; telex 36248; fax (7) 68583.
Ambassador: Salvador Campos-Icardo.
First Secretary (Political): Rodolfo Calixto Reyes.
Diplomatic Attaché: Telma Quintana.

NETHERLANDS

Embassy: 40 rue de Tunis, BP 329, Rabat; tel (7) 33512; telex 31962; fax (7) 33333.
Ambassador: Jongheer Schorer.

NIGERIA

Embassy: 70 ave Omar ibn al-Khattab, BP 347, Agdal, Rabat; tel (7) 71856; telex 31976.
Ambassador: Y. Usman.

NORWAY

Embassy: 4 Jaafar as-Sadik, Agdal, BP 551, Rabat-Chellah; tel (7) 73871; telex 31967.
Ambassador: Aase Speîlberg Danielsen.

OMAN

Embassy: 21 rue Hamza, Agdal, Rabat; tel (7) 71064; telex 31747.
Ambassador: Muhammad bin Salim al-Shanfari.

PAKISTAN

Embassy: 2 blvd Soomat Hassan, Rabat; tel (7) 31791; telex 31918.
Ambassador: Muhammad Safdar.

PERU

Embassy: 16 rue d'Ifrane, Rabat; tel (7) 23236; telex 32659; fax (7) 02803.
Minister Plenipotentiary and Chargé d'affaires: Julian Torres.
First Secretary: Jorge Ramos Marshall.

Consulate: 2 rue des Souvenirs, BP 372, Talborjt, Agadir; tel (8) 24409.
Honorary Consul: María Neyra Faqir.

Consulate: Hôtel Chellah, Tangier.
Honorary Consul: Mohamed Warzazi.

Consulate: 59 blvd Rahal El Meskini, Casablanca; tel 315839.
Honorary Consul: Tahar Mekouar.

PHILIPPINES

Embassy: 11 rue Tiddas, Rabat; tel (7) 67049.
Ambassador: Menandro P. Galenzoga.

POLAND

Embassy: 23 Zankat Oqbah, Agdal, BP 425, Rabat; tel (7) 71791; telex 31003.
Ambassador: Mirosław Wojciechowski.

PORTUGAL

Embassy: 5 rue Thami Lamdouar, Souissi, Rabat; tel (7) 56446; telex 31711.

Ambassador: Jorge Ritto.

QATAR

Embassy: 4 Charia Tarik ibn Ziad, BP 1220, Rabat; tel (7) 65681; telex 31624.
Ambassador: Ali Abd ar-Rahman al-Moftah.

ROMANIA

Embassy: 10 rue d'Ouezzane, Rabat; tel (7) 27899.
Ambassador: Dr Emilian Manciur.

RUSSIA

Embassy: Km 4, route des Zaërs, Rabat; tel (7) 53581; telex 31602.
Ambassador: Yuri M. Rybakov.

Consulate-General: 31 rue Soumaya (Pierre Puget), Casablanca; tel 251873; telex 23775.

SAUDI ARABIA

Embassy: 43 place de l'Unité Africaine, Rabat; tel (7) 30171; telex 32875.
Ambassador: Ali Majed Kabbani.

SENEGAL

Embassy: 17 rue Cadi ben Hamadi Senhaji, Souissi, Rabat; tel (7) 54148; telex 31048.
Ambassador: Gen. Coumba Diouf Niang.

SPAIN

Embassy: 3 Zankat Madnine, Rabat; tel (7) 68638; telex 31073.
Ambassador: Joaquín Ortega Salinas.

SUDAN

Embassy: 5 ave Ghomara, Souissi, Rabat; tel (7) 52863.
Ambassador: Abdalla Maghoub.

SWEDEN

Embassy: 159 ave John Kennedy, Rabat-Souissi; BP 428, Rabat; tel (7) 54740; telex 31041; fax (7) 58048.
Ambassador: Christer Jacobson.
First Secretary: Maikki Lemne.
Second Secretary: Ingalill Trulson.

Consulate: rue de l'Entraide, Agadir; tel (8) 21978.
Consul: Mohamed Ouçama.
Chancellor: Gunilla Maria Ouçama.

Consulate-General: Saida Star Auto, 88 blvd Lalla Yacout, Casablanca; tel 319003; telex 21850; fax 317493.
Consul-General: Omar Benjelloun.

Consulate: c/o Hotel Palais Badia, ave de la Menara, Marrakech; tel (4) 48977; telex 72953.
Consul: M'Hamed Barakat.
Chancellor: Kristina Ester Elise Barakat.

Consulate: ave Allal el Fassi B23, Apt 2, Oujda; tel (68) 5753.
Consul: Lhoussine Kirane.
Chancellor: Gudrun Elisabeth Kirane.

Consulate: Villa Matheron, rue Illal Illane, Safi; tel (46) 442906; telex 71766.
Consul: Gilbert Albert Fête.

Consulate-General: 31 ave du Prince Héritier Sidi Mohamed, Tangier; tel (9) 38730; telex 33674; fax (9) 31729.
Consul-General: Abdelkader Erzini.

SWITZERLAND

Embassy: sq. de Berkane, BP 169, Rabat; tel (7) 66974; telex 31996.
Ambassador: Jean Bourgeois.
First Secretary: Erich Wirth.
Attaché and Head of Chancery: Ruth Zumbühl.

Consulate: 79 ave Hassan II, BP 13005, Casablanca; tel 260211; telex 24050.
Consul: René Fatton.
Vice-Consul and Chancellor: Markus Probst.

TUNISIA

Embassy: 6 ave de Fès, Rabat; tel (7) 30636; telex 31009.
Ambassador: Abderrazak Kefi.

TURKEY

Embassy: 7 ave de Fès, Rabat; tel (7) 62605; telex 36164.
Ambassador: Gün Gür.
First Secretary: Cemil Karaman.

UNITED ARAB EMIRATES

Embassy: 11 ave des Alaouines, Rabat; tel (7) 30975; telex 31697.
Ambassador: Issaa Hamad Bushahab.

UNITED KINGDOM

Embassy: 17 blvd de la Tour Hassan, BP 45, Rabat; tel (7) 20905; telex 31022; fax (7) 20906.
Ambassador: John E. C. Macrae.
First Secretary (Commercial) and Deputy Head of Mission: S. R. H. Pease.
Defence Attaché: Lieut Col C. A. Le Hardy.
Cultural Attaché (British Council Director): E. J. Weston.
Second Secretary (Political/Information): J. P. Bedingfield.
Second Secretary and Consul: A. J. Featherstone.
Assistant Cultural Attaché (British Council Assistant Director): D. T. Baldwin.
Third Secretary (Management): F. Maxton.

Tangier Office: Trafalgar House, 9 rue Amérique du Sud, BP 2122, Tangier; tel (9) 35897.
Vice-Consul: W. A. T. Pulleyblank.

Consulate-General: 60 blvd d'Anfa, BP 13762, Casablanca; tel 221653; telex 22781; fax 265779.
Consul-General: P. C. F. Gregory-Hood.
Consul (Commercial/Information): T. M. Adams.

Consulate: Hôtel Sud Bahia, rue des Administrations Publiques, Agadir; tel (8) 23741; telex 81070.
Honorary Consul: O. Benlahcen.

USA

Embassy: 2 Charia Marrakech, BP 120, Rabat; tel (7) 62265; telex 31005; fax (7) 65661.
Ambassador: E. Michael Ussery.
Deputy Chief of Mission: Richard L. Jackson.
Political Section: Michael C. Lemmon.
Economic Section: David S. Robins.
Consular Section: George W. Brazier III.
Administrative Section: Alphonse López.
Regional Security Officer: Peter Stella.
Public Affairs Officer: Robert Wozniak.
Communications Programme Officer: Victor E. Maffei.
Information Systems Manager: Steven C. Taylor.
Agricultural Section: Andrew A. Duymovic.
Agency for International Development: Dennis M. Chandler.
Office of the Defence Attaché: Col James E. Murphy.
Military Liaison Office: Col Thomas E. Burch.

Consulate-General: 8 blvd Moulay Youssef, Casablanca; tel 264550; fax 204127.
Consul-General: Timberlake Foster.
Political Section: Peter McDevitt.
Economic Section: Allen S. Greenberg.
Commercial Section: Samuel D. Starrett.
Consular Section: Suella Pipal.
Administrative Section: J. Patrick Truhn.
Branch Public Affairs Officer: Elizabeth Thornhill.
Communications Programme Officer: Einar Jarvinen.
Labour Officer: William H. Owen.

YEMEN

Embassy: 11 rue Abou-Hanifa, Agdal, Rabat; tel (7) 74363; telex 32855.

YUGOSLAVIA

Embassy: 23 ave Bni Znassen, Souissi, BP 5014, Rabat; tel (7) 52201; telex 31760.
Ambassador: Dimitrije Babić.

ZAIRE

Embassy: 34 ave de la Victoire, BP 537, Rabat-Chellah; tel (7) 34862; telex 31954.
Ambassador: Mboladinga Katako.

International Organizations

EUROPEAN COMMUNITIES

External Delegation: 2 bis ave de Meknès, BP 1302, Rabat; tel (7) 61217; telex 32620; fax (7) 61156.
Head of Delegation: Ian Boag.

MOZAMBIQUE

ALGERIA

Embassy: CP 1709, Maputo; tel 492070; telex 6554.
Ambassador: Taffar Abdelkader.

AUSTRIA

Consulate: Avda 24 de Julho, 4°, CP 487, Maputo; tel 22344; telex 6319.
Honorary Consul: Klaus Gustav Dieckmann.

BELGIUM

Embassy: CP 1500, Maputo; tel 490077; telex 6511.
Ambassador: Michel Vantroyen.

BRAZIL

Embassy: Avda Kenneth Kaunda 296, Maputo; tel 492388; telex 6454.
Ambassador: Luiz Fernando do Coutto Nazareth.

BULGARIA

Embassy: CP 4689, Maputo; tel 491471; telex 6324.
Ambassador: Ivan Marinov Sokolarski.

CANADA

Office of the Canadian Embassy: 22 Joaquim Lapa, 4°, Rm 4, CP 1578, Maputo; tel 420818; telex 6684; fax 74169.
First Secretary (Development) and Consul: H. Wilson.

CHINA, PEOPLE'S REPUBLIC

Embassy: CP 4668, Maputo; tel 491560.
Ambassador: Xiao Sijin.

CONGO

Embassy: CP 4743, Maputo; tel 490142; telex 6207.
Ambassador: Jacob Okanza.

CUBA

Embassy: CP 387, Maputo; tel 491905; telex 6359.
Ambassador: José Espinosa.

CZECHOSLOVAKIA

Embassy: CP 1463, Maputo; tel 490746; telex 6216.
Ambassador: Ivo Mensik.

DENMARK

Embassy: Avda 24 de Julho 1500, CP 4588, Maputo; tel 420172; telex 6164; fax 420557.
Minister-Counsellor and Chargé d'affaires: Mogens Prehn.
Head of Aid Mission: Stig Barlyng.
Counsellor for Aid: Peter Truelsen.
Aid Attaché: Jens Haarløv.
Attaché: Kirsten Granberg.

EGYPT

Embassy: CP 4662, Maputo; tel 491118; telex 6417.
Ambassador: Mohamed Hindam.

FINLAND

Embassy: Avda Kenneth Kaunda 1202, CP 1663, Maputo; tel 490578; telex 6715; fax 491661.
Development Co-operation Programme Officer: Lauri Parkkali.

FRANCE

Embassy: Avda Julius-Nyerere 2361, CP 4781, Maputo; tel 490444; telex 6307.
Ambassador: Daniel Jouanneau.

Trade Promotion Office: CP 2116, Maputo; tel 742099; telex 6412.

GERMANY

Embassy: Rua de Mapulangwene 506, CP 1595, Maputo; tel 492714; telex 6489.
Ambassador: Reinhart Kraus.

GREECE

Embassy: CP 714, Maputo; tel 490981; telex 6299.
Ambassador: Stelios Rokanas.

GUINEA

Embassy: CP 1125, Maputo; tel 491478; telex 6527.

HOLY SEE

Apostolic Delagation: Avda Julius Nyerere 882, CP 2738, Maputo; tel 491144.
Auditor and Chargé d'affaires a.i.: Mgr Luigi Bonazzi.

HUNGARY

Embassy: Avda Kenneth Kaunda 714, Maputo; CP 1245, Maputo; tel 492343; telex 6431; fax 490880.
Ambassador: Mihály Terjék.
Second Secretary (Consular/Economic/Cultural): Jozsef Szalontai.

INDIA

Embassy: Avda Kenneth Kaunda 167, Maputo; tel 491124; telex 6452.
Ambassador: Surendra Kumar.

IRAN

Embassy: Avda Martires da Machava 1630, Maputo; tel 490700; telex 6159.
Chargé d'affaires: Sayed Moufred.

ITALY

Embassy: Avda Kenneth Kaunda 387, CP 976, Maputo; tel 491605; telex 6442.
Ambassador: Manfredo Incisca di Camerana.

KOREA, DEMOCRATIC PEOPLE'S REPUBLIC

Embassy: CP 4694, Maputo; tel 491482.
Ambassador: Li Zoug Son.

LESOTHO

Embassy: CP 1477, Maputo; tel 492473; telex 6439.
Ambassador: B. Nts'ohi.

LIBYA

Embassy: CP 4434, Maputo; tel 490662; telex 6475.
Ambassador: Muhammad Ahmad al-Amary.

MALAWI

Embassy: CP 4148, Maputo; tel 491468; telex 6300.
Ambassador: Bernard Kachama.

NETHERLANDS

Embassy: CP 1163, Maputo; tel 490031; telex 6178; fax 490429.
Ambassador: A. Hermans.

NICARAGUA

Embassy: CP 4228, Maputo; tel 490810; telex 6245.
Ambassador: Carlos José García Castillo.

NIGERIA

Embassy: 821 Avda Kenneth Kaunda, Maputo; CP 4693, Maputo; tel 492457; telex 6177.
Ambassador: J. O. Odoyen.
Counsellor and Head of Chancery: S. F. Aiyedona.
Counsellor: C. A. Ononye.
Second Secretary: I. I. Onwordi.
Second Secretary: I. A. Paragalda.
Finance Attaché: G. O. David.
Administrative Attaché: A. Ogbada.

NORWAY

Embassy: CP 828, Maputo; tel 491888; telex 6556.
Ambassador: Herman Pedersen.

PAKISTAN

Embassy: CP 4745, Maputo; tel 491265.
Ambassador: Mohammad Nasser Khan.

POLAND

Embassy: Rua D. João IV 22, Maputo; tel 490284.
Ambassador: Mirosław Dackiewicz.

PORTUGAL

Embassy: CP 4696, Maputo; tel 490311; telex 6341.
Ambassador: Francisco Knopfli.

ROMANIA

Embassy: CP 4648, Maputo; tel 742999; telex 6397.
Ambassador: Nasile Musaţ.

RUSSIA

Embassy: Avda Agostinho Neto 1103, CP 4666, Maputo; tel 420091; telex 6635.
Ambassador: Vladimir Vladimirovich Korneev.

Consular Section: tel 28823.

Consulate-General: Rua Roberto Ivence, CP 2064, Beira; tel 311231.

SOMALIA

Embassy: CP 4715, Maputo; tel 6354.
Ambassador: Yusuf Hassan Ibrahim.

SOUTH AFRICA

Trade Mission: Avda Julius Nyerere 745, CP 1120, Maputo; tel 491614; telex 6376; fax 492122.
Trade Representative: D. F. Laubscher.
Deputy Trade Representative: R. J. J. van Vuren.

SPAIN

Embassy: Avda Afonso Henriques 183, CP 1331, Maputo; tel 491519; telex 6579.
Ambassador: Jaime Abrisqueta.

SWAZILAND

Embassy: CP 4711, Maputo; tel 492117; telex 6353.

SWEDEN

Embassy: Rua de Kassuende 118, 1°, CP 338, Maputo; tel 490091; telex 6272; fax 490056.
Ambassador: Lars-Olof Edström.
Second Secretary: Anna-Lisa Trulsson Evidon.
Second Secretary: Lars Wahlund.
Head of Aid Section: Erik Åberg.

SWITZERLAND

Embassy: Avda Julius Nyerere 1213, CP 135, Maputo; tel 421337; telex 6255; fax 421339.
Counsellor and Chargé d'affaires a.i.: Jean-Pierre Ballaman.
Attaché and Head of Chancery: Ernst Steinmann.
Attaché (Development Co-operation and Humanitarian Aid): Jörg Frieden.

TANZANIA

Embassy: CP 4515, Maputo; tel 490110; telex 6295.
Ambassador: Martin Nirkusubila.

UNITED KINGDOM

Embassy: Avda Vladimir I. Lénine 310, CP 55, Maputo; tel 420111; telex 6265; fax 421666.
Ambassador: Maeve Geraldine Fort.
Defence Attaché: Lieut Col C. W. Larkin.
First Secretary, Consul and Deputy Head of Mission: P. January.
First Secretary (Chancery): C. R. G. Pagett.
First Secretary (Commercial and Aid): J. M. Winter.
Second Secretary (Management) and Vice-Consul: J. Fielder.
Third Secretary (Chancery/Aid): K. Shannon.

USA

Embassy: Avda Kenneth Kaunda 193, CP 783, Maputo; tel 490167; telex 6143; fax 490114.
Ambassador: Townsend B. Friedman, Jr.
Deputy Chief of Mission: Michael D. Metelitis.
Political Section: Judy Marie Buelow.
Economic/Commercial/Consular Section: Lucy Tamlyn.
Administrative Section: Michael S. Hoza.
Regional Security Officer: Robert A. Conrad.
Public Affairs Officer: Gerald A. McLoughlin.
Communications Programme Officer: Michael Lamberg.
Agency for International Development: Julius Schlotthauer.
Office of the Defence Attaché: Maj. Richard H. Fritz.

YUGOSLAVIA

Embassy: CP 4759, Maputo; tel 490819; telex 6516.
Ambassador: Miodrag Lekić.

ZAIRE

Embassy: 385 Avda do Martires do Machava; CP 2407, Maputo; tel 492170; telex 6316; fax 492351.
Ambassador: W'Eber M.-B. Angelo.
First Counsellor: Maya Mbongo Mbwanga.
Technical Attaché: Massa Mbo.
Financial Attaché: Tangata Mbassi.

ZAMBIA

Embassy: CP 4655, Maputo; tel 492452; telex 6415.
Ambassador: Goodwill Sizakwe.

ZIMBABWE

Embassy: CP 743, Maputo; tel 490404; telex 6542.
Ambassador: John Moyane.

International Organizations

EUROPEAN COMMUNITIES

External Delegation: 1214 Avda do Zimbabwe, CP 1306, Maputo; tel 490720; telex 6146; fax 491866.
Commission Delegate: Francisco Da Câmara.

MYANMAR

AUSTRALIA

Embassy: 88 Strand Rd, Yangon 802334; tel (1) 78307; telex 21301; fax (1) 71434.
Ambassador: Geoffrey C. Allen.

AUSTRIA

Consulate-General: 16G Thallawaddy Rd, Mayangon, Yangon; tel (1) 61873.
Honorary Consul-General: U Chit Khine.

BANGLADESH

Embassy: 340 Pyi Rd, Yangon; tel (1) 32818; telex 21320.
Ambassador: Mustafa Faruque Mohammed.
First Secretary and Head of Chancery: Mahmood Hasan.

CHINA, PEOPLE'S REPUBLIC

Embassy: 1 Pyidaungsu Yeiktha Rd, Yangon; tel (1) 72087; telex 21346.
Ambassador: Cheng Ruisheng.

CZECHOSLOVAKIA

Embassy: 326 Pyay Rd, Yangon; tel (1) 30515; telex 21337; fax (1) 31613.
Chargé d'affaires a.i.: Vlastimil Samek.
Attaché (Administration): Miroslav Hrenovcik.
Commercial Section: 54 Manawhari Rd, Yangon; tel (1) 21387.
Counsellor (Commercial): Alois Koncal.
Deputy Commercial Attaché: Jan Kouril.

DENMARK

Consulate-General: 65 (A), Kaba Aye Pagoda Rd, POB 365, Yangon; tel (1) 61371; telex 21532.

EGYPT

Embassy: 81 Pyidaungsu Yeiktha Rd, Yangon; tel (1) 81011; telex 21315.
Ambassador: Dr Adel Abbas El-Adawy.

FINLAND

Consulate-General: Yangon.

FRANCE

Embassy: 102 Pyidaungsu Yeiktha Rd, POB 858, Yangon; tel (1) 82122; telex 21314; fax (1) 87759.
Ambassador: Alain Briottet.
Trade Promotion Office: 35 Po Sein Rd, POB 563, Yangon; tel (1) 51311; telex 21404.

GERMANY

Embassy: 32 Natmauk Rd, POB 12, Yangon; tel (1) 50477; telex 21401.
Ambassador: Dr Baron Walther Freiherr Marschall von Bieberstein.

INDIA

Embassy: 545-547 Merchant St, Yangon; tel (1) 82933; telex 21201; fax (1) 89562.
Ambassador: Preet Mohan Singh Malik.

INDONESIA

Embassy: 100 Pyidaungsu Yeiktha Rd, POB 1401, Yangon; tel (1) 81714.
Ambassador: Maj.-Gen. Bernard Paul Makadada.

ISRAEL

Embassy: 49 Pyay Rd, Yangon; tel (1) 22290; telex 21319.
Ambassador: Ori Noy.
Second Secretary: Itzhak Lavie-Bachman.

ITALY

Embassy: 3 Inya Myaing Rd, Golden Valley, Yangon; tel (1) 30474; telex 21317.
Ambassador: Dr Giorgio Bosco.
Attaché (Commercial): Dr Paolo Scimonelli.
Attaché (Economic): Dr Sofia del Curto.
Attaché (Administration): Anna Maria Maurizi.

JAPAN

Embassy: 100 Natmauk Rd, Yangon; tel (1) 52288; telex 21400; fax (1) 52530.
Ambassador: Tomoya Kawamura.

KOREA, REPUBLIC

Embassy: 97 University Ave, Yangon; tel (1) 30655; telex 21324.
Ambassador: Kim Hang-Kyung.

LAOS

Embassy: A1 Diplomatic Quarters, Fraser Rd, Yangon, POB 1550, Yangon; tel (1) 22482; telex 21519.
Ambassador: Chanpang Sihapom.

MALAYSIA

Embassy: 65 Shin Saw Pu Rd, Yangon; tel (1) 20251; telex 21321.
Ambassador: Sallehuddin Abdullah.

NEPAL

Embassy: 16 Natmauk Yeiktha Rd, Yangon; tel (1) 50633; telex 21402.
First Secretary: Suresh Prasad Pradhan.
Attaché: Daman Bahadur Rajbhandari.
Attaché: Indra Kumar Silwal.

PAKISTAN

Embassy: A4 Diplomatic Quarters, Prome Rd, Yangon; tel (1) 22881.
Ambassador: Muhammad Qurban.
Counsellor: Masood Akhtar.

PHILIPPINES

Embassy: 56 Pyi Rd, 6_0 Mile, Yangon; tel (1) 64010.
Ambassador: Rosalinda V. Tirona.

RUSSIA

Embassy: 38 Newlyn Rd, Yangon; tel (1) 72427; telex 21331.
Ambassador: Vadim I. Shabalin.

SINGAPORE

Embassy: 287 Pyi Rd, Yangon; tel (1) 33200; telex 21356; fax (1) 33129.
Chargé d'affaires: Lam Peck Heng.

SRI LANKA

Embassy: 34 Taw Win Rd, POB 1150, Yangon; tel (1) 21509; telex 21352.
Ambassador: S. W. Alawathuwala.
Attaché: M. M. Lyap.

SWEDEN

Consulate-General: c/o U Hla Tun, RA, 53/55 Maha Bandoola Garden St (34th St entrance), POB 175, Yangon; tel (1) 71495; telex 21201.
Honorary Consul-General: U Hla Tun.

THAILAND

Embassy: 91 Pyi Rd, Yangon; tel (1) 21713; telex 21341.
Ambassador: Surapong Posayanond.

UNITED KINGDOM

Embassy: 80 Strand Rd, POB 638, Yangon; tel (1) 81138; telex 21216; fax (1) 89566.
Ambassador: Julian D. N. Hartland-Swann.
Deputy Head of Mission, First Secretary (Commercial) and Consul: Craig S. M. Shelton.
Defence Attaché: Col W. H. Clements.
Cultural Attaché: Ralph H. Isaacs.
Third Secretary (Chancery, Commercial and Information): Victoria J. Robinson.
Third Secretary (Management) and Vice-Consul: J. H. Lock.

USA

Embassy: 581 Merchant St, POB 521, Yangon; tel (1) 82055; telex 21230; fax (1) 80409.
Chargé d'affaires: Franklin P. Huddle, Jr.
Political/Economic Section: Donald L. Jameson.
Commercial Section: Shirlie C. Pinkham.
Administrative Section: Stanley P. Jakubowski.
Regional Security Officer: Bradley C. Lynch.
Public Affairs Officer: William J. Weinhold.
Communications Programme Officer: Millard J. Rollins.
Information Systems Manager: Thomas Smith.
Office of the Defence Attaché: Col David G. Douglass.

VIET-NAM

Embassy: 40 Komin Kochin Rd, Yangon; tel (1) 50361.
Ambassador: Nguyen Van Tiep.

YUGOSLAVIA

Embassy: 39 Shin Saw Pu Rd, POB 943, Yangon; tel (1) 20238.
Ambassador: Dr Svetozar Jovičević.

NAMIBIA

ALGERIA

Embassy: 95 John Meinert St, Windhoek 9000; tel (61) 226521.
Chargé d'affaires: Al Bengueuedda.

ANGOLA

Embassy: Angola House, 3 Ausspann St, PMB 12020, Windhoek 9000; tel (61) 227535; telex 897; fax (61) 221498.
Ambassador: Dr Alberto Do Carmo Bento Ribeiro.

AUSTRALIA

Liaison Office: 5 Raben Rd, Hochland Park, POB 2466, Windhoek; tel (61) 226727; telex 815; fax (61) 36268.

BANGLADESH

High Commission: 98 Klein Windhoek Rd, POB 9123, Windhoek 9000; tel (61) 32301; telex 650.
High Commissioner: A. Y. B. I. Siddiqi (acting).

BOTSWANA

High Commission: 22 Curt von François St, POB 20359, Windhoek 9000; tel (61) 228451; fax (61) 36034.
High Commissioner: Tuelenyana Rosemary Ditlhabi-Oliphant.

BRAZIL

Embassy: 52 Bismark St, POB 24166, Windhoek 9000; tel (61) 37368; telex 498; fax (61) 33389.
Chargé d'affaires: José Augusto Lindgren Alves.

CANADA

High Commission: 111A Gloudina St, Ludwigsdorf, Windhoek; POB 2147, Windhoek 9000; tel (61) 222941; telex 402; fax (61) 224204.
High Commissioner: Wayne N. Hammond.
Attaché (Administration): Roger Lacroix.

CHINA, PEOPLE'S REPUBLIC

Embassy: 39 Beethoven St, POB 22777, Windhoek 9000; tel (61) 222089; telex 675.
Ambassador: Ji Peinding.

CUBA

Embassy: 31 Omuramba Rd, Eros, POB 23866, Windhoek 9000; tel (61) 222952; telex 406; fax (61) 31584.
Ambassador: Angel Dalmau Fernández.
Counsellor: Esther Armenteros.
First Secretary: Alberto Diaz.

DENMARK

Embassy: 29 Van Coller St, POB 20126, Windhoek 9000; tel (61) 224923; telex 461; fax (61) 35807.
Chargé d'affaires: Sven Bille Bjerregaard.

EGYPT

Embassy: 10 Berg St, POB 11853, Windhoek 9000; tel (61) 221501; fax (61) 228856.
Ambassador: Mohammed Hussein Elsadr.

FINLAND

Embassy: Sanlam Centre, 154 Independence Ave, POB 3649, Windhoek 9000; tel (61) 221355; telex 671; fax (61) 221349.
Ambassador: Kirsti Lintonen.
Counsellor (Development Co-operation): Juhani Toivonen.
Attaché: Helena Selkäinaho.

FRANCE

Embassy: 1 Goethe St, POB 20484, Windhoek 9000; tel (61) 229021; telex 715; fax (61) 31436.
Ambassador: Alain Dementhon.

GERMANY

Embassy: Uhland St 11, Klein-Windhoek, POB 231, Windhoek 9000; tel (61) 229217; telex 482; fax (61) 222981.
Ambassador: Harald Ganns.
Legal and Consular Affairs Section: Bülow St 8, 8th Floor, CDM-Gebäude, Windhoek; tel (61) 31741.

GHANA

High Commission: 5 Klein Windhoek Rd, POB 24165, Windhoek 9000; tel (61) 221341; fax (61) 221343.
High Commissioner: Dr Keli Nordor.

INDIA

High Commission: 97 Klein Windhoek Rd, POB 1209, Windhoek 9000; tel (61) 226037; telex 832; fax (61) 37320.
High Commissioner: Shiv Shankar Mukherjee.
First Secretary and Head of Chancery: S. Chakravarti.
Attaché: Vijay Kumar.

IRAN

Embassy: 81 Klein Windhoek Rd, Windhoek 9000; tel (61) 229974; telex 637; fax (61) 220016.
Chargé d'affaires: Ahmad Amoozadeh.

ITALY

Embassy: cnr Gever and Anna Sts, POB 24065, Windhoek 9000; tel (61) 228602; telex 620; fax (61) 228602.
Ambassador: Piero de Masi.
Attaché: Mario Nuvoloni.

JAPAN

Embassy: POB 2710, Windhoek 9000; tel (61) 727500; fax (61) 727769.
Chargé d'affaires: Yukio Rokujo.

KENYA

High Commission: 35 Promenaden Rd, POB 2889, Windhoek 9000; tel (61) 226836; telex 823; fax (61) 221409.
High Commissioner: Jon Davies Odeke Likoko.

KOREA, DEMOCRATIC PEOPLE'S REPUBLIC

Embassy: Coetzee St, Windhoek 9000; tel (61) 41967; telex 631.
Chargé d'affaires: Kim Yong Hwan.

KOREA, REPUBLIC

Embassy: Safari Hotel, Windhoek 9000; tel (61) 38560.
Ambassador: Hak Wong Song.

MALAWI

High Commission: 56 Bismark St, POB 23384, Windhoek 9000; tel (61) 221291; telex 469; fax (61) 221392.
High Commissioner: James D. Kalilangwe (acting).

NIGERIA

High Commission: 4 Omuramba Rd, POB 23547, Windhoek 9000; tel (61) 32103; fax (61) 221639.
High Commissioner: Edward A. Aina.

NORWAY

Embassy: POB 9936, Windhoek 9000; tel (61) 31410; telex 432; fax (61) 222226.
Chargé d'affaires: Rolf W. Hansen.

PORTUGAL

Embassy: 28 Garten St, POB 443, Windhoek 9000; tel (61) 228736; telex 409.
Chargé d'affaires: João José Gomes.

RUSSIA

Embassy: 4 Christian St, Klein Windhoek, POB 3826, Windhoek 9000; tel (61) 228671; telex 865; fax (61) 228671.
Ambassador: Andrei Y. Urnov.
Minister-Counsellor: Pavel D. Pavlov.
Counsellor: Sergei A. Saryguine.
First Secretary: Vladimir V. Makarichtchev.
First Secretary: Yuri G. Lobatchev.
First Secretary: Andrei V. Morev.
First Secretary: Alexei M. Stankin.

SOUTH AFRICA

Representation: RSA House, cnr Jan Jonker and Klein Windhoek Sts, POB 23100, Windhoek 9000; tel (61) 229765; telex 701; fax (61) 224140.
Representative (with rank of Ambassador): J. A. Eksteen.
Deputy Representative: A. P. de V. Eckard.

SPAIN

Embassy: Safari Hotel, POB 21811, Windhoek 9000; tel (61) 223066.
Ambassador: Carlos Sanchez de Boada.

SWEDEN

Embassy: Sanlam Centre, 9th Floor, 154 Independence Ave, POB 23087, Windhoek 9000; tel (61) 222905; telex 463; fax (61) 222774.
Ambassador and Head of Aid Section: Sten Rylander.
First Secretary: Anneli Lindahl Kenny.

SWITZERLAND

Consulate-General: 10 Von Eckenbrecher St, POB 8688, Windhoek 9000; tel (61) 222359; telex 869; fax (61) 227922.
Consul-General: Robert Müller.

UNITED KINGDOM

High Commission: 116a Leutwein St, Windhoek 9000; tel (61) 223022; telex 2343; fax (61) 228895.

High Commissioner: F. N. Richards.
Deputy High Commissioner: R. S. G. Clarke.
First Secretary: R. G. Bowen.
First Secretary (British Council Representative): D. J. Utley.
Second Secretary (Consular/Commercial): S. I. Collier.
Third Secretary (Management/Consular): A. Sealy.

USA

Embassy: Ausspan Bldg, 14 Lossen St, POB 9890, Windhoek 9000; tel (61) 221601; fax (61) 229792.
Ambassador: Genta Hawkins Holmes.
Deputy Chief of Mission: Howard F. Jeter.
Political Officer: Carl F. Troy.
Economic/Commercial Officer: David Nolan.
Defence Attaché: Lieut Col Eugene M. Mensch II.
Administrative Officer: Charles E. Croteau.
Public Affairs Officer: Helen B. Picard.
Director of Agency for International Development: Richard L. Shortlidge.
Peace Corps Director: Kim Ward.
Consular Section: Mary Beth Leonard.
Regional Security Officer: Marilyn M. Wanner.
Communications Programme Officer: George A. Hamic.

VENEZUELA

Embassy: Windhoek.
Ambassador: Alvaro Carnevali.

YUGOSLAVIA

Embassy: Kalahari Sands Hotel, POB 3705, Windhoek 9000; tel (61) 36900; telex 3174; fax (61) 222260.
Chargé d'affaires: Petko Delic.

ZAMBIA

High Commission: 22 Curt von François St, POB 22882, Windhoek 9000; tel (61) 37610; telex 485; fax (61) 228162.
High Commissioner: Lieut-Gen. Benjamin N. Mibenge.

ZIMBABWE

High Commission: POB 23056, Windhoek 9000; tel (61) 228134; telex 866; fax (61) 228659.
High Commissioner: Alban Taka Kanengoni Dete.

NAURU

AUSTRALIA

High Commission: Civic Centre, POB 6, Yaren, Nauru; tel 3356; telex 33084; fax 3027.
High Commissioner: Barry Wyborn.

CHINA (TAIWAN)

Embassy: POB 294, Aiwo District, Nauru; tel 4594; fax 4594.
Counsellor and Chargé d'affaires: George J. Y. Hsieh.

NEPAL

AUSTRALIA

Embassy: Bansbari, POB 879, Kathmandu; tel (1) 411304; telex 2395; fax (1) 417533.
Ambassador: Les B. Douglas.
Consul: A. Uotila.
Vice-Consul: G. P. Fay.

AUSTRIA

Consulate: Hattisar, Naxal, Ward No. 1 GHA 2-200, POB 146, Kathmandu; tel (1) 410891; telex 2322.
Honorary Consul: Thapa Chuda.

BANGLADESH

Embassy: Naxal, Bhagawati Bahal, POB 789, Kathmandu; tel (1) 414265; telex 2420.
Ambassador: Syed Muhammad Hussain.
Counsellor and Head of Chancery: Anwar Husain Choudhury.
Counsellor (Education/Culture/Press): Mohammad Siddique Hossain.
First Secretary (Consular/Commercial): A. S. K. Choudhury.

CANADA

Counsellor (Development): V. Young.

CHINA, PEOPLE'S REPUBLIC

Embassy: Baluwatar, Kathmandu; tel (1) 211289.
Ambassador: Li Debiao.

DENMARK

Consulate-General: Jyoti Bhawan, Kantipath, POB 133, Kathmandu; tel (1) 227044; telex 2264; fax (1) 226314.
Consul-General: Padma Jyoti.

EGYPT

Embassy: Pulchowk, Patan, POB 792, Kathmandu; tel (1) 524844; telex 2225; fax (1) 522975.
Ambassador: Abd el-Hamid Mohamed Tabak.

FINLAND

Consulate-General: Meera Home, Khichapokhari, Kathmandu; tel (1) 211287; telex 2405.
Consul-General: Juddha Bahadur Shrestha.

FRANCE

Embassy: Lazimpat, POB 452, Kathmandu; tel (1) 412332; telex 2209.
Ambassador: Michel Galas.

Trade Promotion Office: POB 1226, Kathmandu; tel (1) 411462; telex 2398.

GERMANY

Embassy: Kingsway, Kanti Path, POB 226, Kathmandu; tel (1) 221730; telex 2213.
Ambassador: Dr Martin Schneller.

INDIA

Embassy: Lainchaur, Kathmandu; tel (1) 410900; telex 2449; fax (1) 413132.
Ambassador: Prof. Bimal Prasad.
Deputy Head of Mission: G. S. Iyer.
Minister: R. Nagarajan.
Minister (Commercial and Project): S. Tripathi.
Military and Air Attaché: Col A. Sharma.
First Secretary (Political): Ashok Tomar.
First Secretary (Economic): A. P. Kala.
First Secretary (Establishment): C. M. Ravindran.
First Secretary and Medical Officer: Dr A. C. Mullick.
First Secretary (Economic and Commercial): U. K. Maitra.
First Secretary (Education): Suresh Dhundia.
Assistant Military Attaché (Records): Lieut Col J. B. Monis.
Assistant Military Attaché: Lieut Col K. J. Singh.
Second Secretary (Information/Culture): Mukta D. Tomar.
Second Secretary (Consular): V. K. Munshi.
Assistant Military and Air Attaché: Capt. J. S. Sandhu.
Second Secretary and Medical Officer: Dr M. Revathy.

ISRAEL

Embassy: Bishramalaya House, Lazimpat, POB 371, Kathmandu; tel (1) 411811; telex 2210; fax (1) 413920.
Ambassador: Shlomo Dayan.
Second Secretary: Ilan Maor.

ITALY

Embassy: Baluwatar, POB 1097, Kathmandu; tel (1) 412743; telex 2311.
Ambassador: Dr Giovanni Cirillo.

JAPAN

Embassy: Panipokhari, POB 264, Kathmandu; tel (1) 410397; telex 2208; fax (1) 419238.
Ambassador: Kazuaki Arichi.

KOREA, DEMOCRATIC PEOPLE'S REPUBLIC

Embassy: Lalitpur, Kathmandu; tel (1) 521084; telex 2330.
Ambassador: An Hui-chong.

KOREA, REPUBLIC

Embassy: Keshar Mahal, Thamel, POB 1058, Kathmandu; tel (1) 211172; telex 2222.
Ambassador: Lee Joung-Binn.

MYANMAR

Embassy: Krishna Galli, Pulchowk, Patan, Kathmandu; tel (1) 521788.
Ambassador: U Aye Pe.

NEW ZEALAND

Consulate: Tiger Tops Bldg, POB 224, Kathmandu; tel (1) 223328; telex 2284.
Honorary Consul: Elizabeth Hawley.

PAKISTAN

Embassy: POB 202, Lazimpath, Kathmandu; tel (1) 410565.
Ambassador: Mohammad Ziaul Haq.
Counsellor: Gul Rehman.
Second Secretary: M. J. Kalim Ullah.
Third Secretary: Amjad Ali Sher.
Third Secretary: Abbas Ahmed.
Defence Attaché: Col Mian Khalid Habib.

RUSSIA

Embassy: Baluwatar, POB 123, Kathmandu; tel (1) 211255; telex 2571.
Ambassador: Felix N. Strok.

Consular Section: tel (1) 411063.

SWEDEN

Consulate-General: Meera Home, Khichapokhari, Kathmandu; tel (1) 220939; telex 2405.
Consul-General: Gajendra Bahadur Shrestha.
Chancellor: Chhabindra Das Shrestha.

THAILAND

Embassy: Jyoti Kendra Bldg, Thapathali, POB 3333, Kathmandu; tel (1) 213910; telex 2373.
Ambassador: Sirajayat Buddhi-Baedya.

UNITED KINGDOM

Embassy: Lainchaur, POB 106, Kathmandu; tel (1) 410583; telex 2343; fax (1) 411789.
Ambassador: Timothy J. B. George.
First Secretary, Consul and Deputy Head of Mission: A. Maclean.
Defence and Military Attaché: Col M. G. Allen.
First Secretary (Development/Commercial Officer): B. W. Money.
Second Secretary (Consular/Management): H. T. F. Jenkins.
Cultural Attaché (British Council Director): R. Hale.

USA

Embassy: Panipokhari, Kathmandu; tel (1) 411179; telex 2381; fax (1) 419963.
Ambassador: Julia Chang Bloch.
Deputy Chief of Mission: Albert A. Thibault, Jr.
Political/Economic Section: Todd R. Greentree.
Commercial Section: Carol T. Reynolds.
Consular Section: Charles M. Parish, Jr.
Administrative Section: Norma L. Kleiber.
Regional Security Officer: Michael Wanagel, Jr.
Public Affairs Officer: Janey Cole.
Communications Programme Officer: Robert Arriaga.
Agency for International Development: Kelly C. Kammerer.
Office of the Defence Attaché: Lieut Col Thomas A. Haase.

THE NETHERLANDS

ALGERIA

Embassy: Van Stolklaan 1-3, 2585 JS The Hague; tel (70) 3522954.

ARGENTINA

Embassy: Javastraat 20, 2585 AN The Hague; tel (70) 3654836; telex 31650.
Ambassador: Julian W. Kent.

AUSTRALIA

Embassy: Koninginnegracht 23/24, 2514 AB The Hague; tel (70) 3630983; telex 32008; fax (70) 3107598.
Ambassador: Donald J. Grimes.

AUSTRIA

Embassy: Van Alkemadelaan 342, 2597 AS The Hague; Postbus 96855, 2509 JG The Hague; tel (70) 3245470; telex 32236; fax (70) 3282066.
Ambassador: Dr Heinrich Pfusterschmid-Hardtenstein.
Minister-Counsellor: Dr Helga Konrad.
Economic Counsellor: Annemarie Vanhoegaerden.
Third Secretary: Peter Janisch.

Consulate-General: Weteringschans 106, 1017 XS Amsterdam; tel (20) 6268033.
Consul-General: Willem Schoemaker.
Honorary Consul: Christine W. Böttger.

BELGIUM

Embassy: Lange Vijverberg 12, 2513 AC The Hague; tel (70) 3644910; telex 31035; fax (70) 3645579.
Ambassador: Dr Luc Ceyssens.
Attaché (Agriculture): Pierre Damen.

BENIN

Consulate: Koningslaan 28, 1075 AD Amsterdam; tel (20) 6764551.
Honorary Consul: Lambertus Van Rooij.

BRAZIL

Embassy: Mauritskade 19, 2514 HD The Hague; tel (70) 3469229; telex 32444.
Ambassador: Alfonso Arinos de Mello Franco.

BULGARIA

Embassy: Duinroosweg 9, 2597 KJ The Hague; tel (70) 3503051; telex 32651; fax (70) 3584688.
Ambassador: Ljuben Gotsev.
Counsellor: Gueorgui Toromanov.
Counsellor: Libert Popov.
Consul and Officer for Press and Cultural Affairs: Krassimir Petrov.

CANADA

Embassy: Sophialaan 7, 2514 JP The Hague; tel (70) 3614111; telex 31270; fax (70) 3561111.
Ambassador: Jacques Gignac.
Minister (Commercial/Economic): P. Théberge.
Counsellor and Consul: G. Plamondon.
Counsellor and Consul: S. Marcoux.
Canadian Forces Attaché: Col N. H. Browne.
First Secretary (Commercial): V. Smith.
Second Secretary (Administration) and Vice-Consul: M. P. Taylor.
Third Secretary (Commercial): R. M. Hoffman.
Attaché: D. A. Doornbos.
Attaché: H. H. Rutinbeck.

Immigration Section: Groot Hertoginnelaan 8, 7th Floor, 2517 EG The Hague; tel (70) 3644825; fax (7) 3561110.
Counsellor (Immigration) and Consul: E. H. Woodford.
First Secretary (Immigration): A. R. Martin.

Consulate: Postbus 305, Maduro and Curiels Bank, N. V., Plaza JoJo Correa 2-4, Willemstad, Curaçao, Netherlands Antilles; tel (9) 61-3515; telex 1127; fax (9) 61-3731.
Honorary Consul: T. S. McCoy.

CAPE VERDE

Embassy: Koninginnegracht 4, 2514 AD The Hague; tel (70) 3469623; telex 34321; fax (70) 3467702.
First Secretary and Chargé d'affaires a.i.: Luís António Valadares Dupret.
Second Secretary: Fernando Jorge Wahnon Ferreira.
Attaché (Administrative Affairs): Dinora de Fátima Burgo Fernandes Barros.

Consulate-General: Mathenesserlaan 326, 3021 HX Rotterdam; tel (10) 4778977; telex 26696; fax (10) 4774553.
Consul-General: Bernardo Oliveira.

CHILE

Embassy: Mauritskade 51, 2514 HG The Hague; tel (70) 3642748; telex 34199; fax (70) 3616227.
Ambassador: Jorge Tapia Valdés.

CHINA, PEOPLE'S REPUBLIC

Embassy: Adriaan Goekooplaan 7, 2517 JX The Hague; tel (70) 3551515; telex 32018; fax (70) 3551651.
Ambassador: Wang Qingyu.
Counsellor: Wang Wenbo.
Commercial Counsellor: Ye Caiwen.
First Secretary (Educational): Liu Dawei.
First Secretary (Administrative): Zhou Linsheng.
First Secretary: Zhang Shuwen.
First Secretary (Cultural): Dong Junxin.
First Secretary (Scientific): Ge Hongsheng.
First Secretary: Liu Weijie.
First Secretary (Commercial): Jiang Deren.
Second Secretary: Shen Yahan.
Second Secretary (Press): Gao Zhansheng.
Second Secretary: Liang Haiying.
Second Secretary: Zhou Yayu.
Second Secretary: Chen Haoqi.
Second Secretary (Consular): Li Yaoquan.
Second Secretary: Xu Xinmin.
Second Secretary (Commercial): Chen Yuxi.
Second Secretary (Commercial): Liu Teping.
Deputy Military, Naval and Air Attaché: Zhang Shuchun.

COLOMBIA

Embassy: Groot Hertoginnelaan 14, 2517 EG The Hague; tel (70) 3614545; telex 31357; fax (70) 3614636.
Ambassador: Dr Ramiro Zambrano.

COSTA RICA

Embassy: Nassau Dillenburgstraat 43, 2596 AC The Hague; tel (70) 3264181; telex 33061; fax (70) 3242062.
Ambassador: Delsa Rangel Salcedo.
Minister-Counsellor and Consul-General: Mario Campos Mohr.
Counsellor and Information Officer: Guillermo F. Rojas Gonzalez.
First Secretary: Mayra Rodríguez Corrales.
Commercial Attaché: Rodrigo Brenes.

Consulate: Melonstraat 122, The Hague; tel (70) 3254857.
Honorary Consul: Paul Just de la Pasiere.

Consulate: Meent 106, 3001 Rotterdam; tel (10) 4130320; fax (10) 4143445.
Honorary Consul: Jean René de Monchy.

CUBA

Embassy: Prins Mauritslaan 6, 2582 LR The Hague; tel (70) 3541417; telex 31318; fax (70) 3520159.
Ambassador: Germán Gustavo Mazorra Hernández.

CZECHOSLOVAKIA

Embassy: Parkweg 1, 2585 JG The Hague; tel (70) 3557566; fax (70) 3514769.
Ambassador: Dr Miroslav Abrahám.

DENMARK

Embassy: Koninginnegracht 30, Postbus 30838, 2500 GV The Hague; tel (70) 3655830; telex 32075; fax (70) 3561433.
Ambassador: Per Søltoft Groot.
Counsellor: Jørgen Hartnack.
Commercial Counsellor: Andrew Jensen.
Agricultural Counsellor: H. Bunk Dybdahl.
Commercial Secretary: W. Kjærby Jensen.
Commercial Officer: Edith Vennix.
Chancellor and Vice-Consul: Ellen ter Poorten.
Export Assistant: Nanna Berg Jensen.
Embassy Chaplain: Rev. Frank Bjørn Christensen.

Consulate-General: De Ruijterkade 139, 1011 AC Amsterdam; tel (20) 234145; telex 12071; fax (20) 223172.
Consul-General: Hans Ivo Møller.
Consular Secretary and Vice-Consul: Hanne Boonstra.

Consulate: Pottebakkersrijge 16, 9718 AG Groningen; tel (50) 136800.
Consul: Peter Johan van Dam.

Consulate: Syndicuslaan 6, 9934 PT Delfzjil; tel (5960) 15820.
Vice-Consul: Cornelis Petrus Sabelis.

Consulate: Zuiderhaven 79, 8861 CM Harlingen; tel (5178) 2831; telex 46092.
Vice-Consul: C. J. van der Meer.

Consulate-General: Westerkade 27, 3016 CM Rotterdam; tel (10) 4360177.
Consul-General: Otto Lambert Oswald de Witt Wijnen.
Consular Secretary and Vice-Consul: D. A. van Maren.

Consulate: Boomstraat 35, 3311 TC Dordrecht; tel (78) 132177; telex 29109.
Vice-Consul: Gerard Maurits de Lange.

Consulate: Julianalaan 3, 4382 AT Vlissingen; tel (1184) 12711.
Vice-Consul: Wilhelmina de Weerd van der Est.

Consulate: 84 Carawaraweg, Willemstad, Postbus 578, Curaçao, Netherlands Antilles; tel (9) 61-4032; fax (9) 81-014.
Consul: Ole Vagn Geisler Hansen.
Vice-Consul: Lionel Capriles.

Consulate: 82 L. G. Smith Blvd, Postbus 189, Oranjestad, Aruba, Netherlands Antilles; tel (8) 24-622; telex 5048; fax (8) 21-627.
Vice-Consul: Eduard de Veer.

EGYPT

Embassy: Borweg 1, 2597 LR The Hague; tel (70) 3542000; telex 32529.
Ambassador: Mohamed Abd-el-Aziz Sharara.

EL SALVADOR

Embassy: Catsheuvel 117, 2517 KA The Hague; tel (70) 3520712; telex 33365.
Ambassador: Arturo Roberto Castrillo Hidalgo.

FINLAND

Embassy: Groot Hertoginnelaan 16, 2517 KH The Hague; tel (70) 3469754; telex 32644; fax (70) 3107174.
Ambassador: Joel Pekuri.
First Secretary: Ritva Koukku-Ronde.
Commercial Counsellor: Ole Silén.
Commercial Secretary: Esko Haavisto.
Attaché: Leena Lankinen-Stanecki.
Chaplain: Toivo Loikkanen.
Defence Attaché: Lieut Col Heikki Ylönen.

Consulate-General: Guido Gezellestraat 12, 1077 WP Amsterdam; tel (20) 6628723.
Honorary Consul: Robert Key.

Consulate-General: Lange Voorhout 86, Apt. 13, 2514 EJ The Hague; tel (70) 3602894.
Honorary Consul-General: Willem van der Vlugt.

Consulate-General: Parklaan 28, 3016 BC Rotterdam; tel (10) 4365500; telex 22241.
Honorary Consul-General: B. K. Brouwerens.

Consulate: Aug. de Meyer, B. V., Zwedenweg 1, 4538 BH Terneuzen; tel (1150) 85000; telex 55023.
Honorary Consul: Anthony Jacob Verbrugge.

Consulate: Nigtevechtseweg 198, 3633 XX Vreeland, Utrecht; tel (2945) 1688; telex 47518.
Honorary Consul: Fredrick Hendrik Bruna.

Consulate: Handelskade West 12, 9930 AA Delfzjil; tel (5960) 16016; telex 53132.
Honorary Vice-Consul: Klaas Matroos.

Consulate: Breedestraat 22, Postbus 3125, Willemstadt, Curaçao, Netherlands Antilles; tel (9) 61-1951.
Honorary Consul: Helga Nieuwkerk-Mensing.

FRANCE

Embassy: Smidsplein 1, 2514 BT The Hague; tel (70) 3469453; telex 31465.
Ambassador: Jean-René Bernard.

Trade Promotion Office: telex 32547.

Consulate-General: Vijzelgracht 2, Postbus 20018, 1000 HA Amsterdam; tel (20) 6428922.

GERMANY

Embassy: Groot Hertoginnelaan 18-20, 2517 EG The Hague; tel (70) 3420600; telex 31012; fax (70) 3651957.
Ambassador: Dr Klaus-Jürgen Citron.

Consulate-General: de Lairessestraat 172, Amsterdam; Postbus 75500, 1070 AM Amsterdam; tel (20) 6623394; telex 10334; fax (20) 6766951.
Consul-General: Winfried Engemann.

Consulate: Parklaan 52, Eindhoven; tel (40) 447725; telex 51180.
Honorary Consul: M. C. A. Klinkenbergh.

Consulate: de Merodestraat 3, 8937 AA Leeuwarden; Postbus 407, 8901 BE Leeuwarden; tel (58) 948494; telex 46191.
Honorary Consul: Gerardus Herman Willem Benes.

Consulate: Papenstraat 8, 6211 LG Maastricht; Postbus 3089, 6202 Maastricht; tel (43) 218202.
Honorary Consul: Peter Meyer Viol.

Consulate-General: Parklaan 36, 3016 BC Rotterdam; tel (10) 4365133; telex 22164.
Honorary Consul-General: Jaques Simon Cornelis Schoufour.

Consulate: OLAU Terminal, Buitenhaven, Vlissingen; Postbus 231, 4380 AE Vlissingen; tel (1184) 88388; fax (1184) 88496.
Honorary Consul: Dieter Hartmann.

Consulate: Scopetstraat 13, Postbus 15, Oranjestad, Aruba; tel (8) 1767.
Honorary Consul: Hans-Günther Jansen.

Consulate: Jan Sofat 202, Postbus 3062, Willemstad, Curaçao, Netherlands Antilles; tel (9) 61-3390; telex 3328.
Honorary Consul: Bastiaan Kooijman.

GHANA

Consulate: Keizersgracht 534, 1017 EK Amsterdam; tel (20) 6209839; telex 12317.

GREECE

Embassy: Koninginnegracht 37, 2514 AD The Hague; tel (70) 3602880; telex 34112; fax (70) 3563040.
Ambassador: Athanassios Exintaris.

HOLY SEE

Apostolic Nunciature: Carnegielaan 5, 2517 KH The Hague; tel (70) 3503363; fax (70) 3521461.
Apostolic Pro-Nuncio: Most Rev. Audrys Juozas Bačkis, Titular Archbishop of Meta.
Counsellor: Mgr Juliusz Janusz.

HONDURAS

Embassy: Catsheuvel 83, 2517 KA The Hague; tel (70) 3540152; telex 32746.
Ambassador: Dr Ramón Valladares Soto.

HUNGARY

Embassy: Hogeweg 14, 2585 JD The Hague; tel (70) 3500404; telex 32147; fax (70) 3521749.
Ambassador: Dr István Csejtei.

ICELAND

Consulate-General: Reved International, Herengracht 176, 1016 BR Amsterdam; tel (20) 6248958; fax (20) 6262658.
Consul-General: Robert Eduard van Erven Dorens.

Consulate: Business Wise BV, Oranje Nassaulaan 45, 1075 AK Amsterdam; tel (20) 6625223; fax (20) 6730380
Vice-Consul: Jacobus Bernardus Mulders.

Consulate: Meyer & Co Scheepvaart Mij. BV, Scheepmakershaven 25, 3011 VA Rotterdam; Postbus 776, 3000 AT Rotterdam; tel (10) 4117580; telex 21188; fax (10) 4117629.
Consul: Johannes A. van Rossum.

INDIA

Embassy: Buitenrustweg 2, 2517 KD The Hague; tel (70) 3469771; telex 33543; fax (70) 3617072.
Ambassador: V. K. Grover.
First Secretary: Ravi Bangar.
First Secretary: K. S. Sastry.
Second Secretary: R. K. Sachdeva.
Second Secretary: B. Prasad.
Attaché: A. P. Bhatia.
Attaché: K. J. Singh.
Attaché: B. S. Rawat.

INDONESIA

Embassy: Tobias Asserlaan 8, 2517 KC The Hague; tel (70) 3469796.
Ambassador: Bintoro Tjokroamidjojo.

IRAN

Embassy: Javastraat 54, 2585 AR The Hague; tel (70) 3469353; telex 33016.

IRAQ

Embassy: Johan de Wittlaan 16, 2517 JR The Hague; tel (70) 3469683; telex 34353.
Ambassador: Safa S. al-Falaki.

IRELAND

Embassy: Dr Kuyperstraat 9, 2514 BA The Hague; tel (70) 3630993; telex 31352; fax (70) 3617604.
Ambassador: Denis O'Leary.
First Secretary: Vincent Herlihy.
Secretary: Nicholas Twist.

Consulate-General: Willemskade 23, 3016 DM Rotterdam; Postbus 520, 3000 AM Rotterdam; tel (10) 4143322; telex 22115.
Honorary Consul-General: Gerard Fontein.

ISRAEL

Embassy: Buitenhof 47, 2513 AH The Hague; tel (70) 3647850; telex 31274; fax (70) 3648870.
Ambassador: M. N. Bavli.

ITALY

Embassy: Alexanderstraat 8, 2514 JL The Hague; tel (70) 3469249; telex 31530.
Ambassador: Antonello Pietromarchi.

JAMAICA

Consulate: Herengracht 316, 1016 CD Amsterdam; tel (20) 243412; telex 15117.
Honorary Consul: Jacques H. Huysser.

JAPAN

Embassy: Tobias Asserlaan 2, 2517 KC The Hague; tel (70) 3469544; telex 32105; fax (70) 3106341.
Ambassador: Kimio Fujita.

KENYA

Embassy: Koninginnegracht 102, 2514 AL The Hague; tel (70) 3504215; telex 33354.

KOREA, REPUBLIC

Embassy: Verlengde Tolweg 8, 2517 JV The Hague; tel (70) 3520621; telex 33291.
Ambassador: Sang-Sup Choi.

KUWAIT

Embassy: Carnegielaan 9, 2517 KH The Hague; tel (70) 3603813; telex 32199; fax (70) 3924588.
Third Secretary: Salem Ghassab Al-Zamanan.
Attaché: Bader Khaled Abdul-Aziz Al-Mufarrej.

LEBANON

Embassy: Frederikstraat 2, 2514 LK The Hague; tel (70) 3658906; telex 32462.
Ambassador: Salah Stétié.

LUXEMBOURG

Embassy: Nassaulaan 8, 2514 JS The Hague; tel (70) 3607516; telex 33174; fax (70) 3563303.

Ambassador: Dr Jean Hostert.
Secretary and Consul: Eugène Goetzinger.

MALAYSIA

Embassy: Rustenburgweg 2, 2517 KE The Hague; tel (70) 3506506; telex 33024.
Ambassador: Datuk Khalid bin Abdul Karim.

MALI

Consulate: Blaak 22, Rotterdam; tel (10) 4136420.
Honorary Consul: Mr van Caldenborgh.

MEXICO

Embassy: Nassauplein 17, 2585 EB The Hague; tel (70) 3602900.
Ambassador: Ezequiel Padilla.

MONACO

Consulate: 2e Weteringplantsoen 21, 1017 DE Amsterdam; tel (20) 6245250.
Consul: Mr Coebergh.

Consulate: Alexander Gogelweg 16, 2517 JH The Hague; tel (70) 3795795.
Consul: C. De Bouter.

Consulate: Mathenesserlaan 233, 3021 HB Rotterdam; tel (10) 4760055.
Consul: L. C. A. van Eijck.

MOROCCO

Embassy: Oranjestraat 9, 2514 JB The Hague; tel (70) 3469617; telex 34163; fax (70) 3614503.
Ambassador: Abdelaziz Jamaï.

NEW ZEALAND

Embassy: Mauritskade 25, 2514 HD The Hague; tel (70) 3469324; telex 31557; fax (70) 3632983.
Ambassador: Graeme Ammundsen.
Counsellor: David McKee.
First Secretary (Commercial): Phillip J. Klap.
Senior Immigration Officer: Lee Wilson.

NICARAGUA

Embassy: Zoutmannstraat 53E, 2518 GM The Hague; tel (70) 3630967.

NIGERIA

Embassy: Wagenaarweg 5, 2597 LL The Hague; tel (70) 3501703; telex 31785.

NORWAY

Embassy: Prinsessegracht 6A, 2514 AN The Hague; Postbus 30826, 2500 GV The Hague; tel (70) 3451900; telex 32265; fax (70) 3659630.
Ambassador: Bjørn Blakstad.

OMAN

Embassy: Koninginnegracht 27, 2514 AB The Hague; tel (70) 3615800; telex 30965.
Ambassador: Abdulaziz bin Abdullah bin Zahor al-Hinai.

PAKISTAN

Embassy: Amaliastraat 8, 2514 JC The Hague; tel (70) 3648948; telex 33696.
Ambassador: Izharul Haque.
Minister: Shahryar Rashed.
Second Secretary: Tasnim Aslam.

Consulate: Debussystraat 2, 3161 WD Rhoon; tel (1890) 30600.
Honorary Consul: Frank Ligterink.

PERU

Embassy: van Alkemadelaan 189, 2597 AE The Hague; tel (70) 3280506; telex 33568.
Ambassador: Jorge Colunge Villacorta.

PHILIPPINES

Embassy: Laan Copes van Cattenburch 125, 2585 EZ The Hague; tel (70) 3604820; telex 33103.
Ambassador: Rosario V. Cariño.

POLAND

Embassy: Alexanderstraat 25, 2514 JM The Hague; tel (70) 3605812; telex 31286; fax (70) 3602810.
Ambassador: Dr Franciszek Morawski.
Counsellor (Political Affairs): Stanisław Czartoryski.
Counsellor (Consular Affairs): Zbigniew Tomkowski.
Military, Naval and Air Attaché: Lieut Col Bohdan Sienkiewicz.
Counsellor (Cultural and Scientific Affairs): Jan Larecki.
First Secretary (Public Relations): Lech Kubiak.

Commercial Section: Van Lennpweg 51, 2597 LG The Hague; tel (70) 3502781; fax (70) 3543966.
Commercial Counsellor: Adam Kucharski.

PORTUGAL

Embassy: Bazarstraat 21, 2518 AG The Hague; tel (70) 3630217; telex 33204.
Ambassador: Francisco Baltasar Moita.

ROMANIA

Embassy: Catsheuvel 55, 2517 KA The Hague; tel (70) 3543796; telex 32189.
Ambassador: Ion M. Anghel.
Counsellor: Emil Mănoiu.
First Secretary: Constantin Rădulescu.
First Secretary (Consular Affairs): Florică Vasiliu.
Counsellor (Economic Affairs): Gheorghe Ududoiu.
First Secretary (Economic Affairs): Gabriel Dumitrescu.
Second Secretary (Economic Affairs): Ion Tamiş.

RUSSIA

Embassy: Andries Bickerweg 2, 2517 JP The Hague; tel (70) 3451300; telex 34585; fax (70) 3617960.
Ambassador: Dr Aleksandr Davidovich Tchikvaidze.
Minister-Counsellor: Alexandr Pankratov.
Counsellor: Victor Koulechov.
Military, Naval and Air Attaché: Col Vladimir J. Boulavinov.
Attaché (Economic/Land Improvement/Water Systems): Vasilii Mamonko.
Agricultural Attaché: Nikolai Ibraguimov.
First Secretary: Vladimir Kareline.
First Secretary: Stanislav Rodtchenkov.
First Secretary: Sergei Sokolov.
Deputy Military, Naval and Air Attaché: Lieut Col Arkadi Bobrov.
Second Secretary: Vladimir Pachedko.
Second Secretary: Vladimir Naidenov.
Second Secretary: Boris Jilko.
Second Secretary: Andrei Poskakouhine.

Consular Affairs Section: Laan van Meerdervoort, 2517 AA The Hague; tel (70) 3467940; telex 34585.
First Secretary and Head of Consular Affairs: Oleg Briouchkov.

Commercial Section: Veluwelaan 22, 1079 RA Amsterdam; tel (20) 6447477; fax (20) 6446643.
Head of Commercial Section: Yuri Kojine.
Deputy Commercial Representative: Valeri V. Iarochenko.
Deputy Commercial Representative: Boris Ous.

SAUDI ARABIA

Embassy: Alexanderstraat 19, 2514 JM The Hague; tel (70) 3614391.
Ambassador: Abdelmohsen Mohammed al-Sudeari.

SOUTH AFRICA

Embassy: Wassenaarseweg 40, 2596 CJ The Hague; Postbus 90638, LP 2509 The Hague; tel (70) 3924501; telex 33610; fax (70) 3458226.
Ambassador: Albertus E. Nothnagel.
Counsellor: R. W. Sherwood.
Counsellor (Trade): C. J. Dahms.
First Secretary: J. M. Krebs.
First Secretary (Administrative): R. du Toit.
Second Secretary: P. Voges.
Second Secretary (Consular): A. de Meyer.
Third Secretary: W. G. F. Geerlings.
Third Secretary (Consular): J. Janse van Rensburg.

SPAIN

Embassy: Lange Voorhout 50, 2514 EG The Hague; tel (70) 3643814; telex 32373.
Ambassador: Manuel Sassot.
Counsellor (Education): José Luis Hernández Marco.
Defence Attaché: Capt. Carlos Rodríguez Casau.

SUDAN

Embassy: Laan Copes van Cattenburch 81, 2585 EW The Hague; tel (70) 3605300; telex 32213; fax (70) 3617975.
Ambassador: Dr Achol Deng.
Counsellor: Mohamed Adam Ismail.
Agricultural Counsellor: Mutasim Ismail Mekki.
Administrative Attaché: Ahmed Osman Ahmed.

SURINAME

Embassy: Alexander Gogelweg 2, 2517 JH The Hague; tel (70) 3650844; telex 32220; fax (70) 3617445.
Ambassador: Cyrill Bisoendat Ramkisor.
Counsellor: Irma Eugenie Loemban Tobing.
First Secretary: Eudia Hillegonda van Frederikslust.
Second Secretary: Djoeminadi Toemin.
Second Secretary: Clyde Ricardo Cummingborg.
Administrative Attaché: Sukram Ajodhia.
Administrative Attaché: Lothar Wim Westzaan.
Administrative Attaché: Guno Erwin Themen.
Administrative Attaché: Winston Franklin Vasconcellos.

Consulate-General: De Cuserstraat 11, Amsterdam; tel (20) 6426717; telex 18879; fax (20) 6465311.
Consul-General: R. Kolader.

SWEDEN

Embassy: Neuhuyskade 40, Postbus 90648, 2509 LP The Hague; tel (70) 3245424; telex 31291; fax (70) 3247911.
Ambassador: Göte Magnusson.
Minister: Kerstin Bothén.
First Secretary and Press Attaché: Herman Gyllenhaal.
Second Secretary: Mikael Lesko.
Vice-Consul: Willem Adrian van Os.
Chancellor: Kerstin Signe Maria Eichperger.

Commercial Section: Zweedse Handelsdelegatie, Zeestraat 71, Postbus 85884, 2508 CN The Hague; tel (70) 3614851; fax (70) 3632722.
Commercial Secretary: Ove Stoltz.

Consulate-General: De Ruyterkade 107/5, 1011 AB Amsterdam; tel (20) 6242699; telex 11859.

Consul-General: Hans Ivo Möller.
Consul: Johanna Cornelia van Hoeken.
Chancellor: Gun Karin Lilienthal.

Consulate-General: Willemskade 12, 3016 DK Rotterdam; tel (10) 4144488; telex 22242; fax (10) 4126324.
Consul-General: Öyvind Riseng.
Vice-Consul: John Lennart Ericson.
Vice-Consul: Kirsten Jaeger.
Vice-Consul: Lillen Grethe Otto.
Vice-Consul: Åke Söderpalm.

Consulate: Plaza Book Shop, 33 Havenstraat, Postbus 425, Oranjestad, Aruba; tel (8) 21821; fax (8) 34317.
Consul: Herman Joseph Somers.

Consulate-General: Franse Bloemweg No. 3, Willemstad, Curaçao, Netherlands Antilles; tel (9) 75-409; telex 3321; fax (9) 37-1425.
Consul-General: Henry Maduro.

SWITZERLAND

Embassy: Lange Voorhout 42, 2514 EE The Hague; Postbus 30913, 2500 GX The Hague; tel (70) 3642831; telex 32705; fax (70) 3561238.
Ambassador: François-Charles Pictet.
First Secretary: Marianne Gramm.
Attaché and Head of Chancery: Ernst Hofstetter.

Consulate-General: Joh. Vermeerstraat 16, 1071 DR Amsterdam; Postbus 50572, 1007 DB Amsterdam; tel (20) 6643811; fax (20) 6755515.
Consul-General: Fridolin Wyss.
Vice-Consul and Chancellor: Rudolf Gauhl.

Consulate-General: c/o A. Reinstein, Groothandelsgebouw, Stationsplein 45, Postbus 29107, 3013 AK Rotterdam; tel (10) 4135070; telex 21111.
Honorary Consul-General: Ricardo Knapp.

TANZANIA

Embassy: Prinsessegracht 32, 2514 AP The Hague; tel (70) 3653800; telex 32065.
Ambassador: Seif Ali Iddi.

THAILAND

Embassy: Buitenrustweg 1, 2517 KD The Hague; tel (70) 3459703; telex 34207.
Ambassador: Suchinda Yongsunthon.

Office of Commercial Counsellor: Delistraat 47, 2585 VX The Hague; tel (70) 3503852; telex 34276; fax (70) 3545108.

TOGO

Consulate: Amsteldijk 319, 1083 AB Amsterdam; tel (20) 6445790.
Consul: Mr Van Den Brink.

TUNISIA

Embassy: Gentsestraat 98, 2587 HX The Hague; tel (70) 3512251; telex 31271; fax (70) 3514323.
First Secretary: Ali Dridi.

TURKEY

Embassy: Jan Everstraat 15, 2514 BS The Hague; tel (70) 3604912; telex 32623.
Ambassador: Bilgin Unan.

UNITED KINGDOM

Embassy: Lange Voorhout 10, 2514 ED The Hague; tel (70) 3645800; telex 31600; fax (70) 3603839.
Ambassador: Sir Michael R. H. Jenkins.
Counsellor and Deputy Head of Mission: R. P. Flower.
Counsellor (Commercial): A. D. Sprake.
Defence and Naval Attaché: Capt. M. Bickley.
Military and Air Attaché: Lieut Col C. P. Cook.
First Secretary and Head of Political Section: P. J. Sullivan.
First Secretary (Political): T. M. Kenwrick-Piercy.
First Secretary (Commercial): M. J. E. Mayhew.
First Secretary (Political and Information): B. M. Bennett.
First Secretary (Management): F. McDermott.
Second Secretary (Economic/Agriculture): G. N. Loten.

Consulate-General: Koningslaan 44, 1075 AE Amsterdam; Postbus 75488, 1070 AL Amsterdam; tel (20) 6764343; telex 15117; fax (20) 6761069.
Consul-General: D. H. Doble.
Consul: T. C. Lamb.

Consulate: Bombadiersweg Z/N, Willemstad, POB 3803, Curaçao, Netherlands Antilles; tel (9) 36-9366; telex 3372.
Honorary Consul: E. J. Wilson.

USA

Embassy: Lange Voorhout 102, 2514 EJ The Hague; tel (70) 3624911; fax (70) 3614688.
Ambassador: C. Howard Wilkins, Jr.
Deputy Chief of Mission: Thomas H. Gewecke.
Political Section: Lawrence G. Rossin.
Economic Section: George Boutin.
Commercial Section: Michael J. Hegedus.
Administrative Section: Timothy E. Roddy.
Regional Security Officer: Robert J. Whigham.
Public Affairs Officer: Arthur S. Berger.
Communications Programme Officer: William J. Linger.
Information Systems Manager: Edward M. Shearer.
Office of the Defence Attaché: Capt. Bruce W. Barker.
Office of Defence Co-operation: Col Charles W. Brewer.
Agricultural Section: Norval Francis.
Labour Officer: William R. Salisbury.
Customs Service (Treasury): Robert L. Gerber.

Consulate-General: Museumplein 19, Amsterdam; tel (20) 6645661; telex 044-16176; fax (20) 6761761.
Consul-General: Kenneth Longmeyer.
Commercial Section: Hilbert C. Engelhardt.
Consular Section: Roger D. Pierce.

Consulate-General: St Anna Blvd 19, Postbus 158, Willemstad, Curaçao, Netherlands Antilles; tel (9) 61-3066; telex 1062; fax (9) 61-6489.
Consul-General: Sharon P. Wilkinson.
Deputy Principal Officer: Marcia E. Cole.
Consular Section: Elizabeth E. Moore.
Regional Security Officer: Kevin Barry.
Legal Attaché: Paul F. Nolan.

URUGUAY

Embassy: Nassaulaan 1, 2nd Floor, 2514 JS The Hague; tel (70) 3609815; telex 32139; fax (70) 3562826.
Ambassador: Mateo Marques Seré.
Counsellor: Manuel G. Vieira Merola.

Consulate-General: Coolsingel 75, 3012 AD Rotterdam; tel (10) 4118382; fax (10) 4129158.
Consul-General: Agustín Ortega.

VENEZUELA

Embassy: Nassaulaan 2, 2514 JS The Hague; tel (70) 3523851; telex 34058; fax (70) 3656954.
Ambassador: Francisco Paparoni.
First Secretary: Silvia C. Dorante D.
Third Secretary: Regulo Burelli Ortiz.
Third Attaché: Franca Baroni de R.
Third Attaché: Nancy López Contreras.
Third Attaché: Carmen Elena Saa Zamora.

Consulate: Amsterdam.

Consulate-General: Paardenbaaistraat 12, Seguros Mansur Gebouw, 2nd Floor, Postbus 78, Oranjestad, Aruba; tel (8) 21078; telex 5085; fax (8) 23317.
Consul-General: Josefina Carrero Prato.
Consul: Ana Mercedes González.

Consulate: Calle Grandi 52, Kralendijk, Postbus 376, Bonaire, Netherlands Antilles; tel (7) 8471; fax (7) 8275.
Consul: Vasco Altuve Febres.
Vice-Consul: Teresa Bustillos.

Consulate-General: Handelskade 12, Willemstad, Curaçao, Netherlands Antilles; tel (9) 61-2449; telex 1118; fax (9) 61-3179.
Consul-General: José Angel Marchena Acosta.
Attaché: Bertha M. Capella Reveron.

YEMEN

Embassy: Surinamestraat 9, 2585 GG The Hague; tel (70) 3653936; telex 33290.
Ambassador: Mohamed Abdul Rehman al-Robaee.

YUGOSLAVIA

Embassy: Groot Hertoginnelaan 30, 2517 EG The Hague; tel (70) 3632397; telex 33199; fax (70) 3602421.

ZAIRE

Embassy: Violenweg 2, 2597 KL The Hague; tel (70) 3547904; telex 32224; fax (70) 3541373.
Chargé d'affaires a.i.: Ndeze Mutarambirwa.
Second Counsellor: Mr Nsingi-zi-Mayemba.
Second Counsellor: Ebonda Bimpele.
Attaché: Kindeki Ambin.

International Organizations

EUROPEAN COMMUNITIES

Bureau: 5 Korte Vijverberg, 2513 AB The Hague; tel (70) 3469326; telex 31094; fax (70) 3646619.
Director: Théo Hustinx.

NEW ZEALAND

ARGENTINA

Consulate-General: Harbour View Bldg, 52 Quay St, POB 2320, Auckland; tel (9) 391-757.
Consul-General: Cesar A. Marquez.
Consul: Manuel Angel Fernández.

AUSTRALIA

High Commission: 72-78 Hobson St, Thorndon, POB 4036, Wellington; tel (4) 473-6411; telex 3375; fax (4) 499-1079.
High Commissioner: R. S. Laurie.
Deputy High Commissioner: Jeremy V. R. Hearder.
Defence Adviser: Group Capt. Ray Gibson.
Counsellor (Commercial): Dr Michael Adams.
Counsellor: Frank C. Ness.
First Secretary (Public Affairs): Julie McDonald.
First Secretary (Consular/Administrative): Peter Puniard.
Second Secretary (Consular): Bruce Kentwell.
Third Secretary: Bruce Jones.
Third Secretary: Sally Noonan.

Consulate-General: Union House, 32-38 Quay St, Private Bag, CPO, Auckland; tel (9) 303-2429; telex 2516; fax (9) 770-798.
Consul-General and Senior Trade Commissioner: Geoffrey M. Hill.
Consul (Commercial) and Trade Commissioner: Ken N. Johnson.
Consul (Immigration): N. Christodoulou.

AUSTRIA

Consulate-General: Security Express House, 2nd Floor, 22-24 Garrett St, POB 6016, Wellington; tel (4) 801-9709; fax (4) 385-4642.
Honorary Consul-General: Otto Tiefenbacher.

Consulate: 4 Ponui Place, Mount Wellington, POB 62080, Auckland 1; tel (9) 276-1735; fax (9) 276-1559.
Honorary Consul: Stanley L. Ellis.

Commercial Office: 7th Floor, 76 Symonds St, POB 310, Auckland; tel (9) 734-078; fax (9) 734-076.
Consul (Commercial): Dr Wilhelm Galathovics.

BELGIUM

Embassy: Robert Jones House, 1-3 Willeston St, POB 3841, Wellington; tel (4) 472-9558; telex 31452; fax (4) 471-2764.
Ambassador: R. K. Coenen.
Attaché (Consular and Trade): Greta J. Fernie-de Brabander.

Consulate: Penthouse, Fisher International Bldg, 18 Waterloo Quadrant, POB 4071, Auckland; tel (9) 799-960; fax (9) 309-9570.
Honorary Consul: Stephen B. Fisher.

Consulate: 56A Clyde Rd, POB 434, Christchurch; tel (3) 348-0969; fax (3) 793-636.
Honorary Consul: J. R. Maddren.

BRAZIL

Consulate: 135 Tamaki Drive, Mission Bay, POB 4356, Auckland 5; tel (9) 528-6681; fax (9) 521-2227.
Honorary Consul: Frank T. Thorpy.
Honorary Vice-Consul: Peter F. Thorpy.

BRUNEI

High Commission: c/o Ministry of Foreign Affairs, Bandar Seri Begawan, Brunei; tel (2) 241177; telex 2292; fax (2) 224709.
High Commissioner: Dato Paduka Lim Jock Seng (resident in Brunei).
First Secretary: Tan Bee Yong.
Second Secretary: Miss Noor Qamar Haji Sulaiman.

CANADA

High Commission: 3rd Floor, 61 Molesworth St, POB 12-049, Thorndon, Wellington 1; tel (4) 739-577; telex 3577; fax (4) 712-082.
High Commissioner: W. Esmond Jarvis.
Counsellor: Leslie A. K. James.
Commercial Counsellor: J. Robert Brocklebank.
Attaché: Monique Lefort.

Consulate: Princes Court, 2 Princes St, Auckland; POB 6186, Wellesley St Post Office, Auckland; tel (9) 309-3689; telex 21645; fax (9) 307-3111.
Consul and Trade Commissioner: Richard D. Pennick.

CHILE

Embassy: Robert Jones House, 12th Floor, 1-3 Willeston St, POB 3861, Wellington; tel (4) 725-180; telex 31034; fax (4) 725-324.
Ambassador: Thomas Rene Hirsch Goldschmidt.
Second Secretary: Eduardo Tapia.
Third Secretary and Consul: Francisco del Campo.
Third Secretary (Commercial): Ricardo Rojas.

Consulate: 21-39 Jellicoe Rd, Panmure, CPO Box 67, Auckland 6; tel (9) 527-8068; fax (9) 570-9511.
Honorary Consul: Helmut Peters.
Honorary Consul: Gerard J. P. Williams.

Consulate: 95 Oxford Terrace, POB 22-633, Christchurch; tel (3) 791-197.
Honorary Consul: M. E. Dormer.

CHINA, PEOPLE'S REPUBLIC

Embassy: 2-6 Glenmore St, Wellington; tel (4) 472-1382; telex 3843; fax (4) 499-0419.
Ambassador: Ni Zhengjian.
Counsellor: Wu Zuqiu.
Counsellor (Commercial): Ruan Jiageng.
First Secretary (Administrative): Zhang Jiasong.
First Secretary (Education): Lin Xinglang.
First Secretary (Press): Wang Xinyuan.
First Secretary (Consular): Xu Zongxi.
First Secretary: Ma Kezheng.
First Secretary (Commercial): Yang Jixiao.
Second Secretary (Cultural): Chen Yongshan.
Second Secretary (Commercial): Cao Jin.
Third Secretary (Science and Technology): Wang Yaohua.

COLOMBIA

Consulate: Wellington.

Consulate: 11 Hopkins Cres., Auckland 5; tel (9) 528-6591; fax (9) 521-3355.
Honorary Consul: Barrie Downey.

COSTA RICA

Consulate-General: Wellington.

CZECHOSLOVAKIA

Embassy: 12 Anne St, Wadestown, POB 2843, Wellington 1; tel (4) 472-3142; telex 31437; fax (4) 472-8268.
Ambassador: Jara David-Moserova (designate).
Chargé d'affaires a.i.: Stanislav Korvas.

DENMARK

Consulate-General: c/o Morrison Morpeth, 18th Floor, MARAC House, 105-109 The Terrace, POB 10-035, Wellington 1; tel (4) 472-0020; telex 30208; fax (4) 472-7017.
Honorary Consul-General: John Bentley Morrison.
Honorary Vice-Consul and Secretary: Edith I. Bradley.

Consulate: 273 Bleakhouse Rd, Howick, CPO Box 619, Auckland 1; tel (9) 537-3099; fax (9) 537-3067.
Honorary Consul: Niels Jaegersborg.

Trade Office: 4th Floor, Harbour View Bldg, 52 Quay St, POB 2154, Auckland 1; tel (9) 793-119; fax (9) 307-5207.
Trade Representative: Jens Peter Klausen.

Consulate: 100 Wainoni Rd, Christchurch 6; tel (3) 895-134; fax (3) 811-646.
Honorary Consul: Jørgen Cort Trap Schousboe.

Consulate: Scotwood Bldg, 12-20 St Andrew St, POB 5675, Dunedin; tel (24) 477-1981; telex 5367; fax (24) 477-1948.
Honorary Consul: Stuart C. Scott.

ECUADOR

Consulate: Wellington.

Consulate: McKay Shipping Ltd, POB 3, Ferry Bldg, 2nd Floor, Quai St, Auckland; tel (9) 309-0229; telex 2554; fax (9) 303-2931.
Honorary Consul: Ian McKay.

EL SALVADOR

Consulate: 24 Seccombes Rd, Epsom, Auckland; tel (9) 524-9376; fax (9) 274-0959.
Honorary Consul: T. K. Weal.

FIJI

Embassy: Level 13, Plimmer City Centre, cnr Boulcott St and Gilmer Terrace, POB 3940, Wellington; tel (4) 473-5401; telex 31406; fax (4) 499-1011.
Ambassador: Edward J. Beddoes.
First Secretary: Ross I. Ligairi.
Second Secretary: Daud Ali.

Consulate-General: 1st Floor, Southpac Tower, 45 Queen St, POB 4284, Auckland; tel (9) 773-955; fax (9) 773-954.
Consul-General: Dr Ahmed Ali.
Vice-Consul: Taniela Vocevoce.

FINLAND

Consulate-General: NZI House, 7th Floor, 25-33 Victoria St, POB 1201, Wellington; tel (4) 472-4924; telex 3221; fax (4) 499-1654.
Honorary Consul-General: Ronald Cameron Macdonald.
Honorary Vice-Consul: John Cameron Macdonald.

Consulate: Max Media Management Ltd, 10 Heather St, Parnell, POB 8553, Auckland; tel (9) 309-2969; telex 60660; fax (9) 357-0466.

Consul: Ari Juhani Hallenberg.

Consulate: Davis Ogilvie and Partners Ltd, 4th Floor, BNZ Bldg, 137 Armagh St, Christchurch; tel (3) 661-653; fax (3) 792-348.
Consul: Peter Yeoman.

Consulate: MFL Bldg, 11 Bond St, POB 141, Dunedin; tel (24) 778-674; telex 5610.
Honorary Consul: John Keith Skinner.

FRANCE

Embassy: Robert Jones Bldg, 13th Floor, 1-3 Willeston St, POB 1695, Wellington; tel (4) 472-0200; telex 3580; fax (4) 472-5887.
Ambassador: Gabriel de Regnauld de Bellescize.
Counsellor: Jean-Louis Rysto.
Defence Attaché: Lieut Col Roger Jargoyhen.
Counsellor (Commercial): Alexandre Troubetzkoy.
First Secretary (Consular): Alain Dubuy.

Cultural Service: POB 53; tel (4) 472-6325.
Counsellor (Cultural): Jean-Pierre Jarjanette.

Economic Section: Eagle Technology House, 150-154 Willis St, POB 11-148, Wellington; tel (4) 384-5042; telex 31309; fax (4) 384-5298.

Consulate: c/o Translink Pacific Shipping Ltd, 5th Floor, Guildford House, 2 Emily Place, Auckland; tel (9) 302-7629; telex 60805; fax (9) 302-7634.
Honorary Consul: Christian Jean-Louis.

Commercial Section: 44 Khyber Pass Rd, Suite II, Eden House, POB 3745, Auckland; POB 8000, Symonds St, Auckland; tel (9) 799-788; telex 60886; fax (9) 302-4043.
Head of Commercial Section: Kevin Bennewith.

Consulate: 15 Bryndwr Rd, Fendalton, Christchurch 5; tel (3) 351-6259; fax (3) 343-0102.
Honorary Consul: E. Lloyd Upton.

Consulate: c/o University of Otago, POB 56, Dunedin; tel (24) 472-8405; fax (24) 479-7906.
Honorary Consul: Dr David V. Fenby.

GERMANY

Embassy: 90-92 Hobson St, Thorndon, POB 1687, Wellington; tel (4) 736-063; telex 30131; fax (4) 736-069.
Ambassador: Dr Gerhard Weber.
Counsellor: Friedrich Neumann.
Second Secretary (Chancery): Karl Emser.
Second Secretary: Herbert Beck.
Third Secretary: Wolfgang Grams.
Third Secretary: Helmut Lörsch.
Attaché: Ingrid Chwolik.
Attaché: Uta Mendelin.

Consulate: Columbus House, 5th Floor, 52 Symonds St, CPO Box 3551, Auckland 1; tel (9) 773-460; telex 2455; fax (9) 393-003.
Honorary Consul: David Rex Brown.

Consulate: Tudor House, 95 Oxford Terrace, POB 1915, Christchurch; tel (3) 793-193; telex 4840; fax (3) 657-360.
Honorary Consul: Allan G. Williams.

GREECE

Consulate-General: 8th Floor, Cumberland House, 237 Willis St, POB 27-157, Wellington; tel (4) 847-556; fax (4) 385-4608.
Consul-General: I. G. Papadopoulos.
Vice-Consul: N. Anagnostopoulos.

Consulate-General: 14-6 Railside Ave, POB 21-033, Henderson, Auckland; tel (9) 837-2798; fax (9) 837-3650.
Honorary Consul: L. J. Nicola.

HOLY SEE

Apostolic Nunciature: 112 Queen's Drive, Lyall Bay, POB 14-044, Wellington 3; tel (4) 387-3470; fax (4) 387-8170.
Apostolic Pro-Nuncio: Most Rev. Thomas A. White, Titular Archbishop of Sabiona.
First Secretary: Rt Rev. Mgr Leopoldo Girelli.

ICELAND

Consulate-General: 88 Oriental Parade, POB 702, Wellington; tel (4) 385-7934; fax (4) 384-4375.
Honorary Consul-General: Denis F. M. Foot.

INDIA

High Commission: Princess Tower, 10th Floor, 180 Molesworth St, POB 4045, Wellington 1; tel (4) 736-390; telex 31676; fax (4) 499-0665.
High Commissioner: C. R. Balachandra.
First Secretary: E. P. P. Baa.
Military, Naval and Air Adviser: Capt. S. K. K. Krishnan.
Attaché: D. C. Barthwal.
Attaché: Harinder Singh.
Attaché: Mahinder Kumar.

INDONESIA

Embassy: 70 Glen Rd, Kelburn, POB 3543, Wellington; tel (4) 475-8697; telex 3892; fax (4) 759-374.
Ambassador: Abdul Irsan (designate).
Minister-Counsellor and Chargé d'affaires a.i.: Ibnu Ash Djamil Siregar.
Defence Attaché: Lieut Col Subagyo Saleh.
Counsellor: Ahlan Bahari Razif.
First Secretary (Administration): Kaspar Hasiaman Siregar.
Second Secretary (Information and Cultural): Tubagus Bastaman.
Second Secretary: Undin Suwarman.
Second Secretary (Consular): Nunung Asriyanti Anggawijaya.
Third Secretary (Administration): Hadi Sapto Pambrastoro.
Third Secretary: Nurtahrir Wongsonegoro.

IRAN

Embassy: POB 10249, The Terrace, Wellington; tel (4) 386-2976; telex 31226; fax (4) 386-3065.
Ambassador: Mohammad Taheri.
First Secretary: Kambiz Sheikh Hassani.
Attaché (Cultural and Commercial): Mr Nadali-Zadeh.
Attaché (Consular): Hamid Noor.
Attaché: Abdollah Allahdad.

IRELAND

Consulate-General: 2nd Floor, Dingwall Bldg, 87 Queen St, POB 279, Auckland 1; tel (9) 302-2867; telex 21437; fax (9) 302-2420.
Honorary Consul-General: Rodney H. C. Walshe.

ISRAEL

Embassy: Plimmer City Centre, 13th Floor, Plimmer Steps, POB 2171, Wellington; tel (4) 472-2362; telex 31221; fax (4) 499-0632.
Ambassador: Shmuel Ovnat.
First Secretary: Ze'ev Luria.
Second Secretary (Administration): Danny Gadot.

ITALY

Embassy: 34 Grant Rd, Thorndon, POB 463, Wellington 1; tel (4) 473-5339; telex 31571; fax (4) 472-7255.
Ambassador: Dr Ottone Mattei.
Attaché (Consular/Administrative): Remo Demicheli.

Commercial Office: 38 Grant Rd; tel (4) 473-6667.
Commercial Officer: Rosamaria Fucile Scialdone.

Consular Agency: 102 Kitchener Rd, Milford, POB 31-194, Auckland; tel (9) 486-1888.
Honorary Consular Agent: Mario M. Magaraggia.

Consular Agency: 48 Seven Oaks Drive, Brynder, Christchurch 5; tel (3) 359-7372.
Honorary Consular Agent: Valerie Mayer.

Consular Agency: 230 Forbury Rd, St Clair, Dunedin; tel (24) 455-8631.
Honorary Consular Agent: Dr Sergio Gian Salis.

JAPAN

Embassy: Norwich Insurance House, 7th-8th Floors, 3-11 Hunter St, POB 6340, Wellington 1; tel (4) 473-1540; telex 3544; fax (4) 471-2951.
Ambassador: Takeo Iguchi.
Minister: Jiro Kobayashi.
First Secretary: Hajime Sasaki.
First Secretary (Cultural) and Director, Information and Cultural Centre: Hyosuke Yasui.
First Secretary (Agricultural and Commercial) and National Fisheries Representative: Shiro Yoshimura.
First Secretary (Consular): Iwao Nakahashi.
Second Secretary: Matahiro Yamaguchi.
Second Secretary: Yukio Tsukagoshi.
Second Secretary (Economic): Ryuichi Kuwajima.

Information and Cultural Centre: Royal Exchange House, 111 Customhouse Quay, Wellington; tel (4) 472-7807.

Consulate-General: 6th Floor, National Mutual Centre Bldg, 37-45 Shortland St, POB 3959, Auckland 1; tel (9) 303-4106; telex 2665; fax (9) 777-784.
Consul-General: Yoichi Hayashi.
Consul: Akio Wada.
Consul: Masaaki Taniguchi.

Consular Office: 764 Colombo St, POB 1469, Christchurch 1; tel (3) 665-680; fax (3) 653-173.
Consular Affairs Officer: Hidero Yaji.

KIRIBATI

High Commission: c/o Ministry of Foreign Affairs, POB 68, Bairiki, Tarawa, Kiribati; tel 21342; telex 177054.
High Commissioner: P. T. Timeon (acting, resident in Kiribati).

Consulate: 32 Tohunga Cres., Parnell, Auckland; tel (9) 732-345; fax (9) 302-0944.
Honorary Consul: P. Ross Cook.

KOREA, REPUBLIC

Embassy: Elders House, 6th Floor, 86-96 Victoria St, POB 11-143, Wellington; tel (4) 473-9073; telex 3352.
Ambassador: Yoon Yeung Yeup.
Counsellor: Chung Shin.
Second Secretary, Consul and National Fisheries Representative: Lee Jong Kug.
Attaché (Administrative) and Vice-Consul: Seo Myung Chul.

Consulate: c/o Price Waterhouse, 119 Armagh St, POB 13-250, Christchurch; tel (3) 790-040; fax (3) 795-677.
Honorary Consul: Clyde L. Sugden.

MALAYSIA

High Commission: 10 Washington Ave, Brooklyn, POB 9422, Wellington; tel (4) 385-2019; fax (4) 385-6973.
High Commissioner: Dato' Anaitullah Karim.
Counsellor: T. Pathmanathan.
First Secretary: Mr Kamarulzaman bin Mohd Murad.
Defence Adviser: Lieut Col Mohd. Ghazali bin Alias.

Attaché (Education): Hj. Mohd Idris b. Hj. Md Yasin.
Second Secretary (Information): Mrs Faridah bt. Awang Ngah.
Second Secretary: Abd. Wahab bin Che Mat.
Second Secretary (Consular and Administration): Abd. Aziz bin Mohd Daud.
Attaché (Education): Abd. Ra'ani bin Ahmad.
Attaché (Education): Abd. Malek bin Bahari.
Attaché (Education): Enah bt. Keli.

Consulate: 14th Floor, 12-26 Swanson St, Auckland 1; tel (9) 307-2948; fax (9) 302-0755.
Honorary Consul: Leo Abbott.

Consulate: 14 Hazeldean Rd, POB 1367, Christchurch; tel (3) 338-9059; fax (3) 338-9828.
Honorary Consul: Sir Robertson Stewart.

MALTA

Consulate: 18 Barlow Place, Birkenhead, Auckland; tel (9) 418-2694; fax (9) 39-1418.
Honorary Consul: Alexander S. Abela.

Consulate: 39 Whitney Se, Auckland 7; tel (9) 886-658; fax (9) 309-0152.
Honorary Consul: Paul A. Micallef.

MAURITIUS

Consulate: 33 Great South Rd, Otahuhu, Auckland; tel (9) 276-3789; telex 2572; fax (9) 276-3342.
Honorary Consul: Gilbert W. Ullrich.

MEXICO

Consulate: Eagle Technology House, 150-154 Willis St, POB 3029, Wellington; tel (4) 385-2145; fax (4) 385-3510.
Honorary Consul: Esme L. Marris.
Honorary Vice-Consul: Martha Compton.

NAURU

Consulate-General: Sheraton Mall, 105 Symonds St, cnr KRD and Symonds St, POB 68-536, Newton, Auckland; tel (9) 799-348; telex 21506; fax (9) 375-222.
Consul-General: Marlene Moses.

NETHERLANDS

Embassy: Investment Centre, 10th Floor, cnr Featherstone and Ballance Sts, POB 840, Wellington; tel (4) 473-8652; telex 3987; fax (4) 471-2923.
Ambassador: G. J. du Marchie Sarvaas.
Counsellor: Walther R. Verhoeven.
Attaché (Administrative): S. M. G. Verdegem.

Migration Office: POB 974.
Attaché (Migration): Willem van der Ree.

Consulate: 6th Floor, Prudential House, 57 Symonds St, POB 3816, Auckland; tel (9) 795-399.
Honorary Consul: Alexander P. van Heeren.
Honorary Vice-Consul: Frank C. Mestrom.

Migration Office: 1st Floor, 21 Queen St, POB 4123, Auckland; tel (9) 798-356.
Emigration Officer: W. J. Walraad.

Consulate: c/o Hart Wool (NZ) Ltd, 161-163 Kilmore St, POB 3041, Christchurch; tel (3) 669-280; telex 4261; fax (3) 793-978.
Honorary Consul: Donald E. Quested.
Honorary Vice-Consul: J. A. Tasman.

Migration Office: tel (3) 662-928.

NORWAY

Consulate-General: 61 Molesworth St, POB 1990, Wellington; tel (4) 471-2503; telex 31015; fax (4) 472-8023.
Honorary Consul-General: P. Malcolm McCaw.

Consulate: 7th Floor, Westpac Securities Bldg, 120 Albert St, POB 25-319, St Heliers, Auckland; tel (9) 771-944; fax (9) 777-638.
Honorary Consul: Frank Ross.

Consulate: c/o McKenzie & Willis Ltd, cnr Tuam and High Sts, POB 22-047, Christchurch; tel (3) 798-980; fax (3) 666-521.
Honorary Consul: Paul Hedley Willis.

Consulate: Dunedin.

PAKISTAN

Consulate: POB 3830, Auckland 1; tel (9) 528-3526; fax (9) 372-238.
Honorary Consul: Brian R. Hunt.

PAPUA NEW GUINEA

High Commission: FAI House, 180 Molesworth St, POB 197, Wellington; tel (4) 473-1560; telex 31353; fax (4) 471-2942.
High Commissioner: Thomas Ritako.
First Secretary: A. Kali.

Consulate: 7th Floor, Stock Exchange Centre, 191 Queen St, POB 8853, Auckland; tel (9) 309-8180; fax (9) 309-3538.
Honorary Consul: Alister M. Martin.

PERU

Consulate: 199-209 Great North Rd, Grey Lynn, POB 28-083, Auckland; tel (9) 780-366; fax (9) 780-650.
Honorary Consul: Ross S. Wales.

PHILIPPINES

Embassy: 50 Hobson St, POB 12-042, Thorndon, Wellington North; tel (4) 472-9848; telex 31297; fax (4) 472-5170.
Ambassador: Ernesto V. Llamas.
Minister-Counsellor and Consul-General: Protasio S. Pablo.
Third Secretary and Vice-Consul: Leah M. Basinang.
Attaché (Administration and Consular): Maria O. Manglo.
Attaché: Leoncia R. Espiritu.

Consulate-General: NZ Dairy Board Bldg, 114 Dominion Rd, Mount Eden, POB 56-127, Auckland 3; tel (9) 623-4803; telex 2358; fax (9) 623-4890.
Honorary Consul-General: Graeme E. Dabb.

POLAND

Embassy: 196 The Terrace, Apt D, POB 10211, Wellington; tel (4) 471-2456; telex 30147; fax (4) 471-2455.

Office of Commercial Counsellor: 17 Upland Rd, Kelburn, Wellington.
Counsellor (Commercial) and Chargé d'affaires a.i.: Stanislaw Amanowicz.
Attaché (Commercial): Andrzej Soltysinski.

PORTUGAL

Consulate: Deloitte Ross Tohmatsu, 61 Molesworth St, POB 1990, Wellington; tel (4) 721-677; telex 31015; fax (4) 728-023.
Honorary Consul: Maxwell W. Downes.

Consulate: 85 Fort St, POB 105, Auckland; tel (9) 309-1545; fax (9) 308-9061.
Honorary Consul: D. C. Silva.

RUSSIA

Embassy: 57 Messines Rd, Karori, Wellington; tel (4) 476-4084; telex 3672; fax (4) 476-3843.
Ambassador: Yuri Mikhailovich Sokolov.
Counsellor (Commercial) and National Trade Representative: Dr Alexandre A. Kovalev.
Counsellor (Political): Dr Rouben M. Azizian.
First Secretary: Stanislav V. Kudriakov.
First Secretary: Sergei V. Garmonin.
Second Secretary: Vladimir Petrov.
Second Secretary (Consular): Vladimir F. Fedotov.
Attaché: Victor I. Malioutine.
Attaché: Vladimir N. Bakalov.

Consular Office: tel (4) 766-742.

Commercial Office: tel (4) 476-7821; fax (4) 476-6205.

Information Section: 233 Willis St, Wellington; tel (4) 384-7190; telex 3213; fax (4) 384-9494.
First Secretary and Head of Information Section: Mikhail Yefimov.

Office of National Fisheries Representative: Southern Cross Bldg, 22 Brandon St, POB 296, Wellington; tel (4) 472-3748; telex 3351.
Attaché and National Fisheries Representative: Arkadi P. Doudenkov.

SINGAPORE

High Commission: 17 Kabul St, Khandallah, POB 29-023, Wellington; POB 13-140, Johnsonville, Wellington; tel (4) 479-2076; telex 3593; fax (4) 479-2315.
High Commissioner: V. K. Rajan.
First Secretary: Leow Siu Lin.
Third Secretary: Yap Beng Ai.

SOLOMON ISLANDS

High Commission: c/o Ministry of Foreign Affairs, POB G10, Honiara, Solomon Islands; tel 21250; telex 66311.

SPAIN

Consulate: POB 71, Papakura, Auckland; tel (9) 298-5176; fax (9) 299-8057.
Honorary Consul: D. E. Lees.

Consulate: Mancan House, cnr Manchester St and Cambridge Terrace, POB 13-637, Christchurch; tel (3) 660-244; fax (3) 669-859.
Honorary Consul: Bartholomew Porta.

SRI LANKA

Consulate: c/o Open Polytechnic, Private Bag, Lower Hutt, Wellington; tel (4) 566-6189; fax (4) 566-5633.
Honorary Consul: Rudra de Zoysa.

SWEDEN

Embassy: Greenock House, 8th Floor, 39 The Terrace, POB 5350, Wellington 1; tel (4) 472-0909; telex 30692; fax (4) 471-2097.
Ambassador: Hans Andén.
First Secretary: Mats Lindström.
Third Secretary: Christina Fridlizius.

Consulate: Level 1, 60 Parnell Rd, POB 37028, Auckland; tel (9) 735-332; telex 3660; fax (9) 735-702.
Honorary Consul and Trade Representative: Hans Erik Björklund.

Trade Council: POB 37542; tel (9) 302-2879.

Consulate: c/o Pyne, Gould and Guinness Ltd, 178 Cashel St, POB 167, Christchurch; tel (3) 650-000; telex 4460; fax (3) 798-616.
Honorary Consul: Arthur Humphrey Gould.

Consulate: Trident House, 40 Jetty St, POB 385, Dunedin; tel (24) 474-0810; telex 5788; fax (24) 479-0448.
Honorary Consul: Ian James Farquhar.

SWITZERLAND

Embassy: Panama House, 7th Floor, 22-24 Panama St, POB 386, Wellington 1; tel (4) 472-1593; telex 31539; fax (4) 499-6302.
Ambassador: Dr Michael von Schenck.

Second Secretary and Consul: Peter Graf.
Attaché and Vice-Consul: Erika Grossenbacher.

Consular Agency: POB 49-019, Auckland; tel (9) 674-725.
Honorary Consul: Arthur W. Muller.

THAILAND

Embassy: 2 Cook St, Karori, POB 17-226, Wellington; tel (4) 768-618; telex 30162; fax (4) 763-677.
Ambassador: Asda Jayanama.
Minister-Counsellor: Chalermchat Tasukon.
First Secretary: Artaporn Puthikampol.
First Secretary: Paradee Siriwat.
Attaché (Administration): Jutarat Chuchart.

TONGA

Agency: Messrs Spedding Ltd, 655 Great South Rd, Penrose, POB 13-166, Onehunga, Auckland; tel (9) 579-7190; telex 63583; fax (9) 579-5661.

TURKEY

Consulate-General: 404 Khyber Pass Rd, Newmarket, Auckland 1; tel (9) 522-2281; fax (9) 522-2281.
Honorary Consul-General: A. N. Kavvas.

TUVALU

Consulate-General: POB 100-375, North Shore Mail Centre, Auckland; tel (9) 410-6463; fax (9) 410-6923.
Honorary Consul-General: Peter L. Jones.

UNITED KINGDOM

High Commission: 44 Hill St, POB 1812, Wellington 1; tel (4) 472-6049; telex 3325; fax (4) 471-1974.
High Commissioner: David J. Moss.
Deputy High Commissioner: I. C. Orr.
Defence Adviser and Senior Defence Liaison Officer: Capt. Michael J. Matthews.
Counsellor (Chancery): Thomas Hugo Preston.
First Secretary (Agriculture and Food): Evelyn A. Blackwell.
First Secretary (Commercial): Peter Rogan.
First Secretary (Chancery/Information): James Robert Setterfield.
Second Secretary (Chancery): Timothy Achille Torlot.
Second Secretary (Consular/Administrative): Raymond Leadbeater.
Attaché (Cultural) and British Council Representative: D. J. Francis King.

Commercial Section: POB 369.

Consulate-General: 17th Floor, Faye Richwhite Bldg, 151 Queen St, Private Bag, Auckland 1; tel (9) 303-2970; telex 2412; fax (9) 303-1836.
Consul-General and Counsellor (Commercial): John F. Holding.
Consul (Commercial): Vernon M. Scarborough.
Vice-Consul (Immigration/Administration): Carol Priestley.

Consulate: 2nd Floor Suite, 173 Cashel St, Christchurch 1; POB 6109, Riccarton, Christchurch 8004; tel (3) 655-440; fax (3) 652-350.
Honorary Consul: Graeme N. Robinson.

USA

Embassy: 29 Fitzherbert Terrace, POB 1190, Thorndon, Wellington; tel (4) 722-068; fax (4) 712-380.
Ambassador: Della M. Newman.
Counsellor: David M. Walker.
Counsellor (Political Affairs): Keith P. McCormick.
Counsellor (Public Affairs): William J. A. Barnes.
Defence Attaché: Capt. Linda J. Balink-White.
Counsellor (Administrative Affairs) and Consul: Landon C. Carter.
Counsellor (Economic Affairs): Ronnie D. Woody.
First Secretary: Robert H. Mills.
First Secretary and Consul: Robert A. Callard.
First Secretary: Theodore H. Jabbs.
Attaché (Agricultural): John T. Hopkins.

Consulate-General: 4th Floor, Yorkshire General Bldg, cnr Shortland and O'Connell Sts, Private Bag, Auckland; tel (9) 303-2724; fax (9) 366-0870.
Consul-General: Michael D. Bellows.
Consul (Commercial): Bobette K. Orr.
Consul: Alma F. Engel.

Consulate: Price Waterhouse Centre, 119 Armagh St, POB 13-250, Christchurch; tel (3) 790-040; fax (3) 795-677.
Consular Agent: J. Malcolm Ott.

Information Service Branch Office: National Mutual Finance House, 2nd Floor, 728 Colombo St, POB 4221, Christchurch; tel (3) 661-097.

URUGUAY

Consulate: 178 Cashel St, POB 167, Christchurch; tel (3) 650-000; telex 4460; fax (3) 798-616.
Honorary Consul: David Cassells.

VANUATU

High Commission: c/o Ministry of Foreign Affairs and Judicial Services, Monford St, Private Mail Bag, Port Vila, Vanuatu; tel 22347; telex 1040; fax 23142.
High Commissioner: Nikenike Vurobaravu (resident in Vanuatu).

WESTERN SAMOA

High Commission: 1A Wesley Rd, Kelburn, POB 1430, Wellington; tel (4) 720-953; telex 31043; fax (4) 712-479.
High Commissioner: Lupematasila Aumua Ioane.
Second Secretary: Elena Peteru.
Second Secretary: Cam Wendt.

Consulate-General: Samoa House, 283 Karangahape Rd, POB 68-147, Newton, Auckland; tel (9) 303-1012; fax (9) 302-1168.
Consul-General: Laulu Fetauimalemau Mata'afa.
Vice-Consul (Immigration): Tafili Tauafiafi Iutoi Tauafiafi.

YUGOSLAVIA

Embassy: 24 Hatton St, Karori, Wellington 5; tel (4) 476-4200; fax (4) 476-6607.
Chargé d'affaires a.i.: Luka Mestrovic.

Consulate: 12th Floor, National Insurance Bldg, 27-35 Victoria St West, CPO Box 6, Auckland; tel (9) 358-3400; fax (9) 358-3401.
Honorary Consul: Rade Ante Vuletic.

NICARAGUA

ARGENTINA

Embassy: Reparto Las Colinas, Pasaje Los Cerros No 111, Apdo 703, Managua, JR; tel (2) 74412; telex 1321.
Ambassador: José Pedro Pico.

AUSTRALIA

Consulate: de los Pipitis 1c abajo, 1/2 al Lago, Managua, JR; tel (2) 664653; telex 1370; fax (2) 26602.
Honorary Consul: Peter Braddock.

AUSTRIA

Consulate-General: Managua, JR.
Development Co-operation Counsellor: Josef Pernerstorfer.

BRAZIL

Embassy: Km 7 3/4, Carretera Sur, Quinta los Pinos, Apdo 264, Managua, JR; tel (2) 50035; telex 1237.
Ambassador: Sergio de Queiroz Duarte.

BULGARIA

Embassy: Reparto Las Colinas, Calle Los Mangos 195, Apdo 1491, Managua, JR; tel (2) 72274.
Ambassador: Stilian Burjanlarski.
Counsellor: Kiril Kirilov.
Counsellor: Mijail Zajariev.
Economic and Commercial Counsellor: Vera Nikolova.
Commercial Attaché: Stoyan Anguelov.

CAMBODIA

Embassy: Managua, JR.
Ambassador: Long Visalo.

CANADA

Consulate: 208 Calle del Triunfo, Frente Plazoleta Telcor Central, Apdo 514, Managua, JR; tel (2) 24541; fax (2) 624923.
Honorary Consul: Alberto Belli.

CHILE

Embassy: Km 13.8 Carretera Sur, 200m a mano izquierda, Apdo 1704, Managua, JR.
Chargé d'affaires a.i.: Eduardo Vega Bezanilla.

CHINA, PEOPLE'S REPUBLIC

Embassy: Managua, JR.
Ambassador: Huang Zhiliang.

COLOMBIA

Embassy: Reparto Los Robles, Apdo 1062, Managua, JR; tel (2) 70247.
Ambassador: Abelardo Duarte.

COSTA RICA

Embassy: Centro Comercial Camino de Oriente, contiguo a AERONICA, Managua, JR.
Ambassador: Jesús Manuel Fernández.

CUBA

Embassy: Las Colinas Sur, 2a entrada, Managua, JR.
Ambassador: Julián López Díaz.

CZECHOSLOVAKIA

Embassy: esq. opuesta donde fue la mansión Teodolinda, Calle Miguel Angel Bonilla, Barrio Bolonia, Apdo 929, Managua, JR; tel (2) 23390.
Ambassador: Zdenek Dlesk.
First Secretary: Bohumil Pikna.
Third Secretary (Culture): Jan Gabor.
Third Secretary (Culture): Natasa Bratkova.
Commercial Counsellor: Eugen Brezina.
Commercial Attaché: Pavol Polenec.
Administrator: Jiri Tupy.

DENMARK

Embassy: Managua, JR.

Consulate-General: Iglesia 'El Carmen', 2c al Oeste no 1610, Apdo 2703, Managua, JR; tel (2) 23189; telex 2387.
Consul-General: Niels Grøn.
Vice-Consul: Dietrich Ernst Günter Zimmermann.

Consulate: Apdo 3, Corinto; tel (342) 337; telex 1292.
Vice-Consul: Rogerio Palazio de Colle.

DOMINICAN REPUBLIC

Embassy: Reparto Las Colinas, Prado Ecuestre 100, con Curva de los Gallos, Apdo 614, Managua, JR.
Ambassador: Miguel Angel Decamps.

ECUADOR

Embassy: Sierritas de Santo Domingo, Managua, JR; tel (2) 23481; telex 2384.
Ambassador: Pablo Yáñez Cossío.

EL SALVADOR

Embassy: Reparto Las Colinas, Avda Las Colinas y Pasaje Los Cerros, Apdo 149, Managua, JR.
Chargé d'affaires a.i.: Joaquín Maza Martelli.

FINLAND

Embassy: del Porton Militar 1c al Lago, 1c y 25 varas abajo, 303, Sucursal Jorge Navarro, Apdo 2219, Managua, JR; tel (2) 22661; fax (2) 663416.
Attaché (Development Co-operation): Inger Hirvelä López.

Consulate: Apdo 1116, Managua, JR; tel (2) 23493; telex 03751005; fax (2) 24801.
Consul: Rodolfo Cardenal Martínez.

FRANCE

Embassy: Km 12, Carretera del Sur, Apdo 1227, Managua, JR; tel (2) 26210.
Ambassador: Richard Narich.

Economic Section: Apdo 2259; tel (2) 22463; telex 1047.

GERMANY

Embassy: Del Parque de la Madre (Plaza España), 1c al Lago, contiguo a la Optica Nicaragüense, Apdo 29, Managua, JR; tel (2) 23343; telex 1070; fax (2) 621191.
Ambassador: Georg Boomgaarden.

Consulate: Casa Cural 101, Corinto; tel (342) 416.
Honorary Consul: Pfarrer Josef Schendel.

GUATEMALA

Embassy: 11 1/2, Carretera a Masaya, Apdo E-1, Managua, JR.
Chargé d'affaires a.i.: Alfonso Aquino S.

HOLY SEE

Apostolic Nunciature: Km 10 y 800 m Carretera Sur, entrada a Quinta Tirrenia, Apdo 506, Managua, JR; tel (2) 50552; telex 2482.
Apostolic Nuncio: Most Rev. Paolo Giglio, Titular Archbishop of Tyndaris.
Secretary: Mgr Baudouin Maunkembe.

HONDURAS

Embassy: Km 7 1/2, Carretera Sur, Reparto Barcelona, Apdo 321, Managua, JR.
Ambassador: Herminio Pineda.

HUNGARY

Embassy: De la Central Sandinista de Trabajadores, 7c al Sur, esq. frente al Terraza, Casa 304, Barrio Bolonia, Apdo 2395, Managua, JR; tel (2) 22343; telex 1398.
Chargé d'affaires a.i.: Gyorgy Abelovszki.
First Secretary: Imre Helyes.
Second Secretary: Sandor Nagy.
Counsellor: Laszlo Gyuro.

ICELAND

Embassy: Managua, JR.

IRAN

Embassy: Calle Vista Alegre 93, Las Colinas, Managua, JR.

ITALY

Embassy: Avda del Guerrillero de Montoya, 1c al Lago, Apdo 2092, Managua 4, JR; tel (2) 662961; telex 1437; fax (2) 664319.
Ambassador: Dr Luigi Mercolini.
Attaché: Fernando Grassi.
Attaché: Luciano Oddo.
Attaché: Paolo Del Monte Oddo.
Attaché: Michelangelo Falino.
Attaché: Maria Vittoria Di Maggio.

JAPAN

Embassy: Del Hospital Militar 1c. al Lago, 1 1/2 c abajo, Mano Izq., Bolonia, Apdo 1789, Managua, JR; tel (2) 623092; telex 2080; fax (2) 627393.
Ambassador: Konishi Yoshizo.
Counsellor: Mochizuki Tadayoshi.
First Secretary: Ueno Hisashi.
Third Secretary: Sato Makoto.
Attaché: Sugisawa Shuji.
Attaché: Nomura Masahiro.

KOREA, DEMOCRATIC PEOPLE'S REPUBLIC

Embassy: De la Central Sandinista de Trabajadores, 2c al Sur y 1c abajo, Managua, JR.
Ambassador: Oh Sung Hwan.

LIBYA

People's Bureau: Mansión Teodolinda, 6c al sur, 1/2c abajo, Managua, JR.
Secretary of the People's Bureau: Ibrahim Mohamed Farhat.

MEXICO

Embassy: Frente Oficinas Telcor de Altamira, Km 4 1/2 a Masaya, Apdo 834, Managua, JR; tel (2) 75275; telex 1241.
Ambassador: Jorge Luis Olivárez Novales.

Office of Development Co-operation Counsellor: de la Plaza España 3c abajo 1c al Lago 11/2c arriba, Apdo 3173, Managua, JR; tel (2) 663316; telex 1093.

MONGOLIA

Embassy: Managua, JR.
Ambassador: G. Dashdaava.

PANAMA

Embassy: Reparto San Juan, Calle El Carmen 619, Managua, JR.
Ambassador: Baltazar Aizpurna.

PERU

Embassy: Barrio Bolonia, Frente a Procuraduría General de Justicia, Apdo 211, Managua, JR; tel (2) 22376; telex 2100; fax (2) 22381.
Ambassador: Manuel Boza Heck.

POLAND

Embassy: 17 Avda Calle S.O. y 13a Avda, Barrio Bolonia, Managua, JR.
Ambassador: Bronisław Wilczak.

RUSSIA

Embassy: Reparto Las Colinas, Calle Vista Alegre 214, entre Avda Central y Paseo del Club, Apdo 249, Managua, JR; tel (2) 79460; telex 2436.
Ambassador: Yevgeni Mikhailovich Astakhov.

SPAIN

Embassy: Avda Central 13, Las Colinas, Apdo 284, Managua, JR; tel (2) 71321; telex 2003; fax (2) 678153.
Ambassador: Miguel Angel Fernández-Mazarambroz Bernabeu.
Counsellor and Deputy Head of Mission: Manuel Hernandez Ruigomez.
Military Attaché: Bernardino Buceta Lopez.
Commercial Counsellor: Jose Ramon Herreros de las Cuevas.
Co-operation Attaché: Jose Echezarreta Bedia.
Attaché: Beatriz Calderon Fornos.
Security Attaché: Ruben Fernandez Escalante.
Communications Attaché: Antonio Castelo Pacio.
Chancellor: Carlos Remacha Elvira.

Consulate: Avda Central 405, León; tel (311) 4376; fax (311) 2042.
Consul: Jose Escudero Gomez.

SWEDEN

Embassy: De la Sub-Estación de Telcor, Las Palmas, 50 varas al Sur, a mano derecha, Casa 2601, Apdo 2307, Managua, JR; tel (2) 660085; telex 1353; fax (2) 666778.
Ambassador: Harald Fälth.
Second Secretary: Anders Kviele.
Second Secretary: Karin Sjöberg.
Head of Aid Office: Carl-Gustav Svensson.

SWITZERLAND

Embassy: Pasaje los cerros Las Colinas, Apdo 166, Managua, JR; tel (2) 74173; telex 2424; fax (2) 72895.
Honorary Consul: Karl Morizzo.

UNITED KINGDOM

Embassy: El Reparto Los Robles 1°, entrada principal de la Carretera de Masaya, 4a Casa al mano derecha, Managua, JR; tel (2) 70034; telex 2166; fax (2) 73827.
Resident Chargé d'affaires and First Secretary: Roger H. Brown.
Third Secretary: P. T. Connolly.

USA

Embassy: Km 4 1/2, Carretera Sur, Apdo 327, Managua, JR; tel (2) 666010; fax (2) 666046.
Ambassador: Harry W. Shlaudeman.
Deputy Chief of Mission: Ronald Dgodard.
Political Section: Edmund F. McWilliams.
Economic Section: Miguel De La Pena.
Consular Section: J. Taylor Blanton.
Administrative Section: Roger E. Burgess, Jr.
Regional Security Officer: Daniel J. Pocus.
Public Affairs Officer: Stedman D. Howard.
Communications Programme Officer: Frederick E. King.
Information Systems Manager: Frederick R. Sadler.
Agency for International Development: Janet C. Ballantyne.
Office of the Defence Attaché: Lieut Col Dennis F. Quinn.

URUGUAY

Embassy: Del portón del Hospital Militar 1 cuadro al Lago, y 1 1/2 abajo, Apdo 3746, Managua, Jr; tel (2) 25542; telex 1348.
Ambassador: Alfredo Lafone.

VENEZUELA

Embassy: Edif. Málaga 2°, Plaza España, Módulo A-13, Apdo 406, Managua, JR; tel (2) 74343; telex 1380; fax (2) 678327.
Ambassador: J. J. Monsant.
Minister-Counsellor: Nelson Barreto.
Counsellor: Marco Tulio Castellanos.
First Secretary: Luis Jorge Narvaez.
Attaché: Raul José Betancourt S.

VIET-NAM

Embassy: Zona Residencial Planetarium, Paseo Saturno, Casa CS10, esq. Vía Láctea, Managua, JR; tel (2) 52186.
Ambassador: Le Duc Cang.
First Secretary: Thai Van Lung.
Third Secretary: Phan Trieu Lap.

YUGOSLAVIA

Embassy: Apdo 3463, Managua, JR; tel (2) 72847.
Ambassador: Dušan Trifunović.

NIGER

ALGERIA

Embassy: ave des Zarmakoye, BP 142, Niamey; tel 72-31-65; telex 5262.
Ambassador: Rachid Aktouf.

BELGIUM

Embassy: BP 10192, Niamey; tel 73-34-47; telex 5329.
Ambassador: Renier Nijskens.

BENIN

Embassy: BP 11544, Niamey; tel 72-39-19.
Ambassador: Mouhammad-Mach'houd Kelani.
Second Counsellor: Viaïnon Fassinou Roger Hayafanme.
Attaché: Vincent Iwikotan.
Attaché: Cyrille Gabriel Vianou.
Attaché: Etienne Sourou.
Secretary to the Ambassador: Marie Chantal Saka.

CANADA

Embassy: Sonara II Bldg, ave du Premier Pont, BP 362, Niamey; tel 73-36-86; telex 5264; fax 73-50-64.
Counsellor (Development) and Consul: A. L. Potvin.
First Secretary (Development): D. Menezes-Dufresne.
First Secretary (Development): G. Montcalm.
First Secretary (Development): D. Provost.
First Secretary (Development) and Consul: J. Couturier.
First Secretary (Development): M. Gagnon.
Second Secretary (Development): T.-B.-M. Pham.

CHINA, PEOPLE'S REPUBLIC

Embassy: rue des Dallols, Quartier Nouveau Plateau, BP 725, Niamey; tel 72-23-32; telex 5452; fax 72-25-28.
Ambassador: Wu Donghe.
Political Counsellor: Zeng Huanfen.
Economic Counsellor: Zhang Kewei.
First Secretary: Sun Qiaocheng.
First Secretary: Liu Yushan.
First Secretary: Zhou Yi.

DENMARK

Consulate: BP 536, Niamey; tel 72-37-96; fax 73-28-81.
Consul: Absi Hamani.

EGYPT

Embassy: Nouveau Plateau, Niamey; tel 73-33-55; telex 5245.
Ambassador: Dr Sobhy Mohamed Nafeh.

FRANCE

Embassy: route de Yantala, BP 10660, Niamey; tel 72-24-31; telex 5220.
Ambassador: Michel Lunven.

Economic Section: BP 12831; tel 73-28-85; telex 5496.

Consulate: place Nelson Mandela, BP 607; tel 72-27-22.

Consulate: Zone urbaine de la Somair, parcelle 3, BP 199, Arlit; tel 45-21-40.

GERMANY

Embassy: 71 ave du Général de Gaulle, BP 629, Niamey; tel 72-25-34; telex 5223.
Ambassador: Sepp-Jürgen Wölker.

ICELAND

Embassy: Niamey.

IRAN

Embassy: ave de la Présidence, Niamey; tel 72-21-98.
Chargé d'affaires: Faghih ali Abadi Mehdi.

LIBYA

People's Committee: BP 683, Rond-Point du Grand Hôtel, Niamey; tel 73-47-92; telex 5429.
Secretary of People's Committee: Ahmed Khalifa Errajel.

MAURITANIA

Embassy: route de Yantala, BP 12519, Niamey; tel 72-38-93.
Ambassador: Mohamed el Houssein Ould Habibou Allah.

MOROCCO

Embassy: ave du Président Lubke, BP 12403, Niamey; tel 73-40-84; telex 5205.
Ambassador: Tahar Nejjar.

NIGERIA

Embassy: BP 11130, Niamey; tel 73-24-10; telex 5259.
Ambassador: Aihaji J. Kogura.

PAKISTAN

Embassy: BP 10426, Niamey; tel 72-35-84; telex 5268.
Chargé d'affaires: Shahryar Rashed.

RUSSIA

Embassy: BP 10153, Niamey; tel 73-27-40; telex 5539.
Ambassador: Vitaly Yakovlevich Litvine.

Consular Section: tel 73-39-62.

SAUDI ARABIA

Embassy: route de Yantala, BP 339, Niamey; tel 72-32-15; telex 5279.
Ambassador: Ghassan Said Sadek Rachach.

SWEDEN

Embassy: Niamey.
Ambassador: Bengt Holmquist (resident in Sweden).

Consulate: Entreprises Henri Georget, Côte Rd, Point des Forces Armées, BP 294, Niamey; tel 73-20-85; telex 5345.
Consul: Henri Rougier Georget.

SWITZERLAND

Embassy: BP 728, Niamey; tel 72-36-90; telex 5505.
Attaché (Development Co-operation/Humanitarian Aid/Consular): Jean-Paul Baerfuss.

TUNISIA

Embassy: ave du Général de Gaulle, BP 742, Niamey; tel 72-26-03; telex 5379.
Ambassador: Rhida Tnani.

UNITED KINGDOM

Embassy: Niamey.

Consulate: BP 11168, Niamey; tel 73-20-51; telex 5244; fax 73-36-92.
Honorary Consul: Barkire Niandou.

USA

Embassy: rue des Ambassades, BP 11201, Niamey; tel 72-26-61; telex 5444.
Ambassador: Carl Copeland Cundiff.
Deputy Chief of Mission: David C. Litt.
Political Section: Philip Bauso.
Economic/Consular Section: Douglas van Treeck.
Regional Security Officer: Wayne E. May.
Public Affairs Officer: Claudia Anyaso.
Communications Programme Officer: Robert A. Lacock.
Security Assistance Office: Maj. Michael Connell.

International Organizations

EUROPEAN COMMUNITIES

External Delegation: rue de l'Afrique - route de Kollo, BP 10388, Niamey; tel 73-23-60; telex 5267; fax 73-23-22.
Commission Delegate: Elio Germano.
Counsellor (Civil): Reinhard Ebersberg.
Counsellor (Rural Development): Robert Chavez.
Counsellor (Rural Development): Jacques Favre.
Counsellor (Economic): Henry Sprietsma.

NIGERIA

ALGERIA

Embassy: 26 Maitama Sule St, SW Ikoyi, POB 7288, Lagos; tel (1) 683155; telex 21676.
Ambassador: El-Mihoub Mihoubi.

ANGOLA

Embassy: 5 Kasumu Ekomode St, Victoria Island, POB 50437, Lagos.
Ambassador: B. A. Sozinho.

ARGENTINA

Embassy: 93 Awolowo Rd, SW Ikoyi, POB 51940, Lagos; tel (1) 682797; telex 21403.
Ambassador: Federico C. Barttfeld.

AUSTRALIA

High Commission: Nurses' House, Plot PC 12, Afribank, Victoria Island, POB 2427, Lagos; tel (1) 618875; telex 21219; fax (1) 618703.
High Commissioner: O. J. Cordell.

AUSTRIA

Embassy: Plot 1656, 7A Olosa St, Victoria Island, POB 1914, Lagos; tel (1) 616081; telex 21463.
Ambassador: Dr Wolfgang Pridun.
Counsellor: Klaus Derkowitsch.
Economic Counsellor: Johann Deutsch.

BELGIUM

Embassy: 1A Bank Rd, Ikoyi, POB 149, Lagos; tel (1) 603230; telex 21118; fax (1) 619683.
Ambassador: Michel Czetwertynski.

BENIN

Embassy: 4 Abudu Smith St, Victoria Island, POB 5705, Lagos; telex 21583.
Ambassador: Patrice Houngavou.

BRAZIL

Embassy: 257 Kofo Abayomi St, Victoria Island, POB 1931, Lagos; tel (1) 610135; telex 23428; fax (1) 613394.
Ambassador: Brian M. F. Neele.

BULGARIA

Embassy: Eleke Crescent, Victoria Island, PMB 4441, Lagos; telex 21567.
Ambassador: P. S. Konstantinov.

BURKINA FASO

Embassy: 15 Norman Williams St, Ikoyi, Lagos.
Chargé d'affaires: Adolphe T. Benon.

CAMEROON

Embassy: 5 Elsie Femi Pearse St, Victoria Island, PMB 2476, Lagos; telex 21343.
Ambassador: Souaibou Hayatou.

CANADA

High Commission: Committee of Vice-Chancellors Bldg, Plot 8A, 4 Idowu-Taylor St, Victoria Island, POB 54506, Ikoyi Station, Lagos; tel (1) 612382; telex 21275; fax (1) 614691.
High Commissioner: Robert L. Elliott.
Counsellor: P. L. K. Hahn.
First Secretary (Commercial): R. H. Merrick.
First Secretary: F. Fullerton.
Second Secretary (Administration): R. Hamilton.
Second Secretary (Commercial): M. C. Danagher.
Attaché: W. Vandermeer.

CENTRAL AFRICAN REPUBLIC

Embassy: Plot 137, Ajao Estate, New Airport, Oshodi, Lagos.
Ambassador: Jean-Paul Mokodopo.

CHAD

Embassy: 2 Goriola St, Victoria Island, POB 70662, Victoria Island, Lagos; tel (1) 613116; telex 21414.
Ambassador: Abdelkerim Mahamat.
First Counsellor: Nodjitoloum Yogangné Joab.
Second Counsellor: Abdallah Mahamoud Arabi.
First Secretary: Allate Detoyna.
Second Secretary: Nourene Abderamane.
Attaché: Salahdine Ali Djouffon.

CHILE

Embassy: Lagos.
Chargé d'affaires: Héctor Vilches-Torres.

CHINA, PEOPLE'S REPUBLIC

Embassy: 19A Taslim Elias Close, Victoria Island, POB 5653, Lagos.
Ambassador: Jin Boxiong.

COLOMBIA

Embassy: 43 Raymond Njoku Rd, POB 2352, Ikoyi, Lagos.
Chargé d'affaires: Dr Bernardo Echeverri.

COTE D'IVOIRE

Embassy: 3 Abudu Smith St, Victoria Island, POB 7780, Lagos; telex 21120.
Ambassador: Desiré Amon Tanoe.

CUBA

Embassy: Plot 935, Idejo St, POB 328, Victoria Island, Lagos; tel (1) 6148.
Ambassador: Juan B. Infante Dilù.

CZECHOSLOVAKIA

Embassy: 2 Alhaji Masha Close, Ikoyi, POB 1009, Lagos; tel (1) 683207.
Ambassador: Václav Bejcek.

DENMARK

Embassy: 4 Eleke Crescent, Victoria Island, POB 2390, Lagos; tel (1) 610537; telex 21349.
Ambassador: Peter Rosting.
Attaché and Vice-Consul: Ebbe Petersen.

EGYPT

Embassy: 81 Awolowo Rd, Ikoyi, POB 538, Lagos.
Ambassador: M. M. Soliman.

EQUATORIAL GUINEA

Embassy: 7 Bank Rd, Ikoyi, POB 4162, Lagos.
Ambassador: A. S. Dougan Malabo.

ETHIOPIA

Embassy: Plot 97, Ahmadu Bello Rd, Victoria Island, PMB 2488, Lagos; tel (1) 613198; telex 21694.
Ambassador: Legesse Wolde-Mariam.

FINLAND

Embassy: 13 Eleke Crescent, Victoria Island, POB 4433, Lagos; tel (1) 610524; telex 21796.
Ambassador: Esko Kunnamo.

FRANCE

Embassy: 1 Queen's Drive, POB 567, Ikoyi, Lagos; tel (1) 603300; telex 21338.
Ambassador: Jacques Thibau.

Economic Section: POB 12665; tel (1) 684392; telex 22654.

GABON

Embassy: 8 Norman Williams St, POB 5989, Lagos; tel (1) 684673; telex 21736.
Ambassador: E. Agueminya.

GAMBIA

High Commission: 162 Awolowo Rd, SW Ikoyi, POB 8037, Lagos.
High Commissioner: Omar Secka.

GERMANY

Embassy: 15 Eleke Crescent, Victoria Island, POB 728, Lagos; tel (1) 611011; telex 21229.
Ambassador: Leonhard Kremer.

Consulate: c/o Western Nigerian Technical Co. Ltd, PMB 5148, 22 Fajuiyi Rd, Dugbe, Ibadan, Oyo State; tel (22) 411291.
Honorary Consul: Helmut-Otto Nau.

GHANA

High Commission: 21-23 King George V Rd, Onikan, POB 889, Lagos; tel (1) 630015.
High Commissioner: Brig. Kwaku Adu-Bediako.
Deputy High Commissioner: Samuel Ansah-Antwi.
Counsellor (Consular): Samuel T. Okantey.
Counsellor and Head of Chancery: Robert K. Gardemor.
First Secretary (Consular): Paul B. Antwi.
First Secretary (Protocol/Welfare): Francis M. Brown.
Second Secretary (Finance): Yaw A. Yirenkyi.
Third Secretary (Administration): Margaret Erskine-Ampah.
Third Secretary (Communications): Anthony K. Adaletey.

GREECE

Embassy: Plot 1644, Oko-Awo Close, Victoria Island, POB 1199, Lagos; tel (1) 611412; telex 21747.
Ambassador: Dr Efstratios I. Mavroudis.

GUINEA

Embassy: 8 Abudu Smith St, Victoria Island, POB 2826, Lagos.
Ambassador: Komo Beavogui.

HOLY SEE

Apostolic Nunciature: 9 Anifowoshe St, Victoria Island, POB 2470, Lagos; tel (1) 613744; telex 22455; fax (1) 618635.
Apostolic Pro-Nuncio: Most Rev. Dr Paul Fouad Tabet, Titular Archbishop of Sinna.
Second Secretary: Rev. Mgr Jean-Marie Speich.

HUNGARY

Embassy: 9 Louis Solomon Close, Victoria Island, POB 3168, Lagos; tel (1) 613582.
Ambassador: Géza Kosai.

ICELAND

Consulate: 16 Burma Rd, POB 3436, Apapa, Lagos; tel (1) 874707; telex 21557.
Consul: Joseph Raymond Raad.

INDIA

High Commission: 107 Awolowo Rd, SW Ikoyi, POB 2322, Lagos; tel (1) 681297.
High Commissioner: Krishnan Rughnati.

INDONESIA

Embassy: 5 Anifowoshe St, Victoria Island, POB 3473, Lagos.
Ambassador: Vice-Adm. Subroto Yudono.

IRAN

Embassy: 1 Alexander Ave, Ikoyi, Lagos; tel (1) 681601; telex 22625.
Ambassador: N. Shodnoosh.

IRAQ

Embassy: Plot 708A, Adeola Hopewell St, Victoria Island, POB 2859, Lagos.
Ambassador: A. A. H. al-Sammarrai.

IRELAND

Embassy: 34 Kofo Abayomi St, Victoria Island, POB 2421, Lagos; tel (1) 615224; telex 21478; fax (1) 615224.
Ambassador: Patrick Cradock.
First Secretary: Eamon Hickey.

ITALY

Embassy: 12 Eleke Crescent, Victoria Island, POB 2161, Lagos; tel (1) 614066; telex 21202.
Ambassador: Dr Stefano Rastrelli.

JAMAICA

High Commission: Plot 77, 303 Rd, Victorian Island Annex, Lagos; fax (1) 612100.
High Commissioner: Dudly Thompson.

JAPAN

Embassy: 24-25 Apese St, Victoria Island, PMB 2111, Lagos; tel (1) 613797; telex 21364; fax 614035.
Ambassador: Yasushi Kurokochi.
Counsellor: Wataru Hayashi.
First Secretary (Medical): Dr Nozomu Nishikawa.
First Secretary (Consular): Minoru Oda.
First Secretary (Administration): Kinzo Higo.
First Secretary (Commercial and Economic): Yuki Yamada.
First Secretary (Economic Co-operation): Hiroshi Betsui.
Second Secretary (Information and Culture): Jiro Usui.
Second Secretary (Political): Masahiko Kiya.

KENYA

High Commission: 53 Queen's Drive, Ikoyi, POB 6464, Lagos; tel (1) 682768; telex 21124.
High Commissioner: Dr I. E. Maluki.

KOREA, DEMOCRATIC PEOPLE'S REPUBLIC

Embassy: 31 Akin Adesola St, Victoria Island, Lagos.
Ambassador: Ahn Kyong-Hyon.

KOREA, REPUBLIC

Embassy: Plot 934, Idejo St, Victoria Island, POB 4668, Lagos; tel (1) 615353; telex 21953.
Ambassador: Chai Ki Oh.

LEBANON

Embassy: Plot 18, Eleke Crescent, Victoria Island, POB 651, Lagos.
Ambassador: M. Salame.

LIBERIA

Embassy: 3 Idejo St, Plot 162, off Adeola Odeku St, Victoria Island, POB 70841, Lagos; telex 23361.
Ambassador: D. Dueh Chieh.

LIBYA

People's Bureau: 46 Raymond Njoku Rd, SW Ikoyi, Lagos; tel (1) 680880.

MALAYSIA

High Commission: 27 Sanusi Fafunwa St, Victoria Island, POB 3729, Lagos; tel (1) 613363; telex 23550; fax (1) 612741.
High Commissioner: Abdul Majid Ahmad Khan.
First Secretary and Head of Chancery: Abdul Aziz Harun.
Second Secretary (Administration and Finance): Musa Rudin Omar.

MAURITANIA

Embassy: 1A Karimu Giwa Close, SW Ikoyi, Lagos.
Ambassador: Mohamed M. O. Weddady.

MOROCCO

Embassy: Plot 1318, 27 Karimu Katun St, Victoria Island, Lagos; tel (1) 611682; telex 21835.
Ambassador: Saad Eddine Taieb.

NETHERLANDS

Embassy: 24 Ozumba Mbadiwe Ave, Victoria Island, POB 2426, Lagos; tel (1) 613510; telex 21327.
Ambassador: L. P. J. Mazairac.

NIGER

Embassy: 15 Adeola Odeku St, Victoria Island, PMB 2736, Lagos; telex 21434.
Ambassador: Lieut Col Tandja Mamadou.

NORWAY

Embassy: 3 Anifowoshe St, Victoria Island, PMB 2431, Lagos; tel (1) 618467; telex 21429; fax (1) 618469.
Ambassador: Harald Høstmark.

PAKISTAN

High Commission: Plot 859, Bishop Aboyade Cole St, Victoria Island, POB 2450, Lagos.
High Commissioner: S. M. A. Khairi.

PHILIPPINES

Embassy: Plot 175, No 51, Kofo Abayomi St, Victoria Island, POB 2948, Lagos; tel (1) 614048; telex 23344.
Ambassador: Purisimo A. de Peralta.

POLAND

Embassy: 10 Idejo St, Victoria Island, POB 410, Lagos; tel (1) 614683; telex 21262.
Ambassador: Mieczysław Cielecki.

PORTUGAL

Embassy: Plot 1677, Olukunle Bakare Close, Victoria Island, Lagos; tel (1) 619037; telex 22424.
Ambassador: Nuno da Cunha e Tavora Lorena.

ROMANIA

Embassy: 30 Raymond Njoku Rd, Ikoyi, POB 595, Lagos; telex 21374.
Ambassador: Vasile Chivulescu.

RUSSIA

Embassy: 5 Eleke Crescent, Victoria Island, POB 2723, Lagos; tel (1) 611381.
Ambassador: Oleg Bocharov.
Consulate: Adjaokuta, Kvara State.

SAUDI ARABIA

Embassy: Plot 1412, Victoria Island, POB 2836, Lagos.
Ambassador: Foud Sadik Mousti.

SENEGAL

Embassy: 14 Kofo Abayomi Rd, Victoria Island, PMB 2197, Lagos; tel (1) 25592; telex 21398.
Ambassador: Cherif Y. Diaite.

SIERRA LEONE

High Commission: 31 Waziri Ibrahim St, Victoria Island, POB 2821, Lagos; telex 21495.
High Commissioner: Umaru Wurie.

SOMALIA

Embassy: Plot 1270, off Adeola Odeka St, POB 6355, Lagos.
Ambassador: M. S. Hassan.

SPAIN

Embassy: 21c Kofo Abayomi Rd, Victoria Island, POB 2738, Lagos; tel (1) 614918; telex 22656; fax (1) 618225.
Ambassador: Carlos Bárcena Portolés.
Counsellor: José Laviña.
Chancellor: José Maria Sáenz de Miera.
Commercial Attaché: Luis Alvarez.
Administrative Attaché: Clotilde Berjillos.
Consular Attaché: Javier Martinez.

SUDAN

Embassy: 2B Kofo Abayomi St, Victoria Island, POB 2428, Lagos; tel (1) 615889; telex 23500.
Chargé d'affaires: Hissim Abdelraziq Saleh.
Second Secretary: Ajang Moyick Ajang.
Third Secretary: Tarig Ali Bakhiet.
Consul: El H. Osman Eltiyib.

SWEDEN

Embassy: 17 Eleke Crescent, Victoria Island, POB 1097, Lagos; tel (1) 610240; telex 21318; fax (1) 617994.
Ambassador: Göran Zetterqvist.
Counsellor: Anders Backman.
First Secretary: Gunnar Sommarin.
Second Secretary: Kristina Östergren.
Consulate: Lagos.

SWITZERLAND

Embassy: 7 Anifowoshe St, Victoria Island, POB 536, Lagos; tel (1) 610183; telex 21597.
Ambassador: Anton Greber.

Third Secretary: Dr Martin Dahinden.
Attaché and Head of Chancery: Ernst Balzli.

SYRIA

Embassy: Lagos.
Chargé d'affaires: Mustafa Haj-Ali.

TANZANIA

High Commission: 45 Ademola St, Ikoyi, POB 6417, Lagos.
High Commissioner: Maj.-Gen. Mirisho Sam Hagai Sarakikya.

THAILAND

Embassy: 1 Ruxton Rd, Old Ikoyi, POB 3095, Lagos; tel (1) 681337.
Ambassador: N. Sathaporn.

TOGO

Embassy: 96 Awolowo Rd, SW Ikoyi, POB 1435, Lagos; tel (1) 617449; telex 21506.
Ambassador: Foli-Agbenozan Tettekpoe.

TRINIDAD AND TOBAGO

High Commission: 6 Karimu Kotun St, Victoria Island, POB 6392, Lagos; tel (1) 612087; telex 21041; fax (1) 612732.
High Commissioner: Dr Randolph R. Peters.
Deputy High Commissioner: Frank C. Sealy.
Financial Attaché: Marilyn J. Collier.

TURKEY

Embassy: 3 Okunola Martins Close, Ikoyi, POB 1758, Lagos; tel (1) 683030.
Ambassador: Orhan Kulin.

UNITED KINGDOM

High Commission: 11 Eleke Crescent, Victoria Island, PMB 12136, Lagos; tel (1) 619531; telex 21247; fax (1) 666909.
High Commissioner: A. Christopher D. S. MacRae.
Deputy High Commissioner and Head of Political Section: R. S. Gorham.
Defence and Military Adviser: Col I. G. Nason.
Naval and Air Adviser: Wing Commdr A. M. Carter.
Counsellor (Commercial): D. Broad.
Counsellor (Political): R. I. S. McGuigan.
Counsellor (Management): P. M. H. Young.
First Secretary (Political): A. D. Kavanagh.
First Secretary (Economic): C. J. B. White.
First Secretary (Information): T. S. Rawlinson.
First Secretary (Political): P. R. Sizeland.
First Secretary (Commercial): C. Jonsen.
First Secretary (Works): G. F. Rundle.
First Secretary (Immigration/Consular): D. B. McAdam.
First Secretary (Management): M. J. Towsey.
Second Secretary (Aid): T. P. Livesey.
Second Secretary (Consular): N. A. Starkey.

Visa Section: Chellaram Bldg, 54 Marina, Lagos; tel (1) 666313.

Deputy High Commission: 2/4 Lamido Rd, PMB 2096, Kaduna; tel (62) 201380; telex 71104.
Deputy High Commissioner: C. K. Woodfield.
First Secretary (Commercial/Information): G. Fairhurst.
Second Secretary (Immigration): D. T. Reynolds.

USA

Embassy: 2 Eleke Crescent, POB 554, Victoria Island, Lagos; tel (1) 610097; telex 23616; fax (1) 635397.
Ambassador: Lannon Walker.
Deputy Chief of Mission: John M. Yates.
Political Section: David E. Kaeuper.
Economic Section: Deborah Ruth Schwartz.
Administrative Section: Robert J. McCanneny.
Communications Programme Officer: Charles Oxendine.
Regional Security Officer: Robert Franks.
Public Affairs Officer: Robert Lagamma.
Agency for International Development: Eugene Chiavaroli.
Office of the Defence Attaché: Col John E. Ryan.
Security Assistance Office: Maj. Sherman L. Gandy.
Agricultural Section: Thomas A. Pomeroy.
Agricultural Trade Office: Joseph Butler.
Labour Officer: Thomas P. Doubleday, Jr.

Consular Section: fax (1) 612218.
Consular Section: Robyn M. Bishop.

Commercial Section: fax (1) 619856.
Commercial Section: Frederic J. Gaynor.

Consulate-General: 2 Maska Rd, POB 170, Kaduna; tel (62) 201070; telex 71617.
Consul-General: Brooke C. Holmes.
Political/Economic Section: Alex Martschenko.
Administrative Section: Larry E. Andre.
Consular Section: Ann Lang Irvine.
Branch Public Affairs Officer: Michael Pelletier.
Communications Programme Officer: Donald J. Connaly.

VENEZUELA

Embassy: 35B Adetokunbo Ademola St, Victoria Island, POB 3727, Lagos; tel (1) 611590; telex 21944.
Chargé d'affaires: Jorge A. Gonzalez G.

YUGOSLAVIA

Embassy: 7 Maitama Sule St, SW Ikoyi, PMB 978, Lagos.
Ambassador: Vlatko Cosić.

ZAIRE

Embassy: 23A Kofo Abayomi Rd, Victoria Island, POB 1216, Lagos; telex 21365.

ZAMBIA

High Commission: 11 Keffi St, SW Ikoyi, PMB 6119, Lagos.
High Commissioner: John B. Shikuboni.

ZIMBABWE

High Commission: 6 Kasumu Ekemode St, POB 50247, Victoria Island, Lagos; tel (1) 619328; telex 22650.
High Commissioner: Isaac L. Nyathi.

International Organizations

EUROPEAN COMMUNITIES

External Delegation: 4 Idowy Taylor St, Victoria Island, Private Mail Bag 12767, Lagos; tel (1) 617852; telex 21868; fax (1) 617248.
Commission Delegate: Marc Zimmer.

NORWAY

ARGENTINA

Embassy: Inkognitogt. 10A, 0244 Oslo 2; tel (2) 55-24-48; telex 19261; fax (2) 44-16-41.
Ambassador: Roberto Vicente Requeijo.
Second Secretary: Jorge Omar Antonio Biga.

AUSTRIA

Embassy: Sophus Liesgt. 2, 0264 Oslo 2; tel (2) 55-23-48; telex 76850; fax (2) 55-43-67.
Ambassador: Dr Franz Palla.
Counsellor (Commercial): Wolfgang Hortlehner.
Secretary (Economic): Alexander Hacker.

Consulate-General: Ullern allé 10, 0351 Oslo 3; tel (2) 52-33-01; fax (2) 52-37-96.
Honorary Consul-General: Thorbjorn Conradi.
Honorary Vice-Consul: Bjorn Conradi.

Consulate: Kong Oscars gate 56, 5000 Bergen; tel (5) 31-21-60; telex 40488.
Honorary Consul: Gerhard Runshaug.

Consulate: c/o Stavanger Roerhandel a/s, Myglabergvn, POB 184, 4033 Stavanger; tel (4) 57-17-20; telex 33004; fax (4) 57-56-35.
Honorary Consul: Olav Gerhard Hestness.

BELGIUM

Embassy: Drammensvn 103C, 0244 Oslo 2; tel (2) 55-22-15.
Ambassador: André Verbist.

BENIN

Consulate: c/o a/s SEMCO, Dicks vei 12, POB 29, 1324 Lysaker, Oslo; tel (2) 53-65-15; fax (2) 53-69-77.
Honorary Consul: Einar Wahlstrøm.

BRAZIL

Embassy: Kristinelundvn 1, 0244 Oslo 2; tel (2) 55-20-29; telex 19495; fax (2) 44-39-64.
Ambassador: Murillo Gurgel Valente.

BULGARIA

Embassy: Tidemandsgt. 11, 0244 Oslo 2; tel (2) 55-40-40; telex 79708; fax (2) 55-40-24.
Ambassador: Dimitar Kissimov.
First Secretary: Roumiana Dermendjieva.

Commercial Section: tel (2) 44-65-60.
Commercial Counsellor: Ivan Vassilev Damianov.

CANADA

Embassy: Oscarsgt. 20, 0244 Oslo 2; tel (2) 49-69-55; telex 71880; fax (2) 69-34-67.
Ambassador: R. H. Graham Mitchell.
Counsellor and Consul: R. C. Smith.
Counsellor (Commercial) and Consul: R. D. Chan.
Forces Attaché: Capt. David E. Pollard.
Third Secretary (Commercial) and Vice-Consul: J. E. J. Hislop.
Attaché (Administration) and Vice-Consul: D. H. Davis.

CHILE

Embassy: Meltzersgt. 5, 0257 Oslo 2; tel (2) 44-89-55; telex 77171; fax (2) 44-24-21.
Ambassador: Alvaro Zúñiga.
First Secretary: Javier Becker.
Third Secretary and Consul: Patricio Utreras.

CHINA, PEOPLE'S REPUBLIC

Embassy: Tuengen allé 2B, 0374 Oslo 3; tel (2) 49-20-52.
Ambassador: Wang Guixin.

COLOMBIA

Embassy: Ikognitogt. 12, 0244 Oslo 2; tel (2) 55-65-79; telex 72130.
Chargé d'affaires: Nazly Lozano Eljure.

COSTA RICA

Embassy: Kongensgt. 1, 0153 Oslo 1; tel (2) 42-56-40.

CYPRUS

Consulate: Brobekkreien 38, POB 98, 0516 Oslo 5; tel (2) 64-90-50; telex 76743.
Honorary Consul: Johan N. Ulrichsen.

CZECHOSLOVAKIA

Embassy: Thomas Heftyesgt. 32, 0244 Oslo 2; tel (2) 55-55-90; fax (2) 55-50-19.
Ambassador: Igor Kratochvíl.
Counsellor: Ivan Jestřáb.
Attaché: Petr Vacek.
Attaché: Zdeněk Koudelka.
Attaché: Miroslav Pidrman.
Commercial Counsellor: Drahomír Macháň.
Commercial Attaché: Vladimír Schlitter.

DENMARK

Embassy: Olav Kyrresgt. 7, 0273 Oslo 2; tel (2) 44-18-46; telex 71275; fax (2) 55-46-34.
Ambassador: Hans Tabor.
First Secretary: Ruben Madsen.
Counsellor: Poul Lembøl.
Attaché: Anni Bang Kjerulff.
Trade Assistant: Niels Albech Andersen.
Trade Assistant: N. J. Abildgaard Hansen.
Export Assistant: Sven-Erik Johannesen.

Consulate: Ole Bulls Plass 13, POB 985, 5001 Bergen; tel (5) 31-10-30; telex 40631; fax (5) 32-24-55.
Consul: Bjarne Rieber.
Vice-Consul: Bente Frimann Dahl.

Consulate: Storgt. 30, POB 54, 8001 Bodø; tel (81) 25-0-95; fax (81) 25-0-59.
Consul: Ole Martin Tjærandsen.

Consulate: Bragernes Torg 13, 3017 Drammen; tel (3) 83-62-53.
Consul: Karsten Hartvig Wahl.

Consulate: Løvli Terrasse 24, POB 343, 1601 Fredrikstad; tel (9) 32-06-44; telex 79237; fax (9) 32-41-20.
Consul: Peter Elias Sæter.

Consulate: Strangata 58, POB 453, 9601 Hammerfest; tel (84) 13-9-77; fax (84) 13-9-79.
Consul: Kjell Gunnar Mikalsen.

Consulate: Samasjøvn 8, POB 961, 9401 Harstad; tel (82) 66-7-22; telex 65800; fax (82) 66-7-30.
Consul: Hugo Flemming Nielsen.

Consulate: Rekavikgaten 18, 5500 Haugesund; POB 248, 5501 Haugesund; tel (4) 72-24-68; fax (4) 72-66-14.
Consul: Theodore Nordbø.

Consulate: Handelens Hus, Rådhusgaten 3, POB 291, 4601 Kristiansand S; tel (42) 25-1-67.
Consul: Thorbjørn Albert.

Consulate: Storgaten 48, POB 1, 3251 Larvik; tel (34) 82-0-30; telex 21541.
Consul: Per Arbo Høeg.

Consulate: Storgaten 57, 2600 Lillehammer; tel (62) 54-0-51; fax (62) 57-0-77.
Consul: Sigmund Thue.

Consulate: Moss Maritime Centre, POB 1022, 1501 Moss; tel (9) 25-50-55; telex 71533; fax (9) 25-43-77.
Consul: Tor Svein Jørgensen.

Consulate: Fagernes, 8500 Narvik; tel (82) 44-0-15; fax (82) 47-7-95.
Consul: Jens Petter Opshaug.

Consulate: Bjørnslettvn 2, POB 60, 3901 Porsgrunn; tel (3) 55-68-15; fax (3) 55-24-80.
Consul: Oddbjørn Solum.

Consulate: a/s Thor Dahl, POB 2010, 3201 Sandefjord; tel (34) 65-2-00; telex 21777; fax (34) 67-2-00.
Consul: Thor Christen Christensen.

Consulate: Lagervn 13, Forus Vest, POB 111, 4033 Forus; tel (4) 80-07-00; telex 33119; fax (4) 57-63-45.
Consul: Leif Hansen.

Consulate: Strantorget 1, POB 353, 9001 Tromsø; tel (83) 82-1-32; fax (83) 58-8-17.
Consul: Karl Jacob Dons.

Consulate: Strandvn 71, 7042 Trondheim; POB 135, 7001 Trondheim; tel (7) 52-40-80; telex 55634; fax (7) 51-20-36.
Consul: Jørgen B. Lysholm.
Vice-Consul: Eva Bache.

Consulate: Storgt. 41, POB 458, 3101 Tønsberg; tel (33) 12-5-03; telex 21948; fax (33) 13-8-68.
Consul: Harald Krogh-Hansen.

Consulate: Sundgt. 6-10, POB 1, 6001 Ålesund; tel (71) 24-6-66; fax (71) 22-2-95.
Consul: Grete Sandvig.

Consulate: Rygene-Smith & Thommesen a/s, 4880 Rykene; tel (41) 93-1-00; fax (41) 93-1-03.
Vice-Consul: Thor Thommesen.

Consulate: Solheimsvh 18, 9900 Båtsfjord; tel (85) 83-1-68.
Vice-Consul: Roar Kristiansen.

Consulate: Joh. Feyersgt. 1, POB 6, 4370 Egersund; tel (44) 90-0-99.
Vice-Consul: Gabriel Albrethsen.

Consulate: POB 23, 4401 Flekkefjord; tel (43) 22-0-22; fax (43) 24-4-07.
Vice-Consul: Asbjørn Egenes.

Consulate: Steinlivn 1, 3770 Kragerø; POB 70, 3771 Kragerø; tel (3) 98-10-55; fax (3) 98-28-17.
Vice-Consul: Sam Lunøe.

Consulate: Fossbekk, 4790 Lillesand; tel (41) 70-9-33.
Vice-Consul: Thorleif Johan Vennesland.

Consulate: Nordre Banegate 26, 4501 Mandal; tel (43) 61-1-22; telex 21359.
Vice-Consul: Hans Christiansen.

Consulate: Per Gyntvei 2-4, POB 7, 1701 Sarpsborg; tel (9) 15-22-22; telex 16504; fax (9) 15-20-88.
Vice-Consul: Bjørn Strømsæther.

Consulate: Kristian 4, gate 2, POB 102, 9951 Vardø; tel (85) 87-7-03.

Vice-Consul: Tor Andreas Kofoed.

EGYPT

Embassy: Drammensvn 90A, 0244 Oslo 2; tel (2) 20-00-10; telex 78405.
Ambassador: Hassan S. Kandil.

ESTONIA

Consulate: Vollsvn 13E, 1324 Lysaker; tel (2) 58-16-10; fax (2) 58-16-15.
Honorary Consul: Arve Røys Stranden.

FINLAND

Embassy: Drammensvn 40, 0244 Oslo 2; tel (2) 43-04-00; telex 76755; fax (2) 43-06-29.
Ambassador: Kaarlo Yrjö-Koskinen.
Defence Attaché: Lieut Col Tapani Hankaniemi.
Consul-General: Harald Tybring-Gjedde.
Vice-Consul: Aimo Repo.
Attaché: Tapio Koskimies.

Commercial Section: Thomas Heftyesgate 1, 0264 Oslo 2; tel (2) 43-04-00; telex 77284; fax (2) 55-22-77.
Secretary (Commercial): Maija-Liisa Tarkkala.
Secretary (Commercial): Ilkka Lukkariniemi.
Secretary (Commercial): Matti Kaskeala.

Consulate: Kongensgate 25, 6000 Ålesund; tel (71) 25-4-02.
Consul: Per Kibsgaard-Petersen.

Consulate: Bratteklev, Tromöy, 4800 Arendal; tel (41) 85-2-11.
Consul: Birger Fredrik Smith-Sörensen.

Consulate: Torgalmenningen 2, POB 826, 5001 Bergen; tel (5) 21-10-00.
Consul: Jan Alfred Løken.

Consulate: Tollbugate 10, 8000 Bodö; tel (81) 20-0-10.
Consul: Erling Sannes, Jr.

Consulate: Bragernes torg 12, 3000 Drammen; tel (3) 83-29-85.
Vice-Consul: Einar Emil Låker, Jr.

Consulate: Havnegate 29, POB 55, 4551 Farsund; tel (43) 90-5-55.
Consul: Gunnar Brøvig.

Consulate: Dues Reisebyrå a/s, Storgt. 5, POB 68, 4891 Grimstad; tel (41) 40-6-66; telex 21405.
Vice-Consul: Carsten Svenn Due.

Consulate: Dyrendalsvn 4, 1750 Halden; tel (9) 18-55-07.
Vice-Consul: Kjell Jarl Jarlsby.

Consulate: Strandgate 32, 9600 Hammerfeet; tel (84) 12-4-11.
Vice-Consul: Paul Helliesen.

Consulate: Heraldsgate 139, 5500 Haugesund; tel (4) 72-30-33.
Consul: Christian Haaland.

Consulate: Storgt. 26, 3190 Horten; tel (33) 41-2-00.
Consul: Rolf Tufte.

Consulate: 9912 Hesseng; tel (85) 98-0-78.
Consul: Johan Wollmann.

Consulate: Kirkegt. 21/3, 4600 Kristiansand S; tel (42) 29-5-96.
Consul: Asbjørn Fredrik Asbjørnen.

Consulate: John Allansgt. 9, 6500 Kristainsund N; POB 97, 6501 Kristiansund N; tel (73) 73-9-58.
Consul: Rolf Arentz-Hansen.

Consulate: Torvet 3, 3250 Larvik; tel (34) 81-9-17.
Consul: Anders Bjarne Stötvig.

Consulate: Ornesvn 5, 8500 Narvik; tel (82) 41-1-50.
Consul: Magne Jostein Schille.

Consulate: POB 40, 1701 Sarpsborg; tel (9) 15-61-11.
Consul: Björn Iversen.

Consulate: Verven 2, 4000 Stavanger; tel (4) 53-20-30.
Consul: Christian Bjelland.

Consulate: Alfheimvägen 31, POB 567, 9001 Tromsø; tel (83) 82-0-60.
Consul: Olaf Jakobsen.

Consulate: Stiklestadvn 3, 7000 Trondheim; tel (7) 52-00-25.
Consul: Harald Setsaas.

Consulate: Havneg. 1, POB 100, 9801 Vadsø; tel (85) 51-2-25.
Vice-Consul: Arnold Dørum Persen.

FRANCE

Embassy: Drammensvn 69, 0244 Oslo 2; tel (2) 44-18-20; fax (2) 56-32-21.
Ambassador: Christian Prettre.

GERMANY

Embassy: Oscarsgt. 45, 0244 Oslo 2; tel (2) 55-20-10; telex 71173; fax (2) 44-76-72.
Ambassador: Harald Hofmann.

Consulate: Tollbugt. 6, 6002 Ålesund; POB 438, 6025 Ålesund; tel (71) 24-0-78; telex 42302.
Honorary Consul: Helge Hagenäs.

Consulate: Strangt. 221, 5004 Bergen; POB 1843, 5024 Bergens; tel (5) 90-23-65; fax (5) 23-20-60.
Honorary Consul: Johan Troye.

Consulate: Sjøgt. 19, POB 394, 8001 Bodø; tel (81) 20-0-31.
Honorary Consul: Carl Johan Jakhelln.

Consulate: Smedesundet 93, POB 263, 5501 Haugesund; tel (47) 23-5-88; telex 42851.
Honorary Consul: Sigurd Haavik.

Consulate: Dr Wesselsgt. 8, 9900 Kirkenes; POB 13, 9901 Kirkenes; tel (85) 91-2-44.
Honorary Consul: Erling M. Saue.

Consulate: Skolebakke 6, 4630 Kristiansand S; POB 36, 4601 Kristiansand S; tel (42) 92-3-40; telex 21964.
Honorary Consul: Odd Birger Nygaard.

Consulate: Strandgt. 78, 6500 Kristiansund N; tel (73) 71-1-11; telex 55202.
Honorary Consul: Halfdan Loennechen Backer.

Consulate: Movn 15, 8520 Ankensstrand; tel (82) 56-7-07.
Honorary Consul: Björn Winther.

Consulate: Søebergtorget 4, 3200 Sandefjord; POB 271, 3201 Sandefjord; tel (34) 62-3-90; telex 21099.
Honorary Consul: Jörgen Jahre.

Consulate: Hagebyvn 26, Graatenmoen, 3700 Skien; POB 2560, 3701 Skien; tel (3) 59-54-66.
Honorary Consul: Erik Tanche Nilssen.

Consulate: Kongsgt. 10, Handelens Hus, 4012 Stavanger; tel (4) 52-25-94.
Honorary Consul: Tore Helliesen.

Consulate: Stakkevollvn 65, 9000 Tromsø; POB 110, 9001 Tromsø; tel (83) 87-5-75; telex 65901; fax (83) 82-3-04.
Honorary Consul: Thor Glaever.

Consulate: Lilleby Smelteverk, Leksvikenc gate 2, 7041 Trondheim; POB 5410-Jarsletta, 7001 Trondheim; tel (7) 52-11-20; telex 55044; fax (7) 51-50-97.
Honorary Consul: Erik Solberg.

GREECE

Embassy: Nobelsgt. 45, 0268 Oslo 2; tel (2) 44-27-28; telex 72189.
Ambassador: Spyridon Mormoris.

HUNGARY

Embassy: Sophus Liesgt. 3, 0244 Oslo 2; tel (2) 55-24-18; telex 78889; fax (2) 44-76-93.
Ambassador: Dr Gábor Nagy.
Counsellor: Sándor Juhász.
Counsellor: Dezső Bartos.
Commercial Counsellor: István Fehér.

Commercial Section: Sofiesgt. 60, Oslo; tel (2) 60-48-98; fax (2) 60-50-04.

ICELAND

Embassy: Stortingsgt. 30, 0161 Oslo 1; tel (2) 83-34-35; telex 19215; fax (2) 83-07-04.
Ambassador: Haraldur Kröyer.
Counsellor: Jon Egill Egilsson.
Secretary: Auđur Rútsdóttir.

Consulate: Sparebanken Möre Torvikplass 224, 6008 Ålemsund; tel (71) 89-0-00; fax (71) 22-6-70.
Consul: Per Oscar Garshol.

Consulate: Fokus Bank, Rådstaplass 2/3, POB 1162, 5001 Bergen; tel (5) 21-89-04; fax (5) 31-83-39.
Consul: Arne Herulf Holm.

Consulate: Strömsö Torg 9, 3044 Drammen; tel (3) 83-54-29.
Consul: Atle Björnli.

Consulate: Strandgt. 162, POB 98, 5501 Haugesund; tel (4) 72-41-11; telex 42203; fax (4) 72-90-50.
Consul: Öivind Wendelbo.

Consulate: Setesdalsvn 17, POB 221, 4601 Kristiansand S; tel (42) 22-9-65; fax (42) 22-6-63.
Consul: Ola Hegg.

Consulate: Strandgt. 10, Moss Maritime Centre, POB 102, 1570 Dilling; tel (9) 25-09-03; telex 71412; fax (9) 25-51-09.
Consul: William Asbjörnsen.

Consulate: Kiellandsgt. 2, POB 327, 4001 Stavanger; tel (4) 52-90-44; telex 33180; fax (4) 53-64-44.
Consul: Jan-Peter Schöpp.

Consulate: Kai 16, Brattöra, 7010 Trondheim; tel (7) 52-45-34; telex 55289; fax (7) 52-56-42.
Consul: Roar C. Hyll.

Consulate: Strandgt. 2/4, 9600 Hammerfest; tel (84) 11-6-22; telex 65866; fax (84) 12-1-27.
Vice-Consul: Odd Evensen.

Consulate: Torvet 2, POB 5, 1701 Sarpsborg; tel (9) 15-50-66; fax (9) 15-54-82.
Vice-Consul: Knut Hans Björge.

Consulate: Sjögt. 16, 9000 Tromsø; tel (83) 83-0-24.
Vice-Consul: Ragnhild Fusdahl Hensen.

INDIA

Embassy: Niels Juelsgt. 30, 0244 Oslo 2; tel (2) 44-31-94; telex 78510; fax (2) 44-07-20.
Ambassador: L. N. Rangarajan.
Deputy Chief of Mission: H. N. Paul.
Attaché: C. Ramachandran.

INDONESIA

Embassy: Inkognitogt. 8, 0258 Oslo 2; tel (2) 44-11-21; telex 72683; fax (2) 55-34-44.
Ambassador: Cyrus Taihitu.
First Secretary (Political Affairs): Saoma Martini.
Third Secretary (Culture and Information): Mutoharul Djanan.
Third Secretary (Consular Affairs): Endang Kuswaya.
Attaché (Administrative Affairs): Hartono Rachmad.
Attaché (Administrative Affairs): Yosef Bandrio Utomo.

IRAN

Embassy: Drammensvn 88E, 0244 Oslo 2; tel (2) 55-24-08.
Ambassador: Jalal Sadatin.

IRELAND

Consulate-General: Kirkevn 7, Oslo 2; POB 5683, Briskeby, 0209 Oslo 2; tel (2) 55-95-10; telex 71159; fax (2) 55-95-15.
Honorary Consul-General: Halvdan Björum.

ISRAEL

Embassy: Drammensvn 82C, 0271 Oslo 2; tel (2) 44-79-24; fax (2) 56-21-83.
Ambassador: Joel Alon.

ITALY

Embassy: Inkognitogt. 7, Oslo; tel (2) 55-22-33.
Ambassador: Giuseppe Scaglia.

JAPAN

Embassy: Parkvn 33B, 0244 Oslo 2; tel (2) 55-10-11; telex 76085; fax (2) 44-25-05.
Ambassador: Shinichiro Asao.

KOREA, DEMOCRATIC PEOPLE'S REPUBLIC

Embassy: Vestheimgt. 4B, 0262 Oslo 2; tel (2) 44-78-63.
Ambassador: Kim Yong Su.

KOREA, REPUBLIC

Embassy: Bjørn Farmannsgt. 1, POB 7572, Skillebekk, 0205 Oslo 2; tel (2) 55-20-18.
Ambassador: Song Sung-Han.

LESOTHO

Consulate-General: Odinsgt. 21, 0266 Oslo 2.
Consul-General: Halfdan Sommerfeldt Jacobsen.

LUXEMBOURG

Embassy: 5 rue Notre-Dame, 2240 Luxembourg; tel (352) 47-82-71; telex 3405; fax (352) 23-1-44.
Ambassador: Paul Peters (resident in Luxembourg).

MALTA

Consulate: 'Vika Atrium', Muntedamsvn 45, 0250 Oslo 2; POB 1923 Vika, 0125 Oslo 1; tel (2) 83-10-48; fax (2) 83-10-48.
Honorary Consul: Jens-Jacob Sander.

MEXICO

Embassy: Drammensvn 108 B1, 0244 Oslo 2; tel (2) 43-11-65.
Ambassador: Tomás Ortega-Bertrand.

NETHERLANDS

Embassy: Oscarsgt. 29, 0244 Oslo 2; tel (2) 60-21-93.
Ambassador: Baron F. M. Van Geen.
Defence, Military and Naval Attaché: Col Charles Receveur.
Air Attaché and Assistant Military and Naval Attaché: Lieut Col Henny J. M. Melkes.

PANAMA

Embassy: Jerikovn 28, 1067 Oslo 10; tel (2) 30-85-88.

POLAND

Embassy: Olav Kyrres pl. 1, 0244 Oslo 2; tel (2) 43-00-15.
Ambassador: Karol Nowakowski.

PORTUGAL

Embassy: Josefinesgt. 37, 0351 Oslo 3; tel (2) 60-62-25; telex 71200.
Ambassador: Luis José de Oliveira Nunes.

ROMANIA

Embassy: Oscarsgt. 51, 0258 Oslo 2; tel (2) 44-15-12.

RUSSIA

Embassy: Drammensvn 74, 0244 Oslo 2; tel (2) 55-32-78; telex 79803; fax (2) 55-00-70.
Ambassador: Anatoly F. Tishchenko.

SOUTH AFRICA

Consulate-General: Drammensvn 88C, 0271 Oslo 2; POB 7588, Skillebeck, 0205 Oslo 2; tel (2) 44-79-10; fax (2) 44-39-75.
Consul-General: W. Bosman.
Vice-Consul: A. Smuts.
Vice-Consul (Administrative): M. L. Geldenhuys.

SPAIN

Embassy: Oscarsgt. 35, 0258 Oslo 2; tel (2) 55-20-15; telex 76641; fax (2) 55-98-22.
Ambassador: Ramón Fernández de Soignie.

SRI LANKA

Consulate: c/o Hydrogas a/s, Ringnesvn 50, POB 23, Haugenstua N 0915, Oslo 9; tel (2) 10-64-10; telex 77505; fax (2) 68-62-21.
Honorary Consul: Jon Reutz.

SWEDEN

Embassy: Nobelsgt. 16, 0244 Oslo 2; tel (2) 44-38-15; telex 71300; fax (2) 55-15-96.
Ambassador: Lennart Bodström.
Minister: Per Anderman.
Counsellor: Hans Ahlberg.
Counsellor (Press): Staffan Björk.
Counsellor (Press): Lars Georgsson.
Military, Naval and Air Attaché: Lieut Col Christer Sterning.
Second Secretary: Eva-Christine Bergström.
Secretary (Trade): Mikael Klingberg.
Chancellor: Birgitta Aadnesen.
Chancellor: Lena Haga.
Chancellor: Eva Sandén.
Chaplain: Örjan Lundqvist.

Consulate: Thommesen-gården, Kirkegt. 5, POB 480, 4801 Arendal; tel (41) 25-1-99; telex 21370.
Consul: Nils Hilmar Thommesen.
Consul: Nils Hilmar Thommesen.

Consulate: Olav Kyrresgt. 11, 5014 Bergen; tel (5) 31-60-32; fax (5) 31-80-23.
Consul: Gert Atle Gundersen.
Chancellor: Inger Jacobsen.

Consulate: Storgt. 7, POB 94, 8001 Bodø; tel (81) 20-1-15.
Consul: Gustav Egil Moe.

Consulate: Brogt. 2, 4550 Farsund; tel (43) 90-2-77; telex 21618; fax (43) 90-6-26.
Consul: Richard Ivar Buch.

Consulate: Mossevn 1, POB 34, 1600 Fredrikstad; tel (9) 31-10-45; telex 78864; fax (9) 31-05-14.
Consul: Jon Erik Brynildsen.

Consulate: c/o Finmark Fylkesrederi og Ruteselkap, POB 308, 9601 Hammerfest; tel (84) 11-6-55; fax (84) 12-7-73.
Consul: Åge Ludvik Olaussen.

Consulate: Kaigt. 1, POB 280, 5501 Haugesund; tel (4) 72-86-15.
Consul: Sverre Pedersen.

Consulate: Dr Wesselgt. 10, POB 140, 9901 Kirkenes; tel (85) 92-8-14; telex 64108; fax (85) 92-0-15.
Consul: Brynjulv Sesseng.

Consulate: Vestre Strandgate 29, POB 251, 4601 Kristiansand S; tel (42) 26-1-60; telex 21063; fax (42) 29-9-78.
Consul: Harald Lunöe.
Chancellor: Olav Jonsson Neset.

Consulate: Nedre Enggate 14, POB 326, 6501 Kristiansund N; tel (73) 71-3-66; telex 15234; fax (73) 72-1-89.
Consul: Jan Backer Heide.

Consulate: Storgt. 50, POB 38, 3251 Larvik; tel (34) 82-0-90; telex 21522; fax (34) 85-7-29.
Consul: Harald Sverdrup Bugge.

Consulate: Rutebilstasjonen, POB 86, 4501 Mandal; tel (43) 62-5-11; fax (43) 65-5-03.
Consul: Aage Morten Bessesen.

Consulate: Gudesgt. 2, POB 313, 1501 Moss; tel (9) 25-12-34; telex 71540; fax (9) 25-47-98.
Consul: Nicolai Vogt.

Consulate: c/o LKAB, Havnegt. 28, 8500 Narvik; tel (82) 41-0-20; telex 64022; fax (82) 44-9-25.
Consul: Kaare Andreas Isachsen.
Chancellor: Börje Gustav Lennart Nilsfor.

Consulate: Gunnar Knudsens veg 144, Borgestad, 3900 Porsgrunn; tel (3) 50-01-00; telex 21297; fax (3) 50-17-00.
Consul: Niels Christian Møller.
Chancellor: Kjell-Jan Fristad.

Consulate: Storgt. 5, 4950 Risör; tel (41) 51-4-95.
Consul: Oddvar Halvorsen.

Consulate: Dronningens gate 1-3, POB 50, 3201 Sandefjord; tel (34) 67-2-30; telex 21526.
Consul: Odd Gleditsch.

Consulate: Hjalmar Wessels vei 10, 1700 Sarpsborg; tel (9) 11-80-00; telex 71400; fax (9) 11-87-70.
Consul: Odvar Arne Borger Thorsen.

Consulate: Kongsgårdbakken 1, POB 44, 4001 Stavanger; tel (4) 52-75-00; telex 33007; fax (4) 53-46-42.
Consul: Charles Racine Bergesen.
Vice-Consul: Rigmor Meidell Krogh.

Consulate: Ogndalsvn 14, POB 25, 7701 Steinkjer; tel (77) 63-5-00; telex 55518.
Consul: Knut Kleven.

Consulate: Storgt. 70, POB 430, 9001 Tromsö; tel (83) 82-0-70; telex 64228; fax (83) 89-9-15.
Consul: Anders Yngvar Aagaard.

Consulate: Fossegrenda 7B, POB 4210-Fossegrenda, 7001 Trondheim; tel (7) 96-77-22; telex 55218; fax (7) 96-48-75.
Consul: Axel Buch.
Chancellor: Aud Larssen.

Consulate: Storgt. 20, POB 160, 3101 Tönsberg; tel (33) 16-2-70; telex 70556.
Consul: Sven Gjeruldsen.

Consulate: St Olav's plass 3, 6002 Ålesund; tel (71) 21-4-47.
Consul: Rolv Berg.

SWITZERLAND

Embassy: Bygdøy allé 78, 0268 Oslo 2; tel (2) 43-05-90; telex 78730; fax (2) 44-63-50.
Ambassador: Hansjakob Kaufmann.
Counsellor: Markus Kummer.
Attaché and Chancellor: Magrit Dudler.

THAILAND

Embassy: Munkedamsvn 59B, 0270 Oslo 2; tel (2) 83-25-17; fax (2) 83-03-84.
Ambassador: Taweebandh Singha.

TURKEY

Embassy: Halvdan Svartesgt. 5, 0244 Oslo 2; tel (2) 44-99-20.
Ambassador: Dr H. Erol Celasun.
Defence Attaché: Capt. Mustafa Ultanur.

UNITED KINGDOM

Embassy: Thomas Heftyesgt. 8, 0244 Oslo 2; tel (2) 55-24-00; telex 71575; fax (2) 55-10-41.
Ambassador: David J. E. Ratford.
Counsellor, Consul-General and Deputy Head of Mission: A. J. K. Bailes.
Counsellor (Economic and Commercial): Dr C. P. Burdess.
Defence and Air Attaché: Wing Commdr J. C. W. Marshall.
Naval Attaché: Commdr G. S. Pearson.
Military Attaché: Lieut Col W. R. de W. Lash.
First Secretary: J. R. Venning.
First Secretary (Economic and Commercial): A. Wotton.
First Secretary (Management): R. H. Tonkin.
First Secretary: T. R. Bevan.

Consulate: a/s Bergens Rørhandel, Carl Konowsgt. 34, Postboks 872, 5001 Bergen; tel (5) 34-85-05; telex 42248; fax (5) 34-32-47.
Honorary Consul: R. C. Hestness.

Consulate: Strandgt. 7, POB 322, 9401 Harstad; tel (82) 63-0-93; fax (82) 67-7-45.
Honorary Consul: T. O. Jacobsen.

Consulate: Sørhauggt. 139, POB 128, 5501 Haugesund; tel (4) 72-30-33; telex 42206; fax (4) 72-30-87.
Honorary Consul: K. Rasmussen.

Consulate: Vagevn 7, POB 148, 6501 Kristiansund N; tel (73) 75-33-3; telex 15019; fax (73) 75-3-52.
Honorary Consul: J. Loennechen.

Consulate: Rygetyønnvn 51, POB 71, 4611 Kristiansand S; tel (42) 24-4-52; fax (42) 23-3-93.
Honorary Consul: J. H. B. Moe.

Consulate: Vassbotnen 6, 4033 Forus, POB 178, 4001 Stavanger; POB 9, 4301 Sandnes; tel (4) 80-16-17; telex 33257; fax (4) 62-22-77.
Honorary Consul: C. W. Peck, Jr.

Consulate: c/o L. Macks Olbryggeri, POB 1103, 9001 Tromsø; tel (83) 84-8-00; fax (83) 58-6-77.
Honorary Consul: H. Bredrup.

Consulate: Sluppenvn 10, POB 6004, 7001 Trondheim; tel (7) 96-82-11; telex 55436; fax (7) 96-54-98.
Honorary Consul: F. Kjeldsberg.

Consulate: Farstadgarden, St Olavs Pl., POB 130, 6001 Ålesund; tel (71) 24-4-60; telex 42755; fax (71) 28-5-30.
Honorary Consul: S. A. Farstad.

USA

Embassy: Drammensvn 18, 0244 Oslo 2; tel (2) 44-85-50; fax (2) 43-07-77.
Ambassador: Loret Miller Ruppe.
Deputy Chief of Mission: Donald J. Planty.
Political Section: Elizabeth P. Spiro.
Economic Section: F. Brenne Bachmann.
Commercial Section: Robert C. Fraser.
Consular Section: Elizabeth J. Berube.
Administrative Section: David W. Mulenex.
Regional Security Officer: Chris Andrews.
Public Affairs Officer: David L. Arnett.
Communications Programme Officer: James McCreary.
Information Officer: John Matel.
Office of the Defence Attaché: Capt. Douglas D. Blaha.
Office of Defence Co-operation: Col William L. Brown.

VENEZUELA

Embassy: Drammensvn 82, 1°, POB 7638, Skillebekk, 0205 Oslo 2; tel (2) 43-06-60; telex 77297; fax (2) 43-14-70.
Ambassador: Rodolfo Molina Duarte.
Minister-Counsellor: Noemy Orsetti Salazar.

YUGOSLAVIA

Embassy: Drammensvn 105, 0244 Oslo 2; tel (2) 44-81-05.
Ambassador: Nenad Radovanović.

International Organizations

EUROPEAN COMMUNITIES

External Delegation: POB 1643, Vika 0119, Oslo 1; Haakon's VII Gate No 6, 0161 Oslo 1; tel (2) 83-35-83; telex 79967; fax (2) 83-40-55.
Head of Delegation: Aneurin Hughes.

OMAN

ALGERIA

Embassy: POB 6942, Ruwi; tel 707337; telex 3749.
Ambassador: Dr Bashir Khadoun.

AUSTRIA

Embassy: Moosa Complex, Bldg 477, 2nd Floor, Way 3109, POB 5070, Ruwi, Muscat; tel 793135; telex 3042; fax 793669.
Ambassador: Dr Ernst Illsinger.
Counsellor: Anton Koppensteiner.

BANGLADESH

Embassy: POB 6959, Ruwi; tel 707462; telex 3800.
Chargé d'affaires: Ahmed Sharful Hussain.
First Secretary (Labour): Khairul Ahsan.
Third Secretary: M. Faizullah.

BRUNEI

Embassy: POB 3091, Ruwi, Muscat; tel 605911; telex 5135; fax 605910.

CANADA

Consulate: Moosa Abdaul Rahman, Hassan Bldg, al-Nboor St, POB 4, Ruwi, Muscat; tel 701566; telex 3222; fax 709091.
Honorary Consul: M. A. Moosa.

CHINA, PEOPLE'S REPUBLIC

Embassy: POB 3315, Muscat; tel 702451; telex 3125.
Ambassador: Zang Shixiong.

DENMARK

Embassy: c/o W. S. Towell, POB 4040, Ruwi, Muscat; tel 708304; telex 3214; fax 707686.
Vice-Consul and Commercial Attaché: Stig E. Jönsson.
Secretary: Ulla V. Rasmussen.

EGYPT

Embassy: POB 5252, Ruwi; tel 600411; telex 5438.
Ambassador: Muhammad Abd al-Khaliq Shalabi.

FINLAND

Consulate: Getco Holdings & Investments, POB 84, Muscat; tel 701454; telex 3278; fax 703826.
Consul: Kamal Mohammed Daud al-Hashim.

FRANCE

Embassy: POB 50208, Medinat Qaboos; tel 604222; telex 5163.
Ambassador: Jean-Pierre Guyot.

Economic Section: POB 5314, Ruwi, Muscat 99250; tel 703753; telex 3551.

GERMANY

Embassy: near Al-Nahda Hospital, Ruwi, Muscat; tel 702164; telex 3440; fax 705690.
Ambassador: Klaus Metscher.

INDIA

Embassy: POB 4727, Ruwi, Muscat; tel 702957; telex 3429; fax 797547.
Ambassador: Ranjit Gupta.
First Secretary: Madhava Chandra.
First Secretary: Ashok Kumar Amrohi.
Naval Attaché: Capt. Mohammed Raza Khan.
Second Secretary: Kul Bhushan.
Second Secretary: Shiva Kumar Singh.

IRAN

Embassy: POB 6155, Ruwi; tel 696944; telex 5066.
Ambassador: Muhammad Arab.

IRAQ

Embassy: POB 4848, Muscat; tel 701349; telex 3471.
Ambassador: Khalid Abdullah as-Samira'i.

ITALY

Embassy: POB 6727, Muscat; tel 560968; telex 5450; fax 564846.
Ambassador: Dr Francesco Sciortino.

JAPAN

Embassy: Medinat Qaboss (West), POB 6511, Ruwi; tel 601028; telex 5087; fax 698720.
Ambassador: Takeshi Ohara.

JORDAN

Embassy: POB 5281, Ruwi; tel 602561; telex 5518.
Ambassador: Samir ar-Rifai al-Hemoud.

KOREA, REPUBLIC

Embassy: POB 5220, Ruwi; tel 702322; telex 3132.
Ambassador: Kang Jong-Won.

KUWAIT

Embassy: POB 4798, Muscat; tel 706444; telex 3455.
Ambassador: Abd al-Wahab Yousuf al-'Adsani.

MALAYSIA

Embassy: POB 6939, Ruwi; tel 698329; telex 5565; fax 605031.
Chargé d'affaires: Wan Yusof Embong.
Third Secretary: M. Rosli H. Saad.

MEXICO

Consulate: Muscat; tel 561804.
Honorary Consul: Sheikh Yaqoub Alharthy.

MOROCCO

Embassy: POB 6125, Ruwi; tel 701977; telex 3033.
Ambassador: Muhammad Faraj ad-Doukkali.

NETHERLANDS

Embassy: POB 6302, Ruwi; tel 705410; telex 3050.
Ambassador: Dr J. T. van Leeuwen.

NEW ZEALAND

Consulate: POB 520, Muscat; tel 794932; telex 3022; fax 706443.
Honorary Consul: Dr Hamed Abdullah al-Riyami.

PAKISTAN

Embassy: POB 5451, Ruwi; tel 603439; telex 5451.

QATAR

Embassy: POB 802, Muscat; tel 701802; telex 3460.
Ambassador: Ahmad bin Ali al-Ansari.

RUSSIA

Embassy: POB 3080, Ruwi, Muscat; tel 602894; telex 5493; fax 602894.
Ambassador: Aleksandr K. Patsev.

SAUDI ARABIA

Embassy: POB 4411, Muscat; tel 701111; telex 3401.
Ambassador: Abd al-Mohsin Saleh al-Ballaa.

SOMALIA

Embassy: POB 4767, Ruwi; tel 701355; telex 3253.
Ambassador: Muhammad Suban Nur.

SRI LANKA

Embassy: POB 50095, Medinat Qaboos.
Chargé d'affaires: Nimal Wijayaratne.

SUDAN

Embassy: POB 6971, Ruwi; tel 708790.
Ambassador: Ghani el-Nour Gawish.

SWEDEN

Embassy: Oman Commercial Centre, Rooms 805-6, POB 3001, Ruwi; tel 708693; telex 3871; fax 794283.
Chargé d'affaires a.i. and Counsellor: Kenneth Stig Allan Bertilsson.
Third Secretary: Marie-Elise Kjerstin Gunterberg.

Consulate-General: Bahwan Business Centre Bldg, Central Business District, POB 169, Ruwi, Muscat; tel 793741; telex 3585; fax 796158.
Consul-General: Suhail Salim Abdullah al-Mukhaini Bahwan.
Chancellor: Alex Borges.

SYRIA

Embassy: Muscat.
Ambassador: Abd al-Karim as-Sabbagh.

THAILAND

Embassy: Villa 33/34 Rd O, Madinat Qaboos East, POB 7028, Mutrah; tel 602684; telex 5210.
Ambassador: Pramual Nuabusya.

TUNISIA

Embassy: POB 5755, Ruwi; tel 704574; telex 3641.
Ambassador: Yousef al-Mokadam.

TURKEY

Embassy: POB 8511, Mutrah, Muscat; tel 697050; telex 5571; fax 697053.
Ambassador: Emin Gündüz.

UNITED ARAB EMIRATES

Embassy: POB 1551, Muscat; tel 600302; telex 3299.
Chargé d'affaires a.i.: Muhammad Sultan al-Oweis.

UNITED KINGDOM

Embassy: POB 300, Muscat; tel 738501; telex 5216; fax 736040.
Ambassador: Sir Terence Clark.
Counsellor and Deputy Head of Mission: N. H. S. Armour.
Defence and Military Attaché: Brig. M. F. Bremridge.
Naval and Air Attaché: Commdr K. A. Harris.
First Secretary (Chancery): N. H. Bates.
First Secretary (Commercial): B. P. Baldwin.
Second Secretary (Management) and Consul: G. H. Davies.
Second Secretary (Commercial): J. A. Begbie.
Third Secretary (Chancery/Information): I. P. Bailey.

Commercial Section: POB 6898, Ruwi; tel 706468; telex 3743; fax 706467.

USA

Embassy: POB 50202, Medinat Qaboos, Muscat; tel 698989; fax 699778.
Ambassador: Richard W. Boehm.
Deputy Chief of Mission: Haywood Rankin.
Political/Economic Section: Mark Scheland.
Political/Military Section: Jeffrey W. Castelli.
Consular Section: Nancy J. Cooper.
Administrative Section: Ellen C. Engels.
Regional Security Officer: Michael T. Manegan.
Communications Programme Officer: Paul R. Million.
Office of Military Co-operation: Col Jewell W. Jeffrey, Jr.

Economic/Commercial Section: tel 699094; fax 604316.
Economic/Commercial Section: Frank R. Adams.

Office of the Defence Attaché: telex 5457.
Office of the Defence Attaché: Col John V. Siebert.

Information Service: fax 699771.
Public Affairs Officer: Steven J. Sharp.

Representative to Omani/American Joint Commission for Economic and Technical Co-operation: POB 6001, Ruwi; tel 703000; fax 797778.
Co-Chairman: Richard W. Boehm.
Agency for International Development Representative: Mark Mathews.

YEMEN

Embassy: POB 3701, Muscat; tel 700091.
Ambassador: Muhammad Oman Abdullah Bassad.

PAKISTAN

AFGHANISTAN

Embassy: 176 Shalimar 7/3, Islamabad; tel (51) 22566.

ALGERIA

Embassy: 20, St 17, F-7/2, POB 1038, Islamabad; tel (51) 820166; telex 5884.
Ambassador: A. S. Bereksi.

ARGENTINA

Embassy: 8, St 17, Shalimar 6/2, Islamabad; tel (51) 821117; telex 5698.
Ambassador: Dr Alberto Naveiro de la Serna.

AUSTRALIA

High Commission: University Rd, POB 1046, Islamabad; tel (51) 822111; telex 5804; fax (51) 820417.
High Commissioner: G. J. Price.

AUSTRIA

Embassy: 13, St 1, Shalimar F-6/3, POB 1018, Islamabad; tel (51) 820137; telex 5531.
Ambassador: Dr Paul Hartig.
Economic Counsellor: Eugen Ruff.
Attaché: Dr Frank Helmut Schiwek.

Consulate: 4 Lawrence Rd, POB 340, Lahore; tel (42) 305061; telex 44580.
Honorary Consul: Mohammed Amin.

BANGLADESH

High Commission: 24, St 28, F-6/1, Islamabad; tel (51) 826885; telex 5615.
High Commissioner: C. M. Shafi Sami.

BELGIUM

Embassy: 39, St 1, Shalimar F-6/3, Islamabad; tel (51) 820131; telex 5865; fax (51) 822358.
Ambassador: Bernard Lauwaert.
First Secretary: Patrick Renault.

Commercial Section: Bungalow No. 108/4, Charlies Fox, 1-5 Clifton, Karachi; tel (21) 531011.

BRAZIL

Embassy: 194 Atatürk Ave, G-6/3, POB 1053, Islamabad; tel (51) 822497; telex 5711.
Ambassador: Antônio Carlos Diniz de Andrade.

BULGARIA

Embassy: 66 Atatürk Ave, Shalimar G-6/3, Islamabad.
Ambassador: Georgi Iliev Bozhkov.

CANADA

High Commission: Diplomatic Enclave, Sector G-5, POB 1042, Islamabad; tel (51) 821101; telex 5700; fax (51) 823466.
High Commissioner: Manfred G. von Nostitz.
Counsellor (Commercial): A. C. H. Smith.
Counsellor (Immigration): P. M. Current.
Counsellor: J. A. Junke.
Counsellor (Development): L. K. Marchand.
Counsellor (Development): B. W. Hunter.
First Secretary (Development): K. C. Smith.
First Secretary (Development): N. Chartrand-Tresch.
First Secretary (Development): W. Quarry.
First Secretary (Administration): S. J. Park.

Consulate: c/o Beach Luxury Hotel, Tamizuddin Khan Rd, Suite 336, Karachi 0227; tel (21) 551031; telex 23899.
Honorary Consul: B. Avari.

CHILE

Embassy: 10, St 62, F-6/3, Islamabad; tel (51) 821813.

CHINA, PEOPLE'S REPUBLIC

Embassy: Diplomatic Enclave, Ramna 4, Islamabad; tel (51) 826667.
Ambassador: Tian Ding.

CUBA

Embassy: 8, St 80, F-7/4, Islamabad; tel (51) 820861.
Chargé d'affaires: María Elena Carballés.

'TURKISH REPUBLIC OF NORTHERN CYPRUS'

Embassy: 315B Kohsar Rd, Margalla Rd, F-7/2, POB 2165, Islamabad; tel (51) 814970; telex 54324; fax (51) 823447.
Ambassador: Bener Erkmen.
First Secretary: Sadettin Topukçu.

CZECHOSLOVAKIA

Embassy: 49, St 27, Shalimar F-6/2, Islamabad; tel (51) 820195; telex 5705.
Ambassador: Stefan Bodnar.

DENMARK

Embassy: 121, St 90, Ramna 6/3, POB 1118, Islamabad; tel (51) 823518; telex 5825.
Chargé d'affaires a.i. and Minister-Counsellor: Jørgen Abrahamsen.
Attaché: Per Christensen.

Consulate-General: c/o Karl Gross Pakistan (Private) Ltd, 1/A, G-22, Block 9, Kehkashan, Khayabane Jami, Clifton, POB 4895, Karachi; tel (21) 534006; telex 28038.
Consul-General: Mohamed Irshad Uddin.
Vice-Consul: Shabanali Mahomedali Shariff.

Consulate: 1st Floor, 8 Alshams Plaza, Davis Rd, Lahore; tel (42) 304133; telex 44439.
Consul: Sheikh Abdul Rahman.

Consulate: Peshawar.

EGYPT

Embassy: 37, 6th Ave, POB 2088, Ramna 6/4, Islamabad; telex 5677.
Ambassador: Mohammad Sani Heila.

FINLAND

Embassy: House 11, St 90, Sector G-6/3, POB 1862, Islamabad; tel (51) 822136; telex 54560; fax (51) 824327.
Chargé d'affaires a.i.: Kimmo Pulkkinen.

Consulate: M/S Interglobe Commerce Pakistan (PVT) Ltd, 72-West, Benazir Plaza, 1st Floor, Sector F-7/G-7, Blue Area, Islamabad; tel (51) 825575; telex 54111.
Consul: Jamil Ansari.

Consulate-General: Finlay House, I. I. Chundringar Rd, POB 4670, Karachi 2; tel (21) 220086; telex 823674.
Consul-General: Ahmed Mahmud.

FRANCE

Embassy: Constitution Ave, Plot 1/6, Diplomatic Enclave, POB 1068, Islamabad; tel (51) 823981; telex 5819; fax (51) 825389.
Ambassador: Jean-Pierre Masset.
First Counsellor: Pascal Maubert.
Counsellor (Commercial): Jean-Paul Huet.
Counsellor (Cultural/Scientific/Technical Co-operation): Pierre Carpentier.
First Secretary: Sylvain Berger.
Second Secretary and Press Attaché: Olivier Richard.
Consul: Michel Roussos.

Economic Section: POB 1078; tel (51) 823551; telex 5715.

Consulate-General: 12A Mohammad Ali Bogra Rd, Bath Island, Karachi 4; tel (21) 532047; telex 25131; fax (21) 533928.
Consul General: Michel Trinquier.

GERMANY

Embassy: Ramna 5, Diplomatic Enclave, POB 1027, Islamabad; tel (51) 822151; telex 5871; fax (51) 826740.
Ambassador: Alfred B. Vestring.

Consulate-General: 90 Clifton, POB 3701, Karachi 6; tel (21) 530806; telex 2772; fax (21) 532445.
Consul-General: Dr Hartmut Wagner.

Consulate: 60 Main Gulberg, POB 3151, Gulberg Post Office, Lahore; tel (42) 874778.
Honorary Consul: Waldemar Kroders.

Consulate: Jamrud Rd, University Post Office, POB 745, Peshawar; tel (521) 50584.
Honorary Consul: Rudolf von Przyborowski.

HOLY SEE

Apostolic Nunciature: St 5, Diplomatic Enclave 1, G-5, POB 1106, 44000, Islamabad; tel (51) 820490; fax (51) 820847.
Apostolic Pro-Nuncio: Most Rev. Luigi Bressan, Titular Archbishop of Severiana.
Second Secretary: Rev. Fr David Malloy.

HUNGARY

Embassy: House No. 12, Shalimar 6/3, POB 1103, Islamabad; tel (51) 824592.
Ambassador: András Dallos.

ICELAND

Embassy: Islamabad.

Consulate-General: House 54, St 1, Shalimar F-6/3, POB 1104, Islamabad; tel (51) 21023.
Consul-General: Khalifa Mahmoodullah.

Consulate-General: Bldg 1-B, 1st Floor, State Life Sq., off I. I. Chundrigar Rd, POB 10062, Karachi; tel (21) 228658; telex 2769.
Consul-General: Naveed A. Khan.

INDIA

High Commission: G-5, Diplomatic Enclave, Islamabad; tel (51) 826718; telex 5849.
High Commissioner: Jyotindra Nath Dixit.

INDONESIA

Embassy: 10-12, St 4, Shalimar 6/3, POB 1019, Islamabad; tel (51) 811291; telex 5679.
Ambassador: Prasodjo Mahdi.

Consulate: E-1.5, Clifton, Karachi 6.

IRAN

Embassy: A3, St 17, F-6/2, Islamabad; tel (51) 822694; telex 5872.
Ambassador: Javaad Mansoori.

IRAQ

Embassy: 1, St 15, F-7/2, Islamabad; telex 5868.
Ambassador: Adil Ahmad Zaidein.

IRELAND

Consulate: POB 12419, 30B Gizri Blvd, Defence Housing Society, Karachi 46; tel (21) 542536; telex 23047; fax (21) 533735.
Honorary Consul: Nadeem S. A. Beg.

ITALY

Embassy: 54 Khayaban-e-Margalla, F-6/3, POB 1008, Islamabad; tel (51) 825791; telex 5861.
Ambassador: Dr Arduino Fornara.

JAPAN

Embassy: Plot No. 53-70, Ramna 5/4, Diplomatic Enclave 1, Islamabad; tel (51) 820181; telex 5805; fax (51) 821009.
Ambassador: Kunio Muraoka.

Consulate-General: 233 Raja Ghazanfar Ali Khan Rd, El Lines, Karachi; tel (21) 511331; telex 2864; fax (21) 514627.
Consul-General: Seiro Kawasaki.

JORDAN

Embassy: 131, St 14, E-7, Islamabad; tel (51) 821782; telex 5701.
Ambassador: Fakhri Abu Taleb.

KENYA

High Commission: 8, St 88, G-6/3, Islamabad; tel (51) 811266.
High Commissioner: G. W. Uku.

KOREA, DEMOCRATIC PEOPLE'S REPUBLIC

Embassy: 9, St 89, Ramna 6/3, Islamabad; tel (51) 822420; telex 5707.
Ambassador: Choe Su Il.

KOREA, REPUBLIC

Embassy: 72 Main Margallah Rd, F-6/2, Islamabad; tel (51) 824926.
Ambassador: Woong Choi.

KUWAIT

Embassy: University Rd, Diplomatic Enclave, Islamabad; tel (51) 822181; telex 5611.
Ambassador: Qasim Omar al-Yaqout.

LEBANON

Embassy: 24, Khayaban-e-Iqbal, Shalimar F-6/3, Islamabad; tel (51) 821022.
Ambassador: Walid A. Nasr.

LIBYA

People's Bureau: Khayaban-e-Iqbal, 8/3, Islamabad; tel (51) 821033; telex 5750.
Ambassador: Muhammad Rashid al-Mugherbi.

MALAYSIA

High Commission: 224, Shalimar 7/4, Islamabad; tel (51) 820147; telex 5801.
High Commissioner: Emam Mohammad Haniff bin Emam Mohammad Hussain.

MALTA

Consulate-General: Gokal Shipping and Trading Corporation (Private) Ltd, Gokal Chambers, Beach Hotel Rd, Karachi; tel (21) 551001; telex 2758.
Honorary Consul-General: Mohammed Bakar Gokal.

MAURITIUS

High Commission: 27, St 26, F-6/2, Islamabad; tel (51) 823345; telex 54362.
High Commissioner: Dhurma Gian Nath.

MOROCCO

Embassy: 6 Service Rd (South), E-7, Islamabad; tel (51) 820820; telex 5718.
Ambassador: Ahmed Drissi.

MYANMAR

Embassy: 12/1, St 13, F-7/2, Islamabad; tel (51) 822460.
Ambassador: U Than Tun.

NEPAL

Embassy: 506, St 84, Atatürk Ave, Ramna 6/4, Islamabad; tel (51) 823642.
Ambassador: Arjun Narsingh Rana.

NETHERLANDS

Embassy: New PIA Bldg, 2nd Floor, Blue Area, POB 1065, Islamabad; tel (51) 814336; telex 5817; fax (51) 822630.
Ambassador: Dr J. J. de Roos.

NEW ZEALAND

Consulate: 110-117 Qamar House, MA Jinnah Rd, Karachi; tel (21) 203153; fax (21) 2410968.
Honorary Consul: Moin Fudda.

NIGERIA

High Commission: 6, St 22, Shalimar 6/2, POB 1075, Islamabad; tel (51) 822465; telex 5875.
High Commissioner: O. I. Yunusa.

NORWAY

Embassy: 15, St 84, G-6/4, POB 1336, Islamabad; tel (51) 822416; telex 5541; fax (51) 825162.

Office of the Narcotics Attaché: fax (51) 822478.

OMAN

Embassy: 440 Bazar Rd, Ramna 6/4, Islamabad; tel (51) 822586; telex 5704.
Ambassador: Salim Muhammad al-Khussaily.

PHILIPPINES

Embassy: 19, St 1, Shalimar 6/3, POB 1052, Islamabad; tel (51) 822720.
Ambassador: Nicasio G. Valderrama.

POLAND

Embassy: St 24, G-4, Diplomatic Enclave, POB 1032, Islamabad; tel (51) 821133.

Ambassador: Dyonizy P. Bilinski.

PORTUGAL

Embassy: 8, St 90, G-6/3, Islamabad; tel (51) 823395; telex 5721.

QATAR

Embassy: 201 Masjid Rd, Shalimar 6/4, Islamabad; tel (51) 824635; telex 5869.
Ambassador: Atiq Masser al-Bader.

ROMANIA

Embassy: 13, St 88, Ramna 6/3, Islamabad; tel (51) 820607.
Ambassador: Iosif Chivu.
First Secretary: Valeriu Arteni.
Second Secretary: Aurel Besliu.

Economic Counsellor's Office: 245/2/H, Block 6, PECHS, Karachi 29; tel (21) 439653; fax (21) 430131.
Economic Counsellor: Marius Vidan.
Second Secretary (Economic): Vasile Baroi.

RUSSIA

Embassy: Khayaban-e-Suhrawardy, Diplomatic Enclave, Ramna 4, Islamabad; tel (51) 824604; telex 54241.
Ambassador: Victor Pavlovich Yakunin.

Consulate-General: 8/26 Flench St, 4 Bleak House Rd, Karachi; tel (21) 512852.

SAUDI ARABIA

Embassy: 1, St 4, F-6/3, Islamabad; tel (51) 820156; telex 5708.
Ambassador: Yusef Motabbakani.

SINGAPORE

High Commission: Islamabad.
High Commissioner: Ton Keng Jin.

SOMALIA

Embassy: 15, St 13, F-7/2, Islamabad; tel (51) 822769; telex 5609.
Ambassador: Abdi Salam Haji Ahmad Liban.

SPAIN

Embassy: 180G, Ramna 6/3, Atatürk Ave, POB 1144, Islamabad; tel (51) 821070; telex 5803.
Ambassador: José García Bañón.

SRI LANKA

High Commission: 19, St 56, F-7/4, Islamabad; tel (51) 820754.
High Commissioner: Austin Jayewardena.

SUDAN

Embassy: 203, Ramna 6/3, Islamabad; tel (51) 820171; telex 5617.
Ambassador: Omar el-Sayed Taha.

SWEDEN

Embassy: 6A, Agha Khan Rd, Markaz Shalimar 6, POB 1100, Islamabad; tel (51) 822557; telex 5806; fax (51) 825284.
Ambassador: Ian Paulsson.
Counsellor: Ulf Håkansson.
Second Secretary: Ingbritt Roche.

Consulate-General: c/o United Liner Agencies of Pakistan Ltd, 5-6 Chartered Bank Chambers, I. I. Chundrigar Rd, POB 5830, Karachi 2; tel (21) 233695; telex 2775.
Consul-General: Mohammed Moonis.

Consulate-General: c/o Packages Ltd, Shahrah-e-Roomi, P. O. Amer Sidhu, Lahore 54770; tel (42) 370158; telex 44866.
Consul-General: Syed Babar Ali.

SWITZERLAND

Embassy: 25, St 19, F-6/2, POB 1073, Islamabad; tel (51) 821151; telex 5815; fax (51) 824872.
Ambassador: Petar A. Troendle.
Third Secretary and Head of Chancery: Urs Berner.
Attaché (Development Co-operation/Humanitarian Aid): Johann Ambühl.

Consulate-General: Clifton 98, Karachi 6; tel (21) 532038; telex 23768; fax (21) 533142.
Consul-General: Peter Felix.
Chancellor: Francesco Ottolini.

SYRIA

Embassy: 30 Hill Rd, Shalimar 6/3, Islamabad; tel (51) 821077; telex 5619.
Ambassador: Saifi Hamwi.

THAILAND

Embassy: 4, St 8, Shalimar 8/3, Islamabad; telex 5527.
Ambassador: Dr Chalerm Acharry.

TUNISIA

Embassy: 426, St 2, Shalimar F-6/3, Islamabad; tel (51) 821576; telex 5676.
Ambassador: Jameleddine Gordah.

TURKEY

Embassy: 42, St 12, Shalimar 6/3, Islamabad; tel (51) 821939.
Ambassador: Baki Ilkin.

UGANDA

High Commission: Islamabad.

UNITED ARAB EMIRATES

Embassy: Plot No. 1-22, Diplomatic Enclave, Islamabad; tel (51) 821373; telex 5831.
Ambassador: Saeed Ali al-Nowais.

UNITED KINGDOM

High Commission: Diplomatic Enclave, Ramna 5, POB 1122, Islamabad; tel (51) 822131; telex 54122; fax (51) 823439.
High Commissioner: Sir Nicholas Barrington.
Deputy High Commissioner: J. C. Harrison.
Counsellor (Economic/Commercial/Aid): P. J. Dun.
Counsellor: J. P. G. Wiseman.
Defence and Military Adviser: Brig. A. E. Berry.
Naval and Air Adviser: Commdr J. D. St J. Ainslie.
First Secretary (Consular/Immigration): S. M. Scaddan.
First Secretary (Commercial/Economic): J. M. Pepper.
First Secretary (Management): G. C. Livesey.
Second Secretary (Works): A. Gillott.
Second Secretary (Aid): R. A. W. Marshall.
Second Secretary (Visits/Information/Chancery): A. J. Walters.
Second Secretary (Chancery/Information): P. Brummell.
Second Secretary (Works): C. B. Gray.

Consulate: c/o ICI Pakistan Ltd, 63 Mozang Rd, Lahore; tel (42) 380892; telex 44851.
Honorary Consul: B. A. Khan.

Deputy High Commission: Shahrah-e-Iran, Clifton, Karachi 75600; tel (21) 532041; telex 24180; fax (21) 530512.
Deputy High Commissioner: D. J. Young.
First Secretary (Commercial): J. G. Lindsay.
Second Secretary (Management/Consular): A. Mills.
Second Secretary (Commercial/Aid): I. M. Dallas.
Second Secretary (Immigration): M. Sim.
Third Secretary (Political/Aid): M. K. Roper.

USA

Embassy: Diplomatic Enclave, Ramna 5, POB 1048, Islamabad; tel (51) 826161; telex 5864; fax (51) 822004.
Ambassador: Robert B. Oakley.
Deputy Chief of Mission: A. Elizabeth Jones.
Political Section: Edward F. Fugit.
Economic Section: Lawrence N. Benedict.
Consular Section: Karen C. Stanton.
Administrative Section: Donald S. Hays.
Regional Security Officer: Wayne S. Rychak.
Public Affairs Officer: William R. Lenderking.
Communications Programme Officer: Raul Holguin.
Information Systems Manager: Roger E. Sawyer.
Office of the Defence Attaché: Col Paul H. Rowcliffe.
Agricultural Section: Frank Coolidge.
Narcotics Assistance Unit: James B. Magnor.
Refugee Co-ordinator: Sandra A. Dembski.
Agency for International Development Representative: Robert N. Bakley.
Military Assistance Advisory Group: Brig. Gen. John D. Howard.

Consulate-General: 8 Abdullah Haroon Rd, Karachi; tel (21) 518180; telex 2611; fax (21) 513089.
Consul-General: Richard C. Faulk.
Political/Economic Section: Nancy C. Mason.
Commercial Section: George A. Kachmar.
Consular Section: Kenneth A. Duncan.
Administrative Section: Jacques Stanitz III.
Regional Security Officer: John Hucke.
Branch Public Affairs Officer: Michael H. Anderson.
Communications Programme Officer: Christopher M. Bonsteel.
Information Systems Manager: James L. Sundstrom.

Consulate-General: 50 Zafar Ali Rd, Gulberg 5, Lahore; tel (42) 870221; fax (42) 872911.
Consul-General: Laurie A. Johnston.
Political Section: Sheila J. Peters.
Economic/Commercial Section: James R. Micsan.
Consular Section: Christopher P. Henzel.
Administrative Section: Jeffry R. Olesen.
Branch Public Affairs Officer: Lois Mervyn.
Communications Programme Officer: Michael A. Cesena.
Agency for International Development: Richard S. Stevenson.

Consulate: 11 Hospital Rd, Peshawar; tel (521) 79801; telex 364; fax (521) 76712.
Principal Officer: Gerald M. Feierstein.
Political/Consular Section: Walter L. Mayo III.
Administrative Section: Allen D. Kobliska.
Agency for International Development: Hank Cushing.
Branch Public Affairs Officer: Michael J. Mingo.

YEMEN

Embassy: 16, St 17, F-6/3, Islamabad 44000; tel (51) 821146; telex 54460; fax (51) 826159.
Ambassador: Abdul Malik Mohammad Wasea al-Tayyeb.

YUGOSLAVIA

Embassy: 14, St 87, Ramna 6/3, Islamabad; tel (51) 821081.
Ambassador: Dr Radoslav Bulajić.

International Organizations

EUROPEAN COMMUNITIES

External Delegation: POB 1605, House N8, Margalla Rd, F 6/3, Islamabad; tel (51) 821828; telex 54044; fax (51) 822604.
Head of Delegation: Thomas Christopher O'Sullivan.

PANAMA

ARGENTINA

Embassy: Edif. del Banco de Iberoamérica, entre Calles 50 y 53, 5°, Apdo 1271, Panamá 1; tel 64-6561; telex 2679.
Ambassador: Juan Bautista Yofre.
Air Attaché: Cdre Marcelo Augusto Conte.
Military and Naval Attaché: Col Jorge Mario Rizo.
First Secretary: Rodolfo Cipriano Cisternas.
Attaché: Magdelena Fuentes Rocha.

AUSTRIA

Consulate-General: Avda Simón Bolivar, Edif. Concreto, Panamá; tel 29-2700; telex 292925; fax 29-2925.
Honorary Consul-General: Robert Zauner.
Honorary Vice-Consul: Reinhilde Monsberger de Moncayo.

BELGIUM

Consulate: Plaza Marbella, Panamá; tel 69-5940.
Consul: Ricardo Alberto Fabrega.

BELIZE

Embassy: Belize.
Ambassador: Ismael Lavrencio Garcia (resident in Belize).

Consulate: Apdo 205, Panamá 9-A; tel 26-4498.
Honorary Consul: Naim Emmanuel Musa G.

BOLIVIA

Embassy: Edif. Bolivia, 1°, Avda Nicanor Obarrio 78, Apdo 8187, Panamá 7; tel 64-3868.
Ambassador: Carlos Montaño Daza.
Attaché: Maria Dolores de Cosulich.

Consulate: Calle 29, 22 Frente a Guardia y Cía, Apdo 7262, Panamá 5; tel 25-1293.
Honorary Consul: Alberto Boyd.

Consulate: Zona Libre, Colón, Apdo 417, Panamá 3; tel 45-2077.
Honorary Consul: Alberto Motta.
Honorary Consul: Jorge Velasco.
Honorary Consul: Julio Antelo Salmon.

BRAZIL

Embassy: Edif. El Dorado 1°, Calle Elvira Méndez y Avda Ricardo Arango, Urb. Campo Alegre, Apdo 4287, Panamá 5; tel 63-5322; telex 3569.
Ambassador: Pedro Paulo Assumpcão.
Military Attaché: Carlos Engelberg Morales S.
First Secretary: Geraldo Alfonso Mozzi.
First Secretary: Luis Antonio Dubeux Fonseca.
Attaché and Vice-Consul: Francisco Carneiro de Almeida.

CANADA

Consulate: Edif. Proconsa, Aero Peru 5°B, Calle Manuel Icaza, Campo Alegre, Panama City; Apdo Postal 3658, Balboa, Panama City; tel 64-7014; fax 23-3508.
Honorary Consul: Ruth Lister de Denton.

CHILE

Embassy: Edif. Grobman 7°, Calle Manuel María Icaza, Apdo 7341, Panamá 5; tel 23-9748; telex 2969.
Ambassador: Wilna Saavedra Córtez.
Counsellor: Hernan Torrealba Pacheco.
Third Secretary: Antonio Pena Mundnich.
Military and Naval Attaché: Col Sergio Pineiro Garcia.

CHINA (TAIWAN)

Embassy: Edif. Torre Banco Unión, 10°, Calle Samuel Lewis, Apdo 4285, Panamá 5; tel 23-3424; telex 3587; fax 63-5534.
Ambassador: Su Pingchao.
Political Counsellor: Lin Chang-Horng.
Economic Counsellor: Kan Pao-Sheng.
Press Counsellor: Tseng Mouchuan.
Defence Attaché: Capt. Chao Chung.
First Secretary: Ching Hsiung Huan.
First Secretary: Jinn-Ming Soong.
Second Secretary: Jeng Chian-Heh Lai.
Second Secretary: Guang-Pu Shyu.
Third Secretary (Commercial): Jaime Chen.
Third Secretary (Consular): Chin-Sheng Lee.
Third Secretary (Press): Hung-Chyi Chou.

Consulate-General: 9085 Calle 9, Avda Roosevelt, Apdo 540, Colón; tel 41-3061.
Consul-General: Liu Chun-Hsiung.

COLOMBIA

Embassy: Edif. Grobman, 6°, Avda Manuel María Icaza, Apdo 4407, Panamá 5; tel 64-9644; telex 3330.
Ambassador: Francisco José J. Safar.
Minister-Counsellor: Hernando Piedrahita Currea.
Counsellor (Commercial): Brig.-Gen. Armando Vanegas Maldonado.
Military, Naval and Air Attaché: Col Luis Eduardo Guiza Valbuena.
Defence Attaché: Capt. Jean Lelong.
Attaché (Political): Col Roso Julio Navarro Franco.
Second Secretary: Amalfi Fernandez de Diaz.
Assistant Attaché (Commercial): Bernardo Marquez Bedoya.
Chancellor: Cecilia Mendez Alzamora.
Chancellor: Maria Victoria Parra Escobar.

Consulate: Calle Eusebio A Morales, al Lado de la Floristeria Las Vegas, Panamá; tel 23-3535.
Consul-General: Francisco Leon Restrepo Acosta.
Consul: Lettfalah Jorge Nader Morales.

Consulate: Edif. Mar del Sur, Apto 5B, Punta Paitilla, Panamá; tel 64-8167.
Consul-General: Dr Miguel Maria Arias Sanabria.
Vice-Consul: Nhora Perfecta Pereiro.

COSTA RICA

Embassy: Edif. Miraflores, Calle Gerardo Ortega, Apdo 8963, Panamá 5; tel 64-2980; telex 2313.
Ambassador: Herbert Wolf Fournier.
Minister-Counsellor: Francisco Hidalgo Brenes.
Minister-Counsellor: Luis Bernal Montes de Oca.
First Secretary: Fabio Ortega Fuentes.
Second Secretary: Maria del Socorro Meza Montoya.

Consulate: Edif. Elizabeth, Apt 6, Avda Argentina, Calle G, Panamá.
Consul: Giovanni Polonio Lobo.
Consul: Ligia Maria Ulloa.
Consul: Otto Roberto Vargas Viquez.
Consul: Danilo Perez Zamora.
Consul-General: Miguel A. Saenz Campos.
Consul: Margarita Cervantes Rivera.
Consul: Juan Flores Badilla.

CUBA

Embassy: Avda Cuba y Ecuador 33, Apdo 6-2291, El Dorado, Panama City; tel 27-5277; telex 2788.
Ambassador: Arnaldo Molina Pérez.
Attaché (Commercial): Oscar Braulio Gutierrez.
Attaché (Economic): Guillermo Mendez Perez.
Consul: José Luis Mendez Mendez.

CYPRUS

Consulate: Apdo 4016, Panamá 5; tel 60-4592.
Consul-General: Nikiforos Constantaki.

DENMARK

Consulate-General: Edif. Diplomatico, Calle Ricardo Arango, Panamá; Apdo 7363, Panamá 5; tel 63-5872; telex 368572.
Consul-General: Svend-Olov Ruben Fahlgren.
Consul: Niels Lykke Pedersen.

Consulate: Roosevelt Ave, Cristobal, Apdo 5025, Colón; tel 45-1155; telex 03788504.
Consul: Adrian Holmes.

DOMINICAN REPUBLIC

Embassy: Edif. Miraflores, 2°, Calle Gerardo Ortega 7, Apdo 6250, Panamá 5; tel 69-4285.
Ambassador: Héctor Pereyra Ariza.
Attaché (Cultural): Elsa Lila Perez de Crespo.

Consulate: Apdo 4543, Panamá 5; tel 64-8630.
Consul-General: Mario Bello Andino.

ECUADOR

Embassy: Edif. Grobman, 3°, Manuel María Icaza y Samuel Lewis, Apdo 8380, Panamá 7; tel 64-2654; fax 23-0159.
Ambassador: Pio Oswaldo Cueva Puertas.
Military Attaché: Col Luis Bolivar Marcial Franco.
Military Attaché: Col Angel Leonardo Alban Delgado.
First Secretary: Claudio Cevallos Berrazueta.

Consulate: Edif. Los Casares, 4 Calle D, El Cangrejo, Panamá; tel 45-2950.
Consul: Miguel Mendez Rueda.

EGYPT

Embassy: Avda 51a Norte, El Cangrejo, Apdo 7080, Panamá 5; tel 63-5020; telex 3572.
Ambassador: Yehia Mohamed Hosny Kabel.
Counsellor: Yousri Youssef Ezzeldin.
Attaché: Abou Bakr Mohamed el-Sayed.
Attaché: Mohamed Mokhamer Mohamed.

EL SALVADOR

Embassy: Edif. Citibank, 4°, Of. 408, Vía España 124, Apdo 8016, Panamá 7; tel 23-3020; telex 3240.
Ambassador: José Fernando S. Olivares.
Counsellor and Consul-General: Aida Mildred Velasco Fagioli.
Defence Attaché: Col Augusto Candelario Maravilla Reyes.
Defence Attaché: Ramon Antonio Morales Ruiz.

FINLAND

Consulate-General: Carretera Transistmicay, Calle 85, Apdo B-2, Panamá 9A; tel 36-3000; telex 3628; fax 36-2875.
Consul-General: Einar Louis Simons.

Consulate: 1 Calle 28, El Cangrejo, Apdo 1673, Balboa, Panama City; tel 52-3123.
Vice-Consul: Hellin Louhi de Shelton.

FRANCE

Embassy: Plaza de Francia 1-06, Apdo 869, Panamá 1; tel 28-7835; telex 2834; fax 28-7852.
Ambassador: Jean-Paul Barre.
Counsellor and Chargé d'affaires: Jean-Claude Nolla.
Counsellor (Finance): Michel Ungemuth.
Defence Attaché: Capt. Yves Pineau.
Second Secretary (Consular): Roger Brattin.
Attaché (Cultural): Henri Tomasini.
Attaché: Jean Benja.
Attaché: Jean-Michel Burgy.
Attaché: Christian Devaux.

Commercial Section: Calle Elvira Méndez y Calle 52, Edif. Vallarino, 8°, Campo Alegre; Apdo 1407, Panamá 1; tel 63-5011; fax 69-6411.
Counsellor (Commercial): Francis Clement.
Attaché (Commercial): Marc Antoine Lopez.

Consulate: Apdo 1100, Colón 3; tel 41-4138.
Honorary Consul: Antonio Chalhoub.

Consulate: Urb. Las Acacias, Calle 1a, Apdo 78, David, Prov. Chiriqui; tel 75-3814.
Honorary Consul: Gustavo de Obaldia.

GERMANY

Embassy: Edif. Bank of America, 6°, Calle 50 y 53, El Obarrio, Apdo 4228, Panamá 5; tel 63-7733; telex 2979; fax 23-6664.
Ambassador: Dr Götz von Boehmer.
Counsellor (Economic/Press): Georg Birgelen.
Second Secretary (Consular/Administrative): Klaus A. Meixner.
Assistant Attaché (Administrative): Torsten Roser.
Assistant Attaché (Administrative): Birgitte Kuba.
Assistant Attaché (Administrative): Marion Mönnich de Rojas.

Consulate: c/o Boyd Steamship Corporation, Apdo 5077, Cristobal, Colón; tel 45-3344; telex 3482031.
Honorary Consul: Jürgen Dorfmeier.

Consulate: Cerveceria Chiricana SA, Via Boquete, Apdo 503, David, Prov. Chiriqui; tel 75-4141.
Honorary Consul: Eckhard Schönleber.

GHANA

Embassy: Panamá.
Ambassador: Kofi Nyidevu Awoonor.

GREECE

Consulate: El Avance 2, Panamá; tel 60-0668.
Honorary Consul: Haralambos Tzanetatos.
Honorary Consul: Panayotis Tzanetatos.

GUATEMALA

Embassy: Edif. Adir, 6°, Of. 6-8, Calle Eric Del Valle y Calle 55, Apdo 2352, Panamá 9A; tel 69-3475.
Ambassador: Col Héctor Rosales Salaverria.
Second Secretary: Aurora Magarita Lopez de Jurado.
Defence Attaché: Col Edgar Eugenio Mendez Lopez.
Attaché (Cultural/Tourism): Maria Isabel Romillo Mendez-Ruiz.

GUINEA

Consulate: Calle Elvira Méndez 30, Edif. Ejecutivo, Apto 4, Panamá; tel 63-5466.
Honorary Consul: Winston Spadafora.

HAITI

Embassy: Edif. Dora Luz, 2°, Calle 1, Urban, Bella Vista, Apdo 442, Panamá 9; tel 63-8728; fax 64-3672.
Ambassador: Michel-Hosé Lapommeray.

HOLY SEE

Apostolic Nunciature: Punta Paitilla, Apdo 4251, Panamá 5; tel 69-3138; fax 64-2116.
Apostolic Nuncio: Most Rev. Osvaldo Padilla, Titular Archbishop of Pia.

HONDURAS

Embassy: Edif. Tapia 3-80, Of. 202, Calle 31 y Justo Arosemena, Apdo 8704, Panamá 5; tel 25-8200; telex 2894; fax 25-3283.
Ambassador: Francisco Salomon Jiménez Munguia.
Attaché (Commercial): Erasmo Williams.
Attaché: Maria Ofelia Alvarez Rodriguez.
Attaché: Rosa Amelia Avila.
Attaché: Aurora Alicia de Tejada.
Attaché: Sandra Larach de Chong.
Attaché: Marianela Mejia Ortega.
Honorary Consul: José Alcides Montemayor Quitero.

ICELAND

Consulate: Apdo 6-666, El Dorado, Panamá; tel 36-1612; telex 3282068; fax 36-1620.
Consul: Alexander Demetrios Psychoyos.

INDIA

Embassy: Via España 120, 5°, Apdo 8400, Panamá 7; tel 64-3043; telex 2273.
Ambassador: Praveen Lal Goyal.
First Secretary: Vinod Behari Lall.
Second Secretary and Consul: N. Narasimhan.
Attaché: Aya Singh.
Attaché: Latteri Srinivasan Viswanathan.
Attaché: M. S. Rao.

ISRAEL

Embassy: Edif. Grobman, 5°, Avda Manuel María Icaza 12, Apdo 6357, Panamá 5; tel 64-8022; telex 2753.
Ambassador: Aryeh Amir.
Counsellor: Gabriel Azoulay.
Second Secretary: Chaim Menachen Shacham.

ITALY

Embassy: Calle Primera Parque Lefevre 42, Apdo 2369, Panamá 9A; tel 26-3111; telex 3374; fax 26-3121.
Ambassador: Dr Enzo Montano.
Attaché (Commercial): Serafino Piacere.

Consulate: Apdo 371, Colón; tel 41-8301.
Honorary Consul: F. Feoli.

JAMAICA

Embassy: Edif. Reprico, Avda Balboa y Calle 26, Apdo 5492, Panamá 5; tel 25-4441.
Ambassador: Tomás Stimpson.
Counsellor: Paul Anthony Robothan.
Attaché (Administrative): Valentine Moseley.
Attaché: Pauline Dias.
Attaché: Andrea Campbell.

Consulate: Edif. Don Tin, Avda Cuba 34-44, 2°, Panamá; tel 25-4441.
Consul-General: Nattan A. Reid.

Consulate: 1422 Avda de los Mártires, Juan B. Sosa, Panamá; tel 28-4674.
Vice-Consul: George Simpson.

Consulate: Agencias Giscome, Calle 9a 8032, Colón; tel 47-6517.
Consul: Oscar Savage.

JAPAN

Embassy: Edif. Don Camilo, Calle 50 y Calle 61, Apdo 1411, Panamá 1; tel 63-6155; telex 2780; fax 63-6019.
Ambassador: Jumpei Kato.
Counsellor: Hiroyuki Kimoto.
Counsellor: Osamu Igami.
First Secretary and Defence Attaché: Fumid Yamazaki.
Second Secretary: Takashi Namba.
Second Secretary: Shigeru Mori.
Second Secretary: Norio Sudd.
Second Secretary: Naomasa Murakoshi.
Second Secretary and Consul: Yoji Nakasu.
Attaché: Katsuhiro Matsumoto.
Attaché: Masayuki Udagawa.

KOREA, REPUBLIC

Embassy: Edif. Plaza, Planta baja, Calle Ricardo Arias y Calle 51-E, Campo Alegre, Apdo 8096, Panamá 7; tel 64-8203; telex 2208.

Ambassador: Sang-Jin Choi.
Counsellor (Political): Byung-Hak Min.
First Secretary (Consular/Information): Park Doo-Hyun.
Second Secretary (Economic): Duck Bo Sim.
Vice-Consul: Kim Kyun Suk.
Vice-Consul: Lee Chan Soo.

LIBYA

People's Bureau: Edif. Republic National Bank, 6°, Vía España y Calle Colombia, Apdo 6-894 El Dorado, Panama City; tel 27-3365; telex 2727.
Head of People's Bureau: Giuma A. Ghali.
Attaché (Finance): Khalid Mohamed Alkilani.
Attaché (Administrative): Mohamed M. Besis.

MEXICO

Embassy: Edif. Bank of America, 5°, Calle 50 y Calle San José, Apdo 8373, Panamá 7; tel 63-5021; telex 2154.
Ambassador: Carlos Planck Hinojosa.
Counsellor: Columba Marisela Calvo Vargas.
Counsellor: José Perez Aburto.
Counsellor: Marisela Calvo Vargas.
Military and Air Attaché: Col Francisco Perez Riojas.
First Secretary (Consular): Juan Victor Manuel Torres Perez.
Third Secretary: Eduardo Francisco Avila Pastrana.
Attaché (Adminstrative): Esperanza Luna Bolaños.
Chancellor: Ricardo de la Peña Flores.

NETHERLANDS

Consulate-General: Calle Manuel Ma. Icaza 4, Edif. ABN, Panamá; tel 65-7257.
Honorary Consul-General: Pieter Hendrik Sharrainga.

NICARAGUA

Embassy: Avda Federico Boyd y Calle 50, Apdo 772, Panamá 1; tel 23-0981; telex 2573; fax 69-2981.
Ambassador: Gilberto Molina Espinosa.
Minister-Counsellor: Dr Mario J. Quintanilla.
Counsellor: Juan Francisco Alvarado.
First Secretary: Rafael Valladares Garcia.
Attaché: Sabrina Arguello de Abaunza.

Consulate-General: Avda Federico Boyd y Calle 48, Edif. Versalles, Apto 5-8, Bella Vista, Panamá; tel 64-6431.
Consul-General: Carmen I. de Irigoyen.
Vice-Consul: Ubalda Vega Carballo.

NORWAY

Embassy: Centro Colón, Paseo Colón, 10°, Colón; tel 57-1414; telex 2245; fax 33-8113.
First Secretary: Oistein Bergh.
Attaché: May Helene Worvik.

Consulate: Calle La Boca 796-X, Apdo 341, Balbao, Panama City; tel 28-1103.
Consul-General: Arne Hauge.

Consulate: Apdo 115, Colón; tel 45-1516.
Consul: Frank Scott.

Consulate: Apdo 2035, Cristóbal.
Consul: Robin Moreland.

Consulate: Calle 35 y Ave, Justo Arosemena, Apdo 5248, Panamá 5; tel 25-5855.
Consul: Terence Ford G.

PAKISTAN

Consulate: Apdo 4881, Edif. Pantrusco, Calle Aquiliono de la Guardia G-17, Panamá 5; tel 64-2186; fax 63-8475.
Consul-General: Ricardo Boyd Chanis.
Honorary Consul: John H. Cogswell Elliott.

PARAGUAY

Consulate: Calle 39 2-89, Bella Visa, Panamá; tel 25-6016.
Honorary Consul-General: Camilo Fabrega Goytia.

Consulate: Via Cincuentenario y Avda 17, 4°, Apdo 347, Panamá; tel 26-6325.
Honorary Consul: Celso C. Carbonell.

PERU

Embassy: Edif. Dilido, 8°, Manuel María Icaza, No 12, Apdo 4516, Panamá 5; tel 23-1112; telex 3548; fax 69-6809.
Ambassador: Guillermo Fernández-Cornejo.
Counsellor (Maritime): Jaime Monge Acuña.
First Secretary: Henry Rizo-Patron.
Second Secretary (Consular): Juan Manuel Tirado.

Consulate-General: Panamá; tel 62-5137.
Honorary Consul-General: Javier Reategui.

Consulate: Colón; tel 41-4194.
Honorary Consul: Humberto Altamirano.

Consulate: Colón; tel 41-4666.
Honorary Vice-Consul: Giovanni Ferrari.

Consulate: Chiriqui; tel 75-4480.
Honorary Consul: Fernando Romero del Puy.

POLAND

Commercial Office: La Cresta, Calle José Gabriel Duque 36, Panamá; tel 63-5067.
Counsellor (Commercial): Andrzej Podkowinski.
Assistant Attaché (Commercial): Tadeusz Janik.

PORTUGAL

Consulate: Edif. Café Durán, Vía Transistmica, Apdo 8307, Panamá 7; tel 63-9522.
Honorary Consul: Pablo Duran.

RUSSIA

Embassy: Panamá.

SAN MARINO

Consulate-General: Apdo 55-0122, Panamá; tel 507-2625.
Consul-General: Rodolfo Garcia de Paredes Chiari.

SAUDI ARABIA

Embassy: Calle 54, Urb. Obarrio Bella Vista, Duplex 9-A, Panamá; Apdo 6-4524, El Dorado, Panama City; tel 69-5867.
Ambassador: Ahmed-Du Sueilem.
First Secretary: Suleiman Tayeb.

SINGAPORE

Embassy: Singapore.
Ambassador: Ridzwan Dzafir (resident in Singapore).

SPAIN

Embassy: Avda Perú y Calle 34, Apdo 1857, Panamá 1; tel 27-4758; telex 2656; fax 27-4926.
Ambassador: Tomás Lozano Escribano.
First Secretary: Javier Herrera.
Commercial Attaché: Juan Antonio Gisbert.
Co-operation Attaché: Jose Maria Berzosa.
Civil Attaché: Felipe Blanco.
Administrative Attaché: Atilano Alonso.

Consulate: Colón; tel 45-0625.
Honorary Consul: Carmen Calonge.

SWEDEN

Consulate-General: Vía José Agustín Arango, Juan Díaz, Apdo 7318, Panamá 5; tel 33-5883; fax 33-5795.
Consul-General: Per Gustaf Ingemar Lundberg.
Vice-Consul: Rudolph Errington Hansen.
Chancellor: Gudrun Alicia Lundberg.

Consulate: c/o Scan Cargo Services SA, Apdo 5037, Cristóbal, Colón; tel 41-5337; telex 8720; fax 41-6837.
Consul: Karsten Haahr Sörensen.
Chancellor: Lamoine Werlein.

SWITZERLAND

Embassy: Edif. Banco Central, 4°, Avda Samuel Lewis y Calle Gerardo Ortega, Apdo 499, Panamá 9A; tel 64-7115; telex 3385; fax 63-8083.
Chargé d'affaires a.i. and Counsellor: Eric Wehrli.
Attaché and Head of Chancery: Helen Kromidakis-Derrer.

TURKEY

Consulate: Calle 4° Norte 170, Augusto Samuel Boyd, Estatua Einstein, Apdo 994, Panamá 1; tel 23-1400.
Consul: Guillermo Andreve.

UNITED KINGDOM

Embassy: Torre Swiss Bank, 4°, Urb. Marbella, Calle 53, Apdo 889, Panamá 1; tel 69-0866; telex 3620; fax 23-0730.
Ambassador and Consul-General: John Grant MacDonald.
Defence Attaché: Lieut Col T. A. Glen.
Commercial Officer: J. Jaen.
Vice-Consul: P. S. Metcalfe.
Management Officer: R. Bemporad.

USA

Embassy: Avda Balboa, entre Calle 37 y 38, Apdo 6959, Panamá 5; tel 27-1777; telex 3583; fax 03-9470.
Ambassador: Deane R. Hinton.
Minister-Counsellor and Deputy Chief of Mission: David R. Beall.
Political Section: Thomas R. Maertens.
Economic Section: John R. Dawson.
Commercial Section: Carlos F. Poza.
Consular Section: Robert Raymer.
Administrative Section: Bohdan Dmytrewycz.
Regional Security Officer: Mark C. Boyett.
Public Affairs Officer: William R. Barr.
Communications Programme Officer: James A. Griffin.
Information Systems Manager: Michael Haftel.
Office of the Defence Attaché: Col Joseph A. McGrath, Jr.
Defence and Naval Attaché: Col Dunbar G. Layton.
Military Assistance Advisory Group: Capt. Michael R. Martinez.
Labour Officer: Harold Baum.
Customs Service (Treasury): Victor Calderon.
First Secretary: John W. Mallett.
First Secretary: Howard Leeb.
First Secretary: Norma R. Harms.
First Secretary and Consul: Brian M. McNamara.
First Secretary and Consul: Ronald A. Harms.
Attaché (Legal): Ruben Muñoz.

Consulate: Edif 1106, Avda Columbus, Cristóbal, Colón; tel 45-0266.

URUGUAY

Embassy: Edif. Vallarino, 5°, Of. 4°, Calle 32 y Avda Justo Arosemena, Apdo 8898, Panamá 5; tel 25-0049; fax 25-9087.
Ambassador: Ernesto Martínez Gariazzo.

VENEZUELA

Embassy: Calle Samuel Lewis, Torre Banco Unión, 5°, Apdo 661, Panamá 1; telex 2758; fax 69-1916.
Ambassador: Luis Ochoa Terán.
Minister-Counsellor: Tibisay Urdeneta Troconis.
Military, Naval and Air Attaché (Defence Co-operation): Col Hugo José Bastidas.
Military, Naval and Air Secretary (Defence Co-operation): Alfredo José Hurtado Figueroa.
Military, Naval and Air Secretary (Defence Co-operation): Antonio Ramon Martinez.
First Secretary: Pablo Herrera Maldonado.
Attaché: Col Jorge Parra Delgado.
Attaché: Celia Anselmi Ramirez.

YUGOSLAVIA

Embassy: Calle 10a Norte, Urb. Los Angeles 30, Apdo 6-91, El Dorado, Panama City; tel 60-4544.
Ambassador: Emir Humo.
Military Attaché: Col Bozidar Tomicevic.
Secretary: Alaz Gosnar.

PAPUA NEW GUINEA

AUSTRALIA

High Commission: POB 9129, Hohola; tel 259333; telex 22109; fax 259183.
High Commissioner: Allan Taylor.

AUSTRIA

Consulate: ANG House, 10th Floor, Hunter St, POB 35, Port Moresby; tel 211977; fax 618905.
Honorary Consul: Harry Beresford Clifford Love.
Honorary Vice-Consul: Günter Trnka.

CHINA, PEOPLE'S REPUBLIC

Embassy: Sir John Guise Dr., POB 1351, Boroko NCD, Port Moresby; tel 259836; telex 23073; fax 258247.
Ambassador: Wang Nongsheng.
Trade and Commercial Counsellor: Wang Mingxia.
First Secretary: Ma Shuxue.
Second Secretary: Liu Youfa.

CYPRUS

Consulate: POB 120, Port Moresby; tel 217607; telex 22274; fax 253441.
Honorary Consul: George Constantinou.

DENMARK

Consulate: 10 Portlock St, POB 698, Port Moresby; tel 211788; telex 23352; fax 212195.
Consul: Brian Denis White.

FINLAND

Consulate: Section 218, Lot 8, Gordon 5, POB 1948, Boroko NCD, Port Moresby; tel 256033; telex 23050; fax 211049.
Consul: Frank Kramer.

GERMANY

Embassy: 2nd Floor, Pacific View Apartments, Pruth St, 3 Mile Hill, POB 3631, Boroko NCD, Port Moresby; tel 252971; telex 23037; fax 251029.
Ambassador: Herbert Kamps.
Deputy Ambassador: Olaf Fitzner.
Third Secretary: Marc-Oliver Urban.
Assistant Attaché: Thorsten Appel.
Assistant Attaché: Sophia Brandl.

HOLY SEE

Apostolic Nunciature: POB 98, Port Moresby; tel 256021; fax 252844.
Apostolic Pro-Nuncio: Most Rev. Giovanni Ceirano, Titular Archbishop of Tagase.
Attaché: James P. Green.

INDONESIA

Embassy: 1, 2/410 Sir John Guisc Drive, Waigani, POB 7165, Boroko NCD, Port Moresby; tel 253116; telex 23311.
Ambassador: Bagus Sumitro.

JAPAN

Embassy: 1st and 2nd Floors, Cuthbertson House, Cuthbertson St, POB 1040, Boroko NCD, Port Moresby; tel 211305; telex 22215; fax 214868.
Ambassador: Yasuo Noguchi.
Consulate-General: Port Moresby.
Consul-General: Kenro Iino.

KOREA, REPUBLIC

Embassy: POB 381, Port Moresby; tel 254735; telex 22399.
Ambassador: Woo Moon-ki.

MALAYSIA

High Commission: Units 1 and 3, 2nd Floor, Pacific View Apartment, Pruth St, Sec. 84, Lot 1, Korobosea, POB 1400, Port Moresby; tel 251506; telex 23240; fax 252784.
High Commissioner: V. Yoogalingam.
Second Secretary and Head of Chancery: Wan Jaafar bin Wan Mahamud.
Second Secretary: Abu Bakar bin Mat.
Third Secretary (Administration): Azlan Haji Ambrose.

NEW ZEALAND

High Commission: Waigani, POB 1144, Boroko NCD, Port Moresby; tel 259444; telex 22191; fax 217158.
High Commissioner: John B. Hayes.
Deputy High Commissioner: Eileen Campbell.
Second Secretary: Richard Rawnsley.
Second Secretary: Rob Macalister.
Attaché: Sheryl Chisholm.
Trade Commissioner: Gavin Young.
Defence Adviser: Lieut Col Neville Reilly.

NORWAY

Consulate-General: c/o Brian Bell & Co. Pty Ltd, POB 1228, Turumu St, Boroko NCD, Port Moresby; tel 255411; telex 22306; fax 211158.
Consul-General: Brian Ernest Bell.

PHILIPPINES

Embassy: POB 5916, Boroko NCD, Port Moresby; tel 256577; telex 23012.
Ambassador: Rodolfo L. Diaz.

RUSSIA

Embassy: Davetari Drive, Section 62, Lot 7, Touaguba Hill, POB 6670, Boroko NCD, Port Moresby; tel 257931; fax 252608.
Ambassador: Evgeni F. Rogov.
Counsellor: Victor V. Rodionov.
First Secretary: Nikolai Sanaikine.
First Secretary: Gennadi K. Frolove.
Third Secretary: Sergei G. Troussov.
Attaché: Vassili G. Koushtchenko.

SWEDEN

Consulate-General: c/o Brian Bell & Co. Pty Ltd, POB 1228, Turumu St, Boroko NCD, Port Moresby; tel 255411; telex 22306; fax 211158.
Consul-General: Brian Ernest Bell.

UNITED KINGDOM

High Commission: Kiroki St, Waigani, POB 4778, Boroko NCD, Port Moresby; tel 251643; telex 22142; fax 253547.
High Commissioner: Noel Levi.
Deputy High Commissioner: A. J. Morris.
Third Secretary (Consular/Management): D. Hansen.

USA

Embassy: POB 1492, Armit St, Port Moresby; tel 211455; telex 22189; fax 213423.
Ambassador: Robert William Farrand.
Deputy Chief of Mission: John W. Vessey III.
Political Section: Oscar W. Clyatt, Jr.
Economic/Commercial Section: Paul Neureiter.
Consular Section: William W. McCulla.
Administrative Section: James R. Doyle.
Public Affairs Officer: Terence J. Spencer.
Communications Programme Officer: Harold E. Mason.
Agency for International Development: Louis H. Kuhn.
Office of the Defence Attaché: Maj. Joseph D. Diloreti.

International Organizations

EUROPEAN COMMUNITIES

External Delegation: 3rd Floor, The Lodge, Bampton St, POB 76, Port Moresby; tel 213504; telex 22307; fax 217850.

Commission Delegate: Dr Arnold E. van Niekerk (also responsible for Kiribati).
Technical Adviser: John M. Loftus.
Economic Adviser: George Gwyer.

PARAGUAY

ARGENTINA

Embassy: Avda Mcal López 2029, Asunción; tel (21) 20-0034; telex 127.
Ambassador: Raul A. J. Quijano.

AUSTRIA

Consulate-General: Edif. 'Internacional Faro', Gral Díaz 525, CC 582, Asunción; tel (21) 44-3910; telex 5323; fax (21) 44-4815.
Honorary Consul-General: Jörg Brunotte.

BELGIUM

Embassy: Edif. Parapití, 5°, O'Leary 509 casi Estrella, Apdo 503, Asunción; tel (21) 44-075.
Chargé d'affaires: Desirée Orens.

BOLIVIA

Embassy: Eligio Ayala 2002, esq. Gral Bruguez, Asunción; tel (21) 22-662.
Ambassador: Dr Raúl Botelho Gonzálvez.

BRAZIL

Embassy: 25 de Mayo y Gral Aquino, Asunción; tel (21) 20-0031; telex 148.
Ambassador: Soares Carbonar.

CANADA

Consulate: El Paraguayo Independiente 995, Entrepiso, Oficinas 1 y 2, Casilla de Correo 883, Asunción; Casilla 2577, Asunción; tel (21) 44-9505; telex 652; fax (21) 44-9506.
Honorary Consul: B. Wiebe.

CHILE

Embassy: Guido Spano 1687, Calle Juan B. Motta, Asunción; tel (21) 66-0344; telex 163.
Ambassador: Jorge F. O'Ryan Balbontin.

CHINA (TAIWAN)

Embassy: Avda Mcal López 1043, Asunción; tel (21) 22-371; telex 702.
Ambassador: Gen. Wang Sheng.

COLOMBIA

Embassy: Avda Mcal López 2240, Asunción; tel (21) 62-162.
Ambassador: Vicente Martínez.

COSTA RICA

Embassy: Lope de Vega casi Venezuela, Asunción; tel (21) 29-3294; fax (21) 29-3294.
Ambassador: Lilliana Falas Valverde.
First Secretary and Consul: Antulio Francisco Lobo Salazar.
Attaché: Ana Lucia Paniagua Campos.

Consulate: Procer Isasi 248, Asunción; tel (21) 66-0861; fax (21) 66-0861.

DENMARK

Consulate-General: Nuestra Señora de la Asunción 766, Casilla 838, Asunción; tel (21) 90-617; telex 458; fax (21) 91-539.
Consul-General: Canuto Rasmussen Niedergesäs.

ECUADOR

Embassy: Edif. Inter-Express, 9°, Of. 901, Herrera 195 esq. Yegros, Asunción; tel (21) 46-150; telex 5160.
Ambassador: Jorge Lasso.

EL SALVADOR

Embassy: Edif. Líder W, 11°, Estrella 692, Calle O'Leary, Apdo 115, Asunción; tel (21) 95-503.

FINLAND

Consulate: Calle Capitan Elias Ayola y Yasu Barrio Villa Guarani Distrito, De Santisima Trinidad, Asunción; tel (21) 29-1175; telex 5134.
Consul: Pehr Guillermo Heikel.
Vice-Consul: Carlos Schauman.

FRANCE

Embassy: España 696, Casilla 97, Asunción; tel (21) 23-111; telex 137.
Ambassador: Robert Rigouzzo.

Economic Section: Casilla 1205; tel (21) 45-442; telex 750.

GERMANY

Embassy: Avda Venezuela 241, Casilla 471, Asunción; tel (21) 24-006; telex 129; fax (21) 21-2863.
Ambassador: Dr Heinz Schneppen.

Consulate: Calle Jorge Memmel 631, Encarnación; tel (71) 2682.
Honorary Consul: Carlos Memmel.

HOLY SEE

Apostolic Nunciature: Calle Ciudad del Vaticano (entre 25 de Mayo y Caballero), CP 83, Asunción; tel (21) 20-0750; fax (21) 21-2590.
Apostolic Nuncio: Most Rev. José Sebastián Laboa, Titular Archbishop of Zaraï.
Secretary: Timothy A. Broglio.

ISRAEL

Embassy: Edif. Líder 2, 3°, O'Leary esq. Gral Díaz, Asunción; tel (21) 95-097; telex 5216.
Ambassador: David Morag.

ITALY

Embassy: Avda Mcal López 1104, esq. Mayor Bullo, Asunción; tel (21) 25-918; telex 618.
Ambassador: Sergio Grimaldi.

JAPAN

Embassy: Avda Mcal López 2364, Casilla 1957, Asunción; tel (21) 60-3682; telex 131; fax (21) 60-6901.
Ambassador: Nakasone Goro.

Consulate: Calle Carlos Antonio López 1290, Casilla 55, Encarnación; tel (71) 2287; telex 887.
Consul: Nuimura Yoshinori.

KOREA, REPUBLIC

Embassy: Rua Dominicana 216 esq. Calle 160, Asunción; tel (21) 20-2651; telex 201.
Ambassador: Kwon Young-Soon.

MEXICO

Embassy: Edif. Parapití, 5°, Estrella y O'Leary, Asunción; tel (21) 44-4421; telex 213; fax (21) 44-1877.
Ambassador: Francisco Correa Villalobos.

PANAMA

Embassy: Calle Eduardo V. Haedo 179, Edif. Betón I, 11B°, Asunción; tel (21) 44-5545; telex 5147; fax (21) 44-6192.
Chargé d'affaires: Augusto Luis Villarreal.

PERU

Embassy: Avda Mcal López 648, Asunción; tel (21) 20-0949.
Ambassador: Jorge Pérez-Garreaud.

SOUTH AFRICA

Embassy: Edif. Sudameris, 4°, Independencia Nacional y Cerro Corá, Asunción; tel (21) 44-331; telex 325; fax (21) 44-5768.
Ambassador: J. G. J. van Rensburg.
Defence Attaché: Col P. D. Uys.

First Secretary: H. B. Lack.
Third Secretary (Administration): L. Lack.

Consulate: Casilla 848, Asunción; tel (21) 92-093.
Honorary Consul: C. von Donner.

SPAIN

Embassy: Yegros 437, Asunción; tel (21) 90-686; telex 473.
Ambassador: Eduardo Cerro Godinho.

SWEDEN

Consulate-General: Coronel Bogado 1039-1047, Casilla 586, Asunción; tel (21) 20-5561; telex 143; fax (21) 21-2021.
Consul-General: Rolf Rieder.
Vice-Consul: Roberto Ignacio Rieder Celle.

SWITZERLAND

Embassy: Edif. 'Parapití', 4°, Ofs 419/23, Juan E. O'Leary 409/esq. Estrella, Casilla 552, Asunción; tel (21) 44-8022; telex 5258; fax (21) 44-5853.
Chargé d'affaires: L. Attenbach.
Attaché and Head of Chancery: Marianne Lässer-Zundel.

UNITED KINGDOM

Embassy: Pdte Franco 706, Casilla 404, Asunción; tel (21) 44-472; telex 139; fax (21) 44-6385.
Ambassador and Consul-General: Michael A. C. Dibben.
Third Secretary: A. J. Sindon.
Commercial/Information Officer: Hernando Silvero.
Management Officer/Accountant: L. Barone.

USA

Embassy: Avda Mcal López 1776, Casilla 402, Asunción; tel (21) 21-3715; telex 203; fax (21) 21-3728.
Ambassador: Timothy L. Towell.
Deputy Chief of Mission: Michael Ranneberger.
Political Section: Rose M. Likins.
Economic/Commercial Section: Jonathan D. Farrar.
Consular Section: Clarence A. Hudson, Jr.
Administrative Section: Carlos Perez.
Regional Security Officer: Maximiliano A. Salazar.
Public Affairs Officer: Patrick D. Duddy.
Communications Programme Officer: Edward M. Smith.
Office of the Defence Attaché: Lieut Col Douglas C. McCary.
Office of Defence Co-operation: Col Paul A. Scharf.

URUGUAY

Embassy: Brasília esq. Rca de Siria, Asunción; tel (21) 25-391; telex 333.
Ambassador: Jorge Pacheco Areco.

VENEZUELA

Embassy: Edif. Delime II, 1°, O'Leary esq. Victor Haedo, Apdo 94, Asunción; tel (21) 44-242; telex 353; fax (21) 49-0515.
Ambassador: Jesus Elias Morrel.
Second Secretary (Technical): Berta Margarita Olivo M.
Second Officer: Nahir Julieta Salas de Saer.

PERU

ALGERIA

Embassy: Avda Angamos Oeste 915, Miraflores, Lima 18; tel (14) 469499; telex 21053.
Ambassador: Abdelaziz Kara.

ANGOLA

Embassy: Lima.

ARGENTINA

Embassy: Avda Arequipa 1155, 7°, Lima; tel (14) 729920; telex 25246.
Ambassador: Anselmo Marini.

AUSTRIA

Embassy: Avda Central 643, 5°, Apdo 853, 100 Lima 27; tel (14) 428851; telex 21128.
Ambassador: Dr Franz Irbinger.
Secretary: Adolf Rieger.

Consulate-General: Emilio Cavenecia 175, Of. 4, Casilla 5804, Lima 18; tel (14) 403073.
Honorary Consul-General: Elfriede Buchner.
Honorary Vice-Consul: Yvonne Erika Mould.

Consulate: Jerusalén 201-E, 2°, Casilla 854, Arequipa; tel (54) 215384.
Honorary Consul: Thomas Laub.

Consulate: Hotel San Augustin, Maruri 390, Cuzco; tel (84) 222322; fax (84) 221174.
Honorary Consul: Raul German Delgado de la Flor Caparo.

BELGIUM

Embassy: Avda Angamos 392, Lima 18; tel (14) 463335; telex 20182.
Ambassador: Willy Tilemans.

BOLIVIA

Embassy: Los Castaños 235, San Isidro, Lima; tel (14) 223418; telex 20275.
Ambassador: Nuflo Chávez Ortiz.

BRAZIL

Embassy: Avda Comandante Espinar 181, Miraflores, Lima; tel (14) 462635; telex 20205.

BULGARIA

Embassy: Avda Salaverry 2555, San Isidro, Lima; tel (14) 409146; telex 25276.
Ambassador: Tsanko Varadinov Grigorov.

CANADA

Embassy: Federico Gerdes 130, (Antes Calle Libertad), Miraflores, Casilla 18-1126, Lima; tel (14) 444015; telex 25323; fax (14) 444347.
Ambassador: James D. Leach.
Counsellor (Commercial) and Consul: W. A. McKenzie.
Counsellor (Development) and Consul: E. W. E. Doe.
First Secretary (Immigration) and Consul: R. W. Herringer.
First Secretary and Consul: C. Winter de Varennes.

CHILE

Embassy: Avda Javier Prado Oeste 790, San Isidro, Lima; tel (14) 403300; telex 20181; fax (14) 419414.
Ambassador: Alejandro Magnet.
Minister-Counsellor: Jorge Iglesias.
Counsellor: Jorge Montero.
First Secretary: Jorge Canelas.

Consulate: tel (14) 407965.
Consul: Luis Goycoolea.

CHINA, PEOPLE'S REPUBLIC

Embassy: Jirón José Granda 150, San Isidro, Lima; tel (14) 400782; telex 25283.
Ambassador: Dai Shiqi.

COLOMBIA

Embassy: Avda Arequipa 2685, Lima; tel (14) 404140; telex 20068.
Ambassador: Jorge Padilla.

COSTA RICA

Embassy: Camino Real 159, Of. 500, San Isidro, Lima; tel (14) 409982.
Ambassador: Tomás Soley Soler.

CUBA

Embassy: Coronel Portillo 110, San Isidro, Lima; tel (14) 227128; telex 25644.
Ambassador: Luis Karakadze Berrayarza.

CYPRUS

Consulate: Malecon Balta 1050, 17°, Miraflores, POB 5037, Lima; tel (14) 810053; telex 25251; fax (14) 816700.
Honorary Consul: Marios A. Constantine.

CZECHOSLOVAKIA

Embassy: Baltazar La Torre 398, San Isidro, Lima 27; tel (14) 400226; telex 25086; fax (14) 424164.
Ambassador: Vasil Mochnac.
Chargé d'affaires and Consul-General: Milan Radek.

Counsellor (Commercial): Pavel Sipka.
Attaché (Administrative): Miroslav Valkovic.

DENMARK

Consulate-General: Bernardo Monteagudo 201, POB 3570, San Isidro, Lima 27; tel (14) 621090; telex 21508; fax (14) 618931.
Consul-General: Dr Manuel Pablo Olaechea.
Vice-Consul: José Antonio Olaechea.

Consulate: Constitución 328, Castilla 252, Callao; tel (14) 293690; telex 20105.
Consul: Raul A. Musso Vento.

Consulate: Calle Arequipa 164, Casilla 4, Mollendo; tel (54) 2928; telex 59653.
Consul: Michael John Flanagan.

DOMINICAN REPUBLIC

Embassy: Lima; tel (14) 710899.

ECUADOR

Embassy: Las Palmeras 356 y Javier Prado Oeste, San Isidro, Lima; tel (14) 409991; telex 25706.
Ambassador: Miguel Antonio Vasco Vasco.

EGYPT

Embassy: Avda Jorge Basadre 1470, San Isidro, Lima; tel (14) 402642; telex 25589.

EL SALVADOR

Embassy: Los Cedros 421-A, San Isidro, Lima; tel (14) 222497.
Ambassador: Roberto Arturo Castrillo Hidalgo.

FINLAND

Embassy: Edif. El Plateado, Apdo 4501, 7°, Los Eucaliptos 291, San Isidro, Lima 100; tel (14) 703750; telex 25436; fax (14) 703748.
Ambassador: Esko Lipponen.

Consulate: Emmel 109, Yanshuara, Apdo 178, Arequipa; tel (54) 223708.
Consul: Edgar Ackermann Chávez.

Consulate: Bolivar 200, Apdo 884, Trujillo; tel (44) 246122; telex 43055.
Consul: Elias Arturo Iturri Urrutia.

FRANCE

Embassy: Plaza Francia 234, Lima; tel (14) 238616; telex 25658.
Ambassador: Jean-François Nougarede.

GERMANY

Embassy: Avda Arequipa 4202, Miraflores, Casilla 18-0504, Lima 18; tel (14) 457033; telex 20039; fax (14) 462348.
Ambassador: Johannes von Vacano.

Consulate: Colegio Peruano, Alemán Max Uhle, Casilla 743, Arequipa; tel (54) 232921; telex 51911; fax (54) 219877.
Honorary Consul: Ulrich Gocht.

Consulate: San Agustin 307, Apdo 1128, Cuzco; tel (84) 235459.
Honorary Consul: Maria-Sophia Jürgens de Hermoza.

Consulate: Fa. Social Mercantil de Norte S.A. Piura, Casilla 106, Piura; tel (74) 322411.
Honorary Consul: Kurt Arens Ostendorf.

Consulate: Calle Estados Unidos 105-7, Urb. 'El Recreo', Trujillo; tel (44) 245903.
Honorary Consul: Dr Guillermo Guerra Cruz.

GUATEMALA

Embassy: Avda del Sur 120, Chacarilla del Estanque, Lima 33; tel (14) 220236.
Ambassador: Edgar Arturo López Calvo.

HAITI

Embassy: Avda Orrantia 910, San Isidro, Lima; tel (14) 223362.
Ambassador: Antoine Bernard.

HOLY SEE

Apostolic Nunciature: Avda Salaverry 6a cuadra, Apdo 397, Lima 100; tel (14) 319436; telex 25751; fax (14) 323236.
Apostolic Nuncio: Most Rev. Luigi Dossena, Titular Archbishop of Capri.
Secretary: Jorge Anibal Rojas Bustamante.

HONDURAS

Embassy: Thomas Edison 215, San Isidro, Lima 27; tel (14) 408881; telex 21383.
Ambassador: Dr Carlos Martínez Castillo.

HUNGARY

Embassy: Avda Orrantia 1580, San Isidro, Lima; tel (14) 409644; telex 25413.
Ambassador: Adolf Szeles.

INDIA

Embassy: Avda Salaverry 3006, San Isidro, Lima 27; tel (14) 621840; telex 25515; fax (14) 610374.
Ambassador: Dilip Lahiri.
Second Secretary and Head of Chancery: A. K. Mudgal.
Third Secretary: Akhilesh Mishra.

ISRAEL

Embassy: Edif. Pacífico-Washington, 6°, Natalio Sánchez 125, Lima; tel (14) 334431; telex 25264.
Ambassador: David Tourgeman.

ITALY

Embassy: Avda Gregorio Escobedo 298, Lima 11; tel (14) 632727; telex 25460.
Ambassador: Massimo Curcio.

JAPAN

Embassy: Avda San Felipe 356, Jesús María, Apdo 3708, Lima; tel (14) 614041; telex 25533; fax (14) 630302.
Ambassador: Masaki Seo.
Consul-General: Tetsuo Hanawa.

KOREA, DEMOCRATIC PEOPLE'S REPUBLIC

Embassy: Lima.
Ambassador: Kim Kyong-Ho.

KOREA, REPUBLIC

Embassy: Avda Principal 190, 7°, Lima 13; tel (14) 704201; telex 25539.
Ambassador: Kim Jae-Hoon.

LEBANON

Consulate: POB 5710, Lima; tel (14) 752707; fax (14) 638987.
Honorary Consul: Dr Elias Chaloubi.

MEXICO

Embassy: Avda Santa Cruz 330, San Isidro, Lima; tel (14) 405465; telex 25417.
Ambassador: Edgardo Flores Rivas.

MOROCCO

Embassy: Nicolás de Riviera 890, San Isidro, Lima 27; tel (14) 417393; telex 21520.
Ambassador: Mohamed Ben Moufti.
First Secretary and Consul General: Abdelkhalek Atrari.
Attaché (Finance): Mohamed Aouad.
Attaché (Administration and Finance): Abdellatif Britel.

NETHERLANDS

Embassy: Avda Principal 190, 4°, Urb. Santa Catalina, La Victoria, Lima; tel (14) 721548; telex 20212.
Ambassador: Henri G. A. Elink Schuurman.

NEW ZEALAND

Embassy: Avda Salaverry 3006, San Isidro, Casilla 5587, Lima 100; tel (14) 621840; telex 20254; fax (14) 610374.
Ambassador: Barry H. Brooks.

Consulate: Miguel Seminario 320, 3°, San Isidro, Lima 100; Casilla 3553, Lima 100; tel (14) 416709; telex 21111; fax (14) 426603.
Honorary Consul: Alfonso Rey.

NICARAGUA

Embassy: Calle Hipólito Unanue 1560, Lince, Lima; tel (14) 710585; telex 25659.
Ambassador: Mauricio Cuadra Schulz.

PANAMA

Embassy: Roma 342, San Isidro, Lima; tel (14) 404874.
Chargé d'affaires: Alexander Cuevas.

PARAGUAY

Embassy: Malecón 28 de Julio 159, Lima 18; tel (14) 462192.
Ambassador: Dr Manuel Avila.

PHILIPPINES

Embassy: Lima.

POLAND

Embassy: Avda Salaverry 1978, Jesús María, Lima; tel (14) 713920; telex 25548.
Ambassador: Bernard Bogdanski.

PORTUGAL

Embassy: Vanderghen 270, Lima 18; tel (14) 409905; telex 25734.
Ambassador: Dr Luis Pazos Alonso.

ROMANIA

Embassy: Avda Orrantia 690, San Isidro, Lima; tel (14) 409396; telex 25624.
Ambassador: Ion Ciucu.

RUSSIA

Embassy: Avda Salaverry 3424, San Isidro, Lima; tel (14) 611775; telex 25608.
Ambassador: Anatoly Filatov.

SAUDI ARABIA

Embassy: Lima.

SPAIN

Embassy: Avda República de Chile 120, Lima; tel (14) 310420; telex 25297.
Ambassador: Nabor García García.

SWEDEN

Embassy: Centro Comercial Camino Real, Torre El Pilar, 9°, Avda Camino Real, San Isidro, Apdo 2068, Lima 1; tel (14) 406700; telex 20245; fax (14) 429547.
Ambassador: Carl-Erhard Lindahl.
Counsellor: Hans Ahlström.
Second Secretary: Ulrika Sundberg.

Consulate: Avda Tacna y Arica 145, Apdo 273, Arequipa; tel (54) 236238; fax (54) 236125.
Consul: Juan Alfredo Guillermo Roberts Billig.

SWITZERLAND

Embassy: Avda Salaverry 3240, San Isidro, Lima 27; Casilla 378, Lima 100; tel (14) 624090; telex 20020; fax (14) 626577.
Ambassador: Sylvia Pauli.
Second Secretary: Bénédict de Cerjat.
Attaché and Office Manager: Ruth Wulff-Fries.
Attaché (Development Co-operation/Aid): Peter Bischof.

UNITED KINGDOM

Embassy: Natalio Sánchez 125, 12°, Plaza Washington esq. Avda Arequipa, Casilla 854, Lima 100; tel (14) 334738; telex 25230; fax (14) 334735.
Ambassador: D. Keith Haskell.
Deputy Head of Mission and Consul: F. Russell C. Thomson.
Defence Attaché: Col Christopher H. van der Noot.
First Secretary: Geoffrey Chalder.
Second Secretary (Chancery/Information): Russell Baker.
Second Secretary (Management) and Vice-Consul: Michael Banham.
Attaché (Culture) and Director British Council: Julian Harvey.
Information Officer: Roxana Castañeda.

Consulate: c/o Hotel San Agustín, Maruri 390, Cusco; tel (84) 222322; fax (84) 231001.
Consul: Dr Raúl Delgado de la Flor.

Consulate: Quesada 107, Yanahuara, Arequipa; tel (54) 211961; telex 51031; fax (54) 214873.
Consul: Reynaldo Roberts.

Consulate: Jesús de Nazareth 312, Trujillo, La Libertad; tel (44) 336220; fax (44) 255818.
Consul: Winston Barber.

Consulate: Ave Grau 760, Casilla 193, Plura; tel (74) 336220.
Consul: Frank William.

Consulate: Jr. Arica 253, Apdo 129, Iquitos; tel (94) 234110; telex 91003; fax (94) 234383.
Consul: Lewis C. J. Power.

USA

Embassy: cnr Avdas Inca Garcilaso de la Vega and España, Casilla 1995, Lima 100; tel (14) 338000; telex 25212; fax (14) 316682.
Ambassador: Anthony C. E. Quainton.
Deputy Head of Mission: Jerrold Mark Dion.
Political Section: Joseph McBride.
Economic Section: David Stebbing.
Consular Section: Wayne Griffith.
Administrative Section: D. Thomas Linville.
Regional Security Officer: Robert Morris.
Agricultural Section: Bill Emerson.
Labour Officer: Kathleen J. Croom.
Agency for International Development: Craig Buck.
Public Affairs Officer: Don R. Hamilton.
Narcotics Assistance Unit: Caesar P. Bernal.
Office of Defence Attaché: Capt. Stephen N. Lombardo.
Military Assistance Advisory Group: Col Patrick McCaslin.
Communications Programme Officer: Gregory J. Tyson.
Information Systems Manager: Luis E. Acosta.

Commercial Section: Larrabure y Unanue 110, Lima 1; tel (14) 330555; telex 20335; fax (14) 311105.
Commercial Section: Richard Lenahan.

URUGUAY

Embassy: Avda Larco 1913, Dptos 201-202, Miraflores, Lima; tel (14) 462047.
Ambassador: Dr Luis Zerbino.

VENEZUELA

Embassy: Avda Arequipa 298, Apdo 3908, Lima 1; tel (14) 314510; telex 2533; fax (14) 338970.
Ambassador: Abel Clavijo Ostos.
Minister-Counsellor: Oscar Pietri Trujillo.
Counsellor: Delma Miralles de T.
Counsellor (Technical): Ana Maria Sanchez V.
Second Secretary: Inocente Quevedo Casas.

YUGOSLAVIA

Embassy: Carlos Porras Osores 360, San Isidro, Lima; tel (14) 404754.
Ambassador: Ladislav Varga.

THE PHILIPPINES

ARGENTINA

Embassy: ACT Tower Condominium, 6th Floor, 135 Sen. Gil J. Puyat Ave, Salcedo Village, Makati, Metro Manila; tel (2) 875655; telex 64666.
Ambassador: Alejandro Horacio Piñeiro.
Counsellor (Economic/Commercial): Roberto Read.
First Secretary and Head of Consular Section: Cristobal Horacio Delfino Costa.
Second Secretary (Commercial): Jaime Juan Goldaracena.

AUSTRALIA

Embassy: Bank of the Philippine Islands Bldg, 18th Floor, Ayala Ave, cnr Paseo de Roxas, Makati, 1200 Metro Manila; tel (2) 8177911; telex 63744; fax (2) 8173603.
Ambassador: Mack Williams.

AUSTRIA

Embassy: 117 Rada St, Prince Bldg, Legaspi Village, POB 1475, Makati, Metro Manila; tel (2) 8179191; telex 23452.
Ambassador: Otmar Koler.
Secretary: Gerhard Erdely.

Consulate-General: 6760 Ayala Ave, POB 589, Makati, Metro Manila 2800; tel (2) 893011; telex 45096.
Honorary Consul-General: Washington Sycip.

Consulate: 513 P. Burgos St, Mandane City, Cebu; PHILAM Life Bldg, Osmena Blvd, Cebu City; tel (32) 83863; telex 24881.
Honorary Consul: Arcadio Alegrado.

BANGLADESH

Embassy: JEG Bldg, 5th Floor, 150 Legaspi St, Legaspi Village, Makati, Metro Manila; tel (2) 8175010.
Chargé d'affaires: Abdul Mannaf.

BELGIUM

Embassy: Don Jacinto Bldg, 6th Floor, cnr de la Rosa and Salcedo Sts, Legaspi Village, POB 968-1299, Makati, Metro Manila; tel (2) 876571; telex 23099; fax (2) 8172566.
Ambassador: Hugo Callebaut.
Counsellor and Deputy Head of Mission: Godelieve van der Bergh.
Third Secretary and Consul: Serge Wauthier.
Attaché (Commercial): Jozef de Clercq.
Attaché (Administrative): Anne-Marie Roelandt.

Consulate: 103-7 Plaridel St, POB 125, Cebu City 6401; tel (32) 93766; telex 24802; fax (32) 52022.
Consul: Enrique Benedicto.

BRAZIL

Embassy: RCI Bldg, 6th Floor, 105 Rada St, Legaspi Village, POB 280 MCC, Makati, Metro Manila; tel (2) 888181; telex 63639.
Ambassador: Raymundo Nonnato Loyola de Castro.

BRUNEI

Embassy: Bank of the Philippine Islands Bldg, 11th Floor, Ayala Ave, cnr Paseo de Roxas, Makati, Metro Manila; tel (2) 8162836; telex 22515; fax (2) 8152872.
Ambassador: Pengiran Mustapha bin Pengiran Metassan.

BULGARIA

Embassy: 1732 Sampaguita St, Dasmariñas Village, Makati, Metro Manila; tel (2) 8179177; telex 64489.
Chargé d'affaires: Georgi Mladenov.

CANADA

Embassy: Allied Bank Center, 9th Floor, 6754 Ayala Ave, POB 971, Makati, Metro Manila; tel (2) 8159536; telex 63676; fax (2) 8159595.
Ambassador: André S. Simard.
Counsellor (Development): C. Latulipe.
Counsellor (Immigration): B. F. de S. O'Connor.
Counsellor (Development): G. Leclerc.
Counsellor (Commercial): D. K. McNamara.
Counsellor and Consul: A. M. McAllister.
Counsellor (Development): J.-C. Lorin.
Counsellor (Commercial): R. G. Shaw-Wood.
Attaché (Medical): Dr B. D. Gushulak.

CHILE

Embassy: Gammon Centre Bldg, 2nd Floor A, 126 Alfaro St, Salcedo Village, Makati, Metro Manila; tel (2) 8150795; telex 66568.
Ambassador: Carlos Desgroux.

CHINA, PEOPLE'S REPUBLIC

Embassy: 4896 Pasay Rd, Dasmariñas Village, Makati, Metro Manila; tel (2) 853148.
Ambassador: Huang Guifang.

COLOMBIA

Embassy: Aurora Tower, 18th Floor, Araneta Center, Quezon City; tel (2) 9212701; telex 40219.
Ambassador: Ramiro Zambrano Cárdenas.

CUBA

Embassy: 51 Paseo de Roxas, Urdaneta Village, Makati, Metro Manila; tel (2) 8171192; telex 63609.
Ambassador: Ana María González Suárez.

CYPRUS

Consulate: 70 Sgt., E.A. Esquezza Ave, Quezon City, 3008 Metro Manila; tel (2) 977051; telex 42018; fax (2) 9213354.
Honorary Consul: Peter Toundjis.

CZECHOSLOVAKIA

Embassy: 14 La Salle St, Greenhills Village, San Juan, Metro Manila; tel (2) 783236; telex 42485.
Ambassador: Rudolf Jakubik.

DENMARK

Embassy: Citibank Center, 10th Floor, 8741 Paseo de Roxas, Makati, 3120 Metro Manila; POB 7707, 1300 Pasay, Metro Manila; tel (2) 8191906; telex 23066; fax (2) 8177577.
Chargé d'affaires a.i. and Minister-Counsellor: Gunnar Blæhr.
Attaché: Jørgen Ledstrup.
Export Assistant: Ole Dybdal Nielsen.
Consul: Kai Kirk Sørensen.

ECUADOR

Consulate: 17 San Pablo St, BGY Batis, San Juan, Metro Manila; tel (2) 702431; telex 27834.
Honorary Consul: Alejandro Padilla.
Vice-Consul: Maria A. Sinjian.

EGYPT

Embassy: 2229 Paraiso cnr Bayan St, Dasmariñas Village, Makati, Metro Manila; tel (2) 880390.
Ambassador: Ahmed Fouad Hosny.

FINLAND

Embassy: Bank of the Philippine Islands Bldg, 14th Floor, cnr Ayala Ave and Paseo de Roxas, Makati, Metro Manila; tel (2) 8162105; telex 22694; fax (2) 8151401.
Ambassador: Timo Jalkanen.
Secretary (Commercial): Antti Heikkinen.

FRANCE

Embassy: Filipinos Life Assurance Bldg, 2nd Floor, 6786 Ayala Ave, cnr Paseo de Roxas, POB 3165, Makati, Metro Manila; tel (2) 8101981; telex 63864; fax (2) 8175047.
Ambassador: Olivier Gaussot.

GERMANY

Embassy: Solidbank Bldg, 6th Floor, 777 Paseo de Roxas, Makati, POB 7703, 1200 Metro Manila; tel (2) 864906; telex 22655; fax (2) 8104703.
Ambassador: Dr Peter Scholz.

HOLY SEE

Apostolic Nunciature: 2140 Taft Ave, POB 3604, 2800 Metro Manila; tel (2) 5210306; telex 65079; fax (2) 5211235.
Apostolic Nuncio: Most Rev. Gian Vincenzo Moreni, Titular Archbishop of Turris in Mauretania.
First Secretary: Very Rev. Paul R. Gallagher.

ICELAND

Consulate: Magsaysay Bldg, 520 T.M. Kalaw St, Ermita, Metro Manila; POB 21, Manila; tel (2) 506611; telex 27830.
Consul: Miguel A. Magsaysay.

INDIA

Embassy: 2190 Paraiso St, Dasmariñas Village, Makati, Metro Manila; tel (2) 872445; telex 63595.
Ambassador: Satish Chandra.

INDONESIA

Embassy: 185 Salcedo St, Legaspi Village, Makati, POB 372, Metro Manila 68; tel (2) 855061.
Ambassador: Suwarso Hardjosudarmo.

Consulate-General: Ecoland Subdivision, POB 156, Mafina, Davao City.

IRAN

Embassy: Don Jacinto Bldg, 4th Floor, cnr Salcedo and de la Rosa Sts, Legaspi Village, Makati, Metro Manila; tel (2) 871561; telex 63711.
Chargé d'affaires: Seyed Kamal Sadjjadi.

IRAQ

Embassy: 1368 Caballero St, Dasmariñas Village, Makati, Metro Manila; tel (2) 856715; telex 45265.
Ambassador: Ali M. Sumaida.

IRELAND

Consulate-General: Max's Restaurant, 2nd Floor, Roxas Blvd, Baclaran, Paranaque, Metro Manila; tel (2) 8321991; telex 27971; fax (2) 8340511.
Honorary Consul-General: Edgardo S. Trota.

ISRAEL

Embassy: Philippine Savings Bank Bldg, Room 538, 5th Floor, 6813 Ayala Ave, Makati, 1200 Metro Manila; tel (2) 885329; telex 22448; fax (2) 8190561.
Ambassador: Yoav Behiri.
Counsellor: Yacov Zahiv.
Military, Naval and Air Attaché: Col Zvi Eadan.
Second Secretary: Shmuel Ravel.

ITALY

Embassy: Zeta Bldg, 6th Floor, 191 Salcedo St, Legaspi Village, Makati, Metro Manila; tel (2) 887632; telex 64142.
Ambassador: Mario Crema.

JAPAN

Embassy: LC Bldg, 375 Gil Puyat Ave, POB 891, Makati, Metro Manila; tel (2) 8189011; telex 22171; fax (2) 8176562.
Ambassador: Tsuneo Tanaka.
Consul-General: Nobuyasu Abe.

Consulate: 3rd Floor, Cluna Bank, Claro M. Recto St, POB 421, Davao City 8000; tel (35) 73781; fax (35) 64923.
Consul: Takeo Shimane.

KOREA, REPUBLIC

Embassy: ALPAP 1 Bldg, 3rd Floor, 140 Alfaro St, Salcedo Village, Makati, Metro Manila; tel (2) 8175705; telex 22157.
Ambassador: Jung Kiro.

LIBYA

Embassy: 4928 Pasay Rd, Dasmariñas Village, Makati, Metro Manila; tel (2) 8173461.
Ambassador: Salem Adem.

MALAYSIA

Embassy: 107 Tordesillas St, Salcedo Village, Makati, Metro Manila; tel (2) 8174581; telex 52758; fax (2) 8163158.
Ambassador: Emam Mohammed Haniff.

MALTA

Embassy: 1 Narra Ave, Forbes Park, Makati, Metro Manila.
Ambassador: Antonio C. Delgado.

Consulate: Zeta Bldg, Suite 32, Salcedo St, Legaspi Village, Makati, Metro Manila; tel (2) 8180051; telex 66826; fax (2) 8183969.
Honorary Consul: Paul A. Aquino.

MEXICO

Embassy: Adamson Centre, 121 Alfaro St, Salcedo Village, Makati, Metro Manila; tel (2) 8124066; telex 23459; fax (2) 8174684.
Ambassador: José Héctor M. Ibarra.
Counsellor: Ismael Orozco.
Chancellor: Rodolfo Cordón.
Chancellor: M. del Socorro Suárez Altamirano.
Attaché (Administrative): Luisa González de Perez.

MYANMAR

Embassy: Basic Petroleum Bldg, 4th Floor, 104 Carlos Palanca Jr St, Legaspi Village, Makati, Metro Manila; tel (2) 8172373; telex 66017; fax (2) 8175895.
Ambassador: U Bo Ni.

NAURU

Consulate: Pacific Star Bldg, 5th Floor, Makati Ave, cnr Gil Puyat Ave, Metro Manila; tel (2) 8175336; fax (2) 8177386.
Consul-General: David Agir.

NETHERLANDS

Embassy: King's Court Bldg, 9th Floor, 2129 Pasong Tamo, Makati, Metro Manila; tel (2) 887753; telex 63551.
Ambassador: P. F. C. Koch.

NEW ZEALAND

Embassy: Gammon Centre, 3rd Floor, 126 Alfaro St, Salcedo Village, POB 2208, Makati, Metro Manila; tel (2) 8180916; telex 63509; fax (2) 8164457.
Ambassador: Alison Stokes.
Counsellor: Warren Searell.
First Secretary: Winton Holmes.
Trade Commissioner: Peter Landon-Lane.
Trade Commissioner: Jo-Anne Maher.

NIGERIA

Embassy: 2211 Paraiso St, Dasmariñas Village, Makati, Metro Manila 3117; tel (2) 8173836; telex 64638.
Ambassador: Aisha Jimeta.

NORWAY

Embassy: Atlantica Bldg, 6th Floor, cnr Salcedo and Herrera Sts, Legaspi Village, Makati, Metro Manila; tel (2) 881111; telex 22503.
Ambassador: Harald Midttun.

PAKISTAN

Embassy: Alexander House, 6th Floor, 132 Amorsolo St, Legaspi Village, Makati, Metro Manila; tel (2) 8172776; telex 64219.
Ambassador: Ahmad Khan.

PANAMA

Embassy: Victoria Bldg, 5th Floor, 429 United Nations Ave, Ermita, Metro Manila; tel (2) 5211233; telex 66420.
Ambassador: Aurelio Chu-Yi.

PAPUA NEW GUINEA

Embassy: 2280 Magnolia St, Dasmariñas Village, Makati, Metro Manila; tel (2) 8108456; telex 22692; fax (2) 8171080.
Ambassador: Stephen N. Igo.

PERU

Embassy: Prince Bldg, 3rd Floor, 117 Rada St, Legaspi Village, Makati, Metro Manila; tel (2) 8187209; telex 22304.
Ambassador: Julio Balbuena López Alfaro.

ROMANIA

Embassy: 1216 Acacia Rd, Dasmariñas Village, Makati, Metro Manila; tel (2) 8176767; telex 45460.
Chargé d'affaires: Valeriu Simion.

RUSSIA

Embassy: 1245 Acacia Rd, Dasmariñas Village, Makati, Metro Manila; tel (2) 595639; telex 63709.
Ambassador: Oleg Mikhailovich Sokolov.

SAUDI ARABIA

Embassy: Insular Life Bldg, 8th Floor, 6781 Ayala Ave, Makati, Metro Manila; tel (2) 8173371; telex 45043.
Ambassador: Faud Muhammad Hassan Faki.

SINGAPORE

Embassy: ODC International Plaza Bldg, 6th Floor, 219 Salcedo St, Legaspi Village, Makati, Metro Manila; tel (2) 894596; telex 63631.
Ambassador: Aziz Mahmood.

SPAIN

Embassy: ACT Tower, 5th Floor, 135 Sen. Gil Puyat Ave, Metro Manila; tel (2) 8183561; telex 45892.
Ambassador: Francisco Javier Conde de Saro.

SRI LANKA

Embassy: Gammon Centre Bldg, 5th Floor, 126 Alfaro St, Salcedo Village, Makati, Metro Manila; tel (2) 8184142; telex 22639.
Ambassador: Dr P. B. G. Kalugalle.

SWEDEN

Embassy: Citibank Center, 15th Floor, 8741 Paseo de Roxas, Makati, Metro Manila; POB 1125, Makati, 1299 Metro Manila; tel (2) 8191951; telex 22029; fax (2) 8153020.
Ambassador: Hans F. Grönwall.
Counsellor: Christer Nilsson.
Second Secretary: Ulf Lindell.

Consulate: c/o Visayan Electric Co., D. Jakosalem St, POB 134, Cebú City, 6000 Cebú; tel (32) 96212; telex 48058; fax (32) 53884.
Consul: José Blanco Sala.

SWITZERLAND

Embassy: V. Esguerra Bldg, 5th Floor, 140 Amorsolo St, Makati, Metro Manila; tel (2) 865591; telex 22339.
Ambassador: Max B. Dahinden.

THAILAND

Embassy: 107 Rada St, Legaspi Village, Makati, Metro Manila; tel (2) 8154220; fax (2) 8154221.
Ambassador: Sarasin Viraphol.

UNITED KINGDOM

Embassy: Locsin Bldg, 15-17th Floors, 6752 Ayala Ave, cnr Makati Ave, Makati, Metro Manila 3116; tel (2) 8167116; telex 63282; fax (2) 8197206.
Ambassador: Keith G. MacInnes.
Counsellor (Commercial) and Deputy Head of Mission: A. S. Collins.
Defence Attaché: Lieut Col J. P. Clough.
First Secretary (Commercial): R. J. Cork.
First Secretary (Political): D. Curran.
Second Secretary (Management): A. A. W. Loosemore.
Attaché (Culture) and British Council Director: N. Bissett.

Consular Agency: 35 Paseo Eulalia, Maria Luisa Estate Park, Banilad, Cebú City 6401; tel (32) 460525; telex 816113; fax (32) 82157.
Honorary Consular Agent: M. P. Jackson.

USA

Embassy: 1201 Roxas Blvd, Metro Manila; tel (2) 5217116; telex 27366; fax (2) 5224361.
Ambassador: Nicholas Platt.
Deputy Head of Mission: Thomas C. Hubbard.
Political Section: John D. Finney, Jr.

Economic Section: John P. Modderno.
Commercial Section: Jonathan M. Bensky.
Adminstrative Section: Robert A. MacCallum.
Consular Section: Bruce A. Beardsley.
Labour Officer: James P. Dodd.
Regional Security Officer: Brendon P. O'Hanlon.
Agricultural Section: Lylc Moe.
Agency for International Development: Malcolm H. Butler.
Public Affairs Officer: Stanley N. Schrager.
Office of Defence Attaché: Col Terry C. Isaacson.
Military Advisory Group: Brig. Robert G. Sausser.
Communications Programme Officer: Renald Grammo.
Information Systems Manager: Brady T. Marking.

Delegation to Asian Development Bank: 2330 Roxas Blvd, POB 789, Manila; tel (2) 807251; telex 5071.
Executive Director: Victor H. Frank, Jr.

Consulate: 3rd Floor, PCI Bank, Gorordo Ave, Lahug, Cebú; tel (32) 211101; telex 6226; fax (32) 52020.
Principal Officer: Mary H. Amaral.
Economic and Commercial Sections: George H. Johnson.
Political Section: Dan J. Larsen.
Branch Public Affairs Officer: Karl G. Nelson.

VENEZUELA

Embassy: Sterling Centre, Dela Rose Cor., 5th Floor, Esteban St, Legaspi Village, Makati, POB 1894, Metro Manila; tel (32) 8185103; telex 63455; fax (32) 8185103.
Counsellor and Chargé d'affaires a.i.: Teofilo Labrador Rubio.

VIET-NAM

Embassy: 554 Vito Cruz, Malate, Metro Manila; tel (2) 500364.
Ambassador: Luu Dinh Ve.

YUGOSLAVIA

Embassy: 2157 Paraiso St, Dasmariñas Village, Makati, Metro Manila; tel (2) 879701; telex 63933.
Ambassador: Zoran Andrić.

POLAND

AFGHANISTAN

Embassy: 02-954 Warsaw, ul. Kubickiego 13; tel (22) 428449; telex 817298.
Ambassador: Khodaedad Basharmal.
Military and Air Attaché: Col Abdurrahim Mustaghni.
Assistant Military and Air Attaché: Col Mohamad Hashem.
Second Secretary: Abdul Samad.
Third Secretary: Mohammad Hussain Naim.

ALBANIA

Embassy: 00-789 Warsaw, Słoneczna 15; tel (22) 498427; fax (22) 484004.
Counsellor and Chargé d'affaires a.i.: Viron Tane.
Counsellor (Commercial): Skënder Pano.
Second Secretary: Tatiana Hajnaj.
Attaché: Dritan Keço.

ALGERIA

Embassy: 03-932 Warsaw, Dąbrowiecka 21; tel (22) 175855; telex 817019.
Ambassador: Mohamed Djeghaba.
Counsellor: El-Hadj Belharizi.
Secretary: Abdelhamid Terki.
Attaché: Abdelaziz Moussaoui.
Attaché: Hamou Belguidoum.
Attaché: Bachir Mokhtari.

ANGOLA

Embassy: Warsaw.
Ambassador: Agostinho André Mendes de Carvalho.

ARGENTINA

Embassy: 03-928 Warsaw, Styki 17/19; tel (22) 176028; telex 812412; fax (22) 177162.
Ambassador: Mario Enrique Burkun.
First Secretary (Consular): Guillermo R. Rossi.

Economic Section: 00-018 Warsaw, ul. Hibnera 6, 19th Floor; tel (22) 275014; telex 817560; fax (22) 276196.
Second Secretary (Economic): Carlos José Albisetti.

AUSTRALIA

Embassy: 03-903 Warsaw, Saska Kepa, Estońska 3/5; tel (22) 176081; telex 813032; fax (22) 176756.
Ambassador: Anthony C. Kevin.
Counsellor (Commercial): John Warnock.
First Secretary (Administrative/Consular): Andre R. Jedreski.
First Secretary (Visas): Gregory Wallis.
Third Secretary: Abigail Rossiter.
Attaché (Administrative): Katherine Anderson.
Attaché (Administrative): Caroline Golding.
Attaché (Administrative): Shane McGrath.
Attaché (Administrative): Stephen Dawes.
Attaché (Administrative): Derek Barker.
Attaché (Administrative): Phillip Burke.
Attaché (Administrative): Ivan Sharp.

AUSTRIA

Embassy: 00-748 Warsaw, ul. Gagarina 34; tel (22) 410081; telex 813629; fax (22) 410085.
Ambassador: Gerhard Wagner.
Counsellor: Helmut Böck.
Counsellor: Michael Weninger.
Counsellor (Administrative): Helmut Legerer.
Air and Military Attaché: Brig. Maximilian Trofaier.
Third Secretary and Vice-Consul: Guido Bruck.
Secretary (Archivist) and Vice-Consul: Hans J. Richter.

Commercial Section: 00-478 Warsaw, al. Ujazdowskie 22; tel (22) 295913; telex 813609; fax (22) 293247.
Counsellor (Commercial): Walter Resl.
Attaché (Commercial): Rudolf Thaler.

Cultural Section: 00-107 Warsaw, ul. Prózna 8; tel (22) 209620; telex 817450; fax (22) 201051.
Counsellor (Cultural): Helga Schmid.
Attaché (Cultural): Helmut Soriat.

Consulate-General: 31-018 Kraków, ul. Św. Jana 12; tel (12) 217829; telex 326597; fax (12) 216764.
Consul-General: Dr Emil Brix.
Consul: Erich Klaus.
Consul (Cultural): Marie Luise Moskart.

BANGLADESH

Embassy: 02-516 Warsaw, Rejtana 15, 20th & 21st Floors; tel (22) 497610; telex 816409.
Ambassador: Khalequzzaman Chowdhury.
Counsellor: Anwarul Bar Chowdhury.

BELGIUM

Embassy: 00-095 Warsaw, ul. Senatorska 34; tel (22) 270233; telex 813340; fax (2) 6355711.
Ambassador: François Ronse.
First Secretary: Philippe de Clerck.
Second Secretary: Geert Myulle.
Attaché (Consular/Administrative): Edgard de Tremmerie.
Attaché (Consular/Administrative): Yves Willaert.
Attaché (Commercial): Guido Scharpe.
Attaché: Christian Hougardy.
Attaché: Maria Looyens.
Attaché: Sylvie Schmitz.
Attaché: Carine van Houtte.
Attaché: Stanislas Morovich.

Military Section: 01-526 Warsaw, ul. Śmiałła 38; tel (22) 393763.
Military, Naval and Air Attaché: Col B. E. M. Walter Mertens.

BRAZIL

Embassy: 03-931 Warsaw, Poselska 11; tel (22) 177177; telex 813748.
Ambassador: João Augusto de Médicis.
Second Secretary: César de Paiva Leite Filho.
Third Secretary: Flávio Lima Rocha.
Third Secretary: Sérgio da Fonseca Costa Couto.
Attaché: Élgeni Lopes Strzeleski.

BULGARIA

Embassy: 00-540 Warsaw, al. Ujazdowskie 33/35; tel (22) 294071.
Minister and Chargé d'affaires a.i.: Miroslav Ivanov.
Counsellor: Anguel Petrov.
Counsellor (Consular): Alexandar Nikolov.
Counsellor: Christo Todev.
Counsellor: Nikolai Petkov.

Military, Naval and Air Attaché: Admiral Dimo Denev.
Second Secretary: Petrouna Kavlakova.
Second Secretary: Ivan Dontchev.
Second Secretary: Valentin Panov.

Commercial Section: 00-586 Warsaw, ul. Flory 9; tel (22) 498151; telex 813322.
Counsellor (Commercial): Detelin Markov.
First Secretary (Commercial): Ivan Kadrinov.
First Secretary (Commercial): Totio Totev.

CANADA

Embassy: 00-481 Warsaw, ul. Matejki 1/5; tel (22) 298051; telex 813424; fax (22) 296457.
Ambassador: Peter J. Arthur Hancock.
Counsellor and Consul: Ronald R. Halpin.
Counsellor (Commercial) and Consul: Anthony J. Coles.
Counsellor and Consul: Renald Dussault.
Forces Attaché: Col John E. Roderick.
First Secretary and Consul: David W. J. Hardinge.
Second Secretary and Vice-Consul: David DeRose.
Second Secretary and Vice-Consul: Peter B. Taylor.
Second Secretary (Administrative) and Vice-Consul: Gregory T. Curry.
Second Secretary and Vice-Consul: Dennis Horak.
Second Secretary and Vice-Consul: Eric Verner.

CHILE

Embassy: 02-932 Warsaw, ul. Morszyńska 71B; tel (2) 6428155; telex 814542.
Ambassador: Maximo Lira Alcayaga.
Second Secretary (Consular): Waldemar Coutts Smart.
Attaché (Cultural/Press): Andrés Koryzma Zep.

CHINA, PEOPLE'S REPUBLIC

Embassy: 00-203 Warsaw, Bonifraterska 1; tel (22) 313836; telex 813589.
Ambassador: Pei Yuanying.
Counsellor: Wang Yan.
Counsellor (Political): Gao Peiyu.
Counsellor (Commercial): Cai Fengshan.
Counsellor (Scientific/Technical): Wang Xi.
Counsellor (Cultural): Dong Songru.
Military, Naval and Air Attaché: Col Li Aimin.
Assistant Military, Naval and Air Attaché: Col Ren Baokai.
First Secretary (Press): Yuan Zongxian.
First Secretary: Chen Zhenhong.
First Secretary: Guo Zenglin.
First Secretary (Administrative): Zhang Yonghong.
First Secretary: Jiang Zhen.
First Secretary (Consular/Protocol): Zhu Yongsheng.
First Secretary (Commercial): Zhang Zichen.
First Secretary (Education): Chen Guozhong.
First Secretary (Cultural): Liang Quanbing.

Consulate-General: 80-236 Gdansk, ul. Grunwaldzka 1; tel (58) 415600.
Consul-General: Chen Shize.

COLOMBIA

Embassy: 03-936 Warsaw, Zwycięzców 29; tel (22) 170973; telex 816496; fax (22) 176684.
Ambassador: Manuel Jaime Guerrero Paz.
First Secretary (Consular): Mauro Hernan Mora Lozano.

COSTA RICA

Embassy: 02-516 Warsaw, Starościńska ul. 1a m. 17; tel (22) 481478; fax (22) 121658.
Ambassador: Carlos Alberto Vargas Solis.
Minister-Counsellor and Consul-General: Manuel Chaves Lizano.
Counsellor and Consul: María A. Castro Franceschi.

CUBA

Embassy: 03-932 Warsaw, ul. Katowicka 22; tel (22) 177108; telex 813588.
Ambassador: Isabel Allende Karan.
Counsellor: Armando Cristóbal Pérez.
Military, Naval and Air Attaché: Capt. Rafael López Rodríguez.
Attaché (Administrative/Protocol): Roque Nápoles Rodríguez.

CZECHOSLOVAKIA

Embassy: 00-555 Warsaw, Koszykowa 18; tel (22) 287221.
Ambassador: Markéta Fialkova.
Counsellor: Zdeněk Chytil.
Counsellor (Economic): Pavel Hrivnák.
Counsellor (Cultural): Ladislav Stindl.
Counsellor: Václav Svatek.
Military and Air Attaché: Gen. Jaroslav Nahálka.
Assistant Military and Air Attaché: Lieut Col Vladislav Raszka.
First Secretary (Consular): Petr Hlaváček.
First Secretary (Economic): Dušan Lojka.
First Secretary (Political): Jan Misiarz.
First Secretary (Economic): Miroslav Novák.
First Secretary: Jindřich Jirásek.

Commercial Section: 00-581 Warsaw, ul. Litewska 6; tel (22) 284051; telex 813585; fax (22) 284055.
Counsellor (Commercial): Jiří Campr.

Consulate-General: 40-058 Katowice, ul. Pawła Stalmacha 21; tel (32) 518576; telex 0312452.
Consul-General: Miloslav Zbořil.

Consulate-General: 71-422 Szczecin, ul. Piotra Skargi 32; tel (91) 225241.
Consul-General: Imrich Sedlák.

DENMARK

Embassy: 02-516 Warsaw, Staróscińska 5; tel (22) 490056; telex 813387; fax (22) 494485.
Ambassador: Niels Peter Georg Helskov.
Counsellor: Nanna Dahlerup.
Counsellor (Commercial): Ole Hjorth Jensen.
Defence Attaché: Col Jørgen Christensen.
Assistant Defence Attaché: Maj. Arne Erik Metzlaff Knippel.
Attaché: Henry Pollas.
Commercial Correspondent: Teresa Kredowska.

Consulate: 70-412 Szczecin, al. Niepodleglości 17; tel (91) 39574; telex 0422381.
Consul: Gunnel Christiansen.

Consular Agency: 81-354 Gdynia, ul. Jana z Kolna; tel (58) 216216; telex 054750.
Consular Agent: Karl-Gustaf Nöjd.

EGYPT

Embassy: 00-570 Warsaw, al. Wyzwolenia 6; tel (22) 280133; telex 813605; fax (22) 298865.
Ambassador: Mahmoud Hassan Farghal.
Counsellor: Ezzat Saad el-Sayed.
Counsellor (Cultural): Ahmed-Aziz M. el-Sharkawi.
First Secretary: Ahmad Ibrahim Ragheb.
Attaché (Administrative): Ahmed Moustafa M. Saleh.
Attaché (Administrative): Mandouh Farahat Ahmed Mansour.
Attaché (Administrative): Wafaa Hassan Sabry.

Commercial Section: 02-516 Warsaw, ul. Starościńska; tel (22) 483336; telex 814238.
Counsellor (Commercial): Mohamed Abdel Ghaffer Hegazi.

Information Office: 00-018 Warsaw, ul. Hibnera 6m. 23; tel (22) 268031; telex 816065.

EQUATORIAL GUINEA

Embassy: 02-516 Warsaw, ul. Starościńska 1m. 21; tel (22) 480167; telex 817404.
Minister and Chargé d'affaires a.i.: Luis Vivar Flores.

FINLAND

Embassy: 00-059 Warsaw, ul. Fr. Chopina 4/8; tel (22) 294091; telex 814286; fax (22) 216010.
Ambassador: Unto Turunen.
Counsellor: Reijo Uuslnleml.
Military, Naval and Air Attaché: Commdr Antti Livonen.
Attaché and Vice-Consul: Karl Salermo.
Attaché: Markku Korpinen.
Secretary/Archivist: Marja Lehti.
Secretary/Archivist: Raija Rodriguez.
Secretary/Archivist: Anna Riitta Lahtela.
Secretary/Archivist: Tiina Maria Kuntsi.

Commercial Section: 00-789 Warsaw, ul. Humańska 10; tel (22) 496633; telex 817731; fax (22) 497534.
Counsellor (Commercial): Juha Metsäntähti.

Consulate: 81-354 Gydnia, ul. Jana z Kolna 25.
Consul: Risto Koistinen.

Consular Agency: 80-952 Gdansk, ul. Grunwaldzka 132a m. 9; tel (58) 415222; telex 0512741; fax (58) 566644.
Consular Agent: Risto Koistinen.

FRANCE

Embassy: 00-477 Warsaw, Piękna 1; tel (22) 288401.
Ambassador: Alain Bry.
Counsellor: Jean-François Terral.
Counsellor: Stéphane Chmelewsky.
Counsellor (Commercial): Christian Saillard.
Counsellor (Cultural/Scientific): Jean-Jacques Beaussou.
Military and Naval Attaché: Col Bernard Aussedat.
Air Attaché: Lieut Col Gérard Muller.
Assistant Military Attaché: Lieut Col Bernard François.
First Secretary (Press): Michel Raineri.
Second Secretary: Didier Chabert.
Second Secretary: Jean-Pierre Gervais.
Second Secretary (Consular): Pierre Lanapats.

Consulate-General: 31-043 Kraków, ul. Stolarska 15; tel (12) 221864.
Consul-General: Alain du Boispean.

Consular Agency: 80-855 Gdansk, ul. Wały Piastowskie 1; tel (58) 314444.
Consular Agent: Annibal Pecorari.

GERMANY

Embassy: 03-932 Warsaw, ul. Dąbrowiecka 30; tel (22) 333488; telex 813692; fax (22) 173582.
Ambassador: Gunter Knoeckstedt.
Minister: Johannes Bauch.
Counsellor (Cultural): Folkmar Stoecker.
Military Attaché: Col Peter Köhler.
First Secretary: Dr Wolfgang Pailer.
First Secretary (Social Affairs): Georg Ziegler.
First Secretary (Administrative): Karl-Heinz Wittek.
Second Secretary: Hubert Knirsch.
Second Secretary: Rüdiger Zettel.
Second Secretary (Cultural): Heidrun Jung.
Second Secretary (Cultural): Joachim Bleicker.
Second Secretary (Press): Matthias Fischer.
Attaché (Press): Monica Josten.

Consular Section: 03-932 Warsaw, ul. Katowicka 31; tel (22) 173021; telex 816306.

Counsellor (Consular): Fritz Rainer Diesem.
Second Secretary (Consular): Jörn Rosenberg.

Economic and Commercial Sections: 03-916 Warsaw, ul. Walecznych 10; tel (22) 179857; telex 825479.
Counsellor (Economic/Commercial): Wolf-dietrich Vogel.

Consulate-General: 50-449 Wrocklaw, ul. Podwale 76; tel (71) 442006; telex 712219.
Consul-General: Bruno Weber.
Consul: Thomas Strieder.

Consulate-General: 80-219 Gdansk, al. Zwyciestwa 23; tel (58) 414366; telex 512374.
Consul-General: Dr Marianne Wannow.
Consul: Dieter Exter.

Consulate-General: 70-485 Szczecin, ul. Krolowej Korony Polskiej; tel (91) 225212; telex 422400.
Consul-General: Rainald Roesch.

GREECE

Embassy: 01-640 Warsaw, Paska 21; tel (22) 173011; telex 813455; fax (22) 173582.
Ambassador: Dr Efstratios J. Mavroudis.
First Secretary: Panayota Mavromichali.
Attaché: Lambros Siozos.
Attaché: Hermes Chatzievagelou.
Attaché: Constantinos Piperidis.
Attaché: Virginia Renieri.
Attaché (Economic/Commercial): Jeanne-Anita Mavromichalis.
Attaché: Theodosia Papagrigoriou-Siozou.

HOLY SEE

Apostolic Nunciature: 00-580 Warsaw, al. I Armii Wojska Polskiego 12; tel (22) 212337; telex 816493; fax (2) 6284556.
Apostolic Nuncio: Most Rev. Józef Kowalczyk, Titular Archbishop of Heraclea.
Auditor: Mgr Celestino Migliore.

HUNGARY

Embassy: 00-559 Warsaw, Chopina 2; tel (22) 284451; telex 814672; fax (22) 218561.
Ambassador: Akos Engelmayer.
Counsellor: Mihály Domszky.
Counsellor: Béla Megyeri.
Counsellor: Dr István Molnár.
Counsellor: Árpád Bende.
Counsellor (Cultural): Dr István Kovacs.
Military and Air Attaché: Col László Bardócz.
Assistant Military and Air Attaché: Lieut Col Ferenc Feld.
First Secretary (Press): Szaboles Szilágvi.
First Secretary: András Asztalos.
First Secretary (Consular): Dr Sándor Dürr.

Commercial Section: 00-646 Warsaw, ul. Szwoleżerów 10; tel (22) 415201; telex 813582; fax (22) 414364.
Counsellor (Commercial): Mihály Györ.
Counsellor (Commercial): Gábor Siklósi.

INDIA

Embassy: 02-516 Warsaw, ul. Rejtana 15; tel (22) 495800; telex 814891; fax (22) 496705.
Ambassador: Jagannath Doddamani.
Counsellor: Sarita Bali.
Military, Naval and Air Attaché: Col Prakash Ramrao Misal.
Second Secretary: Madhusudan Padmakar Gavai.
Attaché: B. Rajagopalan.

Consulate: 81-363 Gydnia, ul. Starowiejska 31; tel (58) 203624.
Honorary Consul: Tarun Kumar Guha.

INDONESIA

Embassy: 00-950 Warsaw, POB 33, Wąchocka 9; tel (22) 171644; telex 813680.
Ambassador: Ambiar Tamala.
Second Secretary: Mr Suhardi.
Second Secretary (Economic): Mr Soetito.
Third Secretary: Teguh Wardoyo.
Third Secretary (Consular): Suprio Utomo Nadir.
Attaché: Tjik Hanan Zaini.

IRAN

Embassy: 03-928 Warsaw, Królowej Aldony 22; tel (22) 171585; telex 813823; fax (22) 178452.
Ambassador: Kiumars Fotouhi-Ghiam.
Second Secretary: Ali Akbar Dabiran.
Third Secretary: Ali Golabi.
Third Secretary: Hassan Hassani.
Attaché: Mahmoud Mehdizadeh.
Attaché: Kazem Mosaffa Tehrani.

IRAQ

Embassy: 03-932 Warsaw, Dąbrowiecka 9A; tel (22) 175773; telex 813918; fax (22) 177065.
Ambassador: Mohammed Fadl Hussain al-Habboobi.
Counsellor (Commercial): Muhammed J. H. al-Nassiri.
First Secretary: Nahd A. S. Alaj.
Second Secretary and Consul: Abdul Malik al-Obaidi.
Third Secretary: Farouk A. Wahib.
Third Secretary (Consular): Sattar A. J. Abbas.
Attaché: Thamir W. Mostaf.
Attaché: Mohammad T. Yousif.
Attaché: Namir Taha Esmail.

IRELAND

Embassy: 00-697 Warsaw, al. Jerozolimskie 65/79, Suite 4023, Warsaw Marriott Hotel; tel (22) 306306; telex 816514; fax (22) 300311.
Ambassador: Richard Anthony O'Brien.
First Secretary: Mairtin O'Fainin.

ISRAEL

Embassy: 02-078 Warsaw, Krzywickiego 24; tel (22) 250028; telex 817660; fax (22) 251607.
Ambassador: Miron Gordon.
Second Secretary: Emanuel Zeev Mahl.
Third Secretary (Administrative): Alexander Livne.
Attaché: David Koren.
Attaché: Edna Livne.
Attaché: Alex Galily.

ITALY

Embassy: 00-055 Warsaw, plac Dąbrowskiego 6; tel (22) 263471; telex 813742; fax (22) 278507.
Ambassador: Vincenzo Manno.
Counsellor: Umberto Colesanti.
Counsellor (Commercial): Guido Larcher.
Military and Air Attaché: Col Savino Onelli.
First Secretary: Pietro Benassi.

Consulate: 81-372 Gdynia, ul. Świetojańska 32; tel (58) 201561; telex 54459.
Honorary Consul: Claudia Filippi Chodorowska.

JAPAN

Embassy: 00-790 Warsaw, Willowa 7; tel (2) 3523485; telex 813349; fax (22) 498494.
Ambassador: Shintaro Yamashita.
Minister: Hideaki Kobayashi.
Military, Naval and Air Attaché: Col Kiyoshi Hirayama.
First Secretary: Akira Hara.
First Secretary (Political): Seija Baba.
First Secretary (Political/Press): Hiroki Tokunaga.
First Secretary (Economic): Toru Takimoto.
Second Secretary (Administrative): Kenji Yazawa.
Second Secretary (Political): Satoru Takahashi.
Third Secretary (Cultural): Yoichi Wada.

KOREA, DEMOCRATIC PEOPLE'S REPUBLIC

Embassy: 00-478 Warsaw, ul. Bobrowiecka 1A; tel (22) 405813; telex 812707.
Ambassador: Han Ui Pyo.
Counsellor: Kim Jong Sul.
Counsellor: Kim So Won.
Counsellor (Science): Pak Chang Col.
Counsellor (Commercial): Li Ho Sik.
Military, Naval and Air Attaché: Col Kim Yong Il.
First Secretary: Li Jong U.
First Secretary (Consular): Cha Ui Sik.
First Secretary (Commercial): Song Du Son.
Second Secretary: Om Sung Chol.
Second Secretary (Commercial): Li Jae Hung.
Second Secretary (Economic): Pak Myong Dok.
Second Secretary (Science): Chong Yong Su.
Third Secretary (Commercial): Kim Gwang Sun.

KOREA, REPUBLIC

Embassy: 02-611 Warsaw, ul. Ignacego Krasickiego 25; tel (22) 483337; telex 817069.
Ambassador: Kyung Chul Kim.
Counsellor: Byung Hyo Choi.
Counsellor: Ki Sang Ahn.
First Secretary (Consular): Hyun Ju Lee.
Attaché: Ha Seob Yun.

LAOS

Embassy: 02-516 Warsaw, ul. Rejtana 15, Apt 26; tel (2) 6484786.
Second Secretary and Chargé d'affaires a.i.: Khouanephet Sayarath.
Third Secretary: Sithong Chitnhothinh.

LIBYA

People's Bureau: 03-934 Warsaw, Kryniczna 2; tel (22) 174822; telex 816233.
Secretary of People's Bureau: Mohamed A. Najah.
Counsellor: Ali T. al-Marmouri.
Counsellor: Mohamed el-Miloudi.
Attaché: Ahmed M. Anemar.
Attaché and Head of Consular Section: Belgasem Omar Gweaan.
Attaché: Khalifa Mohd Gaidi.
Attaché: Ahmed M. Madani.
Attaché: Ahmed A. Aouharba.
Attaché: Mohamed M. Sayah.
Attaché: Ali S. Erzeghi.
Attaché: Abdurrazag Segaier Ghaffar.
Attaché: el-Mehdi O. Sharif.
Attaché: Ahmed Y. Abdelwanis.
Attaché: Abdulgader M. Habib.
Attaché: el-Mabrouk M. el-Wafi.
Attaché: el-Hadi A. Rhuma.
Attaché: Omar Brahim B. Ganga.
Attaché: Ayad A. Ramadan.
Attaché: el-Hadi M. Hamza.

MALAYSIA

Embassy: 03-902 Warsaw, ul. Gruzinska 3; tel (22) 174413; telex 815368; fax (22) 177920.
Ambassador: Tan Koon San.
Counsellor: Mohd Yusof Ahmad.
First Secretary: Rohani Walat.
Third Secretary: Mohd Taib Abdul Samad.

MEXICO

Embassy: 02-516 Warsaw, Starościńska 1B, Apt 4-5; tel (22) 495250; telex 814629.
Ambassador: José Luis Vallarta.
Minister-Counsellor: Eduardo Castellanos Díaz del Castillo.

Third Secretary: Lorenzo Moisés Preciado Murguía.
Attaché: Ricardo Ahuja Hernández.
Attaché (Consular): Micaela Liberato de Sandi.

MONGOLIA

Embassy: 00-478 Warsaw, al. Ujazdowskie 12; tel (22) 281651; telex 814399.
Ambassador: Bajarchugijn Nanzad.
Counsellor: Choin Hunjav.
Attaché: Tsendiin Sambuu.

MOROCCO

Embassy: 02-516 Warsaw, Starościńska 1; tel (22) 496341; telex 813740.
Ambassador: Abdesselam Ouazzani.
Counsellor and Chargé d'affaires: Moulay Driss Zin el-Abidine el-Alaoui.
First Secretary: Abdessadeq Reguig.
Attaché (Finance): Mohamed Benhamou.

NETHERLANDS

Embassy: 00-791 Warsaw, ul. Chocimska 6; tel (22) 492351; telex 813666; fax (22) 488345.
Ambassador: Johan Willem Semeijns de Vries van Doesburgh.
Counsellor: Alfred F. Duyverman.
Counsellor (Agricultural): Leo Braakenburg.
Military, Naval and Air Attaché: Col Leonard H. H. Kuipéri.
Assistant Military, Naval and Air Attaché: Adriaan Corbijn.
Second Secretary (Commercial): Gijsbertus H. C. van der Lingen.
Third Secretary: Willem W. Plomp.
Attaché (Consular/Administrative): Johannes H. M. Niesten.
Secretary/Archivist (Consular/Administrative): Eleonora de Jager.
Secretary/Archivist (Consular/Administrative): Dirk-Peter Trimp.

NIGERIA

Embassy: 00-791 Warsaw, Chocimska 18; tel (22) 486944; telex 814675.
Ambassador: George Ochekwu Ajonye.
Minister-Counsellor: Agnes A. Ilemia.
Second Secretary: Robert I. Edozien.
Second Secretary: Ibrahim F. Ajadi.
Second Secretary: Felix O. Idigbe.

NORWAY

Embassy: 00-559 Warsaw, Chopina 2A; tel (22) 214231; telex 813738; fax (22) 280938.
Ambassador: Arnt Rindal.
Counsellor (Commercial): Finn Lange.
First Secretary: Ole T. Horpestad.
Head of Chancery: Kristin Barsten.
Secretary and Archivist: Inger Christoffersen.

Visa Section: Warsaw, ul. Kubickiego 5; tel (2) 6426733.
Secretary (Chancery/Visa): Kjersti Graudo.

Consulate: Szczecin, al. Niepodleglosci 17; tel (91) 39574.
Consul: Gunnel Christionansen.

Consulate: Gdynia, ul. Jana z Kolna; tel (58) 216216.
Consul: Karl Gustav Nøjd.

PAKISTAN

Embassy: 02-516 Warsaw, ul. Starościńska 1; tel (22) 494808; telex 816063.
Ambassador: S. M. Inaamullah.
Third Secretary: Ayaz M. Khan.

PERU

Embassy: 01-555 Warsaw, Felińskiego 25; tel (22) 399766; telex 814320; fax (22) 399766.
Ambassador: María Salazar Castellanos.
First Secretary: Aurora Luque de Hjorth.
First Secretary (Consular/Commercial): Augusto Lino Cornejo Vásquez.

PHILIPPINES

Embassy: 00-484 Warsaw, ul. Górnośląska 22 m. 5.
Ambassador: Rafael A. Gonzales.
Attaché: Pamela P. Crisol.
Attaché: Roberto F. de los Santos.

PORTUGAL

Embassy: 03-910 Warsaw, Dąbrowiecka 19; tel (22) 176021; telex 815509; fax (22) 176022.
Ambassador: Rui Fernando Meira Ferreira.
Counsellor: Augusto da Ponte Deslandes.
Attaché (Commercial): Ernesto José Ferreira Martins.
Attaché (Consular): Jaime Bello Sucena de Matos.

ROMANIA

Embassy: 00-559 Warsaw, Chopina 10; tel (22) 283156; telex 813420.
Ambassador: Iuliu Dobroiu.
Counsellor: Ilie Ivan.
Counsellor (Economic): Marin Visan.
Counsellor (Political/Press): Dumitru Hampu.
Military, Naval and Air Attaché: Col Mihaiu Margarit.
First Secretary (Political/Consular): Sandu Dan.
First Secretary (Cultural): Constantin Budianu.
First Secretary (Economic): Ovaghim Stroe.

RUSSIA

Embassy: 00-761 Warsaw, Belwederska 49; tel (22) 213453; telex 813530.
Minister-Counsellor: Lev Klepatski.
Minister-Counsellor: Gueli Stoupnev.
Counsellor: Valeri Poliakov.
Counsellor: Mikhail Yuferev.
Counsellor: Anatoly Kovalev.
Counsellor: Nikolai Zakhmatov.
Counsellor: Gennady Podlipniak.
Counsellor: Ivan Arbouzov.
Counsellor: Vladimir Voronkov.
Counsellor: Geuni Korepanov.
Counsellor (Cultural): Fridrikh Loginov.
Counsellor: Boris Beliakov.
Counsellor (Agriculture): Ivan Nikiforouk.
Counsellor: Nikolai Smirnov.
Counsellor: Vladimir Samoussenko.
Counsellor: Valeri Vinogradov.
Counsellor (Scientific/Technical): Yuri Kozyrev.
Counsellor: Vladimir Kouznetsov.
Military, Naval and Air Attaché: Col Alexandre Tenenev.
Assistant Military, Naval and Air Attaché: Col Yevgeny Tovma.
Assistant Military, Naval and Air Attaché: Lieut Col Oleg Soubotchev.
Assistant Military, Naval and Air Attaché: Lieut Col Sergei Khorochilov.
Trade Representative: Georgi Chtchoukine.

Consulate-General: 31-033 Kraków, ul. Westerplatte 11; tel (12) 228400.
Consul-General: Petr Sardatchouk.
Consul: Felix Dovjenok.
Consul: Viktor Kouznetsov.
Consul: Yuri Pavlenko.

Consulate-General: 80-251 Gdansk, ul. Batorego 15; tel (58) 411088.
Consul-General: Vadim Moutski.
Consul: Vladimir Zelenov.
Consul: Valeri Koubanov.
Consul: Boris Rodimov.
Consul: Leonid Rodionov.

Consulate-General: 60-809 Poznán, ul. Świerczewskiego 53a; tel (61) 47523.
Consul-General: Antanas Yurchenas.
Consul: Yuri Alexeev.
Consul: Sergei Koutchine.
Consul: Vadim Roubtsov.

Consulate-General: 71-422 Szczecin, ul. Piotra Skargi 14; tel (91) 221861.
Consul-General: Yuri Ivanov.
Consul: Konstantine Saenko.
Consul: Mikhail Glouchkov.
Consul: Ivan Kourilovitch.

SOUTH AFRICA

Interests Office: 00-697 Warsaw, Hotel Marriott, Room 3827, al. Jerozolimskie 65/79; tel (22) 306306.
Head of Interests Office and Minister-Counsellor: Jurie van Zyl Gryffenberg.

SPAIN

Embassy: 02-516 Warsaw, Starościńska 1B 10, 12 & 14; tel (22) 499926; telex 814515.
Ambassador: José Antonio López Zatón.
Counsellor: María Bassols.
First Secretary: Alfonso Tena.
Attaché (Press): Javier Martínez.
Attaché (Administrative): Juan Batista.

Commercial Section: 00-116 Warsaw, ul. Świetokrzyska 36m. 10; tel (22) 204282; telex 814449; fax (22) 202167.
Counsellor (Commercial): Emilio López Viñuela.

SWEDEN

Embassy: 00-585 Warsaw, ul. Bagatela 3; tel (22) 493351; telex 813457; fax (22) 495243.
Ambassador: Jean-Christophe Öberg.
Counsellor: Bo Emthén.
Counsellor: Per Saland.
First Secretary: Gull-Maj Schollin.
First Secretary: Birgitta Wiberg.
Second Secretary: Jan Amberg.
Second Secretary (Translator): Anders Simonsson.
Third Secretary (Translator): Jan Skagbrant.

Consulate: 70-952 Szczecin 2, BP 535, al. Niepodległości 17; tel (91) 39574; telex 422381; fax (91) 39711.
Consul: Gunnel Christiansen.
Chancellor: Miroslaw Fit.

Consular Agency: 81-354 Gdynia, ul. Jana z Kolna 25; tel (58) 216216; telex 054750.
Consular Agent: Karl-Gustaf Nöjd.

SWITZERLAND

Embassy: 00-540 Warsaw, Ujazdowskie 27; tel (22) 210172; telex 813528; fax (22) 210548.
Ambassador: J. Richard Gaechter.
Counsellor: Rudolf Staub.
Defence Attaché: Col Hans Schmid.
Military and Air Attaché: Col Willy J. Borer.
Attaché and Head of Chancery: Jean-Louis Giddey.
East-European Co-ordinator: Paul Leuenberger.
Attaché: Jean-Pierre Schneuwly.

SYRIA

Embassy: 02-536 Warsaw, Narbutta 19a; tel (22) 491454; telex 815465.
Ambassador: Ahmad Saker.
Minister: Khaled Arslan.
First Secretary (Consular): Hassane Hassane.
Attaché: Mohamed Ihsan Ghandour.
Attaché: Mohamed Oussama Kheir-Bek.
Attaché: Samih Nissafi.
Attaché: Sabet Khseirouf.

THAILAND

Embassy: 02-516 Warsaw, Starościńska 1B; tel (22) 494730; telex 815392; fax (22) 492630.
Ambassador: Somkiati Ariyapruchya.
Minister-Counsellor and Chargé d'affaires: Sewin Sirikul.
First Secretary: Dej Khiao-Narong.
First Secretary: Charnvit Buathongchan.
Third Secretary: Thithayaporn Saranaga.
Attaché: Niyom Sukpinit.
Attaché: Arpasnee Kidmor.

TUNISIA

Embassy: 00-459 Warsaw, Myśliwiecka 14; tel (22) 286330; telex 812827; fax (22) 216295.
Ambassador: Mohamed Fourati.
Counsellor: Béchir Chebanne.
First Secretary: Amel Ben Abdallah.
Third Secretary (Consular/Financial/Administrative): Abdelbaki Dellali.

TURKEY

Embassy: 02-622 Warsaw, Malczewskiego 32; tel (22) 443201.
Ambassador: Hatay Savaşçi.
Counsellor: Tuncay Inkaya.
Counsellor (Commercial): Erkan Özyaşar.
Counsellor (Commercial/Economic): Selçuk Yargici.
Military, Naval and Air Attaché: Lieut Col Necati Ucuzsatar.
First Secretary: Şule Özkaya.
Third Secretary: Imdat Korkmaz.
Attaché: Vahit Özdemir.
Attaché: Mehmet Mert.
Attaché: H. Zafer Çelebi.
Attaché: Halil Erdoğan.
Attaché: Enes Yüksel.

UNITED KINGDOM

Embassy: 00-556 Warsaw, al. Róż 1; tel (2) 6281001; telex 813694; fax (22) 217161.
Ambassador: Michael Llewellyn Smith.
Counsellor and Deputy Head of Mission: Gordon Geoffrey Wetherell.
Defence and Air Attaché: Group Capt. Edward Anthony Harris.
Naval and Military Attaché: Lieut Col Alistair Michael Cumming.
Assistant Military Attaché (Technical): Maj. Jeremy Humfrey York.
First Secretary (Commercial): Michael Alistair Corbett.
First Secretary (Chancery): Peter James McQuibban.
First Secretary (Information): T. Clayden.
First Secretary (Medical Officer): Dr Peter Arthur Eckstein.
First Secretary (Management): David Ernest George Kerly.
Second Secretary (Commercial): John Rutherford.
Second Secretary: Alison Blackburne.
Second Secretary: David Alexander Munroe.
Second Secretary (Know-How Fund): Michael Hayward Davenport.
Third Secretary (Economic): Simon John Banks.
Consulate: 02-061 Warsaw, ul. Wawelska 14; tel (22) 258031; tel 816113; fax (22) 250328.
First Secretary and Consul: A. Stead.

USA

Embassy: 00-540 Warsaw, al. Ujazdowskie 29/31; tel (2) 6283041; telex 813304; fax (2) 6289326.
Ambassador: Thomas W. Simons, Jr.
Deputy Head of Mission: Michael M. Hornblow.
Minister-Counsellor and Consul: Darryl N. Johnson.
Political Section: Daniel Fried.
Economic Section: Paul H. Wackerbarth.
Administrative Section: Mark J. Lijek.
Regional Security Officer: Thomas J. Comiskey.
Office of Defence Attaché: Col Glenn A. Bailey.
Air Attaché: Col Joseph M. Gardewin.
Consular Section: Anthony C. Perkins.
Labour Officer: Patrick G. LaCombe.
Agency for International Development: William R. Joslin.
Agricultural Section: Weyland Beeghly.
Public Affairs Officer: Stephen M. Dubrow.
Communications Programme Officer: Raymond E. Silva.
Information Systems Manager: Susan M. Erlandsen.
First Secretary (Press): Bruce K. Byers.
First Secretary and Consul: Jeannette P. Dubrow.
First Secretary and Consul: William P. Norville.
First Secretary: John J. Boris.
Attaché (Science): Coleman J. Nee.
Trade Centre: Warsaw, ul. Wiejska 20; tel (22) 214515; telex 813934; fax (22) 216327.
Director: Edgar D. Fulton, Jr.
Consulate-General: 31-043 Kraków, ul. Stolarska 9; tel (12) 229764; telex 325350; fax (12) 218292 .
Consul-General: Michael T. Barry.
Political and Economic Sections: Algis Avizienis.
Administrative Section: William A. Slaven.
Branch Public Affairs Officer: Joseph E. Macmanus.
Consulate: Poznán, ul. Chopina 4; tel (61) 529586; telex 413474; fax (61) 530053.
Principal Officer: Christian John Kennedy.
Branch Public Affairs Officer: Thomas Carmichael.
Administrative Section: Michalene F. Kaczmarek.

URUGUAY

Embassy: 02-516 Warsaw, Rejtana 15 m. 12; tel (22) 495040; telex 814647.
Ambassador: Augusto H. Wild.
Second Secretary and Consul: Néstor Canessa.

VENEZUELA

Embassy: 02-011 Warsaw, al. Jerozolimskie; tel (22) 289651; telex 812788; fax (22) 286740.
Ambassador: Jorge Daher Daher.
First Secretary (Cultural/Consular): Jacinta Anato de Bevilacqua.
Attaché (Administrative): Oswaldo Antonio Niño Hernandez.

VIET-NAM

Embassy: 00-468 Warsaw, Kawalerii 5; tel (22) 413369.
Ambassador: Nong The Can.
First Secretary: Pham Nang Dac.
Second Secretary (Cultural/Press): Hoang Binh.
Second Secretary (Protocol/Administrative): Nguyen Thua Bang.
Third Secretary (Consular): Vo Duc Quynh.
Attaché: Nguyen Van Man.
Commercial Section: 00-116 Warsaw, ul. Świetokrzyska 36 m. 32; tel (22) 203499; telex 813908.
Counsellor (Commercial): Le Cong Tam.
Attaché (Commercial): Mai Dinh Hoe.

YEMEN

Embassy: 02-954 Warsaw, ul. Marconich 8; tel (22) 426743; telex 814756.
Ambassador: Mansor Abdul Galil Abdul Rab.
Minister: Nageeb Ahmed Basha.
Counsellor (Consular): Fadl Abbas Ahmed Obeid.
First Secretary (Cultural): Abdulla A. A. Taleb.
Second Secretary: Abdel Ahmed Abdul Bari.
Third Secretary: Hassan Mohamed Esskander.
Attaché (Administrative): Sameera M. A. Sunbol.

YUGOSLAVIA

Embassy: 00-540 Warsaw, al. Ujazdowskie 23/25; tel (22) 285161.
Ambassador: Murat Agović.
Minister-Counsellor: Vladimir Stanimirović.
Military, Naval and Air Attaché: Col Božidar Milinić.
Counsellor (Economic): Zoran Novaković.
First Secretary (Consular): Vlastimir Djuričanin.
First Secretary (Cultural/Press): Dragan Grković.
Third Secretary: Čedomir Labus.
Attaché: Miroslav Pavlović.

ZAIRE

Embassy: 02-954 Warsaw, Kubickiego 11; tel (2) 6422367; telex 816015.
Ambassador: Ipoto Eyebu-Bakand'Asi.
Minister-Counsellor: Boekwa Lokolo-j'Okombe.
Counsellor: Lemba di ne Nkensi-N'Zinga.
Counsellor: Mpozi Mogampyuhyu.

International Organizations

EUROPEAN COMMUNITIES

External Delegation: 00-567 Warsaw, al. Ujazdowskie 14; tel (22) 306306; telex 816514; fax (22) 211290.
Head of Delegation: Alexander Dijckmeester.
Counsellor: Dino Sinigallia.
Counsellor (Economic): Andrew Rasbash.
First Secretary (Press/Cultural): Balthasar O. J. R. Glaubitz.
Attaché (Administrative/Financial): Nigel P. Tucker.
Secretary/Archivist: Christiane Keil Marinković.
Secretary/Archivist: Michelle de Haz.

UNITED NATIONS DEVELOPMENT PROGRAMME—UNDP

Embassy: 00-608 Warsaw, al. Niepodległości 186; tel (22) 255010; telex 825836.
Representative: Gary A. Gabriel.

Other Organizations

PALESTINE LIBERATION ORGANIZATION—PLO

Embassy: 02-516 Warsaw, ul. Starościńska 1m. 7/8; tel (22) 489126; telex 825611; fax (22) 489005.
Ambassador: Abdalla H. A. Hijazi.
Minister-Counsellor: Hafez al-Nemer.
Counsellor: Dr Shoaki Ali al-Omari.
Counsellor (Cultural): Dr Ahmad M. D. Breik.
First Secretary: Moin Abdel Wahab Yasin Haj Moh'd.
First Secretary: A'aish Ali Alokshah.
Second Secretary: Omar M. H. Baji.
Third Secretary: Dawoud I. I. Banlousha.

PORTUGAL

ALGERIA

Embassy: Rua Duarte Pacheco Pereira 58, 1400 Lisbon; tel (1) 616356; telex 15490.
Ambassador: Ahmed Ferhat Zerhowni.

ANGOLA

Embassy: Av. da República 68, 1000 Lisbon; tel (1) 733369; telex 43407; fax (1) 761817.
Ambassador: Rui Alberto Vieira Dias Mingas.

ARGENTINA

Embassy: Av. João Crisóstomo 8 r/c Esq., 1000 Lisbon; tel (1) 797311; telex 13611; fax (1) 774702.
Ambassador: Hipólito Jesús Paz.
Minister: Manuel Maria Pinto.
Minister and Attaché (Commercial): Alberto R. Fernandez Basabilvaso.
Counsellor: Diego Martin Limeres.
Second Secretary and Cultural Adviser: Raul A. Rodriguez Macchi.
Attaché (Administrative): Ana Maria Vaca.

AUSTRALIA

Embassy: Av. da Liberdade 244-2° e 4°, 1200 Lisbon; tel (1) 523066; telex 12536; fax (1) 523928.
Ambassador: Stuart H. R. Hume.

AUSTRIA

Embassy: Rua das Amoreiras 70-3°, 1200 Lisbon; tel (1) 654161; telex 16768; fax (1) 656763.
Ambassador: Nikolaus Horn.
Counsellor (Commercial): Klaus Fabjan.
Secretary: Reinhold Steinberger.

Consulate: Rua Caetano Feu 2, Praia da Rocha, 8501 Portimão Codex; tel (82) 57442; telex 57371.
Honorary Consul: Hugo Stumpf.

Consulate: Praça General Humberto Delgado, 267-s/I, 4000 Oporto; tel (2) 2084757; telex 22174.
Honorary Consul: Oliveira Fernando Pinto.

Consulate: Conjunto Monumental do Infante, Avda Arriaga 73-1, 9001 Funchal Codex, Madeira; tel 21057; telex 72145.
Honorary Consul: França Jorge Ferraz da Veiga.

Consulate: Rua Carvalho Aranjo 12-2, 9500 Ponta Delgada, Azores; tel (96) 27687; telex 82348.
Honorary Consul: Carlos Roberto Botelho.

BELGIUM

Embassy: Praça Marquês de Pombal 14-6°, 1298 Lisbon; tel (1) 549145; telex 12860.
Ambassador: Robert van Overberche.

BOLIVIA

Embassy: Rua Rodrigo da Fonseca 145-5° Esq., 1000 Lisbon; tel (1) 650659.
Ambassador: Clélia Arguedas de Pérez-Luna.

BRAZIL

Embassy: Estrada das Laranjeiras 144, 1600 Lisbon; tel (1) 7267777; telex 12593; fax (1) 7267623.
Ambassador: Luis Filipe Palmeiro Lampreia.

BULGARIA

Embassy: Rua do Sacramento à Lapa 31, 1200 Lisbon; tel (1) 676364; telex 16769.
Ambassador: Boyan Mikhaylov Jordanov.

CANADA

Embassy: Avda da Liberdade 144-156, 2° e 4°, 1200 Lisbon; tel (1) 3474892; telex 12377; fax (1) 3476466.
Ambassador: A. Raynell Andreychuk.
Counsellor (Immigration) and Consul: B. Stipac.
Counsellor (Commercial) and Consul: C. M. Tremblay.
Counsellor (Immigration) and Consul: S. A. Lavoie.
First Secretary and Consul: M. Rancourt.
First Secretary: G. Cormier.
Second Secretary (Administrative) and Vice-Consul: M. McGovern.

Consulate: Rua Frei Lourenço de Sta Maria No. 1, 1°, 8000 Faro; tel (89) 803757; telex 56566; fax (89) 21033.
Honorary Consul: L. Filipe Alfonso.

CAPE VERDE

Embassy: Avda do Restelo 33, 1400 Lisbon; tel (1) 3015271; telex 13765; fax (1) 3015308.
Chargé d'affaires: Raul Jorge Vera-Cruz Barbosa.
First Secretary: Jose Manuel da Cruz.
First Secretary: Francisco de Paula Spencer.
First Secretary: Silvino Lopes.

CHILE

Embassy: Avda Miguel Bombarda 5-1°, 1000 Lisbon; tel (1) 528054; telex 18805.
Ambassador: Patricio Morales.
First Secretary: Rene Rojas.
First Secretary: Eduardo Cisternas.

CHINA, PEOPLE'S REPUBLIC

Embassy: Rua de São Caetano 2, 1200 Lisbon; tel (1) 661882; telex 14762.
Ambassador: Guo Jiading.

COLOMBIA

Embassy: Praça José Fontana 10-5° Dto, 1000 Lisbon; tel (1) 557096; telex 43572; fax (1) 558665.
Ambassador: José Ignacio Villegas Cortes.

COSTA RICA

Embassy: Rua D. Jerónimo Osório 11-1°, 1400 Lisbon; tel (1) 3014667; telex 13493; fax (1) 572353.
Ambassador: María Eugenia Badilla Rojas.

CUBA

Embassy: Rua Pero da Covilhã 14 (Restelo), 1400 Lisbon; tel (1) 3015317; telex 12167.
Chargé d'affaires: Carlos Gomes Owen.

CYPRUS

Consulate-General: Casal de Santa Maria, Colares, 2710 Sintra, Lisbon; tel (1) 9290917; telex 12201; fax (1) 9290465.
Honorary Consul-General: Dr Bodo de Bruemmer.
Consular Assistant: Julio Bruno.

CZECHOSLOVAKIA

Embassy: Rua Pinheiro Chagas 6, 1000 Lisbon; tel (1) 3155628; telex 13406; fax (1) 575553.
Ambassador: Ivan Remenec.
Counsellor: Václav Malý.
Counsellor (Commercial): František Dvořák.
Consul: Pavel Filipek.
Attaché (Administrative): Josef Kubát.

DENMARK

Embassy: Rua Castilho 14-C-3°, 1296 Lisbon Codex; tel (1) 545099; telex 18302; fax (1) 570124.
Ambassador: Axel Buus.
Counsellor (Commercial): Christian Kønigsfeldt.
Counsellor (Agriculture/Government): F. K. Damgaard.
Chancellor and Consul: I. R. Pereira.
Attaché (Commercial): Claus Hofmann Frisch.
Export Assistant: Anne-Marie Bjerre.

Consulate-General: Rua do Alecrim 20F, 1200 Lisbon; tel (1) 361581; telex 13516.
Consul-General: António Eduardo Ferreira Pinto Basto.

Consulate: Rua do Paiol 2, 9000 Funchal, Madeira; tel 47137; telex 72555; fax 72153.
Consul: Rui de Oliverira Dias do Nascimento.

Consulate: Avda Infante D. Henrique 6-1°, 9500 Ponta Delgada, Azores; tel (96) 24291; telex 82161; fax (96) 23619.
Consul: J. W. V. Rieff.

Consulate: Praça Visconde Bivar 4, 8500 Portimão; tel (82) 23131; telex 57390; fax (82) 85935.
Consul: Alberto Cardoso Ribeiro de Azavedo.

Consulate: Rua Eugénio de Castro 280-1°, sala 136, 4100 Oporto; tel (2) 694584; telex 29179; fax (2) 699746.
Consul: Abel Morais Campos.

EGYPT

Embassy: Av. Conselheiro Fernando de Sousa 19-12°, 1000 Lisbon; tel (1) 687143; telex 18394.
Ambassador: Samir Seif el Yazal.

FINLAND

Embassy: Rua Miguel Lupi 12-5°, 1200 Lisbon; tel (1) 607551; telex 13582; fax (1) 604758.
Ambassador: Olli Auero.
Secretary (Commercial): Stephan Strandman.

Consulate: D.A. Knudsen & Ca, Lda, Cais do Sodré 8, 2°, 1200 Lisbon; tel (1) 373501; telex 18319.
Consul: Gunnar Hansen.

Consulate: Villa Finlandia, Vale del Rei, Rio Seco, 8000 Faro; tel (89) 25482.
Consul: Pertti Pohjaniemi.

Consulate: Praça dom João I 28, 2°, 4000 Oporto; tel (2) 320922; telex 25239.
Consul: Rui Thessen Ortigão de Oliveira.

Consulate: Avda de República 133, 8900 Vila Real; tel (59) 43721; telex 56079.
Vice-Consul: Manuel Guerreiro Ramirez.

Consulate: Rua Frei António Chagas 49 r/c Esq., 2900 Setubal; tel (65) 21035; telex 15277.

Vice-Consul: José Manuel Livério Seabra.

FRANCE

Embassy: Rua dos Santos-o-Velho 5, 1293 Lisbon Codex; tel (1) 608121; telex 12367.
Ambassador: Jean Marie Le Breton.

Consulate-General: 123 Calçada Marques de Abrantes, 1200 Lisbon; tel (1) 526206.

Consulate-General: Rua Eugénio de Castro 352, 2°, Quartier Foco, 4100 Oporto; tel (2) 694805.

GERMANY

Embassy: Campo Mártires de Pátria 38, 1100 Lisbon; tel (1) 3523961; telex 12559; fax (1) 3528146.
Ambassador: Alexander Conde York von Wartenburg.

Consulate: Avda da Boavista 5004, 4100 Oporto; tel (2) 610-2336; telex 25324.
Consul: Hans Karl Beste.

Consulate: Avda da República 166, 4°D, Faro; tel (89) 803148; telex 56515.
Honorary Consul: Enzio Freihen Baselli von Süssenberg.

Consulate: Largo do Phelps 6, 1°, Apdo 290, Funchal, Madiera; tel 20338.
Honorary Consul: Elisabeth Gesche.

Consulate: Travessa de Dessterro 18, Ponta Delgada, Apdo 152, São Miguel, Azores; tel (96) 23935.
Honorary Consul: Leo M. Weitzenbaur.

GREECE

Embassy: Rua do Alto do Duque 13, 1400 Lisbon; tel (1) 617133; telex 18832.
Ambassador: Georges Vandalis.

GUATEMALA

Embassy: Rua da Conceição 53-2° Dto, 1100 Lisbon; tel (1) 879917.

GUINEA-BISSAU

Embassy: Rua de Alconene 17-17A, 1400 Lisbon; tel (1) 615371; telex 14326.
Ambassador: Hugo Henrique Galvão dos Reis Borges.

HOLY SEE

Apostolic Nunciature: Avda Luís Bivar 18, 1000 Lisbon; tel (1) 547186; fax (1) 538075.
Apostolic Nuncio: Most Rev. Luciano Andeloni, Titular Archbishop of Vibo.
Secretary: Mgr Augustine Kasujja.

HUNGARY

Embassy: Calçada de Santo Amaro 85, 1300 Lisbon; tel (1) 645928; telex 13385; fax (1) 3632314.
Ambassador: Dr Sándor Árgyelán.

ICELAND

Consulate-General: Rua Rodrigues Sampaio 19, 2°, 1100 Lisbon; tel (1) 546078; telex 12312; fax (1) 575866.
Consul-General: Leif Dundas.

Consulate: Largo do Terreiro 4, 4000 Oporto; tel (2) 322512; telex 22726.
Consul: Paulo Jervell.

INDIA

Embassy: Rua Pero de Covilha, 16 Restelo, 1400 Lisbon; tel (1) 3017291; telex 62670; fax (1) 3016576.
Ambassador: Hardev Bhalla.
First Secretary: Divyabh Manchanda.
Third Secretary: Ashok Das.

IRAN

Embassy: Rua do Alto do Duque 49, 1400 Lisbon; tel (1) 3011560; fax (1) 3010777.
Ambassador: Abdolreza Assadi-Nia.

IRAQ

Embassy: Rua da Arriaga à Lapa 9, 1200 Lisbon; tel (1) 607112; telex 14042.
Ambassador: Mundhir T. al-Wandawi.

IRELAND

Embassy: Rua da Imprensa à Estrela 1-4°, 1200 Lisbon; tel (1) 3961569; telex 13417; fax (1) 67-7363.
Ambassador: Michael Greene.
First Secretary: Martin Greene.

ISRAEL

Embassy: Rua António Enes 16-4°, 1000 Lisbon; tel (1) 570251; telex 12223; fax (1) 3528545.
Ambassador: Colette Avital.
Defence Attaché: Mordechai Alon.
First Secretary and Head of Consular Department: Amram Levy.

ITALY

Embassy: Largo Conde de Pombeiro 6, 1198 Lisbon; tel (1) 546144; telex 12336.
Ambassador: Giovanni Battistini.

JAPAN

Embassy: Rua Mouzinho da Silveira 11, 1200 Lisbon; tel (1) 3523485; telex 12378; fax (1) 537600.
Ambassador: Chiyuki Hiraoka.

KOREA, DEMOCRATIC PEOPLE'S REPUBLIC

Embassy: Rua Jau 62, 1300 Lisbon; tel (1) 646837; telex 18840.
Ambassador: Kim Yong-Nak.

KOREA, REPUBLIC

Embassy: Avda Miguel Bombarda 36-7°, 1000 Lisbon; tel (1) 7937200; telex 13457; fax (1) 777176.
Ambassador: Hynuck In-Lew.

LIBYA

People's Bureau: Av. das Descobertas 24, 1400 Lisbon; tel (1) 616301; telex 43131.
Head of People's Bureau: Omar Saleh Abuarghub.

LUXEMBOURG

Embassy: Rua das Janelas Verdes 43, 1200 Lisbon; tel (1) 675164; fax (1) 60140.
Ambassador: Jean Auguste Joseph Florent Welter.

MALTA

Consulate: Muro dos Bacalheiros 112, 4000 Oporto; tel (2) 2002744; telex 22729; fax (2) 315796.
Honorary Consul: Arlindo Capucho Garcia Fernandes.

MEXICO

Embassy: Rua Castilho 50-4° Esq., 1200 Lisbon; tel (1) 570683; telex 12822.
Ambassador: Roque González Salazar.

MOROCCO

Embassy: Rua Borges Carneiro 32-1°, 1200 Lisbon; tel (1) 679193; telex 62197; fax (1) 3970309.
Ambassador: Ali Benbouchta.

MOZAMBIQUE

Embassy: Avda de Berna 7, 1000 Lisbon; tel (1) 771747; telex 13641; fax (1) 771747.
Ambassador: Esperança Alfredo Machavela.

NETHERLANDS

Embassy: Rua do Sacramento à Lapa 4, 1200 Lisbon; tel (1) 661163; telex 12126; fax (1) 666436.
Ambassador: Jonkheer Maximilien Vegelin.

NIGERIA

Embassy: Rua Fernão Mendes Pinto 50 (Restelo), 1400 Lisbon; tel (1) 3016189; telex 18418.
Ambassador: Agnes L. Imade Onitiri.

NORWAY

Embassy: Av. D. Vasco da Gama 1, 1400 Lisbon; tel (1) 3015344; telex 16505; fax (1) 3016158.
Ambassador: Tore Bøgh.

PAKISTAN

Embassy: Avda da República 20-1°, 1000 Lisbon; tel (1) 538446; telex 64699.
Ambassador: Maj.-Gen. Khurshid Ali Khan.
Counsellor: Sibte Yahya Naqvi.

PANAMA

Embassy: Alameda D. Afonso Henriques 3-7° Dto, 1000 Lisbon; tel (1) 825830; telex 61670.
Ambassador: Elida García de Paredes Aned.

PERU

Embassy: Rua Castilho 50-4° Dto, 1200 Lisbon; tel (1) 570552; telex 64000; fax (1) 570005.
Ambassador: Harry Belevan-McBride.
Counsellor (Culture): Carlos Gamarra Vargas.
First Secretary: Pedro Rey Daly.
Third Secretary: Franca Deza Ferreccio.
Attaché (Civil): Cristina Pérez de Cuellar de Sousa Costa.

Consulate: Rua Sa da Baneira 4814000, Oporto; tel (2) 323435.
Consul: Delfim Alexandre Ferreira.

Consulate: Rua Beal S. Tiago 549000, Madeira; tel 21375.
Consul: Manuel Inocencio de Freitas.

Consulate: Apdo 210-8125, Quarteira; tel 389977.
Consul: Fernanda Pires de Silva.

POLAND

Embassy: Avda das Descobertas 2, 1400 Lisbon; tel (1) 3012350; telex 13393.
Ambassador: Edward Sabik.

ROMANIA

Embassy: Rua de São Caetano 5, 1200 Lisbon; tel (1) 3966463; telex 13377.
Ambassador: Vasile Ileasa.
Counsellor: Ion Floroiu.
Military Attaché: Col Stefan Constantin.
First Secretary (Finance): Ion Nita.

RUSSIA

Embassy: Rua Visconde de Santarém 59, 1000 Lisbon; tel (1) 562424; telex 13420.

Ambassador: Gennadi Gerasimov.

SÃO TOMÉ AND PRÍNCIPE

Embassy: Rua da Junqueira 2, 1300 Lisbon; tel (1) 638242; telex 13796.
Chargé d'affaires a.i.: Dr Raul Aragão.
Third Secretary: Igualdina A. dos Santos.
Attaché (Cultural): Joao Nazare do Espirito Peneta.

SOUTH AFRICA

Embassy: Av. Luís Bivar 10, 1097 Lisbon; tel (1) 535041; telex 12894; fax (1) 545216.
Ambassador: Peter Swanepoel.
Counsellor (Trade): J. C. Pietersen.
First Secretary: P. J. P. Hugo.
First Secretary: H. C. Deacon.
First Secretary: A. Bestbier.
First Secretary: J. du Bruyn.
First Secretary (Administrative): P. J. Els.

Consulate-General: Edif. Torise, Rua Pimenta de Aguiar, Lote C-3 Andar, 9000 Funchal, Madeira; tel 46825; telex 72350; fax 41718.
Consul-General: A. J. P. Figgins.
Vice-Consul (Administrative): S. M. Franken.

Consulate: Rua Eugenio de Castro 280, Sala 238, 4100 Oporto; tel (2) 698968; telex 24171.
Honorary Consul: D. L. de L. Távora e Carnache.

SPAIN

Embassy: Rua do Salitre 1, 1296 Lisbon; tel (1) 3472381; telex 12505; fax (1) 3425376.
Ambassador: José Joaquín Puig de la Bellacasa.

SWEDEN

Embassy: Rua Miguel Lupi 12-2°, 1200 Lisbon; tel (1) 606096; telex 12554; fax (1) 605688.
Ambassador: Göran Hasselmark.
Counsellor: Lars-Erik Grundell.
Second Secretary: Eha Arg.
Secretary (Commercial): Lars Tallroth.

Consulate: Rua da Jasmineiro 6 r/c, 9000 Funchal, Madeira; tel 42222; telex 72291.
Consul: Lennart Edward Hjalmar Cederland.

Consulate: Rua Azevedo Magalhães 314, 4401 Vila Nova de Gaia, Oporto; tel (2) 307966; telex 23774; fax (2) 301432.
Consul: Manuel da Silvas Reis.

Consulate: Rua Judice Bicer 11-4°, Apdo 105, 8502 Portimão Codex; tel (82) 82136; fax (82) 413311.
Consul: Carlos Luis Filipe Gracias.
Chancellor: Birgitta Hallberg.

SWITZERLAND

Embassy: Travessa do Patrocínio 1, 1399 Lisbon Codex; tel (1) 6731212; telex 12893; fax (1) 677187.
Ambassador: Eric-R. Lang.
Counsellor: Thomas Füglister.
Attaché and Head of Chancery: Anne-Marie Chapius.

THAILAND

Embassy: Avda Almirante Gago Coutinho 68-1°, 1700 Lisbon; tel (1) 805359.
Ambassador: Kamtorn Vdomritthirj.

TURKEY

Embassy: Avda das Descobertas 22, 1400 Lisbon; tel (1) 3014275; telex 13392.
Ambassador: Dr Yildirim Keskin.

UNITED KINGDOM

Embassy: Rua de S. Domingos à Lapa 35-37, 1200 Lisbon; tel (1) 3961147; telex 12278; fax (1) 626768.
Ambassador: Hugh J. Arbuthnot.
Counsellor (Commercial) and Deputy Head of Mission: T. T. Macan.
Defence, Naval and Air Attaché: Cdre P. M. Jones.
Military Attaché and Deputy Defence Attaché: Lieut Col P. N. de R. Channer.
First Secretary and Head of Political and Information Section: J. S. Buck.
First Secretary (Political): P. J. B. Roberts.
First Secretary (Commercial): D. H. Turner.
First Secretary (Management): R. Parkinson.
First Secretary and Consul: M. N. Napier.
First Secretary (Political): B. Hopkinson.

Consulate: Avda da Boavista 3072, 4100 Oporto; tel (2) 684789; telex 26647; fax (2) 6100438.
Consul: J. Thomas.

Consulate: Rua de Santa Isabel, 21-1° Esq, 8500 Portimão; tel (82) 27057; telex 58732.
Honorary Consul: Dr J. M. T. G. P. de Azevedo.

Consulate: Largo Vasco Bensaúde 13, 9500 Ponta Delgada, São Miguel, Azores; tel (96) 22201; telex 82401.
Honorary Consul: F. R. Bensaúde.

Consulate: Avda de Zarco 2, Apdo 417, 9000 Funchal, Madeira; tel 21221; telex 72125.
Honorary Consul: R. F. Blandy.

USA

Embassy: Avda das Forças Armadas (Sete Rios), 1600 Lisbon Codex; tel (1) 7266600; telex 12528; fax (1) 7269109.
Ambassador: Everett Ellis Briggs.
Deputy Head of Mission: John H. Penfold.
Political Section: Jeffrey Millington.
Economic Section: David Miller.
Commercial Section: Miguel Pardo de Zela.
Labour Officer: Joseph Sala.
Consular Section: Arturo Macias.
Administrative Section: Thomas M. Widenhouse.
Regional Security Officer: John C. Murphy.
Agricultural Section: Daniel K. Berman.
Agency for International Development: David C. Leibson.
Public Affairs Officer: Gail J. Gulliksen.
Office of Defence Attaché: Col Van C. Sanders, Jr.
Military Assistance Advisory Group: Col Robert A. Young.
Communications Programme Officer: W. Jay Johnson.
Information Systems Manager: Sheila L. Thomas.

Consulate: Rua Julio Dinis 826, 3°, 4000 Oporto; tel (2) 63094; telex 24905; fax (2) 6002737.
Principal Officer: Herb Yarvin.

Consulate: Avda D. Henrique, Ponta Delgada, São Miguel, Azores; tel (96) 22216; telex 82126; fax (96) 27216.
Principal Officer: Mahlon Henderson.

URUGUAY

Embassy: Rua Sampaio e Pina 16-2°, 1000 Lisbon; tel (1) 689265; telex 14591.
Ambassador: Alfredo Platas.

VENEZUELA

Embassy: Avda Duque de Loulé 47-4°, 1000 Lisbon; tel (1) 573803; telex 18402; fax (1) 3527421.
Ambassador: Ildegar Pérez Segnini.
Minister-Counsellor: Ernesto Gonzalez.
Counsellor: Cecilia Pizani U.
Counsellor (Technical): Eugenio Montejo Hernandez A.

Consulate: Rua Rodrigo da Fonseca 82, 1° Esq., 1200 Lisbon; tel (1) 571567; telex 18402; fax (1) 536083.
Consul-General: Regulo Velasco M.

Consulate: Rua de Aljube 27 Andar, 469 Zona Postal, Codigo 9000; tel 24050.
Consul-General: Leya Rodriguez G.

YUGOSLAVIA

Embassy: Avda das Descobertas 12, 1400 Lisbon; tel (1) 3015311; telex 18352; fax (1) 3015311.
Ambassador: Štefan Korošec.

ZAIRE

Embassy: Avda Fontes Pereira de Melo 31-7°, 1000 Lisbon; tel (1) 533126; telex 18438.
Ambassador: Ubiya Magubu Mazobande.

International Organizations

EUROPEAN COMMUNITIES

Bureau: Centro Europeu Jean Monnet, 1-10° Largo Jean Monnet, 1200 Lisbon; tel (1) 541144; telex 0404; fax (1) 554397.
Director: António Bosco Menezes.

QATAR

ALGERIA

Embassy: POB 2494, Doha; tel 662900; telex 4604.
Ambassador: Muhammad Khammar.

BANGLADESH

Embassy: POB 2080, Doha; tel 671927; telex 5102.
Ambassador: Kazi Nasrul Islam.

CHINA, PEOPLE'S REPUBLIC

Embassy: POB 17200, Doha; tel 824200; telex 5120.
Ambassador: Hu Chang Lin.

EGYPT

Embassy: POB 2899, Doha; tel 832116; telex 4321.
Ambassador: Isam ad-Din Hawas.

FRANCE

Embassy: West Bay, POB 2669, Doha; tel 832281; telex 4280; fax 832254.
Ambassador: André Janier.

Trade Promotion Office: POB 4373, Doha; tel 423810; telex 4724.

GERMANY

Embassy: C-Ring Rd, opp. Gulf Cinema, POB 3046, Doha; tel 671100; telex 4528; fax 670011.
Ambassador: Dr Hans-Lothar Steppan.

INDIA

Embassy: POB 2788, Al-Hilal Area, Doha; tel 672021; telex 4646; fax 670448.
Ambassador: Ramesh Chandra Shukla.
First Secretary (Commercial/Consular): S. C. Trehan.
First Secretary (Political/Information): M. L. R. Jafri.
Second Secretary (Labour/Visa): O. P. Aggarwal.
Second Secretary (Head of Chancery): Prabhati Lal.

IRAN

Embassy: POB 1633, Doha; tel 835300; telex 4251; fax 831665.
Ambassador: Nasrollah Mirzaiee Nasir.

IRAQ

Embassy: POB 1526, Doha; tel 662244; telex 4296.
Ambassador: Anwar Sabri Adl ar-Razzaq.

JAPAN

Embassy: Doha West Bay, Diplomatic Area, POB 2208, Doha; tel 831224; telex 4339; fax 832178.
Ambassador: Haruo Hanawa.

JORDAN

Embassy: POB 2366, Doha; tel 832204; telex 4192; fax 832173.
Ambassador: Nayef Saud al-Qadi.

KOREA, REPUBLIC

Embassy: POB 372, Doha; tel 832238; telex 4105.
Ambassador: Nae Hyong Yoo.

KUWAIT

Embassy: POB 177, Doha; tel 832111; telex 4113; fax 832042.
Ambassador: Ahmad Mirshid as-Sulaiman.

LEBANON

Embassy: POB 2411, Doha; tel 444468; telex 4404.
Ambassador: George Siam.

MAURITANIA

Embassy: POB 3132, Doha; tel 670458; telex 4379.
Ambassador: Mafouz Weld al-Morabit.

MOROCCO

Embassy: POB 3242, Doha; tel 329181; telex 4473.
Ambassador: Binaser an-Nasri.

OMAN

Embassy: POB 3766, Doha; tel 449821; telex 4341.
Ambassador: Said bin Ali bin Salim al-Kalbani.

PAKISTAN

Embassy: POB 334, Doha; tel 832237; fax 832227.

RUSSIA

Embassy: POB 15404, Doha; Mansoura, Bahli St 25; tel 410332; telex 5170.
Ambassador: Vladimir I. Vodiakhin.
Counsellor: Mikhail M. Yudin.
Third Secretary: Ilya A. Morgounov.

SAUDI ARABIA

Embassy: POB 1255, Doha; tel 427144; telex 4483.
Ambassador: Sheikh Abd al-Mohsen bin Sulaiman as-Said.

SOMALIA

Embassy: POB 1948, Doha; tel 832181; telex 4275.
Ambassador: Sharif Muhammad Omar.

SUDAN

Embassy: POB 2999, Doha; tel 423007; telex 4707; fax 351366.
Ambassador: Ahmad Yousuf ath-Thani.

SYRIA

Embassy: POB 1257, Doha; tel 421873; telex 4447.
Ambassador: Ahmad Ulayan Tabello.

TUNISIA

Embassy: POB 2707, Doha; tel 421694; telex 4422; fax 426917.
Ambassador: Salem al-Fourati.

TURKEY

Embassy: POB 1977, Doha; tel 865885; telex 4406.
Ambassador: Erdogan Aytun.

UNITED KINGDOM

Embassy: POB 3, Doha; tel 421991; telex 4205; fax 438692.
Ambassador and Consul-General: Graham Hugh Boyce.
First Secretary (Commercial) and Deputy Head of Mission: J. G. Rice.
Second Secretary (Management) and Consul: R. J. Davies.
Third Secretary (Commercial) and Vice-Consul: P. D. G. Cook.
Third Secretary (Vice-Consul): F. A. Drayton.

USA

Embassy: 149 Ali Bin Ahmed St, Fariq Bin Omran, POB 2399, Doha; tel 864701; telex 4847; fax 861669.

Commercial Section: tel 867460.
Ambassador: Mark G. Hambley.
Political/Economic Officer: Donald A. Roberts.
Vice-Consul: Kate Smith.
Administrative Officer: Christa U. Griffin.

Information Service: tel 351207; fax 321907.
Public Affairs Officer: John F. Berry.
Communications Programme Officer: Bruce E. Peters.

Liaison Office: tel 875140.
Liaison Office: Lieut Col Oukrup.

YEMEN

Embassy: POB 3318, Doha; tel 671050; telex 5130.
Ambassador: Abd al-Wahab Nasser Jahaf.

ROMANIA

ALBANIA

Embassy: Bucharest, Str. Modrogan 4; tel (0) 793180.
Ambassador: Piro Vito.
Counsellor (Commercial): Ilir Shijaku.
Third Secretary: Marko Bello.
Attaché: Rezear Xhaxhiu.
Attaché (Commercial): Qemal Gjokutaj.
Attaché: Andon Koci.

ALGERIA

Embassy: Bucharest, Bd. Ana Ipătescu 29; tel (0) 505157.
Ambassador: Haffad Necereddine.
Minister-Counsellor: Rabah Souibes.
Third Secretary: Mohamed Khelili.
Attaché: Tahar Mistiri.
Attaché: Mohand Mezhoud.

ARGENTINA

Embassy: Bucharest, Str. Drobeta 11; tel (0) 117290; telex 11412.
Ambassador: Oscar Eduardo Torres Avalos.
First Secretary: Carlos Ernesto Manteiga.
Second Secretary (Commercial): Carlos José Albisetti.
Attaché (Administrative): Claudio Carlos Pablo Innocenti.

AUSTRIA

Embassy: 70254 Bucharest, Str. Dumbrava Roşie 7; tel (0) 114354; telex 11333.
Ambassador: Christoph Parisini.
Counsellor: Dietmar Fellner.
First Secretary: Ulrike Tilly.
Assistant Attaché: Herbert Pfeiffer.
Assistant Attaché: Hermine Pfeiffer.
Assistant Attaché: Harald Hauptmann.
Assistant Attaché: Elisabeth Reiter.
Assistant Attaché: Anette Stockinger.

Consular Section: Bucharest, Str. Salcîmilor 12; tel (0) 191601.
Secretary (Economic) and Vice-Consul: Paul Mirko Kummer.
Third Secretary (Emigration) and Vice-Consul: Peter Graser.
Attaché (Administrative) and Vice-Consul: Werner Kremnitzer.

Commercial Section: Bucharest, Str. Clopotarii Vechi 4; tel (0) 594590; telex 11291; fax (0) 507600.
Attaché (Commercial): Walter Friedl.

BANGLADESH

Embassy: Bucharest, Bd. Kiseleff 55, Vila 6, Sector 1; tel (0) 171544; telex 10197.
Ambassador: M. Anwar Hashim.
First Secretary: Mohammad Amjad Hossain.

BELGIUM

Embassy: 79359 Bucharest, Bd. Dacia 32; tel (0) 114212; telex 11482.
Ambassador: Jan Hellemans.
Second Secretary: Chris Hoornaert.
Attaché: Patrizio Ventura.
Attaché: Arlette Chevolet.
Attaché: Ingeborg de Feyter.

BRAZIL

Embassy: Bucharest, Str. Praga 11; tel (0) 331110; telex 11307.
Ambassador: Marcel Dezon Costa Haslocher.
First Secretary: Carlos Augusto de Oliveira.

BULGARIA

Embassy: Bucharest, Str. Rabat 5; tel (0) 332150; telex 11329.
Ambassador: Stefan Naumov.
Counsellor: Ivo Todorov.
Counsellor (Commercial): Evgeni Petrov.
Counsellor: Nikola Nikolov.
First Secretary (Cultural): Ivan Dankov.
Second Secretary: Volodja Statkov.
Third Secretary (Press Attaché): Nikolai Iliev.
Third Secretary (Consular): Dimitar Dimitrov.
Attaché: Asen Despotov.

CANADA

Embassy: 71118 Bucharest, Str. Nicolae Iorga 36; POB 2966, Post Office No. 22; tel (0) 506140; telex 10690.
Ambassador: Saul Grey.
Counsellor (Commercial) and Consul: Keith L. McFarlane.
Counsellor and Consul: James H. Holdham.
First Secretary (Immigration): Jeremiah J. Shea.
Attaché (Administration) and Vice-Consul: Lance S. Abbott.
Attaché: Mary Janisch.
Attaché: Timothy Sullivan.
Attaché: Ray Butler.
Attaché: Joseph Arsenault.
Attaché: Desmond Clarke.

CHILE

Embassy: Bucharest, Bd. Ana Ipătescu 8; tel (0) 115691; telex 11197.
Ambassador: Sergio Mimica Bezmalinovic.
Second Secretary: Rodrigo Espinosa Aguirre.

CHINA, PEOPLE'S REPUBLIC

Embassy: Bucharest, Şos. Nordului 2; tel (0) 331925.
Ambassador: Wang Jinqing.
Counsellor: Yang Jiachun.
Counsellor: Chen Guangzhong.
Counsellor (Cultural): Liang Shenxiu.
Counsellor (Commercial): Huang Guozhi.
Counsellor (Economic): Lu Kunbao.
Military, Naval and Air Attaché: Col Chen Bingyue.
Assistant Military, Naval and Air Attaché: Col Wang Shaochuan.
Assistant Military, Naval and Air Attaché: Lieut Col An Zuoshan.
First Secretary (Protocol): Zhang Wenying.
First Secretary: Jiang Xiaohua.
First Secretary: Wu Gansheng.
First Secretary: Zhou Anrong.
First Secretary (Commercial): Lu Shizhao.
First Secretary (Commercial): Gao Delin.
First Secretary (Commercial): Xiong Qingwen.
First Secretary (Commercial): Wu Quanchang.
First Secretary (Science/Technology): Tang Chunyuan.
First Secretary (Economic): Zhou Fuyuan.
First Secretary (Cultural): Cui Nianqiang.
First Secretary: Song Linfang.

Consulate-General: Constanta, Bd. Carpati 7; tel (16) 17833.
Vice-Consul: Su Yanwen.
Vice-Consul: Zhen Shiqin.

COLOMBIA

Embassy: Bucharest, Str. Polonă 35, Ap. 3, Sector 1; tel (0) 115108; telex 10498; fax (0) 114964.
First Secretary, Chargé d'affaires a.i. and Consul: Myriam Elena Beltran de Forero.

CONGO

Embassy: Bucharest, Str. Pictor Mirea 18; tel (0) 170343.
Counsellor and Chargé d'affaires a.i.: Edgard-Philippe Diafouka-Bambelat.
Second Secretary: Félix Mipassi.
Second Secretary: Roger Ondzie.
Attaché: Edouard Akouango.
Attaché: Mr Kouanga-Mboyo.

COSTA RICA

Embassy: Bucharest, Str. Lt. Dumitru Lemnea 3-5, Et. 1, Ap. 4; tel (0) 592008; telex 11939.
Ambassador: Luis Fernando Acosta Mora.
Minister-Counsellor and Consul-General: Ernesto Villavicencio Ruiz.
Counsellor: Renan Corrales Oconitrillo.

CUBA

Embassy: Bucharest, Al. Alexandru 33; tel (0) 796895; telex 11305.
Ambassador: Niel Ruíz Guerra.
Counsellor (Commercial/Economic): Diego Rivero.
Military, Naval and Air Attaché: Lieut Col Sergio Cortina Garcia.
First Secretary: Lazaro Mendez.
First Secretary: Ramón Benitez.
Attaché (Commercial/Economic): Carmen Leonor Marrero.
Attaché: Enrique Torres.

CZECHOSLOVAKIA

Embassy: Bucharest, Str. Ion Ghica 11; tel (0) 159141; fax (0) 159144.
Ambassador: Milan Resutík.
Counsellor: Jaromir Kvapil.
Counsellor: Pavel Sadovský.
Counsellor: Miloslav Krajny.
Counsellor: Pavol Karaffa.
Military Attaché: Ján Hanko.
Deputy Military Attaché: Lubomir Valentin.
First Secretary: Pavol Štibraný.
Third Secretary: Dušan Deván.
Third Secretary: Ján Šoth.

Consulate-General: Constanta, Str. Marii 1; tel (16) 18053.
Consul-General: Karel Dostal.

DENMARK

Embassy: Bucharest, Str. Dr Burghela 3; tel (0) 155419; telex 11325.
Ambassador: Ulrik Helweg-Larsen.
Counsellor (Agriculture): Victor Christian Hjort.
First Secretary: Henrik Kiil.
Attaché: Anne Beck.
Assistant Attaché: Susan Harding Kristensen.

ECUADOR

Embassy: Bucharest, Str. Polonă 35, ap. 1; tel (0) 110503; telex 10836.
Ambassador: Galo Ribadeneira Cueva.
Minister and Chargé d'affaires: Manuel Pesantes Garcia.
Attaché (Administrative): Carlos Eugenio Meza Diaz.

EGYPT

Embassy: Bucharest, Bd. Dacia 21; tel (0) 110138; telex 11549.
Ambassador: Ihab Wahba.
Minister: Lofty Ibrahim Yacoub.
Minister: Asem Fath el-Bab.
Counsellor: Farouk Riad Hassan Mabrouk.
Third Secretary: Khaled Aly Elbakly.
Minister (Commercial): Bahy Eldin Omar Diab.
Third Secretary (Commercial): Inas A. Zedan.
Attaché (Administrative): Ahmed Nagy Ali.
Attaché (Administrative): Ahmed Mohamed Hamed Seleim.
Attaché (Administrative/Commercial): George Elias Awad.
Office of Defence Attaché: Bucharest, Str. Polonă 19; tel (0) 113977.
Defence Attaché: Gen. Hussein M. Abou Elleil.
Assistant Defence Attaché: Maj. Ashraf Aly Arafa.
Press Office: Bucharest, Bd. Magheru 24, et. 9, ap. 48; tel (0) 593896.
Counsellor: Ahmed Youssry Ahmad.
Attaché (Administrative/Press): Hamdy Gomaa Salem.

FINLAND

Embassy: 71271 Bucharest, Str. Atena 2 bis; tel (0) 335440; telex 11293; fax (0) 331790.
Ambassador: Bo Ådahl.
Second Secretary: Marja-Liisa Virtanen.

FRANCE

Embassy: Bucharest, Str. Biserica Amzei 13-15, BP 143; tel (0) 110540; telex 11320; fax (0) 506576.
Ambassador: Renaud Vignal.
Counsellor (Political): Jean Michel Dumond.
Counsellor (Commercial): Gerard Valluet.
Counsellor (Aid/Co-operation): Gilles Carasso.
Military Attaché: Lieut Col René Cagnat.
First Secretary (Political): Gerard Tournier.
Third Secretary: Pascal Delumeau.
Attaché: François Meytraud.
Attaché (Commercial): Jean-Louis Moriniere.
Attaché (Education): Bernard Barbereau.
Attaché (Cultural): Denis Pelbois.
Cultural Section: Bucharest, Str. Cristian Tell 22; tel (0) 502560.
Counsellor (Cultural/Cooperation): Chantal Colleu-Dumond.
Consular Section: Bucharest, Intrarea Cristian Tell 6; tel (0) 110540.
Consul: Gilles Courregelongue.

GERMANY

Embassy: 79449 Bucharest, Str. Rabat 21; tel (0) 792580; telex 11292; fax (0) 796854.
Ambassador: Dr Klaus Terfloth.
Minister-Counsellor: Christiane Geissler-Kuss.
Counsellor (Consular): Dietmar Blaas.
Military, Naval and Air Attaché: Lieut Col Peter Bernd Aretz.
First Secretary (Economic/Commercial): Ulrich-Detlef Grunenberg.
First Secretary: Simon Acker.
Second Secretary: Miguel Berger.
Second Secretary (Press): Klaus Werner Brambach.
Second Secretary and Head of Chancery: Bernhard Rottler.
Third Secretary: Helmut Pfeiffer.
Attaché: Markus Aretz.
Attaché: Michael Grimm.
Attaché: Regina Hamann.
Attaché: Hermann Kötting.
Attaché: Gerhard Lohmeier.
Attaché: Meta Pierau.
Attaché: Peter Schreiner.
Attaché: Horst Wendrich.
Consular Agency: Sibiu, Blocul No. 5, Parcul Tineretului-Parterre; tel (24) 30774; telex 69357; fax (24) 33127.
Consul: Peter-Helmut Finger.

GREECE

Embassy: Bucharest, Str. Orlando 6; tel (0) 503988; telex 11321.
Ambassador: Giorgios Linardos.
Counsellor: Dorothee Douvos.
Military, Naval and Air Attaché: Col Christos Tselouras.
Counsellor (Press): Andreas Papadatos.
Assistant Counsellor (Press): Dimitrios Givalos.
First Secretary (Consular): Michel-Christ Diamessis.
Second Secretary: Thiressia-Paraskevi Angelatou.
Attaché: Nikolitsa Tzafalia.
Attaché: Andonios Perdikoulis.
Commercial Section: Bucharest, Str. Drobeta 4-10; tel (0) 116522.
Secretary (Economic/Commercial): Leonidas Papakonstantinidis.

GUINEA

Embassy: Bucharest, Str. Bocşa 4; tel (0) 111893; telex 10255.
Ambassador: Abel Niouma Sandouno.
First Secretary: Daoro Inapogui.
Attaché: Delamou Inereke.
Consul: Ibrahima Dinn Camara.

HOLY SEE

Apostolic Nunciature: 70764 Bucharest, Str. Pictor C. Stahi 5-7; tel (0) 139490.
Apostolic Nuncio: Most Rev. John Bukovsky, Titular Archbishop of Tabalta.
Secretary: Mgr Ermenegildo Camozzi.

HUNGARY

Embassy: Bucharest, Str. Jean Louis Calderon 63; tel (0) 146621; telex 11323; fax (0) 150089.
Ambassador: Ernő Rudas.
First Counsellor: László Péter.
Military Attaché: József Kis-Benedek.
Counsellor (Political): György Kalmár.
Counsellor (Economic): Károly Bitay.
Counsellor (Foreign Policy): József Nagy.
Counsellor (Cultural): Béla Kálmán.
First Secretary (Political): László Alföldi.
First Secretary (Consular): György Kis.
First Secretary (Political): Dr Béla Szabó.
First Secretary (Press): Dr Miklós Boros.
Commercial Section: Bucharest, Str I. C. Frimu 20; tel (0) 503840.
Commercial Counsellor: László Kónya.

INDIA

Embassy: 71274 Bucharest, Str. Brîncuţei 11; tel (0) 797630; telex 11619.
Ambassador: Julio Francis Ribeiro.
Military, Naval and Air Attaché: Col Amar Singh.
First Secretary: M. V. Sundararaman.
First Secretary: K. Mahadevan.
Attaché: Jasbir Kaur Bharti.
Attaché: P. G. Punnoose.

INDONESIA

Embassy: Bucharest, Orlando 10; tel (0) 507720; telex 11258.
Ambassador: Lamtiur Andaliah Panggabean.
Defence Attaché: Col Abdul Ghani.
Assistant Defence Attaché: Endang Ruchijat.
First Secretary: H. S. Tadjoeddin.
Second Secretary (Press/Cultural): Mascud Effendi Hutasuhut.
Second Secretary (Economic): Deddy Saiful Hadi.
Third Secretary (Administrative): Nur Arifin.
Attaché: I. G. G. Raka Sutarja.

IRAN

Embassy: Bucharest, Bd. Ana Ipătescu 39; tel (0) 334471; telex 11507.
Ambassador: Abdoul Rasoul Mohager Hegeazi.
Second Secretary: Abdolmajid Mozafari.
Second Secretary: Seyed Mohammad Mohsen Emrani.
Attaché: Seyed Ghassem Mousavi.
Attaché: Majid Barparvashan.
Attaché: Seyed Heshmatollah Attarzadeh Niaki.

IRAQ

Embassy: Bucharest, Str. Polonă 8; tel (0) 110835.
Ambassador: Ibrahim Shujaa Sultan.
Minister: Ryadh al-Fadhly.
Counsellor (Cultural): Abdul Rahman Rijab.
Third Secretary and Consul: Mudhir Numan Wahib al-Dury.
Attaché: Abduliatif Hamud Thamir.
Attaché: Hashim M. Khalaf.
Attaché: Mohammed Abbas Keebir.

ISRAEL

Embassy: 73102 Bucharest, Str. Dr Burghelea 5; tel (0) 132633; telex 11685.
Ambassador: Zvi Mazel.
Counsellor: Tamar-Liora Sam-Ash.
Second Secretary and Head of Consular Section: Eliau Sneh.
Commercial Attaché: Rami-Avraham Sam-Ash.
Attaché: Erez Kreiner.
Attaché: Igal Avidan.
Attaché: Guy Bar-Ness.

ITALY

Embassy: Bucharest, Str. I. C. Frimu 7-9; tel (0) 505110; telex 11602.
Counsellor: Paolo Andrea Trabalza.
Military, Naval and Air Attaché: Col Silvio Luccetti.
First Secretary (Commercial/Consular): Mauro Marsili.
First Secretary (Commercial/Consular): Giorgio Marrapodi.
Attaché (Cultural): Prof. Urbano Urbinati.

JAPAN

Embassy: Bucharest, Str. Polonă 4, Sector 1; tel (0) 118525; telex 11322; fax (0) 113658.
Ambassador: Kiyoshi Furukawa.
Counsellor: Kanji Tsushima.
Counsellor: Dr Terutoshi Tanioka.
Defence Attaché: Col Makoto Nasu.
First Secretary: Tetsuo Kunieda.
First Secretary: Taishin Hayashi.
First Secretary: Masanobu Yoshii.
Second Secretary: Katsuaki Yoshimura.
Third Secretary: Ryoji Takekawa.
Third Secretary: Takahiko Watabe.
Attaché: Masahiko Yoshii.
Attaché: Takeo Saito.

Attaché: Yasuhito Fukui.
Attaché: Naoki Nakajima.

JORDAN

Embassy: Bucharest, Str. Dumbrava Roşie 1; tel (0) 104705; telex 11477.
Ambassador: Yasin Istanbuli.
Counsellor: Adel Y. Sweidan.
Counsellor (Cultural): Riad Gharabieh.

KOREA, DEMOCRATIC PEOPLE'S REPUBLIC

Embassy: Bucharest, Şos. Nordului 6; tel (0) 331926.
Ambassador: Mun Biong Rok.
Counsellor: Zu Iăn Cian.
Counsellor (Commercial): Kim Byong Gyu.
Counsellor (Science/Technology): Kim Zin Won.
Military, Naval and Air Attaché: Col Pak Zi Săk.
Second Secretary (Economic): Kim Miăng Riăl.
Third Secretary: Sin Dong Hyong.
Attaché (Press/Cultural): Kim Chun Gil.
Attaché: Kim Sang Gin.

KOREA, REPUBLIC

Embassy: 70412 Bucharest, Bd Nicolae Bălcescu 4, Hotel Intercontinental 217/8/20; tel (0) 146294.
Ambassador: Lee Hyun Hong.
Counsellor (Political): Chay Soo Dong.
Counsellor (Cultural): Jang Kyu Ho.
Second Secretary (Press/Economic) and Consul: Yang Chang Soo.
Attaché (Administrative) and Vice-Consul: Kim Dong Ho.

LEBANON

Embassy: Bucharest, Str. Atena 28; tel (0) 113942; telex 11645.
Ambassador: Emile Bedran.
First Secretary and Consul: Wajib Abdel Samad.

LIBERIA

Embassy: Bucharest, Str. Mihai Eminescu 82-88; tel (0) 193029; telex 11375.
Chargé d'affaires: G. Marcus Kelley.
Second Secretary and Vice-Consul: George P. Masah.

LIBYA

People's Bureau: Bucharest, Bd. Ana Ipătescu 15; tel (0) 505511; telex 10290.
Secretary of People's Bureau: Muhammad al-Baruni.
Member (Political): Ahmed A. Abughula.
Member (Culture/Information): Mohamed A. Masaudi.
Member (Economic): Alsaber A. Khiralla.
Member (Consular): Fathalla M. Ben Khayal.
Member (Administrative): Ayad S. Shawesh.
Member (Administrative): Ahmed M. Khalifa Elmaher.
Member (Finance): Ramadan I. Hamisse.
Member (Finance): Abdalla Ali A. Khalifa.

MALAYSIA

Embassy: Bucharest, Bd. Dacia 30; tel (0) 113801.
Ambassador: Zainuddin bin Abdul Rahman.
Counsellor and Chargé d'affaires: A. Ganapathy.
First Secretary (Commercial): Kamarulzaman Md. Isa.
Third Secretary (Consular/Administrative): Mohd. Arif Kassim.
Third Secretary (Commercial): Ismail Bohran.

MALTA

Embassy: c/o Ministry of Foreign Affairs, Palazzo Parisio, Merchant's St, Valletta, Malta; tel 222407; telex 1100; fax 237822.
Ambassador: Dr Joseph Cassar (resident in Malta).

MAURITANIA

Embassy: Bucharest, Str. Duiliu Zamfirescu 7; tel (0) 592305; telex 10595.
Ambassador: Cheikh Mohamed Fadhel Kane.
Counsellor: Yahya Ngam.
First Secretary (Financial/Consular): Amadou N'Diaye.

MONGOLIA

Embassy: Bucharest, Str. Făgăraş 6; tel (0) 507237; telex 11504.
Ambassador: Osoryn Ghenden.
First Secretary: Dagvin Battulga.

MOROCCO

Embassy: Bucharest, Bd. Dacia 25; tel (0) 192945; telex 11687.
Ambassador: Abdelmajid Bouab.
Counsellor (Political/Economic): Lahcen Saile.
Attaché (Finance): Mohamed Zouiten.
Attaché: Omar Belouali.
Attaché: Latifa Lili.
Attaché: Ahmed Zouhari.

NETHERLANDS

Embassy: 71271 Bucharest, Str. Atena 18; tel (0) 332292; telex 11474.
Ambassador: Coenraad Frederik Stork.
Counsellor (Agriculture): Jan G. Haker.
First Secretary: Kees V. A. van Spronsen.
Third Secretary: Willem A. van Ee.
Attaché (Consular/Administrative): Boy Frank.
Attaché: Mee Lan Frank.

NIGERIA

Embassy: Bucharest, Str. Orlando 9; tel (0) 504050; telex 10478.
Ambassador: L. E. Okogun.
Minister: Okon Effiong.
Second Secretary and Head of Chancery: Enoch Pear Duchi.
Second Secretary (Economic/Cultural/Social): Anthony A. Bosah.
Attaché (Administrative): Saula Bamidele Jimoh.
Attaché (Finance): Kolawole Olarewaju Osisanwo.

NORWAY

Embassy: 71276 Bucharest, Str. Dumbrava Rosie 4; tel (0) 116160; telex 10888.
Ambassador: Rolf Trolle Andersen.
First Secretary: Kjetil Paulsen.
Attaché: Ellen Hausen.

PAKISTAN

Embassy: Bucharest, Str. Barbu Delavrancea 22; tel (0) 177402.
Ambassador: Rasheed Ahmad.
Counsellor: Durray Shahwar Kureshi.

PERU

Embassy: 71249 Bucharest, Str. Paris 45a; tel (0) 331124; telex 11566.
Ambassador: Guillermo Gerdau O'Connor.
Second Secretary: Guido Octavio Toro Cornejo.
Attaché: Celso Rodolfo Ascoy Mendoza.

PHILIPPINES

Embassy: Bucharest, Str. Stirbei Voda 87; tel (0) 137643; telex 10237.
Ambassador: Alicia C. Ramos.
Third Secretary and Vice-Consul: Constancio R. Vingno, Jr.
Attaché: Federico A. Silao, Jr.
Attaché: Rosendo G. Rodriguez.
Attaché: Federico G. Carrasco.
Attaché: Merlita M. Bautista.

POLAND

Embassy: Bucharest, Aleea Alexandru 23; tel (0) 794530; telex 11302.
Ambassador: Zygmunt Komorowski.
Counsellor (Political): Roland Aleksandrowicz.
Counsellor and Consul: Czeslaw Turzanski.
Military, Naval and Air Attaché: Col Jerzy Pawlak.
First Secretary (Consular): Piotr Czyzewski.
Second Secretary (Press): Magdalena Mazinska.
Second Secretary (Administrative): Edward Pokropek.
Attaché: Grzegorz Rzepka.

Commercial Section: Bucharest, Bd. Aviatorilor 24; tel (0) 330202 .
Commercial Counsellor: Wiesław Szymczak.
Attaché (Commercial): Leopold Adamczyk.
Attaché (Commercial): Jerzy Byj.
Attaché (Commercial): Aleksy Mikuc.

RUSSIA

Embassy: Bucharest, Şos. Kiseleff 6; tel (0) 170120.
Ambassador: Felix Petrovich G. Bogdanov.
Minister-Counsellor: Viulen G. Pozdneakov.
Minister-Counsellor (Economic): Ivan P. Kalin.
Counsellor: Leonid B. Polishik.
Counsellor: Mikhail I. Popov.
Counsellor (Consular): Fyodor I. Mailshev.
Counsellor: Anatoly I. Otdelnov.
Counsellor: Yuri M. Ovsiannikov.
Counsellor: Vladimir M. Melnikov.
Counsellor: Alexandr S. Vladimirov.
Military, Naval and Air Attaché: Admiral Gennady A. Mikhailov.
Assistant Military, Naval and Air Attaché: Col Anatoly S. Efrosinin.
Assistant Military, Naval and Air Attaché: Lieut Col Nikolai I. Gremit.
First Secretary: Angara N. Samorukova.
First Secretary: Yuri A. Scerbanin.
First Secretary: Vladimir N. Gubanov.
First Secretary: Rustam S. Djienbaev.
First Secretary: Yuri S. Ceremisin.
First Secretary: Vladimir S. Kiku.
First Secretary: Nikolai G. Maiorov.
First Secretary: Oleg I. Jadetki.
First Secretary: Yuri V. Gherasin.
Third Secretary (Protocol): Victor G. Mokin.
Attaché (Science/Technology): Simion C. Moraru.
Attaché (Cultural): Aurel C. Danila.
Attaché (Agro-Industrial): Nikolai V. Vilko.

Commercial Section: Bucharest, Str. Paris 53; tel (0) 333681.
Commercial Representative: Victor G. Boiko.
Deputy Commercial Representative: Sergei S. Korishev.
Deputy Commercial Representative: Alexandr M. Yakolaev.
Deputy Commercial Representative: Valentin M. Savushkin.
Deputy Commercial Representative: Najmudin R. Abdulaev.
Deputy Commercial Representative: Yuri I. Lisak.

Consulate-General: Constanta, Str. Mihai Viteazu 5; tel (16) 15168.
Consul-General: Vladimir Pavlovich Kulakov.
Consul: Ivan G. Căpătînă.
Secretary: Sergei V. Kamzalov.

Secretary: Igor N. Iniuşkin.

SOMALIA

Embassy: Bucharest, Str. Galaţi 52; tel (0) 110472.
Ambassador: Mohamed Ahmed Abdi Tafadal.

SOUTH AFRICA

Consul-General and Commercial Office: Bucharest, 86 Gregore Alexandrescu.
Consul-General: Petrus J. H. Cilliers.

SPAIN

Embassy: Bucharest, Str. Tirana 1; tel (0) 335730; telex 11508.
Ambassador: Antonio Núñez García-Sauco.
Counsellor: Ramiro Fernandez Bachiller.
Attaché (Administrative): Manuel Santos.
Attaché: Manuela Polo.

Commercial Section: Bucharest, Bd. Dacia 16; tel (0) 156765.
Counsellor and Head of Commercial Section: Luis Alberto Cacho Quesada.

Cultural Section: Bucharest, Str. Paris 34; tel (0) 335354.
Attaché (Cultural): Francisco Bendala Ayuso.

SUDAN

Embassy: Bucharest, Bd. Dacia 35; tel (0) 118352; telex 10855.
Ambassador: Lawrence Modi Tombe.
Counsellor: Mirghani M. Salih Abdalla.
Third Secretary (Press/Cultural): Idris Ismail Farag Alla.
Attaché: Yassin Adam Ahmed.
Attaché: Mooala Said Mooala.

SWEDEN

Embassy: Bucharest, Str. Sofia 5, Pentru Vize 63-10; 71276 Bucharest, CP 63-11; tel (0) 173184; telex 11313.
Ambassador: Nils G. Rosenberg.
Counsellor: Peter Lindgren.
Second Secretary: Pia Bolte.
Assistant Attaché: Eva Ohlsson.
Assistant Attaché: Charlotte Hedberg.

SWITZERLAND

Embassy: 70152 Bucharest, Str. Pitar Moş 12; tel (0) 106475; telex 11579; fax (0) 119327.
Ambassador: Sven Beat Meili.
Third Secretary: Jacques Lauer.
Attaché (Head of Chancery): Rudolf Aregger.

SYRIA

Embassy: Bucharest, Bd. Ana Ipătescu 50; tel (0) 503195; telex 10061.
Ambassador: Hicham Kahaleh.
Counsellor: Hamed Hassan.
Third Secretary: Bakri Nasser.
Attaché: Mohamed Ghazi Abdul-Salam.
Attaché: Mounir Osman.

THAILAND

Embassy: Bucharest, Str. Mihai Eminescu 44-48, Apt. 5, Etaj 2; tel (0) 114686; telex 10247.
Ambassador: Praphot Narithrangura.
Counsellor: Samarn Naruemityarn.
Second Secretary: Sanong Changsobha.
Attaché: Tawin Chullasingh.
Attaché: Songlak Santivacharanurak.

Commercial Section: Bucharest, Bd. Magheru 24; tel (0) 593860; fax (0) 593848.
Counsellor (Commercial): Chead Gasonboonnak.

TUNISIA

Embassy: Bucharest, Str. Mihai Eminescu 50-54; tel (0) 111895; telex 11829.
Ambassador: Rauf Said.

TURKEY

Embassy: Bucharest, Calea Dorobanţilor 72; tel (0) 193625.
Ambassador: Tugay Uluçevik.
Counsellor: Ahmet Gürkan.
Military Attaché: Capt. Rangul I. Halit Çapaner.
Deputy Counsellor (Economic/Commercial): Zafer Sezen.
First Secretary: Sibel Algan.
First Secretary: Yalçin Karlidag.
Attaché: Orhan Yatağan.
Attaché: Faruk Okut.
Attaché: Levent Kadiğlu.
Attaché: Oya Kökver.
Attaché: Osman Zoroğlu.
Attaché: Bülent Gereken.

Consulate-General: Constanta, Bd. Republici 28; tel (16) 11135.
Consul-General: Cahit Özcan.
Attaché: Hasan Akdogan.
Attaché: Kemal Özçakmak.
Attaché: Göksel Topaloglu.
Attaché: Saffet Çagirici.

UNITED KINGDOM

Embassy: 70154 Bucharest, Str. Jules Michelet 24; tel (0) 111634; telex 11295; fax (0) 595090.
Ambassador: Michael W. Atkinson.
Counsellor and Deputy Head of Mission: C. J. Ingham.
Defence, Naval and Military Attaché: Lieut Col P. A. Crocker.
Assistant Defence Attaché: Lieut Michael F. Brown.
Cultural Attaché (British Council): Claus C. Henning.
Assistant Cultural Attaché (British Council): Adrian Odell.
First Secretary (Economic): John N. M. Page.
First Secretary (Commercial): Bernard A. Marshall.
Second Secretary (Chancery/Information): Susan Laffey.
Second Secretary (Management): Robert H. House.
Second Secretary and Consul: J. Fox.
Third Secretary (Chancery): Richard P. Morris.
Third Secretary and Vice-Consul: Susan J. J. Hodgetts.
Third Secretary and Vice-Consul: Joan A. Bennett.

USA

Embassy: Bucharest, Str. Tudor Arghezi 7-9; tel (0) 104040; telex 11416; fax (0) 861669.
Ambassador: Alan Green, Jr.
Deputy Chief of Mission: Larry C. Napper.
Political Section: Brian M. Flora.
Economic Section: Donald E. Booth.
Commercial Section: Kay R. Kuhlman.
Consular Section: Virginia C. Young.
Administrative Section: Anita S. Booth.
Regional Security Officer: Patrick J. Moore.
Communications Programme Officer: Daniel E. Aguayo.
Information Systems Manager: Robert E. Coleman, Jr.
Office of the Defence Attaché: Col Branko B. Marinovich.
Air Attaché: Col Robert P. Kreps.
Naval Attaché: Lieut Commdr Michael Driggers.
Assistant Military Attaché: Kalani E. Cotner.
Press/Cultural Officer: Richard Virden.
First Secretary (Cultural): Agota Kuperman.
First Secretary: Harold J. Nicholson.
First Secretary: Howard J. T. Steers.

URUGUAY

Embassy: Bucharest, Str. Polonă 35; tel (0) 118212; telex 10475.
Ambassador: Domingo Schipani.
First Secretary and Consul: Maria Luisa R. de Veropalumbo.

VENEZUELA

Embassy: Bucharest, Str. Mihai Eminescu 124, Apt 4; tel (0) 110635; telex 10470; fax (0) 113215.
Ambassador: Milos Alcalay Mirkovich.
Commercial Counsellor: María Luisa Cadenas Gauchen.
Second Secretary and Head of Consular Section: Alcides José Rodríguez Alvarez.

VIET-NAM

Embassy: Bucharest, Str. Gr. Alexandrescu 86; tel (0) 116120; telex 11604.
Ambassador: Nguyen Trong Lieu.
Counsellor (Commercial): Pham Hung Chau.
Second Secretary (Political/Cultural): Nguyen Thi Kim Thoa.
Second Secretary (Consular): Tran Van Thani.
Attaché (Commercial): Pham Quang Thu.
Attaché (Press/Protocol): Dinh Quang Dung.

YEMEN

Embassy: Bucharest, Str. Mihai Eminescu 124a; tel (0) 114896.
Ambassador: Ali Abdallah as-Sallal.
Minister-Counsellor: Saeed Muhamad Abdo Dubay.
First Secretary: Molhi Abdul Wahab.
First Secretary: Omar Abdallah al-Mudawi.
Second Secretary: Ali al-Hadrame.
Attaché (Cultural): Abdul Baset Yahya Saleh Gahaf.

YUGOSLAVIA

Embassy: Bucharest, Calea Dorobanţilor 34; tel (0) 119871; telex 92535; fax (0) 191752.
Ambassador: Desimir Jevtić.
Minister-Counsellor (Political): Sreten Aleksič.
Counsellor (Economic): Djordje Koncar.
Military, Naval and Air Attaché: Capt. R. I. Milan Radeka.
First Secretary (Press/Cultural): Veljko Kovacevič.
First Secretary (Consular): Nada Durutovič.
Third Secretary: Vladimir Mirkovič.
Attaché: Branko Bekič.
Assistant Attaché: Zvonimir Pesič.

Consulate-General: Timisoara, Str. Remus 4; tel (61) 17828.
Consul-General: Mirko Atanackovic.
Vice-Consul: Slobodan Kreckovic.
Vice-Consul: Vojislav Risovic.

ZAIRE

Embassy: Bucharest, Al. Alexandru 41; tel (0) 795717; telex 11503.
Ambassador: Musungayi Nkuembe Mampuya.
Counsellor (Economic): Phoba-ki Kumbu.
Counsellor (Economic): Muya-wa Muya-Y.
Counsellor (Consular): Asuma Mboyo.
Counsellor (Cultural): Nkasama Isankunya-Ilonkele.

ZIMBABWE

Embassy: Bucharest, Str. Nicolae Iorga II; tel (0) 506391; telex 10637.
Ambassador: Dzingai C. Chigiga.
Counsellor: Claudius D. Nhema.
First Secretary: Meshack Kitchen.
Second Secretary: Anastasia Ndongwe.

Third Secretary: Jessica M. Chapfiwa.
Third Secretary: Melody Marange.

International Organizations

UNITED NATIONS

Delegation: Bucharest, Str. Aurel Vlaicu 16; tel (0) 115248.
Permanent Representative: Ottorino Jannone.
Deputy Permanent Representative: Pascale Moreau.
Counsellor (Development Programme): Gheorghe Galatchi.
Counsellor (Information Centre): Stelian Ilinoiu.

Other Organizations

PALESTINE LIBERATION ORGANIZATION—PLO

Delegation: Bucharest, Str. Jean-Louis Calderon 46; tel (0) 132549.
Ambassador: Fouad al-Bittar.
Counsellor: Ismail Ahmed Mohammed.
Counsellor (Press): Ziad Abu al-Haija.
Military Attaché: Lieut Col Ali Mahd. Mahd. Bdaiwi.
First Secretary: Mohamed Chreih.
First Secretary: Faisal el-Habbash.
Attaché: Abd. al-Raheem Mahmoud.

RUSSIA

AFGHANISTAN

Embassy: Moscow, per. Sverchkov 3/2; tel (095) 928-50-44; telex 413270; fax (095) 924-04-78.
Ambassador: Muhammad Daoud Razmyar.
Minister: Said Murtaza.
Minister-Counsellor (Political): Bareq Shafii.
Military and Air Attaché: Lieut-Gen. Abdul Baqi.
Assistant Military and Air Attaché: Lieut Col Said Shah.
Assistant Military and Air Attaché: Capt. Mohammad Yasin.
First Secretary (Political): Said Azim Hossainy.
First Secretary: Mir Abdul Shookoor Rauf.
First Secretary (Protocol): Mr Malizai.
First Secretary (Cultural): Omar Rassouli.
First Secretary: Mr Nurullah.
First Secretary: Daoud Mazyar.
Second Secretary (Consular): Abdul Sabur Shahalimi.
Second Secretary: Mr Wares.
Second Secretary: Mr Fazelhaq.
Second Secretary: Abdul Rahman Kouchi.
Second Secretary: Joma Mohammad Nauparwar.
Third Secretary: Mohammadullah Nasiri.
Third Secretary: Ghulam Rabani.
Third Secretary: Said Wali.

Trade and Commercial Section: Moscow, Ulyanovskaya ul. 8; tel (095) 297-89-95.
Minister-Counsellor (Economic/Commercial): Abdul Satar.
Counsellor (Economic/Commercial): Farid Lali.
Third Secretary (Economic/Commercial): Anahita Keshtmand.

ALBANIA

Embassy: Moscow, Mytnaya ul. 3, Kv. 23; (temporary address) Moscow, Oktyabrskaya pl. 1, Kv. 208; tel (095) 230-17-22.
Minister-Counsellor and Chargé d'affaires a.i.: Pertef Hasamataj.
First Secretary: Islam Lauka.

ALGERIA

Embassy: Moscow, Krapivinsky per. 1-A; tel (095) 200-66-42; telex 413273.
Ambassador: Hadj Muhammad Yala.
Minister: Mahieddine Abed.
Minister: Saad Nasri.
Minister: Abdelkader Kasdali.
Counsellor: Samir Bouchemha.
Counsellor (Consular): Ahmed Fekhar.
First Secretary: Toufik Dahmani.
Attaché: Omar Benamoune.
Attaché: Idir Mallek.
Attaché: Mohamed el-Amin Ettayeb.
Attaché: Mohamed Abdou Tebbal.
Attaché: Ali Haddouche.

Defence Mission: tel (095) 200-09-24; telex 413492.
Defence Attaché: Col Ammar Maamri.
Military Attaché: Lieut Col Abderrahmane Khoudir.
Air Attaché: Commdr Laziz Cheloufi.
Naval Attaché: Commdr Abbes Sehaïlia.

ANGOLA

Embassy: Moscow, Olof Palme ul. 6; tel (095) 143-63-24; telex 413402.
Ambassador: Manuel Bernardo de Souza.
Counsellor: Paulino Junior Lutumba.
Military Attaché: Jacinto Pedro Cavunga.
Assistant Military Attaché: Adriano Sebastião Vizado.
Assistant Military Attaché: João Pereira Massano.
Assistant Military Attaché: João Manuel Lopes.
Assistant Military Attaché: Eduardo João Graça.
First Secretary: Afonso Gonçalves.
First Secretary: António Rodrigues Neto.
Second Secretary: Daniel António Rosa.
Attaché (Commercial): José Augusto Albuquerque Barroso.
Attaché (Consular): João António Vidal.
Attaché (Consular): Adriano dos Santos.
Attaché (Political): Irene Maria do Nascimento Neto Paixão.
Attaché (Protocol): Lopes Daniel Adão.
Attaché (Finance): Laurenço Andre Lopes.
Attaché (Cultural): Ana Paula Correa Victor.
Attaché (Administrative): Manuel António Campos.
Attaché (Political): Emilson M'Bidi.

ARGENTINA

Embassy: Moscow, Sadovo-Triumfalnaya ul. 4/10; tel (095) 299-03-67; telex 413259; fax (095) 200-42-18.
Ambassador: Gaston de Prat Gay.
Minister: Joaquín Daniel Otero.
Counsellor: Miguel Angel Cuneo.
Second Secretary: Marcos Bidal D'Asfeld.
Second Secretary: Jorge Luis Gómez.
Attaché: Carlos Alberto Spina.

Military Mission: Moscow, Medvedeva ul. 8, Kv. 1; tel (095) 299-77-24.
Military Attaché: Col D. Hector Olascoaga.
Assistant Military Attaché: Sergio Nicanor Trecaman.

Naval and Air Mission: Moscow, Sadovo-Triumfalnaya ul. 4/10, Kv. 131; tel (095) 299-38-88.
Naval and Air Attaché: Cdre D. Armando E. Buira.
Assistant Naval and Air Attaché: Emilio Antonio Agusti.

Commercial Section: Moscow, Kutuzovsky per. 13, Kv. 125; tel (095) 243-77-82; telex 413004.
Counsellor (Economic/Commercial): Roberto Eduardo Gudiño.
Second Secretary (Commercial): Luis María Villafañe.

AUSTRALIA

Embassy: Moscow, Kropotskinsky per. 13; tel (095) 246-50-12; telex 413474; fax (095) 230-26-06.
Ambassador: C. O. Hogue.
Counsellor: Kyle Wilson.
Counsellor (Commercial): Ian Wing.
First Secretary (Commercial): Gerard Seeber.
First Secretary: Francesca Beddie.
First Secretary: Gerry McGuire.
First Secretary (Administrative) and Consul: Bruce Scott.
First Secretary (Immigration): Olga Wynne.
Second Secretary: Clare Birgin.
Second Secretary (Administrative) and Vice-Consul: Graham Roberts.
Second Secretary (Administrative): John Mitchell.
Second Secretary (Immigration): John Caspersonn.

Third Secretary and Attaché (Cultural): Peter Tesch.
Attaché (Administrative): Chris Martinovitch.
Attaché (Administrative): Eddie Edstein.
Attaché (Administrative): Suzanne Kuhl.
Attaché (Administrative): Andrew Szwajcer.
Attaché (Administrative): Colin Jones.
Attaché (Administrative): John McGrath.
Attaché (Administrative): Peter Freeman.
Attaché (Administrative): Paul Hansson.
Attaché (Administrative): Elenie Kolitis.
Attaché (Administrative): Tracy Laird.
Attaché (Administrative): Margaret Binnie.

AUSTRIA

Embassy: Moscow, Starokonyushenny per. 1; tel (095) 201-73-17; telex 413398.
Ambassador: Friedrich Bauer.
Minister (Cultural): Oswald Soukop.
Counsellor (Economic): Viekoslav Freisitzer.
Counsellor (Cultural): Margit Wästfelt.
Counsellor (Commercial): Friedrich L. Draszczyk.
Defence Attaché: Brig. Maximilian Trofaier.
Second Secretary: Johannes Eigner.
Third Secretary (Administrative): Josef Saiger.
Attaché (Administrative): Susanne Fischer.
Attaché (Commercial): Peter D. Sedlmayer.
Attaché (Commercial): Rudolf Lukavsky.

BANGLADESH

Embassy: Moscow, Zemledelchesky per. 6; tel (095) 246-79-00; telex 413196.
Ambassador: Mustafizur Rahman.
Minister: Ashfaqur Rahman.
Counsellor (Economic/Commercial): Mufazzel Hossain.
First Secretary: Mohammed Hasib Aziz.
Secretary/Archivist: Zainal Abedin Miah.
Secretary/Archivist: Mohd Idris.
Secretary/Archivist: A. K. M. Chowdhury.
Secretary/Archivist: M. Rustum Ali Akond.
Secretary/Archivist: Abul Kashem.
Secretary/Archivist: M. Zafarul Haque.
Secretary/Archivist: A. B. M. Abdul Ghani.
Secretary/Archivist: Abul Kalam Azad.
Secretary/Archivist: M. D. Shaukat Ali.
Secretary/Archivist: Mohd Shahjahan.

BELGIUM

Embassy: Moscow, Stolovy per. 7; tel (095) 203-65-66; telex 413471.
Ambassador: Baron Thierry de Gruben.
Minister-Counsellor: Ingeborg Kristoffersen.
Counsellor (Economic/Commercial): Charles Adriaenssen.
Second Secretary: Danielle Haven.
Second Secretary: Eddy Weyens.
Attaché (Consular/Administrative): Lucien de Wulf.
Attaché (Commercial): Joël Cachet.
Attaché (Commercial): Andreas de Rijck.
Attaché: Elisabeth Piriot.
Attaché: Magda Los.
Attaché: Hilde Ryckx.
Attaché: Isabelle Forrest.
Attaché: Nicole van Roy.
Vice-Consul (Visas): Véronique Marounek.

BENIN

Embassy: Moscow, Uspensky per. 4a; tel (095) 299-23-60; telex 413645; fax (095) 200-02-26.
Ambassador: Babatoundé Constant Koukoui.
Minister-Counselllor (Political): Koffi Mamert Randolph.
Counsellor (Economic/Commercial): Issiradjou I. Gomina.
Counsellor (Culture): Fanou Henri Agossa.
First Secretary (Consular and Protocol): Douéhomè André Tchekonnou.
First Secretary (Information/Press): Hubert Dossou.
Third Secretary (Protocol): Amos Boute.
Attaché (Financial/Administrative): Pascal Tchokponhoue.
Attaché (Administrative): Christophe Richard Atchade.
Attaché (Administrative): Cocou Benoît Noumon.

BOLIVIA

Embassy: Moscow, Elizarovoy per. 10; tel (095) 201-25-08; telex 413356.
Ambassador: Dr Javier Murillo de la Rocha.
Minister-Counsellor: Victor Torres Achá.
Counsellor (Commercial): Mario Salinas Jaldin.
First Secretary: Mauricio Vasquez Prudencio.
Second Secretary: Ivan Antezana Palacios.
Third Secretary: Oscar de la Quitana Rivero.
Military and Air Mission: Moscow, Lopukhinsky per. 5; tel (095) 201-48-46.
Military Attaché: Brig.-Gen. Franklin Chavez Peres.
Air Attaché: Col Dema Fernando Zeballos Luján.

BRAZIL

Embassy: Moscow, ul. Gertsena 54; tel (095) 290-40-22; telex 413476.
Ambassador: Sebastião do Rego Barros Netto.
Minister: Roberto de Abreu Cruz.
Counsellor: Luis Fernando de Andrade Serra.
First Secretary: Maria-Theresa Lázaro.
Second Secretary: Elza Moreira Marcelino de Castro.
Second Secretary: José Roberto Procopiak.
Second Secretary: Elda Maria Alvarez Procopiak.
Second Secretary: João Carlos Parkinson de Castro.
Second Secretary: Roberto Colin.
Second Secretary: Carlos Ricardo Martino Coglia.

BULGARIA

Embassy: Moscow, Mosfilmovskaya ul. 66; tel (095) 147-90-00.
Ambassador: Vladimir Velchev.
Minister-Counsellor (Political): Valentin Radomirski.
Minister-Counsellor: T. Kostadinov.
Minister and Military, Naval and Air Attaché: Rear Adm. I. Nikolov.
Counsellor (Commercial): T. Dakov.
First Secretary: T. Todorov.
Second Secretary: Angel Ganev.
Second Secretary: Andrei Gramenov.
Consulate-General: St Petersburg, W.O., Ryleyeva ul. 27; tel (812) 273-73-47.
Consul-General: Trifon Tikhonov.
Consulate-General: Syktyvkar, Babushikina ul. 10; tel 23-544.
Consul-General: Georgy Karashmalykov.

BURKINA FASO

Embassy: 129090 Moscow, Metchanskaya ul. 17; tel (095) 971-36-94; telex 413284.
Ambassador: Hanitan Jonas Yé.
First Counsellor: Abdoul Karim Salambère.
Counsellor (Culture): Ali Seye.
Chancellor: Alfred A. Guigma.
Attaché (Administrative and Consular): Claire Yé.
Attaché (Culture): Mariam Salambère.

BURUNDI

Embassy: Moscow, Uspensky per. 7; tel (095) 299-72-00; telex 413316.
Ambassador: Ildephonse Nkeramihigo.
Counsellor: Herménegilde Bavakure.
Military Attaché: Charles Kazatsa.
First Secretary: Benoît Bihamariza.

CAMBODIA

Embassy: Moscow, Starokonyushenny per. 16; tel (095) 201-47-36; telex 413261.
Ambassador: Bo Rasy.
Counsellor: Chan Lekha.
First Secretary: Khim Kimhol.
First Secretary: Chhau Se.
Second Secretary: Thai Vanna.
Second Secretary: Dav Savy.
Third Secretary: Khun Komar.
Attaché: Sar Moline.
Attaché: Theam Sothy.

CAMEROON

Embassy: Moscow, ul. Vorovskovo 40; tel (095) 290-65-49; telex 413445.
Ambassador: Alhadji Yérima Souaibou Hayatou.
Counsellor: Ernest Pouhe.
First Secretary: Daniel Dang.
Second Secretary: Peter K. Sunjoh.
Attaché (Cultural): Samuel Becke.

CANADA

Embassy: Moscow, Starokonyushenny per. 23; tel (095) 241-30-67; telex 413401; fax (095) 241-44-00.
Ambassador: Michael R. Bell.
Minister: D. E. F. Taylor.
Minister-Counsellor and Consul: Gerald R. Skinner.
Counsellor and Consul: G. J. Durocher.
Counsellor and Consul: R. W. Todd.
Counsellor and Consul: M. R. Meadows.
Counsellor (Administration) and Consul: J. A. Meadows.
Counsellor (Commercial): J. R. Henry.
Defence Attaché: Col R. J. Donovan.
Military Attaché: Lieut Col J. D. Harris.
Naval Attaché: Commdr Richard M. Williams.
First Secretary and Consul: G. R. G. Breton.
Second Secretary and Vice-Consul: C. Sapardanis.
Second Secretary and Vice-Consul: R. Waschuk.
Second Secretary (Commercial): R. Bale.
Third Secretary (Commercial): L.-P. Dumas.

CAPE VERDE

Embassy: Moscow, Bolshaya Spasskaya ul. 9; tel (095) 208-08-56; telex 413929.
Counsellor and Chargé d'affaires a.i.: Pedro Lopes.

CENTRAL AFRICAN REPUBLIC

Embassy: Moscow, 26 Bakinskikh-Komissarov ul. 9, Kv. 124-5; tel (095) 434-45-20.
Ambassador: Claude Bernard Beloum.
Counsellor: André Doumkodji.
Attaché (Finance): Salomon Nganaré.

CHAD

Embassy: Moscow, Rublevskoye Chaussée 26, Kv. 20-1; tel (095) 415-41-39; telex 413623.
Chargé d'affaires: Brahim Djidah.

CHILE

Embassy: Moscow, pr. Mira 150, Cosmos Hotel, Rm 1638; tel (095) 215-62-91.
Ambassador: Clodomiro Almeyda Medina.
Counsellor: José Miguel Cruz.
Third Secretary (Consular): Jorge Guzmán Gutierrez.
Attaché (Commercial): Guillermo Anguita Pinto.

Attaché (Cultural/Press): Gonzalo García-Huidobro.

CHINA, PEOPLE'S REPUBLIC

Embassy: Moscow, Leninskiye Gory, ul. Druzhby 6; tel (095) 143-15-43; telex 413981.
Ambassador: Wang Jinqing.
Minister-Counsellor: Zhang Zhen.
Minister-Counsellor: Xi Zhaoming.
Minister-Counsellor (Commercial): Lu Shutang.
Counsellor: Pan Zhanlin.
Counsellor: Zhou Yushan.
Counsellor: Zhao Xidi.
Counsellor: Li Fangzhong.
Counsellor (Protocol): Sun Baoli.
Counsellor (Press): Yang Kerong.
Counsellor (Economic): Yang Zhenjia.
Counsellor (Science/Technology): Shen Qingjian.
Counsellor (Education): Jiang Miaorui.
Counsellor: Xing Bingshun.
Military, Naval and Air Attaché: Maj.-Gen. Ning Wenyan.
Assistant Military, Naval and Air Attaché: Col Ji Tongda.
Assistant Military, Naval and Air Attaché: Col Wang Hiayun.
Assistant Military, Naval and Air Attaché: Col Wang Chaingfu.
First Secretary (Commercial): Jiao Haiwen.
First Secretary (Commercial): Zhang Zhenwu.
First Secretary (Commercial): Deng Shunzhi.
First Secretary (Commercial): Qi Zhengxia.
First Secretary: Jiang Kaiyi.
First Secretary: Zhu Zhaoshun.
First Secretary: Wu Dianjun.
First Secretary: Li Yuzhong.
First Secretary: Lu Zhongcheng.
First Secretary: Yuan Zheng.
First Secretary: Liu Wumin.
First Secretary: Liu Chenghai.
First Secretary: Zhang Qingquan.
First Secretary: Guo Linquan.
First Secretary: Jia Fuyun.
First Secretary: Li Hui.
First Secretary: Lu Tianquan.
First Secretary: Yang Huaizhi.
First Secretary: Wang Guoying.

Consulate-General: St Petersburg, W.O., 3-Liniya 12; tel (812) 218-17-21.
Consul-General: Wang Fengxiang.
Consul: Ma Baofeng.
Consul: Chen Huasheng.
Consul: Duan Hehe.
Consul: Lu Gui Cheng.

COLOMBIA

Embassy: Moscow, ul. Burdenko 20; tel (095) 248-30-42; telex 413206; fax (095) 248-30-25.
Ambassador: Ricardo Eastman de la Cuesta.
Counsellor (Consular/Commercial): José Ignacio Mejia Velazquez.
Secretary/Archivist: Jairo Humberto Oviedo Niño.
Assistant Administrative Officer: Carlos Triana Estupiñan.

CONGO

Embassy: Moscow, Kropotkinsky per. 12; tel (095) 246-02-34; telex 413487.
Ambassador: Gabriel Emouengué.
Counsellor (Political): Jean Félix Bouandzi.
Counsellor (Economic/Commercial): Zéphyrin Mafouana-Makosso.
Counsellor (Cultural): Rigobert Kanga-Okoua.
Military, Naval and Air Attaché: Col Juste-Maurice Okemba.
Assistant Military, Naval and Air Attaché: Commdr Sylvian-Raphaël Eba.
First Secretary: Paul Nicolas Abonkelet.
First Secretary (Political): Benoît Gatsé.
First Secretary (Finance): Pascaline Kanga-Okoua.
Second Secretary (Technical): Théodore Ondzié.
Second Secretary (Consul): Ferdinand Kiloko.
Attaché: Madeleine Emouengué.
Attaché (Protocol): Emmanuel M'Bongo.
Attaché: Jacqueline Goma.
Attaché: Raphael Oyolo-Essoua.
Attaché: René Ndoko.

COSTA RICA

Embassy: Moscow, Rublevskoye Chaussée 26, Kv. 58-59; tel (095) 415-40-42; telex 413963.
Ambassador: Arturo Robles Arias.
Minister-Counsellor and Consul-General: Plutarco Hernández Sancho.
First Secretary: Mauricio Alvarado.

COTE D'IVOIRE

Embassy: Moscow, Molochny per. 9/14; tel (095) 201-24-00; telex 413091.
Ambassador: Moïse Aka.
Counsellor: Dr Vazoumana Meite.
Counsellor: Christophe M'Boua.
Second Secretary: Maurice Gouman.
Second Secretary: Koffi N'Bia.

CUBA

Embassy: Moscow, Mosfilmovskaya ul. 40; tel (095) 147-43-12.
Ambassador: José Ramón Balaguer Cabrera.
Minister-Counsellor: Carlos Palmarola Cordero.
Minister-Counsellor: Jesús Renzoli.
Minister-Counsellor (Economic): Raul Donas.
Minister-Counsellor (Commercial): José B. de la Fuente.
Counsellor (Education): Rafael Rolando Vigoa.
Counsellor: Sergio Lopez Briel.
Counsellor: Col Herman Wainshtok.
Counsellor: Lionel F. Borrego.
Counsellor: Winston Lopez Rios.
Counsellor: Alcíbades F. Muños.
Military, Naval and Air Attaché: Ricardo Hernandez.
Assistant Military Attaché: Col Alberto Alvarino.
Assistant Military Attaché: Maj. Juan Valdes.
Assistant Military Attaché: José Pablo Aloma.
First Secretary: Ramon Perera Cumerma.
First Secretary: Lázaro Sardanas.
First Secretary: Ricardo Gonzáles.
First Secretary: Oscar L. González.
First Secretary: Juan R. Perera.
First Secretary: Angel O. Cardoso.
First Secretary: Jorge E. Ortega.
First Secretary: Orlando Obregon.
First Secretary: Miguel González.
First Secretary: José A. Díaz.
First Secretary: Pavel Orencio Díaz.
First Secretary: C. G. Suarez Valdes.
Attaché (Science/Technology): Rosario Expósito.

Consulate-General: St Petersburg, Ryleyeva ul. 37; tel (812) 279-04-92.
Consul-General: Rafael Suárez Tovarez.
Vice-Consul: Melecio Martinez.

CYPRUS

Embassy: 121069 Moscow, ul. Gertsena 51; tel (095) 290-21-54; telex 413477; fax (095) 200-12-54.
Ambassador: Charalambos Christoforou.
Counsellor: Andreas G. Skarparis.
Counsellor and Consul-General: Euripeds L. Evriviades.
Counsellor (Press): Sophoclis Y. Sophocli.
Attaché (Administrative): Vassos Chamberlen.
Attaché (Administrative): Nicolas Andreou.

CZECHOSLOVAKIA

Embassy: Moscow, ul. Yuliusa Fuchika 12/14; tel (095) 251-05-40.
Ambassador: Rudolf Slansky.
Minister-Counsellor (Commercial): Jan Machaj.
Counsellor (Economic): Pavel Svoboda.
Counsellor (Culture/Education/Science): Milan Tokár.
Military and Air Attaché: Col Karel Kluz.
Deputy Military Attaché: Col Milan Cerny.
Deputy Military Attaché: Col Ilko Vološcuk.
Assistant Military Attaché: Col Zdenek Malík.
First Secretary (Economic): Jindrich Pakorny.
First Secretary (Economic): Ivan Marcinov.
First Secretary (Culture/Education/Science): František Král.
First Secretary (Protocol): Ján Kovác.
First Secretary (Political): Josef Macišák.
First Secretary (Political): Jiri Cigroš.
Second Secretary (Political): Oldrich Dosoudil.
Second Secretary (Economic): Jiri Slepicka.
Third Secretary (Political): Jozef Vrabec.
Third Secretary: Miroslav Lajcák.
Third Secretary (Press): Vasil Grivna.
Third Secretary (Consular): Pavel Rezác.
Third Secretary (Administrative): Milan Michalica.
Third Secretary (Culture/Information): Petr Guhl.

Consulate-General: St Petersburg, Smolensky Rayon, Tverskaya ul. 5; tel (812) 271-04-59.
Consul-General: Jaroslav Rek.
Consul: Petr Kubášek.
Vice-Consul: Josef Smetka.

DENMARK

Embassy: Moscow, per. Ostrovskovo 9; tel (095) 201-78-60; telex 413378.
Ambassador: Vagn Egebjerg.
Counsellor: Svend Boje Madsen.
Counsellor (Commercial): Svend Lykke Schmidt.
Secretary: Laurs Holst Nørlund.
Secretary: Uffe A. Balslev.
Attaché (Commercial): Carsten Bennike.
Attaché: Per I. Johansen.
Export Assistant: Carsten Bennike.

ECUADOR

Embassy: Moscow, Gorokhovsky per. 12; tel (095) 261-32-09; telex 413276; fax (095) 291-46-09.
Ambassador: Pedro Saad.
Counsellor: Dr Galor Larenas Serrano.
Second Secretary (Consular): Vladimir V. Jarrin.
Third Secretary: Nela Valdiveso de Ulloa.
Attaché (Cultural): Walter Franco S.

EGYPT

Embassy: Skatertny per. 25; tel (095) 291-62-83; telex 413200.
Ambassador: Ahmed Maher el-Sayed.
Minister (Commercial): Nabil Mohamed Badr Eldin Salem.
Counsellor (Commercial): Mouawad el-Sayed el-Kholy.
Counsellor: Mohamed el-Amir Khalil.
Counsellor: Raouf Adly Saad.
Counsellor: Abdel Wahab Sayed Ahmed.
Counsellor: Maged Abdel Fattah Abdel-Aziz.
Counsellor (Information): Hamdi A. Abdelhamid.
First Secretary: Hadi el-Tonsi.
Second Secretary: Atef Mohamed Salem.
Third Secretary: Hesham Hussein Niaz.
Third Secretary: Sameh M. Abul-Enein.
Third Secretary: Medhat K. el-Meligy.
Third Secretary (Commercial): Ashraf M. Ezz-el-din.
Third Secretary (Commercial): A. Sattar Elsawy.

Head of Industrial Office: Abdel Gawad Gad Omar.
Attaché (Administrative/Industrial): Mahmoud Abouzeid Salim.
Attaché (Administrative/Cultural): Abdel Kader Mohamed.
Attaché (Administrative/Cultural): Mohamed Hussein Ahmed Abu Hussein.

EQUATORIAL GUINEA

Embassy: Moscow, Kutuzovsky prospekt 7/4, kor. 5, kv. 37; tel (095) 243-96-11.
Ambassador: Policarpo Mensuy Mba.
Second Secretary: Pablo Nkoha Nguema.

ESTONIA

Consulate-General: 103009 Moscow, Sobinovsky per. 5; tel (095) 290-50-13; fax (095) 202-38-30.
Consul-General: Sulev Roostar.
Consul: Katrin Koik.
Vice-Consul: Nelly Mihkelsoo.

ETHIOPIA

Embassy: Moscow, Orlovo-Davydovsky per. 6; tel (095) 230-20-36; telex 413980.
Ambassador: Girma Yilma.
Counsellor: Belayneh Mengesha.
Counsellor (Press/Information): Aragaw Worku.
Counsellor (Economic/Commercial): Kassahun Teferra.
Defence Attaché: Col Ayele Feleke.
Assistant Naval Attaché: Tesfaye Wondimagegn.
First Secretary: Getachew Tadesse.
First Secretary: Gougsa Gesahegn Gebru.
Second Secretary: Teruwork Alemu.
Third Secretary: Yimer Endira.
Attaché: Tadesse Bekele.
Attaché: Debebe Janka Worku.
Attaché: Debrework Belachew.

FINLAND

Embassy: 119034 Moscow, Kropotkinsky per. 15/17; tel (095) 246-40-27; telex 413405; fax (095) 230-27-21.
Ambassador: Heikki Talvitie.
Minister-Counsellor (Commercial): Harry Helenius.
Counsellor (Commercial): Timo Laukkanen.
Second Secretary (Commercial): Wladimir Ljapidevskij.
Minister: Yrjö Karinen.
Minister-Counsellor: Kauko Jämsen.
Counsellor (Cultural): Anneli Halonen.
Counsellor (Press): Jukka Savolainen.
First Secretary: Antti Turunen.
Second Secretary: Matti Anttonen.
Second Secretary: Klaus Korhonen.
Second Secretary: Mikko Makkonen.
Second Secretary: Soili Mäkeläinen-Buhanist.
Second Secretary: Terhi Hakala.
Second Secretary: Eeva-Riitta Karhula.
Attaché: Paula Wahlberg.
Secretary (Commercial): Esko Seppälä.
Attaché: Riitta Korpivaara-Mäkelä.
Attaché: Heidi Peltola.
Attaché: Mari Siitari-Mattila.
Attaché: Raimo Taittonen.
Military, Naval and Air Attaché: Col Kalevi Rissanen.
Assistant Military, Naval and Air Attaché: Maj. Pertti Inkinen.
Attaché: Heikki Tani.
Consulate-General: 192194 St Petersburg, ul. Tchaikovskovo 71; tel (812) 273-37-21; telex 121536; fax (812) 273-73-21.
Consul-General: Markus Lyra.
Consul and Secretary (Commercial): Pirja Myyryläinen.
Consul: Kirsti Päällysaho.

FRANCE

Embassy: Moscow, ul. Dimitrova 43/47; tel (095) 236-00-03; telex 413290.
Ambassador: Bernard Dufourcq.
Minister-Counsellor: Michel-Yves Peissik.
Counsellor: Michel Duclos.
Counsellor: Serge Smessow.
Counsellor: Pascal Teixeira da Silva.
Counsellor: Nicolas Chibaeff.
Counsellor (Nuclear): Jean Gourdon.
Defence Attaché: Brig.-Gen. Bruno Elie.
Naval Attaché: Commdr Yves Maillard.
Air Attaché: Lieut Col Alain Grea.
Assistant Military Attaché: Lieut Col Francis Moncaubeig.
Assistant Military Attaché: Lieut Col Michel Lafaille.
Assistant Naval Attaché: Commdr Gérard Oudin.
Assistant Military Attaché: Lieut Col Joël Malavaux.
Assistant Air Attaché: Maj. Alexandre Koplewski.
Assistant Air Attaché: Maj. Marc Rivayrand.
First Secretary: François-Xavier Carrel-Billiard.
First Secretary: Philippe Coquebert.
Second Secretary: Agnès Cukierman.
Second Secretary: Hugues Fantou.
Third Secretary: Jean-Robert Bourdois.
Third Secretary: Marcel Huet.
Third Secretary: Michel Boucher.
Third Secretary: Patrice Piette.
Commercial, Consular, Cultural, Scientific and Technical Sections: Moscow, Kazansky per.; tel (095) 236-00-03.
Minister-Counsellor (Economic/Commercial): Olivier Louis.
Counsellor (Commercial): Isabelle Hausser-Duclos.
Counsellor (Commercial): Philippe Delelis.
Counsellor (Cultural/Scientific/Technical): Philippe Etienne.
Counsellor (Cultural/Scientific/Technical): Olivier Massenet.
Counsellor (Finance): Michel Ungemuth.
First Secretary and Consul: Nicole Girard-Reydet.
Attaché (Agriculture): Patrick Soule.
Attaché (Cultural): Danièle Beaune.
Attaché (Science): Michel Dagonneau.
Head of Cultural Centre: Claude Crouail.
Consulate-General: St Petersburg, Moïka Nab. 15; tel (812) 312-11-30.
Consul-General: Marcel Roux.
Attaché: Michèle Buisson.
Attaché: Marjolaine Carbonnier.
Attaché (Commercial): Dmitri Verdet.

GABON

Embassy: Moscow, ul. Vesnina 16; tel (095) 241-00-80; telex 413245.
Ambassador: Marcel Ondongui-Bonnard.
Counsellor: François Ebibi Mba.
Counsellor (Cultural): Anatôle Mikoungui.
Counsellor and Chancellor: Antoine Mamboundou Madingou.
Second Secretary (Social Affairs): Sylvie Odongui-Bonnard.

GERMANY

Embassy: 123557 Moscow, Bolshaya Gruzinskaya ul. 17; tel (095) 252-55-21; telex 413412; fax (095) 253-92-76.
Ambassador: Dr Klaus Blech.
Minister: Dr Eberhard Heyken.
Minister-Counsellor (Political): Dietmar Stüdemann.
Minister-Counsellor (Economic): Dr Horst Winkelmann.
Counsellor (Political): Norbert Baas.
Counsellor (Political): Thomas Boese.
Counsellor (Press): Hans-Dieter Heumann.
Counsellor (Economic/Commercial/Scientific): Georg-Julius Luy.
Counsellor (Economic/Commercial/Scientific): Ulrich Schöning.
Counsellor (Transport/Telecommunications): Johannes Posth.
Counsellor (Trade): Peter Lorenz.
Counsellor (Economic/Commercial/Scientific): Uwe Meyer.
Counsellor (Cultural): Gerhard Weiss.
Defence Attaché: Brig.-Gen. Wilfried-Otto Scheffer.
Military Attaché: Col Jens-Martin Rohde.
Naval Attaché: Capt. Peter Hammer.
Air Attaché: Col Manfred Diehl.
Head of Chancery: Wilhelm Begemann.
Head of Press: Enno Barker.
First Secretary (Political): Thietmar Bachmann.
First Secretary (Political): Detlef Wolter.
First Secretary (Economic/Commercial/Scientific): Markus Ederer.
First Secretary (Cultural): Christoph Eichhorn.
First Secretary (Cultural): Werner Schaich.
First Secretary (Consular/Legal): Reinhard Ludwig.
First Secretary (Administrative): Wilhelm Begemann.
Second Secretary (Consular/Legal): Ingo Herbert.
Second Secretary (Agriculture): Frank Keunecke.
Consulate-General: St Petersburg, ul. Petra Lavrova 39; tel (812) 273-55-98; telex 121529; fax (812) 279-32-42.
Consul-General: Henning von Wistinghausen.
Deputy Consul-General: Michael Freiherr.
Consul: Dr Ernst Reichel.
Consul: Boris Paul.
Consul: Joachim Ehrhart.

GHANA

Embassy: Moscow, Skatertny per. 14; tel (095) 202-18-70; telex 513475.
Ambassador: Chris Hesse.
Minister-Counsellor (Education/Culture): B. A. Allotey-Babington.
Counsellor and Head of Chancery: Paul K. Aryene.
First Secretary (Consular/Information): R. S. Inusah.
Second Secretary (Finance): Hansen N. Palm.
Second Secretary (Administrative): Eddie W. K. Gbesemete.
Attaché: Emmanuel A. Dompreh.

GREECE

Embassy: Moscow, ul. Stanislavskovo 4; tel (095) 290-22-74; telex 413472; fax (095) 200-12-52.
Ambassador: Elias Gounaris.
Minister-Counsellor: Konstantinos Tritaris.
Counsellor (Press): Artemis Siatra.
Counsellor (Press): Vassilis Papadimitriou.
Counsellor (Economic/Commercial): Leonidas Ananiadis.
Counsellor: Panos Kalogeropoulos.
Military, Naval and Air Attaché: Col Theodoros Kavour.
First Secretary: Nicolas Garilidas.
Second Secretary: Nadine Athanassiadou.
Attaché: Ioannis Boudouris.
Attaché: Vassilios Babaletsos.
Attaché: Ioannis Mouratos.

Attaché: Ioannis Nakos.
Attaché: Anastasios Kappos.
Attaché: George Georgakopoulos.
Attaché: Sophia Koutri.
Attaché: Paraskevas Livadas.
Attaché (Economic/Commercial): Gerasimos Lazaris.
Attaché (Commercial): Nicholas Zevgolis.
Secretary: Irene Zevgolis.

GUINEA

Embassy: Moscow, per Pomerantsev 6; tel (095) 201-36-01; telex 413404.
Ambassador: Cherif Diallo.
Counsellor: Djibril Moriba.
Military Attaché: Capt. Diao Lathyr Sylla.
First Secretary: Caramba Kaba.
Second Secretary: Mariama Sow.
Attaché (Cultural): Aboubacar Soumah.
Attaché (Finance): Anafiou Barry.
Attaché and Consul: Fode Lamine Touré.
Attaché: Aissatou Touré.

GUINEA-BISSAU

Embassy: Moscow, ul. Bolshaya Ordynka 35; tel (095) 231-79-28; telex 413055.
Ambassador: Chérif Turé.
Counsellor: José Gomes Furtado.
First Secretary: Pedro Sebastião de Almeïda.
Attaché: João Gomes.
Attaché: Ansumane Camara.

GUYANA

Embassy: Moscow, II Kazachy per. 7; tel (095) 230-00-13; telex 413071.
Ambassador: Ranji Chandisingh.
Second Secretary: Samuel A. Mann.
Second Secretary: Neisha Bacchus.
Attaché (Finance): Godfrey David.
Attaché (Administrative): Clyde E. Gulliver.
Attaché: Karen Lopes Fraser.

HUNGARY

Embassy: Moscow, Mosfilmovskaya ul. 62; tel (095) 143-86-11; telex 414428; fax (095) 143-46-25.
Ambassador: Sándor Györke.
Envoy and Minister: József Birnbauer.
Minister-Counsellor (Cultural): Pál Fábián.
Counsellor: István Csószik.
Counsellor: Mihály Sári.
Counsellor: Pál Piukovics.
Counsellor: Béla Visontai.
Counsellor: István Zsohár.
Military Attaché: Col Sándor Németh.
Assistant Military Attaché: Maj. István Tóth.
First Secretary: Zoltán Bács.
First Secretary: Péter Holodnyák.
First Secretary: Endre Szalipszky.
First Secretary: József Veress.
Second Secretary: Sándor Molnári.
Third Secretary: Kálmán Manhercz.
Third Secretary: András Tomcsányi.

Commercial Office: Moscow, Krasnaya Presnaya ul. 1/7; tel (095) 252-00-01.
Commercial Representative: János Ambrus.
Counsellor (Commercial): Károly Grichisch.
Counsellor (Commercial): Tibor Borbély.
Counsellor (Commercial): Pál Szües.
Counsellor (Commercial): Mihály Gombkötó.

Consulate: 191025 St Petersburg, Marata ul. 15; tel (812) 312-64-58.
Consul: Lajos Tóth.
Consul: István Varga.

ICELAND

Embassy: Moscow, Khlebny per. 28; tel (095) 290-42-23; telex 413181; fax (095) 200-12-64.
Ambassador: Ólafur Egilsson.
First Secretary: Stefán L. Stefánsson.
Secretary and Archivist: Herga Bertelsen.

INDIA

Embassy: Moscow, Obukha ul. 6-8; tel (095) 297-08-20; telex 413409.
Ambassador: Prof. Alfred S. Gonsalves.
Deputy Head of Mission: P. S. Sahai.
Minister (Economic): Nirupam Sen.
Minister (Political): R. L. Narayan.
Minister (Shipping): A. A. Iyer.
Counsellor: Gurbakhsh Singh.
Counsellor (Political): R. S. Jassal.
Counsellor (Commercial): Manbir Singh.
Counsellor (Co-ordination): Chander Singh.
Counsellor (Science/Technology): Dr Janardan Jha.
Military Attaché: Brig. I. Rikhy.
Assistant Military Attaché: Col K. Sudhakar.
Assistant Military Attaché: Col R. K. Mehta.
Second Secretary (Defence - Military): Maj. B. K. Anand.
Naval Attaché: Cdre P. S. Bawa.
Deputy Naval Attaché: Commdr S. A. O'Leary.
Deputy Naval Attaché: Commdr R. Vaidya.
Assistant Naval Attaché: Lieut Commdr R. Dasari.
Assistant Naval Attaché: Lieut Commdr S. K. Mishra.
Assistant Naval Attaché: Lieut Commdr P. G. Palsule.
Air Attaché: Air Commdr D. N. Rathore.
Deputy Air Attaché: Wing Commdr Devinder Kapoor.
Assistant Air Attaché: Sqn Ldr R. Muthukumar.
Assistant Air Attaché: Sqn Ldr Ravinder Kumar.
Second Secretary (Defence - Air): Sqn Ldr M. M. Pande.
First Secretary and Head of Chancery: M. S. Grover.
First Secretary (Education): S. K. Ganguly.
First Secretary (Consular): Praveen Mehendru.
First Secretary (Technical): Mehendra Sarup.
Attaché (Accounts): M. L. Bhatia.
Attaché (Accounts): Shasheendra Jain.

INDONESIA

Embassy: Moscow, Novokuznetskaya ul. 12; tel (095) 231-95-49; telex 413444; fax (095) 230-22-13.
Ambassador: Janwar Marah Djani.
Minister and Deputy Head of Mission: Djamaris B. F. Suleman.
Minister-Counsellor (Finance): Utoyo Yamtomo.
Minister-Counsellor (Culture/Information): Junor Sunjaro.
Minister-Counsellor (Political): Amiruddin Noor.
Counsellor (Administration): Djemerin Djojomihardjo.
Defence Attaché: Col Suparyatmo.
Assistant Defence Attaché: Col Arifin Razak.
Second Secretary (Political/Consular): Donnilo Anwar.
Third Secretary (Administrative): H. M. Jaeni Tjokrodiwirjo.
Third Secretary (Finance): Abdul Rachman Dudung.
Third Secretary (Culture/Information): Muchlisin Murni.
Third Secretary (Political/Protocol): Priyo Iswanto.
Attaché (Administrative): Sagimin Hadi Susanto.
Attaché (Commercial/Trade): Cornelius Gultom.

IRAN

Embassy: 109028 Moscow, Pokrovsky bul. 7; tel (095) 227-57-88; telex 413493.
Ambassador: Nematollah Izadi.
Military Attaché: Bijan Shafagh.
Assistant Military Attaché: Saeed Mousazadeh.
Second Secretary and Head of Consular Section: Abul Maali.
Third Secretary: Ali Reza Bikdeli.
Third Secretary: Ali Mochtaba Rausbehani.
Third Secretary: Hamid Reza Nafez Arefi.
Third Secretary: Ali Reza Eglim.
Attaché: Miremat Hoseni.
Attaché: Agamehdi.
Attaché: Ghaemi Far.

IRAQ

Embassy: Moscow, Pogodinskaya ul. 12; tel (095) 246-55-06; telex 413184; fax (095) 230-29-22.
Ambassador: Ghafil Jassim Hussain.
Counsellor: Dr Ghalib al-Timimi.
Counsellor (Economic): Abdulhadi K. Abid.
Military Attaché: Staff Brig. Farhan M. Salih.
Assistant Military Attaché: Lieut Col Hitam A. A. Razzak.
Assistant Military Attaché: Maj. Ghaleb K. Majwel.
Assistant Military Attaché: Capt. Hassan A. J. Mohammed.
First Secretary: Abdul Hamid Y. Ibrahim.
Second Secretary: Alaadin H. Ali.
Second Secretary: Aziz A. H. Abed.
Third Secretary: Jamal A. M. al-Jibouri.
Attaché: Maki H. Rasim.
Attaché: Yunis S. Latif.
Attaché: Hasan A. Hamza.

IRELAND

Embassy: Moscow, Grokholsky per. 5; tel (095) 288-41-01; telex 413204; fax (095) 975-20-66.
Ambassador: Patrick McCabe.
First Secretary: Tom Russell.
Secretary: Richard Fallon.
Executive Officer: Ben Poole.

ISRAEL

Embassy: Moscow, B. Ordynka ul. 56; tel (095) 238-27-32; fax (095) 238-13-46.
Ambassador: Arieh Levin.
Consul: Gershon Gorev.
Consul (Political/Cultural): Israel Mey-Ami.
Consul (Economic): Gary Koren.
Consul (Press/Information): Yosef Ben-Dor.
Consul: Maya Gal.
Consul: Alon Reshef.
Consul: Yosef Baler.
Consul: Ehud Balsar.
Vice-Consul (Administrative): Alexander Livne.
Vice-Consul: Edna Livne.
Vice-Consul: Yuval Toren.
Vice-Consul: Michael Levin.
Vice-Consul: Ronen Bar.

ITALY

Embassy: Moscow, ul. Vesnina 5; tel (095) 241-15-33; telex 413453; fax (095) 253-92-89.
Ambassador: Ferdinando Salleo.
Minister-Counsellor: Ferdinando Zezza.
Minister-Counsellor (Finance/Commercial): Gianfranco Facco Bonetti.
First Counsellor: Gerardo Girardo.
First Counsellor: Stefano Stefanini.
First Counsellor: Stefano Benazzo.
Counsellor: Fausto Brunetti.
Counsellor (Administrative): Renata Archini.
Defence and Military Attaché: Brig.-Gen. Gian Giuseppe Santillo.
Naval Attaché: Commdr Franco Paoli.
Air Attaché: Col Rosario Alderisi.
First Secretary: Stefano Pontecorvo.
First Secretary: Diego Ungaro.

Second Secretary: Aldo Amati.
Attaché (Administrative): Giuseppa Cardinale.
Attaché (Science): Guido Piragino.
Attaché (Finance): Paolo Miurin.
Attaché (Cultural): Vito Grasso.
Attaché (Medical): Alessandro Bajardi.

Consulate-General: St Petersburg, Teatralnaya pl. 10; tel (812) 312-28-96; telex 121568.
Consul-General: Gian Ludovico de Martino.
Attaché: Paolo Alimonti.

JAMAICA

Embassy: Moscow, Dobryninskaya ul. 7, kv. 70-71; tel (095) 230-21-20; telex 413358.
Ambassador: Arthur Henry Thompson.
Minister-Counsellor: Paul A. Robotham.
Consul and Accounts Office Manager: Gloria J. H. O'Connor.
Secretary/Archivist: Pauline M. Dias.

JAPAN

Embassy: Moscow, Kalashny per. 12; tel (095) 291-85-00; telex 413141.
Ambassador: Sumio Edamura.
Minister: Hiroshi Shigeta.
Minister (Economic): Kishithiro Amae.
Counsellor (Information): Akio Kawato.
Counsellor (Commercial): Masayoshi Amano.
Counsellor (Agriculture/Fisheries): Minoru Yoneda.
Counsellor (Economic): Shin Maruo.
Counsellor: Kenji Tanaka.
Counsellor (Political): Shotaro Oshima.
Counsellor (Medical): Dr Yoichi Gocho.
First Secretary and Defence Attaché (Air): Col Yuzo Hoshino.
First Secretary and Defence Attaché (Military): Col Masami Goto.
First Secretary and Defence Attaché (Naval): Capt. Kodo Iwata.
First Secretary (Administrative): Akira Tateyama.
First Secretary (Political): Takashi Osanai.
First Secretary (Political/Press): Jiro Kodera.
First Secretary (Political): Takumi Watanabe.
First Secretary (Agriculture/Fisheries): Tetsuya Yedoe.
First Secretary (Consular): Yoshio Shimoda.
First Secretary: Takashi Ayabe.
First Secretary: Toshio Izumikawa.
First Secretary: Takahisa Takahashi.
Second Secretary (Protocol): Kensuke Yoshida.
Second Secretary (Information): Masaru Susaki.
Third Secretary (Information): Keiko Furuta.
Third Secretary (Finance): Hitoshi Sumizawa.
Attaché (Medical): Akiko Aoyagi.

Consulate-General: 692900 Nakhodka, Lunacharskogo ul. 9; tel (423) 56-360; telex 213813.
Consul-General: Koichi Tamaki.
Consul: Terumi Muramatsu.
Consul: Takako Sawa.

Consulate-General: St Petersberg, Nab. Reki Moiki 29; tel (812) 314-14-34; telex 121543.
Consul-General: Shoji Suezawa.
Consul: Shigeatsu Nakajima.

Trade Association: Irkutsk, Gorkovo ul. 31, Kom. 218; tel 24-54-54.
Trade Representative: Yoshio Sato.

JORDAN

Embassy: Moscow, per. Sadovskikh 3; tel (095) 299-96-64; telex 413447; fax (095) 299-43-54.
Ambassador: Dr Mohammed al-Adwan.
Counsellor: Ahmad Mubaydeen.
Counsellor (Cultural): Mustafa Taleb Alodat.
Military Attaché: Brig.-Gen. Ahmed Khamed al-Garalleh.
Assistant Military Attaché: Capt. Mustafa A. R. Sadallah.
First Secretary: Zahi Alsmadi.
Third Secretary: Mohammad Thiab al-Fayez.

KENYA

Embassy: Moscow, ul. Bolshaya Ordynka 70; tel (095) 237-47-02; telex 413495; fax (095) 230-23-40.
Ambassador: Mwabili Kisaka.
Second Secretary (Education): J. K. Gikang'a.
Third Secretary (Consular): S. G. Githieya.
Attaché (Finance): M. W. Kairu.
Attaché (Administrative): P. M. Kuria.

KOREA, DEMOCRATIC PEOPLE'S REPUBLIC

Embassy: Moscow, Mosfilmovskaya ul. 72; tel (095) 143-62-49; telex 413279.
Ambassador: Son Song Pil.
Minister-Counsellor (Political): Kim Hi Su.
Minister-Counsellor (Economic): Li Du Ryol.
Counsellor (Cultural): Li Hyon Bok.
Counsellor (Press): Kim Jae Rok.
Counsellor: Li Cher Gvan.
Counsellor: Tsen Tsen Men.
Military, Naval and Air Attaché: Maj.-Gen. Kim Jong Chan.
Assistant Military Attaché: Col Choe Su Yon.
Assistant Military Attaché: Lieut Col Kim San Sob.
First Secretary (Consular): Kim Kyong Chan.
First Secretary: Li Dong Pal.
First Secretary (Protocol): Hon Zi Sun.
Third Secretary: Choe Yong Myong.
Third Secretary: Pek Chon Kuk.
Trade Representative: Hong Hak Su.
Deputy Trade Representative: Kim Chang Nam.

Consulate-General: Nakhodka, Vladivostokskaya ul. 1; tel (423) 55-310.
Consul-General: Li Yon Sang.

KOREA, REPUBLIC

Embassy: 119121 Moscow, POB 18, ul. Gubkina 14; tel (095) 938-28-02.
Ambassador: Ro-Myng Gong.
Minister: Won-Young Lee.
Minister: Shin Kyu.
Counsellor (Political): Hyun Seop Seo.
Counsellor: Eon-Kee Baek.
Counsellor (Economic): Hwa-Tae Chung.
First Secretary: Sung-Hwan Kim.
First Secretary: Jong-Heub Choi.
First Secretary: Ihl-Song Choi.
First Secretary: No-Byoug Park.
Second Secretary: Bong-Hyun Kim.
Second Secretary and Consul: Joohyeon Baik.
Attaché and Consul: Hyun Han.
Attaché (Administrative): Kee-Young Eom.
Attaché (Administrative): Chang-Sun Kim.
Attaché (Administrative): Hyun-Suk Bae.

KUWAIT

Embassy: Moscow, 3 Neopalimovsky per. 13/5; tel (095) 248-50-01; telex 413353; fax (095) 230-24-23.
Ambassador: Abdulmohsin Y. al-Duaij.
First Secretary: Abdulameer Hassan Ramadhan.
Second Secretary and Consul: Khaled al-Shaibani.
Attaché: Yousef Khaleefah al-Eidan.
Attaché (Cultural): Ali al-Halabi.

LAOS

Embassy: Moscow, ul. Bolshaya Ordynka 18/1; tel (095) 233-20-35; telex 413101.
Ambassador: Khamphong Phanhvongsa.
Counsellor: Koth Sidlakone.
Counsellor (Cultural): Somlith Somvichith.
Deputy Counsellor: Phengsanguan Chounlamany.
Military Attaché: Col Si Inthavong.
Assistant Military Attaché: Capt. Siphanh Phanhthalavong.
Second Secretary: Bountem Santhisouk.
Third Secretary: Sengsanga Vongphouthone.
Third Secretary: Somdi Bounkhoum.
Third Secretary: Darachith Ratsavong.
Third Secretary: Bouavanh Keodara.
Attaché: Phanhmixay Phimdaranoy.
Attaché: Viriya Dalaldy.
Attaché: Liengbounkham Bounkham.

LATVIA

Embassy: Moscow, Chaplygina ul. 3; tel (095) 925-27-07.

LEBANON

Embassy: Moscow, Sadovo-Samotechnaya ul. 14; tel (095) 200-00-22; telex 413120; fax (095) 200-32-22.
Ambassador: Selim Tadmoury.
First Secretary: Gebrael Geara.

LIBYA

People's Committee: Moscow, Mosfilmovskaya ul. 38; tel (095) 143-03-54; telex 413443; fax (095) 143-76-44.
Committee Secretary: Saleh Abdulla Saleh.
Counsellor: Ahmed Mohamed Rhaim.
Committee Member (Cultural): Mohamed A. el-Buaishi.
Assistant Secretary (Military): Eddawi A. Aburas.
Committee Member (Economic): Nureddin M. S. Ejlidi.
Committee Member (Information): Al Hadi I. Sabayee.
Committee Member (Consular): Bashir M. Ashour.

LITHUANIA

Embassy: Moscow, Pisemskovo ul. 10; tel (095) 291-66-98.

LUXEMBOURG

Embassy: Moscow, Krushchevsky per. 3; tel (095) 202-53-81; telex 413131; fax (095) 200-52-43.
Ambassador: Hubert Wurth.
Attaché: Guy Diederich.
Secretary/Archivist: Jeanne Guillaume.

MADAGASCAR

Embassy: Moscow, Kursovoy per. 5; tel (095) 290-02-14; telex 413370.
Ambassador: Simon Raboara Rabe.
Counsellor: Jean Delacroix Bakoniarivo.
Minister-Counsellor: Paul Rakotondramasy.
Attaché (Finance): Raymond Andrianome.
Attaché: Dauphin Rakotonirina.
Attaché: Célestin Rakotondrambola Andriamandimby.
Attaché (Protocol): Berthin Robert Rakotomamonjy.
Attaché (Protocol): Roland Vincent Ratovonirina.

MALAYSIA

Embassy: Moscow, Mosfilmovskaya ul. 50; tel (095) 147-15-14; telex 413478; fax (095) 147-15-26.
Ambassador: Mohamed Haron.
Counsellor: Ahmad Anuar Abdul Hamid.
Counsellor (Commercial): N. Sivarajah.
Counsellor: Hussin Suberi.
First Secretary: Mahinder Singh.
Second Secretary: Mustapah Kamal Sohore.

Third Secretary: Hassim Awang Long.
Third Secretary (Commercial): Amran Awang.

MALI

Embassy: Moscow, Novokuznetskaya ul. 11; tel (095) 231-06-55; telex 413396.
Ambassador: Cheick A. T. Cisse.
Counsellor (Consular): Adama Camara.
Counsellor: Sarata Camara.
Counsellor: Mahamet Boua Keita.
First Secretary: N'Golo Coulibaly.
Second Secretary: Mohamed Cherif Coulibaly.
Attaché (Press): Mamadou Sissoko.

MALTA

Embassy: Moscow, Dobryninskaya ul. 7, kv. 219; tel (095) 237-19-39; telex 413919; fax (095) 237-21-58.
Ambassador: Maurice Lubrano.
First Secretary: Alfred Muscat.

MAURITANIA

Embassy: Moscow, ul. Bolshaya Ordynka 66; tel (095) 237-37-92; telex 413439.
Ambassador: Kamara Aly Gueladio.
Counsellor (Press): Ahmed Deya.
Counsellor (Cultural): Diop Abderrahmane Segueye.
Counsellor: Adama N'Gam.
Counsellor (Consular): Ahmed Bekrine.
Attaché (Finance): Mohamed Mahmoud Ould Abdallahi.
Attaché: Ahmed Moussa.

MEXICO

Embassy: Moscow, ul. Shchukina 4; tel (095) 201-25-53; telex 413125; fax (095) 230-20-42.
Ambassador: Carlos Tello.
Minister: Fernando Escamilla.
Counsellor (Commercial): Carlos Arredondo.
Military and Air Attaché: Brig.-Gen. Jorge Gamboa Solis.
Assistant Military and Air Attaché: Lieut Col Julio Abdón Pedroza Jurado.
Naval Attaché: Vice-Adm. Federico Romero Godínez.
First Secretary: Gerardo Bracho.
Second Secretary: Juan Manuel Nungaray Valadez.
Second Secretary (Cultural/Scientific): Zarina Martínez de Borresen.
Second Secretary (Consular): Laura Olivia Mora-Barreto.
Third Secretary (Press): Juan Pablo Duch.
Attaché: Rocío Schlaepfer Pedrazzini.
Attaché: Irene Ortega Covarrubias.
Attaché: Jorge L. Guadarrama.
Attaché: Iris Alba Ramírez de N.
Attaché: Oscar Esparez Vargas.

MONGOLIA

Embassy: Moscow, ul. Pisemskovo 11; tel (095) 290-3061; telex 414486.
Ambassador: Nyamyn Mishigdorj.
Minister-Counsellor: Jargalsaikhany Enkhsaikhan.
Counsellor: Choindongiin Enebish.
Counsellor: Damdinjavyn Dashnyam.
Counsellor: Lhamtserengiin Zundui.
Counsellor (Administrative): T. Togtokhuu.
Counsellor (Economic): C. Enebish.
Military and Air Attaché: Maj.-Gen. Gembeliin Dugarsuren.
Assistant Military and Air Attaché: Col H. Givaa.
Trade Representative: Khuuvaagiin Bud.
First Secretary and Consul: Khumbyn Zadragchaa.
First Secretary (Political/Bilateral Relations): S. Bud.
First Secretary (Political/Bilateral Relations): Badarchiin Suvd.
First Secretary (Press/Information): T. Batbuyan.
Second Secretary (Student Affairs): B. Havkh.
Second Secretary (Youth Affairs): S. Dagvadorj.
Third Secretary: S. Choilzilaj.
Third Secretary (Protocol): G. Zorigt.
Attaché (Commercial): G. Urtnasan.
Attaché (Commercial): G. Nyamzhav.
Attaché (Commercial): L. Tseesuren.
Attaché (Economic): N. Toleubai.
Attaché (Economic): J. Dorjsuren.

Consulate-General: Irkutsk, Lapina ul. 11; tel 24-23-70.
Consul-General: D. Chimiddorj.

Consulate-General: Ulan-Ude, c/o Embassy, Moscow, Pisemskovo ul. 11.
Consul-General: D. Ulziysaikhan.

MOROCCO

Embassy: Moscow, per Ostrovskovo 8; tel (095) 201-73-51; telex 413446; fax (095) 230-20-67.
Ambassador: Rafik Haddaoui.
Counsellor: Mohamed Majdi.
Counsellor (Economic): Brahim Ounir.
Counsellor (Commercial): Youssef Bentiba.
Counsellor (Press): M'Barek Benbouchaib.
Attaché: Bouchaib Rahmoune.
Attaché: Mohamed Jbira.
Attaché: Omar Aznag.

MOZAMBIQUE

Embassy: Moscow, ul. Gilyarovskovo 20; tel (095) 284-40-07; telex 413369.
Ambassador: José Rui Mota do Amaral.
Military, Naval and Air Attaché: Lieut Col Alfredo Zacarias Chamussora.
Second Secretary: Agotinho Tayali Vakulhavanji.
Secretary: Olga Essita Sambo.
Attaché (Consular): Rafael Pedro.

MYANMAR

Embassy: Moscow, ul. Gertsena 41; tel (095) 291-05-34; telex 413403.
Ambassador: U Tin Tun.
Counsellor: U Ohn Naing.
Military, Naval and Air Attaché: Col Myo Myint.
Second Secretary: U Soe Hlaing.
Third Secretary: Daw Kywe Kywe.
Attaché: U Zaw Win.

NAMIBIA

Embassy: Moscow, ul. Konyushkovskaya 28, kv. 10; tel (095) 252-24-71; telex 413567; fax (095) 253-96-10.
Ambassador: F. N. Malima.
First Secretary (Political): B. Nyamble.

NEPAL

Embassy: Moscow, 2 Neopalimovsky per. 14/7; tel (095) 244-02-15; telex 413292.
Ambassador: Bishweshwar Prasad Rimal.
Military Attaché: Lieut Col Balananda Sharma.
Second Secretary: Prahlad K. Prasai.
Attaché: K. B. Silwal.

NETHERLANDS

Embassy: Moscow, Kalashny per. 6; tel (095) 291-29-99; telex 413442; fax (095) 200-52-64.
Ambassador: Joris M. Vos.
Minister-Counsellor: Jaap Ramaker.
Counsellor (Commercial): Willem Schiff.
First Secretary (Political): Johan F. van Dunné.
First Secretary (Commercial): Clemens H. Capel.
First Secretary and Consul: Wouter H. J. van Rijckevorsel.
First Secretary (Administrative) and Head of Chancery: Elisabeth A. Lieve.
Third Secretary (Political): Frans G. G. M. Timmermans.
Third Secretary (Press/Cultural): Gilles A. Beschoor Plug.
Third Secretary (Commercial): Thymen A. Kouwenaar.
Assistant Attaché (Consular): Tine Kool.
Assistant Attaché (Administrative): Theo M. van Rijn.
Assistant Attaché (Administrative): Paul Thépass.
Assistant Attaché (Communications): Ad van Eil.
Defence Attaché: Brig.-Gen. Adriaan J. van Vuren.
Assistant Defence Attaché: Maj. Cornelis Ros.
Attaché (Agriculture): Herman L. van Wissen.

NEW ZEALAND

Embassy: 121069 Moscow, ul. Vorovskovo 44; tel (095) 290-34-85; telex 413187; fax (095) 290-46-66.
Ambassador: Gerald McGhie.
Counsellor: Tim McIvor.
First Secretary: Brian Sanders.
First Secretary: Ian Duff.
Second Secretary: Phil Lewin.
Attaché: Karen Gilpin.
Attaché: Emily Rickit.
Attaché: Greta Hewitt.

NICARAGUA

Embassy: Moscow, Mosfilmovskaya ul. 50, kor. 1; tel (095) 938-27-01; telex 413264.
Ambassador: Adolfo Evertz Velez.
Minister-Counsellor: Pablo Anselmo Cano Martinez.
Counsellor (Commercial/Economic): Daysi Cristina Pineda Medina.
Counsellor (Cultural/Consular): Roberto Salvador Suárez Delgado.
First Secretary: Patricia Mercedes España Suárez.
First Secretary: Carlos Iván Otero Castañeda.
First Secretary: César Milton Rayo Rayo.

NIGER

Embassy: Moscow, Kursovoy per. 7/31; tel (095) 290-01-01; telex 413180; fax (095) 200-42-51.
Ambassador: Pierre Ausseil.
First Secretary: Labo Kolo Salissou.
Attaché (Administrative): Balkissa Cissé Maïga.

NIGERIA

Embassy: Moscow, ul. Kachalova 13; tel (095) 290-37-83; telex 413489.
Ambassador: Jibrin D. Chinade.
Minister: S. Edem.
Counsellor (Education/Consular): P. I. Elaigwu.
Counsellor (Economic/Commercial) and Head of Chancery: N. O. Davies.
Counsellor (Protocol/Administrative): S. N. Anyanwu.
Defence Attaché: Air Cdre B. F. Osibo.
Deputy Defence Attaché: Lieut Col P. O. Oluleye.
Deputy Defence Attaché: Flight Lieut G. M. Ilyasu.
Second Secretary (Education/Consular): J. K. Adedigba.
Second Secretary (Political): O. A. Akadu.
Second Secretary (Economic/Commercial): I. B. Rabiu.
Second Secretary (Administrative): E. O. Efretuei.
Attaché (Finance): J. U. Enang.
Attaché (Communications): P. N. Orji.
Attaché (Immigration): M. M. Kida.
Attaché (Immigration): T. Wakama.
Attaché (Information/Culture): L. Ndam.

Attaché (Information/Culture): I. Esuabana.
Attaché (Science): A. L. Dauda.

NORWAY

Embassy: Moscow, ul. Vorovskovo 7; tel (095) 290-38-72; telex 413488; fax (095) 200-12-21.
Ambassador: Dagfinn Stenseth.
Minister-Counsellor: Leidulv Namtvedt.
Counsellor: Steinar Gil.
Counsellor (Commercial): Jarle Forbord.
Defence Attaché: Brynjar Nymo.
Military, Naval and Air Attaché: Lieut Col Egil Bjarne Torgersen.
First Secretary: Otto H. Mamelund.
Second Secretary: Geir Westgaard.
Secretary (Commercial): Jan Erik Glimsholt.
Secretary (Commercial): Are Stray.
Attaché (Administrative/Consular): Elisabeth Ellingsen Thue.

OMAN

Embassy: Moscow, ul. Dobryninskaya 7, kv. 197-198; tel (095) 928-56-30; telex 411432; fax (095) 975-21-74.
Ambassador: Nazar Mohammad bin Ali al-Shaikh.
Chargé d'affaires a.i.: Ahmed Mohammed al-Riyami.
First Secretary: Ahmed Ali Shahdad al-Hooti.
Third Secretary: Abdullah Hamad Khalfan al-Hasani.

PAKISTAN

Embassy: Moscow, Sadovo-Kudrinskaya ul. 17; tel (095) 250-39-91; telex 413194.
Ambassador: Ashraf Jahangir Qazi.
Minister: Dr Farouk A. Rana.
Counsellor (Commercial): Javed Syed.
Defence Attaché: Brig. Sultan Habib.
Military, Naval and Air Attaché: Cdre Jamshed Akbar Khan.
First Secretary: Ikramullah Mahsud.
Third Secretary (Political): Qazi M. Khalilullah.
Third Secretary (Consular): Dr Sohail Khan.

PERU

Embassy: Moscow, Smolensky bul. 22/14, kv. 15; tel (095) 248-77-38; telex 413400; fax (095) 230-20-00.
Ambassador: Dr Armando Lecaros de Cossío.
Minister: José Luis Garaycochea Bustamante.
Military Attaché: Brig.-Gen. Julio Valverde Butrón.
Air Attaché: Col Jorge Valencia Mac'Kee.
First Secretary: Diego Alvarado Montoya.
Third Secretary: Librado Orozco Zapata.
Attaché (Civil): Juana Ormeño Quintana.

PHILIPPINES

Embassy: Moscow, Karmanitsky per. 6; tel (095) 241-38-70; telex 413156; fax (095) 230-25-34.
Ambassador: Juan V. Saez.
Minister-Counsellor: Wenceslao J. O. Quirolgico.
Second Secretary: Ernesto N. Diano.
Attaché (Administrative): Rosario C. Diano.
Attaché (Communications): Fernando Y. Mayor.
Attaché (Consular): Socrates O. Lucila.
Attaché (Finance): Cesar C. Cano.
Attaché (Archivist): Manuel Tabada.
Attaché: Francisco C. Magno.

POLAND

Embassy: Moscow, ul. Klimashkina 4; tel (095) 255-00-17; telex 414362; fax (095) 254-22-86.
Ambassador: Stanisław Ciosek.
Minister-Counsellor: Rafał Marszałek.
Minister-Counsellor (Commercial): Jan Giezgała.
Counsellor and Consul-General: Michał Zórawski.
Counsellor (Press/Information): Agnieszka Magdziak-Minszewska.
Counsellor (Education): Henryk Kurowski.
Counsellor: Julian Gazdecki.
Counsellor: Wieslaw Witczak.
Counsellor: Andrzej Nierubiec.
Counsellor: Benedykt Szpyrka.
Counsellor and Deputy Commercial Representative: Zbigniew Balawajder.
Counsellor (Commercial): Edmund Cichowski.
Counsellor (Commercial): Stanislaw Pachota.
Counsellor (Commercial): Marian Pasternak.
Counsellor (Commercial): Ewa Kowalczyk.
Counsellor (Commercial): Jaroslaw Sieradzki.
Military, Naval and Air Attaché: Brig.-Gen. Roman Harmoza.
Military, Naval and Air Attaché: Brig.-Gen. Mieczyslaw Dachowski.
Deputy Military, Naval and Air Attaché: Col Józef Wasik.
Deputy Military, Naval and Air Attaché: Col Stanislaw Kocyk.
Deputy Military, Naval and Air Attaché: Col Maciej Wozniak.
First Secretary (Protocol): Witold Kozub.
First Secretary: Wladyslaw Dabrowski.
First Secretary: Eugeniusz Jablonski.
First Secretary: Jerzy Stepien.
First Secretary: Grzegorz Wisniewski.
First Secretary: Tadeusz Wójcik.
First Secretary: Stefan Piwowar.
Attaché (Finance): Anna Wlodarcyzk.

Consulate-General: St Petersburg, 5-Sovietskaya ul. 12; tel (812) 274-43-31.
Consul-General: Edward Krasowski.
Consul: Alfred Nowak.
Consul: Kazimierz Clapka.
Consul: Aleksander Wasilewski.

PORTUGAL

Embassy: Moscow, Botanichesky per. 1; tel (095) 230-24-35; telex 413221; fax (095) 280-31-34.
Ambassador: Antonío Costa Lobo.
Minister-Counsellor: Manuel Marcelo Curto.
Counsellor (Commercial): Ernesto José Martins.
Third Secretary and Head of Consular Section: Bernardo Luis Fauvevet Ribeiro da Cunha.
Attaché (Consular): Rui Manuel Guedes de Abreu.

QATAR

Embassy: Moscow, Mezhdunarodnaya-2, kom. 930; tel (095) 230-15-77; telex 413728; fax (095) 230-22-40.
Ambassador: Fahd al-Khater.
Counsellor: Reyad Ali al-Ansari.
First Secretary: Fawaz Khalifa al-Ka'bi.

ROMANIA

Embassy: Moscow, Mosfilmovskaya ul. 64; tel (095) 143-04-24; telex 414355.
Ambassador: Vasile Sandru.
Minister-Counsellor: Marius Gheorghui.
Minister-Counsellor (Finance): Aurel Ioncică.
Counsellor: Iancu Râpan.
Counsellor: Nicolae Ciontea.
Counsellor: Neculai Stelian Dăscălescu.
Counsellor: Gheorghe Iancu.
Counsellor: Vasile Buga.
Counsellor: Florin Oniga.
Military, Air and Naval Attaché: Capt. Nicolae Dragnea.
First Secretary: Nicolae Iliescu.
First Secretary: Savian Bulacu.
First Secretary: Marcel Dinu.
First Secretary: Victor Pomponiu.
Second Secretary: Traian Borşan.
Second Secretary: Constantin Ghiţă.
Third Secretary: Gheorghe Enache.
Third Secretary: Alexadru Cornes.

RWANDA

Embassy: Moscow, Bolshaya Ordynka ul. 72; tel (095) 237-32-22; telex 413213.
Ambassador: Anastase Ntezilyayo.
Second Counsellor: Théobald Kabasha.
Second Counsellor: Michel Nzayo.

SENEGAL

Embassy: Moscow, ul. Donskaya 12; tel (095) 236-20-40; telex 413438.
Ambassador: Pascal-Antoine Sané.
Counsellor: Diakha Diallo.
First Secretary: Modou Guèye.
First Secretary: Alioune Sylla.
First Secretary: Ibrahima Lô.
Attaché: Mouhamadou Bassirou Ndiaye.
Attaché: Cheikh Tidiane Ndiaye.

SIERRA LEONE

Embassy: Moscow, ul. Paliashvili 4; tel (095) 203-62-00; telex 413461.
Ambassador: Olu William Harding.
Counsellor: Ibrahim Sorie Conteh.
Counsellor: J. E. S. Summer.
First Secretary: H. J. Summer.
Secretary/Archivist: V. E. A. Barber.

SINGAPORE

Embassy: Moscow, per. Voyevodina 5; tel (095) 241-37-02; telex 413128; fax (095) 230-29-37.
Ambassador: Joseph Francis Conceicao.
First Secretary: Koh Kok Hong.
Third Secretary (Administrative/Consular): Abdul-Rahman bin Hasan.
Secretary/Archivist: Freddie Ong Oon Hua.
Secretary/Archivist: Wong Fook Wah.

SOMALIA

Embassy: Moscow, Spasopeskovskaya pl. 8; tel (095) 241-96-24; telex 413164.
Ambassador: Abdullahi Egal Nur.
Counsellor: Maye Mao Dere.
Counsellor: Abdirahman Mohamed Abdillahi.
Counsellor: Farah Aden Ali.
Counsellor (Cultural): Abdullahi Dualeh Farah.
First Secretary: Safiya Hussein.
First Secretary: Eldarus Elmi Abukar.

SPAIN

Embassy: Moscow, ul. Gertsena 50/8; tel (095) 202-21-61; telex 413220; fax (095) 200-12-30.
Ambassador: José Cuenca Anaya.
Minister-Counsellor: Enrique Panés.
Counsellor (Cultural): Eduardo Alonso.
Counsellor (Commercial): Ana M. Oviedo.
Counsellor (Agriculture): Bernardo Pons.
Military, Naval and Air Attaché: Col Rafael Sánchez.
First Secretary: Gonzalo de Salazar.
First Secretary: Angel Lossada.
First Secretary and Head of Consular Section: José María Ridao Domínguez.
Attaché (Administrative): Miguel Aznar Orti.
Attaché (Protocol): Alberto Quintana.
Attaché (Consular): Jesús García.
Attaché (Consular): Ernesto Collazo.
Attaché (Defence): Javier Montejo.
Attaché (Commercial): Itziar Alberdi.
Attaché (Political): José Miguel Palacios.
Attaché (Political): Andrés Llorente.

SRI LANKA

Embassy: Moscow, ul. Shchepkina 24; tel (095) 288-16-51; telex 413140.
Ambassador: Nissanka Parakrama Wijeyeratne.
Minister-Counsellor: T. B. Maduwegedara.
First Secretary (Commercial): T. Dharmasena.
Attaché (Administrative): M. K. Dayananda.

SUDAN

Embassy: Moscow, ul. Vorovskovo 9; tel (095) 290-39-93; telex 413448.
Ambassador: Ibrahim Mohammed Ali.
Minister: Asmaa Mohamed Ali.
Second Secretary: Abdel Wahab Osman Salih.
Third Secretary: Majak Philemon Majok.
Attaché (Administrative): Mohamed Osman Mahmoud.
Attaché (Administrative): Salah Eldin Mohamed Hassan Agbawi.
Attaché (Administrative): Gasim Idris Hamza.
Attaché (Administrative): Gamal Morgan Hag Ahmed.
Attaché (Administrative): Eltayeb Elsamani Elsheikh.

SWEDEN

Embassy: Moscow, Mosfilmovskaya ul. 60; tel (095) 147-90-09; telex 413410; fax (095) 147-81-88.
Ambassador: Örjan Berner.
Minister: Hans Magnusson.
Counsellor: Berndt Fahlberg.
Counsellor: John-Christer Åhlander.
Counsellor (Cultural): Lars Kleberg.
Military Attaché: Col Johan Palmgren.
Second Secretary: Per Bäckman.
Second Secretary: Hilde Grönblad Kanflo.
Second Secretary: Peter Kanflo.
Second Secretary: Björn Lyrvall.
Second Secretary: Per Wallén.
Third Secretary (Translator): Magnus Dahnberg.
Attaché (Technical Contracts): Rolf Grünbaum.

Consulate-General: 199178 St Petersburg, 10th Line V.O., Dom 11; tel (812) 218-35-26; telex 121550; fax (812) 213-71-98.
Consul-General: Dag Sebastian Ahlander.
Consul: Ulf Sör.
Consul: Håkan Damm.
Consul: Lars Fredén.
Vice-Consul (Translator): Johan Frisell.

SWITZERLAND

Embassy: 107140 Moscow, per. Stopani 2/5; tel (095) 925-52-89; telex 413418; fax (095) 200-17-28.
Ambassador: Francis Pianca.
Minister: Stefan Speck.
Counsellor (Economic): Jean-Marie Souche.
Defence Attaché: Col Hansjürg Uebersax.
First Secretary: Heidi Tagliavini.
Attaché and Head of Chancery: Daniel Blatter.
Attaché: Urs Bucher.
Attaché: Serge François Leuba.

SYRIA

Embassy: Moscow, Mansurovsky per. 4; tel (095) 203-15-21; telex 413352.
Ambassador: Muhamad Issam Naeb.
Minister: Mawia Sheikh Fadli.
Minister: Hisham el-Jundi.
Counsellor: Mounir al-Ali.
Counsellor (Commercial): Aziz Chahoud.
Assistant Military Attaché: Gen. Ismail Ali.
First Secretary: Dr Farouk Taha.
Second Secretary: Dr Majid Khoder.
Second Secretary: Dr Bassam Haj Hussain.
Third Secretary: Abdul Rahman Hassan.
Attaché: Hatem Idriss.
Attaché: Ziyad Kadur.
Attaché (Press): Suleiman Abu Diab.

TANZANIA

Embassy: Moscow, Piatniskaya per. 33; tel (095) 231-81-46; telex 413352; fax (095) 230-29-68.
Ambassador: William Lucas Mbago.
Minister: Mahmoud Issa.
Counsellor (Education/Culture): Emilian P. Henjewele.
Defence Attaché: Brig.-Gen. Oswald C. Liganga.
Attaché (Administrative/Financial): Erasto H. Kibuta.
Attaché (Administrative): Clementia Issa.

THAILAND

Embassy: Moscow, Eropkinsky per. 3; tel (095) 201-48-93; telex 413309; fax (095) 230-20-04.
Ambassador: Kasit Piromya.
Minister: Chamnong Sobhon.
Minister-Counsellor: Vimol Saingchaew.
Second Secretary: Suvat Poopatanapong.
Third Secretary: Wattana Koonwongse.
Third Secretary: Sakdisith Aroonswasdi.
Attaché: Jarun Wansanit.
Assistant Military Attaché: Lieut Col Tut Virulchanya.

TOGO

Embassy: Moscow, ul. Shchuseva 1; tel (095) 290-65-99; telex 413967.
Ambassador: Egoulia Kpanzou.
First Secretary: Elavagnon Agbodji.
Second Secretary: Komlan Agbodji.
Attaché (Finance): Kanyi Agbébavi Kponve.

TUNISIA

Embassy: Moscow, ul. Kachalova 28/1; tel (095) 291-28-58; telex 413449.
Ambassador: Slaheddine Abdellah.
Minister-Counsellor: Monder Jemaiel.
Counsellor (Commercial/Economic): Abdelhamid Erraï.
Military, Naval and Air Attaché: Col Tahar Saïdan.
Secretary (Defence): Mabrouk Ferchichi.
First Secretary: Brahim Aouam.
Second Secretary (Consular): Ghazi Ben Salah.
Attaché (Administrative): Amor Azzabi.
Attaché (Commercial/Economic): Abderrazak Ouanassi.

TURKEY

Embassy: Moscow, Vadkovsky per. 7/37; tel (095) 972-69-00; telex 413731; fax (095) 200-22-23.
Ambassador: Volkan Vural.
Minister-Counsellor: Halil Akinci.
Counsellor (Political): Ahmet Erozan.
Counsellor (Political): Tarik Yalvac.
Counsellor (Commercial/Economic): Bülent Sahinalp.
Deputy Counsellor (Commercial/Economic): Sayer Erbil.
Military Attaché: Col Hasan Memisoglu.
Air Attaché: Col Bilgin Balanli.
Naval Attaché: Husnu Akmusluk.
First Secretary: Reha Keskintepe.
Third Secretary (Cultural/Press): Sevki Mütevellioglu.
Third Secretary and Vice-Consul: Umit Yardim.
Third Secretary: Erhan Ozsoy.
Attaché (Commercial/Economic): Mesut Sapmarztürk.
Attaché (Consular): Akgün Bor.
Attaché (Consular): Tarik Askin.

UGANDA

Embassy: Moscow, per. Sadovskikh 5; tel (095) 251-00-60; telex 413473.
Ambassador: Felix Okoboi.
First Secretary: Fred K. Beyendeza.
Third Secretary: Nicholas Chaka.
Attaché (Administrative): K. C. Muhindo.
Attaché: Phebe Oluka Osiel.

UNITED ARAB EMIRATES

Embassy: Moscow, Olof Palme ul. 4; tel (095) 147-62-86; telex 413547.
Ambassador: Nasser Salman al-Aboodi.
First Secretary: Ahmed Ali Nasser al-Meel.

UNITED KINGDOM

Embassy: Moscow 72, nab. Morisa Toreza 14; tel (095) 231-85-11; telex 413341; fax (095) 233-35-63.
Ambassador: Sir Rodric Quentin Braithwaite.
Minister and Deputy Head of Mission: D. B. C. Logan.
Minister-Counsellor (Internal): G. D. G. Murrell.
Counsellor (Political): D. G. Manning.
Counsellor (Commercial): D. L. Brown.
Counsellor (Culture): T. Sandell.
Counsellor (Science/Technology): Dr P. E. Potter.
Counsellor (Management) and Vice-Consul: N. Holland.
Defence and Air Attaché: Air Cdre P. M. Stean.
Assistant Air Attaché (Technical): Wing Commdr N. Wiseman.
Assistant Air Attaché: Sqn Ldr A. W. Kerr.
Naval Attaché: Capt. W. M. Caswell.
Assistant Naval Attaché: Lieut Commdr Simon Robert Lister.
Assistant Naval Attaché: Lieut Commdr A. R. Davies.
Military Attaché: Brig. P. Jones.
Assistant Military Attaché: Maj. G. R. A. Potter.
First Secretary: A. F. Slatter.
First Secretary: C. K. Bagshaw.
First Secretary (Commercial): L. Duffield.
First Secretary and Attaché (Press): P. A. Leslie-Jones.
First Secretary: R. T. Montgomery.
First Secretary (Information): N. A. S. Jones.
First Secretary (Economic): Dr C. Browne.
First Secretary (Chancery): R. P. Bridge.
First Secretary (Medical Adviser): Dr H. M. Carpenter.
First Secretary (Projects/British Council): K. Ghosh.
First Secretary (ELT/British Council): M. G. Murphy.
Second Secretary (Technical Works Officer): P. J. Phelan.
Second Secretary (Consul): P. F. C. Massey.
Cultural Attaché (British Council): P. Steer.
Assistant Cultural Attaché (British Council): M. G. Bird.

USA

Embassy: Moscow, ul. Chaykovskoyo 19-23; tel (095) 252-24-50; telex 413160.
Ambassador: Robert S. Strauss.
Deputy Head of Mission: James F. Collins.
Minister-Counsellor for Management: Joseph S. Hulings.
Political Section: Raymond F. Smith.
Economic Section: John W. Blaney.
Consular Section: Sandra N. Humphrey.
Administrative Section: Robert D. Austin.
Counsellor (Science): Robert Clarke.
Agricultural Section: David Schoonover.
Public Affairs Officer: John E. Katzka.
Labour Officer: Michael Gfoeller.

Regional Security Officer: Mark Sanna.
Communications Programme Officer: Al Kleinsmith.
Information Systems Manager: Janice J. Fedak.
Counsellor (Regional): David Rolph.
Office of Defence Attaché: Gen. Gregory G. Govan.
Army Attaché: Col John G. Canyock.
Naval Attaché: Capt. Serge Yanov.
First Secretary: Dr LaRae Kemp.
First Secretary: Cesar Beltran.
First Secretary (Press): James Bullock.
First Secretary: Thomas Macklin.
First Secretary: Howard C. Wiener III.
First Secretary: James F. Schumaker.
First Secretary: Judyt Mandel.
First Secretary: Tyrone Kemp.
First Secretary: Ben F. Fairfax.
First Secretary: Judith Deane.
First Secretary: Robert S. Hagen.
First Secretary: Sharon A. Weiner.
First Secretary: Adrienne Stefan.
First Secretary: Eleanor Sutter.
First Secretary: Jackson McDonald.
First Secretary: Frances T. Jones.

Commercial Office: Moscow, ul. Chaykovskogo 15; tel (095) 255-46-60; telex 413205.
Director: James May.

Consulate-General: St Petersburg, ul. Petra Lavrova St. 15; tel (812) 274-82-35; telex 121527.
Consul-General: Jack Gosnell.
Deputy Principal Officer: Jon R. Purnell.
Consul: Paul N. Timmer.
Political and Economic Sections: Douglas B. Wake.
Administrative Section: Robert E. Patterson.
Regional Security Officer: Raymond V. Jarek.
Branch Public Affairs Officer: James Hutcheson.
Information Systems Manager: Richard Carpenter.

URUGUAY

Embassy: Moscow, Lomonosovsky prospekt 38; tel (095) 143-04-01; telex 413238; fax (095) 938-20-45.
Ambassador: Juan José Real.
Second Secretary: Eduardo Rosenbrock.
Third Secretary: Pablo Scheiner.

VENEZUELA

Embassy: Moscow, ul. Ermolovoi 13-15; tel (095) 299-96-21; telex 413119; fax (095) 200-02-48.
Ambassador: Jesús Alberto Fernández.
Counsellor: Alejandro Perera Diaz.
First Secretary: Oscar Garcia Garcia.
Attaché: Leticia Cestari Perez.

VIET-NAM

Embassy: Moscow, Bolshaya Pirogovskaya ul. 13; tel (095) 247-02-12.
Ambassador: Nguyên Manh Câm.
Counsellor: Nguyên van Khiêu.
Minister-Counsellor: Liu van Loi.
Counsellor: Nguyên van Thôi.
Counsellor: Nguyên van An.
Counsellor (Press): Zuong Dac Zung.
Counsellor (Consular): Thai Công Khanh.
Counsellor: Bui Khac But.
Counsellor (Commercial): Dao Chi Công.
Military, Naval and Air Attaché: Col Do Van Phuc.
Assistant Military Attaché: Col Nguyên Tuyên.
Assistant Military Attaché: Col Tran Hiu Thuât.
First Secretary: Nguyên Hiu Toan.
First Secretary: Lê Tiên.
First Secretary: Mai van Vi.
First Secretary: Troung van Chuc.
Second Secretary (Protocol): Doan Khac Tu.
Attaché (Education): Dao Khai Hoan.
Attaché (Education): Tran Ngoc Chuong.
Attaché (Education): Zuong Nang.
Attaché (Education): Nguyên van Cang.
Trade Representative: Phan Xuân Gia.
Deputy Trade Representative: Lê Minh Tâm.

Trade Mission: Nakhodka, Gorkovo ul. 18a; tel (423) 57-034; telex 213819.
Attaché (Commercial): Nguyên Suan Tin.

YEMEN

Embassy: Moscow, 2-Neopalimovsky per. 6; tel (095) 246-15-31; telex 413214.
Ambassador: Ali Abdulla al-Bugery.
Minister: Yahya Ahmed al-Wazir.
Minister: Musaed Obeid Yahia.
Minister: Mehdi Saleh Nasser.
Counsellor: Salem Saeed Ba-Omer.
Counsellor: Saleh Abdulkhabib al-Tamini.
Counsellor (Commercial): Alhugari Ahmed Muhammed.
Military Attaché: Col Hadi Omar Dayan.
Assistant Military Attaché: Col Abdulkarim M. Ali.
Assistant Military Attaché: Col Muftah Abdulla Abad.
Assistant Military Attaché: Lieut Col Hassan Ali Nasser.
Assistant Military Attaché: Capt. Yahya al-Haisami.
Assistant Military Attaché: Capt. Shamlan Mohamed Saleh Ali.
First Secretary: Mohamed Mohamed Ali al-Haisami.
First Secretary: Hamid Shaikh.
Third Secretary (Cultural): Ali Mohamed al-Shami.

YUGOSLAVIA

Embassy: Moscow, Mosfilmovskaya ul. 46; tel (095) 147-41-06.
Ambassador: Anjelko Runic.
Minister-Counsellor: Ibrahim Djikic.
Minister-Counsellor: Milomir Radoevic.
Counsellor: Dragan Djordjevic.
Counsellor: Radojka Fehmovic-Djurakic.
Counsellor: Obrad Koprivica.
Military, Naval and Air Attaché: Col Zoran Lorenzini.
Assistant Military, Naval and Air Attaché: Col Stevo Stojsic.
First Secretary: Grozdana Vitorovic.
Second Secretary: Dusan Tonkovic.
Third Secretary: Bojan Sarkic.
Attaché: Bogola Jonoski.
Attaché: Liliana Yanyushevic.

ZAIRE

Embassy: Moscow, per N. Ostrovskovo 10; tel (095) 201-76-64; telex 413479; fax (095) 201-79-48.
Ambassador: Mitima Kaneno Murairi.
Minister-Counsellor: Omari bin Shindano.
First Counsellor: Kambala Mbiyamuenza.
First Secretary: Muika Mushiya.
Attaché (Administrative): Massamba Meta Bilumbu.
Attaché (Finance): Mr Tshibambe-Kankolongo.

ZAMBIA

Embassy: Moscow, prospekt Mira 52A; tel (095) 288-51-01; telex 413462; fax (095) 975-20-56.
Ambassador: Obino Richard Haambote.
Counsellor: W. J. Moyo.
First Secretary: A. B. Chunda.
First Secretary: Z. S. Nkhowani.
Second Secretary: C. A. M. Millambo.
Third Secretary: F. M. Kabosha.
Third Secretary: B. Nampungwe.

ZIMBABWE

Embassy: Moscow, Serpov per. 6; tel (095) 248-43-67; telex 413029.
Ambassador: Dr Misheck J. M. Sibanda.
Minister: Godfrey Chanetsa.
Counsellor (Political): Martin Chiketa.
Counsellor (Political): Ephraim Chikadaya.
Counsellor (Commercial): Vincent Kwenda.
Defence Attaché: Wing Commdr James P. Machakaire.
Deputy Defence Attaché: Robert Manyanga.
First Secretary: Fred Ngwenya.
Second Secretary (Administrative): Faina Munyariwa.
Second Secretary (Administrative): Faith Mahwehwe.
Second Secretary (Consular): Dorothy Chipomho.
Third Secretary (Administrative): Epiphania Zuze.

International Organizations

EUROPEAN COMMUNITIES

External Delegation (temporary address): c/o Hotel Mezhdunarodnaya 1, 123610 Moscow, 12 Krasnopresnenskaya Nab; tel (095) 253-99-79; fax (095) 253-24-00.
Head of Delegation: Michael Emerson.
Deputy Head of Delegation: Hansjörg Kretschmer.
Counsellor (Economic/Financial): Helmuth Lohan.
Second Secretary and Head of Chancery: Maria Beccarelli.
Second Secretary (Science/Technology): Louis-Victor Bril.
Third Secretary (Press/Information): Catherine Magnant.
Attaché (Administrative): William Dawson.
Assistant Attaché: Claudia Dziersk.
Assistant Attaché: Rita Sigura.

Other Organizations

AFRICAN NATIONAL CONGRESS—ANC

Permanent Mission: Moscow, Konyushkovskaya ul. 28, kv. 9; tel (095) 252-32-95; telex 413583.
Head of Mission: Themba Thabethe.

PALESTINE LIBERATION ORGANIZATION—PLO

Embassy: Moscow, Kropotkinsky per. 26; tel (095) 201-43-20; telex 413126.
Ambassador: Nabil M. Amr.
Envoy and Minister: Said Abu Imara.
Counsellor: Yusef Fadel Irsan Nadji.
Counsellor: Haled M. Miary.
Counsellor: Dr Mussa Mobarek.
Counsellor: Haled A. Arikat.
Counsellor: Tarshahani Mouhamed Abdallah.
Counsellor: Abdul Rakhim Yousef.
Second Secretary: Mahdi Najib al-Ahmad.
Second Secretary: Hanna Abdallah Issa Abu Khilane.

RWANDA

ALGERIA

Embassy: Kigali; tel 85831.
Ambassador: Mohamed Laala.

AUSTRIA

Consulate: Kigali.
Honorary Consul: Michael Zeletzki.

BELGIUM

Embassy: rue Nyarugence, BP 81, Kigali; tel 75554; telex 501.
Ambassador: Luk Darras.

BURUNDI

Embassy: rue de Ntaruka, BP 714, Kigali; tel 75010; telex 536.
Ambassador: Canisius Sambira.

CANADA

Embassy: rue Akagera, BP 1177, Kigali; tel 73210; telex 22592; fax 72719.
Counsellor (Development) and Consul: D. G. Beaudoin.
First Secretary (Development) and Consul: O. Maltais.
Attaché (Administration) and Vice-Consul: M. St-Georges.

CHINA, PEOPLE'S REPUBLIC

Embassy: ave Député Kayuku, BP 1345, Kigali; tel 75415.
Ambassador: Tian Yimin.

DENMARK

Consulate: BP 1525, Kigali; tel 74692; telex 22512; fax 74692.
Consul: Poul Erik Hedelund Jørgensen.

EGYPT

Embassy: BP 1069, Kigali; tel 82686; telex 22585.
Ambassador: Sameh Samy Darwish.

FRANCE

Embassy: 40 ave du Député Kamuzinzi, BP 53, Kigali; tel 75225; telex 522.
Ambassador: Georges Martres.

GERMANY

Embassy: 8 rue de Bugarama, BP 355, Kigali; tel 75141; telex 22520.
Ambassador: Uwe Schramm.

HOLY SEE

Apostolic Nunciature: 49 ave Paul VI, BP 261, Kigali; tel 75293; fax 75181.
Apostolic Nuncio: Most Rev. Giuseppe Bertello, Titular Archbishop of Urbisaglia.
Auditor: Mgr Luigi Pezzuto.

KENYA

Embassy: BP 1215, Kigali; tel 82774; telex 22598.
Ambassador: Peter Kihara Mathanjuki.

KOREA, DEMOCRATIC PEOPLE'S REPUBLIC

Embassy: BP 646, Kigali; tel 75993.
Ambassador: Chon Yong Un.

LIBYA

People's Bureau: BP 1152, Kigali; tel 76470; telex 549.
Secretary of the People's Bureau: Moustapha Masand el-Ghailushi.

RUSSIA

Embassy: ave de la Paix, BP 40, Kigali; tel 75286; telex 22661.
Ambassador: Petr V. Komendant.
Counsellor: Vladimir Priakhine.
First Secretary and Head of Consular Section: Alexander Skorioukov.
Attaché: Sergei Kopyrkine.

SWITZERLAND

Embassy: 38 blvd de la Révolution, BP 597, Kigali; tel 73534; telex 22584; fax 72461.
Attaché (Development Co-operation/Humanitarian Aid/Consular): Jean-Maurice Delèze.
Deputy Attaché (Development Co-operation/ Humanitarian Aid/Consular): Marie-France Renfer.
Deputy Attaché (Development Co-operation/ Humanitarian Aid/Consular): Anne Jüstrich Ilouziech.

TANZANIA

Embassy: ave Paul VI, BP 669, Kigali; tel 76074.
Ambassador: Dorah Ntukano Justina Mbezi.

UGANDA

Embassy: ave de la Paix, BP 656, Kigali; tel 76495; telex 22521; fax 73551.
Ambassador: Jean-Baptiste Katungye Katatumba.
First Secretary: Lewis D. Balinda.
Second Secretary: Richard K. Bamuturaki.
Attaché: Robina Kijjambu.

UNITED KINGDOM

Embassy: Kigali.

Consulate: ave Paul VI, BP 356, Kigali; tel 75219; telex 509.
Honorary Consul: A. D. Wood.

USA

Embassy: blvd de la Révolution, BP 28, Kigali; tel 75601; fax 72128.
Ambassador: Robert A. Flaten.
Deputy Chief of Mission: Sue Ford Patrick.
Economic/Commercial/Consular Section: Thomas Marten.
Administrative Section: Joseph Cuadrado III.
Public Affairs Officer: David Ballard.
Communications Programme Officer: Harry L. Larson, Jr.

Agency for International Development: tel 74719; fax 74735.
Agency for International Development: James A. Graham.

ZAIRE

Embassy: 28 rue Député Kamuzinzi, BP 169, Kigali; tel 75026.
Ambassador and Head of Mission: Kokule Nzongia Kay-Buba.
Minister-Counsellor (Administration): Kimboko Kiasi.
First Counsellor (Cultural/Consular): Ngangala Balade Tongamba.
Attaché (Chancery/Protocol): Dhungula Popoy Kitenge.
Financial Attaché: Kimpir Mbensa.
Cultural Attaché: Kenga Wamba Kwama.
Technical Attaché: Panzo Ngjewuru.
Technical Attaché: Mavinga Vimbu.

International Organizations

EUROPEAN COMMUNITIES

External Delegation: 14 ave du Député Kamuzinzi, BP 515, Kigali; tel 75586; telex 22515; fax 74313.
Commission Delegate: François Bucchini.

SAINT CHRISTOPHER AND NEVIS

CHINA (TAIWAN)

Embassy: Off Taylor's Range, Basseterre; tel 465-2421; telex 6896.

DENMARK

Consulate-General: Basseterre.

UNITED KINGDOM

High Commission: Old Parham Rd, POB 483, St John's, Antigua and Barbuda; tel 465-0008; telex 2113; fax 465-2806.
Second Secretary (Technical Works): I. Agnew.

VENEZUELA

Embassy: POB 435, Delisle St, Basseterre; tel 465-1078; telex 6839; fax 465-5452.
Ambassador: Lisán Strédel Balliache.
Third Secretary: Omar José Touron Unda

SAINT LUCIA

CHINA (TAIWAN)

Embassy: Reduit; tel 45-20643; telex 6278.

DENMARK

Consulate: Halcyon Beach Club, POB 388, Castries; tel 45-25331; telex 6343.
Consul: Peter Kouly.

FRANCE

Embassy: Clarke Ave, Private Box, General Post Office, Vigie, Castries; tel 45-22462; telex 6359; fax 45-27899.
Ambassador: Jean-Paul Schricke.
Counsellor: Emile Guilleminot.
Head of Co-operation and Cultural Mission: Robert Ormand.

GERMANY

Consulate: c/o Peat Marwick, Mitchell & Co., 4 Manoel St, POB 195, Castries; tel 45-22511; telex 6351; fax 45-21061.
Honorary Consul: Lennox Alric Cave.

JAMAICA

Consulate: Stanthur Co. Ltd, 25 Brazil St, Castries; tel 45-21176; telex 6392.
Honorary Consul: Stanley Mullings.

SWEDEN

Embassy: Castries.
Ambassador: Lennart Klackenberg (resident in Sweden).

UNITED KINGDOM

High Commission: Colombus Square, POB 227, Castries; tel 45-22484; telex 6314; fax 31543.
First Secretary and Resident Representative: P. T. Rouse.

VENEZUELA

Embassy: Saint Lucia House, Vigie, Castries; tel 45-24033; telex 6347; fax 45-23647.
Ambassador: Aminta Guacaran T.
Second Secretary: Wolfgang Gonzalez S.
First Officer: Dominga Delgado de R.

SAINT VINCENT AND THE GRENADINES

CHINA (TAIWAN)

Embassy: Indian Bay, Kingstown; tel 45-84706; telex 7596.

DENMARK

Consulate: Corea's Trading Ltd Bldg, Market Sq, POB 114, Kingstown; tel 45-61201; telex 7565.
Consul: Harold David Dear.

GERMANY

Consulate: POB 848, Indian Bay; tel 45-84092.
Honorary Consul: Gisela Balcombe.

UNITED KINGDOM

High Commission: Granby St, POB 132, Kingstown; tel 45-71701; telex 7516; fax 45-62750.
First Secretary and Resident Representative: Geoffrey Greaves.

VENEZUELA

Embassy: Baynes Bros Bldg, Granby St, POB 852, Kingstown; tel 45-61374; telex 7580; fax 45-71934.
Ambassador: Miriam Seil.

SAN MARINO

HOLY SEE

Apostolic Nunciature: P. Le D. Plebis 1, POB 47031, San Marino; tel 992448.
Apostolistic Nuncio: Mgr Pier Luigi Celata.

ICELAND

Embassy: San Marino.

ITALY

Embassy: Via del Voltone 55, POB 47031, San Marino; tel 991271; telex 550889.
Ambassador: Umberto Zamboni di Salerano.
Chancellor: Maria Pia Montanari.

SÃO TOMÉ AND PRÍNCIPE

ANGOLA

Embassy: Avda Kwame Nkrumah 45, São Tomé; tel 22400; telex 227.
Chargé d'affaires: Hermenegildo Torres de Sousa.

CHINA, PEOPLE'S REPUBLIC

Embassy: São Tomé; tel 21323.
Ambassador: Tian Yimin.

CUBA

Embassy: Encarg. Neg. A.I., Avda Amílcar Cabral, São Tomé.
Ambassador: Andrés Silva Díaz.

GABON

Embassy: Avda das Nações Unidas 4, CP 157, São Tomé; tel 21043; telex 222; fax 21043.
Ambassador: Hugues G. Davin.

KOREA, DEMOCRATIC PEOPLE'S REPUBLIC

Embassy: São Tomé.
Ambassador: Kang Sung-Yong.

PORTUGAL

Embassy: Avda Marginal 12 de Julho, CP 173, São Tomé; tel 21130; telex 261.
Ambassador: Eugenio Anacoreta Correia.

RUSSIA

Embassy: Avda Amílcar Cabral 7, CP 60, São Tomé; tel 22419.
Ambassador: Vladimir Nikolayevich Kuznetsov.

SWEDEN

Consulate: c/o Projecto PMI, CP 271, São Tomé; tel 21032; telex 212.
Consul: José Manuel Ramalho Neves.

UNITED KINGDOM

Embassy: São Tomé.
Consulate: c/o Hull Blythe (Angola) Ltd, BP 15, São Tomé; telex 220.
Honorary Consul: J. Gomes.

International Organizations

EUROPEAN COMMUNITIES

External Delegation (Sub-office of Delegation to Gabon): BP 132, São Tomé; tel 21780; telex 224.
Representative: Robert Nelson.

SAUDI ARABIA

AFGHANISTAN

Embassy: Tariq al-Madina, Kilo No. 3, Jeddah; tel (2) 53142.

ALGERIA

Embassy: POB 94388, Riyadh 11693; tel (1) 488-7616; telex 402828.
Ambassador: Abd al-Karim Gharib.

ARGENTINA

Embassy: POB 94369, Riyadh 11693; tel (1) 465-2600; telex 405988.
Ambassador: Mario A. Pepe.

AUSTRALIA

Embassy: POB 94400, Riyadh 11693; tel (1) 488-7788; telex 405944; fax (1) 488-7458.
Ambassador: Alexander J. McGoldrick.

AUSTRIA

Embassy: al Malaz District, 2 blocks North and 2 blocks West from intersection of Sitten and University Sts, POB 94373, Riyadh 11693; tel (1) 476-1299; telex 406333; fax (1) 476-6791.
Ambassador: Dr Gerfried Buchauer.
Counsellor: Michael Brunner.
Third Secretary and Vice-Consul: Günther Wilfinger.
Commercial Section: Dabab St, Chamber of Commerce and Industry Bldg, 5th Floor, Suite 2, POB 94362, Riyadh 11693; tel (1) 404-0334; telex 406555; fax (1) 404-2975.
Commercial Counsellor: Oskar Smrzka.
Commercial Attaché: Dr Carl de Colle.
Consulate: al Ruwais District 1, Muftah al Saad St/Bohour al Elm St, Sector N11 W5, Fitaihi Bldg, 3rd Floor, Apt 8, POB 1706, Jeddah 21441; tel (2) 651-1816; telex 601121; fax (2) 653-3764.
Consul: Friedrich Steinecker.
Vice-Consul: Dr Matthias Prader.

BAHRAIN

Embassy: POB 94371, Riyadh 11693; tel (1) 488-0044; telex 407055.
Ambassador: Issa Muhammad al-Jamea.

BANGLADESH

Embassy: POB 94395, Riyadh 11693; tel (1) 465-5300; telex 406133.
Ambassador: Maj.-Gen. Quazi Golam Dastgir.

BELGIUM

Embassy: POB 94396, Riyadh; tel (1) 488-2888; telex 406344; fax (1) 488-2033.
Ambassador: Pieter Berghs.

BRAZIL

Embassy: POB 94348, Riyadh 11693; tel (1) 488-0018; telex 406711; fax (1) 488-1073.
Ambassador: Luiz Villarinho Pedroso.
Third Secretary: Flavio Marega.

BRUNEI

Embassy: al-Worud Area, behind al-Arouba St, POB 94314, Riyadh 11693; tel (1) 464-6872; telex 407533; fax (1) 464-0953.
Consulate-General: Mushrefah District 3, al-Kawsar St, behind Qasr al-Ameer, Bandar bin Khalid bin Abdul Aziz, Jeddah; tel (2) 665-0565; telex 602688; fax (2) 651-6260.

BURKINA FASO

Embassy: POB 94300, Riyadh 11693; tel (1) 454-6168; telex 403844.
Ambassador: Harouna Koufla.

BURUNDI

Embassy: POB 94355, Riyadh 11693; tel (1) 464-1155; telex 406477; fax (1) 465-9997.
Ambassador: Jacques Hakizimana.
Second Counsellor: Pontien Nzinahora.

CAMEROON

Embassy: POB 94336, Riyadh 11693; tel (1) 488-0022; telex 406688; fax (1) 488-1463.
Ambassador: Mohamadou Labarang.
First Counsellor: Dr Boniface Fontem Nkobena.
First Secretary: Hamidou Mounkambou.
First Secretary: Bello Bouba.
Second Secretary: Reuben Awuh Mbang.
Consulate-General: POB 15517, Jeddah 21454; tel (2) 680-4541; telex 607279.
Consul-General: Ibrahim Abba.

CANADA

Embassy: POB 94321, Diplomatic Quarter, Riyadh 11693; tel (1) 488-0275; telex 404893; fax (1) 488-0137.
Ambassador: Allan N. Lever.
Minister-Counsellor (Commercial): D. P. McLennan.
Counsellor (Commercial): W. M. House.
Counsellor (Commercial): R. M. Bollman.
Counsellor and Consul: D. B. Hutchings.
Second Secretary and Vice-Consul: A. J. Galpin.
Second Secretary (Commercial) and Vice-Consul: A. C. Shisko.
Attaché (Administration) and Vice-Consul: H. Bracken.

Consulate: Headquarters Bldg, Zahid Corporate Group, Jeddah; tel (2) 665-1050; fax (2) 669-0727.
Honorary Consul: T. Y. Zahid.

CHAD

Embassy: POB 94374, Riyadh 11693; tel (1) 465-7702; telex 406366.
Ambassador: al-Hajji Djime Tougou.

CHINA, PEOPLE'S REPUBLIC

Embassy: Riyadh.
Ambassador: Sun Bigan.

DENMARK

Embassy: Main Rd 1, Diplomatic Quarter, POB 94398, Riyadh 11693; tel (1) 488-0101; telex 404672; fax (1) 488-1366.
Ambassador: Ole Wøhlers Olsen.
First Secretary: Sven Gad.
Attaché and Consul: O. Lipholdt Petersen.
Agricultural Counsellor: Tage Jensen.

Consulate: ACE Bldg, 2nd Floor, Palestine St, al-Hamra Area, POB 5333, Jeddah 21422; tel (2) 665-6975; telex 601034; fax (2) 665-1813.
Consul and Commercial Counsellor: Hans H. Ohlsen.
Export Assistant: Esben Nielsen.

Consulate-General: Medina Rd, POB 1049, Jeddah 21431; tel (2) 667-2222; telex 601130.
Consul-General: A. A. Juffali.

DJIBOUTI

Embassy: POB 94340, Riyadh 11693; tel (1) 454-3182; telex 406544; fax (1) 454-3149.
Ambassador: Idriss Ahmed Chirwa.
First Counsellor: Abdourahman Set Selel.
Financial Counsellor: Abdourahman Yacin Mohamed.

Consulate-General: POB 7142, Jeddah 21462; tel (2) 682-8881.
Consul-General: Youssouf Ahmed Djibril.

EGYPT

Embassy: POB 94333, Riyadh 11693; tel (1) 465-2800.
Ambassador: Sayed Kassem al-Masri.

ETHIOPIA

Embassy: POB 94341, Riyadh 11693; tel (1) 477-5285; telex 406633; fax (1) 476-8020.
First Secretary and Chargé d'affaires: Zeleke Alemu.
Third Secretary: Fikru Amdemesekel.
Attaché: Yirga Makonnen.

Consulate-General: POB 495, Jeddah 21411; tel (2) 660-5034; telex 601900; fax (2) 665-3443.
Commercial Counsellor: Shiferaw Tamrat.
Second Secretary and Acting Consul-General: Haileyesus Arbi.
Third Secretary: Teshome Mengiste.
Attaché: Eshetu Gebreyohannes.
Attaché: Tesfaye Damete.

Commercial Section: tel (2) 665-3622.

FINLAND

Embassy: POB 94363, Diplomatic Quarter, Riyadh 11693; tel (1) 488-1515; telex 406099; fax (1) 488-2520.
Ambassador: Pekka Harttila.
Commercial Secretary: Reima Okkola.

Consulate: POB 209, Jeddah 21411; tel (2) 647-8502; telex 600795; fax (2) 647-8502.
Consul: Mohamed Obaied S. Binzagr.

FRANCE

Embassy: POB 94367, Riyadh 11693; tel (1) 488-1255; telex 406966; fax (1) 488-2882.
Ambassador: Jacques Bernière.

Economic Section: POB 2820, Riyadh 11461; tel (1) 488-0880; telex 402680.

Consulate-General: Adham Commercial Centre Bldg, Medina Rd, POB 145, Jeddah 21411; tel (2) 651-0082.

GABON

Embassy: POB 94325, Riyadh 11693; tel (1) 454-9500; telex 406766.

GAMBIA

Embassy: POB 94322, Riyadh 11693; tel (1) 456-0290; telex 406767; fax (1) 456-5958.
Ambassador: Abdallah Bojang.
Counsellor: M. E. Njie.
Second Secretary: B. E. M. Jaiteh.
Translator and Consular Attaché: A. R. Fofana.
Finance Attaché: E. Saidy.

GERMANY

Embassy: Diplomatic Quarter, POB 8974, Riyadh 11492; tel (1) 488-0700; telex 402297; fax (1) 488-0660.
Ambassador: Wolfgang Bente.
Minister-Counsellor: Bernd Westphal.
Counsellor (Economic Affairs): Dr Hans-Cajetan Schmidt-Dahlenburg.
Second Secretary (Cultural/Economic Affairs): Uwe Petry.

Visa Section: telex 407407.

Consulate-General: al Hamra'a District, 6N 17W 5 Sector, al Ibtehal St (49) 2, POB 126, Jeddah 21411; tel (2) 665-3344; telex 601013; fax (2) 667-5964.
Consul-General: Bernhard Döhring.

Visa Section: telex 606553.

GHANA

Embassy: POB 94339, Riyadh 11693; tel (1) 464-1383; telex 406599; fax (1) 462-3089.
Ambassador: Alhaji Mumuni Bawumia.
Minister-Counsellor: Joseph E. Oduro.
Second Secretary: Peter Incoom.

Consulate-General: POB 1657, Jeddah 21441; tel (2) 660-1429; telex 605001; fax (2) 661-1559.
Consul-General: Ahmed Hassan.

GREECE

Embassy: POB 94375, Riyadh 11693; tel (1) 465-5026; telex 406322.
Ambassador: Paul Apostolides.

GUINEA

Embassy: POB 94326, Riyadh 11693; tel (1) 231-0631; telex 404944.
Ambassador: el-Hadj Mamadou S. Sylla.

INDIA

Embassy: POB 94387, Riyadh 11693; tel (1) 477-7006; telex 406077.
Ambassador: Ishrat Aziz.

INDONESIA

Embassy: POB 94343, Diplomatic Quarter, Riyadh 11693; tel (1) 488-2131; telex 406577; fax (1) 488-2966.
Ambassador: E. Soekasah Somawidjaja.
Minister-Counsellor and Head of Political Affairs: Mr Radilas.
Minister-Counsellor and Head of Economic Affairs: Nursin Rigin.
First Secretary and Head of Information: Suherman Obon.
First Secretary and Head of Protocol and Consular Affairs: Mohammad Abduh Dalimunthe.
First Secretary and Head of Administration: Abubakar Madjid.
First Secretary (Administrative Staff): Suparsono Sahir.
Labour Attaché: Prie Sukarno.
Cultural Attaché: Prof. Dr A. Rachman Rachim.
Commercial Attaché: Teddy Setiady.

Consulate-General: POB 10, Khalid bin Wallid St, Jeddah; tel (2) 651-77008; telex 600081; fax (2) 651-7440.
Consul-General: Muslim Syahroni.

IRAQ

Embassy: POB 94345, Riyadh 11693; tel (1) 491-2929; telex 406522.
Ambassador: Abd al-Wahad as-Sabagh.

IRELAND

Embassy: POB 94349, Diplomatic Quarter, Riyadh 11693; tel (1) 488-2300; telex 406655; fax (1) 488-0927.
Ambassador: Declan Connolly.
First Secretary: Aidan Kirwan.

ITALY

Embassy: POB 94389, Riyadh 11693; tel (1) 454-3429; telex 406188.
Ambassador: Francesco Ripandelli.

JAPAN

Embassy: A-11 Diplomatic Quarter, POB 4095, Riyadh 11491; tel (1) 488-1100; telex 405866; fax (1) 488-0189.
Ambassador: Hisahiko Okazaki.

Consulate-General: Palestine Rd, POB 1260, Jeddah; tel (2) 660-4933; telex 601159; fax (2) 667-0373.
Consul-General: Kazuo Wanibuchi.

JORDAN

Embassy: POB 7455, Riyadh 11693; tel (1) 454-3192; telex 406955.
Ambassador: Maj.-Gen. Muhammad Rasoul al-Kilani.

KENYA

Embassy: POB 94358, Riyadh 11693; tel (1) 488-2484; telex 406055.
Ambassador: Ali Muhammad Abdi.

KOREA, REPUBLIC

Embassy: POB 94399, Riyadh 11693; tel (1) 488-2211; telex 405858; fax (1) 488-1317.
Ambassador: Byung Kug-Choo.

KUWAIT

Embassy: POB 2166, Riyadh 11451; tel (1) 488-3401; telex 401301.
Ambassador: Abd ar-Rahman Ahmad al-Bakr.

LEBANON

Embassy: POB 94350, Riyadh 11693; tel (1) 465-1000; telex 406533.

Ambassador: Dr Zafer al-Hassan.

LIBYA

Embassy: POB 94365, Riyadh 11693; tel (1) 454-4511; telex 406399.
Ambassador: Miloud Ramadan Eribi.

MALAYSIA

Embassy: POB 94335, Riyadh 11693; tel (1) 488-7098; telex 406822; fax (1) 482-4177.
Ambassador: Adnan Othman.
Counsellor and Head of Chancery: Haji M. Yusoff Zain.
Counsellor: Haji Ahmad Yusuf Ngah.
Third Secretary: Haji M. Noh Nawi.
Administrative Attaché: Haji Abu Kassim Komeng.
Administrative Attaché: Sobri Daud.

Consulate-General: POB 593, Jeddah 21421; tel (2) 667-4459; telex 601033; fax (2) 660-5874.
Consul-General: Haji Abdul Wahab Harun.

Commercial Section: tel (2) 642-4481; telex 605850; fax (2) 642-0059.
Consul (Trade): M. Zaharil Kassim.

MALI

Embassy: POB 94331, Riyadh 11693; tel (1) 465-8900; telex 406733.
Ambassador: Seicko Soumano.

MALTA

Embassy: POB 94361, Riyadh 11693; tel (1) 463-2345; telex 406422; fax (1) 463-3993.
Ambassador: Joseph Sammut (designate).
First Secretary: Alexander Booker.

Consulate: Palestine Sq., POB 7083, Jeddah; tel (2) 665-7973; telex 604234; fax (2) 665-7980.
Honorary Consul: Dr Mohammed Ahmed Mansouri.

MAURITANIA

Embassy: POB 94354, Riyadh 11693; tel (1) 465-6313; telex 406466.
Ambassador: Baba Ould Muhammad Abdullah.

MEXICO

Embassy: Old Airport Rd, Beta Bugshan Bulg, 5th Floor, next to al-Minhal Hotel, Riyadh; POB 94391, Riyadh 11693; tel (1) 476-1200; telex 406111; fax (1) 478-1900.
Ambassador: Ricardo Villanueva.
Counsellor: Victor Balvanera.
Third Secretary: Jorge Mario Rosas Pineda.
Attaché: Ricardo Ahuja-Hernandez.
Attaché: Rafael Angel Cortes-Armenta.

Consulate: Jeddah; tel (2) 643-3238.
Honorary Consul: Sheikh Seraj Attar.

MOROCCO

Embassy: POB 94392, Riyadh 11693; tel (1) 465-4900; telex 406155.
Ambassador: Dr Ahmad Ramyi.

NEPAL

Embassy: Khazan St, near Prince Musaed Palace, POB 94384, Riyadh 11693; tel (1) 402-4758; telex 406288; fax (1) 403-6488.
Ambassador: Prof. Surenda Bahadur Shrestha.
First Secretary: Subarna Man Shrestha.
Attaché: Shiva Prasad Koirala.

NETHERLANDS

Embassy: POB 21683, Riyadh 11485; tel (1) 488-0011; telex 403820.
Ambassador: Count R. H. van Limburg Stirum.

NEW ZEALAND

Embassy: POB 94397, Riyadh 11693; tel (1) 488-7988; telex 405878; fax (1) 488-7620.
Ambassador: Winston A. Cochrane.
First Secretary: Robert Taylor.
Second Secretary: Barry Glover.
Attaché: Bronwen Williams.
Trade Commissioner: Joe Robinson.

Consulate: c/o Associated Agencies, Sundus Bldg (behind Caravan Shopping Centre), al Madian St, POB 419, Jeddah 21411; tel (2) 651-2109; telex 601025; fax (2) 651-6504.
Honorary Consul: Sheikh A. Raouf Abu Zinadah.

NIGER

Embassy: POB 94334, Riyadh 11693; tel (1) 464-3116; telex 406722.
Ambassador: Abdou M. Moussa.

NIGERIA

Embassy: POB 94386, Riyadh 11693; tel (1) 465-4111; telex 406177.
Ambassador: Prof. Shehu Ahmad S. Galadanci.
Senior Counsellor and Head of Chancery: A. B. Akande.
Second Secretary (Political Affairs): H. S. Shuaib.
Second Secretary (Economic Affairs): I. Mohammed.
Administrative Attaché: A. Kakudi.
Administrative Attaché: I. A. Shehu.
Finance Attaché: S. A. Salami.

Consulate-General: POB 655, Jeddah; tel (2) 671-6865; telex 601079; fax (2) 670-2886.
Consul-General: A. R. Yunusa.

NORWAY

Embassy: POB 94380, Riyadh 11693; tel (1) 488-1904; telex 406311; fax (1) 488-0854.
Chargé d'affaires a.i.: Dagfinn Soerli.

Consulate-General: POB 6251, Jeddah 21442; tel (2) 651-7537; telex 601471; fax (2) 651-8664.

OMAN

Embassy: POB 94381, Riyadh 11693; tel (1) 465-0010; telex 206277.
Ambassador: Hamad H. al-Mo'Amary.

PAKISTAN

Embassy: Shaar-e-Frazdq, Malaz Area, POB 6891, Riyadh 11452; tel (1) 476-7266; telex 406500; fax (1) 477-8563.
Ambassador: Mohammed Waliulla Khan Khaishgi.
Head of Chancery: Liaquat Mahmud.
Counsellor: Javed Hafiz.
Defence Attaché: Maj.-Gen. Mohammad Akram.
Air and Naval Attaché: Group Capt. Ayaz Hussain Tiwana.
Counsellor (Welfare): Dr Sardar Mohammad Habib Khan.
Counsellor (Welfare): Moula Bux Lund Baluch.
First Secretary: Noorullah Khan.
Press Attaché: A. I. Shafaq Hashemi.

Consulate-General: Shar-e-Ibrahim al-Tasan, behind City Centre, off Madina Rd, Jeddah; tel (2) 669-1046.
Consul-General: Ghayoor Ahmed.
Head of Chancery: Mohammad Nawaz Chaudhry.
Director General: Hajj Mohammad Ismail.
Consul (Education): Prof. Dr M. Sharif Memon.
Consul (Welfare): Hafeezur Rehman.
Consul (Commercial): Syed Qaiser Ali Shah.
Vice-Consul (Press): Shah Zaman Khan.
Senior Medical Officer: Dr Abdul Qadir Jatol.

PHILIPPINES

Embassy: Olaya St, opposite Al-Owais Market, Haiyul Malik Fahad District, POB 94366, Riyadh 11693; tel (1) 454-0777; telex 406377.
Ambassador: Abraham A. Rasul.

Consulate-General: Sarhan al-Ajmawi St, Al-Faisaliyyah District 1, POB 4794, Jeddah 21412; tel (2) 660-0348.
Consul-General: B. Gutoc.

PORTUGAL

Embassy: POB 94328, Riyadh 11693; tel (1) 464-4853; telex 404477.
Ambassador: José Manuel Waddington Matos Parreira.

QATAR

Embassy: POB 94353, Riyadh 11461; tel (1) 482-5544; telex 405755.
Ambassador: Abdullah Salih al-Mana.

RUSSIA

Embassy: Riyadh.
Ambassador: Gennady Tarasov.

RWANDA

Embassy: POB 94383, Riyadh 11693; tel (1) 454-0808; telex 406199; fax (1) 456-1769.
Ambassador: Simon Insonere.

SENEGAL

Embassy: POB 94352, Riyadh 11693; tel (1) 454-2144; telex 406565.
Ambassador: Alhaji Amadou Thiam.

SIERRA LEONE

Embassy: POB 94329, Riyadh 11693; tel (1) 463-3149; telex 406744.
Ambassador: Amadou Muhammad Boie Jalloh.

SINGAPORE

Embassy: POB 94378, Riyadh 11693; tel (1) 465-7007; telex 406211.
Chargé d'affaires a.i.: Mushahid Ali.

SOMALIA

Embassy: POB 94372, Riyadh 11693; tel (1) 454-0111.
Ambassador: Abd ar-Rahman A. Hussein.

SPAIN

Embassy: POB 94347, Riyadh 11693; tel (1) 488-0606; telex 406788.
Ambassador: José Luis Xifra de Ocerin.

SRI LANKA

Embassy: POB 96360, Riyadh 11693; tel (1) 463-4200; telex 405688; fax (1) 465-0897.
Ambassador: Al Haj A. C. Markar.
Counsellor: P. Kariyawasam.
Counsellor (Commercial and Economic): D. S. Jayawardena.
Third Secretary: M. I. Aman.
Attaché: I. M. R. Abeysinghe.

SUDAN

Embassy: POB 94337, Riyadh 11693; tel (1) 482-9666.
Ambassador: Omer Yousif Birido.

SWEDEN

Embassy: Collector Rd B, Diplomatic Quarter, Riyadh; POB 94382, Riyadh 11693; tel (1) 488-3100; telex 406266; fax (1) 488-0604.
Ambassador: Steen Hohwü-Christensen.

First Secretary: Peter Björlin.
Second Secretary: Stellan Berg.

Trade Council: tel (1) 488-0736; fax (1) 488-1989.

Consulate-General: 3 Sulaiman al-Tajjel St, al Hamra District 2, POB 2005, Jeddah 21451; tel (2) 665-4735; telex 601464; fax (2) 665-5633.
Consul-General: Göran Zetterström.

Trade Council: POB 6957, Jeddah 21452; tel (2) 665-9687; telex 602066.
Commercial Secretary: Stephan Seidlitz.

SWITZERLAND

Embassy: POB 9265, Riyadh 11413; tel (1) 488-1291; telex 406055; fax (1) 488-0632.
Ambassador: Maurice Jean Renaud.

Consulate-General: Medina Rd, km 2, Alireza Tower, 10th Floor, POB 1016, Jeddah 21431; tel (2) 651 0772; telex 601470; fax (2) 651-9105.
Consul-General: Hans Dornbierer.
Vice-Consul and Chancellor: Michel Zwick.

SYRIA

Embassy: POB 94323, Riyadh 11693; tel (1) 465-3800; telex 406677.
Ambassador: Muhammad Khalid at-Tall.

TANZANIA

Embassy: POB 94320, Riyadh 11693; tel (1) 454-2833; telex 406811; fax (1) 454-9660.
Ambassador: Prof. Abdulkader Abdulwahid Mohammed Shareef.
Minister-Counsellor: Siwajibu Baraka Siwajibu.
Commercial Counsellor: Musa K. Ruji.
Administrative Attaché: Lameck J. Mmbaga.

Consulate-General: POB 15406, Jeddah 21444; tel (2) 665-7528; telex 607350; fax (2) 665-7528.
Minister-Counsellor and Vice-Consul-General: Dr Posanyi Juma Madati.

THAILAND

Embassy: POB 94359, Riyadh 11693; tel (1) 482-6002; telex 406433.
Ambassador: Thongterm Komolsuk.

TUNISIA

Embassy: POB 94368, Riyadh 11693; tel (1) 465-4585; telex 406464.
Ambassador: Kacem Bousnina.

TURKEY

Embassy: POB 94390, Riyadh 11693; tel (1) 464-8890; telex 406206.
Ambassador: Yasar Hyakis.

UGANDA

Embassy: POB 94344, Riyadh 11693; tel (1) 454-4910; telex 406588; fax (1) 454-9260.
Ambassador: al-Haj Prof. Badru Dungu Kateregga.
Second Secretary and Head of Chancery: Emmanuel O. Orinzi.
Attaché: Sully Natovu Naiga.

UNITED ARAB EMIRATES

Embassy: POB 94385, Riyadh 11693; tel (1) 482-6803; telex 406222.
Ambassador: Issa K. al-Huraimil.

UNITED KINGDOM

Embassy: POB 94351, Riyadh 11693; tel (1) 488-0077; telex 406488; fax (1) 488-0623.
Ambassador: Sir Alan Gordon Munro.
Counsellor and Deputy Head of Mission: Derek J. Plumbly.
Commercial Counsellor: Christopher E. J. Wilton.
Defence and Military Attaché: Brig. Michael J. Holroyd-Smith.
Naval Attaché: Commdr Trevor Waddington.
Air Attaché: Wing Commdr John Ambler.
First Secretary (Commercial): Harold B. Formstone.
First Secretary (Economic): Peter O. Gooderham.
Consul-General and First Secretary (Management): Clive H. Woodland.
First Secretary (Chancery): Michael D. K. Halsey.
First Secretary (Defence Supply): Robert M. Regan.
Second Secretary and Consul: Patrick E. Owens.
Second Secretary (Commercial): Peter R. Barklamb.
Second Secretary (Commercial): Philip P. Hagger.
Second Secretary (Management): Paul V. Baines.
Second Secretary (Chancery): Charles J. C. Hollis.
Third Secretary (Information): N. J. R. Abbott.

Consulate-General: POB 393, Jeddah 21411; tel (2) 691-5952; telex 601043; fax (2) 691-8704.
Consul-General: Hugh J. O. R. Tunnell.
Consul (Commercial): R. E. Duggan.
Consul (Management): D. A. Wooten.
Consul (Commercial): C. Parish.

Trade Office: POB 88, Dhahran Airport 31932, al Khobar; tel (3) 857-0595; telex 870028; fax (3) 857-0634.
First Secretary (Commercial): David A. Lloyd.
Second Secretary (Commercial) and Consul: M. G. Plant.

USA

Embassy: Collector Rd M, Riyadh Diplomatic Quarter, POB 9041, Riyadh 11413; tel (1) 488-3800; telex 406866; fax (1) 488-7360.
Ambassador: Charles W. Freeman, Jr.
Deputy Chief of Mission: David J. Dunford.
Political/Military Attaché: William A. Pierce.
Consular Section: Karla Reed.
Regional Security Officer: Frederic M. Krug.
Communications Programme Officer: Michael N. Kuligowski.
Information Systems Manager: Sherrill L. Pavin.
Office of the Defence Attaché: Col J. F. Fields.
Military Training Mission: Maj.-Gen. Donald L. Kaufman.

Information Service: POB 865, Riyadh 11421; fax (1) 488-3989.
Public Affairs Officer: Alan L. Gilbert.

Commercial Section: telex 401363; fax (1) 488-3237.
Commercial Section: Dirck Teller.

Political/Economic Section: fax (1) 488-3278.
Political Section: Richard H. Jones.
Economic Section: David P. Rehfuss.

Administrative Section: fax (1) 488-7360.
Administrative Section: Michael J. McLaughlin.

Representation to Saudi Arabian US Joint Commission on Economic Co-operation: POB 5927, Riyadh; tel (1) 464-0433; telex 201012.
Director: William Griever.
Deputy Director: Larry Bacon.

Consulate-General: between Aramco Headquarters and Dhahran International Airport, POB 81, Dhahran Airport 31932; tel (3) 891-3200; telex 801925; fax (3) 891-3296.
Consul-General: Kenneth A. Stammerman.
Deputy Principal Officer: James P. Bell, Jr.
Economic Section: Todd Schwartz.
Consular Section: Leslie R. Hickman.
Administrative Section: Robert W. Kepler.
Communications Programme Officer: Joseph C. Weller.

Information Service: fax (3) 891-8212.
Branch Public Affairs Officer: Jonathan R. Rice.

Commercial Section: fax (3) 891-8332.
Commercial Section: Carmine D'Aloisio.

Consulate-General: Palestine Rd, Ruwais, POB 149, Jeddah 21411; tel (2) 667-0080; telex 605175; fax (2) 669-3074.
Consul-General: Phillip J. Griffin.
Political/Economic Section: David H. Rundell.
Consular Section: T. Dennis Reece.
Administrative Section: Charles B. Angulo.
Branch Public Affairs Officer: Chris Eccel.
Federal Aviation Administration: Chester Chang.
Geological Survey: Paul Williams.

Commercial Office: tel (2) 667-0040; telex 601459.

Commercial Section: fax (2) 665-8106.
Commercial Section: Michael R. Frisby.

Agricultural Trade Office: tel (2) 661-2408; telex 604683; fax (2) 667-6196.
Agricultural Trade Office: Pitamber Devgon (resident in Riyadh).

URUGUAY

Embassy: POB 94346, Riyadh 11693; tel (1) 455-0146; telex 406611.
Chargé d'affaires a.i.: Barón Dupetit.

VENEZUELA

Embassy: New Sitten Commercial Centre, 4th Floor, Office 4303B, Sitten, POB 94364, Riyadh 11693; tel (1) 476-7867; telex 405599; fax (1) 476-8200.
Ambassador: Norman Pino de Lion.
Counsellor: Abraham Clavero.

YEMEN

Embassy: POB 94356, Riyadh 11693; tel (1) 488-1757.
Ambassador: Ghalib Jamil.

SENEGAL

ALGERIA

Embassy: 5 rue Mermoz, BP 3233, Dakar; tel 22-35-09; telex 3173.
Ambassador: Ahcène Fzeri.

ARGENTINA

Embassy: 34-36 blvd de la République, BP 3343, Dakar; tel 21-51-71; telex 457.
Ambassador: Mario Eduardo Corcuera Ibáñez.

AUSTRIA

Embassy: 24 blvd Pinet-Laprade, entrée rue Malan, BP 3247, Dakar; tel 22-38-86; telex 51611.
Ambassador: Dr Peter Leitenbauer.
Economic Counsellor: Ingeborg Lahr.

BANGLADESH

Embassy: Immeuble Kébé, Appts 11-12, 7e étage, ave André Peytavin, BP 403, Dakar; tel 21-68-81; telex 298.
Ambassador and Head of Mission: Mohiuddin Ahmed.
First Secretary and Head of Chancery: Kazi Emdadul Haque.

BELGIUM

Embassy: route de la Corniche-Est, BP 524, Dakar; tel 22-47-20; telex 265.
Ambassador: Guillaume Metten.

BRAZIL

Embassy: Immeuble Résidence Excellence, 2e étage, 4 ave Roume, BP 136, Dakar; tel 23-25-92; telex 51578.
Ambassador: Lindolfo L. Collor.

BULGARIA

Embassy: Point E, rue 6, BP 419, Dakar; tel 22-18-52.
Chargé d'affaires: M. Zvezdaline Lalov.

CAMEROON

Embassy: 157-9 rue Joseph Gomis, BP 4165, Dakar; tel 21-33-96; telex 1429.
Ambassador: Jerome Mendouga.

CANADA

Embassy: Immeuble Daniel Sorano, 45 blvd de la République, BP 3373, Dakar; tel 23-92-90; telex 51632; fax 23-87-49.
Ambassador: Jacques Bilodeau.
Counsellor (Development): R. Couture.
Counsellor (Development): G. A. Bouchard.
Counsellor (Development): M. Lessard.
Counsellor and Consul: L. R. Daigle.
First Secretary (Development): A. E. Hounzangbé.
First Secretary (Development): A. Létourneau.
First Secretary (Development): R. Drouin.
First Secretary (Development) and Consul: Y. Contamine.
First Secretary (Development): E. Louli.
First Secretary (Development): A. Grandbois.
First Secretary (Development) and Consul: M. Kingsberry.

Co-operation Section: fax 21-24-07.

CAPE VERDE

Embassy: 1 rue de Denain, BP 11269, Dakar; tel 21-18-73; telex 61128.
Ambassador: Victor Fidalgo.
Third Secretary: Daniel Oliveira.
Commercial Attaché: Marcel Moreira.
Consular Attaché: Gualdino Sousa.

CHINA, PEOPLE'S REPUBLIC

Embassy: rue Projetée, Fann Résidence, BP 342, Dakar; tel 22-14-67.
Ambassador: Cang Youheng.

CONGO

Embassy: Mermoz Pyrotechnie, BP 5243, Dakar; tel 24-83-98.
Ambassador: Christian Gilbert Bembet.

COTE D'IVOIRE

Embassy: 2 ave Albert Sarraut, BP 359, Dakar; tel 21-01-63; telex 3170.
Ambassador: Jules Hié Néa.

CZECHOSLOVAKIA

Embassy: rue Aimé Césaire-Fann, BP 3253, Dakar; tel 24-65-26.
Chargé d'affaires: Emil Michalík.

DENMARK

Consulate-General: Km 2 route de Rufisque, BP 191, Dakar; tel 23-30-43; telex 21684; fax 23-87-78.
Consul-General: Frederik Nørgaard.

EGYPT

Embassy: Immeuble Daniel Sorano, 45 blvd de la République, BP 474, Dakar; tel 21-24-75; telex 697.
Ambassador: Hassan Ramadan.

ETHIOPIA

Embassy: BP 379, Dakar; tel 21-75-73; telex 51413.
Ambassador: Mohamed Hamix Ibrahim.

FINLAND

Embassy: Dakar.
Ambassador: Osmo Väinölä (resident in Finland).

Consulate: c/o Ets Buhan et Teisseire, 1 rue des Essarts, BP 119, Dakar; tel 21-39-41; telex 607.
Consul: Jérôme Teisseire.

FRANCE

Embassy: 1 rue El Hadj Amadou Assane Ndoye, BP 4035, Dakar; tel 23-91-81; telex 51597.
Ambassador: Dominique Perreau.

Economic Section: BP 4048; tel 22-36-77; telex 3180.

Consulate-General: BP 330; tel 23-91-73.

Consulate-General: ave Jean Mermoz, BP 183, St Louis; tel 6-11-54.

GABON

Embassy: Villa 7606, Mermoz, Dakar; tel 24-09-95; telex 475; fax 24-15-29.
Ambassador: Simon Ombegue.
First Counsellor: Auguste Mombo Mouele.
First Counsellor (Cultural): Louis Mouloungui-M'Badinga.
First Counsellor (Consular/Chancery): Ernestine Ndiaye-Azizet.
Military Attaché: Comdt-Maj. Irénée Boudd'hou.

GAMBIA

Embassy: 11 rue de Thiong, BP 3248, Dakar; tel 21-44-76; telex 51617.
High Commissioner: El Hadj Abdoulie Sulayman Mboob.

GERMANY

Embassy: 20 ave Pasteur, angle rue Mermoz, BP 2100, Dakar; tel 23-25-19; telex 21686; fax 22-52-99.
Ambassador: Dr Thomas Fischer-Dieskau.

GUINEA

Embassy: km 4.5, route de Ouakam, BP 7123, Dakar; tel 21-86-06; telex 3242.
Ambassador: Facine Bangoura.

GUINEA-BISSAU

Embassy: Point E, rue 6, BP 2319, Dakar; tel 21-59-22; telex 243.
Ambassador: José Pereira Batista.

HAITI

Embassy: Villa Sise face Amicale des Bretons, Corniche-Est, BP 1552, Dakar; tel 22-64-79.
Ambassador: Raymond Mathieu.

HOLY SEE

Apostolic Nunciature: rue Aimé Césaire, angle Corniche-Ouest, Fann Résidence, BP 5076, Dakar; tel 24-26-74; fax 24-19-31.
Apostolic Nuncio: Mgr Antonio Maria Vegliò, Titular Archbishop of Aeclanum.
Auditor: Luigi Pezzuto.

INDIA

Embassy: 5 ave Carde, BP 398, Dakar; tel 21-09-79; telex 514; fax 22-35-85.
Ambassador: Vidya Bhushan Soni.
Second Secretary: Rahul Chhabra.
Attaché: Ram Prakash.

INDONESIA

Embassy: 126 ave Cheikh Anta Diop, angle ave Bourguiba, BP 5859, Fann, Dakar; tel 25-73-16; telex 21644.
Ambassador: Mr Pratjojo.
First Secretary: Dr Suharsono.
Third Secretary: Budhi Rahardjo.
Third Secretary: Mr Rukman.
Attaché: Widi Widjaja Kusuma.

IRAQ

Embassy: Immeuble Kébé, ave Peytavin, Dakar; telex 471.
Ambassador: Bassem al-Bazzaz.

ITALY

Embassy: rue El Hadj Seydou Nourou Tall, BP 348, Dakar; tel 22-05-78; telex 641.
Ambassador: Marco Sorace Maresca.

JAPAN

Embassy: Immeuble Electra II, rue Malan, BP 3140, Dakar; tel 23-74-79; telex 51677; fax 23-73-51.
Ambassador: Mitsuhei Murata.

KOREA, DEMOCRATIC PEOPLE'S REPUBLIC

Embassy: Point E, rue 1 x route A, BP 3862, Dakar; tel 23-09-99.
Ambassador: Sin Byeng Tcheull.

KOREA, REPUBLIC

Embassy: 66 blvd de la République, BP 3338, Dakar; tel 22-58-22; telex 242.
Ambassador: Rew Jong-Hyun.

KUWAIT

Embassy: 36 rue Calmeite, Dakar; tel 21-98-81; telex 3327.
Ambassador: Mohamed Salem al-Balhan.

LEBANON

Embassy: 18 blvd de la République, BP 234, Dakar; tel 22-02-55; telex 61190.
Ambassador: Naji Abouassi.

MALI

Embassy: 46 blvd de la République, BP 478, Dakar; tel 22-04-73; telex 429.
Ambassador: Nfagnanama Kone.

MEXICO

Embassy: Immeuble Sorano, 6e étage, 45 blvd de la République, BP 3830, Dakar; tel 21-51-23; telex 51235.
Ambassador: Santiago Meyer.

MOROCCO

Embassy: ave Cheikh Anta Diop, BP 490, Dakar; tel 24-69-27; telex 51567.
Ambassador: Abdelwahab Chorfi.

NETHERLANDS

Embassy: 37 rue Kléber, BP 3262, Dakar; tel 22-04-83; telex 610.
Ambassador: Rudolph Mulder.

NIGERIA

Embassy: Point E, rue 1 x Fa, BP 3129, Dakar; tel 21-69-22; telex 404.
Ambassador: Alhaji Abubakar Muhammadu Sani Yarima.

PAKISTAN

Embassy: 10 ave Borgnis Desbordes, BP 2635, Dakar; tel 21-20-31; telex 615; fax 21-42-55.
Ambassador: Amin Jan Naim.

PHILIPPINES

Embassy: 41 rue El Hadj Amadou Assane Ndoye, Dakar; tel 22-46-52.
Chargé d'affaires: Supo I Zeyva.

POLAND

Embassy: 7627 route de la Pyrotechnie, BP 343, Dakar; telex 245.
Ambassador: Bolesław Iwankow.

PORTUGAL

Embassy: 5 ave Carde, BP 281, Dakar; tel 23-58-22; telex 61134; fax 23-50-96.
Ambassador: Fernando Pinto dos Santos.
Consul: Antonio Maximo.
Defence Attaché: Col Luis Cadete.
Commercial Counsellor: João Novais da Fonseca.

ROMANIA

Embassy: Point E, blvd de l'Est x rue 4, Dakar; tel 22-19-13; telex 3115.
Ambassador: Geliu Voican-Voiculescu.

RUSSIA

Embassy: angle ave Jean-Jaurès et rue Carnot, BP 3180, Dakar; tel 22-48-21; telex 21432.
Ambassador: Aleksandr Papkin.

SAUDI ARABIA

Embassy: 33 rue Kléber, BP 3109, Dakar; tel 22-23-67; telex 294.
Ambassador: Abdullah A. Altobaishi.

SOMALIA

Embassy: Immeuble Kébé, 17e étage, ave André Peytavin, BP 156, Dakar; tel 22-28-72; telex 61130.
Ambassador: Ali Abdi Gurhan.

SPAIN

Embassy: 45 blvd de la République, BP 2091, Dakar; tel 21-11-78; telex 451.
Ambassador: Ricardo Cortes.

SWEDEN

Embassy: Dakar.
Ambassador: Bengt Holmquist (resident in Sweden).
Consulate-General: 10 rue Huart, BP 2032, Dakar; tel 22-30-74; telex 61362.
Consul-General: Yves Camille Barthélémy Audinot.
Vice-Consul: Karl Inge Leif Ståhl.

SWITZERLAND

Embassy: angle rue René N'Diaye et rue Seydou Nourou Tall, BP 1772, Dakar; tel 22-58-48; telex 411; fax 22-36-57.
Ambassador: Pierre Barraz.
First Secretary: Arnoldo Lardi.
Attaché and Head of Chancery: Margrit Letsch.

SYRIA

Embassy: 66 blvd de la République, BP 348, Dakar; tel 21-62-77; telex 3102.
Chargé d'affaires: Hilal al-Raheb.

THAILAND

Embassy: km 6, ave Cheikh Anta Diop, BP 3721, Dakar; tel 24-30-76; telex 61279.
Ambassador: Sukhum Rasmidatta.

TUNISIA

Embassy: rue El Hadj Seydou Nourou Tall, BP 3127, Dakar; tel 21-47-47; telex 561.
Ambassador: Radia Mestri Gordha.

TURKEY

Embassy: ave des Ambassadeurs, Fann Résidence, BP 6060, Etoile, Dakar; tel 24-58-11; telex 51472.
Ambassador: Nusret Aktan.
Third Secretary: Esra Demir.
Attaché: Cagatay Nadir Sarac.
Attaché: Tahsin Tatar.

UNITED KINGDOM

Embassy: 20 rue du Dr Guillet, BP 6025, Dakar; tel 23-73-92; telex 21690; fax 23-27-66.
Ambassador: Roger Campbell Beetham.
First Secretary and Deputy Head of Mission: R. S. Dewar.
Cultural Attaché and British Council Director: Dr M. D. Cooper.
Assistant Cultural Attaché (British Council): J. H. McCullough.
Second Secretary (Chancery and Information): Viscount Glentworth.
Third Secretary (Management) and Vice-Consul: K. J. Lynch.
Assistant Management Officer and Accountant: A. Stapley.

USA

Embassy: ave Jean XXIII, BP 49, Dakar; tel 23-42-96; telex 21793; fax 22-29-91.
Ambassador: George E. Moose.
Deputy Chief of Mission: Prudence Bushnell.
Political Section: J. Michael Davis.
Economic Section: Alice A. Dress.
Commercial Section: Harold D. Foster.
Consular Section: Helen Bridget Burkart.
Administrative Section: Ned W. Arcement.
Regional Security Officer: Gary T. Denitto.
Communications Programme Officer: John F. Clover III.
Information Systems Manager: Julius Benjik.
Security Assistance Office: Maj. Billy R. Ellis.
Agency for International Development: Julius E. Coles.
Office of the Defence Attaché: Lieut Col Stefan Mytczynsky.
Labour Officer: Ollie P. Anderson, Jr - (resident in USA).
Federal Aviation Administration: Richard L. Hurst.
Information Service: tel 23-11-85.
Public Affairs Officer: Robert J. Palmeri.

ZAIRE

Embassy: ave de l'Ambassade du Maroc, Fann Résidence, BP 2251, Dakar; tel 25-19-79; telex 21661.
Ambassador: Kalenga wa Belabela.

ZIMBABWE

Embassy: km 6, route de Ouakam, BP 2762, Dakar; tel 23-03-25; telex 3231.
Ambassador: Majozi Mthobi Harold Hlabangana.

International Organizations

EUROPEAN COMMUNITIES

External Delegation: 57 ave Pompidou, 2e étage, BP 3345, Dakar; tel 23-13-24; telex 21665; fax 21-78-85.
Commission Delegate: Gabriele von Brochowski.

SEYCHELLES

BELGIUM

Consulate: POB 222, Victoria, Mahé; tel 24240; telex 2374; fax 24456.
Consul: Livio Lang.

CHINA, PEOPLE'S REPUBLIC

Embassy: POB 680, Plaisance; tel 44295.

CUBA

Embassy: Bel Eau; tel 24094; telex 2354.

DENMARK

Consulate: Bodco Bldg, POB 231, Victoria, Mahé; tel 24666; telex 2270; fax 24065.
Consul: Basil John William Soundy.

FINLAND

Consulate: Bodco Bldg, POB 371, Victoria, Mahé; tel 24666; telex 2270; fax 24065.
Consul: Basil John William Soundy.

FRANCE

Embassy: 'Arpent Vert' Bldg, POB 478, Mont Fleuri, Victoria, Mahé; tel 24523; telex 2238.
Ambassador: Jean-Claude Brochenen.

Economic Section: tel 24515; telex 2389.

GERMANY

Consulate: Royal St, Story Bldg, POB 132, Victoria, Mahé; tel 22306.
Honorary Consul: Günter Eichler.

INDIA

High Commission: Le Chantier, Victoria, Mahé; tel 24489; telex 2349.
High Commissioner: Chokila Iyes.

NETHERLANDS

Embassy: Victoria; tel 47100.

RUSSIA

Embassy: Le Niol, POB 632, Victoria, Mahé; tel 21590; telex 2392.
Ambassador: Victor Vitalevich Anisimov.

SWEDEN

Embassy: Victoria, Mahé; tel 24710.
Ambassador: Lars Schönander (resident in Sweden).

Consulate: Bodco Bldg, Harbour Trading Estate, POB 270, Victoria, Mahé; tel 24666; telex 2270; fax 24065.
Consul: Basil John William Soundy.

UNITED KINGDOM

High Commission: Victoria House, 3rd Floor, POB 161, Victoria, Mahé; tel 25225; telex 2269; fax 25127.
High Commissioner: John Sharland.
Deputy High Commissioner: D. P. R. Jenner.

USA

Embassy: Victoria House, POB 251, Victoria, Mahé; tel 25256; fax 25189.
Ambassador: James B. Moran.
Political/Economic Section: Gary E. Anderson.
Consul: Kevin C. Aiston.
Administrative Section: Wayne J. Bush.
Communications Programme Officer: Gilbert Fertado.

International Organizations

EUROPEAN COMMUNITIES

External Delegation (Sub-office of Delegation to Mauritius): POB 530, Victoria, Mahé; tel 23940; telex 2213; fax 66318.

SIERRA LEONE

AUSTRIA

Consulate: 42 Main Motor Rd, Wilberforce, POB 497, Freetown; tel (22) 30495; telex 3489.
Honorary Consul: Klaus Bieber.

CHINA, PEOPLE'S REPUBLIC

Embassy: 29 Wilberforce Loop, Freetown; tel (22) 31797.
Ambassador: Gao Jianchong.

COTE D'IVOIRE

Embassy: 1 Wesley St, Freetown; tel (22) 23983.
Ambassador: Mamadou Touré.

DENMARK

Consulate: c/o Mining & General Services Ltd, 2 Blackhall Rd, POB 68, Freetown; tel (22) 50906; telex 3226.
Consul: Richard Reid Duncan.
Vice-Consul: Ole Flening Thomsen.

EGYPT

Embassy: 37 Percival St, Freetown; tel (22) 31499; telex 3300.
Ambassador: Mohamed Abdel Salam Moussa.

FRANCE

Embassy: 13 Lamina Sankoh St, POB 510, Freetown; tel (22) 22477; telex 3238.
Ambassador: Jacques Nizart.

GAMBIA

High Commission: 6 Wilberforce St, Freetown; tel (22) 225191; telex 3286.
High Commissioner: Boukary Oksubi Fofana.
First Secretary and Head of Chancery: Ansumana E. Ceesay.
Finance and Administrative Attaché: M. Salieu Jallow.
Protocol and Welfare Officer: Seedy K. Ceesay.

GERMANY

Embassy: Santanno House, 10 Howe St, POB 728, Freetown; tel (22) 22511; telex 3248.
Ambassador: Karl Prinz.
Head of Chancery and Deputy Head of Mission: Wolf-Rüdiger Tietz.
Consular Officer: Marianne Schwer.

GUINEA

Embassy: 4 Liverpool St, Freetown; tel (22) 23080.
Ambassador: Djibril Moriba.

IRELAND

Consulate-General: 8 Rawdon St, 1st Floor, POB 234, Freetown; tel (22) 22017; telex 3311; fax (22) 23687.
Honorary Consul-General: Wadi M. Aboud.

ITALY

Embassy: 32A Wilkinson Rd, POB 749, Freetown; tel (22) 30995; telex 3456.
Ambassador: Georgio Peca.

KOREA, REPUBLIC

Embassy: 22 Wilberforce St, POB 1383, Freetown; tel (22) 24269; telex 3313.
Ambassador: Kim Dong Jin.

LEBANON

Embassy: 22 Wilberforce St, POB 727, Freetown; tel (22) 23513.
Chargé d'affaires: Jaoudat Noureddine.

LIBERIA

Embassy: 30 Brookfields Rd, POB 276, Freetown; tel (22) 40322; telex 3229.
Ambassador: Maj.-Gen. A. Karpeh.

NIGERIA

High Commission: 37 Siaka Stevens St, Freetown; tel (22) 24202; telex 3258.
High Commissioner: J. K. Umar.

RUSSIA

Embassy: 13 Walpole St, POB 929, Freetown; tel (22) 23992; telex 3599.
Ambassador: Dr Vladimir S. Novoseltsev.

SWEDEN

Embassy: Freetown.
Ambassador: Bengt Holmquist (resident in Sweden).

Consulate: 12 Wilberforce St, POB 575, Freetown; tel (22) 22834; telex 3452.
Consul: Jonathan Admire Thomas.

SWITZERLAND

Consulate-General: Freetown Cold Storage Co. Ltd, George Brook, POB 99, Freetown; tel (22) 40445; telex 3245.
Honorary Consul-General: Franz Braun.

TURKEY

Consulate-General: 17 Wilberforce St, POB 1284, Freetown; tel (22) 3468.
Honorary Consul-General: Ismail Baydoun.

UNITED KINGDOM

High Commission: Standard Chartered Bank of Sierra Leone Ltd Bldg, Lightfoot Boston St, Freetown; tel (22) 23961; telex 3235.
High Commissioner: David K. Sprague.
Deputy High Commissioner: F. J. Martin.
Management Officer: R. J. Fielder.
Attaché (Consular): J. D. G. Emery.

USA

Embassy: cnr Walpole and Siaka Stevens Sts, Freetown; tel (22) 26155; telex 3509.
Ambassador: Johnny Young.
Deputy Chief of Mission: Gary H. Maybarduk.
Economic/Commercial Section: Thomas M. Newcomb.
Consular Section: Alan B. C. Latimer.
Administrative Section: Johney Brooks.
Regional Security Officer: Raymond J. Fournier.
Public Affairs Officer: Matthew J. McGrath.
Communications Programme Officer: David E. Heil.
Labour Officer: Ollie P. Anderson, Jr (resident in USA).

YUGOSLAVIA

Consulate: 8 Wesley St, POB 552, Freetown; tel (22) 25663; telex 3488.
Honorary Consul: Adonis Abboud.

International Organizations

EUROPEAN COMMUNITIES

External Delegation: Wesley House, 4 George St, POB 1399, Freetown; tel (22) 23975; telex 3203; fax (22) 25212.

SINGAPORE

ARGENTINA

Embassy: 302 Orchard Rd, 10-04 Tong Bldg, Singapore 0923; tel 2354231; telex 23714.
Ambassador: Carlos Lucas Blanco.

AUSTRALIA

High Commission: 25 Napier Rd, Singapore 1025; tel 7379311; telex 21238; fax 7337134.
High Commissioner: Rosaleen McGovern.

AUSTRIA

Consulate-General: 1 Scotts Rd 22-04, Shaw Centre, Tanglin, POB 238, Singapore 0922; tel 2354088; telex 21133.
Honorary Consul-General: Fritz Helmreich.
Honorary Consul: Andreas Meindl.

BANGLADESH

High Commission: 101 Thomson Rd, 06-07 United Sq., Singapore 1130; tel 2550075; telex 23312.
High Commissioner: Maj.-Gen. Moin Ul Hussain Choudhury.

BELGIUM

Embassy: 10 Anson Rd, 09-24 International Plaza, Singapore 0207; tel 2207677; telex 23301; fax 2226976.
Ambassador: Claire Kirschen.
Third Secretary: Dr Frank van de Craen.
Attaché (Commercial): Oscar Cousy.
Attaché (Cultural): Bavo Lievens.
Attaché (Administration): Gilbert Vanderstichelen.

BRAZIL

Embassy: 302 Orchard Rd, 1503/4 Tong Bldg, Singapore 0923; tel 7346777; telex 36204.
Ambassador: A. B. Porto de Oliveira.

BRUNEI

High Commission: 7A Tanglin Hill, Singapore 1024; tel 4743393; telex 24097; fax 4740844.
High Commissioner: Dato Paduka Awang Haji Mohammed Yunos bin Haji Mohammed Hussain.

BULGARIA

Embassy: 15 Scotts Rd, 09-09 Thong Teck Bldg, Singapore 0922; tel 7371111; telex 21204.

CANADA

High Commission: 80 Anson Rd, 14-00 and 15-01 IBM Towers, Singapore 0207; Maxwell Rd, POB 845, Singapore 9016; tel 2256363; telex 21277; fax 2252450.
High Commissioner: Bernard A. Gagosz.
Counsellor (Commercial): D. Comeau.
Counsellor (Immigration): C. Thorlakson.
First Secretary: T. J. Cormier.
First Secretary (Development): R. N. Gold.
First Secretary (Development): R. Ironmonger.
First Secretary (Development): J. Melanson.
First Secretary (Administration): R. G. Blier.
First Secretary (Immigration): P. K. W. Page.
Attaché (Medical): Dr T. Axler.

CHILE

Embassy: 105 Cecil St, The Octagon 14-01/02, Singapore 2159; tel 2238577; telex 34187; fax 2250677.
Ambassador: Carlos Negri Chiorrini.
Second Secretary and Consul: Rolando Drago.
Commercial Attaché: Nestor Riveros.

CHINA, PEOPLE'S REPUBLIC

Embassy: 70-76 Dalvey Rd, Singapore 1025; tel 7343360; telex 36878; fax 7338590.
Ambassador: Zhang Qing.

DENMARK

Embassy: 101 Thomson Rd, 13-01/02 United Sq., Singapore 1130; tel 2503383; telex 24576; fax 2533764.
Ambassador: Jens Peter Larsen.
Attaché: Ulrik Holt Sørensen.
Export Assistant: Steen Thorsted Rasmussen.
Commercial Assistant: Anthony Leong.
Social Attaché: Pastor Ronald Pedersen.

Consulate-General: 6 Raffles Quay, 01-02 Denmark House, Singapore 0104; POB 158, Maxwell Rd, Singapore 9003; tel 2247011; telex 21234; fax 2244932.
Consul-General: Joti Bhokavanij.

EGYPT

Embassy: 75 Grange Rd, Singapore 1024; tel 7371811; telex 23293.
Ambassador: Abbas Zaki.

FINLAND

Embassy: 101 Thomson Rd, 21-02/03 United Sq., Singapore 1130; Newton Post Office, POB 88, Singapore 9122; tel 2544042; telex 21489; fax 2534101.
Ambassador: Erik Heinrichs.
Commercial Secretary: Ensio Pesonen.

FRANCE

Embassy: 5 Gallop Rd, Singapore 1025; tel 4664212; telex 21351; fax 4663296.
Ambassador: Bernard Faubournet de Montferrand.
Counsellor: Hervé Dejean de la Batie.
Defence Attaché: Commdr Jean-Louis Dufour.
Commercial Counsellor: Gilles Della Guardia.
Financial Counsellor: Daniel Besson.
Cultural Counsellor: Dr France Lasnier.
Third Secretary: Jean-Louis Bertrand.
Vice-Consul and Head of Chancery: Philippe Martin.
Technical Defence Attaché: Philippe Tissier.
Deputy Trade Commissioner: Jacques Torregrossa.
Commercial Attaché: Françoise Meley.
Commercial Attaché: Jean-Yves Coulot.
Financial Attaché: Antoine Pozzo di Borgo.
Cultural Attaché: Jan Migot.

Economic Section: 10 Anson Rd, 30-06/07 International Plaza, Singapore 0207; tel 2213033; telex 22121; fax 2259457.

Financial Agency: 10 Collyer Quay, 11-04 Ocean Bldg, Singapore 0104; tel 5324755; telex 55478; fax 5354628.

GERMANY

Embassy: 545 Orchard Rd, 14-01 Far East Shopping Centre, Tanglin POB 94, Singapore 0923; tel 7371355; telex 21312; fax 7372653.
Ambassador: Dr Karl Spalcke.

HOLY SEE

Apostolic Nunciature: 55 Waterloo St 6, Singapore 0718; tel 3372466.
Secretary and Auditor: Mgr George Kocherry.

ICELAND

Consulate-General: c/o Seahorse Pharmaceutical Products Ltd, 0610 The Hong Centre, 4 Leng Kee Rd, Singapore 0315; tel 4740322; telex 56719.
Consul-General: Jón B. Sigurđsson.

INDIA

High Commission: 31 Grange Rd, India House, Singapore 0923; tel 7376777; telex 25526; fax 7326909.
High Commissioner: Y. M. Tiwari.

INDONESIA

Embassy: 7 Chatsworth Rd, Singapore 1024; tel 7377422; telex 21464.
Ambassador: Tuk Setyohadi.

IRELAND

Consulate-General: 541 Orchard Rd, 08-02 Liat Towers, Singapore 0923; tel 7323430; telex 25566; fax 7337250.
Honorary Consul-General: Fergus Healy.

ISRAEL

Embassy: 58 Dalvey Rd, Singapore 1025; tel 2350966; telex 21975; fax 7337008.
Ambassador: Benad Avital.
Second Secretary: Irit Lillian-Cohen.
Counsellor (Economic Affairs): Samy Shmuel Ofri.
Second Secretary (Administration) and Head of Consular Section: Drora Daya.
Attaché: Yacov Katz.
Defence and Military Attaché: Brig.-Gen. Yehuda Peled.

ITALY

Embassy: 101 Thomson Rd, 27-02/03 United Sq., Singapore 1130; tel 2506022; telex 21177; fax 2533301.
Ambassador: Dr Romualdo Bettini.
First Secretary: Dr Pietro Giovanni Donnici.
Cultural Attaché: Prof. Patrizia Raveggi-Djuric.

JAPAN

Embassy: 16 Nassim Rd, Singapore 1025; tel 2358855; telex 21353; fax 7320781.
Ambassador: Wasuke Miyake.

KOREA, DEMOCRATIC PEOPLE'S REPUBLIC

Embassy: 19 Fort Rd, Singapore 1543; tel 3453044; telex 23455.
Ambassador: Yun Chong-Kyu.

KOREA, REPUBLIC

Embassy: 101 Thomson Rd, United Sq., 10-02/04 Goldhill Sq., Singapore 1130; tel 2561188.
Ambassador: Lee Chang-Choon.

MALAYSIA

High Commission: 301 Jervois Rd, Singapore 1024; tel 2350111; telex 21406.
High Commissioner: Dato' K. Tharmaratnam.

MALTA

Consulate: 09-05 Asia Chambers, 20 McCallum St, Singapore 0106; tel 2222100; telex 43011; fax 2228102.
Honorary Consul: Gopalan Mukunnan.

MYANMAR

Embassy: 15 St Martin's Drive, Singapore 1025; tel 7342637; telex 21467; fax 2355963.
Ambassador: U Nyunt Swe.

NETHERLANDS

Embassy: 541 Orchard Rd, 13-01/04 Liat Towers, Singapore 0923; tel 7371155; telex 33815; fax 7371940.
Ambassador: D. H. M. van Woerden.

NEW ZEALAND

High Commission: 13 Nassim Rd, Singapore 1025; tel 2359966; telex 21244; fax 7339924.
High Commissioner: Colin Bell.
First Secretary: Wendy Hinton.
Second Secretary: Brian Chippindale.
Communications Officer: Mark Conroy.
Communications Technician: Dave Moore.
First Secretary: Charles Finny.
Trade Commissioner: Stephen Bryant.
Regional Tourism Director (South East Asia): Fergus Brown.
Defence Adviser and Attaché: Group Capt. K. A. Jones.

NORWAY

Embassy: 16 Raffles Quay, 44-01 Hong Leong Bldg, Singapore 0104; tel 2207122; telex 21225; fax 2247079.
Ambassador: Jens Otterbech.
First Secretary: Anne Rikter-Svendsen.
Attaché (Administration and Consular Affairs): Synnove Holmstad.

Commercial Office: tel 2221316.
Commercial Counsellor (Norwegian Trade Council): Ole Schistad.

PAKISTAN

High Commission: 20A Nassim Rd, Singapore 1025; tel 7376621; telex 36777.
High Commissioner: Salim Nawaz Gandabur (acting).

PANAMA

Embassy: 16 Raffles Quay, 41-06 Hong Leong Bldg, Singapore 0104; tel 2218677; telex 24524; fax 2240892.
Chargé d'affaires a.i. and Consul-General (Merchant Marine): Jorge Luis Alemán.
Vice-Consul: Micaela J. de Oehlers.

PHILIPPINES

Embassy: 20 Nassim Rd, Singapore 1025; tel 7373977; telex 34445; fax 7339544.
Ambassador: Francisco L. Benedicto.

POLAND

Embassy: 100 Beach Rd, 33-10PT/12 Shaw Towers, Singapore 0718; tel 2942513; telex 26355; fax 2950016.
Ambassador: Pawel Ceislar.

ROMANIA

Embassy: 48 Harom Setangkai Rd, Singapore 1025; tel 4683424; telex 22184; fax 4683425.
Chargé d'affaires a.i.: Ioan Ban.

RUSSIA

Embassy: 51 Nassim Rd, Singapore 1025; tel 2351834; telex 23071; fax 7334780.
Ambassador: Anatoly Matfeyevich Dryukov.

SAUDI ARABIA

Embassy: 541 Orchard Rd, 13-03/04 Liat Towers, Singapore 0923; tel 7345878; telex 25318; fax 7374657.
Chargé d'affaires: Mohammad A. al-Hamdan.

SRI LANKA

High Commission: Newton Rd, 1307-1312 Goldhill Plaza, Singapore 1130; tel 2544595; telex 26869; fax 2507201.
High Commissioner: W. M. Janaka B. Nakkawita.

SWEDEN

Embassy: Devonshire Wing, 111 Somerset Rd, 05-08 PUB Bldg, Singapore 0923; Orchard Point POB 292, Singapore 9123; tel 7342771; telex 23450; fax 7322958.
Ambassador: Finn Bergstrand.
First Secretary: Anders Jansson.
Second Secretary: Inga Cederlund Jönsson.
Chancellor: Eva Kristina Ho.

SWITZERLAND

Embassy: 1 Swiss Club Link, Singapore 1128; tel 4685788; telex 21501; fax 4668245.
Ambassador: Dr Kurt O. Wyss.
Third Secretary: Werner Wiedmer.
Vice-Consul and Head of Chancery: Jean-Pierre Baumeyer.

THAILAND

Embassy: 370 Orchard Rd, Singapore 0923; tel 7373372; telex 35891; fax 7320778.
Ambassador: Asda Jayanama.

TURKEY

Embassy: 20B Nassim Rd, Singapore 1025; tel 7329211; telex 34668.
Ambassador: Dr Riza Türmen.

UNITED KINGDOM

High Commission: Tanglin Rd, Singapore 1024; tel 4739333; telex 21218; fax 4752320.
High Commissioner: Gordon A. Duggan.
Counsellor (Economic/Commercial) and Deputy High Commissioner: P. J. W. Le Breton.
Defence Adviser: Group Capt. T. J. Hindmarsh.
Cultural and Educational Adviser: A. G. Webster.
First Secretary and Head of Chancery: T. G. Paxman.
Deputy Cultural and Educational Adviser: G. E. Millington.
First Secretary (Management): J. A. Reeves.
First Secretary (Commercial): D. R. Shaw.
Assistant Defence Adviser: Lieut Commdr M. R. D'Cruz.
Second Secretary: M. Powell.
Second Secretary (Consular): J. D. McDonald.
Second Secretary (Commercial): R. MacKenzie.
Second Secretary: G. G. Causer.
Third Secretary (Science and Technology): G. M. Warrington.

Commercial Department: POB 19, Tanglin, Singapore 1024.

USA

Embassy: 30 Hill St, Singapore 0617; tel 3380251; telex 42289; fax 3384550.
Ambassador: Robert D. Orr.
Deputy Chief of Mission: Arthur L. Kobler.
Economic/Political Section: Thomas H. Martin.
Commercial Section: George F. Ruffner.
Consular Section/Refugee Co-ordinator: Caryl M. Courtney.
Administrative Section: Robert B. Courtney.
Regional Security Officer: Douglas P. Quiram.
Communications Programme Officer: Franklin Pressley, Jr.
Information Systems Manager: Aila K. Long.
Office of the Defence Attaché: Capt. William P. Cooper.
Agency for International Development Auditor: James B. Durnil.
Agency for International Development Inspector: Gordon L. Ransom.
Agricultural Trade Office: Geoffrey W. Wiggin.
Security Assistance Office: Lieut Commdr Richard C. Green.
Customs Service (Treasury): James W. Wilkie.
Drug Enforcement Agency: Harry Fullett.
Federal Aviation Administration: Donald V. Schmidt.
Internal Revenue Service: Charles W. Landry.

Information Service: 15-00 Tung Centre Bldg, 20 Collyer Quay, Singapore 0104; tel 2245233; fax 224-3239.
Public Affairs Officer: Dennis D. Donahue.

Information Service, Commercial Services and Library: 05-12 Colombo Court Bldg, North Bridge Rd, Singapore 0617; tel 3389722; telex 25079; fax 3385010.

Agricultural Office: 541 Orchard Rd, 08-04 Liat Towers Bldg, Singapore 0923; tel 7371233; telex 55318; fax 7328307.

SOLOMON ISLANDS

AUSTRALIA

High Commission: cnr Hibiscus and Mud Alley, POB 589, Honiara; tel 21561; telex 66325; fax 23691.
High Commissioner: John Starey.

CHINA (TAIWAN)

Embassy: Lengakiki Ridge, POB 586, Honiara; tel 22590; telex 66395; fax 21378.
Ambassador: Shih-Cheng Chang.

GERMANY

Consulate: POB 114, Honiara; tel 22588; telex 66313.
Honorary Consul: Gerald Stenzel.

JAPAN

Embassy: National Provident Fund Bldg, Mendana Ave, POB 560, Honiara; tel 22953; telex 66385; fax 21006.
Chargé d'affaires a.i.: Masashi Ikeno.

NEW ZEALAND

High Commission: City Centre Bldg, Mendana Ave, POB 697, Honiara; tel 21502; telex 66322; fax 22377.
High Commissioner: Bernard R. Hillier.
First Secretary: Jan Henderson.
Second Secretary: Ian Goodger.
Attaché: Barbara Shaw.

SWEDEN

Consulate: POB 588, Tambea Village, Honiara; tel 23639; telex 66338; fax 23110.
Consul: Olle Törling.

UNITED KINGDOM

High Commission: Soltel House, Mendana Ave, POB 676, Honiara; tel 21705; telex 66324; fax 21549.
High Commissioner: Raymond F. Jones.
First Secretary: K. A. Neill.
Second Secretary (Aid): E. J. Palmer.
Third Secretary (Aid): C. J. Jones.

USA

Embassy: Mud Alley, POB 561, Honiara; tel 23890; telex 66461; fax 23488.
Deputy Chief of Mission: William Warren.

International Organizations

EUROPEAN COMMUNITIES

External Delegation: 2nd Floor, City Centre Bldg, POB 844, Honiara; tel 22765; telex 66370; fax 23318.
Commission Delegate: Luis Carlos Moreno Abati (also responsible for Vanuatu).

SOMALIA

ALGERIA

Embassy: POB 2850, Mogadishu; tel (1) 81696.
Ambassador: Hamid Bench Erchali.

AUSTRIA

Consulate: J. Hussein Bldg, POB 557, Mogadishu; telex 3723.
Honorary Consul: Jirdeh Hussein.

BELGIUM

Consulate: POB 459, Mogadishu; tel (1) 80784; fax (1) 81903.
Consul: Mohamed A. Mohamed (acting).

BULGARIA

Embassy: Hodan District, Km 5, off Via Afgoi, POB 1736, Mogadishu; tel (1) 81820.
Chargé d'affaires: Peyo Bozov.

CHINA, PEOPLE'S REPUBLIC

Embassy: POB 548, Mogadishu; tel (1) 20805.
Ambassador: Xu Yingjie.

CUBA

Embassy: Mogadishu.

DENMARK

Consulate-General: Somali Prefab Bldg Material, POB 591, Mogadishu; tel (1) 80802; telex 3676.
Consul-General: Ali Sheikh Mohamed.
Vice-Consul: Hussein Ali Sheikh Mohamed.

DJIBOUTI

Embassy: Mogadishu; telex 771.
Ambassador: Abdi Ismael Waberi.

EGYPT

Embassy: Via Maka al-Mukarama Km 4, POB 76, Mogadishu; tel (1) 80781.
Ambassador: Mohamed Shafik Ragab.

ETHIOPIA

Embassy: POB 368, Mogadishu; telex 3089.
Ambassador: Dr Asmamaw Kalimu.

FINLAND

Consulate-General: POB 591, Mogadishu; tel (1) 80802; telex 3676.
Consul-General: Hussein Ali Sheikh.
Vice-Consul: Ali Sheikh Mohamed Hussein.

GERMANY

Embassy: Via Mahamoud Harbi, POB 17, Mogadishu; tel (1) 20547; telex 613.
Ambassador: Dr Helmut Rau.

INDIA

Embassy: Via Jigjiga, Shingani, POB 955, Mogadishu; tel (1) 21262; telex 716.
Ambassador: Krishan Mohan Lal.

IRAN

Embassy: Via Maka al-Mukarama, POB 1166, Mogadishu; tel (1) 80881; telex 616.
Chargé d'affaires: Ali Amouei.

IRAQ

Embassy: Via Maka al-Mukarama, POB 641, Mogadishu; tel (1) 80821; telex 638.
Ambassador: Hikmat A. Sattar Hussain.

ITALY

Embassy: Via Alto Giuba, POB 6, Mogadishu; tel (1) 20544; telex 777.
Ambassador: Mario Sica.

KENYA

Embassy: Via Mecca, POB 618, Mogadishu; tel (1) 80857; telex 610.
Ambassador: John Ole Siparo.

KOREA, DEMOCRATIC PEOPLE'S REPUBLIC

Embassy: Via Km 5, Mogadishu.
Ambassador: Chong Myong-Hwa.

KUWAIT

Embassy: First Medina Rd, Km 5, POB 1348, Mogadishu; telex 608.
Chargé d'affaires: Mattar Thajil al-Salman.

LIBYA

People's Bureau: Via Medina, POB 125, Mogadishu.

NIGERIA

Embassy: Via Km 5, Mogadishu; tel (1) 81362; telex 637.
Ambassador: Dahiru Mohamed Abu Bakar.

OMAN

Embassy: Via Afgoi, POB 2992, Mogadishu; tel (1) 81658; telex 796.
Ambassador: Ahmed Ebrahim Qasim.

PAKISTAN

Embassy: Via Afgoi, Km 5, POB 339, Mogadishu; tel (1) 80856.
Chargé d'affaires: Tahir Iqbal Butt.

QATAR

Embassy: Via Km 4, POB 1744, Mogadishu; tel (1) 80746; telex 629.
Ambassador: Abdul Yusuf al-Jaida.

ROMANIA

Embassy: Via Lido, POB 651, Mogadishu.
Ambassador: Gheorghe Manciu.

RUSSIA

Embassy: Via Repubblica, POB 607, Mogadishu; tel (1) 21909.

SAUDI ARABIA

Embassy: Via Benadir, POB 603, Mogadishu; tel (1) 22087; telex 618.
Ambassador: Abdalla A. Alim.

SUDAN

Embassy: Via Mecca, POB 552, Mogadishu.
Ambassador: Mustafa Hassan Ahmed.

SWEDEN

Consulate-General: Corso Somalia, POB 591, Mogadishu; tel (1) 80802; telex 3676.
Ambassador: Lars Schönander (resident in Sweden).
Consul-General: Ali Sheikh Mohamed.
Vice-Consul: Hussein Ali Sheikh Mohamed.

SYRIA

Embassy: Via Medina, POB 986, Mogadishu; telex 636.
Chargé d'affaires: Shayesh Terkawi.

TURKEY

Embassy: Via Km 6, POB 2833, Mogadishu; tel (1) 81975; telex 784.
Ambassador: Hikmet Sengenc.

UNITED ARAB EMIRATES

Embassy: Via Afgoi, Km 5, Mogadishu; tel (1) 23178; telex 614.
Ambassador: Abdulhadi A. al-Khajah.

UNITED KINGDOM

Embassy: Waddada Hassan Geedi Abtow 7/8, POB 1036, Mogadishu; tel (1) 20288; telex 3617.
Ambassador: Ian McCluney.
Second Secretary: D. P. Gething.

USA

Embassy: Km 5, Afgoi Rd, POB 574, Mogadishu; tel (1) 39959; telex 789.
Ambassador: James K. Bishop.
Deputy Chief of Mission: Joseph J. Borich.
Political/Economic Section: John G. Fox.
Consular Section: Brian H. Phipps.
Administrative Section: Christopher H. Swenson.
Regional Security Officer: David A. Akerman.
Agency for International Development: Michael A. Rugh.
Public Affairs Officer: Karen Aguilar.
Office of the Defence Attaché: Col Kenneth L. Culwell.
Office of Military Co-operation: Col David A. Staley.

YEMEN

Embassy: Via Km 5, POB 493, Mogadishu.
Ambassador: Awadh Abdalla Mashbah.

YUGOSLAVIA

Embassy: Via Mecca, POB 952, Mogadishu; tel (1) 81729; telex 3778.
Ambassador: Dragoljub Kontić.

ZIMBABWE

Embassy: Mogadishu.

International Organizations

EUROPEAN COMMUNITIES

External Delegation: via Makka al-Mukarram, No Z-A6/17 (km 4), POB 943, Mogadishu; tel (1) 81118; telex 628; fax (1) 81118.
Commission Delegate: Donato Chiarini.

SOUTH AFRICA

ARGENTINA

Consulate: 26 Ameshoff St, Braamfontein 2001, Johannesburg; POB 31909, Braamfontein 2017, Johannesburg; tel (11) 339-2382; telex 428302.
Vice-Consul: G. M. Torres Carioni.
Vice-Consul (Maritime): A. E. Nicolás.

AUSTRALIA

Embassy: Mutual and Federal Centre, 4th Floor, 220 Vermeulen St, Pretoria 0002; PB X150, Pretoria 0001; tel (12) 325-4315; telex 322012; fax (12) 323-0557.

Embassy (for Parliamentary session, early January to mid June): BP Centre, 14th Floor, Thibauld Square, Cape Town 8001; POB 4749, Cape Town 8000; tel (21) 419-5425; telex 527898; fax (21) 419-7345.
Ambassador: C. E. McDonald.
Counsellor: D. C. Sprott.
Counsellor (Visas): R. B. Penkethman.
First Secretary: J. R. Monico.
Second Secretary: J. L. Madden.
Second Secretary: T. J. Yeend.
Second Secretary (Visas): D. E. Stewart.
Second Secretary (Visas): I. W. Harrop.
Third Secretary: A. Kalogeropoulos.

AUSTRIA

Embassy: Apollo Centre, 10th Floor, 405 Church St, Pretoria 0002; POB 851, Pretoria 0001; tel (12) 323-3001; telex 320541; fax (12) 322-7793.

Embassy (for Parliamentary Session, early January to mid June): Standard Bank Centre, 622 Main Tower, Hertzog Blvd, Cape Town 8001; tel (21) 216215; telex 526212; fax (21) 253489.
Ambassador: Dr A. Moebiusani.
Counsellor (Administrative/Consular): R. Leu.
First Secretary: B. Oppinger-Walchshofar.
Consul: L. Wundsam.
Honorary Consul: F. Diem.

Consulate-General: Samro House, 9th Floor, 73 Juta St, Braamfontein 2001, Johannesburg; tel (11) 403-1850; fax (11) 339-7802.
Honorary Consul-General: H. E. Krottenberger.
Honorary Consul: Dr W. Kulhanek.

Consulate: 96 Stamford Hill Rd, 1st Floor, Greyville, Durban 4001; POB 3603, Durban 4000; tel (31) 309-1339.
Honorary Consul: E. G. Wegrostek.

BELGIUM

Embassy: 275 Pomona St, Muckleneuk, Pretoria 0002; tel (12) 343-9092; telex 320508; fax (12) 443216.

Embassy (for Parliamentary Session, early January to mid June): 'Northgate', 29 Boshof Ave, Newlands, Cape Town 7700; tel (21) 617376; telex 520944.
Ambassador: E. A. J. D. Kobia.
Counsellor: Y. Hassendonck.
First Secretary: F. de Sutter.
Assistant Attaché (Administrative): P. Duyvejonck.

Consulate-General: Vogue House, 4th Floor, Thibault Sq., Cape Town 8001; POB 2717, Cape Town 8000; tel (21) 419-4690; telex 520944.
Consul-General: E. Kobia (resident in Pretoria).
Vice-Consul (Administrative): W. P. Mertens.

Consulate-General: Traduna Centre, 118 Jorissen St, Johannesburg 2001; POB 31311, Braanfontein 2017; tel (11) 403-2934; telex 424189.
Consul-General: R. D. L. Vanreusel.
Vice-Consul (Administrative): F. van der Sypt.
Vice-Consul (Administrative): A. van den Driessche.
Consular Assistant (Commercial): A. J. A. Bastenia.

Consulate: 37 Jonsson Lane, Durban 4001; POB 29, Durban 4000; tel (31) 323794; telex 9650163.
Honorary Consul: D. J. Cochrane-Murray.

Consulate: 36 Sheerness Rd, Bonnie Doon 5241, East London 5201; POB 658, East London 5200; tel (431) 55300; telex 250606.
Honorary Consul: G. J. J. A. Bodeux.

Consulate: Westhill, 3 Cuyler St, Centrahil, Port Elizabeth 6001; POB 12540, Centrahil, Port Elizabeth 6006; tel (41) 564697; telex 242655; fax (41) 564699.
Honorary Consul: J. M. L. B. Vandenschrik.

BRAZIL

Embassy: 182 Balmoral Ave, Arcadia, Pretoria 0083; POB 3269, Pretoria 0001; tel (12) 435550; telex 321364; fax (12) 342-1419.
Counsellor and Chargé d'affaires a.i.: Luiz Antonio Fachini Gomes.
Administrative Officer: Roberto Porcidônio Silva.
Administrative Officer: Cláudio S. de A. Machado.

CANADA

Embassy: 4-5th Floors, Nedbank Plaza, cnr Church and Beatrix Sts, Arcadia, Pretoria 0083; POB 26006, Arcadia, Pretoria 0007; tel (12) 287062; telex 322112; fax (12) 323-1564.

Embassy (for Parliamentary Session, early January to mid June): Reserve Bank Bldg, 16th Floor, 30 Hout St, Cape Town 8001; POB 683, Capetown 8000; tel (21) 235240; telex 527060; fax (21) 234893.
Ambassador: Ronald S. MacLean.
Minister-Counsellor and Consul: J. R. Schram.
Counsellor (Administration) and Consul: J. A. R. Brazeau.
Counsellor (Development): D. P. Viveash.
Counsellor: J. M. Massey.
Counsellor: B. E. Burton.
Second Secretary and Vice-Consul: D. Fraser.
Third Secretary: H. F. de Pagter.
Attaché (Administration) and Vice-Consul: W. C. Johnson.
Attaché: M. D. Dogterom.
Attaché: R. J. Dogterom.
Attaché: J. R. Hope.
Attaché: G. I. Monette.
Attaché: W. C. Johnson.

CHILE

Embassy: Merino Bldg, 7th Floor, cnr Bosman and Pretorius Sts, Pretoria 0002; POB 2073, Pretoria 0001; tel (12) 326-9387; telex 322567; fax (12) 325-8155.

Embassy (for Parliamentary Session, early January to mid June): 1918 Main Tower, 7th Floor, Suite 712, Standard Bank Centre, Heerengracht, Cape Town; POB 2067, Cape Town 8000; tel (21) 212344; telex 524723.
Counsellor and Consul-General: E. A. Muñoz.
Counsellor (Economic): R. Aguayo.
Military Attaché: Col S. R. Candia.
Naval Attaché: Commdr F. F. Gaete.
Air Attaché: Col R. F. Contreras.
Second Secretary: J. P. Abell.
Third Secretary and Consul: E. Macchiavello.

Consulate: 41 Eastwood Rd, Dunkeld 2196, Johannesburg 2001; POB 61931, Marshalltown 2107; tel (11) 788-9412; telex 485822.
Honorary Consul: R. Aguirre.

Consulate: 333 Smith St, Durban 4001; tel (31) 302-7911.
Honorary Consul: R. J. Barlow.

CHINA (TAIWAN)

Embassy: 1147 Schoeman St, Hatfield, Pretoria 0083; POB 649, Pretoria 0001; tel (12) 436071; telex 320748; fax (12) 435816.

Embassy (for Parliamentary Session, early January to mid June): Main Tower, 7th Floor, Standard Bank Centre, Foreshore, Cape Town 8001; POB 1122, Cape Town 8000; tel (21) 211993.
Ambassador: I-cheng Loh.
Counsellor: Liu Yang-hai.
Counsellor: Hu Tao-huang.
Counsellor (Economic): Shyu Chao-ling.
Counsellor (Press): Li Kun-kun.
First Secretary: Chang Hsu-hui.
Second Secretary: Chi Yung-sheng.
Second Secretary (Economic): Lin Shih-liang.
Second Secretary (Economic): Wang William Ping.
Second Secretary (Press): Liu Tsung-chieh.
Second Secretary (Press): Wang Huey-tarng.
Third Secretary: Su Jen-chung.
Third Secretary: Wu Shao-kai.
Third Secretary: Chou Wei-chung.
Third Secretary: Wang Wen-haw.
Consul-General: Chou Kuo-ruey.

Office of Defence Attaché: tel (12) 342-1288.
Defence Attaché: Col Chen Jia-lim.
Assistant Military Attaché: Lieut Col Kuo Tsu-an.
Assistant Naval Attaché: Commdr Chu Tsong-rong.
Assistant Air Attaché: Lieut Col Wen Ju-ping.

Cultural Office: 310 Brooks St, 0081 Menlo Park; POB 11537, 0011 Brooklyn, Pretoria; tel (12) 342-3090; fax (12) 342-3031.
Counsellor (Cultural): Dr Yeh Chian-kun.
Third Secretary (Cultural): Chen Wu Shao-fen.

Consulate-General: Safren House, 10th Floor, 19 Ameshoff St, Braamfontein 2001, Johannesburg; tel (11) 403-3281.
Consul-General: Tuan George Pei-lung.
Consul: Shih Chiao-tung.
Consul: Chi Jo-chin.
Consul: Shen Pei-hwang.

DENMARK

Embassy: Sanlam Centre, 8th Floor, cnr Andries and Pretorius Sts, Pretoria 0002; POB 2942, Pretoria 0001; tel (12) 322-0595; telex 323133; fax (12) 322-0596.

Embassy (for Parliamentary Session, early January to mid June): Southern Life Centre, 11th Floor, 8 Riebeck St, Cape Town 8001; POB 5596, Cape Town 8000; tel (21) 419-6936; telex 215398; fax (21) 419-9527.
Ambassador: Peter Brüchner.
Attaché: R. S. Haugedal.
Assistant Attaché: D. S. Mikkelsen.

Consulate: Piers Cottage, Piers Rd, 7800 Wynberg, Cape Town; POB 482, 7848 Constantia, Cape Town; tel (21) 797-1789; telex 521512; fax (21) 797-4800.
Consul: Jørgen Dahl.
Vice-Consul: Jøgen Rohleder.

Consulate-General: EAC Graphics Bldg, 19 Eastern Service Rd (Main Pretoria Rd), Eastgate Ext. 6, Sandton, Johannesburg; POB 239, Marlboro 2063, Johannesburg; tel (11) 804-3374; telex 421337; fax (11) 804-3377.
Consul-General: Niels Horn.
Vice-Consul: Ulla Plewman.
Consular Secretary and Vice-Consul: Lis Skouboe Christensen.

Consulate: 215 Loxford House, Hill St, East London 5201; POB 595, East London 5200; tel (431) 481828.
Vice-Consul: Erik Herman Andersen.

Consulate: 119 Grahamstown Rd, Deal Party Estate, Port Elizabeth 6001; POB 12214, Port Elizabeth 6006; tel (41) 432696; fax (41) 436955.
Vice-Consul: Jorgen Erik Jorgensen.

Consulate: Saambou Bldg, 399 Smith St, Durban 4001; POB 101, Durban 4000; tel (31) 3051888; telex 624250.
Consul: G. A. Thygesen.

FINLAND

Legation: 353 Berea St, Muckleneuk Hill, POB 443, Pretoria 0001; tel (12) 343-0275; telex 320715; fax (12) 343-3095.

Legation (for Parliamentary Session, early January to mid June): Southern Life Centre, 9th floor, 8 Riebeeck St, Cape Town 8001; POB 693, Cape Town 8000; tel (21) 419-3520.
Chargé d'affaires: Hannu Uusi-Videnoja.
Second Secretary: E. K. Tuomisto.

Consulate: Trust Bank Centre, Rm 1810, cnr van Riebeeck and Adderley Sts, Cape Town; POB 1911, Cape Town 8000; tel (21) 4181053; telex 527458.
Honorary Consul: Stig-Jörgen Reidar Andersen.
Honorary Vice-Consul: Jouko Tiilikainen.

FRANCE

Embassy: 807 George Ave, Arcadia, Pretoria 0083; tel (12) 435564; telex 321319.

Embassy (for Parliamentary session, early January to mid June): 1009 Main Tower, Cape Town Centre, Heerengracht, Cape Town 8001; tel (21) 212050.
Ambassador: Jacques Dupont.
Counsellor: G. M. Leroux.
First Secretary: C. Dumas-Desselas.
First Secretary: J.-Y. Roux.
First Secretary (Administrative): M. Chauvin.
Second Secretary: J. A. J. Gascuel.
Third Secretary: S. P. Frances.
Attaché (Press/Information): B. Ameil.
Attaché: M. R. Gelin.
Attaché: G. Cuenin.
Attaché: L. Zapparrata.

Trade Promotion Office: POB 1728, Pretoria 0001; tel (12) 218268; telex 320706.
Counsellor (Economic/Commercial): J.-C. Bouchet.
Attaché (Economic/Commercial): R. Schneider.

Cultural Section: 795 George Ave, Arcadia 0083, POB 29086, Sunnyside 0132, Pretoria; tel (12) 435658.
Counsellor (Cultural/Scientific): G. M. Lory.
Attaché (Cultural): G. Lamothe.

Consulate-General: Carlton Centre, 34-35th Floors, Commissioner St, Johannesburg 2001; POB 11278, Johannesburg 2000; tel (11) 331-3468.
Consul-General: A. Couanon.
Consul: J. Bouyal.
Consul (Trade): P. Abelin.

Consulate: 1003 Main Tower, Cape Town Centre, Heerengracht, Cape Town 8000; POB 1702, Cape Town 8001; tel (21) 215617.
Consul: J. Michel.

Trade Promotion Office: 203 Standard Bank Centre, Heerengracht, Foreshaw, Cape Town 8001; POB 6958, Roggebaai, Cape Town 8012; tel (21) 214396; telex 524201.

Consulate: 1022 Sangro House, 417 Smith St, Durban 4001; POB 2231, Durban 4000; tel (31) 62214.
Honorary Consul: B. A. C. Boule.

Consular Agency: 19 Currie St, POB 275, East London 5201; tel (431) 20483.
Honorary Consular Agent: J. P. F. Viaene.

Consular Agency: 17 7th Ave, Summer Strand, Port Elizabeth 6001; tel (41) 532070.
Honorary Consular Agent: N. Bensid.

GERMANY

Embassy: 180 Blackwood St, Arcadia, Pretoria 0083; POB 2023, Pretoria 0001; tel (12) 344-3854; telex 321386; fax (12) 343-9401.

Embassy (for Parliamentary Session, early January to mid June): 825 St Martini Gardens, Queen Victoria St, Cape Town 8001; POB 4273, Cape Town 8000; tel (21) 242410; telex 527799; fax (21) 249403.
Ambassador: Dr Immo Stabreit.
Counsellor: Dr W.-R. Born.
Counsellor: B. H. Borchardt.
Counsellor (Economic): Dr C. Knoop.
Counsellor (Press/Information): M. Schmunk.
First Secretary (Cultural): T. U. Hanckel.
First Secretary (Agriculture): W. Eilers.
Second Secretary: P. von Wesendonk.
Second Secretary: R. D. Preyer.
Second Secretary (Administrative): E. Baumeister.
Attaché (Cultural): B. Scmaus.
Attaché (Press/Information): F. K. Diehm.
Attaché (Administrative): R. A. Hackbarth.
Consul-General: E. G. H. Urmoneit.
Consular Attaché: R. Möcker.

Consulate-General: Community Centre of German Lutheran Church, 5th Floor, 16 Kapteijn St, Hillbrow, Johannesburg 2001; POB 4551, Johannesburg 2000; tel (11) 725-1519; telex 422381; fax (11) 725-4475.
Consul-General: Albrecht Fritzsche.
Consul: F. E. Loeser.
Vice-Consul: I. H. Böhlefeld.
Consular Agent: M. Witzel.

Consulate: 320 West St, 15th Floor, Durban 4001; POB 80, Durban 4000; tel (31) 305-5677; telex 622909; fax (31) 305-1304.
Consul: Johannes Giffels.
Vice-Consul: M. W. P. Müller.
Vice-Consul: P. A. Ernst.

Consulate: Maritime House, Uitenhage Rd, POB 2159, Port Elizabeth 6000; tel (41) 545572; telex 242381; fax (41) 573146.
Honorary Consul: J. Philip Stucken.

GREECE

Embassy: 995 Pretorius St, Arcadia, Pretoria 0002; tel (12) 437351; telex 320520; fax (12) 434313.

Embassy (for Parliamentary Session, early January to mid June): Reserve Bank Bldg, 17th Floor, 30 Hout St, Cape Town 8001; POB 3232, Cape Town 8000; tel (21) 248160.
Ambassador: Pericles Tsamoulis.
Second Secretary: N. Protonotarios.
Attaché (Consular): T. Efthymiadis.
Consul: Ioannis T. Economou.
Consular Attaché: G. Eleftheriadis.

Consulate-General: 116 Marshall St, Johannesburg 2001; POB 3845, Johannesburg 2000; tel (11) 836-7214; fax (11) 834-4431.
Consul-General: John Thomoglou.
Consular Attaché: P. Skourtis.
Consular Attaché (Administrative): C. Zaralis.
Consular Attaché (Administrative): H. Potiriadou-Filippidou.

GUATEMALA

Consulate: 2 Long St, 16th Floor, POB 1661, Cape Town 8001; tel (21) 418-2020; telex 522266; fax (21) 418-1280.
Honorary Consul: M. Serman.

Consulate: Exatrade House, 726 Stirrup Lane, Woodmead Park, Woodmead, POB 782551, Sandton 2199; tel (11) 884-4828; telex 424924; fax (11) 804-4844.
Honorary Consul: M. Rast.

HOLY SEE

Apostolic Delegation: 800 Pretorius St, Arcadia, Pretoria 0083; tel (12) 344-3815; fax (12) 344-3595.
Apostolic Delegate: Most Rev. Ambrose B. De Paoli, Titular Archbishop of Lares.
Counsellor: Rev. Mgr Peter Zurbriggen.

HUNGARY

Permanent Mission: POB 27077, Sunnyside 0132, Pretoria.
Head of Mission and Minister: L. Mohai.
Counsellor (Commercial): G Păkozdy.

ICELAND

Consulate: 15 Landsborough Rd, Robertsham, POB 82298, Southdale, Johannesburg 2135; tel (11) 433-3730; fax (11) 680-3766.
Consul: Hilmar Kristjánsson.

IRELAND

Consulate: 8-10 London House, 21 Loveday St, Johannesburg 2001; tel (11) 836-5869; fax (11) 838-1558.
Honorary Consul: Patrick Ryan.

ISRAEL

Embassy: Dashing Centre, 3rd Floor, 339 Hilda St, Hatfield, Pretoria 0083; POB 3726, Pretoria 0001; tel (12) 421-2222; fax (12) 342-1442.

Embassy (for Parliamentary Session, early January to mid June): Church Sq. House, 3rd Floor, Church Sq., cnr Spin and Plein Sts, Cape Town 8001; POB 180, Cape Town 8000; tel (21) 457201; telex 50009.
Ambassador: Z. Gov-Ari.
Counsellor: A. Granot.
Counsellor (Administrative): D. Livnat.
Counsellor (Economic/Commercial): J. Peri.
Attaché: D. Zach.
Attaché: D. Peretz.
Attaché: Y. Liepaz.

ITALY

Embassy: 796 George Ave, Arcadia, Pretoria 0083; tel (12) 435541; telex 321397; fax (12) 435547.

Embassy (for Parliamentary Session, early January to mid June): 2 Grey's Pass Gardens, Cape Town 8001; tel (21) 235157; telex 527528; fax (21) 245559.
Ambassador: Mario Piersigilli.
First Counsellor: Gian Luigi Mascia.
Second Secretary (Commercial): Alessandro Cortese.
Consul: Francesco Saverio Nisio.

Consulate-General: 3rd Floor, Aloe Grove, 196 Louis Botha Ave, Houghton Estate, Johannesburg 2001; POB 46306, Orange Grove 2119; tel (11) 728-1392; fax (11) 728-3834.
Consul-General: Paolo Massa.
Consular Attaché: G. Semenza.

Consulate: Santam Bldg, Suite 1201, 447 Smith St, Durban 4001; POB 1363, Durban 4000; tel (31) 301-4107; telex 621506; fax (31) 301-8709.
Consul: Mario Cospito.
Consular Attaché: L. C. Capellino.

Consular Agency: POB 1870, East London 5201; tel (431) 52460.
Honorary Consular Agent: M. Marchetti.

Consular Agency: 7 Morrison St, Port Elizabeth 6001; tel (41) 335037.
Honorary Consular Agent: F. S. Vandenschrik.

JAPAN

Consulate-General: 200 Standard Plaza, 440 Hilda St, Hatfield, Pretoria 0083; POB 11434, Brooklyn 0011, Pretoria; tel (12) 342-2100; telex 322134; fax (12) 433922.
Consul-General: Masatoshi Ota.
Consul: Y. Hiraishi.
Consul: Y. Murakami.
Vice-Consul: K. Naganuma.
Vice-Consul: H. Kinoshita.
Vice-Consul: A. Miki.
Vice-Consul: Y. Naito.
Assistant Consular Attaché: K. Sakai.

Consular Office: 1910 Main Tower, Cape Town Centre Heerengracht, Cape Town 8001; tel (21) 251695; fax (21) 418-2116.
Consul: Katsumi Kikkawa.
Vice-Consul: K. Kawaji.

LEBANON

Office of Lebanese Interests: c/o Embassy of France, 7-16th Ave, Lower Houghton, Johannesburg 2196; tel (11) 483-1106.
Officer: C. Abboud.

LESOTHO

Trade Mission: Indent House, 130 President St, Johannesburg 2001; POB 6643, Johannesburg 2000; tel (11) 290751; telex 482985.
Trade Representative: J. K. Mollo.
Deputy Trade Representative: O. T. Maphasa.

LIECHTENSTEIN

Office: c/o Embassy of Switzerland, 818 George Ave, Arcadia, Pretoria 0083; tel (12) 437788; telex 322106; fax (12) 342-1819.

LUXEMBOURG

Office of Luxembourg: c/o Embassy of the Netherlands, 825 Arcadia St, Arcadia, Pretoria 0083; tel (12) 344-3910; telex 321332; fax (12) 343-9550.

Consulate: 7th Floor, Heerengracht, 87 De Korte St, Braamfontein 2001, Johannesburg; POB 31558, Braamfontein 2017, Johannesburg; tel (11) 403-3852; telex 450677.
Honorary Consul: Tom Meredith.

MALAWI

Embassy: Delta Bldg, 1st Floor, 471 Monica Rd, Lynnwood 0081, Pretoria; POB 11172, Brooklyn 0011, Pretoria; tel (12) 477827; telex 322017.
Ambassador: N. T. Mizere.
Counsellor: P. S. Kachipande.
First Secretary: T. J. Mwaya.
Second Secretary (Administrative): S. Kasonda.
Third Secretary: N. Kangulu.
Third Secretary: E. Mhlanga.
Third Secretary (Consular): J. E. Chikaonda.
Third Secretary (Administrative): R. A. Dawa.

Consulate-General: 41 De Korte St, Sable House, Braamfontein 2001, Johannesburg; POB 31752, Braamfontein 2017, Johannesburg; tel (11) 339-1569; telex 424007.
Consul-General: K. E. J. Nsanja.
Deputy Consul-General: R. H. Kalitera.
Consul: S. H. Ng'oma.
Consular Attaché (Immigration): R. G. Matiya.

MOZAMBIQUE

Trade Office: Glencain Bldg, 2nd Floor, 73 Market St, Johannesburg 2001; POB 4635, Johannesburg 2000; tel (11) 234907; telex 484842.
Trade Representative: E. S. Nhavoto.

NETHERLANDS

Embassy: 825 Arcadia St, Arcadia, Pretoria 0083; POB 117, Pretoria 0001; tel (12) 437738; telex 321332; fax (12) 349950.

Embassy (for Parliamentary Session, early January to mid June): 100 Strand St, Cape Town 8001; POB 346, Cape Town 8000; tel (21) 215660; telex 527053; fax (21) 418-2690.
Ambassador: P. A. van Buuren.
Counsellor: H. H. M. Sondaal.
First Secretary and Consul: R. H. Cohen.
First Secretary (Consular): G. J. C. Schulten.
Second Secretary: P. Mollema.
Second Secretary (Social): J. P. M. Peters.
Attaché (Administrative): A. L. van Zijp.
Assistant Attaché (Administrative): J. C. de Bie.
Assistant Attaché (Administrative): K. Marks.
Vice-Consul: W. G. F. M. Veling.

Consulate: 65 Victoria Embankment, 2nd Floor, Durban 4001; POB 1507, Durban 4000; tel (31) 304-1770.
Honorary Consul: W. Valstar.

Consulate: 79 Harewood Drive, East London 5201; POB 8001, East London 5210; tel (431) 352130.
Honorary Vice-Consul: F. B. Staal.

Consulate: Norwich Life Centre, 6th Floor, Market Sq., Port Elizabeth 6001; POB 1396, Port Elizabeth 6000; tel (41) 5624222; telex 243131.
Honorary Consul: H. H. Huijskamp.

NORWAY

Consulate-General: Southern Life Centre, 17th Floor, 8 Riebeeck St, Cape Town 8001; POB 5620, Cape Town 8000; tel (21) 251687; telex 527678; fax (21) 419-3568.
Consul-General: R. O. Berg.
Vice-Consul: A. L. Norhelm.
Vice-Consul (Administrative): A. Thalmann.

Consulate: 75 Winder St, 8th Floor, Cato Creek, Durban 4001; POB 5752, Durban 4000; tel (31) 325611; telex 621002; fax (31) 372986.
Honorary Consul: C. E. Moore.

PAPAU NEW GUINEA

Embassy: c/o Embassy of Australia, Mutual and Federal Centre, 4th Floor, 220 Vermeulen St, Pretoria 0002; tel (12) 325-4315; telex 322102; fax (12) 323-0557.

PARAGUAY

Embassy: 189 Strelizia Rd, Waterkloof Heights, Pretoria 0181; POB 3646, Pretoria 0001; tel (12) 451081; fax (12) 451083.
Ambassador: Raul Dos Santos.
Armed Forces Attaché: Col Sindulfo Fernando Ruiz Ramírez.
Officer: Carlos A. Martínez.

PERU

Embassy: c/o Embassy of Brazil, 182 Balmoral Ave, Arcadia, Pretoria 0083; tel (12) 435559; telex 321364.

POLAND

Interests Office: Pretoria.
Counsellor (Commercial): W. Tomaszewski.
First Secretary: W. Cibor.

PORTUGAL

Embassy: 599 Leyds St, Muckleneuk, Pretoria 0002; tel (12) 341-2340; telex 321365.

Embassy (for Parliamentary Session, early January to mid June): 551 Main Tower, Standard Bank Centre, Heerengracht, Cape Town 8001; POB 314, Cape Town 8000; tel (21) 214560; telex 527461.
Ambassador: J. P. Cutileiro.
Counsellor: A. Chambers de Antas de Campos.
Counsellor (Technology/Energy): J. M. Martins Soares.
Second Secretary: Dr J. A. da Camara.

Consular Section: 701 van Ekron Bldg, 217 Pretorius St, Pretoria 0002; tel (12) 323-5554.
Attaché (Consular/Migration): M. A. M. da Silva.

Commercial Section and Office of Defence Attaché: 410 Unidia, 745 Arcadia St, Arcadia, Pretoria 0083; tel (12) 344-2115.
Counsellor (Commercial): I. S. A. Cordeiro.
Attaché (Commercial): J. M. Salvado Moreira.

Consulate-General: 417 Monex House, Strand St, Cape Town 8001; POB 3433, Cape Town 8000; tel (21) 241454.
Consul-General: Dr F. A. Ruivo Guterres.
Vice-Consul: L. V. Pinto.

Consulate-General: Diamond Corner Bldg, 3rd Floor, 68 Eloff St, Johannesburg 2001; POB 5092, Johannesburg 2000; tel (11) 293826.

Consulate: 320 West St, 16th Floor, Durban 4001; POB 315, Durban 4000; tel (31) 305-7511.
Consul: Dr M. da Silva Pracana Martins.

Consulate: 164 Commercial Rd, Port Elizabeth 6001; tel (41) 431440.
Honorary Consul: J. Vieira.

ROMANIA

Consular and Trade Office (temporary): c/o Trade & Industry, Momentum Life Bldg, PB X84, Pretoria 0001; tel (12) 310-9320.
Consul (Trade): B. Ghinea.

SPAIN

Embassy: 169 Pine St, Arcadia, Pretoria 0083; POB 1633, Pretoria 0001; tel (12) 344-3875; telex 320705; fax (12) 343-4891.

Embassy (for Parliamentary Session, early January to mid June): 37 Shortmarket St, Cape Town 8001; tel (21) 222415; telex 5221049; fax (21) 222328.

Ambassador: Alvaro de Castilla.
Counsellor: Rodrigo Aguirre de Carcer.
Counsellor (Commercial): Sara Alcaide.
Attaché (Administration): Pedro A. Ruiz.

Consulate-General: Southern Life Centre, 2 St George's St, Cape Town 8001; tel (21) 251468; telex 522459.
Consul-General: Alfonso Muñoz-Seca.

SURINAME

Consular Section: c/o Embassy of the Netherlands, 825 Arcadia St, Arcadia, Pretoria 0083; tel (12) 344-3910; telex 321332; fax (12) 343-9950.

SWAZILAND

Trade Mission: 915 Rand Central Bldg, 165 Jeppe St, Johannesburg 2001; POB 8030, Johannesburg 2000; tel (11) 299776; fax (11) 299763.
Trade Representative: B. S. Malinga.
Deputy Trade Representative: P. J. Dlamini.
Assistant Trade Representative: S. F. Dlamini.
Assistant Trade Representative: A. M. Dlamini.

SWEDEN

Legation: Old Mutual Centre, 9th Floor, 167 Andries St, Pretoria 0002; POB 1664, Pretoria 0001; tel (12) 211050; telex 321193; fax (12) 323-2776.

Legation (for Parliamentary Session, early January to mid June): Southern Life Centre, 10th & 17th Floors, 8 Riebeeck St, Cape Town 8001; POB 3982, Cape Town 8000; tel (21) 253988; telex 527434; fax (21) 251016.
Envoy Extraordinary and Minister Plenipotentiary: E. Ingemar Stjernberg.
Counsellor: N. Anders Möllander.
First Secretary: Robert H. Rydberg.
Second Secretary: I. Christina Hoffman de Vylder.
Administrative Assistant: Michaela Wilhelmsson.
Consul-General: Rolf Olav Berg.
Vice-Consul: Aud Lise Norheim.

Consulate: 75 Winder St, 8th Floor, Cato Creek, Durban 4001; POB 5752, Durban 4000; tel (31) 325611; telex 621002; fax (31) 372986.
Consul: Cecil Elliott Moore.

SWITZERLAND

Embassy: 818 George Ave, Arcadia, Pretoria 0083; POB 2289, Pretoria 0001; tel (12) 437788; telex 322106; fax (12) 342-1819.

Embassy (for Parliamentary Session, early January to mid June): NBS Waldorf, 9th Floor, 80 St George's Mall, Cape Town 8001; POB 1546, Cape Town 8000; tel (21) 261201; telex 520063; fax (21) 249344.
Ambassador: Blaise Schenk.
First Secretary: Max Schweizer.
Attaché and Head of Chancery: Monica Camacho-Bandlin.
Consul: Jean Saxod.
Vice-Consul and Chancellor: Barbara Hetzel.

Consulate-General: Swiss House, 86 Main St, cnr Main and Simmonds Sts, Marshalltown, Johannesburg 2001; POB 61230, Marshalltown, Johannesburg 2107; tel (11) 838-5102; telex 489531; fax (11) 838-2648.
Consul-General: Alphons Frey.
Consul: Jörg Feigenwinter.
Vice-Consul and Chancellor: Dirk Meierhofer.

UNITED KINGDOM

Embassy: 'Greystoke', 255 Hill St, Arcadia, Pretoria 0002; tel (12) 433121; telex 320687; fax (12) 433207.

Embassy (for Parliamentary session, early January to mid June): 91 Parliament St, Cape Town 8001; tel (21) 461-7220; telex 527301; fax (21) 461-0017.
Ambassador: Anthony Reeve.
Counsellor and Deputy Head of Mission: J. Poston.
Counsellor: A. A. Rowell.
First Secretary: G. D. Adams.
First Secretary (Chancery): P. Haggie.
First Secretary: R. J. Sawers.
First Secretary (Management): A. E. Gay.
Second Secretary (Chancery): C. B. Farr.
Second Secretary: P. G. Sharp.
Second Secretary (Works): D. J. Evans.
Second Secretary (Information/Aid): D. A. Slinn.
Second Secretary: A. M. Giles.

Consulate: Southern Life Centre, 12th Floor, 8 Riebeeck St, Cape Town 8001; POB 500, Cape Town 8000; tel (21) 253670; telex 527447; fax (21) 251427.
Consul: D. L. S. Coombe.
Vice-Consul (Political/Information): I. K. Morrison.
Vice-Consul (Management): J. A. Dyson.

Commercial Section: POB 1346, Cape Town 8000; tel (21) 217741.
Vice-Consul (Commercial): E. J. McEvoy.

Consulate-General: 19th Floor, Sanlam Centre, cnr Jeppe and von Wielligh Sts, Johannesburg; tel (11) 337-8940; telex 487115; fax (11) 337-7470.
Consul-General and Director of Trade Promotion: J. F. Doble.
Deputy Consul-General: N. A. Ling.
Consul (Commercial): P. J. Bacon.
Consul: M. D. Shipster.
Vice-Consul (Political/Aid): C. D. Wright.
Vice-Consul (Management): A. K. Bubbear.

British Council Office: 76 Juta St, 8th Floor, Braamfontein, POB 30637, Johannesburg; tel (11) 339-3715; telex 426428.
Cultural Attaché (British Council Director): W. L. Radford.

Consulate: c/o Messrs Coopers & Lybrand, First National Bank Bldg, 7th Floor, Union St, East London 5201; tel (431) 25521; telex 250920.
Honorary Consul: J. L. Fletcher.

Consulate: Room 615, Allied Bldg, Main St, POB 213, Port Elizabeth 6001, Cape Province; tel (41) 22423; telex 242326.
Honorary Consul: G. P. Knowles.

Consulate: Fedlife House, 10th Floor, 320 Smith St, POB 1404, Durban 4001; tel (31) 305-2920; telex 622428; fax (31) 307-4661.
Consul: J. Waterton.
Vice-Consul: M. C. Orr.
Vice-Consul (Commercial): D. R. Sparrow.

USA

Embassy: Thibault House, 6th Floor, 225 Pretorius St, Pretoria 0002; tel (12) 284266; telex 322143; fax (12) 219278.
Ambassador: William Lacy Swing.
Deputy Head of Mission: Marshall F. McCallie.
Counsellor (Political): William M. Bellamy.
Counsellor (Economic): Don K. Steinberg.
Consular Section: Julie A. Davidson.
Administrative Counsellor: William J. Hudson.
Regional Security Officer: Michael W. Beckner.
Public Affairs Counsellor (USIS): Kent Obee.
Communications Programme Officer: Robert L. Bright.
Information Systems Manager: Larry D. Huffman.
Counsellor (Agency for International Development): Dennis P. Barrett.
Defence Attaché: Col Michael M. Ferguson.
Agricultural Section: James M. Benson.

Consulate-General: Kine Centre, 11th Floor, Commissioner and Kruis Sts, POB 2155, Johannesburg 2001; tel (11) 331-1681; telex 483780; fax (11) 331-1327.
Consul-General: John L. Hirsch.
Political Section: Ronald A. Trigg.
Economic Section: Thomas Dougherty.
Administrative Section: Thomas P. Trivisani.
Commercial Section: L. Richard Jackson.
Consular Section: Karl I. Danga.
Branch Public Affairs Officer: Emi Yamauchi.
Minerals Officer: Ruth Miles-Henderson.
Communications Programme Officer: Donald W. Goff.
Information Systems Manager: Donald W. Newman.
Labour Officer: John R. Dinger.

Consulate-General: Broadway Industries Centre, Heerengracht, Foreshore, Cape Town 8001; tel (21) 214280; telex 522387; fax (21) 254151.
Consul-General: David Halsted.
Political/Economic Section: Patricia D. Hughes.
Economic Section: Michele Vautrain.
Administrative Section: Barbara Sand.
Consular Section: Melinda Brian.
Branch Public Affairs Officer: Kyra Iberle.
Communications Programme Officer: Jon J. Martino.

Consulate-General: Durban Bay House, 29th Floor, 333 Smith St, Durban 4001; tel (31) 304-4737; fax (31) 301-8206.
Consul-General: Bismarck Myrick.
Consul: Lisa Peterson.
Branch Public Affairs Officer (USIS): John S. Dickson.
Communications Programme Officer: Henry E. Hiker.

URUGUAY

Embassy: Vogue House, 8th Floor, Thibault Square, Cape Town 8001; POB 4774, Cape Town 8000; tel (21) 251847; telex 524176.
Consul-General and Chargé d'affaires a.i.: Joaquin Piriz.

Consulate: 7A Sunny Brae Drive, Westville North 3630, Durban; tel (31) 825706.
Honorary Consul: F. J. Novoa.

Consulate: Johannesburg 2001.

International Organizations

INTERNATIONAL COMMITTEE OF THE RED CROSS

Delegation: 794 Church St, Pretoria 0002; POB 29001, Sunnyside 0132, Pretoria; tel (12) 437335; telex 320680.
Head of Delegation: A. Pfanner.
Deputy Head of Delegation: F. Biancardi.
Delegate: B. Troyon.
Delegate: E. Zumstein.
Delegate: S. A. Fischbach.
Delegate (Eastern Transvaal): D. Fink.
Delegate (Eastern Transvaal): M. Henzelin.
Delegate (Eastern Transvaal): A. S. Lundberg.

SPAIN

ALGERIA

Embassy: General Oráa 12, 28006 Madrid; tel (1) 4116065; telex 41497.
Ambassador: Mohamed Aberkane.

ANGOLA

Embassy: Serrano 64, 3°, 28010 Madrid; tel (1) 4356166; telex 47171.
Ambassador: Kamu de Almeida.

ARGENTINA

Embassy: Paseo de la Castellana 53, 28046 Madrid; tel (1) 4424500; telex 27415; fax (1) 4423559.
Ambassador: José Roberto Dromi (designate).

AUSTRALIA

Embassy: Paseo de la Castellana 143, 2°, Edif. Cuzco 1, 28046 Madrid; tel (1) 2798504; telex 27817; fax (1) 2709026.
Ambassador: Charles Mott.

AUSTRIA

Embassy: Paseo de la Castellana 91, 9°A, 28046 Madrid 16; tel (1) 5565504; telex 22694; fax (1) 5973579.
Ambassador: Michael Fitz.
Counsellor (Commercial): Christian Berlakovits.
Second Secretary: Andreas Melan.
Secretary (Economic): Rudolf Layer.
Attaché (Economic): Karin Franz.

Consulate-General: Calle Mallorca 286, 08037 Barcelona 25; tel (3) 2573614; telex 98322.
Honorary Consul-General: Pedro Jacinto Soler.

Consulate: Avda Zugazarte 37, Las Arenas-Bilbao; tel (4) 4640763; telex 33043.
Honorary Consul: Hermann Diez del Sel Korsatko.

Consulate: Casa INTI, Calle Occidente s/n, Benalmadena Costa, Málaga; tel (52) 441281; telex 79211.
Honorary Consul: Walter Esten.

Consulate: Marqués de Paradas 26, 41001 Sevilla; tel (54) 222162.
Honorary Consul: José Rivas Mulero.

Consulate: Calle Francisco Cubells 43, 46011 Valencia 11; tel (6) 3671658; telex 64562; fax (6) 3670185.
Honorary Consul: Günther Richetti.
Honorary Consul: José H. Garrigos Senchermes.

Consulate: Plaza Olivar 7/2/d, Palma de Mallorca; tel (71) 713949; telex 68826; fax (71) 718872.
Honorary Consul: Miguel Oria Martin.

BELGIUM

Embassy: Paseo de la Castellana 18, 6°, 28046 Madrid; tel (1) 5776300; telex 23715; fax (1) 4318166.
Ambassador: Charles Winterbeeck.

BOLIVIA

Embassy: Paseo de la Castellana 179, 28046 Madrid; tel (1) 2709858; telex 45286; fax (1) 2708393.
Ambassador: Raúl Garafulic Gutiérrez.

BRAZIL

Embassy: Fernando el Santo 6, 28010 Madrid; tel (1) 3080459; telex 23291.
Ambassador: Lindolfo Leopoldo Collor.

BULGARIA

Embassy: Santa María Magdalena 15, 28016 Madrid; tel (1) 4576651; telex 22407.
Ambassador: Ivan Nedev.

CAMEROON

Embassy: Rosario Pino 3, 28020 Madrid; tel (1) 5711160; telex 27772.
Ambassador: André Ngongang Ouandji.

CANADA

Embassy: Núñez de Balboa 35, Edif. Goya, Apdo 587, 28001 Madrid; tel (1) 4314300; telex 27347; fax (1) 4312367.
Ambassador: Julie Loranger.
Minister-Counsellor and Consul: L. S. Clark.
Forces Attaché: Col J. E. Houghton.
First Secretary and Consul: E. Del Buey.
Second Secretary (Administrative) and Vice-Consul: S. I. R. Munro.

Commercial Office: Apdo 117, 28080 Madrid.
Counsellor (Commercial) and Consul: T. G. Cullen (resident in Barcelona).
Counsellor (Commercial): R. B. Noble.

Immigration Office: Apdo 207, 28080 Madrid.
First Secretary (Immigration): K. C. Hosley.

Consulate: Via Augusta 125, Atico 3A, Barcelona; tel (3) 2090634.
Honorary Consul: P. S. Baugh.

Consulate: Edif. Horizonte, Plaza de la Malagueta 3, Apdo 99, 29016 Málaga; tel (52) 223346; telex 73305.
Honorary Consul: J. Schwarzmann.

Consulate: Avda de la Constitución 30, 2°, 41001 Sevilla; tel (54) 229413.
Honorary Consul: J. Garcia Hidalgo.

CHILE

Embassy: Lagasca 88, 6°, 28001 Madrid; tel (1) 4319160; telex 43816.
Ambassador: Juan Gabriel Valdés.

CHINA, PEOPLE'S REPUBLIC

Embassy: Arturo Soria 113, 28027 Madrid; tel (1) 5194242; telex 22808.
Ambassador: Yuan Tao.

COLOMBIA

Embassy: General Martínez Campos 48, 28010 Madrid; tel (1) 4103800; telex 23959.
Ambassador: William Jaramillo Gómez.

COSTA RICA

Embassy: Paseo de la Castellana 166, 5°, 28046 Madrid; tel (1) 4468771; telex 49299.
Ambassador: Antonio López Escarré.

COTE D'IVOIRE

Embassy: Serrano 154, 28006 Madrid; tel (1) 2611607; telex 45971.
Ambassador: Pierre Angoran.

CUBA

Embassy: Paseo de la Habana 194, 28036 Madrid; tel (1) 4582500; telex 23858.
Ambassador: Juan Luis Méndez Morejón.

CYPRUS

Consulate: Alfonso X 3, 28010 Madrid; tel (1) 4100862; telex 42177; fax (1) 4192047.
Honorary Consul: Ignacio Gil Antunano.

CZECHOSLOVAKIA

Embassy: Pinar 20, 28006 Madrid; tel (1) 4111621; telex 22466; fax (1) 5636467.
Ambassador: Pavlína Řezníčková.
Counsellor: Jaromír Mašek.
Military and Air Attaché: Štěpán Krištof.
First Secretary and Attaché (Press and Information): Pavel Micaj.
First Secretary (Culture): Jana Novotná.
First Secretary: Libor Sečka.

Consulate: Pinar 20, 28006 Madrid; tel (1) 4111787; telex 22466; fax (1) 5636467.
Consul: Vladimír Urban.

DENMARK

Embassy: Claudio Coello 91, 4°, 28006 Madrid; tel (1) 4318445; telex 27265; fax (1) 4319168.
Ambassador: Thomas Rechnagel.
Counsellor: Jette Selsø.
Counsellor (Commercial): Jean Christensen.
Counsellor (Agriculture/Government): Birgitte Møller Christensen.
Secretary and Vice-Consul: Birte Secher.
Export Assistant: Christian A. Blikenberg.
Export Assistant: Jørn Mårtensson.

Consulate-General: Carrer de Comte d'Urgell 240, 8°B, 08036 Barcelona; tel (3) 4190428; fax (3) 4190675.
Consul-General and Counsellor (Commercial): Gunner Larsen.
Consul: Hanne Pape.

Consulate: General Peron 38, 17°, 28020 Madrid; tel (1) 5973443; telex 27318; fax (1) 4563673.
Consul: Peter Hertz.

Consulate: Paseo de la Conferencia 11, 17°, Apdo 166, Algeciras; tel (56) 603666; telex 78010; fax (56) 600580.
Consul: Antonio Ruiz Valderrama.

Consulate: Plaza Calvo Sotelo 3, 7°C, 03001 Alicante; tel (6) 5207938; fax (6) 5207983.
Consul: Alejandro Olsen Senante.

Consulate: Muralla del Mar 11, 1° A, Apdo 14, 30202 Cartagena; tel (68) 507000; telex 68105; fax (68) 508969.
Consul: Carlos Augusto Siljeström Schjetlein.

Consulate: Alvarez de Castro 34, 04002 Almería; tel (51) 236724; telex 78826; fax (51) 263714.
Consul: Francisco Pérez Briones.

Consulate: Calle Elcano 24, 48008 Bilbao; tel (4) 4438199; telex 31072.
Consul: Per Erik Lindegaard.

Consulate: Almameda de Apodaca 21, Apdo 105, 11004 Cadiz; tel (56) 221364; telex 76033; fax (56) 225201.
Consul: Joaquin Ramos Diaz.

Consulate: Linares Rivas 18, 2° Dch, 15005 La Coruña; tel (81) 222824; telex 82174; fax (81) 222263.
Consul: Henry H. A. Guyatt.

Consulate: Avda Reina Mercedes 25, 1°B, 41012 Sevilla; tel (5) 4611489; telex 72310.
Consul: Cristina Siljeström.

Consulate: Calle Blasco de Garay, 706°C, 29001 Málaga; tel (52) 226373; fax (52) 225816.
Vice-Consul: Knud Kirstein.

Consulate: Cirilo Amorós 68, 46004 Valencia; tel (6) 3513606; fax (6) 3519116.
Consul: Santiago Juliá.

Consulate: Plaza de Compostela 24, Apto 1505, 36201 Vigo; tel (86) 431092; telex 83184; fax (86) 438899.
Consul: Braulio Román Veiga.

Consulate: Calle Albareda 48, 35008 Las Palmas; tel (28) 264764; telex 95014; fax (28) 267728.
Consul and Secretary: Henning Nielsen.

Consulate: Paseo de Pereda 36, Apdo 141, 39004 Santander; tel (42) 212671; telex 35840; fax (42) 215963.
Consul: Matías Mowinckel von Tangen.

Consulate: Calle Santo Domingo de la Calzada sin, Apto 254, 21080 Huelva; tel (55) 253577; telex 75504.
Vice-Consul: Edmundo Cereceda Gonzalez.

Consulate: Calle de San Francisco 46, 8°, Apto de Correos 17, Ferrol; tel (81) 352102; telex 85512; fax (81) 357983.
Vice-Consul: Carlos Gonzalo Antón Miranda.

Consulate: Pages Oritz 94, 17230 Palamós (Gerona); tel (72) 314400; fax (72) 315450.
Vice-Consul: Andrés Ribera Serra.

Consulate: Calle Apodaca 32, 43004 Tarragona; tel (77) 234105; fax (77) 238095.
Vice-Consul: Juan-Manuel Romeu Sanroma.

Consulate: Manuel Maria Gonzalez 12, 11403 Jerez de la Frontera; tel (56) 340000; fax (56) 332089.
Vice-Consul: Mauricio González-Gordon Diez.

DOMINICAN REPUBLIC

Embassy: Paseo de la Castellana 30, 28046 Madrid; tel (1) 4315395.
Ambassador: Dr Rafael Gautreau.

ECUADOR

Embassy: Príncipe de Vergara 73, 7°, 28006 Madrid; tel (1) 2627215; telex 42038; fax (1) 2613067.
Ambassador: Alfredo Valdivieso Gangotena.

EGYPT

Embassy: Velázquez 69, 28006 Madrid; tel (1) 5776308; telex 42389.
Ambassador: Mohamed Alaa el-Din Barakat.

EL SALVADOR

Embassy: Serrano 114, 28006 Madrid; tel (1) 2628002; telex 23137.
Ambassador: Ernesto Trigueros Alcaine.

EQUATORIAL GUINEA

Embassy: Claudio Coello 91, 5A, Madrid; tel (1) 5772805.
Ambassador: Eduardo Ndong Elo Nzang.

FINLAND

Embassy: Paseo de la Castellana 15, 4°, 28046 Madrid; tel (1) 3196172; telex 22007; fax (1) 3083901.
Ambassador: Eeva-Kristiina Forsman.
Counsellor (Commercial): Hannu Vainio.
Attaché (Science): Juha Koski.

Consulate: Avda Diagonal 613, 8° planta A y B, 08028 Barcelona; tel (3) 4197700; fax (3) 4195136.
Consul: Armi Venermo.
Vice-Consul and Secretary (Commercial): Hannu Seppälä.

Consulate: Calle Blasco de Garay 7, 5°D, 29001 Málaga; tel (52) 212423; telex 79061; fax (52) 212423.
Consul: Ritva Parmi.

Consulate: Alvarez de Castro 34, 1°, 04002 Almeria; tel (51) 243044; telex 78826; fax (51) 234906.
Consul: Alfredo Esteller Rodríguez.

Consulate: Vikingos 4, Benidorm; tel (65) 853599.
Consul: Folke Nyström.

Consulate: San Vincente 8, Edif. 'Albia', 2°, 48001 Bilbao; Apdo 520, 48080 Bilbao; tel (4) 4239036; telex 32734; fax (4) 4236736.
Consul: José María Candida Ezcurdia.

Consulate: Alameda de Apodaca 21, 11004 Cadiz; tel (56) 221364; telex 76033.
Consul: Joaquín Ramos Díaz.

Consulate: Muralla del Mar 11, entlo 30202 Cartagena; tel (68) 507000; telex 68015; fax (68) 68015.
Consul: Carlos Augusto Siljeström Schjetlein.

Consulate: Alvarez Garaya 2, 33206 Gijon; tel (85) 359735.
Consul: Mariano Costales Gomez-Olea.

Consulate: Avda Martín Alonso Finzón 18, 2°, 21003 Huelva; tel (55) 249583; telex 75519.
Consul: Felipe Martinez de Acuña.

Consulate: Sorgintxuli 244, Puerto de Pasajes, 20100 Renteria; tel (43) 512600; telex 36284.
Consul: Ignacio Vega de Seoane Etayo.

Consulate: Paseo de Pereda 35, 39004 Santander; tel (42) 224154; telex 35843.
Consul: Fernando María de Pereda Aparício.

Consulate: Adriano 45, 2°B, 41001 Sevilla; tel (54) 614149; telex 72188; fax (54) 626004.
Consul: Roberto Echevarria Reyes.

Consulate: La Unión 23-1°-2A, 43001 Tarragona; tel (77) 233304; telex 56496.
Consul: Fernando Boada Aragones.

Consulate: De la Paz 27, 46003 Valencia; tel (6) 3320188; telex 62592; fax (6) 3315305.
Consul: Luis Monzó Fletcher.

Consulate: Plaza de Compostela, 14-bajo, 36201 Vigo; tel (86) 222336; telex 83156.
Vice-Consul: Salvador Barreras Masso.

FRANCE

Embassy: Salustiano Olózaga 9, 28001 Madrid; tel (1) 4355560; telex 27798; fax (1) 4356655.
Ambassador: Henri Benoît de Coignac.

Consulate-General: Paseo de la Castellana 79, Edif. UAP, 28046 Madrid; tel (1) 5973267; fax (1) 5972436.

Consulate-General: Paseo de Gracia 11, 08007 Barcelona; tel (3) 3178150.

Consulate-General: 26 Calle Iparraguirre, 48011 Bilbao; tel (4) 4249000.

Consulate-General: 48 Calle Cirilp Amoros, Apdo 745, 46004 Valencia; tel (6) 3524125.

Consulate-General: 1 Plaza de Santa Cruz, 41004 Sevilla; tel (54) 2228967.

Consulate: 27 Calle Virgen del Socorro, 03002 Alicante; tel (65) 264523.

GABON

Embassy: Orense 70, 28020 Madrid 16; tel (1) 2799740; telex 27437.
Ambassador: Jacques Mombo.

GERMANY

Embassy: Fortuny 8, 28010 Madrid; tel (1) 3199100; telex 27768; fax (1) 4105838.
Ambassador: Guido Brunner.

Consulate-General: Paseo de Gracia 111, 08008 Barcelona; Apdo 389, 08080 Barcelona; tel (3) 4153996; telex 54768; fax (3) 4154856.
Consul-General: Dr Karl Friedrich Gansäuer.

Consulate-General: Calle Gobela 1, 1°, Apdo 198, 48930 Las Arenas; tel (4) 4641877; telex 31391.
Consul-General: Walter Wellhausen.

Consulate-General: Avda de Ramón de Carranza 22, 2°, 41011 Sevilla; Apdo 855, 41080 Sevilla; tel (5) 4457811; telex 72446; fax (5) 4282563.
Consul-General: Nikolaus Merten.

Consulate-General: Paseo del Limonar 26, Villa Ibis, 29016 Málaga; tel (52) 227866; telex 77766; fax (52) 309700.
Honorary Consul-General: Hans Hoffmann.

Consulate: Plaza Calvo Sotelo 1-2, 5°, 03001 Alicante; Apdo 486, 03080 Alicante; tel (65) 217060.
Honorary Consul: Dieter Fahnebrock.

Consulate: Centro Comercial Satelites Park HSP, Carretera de Málaga s/n, 04720 Aguadulce; tel (51) 340555; telex 78945; fax (51) 341813.
Honorary Consul: Joachim Prinzen.

Consulate: Calle Gerona 20-22, 4°a, Apdo 31, 17600 Figueras; tel (72) 505954.
Honorary Consul: Hans-Jochem Heinert.

Consulate: Carrer d'Antoni Jaume, 2-2°-9a, Apdo 437, 07800 Ibiza; tel (71) 315763.
Honorary Consul: Ekkehardt Boxberger.

Consulate: Hnos. Sandemann & Cia, Pizarro 10, 11402 Jerez de la Frontera; tel (56) 301100; fax (56) 300007.
Honorary Consul: Jürgen Mundt.

Consulate: Calle Andreu 32, 07703 Mahon, Menorca; tel (71) 361668.
Honorary Consul: Matthias Roters.

Consulate: Avda de Bilbao 39, Apdo 27, 39600 Muriedas; tel (42) 250543.
Honorary Consul: Hans Roever, Jr.

Consulate: Calle Fuenterrabia 15, 3° Izqda, 20003 San Sebastian; tel (43) 421010.
Honorary Consul: Paul Schröder.

Consulate: Calle Lluis Companys 14, 1°, 3a, 43005 Tarragona; tel (77) 230253; telex 56416.
Honorary Consul: Erich Büchen.

Consulate: Avda Primado Reig 70, 10°, 40a, 46010 Valencia; Apdo 67, 46090 Valencia; tel (6) 3614354; telex 62790.
Honorary Consul: Wolfgang Buch.

Consulate: Avda Garcia Barbón 1, Apdo 95, 36201 Vigo; tel (86) 437879; telex 83068; fax (86) 434943.
Honorary Consul: Hans Esser.

GREECE

Embassy: Serrano 110, 28006 Madrid; tel (1) 5644653; telex 44135.
Ambassador: Diamantis A. Vacalopoulos.

GUATEMALA

Embassy: Rafael Salgado 3, 4° Izqda, 28036 Madrid; tel (1) 4577827; telex 48618.
Ambassador: Juan José Dardón Castillo.

HAITI

Embassy: General Martínez Campos 33, 28010 Madrid; tel (1) 3082085.
Ambassador: Lafontaine Saint Louis.

HOLY SEE

Apostolic Nunciature: Avda de Pío XII 46, 28016 Madrid; tel (1) 7668311; telex 47768; fax (1) 7667085.
Apostolic Nuncio: Most Rev. Mario Tagliaferri, Titular Archbishop of Formia.
Secretary: Mgr Bruno Musarò.
Secretary: Mgr Arturo Morelli.

HONDURAS

Embassy: Rosario Pino 6, 4°A, 28020 Madrid; tel (1) 2790251; telex 44136; fax (1) 2797589.
Ambassador: René Arturo Bendaña Valenzuela.

HUNGARY

Embassy: Angel de Diego Roldán 21, 28016 Madrid; tel (1) 4137011; telex 22683.
Ambassador: Attilla Gecse.

ICELAND

Consulate-General: Eurobldg, Of. 15, Juan Ramón Jiménez 8, 28036 Madrid; tel (1) 4578984; telex 46208; fax (1) 2507883.
Consul-General: José Maria Figueras-Dotti.

Consulate-General: Cerdena 229-237, Sobreatico Tercera, 08013 Barcelona; tel (3) 2325810; fax (3) 2312807.
Consul-General: Jose Daurella.
Consul: Luis Balaguer de Palleja.

Consulate: Casa Las Flores, local 13, Avda Mediterranée 2/n, Benidorm; tel (65) 850863; telex 66332.
Consul: Juan José Campus Blanquer.

Consulate: San Vicente 6, Apdo 250, Bilbao; tel (4) 4230679; telex 31249.
Consul: Francisco Sainz Trueba.

Consulate: Paseo Maritimo 25, Málaga; tel (52) 221739; fax (52) 477265.
Consul: Marin Guõrún Briand de Crèvecoeur.

Consulate: Valencia; tel (6) 3517275.
Consul: Luis Miralles Ferrer.

INDIA

Embassy: Avda Pío XII 30-32, 28016 Madrid; tel (1) 4570209; telex 22605; fax (1) 4677996.
Ambassador: Manorama Bhalla.

INDONESIA

Embassy: Agastia 65, 28043 Madrid; tel (1) 4130394; telex 43822.
Ambassador: Mr Utomo.

IRAN

Embassy: Jerez 5, Villa El Altozano (Chamartín), 28016 Madrid; tel (1) 4570112; telex 22322.
Ambassador: Abdullah Zifan.

IRAQ

Embassy: Avda Dr Arce 13, 28002 Madrid; tel (1) 4116417; telex 23806; fax (1) 4116458.

IRELAND

Embassy: Claudio Coello 73, 1°, 28001 Madrid; tel (1) 5763500; telex 23985; fax (1) 4351677.
Ambassador: Patrick Walshe.
First Secretary: Ken Thompson.
Secretary: Aingeal O'Donoghue.

Consulate-General: Torre Oeste, Gran Via Carlos III 94, 10-1A2A, Barcelona 14; tel (3) 3309652; telex 52220.
Honorary Consul-General: José M. Cucurella.

Consulate: Galerias Santa Monica, Entreplanta, General Mola s/n, Fuengirola, Málaga; tel (52) 722504; telex 77659.
Honorary Consul: José M. De La Torre.

Consulate-General: Edif. Hamilton, 3°, Of. Nu 35, Calle de la Marina 7, Santa Cruz de Tenerife; tel (22) 245035; telex 92372.
Honorary Consul-General: Jaime K. Willis.

Consulate: San Miguel 68A, 7°-8°, 07002 Palma de Mallorca; tel (71) 722504; telex 68711; fax (71) 718229.
Honorary Consul: Pedro Pablo Marrero Henning.

ISRAEL

Embassy: Velázquez 150, 7°, 28002 Madrid; tel (1) 4111357; telex 46996; fax (1) 5645974.
Ambassador: Shlomo Ben Ami.

ITALY

Embassy: Lagasca 98, 28006 Madrid; tel (1) 5776529; telex 22414.
Ambassador: Antonio Ciarrapico.

JAPAN

Embassy: Joaquín Costa 29, 28002 Madrid; tel (1) 2625546; telex 27652; fax (1) 2627868.
Ambassador: Toru Ishii.

Consulate-General: Edif. Banca Catalana, Planta 3 Avda, Diagonal 662-664, 08034 Barcelona; tel (3) 2047724; telex 99705; fax (3) 2055718.
Consul-General: Toshikatsu Hatta.

Consulate-General: Santiago Rusiúol 12, Apdo 733, Las Palmas; tel (28) 244012; telex 95301; fax (28) 232348.
Consul-General: Takuzi Ikeda.

JORDAN

Embassy: General Martínez Campos 41, 5°, 28010 Madrid; tel (1) 4191100; telex 23755.
Ambassador: Shaher Bak.

KOREA, REPUBLIC

Embassy: Miguel Angel 23, 4°, 28010 Madrid; tel (1) 3082120; telex 27498.
Ambassador: Chang Myung Kwan.

KUWAIT

Embassy: Paseo de la Castellana 141, 28046 Madrid; tel (1) 5720162; telex 23753.
Ambassador: Jassem Mohammad al-Sabbagh.

LEBANON

Embassy: Paseo de la Castellana 178, 3° Izqda, 28046 Madrid; tel (1) 4571368; telex 45964.
Ambassador: Abbas Fouad Hamiye.

LIBYA

People's Bureau: Pisuerga 12, 28002 Madrid; tel (1) 5635753; telex 27814.
Head of People's Bureau: Nuri Mohamed Abdalla Bet el- Mal.

LUXEMBOURG

Embassy: Claudio Coello 78, 28001 Madrid; tel (1) 5642474; telex 49229; fax (1) 5774826.
Ambassador: Ronald F. C. Mayer.
Secretary and Vice-Consul: Ghislain Bombled.

MADAGASCAR

Consulate: Avda Diagonal 432, 08037 Barcelona.

Consulate: Rúa Padilla 17, 5°, 28006 Madrid.

MALAWI

Consulate: Largo de Don Pedro 8, Madrid; tel (1) 2658659.
Honorary Consul: Pitno Coelho.

MALAYSIA

Embassy: Paseo de la Castellana 91, 5°, 28046 Madrid; tel (1) 5550684; telex 42108; fax (1) 5555208.
Ambassador: H. A. Zaibcdah.

MALTA

Consulate: Girona, 7 Pral, 08010 Barcelona; tel (3) 3176369; telex 81087; fax (3) 1766831.
Honorary Consul: Isidoro Prenafeta Pastor.

MAURITANIA

Embassy: Velázquez 90, 28006 Madrid; tel (1) 5757007; telex 23135.
Ambassador: Cheikh Ould Baha.

MEXICO

Embassy: Paseo de la Castellana 93, 7°, 28046 Madrid; tel (1) 55561263; telex 43186; fax (1) 5971577.
Ambassador: Jesús Silva Herzog.

MOROCCO

Embassy: Serrano 179, 28002 Madrid; tel (1) 5631090; telex 27799; fax (1) 5638228.
Ambassador: Azeddine Guessous.

NETHERLANDS

Embassy: Paseo de la Castellana 178-180, 28046 Madrid; tel (1) 4582100; telex 27316; fax (1) 4582150.
Ambassador: Albertus J. A. M. Nooiy.

NICARAGUA

Embassy: Paseo de la Castellana 127, 1°B, 28046 Madrid; tel (1) 5555510; telex 45382; fax (1) 5555737.
Ambassador: Filadelfo Chamorro Coronel.

NIGERIA

Embassy: Segre 23, Apdo 14.287, 28002 Madrid; tel (1) 5630911; telex 44395.
Ambassador: Yussuf Mamman.

NORWAY

Embassy: Paseo de la Castellana 31, Edif. 'La Pirámide', Apdo 6132, 28046 Madrid; tel (1) 4106863; telex 23331; fax (1) 3190962.
Ambassador: Leif Mevik.

PAKISTAN

Embassy: Serrano 23, 3°D, 28001 Madrid; tel (1) 4315441; telex 41215; fax (1) 4354262.
Ambassador: Naseer Mohammad Shah.
Counsellor (Commercial): Ejaz Ahmad.
First Secretary And Head of Chancery: Humaira Hasan.
Third Secretary: Ayaz Hussain.

Consulate-General: Córcega, 336 Atico, 08037 Barcelona; tel (3) 2180000.
Honorary Consul-General: Juan Escoda Corominas.

Consulate-General: Plaza de las Delicias, 41001 Sevilla; tel (54) 228921.
Honorary Consul-General: Iñigo Moreno.

Consulate: Hurtado de Amezaga, 5°, 48004 Bilbao; tel (4) 220845.
Honorary Consul: José Garibi.

PANAMA

Embassy: Raimundo Fernandez Villaverde 26, 28003 Madrid; tel (1) 5352724.
Ambassador: Jaime Ford Boyd.

PARAGUAY

Embassy: Castelló 30, 1° Izqda, 28001 Madrid; tel (1) 5763186; fax (1) 4358856.

Ambassador: Rubén Sapena Brugada.

PERU

Embassy: Príncipe de Vergara 36, 28001 Madrid; tel (1) 4314242; telex 44112; fax (1) 4351858.
Ambassador: Allan Wagner Tizón.

PHILIPPINES

Embassy: Claudio Coello 92, 28006 Madrid; tel (1) 5765403; telex 41276; fax (1) 5758360.
Ambassador: Juan José Rocha Pérez.

POLAND

Embassy: Guisando 23 bis, 28035 Madrid; tel (1) 3736605; telex 22652; fax (1) 3736624.
Ambassador: Jan Kieniewicz.

PORTUGAL

Embassy: Pinar 1, 28006 Madrid; tel (1) 2617800; telex 22205; fax (1) 4110172.
Ambassador: Carlos Alberto Soares Simões-Coelho.
Minister-Counsellor: João da Silveira Carvalho.
Counsellor: Maria do Carmo Allegro de Magalhães.
Counsellor (Culture): Mário Quartin Graça.
Counsellor (Finance): Manuel Ramires de Oliveira.
Counsellor (Social): José António Galaz.
Counsellor (Press): Pedro d'Anunciação.
Counsellor (Tourism): Nuno Mendes de Almeida.
Counsellor (Commercial): Pedro Feytor Pinto.
Defence Attaché: Capt. António Conde Martins.
Deputy Defence Attaché: Lieut Col Manuel Vizela Cardoso.

Consulate-General: P. General Martinez Campos 11, 1°, 28919 Madrid; tel (1) 4454600; telex 47608.
Consul-General: João Amador.

Consulate-General: Ronda de San Pedro, 7-1°-1a, 08010 Barcelona; tel (3) 3188150.
Consul-General: António Franco.

Consulate-General: Avda del Cid s/n, 41004 Sevilla; tel (54) 4231150.
Consul-General: Manuel Corte-Real.

Consulate: Avda de Francia, 2-1° C, 20012 San Sebastian; tel (43) 276859.
Consul: Dr Alfredo Lope Pires.

Consulate: C. Marqués de Valladares 23-1°, 36201 Vigo; tel (86) 436911.
Consul: Alfonso Texeira da Mota.

QATAR

Embassy: Paseo de la Castellana 15, 28046 Madrid; tel (1) 3198400; telex 48537.
Chargé d'affaires a.i.: Sheikh Fahad Aweada Mohd al-Thani.

ROMANIA

Embassy: Alfonso XIII 157, 28016 Madrid; tel (1) 2504436; telex 22433.
Chargé d'affaires a.i.: Vasile Dan.

RUSSIA

Embassy: Maestro Ripoll 14, 28006 Madrid; tel (1) 4110706; telex 45632; fax (1) 2629712.
Ambassador: Sergei Romanovski.

SAN MARINO

Consulate-General: Paseo de la Castellana 13-3°, Madrid; tel (1) 3193562; telex 27749; fax (1) 4105509.
Consul-General: Antonio Carasol Dieste.
Consul: José Manuel de Mollinedo Martinez.

SAUDI ARABIA

Embassy: Paseo de la Habana 163, 28036 Madrid; tel (1) 4571250; telex 22710.
Ambassador: Mohamed N. Ibrahim.

SOUTH AFRICA

Embassy: Edif. Lista, Claudio Coello 91-6°, 28006 Madrid; tel (1) 4356688; telex 44049; fax (1) 5777414.
Ambassador: Frederich Gustav Conradie.
Counsellor: François Jacques van der Merwe.
Counsellor (Trade): Jacobus Nicolaas Sounes.
First Secretary (Information): Robert Travers Smith.
Second Secretary (Administration): Heinrich Hattingh.
Second Secretary (Consular): Christina Louisa Herbst.

Consulate-General: Avda de las Cortes Catalanas 634, B7 6°, 08007 Barcelona; tel (3) 3180797.
Honorary Consul-General: Enrique Urreta Wood.

Consulate-General: Las Mercedes, 31-4°, Las Arenas, Vizcaya, Bilbao; tel (4) 4641830; telex 34181; fax (4) 4649523.
Honorary Consul-General: Carlos Lerchundi Laidler.

Consulate-General: Albareda 50, 35008 Las Palmas, Gran Canaria; tel (28) 333394; telex 333204.
Honorary Consul-General: Günther Vendt.

SWEDEN

Embassy: Caracas 25, 2°, Apdo 14159, 28010 Madrid; tel (1) 3081535; telex 27405; fax (1) 3081903.
Ambassador: Ulf Hjertonsson.
Counsellor: Linda Fernandez-Corujedo Steneberg.
Counsellor (Press): Jan Sandquist.
Military, Naval and Air Attaché: Lieut Col Claes-Göran Hedén.
First Secretary: Ulla Bohm.
Chancellor: Siv Andersson.
Chancellor: Catharina Skoog.
Secretary (Commercial): Christer Elfverson.

Consulate-General: Avda Diagonal 601, 4°D, Apdo 30210, 08034 Barcelona; tel (3) 4101108; telex 51725; fax (3) 4102501.
Consul-General: Göte Lönnmar.
Consul: Kinna Laraqui.
Vice-Consul and Head of Commercial Office: Inger Maria Weijnitz-Torrell.
Chancellor: Jane Gunnel Håkansson.

Consulate: Explanada de España 29, Apdo 110, 03001 Alicante; tel (65) 218300; telex 66068; fax (65) 5141180.
Consul: Fernando Francisco José Flores Arroyo.

Consulate: Avda l'Aiguera, Edif. Anfiteatro, Portal C, entreplanta, Apdo 289, 03500 Benidorm; tel (65) 5855950; telex 68278; fax (65) 855444.
Consul: José Luis Ripoli Riva.
Chancellor: Araceli Gómez Arandiga.

Consulate: Alda Mazarredo 19, entresuelo, 48001 Bilbao; tel (4) 4248791; fax (4) 4239390.
Consul: Ignacio Marco-Gardoqui Ibánez.

Consulate: Carretera de Alcora Km. 10.5, Inblocas S.A., Apdo 692, 12006 Castellon de la Plana; tel (64) 244574; fax (64) 242592.
Consul: José María Valls Zaballos.

Consulate: Calle Corrida 8, Apdo 67, 33080 Gijon; tel (85) 354643; telex 87371; fax (85) 355310.
Consul: Casimiro González Ayesta.

Consulate: Avda de Linares Rivas 18-21, 2° drcha, 15005 La Coruña; tel (81) 222824; telex 82174; fax (81) 222263.
Consul: Henry H. A. Guyatt.

Consulate: Plaza Frederic Chopin 1-entlo, Apdo 1919, 07080 Palma de Mallorca; tel (71) 725492; telex 68557; fax (71) 712968.
Consul: Els-Marie Eriksson.

Consulate: Avda de Ategorrieta 7, 2°, 20013 San Sebastian; tel (43) 390832; fax (43) 390756.
Consul: Jaime Legarra Belástegui.

Consulate: Paseo de Pereda 36, 39004 Santander; tel (42) 214108; telex 35841; fax (42) 310009.
Consul: Fernando Correa Gutiérrez.

Consulate: Calle de la Unió 23, 1a-2a, Apdo 54, 43080 Tarragona; tel (77) 233304.
Consul: Fernando Boada Aragonés.

Consulate: Calle Chapaprieta 1, 1°B, Apdo 9, 03180 Torrevieja; tel (65) 710985; fax (65) 710985.
Consul: Antonio Conesa Morales.
Chancellor: Mariano Albentosa Conesa.

Consulate: Jorge Juan 10, 1°, 46004 Valencia; tel (6) 3940375; telex 63085; fax (6) 3940376.
Consul: Ramón Ramia de Cap Salvetella.

Consulate: Cánovas del Castillo 22, Apdo 75, 36202 Vigo; tel (86) 431533; telex 83057; fax (86) 438305.
Consul: Alberto Durán Núñez.

Consulate-General: Alameda de Colón 9-4°, 29001 Málaga; tel (52) 215662; telex 77279; fax (52) 220917.
Consul-General: Henry Leo.
Vice-Consul: Francisco Moreno Maldonado.
Chancellor: Inga-Lill Karlsson-Pérez.

Consulate: Avda Virgen del Carmen 29, Edif. Atlantida, Entreplanta, Apdo 249, 11201 Algeciras; tel (56) 660562; telex 78068; fax (56) 661883.
Consul: Juan José Triay.

Consulate: Dr Araez Pacheco 2, Apdo 112, 04004 Almeria; tel (51) 250033; telex 78989; fax (51) 221751.
Consul: Ramón Gómez Vivancos.

Consulate: Alameda de Apodaca 21, Apdo 105, 11004 Cadiz; tel (56) 221364; telex 76033; fax (56) 225201.
Consul: Joaquin Ramos Díaz.

Consulate: Muralla del Mar 11 entlo. dcha, Apdo 14, 30202 Cartegena; tel (68) 507000; telex 68015; fax (68) 508969.
Consul: Carlos Augusto Siljeström.

Consulate: Daoiz 2-10-A, 11701 Ceuta; tel (56) 514706; telex 78375; fax (56) 511592.
Consul: Antonio Bernal Roldán.

Consulate: Plaza Mariana Pineda 7, 6°, Granada; tel (58) 229161; fax (58) 229161.
Consul: Berit Irene Magnusson.

Consulate: Santo Domingo de la Calzada s/n, 21001 Huelva; tel (55) 253577; telex 75504; fax (55) 246178.
Consul: Francisco-José Martin y Alonzo-Martinez.

Consulate: Manuel María González 12, Apdo 1710, 11480 Jerez de la Frontera; tel (56) 340000; telex 75003; fax (56) 332089.
Consul: Guillermo González-Gordon Gilbey.

Consulate: Reina Mercedes 25-1-B, 41012 Sevilla; tel (4) 3611489; telex 72310; fax (4) 232988.
Consul: Cristina Siljeström de Garcia de Samaniego.
Chancellor: Gunilla Ekelund.

SWITZERLAND

Embassy: Nuñez de Balboa 35-7°, 28001 Madrid; Apdo 1317, 28080 Madrid; tel (1) 4313400; telex 23079; fax (1) 5776898.
Ambassador: Roland Wermuth.
Counsellor: Daniel von Muralt.
First Secretary (Economic): Urs Breiter.
Attaché and Head of Chancery: Rudolf Metzler.

Consulate-General: Edificios Trade, Gran Via de Carlos III 94-7°, 08028 Barcelona; tel (3) 3309211; telex 52220; fax (3) 4906598.
Consul-General: Rudolf Hilber.
Vice-Consul and Chancellor: Werner Ziemer.

Consulate: Puerto del Mar 18-6°, Edif. La Vasco, Apdo 7, 29005 Málaga: tel (52) 214729; fax (52) 226736.
Consul: Siegfried Brazerol.
Chancellor: Simone Navarro-Hirschy.

Consulate: Paseo de Mallorca 24, entlo, 07012 Palma de Mallorca; tel (71) 712520; fax (71) 718238.
Consul: Margareta Estermann.

SYRIA

Embassy: Plaza de Platería Martínez 1, 28014 Madrid; tel (1) 4201602; telex 43529.
Ambassador: Mohammad Zuhair al-Aqad.

THAILAND

Embassy: Segre 29, 28002 Madrid; tel (1) 5632903; telex 49044.
Ambassador: Chitrik Sreshthaputra.

TOGO

Consulate: c/o Consulate-General of France, Edif. UAP, Paseo de la Castellana 79, 28046 Madrid; tel (1) 4555450.

Consulate: c/o Consulate of France, Paseo de Gracia 11, 08007 Barcelona; tel (3) 3178150.

TUNISIA

Embassy: Plaza de Alonso Martínez 3, 28004 Madrid; tel (1) 4473508; telex 27672; fax (1) 5938416.
Ambassador: Abdelhamid Fehri.

TURKEY

Embassy: Rafael Calvo 18, 28010 Madrid; tel (1) 3198064; telex 49329; fax (1) 3086602.
Ambassador: Nabi Şensoy.

UGANDA

Consulate: Costa Brava 31, 3°C drcha, 28034 Madrid; tel (1) 7344837.
Honorary Consul: Alfredo Salas Viu.

UNITED ARAB EMIRATES

Embassy: Capitán Haya 40, 28020 Madrid; tel (1) 2701004; telex 42765.
Ambassador: Saeed Ali al-Nowais.

UNITED KINGDOM

Embassy: Calle de Fernando el Santo 16, 28010 Madrid 4; tel (1) 3190200; telex 27656; fax (1) 3190423.
Ambassador: Sir Robin Fearn.
Counsellor (Finance): R. Christopher.
Counsellor (Commercial): D. N. Ridgway.
Minister and Deputy Head of Mission: Ivor A. Roberts.
Defence and Naval Attaché: Capt. Simon Sloot.
Air Attaché: Group Capt. Horace Farquhar-Smith.
Military Attaché: Col Sir William Mahon.
Assistant Military Attaché: Maj. R. D. Peters.
First Secretary and Head of Political Section: Geoffrey Gillham.
First Secretary and Consul-General: Douglas McIntyre.
First Secretary and Consul-General: John Hedley.
First Secretary (Agriculture): Jane Rabagliati.
First Secretary (Management): M. E. J. Herridge.
First Secretary (Press and Information): R. P. Osborne.
First Secretary (Commercial): M. Cumming.
Third Secretary (Economic): H. Elliot.
Attaché (Culture) and British Council Director: Brian Vale.

Consulate-General: Marques de la Ensenada 16, 28004 Madrid; tel (1) 3085201; telex 46664; fax (1) 3080882.
Consul-General: Douglas R. S. McIntyre.

Consulate-General: Alameda Urquijo 2, 48008 Bilbao; tel (4) 4157600; telex 32446; fax (4) 4167632.
Consul-General: A. W. McKenzie.

Consulate-General: Avda Diagonal 477, 08036 Barcelona; tel (3) 4199044; telex 52799; fax (3) 4052411.
Consul-General: D. Joy.

Consulate: Plaza Calvo Sotelo 1-2, 03001 Alicante; tel (65) 216022; fax (65) 140522.
Consul: J. C. A. Dove.

Consulate: Plaza Nueva 8 B, 41001 Sevilla; tel (54) 228875; telex 72107; fax (54) 210323.
Consul: C. Formby.

Consulate: Edif. Cataluña, Luis Morote 6-3°, 35007 Las Palmas; tel (28) 262508; telex 95276; fax (28) 267774.
Consul: P. Nevitt.

Consulate: Edif. Duquesa, Duquesa de Parcent 8, 29001 Málaga; tel (52) 217571; telex 77828; fax (52) 221130.
Consul: M. A. Bartram.

Consulate: Plaza Mayor 3 D, 07002 Palma de Mallorca; tel (71) 712445; telex 69477; fax (71) 717520.
Consul: P. Cross.

Consulate: Calle Real 33, 1°, 1 Apdo 524, 43080 Tarragona; tel (77) 220812.
Honorary Consul: I. Navarro.

Consulate: Paseo Pered 27, 39004 Santander; tel (42) 220000; telex 35832; fax (42) 222941.
Honorary Consul: M. Piñeiro Ceballos.

Consulate: Plaza de Compostela 23, 36201 Vigo; tel (86) 437133; fax (86) 437133.
Honorary Consul: J. M. Cogolludo.

Consulate: Rubicón 7, Arrecife, Lanzarote; tel (28) 815928; fax (28) 814248.
Honorary Consul: B. Key.

Consulate: Avda de las Fuerzas Armadas, 11-1°, 11202 Algeciras; tel (56) 661600; telex 78079; fax (56) 661604.
Vice-Consul: L. A. Forrest de Mas.
Vice-Consul: L. A. Mas.

Consulate: Avda Isidoro Macabich 45, 1°, Ibiza; tel (71) 301818.
Vice-Consul: Jeremy Batey.

Consulate: Torret 28, San Luis, Menorca; tel (71) 366439.
Vice-Consul: R. G. Sheridan.

Consulate: Plaza Weyler 8, 1°, 38003 Santa Cruz, Tenerife; tel (22) 286863; fax (22) 289903.
Vice-Consul: G. K. Hazell.

USA

Embassy: Serrano 75, 28006 Madrid; tel (1) 5774000; telex 27763; fax (1) 5775735.
Ambassador: Joseph Zappala.
Deputy Head of Mission: Edward A. Casey, Jr.
Economic Section: Pierce Bullen.
Commercial Section: Robert Kohn.
Political Section: Walter Clarke.
Political and Military Sections: Martin McLean.
NASA: John South.
Office of Defence Co-operation: Brig. Antonio Maldonado.
Office of Defence Attaché: Capt. Carmine Tortora.
Military Assistance Advisory Group: Rear Adm. Gerald L. Riendeau.
Labour Officer: Charles R. Hare.
Consular Section: Michael L. Hancock.
Administrative Section: Perry W. Linder.
Public Affairs Officer: Jacob Gillespie.
Regional Security Officer: Stanley Bielinski, Jr.
Agricultural Section: Richard T. McDonnell.
Attaché (Science): Ishmael Lara.
Federal Aviation Administration: Robert J. Bernard.
Communications Programme Officer: William Mills.
Information Systems Manager: Frank J. Ledahawsky.
Drug Enforcement Agency: David Herrera.

Consulate-General: Via Layetana 33, Barcelona; tel (3) 3199550; telex 52672; fax (3) 3197543.
Consul-General: Ruth A. Davis.
Commercial Section: Ralph Griffin.
Administration Section: Benjamin H. Castro.
Regional Security Officer: William E. Marsden.
Branch Public Affairs Officer: Guy Burton.

Consulate: Avda Lehenda Kari Agirre 11, 3°, Bilboa; tel (4) 4758300; telex 32589; fax (4) 4761240.
Principal Officer: Heather M. Hodges.

URUGUAY

Embassy: Paseo del Pintor Rosales 32, 1°D, 28008 Madrid; tel (1) 5428038; telex 22441.
Chargé d'affaires a.i.: Pedro Mo Amaro.

VENEZUELA

Embassy: Avda Capitán Haya 1, Edif. Eurocentro, Planta 13, 28020 Madrid; tel (1) 4558452; telex 23699; fax (1) 5971583.
Ambassador: Arturo Hernández Grisanti.
Minister-Counsellor: Nelson Valera Parra.
Counsellor: Gerson Revanales.
Counsellor (Technical): Elisa Lerner.
Counsellor (Technical): Josefina Rodriguez de A.
First Secretary: Maria del Valle Azocar Silva.
Consul-General: Maritza Corredor de M.

Consulate: tel (1) 5558452; fax (1) 5971538.
Consul-General: Leopoldo Linares.

Consulate: Avda Hurtado de Amezaga 27, Planta 9, Edif. Sanreza, Depto 1-2Y, 10 Bilbao; tel (4) 444966; telex 34173; fax (4) 448911.
Consul: José Ramon Dovale.

Consulate: Plaza de José Antonio, Primo de Rivera 16, 3°, Apdo 105, Cadiz; tel (56) 214039.
Consul-General: Francisco Guevara Llovera.

Consulate: Paseo de Ruzafa 20, 1°, Apdo 46002, Valencia; tel (6) 3516977.
Consul-General: Rafael Griman Urbina.

Consulate: Vigo.
Consul-General: Oswaldo Rodriguez Ramos.

Consulate: Calle el Pilar 27, 1°, Apdo 437, Santa Cruz de Tenerife; tel (22) 273310; telex 5292330.
Consul-General: Genaro Verde.

YUGOSLAVIA

Embassy: Velázquez 162, 28002 Madrid; tel (1) 5635045; telex 44208; fax (1) 5630440.
Ambassador: Faik Dizdarević.
Counsellor: Jurica Raos.
Counsellor: Slobodan Bajić.

First Secretary (Economic and Commercial Affairs): Danko Prokić.

Consulate: Numancia 18, Barcelona; tel (3) 4233101; fax (3) 4260665.
Honorary Consul: Roberto Rivera.

ZAIRE

Embassy: Avda del Dr Arce 7, 28002 Madrid; tel (1) 2624710; telex 27816.
Ambassador: Bate Tangale Tomona.

International Organizations

EUROPEAN COMMUNITIES

Bureau: Serrano 41, 5°, 28001 Madrid; tel (1) 4351700; telex 46818; fax (1) 2760387.
Director: Joaquim Portillo Pasqual del Riquelme.

SRI LANKA

AUSTRALIA

High Commission: 3 Cambridge Place, POB 742, Colombo 7; tel (1) 696468; telex 21157; fax (1) 686453.
High Commissioner: Tonia L. Shand.

AUSTRIA

Consulate: 424 Union Pl., POB 903, Colombo 2; tel (1) 691613; telex 21330.
Honorary Consul: Senake Amerasinghe.

BANGLADESH

High Commission: 286 Bauddhaloka Mawatha, Colombo 7; tel (1) 502397; telex 21454.
High Commissioner: Humayun Kamal (acting).

CANADA

High Commission: 6 Gregory's Rd, Cinnamon Gdns, POB 1006, Colombo 7; tel (1) 695841; telex 21106.
High Commissioner: Nancy Stiles.
Counsellor (Development): A. Vinette.
First Secretary: P. Abols.
First Secretary (Immigration): A. M. Robinson.
Second Secretary (Development): C. M. Spoerel.
Second Secretary (Immigration): M. E. Gaillard.
Third Secretary (Administration): R. Beliveau.

CHINA, PEOPLE'S REPUBLIC

Embassy: 191 Dharmapala Mawatha, Colombo 7; tel (1) 596459.
Ambassador: Zhang Ruijie.

CUBA

Embassy: 10 Siri Dhamma Mawatha, Colombo 10; tel (1) 93164; telex 21240.
Ambassador: Olga Chamero Trias.

CZECHOSLOVAKIA

Embassy: 47-47A Horton Place, Colombo 7; tel (1) 94766; telex 21206.
Ambassador: Dr Zdeno Litavsky.

DENMARK

Consulate-General: 264 Grandpass Rd, Colombo 14; POB 161, Colombo 10; tel (1) 547806; telex 21114.
Consul-General: Palle Bjørn Rasmussen.

EGYPT

Embassy: 39 Dickman's Rd, Colombo 5; tel (1) 508752; telex 21127; fax (1) 585292.
Ambassador and Consul-General: Mohamed Said el-Banhawy.
Counsellor and Consul: Awatef Ahmed Mohamed Shalaby.
Third Secretary and Vice-Consul: Khaled Fathy Youssef.
Attaché (Administrative Affairs): Mohamed Ibrahim Ali.
Attaché (Administrative Affairs): Hosni Ahmed Ali.
Commercial Counsellor: Muhsin Farid.
Attaché (Administrative and Commercial): Mostafa Mohamed Aly El Meliguy.

Egyptian Trade Centre: Ceylinco House, 69 Janadhipathi, Mawatha, Colombo 1.
Trade Representative: Reda El-Kherbawy.

FINLAND

Embassy: 81 Barnes Place, POB 1914, Colombo 7; tel (1) 698819; telex 22651; fax (1) 698820.
Counsellor (Development Co-operation): Irma-Liisa Perttunen.

Consulate-General: 264 Grandpass Rd, POB 161, Colombo 14; tel (1) 23171; telex 21114; fax (1) 8031396.
Consul-General: Palle Björn Rasmussen.

FRANCE

Embassy: 89 Rosmead Place, POB 880, Colombo 7; tel (1) 598815; telex 21191.
Ambassador: Christian Lambert.
First Counsellor: Vincent Hommeril.
Defence Attaché: Lieut Col Jacques Schunk de Goldfiem.
Commercial Counsellor: Luc Roudie.
Cultural Counsellor: Claude Berengier.
Vice-Consul: Serge Lacordaire.

Trade Promotion Office: POB 955, Colombo 2; tel (1) 32021; telex 21179.

GERMANY

Embassy: 40 Alfred House Ave, POB 658, Colombo 3; tel (1) 580431; telex 21119; fax (1) 580440.
Ambassador: Klaus M. Franke.

HOLY SEE

Apostolic Nunciature: 220 Bauddhaloka Mawatha, Colombo 7; tel (1) 582554; fax (1) 580906.
Apostolic Pro-Nuncio: Most Rev. François Bacqué, Titular Archbishop of Gradisca.
Second Secretary: Rev. Mgr Jude Thaddeus Okolo.

ICELAND

Consulate-General: 41, WAD Ramanayake Mawatha, POB 1453, Colombo 2; tel (1) 33271; telex 21266.
Consul-General: Ranjit Sujiva Wijewardene.

INDIA

High Commission: 36-38 Galle Rd, Colombo 3; tel (1) 21605; telex 21132.
High Commissioner: Nagendra Nath Jha.

INDONESIA

Embassy: 1 Police Park Terrace, Colombo 5; tel (1) 580113; telex 21223.
Ambassador: R. Sajogo.

IRAQ

Embassy: 19 Barnes Place, POB 79, Colombo 7; tel (1) 596600; telex 21166.
Ambassador: Tariq Ahmed al-Marouf Kudrat.

ITALY

Embassy: 55 Jawatte Rd, Colombo 5; tel (1) 588388; telex 21449; fax (1) 588622.
Ambassador: Luigi Costa Sanseverino.

JAPAN

Embassy: 20 Gregory's Rd, POB 822, Colombo 7; tel (1) 693831; telex 21148; fax (1) 698629.
Ambassador: Isamu Nitta.

KOREA, REPUBLIC

Embassy: 98 Dharmapala Mawatha, Colombo 7; tel (1) 599036; telex 21212.
Ambassador: Kim Bong Kyu.

LIBYA

People's Bureau: 30 Horton Place, Colombo 7; tel (1) 94874.
Secretary of People's Bureau: Yahia Zakaria Y. El-Megadmi.

MALAYSIA

High Commission: 87 Horton Place, Colombo 7; tel (1) 94837; telex 21181.
High Commissioner: Dato' Abdul Karim Marzuki.

MALDIVES

High Commission: 25 Melbourne Ave, Colombo 4; tel (1) 586762; telex 22469.
High Commissioner: Ahmed Abdullah.

MYANMAR

Embassy: 17 Skelton Gdns, Colombo 5; tel (1) 587607; telex 22844; fax (1) 580460.
Ambassador: U Shwe Zin.
Second Secretary: U Soe Aung.
Second Secretary: U Thaung Oo.

NETHERLANDS

Embassy: 25 Torrington Ave, Colombo 7; tel (1) 589626; telex 21308; fax (1) 502855.
Ambassador: J. H. Daman Willems.

NEW ZEALAND

Consulate: c/o Aitken Spence & Co Ltd, POB 5, Colombo; tel (1) 26029; telex 21142; fax (1) 545589.
Honorary Consul: Norman Gunewardene.

NORWAY

Embassy: 34 Ward Place, Colombo 7; tel (1) 692263; telex 21340; fax (1) 695009.
Ambassador: Jon Atle Gaarder.

PAKISTAN

High Commission: 211 De Saram Place, Colombo 10; tel (1) 596301.
High Commissioner: Mir Abad Hussain.

PHILIPPINES

Embassy: 10 Gregory's Rd, Colombo 7; tel (1) 696861; telex 22307.
Ambassador: Virgilio C. Nanagas.

POLAND

Embassy: 120 Park Rd, Colombo 5; tel (1) 581903; telex 23292.
Chargé d'affaires: Stanislaw Zakrzewski.

RUSSIA

Embassy: 62 Sir Ernest de Silva Mawatha, Colombo 7; tel (1) 573555; telex 22751.
Minister-Counsellor and Chargé d'affaires a.i.: Gennady K. Efimov.
Counsellor: Evgeny I. Kolesnikov.
Counsellor: Victor A. Basov.
Commercial Counsellor: German R. Borisov.
Military, Naval and Air Attaché: Vladimir I. Kontchakov.
First Secretary: Vladimir A. Sazanov.
First Secretary: Stanislav K. Tchizov.
First Secretary: Valentin I. Mantourov.
First Secretary: Yuri S. Toumanov.
First Secretary: Alexandre V. Gorban.
Assistant to the Military Attaché: Vladimir V. Stavtsev.

SWEDEN

Embassy: 315 Vauxhall St, POB 1072, Colombo 2; tel (1) 28822; telex 21253; fax (1) 440479.
Counsellor, Head of Aid Section and Chargé d'affaires a.i.: Maj-Britt Amer.
First Secretary: Gunilla von Bahr-Tidbeck.

Consulate-General: 264 Grandpass Rd, POB 161, Colombo 14; tel (1) 27707; telex 21114.
Consul-General: Palle Bjoern Rasmussen.

SWITZERLAND

Embassy: Baur's Bldg, 1st Floor, 7-1/1 Upper Chatham St, POB 342, Colombo 1; tel (1) 438556; telex 21666; fax (1) 447157.
Ambassador: Henri Cuennet.
Third Secretary and Head of Chancery: Werner Michel.

THAILAND

Embassy: 43 Dr C. W. W. Kannangara Mawatha, Colombo 7; tel (1) 697406; telex 22165.
Ambassador: Khajoru Sobhoa.

UNITED KINGDOM

High Commission: 190 Galle Rd, Kollupitiya, POB 1433, Colombo 3; tel (1) 437336; telex 21101; fax (1) 437344.
High Commissioner: John Field.
Deputy High Commissioner: C. M. T. Elmes.
Defence Adviser: Lieut Col I. G. Baillie.
Cultural Attaché (British Council Director): R. A. Jarvis.
First Secretary (Commercial/Economic): J. R. Albright.
First Secretary (Chancery): K. C. James.
Second Secretary (Management): A. J. Mayland.
Second Secretary (Aid): M. R. Foord.
Second Secretary (Immigration/Consular): B. P. McMahon.

USA

Embassy: 210 Galle Rd, POB 106, Colombo 3; tel (1) 448007; telex 21305; fax (1) 437345.
Ambassador: Marion V. Creekmore, Jr.
Deputy Chief of Mission: Donald B. Westmore.
Political Section: Robert Boggs, Jr.
Economic Section: Joseph A. Mussomeli.
Commercial Section/Labour Officer: Elizabeth A. Ewing.
Consular Section: Michael Thurston.
Administrative Section: Raymond J. Pepper.
Regional Security Officer: David J. Benson.

US Information Service: 44 Galle Rd, Colombo 3; tel (1) 421271; fax (1) 449070.
Public Affairs Officer (USIS): William H. Maurer, Jr.
Communications Programme Officer: Robert A. Johnson.

Agency for International Development: 356 Galle Rd, Colombo 3; tel (1) 574333; fax (1) 574264.
Agency for International Development: Richard Brown.
Office of the Defence Attaché: Commdr Vaughn K. Martin.

YUGOSLAVIA

Embassy: 32 Cambridge Place, Colombo 7; tel (1) 599082.
Ambassador: Vancho Andonov.

SUDAN

ALGERIA

Embassy: St 31, New Extension, POB 80, Khartoum; tel (11) 41954.
Ambassador: Laming Bechichi.

AUSTRIA

Embassy: Slavos Bldg, 5 Babiker Badri St, 3rd Floor, Flat 29, POB 1860, Khartoum; tel (11) 77170; telex 22227.
Ambassador: Dr Heimo Kellner.
Commercial Counsellor: Peter Rattinger.

CENTRAL AFRICAN REPUBLIC

Embassy: Africa Rd, POB 1723, Khartoum; tel (11) 45691.
Ambassador: David N'Guindo.

CHAD

Embassy: 21, St 17, New Extension, POB 1514, Khartoum; tel (11) 42545.

CHINA, PEOPLE'S REPUBLIC

Embassy: 93, St 22, POB 1425, Khartoum; tel (11) 222036.
Ambassador: Hui Zhen.

CZECHOSLOVAKIA

Embassy: 39, St 39, POB 1047, Khartoum; tel (11) 43448.
Ambassador: Premysl Kostak.

DENMARK

Embassy: St 18 East, between Baladia St and el Zubeir Basha St, POB 2758, Khartoum; tel (11) 73586; telex 22130.
Chargé d'affaires a.i. and Aid Counsellor: Orla Bakdal.
Project Co-ordinator: Hans Lillelund.
Attaché: Arne Bengt Lauritsen.

EGYPT

Embassy: Al-Gamma St, POB 1126, Khartoum; tel (11) 72836; telex 22545.
Ambassador: Muhammad Taki ad-Din ash-Shirbini.

ETHIOPIA

Embassy: 6, 11A St 3, New Extension, POB 844, Khartoum.
Ambassador: Fili Lamma Lamf.

FINLAND

Consulate: Aboulela Engineering Co., Aboulela New Bldg, Gomhuria St, POB 1696, Khartoum; tel (11) 71053; telex 22071.
Consul: Hisham Mirgani Aboulela.

FRANCE

Embassy: Junction 19th and Ali Dinar Sts, Block 6H, East Plot 2, POB 377, Khartoum; tel (11) 77619; telex 22220.
Ambassador: Pierre Blouin.

Economic Section: Atbara St, el Taha Bldg, POB 1486; tel (11) 71203; telex 22441.

GERMANY

Embassy: 53 Baladia St, Block No. 8DE, Plot No. 2, POB 970, Khartoum; tel (11) 77622; telex 22211; fax (11) 81673.
Ambassador: Thomas Trömel.

GREECE

Embassy: Sharia al-Gamhouria, Block 5, No. 30, POB 1182, Khartoum; tel (11) 73469.
Ambassador: Constantin Ivrakis.

HOLY SEE

Apostolic Nunciature: Kafouri Belgravia, POB 623, Khartoum; tel (11) 74692; telex 26032.
Apostolic Pro-Nuncio: Most Rev. Erwin Josef Ender, Titular Archbishop of Germania in Numidia.
Counsellor: Mgr Inglés Ramiro Moliner.

HUNGARY

Embassy: Block 12AE, House 1, St 1, New Extension, POB 1029, Khartoum; tel (11) 42221; telex 24012.
Chargé d'affaires: Imre Simon.

INDIA

Embassy: 61 Africa Rd, POB 707, Khartoum; tel (11) 40560; telex 22228.
Ambassador: Tangkima Cherpoot.

IRAQ

Embassy: Khartoum; tel (11) 41846; telex 24035.
Ambassador: Tariq Muhammad Yahya al-Ani.

ITALY

Embassy: St 39, POB 793, Khartoum; tel (11) 45326; telex 24034.
Ambassador: Francesco Lo Prinzi.

JAPAN

Embassy: 24, Block AE, St 3, New Extension, POB 1649, Khartoum; tel (11) 44549; telex 24019.
Ambassador: Katsuyoshi Yamano.

JORDAN

Embassy: 25, St 7, New Extension, Khartoum; tel (11) 43264; telex 24047.
Ambassador: Musa Abd al-Hakim al-Kilani.

KENYA

Embassy: St 3, Amarat, POB 8242, Khartoum; tel (11) 40386; telex 24190.
Ambassador: Gideon Nyamweya Nyaanga.
First Secretary: Eric N. Obunyasi.
Second Secretary: Raphael O. Makokha.
Third Secretary: Joshua I. Gatimu.
Third Secretary: Charles O. Manywanda.
Administrative Attaché: Jane A. Nyaware.
Administrative Attaché: Amos A. Mwangi.
Administrative Attaché: Sospeter M. Mulevu.

KOREA, DEMOCRATIC PEOPLE'S REPUBLIC

Embassy: House No. 59, 1, St 31, New Extension, POB 332, Khartoum; tel (11) 75645.
Ambassador: Sim Sang-Il.

KOREA, REPUBLIC

Embassy: House 2, St 1, New Extension, POB 2414, Khartoum; tel (11) 44028; telex 24029.
Ambassador: Park Young Woo.

KUWAIT

Embassy: Africa Ave, near the Tennis Club, POB 1457, Khartoum; tel (11) 81525; telex 24043.
Ambassador: Abdallah Sarie Abdallah Rahman as-Sarie.

LEBANON

Embassy: 60, St 49, POB 1407, Khartoum; tel (11) 45002; telex 22548.
Ambassador: Afif Malas.

LIBERIA

Consulate-General: Khartoum; telex 26047.
Honorary Consul-General: Anis G. Haggar.

LIBYA

People's Bureau: 50 Africa Rd, POB 2091, Khartoum.
Secretary of People's Bureau: Gumma al-Fazani.

MOROCCO

Embassy: 32, St 19, New Extension, POB 2042, Khartoum; tel (11) 43223.
Ambassador: Abd al-Latif Mouline.

NETHERLANDS

Embassy: St 47, House No. 47, POB 391, Khartoum; tel (11) 47271; telex 24013.
Chargé d'affaires: P. C. Feith.

NIGER

Embassy: St 1, New Extension, POB 1283, Khartoum; tel (11) 42427; telex 24031.
Ambassador: Al Haj Omarou Amadou.

NIGERIA

Embassy: St 17, Sharia al-Mek Nimr, POB 1538, Khartoum; tel (11) 79120; telex 22222.
Ambassador: Muhammadu Suleiman.

OMAN

Embassy: St 49, New Extension, POB 2839, Khartoum; tel (11) 45791.
Ambassador: Saied bin Salim an-Nabhani.

PAKISTAN

Embassy: House No. 6, Block 12 AE, St 3, New Extension, POB 1178, Khartoum; tel (11) 42518; telex 24219.
Ambassador: G. K. Panhwer.

POLAND

Embassy: 73 Africa Rd, POB 902, Khartoum; tel (11) 44248.
Chargé d'affaires a.i.: Donant Lawnicki.

QATAR

Embassy: St 15, New Extension, POB 223, Khartoum; tel (11) 42208; telex 22223.
Chargé d'affaires a.i.: Saqr Mubarak Muhammad al-Mansouri.

ROMANIA

Embassy: House 20, Block AE, St 3, New Extension, POB 1494, Khartoum; tel (11) 44298; telex 24188.

Ambassador: Ilie Morodan.

RUSSIA

Embassy: B1, A10 St, New Extension, POB 1161, Khartoum; tel (11) 41315; telex 24304.
Ambassador: Valeri Yakovlevich Sukhin.

SAUDI ARABIA

Embassy: St 29, New Extension, POB 258, Khartoum; tel (11) 41938; telex 24009.
Ambassador: Sheikh Ali Abdalla as-Segaire.

SOMALIA

Embassy: St 23-25, New Extension, POB 1857, Khartoum; tel (11) 44800.
Ambassador: Muhammad Osman Omer.

SPAIN

Embassy: St 3, New Extension, POB 2621, Khartoum; tel (11) 45072; telex 22476.
Ambassador: Tomás Solís.

SWEDEN

Consulate: Babiker Badri St, Slavos Bldg, 1st Floor, Flat 19/1, entrance opposite Sahara Hotel, POB 2206, Khartoum; tel (11) 76308; telex 22290.
Consul: Omer Mohamed Ahmed Salim.
Vice-Consul: Evy Marie-Louise Salim.

SWITZERLAND

Embassy: New Aboulela Bldg, POB 1707, Khartoum; tel (11) 71161; telex 22822.
Chargé d'affaires a.i. and Counsellor: Walter Bopp.
Third Secretary and Head of Chancery: Beat Moser.

SYRIA

Embassy: St 3, New Extension, POB 1139, Khartoum; tel (11) 44663.
Chargé d'affaires a.i.: Mustafa Omran.

TUNISIA

Embassy: 18 Al-Baladiya Ave, POB 8270, Khartoum; tel (11) 70625.
Ambassador: Mansour Ezzedine.

TURKEY

Embassy: 31, St 29, New Extension, POB 771, Khartoum; tel (11) 47194.
Ambassador: N. Aydin Tosun.

UGANDA

Embassy: Plot No. 9, Block 9L, St 35, POB 2676, Khartoum; tel (11) 43049; telex 24137.
Ambassador: J. D. Obina Okumu.

UNITED ARAB EMIRATES

Embassy: St 3, New Extension, POB 1225, Khartoum; tel (11) 44476; telex 24024.
Ambassador: Obaid Salem az-Zaabi.

UNITED KINGDOM

Embassy: St 10, off Al Baladiya St, POB 801, Khartoum East; tel (11) 70760; telex 22189.
Ambassador: Allan J. Ramsay.
Counsellor, Consul-General and Deputy Head of Mission: F. X. Gallagher.
First Secretary (Commercial/Aid): B. M. Dixon.
First Secretary (Management) and Consul: C. P. P. Mulcahy.
Second Secretary (Chancery/Information): F. M. Guy.
Third Secretary (Aid): R. J. Phillips.

USA

Embassy: Ali Abd al-Latif Ave, POB 699, Khartoum; tel (11) 74611; telex 22619.
Ambassador: James Richard Cheek.
Deputy Chief of Mission: Joseph P. O'Neill.
Political Section: Robert E. Downey.
Economic Section: Matthew P. Ward.
Consular Section: Dennis B. Hankins.
Administrative Section: Gerald S. Rose.
Regional Security Officer: W. Christopher Reilly.
Public Affairs Officer: Mary V. Jeffers.
Communications Programme Officer: Rudolph L. Szabados.
Information Systems Manager: Lewis K. Elbinger.
Agency for International Development: Dr Frederick E. Machmer, Jr.
Office of the Defence Attaché: Maj. James P. Gerhard.
Office of Military Co-operation: Col Stephen K. Monsees.
Refugee Co-ordinator: David E. Reuther.

YEMEN

Embassy: St 35, New Extension, POB 1010, Khartoum; tel (11) 43918.
Ambassador: Addi Salam al-Ansi.

YUGOSLAVIA

Embassy: St 31, 79 A, POB 1180, Khartoum 1; tel (11) 41252.
Ambassador: Dr Vladimir Petkovski.
Head of Chancery and Consular Section: Vladan Peric.
Attaché: Zljeko Sabljak.
Administrative Officer: Ljubisa Protic.

ZAIRE

Embassy: St 13, New Extension, Block 12CE, 23, POB 4195, Khartoum; tel (11) 42424; telex 24192.
Ambassador: Kanyanga Fwadi.

International Organizations

EUROPEAN COMMUNITIES

External Delegation: 3rd Floor, The Arab Authority for Agricultural Investment and Development Bldg, Army Rd, POB 2363, Khartoum; tel (11) 75054; telex 23096.

SURINAME

BELGIUM

Embassy: Kwasistraat 10, Paramaribo; tel 99994.
Chargé d'affaires: Dr W. de Smet.

BRAZIL

Embassy: Maratakkastraat 2, Paramaribo; tel 91011.
Ambassador: Sergio da Veiga Watson.

CHINA, PEOPLE'S REPUBLIC

Embassy: Dr Axwijkstraat 45, POB 3042, Paramaribo; tel 51540; telex 197.
Ambassador: Shen Zhihian.

DENMARK

Consulate: Waterkant 92, POB 1849, Paramaribo; tel 71222; telex 128; fax 75718.
Consul: Flip Henry de Vries.

FINLAND

Consulate: Paramaribo.

FRANCE

Embassy: Gravenstraat 5-7 boven, POB 2648, Paramaribo; tel 76455; telex 181.
Chargé d'affaires: Gaston Le Paudert.

GERMANY

Consulate: Coppenamestraat 60, POB 1819, Paramaribo; tel 76963; telex 121; fax 71534.
Honorary Consul: Kurt Rolf Geilert.

GUYANA

Embassy: Gravenstraat 82, Paramaribo; tel 72509; telex 236; fax 72679.
Ambassador: Carl B. L. Morgan.
First Secretary: Barbara Haley.

INDIA

Embassy: Rode Kruislaan 10, Paramaribo; tel 98018.
Ambassador: Indervir Chopra.

INDONESIA

Embassy: Van Brussellaan 3, Uitvlugt, POB 157, Paramaribo; tel 97070; telex 120.
Ambassador: Soekadari Honggowongso.

JAPAN

Embassy: Gravenstraat 23-25, POB 2921, Paramaribo; tel 74860; telex 370; fax 12208.
Ambassador: Tatsuo Ishizaki.

KOREA, REPUBLIC

Embassy: Malebatrumstraat 1-5, POB 1896, Paramaribo; tel 77255.
Ambassador: Kim Kyo Shik.

LIBYA

People's Bureau: Dario Saveedralaan 4, Paramaribo; tel 90717.
Chargé d'affaires: A. Taher Aftees.

NETHERLANDS

Embassy: Mr Dr J. C. de Mirandastraat 10 boven, Paramaribo; tel 77211; telex 125.
Ambassador: Pieter Koch.

RUSSIA

Embassy: Anton Dragtenweg 17, POB 8127, Paramaribo; tel 72387; telex 354; fax 72387.
Ambassador: Yuri A. Dergaoussov.
Counsellor: Valeri V. Chtcherbakov.
First Secretary: Alexandre B. Kireenkov.
Third Secretary and Consul: Alexei S. Borovikov.

SWEDEN

Consulate: Gravenstraat 26, POB 1806, Paramaribo; tel 71100; telex 134.
Ambassador: Lennart Klackenberg (resident in Sweden).
Consul: Albert Jozef Brahim.

UNITED KINGDOM

Consulate: c/o VSH United Bldgs, Van't Hogerhuysstraat, POB 1300, Paramaribo; tel 72870; telex 144.
Honorary Consul: J. J. Healy.

USA

Embassy: Dr Sophie Redmondstraat 129, POB 1821, Paramaribo; tel 72900; telex 373; fax 10025.
Ambassador: John P. Leonard.
Deputy Chief of Mission: Stanley T. Myles.
Political Section: Theodore H. Andrews.
Political/Military Section: Lance Hopkins.
Commercial/Economic Section: Elizabeth Ewing.
Consular Section: Jacob DeRaat.
Administrative Section: Benjamin R. Justesen II.
US Information Service: tel 75051; fax 10025.
Public Affairs Officer (USIS): Carlos Bakota.
Office of the Defence Attaché: Maj. David R. Coven.
Communications Programme Officer: George Bristol.

VENEZUELA

Embassy: AGO-Gebouw, Gravenstraat 25, Paramaribo; tel 75401; telex 146; fax 75602.
Counsellor: Hildemaro Brito Tovar.
First Secretary and Chargé d'affaires: Germán Delgado.

International Organizations

EUROPEAN COMMUNITIES

External Delegation: 239 Dr Sophie Redmondstraat, POB 484, Paramaribo; tel 99322; telex 192; fax 93076.
Commission Delegate: Lutz Salzmann.

SWAZILAND

AUSTRIA

Consulate: Matsapa Industrial Site, POB 232, Malkerus; tel 84529; telex 2239.
Honorary Consul: Guntram Albrecht.

CHINA (TAIWAN)

Embassy: Embassy House, POB 56, Mbabane; tel 42379; telex 2167.
Ambassador: Dominic Chang.

DENMARK

Consulate: Sokhamlio Bldg, cnr Johnson and Walker Sts, POB 815 Mbabane; tel 43547; telex 2018; fax 43548.
Consul: Hans Christian Nøddeboe.

ISRAEL

Embassy: POB 146, Mbabane; tel 42626; fax 45857.
Ambassador: Arye Oded.
Second Secretary: Aliza Bin-Noun Binnewies.

MOZAMBIQUE

Embassy: POB 1212, Mbabane; tel 42904; telex 2248.
Ambassador: António Sumbana.

SOUTH AFRICA

Trade Mission: Standard Bank Pension Fund Bldg, Allister Miller St, POB 2507, Mbabane; tel 44651; telex 2341; fax 46944.
Ambassador and Trade Representative: E. du Toit.
Deputy Trade Representative: N. Wagner.

UNITED KINGDOM

High Commission: Allister Miller St, Mbabane; tel 42581; telex 2079; fax 42585.
High Commissioner: Brian Watkins.
Deputy High Commissioner: R. Milburn.
Defence Adviser: Lieut Col C. W. Larkin.
British Council Director: A. J. Kennedy.
Third Secretary (Management/Consular): B. W. Gard.
Third Secretary (Aid/Commercial): S. A. James.

USA

Embassy: Central Bank Bldg, Warner St, POB 199, Mbabane; tel 46441; telex 2285; fax 45959.
Ambassador: Stephen H. Rogers.
Deputy Head of Mission: Armajane Karaer.
Political, Economic and Consular Sections: John F. Hoover.
Administrative Section: Joseph B. Schreiber.
Agency for International Development: Roger D. Carlson.
Public Affairs Officer: Brooks Robinson.
Communications Programme Officer: Lynn O. Doughty.

ZAIRE

Consulate: Allister Miller St, Empire Bldg, Office No. 3, Mbabane; tel 43984; fax 43984.
Consul: Monsengo Bashwa.

International Organizations

EUROPEAN COMMUNITIES

External Delegation: Dhlan'ubeka Bldg, 3rd Floor, POB A36, Swazi Plaza, Mbabane; tel 42018; telex 2133; fax 46729.
Commission Delegate: Kieran John O'Cuneen.
Technical Adviser: José Pinto Teixeira.
Regional Training Adviser: Anthony Paul Crasner.

SWEDEN

ALBANIA

Embassy: Capellavägen 7, 181 32 Lidingö, Stockholm; tel (8) 731-09-20; fax (8) 767-65-57.
Attaché (Press/Culture) and Chargé d'affaires a.i.: Petraq Proko.
Counsellor (Commercial): Ilir Abdiu.
First Secretary: Dervish Mero.
Second Secretary: Pëllumb Moçka.
Attaché: Kostandin Vardhami.

ALGERIA

Embassy: Danderydsgt. 3-5, POB 26027, 100 41 Stockholm; tel (8) 679-91-40; telex 14734; fax (8) 611-49-57.
Minister-Counsellor: Ferhat Benchemam.
Counsellor: Ramdane Mekdoud.
Attaché: Mohamed Hamada.
Attaché: Mohamed Chérif Hassouna Ounis.

ANGOLA

Embassy: Hagagt. 1, POB 3199, 103 64 Stockholm; tel (8) 24-28-90; telex 12449; fax (8) 34-31-27.
Ambassador: García L. Vaz Contreiras.
First Secretary: Raimundo Quimona.
Second Secretary: Maria Helena Couto de Assis Boavida.
Second Secretary: António Daniel Helena.
Third Secretary: Filomena de Fátima Santana de Sousa Cunha.
Attaché: Lino Marques da Fonseca.
Attaché: José de Aragão Neto.
Attaché: Tolentina Rosaria Sambingo.
Attaché: Horácio Sampaio de Barros.

ARGENTINA

Embassy: Grevgt. 5, POB 14039, 104 40 Stockholm; tel (8) 663-19-65; telex 10029; fax (8) 661-00-09.
Ambassador: Federico Erhart del Campo.
Minister-Counsellor: Oscar Rasmussen.
Minister-Counsellor (Economic): Julio César Raimondi.
Air Attaché: Cdre Walter Domingo Barbero.
First Secretary: Luis Claudio Hashimoto.
First Secretary (Commercial): Eduardo Victor Galotti.
Second Secretary (Consular): Stella Maris Consentino.
Second Secretary (Commercial): Ricardo Nölting.
Second Secretary: Miguel Angel Hildmann.

AUSTRALIA

Embassy: Sergelstorg 12, POB 7003, 103 86 Stockholm; tel (8) 613-29-00; telex 10382; fax (8) 24-74-14.
Ambassador: Robert Stuart Merrilees.
First Secretary: Colin D. MacKenzie.
First Secretary (Consular/Administrative): Mark G. Barber.
First Secretary (Immigration): Cornelia Frederike Siegmund.
Second Secretary: Elizabeth J. Young.
Attaché: Trevor W. Paterson.

AUSTRIA

Embassy: Kommendörsgt. 35, 114 58 Stockholm; tel (8) 23-34-90; telex 10130; fax (8) 662-69-28.
Ambassador: Otto Pleinert.
Counsellor: Dr Michael Miess.
Counsellor (Administrative): Ludwig Kowarzik.
Counsellor (Culture/Press): Dr Liselotte Kitzwegerer.
Defence Attaché: Col Wolfgang Jung.
Consulate-General: Birger Jarlsgt. 67, 113 56 Stockholm; tel (8) 32-25-83; telex 16571.
Honorary Consul-General: Georg Åkerberg.
Consulate-General: Södra Vägen 28, 412 54 Gothenburg; tel (31) 16-10-78.
Honorary Consul-General: Martin Thomas.
Consulate: Grynbodgt. 7, POB 4084, 203 11 Malmö; tel (40) 79-945; fax (40) 23-65-72.
Honorary Consul: Horst Hans William Marschall.

BANGLADESH

Embassy: Sturegt. 6, 4th Floor, 114 35 Stockholm; tel (8) 669-95-55; telex 13158.
Ambassador: A. N. M. Nuruzzaman.
Counsellor: M. Sofiullah.
Counsellor (Economic): Azizur Rahman.

BELGIUM

Embassy: Villagt. 13A, POB 26114, 100 41 Stockholm; tel (8) 11-89-58; telex 17405; fax (8) 10-64-43.
Ambassador: Hugo F. V. Walschap.
First Secretary: Frank Recker.
Attaché (Administrative/Consular): Nora Top.

BOLIVIA

Embassy: Södra Kungsvägen 60, 181 Lidingö, Stockholm; tel (8) 731-58-30; fax (8) 767-63-11.
Ambassador: J. Medardo Navia Quiroga.
Minister-Counsellor (Political/Cultural): Carmen Bascón.
Minister-Counsellor (Economic/Consular): Fernando Calderón.
Attaché (Culture and Press): Ana Maria Velasco Jordán.

BOTSWANA

Embassy: Drottninggt. 56, POB 240, 101 28 Stockholm; tel (8) 723-00-35; telex 16848; fax (8) 723-00-87.
Ambassador: Alfred Uyapo Majaye Dube.
Counsellor: Disa Castro Mothusi Nkgowe.
Second Secretary: Dikgakamatso M. Moremi.
Attaché: Monica Mokgwathi.

BRAZIL

Embassy: Sturegt. 12, 114 36 Stockholm; tel (8) 663-12-85; telex 19132.
Ambassador: Luiz Augusto Pereira Soutomaior.
Naval Attaché: Capt. Jorge de Carvalho.
Air Attaché: Col João Lucio Gatti.
Second Secretary: Luis Eduardo Caracciolo Maya Ferreira.
Second Secretary: Oswaldo Biato Júnior.

BULGARIA

Embassy: Karlavägen 29, 114 31 Stockholm; tel (8) 723-09-38; telex 19369; fax (8) 214-50-30.
Ambassador: Alexander Stresov.
Counsellor (Commercial): Georgi Moussorliev.
First Secretary: Mihail Ninov.
First Secretary: Valentin Solakov.
First Secretary: Orlin Popivanov.
First Secretary (Political/Press): Volodia Neykov.
First Secretary: Dimitar Dokov.
Second Secretary: Krassimir Charkov.

BURUNDI

Embassy: Kommendörsgt. 35, 114 58 Stockholm; tel (8) 663-76-90; fax (8) 667-28-86.
Ambassador: Emmanuel Rwamibango (designate).

CANADA

Embassy: 7th Floor, Tegelbacken 4, POB 16129, 103 23 Stockholm; tel (8) 23-79-20; telex 10687; fax (8) 24-24-91.
Ambassador: Dennis B. Browne.
Counsellor and Consul: L. de Salaberry.
Counsellor (Commercial): E. C. H. Shelly.
Counsellor (Immigration): Richard E. Hetherington.
First Secretary (Administrative) and Consul: H. Knox.
First Secretary: G. M. Gramlick.
First Secretary (Immigration) and Consul: Paul J. Trueman.
Second Secretary (Commercial): Richard Bale.
Second Secretary (Immigration): Caroline Gurmond.

CHILE

Embassy: Kommendörsgt. 35, 114 58 Stockholm; tel (8) 662-04-44; telex 17580.
Ambassador: Carlos Humberto Parra M.
Minister-Counsellor: Carlos Vega.
Second Secretary: Rodrigo Nieto.
Second Secretary (Consular): Fernando Ayala.
Third Secretary: Jorge Norambuena.

CHINA, PEOPLE'S REPUBLIC

Embassy: Bragevägen 4, 114 26 Stockholm; tel (8) 21-75-39; telex 19608; fax (8) 10-80-86.
Ambassador: Tang Longbin.
Counsellor: Zheng Kejun.
Military, Naval and Air Attaché: Col Li Dianchang.
Assistant Military Attaché: Commdr Liu Junying.
Assistant Military Attaché: Col Cao Zhigang.
First Secretary: Lu Rong.
First Secretary: Jia Chengxi.
First Secretary: Gao Feng.
First Secretary: Zhang Zhenduo.
Commercial Section: Ringvägen 56, 181 34 Lidingö, Stockholm; tel (8) 767-40-83.
Counsellor (Commercial): Yang Zhenlun.
First Secretary (Commercial): Wu Tashui.
Cultural Section: tel (8) 11-44-25.
Counsellor (Cultural): Jiang Mingyi.
Consular Section: Baldersgt. 7B, 114 27 Stockholm; tel (8) 20-05-42.
First Secretary (Consular): Tang Chaoyue.
Scientific and Technical Section: Herserudsvägen 51, 181 35 Lidingö, Stockholm; tel (8) 767-75-26.
Counsellor (Scientific/Technical): Zhao Yingfu.

Educational Section: Sköldvägen 10, 182 64 Djusholm; tel (8) 755-23-18.
Counsellor (Education): Lin Xiaoan.

COLOMBIA

Embassy: Östermalmsgt. 46, POB 5627, 114 26 Stockholm; tel (8) 21-84-89; telex 16782.
Chargé d'affaires a.i.: Vilma Piedad Gómez Cano.

COSTA RICA

Embassy: Västra Vägen 1C, 171 46 Solna Stockholm; tel (8) 83-61-71; telex 17019.
Minister and Chargé d'affaires a.i.: Jorge A. Revollo Franco.
First Secretary (Commercial/Consular): Laura Garcia Saenz.

CUBA

Embassy: Karlavägen 49, 114 49 Stockholm; tel (8) 663-08-50; telex 11910; fax (8) 661-14-18.
Ambassador: Dr Leopoldo Ariza Hidalgo.
Counsellor: Miguel Angel Reguero Diaz.
Counsellor (Economic/Commercial): António Tomasi Vergara.
Third Secretary (Culture/Press): Medardo Roca Puente.
Attaché (Consular): Dr Zoraida Léon de Guzmán.
Attaché: Aldo Peña Figueroa.
Attaché: Oscar Torres Arencibia.

CYPRUS

Consulate-General: Kungsgt. 48, POB 3533, 103 69 Stockholm; tel (8) 21-81-84; telex 19397; fax (8) 24-80-94.
Honorary Consul-General: Bertil Sandstrom.

CZECHOSLOVAKIA

Embassy: Floragt. 13, 114 31 Stockholm; tel (8) 24-81-53; fax (8) 24-81-57.
Ambassador: Josef Kruželа.
Counsellor (Commercial): Josef Andel.
First Secretary: Jan Polách.
Second Secretary (Scientific): Karel Janecek.
Third Secretary (Consular): Jan Straka.
Attaché (Commercial): René Vochyan.
Attaché (Culture/Press): Roman Bužek.

DENMARK

Embassy: Gustav Adolfs Torg 14, POB 1638, 111 86 Stockholm; tel (8) 23-18-60; telex 19625; fax (8) 791-72-20.
Ambassador: Otto Rose Borch.
Minister-Counsellor: Niels Aadal Rasmussen.
Counsellor (Commercial): Bent Kristensen.
Counsellor: Jette Egelund.
Defence Attaché: Capt. Kaj Toft Madsen.
Vice-Consul (Consular): Karen Oppelstrup.
Vice-Consul (Commercial): Jørgen Kjørl.
Secretary (Export): Ellen Hansen.

Consulate-General: Linnégt. 7, 413 04 Gothenburg; POB 31075, 400 32 Gothenburg; tel (31) 85-80-00; telex 27509.
Consul-General: Ingvar Harald Fast.

Consulate-General: Södra Promenaden 69, POB 4058, 203 11 Malmö; tel (40) 12-33-44.
Consul-General: Per Bjarne Lindblad.

Consulate: Floatex Glas AB, Industriagt. 9-11, POB 788, 801 29 Gavle-Sandviken; tel (26) 11-51-90; telex 2647151; fax (26) 10-99-02.
Consul: Bertil Fredrik Carlbaum.

Consulate: Norrköpings Stuveri och Terminal AB, Stuvaregränd, POB 6075, 600 06 Norrköpings; tel (11) 25-06-00; telex 64341.
Consul: Stellan Viggo Slåne.

Consulate: Nastagt. 13, POB 9036, 700 09 Örebro; tel (19) 27-22-20; fax (19) 14-65-01.
Consul: Göran Isak Elof Bergholtz.

Consulate: Halmstads Sturveri AB, POB 1, 301 02 Halmstad; tel (35) 10-97-20; telex 38076.
Consul: Per-Olof Svarvar.

Consulate: Sparbanken Alfa Värmland, Kungsgt. 10, POB 56, 651 03 Karlstad; tel (54) 19-80-00; telex 66153.
Consul: Arne Petersson.

Consulate: Stortorget 16, 3 tr., POB 1417, 251 14 Helsingborg; tel (42) 18-33-57; fax (42) 24-03-26.
Consul: Bertil Bertilsson.

Consulate: c/o Stora Hotellet, POB 23, 551 12 Jönköping; tel (36) 11-93-00; telex 70057.
Consul: Bengt Johansson.

Consulate: Godsgt. 5, POB 174, 824 01 Hudiksvall; tel (650) 15-615; telex 71525.
Vice-Consul: Jerker Arndt.

Consulate: c/o Södrs Smålands Stadshypotek, POB 731, 391 27 Kalmar; tel (480) 22-160.
Vice-Consul: Ingemar Lögdahl.

Consulate: Sankt Larsgt. 42, 582 24 Linköping; tel (13) 12-03-07.
Vice-Consul: Sture Gustaf von der Burg.

Consulate: Trädgårdsgt. 20, 951 35 Luleå; tel (920) 15-602.
Vice-Consul: Arne Nyman.

Consulate: AB Nygeverken, 611 02 Nyköping; tel (155) 17-340; telex 64004.
Vice-Consul: Curt Johansson.

Consulate: Södra Långgt. 22, 572 00 Oskarshamn; tel (491) 16-135.
Vice-Consul: Lars Petersson.

Consulate: Södra Järnvägsgt. 49 C, 931 32 Skellefteå; tel (910) 36-475.
Vice-Consul: Bengt O. Gullesjö.

Consulate: S.C.A. Paper AB, POB 846, 851 23 Sundsvall; tel (60) 19-41-63; telex 71003.
Vice-Consul: Berndt Leonard Valdus Norberg.

Consulate: c/o Contactum AB, Renmarkstorget 5D, 902 47 Umeå; tel (90) 11-11-88.
Vice-Consul: Birger Johansson.

Consulate: c/o Rederi AB Gotland, Hamngt. 1, POB 2003, 621 02 Visby; tel (498) 60-500; telex 4133.
Vice-Consul: Eric D. Nilsson.

Consulate: I.C.A. Hakon AB, Sjöhagsvägen 3, 721 84 Västerås; tel (21) 19-30-00; telex 40702.
Vice-Consul: Birger Jarl Persson.

Consulate: Storegt. 6, POB 30, 891 01 Örnsköldsvik 1; tel (660) 10-235; telex 6057.
Vice-Consul: Björn Grundberg.

Consulate: Kyrkgt. 49. POB 3, 831 21 Östersund; tel (63) 12-48-30.
Vice-Consul: Gösta Heilborn.

Consulate: c/o C. Jahn AB, POB 66058, 500 06 Borås; tel (33) 10-01-15; telex 36235.
Vice-Consul: Leif Donald Rosén.

Consulate: Hamnvägen, POB 91, 311 21 Falkenburg; tel (346) 12-116; telex 38228; fax (346) 10-104.
Vice-Consul: Valter Nilsson.

Consulate: Kyrkogt. 25, 440 30 Marstrand; tel (303) 60-040.
Vice-Consul: Bengt Arvid Arvidson.

Consulate: Skaninaviska Enskilda Banken, Kungsgt. 12, 451 16 Uddevalla; tel (522) 36-310; fax (522) 39-784.
Vice-Consul: Lars-Erik Bohwalli.

Consulate: Kungsgt. 24-6, POB 151, 432 01 Varberg; tel (340) 16-130.
Vice-Consul: Carl Anders Lundgren.

Consulate: Vekerumsvägen, POB 85, 374 22 Karlshamn; tel (454) 16-000.
Vice-Consul: Bo Anders Lindqvist.

Consulate: Handelsbanken, Ronnebygt. 47, POB 1017, 371 24 Karlskrona; tel (455) 1-95-10; fax (455) 1-63-07.
Vice-Consul: Roland Aspelund.

Consulate: Kristianstads Sparbank, Ö. Blvden 52, POB 530, 291 25 Kristianstad; tel (44) 13-80-00.
Vice-Consul: Erik Johannesson.

Consulate: Boliden Bergsöe AB, Gasverksgt., POB 132, 261 22 Landskrona; tel (418) 1-61-50; telex 72386.
Vice-Consul: Niels Krarup Basse.

Consulate: Hamngt. 7, 272 00 Simrishhamn; tel (414) 1-18-60.
Vice-Consul: Göran Lundquist.

Consulate: Algt. 40, 231 42 Trelleborg; tel (410) 1-75-90.
Vice-Consul: Frans Jacob Malmros.

Consulate: Sandgärdsgt. 5, 352 33 Växjö; POB 1503, 351 15 Växjö; tel (470) 2-00-00 ; fax (470) 2-03-32.
Vice-Consul: Dick Lennart Söderlund.

Consulate: Hamngt. 16, POB 47, 271 21 Ystad; tel (411) 1-80-80; telex 32396; fax (411) 7-29-60.
Vice-Consul: Fredrik Olsson.

DOMINICAN REPUBLIC

Embassy: Djurgårdsslätten 104 I, 115 21 Stockholm; tel (8) 667-46-11.
First Secretary and Chargé d'affaires a.i.: Abigail Mejía-Ricart.

ECUADOR

Embassy: Engelbrektsgt. 13, POB 26095, 100 41 Stockholm; tel (8) 679-60-43; telex 15141; fax (8) 611-55-93.
Ambassador: Byron Morejón Almeida.
Counsellor: Enrique Arcas.
Second Secretary (Consular): María Gabriela Troya Rodríguez.

EGYPT

Embassy: Strandvägen 35, 114 56 Stockholm; tel (8) 662-96-03; telex 17325.
Ambassador: Abdel Rahman Ahmed Marei.
Minister: Dr Salah Kamel Ibrahim.
Counsellor: Nofal el-Sayed.
Counsellor (Tourism): Abu-Elmagd Abdel-Rahim Omar.
First Secretary: Gamil Said Fayed.
Attaché (Administrative): Helmi Shafik Torky.
Attaché (Administrative): Abdel Rahman Soliman Bassiouny.
Attaché (Administrative): Malek Mohamed Awad.
Attaché (Administrative): Maher Abdel Malek Soliman.

Commercial Section: Grevgt. 13, 114 53 Stockholm; tel (8) 661-58-29.
Counsellor (Commercial): Motaz Abdel Rahman Arafat.

ESTONIA

Embassy: Rådmansgt. 18, 114 52 Stockholm; tel (8) 10-99-86; fax (8) 10-77-44.
Ambassador: Margus Laidre.

ETHIOPIA

Embassy: Östermalmsgt. 34, POB 26116, 114 26 Stockholm; tel (8) 14-35-95; telex 12882; fax (8) 10-70-58.
Chargé d'affaires a.i.: Tekleab Kebede.
First Secretary: Agidew Bogale.
Second Secretary: Kebret Negash.
Third Secretary: Ashagre Kebede.

Attaché: Ayele Tsedekework.

FINLAND

Embassy: Jakobsgt. 6, 111 52 Stockholm; POB 7423, 103 91 Stockholm; tel (8) 24-02-70; telex 19692; fax (8) 20-74-97.
Ambassador: Björn-Olof Alholm.
Minister-Counsellor: Kirsti Lintonen.
Counsellor: Mikko Jokela.
Counsellor (Press): Mika Tapaninen.
Counsellor (Labour): Kaj Laxén.
Military, Naval and Air Attaché: Col Heikki Vilén.
Assistant Military, Naval and Air Attaché: Lieut Col Kaj Wallander.
First Secretary (Culture/Press): Juha Parikka.
Second Secretary (Administrative/Consular): Bo Lindroos.
Attaché (Social Affairs): Gunvor Brettschneider.
Attaché (Science): Jouko Lahtinen.

Consulate-General: Skadinaviska Enskilda Banken, Kungsträdgårdsgt. 8, 106 40 Stockholm; tel (8) 22-19-00.
Consul-General: Curt G. Olsson.

Consulate-General: Götgt. 10, 411 05 Gothenburg; POB 11084, 404 22 Gothenburg; tel (31) 80-10-50; telex 21721; fax (31) 15-70-78.
Consul-General: Tom Söderman.
Vice-Consul and Secretary (Commercial): Paul Aejmelaeus.
Vice-Consul and Secretary (Commercial): Risto Erjanti.

Consulate: Boras Wäfveri AB, Västerbrogt., 502 30 Borås; POB 52, 501 02 Borås; tel (33) 12-70-00.
Consul: Lars L. Mauritzon.

Consulate: F. Ahlgrens Tekn. Fabrik AB, Skeppsbron 26, POB 622, 801 26 Gavle-Sandviken; tel (26) 17-74-00.
Consul: Ove Anonsen.

Consulate: Norrfrys i Haparanda AB, POB 54, 953 00 Haparanda; tel (922) 1-14-10.
Consul: Allan Axel Lehto.

Consulate: Drottning Blankas väg 12, 393 52 Kalmar; POB 950, 391 29 Kalmar; tel (480) 2-06-12.
Consul: Ulf Christer Wahledow.

Consulate: Viscaria AB, POB 841, 981 28 Kiruna; tel (980) 7-16-10.
Consul: Bror Oskar Björnfot.

Consulate: AB Sydsten, Rundelsgt. 14, POB 4072, 203 11 Malmő 4; tel (40) 7-38-40.
Consul: Arne Wehtje.

Consulate: Älvavägen 5, 865 00 Alnö, Sundsvall; tel (60) 55-62-10.
Consul: Lars-Enar Gradin.

Consulate: c/o Saab-Scania AB, 461 80 Trollhätten; tel (520) 7-81-00.
Consul: Bertil Björkman.

Consulate: Fiskars Knivman AB, Stålbrånnaregt. 5, POB 1117, 631 80 Eskilstuna; tel (16) 14-72-50.
Vice-Consul: Jan Olaf Ekman.

Consulate: HDF-Bolagen AB, Svarvaregt. 5, 302 50 Halmstad; tel (35) 11-82-20.
Vice-Consul: Lars Ågren.

Consulate: AB Ramlösa Hälsobrunn, Bunkagårdsgt. 7, 253 68 Helsingborg; tel (42) 29-82-25.
Vice-Consul: Roland Bengtsson.

Consulate: Atteviks bil AB, John Bauersgt. 1, POB 2122, 550 02 Jonköping; tel (36) 16-91-00.
Vice-Consul: Per-Åke Tagesson Löf.

Consulate: Drottinggt. 28, Alice Tegnérs väg 4, 374 35 Karlshamn; tel (454) 1-52-85.
Vice-Consul: Einar Norrsell.

Consulate: Karlskrona Turist- och Konferensbyrå, Södra Smedjegt. 6, 371 83 Karlskrona; tel (455) 8-34-86.
Vice-Consul: Torsten Urban Wikström.

Consulate: W. Weibull AB, Föreningsgt. 217, 261 51 Landskrona; tel (418) 7-80-00.
Vice-Consul: Widar Weibull.

Consulate: TILL-Bryggerier AB, V. Varvasgt. 1, POB 828, 951 28 Luleå; tel (920) 1-04-45.
Vice-Consul: Gustaf Burström.

Consulate: Rud. Jönsson & Co., AB, Saltäangsgt. 33, POB 57, 601 02 Norrköpping; tel (11) 25-08-00.
Vice-Consul: Claes-Iwe Christer Wirström.

Consulate: Södra Aspagt. 1, 892 00 Domsjö, Ornsköldsvik; tel (660) 8-33-52.
Vice-Consul: Tore Erken.

Consulate: Göte Åström AB, Litsvägen 22, POB 578, 831 27 Ostersund; tel (63) 10-47-55.
Vice-Consul: Göte Åström.

Consulate: Curt Thylin AB, Nygt. 55, 931 31 Skellefteå; tel (910) 1-41-74.
Vice-Consul: Curt Thylin.

Consulate: c/o AB J. A. Henriksson & Co., POB 65, 913 00 Holsmund; tel (90) 11-30-13.
Vice-Consul: Claus Henriksson.

Consulate: Strandgt. 19, POB 2070, 621 02 Visby-voir-Gotland; tel (498) 1-26-00.
Vice-Consul: Magnus Wiman.

Consulate: AB Karlberg Bilaffår, Allén 62-4, POB 213, 593 01 Västervik; tel (490) 1-30-80; fax (490) 3-51-37.
Vice-Consul: Johan Karlberg.

Consulate: c/o Nordbanken, Smedjegt. 15, 721 03 Västerås; tel (21) 12-04-40.
Vice-Consul: Roland Hoijar.

Consulate: Vallgt. 8, 352 34 Växjö; tel (470) 1-18-10.
Vice-Consul: Egert Evestål.

Consulate: AB Stephan R. G. Örn, Regementgt. 40, 271 39 Ystad; POB 184, 271 00 Ystad; tel (411) 1-84-00.
Vice-Consul: Stephan Randall Gustaf Örn.

FRANCE

Embassy: Narvavägen 28, POB 10241, 115 23 Stockholm; tel (8) 663-02-70; telex 10864; fax (8) 660-62-90.
Ambassador: Philippe Louet.
First Counsellor: Renaud Levy.
Counsellor (Cultural): Jean-François de Raymond.
Defence Attaché: Lieut Col Thierry Destremau.
First Secretary (Political/Press): Gabriel Jugnet.
Attaché (Agricultural): Benoit Mousse.
Attaché (Tourism): Francine Cacheux.

Consular Section: Linnegt. 78, 115 23 Stockholm; tel (8) 67-01-00; telex 17085.
Second Secretary (Consular): Gilles Cottet Dumoulin.

Commercial and Economic Sections: Storgt. 11, 114 44 Stockholm; tel (8) 667-01-00; fax (8) 662-38-80.
Counsellor (Commercial): Gérard Gerold.

Scientific and Technical Sections: Grevgt. 36-8, 114 53 Stockholm; tel (8) 667-95-75.
Counsellor (Scientific/Technical): Pierre Baruch.

GERMANY

Embassy: Skarpögt. 9, 115 27 Stockholm; tel (8) 663-13-80; telex 19330; fax (8) 661-52-94.
Ambassador: Dr Reinhold Schenk.
Minister-Counsellor: Dr Albert Spiegel.
Counsellor (Cultural/Consular): Klaus Wilde.
Counsellor (Political): Welf Unterholzner.
Counsellor (Agriculture/Forestry): Dr Uwe Kosmack.
Counsellor (Economic): Peter Schönberg.
Defence Attaché: Capt. Jonny Fechtmann.
First Secretary (Social Affairs): Friedhelm Froemer.
Second Secretary (Administrative): Peter Liesenfeld.
Attaché (Press): Sonja Falkvoll.

Berlin Office: Bragevägen 2, 104 32 Stockholm; tel (8) 23-50-30; telex 19163.
Minister: Ursula Wetzl.
Counsellor (Commercial): Amdt Schönherr.
Counsellor: Wolfgang Beyer.
Military, Naval and Air Attaché: Capt. Werner Schanner.
Assistant Military, Naval and Air Attaché: Capt. Sigurd Stecher.
First Secretary (Political): Peter Escher.
First Secretary (Scientific): Jürgen Klotzke.
Attaché (Culture/Press): Hans-Dieter Ziesche.

Consular Section: Verdandigt. 2, 114 24 Stockholm; tel (8) 21-81-22.
Second Secretary (Consular): Hans Tietz.

Office of Counsellor for Transport: Kungsgt. 30, 111 22 Stockholm; tel (8) 10-35-36.
Counsellor (Transport): Gerhard Paul.

Consulate-General: Drottninggt. 63, POB 93, 401 21 Gothenburg; tel (31) 17-83-65; telex 27461; fax (31) 74-08-78.
Consul-General: Dr Alfred van Setten.

Consulate: Stationsgt. 74, POB 209, 301 04 Halmstad; tel (35) 11-86-90; fax (35) 10-45-85.
Honorary Consul: Erik Brolén.

Consulate: Järnvägsgt. 9, c/o Scandinavian Ferry Lines, POB 612, 251 06 Helsingborg; tel (42) 18-60-00; telex 72502; fax (42) 18-60-49.
Honorary Consul: Gunnar Östin.

Consulate: Gula Villan, Torntebogt. 2, POB 44, 551 12 Jönköping; tel (36) 16-91-20; telex 70110; fax (36) 16-91-55.
Honorary Consul: Bo-Erland Sjöberg.

Consulate: Fiskaregt. 12, 392 32 Kalmar; tel (480) 2-62-49; fax (480) 7-69-27.
Honorary Consul: Per Löwstedt.

Consulate: Rattgt. 6, POB 2088, 650 02 Karlstad; tel (54) 11-57-10.
Honorary Consul: Karl-Axel Samuelson.

Consulate: Stora Torget 7, 582 23 Linköping; tel (13) 14-60-30.
Honorary Consul: Harald Schröder.

Consulate: Timotejstigen 7, 954 00 Luleå; tel (920) 5-38-52.
Honorary Consul: Werner Jansen.

Consulate: Lundavägen 142, 212 24 Malmö; Skoogs Företagsgrupp AB, 205 70 Malmö; tel (40) 38-03-80; telex 33119; fax (40) 93-19-85.
Honorary Consul: Gunnar Skoog.

Consulate: c/o Göta Lantmän, Fleminggt. 9, 602 24 Norrköping; tel (11) 12-47-15.
Honorary Consul: Mats Blom.

Consulate: SCA Packaging AB, 851 88 Sundsvall; tel (60) 19-30-00; telex 71000.
Honorary Consul: Börje Nordenö.

Consulate: Johan Kocksgt. 42, POB 134, 231 01 Trelleborg; tel (410) 5-48-95; telex 33540; fax (410) 4-31-76.
Honorary Consul: Rolf Skog.

Consulate: Strömstadsvägen 37, 451 50 Uddevalla; POB 503, 451 21 Uddevalla; tel (522) 3-60-10.
Honorary Consul: Sven-Gunnar Karlsson.

Consulate: Strandgt. 18, 621 56 Visby; tel (489) 1-77-98.
Honorary Consul: Åke Sjöberg.

GREECE

Embassy: Riddargt. 60, 114 57 Stockholm; tel (8) 660-88-60; telex 13110; fax (8) 661-52-94.

Ambassador: Basile C. Patsikakis.
First Secretary: Georgios Paizis.
Second Secretary: Ekaterini-Katia Georgiou.
Attaché: Ilias Kouvelas.
Attaché: Alexander Mourkoyiannis.
Attaché: Marina Kokkalis.

Commercial Section: Linnégt. 65, 114 60 Stockholm; tel (8) 663-38-80.
Counsellor (Commercial): Vassilios Psonis.
Attaché (Commercial): Evagelia Samara-Ångström.

Consular Section: Grev Magnigt. 4, 114 55 Stockholm; tel (8) 661-78-80.

GUATEMALA

Embassy: Wittstockgt. 30, 115 27 Stockholm; tel (8) 660-52-29; telex 12364; fax (8) 660-42-29.
Ambassador: Dr Lars Henrik Pira Pérez (designate).
First Secretary (Consular) and Chargé d'affaires a.i.: María Jimena Diaz Gonzales.

GUINEA-BISSAU

Embassy: Sturegt. 8, 3rd Floor, POB 10141, 100 55 Stockholm; tel (8) 611-73-05; telex 12290.
Ambassador: Pio Gomes Correia.
Third Secretary: Bacar Intchasso.
Attaché (Administrative): Ligia Maria Correia Garcia.

HUNGARY

Embassy: Strandvägen 74, POB 27162, 115 27 Stockholm; tel (8) 661-67-62; telex 15355; fax (8) 660-29-59.
Ambassador: Dr András Hadjú.
Counsellor (Political): Sándor Mátyus.
Second Secretary (Science): Ferenc Molnàr.

Consular Section: Laboratoriegt. 2, 115 45 Stockholm; tel (8) 663-66-39.
First Secretary (Consular): Gyula Szombathelyi.

Commercial Section: Birger Jarlsgt. 37, 111 45 Stockholm; tel (8) 20-86-05.
Counsellor (Commercial): János Müller.
First Secretary (Commercial): Zsolt Monszpart.

Press Section: Torstenssonsgt. 4, 114 56 Stockholm; tel (8) 661-95-10.
First Secretary (Culture/Press): Gabriella Zimboras.

ICELAND

Embassy: Kommendörsgt. 35, 114 58 Stockholm; tel (8) 662-40-16; telex 11921; fax (8) 660-74-23.
Ambassador: Sigrídur Ásdís Snaevarr.
Counsellor (Commercial): Björn Gudmundsson.
First Secretary: Margrét Jónsdóttir.

Consulate-General: Östra Hamngt. 19A, 411 10 Gothenburg; tel (31) 11-68-68; fax (31) 93-54-40.
Consul-General: Gösta Christian Lundholm.

Consulate-General: Gibraltargt. 1, 211 20 Malmö; tel (40) 7-64-60; fax (40) 97-12-45.
Consul-General: Gösta Möllefors.

Consulate: Svenska Cellulosa AB SCA, 851 88 Sundsval; tel (60) 1-93-00; telex 71000; fax (60) 12-72-19.
Consul: Åke Carl Lennart Rietz.

Consulate: Högalundsgt. 19, 564 00 Bankeryd; POB 20, 564 01 Bankeryd; tel (36) 7-22-46.
Consul: Björn Leifland.

Consulate: Wiernergt. 9, POB 11025, 250 11 Helsingborg; tel (42) 11-47-50; telex 72359; fax (42) 14-23-40.
Vice-Consul: Carl Wilhelm Cullman.

Consulate: POB 113, 456 00 Kungshamn; tel (523) 3-09-50; telex 42909.
Vice-Consul: Thorsten Thörnblad.

Consulate: POB 14, 453 00 Lysekil; tel (523) 1-30-00; telex 42049; fax (523) 1-13-08.
Vice-Consul: Kjell Hanson.

Consulate: Kungsgt. 29, 432 44 Varberg; tel (340) 8-01-25.
Vice-Consul: Per-Olof Winquist.

INDIA

Embassy: Adolf Fredriks Kyrkogt. 12, POB 1340, 111 83 Stockholm; tel (8) 11-32-13; telex 11598; fax (8) 24-85-05.
Ambassador: Pushkar Johari.
Counsellor: B. Jaishankar.
Military, Naval and Air Attaché: Col O. P. Nandrajog.
First Secretary: R. K. Tyagi.
First Secretary: G. N. Vyas.

INDONESIA

Embassy: Strandvägen 47 V, 114 56 Stockholm; tel (8) 663-54-70; telex 19371.
Ambassador: Petronella Luhulima.
Counsellor (Political): Tatang Deradjat.
Second Secretary (Consular/Protocol): Septidarmi Affandi-Baroto.
Third Secretary (Administrative): Mr Sukirno.
Third Secretary (Cultural/Information): Linggawaty Hakim.
Attaché (Administrative): Robert Panangian Hutagalung.

IRAN

Embassy: Västra Yttringe Gård, Elfviksvägen, POB 6031, 181 06 Lidingö, Stockholm; tel (8) 765-20-29; telex 17791; fax (8) 765-31-19.
Ambassador: Mehdi Danesh Yazdi.
First Secretary: Abdollah Zarvan.
Third Secretary: Ali Hassani.
Third Secretary (Consular): Abolfazi Taheri-Far.
Third Secretary: Abdollah Edrissi Haghighi.
Attaché: Mashaollah Madani.
Attaché: Rahmatollah Raeisi Filabadi.
Attaché: Djamshid Hassan Pour.

IRAQ

Embassy: Baldersgt. 6A, POB 26031, 100 41 Stockholm; tel (8) 796-79-75; telex 11199; fax (8) 796-83-66.
First Secretary and Chargé d'affaires a.i.: Mohammed Said Al-Hani.
Third Secretary: Abdullah Y. Denkha.
Attaché: Hassan R. Abood.

IRELAND

Embassy: Östermalmsgt. 97, POB 10326, 100 55 Stockholm; tel (8) 661-80-05; telex 11821; fax (8) 660-13-53.
Ambassador: Paul D. Dempsey.
Secretary: Dympna Hayes.

Consulate-General: Scandinavian World Trade Centre, POB 5243, 402 24 Gothenburg; tel (31) 83-69-00; telex 20680; fax (31) 83-69-99.
Honorary Consul-General: Carl Gomer Brunius.

ISRAEL

Embassy: Torstenssonsgt. 4, POB 14006, 104 40 Stockholm; tel (8) 663-04-35; telex 19306; fax (8) 660-44-06.
Ambassador: Dr Moshe Yegar.
Counsellor: Yigal Caspi.
Counsellor (Economic): Hayim Bar-Shai.
Counsellor (Agricultural): Zvi Alon.
Counsellor (Scientific): Dr Yair Sharan.
Defence Attaché: Capt. Dan-Erik Melamed-Lemkov.
Second Secretary (Administrative): Tuvia Israeli.

ITALY

Embassy: Oakhill, Djurgården, 115 21 Stockholm; tel (8) 24-58-05; telex 10453; fax (8) 660-05-05.
Ambassador: Lucio Forattini.
First Counsellor: Venanzio Rapolla.
Counsellor (Commercial): Maurizio Giangolio.
Military, Naval and Air Attaché: Col Gioacchino Insolia.
Attaché (Cultural): Giuseppe Xausa.
Attaché (Scientific): Sergio Dellonte.

JAMAICA

Consulate: Posenbergsgt. 15A, 421 76 Vastra Frolunda; tel (31) 29-56-79.
Honorary Consul: Hyacinth Osterlin.

JAPAN

Embassy: Gärdesgt. 10, 115 27 Stockholm; tel (8) 663-04-40; telex 19948; fax (8) 661-88-20.
Ambassador: Yasushi Murazumi.
Minister-Counsellor: Akio Kawato.
Counsellor: Yuji Ooka.
Defence Attaché: Col Masao Kokubu.
First Secretary: Yoshiyuki Kaseda.
First Secretary: Hiroshi Uno.
First Secretary: Yoshinori Sumi.
First Secretary: Fumiyoshi Kashima.
Second Secretary: Makoto Izumi.
Third Secretary: Tatsukuni Uchida.

KENYA

Embassy: Birger Jarlsgt. 37, POB 7694, 103 95 Stockholm; tel (8) 21-83-00; telex 17811.
Ambassador: Peter J. Ndung'u.
First Secretary (Commercial): S. K. Kuria.
Second Secretary (Consular): P. K. Chege.
Third Secretary (Political): G. C. O. Maroko.
Third Secretary: Lucy C. Chumba.
Attaché (Press): G. Opiyo.
Attaché (Tourism): Wanjiru Muhoho.
Attaché (Financial): R. C. Muturi.

KOREA, DEMOCRATIC PEOPLE'S REPUBLIC

Embassy: N. Kungsvägen 37-39, 181 31 Lidingö, Stockholm; tel (8) 767-38-36; telex 17193.
Ambassador: Yong Jin Chon.
Counsellor: Han Chang Hyop.
Counsellor (Commercial): Pak Du Nam.
Second Secretary (Commercial): Kim Gi Myong.
Attaché: Hong Ryul.
Attaché: Li Chon Ung.

KOREA, REPUBLIC

Embassy: Sveavägen 90, 113 59 Stockholm; tel (8) 16-04-80.
Ambassador: Dong Eui Choi.
Counsellor: Kyu Jung Hwang.
Counsellor: Joon Kil Cha.
Counsellor: Young June Lee.
Military, Naval and Air Attaché: Col Hun Jong Kim.
Second Secretary: Seong Jin Kim.
Attaché: Kwang-Ho Shin.
Attaché (Culture/Information): Kyung-Jin Park.

LAOS

Embassy: Hornsgt. 82B, 1tr., POB 17113, 104 62 Stockholm; tel (8) 668-51-22; fax (8) 669-21-76.
Ambassador: Soutsakhone Pathammavong.
Second Secretary: Thongkhoun Sengphachanh.
Attaché: Khen Sombandith.

LEBANON

Embassy: Kommendörsgt. 35, 114 58 Stockholm; POB 10165, 100 55 Stockholm; tel (8) 665-19-65; telex 16407.
First Secretary and Chargé d'affaires a.i.: Hassan Saad.

LESOTHO

Consulate-General: Artillerigt. 24, 114 51 Stockholm.
Consul-General: Jan Mattson.

LIBYA

People's Bureau: Valhallavägen 74, POB 10133, 100 55 Stockholm; tel (8) 14-34-35.
Chargé d'affaires a.i.: el-Mehdi el-Khabat.
Member of Committee: Salhin Aliwhari.
Attaché: Ali Zaid Ageli.
Attaché (Financial): Abdalla el-Gredi.
Attaché (Consular): Salah Assilini.
Attaché (Commercial): Aisha Tarhuni.

LUXEMBOURG

Embassy: 5 rue Notre Dame, 2240 Luxembourg; tel 478271; telex 3405; fax 23144.
Ambassador: Paul Peters.

MALAYSIA

Embassy: Engelbrektsgt. 5, POB 26053, 100 41 Stockholm; tel (8) 679-59-90; telex 13416; fax (8) 611-31-90.
Ambassador: Datuk Yahya Baba (designate).
Counsellor and Chargé d'affaires a.i.: M. H. Arshad.
First Secretary: Wan Napsiah Salleh.
Third Secretary: Rozalah Hashim.
Attaché (Economic): Othman Ramli.
Attaché: Mohamed Zameri Hassan.

MALTA

Consulate-General: Siab, International Division, 115 86 Stockholm; tel (8) 782-00-00; telex 19986; fax (8) 660-53-48.
Honorary Consul-General: Kurt Nordgren.

Consulate: The Victory Hotel, Lilla Nygt. 5, 111 28 Stockholm; tel (8) 14-30-90; telex 14050; fax (8) 20-21-77.
Honorary Consul: Julian T. de Piro.

Consulate: Swede Chrome AB, POB 50575, 202 15 Malmö; tel (40) 38-88-00; telex 33942.
Honorary Consul: Claes Goran Wahlberg.

MAURITANIA

Consulate: Rasundavägen 158, 171 30 Solna; tel (8) 27-56-53.
Consul: Nils Diding.

MEXICO

Embassy: Grevgt. 3, POB 14058, 104 40 Stockholm; tel (8) 663-51-70; telex 10464; fax (8) 663-24-20.
Ambassador: Agustín García-López Santaolalla.
Counsellor: Benito Andión.
Counsellor (Commercial): Dr José Manuel Martínez Ayala.
First Secretary: Angel Ríos Bernal.

MOROCCO

Embassy: Kungsholmstorg 16, II tr., 112 21 Stockholm; tel (8) 54-43-83; telex 15545; fax (8) 51-97-96.
Ambassador: Saad Baddou.
Counsellor: Abdellatif Boukhari.
Second Secretary: Ali Moussaoui.
Attaché: Abdesselam Lyauk.

Consulate: Barnhusgt. 2, 411 02 Gothenburg; tel (31) 80-13-28.
Honorary Consul: Rune Hennung.
Vice-Consul: Per Håkan Hennung.

MOZAMBIQUE

Embassy: Sturegt. 46 IV, POB 5801, 102 48 Stockholm; tel (8) 666-03-50; telex 10906; fax (8) 663-67-29.
Ambassador: Alberto Massavanhane.
Second Secretary: António Munateia.
Attaché (Administrative): Caetano Filipe James.
Attaché (Consular): José Carlos Orlando Muchanga.

NETHERLANDS

Embassy: Götgt. 16A, POB 15048, 116 46 Stockholm; tel (8) 24-71-80; telex 10541; fax (8) 702-96-83.
Ambassador: Count L. de Marchant et d'Ansembourg.
Counsellor: A. E. Moses.
Counsellor (Agricultural): A. T. van der Struik.
Military and Air Attaché: Col J. G. Haffmans.
Naval Attaché: Lieut Col N. Nommensen.
First Secretary: R. E. Bosch.
Attaché (Consular/Administrative): Willem Weergang.

Consulate-General: Packhusplatsen 2, POB 327, 401 25 Gothenburg; tel (31) 13-04-50; fax (31) 11-87-88.
Consul-General: L. W. Björlin.

NEW ZEALAND

Consulate-General: Arsenalsgt. 8C, POB 16174, 103 24 Stockholm; tel (8) 611-68-24; telex 17990; fax (8) 614-21-50.
Honorary Consul-General: Peter Bonde.

NICARAGUA

Embassy: Sandhamnsgt. 40, 6th Floor, 115 28 Stockholm; tel (8) 667-16-57; telex 15484; fax (8) 662-41-60.
Ambassador: Patricia Delgado Montalvan.
Minister-Counsellor: Enrique Alvarado.
Attaché (Press/Culture): Marie-Thérèse Reichard de Alvarado.

NIGERIA

Embassy: Tyrgt. 8, POB 628, 101 32 Stockholm; tel (8) 24-63-90; telex 17649.
Ambassador: A. E. H. Emenyi.
Minister: A. O. Aderele.
First Secretary: I. K. Nwokike.
First Secretary (Consular/Political): A. Rockson.
Second Secretary: A. M. Bakare.
Second Secretary: M. S. Dole.
Attaché (Administrative): G. O. Azinge.
Attaché (Finance): A. K. O. Etuazim.

NORWAY

Embassy: Strandvägen 113-5, 115 27 Stockholm; tel (8) 667-06-20; telex 10112; fax (8) 782-98-99.
Ambassador: Olav Bucher-Johannessen.
Minister-Counsellor: Truis Hanevold.
Counsellor: Anne K. Lund Larsen.
Military, Naval and Air Attaché: Capt. Werner Johansen.

Commercial Section: Brunnsgt. 21-B, POB 7224, 103 89 Stockholm; tel (8) 24-62-40.
Counsellor (Commercial): Bjørn O. Bjørnsen.

PAKISTAN

Embassy: Grev Magnigt. 6, 114 55 Stockholm; tel (8) 663-59-05.
Ambassador: Arshad Sami Khan.
Counsellor: Akhtar Hussain Kazmi.
Military and Air Attaché: Col Salim Arshad.

PANAMA

Embassy: Östermalmsgt. 59, 114 50 Stockholm; tel (8) 612-12-91; fax (8) 663-04-07.
Ambassador: Tomas Humberto Jácome Díaz.
Attaché (Consular): Joaquín E. Jácome Díaz.

PERU

Embassy: Brunnsgt. 21B, 111 38 Stockholm; tel (8) 11-00-19; telex 16855; fax (8) 20-55-92.
Ambassador: Gustavo Silva-Aranda.
Counsellor: Luis Quesada Incháustegui.
Second Secretary: César de las Casas Díaz.

PHILIPPINES

Embassy: Skeppsbron 22, POB 2219, 103 15 Stockholm; tel (8) 23-56-65; telex 16585; fax (8) 14-07-14.
Ambassador: Luz G. del Mundo (designate).
Attaché and Chargé d'affaires a.i.: Romeo Segins.

Commercial Section: Skeppsbron 22, POB 2092, 103 13 Stockholm; tel (8) 20-67-17.
Attaché (Commercial): Rosalie R. Evangelista.

POLAND

Embassy: Karlavägen 35, 114 31 Stockholm; tel (8) 11-41-32; telex 19847; fax (8) 10-10-69.
Chargé d'affaires a.i. and Counsellor: Stanislaw Szumski.
Counsellor: Dionizy Such.
Military Attaché: Lieut Col Dobroslaw Maka.
First Secretary: Tomasz Jastrun.
First Secretary: Janusz Kutosz.
Second Secretary: Wlodzimierz Sokolowski.
Second Secretary: Janusz Bobek.
Third Secretary: Tadeusz Adamiak.
Attaché (Finance): Wlodzimierz Januszkiewicz.

Commercial Office: Friggagatan 4, 114 27 Stockholm.
Counsellor (Commercial): Jerzy Borowski.

Consulate-General: Prästgårdsgt. 5, 172 32 Sundbyberg; tel (8) 764-48-00; telex 17860; fax (8) 98-35-22.
Consul-General: Jan Turski.

Consulate-General: Adolf Fredriksgt. 13, 217 74 Malmő; tel (40) 26-87-86; telex 331183; fax (40) 91-45-90.
Consul-General: Ireneusz Dworzynski (acting).

PORTUGAL

Embassy: Fredrikshovsgt. 5, POB 27004, 102 51 Stockholm; tel (8) 662-60-28; telex 10118; fax (8) 662-53-29.
Ambassador: Maria Raquel Lopes de Bethencourt Ferreira.
First Secretary: José Manuel Pais Moreira.
Military, Naval and Air Attaché: Commdr Ernesto Correia dos Santos.
Attaché: César Ferreira Faustino.

Commercial Section: Karlaplan 10, 115 22 Stockholm; tel (8) 667-06-15.
Counsellor (Commercial): José António Nolasco Lamas.

ROMANIA

Embassy: Östermalmsgt. 36, POB 26043, 114 26 Stockholm; tel (8) 10-86-03; telex 10166.
Counsellor and Chargé d'affaires a.i.: Ilie Dorobantu.
Second Secretary (Consular): Marin Visan.
Second Secretary (Economic/Commercial): Nicusor Gliga.

RUSSIA

Embassy: Gjörwellsgt. 31, 112 60 Stockholm; tel (8) 13-04-40.
Ambassador: Oleg Grinevsky.

Minister-Counsellor: Dmitri Vassiliev.
Counsellor: Georgi Veremej.
Counsellor: Igor Nikiforov.
Counsellor: Vladimir Samouchine.
Military, Naval and Air Attaché: Gen. Gueorgui Demurin.
Counsellor: Anatoly Novikov.
Counsellor (Scientific): Chamil Souleimanov.
Naval Attaché: Nikolai Mazepa.
Assistant Military, Naval and Air Attaché: Col Gennady Savostiouk.
Assistant Military, Naval and Air Attaché: Lieut Col Vladimir Kondratiev.
Assistant Military, Naval and Air Attaché: Lieut Col Igor Sergoun.
First Secretary (Forestry): Alexandre Garkin.
First Secretary: Vladimir Kharine.
First Secretary: Valeri Lossine.
First Secretary: Sergei Rojenko.
First Secretary (Cultural): Dmitri Berkov.
First Secretary: Sergei Aksenov.
First Secretary: Vladimir Dmitriev.
Third Secretary (Social Affairs/Labour): Evgeni Chiplov.
Third Secretary (Press): Mikhail Skupkov.
Attaché (Agricultural): Dr Anatoli Petrov.

Commercial Section: Ringvägen 1, 181 34 Lidingö, Stockholm; tel (8) 765-11-80.
Commercial Representative: Orest Sossedov.

Consular Section: Kunsgt. 48, 111 35 Stockholm; tel (8) 20-86-52.
Counsellor (Consular): Alexandre Koudinov.

Consulate-General: Sigridsgt. 1, Gothenburg; tel (31) 40-89-00.

SAN MARINO

Consulate-General: Valhallavägen 108, 114 41 Stockholm; tel (8) 62-20-51.
Consul-General: Fredrik Wilhelm Lettstrom.

SAUDI ARABIA

Embassy: Sköldungagt. 5, POB 26073, 100 41 Stockholm; tel (8) 23-88-00; telex 14330.
Ambassador: Abdul-Rahman Ibrahim Alkadi.
Minister and Chargé d'affaires: Marwan Bashir al-Roume.
Third Secretary (Consular): Ali A. al-Yousef.
Attaché (Administrative): Jamil Z. A. Shaldhoom.

SENEGAL

Embassy: Stranvägen 7-B, POB 14025, 104 40 Stockholm; tel (8) 662-58-10; telex 12833.
Ambassador: Joseph Mathiam.
First Counsellor: Laurent Diatta.
First Secretary: Abdoulaye Sarr.
First Secretary: Mohamed Diajhaté Diaw.
Third Secretary: Moustapha Ndiaye.
Attaché: Mamadou Samb.
Attaché: Cheikh Mbaye.

SOMALIA

Embassy: Kommendörsgt. 35, 114 58 Stockholm; tel (8) 667-03-95; telex 12477.
Ambassador: Yusuf Haji Said.
First Counsellor: Mohamed Hussein Jama.
Counsellor (Culture): Ahmed Shire Jama.
First Secretary: Fozia Ali Mire.

SOUTH AFRICA

Embassy: Linnégt. 76, 115 23 Stockholm; tel (8) 24-39-50; telex 12142.
Ambassador: Eugene Myburgh.
Counsellor: Jacob Jacobus J. N. Lötter.
Second Secretary (Administrative): Anton Michael Meiring.
Third Secretary: Hermanus Jacobus van Niekerk.

Consulate: POB 3B, 411 13 Gothenburg; tel (31) 13-13-73.
Honorary Consul: U. Söderpalm.

SPAIN

Embassy: Hazeliusbacken 14, Djurgården, 115 21 Stockholm; tel (8) 662-54-94; telex 17160; fax (8) 663-79-65.
Ambassador: Antonio Serrano de Haro Medialdea.
Minister-Counsellor: Luis Garc'a Cerezo.
Counsellor (Cultural): Pedro Calvo-Sotelo.
Attaché: Guillermo Puerto.
Attaché (Labour): Bernado Diez Rodriguez.
Attaché (Education): Francisco Medina.

Commercial Section: Sergelstorg 12, 115 57 Stockholm; tel (8) 24-66-10.
Counsellor (Commercial): Isidoro Fernandez Valmayor.
Counsellor (Commercial): Alberto Alonso Diaz.

Office of Defence Attaché: Norrlandag 31-3, 111 43 Stockholm; tel (8) 791-75-69.
Defence Attaché: Lieut Col Luis Feliu.

SRI LANKA

Embassy: Strandvägen 39, POB 14053, 104 40 Stockholm 14; tel (8) 663-65-23; telex 12338; fax (8) 660-00-89.
Ambassador: Neville Jayaweera.
Second Secretary: Ahmed A. Jawad.
Third Secretary (Public Relations Officer): D. B. Gamage.
Attaché (Administration): B. U. W. Gunewardena.

SUDAN

Embassy: Centralvägen 12, POB 1341, 171 26 Solna, Stockholm; tel (8) 83-55-74; telex 12609.
Ambassador: Mohamed Zein Elabdeen Mohamed (designate).
Counsellor: Abdelrahman M. A. Dhirar.
First Secretary: Hamza E. Baau.
Attaché (Administrative): Ahmed Abdelgalil Mustafa.

SWITZERLAND

Embassy: Birger Jarlsgt. 64, POB 5616, 114 86 Stockholm; tel (8) 21-72-70; telex 19030; fax (8) 21-15-04.
Ambassador: Alfred Rüegg.
Counsellor: Peter Vogler.
Defence Attaché: Lieut Col Adolf Ludin.
Assistant Defence Attaché: Capt. Martin Schmid.
Attaché and Head of Chancery: Walter Deplazes.

TANZANIA

Embassy: Oxtorgsgt. 2-4, POB 7255, 103 89 Stockholm; tel (8) 24-48-70; telex 10514; fax (8) 10-98-15.
Ambassador: Mohamed Ramia Abdiwawa.
Minister-Counsellor: Hasman Omar Kibelloh.
Second Counsellor (Commercial/Economic): O. Sefue.
Attaché (Administrative): M. H. Mkugwa.

THAILAND

Embassy: Sandhamnsgt. 36, 5th Floor, POB 27065, 102 51 Stockholm; tel (8) 667-80-90; telex 13769; fax (8) 667-62-51.
Ambassador: Birath Israsena.
Counsellor: Mayurin Bhokay Asuphat.
Naval Attaché: Capt. Athikom Hoontrakool.
First Secretary: Preudtipong Kulthanan.
Second Secretary: Chowarit Salitula.
Second Secretary: Voradet Viravkin.

Commercial Section: Oxenstiernsgt. 33, POB 27082, 102 51 Stockholm; tel (8) 783-00-27; fax (8) 667-22-83.
Counsellor (Commercial): Prapan Vonkhorporn.
First Secretary (Commercial): Viroje Muneeunchuleekul.

TUNISIA

Embassy: POB 3219, 103 64 Stockholm; tel (8) 23-64-70; telex 19193; fax (8) 10-86-49.
Ambassador: Youssef Ben Haha.
Minister-Counsellor: Mahmoud Ayadi.
Counsellor: Dr Farouk Kobba Abdennabi.
First Secretary: Sihem Zmerli-Chaouch.
Second Secretary: Mohamed Ali Mansouri.

TURKEY

Embassy: Nobelgt. 19, 115 27 Stockholm; tel (8) 23-08-40; telex 17436.
Ambassador: Erdil K. Akay.
Counsellor: Veka Inal.
First Secretary: M. Akyut Sezgin.
Third Secretary: Namik Güner Erpul.

Commercial Section: Karlvägen 56, 114 49 Stockholm; tel (8) 661-64-83; fax (8) 666-96-25.
Assistant Commercial Counsellor: Firdevs Akyüz.

Culture and Education Sections: Sit Eriksgt. 101, 113 31 Stockholm; tel (8) 30-03-20.
Counsellor (Culture/Information): Tugrul Gülen.
Counsellor (Education): Nuri Demirci.

UGANDA

Consulate: PL 4047, Nybygget, 520 50 Stenstorp; tel (515) 3-10-64.
Honorary Consul: Tosten Johansson.

UNITED KINGDOM

Embassy: Skarpögt. 6-8, 115 27 Stockholm; tel (8) 667-01-40; telex 19340; fax (8) 662-99-89.
Ambassador: Robert L. B. Cormack.
Counsellor (Economic/Commercial): B. P. Austin.
Counsellor, Consul-General and Deputy Head of Mission: M. J. R. Guest.
Defence and Air Attaché: Group Capt. E. D. Stein.
Naval Attaché: Commdr J. J. M. Curtis.
Military Attaché: Lieut Col C. S. Harcourt-Smith.
First Secretary (Commercial): P. Beckingham.
First Secretary (Management) and Consul: N. F. Green.
First Secretary (Political/Information): M. Bradfield.
First Secretary (Political): R. J. Lyne.
Second Secretary (Chancery): R. P. R. Thompson.
Attaché (Culture) and British Council Director: Dr S. M. Lewis.

Consulate-General: Norra Hamngt. 32, 411 06 Gothenburg; tel (31) 80-07-78; telex 27350; fax (31) 80-27-61.
Honorary Consul-General: B. R. Morris.

Consulate: Götgt. 15, 411 05 Gothenburg; tel (31) 11-13-27; telex 28758; fax (31) 15-36-18.
Vice-Consul (Commercial/Consular): A. J. White.

Consulate: Drottninggt. 48, POB 604, 801 26 Gävle; tel (26) 18-03-03; telex 47039; fax (26) 18-32-75.
Honorary Consul: Karl-Erik Högberg.

Consulate: Gnstav Adolfs Torg 8C, 211 39 Malmö; tel (40) 11-55-25; fax (40) 11-02-03.
Honorary Consul: Anders Wixell.

Consulate: SSAB Tunnplåt AB, 951 88 Luleå; tel (920) 9-20-00; telex 50950; fax (920) 9-27-14.
Honorary Consul: J. E. Bergmark.

Consulate: SCA Timber AB, 851 88 Sundsvall; tel (60) 19-32-03; telex 71952; fax (60) 19-38-95.
Honorary Consul: O. Hildingsson.

USA

Embassy: Strandvägen 101, 115 89 Stockholm; tel (8) 783-53-00; telex 12060; fax (8) 661-19-64.
Ambassador: Charles E. Redman.
Deputy Head of Mission: Michael Klosson.
Political Section: Thomas R. Hanson.
Economic Section: Kenneth H. Kolb.
Commercial Section: Robert S. Connan.
Labour Officer: Robert J. Carroll.
Consular Section: Justice B. Stevens.
Administrative Section: Andrea J. Nelson.
Regional Security Officer: Phil A. Whitney.
Agricultural Section: Gordon S. Nicks.
Public Affairs Officer: George F. Beasley.
Office of Defence Attaché: Col John L. Golden.
Naval and Air Attaché: Capt. Daryl L. Kerr.
Military Attaché: Col Carl Gustav Finstrom, Jr.
Assistant Naval and Air Attaché: Capt. Charles C. Cook III.
Assistant Air Attaché: Commdr David N. Anderson.
Attaché (Press): Beatrice Camp.
Communications Programme Officer: James L. Butler.
Information Systems Manager: David C. Summers.

URUGUAY

Embassy: Kommendörsgt. 35, 114 58 Stockholm; tel (8) 660-31-96; telex 15361.
Ambassador: Pedro Vidal-Salaberry.
Second Secretary: Alfredo Raggio.
Attaché: Beatriz Rousserie de Schröder.

VENEZUELA

Embassy: Engelbrektsgt. 35B, POB 26012, 114 32 Stockholm; tel (8) 11-09-96; telex 12339; fax (8) 21-31-00.
Ambassador: Dr Demetrio Boersner.
Minister-Counsellor: José Eugenio Lopez Contreras.
Attaché (Culture): Maria Luisa Sanchez de Wetter.

VIET-NAM

Embassy: Örby Slottsväg 26, 125 36 Älvsjö, Stockholm; tel (8) 86-12-18; telex 10332; fax (8) 99-57-13.
Ambassador: Nguyen Dinh Phuong.
Counsellor: Le Chan Giai.
Counsellor: Doan Ngoc Thanh.
First Secretary: Coa Danh Quyen.
Second Secretary: Do Manh Hung.
Third Secretary: Nguyen Thi Bihn.

Commercial Section: Parkvägen 42, 131 41 Nacka, Stockholm; tel (8) 718-28-41; telex 15716.
Counsellor (Commercial): Doan Ngoc Thani.

YUGOSLAVIA

Embassy: Valhallavägen 70, 114 27 Stockholm; tel (8) 21-84-36; telex 11836.
Ambassador: Zlatan Kikić.
First Counsellor: Dr Dušan Crnogorcevic.
Counsellor (Press/Culture/Education): Djordje Mijalkovic.
Defence Attaché: Lieut Col Zivojin Djordjevic (resident in Yugoslavia).
First Secretary (Consular): Jadran Hocevar.
Second Secretary (Economic): Gordana Sokal.

ZAMBIA

Embassy: Klara Södra Kyrkogt. 1, POB 16148, 103 23 Stockholm; tel (8) 23-16-25; telex 11890; fax (8) 676-03-90.
Ambassador: Wilted Joseph Phiri.
Counsellor: Jackson V. B. Mukupa.
First Secretary: William L. Chintu.
Second Secretary: Fines Mampale Chileka.
Third Secretary: Delphine M. Mabuka.
Third Secretary: Leonard M. Chimedza.

ZIMBABWE

Embassy: Sveavägen 9-11, POB 7319, 103 90 Stockholm; tel (8) 24-66-95; telex 15145; fax (8) 21-91-32.
Ambassador: Dr Ngoni Togarepi Chideya.
Counsellor: Felix Ralph Nyamupinga.
First Secretary: Tatenda Makono.
Second Secretary: Moses Chikanyairo.
Third Secretary: Lucy Chapata-Mutata.

International Organizations

EUROPEAN COMMUNITIES

External Delegation: Hamngt. 6, 111 47 Stockholm; POB 7323, 103 90 Stockholm; tel (8) 611-11-72; telex 13449; fax (8) 611-44-35.
Head of Delegation: Ivo Dubois.
Counsellor: Hans-Jörn Hansen.
Attaché: Claude Lucchini.
Information Officer: Gudrun Waldenström.
Documentalist: Eva Knutsson-Hall.

SWITZERLAND

ALGERIA

Embassy: Willadingweg 74, 3006 Berne; tel (31) 446961; telex 912623.
Ambassador: Amor Benghezal.
Counsellor: Merzak Bedjaoui.
Counsellor: Naceur Boucherit.
Attaché: Merzak el-Gholam.

ARGENTINA

Embassy: Jungfraustr. 1, 2nd Floor, 3005 Berne; tel (31) 443565; telex 911862; fax (31) 440519.
Ambassador: Susana Ruiz Cerutti.
Minister-Counsellor: Carlos Alfredo Carrasco.
Second Secretary: Marcos Antonio Bidal d'Asfeld.
Attaché (Administrative): Guillermo D. Tkaczyk.

Commercial and Economic Section: Spitalgasse 38, 3011 Berne; tel (31) 227061; telex 911862; fax (31) 227073.
Minister-Counsellor (Economic/Commercial): Mario Adolfo Boffi.

AUSTRALIA

Embassy: Alpenstr. 29, 3006 Berne; tel (31) 430143; telex 911992; fax (31) 441234.
Ambassador: John Brook.
First Secretary and Consul: William Jackson.
First Secretary (Immigration): Peter O'Hoy.

Consulate: 56-8 rue de Moillebeau, 1211 Geneva 19; (22) 7346200; telex 414157; fax (22) 7336586.
Consul: Kevin R. Thornton.

AUSTRIA

Embassy: Kirchenfeldstr. 28, 3005 Berne; tel (31) 430111; telex 911754; fax (31) 435664.
Ambassador: Franz Parak.
Minister: Helmut Wessely.
Counsellor (Press/Culture): Otto Schüngel.
Defence Attaché: Brig. Günther Greindl.
Second Secretary: Michael Schwarzinger.
Third Secretary (Administrative): Hartwig Pomper.

Consulate-General: Geneva.
Honorary Consul: Jacques Mayer.

Consulate-General: Minervastr. 116, 8032 Zürich; tel (1) 3837200; telex 816380; fax (1) 3820422.
Consul-General: Aurel Saupe.
Consul: Othmar Wiedenhofer.

Consulate-General: Leimenstr. 1, 4002 Basel; tel (61) 257733; telex 964418; fax (61) 255847.
Honorary Consul-General: Bernhard Maria Menzinger.

Consulate: ave d'Ouchy 66, 1000 Lausanne 6; tel (21) 272894; telex 454452; fax (21) 273585.
Honorary Consul: Carlo de Mercurio.

Consulate: Hirschengraben 13, 6003 Lucerne; tel (41) 234182; telex 865663.
Honorary Consul: Max Turnauer.

Consulate: Via Pretorio 7, 6900 Lugano; tel (91) 235681; telex 844068.
Honorary Consul: Niccoló Lucchini.

Consulate: Quaderstr. 8, Postfach 922, 7000 Chur; tel (81) 229456.
Honorary Consul: Wolfgang Alfred Wunderlich.

Consulate: St Leonhard Str. 20, 4 Stock., 9000 St Gallen; tel (71) 223366.
Honorary Consul: Fredmund Mahk.

BELGIUM

Embassy: Weststr. 6, 3005 Berne; tel (31) 430462; telex 912896; fax (31) 445961.
Ambassador: Roland Burny.
Counsellor: Joris Couvreur.
Military and Air Attaché: Col Willy Vermeerbergen.
Second Secretary: Lucien Wylin.

BELIZE

Consulate-General: BP 106, 1 rue Pedro-Meylan, Geneva 17; tel (22) 7863883; telex 429286; fax (22) 7369939.
Honorary Consul-General: Terence Furey.

BENIN

Consulate-General: Thiersteinallee 12, Postfach 2550, 4002 Basel; tel (61) 206276; fax (61) 3367135.
Consul-General: Louis Chapalay.

BRAZIL

Embassy: Monbijoustr. 68, 3007 Berne; tel (31) 458515; telex 911541; fax (31) 453394.
Ambassador: José Olympio Rache-de-Almeida.
Counsellor: Affonso José Santos.
Second Secretary: Silas Leite da Silva.

BULGARIA

Embassy: Bernastr. 2, 3005 Berne; tel (31) 431455; telex 911786.
Ambassador: Spas Georgiyev.
Minister: Todot Georgiyev Anguelov.
Counsellor (Commercial): Todor Totev Matanov.
First Secretary (Culture): Kamen Mintchev.
First Secretary (Commercial): Mitu Petrov Ouzounov.
Third Secretary (Consular): Plamen Bounzin.
Third Secretary (Science/Technology): Todor Khitov Stoyanov.

CAMEROON

Embassy: Brunnadernrain 29, 3006 Berne; tel (31) 444737; telex 413515.
Ambassador: François-Xavier Ngoubeyou.
Second Counsellor: Victorine Mbette Mbongue.
Military Attaché: Col Marc-Guillaume Nguidjol.
First Secretary: Emmanuel Kita Kejuo.
Attaché (Culture): Athanase Anjongo.

CANADA

Embassy: Kirchenfeldstr. 88, POB 3000, 3005 Berne 6; tel (31) 446381; telex 911308; fax (31) 447315.
Ambassador: Jacques S. Roy.
Counsellor (Commercial) and Consul: Jean-Marc Duval.
Counsellor and Consul: D. Whiteside.
Second Secretary (Administrative) and Vice-Consul: Florence Charbonneau.
Third Secretary (Commercial) and Vice-Consul: P. J. Connors.
Attaché: Gérald L. Bennett.

Immigration Office: Belpstr. 11, POB 1261, 3007 Berne; tel (31) 252261.
Counsellor (Immigration): J. Laurent Gagnon.
First Secretary (Immigration): Bernard Leclerc.
Second Secretary (Immigration) and Vice-Consul: H. O. Mueller.

CHILE

Embassy: Eigerplatz 5, 12th Floor, 3007 Berne; tel (31) 450745; telex 912862.
Chargé d'affaires a.i.: Juan Miguel Heiremanns Etcheberry.
Second Secretary (Consular): Patricio Pradel Elgueta.

CHINA, PEOPLE'S REPUBLIC

Embassy: Kalcheggweg 10, 3006 Berne; tel (31) 447333; telex 912616; fax (31) 434753.
Ambassador: Cai Fangbo.
Counsellor: Pan Haifeng.
Counsellor (Commercial): Sha Wei.
Counsellor (Education): Zhang Zuwang.
Military and Air Attaché: Yu Shuiqing.
Assistant Military and Air Attaché: Zhang Jiuxi.
First Secretary (Science/Technology): Zeng Guanhua.
First Secretary and Head of Chancery: Lu Hongao.
First Secretary (Consular): Wang Xian.
First Secretary: Xing Hua.
First Secretary: Liang Dongbi.
First Secretary (Culture): Yang Deyan.
First Secretary (Commercial): Ling Zhicun.
First Secretary (Commercial): Zhao Peng.
Second Secretary (Culture): Jiang Zhenxiao.
Second Secretary (Administrative): Li Shouqin.

COLOMBIA

Embassy: Willadingweg 27, 3006 Berne; tel (31) 431700; telex 912170; fax (31) 447072.
Ambassador: Enrique Low-Murtra.
Counsellor (Consular): Nancy Lara.
Second Secretary: Jaime Suarez.

COSTA RICA

Embassy: Kornhausplatz 7, 3000 Berne; tel (31) 228438; telex 911145; fax (31) 227829.
Ambassador: Carlos Darío Angulo-Zeledon.
Minister-Counsellor: Nora Ruiz Gonzalez de Angulo.

COTE D'IVOIRE

Embassy: Thormannstr. 51, 3005 Berne; tel (31) 431051; telex 912718.
Ambassador: Joseph-Georges Anoma.
Counsellor (Commercial): Gbizié Gbakayaro.
First Secretary (Consular): Danié Zagba.
Second Secretary (Finance): Charles Daho.

CUBA

Embassy: Gesellschaftsstr. 8, 3012 Berne; tel (31) 242111; telex 912621.
Ambassador: Madeleine Teran Rodríguez.
Counsellor: Rosa Gonzalez Hernandez.

CYPRUS

Consulate-General: Talstr. 83, 8001 Zürich; tel (1) 2213023; telex 813855; fax (1) 2211287.
Honorary Consul-General: Thomas Schmidheiny.

Consulate-General: 25 rue Schaub, 1202 Geneva; tel (22) 7341739.

Honorary Consul-General: Louis Nagel.

CZECHOSLOVAKIA

Embassy: Muristr. 53, 3006 Berne; tel (31) 443645; telex 911415; fax (31) 447502.

Commercial Section: Thunstr. 99, 3006 Berne; tel (31) 443646; fax (31) 434859.
Ambassador: Miloslav Kočárek.
Counsellor: Jiří Jiříček.
Counsellor: Aleš Janku.
First Secretary: Václav Hynek.
Third Secretary: Milan Kovář.
Secretary: Jarmila Madejová.

DENMARK

Embassy: Thunstr. 95, 3006 Berne; tel (31) 445011; telex 911933; fax (31) 432395.
Ambassador: Gunnar Schack Larsen.
Chancellor and Vice-Consul: Ingrid Moergell.
Counsellor (Fisheries): Holger Bak Andersen.

Consulate-General: Bürglistr. 8, 8002 Zürich; Postfach, 8027 Zurich; tel (1) 2016670; telex 816581; fax (1) 2025470.
Consul-General and Counsellor (Commercial): Gunner Tetler.
Vice-Consul and Secretary: Ruth Ruoff.
Export Assistant: Steen Kreinbrink.

Consulate: Küchengasse 16, POB 631, 4100 Basel; tel (61) 231133; telex 963283; fax (61) 236918.
Consul: Knud Rolf Thomsen.
Secretary: Jeanette Nyffenegger.

Consulate: 60 rue du Strand, BP 453, 1211 Geneva 11; tel (22) 206640; telex 423944; fax (22) 284750.
Consul: Poul Rasmussen.

Consulate: ave Marie-Belgia 3, 1006 Lausanne; BP 51, 1000 Lausanne 19; tel (21) 267126; telex 45442.
Consul: Bernard-Louis Ischy.
Vice-Consul and Secretary: Åse Goy-Hovgaard.

Consulate: Via Pioda 8, CP 2105, 6901 Lugano; tel (91) 232358; fax (91) 229527.
Consul: Giovanni Gianola.
Vice-Consul: Hanspeter Stadler.

ECUADOR

Embassy: Helvetiastr. 19A, 3005 Berne; tel (31) 431755; telex 911476; fax (31) 432771.
Chargé d'affaires a.i.: Luis Verdesoto.
Counsellor (Commercial): Patricio Romero (resident in Geneva).
Second Secretary: Martha Parra.

Consulate: Barfusserplatz 14/3, 4051 Basel; tel (61) 256517.
Honorary Consul: Christoph Hodel.

Consulate: Limmatstr. 275, 8005 Zürich; tel (1) 2717995.
Honorary Consul: Peter Brogli.

Consulate: Via della Posta 4, 6900 Lugano; tel (91) 7315289.
Honorary Consul: Gloria Rezzonico.

Consulate: rue de Lausanne 139, 1202 Geneva; tel (22) 7315289.
Chargé d'affaires a.i. (Consular): Santiago Apunte.

EGYPT

Embassy: Elfenauweg 61, 3006 Berne; tel (31) 448012; telex 912210.
Ambassador: Mamdouh Abdel Razek.
Minister: May Mohamed Aboul-Dahab.
Counsellor: Hussein Serry.
Counsellor (Culture): Ahmed el-Borai.
First Secretary: Mohamed Omar Borhan Hassan Said.
Attaché: Hany Moawad Selim.
Attaché (Press/Information): Naela Chahine.

ESTONIA

Consulate-General: 8 chemin des Aulx, 1228 Plan-les-Ouates/Geneva; tel (22) 7061252; telex 429422; fax (22) 7949478.
Honorary Consul-General: Enn Vallak.

FINLAND

Embassy: Weltpoststr. 4, 3015 Berne; Postfach 11, 3000 Berne; tel (31) 433031; telex 912023; fax (31) 433001.
Ambassador: Paavo Kaarlhevo.
Counsellor (Press/Culture): Kaj Virtarinne.
Military and Air Attaché: Lieut Col Esko Lappalainen.
First Secretary: Jukka Tapio Pietkäinen.
Attaché: Pentti Juhani Nuorluoto.
Attaché (Industry): Taavi Hiltunen.
Attaché: Anne-Marie Tuominen.

Consulate-General: Sihlstr. 17, 8001 Zürich; tel (1) 2113692.
Consul-General: Rudolf Lienert.

Consulate: Dufourstr. 24, 8008 Zürich; tel (1) 2621050; fax (1) 2518344.
Secretary (Commercial): Aarni Jaranka.

Consulate: Kornhausgasse 7, 4051 Basel; tel (61) 258850; telex 963183.
Consul: Andre Charles Egg.

Consulate: 25 Grand-Rue, 1211 Geneva 11; tel (22) 218375.
Consul: Olivier Mach.

Consulate: 2 ave Jean-Jacques Mercier, 1003 Lausanne; tel (21) 237460.
Consul: Eugene Ruffy.

Consulate: Via Alla Campagna 2A, CP 157, 6904 Lugano; tel (91) 515645.
Consul: Lorenzo Wullschleger.

Consulate: Meisenweg 9, 6006 Lucerne; tel (41) 313975.
Consul: Martin Arnold.

FRANCE

Embassy: Schosshaldenstr. 46, Postfach 3000, 3006 Berne; tel (31) 432424; telex 912738; fax (31) 252623.
Ambassador: Philippe Cuvillier.
First Counsellor: Bernard Fassier.
Counsellor (Culture/Science): Yves Martial.
Counsellor (Science/Technology): Michel Chauvin.
Forces Attaché: Col Yves Pognat.
First Secretary: Hélène Drougoul.
Third Secretary (Consular): Véra Valenza.
Third Secretary: Jean-Pierre Clément.
Attaché (Agriculture): François Diebold.
Attaché (Culture): François Josephe.

Commercial Section: Sulgeneckstr. 37, 3007 Berne; tel (31) 253364.
Counsellor (Economic/Commercial): Pierre-Louis Labadie.
Counsellor (Commercial): Claude Magand.

Financial Section: Weststr. 4, 3005 Berne; tel (31) 435888.
Counsellor (Finance): Eliane Mossé.

Consulate-General: Elisabethenstr. 33, Postfach 255, 4010 Basel; tel (61) 236318.

Consulate-General: 11 rue Imbert-Galloix, BP 1200, Geneva; tel (22) 296211.

Consulate-General: Mühlebachstr. 7, 8008 Zürich; tel (1) 2518544.

GERMANY

Embassy: Willadingweg 83, 3006 Berne; Postfach 250, 3000 Berne; tel (31) 440831; telex 911565; fax (31) 430861.
Ambassador: Dr Wolfram Dufner.
Minister: Hermann Wentker.
Counsellor: Bodo Karkow.
Counsellor: Götz von Bullion.
Counsellor: Thomas Gläser.
Defence Attaché: Lieut Col Albrecht Freiherr von und zu Egloffstein.
First Secretary: Christine Gläser.
Second Secretary: Erhard Knoop.
Third Secretary (Consular): Hermann Rödel.
Third Secretary (Consular/Economic): Hans-Josef Gerhards.
Third Secretary (Press/Culture): Hubertine Steinhausen.
Third Secretary (Administrative): Karl Schmidt.
Third Secretary (Consular): Michael Haberl.
Third Secretary (Consular/Administrative): Bettina Haupt.

Berlin Office: Brunnaderstr. 53, 3006 Berne; tel (31) 448346; telex 912911; fax (31) 448261.
Minister: Eckhard Bibow.
Counsellor: Arnold Tschirlich.
Counsellor (Commercial): Karl-Heinz Baron.
Military and Air Attaché: Lieut Col Klaus Peter Adam.
Assistant Military and Air Attaché: Lieut Col Uwe Matthäi.
Second Secretary (Science/Technology): Frank Montwill.
Second Secretary (Consular): Ingolf Bierbach.

Consulate-General: Kirchgasse 48, Postfach, 8024 Zurich; tel (1) 2516936; telex 817434; fax (1) 2515616.
Consul-General: Theodor Schmitz.

Consulate-General: Parkweg 12, 4051 Basel; Postfach 3026, 4002 Basel; tel (61) 220822.
Honorary Consul-General: Luzius Gloor.

Consulate: Via Soave 9, 6900 Lugano; Via Maderno 21, 6901 Lugano; tel (91) 227882.
Honorary Consul: Joseph Wick.

GHANA

Embassy: Belpstr. 11, Postfach, 3001 Berne; tel (31) 257852; telex 912993; fax (31) 254941.
Ambassador: Kojo Amoo-Gottfried.
First Secretary and Head of Chancery: Charles Stephen Kwadzo Fenuku.
Second Secretary: Godwin Kofi Seade.

GREECE

Embassy: Jungfraustr. 3, 3005 Berne; tel (31) 441637; telex 912479; fax (31) 440557.
Ambassador: Emmanuel S. Spyridakis.
Counsellor (Press/Information): Stylianos Beys-Kamnarokos.
Second Secretary: Anastassios Petrovas.
Attaché (Consular): Ioanna-Angeliki Pappas-Eskiadou.

Economic and Commercial Sections: Kirchenfeldstr. 31, 3005 Berne; tel (31) 445753.
Counsellor (Economic/Commercial): Ioannis Cambas.
Counsellor (Commercial): Sophie Papadimitriou.

GUATEMALA

Embassy: Aarstr. 98, 3005 Berne; tel (31) 224072; fax (31) 210836.
Ambassador: Julio Palomo Silva.

HOLY SEE

Apostolic Nunciature: Thunstr. 60, 3006 Berne; tel (31) 446040; fax (31) 445064.
Apostolic Nuncio: Most Rev. Edoardo Rovida, Titular Archbishop of Taormina.
Secretary: Jósef Wesolowski.

HUNGARY

Embassy: Muristr. 31, 3006 Berne; tel (31) 448572; telex 912921; fax (31) 432001.
Ambassador: János Hajdú.
Defence Attaché: Col Ferenc Kántor.
First Secretary: László Püspök.
First Secretary: Vince Horváth.
Second Secretary: Tibor Fürtös.
Attaché: Hannelore Püspök.

Commercial Section: Sulgeneckstr. 64, 3006 Berne; tel (31) 454596; telex 911778; fax (31) 457728.
Counsellor (Commercial): Károly Samu.

ICELAND

Consulate: Junkerngasse 23, 3000 Berne 8; tel (31) 229931; telex 912212; fax (31) 222769.
Honorary Consul: Vinzenz Losinger.

Consulate: 8 rue du Mont de Sion, 1206 Geneva; tel (22) 471642; telex 423291; fax (22) 466838.
Honorary Consul: Roland Niklaus.

Consulate: Bahnhofstr. 44, 8023 Zürich; tel (1) 2111338; telex 813353; fax (1) 2118068.
Honorary Consul: Dr Georg Wiederkehr.

INDIA

Embassy: Effingerstr. 45, 3008 Berne; tel (31) 263111; telex 911829; fax (31) 262687.
Ambassador: Madhav Keshav Mangalmurti.
Counsellor: Om Prakesh Shahria.
First Secretary: Rajat Saha.
First Secretary: Mukund Vasudeo Kotnis.
Attaché: Partap Singh Chugh.
Attaché: Prit Pal Singh.
Attaché: Subramaniam Kanakasabesan Tirunelveli.
Attaché: Mahesh Chand Arora.

Consulate-General: 9 rue de Valais, 1202 Geneva; tel (22) 7320859; telex 412651; fax (22) 7315471.
Consul-General: S. K. Tripathi.

INDONESIA

Embassy: Elfenauweg 51, POB 270, 3006 Berne; tel (31) 440983; telex 911525; fax (31) 435283.
Ambassador: Dr Sjahabuddin Arifin.
Counsellor (Economic/Political): Mr Wisnusugriwo.
Second Secretary (Administrative): Sumjan Sjamsuddin.
Second Secretary (Administrative): Siti Partinah Sastroatmodjo.
Second Secretary (Culture/Press): Abdullah Lamrat.
Third Secretary (Economic): Marlina Surachmi.
Third Secretary (Consular): Indra Kesuma Oesman.
Third Secretary (Economic): Marina Estella Anwar Bey.
Third Secretary (Political): Agus Mursito.

IRAN

Embassy: Thunstr. 68, 3006 Berne; tel (31) 430801; telex 912779; fax (31) 435652.
Ambassador: Seyyed Mohammad Hossein Malaek.
Military Attaché: Lieut Col Farajollah Farsiabi.
Second Secretary: Mohammad Hossein Latify.
Third Secretary: Bahman Agharazi Darmani.
Attaché: Majid Tynnejhad.
Attaché: Ebrahim Gardouzadeh.

IRAQ

Embassy: Elfenstr. 6, 3006 Berne; tel (31) 434043; telex 912043.
Ambassador: Abd Ali Hamdan al-Dairi.
First Secretary: Moayed I. al-Mulla Hussain.
Third Secretary: Mohammed Salman Abbas.
Attaché: Hassen Ali Mohammed al-Hadad.
Attaché: Naser Taleb.
Attaché: Mowayad Jeyad.

IRELAND

Embassy: Eigerstr. 71, 3007 Berne; tel (31) 462353; telex 912917; fax (31) 460156.
Ambassador: Dermot Patrick Waldron.
Secretary: William Robinson Henry.

ISRAEL

Embassy: Marienstr. 27, 3005 Berne; tel (31) 431042; telex 912608; fax (31) 441582.
Ambassador: Yehuda Horam.
Counsellor: Arie Avidor.
Defence and Forces Attaché: Col Moredechai Alon.
Attaché: Yossef Alon.
Attaché: Benyamin Mevorach-Levy.

ITALY

Embassy: Elfenstr. 14, 3006 Berne; tel (31) 444151; telex 32202; fax (31) 431026.
Ambassador: Onofrio Solari Bozzi.
First Counsellor: Carlo Ungaro.
Counsellor: Marialetizia Polastro.
First Secretary: Luigi Maccotta.
Attaché (Culture): Carlo Silvio Francescaglia.

Commercial and Social Sections: Willadingweg 23, 3006 Berne; tel (31) 443134.
Counsellor (Commercial): Giovanni Ceruti.
First Secretary (Social Affairs): Arnaldo Abeti.

Military Section: Elfenstr. 3, 3006 Berne; tel (31) 443508; telex 912878; fax (31) 444181.
Military and Air Attaché: Col Bruno Viva.

JAMAICA

Consulate: Guterstr. 141-5, 4000 Basel; tel (61) 344600.
Honorary Consul: Peter Waeckerlin.

JAPAN

Embassy: Engerstr. 43, 3012 Berne; tel (31) 240811; telex 912653; fax (31) 235325.
Ambassador: Toshio Oshima.
Minister: Naotoshi Sugiuchi.
Counsellor: Takafumi Sato.
First Secretary: Riichi Yamakawa.
First Secretary: Toshihiro Tsuboi.
First Secretary: Takeshi Kamiyama.
First Secretary: Shuzo Narita.
Second Secretary: Tadayoshi Hayashi.

Consulate-General: 10 ave de Budé, 1202 Geneva; tel (22) 348400.
Consul-General: Akio Ijuin.

JORDAN

Embassy: Belpstr. 11, 3007 Berne; tel (31) 254146; telex 912945; fax (31) 262119.
Ambassador: Akram Z. Barakat.
Counsellor: Mohammad Ali Qudah.

KOREA, DEMOCRATIC PEOPLE'S REPUBLIC

Embassy: Pourtalèsstr. 43, 3074 Muri/Berne; tel (31) 526621; telex 912457; fax (31) 525704.
Ambassador: Ri Tcheul.
Minister Counsellor: Kim Hung Yong.
Counsellor: Lim Ryong Taek.
First Secretary: Li Sun Gi.

KOREA, REPUBLIC

Embassy: Kalcheggweg 38, 3006 Berne; tel (31) 431081; fax (31) 432657.
Ambassador: Lee Won Ho.
Counsellor: Shim Kyoung-Bo.
Military Attaché: Col Chung Suk Jin.
Third Secretary: Chung Dong Eun.
Attaché: Oh Sung Yong.

Consulate: Villa Miguel, Bonport 19, 1820 Montreux-Territet; tel (21) 9632538.
Honorary Consul: Anna Mayer.

LEBANON

Embassy: Thunstr. 10, 3074 Muri/Berne; tel (31) 522972; telex 912974; fax (31) 528119.
Ambassador: Fouad al-Turk.
Counsellor: Ibrahim Kharma.
First Secretary: Ahmad Abdallah.

LIBYA

People's Bureau: Tavelweg 2, 3006 Berne; tel (31) 433076; telex 912416; fax (31) 440845.
Secretary of Committee and Chargé d'affaires a.i.: Abdulatif H. Mehemed.
Committee Member (Culture/Press): Alhadi Hadeiba.
Attaché (Political): Abdullah Omar Attir.
Attaché (Consular): Abdulwahid Getlawi.
Attaché (Finance): Mohamed Makrouse.
Attaché (Consular): Younes Mohamed Waggad.
Attaché (Economic): Abdurrazag Mohamed Ayed Habeil.
Attaché (Administrative): Abdelgader S. Issa.
Attaché (Administrative): Milad F. Hamouda.
Attaché (Finance): Idries A. Abdulmula.
Attaché (Finance): Suleiman Ahmed Bakkar.
Attaché (Administrative): Bashir M. Abdussalam Abou Sdera.

LIECHTENSTEIN

Embassy: Willadingweg 65, 3006 Berne; tel (31) 448674; fax (31) 449970.
Ambassador: Prince Nicholas de Liechtenstein.
Minister: Mario von Ledebur.
First Secretary: Claudia Fritsche.

LUXEMBOURG

Embassy: Kramgasse 45, 3011 Berne; Postfach 619, 3000 Berne 8; tel (31) 224732; telex 912554; fax (31) 220019.
Ambassador: Julien Alex.
Secretary and Consul: Fernand Vanetti.

MALAYSIA

Embassy: Laupenstr. 37, 3008 Berne; tel (31) 252105; telex 912458; fax (31) 251193.
Ambassador: Dato' Ismail Mohamed Yusof bin Hitam.
First Secretary: Hashim Othman.
Third Secretary: Sellathurai Thuraisingham.

MALTA

Consulate-General: 2 Parc Chateau Banquet, 1202 Geneva; tel (22) 7310580; telex 27978.
Consul-General: Martin Valentino.

Consulate-General: Kuttelgasse 1, 8001 Zürich; tel (1) 2213203; telex 813896; fax (1) 2117887.
Honorary Consul-General: Dr Roland Huber.

Consulate: Via Belvedere 17, 6962 Viganello/Lugano; tel (91) 517589.
Honorary Consul: Albert Huber.

Consulate: Via al Forte 2, 6900 Lugano; tel (91) 233661; fax (91) 233697.
Honorary Consul: G. Castelli.

MEXICO

Embassy: Bernastr. 57, 3005 Berne; tel (31) 431875; telex 912305; fax (31) 433492.
Chargé d'affaires a.i. and Counsellor: Luz Estela Santos de Bruck.
Second Secretary: Hermann Aschentrupp-Toledo.

Consulate: Kaufhausgasse 7, Basel; tel (61) 238833; fax (61) 235716.
Honorary Consul: André Gutwiller.

Consulate: 16 rue Candolles, 1205 Geneva; tel (12) 283921; fax (12) 285242.
Honorary Consul: John Eardley.

Consulate: 4 rue de la Paix, 1003 Lausanne; tel (21) 232696; fax (21) 231765.
Honorary Consul: Phillipe Jaccard.

Consulate: Kirchstr. 38, 8001 Zürich; tel (1) 2511241; fax (1) 2521241.
Honorary Consul: Hans Konrad Rahn.

MONACO

Embassy: Junkerngasse 28, 3011 Berne; tel (31) 222858; fax (31) 228696.
Ambassador: François Giraudon.

Consulate-General: 30 Bundesgasse, 3011 Berne; tel (31) 221321.

Consulate-General: 78 rue du Rhône, 1204 Geneva; tel (22) 213811.

Consulate-General: 51 Isteinerstr., 4021 Basel; tel (61) 262020.

Consulate-General: 10 Salita Chiattine, 6900 Lugano; tel (91) 234337.

Consulate-General: 8701 Küsnacht; tel (19) 110604.

MOROCCO

Embassy: Helvetiastr. 42, 3005 Berne; tel (31) 430362; telex 912997.
Ambassador: Boubker Cherkaoui.
First Counsellor: Ali Bojji.
Counsellor: Abdellatif Benabbad.
First Secretary (Culture/Tourism): Abdallah Elasri.
First Secretary: Abderrazzak Laassel.
Attaché: Abdellatif Abouelfath.
Attaché: Abdelali Lahlou.

NETHERLANDS

Embassy: Kollerweg 11, 3006 Berne; Postfach, 3000 Berne 6; tel (31) 447063; telex 912739; fax (31) 448735.
Ambassador: Arie Bernadus Hoytink.
First Secretary: Hendrik Jan Nijhof.
Attaché (Administrative): Erich Karl Herbert Visscher.

NEW ZEALAND

Consulate-General: 28A chemin du Petit-Saconnex, 1209 Geneva; BP 334, 1211 Geneva 19; tel (22) 7349530; telex 412969; fax (22) 7343062.
Consul-General: Adrian Macey.
Consul: Heather Carew.

NIGERIA

Embassy: Zieglerstr. 45, 3007 Berne; tel (31) 260726; telex 912995; fax (31) 449329.
Ambassador: Sa'ad Abubakar.
Minister-Counsellor: Chioma Sunday Abbey.
First Counsellor: Ahmed Maisaje Usman.

NORWAY

Embassy: Dufourstr. 29, 3005 Berne; tel (31) 444676; telex 912970; fax (31) 435381.
Ambassador: Roald Knoph.
Counsellor: Sölve Steinhovden.

Consulate-General: 2 rue Jargonnant, 1207 Geneva; tel (22) 7361612.
Consul-General: Olivier Dunant.

OMAN

Consulate-General: 28B chemin du Petit-Saconnex, 1209 Geneva; tel (22) 7337320; telex 414182; fax (22) 7401075.
Consul-General: Abdullah al-Farsy.

PAKISTAN

Embassy: Bernastr. 47, 3005 Berne; tel (31) 442992; telex 912856.
Ambassador: Mohammad Sharif Baqir.
Second Secretary: Syed Ibne Abbas.

PERU

Embassy: Spitalackerstr. 20A, 3013 Berne; tel (31) 418359; telex 911359; fax (31) 424906.
Chargé d'affaires a.i. and Counsellor: Doris Sotomayor-Codina.
Minister (Commercial): José Ley-Elias.
First Secretary (Consular): Pedro Rubin.

Consulate-General: 72 rue de Lausanne et 50 rue de Rothschild, 4e étage, 1202 Geneva; tel (22) 7311912; telex 412897; fax (22) 7311347.
Minister-Counsellor: Rosa Esther Silva y Silva.

Administrative Office: 30 chemin des Tuilleries, 1293 Bellevue; tel (22) 7743202.
Administrative Assistant: Mónica Ostolaza.

PHILIPPINES

Embassy: Hallwylstr. 34, 3005 Berne; tel (31) 434211; telex 912493; fax (31) 444341.
Ambassador: Luis V. Ascalon.
Minister-Counsellor: Vesta I. Cuyugan.
Third Secretary (Consular): Calixto V. Espejo.
Attaché: Esmeralda Angob.
Attaché (Commercial): Antonio Paro.

Consulate-General: 47 ave Blanc, 1202 Geneva; tel (22) 7318320; telex 412659; fax (22) 7316888.
Consul-General: Delia Menez-Rosal.

POLAND

Embassy: Elfenstr. 20A, 3006 Berne; tel (31) 440452; telex 912841; fax (31) 443416.
Ambassador: Marek Latynski.
Minister-Counsellor: Ryszard Krol.
Military and Air Attaché: Lieut Col Cezary Lipert.
First Secretary and Consul: Janusz Szczepkowski.
First Secretary: Ryszard Chalupinski.
First Secretary (Press/Culture/Science): Jan Zielinski.
Second Secretary: Jan-Jozef Lyp.

Commercial Office: Elfenstr. 9, 3006 Berne; tel (31) 431935; fax (31) 433457.
Counsellor (Commercial): Andrzej Boguslawski.
Attaché (Commercial): Marian Wojnar.
Attaché (Commercial): Lucjan Zubko.

PORTUGAL

Embassy: Jungfraustr. 1, 3005 Berne; Postfach 5224, 3001 Berne; tel (31) 448602; telex 912837; fax (31) 434432.
Ambassador: Octavio Neto Valerio.
Counsellor (Social Affairs): Victor Manuel Lopes Gil.
First Secretary: Fernando da Silva Gouveia Coelho.
Attaché: Armelin Martin Baptista.

Consulate-General: 220 route de Ferney, Grand-Saconnex, Geneva; tel (22) 7910511.
Consul-General: Domingos Tomaz Vila Garrido Serra.
Vice-Consul: José Dinis Freire.

Consulate-General: Färberstr. 6, Zürich; tel (1) 2613366.
Vice-Consul: Jorge da Silva Loures.

ROMANIA

Embassy: Kirchenfeldstr. 78, 3005 Berne; tel (31) 443522; telex 912634; fax (31) 446455.
Ambassador: Nicolae Iordache.
Counsellor (Commercial): Dumitru Manolache.
Second Secretary: Tudosie Diculescu.

RUSSIA

Embassy: Brunnadernrain 37, 3006 Berne; tel (31) 440566; telex 911297; fax (31) 445595.
Ambassador: Zoya Novozhilova.
Minister-Counsellor: Vladimir Efimov.
Counsellor: Stanislav Makarov.
Counsellor: Yuri Maïorov.
Counsellor: Eduoard Panov.
Counsellor: Viatsheslav Zalomov.
Military and Air Attaché: Col Vladimir Chtcherbakov.
Assistant Military and Air Attaché: Lieut Col Sergei Nerozine.
First Secretary: Boris Skrynnik.
First Secretary: Vladimir Chevtchenko.
First Secretary: Vladimir Fediakhine.
First Secretary: Anatoly Kouzmine.
First Secretary: Alexandre Rybine.
Second Secretary: Vladimir Liventsev.
Second Secretary: Gennady Loukianov.
Third Secretary (Cultural): Victor Borissenko.

Commercial Section: Schanzeneckstr. 19, 3012 Berne; tel (31) 231871.
Commercial Representative: Valentin Kripaitis.

Consulate-General: rue Schaub 24, Geneva; tel (22) 7349083; telex 4122238.

RWANDA

Embassy: Gesellschaftsstr. 30, 3012 Berne; tel (31) 230611; telex 913129; fax (31) 244860.
Ambassador: Ferdinand Kabagema.
First Counsellor: Laurent Uwimana.
Second Secretary: Fabien Singaye Gakuru.

SAN MARINO

Embassy: Monbijoustr. 29, 3011 Berne; tel (31) 252028.

Consulate-General: 2 rue Françoise Bellot, 1206 Geneva; tel (22) 464933; telex 427751.
Consul-General: Roger Canonica.
Consul: Silvano Innocentini.

Consulate: Sternengasse 18, Basel; tel (61) 221400.
Consul: Sergio Macina.

Consulate: Via Calloni 5, 6901 Lugano; tel (91) 548451; telex 841333.
Consul: Silvano Todaro.

SAUDI ARABIA

Embassy: Kramburgstr. 12, 3006 Berne; tel (31) 441555; telex 912482; fax (31) 434581.
Ambassador: Abdulrahman Albaiz.
First Counsellor: Said al-Khayyal.
First Secretary: Abdulkadir al-Farshote.
Third Secretary (Consular): Talal M. H. Anani.
Third Secretary (Administrative): Talal M. H. Khallaf.

SENEGAL

Embassy: Monbijoustr. 10, 3011 Berne; tel (31) 261202; telex 912994.
Ambassador: Alioune Sene.
Minister-Counsellor: Amadou Moustapha Diop.
First Counsellor (Consular/Economic): Mohamed Abdel Razajh Bengeloun.
First Secretary: El Hadji Baba Sakho.
First Secretary (Administrative/Financial): Alassane Cissé.
Attaché: Momar Gueye.
Attaché: Marie-Thérèse Ndong.

SIERRA LEONE

Consulate-General: blvd Georges Favon 8, Geneva.

Honorary Consul-General: Jean E. Kramer.

SOUTH AFRICA

Embassy: Jungfraustr. 1, 3005 Berne; tel (31) 442011; telex 912165; fax (31) 442064.
Ambassador: Johan Frederick Pretorius.
Counsellor: Ignatius Petrus de Swardt.
Counsellor (Technical Agriculture): Gideon Johannes Carstens.
Counsellor (Culture): Richard Behrens.
Military and Air Attaché: Col Louis Philippus Coetzee.
First Secretary (Administrative): Hendrina Margaretha van Heerden.
First Secretary (Press/Information): Linda Glatthaer.
Third Secretary: Annell van Zyl.
Third Secretary: Reimer Göttsche.

Consulate-General: 65 rue du Rhône, 1204 Geneva; tel (22) 7357801; telex 28130; fax (22) 7357973.
Consul-General: A. L. Manley.

Consulate-General: Seestr. 221, 8700 Küsnacht-Zürich; tel (1) 9110660; fax (1) 9100006.
Consul-General: Dr E. Links.
Consul (Finance): D. W. Gernandt.
Consul (Finance): B. R. W. Cameron.
Consul (Trade): G. Peter.

SPAIN

Embassy: Kalcheggweg 24, 3006 Berne; tel (31) 440412; telex 912360; fax (31) 430273.
Ambassador: Joaquín Martínez-Correcher y Gil.
Minister-Counsellor: Alfonso de Borbón y Caralt.
Counsellor (Social Affairs): Antonio Perandones García.
Counsellor (Culture): Mariano Sanz Royo.
Counsellor (Commercial): José María Más Esteve.
First Secretary (Culture): Pilar Ruiz Carnicero.
Attaché (Administrative): María Jesús Cejudo Ruiz.

SWEDEN

Embassy: Bundesgasse 26, 3011 Berne; CP 1004, 3001 Berne; tel (31) 210563; telex 911770; fax (31) 211692.
Ambassador: Hans V. Ewerlöf.
Counsellor: Björn Ingemar Sternby.
Military and Air Attaché: Col Dennis G. N. Harlin.
First Secretary (Consular/Administrative): I. E. Margareta Kjellqvist.
Chancellor: Hjördis Aemmer.
Chancellor: Käthy Grünig.

Consulate: Wiesenstr. 9, 8008 Zürich; tel (1) 3834162; telex (45) 816452; fax (1) 3834632.
Consul-General: Hans Mikael Mott.

Consulate: Neubadstr. 7, 4015 Basel; tel (61) 2810042; telex 962187; fax (61) 235025.
Consul: Staffan Olof Björn.

Consulate: 6 rue François-Bellot, 1206 Geneva; tel (22) 464344; telex 429782; fax (22) 464054.
Consul-General: André de Pfyffer.

Consulate: 70 ave Général-Guisan, 1009 Pully/Lausanne; tel (21) 284000; telex 454702; fax (21) 283630.
Consul-General: Hans Bertil Roland Hagman.

Consulate: 3 Viale Carlo Cattaneo, 6901 Lugano; tel (91) 239071; telex 844052; fax (91) 232331.
Consul: Severo Marco Otto Antonini.

THAILAND

Embassy: Eigerstr. 60, 3rd Floor, 3007 Berne; tel (31) 462281; telex 912445.
Ambassador: Somboon Sangiambut.
Counsellor: Sumniang Chulakanista.
First Secretary: Vithya Sucharitakul.
First Secretary: Apichat Wannayonda.
Second Secretary: Thanikarn Bhadranavik.

TOGO

Consulate: 6 rue Bellot, Geneva; tel (22) 463922.

TRINIDAD AND TOBAGO

Consulate-General: Banque Populaire Suisse, Direction Générale, 3001 Berne.
Honorary Consul-General: Agathan Aerni.

Consulate-General: 37-39 rue de Vermont, 1202 Geneva; tel (22) 7349130; fax (22) 7349138.
Consul-General: Annette Gonzales.

TUNISIA

Embassy: Kirchenfeldstr. 63, 3005 Berne; tel (31) 448226; telex 912620; fax (31) 430445.
Ambassador: Saadeddine Zmerli.
Minister-Counsellor: Mohamed Fekih Ahmed.
Counsellor: Sadok Haouas.
First Secretary (Consular): Mokhtar Amrouche.
Attaché (Consular): Béchir Chennaoui.
Attaché (Administrative/Financial): Mohamed el Hédi ben Moussa.

TURKEY

Embassy: Lombachweg 33, 3006 Berne; tel (31) 431691; telex 911879.
Ambassador: Aydin Yegen.
Counsellor: Dogan Akdur.
Counsellor: Sinan Balkir.
Assistant Counsellor (Economic/Commercial): Nurten Akgül.
Military and Air Attaché: Col Cetin Akyol.
Third Secretary: Ahmet Ulker.
Attaché (Education): Ali Ince.

UNITED KINGDOM

Embassy: Thunstr. 50, 3000 Berne 15; tel (31) 445021; telex 911929; fax (31) 440583.
Ambassador: Christopher William Long.
Counsellor and Deputy Head of Mission: Colin C. Bright.
Counsellor: Charles W. Wainwright.
Defence, Naval and Military Attaché: Lieut Col W. R. Thatcher.
Air Attaché: Wing Commdr H. W. Hughes.
First Secretary (Information): Philip Cole.
Second Secretary (Political): Dr J. E. Mitchener.
Second Secretary (Management) and Consul: P. A. Chatt.
Attaché (Commercial): P. C. Albrecht.

Consulate-General: 37-39 rue de Vermont, 6e étage, 1211 Geneva 20; tel (22) 7343800; telex 414195; fax (22) 7345254.
Consul-General: J. R. Paterson.
First Secretary (Joint Management Officer): P. Newall.
Consul: C. H. Bird.

Consulate-General: Dufourstr. 56, 8008 Zürich; tel (1) 2611520; telex 816467; fax (1) 2528351.
Consul-General and Director of Export Promotions: T. Bryant.
Consul (Commercial): M. F. Smith.
Vice-Consul (Consular/Management): D. L. Cotton.
Vice-Consul (Investment): W. A. Habersaat.

Consulate: Via Motta 19, 6900 Lugano; tel (91) 238606.
Honorary Consul: A. Crevilli.

Consulate: 13 chemin de l'Aubousset, 1806 St Legier/Vaud/Montreux; tel (21) 9433263.
Honorary Vice-Consul: S. Darra.

USA

Embassy: Jubiläumstr. 93, 3005 Berne; tel (31) 437011; telex 912603; fax (31) 437344.
Ambassador: Joseph B. Gildenhorn.
Deputy Head of Mission: John E. Hall.
Counsellor (Political/Economic): Basil G. Scarlis.
Counsellor (Commercial): Arthur J. Reichenbach.
Office of Defence Attaché: Col Henry R. Farrell.
Air Attaché: Col Thomas N. Moe.
First Secretary (Consular): William A. Muller.
First Secretary (Political): Suzanne E. Ziemer.
First Secretary (Political): William G. Perett.
Second Secretary: John C. Campbell.
Second Secretary: David T. Rockey.
Second Secretary: Steven R. Nugent.
Second Secretary: Sigrid Emrich.
Attaché (Administrative): Theodore A. Dawson.
Attaché (Agriculture): Margaret Dowling.
Attaché (Finance): William Quinn.
Public Affairs Officer: Peter Becskehazy.
Regional Security Officer: Henry Jenkins.
Communications Programme Officer: Earle S. Greene.

Consulate and Trade Representation: Botanic Bldg, 1-3 ave de la Paix, 1202 Geneva; tel (22) 7387613; telex 412865; fax (22) 7990880.
Head of Mission: Rufus H. Yerxa.
Deputy Head of Mission: Andrew L. Stoler.
Agricultural Section: Charles J. O'Mara.
Commercial Section: Stephen Arlinghaus.
Communications Programme Officer: William Weatherford.
Information Systems Manager: L. Fred File, Jr.

Consulate-General: Zollikerstr. 141, 8008 Zürich; tel (1) 552566; telex 816830; fax (1) 3839814.
Consul-General: Ruth N. van Heuven.

URUGUAY

Embassy: Kramgasse 63, 3011 Berne; tel (31) 212226; telex 912347; fax (31) 222747.
Ambassador: Mario C. Fernández.
First Secretary: Carlos Baranano.

VENEZUELA

Embassy: Morillonstr. 9, 3007 Berne; tel (31) 453282; telex 912797; fax (31) 450424.
Ambassador: Dr German Carrera Damas.
Minister-Counsellor: Nicolas Emilio Hellmund.
Counsellor: Carlos E. Rios-Scharbaay.
Attaché (Science): Humberto Fernandez-Moran.

YEMEN

Embassy: Kistlerweg 2, 3006 Berne; tel (31) 444885.
Ambassador: Yahya Hamoud Geghman.

YUGOSLAVIA

Embassy: Seminarstr. 5, 3006 Berne; tel (31) 446353; telex 912848.
Ambassador: Jovan Pečenović.
Counsellor (Political/Economic): Pero Janković.
Counsellor (Social Affairs/Economic): Miroslav Buljančević.
Armed Forces Attaché: Col Ivan Umek.
Second Secretary (Consular): Branko Vukmirović.
Attaché (Administrative): Radomir Slijepčević.

Consulate-General: Eidmattstr. 33, 8032 Zürich; tel (1) 3836161; telex 912848; fax (1) 3835101.

ZAIRE

Embassy: Sulgenheimweg 21, 3007 Berne; Postfach 5261, 3001 Berne; tel (31) 453538; telex 911431.

Ambassador: Ndeze Matabaro.
Second Counsellor (Economic): Koyabambi Guga.
First Secretary (Technical): Bateza Mputi.
Second Secretary (Protocol): Fundi Okondi Likita.

International Organizations

EUROPEAN COMMUNITIES

Press and Information Bureau: BP 195, 37-39 rue de Vermont, 1211 Geneva 20; tel (22) 349750; telex 28261; fax (22) 342236.
Head of Delegation: Trãn Van Tinh;
Deputy Head of Delegation: John Beck.

SYRIA

AFGHANISTAN

Embassy: Mezze 5, rue Shafei, East Villas, Damascus; tel (11) 665007; telex 412623.
Ambassador: Abdul Fatah Weidi.
First Secretary: Myr Yahia Mahmood.
Second Secretary: Mr Fariduddin.

ALGERIA

Embassy: Raouda, Imm. Noss, BP 2529, Damascus; tel (11) 411344; telex 411480.
Ambassador: Abdelkader Hadjer.
Minister: Noureddine Ghenim.
Counsellor (Economic/Press): Ramdane Ferhat.
Defence Attaché: Col Abdallah Hannan.
Attaché (Consular): Kheireddine Fourlou.

ARGENTINA

Embassy: Raouda, rue Ziad ben Abi Soufian, BP 116, Damascus; telex 411058.
Ambassador: Andrés Gabriel Ceustermans.

AUSTRALIA

Embassy: 128A rue Farabi, West Villas, Imm. Dakkak, Mezzeh, BP 3882, Damascus; tel (11) 660238; telex 419132; fax (11) 419132.
Ambassador: Ray Spurr.

AUSTRIA

Embassy: Raouda, rue Chafik Mou'ayed, Imm. Sabri Malki, BP 5634, Damascus; tel (11) 247691; telex 411389.
Ambassador: Dr Gerhard Pfanzelter.
First Secretary: Dr Michael Linhart.
Administrative Secretary: Robert Sinnhuber.

Consulate-General: Place de l'Etoile, rue Chawkat Al-Aidi, coin rue R. Mayssaloun 7, BP 3189, Damascus; tel (11) 334585; telex 411949.
Honorary Consul-General: Georges E. Abdini.

Consulate: rue Baron, en face Banque Centrale, Imm. Pères Jésuites, BP 521, Aleppo; tel (21) 214070; telex 331005.
Honorary Consul: Umberto Draghi.

BELGIUM

Embassy: rue Ata Ayoubi, Imm. Hachem, Damascus; tel (11) 332821; telex 411090.
Ambassador: André Vokaer.

BRAZIL

Embassy: 76 rue Ata Ayoubi, Damascus; telex 411204.
Ambassador: Antônio Amaral de Sampaio.

BULGARIA

Embassy: 4 rue Chahbandar, Damascus.
Ambassador: Georgi Yankov.

CANADA

Embassy: Hotel Sheraton, place des Omayades, BP 3394, Damascus; tel (11) 229300; telex 412422.
Ambassador: Martin Collacott.
First Secretary and Consul: G. B. Laurin.
Canadian Forces Attaché: Col G. T. Service.
First Secretary: R. J. Orr.
Immigration Section: tel (11) 330535.
First Secretary and Consul: H. L. Edwards.
First Secretary and Consul: D. L. Clark.
First Secretary and Consul: F. Larochelle.
Second Secretary (Administration) and Vice-Consul: J. B. Christie.

CHILE

Embassy: 43 rue ar-Rachid, Damascus; telex 411392.
Ambassador: Luis Larrain.

CHINA, PEOPLE'S REPUBLIC

Embassy: 83 rue Ata Ayoubi, Damascus.
Ambassador: Zhang Zhen.

CUBA

Embassy: 40 rue ar-Rachid, Imm. Oustwani and Charabati, Damascus; tel (11) 339624; telex 419155.
Ambassador: Jesús Barreiro.

CYPRUS

Embassy: Abd al-Malek al-Marouan, Jaded ar-Rais, Abou Roumaneh, BP 3853, Damascus; tel (11) 332804; telex 411411.
Ambassador: Nicolas Macris.

CZECHOSLOVAKIA

Embassy: place Abou al-Ala'a al-Maari, Damascus.
Ambassador: Alois Reznik.

DENMARK

Embassy: Imm. Patriarcat Grec-Catholique, rue Chekib Arslan, Abou Roumaneh, BP 2244, Damascus; tel (11) 331008; telex 419125.
Ambassador: P. Bent Søndergaard.
First Secretary: Peter Kragh.
Commercial Officer: Ahmad Ayash.
Chancellor and Vice-Consul: Ingrid Saheb.

Consulate: rue Baron, Imm. Jésuites, BP 88, Aleppo; tel (21) 17206; telex 331279.
Consul-Genera: Alfred A. Girardi.

Consulate: BP 140, rue 8 mars, Latakia; tel (41) 34733; telex 451169.
Vice-Consul: Nizar A. Haroun.

EGYPT

Embassy: Damascus.
Ambassador: Moustafa Abd al-Aziz.

ETHIOPIA

Embassy: Damascus.
Ambassador: Abd al-Monem Ahmad.

FINLAND

Embassy: Hawakir, Imm. Yacoubian, West Malki, BP 3893, Damascus; tel (11) 338670; telex 411491; fax (11) 718524.
Ambassador: Arto Kurittu.
First Secretary: Vesa Jaakola.
Administrative Attaché: Anneli Arabi.
Administrative Attaché: Helena Hyyryläinen.

Consulate-General: Al Karameh St, BP 83, Malki, Damascus; tel (11) 210528; telex 419143.
Consul-General: Emile Chaoui.
Consul: Naji Chaoui.

Consulate: 8 March St, BP 14, Latakia; tel (41) 36694; telex 451010.
Vice-Consul: Habib Morcos.

Consulate: Shouhada St, BP 142, Aleppo; tel (21) 223001; telex 331205.
Vice-Consul: Edouard Megarbane.

FRANCE

Embassy: BP 769, rue Ata Ayoubi, Damascus; tel (11) 247992-5; telex 411013.
Ambassador: Daniel Contenay.

Trade Promotion Office: BP 2629, Damascus; tel (11) 213414; telex 411367.

Second Chancery: Khan El Nahassine, BP 768, Aleppo; tel (21) 219823.

GERMANY

Embassy: BP 2237, 53 rue Ibrahim Hanano, Imm. Kotob, Damascus; tel (11) 714995; telex 411065.
Ambassador: Dr Georg-Hermann Schlingensiepen.

Consulate: BP 495, rue de la Banque Centrale, Aleppo; tel (21) 213243; telex 19169.
Honorary Consul: Robert Toutounji.

GREECE

Embassy: 1 rue Farabi, Imm. Tello, Mezzeh, Damascus; tel (11) 244031; telex 411045.
Ambassador: George Constantis.

HOLY SEE

Apostolic Nunciature: 82 rue Masr, BP 2271, Damascus; tel (11) 332601; telex 412824; fax (11) 332446.
Apostolic Pro-Nuncio: Mgr Luigi Accogli, Titular Archbishop of Treba.
Secretary: Mgr Sérapion Bambonanire.

HUNGARY

Embassy: 13 rue Ibrahim Hanano, Imm. Roujoulé, Damascus; tel (11) 337966; telex 419151.
Ambassador: László Kádár.

INDIA

Embassy: 40/46 ave Adnan al-Malki, Imm. Yassin Noueilati, BP 685, Damascus; tel (11) 718203; telex 411377; fax (11) 713294.
Ambassador: Ramesh N. Mulye.
First Secretary: A. Manickam.
First Secretary: S. P. Chibber.
Second Secretary: G. K. Sharma.
Third Secretary: Pratap Singh.
Attaché: H. C. Guglani.
Attaché: K. P. M. Raman.
Attaché: V. V. Narayanan.

INDONESIA

Embassy: 19 rue al-Amir Ezz ed-Din, Sahat Al-Madfa, Abou Roumaneh, BP 3530, Damascus; tel (11) 331238; telex 419188.
Ambassador: Chalid Mawardi.
Second Secretary: As'at Said Ali.
Second Secretary: Judo Prajitno.
Second Secretary: Teuku Sudirman.

IRAN

Embassy: Mezzeh Outostrade, nr ar-Razi Hospital, Damascus; telex 411041.
Ambassador: Hojatoleslam Muhammad Hassan Akhtari.

ITALY

Embassy: 82 ave al-Mansour, Damascus.
Ambassador: Riccardo Leonini.

JAPAN

Embassy: 15 ave al-Jala'a, BP 3366, Damascus; tel (11) 335677; telex 411042.
Ambassador: Ryoji Onodera.

JORDAN

Embassy: rue Abou Roumaneh, Damascus; telex 419161.
Ambassador: Ali Khurais.

KOREA, DEMOCRATIC PEOPLE'S REPUBLIC

Embassy: rue Fares al-Khouri-Jisr Tora, Damascus.
Ambassador: Yi Won-Kuk.

KUWAIT

Embassy: rue Ibrahim Hanano, Damascus; telex 419172.

LIBYA

People's Bureau: 36/37 Abou Roumaneh, Damascus.
Head of People's Bureau: Ahmad Abd as-Salam bin Khayal.

MALTA

Embassy: Palazzo Parisio, Merchants St, Valletta, Malta; tel 222407; telex 1100; fax 237822.
Ambassador: Joseph M. Schembri (resident in Malta).

Consulate: Mouhajirien, Kourtouba Ave, BP 3794, Damascus; tel (11) 718274; telex 411961.
Honorary Consul: Ahmad Houboubati.

MAURITANIA

Embassy: ave al-Jala'a, rue Karameh, Damascus; telex 411264.
Ambassador: Muhammad Mahmoud Ould Weddady.

MOROCCO

Embassy: Damascus.

NETHERLANDS

Embassy: place Abou al-Ala'a al-Maari, Imm. Badr Diab, Damascus; tel (11) 336871; telex 411032.
Ambassador: G. Meihuizen.

NORWAY

Embassy: BP 7703, Damascus; tel (11) 331572; telex 412555; fax (11) 825162.

OMAN

Embassy: Damascus.

PAKISTAN

Embassy: rue al-Farabi, East Villat, BP 9284, Damascus; tel (11) 662391; telex 412629.
Ambassador: S. Azmat Hassan.

PANAMA

Embassy: Malki, rue al-Bizm, Imm. az-Zein, Appt 7, BP 2548, Damascus; tel (11) 224743; telex 411918.
Chargé d'affaires: Carlos A. de Gracia.

POLAND

Embassy: rue Ben Barka, BP 501, Damascus; tel (11) 333010; telex 412673.
Ambassador: Krzysztof Baliński.
Second Secretary (Political Affairs): Jacek Bartosiak.
Military, Naval and Air Attaché: Henryk Bartkowiak.
Third Secretary (Cultural/Consular): Włodzimierz Niedziałek.
Attaché: Władysław Bołoz.
Attaché (Maritime Affairs): Zbigniew Wyszomirski.

Commercial Section: tel (11) 333431.
Commercial Counsellor: Stanisław Wojtaszek.

QATAR

Embassy: Abou Roumaneh, place Madfa, Imm. Allawi No. 20, BP 4188, Damascus; tel (11) 336717; telex 411064.
Ambassador: Fahd Fahd al-Khater.

ROMANIA

Embassy: 8 rue Ibrahim Hanano, Damascus; telex 411305.
Ambassador: Paraschiv Benescu.

RUSSIA

Embassy: Boustan al-Kouzbari, rue d'Alep, Damascus; tel (11) 423156; telex 411221.
Ambassador: Aleksandr Ivanovich Zotov.

Consular Section: Mazraa, Damascus; telex 411671.

Consulate-General: Aleppo; tel (21) 232401.

SAUDI ARABIA

Embassy: ave al-Jala'a, Damascus; telex 411906.
Ambassador: Abdullah bin Saleh al-Fadl.

SOMALIA

Embassy: ave Ata Ayoubi, Damascus; telex 419194.

SPAIN

Embassy: 81 ave al-Jala'a, Imm. Sawaf, Damascus; tel (11) 332126; telex 411253; fax (11) 339506.
Ambassador: Gil Armangue Ruis.
Counsellor (Commercial): Vicente Saval.
First Secretary: Jorge de Lucas y Cadenas.
Attaché: Maria E. Isabel Cifuentes.

SUDAN

Embassy: Damascus; telex 411266.

SWEDEN

Embassy: rue Chekib Arslan, Imm. du Patriarcat Catholique, Abou Roumaneh, BP 4266, Damascus; tel (11) 247261; telex 411339.
Ambassador: Rolf Gauffin.
Counsellor: Ulf Waltré.
Second Secretary: Jan Thesleff.

Consulate: Quartier Azisié, rue Farès, El-Khoury, BP 1312, Aleppo; tel (21) 249945.
Consul: Gaston Homsy.

Consulate: ave 8 de Mars, BP 14, Latakia; tel (41) 36743; telex 451010.
Vice-Consul: Habib A. Morcos.

SWITZERLAND

Embassy: Abou Roumane, 26 rue al-Mehdi ben Baraka, Imm. Chora, BP 234, Damascus; tel (11) 715474; telex 411016; fax (11) 717115.
Ambassador: Eric Pfister.
First Secretary and Head of Chancery: Bruno Ritter.

TUNISIA

Embassy: Villa Ouest, Jaddat Chafei, No. 6 Mezzeh, BP 4114, Damascus; tel (11) 660356; telex 431302.
Ambassador: Muhammad Cherif.

TURKEY

Embassy: 56-58 ave Ziad bin Abou Soufian, Damascus; tel (11) 331370; telex 413086.
Ambassador: Erhan Tunçel.
Minister-Counsellor: Tahsin Özer.
First Secretary: Ayhan Enginar.
Second Secretary: Namik G. Erpul.
Attaché: Memduh Boyra.
Attaché: Ahmet Şahin.
Attaché: Deniz Göktaş.
Attaché: Nihal Sariöz.
Attaché: Edip Bilgin.
Attaché: Haluk Barutçugil.

Attaché: Necati Ölmez.

Consulate-General: Aleppo; tel (21) 331277.
Consul-General: Kaya Inal.

UNITED ARAB EMIRATES

Embassy: rue Raouda No. 62, Imm. Housami, Damascus; telex 411213.
Ambassador: Salim Rashid al-Aqroubi.

UNITED KINGDOM

Embassy: Quartier Malki, 11 rue Muhammad Kurd Ali, Imm. Kotob, Damascus; tel (11) 712561; telex 411049; fax (11) 713592.
Ambassador: Andrew F. Green.
Counsellor and Deputy Head of Mission: I. L. Blackley.
Defence Attaché: Col J. J. Dumas.
First Secretary (Chancery/Information): M. E. Cribbs.
First Secretary (Commercial): M. J. Lowes.
First Secretary (Management and Consul): P. J. Richardson.
Vice-Consul (Immigration): P. J. Blandford.
Vice-Consul (Immigration): S. M. Wadvani.

Consulate: BP 199, Aleppo; tel (21) 332133; telex 331627.
Honorary Consul: G. J. A. Akras.

USA

Embassy: Abu Rumaneh, 2 rue al-Mansour, BP 29, Damascus; tel (11) 330416; telex 411919; fax (11) 718687.
Ambassador: Edward P. Djerejian.
Deputy Chief of Mission: John B. Craig.
Political Section: Kathleen H. Allegrone.
Economic/Commercial Section: Peter Vincent Londano.
Consular Section: Deborah K. Jones.
Administrative Section: Charles R. Allegrone.
Regional Security Officer: Walter B. Deering.

US Information Service: tel (11) 331878.
Public Affairs Officer (USIS): William J. Murphey.
Communications Programme Officer: Judy Chidester.
Office of the Defence Attaché: Lieut Col David J. Anthony.

VENEZUELA

Embassy: Imm. Tabbah, rue Nour Pacha, Abou Roumaneh, BP 2403, Damascus; tel (11) 335356; telex 411929; fax (11) 333203.
Ambassador: José Miguel Quintana Guevara.
First Secretary: Fernando A. Rincon R.

VIET-NAM

Embassy: 236 rue Maksam Ibn Saifai, Damascus; tel (11) 331256.
Ambassador: Le Thanh Tam.
Counsellor: Tran Thi.
Second Secretary: Vu Thi Dung.

YEMEN

Embassy: Abou Roumaneh, Charkassieh, Damascus.
Ambassador: Abdullah Hussain Barakat.

YUGOSLAVIA

Embassy: ave al-Jala'a, Damascus.
Ambassador: Davorin Kotajsek.

International Organizations

EUROPEAN COMMUNITIES

External Delegation: 73 rue al-Rachid, BP 11269, Damascus; tel (11) 247640; telex 412919; fax (11) 420683.
Head of Delegation: Renato Batti.

TADZHIKISTAN

AFGHANISTAN

Consulate-General: Dushanbe, Pushkina ul. 34; tel 27-60-61.
Second Secretary: Mr Zaher.
Third Secretary: Mr Poya.

CHINA, PEOPLE'S REPUBLIC

Embassy: Dushanbe.

IRAN

Embassy: Teheran St, Dushanbe.

USA

Embassy: Dushanbe.

TANZANIA

ALBANIA

Embassy: 93 Msese Rd, POB 1034, Kinondoni, Dar es Salaam; telex 41280.
Ambassador: Mehdi Shaqiri.

ALGERIA

Embassy: 34 Upanga Rd, POB 2963, Dar es Salaam; telex 41104.

ANGOLA

Embassy: POB 20793, Dar es Salaam; telex 41251.
Ambassador: Eusebio Sebastião.

AUSTRIA

Consulate-General: Independence Ave 20 J, POB 312, Dar es Salaam; tel (51) 20417.
Honorary Vice-Consul: Irmgard Gebauer.

BELGIUM

Embassy: NIC Investment House, Wing A, 7th Floor, Samora Machel Ave, POB 9210, Dar es Salaam; tel (51) 20244; telex 41094; fax (51) 20604.
Ambassador: Philippe Henri Arcq.
Third Secretary (Head of Chancery): Theo Dirix.
Head of Development Co-operation Section (First Secretary): Herman Van Den Abeele.
Deputy Head of Section: Pieter Willems.

BRAZIL

Embassy: IPS Bldg, 9th Floor, POB 9654, Dar es Salaam; tel (51) 21780; telex 41228.
Ambassador: José Ferreira Lopes.

BURUNDI

Embassy: Plot. No 10007, Lugalo Rd, POB 2752, Upanga, Dar es Salaam; tel (51) 38608; telex 41340.
Ambassador: Edouard Kadigiri.

CANADA

High Commission: Pan African Insurance Bldg, Samora Machel Ave, POB 1022, Dar es Salaam; tel (51) 20651; telex 41015; fax (51) 35752.
High Commissioner: J. David L. Rose.
Counsellor (Development): L. E. Heuckroth.
Counsellor (Development): J. P. Lobsinger.
Counsellor (Development): R. L. Rose.
Counsellor (Development): R. Groberman.
Counsellor: M. H. White.
First Secretary (Development): J. F. Adams.
First Secretary (Development): S. Barrow.
Second Secretary (Administration): M. Routhier.

CHINA, PEOPLE'S REPUBLIC

Embassy: 2 Kajificheni Close at Toure Drive, POB 1649, Dar es Salaam; telex 41036.
Ambassador: Sun Guotang.

CUBA

Embassy: Plot No. 313, Lugalo Rd, POB 9282, Upanga, Dar es Salaam; telex 41245.
Ambassador: A. Rolando Gallardo Fernández.

CZECHOSLOVAKIA

Embassy: 69 Upanga Rd, POB 3054, Dar es Salaam; tel (51) 22540; telex 41183.
Ambassador: Vilem Pardubsky.

DENMARK

Embassy: Ghana Ave, POB 9171, Dar es Salaam; tel (51) 27077; telex 41057; fax (51) 34789.
Ambassador: Erno Olsen.
Counsellor: Carsten Nilaus Pedersen.
Attaché: Susanne K. Andersen.
Minister-Counsellor and Head of Aid Mission: Knud Kjær Nielsen.
Counsellor for Aid: Finn Christofferson.
Counsellor for Aid: Per Martin Larsen.
Counsellor for Aid: Birger Lorentzen.
Counsellor for Aid: Elsebeth Tarp.
Counsellor for Aid: Flemming West.
Project Administrator: Jakob Vinding Madsen.
Project Administrator: Mette Jacobsgaard.

Consulate: c/o Scan-Tan Tours Ltd AICC, Serengeti Wing, POB 2611, Arusha; tel (57) 6978; telex 42006; fax (57) 7884.
Consul: Geert Lassen Holm.

EGYPT

Embassy: 24 Garden Ave, POB 1668, Dar es Salaam; tel (51) 23372; telex 41173.
Ambassador: Baher M. El-Sadek.

FINLAND

Embassy: NIC Investment House, 9th Floor, Samora Machel Ave, POB 2455, Dar es Salaam; tel (51) 30396; telex 41066; fax (51) 23790.
Ambassador: Kari Karanko.

FRANCE

Embassy: Bagamoyo-Kilimani Rd, POB 2349, Dar es Salaam; tel (51) 34961; telex 41006.
Ambassador: Bernard Lodiot.

Trade Promotion Office: POB 841, Dar es Salaam; tel (51) 22643; telex 41076.

GERMANY

Embassy: NIC Investment House, Samora Machel Ave, POB 9541, Dar es Salaam; tel (51) 23286; telex 41003.
Ambassador: Christel Steffler.

Consulate: c/o Mazao Ltd, off Lema and Mtoni Rd, POB 657, Moshi; tel (55) 2898; telex 43090; fax (55) 4457.
Honorary Consul: Mathias Köhler.

GUINEA

Embassy: 35 Haile Selassie Rd, POB 2969, Oyster Bay, Dar es Salaam; tel (51) 68626.
Ambassador: M. Bangoura.

HOLY SEE

Apostolic Nunciature: Plot 462, Msasani Peninsula, POB 480, Dar es Salaam; tel (51) 68403; fax (51) 41943.
Apostolic Pro-Nuncio: Most Rev. Agostino Marchetto, Titular Archbishop of Ecija.
Secretary: Rev. Mgr William John Morrow.

HUNGARY

Embassy: 40 Bagamoyo Rd, POB 672, Dar es Salaam; tel (51) 34762; telex 41428.
Ambassador: János Zegnál.

INDIA

High Commission: NIC Investment House, Samora Machel Ave, POB 2684, Dar es Salaam; tel (51) 28197; telex 41335.
High Commission: Sharad Kumar Bhatnagar.

INDONESIA

Embassy: 299 Upanga Rd, POB 572, Dar es Salaam; telex 41575.
Ambassador: Hidayat Soemo.

IRAN

Embassy: Plot 685, Masengo Rd, POB 3802, West Upanga, Dar es Salaam; tel (51) 34622.
Ambassador: S. M. A. Lavasani.

IRAQ

Embassy: 355 United Nations Rd, POB 5289, Dar es Salaam; tel (51) 25728; telex 41193.
Ambassador: Fawz Ali al-Bander.

IRELAND

Development Co-operation Office: POB 9612, Dar es Salaam; tel (51) 26917; telex 41222; fax (51) 31578.
First Secretary: Bill Nolan.

ITALY

Embassy: Plot 316, Lugalo Rd, POB 2106, Upanga, Dar es Salaam; tel (51) 29961; telex 41062; fax (51) 29963.
Ambassador: Pasquale Antonio Baldocci.
First Secretary: Stefano Baldi.

JAPAN

Embassy: 1018 Upanga Rd, POB 2577, Dar es Salaam; tel (51) 31215; telex 41065; fax (51) 31219.
Ambassador: Shoichi Nakamura.

KENYA

High Commission: NIC Investment House, POB 5231, Dar es Salaam; tel (51) 31502; telex 41700.
High Commission: D. I. Kathambana.

KOREA, DEMOCRATIC PEOPLE'S REPUBLIC

Embassy: Plot 460B, United Nations Rd, POB 2690, Dar es Salaam.
Ambassador: Chong Nam-Ho.

MADAGASCAR

Embassy: Magoret St, POB 5254, Dar es Salaam; tel (51) 41761; telex 41291.
Chargé d'affaires: Rahdray Desiré.

MALAWI

High Commission: IPS Bldg, 9th Floor, POB 7616, Dar es Salaam; tel (51) 37260; telex 41633; fax (51) 35983.
High Commissioner: L. B. Malunga.
First Secretary: B. M. C. L. Phiri.
Second Secretary: W. M. M'Manga.
Second Secretary: R. N. Savala.
Third Secretary: C. A. Msinja.
Third Secretary: E. M. Chimwala.
Third Secretary: C. S. Kanchiputu.

Third Secretary: J. M. Luwani.

MOZAMBIQUE

Embassy: Dar es Salaam; telex 41214.
Ambassador: António C. F. Sumbana.

NETHERLANDS

Embassy: New ATC Town Terminal Bldg, cnr Ohio St and Garden Ave, POB 9534, Dar es Salaam; tel (51) 26767; telex 41050.
Ambassador: Max Damme.

NIGERIA

High Commission: 3 Bagamoyo Rd, POB 9214, Oyster Bay, Dar es Salaam; telex 41240.
High Commissioner: Yunisa Paiko.

NORWAY

Embassy: Extelcom House, Samora Machel Ave, POB 9012, Dar es Salaam; tel (51) 25195; telex 41221; fax (51) 25197.
Ambassador: Gunnar Garbo.

PAKISTAN

High Commission: 149 Malik Rd, POB 2925, Upanga, Dar es Salaam; tel (51) 27971.
High Commissioner: Imtiaz A. Bhatti.
Counsellor: Amir A. Shadani.

POLAND

Embassy: 63 Alykhan Rd, Upanga, POB 2188, Dar es Salaam; tel (51) 25777; telex 41022.
Counsellor and Chargé d'affaires a.i.: Kazimierz Tomaszewski.
Attaché: Andrzej Pyzinski.

ROMANIA

Embassy: Plot 11, Ocean Rd, POB 590, Dar es Salaam.

RUSSIA

Embassy: Plot No. 73, Kenyatta Drive, POB 1905, Dar es Salaam; tel (51) 36105; telex 41747.
Ambassador: Vladimir N. Kuznetsov.
Minister-Counsellor: Alexandre N. Gogitidze.
Counsellor: Vladimir N. Kharlamov.
Counsellor: Anatoli V. Andreev.
Military Attaché: Alexandre M. Pereliakin.
Deputy Military Attaché: Valeri N. Zaitsev.
First Secretary: Alexandre N. Valentinov.
First Secretary (Cultural Affairs): Yuri Golovin.
Protocol Officer: Andrei I. Nefedov.

Consulate: 6 Kaunda Rd, Zanzibar; tel (54) 32152.
Consul: Vladlen N. Krivonossov.

RWANDA

Embassy: Plot 32, Upanga Rd, POB 2918, Dar es Salaam; tel (51) 30119; telex 41292.
Ambassador: François Bararwerekana.

SPAIN

Embassy: POB 842, 99B Kingsway, Kinondoni Rd, Dar es Salaam; tel (51) 23203; telex 41589.
Ambassador: Javier Navarro.
First Secretary: Ignacio Ybáñez.

SUDAN

Embassy: 'Albaraka', 64 Upanga Rd, POB 2266, Dar es Salaam; telex 41143.

SWEDEN

Embassy: Extelcoms Bldg, 2nd Floor, Samora Machel Ave, POB 9274/9303, Dar es Salaam; tel (51) 23501; telex 41013; fax (51) 33998.
Ambassador: Anders Oljelund.
Counsellor: Åke Peterson.
Second Secretary: Margareta Barvaeus.
Head of Aid Section: Arne Ström.

SWITZERLAND

Embassy: 17 Kenyatta Drive, POB 2454, Dar es Salaam; tel (51) 34772; telex 41322; fax (51) 41054.
Ambassador: Jörg L. Kaufmann.
Third Secretary and Head of Chancery: Stephan Wirth.

Development Section: tel (51) 41823.
Attaché (Development Co-operation and Humanitarian Aid): Max Honegger.

SYRIA

Embassy: POB 2442, Dar es Salaam; tel (51) 20568; telex 41339.
Chargé d'affaires: Kanaan Hadid.

UNITED KINGDOM

High Commission: Hifadhi House, Samora Machel Ave, POB 9200, Dar es Salaam; tel (51) 29601; telex 41004; fax (51) 30365.
High Commissioner: John Thorold Masefield.
Deputy High Commissioner: I. R. Whitehead.
First Secretary (Aid): J. Laurence.
Second Secretary (Commercial): J. D. Knight.
Second Secretary (Consular): L. B. Evans.
Second Secretary (Management): C. Sime.
Second Secretary (Chancery/Information): Alice Walpole.

USA

Embassy: 36 Laibon Rd (off Bagamoyo Rd), POB 9123, Dar es Salaam; tel (51) 37501; telex 41250; fax (51) 37408.
Ambassador: Edmund T. De Jarnette.
Deputy Chief of Mission: Kenneth M. Scott, Jr.
Political Section: Robert N. Bentley.
Economic/Commercial Section: Anne C. Jordan.
Consular Section: Joni E. Baker.
Administrative Section: Jerry L. Baker.
Regional Security Officer: Kevin F. Flanagan.
Public Affairs Officer: Joseph J. Brennig.
Communications Programme Officer: Thomas J. Hettel.
Agency for International Development: Joseph F. Stepanek.

VIET-NAM

Embassy: 9 Ocean Rd, Dar es Salaam.
Ambassador: Tran My.

YEMEN

Embassy: 353 United Nations Rd, POB 349, Dar es Salaam; tel (51) 27891.
Ambassador: Abubaker Saeed Ba-Abbad.

YUGOSLAVIA

Embassy: Plot 35/36, Upanga Rd, POB 2838, Dar es Salaam; tel (51) 23196; telex 41749.
Ambassador: Peter Tos.

ZAIRE

Embassy: 438 Malik Rd, POB 975, Upanga, Dar es Salaam; telex 41407.
Ambassador: Pelendo B. Mawe.

ZAMBIA

High Commission: Ohio St and City Drive Junction, POB 2525, Dar es Salaam; telex 41023.
High Commissioner: S. Akapelwa.

ZIMBABWE

High Commission: POB 20762, Dar es Salaam; tel (51) 30455; telex 41386.
High Commissioner: J. M. Shava.

International Organizations

EUROPEAN COMMUNITIES

External Delegation: Extelcoms House, 9th Floor, Samora Ave, POB 9514, Dar es Salaam; tel (51) 31151; telex 41353; fax (51) 38575.
Commission Delegate: Hugh Swift.

THAILAND

ARGENTINA

Embassy: 20/85 Prommitr Villa, Soi 49/1, off Sukhumvit Rd Soi 49, Bangkok 10110; tel (2) 259-0401; telex 82762.

AUSTRALIA

Embassy: 37 Sathorn Tai Rd, Bangkok 10120; tel (2) 287-2680; telex 82149; fax (2) 287-2029.
Ambassador: Richard William Butler.

AUSTRIA

Embassy: 14 Soi Nandha, off Soi Attakarnprasit, Sathorn Tai Rd, Bangkok 10120; POB 1155, Bangkok 10121; tel (2) 254-6070; telex 82386; fax (2) 287-3925.
Ambassador: Dr Erich Binder.
Counsellor: Gerhard Weinberger.
First Secretary: Dr Ingrid Pech.
Third Secretary and Vice-Consul: Karl Zach.
Secretary (Economic): Christine Moosbrugger.

Commercial Office: Kian Gwan Bldg, 9th Floor, 140 Wireless Rd, POB 495, Bangkok 10330; tel (2) 251-4173; telex 82864; fax (2) 253-3567.
Counsellor (Commercial): Dr Hubert H. Schwetz.

BANGLADESH

Embassy: 6-8 Charoenmitr, Soi 63 Sukhumvit Rd, Bangkok 10110; tel (2) 391-8069; telex 82330.
Ambassador: Moinul Hussain Choudhury.

BELGIUM

Embassy: 44 Soi Phya Phipat, Off Silom Rd, Bangkok 10500; tel (2) 236-0150; telex 82563; fax (2) 236-7619.
Ambassador: Pierre de Mûelenaere.

BOLIVIA

Embassy: 148/4 Soi Kaeng Chuan Nang Linchee Rd, Yanawa, Bangkok 10210; tel (2) 252-2410.

BRAZIL

Embassy: Maneeya Centre Bldg, 9th Floor, 518/5 Ploenchit Rd, Bangkok 10500; tel (2) 252-6023; telex 82742; fax (2) 254-2707.
Ambassador: Paulo Monteiro Lima.

BRUNEI

Embassy: Orakarn Bldg, 14th Floor, Soi Chidlom, Ploenchit Rd, Bangkok 10500; tel (2) 251-5766; telex 20536; fax (2) 252-5851.
Ambassador: Pengiran Setia Raja Pengiran Haji Jaya bin Pengiran Haji Rajid.

BULGARIA

Embassy: 64 Soi Chareonmit, Sukhumvit 63, Bangkok 10110; tel (2) 381-1385.

CANADA

Embassy: Boonmitr Bldg, 11th-12th Floors, 138 Silom Rd, POB 2090, Bangkok 10500; tel (2) 234-1561; telex 82671; fax (2) 236-6463.
Ambassador: Arthur C. Perron.
Counsellor and Consul: D. Dhavernas.
Counsellor (Immigration): K. G. J. Hentschel.
Counsellor (Development): E. Yendall.
Counsellor (Commercial) and Consul: D. G. Summers.
Counsellor (Development): R. G. Belo.
Counsellor (Development): R. Coleman.
Counsellor (Commercial) and Consul: B. Desjardins.
Counsellor (Development): A. L. Potvin.
Attaché (Medical): Dr J. M. Chernin.

CHILE

Embassy: 15 Sukhumvit Soi 61, Bangkok 10110; tel (2) 391-4858; telex 84042; fax (2) 391-8380.
Ambassador: Fernando Gamboa Serazzi.
Second Secretary: Cristian Streeter.

Consulate: 18th Floor, Bangkok Bank Bldg, 333 Silom Rd, Bangkok 10500; tel (2) 233-2177; fax 236-7184.
Honorary Consul: Sutharm Valai-Sathien.

CHINA, PEOPLE'S REPUBLIC

Embassy: 57 Rachadapisake Rd, 10310 Bangkok; tel (2) 245-7032.
Ambassador: Li Shichun.

CZECHOSLOVAKIA

Embassy: Silom Centre Bldg, 21st Floor, 2 Silom Rd, POB 522, Bangkok 10500; tel (2) 234-3942.
Ambassador: Dr Karel Stehno.

DENMARK

Embassy: 10 Soi Attakarn Prasit, South Sathorn Rd, Bangkok 10120; tel (2) 213-2021; telex 87304; fax (2) 213-1752.
Ambassador: Mogens Knud Isaksen.
Counsellor (Agriculture/Government): Carsten Philipsen.
First Secretary: Michael Søndergaard.
Attaché (Commercial): Claus Hermansen.
Chancellor and Vice-Consul: Manoon Laokwansatit.
Commercial Correspondent: Chai Kristhaywin.

Consulate-General: The East Asiatic Co. Ltd Bldg, 53-5 Oriental Ave, POB 228, Bangkok 10500; tel (2) 236-0220; telex 82615.
Consul-General: Henrik de Jonquières.

EGYPT

Embassy: 49 Soi Ruam Rudee, Ploenchit Rd, Bangkok 10500; tel (2) 253-0161; telex 82544.
Ambassador: Mohamed Khalil Azazi.

FINLAND

Embassy: Amarin Tower, 16th Floor, 500 Ploenchit Rd, Bangkok 10330; POB 295, Bangkok 10501; tel (2) 256-9511; telex 82492; fax (2) 256-9310.
Ambassador: Eero Sanlovaara.
Secretary (Commercial): Jukka Orispää.

FRANCE

Embassy: 35 Soi Rong Phasi Kao, Soi 36, Charden Krung, 10500 Bangkok; tel (2) 234-0950; telex 82663; fax (2) 236-7973.
Ambassador: Georges-Emile Vinson.
First Counsellor: Serge Lauroff.
Second Counsellor: Alain Murguet.
Counsellor (Commercial): Jean-Louis Latour.
Counsellor (Culture): Michel Deverge.
Counsellor: Phillipe Dupont.
Defence Attaché: Col Edouard Castagnet-Cazalis.
First Secretary: Hugues Nordi.
First Secretary: Claude Latour.
Second Secretary: Nicole Cheves.
Attaché (Refugees): François Quilichini.
Attaché (Press): Marie Desrousseaux.
Attaché (Culture/Science): Michel Treutenaere.

GERMANY

Embassy: 9 Sathorn Tai Rd, POB 2595, Bangkok 10120; tel (2) 213-2331; telex 87348; fax (2) 287-1776.
Ambassador: Berthold von Pfetten-Arnbach.

GUATEMALA

Embassy: 37/1 Ekamai Sukhumvit Soi 63, Bangkok 10110; tel (2) 391-1617.

HOLY SEE

Apostolic Nunciature: 217/1 Sathorn Tai Rd, POB 12-178, Bangkok 10120; tel (2) 212-5853; telex 20726; fax (2) 212-0932.
Apostolic Pro-Nuncio: Most Rev. Alberto Tricarico, Titular Archbishop of Sistroniana.
Secretary: Mgr George Kocherry.

HUNGARY

Embassy: 28 Soi Sukchai, off Sukhumvit 42, Bangkok 10110; tel (2) 391-2002; telex 82954.
Ambassador: Peter Trunk.

ICELAND

Consulate-General: 59 Soi Navin, Chua Ploeng Rd, Bangkok 10120; tel (2) 249-1300; telex 87304; fax (2) 249-1253.
Consul-General: Jørgen A. Hage.

INDIA

Embassy: 46 Soi Prasarnmitr, 23 Sukhumvit Rd, Bangkok 10110; tel (2) 258-0300; telex 82793.
Ambassador: Vinay Verma.

INDONESIA

Embassy: 600-602 Phetchburi Rd, Bangkok 10400; tel (2) 252-3135; telex 82559.
Ambassador: Gatot Suwardi.

IRAN

Embassy: 602 Sukhumvit Rd, Bangkok 10110; tel (2) 259-0611; telex 82684; fax (2) 259-9111.
Ambassador: Mohammed Mehdi Sazegara.
First Secretary: Seyed Ahmad Hedayat.
First Secretary: Hamid Nazari Tajabadi.
Second Secretary: Bahman Amiari Khamneh.
Third Secretary: Abolfazl Eslami.
Third Secretary: Hamid Aminosharieh Najafi.
Administrator (Finance): Ebrahim Rezaee Shahreza.
Attaché (Cultural): Mohammad Tamhidi.
Attaché (Government Trade Corporation): Seyed Ali Tabibian.

IRAQ

Embassy: 47 Pradipat Rd, Samsen Nai, Phya Thai, Bangkok 10400; tel (2) 278-5335.

IRELAND

Consulate: United Flour Mill Bldg, 11th Floor, 205 Rajawongse Rd, Bangkok 10100; tel (2) 223-0340; telex 82203; fax (2) 221-7699.
Honorary Consul: Plengsadki Prakaspesat.

ISRAEL

Embassy: 31 Soi Lang Suan, Ploenchit Rd, Bangkok 10330; tel (2) 252-3131; telex 87322; fax (2) 254-5518.
Ambassador: Uzi Manor.

ITALY

Embassy: 399 Nang Linchee Rd, Thungmahakek, Bangkok 10120; tel (2) 287-2054; telex 82523.
Ambassador: Dr Giorgio Vecchi.

JAPAN

Embassy: 1674 New Phetchburi Rd, Bangkok 10130; tel (2) 252-6151; telex 87302; fax (2) 253-4153.
Ambassador: Hisahiko Okazaki.

Consular Section: 14 Boonruangrit Rd, POB 77, Chieng Mai; tel (53) 221451.
Consular Agent: Ismau Yamada.

KOREA, DEMOCRATIC PEOPLE'S REPUBLIC

Embassy: Bangkok.

KOREA, REPUBLIC

Embassy: 23 Thiam Ruammit, Huay Kwang, Samsen Rd, Bangkok 10310; tel (2) 247-7537; telex 82824.
Ambassador: Chung Choo-Nyun.

LAOS

Embassy: 193 Sathorn Tai Rd, Bangkok 10120; tel (2) 213-1203; telex 82192; fax 213-1203.
Ambassador: Bounkeut Sangsomsak.
First Secretary (Consular): Khampasong Douangsithi.
First Secretary: Oudom Vorapheth.
First Secretary (Commercial): Khoun Southammakoth.
Second Secretary (Protocol): Mengkham Banchongphanith.
Second Secretary (Administrative): Thongkhoun Phommachack.
Second Secretary (Culture): Somsi Oudomsak.
Third Secretary (Press/Information): Phouttha Khamphavong.

MALAYSIA

Embassy: 35 Sathorn Tai Rd, Bangkok 10120; tel (2) 286-1390; telex 87321.
Ambassador: Dato' Kamarudin Abu.

MEXICO

Embassy: 44/7-8 Convent Rd, Bangkok 10120; tel (2) 235-6367.
Ambassador: Enrique Michel.
Second Secretary: Miguel Angel Vilchis.
Attaché and Head of Consular Section: Adela Marquez.

MYANMAR

Embassy: 132 Sathorn Nua Rd, Bangkok 10500; tel (2) 234-4698; telex 21467.
Ambassador: U Nyunt Swe.

NEPAL

Embassy: 189 Soi 71, Sukhumvit Rd, Bangkok 10110; tel (2) 390-2280; telex 20216.
Ambassador: Ram Chandra Bahadur Singh.

NETHERLANDS

Embassy: 106 Wireless Rd, Bangkok 10500; tel (2) 254-7701; telex 82691.
Ambassador: Thomas Kasteel.
Counsellor: Conrad van Tooren.
Counsellor and Head of Economic and Consular Sections: Michiel den Hond.
First Secretary (Development): Ron Strikker.
Second Secretary: Arnold van Hengel.
Third Secretary: Marie Florence von Es.
Attaché (Administrative/Consular): Alfred Baltgens.

NEW ZEALAND

Embassy: 93 Wireless Rd, Pathumwon, Lumpini, Bangkok 10330; POB 2719, Bangkok 10501; tel (2) 251-8165; telex 81165; fax (2) 253-9045.
Ambassador: Harle Freeman-Greene.
Counsellor: Dr Joan Mosley.
First Secretary (Commercial) and Trade Commissioner: Ian Stockwell.
First Secretary (Administration) and Consul: Peter Cox.
Second Secretary: Linda Rooney.

NORWAY

Embassy: Bank of America Bldg, 1st Floor, 2/2 Wireless Rd, POB 81, Bangkok 10330; tel (2) 255-8210; telex 87309; fax (2) 256-0477.
Ambassador: Johan Dahl.
Second Secretary: Knut Langeland.
Attaché (Administrative/Consular): Berit Gjoelme.
Attaché: Trine Elisabeth Evjen.

PAKISTAN

Embassy: 31 Soi Nana Nua (3), Sukhumvit Rd, Bangkok 10110; tel (2) 253-0288; telex 84774.

PHILIPPINES

Embassy: 760 Sukhumvit Rd, Bangkok 10110; tel (2) 259-0139; telex 34445.
Ambassador: Josue L. Villa.

POLAND

Embassy: 61 Soi Prasanmitr 23, Sukhumvit Rd, Bangkok 10110; tel (2) 258-4112; telex 82074.
Ambassador: Lucjan Mieczkowski.

PORTUGAL

Embassy: 26 Capt. Bush Lane, Charoen Krung Rd, POB 742, Bangkok 10500; tel (2) 234-2123; telex 82866; fax (2) 236-1954.
Ambassador: Sebastião de Castelo-Branco.
Attaché (Culture): Maria Ermelinda Galamba de Oliveira.
Consul: José de Souza.

ROMANIA

Embassy: 150 Soi Charoenporn 1, Pradipat Rd, Bangkok 10400; tel (2) 279-3683; telex 82872.
Ambassador: Petre Mateescu.
Counsellor (Commercial): Marian State.
Second Secretary: Valerica Epure.
Second Secretary: Danut Enescu.
Attaché (Commercial): Cristian Epure.

RUSSIA

Embassy: 108 North Sathorn Nua Rd, Bangkok 10500; tel (2) 234-9824; telex 84693.
Ambassador: Anatoli Ivanovich Valkov.

SAUDI ARABIA

Embassy: Sathorn Thani Bldg, 10th Floor, 90 Sathorn Nua Rd, Bangkok 10500; tel (2) 237-1935; telex 87648.
Chargé d'affaires: Mohammed Mahdi al-Muslih.

SINGAPORE

Embassy: 129 South Sathorn Rd, Bangkok 10500; tel (2) 286-2111; telex 82930; fax (2) 287-2578.
Ambassador: Chin Siat Yoon.

SPAIN

Embassy: 93 Wireless Rd, Bangkok 10500; tel (2) 252-6112; telex 82885.
Ambassador: Tomas Chavarn del-Rivero.
Counsellor: Jorge Sanchez.
Counsellor (Economic) and Head of Commercial Section: Antonio Estevez.

SRI LANKA

Embassy: 48/3 Soi 1, Sukhumvit Rd, Bangkok 10500; tel (2) 251-2788; telex 87019.
Ambassador: H. C. Gunawardena.

SWEDEN

Embassy: Pacific Place, 20th Floor, 140 Sukhumvit Rd, Bangkok 10500; tel (2) 254-4954; telex 87114; fax (2) 254-4914.
Ambassador: Olov Ternstrom.

SWITZERLAND

Embassy: 35 North Wireless Rd, Bangkok 10330; POB 821, Bangkok 10501; tel (2) 253-0156; telex 82687; fax (2) 255-4481.
Ambassador: Gérard Fonjallaz.
Counsellor: Giatgen-Mario Pelican.
Attaché and Head of Chancery: Joseph Koch.
Attaché (Development Co-operation/Aid): Luciano Lavizzari.

TURKEY

Embassy: 153/2 Soi Mahadlek Luang 1, Rajdamri Rd, Bangkok 10330; tel (2) 251-2987; telex 82908; fax (2) 253-2121.
Ambassador: Erdinc Karasapan.
Second Secretary: Cigdem Tenker.
Attaché (Administrative): Mustafa Kursad Somay.
Attaché: Erdal Karaozbek.
Attaché: Hamza Erdogan.
Attaché: Bulent Ahmet Turgay.

UNITED KINGDOM

Embassy: Wireless Rd, Bangkok 10330; tel (2) 253-0191; telex 82263; fax (2) 255-8619.
Ambassador: M. Ramsay Melhuish.
Counsellor and Deputy Head of Mission: D. W. Fall.
Counsellor: R. J. P. Church.
Counsellor: R. E. Darkin.
Defence and Military Attaché: Col R. F. Stewart.
Naval and Air Attaché: Commdr P. S. Buckley.
First Secretary: A. N. George.
First Secretary: S. G. Jaggard.
First Secretary (Management): B. Halliwell.
First Secretary (Commercial): D. Bleakey.
First Secretary (Commercial/Development): G. T. Squires.
First Secretary: P. Matthews.
First Secretary: R. N. G. Wylde.
First Secretary and Consul: J. A. Francis.
Second Secretary (Political): A. M. Hall.
Third Secretary (Political/Information): S. D. Evans.

USA

Embassy: 95 Wireless Rd, Bangkok 10500; tel (2) 252-5040; telex 87008; fax (2) 254-2990.
Ambassador: Daniel A. O'Donahue.
Deputy Chief of Mission: Victor L. Tomseth.
Political Section: Ralph L. Boyce.

Economic Section: John Medeiros.
Commercial Section: Herbert A. Cochran.
Labour Officer: Thomas A. Cadogen.
Consular Section: David L. Lyon.
Administrative Section: Gerald E. Manderscheid.
Regional Security Officer: James A. McWhirter.
Agricultural Section: Richard K. Petges.
Agency for International Development: Thomas H. Reese III.
Public Affairs Officer: Donna Marie Oglesby.
Narcotics Assistance Unit: Albert L. Bryant.
Refugee Co-ordinator: David C. Pearce.
Customs Service: James L. Cable.
Information: James B. Foster.
Defence Attaché: Col William P. Kinnear, Jr.
Joint US Military Advisory Group: Brig. Robert L. Stephens, Jr.
Centre for Disease Control: Edward F. Yacavone.
Communications Programme Officer: Edward B. Wilson.
Information Systems Manager: Jerry D. Helmick.

Consulate: Vidhayanond Rd, Box C, Chieng Mai; tel (53) 252-629; fax (53) 252-633.
Principal Officer: Richard M. Gibson.
Consul and Political Section: James V. Gearhart.
Administrative Section: Dennis A. Droney.
Branch Public Affairs Officer: M. Elizabeth McKay.

Consulate: 9 Sadao Rd, Box S, Songkhla; tel (74) 311-589; fax (74) 324-409.
Principal Officer: Donald B. Coleman.

Consulate: 35/6 Supakitjanya Rd, Box UD, Udon Thani; tel (42) 244-270; fax (42) 244-273.
Principal Officer: Dewey R. Pendergrass.

VIET-NAM

Embassy: 83/1 Wireless Rd, Bangkok 10500; tel (2) 251-5838.
Ambassador: Nguyen Trung.

YUGOSLAVIA

Embassy: 28 Soi 61, Sukhumvit Rd, Bangkok 10110; tel (2) 391-9090; fax (2) 391-9090.
Ambassador: Petar Tolev.

International Organizations

EUROPEAN COMMUNITIES

Headquarters of Delegation for South-East Asia: Kian Gwan House II, 19th Floor, 140/1 Wireless Rd, Bangkok 10500; tel (2) 255-9100; telex 82764; fax (2) 255-9114.
Head of Delegation: Albert Maes.

UNITED NATIONS EDUCATIONAL, SCIENTIFIC AND CULTURAL ORGANIZATION—UNESCO

Office: Darakarn Bldg, 920 Sukhumvit Rd, Bangkok 10110; tel (2) 391-0577.

TOGO

BELGIUM

Embassy: 165 rue Pelletier Caventou, BP 7643, Lomé; tel 21-03-23; telex 5363.
Ambassador: Pierre Vaesen.

Consulate: BP 34, Lomé.

BRAZIL

Embassy: 119 rue de l'Ocam, BP 1356, Lomé; tel 21-00-58; telex 5346.
Chargé d'affaires: Gil de Ouro-Preto.

CHINA, PEOPLE'S REPUBLIC

Embassy: Tokoin-Ouest, BP 2690, Lomé; tel 21-31-59; telex 5070.
Ambassador: Zhou Xianjue.

DENMARK

Consulate: BP 2708, Villa Klouto, blvd de la Paix, Lomé; tel 21-34-45; fax 21-34-45.
Consul: Naja Kalmer Ahialegbedzi.

EGYPT

Embassy: route d'Aného, BP 8, Lomé; tel 21-24-43; telex 5310.
Ambassador: Hassan R. Soliman.

FRANCE

Embassy: 51 rue du Golfe, BP 337, Lomé; tel 21-25-71; telex 5202.
Ambassador: Bruno Delaye.

Consulate: tel 21-25-76.

Trade Promotion Office: BP 4873, Lomé; tel 21-27-78; telex 5390.

GABON

Embassy: Tokoin Super-Taco, BP 9118, Lomé; tel 21-47-76; telex 5307.
Ambassador: Alain Maurice Mayombo.

GERMANY

Embassy: blvd de la République, BP 1175, Lomé; tel 21-23-38; telex 5204.
Ambassador: Hans-Joachim Heldt.

GHANA

Embassy: 8 rue Paulin Eklou, Tokoin-Ouest, BP 92, Lomé; tel 21-31-94; fax 21-77-36.
Chargé d'affaires: J. M. Kwadjo.

ISRAEL

Embassy: Lomé.
Ambassador: Yaacov Revach.

ITALY

Consulate: BP 2105, Lomé; tel 21-08-61.

KOREA, DEMOCRATIC PEOPLE'S REPUBLIC

Embassy: Tokoin-Est, Lomé; tel 21-46-01.
Ambassador: Cho Chun-Hyong.

LIBYA

People's Bureau: blvd du 13 janvier, BP 4872, Lomé; tel 21-40-63; telex 5288.
Chargé d'affaires: Ahmed M. Abdulkafi.

NETHERLANDS

Consulate: BP 347, Lomé; tel 21-63-31.

NIGERIA

Embassy: 311 blvd du 13 janvier, BP 1189, Lomé; tel 21-34-55.
Ambassador: A. G. Gotip.

NORWAY

Consulate: BP 84, Lomé; tel 21-07-13.

RUSSIA

Embassy: route d'Aného, BP 634, Lomé; tel 21-35-78; telex 5409.
Ambassador: Oleg N. Cherny.

SOUTH AFRICA

Representation: BP 3711, Lomé; tel 21-82-63; fax 21-82-63.
Representative: J. W. van Deventer.
Deputy Representative: A. K. van Niekerk.

SWEDEN

Consulate-General: 8 rue Vaubant, BP 7003, Lomé; tel 21-22-31; telex 5290.
Consul-General: Ahlin Sodji.
Vice-Consul: Henri Parviz Dolatabadi.

SWITZERLAND

Consulate-General: 294 blvd du 13 janvier, BP 4851, Lomé; tel 21-56-19; telex 5187.
Consul-General: Margrith Bieri.

TUNISIA

Embassy: rue des Mélinas, BP 2983, Lomé; tel 21-26-37; telex 5356.
Ambassador: Amor Ardhaoui.

UNITED KINGDOM

Consulate: Agence Maritime Atlantique du Togo SARL, 1 rue L'Hôtel Miramar, Ablogame 2, BP 60958 BE, Lomé; tel 21-40-82; telex 5153.
Honorary Consul: Capt. R. A. M. Jones.

Commercial Office: BP 80607, Lomé-Tokoin.
Commercial Officer: G. Fioux.

USA

Embassy: angle rue Pelletier Caventou et rue Vauban, BP 852, Lomé; tel 21-29-91; fax 21-79-52.
Ambassador: Harmon E. Kirby.
Deputy Chief of Mission: Nancy J. Powell.
Political Section: Michael A. D'Andrea.
Economic/Commercial/Consular Section: Donald W. Koran.
Administrative Section: John E. Lange.
Regional Security Officer: Daniel R. Garner.
Public Affairs Officer: Morgan L. Kulla.
Communications Programme Officer: Fredrick Vinson.
Agency for International Development: Mark G. Wentling.

ZAIRE

Embassy: 325 blvd du 13 janvier, BP 102, Lomé; tel 21-51-55; telex 5263.
Ambassador: Lokoka Ikukele Bomolo.

International Organizations

EUROPEAN COMMUNITIES

External Delegation: ave Nicolas Grunitsky, BP 1657, Lomé; tel 21-36-62; telex 5267; fax 21-13-00.
Commission Delegate: Gaspard Dünkelsbühler.

TONGA

AUSTRALIA

High Commission: Salote Rd, Nuku'alofa; tel 21245; telex 66238; fax 23243.
High Commissioner: Howard Brown.

CHINA (TAIWAN)

Embassy: POB 842, Nuku'alofa; telex 66267.
Ambassador: Hugh O'Young.

GERMANY

Consulate: POB 32, Nuku'alofa; tel 23477; telex 66221; fax 23154.
Honorary Consul: Ralph W. Sanft.

NEW ZEALAND

High Commission: cnr Taufa'ahau and Salote Rds, POB 830, Nuku'alofa; tel 23122; telex 66216; fax 23487.
High Commissioner: Nigel Moore.
Second Secretary: Bruce Shepherd.
Attaché: Pat Brown.
Senior Immigration Officer: David Curtis.

UNITED KINGDOM

High Commission: Vuna Rd, POB 56, Nuku'alofa; tel 21020; telex 66226; fax 24109.
High Commissioner: William Lawson Cordiner.
Third Secretary (Consular/Management): M. A. Fidler.

International Organizations

EUROPEAN COMMUNITIES

Sub-Office of Delegation for the Pacific—Fiji: Maile Taha, Taufa'ahau Rd, Nuku'alofa; tel 23820; telex 66207; fax 23869.
Representative: Stefan Zens.

TRINIDAD AND TOBAGO

ARGENTINA

Embassy: 16 Victoria Ave, Port of Spain; tel 628-24586.
Ambassador: Silvio Héctor Neuman.

AUSTRIA

Consulate: 27 Frederick St, Port of Spain; tel 623-5912.
Honorary Consul: Hans Bernd Stecher.

BARBADOS

High Commission: 82 Long Circular Rd, Long Circular, Port of Spain; tel 622-0866.
High Commissioner: Joseph Frank da Silva.

BRAZIL

Embassy: 18 Sweet Briar Rd, St Clair, Port of Spain; tel 622-5779; telex 22550.
Ambassador: Fernando Alves.

CANADA

High Commission: Huggins Bldg, 72 South Quay, POB 1246, Port of Spain; tel 623-7254; telex 22429; fax 624-4016.
High Commissioner: Rodney Irwin.
Counsellor (Commercial): J. B. W. Motta.
First Secretary: D. J. Collier.
Second Secretary (Administrative): A. C. Ricard.
Attaché (Medical): Dr D. Denny.
Attaché (Medical): Br P. Boucher.

Immigration Office: Huggins Bldg, 74 South Quay, POB 565, Port of Spain; tel 625-1941.
Counsellor (Immigration): H. E. Smith.
First Secretary (Immigration): S. Pollin.

CHINA, PEOPLE'S REPUBLIC

Embassy: 39 Alexandra St, Port of Spain; tel 622-6976.
Ambassador: Zhang Ruicong.

COLOMBIA

Embassy: 67 Independence Square, 2nd Floor, POB 664, Port of Spain; tel 623-6601.
Ambassador: Adolfo Fidalgo.

DENMARK

Consulate-General: 72-4 South Quay, POB 179, Port of Spain; tel 623-4700; telex 22431; fax 623 8419.
Consul-General: John William Anthony Alcazar.

FINLAND

Consulate-General: Trinidad Marine Agencies Ltd, 14 Rookery Nook, POB 622, Port of Spain; tel 622-1061; telex 2228; fax 622-7085.
Consul-General: Björn Anders Anderson.

FRANCE

Embassy: Tatil Bldg, 11 Maraval Rd, Newtown, Port of Spain; tel 622-2446; fax 628-2632.
Ambassador: Denis Norto.

GERMANY

Embassy: 7-9 Marli St, POB 828, Newtown, Port of Spain; tel 628-1630; telex 22316; fax 628-5278.
Ambassador: Holger Eberle.
First Secretary: Dr Benedikt Haller.

HOLY SEE

Apostolic Nunciature: 11 Mary St, St Clair, POB 854, Port of Spain; tel 622-5009; telex 22500; fax 628-5457.
Apostolic Pro-Nuncio: Mgr Eugenio S. Barbaro.
Secretary: Dominique Rézeau.

INDIA

High Commission: 6 Victoria Ave, Port of Spain; tel 627-7480; telex 22514; fax 627-6985.
High Commissioner: Chintamani Lakshmanna.
First Secretary: B. Ghosh.

JAMAICA

High Commission: 2 Newbold St, St Clair, Port of Spain; tel 622-4995; telex 22234; fax 628-9180.
High Commissioner: Stafford O. Neil.
Deputy High Commissioner: Gail Mathurin.
Commissioner on Trade: Pamela Wells.
Attaché (Administrative): Marva Taylor.
Attaché: Janice Willingston.

JAPAN

Embassy: 5 Hayes St, St Clair, POB 1039, Port of Spain; tel 622-6105; telex 22441; fax 622-0858.
Ambassador: Mitsuo Iijima.

KOREA, REPUBLIC

Embassy: 61 Dundonald St, Port of Spain; tel 627-6791; fax 627-6363.
Ambassador: Boo Yul Park.
First Secretary and Consul: Byung Kuck Jhung.
Attaché (Administrative) and Vice-Consul: Seon Ho Choi.

NETHERLANDS

Embassy: 3rd Floor, Life of Barbados Bldg, 69-71 Edward St, POB 870, Port of Spain; tel 625-1210; telex 22322.
Ambassador: John Leefmans.

NEW ZEALAND

Consulate: Geo. F. Huggins & Co. Ltd Builiding, 233 Western Main Rd, Cocorite, POB 823, Port of Spain; tel 622-6673; telex 22272; fax 623-8419.
Honorary Consul: George Faria.

NIGERIA

High Commission: 3 Maxwell-Phillip St, St Clair, Port of Spain; tel 622-4002; telex 22390.
High Commissioner: Abubakar Udu.

PERU

Embassy: Maraval Rd, Port of Spain; tel 622-6014.

SWITZERLAND

Consulate-General: 18-20 Pembroke St, POB 905, Port of Spain.
Honorary Consul-General: Fernand Domon.

UNITED KINGDOM

High Commission: Furness House, 3rd and 4th Floors, 90 Independence Square, POB 778, Port of Spain; tel 625-2861; telex 22224; fax 623-0621.
High Commissioner: Brian Smith.
Deputy High Commissioner: D. L. Smallman.
First Secretary: J. J. Penn.
Second Secretary (Commercial): W. E. J. Preston.
Second Secretary (Management/Consular/Immigration/Aid): C. A. Fawcett.
Second Secretary (Chancery/Information): T. R. Knight.

USA

Embassy: 15 Queen's Park West, POB 752, Port of Spain; tel 622-6176; fax 628-5462.
Ambassador: Charles A. Gargano.
Deputy Head of Mission: Lacy A. Wright, Jr.
Political Section: Phillip Antokol.
Economic Section: Judson L. Bruns.
Consular Section: Bruce McKenzie.
Administrative Section: Gary G. Bagley.
Commercial Section: Thomas E. Moore.
Regional Security Officer: Melissa McPeak.
Communications Programme Officer: Ronnie J. Fontenot.

VENEZUELA

Embassy: 16 Victoria Ave, POB 1300, Port of Spain; tel 622-2468; telex 22268; fax 624-2508.
Ambassador: Luis Eduardo Soto Alvarez.
Minister-Counsellor: Pedro Alexis Camacho Sanchez.
Counsellor: Ricardo Mario Rodriguez J.
Second Secretary: Antonio Rangel Barling.

Consulate: 42 Murray St, Port of Spain; tel 82453; telex 624-22268; fax 624-2508.
Consul-General: Elvia Vivas de Lewis.

International Organizations

EUROPEAN COMMUNITIES

Commission Delegation: 2 Champs Elysées, Long Circular, Maraval, POB 1144, Port of Spain; tel 622-6628; telex 22421; fax 622-6355.

TUNISIA

ALGERIA

Embassy: 18 rue de Niger, Tunis; tel (1) 283-166; telex 13081.
Ambassador: Dr Messaoud ait Chaalal.

ARGENTINA

Embassy: 10 rue al-Hassan et Houssaine, al-Menzah, 1004 Tunis; tel (1) 237-313; telex 13053.
Ambassador: Omar Ricardo del Azar Suaya.

AUSTRIA

Embassy: 16 rue ibn Hamdiss, BP 23, al-Menzah, 1004 Tunis; tel (1) 238-082; telex 14586.
Ambassador: Dr Johann Pasch.
First Secretary: Franz Josef Kuglitsch.
Economic Secretary: Ingeborg Vanek.

BAHRAIN

Embassy: 72 rue Mouaouia ibn Abi Soufiane, al-Menzah VI, Tunis; tel (1) 766-812; telex 13733.
Ambassador: Jassim Buallay.

BELGIUM

Embassy: 47 rue du 1er Juin, BP 241002, Tunis; tel (1) 781-655; telex 14342; fax (1) 792-797.
Ambassador: Paul Duque.

BRAZIL

Embassy: 37 ave d'Afrique, BP 64, al-Menzah V, 1004 Tunis; tel (1) 232-538; telex 14560.
Ambassador: Renato Bayma Denys.

BULGARIA

Embassy: 5 rue Ryhane, Cité Mahragène, 1002 Tunis; tel (1) 283-007; telex 15289; fax (1) 791-667.
Ambassador: Stefan Staikov.
Second Secretary: Petar Dragnev.
Third Secretary and Consul: Nikolai Pisanchev.
Attaché: Eugeni Tchaushev.
Financial Affairs: Boris Gueorgiev.

CANADA

Embassy: 3 rue du Sénégal, Place Palestine, BP 31, Belvédère, Tunis; tel (1) 286-004; telex 15324; fax (1) 792-371.
Ambassador: Marius Bujold.
Counsellor and Consul: J.-F. Carle.
Counsellor (Development): P. Giroux.
First Secretary (Commercial) and Consul: J. J. H. Prévost.
First Secretary (Administration) and Consul: R. Tessier.

CHINA, PEOPLE'S REPUBLIC

Embassy: 41 ave Jugurtha, Mutuelleville, Tunis; tel (1) 282-090; telex 12221.
Ambassador: Zhu Yinglu.

COTE D'IVOIRE

Embassy: 84 ave Hédi Chaker, Tunis; tel (1) 283-878; telex 14353.
Ambassador: Collet Philippe Vieira.

CUBA

Embassy: 3 rue Abou Hayane, al-Menzah IV, Tunis; tel (1) 283-555.
Ambassador: Domingo García.

CZECHOSLOVAKIA

Embassy: 98 rue de Palestine, BP 53, Belvédère, 1002 Tunis; tel (1) 280-486; telex 14466; fax (1) 791-183.
Ambassador: Dr Ivo Kubeš.
First Secretary: Stanislav Opiela.
Second Secretary: Ivan Surkoš.
Administrative Attaché: Julian Kvas.
Administrative Attaché: František Šebístek.

DENMARK

Embassy: 5 rue de Mauritanie, BP 254, Belvédère, 1002 Tunis; tel (1) 792-600; telex 14352; fax (1) 790-797.
Chargé d'affaires a.i.: John Kristensen.
First Counsellor (Agriculture): Børge Schou Pedersen.

Consulate-General: 28 rue 8601, Zone Industrielle Charguia, BP 65, 2035 Tunis Carthage; tel (1) 788-100; telex 15158.
Consul-General and Honorary Commercial Counsellor: Roger Bismuth.

Consulate: Monastir.

Consulate: 38 rue Alexandre Dumas, 1er étage, BP 26, Sfax; tel (4) 20552; telex 40802.
Vice-Consul: Hamed Ennouri.

DJIBOUTI

Embassy: 5 rue Fatma al-Fahria, BP 71, Mutuelleville, Tunis; tel (1) 890-589; telex 13148.
Ambassador: Ali Abdou Muhammad.

EGYPT

Embassy: Quartier Montplaisir, Routhi 6, Med V, Tunis; tel (1) 792-233; telex 13992; fax (1) 794-389.
Ambassador: Ali Maher as-Sayed.

FINLAND

Consulate-General: AACC, 5 rue Ibn Rochd, BP 585, 1001 Tunis; tel (1) 243-300.
Honorary Consul-General: Mohammed Rahdhi Kchouk.

FRANCE

Embassy: place de l'Indépendance, BP 689, Tunis; tel (1) 245-701; telex 12553; fax (1) 354-388.
Ambassador: Alain Grenier.

Consulate-General: 1 rue de Hollande, Tunis; tel (1) 245-700.

Trade Promotion Office: 2 rue Gamel Abdel Nasser, Tunis; tel (1) 245-837; telex 14453.

Consulate-General: 9 ave Habib Bourguiba, Sfax; tel (4) 20788.

GERMANY

Embassy: 1 rue al-Hamra, BP 35, Mutuelleville, Belvédère, Tunis; tel (1) 786-455; telex 15463; fax (1) 788-242.
Ambassador: Dr Karl Heinz Kunzmann.

Visa Section: telex 15311.

Consulate: Bungalow 40, Sidi-Mahrez, BP 21, Houmet Essouk, Djerba; tel (1) 57139.
Honorary Consul: François-Joseph Wiels.

GREECE

Embassy: 9 impasse Antelas, Nord Hilton, BP 151, Mahrajane, 1002 Tunis; tel (1) 288-411; telex 13742; fax (1) 789-518.
Ambassador: Constantin Prevedourakis.

HUNGARY

Embassy: 8 rue al-Jahedh, al-Menzah I, 1004 Tunis; tel (1) 233-338; telex 15472; fax (1) 750-620.
Ambassador: Sándor Pamuk.
Second Secretary: Ferenc Gemes.
Attaché: Lászlo Siry.

Commercial Section: 8 rue Ibn Sebain, Notre Dame, Tunis.
Commercial Counsellor: Tibor Havasi.
Second Commercial Secretary: Imre Biro.

ICELAND

Consulate-General: c/o Setcar SA, Zone Industrielle La Charguia, BP 61, Tunis; tel (1) 230-440; telex 15182.
Consul-General: Ferid Abbas.

INDIA

Embassy: 4 place Didon, Notre Dame, Tunis; tel (1) 891-006; telex 13072.
Ambassador: Lakshmi Narasimihan Rangarajan.

INDONESIA

Embassy: 117 ave Jugurtha (ave De Lesseps), Mutuelleville, Tunis; BP 63, al-Menzah, 1004 Tunis; tel (1) 893-127; telex 13173.
Ambassador: Kusnadi Pudjiwinarto.

IRAN

Embassy: Tunis.

IRAQ

Embassy: ave Tahar B. Achour, route X2 m. 10, Mutuelleville, Tunis; tel (1) 890-633; telex 12245.
Ambassador: Nouri Ismail Toha al-Wayes.

ITALY

Embassy: 37 rue Gamal Abd an-Nasser, Tunis; tel (1) 247-486; telex 13501.
Ambassador: Gianfranco Farinelli.

JAPAN

Embassy: 10 rue Mahmoud al-Matri, BP 95, Belvédère, Tunis 1002; tel (1) 285-937; telex 15456; fax (1) 786-625.
Ambassador: Nobuo Nishizaki.

JORDAN

Embassy: 87 ave Jugurtha, Mutuelleville, Tunis; tel (1) 288-401; telex 13745.
Ambassador: Nabih an-Nimr.

KOREA, DEMOCRATIC PEOPLE'S REPUBLIC

Embassy: 10 rue Holima Saodia, al-Menzah, Tunis; tel (1) 231-715.
Ambassador: Li Yong Hak.

KOREA, REPUBLIC

Embassy: 16 rue Caracalla, Notre Dame, 1002 Tunis; tel (1) 894-357; telex 15157.

Ambassador: Chung-Hyun Pyun.

KUWAIT

Embassy: 40 route Ariane, al-Menzah, Tunis; tel (1) 236-811; telex 12332.
Ambassador: Mejren Ahmad al-Hamad.

LIBYA

Embassy: 48 bis rue du 1er Juin, Tunis; tel (1) 236-666; telex 12275.
Ambassador: Abd al-Atti Obeidi.

MALTA

Embassy: Palazzo Parisio, Merchants St, Valletta, Malta; tel 222407; telex 1100; fax 237822.
Ambassador: Alfred A. Zarb (resident in Malta).

MAURITANIA

Embassy: 17 rue Fatma Ennechi, BP 62, al-Menzah, Tunis; tel (1) 234-935; telex 12234.
Ambassador: Muhammad Lamine Ould Yahya.

MOROCCO

Embassy: 39 ave du 1er Juin, Tunis; tel (1) 782-775; telex 14460; fax (1) 787-103.
Ambassador: Abd al-Hakim Iraqui.

NETHERLANDS

Embassy: 6-8 rue Meycen, BP 449, Belvédère, 1025 Tunis; tel (1) 287-455; telex 15260; fax (1) 785-557.
Ambassador: R. J. Mulder.

PAKISTAN

Embassy: 7 rue Ali ibn Abi Talib, al-Menzah, Tunis; tel (1) 234-366.
Ambassador: S. A. D. Bukhari.

POLAND

Embassy: 4 rue Sophonisbe, Notre Dame, Tunis; tel (1) 286-237; telex 14024.
Ambassador: Janusz Fekecz.

PORTUGAL

Embassy: 2 rue Sufétula, Belvédère, 1002 Tunis; tel (1) 788-189; telex 13235; fax (1) 791-008.
Ambassador: Carlos Milheirao.
Vice-Consul: Giuseppe Sergio Pecoraro.

QATAR

Embassy: 2 rue Dr Burnet, Belvédère, Tunis; tel (1) 285-600; telex 14131.
Ambassador: Ali Hussein al-Mufkah.
Third Secretary: Saad Hellal al-Muhannadi.
Third Secretary: Hamad Mohammed al-Khalifa.
Third Secretary: Salah Ali al-Jaber.

ROMANIA

Embassy: 22 rue Dr Burnet, Belvédère, Tunis; tel (1) 281-185; telex 12223.
Ambassador: Gheorghe Arsene.

RUSSIA

Embassy: 31 rue du 1er Juin, Tunis; tel (1) 280-333.
Ambassador: Vladimir Fedorovich Sobchenko.

SAUDI ARABIA

Embassy: 16 rue d'Autriche, Belvédère, Tunis; tel (1) 281-295; telex 13562.
Ambassador: Sheikh Abbas Faik Ghazzaoui.

SENEGAL

Embassy: 122 ave de la Liberté, 1002 Tunis; tel (1) 282 110; telex 15477.
Ambassador: Amadou Moustapha Dior.
First Counsellor: Zapa Ousmane Sèye.
Second Counsellor: Malick Ndaw.
First Secretary and Accountant: Falilou Gueye.
First Secretary and Administrative Accountant: Cheikh Diallo.
Second Secretary and Consular Agent: Vincent Mendy.

SOMALIA

Embassy: 6 rue Hadramout, Mutuelleville, Tunis; tel (1) 289-505; telex 13480.
Ambassador: Ahmad Abdallah Muhammad.

SPAIN

Embassy: 22 ave Dr Ernest Conseil, Cité Jardin, Tunis; tel (1) 280-613; telex 13330.

SUDAN

Embassy: 30 ave d'Afrique, Tunis; telex 13815.
Ambassador: Sayed Sharif Ahmad.

SWEDEN

Embassy: 87 ave Taïeb Mhiri, Belvédère, 1002 Tunis; BP 112, Belvédère, 1012 Tunis; tel (1) 283-433; telex 15258; fax (1) 788-894.
Ambassador: Magnus Faxén.
Counsellor: Jan Olsson.
First Secretary: Cecilia Lithander.

Consulate: 2 rue d'Italie, 4000 Sousse; tel (3) 24274.
Consul: Mahmoud Chaouch.

SWITZERLAND

Embassy: 10 rue Ech-Chenkiti, Mutuelleville, Belvédère, 1002 Tunis; BP 501, 1025 Tunis; tel (1) 280-132; telex 14922; fax (1) 788-796.
Ambassador: Dr Luciano Mordasini.
First Secretary: Werner Gasche.
Head of Chancery: Pierre-Denis Peissard.

SYRIA

Embassy: Cité al-Manor III, No. 119, Tunis; tel (1) 235-577; telex 13890.
Ambassador: Omar as-Said.

TURKEY

Embassy: 47 ave Muhammad V, Tunis; tel (1) 282-060; telex 14067.
Ambassador: Muammer Tuncer.

UNITED ARAB EMIRATES

Embassy: 15 rue du 1er Juin, Mutuelleville, Tunis; tel (1) 783-522; telex 12168.
Ambassador: Hamad Salem al-Maqami.

UNITED KINGDOM

Embassy: 5 place de la Victoire, Tunis; tel (1) 244-805; telex 14007; fax (1) 354-877.
Ambassador and Consul-General: Stephen P. Day.
First Secretary and Deputy Head of Mission: A. Holmes.
First Secretary (Chancery): J. M. Weldin.
Cultural Attaché (British Council Director): D. A. Handforth.
Second Secretary (Commercial/Economic): C. R. Innes-Hopkins.

Consular and Visa Sections: 143 Ave de la Liberté, Tunis; tel (1) 793-322; telex 15218; fax (1) 792-644.,
Vice-Consul and Commercial Officer: V. Zaoui.
Attaché (Management) and Vice-Consul: A. F. McPherson.
Vice-Consul (Immigration): N. R. Martin.

Consulate: Rue de Madagascar, 3000 Bab El Bahr, Sfax; tel (3) 28555; telex 40822.
Honorary Consul: M. Bouricha.

USA

Embassy: 144 ave de la Liberté, Belvédère, 1002 Tunis; tel (1) 782-566; telex 13379; fax (1) 789-719.
Ambassador: Thomas McCarthy.
Deputy Chief of Mission: Shaun E. Donnelly.
Political Section: Janean L. Mann.
Economic Section: Robert L. Glass.
Commercial Section: Elizabeth L. Dibble.
Consular Section: Greta Holtz.
Administrative Section: Stephen T. Smith.
Regional Security Officer: Gregory B. Starr.
Public Affairs Officer: Richard Undeland.
Communications Programme Officer: Richard A. Hoffer.
Information Systems Manager: Robert A. Hall.
Agency for International Development: George Carner.
Agricultural Trade Office: Abdullah A. Saleh.
Office of the Defence Attaché: Col Marc B. Powe.
US Liaison Office: Col MacArthur Deshazer.
Labour Officer: Philo L. Dibble.

VENEZUELA

Embassy: 30 rue de Niger, BP 30, 1002 Tunis; tel (1) 285-075; telex 15091.
First Secretary: Olga Bermudez de C.
Second Officer: Edecia Borges de E.

YEMEN

Embassy: rue Mouaouia ibn Soufiane, al-Menzah VI, Tunis; tel (1) 237-933; telex 13045.
Ambassador: Salah Ali al-Achoual.

YUGOSLAVIA

Embassy: 4 rue de Libéria, Tunis; tel (1) 281-032.
Ambassador: Luan Starova.

ZAIRE

Embassy: 11 rue Tertullien, Notre Dame, Tunis; tel (1) 281-833; telex 12429.
Ambassador: Mboladinga Katako.

International Organizations

EUROPEAN COMMUNITIES

External Delegation: BP 143, Cité el Mahrajene, 1082 Tunis; tel (1) 788-600; telex 13596; fax (1) 788-201.
Head of Delegation: Klaus von Helldorff.

TURKEY

AFGHANISTAN

Embassy: Cinnah Cad. 88, Çankaya, Ankara; tel (4) 1277698.
Chargé d'affaires: Muhammad Anwar Basrar.

ALBANIA

Embassy: Nenehatun Cad. 89, Gaziosmanpaşa, Ankara; tel (4) 1466527; fax (4) 1466526.
Ambassador: Nesip Kaçi.
Counsellor: Akil Payenga.
Attaché: Viron Proko.

Consulate-General: Ömer Rüşkü Paşa, Sokak 3 Teşvikiye, İstanbul; tel (1) 1615726; fax (1) 1616109.
Consul-General: Enver Zeneli.

ALGERIA

Embassy: Şehit Ersan Cad., Ankara; tel (4) 1278700; telex 42053.
Ambassador: Muhammad Kadri.

ARGENTINA

Embassy: İran Cad. 57/1, Çankaya, Ankara; tel (4) 1271322.
Ambassador: Julio César Etchegoyen.

AUSTRALIA

Embassy: Nenehatun Cad. 83, 06680 Gaziosmanpaşa, Ankara 06680; PK 32, Çankaya, Ankara 06552; tel (4) 1361240-5; telex 44248; fax (4) 1361246.
Ambassador: Donald W. Witheford.

Consulate: Tepecik Yolu Üzeri 58, Etiler, İstanbul; tel (1) 1577050.

AUSTRIA

Embassy: Atatürk Bul. 189, 06680 Kavaklidere, Ankara; PK 131, 06661 Küçükesat, Ankara; tel (4) 1342172; telex 42429; fax (4) 1189454.
Ambassador: Dr Friedrich C. Zanetti.
Counsellor: Dr Thomas Wunderbaldinger.
Third Secretary (Administrative/Consular): Gerhard Fittner.
Attaché (Administrative/Consular): Martin Falb.
Commercial Attaché: Wolfgang Wutte.

Commercial Office: Kircicegi Sok. 8/2, Gaziosmanpaşa, Ankara; tel (4) 1361272; telex 42312; fax (4) 1367449.
Commercial Counsellor: Dr Peter Singer.

Consulate-General: Köybasi Cad. 46, 80870 Yeniköy, İstanbul; PK 62, 80212 İstanbul-Tesvikiye; tel (1) 1629315; telex 28026; fax (1) 1622622.
Consul-General: Adolf Klement.

Commercial Office: Halaskargazi Cad. 399-401/A-4, Sisli, İstanbul; tel (1) 1484742; telex 39624; fax (1) 1481607.
Commercial Counsellor: Dr Harald Fiegl.

Cultural Institute: Avusturya Kültür Ofisi, Tesvikiye Cad. 101/2, Belveder Apt, 80200 İstanbul; PK 6, 80212 İstanbul-Tesvikiye; tel (1) 1361581; fax (1) 1580222.
Director of Cultural Institute and Consul: Erwin Lucius.
Consul: Richard Gerstenecker.

Consulate: Gazi Bulv./Sehit Fethi Bey, Cad. 4, PK 160, 35212 İzmir; tel (51) 136123; telex 52257; fax (51) 148127.
Honorary Consul: Muammer Erboy.

Consulate: Namik Kemal Bul. 64, PK 5, 07040 Antalya; tel (31) 151020; telex 56104; fax (31) 151800.
Honorary Consul: Ali Riza Balci.

Consulate: Tarsus Yolu, PK 371, 01322 Adana; tel (71) 281464; telex 63880; fax (71) 281076.
Honorary Consul: Ömer Sabanci.

BANGLADESH

Embassy: Karyağdi Sok. 18, 06690 Ankara; tel (4) 1388396; telex 46068.
Ambassador: Sofi Ahmed Chowdhury.

BELGIUM

Embassy: Nenehatun Cad. 109, Ankara; tel (4) 1361653; telex 42258.
Ambassador: Jan Debergh.

BRAZIL

Embassy: Büyük Esat Mah. Köroğlu Cad., Çayhane Sok. 46, 06700 Çankaya, Ankara; tel (4) 1374401; telex 42657.
Ambassador: Victor José Silveira.

BULGARIA

Embassy: Atatürk Bul. 124, Ankara; tel (4) 1267455; telex 42682; fax (4) 1273178.
Ambassador: Petar Vodenski.
Counsellor: Branimir Petrov.
Counsellor (Commercial/Economic): Evgueni Krouchkov.
Military Attaché: Stayko Christov.
First Secretary (Political/Economic): Vassil Vassilev.
First Secretary (Consular Affairs): Kiril Christov.
Air Attaché: Ivan Nakov.
Third Secretary (Cultural Affairs): Branimir Mladenov.
Third Secretary (Press): Valery Vassilev.
Secretary to Military Attaché: Gueorgui Savov.

Consulate-General: Zincirlikoyu Cad. 44, İstanbul; tel (1) 1690478.
Consul-General: Mr Parouchev.

Consulate-General: Talat Paşa Cad. 31, Edirne; tel 111069.
Consul-General: Mr Momchilov.

CANADA

Embassy: Nenehatun Cad. 75, 06700 Gaziosmanpaşa, Ankara; tel (4) 1361275; telex 42369; fax (4) 1464437.
Ambassador: Paul A. Lapointe.
Counsellor and Consul: J. D. Puddington.
Counsellor (Commercial/Economic): D. B. Collins.
Counsellor (Commercial): M. Wondergem.
Counsellor (Immigration): L. M. C. Verboven.
Canadian Forces Attaché: Capt. J. T. Jones.
Second Secretary (Administration) and Vice-Consul: J. H. Dufresne.

Consulate: Büyükdere Cad. 107/3, Begün Han, Gayrettepe, İstanbul: tel (1) 1725174; telex 26133; fax (1) 1723427.
Honorary Consul: Y. Kireç.

CHILE

Embassy: Cinnah Cad. 78/1, Çankaya, Ankara; tel (4) 1389444.
Chargé d'affaires: Milenko Skoknic Tapia.

CHINA, PEOPLE'S REPUBLIC

Embassy: Yukari Ayranci 8, Durak Hoşdere Cad. 147, Ankara; tel (4) 1264081.
Ambassador: Zhan Shiliang.

'TURKISH REPUBLIC OF NORTHERN CYPRUS'

Embassy: İncirli Sok. 20, Gaziosmanpaşa, 06700 Ankara; tel (4) 1376030; telex 42575; fax (4) 1465238.
Ambassador: Oğuz Ramazan Korhan.
Second Secretary: Mustafa Evran.

Consulate-General: Büyükdere Cad. 81, Kuğu İş Hani, Kat 5 Daire 9, Mecidiyeköy, İstanbul; tel (1) 1752990; fax (1) 1744543.
Consul-General: Münir Muhtaroğlu.

Consulate: Hamidiye Mahallesi, Atatürk Cad., Karadeniz Apartmani 71/3 (Müftü Köprüsü yani), Mersin; tel (741) 16228; fax (741) 132748.
Consul: Mesut Merter.

CZECHOSLOVAKIA

Embassy: Atatürk Bul. 245, Ankara; tel (4) 1265887; fax (4) 1682689.
Ambassador: Benedikt Durmek.

DENMARK

Embassy: Kirlangiç Sok. 42, 06700 Gaziosmanpaşa, Ankara; tel (4) 1275258; telex 42377; fax (4) 1684559.
Ambassador: N. C. Tillisch.
Counsellor: Allan Christensen.
Attaché and Consul: Alice Rostgaard.

Consulate-General: c/o Vitsan, Bilezik Sokak 2, Findikli, 80040 İstanbul; PK 689, Sisli, 80225 İstanbul; tel (1) 1450385; telex 24749; fax (1) 1494434.
Consul-General: Ilkay Bilgisin.
Commercial Officer and Vice-Consul: Sibel Afsar.

Consulate: Akdeniz Cad., Reyent Işhani 1/702, Pasaport, İzmir; tel (51) 195401; fax (51) 255388.
Consul: Ali Nail Kubali.

Consulate: Eski Gümrük Meydani, Güven Ihani, Mersin; tel (741) 39944; telex 67139; fax (741) 22057.
Consul: Hanri Atat.

EGYPT

Embassy: Atatürk Bul. 126, Kavaklidere, 06680 Ankara; tel (4) 1266478.
Ambassador: Aly Shawky el-Hadidy.

FINLAND

Embassy: Farabi Galip Dede Sok. 1/20, Kavaklidere, 06680 Ankara; PK 22, Kavaklidere, 06692 Ankara; tel (4) 1264964; telex 42856; fax (4) 1682507.
Ambassador: Risto Kauppi.
Commercial Counsellor: Pekka Sammallahti.
Second Secretary: Roy Eriksson.
Second Secretary: Pirjo Valinoro.

Consulate-General: Mete Cad. 24, Taksim, 80090 İstanbul; tel (1) 1455880; telex 24052; fax (1) 1492475.

Consul-General: Ural Ataman.

Consulate: Kurtulus Mahallesi 81B, Adana; Akdeniz Nebati Yaglar ve, Tekstil Sanayi Isl. AS, PK 176, Adana; tel (71) 218845.
Consul: Nuri Sabuncu.

Consulate: Gazi Bul. 47-49, İzmir; tel (51) 145470; telex 52583; fax (51) 147001.
Consul: Ergün Özakat.

Consulate: Yapay Jüt AS, Bugday Pazari 5, PK 96, Samsun; tel (361) 11223; telex 82118.
Consul: Akin Balkan.

FRANCE

Embassy: Paris Cad. 70, Kavaklidere, Ankara; tel (4) 1681154; telex 42385; fax (4) 1679434.
Ambassador: François Dopffer.

Trade Promotion Office: PK 1, Kavaklidere, 06692 Ankara; tel (4) 1283175; telex 44429.

Consulate-General: 8 Istiklâl Cad. (Taksim), İstanbul; tel (1) 431852.

GERMANY

Embassy: Atatürk Bul. 114, 06680 Kavaklidere, Ankara; PK 54, 06552 Çankaya, Ankara; tel (4) 1265451; telex 44394; fax (4) 1266959.
Ambassador: Dr Ekkehard Eickhoff.

Visa Section: Güneş Sokak 4, 06690 Kavaklidere-Ankara; tel (4) 1281402; telex 46413.

Branch Office: Kiremit Hane Mahallesi, 123 Sok. No. 8, Andic Apt Blok A, Mersin; tel (741) 76100; telex 67315; fax (741) 76104.

Consulate-General: Inönü Cad. 16-18, İstanbul; PK 355, 80073 İstanbul Beyoğlu; tel (1) 1515404; telex 24234; fax (1) 1499920.
Consul-General: Dr Gerhard Müller-Chorus.

Visa Section: Selim Hatun Camli Cad. 46, İstanbul-Ayazpaşa; tel (1) 1437221; telex 25941.

Consulate-General: Atatürk Cad. 260, 35220 İzmir; PK 156, 35212 İzmir; tel (51) 216995; telex 52654.
Consul-General: Dr Helmut Urbanek.

Consulate: Atatürk Cad. 9, Coskun Apt Kat 5, D9, PK 218, 07050 Antalya; tel (31) 113318; telex 56076.
Honorary Consul: Atalay Tüzün.

Consulate: Cavus Bey Mahallesi, Arif Pasa Cad. 3/3, Edirne; tel (181) 13158; telex 37151.
Honorary Consul: Rifat Culha.

Consulate: Özel Idare Ishani No. 7, Iskenderun; tel (881) 11217.
Honorary Consul: Dr Besim Mülayim.

Consulate: Eski Belediye Sokak No. 7, Sivas; tel (477) 11404.
Honorary Consul: Turhan Akça.

GREECE

Embassy: Zia ül-Rahman 9-11, Gaziosmanpaşa, Ankara; tel (4) 1368860; telex 42146.
Ambassador: Dimitris Makris.

HOLY SEE

Apostolic Nunciature: PK 33, 06552 Çankaya, Ankara; tel (4) 1390041; fax (4) 1402900.
Apostolic Pro-Nuncio: Most Rev. Sergio Sebastiani, Titular Archbishop of Caesarea in Mauretania.
Secretary: Mgr Adolfo Tito Yllana.

HUNGARY

Embassy: Gazi Mustafa Kemal Bul. 10, Kizilay, 06440 Ankara; tel (4) 1186257; fax (4) 1188322.
Ambassador: Dr István Vásáry.
Counsellor: Tamás Gerics.
Commercial Counsellor: István Éliás.
First Secretary: László Pap.

Consulate-General: Poyracik Sok. 35, Tesvikiye, İstanbul; tel (1) 1404275.
Consul-General: József Torma.

Consulate: Rodostó.
Honorary Consul: Erken Erdogan.

ICELAND

Consulate-General: Cinnah Cad. 110/1, Çankaya, Ankara; tel (4) 1388500; telex 42439; fax (4) 1396842.
Consul-General: Faruk Okandan.

Consulate-General: Büyükdere Cad. 13/A, 80260 Sisli, İstanbul; tel (1) 1313406; telex 26974; fax (1) 1467406.
Consul: Kazim Munir Hamamcioglu.

INDIA

Embassy: Cinnah Cad. 77/A, Çankaya, Ankara; tel (4) 1382195; telex 42561; fax (4) 1403429.
Ambassador: K. Sibal.
Counsellor: Francis Vaz.
Military, Naval and Air Attaché: Col P. Mehta.
First Secretary: V. S. Oberoi.
Second Secretary: Y. P. Kumar.

Consulate-General: Cumhuriyet Cad. 257, Kat 3, Harbiye, İstanbul; tel (1) 1484864; telex 22528; fax (1) 1303697.
Honorary Consul-General: Nihat Boytuzun.

Consulate-General: Koyuncuoglu Han Salhane, İzmir; tel (51) 161182; telex 53263; fax (51) 350549.
Honorary Consul-General: Turgut Koyuncuoglu.

INDONESIA

Embassy: Abdullah Cevdet Sok. 10, PK 42, 06552 Çankaya, Ankara; tel (4) 1382190; telex 43250.
Ambassador: Nasrun Syahrun.

IRAN

Embassy: Tahran Cad. 10, Ankara; tel (4) 1274320.
Ambassador: Mohammad Reza Bagheri.

IRAQ

Embassy: Turan Emeksiz Sok. 11, Gaziosmanpaşa, Ankara; tel (4) 1266118; telex 42577.
Ambassador: Rafi Dahham Mujawil.

IRELAND

Consulate: Cumhuriyet Cad., Pegasus Evi 26/A, 80200 Harbiye, İstanbul; tel (1) 1466025; telex 22687.
Honorary Consul: A. Ferruh Verdi.

ISRAEL

Embassy: Farabi Sok. 43, Çankaya, Ankara; tel (4) 1263904; telex 42560.
Chargé d'affaires: Liel Aion.

ITALY

Embassy: Atatürk Bul. 118, Ankara; tel (4) 1265460; telex 42624.
Ambassador: Dr Giorgio Franchetti Pardo.

JAPAN

Embassy: Reşit Galip Cad. 81, Gaziosmanpaşa, Ankara; PK 31, Kavaklidere, Ankara; tel (4) 1361290; telex 42435; fax (4) 1371812.
Ambassador: Takashi Sengoku.

Consulate-General: İnönü Cad. 24, Ayazpaşa/Taksim, İstanbul; tel (1) 1434776; telex 24127; fax (1) 1525864.
Consul-General: Takeshi Tsuruta.

JORDAN

Embassy: Dede Korkut Sok. 10, Çankaya, Ankara; tel (4) 1272362.
Ambassador: D. W. M. Alsadi.

KOREA, REPUBLIC

Embassy: Cinnah Cad., Alaçam Sok. 5, 06690 Çankaya, Ankara; tel (4) 1684822; telex 42680.
Ambassador: Kim Nai-Sung.

KUWAIT

Embassy: Kader Sok. 6/3, Çankaya, Ankara; tel (4) 1274318; telex 43238.
Chargé d'affaires: Abd ar-Razzap al-Attar.

LEBANON

Embassy: Cinnah Cad. 11/3, Çankaya, Ankara; tel (4) 1263729; telex 46063.
Ambassador: Moustapha Zein.

LIBYA

People's Committee: Ebuziya Tevfik Sok. 5, Çankaya, Ankara; tel (4) 1274892; telex 43270.
Secretary of the People's Committee: Omran Issa.

MALAYSIA

Embassy: Köroğlu Cad. 6, 06700 Gaziosmanpaşa, Ankara; tel (4) 1274062; telex 43616; fax (4) 1464130.
Ambassador: B. Rajaram.

MALTA

Consulate: OTIM Ihlamur Sergi Sarayi, Besiktas, 80280 İstanbul; tel (1) 1751212; telex 26254; fax (1) 1720295.
Honorary Consul: Atila Artam.

MEXICO

Embassy: İran Cad. 45/2, 06700 Kavaklidere, Ankara; tel (4) 1675056; telex 42278.
Ambassador: Antonio Deuñas.

MOROCCO

Embassy: Reşit Galip Cad., Incirli Sok. II, Gaziosmanpaşa, Ankara; tel (4) 11376020; telex 42869.
Ambassador: Boubker Cherkaoui.

NETHERLANDS

Embassy: Köroğlu Sok. 16, 06700 Gaziosmanpaşa, Ankara; tel (4) 1460470; telex 42612.
Ambassador: J. T. Warmenhoven.

Consulate: İstiklal Cad. 393, Beyoğlu, İstanbul; tel (1) 1515030.

Consulate: Meydan Apt No. 11/2, Cumhuriyet Meydani, İzmir; tel (51) 211588.

NEW ZEALAND

Consulate: Kizkulesi Sok. 42/1, Gaziosmanpaşa, Ankara; tel (4) 1450556; telex 42076; fax (4) 2306794.
Honorary Consul: Nurettin Soykan.

Office of Commercial Affairs: fax (4) 1450557.
Trade Commissioner: Peter Withers.

NORWAY

Embassy: Kelebek Sok. 18, Çankaya, PK 82, 06692 Kavaklidere, Ankara; tel (4) 1360051; telex 42244; fax (4) 1376430.
Ambassador: Nils Bølset.

PAKISTAN

Embassy: İran Cad. 37, Çankaya, Ankara; tel (4) 1271410.

Ambassador: Mufti Muhammad Abbas.

POLAND

Embassy: Atatürk Bul. 241, 06692 Ankara; tel (4) 1261694.
Ambassador: Mirosław Palasz.

PORTUGAL

Embassy: Kuleli Sok. 26, 06700 Gaziosmanpaşa, Ankara; tel (4) 1461890; telex 42771; fax (4) 1461892.
Ambassador: Francisco de Quevedo Crespo.
Second Secretary: Fernando Teles Fazendeiro.
Military Attaché: Col Fradique da Silva.

Consulate: Talimhane Sehit, Muhtar Cad. 43/3, 80090 Taksim, İstanbul; tel (1) 1501130.
Honorary Consul: J. Abravanel.
Vice-Consul: Aron Nommaz.

ROMANIA

Embassy: Bükreş Sok. 4, Çankaya, Ankara; tel (4) 1271241; telex 42760.
Ambassador: L. Dragut.

RUSSIA

Embassy: Karyağdi Sok. 5, Ashagi Aranci, 06692 Kavaklidere, Ankara; tel (4) 1392122; telex 46151.
Ambassador: Albert Sergeyevich Chernyshev.

Consulate-General: Istiklal Cad. 443, Beyoğlu, İstanbul; tel (1) 1441693.

SAN MARINO

Consulate-General: Cumhriyet Caddesi 247/1, Harbiye, İstanbul; tel (1) 1407525; telex 23466.
Consul-General: Mehmet Bercis Morova.

SAUDI ARABIA

Embassy: Abdullah Cevdet Sok. 18, Çankaya, Ankara; tel (4) 1271587; telex 42456.
Ambassador: Muhammad al-Awadi.

SOMALIA

Embassy: Şehit Ersan Cad. 30/7, Çankaya, Ankara; tel (4) 1275192; telex 43392.
Ambassador: Mohamed Omar Sharif.

SPAIN

Embassy: Abdullah Cevdet Sok. 8, Çankaya, PK 1030, Yenişehir, Ankara; tel (4) 1380392; telex 42551.
Ambassador: Ramón Villanueva Etcheverría.

SWEDEN

Embassy: Kâtip Çelebi Sok. 7, Kavaklidere; PK 3, 06692 Kavaklidere, Ankara; tel (4) 1286735; telex 42230; fax (4) 1685020.
Ambassador: Erik Cornell.
Counsellor: Harald Ernberg.
First Secretary: Ingalill Jonsson.

Consulate-General: Istiklâl Cad. 497, Beyoğlu, İstanbul; PK 125, 80072 Beyoğlu, İstanbul; tel (1) 1435770; telex 24256; fax (1) 1524114.
Consul-General: Kaj Falkman.
Chancellor: Barbro Arguvanligil.

Swedish Trade Council: Özden Konak is Hani Kat 10; Kasap Sokak No. 2, Esentepe, 80280 İstanbul; tel (1) 1740120; fax (1) 1740131.
Consul and Head of Commercial Section: Karl Olov Larson.

Consulate: c/o Ege Yatirim Group, 1378 Sokak No. 4/1 K, 2/201 Kordon Işhani, İzmir; tel (51) 219280; telex 53542; fax (51) 220690.
Consul: Mehmet Haluk Özsaruhan.

Consulate: Inönü Bul., Nakkas Apt, Kat. 5, Daire 10, PK 87, Mersin; tel (741) 11837; telex 67140.
Consul: Mişel Şaşati.

SWITZERLAND

Embassy: Atatürk Bul. 247, PK 25, 06692 Kavaklidere, Ankara; tel (4) 1675555; telex 44161; fax (4) 1671199.
Ambassador: Adolf Lacher.
Counsellor: Benoît Junod.
Attaché and Head of Chancery: Erwin Lüthi.
Defence Attaché: Col René Käser.

Consulate-General: Hüsrev Gerede Cad. 75/3, 2nd Floor, Tesvikiye, İstanbul; PK 122, 80200 Tesvikiye, İstanbul; tel (1) 1591115; telex 23327; fax (1) 1591118.
Consul-General: Rolf Schaufelbühl.
Vice-Consul and Chancellor: Ulrich Schläfli.

SYRIA

Embassy: Abdullah Cevdet Sok. 7, Çankaya, Ankara; tel (4) 1273342; telex 42888.
Ambassador: Bachir al-Kotb.

THAILAND

Embassy: Cinnah Cad. 61/5-6, 06680 Çankaya, Ankara; tel (4) 1391929; telex 46096; fax (4) 386474.
Ambassador: Suchinda Ruangsri.

TUNISIA

Embassy: Kuleli Sok. 12, Gaziosmanpaşa, Ankara; tel (4) 1274536; telex 42215.
Ambassador: Othman Laouani.

UNITED KINGDOM

Embassy: Şehit Ersan Cad. 46/A, Çankaya, Ankara; tel (4) 1274310; telex 42320; fax (4) 1683214.
Ambassador: Sir Timothy Daunt.
Counsellor and Deputy Head of Mission: W. B. McCleary.
Counsellor (British Council/Cultural Affairs): C. W. Perchard.
Defence and Military Attaché: Brig. R. D. H. H. Greenwood.
Naval and Air Attaché: Wing Commdr A. D. K. Campbell.
First Secretary (Political): S. N. Evans.
First Secretary (Chancery): R. H. J. Ashton.
First Secretary (Management): J. M. Brown.
First Secretary (British Council/Cultural Affairs): A. J. Mountford.
First Secretary (British Council/Cultural Affairs): R. L. Varley.
Second Secretary (Chancery/Consular): K. L. Mowbray.
Second Secretary (Commercial): R. Gemmell.
Second Secretary (Commercial): P. J. Karmy.
Second Secretary (Defence Sales): D. E. Bullas.
Third Secretary (Chancery/Information): K. A. Holgate.

Consulate: Ucgen Mahallest Dolaplidere Cad., Pirilti Sitesi, Kati ilit Sauna Karisi, Antalya; tel (311) 177000; fax 177005.
Honorary Consul: H. Pirilti.

Consulate: Iren Sitesi (Turgutreis Rd) No 13, Bodrun; tel (6141) 2343; fax 2289.
Honorary Consul: M. A. Demirer.

Consulate: c/o Messrs Catoni Maritime Agencies, Maresal Cakmak Cad. 28, Iskenderun; tel (881) 30361; fax (881) 30364.
Honorary Consul: H. J. Beard (resident in İstanbul).

Consulate: 1442 Sokak No 49, Alsancak, PK 300, İzmir; tel (51) 211795; fax (51) 212914.
Vice-Consul: A. W. Buttigieg.

Consulate: Haci Imam Sokak No 17, Tepe Mahallesi, Marmaris; tel (6121) 4565; fax (6121) 4384.
Honorary Consul: F. Celikbas.

Consulate: c/o Catoni Maritime Agencies S.A., Mersin Orta Okulu Sokak 3/B, Cakmak Cad., Mersin; tel (741) 12728; fax (741) 30604.
Honorary Vice-Consul: A. Nofal.

Consulate-General: Meşrutiyet Cad. No 34, Tepebaşi, Beyoğlu, PK 33, İstanbul; tel (1) 1447540; telex 24122; fax (1) 1454989.
Consul-General: M. B. Collins.
Deputy Consul-General: B. E. Thorne.
Vice-Consul (Information): R. P. Moore.

Office of the Consul for British Council and Cultural Affairs: Ors Turistik Is Merkezi Istiklal Cad. 251/253 Kat 2, 3, 5 Beyoğlu, 80060 İstanbul; tel (1) 152 7474; telex 23283.
Consul (British Council and Cultural Affairs): W. A. Lockhart.

Commercial Section: tel (1) 1498874.
Vice-Consul (Commercial): R. Salvatore.
Vice-Consul (Commercial): M. K. Oliver.

USA

Embassy: Atatürk Bul. 110, Kavaklidere, Ankara; tel (4) 1265470; fax (4) 1670019.
Ambassador: Morton I. Abramowitz.
Deputy Chief of Mission: Marc Grossman.
Political Section: Michael I. Austrian.
Political/Military Section: Regina M. Eltz.
Economic Section: Charles Jacobini.
Commercial Section: David Katz.
Consular Section: Robert E. Sorenson.
Administrative Section: William C. Kelly, Jr.
Scientific Attaché: Arnold C. Long.
Regional Security Officer: Gerald Kilgore.
Public Affairs Officer: Larry R. Taylor.
Communications Programme Officer: Ron Charles.
Information Systems Manager: Peter K. Jensen.
Agricultural Section: Larry L. Panasuk.
Labour Officer: Nicholas A. Stigliani.
Office of the Defence Attaché: Col Jerry L. Kaffka.
Military Assistance Advisory Group: Maj.-Gen. William Farmen.

Consulate-General: 104-108 Meşrutiyet Cad., Tepebaşi, İstanbul; tel (1) 1513602; telex 24077; fax (1) 1512554.
Consul-General: Thomas J. Carolan, Jr.
Political Section: Daniel B. Smith.
Economic Section: John C. Zimmerman.
Commercial Section: E. Scott Bozek.
Consular Section: Donnie P. Minyard.
Administrative Section: Constance Hammond.
Regional Security Officer: John B. McKennan.
Branch Public Affairs Officer: Harriet L. Elam.
Communications Programme Officer: George L. Escobedo.

Consulate-General: 92 Atatürk Cad., 3rd Floor, Alsancak, İzmir; tel (51) 131369; fax (51) 130493.
Consul-General: Eugene C. Zajac.
Political/Economic Section: Robert L. Norman.
Consular/Administrative Section: Sarah F. Drew.
Branch Public Affairs Officer: Edith Russo.

Consulate: Atatürk Cad., Adana; tel (71) 139106; fax (71) 176591.
Principal Officer: Harry E. Cole, Jr.
Political/Economic Section: Peter J. Secor.
Administrative/Consular Section: Dean Haas.

VENEZUELA

Embassy: Cinnah Cad. 78/2, Çankaya, Ankara; PK 48, Ulus, Ankara; tel (4) 1389440; telex 42453; fax (4) 1406619.

Ambassador: Gustavo Dubuc Leon.

YUGOSLAVIA

Embassy: Paris Cad. 47, Kavaklidere, Ankara; tel (4) 1260354.
Ambassador: Vladislav Jovanović.

International Organizations

EUROPEAN COMMUNITIES

External Delegation: Kuleli Sokak 15, Gaziosmanpaşa, Ankara; tel (4) 1376840; telex 44320; fax (4) 1377940.
Head of Delegation: Johannes Van Rij.

TURKMENISTAN (TURKMENIA)

USA

Embassy: Ashkhabad.

TUVALU

UNITED KINGDOM

High Commission: Funafuti.
Deputy High Commissioner and First Secretary (Consular): R. C. B. Jones.
Second Secretary (Aid): A. C. Hamilton-Walker.
Attaché (Consular/Management): R. Hunter.

UGANDA

ALGERIA

Embassy: POB 4025, Kampala; tel (41) 232918; telex 61184.
Ambassador: Hocine Meghar.

AUSTRIA

Consulate: Entebbe Rd (Bank Lane) Plot 6, POB 11273, Kampala; tel (41) 241558; telex 62163; fax (41) 233002.
Honorary Consul: Karl Wipfler.

BELGIUM

Consulate: POB 7043, Metropole House, Entebbe Rd 8/10, Kampala; tel (41) 233833; telex 61019; fax (41) 259562.
Consul: Walter Hoes.

BURUNDI

Embassy: POB 4379, Kampala; tel (41) 254584; telex 61076.
Ambassador: George Ntzezimana.

CANADA

Consulate: c/o Uganda Bata., Fifth St, POB 422, Kampala; tel (41) 258141; telex 61049; fax (41) 41380.
Honorary Consul: D. Campbell.

CHINA, PEOPLE'S REPUBLIC

Embassy: POB 4106, Kampala; tel (41) 235087; telex 61383.
Ambassador: Xie Youkun.

CUBA

Embassy: POB 9276, Kampala; telex 61174.
Chargé d'affaires: Angel Nicholas.

DENMARK

Embassy: Crusader House, Room 401/2, Plot 3, Portal Ave, POB 11243, Kampala; tel (41) 256687; telex 61409; fax (41) 254979.
Chargé d'affaires a.i. and Counsellor (Aid): Aagaard Andersen.
Counsellor (Aid): Birger Fredriksson.

Consulate: First St 11, POB 6080, Kampala; tel (41) 243364; telex 61037; fax (41) 241625.
Consul: Palle Møller.

EGYPT

Embassy: POB 4280, Kampala; tel (41) 254525; telex 61122.
Ambassador: Samir Abdallah.

FRANCE

Embassy: 9-12 Parliament Ave, POB 7212, Kampala; tel (41) 242120; telex 61079.
Ambassador: Pierre Cornée.

GERMANY

Embassy: Embassy House, 9-11 Obote Ave, POB 7016, Kampala; tel (41) 256768; telex 61005; fax (41) 256767.
Ambassador: Ruprecht Henatsch.

HOLY SEE

Apostolic Nunciature: Mbuya Hill, Chwa II Rd, POB 7177, Kampala; tel (41) 221167; telex 62096; fax (41) 221774.
Apostolic Pro-Nuncio: Most Rev. Luis Robles Díaz, Titular Archbishop of Stephaniacum.
Secretary: Mgr Miguel Maury Buendia.

INDIA

High Commission: 2nd Floor, IPS Bldg, POB 7040, Kampala; tel (41) 257368; telex 61161; fax (41) 254943.
High Commissioner: N. N. Desai.

ITALY

Embassy: POB 4646, Kampala; tel (41) 241786; telex 61261.
Ambassador: Alessio Carissimo.

KENYA

High Commission: POB 5220, Kampala; tel (41) 231861; telex 61191.
High Commissioner: Brig. R. Musonye.

KOREA, DEMOCRATIC PEOPLE'S REPUBLIC

Embassy: POB 5885, Kampala; tel (41) 254603; telex 61144.
Ambassador: Kim Tae Ryong.

KOREA, REPUBLIC

Embassy: Baumann House, POB 3717, Kampala; tel (41) 233667; telex 61017.
Ambassador: Kim Jae Kyu.

NIGERIA

High Commission: 33 Nakasero Rd, POB 4338, Kampala; tel (41) 33691; telex 61011.
High Commissioner: Lieut Col Dagogo Wilcox.

RUSSIA

Embassy: 28 Malcolm X Ave, POB 7022, Kampala; tel (41) 233676; telex 61518.
Ambassador: Stanislav Nikolaevich Semenenko.

RWANDA

Embassy: POB 2468, Kampala; tel (41) 244045; telex 61277.
Ambassador: Claver Kanyarushoki.

SOMALIA

Embassy: POB 7113, Kampala; tel (41) 232823; telex 61252.

SUDAN

Embassy: POB 3200, Kampala; tel (41) 243518; telex 61078.
Ambassador: Taj al-Sirr Abbas.

SWEDEN

Consulate: c/o Grindlays Bank Ltd, 45 Kampala Rd, POB 7131, Kampala; tel (41) 233759; telex 61018.
Consul: John Flemming Murray.

SWITZERLAND

Consulate: Baskerville Ave 1, Kololo, POB 4187, Kampala; tel (41) 241574; telex 61148.
Honorary Consul: Oskar Rothen.

TANZANIA

High Commission: POB 5750, Kampala; tel (41) 256272; telex 61062.
High Commissioner: Joshua Opanga.

UNITED KINGDOM

High Commission: 10/12 Parliament Ave, POB 7070, Kampala; tel (41) 257054; telex 61202; fax (41) 257304.
High Commissioner: Charles A. K. Cullimore.
Deputy High Commissioner: P. R. W. Whiteway.
Defence Adviser: Lieut Col E. J. K. O'Brien.
First Secretary (Chancery): R. N. E. Smith.
First Secretary (Commercial/Aid): M. Frost.
First Secretary (Consular/Management): P. S. Dickson.
First Secretary and British Council Director: S. Moss.
Third Secretary (Chancery/Information): L. C. Morgan.

USA

Embassy: Parliament Ave, POB 7007, Kampala; tel (41) 259792.
Ambassador: John A. Burroughs, Jr.
Deputy Head of Mission: Robert E. Gribbin.
Consular Section: Beatrice McKenzie.
Political Section: Colin Cleary.
Administrative Section: James Webb.
Regional Security Officer: Richard Lubow.
Agency for International Development: Keith Sherper.
Public Affairs Officer: Dudley Sims.
Economic and Commercial Sections: Luther Morris.
Communications Programme Officer: Bruce L. Bortle.

YUGOSLAVIA

Embassy: POB 4370, Kampala.
Ambassador: Slavoljub Aleksić.

ZAIRE

Embassy: POB 4972, Kampala; telex 61284.
Ambassador: Nzapa Kengo.

International Organizations

EUROPEAN COMMUNITIES

External Delegation: Uganda Commercial Bank Bldg, 5th Floor, Plot 12, Kampala Rd, POB 5244, Kampala; tel (41) 233303; telex 61139; fax (41) 233708.
Commission Delegate: Karl Harbo.

UKRAINE

AUSTRIA

Embassy: Kiev.
Chargé d'affaires: Michael Weininger.

BULGARIA

Consulate-General: Kiev, Hospitalnaya ul. 1; tel (44) 255-51-19.
Consul-General: Ivan Ruzhev.

Consulate-General: Odessa, Posmitnovo ul. 9; tel (48) 66-20-15.
Consul-General: Ilya Georgiyev.

CHINA, PEOPLE'S REPUBLIC

Embassy: Kiev.

CUBA

Consulate-General: Kiev, Bethersky per. 5; tel (44) 216-29-30.
Consul-General: Diogenes Hernandez Astorga.
Vice-Consul: Roberto Almeida.
Vice-Consul: Mr Lemes.

Consulate-General: Odessa, Tomasa ul. 7/9; tel (48) 25-14-69.
Consul-General: Arturo Pollo García.
Vice-Consul: Angel Dominges.

CZECHOSLOVAKIA

Consulate-General: Kiev, Yaroslavov Val 34; tel (44) 212-02-10.
Consul-General: Stanislav Hynar.
Consul: Zdenék Huml.
Consul (Commercial): Bohuslav Srna.
Vice-Consul: Vladimir Halenár.
Vice-Consul: Rostislav Hába.

FRANCE

Embassy: Kiev, Reiterskaya ul. 39; tel (44) 228-83-60.
Ambassador: Hugues Pernet.
Vice-Consul: Jean-Ulrich Cillard.
Attaché (Press): Françoise Pernet.
Attaché (Commercial): Philippe Pegorier.

GERMANY

Consulate-General: Kiev, ul. Chkalova 84; tel (44) 216-14-77; telex 131122; fax (44) 216-92-33.
Consul-General: Hennecke Graf von Bassewitz.
Deputy Consul-General: Rolf Welberts.
Consul: Jens Eilers.
Consul: Christa Merk.
Consul: Kurt Schatz.
Consul: Bernd Gliemann.
Vice-Consul: Karl Heinz Gertz.
Vice-Consul: Dr Wolfgang Döke.

HUNGARY

Consulate-General: Kiev, Rejterskaja ul. 33; tel (44) 212-40-94.
Consul-General: András Páldi.
Consul: Vilmos Kocsis.
Consul: András Rajki.

INDIA

Consulate-General: Odessa, Kirova ul. 31; tel (48) 22-43-33.
Consul-General: A. G. Sarma.

MONGOLIA

Consulate-General: Kiev, Kotsyubinskovo ul. 3; tel (44) 216-87-51.
Consul-General: Y. Dashnyam.

POLAND

Consulate-General: Kiev, Yaroslavov Val 12; tel (44) 224-80-40.
Consul-General: Ryszard Polkowski.
Consul: Jerzy Kozakiewicz.
Consul (Commercial): Grazyna Kubiczek.
Vice-Consul: Tomasz Leoniuk.
Vice-Consul: Andrzej Bagdziun.
Attaché: Wlodzimierz Siennicki.

Consulate-General: Lvov, Ivana Franco ul. 110; tel 72-39-42.
Consul-General: Henryk Litvin.

ROMANIA

Consulate-General: Kiev, Mihail Koshubinski ul. 8; tel (44) 24-52-61; telex 131141.
Consul-General: Leontin Pastor.

USA

Embassy: Kiev, Florentsiya ul. 9, 2nd Floor; tel (44) 517-90-01.
Ambassador: Roman Popadiuk.
Political and Economic Sections: John Stepanchuk.

VIET-NAM

Mission: Odessa, Shevchenko per. 23B; tel (48) 63-42-11; telex 232126.
Attaché (Commercial): Nguyên Khanh Kiên.

UNITED ARAB EMIRATES

ALGERIA

Embassy: POB 3070, Abu Dhabi; tel (2) 448943; telex 23414.
Ambassador: Ahmad Ali Ghazali.

ARGENTINA

Embassy: POB 3325, Abu Dhabi; tel (2) 216838; telex 23998.
Ambassador: Alberto Aden.

AUSTRIA

Embassy: Adnic Bldg, 6th Floor, Sheikh Khalifa St, POB 3095, Abu Dhabi; tel (2) 324103; telex 22675; fax (2) 343133.
Counsellor (Commercial): Dr Wolfgang Lanz.
Attaché (Commercial): Konstantin Bekos.

BANGLADESH

Embassy: POB 2504, Abu Dhabi; tel (2) 668375; telex 22201.
Ambassador: Ahmad Fariduddin.

BELGIUM

Embassy: POB 3686, Abu Dhabi; tel (2) 319449; telex 22860; fax (2) 319353.
Ambassador: Claude Misson.

BRAZIL

Embassy: Khalidiya, cnr of Al Nasr and Tariq Bin Ziyad Sts, POB 3027, Abu Dhabi; tel (2) 665352; telex 23815; fax (2) 654559.
Ambassador: José Ferreira-Lopes.
Counsellor: Clovis Abuhamad.
Head of Commercial Section: Celia Barros.

CHINA, PEOPLE'S REPUBLIC

Embassy: POB 2741, Abu Dhabi; tel (2) 211174; telex 23928.
Ambassador: Huang Zhen.

CZECHOSLOVAKIA

Embassy: POB 27009, Abu Dhabi; tel (2) 312800; telex 23797.
Chargé d'affaires: Josef Buzalka.

DENMARK

Embassy: The Blue Tower Bldg, 10th Floor, Sheikh Khalifa St, POB 46666, Abu Dhabi; tel (2) 325900; telex 23677; fax (2) 351690.
Ambassador: Bent Kiilerich.
Counsellor (Commercial): Poul B. Jentzsch.
Attaché: Dorte Kierulff Lops.

Consulate: Masaood Bldg, Baniyas St, 1st Floor, Flat 013, POB 322, Abu Dhabi; tel (2) 772000; telex 22249.
Consul: Abdullah Masaood.

EGYPT

Embassy: POB 4026, Abu Dhabi; tel (2) 445566; telex 22258.
Ambassador: Fakhry Ahmad Osman.

FINLAND

Embassy: Abu Dhabi; tel (2) 328927; telex 23161.
Chargé d'affaires: Aleksi Lahti.

FRANCE

Embassy: cnr Delma and Al Nahayane Sts, POB 4014, Abu Dhabi; tel (2) 331100; telex 22325.
Ambassador: Bernard Poletti.

Chancery: POB 3314, Deira, Dubai; tel (4) 232442.

GERMANY

Embassy: Al Nahayane St, POB 2591, Abu Dhabi; tel (2) 331630; telex 22202; fax (2) 323625.
Ambassador: Dr Günter Held.

Consulate-General: Sharaf Bldg, Al Maukhool Rd, opp. Ramada Hotel, POB 2247, Dubai; tel (4) 523352; telex 47270; fax (4) 528138.
Consul-General: Hansjoachim Neumann.

GREECE

Embassy: POB 5483, Abu Dhabi; tel (2) 316818; telex 24383.
Ambassador: Christos G. Alexandris.

HUNGARY

Embassy: POB 44450, Abu Dhabi; tel (2) 793456; telex 22322.
Ambassador: Balint Gal.

INDIA

Embassy: POB 4090, Abu Dhabi; tel (2) 337700; telex 22620; fax (2) 322403.
Ambassador: Ranjit Sethi.

INDONESIA

Embassy: POB 7256, Abu Dhabi; tel (2) 669233; telex 22253; fax (2) 653932.
Chargé d'affaires: Soesjono Prodjosiswojo.

IRAN

Embassy: POB 4080, Abu Dhabi; tel (2) 447618; telex 22344.
Ambassador: Muhammad Ali Hadi Najaf Abadi.

IRAQ

Embassy: POB 4030, Abu Dhabi; tel (2) 669900; telex 22367.
Ambassador: Taha Rajab Uriem.

ITALY

Embassy: POB 46752, Abu Dhabi; tel (2) 215622; telex 23861.
Ambassador: Giovanni Ferrero.

JAPAN

Embassy: POB 2430, Abu Dhabi; tel (2) 344696; telex 22270; fax (2) 333219.
Ambassador: Yoneyama Tateki.

JORDAN

Embassy: POB 4024, Abu Dhabi; tel (2) 447100; telex 24411.
Ambassador: Awadh M. Abu Obeid.

KENYA

Embassy: POB 3854, Abu Dhabi; tel (2) 666300; telex 24244.
Ambassador: Reuben B. Ryanga.

KOREA, REPUBLIC

Embassy: POB 3270, Abu Dhabi; tel (2) 338337; telex 24237.
Ambassador: Jong Ki Park.

KUWAIT

Embassy: POB 926, Abu Dhabi; tel (2) 446888; telex 22804.
Ambassador: Muhammad Sa'ud Zaban al-Lamia.

LEBANON

Embassy: POB 4023, Abu Dhabi; tel (2) 323863; telex 22206.
Ambassador: Amine R. Assio.

MALAYSIA

Embassy: 17th Floor, Al Suweidi Bldg, Zayed II St, POB 3887, Abu Dhabi; tel (2) 338112; telex 22630.
Chargé d'affaires: Muhammad Tawfiq bin Mohamed Noor.
Third Secretary (Administration): Austin de Alwis.
Consul-General: Tajnadin bin Batatom.

MALI

Embassy: POB 3792, Abu Dhabi; tel (2) 462252; telex 24421; fax (2) 463699.
Chargé d'affaires a.i.: Mohamed Ben Baba Ahmed.
Second Secretary: Issa Sidibe.

MAURITANIA

Embassy: POB 2714, Abu Dhabi; tel (2) 462724; telex 22512.
Ambassador: Moktar Ould Mohammed al Meussa.

MOROCCO

Embassy: POB 4066, Abu Dhabi; tel (2) 345863; telex 22549; fax (2) 313158.
Ambassador: Abd al-Karim Semmar.

NETHERLANDS

Embassy: Al-Ain Ahlia Insurance Bldg, off Hamdan St, POB 46560, Abu Dhabi; tel (2) 321920; telex 23610; fax (2) 313158.
Ambassador: Dr Willem A. Dólleman.
First Secretary: Dr J. C. W. Kruishoop.
Attaché (Administrative): H. R. Betke.
Consul: Tjidelijk Zaakgelastgide.

Consulate: ABN Bldg, Khalid Bin Walled Rd, POB 7726, Bur Dubai; tel (4) 528700; telex 46502; fax (4) 510502.
Consul: J. Bestebreurtje.

PAKISTAN

Embassy: POB 846, Abu Dhabi; tel (2) 447800; telex 23003.
Chargé d'affaires: Syed Zulfiqar Ali Shah.

PHILIPPINES

Embassy: al-Saman Tower, 1st Floor, Hamdan St, POB 3215, Abu Dhabi; tel (2) 345664; telex 23995.
Ambassador: Fortunato Oblena.

POLAND

Embassy: Khalidia Palace Hotel, Rm 202; tel (2) 663470.
Chargé d'affaires: Wojciech Bozek.

QATAR

Embassy: POB 3503, Abu Dhabi; tel (2) 338900; telex 22664.
Ambassador: Hamad Mansour al-Hajeri.

ROMANIA

Embassy: POB 70416, Abu Dhabi; tel (2) 666346; telex 23546.
Ambassador: Nicolae Virgil Irimie.

RUSSIA

Embassy: Halifa ben Zaid, POB 8211, Abu Dhabi; tel (2) 721797; telex 24464.
Ambassador: Konstantin M. Kharchev.

SAUDI ARABIA

Embassy: POB 4057, Abu Dhabi; tel (2) 665700; telex 22670.
Ambassador: Muhammad Abdullah Al-Otaibi.

SOMALIA

Embassy: POB 4155, Abu Dhabi; tel (2) 323800; telex 22624.
Ambassador: Adam Hersi Essa.

SPAIN

Embassy: POB 46474, Abu Dhabi; tel (2) 213544; telex 23340.
Ambassador: Aurelio Pérez Giralda.

SRI LANKA

Embassy: POB 46534, Abu Dhabi; tel (2) 666688; telex 23333.
Ambassador: Muhammad Jameel.

SUDAN

Embassy: POB 4027, Abu Dhabi; tel (2) 772750; telex 22706.
Ambassador: Ali Abd Rahman ar-Nimeiri.

SWEDEN

Embassy: Al Masaood Tower, 10th Floor, Sheikh Hamdan St, POB 2609, Abu Dhabi; tel (2) 337772; telex 23277; fax (2) 332904.
Counsellor and Chargé d'affaires a.i.: Nils Olof Gudmond Naesson.
First Secretary: Lennart Holst.

Consulate-General: c/o Gulf Agency, Dubai Dry Docks Complex, near Port Rashid, POB 9219, Dubai; tel (4) 457716; telex 46662; fax (4) 452439.
Consul-General: Tor Herbert Sandgren.

SWITZERLAND

Embassy: Dhabi Tower, 4th Floor, Hamdan St, POB 46116, Abu Dhabi; tel (2) 335644; telex 22824; fax (2) 216127.
Chargé d'affaires: Emanuel Dubs.
Attaché and Head of Chancery: Pierre Buchs.

Consulate: Dubai World Trade Centre, POB 9300, Dubai; tel (4) 375542; telex 48244; fax (4) 379679.
Consul: Bernhard Meyer.

SYRIA

Embassy: POB 4011, Abu Dhabi; tel (2) 448768; telex 22729; fax 449387.
Ambassador: Mustafa Omran.

TUNISIA

Embassy: POB 4166, Abu Dhabi; tel (2) 661331; telex 22370.
Ambassador: Abd Aziz al-Joular.

TURKEY

Embassy: POB 3204, Abu Dhabi; tel (2) 463372; telex 23037.
Ambassador: Ugurtan Akinci.

UNITED KINGDOM

Embassy: POB 248, Abu Dhabi; tel (2) 326600; telex 22234; fax (2) 341744.
Ambassador: Graham Stuart Burton.
First Secretary, Consul and Deputy Head of Mission: R. T. O. Wilson.
Defence, Naval, Military and Air Attaché: Lieut Col M. A. Cullinan.
First Secretary: I. W. Baharie.
First Secretary (Commercial): L. M. Connor.
Second Secretary (Information): C. P. Bird.
Second Secretary (Commercial): D. Winter.
Second Secretary (Management) and Consul: N. K. Tagg.
Attaché (Culture) and British Council Director: Dr P. J. A. Clark.

Consulate-General: POB 65, Dubai; tel (4) 521070; telex 45426; fax (4) 525750.
Consul-General and Counsellor: R. A. M. Hendrie.
First Secretary (Commercial) and Consul: K. N. Johnson.
First Secretary (Economic): M. J. Regan.
Second Secretary, Vice-Consul and Management Officer: C. W. Francis.
Second Secretary (Commercial): W. W. Magor.
Second Secretary (Works): D. P. Ryan.
Second Secretary (Chancery): K. B. Howell.
Third Secretary (Commercial/Information): A. T. Dimbleby.

USA

Embassy: Al-Sudan St., POB 4009, Abu Dhabi; tel (2) 336691; telex 23513; fax (2) 318441.
Ambassador: Edward S. Walker, Jr.
Deputy Head of Mission: Brian J. Mohler.
Political Section: Juliana Seymour Peck.
Political and Military Sections: Patrick J. Murphy.
Economic Section: William T. Fleming, Jr.
Consular Section: Charles E. Robertson III.
Administrative Section: James Mikel Alderman.
Regional Security Officer: Thomas K. Depenbrock.
Public Affairs Officer: Sami G. Hajjar.
Office of Defence Attaché: Maj. Nathan M. Miyaki.
Liaison Officer: Col Jack McGuinnes.
Communications Programme Officer: Howard L. Keegan.

Commercial Section: Blue Tower Bldg, 8th Floor, Shaikh Khalifa bin Zayed St., Abu Dhabi; tel (2) 345545; telex 22229; fax (2) 331374.
Commercial Section: B. Paul Scogna.

Consulate-General: Dubai International Trade Centre, POB 9343, Dubai; tel (4) 371115; telex 46031; fax (4) 379043.
Consul-General: Joseph Le Brown.
Political Section: Eileen F. Lewison.
Economic Section: Robert W. Richards.
Consular Section: Joseph P. Murphy.
Regional Security Officer: Jacob Wohlman.

YEMEN

Embassy: POB 2095, Abu Dhabi; tel (2) 448454; telex 23600.
Ambassador: Muhammad Hatem al-Khawi.

YUGOSLAVIA

Embassy: POB 3816, Abu Dhabi; tel (2) 665089.
Ambassador: Dr Hasan Dervisbegović.

UNITED KINGDOM

AFGHANISTAN

Embassy: 31 Prince's Gate, London SW7 1QQ; tel (71) 589-8891; telex 916641; fax (71) 581-3452.
Chargé d'affaires and Minister-Counsellor: Taza Khan Wial.
Second Secretary: Mir Abas.

ALGERIA

Embassy: 54 Holland Park, London W11 3RS; tel (71) 221-7800; fax (71) 221-0448.
Ambassador: Abdelkarim Gheraieb.
Minister-Counsellor: Hadi Brouri.
Minister: Mustapha Boukari.
Counsellor: Zahra Bendib.
Counsellor: Lamri Khelif.
Counsellor: Dr Zine el-Abidine Bentabet Dorbani.
Attaché: Abdelduahab Sahroui.
Attaché: Amine Hocine Belkacemi.
Attaché: Azzedine Souidi.
Attaché: Abdellatif Senoussaoui.
Attaché: Mohamed Groussi.

ANGOLA

Embassy: 10 Fife Rd, East Sheen, London SW14 7EL; tel (71) 876-0435; telex 8813258; fax (71) 839-5292.
Ambassador: José Primo.
First Secretary: Maria Teresa Fonsela de Victoria Pereira.
Second Secretary: Santos Bunga.
Third Secretary: Jacinto Rangel Lopes Cordeiro Neto.
Attaché (Press): Dembo do Amaral.
Attaché: Mario Alfredo.
Attaché: Joana das Amarguras Francisco de Jesus.
Attaché: João Makaia.
Attaché: Manuel Candido Adolfo.
Head of Protocol: Emilio Sofia Rosa.
Protocol Officer: Manuela Corrgia de Sousa Camati.

ANTIGUA AND BARBUDA

High Commission: 15 Thayer St, London W1M 5LD; tel (71) 486-7073; telex 8814503; fax (71) 486-9970.
High Commissioner: James A. E. Thomas.
First Secretary: Starret Dickson Greene.
Second Secretary: John Harris.
Attaché: Pauline Sandra Irenie Williams.
Attaché: Gloria Lemoyne Newby.

ARGENTINA

Embassy: 53 Hans Place, London SW1X 0LA; tel (71) 584-6494; telex 913348; fax (71) 589-3106.
Ambassador: Mario Alberto Cámpora.
Minister: Domingo S. Cullen.
Counsellor (Political): Norma Nascimbene Dumont.
Counsellor (Economic): Manuel Benitez de Castro.
Defence Attaché: Capt. Alberto César Secchi.
Second Secretary (Political/Scientific): Ivan Ivanissevich.
Second Secretary (Cultural): Claudio Rojo.
Second Secretary (Press/IMO): Alejandro J. Massucco.
Second Secretary (Administrative/Financial): Gustavo C. Garcia.
Consul-General: Adriana Trotta de Whittam.

Trade Department: 111 Cadogan Gardens, London SW3; tel (71) 730-9334; fax (71) 823-4943.
Minister-Counsellor (Commercial/Financial): Alberto J. Dumont.
Second Secretary (Commercial/Financial): Vicente Salas Martinez.

AUSTRALIA

High Commission: Australia House, The Strand, London WC2B 4LA; tel (71) 379-4334; telex 27565; fax (71) 240-5333.
High Commissioner: Richard J. Smith.
Deputy High Commissioner: Raymond James Greet.
Official Secretary: Desmond Patrick Connors.
Minister: Karina Campbell.
Minister (Health): Dr David de Souza.
Defence Adviser and Head of Defence Staff: Air Cdre Bruce I. Lane.
Minister (Commercial): Robert K. H. Lim.
Minister (Marketing): Ray Anderson.
Minister (Economic): Peter Tormey.
Counsellor (Industry/Science/Technology): Richard B. Gould.
Counsellor (Agriculture): Timothy Roseby.
Counsellor (Liaison): Ian Roy Peterson.
Counsellor (Commercial): Robert John Walters.
Counsellor (Finance): John Nicholson.
Counsellor (Immigration): Vincent Giuca.
Counsellor (Information): James Roy Payne.
Counsellor (Audit): Brett Andrew Kaufman.
Naval Adviser: Capt. James H. Gault.
Army Adviser: Col Colin John Brewer.
Air Adviser: Group Capt. Arthur J. White.
Counsellor (Defence Acquisition and Logistics): Roger H. Houstein.
Counsellor (Defence Science): Dr Anthony D. McLachlan.
Counsellor (Defence): Paul Francis de Cure.
Counsellor (Defence Industry): Denton M. Bocking.
Counsellor (Nuclear): Geoffrey Durance.
First Secretary (Police Liaison): Detective Supt Alan J. Sing.
First Secretary (Consular/Administrative): Anthony B. Davis.

AUSTRIA

Embassy: 18 Belgrave Mews West, London SW1X 8HU; tel (71) 235-3731; telex 28327; fax (71) 235-8025.
Ambassador: Dr Walter F. Magrutsch.
Minister: Helmuth Werner Ehrlich.
Counsellor (Cultural): Dr Peter Margitner.
Counsellor (Administrative): Alois Spitznagel.
Counsellor (Head of Consular Affairs): Othmar Hoerbinger.
Counsellor (Social): Elfriede Kulnig.
Defence Attaché: Brig. Helge Lerider.
First Secretary (Administrative): Peter K. Weissenberger.
First Secretary: Dr René Kurt Pollitzer.
First Secretary: Dr Caroline Gudenus.
Attaché (Cultural): Dr Ernst Peter Brezovsky.
Third Secretary: Alexander Michael Schwarz.

Consulate: 5 Barlows Rd, Edgbaston, Birmingham B15 2PN; tel (21) 454-1197; telex 337475; fax (21) 544-7623.
Consul: Alfred Neumeister.

Consulate: 33-34 Charlotte Sq., Edinburgh EH2 4HF; tel (31) 225-1516; telex 727457; fax (31) 225-9262.
Consul: William Drysdale.

BAHAMAS

High Commission: 10 Chesterfield St, London W1X 8AH; tel (71) 408-4488; telex 892617; fax (71) 499-9937.
High Commissioner and Permanent Representative to the EC: Dr Patricia E. J. Rodgers.
First Secretary and Consul: Wendy Rolle-MacKinnon.
Second Secretary and Vice-Consul: Kent E. Campbell.
Attaché (Maritime): Judith A. Francis.
Attaché (Tourism): Raymond L. Dames.

BAHRAIN

Embassy: 98 Gloucester Rd, London SW7 4AU; tel (71) 370-5132; telex 917829; fax (71) 370773.
Ambassador: Karim Ebrahim Al Shakar.
First Secretary: Rashid Saad Al Dosari.
First Secretary and Consul: Faisal Abdul Rahman Al Dosari.
Second Secretary: Hamed Al Asfour.
Third Secretary (Health): Mohamed Shariff Khonji.
Third Secretary: Fuad Al Maadwdeh.
Attaché (Culture): Hassan Al Monfaradi.

BANGLADESH

High Commission: 28 Queen's Gate, London SW7 5JA; tel (71) 584-0081; telex 918016.
High Commissioner: M. M. Rezgul Karim.
Minister: Ghulam Quader.
Minister (Finance): Syed Rezaul Hayat.
Minister (Press): Abdur Rahim.
Counsellor (Political): Jamil Majid.
Counsellor (Education): Dr Ataur Rahman.
Counsellor: Mohammed Khairuzzaman Zaman.
Defence Adviser: Brig. Saleem Khan.
Assistant Defence Adviser: Lieut Col Mohammed Faizur Rahman Khan.
Assistant Defence Adviser: Lieut Col Mohammed Nazrul Islam Bhuiyan.
Second Secretary (Commercial): Mohammed Shahjahan Majumder.
Second Secretary: Mohammed Shahidullah Miah.
Second Secretary: C. Q. K. Mostaq Ahmad.
Second Secretary: Mohammed Shahidul Haque.

BARBADOS

High Commission: 1 Great Russell St, London WC1B 3NH; tel (71) 631-4975; telex 262081; fax (71) 323-6872.
High Commissioner: Sir William Douglas.
Deputy High Commissioner: Owen Oswald Eversley.
Counsellor (Head of Chancery): Gilbert Delano Greaves.
First Secretary: William Oscar Gooding.
First Secretary: Betty-Anna Allison Warnock.
Attaché: Claudette Veronica Walcott.
Attaché: Gerald Andrew Cozier.
Attaché: Sandra Catherine Springer.

BELGIUM

Embassy: 103-105 Eaton Sq., London SW1W 9AB; tel (71) 235-5422; telex 22823; fax (71) 259-6213.
Ambassador: Herman Dehennin.
Minister-Counsellor (Financial): Johan Maricou.
Minister-Counsellor: Leo Williams.
Counsellor: Marc de Schoutheete de Tervarent.
Counsellor (Agriculture): Joris Vaerewyck.
Military, Air and Naval Attaché: Capt. Guy Henri Arthur Busard.
First Secretary (Political): Ghislain D'Hoop.
Attaché (Consular): Anne Duchêne.
Attaché (Consular): Marc Vinck.
Attaché (Consular): Lodewijk Mariën.
Attaché (Consular): Sylvie Ruttens-Hansenne.
Attaché (Consular): Daniel Ruttens.

BELIZE

High Commission: 10 Harcourt House, 19a Cavendish Sq., London W1M 9AD; tel (71) 499-9728; telex 94082284; fax (71) 491-4139.
High Commissioner: Robert A. Leslie.
First Secretary: Diana M. Locke.

BENIN

Consulate: 125/9 High St, Edgware HA8 7HS; tel (81) 951-1234.

BOLIVIA

Embassy: 106 Eaton Sq., London SW1W 9AD; tel (71) 235-4248; telex 918885.
Ambassador: Maj.-Gen. Gary Prado.
Minister-Counsellor: Jorge Manuel Urquidi-Barrau.
Air Attaché: Col Walter Barron-Garnica.
First Secretary: Marta Bosacoma Bonel.
Second Secretary (Cultural): Patricia Quintanilla.
Attaché (Trade - Minerals): Jaime M. Bueno.
Attaché (Consular): Gabriela Vargas.

BOTSWANA

High Commission: 6 Stratford Pl., London W1N 9AE; tel (71) 499-0031; telex 262897; fax (71) 495-8595.
High Commissioner: Margaret Nasha.
Counsellor: Tunny Violet Innocentia Mosele.
Defence Attaché: Lieut Col Nelson Mokgabo Modiko.
Second Secretary: Charles Theko Mogotsi.
Attaché (Education): Odirile Bagwasi Gabasiane.
Attaché (Administrative): Agnes Elisa Motshelanoka.
Attaché (Commercial): Selebanyo Molefi.

BRAZIL

Embassy: 32 Green St, London W1Y 4AT; tel (71) 499-0877; telex 261157; fax (71) 493-5105.
Ambassador: Paulo-Tarso Flecha de Lima.
Minister-Counsellor: Julio C. Gomes dos Santos.
Minister-Counsellor: Valdemar Carneiro Leão.
Counsellor (Multilateral Affairs): Mara Goes.
Counsellor (Economic/Financial): Paulo Alberto de Silveira Soares.
Counsellor (Commercial): Ilka Maria Lekmkuhl Trinidade Cruz.
Counsellor (Science/Technology): Eduardo dos Santos.
Counsellor: Eduardo Prisco Paraiso Ramos.
Counsellor: Renan Leite Paes Barreto.
Military Attaché: Col Luiz Alberto Rosa Apel.
Second Secretary (Administrative): Regina Maria Cordeiro Dunlop.
Second Secretary (Multilateral Affairs): Tarcisio de Lima Ferreira Fernandes Costa.
Second Secretary (Multilateral Affairs): Guilherme Vasconcellos Coimbra.
Attaché (Petroleum): Antonio Sergio Pizarro Fragomem.

Consular Section: 6 St Alban's St, Haymarket, London SW1Y 4SG; tel (71) 930-4823; telex 892849; fax (71) 839-8958.
Minister (Consular): Frederico Cezar de Araujo.
Counsellor (Consular): Ronaldo Edgar Dunlop.

Cultural Section: 49 Lancaster Gate, London W2; tel (71) 723-9648.
Counsellor (Cultural): Goncalvo de Barros Carvalho e Mello Mourøao.

Office of Naval Adviser: 170 Upper Richmond Rd, Putney, London SW15; tel (71) 788-8111; telex 918551; fax (71) 788-7718.
Naval Attaché: Capt. Jorge de Carvalho Lopes.

Office of Air Adviser: 16 Great James St, London WC1; tel (71) 405-0261; telex 21196; fax (71) 831-8129.
Air Attaché: Group Capt. Marcio Behring Cardoso.

BRUNEI

High Commission: 19/20 Belgrave Sq., London SW1X 8PG; tel (71) 581-0521; telex 888369; fax (71) 235-9717.
High Commissioner: Pengiran Haji Mustapha.
Defence Advisor: Col Pehin Dato Haji Hussin.
First Secretary: Pengiran Haji Yunus.
First Secretary (Finance): Wee Peng Hock.
Second Secretary: Mohammad Murad Haji Paijan.
Second Secretary: Rakiah Abdul Lamit.
Third Secretary (Administrative): Haji Kassim Asmat.
Third Secretary (Protocol): P. H. Kamaruddin P. H. A. Bakar.
Third Secretary (Consular): Abu Bakar Haji Sidup.
Third Secretary: Abdullah Haji Hamid.
Third Secretary: Pengiran Abu Bakar Pengiran Abdul Rahman.
Attaché (Education - Islamic): Pengiran Muhammad Pengiran Mohd Salleh.

BULGARIA

Embassy: 186-188 Queen's Gate, London SW7 5HL; tel (71) 584-9400; telex 25465; fax (71) 584-4948.
Ambassador: Ivan Stancioff.
Minister-Counsellor: Christo Vassilev Halatchev.
Minister: Georgui Manolov Hadjikov.
Counsellor (Political): Goran Stefanov Yonov.
First Secretary (Science): Assen Dimitrov Babanski.
Second Secretary (Press): Assen Sotirov Novatchkov.
Second Secretary: Ivan Totev Piperkov.
Third Secretary (Consular): Vladimir Borissov Popov.
Third Secretary: Svilen Ivanov Iliev.
Third Secretary: Yani Dragoev Dimitrov.
Third Secretary: Latchezar Stoyanov Dimitrov.

BURKINA FASO

Consulate: 5 Cinnamon Row, Plantation Wharf, London SW11 3TW; tel (71) 738-1800; telex 296420; fax (71) 738-2820.
Honorary Consul: Stuart G. Singer.

BURUNDI

Consulate: 19 Kenton Park Crescent, Harrow; tel (81) 907-8985.

CAMEROON

Embassy: 84 Holland Park, London W11 3SB; tel (71) 727-0771; telex 25176; fax (71) 792-9353.
Ambassador: Dr Gibering Bol-Alima.
Counsellor (Economic): Thomas Achu.
Counsellor (Cultural): Samson Negbo Abangma.
Second Counsellor: Che Crecy Tawah.
Second Counsellor: Martin Mpana.
Second Counsellor: Philippe Tsague.
Assistant Military Attaché: Lieut Commdr Emmanuel Babou.
First Secretary (Finance): Anatole Ebanda Alima.
First Secretary: Halidou Garga.
First Secretary (Consular): Jean-Marie Séverin Mbenoun.

CANADA

High Commission: Macdonald House, 1 Grosvenor Sq., London W1X 0AB; tel (71) 629-9492; telex 261592; fax (71) 491-3968.
High Commissioner: Fredrik S. Eaton.
Deputy High Commissioner: Gaetan Lavertu.
Minister (Commercial/Financial): Ronald Berlet.
Minister: J. Thomas Boehm.
Counsellor (Administrative): Lionel Lepage.
Counsellor (Commercial): Robert D. Merner.
Counsellor (Commercial): William Johnston.
Counsellor (Commercial): Pierre Cusson.
Counsellor (Commercial): Gordon Parsons.
Counsellor (Commercial): William Reid.
Counsellor (Commercial/Financial): Robert B. MacKenzie.
Counsellor (Financial): Hugh Young.
Counsellor (Financial): Doug Bieber.
Counsellor (Public Affairs): Len Mader.
Counsellor (Resource Industries): Curtis Copeland.
Counsellor: Greg A. Calkin.
Counsellor: Gary Soroka.
Counsellor: D. MacKinnon.
Counsellor: James Lynch.
Counsellor: Gordon J. Hunter.
Counsellor (Defence Research): P. J. Sutherland.
Counsellor (Defence Research): D. Mabey.
Defence Adviser: Brig. Gen. Colin McDonald Curleigh.
Naval Adviser: Capt. Edward E. Davie.
Army Adviser: David B. Ells.
Air Force Adviser: Col M. Kenneth Kee.
Senior Staff Officer (Administrative/Logistics): Lieut Col Robin D. Cuthbert.
First Secretary (Science/Technology): J. Erle Jones.
Attaché (Investment): Edward A. Walker.
Attaché (Medical): Dr Alan M. Elliot.

Immigration, Passport and Consular Sections: 38 Grosvenor Sq., London W1X 0AA; tel (71) 409-2071.
Minister-Counsellor: Raphael A. Girard.
Counsellor (Immigration): Scott Heatherington.
Counsellor (Consular Affairs): A. Louise O'Connor.

Press, Information, Culture, Tourism and National Archives Section: Canada House, Trafalgar Sq., London SW1Y 5BJ; tel (71) 629-9492.
Counsellor (Culture): René Picard.

Consulate: MacLay, Murray and Spens, Solicitors, 151 St Vincent St, Glasgow G2 5NJ; tel (41) 221-4415; telex 72723; fax (41) 247-5819.
Honorary Consul: D. J. McKichan.

CHILE

Embassy: 12 Devonshire St, London W1N 2DS; tel (71) 580-6392; telex 25970; fax (71) 436-5204.
Ambassador: German Riesco.
Counsellor: Pablo Cabrera.
Naval Attaché and Head of Naval Mission: Rear-Adm. Octavio Bolelli.
Assistant Naval Attaché: Capt. Abel Osorio.
Assistant Naval Attaché: Capt. Victor Wilson.
Maritime Adviser: Capt. Carlos Bastias.

Air Attaché: Col Ricardo Eduardo Bermudez.
Military Air Attaché: Col Roberto Arancibia.
First Secretary and Consul: José Luis Balmaceda.
Attaché (Commercial): Luis Gaston Pascal.
Attaché (Cultural/Press): Florencia Varas.

CHINA, PEOPLE'S REPUBLIC

Embassy: 49-51 Portland Place, London W1N 3AH; tel (71) 636-9375.
Ambassador: Ma Yuzhen.
Minister: Yu Zhizhong.
Counsellor: Wang Yihao.
Counsellor: Yang Xueqian.
Counsellor: Lin Zhiying.
Counsellor: Yuan Shiyin.
Counsellor: Gong Gengquan.
Defence Attaché: Maj.-Gen. Mu Huimin.
Military Attaché: Col Cheng Weiyong.
Naval Attaché: Capt. Sun Yongan.
Air Attaché: Col Chi Naiwen.
Deputy Military Attaché: Lieut Col Zhang Tuosheng.
Deputy Military Adviser: Lieut Col Zhang Jianguo.
Assistant Military Attaché: Maj. Zhang Jichun.
Secretary to Military Attaché: Capt. Zhou Ming.
First Secretary (Shipping): Zhu Xiangbao.

Cultural Section: 28 College Crescent, Hampstead, London NW9; tel (71) 586-9646.
Counsellor (Cultural): Wang Guilin.

Science and Technology Section: 42 Maida Vale, London W9; tel (71) 286-1297.
Counsellor (Science/Technology): Wang Zengrong.
Military Attaché (Science/Technology): Col Ye Lu.

Commercial Section: 56-60 Lancaster Gate, London W2 3NG; tel (71) 262-0253.
Counsellor (Commercial): Zhuang Yulin.
Counsellor (Commercial): Zhang Dimo.
First Secretary (Commercial): Yan Bangsong.

Educational Section: 51 Drayton Green, West Ealing, London W13; tel (81) 991-1649.
Counsellor (Education): Ma Zuyao.
First Secretary (Education): Wang Yongda.
First Secretary (Education): Zhang Taijin.

Maritime Section: 31 Portland Place, London W1N 3AG; tel (71) 636-1835.
Second Secretary (Maritime): Li Guangling.
Second Secretary (Maritime): Miao Hongde.

COLOMBIA

Embassy: Flat 3A, 3 Hans Crescent, London SW1X 0LR; tel (71) 589-9177; telex 916468; fax (71) 581-1829.
Ambassador: Dr Virgilio Barco.
Minister: Ximena Andrade de Casalino.
Counsellor (Coffee): Dr Nestor Osorio.
Military, Naval and Air Attaché: Col German Afanador.
Assistant Naval Attaché (International Maritime Organization): Capt. Larchin Rafael Steer-Ruiz.
First Secretary: Alba Zuluaga.
Third Secretary: Efrain Sánchez.
Attaché (Coffee): Gloria Villaquiran de Barton.
Attaché: Capt. Jorge Luis Pinzon.

COSTA RICA

Embassy: 5 Harcourt House, 19A Cavendish Sq., London W1M 9AD; tel (71) 495-3985; telex 8954798; fax (71) 495-3992.
Ambassador: Luis Rafael Tinoco.
Minister-Counsellor and Consul-General: Damaris Fajardo.
Minister-Counsellor: Miguel A. Carabaguíaz.
Minister-Counsellor: José L. Garmendía.
Counsellor: Alba Domínguez de Farhat.
Attaché (Press): Elke Ruge de Hawilla.

COTE D'IVOIRE

Embassy: 2 Upper Belgrave St, London SW1X 8BJ; tel (71) 235-6991; telex 23906; fax (71) 259-5439.
Ambassador: Gervais Yao Attoungbré.
First Counsellor: Gaoua Georges Ballou.
Counsellor: Colette Gallie.
Counsellor: Marcel Amon-Tanoh.
Second Secretary (Financial): Nestor Ouedo.
Second Secretary: Diomande Siaba.
Attaché (Commercial): Kouame Clement Goli.

CUBA

Embassy: 167 High Holborn, London WC1V 6PA; tel (71) 240-2488; telex 261094; fax (71) 836-2602.
Ambassador: María A. Florez.
Counsellor (Political): Miguel Martínez-Moles.
Counsellor (Commercial): José Miguel Díaz Mirabel.
First Secretary (Political/Press): Roberto de Armas.
Second Secretary (Commercial): Heriberto Ricardo.
Third Secretary: Adrian Delgado.
Attaché (Commercial): Victor Manuel Garcia.
Attaché (Administrative): Aldo Cabrera del Castillo.
Attaché (Diplomatic): José Antonio Pérez.

CYPRUS

High Commission: 93 Park St, London W1Y 4ET; tel (71) 499-8272; telex 263343; fax (71) 491-0691.
High Commissioner: Angelos M. Angelides.
Minister: Michael Spanos.
Counsellor (Commercial): Andreas Mavrogenis.
Counsellor (Legal): Ozer Beha.
Counsellor (Culture): Klitos Avgoustinos.
Counsellor (Press): Sotirios Georgallis.
Counsellor: Stavros Epaminondas.
Attaché (Education): Elli Papaphoti.
Attaché (Welfare): George Vrionis.
Attaché (Welfare): Ntinos Apostolou.
Attaché (Maritime): Rolis-George Lewis.
Attaché (Finance): Charalambos Georgiades.
Attaché (Press): Helen Pateras.
Attaché (Information/Tourism): Orestis Rossides.

Consulate: Edgbaston House, 183 Broad St, Edgbaston, Birmingham B15 1EZ; tel (21) 643-2151.
Honorary Consul: Dr George John Efstathiades.

Consulate: c/o Delta Travel, University Precinct, Oxford Rd, Manchester M13 9RN; tel (61) 273-4321; telex 666223; fax (61) 274-3555.
Honorary Consul: Andreas Demetri Kanaris.

Consulate: 78 Westover Rd, Westbury-on-Trym, Bristol; tel (272) 501655.
Honorary Consul: Pavlos Athanassi Lazarides.

Consulate: Grove Surgery, Charlotte St, Wakefield; tel (924) 372596; fax (532) 687786.
Honorary Consul: Dr Christos Hadjicaritou.

Consulate: 58 West Regent St, Glasgow G2 2QZ; tel (41) 332-7773; telex 779220; fax (41) 331-1406.
Honorary Consul: Sir Reo Stakis.

'TURKISH REPUBLIC OF NORTHERN CYPRUS'

Representation: 28 Cockspur St, London SW1Y 5BN; tel (71) 839-5217; fax (71) 839-5282.
Representative: Reşat Çağlar.
First Secretary: Tahsin Ertuğruloğlu.
Consul-General: Sacit Nereli.
Attaché (Press): Alper Faik Genç.

CZECHOSLOVAKIA

Embassy: 25 Kensington Palace Gardens, London W8 4QY; tel (71) 229-1255; telex 28276; fax (71) 727-5824.
Ambassador: Karel Duda.
Minister-Counsellor: Jaromír Přibyl.
Counsellor (Commercial): Štefan Žiak.
Counsellor: Milan Glozar.
Military and Air Attaché: Col Jaroslav Puchner.
Military and Air Attaché: Lieut Col Ján Sabo.
Assistant Military and Air Attaché: Dušan Zoller.
First Secretary: Roman Janson.
First Secretary: Pavel Šiša.
Second Secretary: Jan Vymětal.
Second Secretary: Miloš Ruppeldt.
Second Secretary: Jan Válek.

Consulate: 26 Kensington Palace Gardens, London W8; tel (71) 727-5824.
Consul and First Secretary: Dr Petr Skácel.

DENMARK

Embassy: 55 Sloane St, London SW1X 9SR; tel (71) 333-0200; telex 28103; fax (71) 333-0270.
Ambassador: Rudolph Thorning-Petersen.
Minister-Counsellor: Hans Michael Kofoed-Peterson.
Minister-Counsellor (Agricultural): Martin Hermansen.
Minister-Counsellor (Commercial): Poul Esseman.
Counsellor (Commercial): Christian François Louis d'Auchamp.
Counsellor (Trade/Social): Birte Johansen.
Counsellor (Fisheries): Jesper Kaae.
Counsellor (Financial): Carsten Søndergaard.
Counsellor (Industrial/Commodities/Taxation): Aili Susanne Koren.
Counsellor (Press/Cultural): Flemming André Axmark.
Defence Attaché: Capt. Erik Fage-Pedersen.
First Secretary (Economic/Consular): Kirsten Rosenvold Geelan.

Consulate: c/o ISS Servisystem, 92 Albert St, Birmingham B5 5LN; tel (21) 643-8831; telex 335532; fax (21) 631-2543.
Consul: Michael Albert Fendt Bizley.

Consulate: Alexandra Rd, New Brighton, Wallasey, Merseyside L45 0JZ; tel (51) 639-8180; telex 629468.
Consul: Ole Toft Christensen.

Consulate: Queens Chambers, 1st Floor, 5 John Dalton St, Manchester M2 6FT; tel (61) 835-1901; fax (61) 834-3393.
Consul: Christian Wewer.

Consulate: c/o D.F.D.S. Ltd, Tyne Commission Quay, North Shields, Newcastle-upon-Tyne NE29 6EE; tel (91) 296-0134; telex 53201; fax (91) 296-0127.
Consul: John McGregor Prescott.

Consulate: 68 James St, Cardiff CF1 6SP; tel (222) 480002; telex 498544.
Consul: Derek Lewis Smithson.

Consulate: 4 Royal Terr., Edinburgh EH7 5AB; tel (31) 556-4263; fax (31) 556-3969.
Consul: Jens Christian Høgel.

Consulate: Magnet House, 59 Waterloo St, Glasgow G2 7BP; tel (41) 204-2209; telex 776353; fax (41) 204-1207.
Consul: John Eadie Milne.

Consulate: Head Line Bldgs, 10/4 Victoria St, Belfast BT1 3GP; tel (232) 230581; telex 74534.
Consul: Michael Walter Savage MacLaran.

Consulate: Portview Rd, Avonmouth, Bristol BS11 9YX; tel (272) 825081; telex 44129.
Consul: Brian Fletcher.

Consulate: c/o D.F.D.S. Ltd, Parkeston Quay, Harwich CO12 4SY; tel (255) 242242; telex 987701; fax (255) 241188.
Consul: Ebbe Søren Køhlen Pedersen.

Consulate: 79 Elveley Dr., West Ella, Hull HU10 7RX; tel (482) 655875.
Consul: Svend Glensmark.

Consulate: New North Quay, St Helier, Jersey; tel (534) 70300; telex 4192560.
Consul: George Raymond Le Moine.

Consulate: 'Les Meunières', Fosse André, St Peter Port, Guernsey; tel (481) 22608; telex 4191445; fax (481) 711385.
Consul: Steen Søren Edward Marcussen.

Consulate: 1-3 Sandgate, Berwick-on-Tweed TD15 1EW; tel (289) 306688.
Vice-Consul: Gordon B. Ayre.

Consulate: 22 Wide Bargate, Boston PE21 6HG; tel (205) 310444; telex 37509; fax (205) 310500.
Vice-Consul: John Bryan Woodcock.

Consulate: Arndale House, 5th Floor, Charles St, Bradford BD1 1ER; tel (274) 733571.
Vice-Consul: Michael James Thorniley-Walker.

Consulate: Limekiln St, Deal, Dover CT17 9EE; tel (304) 201201; telex 96115.
Vice-Consul: James Gregory Ryeland.

Consulate: 48 Arwenack St, Falmouth TR11 3SA; tel (326) 311300; telex 45237.
Vice-Consul: Philip H. Fox.

Consulate: The Docks, Fowey PL23 1AL; tel (726) 833161; telex 45215; fax (726) 833774.
Vice-Consul: John Anthony Samuel.

Consulate: 21/5 Aire St, Goole, Humberside DN14 5RE; tel (405) 2262/4; telex 57609.
Vice-Consul: Jeremy John Kettlewell.

Consulate: Europa House, 40 South Quay, Great Yarmouth NR30 2RL; tel (493) 856831; telex 97477.
Vice-Consul: Malcolm J. Brooks.

Consulate: Bank Chambers, 2 Freeman St, Grimsby DN32 7AD; tel (472) 357521.
Vice-Consul: David R. Smith.

Consulate: Wavenet Chambers, Lowestoft NR32 1BP; tel (502) 572301; telex 97319.
Vice-Consul: Paul William Barlow.

Consulate: York House, Borough Rd, Middlesborough, Cleveland TS1 2HP; tel (642) 243231; telex 58502; fax (642) 223957.
Vice-Consul: Joseph Desmond Cryan.

Consulate: Carlsberg Brewery Ltd, 140 Bridge St, POB 46, Northampton NN1 1PZ; tel (604) 234333; telex 311226.
Vice-Consul: Ebbe Dinesen.

Consulate: 'Chittleburn View', Nettle Hayes, Sherford Rd, Elburton, Plymouth PL9 8BU; tel (752) 401167; telex 45225.
Vice-Consul: Leonard Henry James Underwood.

Consulate: 21 Hampshire Terr., Portsmouth PO1 2PY; tel (705) 753575; telex 86738.
Vice-Consul: Philip Alan Berman.

Consulate: c/o London & Scandinavian Metallurgical Co. Ltd, Fullerton Rd, Rotherham S60 1DL; tel (709) 828500; telex 54581.
Vice-Consul: Geoffrey Cheetham.

Consulate: B. Ackerley & Son Ltd, Canute Chambers, Canute Rd, Southampton SO9 1FJ; tel (703) 227171; telex 47537; fax (703) 223883.
Vice-Consul: Neville J. Fulcher.

Consulate: 44 Lowther St, Whitehaven CA28 7JU; tel (946) 692452; telex 64488; fax (946) 604823.
Vice-Consul: Howard Walwyn Parry-Jones.

Consulate: 59 Marischal St, Aberdeen AB9 8AZ; tel (224) 589921; telex 73134.
Vice-Consul: Ramsey P. H. Pirie.

Consulate: 49 Meadowside, Dundee, Tayside DD1 1EH; tel (382) 23044; telex 76177.
Vice-Consul: David Hillocks Paterson.

Consulate: Winton Bldgs, Ardrossan, Ayrshire KA22 8BY; tel (294) 605284; telex 779814.
Vice-Consul: Christopher John Montgomerie Alpine Mair.

Consulate: Mandal House, South Shore Rd, Grangemouth FK3 8AE; tel (324) 486721; telex 77406.
Vice-Consul: John Ralph.

Consulate: 66 Commercial Rd, Lerwick, Shetland ZE1 0NJ; tel (595) 3057; telex 75295; fax (595) 2781.
Vice-Consul: Charles William Lindsay Aitken.

Consulate: Shore St, Kirkwall, Orkney KW15 1LQ; tel (856) 2961; telex 75498.
Vice-Consul: John Davie Manson Robertson.

Consulate: Sandwick Rd, Stornoway, Isle of Lewis PA87 2SL; tel (851) 2303.
Vice-Consul: Stephen Eriksen.

Consulate: 'Mara Vista', 7 Whitehouse Park, Wick, Caithness; tel (955) 3197.
Vice-Consul: Norman Bremner.

DOMINICA

High Commission: 1 Collingham Gardens, South Kensington, London SW5 0HW; tel (71) 370-5194; telex 881-3931; fax (71) 373-8743.
High Commissioner: Franklin A. Baron.
Minister-Counsellor: Ashworth Elwin.

ECUADOR

Embassy: Flat 3B, 3 Hans Crescent, Knightsbridge, London SW1X 0LS; tel (71) 584-1367; telex 8811087; fax (71) 823-9701.
Ambassador: Dr José Antonio de Correa.
Minister-Counsellor (Commercial): Eulalia Andrade Varea de Sancho.
Naval Attaché: Capt. Hector Ruilova.
Counsellor: Dr Juan Larrea.

EGYPT

Embassy: 26 South St, London W1Y 6DD; tel (71) 499-2401; telex 23650; fax (71) 355-3568.
Ambassador: Mohamed I. Shaker.
Minister and Deputy Head of Mission: S. Mohamed Shaaban.
Counsellor: S. Mohamed Ashraf G. el-Din Rashed.
Counsellor: Hussein Wasfi Saad el-Din.
Counsellor: Yousef Mohamed Mansour.
Counsellor: Moan Omar Mohamed Attia.
Counsellor: Osama Hassan M. Shamaa.
First Secretary: Abdel Magid Mohamed Samaha.
Second Secretary: Bahaa el-Din Mokhtar Mowafi.
Second Secretary: Yousef Ahmed J. el-Shakawy.
Second Secretary: Soha Ibrahim Mohamed Refat el-Far.
Second Secretary: Amgad Maher Abdel Ghaffar.

Consulate-General: 2 Lowndes St, London SW1X 9ET; tel (71) 235-9977; telex 261228.
Consul-General: Aly Mohamed Fahmy el-Karaksy.

Defence Office: 24 South St, London W1Y 6DD; tel (71) 493-2649; telex 893492; fax (71) 499-7948.
Defence Attaché: Maj.-Gen. Aly Ibrahim Awad-Allah.

Agricultural Office: 26 South St, London W1Y 6DD; tel (71) 499-2401; telex 23650; fax (71) 355-3568.
Agricultural Adviser: el-Said Ahmed el-Baz.

Commercial Office: 23 South Street, London W1Y 6DD; tel (71) 499-3002; telex 8952738; fax (71) 493-8110.
Commercial Adviser: Dr Royshdi Mostafa Barakat.
Counsellor (Commercial): Nabila Muhammad Zaki Ragheb.
Counsellor (Commercial): Mostafa Abd el-Latif Nofal.

Cultural Office: 4 Chesterfield Gardens, London W1Y 8BR; tel (71) 491-3002; fax (71) 408-1335.
Cultural Adviser: Dr Younes Ahmed el-Batrik.

Medical Office: 47 Longridge Rd, London SW5 9SD; tel (71) 370-6944; telex 295578; fax (71) 370-3641.
Medical Adviser: Dr Mohamed Ahmed Mohamed Ali.
Medical Attaché: Dr Dawod Ahmed Hamed Dawod.

Press and Information Office: 2 Harewood Place, London W1R 9HB; tel (71) 409-2236; fax (71) 493-7456.
Press and Information Adviser: Dr Ali Abdul Rahman Rahmy.

Tourist Office: 168 Piccadilly, London W1V 9DE; tel (71) 493-5282; fax (71) 408-0295.
Tourism Adviser: Sabri M. Abdul Nabi.
Attaché (Information/Tourism): Khayria Mohammad Bahnas.

EL SALVADOR

Embassy: 1st Floor, 5 Great James St, London WC1N 3DA; tel (71) 430-2141.
Ambassador: Dr Mauricio Rosales-Rivera.
Counsellor: Ernesto Lima.
First Secretary and Consul-General: Carolina Calderón.

ESTONIA

Embassy: 18 Chepstow Villas, London W11 2RB; tel (71) 633-9746; fax (71) 792-0218.
Chargé d'affaires: Eerik-Niiles Kross.

ETHIOPIA

Embassy: 17 Prince's Gate, London SW7 1PZ; tel (71) 589-7212; telex 23681.
Counsellor (Press/Information) and Chargé d'affaires a.i.: Mairegu Bezabih.
Counsellor: Dr Teshome Teklu.
Counsellor: Hailu Kebede Worku.
First Secretary: Mesfin Nigussie.
First Secretary: Mesfin Assegid.
Third Secretary: Eshetu Abayneh.
Attaché: Kassetch Assebegn.
Attaché: Woudenesh Alemu.

Commercial Section: 404-6 Walmer House, 296-300 Regent St, London W1; tel (71) 580-0174.
Counsellor (Commercial): Getahun Leta Toera.

FIJI

Embassy: 34 Hyde Park Gate, London SW7 7DN; tel (71) 584-3661; telex 22408; fax (71) 584-2838.
Ambassador: Brig.-Gen. Ratu Epeli Nailatikau.
Counsellor (Commercial): Sung Kangwai.
First Secretary: Ian Robert Perks.
Second Secretary: Sukulu Maraiwai.

FINLAND

Embassy: 32 Grosvenor Gardens, London SW1W 0DH; tel (71) 235-9531; telex 24786; fax (71) 235-3680.
Ambassador: Leif Blomqvist.
Minister-Counsellor: Jukka Leino.
Counsellor (Political): Anneli Puura-Märkäla.
Counsellor (Economic): Dr Hannu Märkäla.
Counsellor (Cultural): Frank Hellsten.
Counsellor (Press): Jarmo Järventaus.
Counsellor (Industry/Technology): Tuomo Tapani Airaksinen.

Defence Attaché: Commdr Pauli Juhani Kaskeala.
Assistant Defence Attaché: Maj. Risto Tyrväinen.
First Secretary (International Organizations): Pekka Orpana.
Attaché (Scientific): Tuomo Airaksinen.
Attaché (Education): Dr Eino Juhani Lyytinen.
Attaché (Consular): Sickan Park-Lindholm.

Trade Centre: 30-5 Pall Mall, London SW1Y 5LP; tel (71) 839-7262; telex 262360; fax (71) 839-1717.
Counsellor (Commercial): Jyri Muttonen.
Secretary (Commercial): Heli Laukka-Horelli.

Consulate: Nevill Russell Chartered Accountants, Britannia House, 8th Floor, 50 Great Charles St, Queensway, Birmingham B3 2LY; tel (21) 236-7711.
Consul: John Barry Davis.

Consulate: 71 High St, Hull HU1 1QT; tel (482) 25781; telex 592271.
Consul: J. A. Good.

Consulate: c/o Carlbom Shipping Ltd, Dock Offices Bldg, Immingham Dock, Immingham DN40 2NG; tel (469) 72387.
Consul: Anthony Carlbon.

Consulate: 22 Hullet Close, Appley Bridge WN6 9LB; tel (2575) 2684; telex 669017.
Consul: Berndt-Erik Söderström.

Consulate: Trapp & Co., 'C' Floor, Milburn House, Dean St, Newcastle upon Tyne NE99 1DN; tel (91) 261-2711; telex 53113.
Consul: Campbell Yeoman.

Trade Centre: 56 George St, Edinburgh EH2 2LR; tel (31) 225-1295; telex 72282; fax (31) 225-9324.
Trade Commissioner: Timo Auvinen.

Consulate: Walker Timber Ltd, Carriden Sawmills, Bo'ness West Lothian, Edinburgh EH51 9SQ; tel (506) 823331; telex 727489; fax (506) 822590.
Consul: Michael James Walker.

Consulate: Jenkins Shipping Ltd, The Harbour, Warrenpoint, Co. Down.
Consul: Richard Walter Jenkins.

Consulate: Mount Stuart House, Mount Stuart Sq., Cardiff CF1 6QL; tel (222) 480704; telex 498350.
Consul: Christopher Evans.

Consulate: 'Seurasaari', Priory Farm, Station Rd, Portbury, Bristol BS20 9TN; tel (275) 815427.
Vice-Consul: Johan Seward Parsons.

Consulate: Hammond House, Limekiln St, Dover CT17 9EE; tel (304) 201201; telex 96115; fax (304) 240374.
Vice-Consul: James Gregory Ryeland.

Consulate: c/o Barclays Bank Chambers, 9 Church Sq., Hartlepool TS24 7EE; tel (429) 272224; telex 592271.
Vice-Consul: C. Harvey.

Consulate: Burley Place, Kirkstall Rd, Leeds LS4 2PS; tel (532) 460831.
Vice-Consul: J. P. R. Alvin.

Consulate: 20 Park Row, Nottingham NG1 6GW; tel (602) 472038.
Vice-Consul: E. J. Drury.

Consulate: Fairways, Saltergate Lane, Bamford, Sheffield S30 2BE; tel (742) 663084; telex 54115.
Vice-Consul: Mark R. Balfour.

Consulate: Ryde Terr., Southampton SO9 2UL; Latimer St, Southampton SO9 4TU; tel (703) 630966; telex 47629.
Vice-Consul: Michael Thomas Baker.

Consulate: 59 Marischal St, Aberdeen AB9 8AZ; tel (224) 589921; telex 73134.
Vice-Consul: D. G. R. Stroud.

Consulate: Belgary Place, Dundee DD3 8SH; tel (382) 817341; telex 76461; fax (382) 817508.
Vice-Consul: Sinclair Aitken.

Consulate: Shearer Shipping Services Ltd, Garthspool, Lerwick, ZE1 0NF; tel (595) 2556; telex 75176.
Vice-Consul: Laurence John Smith.

FRANCE

Embassy: 58 Knightsbridge, London SW1X 7JT; tel (71) 235-8080; telex 261905; fax (71) 259-6498.
Ambassador: Bernard Dorin.
Minister-Counsellor: Patrick Villemar.
Minister-Counsellor (Finance): Jean de Rosen.
Counsellor: François Barry Martin-Delongchamps.
Counsellor (Press): Anita Limido.
Counsellor: Thierry Vankerk-Hoven.
Counsellor (Social Affairs): Eric Aubry.
Counsellor (Finance): Gilbert Fournier.
Counsellor (Maritime): Jean-Charles Leclair.
Defence and Naval Attaché: Adm. Michel Mollat du Jourdin.
Assistant Naval Attaché: Capt. Robert Alamercery.
Military Attaché: Col Christian Neyron de Saint Julien.
Assistant Military Attaché: Lieut Col Hubert Marchand.
Air Attaché: Col Dominique de Rancourt de Mimerand.
Assistant Air Attaché: Lieut Col Philippe Bricka.
Attaché (Defence Procurement): Chief Engineer Pierre Dumas.
Third Secretary and Head of Administration: Nicole Milliard Natalis.
Attaché (Customs): Marc le Reste.
Attaché (Taxation): Martine Poulin.
Attaché (Agriculture): Jean-Marie Demange.
Attaché (Commodities): Jean-Philippe Guiltat.
Attaché (Economic): Laurence Schloesing-Colchester.
Attaché (Tourism): Patrick Goyet.
Attaché (Civil Aviation): Gérard Le Houx.

Consular Section: 21 Cromwell Rd, London SW7 2EN; tel (71) 581-5292; fax (71) 823-8655.
Counsellor (Consular): Georges Rochiccioli.
First Secretary (Consular): Nicole Tramond.

Commercial Section: 21/4 Grosvenor Place, London SW1X 7HU; tel (71) 235-7080; telex 263093; fax (71) 235-9598.
Minister-Counsellor (Economic/Commercial): Henri le Corre.
Counsellor (Commercial): Dominique Mauppin.

Cultural Section: 23 Cromwell Rd, London SW7 2EN; tel (71) 581-5292; fax (71) 823-8596.
Counsellor (Cultural): Phillipe Guillemin.

Science and Technology Section: 6 Cromwell Place, London SW7 2JN; tel (71) 581-0711; fax (71) 225-3975.
Counsellor (Science/Technology): Michel Ronis.

Consulate-General: Cunard Bldg, Pier Head Water St, Liverpool L3 1ET; tel (51) 236-5520.

Consulate-General: 11 Randolph Crescent, Edinburgh EH3 7TT; tel (31) 225-7954.

Consulate: Philip Le Feuvre House, La Motte St, St Helier, Jersey; tel (534) 26256.

GABON

Embassy: 27 Elvaston Place, London SW7 5NL; tel (71) 823-9986; telex 919418; fax (71) 584-0047.
Ambassador: Vincent Boulé.
Counsellor: Joseph Olivier Menie.
Counsellor: William-André Aguile.
First Secretary: Paulette Nze-Obame.

GAMBIA

High Commission: 57 Kensington Court, London W8 5DG; tel (71) 937-6316; telex 23229; fax (71) 376-0531.
High Commissioner and Counsellor: Bai Ousman Secka (acting).
Second Secretary: Abdoulie M'bye.
Attaché (Finance): Momodou Ceesay.
Attaché (Protocol/Welfare): Mawdo Juwara.
Attaché (Information/Tourism): Momodou M. B. D. Cham.
Attaché (Information/Tourism): Joseph Samuel Gabbidon.
Attaché (Tourism): Sainabou Louisa Ndure.

GERMANY

Embassy: 23 Belgrave Sq., London SW1X 8PZ; tel (71) 235-5033; telex 28191; fax (71) 235-0609.
Ambassador: Dr Hermann Freiherr von Richthofen.
Minister: Helmut Wegner.
Minister-Counsellor: Dr Klaus-Peter Klaiber.
Counsellor: Dr Hans-Jochen Kretschmann.
Counsellor: Matthias von Kummer.
Counsellor: Gerd Pluckebaum.
Counsellor: Dr Hartmut Lang.
Counsellor (Labour): Heinz Pampel.
Counsellor and Head of Economic Dept: Dr Reinhold Huber.
Counsellor (Economic): Karl Albrecht Wokalek.
Counsellor (Agriculture): Dr Richard Peters.
Counsellor (Commodities/Energy): Dr Siegfried Borggrefe.
Counsellor and Head of Press Dept: Friedrich Gröning.
Counsellor (Science): Dietmar Greineder.
Counsellor (Cultural): Dr Reinhard W. Ehni.
Counsellor (Cultural): Hubert Kolb.
Counsellor (Cultural): Roland Herrmann.
Counsellor (Legal/Consular): Bernd Oetter.
Counsellor (Maritime): Dr Peter Seidel.
Defence and Naval Attaché: Rear Adm. Diether Hülsemann.
Air Attaché: Col Kurt Viertler.
Military Attaché: Col Werner Widder.
Assistant Naval Attaché: Commdr Ulf Stickdorn.
Assistant Military Attaché: Maj. Ernst Elbers.
Administrative Officer (Office of Defence Attaché): Flight Lieut Klaus Mai.
Counsellor (Defence Research): Dr Johannes Bakenhus.
First Secretary (Defence Research): Dr Dietmar Binding.
Assistant Attaché (Defence Research): Rainer Wiersch.
First Secretary (Finance): Wolf-Rudiger Bengs.
First Secretary (Press): Hildegard Dunkl.
First Secretary and Head of Administrative Affairs: Ernst Fischer.
Second Secretary (Technical): Gerd Baurmann.

Consulate-General: Norwich House, 8-12 Water St, Liverpool L2 8TA; tel (51) 236-0294; telex 628735.
Consul-General: Franz Goldschmidt.

Consulate: c/o W.H. Doherty & Co. Ltd, Vulcan Rd, Lode Lane Industrial Estate, Solihull B91 2JY; tel (21) 705-9944.
Honorary Consul: Patrick James Mortimore Doherty.

Consulate: 111-7 Victoria St, Bristol BS1 6AX; tel (272) 298040; telex 44220; fax (272) 251528.
Honorary Consul: John Charles Langman.

Consulate: Limekiln St, Dover; tel (304) 201201; telex 96115.
Honorary Consul: David C. Ryeland.

Consulate: c/o G.C. Fox & Co., 48 Arwenack St, Falmouth; tel (326) 311300; telex 45237.
Honorary Consul: Charles L. Fox.

Consulate: c/o Euroatlantic Shipping Services Ltd, Haven House, Albemarle St, Harwich CO12 3HL; tel (255) 56666; telex 987106.
Honorary Consul: Richard Antony Coolen.

Consulate: Redgarth, 6 Newgate, Cottingham HU16 4DT; tel (482) 842511.
Honorary Consul: Andrew Good.

Consulate: 11 New Conduit St, King's Lynn; tel (553) 692233; fax (553) 767318.
Honorary Consul: David Hume.

Consulate: 18 Blind Lane, Shadwell, Leeds LS17 8HE; tel (532) 630505; telex 556237.
Honorary Consul: Hubert Eichinger.

Consulate: 15 Bridge St East, Middlesborough TS2 1NA; tel (642) 230111; telex 587666.
Honorary Consul: James William Cockfield.

Consulate: Norham House, 4th Floor, New Bridge St West, Newcastle upon Tyne NE1 8AD; tel (632) 611063; telex 537192.
Honorary Consul: Lalage Sadler.

Consulate: 16 The Parade, Plymouth PL1 2JT; tel (752) 663444; telex 45247.
Honorary Consul: Edward James Jones.

Consulate: Bowling Green House, 1 Orchard Place, Southampton SO1 1BR; tel (703) 23671; telex 47620.
Honorary Consul: Roger V. Thorton.

Consulate: c/o Commodore Shipping Services Ltd, 28 Conway St, St Helier, Jersey; tel (534) 71263; telex 419-2079.
Honorary Consul: Robert A. Norman.

Consulate: c/o Isle of Sark Shipping Co., White Rock, St Peter Port, Guernsey; tel (481) 24059; telex 419-1549.
Honorary Consul: Peter Drake.

Consulate-General: 16 Eglinton Cres., Edinburgh EH12 5DG; tel (31) 337-2323; telex 727276; fax (31) 346-1578.
Consul-General: Eberhard Boenke.

Consulate: 12 Albert St, Aberdeen AB1 1XQ; tel (224) 643379; fax (224) 643396.
Honorary Consul: Andrew D. F. Lewis.

Consulate: 144 West George St, Glasgow G2 2HG; tel (41) 331-2811.
Honorary Consul: Donald D. M. Frame.

Consulate: Shore St, Kirkwall, Orkney KW15 1LQ; tel (856) 2961; telex 75498.
Honorary Consul: John D. M. Robertson.

Consulate: Shearer Shipping Services Ltd, Garthspool, Lerwick, Shetland ZE1 0NP; tel (595) 2556; telex 75176; fax (595) 5949.
Honorary Consul: Laurence John Smith.

Consulate: Pencoed House, Capel Llanilltern, Cardiff CF5 6JH; tel (222) 890294; telex 49373.
Honorary Consul: Kenneth Martin David Johns.

Consulate: 1 Balleyhampton Rd, Larne BT40 2ST; tel (574) 77777; telex 747466.
Honorary Consul: Douglas Getty.

GHANA

High Commission: 13 Belgrave Sq., London SW1X 8PR; tel (71) 235-4142; telex 21370.
High Commissioner: K. B. Asante.
Deputy High Commissioner: Francis Adjei Danso.
Minister (Trade): James Emmanuel Benjamin Haizel.
Minister-Counsellor (Welfare/Consular): Oliver Kenneth Lawluvi.
Minister-Counsellor (Information): James Kwamena Anaman.
Counsellor (Education): Sam Afrifa-Kyei.
Counsellor (Political/Economic): Yaw Odei Osei.
Counsellor (Information): George Asiedu-Ntow.
Counsellor (Information): Emmanuel Caesar Dzewu.
Counsellor (Finance): Bennaiah Akuetteh Akuffo.
Counsellor (Consular): Kofi Kesse Manfo.
Defence Adviser: Group Capt. John Frank Weir.
First Secretary (Education): Kwasi Obeng-Amoo.
First Secretary (Administrative): Christian Gonçalves Baet.
First Secretary (Finance): Robert Kwatelai Quartey.
First Secretary (Consular): Ernest Sowatey Lomotey.
First Secretary (Consular): Lawrence Kenneth Acheampong.
First Secretary (Recruitment): Jacob Addy Plange.
Second Secretary (Protocol): Andrew Biney.
Second Secretary (Recruitment): Alexander Almond Ackon.
Attaché (Technical): Emmanuel Ofoe Domale.

GREECE

Embassy: 1A Holland Park, London W11 3TP; tel (71) 727-8040; telex 266751; fax (71) 229-7221.
Ambassador: George D. Papoulias.
Counsellor: Aristides Agathocles.
Counsellor (Consular): Anastasios Mitsialis.
Counsellor (Economic/Commercial): George Protonotarios.
Counsellor (Press): John G. Poutos.
Counsellor (Education): Nicholas Voliotis.
Counsellor (Labour): Harilads Hionidis.
Defence Attaché: Capt. Michael Zevelakis.
Assistant Defence Attaché: Commdr Dimitrios Alexandropoulos.
Shipping Attaché: Capt. Spyridon Goros.
Assistant Shipping Attaché: Commdr Pericles Ousantzopoulos.
First Secretary: Alexandros Rallis.
First Secretary (Consular): Aglaia Balta.
Second Secretary: Maria Theofili.
Third Secretary: Dr Constantine A. Papadopoulos.
Secretary (Economic/Commercial): Athanassios Arsenis.
Secretary (Economic/Commercial): Emmanuel Stantzos.
Attaché (Press/Information): Dr Nikos Papadakis.
Attaché (Administrative): Evangelos-John Anagnostou.
Attaché (Administrative): Athina Maria Charalambidis.
Attaché (Administrative): Kyriakos Pantostis.

GRENADA

High Commission: 1 Collingham Gardens, Earls Court, London SW5; tel (71) 373-7808; telex 889183; fax (71) 370-7040.
High Commissioner: Lynton Cosmas Noel.
Counsellor: Maureen Emmanuel.
First Secretary: Ashley David James.
Attaché (Information/Tourism): Christine Maria Noel.
Attaché: Sibyl G. Alexander.

GUATEMALA

Embassy: 13 Fawcett St, London SW10 9HN; tel (71) 351-3042; telex 926556; fax (71) 376-5708.
First Secretary, Consul and Chargé d'affaires a.i.: Dr Magda Antonieta Lopez Toledo.

GUYANA

High Commission: 3 Palace Court, Bayswater Rd, London W2 4LP; tel (71) 229-7684; telex 23945; fax (71) 727-9809.
High Commissioner: Cecil S. Pilgrim.
First Secretary: Arnon Adams.
First Secretary: Jacqueline Too-Kong.
First Secretary: Winston L. A. Henry.
Second Secretary: Orin Alexander.
Attaché: Debra A. L. Collins.

HOLY SEE

Apostolic Pro-Nunciature: 54 Parkside, London SW19 5NF; tel (81) 946-1410; fax (81) 947-2494.
Apostolic Pro-Nuncio: Most Rev. Luigi Barbarito, Titular Archbishop of Fiorentino.
Counsellor: Mgr Abraham Kattumana.

HONDURAS

Embassy: 115 Gloucester Place, London W1H 3PJ; tel (71) 486-4880; telex 296368; fax (71) 486-4880.
Ambassador: Carlos M. Zeron.
First Secretary: Dr Porfirio Garcia.
Military Attaché: Lieut Col Luis Alonso Velasquez-Galeano.
Attaché (Tourism): Iris Paget.
Attaché (Culture): Miguel Angel Ruiz-Matute.
Attaché (Coffee): Norma Leticia Medina.

HUNGARY

Embassy: 35 Eaton Place, London SW1X 8BY; tel (71) 235-4048; fax (71) 823-1348.
Ambassador: Tibor Antalpéter.
Minister: Gábor Bródi.
Minister: Lóránt Czigány.
Counsellor (Commercial): Ede Sziklai.
Second Counsellor (Press): Tünde Vajda.
Defence, Military and Air Attaché: Col Péter Szücs.
Assistant Military and Air Attaché: Lieut Col Imre Szigeti.
First Secretary: Róbert Brósz.
Second Secretary: Gellért Szabó.

Consulate-General: 35b Eaton Place, London SW1X 8BY; tel (71) 235-2664.
Consul-General and Counsellor: Dr Péter Kallós.

ICELAND

Embassy: 1 Eaton Terrace, London SW1W 8EY; tel (71) 730-5131; telex 918226; fax (71) 730-1683.
Ambassador: Helgi Ágústsson.
Minister-Counsellor: Tómas Karlsson.
Secretary: Margrét S. Kristjánsdóttir.
Attaché: Sigrídur Gunnarsdóttir.
Chaplain: Jón A. Baldvinsson.

Consulate: 15 Hazelbank, Kings Norton, Birmingham B38 8BT; tel (21) 458-3435.
Consul: Knud E. H. Teisen.

Consulate: Norwich House, Water St, Liverpool L2 9XR; tel (51) 255-0558; fax (51) 255-0572.
Consul: James A. Brown.

Consulate: The British Linen Bank, 1st Floor, 19-21 Spring Gardens, Manchester M2 1EB; tel (61) 832-4444.
Consul: David G. Wilson.

Consulate: 1/2 Lansdowne Terrace, Gosforth, Newcastle upon Tyne NE3 1HN; tel (91) 213-1010; fax (91) 213-1704.
Consul: W. Gordon McKeag.

Consulate: M. G. H. Ltd, Trelawny House, The Dock, Felixstowe, Suffolk IP11 8TU; tel (394) 676651; telex 85667.
Consul: Jack Derrick Wright.

Consulate: Marr Fishing Vessel Management Ltd, 228 Dock St, Fleetwood FY7 6PA; tel (3917) 3466; telex 67606.
Consul: James Cross.

Consulate: Fylkir Ltd, King Edward VIII House, East Side Rd, Fish Docks, Grimsby, South

Humberside DN31 3NB; tel (472) 241007; telex 527173; fax (472) 355134.
Consul: Jón Olgeirsson.

Consulate: Boyd Line Ltd, Albert Dock, Hull HU1 2DH; tel (482) 24024; fax (482) 23737.
Consul: Thomas W. Boyd.

Consulate: 50 Grange Rd, Edinburgh EH9 1TU; tel (31) 667-2166.
Consul: Snjólaug Thomson.

Consulate: Anderston House, 389 Argyle St, Glasgow G2 8NX; tel (41) 221-6943; telex 77318; fax (41) 221-3191.
Consul: Norman Hamilton.

Consulate: Carleton Bldgs, 59 Marischal St, Aberdeen AB9 8AZ; tel (224) 589921; telex 73134.
Consul: Daniel G. R. Stroud.

Consulate: 66 Commercial Rd, Lerwick, Shetland ZE1 0JO; tel (595) 3057.
Consul: Charles W. L. Aitken.

Consulate: Modref Ltd, Unit 1, Porview Trade Centre, 310 Newtownards Rd, Belfast BT4 1HE; tel (232) 456-484.
Consul: John Gourley Crossen.

Consulate: Limekiln St, Dover, Kent CT17 9EE; tel (304) 201201; telex 96115.
Vice-Consul: David C. Ryeland.

INDIA

High Commission: India House, Aldwych, London WC2B 4NA; tel (71) 836-8484.
High Commissioner: Dr Laxmi Mall Singvi.
Deputy High Commissioner: Salman Haidar.
Minister (Coordination): B. K. Ratnakar Rao.
Minister: Ranjan Roychaudhuri.
Minister: Dhirendra Singh.
Minister (Economic): Madan Prasad Bezbaruah.
Minister (Audit): Ravi Saxena.
Counsellor: Joseph Rosslyn Blah.
Counsellor (Political): Prabhat Prakash Shukla.
Counsellor (Press/Information): Talmiz Ahmad.
Counsellor (Political): Madhusudan Ganapathi.
Counsellor (Trade): Krishna Kant.
Military Adviser: Brig. Hari Mohan Khanna.
Air Adviser: Air Cdre Vinod Patney.
Naval Adviser: Cdre Balchandra Srinivas Karpe.
Deputy Military Adviser: Col Virender Singh Budhwar.
Deputy Technical Adviser (Defence): Col Krishnan Prasad Gupta.
Deputy Naval Adviser: Commdr Shrirang N. Bijur.
Assistant Naval Adviser: Lieut Commdr Girish Luthra.
Director of Acquisitions (Air Cell): Wing Commdr Ramamoorthy Jayaraman.
First Secretary (Press/Information): Rajesh Nandan Prasad.
First Secretary (Passports): Sham Lal Trighatia.
First Secretary (Commercial): Harsh Vardhan Singh Manral.
First Secretary (Consular): Rajesh Mittal.
First Secretary (Visas): Ram Saroop Shrivastava.
First Secretary (Shipping): Shanti Narayan.
First Secretary (Audit): Rekha Gupta.
Second Secretary (Culture): Azad Singh Toor.
Attaché (Hindi/Cultural): Madhu Goswami.

INDONESIA

Embassy: 38 Grosvenor Sq., London W1X 9AD; tel (71) 499-7661; telex 28284; fax (71) 491-4993.
Ambassador: Teuku Mohammad Hadi Thayeb.
Minister and Deputy Head of Mission: Rhousdy Soeriaatmadja.
Minister-Counsellor (Information): Titiek Sitti Aminah Soejono.
Minister-Counsellor (Political): Budiman Darmosutanto.
Counsellor (Administrative): Karso Popon.
Defence Attaché: Col Syam Soemanagara.
Assistant Defence and Air Attaché: Col Suharso.
First Secretary (Administrative): Mr Soepardijono.
First Secretary (Political): Max Pangemanan.
First Secretary (Financial): Nicholas Tandi Dammen.
First Secretary (Consular): Djoko Hardono.
Second Secretary (Financial): Bali Moniaga.
Attaché (Educational/Cultural): Ignatius Suharno.
Attaché (Commercial): Gusmardi Bustami.
Attaché (Communications): Capt. B. J. P. Pitna.

IRAN

Embassy: 27 Prince's Gate, London SW7 1PX; tel (71) 584-8101; telex 23998.
Minister-Counsellor and Chargé d'affaires a.i.: Seyed Shamseddin Khareghani.
First Secretary: Ali Asghar Frashchi.
Second Secretary and Consul: Mahmoud Assadian.
Attaché: Behrooz Azimi.

IRAQ

Interests Section: 21 Queen's Gate, London SW7 5JG; (71) 584-7141; fax (71) 584-7716.
Minister and Head of Interests Section: Zuhair M. Ibrahim.

IRELAND

Embassy: 17 Grosvenor Place, London SW1X 7HR; tel (71) 235-2171; telex 916104; fax (71) 245-6961.
Ambassador: Joseph Small.
Counsellor (Political): Brendan Lyons.
Counsellor (Political): Joe Hayes.
Counsellor (Economic): Michael Fahy.
Counsellor (Agricultural): Vincent Keane.
Counsellor: Paula Slattery.
First Secretary (Political/Press): Sean Farrell.
First Secretary (Press/Information): David Donoghue.
First Secretary (Labour): Paul Cullen.
First Secretary: Paul Murray.
First Secretary: Brendan McMahon.
First Secretary (Labour): Melanie Pine.
Secretary (Administrative): Eamon Gildea.
Secretary (Agricultural): Frank Hayes.
Secretary (Passport Office): Andrew Harwood.

ISRAEL

Embassy: 2 Palace Green, Kensington, London W8 4QB; tel (71) 937-8050; fax (71) 937-5184.
Ambassador: Yoav Biran.
Minister (Financial): Nathan Meyer.
Minister: Nathan Meron.
Minister-Counsellor (Political): Ilan Baruch.
Minister-Counsellor (Administrative): Amnon Hanuka.
Minister-Counsellor (Cultural): Malka Ben-Yossef.
Counsellor (Information): Zvi Rav-Ner.
Counsellor (Press): Dan Ashbel.
Counsellor (Labour): Emanuel Gluska.
Counsellor (Commercial): Zvia Dori.
Counsellor (Agricultural): Zvi Allon.
Defence and Armed Forces Attaché: Brig.-Gen. Yom-Tov Tamir.
First Secretary (Information): Boaz Modai.
First Secretary (Tourism): Shmuel Zurel.

ITALY

Embassy: 14 Three Kings Yard, Davies St, London W1Y 2EH; tel (71) 629-8200; telex 23520.
Ambassador: Giacomo Attolico.
Minister-Counsellor: Livio Muzi-Falconi.
Counsellor: Arnaldo Vittorio Romano de Mohr Sunnegg Morberg.
Counsellor: Norberto Cappello.
Counsellor (Political): Fabio Pigliapoco.
Counsellor: Leonardo Visconti di Modrone.
Counsellor: Stefano Ronca.
Counsellor (Consular): Angelo Gabriele de Ceglie.
First Secretary: Fabrizio Inserra.
First Secretary: Maurizio Massari.
First Secretary (Consular): Raffaele Trombetta.
Second Secretary (Consular/Administrative): Paolo Cartocci.
Maritime Attaché: Felice D'Aniello.
Attaché (Scientific): Dr Giuseppe Roffi.
Attaché (Commodities): Michele Schiavone.
Attaché (Economic): Silverio Mittiga.
Attaché (Finance): Luigi Marini.

Defence Office: 5 Lygon Place, London SW1; tel (71) 730-9011.
Defence and Naval Attaché: Capt. Umberto Cuzzola.
Air Attaché: Col Aldo Olivero.
Military Attaché: Col Ciro Cocozza.

JAMAICA

High Commission: 1-2 Prince Consort Rd, London SW7 2BZ; tel (71) 823-9911; telex 263304; fax (71) 589-5154.
High Commissioner: Ellen Gray Bogle.
Deputy High Commissioner (Trade): John Kenneth Pringle.
Deputy High Commissioner: Douglas Anthony Saunders.
Defence Adviser: Col Torrance Delaney Guiness Lewis.
Minister-Counsellor (Consular): Paul Garth Fitzmaurice Harker.
Counsellor (Financial/Administrative): Enos Thompson.
Counsellor (Political/Economic): Sharon Faith Elizabeth Saunders.
Counsellor (Political/Economic): Leonie Livingston.
Counsellor: Samuel Herbert Parris.
Attaché (Trade): Norman Frederick Rae.
Attaché (Trade): Earl Courtenay Rattray.
Attaché (Information): Wilton Dyer.
Attaché (Finance): Norman Gregory Kitson-Walters.
Attaché (Administrative): Angela V. Brown.

JAPAN

Embassy: 101-104 Piccadilly, London W1V 9FN; tel (71) 465-6500; telex 25638; fax (71) 491-9348.
Ambassador: Hiroshi Kitamura.
Minister: Akira Sugino.
Minister (Finance): Shotaro Miyake.
Minister (Commercial): Hikoharu Kuré.
Counsellor: Yukio Takeuchi.
Counsellor and Medical Attaché: Dr Niro Tode.
Counsellor: Hitoshi Tanaka.
Counsellor: Hiroyasu Ando.
Counsellor (Finance): Sakura Shiga.
Counsellor (Agriculture): Shoji Miyamoto.
Counsellor: Kiyoshi Araki.
Counsellor: Mitoji Yabunaka.
Counsellor: Makoto Mizutani.
Counsellor: Toshio Ohashi.
Counsellor (Transport): Satoru Kanazwaw.
First Secretary: Mitsuaki Ishimura.
First Secretary (Consular): Tetsuo Miura.
First Secretary (Political): Akira Matsuda.
First Secretary (Commercial): Hideo Matsui.
First Secretary (Defence): Capt. Osamu Iizuka.
First Secretary (Transport): Masaru Sakuma.

First Secretary (Telecommunications): Tameyasu Tsukada.
First Secretary (Political/Labour): Kazumi Matsui.
First Secretary (Commercial): Kazuo Kodama.
First Secretary (Political): Kunio Takahashi.
First Secretary (Finance): Toshiyuki Furui.
First Secretary (Political): Atsuro Sasaki.
First Secretary (Science): Nobua Fujishima.
First Secretary (Economic): Akira Kitamura.
First Secretary (Political): Michihiko Takabe.
First Secretary (Political): Mario Miyakawa.
First Secretary (Agriculture): Taiitsu Igarashi.
First Secretary (Information/Culture): Koji Haneda.
First Secretary (Political): Akihiro Kimoto.
Third Secretary (Protocol): Yasukata Fukahori.

JORDAN

Embassy: 6 Upper Phillimore Gardens, London W8 7HB; tel (71) 937-3685; telex 923187; fax (71) 937-8795.
Ambassador: Fouad Ayoub.
Counsellor: Abdullah Madadha.
Military, Naval and Air Attaché: Brig. Hamed Aref al-Rusan.
Assistant Military, Naval and Air Attaché: Lieut Col Rakan Mahmoud Qur'an.
First Secretary: Walid Rifai.
Second Secretary: Omar Bilbeisi.
Third Secretary: Hussein Obeidat.
Attaché (Administrative): Maj. Abdel Fattah Ali Zubi.
Attaché (Administrative): Capt. Nail Hwaimel Farhan al-Zaben.
Attaché (Administrative): Capt. Hikmat Abdallah Elayyan.
Attaché (Administrative): Maj. Mustafa Abdullah Salim Taranneh.
Attaché (Finance): Capt. Atef Mufleh Habahbeh.
Attaché (Finance): Capt. Yousef Mohammed Amin Hijazi.
Attaché (Finance): Capt. Ahmad Salman As'ad Qasem.
Attaché (Medical): Hani Jayousi.
Attaché (Medical): Capt. Suleiman Abdel Salam Hussein.

KENYA

High Commission: 45 Portland Place, London W1N 4AS; tel (71) 636-2371; telex 262551; fax (71) 323-6717.
High Commissioner: Simon B. Arap Bullut.
Counsellor: G. H. O. Josiah.
Counsellor: F. K. Muthaura.
Naval Adviser (Defence Procurement): Brig. J. R. Kibwana.
Defence Adviser: Col F. R. Nthiggah.
Assistant Defence Adviser: Maj. K. A. Shabell.
Attaché: Lieut P. P. M. Muturi.
First Secretary: M. O. Odengo.
Second Secretary: J. V. Awuor.
Second Secretary: P. S. Wamoto.
Second Secretary: D. K. A. Kikaya.
Third Secretary (Protocol): S. K. Maina.
Attaché (Education): P. H. Dido.
Attaché (Coffee): S. R. Onchere.
Attaché (Agriculture): C. M. Kangé.
Attaché (Commercial): C. G. Mkangi.
Attaché (Immigration): S. Mutuku.
Attaché (Finance): P. H. A. Onyuma.
Senior Information/Tourism Officer: D. N. Njau.
Information/Tourism Officer: N. G. Makori.
Legal Adviser: J. K. Kandie.

KIRIBATI

High Commision: c/o Office of the President, POB 68, Bairiki, Tarawa, Kiribati.
High Commissioner: Peter T. Timoen (acting).

Consulate: Faith House, 7 Tufton St, London SW1; tel (71) 222-6952.

KOREA, REPUBLIC

Embassy: 1-4 Palace Gate, London W8 5NF; tel (71) 581-0247; telex 919620; fax (71) 589-9134.
Ambassador: Dr Lee Hong-Koo.
Minister: Choi Keun Bae.
Minister: Hwang Kyu Woong.
Counsellor: Lee Kyung Woo.
Counsellor: Lee Sang Chul.
Counsellor: Cho Sang Hoon.
Defence Attaché: Capt. Yoon Jong-Ku.
Naval Attaché: Choi Lark Jung.
Assistant Defence Attaché: Lieut Col Ahn Sung Hwan.
Second Secretary: Oh Ho Jong.
Third Secretary: Park Hae Yun.
Third Secretary: Lee Key Cheol.
Third Secretary: Kim Jin Hyung.
Attaché (Finance): Chung Duck-Koo.
Attaché (Commercial): Kim Hyo Sung.
Attaché (Press/Cultural): Suh Byung Ho.

KUWAIT

Embassy: 45-46 Queen's Gate, London SW7; tel (71) 589-4533; telex 261017; fax (71) 589-2978.
Ambassador: Ghazi M. A. al-Rayes.
Counsellor (Cultural): Ahmed al-Duwaisan.
First Secretary: Walid al-Khobaizi.
Second Secretary: Ali Khaled al-Sabah.
Third Secretary: Abdul Rahman al-Otaibi.
Attaché: Sameeh Eissa Gohar.
Attaché: Faisal Salem al-Sabah.
Attaché (Consular): Abdul-Rahman Saleh al-Radi.
Attaché: Mohammad al-Sane.
Attaché: Yaqoub Yousef H. al-Mfarrej.
Attaché: Khalid Essa Yousuf al-Essa.
Attaché: Fahad Rashed al-Alban.
Attaché: Jawhar Abdulkareem J. al-Shatti.
Attaché (Cultural): Saud Jaffar.
Attaché: Fahd Majed S. al-Salem.
Attaché: Ali Salem al-Dawai.
Attaché: Faisal Abdulla al-Logani.
Attaché: Khalid Yousef Ali al-Khamées.
Attaché: Abdulwahab Abbas al-Haroun.

Finance Office: St Vedast House, 150 Cheapside, London EC2V 6ET; tel (71) 606-8080.
Attaché (Finance): Sheikh Fahad Mohamed al-Sabah.

Medical Office: 40 Devonshire St, London W1N 2AX; tel (71) 580-8471.
Attaché (Health): Dr Fawzia al-Sayegh.

LATVIA

Embassy: 71 Queensborough Terrace, London W2 3SP; tel (71) 727-1698; fax (71) 221-9740.
Chargé d'affaires: Marie-Anne Zarine.

LEBANON

Embassy: 21 Kensington Palace Gardens, London W8 4QM; tel (71) 229-7265; telex 262048; fax (71) 243-1699.
Ambassador: Mahmoud Hammoud.
Counsellor (Arab League): Assa'ad Moukaddem.
First Secretary: Mohammed Chebli Dib.
First Secretary: Michel Youssef el-Khoury.
Attaché: Ramez Nadim Dimechkie.

LESOTHO

High Commission: 10 Collingham Rd, London SW5 0NR; tel (71) 373-8581; telex 262955; fax (71) 835-2097.
High Commissioner: M. K. Tsekoa.
Counsellor: Peter Nau Khadi.
First Secretary: Mapiti Khabele.
Third Secretary: Moliehi Zityhali.
Attaché (Administrative): Lineo Katleho Taole.
Attaché (Administrative): Ntsivoa E. Makae.

LIBERIA

Embassy: 2 Pembridge Place, London W2 4XB; tel (71) 221-1036; telex 915463.
Minister: George Bardell Cooper.
Minister-Counsellor: Philip D. E. Gbadu.
Second Secretary, Vice-Consul and Chargé d'affaires: Rudolf P. von Ballmoos.
Attaché: Mabel L. Johnson.
Attaché (Education): Priscilla J. Birch.

LIBYA

Interests Section: c/o Embassy of Saudi Arabia, 119 Harley St, London W1; tel (71) 486-8387.
Head of Interests Section: Ahmed Omar Ameish.
Official: Isa Baruni Edaeki.

LITHUANIA

Embassy: 17 Essex Villas, Kensington, London W8 7BP; tel (71) 937-1588.
Ambassador: Vincas Bilickas (designate).
Chargé d'affaires: Kestutis Stankevicius.

LUXEMBOURG

Embassy: 27 Wilton Crescent, London SW1X 8SD; tel (71) 235-6961; telex 28120; fax (71) 235-9734.
Ambassador: Edouard Molitor.
First Secretary: Jean-Jacques Welfring.

MADAGASCAR

Consulate: 16 Lanark Mansions, Pennard Rd, London W12 8DT; tel (71) 746-0133.

MALAWI

High Commission: 33 Grosvenor St, London W1X 0DE; tel (71) 491-4172; telex 263308; fax (71) 491-9916.
High Commissioner: P. Tony S. Kandiero.
Deputy High Commissioner: Ansley Khauyeza.
Counsellor: Dr Francis Moto.
Defence Adviser: Col George Henry Binauli.
First Secretary (Administrative): Joseph Manyusa.
First Secretary (Recruitment): George B. Malunga.
Second Secretary (Administrative): H. C. R. Makawa.
Second Secretary (Consular): Davson Mackina Chikuta.
Second Secretary: Beatrice Pamela Mungomo.
Third Secretary (Administrative): Kennedy W. Nsandu.

Consulate: 17 York Rd, Edinburgh EH5 3EJ; tel (31) 552-2519.
Honorary Consul: Kenneth W. Borthwick.

MALAYSIA

High Commission: 45-46 Belgrave Sq., London SW1X 8QT; tel (71) 235-8033; telex 262550; fax (71) 235-5161.
High Commissioner: Tan Sri Wan Sidek.
Deputy High Commissioner: Ghazzali Sheik Abdul Khalid.
Minister-Counsellor: Mohamed Musa.
Minister-Counsellor: Pahamin Rajab.
Counsellor and Head of Chancery: Mohd Fauzi Yon.
Counsellor (Information): Syed Mohammed Syed Baharum.
Director and Counsellor (Education): Hamzah Haji-Abdul Rashid.
Deputy Director (Education): Hamid Ali.

Defence Adviser: Col Saidi Zakaria.
Assistant Defence Adviser: Maj. Azahar Dato Abu Bakar.
First Secretary (Administrative): Charles Sagayam.
First Secretary: Shahirir Ramlan Zainuddin.
First Secretary: May Yong Ho.
Second Secretary: Mohd Hamdan Hassan.
Third Secretary (Consular): Zainul Zainuddin.
Senior Trade Commissioner: Bahar Bin Ahmad.
Trade Commissioner (Commodities): Abdul Hanan Alang Endut.
Trade Commissioner (Investment): Subramaniam Senivasagam.
Attaché (Administrative): Kamaruzaman Bin Haji Othman.
Attaché (Immigration): Shamsul Kamar Ahmad Tajudin.

MALTA

High Commission: 16 Kensington Sq., London W8 5HH; tel (71) 938-1712; telex 261102; fax (71) 937-8664.
High Commissioner: Salv Stellini.
Counsellor: Victor Sant.
Counsellor: Vincent Sladden.
First Secretary: Carmel M. Mifsud.
First Secretary: Victor Pace.
First Secretary: Constantine Muscat.
Second Secretary: George Cushieri.
Third Secretary: Christopher Grima.

Consulate: 139, Old Dalkeith Rd, Little France, Edinburgh EH16 4SZ; tel (31) 664-1070.
Honorary Consul: George A. Hunter.

MAURITIUS

High Commission: 32-33 Elvaston Place, London SW7 5NW; tel (71) 581-0294; telex 917772; fax (71) 823-8437.
High Commissioner: Dr Boodhun Teelock.
Deputy High Commissioner: Bye Muslim Dilmahamood.
First Secretary: Gajamooghen Thancanamootoo.
Second Secretary: Sohun Ghoorah.
Second Secretary: Satyavatee Ramdoyal.
Attaché (Finance): Keswar Dooraree.
Attaché: Tecknarainsing Purmah.

MEXICO

Embassy: 8 Halkin St, London SW1X 7DW; tel (71) 235-6393; telex 918276; fax (71) 235-5480.
Ambassador: Bernardo Sepúlveda.
Minister: Eduardo Martínez-Curiel.
Minister (Consular): Martin Brito.
Minister (Cultural): Raul Ortiz y Ortiz.
Counsellor (Multilateral Affairs): Leandro Arellano.
Counsellor (Economic): Enrique Alduncin.
Counsellor (Communication/Transport): Ing. Pedro Velazquez.
Counsellor: Manuel de Araoz.
Military Attaché: Maj.-Gen. Juan Manuel Wonchee-Montaño.
Assistant Military Attaché: Lieut Col Rosendo Alfonso Gallardo-Olson.
Assistant Military Attaché: Maj. Victor Manuel Esparza-Ortega.
Naval Attaché: Adm. Tomáas Ortega-Bertrand.
Assistant Naval Attaché: Rear-Adm. Ruben de la Riva Deralta.
First Secretary (Political): José Luis Vivanco.
Third Secretary (Cultural): Elena Uribe de Wood.
Third Secretary (Economic): Agustin García-López.
Attaché (Press): José Ignacio Madrazo.
Attaché (Administrative): Sergio Pérez-Pensado.

Information, Tourism, Commercial and Coffee Sections: 60-1 Trafalgar Sq., London WC2N 5DS; tel (71) 734-1058.
Counsellor (Information/Tourism): Alicia Cazorla de Eckbo.
Counsellor (Commercial): Lic. Augustin R. García-Villa.
Counsellor (Coffee): Lic. Jorge Ortega.

Finance Section: 99 Bishopsgate, 17th Floor, London EC2P 2LA; tel (71) 628-0016.
Counsellor (Finance): Federico Patino.

MONGOLIA

Embassy: 7 Kensington Court, London W8 5DL; tel (71) 937-0150; fax (71) 137-1117.
Ambassador: Choisuregyn Baatar.
Attaché: Davaadelger Luvsanrentsengiin.
Attaché (Commercial): Galsandorj Damba.
Attaché (Cultural): Bazarhand Balchigiin.

MOROCCO

Embassy: 49 Queen's Gate Gardens, London SW7 5NE; tel (71) 581-5001; telex 28389; fax (71) 225-3862.
Ambassador: Khalil Haddaoui.
Counsellor and Chargé d'affaires: Kamal Faqir.
Military, Naval and Air Attaché: Col Mustapha Jabrane.
Counsellor (Political): Mohamed Allam.
Counsellor: Ahmed Ben Abdennebi.
Counsellor (Economic): Ahmed Faouzi.
Counsellor (Social Affairs): Abdelhak Korri.
First Secretary: Latifa Belkhayat Zoukkari.
First Secretary: Abdel Ilah Bennis.
Secretary (Press): Said Safi.
Secretary (Consular): Ahmed Lasfar.
Attaché (Information/Tourism): Hassane Benlamlih.

MOZAMBIQUE

Embassy: 21 Fitzroy Sq., London W1; tel (71) 388-8878; telex 342681; fax (71) 383-3801.
Ambassador: Lieut Gen. Armando Panguene.
Second Secretary (Consular): Maximiano Maxhaeia.
Attaché (Administrative): Chico Vasco Francisco Ferramenta Mendonca.
Attaché (Finance): Samuel Gabriel Monjane.

MYANMAR

Embassy: 19A Charles St, Berkeley Sq., London W1X 8ER; tel (71) 629-9531; telex 267609; fax (71) 629-4169.
Counsellor and Chargé d'affaires a.i.: U Zaw Wynn.
Military, Naval and Air Attaché: Col Tin Oo.
Second Secretary: U Myint Soe.
Third Secretary: U Kyaw Swe Tint.

NAMIBIA

High Commission: Centre Link, 34 South Molton St, London W1Y 2BP; tel (71) 408-2333; fax (71) 495-6157.
High Commissioner: Veiccoh K. Nghiwete.
Deputy High Commissioner and Minister-Counsellor: Pandeleni Shingenge.
First Secretary (Political): Linda A. Scott.
Second Secretary: Anne Zambwe.

NAURU

Consulate: 3 Chesham St, London SW1X 8MD; tel (71) 235-6911; fax (71) 235-7423.
Representative: Martin Weston.

NEPAL

Embassy: 12A Kensington Palace Gardens, London W8 4QU; tel (71) 229-1594; telex 261072; fax (71) 792-9861.
Ambassador: Maj.-Gen. Bharat K. Simha.
First Secretary: Badri Prasad Khanal.
Military Attaché: Lieut Col Lili Jung Gurung.
Attaché: Keshab Thaku.
Attaché: Baikuntha Prasad Ariyal.
Attaché: Rameshwor Paudel.
Attaché: Ghanashyam Lall Joshi.

NETHERLANDS

Embassy: 38 Hyde Park Gate, London SW7 5DP; tel (71) 584-5040; telex 28812; fax (71) 581-3450.
Ambassador: Joop B. Hoekman.
Minister: Edward J. P. Roberts.
Minister: Adriaan Quanjer.
Counsellor (Consular): Georgius J. Schulten.
Counsellor (Press/Culture): Ton Hamoen.
Counsellor: Harmen W. de Boer.
Counsellor: Albert E. Moses.
Defence, Naval and Air Attaché: Capt. Fred van Leeuwen.
Military Attaché: Col Ger Soetermeer.
Assistant to Naval and Air Attaché: Commdr Okko G. W. Tieleman.
First Secretary (Finance): Robert G. de Vos.
First Secretary: Paul A. Menkveld.
First Secretary: Onno D. Kervers.
Second Secretary (Administrative): W. M. van Gennip.
Second Secretary (Consular): Berend Willem Schortinghuis.
Third Secretary (Press/Culture): Henry Kol.
Attaché (Agriculture): Carel J. Heringa.

Consulate: 40 Great Charles St, Queensway, Birmingham B3 2AR; tel (21) 233-1021; fax (21) 200-1548.
Honorary Consul: P. E. Richardson.

Consulate: Euroatlantic Shipping Services Ltd, Havenhouse, Albemarle St, Harwich CO1 23HL; tel (255) 506666; telex 98476.
Honorary Consul: R. A. Coolen.

Consulate: 'Crowle House', 41 High St, Hull HU1 1RJ; tel (482) 224911; telex 592216; fax (482) 224914.
Honorary Consul: T. A. W. Kettlewell.

Consulate: Brown, Geveke and Co. Ltd, Richmond House, Rumford Pl., Liverpool L3 9RT; tel (51) 227-5161; telex 629148; fax (51) 236-3048.
Honorary Consul: A. C. O'Donnell.

Consulate: 41 Spring Gardens, Manchester M2 2BB; tel (61) 832-7290; telex 669489.
Honorary Consul: S. P. Green.

Consulate: c/o Williamson and Co. Solicitors, Williamson House, 63 High Bridge, Newcastle upon Tyne NE1 1DU; tel (91) 261-1431; telex 53440; fax (91) 261-7099.
Honorary Consul: N. Thom.

Consulate: c/o Union Castle House, 100 Canute Road, Southampton SO1 1AG; tel (703) 635211; telex 47444; fax (703) 637215.
Honorary Consul: J. T. Bennet.

Consulate: 18 Grenville St, St Helier, Jersey; tel (534) 74343; telex 192064.
Honorary Consul: R. R. Jeune.

Consulate: 'The Dock', Boston PE21 6BL; tel (205) 62261; telex 37633.
Honorary Vice-Consul: C. L. Butler.

Consulate: c/o Lovell Hodder Whitwill Ltd, Avonmouth Dock, Avonmouth, Bristol BS11 9BH; tel (272) 823251; telex 44168; fax (272) 826272.
Honorary Vice-Consul: M. H. Hazzard.

Consulate: Hammond House, Limekiln St, Dover CT17 9EE; tel (304) 201201; telex 96115; fax (304) 240374.
Honorary Vice-Consul: J. G. Ryeland.

Consulate: 48 Arwenack St, Falmouth TR11 3SA; tel (326) 311300; telex 45237; fax (326) 317913.
Honorary Vice-Consul: P. H. Fox.

Consulate: South Coast UK Ltd, The Docks, Fowey PL23 1AL; tel (726) 833474; telex 45215; fax (726) 833474.
Honorary Vice-Consul: J. A. Samuel.

Consulate: 21/5 Aire St, Goole DN14 5RE; tel (405) 762262; telex 57609; fax (405) 764840.
Honorary Vice-Consul: J. J. Kettlewell.

Consulate: Europa House, 40 South Quay, Great Yarmouth NR30 2RL; tel (493) 856831; telex 97188; fax (493) 857533.
Honorary Vice-Consul: M. J. Brooks.

Consulate: c/o Merchant Marine Shipping Ltd, Enterprise House, Middleplat Rd, Immingham DN40 1AH; tel (469) 571660; telex 527930; fax (469) 571653.
Honorary Vice-Consul: D. E. Emery.

Consulate: c/o Kenneth Bush and Co., 11 New Conduit St, King's Lynn PE30 1DG; tel (553) 692233; fax (553) 767318.
Honorary Vice-Consul: D. W. Hume.

Consulate: Walker Morris Scott Turnbull Solicitors, St Andrew House, 119-21 The Headrow, Leeds LS1 5NP; tel (532) 340795; telex 557455; fax (532) 435483.
Honorary Vice-Consul: C. S. Caisley.

Consulate: 66 Commercial Rd, Lerwick, Shetland ZE1 0JD; tel (595) 2533; telex 75295; fax (595) 2781.
Honorary Vice-Consul: C. R. Duncan.

Consulate: York House, Borough Rd, Middlesbrough TS1 2HP; tel (642) 243231; telex 58502; fax (642) 223957.
Honorary Vice-Consul: J. D. Cryan.

Consulate: 72 Market Jew St, Penzance TR18 2LF; tel (736) 69988; telex 45530.
Honorary Vice-Consul: C. G. B. Bennetts.

Consulate: c/o W. D. Tamlyn and Co. Ltd, Victoria Wharves, Coxside, Plymouth PL4 0RF; tel (752) 663444; telex 45247.
Honorary Vice-Consul: B. J. W. Ellison.

Consulate: 'Norman Piette Ltd', Bulwer Ave, POB 88, St Sampsons, Guernsey; tel (481) 45801; telex 4191107; fax (481) 48542.
Honorary Vice-Consul: G. J. Norman.

Consulate: Taylors Solicitors, The Red Brick House, Tripped Lane, Sheffield S1 4EL; tel (742) 766767; fax (742) 731287.
Honorary Vice-Consul: A. M. Brownlow.

Consulate: 44 Lowther St, Whitehaven CA28 7JU; tel (946) 692453; telex 64488.
Honorary Vice-Consul: H. W. Parry-Jones.

Consulate: Standard Bldgs, 102 Hope St, Glasgow G2 6PW; tel (41) 221-0605; telex 777881; fax (41) 221-4198.
Honorary Consul: W. M. Spence.

Consulate: 16 Union Terrace, Aberdeen AB1 2NJ; tel (224) 639106; telex 739342.
Honorary Consul: D. M. Grant.

Consulate: 26 East Dock St, POB 50, Dundee DD1 9HY; tel (382) 203111; telex 76135; fax (382) 200575.
Honorary Consul: A. D. Chalmers.

Consulate: 10 George St, Edinburgh EH2 2YH; tel (31) 225-8494; telex 727128; fax (31) 225-3142.
Vice-Consul: T. Macgill.

Consulate: 21 Bridge St, POB 2, Kirkwall, Orkney KW15 1HR; tel (856) 2268; fax (856) 5002.
Honorary Vice-Consul: J. W. Spence.

Consulate: Wavency Chambers, Lowestoft NR32 1BP; tel (502) 572301; telex 97319; fax (502) 515915.
Honorary Vice-Consul: T. J. Spurrier.

Consulate: Idwal Williams and Co. Ltd, 113-6 Bute St, Cardiff CF1 6TE; tel (222) 488636; telex 498527.
Honorary Consul: D. I. Williams.

Consulate: British Enkalon Pensions Ltd, 25 Randalstown Rd, Antrim BT41 4LJ; tel (8494) 63535; telex 74667; fax (8494) 63535.
Honorary Consul: I. R. L. Schierbeek.

NEW ZEALAND

High Commission: New Zealand House, Haymarket, London SW1Y 4TQ; tel (71) 930-8422; telex 24368; fax (71) 839-4580.
High Commissioner: George Frederick Gair.
Deputy High Commissioner: John Larkindale.
Counsellor (Economic): John Whitehead.
Counsellor: Vic Wilkinson.
Counsellor: Noel Parker.
Defence and Naval Adviser: Cdre J. G. Leonard.
Assistant Defence Adviser: Commdr K. G. Black.
Assistant Defence Adviser: Wing Commdr P. J. Lacey.
Senior Defence Purchasing Officer and Assistant Defence Adviser: Lieut Col T. O'Reilly.
Second Secretary (Economic): David Walker.
Senior Trade Commissioner: Don Walker.
Trade Commissioner: Alison Fraser.
Tourism Director: Anthony Sturrock.
Chief Migration Officer: Joan Wiltshire.
Immigration Officer: Elizabeth Egan.

NICARAGUA

Embassy: 8 Gloucester Rd, London SW7 4PP; tel (71) 584-4365; telex 269895; fax (71) 823-8790.
Ambassador: Roberto Parrales.

NIGERIA

High Commission: Nigeria House, 9 Northumberland Ave, London WC2N 5BX; tel (71) 839-1244; telex 916814; fax (71) 839-8746.
High Commissioner: George Dove-Edwin.
Deputy High Commissioner: Prof. A. I. Adefuye.
Minister-Counsellor: S. A. Ibi.
Minister-Counsellor: M. U. Mohammed.
Minister-Counsellor: B. S. Ilochi.
Minister-Counsellor: E. F. Udoeyop.
Minister-Counsellor: M. D. Yahya.
Counsellor: I. Abubakar.
Counsellor: R. A. Fatunase.
Counsellor: T. Y. Opantola.
Counsellor: P. J. E. Anegbeh.
Counsellor: A. A. Ahmed.
Counsellor: Dr O. J. Alimole.
Counsellor (Administrative): A. Coker.
Counsellor (Administrative): L. M. Dustin-Ma.
Defence Adviser: Col D. Mohammed.
Deputy Defence Adviser (Navy): Commdr J. M. Ajayi.
Deputy Defence Adviser (Navy): Capt. V. K. Ombu.
Deputy Defence Adviser (Army): Lieut Col G. A. Kpamber.
Deputy Defence Adviser (Army): Lieut Col D. O. Iketubosin.
Deputy Defence Adviser (Finance): Lieut Col S. U. Umusu.
Deputy Defence Adviser (Air): Wing Commdr S. E. Hedima.
First Secretary: A. C. Uzoka-Emejulu.
First Secretary: A. A. Musa.
First Secretary: A. R. L. Jacks.
Attaché (Education): Dr S. A. Adetoro.
Attaché (Education): S. B. Idris.
Attaché (Immigration): H. A. Mahuta.
Attaché (Immigration): P. E. Nkereuwem.
Attaché (Information): L. K. Aridegbe.
Attaché (Commercial): C. R. Ezeokafor.
Attaché (Commercial): M. T. Adamu.

NORWAY

Embassy: 25 Belgrave Sq., London SW1X 8QD; tel (71) 235-7151; telex 22321; fax (71) 245-6993.
Ambassador: Kjell Eliassen.
Counsellor (Press/Cultural): Paul Moe.
Counsellor (Commercial): Viggo Smestad.
Counsellor (Financial): Eva Bugge.
Counsellor (Fisheries/Agriculture): Marius Hauge.
Defence Attaché: Lieut Col Lars Harald Finstad.
Assistant Defence Attaché: Maj. Hans Erling Støvern.
First Secretary (Consular): Wenche Kirkebye.
First Secretary (Political): Rune Aasheim.
First Secretary (Commercial): Erik Berge Wiken.
Second Secretary (Financial): Leif Ingar Engesaeth.
Second Secretary (Press/Cultural/Information): Katja Christina Nordgaard.
Special Adviser (Fisheries): Semund Remøy.

Consulate: A. Straume UK Ltd, Cumberland House, Greenside Lane, Bradford BD8 9TE; tel (274) 491192; telex 51211.
Consul: Arnfinn Straume.

Consulate: Portview Rd, Avonmouth, Bristol BS11 9YX; tel (272) 825081; telex 44129; fax (272) 822912.
Consul: Brian Fletcher.

Consulate: Empire House, Mount Stuart Sq., Cardiff CF1 6QT; tel (222) 488111; telex 498322; fax (222) 491130.
Consul: Mervyn Ralph Pritchard.

Consulate: c/o EIC Ltd, M62 Trading Estate, Rawcliffe Rd, Goole DN14 8JW; tel (405) 720620; telex 57629; fax (405) 765441.
Consul: Robin Leaper Fenton.

Consulate: c/o Bahr Behrend and Co. Ltd, 470 India Bldg, 4th Floor, Water St, POB 28, Liverpool L69 2BW; tel (51) 236-4871; telex 629234; fax (51) 236-1126.

Consulate: Heron House, 2nd Floor, Albert Sq., Manchester M2 5HD; tel (61) 832-8290; telex 667235; fax (61) 832-6042.
Consul: R. Michael Hammond.

Consulate: York House, Borough Rd, Middlesbrough TS1 2HP; tel (642) 243231; telex 58502.
Consul: Joseph Desmond Cryan.

Consulate: Murray Crescent House, The Rath, Milford Haven SA73 3JR; tel (646) 692313; telex 48213; fax (646) 692706.
Consul: Roy Plummer.

Consulate: 2 Collingwood St, Newcastle-upon-Tyne NE1 1JH; tel (91) 232-6358; telex 537955; fax (91) 261-4761.
Consul: Nigel Alistair Westwood.

Consulate: Pearl Assurance House, Friar Lane, Nottingham NG1 6BX; tel (602) 476651; telex 37234; fax (602) 475244.
Consul: Geoffrey Charles Bond.

Consulate: 'Chittleburn View', Nettle Hayes, Sherford Rd, Elburton, Plymouth PL9 8BU; tel (752) 401167; telex 45225; fax (752) 263572.
Consul: Leonard Henry James Underwood.

Consulate: 28 Queens Terrace, Southampton SO9 2UJ; tel (703) 223555; telex 47554; fax (703) 228087.
Consul: George Alan Haswell.

Consulate: 22 Wide Bargate, Boston PE21 6HGH; tel (205) 310444; telex 37509; fax (205) 310500.
Vice-Consul: John Bryan Woodcock.

Consulate: Hammond House, Limekiln St, Dover CT17 9EE; tel (304) 201201; telex 96115; fax (304) 240374.

Vice-Consul: David C. Ryeland.

Consulate: 48 Arwenck St, Falmouth TR11; tel (326) 311300; telex 45237; fax (326) 317913.
Vice-Consul: Philip Hamilton Fox.

Consulate: Powell Duffryn House, Dock Estate, Felixstowe IP11 8RP; tel (394) 674822; telex 98434; fax (394) 673740.
Vice-Consul: William Ewart Gladstone Walton.

Consulate: Waveney Chambers, Waveney Rd, Lowestoft NR32 1BP; tel (502) 572301; telex 97319; fax (502) 515915.
Vice-Consul: Timothy Hall.

Consulate: Basin Rd South, Portslade, Brighton BN4 1WN; (273) 421010; telex 877168; fax (273) 421335.
Vice-Consul: John E. White.

Consulate-General: 86 George St, Edinburgh EH2 3BU; tel (31) 226-5701; telex 727904; fax (31) 220-4976.
Consul-General: Gustav Nikolai Skeie.
Vice-Consul: Per Aksel Karlsson.

Consulate: 59 Marischal St, Aberdeen AB9 8AZ; tel (224) 589921; telex 73134; fax (224) 574410.
Consul: Daniel Gardner Rigden Stroud.

Consulate: Inter City House, 80 Oswald St, Glasgow G1 4PX; tel (41) 204-1353; fax (41) 248-5647.
Consul: Sir Ian John Ferguson Denholm.

Consulate: 84 St Olav St, Lerwick, Shetland ZE1 0ES; tel (595) 2556; telex 5949.
Consul: Frank Garriock (acting).

Consulate: 21 Bridge St, POB 2, Kirkwall, Orkney KW15 1HR; tel (856) 2268; telex 75253; fax (856) 5002.
Consul: James William Spence.

Consulate: Sandwick Rd, Stornoway, Isle of Lewis PA87 2SL; tel (851) 2303.
Consul: Charles Alexander Schau Engebretsen.

Consulate: Winton Bldgs, Ardrossan KA22 8BY; tel (294) 605284; telex 779814; fax (294) 601081.
Vice-Consul: Christopher John Montgomerie Alpine Mair.

Consulate: 49 Meadowside, Dundee DD1 1EH; tel (382) 23044; telex 76177; fax (382) 201383.
Vice-Consul: David Hillocks Paterson.

Consulate: South Side, Western Channel, Grangemouth Docks, POB 11, Grangemouth FK3 9AB; tel (324) 482801; telex 77103.
Vice-Consul: Lawrence Kidd.

Consulate: 54 Broad St, Peterhead AB42 6BX; tel (779) 70638; telex 73114; fax (779) 70638.
Vice-Consul: George Cruickshank Stephen.

Consulate: 22 Bridge St, Wick KW1 4NG; tel (955) 2442.
Vice-Consul: Thomas Paterson Buick.

Consulate: Hurst House, 15-19 Corporation Sq., Belfast BT1 3AJ; tel (232) 242242; telex 74682; fax (232) 235776.
Consul: Michael Francis Ewings.

Consulate: 'Nordben', Harbour House, South Esplanade, St Peter Port, Guernsey; tel (481) 710661; fax (481) 710719.
Consul: Flemming Møller.

Consulate: Petit Bois, La Blinerie Lane, Samares, St Clement, Jersey; (534) 30175; fax (534) 36508.
Consul: Sten Arild Adeler.

OMAN

Embassy: 44A-44B Montpelier Sq., London SW7 1JJ; tel (71) 584-6782; telex 918775; fax (71) 225-0339.
Ambassador: Abdulla Mohamed al-Dhahab.
Counsellor (Economic): Ghassan Ibrahim Shaker.
Counsellor: Dr Omar Zawawi.
Counsellor: Brig. James Timothy Whittington Landon.
Counsellor: Sated Qais bin Tarik al-Said.
Defence Attaché: Salim Hilal Mohammed al-Barwani.
Assistant Military Attaché: Sqn Ldr Ali Abdullah Rashid al-Shukaily.
First Secretary: Mahmood Mohamed Morad al-Raeesy.
First Secretary: Mohamed Ahmed al-Sabaah.
Second Secretary: Ali Abdullah Salim al-Mahrooqi.
Second Secretary: Khalifa Ali Essa al-Harthy.
Second Secretary: Saleh Mohammed Saleh al-Yafaey.
Attaché (Cultural): Abdulla Omar Ahmed.
Attaché (Health): Mohammed Nasser Hamed al-Hinai.

PAKISTAN

High Commission: 34-35 and 39 Lowndes Sq., London SW1X 9JN; tel (71) 235-2044; telex 912783.
High Commissioner: Dr Humayun Khan.
Minister: Khalid Mahmood Shafi.
Minister (Information): Col Mohammad Ismail Khan.
Minister (Medical Liaison Officer): Prof. Nek Mohammed Shaikh.
Counsellor (Commercial): Mohammed Akran Malik.
Counsellor: Mohammad Yousaf Ali.
Counsellor: Azhar Ali Shah.
Counsellor (Legal): Zahid M. Murad.
Counsellor (Education): Dr Mohammad Latif Virk.
Counsellor: Nazir Hussain.
Defence and Army Adviser: Brig. Saeed Ismat.
Naval Adviser: Capt. Sadeed Anver Malik.
Air Adviser: Group Capt. Salim Arshad.
Army Technical Liaison Officer: Col Ghulam Shabbir.
Attaché (Defence Procurement): Commdr Syed Khalid Ali Anwar.
First Secretary: Khurshid Anwar.
First Secretary (Protocol): Muhammad Mahmud.
Second Secretary (Press): Shafiq Zaman.
Attaché (Technical): Faiz Ahmad.
Attaché (Community Welfare): Muhammad Bilal.
Attaché (Welfare): Abdul Rahim Khan.

PANAMA

Embassy: 119 Crawford St, London W1H 1AF; tel (71) 487-5633; telex 8812982; fax (71) 583-0008.
Ambassador and Consul-General: Teodoro F. Franco.
Counsellor (Commercial) and Consul: Eduardo Ernesto Neira.
Counsellor (Commercial/Financial): Salim Kheireddine.
Counsellor (Finance): Eusebio A. Morales.
Attaché (Maritime): Geronimo E. de Obaldia.
Attaché: Marina R. Lewis.

Consulate-General: 24 Tudor St, London EC4Y 0AY; tel (71) 353-4792.

Consulate-General: 42 Stanley St, Liverpool L1 6AL; tel (51) 236-4816.
Consul-General: Gladys E. M. Tufnell.

PAPUA NEW GUINEA

High Commission: 3rd Floor, 14 Waterloo Place, London SW1Y 4AR; tel (71) 930-0922; telex 25827; fax (71) 930-0828.
High Commissioner: Noel Levi.
Counsellor: David Famundi Anggo.
Third Secretary (Administrative): Julie P. Onno.

PARAGUAY

Embassy: Braemar Lodge, Cornwall Gardens, London SW7 4AQ; tel (71) 937-1253; fax (71) 937-5687.
Ambassador: Antonio Espinoza.
First Secretary: G. S. de Jauregui.
First Officer (Consular): T. M. de Castille.

PERU

Embassy: 52 Sloane St, London SW1X 9SP; tel (71) 235-1917; telex 917888; fax (71) 235-4463.
Ambassador: Felipe Valdivieso-Belaúnde.
Minister (Consular): Irma Alicia Fassioli.
Minister (Culture): Carlos Zavaleta.
Minister: Gilbert Chauny.
Counsellor: Julio Jorge Florian.
Naval Attaché: Capt. Juan Francisco Garfias.
First Secretary: Luis Arribasplata.
Second Secretary: María Elvira Velásquez.
Second Secretary: José Ignacio Mariátegui.
Economic/Financial Adviser: Adhemar Montagne.

Office of the Air Attaché: 41 Sloane Street, London SW1; tel (71) 235-9826.
Air Attaché: Col Hernán Fidel Ampuero.
Assistant Air Attaché: Col Fausto Guerra.

PHILIPPINES

Embassy: 9A Palace Green, Kensington, London W8 4QE; tel (71) 937-1600; telex 24411; fax (71) 937-2925.
Ambassador: Manuel T. Yan.
Deputy Head of Mission and Consul-General: Edmundo Libid.
Minister-Counsellor: Estrella A. Berenguel.
Military Attaché: Capt. Augusto Enriquez.
First Secretary: Ernesto Castro.
Second Secretary and Consul: Narciso T. Castañeda.
Attaché: Julieta Posados.
Attaché: Dominga Mahor.
Attaché: Numeriano Aguinaldo.
Attaché: Milagros Agustines.
Attaché: Conrado Paule.
Attaché: Thelma Buenaventura.
Attaché: Fanny Tirol.
Attaché (Commercial): Saleda Ileto.
Attaché: Eduardo Jarque.

POLAND

Embassy: 47 Portland Pl., London W1N 3AG; tel (71) 580-4324; telex 265691; fax (71) 323-4018.
Ambassador: Tadeusz de Virion.
Minister and Counsellor (Commercial): Romauld Szuniewicz.
Minister and Chargé d'affaires: Zdzislaw Rapacki.
Counsellor: Janusz Zwierzchowski.
Counsellor (Culture): Karol Drozd.
Counsellor: Leslaw Zapalowski.
Counsellor: Tadeusz Szumowski.
Counsellor (Maritime): Piotr Jedrzejowicz.
Military, Naval and Air Attaché: Col Kazimierz Cukierski.
Assistant Military, Naval and Air Attaché: Lieut Col Jerzy Szubert.
Assistant Military, Naval and Air Attaché: Lieut Col Jerzy Bednarski.
First Secretary: Janusz Dluzynski.
First Secretary: Wlodzimierz Chraniuk.
First Secretary: Krzysztof Jan Jakubowski.
First Secretary: Barbara Koscielny.
First Secretary: Zbigniew Prochot.
Deputy Finance Attaché: Zofia Skowronska.
Deputy Economic Attaché: Leszek Witold Fabisiak.

Consulate-General: 19 Weymouth St, London W1N 3AG; tel (71) 580-0476; fax (71) 323-2320.
Consul-General: Janusz Kochanowski.

Consulate-General: 2 Kinner Rd, Edinburgh EH3 5PE; tel (31) 552-0301.
Consul-General: Pawel Dobrowolski.

PORTUGAL

Embassy: 11 Belgrave Sq., London SW1X 8PP; tel (71) 235-5331; telex 28484; fax (71) 245-1287.
Ambassador: António Vaz-Pereira.
Minister-Counsellor: Francisco Seixas Costa.
Counsellor (Press): Rui Correia Knopfli.
Counsellor (Culture): Eugenio Lisboa.
Counsellor (Commercial): João Alves Pereira.
Counsellor (Information/Tourism): João Serras Pereira.
Defence, Military and Air Attaché: Col Albano Nogueira Fernandes.
Naval Attaché: Commdr João Pires Neves.
Second Secretary: Antonio Almeida Lima.
Third Secretary: Jorge Torres Pereira.

Consulate-General: Silver City House, 62 Brompton Rd, London SW3 1BJ; tel (71) 581-8722; fax (71) 581-3088.
Consul-General: Duarte Ramalho Ortiga.

QATAR

Embassy: 27 Chesham Place, London SW1X 8HG; tel (71) 235-0851; telex 28469; fax (71) 235-7584.
Ambassador: Abdulrahman Abdulla al-Wohaibi.
Minister: Yousef A. Bobensheat al-Subeai.
Counsellor (Cultural): Mohammed Saleh al-Mannai.
Counsellor: Saqr Mubarak al-Mansouri.
First Secretary: Ibrahim Abdul Aziz Mohamed al-Sahlawi.
First Secretary: Sheikh Fahad bin Mohamed bin Jaber al-Thani.
First Secretary: Abdulhameed Mubarka Khalifa al-Kubaisi.
Second Secretary: Ibrahim Yousef Fakhroo.
Attaché (Press): Leila Fanous.
Attaché (Medical): Khamis Hassan Khamis al-Sulaity.
Assistant Attaché (Medical): Ali Abdulla Saleh al-Humaidi.

ROMANIA

Embassy: 4 Palace Green, London W8 4QD; tel (71) 937-9666; telex 22232; fax (71) 937-8069.
Ambassador: Sergiu Celac.
Minister-Counsellor: Dr Nicu Bujor.
Minister-Counsellor: Valeriu Matache.
Counsellor: Constantin Ghirda.
Counsellor: Gheorghe Duta.
Military, Naval and Air Attaché: Lieut Col Gheorghe Rotaru.
First Secretary: Alexandru Purcea.
First Secretary: Alexandru Puscarciuc.
Second Secretary: Ovidiu Liviu Iancu.
Attaché: Ana Maria Coroianu.

RUSSIA

Embassy: 5-13/16 Kensington Palace Gardens, London W8 4QX; tel (71) 229-3628; telex 261420; fax (71) 727-8625.
Ambassador: Boris Pankin.
Minister-Counsellor: Vladimir V. Ivanov.
Counsellor: Vladimir N. Khanjenkov.
Counsellor: Lev A. Parchine.
Counsellor: Alexei L. Nikiforov.
Counsellor: Kirill Ivanov.
Counsellor: Yuri D. Shevelev.
Counsellor: Gennady I. Fedosov.
Counsellor: Sergei F. Reprintsev.
Counsellor: Valentin F. Fomichev.
Counsellor: Grigory B. Karasin.
Counsellor: Alexander Ivanov-Galitsyn.
Military Attaché: Col Victor I. Kozlov.
Assistant Military Attaché: Lieut Col Yuri K. Yelyutin.
Naval Attaché: Vladimir Kvasov.
Assistant Naval Attaché: Capt. Mikhail G. Zhiltsov.
Assistant Air Attaché: Col Nikolai L. Kolodin.
Assistant Air Attaché: Lieut Col Yevgeny A. Smirnov.
Assistant Air Attaché: Lieut Col Dronov.
First Secretary: Alexandre F. Smaguin.
First Secretary: Nikolai N. Kossov.
First Secretary: Vladimir N. Slavin.
First Secretary: Mikhail N. Polyakov.
First Secretary: Anatoly A. Danilitsky.
First Secretary: Igor M. Kuzmin.

Office of Trade Representative and Agricultural Attaché: 33 Highgate West Hill, London N6; tel (71) 340-3272.
Trade Representative: Stanislav Maslov.
Attaché (Agriculture): Nikolai Z. Jiltsov.

SAINT CHRISTOPHER AND NEVIS

High Commission: 10 Kensington Court, London W8 5DL; tel (71) 937-9522; telex 913047; fax (71) 937-5514.
High Commissioner: Richard Gunn.
Deputy High Commissioner: Edwin Laurent.
First Secretary (Political): Civilia Omelda Dasent.
First Secretary (Consular/Legal): Cenio Elwin Lewis.
Attaché (Trade): Bernard Cornibert.
Third Secretary: Maria Cadet.

SAINT LUCIA

High Commission: 10 Kensington Court, London W8 5DL; tel (71) 937-9522; telex 913047; fax (71) 937-5514.
High Commissioner: Richard Gunn.
Deputy High Commissioner: Edwin Laurent.
First Secretary (Political): Civilia Omelda Dasent.
First Secretary (Consular/Legal): Cenio Elwin Lewis.
Attaché (Trade): Bernard Cornibert.
Third Secretary: Maria Cadet.

SAINT VINCENT AND THE GRENADINES

High Commission: 10 Kensington Court, London W8 5DL; tel (71) 937-9522; telex 913047; fax (71) 937-5514.
High Commissioner: Richard Gunn.
Deputy High Commissioner: Edwin Laurent.
First Secretary (Political): Civilia Omelda Dasent.
First Secretary (Consular/Legal): Cenio Elwin Lewis.
Attaché (Trade): Bernard Cornibert.
Third Secretary: Maria Cadet.

SAN MARINO

Consulate-General: 166 High Holborn, London WC1 6TT; tel (71) 836-7744; telex 264678; fax (71) 240993.
Consul-General: Charles Forte.

SÃO TOMÉ AND PRÍNCIPE

Consulate: 42 North Audley St, London W1A 4PY; tel (71) 499-1995.
Honorary Consul: William Wilder.

SAUDI ARABIA

Embassy: 29-30 Belgrave Sq., London SW1X 8QB; tel (71) 235-0831; telex 918080.
Ambassador: (vacant).
Minister: Ibrahim Mohammed Mosly.
Minister: Saud Ahmed M. Alyahya.
Minister: Abdullah O. Barry.
Counsellor (Islamic Affairs): Dr Ali Abdullah Mughram al-Ghamdi.
Counsellor: Mushtaq Marouf.
Counsellor: Abdullah Ibrahim Ashour al-Jhani.
Defence Attaché: Col Abdulmohsen Hamad al-Bassam.
Naval Attaché: Maj. Abdullah Mohammed Abdullah al-Fozan.
Assistant Defence Attaché (Administrative): Saeed M. A. Kahtani.
First Secretary: Ahmed Mohammed Alzoghaibi.
First Secretary: Ibrahim Abdulaziz al-Kuhaimi.
Second Secretary: Abdullah Ahmed Hamed al-Ghamdi.
Second Secretary: Mohammed I. al-Moghrabi.
Second Secretary: Talal M. S. Abdulsalam.
Second Secretary: Nabil Mohammed Abdul Rahman al-Saleh.
Second Secretary: Mitla Shalah al-Otaibi.
Attaché (Commercial): Saleh A. al-Shibani.
Attaché (Information): Mohammed Ahmed Mohammed Sobaihi.
Attaché (Cultural): Abdullah Mohammed al-Nasser.
Attaché (Administrative): Tamin Taher Radwan.
Attaché (Islamic Affairs): Hmad Abdullah al-Majed.
Assistant Attaché (Islamic Affairs): Mohammed Abdullah Sindi.

Economic Section: Liscarton House, 2nd Floor, 127 Sloane St, London SW1; tel (71) 730-8657.
First Secretary (Economic): Talal M. S. Abdulrahman Daous.

Medical Section: 119 Harley St, London W1; tel (71) 935-9931.
Counsellor (Medical): Dr Mohammad Salah Addin Khater.
Attaché (Medical): Dr Hussein K. Khogah.

SENEGAL

Embassy: 11 Phillimore Gardens, London W8 7QG; tel (71) 937-0925; telex 917119; fax (71) 937-8130.
Ambassador: Seydou Madani Sy.
Counsellor: Abdou Sourang.
Counsellor: Henri Mendy.
First Secretary: Seydou Diop.
First Secretary: Fatou Diallo.
Attaché: Abdou Sakho.
Attaché: Amadou Diop.
Attaché: Madeleine Sow.

SEYCHELLES

High Commission: Box No. 4PE, Eros House, 4th Floor, 111 Baker St, London W1M 1FE; tel (71) 224-1660.
High Commissioner: Louis Sylvestre Radegonde.
Attaché: Jacqueline Moustache-Belle.

SIERRA LEONE

High Commission: 33 Portland Place, London W1N 3AG; tel (71) 636-6483.
High Commissioner: Caleb B. Aubee.
Deputy High Commissioner: Modu Jhegy Sesay.
Counsellor and Head of Chancery: S. Sunda.
First Secretary: A. K. Ballah-Conteh.
Third Secretary: V. A. Jones.
Attaché (Information): S. O. Zack-Williams.
Attaché (Education): A. F. Kamara.
Attaché (Finance): Alpha Kanu Saracouli.
Assistant Attaché (Administrative): W. F. Macfoy.
Assistant Attaché (Trade): A. R. Hamid.

SINGAPORE

High Commission: 9 Wilton Crescent, London SW1X 8SA; tel (71) 235-8315; telex 262564; fax (71) 245-6583.
High Commissioner: Abdul Aziz Bin Mahmood.
Counsellor: Hoy-Cheng Seetoh.
First Secretary: Violet Mui Fang Loo.
First Secretary (Commercial): Hock Chee Tham.
Second Secretary: Charles Joseph Peter.
Third Secretary: Wah Sern Tan.

SOLOMON ISLANDS

Consulate: 17 Springfield Rd, Wimbledon, London SW10 7AL; tel (71) 946-5552.

SOMALIA

Embassy: 60 Portland Place, London W1N 3DG; tel (71) 580-7140; telex 28369; fax (71) 637-9919.
Ambassador: Ali Hassan Ali.
Counsellor: Dahir Tukale Askar.

SOUTH AFRICA

Embassy: South Africa House, Trafalgar Sq., London WC2N 5DP; tel (71) 930-4488; telex 267672; fax (71) 321-0834.
Ambassador: Kent D. S. Durr.
Minister: R. W. Carter.
Minister (Trade): P. M. Pullen.
Counsellor (Trade): Dr J. G. Coetzee.
Counsellor (Agriculture): E. P. Evans.
Counsellor: D. J. Cloete.
Counsellor: P. J. Schabort.
Counsellor: D. Kent-Brown.
Counsellor (Administrative): T. E. M. Eygelaar.
Counsellor (Minerals/Energy): Dr N. J. Grobler.
Counsellor (Culture): Dr L. C. Eksteen.
Counsellor (Labour): C. Fourie.
First Secretary: J. P. Wright.
First Secretary (Trade): H. G. Luttig.
First Secretary: T. E. Claasen.
First Secretary: P. W. Strydom.
First Secretary: J. W. Breytenbach.
First Secretary: J. G. Williams.
Second Secretary: S. G. van Heerden.
Second Secretary: R. S. Lombard.
Attaché (Agriculture): J. F. Kirsten.
Consul (Agriculture): W. Gentle.
Deputy Consul-General: M. W. Marais.
Consul (Migration): J. S. Marais.
Consul (Customs): D. M. van Wyk.
Vice-Consul (Inland Revenue): J. J. Ferguson.

Consulate-General: Stock Exchange House, 69 West George St, Glasgow G2 1BX; tel (41) 221-3114; telex 776221; fax (41) 221-7413.
Consul-General: A. de K. Joubert.
Consul (Administrative): C. J. Claasen.

Consulate: 135 Edmund St, Birmingham B3 2HS; tel (21) 236-7471; telex 338764.
Honorary Consul: R. W. P. Beharrell.

SPAIN

Embassy: 16th Floor, Portland House, Stag Pl., London SW1E 5SE; tel (71) 235-5555; telex 261333; fax (71) 235-9905.
Ambassador: Felipe de la Morena.
Minister-Counsellor: Marquis de Torregrosa.
Counsellor: Juan González-Cebrián.
Counsellor: Fernando de la Serna.
Counsellor: Javier Sangro.
Counsellor: Mariano Borrero.
Counsellor (Finance): Alberto Martínez.
Counsellor (Maritime Transport): Eduardo Cruz-Iturzaeta.
Counsellor (Transport/Tourism): German Porras.
First Secretary: José María Bosch.
Attaché (Transport/Tourism): Faustino Diaz Fortuny.
Attaché (Administrative): Manuel Durban.
Attaché (Legal): Rafael Valls.
Attaché (Administrative): Mariano Rayón.

Commercial Section: 66 Chiltern St, London W1M 1PR; tel (71) 486-0101.
Counsellor and Head of Commercial Office: José Manuel Becerra.
Counsellor (Commercial): Juan Ramon Calabozo Moran.
Counsellor (Commercial): Emilio de la Fuente.
Counsellor (Commercial): José María Luengo-Hernandez.

Consular Section: 20 Draycott Pl., London SW3; tel (71) 581-5921.
Minister (Consular): Ramon Ansoain Garraza.
Counsellor (Consular): José Luis Solano.

Office of the Defence Attaché: 3 Hans Cres., Flat 3, London SW1; tel (71) 589-5731.
Defence and Naval Attaché: Capt. José María Pascual.
Assistant Defence and Naval Attaché: Lieut Commdr Leopoldo López-Eadi.
Military Attaché: Col Juan Ortuño.
Air Attaché: Lieut Col Don Daniel Perez-Cobaleda.

Cultural Section: 102 Eaton Sq., London SW1; tel (71) 235-1484.
Minister (Cultural): Fernando Serrano-Suñer.

Press Section: 24 Belgrave Sq., London SW1; tel (71) 235-7537.
Counsellor (Press): Miguel de Santiago-Juarez.

Education and Labour Sections: 20 Peel St, London W8; tel (71) 727-2462.
Counsellor (Education): Dr Enrique Wulff.
Counsellor (Labour): Bernando Fernandez.

Agriculture, Fisheries and Food Section: 54 Upper Montagu St, London W1; tel (71) 723-9967.
Counsellor (Agriculture/Fisheries/Food): Luis María Esteruelas.
Assistant Attaché (Agriculture/Fisheries/Food): Juan Calvera Vehi.

SRI LANKA

High Commission: 13 Hyde Park Gardens, London W2 2LU; tel (71) 262-1841; telex 25844; fax (71) 262-7970.
Ambassador: Gen. Don Sepala Attygalle.
Deputy High Commissioner: Gamini S. Munasinghe.
Minister-Counsellor (Trade/Economic): N. R. Meemaduma.
First Secretary (Education): P. Abeysekera.
First Secretary (Administrative): K. L. L. Wijeratne.
First Secretary: Maj. K. H. G. Hendawitharana.
Third Secretary: I. Ansar.
Third Secretary (Consular): M. M. Jaffeer.
Third Secretary (Commercial): S. N. Ilangakkone Ekanayaka.
Third Secretary (Information): A. G. C. Algama.
Attaché (Administrative): B. Naiduwa Handi.

SUDAN

Embassy: 3 Cleveland Row, St James's, London SW1A 1DD; tel (71) 839-8080; telex 25195; fax (71) 839-7560.
Minister and Chargé d'affaires: Ahmed Omer Ahmed.
Counsellor: Fadlalla el-Hadi Ibrahim.
Counsellor: Bushra el-Fadil Azrag Mustafa.
Counsellor: Mohamed Hassan Bakhit.
Counsellor: Mohamed el-Hassan Ibrahim Dablouk.
Counsellor: Ahmed Ali Osman.
Counsellor (Information): Abdel Wahab Ahmed Mohamed Osman.
Assistant Military Attaché: Col Omer Ahmed Mohamed Tola.
Second Secretary: Eldirdiri Ahmed Mohamed Hussein.
Second Secretary: Mirghani Abbakar el-Tayeb Bakhit.
Military Attaché: Brig. Mohamed Omer Edreis.
Attaché: Mohamed el-Amin Tayib Mousa.
Attaché: Abdalla Sid Ahmed Ali.
Attaché: Abbass Hassan Mohamed Abu Gabel.
Attaché: Awadia Suleiman Mohamed Abu Salih.
Attaché: Abdel Hameed el-Amin Abdel Hameed.
Attaché: El Hadi Yousif Kabashi.
Attaché: Asaad Buaras Galal Osman.
Attaché: Mahmoud Abd Elmwgoud Mahmoud.
Attaché: Abdel Basit Ismail Amin.
Attaché: Abdel Hadie Mahmoud Abdel Hadie.
Attaché: Abd El Razig Maragan Sayed.
Attaché: Ali Abdalla el-Gadee.

SWAZILAND

High Commission: 58 Pont St, London SW1X 0AE; tel (71) 581-4976; telex 28853; fax (71) 589-5332.
High Commissioner: Mboni N. Dlamini.
First Secretary (Information): Micah M. Dube.
Third Secretary: Solomon D. Hlophe.
Attaché (Administrative): Jessie Mabuza.
Attaché (Trade): Clement T. Mabuza.

SWEDEN

Embassy: 11 Montagu Place, London W1H 2AL; tel (71) 724-2101; telex 28249; fax (71) 753-0486.
Ambassador: Lennart Eckerberg.
Minister: Per Jödahl.
Counsellor: Peter Bruce.
Counsellor: Pontus Järborg.
Counsellor: Ragnar Ängeby.
First Secretary: Anders Elofson.
First Secretary: Hans Pontus Lindbald.
Secretary (Commercial): Mats Nilsson.
Chancellor: Ingrid Agneta Boyd.
Chancellor: Anita McCarthy.
Attaché (Cultural): Torsten Kälvemark.
Attaché (Technical Contracts): Bo Ekström.
Chaplain: Lennart Sjöström.

Consulate: St Philip's House, St Philip's Place, Birmingham B3 2PP; tel (21) 200-3300; telex 339793; fax (21) 200-3330.
Consul: Sidney George Armstrong Roberts.
Chancellor: Veronica Helen Leadbetter.

Consulate: c/o Rathbone Bros & Co., Port of Liverpool Bldg, Pier Head, Liverpool L3 1NW; tel (51) 236-8674; fax (51) 236-3978.
Consul: David Gordon Beazley.

Consulate: 41 Spring Gdns, Manchester M2 2BB; tel (61) 832-7290; telex 669489; fax (61) 832-2655.
Consul: Charles Soren Robert Tattam.

Consulate: 30 Brandling Pl., Newcastle-upon-Tyne NE2 4RU; tel (91) 281-7421; telex 537892; fax (91) 281-8430.
Consul: Christopher David William Souter.

Consulate: 1/9 The Drive, Hove, East Sussex BN3 3JS; tel (273) 29797; telex 877551; fax (273) 24082.
Consul: Agneta Fitch.

Consulate: 1/2 Portview Rd, Avonmouth, Bristol BS11 9YX; tel (272) 825081; telex 44129; fax (272) 822912.
Consul: Brian Fletcher.
Chancellor: Christine Ager.

Consulate: c/o Hammond House, Limekiln St, Dover CT17 9EE; tel (304) 201201; telex 96115; fax (304) 240374.
Consul: James Gregory Ryeland.

Consulate: 89a Queen St, Exeter EX4 3RP; tel (392) 218218; fax (392) 420907.
Consul: Graham Christopher Chester.

Consulate: D.F.D.S. Ltd, Port Agency Office, Harwich CO12 4QG; tel (255) 242242; telex 987550; fax (255) 241096.
Consul: John Ashley Eldridge.
Chancellor: Neil Charles Cray.

Consulate: c/o Carlbom Shipping Ltd, Dock Office Bldg, Immingham Dock, Immingham DN40 2NU; tel (469) 571387; telex 52186; fax (469) 571023.
Consul: Magnus Anthony Axel Carlbom.

Consulate: 236 Marton Rd, Middlesbrough TS4 2HA; tel (642) 243662; telex 58462; fax (642) 243936.
Consul: Norman Peter Clarkson.
Chancellor: Noreen Mary Longstaff.

Consulate: 252 High St, Rochester ME1 1H2; tel (634) 864832; telex 96109; fax (634) 831838.
Consul: David John Bradley.
Chancellor: Maurice Arthur La-Haye.

Consulate: c/o Stewart Shipbrokers Ltd, Northam Iron Works, Princes St, Northam, Southampton SO1 1RP; tel (703) 234232; telex 47649; fax (703) 335884.
Consul: Richard John Hardie.

Consulate-General: 6 St John's Place, Leith, Edinburgh EH6 7EL; tel (31) 554-6631; telex 72114; fax (31) 554-8504.
Consul-General: John Douglas Bottomley.
Chancellor: Maureen Connolly.

Consulate: 228 Clyde St, Glasgow G1 4JS; tel (41) 221-7845; telex 77205; fax (41) 204-2388.
Consul: Alastair Wilson Tear.

Consulate: Carleton Bldgs, 59 Marishal St, POB 60, Aberdeen AB9 8AZ; tel (224) 589921; telex 73134; fax (224) 574410.
Consul: Ramsay Patrick Hendry Pirie.

Consulate: 17/29 Chapel St, Inverness IV1 1NA; tel (463) 233366; fax (463) 711634.
Consul: Ian Crawford Fraser.
Chancellor: Heather Anne Stewart.

Consulate: Birka, Bressay, Lerwick, Shetland ZE2 9EL; tel (595) 82363; telex 75398.
Consul: Magnus Macdonald Shearer.
Chancellor: Magnus John Shearer.

Consulate: Sandwick Rd, Stornoway, Isle of Lewis PA87 2SL; tel (851) 2303; fax (851) 4010.
Consul: Charles Alexander Schau Engebresten.

Consulate: 2 Tesco Precinct, Forestfach, Swansea SA5 4BA; tel (792) 588100; telex 48604.
Consul: William Edward Kervin.

Consulate: 4 Dunraven Cres., Talbot Green, Pontclun, Mid Glamorgan CF7 8JD; tel (443) 222538; telex 445941; fax (443) 222538.
Consul: Leonard David Freeman.
Chancellor: Mary Margaret Ann Freeman.

Consulate: Head Line Bldgs, 10/14 Victoria St, Belfast BT1 3GP; tel (232) 230581; telex 74534; fax (232) 231367.
Consul: Michael Walter Savage Maclaran.

Consulate: 9 Esplanade, St Helier, Jersey; tel (534) 80545; fax (534) 77693.
Consul: Philip Howard Sturgess.

SWITZERLAND

Embassy: 16-18 Montagu Place, London W1H 2BQ; tel (71) 723-0701; telex 28212; fax (71) 724-7001.
Ambassador: Franz E. Muheim.
Minister: Christian M. Faessler.
Counsellor (Economic/Financial): Josef Bucher.
First Secretary (Culture): Livio Huerzeler.
Defence, Naval and Air Attaché: Maj. Gen. Gérard de Loës.
First Secretary (Press/Legal): Marianne Engler.
Second Secretary (Economic): Dr Max H. Schnellmann.
Attaché (Consular/Administrative): Eduard Jaun.
Attaché (Commercial): Max Kuenzle.
Attaché: Roland P. Fischer.
Attaché: Mauro Reino.

Consulate-General: Sunley Tower, 24th Floor, Piccadilly Plaza, Manchester M1 4BT; tel (61) 236-2933; telex 665918; fax (61) 236-4689.
Consul-General: Gilbert Schlaefli.
Consul and Chancellor: Felix Naef.

SYRIA

Embassy: 8 Belgrave Sq., London SW1X 8PH; tel (71) 245-9012; fax (71) 235-4621.
Ambassador: Muhammad Khader.
Minister-Counsellor and Chargé d'affaires: Dr Toufik Salloum.
Counsellor: Rustom al-Zoubi.
Second Secretary: Samir al-Kassir.
Third Secretary: Fawdz Mokaddem.

TANZANIA

High Commission: 43 Hertford St, London W1Y 8DB; tel (71) 499-8951; telex 262504; fax (71) 491-9321.
High Commissioner: Ali S. Mchumo.
Minister-Counsellor: Ulli Kapangala Mwambulukutu.
Minister-Counsellor: Simon U. R. Mlay.
Minister-Counsellor: Fatma Shaaban Abdulla.
Counsellor: Juma Ameir Juma.
Defence Adviser: Brig. Waziri Simba.
Head of Chancery: James Ayub Ram Selengia.
Attaché (Administrative): Waziri R. Lukanza.

THAILAND

Embassy: 29-30 Queen's Gate, London SW7 5JB; tel (71) 589-0173; fax (71) 823-9695.
Ambassador: Tongchan Jokitasthira.
Minister and Deputy Head of Mission: Don Pramudwinai.
Counsellor: Phithak Phrombubpha.
Counsellor: Piseth Pamarapa.
Counsellor (Economic/Financial): Prasit Ujjin.
Defence and Naval Attaché: Capt. Suchart Kolasastraseni.
Assistant Naval Attaché: Capt. Tanoos Suyarnsettakorn.
First Secretary: Yuthika Tansangoan.
First Secretary: Songrit Ratanadilok Na Bhuket.
First Secretary: Chalit Manityakul.
First Secretary (Economic/Financial): Aran Roongsawang.
First Secretary: Siriwan Siriraya.

Office of the Air Attaché: 2 Victoria Rd, London W8 5RD; tel (71) 938-2433.
Air Attaché: Group Capt. Katatip Kunjara.

Office of the Military Attaché: 65 Brondesbury Park, London NW6; tel (71) 589-0209.
Military Attaché: Col Somchai Hiranyasthi.
Assistant Military Attaché: Lieut Col Chainarong Phongsawad.

Education and Information Sections: 28 Prince's Gate, London SW7 1QF; tel (71) 584-4538.
Counsellor (Education): Suwan Xanasongkram.
First Secretary (Education): Somsri Chantaratana.

Commercial Section: 9 Stafford St, London W1X 4RT; tel (71) 493-5749.
Counsellor (Commercial): Nabthong Thongyai.
First Secretary (Commercial): Chulit Stavorn.

Industrial Section: Elysium Gate 19, 126 New Kings Rd, London SW6 4LZ; tel (71) 371-7621; fax (71) 371-7623.
Counsellor (Industrial): Dhawatchai Tangsanga.

TONGA

High Commission: 36 Molyneux St, London W1H 6AB; tel (71) 724-5828; telex 8954094; fax (71) 723-9074.
High Commissioner: Siosaia Tuita.
Counsellor: Mele Lupeha'Amoa Takapautolo.
First Secretary: Kaimana Hauoli 'o Kuini Aleamotu'A.
Third Secretary: Tevita Fe'Aomoelotu Pale Vaipuna.

TRINIDAD AND TOBAGO

High Commission: 42 Belgrave Sq., London SW1X 8NT; tel (71) 245-9351; telex 918910; fax (71) 823-1065.
High Commissioner: P. L. U. Cross.
Deputy High Commissioner: Lingston Cumberbatch.
Senior Counsellor: Calvin Smith.
Counsellor: Vernetta Calvin-Smith.
First Secretary: Razia Ali.
Attaché (Immigration): Anselm Estwick.
Attaché and Vice-Consul: Merlyne Alexander.
Attaché: Mayantee Narine.
Attaché: Dorothy Connell.
Attaché (Finance): Angela O'Brien-Judson.

TUNISIA

Embassy: 29 Prince's Gate, London SW7 1QG; tel (71) 584-8117; telex 23736; fax (71) 225-2884.
Ambassador: Dr Abdelaziz Hamzaoui.
Counsellor (Economic): Hatem Bergaoui.
Military Attaché: Azmi Ben Abdeljelil Mahjoub.
Secretary (Cultural/Social Affairs): Mohamed Bakir.
Secretary (Political/Press): Boutheina Labidi.
Attaché (Finance): Mohamed Lamine Lourimi.
Attaché: Ahmed Ghomrasni.
Attaché: Abdallah Hamouda.

TURKEY

Embassy: 43 Belgrave Sq., London SW1X 8PA; tel (71) 235-5252; telex 916686.
Ambassador: Candemir Önhon.
Minister-Counsellor: Müfit Özdeş.
Counsellor: Osman Cem Ergin.
Counsellor (Press): Ahmet Ersoy.
Counsellor (Education): Yüksel Özer.
Counsellor (Medical): Utku Ünsal.
Counsellor (Finance/Customs): Metin Özşahin.
Counsellor (Economic/Commercial): Avni Özcan.
Counsellor: Dr A. Engin Oba.
Counsellor (Economic/Commercial): A. Firdevs Tuna.
Counsellor: Oğuz Özge.
Counsellor: Hasan Ğogüs.
Counsellor (Information): Mustafa Türkmen.
Assistant Counsellor (Culture/Information): M. Selami Karaibrahimgil.
Assistant Counsellor (Economic/Commercial): M. Serhan Oksay.
Naval Attaché: Capt. Ramis Akdemir.
Air Attaché: Col Ercüment Tokmak.
Military Attaché: Maj. Orhan Akbaş.
Assistant Army Attaché: Capt. Levent Ersoy.
First Secretary: Irfan Acar.
Second Secretary: Taner Karaca.
Attaché (Education): Secil Yazicioglu.
Attaché (Information/Administrative): Nilgün Atalay.

UGANDA

High Commission: Uganda House, 58-59 Trafalgar Sq., London WC2N 5DX; tel (71) 839-5783; telex 915141; fax (71) 839-8925.
Ambassador: George Kirya.
Minister-Counsellor: William Naggaga.

First Secretary (Education): K. M. Nswemu.
Second Secretary: A. N. Kabunga.
Second Secretary: J. Mireego.
Second Secretary: S. Musisi-Mwanje.
Second Secretary: I. Biruma-Sebulime.
Third Secretary: M. Kedisi.
Attaché (Finance): Gabriel Kizza-Kigongo.

Commercial and Coffee Sections: 60-1 Mark Lane, London EC3R 7NE; tel (71) 702-0594.
Attaché (Commercial): I. Luberenga.
Attaché (Commercial): J. C. Biroli.

UNITED ARAB EMIRATES

Embassy: 30 Prince's Gate, London SW7 1PT; tel (71) 581-1281; telex 918459; fax (71) 581-9616.
Ambassador: Essa Saleh Al Gurg.
Counsellor (Consular): Abdul Aziz Merza Amin.
Counsellor: Jassim Ahmed al-Shaikh.
Adviser: Ahmed M. Obaidy.
Military Attaché: Lieut Col Al-Haj Musallam Mefleh al-Mazrouei.
Assistant Military Attaché: Capt. Ali Mohsen al-Hamli.
First Secretary: Abdul Bari Mohamed al-Hashemi.
Second Secretary: Abdulla Mattar Khamis al-Mazroui.
Attaché (Cultural): Abdulrahim Ahmed Moh'd al-Marri.
Attaché (Medical): Dr Juma Bilal.

USA

Embassy: 24-31 Grosvenor Sq., London W1A 1AE; tel (71) 499-9000; telex 266777; fax (71) 409-1637.
Ambassador: Raymond G. H. Seitz.
Deputy Head of Mission: Ronald E. Woods.
Aide to Ambassador: John D. Burley.
Political Section: Bruce Burton.
Political Adviser: James L. Clunan.
Political Officer: Peter M. McKinley.
Attaché and Security Officer: Phillip E. Jornlin.
Economic Section: Ann R. Berry.
Commercial Section: James L. Blow.
Labour Officer: Lester P. Slezak.
Consular Section: Norbert Krieg.
Administrative Section: John Condayan.
Federal Advisory Administration: Patrick Poe.
Internal Revenue Service: Robert Tobin.
Agricultural Section: James P. Rudbeck.
Agricultural Trade Office: Robert D. Fondahn.
Public Affairs Officer: Charles Courtney.
Customs Service: John A. Hurley.
Information Systems Manager: Frederick R. Cook.
Information: Anne Arries.
Consular Officer: Barbara T. Wilson.
Communications Programme Officer: Bernard W. Bies.
Counsellor (Programme Co-ordination): Bertram Dunn.
Counsellor (Economic): Walter B. Lockwood, Jr.
Office of Defence Attaché: Capt. Peter C. Baxter.
Naval Attaché: Capt. Joseph R. McCleary.
Army Attaché: Col James T. Hennessey.
Air Attaché: Col Chester P. Garrison.
Army Attaché: Col Daniel M. Smith.
Military Attaché (Political): James D. Hurd.
First Secretary (Personnel): W. Douglas Frank.
First Secretary (Public Affairs): Brian E. Carlson.
Attaché (Finance): John M. Abbott.
Attaché (Science): James B. Devine.
Attaché (Scientific/Technical): Otis G. Peterson.
Attaché (Security): William S. Trites.
Attaché (Legal): R. John Theriault, Jr.
Attaché (Drug Enforcement Agency): John W. Lee.
Assistant Attaché (Customs): John P. Luksic.
Regional Security Officer: Robert O'Brien.

Consulate-General: Queen's House, 14 Queen St, Belfast BT1 6EQ; tel (232) 328239; telex 747512.
Consul-General: Douglas Archard.

Consulate-General: 3 Regent Terr., Edinburgh EH7 5BW; tel (31) 556-8315.
Consul-General: Donald Holm.

URUGUAY

Embassy: 48 Lennox Gardens, London SW1X 0DL; tel (71) 589-8835; telex 264180; fax (71) 581-9585.
Ambassador: Dr Luis Alberto Solé-Romeo.
Minister-Counsellor: Dr José Luis Remedi.
Military Attaché: Col Juan José Pomoli Gambetta.
Naval Attaché: Capt. Ricardo Hector Medina Ramella.
First Secretary and Consul: Dr Jorge Luis Jure.

VENEZUELA

Embassy: 1 Cromwell Rd, London SW7 2HR; tel (71) 584-4206; telex 264186; fax (71) 589-8887.
Ambassador: Dr Francisco Kerdel-Vegas.
Minister-Counsellor: Jocelyn de Henriquez.
Counsellor (Technical): Elena Mora Monroy.
Second Secretary: Arancha Elorza O.
Third Secretary: Roberto A. Barraez d'Lucca.
Third Attaché: Luis A. Pino Farias.
Vice-Consul: Yolanda Reyna Iribarren.

VIET-NAM

Embassy: 12-14 Victoria Rd, London W8 5RD; tel (71) 937-1912; telex 887361; fax (71) 937-6108.
Ambassador: Chau Phong.
Counsellor (Commercial): Dung Hoang Van.
Second Secretary: Bui Xuan Khoa.
Second Secretary: Yen Nguyen Thi.

YEMEN

Embassy: 41 South St, London W1Y 5PD; tel (71) 629-9905.
Ambassador: Dr Shaya Mohsin Mohamed.
Minister: Mohamed Hazzi Mohamed Ali.
Minister: Abdulwahab Mohamed M. al-Shami.
Counsellor: Kassim Abdulrab Hariz.
Counsellor: Ali Ahmed al-Geraffee.
Counsellor: Ahmed Ahmed al-Aini.
Counsellor: Idress Ahmed al-Shamman.
First Secretary (Consular): Nagmi Mohamed Showdery.
First Secretary: Hani Ali Saleem al-Beedh.
Second Secretary (Finance): Badr Aldin Dawood Gaffer.
Third Secretary: Abdullah Mohamed Ali al-Montser.
Attaché (Commercial): Mohamed Abdulla Zokari.
Attaché (Cultural): Abdulla Abdulla al-Shamahi.
Attaché (Economic): Abdulkarim M. Abu Taleb.
Attaché (Administrative): Naseem Ibrahim Abdullah.

YUGOSLAVIA

Embassy: 5 Lexham Gardens, London W8 5JJ; tel (71) 370-6105; telex 928542; fax (71) 370-3838.
Ambassador: Svetozar Rikanović.
Minister-Counsellor: Feodor Starcevic.
Minister-Counsellor (Economic): Dr Milisav Stankovic.
First Counsellor and Head of Consular Section: Vesna Knezevic.
Defence Attaché: Commdr Zlatko Jazbinsek.
Assistant Defence Attaché: Capt. Drago Markanovic.
Second Secretary: Dragana Ivanovic.
Second Secretary: Aleksandar Brackovic.
Attaché (Economic): Milan Zivkovic.
Attaché (Administrative): Miroslav Savovic.
Attaché (Administrative): Zoran Rancic.

ZAIRE

Embassy: 26 Chesham Place, London SW1X 8HH; tel (71) 235-6137; telex 25651; fax (71) 235-9048.
Ambassador: Liloo Nkema.
Counsellor: Nsangolo Iwula.
Counsellor: Mangaza Luanghy.
Counsellor: Mbingon Mossimi.
Military, Naval and Air Attaché: Col Ngbongolo Mbongo Maduangele.
First Secretary: Liba Balu Mavova-Moses.
Attaché (Finance): Kababo Bushiri.
Attaché (Administrative): Didingo Nzangbe.
Attaché (Maritime): Yisuku Tito.
Attaché (Coffee/Cocoa): Kayoka Mudingay.

ZAMBIA

High Commission: 2 Palace Gate, London W8 5NG; tel (71) 589-6655; telex 263544; fax (71) 581-1353.
High Commissioner: Edward M. Lubinda.
Deputy High Commissioner: J. Muleba.
Trade Commissioner: S. Mutondo.
First Secretary (Administrative): Jojo Angelo Moyo.
First Secretary (Tourism): Josephine Chikwende.
First Secretary (Finance): Noah Clement Tembo.
First Secretary (Education): B. Chomba.
First Secretary: J. M. Mayanda.
First Secretary (Immigration): R. B. Tembo.
Second Secretary (Political/Immigration): O. C. Lungwe.
Second Secretary (Protocol): W. M. Chisuta.
Third Secretary (Communications): Juma Chipeta.

ZIMBABWE

High Commission: Zimbabwe House, 429 The Strand, London WC2R 0SA; tel (71) 836-7755; telex 262014.
High Commissioner: Stephen Cletus Chiketa.
Deputy High Commissioner: Dr Elita T. T. Sakupwanya.
Minister-Counsellor: Godfrey Mwedzi.
Counsellor: Ammon Machingambi Mutembwa.
Counsellor: Martin Pedzisayi Matongo.
Counsellor: Muchechetere Manhuna.
Counsellor (Political): Isaac Moyo.
Counsellor: Violet Tendai Sigauke.
Counsellor: Noah Takawota Joni Mangondo.
Counsellor (Commercial): Samuel Undenge.
Defence Adviser: Lieut Col Christian Mandichamira Katsande.
Assistant Defence Attaché: Ekironi Madzanira.
First Secretary: Shepherd Shingirai Gwenzi.
First Secretary: Samuel Katiyo.
First Secretary (Commercial): Billy Mutoti.
First Secretary (Financial/Administrative): Robson Musekiwa Chinembiri.
First Secretary: Michael Chiwoneso Mukura.
Attaché (Recruitment/Education): Keith C. Chimanikire.
Attaché (Tourism): Wilford Chinenzura.

International Organizations

EUROPEAN COMMUNITIES

Bureau: Jean Monnet House, 8 Storey's Gate, London SW1P 3AT; tel (71) 222-8122; telex 23208; fax (71) 222-0900.
Head of Office: John Drew.
Head of External Affairs: G. Martin.
Deputy Head of External Affairs: W. Wilton.
Head of Media and Information: R. Elphick.
Deputy Head of Media and Information: G. Pau.
Head of Administration: J. C. Marriot.

Belfast Sub-Office: Windsor House, 9-15 Bedford St, Belfast BT2 7EG; tel (232) 240708; telex 74117; fax (232) 248241.
Head of Office: Dennis Kennedy.

Cardiff Sub-Office: 4 Cathedral Rd, Cardiff CF1 9SG; tel (222) 371631; telex 497-727; fax (222) 395489.
Head of Office: Jørgen Hansen.

Edinburgh Sub-Office: 9 Alva St, Edinburgh EH2 4PH; tel (31) 225-2058; telex 727420; fax (31) 226-4105.
Head of Office: Kenneth Alexander Munro.

UNITED NATIONS

Office and Information Centre: 20 Buckingham Gate, London SW1E 6LB; tel (71) 630-1981.
Director: Graeme Maxwell Warner.

UNITED NATIONS ENVIRONMENT PROGRAMME—UNEP

Office: Chelsea College, Octagon Bldg, 459A Fulham Rd, London SW7; tel (81) 693-6902.
Project Leader: Dr B. G. Bennett.

UNITED NATIONS HIGH COMMISSIONER FOR REFUGEES—UNHCR

Office: Suites 7 & 29, Westminster Palace Gdns, Artillery Row, London SW1P 1RR; tel (71) 222-3066.
Representative (UNCHR): Dr F. E. Krenz.
Representative (UNCHR): A. Fortin.

WORLD HEALTH ORGANIZATION—WHO

Office: Ealing Hospital, Uxbridge Rd, Southall UB1 3EV; tel (81) 574 2444.
Consultant (WHO): S. Sundararajan.

UNITED STATES OF AMERICA

AFGHANISTAN

Embassy: 2341 Wyoming Ave, NW, Washington, DC 20008; tel (202) 234-3770; telex 248206; fax (202) 328-3516.
Chargé d'affaires a.i. and Minister-Counsellor: Abdul Ghafoor Jawshan.
Second Secretary and Consul: Mohammad Aqa (acting).

ALGERIA

Embassy: 2118 Kalorama Rd, NW, Washington, DC 20008; tel (202) 265-2800; telex 892443; fax (202) 667-2174.
Ambassador: Abderrahmane Bensid.

ANTIGUA AND BARBUDA

Embassy: Intelsat Bldg, 3400 International Drive, Suite 4M, NW, Washington, DC 20008; tel (202) 362-5122; telex 822-1130; fax (202) 362-5225.
Ambassador: Patrick A. Lewis.
Minister: Paul O. Spencer.
First Secretary: Iva Mendes.
Second Secretary: Debbie Prosper.

Consulate: 121 SE First St, Suite 1004, Miami, FL 33131; tel (305) 381-6762.

ARGENTINA

Embassy: 1600 New Hampshire Ave, NW, Washington, DC 20009; tel (202) 939-6400; fax (202) 332-3171.
Ambassador: Guido José Maria Di Tella.

Consulate-General: 12 West 56th St, New York, NY 10019; tel (212) 397-1400.
Consul-General: Carlos O. Keller Sarmiento.
Deputy Consul-General: Liliana B. Iribarne.
Deputy Consul-General: Elda Sampietro.

Consulate-General: 870 Market St, San Francisco, CA 94102; tel (415) 982-3050.
Consul-General: Simon N. Arguello.
Deputy Consul-General: Alcira Andrea Celoria.
Deputy Consul-General: Jorge José Matas.

Consulate-General: 2000 South Post Oak Rd, Suite 1810, Houston, TX 77056; tel (713) 871-8935.
Consul-General: Fernando Perrone.

Consulate-General: 80 SW 8th St, Suite 1820, Miami, FL 33130.
Consul-General: Orlando R. Rebagliati.
Deputy Consul-General: Ricardo C. Rosselli.
Deputy Consul-General: Marcelo E. Huergo.

Consulate-General: 229 Peachtree, Atlanta, GA.
Consul-General: Juan Carlos Vignaud.
Deputy Consul-General: Eugenio García Santos.

Consulate-General: 915 International Trade Mart, New Orleans, LA 70130; tel (504) 523-2823.
Consul-General: Ramon Villagra-Delgado.
Deputy Consul-General: Alfredo M. Rescic.

Consulate: 3550 Wilshire Blvd, Los Angeles, CA 90010; tel (213) 739-5959.
Consul: Juan V. Sola.
Vice-Consul: Jorge L. Vinuela.
Vice-Consul: Diego de Lara Jauregui.
Vice-Consul: Jorge L. Miranda.
Vice-Consul: Emilio J. Neffa.

Consulate: 20 North Clark St, Suite 602, Chicago, IL 60602; tel (312) 263-7435.
Consul: Ana Luisa Wirth.
Consul: Abraham Rein.
Consul: Jorge L. M. Siri Longhi.

Consulate: 204 Kayser Bldg, Suite 204, 297 East Redwood St, Baltimore, MD 22201; tel (301) 837-0445.
Consul: Arturo Moyano-Molina.

AUSTRALIA

Embassy: 1601 Massachusetts Ave, NW, Washington, DC 20036; tel (202) 797-3000; telex 892621; fax (202) 797-3168.
Ambassador: Michael John Cook.
Deputy Head of Mission: L. Joseph.
Minister (Commercial): G. Thomson.
Counsellor (Commercial): J. Dunn.
Minister (Congressional/Public Affairs): C. Lamb.
Minister (Economic): R. Freney.
Counsellor (Economic): M. Kooymans.
Counsellor (Legal): L. Govey.
Counsellor (Finance): A. Preston Stanley.
Counsellor (Immigration): Dr L. Omelaniuk.
Counsellor (Industry/Science/Technology): Norman Gomm.
Counsellor (Nuclear): Dr J. Harries.
Counselllor (Culture): P. Amberg.
Counsellor (Public Affairs): C. Sweeney.
Counsellor (Agriculture): J. Sault.
Counsellor (Veterinary): Dr S. Kahn.
Counsellor and Head of Political Branch: T. Wilson.
Counsellor (Political): Z. McCarthy.
Counsellor (Political): L. Brown.
Counsellor (Political): N. Campbell.
Counsellor (Political): R. Marshall.
Counsellor (Administrative) and Consul-General: P. Robertson.
Counsellor (Defence Policy): J. Nockels.
Counsellor (Defence Acquisition/Logistics): R. C. Wylie.
Counsellor (Defence Science): Dr R. P. Creaser.
Defence Attaché: Rear Adm. A. M. Carwardine.
Assistant Defence Attaché: Wing Commdr P. J. Bennett.
Military Attaché and Deputy Head of Defence Staff: Brig. J. Robbins.
Assistant Military Attaché: Lieut Col R. W. Crawshaw.
Naval Attaché: Cdre D. J. Campbell.
Assistant Naval Attaché: Commdr P. L. Elliot.
Air Attaché: Air Cdre E. J. Walker.
Assistant Air Attaché: Wing Commdr S. Longbottom.
Defence Industry Attaché: C. Martin.
Attaché (Defence Science): D. Spïvakovsky.
First Secretary (Commercial): M. Dimo.
First Secretary (Commercial): C. Langman.
First Secretary (Finance): N. Williams.
First Secretary (Political): C. Graham.

First Secretary (Political): S. Kentwell.
First Secretary (Administrative): J. Pritchard.
First Secretary (Administrative) and Consul: M. J. Hyam.
First Secretary (Customs): A. Hosking.
Customs Representative: G. Weppner.
Senior Trade Analyst: Helen Freeman.
Trade Commissioner, International Projects: J. Lloyd.
Senior International Projects Analyst: D. Alleva.
Information Officer (Commercial): J. Walpole.
Information and Media Officer: C. Botten.
Attaché (Defence Liaison): C. Williams.
Attaché (Police Liaison): Detective Supt J. Davies.
Staff Officer (Administrative): Maj. L. G. Gittins.

Consulate-General: International Bldg, 636 Fifth Ave, New York, NY 10111; tel (212) 245-4000; fax (212) 265-4917.
Consul-General: Christopher J. Hurford.
Deputy Consul-General (Commercial) and Senior Trade Commissioner: John R. Garran.
Consul (Economic): Mr Horn.
Consul (Public Affairs): T. Miller.
Consul (Information): L. G. Smith.
Consul (Visas/Immigration): Hamish L. Lindsay.

Consulate-General: Quaker Tower, Suite 290, 321 North Clark St, Chicago, IL 60610; tel (312) 645-9494.
Consul-General: K. Gates.
Deputy Consul-General and Trade Commissioner: David B. Moncur.
Consul: Bruce C. Cowled.

Consulate-General: 7th Floor, 1 Bush St, San Francisco, CA 94104; tel (415) 362-6160; telex 340123; fax (415) 986-5440.
Consul-General: David Charles.
Deputy Consul-General and Trade Commissioner: Robert E. Jennings.
Consul (Immigration): Raymond L. Tolley.
Consul: Howard B. Wilson.

Consulate-General: 611 North Larchmont Blvd, Los Angeles, CA 90004; tel (213) 469-4300; fax (213) 469-9845.
Consul-General: John R. Kelso.
Deputy Consul-General and Senior Trade Commissioner: Colin E. Hook.
Consul (Immigration): Ronald Gent.
Consul (Information): T. Grealy.
Consul: Christopher F. Price.

Consulate-General: 1000 Bishop St, Penthouse, Honolulu, HI 96813; tel (808) 524-5050; telex 633128; fax (808) 523-5142.
Consul-General: Robert J. Tyson.
Consul: John J. McAnulty.
Vice-Consul and Communicator: J. Maas.

Consulate-General: 3 Post Oak Central A. H., Suite 800, 1990 Post Oak Blvd, Houston, TX 77056-9998; tel (713) 520-3179; fax (713) 622-6924.
Consul-General: Peter J. Urban.
Consul: Ian C. Lindemann.

Consulate-General: c/o Finnegan and Stanzler, 20 Beacon St, 5th Floor, Boston, MA 02103; tel (617) 248-8655; fax (617) 523-2502.
Honorary Consul-General: Margaret Stanzler.

AUSTRADE: 550 Baltimore Way, Suite 810, Coral Gables, Miami, FL 33134; tel (305) 442-2255; telex 49763650; fax (305) 442-8334.
Senior Trade Commissioner: G. McHugh.
Trade Commissioner: P. Brewer.
Marketing Manager: Richard Phillips.

AUSTRIA

Embassy: 2343 Massachusetts Ave, NW, Washington, DC 20008; tel (202) 483-4474; telex 440010; fax (202) 483-2743.
Ambassador: Friedrich Höss.
Chargé d'affaires: Philipp Hoyos.
Counsellor: Ferdinand Trauttmannsdorff.
Counsellor: Gerhard Reiweger.
Counsellor: Leopold Radauer.
Counsellor (Economic) and Consul-General: Hella Naumann.
Counsellor (Press): Ulf Pacher.
Counsellor (Science): Bernhard Zimburg.
Military and Air Attaché: Brig. Walter Schmit.
Military and Air Attaché: Col Norbert Höber.

Consulate-General: 31 East 69th St, New York, NY 10021; tel (212) 535-5544; telex 147285.
Consul-General: Wolfgang Steininger.
Honorary Consul-General: John Ethelbert Leslie.
Vice-Consul (Social Affairs): Hans Ottermayer.
Consul and Counsellor (Press): Wolfgang Petritsch.

Consulate-General: 11859 Wilshire Blvd, Suite 501, Los Angeles, CA 90025; tel (213) 444-9310; telex 215180.
Consul-General: Franz Cede.
Consul (Press/Culture/Information): Hugo-Maria Schally.

Consulate-General: Wrigley Bldg, Suite 707, 400 North Michigan Ave, Chicago, IL 60611; tel (312) 222-1515; telex 254070.
Consul-General: Clemens Coreth.
Vice-Consul: Paul Jenewein.

Consulate: 860 Lenox Tower, 3355 NE Lenox Rd, Atlanta, GA 30326; tel (404) 264-9858; fax (404) 266-3864.
Honorary Consul: Ferdinand Seefried.

Consulate: 211 Congress St, Suite 400, Boston, MA 02110; tel (617) 426-0330; fax (617) 461-1412.
Honorary Consul: Ira A. Korff.

Consulate: 167 Delaware Ave, Statler Bldg, Suite 828, Buffalo, NY 14202; tel (716) 852-7000.
Honorary Consul: Thomas Martin Dean.

Consulate: 1830 The Illuminating Bldg, 55 Public Square, Cleveland, OH 44113; tel (216) 621-5588.
Honorary Consul: Edward F. Werner.

Consulate: First Interstate Tower South, Suite 2300, 621 Seventh St, Denver, CO 80293; tel (303) 292-900; telex 450711.
Honorary Consul: Arnold C. Wegher.

Consulate: 300 East Long Lake Rd, Suite 375, Bloomfield Hills, MI 48013; tel (313) 645-1444.
Honorary Consul: Aloys Schwarz.

Consulate: 2535 West Loop St, Suite 319A, Houston, TX 77027-9509; tel (713) 623-2233; fax (713) 960-8966.
Honorary Consul: Otmar Kobler.

Consulate: 4505 Madison St, Kansas City, MO 64111; tel (816) 931-8812.
Honorary Consul: Dennis Owens.

Consulate: Republic Bldg, Suite 200, 1454 NW 17th Ave, Miami, FL 33125; tel (305) 325-1561.
Honorary Consul: Arthur W. Karlick.

Consulate: 755 Magazine St, New Orleans, LA 70130; tel (504) 581-5141; telex 584358.
Honorary Consul: Brunswick G. Deutsch.

Consulate: 3 Parkway, 20th Floor, Philadelphia, PA 19102; tel (215) 665-7348; fax (215) 636-9373.
Honorary Consul: Harry C. Schaub.

Consulate: c/o Bosrock & Co. Inc., 2490 MN World Trade Center, 3030 East 7th St, Saint Paul, MN 55101; tel (612) 272-2052; telex 413370; fax (612) 223-8383.
Honorary Consul: Ronald M. Bosrock.

Consulate: 4131 11th NE Penthouse 1, Seattle, WA 98105; tel (206) 633-3606.
Honorary Consul: Walter R. Weber.

Consulate: Oxford Bldg, Suite 3a, 141 North Meramec, Clayton, MO 63105; tel (314) 966-7687.
Honorary Consul: Alexander C. Niven.

Consulate: 5388 Poola St, Honolulu, HI 96821; tel (808) 923-8585; telex 743-0420; fax (808) 528-2800
Honorary Consul: Johann Strasser.

Consulate: Hotel El San Juan and Casino, Isla Verde, Puerto Rico 00913; tel 791-2521.
Honorary Consul: Marie Helene Reinhold.

BAHAMAS

Embassy: 2220 Massachusetts Ave, Suite 865, NW, Washington, DC 20008; tel (202) 319-2660; fax (202) 319-2668.
Ambassador: Margaret E. McDonald.
Deputy Head of Mission: Dr Paulette Bethel.
First Secretary and Consul: Sharon Brennen.
Second Secretary and Vice-Consul: David Cates.
Second Secretary and Vice-Consul: Joseph Curry.

Consulate-General: 9th Floor, 767 Third Ave, New York, NY 10017; tel (212) 412-6420.
Consul-General: Peter Deveaux-Isaacs.

Consulate-General: 25 SE Second Ave, Ingraham Bldg, Suite 818, Miami, FL 33131; tel (305) 319-2668.
Consul-General: Winston Munnings.

BAHRAIN

Embassy: 3502 International Drive, NW, Washington, DC 20008; tel (202) 342-0741.
Ambassador: Ghazi Mohamed Algosaibi.

Consulate-General: 2 United Nations Plaza, 25th Floor, East 44th St, New York, NY 10017; tel (212) 223-6200; fax (212) 319-0687.
Consul-General: Saeed al-Faihani (acting).

BANGLADESH

Embassy: 2201 Wisconsin Ave, NW, Washington, DC 20007; tel (202) 342-8372; fax (202) 333-4971.
Ambassador: A. H. S. Ataul Karim.

Consulate-General: 821 UN Plaza, 8th Floor, New York, NY 10017; tel (212) 867-3434.
Consul-General: Mohammad A. Hannan.

Consulate-General: 321 St Charles Ave, New Orleans, LA 70130.
Honorary Consul-General: Thomas B. Coleman.

Consulate-General: 1915 Grosvenor Center, 733 Bishop St, Honolulu, HI 96813.
Honorary Consul-General: Raymond Y. C. Ho.

Consulate: 10323 Santa Monica Blvd, Suite 105, Los Angeles, CA 90025.
Honorary Consul: Nancy C. Bretzfield.

BARBADOS

Embassy: 2144 Wyoming Ave, NW, Washington, DC 20008; tel (202) 939-9200; telex 64343; fax (202) 332-7467.
Ambassador: Rudi V. Webster.
Minister-Counsellor: A. M. Antony Cave.
First Secretary and Consul: Antoinette A. Forte.
Vice-Consul: Anne M. Blackman.
Second Secretary and Vice-Consul: Donna F. A. Gibson.
Attaché and Vice-Consul: Gladwin J. A. Sargeant.

Consulate-General: 800 Second Ave, 18th Floor, New York, NY 10017; tel (212) 867-8435.
Consul-General: Earl W. Glasgow.
Consul: Anthony Wiltshire.
Consul: Lawson Nurse.
Consul: Charles C. Burnett.
Consul: Hugh C. Riley.

Consulate: Airport Business Center, 34104 NW 72nd Ave, Miami, FL 33126; tel (305) 559-1310.
Honorary Consul-General: Colin S. Mayers.

Consulate: Afro-Carib Inc., POB 593453, Miami, FL 33159; tel (305) 757-1022.
Honorary Consul: William Austin Wynn, Jr.

Consulate: 3440 Wilshire Blvd, Suite 1215, Los Angeles, CA 90010; tel (213) 380-2198.
Vice-Consul: Don R. McCarthy.

Consulate: 6700 South Oglesby, Suite 1603, Chicago, IL 60649; tel (312) 922-7757; fax (312) 922-4093.
Honorary Consul: André Richardson King.

Consulate: 11012 East 13 Mile Rd, Suite 208, Warren, Detroit, MI 48093; tel (313) 751-8840.
Honorary Consul: Dr Lacey Walke.

Consulate: 3935 Flowerland Drive, Atlanta, GA 30319; tel (404) 454-9413.
Honorary Consul: Conrad C. Hunte.

Consulate: 723 Phillips Ave, Toledo, POB 5165, OH 43611; tel (419) 478-5533.
Honorary Consul: Dr Ian D. Murphy.

Consulate: 10202 SE 32nd Ave, Suite 601, Milwaukie, OR 97222; tel (503) 659-0283.
Honorary Consul: Harold Desmond Johnson.

Consulate: 321 St Charles Ave, 10th Floor Suite, New Orleans, LA 70130; tel (504) 586-1979.
Honorary Consul: Peter D. Coleman.

Consulate: 404 Homer St, Newton Center, Boston, MA 02159; tel (617) 427-6175.
Honorary Consul: Dr Henderson Brome.

Consulate: Mentor International, 442 Post St, Suite 800, San Francisco, CA 94102; tel (415) 421-8789.
Honorary Consul: Jerry Levine.

BELGIUM

Embassy: 3330 Garfield St, NW, Washington, DC 20008; tel (202) 333-6900; telex 440139; fax (202) 333-3079.
Ambassador: Juan Cassiers.
Consul: Robert van de Velde.

Consulate-General: 50 Rockefeller Plaza, Rm 1104, New York, NY 10020; tel (212) 586-5110.
Consul-General: Michel L. Dooms.
Deputy Consul-General: Baudouin V. de Callatay.
Vice-Consul: Jean Paul Feyaerts.
Vice-Consul: Leo I. Peeters.
Vice-Consul: Jozef E. Devors.
Vice-Consul: Phil van der Meeren.

Consulate-General: 6100 Wilshire Blvd, 12th Floor West, Los Angeles, CA 90048; tel (213) 857-1244.
Consul-General: Marc Otte.
Vice-Consul: Michel Parys.
Vice-Consul: Mark Bautil.
Vice-Consul: Christine Habig Celestino.

Consulate-General: 333 North Michigan Ave, Suite 2001-13, Chicago, IL 60601; tel (312) 263-6624.
Consul-General: Ronald de Langhe.
Vice-Consul: Jacques Botteman.

Consulate-General: Peachtree Center Cai Tower, Suite 2306, 229 Peachtree St, Atlanta, GA 30303; tel (404) 659-2150.
Consul-General: Ernest L. Staes.
Vice-Consul: Jan Bouchet.

Consulate: 3400 Center Sq. West, 1500 Market St, Philadelphia, PA 19102; tel (215) 972-3400.
Honorary Consul: Thomas Bateman Morris, Jr.

Consulate: 309 South Craig St, Pittsburgh, PA 15213.
Honorary Consul: Anne B. Lackner.

Consulate: 1900 Huntingdon Bldg, Cleveland, OH 44115; tel (216) 781-5470.
Honorary Consul: Ivan Lawrence Miller.

Consulate: St Joseph Bank & Trust Co., 401 Lincoln West Way, Mishawaka, IN 46544; tel (219) 237-5510.
Honorary Consul: Henry J. Nauts.

Consulate: 33 South Gay St, Baltimore, MD 21202; tel (301) 332-4815.
Honorary Consul: Paul F. Connor.

Consulate: 999 South Broadway, POB 5887, Denver, CO 80217; tel (303) 744-4051.
Honorary Consul: Lothar G. Estenfelder.
Honorary Vice-Consul: Michel A. Reynders.

Consulate: 2231 NE 192nd St, Miami, FL 33180; tel (305) 932-8981.
Honorary Consul: Gui Leopold Pierre Govaert.

Consulate: 2516 42nd Ave, Seattle, WA 98199.
Honorary Consul: Herbert Ronald Masnik.

Consulate: 740 18th Ave, Moline, IL 61265; tel (309) 762-7847.
Honorary Consul: Dolores Helen Bultinck.

Consulate: 4600 Bellevue at Gratiot, Detroit, MI 48207; tel (313) 923-7800.
Honorary Consul: Elizabeth A. Stevens.

Consulate: 8956 Moydalgen Rd, St Louis, MO 63124; tel (314) 993-9053.
Honorary Consul: Martine Smith-Cappuyns.
Honorary Vice-Consul: Stephen Brauer.

Consulate: Mulcahy & Wherry, SC Suite 1600, 815 East Mason St, Milwaukee, WI 53202; tel (414) 278-7110.
Honorary Consul: Charles Mulcahy.

Consulate: 1 Maritime Plaza, Suite 1300, San Francisco, CA 94111; tel (415) 399-1255.
Honorary Consul: Richard C. Sears.

Consulate: The Starks Bldg, Suite 475, Louisville, KY 40202; tel (502) 584-8583.
Honorary Consul: Alfred John Welsh.

Consulate: Pacific Bldg, Rm 302, 520 SW Yamhill St, Portland, OR 97204; tel (503) 228-0465.
Honorary Consul: Alfred Jules Herman.

Consulate: International Bldg, Suite 404, 611 Gravier St, New Orleans, LA 70130; tel (504) 522-3591.
Honorary Consul: Dr Paul F. Connor.

Consulate: 300 Commercial St, Suite 29, Malden, Boston, MA 02148; tel (617) 397-8566.
Honorary Consul: Philippe T. Capiau.

Consulate: 5572 Trinity Way, San Diego, CA 92120; tel (619) 945-6132.
Honorary Consul: Patrick J. Sebrechts.

Consulate: 800 Gessner, Suite 1000, Houston, TX 77024; tel (713) 461-7473.
Honorary Consul: Andre Arthur Crispin.

Consulate: 47 East South Temple, Salt Lake City, UT 84150; tel (801) 531-3150.
Honorary Consul: Charles Didier.

Consulate: 508 North Birdneck Rd, Virginia Beach, Norfolk, VA 23451; tel (804) 422-5571.
Honorary Consul: Mia S. Lanese.

Consulate: 1438 Mokolea Drive, Kallua, Honolulu, HI 96734; tel (808) 261-9079.
Honorary Consul: Roger A. Ulveling.

Consulate: 9243 North 81st St, Scottsdale, Phoenix, AZ 85258.
Honorary Consul: Maximilien Litvine.

Consulate: O'Neill, Burke, O'Neill, Leonard & O'Brien Ltd, 800 Norwest Center, 55 East 5th St, St Paul, MN 55101.
Honorary Consul: Patrick H. O'Neill.

Consulate: 1000 Walnut, Kansas City, KS 64106.
Honorary Consul: James Judd.

Consulate: 1031 West 4th Ave, Suite 400, Anchorage, AK 99510-7502.
Honorary Consul: Carl F. Brady, Jr.

Consulate: Banco de Ponce Bldg, Suite 713, 1250 Ponce de Leon Ave, Santurce, San Juan, Puerto Rico 00907; tel 725-3179.
Honorary Consul: Richard Claiborne Durham.

BELIZE

Embassy: 3400 International Drive, NW, Suite 2J, Washington, DC 20008; tel (202) 363-4505; telex 140997; fax (202) 362-7468.
Ambassador: James V. Hyde.

Consulate-General: 1511 'K' St, NW, Suite 425, Washington, DC 20005; tel (301) 983-2220.
Honorary Consul-General: Arthur Lee Quinn.

Consulate: 611 Wilton Plaza, Los Angeles, CA 90005; tel (213) 385-6499.
Honorary Consul: Ernesto Castillo.

Consulate: 1415 Louisiana, Suite 3100, Houston, TX 77002; tel (713) 658-0207.
Honorary Consul: Albert W. Dugan.

Consulate: 27166 Selkirt, Southfield, MI 48076; tel (313) 874-3440.
Honorary Consul: Dr Lennox A. Pike.

Consulate: Palm Beach, FL.
Honorary Consul: Grace T. Meighan.

Consulate: 4521 Elmwood Parkway, Metairie, New Orleans, LA 70003; tel (504) 465-9904.
Honorary Consul: Salvador Figueroa.

BENIN

Embassy: 2737 Cathedral Ave, NW, Washington, DC 20008; tel (202) 232-6656; telex 64155; fax (202) 544-1212.
Ambassador: Candide Pierre Ahouansou.

Consulate: 925 Century Park East, Suite 350, Los Angeles, CA 90067; tel (213) 625-3939.
Honorary Consul: Yvonne Brathwaite Burke.

Consulate: Chrisman-Sawyer Bank Bldg, 201 West Lexington St, 2nd Floor, Independence, MO 64050; tel (816) 252-1000.
Honorary Consul: Keith Wilson, Jr.

BHUTAN

Consulate-General: 2 UN Plaza, 27th Floor, New York, NY 10017; tel (212) 826-1919; telex 224196; fax (212) 826-2998.
Consul-General: Lhatu Wangchuk.
Deputy Consul-General: Leki Wangmo.

BOLIVIA

Embassy: 3014 Massachusetts Ave, NW, Washington, DC 20008; tel (202) 483-4410; telex 440049; fax (202) 328-3712.
Ambassador: Jorge Crespo-Velasco.
Minister-Counsellor: Luis Fernando González.
Counsellor (Economic): Carlos Alberto López.
Counsellor: Gonzalo Bernal Brito.
Counsellor: Erich Kuhn Poppe.
First Secretary: Teresa Menacho Rios.
First Secretary: Juan Peredo.
Second Secretary: Beatriz Bedoya.
Secretary (Consular): Lilian Rocha.
Attaché (Civil): Maria Teresa Campero.
Attaché (Civil): Ximena Hernández-Catá.
Head of Administration: Federico Varela.

Consulate-General: 211 East 43rd St, Suite 802, New York, NY 10017; tel (212) 687-0530; telex 421221; fax (212) 687-0532.
Consul-General: Paul Bruckner.
Vice-Consul: Osvaldo Loza.

Consulate-General: 25 SE 2nd Ave, Suite 545, Miami, FL 33131; tel (305) 358-3450; fax (305) 665-5769.
Consul-General: Martha Valasco de Canelas.
Vice-Consul: Emmy Canido de Chase.

Consulate-General: 870 Market St, Suite 355, San Francisco, CA 94102; tel (415) 495-5173.

Consul-General: Celia Mercado de Trigo.

Consulate: 3399 Garfield St, NW, Washington, DC 20008; tel (202) 298-7133.
Consul: William R. Joyce.

Consulate: 1200 West Superior, Melrose Park, Suite 101, Chicago, IL; tel (708) 366-5037.
Consul: Dr Jaime Escóbar Claros.

Consulate: San Juan Calle San Miguel, Suite 1, Ocean Park, Santurce, Puerto Rico 00911; tel 740-8440.
Consul: Peter E. Mariaca.

Consulate: 2385 East Drew Valley Rd, Atlanta, GA 30319; tel (404) 320-9312; fax (404) 841-2464.
Consul: Gustavo Estenssoro.

Consulate: 15215 South 52nd Ave, Suite 12, Seattle, WA 98188; tel (206) 244-6696; fax (206) 243-3795.
Consul: Ricardo Antezana.

Consulate: 1183 Hampton Park Drive, Saint Louis, MO 63117; tel (314) 241-4744; fax (314) 241-5054.
Consul: Luis Guillermo Zambrana.

Consulate: 8811 Westheimer, Suite 206, Houston, TX; tel (713) 780-8001; fax (713) 780-8738.
Consul: Norah de Walker.

BOTSWANA

Embassy: 3400 International Drive, NW, Suite 7M, Washington, DC 20008; tel (202) 244-4990; fax (202) 244-4164.
Ambassador: Botsweletse Kingsley Sebele.

Consulate: 333 South Hope St, 38th Floor, Los Angeles, CA 90071; tel (213) 626-8484.
Honorary Consul: William Barnum Rudell.

Consulate: 3625 Sacramento St, San Francisco, CA 94118; tel (415) 346-4435.
Honorary Consul: Charles L. Frankel.

Consulate: 4615 Post Oak Blvd, Suite 104A, Houston, TX 77027; tel (713) 622-1900.
Honorary Consul: Stephen V. Vallone.

BRAZIL

Embassy: 3006 Massachusetts Ave, NW, Washington, DC 20008; tel (202) 797-0200; fax (202) 745-2827.
Ambassador: Marcilo Marques Moreira.
Vice-Consul: Eliza Maria de Moraes.
Consular Agent: Francisca de Melo.

Consulate-General: 630 Fifth Ave, Suite 2720, New York, NY 10111; tel (212) 757-3080.
Consul-General: Carlos A. Santos-Neves.
Deputy Consul-General: Marcelo A. de M. Jardim.
Deputy Consul-General: Jorio Salgado Gama Filho.
Deputy Consul-General: Luiz F. de Athayde.
Deputy Consul-General: Eduardo da Costa Farias.
Deputy Consul-General: Luiz C. Villafane Gomes Santos.

Consulate-General: 3810 Wilshire Blvd, Suite 1500, Los Angeles, CA 90010; tel (213) 282-3133; telex 677309.
Consul-General: Celso Diniz.
Deputy Consul-General: Paulo A. V. Wolowski.

Consulate-General: 20 North Wacker Drive, Suite 1010, Chicago, IL 60606; tel (312) 372-2177.
Consul-General: Antonio C. Coelho da Rocha.
Deputy Consul-General: Sergio L. Gomes.

Consulate-General: 777 Brickell Ave, Penthouse, Miami, FL 33131; tel (305) 377-1734.
Consul-General: Luis F. de Oliveira e Cruz Benedini.
Deputy Consul-General: Kywal de Oliveira.

Consulate-General: 650 Poydras St, Suite 2504, New Orleans, LA 70130; tel (504) 588-9167.
Consul-General: Antonio F. da Rocha.
Deputy Consul-General: Sergo R. C. de Lacerda.

Consulate: World Trade Center, 2050 Stemmons, Suite 174, Dallas, TX 75258; tel (214) 651-1854.
Consul: Christovam Araujo.

Consulate: 1700 West Loop South, Suite 1450, Houston, TX; tel (713) 961-3063.
Vice-Consul: Maria J. Dutra Martins.

Consulate: 160 Federal St, 21st Floor, Boston, MA 02110.
Honorary Consul: Salua J. A. Smith.

Consulate: 300 Montgomery, Suite 1160, San Francisco, CA 94104; tel (415) 981-8170.
Consul: João C. de Souza-Gomes.

Consulate: 625 East 45th St, Savannah, GA 31405; tel (912) 234-2266.
Honorary Vice-Consul: John Milton Sayler.

Consulate: 625 Chesopeian Trail, Virginia Beach, Norfolk, VA 23452; tel (804) 340-5820.
Honorary Consul: James Earnest Thompson.

Consulate: 111 North 6th St, POB 52, Lafayette, IN 47902.
Honorary Consul: Eduardo A. Ostergren.

Consulate: 305 Royal Hawaiian Ave, Suite 307, Honolulu, HI 96815; tel (808) 536-5105.
Honorary Consul: John Milton Sayler.

BRUNEI

Embassy: Watergate, Suite 300, 2600 Virginia Ave, NW, Washington, DC 20037; tel (202) 342-0159; telex 904061; fax (202) 342-0158.
Ambassador: Dato Haji Mohammad Suni Idris.

BULGARIA

Embassy: 1621 22nd St, NW, Washington, DC 20008; tel (202) 387-7969; fax (202) 234-7973.
Ambassador: Oganian Pishev.

BURKINA FASO

Embassy: 2340 Massachusetts Ave, NW, Washington, DC 20008; tel (202) 332-5577; telex 440399; fax (202) 265-6972.
Ambassador: Paul-Désiré Kabore.
First Counsellor: Jean Kotie Diasso.
First Secretary: Djeneba Yasmine Traore.
Attaché (Culture): Clarisse Diasso.
Attaché (Consular): Cecile Pare Toe.

Consulate: 10960 Wilshire Blvd, Suite 1908, Los Angeles, CA 90024-3877; tel (213) 824-5100.
Honorary Consul: Allen I. Neiman.

Consulate: 225 Mimosa Drive, Decatur, Atlanta, GA 30030; tel (404) 378-7278.
Honorary Consul: Gary Gunderson.

Consulate: POB 3398, New Orleans, LA 70177; tel (504) 945-3152.
Honorary Consul: John William Ormond.

BURUNDI

Embassy: 2233 Wisconsin Ave, NW, Suite 212, Washington, DC 20007; tel (202) 342-2574.
Ambassador: Julien Kavakure.

Consulate: 854 Castlewood Terr., Chicago, IL 60640; tel (312) 271-2530.
Honorary Consul: Jay Herman Schmidt.

CAMEROON

Embassy: 2349 Massachusetts Ave, NW, Washington, DC 20008; tel (202) 265-8790; fax (202) 387-3826.
Ambassador: Paul Pondi.
First Counsellor: Jean Missoup.
Counsellor (Culture): Dr Nkwenti Ndefru.
Counsellor (Economic): Kesseng A. Mbassa.
Military Attaché: Col Obama.
First Secretary: Battokok Dax.
Second Secretary: Mbulle Vincent.
Second Secretary: Etori A. Zang.
Second Secretary: Boudjiho Regine.

Consulate: 147 Terra Vista, San Francisco, CA 94115; tel (415) 921-5372.
Honorary Consul: Donald Low.

Consulate: 7907 Hilshire Green, Houston, TX 77055; tel (713) 468-3875.
Honorary Consul: Charles Green.

CANADA

Embassy: 501 Pennsylvania Ave, NW, Washington, DC 20001; tel (202) 682-1740; telex 89664; fax (202) 682-7624.
Ambassador: Derek H. Burney.
Minister (Economic) and Deputy Head of Mission: M. Brault.
Minister: M. F. Kergin.
Minister-Counsellor (Commercial): W. A. Dymond.
Minister-Counsellor (Commercial): D. G. Ryan.
Minister-Counsellor: P. R. L. Somerville.
Minister-Counsellor: D. Livermore.
Counsellor (Commercial): H. A. van der Veer.
Counsellor (Commercial): C. Carrière.
Counsellor (Commercial): A. Pregel.
Counsellor (Commercial): J. M. Reid.
Counsellor (Commercial/Agriculture and Fisheries): P. Fawcett.
Counsellor (Commercial/Agriculture and Fisheries): J. A. McNab.
Counsellor (Administrative) and Consul: R. P. Archambault.
Counsellor (Science/Technology): M. St G. Stephens.
Counsellor (Culture): C. L. Barlow.
Counsellor and Consul: I. H. Rankin.
Counsellor: P. R. Anderson.
Counsellor: J. Fried.
Counsellor: J.-P. Gombay.
Counsellor: B. Crossfield.
Counsellor: S. Hibbard.
Counsellor: M. J. McKechnie.
Counsellor: P. D. MacDonald.
Counsellor: G. Tyerman.
Counsellor: A. Smith.
Counsellor: R. B. Snyder.
Counsellor: M. Martin.
Counsellor: R. Glasgow.
Counsellor: J. N. Dawe.
Counsellor (Defence Research): P. Solnoky.
Defence Attaché: Maj. Gen. G. S. Wells.
Assistant Defence Attaché: Lieut Col G. S. Graham.
Military Attaché: Col D. D. Dalziel.
Assistant Military Attaché: Lieut Col R. R. Hoodspith.
Naval Attaché: Cdre E. E. Lawder.
Assistant Naval Attaché: Commdr G. A. Godwin.
Air Attaché: Brig.-Gen. W. J. B. Partington.
Assistant Air Attaché: Lieut Col P. W. Sloan.
Assistant Air Attaché: Lieut Col G. A. Potter.
Attaché (Defence Research): T. D. Drummond.
First Secretary (Defence Production): D. Douville.
First Secretary (Commercial): R. D. Rush.
First Secretary (Commercial): P. H. Drabble.
First Secretary (Commercial): A. C. Aubin.
Second Secretary (Immigration) and Vice-Consul: L. J. Toope.

Mission to the Organization of American States: 501 Pennsylvania Ave, NW, Washington, DC 20001; tel (202) 682-1768; telex 89664; fax (202) 682-7624.
Permanent Representative: Jean-Paul Hubert.
Deputy Permanent Representative: R. J. Wilson.

Consulate-General: 1251 Ave of the Americas, New York, NY 10020-1175; tel (212) 768-2400; telex 126242; fax (212) 768-2440.
Consul-General: Anthony T. Eyton.
Deputy Consul-General: Archie D. McArthur.
Consul and Senior Trade Commissioner: John G. Keale.
Consul and Trade Commissioner: B. T. Giacomin.
Consul and Trade Commissioner: John H. Kern.
Consul and Trade Commissioner: Yves Lemay.
Consul (Investment): David J. Lenihan.

Consulate-General: 412 Plaza 600, Sixth and Stewart, Seattle, WA 98101-1286; tel (206) 443-1777; telex 328762; fax (206) 443-1782.
Consul-General: Roger A. Bull.
Consul and Senior Trade Commissioner: Paul C. Hubbard.
Consul: Richard G. Seaborn.
Consul: Nigel H. Thompson.
Consul: James F. P. Lynn.

Consulate-General: 300 South Grand Ave, 10th Floor, Los Angeles, CA 90071; tel (213) 687-7432; telex 674119; fax (213) 620-8827.
Deputy Consul-General: John E. Kepper.
Consul (Investment): Matthew H. H. Fisher.

Consulate-General: St Paul Place, 750 North St Paul St, Suite 1700, Dallas, TX 75201; tel (214) 922-9806; telex 732637; fax (214) 922-9815.
Consul-General: Carl E. Rufelds.
Deputy Consul-General: John R. Hammill.
Consul and Senior Trade Commissioner: James S. A. Sotvedt.

Consulate-General: 3 Parkway Bldg, Suite 1310, Philadelphia, PA 19102; tel (215) 561-1750.
Commercial Counsellor and Consul: James J. Ganderton.

Consulate-General: 310 South Michigan Ave, Suite 1200, Chicago, IL 60604-4295; tel (312) 427-1031; telex 254171; fax (312) 922-0637.
Consul-General: George Douglas Valentine.
Deputy Consul-General and Senior Trade Commissioner: Gaetan Bruneau.
Consul and Trade Commissioner: Durban C. Morrow.
Consul and Trade Commissioner: George T. Phillips.

Consulate-General: 600 Renaissance Center, Suite 1100, Detroit, MI 48243-1704; tel (313) 567-2340; telex 230715; fax (313) 567-2164.
Consul-General: M. Anne Charles.
Consul and Senior Trade Commissioner: A. B. Bouma.

Consulate-General: One CNN Center, South Tower, Suite 400, Atlanta, GA 30303-2705; tel (404) 577-6810; telex 543197; fax (404) 524-5046.
Consul-General: James A. Elliot.
Deputy Consul-General and Senior Trade Commissioner: Douglas I. Ditto.

Consulate-General: 50 Fremont St, Suite 2100, San Francisco, CA 94105; tel (415) 495-6021; telex 34321; fax (415) 541-7708.
Consul-General: Percy T. Eastham.
Consul and Senior Trade Commissioner: Paul D. Donohue.

Consulate-General: 701 South Fourth Ave, Minneapolis, MN 55415; tel (612) 333-4641; telex 290229; fax (612) 332-4061.
Consul-General: Brian Buckley.
Consul and Senior Trade Commissioner: James E. Graham.

Consulate-General: 3 Copley St, Suite 400, Boston, MA 02116; tel (617) 262-3760; telex 940625; fax (617) 262-3415.
Consul-General: Thomas M. McMillan.
Deputy Consul-General and Senior Trade Commissioner: Terence W. Colfer.

Consulate: 1 Marine Midland Center, Suite 3550, Buffalo, NY 14203-2884; tel (716) 852-1247; telex 247519; fax (716) 852-4340.
Consul and Senior Trade Commissioner: George H. Musgrove.

Consulate: Illuminating Bldg, 55 Public Sq., Cleveland, OH 44113-1983; tel (216) 771-0150; telex 985364; fax (216) 771-1688.
Consul: Lawrence D. Lederman.
Consul and Trade Commissioner: Michael G. Virr.

Consulate: 3935 Westheimer Rd, Suite 301, Houston, TX 77027; tel (713) 627-8079.
Consul and Trade Commissioner: Nick J. Dellavalle.

Consulate: 801 Brickell Ave, 9th Floor, Miami, FL.
Consul and Trade Commissioner: Stewart Beck.

Consulate: The Bemiston Tower, 231 South Bemiston Ave, Suite 843, St Louis, MO 63105.
Consul and Trade Commissioner: André Benoit.

Consulate: 5 Independence Way, Suite 5, Princeton, NJ 08450.
Consul and Trade Commissioner: Barbara T. Giacomin.

Consulate: South Wing Gateway II, 9th Floor, Pittsburgh, PA 15222.
Consul and Trade Commissioner: Ronald J. McLeod.

Consulate: 43500 Lajolla Village Drive, Suite 300, San Diego, CA 92122.
Consul and Trade Commissioner: Anthony B. Bouma.

Consulate: 999 18th St, Suite 1000, Denver, CO 80202.
Consul and Trade Commissioner: William G. McEwen.

Consulate: 273 Ponce de Leon Ave, Hato Rey, San Juan, PR.
Consul and Trade Commissioner: James C. Bradford.

CAPE VERDE

Embassy: 3415 Massachusetts Ave, NW, Washington, DC 20007; tel (202) 965-6820; fax (202) 965-1207.
Ambassador: José Luís Fernandes Lopes.

Consulate-General: 535 Boylston St, Boston, MA 02116; tel (617) 353-0014.
Consul-General: Isildo A. da Silva.
Deputy Consul-General: Julio C. Herbert Duarte Lopes.
Consul: Roque Ramos de Pina.

CENTRAL AFRICAN REPUBLIC

Embassy: 1618 22nd St, NW, Washington, DC 20008; tel (202) 483-7800.
Ambassador: Jean-Pierre Saohong-Kombet.

Consulate: 2330 South Brentwood Blvd, St Louis, MO 63144; tel (314) 961-9825.
Honorary Consul: George Gabriel White.

CHAD

Embassy: 2002 R St, NW, Washington, DC 20009; tel (202) 462-4009; fax (202) 462-4009.
Ambassador: Mahamat Ali Adoum.

CHILE

Embassy: 1732 Massachusetts Ave, NW, Washington, DC 20036; tel (202) 785-1746; fax (202) 887-5579.
Ambassador: Patricio Silva.

Consulate-General: 866 United Nations Plaza, New York, NY 10017; tel (212) 370-1455.
Consul-General: Diego Valenzuela.
Consul: Francisco Vial.
Consul: Maria Cristina Cifuentes.
Honorary Consul: Elba Fuentes.

Consulate-General: 510 West 6th St, Suite 1204, Los Angeles, CA 90014.
Consul-General: Lionel del Solar.
Honorary Consul: Fernando Guzman.

Consulate-General: 1110 Brickell Ave, Suite 616, Miami, FL 33131.
Consul-General: Alberto Labbe.
Consul: Gonzalez Bachelet Artigues.

Consulate-General: 870 Market St, Suite 1062, San Francisco, CA 94102; tel (415) 982-7662.
Consul-General: Maximiliano M. Jarda.
Consul: Hortario Perez D.

Consulate-General: 1360 Post Oak Blvd, Suite 2330, Houston, TX 77056.
Consul: Pedro Aguirre.

Consulate-General: Public Ledger Bldg, 6th & Chestnut, Suites 444-46, Philadelphia, PA 19142.
Consul-General: Daniel Carvallo.
Consul: Luis Winter.

Consulate: 3333 NE Peachtree Rd, Suite 225, Atlanta, GA 30326.
Honorary Consul: W. Taylor Boone, Jr.

Consulate: 79 Milk St, Suite 600, Boston, MA 02109; tel (617) 426-1678.
Honorary Consul: Paul William Garber.
Honorary Consul: Philip C. Garber.

Consulate: 1425 4th Ave, Rm 426, Seattle, WA 98101; tel (206) 624-3772.
Honorary Consul: Kerry N. Monterey.

Consulate: 3500 Oak Lawn Ave, Suite 200, Dallas, TX 75219.
Honorary Consul: Dorothy Reid.

Consulate: 1110 South 150 West Orem, Provo, UT 84057; tel (801) 531-1292.
Honorary Consul: Mario Melendez.

Consulate: 948 Equestrian Drive, Mount Pleasant, Charleston, SC 29464; tel (803) 792-2489.
Honorary Consul: Carlos Salinas.

Consulate: 3517 Bondwood Drive, Columbus, GA 31906; tel (404) 687-6461.
Honorary Consul: Carlos Enrique Urrutia.

Consulate: 701 B St, Suite 2020, San Diego, CA 92101; tel (619) 232-6361.
Honorary Consul: George L. Gildred.

Consulate: 6175 West 38th St, Wheatridge, Denver, CO 80033; tel (303) 424-4022.
Honorary Consul: Maria Soledad Douglas.

Consulate: 4688 Oregon St, La Jolla, CA 92116; tel (619) 298-4160.
Honorary Consul: Patrick J. Ryan.

Consulate: 1376 Johnson St, Menlo Park, Santa Clara, CA 94025; tel (415) 322-6985.
Honorary Consular Agent: Carlos Lopez.

Consulate: 1860 Ala Moana Blvd, Suite 1900, Honolulu, HI 96815; tel (808) 949-2850.
Honorary Consul: Keith E. Adamson.

CHINA, PEOPLE'S REPUBLIC

Embassy: 2300 Connecticut Ave, NW, Washington, DC 20008; tel (202) 328-2500; fax (202) 232-7855.
Ambassador: Zhu Qizhen.

Consulate-General: 520 12th Ave, New York, NY 10036; tel (212) 279-4275.
Consul-General: Weng Fupei.
Deputy Consul-General: Song Youming.
Deputy Consul-General: Cao Pizhong.
Consul: Chen Ruiqiang.
Consul: Wu Jida.
Consul: Huang Zhizheng.
Consul: Feng Changjun.
Consul: Gao Lianyou.

Consul: Yu Changhai.

Consulate-General: 501 Shatto Pl., Los Angeles, CA 90020; tel (213) 380-3105.
Consul-General: Ma Yuzhen.
Deputy Consul-General: Zhang Guoqiang.
Consul: Xue Zhiliang.
Consul: Zhang Pengxiang.
Consul: Fang Haishun.

Consulate-General: 104 South Michigan Ave, Suites 408, 420, 425, 815, 820 & 900, Chicago, IL 60603; tel (312) 346-0287.
Consul-General: Wang Li.
Deputy Consul-General: Xie Junzhen.
Consul: Wang Yingcai.
Consul: Zhou Xingwu.
Consul: Zhao Qun.

Consulate-General: 1450 Laguna St, San Francisco, CA 94115; tel (415) 563-4885.
Consul-General: Zheng Wanzhen.
Deputy Consul-General: Shen Xuezhong.
Consul: Wang Shaohua.
Consul: Zheng Guoxiang.
Consul: Chen Cilan.

Consulate-General: 3417 Montrose Blvd, Houston, TX 77006; tel (713) 524-0780.
Consul-General: Zhu Qiusheng.
Deputy Consul-General: Liu Yibin.
Consul: Wang Yixuan.
Consul: Xie Yougao.
Consul: Tang Dengyin.

COLOMBIA

Embassy: 1825 Connecticut Ave, NW, Suite 218, Washington, DC 20009; tel (202) 332-7573; fax (202) 232-8643.
Ambassador: Jaime García-Parra.

Consulate-General: 10 East 46th St, New York, NY 10017; tel (212) 949-9898.
Consul-General: Luis Toro.
Consul: Santiago Echavarria.
Consul: Alberto Duran.
Consul: Antonio González.
Consul: Ana Catalina del Llano.
Consul: Myriam C. Ramírez.

Consulate-General: 280 Aragon Ave, Coral Gables, Miami, FL 33134; tel (305) 448-5558.
Consul-General: Rafael Guerrero Rodríguez.

Consulate-General: 122 South Michigan Ave, Site 1441, Chicago, IL 60603; tel (312) 341-0658.
Consul-General: Rafael Vanegas.

Consulate-General: 870 Market St, Suite 509, San Francisco, CA 94102; tel (415) 362-0080.
Consul: Miguel S. Mata Alvarez.

Consulate-General: 1844 World Trade Center, 2 Canal St, New Orleans, LA 70130; tel (504) 525-5580.
Consul-General: Rafael Samudio Molina.

Consulate-General: 2990 Richmond Ave, Suite 544, Houston, TX 77098; tel (713) 527-8919.
Consul-General: Abelardo Ramírez.

Consulate-General: Edif. Mercantil Plaza, Hato Ray, Suite 818, San Juan, Puerto Rico 00918; tel 754-1675.
Consul-General: Teresa Berardinelli.

Consulate: 3600 Wilshire Blvd, Suite 1712, Los Angeles, CA 90010; tel (213) 382-1136.
Consul: Douglas Montgomery.

Consulate: 1961 North Druid Hills Rd, NE, Suite 102B, Atlanta, GA 30329; tel (404) 320-9665.
Consul: Claralia Ramírez de Arango.

Consulate: 535 Boylston St, 11th Floor, Boston, MA 02116; tel (617) 536-6222.
Consul: Bertha Olga Ospina.

Consulate: 24901 Northwestern Highway, Horizon Heritage Plaza Bldg, Suite 316B, Detroit, MI 48075; tel (313) 352-4970.
Consul: Alvaro E. Rodríguez.

Consulate: 6800 Telemark Trail, Minneapolis, MN 55436.
Honorary Consul: Dr Fernando Torres Restrepo.

Consulate: 2000 Eoff St, Wheeling, WV 26003; tel (304) 234-8561.
Honorary Consul: Dr Leonidas Castro.

Consulate: 11552 New London Drive, St Louis, MO 63141.
Honorary Consul: Cecilia Henao de Castro.

Consulate: 688 Oriole Drive, Eastlake, OH 44094.
Honorary Consul: Eddy Rosemberg de Herrera.

Consulate: Nine Island Ave, Suite 501, Belle Isle, Miami Beach, FL 33139; tel (305) 534-4733.
Honorary Consul: Victoria Petersson Gildred.

Consulate: 1211 North Westshore Blvd, ADP Bldg, Suite 411, Tampa, FL 33607; tel (813) 875-1499.
Honorary Vice-Consul: Alvaro de Bedout (resident in New Orleans).

COMOROS

Embassy: 336 East 45th St, New York, NY 10017; tel (212) 972-8010; fax (212) 983-4712.
Ambassador: Amini Ali Moumin.

CONGO

Embassy: 4891 Colorado Ave, NW, Washington, DC 20011; tel (202) 726-5500.
Ambassador: Roger Issombo.

COSTA RICA

Embassy: 1825 Connecticut Ave, NW, Suite 211, Washington, DC 20009; tel (202) 234-2945; fax (202) 234-8653.
Ambassador: Gonzalo J. Facio.

Consulate-General: 80 Wall St, Suite 1117, New York, NY 10005; tel (212) 425-2620.
Honorary Consul: Nelson Hernandez-Zamora.

Consulate-General: 1543 West Olympic Blvd, Los Angeles, CA 90015; tel (213) 380-7925.
Consul-General: Hubert Rojas Araya.

Consulate-General: 1633 Filmore St, Suite 100, Denver, CO 80206; tel (303) 377-0050.
Honorary Consul-General: Guillermo E. Aragon.

Consulate-General: 28 West Flagler St, Suite 806, Miami, FL 33130; tel (305) 377-4242.
Consul-General: Oscar Andreoli.

Consulate-General: 8 South Michigan Ave, Suites 1312 & 510, Chicago, IL 60603; tel (312) 263-2772.

Consulate-General: 870 Market St, No. 544-48, San Francisco, CA 94102; tel (415) 392-8488.
Consul-General: Natalia Jimenez Carvajal.

Consulate-General: International Trade Mart, Suite 934, New Orleans, LA 70130; tel (504) 525-5445.
Consul-General: Rodríguez Castro Echeverria.

Consulate-General: 4025 Camino del Rio South, Suite 326, San Diego, CA 92100; tel (619) 280-2308.
Consul-General: Alex Sanchez.

Consulate-General: 3000 Wilcrest, Suite 145, Houston, TX 77042; tel (713) 785-1315.
Consul-General: Francisco Castro.

Consulate-General: 7500 Callaghan Rd, Suite 350, San Antonio, TX 78229; tel (512) 340-8499.

Consulate-General: 5285 86th Ave, North Penellas Park, Tampa, FL; tel (813) 544-1147.

Consulate-General: 7033 Luella Anne Drive, NE, Albuquerque, NM 87109; tel (505) 822-1420.
Vice-Consul: Victoria Beeche de Guirola.

Consulate-General: 1661 Paradise Hill, Rio Piedras, San Juan, Puerto Rico 00926; tel 758-6301.

Consulate: 3815 Presidential Parkway, NE, Suite 102, Atlanta, GA 30340; tel (404) 457-5656.
Honorary Consul: Rose G. Cunningham.

Consulate: 2400 Energy Park Drive, St Paul, Minneapolis, MN 55180; tel (612) 645-3401.
Honorary Consul: Anthony L. Andersen.

Consulate: Security Plaza, 929 Fee Rd, Suite 200, Maryland Heights, St Louis, MN 63043; tel (314) 434-6300.
Honorary Consul: Mark A. Turken.

Consulate: 5436 Mountain View Drive, Las Vegas, NV 89102; tel (702) 878-2175.
Honorary Consul: Rocio M. Quiros de Revello.

Consulate: 5370 Siegle Rd, Lockport, Buffalo, NY 14094; tel (716) 625-9692.

Consulate: 819 Koko Isle Circle, Honolulu, HI 96825; tel (808) 395-7772.
Honorary Consul: Hilda Aguilar de Richardson.

COTE D'IVOIRE

Embassy: 2424 Massachusetts Ave, NW, Washington, DC 20008; tel (202) 797-0300; fax (202) 483-8482.
Ambassador: Charles Gomis.

Consulate-General: 9000 Sunset Blvd, Los Angeles, CA 90069; tel (213) 550-1288.
Honorary Consul-General: Herbert V. K. Hischemoeller.

Consulate-General: Pier 23, San Francisco, CA 94111; tel (415) 391-0176.
Honorary Consul-General: Edgar de Pue Osgood.

Consulate: 901 SW Washington St, Portland, OR 97205; tel (503) 244-2293.
Honorary Consul: Elizabeth Taylor Hamilton.

CUBA

Interests Section: c/o Embassy of Switzerland, 2900 Cathedral Ave, NW, Washington, DC 20008; tel (202) 745-7900.
Official Representative: José Antonio Arbesu Fraga.

CYPRUS

Embassy: 2211 R St, NW, Washington, DC 20008; tel (202) 462-5772; telex 440596; fax (202) 483-6710.
Ambassador: Michael E. Sherifis.

Consulate-General: 13 East 40th St, New York, NY 10016; tel (212) 688-6016; telex 666969; fax (212) 685-7316.
Consul-General: Elias Eliades.

Consulate-General: 42-19 Collidge Ave, Los Angeles, CA 90066; tel (213) 397-0771.
Honorary Consul-General: Andreas C. Kyprianides.

Consulate-General: 205 Crocker Ave, Piedmont, CA 94610; tel (415) 547-5689; fax (415) 428-1450.
Honorary Consul-General: Dr Anastassios K. Simonides.

Consulate: 7714 Langdon St, Philadelphia, PA 19111; tel (215) 928-4290.
Honorary Consul: James Oratis.

Consulate: 2402 Oak Bridge Rd, Fort Wayne, IN 46805; tel (219) 481-6897; fax (219) 481-6880.
Honorary Consul: Prof. Van Coufoudakis.

Consulate: 6680 North Sioux, Chicago, IL 60646; tel (312) 763-5659.
Honorary Consul: Zenon C. Pappas.

Consulate: 15706 Michigan Ave, Dearborm, Detroit, MI 48126; tel (313) 582-1411.
Honorary Consul: Steve Stylianou.

Consulate: 3192 Watson Rd, St Louis, MO 63139; tel (314) 781-7041.
Honorary Consul: Dr Nicolas D. Matsakis.

Consulate: 1790 Muldey Rd, Suite 6-A, Atlanta, GA 30001; tel (404) 941-3764; fax (404) 941-2109.
Honorary Consul: Dr Kyriakos M. Michaelides.

Consulate: Mayer Bldg, Suite 510, 1130 SW Morrison St, Portland, OR 97205; tel (503) 227-1411.
Honorary Consul: Alexander Christy.

Consulate: 5638 Riverbend Blvd, Baton Rouge, LA 70820; tel (504) 388-8701; fax (504) 388-5773.
Honorary Consul: Symeon C. Symeonides.

Consulate: 1336 NE Camelback Court, Rochester, MN 55901; tel (507) 284-2511.
Honorary Consul: Dr Panos P. Kelalis.

Consulate: 1277 East Missouri, Suite 214, Phoenix, AZ 85014; tel (602) 264-9701.
Honorary Consul: Stanley J. Dru.

Consulate: 70-7 Kirkland St, Cambridge, MA 02138; tel (617) 497-0219.
Honorary Consul: Dr John Papajohn.

Consulate: Atlantic Steamers Supply Co. Inc., 320 South 66th St, POB 9049, Houston, TX 77011; tel (713) 928-2264; telex 76760; fax (713) 928-2093.
Honorary Consul: William C. Crassas.

'TURKISH REPUBLIC OF NORTHERN CYPRUS'

Representation: 1667 K St, Suite 690, Washington, DC 20006; tel (202) 887-6198; fax (202) 467-0685.
Representative: Bülent Aliriza.
Second Secretary: Ahmet Erdendiz.

Representation: 821 United Nations Plaza, 6th Floor, New York, NY 10017; tel (212) 687-2350; fax (212) 949-6872.
Representative: Osman Ertuğ.
First Secretary: Aytuğ Plümer.

CZECHOSLOVAKIA

Embassy: 3900 Linnean Ave, NW, Washington, DC 20008; tel (202) 363-6315; fax (202) 966-8540.
Ambassador: Rita Klimova.

DENMARK

Embassy: 3200 Whitehaven St, NW, Washington, DC 20008-3683; tel (202) 234-4300; telex 440081; fax (202) 328-1470.
Ambassador: Peter P. Dyvig.
Minister-Counsellor (Economic): Laurids Mikaelsen.
Minister-Counsellor: Niels Kaas Dyrlund.
Head of Information and Minister-Counsellor: Bent Skou.
Chancellor (Commercial) and Vice-Consul: Evy Jordan.
Counsellor (Finance): Peter Barslund.
Counsellor: Lars Hørmann.
Counsellor: Vibeke Roosen.
Defence Attaché: Brig.-Gen. Kristian Dines Andersen.
Assistant Defence Attaché: Lieut Col Mogens Meyer Pedersen.
Secretary: Anne Meldgaard.
Vice-Consul (Administrative): Niels Erik Andersen.
Agricultural and Government Adviser: L. Ingerslev Madsen.
Agricultural Adviser: Jan Wuff.

Consulate-General: 825 Third Ave, 32nd & 33rd Floors, New York, NY 10022-7519; tel (212) 223-4545; telex 01-25505; fax (212) 754-1904.
Consul-General: Leif Donde.
Consul and Counsellor (Commercial): Niels Carsten Schmidt.
Consul and Fisheries Adviser: Erling Hulgaard.
Consul: Marianne Hoffman.
Vice-Consul and Chancellor (Cultural Affairs): Anita Rasmussen.
Export Assistant: Susan Kirsten Hansen.
Export Assistant: Esben Veng-Christensen.

Consulate-General: 3440 Wilshire Blvd, Suite 904, Los Angeles, CA 90010-2183; tel (213) 387-4277; telex 67-7647; fax (213) 387-9456.
Consul-General: Henning Kristiansen.
Consul and Counsellor (Commercial): Børge Petersen.
Attaché (Industry): Mogens Brabæk Andersen.
Export Assistant: Anne Heiburg-Iürgensen.

Consulate-General: John Hancock Center, Suite 3430, 875 North Michigan Ave, Chicago, IL 60611-1901; tel (312) 787-8780; telex 025-4094; fax (312) 787-8744.
Consul-General: Niels Julius Lassen.
Consul and Counsellor (Commercial): Jørgen Gulev.
Export Assistant: Christian Ingerslev.

Consulate: 3200 National City Center, Cleveland, OH 44114; tel (216) 621-0200.
Consul: H. Stephen Madsen.

Consulate: 22 Townhouse Lane, Corpus Christi, TX 78412; POB 4585, Corpus Christi, TX 78408; tel (512) 991-3012.
Consul: Michael Gersmann.

Consulate: 3200 LTV Center, 2001 Ross Ave, Dallas, TX 75201; tel (214) 970-6200; telex 316565; fax (214) 978-4439.
Consul: Harland Rogers Crow.

Consulate: 1000 Equitable Bldg, Des Moines, IA 50309; tel (515) 245-6789; fax (515) 244-1328.
Consul: William Wimer.

Consulate: 4113 North Woodward Ave, Royal Oak, MI 48072; tel (313) 549-3666.
Consul: Marshall M. Fredericks.

Consulate: 1700 West 12th St, POB 4046, Kansas City, MO 64101; tel (816) 421-0633.
Consul: Elcar A. Nielsen.

Consulate: 9015 W. Maple St, Milwaukee, WI 53214; tel (414) 476-3630; telex 2-6865.
Consul: Barry Nelson James.

Consulate: 7600 Parklawn Ave, Suite 444, Edina, Minneapolis, MN 55435; tel (612) 893-1305; fax (612) 831-7358.
Consul: Gordon A. Johnson.

Consulate: The RAM Companies, 100 NW 63rd St, Suite 300, Oklahoma City, OK 73116; tel (405) 848-8444; fax (405) 848-1062.
Consul: William Woodrow Talley II.

Consulate: 1500 Woodmen Tower, Omaha, NE 68102; tel (402) 344-0500.
Consul: Kenneth Byron Holm.

Consulate: 6515 Page Blvd, St Louis, MO 63133; POB 31, St Louis, MO 63166; tel (314) 727-4010.
Consul: Howard Joseph Behan.

Consulate: Alaska Mutual Bank Bldg, 601 West 5th Ave, Suite 700, Anchorage, AK 99501; tel (907) 276-7401; fax (907) 274-4953.
Consul: Frank A. Danner.

Consulate: 5353 West Dartmouth Ave, Suite 508, Denver, CO 80227; tel (303) 980-9100; fax (303) 989-6610.
Consul: Hans Thyge Nielsen.

Consulate: 2979 Kalakaua Ave, Suite 704, Honolulu, HI 96815; POB 88122, Honolulu, HI 96830; tel (808) 923-8884.
Consul: Paul Bom Krogh.

Consulate: Valley Center, 5th Floor, 241 North Central Ave, POB 71, Phoenix, AZ 85001; tel (602) 261-1254; fax (602) 261-2570.
Consul: Duane Morse Anderson.

Consulate: 1600 Pioneer Tower, 888 SW Fifth Ave, Portland, OR 97204-2099; tel (503) 294-0513; telex 260823; fax (503) 274-8779.
Consul: Ingolf Noto.

Consulate: 231 Edison St, Salt Lake City, UT 84111; tel (801) 355-2135.
Consul: Julius Andersen.

Consulate: 1405 Savoy Circle, San Diego, CA 92107; tel (619) 224-7640.
Consul: William Daniel Larsen.

Consulate: 221 Main St, 14th Floor, San Francisco, CA 94105; tel (415) 243-0705; fax (415) 995-7249.
Consul: Mogens Hubert Lauridsen.

Consulate: 1300 Tower Bldg, 1809 7th Ave, Seattle, WA 98101; tel (206) 682-6101; fax (206) 623-5694.
Consul: Martin D. Metzon.

Consulate: 225 Peachtree St, NE, Suite 201, Atlanta, GA 30303; tel (404) 522-8811; fax (404) 223-0853.
Consul: John C. Portman, Jr.

Consulate: 717 Light St, Suite 400, Baltimore, MD 21230-3807; tel (301) 727-7665; telex 684-9119; fax (301) 727-7667.
Consul: Timothy Connor Spigelmire.

Consulate: 581 Boylston St, Suite 404, Boston, MA 02116; tel (617) 266-8418; fax (617) 536-3497.
Consul: Christian Georg Halby.

Consulate: 28 Broad St, POB 993, Charleston, SC 29402; tel (803) 577-4000; fax (803) 724-6600.
Consul: George Lamb Buist Rivers.

Consulate: 2070 Talleyrand Ave, Office 6, Jacksonville, FL 32206; tel (904) 632-0723; telex 279904; fax (904) 354-4760.
Consul: Claude Leach Collins.

Consulate: Law Offices of Anne-Lise Gustafson, Gables International Plaza, Suite 600, 2655 Le Jeune Rd, Coral Gables, FL 33134; tel (305) 443-3160; fax (305) 447-1190,
Consul: Anne-Lise Dirks Gustafson.

Consulate: 1350 Dauphin St, Mobile, AL 36604; POB 15, Mobile, AL 36601; tel (205) 432-4633; telex 505497; fax (205) 432-8675.
Consul: Martin Horst Cunningham.

Consulate: Vanderbilt University Hospital, D 1120 Medical Center North, Nashville, TN 37232; tel (615) 322-3288.
Consul: Richard Moss Heller.

Consulate: 321 St Charles Ave, 5th Floor, New Orleans, LA 70130; tel (504) 586-8300; fax (504) 586-8300.
Consul: Thomas Kendall Winingder.

Consulate: 1800 Sovran Center, Norfolk, VA 23510; tel (804) 628-5568; fax (804) 628-5568.
Consul: William Edward Rachels, Jr.

Consulate: 956 Public Ledger Bldg, Independence Sq., Philadelphia, PA 19106; tel (215) 625-9900; telex 831477; fax (215) 625-0185.
Consul: Richard Ware Palmer.

Consulate: 801 East Washington St, Tampa, FL 33602; tel (813) 223-1521; telex 53763; fax (813) 221-6406.
Consul: Shirley McKay Savage.

Consulate: c/o Gloucester Shipping & Stevedoring Co., 8 Pond Rd, POB 481, Gloucester, MA 01930; tel (508) 283-5745; telex 94-0323; fax (508) 283-7647.
Vice-Consul: Carl Moores.

DJIBOUTI

Embassy: 1156 15th St, NW, Suite 515, Washington, DC 20005; tel (202) 331-0270; telex 4490085; fax (202) 331-0302.
Ambassador: Roble Olhaye.
Counsellor: Ali Moussa Iye.
Second Secretary: Issa Daher Bouraleh.
Attaché (Finance): Hassan Mohamed Sougal.

DOMINICA

Consulate-General: 820 2nd Ave, Suite 900B, New York, NY 10017; fax (212) 808-4975.
Consul-General: Hyacinth Elwin.

DOMINICAN REPUBLIC

Embassy: 1715 22nd St, NW, Washington, DC 20008; tel (202) 332-6280; fax (202) 265-8057.
Ambassador: Dr Edward Irvin Watty.

Consulate-General: 17 West 60th St, New York, NY 10023; tel (212) 768-2480.
Vice-Consul: Juan Ramon Sencion.
Vice-Consul: Necker Objimovdan.

Consulate-General: 548 South Spring St, Suite 309, Los Angeles, CA 90013; tel (213) 858-7365.

Consulate-General: Lafayette Bldg Associates, Rm 422, 5th & Chestnut Sts, Philadelphia, PA 19106; tel (215) 923-3006.
Vice-Consul: Caperuza Diaz de Almonte.
Vice-Consul: Josefina A. Cantizano Rojas.

Consulate-General: Skinner Bldg, Suite 500, 1326 Fifth Ave, Seattle, WA 98101; tel (216) 622-2195.
Honorary Consul: George James Townsend.

Consulate-General: 1038 Brickell Ave, Miami, FL 33131; tel (305) 358-3221.
Consul-General: Manuel G. Liranzo Ramírez.

Consulate-General: 3228 West North Ave, Chicago, IL 60647; tel (312) 772-6363.
Honorary Vice-Consul: Osvaldo C. Mena y Aristy.
Honorary Vice-Consul: Dr Ramon José Rojas.

Consulate-General: 870 Market St, Suite 982, San Francisco, CA 94103; tel (415) 982-5144.
Consul-General: Miguel A. Jimenez Perez.
Vice-Consul: Hili A. Cordero.

Consulate-General: 1647 ITM Bldg, 611 Gravier St, New Orleans, LA 70130; tel (504) 522-1843.
Consul-General: Joaquin A. Balaguer Ricardo.
Vice-Consul: Augusto Cesar Medina Herasme.

Consulate-General: 755 Boylston St, Boston, MA 02116; tel (617) 267-4630.
Vice-Consul: Georgian Altagracia Michelen Stefan.

Consulate-General: Calle McKinley 30, 2°, Apdo 3067, Marina Station, Mayaguez, Puerto Rico 00708; tel 833-0007.
Consul-General: Felix Luis E. Nuñez.
Honorary Consul: Rafael Diaz Martínez.

Consulate-General: Edif. 'Avianca', Rm 7, Ave Ponce de Leon 1612 Santurce, San Juan, Puerto Rico 00909; tel 725-9550.
Consul-General: Tomas González Santana.
Vice-Consul: Juan Felipe Pena.
Vice-Consul: Ana Gomez Grullon.

Consulate: c/o American White Cross Labs, 52 Webster Ave, New Rochelle, NY 10802.
Honorary Consul: José Marcial, Jr.

Consulate: 4009 Old Shell Rd, Apt E16, Mobile, AL 36608; tel (205) 342-5648.
Consul: Maria T. Dalmasi de Diaz.
Consul: Rufus Brett Lee.

Consulate: 12127 Ridgelake Drive, Dallas, TX 75218; tel (214) 341-3250.
Honorary Consul: Robert D. von Tress.

Consulate: 6363 York Rd, Parma Heights, Cleveland, OH 44130; tel (216) 932-7489.
Honorary Consul: Dr Bolivar Albainy.

Consulate: 2300 Raven View Rd, Timonium, Annapolis, MD 21093; tel (301) 252-4128.
Honorary Consul: Lourdes Fernández Petr.

Consulate: 4501 Ebenezer Rd, Baltimore, MD 21236; tel (301) 539-5051.
Honorary Consul: Oscar Rafael de Moya.

Consulate: 2171 Babcock, Troy, Detroit, MI 48084; tel (313) 643-7022.
Consul: America Lopez de Castillo.
Honorary Consul: Ramon Rodríguez Souffront.

Consulate: 1173 Rico Drive, St Louis, MO 63126; tel (314) 454-0266.
Honorary Consul: Fernando Emilio Peguero.

Consulate: 3566 Monroe St, Lake Charles, LA 70605; tel (318) 477-4506.
Honorary Consul: Glenn Armand Broussard.

Consulate: 316 United Savings Bldg, Corpus Christi, TX 78411; tel (512) 852-1873.
Honorary Consul: Samuel Preston Doughty.

Consulate: 838 Norwest Midland Bldg, 401 South Second Ave, Minneapolis, MN 55401; tel (612) 341-2636.
Honorary Consul: Ralph S. Parker III.

Consulate: 210 SW First Ave, Rochester, MN.
Honorary Consul: Howard Willoughby Blakely.

Consulate: 30 Federal St, Boston, MA; tel (617) 426-8075.
Honorary Consul: Nicholas Vincent Scalli.

Consulate: 1919 Beach Way Rd, Suite 6/0, Jacksonville, FL; tel (904) 398-1118.
Consul: Danilo Tabare González Borrell.
Vice-Consul: Mildred Altogracia de Jimenez.
Vice-Consul: Mercedes Miledys López de Peña.

Consulate: 1530 West 21st St, Sunset Island No. 4, Miami Beach, FL 33140.
Honorary Consul: Ruth E. Gaiz.

Consulate: c/o Fisher Stinson Hardware Co., Panama City, FL.
Honorary Consul: William Russell Kersey.

Consulate: 2901 West Tamiami Circle, Sarasota, FL 33580.
Honorary Consul: Don Ray Spivey.

Consulate: POB 269, Tallahassee, FL.
Honorary Consul: Henry Louis Hill.

Consulate: 3300 Gessner, Suite 113, Houston, TX 77024; tel (713) 467-4372.
Consul: Modesto Lucas Diaz Montano.

Consulate: 6977 Granero Drive, El Paso, TX 79912.
Honorary Consul: Angel Plinio Romero Beltre.

Consulate: Thompson St, Richmond, VA 23221; tel (804) 688-0141.
Honorary Consul: Robert Randolph Jones.

Consulate: 604 East Bay St, Savannah, GA; tel (912) 234-2266.
Honorary Consul: John Milton Sayler.

Consulate: Applewood Knolls Drive, Lakewood, Denver, CO.
Honorary Consul: José Luis Rodríguez Valle.

Consulate: 201 Alhambra Circle, Ponce de Leon Plaza, Suite 1200, Coral Gables, FL 33134.
Honorary Consul: José E. Martínez.

Consulate: POB 143, Gainesville, FL.
Honorary Consul: Fred Marion Cone.

Consulate: Medical Assistance Programs Inc., 317 Main St, POB 50, Wheaton, IL 60187.
Honorary Consul: J. Raymond Knighton.

Consulate: 2490 Paloma, Pasadena, CA 91104.
Honorary Consul: Carmen Olga Reyes de Peralta.

Consulate: 417-83 Standard Bldg, Fort Wayne, IN.
Honorary Consul: Walter Edward Helmke.

Consulate: 4866 Whitehaven St, Baton Rouge, LA.
Honorary Consul: Nelly Mariana Carias Aguilar.

Consulate: 1325 Commerce Title Bldg, Memphis, TN.
Honorary Consul: John M. Heiskell.

Consulate: 3322 Western Ave, Nashville, TN 37205; tel (615) 383-4700.
Honorary Consul: Russell W. Brothers.

Consulate: José de Diego 55, Arecibo, Puerto Rico; tel 878-3207.
Honorary Consul: Dr Antonio Lens-Aresti.

Consulate: Minerva 19, Humacao, Puerto Rico; tel 852-0677.
Honorary Consul: Antonio Roig, Jr.
Honorary Vice-Consul: José Luis Bournigal Mena.

Consulate: Calle A.N. 57, Vista Alegre, Ponce, Juana Diaz, Puerto Rico; tel 842-7884.
Honorary Consul: Virgilio Enrique Larrauri.

Consulate: Calle 4, H-18, University Gardens, Manati, Puerto Rico 00612.
Honorary Consul: Eddy E. Berges Dreyfous.

Consulate: Marginal 303, La Rambla, Ponce, Puerto Rico; tel 842-9004.
Consul: Usino Osvaldo Guzman Liriano.
Consul: Celenia Objio de Lugo.
Consul: Federico C. Franco Diaz.

ECUADOR

Embassy: 2535 15th St, NW, Washington, DC 20009; tel (202) 234-7200; telex 440129; fax (202) 667-3482.
Ambassador: Jaime Moncayo.

Consulate-General: 18 East 41st St, 18th Floor, New York, NY 10017; tel (212) 683-7555.
Consul-General: Manuel Cornejo.
Deputy Consul-General: Guillermo Teran-H.
Consul: Juan Andrade.

Consulate-General: 548 South Spring St, Suite 602, Los Angeles, CA 90013; tel (213) 628-3014.
Consul-General: Patricio E. Baca-Davalas.
Consul: Luis A. Vera.

Consulate-General: 156 Giralda Ave, 2nd Floor, Coral Gables, FL 33134; tel (305) 445-1625.
Consul-General: Rafael E. Guerrero.
Consul: Xavier Rosales.
Consul: Jorge Sosa.
Consul: Jaime Molina.

Consulate-General: 612 North Michigan Ave, Suite 716, Chicago, IL 60611; tel (312) 642-8579.
Consul-General: Eduardo Gomezjurado.

Consulate-General: The Flood Bldg, 870 Market St, Suite 858, San Francisco, CA 94102; tel (415) 391-4148.
Consul-General: Carlos E. Garces Felix.
Honorary Consul: Modesto E. Chacon.
Honorary Consul: Ximena Cordovez-Angotti.

Consulate-General: 1312 International Trade Mart Bldg, 2 Canal St, New Orleans, LA 70130; tel (504) 523-3229.
Consul: Guillermo V. Lara.

Consulate-General: 60 State St, Boston, MA 02109; tel (617) 227-7200.
Honorary Consul-General: Harold Widett.

Consulate-General: 4200 Westheimer, Suite 118, Houston, TX 77027; tel (712) 622-1787.
Consul-General: Cesar R. Robalino Gonzaga.
Consul: Mariela Carolina Zavala Caputti.

Consulate: 1222 Commerce St, Suite 1412, Dallas, TX 75202; tel (214) 747-6329.
Honorary Consul: Mercedes Azua de Penaherrera.

Consulate: 2925 North Charles St, Baltimore, MD 21218; tel (301) 889-4422.
Honorary Consul: Manuel L. V. Aramillo.

Consulate: 16581 Laketree Drive, Fort Lauderdale, FL 33326; tel (305) 389-7195.
Honorary Consul: Ligia Maria R. Landazuri.

Consulate: 132 North Lakeshore Drive, Palm Beach, FL 33408.
Honorary Consul: Doris Cashmore de Mantilla.

Consulate: 136 State St, Pontiac, Detroit, MI; tel (313) 332-7352.
Honorary Consul: Hector A. Bueno.

Consulate: 530 B St, Suite 901, San Diego, CA 92101; tel (619) 233-8640.
Honorary Consul: Francisco Segura Cano.

Consulate: Calle Roosevelt 651, Apt 3A, Miramar Santurce, San Juan, Puerto Rico 00907; tel 781-4408.
Honorary Consul: Carlos Arcos-Moscoso.

EGYPT

Embassy: 2310 Decatur Place, NW, Washington, DC 20008; tel (202) 232-5400; fax (202) 332-7894.
Ambassador: El-Sayed Abdel Raouf El-Reedy.

Consulate-General: 1110 Second Ave, New York, NY 10022; tel (212) 759-7120.
Consul-General: Mohamed S. Derar.
Consul: Samir Mohamed Khalil.
Consul: Soheir S. Zaki.
Consul: Mohamed M. Minessy.
Consul: Maasoum M. Marzouk.
Consul: Mohamed E. Fawzy.
Consul: Hamdi M. Saad El-Din.

Consulate-General: 30 South Michigan Ave, 7th Floor, Chicago, IL 60603; tel (312) 443-5400.
Consul-General: Ismail H. Fahmy.
Deputy Consul-General: Ahmed E. Fahmy.

Consulate-General: 3001 Pacific Ave, San Francisco, CA 94115; tel (415) 346-9700.
Consul-General: Nabil El-Orabi.

Consulate-General: 2000 West Loop South, Suite 1750, Control Data Bldg, Houston, TX 77027; tel (713) 961-4915.
Consul-General: Bedair I. El-Gamrawy.
Consul: Mohamed Mohie Yousef.

EL SALVADOR

Embassy: 2308 California St, NW, Washington, DC 20008; tel (202) 265-9671.
Ambassador: Miguel Angel Salaverria.
Consul-General: José Guillermo Burgos.

Consulate-General: 46 Park Ave, New York, NY 10016; tel (212) 889-3608.
Consul-General: Irma E. García de Borja.
Vice-Consul: José J. Fernandez.

Consulate-General: 2410 7th St, 2nd Floor, Los Angeles, CA.
Consul-General: José M. Angulo.
Vice-Consul: Lucas A. Aguilar.

Consulate-General: 104 South Michigan Ave, Suite 423, Chicago, IL 60603; tel (312) 332-1393.

Consulate-General: 870 Market St, Suite 508, San Francisco, CA 94102; tel (415) 781-7924.
Consul-General: Carlos González.

Consulate-General: 300 Biscayne Blvd, Suite 1020, Miami, FL 33131; tel (305) 371-8850.
Consul-General: Jorge E. Robert Castro.
Vice-Consul: Clotilde Montoya de Iraheta.

Consulate-General: 1136 International Trade Mart, New Orleans, LA 70130; tel (504) 522-4266.
Consul-General: Stella Z. de Gudiel.
Vice-Consul: Mirian Estela Kruger Rodríguez.

Consulate-General: 6655 Hillcroft St, Suite 112, Houston, TX 77081; tel (713) 270-6239.
Consul-General: Astrid M. Salazar de Ariz.
Vice-Consul: Marlene E. Orantes de Salazar.

Consulate: 1161 Rennes Court, NE, Atlanta, GA 30319; tel (404) 252-8425.
Honorary Consul: Margarita E. B. Arrington.

Consulate: Rivergate Plaza, Suite 501, 444 Brickell Ave, Coral Gables, Miami, FL.
Honorary Consul: John P. Corrigan, Jr.

Consulate: 1881 First National Bldg, Detroit, MI 48226; tel (313) 963-8142.
Honorary Consul: James Charles Bruno.

Consulate: 10932 Cloverland Ave, J. & M. International Corporation, Baton Rouge, LA 70809; tel (504) 293-1715.
Honorary Consul: Carlos Guillermo Galluser Aguirre.

Consulate: American National Bank & Trust Co., Mobile, AL.
Honorary Consul: Arthur Banister Pope.

Consulate: 4929 West Van Buren, Phoenix, AZ 85043; tel (602) 269-6621.
Honorary Consul: Tracy R. Thomas.

Consulate: Oakland, CA.
Honorary Consul: Luis Ernest Chaparro.

Consulate: POB 948, San Diego, CA 92112.
Honorary Consul: David Ewing Porter.

Consulate: 565 Petroleum Club Bldg, Denver, CO 80202.
Honorary Consul: Grant William Breuer.

Consulate: 7 North 7th St, St Louis, MO 63101.
Honorary Consul: Michael Jay Bobroff.

Consulate: 733 Highland Park Drive, Billings, MT 59801.
Honorary Consul: Eva Maria Koessler.

Consulate: 119 Bleddyn Rd, Ardmore, Philadelphia, PA 19003.
Honorary Consul: Ana Maria D. Keene.

Consulate: Villa Caparra, Calle K-19, Bayamon, Puerto Rico 00619.
Honorary Consul: Maria Teresa Posada de Estevez.

Consulate: Torrimar Urb., Toledo St 22, Bayamon, San Juan, Puerto Rico 00619.
Honorary Vice-Consul: Adela Calderon de Morell.

EQUATORIAL GUINEA

Embassy: 801 Second Ave, Suite 1403, New York, NY 10017; tel (212) 599-1523.
Ambassador: Damaso Obiang Ndong.

ESTONIA

Embassy: 9 Rockefeller Plaza, Suite 1421, New York, NY 10020; tel (212) 247-1450; fax (212) 262-0893.
Ambassador: Ernst Rudolf Jaakson.
Consul: Aarand Roos.
Vice-Consul: Okke Metsmaa.

Consulate: 500 Union St, Suite 930, Seattle, WA 98101; tel (206) 467-1444; fax (206) 467-8129.
Honorary Consul: Mart Kask.

Consulate: 21515 Vanowen St, Suite 211, Canoga Park, Los Angeles, CA 91303; tel (818) 884-5850.
Honorary Consul: Jaak Treiman.

ETHIOPIA

Embassy: 2134 Kalorama Rd, NW, Washington, DC 20008; tel (202) 234-2281.
Chargé d'affaires a.i.: Girma Amare.

FIJI

Embassy: 2233 Wisconsin Ave, NW, Suite 240, Washington, DC 20007; tel (202) 337-8320; telex 4971930; fax (202) 337-1996.
Chargé d'affaires a.i.: Ratu Finau Mara.
First Secretary: Corinne Yee.

Consulate: 1 United Nations Plaza, 26th Floor, New York, NY 10017; tel (212) 355-7316; fax (212) 319-1896.
Consul: Isilcia R. Savua.

FINLAND

Embassy: 3216 New Mexico Ave, NW, Washington, DC 20016; tel (202) 363-2430; telex 248268; fax (202) 363-8233.
Ambassador: Jukka Vultasaari.
Counsellor (Commercial): Ossi Ragkonen.
Secretary (Commercial): Pekka Lehtonen.

Consulate-General: Finland House, 380 Madison Ave, New York, NY 10017; tel (212) 573-6007; telex 149515; fax (212) 573-6310.
Consul-General: Garth Castren.
Consul and Counsellor (Commercial): Kari Nettamo.
Consul and Counsellor (Science): Göran Lindholm.
Consul and Secretary (Press): Leena Peltola.

Consulate-General: 1900 Ave of the Stars, Suite 1025, Los Angeles, CA 90067; tel (213) 203-9903; telex 674488; fax (213) 203-0301.
Consul-General: Jussi Montonen.
Consul and Counsellor (Press/Culture): Pekka Aalto.
Consul and Trade Commissioner: Per Falenius.
Consul and Attaché (Science): Hannu Leiponen.

Consulate-General: 77 Franklin St, Boston, MA 02110; tel (617) 451-0818.
Consul-General: Leonard Kopelman.

Consulate-General: 333 Bush St, 34th Floor, San Francisco, CA 94104; tel (415) 772-6374; telex 184996; fax (415) 772-6268.
Consul-General: Richard J. Guggenhime.

Consulate and Office of Trade Commissioner: 321 North Clark St, Suite 2880, Chicago, IL 60610; tel (312) 670-4700; telex 253355; fax (312) 670-4777.
Consul and Trade Commissioner: Arto Saarinen.

Consulate and Office of Trade Commissioner: 1300 Post Oak Blvd, Suite 1990, Houston, TX 77056; tel (713) 627-9700; telex 795340; fax (713) 629-5052.
Consul and Trade Commissioner: Matti Rasimus.
Trade Commissioner: Jaako Bask.
Consul and Attaché (Science): Keijo Mutanen.

Consulate: 501 NW Copper Ave, Alburquerque, NM 87102; tel (505) 768-5100.
Consul: Alan B. Clark.

Consulate: 4545 NW 42nd St, Suite 214, Washington, DC 20016; tel (202) 362-6300.
Consul: Sylvan M. Marshall.

Consulate: 550 West 64th Ave, Anchorage, AK 99518; tel (907) 562-3326.
Consul: Wayne A. Stolt.

Consulate: 415 West Marine Drive, Astoria, OR 97103; tel (503) 325-0761.
Consul: Paul D. Thompson.

Consulate: 9240 NE Huntcliffe Trace, Atlanta, GA 30338; tel (404) 993-6696.
Consul: Philip Edwin Nethercut.

Consulate: The World Trade Center, 401 East Pratt St, Suite 800, Baltimore, MD 21202; tel (301) 962-6512.
Consul: Edmond J. Moran, Jr.

Consulate: 6-10 First National Bank Bldg, Butte, MT 59701; tel (406) 723-5411.
Consul: Keith P. Johnson.

Consulate: 3300 South Harlem Ave, Riverside, IL 60546; tel (312) 442-0635.
Consul: Frederick C. Niemi.

Consulate: 33320 Cromwell Drive, Solon, OH 44139; tel (216) 248-4404.
Consul: Walter Maky.

Consulate: POB 619208, D/FW Station, Dallas, TX 75261-9208; tel (214) 556-0500.
Consul: Dan C. Williams.

Consulate: 6855 South Havana, Suite 600, Englewood, CO 80112; tel (303) 649-4000; fax (303) 649-4025.
Consul: Daniel L. Kamunen.

Consulate: 7127 Edinborough Drive, West Bloomfield, MI 48322; tel (313) 626-3618.
Consul: Ruben H. Nayback.

Consulate: 804 Alworth Bldg, Duluth, MN 55802; tel (218) 727-8420.
Consul: Donald Glen Wirtanen.

Consulate: 56 Elm St, POB 2226, Fitchburg, MA 01420-2226; tel (617) 342-6035.
Consul: Edwin E. Kaarela.

Consulate: 2180 North Loop West, Houston, TX 77018; POB 924307, Houston, TX 77292; tel (713) 683-3500.
Consul: Mickey Lane.

Consulate: Stevens Shipping and Terminal Co., 2831 Talleyrand Ave, POB 3336, Jacksonville, FL 32206; tel (904) 354-0883.
Consul: Marcus Carl Lindström.

Consulate: 1 Main Plaza, 4435 Main St, Suite 950, Kansas City, MO 64111; tel (816) 932-8079.
Consul: Hearne Christopher.

Consulate: 706 Lake Ave, Lake Worth, FL 33460; tel (407) 586-2433.
Consul: David Hinsa.

Consulate: 1400 West Ave, Marquette, MI 49855; tel (906) 226-7913.
Consul: Rudolf John Seppälä.

Consulate: 144 Madeira Ave, Coral Gables, Miami, FL 33134; POB 248216, Coral Gables, FL 33124; tel (305) 444-7555.
Consul: Cami E. Green.

Consulate: 10501 Wayzata Blvd, Suite 104, Minnetonka, MN 55343; tel (612) 542-9171.
Consul: Esko E. Ranta.

Consulate: 6913 North Cobblestone Way, Mobile, AL 36608; tel (205) 342-0773.
Consul: Reginald S. Price.

Consulate: 3100 Energy Center, 1100 Poydras St, New Orleans, LA 70163-3100; tel (504) 523-6451; telex 584194.
Consul: James Louis Schupp, Jr.

Consulate: World Trade Center, Suite 820, Norfolk, VA 23510; tel (804) 627-6286.
Consul: T. Parker Host, Jr.

Consulate: 1 Thames Plaza, Norwich, CT 06360; tel (203) 886-8845.
Consul: Carl Dennis Anderson.

Consulate: 112 Christian St, Philadelphia, PA 19147; tel (215) 465-5565.
Consul: Bengt Olof Jansson.

Consulate: 9744 West Bell Rd, Sun City, AZ 85351; POB 1036, Sun City, AZ 85372; tel (602) 876-2718; fax (602) 876-2747.
Consul: Frank R. Smith.

Consulate: 2648 SW Cedar Hills, Portland, OR 97221; tel (503) 292-5994; fax (503) 525-0902.
Consul: Paul M. Niskanen.

Consulate: 79 South Main St, 2nd Floor, Salt Lake City, UT 84111; POB 30006, Salt Lake City, UT 84130; tel (801) 350-5287.
Consul: Spencer F. Eccles.

Consulate: 530 Broadway, Suite 1110, San Diego, CA 92101; tel (619) 238-4433; telex 188910; fax (619) 238-0254.
Consul: Bert J. Salonen.

Consulate: DG No. 6, Torremolinos, Guaynabo, San Juan, Puerto Rico 00657; tel 720-4377.
Consul: Gustavo Adolfo Benitez Badrena.

Consulate: 11045 SE 28th Place, POB 40598, Bellevue, WA 98004; tel (206) 451-3983; fax (206) 451-3983.
Consul: Eric Norman Westerberg.

Consulate: 2907 Bays to Bay Blvd, Suite 310, Tampa, FL 33629; POB 2331, Tampa, FL 33601.
Consul: Howard N. Baron.

Consulate: 608 Turnpike Rd, Golden Valley, MN 55416; tel (612) 544-5961.
Vice-Consul: David James Speer.

FRANCE

Embassy: 4101 Reservoir Rd, NW, Washington, DC 20007; tel (202) 944-6000; fax (202) 944-6072.
Ambassador: Jacques Andréani.
Consul-General: Jean Yves Defay.
Deputy Consul: Anne H. Genoud.

Consulate-General: 934 Fifth Ave, New York, NY 10021; tel (212) 606-3688.
Consul-General: Benoît d'Aboville.
Deputy Consul-General: Annie Cohen-Solal.
Deputy Consul-General: Bernard Thoer.
Deputy Consul-General: Jacques Soppelsa.
Deputy Consul-General: Herve P. Bolot.

Consulate-General: 8350 Wilshire Blvd, Suite 310, Beverley Hills, Los Angeles, CA 90211; tel (213) 653-3120.
Consul-General: Gerard A. M. Coste.
Deputy Consul-General: Jerome Champagne.

Consulate-General: 737 North Michigan Ave, Olympia Center, Suite 2020, Chicago, IL 60611; tel (312) 787-5359.
Consul-General: Yves Lorvellec.

Consulate-General: 285 Peachtree Center Ave, Suite 2800, Marquis Two, Atlanta, GA 30303; tel (404) 522-4226.
Consul-General: Jacky R. Musnier.
Vice-Consul: Antony Nguyen van Ton.

Consulate-General: 3 Commonwealth Ave, Boston, MA 02116; tel (617) 266-9413.
Consul-General: Laurent J. Rapin.

Consulate-General: Worthem Tower, Suite 976, 2727 Allen Parkway, Houston, TX 77019; tel (713) 528-2181.
Consul-General: Bernard Guillet.
Deputy Consul-General: André Bechir.

Consulate-General: 3305 Saint Charles Ave, New Orleans, LA 70115; tel (504) 897-6381.
Consul-General: Didier Destremau.

Consulate-General: 1 Biscayne Tower, Suite 1710, 2 South Biscayne Blvd, Miami, FL 33131; tel (305) 372-9798.
Consul-General: Jean-François Thiollier.

Consulate-General: 540 Bush St, San Francisco, CA 94108; tel (415) 397-4330.
Consul-General: Yvon Roe d'Albert.

Consulate-General: 2 Waterfront Plaza, Suite 300, 500 Ala Moana Blvd, Honolulu, HI 96813; tel (808) 599-4458.
Deputy Consul: Babou Kamichetty.

Consulate-General: Mercantil Plaza, Suite 720, Ponce de Leon Ave, Stop 27, 1/2 Hatorey, San Juan, Puerto Rico 00918; tel 753-1700.
Consul-General: François Bouchet.

Consulate: 31 Inverness Central Parkway, Suite 100, Birmingham, AL 35243; tel (205) 995-0733.
Honorary Consul: Philippe W. Lathrop.

Consulate: 8610 East, Hazelwood, Scottsdale, Phoenix, AZ 85251; tel (602) 946-4185.
Honorary Consul: Claude A. Prosner.

Consulate: 1590 One Union National Plaza, Little Rock, AR 72201; tel (501) 224-1300.
Honorary Consul: Winthrop Paul Rockefeller.

Consulate: 1831 Rockwood Drive, Sacramento, CA 95825; tel (916) 486-7228.
Honorary Consular Agent: Jane R. Wheaton.

Consulate: 2230 4th Ave, Suite B, San Diego, CA 92109; tel (619) 492-8724.
Honorary Consular Agent: Jean-Pierre Paris.

Consulate: 1203 Emory St, San José, CA 95126; tel (408) 429-2198.
Honorary Consul: Hervé Le Mansec.

Consulate: 25 East 16th Ave, Suite 208, Denver, CO 80202.
Honorary Consul: Frieda Sanidas.

Consulate: 120 Laurel St, Bristol, Hartford, CT 06010.
Honorary Consul: Robert R. Maynard.

Consulate: 2006 Woodbrooke Drive, Westwood Manor, Wilmington, DE 19810; tel (302) 475-5964.
Honorary Consular Agent: Danielle Appel Grossman.

Consulate: 1643 Roundelay Lane, Winter Park, Orlando, FL 32789.
Honorary Consul: Robert E. Mignon.

Consulate: The Armstrong House, Bull and Gaston Sts, POB 2139, Savannah, GA 31402; tel (912) 236-2491.
Honorary Consular Agent: Walter C. Hartridge.

Consulate: 3520 Traskwood Lane, Cincinnati, OH 45208; tel (513) 871-8529.
Honorary Consular Agent: Louis Morris Prince.

Consulate: 901 Lakeside Ave, Cleveland, OH 44114.
Honorary Consular Agent: Albert I. Borowitz.

Consulate: 3300 Indianola Ave, Columbus, OH 43214.
Honorary Consular Agent: Richard B. Igo.

Consulate: 1211 North Shartel, Oklahoma City, OK 73103; tel (405) 232-0365.
Honorary Consular Agent: Dr C. Alton Brown.

Consulate: 7666 East 61, Tulsa, OK 74105; tel (918) 254-0471.
Honorary Consul: Burt B. Holmes.

Consulate: 921 SW 6th Ave, Portland, OR 97204.
Honorary Consul: Serge d'Rovencourt.

Consulate: 306 South Second St, Philadelphia, PA 19106.
Honorary Consul: Stanhope S. Browne.

Consulate: 800 Presque Isle Drive, Pittsburgh, PA 15239; tel (412) 327-2911.
Honorary Consular Agent: Jean-Pierre Collet.

Consulate: 15 Broad St, Charleston, SC 29401; tel (512) 480-5605.
Honorary Consul: Xuan-Chi Diep.

Consulate: 5201 Maryland Way, Brentwood, Nashville, TN 37027; tel (615) 373-4242.
Honorary Consul: Thomas Vance Little.

Consulate: 3000 American National Bank, Amarillo, TX 79001; tel (806) 359-1155.

Honorary Consul: Gwendolyn O'Brien Marsh.

Consulate: c/o Graves, Dougherty, Hearon & Moody, 2300 Interfirst Tower, Suite 976, Austin, TX 78701.
Honorary Consul: John M. Harmon.

Consulate: 3407 Hall St, Poston Bldg, Dallas, TX 75219; tel (214) 522-5000.
Honorary Consul: George E. Poston.

Consulate: 175 East 400 South, Salt Lake City, UT 84111; tel (801) 524-1000.
Honorary Consul: Carl W. Barton.

Consulate: 417 Pin Oak Rd, Newport News, Norfolk, VA 23601.
Honorary Consul: Nicole Yancey.

Consulate: 9240 North Sleepy Hollow Lane, Milwaukee, WI 53217; tel (414) 351-3875.
Honorary Consul: Gaston A. Vandermeerssche.

Consulate: 3931 Locarno Drive, Anchorage, AK 99504; tel (907) 582-5713.
Honorary Consular Agent: Colette G. La Rose.

Consulate: POB 700, Mayaguez, Puerto Rico 00708; tel 832-1442.
Honorary Consular Agent: E. Ivan Soler Mari.

GABON

Embassy: 2034 20th St, NW, Washington, DC 20009; tel (202) 797-1000.
Ambassador: Jean Robert Odzaga.

GAMBIA

Embassy: 1030 15th St, Suite 720, NW, Washington, DC 20005; tel (202) 842-1356; telex 204791; fax (202) 842-2073.
Ambassador: Ousman Ahmadou Sallah.
Counsellor: Aminatta Dibba.
Second Secretary: Ramou Sallah.
Attaché (Finance): Kemo Tunkura.

Consulate-General: 10777 Bellagio Rd, Los Angeles, CA 90077; tel (213) 659-2434; fax (213) 471-7424.
Consul-General: Dr Gunther Klaus.

GERMANY

Embassy: 4645 Reservoir Rd, NW, Washington, DC 20007-1998; tel (202) 298-4000; telex 248321; fax (202) 298-4249.
Ambassador: Dr Jürgen Ruhfus.
Consul-General: Hans-Dieter Ziegler.
Vice-Consul: Maria Friedrich.
Vice-Consul: Herbert Czujek.

Consulate-General: 460 Park Ave, New York, NY 10022; tel (212) 308-8700; telex 175382; fax (212) 308-3422.
Consul-General: Leopold Bill von Bredow.
Deputy Consul-General: Horst H. Rinke.
Deputy Consul-General: Dr Eberhard Koelsch.
Deputy Consul-General: Fritz W. Ziefer.

Consulate-General: Marquis Two Tower, Suite 901, 285 NE Peachtree Center Ave, Atlanta, GA 30303-1221; tel (404) 659-4760; telex 154104; fax (404) 659-1280.
Consul-General: Klaus E. Zehentner.
Deputy Consul-General: Hans-Jochen Schmidt.
Consul: Franz-Josef J. Willeke.

Consulate-General: 3 Copley Pl., Suite 500, Boston, MA 02116; tel (617) 536-4414; telex 174038; fax (617) 536-8573.
Consul-General: Dr Walter Gerhardt.
Deputy Consul-General: Dr S. Johannes Trommer.
Consul: Klaus Rainer Schwing.
Consul: Andreas T. Siegel.
Consul: Angelika Voelkel.

Consulate-General: 104 South Michigan Ave, Chicago, IL 60603; tel (312) 263-0850; telex 190160; fax (312) 853-1940.
Consul-General: Günter Wasserberg.
Deputy Consul-General: Karl-Georg Schon.
Consul: Heinz Wirth.
Consul: Klaus D. Hoefel.

Consulate-General: Edison Plaza, Suite 2100, 660 Plaza Drive, Detroit, MI 48226; tel (313) 962-6526; telex 164102; fax (313) 962-7345.
Consul-General: Detlof von Berg.
Consul: Reinhard H. J. Paellmann.
Consul: Peter A. Beerwerth.
Consul: Dirk Veenema.

Consulate-General: 1330 Post Oak Blvd, Suite 1850, Houston, TX 77056-3018; tel (713) 627-7770; telex 166383; fax (713) 627-0506.
Consul-General: Peter Maler-Oswald.
Deputy Consul-General: Stefan C. Gallon.
Consul: Klaus Fleischmann.

Consulate-General: 6222 Wilshire Blvd, Suite 500, Los Angeles, CA 90048; tel (213) 930-2703; telex 215876; fax (213) 930-2805.
Consul-General: Dr Cornelius Metternich.
Deputy Consul-General: Klaus Aurish.
Consul: Renate Friedemann.
Consul: Pius Fischer.
Consul: Siegrid M. Lange.
Consul: Alexander Beckmann.

Consulate-General: 100 North Biscayne Blvd, Miami, FL 33132; tel (305) 358-0290; telex 153159; fax (305) 358-0307.
Consul-General: Klaus-Dieter Sommer.
Deputy Consul-General: Werner Wnendt.
Consul: Rolf-Jürgen Bachman.

Consulate-General: 1960 Jackson St, San Francisco, CA 94109; tel (415) 775-1061; telex 184277; fax (415) 775-0187.
Consul-General: Walter König.
Deputy Consul-General: Dr Volker Anding.
Consul: Michael Koch.
Consul: Lutz F. Lamle.

Consulate-General: 1617 IBM Bldg, 1200 Fifth Ave, Seattle, WA 98101; tel (206) 682-4312; telex 185183; fax (206) 682-3724.
Consul-General: Dr Hans Jürgen Mendel.
Consul: Karl Lothar Schneider.

Consulate-General: 1101 PNB Plaza Bldg, 5th and Market Sts, Philadelphia, PA 19106; tel (215) 922-7415.
Honorary Consul-General: Dr F. Peter Kohler.

Consulate: Messersmith & Schuler, 5700 Harper NE, Suite 330, Alburquerque, NM 87109; tel (505) 822-8826; fax (505) 842-6952.
Honorary Consul: Lanny D. Messersmith.

Consulate: 425 'G' St, Suite 650, Anchorage, AK 99501; tel (907) 274-6537.
Honorary Consul: Bernd Guetschow.

Consulate: 135 Denver Ave, Buffalo, NY 14202; tel (716) 854-4010.
Honorary Consul: Dr Brigitte Barrel.

Consulate: 330 Eastover Rd, Charlotte, NC 28207; tel (704) 373-0774; telex 572467.
Honorary Consul: Eckart Goette.

Consulate: 2310 Star Bank Center, 425 Walnut St, Cincinnati, OH 45202; tel (513) 621-3440.
Honorary Consul: Dean Edward Denlinger.

Consulate: 1100 Huntington Bldg, 9th St and Euclid, Cleveland, OH 44115; tel (216) 696-1100; telex 985384; fax (216) 696-2645.
Honorary Consul: Diana M. Thimmig.

Consulate: c/o Huntington National Bank, 41 South High St, Columbus, OH 43287; tel (614) 463-3623; telex 245475.
Honorary Consul: Frank G. Wobst.

Consulate: 5440 Old Brownsville Rd, POB 4897, Corpus Christi, TX 78469; tel (512) 289-2416.
Honorary Consul: Erich Wendl.

Consulate: 10100 North Central Expressway, Suite 230, Dallas, TX 75231; tel (214) 361-6033; telex 735085; fax (214) 361-6871.
Honorary Consul: Daniel Tomlin.

Consulate: 6th Ave West Office Bldg, 350 Indiana St, Suite 400, Golden, Denver, CO 80401; tel (303) 279-1551.
Honorary Consul: Hans Wiprecht von Barby.

Consulate: 1069 South Beretania St, Honolulu, HI 96814; tel (808) 536-3271.
Honorary Consul: Karl Heinz Oberacker.

Consulate: 2314 North Meridian St, Indianapolis, IN 46208; tel (317) 924-5321.
Honorary Consul: Horst F. Winkler.

Consulate: c/o Deposit Guaranty National Bank, One Deposit Guaranty Plaza, Jackson, MS 39025; POB 1200, Jackson, MS 39125-1200; tel (601) 354-8281; telex 585431; fax (601) 354-8192.
Honorary Consul: Emmerson B. Robinson, Jr.

Consulate: 1510 Talleyrand Ave, POB 3, Jacksonville, FL 32201; tel (904) 353-1741; telex 827-0208; fax (904) 632-1319.
Honorary Consul: John G. McGiffin III.

Consulate: Security National Bldg, One Security Plaza, POB 1250, Kansas City, KS 66117; tel (913) 621-8458.
Honorary Consul: Willard B. Snyder.

Consulate: 925 East Desert Inn Rd, Suite C, Las Vegas, NV 89109; tel (702) 734-9700.
Honorary Consul: Sigrid Sommer.

Consulate: c/o Citizens Fidelity Bank & Trust Co., Citizens Plaza, POB 33000, Louisville, KY 40296; tel (502) 581-3231.
Honorary Consul: E. Frederick Zopp.

Consulate: 100 North Main Bldg, Suite 3002, Memphis, TN 38103; tel (901) 525-8271.
Honorary Consul: David D. Silberberg.

Consulate: 2100 First Bank Place West, 120 South Sixth St, Minneapolis, MN 55402; tel (612) 339-7566; fax (612) 339-9055.
Honorary Consul: Joseph E. Hamilton.

Consulate: 1201 Commercial Guaranty Bank Bldg, POB 2345, Mobile, AL 36601; tel (205) 433-6506.
Honorary Consul: Samuel M. McMillan.

Consulate: 225 Baronne St, POB 61000, New Orleans, LA 70161; tel (504) 569-4289; fax (504) 569-4782.
Honorary Consul: Edwin Lupberger.

Consulate: 142 West York St, Suite 218, Norfolk, VA 23510; tel (804) 627-7283.
Honorary Consul: Dr Rudolf F. Schuster.

Consulate: 4700 Willard, Oklahoma City, OK 73105.
Honorary Consul: Prof. Walter H. Massion.

Consulate: 4250 East Camelback Rd, Suite 120K, Phoenix, AZ 85018-2751; tel (602) 952-9100; fax (602) 840-0476.
Honorary Consul: Berthold K. Koester.

Consulate: c/o Bayer USA Inc., One Mellon Center, 500 Grant St, Pittsburgh, PA 15219-2502; tel (412) 394-5543.
Honorary Consul: Wilheim C. Ostern.

Consulate: 905 First Farwest Bldg, 400 SW 6th Ave, Portland, OR 97204; tel (503) 222-0490.
Honorary Consul: Günther Hoffmann.

Consulate: 455 East 4th South, Suite 40a, Salt Lake City, UT 84111; tel (801) 364-9573.
Honorary Consul: Dr Herwig Glander.

Consulate: 1500 Alamo Bldg, 105 South St Mary's St, San Antonio, TX 78205; tel (512) 224-4455; fax (512) 224-6430.
Honorary Consul: Thomas E. Pawel.

Consulate: 6868 Nancy Ridge Drive, Suite 'I', San Diego, CA 92121; tel (619) 455-1423.
Honorary Consul: Hermann Zilgens.

Consulate: 10733 Sunset Office Drive, Suite 201, St Louis, MO 63126-0509; tel (314) 965-5440; fax (314) 965-3649.
Honorary Consul: Anne Mayer Beck.

Consulate: 4400 Central Ave, St Petersburg, FL 33711; POB 14567, St Petersburg, FL 33733; tel (813) 327-4444; telex 4957-4235; fax (813) 323-4937.
Honorary Consul: Hannes K. Mittermayr.

Consulate: 310 East Bay St, POB 2088, Savannah, GA 31402; tel (912) 232-5581; telex 804702.
Honorary Consul: Frank Kohler Peeples.

Consulate: 290 Montgomery Drive, Spartanburg, SC 29302; POB 5888, Spartanburg, SC 29304; tel (803) 582-5133; telex 530799; fax (803) 579-5930.
Honorary Consul: Paul-Friedrich Förster.

Consulate: 322 Spokane Falls Court, Spokane, WA 99201-0165; tel (509) 838-6630.
Honorary Consul: Hubertus Günther.

Consulate: Sta Bibiana St 1618, Sagrado Corazón, Cupey, Rio Piedras, Apdo 3746, San Juan, Puerto Rico 00936; tel 755-8228; telex 3450494; fax 755-8228.
Honorary Consul: Otto Egon Schulz.

GHANA

Embassy: 3512 International Drive, NW, Washington, DC 20008; tel (202) 686-4520; fax (202) 686-4527.
Ambassador: Eric K. Otoo.

Consulate-General: 19 East 47th St, New York, NY 10017; tel (212) 832-1300.
Consul-General: Charles Baah.
Consul: Ofori Tannor.

GREECE

Embassy: 2221 Massachusetts Ave, NW, Washington, DC 20008; tel (202) 939-5800; fax (202) 939-5824.
Ambassador: Christos Zacharakis.
Consul: Mara Marinaki.
Consul: George Marcantonatos.

Consulate-General: 69 East 79th St, New York, NY 10021; tel (212) 988-5500.
Consul-General: George Assimakopoulos.
Consul: Ioannis Papadimitriou.
Consul: Anthoule A. Balanou.
Consul: Serafim Bourliaskos.
Consul: Capt. Vassilios Tsanakis.
Consul: Dr Efstratios Tsaparlis.

Consulate-General: 168 North Michigan Ave, Chicago, IL 60601; tel (312) 372-5356.
Consul-General: Dimitrios Manolopoulos.
Consul: Fotis Manoussakis.
Consul: Ioannis Kontopoulos.
Consul: Dimitrios Zevelakis.

Consulate-General: 3255 Wilshire Blvd, Suite 1103, Los Angeles, CA 90010; tel (714) 534-0501.
Consul-General: George Zois.
Vice-Consul: Niki Mavriyanni.

Consulate-General: 2441 Gough St, San Francisco, CA 94123; tel (415) 775-2102.
Consul-General: Constantin Yerocostopoulos.
Consul: Vassilis Papadopoulos.

Consulate-General: Tower Place, 3340 Peachtree Rd, NE, Suite 1670, Atlanta, GA 33026; tel (404) 261-3391.
Consul: Efstathios Daras.
Consular Agent: Spiros Vassilikos.

Consulate-General: 20 Park Plaza, Suite 526-9, Stateler Office Bldg, Boston, MA 02116; tel (617) 542-3240.
Consul-General: Vassilis Papaioannou.
Consul: Theodore Passas.

Consulate: 2 Canal St, Suite 2318, International Trade Mart Bldg, New Orleans, LA 70130; tel (504) 523-1167.
Consul: Alexandra Papadopoulou.
Vice-Consul: Dimitrios Kontis.

Consulate: 1360 Post Oak Blvd, Suite 2480, Cigna Tower, Houston, TX 77056.
Consul: Eleftherios Anghelopoulos.

GRENADA

Embassy: 1701 New Hampshire Ave, NW, Washington, DC 20009; tel (202) 265-2561; telex 897029; fax (202) 265-2468.
Ambassador: Denneth Modeste.
Counsellor: Norma Blaize.
Counsellor: Francis Paul.

Consulate-General: 820 Second Ave, New York, NY 10017; tel (212) 599-0301; telex 62081; fax (212) 808-4975.
Consul-General: Mark Isaac.

GUATEMALA

Embassy: 2220 R St, NW, Washington, DC 20008; tel (202) 745-4952; telex 361499; fax (202) 745-1908.
Ambassador: John Schwank Durán.
Consul: Patricia Mendoza-Ibarguen.

Consulate-General: 57 Park Ave, New York, NY 10016; tel (212) 686-3837.
Consul-General: Antonio Aris de Castilla.
Consul: Francisco Enrique Azurdia-García.

Consulate-General: 2500 Wilshire Blvd, Suite 820, Los Angeles, CA 90057; tel (213) 365-9251.
Consul-General: Maynor J. Cuyun-Salguero.
Honorary Consul: John L. Ulmen.

Consulate-General: Coral Gables, 300 Sevilla Ave, Suite 210, Miami, FL; tel (305) 443-4828.
Consul-General: Gustavo A. Lopez.
Consul: Ana Mirza Velasquez-Ochoa.

Consulate-General: 180 North Michigan Ave, Suite 1035, Chicago, IL; tel (312) 332-1587.
Consul-General: Sergio R. Giron Sierra.
Honorary Consul: Willis Ranney, Jr.

Consulate: Westchase Central, 10200 Richmond Ave, Suite 270, Houston, TX 77402; tel (713) 953-9531.
Consul-General: Maria Cristina Alvarez.
Honorary Consul: Dr Carlos Hugo Monsanto.

Consulate: 2153 Meadow Lane Drive, Montgomery, AL 36106; tel (205) 269-2756.
Honorary Consul: José Roberto Ortega-Lopez.

Consulate: 10405 San Diego Mission Rd, Suite 205, San Diego, CA 92108; tel (619) 280-3650.
Honorary Consul: Eugene Herbert Sapper.

Consulate: 3014 Fillmore St, San Francisco, CA 94123; tel (415) 374-7451.
Honorary Consul: Robert J. McCarthy.

Consulate: 530 El Camino Real, Burlingame, San Mateo, CA 94010; tel (415) 344-2728.
Honorary Consul: Dr Juan Aycinena Echeerria.

Consulate: 2200 South Ocean Lane, Suite 1705, Fort Lauderdale, FL 33316.
Honorary Consul: John P. Bauer.

Consulate: 4774 East Conway Drive, NW, Atlanta, GA 30327; tel (404) 261-7234.
Honorary Consul: Maria Teresa Andreu de Fraser.

Consulate: 413 Delaware St, Leavenworth, KS 66048; tel (913) 692-0342.
Honorary Consul: Ralph E. Dix.

Consulate: 1532 World Trade Center, 2 Canal St, New Orleans, LA 70130.
Honorary Consul: Mario Jerez Zachrisson.
Honorary Vice-Consul: Aida de Ojeda.

Consulate: 5803 Loch Raven Blvd, Baltimore, MD 21239; tel (301) 435-6233.
Honorary Consul: Rene Licona Duarte.

Consulate: 9200 Wayzata Blvd, Minneapolis, MN 55426; tel (612) 540-3588.
Honorary Consul: Paul Reimer Nutt.

Consulate: 400 Lodges Lane, Elkins Park, Philadelphia, PA 19117; tel (215) 635-4079.
Honorary Consul: Dr Roberto Rendon Maldonado.

Consulate: 709 Washington Drive, North Hills Estates, Pittsburgh, PA 15229; tel (412) 366-7715.
Honorary Vice-Consul: Margarita Winikoff.

Consulate: 147 Jefferson Ave, Suite 900, Jefferson Plaza, Memphis, TN 38103; tel (901) 527-8466.
Honorary Consul: George E. Whitworth.

Consulate: 1446 Lincoln St, Brownsville, TX 78521; tel (512) 546-6913.
Honorary Consul: George Guy Bevil.

Consulate: 2100 5th Ave, Seattle, WA 98121; tel (206) 728-5920.
Honorary Consul: Elsa O. Smith.

Consulate: Villa Caparra Court Condominiums 3-C, Guaynabo, San Juan, Puerto Rico 00657; tel 782-0249.
Honorary Consul: Carlos Rechani.

GUINEA

Embassy: 2112 Leroy Place, NW, Washington, DC 20008; tel (202) 483-9420; telex 49606982; fax (202) 483-8688.
Ambassador: Moussa Sangare.

GUINEA-BISSAU

Embassy: 918 16th St, NW, Mezzanine Suite, Washington, DC 20006.
Ambassador: Alfredo Lopes Cabral.

Consulate: 211 East 43rd St, Suite 604, New York, NY 10017; tel (212) 661-3977.

GUYANA

Embassy: 2490 Tracy Place, NW, Washington, DC 20008; tel (202) 265-6900.
Ambassador: Dr Cedric Hilburn Grant.

Consulate-General: 866 United Nations Plaza, 3rd Floor, New York, NY 10017.
Consul-General: Gerald Dorway.
Consul: Riley C. A. Abdelnour.
Consul: James W. Ramsahoye.

Consulate: 611 South William Place, Los Angeles, CA 90005; tel (213) 389-7565.
Honorary Consul: Joseph Gabriel d'Oliveira.

Consulate: 655 NW 36th St, Rm 207, Miami, FL 33166.
Honorary Consul: Arnold S. Godette.

Consulate: POB 4362, Waco, TX 767705; tel (817) 799-3611.
Honorary Consul: Theodore Alwyn Talbot.

HAITI

Embassy: 2311 Massachusetts Ave, Washington, DC 20008; tel (202) 332-4090; telex 440202; fax (202) 745-7215.
Ambassador: Jean Casimir.

Consulate-General: 60 East 42nd St, Suite 1365, New York, NY 10017; tel (212) 697-9767.
Honorary Consul: Robert von Tauber.
Vice-Consul: Pierre-Marie Toussaint.

Consulate-General: 259 SW 13th St, Miami, FL 33131; tel (305) 859-2005.
Vice-Consul: Hans P. Lafleur.

Consulate-General: 202 South State St, Suite 1302, Chicago, IL 60604; tel (312) 922-4004.
Consul-General: Jean S. Simeon.

Consulate-General: 15 Court Sq., Suite 860, Boston, MA 02108; tel (617) 723-5211.

Consulate-General: 654 Ave Nunos Rivera, Suite 909, Hato Rey, San Juan, Puerto Rico 00918.
Vice-Consul: Ralph Viard.
Honorary Consul: Joseph E. Binard.

Consulate: 100 Brannan St, San Francisco, CA 94107; tel (415) 957-1189.
Honorary Consul: Oscar Eduardo Carcelen.

Consulate: 621 17th St, Suite 1741, Denver, CO 80293; tel (303) 298-7392.
Honorary Consul: Paul Edward Vranesic II.

Consulate: POB 80340, Atlanta, GA 30366; tel (404) 455-3434.
Honorary Consul: William Gilbert Browning.

Consulate: POB 4200, Evansville, IN 47711; tel (812) 423-8000.
Honorary Consul: Alfred DeCalb Vanhoose.

Consulate: 416 Common St, New Orleans, LA 70130; tel (504) 586-8309.
Honorary Consul: Pierre Benjamin Clemenceau.

Consulate: 2121 First National Bldg, Detroit, MI 48226; tel (313) 965-7962.
Honorary Consul: Ralph Jenkins Osborne.

Consulate: 441 Cloisters Walk, Kirkwood, St Louis, MO 63122; tel (314) 966-5280.
Honorary Consul: Norman Bradford West.

Consulate: First School Bldg, 110 Main Ave, Passaic Park, Trenton, NJ 07055; tel (201) 777-2121.
Honorary Consul: Jean-Claude Levy.

Consulate: 1016 Standard Bldg, Cleveland, OH 44113; tel (216) 771-0280.
Honorary Consul: Henry P. Kosling.

Consulate: 1430 Land Title Bldg, Philadelphia, PA 19110.
Honorary Consul: Albert Momjian.

Consulate: 200 Mahantongo St, Pottsville, PA 17901.
Honorary Consul: John Joseph Curran.

Consulate: 3535 Sage Rd, Houston, TX 77027.
Honorary Vice-Consul: Renato F. Pereira.

HOLY SEE

Embassy: 3339 Massachusetts Ave, NW, Washington, DC 20008; tel (202) 333-7121; telex 440117; fax (202) 337-4036.
Apostolic Nuncio: Most Rev. Agostino Cacciavillan, Titular Archbishop of Amiterno.
Counsellor: Mgr Rino Passigato.
Counsellor: Mgr Leonardo Sandri.
Secretary: Mgr Ivo Scapolo.

HONDURAS

Embassy: 3700 Tilden St, NW, Washington, DC 20008; tel (202) 966-7702; fax (202) 966-9751.
Ambassador: Jorge Ramón Hernández-Alcerro.
Minister and Deputy Head of Mission: Salvador Enrique Rodezno-Fuentes.
Counsellor (Economic/Financial): José Benjamín Zapata.
Counsellor (Legal): Tania Beyl.
Defence, Military, Naval and Air Attaché: Col Juan E. López.
Assistant Defence, Military, Naval and Air Attaché: Lieut Jacqueline Foglia-Sandoval.
Attaché (Culture): Ricardo Jorge Jaar.

Consular Section: 1511 K St, Suite 927, NW, Washington, DC 20005; tel (202) 638-4348.
Consul: Graciamaría Aguero Guevara.

Consulate-General: 80 Wall St, Suite 915, New York, NY 10005; tel (212) 889-3858.
Vice-Consul: Arturo Morales Chavez.
Consular Agent: Edy R. Fajardo.

Consulate-General: 548 South Spring St, Suite 310, Los Angeles, CA 90013; tel (213) 623-2301.
Consul-General: Rene F. Umana.
Honorary Vice-Consul: Susana Martínez de Stevenson.

Consulate-General: 870 Market St, Flood Bldg, Suites 451-53, San Francisco, CA 94102; tel (415) 392-0076.
Consul-General: Jorge A. Moncada.
Honorary Vice-Consul: Henry Langenberg McIntyre.

Consulate-General: 14 NE First Ave, Suite 406, Israel Discount Bank Bldg, Miami, FL 33132; tel (305) 358-3477.
Consul-General: Rene Sagastume.
Honorary Consul: Owen S. Freed.

Consulate-General: 6011 North Kenmore, Apt 212, Chicago, IL 60660; tel (312) 772-7090.
Honorary Vice-Consul: Maura Rosa Alcerro Prudot.

Consulate-General: 203 Carondelet St, Suite 707, New Orleans, LA 70130; tel (504) 522-3118.
Consul-General: Rosamalia M. Pastor.
Honorary Consul: Raul Gregorio Reyes Mazzoni.

Consulate-General: 5803 Loch Raven Blvd, Baltimore, MD 21239; tel (301) 435-6233.
Honorary Consul-General: Rene Licona Duarte.

Consulate: 100 Altura Vista, Los Gatos, Burlingame, CA 95030; tel (408) 379-6156.
Honorary Consul: Raul Arturo Caceres.

Consulate: 525 B St, Suite 2002, Union Bank Bldg, San Diego, CA 92101; tel (619) 533-4515.
Honorary Consul: Ella Isabel Flores Paris.
Honorary Consul: Ondina Pineda de Hiel.

Consulate: 1400 Petroleum Club Bldg, 110 16th St, Denver, CO 80202; tel (303) 629-6118.
Honorary Consul: Zack V. Chayet.

Consulate: 250 Bird Rd, Coral Gables, FL.
Honorary Consul: Federico Alberto Smith.

Consulate: Gainesville, FL.
Honorary Consul: Sonia Mejia de Caceres.

Consulate: 1914 Beachway Rd, Suite 30, Jacksonville, FL 33207; tel (904) 348-3550.
Consul: Antonio J. Valladares.

Consulate: 3091 Chaparral Place, Lythonia, Atlanta, GA 30058.
Honorary Consul: Sonia M. Idiaquez de Siebert.

Consulate: 11017 North Oak Hills Parkway, Baton Rouge, LA 70810.
Honorary Consul: Vilma Cabrera de Calhoun.

Consulate: 486 Beacon St, Suite 2, Boston, MA 02115.
Consul: Graciela Mendizabal Suarez.
Honorary Consul: Hewson A. Ryan.

Consulate: 3620 Shady Lane, Detroit, MI 48216.
Consul: Alma Rosa C. V. de Alonzo.
Honorary Consul: Thomas Roger Mallard.

Consulate: 20 Cygnet Place, Long Lake, Minneapolis, MN 55356; tel (612) 473-5376.
Honorary Consul: Harold Joseph Panuska.

Consulate: POB 158, Marquand, St Louis, MO 63655; tel (314) 473-5376.
Honorary Consul: Francis Doll, Jr.

Consulate: 46 Pinebrook Circle, Pennfield, Rochester, NY 14526.
Honorary Consul: Carolina Srinivasan.

Consulate: 20600 Chagrin Blvd, Suite 400, Cleveland, OH 44122.
Honorary Vice-Consul: Roberto D. Kline.

Consulate: 6315 Rising Sun Ave, Philadelphia, PA 19111; tel (215) 745-9290.
Honorary Consul: Mario H. Romero.

Consulate: 4151 Southwest Freeway, Suite 700, Houston, TX 77027; tel (713) 622-4572.
Consul: Hector E. Medina.

Consulate: 1402 3rd Ave, Suite 1019, Seattle, WA 98101-2110; tel (202) 623-6485.
Honorary Consul: Javier I. Pinel.

Consulate: 1734 Malanai St, Apt 6, Honolulu, HI 96826; tel (808) 944-1647.
Honorary Consul: Lesby Guillermina Billam-Walker.

Consulate: Route 15, Jajome Alto KM 14-3, Cayey, Puerto Rico 00634.
Honorary Vice-Consul: José S. Ergas.

Consulate: Esmeralda Ave 54, Ponce de Leon, San Juan, Puerto Rico 00657.
Honorary Consul: Ricardo A. López Medina.

HUNGARY

Embassy: 3007 Shoemaker St, NW, Washington, DC 20008; tel (202) 966-7702; fax (202) 966-9751.
Ambassador: Jorge Ramón Hernández Alcerro.
Consul: Laszlo Takacs.

Consulate-General: 8 East 75th St, New York, NY 10021; tel (212) 879-4127.
Consul-General: Janos Fodor.
Consul: Gabor Menczel.

ICELAND

Embassy: 2022 Connecticut Ave, NW, Washington, DC 20008; tel (202) 265-6653; telex 248596; fax (202) 265-6656.
Ambassador: Tómas A. Tóminsson.
Secretary: Stefán L. Stefánsson.
Secretary: Hjördís Gunnarsdóttir.
Secretary: Jóna Valdimarsdóttir.

Consulate-General: 370 Lexington Ave (at 41st St), Rm 505, New York, NY 10017; tel (212) 686-4100; telex 234419; fax (212) 532-4138.
Consul-General: Helgi Gíslason.
Vice-Consul: Grétar Már Sigudsson.
Counsellor: Ulfur Sirgurmundsson.

Consulate-General: 16677 Tullie Circle, NE, Suite 507, Atlanta, GA 30329; tel (404) 321-0777; telex 542695; fax (404) 634-9640.
Consul-General: Maurice K. Horowitz.
Vice-Consul: Robert S. Horowitz.

Consulate-General: 221 North La Salle St, Suite 2700, Chicago, IL 60601; tel (312) 782-6872.
Consul-General: Paul Sveinbjorn Johnson.
Vice-Consul: John Thomas Martin.

Consulate-General: 14755 Ventura Blvd, Suite 1604, Shermans Oaks, Los Angeles, CA 91403; tel (213) 474-8485.
Consul-General: Halla Linker.

Consulate-General: 270 Crossway Rd, POB 753, Tallahassee, FL 32302; tel (904) 878-1146; fax (904) 878-6093.
Consul-General: Hilmar S. Skagfield.

Consulate: 5610 NW 20th Ave, Seattle, WA 98107; tel (206) 783-4100; fax (206) 784-8916.
Consul: Jón Marvin Jónsson.

Consulate: 3890 West Northwest Highway, Suite 304, Dallas, TX 75220; tel (214) 352-1035.
Consul: David Henry Watkins.

Consulate: 5220 North Ocean Drive, Hollywood, FL 33109; tel (305) 920-7977; telex 514508; fax (305) 920-6977.
Consul: Þórir S. Gröndal.

Consulate: Bingham Office Park, 30400 Telegraph Rd, Suite 479, Birmingham, MI 48010; tel (313) 540-1044.
Consul: Arthur James Rubiner.

Consulate: 9 Broadview Terrace, San Francisco and Berkeley, CA 94563; tel (415) 254-0169.
Consul: Gunnhildur Lorensen.

Consulate: 2600 Highway Ky 146, POB 265, La Grange, KY 40031; tel (502) 222-1441; telex 204151; fax (502) 222-1445.
Consul: Jón Sigurður Guðmundsson.

Consulate: 7835 SW Northvale Way, Portland, OR 97225; tel (503) 292-6971.

Consul: Sylvia R. Kipnis.

Consulate: 3444 Edmund Blvd, Minneapolis, MN 55406; tel (612) 729-1927.
Consul: Jón H. Björnsson.

Consulate: Gerrity Co. Inc., 90 Oak St, POB 1100, Newton Upper Falls, MA 02164; tel (617) 244-1400.
Consul: J. Frank Gerrity.

Consulate: 2701 Westheimer, Apt 5 A, Houston, TX 77098; tel (713) 523-3336.
Consul: Dr Charles Howard Hallson.

Consulate: 637 Devon Rd, Camp Hill, PA 17011; POB 190, Camp Hill, PA 17001-190; tel (717) 761-8435; fax (717) 761-1499.
Consul: Hubert J. Georges.

Consulate: 2966 Jana Lee Drive, West Jordan, UT 84084; tel (801) 240-1000.
Consul: Thor Leifsson.

Consulate: Capes Shipping Agencies Inc., 1128 West Olney Rd, Norfolk, VA 23507; tel (804) 625-3658; telex 823476.
Consul: Gerald L. Parks.

Consulate: 7100 East 131st St, Grandview, MO 64030; tel (816) 763-2046.
Consul: Vigdís Asdalsteindóttir.

Consulate: Alonso Sobrino Hons Co. Inc., Calle Islandia, POB 2811, Bayamon, Puerto Rico 00619; tel 786-7171; telex 3252306; fax 740-2888.
Consul: Antonio Ruiz Ochio.

INDIA

Embassy: 2107 Massachusetts Ave, NW, Washington, DC 20008; tel (202) 939-7000; fax (202) 939-7027.
Ambassador: Abdul Rachman Ramly.

Consulate-General: 3 East 64th St, New York, NY 10021; tel (212) 879-7800.
Consul-General: Rajendra Kumar.
Deputy Consul-General: Sengupta Dipak.
Consul: George Richard.
Consul: Vishnu Prakash.
Consul: Srinivasachariar Sudarsanam.
Consul: Rahul Kulshreshth.
Consul: Sarv Mitter Trehan.

Consulate-General: 150 North Michigan Ave, Suite 1100, Chicago, IL 60601; tel (312) 781-6280.
Consul-General: Pyare Lal Santoshi.
Consul: K. Joseph Francis.
Consul: Kanwar B. S. Katoch.

Consulate-General: 540 Arguello Blvd, San Francisco, CA 94118; tel (415) 688-0662.
Consul-General: Satinder K. Lambah.
Consul: Biswapati Ghosh.

Consulate-General: 2051 Young St, Honolulu, HI 96826; tel (808) 947-2618.
Honorary Consul-General: Sheila Watumull.

Consulate: 1525 Webster St, New Orleans, LA 70118.
Honorary Consul: George Denegre.

Consulate: 1444 Union Commerce Bldg, Cleveland, OH 44115; tel (216) 696-1144.
Honorary Consul: George Percival Bickford.

INDONESIA

Embassy: 2020 Massachusetts Ave, NW, Washington, DC 20036; tel (202) 775-5200; fax (202) 775-5316.
Ambassador: Abdul Rachman Ramly.

Consulate-General: 5 East 68th St, New York, NY 10021; tel (212) 879-0600.
Consul-General: Arkelaus N. Pantow.
Consul: Chaidir Siregar.
Consul: Salfrida Nasution.
Consul: Koko Wijanarko.

Consulate-General: 2 Illinois Center, Suite 1422, 233 North Michigan Ave, Chicago, IL 60601; tel (312) 938-0101.
Consul-General: Prawirosuhardjo Surahman.
Consul: Hidajat.

Consulate-General: 3457 Wilshire Blvd, Los Angeles, CA 90010.
Consul-General: Djunaedi Sutisnawinata.
Consul: Setijanto Poedjowarsito.
Consul: Otong Hasan.
Consul: Immanuel R. Inkiriwang.
Consul: Sunten Z. Manurung.

Consulate-General: 5633 Richmond Ave, Houston, TX 77057.
Consul-General: Tengku Dahlia Soemolang.
Consul: Hermansyah Joenoes.
Consul: Trijono Marjono.
Consul: Supardjo.

Consulate: 1111 Colombus Ave, San Francisco, CA 94133; tel (415) 474-9571.
Consul: Den Zachrie.

IRAN

Interests Section: 2209 Wisconsin Ave, NW, Washington, DC 20007; tel (202) 965-4990.

IRELAND

Embassy: 2234 Massachusetts Ave, NW, Washington, DC 20008; tel (202) 462-3939; telex 64160; fax (202) 232-5993.
Ambassador: Padraic N. MacKernan.
Counsellor (Political): Brendan Scannell.
Counsellor: Joseph Lynch.
First Secretary (Press/Information): Anne Barrington.
First Secretary (Press/Information): Declan Kelleher.
First Secretary: Timothy P. O'Connor.
Third Secretary: Eamonn McKee.

Consulate-General: 515 Madison Ave, 18th Floor, New York, NY 10022; tel (212) 319-2550; telex 62128; fax (212) 980-9475.
Consul-General: Daithi O. Ceallaigh.
Deputy Consul-General: Denis Malin.

Consulate-General: Chase Bldg, 535 Boylston St, Boston, MA 02116; tel (617) 267-4470; telex 940556; fax (617) 267-6375.
Consul-General: Liam Canniffe.
Vice-Consul: Geoffrey Keating.

Consulate-General: 400 North Michigan Ave, Chicago, IL 60611; tel (312) 337-1868; telex 65040-14610; fax (312) 337-1954.
Consul-General: Gary Ansbro.
Vice-Consul: Niall Burgess.

Consulate-General: 655 Montgomery St, Suite 930, San Francisco, CA 94411; tel (415) 392-4214; telex 65030-73335; fax (415) 392-0885.
Consul-General: John Rowan.
Vice-Consul: Michael Forbes.

Consulate: 65 South 65th St, Bellville, IL 62223; tel (618) 274-0886.
Honorary Consul: Joseph B. McGlynn, Jr.

Consulate: 1900 West Loop St, Houston, TX 77027.
Honorary Consul: John B. Kane.

ISRAEL

Embassy: 3514 International Drive, NW, Washington, DC 20008; tel (202) 364-5500; fax (202) 364-5560.
Ambassador: Zalman Shoval.
Consul: Jacob Perry.

Consulate-General: 800 2nd Ave, New York, NY 10017; tel (212) 351-5200.
Consul-General: Uri Savir.
Consul: Moredechai Yedid.
Consul: Tzion Evrony.
Consul: Yoram Gonen.
Consul: Shmuel Shenhar.
Consul: Bilha Galil.
Consul: Noam Semel.
Consul: Raphael Farber.

Consulate-General: 6380 Wilshire Blvd, Suite 1700, Los Angeles, CA 90048; tel (213) 651-5700.
Consul-General: Ran Ronen.
Consul: Moshe Peer.
Consul: Arie Zomer.
Consul: Eliezer Egosi.

Consulate-General: 220 Bush St, Suite 550, San Francisco, CA 94104; tel (415) 398-8885.
Consul-General: Harry Kney-Tal.
Consul: Dov Kolani.
Consul: Gad Soen.
Consul: Anna Azari.

Consulate-General: 330 Biscayne Blvd, Suite 510, Miami, FL 33132; tel (303) 358-8111.
Consul-General: Moshe Liba.
Consul: Yair Recanati.
Consul: Dvora Ganani-Elad.
Consul: Ruth Raz-Russo.

Consulate-General: 1100 Spring St, Suite 440, Atlanta, GA 30309-2823; tel (404) 875-7851.
Consul-General: Alon Liel.
Consul: Eliezer Hod.

Consulate-General: 111 East Wacker Drive, Chicago, IL 60601; tel (312) 565-3300.
Consul-General: Uri A. Bar-Ner.
Consul: Moshe Fox.

Consulate-General: 1020 Statler Office Bldg, Boston, MA 02116; tel (617) 542-0041.
Consul-General: Yaakov Levy.
Consul: Itzhak Oren.

Consulate-General: 230 South 15th St, 8th Floor, Philadelphia, PA 19102; tel (215) 546-5556.
Consul-General: Israel Peleg.
Consul: Amira Arnon.

Consulate-General: One Greenway Plaza East, Suite 722, Houston, TX 77046; tel (713) 627-3780.
Consul-General: Mordekhai Artzieli.
Consul: Dov Segev-Steinberg.

ITALY

Embassy: 1601 Fuller St, NW, Washington, DC 20009; tel (202) 328-5500; telex 64461; fax (202) 462-3605.
Ambassador: Rinaldo Petrignani.

Consulate-General: 690 Park Ave, New York, NY 10021-5044; tel (212) 737-9100.
Consul-General: Francesco Corrias.
Consul: Gabriella Meneghello Battistello.

Consulate-General: 12400 Wilshire Blvd, Suite 300, Los Angeles, CA 90025; tel (213) 820-0622.
Consul-General: Alberto Bonivar.

Consulate-General: 2590 Webster St, San Francisco, CA 94115; tel (415) 931-4924.
Consul-General: Marcello Griccioli.
Consul: Giancarlo Masini.

Consulate-General: 500 North Michigan Ave, Suite 1850, Chicago, IL 60611; tel (312) 467-1550.
Consul-General: Stefano Maria Cacciaguerra Ranghieri.

Consulate-General: 630 Camp St, Lafayette Place Bldg, New Orleans, LA 70130; tel (504) 524-2271.
Consul-General: Nardo Olivetti.

Consulate-General: 100 Boylston St, Suite 900, Boston, MA 02116; tel (617) 542-0483.
Consul-General: Giuseppe Zaccagnino.
Consular Agent: Alfredo Molinari.

Consulate-General: 421 Chestnut St, Philadelphia, PA 19106; tel (215) 592-7369.
Consul-General: Franco Giodano.

Consulate-General: Allied Bank Towers, 1300 Post Oak Blvd, Houston, TX 77056; tel (713) 850-7520.
Consul-General: Concetta Distefano.

Consulate: 4160 East Shan Drive, Mobile, AL 36609; tel (205) 661-1389.
Honorary Vice-Consul: Italo Manfredo Francalancia.

Consulate: 3838 California St, San Francisco, Berkeley, CA 94118; tel (415) 668-2626.
Honorary Vice-Consul: Piero Oscar Mustacchi.

Consulate: 2409 Merced St, Fresno, CA 93721; tel (209) 268-8776.
Honorary Vice-Consul: Edward LeRoy Fanucchi.

Consulate: 5347 Folsom Blvd, Suite A, Sacramento, CA 95819; tel (916) 456-1950.
Honorary Vice-Consul: Anthony Umberto Virgadamo.

Consulate: 751 7th St, San Diego, CA 92101; tel (619) 231-9111.
Honorary Vice-Consul: Paola F. Deshii.

Consulate: 777 North First St, Suite 600D, San José, CA 95112; tel (408) 971-9170.
Honorary Vice-Consul: Mirella Alterocca Hemp.

Consulate: 8820 West 84th St, Arvada, CO 80005; tel (303) 431-1683.
Honorary Vice-Consul: Caterina Noya Scordo.

Consulate: 945 Wethersfield Ave, Hartford, CT 06114; tel (203) 247-5619.
Honorary Vice-Consul: Concetta R. Di Loreto.

Consulate: 2600 SW Third Ave, Suite 765, Miami, FL 33129; tel (305) 854-1758.
Honorary Consul: Roberto Simoni.

Consulate: 1106 West Peachtree St, NW, Atlanta, GA 30309; tel (404) 875-6177.
Honorary Consul: John Andrew Serafino Fornara.

Consulate: 206 Brotherhood Blvd, Kansas City, KS 66101; tel (913) 281-2222.
Honorary Vice-Consul: Roberto Leopoldo Serra.

Consulate: Kahala Hilton Hotel, 5000 Kahala Ave, Honolulu, HI 96816; tel (808) 734-2211.
Honorary Consul: Louis J. Finamore.

Consulate: 600 Wyndhurst Ave, Suite 250, Wyndhurst Bldg, Baltimore, MD 21210; tel (301) 435-0836.
Honorary Consul: Francesco L. Legaluppi.

Consulate: 535 Griswold, 1840 Buhl Bldg, Detroit, MI.
Consul: Giuseppe Mistretta.

Consulate: 8803 Gravois Ave, St Louis, MO 63123; tel (314) 351-7176.
Honorary Vice-Consul: Maria Ottinger Avila.

Consulate: c/o Bilbray, Carelli & Miller, Attorneys at Law, 302 East Carson, Suite 830, Las Vegas, NV 89101; tel (702) 385-6843.
Honorary Vice-Consul: Paul Vincent Carelli III.

Consulate: 17 Academy St, Newark, NJ 07102; tel (201) 643-1448.
Consular Agent: Antonio de Santis.

Consulate: 359 Hamilton Ave, Trenton, NJ 08609; tel (609) 393-7852.
Honorary Vice-Consul: Guido Luccarelli.

Consulate: 1441 Hertel Ave, Buffalo, NY 14216; tel (716) 874-0912.
Honorary Vice-Consul: Joseph C. Musca.

Consulate: 185 Empire Blvd, Rochester, NY 14609; tel (716) 482-2803.
Honorary Vice-Consul: Arthur Anzalone.

Consulate: 419 Wood St, Pittsburgh, PA 15222; tel (412) 391-7669.
Honorary Vice-Consul: Joseph F. d'Andrea.

Consulate: 294 Washington Ave, Memphis, TN 38103; tel (901) 523-2222.
Honorary Vice-Consul: Lloyd Anthony Deal.

Consulate: 2831 Nagle St, Dallas, TX 75220; tel (214) 350-5784.
Honorary Vice-Consul: Anthony La Barba.

Consulate: 2202 Mechanic St, Galveston, TX 77550; tel (409) 765-7759.
Honorary Vice-Consul: Maurizio Benvenuto Antonelli.

Consulate: Calle Amatista 93, Urb. Golden Gate, San Juan, Puerto Rico 00920-3421; tel 793-5284.
Honorary Vice-Consul: Angelo Pio Sanfilippo.

Consulate: 222 North Central Ave, Phoenix, AZ 85001; tel (602) 351-8099.
Honorary Vice-Consul: Joseph Peter Martori.

Consulate: 1620 East Brundage Lane, Bakersfield, CA 93302; tel (805) 327-9386.
Honorary Vice-Consul: Bernard Sacco.

Consulate: 24 Circle West, Edina, Minneapolis and St Paul, MN 55436; tel (612) 920-3330.
Honorary Vice-Consul: Sarah Rockler.

Consulate: 1712 Old Town Rd, NW, Albuquerque, NM 87104; tel (505) 897-0110.
Honorary Vice-Consul: Paola B. Quargnali.

Consulate: Statler Office Tower, Suite 319, 1127 Euclid Ave, Cleveland, OH 44115; tel (216) 861-1585.
Honorary Vice-Consul: Biagio Parente.

Consulate: 1784 Lawrence Circle, South Jordan, Salt Lake City, UT 84064; tel (801) 254-7573.
Honorary Vice-Consul: Giovanni G. Maschero.

Consulate: 10939 NE 49th St, Seattle, WA 98033; tel (206) 885-3332.
Honorary Vice-Consul: Quinto de Vitis.

Consular Agency: 12301 Johns Rd, Suite 3, Anchorage, AK 99515; tel (907) 564-0664.
Honorary Consular Agent: Vittorio Maurizio Montemezzani.

Consular Agency: 55 River Ridge Rd, Little Rock, AR 72207; tel (501) 225-2827.
Honorary Consular Agent: Dante Paul Jacuzzi.

Consular Agency: 5627 Atlantic Blvd, Suite 4, Jacksonville, FL 32207; tel (904) 724-4441.
Honorary Consular Agency: Anthony F. Marinucci.

Consular Agency: 102 Martinique Ave, Tampa, FL 33606; tel (813) 254-2778.
Honorary Consular Agent: Marina E. Ruffolo.

Consular Agency: 310 East Bay St, POB 2088, Savannah, GA 31498; tel (912) 232-5581.
Honorary Consular Agent: Joseph Mose Cafiero, Jr.

Consular Agency: 720 Van Buren St, South Bend, Indianapolis, IN 46616; tel (219) 233-4021.
Honorary Consular Agent: Pietro Agostino.

Consular Agency: 11 Acushnet Ave, Springfield, MA 01105; tel (413) 734-0575.
Honorary Consular Agent: Giuseppe Polimeni.

Consular Agency: 172 Shrewsbury St, Worcester, MA 01604; tel (508) 755-5990.
Honorary Consular Agent: Aspreno Pietro Ciccarelli.

Consular Agency: East Pier, POB 1689, Gulfport, MS 39502; tel (601) 864-8282.
Honorary Consular Agent: Luigi Scialdone.

Consular Agency: POB 23171, 1569 Chase Ave, Cincinnati, OH 45223; tel (513) 541-2661.
Honorary Consular Agent: Anthony V. Gambino.

JAMAICA

Embassy: 1850 'K' St, Suite 355, NW, Washington, DC 20006; tel (202) 452-0660; telex 64352; fax (202) 452-0081.
Ambassador: Keith Johnson.
Minister-Counsellor: Dr Earl Carr.
Consul: Ransford Athelston Smith.
Consul: Sharon Rosemarie Brown.
Consul: Deborah Ann Lindo.

Consulate-General: 866 2nd Ave, 2 Hammarskjöld Plaza, New York, NY 10017; tel (212) 935-9000; telex 62984.
Consul-General: Derick Heaven.
Consul: Daphne McLeod.
Consul: Effie Marie Morris.

Consulate-General: 842 Ingraham Bldg, 25 SE Second Ave, Miami, FL 33131; tel (305) 374-8431.
Consul-General: Marie Rose Crooks Wray.
Consul: Errol D. James.

Consulate: 3807 Wilshire Blvd, Suite 700, Los Angeles, CA 90010; tel (213) 380-9471.
Honorary Consul: Cleveland Oswald Neil.

Consulate: 22455 Maple Court, Suite 303, Hayward, CA 94542.
Honorary Consul: Dr Horace Alton Penso.

Consulate: 6721 Covington Highway, Lithonia, Atlanta, GA 30035.
Honorary Consul: Sylvia P. Ashley.

Consulate: 28 East Jackson St, Suite 1009, Chicago, IL 60604; tel (312) 663-0023.
Honorary Consul: Lloyd L. Hyde.

JAPAN

Embassy: 2520 Massachusetts Ave, NW, Washington, DC 20008; tel (202) 939-6700; telex 904017; fax (202) 939-2187.
Ambassador: Takakazu Kuriyana (designate).
Minister and Deputy Head of Mission: Takayuki Kimura.
Minister (Political): Kenzo Oshima.
Minister (Economic): Hiroshi Hirabayashi.
Minister (Commercial): Yokiro Kawaguchi.
Minister: Seiichiro Noboru.
Minister (Finance): Yoshiaki Kaneko.
Counsellor (Finance): Toshihiko Amano.
Counsellor (Finance): Keizo Goto.
Counsellor (Economic): Shotaro Yachi.
Counsellor (Economic): Yasuo Suzuki.
Counsellor (Economic Planning): Takafumi Kaneko.
Counsellor (Agriculture): Takashi Kato.
Counsellor (Congressional Affairs): Tsuneo Nishida.
Counsellor (Management): Masakazu Nago.
Counsellor (Political): Shigeru Nakamura.
Counsellor (Information): Hideaki Ueda.
Counsellor (Science): Takashi Kisaka.
Counsellor: Yasuaki Ono.
Counsellor: Sachoro Nanami.
Defence and Military Attaché: Maj. Gen. Takao Sakamaki.
Naval Attaché: Capt. Kazunari Doke.
Air Attaché: Col Yoshishige Hori.
Assistant Defence and Naval Attaché: Commdr Masanori Koga.
Assistant Defence and Military Attaché: Lieut Col Isao Mukunoki.
Assistant Air Attaché: Maj. Kesayoshi Miyashita.
First Secretary (Protocol): Ichiro Namiki.
First Secretary (Construction): Tetsuo Moriuchi.
First Secretary (Economic): Takanobu Teramoto.
First Secretary (Economic): Shunsuke Sugiyama.
First Secretary (Economic): Kazuhide Ishikawa.
First Secretary (Economic): Kenji Kagawa.
First Secretary (Finance): Shinji Sato.
First Secretary (Environment): Yasuhiro Shimizu.

Second Secretary (Press): Noriyuki Shikata.
Second Secretary (Security): Norio Kuboki.

Consulate-General: 299 Park Ave, New York, NY 10171; tel (212) 371-8222; telex 971547; fax (212) 319-6357.
Consul-General: Masamichi Hanabusa.
Deputy Consul-General: Seigi Hinata.
Consul: Kenshiro Fukui.
Consul: Hideaki Suzuki.
Consul: Makoto Kobayashi.

Consulate-General: 250 East First St, Suite 1507, Los Angeles, CA 90012; tel (213) 624-8305; telex 674301; fax (213) 625-2231.
Consul-General: Kiyohiko Arafune.
Deputy Consul-General: Gunkatsu Kano.

Consulate-General: POB 2187, Mobile, AL 36609; tel (205) 433-6951.
Honorary Consul-General: Marion Benjamin Rambeau.

Consulate-General: 601 Union St, Suite 500, Seattle, WA 98101; tel (206) 682-9107; telex 328731; fax (206) 624-9097.
Consul-General: Shinsuke Hirai.
Consul: Keizo Emori.

Consulate-General: 4562 Avondale Blvd, NW, London Square, Canton, Cleveland, OH 44708; tel (216) 477-6977.
Honorary Consul-General: Thomas M. Hague.

Consulate-General: The Denver Post, POB 1709, Denver, CO 80201; tel (303) 820-1359.
Honorary Consul-General: William K. Hosokawa.

Consulate-General: 501 Brickell Key Drive, Suite 300, Miami, FL 33131; tel (305) 374-5505.
Honorary Consul-General: Richard Hill McRae Swann III.

Consulate-General: Olympia Center, Suite 1100, 737 North Michigan Ave, Chicago, IL 60611; tel (312) 280-0400; telex 253431; fax (312) 280-9568.
Consul-General: Takeshi Nakamura.
Deputy Consul-General: Masao Ishikawa.

Consulate-General: 515 Olive St, Suite 1005, St Louis, MO 63101; tel (314) 421-3228.
Honorary Consul-General: Carl Louis Alexander Beckers.

Consulate-General: Suite 2000, 100 Colony Sq. Bldg, 1175 Peachtree St, NE, Atlanta, GA 30361; tel (404) 892-2700; telex 542454; fax (404) 881-6321.
Consul-General: Akira Hayashi.
Consul: Keitaro Sato.
Consul: Hisako Dazai.
Consul: Takeo Shimada.

Consulate-General: 50 Fremont St, Suite 2300, San Francisco, CA 94105; tel (415) 777-3533; telex 34411; fax (415) 974-3660.
Consul-General: Atsushi Tokinoya.
Consul: Hideo Okumura.
Consul: Tatsuro Katsuyama.
Consul: Kazuzo Ebina.

Consulate-General: 2400 First Interstate Tower, 1300 SW Fifth Ave, Portland, OR 97201; tel (503) 221-1811; telex 255939; fax (503) 224-8936.
Consul-General: Akira Watanabe.
Consul: Eizo Kaneyasu.
Consul: Shintaro Nakayama.
Consul: Kuniteru Nishiberi.

Consulate-General: Suite 2050, One Poydras Plaza, 639 Loyola Ave, New Orleans, LA 70113; tel (504) 529-2101; telex 58204; fax (504) 568-9847.
Consul-General: Yasuhiro Hamada.
Consul: Tomoo Hirakawa.
Consul: Yu Takahashi.

Consulate-General: 3154 North 33rd Ave, Phoenix, AZ 85017; tel (602) 275-5111.
Honorary Consul-General: Thomas S. Kadomoto.

Consulate-General: 2049 Loren Rd, St Paul, Minneapolis, MN 55113; tel (612) 626-0931.
Honorary Consul-General: N. L. Gault, Jr.

Consulate-General: Federal Reserve Plaza, 14th Floor, 600 Atlantic Ave, Boston, MA 02210; tel (617) 973-9772; telex 940142; fax (617) 542-1329.
Consul-General: Kensaku Hogen.
Deputy Consul-General: Yoshihiro Nose.
Consul: Takayuki Koike.
Consul: Toshiki Saito.
Consul: Tadahiro Abe.
Consul: Yoshitaka Kitagawa.

Consulate-General: First Interstate Bank Plaza, Suite 5300, 1000 Louisiana St, Houston, TX 77002; tel (713) 652-2977; telex 775341; fax (713) 651-7822.
Consul-General: Masayuki Makiya.
Consul: Koichi Funayama.

Consulate-General: 85 Windsor Ave, Buffalo, NY 14209; tel (719) 684-6100.
Honorary Consul-General: Appleton Fryer.

Consulate-General: 2519 Commerce Tower, 911 Main St, Kansas City, MO 64105-2076; tel (816) 471-0111; telex 42587; fax (816) 472-4248.
Consul-General: Hideo Numata.
Consul: Kazuo Ashizawa.
Consul: Seizaburo Fujisawa.
Consul: Mitsuo Takamatsu.
Consul: Hatsuo Fujishima.

Consulate-General: Bank of America, 450B St, Suite 1900, San Diego, CA 92101.
Honorary Consul-General: James B. Wiesler.

Consulate-General: 10801 East Northwest Highway, Dallas, TX 75238.
Honorary Consul-General: Masashi Kawasaki.

Consulate-General: Nelson Capital Corporation, 3401 West End Bldg, Suite 300, Nashville, TN 37203.
Honorary Consul-General: Edward G. Nelson.

Consulate-General: 550 West 7th Ave, Suite 701, Anchorage, AK 99501; tel (907) 279-8428; telex 25107; fax (907) 279-9271.
Consul-General: Akira Nagasaka.
Consul: Hirozo Ushida.
Consul: Hisashi Endo.

Consulate-General: Suite 604, Guam International Trade Center Bldg, 590 South Marine Drive, Tamuning, Guam 96911; tel 646-1290; telex 6297; fax 646-2620.
Consul-General: Masao Wada.
Consul: Yoshio Koshio.

Consulate-General: 1742 Nuuanu Ave, Honolulu, HI 96817-3294; tel (808) 536-2226; telex 8328; fax (808) 537-3276.
Consul-General: Masaji Takahashi.
Consul: Kazumi Dekiba.
Consul: Masato Katagiri.
Consul: Yukio Yoden.

Consulate-General: POB 3992, San Juan, Puerto Rico 00904; tel 724-2800.
Honorary Consul-General: Manuel San Juan, Jr.

Consular Office: 4th Floor, Nauru Bldg, Susupe, Saipan, Northern Mariana Islands 96950; tel 234-7201; telex 638; fax 234-8764.
Consul: Hideo Okumura.

JORDAN

Embassy: 3504 International Drive, NW, Washington, DC 20008; tel (202) 966-2664; telex 248502; fax (202) 966-3110.
Ambassador: Hussein A. Hammami.
First Secretary: Omar Rifai.
Assistant Air Attaché: Lieut Col Noran Y. al-Maaytah.
Third Secretary: Imad M. Badran.
Attaché (Press/Information): Timoor Daghistani.
Attaché (Education): Hikmat al-Omari.

Information Bureau: 2319 Wyoming Ave, NW, Washington, DC 20008; tel (202) 265-1606; telex 440220; fax (202) 667-0777.
Minister (Press/Information): Dr Marwan J. Muasher.

Consulate: POB 16337, West Palm Beach, FL 33416; tel (305) 655-1844.
Honorary Consul: James Holbrook Kimberley.

Consulate: POB 3727, Houston, TX 77253-3727; tel (713) 224-2911.
Honorary Consul: Sabir Muhammad Amawi.

KENYA

Embassy: 2249 R St, NW, Washington, DC 20008; tel (202) 387-6101.
Ambassador: Denis D. Afande.

Consulate-General: 424 Madison Ave, New York, NY 10017; tel (212) 468-1300.
Consul-General: Nduku N. Mulili.
Vice-Consul: Joseph E. Ojuro.
Vice-Consul: David Waweru.

Consulate-General: 9100 Wilshire Blvd, Los Angeles, CA 90212; tel (213) 274-6635.
Consul-General: Joseph O. Audo.
Consul: Orlando E. Nyakinya.

KIRIBATI

Consulate: 850 Richards St, Suite 503, Honolulu, HI 96813; tel (808) 521-7703; fax (808) 521-8304.
Honorary Consul: William H. Paupe.

KOREA, REPUBLIC

Embassy: 2370 Massachusetts Ave, NW, Washington, DC 20008; tel (202) 939-5600; fax (202) 797-0595.
Ambassador: Park Tong-Jin.
Consul: Suh Yong-Hyun.
Consul: Lee Won Hee.

Consulate-General: 460 Park Ave, New York, NY 10022; tel (212) 752-1700.
Consul-General: Chai Eui-Sok.
Deputy Consul-General: Song Jong Hwan.
Deputy Consul-General: Lee Woo-Sang.

Consulate-General: 3243 Wilshire Blvd, Los Angeles, CA; tel (213) 385-9300.
Consul-General: Park Chong Sang.
Deputy Consul-General: Nam Young Shik.
Deputy Consul-General: Byun Seung Kook.

Consulate-General: 500 North Michigan Ave, Suite 900, Chicago, IL 60611; tel (312) 822-9485.
Consul-General: Kang Dae Wan.
Deputy Consul-General: Kim Chung-Soon.

Consulate-General: 3500 Clay St, San Francisco, CA 94118; tel (415) 921-2251.
Consul-General: Park Choon Vum.
Consul: Yoon Sok Hun.

Consulate-General: 101 Benson Blvd, Suite 304, Anchorage, AK 99503; tel (907) 561-5488.
Consul-General: Cho Myong.

Consulate-General: 201 South Biscayne Blvd, Suite 800, Miami, FL 33131.
Consul-General: Kim Dong-Ho.

Consulate-General: 229 Peachtree St, Suite 500, Cain Tower, Atlanta, GA 30303; tel (404) 522-1611.
Consul-General: Kim Hyun Gon.

Consulate-General: 321 St Charles Ave, New Orleans, LA 70130; tel (504) 586-1979.

Honorary Consul-General: James Julian Coleman.

Consulate-General: 1 Financial Center, 15th Floor, Boston, MA 02111; tel (617) 348-3660.
Consul-General: Park Sang Seek.
Deputy Consul General: Song Young Shik.

Consulate-General: Bank of California Tower, Suite 1330, Portland, OR 97205; tel (503) 222-3531.
Honorary Consul-General: Raymond Mitchel Kell.
Honorary Consul: Rolv Harlow Schillios.

Consulate-General: 1990 Post Oak Blvd, Suite 745, Three Post Oak Central Bldg, Houston, TX; tel (713) 961-0186.
Consul-General: Choi Dae-Hwa.
Consul: Ahn Kyung-Soon.

Consulate-General: 1125 Ual Bldg, 2033 6th Ave, Seattle, WA 98121; tel (206) 682-0132.
Consul: Sung Rak-Hyun.
Consul: Sa Boo.
Consul: Kim Sang-Tae.

Consulate-General: 2756 Pali Highway, Honolulu, HI 96817; tel (808) 595-6109.
Consul-General: Sohn Jangnai.
Consul: Chun Kyu Hak.

Consulate-General: POB 1716, Hato Rey, San Juan, Puerto Rico 00919; tel 751-2255.
Honorary Consul-General: John Brereton Williams.

Consulate-General: GOIC Bldg, Suite 305, Agana, Guam 96910; tel 472-6488.
Consul-General: Choi Yong.
Consul: Rhee Bong Kyu.

Consulate: 31 North Royal St, POB 1628, Mobile, AL 36629.
Honorary Consul: Lee Roe Seifert.

Consulate: 6990 Shea Blvd, Suite 110, Scottsdale, Phoenix, AZ 85254.
Honorary Consul: William Louis Weirich.

Consulate: 1600 Broadway, Suite 600, Denver, CO 80202; tel (303) 830-0500.
Honorary Consul: Dwight Alan Hamilton.

Consulate: 708 Church St, Suite 208, Evanston, IL 60201; tel (312) 263-2016.
Honorary Consul: Paul Chung.

Consulate: 8340 Mission Rd, Suite 107, Prairie Village, Kansas City, KS 66206.
Honorary Consul: John Philip Hilmes.

Consulate: 31151 Stephenson Highway, Madison Heights, Detroit, MI 48071; tel (313) 585-1950.
Honorary Consul: Chester Franklin Mally.

Consulate: c/o Metropolitan Financial Services Inc., 2222 Park Ave, Minneapolis, MN 55404; tel (612) 870-4400.
Honorary Consul: Allison R. Mercer.

Consulate: Pierre Laclede Center, 7811 Carondelet Ave, St Louis, MO 63105; tel (312) 863-2727.
Honorary Consul: Nicholas Phipps Veeder.

Consulate: 711 Leader Bldg, 526 Superior Ave, NE, Cleveland, OH 44114; tel (216) 241-8029.
Honorary Consul: Irvin Myron Miler.

Consulate: 1300 North Broadway, Oklahoma City, OK 73103; tel (405) 235-5621.
Honorary Consul: John E. Kirkpatrick.

Consulate: 2600 Fidelity Bldg, Philadelphia, PA 19109.
Honorary Consul: Harry A. Kalish.

Consulate: 7515 Greenville Ave, Suite 308, Dallas, TX 75231; tel (214) 369-8900.
Honorary Consul: James Weldon Thomas.

Consulate: 8800 Tradeway, San Antonio, TX 78127; tel (512) 822-0694.
Honorary Consul: Roland Magness Dixon, Jr.

KUWAIT

Embassy: 2940 Tilden St, NW, Washington, DC 20008; tel (202) 966-0702; fax (202) 966-0517.
Ambassador: Shaikh Saud Nasir al-Sabah.

LAOS

Embassy: 2222 S St, NW, Washington, DC 20008; tel (202) 332-6416; telex 904061.
Chargé d'affaires a.i.: Linthong Phetsavan.

LATVIA

Consulate-General: 4325 17th St, NW, Washington, DC 20011; tel (202) 726-8213.
Consul-General: Dr Anatol Dinbergs.

Consulate: 1600 El Rito Ave, Glendale, Los Angeles, CA 91208; tel (818) 247-8390.
Honorary Consul: Aivars Leonids Jerumanis.

LEBANON

Embassy: 2560 28th St, NW, Washington, DC 20008; tel (202) 939-6300; fax (202) 939-6324.
Ambassador: Nassib S. Lahoud.

Consulate-General: 9 East 76th St, New York, NY 10021; tel (212) 744-7905.
Consul-General: Victor Bitar.

Consulate-General: 7060 Hollywood Blvd, Suite 510, Los Angeles, CA 90028; tel (213) 467-1253.
Consul-General: Farid C. Abboud.

Consulate-General: 1959 East Jefferson, Suite 4a, Detroit, MI 48207; tel (313) 567-0233.
Consul-General: Hassan M. Saad.

LESOTHO

Embassy: 2511 Massachusetts Ave, NW, Washington, DC 20008; tel (202) 797-5534; fax (202) 234-6815.
Ambassador: William T. Van Tonder.

Consulate: POB 3991, Philadelphia, PA 19146; tel (215) 403-7512.
Honorary Consul: S. McDowell Shelton.

LIBERIA

Embassy: 5201 16th St, NW, Washington, DC 20011; tel (202) 291-0761.
Ambassador: Eugenia A. Wordsworth-Stevenson.
Consul: E. Boima Fahnbulleh.
Consul: Gabriel Randall.
Vice-Consul: Kronyahn Moses Weefur.
Vice-Consul: Edward F. Kawah.
Vice-Consul: Sharon Bee Browne.

Consulate-General: 820 Second Ave, New York, NY 10017; tel (212) 687-1025.
Consul-General: S. Kannah Boons.
Consul: Edith M. Thomas.
Consul: Arnold J. Kandakai.

Consulate-General: 2049 Century Park, East, Suite 890, Los Angeles, CA 90067; tel (213) 277-7692.
Honorary Consul-General: Andrew V. Ippolito.

Consulate-General: 423 East 60th St, Chicago, IL 60637; tel (312) 643-8635.
Honorary Consul-General: Alexander Poley Gbayee.

Consulate-General: 2717 Cascade Rd, SW, Atlanta, GA; tel (404) 753-4754.
Honorary Consul-General: Dr Walter F. Young.

Consulate-General: 20100 Greenfield Ave, Suite 203, Detroit, MI 48235; tel (313) 342-3900.
Honorary Consul-General: Robert Lee Chapman.

Consulate: 2950 Broadway, San Francisco, CA 94115; tel (415) 921-7869.
Honorary Consul: Lia Triff Belli.

Consulate: 913 Maison Blanche Bldg, 921 Canal St, New Orleans, LA 70112; tel (504) 523-7784.
Honorary Consul: Voyce Durling-Jones.

LITHUANIA

Consulate-General: 41 West 82nd St, Apt 5B, New York, NY 10024; tel (212) 877-4552.
Consul-General: Anicetas Simutis.

Consulate-General: 3959 Franklin Ave, Los Angeles, CA 90027; tel (805) 496-5324.
Honorary Consul-General: Vytautas Cekanausal.

Consulate-General: 10000 South Bell Ave, Chicago, IL 60643; tel (312) 233-9122.
Honorary Consul-General: Vaclovas D. Kleiza.

LUXEMBOURG

Embassy: 2200 Massachusetts Ave, NW, Washington, DC 20008; tel (202) 265-4171; telex 64130; fax (202) 328-8270.
Ambassador: André Philippe.
Counsellor: Arlette Conzemius.

Consulate-General: 801 Second Ave, 13th Floor, New York, NY 10017.
Consul-General: Egide Thein.
Attaché (Consular): Anne Bastian.
Honorary Consul: Jacques E. Lennon.

Consulate-General: 516 Avondale Ave, Los Angeles, CA 90049; tel (213) 394-2532.
Honorary Consul-General: Marie-Anne Suzanne Pitz.

Consulate-General: 180 North LaSalle St, Suite 1400, Chicago, IL 60601; tel (312) 726-0355.
Honorary Consul: Richard James Witry.

Consulate-General: One Sansome St, Citicorp Center, Suite 830, San Francisco, CA 94104; tel (415) 788-0816; telex 323-5487; fax (415) 788-0985.
Consul-General: Jean H. Faltz.

Consulate-General: 1429 Atlantic St, North Kansas City, MO 64116; tel (816) 474-4761.
Honorary Consul-General: Robert F. Schaeffer.

Consulate: 200 South Biscayne Blvd, Suite 3240, Miami, FL 33131; tel (305) 373-1300.
Honorary Consul: Jacques Turner.

Consulate: 1900 The Exchange, Suite 440, Atlanta, GA 30339; tel (404) 952-1157.
Honorary Consul: Ralph Oswald Hutchison.

Consulate: 8012 Oak St, New Orleans, LA 70118; tel (504) 861-3743.
Honorary Vice-Consul: Gary J. Mannina.

Consulate: 180 Grove St, Lexington, Boston, MA 02173.
Honorary Consul: Gordon D. MacKay.

Consulate: 2375 University Ave, West, St Paul, MN 55114.
Honorary Consul: Paul R. Heinerscheid.

Consulate: 43043 West 9 Mile Rd, Northville, Detroit, MI 48167; tel (313) 347-0100.
Honorary Consul: William Davidson.

Consulate: 400 First National Bank Bldg, Middletown, OH 45042; tel (513) 4222-4697.
Honorary Consul: Barry J. Levey.

Consulate: 245 Gypsy Lane, Youngstown, OH 44504; tel (216) 746-5991.
Honorary Consul: Joseph E. Gurley.

Consulate: National Steel Center, 20 Stanwix St, Pittsburgh, PA 15222; tel (412) 394-4231.
Honorary Consul: Howard M. Love.

Consulate: 2001 Bryan Tower, Suite 3600, Dallas, TX 75201; tel (214) 746-7200.
Honorary Consul: Robert Ted Enloe III.

Consulate: 12104 NE 141st St, Kirkland, Seattle, WA 98033; tel (206) 237-1280.
Honorary Consul: Fred R. Cerf.

MADAGASCAR

Embassy: 2374 Massachusetts Ave, NW, Washington, DC 20008; tel (202) 265-5525.

Ambassador: Pierrot J. Rajaon-Arivelo.

Consulate-General: 801 Second Ave, Suite 404, New York, NY 10017; tel (212) 986-9491; telex 236545; fax (212) 986-6271.
Consul-General: Blaise Joseph Albert Rabetafika.

Consulate: 867 Garland Drive, Palo Alto, CA 94303; tel (415) 323-7113.
Honorary Consul: Jean-Marie R. de la Beaujardiere.

Consulate: 3000 Two Logan Sq., 18th and Arch Sts, Philadelphia, PA 19103; tel (215) 981-4067.
Honorary Consul: John B. Huffaker.

MALAWI

Embassy: 2408 Massachusetts Ave, NW, Washington, DC 20008; tel (202) 797-1007; telex 64348; fax (202) 265-0976.
Ambassador: Robert B. Mbaya.
Minister: Manuel S. D. Magalasi.
Counsellor: Overtoun S. Mkandawire.
Second Secretary (Administrative): Ivy L. Tembo.
Second Secretary (Finance): Edward E. Zilemba.
Third Secretary (Consular): Stephen P. Kapsua.
Honorary Consul: Dr Donald Brody.

Consulate: 2001 North Soto St, Los Angeles, CA 90032; tel (213) 223-2020.
Consul: Dr J. Clements.

Consulate: 701 Dexter Ave North, Suite 100, Seattle, WA 98109; tel (206) 742-3109.
Consul: Dr Ronald Brody.

MALAYSIA

Embassy: 2401 Massachusetts Ave, NW, Washington, DC 20008; tel (202) 328-2700; telex 440119; fax (202) 483-7661.
Ambassador: Albert S. Talalla.

Consulate-General: 140 East 45th St, 43rd Floor, New York, NY 10017; tel (212) 490-2722.
Consul-General: Kat Meng Tai.
Consul: Suppiah Marappan.
Consul: Mohamed Abdul Halim.
Consul: Kolandavelu Ilankovan.

Consulate-General: World Trade Center, Suite 400, 350 South Figueroa, Los Angeles, CA 90071; tel (213) 621-2991.
Consul-General: Salim Hashim.
Consul: Ber Keat Gan.
Consul: Sulong Haji Tahir.
Consul: Ah Yong Tan.
Consul: Dr Mohyani Razikin.

Consulate-General: 2 Embarcadero Center, 26th Floor, San Francisco, CA 94111; tel (415) 421-4627.
Honorary Consul-General: H. Donald Harris, Jr.

Consulate: First Hawaiian Bank, POB 3200, Honolulu, HI 96847; tel (808) 525-8144.
Honorary Consul: Herbert E. Wolff.

Consulate: 6144 SW 37th Ave, Portland, OR 97221; tel (503) 246-0707.
Honorary Consul: Jay A. Killeen.

MALI

Embassy: 2130 R St, NW, Washington, DC 20008; tel (202) 332-2249.
Ambassador: Mohamed Alhousseyni Touré.

Consulate: 1894 Westbridge Rd, Los Angeles, CA 90049; tel (213) 476-9369.
Honorary Consul: William A. Burke.

Consulate: 339 Union St, Rockland, Boston, MA 02370.
Consul: Warren J. Schjolden.

Consulate: 7600 American Heritage Drive, NE, Albuquerque, NM 87109.
Honorary Consul: Oliver C. Reese.

MALTA

Embassy: 2017 Connecticut Ave, NW, Washington, DC 20008; tel (202) 462-3611; telex 62431; fax (202) 387-5470.
Ambassador: Dr Albert Borg Olivier de Puget.
First Secretary and Consul: Alfred M. Falzon.

Consulate-General: 249 East 35th St, New York, NY 10016; tel (212) 725-2345; telex 62392; fax (212) 779-7907.
Consul-General: Anthony F. Mizzi.

Consulate-General: 25867 Shirley Lane, Dearborn Heights, Detroit, MI 48127; tel (313) 525-9777; fax (313) 562-1657.
Honorary Consul-General: Larry J. Zahra.

Consulate-General: 2562 San Bruno Ave, POB 34-7001, San Francisco, CA 94134; tel (415) 468-4321; fax (415) 468-1461.
Honorary Consul-General: Charles J. Vassallo.

Consulate-General: 2100 First National Bank Bldg, St Paul, MN 55101; tel (612) 228-0935; fax (612) 228-0776.
Honorary Consul-General: Joseph S. Micallef.

Consulate-General: 654 North Belt East, Suite 400, Houston, TX 77060; tel (713) 497-2100.
Honorary Consul-General: Eugene F. Loveland.
Honorary Consul: Dennis L. Kirwin.

Consulate: 5428 East Beverly Blvd, Los Angeles, CA 90022; tel (213) 685-6365.
Honorary Consul: Dame Dolores Galea.

Consulate: 115 Edgecliff Rd, Carnegie, PA 15106; tel (412) 624-5205.
Honorary Consul: Prof. Anthony Debons.

Consulate: 10 Commercial Wharf West, Boston, MA 02110; tel (617) 523-7895.
Honorary Consul: Edward S. Dewey.

Consulate: US Federal Bldg, Suites 201-201A, 301 West Lexington St, Independence, MO 64050; tel (816) 833-0033; telex 379-4273; fax (816) 833-2125.
Honorary Consul: Dr Marcel Dingli Attard de Baroni Inguanez.

MARSHALL ISLANDS

Embassy: 2433 Marshall Ave, NW, Washington, DC 20008; tel (202) 234-5414; fax (202) 232-3236.
Ambassador: Wilfred I. Kendall.
Deputy Head of Mission: Banny de Brum.
Economic Adviser: Frank X. Solomon.
Executive Assistant: Holly M. Barker.

Consulate-General: 1441 Kapiolani Blvd, Suite 1910, Honolulu, HI 96814; tel (808) 942-4422; fax (808) 942-2009.
Consul-General: Justin de Brum.

MAURITANIA

Embassy: 2129 Leroy Place, NW, Washington, DC 20008; tel (202) 232-5700.
Ambassador: Abdellah Ould Daddah.

MAURITIUS

Embassy: 4301 Connecticut Ave, NW, Washington, DC 20008; tel (202) 244-1491; telex 64362; fax (202) 966-0983.
Ambassador: Chitmansing Jesseramsing.

Consulate: 16633 Ventura Blvd, 6th Floor, Los Angeles, CA 91436; tel (818) 788-3720.
Honorary Consul: Bruce E. Dizenfeld.

MEXICO

Embassy: 1019 19th St, NW, Washington, DC 20006; tel (202) 293-1710; telex 248459; fax (202) 234-7739.
Ambassador: Gustavo Petricioli.

Consulate-General: 8 East 41st St, New York, NY 10017; tel (212) 689-3871.
Consul-General: Manuel Alonso-Munoz.
Deputy Consul-General: Juan José Miro Vazquez.
Consul: Mireya Teran-Munquia de Teutli.
Consul: Cesar C. Valdovinos-moya.
Consul: Manuel José Morodo-Fernandez.

Consulate-General: 2401 West 6th St, Los Angeles, CA 90012; tel (213) 624-3261.
Consul-General: José Angel Pescador-Osuna.
Deputy Consul-General: Miguel Angel Lopez Reyes.
Consul: Marco Arturo Ruiz Velasco.
Consul: Alfredo Gaytan Hinojosa.
Consul: José Antonio Ortiz-Pedraza.

Consulate-General: 300 North Michigan Ave, Suite 200, Chicago, IL 60601; tel (312) 855-1380.
Consul-General: Alejandro Carrillo Castro.
Consul: Fernando A. Torres Vasconcelos.
Consul: Maria-Cristina Argudin-Furlong.
Consul: Felipe L. Soria Ayuso.

Consulate-General: 870 Market St, Suite 528, San Francisco, CA 94102; tel (415) 392-5554.
Deputy Consul-General: Alejandro Pescador-Casteneda.
Consul: Sandra G. Claderon Barraza.
Consul: Arturo Balderas Rodríguez.
Consul: Marta Beatriz Navarro-Parada.

Consulate-General: 610 A St, 1333 Front St, San Diego, CA 92101; tel (619) 231-8418.
Consul-General: Enrique Loaeza-Tovar.
Deputy Consul-General: Antonio Hinojosa-Guerrero.
Deputy Consul-General: Martha Orthiz de Rosas Gomez de Carvajal.

Consulate-General: 707 Washington St, Suite A, Denver, CO 80203; tel (303) 830-0523.
Consul-General: Francisco González de Cossio.
Deputy Consul-General: Victor Hugo Ramírez Lavalle.

Consulate-General: 1140 World Trade Center Bldg, 2 Canal St, New Orleans, LA 70130; tel (504) 522-3596.
Consul-General: Raul Castellano-Martínez-Baez.
Deputy Consul-General: Vincente Sanchez Ventura.

Consulate-General: 1349 Empire Central, Suite 100, Dallas, TX 75247; tel (214) 522-9740.
Consul-General: Olivier Albert Farres Martins.
Consul: Luis Eugenio Gama Fernández.
Consul: Alvaro Eduardo Caso Chavez.
Consul: Margarita Flores Diaz.

Consulate-General: 910 East San Antonio St, El Paso, TX 79901; tel (915) 533-3644.
Consul-General: Roberto M. Gamboa-Mascarenas.
Consul: Marie L. B. López Gargallo.
Consul: Alfonso Arriaga y García.

Consulate-General: 3015 Richmond Ave, Houston, TX 77006; tel (713) 524-2300.
Consul-General: Ricardo Ampudia Malacara.
Deputy Consul-General: Leopoldo Octavio Vial Torres.

Consulate-General: 127 Navarro St, San Antonio, TX 78205; tel (512) 227-9145.
Consul-General: Humberto Hernández Haddad.
Consul: Maria del Carmen Romano González.

Consulate-General: Bankers Finance Tower, 654 Avda Munoz Rivera, Suite 1837, San Juan, Puerto Rico 00918; tel 764-0258.
Consul-General: Gustavo Maza Padilla.
Vice-Consul: Mario E. Sosa Castillo.

Consulate: 3151 Hamilton Blvd, Theodroe, Mobile, AL 36582; tel (202) 443-5317.
Honorary Consul: Gastelum Enrique Gomez Palacio.

Consulate: 137 Terrace Ave, Suite 150, Nogales, AZ 85621; tel (602) 287-2521.

Consul: Emerenciano Rodríguez Jobrail.

Consulate: 1990 West Camelback Plaza, Suite 112, Phoenix, AZ 85035; tel (602) 242-7398.

Consulate: 553 South Stone Ave, Tucson, AZ; tel (602) 882-5595.
Consul: Javier Aguilar Rangel.
Vice-Consul: Claudina Saaverdra.

Consulate: 331-3 West Second St, Calexico, CA 92331; tel (619) 357-3863.
Consul: Marco Antonio Tovar Aguilar.

Consulate: 905 North Fulton St, Fresno, CA 93721; tel (209) 233-9770.
Consul: Fernando Rodriguez Romero.

Consulate: 201 East 4th St, Oxnard, CA 93030; tel (805) 483-4684.
Consul: Zoila Arroyo Bartolo.

Consulate: 9845 Horn Rd, Suites 120, 130 & 230, Sacramento, CA 95827; tel (916) 363-3885.
Consul: Nicolas Escalante Barret.

Consulate: 588 West 6th St, San Bernardino, CA 92401; tel (714) 889-9836.
Consul: Juan M. Calderon Jaimes.

Consulate: 406 West 4th St, Santa Ana, CA 92801; tel (714) 835-3069.
Consul: Maria de Lourdes Urbina-Paredes.

Consulate: 380 North First St, Suite 102, San José, CA 95113; tel (408) 294-3414.
Consul: Raul Cardenas-Heraldez.

Consulate: 780 NW LeJeune Rd, Suite 525, Miami, FL 33134; tel (305) 441-8780.
Consul: Enrique Hubbard Urrea.
Deputy Consul: José Antonio Mendoza Labra.

Consulate: 1717 West Cass St, Tampa, FL 33606; tel (813) 254-5906.
Honorary Consul: Olga M. Fidalgo.

Consulate: 410 South Tower, NW, One CNN Center, Atlanta, GA 30303; tel (404) 688-3258.
Consul: Rodolfo Victor Manuel Castresana Rubio.
Consul: Teodoro Maus-Reisbaum.
Vice-Consul: Carlos J. E. Bello Roch.

Consulate: 20 Park Plaza, Boston, MA 02116; tel (617) 426-4942.
Consul: Alberto Lucia Campillo-Saenz.
Consul: Ulises Canchola Gutierrez.

Consulate: 1515 Book Bldg, Washington Blvd, Grand River, Detroit, MI 48226; tel (313) 965-1868.
Consul: José Mendoza-Caamano.
Consul: Federico Moreno-Santos.

Consulate: 1015 Locust St, Suite 922, St Louis, MO 63101; tel (314) 436-3233.
Consul: Humberto A. Zamora Trevino.
Deputy Consul: Maria Prieto-Espinoza.
Consul: Juan Carlos Briz-Figueroa.

Consulate: 401 5th St, NW, Western Bank Bldg, Albuquerque, NM 87102; tel (505) 247-2147.
Consul: Miguel Angel Reyes y Soto.
Consul: Juan Rodrigo Labardini Flores.

Consulate: 1875 Harlem Rd, Buffalo, NY 14212; tel (716) 852-3871.
Honorary Consul: Egon Erich Rassow.

Consulate: 4101 West Blvd, Charlotte, NC 28219; tel (919) 394-2198.
Honorary Consul: Wayne P. Cooper.

Consulate: 545 NE 47th Ave, Suite 317, Portland, OR 97213; tel (503) 233-5661.
Honorary Consul: Fernando de Leon.

Consulate: 575 Philadelphia Bourse Bldg, 21 South 5th St, Philadelphia, PA 19106; tel (215) 922-4262.
Consul: Gonzalo Aguirre-Enrile.
Consul: Raul Salvatore Ramírez-Cossa.

Consulate: 226 Capitol Blvd, Suite 514, Nashville, TN 37219; tel (615) 244-7430.
Honorary Consul: Robert Dudley Smith.

Consulate: 200 East 6th St, Austin, TX 78701; tel (512) 478-2866.
Consul: Luisa Maria Leal Duk.

Consulate: Elizabeth and East 7th Sts, POB 1711, Brownsville, TX 78520; tel (512) 542-4431.
Consul: Carlos Tomas Perez-González.
Consul: Martha Elvia Rosa Rodríguez.

Consulate: 800 North Shoreline Plaza, 410 North Tower, Corpus Christi, TX 78401; tel (512) 882-3375.
Consul: Alicia Abdala y Matuk.

Consulate: 1010 South Main St, Del Rio, TX 78840; tel (512) 775-2352.
Consul: Mario Najera del Valle.

Consulate: 140 Adams St, Eagle Pass, TX 78852; tel (512) 773-9255.
Consul: Leocadio Beytia Vega.

Consulate: One Commerce Plaza, Fort Worth, TX 76102; tel (817) 335-5691.
Honorary Consul: Jerry Murad.

Consulate: 1612 Farragut St, Laredo, TX 78040; tel (512) 723-6360.
Consul: Jesus Preciado García.
Consul: Alicia Arcos Rayon.

Consulate: 511 West Ohio St, Suite 121, Midland, TX 79701; tel (915) 687-2334.
Consul: Ecce Iei Mendoza-Machado.

Consulate: 1418 Beach St, Suite 104, McAllen, TX 78501; tel (512) 686-0243.
Consul: Ernestina Fernández Picazo.
Consul: José Alejandro Aguirre Noriega.

Consulate: 182 South 600 East, Suite 202, Salt Lake City, UT 84102; tel (801) 521-8502.
Consul: Hector Ignacio Mena López.
Deputy Consul: Mauricio Martine Chavez-Medina.

Consulate: 51 East Virginia Beach Blvd, Norfolk, VA 23502; tel (804) 461-4933.
Honorary Consul: Roberto Rodríguez Iturralde.

Consulate: University Park Bldg, 2420 Pemberton Rd, Richmond, VA 23233; tel (804) 747-9200.
Honorary Consul: Walter W. Regirer.

Consulate: 2132 Third Ave, Upper Floor, Seattle, WA 98121; tel (206) 682-3634.
Consul: Raul Lopezlira-Castro.
Consul: M. Marisela Quijano Herrero.
Vice-Consul: Rigoberto Flores Bustamante.

Consulate: 12005 East Sprague Ave, Spokane, WA 99214; tel (509) 926-4713.
Honorary Consul: Carlos Henri Landa.

Consulate: 1818 Fordem Ave, Suite 6, Madison, WI 53704; tel (608) 249-5201.
Honorary Consul: Dr Rudolph Caro Hecht.

Consulate: 2828 Paa St, Suite 2120, Honolulu, HI 96819; tel (808) 833-6331.
Honorary Consul: Ruben Ortiz.

MICRONESIA

Embassy: 1725 N St, NW, Washington, DC 20036; tel (202) 223-4383; telex 292003; fax (202) 223-4391.
Ambassador: Jesse B. Marehalau.
Minister and Deputy Head of Mission: Ringlen P. Ringlen.
First Secretary (Political/Cultural): Kodaro M. Gallen.
First Secretary (Trade/Commerce): James L. Lukan.

Consulate: 3049 Ulalena St, Suite 408, Honolulu, HI 96819; tel (808) 836-4775.
Consul: Kasio E. Mida.

Consulate: 331 South Marina Drive, Suite 20b, Winner Bldg, Tamuning, Guam 96911; tel 646-9154.
Consul: Wilton Mackwelung.

MONACO

Consulate: 888 16th St, NW, Suite 300, Washington, DC 20006; tel (202) 296-8600.
Honorary Consul: Myles Joseph Ambrose.

Consulate-General: 845 Third Ave, New York, NY 10022; tel (212) 759-5227.
Honorary Consul-General: John Dube.
Honorary Consul: Frank Cresci.

Consulate-General: 7449 Melrose Ave, Los Angeles, CA 90046; tel (213) 655-8970.
Honorary Consul: Rupert Mortimer Allan.

Consulate-General: 1 East Superior St, Suite 204, Chicago, IL 60611; tel (312) 642-1242.
Honorary Consul: Robert Leland Steiner.

Consulate-General: 2209 Pacific Ave, San Francisco, CA 94115; tel (415) 362-5050.
Honorary Consul-General: Dagmar Marie-Therese Sullivan.

Consulate-General: 601 Poydras St, Suite 2415, New Orleans, LA 70130; tel (504) 522-5700.
Honorary Consul-General: Carl Fredrick Dahlberg, Jr.

Consulate-General: 1 Federal St, Boston, MA 02110; tel (617) 542-3000.
Honorary Consul-General: John Frederick Collins.
Honorary Consul: Helene Ravera Day.

Consulate-General: POB 4113, San Juan, Puerto Rico 00936; tel 721-4215.
Honorary Consul-General: Guillermo Moscoso.

Consulate: Coastal House, Apt 308, 2200 South Ocean Blvd, Delray Beach, Palm Beach, FL 33444; tel (305) 278-8051.
Honorary Consul: Alfred Joseph Laupheimer, Jr.

Consulate: 925 Bethel St, Honolulu, HI 96813; tel (808) 538-7878.
Honorary Consul: James Vincent Wheeless.

Consulate: 250 Suburban Station Bldg, Philadelphia, PA 19103; tel (215) 665-0152.
Honorary Consul: Curtis P. Laupheimer.

Consulate: 4700 St John's Drive, Dallas, TX 75205; tel (214) 521-1058.
Honorary Consul: Doris Canaan.

MONGOLIA

Embassy: 3636 16th St, NW, Washington, DC 20010; tel (202) 483-1962; fax (202) 983-2140.
Ambassador: Gendengiin Nyamdoo.

MOROCCO

Embassy: 1601 21st St, NW, Washington, DC 20009; tel (202) 462-7979; telex 248378; fax (202) 265-0161.
Ambassador: Mohammed Belkhayat.

Consulate-General: 437 Fifth Ave, New York, NY 10016; tel (212) 758-2625.
Consul-General: Abdelslam Jaidi.

Consulate: 521 North Daroca, San Gabriel, Los Angeles, CA 91775; tel (213) 570-0318.
Honorary Consul: Abdelhak Saoud.

Consulate: 1900 West 47th Place, Suite 208, Westwood, Kansas City, KS 66205.
Honorary Consul: Harry McLear.

Consulate: Lincoln Plaza, 500 North Akard, Suite 2160, Dallas, TX 75201; tel (214) 954-0030.
Honorary Consul: Frank August Schultz.

Consulate: 5607 Indian Circle, Houston, TX 77056; tel (713) 960-8019.
Honorary Consul: Joanne J. Herring Davis.

MOZAMBIQUE

Embassy: 1990 M St, NW, Suite 570, Washington, DC 20036; tel (202) 293-7146; telex 248530; fax (202) 835-0245.
Ambassador: Hipolito Pereira Zozimo Patricio.
Second Secretary (Economy/Trade/Administration): Alberto Maverengue Augusto.
Attaché (Finance/Secretariat): Iveth Venichand Lobo.
Attaché (Consular): Rosario M. Makavaka.
Attaché (Press/Information/Public Relations): Antonio Paulo Elias Jr Matonse.

MYANMAR

Embassy: 2300 S St, NW, Washington, DC 20008; tel (202) 332-9044; telex 248310; fax (202) 332-9046.
Ambassador: U Hla Myint Oo.

Consulate-General: 10 East 77th St, New York, NY 10021; tel (212) 535-1310.
Consul-General: Win Mra.

NAMIBIA

Embassy: 134 Michigan Ave, Washington, DC 20017; tel (202) 234-6047; fax (202) 328-3157.
Chargé d'affaires a.i.: Veiko Nghiwete.

NEPAL

Embassy: 2131 Leroy Place, NW, Washington, DC 20008; tel (202) 667-4550; telex 440085; fax (202) 667-5534.
Ambassador: Mohan Man Sainju.
Counsellor: Narayan D. Shrestha.
Military Attaché: Lieut Col Dilip Karki.
First Secretary: Yug Nath S. Paudel.
Attaché: Ganesh Bahadur Shrestha.

Consulate-General: 820 Second Ave, Suite 202, New York, NY 10017; tel (212) 370-4188.
Consul-General: Mohan B. Panday.

Consulate-General: 1500 Lake Shore Drive, Chicago, IL 60610; tel (312) 787-9199.
Honorary Consul-General: Mary B. Sethness.

Consulate-General: Heidelberg College, Tiffin, OH 44883; tel (419) 448-2202.
Honorary Consul-General: William C. Cassell.

Consulate-General: 909 Montgomery St, Suite 400, San Francisco, CA 94133; tel (415) 434-1111.
Honorary Consul-General: Richard C. Blum.

Consulate-General: 16250 Dallas Parkway, Suite 110, Dallas, TX 75248; tel (214) 931-1212.
Honorary Consul-General: Lucille Gannon Murchison.

Consulate-General: 212 15th St, NE, Atlanta, GA 30309; tel (404) 892-8152.
Honorary Consul-General: Josephine Crawford Robinson.

Consulate-General: 11818 Wilshire Blvd, Los Angeles, CA 90025; tel (213) 473-2122.
Honorary Consul-General: George Pappas.

NETHERLANDS

Embassy: 4200 Linnean Ave, NW, Washington, DC 20008; tel (202) 244-5300; telex 89494; fax (202) 362-3430.
Ambassador: Johan H. Meesman.
Minister (Economic): Jacobus T. Mol.
Minister: Baron Willem O. Bentinck.
Minister: Harold Henriquez.
Minister: Roland O. Wever.
Counsellor (Economic): Cornelis M. Coops.
Counsellor (Culture): Andreas J. Te Boekhorst.
Counsellor (Finance): Frans J. F. M. de Neree Tot Babberich.
Counsellor (Science/Technology): Paul M. Op Den Brouw.
Counsellor (Transport): Eduard V. Sjerp.
Counsellor (Health/Environmental Protection): Dr Bert Metz.
Counsellor (Agriculture/Emigration): Jacob van der Veen.
Counsellor: Cornelis W. Andreae.
Defence and Naval Attaché: Rear Adm. J. S. Tichelman.
Assistant Naval Attaché: Commdr Willem R. Segaar.
Military Attaché: Col Onno S. W. Vollema.
Assistant Military Attaché: Maj. Theodorus J. Alsemgeest.
Air Attaché: Col Wilhelmus J. Sneek.
Assistant Air Attaché: Lieut Col Gerardus L. S. van der Akker.
Defence Co-operation Attaché: Capt. Johan Brink.
Assistant Defence Co-operation Attaché: Maj. Zweitse W. Hofman.
First Secretary (Political): Arnout P. Wegerif.
First Secretary (Economic): Joanna M. P. F. van Vliet.
First Secretary (Administrative): Robert J. C. van der Schatte Olivier.
First Secretary and Consul: Theo H. van der Lugt.
First Secretary: Richard van Rijssen.

Consulate-General: 1 Rockefeller Plaza, 11th Floor, New York, NY 10020-2094; tel (212) 246-1429; fax (212) 333-3603.
Consul-General: Cornelia W. A. de Groot.
Consul: Anthony W. Thone.
Consul: Jan Hesseling.
Consul: Irwin de Jong.
Consul: Jan H. E. Heckman.
Consul: Johannes Wessels.
Consul: Robert van de Graaf.
Consul: Reyer van der Lugt.

Consulate-General: 303 East Wacker Drive, Suite 410, Chicago, IL 60601; tel (312) 856-0110; fax (312) 856-9218.
Consul-General: Steven E. Ramondt.
Consul: Roland B. van der Gaag.

Consulate-General: Central Plaza, Wilshire Blvd, Suite 509, Los Angeles, CA 90010-2270; tel (213) 380-3440; fax (213) 386-6380.
Consul-General: John C. F. von Mühlen.
Consul: Peter Lablans.
Consul: Hendrik J. Schuwer.
Consul: Onno van de Stolpe.

Consulate-General: 2200 Post Oak Blvd, Suite 610, Houston, TX 77056-4783; tel (713) 622-8000; fax (713) 622-3581.
Consul-General: Peter G. M. Zwartkruis.
Consul: Cecile W. A. van der Stelt.
Vice-Consul: Johannes Meijer.

Consulate: POB 8047, Philadelphia, PA 19101-8047; tel (215) 387-2050; fax (215) 387-3827.
Honorary Consul: Yvonne J. G. Orova-Boonacker.

Consulate: c/o Graham & James, 1 Maritime Plaza, Suite 750, San Francisco, CA 94111; tel (415) 981-6454; fax (415) 391-2493.
Consul: Ralph M. Pais.

Consulate: 10051 NE 112th St, Kirkland, WA 98033; tel (206) 827-0584; fax (206) 822-0215.
Honorary Consul: Stephen C. Sieberson.

Consulate: 7350 Young Drive, Walton Hills, Cleveland, OH 44146; tel (216) 232-5100; fax (216) 439-2760.
Honorary Consul: Jack Nicolaas Grooff.

Consulate: c/o Semmes, Bowen and Semmes, 250 West Pratt St, 15th Floor, Baltimore, MD 21201; tel (301) 539-5040; fax (301) 539-5223.
Honorary Consul: William C. Trimble, Jr.

Consulate: 1801 California St, Suite 4100, Denver, CO 80202; tel (303) 297-1118; fax (303) 298-0431.
Honorary Consul: Robert A. Hildebrand.

Consulate: 2041 SW Coral Way (3rd Ave), Suite 103, Miami, FL 33245-2833; tel (305) 858-7617; fax (305) 858-8474.
Honorary Consul: Robert S. Maduro.

Consulate: c/o New York Life Insurance Co., 2000 Town Center, Suite 1200, Southfield, Detroit, MI 48075-1135; tel (313) 352-0620.
Honorary Consul: Paulus Franciscus van der Muysenberg.

Consulate: 562 North Woodlawn, St Louis, MO 63122; tel (314) 965-3533.
Honorary Consul: Richard W. Lodge.

Consulate: Arthur Anderson and Co., Georgia Pacific Center, 133 Peachtree St, NE, Suite 2500, Atlanta, GA 30303; tel (404) 525-4513; fax (404) 658-9177.
Honorary Consul: Johannes W. F. Beerkens.

Consulate: POB 3320, Portland, OR 97208; tel (503) 285-9111; fax (503) 285-9111.
Honorary Consul: Arthur A. Riedel.

Consulate: POB 60643, New Orleans, LA 70160-0643; fax (504) 596-2800.
Honorary Consul: C. J. J. Willems-Charles.

Consulate: c/o Tennant Co., 701 North Lilac Drive, Minneapolis, MN 55440; tel (612) 540-1210; fax (612) 540-1437.
Honorary Consul: Lyle D. Delwiche.

Consulate: 3250 28th St, POB 8709, Grand Rapids, MI 49508; tel (616) 451-4111.
Honorary Consul: M. T. Ruiter.

Consulate: 6 St James Ave, Suite 1001, Boston, MA 02116-3800; tel (617) 542-8452; fax (617) 542-3304.
Honorary Consul: Maarten H. A. M. Janssen.

Consulate: 121 Reist St, Buffalo, NY 14221; tel (716) 633-1818; fax (716) 633-4620.
Honorary Consul: Dr C. J. van Oss.

Consulate: 1128 West Olney Rd, Norfolk, VA 23507-1390; tel (804) 625-3658; fax (804) 625-8154.
Honorary Consul: L. J. Platteel.

Consulate: 5486 Jetport Industrial Blvd, Tampa, FL 33634; tel (813) 888-8200; fax (813) 886-0739.
Honorary Consul: Robert H. Uiterwijk.

Consulate: One Ward Parkway, Suite 138, Kansas City, MO 64112; tel (816) 561-4606.
Honorary Consul: Donald Herman Alexander.

Consulate: 900 University Blvd, North Suite 500, Jacksonville, FL 32211; tel (904) 744-0275; fax (904) 744-3547.
Honorary Consul: M. Frederick Whelan.

Consulate: POB 720, Anchorage, AK 99510; tel (907) 265-3555; fax (907) 265-3545.
Honorary Consul: Daniel H. Cuddy.

Consulate: 345 Queen St, Suite 600, Honolulu, HI 96813; tel (808) 537-1100.
Honorary Consul: G. G. Tom.

Consulate: 540 Broadway, Suite 1116, San Diego, CA 92101; tel (619) 238-2626; fax (619) 557-2372.
Honorary Vice-Consul: Theodora Smit.

Consulate: 153 West, 2nd South St, Salt Lake City, UT 84111; tel (801) 484-2440.
Honorary Vice-Consul: Joseph Leland Teerlink.

NEW ZEALAND

Embassy: 37 Observatory Circle, NW, Washington, DC 20008; tel (202) 328-4848; telex 230-89526; fax (202) 667-5227.
Ambassador: Harold Huyton Francis.
Minister and Deputy Head of Mission: Peter William Trelawny Adams.
Minister (Commercial): David F. Kininmonth.

Counsellor (Political): Elizabeth K. H. Halliday.
Counsellor (Economic): Derek John Gill.
Defence, Military, Naval and Air Attaché: Air Cdre Carey W. Adamson.
Assistant Naval Attaché: Commdr Alan Ross Dudley.
Assistant Military Attaché: Lieut Col Gary Malcolm Corkin.
Assistant Air Attaché: Wing Commdr Desmond Albert Ashton.
First Secretary (Commercial): Kate Sutton.
First Secretary: John Alexander Brandon.
Second Secretary (Political): David L. Taylor.
Second Secretary (Commercial): Jacinta Therese Clark.

Consulate-General: Suite 1530, Tishman Bldg, 15th Floor, 10960 Wilshire Blvd, Los Angeles, CA 90024; tel (213) 477-8241; fax (213) 473-5621.
Consul-General: Kate Lackey.
Vice-Consul: Rama Durie.
Trade Commissioner: Ross Graham.

Consulate: 6810 51st Ave, NE, Seattle, WA 98115; tel (206) 525-9881; fax (206) 525-0271.
Honorary Consul: John Bollard.

Trade Commission: Suite 1206, 432 Park Ave South, New York, NY 10016; tel (212) 447-0550; fax (212) 447-0558.
Trade Commissioner: James Griffiths.

NICARAGUA

Embassy: 1627 New Hampshire Ave, NW, Washington, DC 20009; tel (202) 939-6570; fax (202) 939-6542.
Ambassador: Ernesto Palazio.
Counsellor (Information/Culture): Dr Xavier Arguello.
Counsellor (Economic): Enrique Vanegas.
Counsellor (Commercial): Amilcar Ybarra.
Counsellor (Co-operation): Joaquin Gomez.
First Secretary and Vice-Consul: Eugenio Leal.
Second Counsellor (Co-operation): Leonel Teller.
Consul-General: Dr Mario Melendez.

Consulate: 61 Broadway, Suite 2529, New York, NY 10006; tel (212) 344-4491.
Consul: Sonia Cruz-Baltodano.

Consulate: 2500 Wilshire Blvd, Suite 915, Los Angeles, CA 90057; tel (213) 252-1170.
Consul: Cesar Aviles-Haslam.

Consulate: 8370 West Flagler St, Suite 220, Miami, FL 33144; tel (305) 220-6900.
Consul: Mario Sacsa.

Consulate: World Trade Center, 1937 Canal St, New Orleans, LA 70130; tel (504) 523-1507.
Consul: Mayra Lacayo-Grimaldi.
Consul: Lucia C. Caldera de Newton.

Consulate: J. F. Bldg, 870 Market St, Suite 1050, San Francisco, CA 94102; tel (415) 765-6821.
Consul: Adan Fletes Valle.

Consulate: 6300 Hillcroft, Suite 470, Houston, TX 77081; tel (713) 272-9628.
Consul: Dr Ricardo Reyes.

NIGER

Embassy: 2204 R St, NW, Washington, DC 20008; tel (202) 483-4224.
Ambassador: Moumouni Adamou Djermakoye.

NIGERIA

Embassy: 2201 M St, NW, Washington, DC 20037; tel (202) 822-1500.
Ambassador: Z. M. Kazaure.

Consulate-General: 575 Lexington Ave, New York, NY 10022; tel (212) 715-7200.
Consul-General: Yusufu Usman.
Consul: Gordon M. Ogbedobor.
Consul: Isiaka A. Saliu.
Consul: David Agam D. Osuagwu.
Consul: Odih N. Ewoterai.
Consul: Aminu Nebegu.
Consul: Sylvester A. Ihenyen.

NORWAY

Embassy: 2720 34th St, NW, Washington, DC 20008; tel (202) 333-6000; telex 892374; fax (202) 337-0870.
Ambassador: Kjeld Vibe.
Minister and Deputy Head of Mission: Sven Erik Svedman.
Minister: Per Kristian Pederson.
Counsellor (Security/Defence): Jorg Willy Bronebakk.
Counsellor (Press/Culture): Ingvard Havnen.
Counsellor (Shipping/Civil Aviation): Janne Julsrud.
Counsellor (Fisheries): Kjell Raasok.
Counsellor (Energy): Bjarne Moe.
Counsellor (Trade): Roald Haugen.
Counsellor (Science): Leif E. Westgaard.
Defence Attaché: Rear Adm. Egil Eikanger.
Defence Co-operation Attaché: Lieut Col Cato A. Olsen.
Naval Attaché: Capt. Thor C. Hallin.
Military Attaché and Assistant Defence Attaché: Lieut Col Knut Erik Wedum.
First Secretary (Political): Hans Brattskar.
First Secretary (Economic): Olav Berstad.
First Secretary (Economic): Anne S. Bjelland.
Consul: Eva Vincent.
Attaché (Culture): Bjarne Flolo.

Consulate-General: 855 Third Ave, 38th Floor, New York, NY 10022-7584; tel (212) 421-7333; telex 649740; fax (212) 754-0583.
Consul-General: John Bjoernebye.
Consul: Odd Wibe.
Consul: Olav Land.
Consul: Bjarne Hansen.
Consul: Charles A. Muller.

Consulate-General: 2777 Allen Parkway, Suite 1185, Houston, TX 77019; tel (713) 521-2900; telex 9108-11534; fax (713) 521-9473.
Consul-General: Erik Leikvang.
Honorary Consul: William Douglas Haden III.

Consulate-General: 5750 Wilshire Blvd, Suite 470, Los Angeles, CA 90036; tel (213) 933-7717; telex 371-0287; fax (213) 933-8711.
Consul-General: Per A. Tollefsen.

Consulate-General: Two Embarcadero Center, Suite 2930, San Francisco, CA 94111; tel (415) 986-0766; telex 340940; fax (415) 986-6025.
Consul-General: Dag Mork Ulnes.

Consulate: 1001 North America Way, Suite 205, Miami, FL 33132; tel (305) 358-4386; telex 275361; fax (305) 332-4369.
Consul: Haakon H. Storhaug.

Consulate-General: 229 Foshay Tower, Minneapolis, MN 55402-2961; tel (612) 332-3338; telex 290036; fax (612) 332-1386.
Consul-General: Bjarne Grindem.

Consulate-General: 748 West Algonquin Rd, Arlington Heights, Chicago, IL 60005; tel (312) 956-6969.
Honorary Consul-General: Per Bye Ohrstrom.

Consulate: POB 2191, 399 Michigan Ave, Mobile, AL 36652; tel (205) 432-2672.
Honorary Consul: Leslie Harold Stuart, Jr.

Consulate: 3220 Republic Plaza, 370 17th St, Denver, CO 80202; tel (303) 592-5925.
Honorary Consul: Rita Ehrman.

Consulate: Gabel, McDonald, Anderson & Dees, 112 West Adams St, Suite 920, Jacksonville, FL 32202.
Honorary Consul: George D. Gabel, Jr.

Consulate: 804 South Palafox St, Pensacola, FL 32593; tel (904) 432-0971.
Honorary Consul: Edward Phillips Nickinson, Jr.

Consulate: 801 East Washington St, Tampa, FL 33602; tel (813) 223-1521.
Honorary Consul: Shirley McKay Savage.

Consulate: 3715 Northside Parkway, Bldg 300, Suite 650, Atlanta, GA 30327.
Honorary Consul: John R. McDonald.

Consulate: 2000 Financial Center, Des Moines, IA 50309; tel (515) 243-7100.
Honorary Consul-General: Quentin R. Boyken.

Consulate: 650 Poydras St, Suite 1700, New Orleans, LA 70130; tel (504) 529-5461.
Honorary Consul: Erik F. Johnsen.

Consulate: 19-21 South St, Baltimore, MD 21202; tel (301) 539-5061.
Honorary Consul: Ernest Douglas Levering.

Consulate: 822 Boylston St, Suite 101, Chestnut Hills, Boston, MA 02167.
Honorary Consul: Terje Korsnes.

Consulate: 21624 Grand River, Detroit, MI 48219; tel (313) 477-3103.
Honorary Consul: Norval Eide Engelsen.

Consulate: 10401 Clayton Rd, St Louis, MO 63131; tel (314) 997-6810.
Honorary Consul: Don L. Wolfsberger.

Consulate: 500 Transwestern Plaza II, 490 North 31st St, Billings, MT 59103; tel (406) 252-3441.
Honorary Consul: James P. Sites.

Consulate: One Merrill Lynch Plaza, 10330 Regency Parkway Drive, Omaha, NE 68114; tel (402) 397-2200.
Honorary Consul: Virgil K. Johnson.

Consulate: 10 Roberts St, POB 6017, Fargo, ND 58108; tel (701) 232-8957.
Honorary Consul: Armond G. Erickson.

Consulate: 922 National City Bank Bldg, 629 Euclid Ave, Cleveland, OH 44114; tel (216) 241-6171.
Honorary Consul: Henry Frank Lukas, Jr.

Consulate: 4529 East 29th St, Tulsa, OK 74114; tel (918) 743-7814.
Honorary Consul: Jon R. Stuart.

Consulate: 307 Oregon Pioneer Bldg, 320 SW Stark St, Portland, OR 97204; tel (503) 228-8828.
Honorary Consul: Kjell Lund.
Honorary Vice-Consul: Lorentz Kelly Bruun.

Consulate: 112-24 Christian St, Philadelphia, PA 19147; tel (215) 462-2502.
Honorary Consul: Bengt Olof Jansson.
Honorary Vice-Consul: Jeanne E. Williams.

Consulate: Avda Santiago de los Caballeros, km 2.8, Ponce, Puerto Rico 00732; tel 848-9000.
Honorary Consul: Luis A. Ayala-Parsi.

Consulate: 400 Comercio St, San Juan, Puerto Rico 00903; tel 725-2532.
Honorary Consul: José Octavio Inguez Busto.

Consulate: POB 536, Charleston, SC 29402; tel (803) 577-5782.
Honorary Consul: James Doar Lucas, Jr.

Consulate: 509 South Dakota Ave, Sioux Falls, SD 57102; tel (605) 336-1030.
Honorary Consul: Howard W. Paulson.

Consulate: 5327 North Central Expressway, Dallas, TX 75225; tel (214) 521-2892.
Honorary Consul: Ben Orvell Hindman.

Consulate: US National Bank Bldg, Suite 1000, 2201 Market St, Galveston, TX 77550; tel (409) 766-5400.
Honorary Consul: Arthur Laird McCarthy.

Consulate: 201 East City Hall Ave, Norfolk, VA 23514; tel (804) 446-7300.
Honorary Consul: Rolf Williams.

Consulate: 1402 Third Ave, 806 Joseph Vance Bldg, Seattle, WA 98101; tel (206) 623-3957.
Honorary Consul: Thomas Andersen Stang.
Honorary Vice-Consul: Leif D. Eie.

Consulate: 25 West Main St, Madison, WI 53703; tel (608) 257-0411.
Honorary Consul: Byron Clifford Ostby.

Consulate: 741 North Milwaukee St, Milwaukee, WI 53202; tel (414) 271-7271.
Honorary Vice-Consul: Carl N. Otjen.

Consulate: 820 West 4th Ave, Anchorage, AK 99501; tel (907) 279-5622.
Honorary Consul: Sara Elaine Atwood.
Honorary Vice-Consul: Anton J. Z. Meyer.

Consulate: 1585 Kapiolani Blvd, Honolulu, HI 96814; tel (808) 949-6565.
Honorary Consul: Ruth Rittmeister.

OMAN

Embassy: 2342 Massachusetts Ave, NW, Washington, DC 20008; tel (202) 387-1980; telex 440267; fax (202) 387-2186.
Ambassador: Awadh bin Bader al-Shanfari.

PAKISTAN

Embassy: 2315 Massachusetts Ave, NW, Washington, DC 20008; tel (202) 939-6200; fax (202) 387-0484.
Ambassador: Zulfiqar Ali Khan.

Consulate-General: 12 East 65th St, New York, NY 10021; tel (212) 879-5800.
Vice-Consul: Malik A. Ellahi.

Consulate-General: Los Angeles, CA.
Consul-General: Aziz Ahmad Khan.

Consulate-General: One First National Plaza, Suite 4800, Chicago, IL 60603; tel (312) 853-7630.
Honorary Consul-General: Quincy White.

Consulate-General: 1056 Country Side Trace, Louisville, KY 40223; tel (502) 244-8594.
Honorary Consul-General: William Howard Denhard.

Consulate-General: 745 Boylston St, Boston, MA 02116.
Consul-General: Barry D. Hoffman.

Consulate-General: 555 Del Monte, Houston, TX 77056; tel (713) 963-9110.
Honorary Consul-General: Joanne Herring Davies.

PANAMA

Embassy: 2862 McGill Terrace, NW, Washington, DC 20008; tel (202) 483-1407; telex 64371; fax (202) 483-8413.
Ambassador: Eduardo Vallarino.
Consul-General: Miguel Antonio Corro.

Consulate-General: 1180 Ave of the Americas, New York, NY 10036.
Consul-General: Luis Felipe Clement.

Consulate-General: 1766 Union St, San Francisco, CA 94123.
Honorary Consul-General: Antonio Cucalon, Jr.
Honorary Vice-Consul: Guillermo Crosbi Grimaldo.

Consulate-General: 300 Biscayne Blvd, Suite 1005, Miami, FL 33131.
Consul-General: Libia Ruby Moscoso de Young.
Consul: Nelly Richard de Maduro.

Consulate-General: 260 Peachtree St, NW, Suite 1760, Atlanta, GA 30303; tel (404) 525-2772.
Consul-General: Olmedo A. Rosa.

Consulate-General: 1324 World Trade Center, 2 Canal St, 13th Floor, New Orleans, LA 70130; tel (504) 525-3458.
Consul-General: Diana C. Bares de Fernández.

Consulate-General: 200 South Diary Ashford, Suite 295, Houston, TX 77077; tel (713) 493-5997.
Consul-General: Gabriela de Piad.
Honorary Consul: Fred Rodell.

Consulate: 17341 East Hurley St, Suite 66, La Puente, Los Angeles, CA 91744; tel (818) 912-5790.
Honorary Consul: Elsa A. de Cano del Castillo.

Consulate: 3708 Pickford Ave, Ruskin, Tampa, FL 33570; tel (813) 645-6578.
Honorary Consul: Carlos A. Chiari.

PAPUA NEW GUINEA

Embassy: 1415 New Hampshire Ave, NW, Suite 300, Washington, DC 20009; tel (202) 745-3480; telex 64440; fax (202) 745-3679.
Ambassador: Margaret Taylor.
Counsellor: Veali Vagi.
First Secretary: Magdelene Proansi.

PARAGUAY

Embassy: 2400 Massachusetts Ave, NW, Washington, DC 20008; tel (202) 483-6960; fax (202) 234-4508.
Ambassador: Marcos Martínez Mendieta.

Consulate-General: One World Trade Center, Suite 1609, New York, NY 10048.
Vice-Consul: Mario Medina Oviedo.
Vice-Consul: Carlos Alejandro Weiss López.

Consulate-General: 611 Gravier St, Suite 903, New Orleans, LA 70130.
Consul-General: Luis A. Grenno.

Consulate: 8322 Seaport, Huntingdon Beach, Los Angeles, CA 92646.
Honorary Consul: Maria Alejandrina Vallejos.

Consulate: 870 Markey St, Suite 407, San Francisco, CA 94102.
Honorary Consul: Donald Melvin Haet.
Honorary Vice-Consul: David Leigh Haet.

Consulate: 7205 NW 19th St, Miami, FL 33126.
Consul: Cesar Grillon.

Consulate: 4013 North Milwaukee Ave, Suite 452, Chicago, IL 60641; tel (312) 794-0040.
Honorary Consul: Eulogio Medina.

Consulate: Detroit, MI.
Honorary Consul: Alice Rojas.

Consulate: 1832 Twelfth Ave, Anchorage, AK.
Honorary Consul: Barbara Lorna Deane Dimock.

Consulate: San Jorge 267, Apt 5C, Santurce, San Juan, Puerto Rico.
Honorary Consul: Maria Elena Ponce de Leon de Haszard.

PERU

Embassy: 1700 Massachusetts Ave, NW, Washington, DC 20036; tel (202) 833-9860; telex 197675; fax (202) 659-8124.
Chargé d'affaires a.i.: Jorge Váldez.
Consul-General: Rosa Mendoza de Garibaldi.

Consulate-General: 805 Third Ave, 14th Floor, New York, NY 10022; tel (212) 644-2850.
Consul-General: Hernan A. Couturier.
Deputy Consul: Carlos Pacheco-Queirolo.

Consulate-General: Century Plaza Bldg, 6420 Wilshire Blvd, Suite 1020, Los Angeles, CA 90048; tel (213) 651-0296.
Consul-General: Julio Galindo.
Deputy Consul-General: David González.
Deputy Consul-General: Pablo C. Ontaneda.

Consulate-General: 870 Market St, Suite 579, San Francisco, CA 94102; tel (415) 362-7136.
Consul-General: Humberto Urteaga.
Deputy Consul: Jaime José Perez del Solar Cuculiza.
Deputy Consul: Eugenio M. Risi.

Consulate-General: 444 Brickell Ave, Suite 920, Miami, FL 33131; tel (305) 374-1407.
Consul-General: Juan Luis Reus.
Deputy Consul: Cesar Enrique Bustamante-LLosa.
Deputy Consul: Julio Romero Ojeda.

Consulate: 180 North Michigan Ave, Suite 700, Chicago, IL 60601; tel (312) 853-6173.
Consul-General: Mariano Garcia-Godos.
Honorary Consul: Julio Enrique Vega Guanilo.

Consulate-General: 100 Hamilton Plaza, Suite 1221, Patterson, NJ; tel (201) 278-3324.
Consul-General: Juan F. Villafana.
Honorary Consul: Luis A. Olano.

Consulate-General: 5847 San Felipe Ave, Suite 1481, Houston, TX 77057; tel (713) 781-5000.
Consul-General: Benjamin Ruiz Sobero.
Deputy Consul: Alberto Fernandez-Prada Franco.
Honorary Consul: Bernardo Treistman.

Consulate-General: 7209 NE 149th Plaza Bothell, Seattle, WA 98011; tel (206) 488-4705.
Honorary Consul-General: Victor Schiantarelli.

Consulate-General: Jazmin 1700, Urb. San Francisco, Rio Piedras, San Juan, Puerto Rico 00927; tel 763-0679.
Honorary Consul-General: Bolivar Patino Arca.

Consulate: 6151 Cerrada Tolsa, Tucson, AZ 85718; tel (602) 299-6378.
Honorary Consul: Esteban F. Daranyi.

Consulate: 2742 NE 4th St, Pompano Beach, Fort Lauderdale, FL 33062; tel (305) 946-3646.
Honorary Consul: Walter H. Janke.

Consulate: 1405 South Orange Ave, Suite 601, Orlando, FL 32806; tel (305) 843-8475.
Honorary Consul: Dr Tomas Horna del Rio.

Consulate: 611 Gravier St, Suite 702, New Orleans, LA 70130; tel (504) 861-7827.
Honorary Consul: Raffaele G. F. Beltram Debeuz-Millonig.

Consulate: 745 Boylston St, Boston, MA 02116; tel (617) 267-4050.
Honorary Consul: Thomas Eric Singer.

Consulate: 1034 South Brentwood Blvd, Suite 520, St Louis, MO 63117; tel (314) 726-6610.
Honorary Consul: Rosa Ana Schwarz.

Consulate: 2430 East 41st St, Tulsa, OK 74105; tel (918) 245-5911.
Honorary Consul: Dr Luis Alberto Reinoso.

Consulate: 1031 Maunaihi Place, Suite 802, Honolulu, HI 96822; tel (808) 536-2680.
Honorary Vice-Consul: Luis R. Coronado.

PHILIPPINES

Embassy: 1617 Massachusetts Ave, NW, Washington, DC 20036-2274; tel (202) 483-1414; telex 440059; fax (202) 328-7614.
Ambassador: Emmanuel Pelaez.
Consul-General: Susan O. Castrence.
Consul: Antonio V. Rodríguez.
Consul: MacArthur F. Corsino.
Consul: Generoso de Guzman Calogne.
Consul: Teresita V. G. Barsana.

Consulate-General: Philippine Center, 556 Fifth Ave, New York, NY 10036; tel (212) 764-1330.
Consul: Ruperto M. Dizon.
Vice-Consul: J. Eduardo E. Malaya III.
Vice-Consul: Fe Banzon Fuentebella.

Consulate-General: 3660 Wilshire Blvd, Suite 900, Los Angeles, CA 90010; tel (213) 387-5321.
Consul-General: Victor G. García.
Consul: Ramon C. Munda.

Consulate-General: Philippine Center Bldg, 6th Floor, 447 Sutter St, San Francisco, CA 94108; tel (415) 433-6666.
Consul-General: Alfredo L. Almendrala, Jr.
Consul: Luis L. García.

Consul: Simeon R. Raya.

Consulate-General: Guam International Center, 4th Floor, Marine Drive, Tamuning, Agana, Guam 96910; POB 9880, Tamuning, Guam 96911.
Consul General: Francisco F. Santos.
Consul: Benito B. Valeriano.

Consulate-General: 30 North Michigan Ave, Suite 2100, Chicago, IL 60602; tel (312) 332-6458.
Consul-General: Jaime S. Bautista.
Consul: Gregario Aducayen.

Consulate-General: Texas Commerce Bank Bldg, 5177 Richmond Ave, Suite 1100, Houston, TX 77056; tel (713) 621-8613.
Consul-General: Antonio L. Ramírez.
Consul: Zenaida T. Tolentino.

Consulate-General: United Airlines Bldg, 2033 6th Ave, Suite 801, Seattle, WA 98121; tel (206) 441-1640.
Consul-General: Hermengildo B. García.
Consul: Ruth M. Prado.

Consulate-General: 2433 Pali Highway, Honolulu, HI 96817; tel (808) 595-6316.
Consul: Pedro Chan.
Consul: Edwin D. Bael.

Consulate: 600 B St, Suite 1200, San Diego, CA 92101; tel (619) 544-9058.
Consul: Gloria R. Da Rodda.
Consul: José R. Burgos.

Consulate: 950 East Paces Ferry Rd, NE, Atlanta, GA.
Honorary Consul: Raoul R. Donato.

Consulate: 45 Woodland Shore, Grosse Pointe Shore, Detroit, MI 48236; tel (313) 885-4642.
Honorary Consul: Renato S. Roxas.

Consulate: 378 Balmoral Drive, Cleveland, OH 44143.
Honorary Consul: Victor Vitug.

POLAND

Embassy: 2640 16th St, NW, Washington, DC 20009; tel (202) 234-3800; telex 89480; fax (202) 328-6271.
Ambassador: Kazimierz Dziewanowski.
Minister-Counsellor: Maciej Kozlowski.
Counsellor: Wojciech Adamiecki.
Counsellor: Ryszard Uniwersal.
Counsellor: Jerzy Jaruzelski.
Counsellor: Jerzy Wieclaw.
Counsellor (Cultural): Andrzej Jarecki.
Defence, Military, Naval and Air Attaché: Col Marian Moraczewski.
Assistant Defence, Military, Naval and Air Attaché: Lieut Col Bogdan Sternal.
Assistant Defence, Military, Naval and Air Attaché: Maj. Tomasz Blechman.
First Secretary: Zbigniew Kudas.
First Secretary: Bogumila Wieclaw.
First Secretary: Piotr Starzynski.
Second Secretary: Ryszard Sosinski.
Second Secretary (Cultural): Ewa Konig-Krasinska.
Second Secretary: Pawel Gonera.
Second Secretary: Piotr Szczepanski.
Second Secretary: Zbigniew Kwinta.
Second Secretary (Press/Information): Boguslaw M. Majewski.
Counsellor (Legal): Andrzej Burzynski.
Minister-Counsellor and Head of Consular Section: Wojciech Gilewski.
First Secretary (Consular): Jan Gorecki.

Office of Commercial Counsellor: 820 2nd Ave, 17th Floor, New York, NY 10017; tel (212) 370-5300; telex 141178; fax (212) 818-9623.
Counsellor (Commercial): Wlodzimierz Chodzko.

Office of Financial Counsellor: 2640 16th St, NW, Washington, DC 20008; tel (202) 332-8497; telex 89480; fax (202) 328-6271.
Counsellor (Financial): Krzysztof Krowacki.

Office of Economic Counsellor: 2224 Wyoming Ave, NW, Washington, DC 20008; tel (202) 232-4517; fax (202) 328-2152.
Minister-Counsellor (Economic): Jacek Tomorowicz.

Consulate-General: 233 Madison Ave, New York, NY; tel (212) 889-8360; telex 679-0660; fax (212) 779-3062.
Consul-General: Jerzy Surdykowski.
Consul: Stanislaw Madeja.
Consul: Zbigniew Pilat.
Consul: Henryk Purowski.
Consul: Andrzej Opalinski.
Consul: Zbigniew Siwek.
Consul: Jerzy Szewczyk.

Consulate-General: 1530 North Lake Shore Drive, Chicago, IL 60610-1695; tel (312) 337-8166; telex 254158; fax (312) 337-7841.
Consul-General: Hubert Romanowski.
Consul: Zdzislaw Kominek.
Consul: Jerzy Borowiec.
Consul: Piotr Kozerski.
Consul: Wojciech Jarominski.
Consul: Erwin Klimczak.
Consul: Stanislaw Krauze.

Consulate-General: 3460 Wilshire Blvd, Suite 1200, Los Angeles, CA 90010; tel (213) 365-7900; telex 496-10354; fax (213) 365-7905.
Consul-General: Jan Szewc.

PORTUGAL

Embassy: 2310 Tracy Place, NW, Washington, DC 20008; tel (202) 322-3007; fax (202) 462-3726.
Ambassador: João Eduardo M. Pereira Bastos.
Vice-Consul: Lucas Campos.

Consulate-General: 630 Fifth Ave, Suite 655, New York, NY 10020; tel (212) 246-4580.
Consul-General: João Quintela Paixao.
Vice-Consul: Emilia C. Lopes.

Consulate-General: 3298 Washington St, San Francisco, CA 94115; tel (415) 346-3400.
Consul-General: Antonio A. Carvalho de Faria.
Vice-Consul: Antonio de Sousa Bettencourt.

Consulate-General: 889 Boylston St, Boston, MA 02115; tel (617) 536-8740.
Consul-General: Antonio Lopes da Fonseca.
Vice-Consul: Humberto de Aguiar Fernandes.

Consulate: 1801 Ave of the Stars, Suite 400, Los Angeles, CA 90067; tel (213) 277-1491.
Vice-Consul: Edmundo Aurelio Rebelo de Macedo.

Consulate: 20 East Main St, Waterbury, CT 06702; tel (203) 755-4111.
Honorary Consul: Dr Adriano Seabra Veiga.

Consulate: 1901 Ponce de Leon Blvd, 2nd Floor, Coral Gables, Miami, FL 33134; tel (305) 371-6333.
Honorary Consul: Joseph T. Theriaga.

Consulate: 1955 New England Ave, Chicago, IL 60635; tel (312) 889-7405; telex 332328.
Honorary Consul: Edward Miller Rowley.

Consulate: 628 Pleasant St, Suite 201, New Bedford, MA 02740; tel (617) 997-6151.
Consul: Jorge de M. Serpa Neves.
Vice-Consul: Antonio Magalhaes Pinto.

Consulate: 1180 Raymond Blvd, Suite 222, Newark, NJ 07102; tel (201) 622-7300.
Consul: Julio Vasconcelos de Carvalho.
Vice-Consul: Jorge de sa Araujo de Cardiellos.

Consulate: 427 Chestnut St, Suite 527, Philadelphia, PA 19106; tel (215) 925-3222.
Honorary Consul: Baldimiro Nunes Duarte Soares.

Consulate: 601 Jefferson Ave, Suite 2200, Houston, TX 77002.
Honorary Consul: James H. Westmoreland.

Consulate: 421 San Jovino, Urb. Sagrado Corazon, Rio Piedras, San Juan, Puerto Rico 00926; tel 761-4148.
Honorary Consul: José C. Duarte da Silveira.

Consulate: 700 Bishop St, Suite 1012, Honolulu, HI 96813.
Honorary Consul: John Henry Felix.
Honorary Vice-Consul: Ernest de Sousa Morgado.

QATAR

Embassy: 600 New Hampshire Ave, Suite 1180, NW, Washington, DC 20037; tel (202) 338-0111.
Ambassador: Dr Hamid Abdelaziz al-Kawari.

ROMANIA

Embassy: 1607 23rd St, NW, Washington, DC 20008; tel (202) 232-4747; telex 248960; fax (202) 232-4748.
Ambassador: Virgil Constantinescu.
Minister-Counsellor and Deputy Head of Mission: Mihai Croitoru.
Counsellor: Gheorghe Dumitru.
Counsellor: Ion Tudorache.
Defence, Military, Naval and Air Attaché: Col Dumitru Draghici.
First Secretary (Press/Public Relations): Cornel Dragomirescu.
Second Secretary (Consular): Mihai Delcea.
Second Secretary (Consular): Marian Bordea.
Second Secretary (Culture): Andrei Busuioceanu.
Third Secretary: Adrian Dadalau.
Attaché: Bogdan Badalicescu.
Attaché: Niculae Ionea.

RUSSIA

Embassy: 1825 Phelps Place, NW, Washington, DC 20008; tel (202) 331-1513.
Ambassador: Vladimir Lukin.
Minister-Counsellor and Envoy: Andrei Kolosovsky.
Consul-General: Yevgeny Sergeievich Antipov.
Consul-General: Valentin M. Kamenev.
Consul: Oleg Markovich d'Yachenko.
Consul: Viktor M. Gribanov.

Consulate-General: 9 East 91st St, New York, NY 10021.
Consul-General: Ivan Andreyevich Kuznetsov.

Consulate-General: 2790 Green St, San Francisco, CA 94123; tel (415) 922-6642.
Deputy Consul-General: Gennady Ivanovich Zolotov.
Consul: Aleksandr Dmitrievich Terekhin.
Consul: Vladimir Ivanovich Chernenko.
Consul: Vladimir Ivanovich Azaroushkin.
Consul: Victor Valentinovich Spassky.

RWANDA

Embassy: 1714 New Hampshire Ave, NW, Washington, DC 20008; tel (202) 232-2882; telex 248505; fax (202) 232-4544.
Ambassador: Aloys Uwimana.

Consulate: 666 Dundee Rd, Northbrook, Suite 1401, Chicago, IL 60562; tel (708) 205-1188; fax (708) 205-5617.
Honorary Consul: Glenn L. Felner.

SAINT CHRISTOPHER AND NEVIS

Embassy: 2100 M St, NW, Suite 608, Washington, DC 20037; tel (202) 833-3550; telex 6387679; fax (202) 833-3553.

Chargé d'affaires a.i.: Erstein M. Edwards.
Minister-Counsellor: Irvin R. Sweeney.
Senior Executive Officer: Alice B. Alexis.
Administrative Assistant: L. Brenda Bell.

Consulate: 644 Anbone St, NW, Suite 7, Atlanta, GA 30318.
Honorary Consul: Bernard Porche.

Consulate: 6336 Greenville Ave, Dallas, TX 75206.
Honorary Consul: William R. Ewing.

SAINT LUCIA

Embassy: 2100 M St, NW, Suite 309, Washington, DC 20037; tel (202) 463-7378; telex 6711478; fax (202) 887-5746.
Ambassador: Dr Joseph Edsel Edmunds.
Counsellor: Undine George.
Attaché (Administrative): Thais Edwards.
Attaché (Administrative): Jacqueline Louisy.

Consulate-General: 820 Second Ave, Suites 907-15, New York, NY.
Vice-Consul: Germaine Patricia Louis.
Vice-Consul: Etheline Esma Fricot.

SAN MARINO

Consulate-General: 1899 'L' St, NW, Suite 500, Washington, DC 20036; tel (202) 223-3517; telex 277566.
Consul-General and Minister: Enrico di Portanova.
Consul: Sheila Raab Weidenfeld.

Consulate-General: 350 Fifth Ave, Empire State Bldg, Suite 3107, New York, NY 10118; tel (212) 465-1012; telex 697-3514; fax (212) 465-1014.
Consul-General: Roberto Balsimelli.
Consul: José Riba.

Consulate: 1685 Big-Beaver Rd, Troy, Detroit, MI 48084; tel (313) 528-1190.
Consul: Giuseppe Putti.
Vice-Consul: Diana Paoletti.

SÃO TOMÉ AND PRÍNCIPE

Embassy: 801 Second Ave, Suite 1504, New York, NY 10017; tel (212) 697-4211; fax (212) 687-8389.
Ambassador: Joaquim Rafael Branco.

Consulate: 2125 Biscayne Blvd, Suite 350, Miami, FL 33137; tel (305) 576-5049.
Honorary Consul: William S. Stevens III.

SAUDI ARABIA

Embassy: 601 New Hampshire Ave, NW, Washington, DC 20037; tel (202) 342-3800; telex 440132; fax (202) 944-5983.
Ambassador: Prince Bandar Ibn Sultan.
Assistant to the Ambassador: Abdulaziz A. Nazir.
Counsellor (Information): Habib A. Shaheen.
Counsellor: Ahmed A. Kattan.
Counsellor: Saleh M. al-Rajhy.

Consulate-General: 866 United Nations Plaza, New York; tel (212) 752-2740; fax (212) 688-2719.
Consul-General: Saad Nazir.
Vice-Consul: Saud M. A. Shawwaf.
Vice-Consul: Hazzaa M. Hasher.
Vice-Consul: Fahd M. al-Nassar.
Vice-Consul: Abdullah H. Almobarak.
Vice-Consul: Zaine A. A. Mlebari.
Vice-Consul: Fahad A. H. al-Rashid.

Consulate-General: 5718 Westheimer, Houston, TX; tel (713) 785-5577; fax (713) 785-1163.
Consul-General: Fawaz Kayyal.
Deputy Consul-General: Fuad A. Hafiz.
Deputy Consul-General: Nasser A. Felemban.

Consulate-General: 10900 Wilshire Blvd, Los Angeles, CA; tel (213) 208-6566.
Consul-General: Hassan T. Nazir.
Deputy Consul-General: Ibrahim M. Ammar.
Deputy Consul-General: Altayeb T. al-Hazzazi.
Deputy Consul-General: Zuhair A. Sulaihim.

SENEGAL

Embassy: 2112 Wyoming Ave, NW, Washington, DC 20008; tel (202) 234-0540; fax (202) 352-6315.
Ambassador: Ibra Degenuene Ka.

Consulate-General: 5445 Almeda, Suite 500, Houston, TX; tel (713) 529-3993.
Honorary Consul-General: Arthur Ronald Higgs.

Consulate: 14 NE First Ave, Suite 1400, Miami, FL 33132; tel (305) 371-4286.
Honorary Consul: Michael Stuart Hacker.

Consulate: 931 Martin Luther King Jr Drive, Atlanta, GA 30314.
Honorary Consul: Jacob Robert Henderson.

Consulate: 1803 International Trade Mart, New Orleans, LA 70561; tel (504) 529-7561.
Honorary Consul: William Manchester Ayers.
Honorary Consul: Deborah Ann Adams.

Consulate: 4900 Pilgrim Rd, Baltimore, MD 21214; tel (301) 354-5132.
Honorary Consul: Sandye Jean McIntyre III.

SEYCHELLES

Embassy: 820 Second Ave, Suite 900F, New York, NY 10017; tel (212) 687-9766; telex 220032; fax (212) 808-4975.
Chargé d'affaires a.i.: Marc R. Marengo.

SIERRA LEONE

Embassy: 1701 19th St, NW, Washington, DC 20009; tel (202) 939-9261.
Ambassador: Dr George Carew.

Consulate: 4100 Central Ave, Bldg 3, Atlanta, GA 30321.
Honorary Consul: Therman McKenzie, Sr.

SINGAPORE

Embassy: 1824 R St, NW, Washington, DC 20009; tel (202) 667-7555; fax (202) 265-7915.
Ambassador: S. R. Nathan.
Counsellor: Ong Keng Yong.
Counsellor: Lim Hang Hing.
Defence, Military, Naval and Air Attaché: Col Lee Seng Kong.
First Secretary: Selvadas Govindasamy.
First Secretary (Economic): Michael Chee.
First Secretary (Education): Peter K. S. Ee.
First Secretary (Defence Procurement): Kernail Singh.
Third Secretary (Defence Procurement): Tan Choong Mong.
Third Secretary: Cynthia Chua.

Consulate: 2424 SE Bristol, Suite 320, Santa Ana Heights, CA 92707; tel (714) 476-2330; fax (714) 476-8301.
Honorary Consul: Daryl Arnold.

Consulate: 607 Marquette Ave, Suite 400, Minneapolis, MN 55402; tel (612) 332-8063; fax (612) 332-2089.
Honorary Consul: Stephen Young.

SOMALIA

Embassy: 600 New Hampshire Ave, NW, Suite 710, Washington, DC 20037; tel (202) 342-1575.
Ambassador: Abdikarim Ali Omar.
Consul-General: Mohamud Ali Magan.

Consulate-General: 747 Third Ave, 22nd Floor, New York, NY 10017; tel (212) 687-9877.

Consulate: 8700 Commerce Park, Suite 218, Houston, TX 77036.
Honorary Consul: Harold A. Odom, Jr.

SOUTH AFRICA

Embassy: 3051 Massachusetts Ave, NW, Washington, DC 20008; tel (202) 232-4400; telex 248364; fax (202) 265-1607.
Ambassador: Harry Schwarz.
Minister: E. B. de Montille.
Minister (Economic): E. J. Nyenhuis.
Counsellor: R. G. Desmarais.
Counsellor: D. van Tonder.
Counsellor: H. E. Jansen van Rensberg.
Counsellor: Dr A. H. Lückhoff.
Counsellor: P. A. Vermeulan.
Counsellor (Administrative): J. G. van Niekerk.
Counsellor (Agricultural/Scientific): J. O. Glatthaar.
Counsellor (Science/Technology): N. C. Hauffe.
Counsellor (Minerals/Energy): B. G. Russell.
Defence and Military Attaché: Col J. M. R. van der Riet.
Air Attaché: Col N. C. Parkins.
Assistant Naval Attaché: Lieut Commdr Y. S. Moodley.
First Secretary: R. D. Wilson.
First Secretary: A. S. Weitz.
First Secretary: P. C. Evans.
Second Secretary: W. S. Vosloo.
Second Secretary: C. H. Snyman.
Second Secretary: P. Goosen.
Second Secretary (Administrative): B. C. Eden.
Second Secretary (Consular): E. Bekker.

Consulate-General: 326 East 48 St, New York, NY 10017; tel (212) 371-7997; telex 127549; fax (212) 371-7577.
Consul-General: Pieter H. Viljoen.
Deputy Consul-General: Christiaan C. Badenhorst.
Consul: John A. Davies.
Consul: Louis P. van der Merwe.
Consul: Gerald Anthony Watson.
Consul (Administrative): Mario Carsten van Zyl.

Consulate-General: 50 North La Cienega Blvd, Suite 300, Beverley Hills, CA 90211; tel (213) 657-9200; fax (213) 657-9215.
Consul-General: Stefan C. Buys.
Consul: Johannes H. Roodt.
Consul (Administrative): Lionel Lloyd Wedge.
Consul (Agricultural): Brian W. Young.
Consul (Trade): Hendrik L. Erasmus.

Consulate-General: 200 South Michigan Ave, 6th Floor, Chicago, IL 60604; tel (312) 939-7929; telex 687-1633; fax (312) 939-8748.
Consul-General: Daniel S. Smith.
Consul: Erik F. E. Blumer.
Consul (Administrative): Irene V. Klapwijk.
Consul (Trade): H. C. du Toit.

Consulate-General: 1980 Post Oak Blvd, Suite 1520, Houston, TX 77056; tel (713) 850-0150; telex 203311; fax (713) 850-8738.
Consul-General: Gerhardus P. Pretorius.
Consul: Andrea Snyman.
Consul: Adan D. Weimar.
Consul (Trade): Hendrik T. J. Pretorius.

Consulate-General: 2308 First National Bank Bldg, Mobile, AL 36602; tel (205) 266-7867.
Honorary Consul-General: John H. van Aken.

Consulate-General: New Orleans, LA.

Consulate: 2272 Ridgewood Way, Salt Lake City, UT 84010; tel (801) 266-7867.
Honorary Consul: R. P. Thorn.

Consulate: Boston, MA 02114.

Consulate: Seattle, WA 98145-1115.

SPAIN

Embassy: 2700 15th St, NW, Washington, DC 20009; tel (202) 265-0190; telex 64125; fax (202) 332-5451.

Ambassador: Jaime de Ojeida.
Minister and Deputy Head of Mission: Jorges Fuentes.
Minister (Culture): Dr José Ramón Remacha.
Minister (Economic/Commercial): Manuel de la Cámara.
Minister: Antonio Muñoz-Rojas.
Counsellor (Finance): Rafael Sagrario.
Counsellor (Labour): José A. Zapatero.
Counsellor (Information): Ramón Cercós.
Counsellor: José J. Gomez-Llera.
Counsellor: Santiago Cabanas.
Defence Attaché: Brig. Gen. Gaspar Regalado.
Defence Co-operation Attaché: Capt. Ramón de Velasco.
Military Attaché: Lieut Col Antonio Arregui.
Naval Attaché: Capt. Manuel Rivera.
Air Attaché: Col Jaime Jorge-Raga.
First Secretary: Agustín Santos.
First Secretary: Alfonso López Perona.
First Secretary and Consul: Arturo Spiegelberg-de-Ortueta.

Consulate-General: 150 East 58th St, 16th Floor, New York, NY 10155; tel (212) 355-4080.
Consul-General: Miguel de Aldasoro.
Deputy Consul-General: Javier Collarzabaleta.
Consul: Domingo Reuda.
Consul: Francisco Giron.
Consul: Felix Valdes.
Consul: Mariano Mugla.

Consulate-General: 545 Boylston St, Suite 803, Boston, MA 02116; tel (617) 536-2506.
Consul-General: Jesús J. López Jacoiste.

Consulate-General: 180 North Michigan Ave, Suite 1500, Chicago, IL 60601; tel (312) 782-4588.
Consul-General: Fernando Belloso.
Consul: José L. Perez Sanchez.
Consul: Mario Trinidad.
Consul: Arcadio L. Martínez.

Consulate-General: 2411 Fountain View, Suite 130, Houston, TX; tel (713) 783-6200.
Consul-General: Carlos Reparaz Madinaveita.

Consulate-General: 6300 Wilshire Blvd, Suite 1530, Los Angeles, CA 90048; tel (213) 658-6050.
Consul-General: Eduardo Garriguez.
Consul: Alvaro Renedo.
Consul: Jaime García Murillo.
Consul: Jesus M. Orejas.

Consulate-General: 151 Sevilla Ave, 2nd Floor, Coral Gables, Miami, FL 33134; tel (305) 446-5511.
Consul-General: Erik Martel.
Consul: Alfredo Bonet.
Consul: Julio Rodríguez.

Consulate-General: 2102 World Trade Center, 2 Canal St, New Orleans, LA 70130; tel (504) 525-4951.
Consul-General: Pablo López Teheran.

Consulate-General: 2080 Jefferson St, San Francisco, CA 94123; tel (415) 922-2995.
Consul-General: César González Palacios.

Consulate-General: Edif. Mercantil Plaza, Suite 1101, Hato Rey, San Juan, Puerto Rico 00919; tel 758-6090.
Consul-General: Rafael Márquz Cano.
Consul: Maria-Isabel Dominguez Ayuso.

Consulate: 5912 North Shenandoah Rd, Mobile, AL 36608; tel (205) 342-6977.
Honorary Vice-Consul: John Edward Cartwright Marston.

Consulate: 579 Frogtown Rd, New Canaan, Stamford, CT 06840; tel (203) 966-5363.
Honorary Vice-Consul: George Stevens Moore.

Consulate: Cultural Foundation of Spain in Florida, 2505 Riverside Ave, Jacksonville, FL 32204.
Honorary Vice-Consul: Dr José Lopez Zubero.

Consulate: 8117 Forest Hill Drive, Ellicott City, Baltimore, MD 21043.
Honorary Vice-Consul: Conrado Ferrero.

Consulate: 1012 Baltimore, Suite 702, Kansas City, MO 64105; tel (816) 471-5502.
Honorary Vice-Consul: Eugene Francis Gray.

Consulate: 201 Twelfth St, Albuquerque, NM 87103.
Honorary Consul: Arturo G. Ortega.

Consulate: 23 East 77th St, Cincinnati, OH 45216; tel (513) 821-2100.
Honorary Vice-Consul: Sidney L. Kaufman.

Consulate: 3410 Warden Drive, Philadelphia, PA 19129.
Honorary Vice-Consul: Herminio Muniz.

Consulate: Esteve Brox. & Co. Inc., 3141 Hood St, Lee Park Plaza, Dallas, TX 75219.
Honorary Consul: Eduardo Esteve Campdera.

Consulate: 3816 Mattox, El Paso, TX 79925.
Honorary Consul: Sheldon Hall.

Consulate: 8350 Delphian, Universal City, San Antonio, TX 78148.
Honorary Consul: Isabel de Pedro Marin.

Consulate: 611 Woodward Ave, Detroit, MI 48226.
Honorary Vice-Consul: Louis Betanzos.

SRI LANKA

Embassy: 2148 Wyoming Ave, NW, Washington, DC 20008; tel (202) 483-4025; telex 248312; fax (202) 232-7181.
Ambassador: W. Susantha de Alwis.
Deputy Head of Mission: Prof. Wilfred Mendis.
Minister-Counsellor: B. A. B. Goonetillake.
Counsellor (Commercial): T. G. Ariyaratne.
Officer of Information/Culture: Indra de Silva.

Consulate: 630 3rd Ave, 20th Floor, New York, NY 10017; tel (212) 986-1838.
Consul: A. G. Ranasinghe.

Consulate: 957A 15th Ave, Honolulu, HI 196816; tel (808) 735-1622.
Honorary Consul: G. O. Wickremaratne.

Consulate: 309 Panorama Drive, Bakersfield, Los Angeles, CA 93305; tel (805) 323-8384.
Honorary Consul: Dr Tony Don Michel.

Consulate: 2 East Glen Rd, Denville, Connecticut, NJ 07834; tel (201) 627-7855.
Honorary Consul: J. Liyanage.

SUDAN

Embassy: 2210 Massachusetts Ave, NW, Washington, DC 20008; tel (202) 338-8565; telex 440133; fax (202) 667-2406.
Ambassador: Abdalla Ahmed Abdalla.
Minister: Abdulla Khidir Bashir.
Counsellor: Abubakar Yasin M. al-Shingeiti.
First Secretary: Gaafar Babiker El-Khalifa.
Second Secretary: Ammar Khalafalla Ahmed.
Attaché (Administrative): Salah El-Din Abdel Rahman Ali.
Attaché: Abdalla Abu El-Gasim Ali.
Attaché: Mukhtar Hanfi El-Hag.

Consulate-General: 210 East 49th St, New York, NY 10017; tel (212) 421-2680.

SURINAME

Embassy: 4301 Connecticut Ave, Suite 108, NW, Washington, DC 20008; tel (202) 244-7488; telex 892656; fax (202) 244-5878.
Ambassador: William A. Udenhout.

Consulate-General: 7235 NW 19th St, Suite A, Miami, FL 33126; tel (305) 593-2163.
Consul-General: Dick C. de Bie.
Vice-Consul: Stephanus Marinus Dendoe.

Consulate: 2265 Cascade Rd, SW, Atlanta, GA 30311; tel (403) 753-4753.
Honorary Consul: Dr Walter F. Young.

SWAZILAND

Embassy: 4301 Connecticut Ave, NW, Washington, DC 20008; tel (202) 362-6683; fax (202) 244-8059.
Ambassador: Absalom Vusani Mamba.

SWEDEN

Embassy: 600 New Hampshire Ave, NW, Washington, DC 20037; tel (202) 944-5600; telex 248347; fax (202) 342-1319.
Ambassador: Anders Ingemar Thunborg.
Minister: Sven-Olaf Petersson.
Minister: Percy Westerland.
Counsellor (Political): Staffan Carlsson.
Counsellor (Finance): Jörgen Holmqvist.
Counsellor (Administrative): Tommy Karlsson.
Counsellor (Press): Lars Romert.
Counsellor (Culture): Ingmar Björksten.
Counsellor (Agriculture): Anders Lundin.
Counsellor (Science): Svante Lundin.
Counsellor (Labour): Carin Walldin.
Counsellor: Lars Bjerde.
Defence Attaché (Military): Col P. A. Ringh.
Defence Attaché (Air): Col K. G. Widén.
Defence Attaché (Naval): Commdr Christer Hägg.
Second Secretary (Press): Lena Kjellström.

Consulate-General: One Dag Hammarskjöld Plaza, New York, NY 10017; tel (212) 751-5900; fax (212) 755-2732.
Consul-General: Arne Thorén.
Deputy Consul-General: Bjorn Gosta Sporrong.
Consul: Karin B. Ehnbom-Palmquist.
Consul: Sten J. Ericson.
Consul: Torsten N. Nilsson.
Consul: E. Christine Engfeldt.
Consul: Ann M. Lundgren.
Consul: Anita Siv Nasstrom-Ekman.
Consul: Anne M. Franzen Johnson.
Consul: Gun Inga-Lill Nilsson.

Consulate-General: 150 North Michigan Ave, Suite 1250, Chicago, IL 60601-7593; tel (312) 781-6262; fax (312) 346-0683.
Consul-General: Lave Johnsson.
Consul: Goran T. Rannefors.
Consul: Rolf I. Sandling.

Consulate-General: 10880 Wilshire Blvd, Suite 505, Los Angeles, CA 90024-4314; tel (213) 470-2555; fax (213) 475-4683.
Consul-General: Peter Hammarström.
Deputy Consul-General: Goran P. Larsson.
Consul: Kjell G. Holm.
Consul: Eva B. M. Nilsson.

Consulate-General: 706 Second Ave, POB 2107, Minneapolis, MN 55402; tel (612) 332-6340; fax (612) 332-6340.
Consul-General: Wendell R. Andersson.
Honorary Consul: Phyllis E. Blake.

Consulate-General: 120 Montgomery St, Suite 2175, San Francisco, CA 94104; tel (415) 788-2631; fax (415) 982-7362.
Consul-General: Siri Eliason.

Consulate-General: 5123 Bellaire Blvd, POB 899, Bellaire, TX 77402; tel (713) 295-5747; fax (713) 295-5782.
Consul-General: Robert A. Fowler.

Consulate: 2256 Ashland Place Ave, POB 436, Mobile, AL 36601; tel (205) 829-4047; fax (205) 944-2201.
Consul: Richard W. Overby.

Consulate: 530 Broadway, Suite 1106, San Diego, CA 92101; tel (619) 233-1106; fax (619) 233-9890.
Consul: John H. Norton.

Consulate: 301 West Northern Lights Blvd, POB 100-660, Anchorage, AK 99510-0600; tel (907) 265-2927.
Consul: Edward B. Rasmuson.

Consulate: 2121 South Oneida St, Suite 525, Denver, CO 80224; tel (303) 758-0999; fax (303) 758-1091.
Consul: Glenn D. Peterson.
Honorary Vice-Consul: Donald Glenn Peterson.

Consulate: 9200 North Central Ave, POB 9957, Phoenix, AZ 85068; tel (602) 997-0977.
Consul: Russell O. Allen.

Consulate: c/o Prudential Bache Securities Inc., 28100 US Highway 19 North, Suite 100, Clearwater, FL 34621; tel (813) 799-5540.
Consul: Howard L. Hill.

Consulate: 611 Eisenhower Blvd, 3rd Floor, POB 13094, Fort Lauderdale, FL 33316; tel (305) 467-3507; fax (305) 462-5788.
Consul: John Ira Tureman, Jr.
Honorary Vice-Consul: Guilla A. Lundstrom North.

Consulate: 465 Congress St, Suite 408, Portland, ME 04101; tel (207) 761-2526; fax (207) 761-1791.
Consul: Martin R. Johnson.

Consulate: c/o Sandwell Inc., Suite 100, 9424 Baymeadows Rd, Jacksonville, FL 32256; tel (904) 739-0313; fax (904) 739-3986.
Consul: Lennart Jansson.

Consulate: 10 North Calvert St, Suite L-45, Baltimore, MD 21202; tel (301) 539-5061; fax (301) 539-5055.
Consul: Charles E. Scarlett, III.

Consulate: 3333 Peachtree Rd, NE, Suite 1420-E, Atlanta, GA 30326; tel (404) 261-1187; fax (404) 266-8677.
Consul: Holcombe T. Green, Jr.

Consulate: 6 Saint James Ave, Suite 1001, Boston, MA 02116-3845; tel (617) 426-5558; fax (617) 542-3304.
Consul: Wendell N. Gustafson.

Consulate: 1 Rockwell Ave South, Savannah, GA 31419; tel (912) 927-1126.
Consul: Alexander Pratt Adams.

Consulate: 1290 Maple Rd, POB 1290, Troy, MI 48007-1290; tel (313) 588-3310; fax (313) 588-0718.
Consul: E. Jan Hartmann.

Consulate: 737 Bishop St, Suite 2600, Honolulu, HI 96813; tel (808) 528-4777; fax (808) 523-1920.
Consul: James M. Cribley.

Consulate: J. C. Nichols Co., 310 Ward Parkway, Kansas City, MO 64112; tel (816) 561-3456; fax (816) 561-3456.
Consul: Clarence L. Roeder.

Consulate: 2640 Canal St, New Orleans, LA 70119; tel (504) 827-8600; fax (504) 827-8792.
Consul: William B. Forsyth.

Consulate: 501 North Broadway, POB 14020, St Louis, MO 63178; tel (314) 331-6591; fax (314) 331-6554.
Consul: Richard Oscarson.

Consulate: 700 Service Life Bldg, 1904 Farnam St, Omaha, NE 68102; tel (402) 341-3333.
Consul: Donald H. Erickson.

Consulate: 1800 Liberty Bldg, Buffalo, NY 14202-3686; tel (716) 854-3110; fax (716) 854-1113.
Consul: Roger C. Swanson.

Consulate: 5956 Sherry Lane, Suite 1616, Dallas, TX 75225-6522; tel (214) 363-0800; fax (214) 363-0924.
Consul: J. Robert Alpert.

Consulate: 9-11 East Fourth St, POB 50, Jamestown, NY 14702-0050; tel (716) 484-7195; fax (716) 484-2133.
Consul: John L. Sellstrom.

Consulate: 201 East City Hall Ave, POB 3430, Norfolk, VA 23514-3630; tel (804) 446-7300; fax (804) 625-7854.
Consul: Rolf A. Williams.

Consulate: 1800 Society Bldg, East Ninth and Superior, Cleveland, OH 44114-2688; tel (216) 621-4995; fax (216) 241-0816.
Consul: Michael L. Miller.

Consulate: 1600 SW Fourth Ave, POB 8699, Portland, OR 97207; tel (503) 224-4155; fax (503) 274-2155.
Consul: Leonard A. Forsgren.

Consulate: 1020 Joseph Vance Bldg, Third Ave and Union St, Seattle, WA 98101; tel (206) 622-5640.
Consul: Clifford C. Benson.

Consulate: 112 Christian St, Philadelphia, PA 19147; tel (215) 465-5565; fax (215) 336-3389.
Consul: Bengt O. Jansson.

Consulate: 800 North Marshall St, Milwaukee, WI 53202; tel (414) 273-3393; fax (414) 273-1058.
Consul: Anders Segerdahl.

Consulate: The Commerce Bldg, 465 Congress St, Suite 408, Portland, ME 04101; tel (207) 761-2526; fax (207) 761-1791.
Honorary Consul: Martin Reginald Johnson.

Consulate: POB 2748, c/o Intership, Avda Fernandez Juncos Muelle II, San Juan, Puerto Rico 00936; tel 721-4355; fax 721-4343.
Consul: David R. Segarra, Jr.

SWITZERLAND

Embassy: 2900 Cathedral Ave, NW, Washington, DC 20008-3499; tel (202) 745-7900; telex 440055; fax (202) 387-2564.
Ambassador: Edouard Brunner.
Minister (Economic): Jean-Daniel Gerber.
Minister: Christian Blickenstorfer.
Counsellor: Stephen Nellen.
Counsellor: Michel Gottret.
Defence Attaché: Commdr Hans Dürig.
Assistant Defence Attaché: Col Hansruedi Rüesch.
Head of Armed Services Office: Werner Kälin.
Assistant Head of Armed Services Office: Philipp Marti.
First Secretary: Jean-Jacques de Dardel.
First Secretary: Carlos Orga.
First Secretary: Jürg von Arx.
First Secretary: Maurice Darier.
Second Secretary (Culture): François Barras.
Scientific and Technical Adviser: Dr Christophorus von Arb.
Attaché (Scientific/Technical): Dr Martin Büechi.
Attaché: Hans Hauser.
Consul and Office Manager: Jürg Casserini.

Consulate-General: Rolex Bldg, 665 Fifth Ave, New York, NY 10022; tel (212) 758-2560; telex 220517; fax (212) 207-8024.
Consul-General: Dr Hans-Peter Erismann.
Consul and Chancellor: Franz von Atzigen.
Consul (Culture): Lukas Gloor.
Consul: Jürg Flühmann.
Consul: Eric Pircher.

Consulate-General: 1275 Peachtree St, NE, Suite 425, Atlanta, GA 30309-3533; tel (404) 872-7874; telex 6821127; fax (404) 874-6655.
Consul-General: Paul Heinen.
Consul and Chancellor: Roland Quillet.

Consulate-General: Olympia Center, Suite 2301, 737 North Michigan Ave, Chicago, IL 60611; tel (312) 915-0061; fax (312) 915-0388.
Consul-General: Arthur Burkhardt.
Vice-Consul and Chancellor: Alain Burdet.

Consulate-General: First Interstate Bank Plaza, 1000 Louisiana, Suite 5670, Houston, TX 77002; tel (713) 650-0000; telex 765619; fax (713) 650-1321.
Consul-General: Alfred Killias.
Vice-Consul and Chancellor: Ursula Aarøe-Strasser.

Consulate-General: 3440 Wilshire Blvd, Suite 817, Los Angeles, CA 90010-2176; tel (213) 388-4127; telex 678481; fax (213) 385-4514.
Consul-General: Kurt Welte.
Vice-Consul and Chancellor: Walburga Stadler.

Consulate-General: 456 Montgomery St, Suite 1500, San Francisco, CA 94104-1233; tel (415) 788-2272; telex 67607; fax (415) 788-1402.
Consul-General: Pierre Jordan.
Consul: Jean-Claude Hagmann.
Chancellor: Hans-Ulrich Tanner.

Consulate: 535 Boylston St, Boston, MA 02116; tel (617) 266-2038.
Honorary Consul: Max Josef Steinmann.

Consulate: 3421 North Benzing Rd, Orchard Park, Buffalo, NY 14127; tel (716) 825-3814; telex 926043.
Honorary Consul: André Jaccard.

Consulate: 5301 Lester Rd, Cincinnati, OH 45213-2590; tel (513) 351-3008.
Honorary Consul: Gérard Paroz.

Consulate: 6000 South Marginal Rd, Cleveland, OH 44103; tel (216) 881-2772.
Honorary Consul: Peter Broder.

Consulate: 8516 Thunderbird Lane, Dallas, TX 75238; tel (214) 341-2708.
Honorary Consul: Herbert Haas.

Consulate: 2810 Iliff, Boulder, Denver, CO 80303; tel (303) 499-5641.
Honorary Consul: Walter Wyss.

Consulate: 2129 Austin Ave, Rochester Hills, POB 090040, Detroit, MI 48308; tel (313) 852-0040; fax (313) 853-5107.
Honorary Consul: Karl Pfister.

Consulate: 5018 Main St, Kansas City, MO 64112; tel (816) 561-3440.
Honorary Consul: Marcel Bollier.

Consulate: Sunset Chiropractic Center, 7301 SW 97th Ave, Miami, FL 33173; tel (305) 274-4210; fax (305) 595-6342.
Honorary Consul: Dr Urs Lindemann.

Consulate: Shelard Tower, Suite 651, 600 South County Rd 18, Minneapolis, MN 55426; tel (612) 546-0148; telex 291005.
Honorary Consul: Curt F. Schneider.

Consulate: 1620 8th St, New Orleans, LA 70115; tel (504) 897-6510.
Honorary Consul: John Geiser.

Consulate: 635 Public Ledger Bldg, Independence Sq., Philadelphia, PA 19106; tel (215) 922-2215.
Honorary Consul: Samuel Laeuchli.

Consulate: 1455 South 11th East, Salt Lake City, UT 84105; POB 6154, Salt Lake City, UT 84106; tel (801) 487-0450.
Honorary Consul: Wilford Lieber.

Consulate: 3018 North Scottsdale Rd, Scottsdale, AZ 85251; tel (602) 947-0020; telex 683-5045; fax (602) 481-0081.
Honorary Consul: Max Haechler.

Consulate: c/o SASE Co., 5304 3rd Ave South, POB 81003, Seattle, WA 98108; tel (206) 762-1223.
Honorary Consul: Hans Weder.

Consulate: 176 West Park Drive, Spartanburg, SC 29301; tel (803) 573-2320.
Honorary Consul: Hans H. Kuhn.

Consulate: 105 De Diego, POB 12038, San Juan, Puerto Rico 00912.
Honorary Consul: Christian B. Guex.

Consulate: 4231 Papu Circle, Honolulu, HI 96816; tel (808) 737-5297.
Honorary Consul: Niklaus R. Schweizer.

SYRIA

Embassy: 2215 Wyoming Ave, NW, Washington, DC 20008; tel (202) 232-6313; fax (202) 234-9548.
Ambassador: Walid al-Moulam.

Consulate: 6330 West Loop South 870, Bellaire, Houston, TX 77401; tel (713) 668-1928.
Honorary Consul: Amyan M. Midani.

TANZANIA

Embassy: 2139 R St, NW, Washington, DC 20008; tel (202) 939-6125; telex 64213.
Ambassador: Charles Musama Nyirabu.

THAILAND

Embassy: 2300 Kalorama Rd, NW, Washington, DC 20008; tel (202) 483-7200; telex 64232; fax (202) 234-4498.
Ambassador: Vitthya Vejjajiva.

Consulate-General: 351 East 52nd St, New York, NY 10022; tel (212) 754-1770; telex 961133; fax (212) 754-1907.
Consul-General: Tasanee Bunnag.
Deputy Consul-General: Nibhon Chantarachoti.
Consul: Sopon Jenjirathitikarn.
Consul: Narote Sangkamanee.
Consul: Aran Nilkhamhang.
Consul: Danai Karnpoj.

Consulate-General: 1201 Union Bank Bldg, 60 Commerce St, Montgomery, AL 36104; tel (205) 269-2518.
Honorary Consul-General: Robert F. Henry, Jr.

Consulate-General: 801 North La Brea Ave, Los Angeles, CA 90038; tel (213) 937-1894.
Consul-General: Vidhya Rayananonda.
Consul: Surapol Kotesrimuang.
Consul: Chatsinee Wutimananon.
Consul: Kiartiguna Kitiyakara.

Consulate-General: 580 California St, Suite 1975, San Francisco, CA 94104; tel (415) 781-1650; fax (415) 781-5827.
Honorary Consul-General: Michael Berolzheimer.

Consulate: 3980 Quebec St, Suite 214, Denver, CO 80207; tel (303) 320-4029.
Honorary Consul-General: Donald W. Ringsby.

Consulate-General: 2801 Ponce de Leon Blvd, Suite 550, Coral Gables, FL 33134; tel (305) 445-1477; fax (415) 446-9944.
Honorary Consul-General: Robert M. Holder, Jr.

Consulate-General: 35 East Wacker Drive, Suite 1834, Chicago, IL 60601; tel (312) 236-2447.
Consul-General: Prida Apirat.
Consul: Marwin Tanattanawin.
Consul: Kwanchai Mintrasakdikul.

Consulate-General: 335 Julia St, New Orleans, LA 70130; tel (504) 566-0888; fax (504) 566-0897.
Honorary Consul-General: Arthur Quentin Davis.

Consulate-General: 420 Boylston St, Suite 403, Boston, MA 02116.
Honorary Vice-Consul: Vernon R. Alden.

Consulate-General: 280 Moross Rd, Gross Point Farms, MI 48236; tel (313) 884-7075.
Honorary Vice-Consul: Thomas Benton Stevens.

Consulate-General: 3 Dunford Circle, Kansas City, MO 64112; tel (816) 932-7100; fax (816) 361-6891.
Honorary Consul-General: John Latshaw.

Consulate-General: 7134 South Yale, Suite 600, Tulsa, OK 74136; tel (918) 494-0992.
Honorary Consul-General: Richard H. Hughes.

Consulate-General: 205 SE Spokane St, Portland, OR 97202; tel (503) 238-1814; fax (503) 238-1815.
Honorary Consul-General: Edwin Stanley.

Consulate-General: 1717 Main St, Suite 4100, Dallas, TX 75201.
Honorary Consul-General: W. Forrest Smith.

Consulate-General: 4401 North Mesa, Suite 200, El Paso, TX 79902; tel (915) 533-9511; fax (816) 361-6891.
Honorary Consul-General: Charles Holland Leavell.

Consulate-General: 1 North King St, Suite 200, Honolulu, HI 96817; tel (808) 524-3888.
Honorary Consul-General: Sunao Miyabara.
Honorary Vice-Consul: Colin T. Miyabara.

Consulate: Condominio Avila 11-F, Calle Costa Rica 159, Urb. Pinero, Hato Rey, Puerto Rico; tel 753-7276; fax 753-7276.
Honorary Consul: Rolando J. Piernes Alfonso.
Honorary Vice-Consul: Carmen V. Menendez Piernes.

TOGO

Embassy: 2208 Massachusetts Ave, NW, Washington, DC 20008; tel (202) 234-4212; telex 64129.
Ambassador: Ellom-Kodjo Schuppius.

Consulate-General: 112 East 40th St, New York, NY 10016; tel (212) 490-3455; telex 236453.

Consulate: Southeast Financial Center, Suite 3532, 200 South Biscayne Blvd, Miami, FL 33131; tel (305) 371-4286.
Honorary Consul: Michael Stuart Hacker.

TONGA

Consulate-General: 360 Post St, Suite 604, San Francisco, CA 94108; tel (415) 781-0365; fax (415) 781-3964.
Consul-General: Mele Vikatolia Tuku'aho.
Consul: Emeline U. Tuita.

TRINIDAD AND TOBAGO

Embassy: 1708 Massachusetts Ave, NW, Washington, DC 20036; tel (202) 467-6490; fax (202) 785-3130.
Ambassador: Angus Albert Khan.

Consulate-General: 331-3 Graybar Bldg, 420 Lexington Ave, New York, NY 10017; tel (212) 682-7272.
Consul-General: Learie E. Rousseau.
Deputy Consul-General: John G. S. Gillette.
Consul: Brindsley Peters.
Consul: John Blake.

Consulate: 180 NE Shopping Plaza, Sarasota, FL 33580.
Honorary Consul: Wylene Lam.

TUNISIA

Embassy: 1515 Massachusetts Ave, NW, Washington, DC 20005; tel (202) 862-1850; fax (202) 862-1858.
Ambassador: Dr Abdelaziz Hamzaoui.

Consulate: One Battery Park Plaza, New York, NY 10004; tel (212) 742-6585.
Honorary Consul: Andre O. Backar.

Consulate-General: 3401 Sacramento St, San Francisco, CA 94118; tel (415) 922-9222.
Honorary Consul-General: Proctor Patterson Jones.

Consulate: 7480 Fairway Drive, Suite 206, Miami, FL 33014; tel (305) 556-1079.
Honorary Consul: Deborah B. Jackson.

TURKEY

Embassy: 1714 Massachusetts Ave, NW, Washington, DC 20036; tel (202) 659-8200.
Ambassador: Nuzhet Kandemir.

Consulate-General: 821 United Nations Plaza, New York, NY 10017; tel (212) 949-0160.
Consul-General: Volkan Bozkir.
Deputy Consul-General: Gunes Altan.
Deputy Consul-General: Vefahan Ocak.
Consul: Nejat Akcal.
Consul: Ugur Ariner.

Consulate-General: 4801 Wilshire Blvd, Beverley Hills, Los Angeles, CA 90010; tel (213) 937-0118.
Consul-General: Mehmet Emre.
Vice-Consul: Serdar Kilic.

Consulate-General: 55 Sutter St, Suite 572, Oakland, CA 94104.
Honorary Consul-General: Bonnie Joy Kaslan.

Consulate-General: Southeast Financial Center, 200 Biscayne Blvd, Suite 3532, Miami, FL 33131-2331; tel (305) 371-4286.
Honorary Consul-General: Michael S. Hacker.

Consulate-General: 1100-1 Piedmont Ave, Atlanta, GA 30309; tel (404) 872-9610.
Honorary Consul-General: Ali Yavuz Tarcan.

Consulate-General: 360 North Michigan Ave, Suites 1404-8, Chicago, IL 60601; tel (312) 263-0644.
Consul-General: Mehmet Taser.
Vice-Consul: Emre Yunt.
Consular Agent: Kadir Yuksel.

Consulate-General: 6711 Rainbow, Mission Hills, KS 66208; tel (913) 236-6670.
Honorary Consul-General: Jeffrey P. Hillelson.

Consulate-General: 313 Wendover Rd, Baltimore, MD 21218; tel (301) 889-0697.
Honorary Consul-General: Cenap Remzi Kiratli.

Consulate-General: 1990 Post Oak Central, Houston, TX 77056; tel (713) 622-5849.
Consul-General: Mengu Buyukdavras.
Vice-Consul: Mustafa B. Hizlan.

UGANDA

Embassy: 5909 16th St, NW, Washington, DC 20011; tel (202) 726-7100; fax (202) 726-1727.
Ambassador: Stephen Katenta-Apuli.
Minister-Counsellor: Francis E. S. Katana.
Second Secretary: Albert Mutebi.
Third Secretary: Philip Odida.

UNITED ARAB EMIRATES

Embassy: 600 New Hampshire Ave, NW, Suite 740, Washington, DC 20037; tel (202) 338-6500.
Ambassador: Abdulla bin Zayed al-Nahayyan.

UNITED KINGDOM

Embassy: 3100 Massachusetts Ave, NW, Washington, DC 20008; tel (202) 462-1340; telex 892384; fax (202) 898-4255.
Ambassador: Sir Robin Renwick.
Minister (Commercial): C. J. R. Meyer.
Minister (Economic): D. L. C. Peretz.
Minister (Hong Kong Economic and Trade Affairs): P. Lo.

Minister: A. M. Wood.
Minister (Defence Material): C. V. Balmer.
Counsellor (Congressional) and Head of Chancery: R. P. Ralph.
Counsellor (Press/Public Affairs): N. W. Browne.
Counsellor (Commercial): D. J. Hall.
Counsellor (Management) and Consul-General: A. F. Smith.
Counsellor (Political/Military): K. R. Tebbit.
Counsellor (External Affairs): P. J. Tory.
Counsellor (Science/Technology/Energy): A. W. R. Allcock.
Counsellor (Transport): R. J. Griffiths.
Counsellor (Overseas Development): R. M. Graham-Harrison.
Counsellor (Defence/Science/Equipment): L. N. Large.
Counsellor (Defence Supply): B. J. Limbert.
Counsellor (Hong Kong Economic and Trade Affairs): P. C. Leung.
Counsellor (Economic): M. E. Brown.
Counsellor: J. D. N. R. Clibborn.
Counsellor: J. D. Hansen.
Counsellor: R. J. Nicholls.
Counsellor: Elizabeth Manningham-Buller.
Head of Defence Staff and Defence Attaché: Air Vice-Marshal P. Dodworth.
Joint Warfare and Assistant Defence Attaché: Col D. C. L. Rowe.
Assistant Defence Attaché: Group Capt. D. W. F. Angela.
Naval Attaché and Commander of Navy Staff: Rear Adm. A. P. Hoddinott.
Assistant Naval Attaché: Capt. A. D. E. Pender-Cudlip.
Military Attaché and Commander of Army Staff: Brig. E. F. G. Burton.
Assistant Military Attaché: Col J. G. Hamilton-Russell.
Assistant Military Attaché: Col J. D. Sankey.
Air Attaché and Commander of Air Force Staff: Air Cdre R. G. Peters.
Assistant Air Attaché: Group Capt. T. J. Beney.
Attaché (Defence Supply–SDI): V. Starkey.
Attaché (Civil Air): V. S. Brennan.
Attaché (Atomic Co-ordination): A. C. Parmee.
Attaché (Defence Equipment–Air): C. Jones.
Attaché (Defence Equipment–Maritime): Dr J. M. Williams.
Attaché (Defence Equipment–Land): J. Platt.
Attaché (Defence Equipment–Intellectual Property Rights): M. S. Sedgewick.
Attaché (Defence Supply): J. A. Kenny.
First Secretary (Defence Supply–Sea Systems): H. G. Thomas.
First Secretary (Defence Supply–Air Systems): C. McLaughlin.
First Secretary (Defence Supply–Land Systems): S. Johns.
First Secretary (Political/Military): A. M. Thomson.
First Secretary (Works): J. R. Chandler.
First Secretary (Consul): G. B. Anderson.
First Secretary (Press/Public Affairs): M. A. Price.
First Secretary (Management): D. Clarke.
First Secretary (Science): R. D. Jennings.
First Secretary (Technology): R. Egginton.
First Secretary (Agricultural/Commercial): D. Dawson.
First Secretary (Energy): Dr S. R. Sklaroff.
First Secretary (Economic): P. F. L. Allum.
First Secretary (Commercial): M. K. Page.
First Secretary (Commercial): A. Heath.
First Secretary (Commercial): E. Hosker.
First Secretary (Transport): D. L. McMillan.
First Secretary (Hong Kong Economic and Trade Affairs): R. Chan.
Third Secretary (Royal Visits): C. A. Wilson.

Consulate-General and Trade and Investment Office: 845 Third Ave, New York, NY 10022; tel (212) 745-0200; telex 216756; fax (212) 735-3062.
Consul-General and Director-General of Trade and Investment: A. J. Hunter.
Deputy Consul-General and Counsellor (Joint Management Office): I. C. Sloane.
Deputy Consul-General and Director of Investment: M. E. Frost.
Deputy Consul-General and Director of Trade Development: Guy P. Lockton.
First Secretary (Information/Press/Public Affairs): B. E. Kirk.
Second Secretary (Management): W. G. D. Johnson.
Second Secretary (Computer Manager): J. J. Burton.
Third Secretary (Accountant): M. Douglas-Hiley.
Consul (Commercial): R. A. Cambridge.
Consul (Commercial/Economic): P. W. Hare.
Consul (Investment): R. G. Robinshaw.

Consulate-General: Marquis I Tower, Suite 2700, 245 Peachtree Center Ave, Atlanta, GA 30303; tel (404) 524-5868; telex 240024; fax (404) 524-3153.
Consul-General: B. T. Holmes.
Consul (Commercial): D. L. Hardinge.

Consulate-General: Federal Reserve Plaza, 25th Floor, 600 Atlantic Ave, Boston, MA 02210; tel (617) 248-9555; telex 940994; fax (617) 248-9578.
Consul-General: J. W. Owen.
Deputy Consul-General: A. White.
Vice-Consul (Commercial): M. Harrison.
Vice-Consul (Commercial): N. J. Gaymond.
Vice-Consul (Management): K. M. Tunsley.
Vice-Consul (Information/Public Affairs): A. Kanter.

Consulate-General: 33 North Dearborn St, Chicago, IL 60602; tel (312) 346-1810; telex 254432; fax (312) 346-7021.
Consul-General: F. R. Mingay.
Deputy Consul-General: M. W. Hewitt.
Vice-Consul (Management): R. H. Gordon.
Vice-Consul (Commercial): R. A. Hoffman.
Vice-Consul (Commercial): E. N. Brown.
Vice-Consul (Commercial Publicity): H. Refetoff.
Vice-Consul (Information): C. P. Cracraft.

Consulate-General: 1100 Milam Bldg, Suite 2660, 1100 Milam, Houston, TX 77002-5506; tel (713) 659-6278; telex 762307; fax (713) 659-7094.
Consul-General: B. J. Everett.
Deputy Consul-General and Consul (Commercial): M. B. Magee.
Vice-Consul (Management/Consular): I. C. Kingston.
Vice-Consul (Commercial): S. C. de Steiguer.
Vice-Consul (Information): H. Mann.

Consulate-General: 3701 Wilshire Blvd, Suite 312, Los Angeles, CA 90010; tel (213) 385-7381; telex 759365; fax (213) 381-5450.
Consul-General: R. E. Holloway.
Consul (Commercial): M. T. Jones.
Consul (Internal Investment): J. T. Morrison.
Consul: H. E. Sadler.
Vice-Consul (Information): J. O. Houlton.
Vice-Consul (Public Affairs): A. Mackay.

Consulate-General: 1 Sansome St, Suite 850, San Francisco, CA 94104; tel (415) 981-3030; telex 340628; fax (415) 434-2018.
Consul-General: A. Ford.
Deputy Consul-General and Consul (Commercial): J. A. Elsdon.

Consulate: Lafayette Towers, Suite 1-D, 4601 Mayflower Rd, Norfolk, VA 23508; tel (804) 627-1934.
Honorary Consul: Dr Theodore Bliss.

Consulate: Brickell Bay Office Tower, Suite 2110, 1001 South Bayshore Drive, Miami, FL 33131; tel (305) 374-1522; telex 215851; fax (305) 374-1522.
Consul: P. W. Grice.
Vice-Consul (Commercial): R. Woods.
Vice-Consul (Customs): G. Honey.

Consulate: 55 Public Sq., Suite 1650, Cleveland, OH 44113-1963; tel (216) 621-7674; telex 980126; fax (216) 621-2615.
Honorary Consul: M. C. Gathercole.

Consulate: c/o Hallmark Cards Inc., 2501 McGee Trafficway, Kansas City, MO 64108; tel (816) 274-5400; telex 426115.
Honorary Consul: Stanley A. Hamilton.

Consulate: 625 Skinker Blvd, St Louis, MO 63105; tel (314) 725-5949.
Honorary Consul: V. W. Lammert.

Consulate: 813 Stemmons Tower West, 2730 Stemmons Freeway, Dallas, TX 75207; tel (214) 637-3600; telex 730382; fax (214) 634-9408.
Consul (Commercial): J. D. Clark.
Vice-Consul: B. G. Naifeh.

Consulate: 321 St Charles Ave, 10th Floor, New Orleans, LA 70130; tel (504) 586-8300.
Honorary Consul: J. J. Coleman, Jr.
Honorary Vice-Consul: A. B. Jeffrey.

Consulate: Mather & Co., 226 Walnut St, Philadelphia, PA 19106; tel (215) 925-0118.
Honorary Consul: Charles E. Mather.

Consulate: 3515 SW Council Crest Drive, Portland, OR 97508; tel (503) 227-5669.
Honorary Consul: A. Hay.

Consulate: 820 First Interstate Center, 999 Third Ave, Seattle, WA 98104; tel (206) 622-9255; telex 329602; fax (206) 622-4728.
Consul (Commercial): S. E. Turner.
Vice-Consul and Commercial Officer: L. R. Trousdale.

Consulate: University of Alaska, Anchorage, College of Arts and Sciences, 2311 Providence Drive, Anchorage, AK 99508; tel (907) 786-4848.
Honorary Consul: Dr D. R. M. Hitchins.

Consulate: 1 Taft St, Suite 5E, Santurce, Puerto Rico 00911; tel 728-6715; fax 728-6366.
Honorary Consul: Dr I. Court.

URUGUAY

Embassy: 1918 F St, NW, Washington, DC 20006; tel (202) 331-1313; fax (202) 321-8142.
Chargé d'affaires a.i.: Juan Podesta Piñon.
Consul: Alvaro Enrique González.

Consulate-General: 747 Third Ave, 37th Floor, New York, NY 10017; tel (212) 753-8193.
Consul-General: Julio Tealdi.
Deputy Consul-General: Cristina Carrion.

Consulate-General: Pacific Plaza Tower, 1431 Ocean Ave, Suite 1100, Santa Monica, Los Angeles, CA 90401.
Consul-General: Olga R. Barbarov.

Consulate-General: 25 SE Second Ave, Suite 1050, Miami, FL 33131; tel (305) 236-3369.
Consul: Mercedes M. Rodríguez.

Consulate: 564 Market St, Suite 200, San Francisco, CA 94101.
Honorary Consul: John Bennett Ritchie.

Consulate: 79 West Monroe St, Suite 1310, Chicago, IL 60603-4901; tel (312) 236-3369.
Honorary Consul: Felix Stungevicius.

Consulate: 540 World Trade Center, 2 Canal St, New Orleans, LA; tel (504) 525-8354.

Consulate: 743 Heinel Drive, St Paul, MN 55113.
Honorary Consul: Stanley L. Diesch.

Consulate: Himalaya 254, Monterrey Urb., Rio Piedras, San Juan, Puerto Rico 00926.
Honorary Consul: Josefina Gomez de Hillyer.

VENEZUELA

Embassy: 1099 30th St, NW, Washington, DC 20008; tel (202) 342-2214; telex 440071; fax (202) 342-6801.
Ambassador: Simon Alberto Consalvi.
Minister-Counsellor: Carlos Bivero.
Minister-Counsellor (Technical): William Larralde Paez.
Counsellor: Pedro Emilio Carrillo.
Counsellor: Fidel Garofalo Laya.
Counsellor (Technical): Anibal Ciffoni.
Counsellor (Technical): Ramon Hernández.
First Secretary: Maria E. Perez Vera.
First Secretary: Andres Eloy Rindon T.
First Secretary (Technical): Ana Hernández de P.
Second Secretary: Carlos Amador Perez Silva.

Consulate-General: 7 East 51st St, New York, NY 10022; tel (212) 826-1660.
Consul-General: Guillermo E. Herrera.
Deputy Consul-General: Tatiana Perez de Sucre.
Consul: Claudio Sorio Fermin.
Consul: Cristina García-Metsch.

Consulate-General: 455 Market St, Suite 209, San Francisco, CA 94102; tel (415) 421-5172.
Consul: Guillermo J. Madrid.
Consul: Maria de los A. Chacin Morales.

Consulate-General: 1101 Brickell Ave, Suite 901, Miami, FL 33131; tel (305) 577-3824.
Consul-General: Magda Ruiz Pineda.
Consul: Maria J. Baez-Loreto.

Consulate-General: 20 North Wacker Drive, Suite 750, Chicago, IL 60606; tel (312) 236-9655.
Consul-General: Edna Maria Figuera.
Vice-Consul: Dimas González Snaidero.

Consulate-General: 1006-9 World Trade Center, New Orleans, LA 70130; tel (504) 522-3284.
Consul: José Salvador Briceno Pantin.
Vice-Consul: Omar Calzadilla.

Consulate-General: 111 Water St, Suite 402, Baltimore, MD; tel (301) 962-0362.
Consul-General: Simon A. Faraco.
Consul: Duvis Urdaneta.

Consulate-General: 545 Boylston St, 6th Floor, Boston, MA; tel (617) 266-9355.
Consul-General: Astrid Josefina Consalvi de Lepage.
Consul: Maria Adelaida Manrique de Guerrero.

Consulate-General: New Market at Head House, Suite 303, Philadelphia, PA 19147.
Consul-General: Raul Itriago Toro.
Vice-Consul: Luis A. Farias Tineo.

Consulate-General: 2700 South Post Oak Blvd, Suite 1500, Houston, TX 77027; tel (713) 961-5141.
Consul-General: Violeta Mato de Vazquez.
Consul: Teodoro Thielen.

Consulate-General: Edif. Mercantil Plaza, 6°, Of. 601, Avda Ponce de Leon, Hato Rey, San Juan, Puerto Rico 00907; tel 725-4055.
Consul-General: Felix Poleo.
Consul: José J. Romero.

WESTERN SAMOA

Embassy: 1155 15th St, Suite 510, NW, Washington, DC 20005; tel (202) 833-1743; fax (202) 833-1746.
Ambassador: Tuaopepe Fili Wendt.

Consulate: 5150 Wilshire Blvd, Los Angeles, CA 90036.
Honorary Consul: James Gray Rough.

YEMEN

Embassy: 600 New Hampshire Ave, Suite 840, NW, Washington, DC 20037; tel (202) 965-4760; telex 897027; fax (202) 337-2017.
Ambassador: Mohsin Ahmed Alaini.
Consul-General: Ali Dawod.

Consulate-General: One Parklane Blvd, Suite 1028 West, Dearborn, Detroit, MI 48126; tel (313) 271-0840.
Consul: Abdulrabuh Ali al-Hadad.

Consulate: 388 Market St, Suite 1050, San Francisco, CA 94111; tel (415) 989-3636.
Consul: Abdullah A. M. al-Shaobi.

YUGOSLAVIA

Embassy: 2410 California Ave, NW, Washington, DC 20008; tel (202) 462-6566; fax (202) 797-9663.
Ambassador: Dzevad Mujezinović.
Consul-General: Dusan Paunovic.

Consulate-General: 767 Third Ave, 17th Floor, New York, NY 10017; tel (212) 838-2300.
Consul-General: David Dasic.
Deputy Consul-General: Maja Levi.
Deputy Consul-General: Ivo Segedin.
Consul: Iljir Hasani.
Consul: Milos Nikolic.

Consulate-General: 307 North Michigan Ave, Suite 1600, Chicago, IL 60601; tel (312) 332-0169.
Consul-General: Stanojlo Glisic.
Consul: Petar Soljak.
Consul: Zdravko Stolanovic.
Consul: Kosta Jankovski.

Consulate-General: 1375 Sutter St, Suite 406, San Francisco, CA 94109; tel (415) 776-4941.
Consul: Predrag Backovic.
Vice-Consul: Srdjan Simonovic.
Vice-Consul: Radmila Imamovic.

Consulate-General: Park Center, 1700 East St, Suite 4R, Cleveland, OH 44114; tel (216) 621-2093.
Consul-General: Matjaz Jancar.
Consul: Lence Mitevska-Avramova.

Consulate-General: 625 Stanwix St, Suite 1605, Pittsburgh, PA 15222; tel (412) 471-6191.
Consul: Stojanovic Bozidar.
Vice-Consul: Slobodan Muscic.

Consulate: 1801 Broadway, Suite 1420, Denver, CO 80202.
Honorary Consul: Raymond P. Kogovsek.

Consulate: 419 Carmen St, Jacksonville, FL 32206.
Honorary Consul: Hy W. Kliman.

Consulate: 2958 North 70th Terrace, Kansas City, KS 66109; tel (913) 371-1763.
Honorary Consul: Charles Sugar.

Consulate: 910 Turquoise St, New Orleans, LA 70124; tel (504) 288-6202.
Honorary Consul: Zeljko Franks.

ZAIRE

Embassy: 1800 New Hampshire Ave, NW, Washington, DC 20009; tel (202) 234-7960.
Ambassador: Tatanene Manata.

Consulate-General: 529 Fifth Ave, New York, NY 10017.
Honorary Consul-General: Maurice Tempelsman.

ZAMBIA

Embassy: 2419 Massachusetts Ave, NW, Washington, DC 20008; tel (202) 265-9717; telex 440247; fax (202) 332-0826.
Ambassador: Dr Paul J. F. Lusaka.
Counsellor: Lazarous Kapambwe.
First Secretary (Administrative): Exwell C. Chisambisha.
First Secretary (Economic): Benny Chundu.
Second Secretary (Accounts): Chris S. Sinkala.
Third Secretary (Communications): Ephraim B. Namukombo.
Third Secretary: Edith Muhundika.

ZIMBABWE

Embassy: 1608 New Hampshire Ave, NW, Washington, DC 20009; tel (202) 332-7100; telex 248402; fax (202) 438-9326.
Ambassador: Stanislaus Garikai Chigwedere.
Minister-Counsellor: Mark Gray Marongwe.
Counsellor (Political) and Head of Chancery: Enos Mafemba.
Counsellor (Political): T. P. Chadenga.
Counsellor (Commercial): Norman M. Chakanetsa.
Counsellor (Information): Thomas Bvuma.
Defence, Military and Air Attaché: Lieut Col Michael M. Muchena.
First Secretary: Winpeg Moyo.
Second Secretary (Finance): Thomas T. Musingarimi.
Third Secretary (Administration): Margaret Mateta.
Third Secretary: Bekithemba R. Mhlanga.
Third Secretary: Chiedza Mugari.
Attaché: Cyprian M. Nyashanu.

International Organizations

EUROPEAN COMMUNITIES

External Delegation: 7th Floor, Suite 707, 2100 M St, NW, Washington, DC 20037; tel (202) 862-9500; telex 64215; fax (202) 429-1766.
Head of Delegation: Andreas A. M. van Agt.
Minister and Deputy Head of Delegation: Corrado Pirzio-Biroli.
Counsellor (Agriculture): Jacques Vonthron.
Counsellor (Press and Public Affairs): Peter Doyle.
Counsellor (Science and Technology): Gilbert Fayl.
First Secretary (Commercial Affairs): Richard Wright.
First Secretary (Economic and Financial): Pascal Arnaud.
First Secretary (Transportation, Energy and Environment): Gilbert Dubois.
Second Secretary (Press and Public Affairs): Pierrette Pelhate.
Attaché (Agriculture): John Sinclair.
Attaché (Administration): Jan Bos.

External Delegation: 3 Dag Hammarskjöld Plaza, 305 East 47th St, New York, NY 10017; tel (212) 371-3804; telex 012396; fax (212) 758-2718.
Head of Delegation: Eamonn Gallagher.

Sub-Office attached to Washington: 44 Montgomery St, Suite 2715, San Francisco, CA 94104; tel (415) 391-3476; telex 215107; fax (415) 391-3641.
Head of Office: Bärbel Jacob.

URUGUAY

ARGENTINA

Embassy: Avda Agraciada 3397, Montevideo; tel (2) 393953; telex 863.
Ambassador: Dr Carlos Humberto Perette.

AUSTRIA

Consulate-General: Maldonado 1193/2, 11100 Montevideo; tel (2) 914000; telex 901.
Consul-General: Pedro Slowak.
Honorary Consul: Gertrude Hoffer.

BELGIUM

Embassy: Leyenda Patria 2880, 4°, 11300 Montevideo; tel (2) 701571; telex 22612.
Ambassador: Roger Tyberghein.

BOLIVIA

Embassy: Río Branco 1320, 4°, Of. 401, Montevideo.
Chargé d'affaires: Ana María Siles de Regules.

BRAZIL

Embassy: Blvd Artigas 1328, Montevideo; telex 6310.
Ambassador: Eduardo Moreira Hossannah.

BULGARIA

Embassy: Rambla Mahatma Gandhi 647, 5°, Casilla 502, Montevideo.
Ambassador: Dimitur Markov Marchevski.

CANADA

Consulate: Juan Carlos Gomez 1348-1, Montevideo; tel (2) 958234; telex 829.
Honorary Consul: R. Lannes Clinton.

CHILE

Embassy: Andes 1365, 2°, Montevideo; telex 6418.
Ambassador: Juan Guillermo Toro Dávila.

CHINA, PEOPLE'S REPUBLIC

Embassy: Montevideo.
Ambassador: Yang Xugiang.

COLOMBIA

Embassy: Juncal 1305, 18°, Montevideo; telex 6587.
Ambassador: Dr Santiago Salazar Santos.

COSTA RICA

Embassy: Calle José Martí 3295, Apdo 102, 11300 Montevideo; tel (2) 783645; fax (2) 789714.
Ambassador: Jaime Botey Brenes.
Minister-Counsellor and Head of Consular Affairs: Juan W. Valanzuela.
Counsellor (Economic): Remigio Moreno de la Torre.
Attaché (Commercial): Ligia María Botey.

CUBA

Embassy: Bulevar Artigas 1125, entre Canelone y Maldonado, Montevideo; tel (2) 416512; telex 23031; fax (2) 482140.
Ambassador: Abelardo Curbelo Padrón.
Counsellor: José Fernández Vilela.
Counsellor (Commercial): René Alfonso.
Third Secretary (Consular): Plácido Fernández Méndez.

CYPRUS

Consulate: Avda Gen. Rondeau 2030/27, Apdo 532, Montevideo; tel (2) 233336; telex 22252; fax (2) 237043.
Honorary Consul: Panayiotis Tsakos.
Honorary Vice-Consul: Capt. Demeitrios Linas.

CZECHOSLOVAKIA

Embassy: Luis B. Cavia 2996, Casilla 12262, Montevideo; tel (2) 787808.
Ambassador: Zdeněk Pisek.

DENMARK

Consulate-General: Calle Colonia 981, 5°, Montevideo; tel (2) 915238; telex 26919; fax (2) 983793.
Consul-General: Jørgen Ulrich Larsen.
Vice-Consul: Elizabeth M. Brugnini.

DOMINICAN REPUBLIC

Embassy: Plaza Independencia 838, 5°, Of. 31, Montevideo.
Ambassador: Dr Jesús María Hernández Sánchez.

ECUADOR

Embassy: Rambla República del Perú 1395, 1°, Casilla 1001, Montevideo; telex 845.
Ambassador: Gustavo Cordóvez Pareja.

EGYPT

Embassy: Avda Brasil 2663, Montevideo; tel (2) 781553; telex 22391.
Ambassador: Farouk M. Baraka.

EL SALVADOR

Embassy: Buxareo 1117, Casilla 203, Montevideo; tel (2) 794831; telex 23095; fax (2) 510878.
Ambassador: Leopoldo Canessa.

FINLAND

Consulate-General: Solís 1533, Casilla 248, Montevideo; tel (2) 958463; telex 22025; fax (2) 960059.
Consul-General: Ronald Cooper.

FRANCE

Embassy: Avda Uruguay 853, Casilla 290, Montevideo; tel (2) 920077; telex 6986.
Ambassador: André Cira.

GERMANY

Embassy: La Cumparsita 1417-35, Casilla 20014, Montevideo; tel (2) 908041; telex 23764; fax (2) 923422.
Ambassador: Dr Ludger Buerstedde.

GUATEMALA

Embassy: Blvd España 2921, Casilla 301, Montevideo; tel (2) 782104.
Ambassador: Dr Juan Alfredo Rendón Maldonado.

HOLY SEE

Apostolic Nunciature: Blvd Artigas 1270, Casilla 1503, Montevideo; tel (2) 411410; fax (2) 488949.
Ambassador: Archbishop Francesco de Nittis.
Secretary: Mgr Joseph Marino.

HONDURAS

Embassy: Pagola 3306/501, Casilla 338, Montevideo; telex 22629.
Ambassador: Dr Hernán Antonio Bermúdez Aguilar.

HUNGARY

Embassy: Dr Prudencio de Pena 2469, Montevideo; tel (2) 786173; telex 23232.
Ambassador: Bela Szabo.

ICELAND

Consulate-General: Calle Rincón 531, Of. 401, Montevideo; tel (2) 960296; telex 22421; fax (2) 963660.
Consul-General: Walter R. Koltonski.

ISRAEL

Embassy: Blvd Artigas 1585, Montevideo; tel (2) 404164; telex 26497.
Ambassador: Avraham Toledo.

ITALY

Embassy: José B. Lamas 2857, Casilla 268, Montevideo; tel (2) 785316; telex 22077.
Ambassador: Dr Tommaso de Vergottini.

JAPAN

Embassy: Blvd Artigas 953, Casilla 1273, Montevideo; tel (2) 487645; telex 23807; fax (2) 487980.
Ambassador: Kinnosuke Hirooka.

KOREA, REPUBLIC

Embassy: Jaime Zudáñes 2836, Casilla 12135, 11300 Montevideo; telex 22343.
Ambassador: Tak Ra-Hyoun.

LEBANON

Embassy: Rivera 2278, Montevideo; tel (2) 486365; telex 22257.
Ambassador: Riad Kantar.

MALTA

Embassy: Sarandí 123, 11000 Montevideo; tel (2) 962629; fax (2) 962264.
Ambassador: Dr Raymundo Podesta Wilmart.

MEXICO

Embassy: Juncal 1305, 16°, Montevideo; tel (2) 916890; telex 6473 .
Ambassador: Arturo González Sánchez.

NETHERLANDS

Embassy: Leyenda Patria 2880, 2°, Casilla 1519, Montevideo; telex 22273.
Ambassador: Eldred G. Maduro.

NICARAGUA

Embassy: Rambla República del Perú 1139, Montevideo.

Chargé d'affaires a.i.: Mario Duarte Zamora.

PANAMA

Embassy: Rambla Mahatma Gandhi 509, Casilla 404, Montevideo.
Ambassador: Alexis Cabrera Quintero.

PARAGUAY

Embassy: Blvd Artigas 1526, Montevideo; telex 6440.
Ambassador: Miguel Teófilo Romero.

PERU

Embassy: Soriano 1124, Casilla 126, Montevideo; tel (2) 921194; telex 26985; fax (2) 921194.
Ambassador: Jorge del Campo Vidal.

POLAND

Embassy: Jorge Canning 2389, Montevideo; telex 6447.
Ambassador: Eugeniusz Trzepizur.

PORTUGAL

Embassy: Avda Dr Francisco Soca 1128, Apdo 701, 11300 Montevideo; tel (2) 784061; telex 22318.
Ambassador: Dr Manuel Barreiros Martins.

ROMANIA

Embassy: Ing. Federico Abadie 2940, Casilla 102, Montevideo; telex 23766.
Chargé d'affaires: Anton Donciu.

RUSSIA

Embassy: Blvd España 2741, Montevideo; tel (2) 700722.
Ambassador: Yuri V. Lebedev.

SOUTH AFRICA

Embassy: Dr Prudencio de Pena 2483, Montevideo; tel (2) 790411; telex 22175; fax (2) 790401.
Chargé d'affaires a.i.: Abraham J. Marais.
First Secretary: M. Malan.
Second Secretary (Administrative): D. Barron.

SPAIN

Embassy: Avda Brasil 2786, Montevideo; tel (2) 786010; telex 22439.
Ambassador: Federico Garayalde.

SWEDEN

Embassy: Avda Brasil 3079, 6°, Pocitos, Casilla 12016, Distrito 2, 11300 Montevideo; tel (2) 780088; telex 23151; fax (2) 782489.
Counsellor: Göran Bolin.
Consul: Anna Ingegerd Margareta Axelsdotter Barfod.

SWITZERLAND

Embassy: Calle Federico Abadie 2036/40, Apdo 810, 11°, 11300 Montevideo; tel (2) 704315; telex 23175; fax (2) 715031.
Ambassador: Jacques Rial.
Secretary: Jürg Siegenthaler.

UNITED KINGDOM

Embassy: Marco Bruto 1073, Montevideo; tel (2) 623625; telex 22249 ; fax (2) 627815.
Ambassador: D. A. Lamont.
First Secretary, Consul and Deputy Head of Mission: A. T. J. Lovelock.
Defence, Naval, Military and Air Attaché: Capt. R. A. Highton.
First Secretary (Chancery/Information): R. J. Hutchings.
Second Secretary (Commercial) and Vice-Consul: B. A. McIntyre.

USA

Embassy: Lauro Muller 1776, Montevideo; tel (2) 236061; fax (2) 488611.
Ambassador: Richard C. Brown.
Deputy Head of Mission: John P. Jurecky.
Political Section: Gerard R. Pascua.
Economic and Commercial Sections: John E. Hope.
Labour Officer: Charles W. Evans.
Administrative Officer: John M. Salazar.
Consular Section: Paul M. Doherty.
Regional Security Officer: Richard A. Shoupe.
Public Affairs Officer: Frank L. Jenista.
Agency for International Development: Peter R. Orr.
Office of Defence Attaché: Capt. Marshall W. Bronson.
Military Assistance Advisory Group: Col Curtis S. Morris.
Communications Programme Officer: Kenneth E. Parton.

VENEZUELA

Embassy: Dr Manuel Albo 2675, Montevideo; tel (2) 472788; telex 23035.
Ambassador: Luis La Corte.
Counsellor: Antonieta Arcaya de R.
First Secretary: Maria Eugenia Perez Godoy.

YUGOSLAVIA

Embassy: Blvd España 2697, Montevideo.
Ambassador: Ljubisa Jeremić.

International Organizations

EUROPEAN COMMUNITIES

External Delegation: Edif. Artigas, 1°, Rincón 487, Montevideo; tel (2) 963744; telex 23925; fax (2) 953653.
Head of Office: Franco Teucci.
First Secretary: José Félix Merladet.
Attaché (Administrative): Ingeborg Lohner.

UZBEKISTAN

AFGHANISTAN

Consulate-General: Tashkent, Gogolya ul. 73; tel (371) 33-91-80.
Consul-General: Hafizullah Ebodi.
Second Secretary: Mr Ahgharnoosh.
Third Secretary: Enayatullah Ishaq.

CHINA, PEOPLE'S REPUBLIC

Embassy: Tashkent.

CUBA

Consulate-General: Tashkent, Timiryazeva ul.; tel (371) 35-07-77.

INDIA

Consulate-General: Tashkent, A. Tolstova ul. 5; tel (371) 33-37-82.
Consul-General: A. K. Mukharjee.
Consul: S. K. Behera.
Consul: G. G. Kulkarni.
Attaché: B. S. Saini.

LIBYA

Consulate-General: Tashkent, Engelsa ul. 95; tel (371) 35-20-09.
Consul-General: Mabruk el-Gamoudi Omran.
Consul: Azam Sasi.

MONGOLIA

Consulate-General: Tashkent, Gogolya ul.; tel (371) 33-98-47.
Consul-General: B. Bud.

USA

Embassy: Tashkent.

VANUATU

AUSTRALIA

High Commission: KPMG House, POB 111, Port Vila; tel 2777; telex 1030; fax 3948.
High Commissioner: David Ambrose.

CHINA, PEOPLE'S REPUBLIC

Embassy: Private Mail Bag 071, Port Vila; tel 3598; fax 3598.

FRANCE

Embassy: Kumul Highway, POB 60, Port Vila; tel 2353; telex 1029; fax 2695.
Chargé d'affaires a.i.: Philippe Guerin.

NEW ZEALAND

High Commission: Prouds Bldg, Kumul Highway, POB 161, Port Vila; tel 2933; telex 1121; fax 2518.
High Commissioner: Caroline Forsyth.
Second Secretary: Mary-Anne Crompton.
Second Secretary: Christine Anderson.

SWEDEN

Consulate: Tagabe Roundabout, POB 169, Port Vila; tel 2499; fax 22276.
Consul: Karl Erik Gustav Waldebäck.

UNITED KINGDOM

High Commission: KPMG House, rue Pasteur, POB 567, Port Vila; tel 3100; telex 1027; fax 3651.
High Commissioner: T. J. Duggin.
Second Secretary: D. R. Miller.
Third Secretary (Aid): R. Hyland.

International Organizations

EUROPEAN COMMUNITIES

Sub-Office of Delegation for the Solomon Islands: Pilioko House, 1st Floor, Kumul Highway, POB 422, Port Vila; tel 2501; telex 1093; fax 3282.
Representative: Edwin Vos.

THE VATICAN CITY (THE HOLY SEE)

ARGENTINA

Mission: Palazzo Patrizi, Piazza S. Luigi de' Francesi 37, 00186 Rome; tel (6) 6541701; fax (6) 6879021.
Ambassador: Juan Carlos Enrique Katzenstein.
Minister-Counsellor: Carlos Arturo Spinosa.
Counsellor: Eduardo Mario Mendizábal.
Attaché: César Eduardo Acuña.
Attaché: Fernando Javier Silva.

AUSTRALIA

Mission: Via Paola 24, Apt 10, 00186 Rome; tel (6) 6877688; telex 610165; fax (6) 6896255.
Ambassador: T. B. McCarthy.

AUSTRIA

Mission: Via Reno 9, 00198 Rome; tel (6) 8417427; fax (6) 8543058.
Ambassador: Georg Hohenberg.
Counsellor (Commercial): Martin Bolldorf.
Secretary (Economic): Karl Kühne.

BELGIUM

Mission: Via G. de Notaris 6A, 00197 Rome; tel (6) 3224740.
Ambassador: Ferdinand de Wilde.
Counsellor: Mgr Werner Quintens.
First Secretary: Dirk Loncke.
Attaché: Lucien Grosjean.

BOLIVIA

Mission: Via Archimede 129/7, 00197 Rome; tel (6) 876876; telex 2024; fax (6) 876876.
Ambassador: Daniel Cabezas Gómez.
Adviser (Ecclesiastical): Juan Sansoe Fusero.
Second Secretary: Carmen Bonifaz.

BRAZIL

Mission: Via della Conciliazione 22, 3rd Floor, 00193 Rome; tel (6) 6875252; telex 612269; fax (6) 6872540.
Ambassador: Gilberto Coutinho Paranhos Velloso.
Minister-Counsellor: Carlos Alberto Pessôa Pardellas.
Counsellor: Sergio Elias Couri.
First Secretary: George Ney de Souza Fernandes.

CANADA

Mission: Via della Conciliazone 4/D, 00193 Rome; tel (6) 6547316; fax (6) 6540283.
Ambassador: Théodore Jean Arcand.
Counsellor: Jacques Bélec.
Attaché: Marc Parisien.
Attaché: Nora Valentino.

CAPE VERDE

Mission: Rua Guerra Mendea 1, Praia, Cape Verde.

CHILE

Mission: Piazza Risorgimento 55/20, 00192 Rome; tel (6) 6868925; telex 612032.
Ambassador: Francisco Javier Cuadra Lizana.
Counsellor: Patricio Despouy.
First Secretary: Leonel Searle Couve.

CHINA, PEOPLE'S REPUBLIC

Mission: Via Armando Spadini 9, 00197 Rome; tel (6) 3600865.
Ambassador: Chow Shu-Kai.
Minister-Counsellor: Liu Yu.
Counsellor: Yang Ching-Yeun.
Counsellor: You Tian-Der.

CHINA (TAIWAN)

Mission: Piazza delle Muse 7, 00197 Rome; tel (6) 8083166; telex 610651; fax (6) 8085679.
Ambassador: Hoang Sieou-Je.

COLOMBIA

Mission: Via Cola di Rienzo 285/12, 00192 Rome; tel (6) 3211703; telex 622155; fax (6) 3211703.
Ambassador: Fernando Hinestrosa Forero.
Minister-Counsellor: Manuel Urueta.

COSTA RICA

Mission: Piazza Verbano 16, 00199 Rome; tel (6) 8451210.
Minister and Chargé d'affaires a.i.: Javier Guerra Laspiur.
Counsellor: Iván López Ocampo.

COTE D'IVOIRE

Mission: Via Sforza Pallavicini 11, 00193 Rome; tel (6) 6877503.
Ambassador: Joseph Amichia.
Counsellor: Sérephim Ogou Daix.
Attaché: Augustin Assoa Attoumou.

CUBA

Mission: Via di Porta Angelica 15/2, 00193 Rome; tel (6) 6540789.
Ambassador: Fermin Rodríguez Paz.
Second Secretary: Fernando Faure González Paneque.

DENMARK

Mission: Via Giuseppe Vaccari 53, 00194 Rome; tel (6) 3279900.
Ambassador: Alf C. Jönsson.
Attaché: Jane Jorgensen.

DOMINICAN REPUBLIC

Mission: Lungotevere Marzio 3/6, 00186 Rome; tel (6) 686484.
Ambassador: Rámon Arturo Cáceres.
Secretary: Venera Sanfilippo de London.

ECUADOR

Mission: Borgo Santo Spirito 16, 00193 Rome; tel (6) 6897179; fax (6) 6872826.
Ambassador: Andrés Cárdenas Monge.

EGYPT

Mission: Piazza della Città Leonina 9, 00193 Rome; tel (6) 6865878.
Ambassador: Ismail Mobarak.
Counsellor: Mohamed Elsayed Abbas.
Third Secretary: Ahmed Farouk Tawfik Wahby.

EL SALVADOR

Mission: Via di Villa Ada 24, 00199 Rome; tel (6) 8454008 .
Ambassador: Prudencio Llach Schonenberg.

FINLAND

Mission: Villa Lante, Passeggiata del Gianicolo 10, 00165 Rome; tel (6) 6544604; fax (6) 6542349.
Counsellor: Marjatta Laires.
Vice-Consul: Dorothea Bianchini.

FRANCE

Mission: Villa Bonaparte, Via Piave 23, 00187 Rome; tel (6) 461841; fax (6) 4821507.
Ambassador: Jean-Bernard Raimond.
Counsellor: Toussaint Marcaggi.
Counsellor: Mgr Louis Florin.
First Secretary: Edouard Beslay.

GERMANY

Mission: Via di Villa Sacchetti 4/6, 00197 Rome; tel (6) 879779; telex 610179.
Ambassador: Hans-Joachim Hallier.
Counsellor: Walter Repges.
Counsellor: Rev. Max-Eugen Kemper.
Counsellor: Hans Deetjen.
Second Secretary: Egon Gros.

GREECE

Mission: Via Giuseppe Mercalli 6, 00197 Rome; tel (6) 870786.
Ambassador: Michel-Akis Papageorgiou.
First Secretary: Leonidas Rokanas.
Attaché: Erofili Delaporta Kavalieratou.

GUATEMALA

Mission: Piazzale Gregorio VII 65/A, 00165 Rome; tel (6) 6381630; fax (6) 6381632.
Ambassador: Carlos Alfredo Escobar Armas.
Minister-Counsellor: Maria Lara de Kracht.
First Secretary: Vilma Maria Gálvez Guzmán.
Attaché: Rodolfo Luján Lunsford.

HAITI

Mission: Via Giorgio Vasari 4, 00196 Rome; tel (6) 392285; telex 616398.
Chargé d'affaires a.i.: Magalie Blaise.

HONDURAS

Mission: Via Boezio 45, 00192 Rome; tel (6) 6876051.
Counsellor and Chargé d'affaires a.i.: Grazia Maria Vallone de Grandolini.
Counsellor: Juan Manuel Gálvez Barnes.
Second Secretary: Dolores Méndez Zapata.

HUNGARY

Mission: Via Giulia 1, 00186 Rome; tel (6) 6543463.
Ambassador: Sándor Keresztes.

ICELAND

Mission: Utanríkisráđuneytiđ, Hverfisgötu 115, 150 Reykjavik, Iceland.
Ambassador: Niels P. Sigurđsson (resident in Iceland).

INDONESIA

Mission: Piazzale Roberto Ardigò 42, 00142 Rome; tel (6) 5420441.
First Secretary and Chargé d'affaires a.i.: Kemal Munawar.
Second Secretary: Marxie Dirk Ngantung.
Third Secretary: Yosef Berty Fernandez.

IRAN

Mission: Via Bruxelles 57, 00198 Rome; tel (6) 8552494; fax (6) 8450443.
Chargé d'affaires a.i.: Mohammad Ali Hadizadeh.

IRELAND

Mission: Villa Spada al Gianicolo, Via Giacomo Medici 1, 00153 Rome; tel (6) 5810777; telex 623872; fax (6) 5895709.
Ambassador: Padraig de Paor.
Secretary: Derek Hannon.

ITALY

Mission: Palazzo Borromeo, Via Flaminia 166, 00196 Rome; tel (6) 3200741; fax (6) 3201801.
Ambassador: Emanuele Scammacca del Murgo e dell'Agnone.
Minister-Counsellor: Lucio Alberto Savoia.
Counsellor: Mgr Piero Monni.
Second Secretary: Raffaella Pavani.

JAPAN

Mission: Lungotevere Michelangelo 9/9, 00192 Rome; tel (6) 3211448; telex 610602; fax (6) 3220870.
Ambassador: Masami Tanida.
Counsellor: Aitaka Oshima.
Counsellor: Rev. Jean-Baptiste Itaçaïna.
First Secretary: Toyonori Hayasaka.

KOREA, REPUBLIC

Embassy: Via della Mendola 109, 00135 Rome; tel (6) 3314522.
Ambassador: Kyung-Chul Kim.
First Secretary: Won-Ho Kwak.

LEBANON

Mission: Via Emilio de' Cavalieri 7, 00198 Rome; tel (6) 8419291.
Ambassador: Antoine Jemha.

LIBERIA

Mission: Via Nazionale 172, 00184 Rome; tel (6) 6790922; fax (6) 6785458.
Minister-Counsellor: Giovanni F. Motta.

LITHUANIA

Mission: Via Po 40, 00198 Rome; tel (6) 8554442; fax (6) 844204.

LUXEMBOURG

Mission: Via del Casale di S. Pio V 20, 00165 Rome; tel (6) 6638809; fax (6) 620915.
Ambassador: Jean Wagner (resident in Luxembourg).
Counsellor (Ecclesiastical): Joseph Claude Siebenaler.
First Secretary: Yves Spautz.

MALTA

Mission: Malta.
Ambassador: Alexander Cachia Zammit (resident in Malta).
Counsellor: Rev. Fr Mario Laurenti (resident in Malta).

MEXICO

Mission: Via Ezio 49, 00192 Rome; tel (6) 3230591.
President's Personal Envoy: Agustín Téllez-Cruces.

MONACO

Mission: Largo Nicola Spinelli 5, 00198 Rome; tel (6) 8414357.
Ambassador: César Charles Solamito.

NETHERLANDS

Mission: Piazza della Città Leonina 9, 00193 Rome; tel (6) 6868044; fax (6) 6879593.
Ambassador: Baron Seger Jan Joseph van Voorst tot Voorst.
Counsellor: Martinus Petrus Maria Muskens.

NICARAGUA

Mission: Via F. Bernardini 30, 00165 Rome; tel (6) 3266465; telex 626575; fax (6) 8841695.
Ambassador: Francisco José Fiallos Navarro.
Minister-Counsellor: Adolfo A. Altamirano-Lacayo.
First Secretary: Evangelina Lacayo de Deluca.

PANAMA

Mission: Corso Trieste 159/11, 00199 Rome; tel (6) 8605204; telex 2024; fax (6) 6985278.
Counsellor and Chargé d'affaires a.i.: Porfirio Castillo Meléndez.
Attaché: Carmen I. de Matrone.

PARAGUAY

Mission: Via delle Grazie 3, 00193 Rome; tel (6) 6876941.
Ambassador: Juan Livieres Argañas.
Counsellor (Ecclesiastical): Rev. Luigi Boglioli.
First Secretary: Ignacio Livieres Ocampos.

PERU

Mission: Via del Mascherino 75, 00193 Rome; tel (6) 6548535.
Ambassador: Hubert Wieland Alzamora.
Second Secretary: Arturo Chipoco.
Second Secretary: Daniel Roca Alcázar.

PHILIPPINES

Mission: Via del Sant' Uffizio 29, 00193 Rome; tel (6) 6548020.
Ambassador: Howard Q. Dee.
Second Secretary: Edgardo Manuel.
Attaché (Ecclesiastical): Rev. Francisco Z. Araneta.

POLAND

Mission: Borgo Santo Spirito 16/4, 00193 Rome; tel (6) 6542000.
Ambassador: Henryk Kupiszewski.
Counsellor: Adam Szymczyk.
Second Secretary: Jerzy Florczak.

PORTUGAL

Mission: Villa Lusa, Via S. Valentino 9, 00197 Rome; tel (6) 877012; telex 622293.
Ambassador: João de Sa' Coutinho.
Minister-Counsellor: Pedro Vasconcelos e Castro.
Counsellor: Rev. Arnaldo Pinto Cardoso.
Attaché: Rev. Bento Fernando Dias de Miranda.

RUSSIA

Mission: Via Gaeta 5, 00185 Rome; tel (6) 4941681.
Ambassador: Yuri Yevgenievich Kharlo.

SAINT LUCIA

Mission: Saint Lucia.
Ambassador: Francis Joseph Carasco (resident in Saint Lucia).

SAN MARINO

Mission: Piazza G. Winckelmann 12, 00162 Rome; tel (6) 8390344; telex 613309; fax (6) 8320821.
Ambassador: Prof. Giovanni Glassi.
Minister-Counsellor: Oscar Pasquini.

SENEGAL

Mission: Via dei Monti Parioli 51, 00197 Rome; tel (6) 3217163.
Ambassador: André J. Coulbary.
Counsellor: Charlotte Correa Sow.

SPAIN

Mission: Palazzo di Spagna, Piazza di Spagna 57, 00187 Rome; tel (6) 6784351; telex 610186; fax (6) 6784355.
Ambassador: Jesús Ezquerra Calvo.
Minister-Counsellor: José Manuel Cervera de Góngora.
Counsellor: José Luis Candela Candela.
Attaché: Justo Fernández Alonso.
Attaché: Rev. José Angel Mozo.

SWEDEN

Mission: Via Bertoloni 29, 00197 Rome; tel (6) 870841; fax (6) 870841.
Ambassador: Lars J. T. Bergquist.

TURKEY

Mission: Via Lovania 24, 00198 Rome; tel (6) 8549166; fax 8543986.
Ambassador: Selçuk Korkud.
Counsellor: Selim Karaosmanoglu.
Attaché: Sakire Tosun.

UNITED KINGDOM

Mission: Via Condotti 91, 00187 Rome; tel (6) 6789462; telex 626119; fax (6) 6840684.
Ambassador: Andrew E. Palmer.
First Secretary: P. J. McCormick.

USA

Mission: Villino Pacelli, Via Aurelia 294A, 00165 Rome; tel (6) 6390558; telex 622322; fax (6) 6380159.
Ambassador: Thomas Patrick Melady.
Deputy Chief of Mission: Cameron R. Hume.
Public Affairs Officer (First Secretary): Vincent Chiarello.
Political Officer (Second Secretary): Deborah Graze.
Administrative Section: Douglas B. Leonnig.
Regional Security Officer: Bernhard B. Collins, Jr.

URUGUAY

Mission: Via Antonio Gramsci, 00197 Rome; tel (6) 3218904; telex 621282; fax (6) 3613249.
Ambassador: Juan José Zorrilla.

VENEZUELA

Mission: Via Monte Zebio 32, 00195 Rome; tel (6) 3225916; telex 611191; fax (6) 3204425.
Ambassador: Edilberto Moreno Peña.
Counsellor: Rosa Villa de Tognella.
Attaché: Ana Belkis Rodriguez Jiménez.
Attaché: Nancy Rebolledo Hoyer de Fernández.

YUGOSLAVIA

Mission: Via Antonio Gramsci 36, 00197 Rome; tel (6) 3200897; telex 616303.
Secretary: Davor Rako.

ZAIRE

Mission: Via Alberico II 4, 00193 Rome; tel (6) 6547977.
Ambassador: Mr Atembina-te-Bombo.
Minister-Counsellor: Ikoma Yaliko.
Counsellor: Kafusa wa Mukebo.
First Secretary: Mambu Ndontoni Kapitao.

VENEZUELA

ALGERIA

Embassy: Quinta Aures, Avda Los Mangos, Los Chorros, Caracas; tel (2) 284-8074; telex 21814.
Ambassador: Abderrahim Settouti.

ARGENTINA

Embassy: Centro Capriles, Mezzanina 2, Plaza Venezuela, Apdo 569, Caracas; tel (2) 781-9233.
Ambassador: Francisco Moyano.

AUSTRALIA

Embassy: Quinta Yolanda, Avda Luis Roche entre 6a y 7a Transversal, Apdo 61123, Caracas 1060-A; tel (2) 261-0658; telex 23101; fax (2) 261-3448.
Ambassador: Anthony Frederick Dingle.
First Secretary (Political): James Francis Linsay.
Second Secretary (Consular/Administrative): John Gilbert Judge.

AUSTRIA

Embassy: Edif. Torre Las Mercedes 4°, Of. 408, Avda La Estancia, Chuao, Apdo 61381, Caracas 1060-A; tel (2) 91-3863; telex 23435.
Ambassador: Dr Edgar Selzer.
Counsellor (Economic): Werner Winkler.

Consulate: Edif. Communica, Calle 84 No. 3E-09, Apdo 607, Maracaibo; tel (61) 919199; telex 62443.
Honorary Consul: Vlastimil Ivicic Morton.

BARBADOS

Embassy: Quinta Chapaleta, 9a Transversal, entre 2a y 3a Avdas, Apdo 68829, Altamira, Caracas; tel (2) 262-1820; telex 27106.
Ambassador: John A. Connell.

BELGIUM

Embassy: Quinta La Azulita, Avda 11, entre 6a y 7a Transversales, Apdo del Este 61550, Altamira, Caracas 1060-A; tel (2) 262-0421; telex 21223.
Ambassador: Jacques Ivan d'Hondt.

BOLIVIA

Embassy: Avda Luis Roche con 6a Transversal, Altamira, Caracas; tel (2) 32-3603; telex 27408.
Ambassador: Dr Walter Guevara Arce.

BRAZIL

Embassy: Avda Mohedano con Calle Los Chaguaramos, Centro Gerencial Mohedano, 6°, La Castellana, Caracas; tel (2) 261-4481; telex 25391.
Ambassador: Renato Prado-Guimarães.

CANADA

Embassy: Edif. Torre Europa, 7°, Avda Francisco de Miranda, Apdo 62302, Urb. Campo Alegre, Caracas 1060-A; tel (2) 951-6166; telex 23377; fax (2) 951-4950.
Ambassador: John W. Graham.
Counsellor and Consul (Political/Economic and Cultural Information): Stephen Woollcombe.
Counsellor (Commercial) and Consul: Denis Thibault.
Second Secretary and Vice-Consul (Political/Economic and Cultural Information): Daniel Tremblay.
Second Secretary (Commercial) and Vice-Consul: Nicolas Mesly.
Third Secretary and Vice-Consul (Consular/Passports and Visas): Richard Belair.

CHILE

Embassy: Edif. Torre La Noira, 10°, Calle Paseo Enrique Eraso, Urb. Las Mercedes, Caracas; tel (2) 92-3378; telex 29603; fax (2) 92-0614.
Ambassador: Aniceto Rodríguez A.

CHINA, PEOPLE'S REPUBLIC

Embassy: Prados del Este, Apdo 80665, Caracas 1080-A; tel (2) 978-4424; telex 21734.
Ambassador: Chen Dehe.

COLOMBIA

Embassy: 3a Avda con 3a Calle, Campo Alegre, Plaza la Gran Colombia, Apdo 60887, Caracas; tel (2) 33-1820; telex 23360.
Ambassador: Pedro Gómez Barrero.

COSTA RICA

Embassy: Quinta Poás, 5a Transversal entre Avda Alfredo Jahn y Andrés Bello, Los Palos Grandes, Chacao, Apdo 62239, Caracas; tel (2) 284-4099; telex 23574.
Ambassador: Rafael Paris Steffens.

CUBA

Embassy: Quinta Affise, Avda El Cafetal, Chuao, Caracas 1060-A; tel (2) 92-1124.
Ambassador: Norberto Hernández Curbelo.

CZECHOSLOVAKIA

Embassy: Avda Luis Roche 41, 5a Transversal, Altamira, Caracas; tel (2) 33-9866.
Ambassador: Zdeněk Pulec.

DENMARK

Embassy: Edif. 'Easo', 17°, Avda Francisco de Miranda, Chacaito, Apdo 61-169, Caracas 1060-A; tel (2) 951-4618; telex 23371; fax (2) 951-5278.
Ambassador: John Hartmann Bernhard.
Counsellor (Commercial): Poul Laursen.
Consul-General: Gustavo de la Rosa.
Consul: V. Birch Pedersen.

Consulate: Avda 15 No. 88-78, Las Delicias, Apto 301, Maracaibo; tel (61) 513077; telex 64258.
Consul: Oscar Eduardo d'Empaire.

Consulate: Avda Táchira, Quinta Maninata 50, Apto 319, Ciudad Bolivar; tel (85) 23490.
Vice-Consul: Roberto José Valery Avila.

Consulate: Avda Juan Bautista Arismendi, Centro de Mayorista No. 14, Apto 316, Porlamar, Isla Margarita; tel (95) 24940; telex 618346.
Vice-Consul: Manuel Leiros Silva.

Consulate: Calle Miranda 21, Apto 4365, Puerto La Cruz; tel (81) 23897.
Vice-Consul: Rusella Moya de Fermín.

DOMINICAN REPUBLIC

Embassy: Edif. Humboldt, 6°, Of. 26, Avda Francisco de Miranda, Altamira, Caracas; tel (2) 284-2443; telex 27432.
Ambassador: Bienvenido Hazim Egel.

ECUADOR

Embassy: Centro Andrés Bello, Torre Oeste, 13°, Avda Andrés Bello, Maripérez, Apdo 62164, Caracas 1060-A; tel (2) 781-3180; telex 21047.
Ambassador: Galo Pico Mantilla.

EGYPT

Embassy: Quinta Maribel, Calle Guiacaipuro, Las Mercedes, Caracas; tel (2) 92-6259.
Ambassador: Wahib Fahmy el Miniawy.

EL SALVADOR

Embassy: Quinta Cuzcatlán, Calle Amazonas, final Avda Principal de Prados del Este, Caracas; tel (2) 39-1129.
Ambassador: Jorge Hasfura.

FINLAND

Embassy: Centro Plaza, Torre C, 14°, Avda Francisco de Miranda, Palos Grandes, Apdo 61118, Caracas 1062-A; tel (2) 284-7697; telex 29138; fax (2) 283-2686.
Ambassador: Esko Rajakoski.
Secretary (Commercial): Tom Ryynänen.

Consulate: Fabriven C.A., Calle 146, No. 64-120, 1a etapa, Zona Industrial, Maracaibo; tel (61) 344146; telex 64132; fax (61) 347536.
Consul: María Cristina Mendiri de Cordary.

Consulate: Avda Urdaneta esq. Fuerzas Armadas, Edif. Sudameris, 6°, Puerto Cabello; tel (42) 562-3512; telex 24529; fax (42) 562-5452.
Consul: Ezio Chiarva Strumia.

FRANCE

Embassy: Edif. Los Frailes, Los Frailes, Calle Los Guaritá, Chuao, Apdo 60386, Caracas 1060-A; tel (2) 91-0143.
Ambassador: André-Jean Libourel.

GABON

Embassy: 4 Avda Mohedano, Caracas; tel (2) 283-8849; telex 25532.
Ambassador: Conga Trous Quinta Mogoalla.

GERMANY

Embassy: Edif. Panavén, 2°, Avda San Juan Bosco, esq. 3a Transversal, Altamira, Apdo 2078, Caracas; tel (2) 261-0181; telex 23262; fax (2) 261-0641.
Ambassador: Dr Karl Heinz Neukirchen.

Consulate: Edif. Amazonás, Mezzanina, Local 4, Avda Las Americas, Puerto Ordaz, Ciudad Bolivar; tel (85) 22-2272; telex 86343.
Honorary Consul: Wilfried Eisenfeller.

Consulate: Calle 77, No. 3C-24, Edif. 'Los Cerros', 8°, Apdo 578, Maracaibo; tel (61) 91-2406.
Honorary Consul: Dr Kurt Nagel.

Consulate: Edif. Torovega, Carrera 8, La Concordia, Apdo 358, San Cristobal 5001-A; tel (76) 44-8866; telex 76115.
Honorary Consul: Joachim Funck.

Consulate: Calle 159, No. 106-36, Urb. Guapero, Apdo 3073, Valencia; tel (41) 21-1948; fax (41) 21-4077.
Honorary Consul: Federico Heimbach.

GREECE

Embassy: Quinta La Cañada, la Avda El Casquillo, esq. con Calle Unión, Alta Florida, Caracas; tel (2) 74-0106; telex 29124.
Ambassador: Antoine N. Protonotarios.

GRENADA

Embassy: Edif. Los Frailes, 3°, Of. 34, Calle La Guarita, Urb. Chuao, Edo. Miranda, Caracas 1060-A; tel (2) 91-1237; telex 29606; fax (2) 91-8907.
Ambassador: Fabian A. Redhead.
Attaché: Mark Coutain.

GUATEMALA

Embassy: Edif. Los Frailes, Calle La Guairita, 6°, Chuao, Apdo 80238, Caracas 1080-A; tel (2) 91-8639; telex 29304.
Ambassador: Miriam Cabrera Pasarelli.

GUYANA

Embassy: Quinta 'RORAIMA', Avda El Paseo, Prados del Este, Apdo 51054, Caracas; tel (2) 978-2781; telex 29228; fax (2) 976-3765.
Ambassador: Marylin Cheryl Miles.
First Secretary: Rajendra Mungol.
First Secretary: Lawrence Houston.

Consulate: Quinta Waimi, Urb. Jorge Coll, Redoma San Lorenzo, Pampatar, Margarita; tel (95) 62-2158.
Honorary Consul: Dennis Bourne.

HAITI

Embassy: Quinta Macuro, Calle 12 entre 7a y 8a Transversal, Altamira, Caracas; tel (2) 74-7220; telex 27226.
Ambassador: Paul D. Estime.

HOLY SEE

Apostolic Nunciature: Avda La Salle, Los Caobos, Apdo 29, Caracas 1010-A; tel (2) 781-8939; telex 24040; fax (2) 793-2403.
Apostolic Nuncio: Mgr Dr Oriano Quilici.
Secretary: Francisco Padilla.

HONDURAS

Embassy: 6a Transversal, 2a y 3a Avda Quinta, No 15, Los Palos Grandes, Apdo 68259, Caracas; tel (2) 284-5593; telex 23152.
Ambassador: León Paredes L.

HUNGARY

Embassy: Quinta Budapest, Calle Las Colinas, Lomas de San Rafael, La Florida, Apdo 50888, Caracas; tel (2) 74-3167; telex 21403.
Ambassador: János Dömény.

ICELAND

Consulate-General: Torre Las Mercedes, 2°, Chuao, Apdo 67348, Caracas 1061-A; tel (2) 92-9467; telex 23553; fax (2) 92-6676.
Consul-General: Dr Victor Bentata.

INDIA

Embassy: Apdo 61585, Chacao, Caracas 1060-A; tel (2) 284-5549; telex 25438.
Ambassador: Ranjit Gupta.

INDONESIA

Embassy: Quinta Gibraltar, Avda Río de Janeiro, Chuao, Apdo 67061, Caracas 1061-A; tel (2) 91-2324; telex 25345.
Ambassador: Achmad Hidajat Kusumanegara.

IRAN

Embassy: Quinta Lourdes, Calle El Retiro, El Rosal, Caracas; tel (2) 92-1854; telex 23492.
Chargé d'affaires a.i.: Morteza Tavassoli.

IRAQ

Embassy: Avda San Carlos 404, La Floresta, Caracas; tel (2) 91-5112; telex 23525.
Chargé d'affaires: Doraid A. Salih.

ISRAEL

Embassy: Centro Empresarial Miranda, 4°, Avda Principal de los Ruices cruce con Francisco de Miranda, Los Ruices, Apdo 70081, Caracas; tel (2) 239-4511; telex 25373.
Ambassador: Janan Olamy.

ITALY

Embassy: Edif. Fedecámaras, 3°, Avda El Empalme, El Bosque, Apdo 3995, Caracas; tel (2) 72-3685; telex 21563.
Ambassador: Massimiliano Bandini.

JAMAICA

Embassy: Centro Plaza, Torre A, 11°, Avda Francisco de Miranda 205, Los Palos Grandes, Caracas; tel (2) 283-6933; telex 25462.
Ambassador: Matthew A. C. Beaubrun.
Counsellor: Claudia Barnes.

JAPAN

Embassy: Quinta Sakura, Avda San Juan Bosco, entre 8a y 9a, Transversal, Altamira, Apdo 68790, Caracas 1062-A; tel (2) 261-8333; telex 23363; fax (2) 261-6780.
Ambassador: Jutaro Sakamoto.

KOREA, DEMOCRATIC PEOPLE'S REPUBLIC

Embassy: Caracas.
Ambassador: Pak Chung Kuk.

KOREA, REPUBLIC

Embassy: Quinta Alegría, Avda el Paseo con Calle Occidente, Prados del Este, Caracas; tel (2) 77-0556; telex 23493.
Ambassador: Cho Kwang-Je.

LEBANON

Embassy: Quinta el Cedro del Lebanon, Avda Primera, Colinas Bello Monte, Calle Motatán, Caracas 1050-A; tel (2) 751-5943; telex 29413; fax (2) 752-0726.
Ambassador: Mustapha Hraibeh.
First Secretary: Khaled Salman.

LIBYA

People's Bureau: 3a Avda entre 9a y 10a Transversal, Quinta Los Leones, Altamira, Apdo 68946, Caracas 1060-A.
Ambassador: Ahmed Taher Tabib.

MALAYSIA

Trade Commission: Caracas.
Trade Commissioner: Tham Sing Khow.

MALTA

Consulate-General: Edif. Citibank, 5°, Altagracia a Salas, Caracas; tel (2) 82-6463; telex 26239.
Honorary Consul-General: Dr Lope Tejera Marquez.

MEXICO

Embassy: Edif. Centro Plaza, Torre A, 11°, Avda Francisco de Miranda y Andrés Bello, Los Palos Grandes, Caracas; tel (2) 283-6622.
Ambassador: Jesús Puente Leyva.

NETHERLANDS

Embassy: Centro Banaven, Torre B, 2°, Avda La Estancia, Chuao, Caracas; tel (2) 91-1422; telex 23177.
Ambassador: W. Sinninghe Damsté.

Consulate: Calle Orinoco 134, Apto 109, Ciudad Bolivar; tel (85) 20-020.
Honorary Consul: I. A. Mancini.

Consulate: Avda 19C, No. 97A, Apto 72, Maracaibo 142; tel (61) 21-2950; telex 64105; fax (61) 22-0468.
Honorary Consul: E. W. Rutteman.

Consulate: Calle Puerto Cabello 3-70, Apdo 02, Puerto Cabello; tel (42) 63-103; telex 42465; fax (42) 63-430.
Honorary Consul: R. T. Römer Römer.

Consulate: Calle Guaraguao 1 (Casa de Madera), Apdo 4050, Puerto la Cruz; tel (81) 69-1450.
Honorary Consul: J. M. Echeverria.

Consulate: 'SERVITECNICO', Urb. Zarabon, Calle 7C, Campo 'Maraven' Cardón, Apdo 64, Punto Cardón; tel 40-4211.
Honorary Consul: R. R. Gibson.

Consulate: Centro Comercial el Anil, 3°, Of. 3-3, Urb., Apdo 3348, Valencia; tel (41) 31-2162; telex 46435; fax (41) 31-2183.

NICARAGUA

Embassy: Quinta Teocal, Calle Codazzi, Prados del Este, Caracas; tel (2) 77-2459; telex 24672.
Ambassador: Roberto Leal Campos.

NIGERIA

Embassy: Quinta Hucha, Calle Vaamonde cruce con Las Marias, El Pedregal de Chapellin, Caracas; tel (2) 74-9228; telex 24506.

Ambassador: F. O. Iheme.

NORWAY

Embassy: Edif. EXA, 9°, Of. 905, Avda Libertador, El Rosal, Apdo 60532, Chacao, Caracas 1060-A; tel (2) 262-1506; telex 23310.
Ambassador: Knut Berger.

PANAMA

Embassy: Edif. Los Frailes, 6°, Calle La Guairita, Chuao, Apdo 1989, Caracas; tel (2) 92-9093; telex 27588.

PARAGUAY

Embassy: Quinta Lily, 8a Avda de Altamira norte entre 7a y 8a Transversal, Apdo 80668, Caracas; tel (2) 781-8213.
Chargé d'affaires: Eladio Bueno de los Ríos.

PERU

Embassy: Edif. Centro Andrés Bello, Torre Oeste, 7°, Avda Andrés Bello, Maripérez, Caracas; tel (2) 781-7180; telex 21278.
Ambassador: Alfredo Ramos Suero.

PHILIPPINES

Embassy: Quinta Taray, Avda Tropical, La Floresta, Caracas; tel (2) 284-2006.
Ambassador: Pablo Araque.

POLAND

Embassy: Quinta Ambar, Final Avda Nicolás Copérnico, Sector Los Naranjos, Las Mercedes, Caracas; tel (2) 91-1461; telex 23273.
Ambassador: Edward Polanski.

PORTUGAL

Embassy: Edif. Fedecámaras, 1°, Avda El Empalme, El Bosque, Caracas 1050-A; tel (2) 72-4377.
Ambassador: Pedro de Andrade.

ROMANIA

Embassy: Avda Principal 42, La Castellana, Caracas; tel (2) 33-1770; telex 23176.

RUSSIA

Embassy: Quinta Soyuz, Calle Las Lomas, Las Mercedes, Caracas; tel (2) 92-1164; telex 23397.

SAN MARINO

Consulate-General: Edif. Greco, Calle Vargas, Boleita Norte, Caracas; tel (2) 239-6856; telex 25563.
Consul-General: Giuseppe Attardi Greco.

SAUDI ARABIA

Embassy: Edif. Sucre, Of. 300, Avda Francisco de Miranda, La Floresta, Caracas; tel (2) 284-2622; telex 29398.
Ambassador: Bakr A. Khomais.

SPAIN

Embassy: Avda Mohedano entre 1a y 2a Transversal, La Castellana, Caracas; tel (2) 263-2855; telex 23487.
Ambassador: Alberto de Armas García.

SURINAME

Embassy: 4a Avda entre 7a y 8a Quinta 41, Altamira, Caracas; Apdo 61140, Chacao, Caracas; tel (2) 261-2095; telex 23595.
Ambassador: Ferdinand C. van Dijk.

SWEDEN

Embassy: Torre Europa, 8°, Of. A, Avda Francisco de Miranda, Apdo 61279, Chacaíto, Caracas; tel (2) 952-2111; telex 23419; fax (2) 952-2057.
Ambassador: Karl Wärnberg.
Counsellor: Karin Ehnbohm-Palmquist.
Second Secretary: Yiva Gabrielsson.

Consulate: c/o Edif. Camara de Comercio, 2°, Plaza el Consul, Maiquetia, La Guaira; tel (31) 23-437; fax (31) 22-459.
Consul: Juan Esteban González Fernández.

Consulate: Avda No. 15, No. 88-78, Apdo 301, Maracaibo 4001; tel (61) 52-5136; telex 64258; fax (61) 51-5093.
Consul: Carlos Enrique d'Empaire.

Consulate: Calle Guaraguao No. 1, Apdo 4050, Puerto La Cruz 6023-A; tel (81) 69-1450; fax (81) 66-3134.
Consul: Margaretha Ida Borsten de Echeverría.

SWITZERLAND

Embassy: Torre Europa, 6°, Avda Francisco de Miranda, Campo Alegre, Apdo 62555, Caracas 1060-A; tel (2) 951-4064; telex 23445; fax (2) 951-6201.
Ambassador: Dr Peter Dietschi.
Second Secretary: Dr César Dubler.
Attaché and Head of Chancery: Tiziano Bassi.

SYRIA

Embassy: Quinta Damasco, Avda Casiquare, Urb. Colinas de Bello Monte, Caracas; tel (2) 752-6687; telex 21686.
Ambassador: Raslan Alloush.

TRINIDAD AND TOBAGO

Embassy: Quinta Serrana, 4a Avda entre 7a y 8a Transversal, Altamira, Caracas; tel (2) 261-4772; telex 23234; fax (2) 261-9801.
Ambassador: Christopher R. Thomas.

TURKEY

Embassy: Quinta Turquesa 6, Calle Kemal Atatürk, Valle Arriba, Apdo 62078, Caracas 1060-A; tel (2) 91-0075; telex 23286.
Ambassador: Turgut Tülümen.

UNITED KINGDOM

Embassy: Torre Las Mercedes, 3°, Avda La Estancia, Chuao, Apdo 1246, Caracas 1060-A; tel (2) 751-1022; telex 23468; fax (2) 92-3292.
Ambassador: Giles Eden FitzHerbert.
Counsellor: Michael Hickson.
Defence Attaché: Capt. W. McLaren.
First Secretary: Paul Morris.
First Secretary: Clive Dresser.
First Secretary: William John Roebuck.
British Council Representative: Dr V. A. Atkinson.
Information Officer: Carlos Villalobos.

Consulate: Avda 98 con Calle 66A, No. 66-146, Maracaibo, Estado Zulia; tel (61) 78-642; telex 62246; fax (61) 82-794.
Honorary Vice-Consul: George Podolecki.

Consulate: Pedregosa Media, Conjunto Res., Las Ardillas, Segunda Trans., Calle Las Dantas, Parcela 20A, Mérida 5101; tel (74) 637-6902.
Honorary Vice-Consul: Robert Kirby.

USA

Embassy: Avda Principal de la Floresta, esq. Francisco de Miranda, Apdo 62291, La Floresta, Caracas; tel (2) 285-3111; telex 25501; fax (2) 285-0336.
Ambassador: Michael M. Skol.
Deputy Head of Mission: Robert C. Felder.
Political Section: William Millan.
Economic Section: Frank S. Parker.
Commercial Section: Kenneth Moorefield.
Labour Officer: Robert A. Millspaugh.
Consular Section: Daniel R. Welter.
Administrative Section: Michael A. Boorstein.
Regional Security Officer: Kevin Barry.
Public Affairs Officer: Stephen M. Chaplin.
Internal Revenue Service: Charles Shea.
Office of Defence Attaché: Col William R. Mainord.
Military Group: Col José Muratti.
Legal Attaché: Paul F. Nolan.
Communications Programme Officer: Donald Z. Fisher.
Information Systems Manager: Beth A. Mitchell.

Agricultural Trade Office: Centro Plaza, Torre C, 18°, Los Palos Grandes, Caracas; tel (2) 283-2353; telex 29119.
Agricultural Trade Office: William Westman.
Agriculture Section: Lynn Abbott.

Consulate: Edif. Sofimara, 3°, Calle 77 con Avda 13, Maracaibo; tel (61) 84-253; telex 62213; fax (61) 52-4255.
Principal Officer: Jim E. Wagner.
Administrative Section: Richard Adams.

URUGUAY

Embassy: Edif. Torre Delta, Avda Francisco de Miranda, 8°, Of. A y B, Altamira, Apdo 60366, Caracas 1060-A; tel (2) 31-0013; telex 29778; fax (2) 33-9233.
Ambassador: Alberto Rodríguez-Nin.

YUGOSLAVIA

Embassy: Quinta No. 13, 4 Avda de Campo Alegre, Caracas; tel (2) 33-7995; telex 25488.
Ambassador: Milan Vukos.

International Organizations

EUROPEAN COMMUNITIES

Headquarters of Delegation for Latin America: Calle Orinoco, Las Mercedes, Apdo 768076, Las Americas, Caracas 1061-A; tel (2) 91-5133; telex 27298; fax (2) 91-8876.
Head of Delegation: José Luis Benito Prior.
Head of Information Service: William Forwood.

VIET-NAM

AFGHANISTAN

Embassy: D1, Van Phuc Quarter, Hanoi; tel 53249.
Ambassador: Mohammad Ismail Mahshoor.
Second Secretary: Atiqullah Shahid.

ALBANIA

Embassy: 49 Dien Bien Phu St, Hanoi; tel 54490.
Ambassador: Gezim Dhrima.
Second Secretary: Bashkim Fejzo.

ALGERIA

Embassy: 12 Phan Chu Trinh, Hanoi; tel 53865.
Ambassador: Lamari Mohamed.
First Secretary: Mokrane Ali.
Attaché: Gasmi Abdenour.
Attaché: Terki Djamel.
Attaché: Bouidarene Brahim.

AUSTRALIA

Embassy: 66 Ly Thuong Kiet, Hanoi; tel 52763.
Ambassador: Michael Potts.
Counsellor (Commercial): Peter Ward Bergman.
First Secretary: Dr Janet Mary Gardiner.
First Secretary (Consular/Administrative): Glenn Oliver Conroy.
First Secretary (Immigration): Robyn Martin.
Second Secretary: Roslyn Ann Simms.
Third Secretary (Administrative) and Vice-Consul: Mark Egan.

BELGIUM

Embassy: Khu Van Phuc, Bât. D1, Apt 105-8, Hanoi; tel 52263; fax 57165.
Ambassador: Piet Steel.
Chancellor: Paul de Vos.

BULGARIA

Embassy: 41-3 Trân Phú, Hanoi; tel 52908.
Ambassador: Geno Toshkov.
Counsellor (Economic): Alexander Petkov.
Second Secretary: Atanas Krastin.
Third Secretary: Georgi Vassilev.

CAMBODIA

Embassy: 71 Tran Hung Dao, Hanoi; tel 53788.
Ambassador: Uch Borit.
Counsellor (Political): Eat-Ly Heng.
Military, Naval and Air Attaché: Hing Lang.
Counsellor (Cultural): Pen Saroeun.
Counsellor (Commercial): Say Sokha.
First Secretary: Bun Sambo.
Second Secretary: Sin Dim.

Consulate-General: 41 Phung Khae Khoan St, Ho Chi Minh City; tel 92751.
Consul-General: Suos Sam Nang.
Consul: Sam Than.

CANADA

Diplomatic Office: Hanoi.
Chargé d'affaires a.i.: Marius Grinius.

CHINA, PEOPLE'S REPUBLIC

Embassy: 46 Hoang Dieu, Hanoi; tel 53736.
Ambassador: Zhang Dewei.
Counsellor (Political): Li Jiazhong.
Military, Naval and Air Attaché: Zhao Rui.
First Secretary: Huang Jingye.
First Secretary: Huang Tinghai.
First Secretary: Zhang Dian.
First Secretary: Hu Qianwen.
First Secretary (Commercial): Li Rihong.

CUBA

Embassy: 65 Ly Thuong Kiet, Hanoi; tel 52281.
Ambassador: Armando G. Saucedo Yero.
Counsellor (Political): Ruben Perez Valdes.
Counsellor (Commercial): Wilfredo Blanco Navarro.
Military, Naval and Air Attaché: Lieut Col Miguel San Martin Torriente.
First Secretary: Pedro Moran Tapanes.
Second Secretary: Gabriela Lopez Gabor.
Attaché (Economic): Norge Santana Leiva.

Consulate-General: 124-6 Nguyen Dinh Chieu St, Ho Chi Minh City; tel 95818.
Consul-General: Perfecto Julio Alvarez Dorta.

CZECHOSLOVAKIA

Embassy: 13 Chu van An, Hanoi; tel 54131.
Ambassador: Miroslav Kapoun.
Counsellor: Jozef Haneulak.
Counsellor: Jiri Brozovsky.
Counsellor (Commercial): Alexander Sadovsky.
Military Attaché: Col Oldrich Tureinek.

Consulate-General: 176 Tir Dire St, Ho Chi Minh City; tel 91475.
Consul-General: Jan Kus.
Vice-Consul and Head of Cultural Section: Petr Dokladal.
Head of Commercial Section: Karel Petrzelka.

EGYPT

Embassy: 85 Ly Thuong Kiet St, Hanoi; tel 52909; telex 411448.
Ambassador: Moustafa Hassan Abou Shnief.
Second Secretary (Consular): Mohamed al-Khashab.
Attaché: Abdel Aziz Salama.
Attaché: Maher Fouad Mikky.

FINLAND

Embassy: 1-2 Béb Giang Vo Quarter, Ba Dinh Ward, Hanoi; tel 56754; telex 411443.
Ambassador: Esko Lipponen.
First Secretary: Selma Houkanen.
Attaché: Marjatta Laatu.
Attaché: Annikki Hakala.

FRANCE

Embassy: 49 Ba Trieu, Hanoi; tel 52719; telex 4411.
Ambassador: Claude Blanchemaison.
First Counsellor: Serge Lavroff.
Counsellor (Cultural): Alain Bockel.
Counsellor (Commercial): Jean-Cyprien Linon.
First Secretary: Jean-François Casabonne-Masonnave.
Consul: Roger Abensour.

Consulate-General: 27 Xo Viet Nghe Tinh St, Ho Chi Minh City; tel 97231.
Consul-General: Jean-Paul Dumont.
Vice-Consul: Louis Lescure.

GERMANY

Embassy: 25 Phan Boi Chau, Hanoi; tel 53863; telex 411428; fax 53838.
Ambassador: Jürgen Elias.
Head of Chancery: L. Jeune.

Consulate-General: 15 Phung Khae Khoan St, Ho Chi Minh City; tel 92455.
Consul-General: Erich Zielke.

HUNGARY

Embassy: 47 Dien Bien Phu, Hanoi; tel 52748.
Ambassador: Oszkar Szurovsky.
Counsellor (Commercial): Gabor Kalmár.
Counsellor: Dénes Szász.
First Secretary: Sándor Deesi.

Consulate: Nguyen Dinh Chieu 53, Ho Chi Minh City; tel 99023.
Consul: László Kalmár.

INDIA

Embassy: 58 Tran Hung Dao, Hanoi; tel 53409.
Ambassador: Jagdish Chandra Sharma.
Counsellor (Political): Devasirvatham Jesudas Bell.
Counsellor (Economic): S. Ramani.
Military, Naval and Air Attaché: Col Mohinder Puri.
Second Secretary and Head of Chancery: Sandeep Kumar.
Attaché (Administrative): Gurdeep Singh Bhatia.
Attaché (Consular): N. Chockalingam.

INDONESIA

Embassy: 50 Pho Ngo Quyen, Hanoi; tel 53353; telex 411434; fax 59274.
Ambassador: Mr Aswimarmo.
Minister-Counsellor: Benimo Umar.
Defence Attaché: Lieut Col Sardan Marbun.
Second Secretary: Didik Midiono Muljosantoso.
Third Secretary: Mr Sutadi.

IRAQ

Embassy: 66 Tran Hung Dao, Hanoi; tel 55111.
Chargé d'affaires a.i.: Mahdi Talid Ibrahim.
Attaché: Abbas Fadhil Abid.
Attaché: Khalil S. Afar.
Attaché: Muhammad A. Salman.
Attaché: Naif A. Rasheed.

ITALY

Embassy: 9 Le Phung Hieu, Hanoi; tel 56246; telex 4416.
Ambassador: Maurizio Teucci.
Attaché (Commercial): Gualtiero della Rovere.
Attaché (Administrative): Leonardo de Stefano.
Attaché (Administrative): Biagio Sottile.
Attaché: Pietro Paris.
Attaché: Sergio di Maggio.
Attaché: Salvatore Mulé.

JAPAN

Embassy: E3 Trung Tu Diplomatic Quarter, POB 49, Hanoi; tel 57902; telex 411414.
Ambassador: Kuniaki Asomura.
Counsellor: Rynichi Shoji.
Counsellor: Ineo Suzuki.
First Secretary (Administrative): Hisayoshi Hosokawa.
First Secretary (Administrative): Takashi Tokunaga.
First Secretary: Satoshi Nakajima.
First Secretary: Hisashi Nakatomi.

Second Secretary (Consular): Masato Abe.

KOREA, DEMOCRATIC PEOPLE'S REPUBLIC

Embassy: 25 Cao Ba Quat, Hanoi; tel 53008.
Ambassador: Ri Hong.
Counsellor (Commercial): Han Yang Ki.
First Secretary: Kim Yong Phil.
Third Secretary: Ri Quan Il.
Third Secretary (Commercial): Do Mieng Riong.

LAOS

Embassy: 22 Tran Binh Trong, Hanoi; tel 54576.
Ambassador: Bouasi Chalensouk.
Counsellor (Culture/Education): Thongvanh Souksavath.
First Secretary: Thouane Vorasarn.
Second Secretary (Culture/Education): Thunthongchay Poungpong.
Second Secretary (Economic): Khamkhanh Naphavong.
Second Secretary (Culture/Education): May Manivanh.
Third Secretary (Consular): Khamponh Phaxaynhavong.

Office of Military Attaché: 66 Nguyen Du Sir, Hanoi; tel 53947.
Military, Naval and Air Attaché: Col Khamsay Soukongmy.
Deputy Military, Naval and Air Attaché: Lieut Col Paseuth Soukaseum.

Consulate-General: 181 Iiai Ba Trung St, Ho Chi Minh City; tel 97667.
Consul-General: Bounphieng Luangsichampa.

Consulate-General: 12 Tran Quy Cap St, Da Nang City; tel 22628.
Consul-General: Soukkaseum Senavong.

LIBYA

People's Bureau: Van Phuc Residential Quarter, Hanoi; tel 53379.
Secretary: Saleh al-Hosni.
Committee Member: Abdul Majid Nwelli.
Attaché (Consular): Giumma Sadik Own.
Attaché (Finance): Muftah A. Ramadan.
Attaché: Khairi Namrud.

MALAYSIA

Embassy: A3 Van Phuc Residential Quarter, Hanoi; tel 53371; telex 4412.
Ambassador: Mr Parameswaran.
Counsellor: Shapii bin Abu Samah.
First Secretary: Wan Jaffar Wan Daud.
Second Secretary: Mohd. Ariff Baharom.
Third Secretary: Jahaya bin Jalil.

MONGOLIA

Embassy: 39 Tran Phu, Hanoi; tel 52151.
Ambassador: Niamjavin Baaxanjav.
Counsellor: Gongoryn Bars.
Counsellor (Commercial): Dalhsurenguiin Tserendorj.
Attaché: Dolgorsurengiine Dorjgotov.

MYANMAR

Embassy: A3 Van Phuc Diplomatic Quarter, Hanoi; tel 32056; telex 411427; fax 52404.
Ambassador: U Win Shein.
First Secretary and Chargé d'affaires: U Tmaung Nyunt.
Second Secretary: U Tmant Kyaw.
Third Secretary: U Tmant Zin.
Attaché: U Myint Tmein.
Attaché: U Tint Lwin.

NICARAGUA

Embassy: El Trung Tu Quarter, Hanoi; tel 62214.
Second Secretary: Alejandro J. Orezco C.

PHILIPPINES

Embassy: Diplomatic Compound Bldg, Rooms 305-8, El Trung Tu Diplomatic Quarter, Hanoi; tel 57948.
Ambassador: Cipriano O. Leron.
First Secretary and Consul: Emmanuel J. Contreras.
Attaché: Aluizo D. Lomboy.
Attaché: Miguel T. Mayuga.
Attaché: Ronaldo B. Villanueva.

POLAND

Embassy: 3 Chua Mot Cot, Hanoi; tel 52027.
Ambassador: Stanislaw Gerbala.
Counsellor: Stanislaw Skowron.
Counsellor (Commercial): Miroslaw Jedrzejezak.
Military Attaché: Stanislaw Terlecki.
Attaché (Cultural/Consular): Miroslaw Gajewski.

Consulate: 2B Tran-Cao Van St, Ho Chi Minh City; tel 92215.
Consul: Zozef Rokosik.

ROMANIA

Embassy: 5 Le Hong Phong, Hanoi; tel 52014.
Ambassador: Gheorghe Dumitru.
Counsellor: Simion Diac.
First Secretary: Ion Pitogoi.
Second Secretary: Gheorghe Nica.

RUSSIA

Embassy: 58 Tran Phu St, Hanoi; tel 54631; telex 411440; fax 56177.
Ambassador: Rashit Khamidulin.
Minister-Counsellor: Anatoly Sergeyevich Voronin.
Trade Representative: Victor Mikhailovich Kozlov.
Minister-Counsellor: Boris Vassilyevich Melnik.
Counsellor: Yuri Georgyevich Bykov.
Counsellor: Albert Ivanovich Grichin.
Counsellor: Gennady Victorovich Bouzin.
Counsellor (Technical/Scientific): Anatoly Sergeyevich Soloussov.
Counsellor: Aleftine Ivanovich Levtchenko.
Counsellor: Andrei Markovich Levin.
Counsellor: Yakov Nissonovich Pivavarov.
Counsellor: Andrei Petrovich Chamehin.
Counsellor: Alexei Alexandrovich Sergiev.
Counsellor: Victor Borissovich Deikin.
Military, Naval and Air Attaché: Col Nikolai Vassilievich Lytchak.
Deputy Military Attaché: Lieut Col Yuri Nikolaevich Kobyliatsky.
Deputy Military Attaché: Lieut Col Valery Alexeevich Roumiantsev.
Attaché and Head of Protocol Department: Sergei Alexandrovich Orlov.

Consulate-General: 40 Ba Huyen Thanh Quan St, Ho Chi Minh City; tel 92937; telex 8338.
Consul-General: Rudolf Fedorovich Mukhin.

Consulate-General: 14 Minh Khai St, Hai Phong City; tel 47611; telex 311222.
Consul-General: Dollers Samgunovich Khaliulin.

Consulate-General: 5 Dong Da Sir St, Da Nang City; tel 22543; telex 8119.
Consul-General: Rauf Ali-Zade.
Deputy Trade Representative: Georgi Sergeivich Blinov.

Consulate-General: 54-6 Quang Trung St, Special Zone, Vung Tau-Con Dao Zone; tel 2474; telex 8311.
Consul-General: Anatoly Grigorievich Shmaraev.

SWEDEN

Embassy: So 2, Duong 358, Van Phuc Residential Quarter, Hanoi; tel 54824; telex 411420; fax 32195.
Ambassador: Mats Åberg.
Counsellor and Head of Development Office: Rolf Eriksson.
First Secretary: Svante Kilander.
Second Secretary: Kinna Laraqui.

THAILAND

Embassy: So Nha E1, Khu Ngoai Giao Doan, Trung Tu Residential Quarter, Hanoi; tel 56043.
Ambassador: Surapong Jayanama.
Minister-Counsellor: Chaisak Uthenpong.
Counsellor: Chaibhot Tiravanija.
First Secretary: Nithi Chareonkul.

UNITED KINGDOM

Embassy: 16 Pho Ly Thuong Kiet, Hanoi; tel 52349; telex 411405.
Ambassador: Peter K. Williams.
First Secretary (Commercial), Consul and Deputy Head of Mission: Anthony J. J. Cantor.
First Secretary (Political): Andrew J. Dean.
Third Secretary: John Leonard Parry.
Third Secretary (Management) and Vice-Consul: S. Codd.

YUGOSLAVIA

Embassy: 27B Tran Hung Dao, Hanoi; tel 52343.
Ambassador: Mihajlo Hornjak.
Attaché (Administrative): Zikiea Cirjak.

International Organizations

FOOD AND AGRICULTURE ORGANIZATION—FAO

Office: 3 Nguyen Gia Thieu St, Hanoi; tel 57208.
Permanent Representative: Svetlomir I. Zakhariev.

UNITED NATIONS CHILDREN'S FUND—UNICEF

Office: 72 Ly Thirong Kiet St, Hanoi; tel 52901.
Permanent Representative: Mohammad Tarique Farooqui.

UNITED NATIONS DEVELOPMENT PROGRAMME—UNDP

Office: 27-9 Phan Boi Chau St, Hanoi; tel 57495.
Permanent Representative: David Smith.
Deputy Permanent Representative: F. Tore Rose.
Deputy Permanent Representative: Winston Temple.

UNITED NATIONS HIGH COMMISSIONER FOR REFUGEES—UNHCR

Office: 60 Nguyen Thai Hoc St, Hanoi; tel 56785.
Permanent Representative: Jacques Mouchet.
Deputy Permanent Representative: Erkki Heinonen.

WORLD HEALTH ORGANIZATION—WHO

Office: A1. Van Phuc Quarter, Hanoi; tel 57901.
Permanent Representative: Mario Gonzalez.

WESTERN SAMOA

AUSTRALIA

High Commission: Fea Gai Ma Leata Bldg, Beach Rd, POB 704, Tamaligi, Apia; tel 23411; telex 242; fax 23159.
High Commissioner: Basil J. Teasey.
First Secretary: J. E. Hemsworth.
Third Secretary (Policy): M. Kolobaric.
Administrative Assistant: P. M. Stripsky.

CHINA, PEOPLE'S REPUBLIC

Embassy: Vailima, Apia; tel 22474; telex 232; fax 21115.
Ambassador: Yue Junqing.
First Secretary (Economic/Commercial): Cui Guangrui.
Second Secretary (Administrative): Gong Qiangrui.
Second Secretary: Liu Tianfu.
Attaché (Consular): Li Qun.

GERMANY

Consulate: National Provident Fund Bldg, POB 473, Apia; tel 22695; telex 24; fax 22695.
Honorary Consul: Wilhelm Viktor Albert Keil.

NEW ZEALAND

High Commission: POB 1876, Beach Rd, Apia; tel 21711; telex 222; fax 20086.
High Commissioner: Adrian Simcock.
First Secretary: Julian Ludbrook.
First Secretary: Pam Harrison.
First Secretary: Anne Poulter-Smith.
Attaché: Robyn Glogoski.
Senior Immigration Officer: Rex Heesterman.

SWEDEN

Consulate: Retzlaff Bldg, Ground Floor, Saleuf, POB 1863, Apia; tel 23325; telex 266; fax 23038.
Consul: Hermann Theodor Retzlaff.

UNITED KINGDOM

Office of the Honorary Representative: c/o POB 2029, Apia Kruse Va'ai and Barlow, Apia; tel 21895; fax 21407.
Honorary Representative: R. M. Barlow.

USA

Embassy: POB 3430, Apia; tel 21631; telex 779275; fax 22030.
Deputy Head of Mission: William P. Francisco III.

International Organizations

EUROPEAN COMMUNITIES

Sub-office of Delegation for the Pacific—Fiji: Ioane Viliamu Bldg, 4th Floor, POB 3023, Apia; tel 20070; telex 204; fax 24622.

YEMEN

ALBANIA

Embassy: San'a.
Ambassador: Alkyz Cerga.

ALGERIA

Embassy: POB 509, 14 Ring Rd, San'a; tel (2) 247755.
Ambassador: Khaledi Hasmawi.

CHINA, PEOPLE'S REPUBLIC

Embassy: al Zubeiri St, San'a; tel (2) 275337.
Ambassador: Lin Zhen.

CZECHOSLOVAKIA

Embassy: POB 2501, Safiya Janoobia, San'a; tel (2) 247946; fax (2) 244418.
Ambassador: Václav Skolout.

DENMARK

Consulate: POB 5302, Anam Bldg, Taiz; tel (4) 215170; telex 8804.
Consul: Ahmed Hayel Saeed Anam.

EGYPT

Embassy: Gamal Abd al-Nasser St, San'a; tel (2) 275948.
Ambassador: Abdul Rahman Abd al-Latif Shuma'a.

ETHIOPIA

Embassy: POB 234, Haddah Rd, San'a; tel (2) 208833.
Ambassador: Girma Wolde Mariam.

FINLAND

Consulate: POB 522, al Zubeiri St, San'a; tel (2) 207018; telex 2242.
Consul: Abdussamed Mutahar Said.

FRANCE

Embassy: POB 1286, St 52 off Gamal Abdel Nasser St, al-Baonia, San'a; tel (2) 73169; telex 2248; fax (2) 275996.
Ambassador: Jean-François Nodinot.

GERMANY

Embassy: POB 2562, Outer Ring Rd, West Hadaa, San'a; tel (2) 216756; telex 2245; fax (2) 216758.
Ambassador: Dr Kurt Messer.

Consulate-General: POB 6100, Abyan Beach Rd 49, Khormaksar, Aden; tel (1) 32162; telex 2287.
Consul-General: Adolf Eberhart.

HUNGARY

Embassy: as-Safiya St 5, House No. 9, San'a; tel (2) 248147; telex 3132.
Ambassador: Mihály Bayer.

IRAN

Embassy: POB 1437, Haddah St, San'a; tel (2) 206945; telex 2241.
Chargé d'affaires: Wahid Farmeno.

IRAQ

Embassy: POB 498, South Airport Rd, San'a; tel (2) 244153; telex 2237.
Ambassador: Abd al-Hussain ar-Rafi'i.

ITALY

Embassy: POB 1152, St No. 29, Bldg No. 5, San'a; tel (2) 78846; telex 2560.
Ambassador: Pietro Cordon.

JAPAN

Embassy: POB 817, as-Safiya, al-Gharbiou St 38 off 35 Meter Rd 2, San'a; tel (2) 207356; telex 2345; fax (2) 209531.
Ambassador: Noguchi Masaaki.

JORDAN

Embassy: POB 2152, San'a; tel (2) 216701; telex 2703.
Ambassador: Fakhri Abu Taleb.
Consul and Second Secretary: Muhammad M. H. Kuraan.

KOREA, DEMOCRATIC PEOPLE'S REPUBLIC

Embassy: POB 1209, al-Hasaba, Mazda Rd, San'a; tel (2) 232340; telex 2603.
Ambassador: Choe In Sok.

KUWAIT

Embassy: POB 17036, near Ring Rd 60, San'a; tel (2) 216317; telex 2481.
Ambassador: Musa Sulaiman as-Saif.

LEBANON

Embassy: POB 2283, Haddah St, San'a; tel (2) 203459; telex 2438.
Ambassador: Muhammad Nasrat al-Assaad.

LIBYA

Brotherhood Office: POB 1506, Ring Rd, St No. 8, House No. 145, San'a; telex 2219.
Secretary: M. Albaoush.

MOROCCO

Embassy: POB 10236, West Safiya, San'a; tel (2) 247964; telex 2299.
Ambassador: Abu Bakr Bennouna.

NETHERLANDS

Embassy: POB 463, Hadda Rd, San'a; tel (2) 215626; telex 2429.
Ambassador: J. Wijenberg.

OMAN

Embassy: POB 105, Aser area, al Zubeiri St, San'a; tel (2) 208933; telex 2253.
Ambassador: Awad M. Baktheer.

PAKISTAN

Embassy: POB 2848, Ring Rd, off Hada Rd, San'a; tel (2) 248812.
Ambassador: Faizur Rasool Mohammed Arif.
Second Secretary and Head of Chancery: Mohammed Naeem Khan.

ROMANIA

Embassy: POB 2169, Hadda Rd, San'a; tel (2) 215579; telex 2361.
Chargé d'affaires: Valentin Moraru.

RUSSIA

Embassy: POB 1087, 26 September St, San'a; tel (2) 78272; telex 2952; fax (2) 203142.
Ambassador: Igor G. Ivaschenko.
Minister-Counsellor: Mirgayas M. Shirinsky.
Counsellor (Commercial): Vilen K. Gabashvily.
Military Attaché: Col Vladimir O. Naon.

Consulate-General: POB 6001, Abean Rd, Aden.
Consul-General: Igor Hotsialov.

Consulate-General: POB 8425, Mukalla.
Consul-General: Yakub Y. Islamov.

SAUDI ARABIA

Embassy: POB 1184, Zuhara House, Hadda Rd, San'a; tel (2) 240429; telex 2420.
Ambassador: Ali bin Muhammad al-Qufaidi.

SOMALIA

Embassy: POB 12277, Hadda Rd, San'a; tel (2) 208864; telex 2610.
Ambassador: Abd as-Sallam Mu'allim Adam.

SUDAN

Embassy: POB 2561, 82 Abou al-Hassan al-Hamadani St, San'a; tel (2) 265231.
Ambassador: Taha Makawi Abdelrahman.

SWEDEN

Consulate: c/o Elaghil Trading Co., al Zuberi St, POB 820, San'a; tel (2) 207470; telex 2213; fax (2) 207596.
Consul-General: Ahmed Abdulla Elaghil.

SYRIA

Embassy: POB 494, Hadda Rd, St No. 1, San'a; tel (2) 247750; telex 2335.
Chargé d'affaires: Ahmad Walid Rajab.

TUNISIA

Embassy: POB 2561, Diplomatic area, St No. 22, San'a; tel (2) 240457; telex 2451.
Chargé d'affaires: Mohamed Baatour.

TURKEY

Embassy: POB 12450, as-Safiya, San'a; tel (2) 215478; telex 3159.
Ambassador: Okan Gezer.

UNITED ARAB EMIRATES

Embassy: POB 2250, Ring Rd, San'a; tel (2) 248777; telex 2225.
Ambassador: Saif bin Maktoom al-Mansoory.

UNITED KINGDOM

Embassy: POB 1287, 129 Haddah Rd, San'a; tel (2) 215630; telex 2251; fax (2) 263059.
Ambassador: Mark A. Marshall.
First Secretary (Aid) and Deputy Head of Mission: G. Kirby.
Second Secretary (Commercial): P. D. Sherar.
Second Secretary (Management) and Consul: G. A. D. Ryan.
Second Secretary (Chancery): J. N. G. Bowden.

Consulate-General: 28 Shara Ho Chi Minh, Khormaksar, Aden; tel (1) 645034; telex 11468; fax (1) 659651.
Management Officer and Vice-Consul: K. MacPherson.

USA

Embassy: Dhahr Himyar Zone, Sheraton Hotel District, POB 22347, Sa'awan St, San'a; tel (2) 238842; telex 2697; fax (2) 251563.
Ambassador: Charles F. Dunbar.
Deputy Head of Mission: Bruce D. Strathearn.
Political Section: Bradford E. Hanson.
Political and Military Sections: Frank Scolow, Jr.
Consular Section: Deborah L. Elliott.
Administrative Section: Cornelis M. Keur.
Regional Security Officer: James A. Marek.
Agency for International Development: Philip-Michael Gray.
Public Affairs Officer: Duncan H. MacInnes.
Office of Defence Attaché: Lieut Col Gerald B. Thompson.
Office of Military Cooperation: Col Martin C. Frey.
Communications Programme Officer: Onnie Ogot (acting).

YUGOSLAVIA

AFGHANISTAN

Embassy: 11000 Belgrade, Njegoševa 56/1; tel (11) 4448716.
Ambassador: Sarwar Mangal.

ALBANIA

Embassy: 11000 Belgrade, Kneza Miloša 56; tel (11) 646864; telex 12294.
Ambassador: Kujtim Hysenaj.

ALGERIA

Embassy: 11000 Belgrade, Maglajska 26B; tel (11) 668211; telex 12343.
Ambassador: Ahmed Attaf.

ANGOLA

Embassy: 11000 Belgrade, Tolstojeva 51; tel (11) 663199; telex 11841.
Ambassador: Evaristo Domingos.
Third Secretary: Narciso do Espirito Santo Junior.
Head of Protocol: Martinho Bachi Codo.
Attaché (Administrative): José João Sebastião.
Attaché (Finance): Miguel Carlos da Conceicão.

Office of Military Attaché: Belgrade, Bulevar Jna 99; tel (11) 497175.
Military Attaché: Col João Arnaldo Saraiva de Carvalho.
Assistant Military Attaché: Jaime Eduardo do Couto Cabral.

ARGENTINA

Embassy: 11000 Belgrade, Knez Mihajlova 24/I; tel (11) 623569; telex 12182; fax (11) 622630.
Ambassador: Federico Carlos Barttfeld.
Counsellor: Miguel Alfredo Velloso.
Counsellor: Oscar Horacio Galli.
Attaché: Ramón Francisco Lucero.
Secretary (Commercial): Ricardo Jorge Massot.

AUSTRALIA

Embassy: 11000 Belgrade, Čika Ljubina 13; tel (11) 624655; telex 11206; fax (11) 624029.
Ambassador: Francis W. S. Milne.
Counsellor: Leanne Kerr.
Counsellor (Administrative/Consular): Edward J. Patching.
Counsellor (Commercial): John Hennebry.
First Secretary (Emigration): Kevin Kinna.
Second Secretary: Margaret Twomey.
Second Secretary (Consular/Administrative): Louise Holgate.
Second Secretary (Emigration): Joseph Petyanszki.
Second Secretary (Emigration): Kris Kordzik.

AUSTRIA

Embassy: 11000 Belgrade, Kneza Sime Markovića 2; 11001 Belgrade, POB 839; tel (11) 635955; telex 11456; fax (11) 638215.
Ambassador: Walter Siegl.
Minister: Harald W. Kotschy.
Counsellor (Administrative) and Consul-General: Cyrill Stern.
Military and Air Attaché: Gen. Josef Klamminger.
Assistant Military and Air Attaché: Anton Lutche.
Second Secretary: Markus Wuketich.
Second Secretary: Anna Schmidt.
Attaché (Administrative/Consular): Alfred Handler.

Consulate-General: 6100 Ljubljana, Strekljeva 5; tel (61) 213436; telex 31346; fax (61) 221717.
Consul-General: Jutta Stefan-Bastl.

Consulate-General: 41000 Zagreb, Jabukovac 39; tel (41) 273392; telex 21144; fax (41) 424065.
Consul-General: Andreas Berlakovich.

Culture Institute: 41000 Zagreb, Gunduliceva 3; tel (41) 424628; fax (41) 426195.
Attaché (Culture): Leopold Melichar.

BANGLADESH

Embassy: 11000 Belgrade, Dragorska 4; tel (11) 666153; telex 12459.
Ambassador: Harun Ahmed Chowdhury.

BELGIUM

Embassy: 11000 Belgrade, Proleterskih brigada 18; tel (11) 330016; telex 11747; fax (11) 330016.
Ambassador: Baron Alain Guillaume.

BOLIVIA

Embassy: 11000 Belgrade, Romena Rolana 60; tel (11) 781576.
Ambassador: Raúl Zelada Covarrubias.

BRAZIL

Embassy: 11000 Belgrade, Proleterskih brigada 14; tel (11) 339781; telex 11100.
Ambassador: José Olympio Rache de Almeida.

BULGARIA

Embassy: 11000 Belgrade, Birčaninova 26; tel (11) 646222; telex 11665.
Ambassador: Marko Markov.

CAMBODIA

Embassy: 11000 Belgrade, Gospodar Jovanova 67; tel (11) 631151.
Ambassador: René Vanhon.

CANADA

Embassy: 11000 Belgrade, Kneza Miloša 75; tel (11) 644666; telex 11137; fax (11) 641480.
Ambassador: James B. Bissett.
Counsellor and Consul: L. E. Green.
Counsellor (Immigration) and Consul: B. T. Casey.
Counsellor (Commercial): H. J. Himmelsbach.
Forces Attaché: Col P. M. R. Valois.
Second Secretary (Administrative) and Vice-Consul: R. A. Longtin.
Second Secretary (Immigration) and Vice-Consul: G. J. Kernighan.
Second Secretary (Immigration) and Vice-Consul: N. L. Mathiasen.

Consulate: 41000 Zagreb, Mihanoviceva 1; tel (41) 428783.
Honorary Consul: M. Zmajevic.

CHILE

Embassy: 11000 Belgrade, Vasilija Gaćeše 9A; tel (11) 648340.
Ambassador: Luis Jerez Ramírez.

CHINA, PEOPLE'S REPUBLIC

Embassy: 11000 Belgrade, Kralja Milutina 6; tel (11) 331484; telex 11146.
Ambassador: Zhang Dake.

COLOMBIA

Embassy: 11000 Belgrade, Njegoševa 54/II-5; tel (11) 457246; telex 12530; fax (11) 457120.

CUBA

Embassy: 11000 Belgrade, Kneza Miloša 14; tel (11) 657694.
Ambassador: Zoila Rosales Brito.

CYPRUS

Embassy: 11040 Belgrade, Diplomatska Kolonija 9; tel (11) 663725; telex 12729; fax (11) 665348.
Ambassador: Andrestinos N. Papadopoulos.

CZECHOSLOVAKIA

Embassy: 11000 Belgrade, bul. Revolucije 22; tel (11) 330134; telex 72790; fax (11) 336448.
Ambassador: František Lipka.
Minister-Counsellor: Ján Lehoczký.
Counsellor (Commercial): Ladislav Vodrážka.
Counsellor (Economic): Jiří Urban.
Counsellor (Consular): Eugen Šuhajda.
Military and Air Attaché: Milan Václavík.
Assistant Military and Air Attaché: Jaroslav Jurníček.
First Secretary: Josef Hejsek.
First Secretary: František Vereš.

DENMARK

Embassy: 11040 Belgrade, Neznanog Junaka 9a; tel (11) 667826; telex 11219; fax (11) 660759.
Ambassador: Hans Jespersen.
Counsellor (Commercial): Joachim Rehder.
Attaché and Consul: Kay Erik Sønderup.

Consulate-General: 41000 Zagreb, Pavla Radica 31; tel (41) 277410; telex 21721.
Consul-General: Milan Arko.
Consul: Branko Vukmir.

Consulate: 50100 Dubrovnik, Put Minajla 1, c/o Atlantska Plovidba; tel (50) 22377; telex 27516; fax (50) 20384.
Consul: Pero Musladin.

Consulate: 51000 Rijeka, Zagrebačkka 9/V; tel (51) 211984; telex 24382.
Consul: Djordje Ivkovic.

Consulate: 58000 Split, Put Meja 56; tel (58) 43488; telex 26167.
Consul: Vinko Muscatello.

ECUADOR

Embassy: 11000 Belgrade, Kneza Miloša 16; tel (11) 684876; telex 12751.
Ambassador: Francisco Proaño Arandi.

EGYPT

Embassy: 11000 Belgrade, Andre Nikoliča 12; tel (11) 651225; telex 12074.
Ambassador: Dr Hussein Hassouna.

ETHIOPIA

Embassy: 11000 Belgrade, Knez Mihajlova 6/IV; tel (11) 628666; telex 11818.

Ambassador: Makonnen Gizaw.
Counsellor: Tesfaye Hailemariam.
Second Secretary: Taye Tesfaye.
Third Secretary: Hailemariam Legesse.

FINLAND

Embassy: 11000 Belgrade, Birčaninova 29; 11001 Belgrade, POB 926; tel (11) 646322; telex 11707; fax (11) 683365.
Ambassador: Mauno Castrén.
Secretary (Commercial): Kalevi Uitti.

Consulate: 61001 Ljubljana, Mosa Pijadejeva 29, International Trade Corporation, POB 317-VI; tel (61) 322844; telex 31181.
Consul: Nikolaj Ticar.

Consulate: 71000 Sarajevo, Fuada Midzica 234; tel (71) 35596.
Consul: Osman Djikic.

Consulate: 58000 Split, Saveznicka Obala 1, Jadroagent; tel (58) 45366; telex 26116.
Consul: Peter Hrzic.

Consulate: 41000 Zagreb, Proleterskih brigada 62, Ingra; tel (41) 515355; telex 21239.
Consul: Vanja Kalogjera.

FRANCE

Embassy: 11000 Belgrade, POB 283, Pariska 11; tel (11) 636200; telex 11496.
Ambassador: Michel Chatelais.

Consulate-General: 41000 Zagreb, Sloserove Stube 5, POB 466; tel (41) 272985.

GABON

Embassy: 11040 Belgrade, Dragorska 3; tel (11) 669683; telex 12019.
Ambassador: Emmanuel Mendoume-Nze.

GERMANY

Embassy: 11000 Belgrade, Ul. Kneza Miloša 74-76; tel (11) 645755; telex 11107; fax (11) 686989.
Ambassador: Dr Hansjörg Eiff.

Consulate-General: 41001 Zagreb, POB 1026, Proleterskih brigada 64; tel (41) 519200; telex 21378; fax (41) 518070.
Consul-General: Dr Hans Julius Boldt.

GHANA

Embassy: 11000 Belgrade, Ognjena Price 50; tel (11) 4442401; telex 11720; fax (11) 436314.
Ambassador: Thomas Benjamin Sam.
Minister-Counsellor: Hilary Kwele Ziniel.
Third Secretary: Christina Dei Neequaye.

GREECE

Embassy: 11000 Belgrade, Francuska 33; tel (11) 621443; telex 11361.
Ambassador: Eleftherios Karayannis.

GUINEA

Embassy: 11000 Belgrade, Ohridska 4; tel (11) 431830; telex 11963.
Ambassador: Morou Balde.

HOLY SEE

Apostolic Nunciature: 11000 Belgrade, Svetog Save 24; tel (11) 432822.
Apostolic Pro-Nuncio: Gabriel Montalvo.
Counsellor: Mgr Antonio Lucibello.

HUNGARY

Embassy: 11000 Belgrade, Ivana Milutinovica 74; tel (11) 4440472.
Ambassador: Őszi István.

Consulate: 41000 Zagreb.
Consul: Gábor Bagi.

ICELAND

Consulate-General: 11070 Belgrade, POB 20, 12 Bulevar Lenjina; tel (11) 145351; telex 12184.
Consul-General: Ljubomir Popovic.

INDIA

Embassy: 11070 Belgrade, B-06/07 Genex International Centre, Vladimira Popovića 6; tel (11) 2223325; telex 71127; fax (11) 2223357.
Ambassador: Aditya Narayan Dhairyasheel Haksar.
Counsellor: H. K. Singh.
Military, Naval and Air Attaché: Col Amar Singh.
First Secretary (Commerce): Rajeet Mitter.
First Secretary (Consular): S. Banerjee.
Second Secretary (Information): T. S. Nayar.

INDONESIA

Embassy: 11040 Belgrade, POB 559, bul. Oktobarske Revolucije br. 18; tel (11) 662122; telex 11129.
Ambassador: Atwar Nurhadi.

IRAN

Embassy: 11000 Belgrade, Proleterskih brigada 9; tel (11) 338782; telex 11726; fax (11) 338784.
Ambassador: Nasrollah Kazemi Kamyab.

IRAQ

Embassy: 11000 Belgrade, Proleterskih brigada 69; tel (11) 434688; telex 12325.
Ambassador: Dr Wahbi al-Qaraguli.

ITALY

Embassy: 11000 Belgrade, Birčaninova 11; tel (11) 659722; telex 12082.
Ambassador: Sergio Vento.

JAPAN

Embassy: 11000 Belgrade, Ilirska 5; tel (11) 768255; telex 11263; fax (11) 762934.
Ambassador: Taizo Nakamura.

JORDAN

Embassy: 11000 Belgrade, Kablarska 28; tel (11) 651642; telex 12904.
Ambassador: Hani B. Tabbara.

KOREA, DEMOCRATIC PEOPLE'S REPUBLIC

Embassy: 11000 Belgrade, Dr Milutina Ivkoviča 9; tel (11) 668739; telex 11577.
Ambassador: Chi Jae Ryong.

KOREA, REPUBLIC

Embassy: 11070 Belgrade, Genex International Centre, Vladimira Popovića 6; tel (11) 2223531.
Ambassador: Doo Byong Shin.

KUWAIT

Embassy: 11000 Belgrade, Čakorska 2; tel (11) 664961; telex 12774.
Ambassador: Issa Ahmad al-Hammad.

LEBANON

Embassy: 11000 Belgrade, Vase Pelagića 38; tel (11) 651290; telex 11049.
Ambassador: Dr William Habib.

LIBYA

People's Committee: 11000 Belgrade, General Ždanova 42; tel (11) 644782; telex 11787.
Secretary of People's Committee: Assur Muhamed Karkum.

MALAYSIA

Embassy: 11000 Belgrade, Čakorska 8; tel (11) 660823; telex 12129.
Ambassador: Zainuddin A. Rahman.

MALI

Embassy: 11000 Belgrade, Generala Hanrisa 1; tel (11) 493774; telex 11052.
Ambassador: N'Tji Laico Traore (designate).
Counsellor: Mohamadoun B. Bocoum.
Secretary (Finance): Cherif Abdoulaye Diallo.

MEXICO

Embassy: 11102 Belgrade, Trg Republike 5-IV; tel (11) 638111; telex 12141; fax (11) 629227.
Ambassador: Augustín García-López Santaolalla.
Second Secretary: Eugenia Cabrera Murillo.

MONGOLIA

Embassy: 11000 Belgrade, Generala Vasića 5; tel (11) 668536; telex 12253.
Ambassador: Ludevdorjyn Khashbat.

MOROCCO

Embassy: 11000 Belgrade, Sanje Živanović 4; tel (11) 651775.
Ambassador: Hassan Fassi Fihri (designate).

MYANMAR

Embassy: 11000 Belgrade, Kneza Miloša 72; tel (11) 645420; telex 72769.
Ambassador: U Hla Maung.
Counsellor: U Sai Thaw Da.
Third Secretary: U Tin Aye.

NETHERLANDS

Embassy: 11000 Belgrade, Simina 29; tel (11) 626699; telex 11556; fax (11) 628986.
Ambassador: J. H. W. Fietelaars.
Counsellor: D. R. Hasselman.
Counsellor (Agriculture): I. J. G. Haker.
Defence Attaché: Col W. F. S. van Lingen.
Second Secretary: D. J. L. Werner.
Attaché (Administrative): T. E. Radelaar.

Consulate: 51000 Rijeka, Pino Budicin 1B; tel (51) 213114; telex 24380.
Consul: B. Glavan.

Consulate: 41000 Zagreb, Proleterskih brigada 72; tel (41) 538150; telex 22388; fax (41) 537282.
Consul: J. Janković.

Consulate: 61000 Ljubljana, Titova 52; tel (61) 326961; telex 31314; fax (61) 326158.
Consul: Dr M. Škof.

Consulate: 58000 Split, I. L. Ribar 29; tel (58) 510421; telex 26276; fax (58) 510421.
Consul: S. Kondić.

Consulate: 50000 Dubrovnik, Gruska Obala 22; tel (50) 23469; telex 27524.
Consul: Capt. P. Metković.

Consulate: 91000 Skopje, ul. Partenija Zogravski 41; tel (91) 221735.
Consul: O. Ivanova.

NIGERIA

Embassy: 11000 Belgrade, Geršićeva 14A, POB 1021; tel (11) 413411; telex 12875.
Ambassador: Ezekiel Gotom Dimka.
Minister: Joseph U. Ayalogu.
Minister-Counsellor (Political): Adegboyega I. Boyede.
Senior Counsellor (Economic/Commercial): Tuesday K. Obajuluwa.

First Secretary and Head of Chancery: Valentine I. Ogosi.
Second Secretary (Consular): Stephen V. Chirtau.

NORWAY

Embassy: 11040 Belgrade, Kablarska 30; tel (11) 651626; telex 11668; fax (11) 651754.
Ambassador: Georg Krane.

PAKISTAN

Embassy: 11000 Belgrade, bul. Oktobarske Revolucije 62; tel (11) 661676.
Ambassador: Saidulla Khan Dehlavi.

PANAMA

Embassy: 11000 Belgrade, Strahinjića Baua 51/II-5; tel (11) 620374; telex 11451.
Ambassador: Ricardo T. Pezet H.
Minister-Counsellor: Cristóbal Sarmiento.
Attaché (Consular/Cultural): Zdravka S. de Ilincic.

PERU

Embassy: 11000 Belgrade, Baba Višnjina 26/II-10; tel (11) 452347; telex 12272; fax (11) 454943.
Ambassador: Eduardo Llosa Larrabure.
First Secretary: Benjamin Chimoy Arteaga.
Second Secretary (Consular): Eduardo Rivoldi Nicolini.

PHILIPPINES

Embassy: 11040 Belgrade, Tolstojeva 49, Dedinje; tel (11) 661442; telex 12052.
Ambassador: José U. Fernandez.

POLAND

Embassy: 11000 Belgrade, Kneza Miloša 38; tel (11) 644866; telex 72006; fax (11) 646275.
Ambassador: Jerzy Chmielewski.

PORTUGAL

Embassy: 11110 Belgrade, Stojana Novakovića 19; tel (11) 750358; telex 11648; fax (11) 754421.
Ambassador: João Morais da Cunha Matos.
First Secretary: Hugo Cabral de Moncada.
Attaché (Consular): Carlos Abrantes.
Attaché (Commercial): Carlos Sá Faria.

ROMANIA

Embassy: 11000 Belgrade, Kneza Miloša 70; tel (11) 646071; telex 11316.
Ambassador: Ionel Stanculescu.

RUSSIA

Embassy: 11000 Belgrade, Deligradska 32; tel (11) 657533.
Ambassador: Vadim Loginov.

Consulate-General: 41000 Zagreb, Bosanska 44; tel (41) 575444.

SAN MARINO

Consulate-General: 11070 Belgrade, Hotel Belgrade Intercontinental, Vladimira Popovića 10; tel (11) 134760; telex 12009; fax (11) 131402.
Consul-General: Antonia Fattori.
Consul: Giovanni A. Baggio.

SPAIN

Embassy: 11000 Belgrade, Njegoševa 54/I Apt. 1-3; tel (11) 454777; telex 12864; fax (11) 4440614.
Ambassador: José Manuel Allendesalazar.

SRI LANKA

Embassy: 11000 Belgrade, Lepenička 10; tel (11) 460661; telex 12475.
Ambassador: Razik Zarook (designate).
Third Secretary: M. Renganathan.

SUDAN

Embassy: 11000 Belgrade, Nemanjina 4/V; tel (11) 657960; telex 12479.
Ambassador: Ibrahim A. Hamra.
Military, Naval and Air Attaché: Brig. Kamal A. Maglad.
First Secretary: Ibrahim Ahmed M. Abdel Karim.
First Secretary: Abu Bakr Hussein Ahmed.
First Secretary: Khamis Hagar Zat.
Attaché (Administrative): Ibrahim Ahmed Gornas.

SWEDEN

Embassy: 11001 Belgrade, POB 725, Pariska 7; tel (11) 626422; telex 11595; fax (11) 626492.
Ambassador: Jan af Sillen.
Counsellor: Örjan Landelius.
Defence Attaché: Col Lars-Erik Ström.
Second Secretary: Inger Johannesson.
Second Secretary: Lars-Gunnar Wigemark.
Chancellor: Dragica Andjić.

Consulate-General: 41000 Zagreb, Radićeva 14/2; tel (41) 274446; telex 22354.
Consul-General: Niko Bonetti.

Consulate: 50000 Dubrovnik, ul. Zeljarice 5, c/o Globtour; tel (50) 28144; telex 27550; fax (50) 26322.
Consul: Veljiko Kavurčič.

Consulate: 51000 Rijeka, Palace Jadran, c/o Jadrolinja; tel (51) 30899; telex 24225.
Consul: Nikša Kuiš.

SWITZERLAND

Embassy: 11001 Belgrade, Birčaninova 27, POB 817; tel (11) 646843; telex 11383; fax (11) 657253.
Ambassador: Jean-Jacques Indermühle.
Counsellor: Denis Feldmeyer.
Assistant Defence Attaché: Maj. Samuel Hunziker.
Attaché and Office Manager: Marie-Thérèse Heldner.

Consulate-General: 41000 Zagreb, Bogovićeva 3, POB 471; tel (41) 421473; telex 21550.
Consul-General: Werner Maurer.
Vice-Consul and Chancellor: Monika Styner.

SYRIA

Embassy: 11000 Belgrade, Mlade Bosne 31; tel (11) 430619; telex 11889; fax (11) 453367.
Ambassador: Ismail al-Kadi.
Minister-Counsellor: Mohamed Walid Trabulsi.
Counsellor: Moukhless Pharaon.
Attaché (Public Affairs): As'ad Ahmed Ahmad.
Attaché: Nidal al-Ash'hab.

THAILAND

Embassy: 11000 Belgrade, POB 1024, Molerova 11/V; tel (11) 454053; telex 12657.
Ambassador: Ukirt Durayaprama.
Counsellor (Commercial): Vorathep Supadulya.

TUNISIA

Embassy: 11000 Belgrade, Vase Pelagića 19; tel (11) 652966; telex 11461.
Ambassador: Raouf Said.

TURKEY

Embassy: 11000 Belgrade, Proleterskih brigada 1; tel (11) 335431; telex 12081; fax (11) 331464.
Ambassador: Berhan Ekinci.

UNITED KINGDOM

Embassy: 11000 Belgrade, Generala Ždanova 46; tel (11) 645034; telex 11468; fax (11) 659651.
Ambassador: Peter E. Hall.
Counsellor, Consul-General and Deputy Head of Mission: M. J. Robinson.
Defence and Military Attaché: Col E. D. Powell-Jones.
Naval and Air Attaché: Wing Commdr R. Parker.
First Secretary (Economic): W. L. Jackson-Houlston.
Consul and First Secretary (Management): H. D. Marcelin.
Second Secretary (Political/Information): J. N. Y. Dawbarn.
Vice-Consul and Third Secretary (Management): J. A. Ashdown.

Consulate: 41000 Zagreb, Ilica 12/II, POB 454; tel (41) 424888; telex 21309; fax (41) 420100.
Honorary Consul: B. Jenkins.

Consulate: 58000 Split, Titova Obala 10/III; tel (58) 41464; telex 26497.
Honorary Consul: Capt. A. Mekjavic.

Consulate: 50000 Dubrovnik, Atlas, Pile 1; tel (50) 27333; telex 27515.
Honorary Consul: Sarah Marojica.

USA

Embassy: 11000 Belgrade, POB 5070, Kneza Miloša 50; tel (11) 645655; telex 11529; fax (11) 645221.
Ambassador: Warren Zimmermann.
Deputy Head of Mission: Robert Rackmales.
Political Section: James W. Swigert.
Economic Section: Patrick J. Nichols.
Commercial Section: Peter Noble.
Consular Section: Robert E. Tynes.
Administrative Section: John M. O'Keefe.
Regional Security Officer: Gordon A. Sjue.
Attaché (Science): Thomas Hutson.
Agricultural Section: Clyde E. Gumbmann.
Public Affairs Officer: Bruce R. Koch.
Office of Defence Attaché: Col C. Gene Whisnant.
Communications Programme Officer: Andrew J. Skok.
Information Systems Manager: Steve A. Lauderdale.

Consulate-General: 41000 Zagreb, Brace Kavurica 2; tel (41) 444800; telex 21180; fax (41) 440235.
Consul-General: M. Michael Einik.
Political, Economic and Commercial Sections: Douglas C. Greene.
Consular Section: Theorphilus R. Rose.
Administrative Section: Douglas S. Dobson.
Branch Public Affairs Officer: Mark J. Smith.
Communications Programme Officer: Daniel J. Donoghue.

URUGUAY

Embassy: 11000 Belgrade, Vasina 14; tel (11) 620994; telex 12650.
Ambassador: Dr Fernando Gómez Fyns.

VENEZUELA

Embassy: 11000 Belgrade, Terazije 45/II; tel (11) 331604; telex 12856; fax (11) 330683.
Ambassador: Freddy Christians.
First Secretary: Simón Becerra Farias.
Second Secretary: Federico Dubuc Matos.

Consulate: 41000 Zagreb, Strosmajerov trg 11/II; tel (41) 423651.
Honorary Consul: Anthony Perosch.

VIET-NAM

Embassy: 11000 Belgrade, Lackovićeva 6; tel (11) 663527; telex 11292.
Ambassador: Vo Anh Tulan.
Counsellor: Pham Si Tam.
Second Secretary: Nguyen Viet Canh.
Attaché (Commercial): Tran Hoa Thien.

YEMEN

Embassy: 11000 Belgrade, Vasilija Gaćeše 9C.
Ambassador: Mohamed Mahmood Hassan al-Baihi.

ZAIRE

Embassy: 11000 Belgrade, Oktobarske revolucije 47; tel (11) 668931; telex 11491.
Ambassador: Lundunge Kadahi Chiri-Mwami.

ZAMBIA

Embassy: 11000 Belgrade, Simina 17, POB 1025; tel (11) 637955; telex 12152.
Ambassador: Anderson Henry Kaluya.
Counsellor: G. S. Akafekwa.
Military Attaché: Col Manson P. Mulwanda.
First Secretary: Emmanuel T. Hare.
Second Secretary: Mike Goma.

ZIMBABWE

Embassy: 11000 Belgrade, Perside Milenković 9; tel (11) 647047; telex 11925.
Ambassador: Chimbidzayi E. C. Sanyangare.
Counsellor: Rodney S. M. Kiwa.
Counsellor: Isaac J. Mhaka.
Second Secretary: Tokozile Dlodlo.

International Organizations

EUROPEAN COMMUNITIES

External Delegation: 11040 Belgrade, 29 Kablarsku, Senjak; tel (11) 648666; telex 11949; fax (11) 651458.
Head of Delegation: Marc Janssens.

ZAIRE

ALGERIA

Embassy: 50/52 ave Colonel Ebeya, BP 12798, Kinshasa; tel (12) 22470.
Chargé d'affaires a.i.: Hocine Meghlaoui.

ANGOLA

Embassy: 4413-4429 blvd du 30 juin, BP 8625, Kinshasa; tel (12) 32415.
Ambassador: Miguel Gaspard Neto.

ARGENTINA

Embassy: 181 blvd du 30 juin, BP 16798, Kinshasa; tel (12) 25485.
Ambassador: Werner Roberto Justo Burghardt.

AUSTRIA

Embassy: 39 ave Lubefu, BP 16399, Kinshasa-Gombe; tel (12) 22150; telex 21310.
Ambassador: Dr Hans Kogler.
Secretary (Economic): Gotfried Haffner.

BELGIUM

Embassy: Immeuble le Cinquantenaire, place du 27 octobre, BP 899, Kinshasa; tel (12) 20110; telex 21114; fax (12) 22120.
Ambassador: André Adam.

BENIN

Embassy: 3990 ave des Cliniques, BP 3265, Kinshasa-Gombe; tel (12) 33156.
Ambassador: Pierre Désiré Sadeler.

BRAZIL

Embassy: 190 ave Basoko, BP 13296, Kinshasa; tel (12) 21781; telex 21515.
Ambassador: Ayrton G. Dieguez.

BURUNDI

Embassy: 17 ave de la Gombe, BP 1483, Kinshasa; tel (12) 31588; telex 21655.
Ambassador: Longin Kanuma.

CAMEROON

Embassy: 1175 ave Tombalbaye, BP 10998, Kinshasa; tel (12) 34787; telex 21353.
Ambassador: Jérôme Mendouga.
Second Counsellor: J. B. Charles Foe-Atangana.
Second Counsellor: Justin-Joël Abessolo.
Attaché (Finance): Paul Ngoyong.

CANADA

Embassy: 17 ave Pumbu, BP 8341, Kinshasa I; tel (12) 21801; telex 21303.
Ambassador: Claude Laverdure.
Counsellor and Consul: J. C. Pelletier.
First Secretary (Development) and Consul: J. Savaria.
First Secretary (Development) and Consul: D. Rossetti.
First Secretary (Commercial) and Consul: R. Catellier.

CENTRAL AFRICAN REPUBLIC

Embassy: 11 ave Pumbu, BP 7769, Kinshasa; tel (12) 30417.
Ambassador: J.-G. Mamadou.

CHAD

Embassy: 67-69 ave du Cercle, BP 9097, Kinshasa; tel (12) 22358.
Ambassador: Maitine Djoumbe.

CHINA, PEOPLE'S REPUBLIC

Embassy: 49 ave du Commerce, BP 9098, Kinshasa; tel (12) 23972.
Ambassador: An Guozheng.

CONGO

Embassy: 179 blvd du 30 juin, BP 9516, Kinshasa; tel (12) 30220.
Ambassador: Alexis Oloi.

COTE D'IVOIRE

Embassy: 68 ave de la Justice, BP 9197, Kinshasa; tel (12) 30440; telex 21214.
Ambassador: Gaston Allouko Fiankan.

CUBA

Embassy: 4660 ave Cateam, BP 10699, Kinshasa; telex 21158.
Ambassador: Enrique Montero.

CZECHOSLOVAKIA

Embassy: 54 ave Colonel Tshatshi, BP 8242, Kinshasa-Gombe; tel (12) 34610; telex 21183.
Chargé d'affaires a.i.: František Blažek.
Attaché: Ján Tušim.

DENMARK

Consulate-General: 153 chemin Riviera, Joli Parc, Ngaliema, BP 1446, Kinshasa 1; tel (12) 20260; telex 21339; fax (12) 20648.
Consul-General: Walter Flückiger-Bohren.
Consulate: 1046 ave Mama Yemo, Lubumbashi; tel (2) 2646.
Consul: Jean-Loup Taizard.
Consulate: 3 rue de Vivi, BP 36, Matadi; tel 2166; telex 20406.
Consul: Yves de Biesme.

EGYPT

Embassy: 519 ave de l'Ouganda, BP 8838, Kinshasa; tel (12) 30296.
Ambassador: Aziz Abdel Hamid Hamza.

ETHIOPIA

Embassy: BP 8435, Kinshasa; tel (12) 23327.
Ambassador: Col Legesse Wolde-Mariam.

FINLAND

Consulate: Société d'Evaluation du Diamant au Zaïre, Nouvelles Geleries Prés., 22e étage, No. 22 C, BP 8853, Kinshasa 1; tel (12) 26310; telex 21255.
Consul: Nicholas Charles Davenport.

FRANCE

Embassy: 97 ave de la République du Tchad, BP 3093, Kinshasa; tel (12) 22116; telex 21074.

Ambassador: Henri Rethoré.

GABON

Embassy: ave du 24 novembre, BP 9592, Kinshasa; tel (12) 68325; telex 21455.
Ambassador: Joseph Koumba Mounguengui.

GERMANY

Embassy: 82 ave des Treis, BP 8400, Kinshasa-Gombe; tel (12) 27720; telex 21110; fax (12) 21528.
Ambassador: Dietrich Venzlaff.

Consulate: 25/1 ave Kabare, Muhumba, Zone Ibanda, BP 1240, Bukavu; tel (12) 37074; telex 11; fax 37412.
Honorary Consul: Ulf Behringer.

Consulate: ave Mpale, BP 960, Lubumbashi; tel (2) 224263.
Honorary Consul: Claudia Somville.

Consulate: BP 715, Matadi.
Honorary Consul: Rudolf Obrist.

GHANA

Embassy: 206 ave du 24 novembre, BP 8446, Kinshasa; tel (12) 31766.
Ambassador: Kwaku Adu Bediako.

GREECE

Embassy: 72 ave des 3Z, BP 478, Kinshasa; tel (12) 31189.
Ambassador: Stelio Valsamas-Rhallis.

GUINEA

Embassy: 7-9 ave Lubefu, BP 9899, Kinshasa; tel (12) 30864.
Ambassador: Félix Faber.

HOLY SEE

Apostolic Nunciature: 81 ave Goma, BP 3091, Kinshasa; tel (12) 31419; telex 21527.
Pro-Nuncio: Mgr Alfio Rapisarda.
Secretary: Daniel R. Pater.

INDIA

Embassy: 18-B ave des Batétéla, BP 1026, Kinshasa; tel (12) 33368; telex 21179; fax (12) 263062.
Ambassador: Arun Kumar.
Second Secretary: P. H. Sondhi.
Attaché (Consular): P. P. Sircar.

IRAN

Embassy: 76 blvd du 30 juin, BP 16599, Kinshasa; tel (12) 31052; telex 21429.

ISRAEL

Embassy: 12 ave des Aviateurs, BP 8343, Kinshasa; tel (12) 21201.
Ambassador: Shlomo Avital.
Second Secretary: Dan Golan.

ITALY

Embassy: 8 ave de la Mongala, BP 1000, Kinshasa; tel (12) 23416; telex 21560.
Ambassador: Vittorio Amedeo Farinelli.

JAPAN

Embassy: Bâtiment Marsaveu, 2e étage, ave Col Lukusa, BP 1810, Kinshasa; tel (12) 22118; telex 21227; fax (12) 21817.
Ambassador: Kyoichi Omura.

KENYA

Embassy: 5002 ave de l'Ouganda, BP 9667, Kinshasa; tel (12) 30117; telex 21359.
Ambassador: Mwabili Kisaka.

KOREA, DEMOCRATIC PEOPLE'S REPUBLIC

Embassy: 168 ave de l'Ouganda, BP 16597, Kinshasa; tel (12) 31566.
Ambassador: Yi Hyon Sik.

KOREA, REPUBLIC

Embassy: 2A ave des Orangers, BP 628, Kinshasa; tel (12) 31022.
Ambassador: Chun Soon-Kyu.

KUWAIT

Embassy: Suite 232, Intercontinental Hotel, Kinshasa.

LEBANON

Embassy: 3 ave de l'Ouganda, Kinshasa; tel (12) 32682; telex 21423.
Ambassador: Mustafa Horeibe.

LIBERIA

Embassy: 9 ave de l'Equateur, BP 8940, Kinshasa; tel (12) 21954; telex 21205.
Ambassador: Jalla D. Lansanah.
First Secretary and Consul: L. Llewellyn Witherspoon.

LIBYA

Embassy: BP 9198, Kinshasa.

MAURITANIA

Embassy: BP 16397, Kinshasa; tel (12) 59575; telex 21380.
Ambassador: Lieut Col M'Bareck Ould Bouna Moktar.

MOROCCO

Embassy: 4497 ave Lubefu, BP 912, Kinshasa; tel (12) 30255.
Ambassador: Aboubkeur Cherkaoui.

NETHERLANDS

Embassy: 11 ave Zongo Ntolo, BP 10299, Kinshasa; tel (12) 30733.
Chargé d'affaires: J. G. Wilbrenninck.

NIGERIA

Embassy: 141 blvd du 30 juin, BP 1700, Kinshasa; tel (12) 33342; telex 21173.
Ambassador: Col Dag Wilcox.
Minister-Counsellor: B. C. Okagbare.
Second Counsellor: E. O. Elenwo.
Attaché (Finance): R. A. Koya.

PAKISTAN

Embassy: 4413 blvd du 30 juin, Kinshasa.
Chargé d'affaires: Shafqat Ali Shaikh.

POLAND

Embassy: 63 ave de la Justice, BP 8553, Kinshasa; tel (12) 33349; telex 21057.
Ambassador: Andrzej M. Lupina.
First Secretary: Boguslaw Nowakowski.

PORTUGAL

Embassy: 270 ave des Aviateurs, BP 7775, Kinshasa; tel (12) 24010; telex 221328.
Ambassador: Luís de Vasconcelos Pimentel Quartin Bastos.

ROMANIA

Embassy: 5 ave de l'Ouganda, BP 2242, Kinshasa; tel (12) 30988; telex 21316.
Ambassador: Mircea Andrei.

RUSSIA

Embassy: 80 ave de la Justice, BP 1143, Kinshasa I; tel (12) 33157; telex 21690.
Ambassador: Vladislovas Jonaitis.

RWANDA

Embassy: 50 ave de la Justice, BP 967, Kinshasa; tel (12) 30327; telex 21612.
Ambassador: Antoine Nyilinkindi.

SOUTH AFRICA

Liaison Office: 310 ave de la Gombe, BP 7829, Kinshasa; tel (12) 14676.
Representative (Liaison): H. A. Hanekom.
Deputy Representative (Liaison): K. Pedro.

SPAIN

Embassy: Immeuble de la Communauté Hellénique, 4e étage, blvd du 30 juin, BP 8036, Kinshasa; tel (12) 21844; telex 21401.
Ambassador: Eduardo Junco.
Secretary: Felipe de la Morena.
Chancellor: José Luis Liaño.

Consulate: 26 ave Maniema, BP 1026, Lubumbashi; tel (2) 225216.
Honorary Consul: Angel Manrique.

SUDAN

Embassy: 83 ave des Treis, BP 7347, Kinshasa.
Ambassador: Mubarak Adam Hadi.

SWEDEN

Embassy: Immeuble Botour, 3e étage, rue Ipenge, BP 11096, Kinshasa; tel (12) 21240; telex 21011.
Ambassador: Bengt Rösiö (resident in Sweden).
Chargé d'affaires a.i.: Lars Ekstrom.

Consulate: c/o Atlas Copco, 222 ave Kapenda, BP 2625, Lubumbashi (Shaba); tel (2) 222218; telex 41029.
Consul: Albert Herbigneaux.

Consulate: c/o Conti Lift Zaire, 24 ave de Kinshasa, BP 726, Matadi; tel 2137.
Consul: Walter Margaretha Frederik Van de Werf.

SWITZERLAND

Embassy: 654 ave Col Tshatshi, BP 8724, Kinshasa I; tel (12) 34234; telex 21154; fax (12) 34246.
Ambassador: Robert Mayor.
Secretary: Bernardino Regazzoni.
Attaché and Head of Chancery: Anne Baudois.

TANZANIA

Embassy: 293 ave du Flambeau, BP 1612, Kinshasa; tel (12) 25593; telex 21400.
Ambassador: P. J. C. Ndobho.

TOGO

Embassy: 3 ave de la Vallée, BP 10197, Kinshasa; tel (12) 33397; telex 21388.
Ambassador: Mama Gnofam.
Second Counsellor: M. Dzogbelko.
Attaché (Finance): Zodanou Adotri.
Attaché: Adjagnon A. Essinam.

TUNISIA

Embassy: ave du Cercle, BP 1498, Kinshasa; tel (12) 31632; telex 21171.
Ambassador: Abdel Krim Moussa.

TURKEY

Embassy: 18 ave Pumbu, BP 7817, Kinshasa; tel (12) 32869.

Ambassador: Salih Diler.

UGANDA

Embassy: 177 ave Tombalbaye, BP 1086, Kinshasa; tel (12) 22740; telex 21618.

UNITED KINGDOM

Embassy: 191 ave de l'Equateur, 5e étage, BP 8049, Kinshasa; tel (12) 21327; telex 21689.
Ambassador: Roger Westbrook.
First Secretary, Consul and Deputy Head of Mission: K. W. Oliver.
First Secretary (Commercial): F. G. Geere.
Second Secretary (Works): W. B. Leith.
Second Secretary (Works): M. A. Austin.
Third Secretary (Management): C. W. Crorkin.
Third Secretary (Chancery/Information): D. S. Schroeder.

Consulate: c/o Gecamines, BP 450, Lubumbashi; tel (2) 5130; telex 41034.
Honorary Consul: P. D. Ashman.

Consulate: Sagrim S.P.R.L., 2 ave de la Corniche, BP 190, Goma.
Honorary Consul: Y. G. de Bruyn.

Consulate: BP 504, Kisangani.
Honorary Consul: R. L. F. Seneque.

USA

Embassy: 310 ave des Aviateurs, BP 697, Kinshasa; tel (12) 21532; telex 21405; fax (12) 21232.
Ambassador: William C. Harrop.
Deputy Head of Mission: Marc A. Bass.
Political Section: Gerald W. Scott.
Economic and Commercial Sections: Ralph E. Bresler.
Consular Section: Wanda Nesbitt.
Administrative Section: Philip D. Gutensohn.
Regional Security Officer: Nanette Krieger.
Agency for International Development: Charles Johnson.
Public Affairs Officer: James J. Hogan.
Office of Defence Attaché: Lieut Col Michael A. Peterson.
Military Assistance Advisory Group: Col Robert Huffman.
Communications Programme Officer: Floyd H. Hagopian.
Information Systems Manager: William J. Walls.

Consulate-General: 1029 blvd Kamanyola, BP 1196, Lubumbashi; tel (2) 222324.
Consulate-General: William J. Brencick.
Political Section: William Merkerson, Jr.
Economic, Consular and Commercial Sections: Lucy K. Abbot.
Agency for International Development: Bruce Spake.
Consular Section: Kimberly A. Daley.
Administrative Section: Tara Feret.
Branch Public Affairs Officer: Peter Piness.
Communications Programme Officer: Robert L. Hensley.

YUGOSLAVIA

Embassy: 112 quai de l'Etoile, BP 619, Kinshasa; tel (12) 32325.
Ambassador: Zarko Milutinović.

ZAMBIA

Embassy: 54-58 ave de l'Ecole, BP 1144, Kinshasa; tel (12) 21802; telex 21209.
Ambassador: Aaron William Mulenga.
First Secretary and Head of Chancery: Harry Kachana Mutumba.
First Secretary: Darius Dustin Nyangulu.
First Secretary: John Richard Shaka Bwalya.
Third Secretary (Accounts): Anthony Malambo Lungu.
Third Secretary (Communications): Albert Musonda Chanda.

Consulate-General: BP 596, Lubumbashi; tel (2) 222309.
Consul-General: Rev. Richard C. Nyendwa.

International Organizations

EUROPEAN COMMUNITIES

External Delegation: 71 ave des Treis, BP 2000, Kinshasa; tel (12) 24708; telex 21560; fax (12) 28863.
Commission Delegate: Johan Wallner.

ZAMBIA

ANGOLA

Embassy: Plot 5548, Lukanga Rd, Kalundu, POB 31595, Lusaka; tel (1) 254346; telex 41940.
Ambassador: Pedro Fernando Mavunza.

AUSTRALIA

High Commission: Memaco House, 3rd Floor, Sapele Rd, POB 35395, 10101 Lusaka; tel (1) 229371; telex 44480; fax (1) 218938.
High Commission: Dr Helen Ware.

AUSTRIA

Embassy: 30A Mutende Rd, Woodlands, POB 31094, Lusaka; tel (1) 260407; telex 43790.
Ambassador: Dr H. Schurz.

BELGIUM

Embassy: Anglo-American Bldg, 74 Independence Ave, POB 31204, Lusaka; tel (1) 23251; telex 40000.
Ambassador: Eric Focke.
Second Secretary (Consular): Gérard Uytterhaegen.

BOTSWANA

High Commission: 2647 Haile Selassie Ave, POB 31910, Lusaka; tel (1) 250804; telex 41710.
High Commissioner: Soblem Mayane (acting).

BRAZIL

Embassy: 74 Anglo-America Bldg, Independence Ave, POB 34470, Lusaka; tel (1) 251652; telex 40102.
Chargé d'affaires: Luis Carlos de Oliveira Feldman.

BULGARIA

Embassy: Plot 251, 3 Ngwee Rd, POB 32896, Lusaka; tel (1) 250880; telex 40215.
Ambassador: Dimitar Romanov.

CANADA

High Commission: North End Branch, Barclays Bank Bldg, Cairo Rd, POB 31313, Lusaka; tel (1) 228811; telex 42480; fax (1) 225160.
Counsellor: G. L. Ohlsen.
Counsellor (Development): F. R. Pim.
First Secretary: F. R. Adam.

CHINA, PEOPLE'S REPUBLIC

Embassy: Plot 7430, Haile Selassie Ave, POB 31975, Lusaka; tel (1) 253770; telex 41360.
Ambassador: Zhou Mingji.

CUBA

Embassy: Plot 5509, Lusiwasi Rd, Kalundu, POB 33132, Lusaka; tel (1) 251380; telex 40309.

CZECHOSLOVAKIA

Embassy: Plot 5199, United Nations Ave, POB 30059, Lusaka; tel (1) 254388; telex 40272.
Chargé d'affaires a.i.: Zdeněk Dobiáš.

DENMARK

Embassy: 352 Independence Ave, POB 50299, Lusaka; tel (1) 251634; telex 43580; fax (1) 251634.
Chargé d'affaires a.i. and Minister-Counsellor: Mark V. Jensen.

EGYPT

Embassy: Plot 5206, United Nations Ave, POB 32428, Lusaka; tel (1) 253762; telex 40021.
Ambassador: Sayed Soliman.

FINLAND

Embassy: 74 Independence Ave, 6th Floor, 15101 Ridgeway, POB 50819, Lusaka; tel (1) 228492; telex 43460; fax (1) 254981.
Ambassador: Ilari Rantakari.

FRANCE

Embassy: Anglo-American Bldg, 4th Floor, 74 Independence Ave, POB 30062, Lusaka; tel (1) 212719; telex 41430.
Ambassador: Jean-Pierre Guyot.

GERMANY

Embassy: United Nations Ave 5209, 15101 Ridgeway, POB 50120, Lusaka; tel (1) 229068; telex 41410.
Ambassador: Rüdiger Reyels.

GHANA

High Commission: 7344 Nangwenya Rd, POB 30347, Lusaka; tel (1) 254685.

GUYANA

High Commission: Design House, 2nd Floor, Dar es Salaam Place, POB 34889, Lusaka; tel (1) 228872; telex 42960.

HOLY SEE

Apostolic Nunciature: Saddam Hussein Blvd, POB 31445, Lusaka; tel (1) 251033.
Apostolic Pro-Nuncio: Archbishop Eugenio Barbaro.
Attaché: Ramón Castro.

INDIA

High Commission: 5220 Haile Selassie Ave, POB 32111, Lusaka; tel (1) 228376; telex 41420.
High Commissioner: Satnam Jit Singh.

IRAN

Embassy: Plot 12/2B, Serval Rd, Kabulonga, Lusaka; tel (1) 263941; telex 40434; fax (1) 263945.
Ambassador: Mohsen Pakaein.
First Secretary: Sayed Hussein Mireskandary.

IRAQ

Embassy: Villa No. 33, Mulungushi Village, POB 34191, Lusaka; tel (1) 291640; telex 44150.
Ambassador: Dr Moussa J. al-Soudani.

IRELAND

Development Co-operation Office: 6663 Katima Mulilo Rd, Olympia Park, POB 34923, Lusaka; tel (1) 290650; telex 43110; fax (1) 290482.
First Secretary: Frank Sheridan.

ITALY

Embassy: Plot 5211, Diplomatic Triangle, POB 31046, Lusaka; tel (1) 250341; telex 43380.
Ambassador: Dr G. Cipolloni.

JAPAN

Embassy: Plot 5218, Haile Selassie Ave, POB 34190, Lusaka; tel (1) 228495; telex 41470; fax (1) 254421.
Ambassador: Yoshiki Sugiura.

KENYA

High Commission: Harambee House, Plot 5207, United Nations Ave, POB 50298, Lusaka; tel (1) 227938; telex 42470.
High Commissioner: Jackson Tumwa.

KOREA, REPUBLIC

Embassy: Lusaka.
Ambassador: Song Pil-Chu.

MALAWI

High Commission: Woodgate House, Cairo Rd, POB 50425, Lusaka; tel (1) 228296; telex 41840.
High Commissioner: B. H. Kawonga.

MOZAMBIQUE

Embassy: Mulungushi Village, Villa 46, POB 34877, Lusaka; tel (1) 250436; telex 45900.
Ambassador: Armando Psungo.

NETHERLANDS

Embassy: 5028 United Nations Ave, POB 31905, Lusaka; tel (1) 250468; telex 42690.
Ambassador: S. van Heemstra.

NIGERIA

High Commission: Zambia Bible House, 5th Floor, Cairo Rd, POB 32598, Lusaka; tel (1) 229860; telex 41280.
High Commissioner: B. C. Selchum.

PORTUGAL

Embassy: Plot 25, Yotom Muteya Rd, POB 33871, Lusaka; tel (1) 252996; telex 40010.
Ambassador: A. Lopes da Fonseca.

ROMANIA

Embassy: 2 Leopard's Hill Rd, POB 31944, Lusaka; tel (1) 262182.

RUSSIA

Embassy: Plot 6407, Diplomatic Triangle, POB 3255, Lusaka; tel (1) 252183; telex 40314.
Ambassador: Oleg Semyonovich Miroshkin.

SAUDI ARABIA

Embassy: Premium House, 5th Floor, POB 34411, Lusaka; tel (1) 227829; telex 45550.

SOMALIA

Embassy: G3/377A Kabulonga Rd, POB 34051, Lusaka; tel (1) 262119; telex 40270.
Ambassador: Dr Oman Umal.

SPAIN

Embassy: Lusaka.
Ambassador: José Manuel Paz y Agüeras.

SWEDEN

Embassy: Haile Selassie Ave, POB 30788, 10101 Lusaka; tel (1) 251249; telex 41820; fax (1) 223388.
Ambassador: Per Taxell.
First Secretary: Elisabeth Dahlin.
Second Secretary: Inger Andersson.
Head of Aid Office: Kjell Nyström.

Consulate: Sandvik (Z) Ltd, Plot 1746, Nakambala Rd, Industrial Side, POB 71148, Ndola; tel (2) 650929; telex 34370.
Consul: Stig Svensson.

TANZANIA

High Commission: Ujamaa House, Plot 5200, United Nations Ave, POB 31219, Lusaka; tel (1) 227698; telex 40118; fax (1) 254861.
High Commissioner: Nimrod Lugoe.

UGANDA

High Commission: Kulima Tower, 11th Floor, POB 33557, Lusaka; tel (1) 227916; telex 40990.
High Commissioner: Karakuza Baguma.

UNITED KINGDOM

High Commission: Plot 5201, Independence Ave, 15101 Ridgeway, POB 50050, Lusaka; tel (1) 228955; telex 41150; fax (1) 253421.
High Commissioner: Peter R. M. Hinchcliffe.
Deputy High Commissioner: T. N. Byrne.
First Secretary (Political): D. F. Middleton.
First Secretary (Commercial/Consular): W. F. Somerset.
First Secretary (Development/Economic): M. A. Hammond.
Second Secretary (Political/Information): T. J. Andrews.
Second Secretary (Aid): J. D. Hawkes.
Second Secretary (Management): C. Gibson.
Second Secretary: M. Green.

USA

Embassy: cnr Independence and United Nations Aves, POB 31617, Lusaka; tel (1) 228595; telex 41970; fax (1) 251578.
Ambassador: Gordon L. Street.
Deputy Head of Mission: Jeffrey A. Bader.
Political Section: Robin Hinson-Jones.
Economic and Commercial Sections: Necia L. Quast.
Consular Section: William Fitzgerald.
Regional Security Officer: Alfred Vincent.
Administrative Section: Gordon R. Olsen.
Agency for International Development: Fred Winch.
Public Affairs Officer: Miriam Guichard.
Communications Programme Officer: Margaret A. Carver.

YUGOSLAVIA

Embassy: Plot 5216, Diplomatic Triangle, POB 31180, Lusaka; tel (1) 250247.
Ambassador: Vladislav Drljević.

ZAIRE

Embassy: Plot 1124, Parirenyatwa Rd, POB 31287, Lusaka; tel (1) 213343.
Ambassador: Dr Atende Omwargo.

ZIMBABWE

High Commission: Memaco House, 4th Floor, Cairo Rd, POB 33491, Lusaka; tel (1) 229382; telex 45800.
High Commissioner: Dr A. H. Mtetwa.

International Organizations

EUROPEAN COMMUNITIES

External Delegation: Plot 4899, Brentwood Drive, POB 34871, Lusaka; tel (1) 250711; telex 40440; fax (1) 250906.
Commission Delegate: Jean-Michel Filori.

ZIMBABWE

AFGHANISTAN

Embassy: 26 East Rd, Avondale, POB 1227, Harare; tel (4) 720083; telex 22276.
Ambassador: Mohammed Sakhi Daneshjo.
First Secretary: Tashsinullah Tashin.

ALGERIA

Embassy: 8 Pascoe Ave, Belgravia, POB 2929, Harare; tel (4) 726682; telex 24795.
Ambassador: Mohammed Lamine Allouane.

ANGOLA

Embassy: Doncaster House, 26 Speke Ave, POB 3590, Harare; tel (4) 790070; telex 24195.
Chargé d'affaires: José Augusto Prata.

ARGENTINA

Embassy: Club Chambers Bldg, cnr Baker Ave and Third St, POB 2770, Harare; tel (4) 730075; telex 22284.
Chargé d'affaires: Carlos Chiappe Solozabal.

AUSTRALIA

High Commission: Karigamombe Centre, 4th Floor, 53 Samora Machel Ave, POB 4541, Harare; tel (4) 794591; telex 24159; fax (4) 704615.
High Commissioner: Joe Duncan Thwaites.
Deputy High Commissioner: Dorothy Holt.
First Secretary (Development Assistance): Anthony O'Dowd.
First Secretary (Consular/Administrative): Maxwell G. Brown.
Second Secretary (Development Assistance): Nescha Teckle.
Second Secretary (Development Assistance): Chris Erwin.

AUSTRIA

Embassy: 216 New Shell House, 30 Samora Machel Ave, POB 4120, Harare; tel (4) 702921; telex 22546.
Ambassador: Helmut Scherz.
Secretary: Evelin Fischer-Socher.
Attaché (Development Co-operation): Markus Cornaro.

BANGLADESH

High Commission: 199 Fife Ave, POB 3040, Harare; tel (4) 727004; telex 24806.
High Commissioner: Humayun Kabir.

BELGIUM

Embassy: Tanganyika House, 5th Floor, 23 Third St, POB 2522, Harare; tel (4) 793306; telex 24788; fax (4) 703960.
Ambassador: Bernard Pierre.
Second Secretary and Chargé d'affaires: Koenraad Lenaerts.
First Secretary (Co-operation): Guy Bastiansen.
Attaché (Administrative/Consular): Benoit Standaert.
Attaché (Economic): Michel Bricteux.
Attaché (Co-operation): Herman Boonen.
Attaché (Administrative/Co-operation): Jules van Oeveren.
Attaché (Administrative/Consular): Maryline Collie.

BOTSWANA

High Commission: 22 Phillips Ave, Belgravia, Harare; tel (4) 729551; telex 22663.
High Commissioner: Pheneas M. Makepe.

BRAZIL

Embassy: Old Mutual Centre, 9th Floor, cnr Third St and Jason Moyo Ave, POB 2530, Harare; tel (4) 730775; telex 22205; fax (4) 737782.
Ambassador: Bernardo de Azevedo Brito.
Counsellor: Jorge d'Escragnolle Taunay Filho.
First Secretary: Hélio Póvoas Júnior.

BULGARIA

Embassy: 15 Maasdorp Ave, Alexandra Park, POB 1809, Harare; tel (4) 730504; telex 24567.
Ambassador: Christo Tepavitcharov.
Counsellor (Commercial): Lyudmil Todorov.
First Secretary (Cultural/Consular): Stefan Todorov.
Second Secretary (Political/Press): Boyko Kotzev.
Second Secretary: Todor Largov.
Third Secretary (Political/Information/Protocol): Petko Draganov.

CANADA

High Commission: 45 Baines Ave, POB 1430, Harare; tel (4) 733881; telex 24465; fax (4) 736833.
High Commissioner: Charles Philip Basset.
Counsellor (Development): D. Spearman.
Counsellor (Development): D. A. McMaster.
Counsellor (Development): J. Perlin.
Counsellor (Development): D. Chaplin.
Counsellor (Commercial): M. J. Slig.
Forces Adviser: Col B. T. N. McGraith.
First Secretary (Development): R. J. Schaltz.
First Secretary (Development): G. F. Paine.
First Secretary (Development): F. Malek.
First Secretary (Administrative): B. D. MacKay.
First Secretary (Development): B. J. Dunlop.
First Secretary (Development): J. T. Sykes.
First Secretary (Development): A. Heuchan.
First Secretary (Development): V. Sutherland.
First Secretary (Development): R. M. Harkness.
First Secretary (Development): F. Tuzo.
First Secretary (Administrative): D. H. Dyet.
First Secretary (Development): G. Saint-Cyr.
First Secretary (Development): S. C. Blais.
First Secretary (Development): M. Angers.
First Secretary (Development): V. W. Shtenko.
First Secretary (Development): D. Edwards.

CHINA, PEOPLE'S REPUBLIC

Embassy: 30 Baines Ave, POB 4749, Harare; tel (4) 724572; telex 22569.
Ambassador: Song Quoqing.

CUBA

Embassy: 5 Phillips Ave, Belgravia, POB 4139, Harare; tel (4) 720256; telex 24783.
Ambassador: Eumelio Cabellero Rodríguez.

CZECHOSLOVAKIA

Embassy: 32 Aberdeen Rd, Avondale, POB 4474, Harare; tel (4) 302636; telex 22460.
Ambassador: Dr Bohuslav Hynek.
Head of Chancery: Anton Hajduk.
Trade Officer: Petr Kotršál.

Commercial Section: 104 Jason Moyo Ave, POB 72, Harare; tel (4) 700636.
Counsellor (Commercial): Julius Kudla.

DENMARK

Embassy: UDC Centre, 1st Floor, 59 Union Ave, POB 4711, Harare; tel (4) 732541; telex 24677; fax (4) 790399.
Ambassador: Henning Kjeldgaard.
Counsellor (Aid) and Head of Aid Mission: Jes Boye-Møller.
Counsellor (Aid): Axel Pedersen.
First Secretary: Erik Kjeldgaard.
Attaché and Vice-Consul: Dila Koustrup.
Attaché: Ulla Dreisler.

EGYPT

Embassy: 7 Aberdeen Rd, Avondale, POB A433, Harare; tel (4) 303445; telex 24653.
Ambassador: Ibrahim Aly Badawi el-Sheik.

ETHIOPIA

Embassy: 14 Lanark Rd, Belgravia, POB 2745, Harare; tel (4) 725822; telex 22743.
Chargé d'affaires: Wendemu Kassa.

FINLAND

Embassy: Karigamombe Centre, 3rd Floor, 53 Samora Machel Ave, POB 5300, Harare; tel (4) 704499; telex 4813; fax (4) 736780.
Chargé d'affaires a.i.: Heikki Tuunanen.
Attaché (Commercial): Pekka Kokko.

FRANCE

Embassy: Ranelagh Rd off Orange Grove Drive, Highlands, POB 1378, Harare; tel (4) 48096; telex 24779.
Ambassador: Pierre Garrigue-Guyonnaud.

GERMANY

Embassy: 14 Samora Machel Ave, POB 2168, Harare; tel (4) 731955; telex 24609.
Ambassador: Dr Werner Killian.

GHANA

High Commission: 11 Downie Ave, Belgravia, POB 4445, Harare; tel (4) 738652; telex 24631.
High Commissioner: John K. B. Tettegah.

GREECE

Embassy: 8 Deary Ave, Belgravia, POB 4809, Harare; tel (4) 723747; telex 24790.
Ambassador: Stelios Rocanos.
First Secretary: Helen Sourani-Potamianos.
Second Secretary: Iphigenia Naoum.
Second Secretary: Nicholas Adamakos.
Attaché (Consular): Grigorios Exadactylos.
Attaché: George Tzanakakis.

HOLY SEE

Apostolic Nunciature: 5 St Kilda Rd, Mount Pleasant, POB MP191, Harare; tel (4) 37381; telex 22390; fax (4) 33131.
Apostolic Pro-Nuncio: Most Rev. Giacinto Berloco.
Counsellor: Lorenzo Baldisseri.

HUNGARY

Embassy: 20 Lanark Rd, Belgravia, POB 3594, Harare; tel (4) 733528; telex 24237; fax (4) 730512.
Ambassador: Tamas Gaspar.
Second Counsellor: István Darvasi.

INDIA

High Commission: 12 Natal Rd, Belgravia, POB 4620, Harare; tel (4) 795955; telex 24630; fax (4) 722324.
High Commissioner: Siddharth Singh.
Deputy High Commissioner: L. Prasad.
First Secretary: S. S. Pandey.

INDONESIA

Embassy: 3 Duthie Ave, Belgravia, POB 3594, Harare; tel (4) 732561; telex 24237.
Ambassador: Sularto Sutowardoyo.

IRAN

Embassy: 8 Allan Wilson Ave, Avondale, POB A293, Harare; tel (4) 726942; telex 24793.
Ambassador: Farhad Shahabi.

IRAQ

Embassy: 21 Lawson Ave, Milton Park, POB 3453, Harare; tel (4) 725727; telex 24595; fax (4) 732506.
Ambassador: Issam Abdul Ghani Mahboub.
Counsellor: Ali S. Mohamed.
Third Secretary: Dawood Salman Mari.
Attaché (Financial): Samir H. H. Komona.

ITALY

Embassy: 7 Bartholomew Close, Greendale North, POB 1062, Harare; tel (4) 48190; telex 24380; fax (4) 48199.
Ambassador: Dr Tommaso Troise.

JAPAN

Embassy: Karigamombe Centre, 18th Floor, 53 Samora Machel Ave, POB 2710, Harare; tel (4) 790108; telex 24566; fax (4) 727769.
Ambassador: Ken Ikebe.

KENYA

High Commission: 95 Park Lane, POB 4069, Harare; tel (4) 790847; telex 24266.
Chargé d'affaires: Leonard Ngaithe.

KOREA, DEMOCRATIC PEOPLE'S REPUBLIC

Embassy: 102 Montague Ave, Greenwood, POB 4754, Harare; tel (4) 724052; telex 24231.
Ambassador: Chon Jae-Hong.

LIBYA

People's Bureau: 124 Harare St, POB 4310, Harare; tel (4) 728381; telex 24585.
Secretary of People's Bureau: Fathi Gebril.

MALAWI

High Commission: Malawi House, Harare St, POB 321, Harare; tel (4) 705611; telex 24467.
High Commissioner: Paul Tony Steven Kandiero.

MOZAMBIQUE

Embassy: 152 Herbert Chitepo Ave, cnr Moffat St, POB 4608, Harare; tel (4) 790837; telex 24466.
Ambassador: Lopes Tembe Ndelana.

NETHERLANDS

Embassy: 47 Enterprise Rd, Highlands, POB HG601, Harare; tel (4) 731428; telex 24357; fax (4) 790520.
Ambassador: John Leefmans.
First Secretary: Wouter J. Lok.
Second Secretary: Johannes de Kuiper.
Attaché (Administrative): Eric T. M. Oostveen.

NEW ZEALAND

High Commission: 6th Floor, 57 Jason Moyo Ave, Batanai Gardens, POB 5448, Harare; tel (4) 728681; telex 22747; fax (4) 790693.
High Commissioner: Douglas Law.
Deputy High Commissioner: Peter Aitken.

NICARAGUA

Embassy: 9 Downie Ave, Belgravia, POB 5804, Harare; tel (4) 731520; fax (4) 731520.
Ambassador: Mario Barquero.
First Secretary: Elliette Ortega.

NIGERIA

High Commission: 36 Samora Machel Ave, POB 4742, Harare; tel (4) 790765; telex 24473; fax (4) 36089.
High Commissioner: Mohammed Lameen Mettedem.
Minister-Counsellor and Head of Chancery: Segun Ojerimola.
First Secretary: Jimoh Kitty Lawal.
Second Secretary (Consular/Economic): Iliya Fachanu.
Third Secretary (Administrative): Victor J. Kamto.

NORWAY

Embassy: 92 Montague Ave, POB 4276, Harare; tel (4) 792419; telex 24550; fax (4) 792830.
Ambassador: Herman Pedersen.

PAKISTAN

High Commission: 11 Van Praagh Ave, Milton Park, POB 3050, Harare; tel (4) 720293; fax (4) 722446.
High Commissioner: Rafat Mahdi.

PERU

Embassy: Zimnat House, 8th Floor, Third St and Baker Ave, POB 5570, Harare; tel (4) 736751; telex 22738; fax (4) 736753.
Chargé d'affaires: Henry Rizo-Patron.

POLAND

Embassy: 16 Cork Rd, Belgravia, POB 3932, Harare; tel (4) 732159; telex 22745.
Ambassador: Boguslaw Miernik.
First Secretary: Andrzej Kasprzyk.
Attaché: Robert Ciechonski.
Attaché: Wlodzimierz Sujkowski.

Commercial Office: 7 Downie Ave, Belgravia, POB 5390, Harare; tel (4) 733501; telex 22745.
Counsellor (Commercial): Roman Grzywacz.
Attaché (Commercial): Boguslaw Boczkowski.

PORTUGAL

Embassy: 10 Samora Machel Ave, POB 406, Harare; tel (4) 725107; telex 24714.
Ambassador: Dr Eduardo Nunez de Carvalho.

ROMANIA

Embassy: 105 Fourth St, cnr Montague Ave, POB 4797, Harare; tel (4) 700853; telex 24797.
Chargé d'affaires: Dimitru Ciubotariu.

RUSSIA

Embassy: 66-70 Fife Ave, POB 4250, Harare; tel (4) 720358; telex 22616; fax (4) 700534.
Ambassador: Yuri A. Youkalov.

SOUTH AFRICA

Trade Mission: Temple Bar House, cnr Baker Ave and Angwa St, POB 121, Harare; tel (4) 707901; telex 2332; fax (4) 703559.
Trade Representative: N. M. Nel.
Deputy Trade Representative: L. J. Haasbroek.

SPAIN

Embassy: 16 Phillips Ave, Belgravia, POB 3300, Harare; tel (4) 738681; telex 24173; fax (4) 795440.
Ambassador: José Manuel Paz Agüeras.

SUDAN

Embassy: 4 Pascoe Ave, Harare; tel (4) 725240; telex 26308.
Ambassador: el-Faith Abdullah Yousif.

SWEDEN

Embassy: Pegasus House, 7th Floor, 52 Samora Machel Ave, POB 4110, Harare; tel (4) 702001; telex 24695; fax (4) 702003.
Ambassador: Nils Daag.
Counsellor: Peter Ekelund.
Second Secretary: Catharina Lilliehöök-Jäger.
Head of Aid Office: Birgitta Berggren.
Technical Adviser: Svend Thomsen.
Head of Regional Investigation: Per Arne Ströberg.

SWITZERLAND

Embassy: 9 Lanark Rd, Belgravia, POB 3440, Harare; tel (4) 703997; telex 24669.
Ambassador: Peter Hollenweger.
First Secretary: Fritz Kühni.
Attaché and Head of Chancery: Sibylle Burmester-Hofer.

TANZANIA

High Commission: Ujamaa House, 23 Baines Ave, POB 4841, Harare; tel (4) 721870; telex 24557.
High Commissioner: George Clement Kahama.

TOGO

Embassy: 13 Bath Rd, Avondale, POB A469, Harare; tel (4) 738695; telex 24789.
Chargé d'affaires: Koffi Rinkliff.

TUNISIA

Embassy: 5 Ashton Rd, Alexandra Park, POB 4308, Harare; tel (4) 791570; telex 24801.
Ambassador: Mohamed el-Hedi ben Redjeb.

UNITED KINGDOM

High Commission: Stanley House, Jason Mayo Ave, POB 4490, Harare; tel (4) 728716; telex 24607; fax (4) 728380.
High Commissioner: Walter Kieran Prendergast.
Deputy High Commissioner: N. J. Thorpe.
Counsellor: K. M. Williams.
Defence Adviser: Col R. J. Martin.
First Secretary (Chancery/Information): R. J. Wildash.
First Secretary (Commercial): P. Nessling.
First Secretary (Consular): N. J. Steward.
First Secretary (Aid): D. G. Ward.
First Secretary (Chancery): A. J. Coulson.
First Secretary (Management): F. Pett.
First Secretary (Chancery): D. J. Watson.

USA

Embassy: Arax House, 172 Herbert Chitepo Ave, POB 3340, Harare; tel (4) 794521; telex 24591; fax (4) 796488.
Chargé d'affaires a.i.: Donald Petterson.
Deputy Head of Mission: Raymond Snider.
Political Section: Robert P. Jackson.
Political and Economic Section: Paul B. Larsen.
Consular Section: Sally M. Gober.
Administrative Section: Alphonso G. Marquis.
Regional Security Officer: Walter M. Huscilowitc.
Labour Officer: Harry K. Thomas, Jr.
Agency for International Development: Ted D. Morse.
Public Affairs Officer: Samir M. Kouttab.
Office of Defence Attaché: Lieut Col Richard L. Grauel.
Communications Programme Officer: Dale D. Johnson.
Information Systems Manager: Janet A. Cote.

VIET-NAM

Embassy: 14 Carlisle Drive, POB 5458, Harare; tel (4) 701118; telex 22047.
Ambassador: Vo Anh Tuan.

YUGOSLAVIA

Embassy: 1 Lanark Rd, Belgravia, POB 2446, Harare; tel (4) 724494; telex 27496.
Ambassador: Dusan Litvinović.

ZAIRE

Embassy: 24 Van Praagh Ave, Milton Park, POB 2446, Harare; tel (4) 724494; telex 22265.
Ambassador: Bemboy Baba.

ZAMBIA

High Commission: Zambia House, 48 Union Ave, POB 4698, Harare; tel (4) 790851; telex 24698; fax (4) 790856.
High Commissioner: Nchimunda John Sikaulu.
First Secretary and Head of Chancery: Kaluwe H. Musuumba.
First Secretary: Morgan K. Mutti.
First Secretary: Leonard Hachitapika.
First Secretary: Hilda Bwalya.
Second Secretary: Enock D. Kabila.
Trade Commissioner: Renee B. C. Nguzi.

International Organizations

EUROPEAN COMMUNITIES

External Delegation: NCR House, 10th Floor, 65 Samora Machel Ave, POB 4252, Harare; tel (4) 707120; telex 24811; fax (4) 725360.
Commission Delegate: Santiago Gómez-Reino Lecoq.

THE UNITED NATIONS

AFGHANISTAN

Permanent Mission: 866 United Nations Plaza, Suite 520, New York, NY 10017; tel (212) 754-1191.
Permanent Representative: Khodaidad Basharmal.
Minister-Counsellor: Mohammad E. Roshan-Rawaan.
Minister-Counsellor: G. Sarwar Yourish.
First Secretary: Mohauddin Taeb.
First Secretary: H. M. Razmi.
First Secretary: Ali Ahmad Joushan.
Second Secretary: Mir Mohammadi.

ALBANIA

Permanent Mission: 320 East 79th St, New York, NY 10021; tel (212) 249-2059.
Permanent Representative: Bashkim Pitarka.
Counsellor and Deputy Permanent Representative: Genc Mlloja.
First Secretary: Eqerem Gaxholli.
Second Secretary: Roland Llupa.
Attaché: Fatmir S. Baci.
Attaché: Adeline Llupa.

ALGERIA

Permanent Mission: 15 East 47th St, New York, NY 10017; tel (212) 750-1960; fax (212) 759-9538.
Permanent Representative: Dr Messaoud Ait Chaalal.
Counsellor: Amar Bendjama.
Counsellor (Administrative/Financial): Abdelkader Belleili.
Counsellor: Mouloud Hamai.
Counsellor: Abdallah Laouari.
First Secretary: Sabri Boukadoum.
First Secretary: Sabria Boukadoum.
First Secretary: Abdelaziz Doudou.
First Secretary: Soufiane Mimouni.
Third Secretary: Seddik Saoudi.
Attaché: Mohamed Redjem-Saad.
Attaché: Lahouari Godih.

ANGOLA

Permanent Mission: 125 East 73rd St, New York, NY 10021; tel (212) 861-5656; fax (212) 861-9295.
Permanent Representative: Afonso Van Dunem Mbinda.
Counsellor: Apolinário Jorge Correia.
Second Secretary: Raimundo Sotto-Mayor.
Second Secretary: Damião Fernandes Cristiano, Jr.
Attaché (Finance): Aarão Fernandes dos Santos.
Attaché (Protocol): Antonio Pascoal Gomes Neto.
Attaché: Jerónimo Gaspar de Almeida.
Attaché: José Manuel Paulo.
Attaché: Delfina Abdel Antonio Cordeiro.
Attaché: Samba Luisa Filipe Mbimbi.

ANTIGUA AND BARBUDA

Permanent Mission: 610 Fifth Ave, Suite 311, New York, NY 10020; tel (212) 541-4117; telex 126712; fax (212) 757-1607.
Permanent Representative: Lionel A. Hurst.
Minister-Counsellor and Deputy Permanent Representative: Dr Patrick Lewis.
Counsellor: John W. Ashe.
Attaché (Economic): Telbert King.
Attaché (Science): Dr John William Ashe.
Attaché: Dornella Seth.

ARGENTINA

Permanent Mission: 1 United Nations Plaza, 25th Floor, New York, NY 10017; tel (212) 688-6300; fax (212) 980-8395.
Permanent Representative: Dr Jorge Vázquez.
Minister and Deputy Permanent Representative: Alfredo Chiaradia.
Counsellor: Ernesto S. Martinez-Gondra.
Counsellor: R. Carlos Sersale di Cerisano.
Counsellor: Alejandro Héctor Nieto.
Military Adviser: Brig. Carlos Enrique Corino.
First Secretary: Jorge A. Osella.
First Secretary: Héctor Raúl Pelaez.
Second Secretary: María Fernanda Cañas.
Second Secretary: Estanislao Zawels.
Second Secretary: Alejandro Daneri.

AUSTRALIA

Permanent Mission: 1 Dag Hammarskjöld Plaza, 885 Second Ave, 16th Floor, New York, NY 10017; tel (212) 421-6910; fax (212) 371-5843.
Permanent Representative: Dr Peter Wilenski.
Minister and Deputy Permanent Representative: Howard Bamsey.
Counsellor: Brian Babington.
Counsellor: Jill Courtney.
Counsellor: Gillian Bird.
Counsellor and Military Adviser: Col Bruce Osborn.
First Secretary: David Stuart.
First Secretary: Corinne Tomkinson.
First Secretary: John Griffin.
Second Secretary (Administration): Margaret Wells.

AUSTRIA

Permanent Mission: 809 United Nations Plaza, 7th Floor, New York, NY 10017; tel (212) 949-1840; fax (212) 953-1302.
Permanent Representative: Peter Hohenfellner.
Minister-Counsellor and Deputy Representative: Thomas Hajnoczi.
Minister-Counsellor: Helmut Freudenschuss.
Minister-Counsellor: Irene Freudenschuss-Reichl.
Counsellor: Thomas Stelzer.
Counsellor (Press): Wolfgang Petritsch.
First Secretary: Florian Krenkel.
First Secretary: Gerhard Jandl.
First Secretary: Maria Rotheiser.
First Secretary: Elisabeth Kehrer.

BAHAMAS

Permanent Mission: 767 Third Ave, 9th Floor, New York, NY 10017; tel (212) 421-6925; fax (212) 759-2135.
Permanent Representative: James B. Moultrie.
Minister-Counsellor and Deputy Permanent Representative: A. Missouri Sherman-Peter.
Second Secretary: Sandra P. Carey.
Third Secretary: Sally E. Moss.
Third Secretary: Freddie Tucker.

BAHRAIN

Permanent Mission: 2 United Nations Plaza, 25th Floor, New York, NY 10017; tel (212) 223-6200; fax (212) 319-0687.
Permanent Representative: Dr Muhammad Abdul Ghaffar.
Counsellor: Bibi al-Alawi.
First Secretary: Saeed al-Faihani.
Second Secretary: Jabor al-Romaihi.

BANGLADESH

Permanent Mission: 821 United Nations Plaza, 8th Floor, New York, NY 10017; tel (212) 867-3434; fax (212) 972-4038.
Permanent Representative: Humayun Kabir.
Minister and Deputy Permanent Representative: Dr Iftekhar Ahmed Chowdhury.
Counsellor: Mahbub Kabir.
Counsellor: Nazim U. Chowdhury.
Counsellor: Abdul Hannan.
First Secretary: Dr Khalilur Rahman.
First Secretary: Liaquat Ali Choudhury.
First Secretary: Ahmed Akhtaruzzaman.
Second Secretary: Ismat Jahan.

BARBADOS

Permanent Mission: 800 Second Ave, 18th Floor, New York, NY 10017; tel (212) 867-8431; fax (212) 986-1030.
Permanent Representative: Besley Maycock.
Counsellor: Teresa Ann Marshall.
First Secretary: David O'Wendell Blackman.
Second Secretary: David Mohammed Bulbulia.
Attaché: Muriel Ianthe Jones.

BELGIUM

Permanent Mission: 809 United Nations Plaza, 2nd Floor, New York, NY 10017; tel (212) 599-5250; telex 234370; fax (212) 599-6843.
Permanent Representative: Paul Noterdaeme.
Envoy Extraordinary, Minister Plenipotentiary and Deputy Permanent Representative: Frans van Daele.
Counsellor: Christiaan Tanghe.
Counsellor: Luc Devolder.
Counsellor: Alexis Brouhns.
Counsellor: Alain Cools.
First Secretary: Boudewijn Dereymaeker.
First Secretary: Jana Zikmundova.
First Secretary: Raoul Delcorde.
First Secretary: Machteld Fostier.

BELIZE

Permanent Mission: 820 Second Ave, Suite 922, New York, NY 10017; tel (212) 599-0233; telex 6971679; fax (212) 599-3391.
Permanent Representative: Carl L. B. Rogers.
First Secretary: Steven A. Burn.
Second Secretary: Amalia Mai.
Adviser: Clarine Johnson.

BENIN

Permanent Mission: 4 East 73rd St, New York, NY 10021; tel (212) 249-6014; fax (212) 734-4735.
Permanent Representative: René Mongbe.
Deputy Permanent Representative: Ayité Jean-Claude Kpakpo.
Minister-Counsellor: Georges A. Whannou.
Counsellor: Rogatien Biaou.

First Secretary: Christian C. Missinhoun.
Third Secretary: Bienvenu E. Accrombessi.
Attaché: Pascal Sossou.
Attaché: Gagnon Eke.

BHUTAN

Permanent Mission: 2 United Nations Plaza, 27th Floor, New York, NY 10017; tel (212) 826-1919; telex 224196; fax (212) 826-2998.
Permanent Representative: Ugyen Tshering.
Deputy Permanent Representative and Counsellor: Lhatu Wangchuk.
Second Secretary: Hari K. Chhetri.
Third Secretary: Kunzang C. Namgyel.
Vice-Consul: Sonam Yangchen.
Attaché: Tshering Dorji.

BOLIVIA

Permanent Mission: 211 East 43rd St, 8th Floor, Room 802, New York, NY 10017; tel (212) 682-8132; fax (212) 687-4642.
Permanent Representative: Hugo Navajas-Mogro.
Alternate Permanent Representative: Natalio Fernandez.
Minister-Counsellor and Deputy Permanent Representative: Dr Erwin Ortiz-Gandarillas.
Counsellor: Esther M. Ashton.
Second Secretary: Luis Pablo Ossio-Bustillos.
Attaché (Civil): Evelyn A. Villa-Gomez-Nuñez.
Attaché: Martha V. Montaño.
Attaché: Gabriela Garcia.
Attaché: Juan Carlos Zuleta.
Special Adviser: Moisés Fuentes-Ibañez.

BOTSWANA

Permanent Mission: 103 East 37th St, New York, NY 10016; tel (212) 889-2277; fax (212) 725-5061.
Permanent Representative: Legwaila Joseph Legwaila.
Counsellor: Pholile E. Legwaila.
First Secretary: Samuel O. Outlule.
Second Secretary: Mmamosadinyana P. J. Molefe.
Attaché (Administrative): Margaret Setlhare.

BRAZIL

Permanent Mission: 747 Third Ave, 9th Floor, New York, NY 10017; tel (212) 832-6868; fax (212) 371-5716.
Permanent Representative: Ronaldo Mota Sardenberg.
Deputy Permanent Representative: Luiz Augusto de Araujo Castro.
Air and Military Adviser: Gen. Murillo Santos.
Minister: Flávio Miragaia Perri.
Minister: Adhemar Gabriel Bahadian.
Counsellor: Sérgio Eduardo Moreira Lima.
Counsellor: Maria Elisa de Bittencourt Berenguer.
Counsellor: Edmundo Sussumu Fujita.
Counsellor: Regis Percy Arslanian.
Counsellor: Afonso José Sena Cardoso.
First Secretary: Everton Vieira Vargas.
First Secretary: Vera Regina Delayti Telles.
Second Secretary: Marco Farani.
Second Secretary: Antonio Francisco da Costa e Silva Neto.
Second Secretary: Lauro Eduardo Soutello Alves.
Second Secretary: Demétrio Bueno Carvalho.
Second Secretary: Sylvia Ruschel de Leoni Ramos.
Second Secretary: José Humberto de Brito Cruz.

BRUNEI

Permanent Mission: 866 United Nations Plaza, Room 248, New York, NY 10017; tel (212) 838-1600; telex 422503; fax (212) 980-6478.
Permanent Representative: Dato Paduka Haji Jaya bin Abdul Latif.
Minister-Counsellor and Deputy Permanent Representative: Mr Suyoi Haji Osman.
Counsellor: Pg Hjh Masrainah Bte Pg Hj Ahmad.
Second Secretary: Mr Yahya bin Idris.
Third Secretary: Hj Abdul Majid bin Hj Abdullah.
Third Secretary: Mr Ramlli bin Hj Ahmad.
Third Secretary: Abdul Majid bin Hj Mohamad.
Attaché: Mr Marzuki bin Achee.

BULGARIA

Permanent Mission: 11 East 84th St, New York, NY 10028; tel (212) 737-4790; fax (212) 472-9865.
Permanent Representative: Svetlomir V. Baev.
Minister and Deputy Permanent Representative: Ivan K. Sotirov.
Minister: Todor G. Todorov.
Counsellor: Etien P. Ninov.
Second Secretary: Alexander S. Savov.
Second Secretary: Aliosha I. Nedelchev.
Third Secretary: Peter V. Kolarov.
Third Secretary: Svetlozar V. Panov.
Attaché: Strachil A. Yordanov.
Attaché: Ivan S. Tchomakov.

BURKINA FASO

Permanent Mission: 115 East 73rd St, New York, NY 10021; tel (212) 288-7515; telex 141019.
Permanent Representative: Gaëtan Rimwanguiya Ouedraogo.
First Counsellor: Ambroise Silga.
Second Counsellor: Moussa Nebie.
Counsellor: Awa Ouedraogo.
First Secretary: Macaire Kabore.
Financial Attaché: Marcel Rima.
Attaché: Salamata Téné Rima.
Attaché: Alice Marie Victorine Silga.

BURUNDI

Permanent Mission: 201 East 42nd St, 28th Floor, New York, NY 10017; tel (212) 687-1180; fax (212) 687-1197.
Permanent Representative: Benoît Seburyamo.
Counsellor: Jérémie Ndayiziga.
Counsellor: Melchiade Bukuru.

BELARUS

Permanent Mission: 136 East 67th St, New York, NY 10021; tel (212) 535-3420; fax (212) 734-4810.
Permanent Representative: Gennady N. Buravkin.
Envoy Extraordinary and Minister Plenipotentiary and Deputy Permanent Representative: Oleg N. Pashkevich.
Counsellor: Aleksandr V. Vasilyev.
First Secretary: Vladimir A. Sokolovsky.
First Secretary: Victor A. Akolzin.
Second Secretary: Vladimir N. Gerasimovich.
Second Secretary: Georgi A. Yegorov.
Third Secretary: Aleksandr I. Kotelkin.

CAMBODIA (KAMPUCHEA)

Permanent Mission: 747 Third Ave, 8th Floor, New York, NY 10017; tel (212) 888-6646; fax (212) 980-1041.
Permanent Representative: Prasith Thiounn.
Deputy Permanent Representative: Prince Sirirath Sisowath.
Deputy Permanent Representative: Lapresse Sieng.
Minister-Counsellor: Lonn Toch.
Minister-Counsellor: Kounsaky Ieng.
Counsellor: Bun Thuok Keo.
Counsellor: Khunnal Tep.
First Secretary: Phobol Cheng.
Second Secretary: Kimsan Kep.

CAMEROON

Permanent Mission: 22 East 73rd St, New York, NY 10021; tel (212) 794-2295; fax (212) 249-0533.
Permanent Representative: Pascal Biloa Tang.
Counsellor: Elsie Ngowo Mbella Ngomba.
Counsellor: Dr Michel-Cyr Djiena-Wembou.
Counsellor: Jean-Blaise Konn.
First Secretary: Dr Joseph Atanga.
First Secretary: Mr Ekoumilong.
First Secretary (Finance): Nji Edward Kilo.
Second Secretary (Finance): Pascal Sawalda.

CANADA

Permanent Mission: 866 United Nations Plaza, Suite 250, New York, NY 10017; tel (212) 751-5600; telex 126269; fax (212) 486-1295.
Permanent Representative: Louise Frechette.
Deputy Permanent Representative: Philippe Kirsch.
Minister-Counsellor: David M. Malone.
Counsellor: Richard N. Têtu.
Counsellor (Development): Jeremiah E. Kramer.
Counsellor: Peter A. van Brakel.
Counsellor: Col Douglas A. Fraser.
Counsellor: L. Thomsen.
Counsellor: Russell Merifield.
First Secretary: Marisa J. Piattelli.
First Secretary: Graham N. Green.
Second Secretary: James Trottier.
Second Secretary: Alexandra C. Bezeredi.
Second Secretary (Administrative): Richard W. Hanley.

CAPE VERDE

Permanent Mission: 27 East 69th St, New York, NY 10021; tel (212) 472-0333; fax (212) 794-1398.
Permanent Representative: José Luis Jesus.
Second Secretary: José Armando F. Ferreira Duarte .
Second Secretary: Carlos Alberto Monteiro Pereira.
Attaché (Administrative): Vicência Margarita A. Brito Duarte.
Attaché (Administrative): Custódia Monteiro de Oliveira Lima.
Attaché (Administrative): Helena Tavares Borges.

CENTRAL AFRICAN REPUBLIC

Permanent Mission: 386 Park Ave South, Room 1614, New York, NY 10016; tel (212) 689-6195.
Permanent Representative: Jean-Pierre Sohahong-Kombet.
Counsellor (Economic): Edmond Nzapa-Yeke.
Counsellor (Legal): Philippe Aziz Goundji.

CHAD

Permanent Mission: 211 East 43rd St, Suite 1703, New York, NY 10017; tel (212) 986-0980.
Permanent Representative: Mahamat Ali Adoum.
Counsellor: Ahmat Abderaman Haggar.
Counsellor: Darnace Torou.

CHILE

Permanent Mission: 809 United Nations Plaza, 4th Floor, New York, NY 10017; tel (212) 687-7547; fax (212) 972-9875.
Permanent Representative: Juan O. Somavia.
Deputy Permanent Representative: James Holger.
Counsellor: Pedro Uriarte.
Counsellor: Cristian Maquieira.
Counsellor: José Miguel Cruz.
Counsellor: María Aida Rodríguez.
First Secretary: Jaime Bazan.

First Secretary: Konrad Paulsen.
Third Secretary: Julio Fiol.
Attaché (Cultural): Ana María Palma.

CHINA, PEOPLE'S REPUBLIC

Permanent Mission: 155 West 66th St, New York, NY 10023; tel (212) 787-3838; fax (212) 870-0333.
Permanent Representative: Li Daoyu.
Deputy Permanent Representative: Jin Yongjian.
Minister-Counsellor: Zhao Jihua.
Minister-Counsellor: Li Hongjun.
Minister-Counsellor: Zhang Guanghui.
Counsellor: Liu Zhaodong.
Counsellor: Luo Xu.
Counsellor: Lu Chunlin.
Counsellor: Liu Sha.
Counsellor: Guo Jialu.
Counsellor: Wang Guangya.
Counsellor: Jiang Zhenxi.
Counsellor: Zhu Hongfei.
Counsellor: Jin Tongchao.
Counsellor: Yu Shuning.
Military Adviser: Du Kuanyi.
First Secretary: Wang Suobao.
First Secretary: Li Chuansheng.
First Secretary: Sha Zukang.
First Secretary: Zhang Yesui.
First Secretary: Lin Miaochun.
First Secretary: Zhang Xiamei.
First Secretary: Lu Yongshou.
First Secretary: Chen Yonglong.
First Secretary: Zhang Donghui.
First Secretary: Bai Pu.
First Secretary: Liao Jincheng.
First Secretary: Shen Xingzhong.
First Secretary: Tang Guangting.
First Secretary: Yu Guojin.
First Secretary: Zhou Shanming.
First Secretary: Wang Haizhong.
First Secretary: Wang Songquan.
First Secretary: Kang Yuhe.
First Secretary: Ren Quan.
Third Secretary (Protocol): Shi Weiqiang.

COLOMBIA

Permanent Mission: 140 East 57th St, 5th Floor, New York, NY 10022; tel (212) 355-7776; fax (212) 371-2813.
Permanent Representative: Dr Fernando Cepeda.
Alternate Permanent Representative: Dr Douglas Botero-Boshell.
Minister and Alternate Permanent Representative: Juanita Castaño.
Minister and Alternate Permanent Representative: Jaime Giron.
Minister-Counsellor: Carlos Wolff.
Minister-Counsellor: Luis Fernando Botero.
Minister-Counsellor: Hernendo Clavijo.
Minister-Counsellor: Carmen Escolar.
Counsellor: Gracia Uribe de Lozano.
Counsellor: Fernando Alzate.
Counsellor: Martha Noguera.
First Secretary: Carlos Julio Ardila.
First Secretary: Ana Mercedes Botero.
Second Secretary: Claudia Echavarria.

COMOROS

Permanent Mission: 366 East 45th St, New York, NY 10017; tel (212) 972-8010; fax (212) 983-4712.
Permanent Representative: Amini Ali Moumin.

CONGO

Permanent Mission: 14 East 65th St, New York, NY 10021; tel (212) 744-7840.
Permanent Representative: Dr Martin Adouki.
Counsellor (Economic/Social Affairs): Raymond Serge Bale.
Counsellor: Corneille Edouard Moka.
First Secretary: Désiré Nkounkou.
Second Secretary: Georges Victor Oko.
Third Secretary: David Kounkou.
Third Secretary: Pascal Bazabidila.

COSTA RICA

Permanent Mission: 211 East 43rd St, Room 903, New York, NY 10017; tel (212) 986-6373; fax (212) 986-6842.
Permanent Representative: Cristián Tattenbach.
First Alternate Permanent Representative: José María Borbon.
Second Alternate Permanent Representative: Emilia Castro de Barish.
Third Alternate Permanent Representative: Rodolfo Piza.
Minister: Nazareth A. Incera.
Minister-Counsellor: Elfas Albert Assaf.
Minister-Counsellor: Ana C. Vargas de Zadoff.
Minister-Counsellor: Alfonso Vargas.
Counsellor: Virginia de Rojack.
Counsellor: Ana Matilda Rivera.
Counsellor: Alvaro Herrera.
Counsellor: Milena Herrera.
Attaché (Press): Ronald M. Barish.

COTE D'IVOIRE

Permanent Mission: 866 United Nations Plaza, Room 566, New York, NY 10017; tel (212) 371-7036; fax (212) 935-5347.
Permanent Representative: Jean-Jacques Bechio.
Minister-Counsellor and Deputy Permanent Representative: N'Zi Anet.
Counsellor: Kramo Konan.
Counsellor: Djénébou Kaba.
Counsellor: Emmanuel Amon.
Counsellor: Djabia Joachim Anvire.
Counsellor: Kouassi Florent Ekra.
Counsellor: Marc Georges Sery.
First Secretary (Finance): Gnagoran Thomas N'Cho.
Attaché (Finance): Adama Sanogo.

CUBA

Permanent Mission: 315 Lexington Ave and 38th St, New York, NY 10016; tel (212) 689-7215; fax (212) 779-1697.
Permanent Representative: Ricardo Alarcón de Quesada.
Alternate Permanent Representative: Carlos R. Zamora Rodriguez.
Minister-Counsellor: René Juan Mujica Cantelar.
Counsellor: Pedro J. Lago Gomez.
Counsellor: Abelardo Moreno Fernandez.
First Secretary: Victoria Margarita Delgado Ramirez.
First Secretary: Amado Soto Garcia.
First Secretary: Juan Guillermo Boudy Pizart.
First Secretary: Juan Antonio Hernandez Machado.
First Secretary: José de los Angeles Martinez Cordoves.
First Secretary: Rafael J. Martinez Boue.
Second Secretary: Silvio Gonzalez Lamar.
Second Secretary: Rafael Laguardia Mestre.
Second Secretary: Arturo Moises Jorge.
Second Secretary: Carlos R. Fernandez de Cossio Dominguez.
Second Secretary: Antonio J. Guardado Azaret.
Second Secretary: Rafael Ocaña Santiesteban.

CYPRUS

Permanent Mission (also accredited to Argentina, Barbados, Cuba, Grenada, Guyana, Panama, Saint Lucia, Suriname, Trinidad and Tobago): 13 East 40th St, New York, NY 10016; tel (212) 481-6023; telex 220945; fax (212) 685-7316.
Permanent Representative: Andreas Mavrommatis.
Counsellor: Petros Eftychiou.
Second Secretary: George C. Kasoulides.
Second Secretary: Michalis Stavrinos.
Attaché (Administrative): Ioannis Constantinou.
Counsellor (Economic): Dennis C. Droushiotis.
Attaché (Press): Maria Zoupaniotis.

CZECHOSLOVAKIA

Permanent Mission: 1109-1111 Madison Ave, New York, NY 10028; tel (212) 535-8814; telex 225175; fax (212) 772-0586.
Permanent Representative: Eduard Kukan.
Counsellor and Deputy Permanent Representative: Jaroslav Šuchman.
Counsellor: Alexander Slabý.
Counsellor: Peter Tomka.
Third Secretary: Pavol Šepelák.
Third Secretary: Štefan Fule.
Attaché (Press and Public Relations): Miroslav Sedlák.
Attaché: Stanislav Kadlec.
Attaché: Vladislav Pavelka.

DENMARK

Permanent Mission: 2 United Nations Plaza, 26th Floor, New York, NY 10017; tel (212) 308-7009; fax (212) 308-3384.
Permanent Representative: Bent Haakonsen.
Minister-Counsellor and Deputy Permanent Representative: Hans Klingenberg.
Counsellor (Economic/Financial): Lars Møller.
Counsellor (Human Rights/Legal/Social Affairs): Arnold Skibsted.
Counsellor (Political): Kirsten Nørregaard Rasmussen.
First Secretary (Political): Mette Kjuel Nielsen.
First Secretary (Economic/Development): Anne Ehrenreich.

DJIBOUTI

Permanent Mission: 866 United Nations Plaza, Suite 4011, New York, NY 10017; tel (212) 753-3163; fax (212) 223-1276.
Permanent Representative: Roble Olhaye.
Counsellor: Dysane Abdallah Dorani.
Counsellor: Abdourahman A. Ibrahim.

DOMINICA

Permanent Mission: 820 Second Ave, Suite 900B, New York, NY 10017; tel (212) 949-0853; fax (212) 808-4975.
Permanent Representative: Franklin Andrew Baron.
Deputy Permanent Representative: Simon P. Richards.

DOMINICAN REPUBLIC

Permanent Mission: 144 East 44th St, 4th Floor, New York, NY 10017; tel (212) 867-0833; fax (212) 986-4694.
Permanent Representative: Hector V. Alcantara.
Economic Adviser: Dr Enriquillo A. del Rosario C.
Alternate Permanent Representative: Julia Tavares de Alvarez.
Alternate Permanent Representative: J. M. Roberto Bonetti.
Alternate Permanent Representative: Ana Esther de la Maza.
Alternate Permanent Representative: Placido Ramón Acevedo-Alfau.
Alternate Permanent Representative: Rosa de los Angeles Mota Deler.
Second Secretary: Lourdes Flavia.
Third Secretary: Marlene A. Boves Lopez.
Third Secretary: Elisa de Leon Suaźo.

ECUADOR

Permanent Mission: 866 United Nations Plaza, Room 516, New York, NY 10017; tel (212) 935-1680; fax (212) 935-1835.
Permanent Representative: Dr José Ayala Lasso.
Minister and Deputy Permanent Representative: Abelardo Posso Serrano.
Counsellor: Jenny Almeida de Ribadeneira.
Counsellor: Martha Dueñas de Whist.
First Secretary: Mauricio Montalvo.
First Secretary: Miriam S. Mantilla.
Second Secretary: José R. Sandoval.
Second Secretary: José S. Valencia.
Attaché (Civil): Maritza Piedrahita.

EGYPT

Permanent Mission: 36 East 67th St, New York, NY 10021; tel (212) 879-6300; fax (212) 794-3874.
Permanent Representative: Dr Nabil A. Elaraby.
Minister: Mohamed Noman Galal.
Minister-Counsellor (Press/Information): Abdul Aleem I. Elabyad.
Counsellor: Dawlat Ibrahim Hassan.
Counsellor: Mohamed Assem Ibrahim.
Counsellor: Sameh Hassan Shoukry.
Counsellor: Waguih Said Moustapha Hanafi.
First Secretary: Mahmoud Ismail Elkholy.
First Secretary: Shamuel Elsayed Nasser.
Second Secretary: Somaya Mohamed Saad Hassan.
Third Secretary: Ehab Mostafa Fawzy.
Third Secretary: Aly Ahmed Erfan.
Third Secretary: Mootaz Ahmaidein Khalil.
Attaché (Administrative): Ragai Ramzi Yanni.
Attaché (Administrative): Abdel Maboud Kamel Ebeid.
Attaché (Administrative): Maged Ahmed Ibrahim Osman.
Attaché (Administrative): Essam Eldin Soliman Baddour.
Attaché (Press): Mohamed Said Abdel Ahad.
Attaché (Press/Administrative): Aly Ahmad Fahmy.

EL SALVADOR

Permanent Mission: 46 Park Ave, New York, NY 10016; tel (212) 679-1616.
Permanent Representative: Dr Ricardo G. Castaneda-Cornejo.
Minister and Deputy Permanent Representative: Guillermo A. Melendez-Barahona.
Minister-Counsellor and Alternate Permanent Representative: Antonio Perla-Bustamante.
Minister-Counsellor and Alternate Permanent Representative: Rafael Angel Alfaro-Pineda.
Minister-Counsellor and Alternate Permanent Representative: Alexander A. Kravetz.
Third Secretary: Ana María de Lopez.
Third Secretary (Administrative): Jesús Artiga Hernandez.
Third Secretary (Administrative): Luis E. Alvarado Ramirez.
Attaché: M. Aracely Jovel.

EQUATORIAL GUINEA

Permanent Mission: 57 Magnolia Ave, Mount Vernon, New York, NY 10553.
Permanent Representative: Damaso-Obiang Ndong.
Second Secretary: Jesús-Otunga Nsue Bindang.

ESTONIA

Permanent Mission: 9 Rockefeller Plaza, Suite 1421, New York, NY 10020; tel (212) 247-1450; fax (212) 262-0893.
Permanent Representative: Ernst Rudolf Jaakson.

ETHIOPIA

Permanent Mission: 866 United Nations Plaza, Room 560, New York, NY 10017; tel (212) 421-1830; fax (212) 754-0360.
Deputy Permanent Representative: Haile Mariam Goshu.
Counsellor: Keffyalew Gebremedhin.
Counsellor: Gebre-Medhin Hagoss.
First Secretary: Girmachew Mekonen Eshete.
Second Secretary: Hirut Gebre-Egziabher.
Second Secretary: Meserat Gizaw Kibret.
Third Secretary: Mulumebet Zewdu Engeda.

FIJI

Permanent Mission: 1 United Nations Plaza, 26th Floor, New York, NY 10017; tel (212) 355-7316; fax (212) 319-1896.
Permanent Representative: Ratu Manasa K. Senilou.
Counsellor: Isikia Rabici Savua.
Second Secretary: Apisalome Koroirara Rokotuivuna.

FINLAND

Permanent Mission: 866 United Nations Plaza, Room 222, 2nd Floor, New York, NY 10017; tel (212) 355-2100; telex 234318; fax (212) 759-6156.
Permanent Representative: Wilhelm Breitenstein.
Deputy Permanent Representative: Marjatta Rasi.
Minister-Counsellor and Deputy Permanent Representative (Economic/Social): Tauno Kääriä.
Counsellor and Military Adviser: Cdre Markku Moisala.
Counsellor (Political): Christel Nyman.
Counsellor (Political): Pasi Patokallio.
Counsellor (Budgetary Affairs): Irmeli Mustonen.
Counsellor (Economic): Hannele Tikanvaara.
Counsellor (Press/Culture): Leena Peltola.
First Secretary (Political): Elina Kalkku.
First Secretary (Economic): Anna Liedes.
Second Secretary (Social): Pekka Metso.
Second Secretary: Heli Kanerva.
Attaché (Administrative): Raija Barnes.

FRANCE

Permanent Mission: 1 Dag Hammarskjöld Plaza, 245 East 47th St, New York, NY 10017; tel (212) 308-5700; fax (212) 421-6889.
Permanent Representative: Jean-Bernard Mérimée.
Minister and Deputy Permanent Representative: Jean-Marc Rochereau de la Sabliere.
Minister (Economic/Financial): Paul Lemerle.
Counsellor (Legal): Francis Delon.
Counsellor: Jean Felix-Paganon.
Counsellor: Jacques Boutet.
Counsellor: Christine Robichon.
Counsellor: Pierre Menat.
Counsellor: Laurent Stefanani.
Counsellor: Chantal Poiret.
Counsellor: Michel Tantot.
First Secretary: Jean-Pierre Lacroix.
First Secretary: Patrick Pascal.
First Secretary: Joseph Silva.
First Secretary: Serge Mostura.
First Secretary: Thierry Guiot-Guillin.
Second Secretary (Press): Yves Lo-Pinto.
Representative to the Disarmament Conference: Gérard Errera.

GABON

Permanent Mission: 18 East 41st St, 6th Floor, New York, NY 10017; tel (212) 686-9720; fax (212) 689-5769.
Permanent Representative: Denis Dangue Rewaka.
Counsellor: Dieudonné Ndiaye.
Counsellor: Etienne Mamfoumbi.
Counsellor: Corentin Hervo-Akendengue.
Counsellor: Alba Biffot.
First Secretary: Anne-Marie Mamfoumbi.

GAMBIA

Permanent Mission: 820 Second Ave, Suite 900C, 19th Floor, New York, NY 10017; tel (212) 949-6640; telex 147289; fax (212) 808-4975.
Permanent Representative: Ousman Ahmadu Sallah.
Deputy Permanent Representative: Omar Gibril Sallah.
Counsellor: Baboucar Saho.
Personal Assistant and Secretary: Aminata Segan Saine.
Attaché: Alieu Badou Samba.

GERMANY

Permanent Mission: 600 Third Ave, 41st Floor, New York, NY 10016; tel (212) 949-9200; fax (212) 490-0857.
Permanent Representative: Detlev Graf zu Rantzau.
Deputy Permanent Representative: Dr Hans-Joachim Vergau.
Minister: Dr Karl Borchard.
Counsellor: Kurt-Otto Leonberger.
Counsellor (Budgetary): Ulrich Kalbitzer.
Counsellor: Hans Günter Gnodtke.
Counsellor: Christiane Gnodtke.
Counsellor: Wolfgang Stöckl.
Counsellor (Economic): Ulrich Schönleiter.
Counsellor: Wilfried Grolig.
Counsellor: Helmut Bailek.
Counsellor (Economic/Development): Dr Ursula Schäfer-Preuss.
First Secretary: Dr Peter Wittig.
First Secretary: Dr Axel Berg.
First Secretary: Barbara von Treskow-Klöck.
First Secretary: Rüdiger König.
First Secretary (Administrative): Karl-Heinz Schoer.

GHANA

Permanent Mission: 19 East 47th St, New York, NY 10017; tel (212) 832-1300.
Permanent Representative: Dr Kofi Awoonor.
Minister and Deputy Permanent Representative: Nelson Kojo Dumevi.
Minister-Counsellor: Edward Obeng Kufuor.
Minister-Counsellor: Kwaku Duah Dankwa.
Counsellor: Clifford Nii Amon Kotey.
Counsellor: James Okoe Abubakr Naadjie.
First Secretary: Simon Arthur Nyamikeh.
First Secretary: Lutterodt E. Nater.
Attaché (Protocol): Godfried Adjei Bonsu.
Attaché: Aaron Tsakpoe.
Attaché: Evelina Ababio-Addai.
Attaché: Notei Okwei.

GREECE

Permanent Mission: 733 Third Ave, 23rd Floor, New York, NY 10017; tel (212) 490-6060; fax (212) 490-5894.
Permanent Representative: Antonios Exarchos.
Counsellor and Deputy Permanent Representative: Laonidas Chryssanthopoulos.
Counsellor: Alexandros P. Mallias.
Counsellor (Economic): Dr George Papadatos.
Counsellor (Press): George Hatziioannou.
First Secretary: Nicolaos Dictakis.
First Secretary: Dimitris Platis.
First Secretary: Dr Dimitris Moschopoulos.
First Secretary: Aliki Hadji.
Third Secretary: Filia Poufina.
Third Secretary: Maria Vassiliou.
Adviser (Maritime): Gregory Callmanopoulos.
Attaché (Press): Stelios Korkides.

GRENADA

Permanent Mission: 820 Second Ave, Suite 900D, New York, NY 10017; tel (212) 599-0301; telex 620812; fax (212) 808-4975.
Permanent Representative: Eugene Pursoo.
Counsellor: George B. Brathwaite.

GUATEMALA

Permanent Mission: 57 Park Ave, New York, NY 10016; tel (212) 679-4760; fax (212) 685-8741.
Permanent Representative: Francisco Villagran de León.
Alternate Permanent Representative: Rafael Castellanos-Carrillo.
Alternate Permanent Representative: Antonio Aris de Castilla.
Minister-Counsellor: Francis Eric Aguilar-Hecht.
Second Secretary: Virginia Maria Cabrera-Grijalva.
Third Secretary: Carla C. Garcia Granados.

GUINEA

Permanent Mission: 140 East 39th St, New York, NY 10016; tel (212) 687-8115; fax (212) 687-8248.
Permanent Representative: Zaïnoul Abidine Sanoussi.
Counsellor: François Fall.
Counsellor: Balla Moussa Camara.
First Secretary: Tahirou Diallo.
Attaché (Finance): Aly Camara.
Attaché: Mamadou Saïdou Diallo.
Attaché: Moussa Sano.
Attaché: Abdoulaye Barry.
Attaché: Oria Mara.

GUINEA-BISSAU

Permanent Mission: 211 East 43rd St, Room 604, New York, NY 10017; tel (212) 661-3977; telex 668765; fax (212) 983-2794.
Permanent Representative: Boubacar Toure.
Deputy Permanent Representative: Mario Lopes da Rosa.
Counsellor: Raul de Melo Cabral.
Counsellor: Maria Manuela Lopes da Rosa.
First Secretary: Richard Mantouck.
Attaché: Malam Mane.

GUYANA

Permanent Mission: 866 United Nations Plaza, Suite 555, New York, NY 10017; tel (212) 527-3232; fax (212) 935-7548.
Permanent Representative: Samuel R. Insanally.
Minister-Counsellor: Dr Timothy Nathaniel Crichlow.
Minister-Counsellor: Rawle F. A. Lucas.
Counsellor: June Angela Persaud.
First Secretary: Earl Anthony Manget.
Second Secretary (Administrative): Pamela Anderson.

HAITI

Permanent Mission: 801 Second Ave, Room 300, New York, NY 10017; tel (212) 370-4840; fax (212) 661-8698.
Permanent Representative: Fritz Longchamp.
Deputy Permanent Representative: Roger Ravix.
Deputy Permanent Representative: Nestor Chavannes.
Minister-Counsellor: Antonio Rodrigue.
Minister-Counsellor: Joseph Thevenin.
Counsellor: Serge J. Elien.
Counsellor: Any L. Bernardin.
Counsellor: Nicole Romulus.
Counsellor: Chantal Milord.
Counsellor: Judith Berthaud.
Attaché: Carline N. Mourra.

HONDURAS

Permanent Mission: 866 United Nations Plaza, Suite 417, New York, NY 10017; tel (212) 752-3370; fax (212) 223-0498.
Permanent Representative: Roberto Flores Bermúdez.
Deputy Permanent Representative: Javier Suazo Tome.
Counsellor: Nelson Alexander Valenzuela Soto.
First Secretary: Marco Antonio Suazo Fernandez.
Attaché (Press): Doris Chessman de Avila.

HUNGARY

Permanent Mission: 10 East 75th St, New York, NY 10021; tel (212) 535-8660; fax (212) 734-6036.
Permanent Representative: André Erdös.
Counsellor and Deputy Permanent Representative: Ivan Budai.
Senior Counsellor: Ferenc Gajda.
Counsellor: Dr Zoltan Szedlacsko.
First Secretary: András Dékány.
Second Secretary: Imre Karbuczky.
Third Secretary: György Molnar.
Attaché: Béla Garai.

ICELAND

Permanent Mission: 370 Lexington Ave, 5th Floor, New York, NY 10017; tel (212) 686-4100; fax (212) 532-4138.
Minister-Counsellor and Deputy Permanent Representative: Helgi Gislason.
First Secretary: Grétar Már Sigurdsson.

INDIA

Permanent Mission: 866 United Nations Plaza, Suite 505, New York, NY 10017; tel (212) 751-0900; fax (212) 751-1393.
Permanent Representative: Chinmaya Rajaninath Gharekhan.
Deputy Permanent Representative: T. Prabhakar Menon.
Counsellor: Dinesh Kumar Jain.
Counsellor: Ramaprosad Goswami.
Counsellor: Shyam Chand Mehra.
Counsellor: Yogesh Kumar Gupta.
First Secretary: Sudhir Vyas.
First Secretary and Head of Chancery: Virenda Gupta.
First Secretary: Debebrata Saha.
First Secretary: Nikhil Seth.
First Secretary: Sujata Mehta.
First Secretary: Ranjit Rae.
First Secretary: Tarsem Lal Gill.

INDONESIA

Permanent Mission: 325 East 38th St, New York, NY 10016; tel (212) 972-8333.
Permanent Representative: Nana S. Sutresna.
Deputy Permanent Representative: Nugroho Wisnumurti.
Minister-Counsellor (Political): Isslamet Poernomo.
Minister-Counsellor (Economic): Adian Silalahi.
Minister-Counsellor (Economic/Social Affairs): Saodah B. A. Syahruddin.
Counsellor (Political): Abdul Nasier.
First Secretary (Political): Makmur Widodo.
First Secretary (Political): T. A. Samodra Sriwidjaja.
First Secretary (Economic): Wyoso Prodjowarsito.
First Secretary (Political): Hertomo Reksodiputro.
First Secretary (Political): Sadewo Joedo.
First Secretary (Economic): Resi Gunarto Prasodjo.
First Secretary (Economic/Social Affairs): Indratno Siswoyo.
First Secretary (Administrative/Financial): Mochamad Ridza Sunarta.
First Secretary: Antonius Dasimin Senawi.

IRAN

Permanent Mission: 622 Third Ave, 34th Floor, New York, NY 10017; tel (212) 687-2020; fax (212) 867-7086.
Permanent Representative: Kamal Kharrazi.
Deputy Permanent Representative: Dr M. Javad Zarif.
Ambassador: Gholamali Khoshroo.
Ambassador: Seyed Mohammad Sadegh.
Counsellor: Majid Takht-Ravanchi.
Counsellor: Amir Hossein Zamaninia.
Counsellor: Dr Saied Mirzaee-Yengejeh.
First Secretary (Press): Ramin Rafirasme.
First Secretary: Bahman Naimi-Arfa.
First Secretary: Hossein Sheikh Zeinelddin.
First Secretary: Bozorgmehr Ziaran.
Second Secretary: Mojtaba Amiri-Vahid.
Second Secretary: Ahmad Hadjihosseini.
Second Secretary: Seyed Mehdi Moussavi-Zaree.
Second Secretary: Mahmoud Barimani.

IRAQ

Permanent Mission: 14 East 79th St, New York, NY 10021; tel (212) 737-4434; fax (212) 772-1794.
Permanent Representative: Dr Abdul Amir A. al-Anbari.
Minister and Deputy Permanent Representative: Sabah Talat Kadrat.
Minister: Samir K. K. al-Nima.
Minister: Adnan Malik.
Counsellor: Adnan Ahmed Mohammed.
Counsellor: Mowayad N. Abdulla.
Counsellor: Qasim A. Shakir.
First Secretary: Nadim M. Nail.
Second Secretary: Safa Shihab Ahmed.
Second Secretary: Majeed A. Khalaf.
Second Secretary: Jabir H. Ali.
Third Secretary: Mohammed F. Ahmed.
Third Secretary: Aziz J. Alwan.

IRELAND

Permanent Mission: 885 Second Ave, 19th Floor, 1 Dag Hammarskjöld Plaza, New York, NY 10017; tel (212) 421-6934; telex 420700; fax (212) 752-4726.
Permanent Representative: Francis Mahon Hayes.
Counsellor: John Burke.
Counsellor: Padraic Collins.
First Secretary: Gerry Corr.
First Secretary: Pat Hennessy.
Secretary: Kevin Conmy.
Executive Officer: Gabriel Burke.

ISRAEL

Permanent Mission: 800 Second Ave, New York, NY 10017; tel (212) 351-5200; fax (212) 697-6272.
Permanent Representative: Yoram Aridor.
Deputy Permanent Representative: Ephraim Tari.
Minister: Arie Tenne.
Counsellor: Aaron Jacob.
Counsellor (Administrative): Shmuel Yogev.
Counsellor: Gideon Ezra.
Second Secretary (Press): Yuval Rotem.
Attaché (Administative): Yaakov Markovitz.
Attaché: Avraham Talmor.
Attaché: Amir Takomi.
Attaché: Reuven Gilad.
Attaché: Ziv Barak-Bilaus.

ITALY

Permanent Mission: 2 United Nations Plaza, 24th Floor, New York, NY 10017; tel (212) 486-9191; fax (212) 486-1036.
Permanent Representative: Vieri Traxler.
Deputy Permanent Representative: Mario Scialoja.
Minister: Guido Lenzi.
Counsellor: Vincenzo Petrone.
Counsellor: Sergio Scarantino.
Counsellor: Leonardo Baroncelli.
Counsellor: Saba D'Elia.
Counsellor: Francesco Cottafavi.
Counsellor: Manlio Giuffrida.
First Secretary: Giampaolo Cantini.
First Secretary: Patrizio Fondi.
Second Secretary (Administrative): Giovanni Granata.
Attaché (Legal): Tullio Treves.

JAMAICA

Permanent Mission: 866 Second Ave, 15th Floor, 2 Dag Hammarskjöld Plaza, New York, NY 10017; tel (212) 688-7040; telex 62365; fax (212) 308-3730.
Permanent Representative: Herbert Samuel Walker.
Minister and Deputy Permanent Representative: Maxine Roberts.
Counsellor: Sheila Sealy.
Counsellor: Marcia Thomas.
First Secretary (Administrative): Jean Ashman.
First Secretary: Ava Joy Mignott.
First Secretary: Lylen Ann Marie Scott.
Attaché: Hilary Harker.
Attaché: Mavis Smith.
Attaché (Administrative): Alison Elaine Oliver.
Attaché: Jennifer Angella McPherson-Newman.
Attaché: Hylene Facey.
Attaché: Deborah Lobban.

JAPAN

Permanent Mission: 866 United Nations Plaza, 2nd Floor, New York, NY 10017; tel (212) 223-4300; telex 420414; fax (212) 751-1966.
Permanent Representative: Yoshio Hatano.
Deputy Permanent Representative: Katsumi Sezaki.
Minister and Head of Chancery: Takashi Kiya.
Minister: Hiroharu Koike.
Minister: Yukio Sugano.
Counsellor: Shinya Nagai.
Counsellor: Tadanori Inomata.
Counsellor: Ryo Tagaki.
First Secretary: Ryuichi Shoji.
First Secretary: Chiyoko Teranishi.
First Secretary: Itaro Ogura.
First Secretary: Masahiro Fukukawa.
First Secretary: Satoru Satoh.
First Secretary: Naoto Nikai.
First Secretary: Shigeki Sumi.
First Secretary: Kazuo Minagawa.
First Secretary: Shigehisa Shiraishi.
First Secretary: Takahisa Kawakami.
First Secretary: Satoru Yamazaki.
First Secretary: Hideo Nakajima.

JORDAN

Permanent Mission: 866 United Nations Plaza, Rooms 550-552, New York, NY 10017; tel (212) 752-0135; telex 236380; fax (212) 826-0830.
Permanent Representative: Abdullah Salah.
Minister Plenipotentiary: Samir Naouri.
Minister Plenipotentiary: Mohammed T. A. al-Khalidi.
First Secretary: Abdalla S. Irteimeh.
Second Secretary: Ibrahim Awawdeh.
Third Secretary: Hussein Kheir.

KENYA

Permanent Mission: 866 United Nations Plaza, Room 486, New York, NY 10017; tel (212) 421-4740.
Permanent Representative: Michael George Okeyo.
Counsellor: Robert Kamau Gathungu.
First Secretary (Political): Emma Teresa Shitakha.
First Secretary: R. Ambeyi-Libago.
Second Secretary (Legal): Robert Rufus Hunja.
Second Secretary: Rose Adhiambo Arungu-Olende.
Second Secretary: Joash Oluoch Munda.
Attaché (Press): Philemon Kumbu Chowke.
Attaché (Finance): Patrick M. W. Wafula.
Attaché: Elizabeth Munyiva Nyaunyo.

KOREA, DEMOCRATIC PEOPLE'S REPUBLIC

Permanent Office: 225 East 86th St, New York, NY 10028; tel (212) 722-3536; fax (212) 534-3612.
Permanent Representative: Pak Gil Yon.
Deputy Permanent Representative: Ho Jong.
Counsellor: Kim Chung Nam.
Counsellor: Li Song Jin.
First Secretary: Kim Jae Hon.
First Secretary: Li Chol Jun.
Second Secretary: Kim Mun Dok.
Second Secretary: Pak Ok Ran.
Third Secretary: Li Yong Hui.

KOREA, REPUBLIC

Permanent Office: 866 United Nations Plaza, Suite 300, New York, NY 10017; tel (212) 371-1280; fax (212) 371-8873.
Permanent Representative: Roe Chang Hee.
Deputy Permanent Representative: Shin Kee
Minister: Song Jong Hwan.
Minister: Oh Yoon Kyung.
Counsellor: Keum Jung Ho.
Counsellor: Suh Dae Won.
Attaché (Cultural/Information): Suh Jong Hwan.
Counsellor: Kang Gwang Won.
Counsellor: Choi Jong Moo.
Counsellor: Won Jong Chan.
Counsellor: Yun Byung Se.
First Secretary: Ha Chan Ho.
Second Secretary: Yuh Jae Hong.
Second Secretary: Kim Young Min.
Second Secretary: Choi Jong Moon.

KUWAIT

Permanent Mission: 321 East 44th St, New York, NY 10017; tel (212) 973-4300; fax (212) 370-1733.
Permanent Representative: Mohammad A. Abulhasan.
Deputy Permanent Representative: Mohammad Saad al-Sallal.
Counsellor: Nabeela A. al-Mulla.
Second Secretary: Nasser S. B. al-Sabeeh.
Attaché: Masoud F. M. al-Fehaid.
Attaché: Saleh M. al-Madhahekah.
Adviser: Ziyad Monayair.

LAOS

Permanent Mission: 820 Second Ave, Suite 400, New York, NY 10017; tel (212) 986-0227; telex 234708; fax (212) 750-0039.
Permanent Representative: Saly Khamsy.
Minister-Counsellor: Kanika Phommachanh.
Second Secretary: Bountheung Soumpholphakdy.
Third Secretary: Keó Ounphathai.
Attaché and Press Officer: Hongkham Souvannavong.

LATVIA

Permanent Mission: 115 West 183rd St, New York, NY 10453; tel (212) 933-4500; fax (212) 562-7434.
Permanent Representative: Dr Anatol Dinbergs.

LEBANON

Permanent Mission: 866 United Nations Plaza, Room 531-533, New York, NY 10017; tel (212) 355-5460; fax (212) 838-2819.
Permanent Representative: Khalil Makkawi.
Alternate Permanent Representative: Chawki Choueri.
Counsellor: Nouhad Mahmoud.
Counsellor: Michel Katra.
First Secretary: Jad Said el-Hassan.
Special Adviser: Dr Clovis Maksoud.

LESOTHO

Permanent Mission: 204 East 39th St, New York, NY 10016; tel (212) 661-1690; telex 66273; fax (212) 682-4388.
Permanent Representative: Monyane Paanya Phoofolo.
Counsellor (Political): Tseliso Kolane.
Counsellor (Economic): Ntai E. Makoetje.
First Secretary: Alexander Tasa Ralebitso.
Third Secretary: Kekeletso P. Mosala.
Attaché (Administrative): Hopolang Yolanda Molapo.
Attaché (Information): Baholo G. Moonyane.

LIBERIA

Permanent Mission: 820 Second Ave, 4th Floor, New York, NY 10017; tel (212) 687-1033.
Permanent Representative: William Bull.
Minister-Counsellor: Christian M. Wisseh.
Minister-Counsellor: Youngor S. Telewoda.
Minister-Counsellor: Konah Blackett.
Counsellor: Gabriel N. Fernandez.
First Secretary: Edwin F. Sele.
Second Secretary: Comfort O. Swengbe.
Second Secretary: Moses Y. Harris.

LIBYA

Permanent Mission: 309-315 East 48th St, New York, NY 10017; tel (212) 752-5775; fax (212) 593-4787.
Permanent Representative: Dr Ali A. Treiki.
Deputy Permanent Representative: Ali Sunni Muntasser.
Minister-Counsellor: Dr Ahmed A. Almuakkaf.
First Secretary: Guma I. Amer.
First Secretary: Omar R. Jelban.
First Secretary: Abdussalam S. Sergiwa.
Third Secretary: Mahmoud Y. Azzabi.
Third Secretary: Faisal A. Almabrouk.
Attaché: Saleh A. Shomakhi.
Attaché: Ali M. Elhamroush.
Attaché (Finance): Ramadan S. Ferjani.
Attaché (Finance): Yasein A. Amer.
Adviser: Mustafa J. Zubi.

LIECHTENSTEIN

Permanent Mission: 405 Lexington Ave, Suite 4301, 43rd Floor, New York, NY 10174; tel (212) 599-0220; fax (212) 599-0064.
Permanent Representative: Claudia Fritsche.

LITHUANIA

Permanent Mission: 41 West 82nd St, New York, NY 10024; tel (212) 877-4552; fax (212) 595-8301.
Permanent Representative: Aricetas Simutis.

LUXEMBOURG

Permanent Mission: 801 Second Ave, 13th Floor, New York, NY 10017; tel (212) 370-9850; telex 620241; fax (212) 697-5529.
Permanent Representative: Jean Feyder.
Counsellor and Deputy Permanent Representative: Egide Thein.
First Secretary: Anne Bastian.
Second Secretary: Marc Pierre Baltes.
Second Secretary: Marianne Buschmann.

MADAGASCAR

Permanent Mission: 801 Second Ave, Suite 404, New York, NY 10017; tel (212) 986-9191; telex 236545; fax (212) 986-6271.
Permanent Representative: Blaise Rabetafika.
Minister and Deputy Permanent Representative: Noël Rakotondramboa.
Minister: Raymond Anatole Raoelina.
Counsellor: Martin Rakotonaivo.
Counsellor: Reine Léoncie R. Raoelina.
Counsellor: Claude Randriamalala.
Second Secretary: Yveline Mariette Rakotondramboa.
Attaché: Albert Fety.
Attaché: Perle Ramboasolo.

MALAWI

Permanent Mission: 600 Third Ave, 30th Floor, New York, NY 10016; tel (212) 949-0180; fax (212) 599-5021.
Permanent Representative: Robert B. Mbaya.
Minister: Maweya V. L. Phiri.
Counsellor: W. R. J. Mijoso.
Counsellor: Daniel Dominic Misomali.

MALAYSIA

Permanent Mission: 140 East 45th St, 43rd Floor, New York, NY 10017; tel (212) 986-6310; fax (212) 490-8576.
Permanent Representative: Ismail Razali.
Minister-Counsellor and Deputy Permanent Representative: M. Kushairi Redzuan.
Counsellor: Mohd Isa Rastam.
First Secretary: Haniff Hussein.
First Secretary: Abdul Rahman Mohd Radzi.
First Secretary: Othman Adnan.
First Secretary: Mohamed Baria Kamaruddin.
Second Secretary: Ahmad Zainal Abidin.
Third Secretary: Yeun Meng Wong.
Special Envoy: Bin Hitam Musa.

MALDIVES

Permanent Mission: 820 Second Ave, Suite 800C, New York, NY 10017; tel (212) 599-6195; fax (212) 972-3970.
Second Secretary: Ahmed Khaleel.
Attaché: Hussain Asif.

MALI

Permanent Mission: 111 East 69th St, New York, NY 10021; tel (212) 737-4150; fax (212) 472-3778.
Permanent Representative: Noumou Diakite.
First Counsellor: Cheick Sidi A. T. Diarra.
Second Counsellor: Mahamane A. Maiga.
Secretary and Accountant: Nama Fofana.

MALTA

Permanent Mission: 249 East 35th St, New York, NY 10016; tel (212) 725-2345; fax (212) 779-7097.
Permanent Representative: Victor Camilleri.
Second Secretary: George Vella.
Third Secretary: Anthony F. Mizza.

MARSHALL ISLANDS

Permanent Mission: 1 Dag Hammarskjöld Plaza, 7th Floor, 245 East 47th St, New York, NY 10017-2289; tel (212) 702-4850; fax (212) 207-9888.
Permanent Representative: Wilfred I. Kendall.

MAURITANIA

Permanent Mission: 9 East 77th St, New York, NY 10021; tel (212) 737-7780; fax (212) 472-3314.
Permanent Representative: Mohamedou Ould Mohamed Mahmoud.
Counsellor: Kharass Kane.
Counsellor: Mohamed Mahmoud Ould Cheikh el-Ghaouth.
First Secretary: Brahim Ould Mohamed Abdallahi.
Legal Adviser: Robert W. Thabit.

MAURITIUS

Permanent Mission: 211 East 43rd St, 15th Floor, New York, NY 10017; tel (212) 949-0190; telex 620780; fax (212) 697-3829.
Permanent Representative: Dr Satteeanund Peerthum.
First Secretary: Patrice Eugene Cure.
Second Secretary: Israhyananda Dhalladoo.

MEXICO

Permanent Mission: 2 United Nations Plaza, 28th Floor, New York, NY 10017; tel (212) 752-0220; fax (212) 688-8862.
Permanent Representative: Dr Jorge Montaño.
Deputy Permanent Representative: Antonio Villegas.
Minister: Margarita Dieguez-Armas.
Counsellor: Federico Salas.
Counsellor: José L. Abraham Montes de Oca.
First Secretary: Jorge José Duhalt Villar.
First Secretary: Pablo Macedo.
First Secretary: Arturo Hernandez Basave.
Second Secretary: Adriana Aguilera de Rodriguez.
Third Secretary: Victor Daniel Flores.

MICRONESIA

Permanent Mission: 820 2nd Ave, Suite 800A, New York, NY 10017.
Permanent Representative: Jesse B. Marehalan.

MONGOLIA

Permanent Mission: 6 East 77th St, New York, NY 10021; tel (212) 861-9460; telex 62582; fax (212) 861-9464.
Counsellor and Deputy Permanent Representative: Luvsangiin Erdenechuluun.
First Secretary: Tsagandorjiin Achitsaikhan.
Third Secretary: Ravjaagiin Mounkhou.
Attaché: Galsan Enkhbold.
Attaché: Tudeviin Batchuluun.

MOROCCO

Permanent Mission: 767 Third Ave, 30th Floor, New York, NY 10017; tel (212) 421-1580; fax (212) 980-1512.
Permanent Representative: Ali Skalli.
Ambassador: Abdelslam Jaidi.
Minister-Counsellor: Dr Mohammed Nacer Benjelloun Touimi.
Counsellor: El Hassane Zahid.
Counsellor: Abdelouahab Bellouki.
Counsellor: Mohammed Amar.
Counsellor: Ahmed Amaziane.
Counsellor: Mohammed Chafik el-Khatib.
Counsellor: Raja Ghannam.
First Secretary: Yamina Akhamlich Bennani.
First Secretary: Abdelhakim el-Amrani.
First Secretary: Mohammed Aziz Mouline.
Attaché (Financial/Administrative): Benasser Kassaoui.

MOZAMBIQUE

Permanent Mission: 70 East 79th St, New York, NY 10021; tel (212) 517-4550; fax (212) 517-4553.
Permanent Representative: Pedro Comissario Afonso.
Deputy Permanent Representative: Antonio Deinde Fernandez.
Second Secretary: Filipe Chidumo.
Second Secretary: Tomás João Sales.
Second Secretary: Elias Jaime Zimba.
Attaché (Administrative): Selemane Ossemane.
Attaché: Maria de Lurdes Teodoro.

MYANMAR

Permanent Mission: 10 East 77th St, New York, NY 10021; tel (212) 535-1310; fax (212) 737-2421.
Permanent Representative: Kyaw Min.
Counsellor and Deputy Permanent Representative: Thaung Tun.
First Secretary: Ye Myint.
Second Secretary: Maung Maung.
Third Secretary: Ba Hla Aye.
Attaché: Aung Myint.
Attaché: Nu Nu Aye.

NAMIBIA

Permanent Mission: 135 East 36th St, New York, NY 10016; tel (212) 685-2003; fax (212) 685-1561.
Permanent Representative: Dr Tunguru Huaraka.
Ambassador: Hinyangerwa P. Asheeke.

NEPAL

Permanent Mission: 820 Second Ave, Suite 202, New York, NY 10017; tel (212) 370-4188; fax (212) 953-2038.
Permanent Representative: Dr Jayaraj Acharya.
Minister and Deputy Permanent Representative: Mohan Bahadur Panday.
First Secretary: Binod Prasad Bista.
First Secretary: Lila Prasad Sharma.
First Secretary: Dipendra P. Bista.
Attaché: Shanker Prasad Kattel.

NETHERLANDS

Permanent Mission: 711 Third Ave, 9th Floor, New York, NY 10017; tel (212) 697-5547; fax (212) 370-1954.
Permanent Representative: Robert J. van Schaik.
Minister and Deputy Permanent Representative: Count Jan M. V. A. de Marchant et d'Ansembourg.
Minister (Economic): Frank A. M. Majoor.
Counsellor: Alexander J. Cornelissen.
Counsellor: Kees W. Spaans.
First Secretary: Jan-Jaap van de Velde.
First Secretary: Giovanni R. van der Lugt.
First Secretary: Peter W. Bas Backer.
First Secretary: Kees P. Rade.
First Secretary: Barend C. A. F. van der Heijden.
First Secretary: Peter R. Post.
First Secretary: Bob Hiensch.

NEW ZEALAND

Permanent Mission: 1 United Nations Plaza, 25th Floor, New York, NY 10017; tel (212) 826-1960; fax (212) 758-0827.
Permanent Representative: Terence O'Brien.
Deputy Permanent Representative: Hilary Willberg.
First Secretary: James Kember.
Second Secretary: John Adank.

Second Secretary: Jane Coombs.

NICARAGUA

Permanent Mission: 820 Second Ave, 8th Floor, New York, NY 10017; tel (212) 490-7997; fax (212) 286-0815.
Permanent Representative: Dr Roberto Mayorga-Cortes.
Counsellor: José María Zelaya.
Counsellor: Erich Constantino Vilchez Asher.
First Secretary: Grethel Vargas.
Third Secretary: Bárbara Omier Sharp.
Third Secretary: Norma Elena Castillo Guerrero.
Attaché: Dagmara de la Concepción Araica Duran.
Attaché: Otoniel Barrera Peña.

NIGER

Permanent Mission: 417 East 50th St, New York, NY 10022; tel (212) 421-3260.
Permanent Representative: Col Moumouni Djermakoye.
Counsellor: Ousseini Soumana.
Counsellor: Abdoulaye D. Moumouni.

NIGERIA

Permanent Mission: 733 Third Ave, 15th Floor, New York, NY 10017; tel (212) 953-9130; fax (212) 697-1970.
Permanent Representative: Prof. Ibrahim A. Gambari.
Minister: K. O. Olisemeka.
Minister-Counsellor: Rosaline O. Ogunleye.
Minister-Counsellor: Biodun Owoseni.
Counsellor: Adekunle O. Adeyanju.
Counsellor: Mohammed G. Umar.
Counsellor: Emmanuel N. Agbegir.
First Secretary: Sani L. Mohammed.
First Secretary: Abdullahi A. Omaki.
First Secretary: Thomas C. Onwualia.
First Secretary: Paul N. Uzor.
First Secretary: Chigozie F. Obi-Nnadozie.
Second Secretary: Abdullahi L. Sidi.
Second Secretary: Muntari A. Kaita.
Second Secretary: Ahmed Inusa.
Second Secretary: Okey A. Anigbogu.
Attaché (Finance): Richard O. Omaghomi.
Attaché (Finance): Maryjoan N. Ononaji.

NORWAY

Permanent Mission: 855 Third Ave, 39th Floor, New York, NY 10022-7584; tel (212) 421-0280; fax (212) 688-0554.
Permanent Representative: Martin Johannes Huslid.
Minister-Counsellor: Sverre Bergh Johansen.
Counsellor (Political): Lasse Seim.
Counsellor (Economic/Social Affairs): Ole Kristian Holthe.
Military Adviser: Col Sigurd Friis.
First Secretary (Political): Torgeir Fjaertoft.
First Secretary (Economic/Social Affairs): Ola Brevik.
Second Secretary (Political): Rolf Einar Fife.
Second Secretary (Economic/Social Affairs): Lars Fure.
Attaché (Economic/Social Affairs): Kjersti Roedsmoen.
Attaché (Commercial): Hans Naess Olstad.

OMAN

Permanent Mission: 866 United Nations Plaza, Suite 540, New York, NY 10017; tel (212) 355-3505; fax (212) 644-0070.
Permanent Representative: Salim bin Muhammad al-Khussaiby.
First Secretary: Younes bin Ali Rahma.
First Secretary: Mohammed Abdullah Salim al-Sameen.
Second Secretary: Salim Hamad Saif al-Battashi.
Third Secretary: Ali Abdullah Mahfoodh al-Khasibi.

PAKISTAN

Permanent Mission: 8 East 65th St, New York, NY 10021; tel (212) 879-8600; telex 224186; fax (212) 744-7348.
Permanent Representative: Jamsheed K. A. Marker.
Minister and Deputy Permanent Representative: Shaukat Umer.
First Secretary: Athar Mahmood.
First Secretary: Ashraf Qureshi.
First Secretary: Alamgir Babar.
First Secretary and Head of Chancery: Noor Mohammad Jadmani.
Second Secretary: Tehmina Janjua.
Second Secretary: Faqir Syed Asif Hussain.
Attaché (Press): Mansoor Suhail.

PANAMA

Permanent Mission: 866 United Nations Plaza, Suite 509, New York, NY 10017; tel (212) 421-5240; fax (212) 421-2694.
Permanent Representative: Dr César Pereira Burgos.
Deputy Permanent Representative: Eduardo A. Heart.
Alternate Permanent Representative: Isabel Cecilia Saint Malo.
Counsellor and Alternate Permanent Representative: Noris Elena Ramirez.
Counsellor and Alternate Permanent Representative: Jaime O. Abad.
Attaché: María P. Sgro.
Attaché: Sandra Garcia.

PAPUA NEW GUINEA

Permanent Mission: 866 United Nations Plaza, Suite 322, New York, NY 10017; tel (212) 832-0043; telex 66603; fax (212) 832-0918.
Permanent Representative: Renagi Renagi Lohia.
Counsellor: Alexis O. Maino.
First Secretary: Kappa Yarka.
Third Secretary: Rose Sam.

PARAGUAY

Permanent Mission: 211 East 43rd St, Room 1202, New York, NY 10017; tel (212) 687-3490; fax (212) 818-1282.
Permanent Representative: Alfredo Cañete.
Counsellor: Genaro Vicente Pappalardo.
First Secretary: Pedro Zulin Rojas.
Attaché (Administrative): Hortensia Chammorro de Riba.

PERU

Permanent Mission: 820 Second Ave, Suite 1600, New York, NY 10017; tel (212) 687-3336; fax (212) 972-6975.
Permanent Representative: Dr Ricardo V. Luna.
Minister and Deputy Permanent Representative: José Antonio Arrospide.
Counsellor: Javier Paulinich.
Counsellor: José Antonio Bellina.
Counsellor: Jorge Lazaro.
Second Secretary: Félix Denegri.
Second Secretary: Julio Garro.
Second Secretary: Manuel Talavera.
Second Secretary: Elmer Schialer.
Third Secretary: Carlos Vasquez.
Attaché (Civil): Leddy Chirinos.
Attaché (Civil): Sabina Arita de Alvarado.
Attaché (Civil): Rosa E. de Salinas.

PHILIPPINES

Permanent Mission: 556 Fifth Ave, 5th Floor, New York, NY 10036; tel (212) 764-1300; fax (212) 840-8602.
Permanent Representative: Sedrey A. Ordoñez.
Deputy Permanent Representative: Manuel Mendez.
Deputy Permanent Representative: Ernestina E. Kodikara.
Minister-Counsellor: Gavino Abaya, Jr.
Minister-Counsellor: Cynthia B. Guevara.
Minister-Counsellor: Federico T. Tiongson.
Minister-Counsellor: José Lino B. Guerrero.
Minister-Counsellor: Ruth S. Limjuco.
First Secretary: Nonet M. Dapul.
First Secretary: Virgilio A. Reyes.
First Secretary: Mary Ann O. Arguillas.
Second Secretary: Salvador C. Tolentino.
Second Secretary: Theodore M. Gabriel.
Second Secretary: Cecilia B. Rebong.

POLAND

Permanent Mission: 9 East 66th St, New York, NY 10021; tel (212) 744-2506; telex 220441; fax (212) 517-6771.
Permanent Representative: Dr Robert Mroziewicz.
Minister-Counsellor: Dr Zbigniew Maria Włosowicz.
First Secretary: Aleksander Janowski.
First Secretary: Grzegorz Polowczyk.
Second Secretary: Ryszard Rysinski.
Second Secretary: Maciej Pachelski.
Second Secretary: Jarosław Strejczek.
Second Secretary: Ryszard Morczynski.
Third Secretary: Wojciech Ponikiewski.
Attaché: Adam Skałecki.

PORTUGAL

Permanent Mission: 777 Third Ave, 27th Floor, New York, NY 10017; tel (212) 759-9444; telex 234301; fax (212) 355-1124.
Permanent Representative: Fernando José Reino.
Minister Plenipotentiary and Deputy Permanent Representative: José Caetano da Costa Pereira.
Counsellor (Legal): Adelino Silva.
Counsellor (Economic/Development Affairs): Catulina Soares Guerreiro.
Counsellor (Press): António Amaral Pais.
First Secretary: Maria de Fátima V. de Andrade Mendes.
First Secretary: Francisco Maria de Sousa Ribeiro-Telles.
First Secretary: João Maria Rebelo de Andrade Cabral.
Attaché: Maria Regina Serrão Emerson.
Attaché: Hernani Edmundo Mesquita.

QATAR

Permanent Mission: 747 Third Ave, 22nd Floor, New York, NY 10017; tel (212) 486-9335; fax (212) 758-4952.
Permanent Representative: Dr Hassan Ali Hussain al-Ni'mah.
Minister: Nassir Abdelaziz al-Nasser.
Counsellor: Abdulrahman Mohamed al-Khulaifi.
First Secretary: Khalid Mohammad al-Baker.

ROMANIA

Permanent Mission: 573-577 Third Ave, New York, NY 10016; tel (212) 682-3273; fax (212) 682-9746.
Permanent Representative: Aurel Dragos Munteanu.
Minister-Counsellor and Deputy Permanent Representative: Valeriu Florean.
Minister-Counsellor: Ioan N. Voicu.
Counsellor: Ioan Barac.
First Secretary: Marian-George Dinu.

First Secretary: Viorel-Ovidiu Nuta.
First Secretary: Ionel Gheorghe Calafeteanu.
Third Secretary: Viorel Draghici-Sutic.
Third Secretary: Dorian Popescu.
Attaché: Maria Draghici-Sutic.
Attaché: Aurel Banica.

RUSSIA

Permanent Mission: 136 East 67th St, New York, NY 10021; tel (212) 861-4900; fax (212) 628-0252.
Permanent Representative and Deputy Minister for Foreign Affairs: Yuli M. Vorontsov.
Deputy Permanent Representative: Valentin V. Lozinsky.
Envoy, Minister and Deputy Permanent Representative: Sergei N. Smirnov.
Envoy, Minister and Deputy Permanent Representative: Dimitri V. Bykov.
Envoy, Minister and Deputy Permanent Representative: Eduard V. Kudryavstev.
Envoy, Minister and Deputy Permanent Representative: Aleksandr A. Razvin.
Senior Counsellor: Yuzapas Y. Grigutis.
Senior Counsellor: Gennady I. Slepenkov.
Senior Counsellor: Aleksandr V. Denisov.
Senior Counsellor: Alexei B. Podtserov.
Senior Counsellor: Valery K. Greshnikh.
Senior Counsellor: Rollan G. Dzhikya.
Senior Counsellor: Boris A. Tsepov.
Counsellor: Capt. Aleksandr S. Gorokhov.
Counsellor: Semion A. Dzakhaev.
Counsellor: Leonid I. Verenikin.
Counsellor: Aleksandr N. Ilitchev.
Counsellor: Petr S. Moissa.
Counsellor: Yuri N. Isakov.
Counsellor: Vladimir V. Rumyantsev.
Counsellor: Aleksandre S. Soloviev.
Counsellor: Yuri I. Musienko.
First Secretary: Vadim A. Voytenko.
First Secretary: Boris F. Chuprikov.
First Secretary: Vladimir I. Sergiev.
First Secretary: Yuri P. Chizhik.
First Secretary: Vladimir P. Shishov.
First Secretary: Vladimir D. Khandogy.
First Secretary: Vitaly S. Kalinovsky.
First Secretary: Alexandre N. Avanesov.
First Secretary: Sergei N. Shestakov.
First Secretary: Rashid M. Khalikov.
First Secretary: Vladimir I. Bakhurov.
First Secretary: Andrei A. Dedkov.
First Secretary: Valery D. Arkhipov.
First Secretary: Nikolai M. Anastasyev.
First Secretary: Sergei B. Shestakov.
First Secretary: Yevgeny V. Toropov.

RWANDA

Permanent Mission: 124 East 39th St, New York, NY 10016; tel (212) 696-0644; fax (212) 689-3304.
Counsellor: Corneille Munyampeta.
Counsellor: Chaste Abimana.

SAINT CHRISTOPHER AND NEVIS

Permanent Mission: 414 East 75th St, 5th Floor, New York, NY 10021; tel (212) 535-1234; fax (212) 879-4789.
Permanent Representative: Dr William Herbert.
Minister and Deputy Permanent Representative: Erstein Edwards.
Minister-Counsellor (Economic): Kutayba Y. Alghanim.
Counsellor: Raymond Taylor.

SAINT LUCIA

Permanent Mission: 820 Second Ave, Suites 907-915, 9th Floor, New York, NY 10017; tel (212) 697-9360; fax (212) 808-4975.
Permanent Representative: Dr Charles S. Flemming.
Attaché: Andrew B. Isaac.
Attaché: Germaine Patricia Louis.
Attaché: Sonia Leunce.

SAINT VINCENT AND THE GRENADINES

Permanent Mission: 801 Second Ave, 21st Floor, New York, NY 10017; tel (212) 687-4490.
Permanent Representative: Kingsley Layne.
Minister-Counsellor and Deputy Permanent Representative: James Anton Pompey.
Counsellor: Myron Ewart Dellimore.
Attaché: Diana A. Williams.

SÃO TOMÉ AND PRÍNCIPE

Permanent Mission: 801 Second Ave, Suite 1504, New York, NY 10017; tel (212) 697-4211; fax (212) 687-8389.
Permanent Representative: Joaquim Rafael Branco.
Third Secretary: Adérito d'Apresentação Ramos.

SAUDI ARABIA

Permanent Mission: 405 Lexington Ave, 56th Floor, New York, NY 10017; tel (212) 697-4830; fax (212) 983-4895.
Permanent Representative: Samir S. Shahabi.
Counsellor: Mohammed H. Mirdass al-Kahtany.
First Secretary: Mustafa M. H. Kawthar.
First Secretary: Saleh Radi al-Rehale.
Second Secretary: Prince Mansour bin Khalid al-Farhan al-Saud.
Second Secretary: Said al-Rachach.
Second Secretary: Abdularahman al-Rassi.
Adviser (Finance): Taysir Hussein Badanoro.

SENEGAL

Permanent Mission: 238 East 68th St, New York, NY 10021; tel (212) 517-9030; fax (212) 737-7461.
Permanent Representative: Absa Claude Diallo.
Minister-Counsellor: Mama Balla Sy.
Counsellor: Mamadou Deme.
Counsellor: Mamadou Fall.
Counsellor: Aliou Sene.
Counsellor: Maymouna Diop.
First Secretary: Oumar Cata Cisse.
First Secretary: Ibrahima Diaby.
Attaché: Mouhamadou Diaw.
Attaché: Marie Jeanne Diene.
Attaché (Administrative): Gana Gueye.
Adviser (Technical): Taïbou Amadou Ba.
Special Adviser: Ibrahima Sy.

SEYCHELLES

Permanent Mission: 820 Second Ave, Suite 900F, New York, NY 10017; tel (212) 687-9766; fax (212) 737-7461.
Counsellor and Deputy Permanent Representative: Marc Michael Marengo.

SIERRA LEONE

Permanent Mission: 57 East 64th St, New York, NY 10021; tel (212) 570-0030.
Permanent Representative: Dr Tom Obaleh Kargbo.
Counsellor (Economic) and Head of Chancery: Sheka Abdulai Mansaray.
First Secretary: Andrew G. Bangali.
First Secretary: Thomason D. Lawson.
Third Secretary: Amara Dennis Turay.
Third Secretary: Khadijatu Mansaray.

SINGAPORE

Permanent Mission: 2 United Nations Plaza, 25th Floor, New York, NY 10017; tel (212) 826-0840; fax (212) 826-2964.
Permanent Representative: Dr Chew Tai Soo.
Minister-Counsellor and Deputy Permanent Representative: Mark Hong.
First Secretary: Vanu Gopala Menon.
First Secretary: Iris Chin Choo Geddis.

SOLOMON ISLANDS

Permanent Mission: 820 Second Ave, Suite 800A, New York, NY 10017; tel (212) 599-6190; fax (212) 972-3970.
Permanent Representative: Francis Bugotu.
First Secretary: Beraki Luje Jino.

SOMALIA

Permanent Mission: 425 East 61st St, Suite 703, New York, NY 10021; tel (212) 688-9410.
Counsellor: Fatun Mohamed Hassan.
First Secretary: Abdi Jama Abdulle.
Second Secretary: Ismaël M. Adan.

SOUTH AFRICA

Permanent Mission: 326 East 48th St, New York, NY 10017; tel (212) 371-8154; fax (212) 371-7577.
Permanent Representative: Vernon R. W. Steward.
Minister and Deputy Permanent Representative: Frak H. Land.
Counsellor: Aubrey K. Dwyer.
First Secretary: Hermanus J. van Niekerk.
First Secretary: P. Andre van Zyl.
Third Secretary: Jack Christofides.
Third Secretary: Constantin Ayiotis.
Attaché: Pierre Joubert.

SPAIN

Permanent Mission: 809 United Nations Plaza, 6th Floor, New York, NY 10017; tel (212) 661-1050.
Permanent Representative: Juan Antonio Yañez-Barnuevo.
Minister and Deputy Permanent Representative: Antonio Pedauye.
Minister: Francisco José Viqueira.
Counsellor: Javier Garrigues.
Counsellor: Rafael Fernandez-Pita.
Counsellor: Carles María Casajuana.
Counsellor (Administrative/Financial): Tomás Ramos.
Counsellor: Alfonso María Dastis.
First Secretary: Ana María Menendez.
First Secretary: Pedro Serrano.
Attaché (Administrative): Gregorio Gomez.

SRI LANKA

Permanent Mission: 630 Third Ave, 20th Floor, New York, NY 10017; tel (212) 986-7040; fax (212) 986-1838.
Permanent Representative: Dr Stanley Kalpagé.
Minister-Counsellor and Deputy Permanent Representative: H. K. J. R. Bandara.
First Secretary: N. Sikkander.
Second Secretary: A. G. Ranasinghe.
Attaché: Thompson Bamunuwatte.

SUDAN

Permanent Mission: 210 East 49th St, New York, NY 10017; tel (212) 421-2680; fax (212) 688-1525.
Permanent Representative: Lieut-Gen. Joseph Lagu.
Deputy Permanent Representative: Salah Mohamed Ali.
Counsellor: Kuol Alor Kuol.

First Secretary: Abbas Ahmed Alnur.
First Secretary: Omer Mohamed Ahmed Siddig.
First Secretary: Siraj el-din Hamid Yousif.
Attaché (Finance): Babiker Ahmed Elsheikh.
Attaché (Administrative): Rahamtalla el-Awad Elmaki.
Attaché (Administrative): Mohamed Mohamed Ibrahim Hashim.

SURINAME

Permanent Mission: 866 United Nations Plaza, Suite 320, New York, NY 10017; tel (212) 826-0660; fax (212) 980-7029.
Permanent Representative: Kriesnadath Nandoe.
Second Secretary: Ewald W. Limon.
Second Secretary: Ruth Helen de Miranda.
Attaché (Administrative): Gerhard A. Watson.

SWAZILAND

Permanent Mission: 866 United Nations Plaza, Suite 420, New York, NY 10017; tel (212) 371-8910; telex 620670; fax (212) 754-2755.
Permanent Representative: Dr Timothy L. L. Dlamini.
Counsellor: Carlton M. Dlamini.
First Secretary: Sethabile E. Mdluli.
Third Secretary: Joel Musa Nhleko.
Attaché (Administrative): Nelisiwe P. Dlamini.

SWEDEN

Permanent Mission: 1 Dag Hammarskjöld Plaza, 885 Second Avenue, 46th Floor, New York, NY 10017-2201; tel (212) 751-5900; telex 234150; fax (212) 832-0389.
Permanent Representative: Jan K. Eliasson.
Deputy Permanent Representative: Lars-Göran Engfeldt.
Minister (Economic/Social Affairs): Rolf Andréen.
Minister (Administrative/Budgetary Affairs): Karin Oldfelt Hjertonsson.
Counsellor (Legal/Social Affairs): Staffan Duhs.
Counsellor (Political): Herman af Trolle.
Counsellor (Political): Stefan Noréen.
Counsellor (Political): Catherine von Heidenstam.
Counsellor (Economic/Social Affairs): Lennarth Hjelmaker.
Counsellor and Military Adviser: Col Nils Alstermark.
First Secretary and Special Economic Adviser: Kjell Franzson.
First Secretary (Economic/Social Affairs): Ingrid Hjelt af Trolle.
First Secretary (Political): Anders Lidén.
Second Secretary and Attaché (Press): Annika Wirén.

SYRIA

Permanent Mission: 820 Second Ave, 10th Floor, New York, NY 10017; tel (212) 661-1313; fax (212) 983-4439.
Permanent Representative: Dia-Allah el-Fattal.
Ambassador: Ibrahim Younes.
Minister: Issa Awad.
Minister-Counsellor: Ahmad Hallak.
Minister-Counsellor: Mohammad Adib Khani.
First Secretary: Khalil Abou-Hadid.
First Secretary: Mohammad Najdat Shaheed.
Attaché: Samer Obeido.
Attaché: Abla el-Ali.

TANZANIA

Permanent Mission: 205 East 42nd St, 13th Floor, New York, NY 10017; tel (212) 972-9160; fax (212) 682-5232.
Permanent Representative: Anthony B. Nyakyi.
Ambassador: Conrad S. M. Mselle.
Minister: Samuel A. Mdee.
Counsellor: Stanislaus E. S. Mongella.
Counsellor: Perucy Nyanjula Butiku.
First Secretary: Liberata Rutageruka Mulamula.
First Secretary (Political/Legal): Jerry Elihaki J. Mburi.
First Secretary: Charles A. Sanga.
Attaché (Administrative): George F. Mahimbo.

THAILAND

Permanent Mission: 351 East 52nd St, New York, NY 10022; tel (212) 754-2230; telex 216736; fax (212) 754-2535.
Permanent Representative: Nitya Pibulsonggram.
Minister and Deputy Permanent Representative: Montana Suvarnatemee.
Counsellor: Norachit Sinhaseni.
Counsellor: Piamsak Milintachinda.
First Secretary: Krisana Chandraprabha.
First Secretary: Dr Kantathi Suphamongkhon.
First Secretary: Noppadon Theppitak.
Second Secretary: Paskorn Siriyaphan.
Second Secretary: Vitavas Srivihok.
Third Secretary: Roongruang Ruenrom.
Third Secretary: Piriya Khempon.
Attaché: Surat Nucharoen.
Attaché: Patchara Banyen.
Attaché: Oraphin Singsalai.

TOGO

Permanent Mission: 112 East 40th St, New York, NY 10016; tel (212) 490-3455; fax (212) 983-6684.
Permanent Representative: Soumi-Biova Penaneach.
Counsellor: Latévi Modem Lawson-Betum.
Counsellor: Nolana Ta-Ama.
Third Secretary: Déladie Adéyémi Adjayi.
Attaché (Finance): Agbeko Apetoh-Ankoutse.
Attaché (Protocol): Komlavi Jondoh.

TRINIDAD AND TOBAGO

Permanent Mission: 675 Third Ave, 22nd Floor, New York, NY 10017; tel (212) 697-7620; fax (212) 682-3580.
Permanent Representative: Dr Marjorie R. Thorpe.
Counsellor and Deputy Permanent Representative: Lennox A. Wattley.
First Secretary: Evans King.
First Secretary: Margaret A. King-Rousseau.
Second Secretary: Delia Margaret Chatoor.

TUNISIA

Permanent Mission: 405 Lexington Ave, 65th Floor, New York, NY 10174; tel (212) 557-3344; fax (212) 697-4099.
Permanent Representative: Ahmed Ghezal.
Counsellor: Othman Jerandi.
First Secretary: Lassaad Ben Lamine.
First Secretary: Holla Bachtobji.
First Secretary: Ghazi Jomaa.
First Secretary: Alia Dlimi.
First Secretary: Mohamed Ferid Belhaj.
First Secretary: Mohamed Messaoud.
First Secretary: Abdelaziz Lamouchi.
First Secretary: Moncef Kalthoumi.

TURKEY

Permanent Mission: 821 United Nations Plaza, 11th Floor, New York, NY 10017; tel (212) 949-0150; fax (212) 949-0086.
Permanent Representative: Mustafa Akşin.
Counsellor and Deputy Permanent Representative: Osman Korutürk.
Counsellor and Deputy Permanent Representative: Ali Kocatürk.
Counsellor: Tahsin Burcuoğlu.
Counsellor: Ahmet Acet.
Counsellor: Hayati Güven.
Counsellor: Ahmet Nazif Alpman.
Counsellor: Fuat Tanlay.
Counsellor: Kemal Civelek.
Counsellor: İlhan Lütem.
Counsellor: Yilpar Kaynak.
Counsellor (Legal): Aydin Sefa Akay.
Counsellor: Nizamettin Temel.
First Secretary: Selim Yenel.
Attaché (Press): Nurinisa Bayramoğlu.

UGANDA

Permanent Mission: 336 East 45th St, New York, NY 10017; tel (212) 949-0110; telex 234554; fax (212) 687-4517.
Permanent Representative: Prof. Perezi Karukubiro-Kamunanwire.
Deputy Permanent Representative: Christopher Katsigazi.
First Secretary: David Etuket.
Third Secretary: Martinez Arapta Mangusho.
Third Secretary: Rosemary Semafumu.
Attaché (Administrative): H. V. Kayonjo-Magala.
Attaché: Anne Harriet Zziwa.
Attaché: Alice Babirye Kijjambu.

UKRAINE

Permanent Mission: 136 East 67th St, New York, NY 10021; tel (212) 535-3418; fax (212) 288-5361.
Permanent Representative: Gennady I. Oudovenko.
Counsellor and Deputy Permanent Representative: Victor A. Kryzhanivsky.
Counsellor: Oleksandr M. Bouts'ko.
First Secretary: Anatoly T. Olinik.
First Secretary: Yuri M. Shevchenko.
Second Secretary: Volodimir Y. Eltchenko.
Second Secretary: Sergei V. Koulyk.
Second Secretary: Anatoly G. Kupriyan.

UNITED ARAB EMIRATES

Permanent Mission: 747 Third Ave, 36th Floor, New York, NY 10017; tel (212) 371-0480; fax (212) 319-5433.
Permanent Representative: Muhammad Hussain al-Shaali.
Counsellor: Ali Thani al-Suwaidi.
Counsellor: Mohammad Saeed al-Kindi.
Senior Adviser (Political/Legal): Dr Burhan Wasfi Hammad.
Attaché: Yussef Fayek Kanaan.

UNITED KINGDOM

Permanent Mission: 845 Third Ave, 10th Floor, New York, NY 10022; tel (212) 745-0200; telex 126756; fax (212) 745-0316.
Permanent Representative and Representative on the Security Council: Sir David Hannay.
Minister and Deputy Permanent Representative: Thomas L. Richardson.
Counsellor and Head of Chancery: Christopher O. Hum.
Counsellor (Economic and Social Affairs): John F. R. Martin.
Counsellor: R. Andrew Fulton.
Counsellor (Management): Ian C. Sloane.
Counsellor (Legal Adviser): Anthony I. Aust.
Counsellor: Richard Kinchen.
First Secretary: Robert N. Peirce.
First Secretary: Ian C. Cliff.
First Secretary: W. Alistair Harrison.
First Secretary: Richard M. D. Barrett.
First Secretary: Martin C. Raven.
First Secretary: P. J. Ritchie.
First Secretary: Dr Jan S. C. Priest.
Second Secretary (Management): W. G. Devon Johnson.
Second Secretary: Michael T. Shryane.

Second Secretary (Chancery): Philip M. A. Tissot.
Second Secretary: Caroline M. Cliff.
Second Secretary (Press Officer): Dr Simon D. Harkin.

USA

Permanent Mission: 799 United Nations Plaza, New York, NY 10017; tel (212) 415-4050; fax (212) 415-4443.
Permanent Representative: Edward J. Perkins.
Deputy Permanent Representative: Alexander F. Watson.
Representative to Economic and Social Council: Jonathan Moore.
Alternate Representative for Special Political Affairs: Shirin Tahir-Kheli.
Deputy Representative to Economic and Social Council: Edward Marks.
Political Section: Robert T. Grey.
Regional Security Officer: George McCauley.
Public Affairs Officer: Philip Arnold.
Resources Management: Linda S. Shenwick.
Administrative Section: Dorothy M. Sampas.
International Legal Adviser: Robert B. Rosenstock.
Host Country: Robert C. Moller.
Adviser and Head of Protocol: Brenda Connors.

URUGUAY

Permanent Mission: 747 Third Ave, 37th Floor, New York, NY 10017; tel (212) 752-8240; fax (212) 593-0935.
Permanent Representative: Ramiro Piriz-Ballon.
Minister-Counsellor and Deputy Permanent Representative: Pablo Emilio Sader.
Minister-Counsellor and Deputy Permanent Representative: Dr Carlos Gianelli.
Second Secretary: Adriana Lissidini.
Second Secretary: William Ehlers.
Attaché (Press): Jorge Reiner.
Attaché: Edison N. Wimber.

VANUATU

Permanent Mission: 416 Convent Ave, New York, NY 10031; tel (212) 862-4470; telex 4972163; fax (212) 926-4131.
Permanent Representative: Robert F. van Lierop.

VENEZUELA

Permanent Mission: 335 East 46th St, New York, NY 10017; tel (212) 557-2055; fax (212) 557-3528.
Permanent Representative: Dr Diego Arria.
Ambassador: Dr Emilio Figueredo Planchart.
Military Adviser: Gen. Juan Arraiz.
Counsellor: Guillermina da Silva-Suniaga.
Counsellor (Cultural): Juan Alirio Palacios.
First Secretary: José E. Acosta-Fragachan.
First Secretary: Ramón Enrique Rondon-Musso.
Second Secretary: Alberto J. Armas-Rojas.
Second Secretary: Yasmín Josefina Turuphial.
Second Secretary: Kidder Salazar.
Second Secretary: Luis A. Niño Gomez.
Second Secretary: Lucas Castillo.
Third Secretary: Javier José Diaz Aguilera.
Attaché (Press): Anabel Duran-Schiller.

VIET-NAM

Permanent Mission: 20 Waterside Plaza (Lobby), New York, NY 10010; tel (212) 679-3779; fax (212) 686-8534.
Permanent Representative: Trinh Xuan Lang.
Deputy Permanent Representative: Nguyen Can.
Counsellor: Dinh Thi Minh Huyen.
First Secretary: Pham Van Que.
Second Secretary: Le Khac Trung.
Second Secretary: Thuyen Nguyen Dang.
Third Secretary: Pham Ngoc Quang.
Third Secretary: Nguyen Minh Thong.
Third Secretary: Nguyen Huy Bien.
Third Secretary: Dinh Nguyen Ngok.
Attaché (Press): Le Dung.
Attaché (Legal): Nguyen Troung Giang.

WESTERN SAMOA

Permanent Mission: 820 Second Ave, Suite 800D, New York, NY 10017; tel (212) 599-6190; fax (212) 972-3970.
Permanent Representative: Dr Fili Wendt.
First Secretary: Robin E. G. Mauala.

YEMEN

Permanent Mission: 866 United Nations Plaza, Room 435, New York, NY 10017; tel (212) 355-1730; fax (212) 750-9613.
Permanent Representative: Abdalla Saleh al-Ashtal.
Deputy Permanent Representative: Muhamed Ahmed Muhamed Basalamah.
Ambassador: Hussein Saeed al-Alfi.
Minister: Nabil Khaled Hasson Missary.
Counsellor: Abdelelah Mohamed al-Eryany.
First Secretary: Noria Abdullah Ali al-Hamami.
First Secretary: Abdullah Mohamed Alsaidi.
First Secretary: Ahmed Ali Saleh Muthana.
Attaché: Sheikh Ahmed Nasser.

YUGOSLAVIA

Permanent Mission: 854 Fifth Ave, New York, NY 10021; tel (212) 879-8700; fax (212) 879-8705.
Permanent Representative: Darko Silović.
Minister and Deputy Permanent Representative: Slobodan Kotevski.
Minister-Counsellor: Radmilla Perković.
Counsellor: Zeljko Jerkić.
Counsellor: Dragan Zupanjevac.
Counsellor: Milos Strugar.
Counsellor: Boris Savle.
First Secretary: Borut Mahnić.
Second Secretary: Dejan Sahović.
Second Secretary: Igor Kerstein.
Third Secretary: Vuk Zugić.

ZAIRE

Permanent Mission: 767 Third Ave, 25th Floor, New York, NY 10017; tel (212) 754-1966; fax (212) 754-1970.
Permanent Representative: Bagbeni Adeito Nzengeya.
Minister-Counsellor and Deputy Permanent Representative: Lukabu Khabouji N'Zaji.
Minister-Counsellor: Kibidi Ngovuka.
First Secretary: Zongwe Mitonga M'Puilua.
Second Secretary: Fundi Assani.
Attaché (Finance): Kazadi Biaya Kazzys.

ZAMBIA

Permanent Mission: 237 East 52nd St, New York, NY 10022; tel (212) 758-1110; fax (212) 758-1319.
Permanent Representative: Hannania B. M. Lungu.
Minister-Counsellor and Deputy Permanent Representative: Isaiah Zimba Chabala.
Counsellor (Political): Godwin Mutale S. Mfula.
Counsellor (Economic): Albert Mudenda Muchanga.
First Secretary: William Katongo.
Second Secretary: Bob Mbunji Samakai.
Third Secretary: Mary Phiri.
Legal Adviser: Encyla Sinjela.

ZIMBABWE

Permanent Mission: 19 East 47th St, New York, NY 10017; tel (212) 980-9511; telex 225992; fax (212) 755-4188.
Permanent Representative: Simbarashe Simbanenduku Mumbengegwi.
Minister and Deputy Permanent Representative: Cleophas Johannes Tsokodayi.
Counsellor: Raisedon Zenenga.
Counsellor: Chipo Zindoga.
Counsellor: Godfrey Musafare Dzvairo.
Counsellor: Kesiwe Ndlovu Malindi.
First Secretary: Winston T. Msengezi.
First Secretary: Ronald Tendai Chavunduka.
First Secretary: Catherine M. Piloto.
Second Secretary: Baraka Tirivepi.
Third Secretary: Martha Chikowore.
Third Secretary: Nation Madongorere.
Third Secretary: Kenneth Kanyayi.

Observers

HOLY SEE

Permanent Office: 20 East 72nd St, New York, NY 10021; tel (212) 734-2900; fax (212) 988-3633.
Observer: Archbishop Renato Raffaele Martino.
First Secretary: Mgr Giambattista Diquattro.
Attaché: Mgr Joseph de Andrea.
Attaché: Rev. Michel Amara-Poignet.
Adviser: Karol Krcmery.
Attaché: María Rodriguez-Oliva.

MONACO

Permanent Office: 845 Third Ave, 19th Floor, New York, NY 10022; tel (212) 759-5227; fax (212) 754-9320.
Acting Observer: Francis Cresci.

SAN MARINO

Permanent Office: 745 Fifth Ave, Suite 1208, New York, NY 10151; tel (212) 751-1234; fax (212) 751-1436.
Permanent Observer: Gian Nicola Filippi Balestra.
Deputy Permanent Observer: Ghazi M. Aita.
Counsellor: Livio Capicchioni.
Permanent Delegate (Press) to UNICEF: Camillo de Benedetti.

SWITZERLAND

Permanent Office: 757 Third Ave, 21st Floor, New York, NY 10017; tel (212) 421-1480; fax (212) 751-2104.
Observer: Dieter Chenaux-Repond.
Minister and Deputy Permanent Observer: André Faivet.
Counsellor: Lise Favre.
First Secretary: René Schaetti.
Second Secretary: Walter Wittwer.
Third Secretary: Ivo Sieber.

International Organizations

ASIAN-AFRICAN LEGAL CONSULTATIVE COMMITTEE

Permanent Office: 404 East 66th St, Apt 12C, New York, NY 10021; tel (212) 734-7608.
Observer: K. Bhagwat-Singh.

COMMONWEALTH SECRETARIAT

Permanent Office: 820 Second Ave, Suite 800A, New York, NY 10017; tel (212) 599-6190; fax (212) 972-3970.

EUROPEAN COMMUNITIES

External Delegation: 3 Dag Hammarskjöld Plaza, 12th Floor, 305 East 47th St, New York,

NY 10017; tel (212) 371-3804; telex 012396; fax (212) 758-2718.
Head of Delegation: Eamonn Gallagher.
Counsellor and Deputy Head of Delegation: Arlette Laurent.
Counsellor (Economic): Brian McDonald.
Attaché (Administrative): Susan Besford.

FOOD AND AGRICULTURE ORGANIZATION—FAO

Liaison Office: One United Nations Plaza, Suite DC1-1125, New York, NY 10017; tel (212) 963-6036; fax (212) 888-6188.
Head of Liaison Office: Jean Syrogianis-Camara.
Senior Liaison Officer: Frederick H. Weibgen.
Liaison Officer: Koichi Machidera.
Liaison and Administrative Officer: Toshihiko Murata.

INTERNATIONAL ATOMIC ENERGY AGENCY—IAEA

Liaison Office: United Nations, Room DC1-1155, New York, NY 10017; tel (212) 963-6010; fax (212) 751-4117.
Director and Representative of the Director-General to the United Nations: Berhanykun Andemicael.
Liaison and Public Information Officer: Marlene O'Dell.

INTERNATIONAL COMMITTEE OF THE RED CROSS

Permanent Office: 780 Third Ave, Suite 2802, New York, NY 10017; tel (212) 371-0771; fax (212) 355-3909.
Head of Delegation: Jean-Paul Fallet.
Deputy Head of Delegation: Fred Isler.
Delegate: François Zen Ruffinen.
Assistant: Thérèse Munoz.

INTERNATIONAL FUND FOR AGRICULTURAL DEVELOPMENT—IFAD

Liaison Office: United Nations, Room S-2955B, (212) 963-4444.
Acting Liaison Officer: Kate Starr Newell.
Liaison Assistant: Danielle Maillard-Lejano.

INTERNATIONAL LABOUR ORGANIZATION—ILO

Liaison Office: 820 Second Ave, 18th Floor, New York, NY 10017-4504; tel (212) 697-0150; fax (212) 883-0844.
Deputy Director: Georges Minet.
Public Information Officer: Tuyet Nguyen.

INTERNATIONAL MONETARY FUND—IMF

Liaison Office: One United Nations Plaza, Suite DC1-1140, New York, NY 10017; tel (212) 963-6009; fax (212) 391-9040.
Director: Rattan J. Bhatia.
Deputy Director: Harriet Shugarman.

LEAGUE OF ARAB STATES

Permanent Office: 747 Third Ave, 35th Floor, New York, NY 10017; tel (212) 838-8700; fax (212) 355-3909.
First Secretary: Dr Marwan Selim al-Gharably.
Adviser: Hassan Osman Abdeldaim.
Adviser: Mohamed Morsi.
Attaché: Khalil Hamza.

ORGANIZATION OF AFRICAN UNITY

Permanent Office: 346 East 50th St, New York, NY 10022; tel (212) 319-5490; fax (212) 319-3571.
Observer: Ibrahima Sy.
Deputy Observer (Economic): Dr Victor E. Djomatchoua Toko.
Deputy Observer (Political): Gebre E. Dawit.
Special Political Affairs Officer: Dr Solomon Gomez.
Adviser (Conference/Meetings): Abdoulaye Maiga.
Adviser (Press/Information): Salimatu Khan.
Adviser (Administrative/Financial): Paulette Saint-Lot.
Adviser (Political): Nganatha J. Karugu.
Adviser (Documentation): Mulualem Teferi.
Attaché: Aster Boghossian.
Attaché: Anne-Marie Bungaroo.
Attaché: Louise C. Bailey.
Attaché: Cecile Diomande.
Attaché: Anna Auleley.

ORGANIZATION OF THE ISLAMIC CONFERENCE

Permanent Office: 130 East 40th St, 5th Floor, New York, NY 10016; tel (212) 883-0140; fax (212) 883-0143.
Deputy Observer: Dr Nanguyalai S. Tarzi.
Attaché (Administrative): Yaye N. Samb.

UNITED NATIONS EDUCATIONAL, SCIENTIFIC AND CULTURAL ORGANIZATION—UNESCO

Liaison Office: 2 United Nations Plaza, Suite 900, New York, NY 10017; tel (212) 963-5995; fax (212) 355-5627.
Director: Andri Isaksson.
Deputy Director: Paulos Asrat.
Senior Liaison Officer: Neh Dukuly-Tolbert.
Senior Liaison Officer and Adviser to UNICEF: David Burleson.
Information Officer: Andrew Radolf.
Liaison Officer: Zofia Skowron-Olszowska.
Documentation and Liaison Officer: Somar Wijayadasa.
Associate Expert: Hiroshi Kamiyo.

UNITED NATIONS INDUSTRIAL DEVELOPMENT ORGANIZATION—UNIDO

Liaison Office: One United Nations Plaza, Suite DC1-1110, New York, NY 10017; tel (212) 963-6890; fax (212) 963-7904.
Director: H. Stephen Halloway.
Deputy Director: Hassan H. Bahlouli.
Information Officer: Aurora Rodriguez.
Administrative Assistant: Anne Sifuentes.

WORLD BANK

Office: 747 Thrd Ave, 26th Floor, New York, NY 10017; tel (212) 963-6008; fax (212) 308-5320.
Special Representative: David Loos.
Administrative Officer: Julianne Turner.
Administrative Officer: Priscilla Madrid.

WORLD HEALTH ORGANIZATION—WHO

Liaison Office: Two United Nations Plaza, Suite DC2-0970, New York, NY 10017; tel (212) 963-6005; telex 234292; fax (212) 223-2920.
Director: Ingar Brüggemann.
Principal External Relations Officer: Chin-Min Lee.
Public Information and Liaison Officer: Jery Kilker.
Administrative and Liaison Officer: Cecilia Rose.

Office of Senior Health Adviser: 3 United Nations Plaza, Suite H-8F, New York, NY 10017; tel (212) 326-7385.
Senior Health Adviser (WHO): Dr M. Sathianathan.

WORLD INTELLECTUAL PROPERTY ORGANIZATION—WIPO

Liaison Office: 2 United Nations Plaza, Suite DC2-560, New York, NY 10017; tel (212) 963-6813; fax (212) 963-4801.
Liaison Officer: Jean Anticevic.

Other Organizations

PALESTINE LIBERATION ORGANIZATION

Permanent Office: 115 East 65th St, New York, NY 10021; tel (212) 288-8500; fax (212) 517-2377.
Alternate Observer: Dr M. Nasser al-Kidwa.
Deputy Observer: Dr Riyad H. Mansour.
Counsellor: Maha Giacaman Khoury.
Senior Adviser: Chafic I. Hout.

THE UNITED NATIONS—GENEVA OFFICE

AFGHANISTAN

Permanent Mission: 4 chemin des Hauts Cornillons, 1292 Chambésy; tel (22) 7580220; telex 421802.
Permanent Representative: Mohammad Nabi Amani.
Minister-Counsellor: Mohammad Daoud Shahbaz.
Counsellor: Dr Mohammad Taufiq Mokhtarzada.
First Secretary: Zalmai Damoon.

ALBANIA

Permanent Mission: 32 rue du Môle, Appt. 31, 1201 Geneva; tel (22) 7311143; telex 045412278; fax (22) 7388156.
Counsellor and Chargé d'affaires a.i.: Kadri Çenko.
Third Secretary: Fatos Reka.

ALGERIA

Permanent Mission: 308 route de Lausanne, 1293 Bellevue; tel (22) 7741985; telex 419116.
Permanent Representative: Abdelhamid Semichi.
Minister Plenipotentiary and Deputy Permanent Representative: Hania Semichi.
Minister Plenipotentiary (Administrative/Financial): Abderrahmane Aboura.
Counsellor: Taous Feroukhi.
Counsellor: Hariba Yahia-Cherif.
Counsellor: Fatima Mechiche.
Counsellor: Mohamed Boutouili.
First Secretary: Mourad Adjabi.
Second Secretary: Mohamed Tefiani.

ANTIGUA AND BARBUDA

Permanent Mission: Antigua House, 15 Thayer Street, London W1M 5DL, England; tel (71) 486-7073; telex 8814503; fax (71) 486-9970.
Permanent Representative: James A. E. Thomas.
First Secretary: Starret Greene.
Second Secretary: John Harris.
Attaché: Pauline Sandra Irene Williams.

ARGENTINA

Permanent Mission: 10 route de l'Aéroport, Case Postale 292, 1215 Geneva 15; tel (22) 7981952; telex 22745; fax (22) 7985995.
Permanent Representative: Juan Archibaldo Lanus.
Permanent Representative (Disarmament): Roberto Garcia Moritan.
Minister-Counsellor and Deputy Permanent Representative: Fernando Novillo Saravia.
Minister (Financial): Patricio O'Gorman.
Minister-Counsellor (Economic/Commercial): Néstor Stancanelli.
Minister Plenipotentiary: Hernán Patino Mayer.
Counsellor: Ernesto Paz.
Counsellor: César Fernando Mayoral.
Counsellor (Economic/Commercial): Jorge Vigano.
Counsellor (Economic/Commercial): Jorge Ruiz.
First Secretary: Antonio Trombetta.
First Secretary: Cecilia Barrios Baron.
Second Secretary (Disarmament): Rafael Grossi.

Disarmament Delegation: Case Postale 305, 1215 Geneva 15; tel (22) 7985952.

Economic Bureau: Case Postale 413, 1215 Geneva 15; tel (22) 7988284.

Financial Bureau: 91-93 rue de la Servette, 2e étage, 1201 Geneva; tel (22) 7332197.

AUSTRALIA

Permanent Mission: 56-58 rue de Moillebeau, 1209 Geneva; Case Postale 172, 1211 Geneva 19; tel (22) 7346200; telex 414157; fax (22) 7336586.
Permanent Representative: Ronald Alfred Walker.
Permanent Representative (Commercial): David Charles Hawes.
Permanent Representative (Disarmament): Paul O'Sullivan.
Minister (Commercial): Peter Anthony Hussin.
Special Minister-Counsellor (Labour): William Dejong.
Counsellor (Disarmament): Ron Stanley Morris.
Counsellor and Deputy Permanent Representative: Bill Barker.
Counsellor (Migration): Roseanne Toohey.
Counsellor (Commercial): Miles Jordana.
Counsellor (Commercial): Michael Mugliston.
Counsellor (Commercial): Dr Meredith Anne Borthwick.
First Secretary (Administrative): Barrie James Blackburn.
First Secretary: Dr Palitha Kohona.
First Secretary (Commercial): David Smith.
First Secretary: John Hannoush.
First Secretary (Disarmament): Martine D. Letts.

AUSTRIA

Permanent Mission: 9-11 rue de Varembé, Case Postale 68, 1211 Geneva 20; tel (22) 7337750; telex 414158; fax (22) 7344591.
Permanent Representative: Dr Franz Ceska.
Minister and Deputy Permanent Representative: Dr Christian Strohal.
Minister and Deputy Permanent Representative (Economic/GATT): Dr Richard Hochörtler.
Minister and Deputy Permanent Representative (Economic/AELE): Norbert Faustenhammer.
Minister (Economic): Dr Johannes Potocnik.
Minister-Counsellor: Thomas Michael Baier.
Counsellor (Economic): Michael Reiterer.
First Secretary: Dr Willy Kempel.
First Secretary: Dr Bettina Kirnbauer.
Second Secretary: Gabriele Wallner.
Counsellor (Administrative): Helmut Schörg.
Counsellor (Humanitarian): Dr Franz Josef Homann-Herimberg.
Counsellor (Disarmament): Wolfgang Wosolsobe.

BAHRAIN

Permanent Mission: 31 chemin William Barbey, Case Postale 39, 1292 Chambésy; tel (22) 7582102; telex 419110; fax (22) 7581310.
First Secretary: Adel Sater.
First Secretary: Habeeb Maki Hashim.
Second Secretary: Hakim Bu-Hiji.

BANGLADESH

Permanent Mission: 65 rue de Lausanne, 1202 Geneva; tel (22) 7325940; telex 412644; fax (22) 7384616.
Permanent Representative: R. Osmany (designate).
Minister (Economic): Dr M. Ishaq Talukdar.
Counsellor: Iftikharul Karim.
First Secretary: Nasim Firdaus.

BELARUS

Permanent Mission: 15 ave de la Paix, Case Postale, 1211 Geneva 20; tel (22) 7331870; fax (22) 7344044.
Permanent Representative: Anatoli A. Mardovich.
Second Secretary: Valentine V. Galka.

BELGIUM

Permanent Mission: 58 rue de Moillebeau, 6e étage, Case Postale 473, 1211 Geneva 19; tel (22) 7338150; fax (22) 7345079.
Permanent Representative: Philippe J. Berg.
Permanent Representative (Disarmament): Marcel Houllez.
Counsellor and Deputy Permanent Representative: Marc van Craen.
Counsellor (Disarmament): Marielle ver Elst.
Counsellor: Alex van Meeuwen.
First Secretary: Marc Gedopt.
Second Secretary: Frank Carruet.
Second Secretary (Disarmament): Pierre Dubuisson.
Attaché (Administrative): Marie-Thérèse Houlmont.
Attaché: Justine Gentile.
Attaché: Léona Leppens-Smits.
Attaché (French Community): Jacqueline Lemoine.

BENIN

Permanent Mission: 5 ave de l'Observatoire, 1180 Brussels, Belgium; tel (2) 374-91-92; telex 24568; fax (2) 375-83-26.
Permanent Representative: Edmond Cakpo-Tozo.
Minister-Counsellor: Albert Agossou.
Minister-Counsellor: Omer de Souza.
First Counsellor: Awahou Labouda .
First Counsellor: Christophe Gbegbo.
Second Secretary: Emile Djidohokpin.
Attaché: Marcellin Yevide.
Attaché: Joseph Domingo.
Attaché: Ramanatou Saka.

BHUTAN

Permanent Mission: 17-19 chemin du Champ d'Anier, 1209 Geneva; tel (22) 7987971; telex 415447; fax (22) 7882593.
Permanent Representative: Paljor Jigmi Dorji (designate).
Second Secretary: Yeshey Dorji.

BOLIVIA

Permanent Mission: 7 rue du Valais, 1202 Geneva; tel (22) 7312725; telex 412645; fax (22) 7380022.
Permanent Representative: Jorge Soruco.
Deputy Permanent Representative: Gonzalo de Acha.
Counsellor: Gualberto Rodriguez San Martin.
First Secretary: Wilma Banzer.

BRAZIL

Permanent Mission: 33 rue Antoine-Carteret, 1202 Geneva; tel (22) 7333150; telex 414160; fax (22) 7332834.

Permanent Representative: Celso Luiz Nunes Amorim.
Minister: José Alfredo Graça Lima.
Minister: Armando Sérgio Frazão.
Counsellor: Pedro Motta Pinto Coelho.
Counsellor: Maria Lúcia Santos Pompeu Brasil.
Counsellor: José Eduardo Martins Felício.
Counsellor: Piragibe dos Santos Tarragô.
First Secretary: Frederico S. Duque Estrada Meyer.
First Secretary: Alcides Gastão Rostand Prates.
First Secretary: Marcos Vinicius Pinta Gama.
First Secretary: Eduardo de Mattos Hosannah.
First Secretary: Moira Pinto Coelho.
Second Secretary: Ricardo Guerra de Araujo.
Second Secretary: Maria Izabel Vieira.
Second Secretary: Luiz Antonio Balduino Carneiro.

BRUNEI

Permanent Mission: 46 ave Blanc, 1st Floor, 1202 Geneva; tel (22) 7381144; telex 712347; fax (22) 7381013.
Permanent Representative: Dato Paduka Haji Jaya bin Abdul Latif (resident in USA).
Counsellor: Haji Ahmad Azahari.
Third Secretary (Administrative): Mohammed Ma'eraj Haji Mohammed Sanip.
Attaché: Haji Mahmud Sitinormah.

BULGARIA

Permanent Mission: 16 chemin des Crêts-de-Pregny, 1218 Grand-Saconnex; tel (22) 7980300; fax (22) 7980302.
Permanent Representative: Todor Dichev.
Minister Plenipotentiary and Deputy Permanent Representative: Planen Grozdanov.
Minister Plenipotentiary: Mihail Kolarov.
Counsellor: Dobri Dobrev.
First Secretary: Vladimir Atanassov.
Second Secretary: Guéorgui Dimitrov.
Second Secretary (Commercial): Nikolay Beyazov.
Attaché: Gradimir Kobarelov.
Attaché (Administrative): Marin Marinov.

BURUNDI

Permanent Mission: 3 rue Butini, 1202 Geneva; tel (22) 7383657.
Permanent Representative: Balthazar Habonimana.
First Counsellor and Deputy Permanent Representative: Grégoire Muyovu.
Second Counsellor: Aloys Negamiye.

CAMBODIA

Permanent Mission: Case Postale 608, 1290 Versoix; tel (22) 7790017.
Permanent Representative: Ngo Hac Team.
Special Counsellor: Khek Sysoda.
Minister-Counsellor: Poc Mona.
Third Secretary: Khoeung Bun Ngi.

CAMEROON

Permanent Mission: 6-8 rue du Nant, 1207 Geneva; tel (22) 7362022; fax (22) 7524434.
Permanent Representative: François-Xavier Ngoubeyou.
Second Counsellor: Pierre Ndzengue.
Second Counsellor: William E. Eyambe.
First Secretary: Léonard Eloundou.
Second Secretary: Aaron Moukouri.

CANADA

Permanent Mission: 1 chemin du Pré-de-la-Bichette, 1202 Geneva; tel (22) 7334344; telex 412917; fax (22) 7347919.
Permanent Representative: Gerald E. Shannon.
Permanent Representative (GATT): John M. Weekes.
Minister (Economic) and Deputy Permanent Representative (GATT): Robert G. Wright.
Minister and Deputy Permanent Representative: Paul G. Dubois.
Minister (Disarmament) and Deputy Permanent Representative: Angus W. J. Robertson.
Counsellor (Agricultural): Stewart W. Borland.
Counsellor: John F. Donaghy.
Counsellor: Gerald K. Campbell.
Counsellor: Marc E. Bailey.
Counsellor: Gilles Leblanc.
Counsellor and Consul: François Nadeau.
Counsellor: Geoffrey A. Weir.
Counsellor and Consul: John Ausman.
Counsellor: Robert H. Lawrence.
Counsellor: John S. Gero.
Counsellor (Scientific Research): Mervin C. Hamblin.
Counsellor: David Plunkett.
Counsellor: John C. Sloan.
Counsellor: Jennifer O. Rosebrugh.
First Secretary (Administrative) and Consul: John A. Carisse.

CAPE VERDE

Permanent Mission: 113 Meckenheimer Allee, 5300 Bonn 1, Germany; tel (228) 651604.
Permanent Representative: Antonio Rodrigues Pires (resident in Italy).

CENTRAL AFRICAN REPUBLIC

Permanent Mission: Rheinaustr. 120, Postfach 301080, 5300 Bonn 3, Germany; tel (228) 469724; telex 8861166.
Permanent Representative: Nestor Kombot-Naguemon.
First Counsellor: Jean-Claude Dongopandji.
Administrative and Financial Attaché: Raymond Dekoulou-Dianga.

CHILE

Permanent Mission: 56 rue de Moillebeau, 4e étage, 1209 Geneva; Case Postale 332, 1211 Geneva 19; tel (22) 7345130; telex 22142; fax (22) 7344194.
Permanent Representative: Radomiro Tomic Romero.
Deputy Permanent Representative: Mario Artaza Rouxel.
Minister-Counsellor: Carmen Lynam de Mannakee.
Minister-Counsellor (Economic): Fernando Morales Barria.
Minister-Counsellor (Economic): Carlota Castro.
Counsellor: Raimundo Gonzales.
Counsellor: Francisco Cruz.
Counsellor: Pedro Oyarce.
Counsellor: Jaime Acuña.
First Secretary: Pablo Romero.
First Secretary: Ricardo Babul.
First Secretary (Economic): Gloria Inés Peña de Gonzalez.
Attaché (Culture/Press): Milan Ivelic Kusanovic.
Attaché (Labour): Antonio Mimiza.

Administrative Affairs Bureau: 5e étage, Case Postale 110, 1211 Geneva 19; tel (22) 7346606.

CHINA, PEOPLE'S REPUBLIC

Permanent Mission: 11 chemin de Surville, 1213 Petit-Lancy; tel (22) 7922548; fax (22) 7937014.
Permanent Representative: Fan Guoxiang.
Deputy Permanent Representative (Disarmament): Hou Zhitong.
Minister-Counsellor and Deputy Permanent Representative: Jiang Changqin.
Minister-Counsellor and Deputy Permanent Representative: Wang Tiance.
Counsellor: Fang Ping.
Counsellor: Shan Bingjun.
Counsellor: Yao Ying.
Counsellor: Gu Guoliang.
Counsellor: Zhang Yishan.
First Secretary: Li Enheng.
First Secretary: Yang Weihong.
First Secretary: Yu Pencheng.
First Secretary: Ji Jingyi.
First Secretary: Zhang Yan.
First Secretary: Wu Jinyao.
First Secretary: Liu Shouzhong.
First Secretary: Yu Qingshan.
First Secretary: Zhou Guanshan.
First Secretary: Wang Shichun.

COLOMBIA

Permanent Mission: 17-19 chemin du Champ-d'Anier, 1209 Geneva; tel (22) 7984554; telex 415512; fax (22) 7910787.
Permanent Representative: Eduardo Mestre Sarmiento.
Deputy Permanent Representative: Felipe Jaramillo.
Counsellor: Ligia Galvis.
Counsellor (Commercial): Andrés Espinosa.
First Secretary: Ricardo Melendez.
First Secretary: José Renato Salazar.
Third Secretary: Juan Manuel Cano.

COSTA RICA

Permanent Mission: 89 rue de la Servette, 1202 Geneva; tel (22) 7344106.
Permanent Representative: Rodrigo Barzuna Sauma.
Deputy Permanent Representative: Jorge Rhenan Segura.
Minister-Counsellor: Ronald Saborio Soto.
Minister-Counsellor: Hélène Krygier de Przedborski.
First Secretary: Javier Rodriguez Alpizar.
First Secretary: Gloriana Rodriguez Hernandez.

COTE D'IVOIRE

Permanent Mission: 47 ave Blanc, Case Postale 76, 1211 Geneva 21; tel (22) 7318960; telex 23802; fax (22) 7319338.
First Counsellor and Chargé d'affaires a.i.: Emile M'lingui Keffa.
Counsellor (Economic): Marie Gosset.
Counsellor (Commercial): Kouadio Adjoumani.
Counsellor: N'cho N'takpe.
Third Secretary: Jacques Toure.

CUBA

Permanent Mission: 100 chemin de Valérie, 1292 Chambésy; tel (22) 7582326; telex 419106; fax (22) 7582377.
Permanent Representative: José A. Perez Novoa.
Counsellor: José A. García Lara.
First Secretary (Disarmament): Magda Bauta Soles.
First Secretary (Social/Humanitarian): Marianela Ferriol Echevarría.
First Secretary (Economic/Commercial): Arnaldo Hernández Pérez.
Attaché: Juan González Risco.
Attaché: Félix Hernández Izquierdo.

CYPRUS

Permanent Mission: 34 chemin François-Lehmann, 7e étage, 1218 Grand-Saconnex; tel (22) 7982150; telex 415511; fax (22) 7910084.
Permanent Representative: Vanias Markides.
First Secretary: George Zodiates.
Second Secretary (Press): Patricia Hadjisotiriou Ceri.

Second Secretary (Press): Patricia Hadjisotiriou Ceri.
Attaché (Administrative): Charalambos Theodorou.
Attaché: Popi Christodoulou Emara.

CZECHOSLOVAKIA

Permanent Mission: 9 chemin de l'Ancienne-Route, Case Postale 156, 1218 Grand-Saconnex, Geneva; tel (22) 7989181; telex 415517; fax (22) 7880919.
Permanent Representative: Juraj Králik.
Minister-Counsellor and Deputy Permanent Representative: Zdeněk Venera.
Minister-Counsellor and Deputy Permanent Representative: Zdeněk Pagáč.
Counsellor (Commercial): Richard Wágner.
Counsellor (Commercial): Oto Hlaváček.
First Secretary (Press): Miroslav Musil.
Second Secretary: Miroslav Zich.
Third Secretary: Vladimír Ďuriš.
Third Secretary (Commercial): Milan Hovorka.
Third Secretary: Martin Benko.
Attaché: Ivan Pintér.
Attaché: Vladimír Gašpar.
Attaché: Ivan Pastorek.
Attaché: Otokar Mašín.

Commercial Section: tel (22) 7989065.

DENMARK

Permanent Mission: 58 rue de Moillebeau, 2e étage, Case Postale 435, 1211 Geneva 19; tel (22) 7337150; telex 414166; fax (22) 7332917.
Permanent Representative: Jakob Esper Larsen.
Minister (Disarmament): Knud-Arne Hjerk Eliasen.
Counsellor and Deputy Permanent Representative (GATT): Finn Theilgaard.
Counsellor and Deputy Permanent Representative: Jørgen Maersk Pedersen.
First Secretary: Ole Frijs-Madsen.
Counsellor (Agriculture): Poul Andersen.
Counsellor (Labour): Peter Jørgensen.
First Secretary (Industrial): Lars Koefoed-Johnsen.

DOMINICA

Permanent Mission: 12 rue des Bollandistes, 1040 Brussels, Belgium; tel (2) 733-43-28; telex 29380; fax (2) 735-72-37.
Permanent Representative: Charles Angelo Savarin.
Deputy Permanent Representative: Hugo Lodrini (resident in Geneva).
Second Secretary: Alcid Joseph.

DOMINICAN REPUBLIC

Permanent Mission: 65 rue de Lausanne, 2e étage, 1202 Geneva; tel (22) 7313079.
Minister-Counsellor (Economic) and Chargé d'affaires a.i.: F. Daniel Suazo.
Minister-Counsellor: Mercedes Alfonseca Bursztejn-Lavigne.
First Secretary: Angelina Bonetti Herrera.
First Secretary: Nora Reyes de Ferrer.
Attaché: Jesús Anselmo Paulino Aguilar.
Attaché: Julio Ramón Cordero Espaillat.

ECUADOR

Permanent Mission: 139 rue de Lausanne, 6e étage, 12020 Geneva; tel (22) 7314879; telex 412863; fax (22) 7382676.
Permanent Representative: Eduardo Santos.
Minister and Deputy Permanent Representative: Dr Rubén Rivadeneira.
Counsellor (Commercial): Pilar Andrade.
First Secretary: Santiago Apunte Franco.
Second Secretary: Iñigo Salvador-Crespo.
Attaché: Martha Roman.

Commercial Office: tel (22) 7317222.

EGYPT

Permanent Mission: 49 ave Blanc, 2e étage, 1202 Geneva; tel (22) 7312638; telex 22738; fax (22) 7384415.
Permanent Representative: Dr Nabil A. Elaraby.
Minister Plenipotentiary: Moustapha Omar.
Minister Plenipotentiary (Commercial): Mahmoud el-Falaky.
Counsellor: Naéla Gabr.
Counsellor: Mohammed Rifaah el-Tahtawy.
Counsellor: Dr Mahmoud Karem.
Counsellor: Mahmoud Soliman.
Counsellor (Commercial): Dr Mohsen Helal.
Counsellor (Commercial): Alaa-Eldin Shalaby.
Counsellor (Labour): Dr Naguib Hassan Gheita.
First Secretary: Aleya Aboul-Ezz Halbouny.
Second Secretary: Mohamed Gomaa.
Second Secretary (Commercial): Lofti Ali Mosalem.
Second Secretary: Walid Abdel-Nasser.
Attaché (Administrative): Sayed Shamardy el Sayed.
Attaché (Administrative): Yahia I. el Sawy.

Social and Labour Affairs Bureau: 47 ter route de Florissant, 1207 Geneva; tel (22) 476203.

Commercial Affairs Bureau: 9 rue de Berne, 1201 Geneva; tel (22) 7322248.

EL SALVADOR

Permanent Mission: 65 rue de Lausanne, 2e étage, 1202 Geneva; tel (22) 7327036; telex 412862; fax (22) 7384744.
Permanent Representative: Carlos Ernesto Mendoza.
Minister-Counsellor: Leonora de Sola Saurel.
Minister-Counsellor: Bétida Flor Menjivar.
Minister-Counsellor: Carmen Tobar Sandoval.

ETHIOPIA

Permanent Mission: 56 rue de Moillebeau, Case Postale 338, 1211 Geneva 19; tel (22) 7330750; telex 414170; fax (22) 7401129.
Permanent Representative: Kongit Sinegiorgis.
Counsellor: Gezahegne Tsegaye.
First Secretary: Fikre Mariam Tsehai.
Second Secretary: Negash Kebret.
Second Secretary: Nardos Worku.
Second Secretary: Yeshoalul Gebre Meskel.

FINLAND

Permanent Mission: 1 rue Pré-de-la-Bichette, Case Postale 198, 1211 Geneva 20; tel (22) 7400303; telex 412970; fax (22) 7400287.
Permanent Representative: Antti Hynninen.
Minister-Counsellor (GATT) and Deputy Permanent Representative: Pekka Huhtaniemi.
Minister-Counsellor: Antti Elias Sierla.
Counsellor (Disarmament): Aapo Polho.
Counsellor (GATT): Kim Luotonen.
Counsellor (AELE): Jan Store.
First Secretary (Social Affairs): Anneli Vuorinen.
First Secretary (GATT): Ossi Tuusvuori.
First Secretary: Satu Mattila.
First Secretary (AELE): Hanna Lehtinen.
Second Secretary: Matti Heimonen.
Second Secretary: Silja Ruokola.

FRANCE

Permanent Mission: Villa 'Les Ormeaux', 36 route de Pregny, 1292 Chambésy; tel (22) 7582123; fax (22) 7582449.
Permanent Representative: Bernard Miyet.
Permanent Representative (Disarmament): Gérard Errera.
First Counsellor (Disarmament): Bertrand Besancenot.
First Counsellor: Patrick Bonneville.
Scientific Counsellor (Disarmament): Pierre Canonne.
Second Counsellor: Stéphane Gompertz.
Second Counsellor: Maryse Daviet.
Second Counsellor: Jean-Pierre Allex.
Second Counsellor (Disarmament): Marc Finaud.
First Secretary: Henri Raynaud.
First Secretary: Maryse Delande.
First Secretary: Jean de Souza.
First Secretary: Philippe Delacroix.
First Secretary (Disarmament): Michel Pouchepadass.

Permanent Delegation to GATT: 72 rue de Lausanne, 1211 Geneva 21; tel (22) 311805.

GABON

Permanent Mission: 13 ave de Budé, Case Postale 47, 1211 Geneva 19; tel (22) 7401003; telex 412352.
Permanent Representative: Roger Tchibota-Souamy.
First Counsellor: Manva Nkele.
Counsellor: Jean Ndong-Mboulou.
Counsellor (BIT): Moulomba Nziengui.
Counsellor (Chancery): Raymond Nze-Ndong.

GERMANY

Permanent Mission: 28c chemin du Petit-Saconnex, 1211 Geneva 19; Case Postale 171, 1211 Geneva 19; tel (22) 7301111; telex 412228; fax (22) 7343043.
Permanent Representative: Dr Fredo Dannenbring.
Permanent Representative (Disarmament): Dr Adolf Ritter von Wagner.
Minister and Deputy Permanent Representative: Ulrich Rosengarten.
Minister-Counsellor (Commercial/GATT): Dr Peter Witt.
First Counsellor (Political): Dr Gerhard Fulda.
First Counsellor (Economic): Dr Martin Hecker.
First Counsellor (Disarmament): Klaus Arnhold.
Counsellor (Labour/Social Affairs): Dr Wolfgang Ohndorf.
Counsellor (Economic): Dr Helmut Kruger.
Counsellor (Economic): Peter Bauer.
Counsellor (Political): Hans-Georg Breitenbach.
Counsellor: Dr Werner Daum.
Counsellor (Disarmament): Dr Christoph Muller.
Counsellor (Commercial/GATT): Dr Hans-Christian Reichel.
Counsellor (Disarmament): Dr Bernhard Odernheimer.
Counsellor (Financial): Wolfgang Milzow.
Counsellor (Commercial/GATT): Dr Herbert Neubauer.
Counsellor: Thomas Gotz.
First Secretary (Transport): Dr Karin Kammann-Klippstein.
First Secretary (Economic): Jutta Wolke.
First Secretary (Economic): Dr Norbert Hoekstra.
First Secretary (Disarmament): Rolf Mafael.
First Secretary (Disarmament): Jochen Bauer.
First Secretary (Economic): Joachim Baumgarten.
First Secretary (Administrative): Hasso Vogelgesang.

Disarmament Conference Delegation: 147 rue de Lausanne, 7e étage, appt. 62, 1202 Geneva; tel (22) 7319770; fax (22) 7322348.

Bureau of Multilateral Trade Negotiations Delegation: 49 ave Blanc, 1202 Geneva; tel (22) 7324443; fax (22) 7315153.

GHANA

Permanent Mission: 56 rue de Moillebeau, 1209 Geneva; tel (22) 7349150; telex 414171; fax (22) 7349161.
Permanent Representative: Kojo Amoo-Gottfried.
Minister-Counsellor and Deputy Permanent Representative: Harry Osei Blavo.
Counsellor (Commercial): William Kofi Larbi.
Counsellor and Head of Chancery: Eric Kojo Acquah.
Counsellor (Consular): Fidelis Woenenyo Yao Ekar.
Counsellor and Desk Officer: Kwame Asamoah Tenkorang.
Second Secretary: Raymond Agyeman Bannerman.
Second Secretary: John Dela Dogbegah.
Second Secretary: Ernestina Borkor Agbenuzah.

GREECE

Permanent Mission: 2 rue S. Thalberg, 1201 Geneva; tel (22) 7323356; telex 27035; fax (22) 7322150.
Permanent Representative: Euripide P. Kerkinos.
Minister Plenipotentiary and Deputy Permanent Representative: Vassilios Vassalos.
First Counsellor: Dimitris Iliopoulos.
First Counsellor: Dimitris Yantais.
First Counsellor (Economic): Ioannis Kinnas.
First Counsellor (Economic): Andreas Cambitsis.
First Counsellor (Economic): Jean Tzitzis.
Counsellor (Press): Angelika Perdikari.
Counsellor (Commercial): Hélène Simirioti.
Counsellor (Commercial): Aristotelis-Vassilis Xenakis.
First Secretary: Michel Efstratios Daratzikis.
First Secretary: Christos Iacovou.
First Secretary (Economic): Hélène Yannopoulou.

GUATEMALA

Permanent Mission: 11 rue Butini, 1202 Geneva; tel (22) 7328028; fax (22) 7387103.
Permanent Representative: Federico Urruela Prado.
Minister-Counsellor: Carolina Maria Rodriguez-Fankhauser.
Second Secretary: Blanca María Castro Gutierrez.
Third Secretary: Monica Juarez Martini.

GUINEA

Permanent Mission: 51 rue de la Faisanderie, 75016 Paris, France; tel (1) 45-53-85-45; telex 611745.
Permanent Representative: Marcel Martin (designate).
Second Counsellor: Fara Millimono.

GUINEA-BISSAU

Permanent Mission: 70 ave F. D. Roosevelt, 1050 Brussels, Belgium; tel (2) 647-08-90.
Permanent Representative: Bubacar Ture.

HAITI

Permanent Mission: 12 blvd James-Fazy, 1201 Geneva; tel (22) 7327628.
Minister-Counsellor and Chargé d'affaires a.i.: Joseph Philippe Antonio.

HONDURAS

Permanent Mission: 6 route de Meyrin, 1202 Geneva; tel (22) 7336916; telex 421376; fax (22) 7341608.
Permanent Representative: Mario Fortin.
Permanent Representative (GATT): Carlos H. Matute Irias.
Minister-Counsellor: María Guadalupe Carias Zapata.
First Secretary: Marlen Turcios Diaz.
Attaché: Rita Fabiola Licona Azcona.
Attaché: Mariela Lizette Fernandez.
Attaché: Amanda Gomez Chavarria.

HUNGARY

Permanent Mission: 81 ave de Champel, 1206 Geneva; tel (22) 460323; telex 472980; fax (22) 465861.
Permanent Representative: Tibor Tóth.
Minister Plenipotentiary (Humanitarian): Endre Lontal.
Counsellor (Economic) and Deputy Permanent Representative: Ferenc Bösenbacher.
Counsellor (Human Rights/CICR): Péter Gondor.
First Secretary (BIT/OMS/UIT/OMM): József Szabó.
Second Secretary (Humanitarian): András Gyuris.
Third Secretary (Disarmament): Lajos Bozi.
Attaché (Disarmament): Zóltan Martinusz.
Attaché (Administrative): András Fábián.

Commercial Section and Delegation to GATT: 80 rue de Lausanne, 1202 Geneva; tel (22) 7315136; telex 23750; fax (22) 7384609.
Minister Plenipotentiary and Permanent Representative (GATT): András Szepesi.
Counsellor: Peter Balas.
First Secretary: Dr Sándor Bojtor.
First Secretary: András Lakatos.
First Secretary: Anikó Ivanka.

ICELAND

Permanent Mission: 9-11 rue de Varembé, Case Postale 86, 1211 Geneva 20; tel (22) 7339687; telex 414173; fax (22) 7332839.
Permanent Representative: Kjartan Jóhannsson.
Counsellor and Deputy Permanent Representative: Kristinn F. Árnason.
First Secretary: Stefán Haukur Jóhannesson.
Secretary: Kristín Eva Sigurđsrdóttir.
Secretary: Birna Guđjónsdóttir Rabbath.

INDIA

Permanent Mission: 9 rue du Valais, 6e étage, 1202 Geneva; tel (22) 7320859; telex 412651; fax (22) 7315471.
Permanent Representative: Prakash Shah.
Permanent Representative (GATT): Balkrishan K. Zutshi.
Counsellor: Lakshmi Puri.
Counsellor: Debashish Chakravarti.
Counsellor: Atul Chaturvedi.
First Secretary: Ashok Sajjanhar.
First Secretary: Anil Wadhwa.
First Secretary: Deepa Gopalan Wadhwa.
Third Secretary: Vinay Mohan Kwatra.
Attaché (Administrative): Om Parkash.

INDONESIA

Permanent Mission: 16 rue de Saint-Jean, Case Postale 2271, 1211 Geneva 2; tel (22) 453350; telex 415906; fax (22) 455733.
Deputy Permanent Representative: Jamtono Rahardjo.
Permanent Representative (GATT): Hassan S. Kartadjoemena.
Counsellor (Political): Noer Hassan Wirajuda.
Counsellor (Political): Remy Romauli Siahaan.
Counsellor (Administrative): Rachman Koeslan.
Counsellor (Economic): Johan S. Syahperi.
First Secretary: Susanto Sutoyo.
First Secretary (Administrative): Martedjo Agustono.
First Secretary: Perwitorini Wijono.
Attaché (Commercial): Burham Y. Riyanto.
Second Secretary: Sudjadnan Parnohadiningrat.
Second Secretary: Musma Musa Abas.
Second Secretary: Kusumo Priyo Handriyo.
Second Secretary: Pitono Purnomo.

IRAN

Permanent Mission: 28 chemin du Petit-Saconnex, 1209 Geneva; tel (22) 7333001; fax (22) 7330203.
Permanent Representative: Sirous Nasseri.
Deputy Permanent Representative: Kia Tabatabaee.
Third Counsellor (Disarmament): Hassan Ghahvechi Mashhadi.
First Secretary: Mohammad Homaei-Nejad.
Second Secretary (Administrative): Seyed Mohammad Bagher Modaressi Ghavami.
Third Secretary: Seyed Mohammad Ali Mottaghi-Nejad.
Third Secretary: Morteza Mokhtari-Amin.
Third Secretary: Darvish Ranjbar.
Third Secretary: Bakhtyar Assadzadeh-Sheikhjani.
Attaché: Moshen Chitsaz.
Attaché: Hossein-Ali Tabrizi.
Attaché: Firouz Nassiri Masouleh.
Counsellor (Labour/Social Affairs): Kamran Fanizadeh.

IRAQ

Permanent Mission: 28a chemin du Petit-Saconnex, 1209 Geneva; tel (22) 7340760; fax (22) 7330326.
Permanent Representative: Barzan Ibrahim al-Tikriti.
Counsellor: Dr Abdul Munim al-Kadhi.
First Secretary (CNUCED/Disarmament): Nasir Mahmoud Madhour.
First Secretary (BIT/OMS/CICR): Sami Obaid.
Second Secretary (Human Rights): Shamil A. Mohammed.
Second Secretary (Disarmament): Adil Khalil.
Third Secretary (Administrative): Mamdouh Subhi Mustafa.
Attaché (Financial): Sami Karim.
Attaché (Administrative): Shakir I. Jbarah.
Attaché (Administrative): Yasin H. A. Mousa.
Attaché (Administrative): Shamis al-Din Mahmoud.
Attaché (Administrative): Khalis Jassim.
Attaché (Administrative): Mohammed al-Jibouri.

IRELAND

Permanent Mission: 45-47 rue de Lausanne, 1201 Geneva; Case Postale 2566, 1211 Geneva 2; tel (22) 7328550; telex 412652; fax (22) 7314365.
First Secretary: Clare O'Flaherty.
First Secretary: Colm O'Floinn.
First Secretary: Fergus Clarke.
First Secretary (Agricultural): Kevin Cassidy.
Third Secretary: Eugene Forde.
Attaché (Administrative): Brian Tisdall.

ISRAEL

Permanent Mission: 9 chemin Bonvent, 1216 Cointrin; tel (22) 7980500; telex 415452; fax (22) 7984950.
Permanent Representative: Itzhak Lior.
Minister-Counsellor and Deputy Permanent Representative: Raphael Walden.
Minister-Counsellor and Permanent Representative (GATT/CNUCED): Ariel Kerem.
Minister-Counsellor (Administrative): Michael Pedaya.
Counsellor (Economic): Amichai Perry.
Second Secretary: Itzhak Hasson.
Third Secretary: Shmuel Pinhas Sivan.
Attaché: Armon Limor.
Attaché: Eliézer Doron.

Attaché: Yuda Gerstein.

ITALY

Permanent Mission: 10 chemin de l'Impératrice, 1292 Pregny; tel (22) 7349350; telex 412650; fax (22) 7330783.
Permanent Representative: Giulio di Lorenzo Badia.
Permanent Representative (Disarmament): Andrea Negrotto Cambiaso.
Minister-Counsellor and Deputy Permanent Representative: Alberto Balboni.
First Counsellor (Disarmament): Carlo Selvaggi.
First Counsellor: Adriano Benedetti.
First Counsellor: Giorgio Sfara.
First Counsellor: Giulio Prigioni.
First Counsellor: Laura Mirachian.
First Secretary: Paolo Serpi.
First Secretary (Disarmament): Andrea Perugini.
First Secretary: Antonio Bernardini.
Attaché (Economic): Sebastiano di Gaetano.
Attaché (Economic): Tullio di Pietro.
Attaché (Disarmament): Basilio Cottone.
Attaché (Disarmament): Giuseppe Bacco.

JAMAICA

Permanent Mission: 42 rue de Lausanne, 1201 Geneva; tel (22) 7315780; telex 412653; fax (22) 7384420.
Permanent Representative: Lloyd M. H. Barnett.
Minister-Counsellor: Ransford Smith.
First Secretary: Pamela R. Coke.
Attaché (Administrative): Rudolph Graham.
Attaché: Paulette M. James.
Attaché: Ann-Marie Steele.

JAPAN

Permanent Mission: 10 ave de Budé, 7e étage, Case Postale 19, 1211 Geneva 19; tel (22) 7348400; telex 22024; fax (22) 7332087.
Permanent Representative: Hidetoshi Ukawa.
Permanent Representative (Disarmament): Mitsuro Donowaki.
Minister and Deputy Permanent Representative: Akio Ijuin.
Minister: Kazuo Asakai.
Minister: Yoshinori Miyamoto.
Minister: Zenji Kaminaga.
Minister (Disarmament): Toshio Watanabe.
Counsellor: Kunihiko Makita.
Counsellor: Nobuo Hatakenaka.
Counsellor: Yoji Ishimaru.
Counsellor: Takashi Misumi.
Counsellor: Kanae Saito.
Counsellor: Masanori Hayashi.
Counsellor: Takeshi Nakane.
Counsellor: Hiroyuki Ishige.
First Secretary: Masuo Nishibayashi.
First Secretary (Disarmament): Ken Matsui.
First Secretary: Akitaka Saiki.
First Secretary: Norifumi Ide.
First Secretary: Kunio Mikuriya.
First Secretary: Hisashi Murata.
First Secretary: Nobuyoshi Takabe.
First Secretary: Yasuyuki Hattori.
First Secretary: Shigeo Takakura.
First Secretary: Kunio Naito.
First Secretary: Hiroshi Yamamoto.
First Secretary: Masahiro Tauchi.
First Secretary: Toshiyuki Yamada.
First Secretary: Hiroya Ogata.
First Secretary: Toru Kuramata.
First Secretary: Tsutomu Osawa.
First Secretary: Yukiya Yoshizumi.
First Secretary (Disarmament): Takuji Hanatani.
First Secretary: Akira Yoshikawa.

Disarmament Conference Delegation: 35 ave de Budé, 1202 Geneva; Case Postale 131, 1211 Geneva 19; tel (22) 7330403; telex 414176; fax (22) 7348716.

JORDAN

Permanent Mission: 45-47 rue de Lausanne, Case Postale 463, 1211 Geneva 1; tel (22) 7317134; telex 412655.
Permanent Representative: al Shérif Fawaz Sharaf.
First Secretary: Fakhri Matalgah.
Third Secretary: Omar Nadif.

KENYA

Permanent Mission: 2 chemin des Mines, 1202 Geneva; tel (22) 7327012; telex 412656; fax (22) 7312905.
Permanent Representative: Prof. Thomas Ariba Ogada.
Counsellor: Frost E. O. Josiah.
Counsellor: Njuguna Ngunjiri.
Second Secretary: Michael D. M. Kinyanjui.
Second Secretary: Christopher Muga Chika.
Second Secretary: Nancy Cheluget.
Second Secretary: Daniel K. Mepukori.
Second Secretary: Amina Mohamed.
Second Secretary: Christopher K. Mburu Karumba.
Third Secretary (Financial): Gordon A. Iro.
Third Secretary (Administrative): Daniel Mutellah Maingi.
Third Secretary: Judith A. Okello.
Third Secretary: Ephraim W. Kang'ara.

KOREA, DEMOCRATIC PEOPLE'S REPUBLIC

Permanent Mission: 1 chemin de Plonjon, 1207 Geneva; tel (22) 7354370.
Permanent Representative: Ri Tcheul.
Minister and Deputy Permanent Representative: Han Chang On.
Counsellor: Pak Chang Rim.
Counsellor: Li Chun Song.
Counsellor: Pak Dok Hun.
First Secretary: Kim Tcheul Sou.
First Secretary: Chong Yong Yung.
First Secretary: Tchoe Il.
Attaché: Chong Il Son.
Attaché: Li In Sil.

KOREA, REPUBLIC

Permanent Mission: 20 route de Pré-Bois, Case Postale 566, 1215 Geneva 15; tel (22) 7910111; fax (22) 7910525.
Permanent Representative: Park Soo Gil.
Minister and Deputy Permanent Representative: Park Young Woo.
Counsellor: Oh Haeng Kyeom.
Counsellor: Lee Tae Hyung.
Counsellor: Moon Bong Joo.
Counsellor: Lee Sung Joo.
First Secretary: Kim Chang Yeob.
First Secretary: Kim Jong Il.
First Secretary: Min Dong Seok.
Second Secretary: Kim Choon Hoon.
Second Secretary: Shin Boo Nam.
Second Secretary: Shin Jhong Weon.
Third Secretary: Cho Hyun Dong.
Attaché (Economic): Lee Jong Wha.
Attaché (Financial): Uhm Rak Yong.
Attaché (Agricultural): Chun Joong In.
Attaché (Commercial): Kang Sang Hoon.
Attaché (Press/Cultural): Sohn Woo Hyun.
Attaché (OMPI): Kim Joon Kyu.
Attaché: Kang Dong Sup.
Attaché: Lee Chan Yeun.

KUWAIT

Permanent Mission: 2 ave de l'Ariana, 1202 Geneva; tel (22) 7348330; fax (22) 7337848.
Permanent Representative: Dr Salem Jaber al-Ahmad al-Sabah.
Counsellor: Salah al-Othman.
Second Secretary: Ali al-Sabah.
Third Secretary: Fayez al-Jassim.
Third Secretary: Asaad Abdullazeez al-Bahar.
Attaché: Mohammad Isma'eel Mohammad.

LEBANON

Permanent Mission: 10 ave de Budé, 6e étage, 1202 Geneva; tel (22) 7338140; telex 414178; fax (22) 7401166.
Permanent Representative: Cheikh Amine el Khazen.
First Secretary: Dr Hicham Hamdane.

LESOTHO

Permanent Mission: 66 ave de Cortenbergh, Boîte Postale 5, 1040 Brussels, Belgium; tel (2) 736-39-76.
Permanent Representative: Mabotse Lerotholi.
Counsellor: Ntebeleng M. Mothepu.
Attaché (Customs): Rethabile F. Makhesi.
Third Secretary: Moses M. Sekoli.
Attaché: Thato B. Lehloenya.
Attaché: Puseletso E. Morai.

LIBERIA

Permanent Mission: 9 rue du Valais, 1202 Geneva; tel (22) 7312583; telex 27190.
Minister-Counsellor and Chargé d'affaires a.i.: Fametta R. Osode.
First Secretary: Henry Williamson.

LIBYA

Permanent Mission: 47 ave Blanc, 1202 Geneva; tel (22) 7318203; telex 412377.
Minister and Chargé d'affaires a.i.: Ibrahim Abdul-Aziz Omar.
Minister Plenipotentiary: Milad Mohamed el Meghrawi.
Counsellor (Disarmament): Sedeg Dahmani Elosta.
Second Secretary: Siham Shaheen.
Counsellor (Health): Dr Mohamed Saleh Muafa.
Counsellor (Financial): Abdurrazag T. Aghil.
First Secretary: Elhadi Hussein Ayad.
Attaché: Mohamed el Gatta.

LUXEMBOURG

Permanent Mission: 28A chemin du Petit-Saconnex, 1209 Geneva; tel (22) 7343380; telex 414179; fax (22) 7330996.
Permanent Representative: Julien Alex.
Counsellor and Deputy Permanent Representative: Paul Duhr.
First Secretary: Fernand Vanetti.
Secretary: Odette Wagener.
Secretary: Célestin Lommel.

MADAGASCAR

Permanent Mission: 32 ave Riant-Parc, 1209 Geneva; tel (22) 7401650; telex 415907.
Permanent Representative: Laurent Radaody-Rakotondravao.
Deputy Permanent Representative: Pierre Verdoux.
Special Counsellor (Legal Affairs): Edilbert Razafindralambo.
Counsellor: Jacques Solo Rason.
Counsellor: Phabien Raphaël Edafe.
Second Secretary: Françoise Narove.
Second Secretary: Jean-de-Dieu Antoni.
Attaché: Saholisoa Ratsimbazafy.
Attaché: Koraiche Allaouidine.
Attaché: Roland Guy Razafimahefa.

MALAYSIA

Permanent Mission: International Cointrin Centre, Bât. H, 1er étage, 20 route de Pré-Bois, Case Postale 711, 1215 Geneva 15; tel (22) 7881505.
Permanent Representative: Mohamad Yusof Hitam.
Deputy Permanent Representative: Seni Pakir Syeed Sultan.
Minister (Economic): Manickam Supperamaniam.
Counsellor (Labour): M. bin Abd Muain Sauffee.
Counsellor (Commercial): Merlyn Kasimir.
First Secretary (Chancery): Mat Zakaria.
First Secretary (Economic): Abdul Karim Zulkafli.
First Secretary (Economic): Jayasena Jayasiri.
Second Secretary: Vasudevan Sudha Devi.
Second Secretary: Mohammed Noor Zulkephli.
Third Secretary: Ngah Yahaya.
Third Secretary (Economic): Shafie Rohana.

MALI

Permanent Mission: 86 Basteistr., 5300 Bonn 2, Germany; tel (228) 357048.
Permanent Representative: Modibo Keita (designate).
First Counsellor: Moussa Coulibaly.
First Secretary: Marcel Ky.

MALTA

Permanent Mission: 2 parc du Château-Banquet, 1202 Geneva; tel (22) 7310580; telex 412868; fax (22) 7381120.
Permanent Representative: Charles Vella.
First Secretary: Martin Valentino.
Third Secretary: Simon Pullicino.

MAURITIUS

Permanent Mission: 68 rue des Bollandistes, 1040 Brussels, Belgium; tel (2) 733-99-88; telex 23114; fax (2) 734-40-21.
Permanent Representative: Vijay Singh Makhan (designate, resident in Mauritius).
First Secretary: Sutiawan Gunessee.
Second Secretary: Usha Chandnee Dwarka.
Attaché: Tiagarajen Kalasopatan.

MEXICO

Permanent Mission: 10a ave de Budé, 1202 Geneva; Case Postale 433, 1211 Geneva 19; tel (22) 7338850; telex 412961; fax (22) 7334810.
Permanent Representative: Miguel Marin-Bosch.
Deputy Permanent Representative: Marcelo Vargas Campos.
Permanent Representative (GATT): Jesús Seade Kuri.
Minister: Perla Carvalho de Plasa.
Minister (GATT): Alejandro de la Peña.
Counsellor (Commercial): Armando F. Ortega Gomez.
Counsellor (Commercial): José Félix Poblano.
Counsellor (Commercial): Luis Carlos Tellez.
Counsellor (Commercial): Sergio Soto Nunez.
First Secretary: Armando Arriazola.
Second Secretary: Gerardo Lozano.
Second Secretary: Adela Fuchs.
Second Secretary: Andrea Garcia Guerra.
Second Secretary: Ismael Naveja.
Permanent Mission to GATT: tel (22) 7343031; fax (22) 7331455.
Commercial Section Bureau: 220 route de Ferney, 1218 Grand-Saconnex.

MONGOLIA

Permanent Mission: 4 chemin des Mollies, 1293 Bellevue; tel (22) 7741974; telex 419128; fax (22) 7743201.
Permanent Representative: Damdiny Baljinnyam.
First Secretary (Political/Administrative): Gonchiguin Gongor.
First Secretary (Disarmament): Zagaryn Erendo.
Attaché (Economic/Commercial): Danzannorovyn Boldbaatar.

MOROCCO

Permanent Mission: 18A chemin François-Lehmann, 1218 Grand-Saconnex; tel (22) 7981535.
Permanent Representative: el Ghali Benhima.
Counsellor: Omar Hilale.
Counsellor: Mohamed Laghmari.
Counsellor: Abdeljebbar Brahime.
Counsellor: Abdelkader Lecheheb.
Counsellor: Omar Zniber.
Counsellor: Abderrahim Bendaoud.
Counsellor: Abderrazak Berrada.
First Secretary: Moha Ouali Tagma.
Second Secretary: Moustapha Jebari.
Third Secretary: Fatima Baroudi.
Attaché: Nour-Eddine Cherradi.
Attaché: Ahmed Ouisse.

MOZAMBIQUE

Permanent Mission: 51 rue Florissant, 1206 Geneva; tel (22) 479046; telex 428639.
Permanent Representative: Isaac Murade Miguigy Murargy (resident in France).
Second Secretary: Florêncio Joel Alberto Sele.

MYANMAR

Permanent Mission: 47 ave Blanc, 1202 Geneva; tel (22) 7317540.
Permanent Representative: Tin Kyaw Hlaing.
Deputy Permanent Representative: Win Mra.
First Secretary: Thein Tun.
Second Secretary: Nyunt Swe.
Second Secretary: Yin Yin Myint.
Third Secretary: Win Naing.
Attaché: Than Lwin.

NEPAL

Permanent Mission: 1 rue Frédéric Amiel, 1203 Geneva; tel (22) 444441; telex 415869; fax (22) 444093.
Counsellor and Chargé d'affaires a.i.: Gobardhan Bikram Shah.
Attaché: Narayan Mainali.
Attaché: Ram Babu Dhakal.

NETHERLANDS

Permanent Mission: 11 rue des Anémones, Case Postale 276, 1219 Châtelaine; tel (22) 7975030; telex 418762; fax (22) 7975129.
Permanent Representative: J. F. Boddens-Hosang.
Permanent Representative (Disarmament) and Deputy Permanent Representative: Hendrik Wagenmakers.
Counsellor: Arend Meerburg.
Counsellor: Pim van de Locht.
Counsellor: Toine van Dongen.
First Secretary: Thomas de Bruijn.
First Secretary: Maximiliaan Gevers.
First Secretary: Kees Klompenhouwer.
First Secretary: Geeskelien Wolters.
First Secretary: Adriaan Kooijmans.
Third Secretary: Christina Louise Miedema.
Third Secretary: Dolph Hogewoning.
Attaché (Administrative): Hans de Kleer.

NEW ZEALAND

Permanent Mission: 28a chemin du Petit-Saconnex, Case Postale 334, 1211 Geneva 19; tel (22) 7349530; telex 412969; fax (22) 7343062.
Permanent Representative: Timothy James Hannah.
Deputy Permanent Representative: Tim Groser.
Counsellor (Economic): Adrian Henry Macey.
Counsellor (Political): Peter Rider.
First Secretary (Economic): Joanne Tyndall.
First Secretary (Administrative): Heather Carew.
Second Secretary (Political): Caroline Bilkey.
Attaché: Christine Day.
Administrative Assistant: Irene Groser.

NICARAGUA

Permanent Mission: 16 rue de Roveray, 1207 Geneva; tel (22) 7366644; telex 413262; fax (22) 7366012.
Permanent Representative: Jorge Alaniz Pinell.
Minister-Counsellor and Deputy Permanent Representative: Juan Gazol Salcedo.
Counsellor: Julió César Saborio Arguello.
Third Secretary: Myrna Moncada.

NIGER

Permanent Mission: 78 ave F. D. Roosevelt, 1050 Brussels, Belgium; tel (2) 648-61-40; telex 22857; fax (2) 648-27-84.
Permanent Representative: Adamou Zada (designate).
Counsellor: Daouda Ibrahim.
Second Secretary (Financial): Mallam Harouna Maman.

NIGERIA

Permanent Mission: 1 rue Richard Wagner, 1211 Geneva 2; tel (22) 7342140; fax (22) 7341053.
Permanent Representative: Emeka Ayo Azikiwe.
Minister (Political): Okon I. Udoh.
Minister (Disarmament): Scott O. E. Omene.
Minister (Economic/GATT): Abdulkadir bin Rimdap.
Counsellor: Kabiru Garba.
Counsellor: Olabode Adeola Adekeye.
Second Secretary: Chukwudi J. Ihim.
Second Secretary: Eric A. Bell-Gam.
Second Secretary: George N. A. Agim.
Second Secretary: Julie Green.
Second Secretary: Joy A. Aqua.

NORWAY

Permanent Mission: 58 rue de Moillebeau, 4e étage, 1209 Geneva; Case Postale 274, 1211 Geneva 19; tel (22) 7349730; telex 22574; fax (22) 7339979.
Permanent Representative: Oscar Vaerno.
Permanent Representative (AELE/GATT): Erik Christian Selmer.
Minister (Disarmament) and Deputy Permanent Representative: Torbjørn Aalbu.
Counsellor (Economic): Kjell Lillerud.
Counsellor: Ragne Birte Lund.
First Secretary: Synnøve Fjellbakk Taftø.
First Secretary: Kåre Reidar Aas.
First Secretary: Bente Bingen.
First Secretary: Merethe Nergaard.
First Secretary: Mette Mogstad.
Attaché (Administrative): Björg Valaker.

OMAN

Permanent Mission: 28b chemin du Petit-Saconnex, entrée C, 1209 Geneva; tel (22) 7337320; telex 27733; fax (22) 7401075.
Permanent Representative: Abdullah M. A. al-Farsy.
First Secretary: Ibrahim Mohammed Sharif al-Farsy.
Second Secretary: Mohammed al-Hassan.
Permanent Representative: Ghassan Shaker.
Counsellor: Yehia Omar.

PAKISTAN

Permanent Mission: 56 rue de Moillebeau, Case Postale 434, 1211 Geneva 19; tel (22) 7347760; telex 412934; fax (22) 7348085.
Permanent Representative: Ahmad Kamal.
Counsellor: Mohammad Younis Khan.
Counsellor (Economic): Munir Ahmad.
Counsellor (Disarmament): Mr Shahbaz.
First Secretary: Fauzia Abbas.
First Secretary (Commercial): Asaf Ghafoor.
Third Secretary: Irfan Baloch.

PANAMA

Permanent Mission: 72 rue de Lausanne, 1202 Geneva; tel (22) 7380388; telex 413390; fax (22) 7380363.
Permanent Representative: Dr Osvaldo Velasquez.
Deputy Permanent Representative: Rossana-Luigia Ameglio.
Second Counsellor: Lourdes C. Vallarino.
Counsellor: Sonia M. Ortega.
Deputy Permanent Representative (GATT): Pascal Mahvi.
Attaché: Berta Fabrega de Ballard.

PARAGUAY

Permanent Mission: 2 chemin des Mines, 1202 Geneva; tel (22) 7386515; telex 414184; fax (22) 7382760.
Permanent Representative: Luis Gonzalez Arias.
Deputy Permanent Representative: Pedro Mir Puig.
Attaché: Lucia Monney.

PERU

Permanent Mission: 63 rue de Lausanne, 6e étage, 1202 Geneva; tel (22) 7311130; telex 412897; fax (22) 7311168.
Permanent Representative: Oswaldo de Rivero.
Deputy Permanent Representative: Jaime Stiglich.
Minister: Alvaro Salcedo.
Minister: Rosa Esther Silva y Silva.
Minister-Counsellor (Disarmament): Félix Calderon.
Counsellor: Ruth Saif de Préperier.
Counsellor: Gonzalo Gutierrez.
Minister-Counsellor (Commercial): Ana María Deustua.
Second Secretary: Hubert Wieland.
Second Secretary: Fernando Quiros.
Second Secretary: Mario Lopez.
Attaché (Administrative): Jaime Torres Heredia.

PHILIPPINES

Permanent Mission: 47 ave Blanc, 1202 Geneva; tel (22) 7318320; telex 22160; fax (22) 7316888.
Permanent Representative: Narcisa de Leon Escaler.
Deputy Permanent Representative: Hector K. Villarroel.
Minister-Counsellor: Delia Menez-Rosal.
Second Secretary: Leslie B. Gatan.
Third Secretary: Lourdes O. Yparraguirre.
Third Secretary: Bernarditas de Castro-Muller.
Third Secretary: Calixto V. Espejo.
Attaché (Administrative): Liberato S. Rojas.
Finance Officer and Attaché: Noemi C. Reyes.
Records Officer and Attaché: Arturo C. Arevalo.
Attaché: Teresita L. Concepción.
Communications Officer, Acting Property Officer and Attaché: Pablo T. Mendoza.
Bureau of Labour Affairs Attaché: tel (22) 7314143.
Attaché (Labour): Leo J. Palma.
Bureau of Commercial Attaché: tel (22) 7325964; telex 289010; fax (22) 7317979.
Commercial Attaché: J. Antonio S. Buencamino.

POLAND

Permanent Representation: 15 chemin de l'Ancienne-Route, Case Postale 126, 1218 Grand-Saconnex; tel (22) 7981161; telex 415516; fax (22) 7981175.
Minister Plenipotentiary and Chargé d'affaires a.i.: Stanislaw Przygodzki.
Counsellor and Minister Plenipotentiary: Janusz Kaczurba.
Counsellor: Sylwin Gizowski.
First Secretary: Dariusz Manczyk.
First Secretary: Witold Jozwiak.
First Secretary: Dariusz Grabowski.
First Secretary: Dr Maciej Lebkowski.
Third Secretary: Tadeusz Oliwinski.
Third Secretary: Zygmunt Mazur.

PORTUGAL

Permanent Mission: 1 rue Richard Wagner, 1202 Geneva; Case Postale, 1211 Geneva 20; tel (22) 7333200; telex 23129; fax (22) 7334110.
Permanent Representative: Luis Octávio Roma de Albuquerque.
Counsellor and Deputy Permanent Representative: Luis Cristina de Barros.
Counsellor (Economic): António Pinto de Lemos.
Counsellor (Legal): Adriano Queirós Ferreira.
Counsellor (Social Affairs/Labour): Luis E. Tomé Almeida.
First Secretary: Luis João de Sousa Lorvao.
Second Secretary: José Júlio Pereira Gomes.
Second Secretary: Liliana Mascarenhas Neto.
Attaché (Commercial): Carlos Carvalho Costa.

QATAR

Permanent Mission: 149b route de Ferney, 1218 Grand-Saconnex; tel (22) 7988500.
Permanent Representative: Mohammed Salem Rashid al-Kuwari.
Special Counsellor: William Kazan.
First Secretary: Salman Ahmed al-Hamadi.
Second Secretary: Sheikh Mohamed Ahmed al-Thani.

ROMANIA

Permanent Mission: 6 chemin de la Perrière, Villa 'La Perrière', 1223 Cologny; tel (22) 7521090; telex 422818; fax (22) 7522976.
Counsellor and Chargé d'affaires a.i.: Alexandru Niculescu.
Counsellor: Ion Pacuraru.
First Secretary: Gheorghe Istode.
First Secretary: Sergiu Margineanu.
First Secretary: Florin Rosu.
First Secretary: Vasile Radu.

RUSSIA

Permanent Mission: 15 ave de la Paix, Case Postale, 1211 Geneva 20; tel (22) 7331870; fax (22) 7344044.
Permanent Representative: Evgeny Makeyev.
Permanent Representative (Disarmament): Sergei Batsanov.
Minister Plenipotentiary and Deputy Permanent Representative: Gleb Smirnov.
Minister Plenipotentiary and Deputy Permanent Representative: Valeri Lochtchinine.
Minister Plenipotentiary and Deputy Permanent Representative: Yuri Ryjov.
Minister Plenipotentiary and First Counsellor: Piatras Edmoundas Dapkounas.
First Counsellor: Igor Chtcherbak.
First Counsellor: Igor Markov.
First Counsellor: Alexandre Orlov.
Counsellor: Boris Smirnov.
Counsellor: Stanislav Tcherniavski.
Counsellor: Guennadi Poznoukhov.
Counsellor: Anatoli Sidorkine.
Counsellor: Vladislav Kouvchinov.
Counsellor: Lev Malychev.
Counsellor: Evgueni Kapichine.
Counsellor: Anton Akopian.
Counsellor: Sergei Kossenko.
First Secretary: Sergei Neznanov.
First Secretary: Vitali Dorokhov.
First Secretary: Mikhail Kaitchouk.
First Secretary: Anatoli Kouzine.
First Secretary: Sergei Sedov.
First Secretary: Victor Yuriev.
First Secretary: Yuri Pohilko.
First Secretary: Vassili Orekhov.
First Secretary: Vladimir Skliarov.
First Secretary: Sergei Vesselovski.
First Secretary: Guennadi Pachanine.
Delegation to Disarmament Conference: 4 chemin du Blé, 1292 Chambésy; tel (22) 7581012.

RWANDA

Permanent Mission: 30 Gesellschaftsstr., 3012 Berne; tel (31) 230611; telex 913129; fax (31) 244860.
Permanent Representative: Ferdinand Kabagema.
First Counsellor: Evariste Nsabimana.
Second Secretary: Fabien Singaye Gakuru.

SAUDI ARABIA

Permanent Mission: 263 route de Lausanne, 1292 Chambésy; tel (22) 7582441; telex 412294; fax (22) 7384128.
Permanent Representative: Sheikh Ahmed Abdul-Jabbar.
Second Secretary: Jassim M. Abu-Oshba.
Third Secretary: Majid A. Aldrees.
Attaché: Sulaiman Budair.
Commercial Attaché: Issam al-Mubarak.
Attaché (GATT): Mussad M. S. al-Eshawi.
Special Counsellor: Dr Mehdat Sheikhelard.
Counsellor (Research): Dr Omar Haliq.
Special Counsellor: Hassan Chabib.
Legal Counsellor: Faysal Assaly.
Counsellor: Dr Mohammed Salah Addin Khater.
Bureau of Commercial Attaché: 139 rue de Lausanne, 1202 Geneva; tel (22) 7327401.
Bureau of GATT Affairs Attaché: 46 ave Blanc, 1202 Geneva; tel (22) 7383030.

SENEGAL

Permanent Mission: 93 rue de la Servette, 1202 Geneva; tel (22) 7345300; telex 414187; fax (22) 7400711.
Permanent Representative: Alioune Sene.
First Counsellor: Moussa Bocar Ly.
First Counsellor: Balla Mandaw Dia.
First Counsellor (Commercial): Mamadou Mansour Diop.
Second Counsellor (Social Affairs): Marie Angélique Diatta.
Second Secretary: Assane Gaye.
Second Secretary: Galo Diop.

SINGAPORE

Permanent Mission: 6 bis rue Antoine Carteret, 1202 Geneva; tel (22) 447330.
Permanent Representative: See Chak Mun.
Counsellor: Margaret Liang.
First Secretary (Economic): Yong Siew Min.
Second Secretary: Tong Tek Liong.

SOMALIA

Permanent Mission: 9 rue du Valais, 1202 Geneva; tel (22) 7315450.
Minister-Counsellor: Mohamed Omar Dubad.
Counsellor: Ahmed Abdi Isse.
Counsellor: Najib Mohamed.

First Secretary: Hassan Abdirahman Jama Barre.
Third Secretary: Amina Aden Serear.

SOUTH AFRICA

Permanent Mission: 65 rue du Rhône, 1204 Geneva; tel (22) 7357803; telex 421685; fax (22) 7352032.
Permanent Representative: Albert Leslie Manley.
Minister and Deputy Permanent Representative: Hendrik Jacobus du Toit.
Minister (Economic): Ernst Hendrik Els.
Counsellor (Economic): Johannes Hendrik Human.
Counsellor (Agricultural Trade): Adriaan Jakobus van der Merwe.
Counsellor (Social Affairs): Dr F. Gustaaf Volvaardt.
Counsellor: André François Jacobs.
First Secretary: Andrew Bradley.
First Secretary (Administrative): Annemarie Kruger.
Third Secretary (Economic): Jens Triebel.
Third Secretary: Hermanus S. van Roy.
Third Secretary: Pieter du Plessis.
Attaché (Labour): Gerhardus Jacobus van Zyl.

SPAIN

Permanent Mission: 53 ave Blanc, 1202 Geneva; tel (22) 7312230; telex 412776; fax (22) 7315370.
Permanent Representative: Emilio Artacho Castellano.
Permanent Representative (Disarmament): Joaquin Perez-Villanueva.
Minister Plenipotentiary and Deputy Permanent Representative: Pablo Barrios Almazor.
Deputy Permanent Representative (Commercial): Juan Antonio Castillo Urrutia.
Counsellor: José Luis los Arcos Galbete.
Counsellor: Fernando Garcia Casas.
Counsellor: Angel Losada.
Counsellor (Disarmament): Félix Gonzales Jimenez.
Counsellor (Commercial): Eduardo Moya Lopez.
Counsellor (Commercial): Gonzalo Avila.
Counsellor (Financial/Fiscal): Manuel Goizueta Sanchez.
Counsellor (Social Affairs): Joaquín Albalate Lafita.
Counsellor (Agricultural/Fisheries/Food): José-Ramón Prieto Herrero.
Counsellor (Agricultural Trade): José María Romero Ordeig.
Deputy Counsellor (Agricultural/Fisheries/Food): Primitivo Gomez Toran.
Counsellor: José María Campa de Blanes.
First Secretary: Maria Saenz de Heredia Alonso.

Delegation to Disarmament Conference: tel (22) 7384324.

Commercial Affairs Bureau: 49 ave Blanc, 1202 Geneva; tel (22) 7328593; fax (22) 7386476.

Agricultural Affairs Bureau: tel (22) 7384206.

Financial and Fiscal Affairs Bureau: tel (22) 7384527.

Social Affairs Bureau: tel (22) 7352318.

SRI LANKA

Permanent Mission: 56 rue de Moillebeau, Case Postale 436, 1211 Geneva 19; tel (22) 7349340; telex 414188; fax (22) 7349084.
Permanent Representative: Dr Warnasena Rasaputram.
Minister (Economic/Commercial): L. P. Douglas Pemasiri.
First Secretary: Siripala Palihakkara.
First Secretary (Economic/Commercial): Ranjan N. Abeysekera.
Second Secretary: Aruni Y. Dewaraja.
Attaché: Haupage Don Ariyaratna.

SUDAN

Permanent Mission: 56 rue de Moillebeau, Case Postale 335, 1211 Geneva 19; tel (22) 7332560; telex 414124; fax (22) 7344887.
Permanent Representative: Omar Alim.
Minister Plenipotentiary and Deputy Permanent Representative: Ahmed Abdelwahab Gubartalla.
Second Secretary: Omer Ibrahim el Turabi.
Third Secretary: Siddieg M. Abdalla.
Third Secretary: Abdel Gani al Naim.
Attaché (Administrative): Mustapha Elkheir Abu Bakr.

SWEDEN

Permanent Mission: 9-11 rue de Varembé, Case Postale 190, 1211 Geneva 20; tel (22) 7343600; telex 22112; fax (22) 7331227.
Permanent Representative: Lars Anell.
Deputy Permanent Representative: Arnold Willén.
Minister: Mikael Lindström.
Counsellor: Mårten Grunditz.
Counsellor: Mikael Dahl.
Counsellor: Arne Rodin.
First Secretary: Claes Ljungdahl.
First Secretary: Lars T. L. Tillfors.
First Secretary: Anders Ahnlid.
Second Secretary: Lena Mirow.
Permanent Representative (AELE): Vidar Hellners.

Disarmament Delegation: 62 rue de Vermont, Case Postale 97, 1211 Geneva 20; tel (22) 7344400; telex 23526; fax (22) 7348164.
Permanent Representative (Disarmament): Carl-Magnus Hyltenius.
Counsellor (Disarmament): Johan Molander.
First Secretary (Disarmament): Christer Elm.
First Secretary (Disarmament): Klas Gierow.
Military Counsellor (Disarmament): Commdr Lennart Grenstad.

SYRIA

Permanent Mission: 72 rue de Lausanne, 3e étage, 1202 Geneva; tel (22) 7326522; telex 412643; fax (22) 7384275.
Permanent Representative: Ahmad Fathi al-Masri.
Minister Plenipotentiary: Nabila Chaalan.
Minister-Counsellor: Clovis Khoury.
Counsellor (Legal): Badr Kasme.
First Secretary: Line al Khayer.
Second Secretary: Mohammad Bassam Imadi.
Second Secretary: Nabih Hussami.
Second Secretary: Chaghaf Kayali.
Third Secretary (Economic): Abdul-Wahab Barakat.
Third Secretary: Ghassan Haidar.
Attaché: Dereid al Assad.
Attaché: Salah Aldeen al Ayoubi.

TANZANIA

Permanent Mission: 47 ave Blanc, 1202 Geneva; tel (22) 7318920; telex 412661; fax (22) 7328255.
Permanent Representative: Amir Habib Jamal.
Minister Plenipotentiary: Dr Augustine Philip Mahiga.
Minister-Counsellor (Economic): Marcel W. Namfua.
First Counsellor (Economic): Khamis Juma Suedi.
Counsellor (Commercial): Marwa J. Kisiri.
Second Counsellor (Financial/Administrative): Christopher M. Mukama.
Second Secretary: Evelyn Rose Ley.

THAILAND

Permanent Mission: 28b chemin du Petit-Saconnex, 1209 Geneva; tel (22) 7342010; telex 414193; fax (22) 7333678.
Permanent Representative: Tej Bunnag.
Minister: Kriengsak Deesrisuk.
Minister-Counsellor (Commercial): Somchin Suntavaruk.
Counsellor: Vipawan Nipatakusol.
First Secretary: Somsakdi Suriyawongse.
First Secretary: Jade-Sada Chavarnbhark.
First Secretary (Commercial): Srirat Rastapana.
First Secretary (Commercial): Chutima Bunyapraphasara.
Second Secretary: Manasvi Srisodapol.
Second Secretary: Chutintorn Gongsakdi.
Second Secretary (Commercial): Boonyarit Kalayanamit.
Attaché: Jittima Tusueyong.
Attaché: Phanthip Thamakul.

Bureau of Commercial Counsellor: 28 chemin Colladon, 1209 Geneva; tel (22) 7980576; fax (22) 7910166.

TOGO

Permanent Mission: 1 rue Miollis, 75732 Paris Cedex 15, France; tel (1) 45-68-34-89; telex 204461; fax (1) 47-83-71-12.
First Counsellor and Chargé d'affaires a.i.: Mensavi Koffi Kpotogbey.
Attaché (Financial): Dometo Kafui Degboe.

TRINIDAD AND TOBAGO

Permanent Mission: 37-39 rue de Vermont, 1202 Geneva; tel (22) 7349130; telex 27802; fax (22) 7349138.
Permanent Representative: Rabindranath Permanand.
Counsellor and Deputy Permanent Representative: Annette Gonzales.
Second Secretary: Laurence Placide.
Second Secretary: Donna Henry.
Attaché: Lynn Paul-Joseph.

TUNISIA

Permanent Mission: 58 rue de Moillebeau, Case Postale, 1211 Geneva 19; tel (22) 7348450; fax (22) 7340663.
Permanent Representative: Dr Souad Lyagoubi-Ouahchi.
Minister Plenipotentiary and Deputy Permanent Representative: Hamid Zaouche.
Counsellor: Abderrazak Azaiez.
Counsellor: Sadok Haouas.
Secretary: Fakhreddine Laroui.
Secretary: Habib Tebourbi.
Secretary: Khaled Khiari.
Secretary: Ali ben Malek.
Secretary: Azouz Rafrafi.

TURKEY

Permanent Mission: 28 chemin du Petit-Saconnex, Case Postale, 1211 Geneva 19; tel (22) 7334894; telex 414194; fax (22) 7340859.
Permanent Representative: Cem Duna.
Minister-Counsellor and Deputy Permanent Representative: Onur Gokce.
Deputy Permanent Representative: Yener Dincmen.
First Counsellor (Economic/Commercial): Cüneyt Elker.
Counsellor (Economic/Commercial): Ismail Hakki Gucuk.
Counsellor: Tomur Bayer.
Deputy Counsellor (Social Affairs/Labour): Osman Terzi.
Counsellor (Economic/Commercial): Vasia Sade.
Counsellor: Alphan Solen.

Counsellor: Oguz Demiralp.
Counsellor: Hasan Servet Oktem.
Counsellor: Ercüment Ahmet Enc.
First Secretary: Haluk Ilicak.
Deputy Counsellor (Economic/Commercial): Recep Hakan Ozyildiz.

UGANDA

Permanent Mission: 317 ave de Tervuren, 1150 Brussels, Belgium; tel (2) 762-58-25; telex 62814; fax (2) 763-04-38.
Permanent Representative: Charles K. Katungi.
Deputy Permanent Representative: Stephen S. Nabeta.
Second Secretary: Peter Nkurunziza.
Second Secretary: John W. K. Magoba.
Third Secretary: Roland Mugabi.
Attaché: Ruth N. F. Musisi.

UKRAINE

Permanent Mission: 15 ave de la Paix, Case Postale, 1211 Geneva 20; tel (22) 7331870.
Permanent Representative: Andrei Ozadovski.
Second Secretary: Nikolai Maimeskoul.

UNITED ARAB EMIRATES

Permanent Mission: 58 rue de Moillebeau, 1209 Geneva; tel (22) 7334330; fax (22) 7345562.
Permanent Representative: Abdul Reda Abdulla Mahmoud.
First Secretary: al Asri al Dhahiri.

UNITED KINGDOM

Permanent Mission: 37-39 rue de Vermont, Case Postale, 1211 Geneva 20; tel (22) 7343800; telex 414195; fax (22) 7345254.
Permanent Representative: Martin R. Morland.
Deputy Permanent Representative: Gavin W. Hewitt.
Deputy Permanent Representative (Economic): Anne E. Stoddart.
Counsellor: Richard B. Dearlove.
First Secretary: Anthony W. Dell.
First Secretary: E. Carol Robson.
First Secretary (Press): Andrew A. Cooper.
First Secretary (GATT): David Hayes.
First Secretary: David I. Campbell.
First Secretary (Administrative): Peter Newall.
First Secretary: Stephen M. McDadd.
First Secretary (UNCTAD): David O. Hay-Edie.
First Secretary: Michael J. Lonsdale.
Second Secretary: Steven J. Phillips.

Delegation to Conference on Disarmament: tel (22) 7332385.
Permanent Representative (Disarmament): Tessa A. H. Solesby.
Counsellor (Disarmament): Ian R. Kenyon.
Counsellor (Disarmament): Col Terence T. Taylor.
First Secretary (Disarmament): Dr Graham H. Cooper.
First Secretary (Disarmament): C. J. Ferguson.
First Secretary (Administrative): Peter Newall.

USA

Permanent Mission: 11 route de Pregny, Case Postale, 1292 Chambésy; tel (22) 7990211; telex 412865; fax (22) 7990880.
Permanent Representative: Morris B. Abram.
Permanent Representative (Disarmament): Stephen J. Ledogar.
Minister-Counsellor and Deputy Permanent Representative: H. Clarke Rodgers, Jr.
Minister-Counsellor (Agricultural): Charles J. O'Mara.
Counsellor: Charles E. Rushing.
Counsellor (Public Affairs): John D. Garner.
Counsellor (Economic): George Clay Nettles.
Counsellor (Programmes Co-ordination): Montgomery L. Rogers.
Counsellor (Political): Anne Patterson.
Counsellor (Administrative): Franklin D. English.
Counsellor (Migration/Refugees): Allan G. Jury.
First Secretary: Richard T. Booth.
First Secretary: David R. Patterson.
First Secretary: Arthur L. Skop.
First Secretary: John G. Cook.
First Secretary: Clayton F. Ruebensaal.
First Secretary: Jerold H. Klaimon.
First Secretary: Thomas Henry Carter.
First Secretary: Eric J. Carlson.
First Secretary: Joyce E. Leader.
Attaché (Agriculture): Mary E. Revelt.
First Secretary: E. Craig Lineburger.
First Secretary: Frances Culpepper.
First Secretary: Gail Dennise Mathieu.

URUGUAY

Permanent Mission: 65 rue de Lausanne, 4e étage, 1202 Geneva; tel (22) 7328366; fax (22) 7315650.
Permanent Representative: Julio A. Lacarte-Muro.
Minister-Counsellor: Inès Rodriguez.
Counsellor: Cristina Figueroa.
First Secretary: Carlos Amorin.
Second Secretary: Ricardo Gonzalez-Arenas.
Second Secretary: Nelson Chaben.
Third Secretary: Maria Cassarino.

Bureau of Economic and Commercial Affairs: tel (22) 7319613.
Minister-Counsellor (Economic/Commercial): José Pedro Buda Olivera.

VENEZUELA

Permanent Mission: 18a chemin François-Lehmann, 1218 Grand-Saconnex; tel (22) 7982621; telex 415518; fax (22) 7985877.
Permanent Representative: Horacio Arteaga Acosta.
Minister-Counsellor (GATT): Juan Francisco Misle Giraud.
Counsellor: Lourdes Molinos Abreu.
Counsellor: María Esperanza Ruesta de Furter.
First Secretary: Ana Esther Hernandez Correa.
Second Secretary: Jenny Clauwaert Gonzalez.
Second Secretary: Oscar Fornoza Fernandez.
Second Secretary: Wilmer A. Mendez Graterol.
Third Secretary: Carlos R. Pestana Macedo.
Third Secretary: Nancy Meza Cuello.
Attaché: Lesbia Angulo Escobar.

VIET-NAM

Permanent Mission: 34 chemin François-Lehmann, 1218 Grand-Saconnex; tel (22) 7982485; telex 415451; fax (22) 7980724.
Permanent Representative: Nguyen Luong.
First Secretary: Vu Xuan Truong.
Second Secretary: Le Luong Minh.
Second Secretary: Nguyen Thanh Long.
Third Secretary: Nguyen Thi Nha.
Third Secretary (Economic): Tran Minh Tuan.

YEMEN

Permanent Mission: 19 chemin du Jonc, 1216 Cointrin; tel (22) 7985333; telex 415699; fax (22) 7980465.
Permanent Representative: Yahya Hamoud Geghman.
Counsellor: Mohamed al-Qutaish.
General Counsellor: Dr Adnan Tarcici.
Minister Plenipotentiary: Saeed Taleb Mokbil.
First Secretary: Abdullah Noman.
First Secretary: Nagiba Ahmed Kaid.

YUGOSLAVIA

Permanent Mission: 5 chemin Thury, 1206 Geneva; tel (22) 464433; fax (22) 464436.
Permanent Representative: Naste Calovski.
Minister-Counsellor and Deputy Permanent Representative: Mustafa Bijedic.
Minister-Counsellor: Nebojsa Dimitrijevic.
Counsellor (GATT): Olga Lazic-Djerdj.
Counsellor (Human Rights/BIT/OMS/HCR): Mirjana Radic.
First Secretary: Borislav Vukovic.
First Secretary: Jure Gasparic.
Third Secretary: Olga Spasic.
Attaché: Predag Matovic.

ZAIRE

Permanent Mission: 45A-47A rue de Lausanne, 1211 Geneva 2; Case Postale 2595, 1211 Geneva 2 Dépôt; tel (22) 7383372; telex 412686; fax (22) 7382873.
Permanent Representative: Mutuale Kikanke.
First Counsellor: Maliyabwana Kirongozi.
Second Counsellor: Ngimbi Mak Mantuba.
First Secretary: Lokwa Bula.
Second Secretary: Yamboko Fangbi.
Attaché (Financial): Mulume Marume.
Attaché (Technical): Luminuku Biasalua.

ZIMBABWE

Permanent Mission: 250 route de Lausanne, chemin du Rivage, 1292 Chambésy; tel (22) 7320119; telex 28781.
Permanent Representative: Dr Agrippah Tshabalala Mugomba.
Minister and Deputy Permanent Representative: Misheck Chenyika Hove.
Counsellor (Economic): Dr Godfrey Majoni Chipare.
First Secretary: Peter Chali.
First Secretary (Commercial): Calson Mbegabolawe.
First Secretary: Sibusiso Khumalo.
First Secretary: Herbert Dzvimbo.
Second Secretary: Madzorera Meki.
Third Secretary: Rosemary Magara.

Observers

HOLY SEE

Permanent Office: 16 chemin du Vengeron, Case Postale 28, 1292 Chambésy; tel (22) 7581728; telex 419114; fax (22) 7581729.
Apostolic Nuncio and Permanent Observer: Mgr Justo Mullor Garcia, Titular archbishop of Mérida Augusta.
Counsellor: Mgr Diego Causero.

SAN MARINO

Permanent Office: 21 ave Jean Trembley, 1209 Geneva; tel (22) 7401231; telex 412625; fax (22) 7401239.
Observer: Dieter E. Thomas.
Deputy Observer and Deputy Permanent Representative: Huguette Zeiler-Werbrouck.

SWITZERLAND

Permanent Office: 9-11 rue de Varembé, Case Postale 194, 1211 Geneva 20; tel (22) 7335200; telex 414192; fax (22) 7337985.
Observer: Bernard de Riedmatten.
Permanent Representative (CNUCED/CEE/AELE/GATT): William Rossier.
Permanent Representative (Disarmament): Herbert von Arx.
Minister, Deputy Observer and Deputy Permanent Representative: Dominik Alder.

Minister and Deputy Representative (AELE): Josef Doswald.
Deputy Representative (GATT): Dr Rudolf Ramsauer.
Counsellor: Anne Bauty.
Counsellor (Economic): Ruth Flint-Ledergerber.
Counsellor (Economic): Wilhelm Meier.
Counsellor (Legal): Amadeo Perez.
Third Secretary: Alain Guidetti.
Third Secretary: Martin Strub.
Third Secretary: Liliane Vandervorst.
Third Secretary (Accreditation Cards and Matriculation): Marianne Aeschbach.

International Organizations

EUROPEAN COMMUNITIES

External Delegation and Information Office: 37-39 rue de Vermont, Case Postale 195, 1211 Geneva 20 CIC; tel (22) 7349750; telex 28261; fax (22) 7342236.
Head of Delegation: Trân Van-Thinh.
Deputy Head of Delegation: John R. Beck.
Minister-Counsellor: Ivan Klaric.
Counsellor (Agricultural): Helmut Stadler.
Counsellor (Legal): Christoph Bail.
First Secretary: Wolfgang Plasa.
First Secretary (Agricultural): Jean-Jacques Bouflet.
First Secretary (CNUCED): Richard Wyatt.
First Secretary: George Bicknell.
First Secretary: Karl-Friedrich Falkenberg.
Attaché (Administrative): Annick Auzat.
Attaché (Agricultural): Lars Berner.

Liaison Bureau of Secretariat-General of Council of European Communities: 2 chemin Louis-Dunant, Case Postale 29, 1211 Geneva 20 CIC; tel (22) 7342720; fax (22) 7335079.
Head of Liaison Bureau: Klaus-Dietrich Jagstaidt.
Deputy Head of Liaison Bureau: Jacques Brodin.
Counsellor: Marcel Gleizes.
Second Secretary: Angela Marques de Atrayde.

LEAGUE OF ARAB STATES

Permanent Delegation: 9 rue du Valais, 1202 Geneva; tel (22) 7323030.
Deputy Observer: Ahmed Harguem.
Counsellor (Information): Subhi Khidhair.
First Secretary: Abdellah Ould Babacar.
Second Secretary: Yusri Mahmoud Helmi.
Counsellor (Economic): Waêl Fahmy.
Attaché (Economic): Ala al Moman.
Attaché (Legal/Social Affairs): Osman el Hajje.
Attaché (Information): Mohamed Dayri.
Attaché: Najib Chakroun.
Minister Plenipotentiary: Misbah Oreibi.

ORGANIZATION OF AFRICAN UNITY

Permanent Delegation: 220 route de Ferney, 1218 Grand-Saconnex; tel (22) 7881660.
Observer: Noureddine Hached.
Deputy Observer (Political/Information): Amr A. Moukhtar.
Deputy Observer (Economic): Usele Mawisa.
Counsellor (Economic): Mohamed Hafiz Tunis.
Counsellor (Labour): Abdelaziz Farag.
Counsellor (Political/Information): Desta Negousse.
Attaché: Samuel Muganda.
Attaché: Hamet Dansoko.
Attaché: Akalework Tersit.

Other Organizations

PALESTINE LIBERATION ORGANIZATION—PLO

Bureau of Permanent Observer: 96 route de Vernier, 1219 Châtelaine; Case Postale 1828, 1211 Geneva 1; tel (22) 7967607; telex 418755.
Permanent Observer: Nabil Ramlawi.
First Secretary: Tayssir al-Adjouri.
First Secretary: Ahmad Abdel Hadi.
Second Secretary: Ibrahim Musa.
Second Secretary: Rana Balawi.

THE EUROPEAN COMMUNITY

Member States

BELGIUM

Permanent Representation: 62 Belliardstraat, 1040 Brussels; tel (2) 233-21-11; fax (2) 231-10-75.
Permanent Representative: Philippe de Schoutheete de Tervarent.
Deputy Permanent Representative, Envoy Extraordinary and Minister Plenipotentiary: Marc Lepoivre.
Minister Plenipotentiary (Ministry of Foreign Affairs, External Trade and Development Co-operation): Dominique Laloux.
Director-General (Ministry of Finance): Gaston Meuleman.
Director (Ministry of Economic Affairs): Claude Cheruy.
Director (Ministry of Economic Affairs): Jozef Nackaerts.
Director (Ministry of Communications) and Counsellor (Ministry of Transport): Roger de Borger.
Inspector-General (Ministry of Finance): Sylvain Haber.
Finance Inspector (Ministry of Finance): Yves Van Honacker.
Deputy Inspector (Ministry of Finance: Financial Affairs): Paul Annicaert.
Minister-Counsellor (Ministry of Foreign Affairs, External Trade and Development Co-operation): Lucien De Groote.
Counsellor (Ministry of Foreign Affairs, External Trade and Development Co-operation): Rafaël Van Hellemont.
Counsellor (Ministry of Foreign Affairs, External Trade and Development Co-operation): Jean-Michel Veranneman de Watervliet.
Counsellor (Ministry of Foreign Affairs, External Trade and Development Co-operation): Raoul Van Landuyt.
Counsellor (Ministry of Finance): Bruno G. Guiot.
Counsellor (Ministry of Agriculture): Jozef Van Mullem.
Counsellor (Ministry of Employment and Labour): François Van Damme.
Counsellor (National Bank): Dominique Servais.
Deputy Counsellor (Ministry of Foreign Affairs, External Trade and Development Co-operation): Robert Remy.
Deputy Counsellor (Ministry of Foreign Affairs, External Trade and Development Co-operation): Thérèse Willekens.
Deputy to Counsellor (Ministry of Agriculture): Pierre de Grand Ry.
First Secretary (Ministry of Foreign Affairs, External Trade and Development Co-operation): Dirk Wouters.
First Secretary (Ministry of Foreign Affairs, External Trade and Development Co-operation): Bénédicte Frankinet.
First Secretary (Ministry of Foreign Affairs, External Trade and Development Co-operation): Alex Van Meeuwen.
First Secretary (Ministry of Foreign Affairs, External Trade and Development Co-operation): Ludovic Dieltjens.
First Secretary (Ministry of Foreign Affairs, External Trade and Development Co-operation): Vincent Mertens de Wilmars.
Secretary (Ministry of Foreign Affairs, External Trade and Development Co-operation): Danielle del Marmol.

DENMARK

Permanent Representation: 73 rue d'Arlon, 1040 Brussels; tel (2) 233-08-11; telex 64434; fax (2) 230-93-84.
Permanent Representative: Jakob Rytter.
Deputy Permanent Representative, Envoy Extraordinary and Minister Plenipotentiary: Niels Henrik Sliben.
Minister-Counsellor (Ministry of Foreign Affairs): Klaus Dahlgaard.
Counsellor (Ministry of Foreign Affairs): Ole Lisborg.
Counsellor (Ministry of Foreign Affairs): Ole Samsing.

Counsellor (Ministry of Foreign Affairs): Kaare Janson.
Counsellor (Ministry of Foreign Affairs): Ove Ullerup-Petersen.
Counsellor (Ministry of Foreign Affairs): Søren Halskov.
Counsellor (Ministry of Agriculture): Jens Hauge Pedersen.
Counsellor (Ministry of Fisheries): Michael Roitmann.
Counsellor (Ministry of Fisheries): Lars Touvdal Christensen.
Counsellor (Ministry of Education and Research): Holger Rasmussen.
Counsellor (Ministry of Culture): Henrik Bering Liisberg.
Counsellor (Ministry of Finance): Ernst O. Kristensen.
Counsellor (Ministry of Finance): Peter Brix Kjelgaard.
Counsellor (Ministry of Inland Revenue): Erik Jørgensen.
Counsellor (Ministry of Employment and Social Affairs): Søren Hess.
Counsellor (Ministry of Energy): Brian Juel Jensen.
Counsellor (Ministry of Health): Marianne Lauridsen.
Secretary (Ministry of Foreign Affairs): K. Sandberg.
First Secretary (Ministry of Foreign Affairs): Kjeld Juel Petersen.
First Secretary (Ministry of Foreign Affairs): Carl Balle Petersen.
Attaché (Ministry of Justice): Helle Lindegaard.
Attaché (Ministry of the Environment): Axel Kristiansen.
Attaché (Ministry of Communication): Finn Petersen.
Attaché (National Bank): Ove Steen Jensen.

FRANCE

Permanent Representation: 67-71 rue Ducale, 1000 Brussels; tel (2) 511-49-55; telex 21265; fax (2) 514-53-09.
Permanent Representative: Jean Vidal.
Deputy Permanent Representative: Jean Cadet.
Minister Plenipotentiary: Bernard Prague.
Counsellor (Ministry of Foreign Affairs): Yves Doutriaux.
Counsellor (Ministry of Foreign Affairs): Philippe Etienne.
Counsellor (Ministry of Foreign Affairs): François-Xavier Deniau.
Counsellor (Ministry of Foreign Affairs): François Saint-Paul.
Counsellor (Ministry of Foreign Affairs): Francis Etienne.
Counsellor (Legal Questions): Alain Sortais.
Counsellor (Ministry of Economic and Financial Affairs and the Budget: Finance): Michel Thérond.
Counsellor (Ministry of Economic and Financial Affairs and the Budget: Finance): Jean-Marie Metzger.
Counsellor (Ministry of Economic and Financial Affairs and the Budget: Commerce): Philippe Coste.
Counsellor (Ministry of Industry and Town and Country Planning: Industrial Affairs): Gérard Tagliana.
Counsellor (Atomic Energy Commission): Pierre Bernhard Frigola.
Counsellor (Ministry of Research and Technology: Scientific Matters): Jean-Pierre Chevillot.
Counsellor (Ministry of Labour, Employment and Vocational Training and Ministry of Solidarity, Health and Social Security: Social Affairs): Hélène Marsault.
Counsellor (Ministry of Labour, Employment and Vocational Training and Ministry of Solidarity, Health and Social Security: Social Affairs): Marc Boisnel.
Counsellor (Customs Matters): Ralph Dassa.
Counsellor (Ministry of Transport and the Sea: Transport): Philippe Citroën.
First Secretary (Ministry of Foreign Affairs): Gérard Guillonneau.
Attaché (Ministry of Industry and Town and Country Planning): Henri Brewil.
Attaché (Ministry of Agriculture and Forestry: Agricultural Affairs): Patrice de Laurens de Lacenne.
Attaché (Ministry of Agriculture and Forestry): Yves Discors.
Attaché (Ministry of Agriculture and Forestry): Pierre Amidey.
Delegate for Regional Planning (Ministry of Industry and Town and Country Planning): Fernand Burn.
Delegate (Ministry of Research and Technology: National Centre for Scientific Research): Gérard Rivière.
Delegate (Ministry of Agriculture and Forestry: Agricultural Affairs): Jean-Claude Trunel.

GERMANY

Permanent Representation: 19-21 rue Jacques de Lalaing, 1040 Brussels; tel (2) 238-18-11; telex 21745; fax (2) 238-19-78.
Permanent Representative: Dr Jürgen Trumpf.
Deputy Permanent Representative and Minister Plenipotentiary (Minister of Economic Affairs): Jochen Grünhage.
Minister-Counsellor (Ministry of Foreign Affairs): Johannes Dohmes.
First Counsellor (Ministry of Economic Affairs): Sigrid Selz.
First Counsellor (Ministry of Finance): Peter Jabcke.
First Counsellor (Ministry of Food, Agriculture and Forests): Klaus Jörg Heynen.
First Counsellor (Ministry of Labour and Social Affairs): Franz Burger.
First Counsellor (Ministry of Transport): Hans-Joachim Preker.
First Counsellor (Ministry of Scientific Research, Technology, Education and Science): Henning Eikenberg.
First Counsellor (Ministry of Youth, Family and Health): Werner Siebenpfeiffer.
Counsellor (Ministry of Foreign Affairs): Elmar Timpe.
Counsellor (Ministry of Foreign Affairs): Georg Birgelen.
Counsellor (Ministry of Foreign Affairs): Reinhard Silberberg.
Counsellor (Ministry of Foreign Affairs): Reinhard Krapp.
Counsellor (Ministry of Foreign Affairs): Werner Wnendt.
Counsellor (Ministry of Economic Affairs): Ulrich Mohrmann.
Counsellor (Ministry of Economic Affairs): Rolf Hochreiter.
Counsellor (Ministry of Economic Affairs): Günter Waschke.
Counsellor (Ministry of Economic Affairs): Guido Peruzzo.
Counsellor (Ministry of Economic Affairs): Herbert Krumbein.
Counsellor (Ministry of Finance): Franco Bettin.
Counsellor (Ministry of Finance): Dietrich Jahn.
Counsellor (Ministry of Food, Agriculture and Forests): Till Cramer.
Counsellor (Ministry of Food, Agriculture and Forests): Rudolf Wendt.
Counsellor (Ministry of Scientific Research, Technology, Education and Science): Dietlind Jering.
Counsellor (Ministry of Youth, Family and Health): Gerd Johannes.

GREECE

Permanent Representation: 71 ave de Cortenberg, 1040 Brussels; tel (2) 739-56-11; fax (2) 735-59-79.
Permanent Representative: Constantinos Lyberopoulos.
Deputy Permanent Representative and Minister-Counsellor: Haris Carabarbounis.
First Counsellor (Ministry of Foreign Affairs): Dimitrios Contoumas.
First Counsellor (Ministry of Foreign Affairs Special Counsellors: Relations with European Parliament): Eleftherios Pottakis.
First Counsellor (Ministry of National Economy: Economic and Financial Affairs): Ioannis Drymoussis.
First Counsellor (Ministry of National Economy: Economic Affairs): Athanassios Kargalakis.
First Counsellor (Ministry of Finance: Internal Market, Other Policies): Stergios Stagos.
First Counsellor (Ministry of Agriculture): Christos Economou.
First Counsellor (Ministry of Industry, Research and Technology: Scientific Policy): Alkibiadis Grecos.
Commercial Counsellor (Ministry of Trade): Stylianos Liagis.
Counsellor (Press Office): Léonidas Antonakopoulos.
Second Counsellor (Ministry of National Economy: Industrial Policy): Evgenia Anaguostopouloy.
Second Counsellor (Ministry of National Economy: Economic Affairs): Constantinos Costopoulos.
Second Counsellor (Ministry of National Economy: Economic Affairs): Anastassios Protopappas.
Second Counsellor (Ministry of Finance: Customs Matters): Popi Mouzaki.
Second Counsellor (Ministry of Finance): Athanassios Sagos.
Second Counsellor (Ministry of Finance: Budget, Public Finances): Loukas Samartzis.
Second Counsellor (Ministry of Agriculture: Organization of Markets): Constantinos Alexandropoulous.
Second Counsellor (Ministry of Agriculture: Organization of Markets): Apostolos Chronis.
Second Counsellor (Ministry of Agriculture): Anastassios Gogos.
Second Counsellor (Ministry of Agriculture: Organization of Markets): Ioannis Kariofilis.
Second Counsellor (Ministry of Agriculture: Fisheries, Agriculture, External Relations): Antonios Kountouris.
Second Counsellor (Ministry of Agriculture: Agricultural Structures and Forestry): Vassilios Mouzakitis.
Second Counsellor (Ministry of Labour: Employment, Social Affairs): Evangelia Hautziantoniou-Karaamitzani.
Second Counsellor (Ministry of Industry, Research and Technology: Telecommunications, Audio-Visual): Ioannis Samouilidis.
Second Counsellor (Ministry of Industry, Research and Technology): Eleftherios Spithas.
Second Counsellor (Ministry of the Environment, Regional Planning and Public Works: Environment): Miltiadis Vassilopoulos.
First Secretary (Ministry of Foreign Affairs): Petros Avierinos.
First Secretary (Ministry of Foreign Affairs): Georgis Dimitriadis.

First Secretary (Ministry of Foreign Affairs): Michel Koukakis.
First Secretary (Ministry of Foreign Affairs: seconded to European Political Co-operation Secretariat): Tryphon Paraskevopoulos.
First Secretary (Ministry of Foreign Affairs Special Counsellors: Anti-dumping): Alikivradis Pappas.
First Secretary (Ministry of Foreign Affairs Special Counsellors: Legal Affairs): Panayotis Panayotopoulos-Tsiros.
First Secretary (Ministry of Foreign Affairs Special Counsellors: External Relations): Marianna Papadopoulou.
First Secretary (Ministry of National Economy: Regional Policy, Tourism): Dimitrios Kolios.
First Secretary (Ministry of National Economy: Programmes of Structural Funds): Angeliki Makropoulu.
First Secretary (Ministry of National Economy: Insurance): Nikolaos Stratis.
First Secretary (Ministry of National Economy: Insurance): Stavria Vamvouka.
First Secretary (Ministry of Finance: Foodstuffs, Pharmaceuticals, Dangerous Substances): Irina Hatzidaki.
First Secretary (Ministry of Finance): Petros Petrof.
First Secretary (Ministry of Finance): Angeliki Tsatsou-Dritsa.
First Secretary (Ministry of Agriculture: Vegetable Products): Chryssi Savvopoulou-Papafili.
First Secretary (Ministry of Industry, Research and Technology: Standardization Policy, Public Markets): Michel Kyriakidis.
First Secretary (Ministry of Merchant Shipping): Andreas Syrigos.
First Secretary (Ministry of Education and Religious Affairs): Nicolaos Antoniou.
Commercial Secretary (Ministry of Trade): A. Pappas.
Commercial Secretary (Ministry of Trade): Dimitrios Chalepidis.
Commercial Secretary (Ministry of Trade: Textiles): Georgios Mermingis.
Attaché (Press Office): Loucas Panoussis.

IRELAND

Permanent Representation: 5 ave Galilée, bte 22, 1030 Brussels; tel (2) 218-06-05; telex 26730; fax (2) 218-13-47.
Permanent Representative: John H. F. Campbell.
Deputy Permanent Representative and Minister Plenipotentiary: Antoin Mac Unfraidh.
Counsellor (Department of Foreign Affairs: Mediterranean and Gulf Policy): Art Agnew.
Counsellor (Department of Foreign Affairs): Tony Mannix.
Counsellor (Department of Finance: Economic and Monetary Matters and Regional Policy): Seán Connolly.
Counsellor (Department of Agriculture): Donal Russell.
Counsellor (Department of Labour): Mairéad Redmond.
Counsellor (Department of Energy: Energy Policy, Euratom, Coal, Oil, Nuclear, Forestry, Post, Communications)): Martin Brennan.
Counsellor (Department of Tourism and Transport: Tourism and Road, Rail, Air and Maritime Transport): John Brown.
Counsellor (Department of Industry and Commerce: General and Eastern European Trade): Eamonn Carey.
Counsellor (Department of the Environment): Mary Moylan.
Counsellor (Institutional Affairs and Administration): James Brennan.
First Secretary (Department of Foreign Affairs: Fisheries Questions, and Department of the Marine): Eugene Hutchinson.
First Secretary (Department of Finance: Fiscal and Customs Questions): Robert Bradshaw.
First Secretary (Department of Finance): Patrick Barry.
First Secretary (Department of Agriculture): Richard Healy.
First Secretary (Department of Industry and Commerce: Research and Technology, Industry, State Aids): Michael English.
First Secretary (Department of Industry and Commerce: Internal Market, Export Credit, Competition): Eamonn T. McHale.
First Secretary (Department of the Marine): Michael Prendergast.
First Secretary (Institutional Affairs and Administration): Robert McDonagh.
First Secretary (Press and Information): Dan Mulnall.
Third Secretary (Department of Industry and Commerce: EFTA, Consumer Affairs, Commodities): Philip Lynch.
Third Secretary (Institutional Affairs and Administration): Pearse O'Donohue.
Attaché (Institutional Affairs and Administration): John Boyd.

ITALY

Permanent Representation: 74 rue de la Loi, 1040 Brussels; tel (2) 230-81-70; telex 01121462.
Permanent Representative: Federico di Roberto.
Deputy Permanent Representative and Minister Plenipotentiary: Enrico Pietromarchi.
First Counsellor (Ministry of Foreign Affairs): Ludovico Tassoni Estense di Castelvecchio.
First Counsellor (Ministry of Foreign Affairs): Paolo Garofalo.
First Counsellor (Ministry of Foreign Affairs): Rocco Antonio Cangelosi.
First Counsellor (Ministry of Foreign Affairs): Emanuele Pignatelli.
First Counsellor (Ministry of Foreign Affairs): Giovan Battista Verderame.
Counsellor (Ministry of Foreign Affairs): Alessandro Fallavollita.
Counsellor (Ministry of Foreign Affairs): Maurizio Melani.
Counsellor (Ministry of Foreign Affairs): Giovanni Manfredi.
Counsellor (Ministry of Foreign Affairs): Roberto Spinelli.
First Secretary (Ministry of Foreign Affairs): Claudio Vozzi.
First Secretary (Ministry of Foreign Affairs): Stefano Mistretta.
First Secretary (Ministry of Foreign Affairs): Domencio Giorgi.
First Secretary (Ministry of Foreign Affairs): Efisio Luigi Marras.
Attaché (Ministry of the Interior: Legal Affairs): Emilio d'Acunto.
Attaché (Ministry of Finance: Fiscal Affairs): Andrea Corvo.
Attaché (Treasury: Financial Affairs): Alfonso Acierno.
Attaché (Treasury: Financial Affairs): Renzo Antonini.
Attaché (Treasury: Economic and Monetary Affairs): Nuncio Guglielmino.
Attaché (Ministry of Agriculture): Raffaele Mezzacapo.
Attaché (Ministry of Transport): Luigi Lauretti.
Attaché (Ministry of Industry): Paolo Falciani.
Attaché (Ministry of Industry): Francesco Tetamo.
Attaché (Ministry of Labour: Social Affairs): Benito Gazzé.
Attaché (Ministry of Foreign Trade): Manlio Condemi de Felice.
Attaché (Ministry of Foreign Trade): Sandro Fanella.
Attaché (Ministry of the Merchant Navy): Biagio Amoroso.
Attaché (Ministry of Health): Romano Marabelli.
Attaché (Bank of Italy: Monetary Affairs): Giuseppe Godano.
Attaché (Legal Affairs): Prof. Antonio Tizzano.
Chancellor (Chancery): Eugenio Ladovaz.

LUXEMBOURG

Permanent Representation: 211 rue du Noyer, 1040 Brussels; tel (2) 735-20-60; telex 21707; fax (2) 736-14-29.
Permanent Representative: Joseph Weyland.
Deputy Permanent Representative and Counsellor: Thierry Stoll.
First Counsellor (Ministry of Finance): Jean-Pierre Lahire.
Counsellor: Jim Cloos.
First Secretary: Jean-Marc Hoscheit.

NETHERLANDS

Permanent Representation: 46 ave des Arts, 1040 Brussels; tel (2) 513-77-75; telex 26125; fax (2) 513-08-29.
Permanent Representative: P. C. Nieman.
Deputy Permanent Representative and Minister Plenipotentiary: C. R. van Beuge.
Counsellor (Ministry of Foreign Affairs): O. W. C. Hatting van't Sant.
Counsellor (Ministry of Foreign Affairs): G. M. Borchardt.
Counsellor (Ministry of Foreign Affairs): H. E. G. de Boer.
Counsellor (Ministry of Foreign Affairs): E. Kronenburg.
Commercial Counsellor (Ministry of Economic Affairs: Commerce): H. Demper.
Counsellor (Ministry of Finance: Finance): W. T. van Ballekom.
Counsellor (Ministry of Finance: Fiscal and Customs Affairs): E. A. Bosch.
Counsellor (Ministry of Transport and Public Works): A. van der Noordt.
Counsellor (Ministry of Agriculture and Fisheries): A. J. M. van Poppel.
Counsellor (Ministry of Social Security): F. Schumacher.
Counsellor (Ministry of Welfare, Health and Cultural Affairs): M. van Erkel.
Counsellor (Netherlands Antilles Affairs): R. S. J. Martha.
First Secretary (Ministry of Foreign Affairs): J. L. I. van Hoorn.
First Secretary (Ministry of Foreign Affairs): J. Kraak.
First Secretary (Ministry of Foreign Affairs): Baroness van Lynden-Leijten.
First Secretary (Ministry of Economic Affairs: Commerce): R. C. J. M. Cornelissen.
First Secretary (Ministry of Economic Affairs: Commerce): R. S. A. van der Kraan.

PORTUGAL

Permanent Representation: 11-13 rue Marie-Thérèse, 1040 Brussels; tel (2) 211-12-11.
Permanent Representative: José César Paylovro das Neves.
Deputy Permanent Representative and Minister Plenipotentiary: Vasco Valente.
Minister Plenipotentiary (Political Affairs and External Relations): João Valera.
Counsellor (Political Affairs and External Relations): António Augusto Jorge Mendes.
Counsellor (Political Affairs and External Relations): Alda Medeiros Fernandes.

Counsellor (Political Affairs and External Relations): José de Freitas Ferraz.
Counsellor (Agriculture): Luís Felipe Vieira Frazão Gomes.
Counsellor (Agriculture): Maria Rita de Oliveira Horta.
Counsellor (Agriculture): Luis Cardoso de Albuquerque.
Counsellor (Agriculture): José Paulo Mendonça da Silva Carvalho.
Counsellor (Agriculture): Maria Ana Nunes da Silva Rendeiro Marques.
Counsellor (Fisheries): Luis Pereira da Silva.
Counsellor (Commercial and Industrial Affairs): Pedro de Almeida e Vasconcelos Alvares.
Counsellor (Commercial and Industrial Affairs): Fernando Sérgio de Abreu Duarte Fonseca.
Counsellor (Commercial and Industrial Affairs): Rosa Barreto.
Counsellor (Commercial and Industrial Affairs): Pedro Manuel Almeida Vitorio.
Counsellor (Internal Market): Luis Fernando Godinho Varandas.
Counsellor (Economic and Financial Affairs): Carlos da Silva Costa.
Counsellor (Economic and Financial Affairs): Paulo José Queiroz de Magalhães.
Counsellor (Economic and Financial Affairs): Raúl Jorge Correia Esteves.
Counsellor (Economic and Financial Affairs): António Eduardo de Vasconcelos Calado Lopes.
Counsellor (Economic and Financial Affairs): Maria Graça Dias Damião.
Counsellor (National Bank): Carlos Maggiolo Saldanha do Valle.
Counsellor (Social Affairs, Education and Health): António Valadas da Silva.
Counsellor (Social Affairs, Education and Health): Manuel Adelino Vieira Paisana.
Counsellor (Regional Affairs, Research and Environment: Regional Affairs): Guilherme Luis Faria Câncio Martins.
Counsellor (Regional Affairs, Research and Environment: Environment): Fernando Faria Almiro do Vale.
Counsellor (Regional Affairs, Research and Environment: Research, Consumer Affairs and Civil Protection): Orlando Quintas Gomes Veiga.
Counsellor (Transport and Telecommunications): José Osorio da Gama de Castro.
Counsellor (Legal Affairs): Martinho Martins de Almeida Cruz.
Counsellor (Legal Affairs): João Maria de Lemos de Menezes-Ferreira.
Attaché (Press and Tourism): Nuno Jonet.
Attaché (Staff and Administration): João Arlindo Andrade Sena.
Attaché (Staff and Administration): Luis Salvador de Vasconcelos Domingues.
Attaché (Staff and Administration): João da Silva Ferreira.
Attaché (Protocol): Reinaldo Barreiros.

SPAIN

Permanent Representation: 52 blvd du Régent, 1000 Brussels; tel (2) 509-86-11.
Permanent Representative: Carlos Westendorp y Cabeza.
Deputy Permanent Representative and Minister Plenipotentiary: Francisco Javier Elorza Cavengt.
Minister Plenipotentiary (Foreign Affairs): Antonio Bellver Manrique.
Counsellor (Foreign Affairs): Antonio López Martínez.
Counsellor (Foreign Affairs): Miguel Fuertes Suárez.
Counsellor (Foreign Affairs): Ignacio García-Valdecasas Fernandez.
Counsellor (Foreign Affairs): Miguel Angel Navarro Portera.
Counsellor (Foreign Affairs): Emilio Fernández Castaño y Díaz-Caneja.
Counsellor (Foreign Affairs): Fernando Carderera Soler.
Counsellor (Information): José Luis Fernandez.
Counsellor (Administrative Questions): José Reina Cantalejo.
Counsellor (Financial Affairs): Luis Fernando Alemany Sanchez de Léon.
Counsellor (Financial Affairs): José Luis Torres Fernández.
Counsellor (Financial Affairs): Luis Romero Requena.
Counsellor (Customs Questions): Manuel Rubias Rodríguez.
Counsellor (Customs Questions): Javier Goizueta Sanchez.
Counsellor (Economic and Commercial Affairs): Angel Rodríguez-Mata Salcedo.
Counsellor (Economic and Commercial Affairs): Angel Gutierrez Escudero.
Counsellor (Economic and Commercial Affairs): José Antonio Lopez-García.
Counsellor (Economic and Commercial Affairs): José Gasset Loring.
Counsellor (Agricultural Questions and Fisheries): Francisco Javier Matut Archanco.
Counsellor (Agricultural Questions and Fisheries): Eduardo Diez Patier.
Counsellor (Agricultural Questions and Fisheries): Cesáreo Goicoechea Goicoechea.
Counsellor (Agricultural Questions and Fisheries): Ramón Gimenez Peris.
Counsellor (Agricultural Questions and Fisheries: Fish): Juan Bautista Herrero Huerta.
Counsellor (Agricultural Questions and Fisheries): Joaquín Serna Hernández.
Counsellor (Industrial Questions and Energy): Gabriel Vidal Comas.
Counsellor (Industrial Questions and Energy): Germán Dominguez Rodriguez.
Counsellor (Social Questions): Celia Abenza Rojo.
Counsellor (Public Works and Environment): Hilario Dominguez Hernández.
Counsellor (Transport and Communications): Carlos Ibarz del Olmo.
Counsellor (Health and Consumer Questions): Pedro Angel García Gonzalez.
Counsellor (Scientific Questions): Miguel Royo Macia.

UNITED KINGDOM

Permanent Representation: 6 rond-point Robert Schuman, 1040 Brussels; tel (2) 230-62-05; telex 24312; fax (2) 230-83-79.
Permanent Representative: Sir John O. Kerr.
Minister and Deputy Permanent Representative: D. R. C. Durie.
Minister (Agriculture): V. Kate Timms.
Counsellor (External Relations): Hon. Michael Pakenham.
Counsellor (Political and Institutional Affairs): John R. de Fonblanque.
Counsellor (Industry): Jonathan N. Rees.
Counsellor (Economics and Finance): Robert J. Bonney.
Counsellor (Social Affairs, Environment, Regional Policy and Transport): D. J. Crawley.
Counsellor (Legal Adviser): I. Hendry.
First Secretary (Institutions): Richard E. Makepeace.
First Secretary (Economics and Finance): Nick G. F. Baird.
First Secretary (External Relations): David F. Richmond.
First Secretary (Developing Countries): R. C. Calvert.
First Secretary (Transport): N. D. J. Denton.
First Secretary (Energy): Peter J. Millett.
First Secretary (Regional Policy and Right of Establishment): W. D. A. Haire.
First Secretary (Information and Press): C. R. V. Stagg.
First Secretary (Customs and Excise): Mike W. Norgrove.
First Secretary (Agriculture): R. E. Rawling.
First Secretary (Environment): Simon M. Featherstone.
First Secretary (Social Affairs): Keith Masson.
First Secretary (External Relations): John D. K. Grant.
First Secretary (Fisheries and Food): D. Matthew Hudson.
First Secretary (Economics and Finance): H. R. Quinn.
First Secretary (Budget and Fiscal): M. Neilson.
First Secretary (Industry and Competition): Catherine Bradley.
First Secretary (Commercial): Jett Harrod.
First Secretary (Industry): J. C. Farrel.
First Secretary (External Relations): S. J. Butt.
First Secretary (Assistant Legal Adviser): I. MacLeod.
Second Secretary (Agriculture and Food): H. Robinson.
Second Secretary (Community Staffing): M. Clark.
Third Secretary (Institutions): M. H. Lamport.
Third Secretary (Management): S. A. Huckle.
Third Secretary and Conference Officer: Jean Harrod.
Third Secretary (Management): Dick J. Bryant.

Non-Member States

AFGHANISTAN

Permanent Mission: 32 ave Raphaël, 75016 Paris, France; tel (1) 45-25-05-29; telex 642474; fax (1) 45-24-46-87.
Chargé d'affaires and Minister-Counsellor: Fahim Ada.
First Secretary: Kadir Mahboub.
Third Secretary: Abdul Aziz.

ALBANIA

Permanent Mission: Brussels.

ALGERIA

Permanent Mission: 209 ave Molière, 1060 Brussels; tel (2) 343-50-78; telex 64142.
Permanent Representative: Noureddine Kerroum.
First Counsellor: Abdel Kader Riame.
Counsellor: Mohamed Larguem.
First Secretary: Mahmoud Baba Ali.
First Secretary: Tewfik Abada.
Second Secretary: Mahieddine Djeffal.
Second Secretary: Djihed-Eddine Belkas.
Civil Administration: Labidi Dhif.
Attaché: Abdellah Chikhi.
Attaché: Nahimane Rifi.

ANGOLA

Permanent Mission: 182 rue Franz Merjay, 1180 Brussels; tel (2) 344-49-80; telex 63170.
Permanent Representative: Emílio José de Carvalho Guerra.
First Secretary: Joana Antónia Henriques de Barros Aires.
Third Secretary: Joaquim Feliciano dos Santos Sobrinho Junior.
Attaché: Manuel Agostinho Salvador Ribeiro.
Attaché: Faustino Van-Dunem Ferreira Junior.
Attaché: Benjamin Pereira Bravo Neto.
Attaché: Moniz Manuel Francisco.

ANTIGUA AND BARBUDA

Permanent Mission: Antigua House, 15 Thayer St, London W1M 5DL, England; tel (71) 486-7073; telex 8814503.
Permanent Representative: James A. E. Thomas.
Attaché: Althea van der Poole.

ARGENTINA

Permanent Mission: 225 ave Louise, 7e étage, BP 2, 1050 Brussels; tel (2) 648-93-71; telex 23079.
Permanent Representative: Diego Ramiro Guelar.
Minister Plenipotentiary: Emilio R. Pardo.
Minister Plenipotentiary: Alberto M. dc Nuñez.
Counsellor: Horacio Salvador.
Second Secretary: Hugo Javier Gobbi.
Second Secretary: Héctor Marcelo Cima.
Economic Section: 8e étage, BP 6; tel (2) 648-46-82; fax (2) 642-91-87.
Minister-Counsellor for Economic and Commercial Affairs: Felipe Frydman.
First Secretary for Economic and Commercial Affairs: Jorge Alberto Biglione.
Agricultural Section: BP 8; tel (2) 640-04-89; fax (2) 646-24-13.
Agricultural Minister-Counsellor: Guillermo E. Nielsen.

AUSTRALIA

Permanent Mission: Guimard Centre, 6/8 rue Guimard, 1040 Brussels; tel (2) 231-05-00; telex 21834.
Permanent Representative: Peter C. J. Curtis.
Commercial Minister: Peter Gallagher.
Minister: J. G. Oliver.
Counsellor for Commercial Affairs: Peter Appelton.
Counsellor for Commercial Affairs: I. Dickie.
Counsellor for Agricultural Affairs: M. C. Todd.
Counsellor for Veterinary Affairs: K. J. Dunn.
Counsellor for Customs Affairs: D. A. Nancarrow.
Counsellor for Financial Affairs: Bertrand Buchler.
Counsellor for Industrial, Scientific and Technological Affairs: R. Gould.
Counsellor for Labour, Educational and Social Affairs: Kerry Keogh.
First Secretary: G. Polson.
First Secretary: Hugh Borrowman.
First Secretary (Administration): G. E. C. Swift.
First Secretary (Customs Affairs): Peter Gulbransen.
First Secretary (Information): Lyn Drummond.
First Secretary (Customs Affairs): A. Hall.
First Secretary (Emigration): G. Smith.

AUSTRIA

Permanent Mission: 35-36 ave des Klauwaerts, 1050 Brussels; tel (2) 649-00-83; telex 21407; fax (2) 640-39-14.
Permanent Representative: Dr Wolfgang Wolte.
Minister and Deputy Head of Mission: Simon Hausberger.
Minister-Counsellor: Dr Elisabeth Slavkoff.
Counsellor: Franz Cermak.
Counsellor: Christoph Querner.
Minister: Dr Franz Urlesberger.
Second Secretary: Irmfried Stampfl.
Counsellor for Administrative Affairs: Heinz Hakenberg.
Counsellor for Industrial and Commercial Affairs: Léopold Maurer.
Financial Affairs Attaché: Dr Kurt Pribil.

BAHAMAS

Permanent Mission: Bahamas House, 10 Chesterfield St, London W1X 8AH, England; tel (71) 408-4488; telex 892617; fax (71) 499-9937.
Permanent Representative: Dr Patricia Elaine Joan Rodgers.
First Secretary and Consul: Wendy Rolle-MacKinnon.
Second Secretary and Vice-Consul: Kent E. Campbell.
Maritime Attaché: Judith Francis.
Second Secretary: Sylvia Davis-Stubbs.

BANGLADESH

Permanent Mission: 29-31 rue Jacques Jordaens, 1050 Brussels; tel (2) 640-55-00; telex 63189.
Permanent Representative: A. K. M. Kamaluddin Choudhury.
Political Counsellor: Akramul Qader.
Administrative Counsellor and Head of Chancery: Mohammed Muhaddes.
First Political Secretary: Taher Ahmed.
Minister for Press: M. Tajul Islam.
Minister for Customs Affairs: Abul Hussain.
Commercial Counsellor: Zakir Ahmed Khan.
First Secretary for Economic Affairs: Kazil Priya Barua.

BARBADOS

Permanent Mission: 162 ave Louise, 1050 Brussels; tel (2) 648-12-28; telex 63926.
Permanent Representative: Rashid Orlando Marville.
Counsellor: Carl Jackson.
Second Secretary: Hughland St Clair Allman.
Attaché (Administrative Affairs): Beulah Sicily Scantlebury.
Attaché: C. Gaile Thompson.

BELIZE

Permanent Mission: 10 Hardcourt House, London W1M 9AD, England; tel (71) 499-9728; telex 8814503; fax (71) 266-3486.
Permanent Representative: Sir Henry Edney Conray Cain.

BENIN

Permanent Mission: 5 ave de l'Observatoire, 1180 Brussels; tel (2) 374-91-92; telex 24568; fax (2) 375-83-26.
Permanent Representative: Edmond Cakpo-Tozo.
Minister-Counsellor: Albert Agossou.
Minister-Counsellor: Omer de Souza.
First Counsellor: Awahou Labouda.
First Counsellor: Christophe Gbegbo.
Second Secretary: Emile Djidohokpin.
Attaché: Marcellin Yevide.
Attaché: Joseph Domingo.
Attaché: Ramanatou Saka.

BHUTAN

Permanent Mission: 17-19 chemin du Champ-d'Anier, 1209 Geneva, Switzerland; tel (22) 7987971; telex 415447; fax (22) 7882593.
Permanent Representative: Dasho Paljor J. Dorji.
Second Secretary: Yeshey Dorji.

BOLIVIA

Permanent Mission: 176 ave Louise, BP 6, 1050 Brussels; tel (2) 647-27-18; telex 63494; fax (2) 647-47-82.
Permanent Representative: Eduardo Ruíz-García.
First Secretary: Arturo Suarez Vargas.
Minister-Counsellor: Javier Villa-Alvarez.

BOTSWANA

Permanent Mission: 169 ave de Tervuren, 1150 Brussels; tel (2) 735-20-70; telex 22849; fax (2) 735-63-18.
Permanent Representative: Sipho Ernest Mpofu.
Counsellor: Caesar Lapologang Lekoa.
First Secretary: T. V. Mosele.
Commercial Affairs Attaché: F. Mogatusi.
Second Secretary: M. M. B. Sebele.
Administrative Affairs Attaché: P. S. Bale.

BRAZIL

Permanent Mission: 350 ave Louise, 6e étage, 1050 Brussels; tel (2) 640-20-40; telex 24676; fax (2) 648-80-40.
Permanent Representative: Geraldo Egídio da Costa Holanda Cavalcanti.
Minister-Counsellor: Genaro António Mucciolo.
Counsellor: Washington Luís Pereira de Sousa.
Counsellor: Roberto Pessoa da Costa.
Counsellor: Roberto Pires Coutinho.
Counsellor: Fernando Jacques de Magalhaes Pimenta.
First Secretary: José Carlos de Araujo Leitão.
Second Secretary: Carlos Alberto Michaelsen Den Hartog.

BRUNEI

Permanent Mission: Brunei House, 49 Cromwell Rd, London SW7 2ED, England; tel (71) 581-0521; telex 888369; fax (71) 225-0804.
Permanent Representative: Pengiran Haji Mustapha.
First Secretary: Pengiran Haji Yunus.
Second Secretary: Mohammad Murad Haji Paijan.
Second Secretary: Rakiah Abdul Lamit.
Defence Adviser: Col Pehin Dato Haji Hussin.
Third Secretary: Haji Kassim Haji Asmat.

BULGARIA

Permanent Mission: 58 ave Hamoir, 1180 Brussels; tel (2) 374-59-63.
Permanent Representative: Atanas G. Guinev.
Counsellor: Nikolay Stoyanov Stefanov.

BURKINA FASO

Permanent Mission: 16 place Guy d'Arezzo, 1060 Brussels; tel (2) 345-99-11; telex 22252; fax (2) 345-06-12.
Permanent Representative: Salifou Rigobert Kongo.
First Counsellor: Alain Francis Gustave Ilboudo.
Economic Counsellor: Daniel Ouedraogo.
Financial Affairs Attaché: Hati Alexis Ouedraogo.
Consular Affairs: Awa Dorothée Ouedraogo.

BURUNDI

Permanent Mission: 46 square Marie-Louise, 1040 Brussels; tel (2) 230-45-35; telex 23572.
Permanent Representative: Julien Nahayo.
Second Counsellor: Célestin Niyongabo.
Second Counsellor: Hermenegilde Nimbona.
Second Counsellor: Jean Ngendanganya.
Second Secretary: Louis Sindayigaya.

CAMEROON

Permanent Mission: 131-133 ave Brugmann, 1060 Brussels; tel (2) 345-18-70; telex 24117.
Permanent Representative: Isabelle Bassong.
Minister-Counsellor: Jules Mevaa.
Second Counsellor: Blaise Banoum.
Second Counsellor: Augustine Gang Beng'yela.
First Secretary: France Linonge Kinge.
Second Secretary: Gabriel Dang.
Cultural Counsellor: Casimir Ndjodo.
Cultural Attaché: Lucien Félix Azola.
First Financial Secretary: Antony Garba Ezudogu.
Financial Affairs Attaché: Peter Félix Mba Ebong.
Economic and Commercial Delegation: 57 ave F. D. Roosevelt, 1050 Brussels; tel (2) 640-98-04; telex 26933.

Economic Counsellor: Emmanuel Ngollo Ngama.
Economic Counsellor: Georges Tanwo.

CANADA

Permanent Mission: 2 ave de Tervuren, 1040 Brussels; tel (2) 735-91-25; fax (2) 735-33-83.
Permanent Representative: Daniel Molgat.
Deputy Head of Mission and Minister-Counsellor: Thomas A. MacDonald.
Counsellor (Science and Technology): P. L. Eggleton.
Counsellor (Fisheries): E. Wiseman.
Counsellor (Commercial): F. Veenema.
Counsellor: René P. Bersma.
Counsellor: Jean Ouellet.
Counsellor (Agriculture): Philip D. Jensen.
Counsellor (Administration): Richard J. P. Renaud.
Counsellor: J. Mundy.
Counsellor: Randle Wilson.
Attaché (Agriculture/Food): D. Cumming.
Attaché (Customs): J. Gove.
Attaché (Customs): D. F. Herbst.
Attaché (Customs): Louis Nadon.
Attaché (Customs): A. A. Bradley.

CAPE VERDE

Permanent Mission: 44 Koninginnegracht, 2514 AD The Hague, Netherlands; tel (70) 50-59-50; telex 34321; fax (70) 346-77-02.
Permanent Representative: Luís de Matos Monteiro da Fonseca.
First Secretary: Luís António Valadares Dupret.
Second Secretary: Fernando Jorge Wahnon Ferreira.
Administrative Affairs Attaché: Dinora de Fátima Burgo Fernandes Barros.

CENTRAL AFRICAN REPUBLIC

Permanent Mission: 416 blvd Lambermont, 1030 Brussels; tel (2) 242-28-80; telex 0222493.
Permanent Representative: Jean-Louis Gervil-Yambala.
First Counsellor: Jacques Siolo.
First Counsellor: Grégoire Willybiro-Ngoutou.
Counsellor for Agriculture and Economics: Jacky-Alphonse Tchabassimy.
Economic and Commercial Counsellor: Germain Gresenguet.
Administrative and Financial Attaché: François Kossi.
Cultural Attaché: Patrice Kamba.

CHAD

Permanent Mission: 52 blvd Lambermont, 1030 Brussels; tel (2) 215-19-75.
Permanent Representative: Abdoulaye Lamana.
First Counsellor: Mahamat Warou.
Second Counsellor for Economic Affairs: Mbai-Arebeye Tambert.
First Secretary: Idriss Adjideye.

CHILE

Permanent Mission: 326 ave Louise, bte 22, 5e étage, 1050 Brussels; tel (2) 649-94-83; telex 61442; fax (2) 649-19-50.
Permanent Representative: Mariano Fernandez.
Minister-Counsellor: Manuel Cardenas.
Minister-Counsellor: Raquel Flisfisch.
Economic Counsellor: Gonzalo Arenas.
Second Secretary: Patricio Victoriano.
Second Secretary: Francisco Telleria.

CHINA, PEOPLE'S REPUBLIC

Permanent Mission: 445 ave de Tervuren, 1150 Brussels; tel (2) 771-58-57.
Permanent Representative: Xia Daosheng.
Counsellor: Wu Jianmin.
Counsellor: Shi Yanhua.
Counsellor: Zhou Zizhong.
Counsellor: Xu Daijie.
Counsellor: Wang Guidong.
First Secretary: Tian Wenhuang.
First Secretary: Li Binghao.
First Secretary: You Songxi.
Second Secretary: Cheng Junhui.
Second Secretary: Liu Zhiming.
Commercial Section: 21 blvd Général Jacques, 1050 Brussels; tel (2) 640-40-06.
Commercial Counsellor: Li Wenqun.
Second Secretary: Qu Guoxiang.
Customs Section: 30 square Ambiorix, BP 57, 1040 Brussels; tel (2) 736-66-09.
Counsellor for Customs Affairs: Tao Jisheng.
Scientific and Technical Section: tel (2) 771-23-03.
Counsellor: Yu Ying.
Second Secretary: Shi Yidong.
Cultural Section: tel (2) 771-02-12.
Counsellor: Zhang Wenmin.
Education Section: 408 ave de Tervuren, 1150 Brussels; tel (2) 771-01-57.
First Secretary: Xu Baofa.

COLOMBIA

Permanent Mission: 44 rue Van Eyck, 2e étage, BP 5-6, 1050 Brussels; tel (2) 649-56-79; telex 25254.
Permanent Representative: Manuel José Cardenas.
Minister Plenipotentiary: Teresa Ivars Benalcazar.
First Secretary: María Victoria Duran Restrepo.
Attaché: Jorge Zaldua Caro.

COMOROS

Permanent Mission: 15 rue de la Neva, 75008 Paris, France; tel (1) 47-63-81-78; telex 651390; fax (1) 40-67-72-96.
Permanent Representative: Ali Mlahaili.
First Counsellor: Bourhane Abdourazak.
Counsellor (Political Affairs): Salim Djohar.
Counsellor (Cultural Affairs): Ahmed Kalidanse.
Counsellor (Financial Affairs): Said Amadi.
Attaché and Accountant: Said Oussoufa.

CONGO

Permanent Mission: 16 ave F. D. Roosevelt, 1050 Brussels; tel (2) 648-38-56; telex 23677; fax (2) 648-42-13.
Permanent Representative: Ambroise Gambouele.
Economic Counsellor: Jacques Obia.
Counsellor for Forestry Affairs: Bernard Ekaba-Itoua.
Third Secretary: Gabrielle Olea.
Secretary (Economic Affairs): Cécile Nkouelolo.
Secretary: Faustin Lawson.
Attaché: Thérèse Gabrielle Peya.

COSTA RICA

Permanent Mission: 489 ave Louise, 12e étage, bte 23, 1050 Brussels; tel (2) 640-55-41.
Commercial Counsellor: Félix Przedborsky.
First Counsellor: Manuel Antonio Barrantes Rodríguez.
Counsellor: José Francisco Oreamuno.
Counsellor: María Eugenia Cortes de Bourla.
Counsellor: Silvia Reyes.

COTE D'IVOIRE

Permanent Mission: 234 ave F. D. Roosevelt, 1050 Brussels; tel (2) 672-95-77; telex 21993.
Permanent Representative: Charles Valy Tuho.
First Counsellor: Kouébi Patrice Sery.
Counsellor: Guillaume Christ Ahipeaud.
Counsellor: Charles Darius Atchimon Ake.
Counsellor for Customs Affairs: J. B. Kouadio Malan.
Counsellor for Agricultural Affairs: Kouamé Apporture Kouakou.
Counsellor for Maritime Affairs: Laye Koutoub Fadika.
Secretary for Consular and Cultural Affairs: Yao Amédée Yobouet.
Financial Attaché: Marc Ketekre.
Commercial Section: Centre Commercial International d'Abidjan (CCIA), 35 blvd Louis Schmidt, BP 16, 1040 Brussels; tel (2) 736-63-63; telex 24223.
Counsellor for Commercial Affairs: Tiémélé Sainy.

CUBA

Permanent Mission: 77 rue Robert Jones, 1180 Brussels; tel (2) 343-00-20; telex 21495; fax (2) 344-96-91.
Permanent Representative: Teresita Averhoff Purón.
Counsellor for Political Affairs: Rafael Fernández Hernández.
Counsellor for Commercial Affairs: José Joaquin Alvarez Portela.

CYPRUS

Permanent Mission: 83-85 rue de la Loi, 4e étage, 1040 Brussels; tel (2) 230-12-95; telex 25172.
Permanent Representative: Nicos Agathocleous.
First Counsellor: Stavros Orphanou.
Secretary: Christos Petrou.
Attaché for Administrative Affairs: Leontios Leontiou.
Commercial Counsellor (Ministry of Commerce and Industry): Demos Spatharis.

'TURKISH REPUBLIC OF NORTHERN CYPRUS'

Permanent Mission: 284-286 ave Louise, BP 10, 1050 Brussels; tel (2) 648-48-70; fax (2) 48-70-88.
Permanent Representative: Ayer Kaşif.
First Secretary: Zeki Gazioğlu.

CZECHOSLOVAKIA

Permanent Mission: 152 ave Adolphe Buyl, 1050 Brussels; tel (2) 647-68-09; telex 21455; fax (2) 647-91-81.
Permanent Representative: Karel Lukáš.
Commercial Counsellor: Milan Černohubý.
Counsellor: Václav Kodiš.
Commercial Attaché: Ladislav Valášek.

DJIBOUTI

Permanent Mission: 24 ave F. D. Roosevelt, 1050 Brussels; tel (2) 646-41-51; telex 27242; fax (2) 646-44-59.
Permanent Representative: Hassan Idriss Ahmed.
First Counsellor: Ahmed Mohamed Ismael.
Second Counsellor: Doualeh Ali Ahmed.
Counsellor: Hassan Said Idriss.
Financial Attaché: Mohamed Ali Barreh.
Attaché: Mohamed Ismaël Ali.
European Promotion Office: tel (2) 646-27-77; telex 27242; fax (2) 646-44-59.
Director: A. M. Ismaël.
Secretary-General: Francis Henrion.
External Relations and Press Attaché: Tina Antonsen.
Culture, Co-operation and Development: Elisabeth Speeckaert-Cornet d'Elzius.

DOMINICA

Permanent Mission: 12 rue des Bollandistes, 1040 Brussels; tel (2) 733-43-28; telex 29380; fax (2) 735-72-37.
Permanent Representative: Charles Angelo Savarin.
Second Secretary: Alcid Joseph.

DOMINICAN REPUBLIC

Permanent Mission: 160A ave Louise, bte 19, 1050 Brussels; tel (2) 646-08-40; fax (2) 640-95-61.
Chargé d'affaires and Minister-Counsellor: Renso Herrera Franco.
Attaché (Economic Affairs): Escipion Joaquin Oliveira Gomez.

ECUADOR

Permanent Mission: 70 chaussée de Charleroi, 1060 Brussels; tel (2) 537-91-30; telex 63292.
Permanent Representative: Xavier Pérez Martínez.
Minister: Raul Mantilla.
First Secretary: Juan Leoro Almeida.
First Secretary: Xavier Bustamante.
Commercial Section: tel (2) 537-50-86.
Commercial Minister-Counsellor: Ecuador Rodríguez Bustamante.

EGYPT

Permanent Mission: 44 ave Léo Errera, 1180 Brussels; tel (2) 345-50-15; telex 23716; fax (2) 343-65-33.
Permanent Representative: Hussein Mohamed Elkamel.
Minister Plenipotentiary: Mohamed Chérif Sadek.
Minister Plenipotentiary: Samiha Abou-Steit.
Counsellor: Mokhless Kotb.
Second Secretary: Yasser Morad Hossny.
Third Secretary: Ashraf Hamdy Saad.
Third Secretary: Alaa El Din Youssef.
Commercial Section: 522 ave Louise, BP 4, 1050 Brussels; tel (2) 647-32-27; telex 64809; fax (2) 646-45-09.
Minister Plenipotentiary: Fikry el Kallini.
Counsellor (Commercial Affairs): Kamal Eldin Aly Rezk.
Attaché (Commercial Affairs): Ahmed Tallat Mohamed.
Press and Information Section: 42 blvd Général Jacques, 1050 Brussels; tel (2) 640-35-01; telex 64565; fax (2) 646-45-32.
Press Counsellor: Asma el-Meligui.

EL SALVADOR

Permanent Mission: 3 blvd Saint-Michel, 1150 Brussels; tel (2) 733-04-85; fax (2) 735-02-11.
Permanent Representative: Ana Cristina Sol.
Minister-Counsellor: Luis Menendez Castro.
Minister-Counsellor and Head of Consular Affairs: Mathilde Abastado de Craik.
Third Secretary: Astrid W. de Amador.

EQUATORIAL GUINEA

Permanent Mission: 6 rue Alfred de Vigny, 75008 Paris, France; tel (1) 47-66-44-33.
First Secretary: Victorino Nka Obiang Maye.
Second Secretary: José Edjang Nguema Oyana.

ETHIOPIA

Permanent Mission: 32 blvd Saint-Michel, 1040 Brussels; tel (2) 733-49-29; telex 62285; fax (2) 732-18-51.
Permanent Representative: Wolde Emanuel Hailu.
Counsellor: Abebe Andualem.
Counsellor: Sultan Samuel.
Second Secretary: Berhanu Kebede.
Attaché: Genet Kiflevesus.

FIJI

Permanent Mission: 66-68 ave de Cortenberg, 7e étage, bte 7, 1040 Brussels; tel (2) 736-90-50; telex 26934; fax (2) 736-14-58.
Permanent Representative: Kaliopate Tavola.
Counsellor: Josaia Maivusaroko.
First Secretary: Waisale Rai.
Third Secretary: Munesh Naidu.

FINLAND

Permanent Mission: 489 ave Louise, 1050 Brussels; tel (2) 648-84-84; telex 23099; fax (2) 640-18-58.
Permanent Representative: Leif Blomqvist.
Minister-Counsellor and Deputy Head of Mission: Antero Viertiö.
Counsellor: Antti Kuosmanen.
Counsellor for Economic Affairs: Reino Hjerppe.
Counsellor for Customs Affairs: Hannu Aarnio.
Counsellor for Agricultural Affairs: Hannu Esko Vesa.
Counsellor for Labour and Social Affairs: Tuuli Raivio.
Counsellor for Scientific and Technological Affairs: Hannu Jarvinen.
Counsellor for Press Affairs: Risto Makkonen.
Counsellor for Transport Affairs: Ismo Koskinen.
Second Secretary: Nina Vaskunlahti.
Second Secretary: Juha Virtanen.
Second Secretary: Jaana Pirinen.

GABON

Permanent Mission: 112 ave Winston Churchill, 1180 Brussels; tel (2) 343-00-55; telex 23383.
Permanent Representative: Marcel Eugène Ibinga Magwangu.
First Counsellor: Henri Bekalle-Akwe.
First Counsellor: Jean Roch Renamy.
First Counsellor for Press and Information: René Boissin.
First Counsellor for Economic and Commercial Affairs: François Ondo Bekale.
Counsellor: Charles Guy Mandji.
Counsellor: Jean-Pierre Doucka.
Counsellor for Academic Affairs: Monique Odongui-Bonnard.
Second Counsellor: Pascal Obame Ngoua et Obame.
First Secretary for Consular Affairs and Protocol: Anne-Marie Kazmierczak.

GAMBIA

Permanent Mission: 126 ave F. D. Roosevelt, 1050 Brussels; tel (2) 640-10-49; telex 24344.
Permanent Representative: Ruth Adjua Sowe.
Counsellor: Ebrima O. Camara.
First Secretary: William John Joof.
Attaché for Financial and Administrative Affairs: Omar L. Dibba.

GHANA

Permanent Mission: 7 blvd Général Wahis, 1030 Brussels; tel (2) 245-82-20; telex 22572; fax (2) 245-64-53.
Permanent Representative: Alex Ntim Abankwa.
Counsellor: Kingsley Ebow Derby.
First Secretary: Beatrice Rosa Brobey.
First Secretary: Robert Kofi Badu.
Second Secretary: Stephen Yaw Ofori.
Second Secretary: Daniel Komla Alifo.
Third Secretary: Elizabeth Modey.

GRENADA

Permanent Mission: 24 ave des Arts, BP 2, 1040 Brussels; tel (2) 230-62-65; telex 64015.
Permanent Representative: L. C. Noel.
Counsellor and Chargé d'affaires a.i.: Samuel Orgias.

GUATEMALA

Permanent Mission: 53 blvd Général Wahis, 1030 Brussels; tel (2) 736-03-40; telex 25130.
Permanent Representative: Carlos Humberto Jiménez-Licona.
First Secretary: Carla Maria Rodríguez Mancia.
Third Secretary: Julio Oliva Fernández.

GUINEA

Permanent Mission: 75 ave Roger Vandendriessche, 1150 Brussels; tel (2) 771-01-26; telex 64731.
Permanent Representative: Mamadou Bobo Camara.
Financial Counsellor: Djigui Camara.
First Secretary: Ibrahima Fofana.
Second Secretary: Makhissa Camara.
Financial Attaché: Cherif Mamadou Diallo.
Protocol Attaché: Thierno Abdel Aziz Sakho.
Attaché: Nabi Camara.

GUINEA-BISSAU

Permanent Mission: 70 ave F. D. Roosevelt, 1050 Brussels; tel (2) 647-08-90; telex 63631.
Permanent Representative: Fali Embalo.
Counsellor for Economic Affairs: Filomena Araujo Embalo.
Counsellor: José Filipe Fonseca.
First Secretary for Consular Affairs: Oscar Batica Ferreira.

GUYANA

Permanent Mission: 21-22 ave des Arts, 1040 Brussels; tel (2) 230-60-65; telex 26180.
Permanent Representative: James Henry E. Matheson.
Counsellor: David T. A. Hales.
First Secretary for Commercial Affairs: James William Ramsahoye.
Administrative Attaché: Pamela Anderson.
Attaché: Joycelyn B. Anderson.

HAITI

Permanent Mission: 160A ave Louise, BP 4, 1050 Brussels; tel (2) 649-73-81.
Minister-Counsellor and Chargé d'affaires a.i.: Maryse Penette-Dominique.

HOLY SEE

Apostolic Nunciature: 5-9 ave des Franciscains, 1150 Brussels; tel (2) 762-20-05.
Apostolic Nuncio: Mgr Giovanni Moretti.
Counsellor: Mgr Joseph Chennoth.

HONDURAS

Permanent Mission: 3 ave des Gaulois, 5e étage, 1040 Brussels; tel (2) 734-00-00; telex 63175.
Permanent Representative: Manuel López Luna.
Counsellor for Economic Affairs: Fanyna Edith Glynn Ferrera.
Cultural Attaché: Sofia Daisy Pérez Cadalso.

HUNGARY

Permanent Mission: 57 rue Mignot Delstanche, 1060 Brussels; tel (2) 343-50-44; telex 21428; fax (2) 344-30-74.
Minister Plenipotentiary and Head of Mission: Prof. Iván Szász.
First Counsellor (Political Affairs) and Deputy Head of Mission: László Ság.
Counsellor (Economic Affairs): György Mikósdi.
First Secretary (Commercial and Agricultural Affairs): Péter Gottfried.

First Secretary (Legal Affairs): Egon Dienes-Oehm.
Second Secretary: László Horváth.
Third Secretary: Zsolt Becsey.

ICELAND

Permanent Mission: 5 rue Archimède, 8e étage, 1040 Brussels; tel (2) 231-03-95; telex 29459; fax (2) 230-81-46.
Permanent Representative: Einar Benediktsson.
Minister-Counsellor and Deputy Head of Mission: Gunnar Snorri Gunnarsson.
First Secretary: Thórdur B. Gudjónsson.
Commercial Counsellor: Tómas Oli Jónsson.

INDIA

Permanent Mission: 217 chaussée de Vleurgat, 1050 Brussels; tel (2) 640-91-40; telex 22510.
Permanent Representative: M. G. V. Ramakrishna.
Minister and Deputy Head of Mission: Surinder Singh Gill.
Counsellor: Om Prakash Goel.
Counsellor: A. K. Banerjee.
First Secretary: A. K. Pandey.
First Secretary: Muktesh Raghupathi.
First Secretary: Amit Dasgupta.
First Secretary: Satya Pal Mann.
First Secretary: Kanwar Sharma.
First Secretary (Agricultural Produce): N. M. N. Rahman.
Third Secretary: Rahur Chhabra.

INDONESIA

Permanent Mission: 294 ave de Tervuren, 1150 Brussels; tel (2) 771-20-14; telex 21200; fax (2) 771-22-91.
Permanent Representative: Atmono Suryo.
Minister and Deputy Head of Mission: Tetty C. A. Latupapua.
Minister-Counsellor: Abdul Rahman Siata.
Minister-Counsellor: Mr Aroeman.
Counsellor for Administrative Affairs: Imam Patmavidjaja.
First Secretary: Abdurrachman Mattalitti.
First Secretary: Abdulmanan Sulaiman.
First Secretary: Deddy Sumjadi.
Second Secretary: Danto Ntoma.
Third Secretary: Elias Ginting.
Third Secretary: Adhy Soesanto.
Third Secretary: Benny Bahanadewa.

Commercial, Agricultural and Industrial Section: 7 ave Tedesco, 1160 Brussels; tel (2) 675-32-50.
Commercial Attaché: Hatanto Reksodipoetro.
Agricultural Attaché: Husin Anang.
Industrial Attaché: Asahon Siregar Siagian.

Financial Attaché's Office: 190 ave de Tervuren, 1150 Brussels; tel (2) 763-32-50.
Financial Attaché: Roy Ronald Lino.

IRAN

Permanent Mission: 415 ave de Tervuren, 1150 Brussels; tel (2) 762-37-45.
Permanent Representative: Mohamed Reza Bakhtiari.
First Secretary: Hassan Tajk.
First Secretary: Ahmad Shahvary.
First Secretary: Seyed Hossein Enayat.
Attaché: Moraol Alj Gholami.
Third Secretary: Gholamreza Ebrahim-Pour.
Third Secretary: Said Khalozadeh.

IRAQ

Permanent Mission: 131 ave de la Floride, 1180 Brussels; tel (2) 374-59-91; telex 26414; fax (2) 374-76-15.
Permanent Representative: Dr Zaid Hwaishan Haidar.
First Secretary: Naffa M. Mahdi.
Second Secretary: Hameed Hamed.
Attaché: Ramzi M. A. Hamid.
Attaché: Saeed Jassim.
Attaché: Fatihi Saleh.
Third Secretary: Khalil al-Hadithy.
Third Secretary: Thamir Khalaf.
Commercial Attaché: Nabil M. A. Sharif.

ISRAEL

Permanent Mission: 40 ave de l'Observatoire, 1180 Brussels; tel (2) 374-90-80.
Permanent Representative: Avraham Primor.
Minister-Counsellor and Deputy Head of Mission: Lydia Chouk-Ron.
Counsellor for Press, Information and Parliamentary Affairs: Rafaël Barak.
Counsellor for Agricultural Affairs: Eva Gover.
Counsellor: Yehoshua Krith-Man.
First Administrative Secretary: Arieh Danon.
First Secretary for Economic Affairs: Ilan Nave.

JAMAICA

Permanent Mission: 83-85 rue de la Loi, 5e étage, 1040 Brussels; tel (2) 230-11-70; telex 26644.
Permanent Representative: Leslie Armon Wilson.
Minister-Counsellor: Yvette Cross.
First Secretary: Charlane Edwards.
First Secretary: Gail Marie Applewhaite.
Attaché: Robert Miller.

JAPAN

Permanent Mission: 58 ave des Arts, 7e étage, BP 13-14, 1040 Brussels; tel (2) 513-92-00; telex 22174; fax (2) 513-32-41.
Permanent Representative: Takehiko Nishiyama.
Minister: Kojiro Takano.
Counsellor: Mutsuo Mabuchi.
Counsellor: Kozo Oikawa.
First Secretary: Wataru Nishigahiro.
First Secretary: Kenji Tsunekawa.
First Secretary: Kazuyuki Sugimoto.
First Secretary: Yoshihisa Ito.
First Secretary: Shuichi Inada.
First Secretary: Juichi Takahara.
First Secretary: Yukata Kiyokawa.
First Secretary: Kazuo Haraguchi.
First Secretary: Yasuhei Gomi.
First Secretary: Shinya Wakimoto.
First Secretary: Akira Konishi.
Second Secretary: Toshihide Tsumagari.
Second Secretary: Hiroshi Yamamoto.
Second Secretary: Hiroya Michigami.
Second Secretary: Kenji Wani.

Luxembourg Chancery: 2 rue des Girondins, Luxembourg; tel 44-85-11.
Counsellor: Yoshitomo Tsunekawa.
Second Secretary: Yukihiro Tsunai.

JORDAN

Permanent Mission: 104 ave F. D. Roosevelt, 1050 Brussels; tel (2) 640-77-55; telex 62513.
Second Secretary: Nabil Masarweh.

KENYA

Permanent Mission: 1-5 ave de la Joyeuse Entrée, 1040 Brussels; tel (2) 230-30-65; telex 62568.
Permanent Representative: Francis Kirimi Muthaura.
First Secretary for Commercial Affairs: G. K. Muriithi.
Second Secretary (Information): Simeon Jagongo Ayieko.
Second Secretary (Consular Affairs): D. M. O. Okemwa.
Second Secretary: A. O. Ang'awa.
Second Secretary: A. Odera.
Financial Attaché: C. O. Olando.
Administrative Attaché: M. D. Okello.
Administrative Attaché: E. W. Odingo.

KIRIBATI

Embassy: c/o Ministry of Foreign Affairs, POB 68, Bairiki, Tarawa, Kiribati.
Permanent Representative: I. T. Tabai.

KOREA, REPUBLIC

Permanent Mission: 249 ave de Tervuren, 1150 Brussels; tel (2) 772-32-00; fax (2) 772-30-51.
Permanent Representative: Kwun Tong Man.
Counsellor: Shin Jangbum.
First Secretary: Kim Kwang Dong.
First Secretary: Yoon Jong Kon.
Commercial Attaché: Noh Jang Wooh.
Agricultural Affairs Attaché: Lee Kwan Yong.
Commercial Affairs Attaché: Park Ingu.
Scientific Attaché: Lee Hun Gyu.
Second Secretary: Lee Hye Min.
Second Secretary: Hahn Myungjae.
Communications Attaché: Park Kun Woong.
Financial Affairs Attaché: Lee Chong Hoon.

KUWAIT

Permanent Mission: 43 ave F. D. Roosevelt, 1050 Brussels; tel (2) 647-79-50.
Permanent Representative: Ahmad A. el-Ebrahim Ibrahim.
Counsellor: Ali Husain al-Sammak.
Attaché: Abdullah al-Askar.
Attaché: Zakaria Ahmad M. S. al-Khamis.

LAOS

Permanent Mission: 74 ave Raymond Poincaré, 75116 Paris, France; tel (1) 45-53-70-47; telex 610711.
Permanent Representative: Phoune Khammounheuang.
Second Secretary: Southam Sakonhninhom.

LEBANON

Permanent Mission: 2 rue Guillaume Stocq, 1050 Brussels; tel (2) 649-94-60; telex 22547.
Permanent Representative: Saïd al-Assaad.
Counsellor: Michel Geahchan.
First Secretary: Mourad Jammal.

LESOTHO

Permanent Mission: 66 ave de Cortenberg, BP 5, 1040 Brussels; tel (2) 736-39-76; telex 25852.
Permanent Representative: Mabotse Lerotholi.
Counsellor: Ntebaleng Malebenya Mothepu.
Customs Attaché: Rethabile Fraser Makhesi.
Third Secretary: Moses Mphohle Sekoli.
Administrative Attaché: Mojabeng Bolae.
Attaché: Edith Puseletso Morai.

LIBERIA

Permanent Mission: 18 ave des Touristes, 1640 Rhode-St-Genese, Brussels; tel (2) 385-45-39; telex 61384.
Minister-Counsellor and Chargé d'affaires a.i.: Jarjar M. Kamara.
Counsellor: Catherine N. Watson Khasu.

LIBYA

Permanent Mission: 28 ave Victoria, 1050 Brussels; tel (2) 649-21-12; telex 23398.
Permanent Representative: Mohamed S. Alfaituri.
Attaché (Economic Affairs): Abdessalam Sergiwa.
Attaché (Customs Affairs): Salem Azabi.

MADAGASCAR

Permanent Mission: 276 ave de Tervuren, 1150 Brussels; tel (2) 770-17-26; telex 61197.
Permanent Representative: Christian Rémi Richard.
First Counsellor: Henry Rabary-Ndrano.
Counsellor: Cyrille Fida.
Counsellor: Ignace Ratovoherison.
Counsellor: Mélanie Chan Mane.
Counsellor: Henri Roderic Rajaofera.
Counsellor: Cyril Rabarihoela.
Secretary: Pierre Rabarivola.
Attaché: Fama Rakotoaly.
Attaché: André Andriamasy.

MALAWI

Permanent Mission: 15 rue de la Loi, 1040 Brussels; tel (2) 231-09-80; telex 24128.
Permanent Representative: Lawrence P. Anthony.
Counsellor: C. S. M. Jere.
First Secretary: C. J. Kambauwa.
Second Secretary: A. K. Numero.

MALAYSIA

Permanent Mission: 414A ave de Tervuren, 1150 Brussels; tel (2) 762-67-67; telex 26396; fax (2) 762-50-49.
Permanent Representative: Dato Dali Mahmud Hashim.
Minister-Counsellor: Kamal Ismaun.
Minister-Counsellor (Customs): Wan Yeop Abdul Shukor Bin Wan Din.
Minister-Counsellor (Trade): Kalsom Bte Abdul Rahman.
First Secretary: Fauziah Mohd Taib.
First Secretary: Mohd Hatta Abdul Aziz.
Trade Commissioner: Abdul Kabur Bin Mohd Ibrahim.
Second Secretary (Administration): Abu Bakar Bin Hanif.
Attaché (Administration): Ahmad Apandi Bin Samsudin.

MALDIVES

Permanent Mission: 212 East 47th St, New York, NY 10017, USA; tel (212) 688-0776; telex 960945.

MALI

Permanent Mission: 487 ave Molière, 1060 Brussels; tel (2) 345-74-32; telex 22508; fax (2) 344-57-00.
Permanent Representative: Lamine Keïta.
First Counsellor: Amadou Fidiane Dia.
Second Counsellor: Demba Macalou.
Secretary: Dioflo Coulibaly.

MALTA

Permanent Mission: 44 rue Jules Lejeune, 1060 Brussels; tel (2) 343-01-95; telex 26616; fax (2) 343-01-06.
Permanent Representative: Dr Joseph Licari.
First Secretary: Charles Inguanez.
First Secretary: Dr Paul Saliba.

MAURITANIA

Permanent Mission: 6 ave de la Colombie, 1050 Brussels; tel (2) 672-47-47; telex 26034.
Permanent Representative: Taki Ould Sidi.
First Counsellor: Lafdal Ould Abeih.
First Counsellor: Yéro Fall.
Second Secretary: Oumar Samba Bâ.
Third Secretary: Mohamed Ould Mahmoud.

MAURITIUS

Permanent Mission: 68 rue des Bollandistes, 1040 Brussels; tel (2) 733-99-88.
Permanent Representative: Raymond Chasle.
Counsellor: Satiawan Gunessee.
Second Secretary: Usha Chandnee Dwarka.
Attaché: Tiagarajen Kalasopatan.

MEXICO

Permanent Mission: 164 chaussée de la Hulpe, 1170 Brussels; tel (2) 676-07-11; telex 22355; fax (2) 676-07-77.
Permanent Representative: Alfredo del Mazo González.
Deputy Head of Mission: Luis Antonio de Pablo Serna.
Minister: Vicente Montemayor.
Minister: Juan José Huerta Flores.
Counsellor: Rodolfo Sandoval.
Counsellor: Eduardo Martínez.
Counsellor: Miguel Angel Herrerias.
Counsellor and Attaché for Culture and Information: Daniel Leyva y Santiago.
Economic Counsellor: José Guadalupe Barrera Flores.
Commercial Counsellor: Reynaldo Alejandro Cruz Serrano.
Counsellor for Agricultural and Forestry Affairs: Sergio Osorio Romero.

MONGOLIA

Permanent Mission: 5 ave Robert Schumann, 92100 Boulogne-Billancourt, France; tel (1) 46-05-28-12.
Permanent Representative: Luvsandorjiin Mundagbaatar.

MOROCCO

Permanent Mission: 29 blvd Saint-Michel, 1040 Brussels; tel (2) 736-11-00; telex 21233; fax (2) 734-64-68.
Permanent Representative: Abdellah Lahlou.
First Counsellor and Deputy Head of Mission: Jaafar H. Alj.
First Counsellor: Abdesslam Alem.
Counsellor: Mina Tounsi.

MOZAMBIQUE

Permanent Mission: 97 blvd Saint-Michel, 1040 Brussels; tel (2) 736-25-64; telex 65478; fax (2) 735-62-07.
Permanent Representative: Frances Vitória Velho Rodrigues.
Counsellor: Roque José Loforte.
First Secretary: Francisco Joaquim Paindane.
Second Secretary: Benedito Nassone.
Attaché: Guida Baptista Gonçalves Alegre.

MYANMAR

Permanent Mission: 5300 Bonn 1, Schumannstr. 112, Germany; tel (228) 210091; telex 8869560; fax (228) 219316.
Permanent Representative: U Wing Aung.
Counsellor: U Nyi Nyi Than.
First Secretary: U Kyaw Nyunt Hman.
Second Secretary: Daw Maw Maw.
Attaché: U Sein Nyunt.

NAMIBIA

Permanent Mission: Sq. Stéphanie Business Centre S.A., 65 ave Louise, 1050 Brussels; tel (2) 535-78-01.

NEPAL

Permanent Mission: 53 Bonn-Bad Godesberg, Im Hag 15, Germany; tel (228) 343097; telex 8869297.
First Secretary: Madhav Ji Shrestha.
First Secretary: Bhagirath Basnyat.
Attaché: Jaya B. Rai.

NEW ZEALAND

Permanent Mission: 47-48 blvd du Régent, 1000 Brussels; tel (2) 512-10-40; telex 22025; fax (2) 513-48-56.
Permanent Representative: David L. Gamble.
Counsellor: Maarten L. Wevers.
Counsellor (Veterinary): Dr Barry D. O'Neil.
First Secretary (Customs): Michael A. Spong.
First Secretary: John N. Goodman.
First Secretary: Julie MacKenzie.

NICARAGUA

Permanent Mission: 55 ave de Wolvendael, 1180 Brussels; tel (2) 375-64-34; telex 63553; fax (2) 375-71-88.
Permanent Representative: Sergio Mario Blandon Lanzas.
Minister-Counsellor: Lester Mejia Solis.

NIGER

Permanent Mission: 78 ave F. D. Roosevelt, 1050 Brussels; tel (2) 648-61-40; telex 22857.
Permanent Representative: Amadou Zada.
Counsellor: Gany Diaroumeye.
Second Secretary for Financial Matters: Mallam Harouna Maman.

NIGERIA

Permanent Mission: 288 bis ave de Tervuren, 1150 Brussels; tel (2) 762-98-31; telex 22435.
Permanent Representative: Maurice Bisong Ekpang.
Minister-Counsellor: George O. Adetuberu.
Administrative Attaché: S. B. Gada.
Administrative Attaché: O. S. Nwabueze.
Counsellor for Consular Affairs: M. K. Ibrahim.
First Secretary: P. U. Iweze.
Second Secretary: O. G. Nnaji.
Second Secretary: A. C. Uche.
Attaché: A. O. Olukemi.
Customs Attaché: K. O. Ajidele.
Commercial Attaché: I. E. Enyenihi.
Commercial Attaché: O. McEwen.

NORWAY

Permanent Mission: 17 rue Archimède, 1040 Brussels; tel (2) 230-78-65; telex 21071; fax (2) 230-36-84.
Permanent Representative: Eivinn Berg.
Minister and Deputy Head of Mission: Arne Sivertsen.
Counsellor: Stein Vegard Hagen.
Counsellor: Tarald Osnes Brautaset.
First Secretary: Thomas Hauff.
First Secretary: Dag Wernø Holter.
Counsellor for Labour, Social and Environmental Affairs: Tore Malterud.
Counsellor for Economic and Monetary Affairs: Per Christiansen.
Counsellor for Transport Affairs: Andreas Dalstø Lothe.
Counsellor for Agricultural Affairs: Leif Forsell.
Counsellor for Fisheries: Dag Erling Stai.
Attaché for Scientific Affairs: Knut Reintz.

OMAN

Permanent Mission: 50 ave d'Iéna, 75116 Paris, France; tel (1) 47-23-01-63; telex 613765.
Permanent Representative: Munir bin Abdulnabi bin Yousuf Makki.
First Secretary: Jihad al Taie.
Second Secretary: Abdullah Saleh Hilal.

PAKISTAN

Permanent Mission: 57 ave Delleurs, 1170 Brussels; tel (2) 673-80-07; telex 61816; fax (2) 675-31-37.
Permanent Representative: Munir Akram.

Minister and Head of Chancery: Toheed Ahmad.
Minister (Economic): Shuja Shah.
Minister (Customs): Tahir Mahmood.
First Secretary: Mr Sanaullah.
First Secretary: Fauzia M. Sana.

PANAMA

Permanent Mission: 8 blvd Brand Whitlock, BP 6, 1040 Brussels; tel (2) 733-90-89; telex 25169; fax (2) 733-77-79.
Permanent Representative: Roberto Alemán Healy.
Deputy Head of Mission: Carlos Ernesto González Ramírez.
Counsellor for Economic Affairs: Navidad Moron Zanet.

PAPUA NEW GUINEA

Permanent Mission: 17-19 rue Montoyer, 1040 Brussels; tel (2) 512-31-26; telex 62249.
Counsellor and Chargé d'affaires a.i.: Joseph Gabut.
First Secretary: Lucy Bogari.
Second Secretary: Samuel Neine Abal.

PARAGUAY

Permanent Mission: 42 ave de Saturne, 1180 Brussels; tel (2) 374-87-48; telex 26535.
Permanent Representative: Dido Florentin-Bagado.
First Secretary: Jorge Antonio Colman.
First Secretary: Myriam Scorza de Zea.

PERU

Permanent Mission: 179 ave de Tervuren, 1150 Brussels; tel (2) 733-33-19; fax (2) 733-48-19.
Permanent Representative: Julio Ego-Aguirre-Alvarez.
Minister: Domingo Da-Fieno Gandolfo.
Minister-Counsellor: Alberto Carrion Tejada.
Second Secretary: Fortunato Ricardo Quesada Seminario.
Third Secretary: Carlos Amezaga R..
Third Secretary: Maria del Rocio Bedoya.
Attaché: Gabriela Basurco.

Commercial Section: tel (2) 735-24-00; telex 25079.
Commercial Counsellor: Lita Vaisman K..

PHILIPPINES

Permanent Mission: 85 rue Washington, 1050 Brussels; tel (2) 533-18-11; telex 23631; fax (2) 538-35-40.
Permanent Representative: Roberto R. Romulo.
Minister: Jose A. Zaide, Jr.
Second Secretary and Consul: Ricardo M. Endaya.
Second Secretary and Consul: Libran N. Cabactulan.
Second Secretary and Consul: Alejandrino A. Vicente.
Administrative Officer and Attaché: Reynaldo G. Cardenas.
Property/Records Officer and Attaché: Virgilio G. Cajaljal.
Finance Officer and Attaché: Norma C. Tuiza.
Secretary to Ambassador and Attaché: Maria Victoria V. Ortiz-Dony.
First Secretary (Information): Alejandro D. del Rosario.

Commercial Section: tel (2) 347-46-40; fax (2) 344-27-10.
Commercial Counsellor: Cristina G. Ortega.

Agricultural Section: tel (2) 345-74-57; fax (2) 345-74-57.
Agricultural Attaché: Horacio M. Carandang.

POLAND

Permanent Mission: 18 ave de l'Horizon, 1150 Brussels; tel (2) 771-32-62; telex 20555; fax (2) 771-49-10.
Permanent Representative: Jan Kułakowski.
Counsellor and Minister Plenipotentiary: Jan Truszczynski.
Counsellor: Tomasz Wasilewski.
First Secretary: Romuald Daniel.
First Secretary: Anna Stępniewska.
First Secretary: Roman Sobierski.

QATAR

Permanent Mission: 71 ave F. D. Roosevelt, 1050 Brussels; tel (2) 640-29-00; telex 63754.
First Secretary and Chargé d'affaires a.i.: Ali Hassan al-Hamadi.
Second Secretary: Mohamed Fraish M. S. al-Adawi.
Second Secretary: Sheikh Mubarak Fahed Jassim al-Thani.

ROMANIA

Permanent Mission: 37a rue Washington, 1050 Brussels; tel (2) 647-96-14.
Permanent Representative: Constantin Parvutoiu.
Counsellor: Lazar Comanescu.

RUSSIA

Permanent Mission: 56 ave Louis Lepoutre, 1060 Brussels; tel (2) 343-03-39; fax (2) 346-24-53.
Permanent Representative: Lev A. Voronine.
Minister Plenipotentiary and Deputy Head of Mission: Valentin M. Bogomazov.
First Counsellor: Valentin A. Zimine.
Counsellor: Pavel S. Smirnov.
Second Secretary: Yuri A. Gloukhov.
Third Secretary: Tatiana D. Valovaya.

RWANDA

Permanent Mission: 1 ave des Fleurs, 1150 Brussels; tel (2) 763-07-21; telex 26653.
Permanent Representative: François Ngarukiyintwali.
Second Counsellor: Anastase Nderebeza.
Second Counsellor: Gratien Musigazi.
Second Counsellor: Charles Sindabimenya.
First Secretary: Benoît Habiyakare.

SAINT CHRISTOPHER AND NEVIS

Permanent Mission: 10 Kensington Court, London W8 5DL, England; tel (71) 937-9522; telex 913047; fax (71) 937-5514.
Permanent Representative: Alan Richard Gunn.
Deputy Permanent Representative: Edwin Laurent.
First Secretary (Political): Civilia Omelda Dasent.
First Secretary (Consular and Legal Affairs): Cenio Elwin Lewis.
Attaché (Trade): Bernard Cornibert.
Third Secretary: Maria Cadet.

SAINT LUCIA

See entry on Saint Christopher and Nevis above.

SAINT VINCENT AND THE GRENADINES

See entry on Saint Christopher and Nevis above.

SAN MARINO

Permanent Mission: 44 ave Brugmann, 1060 Brussels; tel (2) 344-60-67; fax (2) 347-17-08.
Permanent Representative: Gian Nicola Filippi Balestra.

SÃO TOMÉ AND PRÍNCIPE

Permanent Mission: 42 ave Brugmann, 1060 Brussels; tel (2) 347-53-75; telex 65313.
Counsellor: Francisco Paesa Sanchez.
First Secretary and Chargé d'affaires a.i.: Carlos Gustavo dos Anjos.
Second Secretary for Commercial Affairs: António Albertino Afonso Días.

SAUDI ARABIA

Permanent Mission: 45 ave F. D. Roosevelt, 1050 Brussels; tel (2) 649-57-25; telex 61600.
Permanent Representative: Prince Muhammad ibn Nawaf ibn Abd al-Aziz as-Sa'ud.
Minister-Counsellor: Omar Yeslam Bamanie.
First Secretary: Abbas M. Baswari.
First Secretary: Fawaz H. Joukhdar.
First Secretary: Naser F. M. Alsharif.
Secretary: Abdullah Almadhi.
Second Secretary: Ali Mohamad Alhamdan.
Third Secretary: Abdallah M. R. al-Salama.
Attaché: Abdallah al-Rowaily.

Economic Section: 380 ave Louise, 1050 Brussels; tel (2) 647-40-80; telex 20953.
First Secretary: Faisal H. Trad.
First Secretary: Mohammad H. A. Ahmed.
Attaché: Nezar H. M. Basheer.

Cultural Section: 9 rue André Pascal, 75767 Paris Cedex 16, France; tel (1) 46-47-90-80; telex 614119.
Cultural Attaché: Ibrahim A. H. al-Sheikh.

SENEGAL

Permanent Mission: 196 ave F. D. Roosevelt, 1050 Brussels; tel (2) 673-00-97.
Permanent Representative: Falilou Kane.
First Counsellor: Mamadou Sow.
First Counsellor: Demba Konté Niare.
First Counsellor for Customs Affairs: Raphaël Diouf.
Counsellor for Economic and Commercial Affairs: Papa Amadou Fall.
Counsellor: Sidy Mbaye Mbaye.
Counsellor: Elymane Ly.
First Secretary for Financial Affairs: Birago Diene.
First Secretary: Daouda Ndoye.
Secretary: Amadou Diaw.
First Secretary for Consular Affairs: Libasse Lo.
Third Secretary: Mame Diarra Fall Sambe.

SEYCHELLES

Permanent Mission: 53 bis rue François 1er, 75008 Paris, France; tel (1) 47-23-98-11; telex 649634.

SIERRA LEONE

Permanent Mission: 410 ave de Tervuren, 1150 Brussels; tel (2) 771-00-52; telex 63624.
Permanent Representative: Marian Judith Tanner Kamara.
Counsellor: Henri L. Tucker.
Counsellor: Felicia Ajuah Fyne.
First Secretary: Juliana M. Dimoh.
First Secretary: Ahmed Lans Kumalah.

SINGAPORE

Permanent Mission: 198 ave F. D. Roosevelt, 1050 Brussels; tel (2) 660-30-98; telex 26731; fax (2) 660-86-85.
Permanent Representative: Jayalekshimi Mohideen.
Minister-Counsellor: Dr Vincent Yip.
Second Secretary: Olivia Joseph.
Third Secretary: Sun Chun Lee.

SOLOMON ISLANDS

Permanent Mission: c/o Ministry of Foreign Affairs, Honiara, Solomon Islands; tel 22223; telex 66311.
Permanent Representative: Wilson Ifunaoa.

SOMALIA

Permanent Mission: 66 ave F. D. Roosevelt, 1050 Brussels; tel (2) 640-16-69; telex 24807.
Permanent Representative: Ahmed Shire Mohamud.
Second Counsellor: Ali Abdi Mohamed.
First Secretary: Dahir Tukale.
First Secretary: Shamso Hassan-Said.

SOUTH AFRICA

Permanent Representation: 26 rue de la Loi, BP 14/15, 1040 Brussels; tel (2) 231-17-25; telex 63060; fax (2) 230-80-32.
Permanent Representative: Dr Bhadra Galu Ranchod.
Minister and Deputy Permanent Representative: W. J. V. Baker.
Minister (Economic): W. J. Smalberger.
Counsellor (Economic): Dr W. Brümmerhoff.
Counsellor (Administration): Zacharias Johan Prinsloo.
Counsellor (Agriculture): G. J. Joubert.
First Secretary: J. H. van Jaarsveld.
Third Secretary (Economic): D. J. Kruger.

SRI LANKA

Permanent Mission: 21-22 ave des Arts, 1040 Brussels; tel (2) 230-48-90; telex 26927.
Permanent Representative: Tyrrel Derric Samuel Alaric Dissanayaka.
Minister-Counsellor: Nimal Wijayaratne.
Counsellor for Commercial Affairs: Nande Rupesiri Meemeduma.
Attaché: Thompson G. Jayasekera.
Attaché: Christie Oliver Liyanage.

SUDAN

Permanent Mission: 124 ave F. D. Roosevelt, 1050 Brussels; tel (2) 647-51-59; telex 24370; fax (2) 648-34-99.
Permanent Representative: Saeed Saad Mahgoub Saad.
Minister Plenipotentiary: Nureldin Mohamed Hamed Satti.
Counsellor for Economic Affairs: Omer Mohamed Abdelsam.
First Secretary: Rahamtalla Mohamed Osman.
First Secretary: Abu Bakr Hussein Ahmed.
Administrative Attaché: Mohamed Dahab Mohamed.

SURINAME

Permanent Mission: 379 ave Louise, BP 20, 1050 Brussels; tel (2) 640-11-72.
Permanent Representative: Donald Aloysius McLeod.
Counsellor and Deputy Head of Mission: Joan H. Antonius.
First Secretary: Rudi Alihusain.

SWAZILAND

Permanent Mission: 71 rue Joseph II, 5e étage, 1040 Brussels; tel (2) 230-00-44; telex 26254; fax (2) 230-50-89.
Permanent Representative: John Bongani Jourbet Solomon Dlamini.
Counsellor: Prince Churchill B. Dlamini.
First Secretary: Christian M. Nkambule.
Third Secretary: Mlungisi Dlamini.
Administrative Secretary: Harriet B. Dludlu.

SWEDEN

Permanent Mission: 6 rond-point Robert Schumann, 1040 Brussels; tel (2) 237-01-11; telex 26126; fax (2) 230-77-57.
Permanent Representative: Stig Brattström.
Minister Plenipotentiary and Deputy Head of Mission: Anders Olander.
Counsellor: Lennart Nilsson.
Counsellor: Magnus Wernstedt.
Counsellor: Sven Backlund.
Counsellor: Ninna Rösiö.
First Secretary: Arne Kallin.
Counsellor for Economic Affairs: Gustaf Adlercreutz.
Counsellor for Agricultural Affairs: Jerzy Glücksman.
Counsellor for Scientific and Technological Affairs: Göran Belfrage.
Counsellor for Education: Ulf Lundin.
Counsellor for Press Affairs: Christian Andersson.
Counsellor for Labour and Social Affairs: Margit Wallsten.
Customs Affairs Attaché: Bertil Legnestedt.
Attaché for the Working Environment: Rolf Dahlström.
Second Secretary: Anders Wollter.

SWITZERLAND

Permanent Mission: 53 rue d'Arlon, BP 9, 1040 Brussels; tel (2) 230-14-90; telex 21660; fax (2) 230-45-09.
Permanent Representative: Dr Bénédict de Tscharner.
Minister and Deputy Head of Mission: Dr Bruno Spinner.
Counsellor: Michel Besson.
Counsellor: Aldo Matteucci.
Counsellor: Dr Charles-Edouard Held.
First Secretary: Dr Jacques de Watteville.
First Secretary: Rolf Stücheli.
Counsellor for Telecommunications: Patrice Haldemann.
Head of Chancery: Odile Weisgerber.

SYRIA

Permanent Mission: 3 ave F. D. Roosevelt, 1050 Brussels; tel (2) 648-01-35; telex 26669.
Permanent Representative: Siba Nasser.
First Secretary: Anwar al-Fadel.
Third Secretary for Commercial Affairs: Fatima Ghada Talas.
Attaché: Hamzeh Dawalibi.
Attaché: Moustafa Sallakh.

Press and Information Section: 106 ave F. D. Roosevelt, 1050 Brussels; tel (2) 648-51-76.
Counsellor: Haidar Koudmani.
First Secretary: Tahsine Eldin Ali Hilal.

TANZANIA

Permanent Mission: 363 ave Louise, 7e étage, 1050 Brussels; tel (2) 640-65-00; telex 63616.
Permanent Representative: Abdi Hassan Mshangama.
Minister Plenipotentiary: J. A. T. Muwowo.
Minister-Counsellor: A. U. T. Kanyenye.
Counsellor: R. A. Bitungwa.
First Secretary: G. R. Mbunda.
Administrative Attaché: I. B. Kassege.
Administrative Attaché: Sanifa Lyimo.
Financial Attaché: F. Z. Luambano.

THAILAND

Permanent Mission: 2 square du Val de la Cambre, 1050 Brussels; tel (2) 640-68-10; telex 63510; fax (2) 648-30-66.
Permanent Representative: Danai Tulalamba.
Minister-Counsellor: Chirasak Moodhitaporn.
Counsellor: Thinakarn Kanusata.
First Secretary: Choosak Ramabutr.
First Secretary: Takerngsak Lekklar.
Second Secretary: Panpimon Suwannapongse.
Second Secretary: Vimon Kidchob.
Second Secretary: Maris Sangiampongsa.
Third Secretary: Poowadol Weerawedphisai.
Attaché: Sunee Cherdsukjai.
Attaché: Potjana Satapana.

Commercial Section: tel (2) 640-59-50.
Counsellor: Tong Indharameesup.
First Secretary: Meechai Boonyamarn.
Second Commercial Secretary: Boon Intiratana.

Customs Section: 59 ave du Pérou, 1050 Brussels; tel (2) 660-58-35.
Counsellor: Sathit Limpongpan.
Second Secretary: Chutinat Watanaphol.
Third Secretary: Narin Kalayanamit.

Scientific and Technical Section: 366 ave Louise, 1050 Brussels.
Counsellor: Chobvit Lubpairee.
Second Secretary: Krisada Tharasook.

TOGO

Permanent Mission: 264 ave de Tervuren, 1150 Brussels; tel (2) 770-17-91; telex 25093; fax (2) 771-50-75.
Permanent Representative: Eboué Assiongbon A. Agbenou.
Counsellor: Déma Kodjo.
Second Secretary: Bayédzè Komi Dagoh.
Attaché: Abouya Fafa Semedo.
Attaché: Alangba Assoum-Toko Talboussouma.
Attaché: Appoh Amabley.
Attaché: Latré Kayi Lawson.

TONGA

Permanent Mission: New Zealand House (12th floor), Haymarket, London SW1Y 4TE, England; tel (71) 839-3287; telex 8954094.
Permanent Representative: Siosaia Ma'ulupekotofa Tuita.
Counsellor: Tevita Uasi'ahokovi.
First Secretary: 'Akosita Fineanganofo.
Third Secretary: K. T. Tiliti.

TRINIDAD AND TOBAGO

Permanent Mission: 14 ave de la Faisanderie, 1150 Brussels; tel (2) 762-94-00; telex 23539; fax (2) 772-27-83.
Permanent Representative: Terrence Baden-Semper.
Counsellor: Rawlston Gonourie.
First Secretary: Carl Francis.
Commercial Attaché: Richardson Andrews.

TUNISIA

Permanent Mission: 278 ave de Tervuren, 1150 Brussels; tel (2) 771-73-95; telex 22078; fax (2) 771-94-33.
Permanent Representative: Rachid Sfar.
Minister Plenipotentiary: Honcine Longo.
Counsellor: Abdelwahed Bouzouita.
Counsellor: Abdelaziz Ghodbane.
Secretary: Mohamed Ridha Farhat.
Secretary: Zine El Abdine Terras.

TURKEY

Permanent Mission: 4 rue Montoyer, 1040 Brussels; tel (2) 513-28-36.
Permanent Representative: Özdem Sanberk.
Minister-Counsellor and Deputy Permanent Representative: Mithat Balkan.
Deputy Permanent Representative: Ünal Altintas.
Chief Counsellor for Economic and Commercial Affairs: Mehmet Haluk Özelçi.
Counsellor for Financial and Customs Affairs: Saim Kirgoz.

Counsellor: Ahmet Akses.
Counsellor: Ahmet Umit Danişman.
Counsellor for Economic and Commercial Affairs: Osman Merih Dogangun.
Counsellor for Economic and Commercial Affairs: Nejat Eren.
Deputy Counsellor for Economic and Commercial Affairs: Mehmet Haluk Nuray.
Deputy Counsellor for Economic and Commercial Affairs: Levent Tekin.
Deputy Counsellor for Economic and Commercial Affairs: Ayse Firdevis Akdag.
Deputy Counsellor for Economic and Commercial Affairs: Ziya Altan Alpay.
Deputy Counsellor for Economic and Commercial Affairs: Fisum Aktug-Özen.
Administrative Attaché: Nevin Demir.

UGANDA

Permanent Mission: 317 ave de Tervuren, 1150 Brussels; tel (2) 762-58-25; telex 62814.
Permanent Representative: Charles Kakuru Katungi.
Political Counsellor: Joshua W. Sempebwa.
Second Secretary for Economic Affairs: Peter Nkurunziza.
Financial Attaché: John Magoba.
Attaché: Ruth F. Musisi.

UNITED ARAB EMIRATES

Permanent Mission: 73 ave F. D. Roosevelt, 1050 Brussels; tel (2) 640-60-00; telex 26559; fax (2) 646-24-73.
Permanent Representative: Salem Rached Salem al-Agroobi.
Counsellor: Marzouk Falah Jaber al-Hababi.
Second Secretary: Moosa Abdul Wahid al-Khajah.

USA

Permanent Mission: 40 blvd du Régent, BP 3, 1000 Brussels; tel (2) 513-44-50; telex 21336; fax (2) 511-20-92.
Permanent Representative: James F. Dobbins.
Deputy Chief of Mission: Michael E. C. Ely.
Political Counsellor: Joanna W. Martin.
Economic Counsellor: Joel S. Spiro.
Commercial Section: James L. Blow.
Public Affairs Counsellor: David Michael Wilson.
Scientific and Technological Affairs: Anthony F. Rook.
STF: Karen S. Brown.
Customs Attaché: Alice M. Rigdon.
Trade Policy Officer: Christopher P. Marcich.
Industry Officer: Alan R. Tousignant.
Agricultural Minister-Counsellor: Edmund L. Nichols.
Labour Officer: Paul W. Hilburn, Jr.

URUGUAY

Permanent Mission: 437 ave Louise, 1050 Brussels; tel (2) 640-11-69; telex 24663; fax (2) 648-29-09.
Permanent Representative: José María Araneo.
Minister-Counsellor: Duncan B. Croci.
First Secretary: Carlos Sgarbi.

VENEZUELA

Permanent Mission: 5 sq. Vergote, 1200 Brussels; tel (2) 736-10-23; telex 61742; fax (2) 732-24-87.
Permanent Representative: Julio César Gil.
Counsellor: Amadeo Volpe-Giacoboni.
First Secretary: Beatriz Davila Barrios.
Third Secretary: María Milagros Gil Quintero.

WESTERN SAMOA

Permanent Mission: 95 ave F. D. Roosevelt, 1050 Brussels; tel (2) 660-84-54; telex 25657; fax (2) 675-03-36.
Permanent Representative: Afamasaga Faamatala Toleafoa.
First Secretary: Tina Hellesoe.

YEMEN

Permanent Mission: Surinamestraat 9, 2585 GC The Hague, Netherlands; tel (70) 365-39-36; telex 33290.
Permanent Representative: Mohammed Abdul Rehman al-Robaee.
Counsellor: Abdulwhab Mohamed.
Counsellor: Ahmed Ali Kalaz.
Counsellor for Economic Affairs: A. A. al-Mekhlafi.

YUGOSLAVIA

Permanent Mission: 11 ave Emile de Mot, 1050 Brussels; tel (2) 649-83-65; telex 26156; fax (2) 649-08-78.
Permanent Representative: Mihailo Crnobrnja.
Minister-Counsellor: Ivan Mrkić.
Counsellor: Marija Bedenik.
Secretary: Duško Lopandić.

ZAIRE

Permanent Mission: 30 rue Marie de Bourgogne, 1040 Brussels; tel (2) 513-66-10; telex 21983.
Permanent Representative: Kimbulu Moyanso wa Lokwa.
Minister-Counsellor and Deputy Permanent Representative: Zulu Kilo-abi.

ZAMBIA

Permanent Mission: 469 ave Molière, BP 2, 1060 Brussels; tel (2) 343-56-49; telex 63102.
Permanent Representative: Kapembé Nsingo.
Counsellor for Economic Affairs: P. N. Sinyinza.
First Secretary for Political Affairs: Chipili B. C. Nkonga.
First Secretary for Administrative Affairs: W. Y. Zulu.
Second Secretary for Financial Affairs: William Njobvu.
Secretary: P. V. Kabwe.

ZIMBABWE

Permanent Mission: 11 sq. Josephine-Charlotte, 1200 Brussels; tel (2) 762-58-08; telex 24133.
Permanent Representative: Andrew Hama Mtetwa.
Minister-Counsellor: C. T. Mavodza.
Counsellor for Political Affairs: Lucia Muvingi.
Counsellor for Customs Affairs: Wilfred J. Ndanga.
First Secretary for Commercial Affairs: Herbert Dzvimbo.
First Secretary for Commercial Affairs: Sibongile N. Gumede.
First Secretary: Charity Nzenza.
First Secretary: Charles C. Z. Musumhi.
Second Secretary: Alexander Dzenga.
Third Secretary: Andrew Tapomwa.
Third Secretary: Nyaradzo Mabugu.
Third Secretary: Faith R. Sagwete.

International Organizations

COUNCIL OF EUROPE

Liaison Office: Résidence Palace, 155 rue de la Loi, BP 3, 1040 Brussels; tel (2) 230-41-70; fax (2) 230-94-62.
Head of Office: Thomas Ouchterlony.
Deputy Head of Office: Gianluca Brunetti.
Documentation: Chantal Tiphaigne.

EUROPEAN FREE TRADE ASSOCIATION—EFTA

Liaison Office: 118 rue d'Arlon, 1040 Brussels; tel (2) 231-17-87; fax (2) 230-34-75.
Head of Office: Christoph Querner.
Officer: Anders Wollter.
Officer: Lars Erik Nordgaard.

INTERNATIONAL LABOUR ORGANIZATION—ILO

Liaison Office: 40 rue Aimé Smekens, 1040 Brussels; tel (2) 736-59-42; telex 25307; fax (2) 735-48-25.
Director: Gérard Fonteneau.

UNITED NATIONS

Liaison Office: 40 ave de Broqueville, 1200 Brussels; tel (2) 770-50-47; telex 62966.
Director: Salah Cherif.

UNITED NATIONS HIGH COMMISSIONER FOR REFUGEES—UNHCR

Liaison Office: 11a rue Van Eyck, BP 3, 1050 Brussels; tel (2) 649-01-51; telex 64352.
Director: Michel Moussalli.

NORTH ATLANTIC TREATY ORGANIZATION—NATO

BELGIUM

Permanent Representation: 9 blvd Léopold III, 1110 Brussels; tel (2) 728-60-11; telex 23689; fax (2) 728-60-90.
Permanent Representative: Prosper Thuysbaert.
Minister-Counsellor and Deputy Permanent Representative: M. Servais.
Counsellor: R. Schellinck.
Secretary: T. Baekelandt.
Secretary: P. Martin.
Military Counsellor: Col G. Bastien.
Financial Counsellor: F. Wauters.
Economic Counsellor: J. P. Godfurnon.
Permanent Military Representative (Army): Lieut-Gen. A. Everaert.
Deputy Military Counsellor: Col E. van de Putte.
Counsellor for Military Budget: Lieut Col M. Thijs.
Counsellor for Infrastructure: Col M. Halon.
Counsellor for Armament and Production: Capt. F. Gevers.
Deputy Counsellor for Armament and Production: Lieut Col J. C. Willem.
Chancellor: N. de Clippele.
Deputy Counsellor for Press and Information: M. Riga.
Security Officer: J. van Roy.

CANADA

Permanent Representation: blvd Léopold III, 1110 Brussels; tel (2) 216-03-46; telex 23867; fax (2) 245-24-62.
Permanent Representative: James K. Bartleman.
Minister-Counsellor and Deputy Permanent Representative: R. J. Lysyshyn.
Counsellor: R. P. McDougall.
Counsellor: P. Meyer.
Permanent Military Representative (Army): Lieut-Gen. R. Evraire.
Counsellor (Defence Production): J. A. Holt.
Counsellor (Defence Planning and Policy): Col G. Brown.
Counsellor (Finance): R. J. Sutherland.
Counsellor (Finance): J. C. Hunter.
Counsellor (Armaments): Lieut Col L. W. Bentley.
Attaché (Emergency Measures): H. Sampson.
First Secretary (Finance): R. W. Adams.
First Secretary: Maj. A. B. Bowles.
Second Secretary: J. Jonk.
Second Secretary (Administration): J. Dufault.

DENMARK

Permanent Representation: blvd Léopold III, 1110 Brussels; tel (2) 728-61-11; telex 23595; fax (2) 728-61-15.
Permanent Representative: Ole Bierring.
Minister-Counsellor: Per Carlsen.
Minister-Counsellor (Defence): B. Jacobsen.
First Secretary: Svend Waever.
First Secretary: Lars Kjaer.
First Secretary: Carl C. Hasselbalch.
Permanent Military Representative (Army): Lieut-Gen. P. B. Krogen.
Military Counsellor: Vice-Admiral Jørgen Frits Bork.
Counsellor (Communications): Lieut Col Jørgen Henrik Kimose.
Counsellor (Air Defence, Nuclear Weapons and Planning): Lieut Col Esben Høholt Larsen.
Counsellor (Materials and Logistics): Commdr Erik Rode.
Counsellor (Budget and European Organizations): Lieut Col Niels Jørgen Bundgaard.
Counsellor (Infrastructure): John Stanley Rasmussen.

FRANCE

Permanent Representation: blvd Léopold III, 1110 Brussels; tel (2) 728-41-11; telex 23867; fax (2) 728-45-79.
Permanent Representative: Gabriel Robin.
Head of Military Mission (Air): Maj.-Gen. Yves Aubert.

GERMANY

Permanent Representation: blvd Léopold III, 1110 Brussels; tel (2) 728-41-11; telex 23867; fax (2) 728-45-79.
Permanent Representative: Dr Hans-Friedrich von Ploetz.
Permanent Military Representative (Army): Lieut-Gen. R. A. Hüttel.

GREECE

Permanent Representation: 1110 Brussels; tel (2) 728-41-11; telex 23867; fax (2) 728-45-79.
Permanent Representative: Ioannis Bourloyannis-Tsangaridis.
Permanent Military Representative (Navy): Vice-Admiral I. Maniatis.

ICELAND

Permanent Representation: 1110 Brussels; tel (2) 215-10-35; telex 23763; fax (2) 242-23-31.
Permanent Representative: Sverrir Haukur Gunnlaugsson.
Deputy Permanent Representative: Róbert T. Árnason.
Secretary: Thórdur Aegir Óskarsson.
Secretary: Sigrídur Jónsdóttir.
Secretary: Anna Sigrídur Alfredsdóttir.

ITALY

Permanent Representation: 1110 Brussels; tel (2) 728-41-11; telex 23867; fax (2) 728-45-79.
Permanent Representative: Francesco Paolo Fulci.
Permanent Military Representative (Navy): Vice-Admiral M. Castelletti.

LUXEMBOURG

Permanent Representation: 1110 Brussels; tel (2) 241-35-50; telex 23720; fax (2) 245-54-60.
Permanent Representative: François Bremer (acting).
Permanent Military Representative (Army): Lieut Col J. P. Heck.

NETHERLANDS

Permanent Representation: 1110 Brussels; tel (2) 728-41-11; telex 23867; fax (2) 728-45-79.
Permanent Representative: Adriaan Jacobovits de Szeged.
Permanent Military Representative (Army): Lieut Col A. A. Herweiler.

NORWAY

Permanent Representation: Bâtiment B, 3e étage, autoroute de Zaventem, 1110 Brussels; tel (2) 215-18-34; telex 23702; fax (2) 243-04-30.
Permanent Representative: Bjørn Inge Kristvik.
Permanent Military Representative (Air): Lieut-Gen. A. Granviken.

PORTUGAL

Permanent Representation: 1110 Brussels; tel (2) 728-41-11; telex 23867; fax (2) 728-45-79.
Permanent Representative: José Gregorio Faria.
Permanent Military Representative (Navy): Vice-Admiral A. C. Fuzeta da Ponte.

SPAIN

Permanent Representation: 1110 Brussels; tel (2) 728-41-11; telex 23867; fax (2) 728-45-79.
Permanent Representative: Máximo Cajal.
Permanent Military Representative (Army): Lieut-Gen. F. Pardo de Santayana.

TURKEY

Permanent Representation: 1110 Brussels; tel (2) 728-41-11; telex 23867; fax (2) 728-45-79.
Permanent Representative: Ünal Ünsal.
Permanent Military Representative (Air): Lieut-Gen. E. Calasin.

UNITED KINGDOM

Permanent Representation: autoroute Bruxelles Zaventem, Evere, 1110 Brussels; tel (2) 242-67-75; telex 23774; fax (2) 728-45-79.
Permanent Representative: D. J. Weston.
Minister and Deputy Permanent Representative: D. Beattie.
Counsellor and Head of Chancery: J. M. Cresswell.
Counsellor (Defence): D. R. Fisher.
Counsellor (Finance and Infrastructure): J. Elliott.
Permanent Military Representative (Navy): Admiral Sir Richard Thomas.
First Secretary (Eurogroup): J. S. Day.
First Secretary (Arms Co-operation): G. D. Magnus.
First Secretary (Nuclear Matters): J. F. M. Tesh.
First Secretary (Civil and Military Budgets): R. M. Milton.
First Secretary (Infrastructure): S. C. Routh.
First Secretary (Infrastructure): D. Whitlock.
First Secretary (Information/Chancery): D. Skingle.
First Secretary (Political): R. V. Court.
First Secretary (Defence Policy): P. H. Tipple.

Second Secretary (Arms Co-operation): A. J. S. Merrill.
Second Secretary (Chancery): G. D. H. Whitaker.

USA

Permanent Representation: autoroute de Zaventem, 1110 Brussels; tel (2) 242-52-80; telex 21336; fax (2) 511-20-92.
Permanent Representative: William H. Taft IV.
Deputy Permanent Representative and Deputy Chief of Mission: John C. Kornblum.
Political Adviser: Craig G. Dunkerley.
Economic Adviser: E. Mark Linton.
Administrative Adviser: Henry M. Reed II.
Public Affairs Adviser: Barry Fulton.
Communications Programme Officer: Thomas A. Bell.
Permanent Military Representative (Navy): Admiral J. R. Hogg.
Defence Adviser: David R. Nicholas.
Information Service: fax (2) 242-06-96.
Supreme Headquarters Allied Powers Europe - SHAPE: 7010, Belgium; tel (65) 44-50-00.
Political Adviser: Kent N. Brown.

ORGANIZATION FOR ECONOMIC CO-OPERATION AND DEVELOPMENT—OECD

AUSTRALIA

Permanent Delegation: 2 rue André-Pascal, 75775 Paris Cedex 16; tel (1) 45-24-82-00; telex 620160; fax (1) 45-24-85-00.
Head of Permanent Delegation: Ed Visbord.

AUSTRIA

Permanent Delegation: 3 rue Albéric Magnard, 75116 Paris; tel (1) 45-20-74-45; telex 611946; fax (1) 40-50-87-05.
Head of Permanent Delegation: Dr Georg Lennkh.
Minister: Franz Troji.
Counsellor: Dr Otto Hellwig.
Counsellor: Dr Gernot Schnabl.
Science Attaché: Dr Christian Wild.
Finance Attaché: Dr Norbert Schuh.

BELGIUM

Permanent Delegation: 2 rue André-Pascal, 75775 Paris Cedex 16; tel (1) 45-24-82-00; telex 620160; fax (1) 45-24-85-00.
Head of Permanent Delegation: Juan Cassier.

CANADA

Permanent Delegation: 15 bis rue de Franqueville, 75116 Paris; tel (1) 45-24-98-12; telex 620160; fax (1) 45-20-30-08.
Head of Permanent Delegation: L. Michael Berry.
Deputy Permanent Representative and Minister-Counsellor: D. C. Elder.
Counsellor: D. E. Hobson.
Counsellor: P. Gusen.
Counsellor (Development): I. Wright.
First Secretary: K. D. O'Shea.
First Secretary: Y. Brodeur.

DENMARK

Permanent Delegation: 6 rue Jean Richepin, 75116 Paris; tel (1) 45-04-12-70; telex 620662; fax (1) 45-04-81-21.
Head of Permanent Delegation: Jens Christensen.
Counsellor: Erik Hedegaard.
Attaché (Agriculture): Niels Sønderbye.
Financial Counsellor: Steen Ryd Larsen.
Attaché (Energy): Knud Pedersen.

FINLAND

Permanent Delegation: 6 rue de Franqueville, 75116 Paris; tel (1) 45-24-99-96; telex 620942; fax (1) 45-20-63-04.
Head of Permanent Delegation: Wilhelm Breitenstein.

FRANCE

Permanent Delegation: 21 rue Octave Feuillet 75116 Paris; tel (1) 45-20-77-56; telex 620160; fax (1) 45-24-85-00.
Head of Permanent Delegation: Bernard Bochet.

GERMANY

Permanent Delegation: 5 rue Léonard-de-Vinci, 75116 Paris; tel (1) 45-01-73-88; telex 611010; fax (1) 45-01-29-77.
Head of Permanent Delegation: Dr Klaus Meyer.

GREECE

Permanent Delegation: 2 rue André-Pascal, 75775 Paris Cedex 16; tel (1) 45-24-82-00; telex 620160; fax (1) 45-24-85-00.
Head of Permanent Delegation: Dimitris Koulourianos.

ICELAND

Permanent Delegation: 124 blvd Haussmann, 75008 Paris; tel (1) 45-22-81-54; telex 290314; fax (1) 42-93-42-95.
Head of Permanent Delegation: Albert Guđmundsson.
Deputy Head of Permanent Delegation and Counsellor: Benedikt Jónsson.

IRELAND

Permanent Delegation: 2 rue André-Pascal, 75775 Paris Cedex 16; tel (1) 45-24-82-00; telex 620160; fax (1) 45-24-85-00.
Head of Permanent Delegation: Tadhg O'Sullivan.

ITALY

Permanent Delegation: 2 rue André-Pascal, 75775 Paris Cedex 16; tel (1) 45-24-82-00; telex 620160; fax (1) 45-24-85-00.
Head of Permanent Delegation: Luigi Fontana Giusti.

JAPAN

Permanent Delegation: 7 ave Hoche, 75008 Paris; tel (1) 47-66-02-22; telex 644493; fax (1) 42-27-66-29.
Head of Permanent Delegation: Hiroaki Fujii.

LUXEMBOURG

Permanent Delegation: 33 ave Rapp, 75007 Paris; tel (1) 45-55-13-37; telex 204711; fax (1) 45-51-72-29.
Head of Permanent Delegation: Pierre Wurth.
Deputy Head of Permanent Delegation: Pierre Gramegna.
Secretary: Fernand Schritz.

NETHERLANDS

Permanent Delegation: 2 rue André-Pascal, 75775 Paris Cedex 16; tel (1) 45-24-82-00; telex 620160; fax (1) 45-24-85-00.
Head of Permanent Delegation: A. G. O. Smitsendonk.

NEW ZEALAND

Permanent Delegation: 2 rue André-Pascal, 75775 Paris Cedex 16; tel (1) 45-24-82-00; telex 620160; fax (1) 45-24-85-00.
Head of Permanent Delegation: Judith Trotter.
Deputy Head of Permanent Delegation: George Troup.
Counsellor (Economic): Deborah Roseveare.
First Secretary (Agriculture): Neil Fraser.

NORWAY

Permanent Delegation: 19 rue de Franqueville, 75775 Paris Cedex 16; tel (1) 45-24-97-84; telex 620013; fax (1) 45-20-08-82.
Head of Permanent Delegation: Bjørn Barth.

PORTUGAL

Permanent Delegation: 2 rue André-Pascal, 75775 Paris Cedex 16; tel (1) 45-24-82-00; telex 620160; fax (1) 45-24-85-00.
Head of Permanent Delegation: Fernando dos Santos Martins.

SPAIN

Permanent Delegation: 2 rue André-Pascal, 75775 Paris Cedex 16; tel (1) 45-24-82-00; telex 620160; fax (1) 45-24-85-00.

Head of Permanent Delegation: Eloy Ibáñez.

SWEDEN

Permanent Delegation: 19 rue de Franqueville, 75116 Paris; tel (1) 45-24-98-60; telex 611977; fax (1) 45-24-67-74.
Head of Permanent Delegation: Staffan Sohlman.
Counsellor: Staffan Åberg.
First Secretary: Viveka Bohn.
First Secretary: Anita Melin.
Financial Counsellor: Lars-Olof Lindgren.
Industrial Counsellor: Birgitta Råland.
Educational Counsellor: Ulf Lundin.

SWITZERLAND

Permanent Delegation: 28 rue de Martignac, 75007 Paris; tel (1) 45-50-34-46; telex 620160; fax (1) 45-51-01-49.
Head of Permanent Delegation: Dr Eric Roethlisberger.
Minister: Dr Jean-Daniel Clavel.
Counsellor: Dr Anton Thalmann.
Counsellor: Dr Walter Frunz.
Counsellor: Rodolfo Laub.
First Secretary: Felix Andrist.
Second Secretary: Dr Dominik Furgler.
Attaché and Head of Chancery: Christiane Thommen.

TURKEY

Permanent Delegation: 2 rue André-Pascal, 75775 Paris Cedex 16; tel (1) 45-24-82-00; telex 620160; fax (1) 45-24-85-00.
Head of Permanent Delegation: Mustafa Asula.

UNITED KINGDOM

Permanent Delegation: 19 rue de Franqueville, 75116 Paris; tel (1) 45-24-98-28; telex 620160; fax (1) 45-24-98-37.
Head of Permanent Delegation: J. W. D. Gray.
Deputy Permanent Representative and Counsellor (Economic and Financial): J. Thomas.
Counsellor (Management): D. H. Cooper.
First Secretary: T. J. Craddock.
First Secretary: M. D. Reilly.
First Secretary: R. A. E. Gordon.
Third Secretary: J. J. Gimblett.

USA

Permanent Delegation: 19 rue de Franqueville, 75016 Paris; tel (1) 45-24-74-77; telex 643964; fax (1) 45-24-74-80.
Head of Permanent Delegation: Alan Philip Larson.
Deputy Head of Permanent Delegation: Stephen Ecton.
Economic/Financial Section: John Lange.
International Economic Section: John P. Spillane.
Labour/Manpower/Agricultural Section: Robert C. Friel.
Trade Division: John M. Hoover.
Administrative Officer: Barbara F. Hughes.
Public Affairs Officer (acting) and Delegation Secretary: James M. Roberts III.
Science/Environment/Industry Section: Daniel L. Dolan.
Energy/Science Adviser: Peter P. Jodoin.
Representative on Development Assistance Committee: Martin V. Dagata.
Development Assistance Committee Chairman: Joseph C. Wheeler.
Industry/Commerce Section: Robin R. Layton.
Investment Adviser: James T. Heg.
Energy Adviser: C. David Trotter.
Security Trade Control: Ronald D. Flack.

Participants with Special Status

YUGOSLAVIA

Permanent Delegation: 54 rue de la Faisanderie, 75016 Paris; tel (1) 45-04-38-01; telex 620160; fax (1) 45-04-09-85.
Head of Permanent Delegation: Žarko Papić.
Counsellor: Nemanja Jović.
Attaché (Science/Technology/Environment/Education/Management/Information): Nikola Lukić.
Special Adviser: Beno Lukman.

EUROPEAN COMMUNITIES

Permanent Delegation: 61 rue des Belles-Feuilles, 75782 Paris Cedex 16; tel (1) 45-01-58-85; telex 630176; fax (1) 47-27-08-02.
Head of Delegation: Raymond Phan Van Phi.
Adviser: Adolfo Comba.

EUROPEAN FREE TRADE ASSOCIATION— EFTA

AUSTRIA

Permanent Delegation: 9-11 rue de Varembé, 1211 Geneva 20; tel (22) 7337750; telex 22471; fax (22) 7344591.
Head of Permanent Delegation: Dr Franz Ceska.
Minister: Dr Norbert Faustenhammer.
Attaché: Dr Ingrid Frasl.

FINLAND

Permanent Delegation: 9-11 rue de Varembé, 1211 Geneva 20; tel (22) 7491111; telex 22660; fax (22) 7339291.
Head of Permanent Delegation: A. Hynninen.

ICELAND

Permanent Delegation: 9-11 rue de Varembé, 1211 Geneva 20; tel (22) 7491111; telex 22660; fax (22) 7339291.
Head of Permanent Delegation: Kjartan Jóhannsson.
Deputy Head of Permanent Delegation and Counsellor: Kristinn F. Árnason.

NORWAY

Permanent Delegation: 58 rue Moillebeau, Case Postale 274, 1211 Geneva 19; tel (22) 7349730; telex 414181; fax (22) 7339979.
Head of Permanent Delegation: Erik Selmer.

SWEDEN

Permanent Delegation: 9-11 rue de Varembé, 1211 Geneva 20; tel (22) 7491111; telex 22660; fax (22) 7339291.
Head of Permanent Delegation: L. Anell.

SWITZERLAND

Permanent Delegation: 9-11 rue de Varembé, Case Postale 194, 1211 Geneva 20; tel (22) 7491111; telex 22660; fax (22) 7339291.
Head of Permanent Delegation: William Rossier.
Counsellor: Josef Doswald.
Counsellor: Dr Rudolf Ramsauer.
First Secretary: William Frei.
Head of Chancery: Anne Antunes Garrido-Bonzon.

INDEX BY COUNTRY OF ORIGIN

INDEX BY COUNTRY OF ORIGIN

Afghanistan

Albania

Algeria

Angola

Antigua and Barbuda

Argentina

Australia

Austria

Bahamas

Bahrain

Bangladesh

Barbados

Belarus

Belgium

Belize

Benin

Bhutan

Bolivia

Botswana

Brazil

Brunei

Bulgaria

Burkina Faso

Burundi

Cambodia

Cameroon

Canada

Cape Verde

Central African Republic

Chad

Chile

China, People's Republic

China (Taiwan)

Colombia

Comoros

Congo

Costa Rica

Côte d'Ivoire

Cuba

Cyprus

'Turkish Republic of Northern Cyprus'

Czechoslovakia

Denmark

Djibouti

Dominica

Dominican Republic

Ecuador

Egypt

El Salvador

Equatorial Guinea

Estonia

Ethiopia

Fiji

Finland

France

Gabon

Gambia

Germany

Ghana

Greece

Grenada

Guatemala

Guinea

Guinea-Bissau

Guyana

Haiti

Honduras

Hungary

Iceland

India

Indonesia

Iran

Iraq

Ireland

Israel

Italy

Jamaica

Japan

Jordan

Kenya

Kiribati

Korea, Democratic People's Republic

Korea, Republic

Kuwait

Laos

Latvia

Lebanon

Lesotho

Liberia

Libya

Liechtenstein

Lithuania

Luxembourg

Madagascar

Malawi

Malaysia

Maldives

Mali

Malta

Marshall Islands

Mauritania

Mauritius

Mexico

Micronesia

Monaco

Mongolia

Morocco

Mozambique

Myanmar

Namibia

Nauru

Nepal

Netherlands

New Zealand

Nicaragua

Niger

Nigeria

Norway

Oman

Pakistan

Panama

Papua New Guinea

Paraguay

Peru

Philippines

Poland

Portugal

Qatar

Romania

Russia

Rwanda

Saint Christopher and Nevis

Saint Lucia

Saint Vincent and the Grenadines

San Marino

São Tomé and Príncipe

Saudi Arabia

Senegal

Seychelles

Sierra Leone

Singapore

Solomon Islands

Somalia

South Africa

Spain

Sri Lanka

Sudan

Suriname

Swaziland

Sweden

Switzerland

Syria

Tanzania

Thailand

Togo

Tonga

Trinidad and Tobago

Tunisia

Turkey

Tuvalu

Uganda

Ukraine

United Arab Emirates

United Kingdom

United States of America

Uruguay

Vanuatu

The Vatican City (The Holy See)

Venezuela

Viet-Nam

Western Samoa

Yemen

Yugoslavia

Zaire

Zambia

Zimbabwe

INTERNATIONAL ORGANIZATIONS

Asian-African Legal Consultative Committee

Commission for the Conservation of Antarctic Marine Living Resources—CCAMLR

Council of Europe

European Communities

European Free Trade Association—EFTA

Food and Agriculture Organization—FAO

International Atomic Energy Agency—IAEA

International Committee of the Red Cross—ICRC

International Fund for Agricultural Development—IFAD

International Labour Organization—ILO

International Monetary Fund—IMF

League of Arab States

Organization of African Unity—OAU

Organization of the Islamic Conference—OIC

South Pacific Forum Secretariat

United Nations

United Nations Children's Fund—UNICEF

United Nations Development Programme—UNDP

United Nations Educational, Scientific and Cultural Organization—UNESCO

United Nations Environment Programme—UNEP

United Nations High Commissioner for Refugees—UNHCR

United Nations Industrial Development Organization—UNIDO

United Nations Peace-Keeping Force in Cyprus—UNFICYP

World Bank

World Health Organization—WHO

World Intellectual Property Organization—WIPO

OTHER ORGANIZATIONS

African National Congress—ANC

Palestine Liberation Organization—PLO